The New
Encyclopedia of
UNBELIEF

The New Encyclopedia of
UNBELIEF

Edited by
TOM FLYNN

Foreword by
RICHARD DAWKINS

Publisher
PAUL KURTZ

Prometheus Books

59 John Glenn Drive
Amherst, New York 14228–2119

Published 2007 by Prometheus Books

Inquiries should be addressed to
Prometheus Books
59 John Glenn Drive
Amherst, New York 14228-2119
VOICE: 716-691-0133, ext. 210
FAX: 716-691-0137
WWW.PROMETHEUSBOOKS.COM

11 10 09 08 07   5 4 3 2 1

Library of Congress Cataloging-in-Publication Data

The new encyclopedia of unbelief / ed[ited] by Tom Flynn.
  p. cm.
Includes bibliographical references and index.
ISBN 978-1-59102-391-3 (hardcover : alk. paper)
  1. Rationalism—Encyclopedias. 2. Free thought—Encyclopedias. 3. Atheism—Encyclopedias.
4. Agnosticism—Encyclopedias. 1. Flynn, Tom, 1955-.

BL2705.N49 2006
211'.803—dc22

2006012121

Printed in the United States of America on acid-free paper

Prometheus Staff

EDITORIAL ADVISORY BOARD

INDEX OF CONTRIBUTORS

David Adams is professor of French Enlightenment studies at the University of Manchester (UK). He has published many articles and books on the literature and thought of the period, and is now working on the relationship between illustrated books and the society of the ancien régime.

Michael Adcock, an independent freethought historian and researcher, was formerly a Christian fundamentalist activist. He is currently working on a biography of Charles Chilton Moore, a notable regional freethought propagandist of the nineteenth century.

Norm R. Allen Jr. is deputy editor of *Free Inquiry* magazine and editor of *African American Humanism: An Anthology* and *The Black Humanist Experience: An Alternative to Religion.* He is the executive director of African Americans for Humanism (AAH), and has traveled throughout Africa, Europe, North America, and Latin America as a spokesperson for the Council for Secular Humanism.

W. Michael Ashcraft is an associate professor of religion at Truman State University. He is the author of *The Dawn of the New Cycle: Point Loma Theosophists and American Culture* (2002) and coeditor of *New Religious Movements: A Documentary Reader* (2005).

Hector Avalos is associate professor of religious studies and director of the US Latino/a Studies program at Iowa State University. The author of six books and numerous articles, Avalos received his BA in anthropology from the University of Arizona and a PhD in biblical and Near Eastern studies from Harvard.

A. J. (Jim) Baker taught philosophy for many years at Australia's Sydney, Waikato, and Macquarie universities. In Sydney, he was a student of John Anderson and later a colleague of both he and John Mackie. He was also a leading member of the Libertarian Society and the radical bohemian "Sydney Push."

William Baker is presidential research professor at the Department of English and University Libraries, Northern Illinois University. He edits *George Eliot–George Henry Lewes Studies.* His coauthored *George Eliot: A Bibliographical History* was published by Oak Knoll/British Library in 2002.

Joe Edward Barnhart is professor of philosophy and religion studies at the University of North Texas. He has published in leading journals and is author of *The Study*

of Religion and Its Meaning: New Explorations in Light of Karl Popper and Emile Durkheim, Religion and the Challenge of Philosophy, The Billy Graham Religion, and other books.

Lawrence I. Berkove is emeritus professor of English at the University of Michigan–Dearborn. Among his frequent publications on Twain is Modern Library's edition of the *Best Short Stories of Mark Twain* (2004). He is presently writing a book on Twain's religion and is current president of the Mark Twain Circle of America.

David Berman is an associate professor of philosophy and a fellow of Trinity College, Dublin, where he has been teaching since 1968. He is author of *A History of Atheism in Britain* (Routledge, 1990), *George Berkeley: Idealism and the Man* (Oxford, 1996), *Berkeley: Experimental Philosophy* (Phoenix, 1997), and *Berkeley and Irish Philosophy* (Continuum, 2005).

Ray Billington was a Methodist minister until 1971, when he was expelled for heresy over his book *The Christian Outsider.* A relative rarity, a living officially declared heretic, he rose to be head of philosophy at the University of the West of England. Since retirement he teaches at Oxford and Bath.

Timothy Binga, director of the Center for Inquiry Libraries, received his MLS in 1995, and is a member of the American Library Association and the New York Library Association. His original cataloging of many rare freethought works held nowhere else but at the Center for Inquiry led to his article "Preserving Our Freethought Heritage Redux" (*Free Inquiry*, Spring 2003).

Rebecca Bizonet, MSI, is an archivist at the University of Michigan Special Collections Library, where she arranges and describes collections of manuscripts, personal papers, and organizational records ranging from a trove of poet A. C. Swinburne's manuscripts and letters to anarchist papers from the renowned Labadie Collection of social protest materials.

Dan Bollinger is executive director of the International Coalition for Genital Integrity (Santa Cruz, CA). He is a men's issues researcher and instructor for men's personal growth workshops.

Robert Boston is the assistant director of communications for Americans United for Separation of Church and State in Washington, DC. He is the author of three books on church-state separation, including *Why the Religious Right Is Wrong about Separation of Church & State* (second edition, 2003).

Roderick Bradford is the author of a 2006 biography, *D. M. Bennett: The Truth Seeker*, a life of the founder of America's longest continually published freethought publication. He is a documentary video producer and writer whose articles have appeared in *American History* magazine, *American Atheist, The Truth Seeker*, and *The Quest*, the official journal of the Theosophical Society in America.

Graham Bradshaw is professor of English at Chuo University, Japan. He is senior editor of the Shakespearean International Yearbook and the author of *Shakespeare's Scepticism* and *Misrepresentations: Shakespeare and the Materialists*. His most recent book, written with Tetsuo Kishi, is a study of Shakespeare in Japan.

Paul Sydney Braterman moved in 1988 from a readership at Glasgow University to the University of North Texas, where he is a regents professor of chemistry. He has published over 120 scientific publications, and is a member of the editorial board of *Origins of Life and Evolution of Biospheres*.

Emeritus Professor Anthony Briggs, a senior research fellow at Bristol University, has written widely on Russian literature and English poetry, including several books and articles on Alexander Pushkin and some verse translations. His new translation of Tolstoy's *War and Peace* was published recently by Penguin Books (UK) and Viking (USA).

Gary Brill is an instructor in psychology at Rutgers, the State University of New Jersey. He is a longtime humanist and one of the original members of the HumanLight Committee.

George Broadhead is a founding member of the Gay and Lesbian Humanist Association (GALHA), based in the UK, and has been its voluntary administrator almost since its founding in 1977.

Ed Buckner leads the Atlanta Freethought Society and was formerly executive director of the Council for Secular Humanism. He coedited with his son Michael E. Buckner *Quotations That Support the Separation of Church and State* (1995) and contributed the concluding chapter to *Fundamentals of Extremism: The Christian Right in America*, ed. Kimberly Blaker (2003).

Vern L. Bullough, PhD, DSci, RN, was a former co-president of the International Humanist and Ethical Union (IHEU) and one of the founders of the Council for Secular Humanism. He was author or editor of more than fifty books and was a State University of New York distinguished professor emeritus. A longtime activist in the struggle for civil rights and civil liberties, much of his later research concentrated on sex and gender issues.

David Bumbaugh, minister emeritus of the Unitarian Church in Summit, New Jersey, is president of the Unitarian Universalist Historical Society and professor of ministry at Meadville Lombard. He is the author of two books: *The Education of God* and *Unitarian Universalism: A Narrative History.*

Kenneth W. Burchell is president of the Thomas Paine Institute and a past association historian and trustee of the Thomas Paine National Historical Association. A professional appraiser of fine gems, jewelry, and antiquarian books, he devotes his personal time to research and writing on American reform and freethought.

Bruce E. Cathey is an independent scholar writing two large-scale freethought bibliographies. He has visited dozens of national and university research libraries, public and special libraries, rare book collections, and freethought libraries in six countries and on three continents. He is also an acquisitions consultant to the Center for Inquiry Libraries (Amherst, New York).

Virginia Clark was reference librarian at Kenyon College (Ohio) and editor of the journal *Choice*. She spent much of her widowed retirement in London, volunteering at the Women's Library and the Conway Hall Humanist Centre. She completed research for her entry in this work one week before her sudden death.

William Raymond Clark received his PhD from the University of California–Berkeley. He is professor emeritus of French at Salem State College (Massachusetts). He has written on the unbelief of Stendhal, Mérimée, Clemenceau, and Littré.

Edmund D. Cohen is the author of *The Mind of the Bible-Believer, C. G. Jung and the Scientific Attitude*, and many articles. He is an attorney and a PhD psychologist. He was a pioneer in the videotaping of Religious Right leaders' television broadcasts, using their own recorded utterances to discredit them.

Heather J. Coleman is associate professor and Canada research chair in imperial Russian history in the department of history and classics at the University of Alberta, Edmonton, Canada. She is the author of *Russian Baptists and Spiritual Revolution, 1905–1929* (Indiana, 2005).

Bill Cooke is senior lecturer at the School of Visual Arts, University of Auckland at Manukau (New Zealand), visiting assistant professor of philosophy at the University of Buffalo (2003–2006), and a fellow of the Committee for the Scientific Examination of Religion.

Robert M. Cutler is senior research fellow at the Institute of European and Russian Studies, Carleton University (Canada). He is translator and editor of the acclaimed anthology *The Basic Bakunin* (Prometheus Books, 1992) as well as a number of articles on Bakunin's life and thought. He also maintains a Bakunin-oriented Web site.

Austin Dacey is vice president and United Nations representative of the Center for Inquiry. He is executive editor of *Philo*, the journal of the Society of Humanist Philosophers, and was an associate editor of *Free Inquiry* magazine.

Sarah Darby is a PhD candidate in the philosophy department at Stanford University. She is writing a dissertation about Nietzsche's analysis of the relationship between authority and value in Christianity and how he thought that relationship would be transformed in the process of creating new values.

Richard Dawkins is Charles Simonyi professor of the public understanding of science at Oxford University. His books, *The Selfish Gene*, *The Extended Phenotype*, *The Blind Watchmaker*, *River Out of Eden*, *Climbing Mount Improbable*, *Unweaving the Rainbow*, *A Devil's Chaplain*, and *The Ancestor's Tale*, many of them bestsellers, have earned him the humorously Huxleyan accolade of "Darwin's Rottweiler." His 2006 *The God Delusion* became a major bestseller. His most valuable prizes are the International Cosmos Prize (Japan) and the Kistler Prize (US). He holds honorary degrees in literature as well as science and is a fellow of the Royal Society as well as of the Royal Society of Literature.

Kathleen De Grave is a professor of American literature and codirector of creative writing at Pittsburg State University. Her publications include *Swindler, Spy, Rebel: The Confidence Woman in 19th-Century America* and *Company Woman*, a novel. She also wrote the introduction to the recent unexpurgated edition of Upton Sinclair's *The Jungle*.

Tim Delaney is a social theorist who teaches sociology courses at the State University of New York at Oswego. He has published seven books including *Classical Social Theory: Investigation and Application* and *Contemporary Social Theory: Investigation and Application*. He regularly presents papers at regional, national, and international conferences.

Hans van Deukeren is a science and historical writer. He served as office manager at the Humanist Archives in the Netherlands (1998–2005) and has published a history of the International Humanist and Ethical Union (2002).

Christopher W. diCarlo is lecturer in philosophy at the University of Ontario Institute of Technology. He has spoken and written on topics from bioethics to cognitive evolution. A past visiting research scholar at Harvard University, his forthcoming book is *How to Become a Really Good Pain in the Ass: A Practical Guide to Thinking Critically*.

Edd Doerr, president of Americans for Religious Liberty and immediate past president of the American Humanist Association, is the author, coauthor, editor, or translator of twenty-five books on church-state issues, fiction, and poetry. He has also authored over two thousand published articles, reviews, and letters and has served on the boards of NARAL, the Maryland ACLU, and other organizations.

George Donaldson is lecturer in English and deputy head of the department of English at the University of Bristol. He has teaching and research interests in Shakespeare, Shelley, and Lawrence; eighteenth-, nineteenth-, and twentieth-century novel, poetry, and literary criticism; and Freud, psychoanalysis, and literature. He has published on Shelley and Lawrence.

Theodore Drange is professor emeritus of philosophy at West Virginia University and is the author of *Type Crossings: Sentential Meaninglessness in the Border Area of Linguistics and Philosophy* (1966) and *Nonbelief and Evil: Two Arguments for the Nonexistence of God* (1998). Several of his essays and debates appear on the Internet.

Dan Dugan is known in audio engineering as the inventor of the automatic microphone mixer. His equipment is used in churches, courtrooms, conferences, and television shows. In addition to engineering, Dugan has a lively interest in the philosophy of science and current controversies about scientific paradigms and alternative medicine.

Sanal Edamaruku is president of the Indian Rationalist Association and of Rationalist International. He edits Rationalist International's Internet publication that appears in English, French, German, Spanish, and Finnish. He has convened three international rationalist conferences (1995, 2000, and 2002) and is a well-known campaigner against superstitions and obscurantism.

Taner Edis is associate professor of physics at Truman State University, author of *The Ghost in the Universe* (Prometheus Books, 2002), and coeditor of *Why Intelligent Design Fails* (Rutgers University Press, 2004). His recent books include *Science and Nonbelief* (2005) and *An Illusion of Harmony: Science and Religion in Islam* (2007). He is an active critic of supernatural and paranormal claims.

Fred Edwords was formerly editor of *The Humanist* magazine and executive director of the American Humanist

Association (AHA). He has been recognized as Rationalist of the Year by the American Rationalist Federation and as a Humanist Pioneer by the AHA. His start in freethought included working for the fourth publisher of *The Truth Seeker*, James Hervey Johnson, which gave him access to records now scattered or destroyed.

Allen Esterson is a former lecturer at Southwark College, London, and author of *Seductive Mirage: An Exploration of the Work of Sigmund Freud* (1993) and varied articles on Freud and the history of psychoanalysis.

Yolanda Estes is professor of philosophy at Mississippi State University. She specializes in ethics and German idealism, particularly J. G. Fichte's philosophy. Her publications include *Marginal Groups and Mainstream American Culture* (University Press of Kansas) and *J. G. Fichte and the Atheism Dispute, 1798–1800* (Ashgate Publishing Company).

Charlotte Eulette, national director of the Celebrant USA Foundation and Institute, hails from Oak Park, Illinois. For twenty years an executive in high technology companies and Internet advertising firms, her life changed in 2001 when, together with her partner Gaile Sarma, she brought Celebrancy to the US and started the Celebrant USA Foundation—the US arm of a worldwide phenomenon in secular ceremonies that began thirty years ago and has flourished throughout North America.

Wayne Facer cofounded the University of Auckland (New Zealand) Humanist Society and was its chairman from 1965 to 1970. He has made media appearances and participated in social reforms concerning family planning and abortion. He currently researches New Zealand Unitarian and freethought history. He belongs to the New Zealand Association of Rationalists and Humanists.

Grace Farrell, Rebecca Clifton Reade professor at Butler University, publishes on American fiction. Her books include *From Exile to Redemption: The Fiction of Isaac Bashevis Singer, Isaac Bashevis Singer: Literary Conversations, Critical Essays on Isaac Bashevis Singer*, the recovered edition of Blake's *Fettered for Life*, and *Lillie Devereux Blake: Retracing a Life Erased*.

Jose Manuel Fernandez Santana earned his law degree from the University of Buenos Aires. He organized the First International Exhibition of Literature for Nonbelievers (Stockholm-Oslo) and founded the Humanist and Ethical Union of Sweden. The Argentine Society of Writers (SADE) named his book *Miramar Memories* as the best biographical book of 1999.

Carlos Fiolhais is professor of physics and director of the general library at the University of Coimbra in Coimbra, Portugal. He has authored several books including *A coisa mais preciosa que temos* (*Our Most Precious Thing*) and has received a national prize for scientific excellence.

Antony Flew was born in London and educated in Kingswood School, Bath, and Oxford University, where he earned a First Class degree as well as the university prize in philosophy. Married, he has two daughters and one granddaughter. He has held various professorial appointments in England and North America and has written twenty-six books and edited twelve anthologies.

Ronald B. Flowers is John F. Weatherly emeritus professor of religion at Texas Christian University, Fort Worth. He is the author of *That Godless Court? Supreme Court Decisions on Church-State Relationships* (second edition, 2005). He has served as president of the American Academy of Religion/Southwest and is a member of the editorial council of the *Journal of Church and State*.

J. M. Floyd-Thomas teaches US and African American history at Texas Christian University (Fort Worth) and is working on a book about Rev. Ethelred Brown's life and career titled *Creating a Temple and a Forum: Religion, Culture, and Politics in the Harlem Unitarian Church, 1920–1956*.

Tom Flynn is editor of the *New Encyclopedia of Unbelief*; editor of *Free Inquiry*, the world's largest-circulation English-language secular humanist magazine; and designer and director of the Robert Green Ingersoll Birthplace Museum, America's only freethought museum. He is author of *The Trouble with Christmas* (1993) and two irreverent science fiction novels, *Galactic Rapture* (2000) and *Nothing Sacred* (2004). His antireligious short play best known as *Messiah Game* enjoyed several productions, including an off-off-off-Broadway debut in 2002. A video producer and a student of visual effects and photographic deception, Flynn has performed photo/video analysis in numerous television programs and has written on photography and the paranormal in Gordon Stein's *Encyclopedia of the Paranormal* (1996).

Joe Fox is an activist involved with many humanist, freethought, skeptical, and civic/political activist groups. He is currently vice president of the New Jersey Humanist Network and serves on the boards of other humanist groups. He is also cocreator of HumanLight, a new December humanist holiday.

Kendrick Frazier is editor of *Skeptical Inquirer*, the Magazine for Science and Reason. He is editor of five anthologies, including *Science Confronts the Paranormal* and *Encounters with the Paranormal: Science, Knowledge, and Belief*. He is also a science writer with interests in astronomy, space exploration, and the philosophy of science.

Andrea Frova is presently full professor of physics at the University of Rome "La Sapienza." He has been a research scientist at AT&T Bell Labs and a visiting professor at the Universities of Illinois, Stuttgart, California, and Polytechnic of Lausanne. He has authored more than one hundred fifty scientific papers, two hundred popular articles, and numerous books, including (with Mariapiera Marenzana) *Thus Spoke Galileo* (2006).

Mark Furner's curiosity for history and subversive ideas led him to study Switzerland's religious underground and turned him from mild agnostic to atheist. Since the late 1990s he has belonged to the Swiss Freethinkers Society (FVS) and its national committee, where he assists Jean Kaech in international affairs.

James Garvey teaches philosophy at the University of Nottingham, England, and is secretary of the Royal Institute of Philosophy. He has published papers and reviews on metaphysics and epistemology.

Bert Gasenbeek is director of the Humanist Archives and of the Library of the University for Humanistics in Utrecht, the Netherlands. He has been research fellow for history and theory of humanism since 2002. His main field of interest is the history of the humanist movement in the Netherlands.

Annie Laurie Gaylor is copresident of the Freedom From Religion Foundation and editor of its newspaper, *Freethought Today*, as well as the anthology of women freethinkers, *Women without Superstition: No Gods—No Masters* (1997). She is also author of *Woe to the Women—The Bible Tells Me So* (1981, revised 2004).

Elizabeth M. Gerber is a regional freethought activist and an amateur archivist of freethought history. British-born, she has lived in Kansas City, Missouri, since 1976. Her special research interest concerns women in freethought history; she is currently compiling a biographical dictionary of nineteenth-century women freethinkers.

Lloyd Gerson is professor of philosophy at the University of Toronto. His works on ancient philosophy include *Knowing Persons: A Study in Plato*, *Neoplatonic Philosophy: Introductory Readings* (with John Dillon), and *Aristotle and Other Platonists*. His translations of Sextus Empiricus can be found in *Hellenistic Philosophy: Introductory Readings* (with Brad Inwood).

Lawrence B. Goodheart is professor of history at the University of Connecticut. He is the author of *Abolitionist, Actuary, Atheist: Elizur Wright and the Reform Impulse* (1990). Most recently, he has coedited *Murder on Trial* (2005) and is now working on a manuscript titled "The Death Penalty in Connecticut, 1636–2005."

A. C. Grayling is professor of philosophy at the University of London and an honorary associate of the British Humanist Association.

Karen Green is an associate professor at Monash University (Australia) where she teaches existentialism, philosophy of language, and history of women's ideas. Her publications include *The Woman of Reason: Feminism, Humanism, and Political Thought* (1995), *Dummett: Philosophy of Language* (2001), and, with Constant J. Mews, *Healing the Body Politic: The Political Thought of Christine de Pizan* (2005).

Jason Grinnell received his PhD in philosophy from Bowling Green State University. He has taught at Adrian College (Michigan) and has served as a visiting assistant professor at the University of Toledo (Ohio). His research interests include ancient philosophy, social philosophy, and the philosophy of biology.

Philippe Jean Florencio Grollet is a barrister in Brussels, Belgium. Since 1977 he has been a trustee of the *Centre d'action laïque*. He was president of "*Brussels laïque*" (1980–86) and has been president of *Centre d'action laïque* since 1988. He is author of *Laïcité, Utopia, and Necessity* (Brussels, 2005).

Horst Groschopp has studied the history of labor culture, German freethought, and modern humanism. For twenty-five years a lecturer at Berlin's Humboldt University, since 2000 he has been an associate of the Institute for Humanist Life in Berlin, director of the Humanist Academy, and editor of the magazine *Humanismus Aktuell* (Humanism Today). Since 2003 he has been one of the national leaders of the HVD (Humanist Federation of Germany).

Melinda Grube, a doctoral candidate at the Union Institute and University, teaches history at Cayuga Community College in Auburn, New York.

Stewart Elliott Guthrie is emeritus professor of anthropology at Fordham University. His research, which began with fieldwork in Japan, centers on anthropomorphism and religion. It approaches these as by-products of a perceptual strategy for an ambiguous world. That strategy is: Look first for what matters most.

Brean Hammond is professor of modern English literature at the University of Nottingham. He is the author of *Bolingbroke and Pope: A Study in Friendship and Influence* (1983), which considers the question of deism in the two authors.

Glenn Hardie was a founding member of the British Columbia (Canada) Humanist Association. Holding degrees in philosophy and education and diplomas in construction economics and property appraisal, he has published three books on building technology and one titled *The Essence of Humanism*. He and his wife of forty years, Lorraine, live in Vancouver.

Peter H. Hare taught at the University at Buffalo until his retirement as SUNY distinguished service professor of philosophy. He is author, coauthor, or editor of several books in the history of American philosophy, philosophy of religion, epistemology, and metaphilosophy. For more than thirty years he has coedited *Transactions of the C. S. Peirce Society*.

Erkki Hartikainen, a teacher, introduced the subject "View of Life" (worldview, lifestance) in Finland's schools. He is a past secretary-general and current chair of the Union of Freethinkers of Finland and chair of the Atheist Association of Finland. He is editor-in-chief of the magazine *Vapaa Ajattelija* (Free Thinker).

Van A. Harvey is an emeritus professor of religious studies at Stanford University. After serving in the US Navy during World War II, he earned his PhD at Yale University. Twice a John Simon Guggenheim fellow, he is the author of *A Handbook of Theological Terms*, *The Historian and the Believer*, and the award-winning *Feuerbach and the Interpretation of Religion*. He is a fellow of the Committee for the Scientific Examination of Religion's Jesus Project.

Robert P. Helms is an independent historian, presently writing a book on the early anarchists of Philadelphia. He edited and was the principal author of *Guinea Pig Zero: An Anthology of the Journal for Human Research Subjects* (New Orleans, 2002), has published many articles on anarchism, and edited and annotated the forthcoming translation of anarchist Chaim L. Weinberg's 1930 Yiddish memoirs.

Julie Herrada is curator of the Labadie Collection, part of the Special Collections Library at the University of Michigan, where she has worked since 1994. The Labadie Collection is one of the top research libraries in the world on topics relating to radical social protest. Herrada holds an MLS with a certificate in archival administration from Wayne State University.

Jim Herrick is the former editor of *The Freethinker*, *International Humanist News*, and *The New Humanist*. He is author of *Vision and Realism: A Hundred Years of The Freethinker* (1982), *Against the Faith: Some Deists, Sceptics and Atheists* (1985), and *Humanism: An Introduction* (2003).

Alberto Hidalgo Tuñón, Spanish materialist philosopher, was president of the *Sociedad Asturiana de Filosofía* (1981–2000) and is a laureate of the Interna-

tional Academy of Humanism. Author of over three hundred articles and eleven books, his high school textbook *Symploké* (Jucar, 1987) was censored; in 2003 he was denied a philosophy professorship at La Coruña University by an Opus Dei veto.

Finngeir Hiorth was born in Indonesia. His Norwegian parents were Salvation Army missionaries, but he ceased believing in God at age nineteen. He was lecturer, then senior lecturer, in philosophy at the University of Oslo from 1963 to 1993. His books deal with linguistics, freethought, humanism, atheism, materialism, rationalism, metaphysics, Marxism, and ethics.

Christopher Hitchens is columnist and contributing editor at *Vanity Fair*, visiting professor at the New School for Social Research, and columnist at *Free Inquiry*. His books include *Thomas Jefferson: Author of America* (2005); *Thomas Paine's* Rights of Man: *Books That Changed the World,* and a best-selling critique of religion titled *God Is Not Great: How Religion Poisons Everything* (2007).

R. Joseph Hoffmann is senior vice ppresident for academic affairs at the Center for Inquiry, chair of the Center for Inquiry's Committee for the Scientific Examination of Religion (CSER), and director of CSER's Jesus Project. Prior to that he was Campbell professor and chair of the department of religion at Wells College, New York. He taught at the University of Michigan, Oxford, and the American University of Beirut, and was a Fulbright exchange scholar in Malawi and Zimbabwe. A specialist in the social and intellectual history of early Christianity, he has published, among his other writings, reconstructions of the writings of Celsus (1987), Porphyry (1996), and Julian the Apostate (2004).

Aaron Holland teaches logic and philosophy at Mesa Community College in Mesa, Arizona.

Ted Honderich, Great Britain's outstanding progressive philosopher, was recently interviewed for *CounterPunch* by Paul de Rooij. One of his past books is titled *Punishment, the Supposed Justifications*. Another is the funny and deadly examination of a political tradition, *Conservatism*, and a third is titled *Violence for Equality: Inquiries in Political Philosophy*. His new book is *After the Terror* (Edinburgh University Press, Columbia University Press).

Lawrence Westerby Howe is associate professor of philosophy at the University of West Florida. Aside from numerous publications on Bergson, he has also published papers in environmental ethics, the history of philosophy, and the philosophy of time.

Wesley V. Hromatko holds degrees from the University of Minnesota and Meadville/Lombard. Admitted to the

Unitarian Universalist Ministerial Fellowship, he belongs to the Collegium of the Unitarian Universalist Ministers' Association and the Unitarian Universalist Historical Society (UUHS). His publications include articles and contributions to the UUHS Biographical Dictionary.

Richard T. Hull is professor emeritus of philosophy at the State University of New York at Buffalo. He has held visiting positions at Tarleton State University, Texas State University, and the University of Montana, and he has served on various hospital ethics committees. He has published extensively on issues in bioethics.

Inge Hüsgen studies German and English language and literature. She has worked at the Heinrich-Heine-Insititut, Düsseldorf, and is now editor of the German magazine *Skeptiker*. She has contributed journalistic articles to various papers and magazines.

Innaiah Narisetti is director of the Center for Inquiry, India. He has taught philosophy of science at Osmania University (India) and written books and articles on humanism and child abuse by religions in English and Telugu. An active participant in the humanist movement, he has translated books by Paul Kurtz, M. N. Roy, A. B. Shah, Agehananda Bharati, V. B. Karnik, Shib Narayan Ray, and Ibn Warraq into Telugu.

Susan Jacoby is the author of *Freethinkers: A History of American Secularism* (2004) and seven other books, including *Half-Jew: A Daughter's Search for Her Family's Buried Past* and *Wild Justice: The Evolution of Revenge*. She is a frequent contributor to magazines and newspapers.

S. T. Joshi is the author of *God's Defenders: What They Believe and Why They Are Wrong* (2003) and the editor of *Atheism: A Reader* (2000) and *H. L. Mencken on Religion* (2002). He has also written *The Weird Tale* (1990), *H. P. Lovecraft: A Life* (1996), and other critical and biographical studies.

Jean Kaech joined the Swiss Freethinkers Society (FVS) in 1951. He has held various offices on FVS's local committee, including section president. Since 1969 he has served FVS's national committee, for several years, as copresident. Since 1979 he has served on the board of the World Union of Freethinkers.

Bernard Katz was a contributing editor of *The American Rationalist* from 1982 until 2006. He is author of *A Different Point of View: Debunking Religion*, *The Ways of an Atheist*, and *Superstocks*.

David Kelley is founder and senior fellow of the Objectivist Center and author of many articles and books in theoretical philosophy, social issues, and public policy. His works include *The Art of Reasoning*, a widely used logic textbook, and *The Contested Legacy of Ayn Rand: Truth and Toleration in Objectivism*.

Robert Kirk is emeritus professor of philosophy at the University of Nottingham. He has published widely on topics in the philosophy of mind and the philosophy of language, including the books *Translation Determined* (1986), *Raw Feeling* (1994), *Relativism and Reality* (1999), and *Mind and Body* (2003).

Barry Klassel holds degrees in psychology and theater and has been a Certified Celebrant (Celebrant USA) since 2003. An actor and theater director, he advocates greater prominence for the arts in humanism because the arts explore the full range of human experience and are a springboard for examining dynamic themes of human life.

David Koepsell is executive director of the Council for Secular Humanism. He earned a law degree and a doctorate in philosophy at the State University of New York at Buffalo. His publications include articles in scholarly journals and the books *The Ontology of Cyberspace* and *Searle on the Institutions of Social Reality*, which he coedited with Laurence Moss.

Carol Kolmerten is professor of English at Hood College, Frederick, Maryland, where she has taught for twenty-seven years. Her books include *Women in Utopia: The Ideology of Gender in the American Owenite Communties* (1990) and *The American Life of Ernestine L. Rose* (1999).

Paul Kurtz is professor emeritus of philosophy at the State University of New York at Buffalo, founder and chair of the Committee for Skeptical Inquiry (formerly CSICOP) and the Council for Secular Humanism, and editor-in-chief of *Free Inquiry* magazine. He is author or editor of forty-eight books and eight hundred articles. He is also founder and chair of the Center for Inquiry/Transnational, founder and chair of Prometheus Books, a fellow of the American Association for the Advancement of Science, a past copresident of the International Humanist and Ethical Union, and president of the International Academy of Humanism.

Alan Lacey was born in Birmingham in 1926 and studied at Cambridge from 1946 to 1952. After two years at Manchester, he lectured in London at Bedford College (1954–84) and King's College (1984–91). His main publications are a dictionary of philosophy and books on Bergson and Nozick.

John Lachs is centennial professor of philosophy at Vanderbilt University. He received bachelor's and master's degrees from McGill University, and a PhD from Yale.

His books include *A Community of Individuals* (2003) and *On Santayana* (2005).

Roberto La Ferla, a physical chemist by training, works in basic and applied science research. He served for several years as secretary of the "Giordano Bruno" Italian National Freethought Association and as coeditor of its publications *La Nuova Ragione* and *Libero Pensiero*. He is a member of the executive board of the World Union of Freethinkers (Paris).

Ann J. Lane is professor of history and women and gender studies at the University of Virginia. She has previously taught at Rutgers University, Sarah Lawrence College, and elsewhere. She has written a biography of Charlotte Perkins Gilman and edited and published Gilman's feminist utopian novel *Herland* and *The Charlotte Perkins Gilman Reader.*

Lavanam (Goparaju) is director of the Atheist Centre in Vijayawada, India, which was founded by Gora in 1940. He has participated in the Indian freedom movement, the post-Gandhian movement, and Sarvodaya. He also chairs Samskar, an organization for social and criminal reform. He has traveled as an atheist goodwill ambassador worldwide. Coeditor of the Atheist Centre's English-language monthly *Atheist*, he has published ten books and five hundred articles on atheism, humanism, Gandhism, and social change.

Earl Lee is a librarian at Pittsburg State University (Kansas) and has written for *The Humanist* and *The Truth Seeker*. His books include *Libraries in the Age of Mediocrity* and parodies of the fundamentalist *Left Behind* series, including *Kiss My Left Behind* and *Kiss My Left Behind 2: The Tribulation Farce.*

Michel Le Normand is professor emeritus of botany at the National Higher Agronomic School of Rennes, France. He served for three years as president of the Rennes freethought group *Association Joseph Turmel*. In December 2003, the association organized a memorial colloquium to mark the sixtieth anniversary of Turmel's death. He serves as the chief editor of Turmel's collected works.

Neil Levy is a research fellow at the Centre for Applied Philosophy and Public Ethics, University of Melbourne. He is the author of four books, including *Sartre* (2002) and *What Makes Us Moral* (2004), as well as many articles in all areas of philosophy.

Alison M. Lewis is the humanities/social sciences librarian at Drexel University. Her research interests have focused on the intersection of modernism and mystical beliefs, particularly in the works of D. H. Lawrence and Virginia Woolf.

Terry Liddle writes and lectures on radical history including freethought history. He is secretary of the Freethought History Research Group and a member of the National Secular Society, South Place Ethical Society, and the Thomas Paine Society. He is author of *Deptford's Red Republican*, a biography of the Chartist George Harney.

Georges C. Liénard was born in Brussels, Belgium. A PhD in chemistry, he spent his career doing fundamental research in heterogeneous catalysis. Between 1975 and 1983 he was president of *Centre d'action laïque*, a Belgian humanist umbrella association. Since 2000 he has been general secretary of the European Humanist Federation.

Ronald A. Lindsay is legal director of the Center for Inquiry / Office of Public Policy in Washington, DC. By training both a philosopher and a lawyer, he has published articles on bioethics, the philosophy of religion, and constitutional law in various publications, including the *Kennedy Institute of Ethics Journal*, the *Journal of Law, Medicine, & Ethics*, and *Free Inquiry.*

James C. Livingston is professor emeritus of religion at the College of William and Mary, where he was the founding head of the department of religion. He is the author of nine books and a fellow of the American Council of Learned Societies, the National Endowment for the Humanities, the Woodrow Wilson International Center for Scholars, and Clare Hall, Cambridge University.

Jeannette Lowen, a student of human behavior, worked as a social worker and educator and in retirement discovered the study of philosophy. She has had articles published in *Free Inquiry* and two books critically acclaimed by anthropologist Ashley Montagu. Lowen continues writing and lecturing for a humanistic social psychology.

John M. Lynch is a lecturer at Arizona State University, where he is affiliated with the Center for Biology and Society and the history and philosophy of science program. He currently researches Catholic reactions to evolution and is the editor of the *Dictionary of Evolutionary Thought* (2007).

Sherrie Lyons teaches at Empire State College. She received her PhD at the University of Chicago and is the author of *Thomas Henry Huxley: The Evolution of a Scientist* (1999). Her current research examines three cases of marginal science in the Victorian period to explore issues of scientific marginality and legitimacy.

Tibor R. Machan is the R. C. Hoiles professor of business ethics at Chapman University in Orange, California.

He is research fellow at the Hoover Institution and advises Freedom Communications, Inc., on libertarian issues.

Timothy J. Madigan teaches philosophy at St. John Fisher College and was editorial director of the University of Rochester Press from 1999 to 2004. Since 1987 he has served on the editorial board of *Free Inquiry* magazine; he served as its editor from 1997 to 1999. For many years he has been active in the Bertrand Russell Society.

Lois N. Magner, professor emerita at Purdue University, taught courses in the history of medicine and life sciences. Her publications include *A History of the Life Sciences* (third edition, 2002), *A History of Medicine* (second edition, 2005), and *Doctors, Nurses, and Medical Practitioners: A Bio-Bibliographical Sourcebook* (1997).

Mariapiera Marenzana graduated from the University of Pavia and undertook advanced study in psychology at the Universities of Illinois and California. Now retired, she was for decades a teacher in Italian senior high schools. She has written freelance articles in Italian cultural magazines and coauthored with Andrea Frova the book *Thus Spoke Galileo* (2006).

Kenneth Marsalek is a founding member and past president of the Washington Area Secular Humanists and a former board member of the Council for Secular Humanism. He has written on the humanism of *Star Trek* creator Gene Roddenberry in *Free Inquiry* magazine.

Michael Martin is professor of philosophy emeritus, Boston University, author of *Atheism: A Philosophical Justification, The Case Against Christianity, The Big Domino in the Sky,* and *Atheism, Morality, and Meaning.* He is coeditor with Ricki Monnier of *The Impossibility of God* and editor of the *Cambridge Companion to Atheism.*

James McCollum, the son of Vashti Cromwell McCollum, is retired from a thirty-four-year law practice but currently works as a computer specialist and instructor at Southern Arkansas University. He is active with Americans United for Separation of Church and State and the South West Unitarian Universalist Conference.

Wendy McElroy is the editor of ifeminists.com, a weekly columnist for Fox News, and a research fellow for the Independent Institute in Oakland, California. She is author and editor of many books and articles, including *Liberty for Women: Freedom and Feminism in the 21st Century* (2002).

Mario Mendez-Acosta is a science writer, journalist, and civil engineer. He heads the Mexican Skeptical Research Society. He is a columnist for *Ciencia y Desarrollo*, the journal of the Mexican government science agency, and heads the Journalist's Club of Mexico City. He has authored several books on science and skepticism.

James Moore is a historian of science at the Open University in England. He has taught at Cambridge, Harvard, Notre Dame, and McMaster universities. His books include *The Post-Darwinian Controversies* (1979), *The Darwin Legend* (1994), and with Adrian Desmond the best-selling biography *Darwin* (1991). Moore is working on a biography of Alfred Russel Wallace.

Robert W. Morrell, MBE, is a retired local government officer and founder, in 1963, of the Thomas Paine Society. He has published many articles on freethought history and Paine studies. Editor of the *Journal of Radical History*, he wrote a short biography of former NSS president F. A. Ridley and the only English-language biography of Egyptologist Sir E. A. Wallis Budge.

Mario Murzi is a member of the Italian Philosophical Society and editor of the journal *Notiziario di informatica*. His primary area of research interest is the history and philosophy of science. He has written on Carnap, Hempel, Reichenbach, and logical positivism in the *Internet Encyclopedia of Philosophy* and on Reichenbach in the *MacMillan Encyclopedia of Philosophy*, second edition.

Jo Nabuurs was born in 1936 in the Netherlands. He studied philosophy and history at the University of Leiden and later taught at the Hogeschool of Rotterdam. Since 1999 he has been a research worker at the University of "Humanistiek" and at the Humanist Archive, both in Utrecht.

Joe Nickell is senior research fellow of the Committee for Skeptical Inquiry (formerly CSICOP). A former stage magician, private investigator, and university writing teacher, Nickell is author, coauthor, or editor of more than twenty books, including *Looking for a Miracle* and *Crime Science*. His Web site is www.joe nickell.com.

Kai Nielsen is emeritus professor of philosophy at the University of Calgary and adjunct professor of philosophy at Concordia University, Montreal. He has also taught at Amherst College, New York University, and Ottawa University. He is a member of the Royal Society of Canada. He is author of (among other works) *Ethics without Religion, Philosophy and Atheism,* and *Naturalism without Foundations.*

David C. Noelle is assistant professor of computer science and psychology at Vanderbilt University and an investigator at Vanderbilt's Center for Integrative and Cognitive Neuroscience. His research involves the construction, analysis, and evaluation of computational models of human behavior and brain function, focusing on learning mechanisms.

Robert Nola is professor of philosophy at the University of Auckland. He works in philosophy of science, metaphysics, epistemology, and the sociology of science and science education. He is author of *Rescuing Reason* (2003) and coeditor of *After Popper, Kuhn, and Feyerabend* (2000). His current work concerns the scientific method.

Graham Oppy is associate dean of research in the faculty of arts and heads the School of Philosophy and Bioethics at Monash University, Australia. He has published on a wide range of topics in philosophy of religion, including a monograph on ontological arguments.

T. Peter Park earned his PhD from the University of Virginia, writing as his dissertation *The European Reaction to the Execution of Francisco Ferrer*. A librarian from 1972 to 1997, he is now a freelance researcher and writer. His specialties include Thomas Carlyle's social thought, Estonian history, religion, philosophy, astronomy, and the paranormal.

Frank L. Pasquale received his PhD from Northwestern University. He is a cultural anthropologist engaged in research on the nonreligious in the United States. He has contributed articles on humanism, morality and ethics, and church-state separation to *Free Inquiry* and other publications.

Joanne Passet is an assistant professor of history at Indiana University East and the author of *Sex Radicals and the Quest for Women's Equality*. Her current research explores the life of Jeannette Howard Foster (1895–1981), a freethinking librarian and the author of *Sex Variant Women in Literature*.

Gregory Paul, an independent paleontologist and evolutionary scientist, wrote and illustrated *Dinosaurs of the Air* (Johns Hopkins) and edited the *Scientific American Book of the Dinosaur*. He now conducts sociological research at the junction of religion, science, and society. His study in the online *Journal of Religion and Society*—demonstrating a positive link between secularism and measures of social improvement—received global coverage; Paul was labeled the "public enemy No. 1" of the churches by MSNBC.

Manuel Paz-y-Miño holds two degrees in philosophy from San Marcos National University (Lima, Peru). He has taught in several Peruvian colleges. He has authored six books, including *Does God Not Exist?* In addition he has translated, edited, or published another twenty works for the Peruvian *Journal of Applied Philosophy*'s Publishing House Association.

Jean-Claude Pecker, a humanist and skeptical activist, is professor of theoretical astrophysics at the Collège de France. He is a member of the *Académie des Sciences* (Paris) and a laureate of the International Academy of Humanism. His books and many papers concern astronomy popularization, astrophysics, cosmology, the history of science, human rights, pseudosciences, poetry, and studies in art and literature.

Mark Perakh is professor of physics emeritus at California State University, Fullerton. He has to his credit nearly three hundred scientific publications, a number of patents, and a number of prizes for his research. He has also been active in the anticreationism debate; his recent book is *Unintelligent Design* (2004).

Mark Philp is head of the department of politics and international relations at the University of Oxford and a fellow of Oriel College. He is the general editor of *The Collected Works of William Godwin* and has written widely on political theory and late eighteenth-century history.

Massimo Pigliucci is a professor of evolutionary biology at the State University New York at Stony Brook. He has written several books on evolution and skepticism, including *Denying Evolution* (2002). He has contributed articles to *Free Inquiry*, *Skeptical Inquirer*, and *Philosophy Now* and publishes a popular monthly e-column, "Rationally Speaking."

Lois Porter cofounded the Washington Area Secular Humanists (WASH) in 1989. She served as its president for four years and was for more than a decade the assistant editor of its newsletter, *WASHline*. She has contributed articles to *Free Inquiry*, *WASHline*, and to two WASH publications.

Alan R. Pratt is professor of humanities at Embry-Riddle Aeronautical University. He is author of articles on nihilism and culture, compiler of the nihilistic collection *The Dark Side: Thoughts on the Futility of Life*, and editor of *Black Humor: Critical Essays* and *The Critical Response to Andy Warhol*.

John Valdimir Price is the author of several works on David Hume, the Scottish Enlightenment, and other aspects of eighteenth-century life and literature. Formerly a senior lecturer and research fellow at the University of Edinburgh, he is now retired and works as an independent scholar and antiquarian bookseller.

Robert M. Price lives with his wife and daughters in North Carolina. He holds PhD degrees in Systematic Theology (1981) and New Testament (1993) from Drew University. He is author of *Deconstructing Jesus* and *The Incredible Shrinking Son of Man* and editor of the *Journal of Higher Criticism*. He is a fellow of the Committee for the Scientific Examination of Religion's Jesus Project.

Jesús Puertas Fuertes taught philosophy in Spain. His academic background included history, philosophy, and computer science. He was a lecturer and author of articles on humanist and skeptical topics. He coedited of *Racionalismo y Evolucionismo* (1998).

Benjamin Radford is managing editor of the science magazine *Skeptical Inquirer* and director of publications at the Center for Inquiry/Transnational. He has written on topics including urban legends, mass hysteria, mysterious creatures, and media criticism. He is the author or coauthor of two books on related topics.

Gino Raymond is a professor of French studies at the University of Bristol in the UK. His research focuses on the emanations of France's political culture in all its aspects, from literary production to the language of contemporary politics. His books include *France during the Socialist Years* (1994), *André Malraux: Politics and the Temptation of Myth* (1995), and *Structures of Power in Modern France* (1999).

Katharine M. Rogers, professor emerita of English, City University of New York, is the author of *L. Frank Baum: Creator of Oz* (2002) and editor of *Policeman Bluejay*. She discusses traditional Christian churches' callousness toward animal welfare in her *Cat and the Human Imagination* (1998) and *First Friend: A History of Dogs and People* (2005).

Born in Spa, Belgium, **Jacques G. Ruelland** emigrated to Canada in 1969. He completed three MA degrees in philosophy, history, and museology, becoming a PhD in the history of sciences. He currently teaches in the department of history at the University of Montreal. He has authored more than twenty-five books.

Herbert K. Russell is a former college English teacher and director emeritus of John A. Logan College's public relations unit. Previous publications on Edgar Lee Masters include entries in the *Dictionary of Literary Biography* and *Dictionary of Midwestern Literature*. Russell's *Edgar Lee Masters: A Biography* was published by the University of Illinois Press in 2001.

Susan Sackett is president of the Humanist Society of Greater Phoenix and a humanist celebrant. She was for seventeen years executive assistant to *Star Trek* creator Gene Roddenberry, and cowrote several episodes of the TV series *Star Trek: The Next Generation*. Her eleven books include the memoir *Inside Trek*.

William J. Scheick holds the J. R. Millikan centennial professorship at the University of Texas at Austin. His books include *The Splintering Frame: The Later Fiction of H. G. Wells* (1984), *Fictional Structure and Ethics: The Turn-of-the-Century English Novel* (1990), and *The Ethos of Romance at the Turn of the Century* (1994).

John R. Shook is director of the Naturalism Research Project at the Center for Inquiry/Transnational. Formerly associate professor of philosophy and director of the Pragmatism Archive at Oklahoma State University, he authored *Dewey's Empirical Theory of Knowledge and Reality*, edited *Pragmatic Naturalism and Realism*, coedited the *Blackwell Companion to Pragmatism*, and edited the *Dictionary of Modern American Philosophers*.

Vladimir Shtinov is a freelance scholar who holds a doctorate in philosophy from Moscow State University. His interests include the history of philosophy and social and political thought. He has published a number of articles in scholarly publications both in Russia and in the United States.

Gary Sloan holds a PhD in American literature from Texas Tech University. In 1999 he retired from Louisiana Tech University, where he was George Anding professor of English. In retirement he has written for such magazines as *Free Inquiry*, *Skeptic*, *Skeptical Inquirer*, *The Humanist*, *American Atheist*, and *The Freethinker*.

J. J. C. Smart is an emeritus professor of Adelaide and Australian National universities. At present he is an honorary research fellow of Monash University. He is an honorary fellow of Corpus Christi College, Oxford. His main interests have been in metaphysics (including philosophy of mind), philosophy of science, and ethics.

Barbara Smoker was born into a devout Roman Catholic family in London, England. She converted to atheism by reading and thinking. From 1971 to 1996 she was the "hands-on" president of Britain's National Secular Society. Publications include a school textbook, *Humanism* (1973), with three updated editions.

Stefan Lorenz Sorgner teaches philosophy and applied ethics at Friedrich-Schiller University, Jena, Germany. He is author of *Metaphysics without Truth* (Munich: Utz, 1999) and coeditor of (with Oliver Fuerbeth) *Musik in der deutschen Philosophie* (Stuttgart: Metzler, 2003), (with Nikolaus Knoepffler and Dagmar Schipanski) *Humanbiotechnologie als gesellschaftliche Heraus-*

forderung (Freiburg: Alber, tbp), and (with H. James Birx and Nikolaus Knoepffler) *Eugenik und die Zukunft* (Freiburg: Alber, tbp).

Barbara Stanosz retired as professor of philosophy from Warsaw University, Poland. She is the founder and the first editor-in-chief of the journal *Bez Dogmatu* (Without Dogma).

David Ramsay Steele grew up in Birmingham, England. He holds a BA in sociology and a PhD from the University of Hull. He wrote *From Marx to Mises* (1992) and coauthored (with Michael Edelstein) *Three Minute Therapy* (1997). He is editorial director of Open Court Publishing Company, Chicago.

Vic Stenger is emeritus professor of physics at the University of Hawaii and adjunct professor of philosophy at the University of Colorado. He has published six books that interface between physics and cosmology and philosophy, religion, and pseudoscience, most recently *God: The Failed Hypothesis* (2007).

Walter Stephens is the Charles S. Singleton professor of Italian studies at Johns Hopkins University. His books include *Demon Lovers: Witchcraft, Sex, and the Crisis of Belief* (Chicago, 2002) and *Giants in Those Days: Folklore, Ancient History, and Nationalism* (Nebraska, 1989). He has written extensively on Renaissance literature.

Barbara Stocker grew up without heavy indoctrination into religion and began to doubt the efficacy of prayer when forced to pray in public schools. She was business manager for *American Rationalist* and the longtime editor of *Secular Subjects*, the newsletter of the Rationalist Society of St. Louis, Missouri.

Harry Stopes-Roe studied physics at Imperial College London but switched to philosophy at Cambridge University, receiving his PhD. While a lecturer in science studies at Birmingham University, he decided that science fatally undermined religion and its morality, and his main attention turned to the problems of making sense of life on naturalistic foundations—that is, humanism.

William Sweet is professor of philosophy at St. Francis Xavier University (Canada). The author of *Idealism and Rights* (1997; 2005), he has published several collections of scholarly essays, including *Philosophy, Culture, and Pluralism* (2002), *Philosophical Theory and the Universal Declaration of Human Rights* (2003), and other works.

Robert B. Talisse is assistant professor of philosophy at Vanderbilt University. His research is focused on contemporary political philosophy. Much of his work draws upon the classical pragmatists, especially the epistemology of Charles Peirce. His most recent book is *Democracy after Liberalism* (2004). He is also the coeditor of *Aristotle's Politics Today* (2007).

Robert B. Tapp is dean of the Humanist Institute and professor emeritus of humanities, religious studies, and South Asian studies at the University of Minnesota. He is an executive board member of the Committee for the Scientific Examination of Religion, author of *Religion among the Unitarian Universalists: Converts in the Stepfathers' House*, and editor of *Multiculturalism* and *Ecohumanism*.

Ann Thomson, professor at Paris 8 University, is a specialist on intellectual history and has published widely on eighteenth-century materialism and irreligious thought. Works include *Materialism and Society in the Mid-Eighteenth Century: La Mettrie's "Discours préliminaire"* (1981) and *La Mettrie, Machine Man, and Other Texts* (1996).

Rob A. P. Tielman is a sociologist, a laureate of the International Academy of Humanism, and emeritus professor in humanism at the University of Utrecht (Netherlands). He was president of the Dutch Humanist League and the International Humanist and Ethical Union, and is president of the Dutch Pluralist Schools Network and the Dutch Humanist Archives. He was knighted by the Queen of the Netherlands in 1987.

Michael Tooley, formerly professor of philosophy at the University of Western Australia and senior research fellow at the Australian National University, is professor of philosophy at the University of Colorado at Boulder. His books include *Abortion and Infanticide* (1983), *Causation* (1987), and *Time, Tense, and Causation* (1997).

Miguel A. De La Torre is associate professor of social ethics at Iliff School of Theology and director of Iliff's Justice and Peace Institute. He has published nine books over the past six years, three of which exclusively deal with Cuban religiosity: *The Quest for the Cuban Christ*, *La Lucha for Cuba*, and *Santería*.

David Tribe is a polymath author, journalist, lecturer, broadcaster, poet, and artist. He has served as president of the National Secular Society, chair of Humanist Group Action, and editor of *The Freethinker* (all UK). An honorary associate of the Rationalist Press Association, he now resides in Australia.

Gopi Upreti is director of the Center for Inquiry/Nepal and founding president of the Humanist Association of Nepal (HUMAN). A professor at Tribhuvan University, Nepal, he teaches ecological agriculture and horticulture at the Institute of Agriculture and Animal Sciences and is a founder of the Nepal Institute of Health Sciences (NIHS) at Purbanchal University.

Vijayam (Goparaju) is executive director of the Atheist Centre in Vijayawada, India, which was founded by Gora in 1940. He is a lecturer in political science at Andhra University and director of research at the Gandhi Peace Foundation, New Delhi. He is the author of five books and four hundred articles on atheism, humanism, science, environment, and social change and editor of the Atheist Centre's English-language monthly *Atheist*.

Sally Roesch Wagner, executive director of the Matilda Joslyn Gage Foundation, is one of the first women to receive a doctorate for work in women's studies and a founder of one of the country's first women's studies programs. The author of numerous books and articles, she appeared in Ken Burns's documentary *Not for Ourselves Alone: The Story of Elizabeth Cady Stanton and Susan B. Anthony*.

G. A. Wells is emeritus professor of German at the University of London, where he taught German language, literature, and philosophy for forty-two years until his retirement in 1991. He holds degrees in these subjects and in natural sciences. His books include works on German thinkers and on the origin of language, as well as on Christian origins.

Ruth Whelan is the professor of French and head of the department of French at the National University of Ireland, Maynooth, and a member of the Royal Irish Academy. She is the author of *The Anatomy of Superstition: A Study of the Historical Theory and Practice of Pierre Bayle* (1989) and related works and one of the editors of the *Encyclopedia of the Enlightenment* (2003, 4 vols.).

David White has been active in philosophy for over forty years. A past president and present vice president of the New York State Philosophical Association, he has completed his editing of the works of Bishop Butler for the University of Rochester Press. For many years he has been active in the Bertrand Russell Society.

Fred Whitehead, who with Verle Muhrer edited *Freethought on the American Frontier* (1992), retired in 2000 from the administrative staff of the University of Kansas School of Medicine. For several decades he has collected scarce materials on American cultural history, especially concerning labor, radicalism, and intellectual controversy, and he has published extensively on these subjects. He is the editor of *Freethought History*.

Rabbi Sherwin T. Wine is the founder of Humanistic Judaism and its flagship congregation, the Birmingham Temple, which he established in 1963. He also established the Society for Humanistic Judaism and helped to create the International Federation of Secular Humanistic Jews. He is author of *Humanistic Judaism, Judaism beyond God*, and other books.

Kwasi Wiredu is distinguished professor of philosophy at the University of South Florida, Tampa. He was born in Ghana and studied philosophy at the University of Ghana and at Oxford. He taught philosophy in Ghana for twenty-three years. His publications have focused on the philosophy of logic, epistemology, and African philosophy.

Frieder Otto Wolf taught philosophy since 1966 at Saarbrücken, Coimbra, and Berlin universities. Active in politics, he was a Member of the European Parliament from 1994 to 1999. He is vice president of the German humanist organisation *Humanistischer Verband Deutschland* and president of the Humanist Academy of Berlin.

Paul Woodruff teaches philosophy and classics at the University of Texas at Austin. He has published translations of work by Thucydides, Sophocles, Euripides, and Plato, while pursuing his interest in the Greek enlightenment of the fifth century BCE.

Martin D. Yaffe is professor of philosophy and religion studies at the University of North Texas. He is author of *Shylock and the Jewish Question* (1997), cotranslator of Thomas Aquinas's *Literal Exposition on the Book of Job* (1989), editor of *Judaism and Environmental Ethics: A Reader* (2001), and translator of Spinoza's *Theologico-Political Treatise* (2004).

Matt Young is senior lecturer in physics, Colorado School of Mines, and former physicist with the National Institute of Standards and Technology. He is author of *No Sense of Obligation: Science and Religion in an Impersonal Universe* (2001) and coeditor of *Why Intelligent Design Fails: A Scientific Critique of the New Creationism* (2004).

ACKNOWLEDGMENTS

As should be obvious, I owe an incalculable debt to the late Gordon Stein for conceiving the original *Encyclopedia of Unbelief*, and for organizing and editing this work's precursor so expertly. I gratefully acknowledge also the leadership and support of Paul Kurtz, who played a seminal role in creating Stein's original encyclopedia and whose idea the *New Encyclopedia* was.

I am obliged to the Council for Secular Humanism and the Center for Inquiry, where my career has unfolded since 1989. In my work I have enjoyed the immense privilege of meeting and networking with unbelieving academics, activists, pundits, social critics, and other leaders of thought worldwide. This experience made it possible to bring together such diverse and illustrious individuals—first as members of the Editorial Advisory Board, and then, of course, as contributors.

I appreciate the work of the members of the Editorial Advisory Board, whose prized input helped to shape the present work, especially insofar as its structure departs from that of the 1985 *Encyclopedia*.

I am grateful to Tim Binga, Gordon Stein's successor as director of the Center for Inquiry Libraries, who provided outstanding reference support throughout the compilation process and who put obscure freethought tomes at my disposal whenever I needed them. Kevin Christopher provided custom entry management software. I am equally appreciative of my "serial contributors," each of whom shouldered the burden of authoring numerous entries:

Norm R. Allen Jr.	Jim Herrick
Hector Avalos	Finngeir Hiorth
Joseph Barnhart	Paul Kurtz
Timothy Binga	Timothy J. Madigan
Vern L. Bullough	Robert M. Price
Bill Cooke	Robert Tapp
Annie Laurie Gaylor	David Tribe
Robert Helms	Fred Whitehead
Julie Herrada	

Special thanks to Gwen Brewer for ably proofreading the many entries by her late husband, Vern Bullough. Of course I owe a debt to all of the *New Encyclopedia*'s contributors. It is worth noting that each was solicited as a volunteer. In contrast to more mainstream reference works that can offer token (and sometimes not-so-token) payments for each article, the *New Encyclopedia* approached its authors with nothing more than the promise of intellectual gratification and a complimentary copy of the work. So the *New Encyclopedia* should be recognized as a labor of love on the part of a great number of people.

I am beholden to Steven L. Mitchell and Jonathan Kurtz of Prometheus Books for their support of the project and their forbearance with the numerous delays that seem endemic in an undertaking of this scope, and to Meg French, my indefatigable editor.

Finally, I gratefully acknowledge the work of my successive editorial assistants, who expertly discharged a daunting variety of tasks during the *New Encyclopedia*'s long gestation. Ranjit Sandhu provided administrative support for the creation of the Editorial Advisory Board, the topic selection process, and the first rounds of contributor invitations. Matt Cravatta assumed this role thereafter, and I cannot say enough about his dogged and precise work in maintaining relations with the numerous contributors, answering information requests, keeping track of completed and delinquent entries, and most of all his determination and willingness to innovate when peculiar problems leapt for our throats in the shadow of deadlines. Well done!

FOREWORD

RICHARD DAWKINS

The term *unbelief* sounds negative. One might ask, "How can you have an encyclopedia of anything defined as an absence?" There are encyclopedias of music, but who would buy an encyclopedia of tone deafness? I have seen and enjoyed an encyclopedia of food, but never an encyclopedia of hunger.

The first thing wrong with these comparisons is that both music and food have positive associations. Tone deafness is an absence of something valued. So is hunger. Among the many things this encyclopedia demonstrates is that religious unbelievers are not similarly deprived. For many—and I shall return to this—unbelief serves as a liberating gateway to a more fulfilled life.

The second thing that might give us pause about unbelief is that there exists an all but infinite number of things in which we don't believe, but we don't go out of our way to say so. I am an unbeliever in fairies, unicorns, werewolves, Elvis on Mars, spoon bending by mental energy, the Easter Bunny, green kangaroos on Uranus . . . the list could be expanded trivially and without end. We don't bother to declare ourselves unbelievers in all the millions of things that nobody else believes in. It is only worth bothering to declare unbelief if there is a default assumption that we all must believe in some particular hypothesis unless we positively state the contrary.[1] Manifestly, and in spades, that is the common assumption over the hypothesis of divine intelligence.

Divine intelligence is not the only thing that is both widely believed and widely doubted. The word *skeptic* rather than *unbeliever* is commonly applied to those who doubt the widespread claims of astrology, homeopathy, telepathy, water divining, clairvoyance, alien sexual abduction, and communication from beyond the grave. Skeptics in this sense do not necessarily deny the validity of these claims; instead, they demand evidence and sometimes go out of their way to set up the rather stringent conditions—much more stringent than supporters usually realize—that proper evidence requires. Supporters of homeopathic medicine or dowsing, for example, seldom understand the need for statistically analyzed, double-blind controlled experiments to guard against chance effects, placebo effects, and the unwitting suggestibility of the believing mind. It is a matter of convention that *skeptic* has come to be associated with those matters, while the superficially synonymous *unbeliever* implies *religious* unbelief. The two kinds of skepticism/unbelief often go together, but you can get into trouble if you simply assume that they do.

There is further ambiguity over whether "unbelief" signifies positive disbelief or a mere lack of belief. The dictionary definition allows either. In the original 1985 *Encyclopedia of Unbelief*, its editor, Gordon Stein, interpreted *unbelief* to mean a definite belief that deities (from now on, for brevity, I shall use *God* to stand for supernatural deities in general) do *not* exist. Others could easily mean something more agnostic. Within agnosticism there are those who feel that, because we can neither prove nor disprove the existence of God, existence and nonexistence are therefore completely undecidable hypotheses, on an exactly equal footing with each other and having equal probability. Then, of those agnostics who forswear such "equal probability" impartiality, there is a spectrum of those who lean one way or the other. The following five representative propositions span the spectrum:

1. **Strong Theist.** In the words of C. G. Jung, "I do not believe, I *know.*"
2. **Agnostic, Leaning toward Theism.** I cannot know for certain, but I think the existence of God is highly probable.
3. **Truly Impartial Agnostic.** It is impossible to prove or disprove the existence of God. This is often illogically taken to imply that his existence and his nonexistence constitute equally probable hypotheses.

4. **Agnostic, Leaning toward Atheism.** It is impossible to disprove God, but he is just as improbable as fairies or unicorns.
5. **Strong Atheist.** I know there is no God, with the same conviction as Jung "knows" there is one.

I suspect that most contributors to this encyclopedia, including me, would place themselves somewhere around 4 or 4.5 in the spectrum, while most thinking churchgoers would not stray far beyond position 2 or 1.5 at the other end. Positions 1 and 5 are too strong for most reasonable people. This really is a spectrum, by the way. A research questionnaire to measure religious belief could sensibly invite participants to place themselves along a continuously scalar graph, with these five positions serving as guideposts.

Religious belief itself is subject to ambiguity and misunderstanding. Here is another spectrum of statements, all of which might be claimed as "religious" by those who utter them.

1. **Strong Theism.** God is a personal being whose exact nature is specified in my holy book (as opposed to yours!): an intelligence who created the universe, who can see into your mind, who cares about your vices and virtues, and who will punish or reward you for all eternity after you die.
2. **Deism.** God is some kind of supernatural intelligence who laid down the laws of physics and started the universe off, but then stood back and intervened no more in its subsequent development and evolution.
3. **Einsteinian "Religion."** God does not exist as a personal intelligence at all, but the word may be used as a poetic metaphor for the deep laws of the universe that we don't yet understand.

Once again the spectrum is continuously distributed, and people who call themselves religious might be invited to locate themselves using a pencil mark on a graphical axis with my three propositions as guide posts. My own position would be 3, except that I deplore the use of the word *God* itself in the Einsteinian sense (or in the sense of Stephen Hawking's "For then we should know the mind of God") because I think it has actively confused many people. I prefer to limit the word "religious" to 1 and 2. Einstein called himself religious, but if Einstein was religious it is hard to imagine who is not: no sensible person denies that there are deep laws and principles underlying the universe.

An American student asked her professor whether he had a view about me. "Sure," he replied. "He's positive science is incompatible with religion, but he waxes ecstatic about nature and the universe. To me, that is religion!" But is *religion* the right word to use? Words are our servants, not our masters, but there are many people out there, passionate believers in supernatural religion, who are only too eager to misunderstand.

There is a tactical, political point to be made here. Maybe Einsteinian "religion" provides a useful way for atheists to euphemize their way into American society and lessen the grip of fundamentalist theocracy. In the twenty years since the original *Encyclopedia of Unbelief* was published, the expected decline in religiosity has continued apace in western Europe, but the reverse has happened in North America and the Islamic world. The hapless European sometimes feels cornered in a nightmarish pincer movement between Islamic and Christian jihadists in holy alliance. The United States is now suffering an epidemic of religiosity that seems almost medieval in its intensity and positively sinister in its political ascendancy (See DEMOGRAPHICS OF UNBELIEF). At various times in history it has been impossible for a woman, a Jew, a homosexual, a Roman Catholic, or an African American to gain high political office. Today this negative privilege is pretty much restricted to atheists and criminals. The actress Julia Sweeney, in her beautiful theatrical monologue "Letting Go of God," recounts with black humor her parents' response to her own gentle atheism.

My first call from my mother was more of a scream. "Atheist? ATHEIST?!?!"

My dad called and said, "You have betrayed your family, your school, your city."
It was like I had sold secrets to the Russians. They both said they weren't going to talk to me anymore. My dad said, "I don't even want you to come to my funeral." After I hung up, I thought, "Just try and stop me."

I think that my parents had been mildly disappointed when I'd said I didn't believe in God anymore, but being an *atheist* was another thing altogether.

Well, that's just one woman's parents. But the mischief reaches all the way to the top. On a now notorious occasion in 1987, the following dialogue is alleged to have taken place between George Herbert Walker Bush and Robert Sherman, one of the reporters at a news conference held by the then–vice president and soon to be successful presidential candidate:

Sherman: What will you do to win the votes of the Americans who are atheists?

Bush: I guess I'm pretty weak in the atheist community. Faith in God is important to me.

Sherman: Surely you recognize the equal citizenship and patriotism of Americans who are atheists?

Bush: No, I don't know that atheists should be considered as citizens, nor should they be considered patriots. This is one nation under God.

Sherman (somewhat taken aback): Do you support as a sound constitutional principle the separation of state and church?

Bush: Yes, I support the separation of church and state. I'm just not very high on atheists.

The tone in which Bush uttered these disgracefully bigoted words—just try substituting the word *Jew* for *atheist* in the above dialogue—is not recorded. I imagine it as condescendingly jocular, which makes it even more deplorable. Again, try the experimental *Jew* substitution, and see whether a humorous tone makes it sound any better. It doesn't.

Disgraceful as it may be, it is indicative of the standing of atheism in modern America. One can argue that the problem lies in the ludicrously demonized word *atheist* itself. Julia Sweeney's parents made this more or less explicit. If Robert Sherman had quoted Einstein and asked Bush his attitude to those Americans who do not believe in a personal God but harbor a deep reverence and awe for the majestically deep mysteries of the universe, he would have received a far more sympathetic and civilized answer. Yet if you look at the detail of what Einstein said, notwithstanding his God-encumbered language he was just as much of an atheist as, say, Bertrand Russell or Robert Green Ingersoll or any typical Fellow of the Royal Society or the National Academy of Sciences. Einsteinian euphemisms have probably enabled more than one intelligent, thinking person to achieve election to high office.

Some see this as a tactical argument for ditching the word *atheist* altogether, and calling ourselves *Brights*, analogous with the way homosexuals positively rebranded themselves as *gays*.[2] Various more or less attractive attempts are made to turn Einstein-style pantheism into organized quasi religions with names like Religious Naturalism[3] or World Pantheism;[4] and perhaps this, or Universism,[5] is the politically expedient way to go. Others prefer to tough it out and call a spade a spade, while making consciousness-raising efforts to rehabilitate the word *atheist* itself.

Maybe "politically expedient" is too cynical. Carl Sagan's ringing declaration in *Pale Blue Dot* can be read as positively inspiring:

How is it that hardly any major religion has looked at science and concluded, "This is better than we thought!" "The Universe is much bigger than our prophets said, grander, more subtle, more elegant"? Instead they say, "No, no, no! My god is a little god, and I want him to stay that way." A religion, old or new, that stressed the magnificence of the Universe as revealed by modern science might be able to draw forth reserves of reverence and awe hardly tapped by the conventional faiths. Sooner or later, such a religion will emerge.

Back to liberation: we experience liberation only by comparison with captivity. Nobody today feels liberated by unbelief in Thor's hammer or Zeus's thunderbolts, though our ancestors might have done so. Today, huge numbers of people are brought up to treat belief in—depending on an accident of birth—Christianity, Islam, Judaism, or Hinduism as an expected norm, departure from which is a grievous and onerous decision (to put it no more strongly: the official Islamic penalty for apostasy is death). Women, in many parts of the world, have additional reasons to regard the end of religion as a liberation (see WOMEN AND UNBELIEF).

I frequently receive letters from readers of my books, thanking me for liberating them from the bondage of religion. I'll quote just one example, renaming the author Jerry because—reasonably enough, given Julia Sweeney's experience—he is deeply worried lest his parents discover his newly gained unbelief. Jerry's youthful indoctrination as an evangelical Christian was depressingly successful. He recounts how, in his last year at school,

> the headmaster chose a small group of brighter boys to study philosophy with him. He probably regretted selecting me, as I made it perfectly clear during class debates that there really was no need for such discussions—the answer to all life's problems was simple, and it was Jesus.

Jerry's liberation had to wait until his postgraduate years:

> My postgraduate studies, however, opened my mind to a world of ideas I barely knew existed. I met highly intelligent fellow students who had applied their rationality to all aspects of their lives, and come to the conclusion that there was no God. And, amazingly, they were happy, they enjoyed life, they didn't feel the "God-shaped hole" that I had warned people about so often [Jerry had done a stint as a missionary, financed by well-meaning donations from his home church]. . . .
>
> For the first time in my life, I was willing to be challenged. "Bliss was it in that dawn to be alive." I craved more intellectual meat . . . and so I spent the summer of 1998 devouring book upon book.

Among the books he devoured were two of mine, which explains his writing to me. He went on to expound his reaction to these and other books:

> The dawning realization that I could safely jettison my increasingly tenuous faith, and that a world without God wouldn't be the joyless hell I had always imagined it would be, was overwhelming. I felt liberated. All the benefits of Christianity that I had promoted—that faith brings you freedom, meaning, purpose, joy etc.—I now discovered for real, but on the wrong side!

How are we liberated when we forsake religion? Let me count the ways! Morally we are freed—to a greater or lesser extent, depending on the religion—from an ominous burden of guilt and fear. The awful notion of private "sin" is never far from the minds of the pious, and we cannot but feel joyous release when we shake it off and replace it by the open good sense of moral philosophic reasoning. In place of private "sin," we choose to behave in such a way as to avoid causing suffering to others and increase their happiness.

Practically we are freed, depending on the details of the particular faith in which we were raised, from the fatuity and inconvenience of time-wasting rituals: freed from the necessity to pray five times a day; freed from the duty to confess our "sins" to a priest; freed from having to buy two refrigerators, lest meat and milk should meet; freed from enforced laziness on Saturdays to the point of being unable to move a light switch or lift a telephone; freed from having to wear uncomfortable and unbecoming clothes lest a flash of forbidden skin should be exposed; freed from the obligation to mutilate children too young to defend themselves.

Intellectually, we are freed to pursue evidence and scholarship wherever it might lead, without constantly looking over our spiritual shoulder to check whether we are straying from the party line. "Party line" is right, even when it is not dictated by living priests, elders, or ayatollahs, but fossilized in a book (actually a motley collection of arbitrarily stitched-together fragments whose anonymous authors were writing in different times and to different audiences, reflecting different local and long-dead issues).

Personally, we are freed to direct our lives toward a worthwhile fulfillment, in the full knowledge and understanding that this is the one life we shall ever have. We are freed to exult in the privilege—the extraordinary good fortune—that we, each individual one of us, enjoy through the astronomically improbable accident of being born. The measure of the privilege you and I enjoy through existing is the number of possible people divided by the number of actual people. That ratio—too large for decent computation—should be the measure of our gratitude for life and our resolve to live it to the full. Well might the newly liberated unbeliever quote Wordsworth and his blissful dawn.

NOTES

1. When a young woman of my acquaintance was admitted to hospital, a nurse came round to fill in her personal details form. To the nurse's question "Religion?" my friend answered, "None." Later she overheard a pair of nurses gossiping about her: "She doesn't *look* like a nun!" Isn't it bizarre that such official forms always ask our religion, and assume that we have one? Why not note down our political persuasion, our taste in music, or our favorite color?

2. The Brights Web site, http://www.the-brights.net.

3. Coined by Ursula Goodenough.

4. Pantheism: The World Pantheist Movement, http://www.pantheism.net.

5. Universist Movement, http://universist.org.

INTRODUCTION

AGAINST THE SEDUCTIONS OF MISBELIEF

Tom Flynn

The volume before you is the successor to *The Encyclopedia of Unbelief*, which was edited by Gordon Stein and published by Prometheus Books in 1985. The original *Encyclopedia* was something that had never before existed: a comprehensive reference to unbelief in religion.[1] Stein was his generation's foremost historian, bibliographer, and literary collector in atheism, agnosticism, freethought, and related domains. He was the perfect choice to edit the original *Encyclopedia*, which enjoyed the success it richly deserved and immediately became the field's standard reference.

SO, WHY A *NEW ENCYCLOPEDIA*?

There are several reasons why I believe this volume was not just important, but necessary:

First, the twenty-two years since the original work appeared have seen more than their share of history unfold. On the world stage, the fall of Communism utterly reshaped the context in which religious unbelief is understood. The United States, too, has seen significant developments, from the grisly death of raucous atheist activist Madalyn Murray O'Hair[2] to the rise of a vigorous, academically respected secular humanist movement.[3]

Second, there have been multiple reorientations as regards the role of religion in society worldwide. Once again, there was the fall of Communism. With the collapse of regimes committed to dialectical materialism and the near-disappearance of Marxist academics, Western atheists and humanists found themselves more nearly alone on the barricades of unbelief than they had been in more than a century. Meanwhile, western Europe was freed from the intellectual and physical threat entailed in its immediate proximity to the Soviet empire. It responded by becoming openly post-Christian; the United States moved in the opposite direction, and is now the only first world society that displays third world levels of religiosity.[4] Strong growth in public piety, brazen reentanglement of religion and government, and heightened acceptance for strident religious expression in public venues came to dominate the American scene after 1990. Yet during the same period, the number of Americans who told pollsters and social scientists that they reject any formal religious affiliation more than doubled. While all of this was taking place, radical Islam greatly expanded its influence, becoming a focus of social turmoil not only in the Middle East but across Indonesia, the Indian subcontinent, Africa, and Europe, even as it furnished the worldwide background for the so-called war on terrorism. During the same years, Christianity, Hinduism, Judaism, and Islam all began to exhibit a disturbing trend: In areas where religious practice *was* expanding, the type of religious practice that expanded most rapidly tended to be socially and doctrinally conservative and theologically literalistic. Often such expansion occurred at the expense of more historically and scientifically sophisticated, theologically moderate outlooks. It was as though in all four traditions, great ages of liberal secularism were drawing to a simultaneous close. In the United States Christian fundamentalists and evangelicals shouldered aside "mainline" Protestant denominations and sharply marginalized religious liberalism. In India an aggressively nationalistic Hindu fundamentalism threatened to supplant progressive, secularizing viewpoints prevalent since the days of Nehru.[5] Across the Jewish Diaspora, Orthodoxy—which had not long before seemed poised for extinction—regained robust vigor; in Israel Orthodoxy and ultra-Orthodoxy attained a position from which they often oppressed more liberal forms of Judaic practice. In the Muslim world secularizers in the mold of Kemal Atatürk were reviled by fundamentalists and in some countries dared not raise their heads.[6] If the religious environment has changed so radically, then irreligion too deserves fresh scrutiny.

The third and final reason to compile a new encyclopedia is less high-flown: there were just some things about the 1985 *Encyclopedia* that I (or members of the Editorial Advisory Board) wished to approach differently. Compared to its precursor, the current work relies less heavily on survey articles. There are more biographical entries. A greater effort has been made to place unbelief—in particular, nineteenth-century freethought—into a richer context vis-à-vis its companion radical reform movements, including anarchism, socialism, labor reform, feminism and woman suffrage, sex radicalism, and even Spiritualism.[7] Care was also taken to present a balanced portrait of twentieth-century American unbelief, including the unsavory digressions some activists made into eugenics, racism, and fiscal opportunism.[8]

Over the years since the original *Encyclopedia*'s release, some parts of it aged better than others. Stein included as appendices directories of unbelieving groups and publications; these became obsolete too quickly in an otherwise enduring work. For that reason, and because directory-style information is now so easily obtained from the Internet, tables of groups and publications have been omitted from the *New Encyclopedia*. Another appendix to the 1985 work combined a bibliography of unbelief and a directory of publishers. In view of the pending release of Bruce Cathey's mammoth worldwide bibliography of unbelief, whose scope far exceeds anything that could have been attempted here, the present work contains no bibliographic appendix.

WHY "UNBELIEF"?

The word strikes some as clumsy and negative. Why call this volume—or its predecessor— an encyclopedia of *unbelief*? It is a question I heard often, and one that Stein anticipated in his introduction to the 1985 work:

> In the English language about the closest synonym for *unbelief*, as it is being used here, is *heterodoxy*. That word, in turn, can be said to mean "not holding orthodox beliefs or traditional opinions"—on religious matters, in our context. . . . This is the history of heresy, blasphemy, rejection of belief, atheism, agnosticism, humanism, and rationalism. In many respects, it is also the history of the intellectual progress of the human race.[9]

In a movement with a rich, sometimes contentious sectarian history, *unbelief* is one of the few labels no major faction ever claimed. For that reason one hopes it can be equally inclusive toward atheists and agnostics, deists and freethinkers, religious humanists and secular humanists, Ethical Culturists and infidels. *Unbelief* covers the conceptual floor they all share, heedless of disputes between reductive materialists and rational mystics, deaf to the arguments between moral nihilists and secular humanists who claim objective validity for their ethical moral codes. Despite their differences, they all share a foundational disbelief in any religious system or supernatural domain. They're all unbelievers, and the *New Encyclopedia* is for—and about—them.

POLICIES

A few notes are in order concerning the policies that shaped the *New Encyclopedia*'s structure, compilation, and editing.

As a rule, articles do not cite online sources. This decision was made because of the work's long anticipated shelf life relative to the ephemerality of Internet addresses.

In order to qualify for a discrete, named biographical entry, individuals must be deceased. Individuals who died after November 2005 could not be included. In order to qualify for a discrete, named subject entry, organizations and institutions must be defunct, or must have operated continually for more than fifty years as of November 2005. This is intended to prevent the accumulation of evanescent directory-style information about current groups and institutions. Individuals and organizations denied coverage in freestanding entries may of course be discussed in other entries, and may be located using the index.

Certain issues regarding unbelief are controversial among unbelievers. On several such matters the *New Encyclopedia* unabashedly reflects a "house stance," though contributed articles expressing divergent positions have been welcomed. For example, the *New Encyclopedia* accepts the definitions of the words *atheism* and *agnosticism* defended by Stein in the 1985 work and elsewhere.[10] It interprets *a-theism* in accord with its Greek roots: the absence of belief in a supernatural being. On this view, in order to be an atheist one need not deny the existence of God; it is enough to be without belief that God (or, by extension, a supernatural order) exists. This position has interesting implications. For one, it rejects the popular view of atheism and agnosticism as adjacent points along a single continuum of religious belief and disbelief. This is the notion that underlies flippant accusations that atheists are just agnostics who have grown too sure of themselves, or that agnostics are atheists who don't trust their own judgment. In contrast, this work views atheism and agnosticism as independent qualities. Atheism pertains to the belief or disbelief that a god or a supernatural order exists: a question of fact. In contrast, agnosticism pertains to whether we can have *reliable knowledge* that a god or supernatural order exists: what philosophers call a question of epistemology. From this it follows that a person can be simultaneously an atheist and an agnostic without contradiction. The *New Encyclopedia*'s view is not shared by all the authorities, or even by all of its contributors. Some explicitly characterize atheism and agnosticism as adjacent points on the same continuum, or hold that to be an atheist one must actively deny the existence of a god. Where a distinguished contributor holds such a view, compliance to the "house line" is not demanded—only internal consistency and integrity of argument.

Other "house stances" include:

1. Secular humanism is in no sense a religion.
2. Religion, properly understood, necessarily entails supernaturalism. This rejects Paul Tillich's identification of religion with any "ultimate concern," under which even such things as a passion for fly fishing might be spoken of as one's religion. Similarly rejected is John Dewey's attempt to endow the words *religion* and *religious* with independent meanings, such that any deeply felt commitment might be termed "religious." The *New Encyclopedia* relies on a definition of religion that I offered in 1996: Religion is "a life stance that includes at minimum a belief in the existence and fundamental importance of a realm transcending that of ordinary experience."[11]
3. Science and religion can genuinely stand in conflict. This rejects Stephen Jay Gould's view that, properly understood, religion and science occupy "non-overlapping magisteria" whose agendas never collide. On the contrary, in the *New Encyclopedia*'s view, religion and science offer competing, mutually exclusive accounts in many areas, including cosmology, the origins of life, and even certain moral conundrums.[12]
4. So-called religious humanism merits coverage in this work—even though to the degree that it *is* religious as defined above, it is not a form of unbelief.[13] One reason for this inclusion is historical. From deism to Unitarianism, Universalism, and Ethical Culture, among others, movements that fell short of full "unbelief" have played key roles in countering orthodoxy and in opening social spaces wherein religious doubt could openly be expressed. The second reason to include religious humanism is that many of the contemporary movements and personal commitments that accept the religious humanist label in fact carry no supernatural content. Think of a Unitarian Universalist humanist who has no belief in a cosmic designer, an immortal human soul, or the efficacy of prayer; much as he or she might self-describe as a "religious humanist," such a person simply *isn't* in any rigorous sense religious.[14] A label that includes that word might bring comfort or improve one's perceived standing in others' eyes, but it is a misnomer. For both of these reasons the *New Encyclopedia* includes substantial coverage of religious humanism, undeterred by the handful of its contemporary expressions that truly are religious in the rigorous sense embraced here. These include forms of humanist practice that consider a glorious future for the human species guaranteed (not knowable through purely natural means); that effectively elevate humanity to godlike status (rare); that endorse paranormal claims including divination, astrology, extrasensory perception, and traditional

healing; or that impute independent agency or quasi-supernatural powers to such abstractions such human love, élan vital, or the march of history. Historical examples of genuinely "religious" humanisms would include Comtean positivism and pre-Soviet Marxism. Naming contemporary examples here would be needlessly provocative.

The reader who peruses multiple *New Encyclopedia* entries and comes away with the impression that issues of this character are being treated inconsistently will often be correct, but this divergence reflects actual diversity of opinion on these subjects among unbelievers—and contributors. *Caveat lector.*

WHY DOES A *NEW ENCYCLOPEDIA OF UNBELIEF* MATTER?

In my personal opinion, it matters because unbelief itself matters—admittedly a contentious stance. Many Americans might disagree, noting that religiosity seems so pervasive and is rapidly expanding throughout public life. Some Europeans might disagree also, noting that religiosity has shriveled and now seems socially irrelevant. The very fact that unbelief seems unimportant for opposing reasons—and that merely within the confines of Western culture—should give us pause before we consign unbelief to history's bulging dustbin. It is true that many of unbelief's most prestigious recent advocates—labor reformers, political revolutionaries, and academic Marxists—have largely melted away. It is true, and already noted here, that atheists, agnostics, secular humanists, old-line freethinkers, and anticlericals stand increasingly alone on the barricades of radical reform. Despite these historical developments, the fundamental stance that all unbelievers share, the conviction that the everyday world of matter, energy, and their interactions is either *all that exists* or *all that matters*, has an inescapable significance.

We can grasp this significance by considering how important it would be if unbelievers' naturalistic worldview were definitely proven wrong—say, by some demonstration that one of the conventional theistic worldviews was inarguably true. Imagine for the sake of argument that the core contentions of Christianity were somehow proven correct beyond any possibility of question. If the universe really is intentionally designed, and the designer knows and cares for us—if each of us truly hosts an immortal soul that will know an eternity of ecstasy or pain determined by our behavior during an eyeblink sojourn on earth—if this and the rest of the Christian worldview is true, then *the knowledge that this is true* is the most important item of knowledge any human being could possess. No scientific discovery, no mathematical theorem, no artistic expression, no secret to success, no avowal of love could ever be as significant as the knowledge that gave us *accurately* the key to eternity.

But now imagine (as unbelievers hold to be the case) that *no* conventional theistic worldview is true—but that millions of people still order their lives, allocate their resources, and make decisions as though some form of theism *were* true. Knowing this is terribly important, too, if for a different reason. To believing readers, I propose a thought experiment. Suppose for a moment that unbelievers *are* correct. Suppose that each human being is nothing more than an accidental and temporary convergence of pattern . . . that nothing is eternal . . . that the only values we can hold authentically are the ones we create and embrace for ourselves. Suppose most of all that *this life is the only one that any of us will ever have.* If those things are true, then the most important item of knowledge any religious believer could ever possess is the knowledge that his or her faith is groundless. Denied that knowledge, ardent believers—perhaps we should think of them as *mis*believers—will go on squandering the precious hours and days of their only lives pursuing otherworldly rewards that will—that *can*—never be theirs. In addition to making empty investments in ineffectual prayer and ritual, misbelievers may forsake harmless pleasures (think Mormons and coffee) or even disdain highly beneficial practices (think Christian Scientists and medical care, or Muslims and commercial credit). Recall again that the fastest-growing pieties tend to be literalistic and retrograde, and to grow at the expense of liberal strands within the same faith community. Mere decades ago, religious liberalism held out the promise that it might tame religious conviction, making of it something with which naturalists could effortlessly coexist. Sadly, religious liberalism no longer commands much momentum; in almost every religious community the momentum lies much further to the right. The odds are greater today than at any time in nearly a century that a randomly chosen believer will be a literalist, if not an outright fundamentalist, within whatever tradition he or she inhabits. If false beliefs are so likely to be taken so seriously by so many, then we cannot avoid this harrowing conclusion: if unbelief is true, countless misbelievers are stunting their only lives in tragic and eventually irremediable ways. Consider the deep-felt pain of men and women who have thought their way from piety to atheism, but achieved this only in their old age—there is no reclaiming a lifetime dissipated in service to a god who never was. That is one reason why unbelief matters very much.

Or consider this: Across our world, billions embrace one religion or another. Tens of billions of person-hours, hundreds of billions of dollars, are devoted to affairs of faith. How much might the human prospect have been improved had this energy and these resources been even partially redirected down the centuries toward improving the human prospect in *this* world? What technological innovations do we live without today, what medical breakthroughs remain undiscovered, what dazzling philosophical and artistic ideas remain unconceived? (Keep in mind that I'm not even talking about the way some faiths engender hostility toward scientific discovery or the social application of its products—for now I'm focused solely on the diversion of resources.) If unbelievers are right and no religion is true, why wait another moment before striving to deflect so much human passion and wealth into channels at whose end some *real* benefit can result?

Finally, consider how much we might learn about the human brain and "human nature" by studying the cognitive mechanisms through which religions exert their extraordinary power.[15] What is it that endows religious ideas—all of them, on this view, untrue—with a compelling psychological resonance so far exceeding that wielded by any of the other sorts of untruths and wild surmises that human beings have seen fit to make up over the ages? Why does religion tug at us (at least, some of us) so urgently? Equally important, why does religion leave some individuals cold? Why does the size of the apparently "faith-resistant" population vary so widely between cultures? (Think of the United States, with its relatively modest unbelieving population, compared to western Europe or Japan, where strong faith is quite exceptional.) From my vantage at the dawn of the twenty-first century, it is difficult to imagine more important questions for the social sciences to examine.[16]

Believers may find these suggestions shocking—which merely underscores the significance of the gulf between the ways believers and unbelievers look at the world. Most (though not all) believers see human nature as a duality of body and spirit; they see their brains not as what they *are* but as things they *have*. They see the universe as planned and purposive, as something understood in its totality by a force that is essentially benign.[17] Many see morality as definite, inflexible, and ordained. Most view reality as eternal and attach primary significance to the countless eons that they expect will come after our earthly sojourn. While unbelievers are far from homogeneous, most would disagree with this cluster of views. Most unbelievers see human nature as monistic; consciousness is simply what goes on in our brains as viewed from the inside, and, yes, Virginia, we *are* our brains. Many reject any idea of "spirit" or immaterial causation; everything *is* physics. Most unbelievers see the universe as unplanned, as purposeless, as something that has never been understood in toto and probably never will be, unless one day human beings (or other intelligences of equally natural origin) rise to meet that challenge. Far from benign, unbelievers see the universe as coldly neutral—or they may discern, as Bertrand Russell did, a mute hostility in the relentless, uncaring order of the cosmos. On morality, opinion is diverse. Some unbelievers feel that morality must be utterly flexible and relative. Some argue that without God all things are possible, so we should launch ourselves headlong into every possible alternative, run every experiment, test every option, break every barrier. Others conclude that we can discern the outlines of an objective moral code that best serves the welfare of human communities because it is best fitted to the way humans think and interact. What almost all unbelievers agree on is that no part of morality has been ordained, there being no entity in a position to do the ordaining. As for cosmology, unbelievers generally draw their cosmic outlooks from science, which says that our universe had a distinct beginning and predicts it will one day end. On the best available evidence, eternity is not in the cards. This brings us to what is perhaps the most fundamental difference between believers and unbelievers: whereas most traditional religious believers claim to attach primary importance to eternity, unbelievers necessarily attach primary—indeed, sole—importance to *this* life. Hence the sick anguish so many of us feel as we watch our believing fellow citizens throw away vast chunks of their only lives—lives whose very solitary and precioius finitude their faiths render them impotent to grasp.

Believers often have enormous difficulty "getting their heads around" the way unbelievers see the world—so much so that in countries as generally devout as the United States, it may seem convenient to deny that unbelievers actually exist in anything more than token numbers. By contrast, unbelievers seem to have less difficulty internalizing the believer's mind-set, perhaps because so many unbelievers were once believers themselves; in their lives they've seen both sides (I number myself in this group). Yet in reality, unbelievers exist in great numbers. Even in the pious United States, unbelievers form one of the largest identifiable minority groups. Around the world, despite the fall of "official" atheism in the Communist bloc, unbelief in all its forms continues to gain ground. No religion—not even Islam in its militant youth—has enjoyed sustained growth on the scope that unbelief has experienced since the turn of the twentieth century.[18]

Unbelief, I conclude, matters very much. Its contentions, its implications, and its history merit study. Its findings deserve respect and broader advocacy. If I have succeeded in my work as editor of this *New Encyclopedia of Unbelief*, I hope that it has done some small justice to the importance of its subject. Perhaps it will be a portal through which at least some believers can better come to understand how unbelievers see the universe. And perhaps it will aid in liberating a few more human beings from the seductions of misbelief.

NOTES

1. The most comprehensive prior works were Samuel Porter Putnam, *Four Hundred Years of Freethought* (New York: Truth Seeker Company, 1894); and George E Macdonald, *Fifty Years of Freethought*, 2 vols (New York: Truth Seeker Company, 1929). Both are widely cited by *New Encyclopedia* contributors writing on nineteenth- and early twentieth-century freethought, but they are limited by their focus on freethought, a significant "sect" within unbelief, but still only one sect.

2. See O'HAIR, MADALYN MURRAY; UNITED STATES, UNBELIEF IN THE.

3. See SECULAR HUMANISM.

4. For this and all demographic claims made in this introduction, see DEMOGRAPHY OF UNBELIEF.

5. See INDIA, UNBELIEF IN.

6. See ISLAM, UNBELIEF WITHIN.

7. See ANARCHISM AND UNBELIEF; BIRTH CONTROL AND UNBELIEF; LABOR AND UNBELIEF; SEX RADICALISM AND UNBELIEF; SOCIALISM AND UNBELIEF; SPIRITUALISM AND UNBELIEF; WOMAN SUFFERAGE MOVEMENT AND UNBELIEF.

8. See AMERICAN ASSOCIATION FOR THE ADVANCEMENT OF ATHEISM; JOHNSON, JAMES HERVEY; SMITH, CHARLES LEE; TELLER, WOOLSEY; *TRUTH SEEKER, THE*; O'HAIR, MADALYN MURRAY.

9. Gordon Stein, introduction to *The Encyclopedia of Unbelief*, ed. Gordon Stein (Amherst, NY: Prometheus Books, 1985).

10. See particularly Gordon Stein, "Atheism," in *The Encyclopedia of Unbelief*.

11. Tom Flynn, "Why Is Religious Humanism?" *Free Inquiry* (Fall 1996). See also Flynn, "Watching Our Language," a sidebar to "A Secular Humanist Definition: Setting the Record Straight," *Free Inquiry* (Fall 2002). See also RELIGION.

12. See DARWINISM; EVOLUTION AND UNBELIEF; REGLION IN CONFLICT WITH SCIENCE; DRAPER, JOHN WILLIAM; WHITE, ANDREW DICKSON.

13. See RELIGIOUS HUMANISM; ETHICAL CULTURE; JUDAISM, UNBELIEF WITHIN; UNITARIANISM TO 1961; UNIVERSALISM TO 1961; UNITARIAN UNIVERSALISM; SOUTH PLACE ETHICAL SOCIETY; AMERICAN HUMANISM ASSOCIATION.

14. In many US Unitarian Universalist churches, naturalistic humanism—powerful since the early twentieth century—has been or is being supplanted by neo-paganism, Wicca, generic "spirituality," and in some congregations a resurgent Christianity.

15. See COGNITIVE SCIENCE AND UNBELIEF.

16. In this connection the entry UNBELIEF, EMPIRICAL, NEGLECT OF IN THE BEHAVIORAL AND SOCIAL SCIENCES is most provocative.

17. See EXISTENCE OF GOD, ARGUMENTS FOR AND AGAINST.

18. Once again the reader is directed to DEMOGRAPHY OF UNBELIEF.

ABBOT, FRANCIS ELLINGWOOD (1836–1903), American secularist and philosopher. A dissident Unitarian minister, Abbot argued for a scientific theism that he felt would strip away the superstitious hull and leave the spiritual kernel, a rational deity at home in a Darwinian world.

Early Life. Francis Ellingwood was born in Boston on November 6 to Joseph Hale, a schoolmaster, and Fanny Ellingwood Abbot. He attended Boston Latin School, graduated from Harvard University in 1859, and received a ministerial certificate in 1863 from Meadville Theological School in Pennsylvania. He married Katharine Fearing Loring in 1859; the difficult birth of a daughter in 1872 left her an invalid. Abbot's controversial dismissal in 1868 from a Dover, New Hampshire, pulpit for heterodox views—a decision sustained by the state supreme court—made him sensitive to the collusion of church and state.

Reform Career. Abbot's iconoclastic thought led inevitably to a break with Unitarianism, which he indicted as creed-bound. In 1867 he joined with other dissenters to found the Free Religious Association, an organization dedicated to creating a universal "Religion of Humanity." On January 1, 1870, he published the first issue of his anticlerical newspaper, the *Index*, in Toledo, Ohio (see PERIODICALS OF UNBELIEF). Relocating to Boston in 1873, Abbot issued "The Nine Demands of Secularism," the principles that guided the formation of the NATIONAL LIBERAL LEAGUE in Philadelphia on July 4, 1876. That pioneering freethought organization was dedicated to First Amendment guarantees of free speech and complete separation of church and state. Abbot, however, withdrew from the organization after its heated 1878 convention in Syracuse, over the league's blanket condemnation of the repressive Comstock Act (1873; see COMSTOCK, ANTHONY, AND UNBELIEF) and support of sexual reformers. An opponent of what was termed "free-love" (see FREE-LOVE MOVEMENT AND UNBELIEF), he created a rival organization, the National Liberal League of America (later the American Liberal Union). In 1881 he received a doctorate in philosophy from Harvard, where a decade later Josiah Royce sharply criticized his radical religious thoughts. On the tenth anniversary of his wife's death (October 23) and on the completion of a major manuscript (*The Syllogistic Philosophy*), he committed suicide by poison on her grave.

BIBLIOGRAPHY

Ahlstrom, Sydney E., and Robert Bruce Mullin. *The Scientific Theist: A Life of Francis Ellingwood Abbot.* Macon, GA: Mercer University Press, 1987.

Goodheart, Lawrence B. "The Ambiguity of Individualism: The National Liberal League's Challenge to the Comstock Law." In *American Chameleon: Individualism in Trans-National Context*, edited by Richard O. Curry and Lawrence B. Goodheart. Kent, OH: Kent State University Press, 1991.

LAWRENCE B. GOODHEART

ADAMS, ROBERT CHAMBLET (1839–1892), Canadian freethinker. Robert C. Adams was born in Boston, Massachusetts, to a family that espoused fundamentalist Christian values common in that area at that time. His father was a preacher and Robert was a Sunday school teacher for a short time. Upon leaving school at age fourteen, he went to sea. For the next fifteen years, he rose from cabin boy to captain, traveled twice around the world, and visited many different countries. It was during this period that his religious beliefs came into direct conflict with his life experiences, and he began to have doubts about much of what he had been taught as a boy. Among other influences, he also read *The Age of Reason* by Thomas PAINE. A book about that part of his life is titled *On Board the Rocket*.

Around 1870 he settled in Montréal, Québec, Canada, where he became involved in several speculative developments, mining phosphate and mica in Ontario and silver and gold in British Columbia. Among other appointments, he was president of the Geological Mining Association of Québec and a director of the Sailor's Institute in Montréal. He married Mary Emily Job, who came from Liverpool, England. Politically he was a liberal, favoring free trade and Canadian reciprocity with (and even annexation to) the United States. During his time in Montréal, he consolidated his disbelief in religion. His SKEPTICISM stemmed primarily from the divergence he observed between what believers say and what they do. He became the president of the Montréal Pioneer FREETHOUGHT Club and was involved with the Montréal Secular Union.

He gave several public lectures, some of which were published, notably one titled "Evolution" (see EVOLUTION AND UNBELIEF) in 1883, in which he dealt with natural selection, and one titled "RATIONALISM" in 1884, in which he asserted that "[m]orality is independent of religion" and that "[t]he only cause is nature's laws." He also questioned the contribution of most believers to society, observing that such people seem to be opposed to almost everything except their own parochial views. But perhaps the best source of information about this freethinker is his autobiography titled *Travels in Faith: Tradition to Reason.* In it, he said, "Anyone who wishes to keep faith should not travel or read secular books." Another title, *Good without God*, was published posthumously by Peter Eckler of New York in 1902. After a relatively short but productive life, he died in Sedgewick, Maine.

BIBLIOGRAPHY

Adams, Robert. *Evolution*. New York: G. P. Putnam & Son, 1883.

———. *Good without God*. New York: Peter Eckler, 1902.

———. *Lectures in Rationalism*. New York: Truth Seeker Company, 1889.

———. *Travels in Faith—Tradition to Reason.* New York: G. P. Putnam & Son, 1884

GLENN HARDIE

ADDAMS, JANE (1860–1935), American social reformer. Cowinner of the Nobel Peace Prize in 1931 (with Nicholas Murray Butler), Jane Addams is best remembered for her association with Hull House, one of the first social "settlements" in the United States. Born in Cedarville, Illinois, Addams graduated from Rockford College in Rockford, Illinois, in 1881. She then entered Woman's Medical College in Philadelphia but had to leave because of ill health. After her recovery, she traveled extensively in Europe, and in London visited the Toynbee Hall "settlement." Impressed with its program, on her return she joined with Ellen Gates Starr to found Hull House in 1889 in the old Hull Mansion in Chicago. Originally conceived as a community center for the neighborhood poor, with many social reformers as residents, Hull House increasingly became a center for all kinds of reform. It became a model for other such settlements across the United States. Among other things a social activist, Addams was a leader in the woman suffrage movement (see WOMAN SUGGRAGE MOVEMENT AND UNBELIEF) and an active pacifist. She was chairman of the International Congress of Women at The Hague in the Netherlands in 1915, out of which arose the Women's International League for Peace and Freedom, of which she was the first president. She was the first woman president of the National Conference of Social Work (1910) and took an active part in the Progressive Party presidential campaign in 1912 with Theodore Roosevelt. She campaigned for social justice for immigrants, for Negroes, for labor, and agitated for the establishment of juvenile courts, tenement house regulation, and for the rights of women and children in every setting. In 1916 Addams urged aspiring publisher Emanuel Julius, about to marry her niece, Marcet Haldeman, to flout social convention by hyphenating his name with his wife's maiden name placed first; as Emanuel HALDEMAN-JULIUS he achieved fame as a pioneering FREETHOUGHT publisher.

Freethinking chronicler Joseph MCCABE said Addams was reticent about expressing her religious views, careful not to alienate her religious supporters; yet her nephew J. W. Linn wrote in his 1935 biography of Addams that she never departed from the RATIONALISM that her father taught her, and that she joined the Congregational Church out of duty, as one might join a labor union. She also attended All Souls Unitarian Church in Chicago, a center of the emerging humanist movement (see HUMANISM) and was briefly an interim lecturer at the ETHICAL CULTURE Society in Chicago. Her funeral by her own specifications was nonsectarian.

She wrote two autobiographies, *Twenty Years at Hull House* (1910) and *The Second Twenty Years at Hull House* (1930). There is a vast collection of articles and books about her.

BIBLIOGRAPHY

Farrell, John C. *Beloved Lady: A History of Jane Addams.* Baltimore, MD: Johns Hopkins University Press, 1967.
Linn, James W. *Jane Addams: A Biography.* New York: Appleton Century, 1935.
Tims, Margaret. *Jane Addams of Hull House.* London: Allen & Unwin, 1961.

VERN L. BULLOUGH

ADLER, FELIX (1851–1933), German religious reformer. Felix Adler was the creator of ETHICAL CULTURE, a nontheistic religious movement that had its roots in the Jewish world. His early career coincided with the period of time when FREETHOUGHT and SECULARISM found wide support in intellectual circles and among some of the masses. His work was also contemporary with the rise of liberal Protestantism at the end of the nineteenth century. The new mainstream Protestant message ignored salvation and the afterlife and substituted the "social Gospel," with its emphasis on morality and social justice, as the heart of the Christian religion.

The end of the nineteenth century was also the time when emancipated German Jews in North America embraced radical Reform. This Jewish religious radicalism tossed most of traditional Jewish ritual into the dustbin of history and proclaimed morality the heart of religion. It also rejected Jewish ethnicity and parochialism and defined Judaism as a universal faith (see JUDAISM, UNBELIEF WITHIN). Having rejected traditional culture, the radical rabbis chose the music and lecture formats of the new liberal Protestantism.

Felix was born in Germany in 1851. His father, Samuel Adler, was a rabbi who joined the radical reformers. Since Germany after 1848 was not a comfortable place for political or religious radicals, Samuel immigrated to America, where he became the powerful leader of the Temple Beth El in New York, which later merged with the prestigious Temple Emmanuel. Educated in both the Columbia Grammar School and Columbia College, Felix was sent to the University of Berlin. Slated for the Reform rabbinate, Felix was also enrolled in the newly organized seminary for the training of liberal rabbis, the *Hochschule fur die Wissenschaft des Judentums*. This school was created by Abraham Geiger, Germany's most famous Reform pioneer. At the seminary Felix was confronted with the two dilemmas of Reform Judaism: If religion is essentially ethics, what difference does it make whether you think of yourself as religious or not, as long as you are ethical? And if Judaism is essentially universalistic, what is the point of preserving a particularistic Jewish identity?

Adler studied in a German intellectual environment

dominated by the ideas of the German philosopher Immanuel KANT. Kant had demonstrated that reason could not prove either the existence or the nonexistence of God. Only an absolute ethics could be reasonably demonstrated to be real. These affirmations of Kant would serve as a foundation of Adler's own philosophy of life. This worldly religion calling for social justice was to become the passion of the young Felix.

When Adler returned to New York he was invited to preach at Temple Emmanuel on October 11, 1873. His debut in the Reform pulpit was not a great success. He had moved beyond Judaism into the realm of a theological agnosticism. It appeared that the world of organized religion was not for him. With the help of the Jewish banker Joseph Seligman he was hired in 1874 by Andrew Dickson WHITE, the president of the newly formed Cornell University, to be a nonresident professor of Hebrew and Oriental literature.

But an influential group of German Reform Jews led by Julius Rosenbaum was inspired by Adler's message. They wanted to follow him into a new philosophical and religious adventure that would resolve the dilemmas of Reform Judaism and would break down the denominational barriers that prevented liberal people from uniting under the banner of ethics. Adler was persuaded to lecture about this possibility on May 15, 1876. Shortly after this talk the New York Society for Ethical Culture was founded. Most of its members were German Reform Jews. The movement that would emerge from this organization would be dominated by Jews for many decades. Some Jews thought of Ethical Culture as an extension of Judaism. But there was nothing about the official ideology that revealed any Jewish connection. Adler himself viewed Jewish identity as purely religious. Like most of his German Jewish contemporaries in America, Adler maintained that Jewish identity was only a matter of belief. To affirm Ethical Culture was to cease to be Jewish.

The name "Ethical Culture" was awkward in English. In German *Ethische Kultur* was a more felicitous phrase. But the puzzling name was irrelevant. Adler had found the path that would arouse his strongest passions, utilize his best talents, and provide him with the pleasures of fame and recognition. For the next fifty years Adler was on a fast train of achievement. He pioneered a new kind of religion, a religion without God. He became the leader of the Free Religion movement. He established the New York Society for Ethical Culture as a major voice for liberal ideas and social justice on the East Coast. He mobilized thousands of people for social action in the New York area. He created new schools for ethical education, which turned into his most lasting achievements. He taught ethics and philosophy to thousands of students at Columbia University (from 1902). He helped to create sister societies to the New York congregation in Chicago, Philadelphia, and St. Louis—even in Vienna.

He wrote many books that influenced the worlds of religious ideas and education. There were *Creed and Deed* (1877), *The Moral Instruction of Children* (1892), *Prayer and Worship* (1894), *An Ethical Philosophy of Life* (1918), and *Reconstruction of the Spiritual Ideal* (1924). All of them emphasized the following basic ideas: (1) Ethics is the heart of religion; (2) religion does not need God; (3) action is more important than belief; and (4) the human mind and its ethical aspirations are part of a spiritual reality that transcends the material world. Adler was close to HUMANISM and secularism. But he was not wholly comfortable with them.

Adler was not comfortable with MARXISM because it was too materialistic. He was not happy with Freudianism (see FREUD, SIGMUND) because it demeaned human motivation. He was not tolerant of conventional freethinking because it was too aggressively atheistic. There was at times something prudish, ethereal, and dogmatic about him as he hovered between the old world of religion and the new world of science and freedom.

Adler's death in 1933 was ironic. It was the year that Adolf Hitler came to power. The new anti-Semitism was to disrupt Ethical Culture and to inhibit its growth. Hitler restored Jewish ethnicity to the center of the Jewish world. The old universalism faded away. The Jewish population that had offered its allegiance and support to Adler's endeavors was now recruited to other enterprises. The old optimism yielded to fear and parochialism. Christian Unitarianism (see UNITARIAN UNIVERSALISM) was to pick up his message of ethics without God. Two decades later, Ethical Culture, the movement Adler founded, openly embraced ethical humanism.

SHERWIN WINE

AFRICA, UNBELIEF IN. Exaggerated notions of African religiosity are standard in African studies. Yet it is not clear in what sense the concept of religion applies to any aspect of African culture. There is, certainly, among the *generality* of traditional African peoples a belief in a supreme being. But it is arguable that this being is not conceived of as a creator ex nihilo, but rather as a divine architect of the *order* (as distinct from what, in some alien conceptual frameworks, might be called the sheer *existence*) of the world. Moreover, there is generally no such thing as an institution of God worship or an eschatology of eternal reward and punishment. Nor, connected with this, is there a priesthood entrusted with the moral and metaphysical guidance of its flock. Metaphysical enlightenment is left to native aptitude and wise conversation, while moral education is for the home. If belief in a supreme being in such institutional vacuum constitutes a religion, then it does so in a very minimal sense.

Even more important for our purposes here is the fact

that there were and still are religious skeptics in African traditional society. The African belief in the supreme being or God in the specified sense is one entertained by the generality of Africans, but not by all of them. Skeptics have been known in traditional culture. In the indigenous language of the present writer, Akan, they are called *akyinyegyefo*, literally, "those who question things or are given to disputing." They are not skeptics in the Western classical sense of doubting the very possibility of knowledge, but they are skeptics in the sense that they are apt to subject generally received beliefs to rigorous ratiocinative scrutiny, rejecting those that fail to hold up (see Skepticism). Belief in God was one such object of scrutiny. So also was the belief in the continued existence of the ancestors and kindred spirits, of whom more below.

One knows the existence of such skeptics by direct personal experience. They live, move, and have their discourses in traditional society without let or hindrance, illustrating a milieu of free thought and expression that in the West was attained only with blood and tears. Until the late Kenyan philosopher Odera Oruka's *Sage Philosophy: Indigenous Thinkers and Modern Debate on African Philosophy* (1990), evidence for the claim that there are traditional skeptics was largely anecdotal. But in that book Oruka provided direct quotes from such thinkers in print. Here are some examples. They come from indigenous thinkers in Kenya that Oruka sought out and interviewed at length. One of them, Oruka Rang'inya, expresses himself as follows about God: "It is quite wrong to personalize him. He is an idea, the idea which represents goodness itself. God is thus a useful concept from a practical point of view." (This is Oruka's translation of taped remarks by Rang'inya.) This sage, as Oruka called him and others he interviewed, had no Western-style education, and it is just as unlikely that he borrowed this view from John Dewey's notion of God as "the unity of all ideal ends arousing us to desire and action," which was expounded in his *A Common Faith* (1934), as that Dewey borrowed the concept from him.

Another of Oruka's sages, Simiyu Chaungo, remarks: "I think that God, in fact, is the Sun. . . . Well, the doings of the Sun are big. It heats the land all day, and its absence cools the land all night. It dries things: plants use it to grow. Surely, it must be the God we talk about."

For his part, Stephen M'Mukindia Kithanje explains, "When I try to have an idea of God, he appears to me as a mixture of heat and cold. When these two merge (fuse) there comes up life. . . . The act of fusion, which brings forth life, is what we call God. And that is what we mean when we say that God created the universe."

More straightforwardly atheistic is Njeru wa Kinyenje. In his opinion, Christianity is the white man's witchcraft. He comments, "This witchcraft has triumphed over the traditional African witchcraft. Today I recognize its *victory*, but not its *truth*. I do not pray to

God nor do I consult witch doctors. Both religion and witchcraft . . . have no truth in them. My greatest wish is that I should be spared interference from religion and witchcraft."

The early practice in the study of African thought was to identify African philosophy with African folk philosophy. Because of this, the existence of the class of thinkers mentioned above was rarely noted. These thinkers were aware of the folk or communal thought of their societies. They knew, for example, that the folk cosmology is generally theistic, but in regard to their own thinking they had no qualms in following wherever the argument led, whether into theistic or atheistic waters.

It was noted above that African folk theism tends not to involve the notion of a creator ex nihilo. One reason, possibly the principal one, for this is that the concept of *existence* in at least many African languages includes a spatial contextualization. For example, in Akan, to exist is to *wo ho* (be there, at some place). According to the Rwandan philosopher and linguist Alexis Kagame, the peoples of the Bantu zone, who by his estimate occupy about one third of the African continent, render the concept of existence in an intriguingly similar manner. To exist is to *liho* or *baho*, to be there, at that place. The *ho*, exactly as in Akan, functions as an adverb of place. This spatial conception of existence has widespread reverberations in African metaphysical thinking. To take the question of creation out of nothing: If to exist is to be at some place, then *nothingness* will be a relative concept. "Nothing" can only mean the circumstance of there not being any item, as defined by a given universe of discourse, at some point of space. In that case *something* is logically prior to *nothing*, and the transcendental notion of creation out of nothing falls by the wayside. Incidentally, cognizant of this conceptual situation, an Akan metaphysician, certainly the present one, cannot be browbeaten in this matter with any faith-based (mis)interpretations of Big Bang cosmology.

The spatial conception of existence just commented upon is, in general, connected with a feature of African thought that might be called in broad terms empirical. As used here that word is only a characterization of the conceptual framework of African thought; what it means is that this framework of thought does not accommodate concepts that are not derivable from experience. It is easy to see that in this way of thinking the basic illusion of design can only yield a divine architect. But the empirical orientation could, conceivably, facilitate the avoidance of such a hypothesis too. And this happens, according to Okot p' Bitek, in the thought of the Central Luo in parts of Uganda and Kenya. There is, he says, no concept of a supreme being among them. In their language a question like "Who created the world?" is unintelligible. Despite this, in Christian missionary discourse a concept of God as creator of the universe was ascribed to the Luo, complete with the Luo name *Rubanga*. Okot p' Bitek in his classic *African Religions in Western Scholarship* (1970) explains how this happened:

In 1911 Italian Catholic priests put before a group of Acholi elders the question "Who created you?" and because the Luo Language does not have an independent concept of create or creation, the question was rendered to mean "Who moulded you?" But this was still meaningless, because human beings are born of their mothers. The elders told the visitors they did not know. But we are told that this reply was unsatisfactory, and the missionaries insisted that a satisfactory answer must be given. One of the elders remembered that, although a person may be born normally, when he is afflicted with tuberculosis of the spine, then he loses his normal figure, he gets "moulded." So he said "Rubanga is the one who moulds people." This is the name of the hostile spirit which the Acholi [a Luo people] believe causes the hunch or hump on the back. And instead of exorcising those hostile spirits, the representatives of Jesus Christ began to preach that *Rubanga* was the Holy Father who created the Acholi.

This may be amusing, but it is also instructive; it illustrates the superimposition during the colonial period of alien concepts on African thought structures, damn all the incongruities. *Religion* may be one such alien concept. Although, as noted above, African cultures generally feature a belief in some kind of supreme being, so that Luo a-theism is something of an exception, a foreign superimposition is responsible for an overloading of the concept of *African religions*. Christian missionaries described African religions as consisting mainly in the worship of a great assortment of spirits apart from God. These included the ancestors, lesser deities, and other, less glorious beings. And this has become among scholars a popular way of looking at African religions.

In fact, however, it is doubtful whether there is a word *or paraphrase* for either "religion" or "worship" in any indigenous African language. More decisively, the spirits in question are taken to be as much a part of the world *order* as human beings, for example. They are regarded in many cases as beings and powers that can be exploited to the advantage of humans if they know how. Evidently, the technique includes the use of flattery and offerings of all kinds. The procedures involved have been called *rituals* in the study of African religions. But the religious connotation of the word is open to question. These procedures are purely utilitarian. If the expected utility consistently fails to materialize, these alleged gods can be condemned to death. This certainly is how, as a rule, the African perceives the matter. The notion that these procedures are religious is much encouraged by the assumption that they involve a relationship with the supernatural. But this concept and the distinction between the natural and the supernatural that it presupposes carry any appearance of intelligibility at all only from Christian and like-minded Western points of view.

The term *spirit* also has proved conducive to the misunderstanding of African thought in relation to religion. In one sense it means an entity that is physical in terms of imagery but is exempt from the ordinary laws of motion and vision. Ghosts are spirits in this sense. They are supposed to be (very) occasionally perceptible, though they can apparently never be pinned down. If such entities exist, their existence can be discovered only by quasi-empirical cognition. Both African and Western cultures are replete with people who believe in the existence of such quasi-physical beings. Hopefully, the march of science will someday make that belief extinct. But *spirit* has another sense more resistant to scientific probing. It is the sense according to which a spirit is a nonextended, completely immaterial substance. This is what might be called the Cartesian sense of the concept of spirit. It is in this sense that René DESCARTES supposed that the mind or soul is spiritual. The struggle over the contradiction of how such a "substance" can reside in the material body is part of Descartes's legacy to Western thought. Africa is innocent of such a conundrum. If to exist is to be spatial, Cartesian spirituality is an incoherence. The claim, then, that African life is full of religious trafficking in *spiritual* things needs to be taken with at least a pinch of analysis.

So far we have discussed African belief or unbelief with respect to the oral tradition. There is a written tradition which will be commented on below. But it should be noted that the oral tradition has two layers, namely, the communal and the individualized. The worldview of the community is to be found at the communal layer, and the technical, speculative thought of individuals of an abstract inclination in the individualized layer. Of course, even the communal thought is the result of the discourse of individuals; it is what remains in the public memory, in an inevitably abridged and synthetic form, of the talk of remarkable individual thinkers in the community. And these are found in proverbs, poems, myths, and other media for preserving thought and information in an oral tradition. Oruka's skeptical sages belong to the individualized category, while Okot p' Bitek's account of Luo a-theism appertains to the communal. In Oruka's case the individualized reflections of the philosophical sages are captured and perpetuated in print. But there is also a traditional way of doing something similar. African talking drums have been used not only to disseminate information but also to communicate reflection. Among the Akans, for example, sage drummers have left philosophical riddles and epigrams in standardized forms that are quite appropriately called "drum texts." They are a perpetual challenge to analysis, interpretation, and evaluation. For another example, in the Yoruba system of Ifa Divination in Nigeria, there are vast numbers of such incentives to reflection.

Some of the Akan drum riddles are distinctly skeptical. Consider: "The creator created death, and death killed him." What does this mean? In Akan society one of the criteria of intellectual ability is being able to propose plausible interpretations of such texts. To the present writer the most plausible interpretation of this one is that the world order is defined by regular laws, that is, by indefeasible laws. This rules out immediately, for example, the idea of miracles. Such cosmic surds are ruled out, in any case, by the seamless African ontology in which, as previously hinted, there is no distinction between nature and supernature.

Or take another riddle. The supreme being is likened to a bagworm and it is queried whether it wove the bag before getting into it or got into it before weaving it. The contradiction in the first disjunct is plain: It couldn't have gotten into a nonexistent bag. But there is a contradiction in the first disjunct, too: If the bagworm wove the bag beforehand, then there was no bagworm to start with, and how does a nonexistent bagworm weave anything? In either case, therefore, there is a contradiction! The corresponding cosmological antinomy is this: Either God was somewhere when he created everywhere, or he was nowhere when he created everywhere. Given a spatial concept of existence, a contradiction follows either way. Intended lesson: It is conceptually ill advised to speak of creation (out of nothing).

An even better-known riddle is in the following drum verse.

Who gave word?
Who gave word?
Who gave word?
Who gave word to Hearing
For Hearing to have told the Spider
For the Spider to have told the Creator
For the Creator to have created things?

The question in this final riddle is: If the world was ever created by decision, then from what considerations or circumstances were the reasons derived? "Hearing" stands for understanding, conception, reasoning. The thought seems to be that it is circular to think of creation as a volitional act. Such an act would require purpose and in this case ingenuity, and a purpose already presupposes a causal order of objects and events. (Incidentally, the Spider, *Ananse*, is the hero of countless Akan folk tales, in which it represents ingenuity and originality. Indeed, God himself is sometimes called the Stupendous Spider, *Ananse Kokroko*.) Although Akan communal thought is theistic, albeit in a nontranscendental sense, this drum text, which is famous among the Akans, suggests, at best, some form of pantheism (see PANTHEISM AND UNBELIEF)—which, in plain language, is a kind of reverential ATHEISM. Presumably, this happens in all cultures. Abstract thinkers do not feel called upon to repeat communal commonalities.

This is even more evident in a written tradition of philosophy. The written tradition of philosophy in Africa, though it goes back to ancient Egypt, is not evenly spread over Africa. Ethiopia is perhaps the best endowed in this regard. The most illustrious philosopher of that country was a remarkable individual called Zara Yacob, a contemporary of Descartes. Both were ignorant of each other, though each placed his trust in reason. Yacob was, however, more uncompromising in his reliance on reason and was apt to declare various religious edicts, whether Christian or Islamic, absurd on grounds of irrationality. "God" he said, "does not order absurdities." Of course, what is absurd or otherwise was to be determined by each individual's reason. In Yacob's exercise of reason he came to the conclusion, for example, that the Muslim permission of polygamy could not possibly have come from God, since "it ruins the usefulness of marriage." Nor could the observance of the Sabbath be a commandment of God, "for our reason says nothing of the observance of the Sabbath." On the other hand, the Golden Rule is dictated by reason, and therefore any imperatives deducible from it are the will of God.

Zara Yacob did, however, believe in God on the basis of what he regarded as rational grounds. But though he cannot therefore be called an unbeliever, his RATIONALISM evidently rendered God logically superfluous to the foundations of morality. This, contrary to frequent suggestion, is generally the case in African indigenous thought. What is right is conceived as what conduces to the harmonization of the interests of the individual and the community. Any policing influence that the will of God or the ancestors or living elders might be thought to have on the conduct of those of a weak moral fiber is of a secondary significance in African ethics.

In North Africa there is an old tradition of written philosophy, but (outside of ancient Egypt) it is mostly Islamic. One might, of course, mention the contributions of Africans such as Origen, Tertullian, and Augustine to Christian doctrine. But that is far distant from unbelief. However, there is a lesser-known tradition of written philosophy in West and East Africa. Its manuscripts are only now being translated from the Arabic. But so far, it is Islamic and unskeptical. As for ancient Egyptian cosmology, it was subtle and intricate and defies brief accounting. At all events, however, one thing can be said: It had no use for the concept of a creator ex nihilo.

This discussion has been mainly occupied with the question of unbelief in traditional and historical Africa. In contemporary Africa, unbelief tends to be the result of de-conversion from one of the so-called world religions. Greater attention to indigenous African thought would probably reinforce that process.

BIBLIOGRAPHY

Dewey, John. *A Common Faith*. New Haven, CT: Yale University Press, 1934.

Masolo, D. A. "African Philosophers in the Greco-Roman Era." In *A Companion to African Philosophy*, edited by Kwasi Wiredu. Malden, MA: Blackwell, 2004.

Obenga, Theophile. "Egypt: Ancient History of African Philosophy." In *A Companion to African Philosophy*, edited by Kwasi Wiredu. Malden, MA: Blackwell, 2004.

Oruka, H. Odera. *Sage Philosophers: Indigenous Thinkers and Modern Debate on African Philosophy.* Leiden: Brill, 1990.

p' Bitek, Okot. *African Religions in Western Scholarship.* Nairobi, Kenya: East African Literature Bureau, [1970].

Sumner, Claude. *Classical Ethiopian Philosophy.* Los Angeles: Adey, 1994.

Wiredu, Kwasi. *Cultural Universals and Particulars: An African Perspective.* Bloomington: Indiana University Press, 1996.

———. "Morality and Religion in Akan Thought." In *African-American Humanism*, edited by Norm Allen Jr. Amherst, NY: Prometheus Books, 1991.

KWASI WIREDU

AFRICAN AMERICANS AND UNBELIEF. According to every major poll on religion in the United States, African Americans are among the nation's most intensely religious minority groups. In August 2004 the Barna Group—a California-based consulting firm headed by Christian researcher George Barna—found that 91 percent of African Americans said they had prayed to God in the previous week. The comparable figure for Latinos was 86 percent; for whites, 81 percent; and for Asians, 46 percent. Fifty-nine percent of African Americans had read the Bible in the previous week. Among Latinos the figure was 39 percent; among whites, 36 percent; and among Asians, 20 percent. Forty-eight percent of African Americans said they had attended a worship service in the previous week. Among whites the attendance was 41 percent, 38 percent among Hispanics, and 23 percent among Asians. Blacks were also the group most likely to believe that the Bible was inerrant.

What, then, could be said about African Americans and unbelief? In truth, it would be odd if there were nothing to say on this topic. For despite African Americans' intense religiosity—or because of it—they have been historically at or near the bottom of every important quality-of-life indicator.

Despite their constant prayers, African Americans become sick more often and die far sooner than their counterparts in other groups. The supposed healing power of God obviously has no positive effect on the collective health and life span of African Americans. Though they only make up about 12 percent of the US population, African Americans make up 35 to 40 percent of those awaiting organ transplants. Blacks are generally twice as likely to die early as whites. Blacks have a life expectancy of seventy-two years, compared to seventy-eight years for whites. As talk show host Tony Brown says, "We lead in categories no one wants to lead in."

Biblical teachings profoundly influenced the enslavement of African Americans. Secular humanist William Sierichs Jr. explored the Christian origins of racism and the Christian defenses of slavery. Long before Sierichs, the great nineteenth-century freethinker Robert Green INGERSOLL pointed out that white men quoted the Bible in every phase of the slaves' experience—from the moment they were captured to the time they were sold.

The great abolitionist Frederick DOUGLASS said that religious overseers were generally the most brutal, despite the contradictory gentle messages of the Bible. Moreover, he remarked that he never had enough religion to prevent him from running away from slavery—and that atheism was preferable to the harsh Christianity of religious overseers.

Slaves must have experienced great cognitive dissonance. After all, the Bible taught them to be obedient to their masters (Eph. 6:5–6). On the other hand, though the "Good Book" says that masters must extend justice and fairness to their slaves (Col. 4:1), Luke 12:47–48 says that masters may beat their disobedient slaves with many lashes.

It must also have been difficult for slaves during the planning of rebellions. For example, though biblical teachings inspired Denmark Vesey to lead a major slave uprising, George Wilson and another religious slave betrayed him and told the master about the plot. It would be easy to deem these religious slaves traitors to their people. However, is not obedience to the word of God far greater than allegiance to mere mortals, regardless of the color of their skin?

There was also the problem of hunger. The Bible teaches that stealing is a sin. However, slaves often went hungry, and some would steal food from their masters. That is to say, in the cruelest sort of irony, they had to commit a sin against God in order to stay alive.

Because of these kinds of moral dilemmas, some slaves must have had doubts regarding the existence of God. In *Why, Lord? Suffering and Evil in Black Theology*, secular humanist scholar Anthony B. Pinn argues that black suffering cannot be reconciled with the notion of a perfect God. No doubt some slaves had to be of the same opinion.

In *By These Hands: A Documentary History of African American Humanism*, Pinn includes a short story in which a slave named James Hay rejects Christianity. In the same book, religious humanist William R. Jones persuasively argues that blacks come to HUMANISM for different reasons than their white counterparts. Whites generally embrace a humanist LIFE STANCE because they are attracted to Enlightenment ideals (see ENLIGHTENMENT, UNBELIEF DURING THE), revolutions in science (see RELIGION IN CONFLICT WITH SCIENCE), philosophy, and so forth. However, black unbelievers, Jones contends, find themselves in a state of oppression and cannot make sense of their plight by believing in the God of Christianity.

African American unbelievers exist, and some of them have made enormous contributions to the arts, intellectualism, activism, and numerous other areas of human endeavor. Moreover, they have had a tremendous impact upon the ideas and actions of religious people throughout the world.

However, organized humanism, ATHEISM, or FREETHOUGHT among African Americans has been rare. Aside from the national organization African Americans for Humanism (AAH), a project of the Council for Secular Humanism, there has never been a well-known, concerted national effort to bring African Americans into organized humanism. Furthermore, there have been few major efforts among African American unbelievers to organize among themselves.

That during the history of organized freethought some influential white unbelievers were thoroughly racist certainly did not help matters. Some leading mid-twentieth-century white freethinkers wrote and spoke disparagingly against black people. James Hervey JOHNSON, the former editor of THE TRUTH SEEKER, and essayist Woolsey TELLER were among the worst offenders. In 1945 the Truth Seeker Company published Teller's *Essays of an Atheist*. Teller wrote five especially racist essays: "Grading the Races," "Brains and Civilization," "There Are Superior Races," "Shall We Breed Rationally?" and "Natural Selection and War." In "Grading the Races," Teller discusses an essay by the African American atheist and historian John G. Jackson (1907–93) called "Ethiopia and the Origin of Civilization." Teller calls Jackson "a mulatto" and argues that "the ancient Egyptians were dominantly Caucasian." Moreover, he argues that the "Caucasian skull, anatomically considered, is the highest in the world." In "Brains and Civilization" Teller compares the brains of the "White Race," the "Yellow-Brown Race," and the "Black Race." (Apparently, these are the only "races" he recognizes.) He again concludes that the brain of the white race is larger, with more convolutions than the brains of the other two inferior races. In "There Are Superior Races," the writer dismisses the notion of biological equality among the races. He claims that there is an "aristocracy of brains" that favors the white race. However, he also argues that whites have maintained "cultural supremacy." In "Shall We Breed Rationally?" Teller argues against "miscegenation." He is especially concerned that whites not breed with the lower races. In "Natural Selection and War" he refers to himself as "a Darwinian" (see DARWINISM), and defends "natural selection as an operative factor throughout the organic world." In the name of RATIONALISM he argues in favor of white supremacy.

Despite the racism some influential white freethinkers displayed, some blacks were still attracted to freethought,

and others were deeply influenced by it. The great freethinker and black intellectual giant Hubert H. HARRISON wrote for *The Truth Seeker*. John G. Jackson became an influential member of American Atheists. He began writing for *The Truth Seeker* in 1930. He lectured on African history at the Ingersoll Forum in New York for several years. Furthermore, he lectured in universities throughout the northeastern part of the United States.

A. Philip RANDOLPH and Chandler Owen were attracted to freethought and wrote strong critiques of religion. The historian and anthropologist Joel Augustus ROGERS came under the sway of freethought, as did Claude McKAY and the black conservative George S. Schuyler.

Jackson and Rogers wrote numerous books to combat the racist onslaught from writers such as Teller. The February 1987 issue of *American Atheist* featured "Atheists of a Different Color." Many African American street vendors and bookstores throughout the United States still sell photocopies of this issue. The issue features biographical information on Rogers, Randolph, Jackson, Schuyler, and others. There are also writings on two of the leading Afrocentric scholars: Yosef A. A. ben-Jochannan (aka Dr. Ben) and the late John Henrik Clarke.

Clarke and Dr. Ben were associates of Malcolm X, and might have influenced his thinking, as did the works of Rogers. Clarke and Dr. Ben believed that Islam and Christianity were highly detrimental to people of African descent. Indeed, in 1984, during Jesse Jackson's historic run for president, Minister Louis Farrakhan of the Nation of Islam (NOI) referred to Judaism as it was practiced by white Jews as a "gutter" religion (according to some reports, the actual words were "dirty religion"). Farrakhan and his apologists tried to rationalize the statement. However, Dr. Ben—a nominal Ethiopian Jew—stated that Farrakhan was absolutely correct to speak of Judaism in this way. He simply wished that Farrakhan had included Christianity and Islam along with his denunciation of Judaism. As far as he was concerned, they are *all* gutter religions.

Dr. Ben and Clarke wrote and spoke about the prebiblical origins of Judaism, Christianity, and Islam. Indeed, much Afrocentric thought centers around the human origins of these three world religions. Afrocentric scholars pointed out the remarkable similarities between the wisdom, philosophy, theology, religious practices, and moral ideas in the religious texts of Judaism, Christianity, and Islam, and those found among the ancient Egyptians and other civilizations. For example, Clarke used to say that if Moses came down from the mountain with the Ten Commandments, it was only because he carried them up the mountain with him in the first place. Clarke taught that long before the Hebrews had the Ten Commandments, the Egyptians had the "Negative Confessions," the "Declarations of Innocence" in the Book of the Dead, and the Book of Coming Forth by Day into

Night. Examples of the declarations included "I will not commit murder," "I will not steal," "I will not commit adultery," and the like.

Dr. Ben would say, "Heaven is between a Black woman's thighs." That is to say, the black woman not only gives sexual pleasure, but the first women probably came from sub-Saharan Africa and gave birth to our ancestors. For that reason, he said, "the Black woman is the only God we know. Everything else is just our opinion."

Black militants such as those from the NOI presented harsh critiques of Christianity, leading some African Americans to embrace freethought. Many black militants denounced Christianity as a white man's religion. They pointed out that white Christians enslaved and oppressed black people in the name of Christ.

Members of the NOI were especially critical of Christ's command to turn the other cheek. As blacks were turning the other cheek, white racists were beating and killing them. NOI members found this kind of hypocrisy unacceptable and detrimental to the survival of black people. Some blacks, however, reasoned that if Christianity is false, many of the theistic claims of the NOI must also be false, and that all theistic truth claims are dubious.

The Harlem Renaissance was especially critical in the history of black humanism. Indeed, this was a deeply humanistic movement. During this creative period, Nella Larsen wrote the humanistic/atheistic novella *Quicksand*. In this story, Larsen compares religionists to rapists. Helga, the central character, is forced to edify blind faith in God's representatives on Earth (i.e., Christian ministers). However, in the end Helga rebels, angrily rejects theism, and understands that theism has been used historically to oppress black people in the United States.

In 1923 Jean Toomer wrote *Cane*, considered by many to be the greatest literary masterpiece of the Harlem Renaissance. It is a brilliant collection of poems, sketches, and stories about black life in the United States. In his poem "Cotton Song," Toomer repeatedly advises his people not to wait for Judgment Day. He advocates human action and hard work. Humanistic themes permeate *Cane* and give the novel its vibrancy and power. Toomer was not only concerned with racial issues; he studied atheism, naturalism, history, biology, psychology, and many other subjects. He once heard a lecture by the agnostic Clarence Darrow that destroyed his faith in a universe run according to God's immutable laws. In the story "Kabnis," Toomer compares Christian preachers unfavorably to buzzards. The character Kabnis considers them ignorant and arrogant. He complains that blacks are a "preacher-ridden race," controlled by black preachers who are in turn controlled by whites. Another character, Layman, says *all* preachers are parasites. He says that the church is filled with sinners and obnoxious hypocrites.

The freethinker James Weldon Johnson was one of the most productive writers of the Harlem Renaissance. Johnson was a lawyer and served as US consul at Venezuela and Nicaragua from 1906 to 1913. He was the secretary of the NAACP from 1920 to 1930. Johnson wrote *The Autobiography of an Ex-Coloured Man* in 1912. It is published anonymously, but was republished with attribution in 1927,when the Harlem Renaissance was at its zenith. It was considered to be the first first-person novel ever written by a black. The book became a sensation. It is narrated by a man who has the ability to "pass" for white, and who struggles with his racial identity. Ironically, Johnson, an avid reader of agnostic orator Robert Green Ingersoll, was also famous for writing a book called *God's Trombones*, as well as "the Negro National Anthem," called "Lift Every Voice and Sing." Johnson vied with W. E. B. Du Bois for recognition as the most accomplished African American of his day.

In 1929 Wallace Thurman wrote *The Blacker the Berry.* . . . The novel is a satire about a dark-skinned black woman victimized by intraracial bigotry. However, most people—including scholars and intellectuals—still believe the story is to be taken seriously. It was one of the most widely read black novels of its day, and is still required reading in many Black Studies departments.

Sterling Brown was a major Harlem Renaissance poet. His poem "Slim in Hell" beautifully and hilariously explores racism in the Deep South. A black man named Slim Greer dies and goes to heaven. Saint Peter greets him, gives him angel wings, and tells him to report on what is happening in hell. He then will be permitted to stay in heaven. Slim cannot tell the difference between hell and Dixie, and winds up getting the surprise of his life.

There have been important black humanist writers and thinkers since the Harlem Renaissance. In 1973 the aforementioned philosopher William R. Jones of Florida State University wrote a book titled *Is God a White Racist? A Preamble to Black Theology*. Jones argued that the claim that God cares about black people must be supported by strong evidence. Otherwise, it could be persuasively argued that God is a white racist, considering the ongoing plight of black people. Jones described himself as a human-centered or "humanocentric" theist. Others have described him as a "religious secular humanist." He had a close relationship with the Unitarian Universalist Church (see Unitarian Universalism), an institution that has embraced liberal and radical theists, deists, agnostics, Wiccans, atheists, secularists, freethinkers, rationalists, naturalists, and others. Jones was highly critical of the leading humanist Paul Kurtz, claiming that Kurtz had abandoned the ideals of Socrates. (Kurtz has always denied the charge.) In 1989, shortly after the founding of African Americans for Humanism, this writer met with Jones and other black Unitarian Universalist ministers at historically black Howard University in Washington, DC. Though Jones signed African Americans for Humanism's African American Humanist Declaration, he had reservations about the document. He believed that its emphasis upon black self-help was tantamount to "blaming the victim," and succeeded in persuading the other ministers in attendance to share his concern. After the meeting, Jones attacked the declaration again and ceased contact with AAH. Jones shared his "grid of oppression" with humanist and nonhumanist audiences. He argued that powerful whites had control of all of the most important institutions in America, and that consequently, blacks were powerless to effect meaningful change by themselves. He was obsessed with government intervention as a means for significantly improving the lives of blacks.

Like James Cone and other black scholars, Jones argued that the blues is a nontheistic art form. Unlike the spirituals, it does not call upon God to address racism and oppression. Moreover, the black church and Jesus Christ are equally unimportant in this musical genre. Not surprisingly, many—if not most—staunch black religionists opposed the blues. They referred to the tunes as "devil songs," and warned people about their allegedly corrupting influences. In *Why, Lord?* Pinn notes that blues musicians often dealt with themes that many black religionists found embarrassing. He further contends that the blues presented challenges to important religious ideas, dealing critically with Christian hypocrisy and quietist ideas. Some blues songs even questioned the existence of God.

Jones opposed the attempts by black religious scholars to construct one monolithic religious model for African Americans. He believed that while it was important to recognize the Christian tradition in black culture, there was also a nontheistic black tradition that had to be recognized and studied.

Though white humanists and black humanists have much in common, Jones believed that blacks and whites arrive at a humanist life stance for different reasons. Most white humanists consider themselves children of the Enlightenment; according to Jones, most blacks embrace humanism as a result of contemplating black suffering in a racist world. That is to say, black humanism is firmly rooted in the black experience. Therefore, it is erroneous to claim that black humanists have been simply tricked into accepting a Eurocentric worldview.

Jones believed that one of the main functions of black humanism is to challenge the popular notion that black Christianity is necessarily authentic. Much of black Christianity—if not most of it—is simply copied from the Christianity of white oppressors. Therefore, the black humanist must challenge "black" Christianity, because it often aids and abets black oppression. In this way, black humanists are doing the important work that black theologians are unable or unwilling to do.

Linton Kwesi Johnson is one of only two living poets to have work published in the Penguin Modern Classics series. He was born in Jamaica on August 24, 1952. He attended Goldsmith's College, University of London, and eventually joined the Black Panthers (see CLEAVER, ELDRIDGE). Having read *The Souls of Black Folk* by W. E. B. Du Bois and deciding to become a poet, he joined a group of poets and drummers. The journal *Race Today* published his first poetry collection, *Voices of the Living and the Dead*, in 1974. His second anthology, *Dread Beat An' Blood*, was published the following year. Virgin Records released a record of the same name in 1978. Johnson has gone on to produce many more records and has received numerous awards. His biggest audience consists of Jamaican immigrants in Britain. In the 1970s his poetry was intensely political and focused on racism and injustice. Johnson attended a Baptist church in Jamaica as a child, but asked difficult questions, earning him stern words from his pious grandmother. When he moved to Britain at age eleven, he attended a Methodist church and sang in the choir. Johnson began to doubt religion after reading *Capitalism and Slavery* by Eric Williams. He learned that religion was essential in the enslavement of black people. He learned that Spaniards and Portuguese Catholics had agreed to divide and conquer Africa. Moreover, he learned that Wesley of the Methodist Church was a slavery advocate. In college, he read MARX and was further convinced that religion enslaves the masses. After discovering Rastafarianism, Johnson moved toward AGNOSTICISM. Though he embraced black consciousness, he never accepted the NOI. The Panthers strongly opposed the NOI's reactionary black nationalism and its racialist theology. Moreover, the NOI had assassinated Malcolm X, and that, for Johnson, confirmed its moral bankruptcy. Johnson discovered that, contrary to popular opinion, many of the atheists he met were good people. Conversely, many of the Christians he had known were "hypocrites." Today he embraces a humanist life stance and continues to write poetry and give performances.

Two black women have been selected "Humanist of the Year" by the AMERICAN HUMANIST ASSOCIATION (AHA)—Alice Walker and Faye Wattleton. Walker won the Pulitzer Prize for *The Color Purple*. Anthony Pinn includes a chapter on Walker in *By These Hands*. The essay is titled "The only reason you want to go to heaven is that you have been driven out of your mind." It begins with Genesis 3:16, in which the reader is informed that God has cursed "the woman" with servitude to her husband. Walker bemoans the fact that so-called men of God often worship a God of sexism and violence against women. She is critical of the blond, blue-eyed Jesus and prefers to worship the earth. She says that too many people love and worship a God that does not love and worship them in return. Wattleton is the past president of Planned Parenthood Federation of America (1978–92). She is a brilliant debater and forthright defender of sex education and reproductive rights, aiding in the implementation of family planning programs in numerous developing countries. In 1989 this writer contacted her and asked her to become involved with AAH. Though she applauded the humanist group's efforts, she declined the offer to join. She had already received numerous death threats in her capacity as the head of Planned Parenthood, and she thought it unwise to become an easier target by becoming a member of an openly humanist organization. In 1993 Wattleton was inducted into the National Women's Hall of Fame. Today she is the president of the Center for the Advancement of Women. In 2005 she was a spokesperson at "The State of the Black Union: Road to Health and Defining the African American Agenda" at New Birth Missionary Baptist Church in Lithonia, Georgia. The one-day symposium, carried live by CSPAN, featured such luminaries as Minister Louis Farrakhan, Rev. Jesse Jackson Sr., Cornel West, Rev. Al Sharpton, Michael Eric Dyson, and many others.

African Americans and Organized Humanism. It should be absolutely clear that unbelief has had a profound impact upon African American intellectualism, activism, life, and culture. However, as previously noted, there have not been many successful efforts at *organized* humanism, freethought, atheism, and the like among African Americans.

In his heyday, Hubert H. Harrison headed a small group of atheists in Harlem. However, he was the only black member in the group. In the late 1980s and early 1990s, a man named Al Brown headed the Afro-American Atheist Association in Florida, but it consisted of only Brown and one other person. In the mid-1990s, Eugene Charrington of Brooklyn headed the Harlem Atheist Association. That group did not have many members, and eventually disbanded. There was a vibrant chapter of African Americans for Humanism associated with the former Center for Inquiry–Midwest in Kansas City, Missouri. However, the center no longer exists.

There was also an attempt by little-known Northern California hip-hop artists to popularize humanism through music. Furthermore, there have been similar attempts by big-name hip-hop artists. KRS-One, a major rapper during the late 1980s and early 1990s, promoted a conception of religious humanism. However, his conception of humanism was homophobic. In any case, it did not catch on with his fans. In Portland, Oregon, a hip-hop group called Lifesavas rejects religion and promotes a secular worldview. They believe in drawing upon their inner human strength to find solutions to the world's problems. Yet they do not try to force their views on their listeners in a preachy way.

There have been other attempts to attract large numbers of blacks to organized humanism, all to no avail. However, freethought hope springs eternal. Reginald Finley, who helms an Internet radio show as the Infidel Guy, is a former "psychic." He and his wife worked for a psychic hotline and persuaded many callers that they possessed psychic powers. He shared some of his secrets at a Center for Inquiry conference in Atlanta in 2001. He

hosts a Web site that attracts many black freethinkers, and he has traveled to different US cities promoting freethought among African Americans.

By far, AAH is the organization in the best position to promote organized humanism among people of African descent. Headquartered near Buffalo, New York, since 1989 AAH has had representatives on major programs in the US media, at institutions of higher learning, and in newspapers and other print media. Today, local AAH groups operate in Harlem and in Albany, New York. There are currently plans to start one in the Washington, DC, area and to eventually branch out into other US cities.

In Albany, McKinley Jones and Taunya Hannibal-Williams are engaged in an ambitious effort to explore and document the role of humanism in the civil rights movement. They will tap into law, literature, the arts, social science, and political science. Ultimately, they would like to make course materials available and give lectures, exhibits, and presentations.

Ironically, perhaps the best model for organized humanism and freethought for blacks comes from Africa. Some forty-five humanist and freethought groups exist in Congo, Ghana, Kenya, Guinea, Gambia, Uganda, Rwanda, Zambia, Liberia, Nigeria, Cameroon, Ethiopia, Tanzania, South Africa, and Sierra Leone.

AAH helped form the African Humanist Alliance, an organization of African humanist groups that now operates with great support from the INTERNATIONAL HUMANIST AND ETHICAL UNION (IHEU), headquartered in England. The alliance plans to have at least one humanist group in all fifty-three African nations.

The Nigerian Humanist Movement—headed by Leo Igwe of Ibadan, Oyo State, Nigeria—received strong words of encouragement from Nobel laureate Wole Soyinka in 2001. In October of that year, the Nigerian Humanist Movement and the Council for Secular Humanism cohosted the first major humanist conference in sub-Saharan Africa. Soyinka, also a laureate of the International Academy of Humanism, sent a letter to be read at the conference. He acknowledged the importance of humanism in Nigeria and discussed the importance of SECULARISM.

Soyinka has long been an outspoken advocate of secularism. He has defended Salman Rushdie, Taslima NASRIN, and other alleged blasphemers (see BLASPHEMY). Moreover, he has been imprisoned and threatened with death many times for calling for democracy in Nigeria. He dedicated his book *The Open Sore of a Continent* to the outspoken atheist, educator, humanitarian, and prodemocracy activist Tai SOLARIN. In November 2001 Soyinka was the keynote speaker at the Center for Inquiry's conference "Science and Religion: Are They Compatible?" The Council for Secular Humanism presented him with the Distinguished Humanist Award.

The Committee for the Scientific Investigation of Claims of the Paranormal (CSICOP) is also affiliated with the Center for Inquiry. The work of CSICOP is of great interest to African humanists. Most African humanists are combating juju, ritual killings, and other paranormal phenomena. CSICOP provides rational explanations for these kinds of beliefs and actions.

There is also interest in humanism in the Caribbean. In the earlier part of the twentieth century, many Jamaican humanists belonged to the RATIONALIST PRESS ASSOCIATION, based in Britain. In the 1990s there was a humanist group in Haiti. Today, AAH has plans to help start a group in Barbados.

If more black unbelievers would come out of the closet, much greater progress could be made in attracting larger numbers of blacks to organized unbelief. However, whereas religionists loudly and proudly acknowledge their religious beliefs—no matter how bizarre they might be—most unbelievers prefer to keep their unbelief hidden. It is hoped that this encyclopedia will encourage more unbelievers to become part of a great and proud legacy.

Moreover, humanist and freethought leaders must do more to take into consideration differences in class and culture between whites and blacks. As this volume makes clear, different people—and different groups— come to unbelief for different reasons. For example, the AAH group in Kansas City attracted large numbers of blacks by featuring jazz, blues, soul food dinners, and poetry. For unbelief to grow, it cannot appeal only to scholars and well-read educated intellectuals.

Race, ethnicity, or geography will never restrict the development of humanism, atheism, freethought, and rationalism. As long as people think for themselves, there will be freethinkers. Moreover, there will always be courageous efforts—somewhere—to bring them together for a shared sense of community.

BIBLIOGRAPHY

Brown, Sterling. "Slim in Hell." In *The Black Poets*, edited by Dudley Randall. New York: Bantam, 1971.

Johnson, James Weldon. *The Autobiography of an Ex-Coloured Man*. New York: Vintage Books, 1989.

Jones, William. *Is God a White Racist? A Preamble to Black Theology*. Garden City, NY: Anchor Press/Doubleday, 1973.

———. "Religious Humanism: Its Problems and Prospects in Black Religion and Culture." In *By These Hands: A Documentary of African American Humanism*, edited by Anthony Pinn. New York: New York University Press, 2001.

Larsen, Nella. *Quicksand*. In *An Intimation of Things Distant: The Collected Fiction of Nella Larsen*, edited by Charles R. Larson. New York: Anchor Books, 1992.

Pinn, Anthony, ed. *By These Hands: A Documentary of African American Humanism*. New York: New York University Press, 2001.

———. *Why, Lord? Suffering and Evil in Black Theology*. New York: Continuum, 1995.

Ragland, John. "Atheists of a Different Color." *American Atheist*, February 1987.

Seaman, Ann R. *America's Most Hated Woman: The Life and Gruesome Death of Madalyn Murray O'Hair*. New York: Continuum, 2005.

Sierichs, William. "The Christian Origin of Racism: That Old Black Devil." *AAH Examiner* 12, no. 4 (Winter 2002–2003).

———. "The Christian Origin of Racism: 'For They Are Heathens . . . .'" *AAH Examiner* 13, no. 1 (Spring 2003).

———. "The Christian Origin of Racism: The Christian Defense of Slavery." *AAH Examiner* 13, no. 2 (Summer 2003).

———. "The Christian Origin of Racism: Atheist Abolitionist Serpents in Slaves' Eden." *AAH Examiner* 13, no. 3 (Fall 2003).

Teller, Woolsey. *Essays of an Atheist*. New York: Truth Seeker Company, 1945.

Toomer, Jean. *Cane*. New York: Liveright Publishing, 1975.

NORM R. ALLEN JR.

AGATHONISM. Agathonism is a system of humanistic ethics devised by the philosopher Mario Bunge that balances duties with rights and centers around what is good. Agathon (c.450–400 BCE) was an Athenian tragedian, but *agathon* is also the Greek word for "good," and it is in this context that Bunge uses the word. Agathonism is a refinement of the Golden Rule, which has served as a moral maxim to virtually every system of belief ever devised. Despite its ubiquity, some philosophers have detected logical problems with the Golden Rule. For instance, is it right for a masochist to inflict pain on others because he might want pain inflicted on him? Bunge has devised the notion of agathonism as a reliable method for determining humanist ethics. The two base postulates of agathonism are as follows:

1. Whatever contributes to the welfare of an individual, without jeopardizing the basic rights of any others, is both good and right.
2. Everyone has the right to enjoy life and the duty to help others enjoy life.

Agathonism can be simplified to the maxim "Enjoy life and help live an enjoyable life." Agathonism is specifically realist and materialist and thus can be employed in the real world. It balances selfishness and altruism and places a premium on the moral equality of people and on the principle of fairness. In addition, its simplicity makes it accessible to everyone. Agathonism has the intellectual clarity and humanitarian simplicity to become the foundation for any humanist ethics.

BIBLIOGRAPHY

Bunge, Mario. *Philosophy in Crisis: The Need for Reconstruction*. Amherst, NY: Prometheus Books, 2001.

BILL COOKE

AGNOSTICISM. Agnosticism is an epistemological term (from the Greek *agnosis*, meaning "without knowledge") that connotes a form of SKEPTICISM concerning the existence of God. According to agnosticism, the existence of God is unknowable, either because this metaphysical claim lies beyond the reach of human cognitive faculties, or because neither the evidence for nor the evidence against the existence of God is epistemically superior. For these reasons, agnosticism normally involves a suspension of belief concerning God's existence as well.

Origin of Agnosticism. Historically, Thomas Henry HUXLEY is credited with coining the term *agnostic* in 1869 CE in order to distinguish his view from ATHEISM and theism. In his undergraduate years, Huxley had read from the texts of the ecclesiastical sect known as the Gnostics, a group famous for claiming to possess fundamental knowledge of the universe. To separate his position from the dogmatism of the Gnostics, Huxley adopted the term *agnostic* to emphasize his lack of knowledge and to endorse a cautious methodological modesty in his approach to answering the question of God's existence. Accordingly, he wrote: "[I]t is wrong for a man to say that he is certain of the objective truth of any proposition unless he can produce evidence which logically justifies that certainty. This is what agnosticism asserts and, in my opinion, is all that is essential to agnosticism . . . the application of the principle results in the denial of, or the suspension of judgment concerning, a number of propositions respecting which our contemporary ecclesiastical 'gnostics' profess entire certainty."

Huxley gave serious weight to the appraisal of evidence for God's existence, and claimed that the inability to provide sufficient justification for belief in God should result in suspension of judgment. Although he suggested that the existence of God may reach beyond our cognitive faculties and is unknowable, Huxley also doubted that he knew this to be the case, that rather, such a matter is probably unknowable. Thus, paradoxically, Huxley is "agnostic" about his own agnosticism.

Interpretations of agnosticism began to diversify in the decades after Huxley before reaching their pinnacle of ambiguity in philosophy of religion today. For example, in the late 1800s the famous Scopes trial attorney Clarence DARROW, a self-proclaimed agnostic, wrote: "An agnostic is a doubter. The word is generally applied to those who doubt the verity of accepted religious creeds or faiths. . . . Anyone who thinks is an agnostic about something, otherwise he must believe that he is possessed of all knowledge. And the proper place for such a person is in the madhouse or the home for the feeble-minded." Darrow seems to have given teeth to Huxley's cautious methodological modesty; however, this haughty interpretation of agnosticism is scarcely found in the twentieth century.

Contemporary Agnosticism. Modern agnosticism naturally overlaps many elements of the Huxleyan agnosticism discussed above, however imprecisely it is defined in common usage. Upon survey one will find that those who consider themselves agnostics may differ significantly in their views with respect to methodology of inquiry, the conditions for justification of belief, and the limits of knowledge. Strictly speaking, there is no orthodox interpretation of agnosticism; no single set of necessary and sufficient conditions for agnosticism can be articulated. What follows is a concise yet broad mapping of the landscape within agnosticism.

First, in its weakest sense, agnosticism may be attributed to someone who merely professes personal ignorance with respect to the claims that God does or does not exist. This form of agnosticism is quite popular among the general population. It clearly emphasizes Huxley's methodological modesty; however, it arguably goes too far. Those who are intellectually lazy, failing to seriously inquire into the evidence presented for and against God's existence, nonetheless help themselves to a lofty title. While it is true that such agnostics suspend belief, a common component of many versions of agnosticism, their suspension is due to cognitive lethargy. Therefore, perhaps critics are fair in pointing out that such people are deserving of no title at all.

A second, stronger form of agnosticism may be attributed to those who claim that the existence of a deity is unknowable due to a balance of evidence (see EXISTENCE OF GOD, ARGUMENTS FOR AND AGAINST). According to the parity agnostic, the evidence for and against God's existence is sufficiently balanced such that neither belief nor disbelief is epistemically preferable. Given the parity of evidence resulting in suspension of belief, knowledge is taken to be unattainable. While parity agnosticism vaguely expresses a widely held opinion that both theism and atheism each have plausible considerations in their favor, it is up to the parity agnostic to show us exactly how this evidence is so nicely balanced. If the arguments on one side are even marginally superior to those on the other, the parity agnostic must answer why suspension of belief is preferable to a diffidently held belief or disbelief.

Third, a close relative to the parity agnostic known as the *sans*-evidence agnostic maintains that there is no evidence for, as well as no evidence against, the existence of God. Since there is no evidence for either side, alleges the *sans*-evidence agnostic, neither belief nor disbelief is adopted. Just as with the parity agnostic, a balance of evidence must be shown, but in this case there must be close to zero evidence for each side. Many inquirers will find it difficult to accept that both theists and atheists have absolutely nothing persuasive in defense of their respective views, and this relegates the *sans*-evidence agnostic to an uncomfortable position. If adopted, both the parity and *sans*-evidence strands of agnosticism are no longer seen as a third, more modest alternative to theism and atheism. Huxley's methodological modesty has been abandoned, although the latter two versions of agnosticism are certainly innocent of intellectual laziness.

Fourth, some agnostics focus on the unknowability of the metaphysical claims to God's existence or nonexistence, but allow that belief or disbelief is nonetheless permissible. It is important to note that this interpretation of agnosticism is compatible with theism or atheism, since it is only asserted that *knowledge* of God's existence is unattainable. This agnosticism is also compatible with both a modest and an immodest methodology. For example, agnostics such as Leslie D. Weatherhead can believe in the existence of God, yet acknowledge limitations of our cognitive faculties. He writes: "But surely, in so many matters, a reverent agnosticism is the only place where the Christian can rest his mind, remembering that the gap between a child's comprehension and his father's activities is nothing compared with the gap between wisest man's understanding and the scope of God's activity."

Weatherhead and other theistic agnostics may often emphasize the inability of humans to know of God's existence, for this condition of ignorance leaves ample room for religious faith. Agnosticism of this flavor may be referred to as a fideistic agnosticism. Immanuel KANT is a comfortable fit for this category. While Kant expressly denies metaphysical knowledge of many sorts, including of God's existence, he elects to postulate the existence of God to make sense of our moral experience.

Alternatively, one might agree with Kant and Weatherhead that knowledge of God's existence is unattainable, yet disbelieve in the existence of God. Atheists may seize upon the opportunity to count these agnostics as atheists so long as atheism is broadly construed to include everyone who is not a theist. If the label *atheist* simply means not a theist, just as *amoral* means not moral and *atypical* means not typical, then the set of atheists is much larger that one might have thought. However, this imperialistic tendency ought to be resisted. Those preferring the appellation of agnostic in this case may be doing so because they prefer to emphasize the limitations of knowledge, rather than to highlight their disbelief, which often is taken to have a negative stigma.

Contemporary thinkers favoring a form of philosophical NATURALISM that is thoroughly dismissive of metaphysics altogether may be atheistic agnostics of this sort. Such naturalists may claim that knowledge of metaphysical claims is unattainable, yet still disbelieve in the existence of God. To some it might seem inconsistent to shun metaphysics yet advocate the metaphysical belief of God's nonexistence in one's next breath. Thus, it appears that the naturalists' views are self-contradictory.

However, though it is a metaphysical claim to deny the existence of deities, it seems unreasonable to expect the naturalist to suspend belief in these cases rather than disbelieve. This unreasonableness is clearly seen when we emphasize that agnosticism often connotes a middle ground between belief and disbelief. It is often a position held because neither side is more reasonable than the other. Thus, the naturalist may point out that it would be odd for someone to be agnostic about belief in the existence of Zeus; maybe Zeus exists, maybe not. So, even though the naturalist admits that knowledge of Zeus's nonexistence is unattainable, this does not commit the naturalist to a suspension of *belief*. It is open for the naturalist to claim that belief in Zeus, or any other deity, arises from normatively problematic belief-forming processes. Thus, it is far from clear that an atheistic agnosticism arising from a philosophical naturalism is self-contradictory.

One additional version of agnosticism that focuses on the unknowability of the claim that God exists is one that is conjoined with neither belief nor disbelief. Instead, agnostics of this sort are skeptics with regard to knowledge of God's existence, but also insist that one must suspend belief as well. David HUME, for instance, is notoriously hostile toward metaphysics. Famously, he wrote: "If we take in our hand any volume; of divinity or school metaphysics, for instance; let us ask, *Does it contain any abstract reasoning concerning quantity or number?* No. *Does it contain any experimental reasoning concerning matter of fact and existence?* No. Commit it then to the flames: For it can contain nothing but sophistry and illusion."

However, Hume, unlike Kant, seems to advocate that one must suspend judgment. Although Hume sometimes concealed his views by writing in dialogue form, a notable exception is found in the concluding words of his *The Natural History of Religion*: "The whole is a riddle, an enigma, an inexplicable mystery. Doubt, uncertainty, suspense of judgment appear the only result of our most accurate scrutiny, concerning this subject." Hume can be plausibly interpreted as representing a form of agnosticism containing a mixture of several elements already mentioned. He shares an opposition to metaphysics alongside Kant and contemporary naturalists, yet he advocates neither belief nor disbelief. His comments echo some of the claims of the parity and *sans*-evidence agnostics when he concludes that suspense of judgment is the "result of our most accurate scrutiny, concerning this subject."

To conclude, it should be apparent that agnosticism is employed in many different ways. When approaching an agnostic in public, it might be useful to ascertain whether such a person is an agnostic of the aforementioned weak variety, for if so it is unlikely that a worthwhile conversation will ensue. But if the agnostic is claiming more than just personal ignorance due to cognitive lethargy, then one will have to discover what position is taken with respect to the evidence for and against the existence of God. Does the agnostic think the evidence is balanced? Is there no good evidence for or against God's existence? And furthermore, one will need to determine what the self-proclaimed agnostic thinks with respect to the possibility of knowledge of God's existence. And even if such knowledge is not possible, it is still open as to whether or not belief is permissible. Some agnostics, such as those resembling Kant or Weatherhead, may allow that one believe even though knowledge is not possible. On the other hand, suspension of belief may be advocated, as suggested by Hume, or perhaps disbelief might be adopted. In short, there is no single, straightforward understanding of agnosticism.

BIBLIOGRAPHY

Darrow, Clarence. "Why I Am an Agnostic." In *Why I Am an Agnostic and Other Essays.* Amherst, NY: Prometheus Books, 1995.

Holland, Aaron. "Consistency in Presuming Agnosticism." *Philo* 4 (2001).

Hume, David. *An Enquiry concerning Human Understanding.* Edited by Tom L. Beauchamp. Oxford: Oxford University Press, 1999.

———. *The Natural History of Religion.* In *Writings on Religion,* edited by Antony Flew. LaSalle, IN: Open Court, 1992.

Huxley, Thomas. "Agnosticism and Christianity." In *Collected Essays,* vol. 5. New York: Appleton, 1894.

Nielsen, Kai. *Naturalism without Foundations.* Amherst, NY: Prometheus Books, 1996.

Pojman, Louis. "Agnosticism." In *The Cambridge Dictionary of Philosophy.* Cambridge: Cambridge University Press, 1995.

Scriven, Michael. *Primary Philosophy.* New York: Random House, 1971.

Smith, George H. *Atheism: The Case against God.* Los Angeles: Nash, 1974.

Weatherhead, Leslie D. *The Christian Agnostic.* Nashville, TN: Abingdon, 1965.

Zuurdeeg, Willem E. *An Analytical Philosophy of Religion.* Nashville, TN: Abingdon, 1958.

AARON HOLLAND

AGNOSTICISM AND ATHEISM. Definitional Issues. The terms *ATHEISM* and *AGNOSTICISM* lend themselves to two different definitions. The first takes the privative *a* both before the Greek *theos* (divinity) and *gnosis* (to know) to mean that atheism is simply the absence of belief in the gods and agnosticism is simply lack of knowledge of some specified subject matter. The second definition takes atheism to mean the explicit denial of the existence of gods and agnosticism as the position of someone who, because the existence of the gods is unknowable, suspends judgment regarding them (see EXISTENCE OF GOD, ARGUMENTS FOR AND AGAINST).

Each definition has its advantages and disadvantages. The first is the more inclusive and recognizes only two alternatives: Either one believes in the gods or one does not. Consequently, there is no third alternative, as those who call themselves agnostics sometimes claim. Insofar as they lack belief they are really atheists. Moreover, since absence of belief is the cognitive position in which everyone is born, the burden of proof falls on those who advocate religious belief. The proponents of the second definition, by contrast, regard the first definition of atheism as too broad because it includes uninformed children along with aggressive and explicit atheists. Consequently, it is unlikely that the public will adopt it. They also see some advantages in preserving the term *agnostic* for those who wish to claim the suspension of judgment as a third alternative between belief and disbelief.

It is usually unproductive to argue about the definitions themselves rather than dealing with those complex issues that anyone using either of the definitions ultimately has to discuss: the various types of explicit atheism in Western culture as well as the rationale that those who call themselves agnostic give for their suspension of both belief and disbelief. In what follows, I will be dealing with the most important contemporary types of atheism, even though the phenomenon goes back to the ancient world. Since these types have been principally formulated over against the monotheism common to the three major religious traditions—Christianity, Islam, and Judaism—it is with these types that I will be concerned. Then I will turn my attention to the phenomenon of agnosticism, especially the issues that arise in Thomas Henry HUXLEY's formulation of it.

Types of Atheism. Although atheists agree in denying the existence of gods however conceived, they often give quite different reasons for this denial. These differences are, in turn, often grounded in the worldview or philosophical beliefs of the individual atheist. Some atheistic denials, for example, spring from an alternative metaphysical system, as was the case of Baron d'HOLBACH, who, in 1770, developed one of the first materialistic systems (see MATERIALISM, PHILOSOPHICAL; ENLIGHTENMENT, UNBELIEF DURING THE). A great deal of modern atheism, on the other hand, rests on the conviction that theism of any sort is incompatible with modern science, especially Darwinian evolution and contemporary cosmologies (see DARWINISM; ANTHROPIC PRINCIPLE). Still another form of atheism reflects Friedrich NIETZSCHE's view that all otherworldly beliefs, whether metaphysical or religious, are an expression of psychological weakness. Sometimes the rejection of theism is based on highly technical logical arguments typical of the discourse of professional philosophers, while at other times it is a part of a synthesis of a range of convictions and beliefs characteristic of modernity, as in the case of secular humanism. Because of this variety of types of atheism, it would be more useful to forgo generalization about it in favor of depicting certain influential types.

Atheism as Counterinterpretation of Religion. Although atheism is found in the ancient world—one thinks of EPICURUS (341–270 BCE)—the characteristic forms of modern atheism are rooted in the eighteenth-century Enlightenment with its newfound confidence in reason and the sciences, its distrust of appeals to revelation, its demand for freedom of expression, and its correlative hostility to political and ecclesiastical authority. The first intellectual result of this Enlightenment ethos was DEISM, even among such radical critics of Christianity as VOLTAIRE. But it was not long before deism itself was subjected to devastating criticism by David HUME. As a consequence, the intellectual in the Western world was for the first time confronted with not only the possibility of skepticism but the explicit atheism propounded by such radical French thinkers as d'Holbach.

Although it is debatable whether Hume was himself an atheist, he constructed a type of argument concerning religion that has been extraordinarily influential in contemporary atheistic circles. He proposed a thesis shocking to the eighteenth-century world, namely, that one could write a natural history of religion. In doing this he did not so much propose philosophical objections to religious beliefs as provide what seemed to be a more plausible explanation for these beliefs than theists could themselves offer. The belief in supernatural gods, he argued, can best be explained by the propensity of human beings to personalize the unknown causes that impinge on them and cause them anxiety. The significance of this type of proposal is that it does not depend simply on a rejection of the arguments of theists but attempts to offer a counterinterpretation of the origins and the persistence of theism.

Hume's argument is put in very general terms but it is the forerunner of atheistic arguments elaborated in the nineteenth century. Perhaps the most powerful use of this type of counterinterpretation is to be found in the writings of Ludwig FEUERBACH, who argued that the self is immersed in and absolutely dependent upon the forces of nature. Out of its feeling of dependence and the anxiety that follows from it, the imagination takes over and personifies these forces. This yields polytheism in more primitive cultures, but monotheism results in more developed civilizations in which nature is seen as a unified whole. A god, Feuerbach argued, is essentially a being who is concerned for the individual's welfare and can protect her from suffering and death.

A similar although less developed theory was advanced by Nietzsche, who argued that the inveterate tendency of the human mind under the pressure of a language constructed around subjects and predicates is to see a "doer" behind every event and so to create a "true world" behind the apparent world. This phenomenon would not in itself be particularly deleterious did it not provide the occasion for sufferers and the psychologically weak to long for this better, truer world in order to avoid the evils of the apparent, real world. Priests then capitalize on this longing and constitute themselves the necessary gatekeepers to this truer world.

This counterinterpretation of religion does not stand alone but is buttressed by explicit philosophical and ethical criticisms of theism. Philosophically, for example, Feuerbach argued that the god of Christian theism has mutually incompatible predicates: the anthropomorphic, to which the naively religious cling, and the metaphysical, to which the theologians retreat in order to avoid the embarrassment of the anthropomorphism. Theism is also always threatened by scientific explanations. Ethically, both Feuerbach and Nietzsche argued that religious faith corrupts both the moral and the truth sense: The moral sense, because faith is set above moral and ethical considerations; the truth sense, because it rests on the conviction that the deity revealed itself only to a particular group. For both of them, religious faith is a kind of diseased *eros*, a desire on the part of the individual to avoid suffering and to live forever.

This type of atheism has found contemporary expression in the twentieth century in the writings of Sigmund FREUD and anthropologists such as Weston La Barre and Melford Spiro. Freud argued that primitive people and children live under the principle of the "omnipotence of thoughts" and attribute immense importance to wishes, as can be seen in magic and play. This, in turn, reflects a fundamental narcissism that is dealt with in defensive reactions designed to ward off disaster and death. The basic argument, then, is that the human self coming to self-consciousness tends to personify the forces that impinge upon it and then interprets these forces in parental terms, as a nurturing mother and, later, the father. Through the long period of human dependency the child becomes accustomed to calling on these figures in times of stress. It is natural, then, that when danger and stress arise and no parent is available, the person is driven to perceive the nonhuman environment in terms of this infantile prototype.

Atheism as Rooted in an Ethics of Belief. Another influential precursor to a type of contemporary atheism is to be found in the writings of the British mathematician and philosopher William Kingdon CLIFFORD. Clifford was less concerned to criticize the concept of God than he was to argue that any belief not based on evidence corrupts both the individual and society. It corrupts the individual because when we let ourselves believe for reasons not based on evidence we weaken our powers of self-control, of doubting, and of fairly seeking evidence (see EVIDENTIALISM). It corrupts the society because the progress of society depends upon individuals who exercise these faculties of judgment. Unreasoned belief makes a society credulous and lazy. Consequently, he concluded that everyone has the duty to guard the purity of his belief. Indeed, "it is wrong always, everywhere, and for anyone, to believe anything on insufficient evidence." Insofar as religious beliefs are not founded on evidence, it is wrong to hold them, and Clifford was particularly critical of the Roman Catholic priesthood for promoting the doctrines of original sin, vicarious suffering, and eternal punishment.

Atheism as a General Worldview. Perhaps the most representative form of atheism in the Anglo-Saxon world is the atheism built upon more general and nontechnical assumptions about the relationships among critical intelligence, religious skepticism, science, and a healthy society. This type of atheism is characteristic of the movement called SECULAR HUMANISM. Although a representative document "A Secular Humanist Declaration" does not explicitly endorse atheism and even welcomes religious believers who share its values, it notes more aggressively that it finds the traditional view of God as either meaningless or undemonstrated and rejects religious experience as having anything to do with the supernatural. Men and women are said to be responsible for their own destinies and cannot look toward some transcendent being for salvation.

As in the case of Clifford, the driving impulse of the secular humanist movement is the conviction that a flourishing human civilization depends upon free intellectual inquiry and, consequently, it rejects any attempt, whether civil or ecclesiastical, to restrict this inquiry. Moreover, this inquiry necessarily assumes the discipline of rejecting appeals to faith and revelation in contrast to logic and science. Although it acknowledges the imperfections of the scientific method, it argues that it is the most reliable way of understanding the world.

Secular humanism is especially concerned to argue, as Pierre BAYLE did centuries ago, that atheism and agnosticism do not lead to immorality, as religious authorities have tended to argue. It argues that ethics can and has been intellectually separated from the claims of religion, as can be seen in a long philosophical tradition extending back from John DEWEY to ARISTOTLE. Just as critical reason is to be employed in the sphere of knowledge, so too should it be employed in ethics. Its aim is to cultivate an appreciation for social justice and the individual's obligations toward others.

Philosophical Atheism. The atheism of secular humanism, as I have noted, is formulated in nontechnical terms, but it includes among its proponents many professional philosophers who would justify their atheism on what they consider to be strictly philosophical and logical arguments. As a result, this form of atheism necessarily adopts the style and technique of academic philosophy. A well-known example of this type of atheism is J. L. MACKIE's *The Miracle of Theism: Arguments For and Against the Existence of God.* In this book, Mackie carefully considers and rejects all of the classical arguments for the existence of God—the ontological, cosmological, moral, and teleological (the argument from design)—and also takes up the argument from con-

sciousness, the problem of evil, religious experience, and the claim that religious faith is a "leap." He even considers and rejects the modern view attributed to Ludwig WITTGENSTEIN and R. B. Braithwaite that Christianity is not to be understood as a series of beliefs at all, but rather as a way of life associated with certain stories. Since it is not a series of beliefs, it is said not to be subject to the rational attacks of philosophers.

Just because these arguments against theism are so technical and complex, it is not possible to discuss them here. But it is important for laypeople to understand that Mackie does not argue that the failure of theist arguments itself entails atheism; rather, he argues that when all the various arguments he has considered are taken together, "the balance of probabilities . . . comes out strongly against the existence of a god." And this probability is increased when we consider that one can, like Hume and Feuerbach, provide a natural explanation for the origin and persistence of religious belief.

A great deal of the contemporary professional discussion in philosophy between theists and atheists revolves around the problem of evil (see EVIL, PROBLEM OF). Most philosophers would agree that evil constitutes the most important objection to classical theism, although it would not be a devastating criticism if God were limited in some fashion, as John Stuart MILL has argued. The objection, which is an ancient one, is that either God can do something to prevent the manifest evil in the world but will not, or God wishes to prevent or mitigate evil but cannot. Christian theists, especially, are not lacking for some replies to this dilemma, most of them being some variant of the view that the manifest evil in the world is permitted by God as necessary for some higher good. And of these higher goods, theists point to the existence of creatures with free will (see DETERMINISM). If there is to be free will, they argue, then there must be the possibility that some will choose evil. Atheists, by contrast, find this solution unconvincing. First of all, it does not consider the chaos and suffering that has nothing to do with human choice. Second, if the deity has created people who can sometimes prefer the good, it could have created them so that they always choose the good. For Christians to argue that this is impossible is unconvincing because their own view of heaven refers to just such a situation in which the good is always chosen.

In contemporary debate, some Christian theists have interjected the notion of the hiddenness of God as one of the necessary conditions for the exercise of free choice. God, so to speak, has placed his creatures at an "epistemic distance," a distance that is logically necessarily for two reasons: (a) so that persons will not be, as it were, forced to believe in him, and (b) so that their moral choice to be obedient is not based on hope of reward. In short, God is hidden to preserve both our cognitive and our moral freedom to form our character for good or ill.

Atheists, of course, regard these arguments as unconvincing. The notion that any knowledge of God would jeopardize our cognitive freedom has first to settle the issue whether belief is voluntary or not and whether moral choice is better when made in ignorance rather than with knowledge. At least one philosopher, J. L. Schellenberg, has turned the argument for the hiddenness of God against the theist and in support of atheism. His argument goes something like this: (1) If there is a god, he is perfectly loving; (2) if a perfectly loving god exists, reasonable nonbelief would not occur; (3) but reasonable nonbelief does occur; (4) so no perfectly loving god exists; therefore, (5) there is no god.

Atheism as Incompatible with Science. These philosophical arguments are exceedingly abstract and their persuasiveness and validity often depend on technical premises that are themselves debated by philosophers. It is not surprising, then, that there are atheists like Taner Edis, who, in his book *The Ghost in the Universe*, argues that these abstract, metaphysical arguments too often obfuscate rather than illuminate. The arguments are interminable and there are no possible and tangible verifications of them. He regards them as philosophical wheel spinning, claiming that we need a different kind of debate in which we take the claims of an existing religion whose metaphysical claims are normally connected to potentially embarrassing supernatural claims and examine them in the light of our best scientific knowledge. He then engages in a detailed discussion of the theory of creation versus the theory of evolution, the idea of God and modern physics, the religious claims about the Bible, Jesus Christ, and miracles, as well as mysticism and the nature of faith. His conclusions are atheistic, although he argues for a kind of poetry that has its roots in our historic religions but that does not tell us how things really are.

Atheism as Revolt. There is still another type of atheism worth noting that emerged after World War II and is sometimes associated with EXISTENTIALISM. This atheism is championed not because it is incompatible with science, but in the interest of the enhancement of the inner life. It argues that religious faith relieves the person from the burden of freedom, and that the rejection of absolutes of any kind is what gives life its value and, spread over a lifetime, restores majesty to that life. A powerful literary expression of this type of atheism is found in the writings of the French journalist Albert CAMUS. In his essay "The Myth of Sisyphus," he was concerned with the issue of why anyone should commit suicide, as some did, because they thought life had no higher meaning. He understood how such a question could arise because there are unavoidable experiences in life that prompt this question, especially when one has experienced a sense of the groundlessness and contingency of everything. The history of Western thought and religion may be understood as a series of attempts to discover some such ultimate meaning. But Camus concluded that any candid history of these attempts since PLATO reveals a series of impotencies. The human mind yearns for some final answer, but the world yields none. It is this incommensurability between the desire for meaning and the indifference of the universe that he labels "the Absurd." He argues, however, that instead of trying to escape the Absurd by suicide, religion, or philosophy, it is better to live with the conscious awareness of the lack of any transcendent meaning. It is better to live in revolt than in religious faith: whereas hope and faith relieve individuals of the weight of their lives, revolt casts them back on themselves and on the significance of every moment.

Agnosticism. The term *agnosticism* was coined by T. H. Huxley in the nineteenth century and soon was widely adopted by those who wanted to be neither theists nor aggressive atheists. Huxley later wrote that he coined the term because when he achieved intellectual maturity and noted that most of his colleagues were "-ists" of some kind—materialists, idealists, or atheists—he discovered that what separated him from them was that they all claimed to have *gnosis*, or knowledge, concerning the deepest issues of human existence, whereas he did not. And so he coined the privative *agnostic* to signify that he, for one, just did not know.

Actually, Huxley's position, when analyzed, involves more than simply the claim not to know. It is, as he makes clear, a commitment to a principle or method, a method that may be stated both positively and negatively. Positively, it means that we should follow our reason as far as it will take us in all matters of the intellect without regard to any other consideration. Negatively, it means that in matters of the intellect we should not pretend that conclusions that are neither demonstrated nor demonstrable are certain.

To say that the conclusions in the case of theism are not demonstrable reflects Huxley's obvious debt to the philosophy of Immanuel KANT, whose critique of classical metaphysics yielded the conclusion that the human mind by virtue of its very constitution was limited to knowledge of the world of sense experience. The mind was quite incapable of knowing anything that transcended that sense experience. But Kant did not deny the existence of God. Indeed, he argued that the idea of God was a "postulate" of the pure reason, and even though pure reason could not say that this postulate referred to an actual existing being, the moral or practical reason was compelled to posit God's existence. He wrote that he had limited reason in order to make room for faith.

Religious Agnosticism? The Kantian position that the divine is unknowable but nevertheless can be the legitimate object of belief is one of the reasons it is argued that agnosticism is not itself a third alternative to belief and unbelief. One might hold that the divine is unknowable and yet either believe or not believe. Indeed, there were prominent Protestant theologians in the nineteenth century—Friedrich Schleiermacher, Albrecht Ritschl, and Bishop Henry Mansel—who, under the influence of

Kant, argued that the divine was unknowable and that Christian theology was not a science of the divine but a description of the religious feelings or the value judgments of the community.

Huxley, however, would probably have refused to permit these theologians to claim the term *religious agnostic* for their position. He undoubtedly would have argued that these religious feelings and value judgments of the religious community were grounded in a certainty that a supernatural reality existed, and it was just such a certainty that his ethic of belief proscribed. Huxley's agnosticism was driven by the judgment that it was morally wrong to hold propositions for certain that were neither demonstrated nor demonstrable. For him, then, the notion of religious agnosticism was an oxymoron.

The most interesting philosophical question here is not how we are to define agnosticism, but how one formulates an ethics of belief that proscribes religious belief. Huxley seems to have formulated his ethics of belief in two slightly different ways. The first is "that it is wrong for a man to say that he is certain of the objective truth of any proposition unless he can produce evidence which logically justifies that certainty." In this formulation, the accent falls on the issue of certainty. It is because the religious believer holds his doctrines to be certain even though evidence is lacking that Huxley is critical. But there is a second, stronger formulation. In this instance, Huxley argues that the agnostic must repudiate as immoral the claim "that there are propositions which men ought to believe, without logically satisfactory evidence; and that reprobation ought to attach to the profession of disbelief in such inadequately supported propositions." In this formulation, it is not the claim to certainty that is condemned but the very act of believing propositions unsupported by evidence.

Agnosticism and the Ethics of Belief. W. K. Clifford's formulation of this ethics of belief leaves no room for such an ambiguity. Clifford simply states that "it is wrong, everywhere, and for anyone to believe anything on insufficient evidence." If the religious believer claims that he does not know but nevertheless believes "by faith," Clifford believes this is a "sin against mankind." This prohibition, in turn, is linked with the duty to inquire about anything that is proposed for our assent. If someone says that they do not have the time for such an inquiry, then Clifford replies that they should have no time to believe.

Many contemporary philosophers not unfriendly to either atheism or agnosticism argue that however high-minded Clifford's ethics of belief seems, it nevertheless rests on an erroneous view concerning our epistemic situation. They argue that we do not acquire our beliefs through inquiry or by the weighing of evidence for every proposition recommended to us. Rather, our culture teaches us to organize our experience in certain ways by giving us conceptions, rules of use, names, and the like. We acquire a loosely connected network of propositions in which the consequences and premises are mutually supporting, a picture of the world. And among the propositions we acquire, many are not empirical or grounded in evidence, although this has nothing to do with either stupidity or credulity. We do not acquire them through testing or investigation but simply by belonging to a community bound together by education and science. It is against this background that doubt arises, either because we find ourselves entertaining propositions whose consequences are contradictory or because they contradict our picture of the world. We begin by believing and we must have grounds for doubting.

If we were to assume some such situation as this, then someone might reformulate the basis for something like agnosticism in two slightly different ways. First, one might say that the rules of the community bound together by education and science are such that one simply cannot assess the truth or falsity of theistic belief. One just does not know and one decides to be neither a denier nor a believer. He or she is an agnostic. But there is a second formulation that preserves more of the intellectual ideal of Clifford. Here one decides to live as lucidly as possible, and this means actively willing to live within the limits of what seems evident to our community of education and science. The ideal is to keep one's mind as unclouded as possible by nostalgic desires and appeals to the absolute. One accepts the relativity of one's place in history and refuses to go beyond that complicated nest of propositions that our community has taught us constitutes reasonable belief. Perhaps many of these beliefs will be regarded by some future community as erroneous and theism may even come to seem more reasonable than it now is. But we will only arrive at this future reasonable community if we adopt those norms and procedures of inquiry that have produced what we now consider to be acceptable knowledge. Therefore, one does not now actively believe there is a deity but one does not claim that it does not exist. Under one definition, this is atheism; under another, it is called agnosticism.

BIBLIOGRAPHY

Camus, Albert. *The Myth of Sisyphus and Other Essays.* Translated by Justin O' Brien. New York: Knopf, 1955.

Clifford, W. K. *The Ethics of Belief and Other Essays.* Amherst, NY: Prometheus Books, 1999.

Edis, Taner. *The Ghost in the Universe.* Amherst, NY: Prometheus Books, 2002.

Feuerbach, Ludwig. *Lectures on the Essence of Religion.* Translated by Ralph Manheim. New York: Harper & Row, 1967.

Harvey, Van A. *Feuerbach and the Interpretation of Religion.* New York: Cambridge University Press, 1995.

Huxley, T. H. *Selections from the Essays of T. H. Huxley.*

Edited by Alburey Castel. New York: Appleton-Century-Crofts, 1948.

Mackie, J. L. *The Miracle of Theism: Arguments For and Against the Existence of God*. Oxford: Clarendon, 1982.

Schellenberger, J. L. *Divine Hiddenness and Human Reason*. Ithaca, NY: Cornell University Press, 1993.

A Secular Humanist Declaration. Drafted by Paul Kurtz and Endorsed by Fifty-eight Prominent Scholars and Writers. Amherst, NY: Prometheus Books, 1980.

Smith, George H. *Atheism: The Case against God*. Amherst, NY: Prometheus Books, 1989.

VAN A. HARVEY

ALLEN, ETHAN (1739–1789), American soldier and author. A courageous and intrepid hero of the Revolutionary War, Allen survived three years as a prisoner of the British and wrote the first sustained defense of DEISM in the United States. He grew up in a New England farming family and experienced the uncertainties and hardships typical of that era. In the 1760s he became a close friend of a physician Thomas Young, with whom he explored ideas arising from the deist tradition of John TOLAND and others. Allen and Young decided to write a book on this subject, but apparently did not complete it at the time—though Allen would later use some manuscript material from this collaboration.

By 1770 Allen had become active in the formation of the Green Mountain Boys, a militia of farmers who opposed attempts of Governor William Tryon of New York to thwart their claims to lands in what is now the state of Vermont. During this time Allen developed a well-earned reputation for hardheaded tenacity and exuberant profanity. When the Revolutionary War erupted, Allen and a group of his men marched to Fort Ticonderoga, where they surprised the heavily outnumbered British garrison. Allen demanded their surrender "in the name of the great Jehovah and the Continental Congress." This victory was a considerable morale booster for the rebels. But when Allen led an invasion of Canada, he was captured at Montréal and underwent severe treatment as a prisoner of war. His captors often cursed him and his fellow prisoners, threatening them with being hanged as traitors. Taken to England, Allen was displayed in chains in Falmouth, but was later transferred back to America. In New York City he witnessed the starvation of hundreds of American soldiers at the hands of the British. Upon release, Allen went to Valley Forge, where Gen. George Washington acclaimed his valor. His *Narrative of Colonel Ethan Allen's Captivity* was published in Philadelphia in 1779, while the outcome of the war was yet to be decided. Written in a vivid, homespun style, the *Narrative* presents a dramatic picture of his seizure of Ticonderoga, and the hardships he and his comrades suffered as prisoners.

After the victory of the Revolution in 1781, Allen continued to agitate for the admission of Vermont to the Union (not attained until 1791, after his death), and against what he viewed as tyrannical tendencies in the new republic. However, he soon decided to retire from active political life, and to complete the book he and Young had projected decades before.

Reason, the Only Oracle of Man was published in 1784 at Allen's own expense, though the printer refused to release it for two years. From an edition of perhaps fifteen hundred, only two hundred were sold before a fire destroyed most of the rest. Hence, the book became both scarce and notorious, even in Allen's lifetime.

In his preface, Allen writes: "I have generally been denominated a Deist, the reality of which I never disputed, being conscious I am no Christian, except mere infant baptism make me one; and as to being a Deist, I know not, strictly speaking, whether I am one or not, for I have never read their writings." Today, scholars tend to concur that a great part of Allen's book was probably written by his friend Young, who must have read at least some previous deist literature.

In thirteen chapters, *Reason, the Only Oracle of Man* takes up a number of ideas that would become standard fare in subsequent deist and FREETHOUGHT writing even to the present day. In common with deists, Allen argues that God represents a First Cause of the universe, and that the existence of this kind of deity can logically be inferred from the consistency of the laws of nature. Thus, like SPINOZA and Newton, Allen holds that God is for all practical purposes nearly equivalent to Nature. "God, the great architect of nature," he writes, "has so constructed its machinery, that it never needs to be altered or rectified." Like David HUME, Allen further argues that miracles, being by definition exceptions to the laws of nature, are generally fantastic and unbelievable on their face. "Nothing is more evident," Allen concludes, "to the understanding part of mankind, than that in those parts of the world where learning and science has prevailed, miracles have ceased."

Allen denounces episodes of demonic possession such as were experienced during the Salem witch trials: "Great numbers of the inhabitants of both sexes were judicially convicted of being wizards and witches, executed accordingly; some of whom were so infatuated with the delusion, that at their execution they confessed themselves guilty of the sorcery for which they were indicted." With satisfaction, Allen notes that in British jurisprudence, the laws against witches enacted during the reign of James I were repealed in 1739. Even so, Allen observes that various fantastic claims were entertained by the Shakers in his own times, under the misguided leadership of their "Elect Lady," Ann Lee. Allen wastes little time on the devil, mocking the large numbers of those who superstitiously credit that he actually exists (see DEVIL, UNBELIEF IN THE).

In the line of common deistic argument soon taken up by Thomas PAINE in his *Age of Reason*, Allen contends that the Mosaic account of creation is inconsistent and that the multiplicity of claims to ultimate truth by particular religions tends in the long run to cancel them all out. None is worthy of a vast, impersonal First Cause. Hence all forms of divine revelation are untenable, as are claims to Christ's divinity. Allen easily shows that the Bible itself is a historic document; its manuscripts were originally various, and translations equally so.

Moving toward his conclusion, Allen admits that "such of mankind, as break the fetters of their education, remove such other obstacles as are in their way, and have the confidence publicly to talk rational, exalt reason to its just supremacy, and vindicate truth and the ways of God's providence to men, are sure to be stamped with the epithet of irreligious, infidel, profane and the like." In response, he concludes, "all the satisfaction the honest man can have while the superstitious are squibbling hell fire at him, is to retort back upon them that they are priest ridden."

In spite of what he already perceived as social marginalization, Allen disdained to soften his views; like a soldier, he was prepared to take the consequences of telling the truth as he saw it. Having defied the king, he was not going to accept the king's tyrannical God, and he placed his hope for the republic in the steady advance of reason.

In retirement, Allen lived quietly until his death, at which time there was no religious ceremony, though the stone placed over his grave included a verse thus: "His spirit tried the mercies of his God, / In whom he believed, and strongly trusted." In 1855 a monument to his memory was erected in Burlington, Vermont.

BIBLIOGRAPHY

Bellesiles, Michael A. *Revolutionary Outlaws: Ethan Allen and the Struggle for Independence on the Early American Frontier*. Charlottesville: University Press of Virginia, 1993.

Walters, Kerry S. *The American Deists: Voices of Reason and Dissent in the Early Republic*. Lawrence: University Press of Kansas, 1992.

———. *Rational Infidels: The American Deists*. Durango, CO: Longwood Academic Press, 1992.

FRED WHITEHEAD

ALLEN, STEVE (1921–2000), American entertainer and author. Steve Allen was a unique figure in popular American culture, particularly in the media, for he was an outstanding defender of humanism and skepticism. His talents were multidimensional. He has been heralded by the entertainment industry as a gifted raconteur, comedian, performer, television pioneer, author of songs, plays, short stories, and novels, among other achievements.

He also had a serious side. A man deeply interested in ideas, he stands out as one of the few skeptical and agnostic intellectuals able to survive in the mass media

(see SKEPTICISM; AGNOSTICISM). Allen was a defender of often-unpopular causes—he was a consistent liberal in politics, a humanist and skeptical critic of religion and the paranormal, an exponent of rationality, and a severe opponent of raunch in TV and radio. This latter position provoked criticism from his liberal friends because he seemed to have allied himself with conservatives.

His award-winning TV series *Meeting of Minds*, which he wrote and produced in cooperation with his wife, Jayne Meadows, stood out in comparison with the generally mundane wasteland of TV fare. This series pitted SOCRATES, Marie Antoinette, Sir Thomas More, Tom PAINE, Karl MARX, Attila the Hun, Emily Dickinson, Thomas Aquinas, GALILEO, Charles DARWIN, and other historical figures in dialogue and disputation. Allen published fifteen books with Prometheus Books, including four volumes of the scripts from *Meeting of Minds* and several titles critical of American popular culture, such as *Dumbth: The Lost Art of Thinking with 101 Ways to Reason Better & Improve Your Mind* (1998), which dealt with the dumbing down of American life; and *Vulgarians at the Gate: Trash TV and Raunch Radio: Raising Standards of Popular Culture* (2001), which criticized vulgarity in the media.

Two of his books stand out for their contributions to biblical criticism and freethought: *Steve Allen on the Bible, Religion, & Morality* (1990) and *More Steve Allen on the Bible, Religion, & Morality* (1993). These books were issued at a time when the fundamentalist political movement in America was growing through organizations like the Moral Majority and challenging American secular values.

In his preface to the first volume, Allen said that although it had been his original intention to publish his studies after death, he decided to permit the publication earlier "because an element of emergency has entered the public dialogue." Steve Allen's books on the Bible, religion, and morality were unique, for they were virtually the only critical commentaries on the Bible published by a leading media celebrity containing not simply praise for Jesus but recognition of scripture's many factual errors, inconsistencies, and moral limitations. For example, Allen states: "The proposition that the entire human race—consisting of enormous hordes of humanity—would be placed seriously in danger of a fiery eternity characterized by unspeakable torments purely because a man disobeyed a deity by eating a piece of fruit offered him by his wife is inherently incredible."

Martin Gardner, in the preface to the book, said, "No other work by an American can be likened more favorably to Tom Paine's classic, *The Age of Reason*, than Steve Allen's book"—a compliment of the highest order coming from one of America's leading critical essayists. Indeed, Allen's two volumes could also be likened to the writings of Robert Green INGERSOLL, America's leading orator and agnostic of the nineteenth century. Allen was not an atheist (see ATHEISM), but he was a freethinker in the best sense of the word (see FREETHOUGHT), for he attacked fanatic and dogmatic religion at a time when he felt that this kind of criticism was necessary. He admitted that he was an agnostic.

Steve Allen also participated in many conferences of the Committee for the Scientific Investigation of Claims of the Paranormal (CSICOP), the Council for Secular Humanism, and the Center for Inquiry. He joined CSICOP's Council for Media Integrity in order to persuade television producers and writers to include more scientific content in their programs and to avoid confusing pseudoscience with genuine science. He thought that the campaign for scientific literacy was crucial to the future of the United States, for its scientific and technological development depended in part upon the public understanding of science.

He was elected a Laureate of the International Academy of Humanism in recognition of his commitment to science, reason, the cultivation of free inquiry, and humanist values.

PAUL KURTZ

AL-MA'ARRI (also known as ABU'L-'ALA AHMAD bin ABDALLAH; 973–1058), Islamic thinker. Al-Ma'arri, sometimes called the Eastern LUCRETIUS, is one of the great freethinkers of Islam. Born in Syria not far from Aleppo, Al-Ma'arri (or Abu'l-'Ala, as he is sometimes called) was struck at an early age with smallpox, which was eventually to lead to his total blindness. He studied in Aleppo, Antioch, and other Syrian towns before returning to his native town of Maara. As a young poet Al-Ma'arri was attracted to the famous cultural center of Baghdad, to which he traveled in 1008, but stayed only eighteen months.

Returning home, he lived in semiretirement for the next fifty years until his death. Such was his fame, however, that eager disciples flocked to Maara to listen to his lectures on poetry and grammar. His poetry is deeply affected by a pervasive pessimism. He constantly speaks of death as something very desirable, and regards procreation as a sin. At times, at least, he denies the resurrection. As for religion, he argues that all people unquestioningly accept the creed of their forebears out of habit, incapable of distinguishing the true from the false.

For Al-Ma'arri, religion is a "fable invented by the ancients," worthless except for those who exploit the credulous masses. At other times he refers to religions as "noxious weeds":

Among the crumbling ruins of the creeds
The Scout upon his camel played his reeds
And called out to his people—"Let us hence!
The pasture here is full of noxious weeds."

He clearly puts Islam on the same level as all other creeds, and believes not a word of any of them:

What is religion? A maid kept close that no eye
    may view her;
The price of her wedding-gifts and dowry baffles
    the wooer.
Of all the goodly doctrine that I from the pulpit
    heard
My heart has never accepted so much as a single
    word.

"Do not suppose the statements of the Prophets to be true; they are all fabrications. Men lived comfortably till they came and spoiled life. The 'sacred books' are only such a set of idle tales as any age could have and indeed did actually produce. What inconsistency that God should forbid the taking of life, and Himself send two angels to take each man's! And as for the promise of a second life—the soul could well have dispensed with both existences."

On Al-Ma'arri's view, Islam possesses no monopoly on truth; as for the *ulama*, the Muslim "clergy" or divines, Al-Ma'arri has nothing but contempt for them. Al-Ma'arri is a supreme rationalist (see RATIONALISM) who everywhere asserts "the rights of reason against the claims of custom, tradition and authority," mercilessly attacking every kind of superstition—astrology, augury, belief in omens, the custom of exclaiming "God be praised" when someone sneezes, and the like. He ridicules beliefs that the patriarchs lived to be hundreds of years old or that holy men walked on water or performed miracles.

Al-Ma'arri further offended Muslim sensibilities by composing "a somewhat frivolous parody of the sacred volume" (the Qur'an) and declaring that "in the author's judgment its inferiority was simply due to the fact that it was not yet polished by the tongues of four centuries of readers."

Another remarkable feature of Al-Ma'arri's thought was his belief that no living creature should be injured or harmed in any way. He adopted vegetarianism in his thirtieth year and held all killing of animals, whether for food or sport, in abhorrence. In his poetry, Al-Ma'arri firmly advocates abstinence from meat, fish, milk, eggs, and honey on the ground that it is an injustice to the animals concerned. Animals are capable of feeling pain, and it is immoral to inflict unnecessary harm on our fellow creatures. And even more remarkably, Al-Ma'arri protests against the use of animal skins for clothing, suggests wooden shoes, and reproaches court ladies for wearing furs. Von Kremer has justly said that Al-Ma'arri was centuries ahead of his time.

Al-Ma'arri was charged with HERESY during his life, but was neither prosecuted nor punished, for reasons that Von Kremer and Nicholson have carefully analyzed. Al-Ma'arri himself tells us that it is often wise to dissimulate, and thus we find in his poetry many orthodox passages meant to throw the sniffers of heresy off the scent. At heart, he seems to have been a thorough skeptic who managed to ridicule practically every dogma of Islam.

BIBLIOGRAPHY

Nicholson, R. A. *Studies in Islamic Poetry*. Cambridge: Cambridge University Press, 1921. All the translations of Al-Ma'arri and all quotations in the above text are drawn from this work.

IBN WARRAQ

AL-RAZI, ABU BAKR MUHAMMAD BIN ZAKARIYA (865–925), Islamic thinker. Perhaps the greatest freethinker (see FREETHOUGHT) in the whole of Islam was al-Razi, known as Rhazes in medieval Europe and as Razis by Chaucer. Al-Razi was a native of Rayy, near Tehran, where he studied mathematics, philosophy, astronomy, literature, and perhaps alchemy. He learned his medicine in Baghdad.

Al-Razi is credited with at least two hundred works on a wide variety of subjects excluding only mathematics. As a physician, al-Razi was a thorough and undogmatic empiricist. This is evident from his extant clinical notebook, in which he carefully recorded the progress of his patients, their maladies, and the results of their treatment. He wrote what was perhaps the earliest treatise on infectious diseases—smallpox and measles—based on his own painstaking empirical observations.

Most unusually, in *The Spiritual Physick*, his treatise on ethics, al-Razi refers not once to the Qur'an, the sayings of the Prophet, or any specific Muslim doctrine. The scholar Arberry describes his attitude as "tolerant agnosticism" and "intellectual hedonism." In the *Physick* al-Razi advocates moderation, disapproves of asceticism, and enjoins control of one's passions by reason. On life after death he reserves judgment, seeking to use reason to allay the fear of death, in a manner reminiscent of EPICURUS.

Al-Razi sees no possibility of a reconciliation between philosophy and religion. In two heretical works (see HERESY), one of which may well have influenced the European freethought classic *De Tribus Impostoribus* (see ITALY, UNBELIEF IN), al-Razi gives vent to his hostility toward the three revealed religions of the West. Al-Razi's heretical book *On Prophecy* has not survived, but we know that it maintained the theses that reason is superior to revelation and that salvation is possible only through philosophy.

In another work, al-Razi maintains that all men are by nature equal and equally endowed with the faculty of reason, which must not be disparaged in favor of blind faith; reason further enables men to perceive scientific truths in an immediate way. The prophets—"these billy goats with long beards"—cannot claim any intellectual or spiritual superiority; they pretend to come with a message from God, exhausting themselves in spouting their lies and imposing on the masses blind obedience to the "words of the master." Either the miracles of the prophets are impostures based on trickery, or the stories regarding them are lies. The falseness of what all the prophets say is evident in the fact that they contradict one another—one affirms what the other denies, and yet each claims to be the sole depository of the truth. Thus the New Testament contradicts the Torah, and the Qur'an the New Testament. As for the Qur'an, it is but an assorted mixture of "absurd and inconsistent fables" that has ridiculously been judged inimitable when in fact its language, style, and much-vaunted "eloquence" are far from faultless. Custom, tradition, and intellectual laziness lead men to blindly follow their religious leaders. Religions have been the sole cause of the bloody wars that have ravaged humankind. Religions have also been resolutely hostile to philosophical speculation and to scientific research. The so-called holy scriptures are worthless, and have done more harm than good, whereas "the writings of the ancients like PLATO, ARISTOTLE, Euclid, and Hippocrates have rendered much greater service to humanity."

In his political philosophy, al-Razi believed one could live in an orderly society without being terrorized by religious law or coerced by the prophets; that only through philosophy and human reason could human life be improved. Finally, al-Razi believed in scientific and philosophical progress, holding that the sciences progressed from generation to generation. He believed that one day they would be superseded by even greater minds than his.

BIBLIOGRAPHY

Al-Razi. *The Spiritual Physick*. Translated by A. J. Arberry. London: John Murray, 1950.

Hunter, M., and D. Wootton, eds. *Atheism from the Reformation to the Enlightenment*. Oxford: Oxford University Press, 1992.

Kraus, P., and S. Pines. "Al-Razi." In *Encyclopaedia of Islam*. Leiden: Brill, 1913–14.

Pines, S. "Philosophy." In *Cambridge History of Islam*, vol. 2B, edited by Holt, Lambton, Lewis. Cambridge, Cambridge University Press, 1970.

IBN WARRAQ

AMERICAN ASSOCIATION FOR THE ADVANCEMENT OF ATHEISM. This quixotic American FREETHOUGHT organization, usually known as "the 4As," was founded in 1925 by freethinking lawyer Charles L. SMITH and Freeman Hopwood, the grandson of a prominent frontier evangelist. New York briefly denied the group permission to incorporate on grounds that its purpose was (in its own words) "purely destructive . . . a wrecking company" whose "object . . . is to abolish belief in god, together with all forms of religion based upon that belief." Its goals included taxing churches, ending paid chaplaincy in government and the armed forces, ending state recognition of religious festivals, ending religious oaths in courts and upon assumption of public office, and ending legal recognition of the Sabbath. Incorporation was secured by 1926.

Lacking resources and popular support, the 4As set out to achieve what it could by bluster. Smith gained wide publicity by announcing a scheme to spread ATHEISM among young Americans. Within eighteen months some twenty college atheist groups formed, taking colorful names like the University of North Dakota's Legion of the Damned. A Junior Atheist League organized groups in high schools; in Los Angeles an atheist Sunday school was held.

By 1927 the Ku Klux Klan was worried enough to proclaim a list of states in which it would not allow 4As representatives to speak. At its peak, the 4As had about three thousand off-campus members nationwide. Local groups operated in New York City; San Francisco; Fort Worth, Texas; Rochester, New York City; and Los Angeles, where the prodigiously capable child atheist activist Queen SILVER had been recruited to the Junior Atheist League. In a weird bit of cultural fallout, Cecil B. DeMille's last silent film, *The Godless Girl* (1929), concerned a Junior Atheist League–style high school atheist club whose charismatic female leader was modeled after Silver.

The 4As held annual conferences and held weekly lectures in New York. It sued to abolish paid congressional chaplains and the motto "In God We Trust," but failed to fund appeals after losing in lower courts. Ultimately its student atheism project sputtered, groups failing to survive their founders' graduations. The Depression devastated 4As finances. After 1933 it was little more than the publisher of the *4A Bulletin*, a newsletter edited by Woolsey TELLER.

Smith merged the 4As with the TRUTH SEEKER organization. The *4A Bulletin* continued separate publication, changing its name to the *Atheist* in 1947. Following Teller's death in 1954 the *Atheist* was edited by successive editors of *The Truth Seeker*, first Smith, then James Hervey JOHNSON, who had purchased *The Truth Seeker* and the 4As from Smith in 1964. With Johnson's death in 1988, the 4As essentially dissolved, though it and a sister group, the National League for the Separation of Church and State, maintained a vestigial online presence into the early twenty-first century.

BIBLIOGRAPHY

Croy, Homer. "Atheism Beckons to Our Youth." *World's Work* 54 (1927).
———. "Atheism Rampant in Our Schools." *World's Work* 54 (1927).
McElroy, Wendy. *Queen Silver: The Godless Girl.* Amherst, NY: Prometheus Books, 2000.
Pankhurst, Jerry G. "Propaganda, Antireligious." In *The Encyclopedia of Unbelief*, edited by Gordon Stein. Amherst, NY: Prometheus Books, 1985.
Stein, Gordon. "Charles Lee Smith: 1887–1964." *American Rationalist*, May–June 1984.
———. "Smith, Charles Lee." In *The Encyclopedia of Unbelief*, edited by Gordon Stein. Amherst, NY: Prometheus Books, 1985.

TOM FLYNN

AMERICAN FREETHINKERS LEAGUE. See HALDEMAN-JULIUS, EMANUEL.

AMERICAN HUMANIST ASSOCIATION. Early organized HUMANISM in the United States was at first closely associated with the Unitarian Church (see UNITARIAN UNIVERSALISM), but it had other sources as well. Auguste COMTE described three ages of religion in human history. The first, he said, was the *theological*, in which humans ascribed to the supernatural whatever they did not understand. This was followed by the *metaphysical*, in which ideas were thought to be the key to natural phenomena. Finally came the *positive*, in which phenomena were—and are—understood using the scientific method. Positivist clubs were formed in Europe and in the Americas. A Church of POSITIVISM was even established in Brazil in 1881.

Other groups had ideas resembling Comte's; a group calling itself the Humanistic Religious Association formed in London in 1853. Its members proclaimed themselves free from the ancient compulsory dogmas, myths, and ceremonies of the past. They met regularly for cultural and social meetings, provided education for their children, and assisted members in need. Charles BRADLAUGH, an avowed atheist, brought together freethinkers (see FREETHOUGHT) to form the NATIONAL SECULAR SOCIETY in 1866. In 1859 a new liberal Christian denomination, the *Bund Frierreligose Gemeinden Deutschlands* (Federation of Free Religious Congregations of Germany) was established. In the United States, dissenters from creedalism within the Unitarian Church, led by Ralph Waldo EMERSON, founded the Free Religious Association, which included individuals of Jewish as well as Unitarian background. It promoted the idea of humanistic theism, but ceased to exist shortly after the beginning of the twentieth century. One of its supporters, Rabbi Isaac M. Wise, was a major force in organizing Reform Judaism, while another, Felix ADLER, founded ETHICAL CULTURE in 1876. Ethical Culture made social service a central focus, emphasizing the need to concentrate on this world and life. Adler's ideas were picked up by others who founded congregations in Chicago, Philadelphia, and St. Louis, among other places.

Moncure CONWAY, the American minister of a Unitarian chapel in London, began guiding his congregation in a specifically ethical direction. In 1887 his church became the SOUTH PLACE ETHICAL SOCIETY. In 1896 the International Ethical Union was established with congregations in the United States, the UK, Germany, Switzerland, Austria, and New Zealand.

The first reference to the concept of humanism in any of these groups came in the writing of Frederick J. Gould, a British Ethical Culture leader and editor of the *Leicester Reasoner*, who used the term *humanist* in an article in that paper to denote a belief and trust in human effort. After reading the article, John H. Dietrich, a Unitarian minister in Minneapolis, Minnesota, felt humanism was the best name for his new, fully naturalistic religious outlook. His conception of this term was adopted by other freethinkers—including Edward Howard Griggs, author of *The New Humanism: Studies in Personal and Social Development* (1899), and Frank Carleton Doan, who defended humanism and modernism in his *Religion and the Modern Mind* (1909)—as a way to explain their viewpoint.

These developments at the turn of the twentieth century marked a time when the Unitarian clergy was badly split between those who wanted a creed that would exclude both nontheists and other Christian dissenters from the denomination, and those who were opposed to creeds. It was not until a 1917 meeting of the Western Unitarian Conference, during which Dietrich and Curtis Reese combined their efforts to get the humanist movement under way within the Unitarian Church, that humanism began to gel as an organized movement. Progress was slow, however, until 1927, when a number of Unitarian professors and seminarians at the University of Chicago and Meadville Seminary (a Unitarian seminary that had recently moved from Pennsylvania to Chicago) organized to form a humanist fellowship. In 1928 the group launched a magazine titled the *New Humanist* (not to be confused with the present-day British publication of that name) to carry the message of a growing humanist movement. Edmund Wilson and Harold Buckman served as owners and publishers. The movement finally had a regular voice, which served briefly to unify "schismatic" ministers within the Unitarian Church.

Humanist ministers began again to leave the Unitarian Church, as Charles Francis Potter did in 1929 to form the First Humanist Society of New York. Still, the struggling humanist movement lacked focus until 1933, when thirty-four intellectual and ministerial leaders formulated and signed a document titled "A Humanist Manifesto," published in the *New Humanist*. Raymond Bragg and Ed Wilson took the lead in this initiative. Signers included the philosopher John DEWEY and the historian Harry Elmer Barnes, but most were leaders of Unitarian and Universalist societies. Still, the movement was a tenuous one. The *New Humanist* ceased publication due to lack of funds in 1936; in an effort to hold the movement together, Wilson began publishing a newsletter, the *Humanist Bulletin*, using his own funds.

Out of this ferment would emerge the American Humanist Association. Its immediate precursor, the Humanist Press Association, was organized in 1935. Modeled on the RATIONALIST PRESS ASSOCIATION (RPA)

of the UK, it was designed to encourage publication of information about humanism. It took over publishing the *Humanist Bulletin* in 1938, though Wilson remained as editor. Its president, Curtis W. Reese, suggested changing the association's name to the broader American Humanist Association, and the organization was so incorporated in 1941. To signify this change, the *Humanist Bulletin* published its last issue in January 1942, and changed its name to the *Humanist*. The first issue of the new magazine appeared in the spring of 1942. Wilson was the dominant force in the organization, serving both as publisher of the journal and as administrator of the AHA while also serving as a Unitarian minister, first in Schenectady, New York, and later in Salt Lake City before establishing a headquarters at Yellow Springs, Ohio. Wilson edited the *Humanist* until 1956 and served a second temporary term as editor from 1963 to 1964. He served as executive director of the AHA until he was succeeded by Toby McCarroll in 1965.

The editorship of the *Humanist* and the executive directorship of AHA were generally kept separate after Wilson stepped down. Philosopher Paul Kurtz served as editor of the *Humanist* from 1967 to 1978, when Lloyd Morain assumed the position. He was succeeded by Fred Edwords. The positions of editor and executive director were combined again under Edwords in 1994 before being separated once more at the beginning of the twenty-first century.

Overseeing the affairs of the AHA is a board of directors chosen by ballot vote from its members. The board at times has been rather cantankerous and has fueled considerable change in the organization's direction. As humanism changed, so did the AHA. One sign of this was the new manifesto, *Humanist Manifesto II*, drafted by Paul Kurtz with the assistance of Roy Fairfield, Ed Wilson, and others. Issued in 1973, *Manifesto II* was signed by several hundred individuals. Other humanist organizations also began to appear, many of them local groups not affiliated with the AHA, although some of their individual members were also members of the AHA. Some of these groups later went national and international, but the most successful was a national organization from its inception. Now known as the Council for Secular Humanism, it was founded by Paul Kurtz and others in 1980 as the Council for Democratic and Secular Humanism. It publishes *Free Inquiry* magazine. Interorganizational rivalries peaked in the late 1990s over a document drafted by Kurtz which was to be called *Humanist Manifesto III*. The AHA claimed copyright in *Humanist Manifestos I* and *II* and thus claimed that only the AHA could issue a manifesto titled *Manifesto III*. Though this claim was questionable, the council chose to issue its completed statement in 1999 under the title *Humanist Manifesto 2000*. This document set forth a new vision of a planetary humanism, but in the process the split between the AHA and the Council for Secular Humanism sharpened. The AHA finally published its own *Humanist Manifesto III* in 2004, but it was quite different from the earlier ones. Rather than listing specific goals, it made general statements without going into detail.

Now headquartered in the Washington, DC, area, the AHA has chapters in most major population centers of the United States. It was very active in the formation of the INTERNATIONAL HUMANIST AND ETHICAL UNION (IHEU) in 1952. Many of the individuals involved in this were also involved in the founding of the United Nations, and many of the humanist principles promoted by the AHA and the IHEU found expression in the international rights conventions of the UN. While the AHA is no longer the largest organization of humanists in the United States, it continues to grow slowly. Though there is not much programmatic difference between the AHA and the Council for Secular Humanism, the board of directors of the AHA is democratically elected, while the council has a self-perpetuating board, filling vacancies by board vote. The AHA is much closer to the Unitarian Universalist Church than is the council, and is a religious organization for tax purposes while the council holds educational status. Many humanists belong to both groups.

BIBLIOGRAPHY

Wilson, Edwin. *The Genesis of the Humanist Manifesto.* Amherst, NY: Humanist Press, 1995.

VERN L. BULLOUGH

AMERICAN LITERATURE, UNBELIEF IN. Religious SKEPTICISM, ANTICLERICALISM, and radical thought have shaped American literature through the centuries. Often the voices of dissent come from those who have had the least power: women, slaves and free blacks, and Native Americans. These voices and the voices of others who refuse to accept the status quo have given American literature its distinctive flavor, changing in focus from era to era but always standing for religious freedom and human rights.

Dissent has been a part of American literature from the beginning. Puritan tracts of the seventeenth century may be considered the start of American literature, but even in that theocratic society, some people refused to believe what they were told. Anne Hutchinson could be considered the first anticlerical figure in American literature (see ANTICLERICALISM), because she insisted on following her own spiritual path despite being thrown in prison and finally banished. Hutchinson herself did not write much, but she recurs as a figure in American literature, representing the woman in opposition. In John Winthrop's *Journal*, she represents what happens when anyone questions the official religion—her child is still-born, a "monstrous birth," and she later dies violently. Two centuries later, Nathaniel Hawthorne used Anne Hutchinson in *The Scarlet Letter* as the emblem of dissent against a repressive society.

Even as the Puritans were establishing their voice, Native Americans created oral tales and songs, and, later, slaves began to write their narratives. Contemporary literature by African American writers and by Native Americans has its roots in Puritan times or before and is by its nature a dissenting voice. American literature has always had a radical element, changing focus and forms over the centuries but ever vigilant against the hypocrisies and tyrannies of religion and the society that upholds it.

The Eighteenth Century, the American Enlightenment. The eighteenth century was the most radical in American history, leading to a revolution against monarchy and established religion. The great writers of the time, Benjamin FRANKLIN, Thomas JEFFERSON, and Thomas PAINE, were political figures, writing public papers in which they argued their radical thought. All three were outright in their anticlericalism, their religious SKEPTICISM, and their revolutionary ideas about politics and society. And all three were self-professed deists (see DEISM).

Benjamin Franklin wrote a humorous description in his *Autobiography* (1790) of turning to deism as a teenager by reading the arguments against it. However, as an adult, he gave his "mite" to many local churches, not because he had changed his mind, but because he believed that deism as a general principle wasn't "useful" for most people, whom he thought needed the coercive force of religion to keep them honest. He was willing to accept any religion as long as it fostered "Truth, Sincerity, and Integrity." His religious views were so rigorously tolerant that he convinced Philadelphians to build a meeting house for any speaker to use, "so that even if the Mufti of Constantinople" wanted to send a preacher, he would have a pulpit. This was a major shift away from the single-minded theocracy of the century before.

Franklin devised his own moral system, the "Thirteen Virtues," based on a spiritual pragmatism that considers frugality as important as humility. Nowhere in his "bold and arduous Project of arriving at moral Perfection" does Franklin include religious observance. Rather, his ethical project is rational and humanist (see HUMANISM).

Thomas Jefferson went further than Franklin in his attack on religious tyranny by writing religious freedom into law. In 1776 he helped change the laws of Virginia to protect every person's "natural right" to freedom of religion (see CHURCH, STATE, AND RELIGIOUS FREEDOM). Before that, the state practiced what Jefferson called "religious slavery," under which anyone who fell away from Christian beliefs would lose the right to hold office, be unable to sue, lose custody of children, and, in the most extreme case, be imprisoned for three years. Jefferson wrote an impassioned defense of religious freedom in his *Notes on the State of Virginia* (1784),

Query XVII. In his personal letters, Jefferson is vigorously anticlerical, particularly rejecting "priestcraft" in his letters to John Adams. In a letter to Adams dated April 11, 1823, he expresses his anger toward the Puritan religion that still lingered in American culture. He calls Calvin an "atheist" and Calvinism "daemonism." Jefferson's deism appears in this letter, in which he argues for "an ultimate cause." In a letter to William Short in 1819, Jefferson says that he follows the ideas of Epictetus and EPICURUS for self-government and considers Christ a "benevolent moralist." Christianity, on the other hand, is full of "bigotry and fanaticism" that has "deeply afflicted mankind." The "artificial systems" of religion are an evil that must be constantly guarded against in the new democracy.

Thomas Paine, likewise a strong proponent of deism, wrote *The Age of Reason* (1794) as a condemnation of the hypocrisies and cruelties perpetrated by believers in the Bible. Like Jefferson, Paine saw Christ as a man to be admired, calling him a "virtuous reformer and revolutionist," "an amiable man" whose vision has been distorted by "Christian mythology." He wrote with wry humor and elegant rationality as he shows the errors of religious superstition, and his rhetoric soars when he describes the deist vision. In contrast is the Bible, filled with "obscene stories," "voluptuous debaucheries," and "unrelenting vindictiveness." In France, Paine was imprisoned for defending deism as a natural religion; in America he was buried in dishonor, with Jefferson the only friend at the graveside, because he was popularly considered to be, as Theodore Roosevelt would later incorrectly call him, a "filthy little atheist." Still, *The Age of Reason* became the central text for philosophers who believed that "priestcraft" and tyranny went hand in hand.

In *The Rights of Man* (1791–92), Paine defends the right of every new generation to choose its own government. He shows that "by distortedly exalting some men, . . . others are distortedly debased" and, thus, that an aristocracy of wealth cannot succeed. Paine argues that the rights of man are fundamental and that unless a government is based on those rights it must fail.

In America in the eighteenth century, the three main human rights questions concerned slavery, the treatment of the American Indian, and the status of women. Although Franklin, Jefferson, and Paine agreed on the tenets of deism and democracy, they were not in accord on other human rights issues. Paine wrote an essay condemning slavery in America, and Jefferson argued against the slave trade in the Declaration of Independence. Franklin, late in life, came to hate slavery, also. But both Jefferson and Franklin owned slaves, and Jefferson wrote in Query XIV of *Notes on the State of Virginia* a "scientific" analysis of the inferiority of blacks to whites, including on grounds of appearance and intellect, arguing that the black race does not excel in any art and infamously declaiming that "religion could produce a

Phyllis Whately [*sic*], but it could not produce a poet."

Phyllis Wheatley, the first African American poet, consistently made a stand for freedom. She had to write indirectly about slavery to be published, but she was clear in her hatred of "the iron chain," "wanton Tyranny," and the "lawless hand." In her epistle to the Earl of Dartmouth (1773), Wheatley says, "Should you . . . / Wonder from whence my love of Freedom sprung," just remember that she was "snatch'd" from Africa and her father's arms. Although a Christian, Wheatley raises a radical issue in "On Being Brought from Africa to America" (1773): "Remember, Christians, Negroes, black as Cain, / May be refined, and join the angelic train." To claim that blacks are equal to whites in heaven was daring in slave-bound America.

Another strong antislavery voice is Olaudah Equiano in *The Interesting Narrative of the Life of Olaudah Equiano* (1789), the first significant slave narrative. Like Wheatley, Equiano takes a Christian stance, but he calls Christianity and the profit motive into question when he describes the horrors of the slave ship he was forced onto as a child. In chapter 2, he describes in chilling detail the "stench" of the hold, the way people were "so crowded that each had scarcely room to turn himself," the "galling of the chains," and children falling into "the filth of the necessary tubs." In a radical reversal of the captivity narrative, Equiano describes his European captors as "bad spirits" with "horrible looks, red faces, and long hair." A child at the time, Equiano was afraid they would eat him. At the end of this chapter, Equiano writes in lofty disdain, "O, ye nominal Christians! might not an African ask you—Learned you this from your God? . . . Surely, this is a new refinement in cruelty."

On the other question of race, how to interact with the Native American, Jefferson and Franklin were ahead of their times. Franklin wrote a satirical piece in support of the Native American, "Remarks concerning the Savages of North America," in which he showed the Native Americans as more civilized than the whites. In the piece, a chief of the Six Nations politely explains that the Native Americans do not want their sons to go to the white colleges because when their young men come back to them "they [are] bad Runners, . . . unable to bear either cold or hunger . . . [are] therefore neither fit for Hunters, Warriors, or Counsellors; they [are] totally good for nothing." He suggests instead that the whites should have their sons educated by the Native Americans, who would "make *Men* of them." At the end of the essay, the speaker tells a story about a white man who offers him four shillings for a pound of beaver before going to church, but only three shillings and some pence afterward. "This made it clear to me," he says, "that whatever they pretended of Meeting to learn *good things*, the real Purpose was to consult, how to cheat Indians in the Price of Beaver."

Jefferson likewise extols the virtues of Native Americans in his *Notes on the State of Virginia*, Query VI, finding them brave, intelligent, and advanced in the art of oratory, and in no way inferior to whites were they given the same education. Meanwhile, the Native Americans themselves gave stirring speeches in defense of their rights, an oral literature only recently recognized for its literary value.

The third human rights issue of the times was the rights of women. Franklin often took a woman's persona in his humorous essays, such as in "The Speech of Miss Polly Baker" (1747). Polly argues that she should not be punished for conceiving children out of wedlock, but should be paid by the state for populating the colony with the bastard children of its leaders. Although Polly is a strong female character, this is not a consciously feminist tract. Franklin did not believe in women's rights or in advanced education for girls. Jefferson is more outright in his misogyny, specifying in his letters to his daughter the limited education he considered appropriate for her. Jefferson believed that women should learn how to keep household accounts, speak French, and play the piano. He reserved any advanced education strictly for boys, although he was ahead of his time in including the top 10 percent of lower-class boys in this vision.

Thomas Paine, reliably on the liberal side of any argument, made a bow in the direction of equal rights for women, and his *Rights of Man* inspired the *Vindication of the Rights of Women* (1799) by English feminist Mary WOLLSTONECRAFT. Some eighteenth-century American women argued for women's rights, notably Judith Sargent Murray in "On the Equality of the Sexes" (1790). Tabitha Gilman Tenny's satiric novel *Female Quixotism* (1801) is remarkable: In an age when the only novels written in America were imitations of the English sentimental novel, *Female Quixotism* turns the sentimental novel upside-down. The novel's heroine, Dorcasina, tries her best to have a romantic encounter, but fails. The ostensible theme of the novel is that reading novels is pernicious for women, but the serious subtext argues for a wider education for women and more freedom to control their own lives.

Two other significant writers from this time period are J. Hector St. John De Crèvecoeur and Phillip Freneau. In his *Letters from an American Farmer* (1782), De Crèvecoeur describes the best in the American character (Letter III, "What Is an American"), including fairness to everyone and "decent" living. His vision for the future is that "religious indifference is imperceptibly disseminated from one end of the continent to the other." Gone will be "persecution, religious pride," and "the love of contradiction." But De Crèvecoeur also sees the negatives in America. In Letter IX, "Description of CharlesTown; Thoughts on Slavery," De Crèvecoeur describes a slave in a cage hanging from a tree, the birds pecking out his eyes. The man is in such pain that the narrator wishes to shoot him, but cannot. The narrator leaves the slave hanging there and goes to the home of the owner, who considers himself religious, only to hear the usual justifications for this barbarity. De Crèvecouer, seeing the vast wealth of Charlestown built on the backs of slaves, says, "[T]heir hearts are hardened; they neither see, hear, nor feel for the woes of their poor slaves. . . . The chosen race eat, drink, and live happy, while the unfortunate one grubs up the ground."

At the end of the century, Phillip Freneau wrote poems in support of human rights, such as "On Mr. Paine's *Rights of Man*" (1795), and in support of a "natural religion." In "On the Religion of Nature" (1815), Freneau praises a rationalist religion, believing that people are innately inclined toward "[t]he path of right." Because organized religion "dooms [mankind] to perpetual grief" and is built on "fraud, design, and error," we will find joy only by returning to our natural goodness.

The Nineteenth Century: Transcendentalism, Romanticism, and Realism. At the beginning of the nineteenth century, James Fenimore Cooper and Catherine Sedgwick picked up on the image of the strong, intelligent Native American drawn by Franklin and Jefferson. In contrast with the popular urge to demonize the enemy, their native characters are passionate, smart, and fiercely loyal to their friends.

A decade later came the great burst of dissent that was Transcendentalism. Ralph Waldo EMERSON, Henry David Thoreau, Margaret Fuller, and Walt WHITMAN, four leading Transcendentalists, were all radical thinkers of the nineteenth century. Emerson was barred from speaking at Harvard after he gave his "Divinity School Address" (1838), a graduation speech for new ministers in which he denied miracles, saying that Christ used the term miracles because "he felt that man's life was a miracle, . . . and he knew that this daily miracle shines." Emerson also said that all humans are divine and that Christ is God only in the same way that all of us are. Influenced by Eastern religions, Emerson posited an Over-Soul, rather than the God of the Bible. In "Nature," he argues that we are all "part and particle of God." Although the Transcendentalists reject the biblical God, they do believe in the "unseen in the seen."

Transcendentalists were not rationalists (see RATIONALISM). They were, however, social radicals. Thoreau wrote *Resistance to Civil Government* (1849), the little book that became the basic text for civil disobedience, first influencing Mahatma Ghandi in 1906 and later Martin Luther King Jr. in the 1960s. In this long essay, Thoreau declares that the strong individual will follow a "higher law" of his own devising when the civil law goes awry. "Unjust laws exist: shall we be content to obey them . . . or shall we transgress them at once?" King would quote Thoreau a hundred years later in his "Letter from Birmingham Jail" as he agrees that, when a law is unjust, "the true place for a just man is also a prison." Thoreau himself went to jail for one night to make his point against slavery and the Mexican War. In *Walden* (1854), Thoreau critiques capitalist values by stating that people don't own property as much as property owns them. "The mass of men lead lives of quiet desperation," he tells us in chapter 1, "Economy," because they work for wages or work to develop property, losing their humanity in the process.

Among the Transcendentalists, Margaret Fuller was the only prose writer who considered women equal to men and equally in need of a revolution in their lives. In *Woman in the Nineteenth Century* (1845), Fuller calls for a new social structure in which women can be fully human, not defined by marriage. Until society gives women full human rights, she says in "The Great Lawsuit," strong and imaginative women like George Sand and Mary Wollstonecraft will be "outlaws." Fuller's radical vision of gender is that men and women are androgynous and should develop according to their talents. In the chapter titled "The Great Radical Dualism," she calls on women to forgo marriage until they become "units" in themselves. She declares "celibacy as the great fact of the time" as women struggle to develop themselves.

Unlike Emerson and Thoreau, Walt Whitman embraced the idea of equality for women. His *Leaves of Grass* (1855, 1881), a cycle of poems with a preface, celebrates egalitarianism of all kinds. In "Song of Myself," Whitman equates senators with slaves and the working poor. He "celebrates" women, blacks, Native Americans, the sick, the mentally deranged, sailors, farmers, and seamstresses. He "sings America" as he sings himself: "Of every hue and caste am I, of every rank and religion" (sec. 16). Whitman also introduces a liberal view of sexuality, a daring idea for the Victorian nineteenth century. He "sings the body electric," saying, "I am the poet of the Body and I am the poet of the Soul / . . . / I am the poet of the woman the same as the man, / And I say it is as great to be a woman as to be a man" (sec. 21). Likewise, Whitman confronts death with a positive view: "All goes onward and outward, nothing collapses, / And to die is different from what any one supposes, and luckier" (sec. 6); "It is not chaos or death—it is form, union, plan—it is eternal life—it is Happiness" (sec. 50). This is not rationalist, but it is radical.

In this poem, Whitman is outspoken on religion. "Divine am I inside and out, and I make holy whatever I touch . . . / The scent of these arm-pits aroma finer than prayer, / This head more than churches, bibles, and all the creeds" (sec. 24). Whitman puts himself outside religion by embracing all forms, from "Making a fetich [*sic*] of the first rock or stump," to "minding the Koran," to "Accepting the Gospels." But he is with the "doubters," too (sec. 43). As to God, he tells us, "Be not curious about God / . . . I hear and behold God in every object, yet understand God not in the least, / Nor do I understand who there can be more wonderful than myself" (sec. 48). At last he says, "It is time to explain myself / . . . I launch all men and women forward with me into the Unknown" (sec. 44). This is the ultimate affirmation of radical thought.

The 1840s and 1850s are considered the romantic era in American literature. Of the romantics, the writer most

clearly an unbeliever is Herman Melville. Like the Transcendentalists, Melville admitted the unseen behind the seen, but what he saw was "the blackness of darkness." Raised in the Calvinist tradition, Melville wrote *Moby Dick* (1851) with a religious question in mind: Might the Calvinist God represent all "the demonism in the world"? The symbol of this god is Moby Dick himself. Ahab, the egomaniac captain of the *Pequod*, identifies "all evil" with the white whale. At the end of the novel, when Ahab strikes at the whale with his harpoon, he cries, "[T]o the last I grapple with thee; from hell's heart I stab at thee." Melville's first book, *Typee* (1846), brought Melville into trouble with the religious establishment because it assailed missionaries for ruining the cultures they meet and argued for religious tolerance. This tolerance is prominent in *Moby Dick*, too. Ishmael has a close bond with Queequeg, the pagan harpooneer. Ishmael reasons that since he is supposed to do unto others as he would want them to do unto him, and since he would like Queequeg to join him in his Presbyterianism, it follows that to make Queequeg happy he must join him in his religion: "Ergo, I must turn idolator," he says.

Although Melville does not address slavery in America directly, the race issue is at the fore in many of his novels and short stories, such as in "Benito Cereno" (1856), the story of a slave ship taken over by the wit and strength of the slaves. Melville consistently shows the evils of imperialism abroad and capitalism at home. His "Bartleby the Scrivener" (1856) depicts Bartleby, a clerk in a law office, refusing the dehumanizing tasks he is asked to perform. He "prefers not to" participate any longer in a system that treats him like a piece of property. One of the darkest of Melville's works, this story ends with Bartleby "preferring not" to live.

Melville's contemporary, Nathaniel Hawthorne, was not such an iconoclast, although he criticized the Puritan heritage both in his own family and in society at large. In *The Scarlet Letter* (1850), he created the great Hester Prynne, who, like Margaret Fuller, questions a social system that twists relationships between men and women. In "Another View of Hester," Hester considers how "the whole system of society is to be torn down, and built up anew." But Hawthorne recants when he has Hester return to the Puritan society that cast her out, to live the rest of her days in atonement.

Not a romantic, but writing at the same time, is Frederick DOUGLASS, whose *Narrative of the Life of Frederick Douglass* (1845) makes clear the connection between slavery and established religion. Douglass, an escaped slave, says in chapter 9 that the worst slave owners were the religious ones, with their "pretensions to piety."

Meanwhile, Protestant Christianity was the norm, and popular novelists promoted Christian ideology with its belief in the submission of women and often acceptance of slavery. Another Protestant issue was the fear of

Catholicism that grew from the massive numbers of Catholics immigrating at that time. Although some literary writers expressed anti-Catholic sentiments—Edgar Allen Poe criticized the Inquisition in "The Pit and the Pendulum" (1845) and Melville linked slavery with Catholicism in "Benito Cereno"—most anti-Catholicism arose in the popular literature. *The Awful Disclosures of Maria Monk* (1836), the purported tale of a young woman's experiences in a Canadian convent, sold over three hundred thousand copies before the Civil War. Many similar books in America had a broad audience, mainly because of the sexually explicit descriptions and sadomasochistic themes.

In the 1860s it was Emily Dickinson who questioned religion and the existence of God. Often mistakenly read as a Christian writer, Dickinson remains a prominent doubter in American letters. Dickinson's poems, deceptively simple, ask deep questions. In Poem 501 ("This World Is Not Conclusion"), the speaker runs through the arguments for an afterlife then ends with the line, "Narcotics cannot still the Tooth / That nibbles at the soul—." The well-known "I heard a fly buzz when I died" (poem 465) questions what happens at the moment of death. A dying person expects "the King" to appear and instead "there interposed a fly," the last vision not God but an insect, buzzing. Dickinson is skeptical of most "truths" she is handed. "I like a look of agony," one of her speakers says (poem 241), "Because I know it's true—. / Men do not sham convulsion, / Nor simulate, a Throe—." It is ironic that Dickinson's poetry, which ruthlessly uncovers religious hypocrisy and is keenly skeptical, now sells as light reading.

The romantic era ends with the Civil War. From that point onward, most writers are realists. Mark Twain (see CLEMENS, SAMUEL LANGHORNE) was a realist who satirized "sivilization" and religious humbug. In *The Adventures of Huckleberry Finn* (1884), a scoundrel at a camp meeting claims to be a missionary and bilks the fervent crowd, the Duke and the King pretend to be religious men even as they steal gold from a bereaved family and sell a whole family of slaves downriver, and Huck Finn determines to go against what civilization has taught him: He will try to save his slave friend Jim. If it's wrong to steal a slave out of slavery, he decides, "Then I'll go to hell!" In this novel, too, the Grangerfords pray every night and take their guns to church every Sunday, yet participate in a feud that kills children for "honor's" sake. Twain also wrote *Letters from the Earth* in 1909, a collection of humorous pieces of religious skepticism that were published posthumously.

In the last decade of the nineteenth century, realism turned to naturalism, with such writers as Stephen Crane and Theodore DREISER writing about humanity's lack of free will. In the wake of Charles DARWIN and Karl MARX, our lives seemed determined by biology and our economic class. In Crane's "The Open Boat" (1897), the narrator, a shipwreck survivor, is so frustrated that he

"wishes to throw bricks at the temple." But at last he realizes that "there are no bricks and no temples." One of the most striking images in Crane's *The Red Badge of Courage* (1895) is of a dead soldier sitting under a beautiful tree, being devoured by insects. Naturalists understood the indifference of nature and refused to hold to a religious belief in contradiction of what they saw. However, Crane, like Melville before him, argued for the positive value of "the subtle brotherhood of men."

Similarly, Theodore Dreiser argued against free will by showing the role of chance and "chemisms" in our actions. In *Sister Carrie* (1900) a mixture of lust, greed, and chance drive a man to steal the money that will be his downfall. *Sister Carrie* was denounced as a godless book because Carrie, a "fallen woman" moving from man to man, successfully climbs the social scale. Another such success is Undine Spragg, in Edith Wharton's *The Custom of the Country* (1913), a skeptical analysis of capitalism and romance in America. The end of the nineteenth century brought Kate Chopin, ostracized because of her dissenting opinions about women, sex, and motherhood. It also produced Charlotte Perkins GILMAN, whose "The Yellow Wallpaper" (1892) is an exposé of "the rest cure" and society's repressive expectations of women. Gilman later wrote *Women and Economics*, a radical economic analysis.

At the turn of the century, W. E. B. DuBois wrote *The Souls of Black Folk*, which includes an indictment of the established religions in America that perpetuate racial discrimination and of a political system that allows some people to grow rich on the backs of the poor. Socialists Jack London and Upton SINCLAIR (*The Jungle*, 1904) wrote their critiques of capitalism then, also.

The Twentieth Century: Modernism, Postmodernism, and Ethnic Literature. Of all the centuries in American literature, the twentieth can be named the century of unbelief. Beginning with the modernists from the 1920s to the 1940s, a general skepticism swept American letters. World War I undermined our political illusions, and science showed how our biology, our subconscious drives, and our social class control us. With Friedrich NIETZSCHE, the modernists agreed that "God is dead." Many modernists became expatriates, shunning American consumerist values and feel-good religion. Among the poets, T. S. Eliot depicts the emptiness of twentieth-century life in *The Waste Land* (1922), which ends with the Hindu precepts: Give, Sympathize, and Control. "H.D." (Hilda Dolittle) likewise turned away from Christianity to consider Egyptian religions in *The Walls Do Not Fall* (1944), and Ezra Pound studied the moral systems of the Chinese. Robert Frost (who stayed in America) is, like Emily Dickinson, often misread as a nature poet. However, poems like "Design" (1922) go beneath nature to ask an ultimate question: In this case, what would lead a white moth to a white flower in order to be killed by a white spider? "What but design of darkness to appall?— / If design govern in a thing so small."

Wallace Stevens suggested that there is no design other than the design an artist makes. In "The Idea of Order at Key West" (1936), chaos is ordered by a woman singing, emblem of the poet creating order through language. In the satiric "next to of course god america i," e. e. cummings used language play to explore the junctures among consumerism, patriotism, and religion.

In fiction, Ernest Hemingway posited a "code hero" instead of a set of religious values. "The Snows of Kilimanjaro" (1936) deals with a man dying for an absurd reason, but dying with dignity, facing the errors of his life with poise, even as the hyenas approach. Taking a different tack, Katherine Anne Porter wrote "The Jilting of Granny Weatherall" (1935), in which Granny, confidently Catholic, discovers at the moment of death that she is jilted when God does not show up. Granny stands up to the situation, saying, "there's nothing more cruel than this—I'll never forgive it." In these same years, Sinclair LEWIS wrote *Elmer Gantry* (1927), a satiric portrayal of a preacher, and Djuna Barnes questioned gender roles in *Nightwood* (1936).

If modernism connotes despair and disillusionment because there is no central truth, postmodernism connotes joy for the same reason. With no truth, there is no hierarchy. Relativism becomes "infinite play" for the postmodernists, and life is a game. Absurdists like Edward Albee (*Who's Afraid of Virginia Woolf*, 1962) saw the dark humor of meaninglessness. Postmodernists turned meaninglessness into play. Thomas Pynchon's *The Crying of Lot 49* (1966) has Oedipa Maas search for the "truth" about an elusive and secret postal service, her quest leading her into wild company and hilarious scenes. The search, of course, ends nowhere. An offshoot of postmodernism in the 1960s and 1970s was "metafiction," fiction that plays a game with literary convention. Metafictionists like John Barth in *Lost in the Funhouse* (1968) were so far beyond worrying about meaning that they questioned even the last stronghold of the serious literary writer—the moral effectiveness of literature. Metafiction shows how meaning deconstructs before it begins.

While the postmodernists were arguing that nothing has meaning, the civil rights era of the late 1960s brought about a countermovement. Blacks in America had been skeptical about traditional religion and its attendant social values from the beginning, since Christianity was the religion of the slave owners (see AFRICAN AMERICANS, UNBELIEF AND). By the mid-twentieth century, many black writers saw that the cross had become the symbol of the Ku Klux Klan and the profit motive had built the ghettos and fueled lynchings. Richard WRIGHT, Langston HUGHES, and Ralph Ellison, African American writers of the 1940s and 1950s, wrote passionate denunciations of American society in such works as *Invisible Man* (1952) and *Native Son* (1940). All three dabbled in communism until they discovered that it was as racist as American capitalism was. By the time the

riots occurred in the long hot summers of the late 1960s, black writers had stopped trying to assimilate to Euro-American ideals and had created the Black Arts Movement. This movement called for a new aesthetic that would destroy the old belief systems and imagine a new literature and a new culture based on black experience and community.

An upsurge in literature by marginalized ethnic groups began soon after. The Black Arts Movement led to the Native American Renaissance, which in turn opened the door for Asian American and later Latino writers. The writers on the cutting edge of American literature today come from these ethnic groups and from the gay community (for instance, David Hwang with *M. Butterfly* [1988] and Terrence McNally with *Andree's Mother* [1990]). These authors reject the mainstream American values that claim anyone "different" is wrong. Instead, they work from a value system born of their home cultures. Native American writers like N. Scott Momaday in *House Made of Dawn* (1968) and Leslie Marmon Silko in *Ceremony* (1977) describe a belief system that is not Christian but Navajo or Laguna Pueblo. For Native American writers, there is another plane of existence that affects our own, and the trickster, the ancient transformer/bringer of chaos, is alive and well. This is unbelief turned on its head. Likewise, Nobel Prize winner Toni Morrison wrote *Beloved* (1988), in which the title character is both woman and ghost. She represents the "60 million" who were enslaved. Maxine Hong Kingston has ghosts in her novel *The Woman Warrior* (1975), based on the Asian tradition, as does August Wilson, the African American playwright, in *The Piano Lesson* (1990). All of these works argue for a radical restructuring of the American value system and create new forms for American literature.

Obviously, "unbelief" in American literature is a complex consideration. But unbelief in some form has been a defining concept from the beginning.

KATHLEEN DE GRAVE AND EARL LEE

AMERICAN RATIONALIST. For half a century, the US periodical publication the *American Rationalist* has dared to criticize the absurdity of religious beliefs and to defy tradition, convention, church, and state.

Its founding publisher was Rationalist Publications, a nonprofit publishing venture established to promote the rationalist movement (see RATIONALISM). *American Rationalist* was envisioned as a channel for ideas, suggestions, problems, and solutions that would further the movement. The first editor was Arthur B. Hewson of Chicago. The premiere issue in May 1956 featured a photo of the Freie Geminde Building in St. Louis, former home of a German-speaking FREETHOUGHT group (see FREIE GEMEINDEN).

The publication was first produced and distributed from Chicago and was later moved to St. Louis. A dedicated group of rationalists agreed to use their own resources to keep the publication afloat until it was self-supporting. It has always been a shoestring operation. In time, enough donations and bequests were contributed to assure continued publication while keeping subscription rates at very affordable levels.

Over the years the publication had several editors, including Edd Doerr, Walter HOOPS, and Eldon Scholl. Of note as editor was Gordon STEIN, who brought the magazine an edgy character by including articles on biblical criticism and little-known historical freethinkers. The current editor, Kaz Dziamka, has continued this practice.

Another goal of the *American Rationalist* was to provide a book service offering rationalist books, pamphlets, tracts, and other literature by mail order. Walter Hoops ran this service for many years, using its earnings to support the organization.

From the beginning *American Rationalist* was a low-tech, volunteer operation. For many years Eldon Scholl and his wife, Norma, prepared each issue for mailing from their home using typed name sheets photocopied onto labels. After Scholl died, the Rationalist Society of St. Louis did the work as a group taking an afternoon folding, gluing, and sorting to get them ready for mailing.

In 1996 ownership of the *American Rationalist* was transferred to the Center for Inquiry, where it should remain a viable publication for many years to come.

BARBARA STOCKER

AMERICAN RATIONALIST FEDERATION. The Jan Hus Memorial Hall of Chicago provided the venue on November 19–20, 1955, as twelve organizations joined efforts in the cause of RATIONALISM. Several ethnically German groups from Milwaukee and St. Louis supported this effort, quickly joined by Czech rationalists. The constitution of the American Rationalist Federation (ARF) stated that its purpose was "to coordinate on a national scale the efforts of local, autonomous, Rationalist, Secularist, FREETHOUGHT and like-minded organizations in preserving the principles of separation of church and state and to promote Rationalism, which is defined as the mental attitude which unreservedly accepts the supremacy of reason and aims at the establishment of a system of philosophy and ethics verifiable by experience, independent of all arbitrary assumptions or authority." The formation of the ARF was reported in the first issue of the new journal, the *AMERICAN RATIONALIST*, in May 1956. There was no formal connection between the ARF and the journal, though over the ensuing years reports of ARF activities and conventions regularly appeared in its pages, usually authored by Eldon Scholl of St. Louis, where the ARF had its headquarters in that city's Freie Gemeinde building (see FREIE GEMEINDEN).

The ARF's conventions were a focus of its work, and prominent activists were often the featured speakers. In 1962 Madalyn Murray O'HAIR gave a spirited defense of materialism; but by 1965 the ARF had withdrawn its support of O'Hair's efforts, alleging a lack of information regarding her finances. In that same year, the ARF established the Foundation of Rational Endeavor, to provide material support to educational work. The 1968 convention featured a talk by H. B. Dodd, an African American who had initiated a series of radio broadcasts in the cause of humanism in Beaumont, Texas. The foundation supported his project, but was later critical because of a lack of information on contacts made via the broadcasts. Occasionally, ARF meetings attracted sizable numbers; in 1969, some six hundred attended a debate on EVOLUTION and related topics between a Harding College professor and a rationalist.

But the next year, as an editorial in the *American Rationalist* lamented, delegates from only three organizations showed up in St. Louis, "and their reports were on the pessimistic side. Membership is falling off and new adherents are hard to find, especially among the two main ethnic groups represented in the AFR: the Czechs and Germans."

Even so, the *American Rationalist* continued to appear steadily. By the late 1970s it was reporting on the growth of the Freedom From Religion Foundation (FFRF), which had emerged in a split from O'Hair's American Atheists. So while the ARF was slowly dwindling, other similar organizations were rising to the fore. In 1987, seventy-two people from ten states registered for the annual convention. But shortly afterward the ARF apparently ceased to exist, though the Rationalist Society of St. Louis continued to operate on a local basis.

In its thirty years, the ARF sustained the rationalist cause under difficult circumstances, from its foundation in the middle of the McCarthy era through the turbulence of the 1960s. Notable among ARF officers were Walter Hoops and Eldon Scholl; their deaths paralleled the end of the organization, though their latter years were brightened by the vitality of the FFRF, the Council for Democratic and Secular Humanism (later the Council for Secular Humanism), and, later, the Atheist Alliance.

FRED WHITEHEAD

AMERICAN SECULAR UNION. In October 1885 the NATIONAL LIBERAL LEAGUE (NLL) met in Cleveland, Ohio, and renamed itself the American Secular Union (ASU). It had been the intention of the league to become a voice for moderate secular opinion (see SECULARISM) in America. This had not happened, largely thanks to successful stereotyping of secularists as radicals by religious rivals. Organizers hoped the new name would reassure middle-of-the-road Americans that the organization was respectable. The word *secular* was then at the height of its authority and implied sensible, nonradical views on issues like the separation of church and state. Robert Green INGERSOLL, who had resigned from the NLL, was persuaded to return as the president of the newly formed ASU. The high point of his tenure was the presentation of his address "A Lay Sermon" at Chickering Hall, New York, at the ASU's second congress in 1886.

Though anxious to claim the middle ground, the ASU was loyal to its progressive ethos when it elected Mattie KREKEL as vice president in 1885, noting that women "have to suffer a little more punishment than men, being amenable to social laws that are more exacting and tyrannical than those passed by Legislatures." But the real power behind the reformed organization was Samuel Porter PUTNAM, who served as the group's president and secretary at various times.

One of the ASU's greatest successes was a legal suit brought against the Catholic archbishop of Chicago, who was found to have directed public funds to sectarian institutions. The church had to repay what was then the enormous sum of $60,000. These successes were not without cost, however, because they only made more difficult the attempt to shake off the negative public stereotype of freethinkers (see FREETHOUGHT) as radicals. When the ASU met in Pittsburgh in 1888, its leaders narrowly avoided arrest on the grounds of their unbelief. At that congress, members elected the former Presbyterian minister Richard Westbrook as president. Westbrook oversaw the publication of a manual of morality called *Conduct as a Fine Art*, by N. P. Gilman (father of Charlotte Perkins GILMAN) and E. P. Jackson.

In 1891 the radicals, tired of what they saw as a pointless policy of trying to appease the clergy, broke off, and founded a rival freethought body in Chicago. This led to the intervention, once again, of Samuel Putnam, who effected a union of the ASU and another group, the Freethought Federation, in 1894. While Putnam remained active, the ASU & FF—as the organization was now known—achieved a relatively high profile. Putnam's greatest political success was his effort to defeat an 1896 proposal to alter the US Constitution by inserting a mention of God. Putnam's speech before the Joint Judiciary Committee of the House on March 11 of that year helped to kill the bill, a fact his Christian opponents acknowledged.

The untimely death of Putnam in December 1896 spelled the end of the ASU & FF as a significant force in American society. It continued as a freethought organization for another twenty years, largely due to the tireless leadership of John Eleazer REMSBURG as president and E. C. Reichwald at secretary. After the deaths of Remsberg and Reichwald in 1919, the organization withered away.

BIBLIOGRAPHY

Macdonald, George E. *Fifty Years of Freethought*. New York: Truth Seeker Company, 1972.

Putnam, Samuel P. *Four Hundred Years of Freethought*. New York: Truth Seeker Company, 1894.

BILL COOKE

ANARCHISM AND UNBELIEF. Anarchism and unbelief are inseparable wherever capitalism, private property, social hierarchies, or slavery are justified by theology.

Being attractive to people who question any prevailing hierarchy, anarchism can coexist with atheistic or dissenting religious views, and in both cases has been in a continuous conflict with organized religion. In 1609 British investors drafted Laws Divine, Moral, and Martial, providing for the torture and execution of their personnel in Virginia and Bermuda who were caught escaping from plantations to join the anarchistic native societies of those lands. In Boston during the 1630s the Antinomian intellectual Anne Hutchinson was absolutely devoted to Christianity, but in Monday-night meetings at her home she discussed the previous day's sermon with neighbors, and took the anarchistic position that any person who was with God was equal in all ways to any other person (male or female) who was with God. With her obvious intellectual eminence adding to the displeasure of Puritan authorities, Hutchinson endured a humiliating trial, house arrest, and then banishment from the colony. Views similar to hers were developed in the fight against slavery during the 1830s, by then usually called Immediatism, or the immediate and direct government of God over each human being with no intermediary such as a professional clergy or state institutions. This meant that a master usurped the authority of God by making moral choices for a slave, and it defied government authority. William Lloyd Garrison professed "nonresistance" as a guiding principle for abolitionists: the New Testament forbids the use of force (counseling instead that believers "turn the other cheek"), government is upheld by force, and thus a Christian must abstain from government. The fact that the New England Non-Resistance Society (of which Garrison was the leader) allowed infidels among its members was as controversial among abolitionists as its inclusion of women and Negroes.

Most important nineteenth-century anarchist theorists agreed that people acquire the habit of obedience to the state from the persuasion of theistic religion. Mikhail BAKUNIN wrote that "there is not, there cannot be, a State without religion," and also that "if God existed, it would be necessary to abolish him." Pierre-Joseph PROUDHON wrote that "if God exists, he is Man's enemy." Both viewed the belief of privileged classes that they are nearer to or more favored by God as the chief pretext for their exercise of human authority. None of them, however, opposed freedom of religion: it was the monopoly of theology that presented a societal problem. Max STIRNER, whose 1845 book *The Ego and His Own* has remained a foundation-stone of anarchist individualism, wrote, "I no longer do anything for [the world] 'for God's sake,' I do nothing 'for Man's sake,' but what I do, I do 'for my sake.'" Stirner felt that he was entitled to overthrow all deities "if I can. If I cannot, then these gods will always remain in the right and in the might against me." He held that religious thought was just one of the avenues by which laws are created, along with the concept of "rights" brought up in popular revolution. His egoism rejected anything that made laws, because all laws created a "sacred" boundary, interfering with the interests of the individual.

The French anarchist outlaw known by his maternal surname, Ravachol, had a violent career of reprisals against state violence that included the strangling of an elderly hermit-monk who hoarded money. In 1892 he walked to the guillotine singing the anticlerical anthem (see ANTICLERICALISM) "Pere Duchesne," but the blade fell as he sang its penultimate verse: "If you want to be happy, god damn it, / hang your landlord, cut the priests in two, god damn it! / Knock the churches to the ground, bloody god! / bury the good god in shit, god damn it!" The song is still popular today among French anarchists.

Jewish anarchists of the late 1880s were prominent in a public antireligious campaign, with atheist-Talmudists lecturing against the religion and holding Yom Kippur Balls on that most solemn holiday when all nonreligious activities halt. This developed from a more discreet tradition by which radical groups held secular social gatherings so there would be something else to do on the high holidays other than stay home or pray. Taking it a step further, in London and several US cities they announced public dancing and drinking parties for which they printed special atheist brochures written by gifted anarchists including the songwriter David Edelstadt. The balls drew violent opposition from religious Jews and suppression by authorities through the midnineties, yet Jewish anarchists were involved in atheist events on high holidays as late as 1905. Speaking at some of the Yom Kippur Balls was the (non-Jewish) German anarchist leader Johann Most, whose popular 1883 pamphlet "The God Pestilence" uses his typically harsh language: "If a person is once in the clutches of the priests, his intellect becomes barren . . . and instead, religious maggots and divine worms wriggle through his brain. He resembles a sheep that has the staggers."

Anarchist novelists and playwrights have produced masterful works of unbelief. Examples include the autobiographical novel *Sebastien Roche* (1890) by Octave Mirbeau, which describes a boy student at a Jesuit school who is raped and psychologically devastated by a priest. More recently the novel *La Petite Écuyère a Café* (1996) by Jean-Bernard Pouy, whose villains are murderous Catholic antiabortion crusaders undone by an independent anarchist investigator, began the "Le Poulpe" series of dissident pulp fiction by hundreds of (often anarchist) authors. Other examples use an anarchist but nonatheist plot, such as Ursula K. Le Guin's science fiction novel *The Word for World Is Forest* (1976). The people of a certain planet repel an invasion by capitalist plunderers who have enslaved them. One of the forest dwellers temporarily becomes a god, only for

the period when the rebellion and a leader are necessary. After the war, he returns to his life with no title or special status.

Turning to theater, Octave Mirbeau's debut as a playwright was *Les Mauvais Bergers* (The bad shepherds, 1898). The lead character is an anarchist militant who leads a long and difficult strike. The workers turn against him and are about to lynch him on a "Calvary," when his lover, Madeleine (played by Sarah Bernhardt), pleads for his life and turns the workers back to the strike, which ends in a bloodbath. The plot depicts all leaders (religious, capitalist, political, and even anarchist) as similarly bad. One year later, Mirbeau's dedication to the novel *Torture Garden* says it again: "To the priests, the soldiers, the judges / to those people who educate, instruct and govern men / I dedicate these pages of Murder and Blood." The intense interest of anarchist critics and theater groups was critical in promoting the iconoclastic playwright Henrik Ibsen to international audiences.

The explicitly atheist-anarchist songs of the Yiddish "sweatshop poet" David Edelstadt were so popular, and the man himself so deeply mourned after his death in 1892 at age twenty-six of tuberculosis, that there were Edelstadt singing clubs in many cities for some sixty years after his death. Voltairine DE CLEYRE was one among many Anglophone anarchist-FREETHOUGHT poets. Her "Nameless" (1889) gave voice to a desperately poor woman who has already lost her husband and baby son who, on her own deathbed, ridicules a minister who has come "to pray my soul through the gates of gloom." She asks the minister, "[W]ould you care to preach for seventeen hours at thirty-five cents a day? / It wasn't often I'd make that much, for sewing without a fire, / in dead of winter, is fearful work, and your stiffened fingers tire." In her last minute of life she says, "No! Your prayers would be useless. I asked for bread, and your Christ gave me a stone."

After the 1901 killing of US president William McKinley by Leon Czolgosz, an emotionally depressed workingman who had attended a few anarchist meetings, religious leaders launched furious attacks against anarchists. Among the countless examples was Rev. Russell H. Conwell, leading Philadelphia Baptist and founder of Temple University, who said from his pulpit that "either the anarchists must be exterminated from the country or the government must die. There is no middle ground. . . . We must keep out of the country, or send out of the country, or hang from the gallows every man who does not believe in a government founded on the Ten Commandments and the moral law established by Jesus Christ. He has no right to live, he is an enemy to Society."

Anticlerical anarchism colored the economic depression of 1907–1908. On February 23, 1908, Giuseppe Alia, a poor Sicilian anarchist living in Denver, shot a Catholic priest dead at the altar after spitting the communion wafer to the floor. Alia had been driven from his village and family for his ATHEISM, and the dead priest was wearing "scourges" (a girdle and armlets fitted with hooks) to continuously mortify his flesh. In the preceding weeks, rallies of unemployed men in Chicago and Philadelphia had been attacked by police and anarchists needlessly arrested. Then, on March 2, an apolitical Russian Jew named Lazarus Averbuch was killed in Chicago, on the assumption that he was an Italian anarchist. This was only a moderately high point in an age when anarchist scares (often involving the clergy) were commonplace in mainstream daily papers.

The struggle between secularists and the church for control over education climaxed with the martyrdom of anarchist Francisco FERRER, the guiding spirit of the International League for the Rational Education of Children and head of Barcelona's Escuela Moderna. After a ruthless campaign against Ferrer and his work, Catholic and Spanish authorities conspired clumsily to frame him for involvement in an insurrection. His execution on October 13, 1909, sparked worldwide outrage (with demonstrations and riots in many cities), and the educator became a clear martyr for his cause. The affair intensified the anticlerical movement (see ANTICLERICALISM); Ferrer Modern Schools were established by anarchists all over the world, most successfully in the United States. Ferrer's anarchism, however, was itself a bone of contention within the secular movement, with shouting matches erupting between pro-Ferrer speakers and anti-anarchists at secularist meetings.

Other episodes in the war between Spain's anarchists and the church included the battles between Catholic-run "Free Unions" (puppet unions whose grievance process was prayer) and anarchist unions from the early 1920s, marked by many assassinations on each side. The early months of the Spanish Civil War in 1936 saw extreme actions on both sides. In the "anticlerical fury," several thousand priests (and some nuns) were lynched in the Republican zone, most frequently in areas held by anarchist militias. Crowds spontaneously set fire to churches; the tombs of clergy were opened, the nuns' skeletons propped against walls with cigarettes in their mouths so as to mimic prostitutes; the skull of one saint, removed from his casket on the altar, was used as a soccer ball in front of the church bearing his name. In the Nationalist zone, priests wearing sidearms demanded "confessions" from anarchists and other "reds" who waited to be executed by the thousands. To this day there are fierce denials that one's own side did these things, but the evidence is ample.

In the early decades of the Christian-capitalist war against perceived demons under the Comstock Postal Act of 1873 (see COMSTOCK, ANTHONY, AND UNBELIEF), the best known among its thousands of targets were anarchist writers, editors, and publishers for discussing human sexuality on rationalist terms (see SEX RADICALISM AND UNBELIEF). This included the arrests (some-times leading to prison terms) of Lois WAISBROOKER (1894, 1902), Ezra HEYWOOD (1878, 1882, 1890), and Moses HARMAN (1887, 1890, 1896, 1905), who published the weekly anarchist-freethought journal *Lucifer, the Light-Bearer*. LILLIAN HARMAN and Edwin C. Walker were imprisoned in 1887 in Kansas for declaring a "free marriage" to each other on their own authority.

The French individualist-anarchist André LORULOT was also a major proponent of atheism. He published and edited newspapers including *l'Action Antireligieuse* (Antireligioius action), *La Libre Pensée* (Freethought), and the satirical monthly *La Calotte* (double meaning: the clergy/the slap), which began as pamphlets printed clandestinely under Nazi occupation. Lorulot served in official capacities in national and international freethought organizations before and after World War II.

Some anarchists understand famous religious personalities as anarchists. Ross Winn of the southern United States believed that the teachings attributed to Jesus were generally similar to his own moral values, but that church and state had twisted them into instruments of control. "I suppose some people will object if I call Jesus an anarchist," Winn wrote in 1902, "but I am sure the whole world would call him that if he lived today, and preached such doctrines." In some cases, distinct varieties of anarchism develop around a Jesus fixation and may blur the point at which the freethought ends and religion begins. The writings of Lev TOLSTOY in his late years had this effect within the anarchist movement, attracting many distinguished thinkers and having a vast influence worldwide against violence, militarism, and patriotism. Another major anarchist leader who held mystical, Christian-derived convictions was the French geographer Élisée Reclus, though his convictions never conflicted with his anarchism. Also, the Catholic Worker movement is usually understood to be anarchist. Founded by the lay Catholics Dorothy Day and Peter Morin in 1933, members of that faith-based antipoverty movement today are not connected in any way to the Vatican, and many have no Christian background whatsoever. The movement consists of small, task-oriented groups with a major focus on nonviolent methods. A group needs no permission to call itself Catholic Worker and establish an operation under the name.

Anarchism has always been generally atheistic, with most of its periodicals holding secular editorial positions. The idea is commonly identified, in many languages, with the slogan "No God, No Master."

BIBLIOGRAPHY

Avrich, Paul. *The Modern School Movement: Anarchism and Education in the United States*. Princeton, NJ: Princeton University Press, 1980.

Blatt, Martin Henry. *Free Love and Anarchism: The Biography of Ezra Heywood*. Urbana: University of Illinois Press, 1989.

Carr, Reg. *Anarchism in France: The Case of Octave Mirbeau*. Montreal: McGill-Queens University Press, 1977.

Conwell, Russell H. "Responsibility for Belief." *Temple Review* (Philadelphia), September 20, 1901.

Crowder, George. *Classical Anarchism: The Political Thought of Proudhon, Bakunin, and Kropotkin*. Oxford: Oxford University Press, 1991.

De Cleyre, Voltairine. "Nameless." *Justice* (Philadelphia), January 27, 1889.

Eltzbacher, Paul. *Anarchism: Exponents of the Anarchist Philosophy*. Translated by Stephen T. Byington. New York: Benjamin R. Tucker, 1908.

Hall, David D., ed. *The Antinomian Controversy: A Documentary History*, 2nd ed. Chapel Hill: University of North Carolina Press, 1990.

Linebaugh, Peter, and Marcus Rediker. *The Many-Headed Hydra: Sailors, Slaves, Commoners, and the Hidden History of the Revolutionary Atlantic*. Boston: Beacon, 2000.

Lorulot, André. *Porquoi Je Sius Athée!* [Why I am atheist!]. Herblay, France: n.p., 1957.

Michel, Pierre, and Jean-François Nivet. *Octave Mirbeau: l'Imprécateur au Coeur Fidèle* [Octave Mirbeau: The curse-maker with a faithful heart]. Paris: Editions Seguier, 1990.

Mirbeau, Octave. *Théâtre Complet* [Complete plays]. Edited by Pierre Michel. Saint-Pierre-du-Mont: Euredit Broché, 1999.

Most, Johann. *Die Gottespest/The God Pestilence*. Tuscon, AZ: The Match!, 1992.

Paz, Abel. *Durruti: The People Armed*. New York: Free Life Editions, 1977.

Perry, Lewis. *Radical Abolitionism: Anarchy and the Government of God in Antislavery Thought*. Ithaca, NY: Cornell University Press, 1973.

Sanchez, José M. *The Spanish Civil War as a Religious Tragedy*. Notre Dame, IN: University of Notre Dame Press, 1987.

Sears, Hal D. *The Sex Radicals: Free Love in High Victorian America*. Lawrence: Regents Press of Kansas, 1977.

S[lifer], Shaun, Ally Greenhead, Sunfrog, Robert P. Helms, and Ross Winn. *Ross Winn: Digging Up a Tennessee Anarchist*. Pittsburgh: Firebrand Collective, 2004.

Tolstoy, Lev. *Government Is Violence: Essays on Anarchism and Pacifism*. London: Phoenix, 1990.

ROBERT P. HELMS

ANCIENT WORLD, UNBELIEF IN. The earliest traces of unbelief are very difficult, if not impossible, to detect prior to the advent of writing at the end of the fourth millennium BCE in the ancient Near East. Based on observations of nonliterate and premodern societies, the anthropologist Mary Douglas concludes that persons we would recognize as secularists or humanists probably existed in every type of human society, modern or ancient (see SECULARISM; HUMANISM). In this article we shall discuss unbelief in specific religious traditions (see ATHEISM)—as well as a more general unbelief in supernatural forces, entities, and causes—within the major cultural areas of the ancient Near East, from the dawn of writing to the fall of the Roman Empire.

Mesopotamia. Mesopotamia, the land between the Tigris and Euphrates rivers in what is now Iraq, contains some of the earliest known written records of human thought about religion, dating to the end of the fourth millennium BCE. The first extensive description of a seemingly nonreligious life is found in a collection of tablets called *Ludlul bēl nēmeqi* (I will praise the lord of wisdom) dated to the middle of the second millennium BCE. The work apparently describes the suffering of a sick man, who complains that his religious rituals are not having the expected results:

> I called to my god, but he did not show his face,
> I prayed to my goddess, but she did not raise her
>   head.
> The diviner with his inspection has not got to the
>   root of the matter,
> Nor has the dream priest with his libation eluci-
>   dated my case.

The author then complains that he is being treated like someone who does not worship the gods at all:

> Like one who has not made libations to his god,
> nor invoked his goddess at table,
> does not engage in prostration, nor takes cog-
>   nizance of
> bowing down; From whose mouth supplication
>   and
> prayer is lacking, who has done nothing on holy
>   days,
> and despised sabbaths, who in his negligence has
>   despised
> the gods' rites, has not taught his people reverence
>   and worship,
> but has eaten his food without invoking his god.

Even if the author is not an atheist, he seems to recognize the existence of people who seemingly live a nonreligious life. The author himself suggests that not all religious rituals may work in solving real-world problems, illness being one of the most intractable among them. Otherwise, no known writer in ancient Mesopotamia made any coherent defense of unbelief in the gods.

Egypt. Ancient Egypt had a complex civilization by the end of the fourth millennium BCE. No one will mistake Egypt for a secular society, given the myriad religious practices uncovered through archaeology. Perhaps best known are Egypt's extensive royal funerary rituals, which signaled a deep belief in the afterlife. The famous gods of Egypt include Osiris and Isis, not to mention a legion of minor deities and demons. However, even in such a religious environment, there are indications that some people could look at the world without reference to the supernatural.

One example of apparent NATURALISM is the Edwin Smith Surgical Papyrus, named after an American collector who reportedly acquired it in 1862. James Henry Breasted, the eminent Egyptologist who published a definitive edition of the Papyrus, dates the current copy to the seventeenth century BCE, and says: "In this document, therefore, we have disclosed to us for the first time the human mind peering into the mysteries of the human body, and recognizing conditions and processes there as due to intelligible physical causes." The papyrus, indeed, lists physical conditions in a very objective manner, and then prescribes remedies, usually without any reference to supernatural phenomena.

A more complex case of unbelief is illustrated by IKHNATON, the Egyptian pharaoh who around 1375 BCE decided to abandon the worship of traditional Egyptian gods in favor of only Aton, the personification of the sun. Ikhnaton built a new city, Amarna, devoted to the worship of Aton. On the one hand, Ikhnaton may have thought that Aton should be the only name used for all of the gods; or that other gods were manifestations of Aton. However, an inscription from the time of Tutankhamen indicates that Ikhnaton did not believe in all the gods. Tutankhamen boasts that he has restored all of the temples left in ruins by Ikhnaton, and vows to benefit "all the gods," perhaps a criticism of Ikhnaton's unbelief in polytheism. Otherwise, we find no systematic defense of unbelief in the supernatural in ancient Egypt.

Israel. Frank Moore Cross, the famed Harvard biblical scholar, has argued that ancient Israel represents a trend toward secularization relative to other ancient Near Eastern cultures. He cites a movement away from personifying nature and toward a more transcendent and elusive god as a mark of that secularization. While Cross may be overstating his case, there are a number of indications that unbelief was a constant concern for biblical authors. The object of unbelief, however, was not all supernaturalism, but rather specific gods, cults, or practices. In fact, in the ancient Near East a belief in "God" was seldom spoken of, but rather of belief in specific gods or in "the gods" as a collective.

One oft-cited verse used to support the presence of atheists in ancient Israel is Psalm 14:1: "Fools say in their hearts, 'There is no God.' They are corrupt, they do abominable deeds; there is no one who does good." However, the translation may be misleading insofar as the term translated "God" can actually refer to the specific god named Elohim. Thus, a better translation may be "A fool says in his heart, 'Elohim is not (present here).'" Nonetheless, the idea that Elohim is not present might lead logically to denying that Elohim exists at all.

Advocates of Yahweh, the principal name for the Hebrew god, had a particular problem because his characteristics and actions were similar to those claimed for another god named Baal. The latter had a much longer history in the ancient Near East, and many scholars believe that Yahweh is a Hebrew adaptation of Baal. In any case, Yahweh enthusiasts had to convince the populace that it was Yahweh, not Baal, who provided some of the benefits they enjoyed. This is clear in a complaint against Israel, personified as an errant wife, in Hosea 2:10: "She did not know that it was I who gave her the grain, the wine, and the oil, and who lavished upon her silver and gold that they used for Baal."

Another source of unbelief involved war. Many Near Eastern cultures measured the existence and effectiveness of gods by whether their worshipers won or lost wars. According to 2 Kings 18:33–34, the Assyrians, whose Mesopotamia-based empire reached its height in the early first millennium BCE, used their victories as arguments against the existence or efficacy of the gods of their victims: "Has any of the gods of the nations ever delivered its land out of the hand of the king of Assyria? Where are the gods of Hamath and Arpad? Where are the gods of Sepharvaim, Hena, and Ivvah? Have they delivered Samaria out of my hand?"

Of course, there were strategies that helped believers to cope with military losses without giving up belief in their gods. A Hebrew author might say that Yahweh was using the Assyrians as his instrument (see Isa. 10:5), or that Yahweh was angry with Israel, and so did not respond.

Prophecy was particularly crucial in proving the existence or power of favored gods. The basic premise is that only a true god could predict events with an accuracy not expected of human beings. However, the Hebrew Bible reflects how troublesome belief in prophecy could be. Consider Deuteronomy 18:21–22: "You may say to yourself, 'How can we recognize a word that the LORD has not spoken?' If a prophet speaks in the name of the LORD but the thing does not take place or prove true, it is a word that the LORD has not spoken. The prophet has spoken it presumptuously; do not be frightened by it."

The fact that the author is addressing the question of how to recognize communications from Yahweh indicates that he acknowledges the existence of a corresponding SKEPTICISM. The criterion provided by the biblical author, however, is weak because it does not address cases in which two different gods predict the same event. For example, suppose that a prophet of Yahweh predicted rain in seven days, and that a prophet of Baal also predicted the same. Using the criterion outlined above, one would not be able to distinguish which god actually provided the correct information. Others recognized that the frequency of an event should also be cause for skepticism in prophecy, as indicated in the complaint of Jeremiah, the Hebrew prophet (Jer. 28:8–9): "The prophets who preceded you and me from ancient times prophesied war, famine, and pestilence against many countries and great kingdoms. As for the prophet who prophesies peace, when the word of that prophet comes true, then it will be known that the LORD has truly sent the prophet."

In short, frequent events, such as wars, were useless as indicators of true prophecy because they were bound to occur no matter which god's prophets predicted them. Improbable events, like peace, now were touted as better indices of true prophecy.

But even such a refinement did not end the skepticism. In 1 Kings 22, we find the story of a prophet of Yahweh named Micaiah, who usually predicts disaster for the king of Israel. Other prophets of Yahweh predict that the king of Israel will win a war with the Syrians, and Micaiah repeats that prediction. However, upon further inquiry, Micaiah reverses himself, and says that Yahweh has actually told him that the king would lose the battle. Micaiah's first prediction, therefore, was a lie. Moreover, Micaiah claims that Yahweh has actually incited other prophets of Yahweh to lie (1 Kings 22:22–23). The whole narrative appears to be an effort to address unbelief in the accuracy and/or consistency of Yahweh's prophets.

The belief that scriptures contained the word of God was also a target of biblical authors. One interesting example is in Jeremiah 8:8: "How can you say, 'We are wise, and the law of the LORD is with us,' when, in fact, the false pen of the scribes has made it into a lie?" In other words, the biblical author acknowledges that scribes could manufacture the illusion of sacred scripture. The author, however, is ultimately powerless in distinguishing true and false scripture on anything other than his own subjective opinion.

Ecclesiastes, whose authorship is uncertain but which may date to the Hellenistic era, sometimes has been hailed as a secular humanist manifesto. In some cases, the author's ideas were certainly perceived to be so skeptical that the text or translation was changed to soften that skepticism. In Ecclesiastes 2:24–25, the New Revised Standard Version translates as follows: "There is nothing better for mortals than to eat and drink, and find enjoyment in their toil. This also, I saw, is from the hand of God; for apart from him who can eat or who can have enjoyment?" Yet the Hebrew text actually says "for apart from *me*, who can have enjoyment?" (emphasis added). In other words, the author is quite human centered in his pursuit of happiness. The author of Ecclesiastes does question many commonplace beliefs. Note, for example, the author's skepticism about the afterlife (Eccl. 3:20–21): "All go to one place; all are from the dust, and all turn to dust again. Who knows whether the human spirit goes upward and the spirit of animals goes downward to the earth?" The author's question suggests that no one knows the answer about the fate of any immaterial components of one's life (or the fate of the actual physical breath that ceases at death). The only phenomenon one observes is the decomposition of

bodies into dust. In fact, the author suggests that it is futile to speculate about the fate of the life-breath, and so he provides more advice in verse 22: "So I saw that there is nothing better than that all should enjoy their work, for that is their lot; who can bring them to see what will be after them?"

The book of Job, whose authorship and exact date of composition are uncertain, contains some of the boldest skeptical questions about God found in the entire Bible. The book itself is premised on the idea that Yahweh can allow people to be destroyed "for no reason" (see Job 2:3). Job, indeed, is tortured because of a wager made between Yahweh and a figure called The Satan, which should not be confused with the archenemy of God in later Christian tradition. The author does seem to advocate the idea that human beings have no right to know Yahweh's reasons, and Job is never told the reasons for his misfortune. But most scholars overlook the radical question found in Job 7:20: "If I sin, what do I do to you, you watcher of humanity?" In other words, why should the actions of a worthless lump of clay (as human beings are conceived in Job) be of any consequence to an omnipotent being? In more concrete terms, why should Yahweh care if a human being commits adultery, lies, or steals, any more than a human being cares if ants or other lower forms of life misbehave? In short, Job questions the very notion of sin itself. As such, Job may contain one of the most subversive critiques of sin found in any prior work of literature in the ancient Near East. Otherwise, biblical authors may express unbelief in particular gods and practices (e.g., Isa. 40:17–28), but none can be seen as advocating unbelief in all supernatural phenomena.

Greece. The first systematic rational and secularized philosophies appeared by the middle of the first millennium BCE in Greece, understood here broadly as encompassing areas where Greek was a dominant language of philosophical discourse and including at that time what is now western Turkey and southern Italy. Unfortunately, we usually have to reconstruct the supposed teachings of early Greek philosophers from later writers whose surviving manuscripts often actually date to medieval times. We often cannot verify that those later writers are transmitting much very faithfully. Consider the case of Anaxagoras, who is portrayed by Saint Augustine in his *City of God* as a believer in some form of an indwelling divine mind. Yet Irenaeus, another early Church father, specifically portrays Anaxagoras as an "atheist." Our survey, therefore, must be seen in light of these problems. Greece, of course, produced many philosophers of lasting influence including PLATO and ARISTOTLE. Aristotelian logic, with its emphasis on the syllogism and law of noncontradiction, still permeates modern science. Frederick Copleston, the famed Jesuit historian of philosophy, sees Plato and Aristotle as theists, but even he cannot deny that their view of theism is not always what we may envision. It is debatable if Aristotle's Prime Mover, the cause that set the universe into motion, is a personal god or not. Accordingly, in order to find ideas that approximate those of modern secularists, we have to look more closely at some of the lesser-known philosophers. According to CICERO, the famous Roman author and philosopher of the first century, in his *De Natura Deorum*, Diagoras of Melos and Theodorus of Cyrene (now Libya) "held that there are no gods at all." If Cicero is preserving an authentic tradition, these figures, who are usually thought to have lived before the end of the fifth century BCE, would be some of the earliest explicit atheists on record.

Naturalistic explanations for the origin of the universe are already evinced in a group of philosophers living in Ionia (now western Turkey) and known as the pre-Socratics because they were active in the seventh and sixth centuries BCE, before the rise of SOCRATES, the benchmark of Greek philosophy. Although some scholars have claimed that the pre-Socratics were opposed to all theology, the fragmentary nature of the sources should caution us against such generalized statements. The sources we do have indicate that later writers thought that at least some of these pre-Socratics advocated completely naturalistic explanations for the origin of the universe (see NATURALISM, PHILOSOPHICAL).

Thales, for example, believed water to be the primary element underlying the entire universe. In part, Thales reached this conclusion because water had the ability to become a gas when heated, and a solid when cooled. If so, the three basic states of all matter (solid, liquid, and gas) could be seen as different forms of water. In actuality, the idea that water is a primordial component of the universe can be found also in Genesis 1:1–3, and in the Babylonian work known as the *Enuma elish*, which dates as early as 1500 BCE. Both of those stories began with a chaotic mass of water that was reshaped. The difference is that Thales made no reference to gods shaping the water.

Anaximander had quite a sophisticated cosmogony, which posited that the universe arose from the everlasting motion of the *apeiron*, perhaps understood as "a huge, inexhaustible, mass stretching away endlessly in every direction." Anaximander describes something akin to a Big Bang theory in hypothesizing that this *apeiron* grew into a fiery sphere that then differentiated into the basic elements of the universe that we observe today. Anaximander also outlined a very crude theory of evolution whereby land animals originated in fish. As did many later Greek philosophers, Anaximander already postulated that the earth was suspended in space (or midair).

PROTAGORAS of Abdera is famous for an epistemology which was completely human centered, as indicated in his famous dictum, "Of all things the measure is Man." He is also credited with a frankly agnostic stance (see AGNOSTICISM) when he said: "About the gods, I am not able to know whether they exist or do not exist, nor what they are like in form; for the factors preventing knowl-

edge are many; the obscurity of the subject, and the shortness of human life." Cicero reports that Protagoras's ideas resulted in his exile and in his books being burned. If Cicero's report is true, it could be the earliest known instance of burning the books of skeptics/agnostics in the historical record.

XENOPHANES of Colophon is famous for outlining a theory for the origin of religion that would recur in the works of Ludwig FEUERBACH, among others. Xenophanes argued that the portrayal of gods was culturally conditioned because the physical characteristics and behaviors of the gods depended on the culture in which they originated. As Xenophanes phrased it: "Aethiopians have snub-nosed gods with black hair; Thracians have gods with grey eyes and red hair." In making this observation, Xenophanes was criticizing more particularly the anthropomorphic views of the gods found in Homer and Hesiod, some of the most revered early Greek poets.

Critias of Athens is perhaps the first writer to express the idea that the gods were invented for purposes of social and political manipulation. The idea cannot actually be attributed to Critias because it is placed in the mouth of the title character in his play, *Sisyphus*, as follows: "A wise and clever man invented fear (of the gods) for mortals that there might be some means of frightening the wicked, even if they do or think anything in secret. Hence he introduced the Divine (religion). In saying these words he introduced the pleasantest of teachings, covering up the truth with false theory." This idea was later echoed by the medieval anticlerical writer named Marsilius of Padua and by a host of Enlightenment thinkers.

The existence of unbelief can also be found in accusations reported in various sources. Plutarch reports that Anaxagoras of Clazomenae, a friend of Pericles, the famed Athenian ruler, was accused of violating a decree against those "who do not believe in the gods." Anaxagoras, among other things, is reported to have denied that the sun is a god. According to Plato's *Apology*, Socrates was tried and convicted, in part, because he was teaching youth "not to believe in the gods the state believes in, but in other new spiritual beings."

THUCYDIDES exemplifies a more systematic critique of belief in written reports. He complains that people are too willing to believe in ancient reports "composed with a view rather of pleasing the ear than of telling the truth." Such a critique, of course, could also lead to unbelief in the claims of the Bible and other sacred scriptures outside of Greece. We should note that Thucydides was quite self-serving in wanting readers to believe what he wrote even though his reports are sometimes no more well substantiated than his targets of complaint.

Healthcare was an area in which unbelief in supernatural explanations was clearly manifested, especially in the corpus of works attributed to an otherwise obscure man named Hippocrates. Simple observations and analogies served to promote nonsupernatural explanations for disease. For example, in a treatise on *Breaths*, the Hippocratic corpus observed that anything that made human beings suffer should be classified as a disease. Hunger was a disease under such a definition since it made human beings suffer. The treatise further observed that hunger was clearly due to a lack of food. The cure for hunger is the addition of food. By extending this analogy of hunger to other diseases, the Hippocratic corpus reasoned that all diseases were due to an excess or lack of something. The cure, therefore, is to add what is lacking and subtract what is in excess. In short, no supernatural causes or cures were even contemplated once one established that other conditions also qualified as "diseases" caused by imbalances in particular substances.

In the treatise *On the Sacred Disease*, the Hippocratic corpus leveled the most systematic attack on supernatural causation ever seen in ancient medicine. The focus is on the condition that has been identified as epilepsy, which was commonly diagnosed as a specifically supernatural disease. The author explicitly lays out his thesis: "This disease is in my opinion no more divine than any other; it has the same nature as other disease, and the causes that gives rise to individual diseases."

The attack on supernatural causation centers on the observation that there were observable conditions correlated with the incidence of the disease. For example, the author notes that the disease is more common in so-called phlegmatic people than in so-called bilious people. The author also notes that climate correlates with the frequency of mortality from the disease, with the highest tolls being in winter. If gods were causing the disease, then we would not expect that they would be deterred by the seasons. In fact, the author hypothesizes that the disease is centered in the brain.

After Aristotle, Greek philosophy developed a number of schools, some of which contributed to later secularist ideas even if these schools did not always see themselves as atheistic. The Stoics, founded by Zeno of Citium, advocated an ancient version of intelligent design in positing that the world was divinely purposed for the benefit of humanity (see STOICISM). However, Stoics also emphasized that all knowledge should be based on sense perception, something crucial to most modern atheistic scientific outlooks. A school of Skeptics, represented by, among others, Pyrrho of Elis (see PYRRHONISM) and Carneades of Cyrene, advocated agnosticism and relativism about every proposition, ethical or factual. Carneades is also credited by Cicero as controverting the idea that the earth contains features designed by the gods for the use of mankind. But the most coherent advocates of unbelief are the Epicureans, named after the Greek philosopher EPICURUS, a native of the island of Samos who founded his school of philosophy at Athens. Actually, the most prominent Epicurean author was a Roman named LUCRETIUS, whom we discuss further below. But, in general, the Epicureans centered their philosophy on

achieving the highest possible happiness and quality of life. Gods exist, but they are unconcerned with human affairs and they are themselves made of material substances. Death represents simply the dispersal of the physical elements that constitute the body. Human beings should make the best of the life they have rather than be concerned about an afterlife. Thus, Epicureans approach what we would later call deists (see DEISM).

The Roman Empire. Given our overlapping discussion of Christianity in the next section, the period of the Roman Empire discussed here is mostly from the first century BCE to the second century CE. Generally, Roman philosophy was an adaptation or continuation of the varieties of Greek philosophy. Within those schools, the most prominent advocates of unbelief in traditional religion were the Epicureans. According to Cicero, who exemplified an eclectic approach to philosophy, "Epicurus really abolished the gods, but nominally retained them in order not to offend the people of Athens." Lucretius, the foremost representative of Epicureanism, devised the most systematic use of naturalistic explanations conjoined with a critique of supernatural explanations in his *De Rerum Natura* (On the nature of things). Lucretius opined that priestly groups promote belief in superstition in order to facilitate social control. Lucretius expressed hopes that if people saw the folly of divine retribution in the afterlife, then "they would have the power to defy the superstitions and threatenings of the priests."

Lucretius outlined several criticisms of common religious institutions such as temples, which were generally viewed as the home of the gods. Lucretius reasons that any gods who exist are in no need of material homes since their nature, even if material, is so different that temples would be unnecessary.

Lucretius outlined a thorough and systematic naturalistic cosmology which views the origin of the universe as the result of random physical processes. Lucretius also offers one of the first extended critiques of what today would be called intelligent design (see INTELLIGENT DESIGN THEORY), the idea that there is observable and rational evidence that the universe was designed for the benefit of human beings. Lucretius specifically observes that such an idea, popular among the Stoics, must also contend with all of the flaws that exist in the universe.

Cicero, whose work we have been quoting, was himself a theist, but he recorded in his *De Natura Deorum* the arguments of many unbelievers in the supernatural. Cicero notes that the existence of contradictory opinions among the greatest philosophers about the gods has itself been used to advocate unbelief in the gods. In order to counter the Stoic idea that universal opinion constitutes proof of the existence of the gods, Cicero claims that "there are many nations so uncivilized and barbarous as to have no notion of any gods at all." In addition, Cicero composed a systematic discussion of belief and unbelief in prophecy in his treatise *De Divinatione* (On divination), wherein he notes the importance of prophecy in establishing the existence of the gods.

In his work *On Superstition*, Plutarch, the Greek writer and priest of the temple of Delphi, condemns both superstition and atheism. For Plutarch, superstition is rooted in fear, and he claims that superstition, not "true" religion, is the real cause of atheism. The works of Juvenal, the Roman satirist, also show how more popular forms of literature could be used as vehicles for unbelief. Otherwise, the Roman Empire is another of many Near Eastern examples of governments that sponsored and encouraged the worship of the gods of the state.

Early Christianity. In the first century, a sect of Jews broke with traditional Jewish teachings and developed into a collective we call Christianity. By 476, the traditional date for the fall of the Roman Empire, Christianity had become the empire's official religion. This period is notable because it initiated the most systematic and extensive dialogue between belief and unbelief in world history. Christian apologists and their opponents set the agenda for debates that continue today. As such, these debates also sometimes contributed to unbelief in all religion. The earliest teachings of Christianity are difficult to decipher—all extant documents about Christianity come from no earlier than the second century, by which time it was already a very differentiated phenomenon. Some self-described followers of Christ believed that he was God and others did not. Some Christians believed that Christ had resurrected from the dead, and some did not. Perhaps their only common denominator was their claimed adherence to the teachings of the figure called Christ. To complicate matters, Justin Martyr, the famed early Christian father, tells us in his *First Apology* that the term *atheist* was applied to Christians to signify their unbelief in the gods of the Roman Empire. Some of the first reports of skepticism regarding Christian supernatural claims appear within the New Testament itself. Matthew 28:11–15 reports that the belief in the resurrection of Jesus was being combated by using an alternative and naturalistic explanation of body theft. The letters attributed to Paul contain many complaints of unbelief among both Jewish and Gentile listeners (see 1 Cor. 1:20–23). Throughout the New Testament there are repeated threats and complaints about unbelief even among Christians (for example, Matt. 28:17, John 20:25).

Outside of the New Testament, we find a number of important writers against religion who use Christianity as a principal example (see CHRISTIANITY, RESISTANCE TO IN THE ANCIENT WORLD). Lucian of Samosata is sometimes called the VOLTAIRE of his time because of his wide-ranging indictment of religious belief. In *The Passing of Peregrinus*, Lucian relates the story of a Cynic philosopher, Peregrinus, who experiments with Christianity but is rejected by the Christians after he apparently violates some of their regulations. Lucian complains that Christians are gullible in adopting beliefs without evidence, especially when those beliefs can lead to the very death of Christians.

One of the most important substantive attacks on Christianity is recorded in *Contra Celsum* (Against Celsus), the Christian apologetic handbook attributed to the church father Origen. Celsus was an anti-Christian and anti-Jewish writer whose origin and philosophical affiliations are still disputed. His writings did not survive; our main record of Celsus's major work, *The True Discourse*, is preserved in Origen's quotations. In addition to attacking the belief in the resurrection of Jesus, Celsus attacked a wide range of biblical beliefs with arguments that are still used today in some form. Indeed, Celsus was among the first to refute specifically the young-earth chronology of Genesis, and he posited that our eternal planet had experienced a series of cataclysms, the latter being an idea that persists in modern geology. In general, evaluating the validity of beliefs centered on their antiquity in most premodern literature. The more ancient a belief, the more credibility it had for philosophers. Celsus was no exception, and he strove to show that there were non-Christian traditions that were much older than Christianity. Celsus used extensive parallels to show that Christian claims, while historically more recent, were not unique, but rather could be seen as a type of plagiarism from or adaptation of non-Christian beliefs. In particular, Celsus cited stories of births caused by the union of gods and human women in Greek traditions (for instance, Apollo is reported to have fathered Plato after a union with his human mother, Amphictione) to counter the story of the virgin birth of Jesus. Celsus also proposed a naturalistic alternative in claiming that the Christian story was contrived to explain away Mary's sexual liaison with a Roman soldier named Panthera. Other ulterior motives are ascribed to gospel stories, such as when Celsus hints that Jesus operated some sort of sex cult because so many women were willing to follow him into deserted areas.

More direct attacks on the Christian god by Celsus centered on theological contradictions. The idea that God can do "all things," as stated in Mark 10:27, would mean that God is able to cease being God or be able to do ungodly things. An omniscient god would not have been so easily betrayed as Jesus was by Judas. An omnipotent god would not have needed an angel to roll away the stone sealing Jesus's tomb, as is claimed in Matthew 28:2. The idea that God "comes down" (see Gen. 11:5) contradicts his omnipresence, since one does not come down to where one already is present. The incarnation is incompatible with God's immutability. In all fairness, some of the skepticism evinced by Celsus can be viewed as ad hominem attacks. This would include the idea that Christianity is untrue because it derives from a religion (Judaism) that Celsus viewed as "barbarous in origin." Celsus claimed that the apostles should not be believed because they were in dishonorable professions such as tax collecting and sailing.

Elsewhere, Celsus uses the Bible's own description of unethical behavior by Yahweh and Hebrew heroes to impugn the credibility of biblical information. In *Contra Celsum* 4.33, Celsus apparently alludes to biblical reports that Abraham lied about Sarah being his sister (Gen. 12:19) and that Jacob deceived his father (Gen. 27:18–40). Accordingly, Celsus concludes that we ought not believe anything else these patriarchs say. Celsus notes the amount of unjustified violence endorsed by the god of the Bible, and he reasoned that such violence was unworthy of a loving god. From the works of Philo, an Alexandrian Jewish writer of the first century CE, we know that objections to the Hebrew Bible were already being launched on the basis of the unjustified violence endorsed therein against the Canaanites and other native inhabitants of ancient Palestine.

Justin Martyr, another important early Christian apologist, records other attacks on Christianity, especially those made by Jews. It is clear that some Christian supernatural claims were being disputed on the basis of linguistics. For example, Jewish scholars noted that many events claimed by Christians as fulfillments of biblical prophecy were actually based on misunderstanding the Hebrew text. One example is Psalm 22, which speaks of the sufferings of the author. Christians believe Psalm 22 speaks of the sufferings of Christ. However, the Book of Psalms was written, according to traditional dating, about one thousand years before Christ, and the Psalmist uses the equivalent of the English past tense to describe these sufferings. Therefore, Jewish exegetes could argue, the Psalmist could not be referring to anyone in the first century.

Most known participants in debates between Christian believers and their opponents were men. Less certain is the role that unbelief played in the work of HYPATIA, a mathematician and astronomer from Alexandria. While most available sources report her murder by Christians, it is not certain whether the cause was her anti-Christian belief, or whether it was because of her role in a rivalry between Cyril, the bishop of Alexandria, and Orestes, a government official and friend of Hypatia. In any case, Hypatia remains one of the few women who is recorded as having any sort of unbelief or trouble with Christianity in the ancient world.

Julian "the Apostate" was the last Roman emperor to attempt to dismantle the Christian empire created by Constantine. But Julian was no unbeliever; he would never have abandoned supernaturalism as he was devoted to his Roman gods. By the time of Augustine, the most important Christian theologian near the fall of the Roman Empire, most types of objections to Christianity had been voiced in some form. Nonetheless, Augustine mounted a systematic defense in his *City of God*. The ascent of Constantine, the first Christian emperor, and the subsequent rise of Catholic and Protestant kingdoms, meant that Christians increasingly moved away from debate with unbelief to persecution and suppression of unbelief for the next fifteen hundred years or so.

Conclusion. Unbelief has existed in some form since the dawn of recorded history. However, it is useful to distinguish at least two types of ancient unbelief: (1) unbelief in specific religious traditions and practices (such as unbelief in Christianity or even certain forms of Christianity); and (2) unbelief in all gods and supernatural phenomena. This also explains why the term *atheist* can have at least two meanings in the ancient world: (1) unbelief in all gods; and (2) unbelief in specific gods (for example, Romans calling Christians "atheists" because the latter did not believe in the Roman gods).

These distinctions become more significant when we realize that, while the first type of unbelief still retains belief in supernaturalism generally, it nonetheless carries the potential seeds of unbelief in all religion. The main reason is that the objections made against specific religions could often be extended to all religions. Thus, if one questions the ethics of the Christian god, then one could also question the ethics of all the gods. If one argued that Christianity was unworthy of belief because its supernatural claims could not be verified, then one could just as well extend this rationale to the claims of all religions.

Our survey reveals that all the main types of objections to religion in existence today had already been voiced by the beginning of the Roman Empire. Among the most important types of arguments for unbelief were: (1) lack of empirical evidence; (2) internal contradictions in theology; (3) alternative natural/historical explanations; (4) undesirable ethical and social consequences. Other arguments, which would not be regarded as highly today, include: (1) the "cultural" level of the believers ("barbarous" versus "civilized") and (2) anecdotes about misbehavior of adherents.

What has changed since ancient times is the quality and relative importance of some types of arguments. For example, in the vast majority of premodern literature, the antiquity of a belief was used to support its credibility. Today, "recent and up-to-date" information is usually regarded as more credible, and an old belief can be dismissed as being outdated. In the period we surveyed, women who advocated unbelief were practically invisible. Today, while their proportions are still not equal to those of men, there have been some notable women advocates of secularism. Among some ancient authors, atheism was a characteristic of uncivilized and uneducated peoples, but today atheism is not deemed to be characteristic of any nonliterate or nonindustrialized society. In almost every culture and historical period we find at least three strategies for combating unbelief: (1) civil debate; (2) apathy (in the hope that unbelief will disappear); and (3) persecution, which could take forms ranging from loss of certain rights to outright killing or exile. But while there were always instances of persecution of unbelievers, there has been nothing so sweeping and violent as the policies against unbelief expressed in the Hebrew Bible and the New Testament, whose consequences we are still witnessing today.

Perhaps the most important lesson of all is that unbelief has persisted even amid the most ardent opposition. Epicurus and Lucretius, in particular, demonstrate that simple reason and the amount of information already available in their time were sufficient to justify a life free from presumptions of supernatural causation. The history of ancient unbelief teaches us that unbelief will probably always survive, but its level and intensity will probably depend, as it always has, on a host of factors ranging from politics to education.

BIBLIOGRAPHY

Augustine. *The City of God, Against the Pagans.* Translated by George E. McCracken et al. 7 vols. Loeb Classical Library. Cambridge, MA: Harvard University Press, 1957–72.

———. "Reply to Faustus." In *The Nicene and Post-Nicene Fathers*, edited by Philip Schaff. 14 vols. Grand Rapids, MI: Eerdmans, 1996–.

Breasted, James Henry, ed. *The Edwin Smith Surgical Papyrus.* 2 vols. Chicago: University of Chicago Press, 1930.

Buckley, Michael J. *At the Origins of Modern Atheism.* New Haven, CT: Yale University Press, 1987.

Cicero. *De Natura Deorum.* Translated by H. Rackham. Loeb Classical Library. Cambridge, MA: Harvard University Press, 1979.

Copleston, Frederick. *A History of Philosophy: Greece and Rome.* Westminster, MD: Newman, 1966.

Cross, Frank Moore. "The History of Israelite Religion." *Biblical Archaeology Review* 31, no. 3 (May/June 2005).

Douglas, Mary. *Natural Symbols: Explorations in Cosmology.* New York: Pantheon, 1970.

Dzielska, Maria. *Hypatia of Alexandria.* Translated by F. Lyra. Cambridge, MA: Harvard University Press, 1996.

Freeman, Kathleen, ed. *Ancilla to the Pre-Socratic Philosophers: A Complete Translation of the Fragments in Diels*, Fragmente der Vorsokratiker. Cambridge, MA: Harvard University Press, 1966.

Hippocrates. Translated by W. H. S. Jones. 4 vols. Loeb Classical Library. Cambridge, MA: Harvard University Press, 1923–31.

Irenaeus. *Against Heresies.* In *The Ante-Nicene Fathers*, edited by Alexander Roberts and James Donaldson. 10 vols. Grand Rapids, MI: Eerdmans, 1994.

Kahn, Charles H. *Anaximander and the Origins of Greek Cosmology.* New York: Columbia University Press, 1964.

Lambert, W. G. *Babylonian Wisdom Literature.* Oxford: Clarendon, 1960.

Larue, Gerald A. *Freethought across the Centuries: Toward a New Age of Enlightenment.* Amherst, NY: Humanist Press, 1996.

Lucretius. *De Rerum Natura.* Translated and edited by W. H. D. Rouse and M. F. Smith. Loeb Classical Library. Cambridge, MA: Harvard University Press, 1982.

Martyr, Justin. *First Apology of Justin.* In *The Ante-Nicene Fathers*, edited by Alexander Roberts and James Donaldson. 10 vols. Grand Rapids, MI: Eerdmans, 1994.

Murnane, William J. *Texts from the Amarna Period in Egypt.* SBL Writings from the Ancient World Series 5. Atlanta: Scholars, 1995.

Origen. *Contra Celsum.* In *The Ante-Nicene Fathers*, edited by Alexander Roberts and James Donaldson, 10 vols. Grand Rapids, MI: Eerdmans, 1994.

Plato. *Euthyphro, Apology, Crito, Phaedo, Phaedrus.* Translated and edited by H. N. Fowler. Loeb Classical Library. Cambridge, MA: Harvard University Press, 1982.

Plutarch. *Plutarch's Lives: Pericles and Fabius, Maximus, Nicias, and Crassus.* Translated by Bernadotte Perrin. Loeb Classical Library. Cambridge, MA: Harvard University Press, 1967.

Thucydides. Translated by C. F. Smith. Loeb Classical Library. Cambridge, MA: Harvard University Press, 1975.

Unless noted otherwise, all of the author's biblical quotations are those of the New Revised Standard Version, National Council of Churches of Christ in the United States of America. Nashville: Thomas Nelson, 1989.

HECTOR AVALOS

ANDERSON, JOHN, (1893–1962), Australian atheist philosopher. Coming from Scotland to Sydney in 1927, Anderson became the leading Australian philosopher of his time, also gaining fame as an uncompromising critic of prevailing uncritical beliefs, especially those of religion.

Anderson criticized religion not only for the content of its beliefs but for its promotion of credulity. Consider his view of the unscientific character of religious faith: "A belief from which we cannot depart, which is not founded on inquiry, but, on the contrary, stops it at its source—such a belief is credulous." That is why, he noted, the principle of Christianity is subjectivity, whereas the principle of science and of empiricist philosophy is objectivity.

In 1943 Anderson gave a reasoned address titled "Religion in Education" that led to a famous public controversy, in the course of which Anderson was condemned by the New South Wales Parliament and publicly cursed by a clergyman. Anderson's argument was that since religion seeks to close down inquiry, there is no place for it in education. At one point, for instance, he noted that when a child is told that God made everything and the child responds, "But who made God?" the child is proceeding sensibly by connecting it with his experience, as he knows what it is for something to be made. Anderson said the best approach to religion in education for children was to dispense with the notion of "sacredness" and treat religious writings as *literature*—coupled, for example, with the study of the legends of the Greeks, which "have always seemed to me to be much more interesting than the Christian stories—perhaps because they are connected with the life of a highly cultured people."

In general, Anderson opposed religious dogma because of its promotion of unintelligibility and because of its "servile ethic." Influenced in part by G. E. MOORE and G. Sorel, he developed an objective, nonprescriptive theory of ethics according to which positive ethical goodness is a quality of inquiring, artistic, and other productive/enterprising social activities. In terms of this he criticized the Christian attitudes of dependence, renunciation, and consolation. As he once put it, "As Sorel has pointed out, Christianity takes the standpoint of the individual recipient of benefits and has no sense of the organization involved in scientific, artistic and productive activity; it exalts 'humble virtue' at the expense of the achievements of culture which alone can be called good."

On the side of the content of Christian belief, Anderson followed philosophers such as David HUME and Immanuel KANT in demonstrating the logical failure of theistic arguments. But while recognizing that there exist no God or gods, he took ATHEISM to be only a particular application of his basic "ontological egalitarianism." Contrary to much of the metaphysics in the history of philosophy, he held that there are no *necessary*, *ultimate*, or *all-explaining* ontological beings or realities. This position, which he defended by trenchant criticisms of philosophical monism, dualism, and atomism, is summed up by saying that there is neither the One nor the Two nor the Many, but only the None—that is to say, no ultimate realities.

BIBLIOGRAPHY

Anderson, John. *Education and Inquiry.* Edited by D. Z. Phillips. Oxford: Basil Blackwell, 1980.
———. *Studies in Empirical Philosophy.* Sydney: Angus & Robertson, 1962.
Baker, A. J. *Australian Realism: The Systematic Philosophy of John Anderson.* Cambridge: Cambridge University Press, 1986.

A. J. BAKER

ANNEKE, MATHILDE FRANZISKA GEISLER (1817–1884), German freethought editor and feminist. Born on April 3, 1817, Mathilde Franziska was the first of twelve children born to a prosperous family in Westphalia. Mathilde was raised a devout Roman Catholic. At nineteen, she married a French wine merchant. After a battle over her daughter, Fanny, her marriage was annulled, and

Mathilde turned more fervently to her faith. In 1847 she married Prussian artillery officer Fritz Anneke. She published a censored revolutionary journal while he was imprisoned for revolutionary acts, meeting Karl MARX and Mikhail BAKUNIN. Mathilde became a radical freethinker.

After Fritz fought in the failed German revolutions of 1848 and 1849, the couple fled to the United States with other German "Forty-Eighters" (see GERMANY, UNBELIEF IN; FREIEN GEMEINDEN, DIE). Settling briefly in Milwaukee, Mathilde published *Deutsche Frauenzeitung*, a radical monthly freethought journal dedicated to women's complete emancipation. Although the German-language press jibed her feminism, she continued to publish the periodical for two and a half years after the couple moved to New Jersey. She also edited *Newark-erzeitung*, a German-language paper of local news.

Mathilde spoke at the first woman's rights convention she ever attended, with atheist Ernestine L. ROSE translating, during the infamous "mob convention" of 1853 when clergy disrupted proceedings.

After three of her six children died of smallpox in 1858 (fearful of inoculation, Mathilde had not had them vaccinated), she went abroad while her husband worked as a foreign correspondent. She remained in Switzerland with their surviving children when Fritz returned to America to fight in the Civil War. In 1865 Mathilde returned to Milwaukee without her husband. An activist, she worked for temperance and anticlericalism, and opposed nativist propaganda. She cofounded Wisconsin's major suffrage group in 1869. She also opened the Milwaukee *Tochter Institut*, a highly regarded German-language girls' school. The tireless worker also lectured, wrote, and sold insurance on the side to supplement family income.

Anneke addressed the 1869 national Equal Rights Association convention in New York, where she called scientific knowledge "that fountain of all peacefully progressing amelioration in human history." She added: "There does not exist a man-made doctrine, fabricated expressly for us, and which we must learn by heart, that shall henceforth be our law. Nor shall the authority of old traditions be a standard for us—be this authority called Veda, Talmud, Koran, or Bible. No. Reason, which we recognize as our highest and only law-giver, commands us to be free."

Mathilde Anneke died on November 25, 1884.

BIBLIOGRAPHY

James, Edward T., ed. *Notable American Women: 1607–1950: A Biographical Dictionary.* Vol. 1. Cambridge, MA: Belknap Press, 1971.
Stanton, Elizabeth Cady, Susan B. Anthony, and Matilda Joslyn Gage, eds. *The History of Woman Suffrage.* Vols. 1–3. Rochester, NY: Susan B. Anthony, 1886–89.

ANNIE LAURIE GAYLOR

ANNET, PETER (1693–1769). British deist. Peter Annet was at one time a schoolteacher but later moved to London, where he joined the Robin Hood Society, a radical debating group, and wrote a number of freethinking polemics. His exact position on the theological spectrum is difficult to assess, as he published many of his essays anonymously; also, some essays occasionally attributed to him have more tinges of ATHEISM than of DEISM. His first publication was *Judging for Ourselves: Or, Free-Thinking the Great Duty of Religion* (1739), in which he articulated criticisms of Christianity based on the inconsistencies in biblical texts. Unlike Charles Blount, who raised questions about New Testament canonicity, Annet focused his skeptical and historical assessments on established texts. In 1744, stimulated by such works as Henry Dodwell's *Christianity Not Founded on Argument* (1742) and works by John Leland and George Benson, Annet published his *Deism Fairly Stated* (1744). Here he asserted that "Deism, properly so called, whatever ill usage it may have met with, is no other than the Religion essential to Man, the true, original Religion of Reason and Nature; such as was believed and practised by SOCRATES, and others of old, who were as great Ornaments, and did as much Honour to Human Nature, as any Christians ever did. . . ." This statement of what constitutes deism goes further than any claim made by previous deists such as Blount, Anthony COLLINS, Matthew TINDAL, and John TOLAND. Among conventional theological principles that Annet rejected were free will (his orientation here was fairly deterministic; see DETERMINISM), revelation, the Trinity, and resurrrection; on the question of evil (see EVIL, PROBLEM OF), he more or less restated the argument of EPICURUS.

In 1750 (the publication date is sometimes given as 1768, but this is unlikely), Annet published *A Collection of the Tracts of a Certain Free Enquirer, Noted by His Sufferings for His Opinions*. His posthumous reputation rests on this volume, which gives an accurate summation of his ideas. Annet was a careful and consistent thinker, but the aggressiveness of his style, amounting often to sarcasm, often diminished the shrewdness of his arguments. All the tracts in this volume are on theological topics, except for one titled *Social Bliss Considered*, in which Annet cast doubt upon marriage without a prospect of divorce.

Between October 7 and December 12, 1761, Annet was the editor and publisher of a periodical called *Free Enquirer*. Here his skepticism about the historical accuracy of the Old Testament led to a prosecution for blasphemous libel (see BLASPHEMY), which his earlier publications also seemed to invite. He was imprisoned for a month at the age of sixty-eight, and was forced to stand twice in the pillory. He died on January 18, 1769.

BIBLIOGRAPHY

Annet, Peter. *A Collection of the Tracts of a Certain Free Enquirer, Noted by His Sufferings for His Opinions*. London, 1750. Reprint, London: Routledge/Thoemmes Press, 1995.

Twyman, Ellen. *Peter Annet, 1693–1769*. London: Pioneer Press, 1938.

JOHN VALDIMIR PRICE

ANTHROPIC PRINCIPLE, THE. The Anthropic Coincidences. In 1919 mathematician and physicist Hermann Weyl puzzled why the ratio of the electromagnetic force to the gravitational force between two electrons is such a huge number, $N_1 = 10^{39}$. Weyl wondered why this should be the case, expressing his intuition (and nothing more than that) that "pure" numbers like π—that is, numbers that do not depend any system of units—when occurring in the description of physical properties, should most naturally occur within a few orders of magnitude of unity. Why 10^{39}? Why not 10^{57} or 10^{-123}? Some principle, Weyl thought, must select out 10^{39}.

In 1923 astronomer Arthur Eddington agreed: "It is difficult to account for the occurrence of a pure number (of order greatly different from unity) in the scheme of things; but this difficulty would be removed if we could connect it to the number of particles in the world—a number presumably decided by accident." He estimated that number, now called the Eddington number, to be $N = 10^{79}$. Well, N is not too far from the square of N_1.

In 1937 physicist Paul Dirac noticed that N_1 is the same order of magnitude as another pure number, N_2, which gives the ratio of a typical stellar lifetime to the time light requires to traverse the radius of a proton. That is, he found two seemingly unconnected large numbers to be of the same order of magnitude. If one number being large is unlikely, how much more unlikely is it that another will come along with about the same value?

In 1961 astrophysicist Robert Dicke pointed out that N_2 is necessarily large in order that the lifetime of typical stars can be sufficient to generate heavy chemical elements such as carbon. Furthermore, he showed that N_1 must be of the same order of N_2 in any universe with heavy elements. This became the first of what are called the anthropic coincidences, connections between physical constants that seem to be necessary for the existence of life in the universe.

While many examples of claimed anthropic coincidences can be found in the literature, here are the most significant:

1. The electromagnetic force is 39 orders of magnitude stronger than the gravitational force. If they were more comparable in strength, stars would have collapsed long before life had a chance to evolve.

2. The vacuum energy density of the universe is at least 120 orders of magnitude lower than some theoretical estimates. If at any time it were as large as these calculations suggest, the universe would have quickly blown apart.

3. The electron's mass is less than the difference in the masses of the neutron and proton. Thus, a free neutron can decay into a proton, electron, and antineutrino. If this were not the case, the neutron would be stable, in which case most of the protons and electrons in the early universe would have combined to form neutrons, leaving little hydrogen to act as the main component and fuel of stars.

4. The neutron is heavier than the proton, but not so much heavier that neutrons cannot be bound in nuclei, where conservation of energy prevents the neutrons from decaying. Without neutrons we would not have the heavier elements needed for building complex systems such as life.

5. The carbon nucleus has an excited energy level at around 7.65 million electron-volts (MeV). Without this state, insufficient carbon would be manufactured in stars to form the basis for life. Using anthropic arguments, astronomer Fred Hoyle was able to predict this energy level before it was confirmed experimentally.

The Three Anthropic Principles. In 1974 astronomer Brandon Carter introduced the notion of the anthropic principle, which hypothesized that the anthropic coincidences are not the result of chance but are somehow built into the structure of the universe. He proposed two versions. His weak anthropic principle (WAP) states: "We must be prepared to take into account the fact that our location in the universe is necessarily privileged to the extent of being compatible with our existence as observers." Carter's strong anthropic principle (SAP) says: "The Universe (and hence the fundamental parameters on which it depends) must be such as to admit the creation of observers within it at some stage."

Other authors have presented their own versions of anthropic principles, more than thirty being available in the literature. I will mention only three more versions—those proposed by mathematician John Barrow and physicist Frank Tipler in their tome on the subject. The first two are rephrases of Carter's wording. The Barrow and Tipler WAP reads: "The observed values of all physical and cosmological quantities are not equally probable but take on values restricted by the requirement that there exist sites where carbon-based life can evolve and by the requirement that the Universe be old enough for it to have already done so." Note that Barrow and Tipler require the existence of "carbon-based life," while Carter simply refers to the existence of "observers." This is better phasing, since many of the coincidences have to do with carbon, directly or indirectly.

Barrow and Tipler's SAP reads: "The Universe must have those properties which allow life to develop within it at some stage in its history." Note that all three authors say that the universe "must" have the properties that allow for the creation of life, or at least observers. Thus, the SAP seems to imply some intent or purpose within the universe.

Barrow and Tipler round out their trio of anthropic principles with what they term the final anthropic principle (FAP): "Intelligent information processing must come into evidence in the Universe, and, once it comes into existence, it will never die out."

Note that the term *anthropic principle* is a misnomer, as is *anthropic coincidence*. While singling out our kind of carbon-based life, none of the coincidences require *human* life or demand that carbon-based life develop intelligence.

Implications. The WAP is considered by most physicists and cosmologists to be a simple tautology. Of course the constants of nature are suitable for our form of life. If they were not, we would not be here to talk about it.

Still, the anthropic coincidences strike most people as puzzling; what might they imply about the nature of the universe? Barrow and Tipler suggest three different possible implications of the SAP:

(A) There exists one possible universe "designed" with the goal of generating and sustaining "observers."

(B) Observers are necessary to bring the Universe into being.

(C) An ensemble of other different universes is necessary for the existence of our universe.

Authors with religious agendas have interpreted (A) as evidence for a creator God, in particular, the God they happen to worship (see EXISTENCE OF GOD, ARGUMENTS FOR AND AGAINST). They ask: How can the universe possibly have obtained the unique set of physical constants it displays, so exquisitely fine-tuned for life as they are, except by purposeful design—design with life and perhaps humanity in mind (see INTELLIGENT DESIGN THEORY)?

However, nothing in the above discussion requires that this God be the one of any particular faith. Indeed, "design" might be interpreted as a purely natural process, perhaps an evolutionary one akin to the design inherent in Darwinian natural selection (see DARWINISM) or just some structure built into the universe that science has not yet explained.

Possibility (B) arises from a mystical misinterpretation of quantum mechanics. Though it has formed the basis of a large popular literature in recent years, few physicists take it very seriously.

Possibility (C) presents the notion that multiple universes exist and so we happen to just live in a universe that is suitable for the evolution of our kind of life. We will consider this possibility below.

Fine-Tuning in the Eye of the Beholder. The strength of the electromagnetic force is determined by the value of the unit electric charge—the magnitude of the charge of an electron—designated by e. The claim is that e is a constant that has been fine-tuned far from its natural value in order that stars will live long enough for life to evolve (coincidence 1, above).

However, e is not a constant. We now know from the highly successful standard model of particles and forces that e and the strengths of the other elementary forces vary with energy, and changed very rapidly in the first moments of the Big Bang. According to current understanding, in the very high-energy environment at the start of the Big Bang, the four known forces were unified as one force, just as Weyl anticipated should happen "naturally." That is, e began with its natural value. Then, as the universe cooled, the forces separated by a process called spontaneous symmetry breaking into the four basic forces (electromagnetic, gravitational, strong nuclear, and weak nuclear) that we experience at much lower energies today, with e and the other force strengths having evolved to their current stable values. Stellar formation, and thus life, had to simply wait for the forces to separate sufficiently. Actually the wait was a just tiny fraction of a second.

Only four parameters are needed to specify the broad features of the universe as it exists today: the masses of the electron and proton and the current strengths of the electromagnetic and strong interactions. I have studied how the minimum lifetime of a typical star depends on the first three of these parameters. Varying them by ten orders of magnitude around their present values, I find that more than half the stars will have lifetimes exceeding a billion years.

Large stars need to live tens of millions of years or more to allow for the fabrication of heavy elements. Smaller stars, such as our sun, also need about a billion years to allow life to develop within their solar systems of planets. Earth did not even form until nine billion years after the Big Bang. The requirement of long-lived stars is easily met for a wide range of possible parameters. The universe is certainly not fine-tuned for this characteristic.

One of the many major flaws with most studies of the anthropic coincidences is that the investigators vary a single parameter while assuming all the others remain fixed. They further compound this mistake by proceeding to calculate meaningless probabilities based on the grossly erroneous assumption that all the parameters are independent. In my study I took care to allow several parameters to vary at the same time.

In a very impressive paper, physicist Anthony Aguire has independently examined the universes that result when six cosmological parameters are simultaneously varied by orders of magnitude and found he could construct cosmologies in which "stars, planets, and intelligent life can plausibly arise."

The standard model contains about twenty parameters that are not determined by theory but which must currently be inferred from experiment. However, only four are needed to specify most properties of matter. These are the masses of the electron and the two quarks ("up" and "down") that constitute protons and neutrons, and a universal strength parameter from which the value e and the other force strengths are determined. Ultimately, it is hoped that all the basic parameters will be determined by theories that unify gravity with the standard model, for example, string theory. We must wait to see if the calculated masses of the electron and neutron come out to satisfy coincidences 3 and 4, above. Another possibility, which we will consider below, is that these parameters are random.

Many of the examples of anthropic coincidences found in theological literature result from simple misunderstanding of physics. For example, any reference to the fine-tuning of constants like the speed of light (c), Planck's constant (h), or Newton's gravitational constant (G) are irrelevant, since these are all arbitrary constants whose values simply define the system of units being used.

Also, some of the "remarkable" precision people talk about is highly misleading, depending on the arbitrary choice of units. For example, theologian John Jefferson Davis asserts, "If the mass of neutrinos were 5×10^{-34} instead of 5×10^{-35} kg, because of their great abundance in the universe, the additional gravitational mass would result in a contracting rather than expanding universe." This sounds like fine-tuning by one part in 10^{35}. However, as philosopher Neil Manson points out, this is like saying that "if he had been one part in 10^{16} of a light-year shorter (that is, one meter shorter), Michael Jordan would not have been the world's greatest basketball player."

Incidentally, Davis's estimate of the neutrino mass is not accurate. In fact, the individual masses are not known, with experiments so far measuring only mass differences. Furthermore, if the mass of neutrinos were ten times greater, there likely would be ten times fewer of them in the cosmos and the gravitational effect would be the same. So this fine-tuning claim collapses on several fronts.

Let us next consider coincidence 5, which asserts fine-tuning is needed to produce carbon. Nobel laureate physicist Steven Weinberg has shown that the production of carbon in stars is not strongy dependent on the 7.65 MeV nuclear energy level predicted by Hoyle. Rather it hinges on the radioactive state of a carbon nucleus formed out of three beryllium nuclei. This misses being too high for carbon production by 20 percent, which, as he says, "is not such a close call after all."

In short, much of the so-called fine-tuning of the parameters of microphysics is in the eye of the beholder, a beholder not always sufficiently versed in physics who plays with the numbers until they seem to support a prior belief that was based on something other than objective scientific analysis.

The Cosmological Constant Problem. Although we normally think of the vacuum as empty of matter and energy, gravitational energy can be stored in the curvature of empty space. Futhermore, quantum mechanics implies that a vacuum will contain a minimum zero-point energy.

Weinberg was perhaps the first to highlight the vacuum energy problem (coincidence 2). He referred to it as the cosmological constant problem, since any vacuum energy density is equivalent to the parameter in Einstein's theory of general relativity called the cosmological constant that relates to the curvature of empty space.

Calculations gave a value for the vacuum energy density that is some 120 orders of magnitude greater than the maximum value possible from observations. Since this density is constant, it would seem to have been fine-tuned with this precision from the early universe to ensure that its value today would allow for the existence of life.

Until recently, it was thought that the cosmological constant was probably exactly zero, in which case there was no need for fine-tuning. However, in 1998, two independent research groups studying distant supernovae were astonished to discover that the current expansion of the universe is in fact accelerating. More recent observations have confirmed this result. The universe is falling up! The source of this cosmic acceleration is some still-unidentified dark energy, which constitutes 70 percent of the mass of the universe. One possible explanation is gravitational repulsion by means of the cosmological constant, that is, by way of the vacuum energy field that is allowed by general relativity.

If that is the case, then the cosmological constant problem resurfaces. In the meantime, we now can argue plausibly that the original calculation was incomplete and a proper calculation will give zero for the vacuum energy density. Until these newer estimates are shown to be wrong, we cannot conclude that the vacuum is fine-tuned for life and have no particularly strong need to invoke a designer deity.

But what, then, is responsible for cosmic acceleration? What is the nature of the dark energy? A cosmological constant is not the only possible source of gravitational repulsion. According to general relativity, any matter field will be repulsive if its pressure is sufficiently negative. Theorists have proposed that the dark energy may be a matter field, called quintessence, which requires no fine-tuning.

Is Our Form of Life the Only One Possible? Consider the fact that we live on Earth, rather than Mercury, Venus, Mars, or some other planet in the known solar system. Mercury and Venus are too hot and Mars is too cold to support life of our kind. Mercury has no atmos-

phere, while the atmosphere of Venus is too thick for the sun's rays to penetrate to the surface and the atmosphere of Mars is too thin to provide sufficient oxygen and water.

The temperature range and other properties of Earth are just right for life. For example, Earth's atmosphere is transparent to the same spectrum of light to which our eyes are sensitive. Anthropic reasoning would have it that the atmosphere was fine-tuned so that humans and other animals could see at a distance. The transparency also happens to match the spectral regions within which the electromagnetic radiation from the sun is maximal. Again, anthropic reasoning would attribute this to design with humans in mind.

But, rather obviously, life evolved on Earth *because* conditions here were right. The type of life that evolved was suitable for those conditions.

With 100 billion stars in 100 billion galaxies in the visible universe, and countless others, according to current cosmological theory, likely to lie beyond our horizon, the chances of some form of life developing on some planets seems very good. Indeed, many of the chemical ingredients of life such as complex molecules have been observed in outer space. Of course, we will not know for sure until we find such life.

Still, we expect any life found in our universe to be carbon based, or at least based on heavy element chemistry. The fine-tuning argument implies that this is the only form of life that is possible, but that is a huge, unwarranted assumption. Even if all the forms of life in our universe turn out to be of this basic structure, it does not follow that life is impossible under any other arrangement of physical laws and constants. This fact alone is fatal to the fine-tuning argument.

Carbon would seem to be the chemical element best suited to act as the building block for the type of complex molecular systems that develop lifelike qualities. Even today, new materials assembled from carbon atoms exhibit remarkable, unexpected properties, from superconductivity to ferromagnetism. However, we have no reason to assume that only carbon-based life is possible.

Given the known laws of physics and chemistry, we can imagine life based on silicon or other elements chemically similar to carbon. While carbon may be optimum for the parameters of our universe, silicon might be better if the parameters were slightly different. However, whatever elements are used, they still require cooking in stars and thus a universe old enough for stellar evolution.

We can only speculate what form life might take on another planet, with different conditions. It would be wonderful to have more examples of life, but we do not. And any speculation about what form life might take in a universe with a different electron mass, electromagnetic interaction strength, or different laws of physics is even more problematical. We simply do not have the knowledge to say whether life of *some* sort would not occur under different circumstances.

Multiple Universes. We have seen that cosmological parameters, such as the cosmological constant, need not have been fine-tuned for life. We also have a plausible scenario in which the strengths of the four forces evolved to their current values, and recognize that long-lived stars can be expected over a large range of these and other physical parameters. The hope is that a future theory that unifies gravity and microphysics will enable the calculation of the few parameters that are needed to define the fundamental structure of matter. However, even if this hope is not realized, current theories already suggest another possible answer to the anthropic coincidences.

For example, our universe may be just one of a huge number of other universes within some super universe called the multiverse. Fundamental parameters may be randomly distributed among universes, and we simply live in the one where the parameters happen to be suitable for the evolution of our form of life.

Theists have scoffed at the idea of multiple universes, arguing that we have no evidence for the existence of any but our own. But we have no evidence for their God, either. At least in the case of multiple universes we have physical theories, based firmly on empirical data within our own universe, pointing to their existence. The highly successful cosmological inflation model implies that the spontaneous event that created our universe would have been repeated many times. While this may still be classified as speculation, it is speculation based on good science and observational data. The speculation that a creator God exists is based on no science and no data.

Several commentators have argued that a multiverse cosmology violates Occam's razor. This is wrong. The entities that Occam's law of parsimony forbids us from "multiplying beyond necessity" are theoretical hypotheses, not universes. Although the atomic theory of matter multiplied the number of bodies we must consider in solving a thermodynamic problem by 10^{24} or so per gram, it did not violate Occam's razor. Instead, it provided for a simpler, more powerful, more economic exposition of the rules that were obeyed by thermodynamic systems.

The existence of many universes is in fact consistent with all we know about physics and cosmology. No new hypotheses are needed to introduce them. It takes an added hypothesis to rule them out—a superlaw of nature that says only one universe can exist. That would be an uneconomical hypothesis. Putting it another way, we have no basis for assuming that only a single universe exists. The theist argument requires two hypotheses that are unwarranted by data or theory: (1) only one universe exists and (2) God exists.

A Life Principle? Despite the apparent uncongeniality of the universe to life, life is present and some people still insist that this is remarkable. Physicist Paul Davies suggests a life principle is "written into the laws of physics" or "built into the nature of the universe."

Of course, nowhere in current physics, chemistry, or biology do we see any sign of a fundamental life principle, some *élan vital* that distinguishes life from nonlife. Davies speculates: "[A] felicitous mix of law and chance might be generalised to cosmology, producing directional evolution from simple states, through complex, to life and mind." Davies shares this notion with Nobel laureate biochemist Christian de Duve and biologist Stuart Kauffman. These authors all seem to view the life principle as some previously unrecognized, holistic, teleological law of nature. Nancey Murphy and other theologians who admit that the traditional notion of a separate soul and body is no longer viable given the evidence from neuroscience (see COGNITIVE SCIENCE AND UNBELIEF), have termed this notion "nonreductive physicalism." They think they can find a place for God and the soul therein.

However, computer simulations indicate that complexity evolves from simplicity by familiar, purely reductive physical processes without the aid of any overarching holistic guiding principle. The life principle, if it exists, may be one of the type of so-called emergent principles found in chaos and complexity theory that naturally arise from the nonlinear, dissipative, but still purely local interactions of material particles. These cannot be called new laws of physics since they follow from already existing laws, if not by direct, mathematical proof, then by computer simulation.

A Tiny Pocket of Complexity. Perhaps any random universe, regardless of its properties, will naturally develop at least some tiny pockets of complexity within a vast sea of randomness, which is just what we see in our universe. Complexity is not so ubiquitous in our universe as most people seem to think. The photons in the Cosmic Microwave Background, a billion times more common than hydrogen atoms, are random to one part in a hundred thousand. The visible matter we see around us and in the sky, which impresses us so much by its complexity, constitutes one-half of 1 percent of the mass of the universe. Perhaps we do not need either a designer or multiple universes to explain such small deviation from chance behavior.

I find it rather amusing that theists make two contradictory arguments for life requiring a creator. Sometimes you hear these from the same people. In the fine-tuning argument, the universe is so congenial to life that the universe must have been created. But if it is so congenial, then we should expect life to evolve by natural processes. In the second argument, which one hears from creationists and antievolutionists, the universe is so uncongenial to life that life must have been created. In that case it is too unlikely for life to have evolved by natural processes and so must have been produced by an intelligent designer. But then life could very easily have been an improbable accident.

The universe looks just as it would be expected to look if it were not created by God. From this we can conclude, beyond a reasonable doubt, that such a God does not exist.

BIBLIOGRAPHY

Aguire, Anthony. "The Cold Big-Bang Cosmology as a Counter-Example to Several Anthropic Arguments." *Physical Review* D64 (2001): 083508.

Barrow, John D., and Frank J. Tipler. *The Anthropic Cosmological Principle*. Oxford: Oxford University Press, 1986.

Bostrom, Nick. *Anthropic Bias: Observation Selection Effects in Science and Philosophy*. New York: Routledge, 2002.

Carter, Brandon. "Large Number Coincidences and the Anthropic Principle in Cosmology." In *Confrontation of Cosmological Theory with Astronomical Data*, edited by M. S. Longair. Dordrecht: Reidel, 1974. Reprinted in John Leslie, ed., *Physical Cosmology and Philosophy*. New York: Macmillan, 1990.

Davies, Paul. *The Cosmic Blueprint*. Radnor, PA: Templeton Foundation Press, 2004.

Davis, J. J. "The Design Argument, Cosmic 'Fine Tuning,' and the Anthropic Principle," *Philosophy of Religion* 22 (1987).

De Duve, Christian. *Vital Dust*. New York: Basic Books, 1995.

Dicke, R. H. "Dirac's Cosmology and Mach's Principle." *Nature* 192 (1961).

Dirac, P. A. M. *Nature* 139 (1937).

Drange, Theodore M. "The Fine-Tuning Argument Revisited." *Philo* 3, no. 2 (2000): 38–49.

Eddington, A. S. *The Mathematical Theory of Relativity*. London: Cambridge University Press, 1923.

Hoyle, F., D. N. F. Dunbar, W. A. Wensel, and W. Whaling. "A State in C12 Predicted from Astrophysical Evidence." *Physical Review Letters* 92 (1953).

Kane, Gordon. *The Particle Garden: Our Universe as Understood by Particle Physicists*. New York: Addison-Wesley, 1995.

Kauffman, Stuart. *At Home in the Universe: The Search for the Laws of Self-Organization and Complexity*. New York: Oxford University Press, 1995.

Manson, Neil A. "There Is No Adequate Definition of 'Fine-Tuned for Life.'" *Inquiry* 43 (2000).

Smith, Quentin. "A Natural Explanation of the Existence and Laws of Our Universe." *Australasian Journal of Philosophy* 68 (1990).

Smolin, Lee. "Did the Universe Evolve?" *Classical and Quantum Gravity* 9 (1992).

———. *The Life of the Cosmos*. Oxford: Oxford University Press, 1997.

Stenger, Victor J. "Natural Explanations for the Anthropic Coincidences." *Philo* 32 (2001).

———. *The Unconscious Quantum: Metaphysics in Modern Physics and Cosmology*. Amherst, NY: Prometheus Books, 1995.

Weinberg, Steven. "The Cosmological Constant Problem." *Reviews of Modern Physics* 61 (1989).

———. "A Designer Universe?" *New York Review of Books*, October 21, 1999. Reprinted in *Skeptical Inquirer* (September–October 2001).

Weyl, H. *Ann. Physik* 59 (1919).

VICTOR J. STENGER

ANTHROPOMORPHISM AND RELIGION. Anthropomorphism commonly is defined as the attribution of human characteristics to nonhuman things and events. RELIGION, in contrast, has defied any common definition. Attempts to define religion range from those of adherents, who may, for example, refer to it as an engagement with something sacred or transcendent, to those of skeptics, who may see it as anthropomorphism. The view that all religions do, in fact, anthropomorphize is somewhat less controversial. It is based on a near consensus that religions universally postulate the existence of some important nonhuman, yet humanlike, being or beings. The significance of this, however, is widely debated.

The relationship of anthropomorphism and religion historically has been contested, especially in Judaism, Christianity, and Islam. From as early as the Greek writer Xenophanes, observers have noted that religions include representations of gods as humanlike beings. These often resemble the religion's adherents mentally, physically, or both. Xenophanes pointed out, for example, that Ethiopians represented their gods as black, while Thracians conceived theirs as having red hair; and the Bible presents a God with face, hands, jealousy, and other human features. Jewish, Christian, and Muslim theologians, however, have tried to minimize the importance of human features in these representations, maintaining that they are merely the attempts of a limited human mind to understand a being that is wholly other. Dissenting scholars reply that if human features are deleted from our conceptions of gods, almost nothing remains.

Theories of Religion. Understanding the relation of anthropomorphism and religion may help illuminate a perennial question: Why are religious thought and action so pervasive in human life? The question arises because something identifiable as religion, though highly variable, seems to exist in every human society, yet independent evidence supporting essential religious ideas is tenuous. The question persists, moreover, because despite centuries of scholarly inquiry into the basis of religious belief and behavior, no general consensus has emerged. Instead, theories of religion are divergent, without so much as an agreement on a definition of religion itself.

Most broadly, these theories may be divided into two camps: those of religious believers and those of unbelievers. The theories of believers may be further divided into two groups: those that aim to give a single account for all religions, and those that give one account for some religion regarded as true, and another for all the rest.

Neither group offers a convincing general theory—that is, one that accounts for religion in general. Those theories that account for the "true" religion in one way (e.g., as the result of revelation) and for other religions in another way (e.g., as the result of ignorance) are, by definition, not general but special. On the other hand, theories that aim at a single account for all religion can achieve it only by great abstraction, because religious beliefs and practices are so diverse. Indeed the authors of such theories (e.g., Friedrich Schleiermacher, Rudolf Otto, and Mircea Eliade) often regard specific beliefs and practices as irrelevant and claim that what counts is a certain ineffable religious experience (see RELIGIOUS AND MYSTICAL EXPERIENCES).

This experience supposedly is universal. Because it is unique and autonomous, however, it cannot be corroborated or compared. The resulting accounts necessarily are vague and even incoherent. They are accessible only to those who have had the experience, and offer no way to know whether one's own experience is the same as that of another.

The theories of skeptics also are both divergent and problematic. The idea that religious beliefs are mistaken is almost their only consensus. These theories may be divided loosely into three groups: wishful thinking, social glue, and intellectualist. These three also may be combined in varying ways.

Wishful thinking theories describe religion as an attempt to assuage our anxieties and discontents by imagining a better world. In such a world, we are aided by superhuman beings and rewarded for good behavior (often in a future life), while our enemies are punished. Variants of the wishful thinking approach go back to Greek and Roman times and continue to the present, but the best-known advocate is the late nineteenth- and early twentieth-century writer Sigmund FREUD. Freud saw humans as enmeshed in existential difficulties and as desperately needing the reassurance that they supposedly find in religion.

While wishful thinking may perhaps be involved in religion, at least two facts suggest that it is insufficient as an explanation. First, most religions have beliefs with components that we probably would not choose: hells, purgatories, angry and jealous gods, and the like. Second, even if all features of religious belief were sanguine, the theories still would have to say why anyone would believe them. In other areas of life, we do not simply believe whatever would feel good. Hungry people, for example, do not content themselves with imagining that they have just eaten.

Social glue theories hold that the function of religion is to satisfy a society's need for cohesion and solidarity. This approach, too, may be traced back to antiquity, but its most influential exponent is the French sociologist Emile Durkheim, roughly a contemporary of Freud.

According to Durkheim, religion aids social cohesion by providing a symbolic image of society, such as a god or a flag, which represents its essential elements, especially its ethics. This image underscores society's value for its members and the primacy of its demands on them. The symbolic image may or may not take the form of a deity, since its defining characteristic is only that a society's members regard it as sacred.

Social glue theories, like wishful thinking theories, doubtless make valuable points. Again, however, they have crucial limitations. First, they provide no good explanation of what motivates people to think and act religiously. Second, the religions of some societies, such as those of hunter-gatherers, are not clearly linked to their ethics. Third, although religion sometimes unites groups, it sometimes divides them as well.

The third or intellectualist (now often called cognitivist) group of theories presents religion as an attempt to understand the world as a whole and to act accordingly. Its lineage extends back at least to Benedict de SPINOZA in the seventeenth century and continues with David HUME in the eighteenth and E. B. Tylor in the nineteenth. At present it is perhaps the leading approach among skeptics.

Most members of this group hold that the common characteristic of religion is the view that the world is shaped in important ways by humanlike, though nonhuman, beings. For example, all manner of phenomena—from windstorms to butterfly wings to the starry firmament—may be seen as the actions or products of humanlike agents, usually acting behind the scenes. Writers in this group note that even Buddhism, often cited as a "godless religion," in fact has a pantheon of deities, often including the Buddha himself. Although there are, to be sure, Buddhist philosophies and psychologies in which gods are absent, these are no more diagnostic of Buddhism in general than are demythologized Christianity or Judaism of those religions.

The humanlike agents postulated by believers may or may not be described in detail. They may be as fully fleshed out as Krishna or Christ, or as allusive as "intelligent design" (see INTELLIGENT DESIGN THEORY) or Tillich's "ground of being." In either case, the intellectualists hold, religions anthropomorphize natural phenomena, though varying in the human features emphasized (usually mental features but often physical ones as well) and in the level of detail.

That religion anthropomorphizes is not really in question. Even theologians admit, if reluctantly, that it inevitably does so. The question is, rather, why it does and what this implies. For the theologians, as noted, anthropomorphism merely marks the limits of the human mind in trying to grasp a transcendent Other. For the skeptical theorists as well, it marks human limits, but these are limits in understanding the natural world, not a divinity. Encountering our limits, we invoke humanlike models for nonhuman phenomena.

Theories of religion as anthropomorphism have not been convincing, however, because they have not successfully explained anthropomorphism itself. This may be because they have looked mainly at anthropomorphism only in religion, not in general. This is a major oversight, because anthropomorphism itself is highly general.

Explanations of anthropomorphism have been of two sorts: wishful thinking and familiarity. Although each is useful, neither is sufficient. Wishful thinking was mentioned above as a theory of religion. As a theory of anthropomorphism, it holds similarly that a nonhuman world is frightening and lonely, and that we therefore populate it with supportive quasi-human beings. The problem with this explanation is that many imagined humanlike beings, like many humans, are not supportive but threatening—for example, sasquatches, goblins, and Frankenstein's monster. Likewise, when we find ourselves in a lonely place after dusk and mistake a tree stump or a shadow for a threatening figure, we are anthropomorphizing but not reassuring ourselves.

A second explanation of anthropomorphism (offered by both Spinoza and Hume) is that we simply wish to understand the world, which is vast and mysterious, and that to do so we employ the most familiar available model. That model is ourselves. The problem with this explanation is that we anthropomorphize not only unfamiliar things and events but also ones that are as familiar to us as we ourselves: dogs and cats, cars and computers. Although we may feel that we are even more familiar with ourselves than with such other things, writers including Shakespeare and Freud note that we know ourselves but slenderly. Our self-knowledge then is not necessarily more direct or reliable than our knowledge of not-self. Since we already have models for cats, cars, and computers that are as adequate intellectually as our models of ourselves, something else must explain why we insert humanlike features.

Anthropomorphism and Animism: A New Account. A more adequate explanation of anthropomorphism begins with the realization that religion is only a small part of its manifestations. Together with a closely related phenomenon, animism—here defined as attributing characteristics of life to biologically inanimate things and events—anthropomorphism appears throughout human thought and action: in daily life, in the arts, and even in the sciences.

In daily life, for example, we find faces in clouds and in wood grain, and do so without thinking. When we hear a door slam somewhere in the house, we wonder who is there, even though we expect no one and know that it is windy outside. When we see a windblown leaf or dust ball scurry erratically across a surface, we look twice, thinking it is an insect or spider. Graphic art and literature also regularly personify and animate both natural phenomena and human artifacts. Shakespeare in *As You Like It*, for instance, finds "tongues in trees";

Homer's spears thirst for blood. Even the sciences, which abjure anthropomorphism, inadvertently employ humanlike models. Charles DARWIN, for example, described Nature as diligently improving her progeny.

Moreover, anthropomorphism and animism both are durable, worldwide, and diverse. Paleolithic cave paintings display them, and today people cross-culturally continue to see human and animal shapes everywhere, for example, in such landforms as mountains and stalactites. We think we see not only physically human forms but also, and more importantly, mental features such as intention. Stuck drawers appear obstinately to resist us. Developmental psychologists such as Jean Piaget and Deborah Kelemen have shown that even young children assume that the world manifests design and purpose: clouds are for raining, and lions are to put in zoos. Nonetheless, we fail to appreciate the pervasiveness of anthropomorphism and animism, because (like most mental processes) they remain primarily unconscious.

If wishful thinking and familiarity do not account for the omnipresence of anthropomorphism and animism, what does? The apparent answer lies in the uncertainty of our knowledge of the world, in the importance to us of humans and other animals, and in our strategy for dealing with this uncertainty and this importance.

As Spinoza, Hume, and other philosophers have noted, and as contemporary cognitive psychology affirms, uncertainty in perception and cognition is pervasive and chronic. Perception is uncertain because any given sensation, such as a tickle on our skin, a booming noise, or a dark shape in an alley, has more than one possible cause. The tickle may be a loose thread or a spider, the noise may be a firecracker or a gunshot, and the shape may be a sack of garbage or a lurking figure. Thus, phenomena do not declare their own meanings but must be construed. The world we hear, see, and feel is not transparent but must be interpreted. Because we typically do not have enough timely information for certainty, our interpretations are bets.

The interpretive bets we make are neither random nor based primarily on probability. Rather, we bet primarily on significance—that is, on information important to us, even if that information is improbable. Thus we bet on the most significant possibilities we know that might fit the stimulus: the spider not the thread, the gunshot not the firecracker, and the figure not the sack. If these bets are right, we gain much. Most important, we are prepared for appropriate action. If the bets are mistaken, we have lost little.

Among things and events we might bet on, the most important to us usually are the most highly organized, which is to say, living organisms. These constitute hot spots of significance: of energy, of motion, of things that we might eat or that might eat us. Correctly interpreted, organisms (and traces of them) also deliver big packages of information, not only about themselves but also about their environments. Snakes may mean painful bites, birds screaming in a tree may mean a snake, and the disappearance of birds may mean environmental toxins.

Although complex animals such as snakes and birds are important to us, the most highly organized animals, our fellow humans, are more important still. This is not a result of our egotism but of our practicality, since humans are the most potent creatures we know. Thus they may be our best friends, our worst enemies, or something in between. Hence, although we are sensitive to the presence of any animals, we are with good reason especially sensitive to the presence of humans.

However, our sensitivity to animals and humans does not give us certainty about their presence or absence. The inherent ambiguity of perception is exacerbated by natural deception in the case of nonhuman animals and by deliberate deception in the case of humans. By virtue of their highly evolved camouflage, almost all wild animals in their natural habitats are difficult if not impossible to see until they move. With a few exceptions, such as animals in mating plumage, they do not stand out like a black-and-white cow in a green pasture, but merge imperceptibly with their environments. Humans may choose similarly to remain unseen and may use even more elaborate deceptions than those of animals.

As a result of such deception, our sensitivities to the presence of any and all agents are especially finely honed and on a hair trigger. Special sensitivities of several kinds, apparently innate, reveal our evolved preoccupation with detecting animals, including humans. Visual sensitivities alone include sensitivities to motion (especially motion that appears self-initiated or goal directed), symmetry (especially bilateral symmetry), eyespots (black disks resembling eye pupils), faces, and spectrally pure color (such as that of coral snakes). Any of these catches our attention. We also have apparently innate sensitivities to evidence of characteristically human capacities and activities: to seeming design and purpose, social intention, and symbolic communication. Thus we look for meaning everywhere and see comets as portents, evolution as design, and plagues, including AIDS, as punishments.

Since all these sensitivities are on a hair trigger, they are especially susceptible to mistakes. Doors slammed by the wind are not persons, yet we persistently hear them as such. Nor are plagues punishments, storms angry, or the universe a result of design. Yet for thousands of years people have thought they were, and today many still find such thinking natural. In our perceptual situation, this kind of mistake is inevitable. Our perceptual and cognitive stances are not neutral, but rather biased toward discovering animals and particularly people. Correspondingly, we often mistakenly find them where they do not exist. Thus our world chronically appears to us more alive, more personal, and more purposeful than it is.

Although anthropomorphism and animism are by definition mistakes, the proclivity that gives rise to them—the proclivity to find agents wherever they exist—is not a mistake. Rather, it is an evolved strategy that copes with the natural environment, one in which most agents conceal themselves. The central principle of this strategy is "better safe than sorry." It is better that we mistake a stick for a snake than the other way around. Although nine of ten such identifications may be mistaken, the single correct one makes betting high a good strategy.

Religion as Systematized Anthropomorphism. The strategy of betting high has, as noted, been built into our perceptual sensitivities, and we therefore interpret the world as alive and humanlike. Not all such interpretations, of course, constitute religion. Some mistaken interpretations are quickly discovered and tacitly dismissed as anthropomorphism or animism: I thought that was an animal on the road but now I see it's a piece of a tire. Others linger but do not become part of a larger system: artifacts in advertisements, for example, may be humanized so subtly that we are not consciously aware of it, but their significance ends with consumer behavior. Still others influence larger-scale expectations and behavior, and may be quasi-religious. Our expectation that the world show design and purpose, for example, has made plausible Adam Smith's notion that market systems operate for the general well-being, as an "invisible hand." This notion, and the expectation that makes it seem natural, encourage laissez-faire policy.

What we call religion, however, is a still more comprehensive and more systematic form of anthropomorphism. In a religious worldview, most, if not all, events may be attributed to the consistent, elaborated will or workings of humanlike beings operating offstage. Indeed, a religious view may rule out the very notion of accident.

A religious worldview may be put to varied uses. People may be reassured by having some encompassing account of the world, even if this is a harsh or gloomy one. Rulers of stratified societies, such as chiefdoms and states, may use religion to bolster their regimes, as by asserting that gods support them or that their subjects will be rewarded or punished in a later life. Although the uses to which religion can be put may explain why religions are actively promulgated, however, they do not explain what gives rise to religion and makes it plausible. What does so is that human beings are spring-loaded to see human characteristics, both physical and mental, in the world at large.

Conclusion. Religion, then, may be described as a system for interpreting and influencing the world, built on an anthropomorphic premise. So described, religion has borders with other sorts of thought and action that are not sharp but gradual. Continuous as it is with other thought and action, including common sense and science, religion is not sui generis but has the same topic (the world), the same aims (influence and interpretation), and the same methods (conjecture and criticism) as they. Although distinctions can usefully be made, they are distinctions of degree, not kind.

The relation of anthropomorphism and religion thus is both close and complex. Anthropomorphism is central to religion but not unique to it. All religion is anthropomorphic, but grades into other phenomena, such as philosophy and psychology, that typically are not. Religion has at its heart a misapprehension, but the impulse that gives rise to that misapprehension is no mistake. Rather, it is a necessary component of our orientation to the world.

BIBLIOGRAPHY

Durkheim, Emile. *The Elementary Forms of the Religious Life*. Translated by Karen E. Fields. New York: Free Press, 1995.

Eliade, Mircea. *The Sacred and the Profane: The Nature of Religion*. New York: Harper & Row, 1961.

Freud, Sigmund. *The Future of an Illusion*. Garden City, NY: Anchor, 1927.

Guthrie, Stewart. *Faces in the Clouds: A New Theory of Religion*. New York: Oxford University Press, 1993.

Hume, David. *The Natural History of Religion*. Edited by H. E. Root. Stanford, CA: Stanford University Press, 1957.

Kelemen, Deborah. "Are Children 'Intuitive Theists'? Reasoning about Purpose and Design in Nature." *Psychological Science* 15, no. 5 (2004).

Otto, Rudolf. *The Idea of the Holy*. New York: Oxford University Press, 1950.

Piaget, Jean. *The Child's Conception of the World*. London: Routledge & Kegan Paul, 1929.

Schleiermacher, Friedrich. *On Religion*. Cambridge: Cambridge University Press, 1988.

Spinoza, Benedict de. *The Chief Works of Benedict Spinoza: On the Improvement of the Understanding; The Ethics; Correspondence*. Translated by R. H. M. Elwes. New York: Dover, 1955.

Tylor, E. B. *Primitive Culture*. London: John Murray, 1873.

STEWART ELLIOTT GUTHRIE

ANTHROPOSOPHY. An international religious sect following the teachings of Rudolf Steiner (1861–1925), also called Spiritual Science. Activities include Waldorf education, Anthroposophical medicine, pharmaceuticals, Camphill communities for the developmentally disabled, biodynamic agriculture, Eurythmy (a spiritual dance), art schools, psychotherapy, elder care, the Christian Community (a formal church), financial institutions, publishing, and politics (Steiner's "threefold social order"). The world headquarters of the Anthroposophical Society is the Goetheanum in Dornach, Switzerland.

History. Steiner followed the technical education track in his native Austria, and supported himself by private tutoring and lecturing at a workers' institute. He was engaged to edit GOETHE's scientific works for a new edi-

tion. In recognition of this work Steiner was given a doctorate, conferred in a special dispensation by a university professor.

In 1894 Steiner published his chef d'oevre in philosophy, *The Philosophy of Freedom* (also translated as *The Philosophy of Spiritual Activity*). It failed to establish Steiner in the academic world.

Steiner was appointed head of the German section of THEOSOPHY by Annie BESANT in 1902 after his lectures made a strong impression at a Theosophical congress. He had found his life's work. He was a charismatic leader, and the sect thrived. Around 1912 Charles Leadbeater at Theosophy's center in India convinced other Theosophical leaders that a boy he admired, Krishnamurti, was a reincarnation of Christ. Steiner had already integrated Christ into his cosmological system, and Krishnamurti had no place in it.

Steiner split with Theosophy (knowledge of God) to form his own group, which he called Anthroposophy (knowledge of man). Most of the German section defected with him, forming an instant cult. Later he claimed to have been teaching Anthroposophy all along, and Anthroposophical presses sometimes change "Theosophy" to "Anthroposophy" in editions of his earlier books. He taught a self-hypnotic meditation technique that engenders feelings of wisdom and superiority.

Worldview. Anthroposophy synthesizes a wide range of spiritual traditions, claiming to reveal comprehensive truths that are only present in fragments in other religions. At its foundation are the concepts of REINCARNATION, karma, and polytheism, which derive from Buddhism and Hinduism. Steiner was something of a fundamentalist Platonist, holding that the real world was all illusion and objects but reflections of eternal essences in the spiritual world. He also espoused Plato's political philosophy, and may well have imagined himself as a philosopher-king. He took the dual gods of light and dark from the ancient Persian religion Zoroastrianism, identifying the light god as Lucifer, and created his own trinity of Lucifer, Ahriman (the dark god), and a Gnostic and Manichean conception of Christ, usually referred to as "the Christ Spirit." Steiner, who claimed to be able to see the past and future written in the "akashic record," wrote *The Fifth Gospel* to explain what really happened in the life of Christ.

To this rich mix Steiner added European occult traditions: Cabbalism, numerology, white magic, alchemy, Rosicrucianism and Masonry, and spiced it with vegetarianism, astrology, herbalism, and homeopathy. Steiner claimed to make "exact scientific observations" in the spiritual world, so it is impossible to question the veracity of his authoritative pronouncements without questioning the foundations of Anthroposophy.

Racism. Steiner lectured extensively on evolution, a popular topic at the beginning of the twentieth century, but his theory was explicitly opposed to Charles DARWIN's. He taught that humans have always been present, and that the nonhuman animals evolved out of humanity, separating out overspecialized qualities (the eagle's vision, the gazelle's speed) so that humanity could be perfectly balanced.

Evolution in Anthroposophy also involves personal development as souls reincarnate in successively higher races. Anthroposophy follows the Theosophical system, derived in turn from Hinduism, of cycles within cycles. Steiner taught that mankind should have advanced together from race to race, but the "adversary" gods Lucifer and Ahriman interfered, and so races that should have died out are still hanging around. Steiner changed the Theosophical terminology from "root races" to "cultural epochs," but made it clear that skin color was a definitive indicator of spiritual potential. Black skin belongs to survivors of the Lemurian root race, and yellow skin to Atlanteans who failed to progress. Native Americans are a remnant destined for extinction, and the survival of the Jews is "a mistake of history." The present time period belongs, unsurprisingly, to the white "Aryans." Anthroposophists find these doctrines embarrassing, but they construct elaborate evasions and denials rather than simply repudiating Steiner's words.

Anthroposophy and the Nazis. During and after World War I, Steiner was active politically. He proposed his "threefold social order" to the leaders of Europe, but could not find a receptive audience. He sent agents to influence the election in Upper Silesia, and at one point had a weekly newspaper in Stuttgart. The growing Nazi movement regarded Anthroposophy as a rival for the hearts and minds of the German people.

Steiner died in 1925, eight years before Hitler came to power. During the Nazi period, Anthroposophy and its works were controversial in the Nazi party. There was a clear majority against the Anthroposophical Society itself, since it was a political rival, and it was banned in 1935. Other Anthroposophical activities like biodynamic agriculture and the Waldorf schools collaborated, and were protected by supporters in the party. Jewish teachers left or were dismissed from Waldorf schools, and a German Waldorf school association was formed that claimed the schools were teaching National Socialist ideals. Waldorf schools were harassed by local officials, but many survived until Rudolf Hess, a strong supporter of Anthroposophy, flew to Scotland. After that it was open season on occultists and the last schools were closed. Biodynamic agriculture remained a successful collaboration.

Anthroposophy Today. Working in the world doesn't secularize Anthroposophy; rather Anthroposophy attempts to spiritualize the world. These worldly activities are usually referred to in Anthroposophical jargon as "initiatives," based on Steiner's "impulses." They are claimed as Anthroposophical activities when it is desired to glorify Anthroposophy, but denied and called independent free associations when scandals arise or outsiders question their connection to problematic Anthro-

posophical doctrines. Each activity will, of course, have its own local nonprofit corporation, but they are all carried out under Anthroposophical direction, ultimately taking guidance from departments in the Dornach headquarters (near Basel, Switzerland).

Waldorf Education. Waldorf schools, also called Steiner Schools and Free Schools, are named after the original school that Steiner founded in Stuttgart, Germany. The school was for the children of the workers at the Waldorf-Astoria cigarette factory, thus the name. The movement calls itself the largest nonsectarian school system in the world, but pervasive Anthroposophical doctrine vitiates its claim of being nonsectarian. Waldorf education is guided by Steiner's theory of child development, which is based on reincarnation. In this scheme, the physical body is born at birth, the "etheric body" at age seven, the "astral body" at age fourteen, and the "I," the immortal member, at age twenty-one. Teachers classify students according to the ancient "four temperaments." Teachers are trained in a two- or three-year Anthroposophical seminary program in which the first year, called the foundation year, consists entirely of the study of Anthroposophy.

Anthroposophical pseudoscience is easy to find in Waldorf schools. "Goethean science" is supposed to be based only on observation, without "dogmatic" theory. Because observations make no sense without a relationship to some hypothesis, students are subtly nudged in the direction of Steiner's explanations of the world. Typical departures from accepted science include the claim that Goethe refuted Newton's theory of color, Steiner's unique "threefold" systems in physiology, and the oft-repeated doctrine that "the heart is not a pump" (blood is said to move itself).

Anthroposophical Medicine. Medicine is one of the more visible activities of Anthroposophy in Europe. Physicians are required to have medical degrees before training in Anthroposophical medicine, but that training denies and contradicts evidence-based medicine. Steiner's method uses homeopathic remedies, but abjures the homeopathic method of testing a proposed therapeutic substance by observing the effects of the undiluted substance on a volunteer. The symptoms the subject experiences are supposed to indicate the diseases that the diluted substance will cure. This was too scientific for Steiner, who preferred to rely on the traditional herbalistic method of recognizing the application of a remedy from its appearance. For example, his remedy for cancer is mistletoe, because mistletoe grows radially rather than toward the sun as other plants do, and cancer grows radially. The Anthroposophical cancer remedy Iscador, prepared in a magical process from mistletoe, is in common use in Europe despite a lack of sufficient evidence for efficacy.

Camphill. Camphill communities are Anthroposophically inspired residential programs for developmentally disabled children and adults. Completely contained enclaves, they are worthy of study as models of life in an Anthroposophical world. Since only cooperative inmates are retained, the atmosphere is artificially idyllic, and an ostensible "village" structure conceals strict authoritarianism.

DAN DUGAN

ANTICLERICALISM. Opposition to the power and pretensions of the Roman Catholic Church. In its narrower sense anticlericalism connotes opposition to reactionary political and social views favored by the Roman Catholic Church in countries where its influence was strong, in particular, Italy, France, Belgium, Spain, and the nations of Latin America. The classical period of anticlericalism extended from the 1850s to the 1910s, although it remains influential in all of these countries and regions to the present day.

Catholic doctrine claims that because Catholicism is the only true religion, it enjoys a unique right to exercise leadership in society. Boniface VIII outlined this attitude clearly in the 1302 encyclical message *Unam Sanctam*, in which he decreed: "We declare, affirm, and define as a truth necessary for salvation that every human being is subject to the Roman pontiff." For centuries to come, many who served the papacy felt justified in seeing their own political preferences as also being those of God, which in turn justified harsh measures against those who would dissent. Countries with large Catholic majorities have long been resigned to clerical interference in politics, education, and cultural affairs, whether directly or behind closed doors. And those who oppose such measures must, so this thinking goes, work from ignoble or even satanic motivations. There was a certain softening of this stance as a result of the Second Vatican Council (1962–65), but during the pontificate of John Paul II there was a partial return to the earlier hard-line position.

Anticlericalism is not the same as anti-Catholicism. To be anticlerical is to oppose the presumed right of Catholic churchmen to participate at a senior and unelected level in government decisions or in the cultural life of one's country. Anti-Catholicism, by contrast, is the opposition to all aspects of the Roman Catholic Church, not simply its interference in government. At its worst, anti-Catholicism includes the disparagement of Catholics as people. The old Protestant fears of "popery" and the fear of the "whore of Babylon" are informed more by theological than by political concerns. Protestant anti-Catholicism is concerned with what Protestants see as the Catholic betrayal of the original message of Christ, which they— the Protestants—are proclaiming in pure form once again. Laced with such theological fears were social fears of Catholics as being unreasonably prolific, uneducated, and a danger to the moral stability of the nation. For anti-Catholic Protestants, clerical mismanagement is only a symptom of popish falling away from the New Testament, but for anticlericals, it stands as a failing in its own

right. Anticlericals might or might not be anti-Catholic in the broader sense. Indeed, many anticlericals have considered themselves to be sincere Catholics, and others have supported a variety of religious viewpoints. In particular, many anticlericals have been Masons. More recently, some of the most effective anticlerical groups have been Catholic reform organizations.

Anticlericalism, understood in the narrower sense, was provoked by the rise of Ultramontane Catholicism, a staunchly conservative form of Catholicism that grew out of the shock of the French Revolution and the subsequent temporal humiliation of the papacy. *Ultramontane* means "beyond the mountains," from the view of Europeans residing west of the Alps, a reference to Rome. In reaction to the Enlightenment values of reason, natural religion, confidence in the future, and in the possibility of building a better future (see ENLIGHTENMENT, THE, UNBELIEF WITHIN), Ultramontanism was bitterly antirationalist, even antimodern. It preferred a sentimental, unthinking piety centered around church, home, and hearth. Moreover, Ultramontanism spoke of Rome as the sole source of God's wisdom, indeed of any wisdom worth the title. Ultramontanism was also a response to Gallicanism, a powerful trend among national churches in the three centuries prior to the French Revolution to assert local control over their own affairs while conceding to Rome supremacy in the spiritual domain.

Whereas Gallicanism was confined to ecclesiastical elites, the confidence to criticize the actions of the church extended during the Enlightenment to the educated middle classes. And, and in many cases, these new critics were less prepared to offer lip service to the supremacy of the papacy over spiritual matters. The church made a series of blunders that seriously compromised its claim to exercise spiritual authority that could plausibly be seen as the will of God. In particular, the long record of persecution of progressive-minded people, from Galileo GALILEI to Denis DIDEROT, editor of the influential *Encyclopedie*, excited opposition from the general population. And the Calas case (1761–62), which VOLTAIRE turned into a cause célèbre of the underdog fighting against an unrepresentative tyranny, further undermined the moral authority of the church in the eyes of many people. But if the middle classes were critical of the church during the Enlightenment, the French Revolution extended that spirit of independence to the working people. French Catholicism suffered serious reverses in the years following the revolution. Its position was only partially restored by Napoleon, and then only as a political gambit rather than through any genuine sense of piety.

In the years after Napoleon's defeat, the Catholic Church in Europe forged close links with reactionary monarchies in an attempt to prevent the recurrence of such popular agitation as had occurred in France. While the church allied with reactionary regimes, progressive-minded people were more inclined to express their confidence in the future in increasingly secular terms (see SECULARISM). Anticlerical views played a significant role in moving progressive opinion along by concentrating attention on the largest single obstacle to their dreams: the Roman Catholic Church.

The quintessential anticlerical politician was Leon Gambetta, an architect of contemporary French democracy. Born in modest circumstances, Gambetta was the child of a Frenchwoman and an Italian immigrant to France. Gambetta's talents moved him toward politics, and in 1869 he was elected as a deputy to the French parliament. After France's defeat by the Prussians in 1871 he became an important spokesman for the opposition to the hapless Emperor Napoleon III. Gambetta's courage during the war, and his dramatic escape from Paris in a balloon, inspired his countrymen at a dark time. So important did Gambetta become that although he only briefly held the position of premier, he is seen as one of the most important figures in the creation of the Third Republic. He was a very significant presence behind the 1875 Republican Constitution.

Gambetta led the struggle against clerical reaction between 1871 and 1879. His slogan was "Clericalism: there is the enemy!" He was a leading influence behind what are known as the Ferry Laws of 1881–82, which established free secular education, the right to civil marriage, and limited access to divorce. Each of these reforms was gained in the face of bitter clerical opposition. To this day there is hardly a town in France which does not have a Rue Gambetta.

The greatest victory of the French anticlericals was the formal separation of church and state in 1905. Prior to 1905, priests were habitually employed as teachers in state schools, where Catholicism was taught as the only religious option available. French Catholicism was also strongly anti-Semitic, reaching a fever pitch during the lengthy case involving the French soldier Alfred Dreyfus, a Jew who was falsely accused of treason in 1894 and not fully cleared of the trumped-up charges against him until 1906. The role played by anticlericals in these two series of events constitute anticlericalism's finest hour.

In Italy, anticlericalism took on a slightly different form, taking its definitive shape in opposing the tyranny in the Papal States. The pontificate of Pius IX in particular pitted the papacy, and thus Catholicism, against all the trends of the century: national unity, secular education, and the growth of science. Italian anticlericals saw the Catholic Church as standing squarely against progress. Nowhere was this more evident than in the Papal States. Until 1870 the pope ruled a large slice of central Italy, from the Gulf of Gaeta north of Naples to the delta of the Po on the Adriatic, several hundred miles to the north. The Papal States were chronically misruled, with standards of education, health, and civic amenities among the poorest in Europe. A call by European leaders at the Congress of Paris in 1856 for the pontiff to reform his lands was ignored.

The growing sense of a common Italian identity lay behind a drive to unite the peninsula into a united nation. But against this, the papacy claimed to hold legal tenure of its dominions going back to the Roman emperor Constantine, who was supposed to have donated that territory, as well as moral authority over all western Europe, to Pope Sylvester in perpetuity. In fact, the humanist scholar Lorenzo Valla had proved these documents, known collectively as the Donation of Constantine, were an eighth-century forgery. Valla had taught the popes to fear learning they could not control; later the near demise of the papacy at the hands of the revolutionary French in the years before Napoleon had taught them a lasting fear of radical politics. For a while Pius IX gave signs of being ready to embrace change, but he was so shocked by the revolts and unrest in 1848 that he quickly became more reactionary than his predecessors. His long pontificate was the principal breeding ground for contemporary anticlericalism, in Italy and abroad.

As a united Italy was being formed all around him, Pius IX retained his hold over the Papal States only because of the French, who stationed a large contingent of troops in Rome to quell the growing unrest. Across the rest of the country, the growing fervor of Italian nationalism grew in direct proportion to popular hostility toward the reactionary papacy. In 1850 the Kingdom of Piedmont passed a series of laws that drastically curtailed the power of the church. This legislation was a victory for anticlericals, who had little difficulty in portraying the papacy as the biggest obstacle to the future of Italy. Piedmont became the leading force in the drive for Italian unity, with the temporal power of the papacy as its target.

The true flag bearer for Italian anticlericalism, however, was Giuseppe Garibaldi. Even more of an adventurer than Gambetta, Garibaldi fought actively to unite Italy between 1859 and 1870. Garibaldi spoke of the papacy as the "sacred shop." It was the prospect of Garibaldi's soldiers, marching north from Sicily in 1860, that provoked a popular uprising in the Papal States. A motley papal defensive army was quickly defeated, leaving only Rome and its environs under papal control, and this due only to the continuing presence of French troops. All the other provinces voted overwhelmingly to throw off allegiance to the pope and to join the newly created Kingdom of Italy. Four years after this defeat, on December 8, 1864, Pius IX decreed the Syllabus of Errors, which roundly condemned virtually every tenet of modernity. For opponents of the Catholic Church, the Syllabus confirmed all their suspicions that the church was hopelessly reactionary (see DRAPER, JOHN WILLIAM).

Italy was finally able to march into Rome in 1870. The French withdrew in April, and in September the Italians marched in. Once again there was a plebiscite and the vote was overwhelmingly in favor of union with Italy. Rome became Italy's capital and Pius IX retreated to the Vatican, claiming he was a prisoner. Pius then convened the first Vatican Council, which established the dogma of papal infallibility. This did nothing to reassure the anticlericals. After the heady years of the unification of the country, Italian anticlericalism lost its force as an agent for progressive change, while Italian politics declined into a corrupt merry-go-round of short-lived governments.

In Spain the situation was different yet again because of the uniquely pervasive role that the Catholic Church had forged for itself in the life of the country. For many people, to be Spanish meant to be Catholic, which in turn meant that opposition to the church could be equated with hatred of Spain. Much of this had grown out of the lengthy reconquest of the country from the Muslims and the subsequent campaigns to eradicate Judaism and Islam from national life. The strength and ubiquity of Spanish Catholicism provoked a proportionately intense anticlerical reaction to it. Successive nineteenth-century liberal governments enacted progressive legislation, only to see it repealed by the reactionary regimes that followed them. These changes were punctuated by recurrent violence against churches, seen by the poor as bastions of privilege, license, and corruption. Later in the century, Spanish anticlericalism became tinged with radical anarchism (see ANARCHISM AND UNBELIEF). Partly in reaction to the nationalist flavor Spanish Catholicism had assumed, the anarchists responded by renouncing nationalism in favor of a militant internationalism. This lent fire and commitment to the anticlerical cause, but the inability of anarchism to articulate a plausible alternative limited its appeal.

A significant figure in Spanish anticlericalism who did offer a positive alternative was the educator Francisco FERRER. After beginning his career as a revolutionary, Ferrer spent many years in exile in Paris, where he abandoned violent means and turned his energies to education. He returned to Spain and established a school with a strictly secular curriculum. Ferrer's policy of educating girls on equal terms with boys scandalized Catholic opinion. The schools were popular and eventually he had about forty of them around Catalonia.

When King Alfonso XIII was the target of an assassination attempt in 1906, the authorities took their opportunity. Ferrer was arrested and his schools closed down. The gambit failed, however, as Ferrer was acquitted of any involvement in the attack. During renewed unrest in 1909, there was serious rioting in what became known as the Tragic Week, and Ferrer's enemies saw an opportunity to saddle him with the blame. He was charged with fomenting the riots, and after a travesty of a trial Ferrer was shot on October 13, 1909. Ferrer's death brought about the downfall of the conservative Spanish government amid a storm of international criticism. Oblivious to this, Pope Pius X sent to the military prosecutor responsible for Ferrer's death an engraved, gold-handled sword as a reward.

The church's determination to retain its privileges and the intransigent opposition of the anticlericals, now joined by Communists, led the country into its disastrous civil war followed by the lengthy rule of Francisco Franco, which persisted until 1975. At the turn of the twenty-first century, however, the initiative rests once again with the anticlericals (see SPAIN, UNBELIEF IN). Emblematic of this was the Spanish government's 2005 decision to extend civil rights to homosexuals in the face of bitter church opposition.

In South and Central America, anticlericalism has had a long and varied career. Anticlericalism wedded in turn with liberalism, POSITIVISM, and MARXISM as respective vehicles by which the church could be challenged and its power curtailed. In the century after the South American countries secured their independence from Spain and Portugal, the church exhibited a distinct preference for autocratic regimes and looked to preserve its privileges. With some notable exceptions, the same had been true with respect to local independence struggles. Until shortly before Spain finally lost control of the continent, the papacy lent support to colonial powers. It was forced into an embarrassing reversal of this policy shortly afterward, in the face of a newly independent continent.

The precedent for Latin American anticlericalism was set by Simón Bolívar, the person who, more than anyone else, can be credited as the liberator of the continent from colonial rule. Bolívar, who had been in Paris at the time of the French Revolution, brought progressive and anticlerical ideas back to Latin America with him. Leaders keen to build their societies usually had to reckon with a powerful and deeply conservative Catholic Church that inevitably bred anticlerical attitudes. Powerful examples include Victorino Lastarria, who devoted his life to building up secular education, a free press, and an end to clerical privilege in Chile.

In Mexico the clerical reaction was so pronounced that the anticlericalism it provoked was among the most radical. The principal figure here was Benito Juárez. Shortly after becoming president in 1858, Juárez enacted a series of laws sharply separating church from state, confiscating church property, and suppressing religious orders. The Catholic Church had grown very powerful and corrupt and habitually supported reactionary leaders. Late in 1862 French troops landed in Mexico with the intention of restoring a reactionary government to power. In 1864 the French installed Archduke Maximilian of Austria as emperor of Mexico. Resistance to Maximilian, who had the support of the church, intensified until an uprising in 1867 overthrew him and restored Juárez to power. The Mexican Revolution of 1910 further entrenched the anticlerical reforms by drastically curbing the political power of the church. Guatemala's story is less happy. Francisco Morazán, now often spoken of as the Father of the Country, was executed by his clerical enemies after enacting a wide range of progressive legislation.

In many Latin American countries the optimistic confidence in their future took the form of Positivism, inspired by the French thinker Auguste COMTE. Positivism brought together Comte's ideas with the progressionist evolutionism of Herbert SPENCER and anticlericalism. Typical of these reformers was Antonio Guzmán Blanco, who ruled Venezuela for almost two decades. Guzmán Blanco is known as "the Regenerator" for his role in building his country. He confiscated church property, established a national church—one less directly dependent on either Rome or Spain—and built much of the young country's infrastructure.

After World War I, Positivism declined in favor of Marxism as the preferred vehicle for anticlerical activity. But by midcentury, much of the initiative had passed from the anticlericals to Catholic radicals who espoused variations of liberation theology. But as these theologians have been progressively squeezed out by church authorities or left the church of their own accord, there may be a revival of anticlericalism, particularly as the church is once again defending a starkly authoritarian position. By and large, Latin American anticlericals succeeded in establishing mainly secular political institutions, but they were less successful in exporting those secular attitudes to large sections of the population. To address this imbalance, contemporary anticlericalism needs to be informed principally by HUMANISM.

Turning to the humanist movement, we see that, for the most part, it has avoided the less helpful excesses of anti-Catholicism employed by Protestant critics. The most significant critic of the Catholic Church in the twentieth century was Joseph MCCABE, who wrote approximately forty-nine books on this theme. Even in his later works, which were more openly adversarial—he described them as his *advocatus diaboli* (devil's advocate) works—McCabe confined his criticism to the workings of the papacy and the writings of its apologists. In a vast body of work spanning more than half a century, there are very few expressions or judgments which could be seen as anti-Catholic in the pejorative sense. The same can be said of most other significant humanist critics of the Catholic Church such as Paul BLANSHARD in the United States. These critics opposed the Roman Catholic Church without being purveyors of a simple anti-Catholicism. A couple of lesser writers, like Avro Manhattan and F. A. Ridley, were more prone to conspiracy theory hysteria reminiscent of older Protestant critics of Rome. This was evident in Manhattan's case, when his later works were published by Protestant publishers linked to the rabid Northern Ireland anti-Catholic Rev. Ian Paisley.

The vast majority of humanist criticism of Roman Catholicism, then, can be seen to fit in the tradition of robust anticlericalism from the standpoint of having rejected the truth claims the church makes about itself and the world. This is a credible viewpoint, and is very different from the simpler anti-Catholicism in which Catholics as people are disparaged or slighted.

And finally, attention should be directed to the literature that has been inspired by anticlerical themes and has been as influential as anticlericalism in politics. The dissolute priest, the scheming cardinal, and the woman whose sexuality has been skewed by repressive dogma have become staples of literature. Denis Diderot probably deserves credit for stimulating this genre, with works like *The Nun* (1796), an account of a woman's life broken by the shackles of convent life. A century later Emile Zola's trilogy, *Rome*, *Lourdes*, and *Paris* (1894–98), and some of the works of Anatole France, in particular *Penguin Island* (1908), became classics of anticlerical literature. Other novels with anticlerical tones could include *A Portrait of the Artist as a Young Man* (1916) by James Joyce; *A.M.D.G.* (1910) by the Spaniard Ramón Pérez de Ayala (see SPANISH LITERATURE, UNBELIEF IN); *The Brothers* (1938) by H. G. Wells; and, more recently, *The Troublesome Offspring of Cardinal Guzman* (1992) by Louis de Bernières. At a more popular level, Dan Brown's runaway bestseller *The Da Vinci Code* (2003) would also figure here. And there have been some important memoirs on Catholic upbringings, from the belligerent *Gathering Evidence* (1982) by Thomas Bernhard, through *Angela's Ashes* (1996) by Frank McCourt, to the gentler—though no less critical—autobiographical works of Karen Armstrong and Anthony Kenny. Films like *Dogma* (1999) and *The Magdalene Sisters* (2002), cartoon series like *Popetown*, and comic characters like Knuckles the Malevolent Nun by Cornelius Stone carry on the tradition in their respective media. These various styles of anticlerical criticism are probably more effective, and certainly better known, than the earlier nonfiction accounts.

BIBLIOGRAPHY

Arciniegas, Germán. *Latin America: A Cultural History*. New York: Knopf, 1967.

Blanshard, Paul. *American Freedom and Catholic Power*. Boston: Beacon, 1949.

Cooke, Bill. *A Rebel to His Last Breath: Joseph McCabe and Rationalism*. Amherst, NY: Prometheus Books, 2001.

McCabe, Joseph. *Crises in the History of the Papacy*. London: Watts, 1916.

———. *A History of the Popes*. London: Watts, 1939.

Sanchez, M. Jose. *Anticlericalism: A Brief History*. Notre Dame, IN: University of Notre Dame Press, 1972.

BILL COOKE

ARISTOTLE (384–322 BCE), Greek philosopher. In the system set out in his *Metaphysics*, Aristotle invokes the idea of something that provides motive force for movement and change in the universe, and again something that serves as that to which everything tends, which he defines as "pure thought thinking about itself"; and he identifies these two somethings as the same thing, which his translators render as "God." Some then invoke this as proof that Aristotle shares with conventional theists belief in a deity similar to the God of revealed Judeo-Christian religion.

Religious apologists are eager to interpret references to deity in the works of the "pagan" philosophers as supporting their own theologies. To take another and similar example, they read the Stoics (see STOICISM) as being committed to a god like their own because the Stoics invoked the idea of a principle of rational order in the universe which they variously called *logos*, reason, god, and other names.

But in all these cases, whether of Aristotle, the Stoics, or others, the attempted appropriation of the entities or agencies they postulated in their metaphysical systems are not the deities variously invoked by Jewish, Christian, and Muslim believers. These gods are personal deities who created the world and have a particular interest in the behavior of the human beings in it, commanding obedience to their laws and punishing or rewarding people accordingly as they conform or otherwise. This is very remote from the metaphysical conceptions of Aristotle or the Stoics.

For this reason it is a mistake at best, and intellectually dishonest at worst, to include Aristotle among those who "believed in God" in the sense in which this phrase is used by theists in the Judeo-Christian tradition. A sketch of his system shows clearly why this is so.

Aristotle's *Metaphysics* is the work in which he deals with the question of existence, or, as he puts it, with "being *qua* being." In it he asks what existence is and what its essential attributes are. The key objective in his inquiry is identifying the nature of the primary substance of the universe, this being that which exists in its own right independently of anything else. He defines it as the merging of matter and form. Matter is the basic stuff of things, without specific qualities of its own, but capable of being actualized when merged with form, whereupon it takes on the definite character of an individual thing. Before this it is the purely potential basis of change, growth, and decay.

The transition of potentiality (*dynamis*) to actuality (*entelecheia*) is a principal theme of Aristotle's *Metaphysics*. Potentiality is incomplete and therefore imperfect; actuality in its ideal fulfillment is complete and perfect. Potentiality is determinable (what can be determined or shaped); actuality is determining (what determines). The duality of matter and form is accordingly to be understood as follows: matter is the determinable, form the determining.

Aristotle explains the transition of potentiality to actuality by means of the four kinds of cause that act on things: the material cause, which is what something consists of (such as the wood that is the material out of which a table is made); the efficient cause, which is the work that brings about the actualization of a potential (such as the work done by the carpenter to fashion the wood into a table); the formal cause, which is what determines the nature of an individual thing as the thing it is (such as the plan or design followed by the carpenter in making the table); and the final cause, the aim, end, or purpose for which the thing exists (such as the purpose of eating off or writing on for which the table was brought into existence).

In summary characterization, the four causes can be described as matter, form, agent, and end—the agent being the efficient cause, the end being the final cause.

Of these four causes, the two most important for grasping the nature of any individual thing are the formal and final causes. A full account of anything would invoke all four causes, but these two give the explanation of *what* and *why* a thing is.

For Aristotle, motion and change are eternal in the universe. (This view stands in conscious opposition to the Parmenidean claim that the universe is a single eternal unchanging thing, and that change and motion, as perceived by our finite senses, are illusory). Motion and change are eternal; there cannot have been a first motion, because it would itself have required a preceding motion to set it off—and so on, in infinite regress. But although there cannot have been a first motion, there must be something that keeps the eternal motion of things going—an efficient cause of the sustaining (not the origin) of motion. But this thing cannot itself be moved, because it would require something to move it. So the mover must be unmoved. And this Aristotle therefore calls "the Unmoved Mover."

On some readings of the *Metaphysics* there is not one but many unmoved movers, one each for each of the movements in the spheres constituting the heavens.

This same thing Aristotle defines as the final cause of things too, for it is what everything tends toward in its highest and final realization, for it is "pure thought" thinking about the highest and most perfect thing there is, pure thought—and hence it is pure thought thinking about itself (*noesis noeseos*). As one might expect from a philosopher, Aristotle regarded thinking, and correlatively the contemplative life, as the best and highest activity, from which it naturally follows that the best thing contemplating the best thing must be "thought thinking about thought." Moreover, the only thing that could satisfy the description of being pure actualization, pure activity, without any residual potentiality in it, and therefore without any trace of *materia prima* (primary matter), must be pure thought thinking about itself.

It is hard to see the logic behind Aristotle's identification of the Unmoved Mover (or Movers) with "pure thought thinking about itself," but so he does; and he ventures no explanation of how pure thought can have the mechanical effect of imparting motion and inducing change in things whose causes are, by the definition of causality, material causes. But for those eager to pounce on apparent similitudes to their own conception of deity, the poetic-sounding "pure thought thinking about itself" moves them to say such things as, "According to this theory God never leaves the eternal repose in which His blessedness consists." Thus do the overlays of conventional religion distort the business of classical metaphysics.

Aristotle would doubtless have been astonished to find his Unmoved Mover(s) being identified with deities to whom prayer and sacrifice are directed, which demand obedience, which reward and punish, and which above all make it the greatest sin to question, doubt, think for oneself (this being the sin of pride), and seek knowledge (the tree of knowledge was forbidden in Eden's garden). Indeed, as regards thinking and seeking knowledge, Aristotle would be not just astonished but disgusted—and would surely point out that if his "god" is the highest ideal thing, that is, thought, doing the highest ideal thing, that is, thinking, it is an extraordinary contradiction to identify it with a God who says that thinking is sinful and demands unthinking obedience in its place.

The appropriation of Aristotle into Christian theology is chiefly the work of Saint Thomas Aquinas, the "Angelic Doctor." In his *Summa Theologica* he praises Aristotle's conception of "the Godhead," but observes that this is not a personal deity with a "loving care and interest in His creation" (this leaves aside the fact that the Mover is not for Aristotle a creator). And this means that Aristotle's god will not do as "God," because (as the *Catholic Encyclopedia* puts it) his god is not one "to Whom all rational beings are responsible for their every thought, word and act"; it is not "the God of Faith and Revelation, the God of the Nicene Creed, in substance One, in personality Three."

These remarks speak for themselves, since the Unmoved Mover of Aristotle is at least not the amalgam of credulity, superstition, and contradiction, which is what the last eighteen words of the preceding paragraph denote. It is instead a metaphysical entity postulated to fit and complete a metaphysical structure; and its intelligibility stands or falls with that structure.

A. C. GRAYLING

ARNOLD, MATTHEW (1822–1888), English poet and essayist. One of the most influential English poets and essayists of the nineteenth century, Matthew Arnold was born on Christmas Eve 1822, at Laleham, England. He was the son of Thomas Arnold, a prominent Church of England clergyman who made his reputation as headmaster of Rugby School. Matthew was educated at Rugby and Oxford. Much of his working life was spent as an inspector of schools, which gave him insights into the important changes Victorian Britain was undergoing.

Arnold's real vocation, however, was as a poet and critic. Though his period of poetic creativity was relatively short—he wrote little of significance after he was thirty-five years old—Arnold captured the Victorian crisis of faith as few others were able to do. By the time Arnold was appointed professor of poetry at Oxford in 1857, his career as poet was coming to an end, but his second career, as critic and essayist, was about to begin.

Arnold's genius was to understand and articulate the shifting tide of belief in Victorian England, in particular the decline of conventional piety. He understood, because he felt himself, the rootlessness and uncertainty of the new society that was emerging. If Arnold had little use for the dogmas then declining, he nonetheless felt their departure keenly. Arnold was without belief in a personal God or immortality and was actively uninterested in the details of dogma. He addressed this in his poem "Pis-Aller" (1867), in which a dogmatist asserts a range of things, ending, "Without that, all's dark for men / That, or nothing, I believe" and to which Arnold retorts, "For God's sake, believe it then!"

For many years Arnold was best known for his popular work *Culture and Anarchy* (1869), which argues for the value of a cultural knowledge as a bulwark against anarchy and loss of certainties. Arnold's critics have accused him of an elitist despair at the inability of the mass of the people to appreciate the glories of classicism. There is an element of truth to this charge, although Arnold deprecated philistinism from whatever class it originated.

More recently, his poem "Dover Beach" (written in 1851, published in 1867) has become Arnold's most emblematic work. "Dover Beach" is a lament on the decline of religion in Europe and features the phrase "sea of faith," which was taken up by the heretical English theologian Don Cupitt and used as the name of a religious humanist network in England, with important offshoots in Australia, Canada, and New Zealand (see RELIGIOUS HUMANISM).

Matthew Arnold died on April 15, 1888, while on his way to Liverpool to see his daughter, who was returning from New York.

BIBLIOGRAPHY

Arnold, Matthew. *Culture and Anarchy*. Cambridge: Cambridge University Press, 1960.
———. *Literature and Dogma*. London: Macmillan 1898.
———. *The Works of Matthew Arnold*. Ware, UK: Wordsworth, 1995.

BILL COOKE

ARTS, UNBELIEF AND THE. It is more important than usual in a topic such as this to first define our terms. *Unbelief* is the more problematic term because, by its very nature, it is defined in negative terms. There are two senses in which unbelief will be relevant here. On the one hand it is a loose, umbrella term to cover all world-views that are grounded in the natural world, as opposed to the many varieties of belief that are supernaturalist in orientation. And on the other hand unbelief suggests an opposition to all forms of orthodoxies, be they religious or secular. The principal feature both understandings of unbelief have in common, then, is their opposition to all attempts to straitjacket free inquiry. After this common-ality has been acknowledged, unbelievers have very little in common, because, having rejected strait-jackets—be they political, social, religious, or intellec-tual—they then proceed to believe a great many things. With respect to supernaturalism alone, an unbeliever may be an atheist, agnostic, deist, pantheist, or any other variety of heterodox belief (see ATHEISM; AGNOSTICISM; DEISM; PANTHEISM AND UNBELIEF; and CONTROVERSIES: ATHEISM, PANTHEISM, SPINOZA). The sole guiding motif of unbelief, then, is the imperative for freethinking. With that in mind, this entry will speak of FREETHOUGHT instead of unbelief.

Turning to art, we can begin with the conventional understanding as referring to all styles of visual art, per-forming art, and music. What is needed now are some formulas by which we can continue our investigation. For this we can turn to the Australian philosopher John Passmore, who distinguished three forms of art. There is entertainment art, which is designed to create a high level of excitement or an easy level of listenability, as a means of escape. Then there is what he called telic art, which induces us to care about some cause, religion, movement, or philosophy. And then there is serious art, which Passmore defines negatively and simply as art that is largely independent of the other strands.

Passmore acknowledges that there is no sharp distinc-tion between these three, and that any piece of art can involve more than one category at once. However, he goes on to say that serious art is absolutely serious, in the way that entertainment art is not absolutely entertain-ment or telic art absolutely telic. The term *serious art* is an unfortunate one, which can give the wrong impres-sion. Contrary to first impressions, serious art can excite, divert, and amuse, in the manner of entertainment art. And it can inspire, even preach, in the manner of telic art. The point is that serious art is not limited or bound by these qualities.

A clear illustration is Picasso's *Guernica*, which was created with a view to inducing the viewer to care about the German destruction of the Spanish town of that name during the Spanish Civil War and, more generally, to abhor the brutality of war. In this sense, *Guernica* is telic art. But long after the passions aroused by the Spanish Civil War have eased, *Guernica* is still a moving work of art. In Passmore's categories, *Guernica* was created as telic art and has since made the transition to serious art with telic overtones.

Passmore's distinctions are useful for our purposes. It is clear that all art commissioned in the service of a ruling orthodoxy, whether religious or secular, is going to have significant characteristics of telic art. In some cases, the genre is so stifling that it is next to impossible for serious art to emerge from it, socialist realism being a prime example. Relatively few works of telic art are able to make the transition *Guernica* has achieved.

Turning more specifically to the relations between reli-gion and art, we need at this stage to introduce another series of distinctions. Diane Apostolos-Cappadona has identified five basic types of relation between religion and art. These relations run along a spectrum from, at the negative end, the authoritarian relation, where religion dominates art, through the oppositionist relation, where both are in relations of equality but are seeking to domi-nate each other. In the middle is the mutual relation, where art and religion are in relations of equality and are working symbiotically. Then there is the separatist rela-tion, where religion and art operate without reference to each other. And finally, Apostolos-Cappadona cites what she calls the unified relation, where religion and art operate as one identity with no attempt to make distinc-tions. It is clear that Apostolos-Cappadona sees this uni-fied relation as the highest of the forms of interaction between religion and art.

This is a thoughtful framework, but it has conse-quences for which Apostolos-Cappadona made no allowance, principally the imbalance of evidence for each of these relations. Sadly, history is replete with evi-dence of the authoritarian relation at work, whereas the unified relation remains a pipe dream. Remaining with Apostolos-Cappadona's framework, we can say that the mutual relation may well be the ideal one, but the sepa-ratist relation is probably the best that can realistically be managed. And it follows from this that for either of these relations to flourish, the society needs to be thoroughly secular, if not operating on a formal separation of church and state (see SECULARISM). Telic art has thrived in soci-eties that are not open societies, in the sense by which Karl POPPER understood that term. Popper spoke of an open society as one where people are presented with choices as a normal part of their life experience. An open society has a transparent mechanism by which govern-ments can be replaced by the people. Such a society has institutions for which the individual can work by virtue of merit, or transact business by virtue of citizenship. Closed societies, by contrast, have no reliable mecha-nism by which leaders are replaced, and institutions are hedged in by limitations of class, creed, or culture. It is central to telic art that only one credible choice should be urged on the viewer, and it has traditionally been the role of the closed society to limit or even persecute all paths save the officially sanctioned one. In short, there has long been a symbiotic relation between telic art and the closed society, which is expressed most clearly in the authoritarian relation between art and religion.

We need now to examine closely the sources of this preference for the authoritarian relation between religion and art. For the time being, by *religion*, I will be referring only to the Western monotheistic faiths and to universalizing ideologies, be they secular or religious. Among many defenders of orthodoxy, there has long been a suspicion of serious art. For the defenders of orthodoxy, art not commissioned for the instruction of the people is art to fear and to control. It has long been noted that the more stern the upholders of supernaturalism are, the more likely are such thinkers to take a dim view of the arts. The classic example is PLATO, who saw artists and poets as a danger to the ideal republic he dreamed of. Plato has SOCRATES insisting that if poets cannot portray good character in their poems, they should refrain from writing. Socrates goes further: We "must issue similar orders to all artists and craftsmen, and prevent them portraying bad character, ill-discipline, meanness, or ugliness in pictures of living things, in sculpture, architecture, or any work or art, and if they are unable to comply they must be forbidden to practise their art among us." Plato's objection to art was that it seduced people to be satisfied with a thirdhand representation of reality. The artist's representation of an object is one step removed from the actual object, which itself is one step removed from the archetypal form of that object. And it is the archetypal form of the object that should be the object of our contemplation, not the mere physical representation of it, and certainly not the artistic representation of the physical representation.

In Plato's mind, art's only justifiable use is to produce propaganda, much like Stalinist socialist realism; it has to sing the praises of the state, decry the follies of foreigners, and tell us how happy and lucky we are. Unless the arts are managed in this way, Plato saw only trouble ahead because artists know nothing of the truth and can only indulge in superficiality.

Significant elements of Plato's distrust of the arts were taken up by the Christian religion, and, later again, by Islam. More precisely, these Platonist fears merged with a suspicion of art that was indigenous to the monotheistic religions. For the monotheistic religions, the suspicion of art had more of a moral tinge than the intellectual fear on which Plato concentrated. Plato was not distrustful of beauty so much as unconvinced that artists were capable of grasping the ethereal majesty of the abstract beauty as he understood it. For Christians and Muslims, beauty was the inevitable product of their creator God. This meant that ugliness, depravity, or any message suggestive of sedition or laxity of morals had to derive from some alternative source. These usually turned out to be some combination of the hubris of the unbeliever or the malice of Satan, or, more usually, a combination of these.

The prophet Amos gave voice to this suspicion when he declared: "I hate, I despise your feasts, and I will not smell the savor of your assemblies. . . . Take thou away from me the noise of thy songs; for I will not hear the melody of thy viols. But let judgment roll down as waters and righteousness as an ever-flowing stream." This deep suspicion of the arts and the levity it is thought to bring in its train has been echoed right down through the history of monotheist religions. From the iconoclasts to the Puritans to today's religious conservatives in the culture wars, all follow in the footsteps of Amos.

The situation is no less fraught with respect to the Christian religion, for the second commandment forbids making images for worship: "You shall make for yourself no idol in the likeness of anything in the heavens above or on the earth below or in the waters under the earth. You shall not bow down to them or serve them; for I, the Lord your God, am a God who brooks no rival. . . ." (Exod. 20:4–5). The prohibition against idols is broadly conceived and fiercely worded. The sin of hubris in making the idol is compounded by the sin of turning away from the true god.

Christian history has seen successive waves of Puritanism that took this commandment at face value. The iconoclasts during the Byzantine Empire of the eighth century CE took the movement to the extremes of systematic destruction of what they saw as idolatrous images standing in between the individual and God. And the very music that now inspires believers was once held in deep suspicion. In 1322 Pope John XXII denounced the use of counterpoint in church services, declaring such musical harmony fit only for profane uses. During the Reformation followers of Huldrych Zwingli's brand of Protestantism whitewashed church walls to ensure the faithful would have no idolatrous image to distract their attention from the word of God as given by the sermon. John Calvin shared a similar hostility to religious imagery. God, Calvin believed, could not be represented pictorially, so any attempt to do so would be bound to fail, and the moral and spiritual consequences of that failure were too fearful to contemplate. For Calvin, attempts to render God pictorially would inevitably result in idolatry, which ran up against the proscriptions in the book of Exodus. The effect of Calvin's censorship was to force art into producing openly telic work, or to sidestep the issue by focusing on landscapes and domestic environments, much of which was little more than entertainment art.

This deep hostility to images is shared by Muslims, who see Allah as incomparably unique and insist on an unbridgeable gulf between the creator and his creatures. Any attempt to intercede between humanity and Allah is bound to fail and bound to be tinged with wickedness. Following on from this, any attempt to portray Allah by human hands is bound to produce only the worst form of blasphemous idolatry: "Who is he that can intercede with Him but by His permission? He knows what is before them and what is behind them. And they encompass nothing of his knowledge except what He pleases." Very much in the manner of Amos, the Qur'an asks rhetorically: "Is one decked with ornaments and unable to make plain speech in disputes a partner with God?" And again: "Shall I inform you upon whom the devils descend? They descend upon every lying, sinful one— They give ear, and most of them are liars. And the poets—the deviators follow them." It is not that Islam is hostile to art as a whole, but like other monotheistic religions, Islam insists on the right to circumscribe art until it conforms to its view of the world. This means that while beautiful telic art can still be made in conformity with Islam, it is not as straightforward for serious art.

This is not to say that all religions hold to this suspicion of images and image makers; Roman Catholic and Orthodox Christianity—and significant strands within Hinduism and Buddhism—have been awash with artistic representations, though, as if to confirm the fears of the Protestants, the images have often been the focus of veneration in themselves. And in the case of Catholic and Orthodox Christianity, their greater ease with images has not meant they have avoided the authoritarian relation between religion and art.

When we turn our attention specifically to freethought and art, we can see that the situation is considerably more simple. If religious attitudes toward art range from ambivalence to downright hostility, freethinkers have taken unalloyed joy in the arts. It has been a staple of humanist thinking that, in the absence of a preordained cosmic purpose, people must determine meaning and value in their own lives (see ETHICS AND UNBELIEF; MORALITY FROM A HUMANIST POSITION; and LIFE STANCE). Appreciation of the arts has always been an important component in that process. To take one example, pretty much at random, the Chinese sage CONFUCIUS said that the arts were an integral part of understanding the Way, or the core reality of life: "I set my heart on the Way, base myself on virtue, lean upon benevolence for support and take my recreation in the arts." Elsewhere it was reported that Confucius was once so transfigured by the beauty of some music he heard that he failed to notice the taste of the meat he ate for three months.

Freethinkers appreciate art for precisely the reason Plato feared it. Plato saw artists as almost constitutionally dishonest for providing people with pleasing images that serve to lessen our zeal for the disembodied form of the Good. In rejecting that and other supernaturalist abstractions—what Daniel Dennett called skyhooks—freethinkers relish the opportunity to have the universe drawn for them anew by artists. In an interesting dialogue on art, Iris Murdoch has her Plato decry art's dishonesty while another character, Acastos, argues for art's role as a vehicle for profound meaning without imposing the duty on artists to do nothing but provide meaningful art. The duty of artists, Acastos says, is to be good artists. It is up to everyone else to determine the extent and nature of the message they glean from art. Murdoch has her Socrates conclude by saying we should be thankful for great artists who "draw away the veil of anxiety and selfishness and show us, even for a moment, another world, a real world, and tell us a little bit of truth."

Freethinkers recognize that truth needs to be sought out by curious humans, rather than discovered intact through passive worship or prayer. The length and strength of the hostility between monotheistic religions and open-ended artistic creativity brings to mind the no less long-standing conflict between science and religion (see RELIGION IN CONFLICT WITH SCIENCE). Monotheistic religion is by its very nature hostile to the NATURALISM of science, because it undermines the anthropocentric foundations of religious belief. Many philosophers have noted that art and science have more in common than art and religion. Art and science are both truth-seeking pursuits, and both flourish best in an open society. Art and science both want to understand the world on its own terms and not according to some prearranged formula. Telic science is even more unhelpful than telic art, as the examples of Lysenkoism in the Soviet Union or "intelligent design" in the United States (see INTELLIGENT DESIGN THEORY) amply demonstrate. And unlike telic art, telic science will never be able to climb out of its intellectual hole and make a serious contribution.

Art and science are both exercises in human creativity. We need now to consider the relation between unbelief and creativity. When thinking of some of the most creative periods of human history, periods that used to be called golden ages, several features can be found in common. Chief among these is an attitude of confidence about the values of one's own culture without this descending into paranoia about foreigners. Then there is economic prosperity that enables the wealthy to patronize the arts and humanities. We can find important commonalities here between fifth-century Athens, Florence during the Renaissance, the T'ang dynasty in China, England in the century after the Armada, and Holland in the seventeenth century.

In each of these ages, we find greater levels of intellectual freedom, artistic activity, and religious heterodoxy. These are what make a golden age. Looking briefly at two examples, the T'ang dynasty in China is generally recognized as the dynasty most open to foreign influences. T'ang military and diplomatic power stretched all the way to central Asia and Persia and south to Vietnam and beyond. Merchants, diplomats, and adventurers of all stripes lived in the T'ang capital of Ch'ang-an, practicing their religions freely and discussing their views with one another. It was also known for unsurpassed levels of artistic creativity. The T'ang golden age began to fade after—something unusual for China—a series of persecutions against foreign beliefs. The persecutions were successful, and the heresies were largely extirpated, but the intellectual ferment their existence had helped to facilitate ended with them. The art of the Sung dynasty that followed was more self-contained, drawing inspiration from within its own culture. But once the wellsprings of creativity from within had drained, the Ming and Ching dynasties which followed produced art no less skillfully executed, but which was derivative of earlier forms.

We can see a similar pattern with respect to the Italian Renaissance. Each of the milestones commonly cited as significant diminutions of the Renaissance spirit were made in the name of defending some version of orthodoxy. From the puritanical rantings of Savonarola—very suggestive of Amos—to the sacking of Rome in 1527, to the enforcement of the Counter-Reformation with the Council of Trent, each of these helped crush the spirit of optimism and inquiry. And with the effective strangulation of those motive forces, the artistic spirit was severely circumscribed.

Despite the evidence of history, it has long been a staple of popular Christian apologetics to assert the essential link between art and religion. In the West, the Renaissance artists are most frequently pointed to as evidence. But Renaissance art tells us more about power relationships—Apostolos-Cappadona's authoritarian relationship, to be specific—than it does about links of this sort. That an artist is responsible for a beautiful work on the Virgin and child is no evidence that he was motivated by Christian piety. In a culture where the church commissioned most of the important work, it is hardly surprising that most art of the time reflected its beliefs and taste. And if a gifted artist is to be credited with Christian religiosity for his sensitive rendering of a Christian theme, then he needs also to be praised for his authentic paganism for producing a brilliant work on a theme from Greek mythology.

Freethought is important not merely for providing the best cultural backdrop for artistic flowering; in some important cases it is integral to its survival. It has frequently been observed, for instance, that monotheistic religion is antithetical to the spirit of tragedy because the religious promise of redemption drains tragedy of its meaning. The implications for this are manifold, because tragedy has played a disproportionately important role, at least in European art. From the Greek playwrights through to Shakespeare, to say nothing of the visual art and music that tragic themes have inspired, tragedy has been an ongoing strand by which artists have explored the dilemma of being human. Friedrich NIETZSCHE viewed Attic tragedy as the apotheosis of the Apollonian and Dionysian forms of art. Art, Nietzsche wrote, "raises its head where the religions relax their hold." For Nietzsche, art takes over a whole range of moods and feelings that religions cannot understand or sympathize with, infusing them with new and more powerful meanings. Tragedy speaks of the fatal flaw in human nature: the tragic hero is greater than the rest of us, but his flaws are also larger than life, and lead inevitably to his ruin. The simplistic binary of good and evil is corrosive of the more nuanced understanding of human nature that tragedy grasps. And the illusion of eternal reward

directly undermines the tragic impulse. On this understanding, tragedy is the most profound manifestation of humanist aesthetics. The enlightened acceptance of what life deals us, and of our inevitably flawed and frequently counterproductive responses to life's challenges, constitutes the core of the human experience.

It is one thing to acknowledge that freethought is an important precondition for major forms of art such as tragedy. But what about the many artists who have been motivated by religious beliefs? The fact that many artists have been inspired by religious beliefs only strengthens the bonds between freethought and art. It is important to note what is not being asserted here. Clearly, it is not that artists need to be unbelievers in order to function. Rather, the argument is that the spirit of free inquiry is a precondition of artistic creativity and the surest guarantee that serious art, whether created by religious or nonreligious artists, will not lapse into telic or entertainment art. We have seen that artistic golden ages were frequently also periods of unusual acceptance of the right to free inquiry. And it should also be noted that many artists' religiosity is of a distinctly heterodox character. Ludwig van Beethoven, to take one prominent example, is thought by many to be the greatest composer of all time. His musical repertoire consists of nine symphonies, five piano concertos, thirty-two piano sonatas, and sixteen string quartets. Beethoven was not a churchgoer and was suspicious of any sort of orthodoxy, religious or secular. He composed very little religious music, in the narrower sense of the term. His most ostensibly religious piece was *Missa Solemnis*, which was first completed in 1824 and played in St. Petersburg soon after. The *Missa Solemnis* is, in fact, a hymn to DEISM, and evokes the ideal not of humanity managing to qualify for entrance into a distant heaven above, but of humanity living authentically and fully here on earth. Examples such as this could be multiplied. Among painters we could range from the mystical THEOSOPHY of Wassily Kandinsky to the Zen Buddhism of Ad Reinhardt; from the Jungianism of Jackson Pollock to the atheism of Francis Bacon, from the antirationalism of Donald Judd to the pseudo-Wittgensteinianism of the conceptual artists (see WITTGENSTEIN, LUDWIG); they all needed a minimal level of outside ideological constraint before they could produce serious art.

And finally, it is worth noting how many significant artists have been unbelievers in whichever brand of supernaturalism was dominant in their culture. Take the example of nineteenth- and twentieth-century novelists. People as different in other respects as Thomas HARDY and Philip Pullman, H. G. WELLS and Fay Weldon, Arnold Bennett and Iain Banks, Somerset Maugham and Iris Murdoch, Mark Twain (see CLEMENS, SAMUEL LANGHORNE) and V. S. Naipaul are all unbelievers in conventional religion. Examples among playwrights and musicians could also be given. The fact of the diversity of religious views among artists is a strong argument for seeing the separatist relation between art and religion in more positive terms than Apostolos-Cappadona assumed. Indeed, it can reasonably be claimed that the separatist relation between religion and art is the best guarantee of unfettered artistic creativity.

The conclusion that can be drawn from all this is that the bonds linking art and freethought are comprehensive and inevitably intertwined. Freethought is about life freed from the transcendental temptation. A life with no reference to the supposed promise of an afterlife needs to be made as meaningful and delightful as possible, and art clearly has a crucial role in achieving that. In the absence of truths being imparted to us on tablets of stone, art can help us search for truth in any number of different ways. And *truth* in this context should not be confused with a set of commands. Freethinking can have no truck with telic art, in Passmore's usage, or the authoritarian relation, to use Apostolos-Cappadona's. The relation between freethought and art is entirely symbiotic. Art needs the conditions of free inquiry in order to thrive, and freethought needs art to give meaning and color to life in the here and now. Here is Apostolos-Cappadona's mutual relation in action, no pipe dream after all.

There is no limit to the way people can find meaning, purpose, contentment, and peace of mind in their lives. There is no formal body of dogma that must be protected from art's searching gaze. There are no sensitive issues that need to be deemed no-go zones. Artistic creativity requires freedom; freedom requires an open society; and an open society requires at the very least the absence of the authoritarian relation between religion and art. This condition is best achieved in a society imbued with the humanist principles of toleration, secularism, and freethought.

BIBLIOGRAPHY

Apostolos-Cappadona, Diane. "Religion and Art." In *The Dictionary of Art*, edited by Jane Tuner. Vol. 26. London: Macmillan, 1996.

Columbine, W. B. "Will Rationalism Destroy Art?" *Agnostic Annual 1905*. London: Watts, 1905.

Confucius. *The Analects*. Translated by D. C. Lau. London: Penguin, 1987.

Herrick, Jim. "Art, Atheism and Reform." *International Humanist News* (February 2005).

Kurtz, Paul. "Do the Arts Convey Knowledge?" In *Skepticism and Humanism: The New Paradigm*. New Brunswick, NJ: Transaction, 2001.

Lipson, Leslie. *The Ethical Crises of Civilization*. Newbury Park, CA: Sage, 1993.

Macy, Christopher, ed. *The Arts in a Permissive Society*. London: Pemberton, 1970.

Murdoch, Iris. *Acastos: Two Platonic Dialogues*. London: Penguin, 1987.

———. *The Fire and the Sun: Why Plato Banished the Artists*. London: Chatto & Windus, 1977.

Nietzsche, Friedrich. *The Birth of Tragedy*. London: Penguin, 1993.

———. *Human, All Too Human*. Cambridge: Cambridge University Press, 1988.

Nott, Kathleen. "Humanism and the Arts," In *The Humanist Outlook*, edited by A. J. Ayer. London: Pemberton, 1968.

Passmore, John. *Serious Art*. London: Duckworth, 1991.

Plato. *The Republic*. Translated by Desmond Lee. London: Penguin, 1987.

Popper, Karl. *The Open Society and Its Enemies*. London: Routledge, 1963.

Steiner, George. *The Death of Tragedy*. New York: Hill & Wang, 1969.

Taubes, Timothy. *Art and Philosophy*. Amherst, NY: Prometheus Books, 1993.

BILL COOKE

ASIMOV, ISAAC (1920–1992), American author. One of the most prolific and versatile writers in recorded history, Isaac Asimov was the greatest popularizer of science of his generation.

Asimov was born in Petrovichi, Russia, two years before the formation of the USSR. When Isaac was three years old, his family immigrated to Brooklyn, New York, where his father operated a candy store. The oldest of three children, Isaac taught himself to read English before starting school.

Although Asimov's parents were Orthodox Jews, they did not impart their religious beliefs to him. His ATHEISM was not, therefore, an act of rebellion. Rather, unencumbered by a religious upbringing, Asimov's insatiable curiosity and love of reading steered him toward a rational, secular worldview. Reading Greek and Norse mythology convinced him that the Bible was Hebrew mythology.

Education and Family. Trained as a biochemist, Asimov earned a doctorate in chemistry at Columbia University in 1948, where he began writing science fiction. During World War II, he served in the army and worked as a chemist at the Naval Air Experimental Station in Philadelphia. He suffered from acrophobia, and his time in the service was the only time in his life that he ever flew. Asimov had a son and a daughter from his first marriage, which ended in divorce. In 1973 he married Dr. Janet Jeppson.

Writing. Asimov wrote or edited about five hundred books, including popular books on numerous branches of science, science fiction, history, literature, mysteries, religion, mathematics, and books for children. At the age of eighteen, he began submitting short stories to science fiction magazines, making his first sale in 1938 to *Amazing Stories*. "Nightfall," published in 1941, explored the conflict between science and myth on a planet with six suns that experiences darkness once every

2,049 years. The Science Fiction Writers of America voted it the best short story ever written in the genre. In 1949 Asimov joined the faculty at the Boston University Medical School, and in Boston he wrote his first novel, *Pebble in the Sky*. He began writing full time in 1958.

Asimov is best known for his science fiction, particularly his Foundation Trilogy, for which he won the Hugo Award in 1966 for Best All-Time Science Fiction Series, and for his robot novels. Asimov lived to write, and wrote to explain the world to everyone else. When asked what he would do if he learned he was shortly going to die, he responded that he would type faster.

Humanism. Through his writings, Asimov presented the excitement of science, promoted skepticism, and critiqued the paranormal, pseudoscience, and creationism. But perhaps his greatest contribution was in showing that there are many different areas of study that can lead toward a secular and humanistic philosophy. *Asimov's Guide to the Bible*, written from a strictly humanist viewpoint, was published in 1968. *In the Beginning*, published in 1981, compares the Genesis myth unfavorably with the scientific account of origins.

Asimov's humanism was further evidenced by the causes he supported and publicized, including human and civil rights. He warned against the dangers of overpopulation and fought against censorship. Asimov was a signatory of *Humanist Manifesto II*, published in 1973. He was named Humanist of the Year in 1984 by the AMERICAN HUMANIST ASSOCIATION (AHA), and served as AHA president from 1985 to 1992.

Asimov was never tempted toward religion, nor did he report experiencing a spiritual void. As a rationalist, he found a worldview without the supernatural totally satisfying. He wrote that he found atheism liberating, because it removed the fear of death and hell. He said he did not worry about death, because every idea he ever had was published. This, along with his children, was the only immortality he desired. He died in 1992, four months after the dissolution of the Soviet Union.

BIBLIOGRAPHY

Asimov, Isaac. *Asimov's Guide to the Bible*. 2 vols. New York: Doubleday, 1968–69.

———. *The Foundation Trilogy: Foundation; Foundation and Empire; Second Foundation*. New York: Doubleday, 1951–53.

———. *I, Asimov: A Memoir*. New York: Doubleday, 1994.

———. *In Joy Still Felt: The Autobiography of Isaac Asimov 1954–1978*. New York: Doubleday, 1980.

———. *In Memory Yet Green: The Autobiography of Isaac Asimov 1920–1954*. New York: Doubleday, 1979.

———. *In the Beginning*. New York: Crown, 1981.

———. *Nightfall and Other Stories*. New York: Doubleday, 1969.

———. *Pebble in the Sky*. New York: Doubleday, 1950.

KENNETH MARSALEK

ATENEOS. These nineteenth- and twentieth-century cultural associations of Spain and Latin America took their name from the Athenaeums founded by French Enlightenment thinkers of the eighteenth century (see ENLIGHTENMENT, THE, AND UNBELIEF). Their concept of the Atheneum was inspired by the advanced school founded by the Spanish-born Emperor Hadrian at Rome around 135 to encourage literary and scientific study, itself based on the pagan and arguably rationalist inspiration of the Ateneum, the temple at Athens, Greece, erected in honor of Pallas Athena, goddess of reason and the inventor of the arts, agriculture, and industry.

In Spain the Ateneos were successor institutions to the eighteenth-century Sociedades Económicas de Amigos del País (Economic societies of friends of the country). The Ateneos played an important role in familiarizing the cultured circles of society with the bourgeois and secularizing ideals of the French Revolution. Already these ideals had shaped the liberalizing Constitution of Cadiz of 1812. The Ateneo of Madrid was founded in 1820 to "calmly and amicably discuss matters about legislation, politics, economy, and, in general, about everything which may be considered of *public usefulness*." The restoration of absolute monarchy by Ferdinand VII prompted its closure between 1823 and 1835, when it resumed its activities in a new headquarters and under the presidency of the duke of Rivas.

This Ateneo, with its divisions devoted to the sciences, arts, and humanities, its lending library, and its theatre and exhibition halls was greatly admired, prompting the creation of local Ateneos across Spain (including Cádiz in 1858, Barcelona in 1860, Zaragoza in 1864, Sevilla in 1877, and Valencia in 1879). Ateneos were also established across Latin America, including the Ateneo de la Plata of Buenos Aires in 1858, Puerto Rico in 1876, Santiago de Cuba in 1879, Uruguay in 1881, Lima in 1886, and México in 1909. Generally opposed to the thinking and social policies of the Roman Catholic Church, the *Ateneos liberales* (liberal Atheneums) represented the ideals of HUMANISM, RATIONALISM, and the Enlightenment across the Spanish-speaking world.

During the nineteenth century, the Ateneos helped to transmit emerging ideas such as DARWINISM, utopian and scientific socialism, and women's equality. Linked with the Ateneo of Cádiz, for example, was the fortnightly magazine *El Pensil Gaditano* edited by María Josefa Zapata, which celebrated human progress and spotlighted the necessity of overcoming social inequalities. The magazine championed equality between the sexes, opposed the double exploitation of working women who are also homemakers, and attacked the bourgeois marriage institution as "a buying and selling between father and husband." *El Pensil Gaditano* was censored by the bishop of Cádiz, who ordered its closure in 1859.

Contributing to the progress of the arts, science, and literature, the Ateneos achieved enormous political, social, and cultural influence. Following the Revolution of 1868 the Ateneo of Madrid supported the development of a theory of liberal monarchy. During the First Republic the intellectual superiority of "the devil of the critic" over the "sweet traditional faith" was there proclaimed in 1878. It was the scene of significant debates about protectionism and customs duties reform, the anticholera vaccine discovered by Jaime Ferrán, and others. But if the nineteenth-century Ateneo was intellectually adventurous, it also tended to be elitist and socially exclusive. For example, it lent ideological support by the restoration to Antonio Cánovas del Castillo, who helped restore the Bourbon monarchy and was a dominant conservative force in Spanish politics during the later nineteenth century. This elitism drove the formation of the *Ateneos Obreros* (Working-class Atheneums). These associations dedicated themselves to teaching working people to read and write and to instill the habit of reading in the masses, in part to facilitate the development of trade unions.

The special significance of pedagogic movements such as the Institución Libre de la Enseñanza in Madrid; the Extensión Universitaria in Oviedo, the oldest in Spain; and the Escola Moderna in Barcelona (see FERRER, FRANCISCO; ANARCHISM AND UNBELIEF) at the beginning of the twentieth century encouraged the *Ateneos burgueses* (bourgeois Atheneums) to redouble their efforts in order to encourage scientific culture. At the same time the *Ateneos Obreros* agitated for free, high-quality public education. In 1914 Barcelona's city council opened a local schools network for teaching the working classes to read and write under the pressure from the anarchist-oriented *Ateneos libertarios* (libertarian Atheneums). These Ateneos proliferated with the advent of the Second Republic (1930–36) at the same time as the Ateneo of Madrid, under the presidency of Manuel Azaña, adopted a more radical position in its fight for public education and against the privileges of the Catholic Church.

During Franco's dictatorship the Ateneos declined or disappeared, but with the advent of the democracy in 1976 they flourished again. In 1994, in collaboration with the INTERNATIONAL HUMANIST AND ETHICAL UNION, a conference called "Humanism and Ethics" was organized at Madrid. Today there are some fifty functioning Ateneos across the Hispanic world, fifteen of them in Spain. Its current president, Carlos París, advocates radical humanism.

BIBLIOGRAPHY

Alba, Fraterno. *La labor cultural de los ateneos.* Barcelona: Gráficas Alfa, 1930.

Azaña, Manuel. *Tres generaciones del Ateneo.* Madrid: Imp. Sáez Hnos., 1930.

Bajatierra, Mauro. *Los ateneos libertarios: su orientación.* Madrid: Bib. Plus Ultra, 1931.

De Labra, Rafel M. *El Ateneo de Madrid. Sus orígenes, desenvolvimiento, representación y porvenir.* Madrid, 1878.

Garrorena Morales, Angel. *El Ateneo de Madrid y la teoría de la monarquía liberal (1836–1847).* Madrid: Instituto de Estudios Pol"ticos, 1974.

Guereña, Jean-Louis, and Alejandro Tiana, eds. *Clases populares, cultura, educación. Siglos XIX–XX.* Madrid, 1989.

Miranda, Ledesma. *El Ateneo en su antiguo marco: ambiente, ideas y figuras.* Madrid: Ateneo, 1961.

Tuñon de Lara, Manuel. *Medio siglo de cultura española (1885–1936).* 3rd ed. Madrid: Taurus, 1984.

Villacorta Baños, Francisco. *El Ateneo científico, literario y artístico de Madrid (1885–1912).* Madrid: CSIC, 1985.

ALBERTO HIDALGO TUÑÓN

ATHEISM.

INTRODUCTION

In its broadest sense *atheism*, from the Greek *a* ("without") and *theos* ("deity"), standardly refers to the denial of the existence of any god or gods. In contrast to this strong or positive sense of atheism there is a weak or negative sense that is also compatible with its Greek roots. To be "without" god is not necessarily to deny the existence of any deity; it can simply mean not having a belief in any. Although atheism is often contrasted with AGNOSTICISM—the view that one cannot know whether or not any deity exists and hence one should suspend belief—agnosticism entails this latter type of negative atheism (see AGNOSTICISM AND ATHEISM).

Historically, *atheism* has sometimes been used as a term of abuse to refer to religious positions that the speaker opposes. Thus, the first Christians were called atheists because they denied the existence of the Roman deities. However, in Western society the term atheism has most frequently been used to refer to the denial of theism, in particular Judeo-Christian theism. This is the position that a being that is all-powerful, all-knowing, and all-good exists who is the creator of the universe and who takes an active interest in human concerns, and guides his creatures by revelation. Theism, however, is not a characteristic of all religions. While the theistic tradition is fully developed in Hinduism in the Bhagavad-Gita, the earlier Upanishads teach that ultimate reality, Brahman, is impersonal. Theravada Buddhism and Jainism also reject a theistic creator god, but they accept numerous lesser gods. At most they are atheistic in the narrow sense of rejecting theism.

Positive atheists reject the theistic God and with it belief in an afterlife, in a cosmic destiny, in a supernatural origin of the universe, in an immortal soul, in the revealed nature of the Bible and Qur'an, and in a religious foundation of morality. Positive atheism in its broadest sense also rejects both the theistic and the pantheistic aspects of Hinduism as well as the lesser gods of Theravada Buddhism and Jainism.

In the Western world, nonbelief in the existence of God is a widespread phenomenon with a long and distinguished history. Philosophers of the ancient world such as LUCRETIUS were nonbelievers, and leading thinkers of the Enlightenment such as Baron D'HOLBACH and DIDEROT were professed atheists. Even in the Middle Ages there were skeptical and naturalistic currents of thought. Expressions of nonbelief are found, moreover, in the literature of the Western world: in the writings of Percy Bysshe SHELLEY, Lord BYRON, and Thomas HARDY; VOLTAIRE and Jean-Paul SARTRE; Ivan Turgenev, Mark Twain (Samuel CLEMENS), and Upton SINCLAIR. In the nineteenth century the most articulate and best-known atheists and critics of religion were Ludwig FEUERBACH, Karl MARX, Arthur SCHOPENHAUER, and Friedrich NIETZSCHE. Bertrand RUSSELL, Sigmund FREUD, and Sartre were among the twentieth century's most influential atheists. At the end of the twentieth century, nonbelievers were found from the Netherlands to New Zealand, from Canada to China, from Spain to South America. It was estimated in the 2002 *New York Times Almanac* that there were about 222 million professed atheists in the world, comprising approximately 4 percent of the world's population. Add to that figure people who are agnostic, who profess no religion, and who are indifferent to religion, and the total is 887 million people, or approximately 15 percent of the world's population.

There are several prevalent misunderstandings of atheism, among them that atheists are immoral; that morality cannot be justified without belief in God; and that life has no purpose without belief in God. However, there is no evidence to suppose that atheists are any less moral than believers; many moral systems have been developed that do not presuppose the existence of supernatural beings; and the purpose of life can be based on secular goals such as the betterment of humankind. Indeed, atheism has wide-ranging implications for the human condition, for most versions of atheism entail that ethical goals must be determined by secular aims and concerns, that human beings must take charge of their own destiny, and that death is the end of human existence.

Atheism has sometimes been associated with MATERIALISM, communism, and RATIONALISM. However, there is no necessary relation between it and these other positions. Some atheists have been opposed to communism and some have rejected materialism. Although all contemporary materialists are atheists, EPICURUS, an ancient materialist, believed that the gods were made of atoms. Rationalists such as René DESCARTES have believed in God, while atheistic existentialists such as Sartre are not considered to be rationalists. Atheism has also sometimes been associated with systems of thought that reject authority, such as anarchism and existentialism, but again there is no necessary connection to these other positions. The analytic philosopher A. J. AYER was an atheist who opposed existentialism, while Søren KIERKEGAARD was an existentialist who accepted God. In turn, Marx was an atheist who rejected anarchism but Lev TOLSTOY, a Christian, embraced it.

In contemporary philosophical thought, atheism has been defended by, among others, Paul Edwards, Antony Flew, Paul Kurtz, John MACKIE, Michael Martin, Kai Nielsen, Michael Scriven, and J. J. C. Smart. Leading organizations of unbelief in the United States include American Atheists, the International Academy of Humanism, the AMERICAN HUMANIST ASSOCIATION, the AMERICAN RATIONALIST FEDERATION, Atheists United, the Council for Secular Humanism, the Freedom From Religion Foundation, the Committee for the Scientific Study of Religion, and the Internet Infidels.

JUSTIFICATION OF NEGATIVE ATHEISM

Philosophically, atheism is justified in two different ways. Negative atheists attempt to establish their position by showing that the standard arguments for the existence of God are unsound. Positive atheists attempt to show that there are good grounds for disbelieving in God. Let us consider first the most important arguments for the existence of God (see EXISTENCE OF GOD, ARGUMENTS FOR AND AGAINST).

The Cosmological (First Cause) Argument. Three versions of the Cosmological Argument can be distinguished. Aquinas in his Third Way argued that since there are contingent beings there must be a necessary being, namely, God, that is distinct from the universe itself. However, this argument seems to commit the fallacy of composition—of assuming that the whole of the universe cannot be necessary since it is made of contingent parts—and, once explicated, contains several other dubious premises. Aquinas's argument also assumes without warrant that a necessary being must have all of the attributes of God.

The Kalam Cosmological Argument, associated in contemporary thought with William Lane Craig, assumes that the universe has a beginning in time and that God caused this beginning. To be sure, Big Bang cosmology teaches that there is a temporal beginning to the universe. However, this provides no support for theism. First of all, the universe could have arisen spontaneously; that is, "out of nothing." Several well-known cosmologists have embraced this view, and it is not to be dismissed as impossible. Second, the cause of the universe need not be God. It could be a malevolent being or an impersonal force. Third, it is unclear how God could have caused the Big Bang since time was supposed to have been created in the Big Bang. God could not have caused the universe in any sense we understand since a cause is temporally prior to its effect. In particular, intentions and desires are temporally prior to their effects. How then could God's intentions cause the Big Bang?

A third version of the Cosmological Argument is based on Leibniz's principle of sufficient reason, namely, that there must be a sufficient reason for everything, and since there cannot be an infinite regress of reasons, there must be a being that is the reason for its own existence and for everything else. However, there is no good reason to accept the principle of sufficient reason, and no good reason to suppose that even if there is a being that is the reason for its own existence, it would have to be God.

The Teleological (Design) Argument (see INTELLI-GENT DESIGN THEORY). This argument also fails, since it at most proves the existence of a designer or designers and this is compatible with deism, polytheism, or a finite god. Let us consider first the version of William Paley, an eighteenth-century churchman. Paley's argument is an inductive argument from analogy. He maintained that since the universe is analogous to a machine and machines are created by intelligence, the universe is probably created by an intelligence. However, David HUME showed that if we take the analogy seriously, we are justified in drawing conclusions that are incompatible with traditional theism. For example, since in our experience a machine is created by many imperfect beings with bodies from preexisting material, we should infer that the universe was probably created by many imperfect beings with bodies from preexisting material. Hume's main point was that advocates of the teleological argument do not take seriously the *empirical* nature of the argument. We are justified only in inductively inferring from what is found in experience, and in terms of our experience we would have to infer that the creator is less than perfect. Hume did not say that experiences allow us to infer that the creator of the universe is totally evil, only that the creator is *less* than perfect. This inference is justified from our experience and is in conflict with Christian theism.

The fine-tuning version of the Teleological Argument, used by contemporary philosophers such as Richard Swinburne and Craig, maintains that there is an extremely large number of possible values for the physical constants in the universe, yet only a very narrow range of those possible values are compatible with human life; consequently, it is extremely improbable that human life occurred by chance. However, this fine-tuning argument is valid only if one makes the unjustified assumption that all possible values are equally probable. None of our current probability theories—classical, frequency, or propensity—can be applied to the beginning of the universe nonproblematically. Moreover, if human life in the universe is caused by design, why is it so rare and why did it arrive so late? As far as we know, human life exists now on only one insignificant planet and did not exist at all for about ten billion years.

The Ontological Argument. This argument, used by Saint Anselm and Descartes, represents an attempt to show that God—a perfect being, or a necessary being, or a being such that no greater being can be conceived—exists by definition. It has taken many different forms but all have proved to be unsound after examination. Moreover, even if the argument were sound, it would fall short of proving the existence of the theistic god, for the god of this argument need not be a person or reveal himself through miracles and scripture.

The Argument from Miracles (see MIRACLES, UNBE-LIEF IN; MIRACULOUS PHENOMENA). Many Catholic theologians attempt to argue from allegedly miraculous events such as the "cures" at Lourdes to the existence of God. However, this argument also fails to prove theism; at most it demonstrates a supernatural miracle worker or workers. Moreover, it assumes that there is evidence of miracles in the form of events that can never be explained by scientific theories. But we do not know of any such events. Alleged miracles such as Jesus's resurrection and the "cures" at Lourdes need strong evidence to be believed and this is lacking.

The Argument from Religious Experience. This argument, used by Richard Swinburne, provides no reason for belief in the theistic God, since there is no good reason to suppose that any religious experiences are veridical. Indeed, we know that some of them are not, since they conflict with those reported by others. In particular, there is no reason to suppose that religious experiences of a theistic God are veridical and that conflicting nontheistic religious experiences are not.

The Argument for Morality. The basic idea of the argument used by the English philosopher Hastings Rashdall is that because there is an absolute standard of morality, we must assume, or at least act as if, there is a being that provides this standard, namely, God. There are three main problems with this argument. First, it is simply assumed that there is an absolute standard and that if there were no standard, moral anarchy would reign. But a nonabsolute ethical standard need not entail moral anarchy: human beings can have good prudential reasons to create moral systems with prohibitions against murder, stealing, and so on. Second, absolute moral standards are compatible with atheism. Finally, it is doubtful that theism can provide any absolute moral standards in actual practice. Different theistic religions, for example, Christianity and Islam, are committed to conflicting absolute standards and there seems to be no objective way to reconcile them. Moreover, even within the same religious tradition, there are different interpretations of what one should do. For example, with respect to the death penalty, Christian thought ranges from advocating complete abolition to advocating the death penalty for homosexuality and for working on the Sabbath.

Pascal's Pragmatic Argument (see PASCAL'S WAGER). Pascal maintained that it was a good bet to believe in God: If one believes and God exists, one will obtain heaven; but if one fails to believe and God exists, one goes to hell; but if God does not exist, one has gained little if one fails to believe and has lost little if one believes; hence, it is in one's interest to believe in God. This argument fails since it gives us no reason to believe in the theistic God rather than in other kinds. Moreover, it does not acknowledge that God may take a dim view of one's betting on his existence. In any case, pragmatic arguments at most show that it is useful to believe in God—not that the belief is true or probable.

Plantinga's Argument from Basic Belief. Alvin PLANTINGA has argued that the theistic belief in God is a properly "basic" belief. Like simple perceptual beliefs and simple mathematical beliefs, it is rationally held, yet not inferentially based on more basic beliefs. However, this analysis not only allows conflicting religious beliefs to be properly basic, but also provides no clear non-question-begging criteria for excluding astrological and magical beliefs as properly basic.

THE JUSTIFICATION OF POSITIVE ATHEISM

Although the above arguments do not exhaust all of the arguments for the existence of God, they do cover the most important ones. Thus, their failure does provide some grounds for negative atheism. However, are there any reasons to disbelieve in God? Let us consider some reasons.

The Argument from Incoherence (AFI). One good reason not to believe that God exists is that the concept of God is incoherent; that is, the concept of God is like that of a round square or the largest number. The AFI can be made in two ways: First, it can be shown that some of the properties attributed to God in the Bible are inconsistent. For example, God is said to be invisible (Col. 1:15, 1 Tim. 1:17, 6:16), a being that has never been seen (John 1:18, 1 John 4:12). Yet several people in the Bible report seeing God, among them Moses (Exod. 33:11, 23), Abraham, Isaac, and Jacob (Gen. 12:7, 26:2, Exod. 6:3). God is supposed to have said, "You cannot see my face, for no one can see me and live" (Gen. 32:30). However, Jacob saw God and lived (Gen. 32:30). In some places God is described as merciful and in other places as lacking mercy; in some places as a being who repents and changes his mind, in other places as a being who never repents and changes his mind; and in some places as a being who deceives and causes evil, and in other places as a being who never does; in some places as one who punishes children for their parents' wrongdoing and in other places as one who never does.

Second, AFI can also be made by showing that the attributes of omniscience, omnipotence, and divine freedom specified in philosophical accounts of God are either in conflict with one another or internally inconsistent. Consider some arguments connected with omniscience.

a. In one important sense, to say that God is omniscient is to say that God is all-knowing and to say that God is all-knowing entails that he has all the knowledge that there is. Now philosophers have usually distinguished three different kinds of knowledge: propositional, procedural, and knowledge by acquaintance. Briefly, propositional or factual knowledge is knowledge that something is the case and is analyzable as true belief of a certain kind. In contrast, procedural knowledge or knowledge *how* is a type of skill, and is not reducible to propositional knowledge. Finally, knowledge by acquaintance is direct acquaintance with some object, person, or phenomenon. For example, to say "I know Mr. Jones" implies that one has not only detailed propositional knowledge about Mr. Jones but direct acquaintance with Mr. Jones. Similarly, to say "I know poverty" implies that, besides detailed propositional knowledge of poverty, one has some direct experience of it.

b. To say that God is all-knowing, then, is to say that God has all knowledge where this includes propositional knowledge, procedural knowledge, and knowledge by acquaintance. However, the implications of this account for the existence of God have usually not been noticed. God's omniscience conflicts with his disembodiedness. If God were omniscient, then on this definition God would have all knowledge, including that of how to swim. Yet only a being with a body can have such knowledge in the procedural sense, that is, actually have the skill, and by definition God does not have a body. Therefore, God's attribute of being disembodied and his attribute of being omniscient are in conflict. Thus, if God is both omniscient and disembodied, God does not exist. Since God is both omniscient and disembodied, he does not exist.

c. The property of being all-knowing not only conflicts with the property of being disembodied, but also with certain moral attributes usually attributed to God. If God is omniscient, he has knowledge by acquaintance of all aspects of lust and envy. But one aspect of lust and envy is the feelings of lust and envy. However, part of the concept of God is that he is morally perfect and being morally perfect excludes these feelings. Consequently, there is a contradiction in the concept of God. God, because he is omniscient, must experience the feeling of lust and envy. But God, because he is morally perfect, is excluded from doing so. Consequently, God does not exist.

d. In addition, God's omniscience conflicts with God's omnipotence. Since God is omnipotent, he cannot experience fear, frustration, and despair. For in order to have these experiences, one must believe that one is limited in power. But since God is all-knowing and all-powerful, he knows that he is not limited in power. Consequently, he cannot have complete knowledge by acquaintance of all aspects of fear, frustration, and despair. On the other hand, since God is omniscient, he must have this knowledge.

Various objections to these three arguments can, of course, be imagined. Although these objections can be met, it is useful here to mention the most commonly voiced criticism. The coherence of God is often defended on the grounds that God's knowledge should not include knowledge by acquaintance and all knowledge how but should be limited to factual knowledge. The trouble with this defense, however, is that it makes it logically impossible for God to have knowledge that humans have. This is paradoxical to say the least. One normally supposes that the following is true:

(1) If person P is omniscient, then P has knowledge that any nonomniscient being has.

Furthermore, one normally supposes that the following is true:

(2) If God exists, God has all knowledge that humans have.

But both (1) and (2) are false given the restriction of God's knowledge to factual knowledge. Furthermore, even if we restrict God's knowledge to propositional knowledge, the concept of God is still incoherent. Consider one argument that can be adduced to show that it is logically impossible for God to be omniscient in this sense.

If P were omniscient, then P would have knowledge of all facts about the world.

Let us call this totality of facts Y. So if P is omniscient, then P knows Y. One of the facts included in Y is that P is omniscient. But in order to know that P is omniscient, P would have to know something besides Y. P would have to know:

(Z) There are no facts unknown to P.

But how can Z be known? It can be argued that Z cannot be known since Z is an unrestricted negative existential statement. It can be admitted that it is possible to know the truth about those negative existential statements that are restricted temporally and spatially. But Z is a negative existential that is completely uncircumscribed. Knowing Z would be like knowing it is true that no centaurs exist anywhere at any time.

But why could not God with his infinite power search all of space and time and conclude that there are no centaurs? Similarly, why could not God search all space and time and conclude there is no more factual knowledge that he can acquire? This could be answered by saying

that God could not exhaustively search space and time because they are both infinite. No matter how much God searched, there would be more space and time to search. Consequently, it is possible that there are facts he does not know. Thus, for God to know that he knows all the facts located in space and time is impossible, and since omniscience entails such knowledge, omniscience is impossible.

Now it may be objected that God will know Z because he is the sole creator of the totality of facts (other than himself). But this reply begs the question. How could God know that he is the sole creator of the totality of facts unless he also knows Z? But since Z cannot be known, God cannot know he is the sole creator of the totality of facts.

This reconstruction turns on the factual assumptions that space and time are infinite, but some scientists have claimed that space is finite but unbounded. The infinite nature of time is also controversial. At most, then, the argument proves that *if* space and time are infinite, *then* God is not omniscient. But since God is omniscient by definition, he cannot exist if space and time are infinite.

However, there is a realm that is uncontroversially infinite. If God were omniscient, he would know all mathematical facts and know that there are no mathematical facts that he did not know. In order to know all mathematical facts however, it would be necessary to investigate all mathematical entities and the relations between and among them. But the number of mathematical entities and relations is infinite. So even God could not complete such an investigation.

We can conclude, then, that given the existence of an infinite number of mathematical entities, God is not omniscient; hence, if omniscience is an attribute of God, he does not exist. Since omniscience is an attribute of God, he does not exist.

The Argument from Evil (AE) (see EVIL, PROBLEM OF). Another good reason to disbelieve in God is the existence of a large amount of evil in the world. How can a perfectly good and all-powerful being allow this evil? The simplest and most probable explanation of this evil is that God does not exist. With respect to moral evil—the evil brought about by human beings—the free-will defense (FWD) is used to overcome the difficulty. This is the familiar strategy of arguing that moral evil is not to be blamed on God, but is the result of humans' misuse of their free will. This defense is severely flawed.

a. The FWD presupposes contracausal freedom (CCF), the position that human decisions are not caused by any events in our brains or nervous systems. However, there is no scientific reason to suppose that CCF is true.

b. God could have created human beings with a tendency to do good. This would be compatible with CCF, and would have produced less evil.

c. God could have produced human beings with CCF

who would be less vulnerable to physical attack; for example, human beings with bulletproof skin.

d. God could have made natural laws in such a way that would have made it harder for human beings to inflict harm on one another; for example, laws that prevented the making of explosives. This also would have been compatible with CCF and would have prevented much evil.

e. There is a distinction between the decision D to do an act A, and the outcome O of A. God could have allowed people to exercise their CCF in D and yet have ameliorated the harmful outcome O by divine intervention.

f. The FWD assumes that the exercise of free will is worth the price of millions of deaths and untold suffering. This is a doubtful assumption.

g. Although God is not directly responsible for evil on the FWD defense, he is indirectly responsible. Presumably he has foreknowledge and knows that his creatures will misuse their CCF. In this case, God is reckless. Moreover, if he does not have foreknowledge, he knows at least that this misuse is possible and takes no safeguards to prevent it. In this case, God is negligent.

A variety of strategies have been proposed for solving the problem of natural evil—that is, evil not brought about by human action, for example, earthquakes, tidal waves, or severe mental retardation. For example, it might be suggested that natural evil is necessary for moral perfection, that demons cause natural evil, that natural evil is warning that greater evil will follow, and that evils such as the suffering of animals are necessary in the present state of the world. I am afraid that none of these suggestions will do.

a. Natural evil may be necessary in the present state of the world, but an all-powerful God need not be limited to this world, and is capable of actualizing a possible world with different laws, including a world where animals would not suffer.

b. The suggestion that demons cause natural evil simply assimilates the problem of natural evil to the problem of moral evil: it makes natural evil the result of the free will of demons. In this case, all of the problems of the FWD apply.

c. The suggestion that evil is a warning has at least two problems. First, it is difficult to see how evils such as genetic birth defects are a warning to the innocent children who have them, or even to the parents of the children who may have led morally upright lives. Second, an all-powerful God could warn people in ways that are not so destructive and that are less ambiguous. For example, he could speak to directly to them, or send heavenly messengers.

d. The idea that evil is necessary for moral perfection also has great problems. First, a flood or tidal wave that kills thousands of children is hardly building the character of these children. With respect to other people who survive, for example, the parents of the children, instead of strenthening their character, the trauma may just as well crush them beyond recovery. Second, an all-powerful God could have provided opportunities for moral development without causing so much pain and suffering, including the killing of the innocent.

The Argument from Nonbelief (ANB). Still another reason for disbelieving in God is the large number of disbelievers in the world. ANB is especially telling against evangelical Christianity, although it has some force against other religions, for example, Orthodox Judaism.

Evangelical Christianity is the view that (1) God is a merciful and all-loving God, compassionate and caring toward humanity, (2) the Bible and only the Bible is *the* source of God's word, (3) God wants all humans to be saved, and (4) a necessary condition for being saved is becoming aware of the word of God and accepting it. Supposing evangelical Christianity is true, it is difficult to understand why there are nearly one billion nonbelievers in world. How can a merciful God, a God who wants all humans to be saved, not provide clear and unambiguous information about his word to humans when having this information is necessary for salvation? Yet, as we know, countless millions of people down through history have not been exposed to the teaching of the Bible and those who have been exposed are often exposed in a superficial and cursory way, a way that is not conducive to acceptance. Even today there are millions of people who, through no fault of their own, either remain completely ignorant of the Christian message or, because of a serious lack in their education, reject it. One would expect that if God were rational, he would have arranged things in such a way that there would be more believers.

Here are a few obvious ideas about how this could have been done:

a. God could have made the Bible more plausible. He could have made it free from contradictions and factual errors. It could contain clear and unambiguous correct prophecies and no false and ambiguous ones.

b. God could have provided people with exposure to the Bible's message by having Bibles appear in every household in the world written in a language that the occupants could read.

c. God could have spoken from the heavens in all known languages so that no human could doubt his existence and his message.

d. God could have sent angels disguised as human preachers to spread his word and given them the power to perform unambiguous miracles and works of wonder.

e. God could have implanted belief of God and his message in every person's mind.

f. In recent times, God could have communicated with millions of people by interrupting prime-time TV programs and broadcasting his message.

These ideas and countless others would have increased the number of believers and presumably the number of saved people. Yet God has used none of them.

There are a number of defenses against ANB that I should briefly mention.

The Free Will Defense. Theists might argue that God wants his creatures to believe in God without any coercion. The above suggestions, it might be said, involve making people believe in God and this would interfere with their free will.

However, none of the above suggestions about how God could have increased people's belief in God interfere with their free will. For example, providing people with clear and unambiguous evidence of his existence hardly interferes with their free will, since they can reject this evidence. In fact, in the Bible God is said to have performed spectacular miracles that influenced people to believe in him. For example, in Exodus 7:5 God performed a miracle to demonstrate to the Israelites that he was the true God. Even if God implanted belief in God into people's minds, they could reject the implanted idea. Moreover, it makes no sense to suppose that a rational God would create human beings in his own image and yet expect them to believe in him without strong evidence; that is, to be irrational.

The Testing Defense. One defense that is used by evangelical Christians is that evidence for God is clear and unambiguous but humans have rejected it because of a spiritual defect such as false pride. Those who accept the evidence pass the test and those who don't fail the test.

However, there is no reason to suppose that evidence for God is convincing but that people reject it because of a spiritual defect. There is another, more plausible hypothesis: the evidence of God is utterly unconvincing. In addition, even if it were convincing, billions of people, because of their backgrounds or circumstances, have not been exposed to it. Moreover, if the Bible is convincing in principle and humans have been exposed to it, they may not see this because of faulty reasoning. It is grossly unfair to punish people for not believing in God either because they have not been exposed to his teachings or because of an error of reasoning.

The Unknown Purpose Defense. Theists might argue that God has some unknown reason for permitting so many nonbelievers. In reply to this defense one could argue that theists have the burden of proof of showing that there is an unknown purpose. First, God commanded all people to love him and to believe in his son. Second, the Bible says that the commandment to love God is the greatest of all commandments—not to be overridden by another. Third, Jesus said he came to the world to testify to the truth—the gospel message. Again

his mission is presumably not to be overridden by other purposes. These reasons indicate that there is strong scriptural support for there being no unknown reason for the existence of so many nonbelievers.

In addition, God has further properties that make his having an unknown purpose for permitting so much nonbelief implausible. For example, according to evangelical Christianity, God wants humans who love him. Since loving him presupposes being aware of his message, how can he want this and yet fail to make billions of humans aware of the gospel message? The appeal to unknown purposes at worst makes God appear irrational and at best creates a mystery that detracts from the explanatory power of theism.

In addition to providing general arguments against the existence of God, atheists have also been critical of the historical evidence used to support the major theistic religions. For example, they have argued that a lack of good evidence casts doubt on doctrines of Christianity such as the Resurrection and the Virgin Birth. On the one hand, it is said that since these events are miracles, claims of their occurrence should be rejected unless there is extremely strong evidence to support them. On the other hand, it is held that the available evidence in their favor from biblical, pagan, and Jewish sources is weak.

ATHEISM VERSUS AGNOSTICISM

From the point of view of the world at large, atheism's greatest rival is theism, but from the point of view of the world of nonbelievers, its greatest rival is agnosticism (see AGNOSTICISM; AGNOSTICISM AND ATHEISM). What can atheism say in its defense? First of all, the case for positive atheism presented above is indirectly a case against agnosticism. If one can show that there are good reasons to disbelieve in God, then agnosticism is indirectly refuted. However, agnostics have arguments for rejecting atheism that must be addressed.

Thomas Henry HUXLEY said that one should not pretend to conclusions one cannot demonstrate. Although Huxley did not actually do this, he might have gone on to say that atheists pretend to the conclusion that God does not exist, but cannot demonstrate it. There are some problems, however, with this sort of argument. To begin with, it begs the question by supposing that there are no atheistic arguments that demonstrate God's nonexistence. Furthermore, if by *demonstrate* one means a deductive proof or disproof of the kind found in mathematics, then science is at fault, for scientists accept conclusions they cannot demonstrate. Inductive reasoning does not yield demonstrative conclusions, and yet it is intellectually respectable.

A variation of this theme is that atheism is not justified since one cannot be certain that God does not exist. But stated more formally, the Argument from Certainty is: Since only certainty can justify disbelief in God, atheism is not justified and agnosticism is justified. However, although some atheists claim to be certain that God does not exist, this is not essential to their position. For positive atheism to be rationally justified it is necessary only that either it be more probable than not or at least more probable than theism. Certainty is no more required in the case of atheism than it is in the case of scientific theories.

Another common argument agnostics adduce is that in claiming to have knowledge that God does not exist, atheists have transcended the limits of reason; hence, their conclusion is not acceptable. Moreover, the claim assumes what must be shown, in that atheists have claimed to show that one can have knowledge that God does not exist.

Another agnostic argument against atheism is that any atheist thinker knows that many theists who are intelligent enough to know all of the atheistic arguments against the existence of God reject them. Should not the existence of such theists cause atheists to reconsider their position? Indeed, should not their existence induce atheists to retreat to agnosticism? This argument is not, however, persuasive. First, the existence of such theists does not mean that agnosticism is justified. Intelligent and knowledgeable theists might induce atheists to reexamine their arguments, but if, on careful examination, the atheistic arguments hold up to criticisms, atheists are justified in maintaining their position. Second, this argument proves too much. After all, intelligent and even brilliant scientists who know the arguments of their critics have held all manner of crank and outlandish theories. This argument would have the absurd implication that other scientists should be agnostic with respect to these theories.

Another argument for agnosticism starts from the premise that one can look at atheism from an external point of view and try to determine the causal factors that bring about atheism and the acceptance of the arguments that are used to justify it. Viewed in this way, atheistic beliefs, values, and attitudes are dependent on social, historical, and psychological factors. Thus, for example, if the present writer had been raised in a strict fundamentalist home, he might not have accepted the atheistic argument that he readily accepts today. Thus, the fact that he is an atheist today rather than a theist is a matter of luck or accident, in that is depends on where he was born and on other early influences. Given this insight, one might argue that the only rational stance to take is agnosticism, a position that avoids the possible biases of the accidents of birth.

The first problem with this argument is that if it were taken seriously it would generate widespread skepticism in all fields, including science. For example, there are usually conflicting theories in physics. On this view whether a person accepts one theory of physics rather than an alternative will depend on historical, social, and psychological factors. But surely it is absurd to suppose that agnosticism in relation to these theories is always justified. Sometimes the evidence for one theory is so much stronger than it is for any of its rivals that it justifies belief in one theory and rejection of its rivals. Second, agnosticism is no less dependent than atheism on social, historical, and psychological factors. One might argue that had Thomas Huxley been born in different circumstances, his famous essay on agnosticism would never have been written. Does this mean that we should neither believe nor disbelieve the major theses of his essay? It is also worth noting that not all atheists are born into atheistic families. Many atheists are former religious believers who have somehow transcended their religious heritage. To be sure, the fact that what we believe about the existence of God is partly a function of our social, historical, and psychological background should alert us to possible biases and induce us to review our arguments. Nevertheless, after careful review we may justifiably decide that our arguments hold.

Yet another agnostic claim is that atheism is a dogmatic view characterized by an authoritative, arrogant assertion of unproved or unprovable principles. It is maintained that since such dogmatic views should be avoided, atheism should be as well. In contrast, agnosticism is characterized as being tentative, flexible, and open-minded. Since these characteristics are to be encouraged, agnosticism is to be preferred to atheism. However although there have been dogmatic atheists, there is no necessary connection between atheism and dogmatism. Atheists can be tentative, flexible, and open-minded in their position, willing to consider objections to their arguments and to give up their views in the light of new evidence. On the other hand, agnostics can stubbornly cling to their rejection of atheism in spite of strong evidence to the contrary, unreasonably sticking to their claim that there is no good evidence for disbelief.

Finally, many appear to advocate agnosticism instead of atheism because of atheism's "bad name." They believe it is bad public relations to bill oneself as an atheist, since people tend to reject the views of an avowed atheist out of hand. They say that in order to get one's views accepted, one should advocate the less controversial and more socially acceptable label "agnostic" over the more controversial and less socially acceptable label "atheist."

However, although this may be a good argument for pretending to be an agnostic, it is not a good argument for actually being one. In fact, if pushed to its logical conclusion, it would justify pretending to be a theist. After all, although agnostics may have better reputations than atheists, they do not have as good reputations as theists. It has been said that in the United States a professed atheist could never be elected president. But could a professed agnostic?

BIBLIOGRAPHY

Drange, Theodore M. *Nonbelief and Evil: Two Arguments for the Nonexistence of God.* Amherst, NY: Prometheus Books, 1998.

Everitt, Nicholas. *The Non-existence of God*. London: Routledge, 2004.

Mackie, J. L. *The Miracle of Theism: Arguments For and Against the Existence of God*. Oxford: Clarendon, 1982.

Martin, Michael. *Atheism: A Philosophical Justification*. Philadelphia: Temple University Press, 1990.

———. *Atheism, Morality, and Meaning*. Amherst, NY: Prometheus Books, 2002.

———. "Atheism v. Agnosticism." *The Philosophers' Magazine* 19 (Summer 2002).

Martin, Michael, and Monnier, Ricki, ed. *The Impossibility of God*. Amherst, NY: Prometheus Books, 2003.

Schellenberg, J. L. *Divine Hiddenness and Human Reason*. Ithaca, NY: Cornell University Press, 1993.

Weisberger, A. M. *Suffering Belief: Evil and the Anglo-American Defense of Theism*. New York: Peter Lang, 1999.

MICHAEL MARTIN

AUSTRALIA, UNBELIEF IN. As is seen with other social trends, belief and unbelief in Australia display characteristics of both their British and their American counterparts.

Australia has inherited most British religious and irreligious institutions and attitudes. Nominal Christian belief has passed from the Church of England (now Anglican) leavened with Nonconformism (that is, non-Anglican Protestantism) to a situation where Roman Catholic Church membership approximately equals the population of Anglicans plus members of the Uniting Church (Methodist, Congregationalist, and ecumenical Presbyterian). Meanwhile the targets of campaigning unbelievers have changed to address the theological and social claims of whichever denomination has appeared most threatening at the time. Latterly, concern has extended to fundamentalist Islam. Britain has inspired freethought labels from SECULARISM (curiously blended with Spiritualism) to RATIONALISM to HUMANISM; but whereas the first is still prominent in Britain, it has all but vanished in Australia. Yet demands for secularity and the spontaneous growth of secularization are common to both countries (see SECULARISM; DEMOGRAPHY OF UNBELIEF). Politically, Australia and Britain share the same monarch as head of state, a republican tradition opposed to that monarchy, and the Westminster system of choosing members of the lower house of Parliament and the executive government.

In other respects, Australia has followed the United States. Both have long been immigrant countries facing the challenge of multiculturalism; both have known slavery and quasi slavery (in northeast Australia, Pacific Islanders); both are federations with a state-based upper house of the legislature and a written secular constitution. Yet whereas the United States has upheld its secu-

larity more conscientiously, it is paradoxically better noted for public and private piety. Most Americans patronize church, chapel, mosque, temple, or synagogue, while many unbelievers may see a sociopolitical need to embrace UNITARIAN UNIVERSALISM (see DEMOGRAPHY OF UNBELIEF). In Australia, God is rarely invoked by politicians save in opening Parliament, and in the 2001 census 15.3 percent of Australians claimed "no religion" while 9.7 percent declined to state a religion.

HISTORY OF AUSTRALIAN UNBELIEF

As each Australian state has a different educational and legal system, so each (apart from unorganized Tasmania) has fostered separate freethought organizations to respond to local challenges, though federal coalitions may exist to coordinate campaigns of national interest. Australia's small population and vast area, plus the traditional independence of freethinkers, have combined to keep these bodies small and often ineffective, factionalized, and evanescent. Freethought within religious denominations has largely arisen spontaneously to produce "lapsed" believers rather than active unbelievers.

The greatest lapsing has occurred in the indigenous animistic faith, which had lasted for around fifty thousand years before the white occupation. Aboriginal belief systems varied in detail from place to place in a vast continent with little precontact communication, but essentially involved black and white magic performed by a *kurdaitcha* man (witch doctor), and beliefs in Dreamtime ancestors, animals, and spirits with supernatural powers to shape the landscape and tribal lore. Then Christians—chiefly Catholic, Lutheran, Uniting Church, and Seventh-Day Adventist—established missions to eradicate "primitive" Aboriginal beliefs. Secularization virtually completed the process, though freethought bodies have been in the forefront of support for the maintenance of Aboriginal identity and land rights and for Aboriginal reconciliation with the nonindigenous population. While traditional stories are perpetuated in Aboriginal art and dance, all but a few remote tribal elders regard them as that: just stories.

Australia's first white settlers, the 1788 "First Fleeters"—overwhelmingly convicts and soldiers sent from Britain to serve out their time—often displayed the rootlessness, licentiousness, and simulated piety usually associated with such groups. This mix of rebelliousness and authoritarianism within a governmental framework of social conservatism and cultural cringe toward the "Mother Country" survived largely intact for 180 years, though the arrival of Irish political prisoners from the end of the eighteenth century brought people with deep religious or nonreligious views. After 1840 almost all arrivals were free settlers with their own religious and other traditions but a strong, if declining, desire to fit into the prevailing ethos. Nevertheless, freed from entrenched class systems in their countries of origin and fortified by geographical isolation, they made Australia (together with New Zealand) a pioneer in civil liberties.

Nineteenth Century. Throughout the nineteenth century, the leading freethinkers in Australia were English immigrants of Protestant derivation; often they originally intended careers in the ministry. To earn a living lecturing, especially during economic depressions, they were forced to travel throughout the six Australian colonies and New Zealand, though they preferred to keep one city as a base. There they often established their own newspaper or magazine, however short-lived. Disputes over the need for militancy, or AGNOSTICISM versus ATHEISM, were fewer than in the United Kingdom, and the major confrontation was between PHILOSOPHICAL MATERIALISM and Spiritualism (see SPIRITUALISM AND UNBELIEF). The first notable unbelieving settler was Charles SOUTHWELL. Maneuvered out of a legacy and secularist prominence in England by George Jacob HOLYOAKE, he settled in Melbourne in 1855, then New Zealand in 1856.

The earliest freethought society known in Australia was established in Newcastle, New South Wales, in 1862, with the Chartist Daniel Wallwork becoming its secretary in 1865. In Melborne, W. H. Terry founded the *Harbinger of Light* in 1870 and became treasurer of the Victorian Association of Progressive Spiritualists in 1872. In 1871 William Lorando Jones was convicted of BLASPHEMY in Sydney and sentenced to two years in jail and fined for saying the Bible was immoral, but a public protest secured his release on bond. By 1874 Melbourne had a Progressive Lyceum and a Free Discussion Society, Brisbane a Freethought Association, and Sydney a Freethought Progressive Society. Six years later Sydney had a Progressive Secular Lyceum for secularists and spiritualists under Ebenezer Skinner. All the leading freethought lecturers of the 1870s—John Tyerman, Thomas WALKER, Dr. James Peebles, Mrs. Emma Hardinge Britten, and Charles Bright—were spiritualists, and the *Harbinger* solemnly recorded all supposed "manifestations" from the spirit world. Walker began his Australian career in Sydney in 1877 allegedly "controleed" by four spirit guides, including Giordano BRUNO, but abandoned them and went to wealthier Melbourne, where he tried to secularize its lyceum, which had fallen under the control of Spiritualists.

Faced with emergent SKEPTICISM, the spiritualists formed the Liberal Association of New South Wales in 1881 to fuse religious and atheistic thought into one "party of progress," but the secularists soon bridled at Spiritualism's dominance. In 1882 Walker and others launched in Melbourne the Australasian Secular Association (theoretically embracing New Zealand), with the *Reformer* as its journal; but when Terry revealed his Canadian past (see WALKER, THOMAS) he left Melbourne to become president of the Sydney branch of the Australasian Secular Association. To take his place in Melbourne, the Australasian Secular Association requested a lecturer from England. Disappointed that Edward B. AVELING and not himself had taken the place of the jailed George William FOOTE as editor of the British magazine the *FREETHINKER*, Joseph SYMES came to Melbourne with Charles BRADLAUGH's blessing in 1884. He was soon joined by William Willis, who later established a freethought bookstore in Sydney. An Australasian Freethought Conference there inspired the formation of freethought societies in South Australia and major country centers. Symes became president of the parent Australasian Secular Association, with Bright and Walker as vice presidents, and established the republican and atheistic *LIBERATOR: A Weekly Radical Freethought Paper.* Also in 1884 the *Liberal*, edited by Bright, was established in Sydney, and a short-lived *Young Secularist* in Melbourne. An Australasian Freethought Union was formed in Sydney; its radical secularist agenda served as a counterweight to the Australasian Secular Association.

In 1885 Walker resigned his presidency and was expelled from the Australasian Secular Association's Sydney branch, but became president and lecturer of the Australasian Freethought Union and editor of its *Reflector.* The Australasian Secular Association sent another call to England for a Sydney lecturer, and received William Whitehouse COLLINS. Collins founded and edited the *Freethinker and New South Wales Reformer*, which soon merged with the *Liberator.*

In 1886 Sir Alfred Stephens introduced into the New South Wales Legislative Assembly a liberal divorce-extension bill, which finally passed in 1887 with the support of Walker, then a member of the legislative assembly. The editor of the *Australian Christian World* asked the premier of New South Wales, Sir Henry Parkes, to ban Symes's *Ancient and Modern Phallic or Sex-Worship* (1886) for "blasphemy and obscenity." Instead, Parkes stopped Sunday lecturing in Sydney theaters. Collins was unsuccessfully prosecuted for selling Annie BESANT's contraceptive tract *Law of Population* (1877); deprived of his main income source, he went to Brisbane.

In Melbourne, some Australasian Secular Association executive members accused Symes of autocracy, while others were shocked by his writing on phallic worship. Yet others abandoned his Bradlaughite liberalism for emerging MARXISM or anarchism (see ANARCHISM AND UNBELIEF). Symes called a "showdown" meeting at which, he asserted, the other association officers (who were also trustees of assets) were dismissed and new ones elected. The trustees claimed they had walked out and the elections were invalid. On Australasian Secular Association land, Symes built a Hall of Science that opened in 1889; he ran unsuccessfully for Parliament. In Sydney an Australasian Secular Friendly Benevolent Society was formed; Collins established *Freedom* and laid the foundation stone for a new Sydney Lyceum before leaving on a lecture tour of New Zealand, and settling there till 1917.

Throughout Australia, secularists were so successful in flouting Sunday observance laws with their paid-admission lecture events that museums, art galleries, libraries, excursions, and other entertainments were eventually permitted to operate on the Sabbath. Unfortunately for the secularists, these provided competition for their lectures. In the 1890s the situation worsened with a depression which caused unemployment for the artisans and bankruptcies for the small businessmen on whom the secularist movement depended. Many went to remote mining centers in New South Wales and Western Australia looking for work.

In 1890, members of an anarchist anti-Symes faction invaded his hall but were driven back by supporters led by its socialist caretaker, Joseph Skurrie. The following year, Australasian Secular Association trustees obtained a court order for possession of the hall Symes had erected on their land. Symes was forced to lecture in a city theater; Skurrie to become an itinerant lecturer, then a miner; Walker, after a shooting incident, to leave the parliament of New South Wales and become a temperance lecturer. Symes again ran unsuccessfully for Parliament in 1892; Skurrie was fined for obstruction, profanity, and trespass in 1893; and Willis went to Tasmania in 1894, but died suddenly. Though closure of the impoverished *Liberator* was announced that year, Symes kept it alive for ten years with help from his second wife, Agnes Wilson SYMES. Sentenced to jail for criticizing a jury appointment, Symes resigned as president and trustee of his rival Australasian Secular Association in 1895, formed the Melbourne Freethought Society in 1897, bought back the old hall, and renamed it Freethought Hall.

Twentieth Century. Becoming law at the beginning of the new century, the flawed Australian Constitution gave the Commonwealth Government powers over trade, commerce, and the mails. Under enabling acts, these facilitated censorship of blasphemous, indecent, obscene, or immoral material, including advertisements relating to pregnancy, impotence, venereal disease, or abortion. It was the launch of Australian "wowserism" (WOWSER: We Only Want Social Evils Rectified). But section 116 of the constitution stated: "The Commonwealth shall not make any law for establishing any religion, or for imposing any religious observance, or for prohibiting the free exercise of any religion." Symes was only one observer to note the implicit contradiction.

Having failed to convert the Melbourne Freethought Society into an Australasian one, Symes retired in 1904. Harry Scott BENNETT, the first notable Australian-born freethinker, served one term in Victoria's legislative assembly and in 1907 began lecturing for the Victorian Socialist Party, which Symes had blamed for the "White Australia" policy implicit in the 1901 Immigration Restriction Act.

Under the banner of secularism or freethought, organized unbelief had grown moribund. It took RATIONALISM to breathe new life into it. In 1899 some National Secular Society dissidents and academic freethinkers formed the RATIONALIST PRESS ASSOCIATION (RPA) in London to bring classics of unbelief to a wider public. It soon attracted a significant overseas membership, which coalesced to form local associations and from which the RPA selected honorary local secretaries. In Australia rationalist associations appeared in Melbourne (1906), Sydney (1910), Brisbane (1914), and Perth and Adelaide (1918). The best-known figures were businessman William John Miles, New South Wales secretary from 1913, and H. A. Layman, director of the Queensland Museum and founding president of the Queensland rationalist society. Visits by English ex-priest Joseph MCCABE in 1910 and 1913 boosted these groups.

During World War I, three unbelievers—the socialist suffragette Adele Pankhurst, Dr. Vida Goldstein, and Celia Johns—formed the Women's Peace Army to fight conscription. In 1915 Skurrie returned to Melbourne and a fine and jail for saying that no thinking man would enlist. Robert S. Ross, leader of the Victorian Socialist Party, began *Ross's Magazine of Protest Personality and Progress*, supported by Miles, to oppose the war. It was prosecuted for blasphemy and confiscated in 1916 for printing an abstract of Skurrie's lecture "Gods, Ghosts, and Devils." Prime Minister William Morris (Billy) Hughes, an atheist, sponsored unsuccessful referenda on conscription in 1916 and 1917 and was expelled from the Australian Labor Party, but continued in office till 1923. Miles tried unsuccessfully to establish an Advance Australia League with the slogan "Australia First."

The first president of the Western Australian Rationalist Association (WARA) in Perth was Walker, who finally gained stability in the west as a goldfields journalist, newspaper proprietor, farmer, lawyer, legislative assembly member, and cabinet minister. John Samuel Langley was the association's secretary. When Melbourne industrialist Walter D. Cookes visited Perth, he persuaded Langley to return with him to Melbourne in 1919 to lead a Rationalist Society of Australia. Presently it became the Rationalist Association of Victoria and, in 1923, the Rationalist Association of Australia, with its publication the *Rationalist*. Two years later, to protect a bequest the Rationalist Association of Australia had received, a holding company was formed, the Rationalist Association of Australia Ltd. The Rationalist Association of Australia's assets and five members, who became directors, were transferred to the Rationalist Association of Australia Ltd. For the other Rationalist Association of Australia members and new recruits, a propagandist Rationalist Society of Australia was formed in 1926. Langley was secretary and lawyer Alfred Foster was chairman/president of both new bodies, which attracted the support of leading Melbourne writers, scientists, and judges.

Meanwhile, in Sydney two short-lived *Liberators* (1918 and 1923) were formed and Miles, believing McCabe was a British secret agent, quarreled with the

RPA and retired as secretary of the Rationalist Association of New South Wales. In 1930 the Sydney University Society for Freethought was formed by John ANDERSON, a Scottish immigrant, disillusioned Marxist, and Australia's most influential professor of philosophy. In 1931 he said that "State, Nation, King and Country, and loyalty" were superstitious terms appealing to prejudice, and incurred criticism in New South Wales's legislative assembly and censure by the university senate. Having retired from business, Miles began the *Independent Sydney Secularist* (1935) and, with the help of Queensland atheist writer Percy Reginald (Inky) Stephensen, the *Publicist: The Paper Loyal to Australia First* (1936). Though right-wing and chauvinistic, this paper was pro-monarchy. As Melbourne abounded in freethinking socialist lecturers, with Langley's blessing and financial aid Scott Bennett came to Sydney as secretary-lecturer of the Rationalist Association of New South Wales.

Moderately left-wing, Langley objected to Cookes's distributing Australia First literature on rationalist premises, and to the undemocratic nature of the Rationalist Association of Australia Ltd. Cookes, Foster, and most of the other directors (now eleven in total) objected to Langley's administrative inefficiency, extravagance, and autocracy, wrongly accused him of alcoholism, and expelled him in 1938. As with Symes, Skurrie supported Langley in his unsuccessful legal action for reinstatement. Langley retained support from the Rationalist Society of Australia, but when the Rationalist Association of Australia Ltd. formed a new Rationalist Society of Australia with W. Glanville Cook as secretary and *Rationalist* editor, Langley was legally forced to change its name to Freethought Society of Australia.

During World War II Stephensen became founding president of the Australia First Movement (1941). Criticizing the timing, Miles did not join. In 1942 Laurence Frederick Bullock and three other Perth members called for "a negotiated peace with the Japanese" and announced an alternative, pro-Japanese Australian government and a "liquidation" list of officials who had taken a hard line on Japan. Despite claiming these proclamations were drunken jokes, two members were jailed for conspiracy under the broadly written Crimes Act. Totally unaware of the Perth initiative, Stephensen, Pankhurst, and other eastern members were interned for various periods. In 1943 Anderson declared that religious doctrines assaulted a child's common sense and was denounced in the New South Wales parliament, but the university senate this time upheld academic freedom.

After the war a mild form of McCarthyism under Catholic auspices flourished. Claiming the trade unions and Australian Labor Party were communist dominated, lawyer B. A. Santamaria and Melbourne archbishop Daniel Mannix formed cells of the Movement, a Catholic group, inside both, and then established the Democratic Labor Party (1956). This attracted some non-Catholic supporters and kept conservative parties in power till 1972. Reactively, most freethinkers gravitated toward the Australian Labor Party.

With the death of Scott Bennett in 1959, the heyday of New South Wales rationalism ceased. As well as disdaining open-air "Bible-bashing," many Sydney freethinkers deemed the Rationalist Association of New South Wales Marxist dominated and in 1960 formed the New South Wales Humanist Society with its publication *Viewpoints* (1963), under William and Daphne Weeks. It published a number of tracts on civil liberties and BIOETHICS, and spawned a Secular Education Defense Committee (1962), a Council for Civil Liberties (1963), and an Abortion Law Reform Association (1969). Humanist societies were soon formed in other states: Victoria, with its publication *Victorian Humanist*, under Clive Sandy and Myfanwy M. Beadnell (1961); South Australia under Bruce Muirden (1962); Canberra (1964); Queensland, with its publication *Queensland Humanist*, under Tup and Margaret Baxendell (1964); and Western Australia (1965). The Council of Australian Humanist Societies was formed under Ian Edwards in 1965, and *Australian Humanist* became its organ.

In most Australian states a weakened rationalist association, with *Rationalist News* in New South Wales, survived; but in Queensland it was taken over. After internment in South Australia, Bullock revived the South Australian Rationalist Association in 1968. In 1970, inspired by the Indian atheist activist GORA, Bullock transformed it into the Atheist Foundation of Australia, with its publication *Australian Atheist*. An offshoot Atheist Association, with its *Atheist Journal*, then emerged under Frederick Swann, Bullock, and Alan Rickard. A Freethinkers Association of New South Wales under Charles King (1973) and a Victorian Secular Society under Harry H. Pearce and Nigel Sinnott (1978) came and went, but the Australian Skeptics with their journal *Skeptic* came into being under controversial solicitor Mark Plummer (1981) and continues to flourish under Barry Williams.

In recent decades unbelievers in Australia have been active but unsuccessful in defending its secular constitution as state aid to church schools mushrooms under all governments, as religion and CREATIONISM creep into state schools, and as medical and social services are outsourced to "faith" institutions. The Council for the Defense of Government Schools challenged state aid to religious schools in 1973, but lost in the High Court in 1981. A new challenge is being considered. In 1997 the Northern Territory parliament passed a voluntary euthanasia act, which the commonwealth vetoed; today humanist Dr. Philip Nitschke offers practical advice to those wishing to end lives shadowed by terminal disease. Faced with declining support and impact, the Rationalist Association of New South Wales contemplated merger with the the Humanist Society of New South Wales in 2006 to form the Humanist and Rationalist Association of New South Wales.

BIBLIOGRAPHY

Biddington, Ralph. *The Supremacy of Reason: Episodes in Victoria's Rationalist History, 1880–1972.* Unpublished manuscript, 2001.

Dahlitz, Ray. *Secular Who's Who.* Melbourne: R. Dahlitz, 1994.

Edwards, Ian. *A Humanist View.* Sydney: Angus & Robertson, 1969.

Muirden, Bruce. *The Puzzled Patriots: The Story of the Australia First Movement.* Melbourne: Melbourne University Press, 1968.

Smith, F. Barrymore. *Religion and Freethought in Melbourne 1870–1890.* Unpublished thesis, 1960.

Tribe, David. *100 Years of Freethought.* London: Elek, 1967.

DAVID TRIBE

AVELING, EDWARD BIBBINS (1849–1898). English author and lecturer. Despite great talent and literary output, he is recalled negatively: unoriginal, unstable, and unprincipled.

Son of Congregationalist minister Thomas Aveling, Edward was born in Stoke Newington, London, on November 29, 1849. Educated in Taunton, he enrolled as a medical student at University College, London, but switched to science, graduating with honors in zoology (1870). After a stint as physiology assistant at Cambridge University he returned to London to marry heiress Isabel Frank in July 1872, but they separated after two years of high living. From 1872 to 1876 he taught physics and botany at a girls' school, then gained a doctorate, a fellowship in the Linnean Society, and a lectureship in comparative anatomy at London Hospital.

While lecturing at the City of London College in 1879, he met Annie BESANT and began writing pseudonymously for Charles BRADLAUGH's *NATIONAL REFORMER*. In July of that year he publicly revealed himself and abandoned his application for a professorship at University College. Claiming he had also lost his lectures at City of London College, he persuaded Bradlaugh to let him create formal classes under official Science and Art Department auspices at the NATIONAL SECULAR SOCIETY's Hall of Science. There he successfully taught botany, Latin, chemistry, mathematics, French, and advanced science, which he also wrote about in *The Student's Darwin* (1881) and other textbooks. Now a National Secular Society (NSS) vice president and a Bradlaugh lieutenant, he edited the *FREETHINKER* and *Progress* in 1983–84 while George W. FOOTE was in jail. Meanwhile, he was elected to the London School Board and joined H. M. Hyndman's (Social) Democratic Federation (SDF). Because of numerous unpaid debts and philanderings Bradlaugh forced him to resign from the NSS and return Besant's love letters.

By 1884 he had begun living with Eleanor Marx, Karl MARX's daughter; he abandoned the SDF for the Socialist League, which he left in 1885. After an extravagant lecture tour of North America in 1886, he promoted the "new unionism," the eight-hour workday, and the International Labor League. He was the first to publish Marx's *Kapital* (1867) in English (1887) and he also published *The Student's Marx* (1892), an influential text of the day. He joined the Independent Labor Party in 1893 but was expelled in 1894. From 1885 to 1896 he was also involved with the theater as drama critic, playwright, actor, and producer. In 1897 he secretly married actress Eva Frye and left Eleanor, but, ill and cash-strapped, rejoined her. In 1898 she committed suicide, and he died in Battersea on August 2.

BIBLIOGRAPHY

Kapp, Yvonne. *Eleanor Marx.* 2 vols. London: Lawrence and Wishart, 1972–73.

Tribe, David. *President Charles Bradlaugh, M.P.* London: Elek, 1971.

DAVID TRIBE

AVERRÖES (Ibn Rushd; 1126–1198), Muslim philosopher and commentator. Abu al-Walid Muhammad bin Ahmad ibn Rushd, originally known in the West as Averröes, came from a family of jurists. Trained in the legal sciences, he served as a judge in Seville and Cordoba, Spain. He also studied medicine and philosophy, and is considered one of the greatest commentators on ARISTOTLE. His philosophical and religious views are the subject of furious debate among specialists; the nonspecialist should tread with care. No area of his thought is more sharply contested than his actual position on the relation between philosophy and religion.

Averröes may be most important as one of the conduits through whom ancient Greek and Hindu learning preserved during the Islamic Renaissance (eighth to tenth centuries CE) was retransmitted to the West, shaping the growth of science and philosophy during Europe's Renaissance. To better appreciate his role—and the context in which he is often misinterpreted—it is appropriate to review the process by which ancient learning was acquired, and to a limited degree resynthesized, by Muslim intellectuals.

Greek Philosophy and Science and Their Influence on Islam. The many words of Arabic origin that have entered European philosophy, science, and mathematics reveal the extent to which Islamic civilization influenced later European thought. This Islamic learning was founded on the works of the ancient Greeks, and the Muslims are important as the preservers and transmitters of ancient learning that might otherwise have been lost. Although Islamic thinkers seldom improved substantially on the works of the Greeks, they did make original contributions to trigonometry, for example, inventing plane and spherical trigonometry, which did not exist among the Greeks. Islamic work on alchemy, magic, and astrology also played an important part in the development of European science—the idea of power over nature stimulated research and experimentation.

The period during which the heritage of classical antiquity was assimilated into Islam is known as the Islamic Renaissance. As the scholar F. R. Rosenthal forthrightly reminds us: "Islamic rational scholarship, which we have mainly in mind when we speak of the greatness of Muslim civilisation, depends in its entirety on classical antiquity, down to such fundamental factors as the elementary principles of scholarly and scientific research. More than that, the intellectual life of Islam in its most intimate expressions bowed to the Greek spirit."

To study this assimilative process is to confront the seeming oxymoron of Islamic philosophy. For to many Western scholars, and more importantly, to many Muslims, the very idea of "Islamic philosophy" is a contradiction in terms. Surely orthodox Sunni Islam never welcomed philosophic thought. Traditionalists denounced philosophy as a "foreign science," which they claimed must lead to heresy, doubt, and total unbelief. In this, traditionalist fears were well founded, for many Islamic philosophers developed views that were far from orthodox, while others, especially those hostile to the rising Sunni hierarchy, openly embraced the unfettered guidance of REASON as understood in Greek philosophy, offering but lip service to their religion. Thus the story of Islamic philosophy is, in part, the story of the tension between reason and revelation.

Although translation of Greek works may well have started in the seventh century under the first caliphate dynasty, the Umayyads, it was a caliph of the succeeding dynasty, the Abbasid al-Mamun (ruled 813–833), who strongly encouraged the translation of Greek philosophy and science. Al-Mamun went so far as to establish an institution called the House of Wisdom as a center for research and translation. The initial impulse for translating ancient works was practical—the need for medical and astronomical knowledge. But prestige and, later, genuine intellectual curiosity also played a part in what became a feverish activity.

The Greek philosophers translated included ARISTOTLE and his commentators such as Themistius, Simplicius, and Alexander of Aphrodisias; PLATO, particularly the *Timaeus*, *Republic*, and *Laws*; Plotinus and Neoplatonists such as Proclus and Porphyry; pre-Socratics; Galen, Hippocrates, Archimedes, Euclid, and Ptolemy.

The West's Discovery of Averröes. The first period of Islamic philosophy took shape in the East between the ninth and eleventh centuries with al-Kindi, al-Farabi, and Ibn Sina (Avicenna). It was this deposit of ancient learning that Averröes would play a special role in retransmitting to Europe, in the process inspiring widely divergent perceptions as to his own views.

First to present Averröes to the Christian West was Michael Scott, who under the patronage of the House of Hohenstaufen began around 1230–40 a Latin translation of the Arabic text of Averröes. The commentaries of Averröes were first translated into Hebrew by a group led by Jacob ben Abba Mari Anatoli of Naples in 1232. The scholars Augustinus Niphus and Marc-Antonio Zimara made some improvements in these translations. Newer translations based on the Hebrew text would later be made by Jacob Mantino of Tortosa. The two best Latin editions of Averröes are those of Niphus (1495–97) and of the Juntas (1553).

Averröes and His Modern Interpreters. The French biblical scholar Ernest RENAN viewed Averröes as a supreme rationalist (see RATIONALISM) opposed to all religious dogmas, who used his theological writings as smokescreens to hide his true views from the intolerant orthodox doctors of law. Twentieth-century scholars preferred to call him by his Arabic name, Ibn Rushd, and they have rejected this view of him as a clandestine soldier of the Enlightenment. Today Ibn Rushd is more often seen as a sincere Muslim, convinced that philosophy and revelation were both true.

Nor do modern scholars accept the idea that Ibn Rushd propounded the theory of "double truth"—the teaching that there exists one (usually religious) truth for the uneducated masses and another, less superstitious truth for the cultured few. For Ibn Rushd, there existed a religious truth that is true for all persons regardless of their education, status, or level of understanding. But he wrote that the sharia (Islamic law) commands the study of philosophy only for those capable of understanding and using Aristotle's demonstrative method. He held that the Qur'an contains passages that require interpretation, but this should only be attempted by those with a solid grounding in scholarship. Other parts of the Qur'an, as well as other texts that form a part of the sharia, must be taken literally. To interpret them would amount to unbelief and heretical innovations.

Western scholars also differ regarding Ibn Rushd's views on the resurrection of the dead. Over his productive life he seems genuinely to have changed his mind, or at least refined his theory. De Boer thought Ibn Rushd believed in the "perishable nature of all that is individual, by which theory individual immortality is also taken away," whereas George Hourani attributed to Ibn Rushd the view that "our physical bodies are dissolved at death, but we may receive new celestial ones in a resurrection, and these would hold our reconstituted individual souls." Meanwhile, Marmura holds that in his technical writings, such as his commentaries on Aristotle, Ibn Rushd's thought left no room for the immortality of individual souls. Yet in his other writings, Ibn Rushd "affirms a doctrine of individual immortality, whether this is confined to the soul or involves bodily resurrection." And in yet another work, Ibn Rushd affirms a doctrine of bodily resurrection. For Fakhry, Ibn Rushd's theory entails that "the only form of survival possible is intellectual, i.e., that of the material or 'possible' intellect, once it is reunited with the active intellect," Hourani, Marmura, and de Boer seem to agree that Ibn Rushd's theory would not have been acceptable to the orthodox clergy; Mamura even goes back to a Renan-like hypothesis, claiming that Ibn Rushd may have sought to protect himself against charges of unbelief in presenting different arguments to different audiences.

On another important issue, the position of women in Islam, Ibn Rushd's opinion must have driven the orthodox to fury: as interpreted by De Boer, he wrote that much of the poverty and distress of his day arose from the fact that women are kept like "domestic animals or house plants for purposes of gratification, of a very questionable character besides, instead of being allowed to take part in the production of material and intellectual wealth, and in the preservation of the same."

The Impact of His Thought. Averröes, as he became known, exerted profound influence on the Latin philosophers and scientists of the thirteenth century. A school of Averroists arose at the University of Padua, among whom Averröes's work on Aristotle sparked the very development of the inductive, empirical sciences.

Despite the almost incalculable importance of Averröes for Western learning, Ibn Rushd would have no influence whatever on the development of Islamic philosophy. After his death, he was practically forgotten in the Islamic world. Philosophy itself went into a decline within Islam, which came under the domination of Ash'arism, with its attendant petrifying dogma. There was a rather misguided attempt by the early twentieth-century Islamic renaissance movement, the Nahda, to take Averröes on board as an out-and-out rationalist who advocated a secular state. The movement was much influenced by Renan's interpretation of Averröes, an interpretation that overemphasized Averröes's rationality and belittled his religious and juridical work.

BIBLIOGRAPHY

Arnaldez, R. "Ibn Rushd." In *The Encyclopedia of Islam*, 2nd ed. Leiden: E. J. Brill, 1999.

De Boer, D. T. J. *History of Philosophy in Islam*. Translated by Edward R. Jones. London: Luzac and Company, 1903.

Fakhry. *A History of Islamic Philosophy*, 2nd ed. New York: Columbia University Press, 1987.

Hourani, George. "Ibn Rushd." In *The Encyclopedia of Religion*, edited by Mircea Eliade. New York: Macmillan, 1995.

Marmura, M. E. "Falsafa." In *The Encyclopedia of Religion*, edited by Mircea Eliade. New York: Macmillan, 1995.

Rosenthal, F. R. *The Classical Heritage of Islam*. Berkeley and Los Angeles: University of California Press, 1965.

Warraq, Ibn. *Why I Am Not a Muslim*. Amherst, NY: Prometheus Books, 1995.

IBN WARRAQ

AYER, ALFRED JULES (1910–1989), English philosopher. A. J. Ayer was born in London on October 29, 1910, into a well-connected family with a continental past, went to the great private school Eton and then to Oxford, wrote the book *Language, Truth and Logic* when he was twenty-four, and won celebrity and some notoriety for it. After serving in World War II as an intelligence officer, he became the Grote Professor of the Philosophy of Mind and Logic at University College London, and then the Wykeham Professor of Logic at Oxford. He was known as England's logical positivist for his youthful work.

Ayer was a dutiful teacher, and in philosophical discussions he invigorated and indeed inspired students and younger colleagues. As a result of numerous broadcasts on the BBC he became the best known of British philosophers, and was knighted.

More than any of that, Ayer was the greatest of the twentieth-century philosophers who definitely fit into the tradition established by David HUME in the eighteenth century, perhaps the greatest of philosophical traditions. Ayer was the antithesis of the philosopher of mystery and intimation, and his work was refreshingly free of technicality.

He lived assertively and was vain and cocksure—at some cost to his philosophical reputation, since other philosophers were no less human in their judgments on him. He was also honest, humane, and more or less on the Left in politics. He enjoyed society, was a man of many women, came to be self-judging, and after some sadness died bravely on June 27, 1989. He lived and died an atheist (see ATHEISM).

If Ayer's connection to Hume is a matter of more than one fact, the heart of *Language, Truth and Logic*, no doubt the best-known expression of logical positivism, is a proposal with an antecedent in the resolute and resonant words of Hume. It gives philosophical expression to a hardheadedness and SKEPTICISM that also turn up elsewhere, certainly in much science and common sense.

The verification principle (see VERIFICATIONISM), the foundation of logical positivism, contends that any statement that is true or false must either be necessarily true or self-contradictory, or verifiable by sense experience. Hence utterances of logic and mathematics and utterances of empirical science, and similar utterances of both kinds in ordinary life, have the important standing of being statements, while utterances of religion, metaphysics, and ethics do not, and are to be understood as merely expressions of feeling. This doctrine was sometimes overstated as being to the effect that the latter utterances have no meaning at all, which in fact Ayer did not and of course could not believe. It is of about as much effect that they do not come up to the level where utterances can be judged true or false.

In *Language, Truth and Logic* Ayer very much gives the impression—and sometimes says outright—that the verification principle is a *premise* or *basis* from which there follows, or on which there rests, the *conclusion* that the utterances of religion, metaphysics, and a kind of morality are neither true nor false. This is a matter, as already remarked, of their being in certain senses neither logical nor empirical. Ayer promises at the beginning of his book that he will provide a demonstration—or proof—of the verification principle.

It is also possible to wonder, more radically, whether the whole philosophical situation in which Ayer involves us is otherwise. At any rate, is it better described in a very different way? Does the whole argument really go in the other direction? Might it be that the supposed premise or basis mentioned above is the conclusion, and the supposed conclusion is the premise or basis? That is, an examination without presupposition of particular utterances of religious believers, metaphysicians, moralists, and the like shows these utterances to be *other than* statements or propositions, *other than* true or false. And this is summed up in—or provides good reason for—the generalization that is the verification principle.

It was said at the beginning of these reflections that Ayer is the greatest twentieth-century philosopher within a definable tradition established by Hume in the eighteenth century, and that this is arguably the greatest of philosophical traditions. That tradition can be understood in a certain way.

It has in it certain problems—those that are forced us on by our world and our common existence in it, and thus are not factitious. As important as any among these problems are those spoken of earlier as having to do with reality, knowledge, and perception. Also, this tradition is one of clearheaded reasoning, something carried forward in the light of experience and of theory close to it, not given to flying above it or being visionary about what lies under it. It is definitely not what we might call performance philosophy. Further, this tradition is not one of any specialism, but of the use of our shared intelligence, including our moral intelligence, in a general way. It is not just the philosophy of science or of mathematics or of any other department that makes a contribution to the subject of philosophy. It is not obscured or constrained by formalisms, or by science, whatever good use it makes of them.

It is not necessary to my judgment of Ayer's greatness, as you may anticipate, that Ayer's philosophy is now paid as much attention as, say, that of Willard Van Orman Quine. To be cited today but not tomorrow is a common fate of philosophers, scientists, novelists, and others. There is the fact of fashion in philosophy, and of oversight corrected later. It needs to be remembered that Hume was passed over for the chairs of philosophy at Edinburgh and Glasgow, and that little was heard thereafter of Mr. Cleghorn and Mr. Clow, deemed to be his superiors.

TED HONDERICH

BAKUNIN, MIKHAIL ALEKSANDROVICH (1814– 1876), European revolutionary socialist and collectivist anarcho-federalist. Mikhail Bakunin, sometimes called the "father of Russian anarchism," was born to a Russian noble family in Tver Province. After two international revolutionary careers of the highest and still-continuing significance, he died in Berne, Switzerland, where he is buried. Bakunin's ATHEISM was most clearly expressed in two pamphlets published during his lifetime: *Federalism, Socialism, and Anti-Theologism* (1867) and *The Political Theology of Mazzini and the International* (1871), and also the posthumous *The Paris Commune and the Idea of the State* (1878) and *God and the State* (1882). He called his atheism "antitheologism" in riposte to Giuseppe Mazzini's program for Italy's national unification. Mazzini advocated an overtly religious concept of the state in the form of a bourgeois republic, a theocracy supposedly democratized by the people's spiritual unity, itself in turn reified as a unitary mass consciousness. Mazzini's ideas were thus anathema not only to Bakunin's antistatism, but also to his anthropocentric moral philosophy.

Bakunin's Road to Atheism. The first translator of both J. G. FICHTE and G. W. F. Hegel into Russian, Bakunin journeyed to Berlin to study philosophy in 1840. Two years later he caused his first sensation in Europe with the pseudonymous article "The Reaction in Germany." There he declared the negative rather than the positive to be the motive force in dialectical change, and drew the conclusion that revolutionaries should never compromise in the pursuit of social change. An advocate of Polish nationalism and then of Pan-Slav federalism in the 1840s, he participated in the 1848 February Revolution in Paris, then also in the insurrections in Prague (June 1848) and Dresden (May 1849). His arrest in the aftermath of the last ended the first of his revolutionary careers in Europe.

Bakunin's second revolutionary career in Europe began in 1862, following a dozen years of imprisonment and Siberian exile, from which he escaped and sensationally circumnavigated the globe. Landing in London in late 1861, he sought to continue where he had left off after his arrest in 1849. His atheism came to the fore with his transition from Pan-Slav federalism to international anarchism (see ANARCHISM AND UNBELIEF) following the czar's bloody suppression of the 1863 Polish rebellion. Reflecting that broadened scope, Bakunin moved in 1864 to Italy, where the confrontation with Mazzini sharpened his ideas on atheism.

Bakunin as Moral Philosopher. The significance of Bakunin's moral philosophy is only now being recognized. Its cornerstones were freedom and the individual's interdependence with society; from them, it followed that any individual's freedom required every individual's freedom. Influenced by Ludwig FEUERBACH, Bakunin saw human history as a progression from animality to humanity. Man's capacity for abstraction marked the distinction between animal and human and was the key feature of human existence. Unfortunately, it also made possible the creation of such institutions as state and church. Bakunin's writings mercilessly contrasted religious pieties with the actual effects of religious institutions upon people's real lives.

Bakunin's atheism included a refutation of theism by reductio ad absurdum turning upon the theodicy problem (see EVIL, PROBLEM OF). More significantly, it was a corollary of his uncompromising opposition to hierarchical authority of any kind. Wherever any external source of law, whether human or divine, sought to impose itself on human society, Bakunin saw society's resistance as merely a manifestation of its own inherent natural laws. Theologism, that is, a theological doctrine institutionalized through social structures characterized by privilege and oppression, was contrary to natural law. From this followed Bakunin's "antitheologism," perhaps best encapsulated in two of his best-known aphorisms: "If God really existed, it would be necessary to abolish him" and "The State is the younger brother of the Church."

BIBLIOGRAPHY

Bakunin, Michael. *God and the State*. New York: Dover, 1970.

Cutler, Robert M., trans. and ed. *The Basic Bakunin: Writings, 1869–1871*. Amherst, NY: Prometheus Books, 1992.

Dolgoff, Sam, ed. *Bakunin on Anarchism*, 2nd ed. Montreal: Black Rose Books, 1980.

Lehning, Arthur, ed. *Michael Bakunin: Selected Writings*. New York: Random House, 1974.

McLaughlin, Paul. *Mikhail Bakunin: The Philosophical Basis of His Anarchism.* New York: Algora, 2002.

Morris, Brian. *Bakunin: The Philosophy of Freedom.* Montreal: Black Rose Books, 1993.

Ravindranathan, T. R. *Bakunin and the Italians*. Kingston and Montreal: McGill-Queen's University Press, 1988.

ROBERT M. CUTLER

BALLANCE, JOHN (1839–1893), New Zealand politician, newspaper owner and editor, prominent freethinker. John Ballance's father's political activities in Ireland gave him an early introduction to political life. His religious views were shaped by the experience of sectarian rioting in Belfast together with his mother's nonconformity. These, in conjunction with his belief in the importance of education and critical thought, led Ballance to an advocacy of secularism.

Ballance was born on March 27, 1839, at Glenavy, County Antrim, Northern Ireland, the eldest son of Samuel Ballance, a tenant farmer descended from Puritan immigrants from England, and his wife, Mary, a Quaker. Ballance was educated at Glenavy National School and at Wilson's Academy, Belfast. He left school before completing his education and from the age of fourteen was apprenticed to a Belfast ironmonger for four years. He then went to work in the ironmongery business in Birmingham, then a center of radicalism and the home of self-education. He attended classes at the Birmingham and Midland Institute, studying politics and history. There he was exposed to the ideas of Robert OWEN and the secularist movement. He also belonged to literary and debating societies and wrote articles for the press.

Ballance married Fanny Taylor in 1863 and migrated to New Zealand in 1866, settling in Wanganui, where his brother-in-law lived. Fanny died in 1868; two years later Ballance married Ellen Anderson.

In 1867 Ballance and Archibald Dudingston Willis established the *Wanganui Herald*. Early editorials in the *Herald* criticized the church, especially over unscrupulous land deals, and warned of the "evils of ecclesiasticism" in the colony. The establishment of the Wanganui Freethought Association by Balance and Willis in 1883 was a major development for the secularist cause. That same year the monthly *Freethought Review* was started, with Willis as publisher and Ballance as editor. It continued for two years until October 1885 and for a time was the only local freethought paper in New Zealand. In March 1884 a national conference of seven secular societies in Dunedin established the New Zealand Freethought Federal Union with Ballance's friend Sir Robert STOUT as president and Ballance himself as vice president. Resolutions were passed supporting the Oaths Abolition Bill, Charles BRADLAUGH's struggle in Britain, and opposing the legislation on BLASPHEMY. Although the union never met again, it assisted with the itineraries of visiting speakers for some time.

When Ballance entered politics his secularist views were not used against him by opponents. Occasionally an outburst of letter writing called for defeat of the "infidel." He took this in his stride and remarked that religion and politics should be kept separate. In 1875 Ballance was elected to the House of Representatives. In 1878 he was appointed commissioner of customs, minister of education, and colonial treasurer. He was involved in debates about land nationalization and the land tax.

After regaining his seat which he had lost in 1881, between 1884 and 1887 Ballance joined the administration led by fellow freethinker Robert Stout, holding the portfolios of Lands, Native Affairs, and Defense. One of his important achievements was the creation of a sixty-six-thousand-acre national park in the central North Island, which involved a gift of land by local Maori.

In parliamentary opposition between 1887 and 1890, Ballance proved to be an outstanding leader. During this time he adapted the work of English social theorists to

New Zealand's problems and concentrated on building a base among the urban working class. Ballance led the Liberals to victory in the December 1890 election. In January 1891 he formed the country's first Liberal government, becoming premier, colonial treasurer, and commissioner of customs.

The new administration moved quickly to introduce direct taxation and other tax reform. His government introduced legislation for which New Zealand would become famous: a new Factory Act, an Employers' Liability Act, and other acts to improve working conditions. It ran into opposition in the Legislative Council, New Zealand's upper house, which rejected a number of important measures, including the Industrial Conciliation and Arbitration Bill introduced by Ballance's friend and fellow secularist William Pember Reeves, who was the country's first minister of labor. To overcome the Legislative Council, which had been "stacked" with appointments by the outgoing government, Ballance asked the governor to make new appointments. When this was refused he appealed to the secretary of state for the colonies, who ruled in his favor, thus ensuring that the legislation was eventually passed.

Like his wife Ellen, who was a prominent feminist, Ballance strongly supported the female franchise and introduced a bill to this effect in 1892. However he did not live to see it implemented, becoming increasingly ill during 1892. He died on April 27, 1893, the first premier to die in office. He was succeeded as the member for Wanganui by his friend and fellow freethinker A. D. Willis. In 1991 Ballance House, the restored family home in Northern Ireland, was opened to the public to commemorate this famous man.

BIBLIOGRAPHY

Dakin, Jim. "New Zealand's Freethought Heritage Chapter 5: Early Freethought in Wellington and Other Centres." *N.Z. Rationalist and Humanist* 74, no. 4 (2001).
McIvor, Timothy. *The Rainmaker.* Auckland: Heinemann Reed, 1989.
Ross, Angus. "Balance, John (1839–93)." *An Encyclopedia of New Zealand.* Vol. 1. Wellington: R. E. Owen, Government Printer, 1966.
Scholefield, G. H. *Notable New Zealand Statesmen.* Auckland: Whitcombe & Tombs, 1946.
Springer, Randal. "Willis, Archibald Dudingston 1842–1908." *Dictionary of New Zealand Biography.* Vol. 2. Wellington: Bridget Williams Books with the Department of Internal Affairs, 1993.

WAYNE FACER

BALLOU, HOSEA (1771–1852), American Universalist leader. Hosea Ballou persuaded most Universalists of the truth of Unitarian theology, the doctrine that God is one.

Ballou's Unitarianism was readily accepted by most Universalists, who held that all men are saved (see UNITARIAN UNIVERSALISM). He was the last of eleven children born to a Calvinist Baptist preacher and farmer living in Richmond, New Hampshire. While he was a baby, his mother, Lydia Harris Ballou, died. After being tutored by his father, he briefly attended a Quaker school and Chesterfield Academy. Rejecting eternal damnation, he became an itinerant preacher in 1791. He married Ruth Washburn on September 5, 1795, and they had eight children. After early settlements he spent thirty-five years in Boston and died a respected Universalist leader.

Ten years before the 1805 Unitarian Controversy over the election of the supernatural rationalist Henry Ware to a divinity chair at the Congregationalist Harvard, Ballou opposed the doctrine of the Trinity. By then, he had convinced most Universalists of theological Unitarianism. That year Ballou published *A Treatise on Atonement*, his theory of universal salvation and Unitarian theology. Christ's mission, he held, was to reconcile humanity to God, not God to humanity. The Vermont deist (see DEISM) Ethan ALLEN's denial of infinite sin, Ferdinand Petitpierre's DETERMINISM, and Arminian Charles Chauncy's argument against eternal punishment influenced the book. There were two significant changes in Ballou's ideas between the 1805 edition of *A Treatise on Atonement* and that of 1832. His early Christology was Arian, but by 1832 he believed Jesus an ordinary human who had been assigned a divine task. While at first undecided about corrective punishment after death, by the second edition he definitely rejected it for punishment in this life, anticipating Ralph Waldo EMERSON's idea of "compensation."

In 1819 Ballou became editor of the *Universalist* magazine. As he did not believe in the Trinity, the magazine reflected his interest in Unitarian ideas. He published an account of Servetus's martyrdom in Calvinist Geneva, selections from Charles Chauncey's *Salvation of All Men* and Joseph PRIESTLEY. Priestley was an English Unitarian and a friend of Thomas Jefferson. Ballou also reprinted writings of Priestley associate Thomas Belsham and portions of William Ellery Channing's Baltimore sermon "Unitarian Christianity." The *Universalist* magazine introduced upper-middle-class and upper-class Unitarianism to a wider audience of ordinary people. As an editor Ballou avoided controversy, except in religion. He opposed the Standing Order, the tax-supported Congregational churches. Although he did not address most social questions, believing that only the triumph of Universalism would transform the world, he favored temperance and in old age he opposed capital punishment and slavery.

BIBLIOGRAPHY

Ballou, Hosea. *A Treatise on Atonement.* Boston: Skinner House, 1986.

Cassara, Ernest. *Hosea Ballou: Challenge to Orthodoxy.* Boston: Beacon, 1961.

Miller, Russell E. *The Larger Hope: The First Century of the Universalist Church in America, 1770–1870.* Boston: Unitarian Universalist Association, 1979.

Robinson, David. *The Unitarians and the Universalists.* Westport, CT: Greenwood, 1985.

WESLEY V. HROMATKO

BARLOW, JOEL (1754–1812), American poet and diplomat. Born March 24, 1754, in Redding, Connecticut, Joel Barlow likely wanted most to be remembered as a poet, especially as the author of *The Columbiad*, a long epic he worked on for years and envisioned as the great American poem. *The Columbiad* got mixed reviews then and has not since become the basis for literary fame. An earlier version, *Vision of Columbus*, produced more acclaim when published in 1787. Barlow, a member of a group calling itself the Connecticut Wits, served as an American chaplain at the end of the Revolutionary War after graduating from Yale in 1778. He is best known now for "The Hasty Pudding," a short satirical mock epic poem that may have inspired Harvard University's famous club of the same name, and as the author and negotiator of a treaty with Tripoli (1796–97) that declared the US government was "not in any sense founded on the Christian Religion" (see TREATY OF TRIPOLI).

Barlow also wrote radical political philosophy, publishing "Advice to the Privileged Orders" (1792) in London, which the British government proscribed, and later publishing political essays in France. Thomas PAINE entrusted his draft of the first part of *The Age of Reason* to his friend Barlow just as the guards of the French Revolution hauled Paine off to prison in 1793, and Barlow assisted later with getting *Age of Reason* published. Barlow also corresponded with Thomas JEFFERSON.

Barlow died in Poland while on a diplomatic mission from the United States to Napoleon. As he drew near Napoleon, the French army was in retreat from the Russians, and Barlow died of pneumonia amid the exodus. His tombstone inscription in Poland roughly translates as "Joel Barlow, diplomat from the United States of America to the Emperor of France and the Queen of Italy; died here while traveling." He was fifty-eight.

BIBLIOGRAPHY

Barlow, Joel. "Preface and Postscript to *The Columbiad*." In *The Annals of America, Volume 4, 1797–1820: Domestic Expansion and Foreign Entanglements.* Chicago: Encyclopedia Britannica, 1968.

Boston, Rob. "A Tangled Tale of Pirates, a Poet and the True Meaning of the First Amendment." *Church & State* 50, no. 6 (1997).

Woodress, James. *A Yankee's Odyssey: The Life of Joel Barlow.* Philadelphia: Lippincott, 1958.

ED BUCKNER

BAUER, BRUNO (1809–1882), theologian and gospel critic. Having studied with both G. W. F. Hegel and Friedrich Schleiermacher, Bruno Bauer was a pioneer of biblical criticism. For all its incisiveness (and indeed no doubt because of it), his work has been largely forgotten, at least in Christian-dominated Western circles. Bauer's scholarly legacy was, however, championed in the East thanks to his protégé Karl MARX. Bauer's theories became enshrined as the official Soviet ideology on the "historical" Jesus. Even today, Bauer's thick, erudite works on the New Testament (which got him discharged from his teaching post in 1842) are frustratingly, even glacially slow to appear in English translation, largely because few wish to hear what he had to say. Albert Schweitzer's friendly reviews of his books in *The Quest of the Historical Jesus: From Reimarus to Wrede* and *Paul and His Interpreters* seem to have inoculated Christian scholarship against wanting to hear more from Bauer, much less allowing the virulent germs of his ideas to spread among vulnerable theology students.

Bauer took up and significantly carried forward the work of two slightly earlier contemporaries, David Friedrich STRAUSS and Ferdinand Christian Baur, both of whom are usually denominated as radical critics. But in Bauer's estimation, each man, while courageously blazing a trail, lacked either the vision or the courage to pursue it to its end. This Bauer was determined to do with his eyes wide open. In his *Kritik der evangelischen Geschichte des Johannes* (1840) Bauer sided with Strauss, demonstrating the purely literary, theological, and unhistorical character of the Gospel of John. Soon, in his *Kritik der evangelischen Geschichte der Synoptiker* (three volumes, 1841–42), Bauer had realized that the earliest gospel, Mark, was no less likely to be a piece of edifying fiction. Like almost all modern scholars, Bauer recognized the dependence of both Matthew and Luke upon Mark (though he saw Luke as a rewrite of Mark, then Matthew as a rewrite of both Mark and Luke). In all this, Bauer made critical advances from which almost all scholars at the time and since have recoiled in loathing. Only today, busy reinventing the wheel, are some researchers coming independently to recapitulate his results, though very few even of these seem to understand the broader implications of the individual insights. Given that, on the one hand, Mark would seem to have been the sole source of "information" about Jesus, even for the ancients, and, on the other, that Mark appears to be fictitious, we must seriously question whether the very figure of Jesus is fictive. Bauer concluded that he was.

Bauer anticipated the whole trend of form criticism by recognizing how saying after saying of the gospel material reflected the life context of the Christian community, not that of Jesus and his contemporaries. One major instance would be the constant summonses to be ready for persecution, a retrojection of the ill fortunes of the church in subsequent generations. The missionary instructions preceding the sending out of the disciples (Mark 6:7–13; Matt. 10:5–42; Luke 9:1–6) likewise anticipate future church history while conspicuously lacking any specific instructions appropriate to the mission the disciples are ostensibly on the point of undertaking. The supposed sermons of Jesus are instead mere collections of unrelated maxims and parables (not that these cannot have gone back to a historical Jesus, but their atomistic character reveals the fictitious native of the picture of a preaching or discoursing Jesus).

Bauer's insights on the Messiah doctrine were among his most radical. First, he noticed that the first version of the Jesus story, Mark's, did not imagine Jesus coming forward proclaiming himself as the Messiah; indeed, just the opposite, since the Caesarea Philippi scene (Mark 8:27–30) reveals that no one, even among his many followers, held such an idea concerning him—something scarcely possible if he had been teaching that very thing! Subsequent evangelists obscure this Markan theme, reading their own faith even more directly into the story, by having Jesus preach his messiahship from the first.

Beyond this, Bauer suggested that the very notion of "the Messiah" was a Christian invention later adopted by Jews. As the subsequent studies of Sigmund Mowinkel, Helmer Ringgren, and others have made even clearer, Old Testament passages cited by Christians as "messianic prophecies" not only have no discernible connection with Jesus, but do not even transcend reference to the ancient Jewish monarchy (and its anticipated restoration). Intertestamental Jewish writings predict a millennial age of redemption, but the Messiah is conspicuous by his absence—or else appears to owe his position to later Christian interpolators (e.g., Similitudes of Enoch, 4 Ezra).

Christianity began in Alexandria, as Bauer envisioned it, among the mystical ascetic Jews whom Philo calls the Theraputae. Philo's own doctrine of the Logos (the divine Word, a piece of Stoicism read into the Bible) provided the mytho-theological undergirding for the Christ concept. The moral content came from Hellenistic Roman sources, especially from Seneca. In *Christ and the Caesars* (1877), Bauer described how Seneca advised that the person who sought moral maturity ought to choose for himself an ideal guide and companion to accompany him, in imagination, each day and every hour. One ought to envision such a person's reactions to one's contemplated actions and thus one might keep to the straight and narrow. This suggestion, Bauer decided, must have been what catalyzed Mark's decision to concretize the collective experience of the Christian community into a literary character, Jesus Christ, who thus turns out to be equivalent to John Bunyan's protagonist Pilgrim. (Again, Johannes Weiss and, after him, Rudolf Karl Bultmann and the form critics, vindicated in ample detail Bauer's contention that saying after saying, story after story, represented not the *Sitz-im-Leben Jesu*, or "life setting of Jesus," but rather the *Sitz-im-Leben Kirche*, the "life setting of the church.")

The melding of Jews and (mainly underclass) Romans to produce Christianity was not entirely smooth. The Greek side issued in law-free Gnosticism, which chafed at Christian Jews' insistence that Christians must keep the Torah. As Bauer argued in his *Kritik der Paulinischen Briefe* (three parts, 1850–52), the Acts of the Apostles was produced by the Jewish side, appealing to Paul (a dubiously historical champion) in behalf of legalism, while the Epistles were the response of Greek Christians of an antinomian, Gnostic bent. The historical Paul, if there was one, had nothing to do with any of them. This Bauer (and his successors among the so-called Dutch Radical School, especially W. C. van Manen) showed by applying the same critical criteria that had led F. C. Baur to deny Paul all but the *Hauptbriefe*, the "principal epistles": Romans, Galatians, 1 and 2 Corinthians. Baur repudiated Bauer, and by the time of Bultmann, supposedly critical scholars had backslid to consider Philippians, 1 Thessalonians, and Philemon authentically Pauline also. Today, the theories of Bauer and the Dutch Radicals are advanced by a tiny group including Hermann Detering, Darrell Doughty, and the present writer.

BIBLIOGRAPHY

Bauer, Bruno. *Christ and the Caesars: The Origin of Christianity from Romanized Greek Culture.* Translated by Frank E. Schacht. Charleston, SC: Alexander Davidonis, 1998.

———. *An English Edition of Bruno Bauer's 1843 Christianity Exposed: A Recollection of the Eighteenth Century and a Contribution to the Crisis of the Nineteenth Century.* Edited by Paul Trejo. Translated by Esther Ziegler and Jutta Hamm. Lewiston, NY/Queenston, ON: Edwin Mellen Press, 2002.

———. *Kritik der Apostelgeschichte.* 1850.

———. *Kritik der Evangelien.* Berlin, 1850–51.

———. *Kritik der evangelische Geschichte des Johannes.* Bremen, 1840.

———. *Kritik der evangelischen Geschichte der Synoptiker.* Leipzig, 1841–42.

———. *Kritik der Paulinischen Briefe.* Berlin, 1850–52.

———. *Philo, Strauss, Renan und das Urchristentum.* Berlin, 1874.

ROBERT M. PRICE

BAUM, L. FRANK (1856–1919), American author. L. Frank Baum, author of the Oz books (1900–1920) and other fantasies for children, pointedly omitted religion from the marvelous worlds he created. Oz is a utopia where people are naturally inclined to help and respect each other because they are happy. Laws are minimal and reasonable, and law enforcement is no problem because people have no motive to disobey. When confronted with difficulties, the characters draw on their own enterprise, ingenuity, and common sense to solve them. There is no mention of divine sanctions, because none are needed.

Born in upstate New York, Baum grew up in a pious Methodist household in which his mother strictly enforced observance of the Sabbath. But by his midthirties, when he was editing a South Dakota newspaper, the *Aberdeen Saturday Pioneer*, Baum was a committed unbeliever. He was probably influenced by his mother-in-law, the eminent suffragist Matilda Joslyn GAGE, who maintained that the established churches were "the bulwark of woman's slavery" (see also WOMAN SUFFRAGE MOVEMENT AND UNBELIEF). In the very first issue of the *Pioneer*, Baum celebrated "the age of Unfaith." *Unfaith* did not mean ATHEISM but THEOSOPHY, a theistic system that satisfied the intellectual and emotional needs of people like Baum and Gage, who could not accept orthodox religion and blind faith, but also needed to believe in something beyond the material world. Theosophists aimed to investigate the spiritual world (see SPIRITUALISM AND UNBELIEF) exactly as scientists investigate the physical world, and they believed that people should look for strength within themselves rather than praying to God for help. Nine months after his first editorial, Baum proceeded to an open attack on conventional religion. "Fully two thirds" of the American people are unchurched, he declared. And this percentage will become greater because "[t]he people are beginning to think," therefore they will reject "the same old superstitions, the same blind faith in the traditional bible, the same precepts of salvation and damnation" that the church persists in teaching.

Baum indirectly mocked orthodox piety in two non-Oz fantasies, where he allegorically satirized the orthodox concept of heaven. Among the marine creatures introduced in *The Sea Fairies* (1911) are mackerel who eagerly take the bait and the hook because they are convinced that when one of them is jerked out of the water and disappears "he has gone to glory—which means to them some unknown, but beautiful sea."

Baum's most detailed satire on the orthodox concept of heaven appears, remarkably, in *Policeman Bluejay* (1907), a book for small children. The story is set in a forest where owls kill to eat and human hunters slaughter animals for fun. In its center is the Land of Paradise, appropriately populated entirely by birds of paradise, which is blissfully free of the need, conflict, and suffering that dominate life on the outside. Bathed in rosy light and filled with flowers and fruits that constantly regrow, this land is indeed a paradise in its sharp contrast to the stressful life of the forest. It represents the biblical Garden of Eden—humankind once lived there, "but for some unknown crime was driven away"—and perhaps heaven as well. The King Bird of Paradise, who exists solely to be perfect and to be admired

by his beautiful and sinless subjects, does bring to mind God surrounded by the heavenly hosts who sing hosannas all day long. In either case, it is far from the ideal place of orthodox Christian doctrine. Baum's unfallen creatures are vacuous and complacent, doing no evil because they have no temptation. This is very different from the Theosophist heaven, where souls actively strive for improvement of themselves and the world. It also contrasts strongly with the rich variety of Oz, where conflicts arise between diverse individuals and characters must make an effort to be good and achieve success.

Baum should not, perhaps, be described as a secular humanist, for he believed in the reality of things unseen and in universal moral as well as physical laws. But he rejected the idea of a divine lawgiver imposing laws on nature. And in Oz he created an ideal world that works very well using only human wisdom, human effort, and human goodwill.

BIBLIOGRAPHY

Baum, L. Frank. *The Twinkle Tales* (includes *Policeman Bluejay*). Lincoln: University of Nebraska Press, 2005.
Rogers, Katharine M. *L. Frank Baum, Creator of Oz*. New York: St. Martin's, 2002.

KATHARINE M. ROGERS

BAYLE, PIERRE (1647–1706), French Protestant writer. Freethinker, journalist, the most important skeptic of the late seventeenth century, and a promoter of toleration, Pierre Bayle's influence on the development of unbelief was enormous. It is by no means clear, however, that Bayle himself espoused unbelief.

Early Life. The son and brother of Protestant pastors, Bayle grew up in Le Carla, a small village in southwestern France. He entered adulthood as the anti-Protestant legislation of the regime of Louis XIV gained momentum. He studied briefly at the Protestant Academy in Puylaurens (1668), but without telling his family, he transferred to the Jesuit College in Toulouse, where, on March 19, 1669, he converted to Roman Catholicism, which, for a brief period, he came to believe was the true church. Shortly after defending his MA in August 1670, however, he returned to the Protestant faith, which made him liable to the severe penalties meted out to lapsed Catholics under French law. He fled France for Geneva, completed his theological and philosophical studies there, and in 1674 returned to France under an assumed name, working as a private tutor in Rouen and Paris, and from 1675 as professor of philosophy at the Protestant Academy in Sedan, until it was closed down by royal decree in July 1681. Bayle then moved to Rotterdam, where he was professor of history and philosophy at the *École Illustre*; but this post was abolished on October 30, 1693. At that point, Reinier Leers, Bayle's friend and publisher, paid him a small annuity, which made it possible for him to devote his life to scholarship. However, Bayle's pursuit of what he believed was the truth, whether in history, philosophy, or theology, brought him into conflict with the orthodoxies of his time and with those who defended them. In 1697 the authorities of the Walloon (French Protestant) Church in Rotterdam formally censured Bayle for what they described as the scandalous and reprehensible way he had written about ATHEISM, the Bible, the problem of evil (see EVIL, PROBLEM OF), and SKEPTICISM in the two volumes (later four) of the first edition of his biographical *Dictionnaire historique et critique* (Historical and critical dictionary; first ed., 1697; second ed., 1702).

Atheism. In his writings, and especially in the *Dictionnaire*, Bayle drew sympathetic portraits of atheists, the prototype being Baruch SPINOZA, to whom Bayle devoted the longest of his biographical entries. In the early modern period, atheism was presumed to lead to immorality and social disorder because atheists had no fear of God or divine retribution, attitudes believed necessary to morality and the maintenance of civil society. As early as 1682, in his writing about the comet, Bayle advanced what was a notorious paradox for its time, namely, that atheists could live together morally and peaceably in society, while people of religious principle often lived immorally and could be a menace to social order. His argument was based on the assertion that human beings are motivated less by principles or belief than by their dominant passions, temperament, self-love, self-interest, or education. However, Bayle also believed that the first principles of morals are available to human reason independently of knowledge of God and that people could behave morally out of a love of virtue for its own sake. This opens up at least the possibility that atheists may embody an irreproachable and genuine morality that is consistent with rational ethical principles.

The Bible. The authorities of the Walloon Church also took issue with Bayle for the negative way he presented important figures from the Old Testament in the *Dictionnaire*. In the triptych Bayle devoted to Abraham, Sarah, and Hagar, or in the longer and polemical article on David, he dwelled at length on their immoral behavior, pointing to the lies, sexual aberrations, cruelties, and political chicanery of these figureheads of the Jewish and Christian traditions. Commenting on the life of David, Bayle famously observed, "He is a Son of Holiness in the Church . . . but that Sun had its Spots," which he proceeded to enumerate and censure. VOLTAIRE harnessed Bayle's biblical articles to his own jocose irreverence in his *Dictionnaire philosophique* (Philosophical dictionary), making it difficult for them to be read as anything but an ironic onslaught on religious belief. Yet Bayle's position is more complex. He believed that all conduct, whether that of atheists or believers, is to be judged in the light of the ethical principles available to reason. The result is certainly iconoclastic but it is not inconsistent with a broadly defined Calvinist tradition of

biblical interpretation on which Bayle explicitly draws. He also has a political motivation. By making scripture subject to ethical scrutiny, and arguing that any interpretation that involved committing a crime was false, Bayle was seeking to undermine the way Saint Augustine (and those who followed him) interpreted scripture to justify coercing the consciences of those deemed heretical or heterodox. However, Bayle's insistence on the criteria of reason and ethics in biblical exegesis provided him with his greatest—and, to his contemporaries, most scandalous—conundrum.

The Problem of Evil. Bayle states the problem in the *Dictionnaire*: "the manner of introducing evil under the empire of a sovereign being, infinitely good, infinitely holy, and infinitely powerful is not only inexplicable but also incomprehensible." And he did not flinch from demonstrating just how inexplicable it is. For example, putting words into the mouth of an *abbé philosophe*, he applies the criteria of reason and ethics to the problem and, by ironic implication, finds God wanting: "It is evident that evil ought to be prevented, if it be possible, and that it is a sinful thing to permit it when it can be prevented. Nevertheless, our Theology shews us that this is false. It teaches us that God does nothing but what becomes his perfections, when he permits all the disorders that are in the world, and which might easily have been prevented." Bayle pointed to the miseries, misfortunes, and catastrophes of human beings and the world they inhabit, arguing that dualism—the view that if God is good, then evil originates from a rival force at war with God—was more consistent with the evidence than theism. And he was adamant that no theodicy (philosophical effort to reconcile God's goodness with the existence of evil in the world) could resolve the dilemma of the undeniable existence of natural, personal, and systemic evil in a world that believers held was created and sustained by a good and all-powerful God. REASON and faith, philosophy and theology, are irreconcilable on this issue.

Skepticism and Fideism. Bayle's radical critique of theodicy is part of a series of articles in the *Dictionnaire* in which he revived skeptical themes in an attempt to undermine the dogmatic claims of all metaphysical systems. Among these Cartesianism was a favorite target, with its criterion of self-evidence, clear and distinct ideas, mind-body dualism, distinction of primary and secondary qualities, and mathematical explanation of space (see DESCARTES, RENÉ). But Bayle also precipitated a skeptical crisis in Christian dogmatics by the way he applied self-evident principles to certain doctrines, notably those of the Trinity, the immortality of the soul, and transubstantiation, only to find them wanting. Bayle consistently argued, however, that his skeptical critique of rational and religious certitudes had a preparatory function. He claimed that his purpose was to liberate readers from all forms of dogmatism and lead them to faith. The fact that such faith is sometimes at odds with what we know to be true or right (as in the case of the problem of evil) or has no rationally demonstrable content has led many critics to interpret Bayle's fideism as an ironic, self-protective device. Skeptical doubt and religious belief are not mutually exclusive in Bayle's worldview, however. Throughout his writings he argues for the possibility of true knowledge and a degree of certainty, provided they are held as probable and provisional, open-ended and always subject to revision. This attitude is inspired by the skeptical Christian HUMANISM of the Renaissance, which Bayle admired, with its ideal of moral, moderate, and tolerant religious belief and practice.

The Baylean Footnote. Bayle's *Dictionaire*—a massive four volumes in folio in its final form—is a monument of learning, which became an unlikely best-seller in the eighteenth century. The text of each biographical entry has three levels: a narrative at the top of the page; two columns of footnotes in smaller print underneath, linked into the narrative by the capital letters of the alphabet; and down the left- and right-hand margins, citations of sources in tiny print, attached to the narrative by the lowercase letters of the alphabet and to the footnotes by numbers. The footnotes provide a running commentary on the narrative, and are laden with mind-numbing erudition, which Bayle sought to enliven with philosophical and theological conundra, ironic commentaries on the vagaries of human life, and salacious anecdotes. According to a tenacious myth among readers of the *Dictionaire*, Bayle put his most scandalous, heterodox, and irreverent comments in the footnotes in order to hide them from censorship. Recent research has shown, however, that both the narrative and the footnotes are animated by the same personal, ironic, and philosophical tone. Besides, Bayle's critics and censors "were also habitués of works of erudition, expert explorers of scholarly apparatus. No nook or cranny in a suspect commentary could escape their attention," to quote Anthony Grafton. In fact, the organization of the articles in the *Dictionnaire* reflects Bayle's understanding of knowledge as an essentially dialogic, even polyphonic, engagement with a multiplicity of unmerged voices and consciousnesses in the quest for truth. He constructed his *Dictionnaire* as a virtual library in the early modern manner, that is, a place of encounter and discussion, where the books cited in the margins were opened and read into the articles as a prelude to scholarly disputation and interaction. His own models for this open-ended, always unfinished quest were humanist, but his *Dictionnaire* helped to shape the discursive and collaborative models of knowing that characterize the Enlightenment.

Bayle and Unbelief. Many of Bayle's readers, then and now, think of him as an unbeliever attempting to undermine faith by making it seem irrational and ridiculous. Others argue that he was a "speculative atheist," who rejected all proofs and demonstrations of God, and therefore, by logical implication, God's existence. However, Bayle's critique of human knowing and pretensions to rational, dogmatic certitude, whether philosophical or religious, is compatible with his Calvinist conviction that God is rationally inscrutable and ultimately incomprehensible. It is also part of Bayle's lifelong attempt to subvert certainty—wherever he met with it—in order to counter its violence and undermine the way it was used to justify the persecuting society. He was adamant that tolerance—of people of all beliefs or of none—is the basis of both civil society and social stability. In sum, Bayle was a person given to paradoxes, whose life, thought, and influence make him both freethinker and Protestant.

BIBLIOGRAPHY

Grafton, Anthony. *The Footnote*. London: Faber & Faber, 1997.

Kors, Alan C. "Atheism." In *Encyclopedia of the Enlightenment*, edited by A. C. Kors et al. New York: Oxford University Press, 2003.

Labrousse, Élisabeth. *Bayle*. New York: Oxford University Press, 1983.

———. *Pierre Bayle*, 2nd ed. 2 vols. La Haye: M. Nijhoff, 1985, 1996.

Mason, Haydn T. *Pierre Bayle and Voltaire*. Oxford: Oxford University Press, 1963.

Mori, Gianluca. *Bayle philosophe*. Paris: Champion, 1999.

Paganini, Gianni. "Fidéisme ou 'modica theologia'? Pierre Bayle et les avatars de la tradition érasmienne." In *Critique, savoir et érudition à la veille des Lumières. Le Dictionnaire historique et critique de Pierre Bayle (1647–1706)*, edited by H. Bots. Amsterdam and Maarssen: APA–Holland University Press, 1998.

———. "Skepticism." In *Encyclopedia of the Enlightenment*, edited by A. C. Kors et al. New York: Oxford University Press, 1998.

Rétat, Pierre, "La remarque baylienne." In *Critique, savoir et érudition à la veille des Lumières. Le Dictionnaire historique et critique de Pierre Bayle (1647–1706)*, edited by H. Bots. Amsterdam and Maarssen: APA–Holland University Press, 1998.

Rex, Walter E. *Essays on Pierre Bayle and Religious Controversy*. The Hague: M. Nijhoff, 1965.

Whelan, Ruth. *The Anatomy of Superstition, a Study of the Historical Theory and Practice of Pierre Bayle*. Oxford: Voltaire Foundaton, 1989.

———. "Bayle, Pierre." In *Encyclopedia of the Enlightenment*, edited by A. C. Kors et al. New York: Oxford University Press, 1998.

———. "The Wisdom of Simonides: Bayle and La Mothe Le Vayer." In *Scepticism and Irreligion in the Seventeenth Century*, edited by R. H. Popkin and A. Vanderjagt. Leiden: Brill, 1993.

RUTH WHELAN

BEAUVOIR, SIMONE DE (1908–1986), French feminist philosopher and author. Born into a bourgeois Parisian family at the beginning of the twentieth century, Simone de Beauvoir would not have been encouraged to pursue a career were it not for the relative impoverishment of her family. She was educated at a Catholic girls' school and was tempted by mysticism until the age of fourteen, when she lost her faith. Having studied philosophy at the Sorbonne, she passed the *aggregation* in philosophy in 1929, coming second to Jean-Paul SARTRE, who had become her lover. During the 1930s she taught philosophy at lycées in Marseille, Rouen, and Paris, and it was not until 1943 that she published her first novel *She Came to Stay* (*L'Invitée*). After the war she helped set up the journal *Modern Times* (*Les Temps Modernes*) with Sartre, Maurice Merleau-Ponty, and Albert CAMUS. In an article in this journal titled "Littérature et Métaphysique," she explained her desire to write philosophical novels in which the abstract truths of a philosophy would be clothed in concrete detail so that they expressed a living, emotional truth. She did not consider herself to be an original philosopher, since she reserved the term *philosopher* for those like Sartre and Martin Heidegger, who had developed an all-encompassing abstract system. Nevertheless, as well as publishing five novels, a play, short stories, and four volumes of memoirs during her lifetime, she also published a number of philosophical essays. Of these, *The Second Sex* (*Le deuxième sexe*), her account of the situation of women examined from the point of view of an existentialist ethic, has been by far the most influential.

In *The Second Sex* Beauvoir set out to answer the question: How it is that women, though free conscious beings like men, came to be dominated by men so that all culture, history, and religion seemed to have been created by them? She criticized all deterministic accounts of women's inferior social situation, arguing that neither biology, nor psychoanalysis, nor Marxist materialism sufficed to explain women's acceptance of a position of social secondariness. In place of these explanations, and supplementing them, she drew on G. W. F. Hegel's claim that there is a fundamental conflict between consciousnesses. A quote from Hegel, "[E]very consciousness seeks the death of every other consciousness," introduced the French edition of Beauvoir's *She Came to Stay*, and this novel develops, in its account of a love triangle, the conflicts between conscious beings that are explored at a social level in *The Second Sex*. In the introduction to *The Second Sex*, Beauvoir sums up her analysis of the situation of women by asserting that man is the subject, woman the other. Woman finds herself in a situation where her consciousness is transcended by another consciousness, and she is "the inessential." Beauvoir seems to vacillate over the question of whether woman's acceptance of her role as the other of man is due to oppression or to the moral fault of bad faith. She says that falling

into the role of the other constitutes oppression if it is forced on one, but bad faith if, out of a fear of freedom, one consents to it. Her attempt to show how oppression and nonreciprocal relations between humans derives from fundamental features of consciousness was influenced by the US black activist Richard WRIGHT. It is also structurally similar to the account of the oppression of the Jews in Sartre's *Anti-Semite and Jew* (*Réflexions sur la question Juive*), which itself may have been influenced by Beauvoir's earlier reading of Hegel and her development of Hegelian ideas during the war. Because the translation of *The Second Sex* into English was philosophically illiterate, and because many English-speaking readers knew little of existentialism, Beauvoir's text has mistakenly been read as a sociological account of gender construction and not as an essay in existentialist ethics.

In the period just after the war, Beauvoir wrote two philosophical essays. These attempted to demonstrate that existentialism is not a moral nihilism, and that it is possible to create an ethics of ambiguity that does not deny a priori that separate existences can at the same time be connected. Such an ethics would show how individual liberties can forge laws valid for all. The first of these essays, *Pyrrhus et Cinéas*, has only recently been published in English; the second, *An Ethics of Ambiguity* (*Pour une morale de l'ambiguité*), is a major source for Beauvoir's own reading of the meaning of existentialism. However, in her autobiography, written when she had moved closer to Marxism, she criticized this work for its idealism and lack of a philosophy of history. Nevertheless, it has become an important tool for those interested in Beauvoir as an original thinker. In it she raises the problem that childhood poses for any existentialism, such as Sartre's, that proposes that every consciousness is free and is in bad faith insofar as it flees its freedom. Clearly a child, though in some sense conscious, is not free. By the early 1960s, when he wrote *Words* (*Les Mots*), Sartre too had come to recognize the importance childhood has in determining one's worldview. He wrote an amusing account of how the beliefs of the philosopher of absolute freedom were determined by a childhood milieu that fated him to follow a path leading to faith in the value of freedom and literature.

From the late 1950s Beauvoir wrote a series of autobiographical memoirs that crafted her life story as an existential quest. In these memoirs, which mixed biographical details with a discussion of philosophical works, political movements, and events, Beauvoir found a medium that perfectly suited her desire to fuse philosophy with an account of a singular reality. Here she achieves her early stated intention by clothing the abstract truths of existentialism with the living, emotional truth of a single individual attempting to live out an authentic existence. This project can also be seen to infuse the novels for which she is most famous, *The Blood of Others* (*Le sang des autres*, 1945), *All Men Are Mortal* (*Tous les hommes sont mor-*

tels, 1946), and *The Mandarins* (*Les Mandarins*, 1954), for which she received the Prix Goncourt. By writing philosophy in the guise of literature and essays directed at a broad, engaged public, Beauvoir has come to have a far greater impact on contemporary attitudes, particularly in the realm of relations between the sexes, than have many male philosophers who have concerned themselves with constructing abstract systems.

BIBLIOGRAPHY

Beauvoir, Simone de. *Le deuxième sexe*. 2 vols. Paris: Gallimard, 1949.

———. *La Force des choses*. Paris: Gallimard, 1963.

———. *La Force de l'age*. Paris: Gallimard, 1960.

———. *L'Invitée*. Paris: Gallimard, 1943

———. Littérature et Métaphysique." *Les Temps Modernes* (1946).

———. *Les Mandarins*. Paris: Gallimard, 1954.

———. *Mémoires d'une jeune fille rangée*. Paris: Gallimard, 1958.

———. *Pour une morale de l'ambiguité*. Paris: Gallimard, 1947.

———. *Pyrrhus et Cinéas*. Paris: Gallimard, 1944.

———. *Tous les hommes sont mortels*. Paris: Gallimard, 1946.

KAREN GREEN

BELGIUM, UNBELIEF IN. Since Belgium gained independence in 1830 it has undergone a progressive de-Christianization, so that as of 2003 less than 10 percent of the population in the principal towns attends religious services weekly. In the capital, Brussels, the figure is less than 5 percent. An ever-increasing part of the population is not concerned with religion, and in everyday life does not obey the instructions of any church regarding divorce, abortion, and family and ethical questions. Such disinterest is especially obvious among Catholics.

Belgium has become de-Christianized without a revolution and without any religious war. Strangely, Catholic schools managed by the Catholics still enroll a majority of pupils in Flanders (the northern, Flemish-speaking half of the country) and a large part of pupils in Wallonia (the southern, French-speaking half of the country), but many of these schools are Catholic in name only. This is especially ironic because the division between supporters of the Catholic schools and defenders of public education has been a principal point of conflict between religiously orthodox conservatives and reformers who tended to be heterodox or irreligious. Today, many in the latter group are atheists (see ATHEISM), but this was not always so.

When the public schools movement began in the nineteenth century, most Belgians believed in a deity and even took part in religious services, but they wanted to free themselves from the constraint of the dominant Catholic Church and of its clerical authoritarianism. They were not so much antireligious as anticlerical (see ANTICLERICALISM).

In the mid-nineteenth century Belgium's first FREETHOUGHT organizations, humanist leagues (see HUMANISM), and people's universities were established around the principle of giving the public authorities and society as a whole greater independence from the churches. The oldest of these organizations was the Ligue de l'Enseignement (Teaching league), a pressure group and think tank that has spearheaded defense of the public schools since its foundation in 1864 until today.

Reformers, originally deeply anticlerical and later progressively nonreligious circles, sought to increase the public sector's autonomy relative to the churches. They drew upon the concept of *LAÏCITÉ* as it had developed in France (see FRANCE, UNBELIEF IN) and embraced the "separation of churches and state" as a model for institutional relations in Belgium.

During the second half of the twentieth century, numerous explicitly humanist organizations were established with the aim of defending and expressing humanist values in such varied fields as lifelong education, radio and television broadcasting, moral counseling in prisons and hospitals, international development—in short, all of the fields in which the de facto monopoly of the dominant religious ideology remained to be broken down. More radical humanist organizations offered contraceptive education and devices (still a taboo as late as the 1960s and illegal until 1973), later establishing fully equipped abortion clinics that operated with perfect medical safety—though completely illegally.

Legal Recognition. A feature common to church-state relations both in Belgium and in France is the remuneration of chaplains in hospitals, prisons, and the army in order to "ensure the free practice of religions." In Belgium as in several French *départements* (provinces), ministers of religion are paid by the state though there is no established state religion. By the mid-twentieth century it was clear that such a system constituted grave discrimination against unbelievers. It is as though atheists, agnostics, and other nonreligious people—in a hospital, in the army, or in everyday life—do not have to face problems, too, and do not need to receive support corresponding to their LIFE STANCE, which would mean for nonreligious persons support that is not based upon a religion or a belief in God.

That is why, in Belgium as in other European countries, humanists and other unbelievers have demanded "equal treatment by the state" for all life stances and worldviews, whether religious or not. Such a demand corresponds to the notion of a secular state that is truly impartial with regard to the worldviews of all its citizens.

Since 1964 the first foundation was registered in Belgium to provide nonreligious, humanist moral counseling to prisoners. Since then a number of so-called nonconfessional organizations have been set up to provide a nonreligious parallel to clerical counseling throughout Belgian society. In the early 1970s, coordinating bodies were formed to facilitate the work of nonconfessional organizations. In Flanders was formed the Unie Vrijzinnige Verenigingen (Union of Freethinker Organizations); in Wallonia, the Centre d'Action Laïque (Center for Secular Action). That organization is entirely democratic in its structure.

Together, the two organizations represent the class of nonconfessional organizations before the public authorities. They have pursued two major strategic objectives: first, to obtain for official recognition of nonconfessional organizations by the state, securing the same treatment given to any of the churches; and second, promoting secularism within public institutions so that laws, political decisions, and the like do not favor a particular religion or worldview over others.

Objectives. As early as 1970, the Fondation pour l'assistance morale laïque (Foundation for Secular Moral Counseling) was created in order to provide humanist moral counseling to hospital patients. But it took more than twenty years of activism and lobbying until, in 1993, the Belgian parliament approved an article of the nation's constitution providing that "the salaries and the pensions of the organizations, recognized by the State, providing moral counseling according to a philosophical non-confessional life stance, are taken charge of by the State."

This entailed the official recognition of an organized community of "nonconfessional persons" whose counselors are paid by public authorities. The law of June 21, 2002, determined the levels of payment and allocated specific public resources for direct payment of salaries for humanist delegates spread out across the country. There are currently 230 such delegates who provide professional support for local humanist associations as well as individuals.

Especially in light of this reform, it must be emphasized that the philosophical nonconfessional communities are not churches, and secularism is not a religion but a life stance. Indeed, it is a life stance of great social importance; while it has proven difficult to estimate the number of atheists and other nonbelievers precisely, it is generally acknowledged that they form the second-largest life stance community after Roman Catholicism.

The second major objective of the nonconfessional movement addresses society as a whole: it is the campaign to promote a secular society. This is a somewhat more radical goal than secularizing of the schools or building counseling networks to parallel the clergy. It seeks nothing less than to build a fraternal, progressive, and just society, endowed with impartial public institutions that guarantee human rights and the dignity of persons, ensuring for everyone freedom of thought and expression as well as the equality for all before the law without any distinction of sex, origin, culture, or worldview.

One must recognize that the majority of those who have defended this principle in the past were nonreligious, atheist, agnostic, or religiously indifferent. This situation has changed, and today many Catholics have come to embrace the principle that society should be organized so as not to discriminate according to worldview.

The results that have been obtained on the legislative and political level during the last twenty years bear witness to the movement's success in bringing about the secularization of Belgian public institutions.

That situation has considerably reduced the influence of the churches, particularly the Catholic Church, in the nation's political life. Consequently, a number of policies opposed by the Vatican, like abortion, euthanasia, and marriage and adoption of children by homosexuals, have been implemented with large political majorities, making Belgium (with the Netherlands) a particularly progressive country.

Participation. Let us examine the organization of nonconfessionals in Wallonia, the French-speaking part of Belgium, which has about 4.5 million inhabitants. The Centre d'Action Laïque (CAL) is the federation of French-language nonconfessional organizations. It coordinates the activities of its federated organizations across seven administrative regions. The federated organizations develop activities in their particular fields: international development, moral counseling for prisoners and hospital patients, audiovisual production, education, humanist housing, humanist ceremonies (see RITUAL, CEREMONIAL, AND UNBELIEF), and many others.

The administrative regions also serve some 330 local organizations, which set up varied activities, often lectures, but also service projects such as family planning centers.

The essential part of the actions undertaken by the CAL and its regional sections consists in promoting active citizenship based on the personal elaboration of a life stance founded on human experience and excluding any confessional, dogmatic, or supernatural reference.

The organization, on a federal basis, of cooperating humanist organizations that were previously scattered has turned out to be very useful to reply to those who advocate dogmatic ideologies. It also serves to remind the state of its responsibilities, so that the public sphere remains large, free, and open to all without distinction. Finally, this development has put Belgians of religious and humanistic convictions on a more equal footing.

GEORGES C. LIÉNARD
TRANSLATED BY EDITH NAGANT

BELIEF AS A PSYCHOLOGICAL PHENOMENON.
Believing and Beliefs. Believing as a psychological and biological process can be distinguished from beliefs themselves. While all individuals engage in believing, they do not share all the same beliefs. Believing is, among other things, the process of having expectations. People sometimes differ sharply in what they expect from various aspects of their physical and social environment. Animals have expectations and can correct many of them, even though they cannot describe them in words.

Skepticism. Doubting is an essential ingredient of believing or expecting. To expect the social and physical environment to behave in certain ways is to doubt that it will behave in certain other ways. While believing as a psychological phenomenon proves necessary to living, not every belief or expectation is necessary. Some are required for survival, others are lethal if acted upon, while some prove either helpful, harmful, or negligible.

Skepticism, like believing, does not exist in the abstract. It is always relative to a given claim or expectation. Healthy skepticism develops through the trials and errors of both one's own experiences and those of others. Caution develops as we fine-tune specific claims and reflect on the actions based on those claims. Like reckless believing, excessive caution carries its own dysfunctional consequences.

Believing In and Believing That. In most, if not all, cases of believing in something, we believe that certain relevant claims are true. If we believe *in* our family doctor, for example, we believe *that* she will tell us the truth about our condition as best she can, *that* she is in good standing with the medical profession, *that* she does not engage in certain shady practices, and so on. We expect that she will recommend a specialist if needed, but not that she will lend us the money to pay our hospital bills. To believe in prayer is in some cases to expect *that* certain things will or will not come about because of the prayers. To avoid having to acknowledge that prayer expectations or predictions fail to materialize, believers sometimes either (1) avoid being specific about what is expected or (2) pretend that no answer is an answer.

In other cases, those professing to believe in prayer think that the prayed-for result *might* come about, which is to say it also might not. This is not so much an expectation or prediction as a hope. The word *faith* (which is a cognate of *belief* in ancient Greek) is often used to mean "hope."

It is useful to ask, What does a believer imply about a putative god who allegedly answers relatively trivial prayers but declined to answer the prayers of suffering Jews in Buchenwald or Auschwitz? In 1980 Bailey Smith, the president of the Southern Baptist Convention, stated, "God Almighty does not hear the prayer of a Jew." To believe *in* this version of a putative omnipotent being is thus to believe *that* he did not desire to rescue the Jews from their Nazi captors.

Implicit and Explicit Beliefs. Certain beliefs imply other beliefs. An implicit belief or expectation is one we would consciously recognize if we were consistent. Some Christians who believe in the "ultimate harmony" imply that the sufferings of the majority of the human race in the endless Auschwitz called hell will contribute significantly to the happiness of those in heaven. To believe in this cosmic system is to imply further that the inmates of hell perpetually pay the supreme sacrifice. Their endless agony is necessary to the entire scheme.

The sufferings of Jesus pale by comparison.

In some cases, we resist making some of our implicit beliefs explicit. Friends, therapists, and opponents may help us to explicate our implicit beliefs. Often when our decisions and actions come into conflict, we recognize that some of our background beliefs stand at odds with one another. Bernard J. Paris points out that many of Shakespeare's plays are about people who, having made dysfunctional bargains with their environment, suffer the consequences of either their inability to correct their mistakes or their waiting too long to forestall the destructive consequences of their unrealistic expectations. Macbeth believed he could both commit murderous treachery and subsequently gain the loyalty of those who had remained loyal to King Duncan. King Lear mistakenly expected to receive love, devotion, and admiration from his two Machiavellian daughters, Goneril and Regan. In many ways, King Lear's great tragedy unfolds largely because of actions taken upon delusional beliefs about himself and those surrounding him. The play is a clinical study of highly destructive beliefs or expectations that remained acted upon, unexplicated, and therefore not understood until it was too late.

The Psychology of the Implicit. The so-called subconscious mind is mostly the process of acting on implicit beliefs. Much, if not most, of life has to be lived in this way. The most conspicuous way of explicating beliefs is to verbalize them in a public language. Musicians in practice sessions and during music lessons become more explicit than when performing. Playing the instrument is different from talking about playing. Subvocal talking in private is the implicit becoming more explicit.

Resistance to explication in some cases stems from a vague awareness that certain beliefs and the actions linked to them will have to be changed. Explication can expose foolish expectations. Some people build a significant portion of their lives around foolish and contradictory beliefs. To sustain this aspect of their lives, they often find a group of fellow believers who share their beliefs. To maintain this social network, the participants must reinforce one another in a variety of ways. The group may serve also to restrain some of the believers from taking their beliefs too seriously, that is, from acting on them. To talk about the imminent return of Jesus, for example, and to reinforce one another for talking in this way is one thing. It is another to cash in insurance policies and liquidate investments for financing last-minute missionary and evangelistic activities. If action is the indicator of genuineness of a strong belief, most of those who speak of Christ's imminent second coming appear not to expect it to happen soon but to hope it will or think it might. Evangelist Mordecai Ham, after years of preaching the imminent return of Jesus, advised a young Billy Graham to ease up on specifying dates for the return. In *Reading the Signs*, T. C. Smith notes that some of the first-century Christians had to revise their account of Christ's pending return to earth. By in effect making explicit their expectation, they came to see that their belief had been falsified. While the last New Testament book to be written, 2 Peter, still clings to the expectation of Jesus's physical return, its author apparently felt the need to explain why the earlier predictions had failed.

The Psychology of Magical Beliefs. The world-famous Polish anthropologist Bronislaw Malinowski did his field work in the Trobriand Islands of Melanesia between the two world wars. He noted that the Trobriand Islanders drew a clear line between their work and their magical rituals. Their garden work and canoe building proceeded along rational paths of learning from experience and revising their technology to solve specific problems. Their complex system of principles of sailing included a rich terminology and a tradition of know-how. When navigating in the dangerous open sea and when encountering incalculable tides, sudden gales, unknown reefs, and other unmanageable contingencies, they resorted to magic. In warfare the natives relied on strength, courage, and agility. Magic came into play when predictability waned and the natives had to deal with luck and chance.

The growth of science can be studied as a movement from the anthropomorphic paradigm to one in which natural events occur in regularities that are not discovered through, or related to, supernatural purposes and activities. God-talk continues to run *parallel* to discourse in nonsupernatural categories. Attempts to make the two realms of discourse interact systematically, however, have gained limited support in North America and Europe (see RELIGION IN CONFLICT WITH SCIENCE). Businesses, the sciences, medicine, and banking proceed without attempts to negotiate with supernatural forces. Recent attempts to mix theological claims with political goals appear to have increased magical expectations in both church and state.

Belief in Causality. Technology, magic, and religion operate under the assumption that events are caused. The telephone is a product of technology. Telepathy resorts to magic in the sense of positing causal connections that do not exist. In some cases, the line between technology and magic is difficult to draw. Technology progresses by not only keeping careful records of successful predictions, but also recording failures and making physical adjustments.

Among anthropologists, functionalists have argued that magical rituals help a community bond together. In areas of relative desperation where technology and common sense cannot either bring about certain desired events or prevent undesired events, magic becomes symbolic and ritualistic activity that helps the community feel that it has *some* control over events. Performing the prescribed activities provides a sense of bonding and of not being alone. Magic may be seen as an attempt to overcome the sense of futility, weakness, and fatalism. Given that the human race continued for centuries with

little or no science, it is understandable that elaborate delusions and erroneous beliefs emerged and thrived. In some respects, magic is to technology what myth is to science. Science began in myth and in the process developed testable theories and hypothesis. Technology began as magical attempts to change events and in the process developed methods for testing, correcting, and improving its attempts.

Some versions of magic are a bet that *words* variously arranged can have a significant impact on whatever forces or beings affect human life. Words may in many cases combine with *bodily movements* that are also believed to be efficacious despite there being no apparent direct contact with the reality to be influenced. In chapter 9 of the book of Exodus, the god Yahweh instructs Moses to stretch out his hand over Egypt. When Moses stretched out his staff, a wind brought in locusts from the east. Earlier in the tale, Pharaoh's magicians and sorcerers use their spells to bring about extraordinary results, including turning a staff into a serpent. The contest between Moses and Pharaoh's magicians continues until Moses wins in chapter 14. The narrator of the tale emphasizes that Yahweh is the real controlling power. Some interpreters see religion as an attempt to remove the magicians' power by giving it to a god who as the conscious, primary casual power selects finite creatures (e.g., a prophet or Balaam's ass) to carry out his purposes.

Belief in Preternatural Agents. Most of the human species has believed in the existence of agents presumed to be either invisible or not visible to the naked eye. The anthropomorphic paradigm spawned an entire cosmic zoo of demons, angels, gods, spirits, and other conscious, purposive agents that caused a range of effects from health and pregnancy to storms, plagues, and earthquakes. Believing that these agents influenced human and natural happenings, our forebears sought ways to negotiate with and influence them. By contrast, the philosopher Democritus conjectured that the world was made up of tiny, constantly moving particles, imperceptible to the senses but indivisible (*atom*) and indestructible. Since no technology existed for testing this theory, it remained dormant for centuries. Alchemy, though largely symbolic and cryptic, evolved eventually into chemistry, which put to rest the belief in the transmutation of elements. The French chemist Louis Pasteur raised medicine to a new level by his experiments with crystals and bacteria. Boiling hot water to sterilize instruments slowly replaced the boiling of heretics. Inoculations in most cases replaced exorcisms. Even though some individuals in North America and Europe profess to believe in demons or the devil, they have revised their expectations. For many contemporary Christians, Satan is viewed as either a deflated myth or an ignored lame duck not worth mentioning.

Fanaticism. Anglican minister and noted sociologist David Martin studied the advantages and disadvantages of the community aspect of religion: "Faith is good for neighborliness, peace of mind, children's homes, and social ambulance work, bad for peace in the Balkans, the Middle East, India, and parts of Africa." Historically, religions have contributed to both community bridge building and lethal fanaticism. This is largely because religion reflects our common biological propensity to divide ourselves into insiders and outsiders. Apocalyptic thinking develops this propensity into a cosmic dualism with the righteous on one side and the wicked on the other. G. A. WELLS points out that, given our human finitude and diverse backgrounds, we human mortals will continue to have strong disagreements on important matters. Hence, it becomes imperative to cultivate ways to maintain an open society wherein people can cooperate with one another and explore common values. This requires resisting fanaticism's temptation to indulge in intimidation and persecution: "To create this moral approval [of cruelty] it is necessary to define the polluting enemy as nonhuman or inhuman, that is, outside the range of human beings to whom one owes the slightest obligation as fellow creatures. . . . [R]egularized and routinized cruelty may have been the most important contributors to human suffering."

The Soviet and Chinese version of Marxism turned the secular state into totalitarian fanaticism with its own rationalization of torture and dehumanizing cruelty. As Eric Hoffer notes, the adherent of every ideology must deal with the temptation to succumb to fanaticism, to become the true believer at the expense of other believers and unbelievers.

The Impact of Beliefs. Beliefs in the form of theories and conjecture about aspects of the world have a psychological impact. Even beliefs that correspond with no reality are themselves a cultural reality. Erroneous beliefs have exerted a major influence on human history. Human beings build theories and live by them just as beavers build dams and live in them. Beliefs can function in significant ways as instincts or powerful drives. Far from being dispassionate, scientists are driven by the belief that better explanatory theories are possible, that an open exchange of argument and information frees the imagination to invent new and possibly better theories, and that rigorous, severe tests can often expose real and possible flaws in those theories. In short, science is driven by many beliefs, including the expectation of intellectual progress in an environment where freedom is vigilantly protect and cultivated.

BIBLIOGRAPHY

Barnhart, Joe. *The Study of Religion and Its Meaning: New Explorations in Light of Karl Popper and Emile Durkheim.* New York: Mouton, 1977.
La Barre, Weston. *The Ghost Dance: The Origins of Religion.* New York: Dell, 1972.
Lehman, Arthur C., and James E. Myers, eds. *Magic, Witchcraft, and Religion: An Anthropological Study of the Supernatural.* 4th ed. Mountain View, CA: Mayfield, 1985.
Moore, Barrington, Jr. *Moral Purity and Persecution in History.* Princeton, NJ: Princeton University Press, 2000.
Paris, Bernard J. *Bargains with Fate: Psychological Crises and Conflicts in Shakespeare and His Plays.* New York: Plenum, 1991.
Smith, T. C. *Reading the Signs.* Macon, GA: Smyth and Helwys, 2002.
Wells, G. A. *Can We Trust the New Testament? Thoughts on the Reliability of Early Christian Testimony.* Chicago: Open Court, 2004.

JOE EDWARD BARNHART

BELINSKII, VISSARION (1811–1848), Russian critic and radical journalist. Vissarion Belinskii was born into the family of a poor provincial doctor. His grandfather was a priest; his father was known as a "godless one" (*bezbozhnik*), though he may have earned this epithet only because he was rude to his neighbors, drank too much, and did not go to church.

By the age of twenty-one Belinskii had failed to graduate from two different high schools. Even so, he was a gifted student and was admitted to Moscow University on scholarship. After two years of study—and his writing of a play critical of serfdom—he was expelled. The official reason was "an unsound health and limited capabilities." To his radical friends, losing the opportunity to study at Moscow University was no great loss. Belinskii himself recognized later that both his own lack of diligence and poor teaching at the university contributed to his expulsion. Despite the university's dim view of his prospects, Belinskii found work at one of the leading Russian journals as a writer (*literator*) and soon became one of the most influential literary critics in Russia.

By that time he was quite skeptical about his religious beliefs. Throughout his life Belinskii had no stable source of income, and his life was quite miserable. When his mother advised him "to visit all Moscow churches" in order to get support in his life struggle, he replied to her that he had better things to do besides becoming a "devout itinerant pilgrim." By this time Belinskii was soundly under the influence of the German philosophy, especially that of Hegel, but he did not yet criticize traditional religious beliefs. That turning point came in 1842, when his friend Botkin introduced him to Ludwig FEUERBACH.

The only foreign language Belinskii knew was French. However it is reliably attested that friends translated some excerpts from Feuerbach for him, and he was deeply impressed with the German philosopher's ideas. In a letter to the anarchist Mikhail BAKUNIN dated November 28, 1842, Belinskii wrote, "What is a human being without God? It is a cold body. His life is in God, in Him he dies and rises from the death, suffers and states in bliss. And what is God if not a human *idea* of God?" This sounds clearly Hegelian and indeed bears the stamp of Feuerbach. Still Belinskii did not share his new views with the reading public. Within his circle of friends, he was more open and tried to advocate for his unbelief in God. In his later memoirs, Dostoyevski wrote of a meeting with his friend Belinskii in or around the year 1846: "I found him as a passionate socialist, and he began [discussion] straight from atheism."

Belinskii's most famous statement of his anticlerical and antireligious views is his "Letter to Gogol" dated July 17, 1847. The letter contains open criticism of the Russian Orthodox Church and the official ideology of nineteenth-century Russia. Though published only after the Russian Revolution of 1917, it circulated widely among nineteenth-century Russian radicals as a hand-written document. Possessing or reading the Letter was a crime—for example, it was the crime for which Dos-toyevski was initially sentenced to death, subjected to a mock execution, imprisoned, and remanded to compul-sory military service. Belinskii wrote in the letter, "Russia sees her salvation not in mysticism or asceticism or pietism, but in the successes of civilization, enlighten-ment, and humanity. What she needs is not sermons (she had heard enough of them!) or prayers (she had repeated them too often!), but the awakening in the people a sense of their human dignity, lost for so many centuries amid dirt and refuse (*nevolya*); she needs rights and laws con-forming not to preaching of the church, but to common sense and justice, and their strict possible observance." The letter expresses a sincere belief in Christ as a social prophet, quite common among social radicals at that time.

Eight months later Belinskii died from tuberculosis.

VLADIMIR SHTINOV

BENNETT, DEROBIGNE MORTIMER (1818–1882), American freethought publisher and editor. D. M. Ben-nett published FREETHOUGHT literature and philosoph-ical, biographical, and scientific books and pamphlets. Bennett's HUMANISM, iconoclasm, and persecution by Christian zealots earned him mythic stature among unbe-lievers around the world. Admirers referred to him as "Nature's Nobleman" and the "American VOLTAIRE."

Bennett was an outspoken free-speech advocate who promoted women's rights (see WOMAN SUFFRAGE MOVE-MENT AND UNBELIEF) and labor reform (see LABOR MOVEMENT AND UNBELIEF). His hard-fought battle against censorship culminated in one of the most publi-cized and historically significant freedom of the press trials in the United States. Bennett's irreverent "An Open Letter to Jesus Christ" and his incendiary debates with some of America's leading clergymen, which he printed and sold as tracts, infuriated religionists, who called him "the Devil's Own Advocate."

Early Life. Bennett was born on December 23, 1818, in Springfield, New York. At age fifteen he escaped a poverty-stricken family by joining the United Society of Believers in Christ's Second Appearing, commonly known as the Shakers. The Shakers were a strict reli-gious sect and the most enigmatic and successful utopian movement in America. Bennett was a devout member of this celibate communitarian society for thirteen years and worked as an herbalist, physician, and ministry-appointed journalist. Bennett recorded "divinely inspired" messages during the Shakers' decade-long spiritualistic revival period, the Era of Manifestations. When the revival subsided, some of the younger mem-bers including Bennett and his future wife, Mary Wicks, began to lose their religious fervor (see SPIRITUALISM AND UNBELIEF). In 1846 Bennett and Wicks eloped.

Soon after leaving the Shakers, Bennett read his first "infidel" publication and subsequently studied the scien-tific and philosophical works of Charles DARWIN, Thomas Henry HUXLEY, Herbert SPENCER, John Stuart MILL, Voltaire, and Thomas PAINE. It was Paine's *Age of Reason* that converted the former devout Christian to a freethinker and unremitting skeptic.

The Truth Seeker. For the next twenty-seven years the couple moved around the country. Bennett invested in various business ventures, owned drugstores, and success-fully marketed his Dr. Bennett's Family Medicines. In 1873, while living in Paris, Illinois, Bennett got into a spirited debate with clergymen over the efficacy of prayer. After the local newspapers refused to print some of his "infidel" letters to the editor, Bennett founded *The TRUTH SEEKER* as an alternative to the Christian-controlled press. The Shaker-turned-freethinker devoted his "little sheet" to "Science, Morals, Freethought and Human Happiness."

Later that year, Bennett moved *The Truth Seeker* to New York City, where it would remain for nearly a cen-tury. Within a few years he transformed his prairie monthly into the nation's most influential reform weekly, with fifty thousand readers. Thomas Edison, Samuel Langhorne CLEMENS (Mark Twain), Harry Houdini, and Clarence DARROW were among the illustrious subscribers. *The Truth Seeker* was the official organ of the NATIONAL LIBERAL LEAGUE, an association of freethinkers devoted to complete separation of church and state. Bennett served as vice president along with Robert Green INGERSOLL, the famous agnostic attorney and orator.

A lightning rod for controversy, Bennett was both the most revered *and* the most reviled publisher of the Gilded Age. He was brazen and sweeping in his condem-nation of Christianity: "We humbly believe Christianity to be false, to be the greatest sham in the world, without truth in its history, without loveliness in its doctrines, without benefit to the human race, and without anything to sustain it in the hold it has upon the world." Bennett opposed dogmatic religions and took great pride in debunking the Bible and exposing hypocritical cler-gymen. (He was the first editor in America to routinely report misdeeds by the clergy, publishing the collected reports as *Sinful Saints and Sensual Shepherds.*) Bennett reminded Americans that the government of the United States was "*not in any sense* founded on the Christian religion" (see TREATY OF TRIPOLI). He argued that Abraham Lincoln and many of the Founding Fathers were, like his hero Thomas Paine, deists or infidels, the most noteworthy being Benjamin FRANKLIN, Thomas JEFFERSON, and George Washington.

In 1877 Bennett became the target of Anthony Comstock, America's self-appointed arbiter of morals (see COMSTOCK, ANTHONY, AND UNBELIEF). Comstock was a "special agent" for the US Post Office and secretary and chief vice hunter for the New York Society for the Suppression of Vice, an organization that was part of the social purity crusade. This self-described "weeder in God's garden" waged war on "obscene" books (including some classic works of literature) and freethinking writers and publishers. Comstock judged Bennett to be "everything vile in blasphemy and infidelity."

Free-Speech Advocacy. Some of the country's most powerful and pious citizens backed Comstock, who bragged about driving fifteen people to suicide in his Christian-sanctioned mission to "save the young" (see CRADDOCK, IDA). There was little protest in the nation's newspapers and magazines against the puritanical and ill-defined Comstock Laws. Like the politicians, most publishers felt that opposing the crusader and his often ballyhooed "fight for the young" might be interpreted as tolerating crime. Censorship and church hypocrisy, however, were two of Bennett's favorite subjects. In Comstock and his "Vice Society" as the editor dubbed it, he found both. While other periodicals occasionally scolded Comstock, Bennett persistently challenged and lampooned "Saint Anthony" and his wealthy sponsors (including Samuel Colgate, the soap tycoon) in books, pamphlets, and countless pages of *The Truth Seeker*. Prominent abolitionists, reformers, and suffragists supported Bennett's "cause" for "free speech, a free press, and mails free from espionage and Comstockism."

"The charge is ostensibly 'obscenity,'" Bennett wrote after being arrested by Anthony Comstock. "But the real offense is that I presume to utter sentiments and opinions in opposition to the views entertained by the Christian Church." Bennett's first arrest was for his "Open Letter to Jesus Christ" and a scientific tract written by a former minister. (The charges were dropped after Ingersoll interceded on Bennett's behalf.) His second arrest was for selling *Cupid's Yokes*, a free-love pamphlet (see SEX RADICALISM AND UNBELIEF) at a freethought convention in Watkins Glen, New York. Bennett was arrested a third time, convicted, and imprisoned for sending *Cupid's Yokes* through the US Mail. Bennett's 1879 obscenity trial was a travesty of justice. The Hicklin rule (an ambiguous common-law "test" for obscenity that permitted work to be judged by introducing only isolated passages without regard for the intention of the author)

was used to convict Bennett, and became the obscenity standard in US law until it was overturned in 1957.

Bennett spent almost a year in the Albany Penitentiary, where he nearly died from harsh prison conditions and the stigma attached to selling "obscenity." A petition with more than two hundred thousand names (the largest petition campaign of the nineteenth century) was sent to President Rutherford B. Hayes, asking for a pardon for the elderly editor. Hayes (who, ironically, had earlier pardoned Ezra HEYWOOD, author of *Cupid's Yokes*) also received petitions from Comstock that were signed by religious leaders and Sunday school children. Mrs. Hayes, a pious Christian, adamantly opposed absolving the publisher of *The Truth Seeker*. Hayes denied the pardon, although he would later admit in his diary that *Cupid's Yokes* was not "obscene."

While in jail, Bennett wrote *From behind the Bars: A Series of Letters Written in Prison* (1879) and *The Gods and Religions of Ancient and Modern Times* (1879). Soon after serving his sentence, Bennett traveled to Europe to represent American liberals at the Congress of the Universal Federation of Freethinkers in Brussels, Belgium. In Europe he wrote *An Infidel Abroad*, also titled (to reach a wider audience) *A Truth Seeker in Europe: A Series of Letters Written Home during a Ten Week's Visit* (1881). Bennett traveled abroad a second time and chronicled his trip in a four-volume work, *A Truth Seeker around the World: A Series of Letters Written While Making a Tour of the Globe* (1882). During his yearlong journey (paid for by thousands of supporters) he was given a hero's welcome in numerous cities.

Bennett's Legacy. Bennett died on December 6, 1882, a few months after returning home from abroad. Obituary writers expressed varied opinions. The *New York Times* minimized Bennett's free-speech advocacy, writing that he was a "a pronounced free-thinker" who "obtained some notoriety in 1878 by reason of his arrest upon the charge of sending indecent publications through the mails." Like most "secular" newspapers in the nineteenth century, the *Times* was Christian, conservative, pompous, and essentially a guardian of repressive Victorian morality. Other newspapers characterized him as "the leader of Atheism in the United States" and the "Luther of the nineteenth century." According to the *Dictionary of American Biography*, Bennett was "an amalgam of quack, crank, and idealist" and "an effective popular spokesman for liberal ideas in religion and ethics."

The Truth Seeker continued to provide a forum for freethinkers long after Bennett's death. Although Bennett's significance looms large in the annals of unbelief, his contribution to free speech has yet to be recognized. There have been several celebrated obscenity trials in America, but few if any of the defendants suffered the injustice and severe consequences as the courageous editor of *The Truth Seeker*. "Mr. Bennett was a man wholly extraordinary, and his career was not less so," wrote James Parton, the famous nineteenth-century biographer. "He embraced an unpopular cause; he made it less difficult for others to do so."

Two years after D. M. Bennett's death, a thousand friends erected a massive and controversial monument to "the Defender of Liberty and Its Martyr" in New York. The granite memorial, still standing today in Brooklyn's Greenwood Cemetery, is inscribed with Bennett's philosophical principles and the proclamation: "When The Innocent Is Convicted, The Court Is Condemned."

BIBLIOGRAPHY

Bennett, DeRobigne Mortimer. *The World's Sages, Infidels, and Thinkers*. New York: Liberal and Scientific Publishing House, 1876, 1880.

Bradford, Rod. *D. M. Bennett: The Truth Seeker*. Amherst, NY: Prometheus Books, 2006.

Broun, Heywood, and Margaret Leech. *Anthony Comstock: Roundsman of the Lord*. New York: Albert and Charles Boni, 1927.

Hoogenbloom, Ari. *Rutherford B. Hayes: Warrior and President*. Lawrence: University Press of Kansas, 1995.

Macdonald, George Everett Hussey. *Fifty Years of Freethought: Story of* The Truth Seeker *from 1875*. 2 vols. New York: Truth Seeker Company, 1929, 1931.

Warren, Sidney. *American Freethought, 1860–1914*. New York: Gordian, 1966.

ROD BRADFORD

BENNETT, HENRY SCOTT GILBERT (HARRY SCOTT)

(1877–1959), Australian lecturer and organizer. Harry Scott Bennett was the first notable Australian-born freethinker (see FREETHOUGHT) and, despite his controversial views, was a respected figure in Australia, the United States, and New Zealand.

Bennett was born in Chilwell (Geelong), Victoria, Australia, on June 1, 1877, to a freethinking socialist mother (see SOCIALISM AND UNBELIEF). He embraced RATIONALISM and republicanism through Joseph SYMES. While working as a draper's assistant in Melbourne, he was "discovered" by visiting British socialist Tom Mann. With Mann and another British socialist, Henry Hyde (Harry) Champion, Bennett founded the Victorian Socialist League in 1897 and the Victorian Socialist Party (VSP) in 1906. In 1902 he began lecturing for the Political Labor Council (PLC) and was elected to the Victorian Legislative Assembly as the PLC's candidate in 1904. In parliament he spoke for railway workers, miners, the unemployed, and animals, and against corporal punishment in schools, but claimed there were issues that caucus prevented his raising. Probably these included the parochialism and racialism of Australians at the time. So Bennett did not run for reelection in 1907, broke with the PLC, and instead began lecturing for the VSP.

Later that year he went to Sydney to be a mainstay of the International Socialist Club. In 1909 he went to New Zealand to lecture under the auspices of the New Zealand Socialist Party. Bennett supported the Federation of Labor ("Red Feds") but found time for rationalism, and by 1914 was giving weekly freethought addresses in Auckland. In January 1915 he was appointed organizer for the New Zealand Social Democratic Party, but went to the United States in September to lecture for the Rationalist Association of America.

Upon his return to Australia in 1917, Prime Minister Billy Hughes made Bennett an attractive offer to promote enlistment or conscription for the armed forces, but he rejected the offer and opposed conscription during the 1917 referendum. He became a founding member of the Y Club (1918), a sociable "think tank" of what the Melbourne *Age* called "revolutionary conspirators." As organizer of the VSP, he lectured throughout eastern Australia from 1917 to 1920, when he resigned to devote himself to rationalism, briefly in New Zealand, then Victoria again. He was principal lecturer of the Social Science Forum (1935–36) before moving to Sydney as secretary-lecturer of the New South Wales Rationalist Association until his death on May 24, 1959.

BIBLIOGRAPHY

Osborne, Graeme. "Henry Gilbert Bennett." *Australian Dictionary of Biography*. Vol. 7. Melbourne: Melbourne University Press, 1979.

Walker, Bertha. "Harry Scott Bennett: An Appreciation." *Labour History* 16 (May 1969).

DAVID TRIBE

BENTHAM, JEREMY (1748–1832), English philosopher, social reformer, and utilitarian. Jeremy Bentham is perhaps more famous for being dead than being alive. His embalmed body, seated in a chair and dressed in his finest clothes, may still be seen in the main hall of the institution he helped to found, University College London. Like everything else associated with Bentham, there was a practical reason for this—he wished to encourage people to donate their bodies for the good of science, and to take away the stigma (primarily of religious origin) that prevented corpses from being used to further medical knowledge. In an era infamous for grave robbers like the notorious William Burke and William Hare, who sold bodies to surgeons unable to get them any other way, Bentham's gesture, shocking though it may be, was perfectly reasonable.

Bentham is credited with founding the philosophy of utilitarianism (the view that ethical actions should be based upon what would bring about the greatest good for the greatest number). Coming from a family of attorneys, and trained in the law himself at Oxford University, he inherited a large sum of money and was thus not required to practice law as a profession. He had the luxury, rare for most philosophers, of devoting himself entirely to a life of thought. But his thought was very much action oriented. Bentham was one of the foremost social reformers of his time.

Bentham's most important work of political theory was *An Introduction to the Principles of Morals and Legislation*, published in 1789. In it, he attempted to deduce legal matters not from tradition, natural law concepts, or accepted precedents, but from universal principles of reason. Bentham revived the classic doctrine of Epicureanism (see EPICURUS), arguing that the prime motivating factor for human beings was the desire to minimize pain and maximize pleasure. His "hedonic calculus" was designed to determine which actions would bring about the best results for the general populace. Utility, or usefulness, should be the basis for action. While his work was deemed highly controversial in his native England, it was embraced by the revolutionists in France, who made Bentham an honorary citizen in 1792. Unlike Thomas PAINE, Bentham wisely decided not to venture to Paris to receive his honor. He spent the remainder of his life in his native country, where he fought for such social causes as prison reform (he designed a model jail, called the "panopticon," where prisoners could be viewed at all times); increasing the number of voters by basing eligibility on population rather than wealth; raising the age of factory workers and limiting the number of hours they were required to work; and secularizing public education through opening accessibility to Catholics, Jews, and other nonconformists. On the latter issue, he donated a large sum of money for the founding of University College, the first institution of higher learning in England which was strictly nondenominational.

While never referring to himself as an atheist, it is clear from his writings on religion that Bentham was an unbeliever, as well as a sharp critic of the established churches of his time. Religion, he argued, does not promote the cause of utilitarianism. It usually denies people the right to pursue pleasurable activities, makes a fetish of denial and suffering, and castigates as immoral and evil anyone who dares question its authority. The God of the Bible is a despotic figure who creates human beings for the sole purpose of tormenting them. His 1818 "The Church of England Catechism Explained" is a step-by-step demolition of the absurdities of Anglican doctrines, and his "The Influence of Natural Religion on the Temporal Happiness of Mankind," posthumously published and added to by the jurist George Grote, is a merciless lawyer's brief on the harm which superstition and dogmatism have inflicted upon humankind.

Bentham was a colleague of James Mill, and helped his friend to raise his son John Stuart MILL, who was to further the cause of utilitarianism by distancing it from Bentham's extreme brand of RATIONALISM. J. S. Mill came to feel, ironically enough, that his upbringing was insufficiently hedonistic, as both his father and Bentham had failed to appreciate the importance of emotions and physical pleasures in one's life. Bentham's hedonic calculus—in which pleasures and pains were tallied up based upon such measures as which were most long-lasting, immediate, or ephemeral—proved too crude a formula to capture the richness of human experience. Still, his work advanced the cause of moral reasoning by making it less of an abstract art or theological concern, focusing instead on the concrete question of what will bring about the greatest happiness for all those whose interests will be impacted upon by any given action.

BIBLIOGRAPHY

Atkinson, Charles Milner. *Jeremy Bentham: His Life and Work.* Honolulu: University Press of the Pacific, 2004.
Harrison, Ross. *Bentham.* New York: Routledge and Kegan Paul, 1983.
Postema, Gerald L. *Bentham and the Common Law Tradition.* Gloustershire, UK: Clarendon, 1986.

TIMOTHY J. MADIGAN

BERGSON, HENRI (1859–1941), French philosopher. Henri Bergson was born in the same year as John DEWEY and Edmund Husserl. It is noteworthy that this is the same year that Charles DARWIN's *The Origin of Species* appeared (see EVOLUTION AND UNBELIEF), since evolutionary thought was to bear a profound influence on Bergson's philosophical work. Against this background, Bergson entered the Collége de France, where he would write a novel chapter in the history of French philosophical thought.

Bergson's major contribution to philosophy was his theory of duration, first presented in his 1889 doctoral dissertation titled *Essai sur les donnees immediates de la conscience*, translated into English as *Time and Free Will*. This is the most important work of Bergson's early career. Like many of his works to follow, he tackles a philosophical problem by laying out the contemporary landscape, analyzing the conceptual confusions that have caused the problem, and then presenting his solution to the problem in the light of his analysis. For instance, *Time and Free Will* critiques the concept of time as nothing more than a measure of quantitative homogeneous units; he then introduces his theory of time as duration and goes on to show that free will is possible for humans when we realize that psychological motives are not separate atomic states of minds, as held by the associationist school in psychology; rather they involve a heterogeneous interpenetration of psychological qualities so organically interwoven that one's actions issue immediately from the agent. He points out that it is only "after the fact" that our motives are separated and dissected as divisible units, producing the illusion of DETERMINISM, which assumes that all human acts are, at least in theory, predictable events unfolding in accordance with causal laws of nature.

This methodology is applied throughout his works, the idea being that traditional problems of philosophy and related fields of science can be treated by reconsidering the immediate data of experience as durational rather than temporal in the classical Newtonian sense. Duration, Bergson held, is the intuitive awareness of change as an indivisible and continuous succession of events, that are only numerically demarcated as a plurality of "events" after the subject has come to reflect on them, albeit with particular pragmatic interests.

Though Bergson rejected the materialism of his age (see MATERIALISM, PHILOSOPHICAL), especially the version championed by Herbert SPENCER, he studied science meticulously. He believed that scientific data could be understood more fully when one accepts the reality of duration at the core of existence. In this sense Bergson anticipated the twentieth-century school of thought known as process philosophy and greatly influenced the philosophy of, among many others, A. N. Whitehead. For Bergson, the processes of nature are the fundament of reality, and any attempt to tackle metaphysical problems must recognize the reality of change.

In an entry of this brevity, justice cannot be done to the widespread influence Bergson's thought exerted on the intellectual world in the first part of the twentieth century. We can however take an overview of some of the fields he treated in his main works other than *Time and Free Will*.

In his most popular work, *L'Evolution creatrice* (Creative Evolution, 1907), he shows that in biology mechanistic explanations cannot account for the change necessary for the emergence of vital processes. Such explanations, he argues, result from the intrusion of ideas fabricated by pragmatic intelligence that are used as theoretical applications to the growth and development of living forms. His view is often termed *vitalism*, as opposed to mechanism, since it posits an *élan vital* the essence of which is duration. To better understand Bergson's methodology one cannot overlook his influential 1903 essay "Introduction a la metaphysique" (An Introduction to Metaphysics). To briefly summarize this work, composed prior to *Creative Evolution*, Bergson draws a sharp distinction between two ways of knowing a thing: one way is through analysis, the other is through intuition. The goal of analysis is to reduce its objects to elements common with other elements in other objects. Analysis breaks a whole into parts. Further, it uses symbols (words) to reconstruct the object; thus analysis implies reduction into parts and reconstruction back into wholes. But the reconstructed whole is artificial since it depends on the commonality of parts. In the final account the goal of analysis is not truth, but utility and workability of the objects in our surrounding world. Intuition, on the other hand, has truth for its end, and is found in the interior of an object where duration is prominent. It is the preferred method of metaphysics.

Bergson's other works share the same approach and methodology, starting with critique of entrenched contemporary theories and ending with novel insights that shed new light on old philosophical problems. As suggested above, the theory of duration, as opposed to "clock time," is held to reveal the structure of reality. The method of intuition, largely an appeal to overcome ordinary habits of thinking, is the method Bergson uses to disclose process and duration in all strata of existence from matter to life to mind.

One of France's greatest philosophers, Bergson was awarded the Nobel Prize in Literature in 1927. He was not able to accept the award in person due to his severe arthritis, which plagued him until his death in 1941.

BIBLIOGRAPHY

Bergson, Henri. *Creative Evolution*. New York: Random House, 1944.
———. *An Introduction to Metaphysics*. New York: Liberal Arts Press, 1949.
———. *Time and Free Will*. New York: Harper & Row, 1910.

LAWRENCE WESTERBY HOWE

BESANT, ANNIE (1847–1933), British freethought activist. Brought up a devout Anglican, Annie Wood was born on October 1, 1847. Her upbringing was genteel and sheltered, though the family had fallen on hard times. While still only twenty, Annie married Frank Besant, a dour and brutish clergyman. Like many young women of her generation, Annie learned the facts of life on her wedding night. Religious doubts soon crept into her life, partly from the behavior of her husband, partly because of the suffering of her infant daughter, Mabel, during an illness. By the time she secured a separation from her husband in 1873, Besant was a convinced freethinker (see FREETHOUGHT). She joined the NATIONAL SECULAR SOCIETY in 1874 and quickly became an active writer and speaker for the freethought movement. In 1877 Besant became coeditor of Charles BRADLAUGH's paper, the NATIONAL REFORMER, in recognition of her ability and value to the movement.

Besant soon acquired a nationwide reputation for her defense alongside Bradlaugh of the birth control pamphlet *The Fruits of Philosophy*, written by the American physician Charles KNOWLTON. The discussion in public of birth control (see BIRTH CONTROL AND UNBELIEF) was unheard of, and in 1877 Bradlaugh and Besant were prosecuted for publishing obscene literature and sentenced to six months' imprisonment, but released on a technicality. Although deeply committed to the principle of birth control, neither Bradlaugh nor Besant was uncritically supportive of Knowlton's book. It was the principle of free speech they were concerned to defend, at least as much as the topic at hand. The year after their prosecution, Besant wrote *The Law of Population*, which she intended to replace Knowlton's work. Besant's achievement was to bring the subject of birth control into the open, and to make its principles available to the general reader.

As a result of the publicity attracted by this case, Frank Besant, who had been granted custody of their son, Digby, was also able to wrest control of Mabel, who had been granted to Annie's care. The courts agreed that Annie's support for birth control proved her unsuitable as a mother. (It is worth noting that later, when they were able to choose for themselves, both children opted to live with their mother.)

Undeterred by these reverses, Annie Besant went on to collaborate with Bradlaugh during his prolonged campaign to take his seat in Parliament. Bradlaugh won the seat of Northampton in 1880, but was soon involved in a protracted struggle over his original refusal to swear his oath of allegiance on the Bible. Over the next six years Bradlaugh was reelected four times by the electors of Northampton before Parliament finally allowed him to take his seat. Besant continued to suffer for her beliefs during this campaign, being subjected to several demeaning persecutions. She was refused leave to use the garden of the Royal Botanic Society, the reason being given that the daughters of the curator used it. And in 1883 Besant was refused admittance to the practical botany classes at University College on grounds of her supposed immorality. During her atheist period (see ATHEISM), Besant wrote some essays that have remained classic popular freethought polemics, which were gathered as a collection titled *My Path to Atheism* (1877).

Besant was also active during these years as a socialist agitator (see SOCIALISM AND UNBELIEF), a trend the liberal and individualist Bradlaugh did not support. Her drift toward socialism reflects the influence of George Bernard SHAW. Besant had joined the Fabian Society in 1885. In 1888 she took a brave stand in support of a group of girls being shamelessly exploited while the company they worked for announced record profits. The girls were employed by Bryant and May to make matches, and the strike became a cause célèbre for the exploitation of labor in England. A year later, and largely on the strength of that success, Shaw invited Besant to contribute an essay to *Fabian Essays on Socialism*, which went on to become very influential in establishing the intellectual credentials of socialism.

But another event from 1889 proved to be even more significant for her long-term future as a leader of the freethought movement. That year Shaw—though other accounts say it was the journalist W. T. Stead—gave Besant a copy of Madame Helena Blavatsky's esoteric work *The Secret Doctrine* to review. To everyone's surprise, she found the work convincing and was converted. Madame Blavatsky claimed to have traveled through Tibet, where wise mahatmas had revealed to her the secrets of life. In fact, THEOSOPHY was an eccentric compendium of ideas drawn from Western mysticism, the newer vogue of spiritualism (see SPIRITUALISM AND UNBELIEF), and the still newer interest in the Asian traditions being brought to light by studies in comparative religion, a discipline then in its infancy. Mysticism bequeathed ideas of the nonpersonal godhead. From spiritualism came the idea of the reality of the unseen and our ability to communicate with it. And from Hinduism came the belief in reincarnation. Theosophy is the parent of all contemporary New Age beliefs.

In February 1890 Besant resigned as vice president of the National Secular Society. By 1896 she was a major leader of the Theosophical movement, which she remained for the rest of her life. Besant argued that her transition to Theosophy was not the volte-face her former colleagues saw it to be. She remained opposed to notions of a personal god, and over her long career in Theosophy she led that movement to deemphasize its supernatural tendencies. This said, Besant claimed fifty earlier reincarnations, from mineral to vegetable and then from a variety of primal beings to HYPATIA and Giordano BRUNO. Her extensive writings became increasingly eccentric as she got older. Her best books from this stage in her life are *The Ancient Wisdom* (1897) and *Esoteric Christianity* (1898). Besant was also, as Bradlaugh had been before her, a staunch supporter of Indian independence. She moved to India in 1893 as part of her deepening interest in Theosophy, and spent most of the last three decades of her life there. In 1907 she became president of the Theosophical Society and, in 1913, the first woman president of the Indian National Congress. It was Besant who bestowed on Mohandas Gandhi the honorific *Mahatma*, or "great soul."

On the negative side, Besant gave close support to fellow Theosophist Charles Leadbetter, whose sexual exploitation of boys in his care provoked widespread outrage and did much to damage the movement. Besant was also party to the exploitation of the Indian youth they named Krishnamurti, whom Besant and Leadbetter were grooming as the future leader of the movement. In 1931, six years after the two proclaimed him the Messiah, Krishnamurti renounced his ties with Theosophy and moved to California, where he had a long and successful career as a public guru. Besant's longest-lasting positive contribution from these later years was her consistent advocacy of Indian independence. She died on September 20, 1933.

BIBLIOGRAPHY

Besant, Annie. *An Autobiography*. London: T. Fisher Unwin, 1893.

———. *My Path to Atheism*. London: Freethought Publishing, 1877.

Nethercot, Arthur H. *The First Five Lives of Annie Besant*. London: Rupert Hart-Davis, 1961.

———. *The Last Four Lives of Annie Besant*. London: Rupert Hart-Davis, 1963.

Shaw, George Bernard, ed. *Fabian Essays in Socialism*. London: Walter Scott, 1889.

Washington, Peter. *Madame Blavatsky's Baboon*. New York: Schocken, 1995.

BILL COOKE

BIBLICAL CRITICISM. Criticism of scripture—not in the sense of faultfinding, but of serious study undertaken in the way any other ancient manuscript might be studied—can be considered in five major forms: historical criticism, source criticism, form criticism, redaction criticism, and criticism centering on the historical Jesus.

Historical Criticism. Historical criticism of sacred texts may be said to have begun with the determination in 1440 by Lorenzo Valla that the Donation of Constantine, by which the first Christian emperor had supposedly ceded the Papal States to the church in perpetuity, was a pious fraud. This was a harbinger of things to come, and in the next century we begin to see the same sort of scrutiny applied to the central documentation for the imperious claims of the church: the scriptures themselves. The Renaissance humanists including Desiderius ERASMUS, Thomas Cardinal Cajetan, and John Colet insisted that the Bible be interpreted and studied in a fashion no different from that applied to other documents of antiquity then being scrutinized: namely, rationally and in their original historical sense. Martin Luther agreed; he argued for the grammatico-historical method, whereby the biblical text must be studied as any other ancient writing, according to the normal rules of grammar and in historical context. This way he sought to counter the spiritualizing allegory used by the church to import its dogmas into an unsuspecting Bible. Though Luther substituted "*was Christum triebt*" (whatever conveys Christ) for Erasmus's criterion of REASON, and so could never quite refrain from a bit of spiritualizing (especially in the case of the Old Testament), his grammatico-historical method was clearly the precursor to the modern historical-critical method (as James Barr and others have noted).

The sixteenth-century astronomers Andreas Osiander, Nicolaus Copernicus, and Johannes Kepler (whom Luther called "this mad fellow") dared to approach their mapping of the planets and stars apart from biblical cosmology—though to protect himself, Kepler troubled to harmonize the text with his results, claiming he had merely shown the "correct" interpretation of the Bible, what it meant all along, waiting for us to catch up with it. He had freed critical inquiry, by an inch or so at least, from the hegemony of the doctrine of scriptural authority.

Parisian Benedictine Jean Mabillon wrote *Acta Sanctorum* (1668), in which he set forth criteria for determining the actual date and authenticity of ancient documents, a critical element in historical criticism. Another key weapon in the arsenal of criticism was the principle of methodological doubt (see SKEPTICISM) applied to philosophical epistemology (the question of how we know things) by René DESCARTES. It would prove equally indispensable in historical matters, too. Fellow rationalist Baruch SPINOZA did give explicit attention to the Bible, suggesting that it contained no true revelation—none different at any rate from that revealed by human reason—and that the miracles of the Bible were metaphors, expressing the pious tendency to trace all events back to God. He stressed that scripture ought to be studied like any other text and asked why the guardians of orthodoxy feared such scrutiny. "Do they think," asked Spinoza, "that piety can only be maintained through ignorance? If so, they have but a timid trust in scripture."

Richard Simon, determined to vindicate Catholic reliance on tradition, sought to show the inadequacy of the Protestant principle of *Sola Scriptura* ("Scripture alone" as the arbiter of faith and practice) by showing the ambiguity and unreliability of the Bible. He denied that Moses had authored the first five books of the Old Testament, the Pentateuch. Further, he stressed the nature of many biblical books as compilations of traditions gathered long after the events they purported to describe, the corrupt state of the text, and the equivocality of the books' literal sense, such that no doctrine could depend upon it. His efforts were appreciated by his Popish masters as little as those of modernist Alfred Firmin LOISY two centuries later.

John LOCKE introduced another critical principle for the historical endeavor when, as against Descartes and the rationalists (see RATIONALISM), he stressed the historical character of all human knowledge. There are no "innate ideas," but rather all knowledge is a matter of empirical data gathered and processed by inference. Ultimately, then, historical-critical method is simply a special case of general epistemology. Consciousness itself is historical as well, since it is a serial process in history, in the flow of experience. Locke had progressive views on the Bible specifically, as well. He thought the Bible should be interpreted by reason (see his *The Reasonableness of Christianity*, 1695), since the true revelation granted men by their creator was reason. Thus what in the Bible did not accord with reason could be safely rejected. This criterion was uppermost in the minds of deists (see DEISM) like Ethan ALLEN (*Reason: the Only Oracle of Man*, 1784) and Thomas Paine (*The Age of Reason*, 1795) writing about a century after Locke.

Locke felt that the epistolary genre was, strictly speaking, tangential to rational revelation, since the epistles were historically occasioned and thus represented a secondary application of the truth, not a straightforward statement of it. In this he resembled his near contemporary Gotthold LESSING who carved the "ugly ditch," pointing out that "[t]he accidental truths of history can never establish the necessary truths of reason." For Locke, epistles were the former, not the latter. But this freed him to deal with the epistles in a realistic manner, refusing to take individual verses out of the context of the argument; insisting on reading the letter according to the occasion that called it forth; and seeking after the author's intent, which must have been of such a nature that readers in their day could possibly have made some sense of it.

Lessing, too, made positive contributions to biblical science. He published Hermann Samuel Reimarus's fragments (see below) and probed ancient "reader response" to the Bible as a check on the anachronistic readings of later orthodox theologians. For instance, he noted that the early Jewish Christian sect of the Nazoreans used, of the four gospels, only Matthew; and that they held an "adoptionist" Christology (the view that Jesus was a righteous man adopted by God as his honorary "son"). Lessing suggested that perhaps this was because when read without Trinitarian lenses, Matthew's text permitted only such a Christology.

David HUME, an empiricist following in the train of Locke, made an epochal contribution with his argument against miracles (see MIRACLES, UNBELIEF IN). Though unfairly characterized by later apologists like C. S. Lewis and even genuine historians like Robin George Collingwood as an antisupernaturalist scientific positivist (see POSITIVISM), Hume was actually an early proponent of the principle of analogy. He observed that the universal testimony of mankind (by which, in context, he seems to mean the testimony of our contemporaries) tells us two things. First, we do not observe the occurrence of miracles ourselves. Second, whenever we do hear reports of such things, we sooner or later trace them down to the well-known human tendency to exaggerate, to rumormongering, or to simple error or delusion. Given these facts, it will never be more likely that an ancient or a modern report of a miracle is a fact than that it is a rumor or legend. Hume is not talking about what *can* occur, but rather what *seems* to occur, and what can and cannot be considered as *probably* having occurred.

Within the realm of biblical studies more narrowly drawn, we may trace the development of historical criticism by means of a catalogue of scholarly saints beginning with Johann Salomo Semler, who distinguished between scripture (documents found in the Bible by the mere fact of ecclesiastical decision) and the word of God, which makes us wise unto salvation. Thus freed of a superstitious regard for the text, we may dare to touch the ark; and so Semler called for a commentary on scripture that would be purely scientific, not edifying. Similarly, another eighteenth-century critic, Karl August Gottlob Keil, called for the exegete to think the biblical author's thoughts after him, passing no judgment of truth or falsity, neither criticizing nor apologizing, a purely descriptive treatment.

French physician Jean Astruc about the same time set source criticism (see next section) on its way, delineating four (as he thought, pre-Mosaic) sources in the Pentateuch, identifiable by the different divine names used. Johann Gottfried Eichhorn and Johann David Michaelis wrote the first critical *Introduction to the New Testament* (1750), while Johann Philipp Gabler wrote the first "biblical theology" of the New Testament, a purely descriptive account of what the ancient writers believed, free of the falsifying influence of what modern readers may wish to find there. Gabler and Georg Lorenz Baur first spoke of myth in the New Testament, and Baur embarked on a course of what would later be called demythologizing it.

Hermann Samuel Reimarus's 1778 work *On the True Intention of Jesus and His Disciples* (fragments of which had been published by Lessing) was the first critical life of Jesus. David Friedrich Strauss (*The Life of Jesus Critically Examined*, 1835) would more fully develop both the idea of gospel myth and that of its application to the life of Jesus. He demonstrated in exacting detail the bankruptcy of both orthodox literalism (construing miracles as actual supernatural events) and rationalism (construing miracles as contrived or misunderstood natural occurrences). Strauss showed that the miracle stories are myths and legends characteristic of the ancients.

Barthold Georg Niebuhr wrote the first truly critical history of Rome, employing the methods soon to be applied with dazzling effect to the New Testament by Ferdinand Christian Baur. Niebuhr observed that the historian must first ask what is the evidence, then how good is the evidence, and then seek to make sense of the evidence even where what it tells us is false. Can we discern the *Tendenz* (the tendency or ax-grinding "spin") of the writer? Why is he telling us the falsehood he is telling us? If we can discover this, we will know even more about him and his purpose in writing than he wanted us to know. Baur applied these canons to the history of the early church, realizing that the interpreter must first place each document in its correct historical context. Where is it to be placed along the trajectory of the development of Christian thought? Baur plotted out this process as the antithetical struggle between Paulinist Gentile Christianity and Petrine Jewish Christianity, followed by a period of Catholicizing harmonization. Luke, in his Acts of the Apostles, was shown to have rewritten the history of the church in accord with his later catholicizing agenda.

F. H. Bradley (*The Presuppositions of Critical History*, 1874) wrote in defense of Baur and Strauss. He argued that the historian is not a slave of his sources. He must make himself, as the son of his age, the criterion of what he will accept as historical and reject as legendary or tendentious. What else can he do? He has no recourse except to the observed experience of himself and his contemporaries. We cannot accept a report of a prodigy if it is unparalleled in the experience of anyone we know or unless we can verify it for ourselves. If suddenly we were to verify the occurrence of paranormal phenomena like exorcism or the stigmata, then we could in principle accept ancient reports of these things, however we might want to explain them. But unless we make our own experience the norm—that is, unless we assume methodologically the uniformity of nature and history—no inference is possible at all. And equally, nothing could be judged more probable than anything else. Our only alternatives would be utter skepticism or utter credulity.

R. G. Collingwood, in his posthumously published *The Idea of History* (1956), reviewed the necessary evolution of history, from a mere compiling and harmonizing of documents as "authorities" whose word about past events is to be believed without question into what he termed "critical history." In the latter, the historian himself has become the authority, his documents mere sources. (Here, as often, Collingwood merely recapitulates Bradley, selling the latter short in the process.) He says that the difference between a precritical historian and a scientific historian is that the former is a mere cut-and-paste compiler, weeding out the lying sources, but simply passing on what the truthful ones tell him. The scientific historian on the other hand is able to use false testimony as genuine evidence anyway (just as Niebuhr did), thinking himself back into the mind-set of the ancient writer so as to discern the tendency or belief that caused him to give us the false statement. It may have been sexist bias, in which case we can use his distortions as evidence in a history of sexism. Again like F. H. Bradley, Collingwood notes that historical reconstruction is largely a matter of causal inference traced between coordinates provided by a set of facts. But the "facts" themselves are established as such by virtue of the historian's judgment. Collingwood says that the criterion the historian uses is a general picture of the past, a paradigm that he both infers from the evidence and uses to make fuller sense of the evidence.

Van A. Harvey (*The Historian and the Believer*, 1972) set himself the task of vindicating Ernst Troeltsch's three principles of criticism (no historical judgment can ever be any more than probable and provisional), analogy (the experience of the past must be assumed to be not radically different from that observed today), and correlation (events are to be set in a sequence of cause and effect and historical conditioning) against the charges of theological apologists that the three principles are the function of arbitrary "naturalistic presuppositions," for example, the philosophical exclusion of the very possibility of miracles. Harvey shows that this is not so. First he shows that there is not one unique type of "historical" judgment call; rather, the field of historical study encompasses various different logical fields of argument in which very different bodies of data, warrants for conclusions inferred from the data, challenges to warrants, rebuttals, and the like, function. The historian must deal with them all. Each warrant appropriate to the evaluation of a particular historical claim is in turn based on certain truisms, generalizations about what everyone recog-

nizes as the truth, what the burden of proof would be on one to deny. Thus no universal laws of nature or anything else are called upon. Nor need they be, since the historian is not a clairvoyant in reverse, dogmatizing on what happened. Rather he is merely inferring what *would* have happened in the past, "all things being equal." The name of the game is probability. As F. C. Baur said, Anything is possible, but what is probable? The real problem for apologists is not the use of a dogmatic presupposition by critics (that miracles can't happen) but rather their lack of one (the believer's presupposition that scripture is factually inerrant). Only so can we explain the special pleading in which the apologists indulge.

Source Criticism. Source criticism disputes both traditional ascriptions of authorship and the literary integrity of the books of the Bible. The first major bombshell dropped by source critics (the greatest of whom was Julius Wellhausen) was that the Pentateuch (first five books, the Torah proper) was not written by Moses, something that ought to be obvious from the fact that the narration several times refers to conditions long after the time of Moses (Gen. 36:40–43; Exod. 12:6), who is already regarded as an ancient figure even in Deuteronomy (34:6,10). Rather, the Pentateuch is a compilation of earlier narrative and legal sources probably assembled in the fifth century BCE or later: collections of legends and laws. It is fairly simple to tell the sources apart, even in English translation, once one knows what to look for.

The earliest of these underlying documents, as well as the most stylistically beautiful, is the J source, so called because it uses the name Yahve (or Yahweh, or Jehovah represented in English Bibles as "LORD" or "GOD") the whole way through, and it is a collection of material from the southern Hebrew kingdom, Judah (Yehudah). (German scholars discovered all this, and Germans pronounce *J* like our English *Y*.) J gives us raw mythology unretouched (Yahve often appears as a character on stage)—entertaining portraits of biblical characters not yet "sanitized" as holy saints. J is anachronistic, paying little attention to when various laws actually began to be observed in Israel, sometimes describing the ancients as if they followed the customs of J's own day. J's story begins with the creation (the Garden of Eden story, Gen. 2:4b–chap. 3) and continues on through Moses. J may have compiled his epic, at the earliest, in Rehoboam's reign (just after Solomon), but it may even date to as late as post-Exilic times.

The second source is a collection of similar materials, the E source, so called because it calls the deity Elohim ("God") until the burning bush story (Exod. 3:13–16), after which it adds "Yahve." It was a collection of stories from the northern Hebrew kingdom, Israel or Ephraim. E is more conservative in its depiction of God, having him speak from offstage in dreams or visions. It also tries to clean up the faults of the characters, as we can see by comparing the J and E versions of the same story

(Gen. 16 [J] vs. 21 [E]; 12:10–20 [J] vs. 20 [E]). E begins with Abraham and extends through Moses. E is later than J and may come from the ninth century—the dawn of the prophets—since it calls Abraham a prophet. But it may date from much later.

The third source is D, the basis of the Book of Deuteronomy, consisting of the sermons fictively ascribed to Moses from chapters 4 through 34. Though it seems to incorporate sermonic material from the old Shiloh shrine in the north, this book was put together by prophets and priests (Hilkiah, Huldah, Jeremiah?) in the seventh century BCE. Someone later added a historical preface (Deut. 1–3), a summary of the Moses/Exodus sections of J and E, already combined.

Like D, the fourth source is mainly a vast law code, or a set of them—called P, or the Priestly Code—compiled by the exiled Jewish priests while in Babylon in the sixth century BCE. It contains the sketchiest summary of Israelite history, beginning with the six-day Creation (Gen. 1:1–2:4a) and going on through Moses. The Creation, Flood, and Moses stories are told at some length. But by far most of P is legal materials. We do not know to what extent these were actual laws that governed Israel and Judah, or whether they may have been an ideal blueprint like Plato's *Republic* or Thomas More's *Utopia*.

Source-critical study also disclosed to the satisfaction of all but fundamentalist apologists the late and multiple authorship of Isaiah, Daniel, Ezekiel, Zechariah, and Job, as well as the gospels (Matthew and Luke both having rewritten the earlier Q source [see below] and the Gospel of Mark) and the epistles, especially 2 Corinthians.

Form Criticism. Form criticism (*formgeschichte*), or form history, appeared in biblical studies in the work of Hermann Gunkel. He pointed out, as against Julius Wellhausen, whose source analysis he accepted in broad outline, that the J and E sources were not the work of writers in any modern sense, but rather of collectors and compilers of ancient oral traditions, which they modified very little except for writing them down. Gunkel picked out five major types of stories/legends in Genesis, though we find many of them throughout the Bible. They are differentiated according to what question the ancients were seeking to answer in a prescientific yet ingenious and inventive way.

Etiological stories are narrative attempts to explain why remarkable things are the way they are: how they came about. Why is there death (Gen. 3:19)? Why do we wear clothes (Gen. 3:7)? Why must we work for a living (Gen. 3:17–19a)? Why do people hate snakes (Gen. 3:14–15)? What is the rainbow (Gen. 9:12-17)? Why do spiders spin webs (see the Greek myth of Arachne the seamstress)?

Etymological stories seek to explain, by means of puns, the supposed origins of names no one understood anymore, or that had unsavory pagan origins and needed a more wholesome Hebrew explanation. Such fanciful name origins are supplied for Moses (Exod. 2:10), Cain

(Gen. 4:1), Jerubbaal (Judg. 6:32), Ishmael (Gen. 16:11), Isaac (Gen. 21:3–16), Jacob (Gen. 25:26), Perez (Gen. 38:29), and many others, as well as for sacred places like Beer-lahai-roi (Gen. 16:13–14) and Bethel (Gen. 28:17–18).

Ethnological stories depict the relations of nations, tribes, groups existing in the narrator's day—symbolizing each group as a fictive ancestor who has the stereotype traits of the group. Why do the Israelites and the Edomites always fight, despite being neighbors and even kin? Because Esau and Jacob got off to a bad start (Gen. 27:1–41), and now it's in the blood. What justified Israelite intermarriage with Philistines and their joint subjugation of the Canaanites? Noah's prophetic curse (Gen. 9:20–27).

Geological stories explain the origin of remarkable features of the landscape, whether oases (Exod. 17:6), springs (Judg. 15:18–19), wind-eroded rock formations, man-made cairns (Gen. 31:44–54; Joshua 4:1–7; 7:25–26), glacial megaliths, and so on. The most famous is the salinization of Mrs. Lot (Gen. 19:26).

Ceremonial stories are told to supply a rationale for performing some ritual or custom that was either so archaic that no one remembered why it was first done, or else pagan in origin and thus requiring a new "orthodox" rationale. The Passover story (Exod. 12:21–27), that of Jacob wrestling with a god (Gen. 32:13–31, accounting for a dietary taboo), God attacking the uncircumcised Moses (Exod. 4:24–26, justifying the changeover from puberty to infancy circumcision), and many others are of this type. Most of the stories of Moses and Israel in the wilderness establish ceremonial and legal precedents.

To these five we might add another, suggested by anthropologist Bronislaw Malinowski: *Legitimization stories.* In order to reinforce a society's laws and customs, a story tells how, at the dawn of creation, God or the gods decreed that it be this way. Who are we to change it now? Of course, the story is told after human beings have created the custom, not before. The subordination of women to men in Eden is a prime example.

Many biblical stories fall into more than one of these categories, doing double or triple duty to answer many questions. Perhaps the stories grew in the telling, as each telling prompted new questions from the audience.

Form criticism also allowed the first intelligible reading of the Psalms, placing them as the lyrics of various kinds of laments, hymns, petitions, and ceremonial songs to be performed by the king and the Levitical choristers in the Jerusalem temple.

This approach passed over into New Testament studies once Karl Ludwig Schmidt demonstrated that the chronology of the Gospel of Mark was wholly artificial, and had served merely as a skeleton on which to arrange various individual, originally independent oral traditions. Previously scholars had relied heavily upon the Markan outline for their highly imaginative "lives of Jesus." Now that prop was kicked away. The most important work in the field was immediately undertaken by Rudolf Karl Bultmann (*History of the Synoptic Tradition*, 1921), Martin Dibelius (*From Tradition to Gospel*, 1933), and Vincent Taylor (*Formation of the Gospel Tradition*, 1935). The main premise governing all gospel form criticism (and one which seems to survive the controversies discussed below) is that the gospel tradition was passed down orally in the form of separate units, streamlined in transmission. Nothing was preserved that did not have a practical (theological, polemical, liturgical, etc.) use. Within a specific *pericope* (a unit of material such as an individual miracle story, aphorism, parable, and the like), no detail was preserved unless it met some need, served some purpose. Further, each specific form had a set function. For instance, genealogies (Matt. 1:1–17; Luke 3:23–38) serve to legitimate, in this case, Jesus's Messianic lineage (just as those in 1 Chronicles serve as pedigrees for priestly families). The result of all this is that the form critic's task is to creatively reconstruct the *Sitz-im-Leben* (the socioreligious matrix in which each piece of tradition was preserved or created by the early community).

Pronouncement stories (Taylor) or *paradigms* (Dibelius) or *apophthegms* (Bultmann, using the term conventional in the study of such anecdotes told of the Greek philosophers) are brief tales that issue in a memorable saying ("pronouncement") of Jesus. Only enough is told to provide an interpretive context for the saying, and the stories likely arose in order to interpret originally unattached sayings. Dibelius thought these stories were sermon illustrations ("paradigms"). More likely they were used in intra-Christian polemic over the issues treated in them such as Sabbath observance rules. Should we pick grain (Mark 2:23–28), heal (Mark 1–5), or carry mats (Mark 2:1–12) on the Sabbath? Must we pay the two-drachma tax (Matt. 17:24–27)? *Aphorisms* serve much the same purpose, but may also be used simply as proverbs to guide one's conduct. These are like pronouncement stories, only with no story attached.

Miracle stories were probably used as evangelistic propaganda to create faith in the divine savior, much as the testimonials of the miracles of the Hellenistic healing god Asclepius were posted for perusal at the shrine of Epidauros. But the third-century CE church father Origen gives us an important clue as to the function of the healing and exorcism stories, when he tells us that in his day they were read on the occasion of attempted exorcisms and healings. Dibelius had surmised as much. The research of Claude Lévi-Strauss on healing chants among the Kuna, and of Raphael Patai on medieval exorcism stories, would confirm the same. The preservation of the magical techniques used by Jesus, as well as his exact Aramaic words (Mark 5:41; 7:34) is thus explained: the would-be Christian exorcist/healer wanted to ape Jesus as exactly as possible.

Law words are legislation for the early church on various topics on which it had come to differ from Judaism. Many are simply given in didactic form, some of these to be found in Matthew 18–19. Others must be identified as such by subject, since as to form they are pronouncement stories. They may also be garnished with scripture citations (as the story about plucking grain on the Sabbath) or with a rule miracle (as Gerd Thiessen calls them in his *The Miracle Stories of the Early Christian Tradition*, 1983), as in the story where Jesus proves the community's right to pronounce forgiveness of sins when he heals the paralytic lowered through the thatching. The tradition also abounds in *wisdom sayings*, Christological "*Ich-wörter*" ("I" sayings—portentous self-revelations, as of a hitherto incognito god), *prophecies* of Roman conquest, *apocalyptic predictions* of the coming of the Son of Man and the Kingdom of God, and the like.

Some of the presuppositions of the earliest form critics (perhaps Bultmann rather less than the rest) have come under fire in recent years from Eberhardt Güttgemanns (*Candid Questions concerning Gospel Form Criticism*, 1970) and others. Güttgemanns and Ulrich Wilckens assailed Dibelius's assumption that the forms, especially the paradigms, originated as either preaching texts or sermon illustrations. Dibelius thought that Acts preserved what Luke intended as models for Christian preaching drawn from traditions of the preaching of the apostles. Though Dibelius (see his collection *Studies in the Acts of the Apostles*, 1956) knew better than anyone else that the sermons were anything but transcripts, he thought they represented the general *kind* of thing once preached. But Wilckens pointed out that even if this were so, and it probably was not, these so-called sermons do not in fact use paradigms and scarcely hint of miracles in any more than general terms. No, Dibelius had unwittingly smuggled the modern Lutheran preaching he heard in church back into the gospels. (For his part, Bultmann had already expressed doubt as to this Dibelian axiom.)

Pressing on further, Güttgemanns denied the common form-critical assumption that the gospel materials ultimately stemmed from the earliest preaching of the death and resurrection of the Son of God. Dibelius was no doubt correct that the materials are thoroughly religious propaganda, not products of historical research, but he never demonstrated how any of them, outside of the Passion narrative, had anything to do with the *kerygma* (the early Christian message). What did exorcisms, law words, walking on the water, and the like, have to do with the kind of thing we read in 1 Corinthians 15:1–11? Paul needed miracles so little that he never mentions them. The same is true with the teachings of the Risen One, with one or two possible exceptions.

C. H. Dodd (*The Apostolic Preaching and Its Developments*, 1935) had already tried to clarify things by distinguishing the *kerygma* (in his model, the saving message of the cross and resurrection) from the *didache* (subsequent catechism on secondary matters), but this was only to concede that most of the material had nothing really to do with the allegedly all-important *kerygma*. Certainly Ernst Käsemann, Bultmann's disciple, was off target with his claim that the rest of the tradition was necessary to keep the *kerygma* from fading into Docetism (the denial that Jesus had ever assumed a fleshly body). Was Paul, who wrote of the risen Christ but scarcely ever of the man Jesus, then a Docetist?

Recently, Burton L. Mack (*A Myth of Innocence*, 1988) has taken this insight much farther, indeed to its logical conclusion. For the material that seems unconcerned or ignorant of a *kerygma* of a dead and risen Christ we must postulate a religious community in which these supposed events were either unknown or unimportant. Whatever community compiled the Q-source of sayings (the sayings common to Luke and Matthew, but not Mark) must have been unconcerned with Jesus's supposed atonement and resurrection, since Q makes no reference to these things. The Q community, therefore, would perhaps have denied them had they heard of them. Conversely, the *kerygma* belonged to the Christ Cult, which venerated a Christ analogous to the shadowy *Kurioi* ("Lords," saviors and demigods) of the Hellenistic mystery religions.

Dibelius and Gunkel had been much influenced by the theories of Johann Gottfried von HERDER on folklore and folk poetry. Herder had maintained that such poetry stemmed from a primitive *Volk* lacking either artistic sophistication or any polemical ax to grind. This was all of a piece with Rousseau's popular "noble savage" idea. Artistic craft was seen as a poor substitute for the authentic poetic inspiration of the pristine and unspoiled, because unsophisticated, *Volk*. In Dibelius this translated into the convenient notion that the early gospel material (paradigms and paradigmatic miracle stories) came fresh from the collective matrix of "the early community," a blessed band innocent of both contrived artistry and ax grinding. Their simplicity was a mark and a proof at once of historical truth and of naive poetic beauty. And, just as Herder thought the unspoiled poetic consciousness of the *Volk* was transparent to God, Dibelius put the historical Jesus in God's place. Form critic Vincent Taylor, more of a rationalist and an apologist, sought to buttress the case for gospel authenticity by in effect placing the apostles and eyewitnesses as guards at the tomb of the tradition, guaranteeing that the fancy-flights of the early community did not carry off the truth about the historical Jesus. But, as Güttgemanns shows, the fantasy of the poetic *Volk* was soon seen in wider literary circles for what it was: the product of Herder's Romantic sentimentality. Again, we have Mack to thank for a consistent application of this insight. He shows us that the artistry of any pericope is evidence for a highly sophisticated and intentional crafting by educated people. The apophthegms, far from being simple recollections by the pristine Galilean peasants, were more likely the products of a school exercise to show how well one had grasped the thought of an important figure. Hellenistic students were educated in the art of creating appropriate sayings to attribute to philosophers they studied.

Can we determine the authentic words of Jesus? Bultmann thought this improbable, indeed nearly impossible. But in light of research into oral tradition as it functions today, it is rather simply out of the question given the nature of the case. Homer scholar Albert B. Lord (*The Singer of Tales*, 1960) recorded oral recitations of epics by Balkan singers, and he showed that each such recitation, especially with any innovations it incorporates, is intended and must be appreciated as a new "original," each performance having its own integrity. Similarly, no reviewer thinks one judges the merits of the various screen versions of *Hamlet* simply by virtue of how many of William Shakespeare's words have been left unchanged or left out. That is the whole idea of an adaptation or, in music, of a new arrangement. To seek the "original words" of Jesus is to make nonsense of the tradition as we now have it, to interpret it against its own intent. The early form critics were guilty of the logocentric fallacy, seeking some true original intent as if it hovered like a ghost at a seance somewhere above the extant versions. As anthropologist Jan Vansina (*Oral Tradition as History*, 1985) shows, the very notion of an original version when we are talking about oral literature is itself highly questionable.

Form critics like Dibelius and Joachim Jeremias (*The Parables of Jesus*, 1954) underestimated the extent to which oral transmission is a process of incremental evolution. A particular pronouncement story or miracle story is like a biological species: it didn't just appear full-blown one morning. Rather, so many little changes accumulated over time that eventually it was a whole new beast. Even so, we must suppose that individual motifs, themes, details, and so on, gradually were added and dropped out, until one story turned into another. And we cannot know where the process began. What was the first form of the Prodigal Son story? Well, what was the first bird? The Pteranodon? It had wings. Archaeopteryx? It had feathers. Or do you want to wait until the eagle? It's all arbitrary.

Vansina shows that oral transmission need not proceed along the kind of unidirectional, linear trajectory that Jeremias thought he could chart. A piece of tradition may well double back on itself; interact with written versions before it returns to orality; or be cross-fertilized with other tellings, harmonizing details as it goes. The process might be compared to textual transmission/corruption of biblical manuscripts. Our only hope of straightening out the whole mess is to have plenty of manuscript evidence to work with, and with the *pericopae* of the gospels, that is precisely what we do not have in most cases. Güttgemanns attacked the form-critical insistence that the compilation of the gospels in written form was merely the extension of the same oral tradition process, a further step on the same trajectory. Güttgemanns showed from Lord's research how the stage of writing down must have occasioned a fundamental change in the hitherto oral material (on this see further Werner Kelber, *The Oral and the Written Gospel*, 1983).

Güttgemanns argues that the critics were wrong in denying any authorial role to the Synoptic collectors, making them out to be cut-and-paste editors, a myopia that resulted in the ridiculous spectacle of critics seeking a traditional basis for obviously redactional items like the Markan Passion predictions (Mark 8:31; 9:12, 31; 10:33–34). No, shortsightedness like this only stops us from seeing the forest for the trees. The gospels *as wholes* could not be understood until the advent of redaction criticism, and later of literary, narrative criticism.

Redaction Criticism. Redaction criticism takes up where form criticism left off. It focuses on the designed and tendentious alteration of their source material by the evangelists. The science of *Redactionsgeschichte* was pioneered by Willi Marxsen (*Mark the Evangelist*, 1969); Hans Conzelmann (*The Theology of Saint Luke*, 1960); and Günther Bornkamm, Gerhard Barth, and Hans Joachim Held (*Tradition and Interpretation in Matthew*, 1963). The method of redaction criticism differs as to whether one has the redactor's sources available for comparison. If we do, then redaction criticism proceeds directly from source criticism, as when we compare either Matthew or Luke with their sources: Mark and the reconstructed Q. If we do not have the prior source in any independent form, then redaction criticism works on the basis of form criticism, together with a few other tricks. For example, we may try to reconstruct what Mark did to his source material by trying to recognize the original outlines of the pericopae he had to work with from tradition. A classic example would be Wilhelm Wrede's *The Messianic Secret* (1901). His work preceded form and redaction criticism, but anticipated the results of both. He could see that the secrecy theme ill fit most of the texts upon which Mark seems to have imposed it, the clearest being the resurrection of Jairus's daughter. From a form-critical standpoint we would expect the story to end with an acclamation of the miracle worker, which is what we do usually find, even elsewhere in Mark (e.g., 1:27; 2:1; 4:41; 6:51; 7:37). But instead, here (Mark 5:43) Jesus sternly warns the parents to tell no one—even though the house is circled by mourners who know their daughter is dead! Is she to grow up confined to her room in order to maintain the pretense that she's dead?

Wrede noticed a recurrent pattern of such silencings (Mark 1:25, 34, 44; 3:12; 4:11–12; 7:36; 8:26, 30; 9:9) and decided that Mark had been anything but a simple compiler. Rather, he had rewritten the whole story in order to harmonize two conceptions of Christology: Had Jesus only been made Messiah upon his resurrection (Rom. 1:3–4; Acts 2:36; 13:33)? Or had he been Messiah during his whole ministry, ever since the baptism? Both! Mark has Jesus become Messiah at the baptism (Mark 1:11), yet keep it hidden until the Resurrection (Mark 9:7, 9), so that most only became aware of the fact then, understandably to infer that only then was he entering into messiahship.

Sometimes the redaction critic must be on the lookout for "redactional seams" that seem to hint at editorial work on material he can no longer compare with the final product. These include abrupt discontinuities, as when Jesus's prediction of his resurrection at the Last Supper in Mark (14:28) seems to go unheard as Peter responds (14:29) to what Jesus had said immediately *before* (14:27). No doubt Mark added the prediction. Another obvious type of seam is the repetition of a sentence after an apparently interruptive digression, as if the redactor, after adding new material, felt the need to duplicate the hook on which the ensuing text originally hung (e.g., 2 Cor. 6:13; 7:2).

Perhaps the greatest systematic use of redaction criticism is the work of Conzelmann on Luke, focusing on Luke's redaction of the eschatological teaching in Mark. In several places Luke has toned down Mark's imminent expectation of the end of the age, in others eliminating it altogether. Gone is the initial proclamation of Jesus entering Galilee: "The time is fulfilled. The Kingdom of God is at hand" (from Mark 1:15). Luke replaces it with the Nazareth sermon (Luke 4:16–30), transferred from a later point in Mark (6:1–6), as even its Lukan context shows by its reference to previous miracles in Capernaum (Luke 4:4–23), which cannot have yet occurred in Luke's timeline. After the confession of Peter, Mark had Jesus promise that at least some of the disciples would live to see the Kingdom of God come "in power" (Mark 9:1), a phrase which often in the New Testament denotes eschatological (end-time) resurrection (Romans 1:4; 1 Cor. 15:43; Mark 6:14). But since all the twelve are now sleeping beneath the sod, Luke 9:27 omits "in power" to leave room for some metaphorical or other invisible mode of the arrival of the kingdom.

At the Sanhedrin trial, Mark had Jesus promise his accusers that "[y]ou will see the Son of Man sitting at the right hand of power and coming with the clouds of heaven" (14:62). But in Luke's time the Sanhedrin members are dead without exception, so he has Jesus say to them, "From now on the Son of Man will be seated at the right hand of the power of God" (Luke 22:69)—nothing about anyone seeing him. In the Olivet Discourse, Mark (13:6) had Jesus predict pseudoprophets who falsely announce "I am he!" But Luke (21:8) adds to their falsehoods something that was true for Mark's Jesus, namely, "The time is at hand!" In the same context, Mark had Jesus predict the fall of Jerusalem and the temple in a lurid apocalyptic cipher derived from Daniel (9:27; 11:31; 12:11): "the abomination of desolation" (Mark 13:14). But the antiapocalyptic Luke does not want the destruction of the temple to be seen as a portent of an immediate end (since in fact it wasn't!), so he historicizes the event, making overt references to Roman siege tactics (Luke 21:20). If Josephus made Vespasian into the Christ, Luke at least absolved Titus of being the Antichrist! And so little can the events of 70 CE presage the end that Luke inserts into the discourse a new dispensation, "the times of the Gentiles," which must be fulfilled before the end can be near (21:24). Into this compartment he will place the whole of the Acts and any future history as well.

But this is not enough for Luke. Into his narrative he places no less than three strategic questions intended to explode the notion of the soon-coming kingdom, a fanatical view he knows some readers still hold. In Luke 17:20 Jesus is "asked by the Pharisees when the Kingdom of God was coming." This question thus throws the following saying into new perspective as a denial of any calculability or temporality of the coming of the End: "The Kingdom of God is not coming with observation, nor will they say, 'Lo, here it is!' or 'Lo, there!' But the Kingdom of God is within you/in your midst."

Again, in Luke 19:11–27 Jesus is made to tell the parable of the Minas (in Matt. 25:14–30, the Talents) in order to deflate the mistaken notion that "the Kingdom of God was to appear immediately" (v. 11), and the parable is expanded to include the episode of a lord going away to receive kingly authority. He must make a *long* journey and thus will be gone a *long* time, so his return as king surely cannot be soon.

Third, in Acts 1:6, the disciples, apparently none the wiser after a full forty days of presumably juicy post-Resurrection revelations, are still dumb enough to ask, "Lord, will you at this time restore the kingdom to Israel?" He replies by both temporizing and spiritualizing the kingdom: "It is not for you to know the times and seasons the Father has fixed by his own authority, but you will receive power when the Holy Spirit is come upon you."

Discerning patterns like these, Conzelmann was able to postulate a unique historical interest for Luke. Luke did not think Christians ought to wait for an *eschaton* that had already been embarrassingly delayed more than once. Picking up certain other hints, Conzelmann was able to construct a Lukan periodization of history that made room for an ongoing age of the church in which he himself stood and sought to do constructive work. First, Luke prefaces the story of Jesus with sections on John's and Jesus's nativities, which are closely modeled on Old Testament accounts of the birth of Samuel and his recognition by Eli (1 Sam. 1–3). Eli's place is taken here by Simeon and Anna, who embody the previous Old Testament dispensation, the time of Israel. This period will continue petering out till the appearance of John the Baptist, whom Luke robs of his Markan position as the apocalyptic Elijah-prophet, relegating him to a mere pre-Christian prophet, albeit the last in the series: "The Law and the Prophets prophesied until John; since then the Kingdom of Heaven is evangelized." So the "middle of time" (Conzelmann's original title for this book) begins, the time of Jesus, a Satan-free period of ideal fellowship with God's Messiah. Once Jesus banishes Satan in the wilderness, the tempter departs "until an opportune

time" should present itself (Luke 4:13), which it does at Gethsemane (hence no "get behind me Satan" rebuke in Luke's version of the confession of Peter, 9:18–21). The disciples may travel and preach the news of the Kingdom without fear of persecution or molestation. But this is over at the Last Supper, when Jesus recalls those halcyon days: "Remember when I sent you out without provisions? Did you lack anything? I thought not. But now I tell you, if you lack a sword, go sell your cloak and buy one" (Luke 22:35–36). Hard times ahead! The middle of time will end, and even as Jesus speaks these words they are being fulfilled, as the Satan-possessed Judas leads the temple police to arrest Jesus.

But the period of the church dawns bright and sunny on Easter when at the end of the gospel and the start of Acts Jesus gives the disciples their marching orders (take the Gospel to Galilee, Samaria, and Rome—the ground plan of Acts) before he ascends to heaven from whence he may occasionally be seen by the likes of Stephen (Acts 7:55) and Paul (Acts 9:4–5; 22:17–21) during the time of the church. Parenthetically, it is significant that this schematization extends even to the exclusion of the latecomer Paul from the ranks of the apostles, since to qualify for that select college one must have been present with Jesus during the whole of the middle of time (Acts 1:21–22). Those who were functioned much as they do in Irenaeus, as guarantors of the doctrine traced by their supposed successors, the bishops, to that golden time (Acts 10:39; 13:31).

The Historical Jesus. As already anticipated, these critical methodologies have been honed as tools for the task of rediscovering the historical Jesus (see JESUS, HISTORICITY OF). Why has this search gone on for so long, and with such mixed and negligible results? Our difficulties stem from the state and character of the evidence for Jesus, or what at first appears to be such evidence. We have four canonical—and more noncanonical—gospels, which, insofar as they agree in any detail, seem to be mutually interdependent rather than serving as multiple witnesses. And insofar as they disagree, they seem to wildly contradict one another. Any semblance of a coherent unity is a dogmatic synthesis imposed on the texts by centuries of harmonization of the canonical four and suppression of the others. Add to this fact that we have no early material, so far as we know. No source definitely attests that the canonical gospels existed until Irenaeus, late in the second century. Even if we knew we had early sources, they are based on floating oral tradition which transmogrifies as often as it gets repeated; the more often it seems to have been repeated, the more luridly it is embellished. The accounts could have changed many times within weeks of the events, let alone years. And how much more so when we are dealing with reports of supposed miracles? Recent psychological research has demonstrated that eyewitness memory is at its most unreliable when it comes to extraordinary events.

Many sayings and stories in the gospels so closely mirror similar materials to be found among the fund of Rabbinic and Hellenistic lore that we must assume that some of each has ended up attributed to the other, and it is now impossible to trace the direction or the extent of influence. However, Christian borrowing from pagan and Jewish sources is more probable in the nature of the case, and likely to be more extensive. This is simply because Christianity is the younger phenomenon, hence more likely the recipient of converts from its rivals than a contributor of them to its rivals. New converts must have brought with them their cherished myths and sayings, now attributed to their new savior. Anachronisms such as the frequent presence of Pharisees in Galilee in the 20s CE shake our confidence further.

Many sayings are clearly tendentious, obviously made to order to settle some later church dispute, such as the unequivocal Great Commission aimed at settling the vexing question of the Gentile mission long after Jesus (an end also served by those stories where Jesus reluctantly heals the children of Gentiles, code for the Gentile mission bringing Jesus to Gentiles in the subsequent generation). Or: "Think not that I have come to abolish the Law and the Prophets. I have not come to abolish them but to fulfill them" (Matt. 5:17–19). This looks back on the life of Jesus in such a way (as do all the "I came to . . ." or "The Son of Man came to . . ." sayings) as to sum up his whole historical career. And it is manifestly an intended corrective to a libertine opinion held by radical Paulinists, a party of Christians who say Jesus "came to" do away with the law.

Though critics and historians have invented various criteria to help us arrive at what Jesus did or said, they are of little help. Not only do they present us with wildly varying results, but their criteria cancel one another out. Norman Perrin calls one of these widely used canons, used also by Bultmann and others, the criterion of dissimilarity. That is, we can be pretty sure that a saying goes back to Jesus only if it does not too closely mirror the belief or practice of either the early church (for otherwise the church belief may have been retrojected onto Jesus) or that of contemporary Judaism (for otherwise it may have been Jewish in origin and attributed to Jesus later). Perrin's caveats are quite well founded, but they leave us with near-total skepticism. This is because the criterion of dissimilarity runs afoul of the central axiom of form criticism: that nothing, nothing at all, was transmitted unless it represented the usage of some quarter of the church. This, too, is likely to be true. But then it means nothing at all can be safely traced back to Jesus. Does Mark 2:16ff. tell us *not* to fast, while Matthew 6:16ff. tells us *how* to fast? We must assume that each represents the praxis of a different faction within the church.

James Breech speaks of the criterion of embarrassment, a good new name for a well-worn tool. John Dominic Crossan calls it "theological damage control"—even better. If an item embarrassed the church, the church could hardly have created it. But this ignores the fact that what was embarrassing to one generation or sector of the church was not embarrassing to another. As apologist John Warwick Montgomery once quipped, everything Jesus said offended *somebody* in the early church! Matthew and Luke found the spittle magic of Jesus in Mark to be embarrassing, but that need not mean that Mark was right in having Jesus do it. It may be that earlier Christians, casting out spirits in the name of their cult deity Jesus, created stories which attributed to him the current conventions of exorcism.

Does Mark 12:35ff., with its clear denial of the Davidic descent of the Messiah, embarrass the creators of the Davidic genealogies of Matthew and Luke? Yes, but it is most likely the creation of earlier Christians who knew Jesus wasn't Davidic and decided to challenge this troublesome premise of Jewish critics. It appears in the Epistle of Barnabas with no attribution to Jesus.

Even the "I will destroy this temple made with hands and in three days raise up another not made with hands" (Mark 14:58) saying began as a theological *vaticinium ex eventu* (prediction after the fact) coined by Christians, meaning that the temple was destroyed because Jews rejected Jesus, and that Christianity erected a spiritual temple on its ruins. It only became too hot to handle once it occasioned persecution by Romans later.

The criterion of multiple attestation means to vindicate sayings of Jesus found in more than one independent gospel source. Such multiple occurrence makes it less likely that a particular saying is the coinage of some lone wolf prophet or of the evangelist himself. (The criterion is exactly analogous to that of "catholicity" in the case of the New Testament canon: only widely attested writings were eligible.) If a saying went back to Jesus, it should have had more time to circulate and would have found purchase in more than one place. But rumors and inauthentic, misattributed sayings can make the rounds, too. Can we discern the life settings of various elaborations and embellishments of this or that pericope, and thus tell when and where in the history of the community they were added? Yes: Bultmann and Jeremias do this quite effectively in many cases. But as Jan Vansina points out, one can only show in this way that a saying is *in*authentic. One may not be able to show the saying or story is spurious from its beginning, but this may be because we can't trace it all the way back. The burden of proof is on the defender of authenticity, and it seems a burden that no scholarly Atlas can bear. Thus, though there may once have been a historical Jesus, a Jesus who lived, there is no historical Jesus any more. None is available to us with any real degree of probability. Guesses may be made— and guesses have continued to be made—but guesses are all they are; and too often they are the reflections, as Modernist George Tyrrell observed long ago, of the face of each "quester." We may survey some of the guesses of recent experts in the field.

Geza Vermes (*Jesus the Jew*, 1973; *The Religion of Jesus the Jew*, 1993) notices the similarity between many aspects of the Jesus story in the gospels and tales told of Galilean Hasidim like Honi (Onias) the Circle-Maker and Hanina ben-Dosa. Heavenly voices claimed all these men as "my son." All were in trouble with more orthodox scribes for lax observance of Halakah (Rabbinic rules of conduct and ritual) at certain points. All were effective exorcists of demons, their name alone sufficing to put them on the run. All worked miracles. All addressed God as *Abba* ("Father"). Vermes's essential case is that Jesus was a Galilean Hasid (charismatic holy man). But Vermes is too trusting both of Hasidic and Christian legends. He might effectively argue that Galilean Christians employed such legends to interpret Jesus, but that's all. Surely no one actually heard a heavenly voice claiming any of these men as sons of the Almighty. It is a legend in all cases. And did Jesus call God *Abba* at all? We find this only in the Gethsemane story (Mark 14:36) where all possible witnesses are asnooze. Mark has simply attributed Christian prayer language (Gal. 4:6), inherited from the Aramaic church, to Jesus.

Ben P. Meyer (*The Aims of Jesus*, 1979) just dishes up warmed-over Jeremias. He has Jesus as a Messiah and would-be spearhead of a movement of national repentance. He is recognizably the orthodox Protestant Christ, going to the cross with eyes open. This book is a throwback to the lives of Jesus written around World War II by Jeremias, Vincent Taylor, T. W. Manson, William Manson, A. M. Hunter, and Oscar Cullmann. Like them, Meyer accepts altogether too much as authentic which is demonstrably redactional—for example, the Matthean antitheses (Matt. 5:21–48), on the basis of which Meyer makes Jesus challenge scripture itself with Christological authority. Like his predecessors, Meyer pretends to be a critic, agreeing to place some gospel items on the shelf but retaining those bits which contain only a residual wash of Christian dogma. Meyer then claims that since what he has left is more modest Christologically, then it is early and authentic, and since it contains implicitly or by hint what the bracketed materials say explicitly, then we can go on and accept as authentic the explicit features of the rest, too. Pure sleight of hand! Meyer also makes use of the argument from silence when it suits him (Jesus must have aimed at collective national repentance because it is a common Jewish notion, even though Jesus never explicitly mentions it), but he rejects it when it does not. He even makes Jesus satirize the idea of Gentile destruction in the eschaton—by ignoring it!

Juan Luis Segundo (*The Historical Jesus of the Synoptics*, 1982) makes Jesus an agitator of class conflict. His argument, however, is a chain of weak links. The Lukan beatitude on the poor (Luke 6:20) is taken in a classist sense, though a Cynic frame of reference makes at least as much sense (see below). He assumes a climate of unrest in Galilee that Sean Freyne, Richard A.

Horsley, and others have shown is anachronistic. He makes much of Jesus offering the kingdom to the poor en masse, by doing miracles for individuals when he could not have known whether they were pious Jews or not. But this assumes that Jesus regarded his healings (if he did any) as signs of the in-breaking kingdom, as in the saying, "But if I cast out demons by the finger of God, then the kingdom of God has come upon you" (Luke 11:20). Alas, this is probably a subsequent cloaking of the original magical character of the Beelzebul story, in which Jesus defended the practice of binding the Strong Man Beelzebul so as to use his demonic power to divide his kingdom, conquer him, and free his hostages.

Segundo makes the entry into Jerusalem a messianic provocation, though the earliest gospel, Mark, carefully refrains from having the crowd acclaim Jesus as the Davidic King. The later gospels rewrite it adding "Hosanna to the King (or the Son of David)." Segundo accepts Jeremias's fraudulent equation of the *haberim* (pious dining clubs), the Pharisees, and the Javneh rabbis on the one hand, and the equation of the "sinners" with the common people on the other, which he needs to do if he is to cast Jesus as a champion of the downtrodden poor against their legalistic Pharisee oppressors. He takes even Acts 1:6 seriously as history, so he can say the disciples must have had a political understanding of the kingdom, and that they must have derived it from the pre-Easter Jesus. Unconvincing.

E. P. Sanders (*Jesus and Judaism*, 1985) does a wonderful job in dismantling the anti-Semitic confusions and deceptions of Jeremias and others who made a caricature of Judaism. He shows how, in view of the work of Jacob Neusner and others, we cannot attribute to the Pharisees all the niceties of the Mishnah. We cannot attribute to them the purity vows of the *haberim*, nor can we ascribe to the *haberim* a contempt for outsiders who did not choose their supererogatory discipline. We must not attribute to the Pharisees either the excommunicatory power of the Javneh rabbis, nor any perverse opposition to Jesus's preaching of grace and mercy to repentant sinners. No such Pharisees existed until Christian polemic created them, and certainly Jesus was not condemned for preaching grace and repentance. To explain why Jesus died, Sanders falls back on the model of Jesus as a proclaimer of the end and a predictor of the destruction and replacement of the temple. This plus the cleansing of the temple sealed his doom. But Burton L. Mack has shown anew that we cannot take for granted the historicity of the temple act, and certainly not that of the temple saying (see above).

Sanders also builds a case for an eschatological Jesus on dubious sayings such as "But whoever is least in the Kingdom is greater than [John]" (Matt. 11:11/Luke 7:28) and the promise that his followers will sit on thrones to judge Israel (Matt. 19:28/Luke 22:29–30). The former is obviously a polemical corrective to what was later seen as overpraise of a competitor, while the latter was a saying of a Christian prophet (cf. Rev. 2:26–27).

James Breech (*The Silence of Jesus*, 1983) completely dehistoricizes Jesus, making him mouth Nietzscheanisms (see Friedrich NIETZSCHE), codependency jargon, and late-twentieth-century academic sophisms. Can Jesus really have defined the Kingdom of God as that power that generates the being of individuals as free individuals? Here all distinction between exegesis (what the text meant to its first readers) and hermeneutics (what it might imply for modern readers) has been left far behind. Breech is quite helpful, though, in his indications of the inauthenticity of the seed/growth parables (Mark 4:26–32; Matt. 13:33) insofar as they seem to be fictive "predictions" of the later spread of the Christian Church. Also, his case that the interpretive frame for the parables, "The Kingdom of God is like . . . ," is in every case secondary is quite worth considering.

Marcus Borg (*Conflict, Holiness and Politics in the Teaching of Jesus*, 1984; and *Jesus: A New Vision*, 1987) is another "perilous modernizer" of Jesus. His Jesus is Vermes's Galilean charismatic made into the leader of John G. Gager's (*Kingdom and Community*, 1975) revitalization movement, preaching in contrast to traditional Jewish nationalism a "grounding in Spirit rather than in culture," teaching this phantom sophistry by means of parables interpreted along the perversely modern lines of Breech and Crossan.

Morton Smith's *Jesus the Magician* (1978) shows that not only is Jesus reputed to have been a sorcerer by his opponents both within and without the gospels (including the Talmud and Celsus), but he is shown in the gospels using magical techniques, such as spittle (contagious magic), finger manipulation (imitative magic), groaning to muster psychic power, and silencing the demons. Granted, John M. Hull had shown most of this in his *Hellenistic Magic and the Synoptic Tradition* (1974), but Smith shows how even the descent of the Spirit story reflects the coming of the magician's familiar spirit in the form of a bird. The wilderness testing with spirits approaching under the guise of animals is a typical shamanic initiation. When the Centurion recognizes that Jesus's word of command will be effective (Matthew 8:8–9), he must know that Jesus commands spirits. Thus Jesus had a reputation as a magician.

John Dominic Crossan (*The Historical Jesus*, 1991) seems to accept most of Smith's case. He combines it with material drawn from Richard A. Horsley (*Jesus and the Spiral of Violence*, 1987) and Gerald Downing (*Christ and the Cynics*, 1988; *Cynics and Christian Origins*, 1992) to arrive at a Jesus who was part Cynic philosopher, part sorcerer, and whose only real revolutionary activity was to have potluck suppers with the socially outcast. This vast book should have been much thinner. Its picture of Jesus seems to be mostly a function of the scholarly categories used to analyze him, an unwieldy composite. It has much in common with certain portions of Burton Mack's *A Myth of Innocence*.

Mack, too, sees a good deal of similarity between Jesus as portrayed in certain gospel materials (especially the Mission Charge, Mark 6:12–11, and the early portions of the Q source) and the Cynics. Indeed the similarities are striking. The Cynics preached ideal kingship, the "government of Zeus," and the regulation of life by nature. They preached that one should love one's persecutors. They upbraided the crowd. They begged. They wandered as sons of men for whom nature provided, unlike foxes and birds, no natural habitats.

Mack's great insight is that the various Jesus and Christ images presupposed in various gospel materials do not readily fit together. A parable-spinning exorcist? A halakah-spouting redeemer? And where in all his Galilean wanderings does he ever utter a word relevant to what finally happened at the temple? Jesus's life as well as his death must remain unknown to us, Mack says. The variegated traditions, combined against their original intents by Mark and variously reshaped by others, stem from incompatible religious movements that used their diverse traditions as legitimation charters. In this way, Jesus turns out to be a cameo or a microcosm of the Bible as a whole.

BIBLIOGRAPHY

Baur, Ferdinand Christian. *Paul the Apostle of Jesus Christ: His Life and Works, His Epistles and Teachings; A Contribution to a Critical History of Primitive Christianity*. 2 vols. Translated by Allan Menzies. London: Williams & Norgate, 1873–75.

Bornkamm, Günther, Gerhard Barth, and Heinz Joachim Held. *Tradition and Interpretation in Matthew*. Translated by Percy Scott. New Testament Library. London: SCM, 1963.

Bultmann, Rudolf. *History of the Synoptic Tradition*. Translated by John Marsh. 2nd ed. Oxford: Basil Blackwell, 1968.

Conzelmann, Hans. *The Theology of St. Luke*. Translated by Geoffrey Buswell. New York: Harper & Row, 1960.

Dibelius, Martin. *From Tradition to Gospel*. Translated by Bertrram Lee Woolf. New York: Scribner's, 1934.

Fowler, Robert M. *Let the Reader Understand: Reader-Response Criticism and the Gospel of Mark*. Minneapolis: Fortress, 1991.

Gunkel, Hermann. *Genesis*. Translated by Mark E. Biddle. Macon, GA: Mercer University Press, 1997.

Lohfink, Gerhard. *The Bible: Now I Get It! A Form-Criticism Handbook*. Translated by Daniel Coogan. Garden City, NY: Doubleday, 1979.

Marxsen, Willi. *Mark the Evangelist: Studies on the Redaction History of the Gospel*. Translated by James Boyce, Donald Juel, William Poehlmann, and Roy A. Harrisville. New York: Abingdon, 1969.

Mowinckel, Sigmund. *The Psalms in Israel's Worship*. Translated by D. R. Ap-Thomas. Oxford: Basil Blackwell, 1962.

Perrin, Norman. *What Is Redaction Criticism?* Guides to Biblical Scholarship, New Testament Series. Philadelphia: Fortress, 1969.

Reventlow, Henning Graf. *The Authority of the Bible and the Rise of the Modern World.* Translated by John Bowden. Philadelphia: Fortress, 1985.

Schmidt, Karl Ludwig. *The Place of the Gospels in the General History of Literature.* Translated by Byron R. McCain. Columbia: University of South Carolina Press, 2002.

Schweitzer, Albert. *The Quest of the Historical Jesus: A Critical Study of Its Progress from Reimarus to Wrede.* Translated by W. Montgomery. London: A. & C. Black, 1910.

Strauss, David Friedrich. *The Life of Jesus Critically Examined.* Translated by George Eliot. 2nd ed. London: Swan Sonnenschein, 1892.

Streeter, Burnett Hillman. *The Four Gospels: A Study of Origins, Treating of the Manuscript Tradition, Sources, Authorship & Dates.* London: Macmillan, 1924.

Talbert, Charles H., *What Is a Gospel? The Genre of the Canonical Gospels.* Philadelphia: Fortress, 1977.

Taylor, Vincent. *The Formation of the Gospel Tradition: Eight Lectures.* London: Macmillan, 1933.

Wellhausen, Julius. *Prolegomena to the History of Israel.* Translated by J. Sutherland Black and Allan Menzies. Edinburgh: A. & C. Black, 1885.

Wrede, Wilhelm. *The Messianic Secret.* Translated by J. C .G. Greig. London: James Clarke, 1971.

ROBERT M. PRICE

BIBLICAL ERRANCY. The Theory of Infallibility.

In the first decade of the twentieth century, various Protestant scholars began contributing articles to *The Fundamentals*, an influential conservative Christian anthology, to counter what they regarded as the dangers of modern BIBLICAL CRITICISM. Professor James Orr expressed their sentiments when he wrote that the Bible was the repository of a true revelation of God and an infallible guide. By following scripture, one could, he insisted, find salvation, the purpose of living, and the scheme of divine grace. In the second half of the twentieth century, the phrase *biblical inerrancy* expressed the belief that the Bible in its original autographs stood free of error. Whereas the third-century church father Tertullian contended that only the church had the right to interpret scripture, Protestants later rejected the doctrine of papal infallibility to affirm the thesis that believers in fellowship with other believers were free to interpret scripture provided the Holy Spirit guided them.

Relentless Biblical Scholarship. For the past century and a half, the conjecture of biblical inerrancy has steadily yielded ground to biblical scholarship's relentless inquiries into the historical sources, diverse literary genres, rhetorical strategies, and redaction processes. Arranged by topic with cross-references, C. Dennis McK-insey's *Biblical Errancy: A Reference Guide* focuses on biblical contradictions, errors, fallacies, and significant dilemmas. McKinsey is also editor and publisher of *Biblical Errancy Newsletter* and author of *The Encyclopedia of Biblical Errancy*.

Bart D. Ehrman's *The Orthodox Corruption of Scripture* argues that certain orthodox Christians altered various texts of the Bible to suit their theological doctrines. Gerald A. Larue's *Ancient Myth and Modern Life* casts important light on the emergence of religious traditions. In *Can We Trust the New Testament?* G. A. Wells spells out in readable, scholarly detail reason for concluding that the New Testament as a historical document is largely unreliable. Like Wells in his several books on the historical Jesus question, Robert M. Price argues in his *The Incredible Shrinking Son of Man* that the New Testament provides meager information for reconstructing a trustworthy representation of a historical Jesus. *The Empty Tomb: Jesus beyond the Grave* (edited by Price and Jeffery Jay Lowder) deals with severe problems in the various stories of Jesus's resurrection among first-century Christians.

BIBLIOGRAPHY

Green, Ruth Hurmence. *The Born-Again Skeptic's Guide to the Bible.* Madison, WI: Freedom From Religion Foundation, 1979.

JOE EDWARD BARNHART

BIBLE, THE, AND VIOLENCE.

The Bible is not so much one book as a confluence of genres and redactions giving voice to a family of themes, guided roughly by a highly anthropomorphic model of the universe. Violence in the text, which is ample, tends to appear under several broad headings.

Extermination. Since the Hebrew version of the book of Esther does not mention a deity, some rabbis opposed its reception into scripture. To counter its secular tone, the Greek version reconstructed the story with additions providing explicit religious, apocalyptic, and cosmic elements. In both the Hebrew and Greek versions, the story tells of King Ahasuerus's edict to exterminate all the Jews throughout the provinces. Because of the political maneuvers of Esther and her Uncle Mordecai, the king reversed his edict by issuing a decree permitting the Jews to exterminate all who might attack them. This included the liquidation of enemy women and children. Their goods were confiscated on this "day of vengeance," and Uncle Mordecai acquired the king's blessing and an imposing golden crown. Thereafter, many of the people of Susa professed Judaism "because fear of the Jews had fallen on them" (8:17).

In *War in the Hebrew Bible: A Study in the Ethics of Violence*, Old Testament scholar Susan Niditch notes that the Boston Puritan preacher Cotton Mather partially justified killing the natives by using examples of Israel's alleged extermination of Amalekites, Canaanites, Midianites, and other enemies. "The particular violence of the Hebrew Scriptures has . . . served as a model . . . for persecution, subjugation, and extermination for millennia."

The Amity-Enmity Complex. Various theories have been advanced to help to explain the prevalence of approved violence in the Old Testament. Philosopher Herbert SPENCER, drawing partly from Charles DARWIN's study of animal behavior, noted that numerous species appear to live by a dual code. According to the first code, members of the social unit bond for support, defense, and affection. According to the second code, the group expresses hostility and aggression toward outsiders of the same species. The insiders-versus-outsiders syndrome runs throughout both testaments of the Bible. The New Testament apocalypse, for example, features intense and undying aggression toward the enemy. The book of Revelation portrays the enemy, including the Roman government, as the emanation of Satan, who will not be exterminated but given a worse sentence, namely, everlasting torture. Borrowing from such passages as Enoch 10:4 and Jubilees 48:15, the author of the New Testament apocalypse yearns for the day of fierce revenge. Unlike the Christ who cries out from the cross, "Father forgive them; for they do not know what they are doing," the martyrs in the book of Revelation cry out for vengeance.

Apocalyptic thinking in the New Testament projects both stark dualism and the amity-enmity complex onto its version of the deity. Its deterministic outlook in some cases presents a deity who predestines some human instruments to receive his love and others to become the objects of his hatred. Before the twin boys in Rebecca's womb were born, God loved one and hated the other. Jacob became the recipient of amity, whereas Esau was created to serve as the object of divine enmity (Rom. 9:11–24).

Pathological Wrath. A surprisingly large portion of the Old Testament purports to be accounts of violence and mayhem that the god Yahweh commanded, supported, or carried out directly. In 1 and 2 Samuel, he appears as Israel's king and chief warrior. Yahweh exemplifies pathological violence in various sections of biblical literature. The most bizarre is his disgust with the human race to the point of drowning every man, woman, and child except for eight individuals. His rage becomes so out of control that he destroys most of the animal kingdom, which presumably was guilty of no sin. Whereas Yahweh in Genesis promises never again to destroy the earth with floods, the god of the New Testament apocalypse resorts to fire, hail, earthquake, and pestilence to bring about mayhem and agony. The promise of Genesis 9 turns out merely to restrict the means of mass destruction.

Cosmic Dualism. Various attempts have been made to reframe the apocalyptic cruelty in the New Testament. According to the apocalyptic writers, the targets of vio-lence bring it upon themselves. By offering a cosmic version of the insiders-versus-outsiders motif, the author of the book of Revelation views all human beings outside his religion as mystically connected to evil personified, to a cosmic Satan. The same dualism appears in the Gospel of John, where Jesus stands in deep conflict with "the Jews," who do not believe in him. He says to them, "Your father is the devil and you choose to carry out your father's desires. He was a murderer from the beginning" (John 8:44–46).

Earlier, this gospel advanced the thesis that everyone is condemned already. Only those who come to believe that Jesus is God's only begotten son can escape everlasting wrath. Unbelievers are thus regarded not as individuals harboring honest disagreement, but as agents of evil who prefer darkness to light (3:18–19). The writer of this gospel appears to have incorporated the amity-enmity model, extolling love for believers and exuding malice toward unbelieving outsiders.

The First Epistle of John also extols love, most of it reserved for fellow believers. "God is love," and whoever loves God must love fellow believers. If a believer "does not love a fellow-Christian whom he has seen, he is incapable of loving God whom he has not seen" (1 John 4:20). This writer seems unable to acknowledge, however, that love exists outside the Christian circle. Like the book of Revelation, 1 John is thoroughly dualistic, insisting that except for believing Christians "the whole world lies in the power of the evil one" (5:19). Non-Christians are "the spirit of antichrist" (4:3). The dualism that pervades this epistle becomes vitriolic. Anyone who does not think Jesus is the heaven-sent Messiah is called a liar: "He is the antichrist" (2:2).

Violence Turned upon the Chosen. One of the most perplexing aspects of the Old Testament is the violence Yahweh is said to have frequently inflicted on Israel. The prophets and the Deuteronomic tradition had advanced the theory that Yahweh controlled all human events. The conspicuous defeats and suffering that came to the people of Israel—often at the hands of foreign armies—created serious challenges to this theological theory. What advantage did people enjoy in being the chosen of Yahweh if he could not protect them? It seemed that either there was no advantage or the idea of a chosen people was a delusion.

According to some interpreter of 2 Samuel 24, after becoming angry with Israel for no apparent reason, Yahweh incited David to commit the sin of taking a census of the people so that he (Yahweh) could have a reason to inflict a punishment on either David or his subjects. The punishment came in the form of a plague that liquidated seventy thousand citizens. The destruction would have continued, according to the story, had David not offered appropriate burnt animals to appease Yahweh (2 Sam. 24:18–25). Earlier in the story, a three-year famine in the land ended as soon as David turned Saul's male descendants over to the Gibeonites to be crucified or dismembered as a sacrifice to Yahweh on the mountain of Yahweh (2 Sam. 21:1–14). This human sacrifice satisfied the Gibeonites, who wanted revenge for what Saul had done to them generations earlier. The redactor of this grim story says the famine did not end until David retrieved and buried the bones of the men he had earlier delivered to be executed. This redaction does not state explicitly that in handing over the male descendants of his predecessor on the throne, David conveniently liquidated most of his rivals to the throne.

Other Interpretations. Entirely different accounts of the prophetic and Deuteronomic theological interpretation of those macabre events are possible. According to a more secular version, the death of thousands of Israelites came about by natural causes and conditions. The epidemic eventually subsided, but not by David's deeds or the execution of Saul's descendants. According to the monotheistic redactor of 1 and 2 Samuel, several popular stories can be reshaped and woven in with other materials, provided the chief concerns guide the overall narrative. First, Yahweh must always be portrayed as in control of all lives and events. Second, David must appear as Yahweh's chosen king-Messiah of all Israel and Judah. The following is the extension of this rewrite. (1) Yahweh rejected not only King Saul (giving him an evil spirit), but also all the claims of Saul's heirs to the throne. (2) Contrary to what many have said, David did not murder his rivals to the throne but handed them over to the Gibeonites to satisfy their just claim for justice and blood revenge. (3) Although David did have Uriah murdered so that he could have intercourse with Bathsheba (who eventually became the mother of King Solomon), he did not murder Abigail's husband, but rather married Abigail only after Yahweh killed the husband. (4) David in his magnanimity honored Saul by reclaiming his bones and those of his butchered descendants and burying them in a friendly land. (5) David's righteous deed and his offering of a blood sacrifice induced Yahweh to restrain his wrath sufficiently to end the plague and the draught.

Without the redactor's theological reconstruction, the epidemic does not appear as a purposive act of violence by a wrathful god. Much of the violence that needs to be explained turns out to have been carried out by David and his band of outlaws and malcontents who resorted to extortion, spying, treachery, terror, murder, and large-scale thievery to gain power, territory, and eventually David's replacement of Saul and his heirs to the throne.

Many Old Testament scholars view Saul and David as something like Mafia chieftains who operate through coercion, presenting citizens with offers they cannot refuse. The world of the Deuteronomic tradition was fraught with danger, strewn with chaotic forces, including enemies, traitors (like David), criminals, sociopaths, opportunists, and dysfunctional families. In short, much of early Hebrew life approximated a Hobbesian "state of nature" in which life was nasty, brutish, and short. In *Leviathan*, Thomas HOBBES contends that the turbulent,

violent condition in which Hebrews had to live at the time of Saul and David required a king with absolute authority to secure the Hebrews' safety. Royal violence thus became a necessary evil to restrain the mayhem that prevailed at the time.

The Ban (*Hērem*). The grimmest of the rules of Israelite holy war was the *hērem*, or ban, which is nothing less than genocide. According to 1 Samuel 15, Yahweh ordered King Saul to liquidate the entire Amalekite population: "Spare no one. Put them all to death, men and women, the children and babes in arms, herds and flocks, camels and asses" (1 Sam. 15:2). When Saul spared the life of the Amalekite king, Samuel the seer became enraged and personally executed the king by hewing him into pieces "before Yahweh at Gilgal." In doing this before Yahweh, Samuel apparently believed he was completing a human sacrifice. The entire ban or extermination of the Amalekites was considered a sacrifice to Yahweh. The concept of *hērem* as Yahweh's portion of the kill was deeply rooted in ancient Israel. The apparently wanton, meaningless destruction of human and animal life took on theological meaning when viewed as a sacrifice. While one part of the Hebrew tradition condemned the sacrifice of human children to Yahweh, another part held that it was accepted.

Sacrificing Children to God. Whatever the historical facts of the Hebrews in Egypt and their departure were, the writer of Exodus claimed that the god Yahweh, after presumably hardening Pharaoh's heart or mind, slaughtered the firstborn of all Egyptian families, including the cattle. This was presumably a way to pass judgment on the Egyptian gods (Exod. 11–12). Some Old Testament passages indicate the belief that Yahweh owned the firstborn of everything, as well as the first fruit. Yahweh referred to Israel as his firstborn son (Exod. 4:22).

Two inscriptions from Upper Mesopotamia dating to the tenth century BCE allude to the burning of seven of the blasphemer's sons as punishment for having defaced the name of the royal family. Seventh-century BCE contracts include burning the eldest son in the sacred precinct of Adad as punishment for violating the contract. According to Genesis 22, Abraham believed he heard Yahweh tell him to sacrifice his firstborn son (at least the firstborn to his wife) on the altar. Later in the story, Yahweh revealed he had not really meant it. Later, some rabbis as well as Christian and Muslim theologians praised Abraham for his *willingness* to offer Isaac as a burnt offering.

Conflicting Views regarding Blood Sacrifice. The eighth-century prophet Micah appeared to believe that Yahweh required not calves, rams, oil, or "my eldest son for wrongdoing," but justice, humility, and loyalty (6:8). The Hebrew tradition struggled with the moral problem implicit in human sacrifice. In *Abraham on Trial*, Carol Delaney deals with Jewish, Christian, and Muslim attempts to transform human sacrifice into something well pleasing to a deity. As if to shift the focus from the moral contradiction (euphemistically labeled a paradox by some Kierkegaardians), various interpreters have written about Isaac as the archetypal martyr, the beloved son who freely submits to his father's and Yahweh's murderous intent. The apostle Paul and the author of the Epistle to the Hebrews viewed the crucifixion of the beloved Son of God as a willing sacrifice essential to bringing about forgiveness. When the doctrine of vicarious atonement portrayed god as persecuting his only begotten son because of humanity's sin, it raised questions about the character of the god demanding the violence. The doctrine portrays him as taking part with the group in killing the victim. René Girard and others advance the thesis that the whole process of creating moral approval for cruelty and liquidation gave birth to a conviction that the victims, far from being genuine human beings, were the poisonous agents of contagion and pollution. Much of the Bible appears deeply involved in notions of ritual impurity.

Unending Violence. By the first century CE, the idea of everlasting torment had become a part of some branches of Judaism and emerging Christianity. The Greek word *Gehenna* referred to the garbage area outside Jerusalem and became a symbol of the place where the unclean or the unbelievers would be cast. Since unbelievers were seen as unholy and impure, many believers felt that holiness required unbelievers to suffer perpetual torment in the eternal garbage pit where the worm would not die and the fire would never be extinguished. Various attempts to spiritualize the fire have been motivated by the desire not to reduce the amount of human torment, but to escape the conclusion that the torment springs from God's perpetual acts of unprecedented, relentless violence against his creatures.

Historically, the word *Gehenna* derived from the Hebrew *ge-hinnom*, the valley of Hinnom, where various kings of Judah engaged in human sacrifice by fire (2 Chron. 28:3, 33:6; Jer. 7:31). The prophet Jeremiah denounced it as foreign to the mind of Yahweh. King Josiah regarded the practice as wicked and ended it. Ironically, many Jewish and Christian believers of the first century embraced the idea of human sacrifice by fire. According to various Old Testament passages (Gen. 8:21; Exod. 29:19–25; Lev. 8:21, 23:13; Num. 15:10, 28, 22–24), the god Yahweh apparently required certain select animals to be cooked over open flame. The pleasing aroma ascending to heaven would bring him great satisfaction. Some portions of the New Testament portray the crucifixion of Jesus as a satisfying sacrifice to god: "Christ gave himself up for us, a fragrant offering and sacrifice to God" (Eph. 5:2).

The idea of human sacrifice by fire persists in some branches of Christianity. *Gehenna*'s inmates become a perpetual sacrifice to the god's presumed holiness. By never allowing the inmates to lose consciousness, this god established human sacrifice in perpetuity. Ironically, if taken to its logical conclusion, the doctrine of everlasting *Gehenna* would render the sacrifice of Jesus to have been slight when compared with the sacrifice made endlessly by any one of the unbelievers. Some Christians who reject the doctrine of everlasting torment interpret the flames of *Gehenna* to be the burning enmity and hostility within the hearts of some of their fellow believers.

BIBLIOGRAPHY

Alter, Robert. *The David Story*. New York: Norton, 1999.

Baker, Raymond William. *Islam without Fear*. Cambridge, MA: Harvard University Press, 2003.

Delaney, Carol. *Abraham on Trial*. Princeton, NJ: Princeton University Press, 1998.

Friedman, Daniel. *To Kill and Take Possession: Law, Morality, and Society in Biblical Stories*. Peabody, MA: Hendrickson, 2002.

Green, Amanda Aldhouse. *Dying for the Gods*. Charleston, SC: Tempus, 2002.

Hamerton-Kelly, Robert G. *Sacred Violence*. Minneapolis: Augsburg Fortress, 1992.

Kirsch, Jonathan. *God against the Gods*. New York: Viking Compass, 2004.

Kugel, James L. *The God of Old*. New York: Simon & Schuster, 2003.

Levenson, Jon D. *The Death and Resurrection of the Beloved Son*. New Haven, CT: Yale University Press, 1993.

McKenna, Andrew J. *René Girard and Biblical Studies, Semeia 33*. Decatur, GA: Scholars Press, 1985.

Moore, Barrington, Jr. *Moral Purity and Persecution in History*. Princeton, NJ: Princeton University Press, 2000.

Niditch, Susan. *War in the Hebrew Bible*. New York: Oxford University Press, 1993.

Rundin, John S. "Pozo Moro, Child Sacrifice, and the Greek Legendary Tradition." *Journal of Biblical Literature* 123, no. 3 (Fall 2004).

Segal, Alan F. *Life after Death: A History of the Afterlife in Western Religion*. New York: Bantam Doubleday Dell, 2003.

JOE EDWARD BARNHART

BIOETHICS AND UNBELIEF. On the face of it, bioethics without belief is mostly bioethics, for much of contemporary thinking about bioethics has been developed without the explicit and obvious derivations of principles from religious assumptions. The leading bioethics text of the twentieth century, Tom Beauchamp and James Childress's *Principles of Biomedical Ethics*, was written with the idea that whatever religiously derived principles the one (Childress) might offer, the other (Beauchamp) could demonstrate from nonreligious beginnings.

That work, now part of the core of bioethics literature, follows various professional organizations and federal commissions in endorsing a set of four principles from which various rules and guidelines are derived for more specific situations. They are the principle of nonmaleficence, the principle of beneficence, the principle of autonomy, and the principle of justice.

The principle of nonmaleficence enjoins healthcare practitioners to avoid being the causes of harm to patients and others. It is the oldest and primary principle of the medical ethics found in the writings of Hippocrates, a Greek physician born in 460 BCE, which dominated the practice of medicine in subsequent centuries. Though contemporary bioethics has preserved this ancient principle, because of the growing power of medical intervention and the cultural drift away from unitary conceptions of human good and harm, nonmaleficence as a principle has been placed on equal footing with the principle of autonomy.

The principle of autonomy recognizes the importance of the values and wishes of patients in determining the direction and extent of medical interventions. The principle is clear enough for the competent patient with full capacity to understand the consequences of a choice among the alternatives offered by medicine (including the possibility of no action). This principle is the basis for the requirement, in both medicine and research, of *informed consent*, generally interpreted as a requirement to present to the patient or subject the proposed treatment or research protocol, the alternatives that fall under standard practices of the profession for the malady or injury in question, and the potential consequences of each alternative and their likelihood of occurring. Patients may then, with assistance, compute the expected value of each alternative and its probable consequences weighted by their own personal values. Healthcare professionals, given the patients' choices, may then elect to comply or to leave the therapeutic relationship (under certain conditions), thereby preserving their own autonomy. In the research context, potential subjects must be provided with explanations of the research protocol and its attendant risks given in language appropriate for the individual's level of education and must be provided with the opportunity to exit the protocol at his or her choosing.

But the capacities of many patients are severely diminished—by dementia; by psychoses and neuroses; by infancy or youthfulness; or by coma, persistent vegetative states, and other neurological disorders. For such patients, concurrent informing and consultation is usually not possible; various alternative strategies have been devised that seek to make an approximation of the patient-centered decision process. Advance directives given formally to caregivers or through written documents, or informally to friends and relatives, are typically sought. Where they cannot be found, substituted judgments based on what is known of the patient's values and beliefs are often sought. Where those are unknown or insufficient, various rational-person standards, either culturally explicit or culturally neutral, are

employed. The ethics committees of hospitals and other institutions devote much time to grappling with these difficult decisions, which are often complicated by the emotions, interests, and values of family members, friends, and healthcare providers. Sometimes this spills over into the public arena accompanied by the posturings of politicians and special interest groups. The now-infamous Terri Schiavo case illustrates how explosive these decisions can become.

The principle of beneficence provides both the general motivation to provide medical services to patients, and for seeking to advance medical practice through basic and applied research. Beneficence is understood as implying both a duty to remove and to prevent natural harms, and—more controversially—a duty to provide positive enhancements to ordinary lives. Beneficence as harm prevention prompts widespread vaccination and inoculation programs; beneficence as harm removal prompts research into development of new surgical techniques, artificial organs, prosthetic devices, and even of fields such as genomics and proteonomics in order better to understand and adjust treatment to the individual's responses to potential therapies. Beneficence as enhancement prompts research that aims to improve the individual's naturally occurring qualities, including selection of characteristics in potential offspring, the use of surgery and other treatments to augment appearance through implants and various injections, and even off-label uses of steroids and other drugs and techniques to enhance performance of athletes. This third, most controversial type of application of the principle of beneficence arises out of what has been called the technological imperative, the position that what is technologically possible ought to be tried. It further reflects the pressure of a society that funds medical research and education in order to serve more than just its health needs as traditionally conceived.

Finally, the principle of justice seeks to remind practitioners—as well as the social and economic constructs that cover the costs of their services—that fundamental respect for human dignity requires that at least basic medical services be available to all, regardless of any patient's ability to pay for them. Further, the principle of justice requires that the burdens of research be borne by the full range of individuals who have the potential to benefit from its results, and not by elements of a society that, because of particular vulnerabilities, present tempting populations for exploitation. This principle is thought by some to imply a moral requirement for universal health insurance; minimally, it implies an obligation on the part of hospitals and providers to provide treatment in emergency situations without regard to the patient's ability to pay.

Bioethicists generally agree on these principles, although some caution against applying them too rigidly. They may cite the enormous variability in human circumstances, social structures, and belief systems as reasons why reasoning based on principle is often inadequate to the problems of bioethics. Others insist that the goal of bioethics ought not to be to articulate principles and rules underlying bioethics, but rather to articulate the qualities of character, or virtues, required of good physicians and other healthcare professionals. But the greatest disagreements within bioethics are rooted in the background metaphysical presuppositions and beliefs held by the practitioners of bioethics.

Religious Approaches. Religious traditions locate the warrant for the principles of justice, beneficence, nonmaleficence, and autonomy in natural rights: that is, rights of humans arising from their natures as creatures of a supreme being who is often characterized in terms of analogies with human roles. Thus, the supreme being is characterized as a lawgiver, a father to human children, and an all-knowing, omnipotent, perfectly good being. Many traditions teach that this being is engaged in a struggle with a powerful but malevolent lesser being; human disease and suffering are often laid at the door of this diabolical one. So on the religious view, the warrant for bioethical principles lies in the nature of humans as creatures of a supreme being, beings who possess free will and who reside in a world characterized by the evil machinations of a would-be tyrant; in such a world, the mandates of medicine lie in that profession's efforts to ameliorate suffering and restore health as the natural and optimal state of a creature in a theocratic struggle between good and evil. Even without the postulation of satanic forces, traditional religious bioethics recognizes the tension between what humans may will or wish and what is acceptable to their creator. The *rapprochement* between religious and secular ethics has often turned on the question of what it is that makes the supreme being's wishes good (see ETHICS AND UNBELIEF). If that being wills something *because* it is good, then there must exist a standard for good that preexists and is independent of the divine will, some standard which is potentially as discoverable by reason as it is through revelation.

Nonreligious Approaches. Various nonreligious traditions provide a range of options for grounding bioethics. Utilitarians generally accept the primacy of pleasure or happiness for humans as a universally shared, primary motive, and see the pursuit of scientific knowledge and technology as serving the maximization of happiness and the minimization of suffering through a common duty of all humans. That common duty to produce the greatest balance of benefit over disbenefit for all those affected by your actions is itself explained in various ways: through a theory of natural moral sentiments; through an analysis of the logic of the nature of each human as a rational, purposive agent; or through a sober agreement to constrain self-promotion in recognition of the dangers of such a policy gone rampant.

Hence, there is no general ethical theory of unbelief, unitary in its core assumptions, that can provide a single positive account of the principles of bioethics. Part of the genius of Beauchamp and Childress's work lies in the effort to settle on a common ethics of healthcare *despite* the diverse origins of its principles in various religious and nonreligious traditions. In a pluralistic society, such an achievement is an admirable lesson in mutual respect and cooperative accommodation.

When Religion Matters. Nonetheless, there are two major arenas of bioethics in which the presence or absence of religious presuppositions seems to make a major difference in conclusions regarding how medicine ought to comport itself, and regarding what is to be regarded as morally permissible in options offered to patients. One is the arena of conception, with its attendant issues of abortion and fetal stem cells. The other is the arena of death and dying. That is, at beginning and ending points of human life, we find that prior religious metaphysical assumptions typically result in the advocacy of markedly different outcomes from those advocated by persons whose values are not grounded in religiously dictated beliefs.

The metaphysical presuppositions of religiously guided bioethics are typically associated with the concept of the presence of a *soul*, a hypothesized entity held both to explain the orderly development of the unique qualities of the human being through gestation and maturation and to tie the mandates of religious commands to eventual consequences of reward or punishment. A common position is that the individual's immortal soul is present within the body from the "point" or "moment" of fertilization until the "moment" of death. From this premise, together with the assumption that fundamental human rights are bestowed on every being with a soul, it follows that the right to life is present from the very earliest point of human development. Hence, any action that destroys the resultant embryo, whether in an act of abortion or in pursuit of stem cells for research or medical treatment, is a violation of the individual human being's right to life.

Associated rights to being conceived in a natural way—that is, between married parents who experience the unitive and procreative aspects of sexual intercourse—are found in the religious and metaphysical presuppositions underlying much of religious bioethics, a view conspicuously espoused by the then-cardinal Josef Ratzinger, now Pope Benedict XVI. From these doctrines arise the standard prohibitions against conceptive-preventive measures insofar as these are conceived as thwartings of divine purposes.

Dilemmas of Twinning and Cloning. Those holding such a religious view must make various ad hoc arrangements to handle such issues as twinning and cloning. If future persons are endowed with souls at the earliest moment of conception, how are cases in which later bifurcation will occur held to be accommodated? On the most "conservative" view, a fertilized ovum that is destined later to become twins has two souls infused into it at fertilization, as recently argued by Rose Koch. A fertilized human ovum not so destined cannot be made into twins; the fact that fertilized ova of other species are capable of such artificial cleavage into twins is not evidence of such possibilities for humans, as it is the infusion of the soul (presumably, solely an endowment of humans) that completes the individuation of the human embryo into a given person.

Somewhat surprisingly, this view implies predictions that make it, at least in the version as described, capable of being tested—although the ethics of attempting any such test poses deep difficulties for the religious viewpoint. First, given that a particular embryo not destined for twinning has already been endowed with but a single soul, it should not be possible to subject that embryo to an artificial process of twinning—that is, to render it mechanically into two or more undifferentiated bundles of totipotent cells each of which can then proceed through normal gestation and development. For the role of the unique soul is to produce a unique individual; even in the case of natural identical twins, the view is that they are preordained to emerge by some supernatural power that foresees, if not determines, the twinning; in such cases two souls are associated from the start. Given other assumptions about the independence of human action, a deliberate, artificial twinning should be physically unable to produce two viable offspring. Conversely, if such an artificial twinning were successfully to occur, that would constitute evidence that a single, indivisible soul had not been associated with the embryo from its earliest stages.

Second, given that two embryos each have an individual soul implanted within from the earliest stages of development, it should not be possible for those embryos to fuse and produce a single individual. Ad hoc adjustments are, of course, possible even here; one might hold that in the case of natural fusion, the fused individual was preordained and one of the embryos lacked the requisite soul, or perhaps lost it in the process of fusion. But the possibility of artificial fusion, given the standard assumptions about human authority for human actions, would imply that this ad hoc adjustment could not be extended to artificial fusion. That is, given two embryos each with a soul, it ought not to be possible for them to be deliberately fused into a single ball of totipotent cells that can then become implanted and develop into a single human being, albeit with some untypical characteristics: perhaps both male and female external sex organs, perhaps two distinct blood types, and perhaps with different cells in the same organ or tissues showing XX and XY chromosomes. That such chimeric humans occur naturally is beyond dispute.

Finally, the possibility of cloning an individual human from the somatic cells of another human, thereby bypassing the process of fertilization altogether, places yet another burden on the proponent of traditional religious ontology. Should the cloning of human cells eventuate in an embryo, the question of when a soul is infused becomes even more tenuous. The soul associated with the individual from whom the skin cell was taken presumably remains with that individual; also, nothing occurs that is like the union of previously disparate genetic material which is traditionally held to constitute the creation of the receptacle for the soul. Again, an ad hoc adjustment in the account is necessary, and again human agency challenges the theocentric account of the creation of unique individuals.

The view that humans are possessed of a divinely given soul characterizes the differences between religious bioethics and the bioethics of unbelief as well. Traditionalists reject the idea that your life is your property, with the consequence that, under conditions of extreme suffering and despair, ending it actively—with or without the assistance of a physician—is morally impermissible. This prohibition stands with the notion that, as creatures of a supreme being, we live at his pleasure in accordance with his plans, and that we therefore lack the authority—outside of self-defense justifications—to end our lives. In its most extreme forms, religious bioethics even prohibits killing a fetus to save the life of the mother where the threat to the mother's life is innocent of malevolent intent. Only where normal medical treatment, such as the necessary removal of a cancerous uterus, foresees but does not intend the death of the fetus is a medical act resulting in death permissible. On the traditional view intentional suicide and active euthanasia are always impermissible; under some conditions, withholding burdensome treatment that prolongs dying but does not hold significant promise of cure or return to meaningful activity is permissible even if death is thereby hastened, as is treatment of suffering where such treatments may have, as a foreseeable but unintended consequence, the hastening of death.

Implications of Unbelief for the Value of Human Life. Divorced from the trappings of religious metaphysics, mere human biological life—where the human person has either not developed or is no longer functional—comes to have at best only utility value. Tempting though it is to attach great significance to the potential for the emergence of personhood, that significance is typically tempered by considerations of probability or likelihood of successful emergence, by costs to those charged with its development, and by the prognosis for the potential human person's burdens and capacities. The utility value of the earliest states of human existence and the final stages lies with their potential as sources of organs and tissues for transplantation and research. Absent a person in whom there is a socially principled recognition of rights, it makes no sense to speak of a right to life that overrules other interests.

Among nonbelievers, there still remain substantial divisions over what is permissible in these arenas of medical decision. Some secularists have seized upon the potential of abuse in legalized physician-assisted suicide, holding that the dangers of creeping justifications and social pressures endanger the interests of the elderly and the handicapped. Organizations such as Not Dead Yet have opposed liberalized laws, such as that in Oregon, which permit physician-assisted suicide under defined conditions as an open door to unscrupulous nursing home operators and weary family members eager to unshoulder their burdens. Often these protests lose sight of the far wider burdens to patients of an inescapable status quo, and the medical community has been slow to respond to calls for better management of patient suffering.

Nonetheless, unbelievers generally claim a right to determine, for themselves, the time and manner of their deaths. Articulate individuals such as those depicted in the film and play *Whose Life Is It Anyway?* have advanced a powerful challenge to traditional attitudes toward unwanted life, advancing the thesis that the autonomous individual with capacity should have the choice between ending life while still with capacity, having life ended after capacity is lost but while organic life is still ongoing, and allowing the process of dying to run its natural course with or without artificial extension. Physicians such as Timothy Quill and Jack Kevorkian have responded to the requests of their patients for greater control over the end of life in a variety of ways. While, due to various complexities in the physician-patient relationship, the results have not led to federal courts recognizing a general right to assisted suicide, the effect has been to return legislation on these issues to the states, allowing for the effective emergence, state by state, of policies and practices reflecting the will of the majority of voters.

Regulation, not prohibition, has emerged as the key to avoiding a slide from the abuses of prolonged dying into abuses of hastened dying. The Oregon Death with Dignity law, now in place for nine years, has seen a gentle increase in the use of physician-prescribed lethal medication by patients with terminal diagnoses. So far in Oregon, only patients with decision-making capacity have been allowed to receive such terminating measures. In Holland and other European countries that have also permitted physician-assisted death, somewhat looser standards have seen the practices extended to formerly competent patients who have elected termination to be initiated after losing competence; in some cases euthanasia has been practiced on the assurances of family members that such is consistent with patient wishes, even if not formally recorded.

These and similar considerations have led ethicist Peter Singer recently to predict that, in the next thirty-five years, the traditional view of the sanctity of human life from conception will collapse and be replaced by a concept of personhood that will assume the primary role in questions of ending human life. Mere membership in the species *Homo sapiens* will not be the ground of rights, but rather possession of the qualities of personhood that make in the intact person for autonomy and the possession of morally significant interests. Singer writes: "We will understand that even if the life of a human organism begins at conception, the life of a person—that is, at a minimum, a being with some level of self-awareness—does not begin so early. And we will respect the right of autonomous, competent people to choose when to live and when to die."

BIBLIOGRAPHY

Beauchamp, Tom L., and James F. Childress. *Principles of Biomedical Ethics*. 5th ed. New York: Oxford University Press, 2001.

Congregation for the Doctrine of the Faith (Cardinal Josef Ratzinger). *Instruction on Respect for Human Life in Its Origin and on the Dignity of Procreation: Replies to Certain Questions of the Day*. Boston: St. Paul Editions, 1987.

Department of Human Services, Offices of Disease Prevention and Epidemiology. "Seventh Annual Report on Oregon's Death with Dignity Act," March 10, 2005.

Hull, Richard T., ed. *Ethical Issues in the New Reproductive Technologies*. 2nd ed. Amherst, NY: Prometheus Books, 2005.

Koch, Rose. "A Hylomorphic Account of the Origin of the Human Being," PhD dissertation, State University of New York at Buffalo, 2005.

Singer, Peter. "The Sanctity of Life: Here Today, Gone Tomorrow." *Foreign Policy*, September/October 2005.

RICHARD T. HULL

BIRTH CONTROL AND UNBELIEF. Though various methods of birth control have been tried throughout history, those methods were not usually mentioned in medical literature. Rather, they were more or less secret information, passed from midwives to their patients or even from woman to woman. Such knowledge was often thought to depend upon witchcraft, and some women were scapegoated for possessing alleged knowledge of ways to prevent pregnancy or induce abortion. In Western culture, this became particularly the case after Pope Innocent VIII, in a bull, or policy statement, issued December 5, 1494, stated it had been called to his attention that members of both sexes were using incantations, charms, and conjurations to "suffocate, extinguish, and cause to perish the births of women" or to "impede the conjugal actions of men and women." Such alleged practices came to be associated with witchcraft, and witches came to be viewed as the causes or sources of impotence, infertility, abortion, and preventing pregnancy. In the case of birth control, the witches were said to have secret recipes for emmenagogic medicines—recipes believed to stimulate the menstrual flow and bring about miscarriages—or, in stronger words, abortions. Some seventeenth- and eighteenth-century investigators of witchcraft went so far as to claim that the better the midwife the better the witch, an unsupported exaggeration undoubtedly, but one that emphasizes the reliance of women upon other women for information. It is no accident that among the women accused of witchcraft in the Salem witch trials in seventeenth-century New England, two were midwives. Midwives in many areas of Europe were required to take an oath that they would not use any witchcraft or charms in their practices, an oath that emphasizes the association of their calling with contraception and abortion.

Since the Christian Church in much of the Western world set the moral agenda in terms of sexuality (see SEXUAL VALUES, IMPACT OF UNBELIEF ON), it was perhaps inevitable that most modern advocates of birth control were freethinkers (see FREETHOUGHT) opposed to church dominance and to the hostility the religious establishment had characteristically displayed toward birth control, let alone abortion.

One early freethinking advocate of birth control in the United States was Charles KNOWLTON. Early in his career as a physician he began giving out information about birth control, and soon wrote up his recommendations into a self-published booklet titled *Fruits of Philosophy, or the Private Companion of Young Married People, by a Physician*. His solution was for women to douche right after the emission of sperm into the vagina. The effectiveness of this depended on the douching solution, since simple douching would not eliminate the semen. He recommended two solutions. One involved alum, which is a spermicide, and could have been fairly effective if the mixture was right. He also recommended the use of sulfite of zinc, which would not have worked at all.

Finding it difficult to get his book accepted for publication, Knowlton decided to publish it on his own. He toured nearby communities in Massachusetts, giving lectures and selling his book. He was fined in 1832 in Taunton, Massachusetts, and in 1838 he was jailed at Cambridge for three months for attempting to distribute it. The net effect was to give broader publicity to his book; *Fruits of Philosophy* soon sold ten thousand copies. The book continued to be published throughout the nineteenth century by a variety of freethought presses, and was also incorporated into a variety of books on home remedies.

The attempt to distribute *Fruits of Philosophy* in England led to one of the more famous trials of the nineteenth century, the 1877 trial of the freethinkers Charles BRADLAUGH and Annie BESANT. Though Knowlton's book had gone through several previous printings in England, the authorities suddenly clamped down. Bradlaugh in fact had previously published articles on the same topic by freethinker George Drysdale in his own newspapers. Drysdale had edited an updated British version of Knowlton's book, adding discussions of contraceptive use of the sponge, the utilization of the safe period (which he said was from two to three days before menstruation to eight days after), coitus interruptus (which Drysdale felt was "physically injurious"), and the condom. Drysdale's edition was seized by authorities in Bristol in 1876 and the bookseller sentenced to two years in jail. Though the original Knowlton book had been sold in London for many years, Bradlaugh and Besant seized on the Bristol case to publish Drysdale's revision of Knowlton's book and confront the authorities. Emboldened by the Bristol case, London authorities responded by arresting the two. During the subsequent trial Bradlaugh and Besant were tried and found by the jury to have published a book calculated to deprave public morals. Yet at the same time the jury declared that the defendants should be exonerated from "any corrupt motives" in publishing the book. What this meant was unclear. Besant held that the decison amounted to saying: "Not guilty, but don't do it again."

The judge took it as a guilty verdict. The two activists were sentenced to six months' imprisonment, fined two hundred pounds, and required to each post five hundred pounds as a bond that they would not publish the book again for a period of two years. On appeal, they were acquitted on a technicality, and though warned not to do so, continued to publish the revised *Fruits of Philosophy* without interference.

Prior to the London trial, the American freethinker and birth control advocate Edward Bliss FOOTE (1829–1906) published a book titled *Medical Common Sense* (1864) that included much better information on contraception than that offered by Knowlton. Foote discussed at length four methods that he claimed to have invented: (1) the "membrainous envelope," a type of condom made from fish bladders; (2) the "apex," a rubber penis cap; (3) a "womb veil," a rubber diaphragm; and (4) an electromagnetic preventive machine that supposedly altered the partner's electrical conditions during intercourse. The first three would have been as effective as any other means of birth control then available; the fourth is indicative of the great degree to which quackery pervaded much nineteenth-century medical practice. Foote's wife, Dr. Mary Bond Foote, was also a freethinker and an advocate for birth control, as was his son, Edward Bond FOOTE.

Though the passage of the Comstock Act (see COMSTOCK, ANTHONY, AND UNBELIEF) prevented Foote from sending his book through the mail, and though many states enacted their own laws against the dissemination of contraceptive information, *Medical Common Sense* still managed to attain steady sales, reflecting bootlegging of copies into other states and Foote's own sales of the book in New York.

Probably the most notorious of the freethinking birth control advocates was Emma GOLDMAN, who used lectures on birth control to attract audiences for her more radical views on the social reorganization of society (see ANARCHISM AND UNBELIEF). She also issued pamphlets based on Foote and others. She was later expelled from the United States; for a time she lived in Russia, where she became disillusioned with Stalinism, and she finally settled in Canada, where she died.

Margaret SANGER, the daughter of a freethinker and in her early years a radical socialist (see SOCIALISM AND UNBELIEF) as well as a freethinker, was the dominant voice for birth control in the United States during much of the twentieth century. The culmination of her career was her sponsorship with Katherine McCormick of the research that led to the development of the commercial birth control pill by another freethinker, Gregory Pincus.

Ben Reitman, a freethinker and radical, complained in a poem that "the physicians, Social Scientists, Clergy & etc." only became interested in birth control "after the radicals had broken the ground. And gone to jail." He was essentially correct. The history of birth control in the United States, England, and elsewhere demonstrates that the vanguard in propagating information about conatraceptives was made up of freethinkers, secular reformers, utopians, sex radicals (see SEX RADICALISM AND UNBELIEF), socialists, and others. Effective birth control and, later, safe and effective abortions are among the major contributions to society for which freethinkers deserve primary credit.

At the beginning of the twenty-first century, some churches still remain hostile to information about sex and the dissemination of contraceptives. Yet even in the conservative Roman Catholic Church, there is strong lay support for contraception and even for abortion rights. Though freethinkers were probably the dominant force, it would be a mistake to think they were alone in their efforts to change attitudes about contraception and abortion. They were often joined by individuals and even groups representing organized religion, and by members of such groups as the Quakers, Unitarians (see UNITARIANISM TO 1961), Episcopalians, Unitarian Universalists (see UNITARIAN UNIVERSALISM), and others.

BIBLIOGRAPHY

Brodie, Janet Farrel. *Contraception and Abortion in Nineteenth Century America.* Ithaca, NY: Cornell University Press, 1994.

Bullough, Vern L. "A Brief Note on Rubber Technology: The Diaphragm and the Condom." *Technology and History* 22 (January 1981).

———, ed. *Encyclopedia of Birth Control.* Santa Barbara, CA: ABC Clio, 2001.

———. *Sexual Variance in Society and History.* Chicago: University of Chicago Press, 1976.

Chesler, Ellen. *Woman of Valor: Margaret Sanger and the Birth Control Movement in America.* New York: Simon & Schuster, 1992.

Drinnon, Richard. *Rebel in Paradise: A Biography of Emma Goldman.* Chicago: University of Chicago Press, 1961.

Fryer, Peter. *The Birth Controllers.* London: Seckeer and Warburg, 1965.

Goldman, Emma. *Marriage and Love.* New York: Mother Earth, 1911.

Gordon, Linda. *Woman's Body, Woman's Rights: Birth Control in America.* New York: Penguin, 1990.

Himes, Norman. *Medical History of Contraception.* New York: Schocken Books, 1970.

Knowlton, Charles. *Fruits of Philosophy.* Mount Vernon, NY: Peer Pauper Press, 1936.

VERN L. BULLOUGH

BJØRNSON, BJØNSTJERNE. See NORWAY, UNBELIEF IN.

BLAKE, LILLIE DEVEREUX (1833–1913), American suffragist, novelist, and freethinker. Lillie Devereux Blake's critique of Christian belief systems resulted from her feminism. In novels, essays, and lectures, Blake exposed "all the false arguments which [Christian] enthusiasts" have brought to the subjugation of women.

Blake was descended from Puritan divine Jonathan Edwards, to whose essays she responded, "What wretched hair-splitting!" Raised by her widowed mother in New Haven, Connecticut, Elizabeth Devereux married attorney Frank Umsted in 1855, bore two daughters, and lost her husband to an apparent suicide in 1859. She then worked as a journalist and novelist. She married Grinfill Blake in 1866, settling in New York City. By the 1870s Lillie Blake had become a highly successful lecturer and political organizer for the suffrage and labor movements (see WOMAN SUFFRAGE MOVEMENT AND UNBELIEF). She initiated actions that led to the founding of Barnard College of Columbia University, and she attained such prominence in the woman suffrage movement that in 1900, Elizabeth Cady STANTON supported her to succeed Susan B. Anthony as president of the National American Woman Suffrage Association.

Blake's childhood world was populated by Christian apologists. Her cousin, Yale University president Theodore Woolsey, lectured on the positive effects of Christianity on the social position of women. But Blake early rebelled against what she termed "this man-made Church" that degraded rather than uplifted women; the nonbelieving heroine of her first novel, *Southwold* (1859), denies that women "owe any special debt of gratitude to Christianity. . . . I can scarcely imagine it to be necessary to the maintenance of a true faith that we should believe all the false arguments which enthusiasts have adduced in its support."

In 1883 Blake was enraged by Reverend Morgan Dix, rector of New York City's Trinity Church, who argued that the status of women was elevated by the teachings of the Christian Church. Blake referred to him as "this clerical dictator." Each Friday in Lent Dix lectured, and each Sunday evening Blake responded. To packed halls, she refuted him on historical fact and peppered her own history of woman's condition with citations from Livius, Quintilian, and Valerius Maximus. She correlated the contraction of woman's status with the rise of the celibate priesthood, arguing that in order to sustain "this hideous doctrine . . . women were declared to be by nature inferior, to be unfit to associate with men, to be unworthy and degrading in their influence. . . ." Her lectures were published as *Woman's Place To-Day.*

In 1886 Blake collaborated with Elizabeth Cady Stanton on *The Woman's Bible,* which contextualized biblical stories with non-Christian cultural myths and may well have found its inspiration in *Woman's Place To-Day.*

BIBLIOGRAPHY

Blake, Katherine Devereux, and Margaret Louise Wallace. *Champion of Women: The Life of Lillie Devereux Blake.* New York: Fleming H. Revell, 1943.

Blake, Lillie Devereux. *Fettered for Life.* New York: Sheldon, 1874, 1885.

———. *Southwold.* New York: Rudd and Carleton, 1859.

———. *Woman's Place To-day.* New York: J. W. Lovell, 1883.

Farrell, Grace. *Lillie Devereux Blake: Retracing a Life Erased.* Amherst: University of Massachusetts Press, 2002.

GRACE FARRELL

BLANSHARD, BRAND (1892–1987), American philosopher, son and grandson of Protestant clergymen. Only midway through his graduate studies did Brand Blanshard abandon his plan to make a career in the ministry. Educated at Michigan, Oxford (as a Rhodes scholar), Columbia, and Harvard, he taught philosophy at Michigan, Swarthmore, and Yale. During the middle decades of the twentieth century he was the only American philosopher of the first rank to subject Christian thought to detailed yet respectful criticism. Other philosophers at elite universities who won highest honors in the profession either ignored religion or dismissed it in brief polemics. Blanshard painstakingly marshaled thousands of cogent arguments in lucid and graceful prose. A love of sermons developed in childhood showed in all his writing. Sharply critical of logical empiricism and linguistic analysis, the forms of philosophical analysis dominant in his time, Blanshard's own brand of analysis was universally respected as subtle and penetrating. Still more atypical in the mid-twentieth century, his analytic method was employed in the construction of a philosophical system comparable in scope to the systems found in earlier centuries of Western philosophy. He was both a sage of old and a master of twentieth-century logical techniques.

Central to Blanshard's philosophy of religion was an "ethics of belief." Although he was critical of William James as too permissive of belief beyond the evidence, he stressed more than William K. CLIFFORD did the need to act on probabilities and working hypotheses. "The indulgence" of belief "when not under constraint by the evidence is defensible on neither moral nor rational grounds." His advocacy of "the rational temper" avoided the excesses of skepticism often found in the history of "RATIONALISM."

Blanshard's intention was never to debunk all forms of religion. Rather, he wished to formulate naturalistic concepts of the religious. Fundamental to his notion of naturalistic religion was "the service of REASON." God, for him, was not an existent being but rather "the immanent end which realizes or incarnates itself in the process of advance." Religion is "man's attempt to adjust himself to ultimate reality." This, he said, "leaves religion with meaning and importance; it keeps reverence alive, even while redirecting it . . . and makes religion not only a live option but an unavoidable one."

BIBLIOGRAPHY

Blanshard, Brand. *Four Reasonable Men: Marcus Aurelius, John Stuart Mill, Ernest Renan, and Henry Sidgwick.* Middletown, CT: Wesleyan University Press, 1984.

———. *The Nature of Thought.* 2 Vols. London: George Allen & Unwin, 1939; New York: Macmillan, 1940.

———. *On Philosophical Style.* Bloomington: Indiana University Press, 1954.

———. *Reason and Analysis.* La Salle, IL: Open Court, 1962.

———. *Reason and Belief.* London: George Allen & Unwin, 1974.

———. *Reason and Goodness.* London: George Allen & Unwin; New York: Macmillan, 1961.

———. *The Uses of a Liberal Education and Other Talks to Students.* Edited by Eugene Freeman. La Salle, IL: Open Court, 1973.

Howie, J. "Brand Blanshard." In *American National Biography,* edited by J. A. Garraty and M. C. Carnes. New York: Oxford University Press, 1999.

Idealistic Studies 20 (May 1990).

"Internal Relations and Their Importance in Philosophy." *Review of Metaphysics* 21 (December 1967).

Schilpp, P. A., ed. *The Philosophy of Brand Blanshard.* La Salle, IL: Open Court, 1980.

"Truth and Reason." *Idealistic Studies* 4 (January and May 1974).

PETER H. HARE

BLANSHARD, PAUL (1892–1980), American writer and crusader for liberal causes. Paul Blanshard was born on April 27, 1892, along with his twin, Brand, who went on to a distinguished career as a philosopher at Yale University. The twins' parents died when they were very young, and they were brought up by their father's family, who were strict Methodists. Despite this, the twins grew up firmly committed to liberal causes and values. They graduated from the University of Michigan in 1914 and Paul began a restless search for his place in the world. He was for a while a Congregationalist minister, as his deceased father had been. He was then a student at Union Theological Seminary before rejecting Christian belief altogether. Blanshard described himself as a "humanist atheist" (see ATHEISM; HUMANISM).

Having abandoned organized religion, Blanshard worked for several years in the union movement before moving to New York, where he worked for Mayor Fiorello LaGuardia and oversaw the prosecution of many corrupt Tammany politicians. During World War II, Blanshard worked for the State Department as an adviser on the situation in the West Indies.

Blanshard's reputation was made with his controversial book *Freedom and Catholic Power* (1949), which argued that the dogmas of Roman Catholicism are incompatible with democracy and pluralism. After ten publishing houses rejected it, Beacon Press, owned by the Unitarian Church, agreed to publish the book. Despite the refusal of most important media outlets to review it, *Freedom and Catholic Power* generated a storm of controversy and sold more than a quarter of a million copies in hardcover alone. A revised version was sold in Great Britain in 1951, but generated less controversy there. The Roman Catholic Church vigorously opposed the book and placed it on its Index of Forbidden Books.

Blanshard went on to write fourteen more books, but none achieved the publicity of *Freedom and Catholic Power*. He wrote several sequels, which focused on Catholicism in various parts of the world and replied to his critics. Other works included *The Right to Read* (1955), a criticism of censorship; *God and Man in Washington* (1960); an edited work called *Classics of Free Thought* (1977); and, in 1973, an autobiography. Paul Blanshard died in St. Petersburg, Florida, in 1980, aged eighty-seven.

BIBLIOGRAPHY

Blanshard, Paul. *Freedom and Catholic Power*. Boston: Beacon Press, 1949.
———. *Personal and Controversial*. Boston: Beacon Press, 1973.

BILL COOKE

BLASPHEMY. The core meaning of *blasphemy* is a legal or moral offense consisting of statements that disparage a deity, the deity's attributes, or some person or object considered sacred because of close association with a deity (such as Muhammad or the Bible). Those who deny the existence of deities are, therefore, inclined to regard blasphemy as a victimless offense. However, until recently most persons and societies have considered blasphemy a very serious wrong meriting severe punishment. Indeed, Leviticus 24:16 prescribes death by stoning as the punishment for blasphemy, and Thomas Aquinas characterized blasphemy as the greatest sin.

Blasphemy in Early Cultures. Although necessarily scant, there is evidence that many early cultures regarded statements expressing contempt for a deity as, at best, highly inadvisable and, at worst, a grave offense. The Egyptian Book of the Dead specifies a list of actions that the deceased must assert he has not committed if he hopes to gain immortality. Among other things, the deceased must assure Osiris that he has "not blasphemed a god." Legal codes from ancient cultures are only partially preserved, so it is difficult to discern the extent to which blasphemy was considered a crime or how severely it was punished. However, fragments from an Assyrian code suggest it was a very serious crime, as a false accusation of blasphemy resulted in the accuser being beaten with a staff forty times. On the other hand, the Code of Hammurabi contains no prohibition of blasphemy. Whether this implies that blasphemy was not regarded as an unlawful act or that blasphemy was addressed by other means (for example, by religious tribunals) remains unclear. One problem in determining the extent to which blasphemy was considered a crime in early cultures is that these societies usually did not have anything resembling what we would consider a comprehensive criminal code. Another problem in determining the extent to which blasphemy was punished is that there was often no clear distinction between blasphemy and sacrilege, which encompasses any action offensive to a deity, such as stealing from a temple.

The Old Testament indicates that the ancient Jews considered blasphemy a serious offense. In Jewish thought, the gravity of blasphemy was connected to the sacred character of God's name. To invoke God's name inappropriately was bad enough; to curse God was a horrific act. Moses decreed death by stoning as the appropriate punishment for "he who blasphemes the name of the Lord." Significantly, this penalty applied equally to foreigners and to the Jews themselves. The Old Testament also indicates how a false accusation of blasphemy could be used for nefarious ends. King Ahab and his wife, Jezebel, were able to have Naboth killed and secure his land by bringing against him trumped-up charges of blasphemy (Kings 21: 8–14). One might think that since their own scriptures confirmed how easily a charge of blasphemy could be misused, the Jews would be reluctant to continue to treat blasphemy as a capital crime, but apparently, the risk of offending the deity outweighed the dangers of a law so liable to abuse.

Surviving myths and stories from ancient cultures strongly suggest that blasphemy was highly disfavored even when not subject to criminal proscription. In the

Sumerian epic of Gilgamesh, the friend of Gilgamesh, Enkidu, is killed after the two heroes insult the goddess Ishtar. Numerous Greek myths (such as the myths of Arachne, Niobe, and Pentheus) also attest to the severe consequences that follow from uttering words that show disrespect for a deity. Interestingly, however, in these myths it is the deity that exacts punishment. Indirectly, these myths present one of the paradoxes of blasphemy when it is made a crime against human laws: If blasphemy offends a deity, why not leave it to the offended deity to impose punishment? Indeed, it would seem blasphemous to suggest that a deity cannot assume responsibility for defending him or herself.

Blasphemy Prosecutions in Greece And Rome. One justification for human punishment of blasphemy is that the blasphemer places his or her community at risk, for example, if the offended deity no longer supports the community that harbors the blasphemer. This rationale appealed to the Greeks and Romans of classical times, who emphasized the need to maintain a harmonious relationship with their numerous deities. If the community encountered disasters, an angry deity was the likely explanation for these unfortunate events, and it was believed that deities, much like their human worshipers, were angered by insults. Blasphemers had to be punished for the sake of the community.

One of the earliest examples of a law punishing blasphemy was the Athenian decree adopted at the urging of Diopeithes around 440 BCE. This decree prohibited "impiety," which encompassed denying the existence of the gods and explaining celestial phenomena without reference to the gods. Several prominent philosophers, artists, writers, and scientists were prosecuted under this law, including Anaxagoras, PROTAGORAS, and EURIPIDES. The prosecution against Euripides was unsuccessful; Anaxagoras was either imprisoned or exiled; Protagoras was either exiled or condemned to death, and died by drowning after fleeing Athens. The principal motivations for both the decree and the various persecutions appear to be the stresses experienced by Athens during this time (including, of course, the Peloponnesian War) and the very public religious skepticism of certain individuals. The two sets of phenomena were linked in the minds of many. Just as contemporary fundamentalists in the United States attribute everything from AIDS to tornadoes to taking "God out of the classroom," so too ancient Athenians were likely to attribute perceived social ills and natural disasters to "impiety." Socrates was the most famous victim of this law. As is well known, he was convicted and sentenced to death. Less well known is that about seventy years later, in 323 BCE, Aristotle was similarly charged with impiety; he fled Athens so "Athens would not sin against philosophy twice."

For most of Rome's existence as a city, nation, and empire, Roman law was much more concerned with magic and sacrilege than blasphemy per se. Extant provisions of the Twelve Tables are silent on blasphemy,

although they provide the death penalty for anyone who sings or composes an incantation that harms another. It was not until fairly late in the imperial era that references to anything resembling a prohibition on blasphemy can be found in Roman legal treatises. However, one should not be too quick to infer that blasphemy, understood as an insult to the gods, went unpunished by the Romans merely because no specific prohibition of it can be found in earlier law. Although Roman civil law, dealing with property, marriage, and the like, was impressively detailed, Roman criminal law was not. Magistrates had wide discretion not just with respect to punishment, but also with respect to what could be regarded as a criminal offense. Moreover, criminal charges were typically not initially lodged by a government official. Private persons brought the charges.

The persecution of Christians must be understood in this context. Christians were subject to criminal prosecution even though, until the time of Decius, there were no specific laws directed against Christianity and only the vaguest of legal references to offenses against the gods. As scholar Geoffrey E. M. de Ste. Croix has noted, it is a mistake to look for an express legal foundation for the early persecutions of Christians. The only foundation necessary was "a prosecutor, a charge of Christianity, and a governor willing to punish on that charge." Christians were persecuted because they were Christians, or, to be more precise, because as Christians they openly proclaimed either that the pagan gods did not exist or, more commonly, that the pagan gods were demons, not deities. These insults to the gods earned them the enmity of the vast majority of the population, who thought it critical to keep the deities in a favorable state of mind.

An understanding of Roman law is useful for analyzing the purported trial and execution of Jesus of Nazareth (see JESUS, HISTORICITY OF). Given the accretion of myth and legend surrounding this story, it is unlikely we will ever have any certainty about what actually happened. Those who accept the story in the Gospels of Mark and Matthew insist that Jesus's trial before the Sanhedrin was the most infamous blasphemy case in history. Others point out that nothing Jesus reportedly uttered would have been regarded as blasphemous under Jewish law; that he did not receive the penalty for blasphemy under Jewish law (stoning); that the Sanhedrin had not previously tried anyone for blasphemy; and that the Romans, who executed him though crucifixion, would hardly have been troubled by blasphemy against a Jewish deity. Their conclusion is that Jesus, if he was executed at all, must have been executed because of a political crime against Rome. Reviewing what objective evidence there is, it does appear that the blasphemy charge is probably a fiction, explicable as a backward projection of early Christian theology. However, this does not imply that Jesus must have been some sort of political revolutionary, guilty of sedition or treason. The reality is that given the discretion Pilate had, he could have executed Jesus merely because he was convinced Jesus was disturbing the peace of his province.

Blasphemy under Christianity. Christianity eventually became the official religion of the Roman Empire, and it almost immediately used its position to oppress those who refused to accept church doctrine. Both HERESY and blasphemy became crimes. The Code of Justinian (529 CE) provided the death penalty for blasphemy and in doing so explained that failing to punish blasphemy would provoke God's wrath. Although this code was officially enforced only in the Byzantine Empire, it influenced Christian states in the West as well. From the early Middle Ages until the Enlightenment, blasphemers were severely punished, although they sometimes escaped death. Alternative penalties included cutting or slitting the lips or cutting out the tongue.

Thomas Aquinas provided a succinct rationale for the severe punishment of blasphemy. He argued that blasphemy is a greater sin than murder because it is committed "directly against God" whereas murder is merely "a sin against one's neighbor." Of course, the blasphemer cannot actually harm the deity, but this does not matter because "the gravity of a sin depends on the intention of the evil will rather than on the effect of the deed." In this passage, Aquinas manifests the thought process of many religious believers through the ages.

The Reformation did not diminish the severity with which blasphemy was punished. In fact, early Protestants brought at least as many blasphemy prosecutions as Catholics did, in part because Protestants generally disfavored accusations of "heresy"—this was, after all, the accusation Catholics made against them. Thus Protestants tended to characterize unacceptable religious views as blasphemous rather than heretical. The distinction presumably made little difference to those executed, maimed, or imprisoned for making assertions regarded as offensive to the Christian deity. Fire burned as hot for blasphemers in Protestant lands as it did for heretics in Catholic lands.

Blasphemy in Great Britain and the United States. The seventeenth century witnessed two developments in blasphemy law in Britain, one of which was to have important implications for blasphemy law in the United States. First, both England and Scotland adopted statutes making blasphemy a crime. The Scottish statute, adopted in 1661, resulted in the last execution of anyone for blasphemy in Great Britain. Interestingly, Thomas Aikenhead, the unfortunate person executed in 1697, was not properly prosecuted under the statute, since the law forbade an *unrepentant* denial of the Trinity or God and Aikenhead, a deist (see DEISM), had recanted following his arrest. England adopted its own statute prohibiting blasphemy in 1695.

This law remained in force until 1967, but its repeal was meaningless because, curiously, no one had ever been prosecuted under the statute. Instead, blasphemers were prosecuted in England under the common law, that is, judge-made law. In the notorious case of John Taylor in 1676, Thomas Hale, the chief justice of England, decided that Taylor could be punished for calling Christ a "whore-master" and religion a "cheat" because Christianity was "parcel" of the English common law. Hale's reasoning was obscure, but whatever the weakness of his reasoning, blasphemy became an English common law crime, which it remains to this day.

Scores of English men and women have been prosecuted for blasphemy since Hale's decision. None of these was executed, but some did suffer significant terms of imprisonment. In the early 1800s Richard CARLILE spent six years in prison for blasphemy; his principal offense was publishing and selling Thomas PAINE's *Age of Reason*. One interesting aspect of Carlile's case is that during this litigation, the crown adopted a new rationale for punishing blasphemy. Blasphemy was held to be a crime not because it offended a deity but because it sapped the faith of the lower and illiterate classes and threatened to undermine accepted morality. This rationale could have been provided by Karl MARX.

Because English common law was accepted in the United States, except where modified by statute, blasphemy was initially regarded as a common law crime in the United States as well. Some early decisions (such as the 1811 New York case *People v. Ruggles*) stated that blasphemy could be prosecuted because, and only if, the blasphemer expressed his thoughts offensively. Blasphemy laws did not inhibit free speech, but rather prevented disturbances of the peace. (Ruggles had called Jesus a "bastard" and his mother a "whore.") However, later blasphemy cases were brought against individuals who did not simply insult or ridicule accepted deities. In the 1838 case of *Commonwealth v. Kneeland*, writer and lecturer Abner KNEELAND was convicted of blasphemy even though he had expressed a reasoned disbelief in the divinity of Jesus and in miracles.

Overall, the number of blasphemy prosecutions and convictions in the United States was far fewer than in Britain. The last American blasphemy conviction of any significance occurred in 1928 when Charles Lee SMITH, the president of the AMERICAN ASSOCIATION FOR THE ADVANCEMENT OF ATHEISM, was convicted in Arkansas. However, he never served his ninety-day sentence and the charges were eventually dropped.

It is important to bear in mind that earlier in American history, states could prosecute blasphemy despite the First Amendment because the Bill of Rights did not apply to the states. In other words, the First Amendment restrained the actions of the federal government only. However, once the Supreme Court began to apply the Bill of Rights to the states—a process that started in 1925—blasphemy laws effectively became dead letters. In 1970 the Maryland Court of Special Appeals found Maryland's blasphemy statute unconstitutional precisely because it conflicted with the First Amendment.

As indicated, blasphemy remains illegal in England. Indeed, the law has arguably become more strict in recent decades. In the 1883 prosecution of freethinker George William FOOTE, the courts appeared to declare that a person could be convicted of blasphemy only upon a showing of intent to shock or outrage. English courts in the 1977 *Gay News* case (see GAY HUMANISM) repudiated that interpretation of the law, holding that intent to shock or outrage was not an element of the crime. (The convicted publisher in *Gay News* had printed a homoerotic poem depicting Jesus receiving fellatio.)

The *Gay News* case led to a number of efforts to repeal the law on blasphemy in England. To date, all have been unsuccessful. Indeed, some in England have argued for expanding the law so that all religions are protected. As the Salman Rushdie affair reminded many, in England only remarks that offend Christians are prohibited. The rationale offered by those who favor retention or expansion of the law is that the sensibilities of all religious believers merit protection from offensive statements.

The Contemporary Situation. England is not the only Western democracy that retains a law penalizing blasphemy, but fortunately, for the most part these laws are now legal relics. They remain potential hazards, but they cannot be regarded as posing much of an actual threat to free speech.

Unfortunately, the same cannot be said for other countries, especially Islamic countries. Even relatively progressive Islamic countries, such as Malaysia, retain and enforce blasphemy laws. The rigor with which blasphemy laws are enforced in these countries varies greatly, but prosecutions are frequent enough and penalties severe enough to present a grave danger to freedom of conscience. For example, since 1986, when its current blasphemy law was adopted, more than four thousand people have been accused of blasphemy in Pakistan. Some have been convicted and sentenced to death (although no death sentence has been carried out). Iran has the most intolerant regime, with hundreds of individuals convicted of blasphemy since the Khomeini revolution of 1979; dozens have been executed. Justifications of laws against blasphemy in Islamic counties are not typically based on the more modern rationales of the need to preserve peace or protect the religious from offense; rather, they hark back to the medieval and ancient views that statements disparaging a deity are intrinsically evil. These harsh sanctions serve as a reminder that FREETHOUGHT and free speech are at risk whenever there are those who remain in thrall to the supernatural and believe that failing to respect their deities is the greatest sin.

BIBLIOGRAPHY

Aquinas, Thomas. *Summa Theologica*. Translated by Fathers of the English Dominican Province. New York: Benziger Brothers, 1947.

Levy, Leonard W. *Blasphemy*. New York: Knopf, 1993.

Nokes, George. *A History of the Crime of Blasphemy*. London: Sweet & Maxwell, 1928.

Ste. Croix, Geoffrey E. M. de. "Why Were the Early Christians Persecuted?" In *Studies in Ancient Society*, edited by Moses I. Finley. London: Routledge & Kegan Paul, 1974.

United States Commission on International Religious Freedom. *Annual Report*. Washington, DC: US Government Printing Offices, 2004.

RONALD A. LINDSAY

BOLINGBROKE, LORD (HENRY ST. JOHN, VISCOUNT BOLINGBROKE; 1678–1751), English politician and deist. Alive, Henry St. John was a controversial politician. Secretary of state in Queen Anne's Tory ministry, he condemned himself to a life of exile and opposition when, an opponent of the Hanoverian succession, he fled to France in 1715 in support of the Jacobite cause. Dead, Lord Bolingbroke provoked even more controversy when the posthumous publication in 1754 of his collected works proved the extent of his philosophical unorthodoxy. In the *Letter to Mr. Pope* that introduces his philosophical writings, Bolingbroke explains that he is not a "freethinker"; that is, he does not think that men have the right to create instability in a country by freely publishing their thoughts. They are free to *think* them, but not to *publish* them, which is why he never did so in his lifetime. Despite his hostility to organized religion, Bolingbroke considered it useful socially and politically, and he did not encourage law breaking.

Bolingbroke defined himself as a "theist," in opposition to "divines" on the one hand and "atheists" on the other (see ATHEISM), but his central convictions were broadly in line with the tradition of DEISM.

Bolingbroke's philosophical writings were composed as a series of conversational and ironic "essays" and "fragments." Some of these were addressed to the poet Alexander Pope, and heavily influenced Pope's *Essay on Man*. In his writings Bolingbroke asserted that we cannot know more of God than can be inferred from the natural world. "Revealed religion," to which we have access through the Bible, is untrustworthy and implausible. The Bible is not incontrovertibly the word of God, because it does not stand the test of reason. Those whom he called "divines," by which he usually meant clergymen of all Christian communions, have erected upon the Old Testament and the early Christian gospels a body of doctrine—"artificial religion"—that is self-serving and obscurantist. Bolingbroke dismissed much organized religion as a trade carried on for the profit of its practitioners. He anticipated later thinkers such as Karl MARX in arguing that in all organized faiths, one set of views is purveyed to ordinary believers and an entirely different set of views is actually believed by the hierarchs. An Englishman of his time, Bolingbroke was especially quick to spot examples of pious fraud in Roman Catholicism, though he was equally hostile to the biblical claim of Jews to be a chosen people.

Paragraph 42 of the *Fragments* offers a good example of Bolingbroke's characteristic style and content. Opposing the view promulgated by the Newtonian physicotheologists that the discomfort of this world can only be justified if there is a perfect world beyond the grave, Bolingbroke contends that this is impiety, because it implies that God owes us something. In a wide scholarly sweep that embraces LUCRETIUS, Ovid, PLATO, Michel de Montaigne, and Pliny, Bolingbroke argues that the hopefulness and the hopelessness of the human condition are routinely exaggerated, and that the truth lies in a middle position.

God's attributes, Bolingbroke everywhere contends, are unknowable. Our knowledge of God does not extend beyond the evidence of the created universe, and does not form a basis for the moral law. Self-love guided by reason leads men to benevolence and sociability, not the promise of judgment and eternal happiness beyond the grave.

BIBLIOGRAPHY

Henry St. John, Viscount Bolingbroke. *The Works of Lord Bolingbroke*. 4 vols. 1841. Reprint, Hampshire: Gregg International Publishers, 1969.

Dickinson, H. T. *Bolingbroke*. London: Constable, 1970.

Hammond, Brean S. *Pope and Bolingbroke: A Study of Friendship and Influence*. Columbia: University of Missouri Press, 1984.

Kramnick, Isaac. *Bolingbroke and His Circle: The Politics of Nostalgia in the Age of Walpole*. Cambridge, MA: Harvard University Press, 1968.

BREAN HAMMOND

BONNER, HYPATIA BRADLAUGH (1858–1935), British editor, lecturer, and activist. Though a significant exponent of unbelief in her own right, as the only surviving child of Charles and Susannah BRADLAUGH, Hypatia is chiefly remembered for supporting her father in life and death.

She was born in Hackney, London, on March 30, 1858, two years after her sister, Alice, and educated at private London schools and in Paris. When the family split up in 1870, Susannah and the girls went to live with grandparents in Sussex, but came to London alternately to give Charles secretarial help. After Susannah died in 1877 they lived with Charles in St. John's Wood, London.

Bradlaugh hoped Hypatia would read law at London University, and she studied law privately, but at the City of London College she took political economy and, under Edward Bibbins AVELING, science, before women were excluded. In 1879 Aveling established formal classes under Science and Art Department auspices at the NATIONAL SECULAR SOCIETY's Hall of Science, and Hypatia studied botany, Latin, and chemistry, also acting as secretary. In 1881 she matriculated and was recognized as a teacher of mathematics and chemistry, publishing four lectures as *Chemistry of Home* (1882). As mathematics teacher and student union vice president she met student Arthur Bonner and married him in June 1885. He became Charles Bradlaugh's printer, and she bore two sons: Kenneth, who died in infancy, and Charles.

Already a National Secular Society (NSS) vice president and congress delegate, she joined the NSS's corps of lecturers and wrote for her father's *NATIONAL REFORMER* and Annie BESANT's *Our Corner*. The Bonners also loved music, art, and literature, and Hypatia wrote children's stories, collected in 1886. She lost her elder sister, Alice, in 1888 and her father in 1891; so, as Aveling and Besant had also departed, she closed the Hall of Science classes. From Bradlaugh the Bonners inherited the Freethought Publishing Company, and its debts. They managed to pay these, but the *National Reformer* folded in 1893. Disliking George W. FOOTE, Bradlaugh's successor as president, Hyatia left the NSS in 1891. In defending her father's memory, she quarreled with Foote, George Jacob HOLYOAKE, and Joseph MCCABE.

In 1897 she established and edited a monthly, *Reformer*, which lasted until 1904. She was on the executive of the nonviolent female-suffrage Women's National Liberation Federation, the International Arbitration and Peace League, and the Humanitarian League, and in 1910 became founding chair of the Rationalist Peace Society (RPS), an independent offshoot of the RATIONALIST PRESS ASSOCIATION (RPA), for which she was a principal lecturer. World War I caused dissension within the RPS, suspension in 1917, relaunch in 1918, and dissolution in 1921.

She became an RPA honorary associate in 1912 and a director in 1916. A persistent campaigner against British BLASPHEMY laws, she wrote *Penalties upon Opinion* (1912). When her voice failed in 1924 she ceased lecturing, but served as a London magistrate from 1921 to 1934. She died in Tooting Bee, London, on August 25, 1935, four years before Arthur.

BIBLIOGRAPHY

Bonner, Arthur, and Charles Bradlaugh Bonner. *Hypatia Bradlaugh Bonner: The Story of Her Life*. London: Watts, 1942.

Cooke, Bill. *The Blasphemy Depot*. London: Rationalist Press Association, 2003.

Tribe, David. *President Charles Bradlaugh, M.P.* London: Elek, 1971.

DAVID TRIBE

BOSTON INVESTIGATOR. This American liberal newspaper was founded in February 1831 by Abner Kneeland, a former Baptist minister who had lost his faith and become an agnostic (see AGNOSTICISM) and liberal. Prior to establishing the *Investigator*, Kneeland had been an active Universalist (see UNIVERSALISM TO 1961). He edited the Philadelphia *University Magazine* between 1821 and 1823 and the *Olive Branch* in 1828. Soon after his arrival in Boston at the end of 1830, Kneeland launched the *Boston Investigator* with the general aim to "improve the condition of Man." This would be done by exposing corporate and government fraud, airing criticism of monopolies, and advancing causes such as the abolition of slavery, women's emancipation, and the rights of the working classes.

In 1834 Kneeland served a prison term for BLASPHEMY. His actual crime was to say publicly that he did not believe in God. While Kneeland was in prison the *Investigator* was run by Horace SEAVER, a native Bostonian. Seaver was an atheist and materialist in the manner of Ludwig BÜCHNER and a man proud of his working-class roots. When Kneeland abruptly retired as editor in 1838, Seaver began an extraordinary fifty-year period as editor, retaining the post until his death. Much of this time he coedited the *Investigator* with J. P. MENDUM, who became sole owner of the paper in 1840. After Seaver's death, Lemuel K. WASHBURN took over the position, becoming the third and last editor of the *Investigator*. Washburn had for many years been a Unitarian minister before losing his faith and becoming a freethinker in the manner of Robert Green INGERSOLL and Thomas PAINE. But by now the *Investigator* was struggling to bring in a new generation of readers. Washburn supplemented his, and the *Investigator*'s, income through much of the 1890s by lecturing to FREETHOUGHT societies. Changing times began to take their toll on the paper, which suspended publication on July 30, 1904, and turned its subscription list over to THE TRUTH SEEKER.

The *Boston Investigator* was an extraordinary achievement. Over its seventy-three-year life, the paper had only three editors and as a result was able to achieve a remarkable continuity. Ingersoll once said that the distribution of the *Investigator* was what made it possible for him to travel around the country and lecture on freethought.

BIBLIOGRAPHY

Macdonald, George E. *Fifty Years of Freethought*. New York: Truth Seeker Company, 1972.
Putnam, Samuel P. *Four Hundred Years of Freethought*. New York: Truth Seeker Company, 1894.

BILL COOKE

BRADLAUGH, CHARLES (1833–1891), English atheist, reformer, and politician. As Britain's leading secularist (see SECULARISM) and an inspiration for similar movements in other countries, Charles Bradlaugh stands in the forefront of world freethinkers. Through his legal struggle to take his parliamentary seat; his leadership of the secularist wing of British republicanism, which advocated abolition of the monarchy, the House of Lords, and other manifestations of hereditary privilege; and his trial with Annie BESANT for publishing a contraceptive manual, he colors British political and social history.

Early Life. The eldest of seven children, Charles was born to a solicitor's clerk and a former nursemaid in Hoxton, London, on September 26, 1833. Sent to a brutal British Quaker school and two private schools until he was eleven, he received little formal education beyond the "four Rs." He found work as an office boy, wharf clerk, and cashier to a coal merchant, and was a Sunday school teacher at the local Anglican church. For a confirmation visitation by the bishop of London, its priest in charge asked him to study the Thirty-nine Articles of the Anglican faith. He conscientiously extended his study to their biblical source and found discrepancies, which he asked his pastor to explain. Branding this questioning as ATHEISM, the Reverend J. G. Packer suspended him from Sunday school duties. Absenting himself from church, too, Bradlaugh spent Sundays with Chartists and Owenites (see OWEN, ROBERT), who debated political and religious themes. They gave him Robert TAYLOR's deistic *Diegesis* (1829), which he sent to Packer for comment. Instead he received an ultimatum to change his views within three days or lose his home and job. Before the time was up, he left both.

He found refuge with an old Chartist and then the widowed partner of atheist republican Richard CARLILE. Eliza Sharples (see CARLILE, ELIZA SHARPLES) ran a coffee room in front of a temperance hall, where Bradlaugh socialized with radical freethinkers, lost his Christian faith, and embraced teetotalism. One new friend was James Savage, who taught him Hebrew to facilitate his biblical studies. Savage knew the well-known Chartist and Owenite George Jacob HOLYOAKE, who chaired Bradlaugh's first lecture on the past, present, and future of theology. He had also begun to write and distribute political poems and anti-Christian tracts, but his first bylined publication was *A Few Words on the Christians' Creed* (1850). To earn a living he set up as a coal merchant, but lack of capital and his infidel reputation killed the business. Selling buckskin braces for an admirer was equally profitless, and he fell into debt. Greatly influenced by Ralph Waldo EMERSON's essay "Self-Reliance" (1841) he declined charity and in December 1850 took the "Queen's shilling" (actually six pounds, ten shillings) and joined the Seventh (Princess Royal's) Dragoon Guards, stationed in Ireland. There he saw the oppression of British imperialism and first became an advocate of Irish home rule within the United Kingdom. Resenting military drill and discipline, he found life tolerable only through friendship with an army schoolmaster and poet, James Thomson. He had become reconciled with his parents, and his widowed mother purchased his discharge with a legacy in 1853. Mellowing afterward, he applied military discipline to his political demonstrations and steadfastly supported soldiers' rights.

Making a Mark. Back in London Bradlaugh found that Holyoake had launched a new movement to take the place of both Chartism and Owenism, which were in terminal decline. This was SECULARISM, a reformist and ethical commitment to "this world" as the only one we know. Reversing his earlier positions, Holyoake now wished to avoid theological confrontation. Influential freethinkers disagreed with and were defrauded by him.

Bradlaugh obtained employment as an office boy with solicitor Thomas Rogers and rapidly rose to common-law manager. At Rogers's request, Bradlaugh adopted a pseudonym for his secularist propaganda and chose "Iconoclast," which he maintained until 1870. Earning one hundred pounds a year from Rogers and a building society, he felt able in June 1855 to marry Susannah Lamb Hooper, daughter of a freethinking republican father and conventional mother. Three children were born: Alice in 1856, Hypatia in 1858, and Charles in 1859.

After years of neutrality within the secularist movement, Bradlaugh took the side of Robert Cooper and other dissidents against Holyoake. In 1858 he became editor of Cooper's *Investigator* and president of the London Secular Society after Holyoake resigned. Thereafter the secularist movement adopted Bradlaugh's radical anticlerical stance. A profession of atheism was never required for secularist membership. Bradlaugh himself said, "I do not deny God," and sometimes—after Baruch SPINOZA and Ernst HAECKEL—called himself a monist, monism being a naturalism that posits the physical as the sole realm that exists, contrary to dualism or pluralism. Yet Bradlaugh always said that "atheist" best represented the freethought position. And he believed the movement should be actively engaged in popular protests and political demonstrations in support of civil liberties, neo-Malthusianism (family planning) promotion, and republicanism.

He supported French and Italian, and later Spanish and Russian, revolutionaries and was admitted to the Masonic *Loge des Philadelphes*, founded by Continental émigrés; but he still sought a legal career. While Rogers had allowed him to argue cases in court, though unqualified, when he asked to be articled for training as a solicitor, he was refused an eighty-pound loan to pay for his stamp duty, a necessary government registration fee. So he turned to a more obliging solicitor and company promoter, Thomas Harvey. He now felt able to leave the East End of London. Weekends were occupied with exhausting provincial lectures and debates. He always charged lecture admission and underwrote all expenses, which initially exceeded takings.

In 1859 the *Investigator* folded, but a Reformer Newspaper Co., Ltd., launched the *National Reformer*, with

Bradlaugh and Joseph Barker as coeditors, in 1860. After much bickering over Bradlaugh's support for George Drysdale's contraceptive tract *Elements of Social Science* (1854), Barker was deposed and Bradlaugh became sole editor and, later, proprietor. In 1861 he left Harvey's employ just before the latter was imprisoned for debt, and joined Montague Leverson, another solicitor and company promoter. In 1863 he left Leverson just before, under investigation for fraud, the latter decamped. Realizing that an association with two disgraced solicitors meant the end of his legal career, he became a City "merchant," company secretary, insurance agent, loan broker, and general financier. In 1863, when "his health broke down," he handed over the *Reformer* editorship to a capable but uninspiring young freethinker, John WATTS, and joined his local Tottenham parish vestry and Masonic lodge in 1864. Unfortunately, in 1866 Watts fell terminally ill and Bradlaugh had to resume editorship. He also resumed political activism and became a founding vice president of the National Reform League, which sought to extend the franchise.

Years of Achievement. Most significant in 1866 was the formation of the NATIONAL SECULAR SOCIETY under Bradlaugh's presidency. As well as promoting freethought, the National Secular Society acted as coordinator for his political and legal agitation. This included defying "security laws" (which demanded costly bonds against seditious or blasphemous libels in newspapers) in 1868. His vigorous legal and journalistic fight against prosecution led to their repeal in 1869. Contemporaneously, in a civil action he obtained the right of unbelievers to affirm in law courts.

In 1870 his business finally failed, but he avoided bankruptcy and eventually paid off his debts. Most household contents were sold and the family split up. His wife, now alcoholic, and daughters went to her parents' home; his son to an army tutor; and he to two rooms in Stepney.

This was another year of revolutions in Europe, and Louis Napoleon was overthrown during the Franco-Prussian War. Bradlaugh supported Republican France and was invited to act as an unofficial mediator in peace talks between the Paris Commune and Versailles government in 1871. Yet greater challenges emerged at home, with an upsurge of republicanism inspired by France, fueled also by anger at the dissolute Prince of Wales and Queen Victoria's decade of costly nonperformance as the "widow of Windsor." Wishing to be "prepared for any event," Bradlaugh declined nomination as president of the National Secular Society; contrary to some accounts, it did not "collapse"; rather, it was transformed into a network of republican clubs. Bradlaugh became president of the London Republican Club and wrote a bestselling *Impeachment of the House of Brunswick*. In 1873 he was the National Republican League's emissary to Republican Spain and, during the first of three American lecture tours, the *New York Herald* proclaimed him "[t]he Future President of England." It was very premature. The republican movement was a warring coalition of radicals, Christian socialists, social democrats, Marxists, anarchists, and adventurers that collapsed when Victoria regained popularity in 1874. Secularism then resumed centrality in his life.

This was when Besant, the separated wife of an Anglican clergyman, joined the National Secular Society, soon demoting lieutenants Charles WATTS and George William FOOTE. In 1876 a Bristol bookseller was prosecuted for selling a provocatively illustrated edition of Charles KNOWLTON's contraceptive tract *Fruits of Philosophy* (1832). The publisher was Watts, secretary of the National Secular Society and Bradlaugh's uncontracted subeditor, printer, and publisher. Arrested himself in 1877, Watts pleaded guilty to obscene libel against the wishes of Besant and Bradlaugh, and was summarily dismissed from the last three positions. Besant and Bradlaugh formed a Freethought Publishing Company to republish the (slightly modified) book, and were arrested, tried, convicted, and sentenced to six months in jail, but escaped on a legal technicality. Watts, Foote, and Holyoake then formed a British Secular Union, which just survived until 1884.

Despite this saga and three previous electoral failures (one in 1868 and two in 1874) as Radical candidate for Northampton, Bradlaugh was elected as one of Northampton's members of Parliament in 1880. When he asked to affirm rather than swear an oath of office before taking his seat, a select committee declared the 1869 reform, which permitted replacing oaths in law courts by affirmations, did not apply to Parliament. He then asked to take the oath, but another select committee said atheists were ineligible to swear an oath but that Bradlaugh should be allowed to affirm. After first rejecting this recommendation and imprisoning him, the House allowed it "subject to any liability by statute" (fines for voting without swearing). He then faced six years of self-conducted litigation, physical expulsion, another general election (1885), and three by-elections (1881, 1882, and 1884) before a new Speaker allowed him to take oath and seat in 1886.

Inside Parliament, his greatest success was the 1888 Oaths Act allowing universal affirmation; but he was largely responsible for the Royal Commission on Market Rights and Tolls (1887) to benefit small traders and consumers, and sat on the Royal Commission on Vaccination (1889) and Select Committees on the Employers' Liability Bill (1886), Perpetual Pensions for the aristocracy (1887), Immigration of Destitute Aliens (1888), and the Friendly Societies Act (1888). Internationally he was known as the "member for India," which he visited in 1889. It was believed that Gladstone intended to make him undersecretary of state for India.

He also advocated proportional representation, land-law and penal reform, international and industrial arbitration, colonial freedom, bimetalism, and a channel tunnel. But the issue which most occupied his final years was "scientific socialism." All his life he had optimistically promoted self-help and cooperative retail, building, benevolent, and insurance societies, so it was inevitable he would oppose both utopian socialism and MARXISM. While his opposition to an eight-hour workday and widespread government regulation of industry is now seen as reactionary, his criticism of the violent revolution, tyranny, censorship, lack of enterprise, and economic stagnation that he said would be consequences of socialism was prescient. He died of chronic renal disease and uremia on January 30, 1891.

BIBLIOGRAPHY

Arnstein, Walter L. *The Bradlaugh Case: A Study in Late Victorian Opinion and Politics.* Oxford: Oxford University Press, 1965.

Bonner, Hypatia Bradlaugh, and John M. Robertson. *Charles Bradlaugh: A Record of His Life and Work, with an Account of His Parliamentary Struggle, Politics, and Teachings.* 2 vols. London: Fisher Unwin, 1894–95.

Bradlaugh, Charles. *The Autobiography of C. Bradlaugh.* London: Austin Holyoake, 1873.

Gilmour, J. P., ed. *Champion of Liberty: Charles Bradlaugh.* London: Watts, 1933.

Tribe, David. *President Charles Bradlaugh, M.P.* London: Elek Books, 1971.

DAVID TRIBE

BRANDES, GEORG MORRIS COHEN (1842–1927),

Danish literary critic, scholar, and historian. Georg Morris Cohen Brandes was born in Copenhagen to middle-class nonreligious Jewish parents.

Though he received his master's degree in aesthetics from the University of Copenhagen in 1864, Brandes was refused the chair in aesthetics there in 1870 because, among other reasons, he was a well-known atheist. Afterward he worked as a lecturer and drama critic, becoming the principal leader of the naturalistic movement in Scandinavian literature.

Brandes introduced POSITIVISM and DARWINISM in Denmark and taught that the most significant literature in Germany, France, and England from 1789 to 1848 was indebted to the French Revolution, which had introduced the freedom of thought without which a significant literature could not thrive. His thought was influenced by Friedrich NIETZSCHE, John Stuart MILL, Hippolyte-Adolphe Taine, and Ernest RENAN, with whom he corresponded, resulting in a critical position about religion. When he wrote "Sagnet om Jesus" (Jesus, a Myth, 1925), his work provoked wide protests and gained him many enemies.

Even today his words are considered deeply controversial within conservative circles. Noteworthy passages include: "The Christian god is blood thirsty." "The working classes intend not to create a paradise of ignorance but a cultural and scientific one." "George Sand debates the question of marriages, VOLTAIRE, BYRON and FEUERBACH debate religion, PROUDHON private property. . . . Literature should be an organ of the great thoughts of liberty and progress of humanity. For a literature not to raise any question for debate is the same as for it to set out to lose all significance." "Writers should reject abstract idealism and work in the service of progressive ideas and the reform of modern society, deal with atheism, marriage, etc."

With his brother Edward, Brandes published the magazine *Det Nittende Aarhundrede* (The Nineteenth Century) between 1874 and 1877. His literary works include *Critiques and Portraits* (1870), *Main Currents in Nineteenth-Century Literature* (1872–90 and 1901–05), *The Contemporary French Aesthetics* (1870), *Naturalism in England* (1875), and biographies of Voltaire, GOETHE, Byron, Napoleon, Garibaldi, and others.

JOSÉ MANUEL FERNÁNDEZ SANTANA

BRANN, WILLIAM COWPER (1855–1898), American journalist. Founder and principal author of the *Iconoclast*, published in Waco, Texas, William Cowper Brann battled that state's Baptists until martyrdom ended his colorful life. He was born in Coles County, Illinois, the son of a Presbyterian minister; however, after his mother died when he was only two, he was taken to be raised by a local farm family. Brann left the farm at age thirteen, carrying a single box of his belongings. He worked a variety of jobs until his natural talent for language secured him a position as a newspaper reporter and, later, an editorial writer. Though the first thirty-nine years of Brann's life were marked by "the harassing annoyances of extreme poverty," a love of reading richly equipped his mind, which, combined with a fiery temperament, produced "an inexhaustible vocabulary, from which he could always find the words best fitted to convey his meaning at the moment they were most needed, and every sentence was resplendent with an order of wit, humor, and satire peculiar to a style original with himself."

Brann moved to Waco, Texas, where, after further work on newspapers, he commenced the publication in 1891 of the *Iconoclast* as a monthly magazine, which lasted only two faltering years. Successful engagements as a lecturer convinced him to revive it in 1895. Fiercely independent and sharply critical of many Texas and national institutions as well as outworn attitudes, this magazine soon attained a circulation of ninety thousand, with subscribers across the country and around the world.

Paralleling the ferment of the populist movement of that era, Brann attacked "plutocrats," the Associated Press ("the champion toad-eater of the universe"), and the anti-Catholic American Protective Association (the "Aggregation of Pusillanimous Asses"), as well as the locally powerful Baylor University, a theological center of the Baptist church. Dr. J. B. Cranfill, editor of the monthly *Baptist Standard*, was a leader of the anti-Brann faction.

Brann had an unusually colorful, complex, and contradictory personality: he was a self-proclaimed freethinker (see FREETHOUGHT) but had little use for ATHEISM; he defended Catholics and Jews but expressed a pathological hatred of African Americans. Finally, Brann's feud with Baylor provoked a beating and near lynching at the hands of an enraged mob of students in 1897, and the next year, his assassination on the streets of Waco. Brann's marble monument, featuring a carved profile and a lamp of "Truth," was later defaced by bullets.

BIBLIOGRAPHY

Brann, William Cowper. *Works*. 12 vols. New York: Brann Publishers, 1919.

Carver, Charles. *Brann the Iconoclast.* Austin: University of Texas Press, 1957; reprinted 1987.

FRED WHITEHEAD

BRECHT, BERTHOLT (1898–1956), German playwright and poet, and spokesman for the so-called Lost Generation whose lives were destroyed or ruined by World War I. Bertholt Brecht was born on February 10, 1898, in Augsburg, Bavaria, the son of a paper manufacturer. His education was in medicine but his heart was with the theater. Brecht was an early rebel against the bourgeois values with which he was raised. His experiences as a medical orderly in the last year of World War I only strengthened his sense of alienation.

In the years between the wars Brecht wrote some of the most powerful plays and poems of the period. Brecht understood the destruction of the old values the war had wrought, and, when at his best, articulated in their place a powerful, raw HUMANISM. In opposition to the tired nostrums of nation and religion, Brecht gave voice to an intense joy in the existential business of living (see EXISTENTIALISM). Works like *The Threepenny Opera* (1928) and *The Rise and Fall of the Town of Mahoganny* (1930) established Brecht's standing as one of Weimar Germany's leading playwrights and poets.

Brecht's left-wing politics and his role as cultural icon in Weimar Germany meant that he could not stay in Germany after the Nazis came to power. Within weeks of their accession, Brecht went into exile in Denmark. But that country's vulnerability to the Nazis forced Brecht to move once again, this time to Sweden in 1939, then to Finland the following year, and on to the United States via the Soviet Union in 1941.

The first years of Brecht's exile inspired another wave of important work, most notably *Galileo* (1938), *Mother Courage and Her Children* (1939), *The Good Woman of Szechwan* (1943), and *The Caucasian Chalk Circle* (1944). Brecht found life as an exile in the United States difficult and, after a brush with the House Un-American Activities Committee in 1947, he returned to West Germany. However, he was denied permission to settle there and in 1949 he moved to East Germany, where he spent the rest of his life. His last years were sad ones, as he saw firsthand the reality of the Communist society he had spent his life advocating. After warning of the low value of Nazi poetry that lauded Hitler, he wrote similar material in praise of Stalin. Brecht died in East Berlin on August 14, 1956.

BIBLIOGRAPHY

Arendt, Hannah. *Men in Dark Times*. London: Penguin, 1973.
Willett, J. *The Theater of Bertolt Brecht*. London: Methuen, 1967.

BILL COOKE

BRITISH HUMANIST ASSOCIATION, THE. The organization now known as the British Humanist Association (BHA) was founded in 1896 as the Union of Ethical Societies, soon becoming the Ethical Union, taking the name BHA in 1967. According to one of the early BHA activists, Dr. Peter Draper, "Humanists believe that this is our world, our responsibility, our possibility." It is within such very wide premises that the BHA operates (see HUMANISM).

In the 1950s there was a growing feeling that it was divisive and wasteful to have several organizations with similar ambitions operating side-by-side in British life. The Ethical Union approached the RATIONALIST PRESS ASSOCIATION (RPA) to negotiate cooperation, with Harold J. Blackham playing a leading role. A coordinating body called the Humanist Council was set up in 1950, encompassing the RPA, the Ethical Union, and the SOUTH PLACE ETHICAL SOCIETY (SPES); this was done on the initiative of Hector HAWTON, then connected with the SPES. In 1955 the RPA and the Ethical Union set up a Joint Development Committee; at the 1957 world congress of the INTERNATIONAL HUMANIST AND ETHICAL UNION (IHEU), held in London, a Humanist Association was formed in order to investigate amalgamation. Its members agreed on action on unilateral disarmament for nuclear tests, opposition to racial discrimination, and support for work on behalf of underdeveloped countries.

There were obstacles to a merger, including the matter of how bequests meant for a constituent organization might flow to a new organization and whether the new organization would have charitable status (since British charity law does not permit a charitable body to undertake political activity). The Humanist Association was replaced in 1959 by a new body, which reverted to the earlier name of the Humanist Council, the only significant difference being that the NATIONAL SECULAR SOCIETY was briefly a member. By 1963 the RPA and

Ethical Union decided jointly to sponsor a new British Humanist Association, with the RPA directing publications and the Ethical Union dealing with branch activities, conferences, and education. An inaugural meeting of the BHA took place on May 17, 1963, at the House of Commons, hosted by the sympathetic Member of Parliament Laurie Pavitt. Also in attendance were Sir Julian HUXLEY; philosopher Alfred Jules AYER; Baroness Barbara Wootton, a leading Labour member of the House of Lords; and Kingsley Martin, a well-known left-wing journalist and writer.

Administrative problems arose among the three cooperating organizations (the RPA, the Ethical Union, and BHA). There was the difference, which remained longstanding for the BHA, between those wanting action against religion (see ATHEISM; SECULARISM; FREETHOUGHT) and those prepared to go along with "ultimate concerns, religious humanism," spiritual humanism, and the like (see RELIGIOUS HUMANISM). The RPA withdrew when the Ethical Union lost its charitable status, and in 1967 the Ethical Union changed its name to the British Humanist Association. The long gestation preceding the birth of the BHA was finally over.

Among the early aims of the BHA were repeal of the Sunday observance laws, which prohibited the opening of shops and performances in theatres on Sunday; and reform of the 1944 Education Act's clauses on religion in schools, which enforced religious worship and religious education. More generally, the BHA wished to defend freedom of speech, supported the elimination of world poverty, and pressed for removal of privileges held by religious groups. In 1977 it was pronounced that the BHA "aimed to make humanism available and meaningful to the millions who have no alternative belief."

Harold Blackham, who can be considered the founding father of the BHA and was its first director, retired as director in March 1968. As a philosopher and organizer, a diplomat and plain speaker, he was a leading figure in British and world humanism in the twentieth century.

During its nearly forty years' existence the BHA continued a twin role of political lobbying and public reflection on philosophical—especially ethical—issues. It regained charitable status, to great financial advantage and without hindering any area of its activity. Its sumptuous premises in 13 Prince of Wales Terrace, Kensington, London, had been purchased by the Ethical Union after the sale of the Ethical Church in Bayswater, London. However there were later financial problems and the BHA moved to premises in Lamb's Conduit Passage as tenants of SPES, attached to Conway Hall (Red Lion Square, London), and then as tenants of the National Secular Society in Bradlaugh House in Theobald's Road in conjunction with the NSS, the RPA, and the IHEU. However, these premises were not considered adequate and the BHA moved (with the RPA and the IHEU) in 2003 to 1 Gower Street (Bloomsbury, London) where it now remains.

An essential aspect of the BHA has been support of local groups (up to about one hundred at the peak), and the development of a network of humanist officiants able to offer nonreligious funerals, weddings, naming ceremonies, and gay and lesbian affirmations (see RITUAL, CEREMONIAL, AND UNBELIEF). Educational issues have been very important. There have been efforts to abolish daily worship in schools and to change legally required religious education (RE) in public schools so that it included something about humanism as an alternative LIFE STANCE (a phrase introduced by Dr. Harry Stopes-Roe, which has had staying power). *Objective, Fair and Balanced* (1975) was a key pamphlet in developing the idea of acceptable RE, and in 2004, partly as a result of BHA lobbying, the government agreed that the national framework for RE should include humanism. Gaining recognition for humanism as a valid life stance has been a constant theme, and since Britain's 1998 Human Rights Act came into force, the BHA has campaigned for rights in law for humanism as a nonreligious belief equal to those given to religions.

Social concerns have persisted in the BHA's programming—the Social Morality Council, which brought together believers and unbelievers, was concerned with a moral outlook in society and moral education. The BHA has been active in arguing for voluntary euthanasia and the right to obtain an abortion. It has always sought an open society—the term popularized by Sir Karl POPPER—in which people of fundamentally different views cooperate in shared and neutral institutions for the common good. The Humanist Housing Association attempted to provide accommodation for needy, elderly humanists; the Agnostics Adoption Society worked to gain adoption rights for the nonreligious; the Humanist Counselling Group pioneered in nondirective counseling; Humanist Holidays organized vacations for humanists; while the World Order Group seemed to face an impossible task. Barbara Wootton criticised the BHA for aims which were too vague and unrealistic. Distinguished Advisory Council Members have included E. M. FORSTER, Harold Pinter, Julian Huxley, A. S. Neil, Karl Popper, Vanessa Redgrave, Richard Dawkins, and Bernard Crick.

A survey of members in 1971 indicated that members were largely middle class, male, elderly, left wing, and passionately concerned with social problems. The sociologist and active humanist Dr. Colin Campbell considers that humanism cannot be just antireligious but must be predicated on "the value of rationality, individual responsibility, and human-self-sufficiency." Today the BHA persists with its activity, especially in education, philosophical research, local groups, a network of nonreligious officiants, and a regular newsletter. It is the largest membership organization in the British humanist movement, with more than four thousand members. Although it has financial problems, it appears set to continue its work throughout the twenty-first century.

BIBLIOGRAPHY

Blackham, Harold. *Humanism.* Harmondsworth, UK: Penguin, 1968.

Budd, Susan. *Varieties of Unbelief: Atheists and Agnostics in English Society, 1850–1960.* London: Heinemann, 1977.

Campbell, Colin. *Towards a Sociology of Irreligion.* London: Macmillan, 1971.

Cooke, Bill. *The Blasphemy Depot: A Hundred Years of the Rationalist Press Association.* London: Rationalist Press Association, 2003.

JIM HERRICK

BROWN, ETHELRED EGBERT (1875–1956), African American Unitarian leader. Ethelred Brown was born on July 11, 1875, in Falmouth, Jamaica, the oldest of James and Florence Brown's five children. He entered the Jamaican civil service after taking the exam in 1894. Five years later he became the first clerk of the treasury and he remained in that post until 1907, when he was dismissed under questionable circumstances in connection with an allegation of missing funds. After leaving the civil service, he accepted his call to ministry. During his youth, Brown had many doubts theologically and found himself greatly attracted to Unitarianism after reading the writings of notable Unitarians including William Ellery Channing (see UNITARIANISM TO 1961). Despite his growing interest, no Unitarian fellowship for blacks existed in his native Jamaica, severely limiting his theological options. Brown could have sought ordination in the African Methodist Episcopal (AME) Church, of which he had been an active member and sometime organist, but he felt compelled to develop his faith along Unitarian lines.

Brown wrote a letter expressing his interest in becoming a Unitarian minister, which reached Franklin Southworth, president of the Meadville Theological School. Southworth replied discouragingly, noting that white churches needed white ministers and there were no prospects for organizing a black or interracial Unitarian church. Despite such dissuasion, and despite the considerable hardships borne by his wife, Ella, and their six children, Brown eventually received his theological preparation at Meadville Theological School as a special two-year student to the seminary. On June 4, 1912, he was ordained to the ministry of the Meadville Unitarian Church. Due to immigration problems, Brown was deported back to Jamaica. Upon returning to his homeland, he became a Unitarian missionary and formed a Unitarian Lay Center in Montego Bay; this lasted for nearly three years with meager support from the American Unitarian Association (AUA) as well as the British and Foreign Unitarian Association (B&FUA). Brown subsequently served as a minister of the Unitarian Church in the city of Kingston for six years at the behest of the AUA. Financial support for Brown's ministry was abruptly cut by the two associations based on a critical report by the Unitarian minister Hilary Bygrave. In an effort to restore his funding, Brown pleaded his case directly with Samuel Eliot, president of the AUA. Though he felt that Eliot was condescending toward black people, Brown refused to believe that the AUA was antagonistic toward him or his ministerial efforts. Although the AUA briefly provided more funding, the leadership of the denomination was halfhearted about Brown's prospects of organizing a Unitarian church among black congregants and finally withdrew its support by 1917.

In February 1920 Brown left Jamaica with his wife and family to seek greater opportunity in New York City. Along with several other Afro-Caribbean immigrants, he founded the Harlem Community Church, which by the end of the decade had been renamed the Harlem Unitarian Church despite the fact that it had received virtually no backing from the AUA. Lacking significant financial support for nearly twenty years, Brown held a wide variety of jobs including elevator operator in order to provide for his family. For several decades, his relations with the denomination were strained, until in 1937 the Harlem Unitarian Church was officially recognized as an AUA congregation. This change in status also made it possible for Brown to receive a pastoral support and a pension for his years of ministerial service.

For more than twenty years, Brown was an active member of the Socialist Party, which employed him as an organizer and speaker. He was also chairman of the Board of the Jamaica Benevolent Association and president of the Jamaica Progressive League, a political society that secured a new constitution for Jamaica in 1944. One of the great fights of his life was the battle to make the promise of racial equality in America and worldwide a reality, but this struggle took a great toll on him and his family; his wife became mentally ill after suffering a nervous breakdown and a son committed suicide. Brown remained as the pastor of the church he had helped to found until his death on February 17, 1956.

JUAN FLOYD-THOMAS

BROWN, GEORGE (1858–1915), English cobbler, anarchist, and atheist. Born April 16, 1858, at Raunds, England, the son of a freethinking shoemaker, George Brown began as a public speaker by stumping for Charles BRADLAUGH, then campaigning for Parliament. Brown's education was limited almost entirely to debates in gatherings of the NATIONAL SECULAR SOCIETY and labor unions. Around 1881 he began a five-year stint in India, where native noncooperation with capitalism at a boot factory further radicalized him. Arriving in Chicago in early 1886, Brown was present at the Haymarket police riot, and following that case he converted to philosophical (nonviolent) anarchism (see ANARCHISM AND UNBELIEF). He settled in Philadelphia around 1891, where he made a free-love union with the anarchist poet Mary Hansen that lasted twenty-four years (see SEX RADICALISM AND UNBELIEF). Both were leading members of the city's anarchist-liberal clubs, and the couple was always quite poor. Brown lectured on labor activism, modern literature, and the morality of free-love, mostly in Philadelphia. From 1899 he contributed essays to anarchist and socialist journals. In 1910 he cofounded the city's Ferrer Modern School (see FERRER, FRANCISCO).

From 1908 the Browns spent their summers at the Single Tax colony at Arden, Delaware, and in 1911 an ongoing feud there escalated into a national news item. Brown's rivals, loyal to the colony's affluent trustees, had the shoemaker arrested for disturbing the peace after he repeatedly raised local issues at club meetings. He spent four days in jail, then retaliated by swearing out warrants against eleven neighbors, including Upton SINCLAIR, for violating the blue laws by playing ball on Sunday. The trial at Wilmington, Delaware, on August 1 gave Brown the platform of his lifetime. The crowd went wild as he calmly testified, reversing every word he had been shouting from rostra and street corners all his life, in order to demonstrate the absurdity of law.

"I want the Sabbath day to be one of peace," Brown said. "[I]t is a day when the workman . . . should have his peace and quiet . . . the slang used on the ball field shocks me." He said that while breaking rocks at the jail, he "came to see a great light; that the Law is supreme and must be obeyed." The result was an eighteen-hour sentence in the same jail for ten men, which brought on a public campaign for prison reform by Sinclair, to say nothing of embarrassing public exposure of the colony's internal disputes and gossip.

Summoned for jury duty the following year in Philadelphia, Brown asked to be excused, telling the judge, "I do not believe in Religion or Law. If there were no law there would be no poverty, and if there were no poverty there would be no crime, and we would need no courts." The judge ruled that Brown was not excused but unfit to be a juror, and regretted having no excuse to commit him to an asylum. Brown died from blood poisoning on February 14, 1915, the result of a splinter in his hand received three months earlier.

BIBLIOGRAPHY

"Anarchist Offers Jobs at Stone Pile to Arden Colonists." *Philadelphia North American*, July 31, 1911.

"Arden Anarchist Dies in Hospital." *Wilmington Evening Journal*, February 16, 1915.

"Ardenite Leader Opens Fire upon Delaware's Jails." *Philadelphia Evening Telegraph*, August 5, 1911.

Avrich, Paul. *An American Anarchist: The Life of Voltairine de Cleyre.* Princeton, NJ: Princeton University Press, 1978.

"Brown Gone, Leaving Jail without Bald Headed Man." *Wilmington Evening Journal*, July 29, 1911.

"Doesn't Believe in the Law or Religion." *Philadelphia Evening Item*, December 2, 1912.

Elliott, James B. "George Brown." *Mother Earth* (April 1915).

"R-R-Revenge! Brown Sends Arden Foes to the Stone Pile." *Philadelphia North American*, August 2, 1911.

Traubel, Horace Logo. "George Brown." *Conservator* (June 1915).

ROBERT P. HELMS

BRUNO, GIORDANO FILIPPO (1548–1600), Italian philosopher and Inquisition victim. Giordano Bruno was born in the town of Nola, located near Naples, Italy. He was an outspoken youth and eventually became an outspoken Dominican monk. During his tenure as a Dominican, it was suggested that he had read some of the "forbidden works" of Desiderius ERASMUS. This, along with his unorthodox views of Christianity, prompted the Catholic Church to issue an indictment of HERESY against Bruno in 1578. On learning the indictment was imminent, Bruno fled to France, beginning a life as an intellectual nomad.

It was not uncommon for intellectuals to wander from university center to university center, but it was uncommon for them to be forced to move. Bruno's outspoken critiques and attacks upon orthodox views made him welcome at these university centers only for a short time. He began his wanderings by going to Geneva, followed in turn by France, England, France again, Germany, and then Venice.

Bruno returned to Italy in 1591 and stayed in Venice, at the insistence of Giovanni Moncenigo, in order to teach some of his "natural magic of memory training." Bruno also could have been homesick, or trying to reach the Vatican in order to win the pope's support for some of his controversial ideas. Nonetheless, Moncenigo turned him over to the Venetian Inquisition. Bruno was held for more than a year in Venice; Roman authorities insisted that he be turned over to them, which he was in February 1593. Bruno was imprisoned for more than six years without writing materials and without any explanation for the delay in his trial. In January 1600 he was handed over to the Grand Inquisitor, convicted, and turned over to the secular authorities to carry out the Inquisition's sentence. The decree was that Bruno be burned at the stake by the governor of Rome (the Inquisition commonly handed over its victims to the secular authorities to dispatch). On February 17, 1600, Bruno was led to Campo de Fiori, where he was burned at the stake before the crowds visiting Rome for the Jubilee Year.

Bruno and his works were largely ignored until eighteenth-century deists (see DEISM) started reading his works and making him their champion. In the nineteenth century, Italy's freethinkers also adopted Bruno as a martyr to the cause of FREETHOUGHT. A statue of Bruno was placed at the spot of his death and dedicated on June 9, 1889. On every February 17 thereafter, freethinkers have gathered in Campo de Fiori to celebrate Bruno's life.

There are no clear indications as to the exact reason for Bruno's execution. Some scholars have attributed it to his knowledge of magic and Hermetic philosophy; others have attributed it to his belief in the Copernican system. In *The Catholic Encyclopedia*, it is stated that it was for his errors in theology, which included the idea that Christ was a master magician and that he believed transubstantiation to be impossible. After hearing the judgment of the Inquisition, Bruno is quoted as saying, "Perchance your fear in passing judgment on me is greater than mine in receiving it."

BIBLIOGRAPHY

Birx, H. James. "Giordano Bruno: From a Closed Cosmos to an Infinite Universe." *New Zealand Rationalist and Humanist* (Summer 1997–98).

Singer, Dorothea Waley. *Giordano Bruno, His Life and Thought.* New York: Henry Schuman, 1950.

Turner, William. "Giordano Bruno." In *The Catholic Encyclopedia,* vol. 3.

Yates, Frances A. "Giordano Bruno." In *The Encyclopedia of Philosophy,* vol. 1, edited by Paul Edwards. New York: Macmillan, 1967.

TIMOTHY BINGA

BÜCHNER, GEORG (1813–1837), German writer, social revolutionary, and physician.

Life. Born in 1831 in Goddenau near Darmstadt as the son of a physician, Georg Büchner studied medicine in Strassburg, Giessen, and Zürich. In 1833 he cofounded a section of the *Gesellschaft der Menschenrechte* (Society for Human Rights) in Giessen. This secret oppositional group espoused an egalitarian, early communist position.

In 1834 Büchner moved to Darmstadt, where he wrote and distributed rabble-rousing pamphlets. Denounced, he fled to Strassburg in 1835. He died at Zürich at the age of twenty-three, shortly after completing his PhD. Georg Büchner was the brother of philosopher and physician Ludwig BÜCHNER.

Major Works. In his time, Büchner was among the lesser-known authors. Only since the early twentieth century he has been acknowledged as a forerunner of NATURALISM and expressionism. His first play, *Danton's Death (Dantons Tod)*, written in 1835, presents the French Revolution's key figures as resigned men, disillusioned after their attempt to change the course of history. Erroneously equating the characters' position with the author's, philologists used to interpret the text as antirevolutionary and nihilistic; today its revolutionary appeal is undisputed.

An overtly social revolutionary publication was the pamphlet "Hessian Courier" (*Hessischer Landbote*), written by Büchner and Friedrich Ludwig Weidig to oppose the staggering tax burden borne by peasants and artisans to subsidize the grand duke's inflated administrative machinery. Published anonymously, it marked the peak of journalism in the *Vormärz*, the years between the German war of independence (1813–1915) and the 1848 revolution.

In his novella *Lenz* (1839), Büchner criticized Christianity for discouraging reform in this life by offering the consolations of the hereafter. The work was based on the life and descent into madness of writer Jakob Michael Reinhold Lenz, who suffered from schizophrenia. Büchner's source was a report by the priest, social reformer, and educator Johann Friedrich Oberlin, with whom Lenz spent some time in a Vosges village. Unlike Oberlin, Büchner does not blame Lenz's illness on his "immoral lifestyle," but merely describes it as a feeling of overwhelming isolation.

Büchner's fragmentary play *Woyzeck* is considered the beginning of German social drama and has meanwhile become one of the most widely read and performed nineteenth-century German plays.

BIBLIOGRAPHY

Hauschild, Jan Christoph. *Georg Büchner: Biographie.* Reinbek: Rowohlt, 2004.

Lehmann, Susanne. *Georg Büchner: Revolutionär, Dichter, Wissenschaftler 1813 bis 1837* (Der Katalog. Ausstellung Mathildenhöhe, Darmstadt, 2. August bis 27. September 1987). Basel, Frankfurt a.M.: Stroemfeld, Roter Stern, 1987.

Mayer, Thomas Michael, ed. *Georg Büchner Jahrbuch.* Frankfurt a. M.: Europäische Verlagsanstalt, 1981–88; Tübingen: Hain, 1991ff.

Patterson, Michael. *Büchner: The Complete Plays: Danton's Death, Leonce and Lena, Woyzeck, The Hessian Courier, Lenz, On Cranial Nerves, and Selected Letters.* London: Methuen, 1987.

INGE HÜSGEN

BÜCHNER, LUDWIG (1824–1899), German physician and philosopher. Together with Carl Vogt and Jacob Moleschott, Ludwig Büchner continued in Germany the development of French eighteenth-century materialism. Büchner, Vogt, and Moleschott advocated what may be called physicalistic materialism (see PHYSICALISM), quite distinct from the social and political ATHEISM and MATERIALISM of Karl MARX, Friedrich Engels, and Vladimir Ilyich Lenin.

Büchner, Moleschott, and Vogt were mainly influenced by developments in chemistry, physiology, and zoology. Their materialism represented an extrapolation of scientific results to a philosophical level. This was particularly the case with Büchner, who in 1855 published his sensational *Kraft und Stoff* (Force and Matter). The title of this book was taken from a chapter of a book which Moleschott, originally from Holland, had published in 1852.

Büchner's *Kraft und Stoff* has sometimes been compared to a similar book of French materialism, Paul Heinrich Dietrich d'HOLBACH's *Système de la nature* (*System of Nature*, 1770), sometimes called "the Bible of French materialism." But as a philosopher, Holbach was more accomplished and wide ranging than Büchner.

In *Kraft und Stoff*, Büchner attempted to compensate for his limited philosophical knowledge by spewing derogatory remarks about philosophers. Büchner later acquired a deeper understanding of philosophical problems, but he never reached the same level as Holbach. In fact, Holbach may well be ranked with the great philosophers of the past, whereas Büchner was less important. Still, as a philosopher Büchner has often been underrated.

Büchner was not only active as a physician and a theorist. Together with eleven other intellectuals, Büchner played an active role in founding the World Union of Freethinkers in 1880. He was also instrumental in founding the German Freethinker Association (Deutscher Freidenkerbund) in 1881.

BIBLIOGRAPHY

Bunge, Mario. *Scientific Materialism.* Reidel: Dordrecht, 1981.

Dreisbach-Olsen, Jutta. "Ludwig Büchner." PhD thesis, Marburg/Lahn, 1969.

Gregory, Frederick. *Scientific Materialism in Nineteenth-Century Germany.* Reidel: Dordrecht, 1977.

Hiorth, Finngeir. *Introduction to Atheism.* Oslo: Human-Etisk Forbund, 2002.

Kahl, Joachim, and Erich Wernig, eds. *Freidenker, Geschichte und Gegenwart.* Köln: Pahl-Rugenstein, 1981.

FINNGEIR HIORTH

BUDDHISM, UNBELIEF WITHIN. What Is Buddhism? Buddhism is a religion, a philosophy, and a body of practices that originated in India in the fifth century BCE. Its founder is ordinarily said to be Siddhartha Gautama, often believed to have lived between 563 and 483 BCE. An alternative date of death based on Chinese sources is 368 BCE. Sources agree that Gautama died at eighty years old. He is traditionally called the Buddha, the "enlightened one." Buddhism teaches salvation through escape from samsara, an endless cycle of birth and rebirth that Buddhists ordinarily take for granted.

In Hindu and Buddhist belief, samsara is a bondage of life, death, and rebirth dictated by karma. Karma is a universal law of cause and effect as applied to the deeds of people. A deliberate good or bad deed leads a person's destiny in the appropriate direction. The ripening of the deed may take more than one lifetime, tying the agent to the cycle of rebirth as dictated by samsara. Only deeds free from desire and delusion are without consequences for karma.

Buddhists ordinarily say that there are Four Noble Truths, the four great truths of Buddhism. The first says that all existence is afflicted with suffering. The second truth identifies desire, thirst, or craving as the source of suffering that binds beings to samsara, the cycle of existence. The third truth asserts that through the elimination of craving, suffering can be brought to an end. The fourth truth identifies an eightfold path as the means to eliminate suffering and escape from samsara.

The eightfold path, the last of the four noble truths of Buddhism, is the key to release from suffering. Its elements are: (1) The right or perfect view of the four noble truths and of the nature of the self (atman). (2) Perfect resolution in favor of renunciation and ahimsa, or nonviolence. Ahimsa is an ethical principle forbidding injury to all living creatures, implying vegetarianism and pacificism. (3) Perfect speech, that is, avoidance of lying and slander. (4) Perfect conduct. (5) Perfect livelihood, including avoidance of harmful professions. (6) Perfect effort. (7) Perfect mindfulness or control of thought. (8) Perfect concentration, or attainment of the contemplative ideal.

The eightfold path is not intended to be followed in a linear way, but gives the different elements needed to live a life that leads to release from suffering.

The first step in the eightfold path states the need to have the right view of the nature of the self or atman. In Hindu thought atman is believed to be an eternal soul, at death transmigrating to another body, not necessarily human. Buddhism denies the existence of atman as an eternal soul. It subscribes to the doctrine of *anatman* (*anatta*), the view that there is no permanent soul. There is no ongoing owner of the fleeting perceptions and experiences that make up our lives.

The doctrine of *anatman* has often been praised as a precursor of the so-called bundle theory of the mind or self, a theory advocated by the Scottish philosopher David HUME. According to the bundle theory, we have no reason to think in terms of a single unified self that owns a variety of experiences or states. We only have access to the succession of experiences. The enduring self is a fiction of the imagination. This sounds very much like the doctrine of *anatman* found in Buddhism. But in Buddhism it is combined with a doctrine of karma and rebirths, which is not the case in Hume's thought.

The cycle of births and rebirths is not necessarily unending. By accepting the four noble truths and practicing the eightfold path, it is possible to escape from the cycle of births and rebirths and reach nirvana. Nirvana is posited as the final and total release from cyclic existence, without further rebirths and their attendant miseries. Nirvana is, in Buddhist thinking, ordinarily conceived as the complete extinction of individuality, but without total loss of consciousness. It is invariably described as a condition in which all pain, suffering, mental anguish, and above all, samsara, have ceased. Whereas an atheist (see ATHEISM) ordinarily believes that with death all consciousness, all pain, and all happiness end, Buddhists tend to believe that all *painful* kinds of consciousness disappear, but that there still is room for some bliss or happiness, perhaps even a form of bliss that is impossible in samsara.

Critique of Buddhism. We have so far given an account of the more basic aspects of Buddhism. We have mentioned speculative beliefs in karma, in samsara with its "unending" cycle of births and rebirths, and in nirvana. Buddhism in fact contains an immense amount of speculation. But Buddhism does not postulate an almighty God who created everything. In this way, Buddhism may remind one of modern atheism. But taken as a whole, Buddhism is quite remote from most forms of modern atheism.

The early Buddhists accepted the views of the universe generally held in India at that time. These views implied that the universe is not created out of nothing at a particular time, nor will it be completely destroyed at another time. The universe has always existed and will always exist.

This sounds like a modern kind of cosmology, albeit one without a Big Bang. It is therefore sometimes supposed that Buddhism is compatible with modern atheism or that it is an atheistic religion. This does not hold for traditional Buddhism, which takes polytheism for granted. A modern Buddhist can reject the existence of gods, but in doing so he or she deviates from traditional Buddhism.

Traditional Buddhism has a mythology with six realms or destinations in which it is possible for rebirth to take place: (1) the heavens, that is, the realms of gods and other "higher" beings, plus some rarefied regions above them; (2) the realm of the *asuras* or titans, that is, bellicose gods; (3) the realm of humans; (4) the realm of animals; (5) the realm of hungry ghosts; and (6) the hell realms, which in Buddhist writings are numerous and exceedingly painful.

Siddhartha Gautama himself left no writings. His beliefs were orally transmitted for about four hundred years before being written down. Serious quarrels arose among the successive generations of adepts. Many schools of Buddhism arose. Of these Theravada, Mahayana, and Tantrayana survive and are divided into many sects and groups. They all appeal to the Buddha as their authority. But strictly speaking, nothing is known as to what the Buddha himself believed.

As a whole there is not much unbelief *within* Buddhism.

Buddhism, like theistic religions and philosophies, is highly speculative. An atheist may feel at home in Buddhism, and there almost certainly are many atheists among the Buddhists. But so are there many atheists among nominal Christians, Muslims, and Hindus. Buddhism as whole is hardly more atheistic than the theistic religions.

BIBLIOGRAPHY

Conze, Edward. *Buddhism: Its Essence and Development.* New York: Harper & Row, 1975

Dasgupta, Surendranath. *A History of Indian Philosophy.* Cambridge: Cambridge University Press, 1969.

Hiorth, Finngeir. *Atheism in India.* Oslo: Human-Etisk Forbund, 1999.

Radhakrishnan, Sarvepalli, and Charles A. Moore, eds. *A Sourcebook in Indian Philosophy.* Princeton, NJ: Princeton University Press, 1957.

Robinson, Richard H., and Willard L. Johnson. *The Buddhist Religion: A Historical Introduction.* Encino, CA: Dickenson, 1977.

Snelling, John. *The Elements of Buddhism.* Longmead, UK: Element Books, 1990.

Stutley, Margaret, and James Stutley, eds. *A Dictionary of Hinduism.* London: Routledge & Kegan Paul, 1977.

FINNGEIR HIORTH

BUFFON, GEORGES-LOUIS LECLERC, COMTE DE (1707–1788), French naturalist and freethinker. Georges-Louis Leclerc was born to a wealth family in Montbard, France, on September 7, 1707. His father, Benjamin, wanted his son to study law, which he did until 1727, when his interest in mathematics became strong. Georges-Louis studied mathematics as well as botany at Angers University until he was forced to leave as a result of a duel in 1730. Buffon (as he began calling himself) studied in other places at this time, including Italy, until he inherited his mother's estate and became an important gentleman. As a result of his background in botany and mathematics, he was asked to improve shipbuilding for the French navy by testing the mechanical properties of wood. This eventually led to his appointment to the Jardin du Roi (which later became the Jardin des Plantes) as a member of the French Academy of Sciences. In this position, he began his *Histoire naturelle, générale et particulière* in 1749.

Histoire naturelle, an epic work written to unify the sciences of natural history, geology, anthropology, and botany, was originally conceived to be a fifty-volume work, but Buffon died in 1788 after only thirty-six volumes (eight were published posthumously). These volumes are thought to have provided influences upon the thought of Charles DARWIN, Alfred Russel WALLACE, and Lamarck, concerning the evolution of species. Buffon proposed no "mechanism" for evolution, but he pointed out generally that man and ape may have descended from a similar ancestor, as well as the idea that animals and plants both undergo "modifications" over time that produce different varieties, and these changes can be seen if one studies nature.

The environment in France at the time when the first several volumes of *Histoire naturelle* were published became problematic for Buffon. Buffon was a man of means, and as such, was supposed to hold to orthodox thought on the state religion. The Sorbonne (at that time, the Faculty of Theology, Paris) condemned parts of his work, especially those presenting Buffon's least orthodox proposals. The Sorbonne was in a difficult way itself; *Histoire naturelle* was an official publication of the crown and it could not publicly oppose a work of the King. Buffon was censured, but in the following volume of *Histoire naturelle*, he published all the correspondence that had occurred over this incident as a way to appease the Sorbonne. This included letters that Buffon had written affirming his belief in the official state religion, particularly creation as it was written in the Bible. It is believed that Buffon only wrote this to appease the religious regime of France at that time. In later correspondence Buffon seems to retract these letters; thereafter his writings were crafted with particular care so as not to create controversy.

Despite his being a friend of Denis DIDEROT, Buffon was not included in *L'Encyclopédie* (see ENCYCLOPÉDIE L', AND UNBELIEF), other than seeing proofs from time to time. *L'Encyclopédie* was written during the same time Buffon was writing his *Histoire naturelle*, and the two works display many similar passages within their texts. *L'Encyclopédie* attracted close official scrutiny for its heterodoxy; it is likely that Buffon escaped much of the controversy that might have embroiled him if *L'Encyclopédie* was not keeping would-be censors so busy.

Buffon's writing style was unusually open and nontechnical, and his works had a significant impact in promoting interest in the natural sciences in France. His writings were another stepping-stone that eventually led to the theory of evolution as we know it today (see EVOLUTION AND UNBELIEF).

BIBLIOGRAPHY

Buffon, Georges Louis LeClerc, Comte de. *Histoire naturelle, générale et particulière.* Paris: Imprimeries royale, 1749–88.

Roger, Jacques. *Buffon: A Life in Natural History.* Translated by Sarah Lucille Bonnefoi. Edited by L. Pearce Williams. Ithaca, NY: Cornell University Press, 1997.

TIMOTHY BINGA

BULLOUGH, BONNIE (1927–1996), American humanist writer. Bonnie Bullough became a humanist (see HUMANISM) in her teens. She was a laureate of the International Academy of Humanism; a contributing editor of the secular humanist magazine *Free Inquiry*; and author, coauthor, or editor of more than thirty books, a hundred or so refereed articles in scholarly journals, and an equal number in popular journals.

Bonnie never knew her father, and although she was named Louise Larsen at birth, she soon came to be called Bonnie; when her mother remarried she became Bonnie Dempsey. In her early teens she was adopted by a bachelor uncle after her mother abandoned the family. Thus her full name was Bonnie Louise Larsen Dempsey Uckerman. When she married, Bullough became the surname she preferred. She might be called a survivor who blossomed as an adult. Badly burned at age four, she spent most of her childhood summers in the hospital undergoing plastic surgery, and still retained some scars as an adult. She entered nursing through the Cadet Corps during World War II and graduated from the University of Utah. She later went on to get a master's degree in nursing, as well as master's and doctorate degrees in sociology from UCLA.

She was one of the pioneers in the nurse practitioner movement, helping to launch and serving on the editorial staff of several nurse practitioner journals. She was on the faculty at UCLA and at California State University, Long Beach, before becoming dean of nursing of the State University of New York at Buffalo, where she became a full professor. After retiring from Buffalo in 1993, she became a professor at the University of Southern California, a position she held until her death.

She lectured and traveled all over the world, making many presentations to humanist groups, including lectures in Egypt, Ghana, the USSR, China, Greece, Croatia, and Australia. Many of her other presentations were to nursing groups, which she addressed in almost every state in the United States. She was a member of the American Academy of Nursing.

Much of her research in her later years was devoted to sex and gender issues, as were many of her publications. She and her husband, Vern Bullough, received the Kinsey Award for their research and publications in the field. She was the mother of five children, three of them adopted. Her eldest son was murdered while in his early teens during a visit to Palestine. She had one granddaughter.

BIBLIOGRAPHY

Bullough, Vern L., and Bonnie Bullough. *Contraception: A Guide to Birth Control Methods*. Amherst, NY: Prometheus Books, 1990.
———. *Sin, Sickness, and Sanity*. New York: New American Library, 1977.
———. *The Subordinate Sex*. New York: Penguin, 1974.

VERN L. BULLOUGH

BUTLER, SAMUEL (1835–1902), English satiric novelist. Though Samuel Butler was the son of a country vicar and grandson of an influential bishop, he became hostile to orthodox Christianity, especially as practiced in the Anglican Church. In the preface to his *Erewhon Revisited* he described himself as "the broadest of broad churchmen." In nineteenth-century parlance a broad churchman was one who believed very little of the Christian story and metaphysics, but saw the church as an instrument of good works and social control. In his *Notebooks* he referred to "The Scylla of Atheism and the Charybdis of Christianity." This suggests that he was some sort of noncommittal theist or perhaps an agnostic. Butler had an unhappy boyhood with a hypocritical and unpleasant father, but at St. John's College, Cambridge, he was happy and successful. He declined to take holy orders and for a time took up sheep farming in New Zealand, whose topography suggested the fictional setting of his *Erewhon* ("Nowhere" backwards). In Erewhon, ill people are treated with contempt and criminals are treated with great sympathy. Criminals go to "straighteners" who give them pain and unpleasant prescriptions, much as surgeons and physicians do to us, in a neat satire of our penal systems. In Erewhon machinery is banned because of fear that it would evolve to enslave us, foreshadowing concerns some people hold today about computers. Higgs, the traveler to Erewhon, escapes in a balloon attended by storks. In *Erewhon Revisited*, Higgs's son goes to Erewhon to find that a religion of the Sunchild had grown up, because the older Higgs was said by the credulous to be the Sunchild and to have ascended to his father, the Sun, accompanied by angels. A more direct, but ironically stated, critique of the Christian resurrection story is given by Butler in his book *The Fair Haven*. Charles DARWIN admired this book, but in general disapproved of Butler on account of the latter's amateurish attacks on the theory of natural selection. This made Butler hostile to what he conceived of as dogmatic science no less than to dogmatic theology. Probably Butler's greatest book was his posthumously published *The Way of All Flesh*. This great novel in part reflects Butler's own upbringing and loss of faith. Butler was praised by George Bernard SHAW in the preface to *Back to Methuselah*, but for the wrong reason, Butler's Lamarckianism.

J. J. C. SMART

BYRON, GEORGE GORDON, LORD (1788–1824), British poet, once the most celebrated literary figure in Europe. Handsome and charismatic, George Gordon, Lord Byron, was the darling of polite society, the cynosure of salons, a pacesetter in fashion and manners, the observed of all observers. Smitten debutantes, madams, and maidservants vied for the attention of the dashing peer of the realm. Men envied him. *Childe Harold's Pilgrimage*, published when the poet was twenty-four, captivated the romantic imagination of a continent. "I awoke one day," said Byron, "and found myself famous." Despite his demurrals, readers fused him with Childe Harold—a brooding, enigmatic pariah haunted by a dark past and nameless guilt.

Byron was an amalgam of disparate traits: cruelty and kindness, misanthropy and philanthropy, cynicism and idealism, affectation and sincerity, arrogance and self-mockery, pettiness and magnanimity, intemperance and asceticism, self-pity and courage. On balance, the virtues trumped the vices. Despite sporadic vulgarities, tawdry liaisons, and a studied flippancy, Byron was a loyal friend and a bold leader.

Influence of Calvinism. Byron could never quite shake off an early indoctrination in Calvinism. Harangued by a pious, domineering mother and cate-chized by a string of Presbyterian tutors and scripture-quoting nurses, young Byron perversely deduced that he was irremediably damned. A clubfoot (his mark of Cain), the mockery of playmates, and the early loss of his father confirmed his perceived reprobate status. Possessing a Puritan conception of wickedness, Byron was suscep-tible to bouts of Olympian debauchery, oscillating between "ungodly glee" and remorse.

His sense of unmerited reprobation led him to identify with Lucifer and Cain: "Souls who dare look the Omnipo-tent tyrant in / His everlasting face, and tell Him that / His evil is not good." In *Cain*, a closet drama on the theme of the Fall, the scofflaws collaborate on an indictment of the Almighty. Jehovah, Lucifer tells Cain, wanted humans to live as benighted beasts in "A Paradise of Ignorance, from which / Knowledge is barred as poison."

Critic of Christian Doctrine. In letters to friends, Byron could sound the note of an Enlightenment ratio-nalist (see ENLIGHTENMENT, THE, AND UNBELIEF; RATIO-NALISM). "In morality," he said, "I prefer Confucius [see CONFUCIANISM] to the Ten Commandments and SOCRATES to St. Paul." He disdained revelation and mys-tery: "God would have made his Will known without books," he told his lifelong friend Francis Hodgson, a cleric, "considering how very few could read when Jesus of Nazareth lived, had it been His pleasure to ratify any peculiar mode of worship."

On miracles, he sided with the skeptics: "I agree with HUME that it is more probable men should lie or be deceived than that things out of the course of nature should so happen." Resurrection was illogical: "If people are to live, why die? And are our carcasses worth raising? I hope, if mine is, I shall have a better pair of legs than I have moved on these two-and-twenty years, or I shall be sadly behind in the squeeze into Paradise." Like eternal punishment, eternal bliss was unjust: "All the pious deeds performed on Earth can never entitle a man to everlasting happiness." The Christian scheme of salvation was superfluous: "Christ came to save men, but a good Pagan will go to heaven and a bad Nazarene to hell. If mankind who never heard or dreamt of Galilee and its prophet may be saved, Christianity is of no avail. And who will believe God will damn men for not knowing what they were never taught."

Byron anticipated Sigmund FREUD's "moral fallacy" of Christianity: "The basis of your religion," he wrote to Hodgson, "is injustice. The Son of God, the pure, the immaculate, the innocent, is sacrificed for the guilty. This proves His heroism; but no more does away with man's guilt than a schoolboy's volunteering to be flogged for another would exculpate the dunce from neg-ligence or preserve him from the rod." Byron thought religions were best judged by the moral character of their adherents. On that score, Christianity did not impress him: "Talk of Galileeism? Show me the effects—are you better, wiser, kinder by your precepts? I will bring you ten Mussulmans shall shame you in all good will towards men and duty to their neighbors."

Uneasy Agnostic. While a student at Cambridge, Byron had read enough of Hume and the Voltairian skeptics (see VOLTAIRE) to unsettle his faith in Christian dogma, both Catholic and Protestant, but he was never secure in his apostasy. Percy Bysshe SHELLEY, his atheistic neighbor and fellow exile in Switzerland, bemoaned his inability to unfetter Byron from the delusions of Christianity and rid himself forever of the specter of Calvinism. Apparently, Byron went to his grave in a state of incertitude.

BIBLIOGRAPHY

Eisler, Benita. *Byron: Child of Passion, Fool of Fame.* New York: Knopf, 1999.

Garrett, Martin. *George Gordon, Lord Byron.* New York: Oxford University Press, 2000.

Marchand, Leslie A., ed. *Byron's Letters and Journals.* 13 vols. Cambridge, MA: Belknap Press, 1973–94.

Sloan, Gary. "Lord Byron: The Demons of Calvinism." *American Atheist* 40, no. 4 (2002).

GARY SLOAN

CALDERONE, MARY STEICHEN (1894–1998), Amer-ican humanist and sex educator. The daughter of well-known photographer Edward Steichen, Mary Calderone made her reputation as a sex educator and counselor. A graduate of the medical school at the University of Rochester, she was married to another physician, Frank Calderone. The two separated in 1979 but never divorced. A nominal Quaker, she was much honored in humanist circles, and was named Humanist of the Year in 1974 by the AMERICAN HUMANIST ASSOCIATION.

She entered the sex field as a professional when she was appointed medical director of the Planned Parent-hood Federation of America in 1953. As director she tried to take the federation into the field of sex education, believing that as a result of the research of Alfred Kinsey and others, there was a need for large-scale public educa-tion about sex. Her efforts at Planned Parenthood were opposed by Alan F. Guttmacher, who headed up research for Planned Parenthood and who believed that any public education program would weaken the organization. Con-traceptive planning itself, he held, was controversial enough without the organization taking on further causes.

Discouraged, she and Lester KIRKENDALL, a humanist and longtime family life educator, joined to form SIECUS (Sex Information and Education Council of the United States) in 1964. Resigning from Planned Parenthood, Calderone became executive director of the new organization. Under her leadership SIECUS developed a public health approach to sex, focusing on awareness and education. It soon assumed a leading role in introducing sex education into the schools. She and the organization quickly became a target of virulent attacks from opponents of sex education such as the John Birch Society and the Christian Crusade; among other things, she was accused of being a tool of the Communist Party. Calderone became president of SIECUS in 1975; in 1980 she received the Margaret SANGER Award from Planned Parenthood, marking a change of attitude in that organization.

Calderone was a very effective public speaker. One of her favorite questions to young audiences was to ask for a four-letter word ending in *k* that among other things meant sexual intercourse. When they tittered, she answer the word was *talk*, emphasizing that human sexuality went far beyond the sex act but rather was a multifaceted aspect of life that should not be hidden in a shroud of secrecy or lowered only to the level of erotic expression. Among her books are *Talking with Your Child about Sex* (1982) and *The Family Book about Sexuality* (1987).

She received honorary doctorates from twelve institutions, and had numerous awards from groups such as the American Public Health Association, the Society for the Scientific Study of Sex, and the Scheslinger Library. She was the mother of three daughters, a grandmother of three, and a great-grandmother of three. She was named by various publications as one of the fifty most influential women in America, in another as one of the seventy-five most important women, and in the *World Almanac* she was listed as among the two hundred most influential people in the world.

VERN L. BULLOUGH

CAMUS, ALBERT (1913–1960), French novelist and existentialist. Albert Camus surged upon literary Paris in 1942 with the novel of his generation, *The Stranger.* He had first to open the door to the *absurd*, so he could pass beyond it to the concept of *revolt* and, ultimately, to the *seeking of the moral act.* Camus wove these themes into a philosophy of life (see EXISTENTIALISM) that later would inform his novels, plays, and essays, and his commitment to social activism.

World of Silence. Born in Algeria, he was raised by his grandmother; his mother, whom he adored, but who rarely spoke or made a gesture of affection; and his uncle, who was partially mute. His father was killed in World War I when Camus was an infant. The family lived in a world of silence. He would later confront the duality within himself (as he writes in *The First Man,*

posthumously published in 1995), the split between his love for the land of the unknown—the heat, the sun— and the man he became, an author who won fame, a luminary in Parisian intellectual circles. The young boy's intelligence and fervor, his hunger for knowledge, created a chasm within him, making him ever an outsider. He espoused views, often controversial, in defense of his native Algerians. Camus was tragically killed in a car crash in 1960.

The Absurd. To challenge the NIHILISM of his age, Camus developed the concept of the absurd, which he defines in *The Myth of Sisyphus* as the encounter between the human being's innate need for order and purpose and the blank indifference of the universe. To live in such a world and to salvage meaning from it, he urges, one must live with the conviction that absurdity, in the sense of recognizing and accepting the fact that there are no metaphysically guaranteed directives for conduct, can generate a positive ethic. Only by this recognition, and this acceptance, insists Camus, and only by the conscious espousal of human purpose and action, can we transform nihilism from a passive despair into a way of *revolting against* and of transcending the world's indifference to the human being.

Revolt. Camus introduces his principle of *revolt* in his novel *The Plague.* Refusing the world for what it is does not mean that one gives up and flees it, but rather that one lives in it under different terms, under the concept of revolt. Once we discover finitude and uncertainty and the old certitudes and confidence and ease have passed away, although we may despair of such a world, Camus reassures, this does not mean that we despair of ourselves, or of the validity of our own demands and aspirations. Moving away from the nihilism of *The Stranger* toward the HUMANISM of his subsequent works, Camus is leaving a solitary world for one in which the individual is concerned with the problems of the human being living with other human beings, and the need for finding meaning in life. Still living in the world of the absurd, but having discovered that he is no longer alone, and that we are *all* in trouble, he can challenge the world, if not remake it. Camus thus initiates a philosophy of rebellion.

In the words of the Nobel Prize in Literature that he was awarded in 1957, "Albert Camus illuminated the problems of the human conscience in our time." Rejecting older views and absolute values led some to individualism, often carelessly attributed to the existentialists—an error that Camus (and Jean-Paul SARTRE) tried to refute. There is a standard of values intrinsic to the human condition, Camus responds.

As Humanist. In his last and most controversial novel, *The Fall,* Camus decries our moral ambivalences. He is making an appeal for humanism. Unlike most spokespersons of the twentieth century, once Camus subscribes to the human being's *aloneness,* he will not stop here: we need not struggle alone, we can seek out what we share in common as a solidifying base between us. We cannot change the absurdity, Camus knows, but we can change the way we live in it; we can change how we live with one another. It was Camus's vision that by working together we can create new values, "a new humanism."

Camus is said to have possessed that rarest of gifts, moral authority. He was the hero of many, and the object of incessant controversy. He found solidarity with fellow exiles and with victims of persecution everywhere. He won the respect of contemporaries, and from the reading public, for the stands he took (yet often in dispute), and for his lyrical prose. Albert Camus is considered perhaps the most important moral voice in literature since Lev Nikolayevich TOLSTOY.

BIBLIOGRAPHY

Camus, Albert. *Lyrical and Critical Essays*. New York: Vintage, 1970.
———. *Resistance, Rebellion, and Death*. New York: Vintage, 1974.
Lowen, Jeannette. "How Can We Live in the World of the Absurd?" *Free Inquiry* (Fall 1994).
——— "The Search for Connection between Two Worlds." *Free Inquiry* (Winter 1996–97).

JEANNETTE LOWEN

CANADA (ANGLOPHONE), UNBELIEF IN. Colonized primarily by the French and English during the seventeenth century, early Canada was dominated by the Roman Catholic and Protestant faiths. By the time of Confederation in 1867, however, economic and population growth was producing an expanding middle class. This expansion had considerable impact on the belief systems of Canadians. As technological innovation and material wealth increased, middle-class Canadians began to embrace the view that there is an essential goodness in humans and that progress is a desirable goal of human striving. This view differed significantly from the central Christian view of humanity, which holds that all are born in sin and that release from human suffering and toil comes only in a heavenly afterlife. This new, emerging perspective on human possibility emphasized education and moral training as keys to reforming society. Middle-class reformers of the mid-nineteenth century tended to view criminals, the poor, and the insane as people who might be treatable and possibly even curable. Model prisons, houses of industry, and asylums were established to provide treatment, rehabilitation, and work skills. Meanwhile, science was becoming increasingly popular in academia; by the 1860s most Canadian universities had science faculties. And many Canadians, like their neighbors to the south, very much appreciated the novelty and laborsaving practicality of technological inventions. Still maintaining

close ties to Britain, Anglophone Canada's middle class was influenced to some degree by Charles DARWIN's publication of the *Origin of Species* in 1859 (see DARWINISM; RELIGION IN CONFLICT WITH SCIENCE). Although many universities had ties to churches, their dependence on sponsoring churches diminished as they became more and more secularized. The presence of news services can also be considered as a major contributing factor to the gradual secularization of Anglophone Canada. By 1866 the Atlantic cable had been successfully placed, connecting Canada with Europe. Information could now be received and disseminated in a matter of minutes rather than weeks. Although newspapers were largely sustained by political parties and religious denominations, the eventual use of advertisements gradually displaced such control.

Freethought in Canada. One of the first strong indications of FREETHOUGHT activity in Canada came when Charles WATTS and his wife, Kate Eunice WATTS, emigrated to Toronto from England in 1883. Watts was a special lecturer of England's NATIONAL SECULAR SOCIETY; in 1876 he had become editor, printer, and publisher of a prominent freethought paper, the London-based *NATIONAL REFORMER*. He would eventually produce works ranging from *The Freethinker's Text Book* by Charles BRADLAUGH and Annie BESANT to his own *Freethought: Its Rise, Progress and Triumph.* When Watts first visited Toronto in 1882 to lecture before the Toronto Secular Society, he was invited to take up residence there. He returned in 1883 and led the secularist movement in Canada (see SECULARISM). It should be noted that a group called Freethinkers of Canada already existed, and had held a successful convention in Toronto in September 1888. Yet in that same year, the Canadian government refused to charter Watts's Secular Thought Publishing Company. Notwithstanding, during his time in Canada Watts managed to produce his Canadian journal publication *Secular Thought*, which was circulated from 1888 until around 1909. Watts's wife accompanied him on his lecture tours, emerging as a freethought activist and writer in her own right. She wrote several pamphlets, including "The Education and Position of Women" and "Reasons for Not Accepting Christianity," and a book published in Toronto, *Christianity Defective and Unnecessary.*

Still, for various personal, socioeconomic, and political reasons, religious influence—specifically Catholic influence—over Canadian life would not decline until almost a century later. But then it would dwindle sharply. Such phenomena of the 1960s as the Second Vatican Council, the emerging human and women's rights movements, reform on abortion laws, and the advent of reliable birth control in the form of "the pill" (see SEXUAL VALUES, IMPACT OF UNBELIEF ON; BIRTH CONTROL AND UNBELIEF) contributed considerably to the secularization of Anglophone Canada.

It is not surprising, then, that most of the prominent

persons and organization that have contributed to the rise of unbelief in Anglophone Canada since the day of Charles and Kate Eunice Watts appear in the twentieth century. The rest of this article offers a descriptive list of these individuals and groups.

The Humanist Association of Canada (HAC; 1968–). Organized humanism in Canada began around the middle of the twentieth century. Dr. Ernest Poser, a member of Britain's RATIONALIST PRESS ASSOCIATION (RPA), emigrated to Canada in 1941. He married a freethinker, Dr. Maria Jutta Cahn, and in 1954 they moved to Montreal. Later that year, Dr. R. K. Mishra, a research physician at the University of Montreal, placed an advertisement in the *Montreal Star* inviting area members of the RPA to begin a humanist group. The three met and eventually founded the Humanist Fellowship of Montreal. This group had two official patrons: Lord Bertrand RUSSELL and Dr. Brock CHISHOLM, a Canadian psychiatrist and first director of the World Health Organization. Chisholm often addressed the fellowship on public occasions. In 1968 the Humanist Fellowship of Montreal, the Victoria (British Columbia) Humanist Association, and several smaller local or regional humanist organizations merged to form the Humanist Association of Canada. Membership rose, and by the early 1970s there were approximately 350 members. The organization would spawn the development of Humanist groups across Canada, including those in Ottawa, Toronto, Guelph, Kitchener-Waterloo, Cambridge, Windsor, Winnipeg, Calgary, Vancouver, and Victoria. In 1996 the HAC was granted permission by the government of Ontario to perform legally recognized marriages. Two of the HAC's most influential leaders were past president Dr. Henry Morgentaler and current president Dr. Robert Buckman (see below).

Henry Morgentaler (1923–). Dr. Henry Morgentaler is a medical doctor and longtime abortion activist from Montreal. Polish-born, Morgentaler survived the Holocaust and emigrated to Canada in 1950. He began practicing medicine in Montreal. On October 19, 1967, he provided public testimony before a government of Canada committee stating that any pregnant woman should have the right to a safe abortion. Recognizing that there were limited options for unwanted pregnancies in Canada, in 1969 Morgentaler gave up his family practice and began performing illegal abortions. By 1970 he was arrested in Quebec for performing an illegal medical act. By 1973 Morgentaler claimed to have performed five thousand illegal abortions and was again arrested. Although he was acquitted by a jury in the court case, the verdict was overturned by five judges on the Quebec Court of Appeal in 1974 and he was sent to prison. His lawyer appealed and Morgentaler was again acquitted. In 1983 Morgentaler was charged again in Ontario for procuring illegal miscarriages. Although he was acquitted by a jury, the verdict was reversed by the Ontario Court of Appeal and was then sent to the

Supreme Court of Canada. Here, Morgentaler was acquitted once again, and the Canadian Supreme Court declared the law unconstitutional (*Morgentaler et al. v. Her Majesty The Queen* 1988 [1 S.C.R. 30]).The power and breadth of this ruling contributed greatly to the end of all statutory restrictions on abortion in Canada.

However, in 1992 Morgentaler's Harbord Street abortion clinic in Toronto was bombed. In December 1995 Morgentaler sent an open letter to Pope John Paul II, pleading with him to find a peaceful resolution to the hate propaganda and violence directed not only at himself and his clinics but other clinics throughout the world.

Currently, Dr. Morgentaler is attempting to open several abortion clinics in the Canadian Arctic. He served as the first president of the Humanist Association of Canada. And on June 16, 2005, the University of Western Ontario awarded him his first honorary Doctor of Laws degree, in the face of considerable protest.

Robert Buckman (1955–). Dr. Robert Buckman is a medical oncologist at the Toronto-Sunnybrook Regional Cancer Centre and associate professor in the Department of Medicine at the University of Toronto. He graduated as a physician from Cambridge University in 1972 and completed his training in medical oncology at the Royal Marsden Hospital in London. He emigrated to Toronto in 1985. He is also an author, television personality, documentarian, and communications expert who has written over a dozen books and has been featured in award-winning television documentaries. He also writes and presents a series of medical information videos with Monty Python's John Cleese. Dr. Buckman is currently the president of the Humanist Association of Canada. He has appeared on numerous television and radio programs worldwide promoting the secularist humanist cause. He recently hosted a national documentary titled *Without God*, which follows the theme of his book *Can We Be Good without God?*

Ontario Skeptics Society for Critical Inquiry. This society defines itself as being comprised of "diverse individuals who share a common interest in promoting the understanding and application of critical thinking skills and scientific methodology in the explanation of human experience—from the seemingly mundane to the alleged paranormal." The society is committed to the maintenance of five fundamental tenets: activism for critical inquiry, provision of information to interested individuals and organizations, communication in the form of a "watchdog" approach to misinformation, education of critical thinking skills at all levels of education by means of the media, and philosophical reflection regarding scientific methodologies and their relevance to specific components of understanding human nature.

Pierre Berton (1920–2004). Born in Whitehorse, Yukon Territory, Berton was one of Canada's most prolific and best-known authors. During an extremely distinguished career which included the authoring of fifty books, hundreds of daily columns for the *Toronto Star*, and television shows like *Front Page Challenge*, Berton sparked controversy by openly expressing freethought views on everything from the nonexistence of God to racism, premarital sex, and the finer points of rolling a marijuana cigarette. Berton had also received more than thirty literary awards and twelve honorary degrees. In 1986 he was appointed as a companion of the Order of Canada.

Evelyn Martens (1932–). Evelyn Martens was born and raised in Alberta, Canada. In the early part of the 1990s, Evelyn became quite active in the Right to Die Society, which provides terminally ill patients with information allowing them to end their lives safely. In 2002 Evelyn Martens was charged with counseling and aiding former nun Monique Charest to commit suicide in British Columbia. She also faced charges related to the June 26, 2002, death of Vancouver schoolteacher Leyanne Burchell. Facing as much as fourteen years' imprisonment, Martens was eventually acquitted of both charges on grounds that Charest and Burchell had voluntarily taken their own lives. An Evelyn Martens Defence Fund was established and successfully raised money for her court costs. In June 2005 Martens was presented with the Humanist of the Year Award by the Humanist Association of Canada.

Jan Narveson (1936–). Jan Narveson was educated at the University of Chicago, spent a year at Oxford (1959–60) on a traveling fellowship, and earned a PhD at Harvard in 1961. He initially taught at the University of New Hampshire until he was recruited in 1963 to help start up the philosophy department at the University of Waterloo in Ontario, from which he retired in 2005. He has published dozens of articles in professional journals and has written several books. His main professional interests lie in moral and political philosophy, specifically dealing with notions of personal and social liberty. Narveson is an avowed atheist (see ATHEISM) and a fierce debater in professional and social circles. He was the second atheist invited to the World Religions Conference held annually in Waterloo. One of Narveson's most succinct critiques against the existence of God came during a debate in 1996 against prominent Christian apologist debater William Lane Craig at the University of Toronto in January 1996. In 1989 Narveson was elected to membership in the Royal Society of Canada.

Michael Persinger (1945–). Michael Persinger attended Carroll College (1963–64), and then graduated from the University of Wisconsin, Madison, in 1967 with a major in psychology. He then received an MA in physiological psychology from the University of Tennessee and his PhD from the University of Manitoba in 1971. Since 1971 he has been a professor at Laurentian University in Sudbury, Ontario. He has published more than two hundred technical articles in referred journals and has written six books. Much of Persinger's work as a neuroscientist focuses on the subtle interactions between the geophysical and meteorological environment and human behavior, especially the effects of magnetic fields on human behavior. This has led him to search for neurological explanations regarding illusory accounts of causal relationships—specifically, the psychology by which persons attribute causation to unseen forces. In his book *The Neuropsychological Base of God Beliefs* (1987), he described the use of complex electromagnetic fields to discern the patterns that will induce experiences (sensed presence) that people often attribute to various perceived intrusions ranging from aliens to gods. Persinger has devised a helmet that applies weak magnetic fields across the right and left brain hemispheres, specifically the temporal lobes, often triggering pseudomystical experiences in the wearer. Persinger believes that naturally occurring electromagnetic fields arising from geophysical activity may be the cause of some religious or mystical experiences (see COGNITIVE SCIENCE AND UNBELIEF; RELIGIOUS AND MYSTICAL EXPERIENCES).

Svend Robinson (1952–). A controversial figure in Canadian politics, Svend Robinson represented the progressive New Democratic Party in Burnaby, British Columbia, from the age of twenty-seven and remained undefeated in the next six elections. In 1983 he was temporarily stripped of his title as justice critic—minority-party commentator on the work of the Ministry of Justice—after he commented to a Vancouver TV show that he supported the establishment of red-light districts and houses of prostitution. In 1988, at the age of thirty-five, Robinson announced on national television that he was gay and pledged to push for expansions in gay rights. In so doing he became the first openly gay member of the House of Commons. In 1999 Alexa McDonough, leader of the NDP, relegated Robinson to the backbenches in the House of Commons after he presented a petition calling for the word *God* to be removed from the preamble of the Canadian Charter of Rights and Freedoms. In 2002 Robinson traveled to the Middle East and attempted unsuccessfully to visit with Palestinian leader Yasser Arafat at his compound in Ramallah. Robinson is quoted as saying upon his return that "[t]he Israeli government and the Israeli military are guilty of torture and murder." Robinson was also quite active in the dying with dignity movement and aided high-profile patient Sue Rodriguez in her battle to convince the Supreme Court of Canada to grant her the right to a doctor-assisted suicide. Robinson is currently employed by the British Columbia Government and Service Employees Union as both an arbitrator and an advocate.

Michael Ruse (1940–). Michael Ruse was born on June 21, 1940, in Birmingham, England. A philosopher of science and professor of philosophy and zoology, he taught at the University of Guelph for thirty-five years and is currently the Lucyle T. Werkmeister Professor of Philosophy at Florida State University. Ruse is a worldrenowned author and champion of Darwinian evolutionary theory. With David Hull he developed the field now known as philosophy of biology. The author of dozens of journal articles and more than twenty books, he is also the founder and editor of the journal *Biology and Philosophy*. In 1981 Ruse was a state witness in the appeal of a state law in Arkansas that mandated the teaching of so-called creation science in public schools (see CREATIONISM). The law was ruled unconstitutional. In the preface to the second edition of his book *Taking Darwin Seriously*, Ruse stated: "The fact that we are the contingent end-products of a natural process of evolution, rather than the special creation of a good god, in his own image, has to be just about the most profound thing we humans have discovered about ourselves."

BIBLIOGRAPHY

Berton, Pierre. *1967: The Last Good Year.* Toronto: Doubleday, 1997.

Finkel, Alan, and Margaret Conrad. *History of the Canadian Peoples: 1867 to the Present.* Toronto: Addison Wesley Longman, 2002.

Narveson, Jan. *Respecting Persons in Theory and Practice.* Lanham, MD: Rowman and Littlefield, 2002.

Persinger, Michael. *The Neuropsychological Base of God Beliefs.* Westport, CT: Greenwood, 1987.

Ruse, Michael. *The Evolution Wars: A Guide to the Debates.* Piscataway, NJ: Rutgers University Press, 2001.

Watts, Kate Eunice. *Christianity Defective and Unnecessary.* Toronto: Secular Thought Office, 1900.

———. "The Education and Position of Women." *Secular Review*, September 27, October 4 and 18, 1879.

———. *Reasons for Not Accepting Christianity.* London: Watts, [1877].

CHRISTOPHER DICARLO

CANADA (FRANCOPHONE), UNBELIEF IN. The FREETHOUGHT tradition in Quebec started in 1776 with the arrival of Fleury Mesplet, Montreal's first printer, librarian, and publisher. He also founded two newspapers and an academy named for VOLTAIRE. Until his death in 1794, Mesplet promoted Enlightenment ideals of tolerance and freedom and even the more radical thinking of the American and French revolutions (see ENLIGHTENMENT, UNBELIEF DURING THE). He was twice imprisoned for his ideas. By the end of the eighteenth century, Montreal's intelligentsia were infused with the ideas of the encyclopedists, as is clearly seen, for example, in the reading notes and correspondence of lawyer and politician Joseph Papineau.

The prominent politician Louis-Joseph Papineau, Joseph's son, inherited his father's ideals. In 1844 he founded the Institut canadien, an establishment that advocated sovereignty for French Canada, universal suffrage, the separation of church and state, and legal reform. Its library contained works of the philosophes and contemporary authors like Victor Hugo.

The Clerical Environment. French Canadian freethought bears the stamp of the suffocating power exercised by the Roman Catholic Church in nineteenth-century Quebec, as well as the persistent struggles between a largely Catholic population and the province's English Protestant rulers. Montreal bishop Ignace Bourget doggedly opposed the Institut canadien, railing against the "evil books" it contained and threatening its members with excommunication. In 1858 Bourget, writing "on behalf of God," urged his flock not to read books not approved of by the church and actually forbade the purchase of any book not approved by his office. "We were permitted to have books," wrote the journalist Louis-Antoine Dessaulles—Papineau's nephew—"as long as we read only those consecrated to divine right . . . religious intolerance" and "coercive thinking." Bourget had as little use for "evil newspapers" as he had for the Institut. In a pastoral letter of May 1858 Bourget condemned what he termed the heretical, irreligious, immoral, impious, and liberal press, adding that freedom of opinion is but a misguided freedom that kills the soul.

When the typographer Joseph Guibord, a member of the Institut, died in 1869, Bourget denied him Christian burial. In 1875 an order from the privy council of London—enforced by a thousand British soldiers—finally secured Guibord's burial. Bourget responded by damning the grave. Journalist Arthur Buies wrote that Bishop Bourget "wanted absolute docility, the suppression of free opinion, and submission to ecclesiastic authority."

Bourget was not alone; as late as the turn of the twentieth century, the cleric Oblate Zacharie Lacasse stated in his brochure *Autour du drapeau de l'Église* (Around the Flag of the Church) that real freedom consisted in recognizing the church as one's sole authority in all things.

Educational Controversies. Controversies over public—that is, Protestant—schools proliferated between 1846 and 1867 in the context of recurrent peasant uprisings. On several occasions Catholic peasants burned schools. The government ordered municipalities to contribute financial support for opening new public schools, sparking sharp protests by the church. By 1867 the church had managed to seize effective control of public schools and ceased to oppose them. It could afford to, having purged the schools of any vestige of freedom of thought. In his *Lettre sur le Canada* of February 9, 1867, Buies lamented that "intolerance is sanctified . . . teachers are no longer free . . . they are all under the rod of the village priest who manages the school at his whim and whom one must obey to avoid persecution, criticism, and loss of employment." By 1875 the church was even able to have the Ministry of Public Instruction, the government body responsible for public schools, abolished. As late as 1945 Jean-Charles Harvey could write in *Le Jour* that "Québec is the only province where all instruction is under clerical monopoly." Its schools underperformed all others in

North America. (The Ministry of Public Instruction would not be reestablished until 1963.)

From 1867 forward the church banned Quebec newspapers wholesale: *La Lanterne*, *L'Indépendant*, and *Le Réveil*, edited by Arthur Buies; *Le Bien public*, edited by Louis-Olivier David; *La Sentinelle*, edited by Aristide Filiatrault; *L'Électeur*, edited by Wilfrid Laurier; *La Semaine*, edited by Gustave Comte; *L'Action* and *L'Ordre*, edited by Olivar Asselin; *Le Pays*, edited by Godfroy Langlois; and *Le Jour*, edited by Harvey.

In 1902 the Ligue de l'enseignement (League for Teaching), established by Olivier Faucher, Godfroy Langlois, and Honoré Gervais, attempted to secularize the school system. Two years later the Ligue was destroyed by Archbishop Jean Bruchési; nothing would replace it until 1961. Until 1959 the Catholic Church exercised harsh control over educational institutions. Dissenters were attacked as atheists, though many of them were seeking only freedom in the context of excessive religious and state controls.

On the pretext of protecting Quebec against communism, on March 17, 1937, Premier Maurice Duplessis passed a law on the ideological control of dissidents. Without defining communism, the law allowed the province to declare any person a communist. As general prosecutor, Duplessis became at once plaintiff, judge, sheriff, and executioner. The law authorized him to "padlock" for a year any establishment suspected of harboring communists. It was forbidden to print, publish, or distribute any writing tending to propagate communism. All offenders were liable to at least three months' imprisonment, plus prosecution expenses or one month's additional imprisonment. During the Padlock Law's adoption, Duplessis declared that he was acting to satisfy the archbishop of Quebec, Cardinal Rodrigue Villeneuve. In *Le Jour* (March 12, 1938), Jean-Charles Harvey demonstrated abuses of the law to violate homes, pillage private libraries, and exercise harsh reprisals, all without the possibility of defense. During the "reign" of Duplessis freethinking was severely repressed. On March 8, 1957, the Supreme Court of Canada declared that the law that had given Duplessis such broad discretionary powers was contrary to freedom of thought, speech, and action.

The death of Duplessis in 1959 was the starting signal for the Quiet Revolution, during which Quebec abruptly shrugged off much of its Catholic heritage. The most important achievement of this movement, for which Harvey and the freethinkers never ceased to claim credit, was the reestablishment in 1963 of the Ministry of Public Instruction, which had been abolished in 1875. It was a victory for the Mouvement laïque de langue française (French-language Secularization Movement). Even so, the school system remained under church control until 1997.

Since 1960 Québecois reformers have agitated openly for numerous freedoms: the secularization of public institutions (for example, eliminating crucifixes from public classrooms, hospitals, courtrooms, city halls, and the like); the eradication of religious, racial, and gender discrimination; the right to death with dignity; safe and legal abortion; same-sex marriage; and so on. In 1975 Quebec's adoption of a Charter of Human Rights and Freedoms was seen as a victory for freethinkers. However, the charter did not fully meet the demands of civil libertarians; neither did the Canadian Charter of Rights and Freedoms, adopted in 1982.

In 1981, the Mouvement laïque québécois (MLQ, Secular Movement of Quebec) succeeded the Association québécoise pour l'application du droit à l'exemption religieuse (Quebec Association to Apply the Right of Religious Exemption, 1976–81), its first presidents being Norma Legault, Daniel Baril, and Micheline Trudel. Today this association publishes a journal, *Cité laïque* (Secular City). Another association, La Libre Pensée Québécoise (Freethought Quebec), founded in 1982, closed at the end of the century. Its journal, *La Libre Pensée*, was published twice yearly from 1984 to 1991. Its first presidents were Bernard La Rivière, Henry Morgentaler, and Danielle Soulières. Since the early 1970s Morgentaler has championed the right of Canadian women's to safe and legal abortion (see CANADA [ANGLOPHONE], UNBELIEF IN).

Created on June 10, 2005, by Normand Baillargeon, Bernard Cloutier, and Michel Virard, the Humanist Association of Quebec aims to promote critical thinking and humanist values in Quebec. It revives the late Libre Pensée québecoise with a new basis.

Today, many Quebec historians, like Dr. Jean-Paul de Lagrave, place their emphasis upon rights and freedoms. In spite of the media conformism and religious orthodoxy, in Quebec freethinking is now considered a precious heritage. Dr. Morgentaler, Dr. de Lagrave, Dr. Baillargeon, the MLQ, and many community groups are involved in recognizing and expanding civil and moral liberties. They consider religion a personal affair, not a matter of state. More tolerant than irreligious, they are building slowly but surely a modern, multiethnic, and happy society.

BIBLIOGRAPHY

de Lagrave, Jean-Paul. "Les combats de la libre pensée au Québec." *La Libre pensée* 7 (1987).

———. *Voltaire's Man in America*. Montreal: Robert Davies Multimedia, 1997.

de Lagrave, Jean-Paul, and Jacques G. Ruelland. *L'Imprimeur des Libertés: Fleury Mesplet (1734–1794). Roman historique.* Montreal: Pointe de fuite, 2001.

———. *Valentin Jautard (1736–1787), premier journaliste de langue française au Canada.* Quebec: Le Griffon d'argile, 1989.

Dutil, Patrice. *L'Avocat du diable. Godfroy Langlois et le libéralisme progressiste dans le Québec de Wilfrid Laurier.* Montreal: Robert Davies, 1994.

Gragnon, Marcel-Aimé. *Jean-Charles Harvey, précurseur de la Révolution tranquille.* Montreal: Beauchemin, 1970.

Lamonde, Yvan. "Les archives de l'Institut Canadien de Montreal (1844–1900): historique et inventaire." *Revue d'histoire de l'Amerique française* 28, no. 1 (1974).

Ruelland, Jacques G. *Figures de la philosophie québécoise à l'époque de la Révolution française.* Quebec: Presses de l'Université du Québec, 1989.

———. "La philosophie des Lumières à la fin du XVIIIe siècle au Québec." In *Essais de philosophie politque québécoise, XVIIIe–XIXe siecles*, edited by Harel Malouin. Quebec: Presses de l'Universite du Québec, 1992.

JACQUES G. RUELLAND
TRANSLATED BY JEANNE POULIN

CARLILE, ELIZA SHARPLES (1805?–1852), English freethinker. A courageous FREETHOUGHT campaigner, Elizabeth Sharples was born into a modestly prosperous family in Bolton, Lancashire, England. The Sharples family was deeply religious, and Elizabeth grew up fervently evangelical. She later said she "prayed [her]self into the grave almost." As a young woman, she was told about a wicked agitator named Richard CARLILE. Being of an independent nature, Sharples took an interest in this person who attracted such disapproval at home. She familiarized herself with Carlile's writings and with the radical politics he was involved in, and was soon as committed to the cause as she was to him as her mentor.

Showing extraordinary courage for a young, unattached woman, Sharples left Bolton in January 1832 without her family's permission and headed for London, where she visited Carlile in jail. Two weeks later, on January 29, she gave her first freethought lecture. This is thought to be the first freethought lecture given by a woman. The following month she began a freethought journal called *Isis*, which championed the causes of radical politics, gender equality, and freethought. While formally denying she was an atheist (see ATHEISM), her understanding of God as a first cause was so nominal as to count for nothing. "God," or "first cause," were, she argued, "mere covers for our ignorance." *Isis* folded in December of the same year. After Carlile's release from prison, Elizabeth moved in and became his common-law wife. From about 1834 she called herself Eliza Sharples Carlile. In the face of bitter criticism about her marital situation, she was defiant, writing that a "marriage more pure and moral was never formed and continued in England."

Eliza was an indispensable companion to her husband, taking up an ever-greater burden of work as his health declined. She also had four children by Richard Carlile. The three who survived were given the faultlessly heretical names of Julian, Hypatia, and Theophilia. All three migrated to the United States, where Julian died young in active service in the Civil War. Hypatia died in poverty in Chicago. Only Theophilia lived to anything like old age, dying in California in 1913.

After Richard Carlile's death in 1843, Eliza slowly drifted into complete penury. In 1849 she was rescued by some freethought friends and installed in a large building in London's East End where a coffee room was established. But Eliza had no head for business and the project failed. For a while the young Charles BRADLAUGH stayed in the same building, where he fell in love with Hypatia, although the love was unrequited. Eliza Sharples Carlile died penniless in London in 1852.

BIBLIOGRAPHY

Bonner, Hypatia Bradlaugh. *Charles Bradlaugh: A Record of His Life and Work.*1894. Reprint, London: T. Fisher Unwin, 1908.

———. "Richard Carlile: A Stalwart of Liberty." *The R. P. A. Annual.* London: Watts, 1924.

Priestman, Martin. *Romantic Atheism.* Cambridge: Cambridge University Press, 2000.

BILL COOKE

CARLILE, RICHARD (1790–1843), English FREETHOUGHT pioneer and martyr for freedom of expression. Richard Carlile is known principally for his courageous struggle for a free press in England. He was born in modest circumstances on December 9, 1790, in Ashburton, Devon, where he attended charity schools. At the age of twenty-three he moved to London and quickly became associated with the radical movement. Between 1817 and 1835 Carlile spent more than nine years in prison for publishing freethought material. In 1819 the Society for the Suppression of Vice led a prosecution against Carlile for republishing Thomas PAINE's *Age of Reason.* Carlile insisted on reading the entire book to the court, so that they may know what he was being prosecuted for. He was fined fifteen hundred pounds and sentenced to three years' imprisonment. The fine was impossibly steep and Carlile had no hope of paying it, so his term in prison was extended to six years.

What followed was one of the most outstanding episodes of freethought history. While Carlile was incarcerated, colleagues and employees continued to publish heretical works, and each in turn was imprisoned. Jane Carlile, Richard's wife, was sentenced to two years' imprisonment in November 1819, followed by Richard's sister Mary Ann in 1821. By 1824 approximately 150 people had come, unbidden, to Carlile's shop, in full knowledge that their working there would mean certain imprisonment. But still they came. One such person, Susannah Wright, was imprisoned for eighteen months and fined one hundred pounds. While conducting her defense she was continually interrupted by the prosecution and the judge. What alarmed the judges in each of these cases was not so much the offending material, but that it was directed at the "lower orders," whose servility to their masters, it was feared, would be jeopardized by exposure to such material.

Carlile's persecution attracted the attention of Julian HIBBERT, a wealthy liberal freethinker who provided generous financial assistance for his publishing ventures. It is said that Carlile did not use Hibbert's gift to pay his fine and thus secure release because he found imprisonment preferable to living with his wife. Their marriage ended in 1827. Carlile's later struggles were shared with Eliza Sharples CARLILE, who became his common-law wife in about 1834. In Carlile's decline, he lapsed into a theistic mysticism. He died on February 10, 1843, and was given an Anglican burial, notwithstanding the objections of his sons.

Freethinkers of all persuasions owe Richard Carlile a huge debt. The right to freely publish, circulate, and discuss heretical material was won by his lengthy spells of imprisonment. And thanks to Carlile, it was no longer possible to contrive a successful charge of BLASPHEMY against someone who denied the truth claims of Christianity. From then on, the anti-Christian item had to be specifically abusive or offensive before it could be deemed blasphemous. Carlile should also be remembered as a brave pioneer for birth control (see BIRTH CONTROL AND UNBELIEF).

BIBLIOGRAPHY

Bonner, Hypatia Bradlaugh. *Penalties upon Opinion.* London: Watts and Company, 1912.
———. "Richard Carlile: A Stalwart of Liberty." *The R. P. A. Annual.* London: Watts and Company, 1924.
Cole, G. D. H. *Richard Carlile 1790–1843.* London: Victor Gollancz, 1943.

BILL COOKE

CARVAKA. A Sanskrit word variously derived from *carv*, to eat, or *caru-vaka*, sweet-tongued, Carvaka is often assumed to be the name of a philosopher and teacher who advocated ATHEISM and materialism (see INDIAN MATERIALISM, ANCIENT). The name is also given to that movement of thought, and to its adherents. What may have been a principal work of the system, the *Brhaspati Sutra*, is lost. Two schools of Carvaka have been distinguished: *Dhurtta* and *Susiksita.*

The Carvakas held that earth, water, fire, and air are the ultimate elements. Only the perceived exists; the unperceived does not exist. There exists no cause except nature. There is no world other than this. There is no heaven and no hell, only mundane pleasure and pain exist. The only supreme is the earthly monarch, whose existence all men can plainly see. The only liberation is the dissolution of the body. From the four ultimate elements, the body and intelligence are produced by mixing the ingredients. When the body is destroyed, intelligence is destroyed. The *Vedas*, the oldest sacred scriptures of the Hindus, are tainted by the three faults of untruth, self-contradiction, and tautology. The Vedic *pandits* (wise men of ancient

times) are impostors. The mystical realms of the God Shiva and the like are inventions. The enjoyment of heaven lies in eating delicious food, keeping company of young women, having fine clothes and perfumes, and the like. The pain of hell lies in the troubles that arise from enemies, weapons, and diseases. Liberation (*moksa*) is death, which is the cessation of life-breath.

Carvaka is also known as *lokayata*, "that which is found among people in general" or "materialist," "atheist," "adherent of the Carvaka school." *Loka* means "space," "room," or "world." Together with Buddhism and the Jaina religion, Carvaka has ordinarily been counted as an old heterodox Indian school, as distinct from the six main Hindu schools, which were the orthodox schools. Carvaka philosophy is also known as *barhaspatya.* As a philosophical school it may be almost as old as the oldest Indian religions, but next to nothing is known about its historical development.

BIBLIOGRAPHY

Hiorth, Finngeir. *Atheism in India.* Oslo: Human-Etisk Forbund, 1999.
Hiriyanna, M. *Outlines of Indian Philosophy,* Mumbai: George Allen & Unwin, 1973.
Radhakrishnan, Sarvepalli, and Charles A. Moore, eds. *A Sourcebook in Indian Philosophy.* Princeton, NJ: Princeton University Press, 1957.
Stutley, Margaret, and James Stutley, eds. *A Dictionary of Hinduism.* London: Routledge & Kegan Paul 1977.

FINNGEIR HIORTH

CHAPPELLSMITH, MARGARET REYNOLDS (1806–1883), English feminist pioneer. Margaret Reynolds was the daughter of a master mechanic and was raised Baptist. According to freethinker Moncure D. CONWAY, she apparently became the first of the English female Owenites (sometimes referred to as "English Communists") to lecture after she joined Robert OWEN's community near Broughton known as Harmony Hall. According to a letter Chappellsmith wrote to her biographer, Sara A. Underwood, she spoke on a variety of topics, including "Education of Women," "My Reasons why I, having been a Calvinist, have Become an Infidel," as well as five lectures on the Protestant Reformation, and, perhaps most controversial, on the subjects of marriage and divorce (see SEX RADICALISM AND UNBELIEF). She married John Chappellsmith, who endeared himself to feminists by occasionally pouring tea at his wife's public gatherings.

"I frequently took part in public discussions on religion, taking the Infidel side," Chappellsmith recalled. She spoke in London, the midland and northern parts of England, and Scotland. Feminist Owenites were routinely heckled at public meetings by religious opponents quoting scriptural edicts that women should "be in silence." She and other women lecturers, such as freethinker Emma MARTIN, were called witches and whores. In Scotland, a Paisley newspaper called Chappellsmith a "she-devil"; a mob of women once gathered around her and threw stones. John Brindley, editor of the *Antidote, or the Anti-Socialist Gazette,* focused on Chappellsmith, making scurrilous accusations that she had deserted her husband and promiscuously taken lovers. Brindley went so far as to seek out her husband, who defended his wife's reputation. In disgust, Brindley then wrote that John was as immoral as that "filthy female lecturer." Thanks to such slander, Margaret was mobbed in South Shields by a group of women and children, who taunted her by asking, "Are you her with the seven husbands?" She wrote, "Poor creatures, they might well be angry with me, since they have been taught to believe me such a monopolizer." Yet Chappellsmith and her sister lecturers were also lauded by many women in their audiences for advocating "new and rational arrangements" of marriage and women's emancipation.

Chappellsmith had had to be induced to lecture, and gratefully ceased her public life by 1843. She and John went into bookselling and emigrated to New Harmony, Indiana (see OWEN, ROBERT DALE). They both continued to write, contributing some three hundred articles to the freethinking *BOSTON INVESTIGATOR.*

BIBLIOGRAPHY

Taylor, Barbara. *Eve and the New Jerusalem: Socialism and Feminism in the Nineteenth Century.* New York: Pantheon, 1983.

Underwood, Sara A. *Heroines of Freethought.* New York: Charles P. Somerby, 1876.

ANNIE LAURIE GAYLOR

CHILD, LYDIA MARIA (1802–1880), American abolitionist and freethinker. In her fifty-five-year career, Lydia Maria Child was one of the most prolific and popular authors of her day, addressing such diverse concerns as abolition, women's history, and comparative religious studies. As an activist author, her freethought intellectual achievements were a primary resource for those working toward racial and sexual equality throughout the nineteenth century.

Early Life. The youngest child in a successful baker's family in Medford, Massachusetts, Lydia's strongest early influence was her Harvard-educated brother, Convers. When Convers became the minister of a Unitarian church in Watertown, Massachusetts, Lydia moved in with him and was baptized a Unitarian despite her tendency toward religious skepticism. Her association with her brother's friends Ralph Waldo EMERSON and Theodore Parker further encouraged her religious questioning. Doubting even these friends' liberal interpretations of faith, she would remain a religious skeptic for the rest of her life.

Abolition and Racial Equality. Beginning with her first book, *Hobomok,* a novel challenging racial and religious intolerance against indigenous Americans, Child embarked on a writing career that consistently challenged the supremacy of white American Protestantism. After meeting William Lloyd Garrison in 1830, she dedicated her talents to the abolitionist cause, writing several monographs, most notably *An Appeal in Favor of That Class of Americans Called Africans* (1833). Noteworthy for its support of immediate emancipation, *An Appeal* also called for an end to Northern racism and praised the achievements of African peoples. She paid for this radicalism when subscribers to Child's financially successful *Juvenile Miscellany,* a children's literature periodical published since 1826, canceled their subscriptions in protest, leading to its failure in 1834.

Women's History. Child's contribution to women's history remains underestimated. After writing about the lives of several famous women, Child researched the history of ordinary women to produce *The History of the Condition of Women, in Various Ages and Nations* (1835). This work would inspire and inform a younger generation of women's rights historians and theorists, including Elizabeth Cady STANTON and Matilda Joslyn GAGE, who would use Child's history as a resource to support women's rights and suffragist appeals.

Comparative Religion. During her years as an abolitionist, Child did not forget her early years of religious questioning. The publication of *The Progress of Religious Ideas, Through Successive Ages* (1855) presented the formerly inaccessible academic perspectives of comparative religious and biblical scholarship to a larger popular audience, further undermining Christianity's claim to divine revelation and religious supremacy by exploring connections between Christian and non-Christian mythologies. Her interest in Eastern and pagan spiritualities would deepen and intensify in the following decades providing further inspiration for her life's work fighting racism and religious bigotry.

Until the end of her life, Child remained steadfastly committed to the advancement of women and to the end of discrimination against Asian, African, and Native Americans. As a freethinker, her intellectual openness to religious diversity coupled with her native skepticism enhanced her commitment to the defense of human diversity and equal rights. As one of the most-read authors of the nineteenth century, her liberal influence has been widely felt by generations of liberal reformers.

BIBLIOGRAPHY

Karcher, Carolyn L., ed. *A Lydia Maria Child Reader.* Durham, NC: Duke University Press, 1997.

———. *The First Woman in the Republic: A Cultural Biography of Lydia Maria Child.* Durham, NC: Duke University Press, 1994.

MELINDA GRUBE

CHINA, UNBELIEF IN. The word universally acknowl-edged to characterize Chinese thought and values over three millennia is HUMANISM. The connotation of this word is important. It is not to be confused with the phi-losophy of Western humanist societies, whose aim is to express moral values without recourse to theistic con-cepts—though Chinese humanism includes this consid-eration. Equally, it should not be associated with the Christian humanism of the early Reformation period, when the attempt was being made to establish a more academic ethos in Christianity than had been previously manifested—though the pursuit of knowledge for its own sake is a major strand in Chinese culture. Rather, the humanism of China is characterized by an unam-biguous assertion of the intrinsic value of life on earth. Whatever the world provides—food, culture, human relationships, nature—is for the present benefit and enjoyment of human beings. It can consequently be con-trasted with two widespread and divergent theories of the universe.

The first of these is the Hindu concept of *maya*, whereby whatever the world provides is held to be ulti-mately delusory because it will not endure forever. The Hindu aim is to seek enlightenment (*moksha*) by real-izing the union of the basic self (atman—what Immanuel KANT might have termed the nominal self) with the ground of being, brahman. The second contrasting theory is the theistic view that this world and its activi-ties are no more than an antechamber to heaven. This leads, to a greater or lesser extent, to the development of what Friedrich NIETZSCHE was to describe as "other-worldspeople," who assess moral behavior according to its reflection of the allegedly perfect standards of heaven, and consequently hold the view that human desires and needs must, if necessary, be sacrificed to these "higher" standards. Theists—Jews, Christians, Muslims—are therefore encouraged to look beyond the reality of the present age and view all their activities *sub specie aeternitatis*. Chinese philosophy offers a clear-cut alternative to both of these worldviews by expressing itself comprehensively in terms of this world and its rewards.

It is important to note that, unlike Western humanism, which emphasizes individual freedom and personal ful-fillment, Chinese humanism sets greater store on rela-tionships between, on the one hand, individuals and their fellows, and, on the other, human beings and the natural world. The former is expressed primarily (though by no means exclusively) in CONFUCIANISM, the latter in Taoism (see TAOISM, UNBELIEF WITHIN).

Confucius. Confucius held that society could function harmoniously only if everyone recognized and lived consistently within the confines of his or her station. He outlined the five relationships which he affirmed to be the key to social contentment: between husband and wife, father and son (or daughter), older brother and younger brother, older friend and younger friend, and ruler and subject. In all these, he suggested, the first-named should assume the yang (dominant or initiating) role, and the second the yin (secondary or responsive). Most people will thus play a yang role in some of their relationships, a yin in others. Confucius's emphasis on the primacy of age and the male sex stamp him as a man of his era; where he looks beyond not only his own age but also that of many centuries later, is by his refusal to seek authority for his social theories via some kind of divine or nominal inspiration. He rejected the view that excessive attention should be paid to the dead, telling his followers (or students) that their energies and abilities would be comprehensively employed by concerns for the living. When asked whether it was important for people to cultivate the spirits, he replied that they would find quite enough that was worthwhile by developing their minds and keeping their bodies fit. When asked whether people should seek to observe the will of heaven, his answer was that they would find life ade-quately fulfilling by being involved in earthly matters, without the distractions presented by extraterrestrial concerns. It is true that he frequently spoke of the "way of heaven" (*tsien*), a word in common use in his time, but his usage is metaphorical: the way of heaven signi-fied the highest peak of human behavior. Any hint of the supernatural, such as the belief that by prayer the will of heaven could be mollified or that moral dilemmas could be resolved by divine intervention, seemed to him absurd. Certainly, people would have stories of their ancestors for inspiration, but that is a quite different matter from believing in their spiritual presence and influence.

Two basic features of Chinese thought follow from this Confucian emphasis. First, philosophy and religion are not separated from each other as in the West. Both are concerned with values, answering the question of what is worthwhile. Since no extraterrestrial element is introduced into this discussion, there is simply no need for two separate areas of inquiry, religious and philo-sophical, as in the West. One significant bonus arising from this circumstance is that the conflict between the two forms of thought often experienced in the West is not found in Confucianism.

Second, philosophy is accepted as a natural facet of life, relevant, as we shall see in particular as related to Taoism, to even the most mundane of activities. Whether one is preparing a meal, choosing one's clothes, or planning a home (feng shui), these apparently routine functions are imbued with significance, since they all are capable of adding to or reducing the individual's well-being, It may be an exaggeration to say that for the Chinese "you are what you eat," but if it is the case that the ideal Indian is a guru, the ideal Chinese could well be a chef.

Taoism. Taoism is second only to Confucianism among the major schools of China. Like Confucianism, it expresses no belief in a God, an immortal soul, or a life after death. The aim in life for a Taoist is to discover the Tao, the Way, which is the harmony of the twin forces of yin and yang, the negative and positive, the dark and the light, the feminine and the masculine, the submissive and the assertive. Some have suggested that these ideas are not alien to a theistic view of life (for "Tao" read "God") but the Taoist classic the *Tao Te Ching* (Classic of the Way and Its Power) states unequivocally from the first line that the Tao cannot be known or discussed. It cannot even be described as "the unknowable origin of the universe" since it is even more remote than that. The origin of the universe is chi, or vital breath, a word that can also be translated as wind, or spirit. The Tao is the origin of chi, which can be apprehended through its twin manifestations, yin and yang.

We reflect below more directly on the philosophy of these concepts. At this stage we need only state that this means living as closely as possible on natural lines: not trying to outshine nature by outshining one's fellows; recognizing that one is merely an infinitesimal part of the universal processes; above all, treating nature naturally by not interfering with it, a process described as being like an unplaned piece of wood (*pu*). Interference brings harm, not least to the one who interferes. It is in any case not only destructive but also superfluous, like gilding a lily or painting legs on a snake.

A significant outcome of Taoism's advocacy of intuitive living is its rejection of any kind of overriding moral code such as the Ten Commandments or the *Communist Manifesto*. Different circumstances may require different actions: aggression may be the right quality to use when facing a mob, but not when addressing young children in a classroom. This is thoroughgoing moral relativism, which was unambiguously expressed by Chuang-Tzu. Among the Taoist masters he is second in esteem only to Lao Tzu, traditionally held to be the author of the *Tao Te Ching*. Chuang-Tzu argued that nobody could possibly know everything; everyone was blinkered in some way. Consequently, people would show wisdom by being slow to criticize alleged wrongs in others and by being even slower to affirm their own convictions as absolutely true (there is a clear foretaste of John LOCKE here). In a world where values differ inevitably from person to person and from society to society, he said in a famous passage, the impartial arbiter simply does not exist. In words that are hauntingly relevant two and a half millennia later, he argued that there was no such entity as absolute truth: in fact, he throws into question the use of the word *truth* at all when discussing ideas. In this respect he figures as not only a supreme relativist but also an early, if not the earliest, postmodernist.

It should be made clear that this has been a description of philosophical Taoism, *tao-chia*, not magical—sometimes called religious—Taoism, *tao-chiao*. This latter is a more popular expression of the philosophy, and aims,

(1) through consuming certain elixirs, (2) by using particular breathing patterns, and (3) by engaging in certain sexual practices, to achieve longevity. But even this school of Taoism seeks longevity on earth, not eternity in heaven. *Tao-chiao* speaks of "immortals," but these are legendary figures, introduced to encourage followers of the way to remain steadfastly on the path.

Yin and Yang. The yin-yang school is older than both Confucianism and Taoism, and has had a marked influence on both. The yin and yang were originally the dark and light sides of a mountain, the significant points being that (1) neither can be dispensed with, (2) each has its period of predominance followed by one of subservience, and (3) each is continuously moving into the other, as day into night into day, summer into winter into summer. Applying this philosophy in human life means learning to recognize when the positive, assertive yang qualities are needed and when the negative, submissive yin; when to speak and when to be silent; when to act and when to do nothing. This is an intuitive, rather than a rational process (yin rather than yang), though both qualities are likely to be needed in various situations. The two forces reach out into every aspect of life—the food we eat, the way we spend our time (actively and passively), managing change in individual and community life, conducting relationships, including marriage. There is no divine guidance for this process: it is entirely a matter of "reading the signs of the times" and proceeding accordingly.

The fascinating outcome of these emphases is that there are no ivory towers for Chinese philosophers: their podium is the marketplace, their campus the home. For example, a major philosophical issue is the content and preparation of meals, which should contain a mixture of both yin and yang foods: too much yin (as with vegans, for example) is likely to create weaklings; too much yang (huge steaks two or three times a day as in the United States, for example) will make for aggressive, if not violent, behavior. Marital relationships will be more harmonious if each partner accepts that in some areas he or she will play the yin role, in others the yang, leaving the complementary role to his or her partner. If both husband and wife always try to express the yang element, the result will be a battlefield; if both settle for the yin, the marriage will be more like a graveyard. Above all, to know—intuitively—whether the yin or the yang should be acknowledged as dominant at any particular moment is to be at one with the Tao and in harmony with nature.

The natural successors to the founders of Confucianism and Taoism—Mencius and Chuang-Tzu—both advocated that human beings engage regularly in periods of quiet contemplation; but it would be wrong to identify this concern as a return to or discovery of religious principles, in the sense that religion necessarily includes a belief in the supernatural. Both teachers bore testimony to an inner awareness, maybe even a transcendental experience, but would have been shocked had these affirmations been offered as evidence that they were religious in the conventional sense of the word. Their conviction was that there was indeed a transcendental aspect to both nature and humanity, but that this did not imply any otherworldly dimension. They spoke of what they knew or had experienced, and this led them to the realization that human beings, far from needing to rely on God or any other supernatural being in order to make their way through life, could control their own destinies through their own moral decision making. The power of "the spirits" was therefore supplanted by human virtue and human effort.

Other schools in China are more obviously philosophical in a Western sense. The School of Names involves the analysis of words and their meaning, aiming at the avoidance of logical errors in language. The Legalistic School was concerned with the question of effective government and how this was best achieved by using the law to control the people. Mohism (founded by Mo Tzu) was for a period a rival to Confucianism, particularly apropos of Mo's insistence (against Confucius's stress on ever-widening circles of personal responsibility) that everyone everywhere had an equal call on a person's goodwill—an early form of utilitarianism. Some commentators have identified in Mo's doctrine of universal love, or goodwill, an early expression of Christian *agape*. The important point here is that Mo viewed love as a totally human quality, and would have been disturbed to be described as (in the traditional sense) religious. It is worth adding that agape itself is in fact a thoroughly human quality.

With the declaration of a Communist state in October 1949, Chinese schools abandoned the teaching of all Chinese classical writers. This was because of the occasional suggestion in their writings that there were values to be discovered other than the material: For a regime that proclaimed dialectical materialism to be not just the Zeitgeist but also the perpetual philosophy of the people, this teaching seemed a prima facie example of outdated delusions. It was gradually realized, however, that this was a misunderstanding of the classics, and, facilitated by the death of Mao Tse-tung in 1976, Confucianism was restored to every school's curriculum. This restoration did not apply to Taoism, not because of any secret supernatural doctrines which its writings might be held to contain, but because of its seemingly anarchic, if not totally seditious, emphases, particularly as expressed by Chuang-Tzu, whose advice to anyone wishing not to be called upon for government service was the not entirely negative suggestion that they pretend to be totally incompetent. But maybe this is a form of unbelief not relevant in this context.

RAY BILLINGTON

CHISHOLM, GEORGE BROCK (1896–1971), Canadian humanist and cofounder of the WHO. Brock Chisholm was born into a Christian family in semirural Ontario, Canada. His military experiences in World War I, during which he was wounded, affected him profoundly. He enrolled in medical school, graduating in 1924. He established a general practice, which he later developed into the first psychiatric service in Toronto. During this period, he testified for the defense in an early court case about family planning (see BIRTH CONTROL AND UNBELIEF).

In 1939 Chisholm was appointed director of medical services for national defense. He developed a successful assessment test for personnel placement. In 1944 he was appointed deputy minister of public health. Among other things, he gave lectures on the relationship of physical to mental health. In one of these, he remarked that the Santa Claus myth damaged the ability of children to think properly. This sparked an outburst of negative responses from intolerant critics, which he simply ignored.

In 1946 Chisholm was appointed to the UN Commission on World Health. He developed its secretariat, constitution, and standards for appointments, and in 1948 became the first director of its successor, the World Health Organization (WHO). His most difficult task was to get the necessary twenty-six countries to sign on to establish a new organization. Later, he focused on three main goals: strengthening national health services, integrating international health work, and developing an epidemic warning system. He promoted Esperanto as a universal language and warned about the dangers of overpopulation.

Chisholm described himself as a humanist (see HUMANISM). He advocated telling children that there are many competing worldviews. Asked to define God, he said, "I have no such definition, and have not felt the need of one since childhood." He once declined to meet with the pope because policies of the Roman Catholic Church conflicted with those of the WHO. In retirement, he moved to Victoria, British Columbia, where he was in great demand as a lecturer. In 1957, at the invitation of Bertrand RUSSELL, he attended the first Pugwash Conference hosted by Cyrus Eaton in Nova Scotia.

Chisholm published two books and numerous essays and papers. Among many honorary awards, he was named Canadian Humanist of the Year in 1959 and appointed a Companion of the Order of Canada in 1967. He was honorary president of the Humanist Association of Canada in 1968, the same year that Dr. Henry Morgentaler was its president. He died in Veterans Hospital in Victoria in 1976.

BIBLIOGRAPHY

Chisholm, Brock. *Can People Learn to Learn?* New York: Harper Brothers, 1958.
———. *Prescription for Survival.* New York: Columbia University Press, 1957.
Hardie, Glenn. "Brock Chisholm, Canadian Humanist." *Humanist in Canada* 107 (Winter 1993–94).

GLENN HARDIE

CHRISTIANITY, RESISTANCE TO IN THE ANCIENT WORLD.

INTRODUCTION: HISTORICAL APPROACHES TO CHRISTIAN ORIGINS

Since the pioneering history of the decline of Rome by the rationalist historian Edward GIBBON in 1776, the study of early resistance to the spread of Christianity has been shaped by competing schools of thought, theological and positivist (see POSITIVISM). Prior to Gibbon, church historians, especially those working in the European tradition and drawing largely on the work of the so-called church fathers, saw the "triumph" of Christianity as being due to divine providence. Typical of this view was the belief that Christianity itself was a final revelation of God within history, and as such was destined to supplant all other forms of belief, ranging from Judaism to the pagan religions, Christian HERESY, and competing religious traditions such as Manichaeism and Islam. "Triumphalist historiography," whether Protestant or Catholic theologically, was careless of details, sociologically naive, and subservient to the colonial agendas of the post-Renaissance period. It was shaped by the doctrine that the spread of Christianity was supported by a divine mandate (Matt. 28:19; Mark 13:10) that required the conversion of the world to the Christian faith. The collapse of imperial Christianity ("Christendom"), the fragmentation of the church and its mission after the Reformation of the sixteenth and seventeenth centuries, and above all the Enlightenment of the eighteenth century (see ENLIGHTENMENT, UNBELIEF DURING THE), made the older, providential view of Christianity's success untenable. While the effects of the critical view of history, foreshadowed in the fifteenth-century work of Lorenzo Valla, were not felt immediately nor everywhere at the same time, historians outside the theological establishment gradually awakened to the fact that the early years of the church's existence were fraught with uncertainty and internal conflict and that the eventual success of Christianity as a missionary religion could more easily be explained by social and political factors than by supernatural ones. This recognition in itself was devastating to the Catholic position that orthodox Christianity was the product of an unbroken development of authority from the time of the apostles onward (*traditio apostolica*, or apostolic tradition). Valla himself paved the way for later rationalists in his famous 1440 *Declamation on the Donation of Constantine*, in which he showed that a document, used by the popes for centuries to support the doctrine of supreme papal secular authority, could not have been written as early as the fourth century and was instead a medieval forgery. Valla also challenged another cornerstone of Christian belief by demonstrating that the document known as the Apostle's Creed had not been composed by the twelve apostles, a view that caused him to be referred to the Inquisition as a heretic. Ironically, the process of retelling the history of the church was helped by the work of Catholic critics and Protestant reformers, many reared in the classical tradition, who challenged prevailing views of how the church had departed from the teaching of Jesus in structure, polity, and belief. In addition, significant new translations of the biblical texts ranging from Desiderius ERASMUS's New Testament (Greek) in 1516 to Martin Luther's German edition in 1522 and that of the Oxbridge translators (authorized by James I in 1611) contributed inadvertently to a new interest in Christian origins, the reliability of ancient texts, and the cultural context of the world within which Christianity grew to maturity. The competing historical interests that spurred research into the history of texts and the evolution of doctrines would eventually undermine the belief that the earliest period of the Christian church was one of pristine innocence and uniform belief.

By the eighteenth century, discussion of the church's beginnings had moved from a purely internal one among Christian historical theologians to the new "professional" class of scholars who took their inspiration from the encyclopaedist tradition of free and critical inquiry (see *ENCYCLOPÉDIE, L'*, AND UNBELIEF). Scholars of this new breed were unencumbered by dogmatic concerns and unconcerned with the disapproval of church authority and often, as in the case of Denis DIDEROT and VOLTAIRE, outwardly satirical and skeptical in dealing with the claims of the old historiography. Gibbon himself represented a school of thought that understood the ultimate success of Christianity as being due to both extrinsic and instrinsic causes. Like many intellectuals of his day, he regarded much of the dogmatic tradition of Christianity as little better than superstition. He debunked the myth of Christian martyrdom by deconstructing official church history that had been perpetuated for centuries. Because the Roman Catholic Church had a virtual monopoly on its own history, its own Latin interpretations were considered sacrosanct, and as a result the church's writings had rarely been subjected to scrutiny. For Gibbon, however, they were secondary sources: the same Latin documents merely translated by previous apologists. Gibbon eschewed these, and never referred to them in his own history. According to Gibbon, Romans were far more tolerant of Christians than Christians were of one another, especially once Christianity gained the upper hand. Christians inflicted far greater casualties on Christians than were ever inflicted by the Roman Empire. He extrapolated that the number of Christians executed by other Christian factions far exceeded all the Christian martyrs who died during the three centuries of Christianity under Roman rule. This was in stark contrast to Catholic church history, which insisted that Christianity won the hearts and minds of people largely because of the inspirational example set by its martyrs. Gibbon proved that the early church's custom of bestowing the title of martyr ("saint") on all confessors of faith grossly inflated the actual numbers. Christianity succeeded by default: because of the wide appeal of its superstition, the "decadent" condition of Roman religion (his most speculative point), and the intolerance of its propagandists. Opposition to his work (labeled "paganist" by his challengers) was an episode in intellectual history second only to the opposition to Charles DARWIN in the following century (see DARWINISM; EVOLUTION AND UNBELIEF).

The advances in historical criticism of the nineteenth century and beyond saw an emphasis on situating Christianity among the religions and cultural movements of the Roman Empire. The work of scholars such as F. C. Baur, Franz Cumont, Wilhelm Bousset, Richard Reitzenstein, Adolph von Harnack, and perhaps most importantly Walter Bauer and Martin Werner paved the way for modern assessments of the critical period in Christian origins. In conjunction with the work of classical, "crossover," and Near Eastern historians such as E. R. Dodds, Werner Jaeger, A. Travers Herford, and A. D. Nock, trendsetting studies appeared leaving almost no aspect of Christianity's association with the mystery religions, hellenistic Jewish traditions, and rival philosophical schools unexamined. The summation that follows draws on the work of these and more recent scholars, with special reference to (a) Jewish resistance to Christianity and (b) the Roman-pagan intellectual and moral critiques of the Christian religion between the second and fourth centuries.

JEWISH RESISTANCE

Christianity's dependence on Judaism for its core doctrines—belief in a Messiah who would deliver his people and a spiritual view of God's salvation of his people through an atoning sacrifice—was never denied in the early church. The New Testament writers drew freely on the Hebrew Bible to support its notion that Jesus had been the fulfillment of the prophecies of the Old Testament. They made equally liberal use of Jewish eschatology and apocalyptic ideas, which placed believers at an "end time" in relation to world history and envisioned God as a severe judge of the enemies of his chosen people (Ezek. 36). Greco-Jewish ideas of eternal reward or "afterlife," the suffering of the unrighteous (Ezek. 33), the judgment of the world, and the deliverance (salvation) of the righteous, were integral to apocalyptic ideology, which completely suffused Christian thinking in the first decades of the sect's existence. Christianity differed from Judaism largely in making Jesus the unique espouser of ideas completely familiar to hellenistic rabbis, a fact that led both Jewish and pagan critics of the new religion to harangue Christian preachers for their unoriginality. One of the earliest examples of a Christian dispute is the (fictional) debate between Justin Martyr, a Syrian theologian, and a Jewish teacher named Trypho,

dating from around 170 CE. From it and scattered references in other pieces of early Christian literature we are able to trace the main lines of Jewish hostility to the early Christian church. Some of these criticisms occur later on in the writings of Roman intellectuals, who seem to have given a fair hearing to both sides in disputes such as the one created at the end of the second century by Justin.

Resurrection and the Resurrection of Jesus. The belief in resurrection was not a uniform doctrine in the sectarian Judaism of the first century CE. Some Jews, especially those in the rabinnical tradition called Pharisaism, seemed to hold to the view that the dead would rise in order to be judged by God on the last day. Others, namely, the sect of the Sadducees and other unaligned traditionalists, held the view that the idea of resurrection had been imported into Judaism through Greek-inspired interpretations of the Hebrew bible, especially the book of Ezekiel (36:26–37:28) dating from perhaps the sixth century BCE. Neither tradition was in complete harmony with the Greek-Platonic belief in the immortality of the soul, which argued vigorously in favor of the decadence of the body. The earliest Christian preaching seems broadly to conform to the Pharisaic view of resurrection, but exceeds it in the belief that Jesus, with Elijah and perhaps Moses (the attendants of Jesus in the story of the "transfiguration," Mark 9:4f.), had survived death and would come again as the expected judge of the world (Dan. 7:11–13; Mark 13). The story of the resurrection of Jesus, probably the earliest element of the Jesus tradition to circulate and win a hearing, was widely if not universally (1 Cor. 15:12) understood to mean that all Christians would share his fate, a spectacular claim even in an acutely religious era. Paul, writing in the fifties of the first century, expresses the view that the Christian faithful will be "awakened" by the sound of a trumpet, joining those who are still alive at the time of the event to be judged by the "Lord in the sky." (1 Thess. 4:15ff.). Significantly, for the early missionaries, Christianity was a "resurrection faith," and without an explicit belief in the bodily resurrection of the dead, incorporating the resurrection of Jesus Christ as its model, one was not entiled to be called Christian (1 Cor. 15:12–34). While many of the so-called mystery religions of the Roman world preached a belief in immortality, Christianity was unique in its emphasis on the material and physical nature of the afterlife.

Jewish hostility toward the early preaching centered therefore on the Christian doctrine of resurrection, and seems to have come largely from the Pharisaic side, as mediated by the rabbis after the destruction of the Jewish temple in 70 CE. Where the Pharisaic belief was speculative, symbolic, and nuanced, Christian belief in resurrection, as conveyed in their stories, was crude and specific. The earliest stratum of Judeo-Christian belief in the resurrection seems to have arisen from the view that Jesus was a completely "righteous" man, one whose situation in relation to Jewish law made him innocent of sin and hence worthy to be spared the "punishment of death," widely thought in Jewish theology to be the consequence of sin (Gen. 6:3). In the synagogues where Paul and other missionaries preached with variable success, they began with the simple asseveration that Jesus "had not been abandoned to Hades, nor did his flesh see corruption," as a sign of his special status, or "divinity" in the hellenistic lexicon (Acts 2:31). This preaching was often joined to the belief that the resurrection of Jesus corroborated his status as "Kyrios" ("Lord," an honorific title ambiguous enough to cause offense to some listeners and not to others) and "Christ," a term loosely equated with the Jewish idea of Messiah, but also with the idea of divine sonship or kingship—an "anointed man," set aside for a specific role. The title that seems to have caused the greatest offense to Jewish audiences was the use of the Greek phrase "son of God," also employed by the emperors in token of their divine status, as a title for Jesus (Matt. 26:63).

Synagogue leaders first tried persuasion to prevent the missionaries from interpreting scripture in unacceptable ways (cf. Luke 4:16–30). When this failed, they resorted to more extreme measures, ranging from flogging, as happened to Paul on a number of occasions (2 Cor. 11:23–26), and occasionally to execution by stoning, a remedy Paul himself prescribes for certain forms of apostasy (1 Cor. 5:2; Luke 4:29). The purging of Christians from synagogues seems to have begun systematically in the mid-first century, though there is evidence that eastern Christians continued occasionally to attend synagogue meetings well into the third century. The language Paul uses to describe his own efforts to roust cells of Jesus believers from synagogues in Asia Minor suggests a program dating at least from the forties (Gal. 1:13–15). While there is no evidence prior to the end of the first century that Christianity was driven underground by these measures, Jewish hostility on all sides seems to have caused fractures in the movement. As a result, a Jerusalem faction headed by Jacob, or "James," the brother of Jesus, arose sometime in the forties of the first century and was characterized by a type of preaching designed to conciliate the rabbis and perhaps also to mitigate some of the more extravagant messianic claims made on behalf of Jesus. This James "party" may never have had an official sectarian status—Josephus, for example, knows nothing of them—but seems to have held to a fairly rigid ethical code, to have practiced circumcision, kept the dietary laws, and retained sabbath practice as the core of their corporate life (Acts 3:40). They do not seem to have had any teaching regarding the birth of Jesus (the party was headed by a caliph, Jesus's closest biological relative) and their exact views on the resurrection are unknown. They were undoubtedly aligned with the more extreme apocalyptic sects and hence may have run afoul of Roman authority because of their prior association with an executed dissident. A

quite separate faction, brought into fictional harmony with the James faction in the Acts of the Apostles (written around 100 CE) minimized Jewish tradition, abandoned sabbath regulations by inventing a new feast for celebrating the resurrection of Jesus, the *dies domini* or day of the Lord, and deliberately emphasized the significance of Jesus as a savior god, comparable to those found in all corners of the Roman world. This party seems to have attempted conciliation with the Jerusalem church throughout the fifties and sixties of the first century, but then to have positioned itself politically and theologically to take advantage of growing Roman hostility toward the Palestinian client kingdom of Judaea. Paul's letters provide the basic documentation for the success of this faction. While the Jerusalem church was destined for extinction, the church outside Palestine survived to tell the story of Jesus in its own and intensively anti-Jewish way.

Resistance Following the Destruction of Jerusalem. The end of an independent Palestinian Judaism ended only the internal struggle between the rival forms of messianic faith. No longer able to punish the "Nazarenes" as homegrown apostates in official tribunals, Judaism also lost what influence it may have had over the more extreme forms of Christian messianism. Much of the evidence for Jewish resistance post-70 is discernible from Christian lines of defense in the New Testament, especially the gospels, and falls broadly into three categories: attacks on a discredited Christian apocalyptic message; historical criticism of the resurrection; and attacks on Christian abuse of Hebrew prophecy. A fourth and less significant line of resistance, dating from the Talmudic period but expanded throughout late antiquity and the early Middle Ages, comprised literary attacks on the moral character of Jesus and his family, a polemical device familiar in antiquity and identical in purpose to later Christian slanders concerning the life and character of Muhammad.

The attack on Christian apocalypticism dates from before the destruction of the temple, since earliest Christian belief seems to have included the idea that the return of Jesus from heaven would be swift and sure, or at least within the lifetime of many who had heard him (Mark 9:1, 13:20; 1 Thess. 4:15; Matt.10:23). The specificity of this belief was subject to interpretation, recasting, rationalization, and disconfirmation. From the Jewish standpoint (for instance, Isa. 65:17) the apocalyptic catastrophe was often seen as a way of purging the earth rather than a way of annihilating creation. By the time the polemical New Testament letter known as 2 Peter appears (around 110–120 CE), a strong element of Jewish skepticism toward the inevitability of the judgment had developed, making the Christian belief a matter for ridicule. There an unnamed critic is described as complaining, "And now where is the promise of his coming [again]? Ever since our ancestors fell asleep, things have continued just as they were at the beginning of creation." Indeed 2 Peter caps a skeptical tradition dating from fifty years earlier when Paul confronted sarcasm about the second coming of Jesus in the Christian community at Thessalonike, a situation probably instigated by Jewish and possibly even Jewish-Christian teachers attempting to discredit him (1 Thess. 4:1–13).

According to Jewish detractors therefore the most obvious deficiency of the Christians was their inability to corroborate Jesus's promise to return to reveal his true identity and their apparent readiness to invent various stratagems to explain the failure away. These stratagems would have arisen in reponse to particular charges leveled by Jewish teachers: Christians argued, for example, that before the last days the gentiles would be converted (Mark 13:10), that the power of the emperor would fade (Rom. 16:20), that a cosmic battle between the powers of good and evil would take place (2 Thess. 2:2–10), and in what may be the earliest level of attack and defense (since it violates earlier prophecies of Jesus), that Jesus himself had professed ignorance of the time (Mark 13:32) and later, that he had refused to speculate about the signs of the last days (Mark 8:11–12; cf. 1 Thess. 5:1–7).

A consistent feature of Christian defense was the belief that the crucifixion and resurrection of Jesus formed a transition between two ages, an old and corrupt period characterized by sin, and a new age that would see the dawn of redemption (Luke 12:49–56, 17:22–37; Matt. 12:38–42). Accordingly, Jewish rhetoric emphasized that the death of Jesus did not conform to any prophecy of their tradition and that the resurrection story had been fabricated by his followers to escape humiliation. The first of these assertions—that Christianity mangled Jewish prophecies and twisted the original meanings of the oracles—was potentially devastating for the new cult. The messianic status of Jesus, the doctrine of the last days, and the honorific titles "Messiah," "Son of Man," and "son of David" had specific reference to Jewish history. In the *Dialogue with Trypho* (ca. 168) the Christian Justin represents the Jewish teacher as conceding every objection except the idea that the Messiah was destined to suffer and die. This suggests that of all points of discussion, the Jews were the most insistent that Christianity was a perversion of their messianic hopes, which after the destruction of Jerusalem tended to become future-oriented in contrast to Christian belief that the savior had already appeared. In close connection was Jewish emphasis that the death of Jesus had been humiliating and final, and that the resurrection itself had been fabricated to support Christians' already eccentric glosses of prophecy. What "Christian" prophecy was in supporting the belief that the death of Jesus unfolded by divine plan, the resurrection and the corollary doctrine of a second coming were in revealing his "true" identity and making sense of his suffering. The poetic language of Isaiah 52:13–53:12, sometimes called the Fourth Servant Song and applied by the Hebrew prophets to the disfigurement of Israel at the hands of its oppressors,

was taken over by Christian teachers and applied to the death of Jesus. Equivalent misuse of the Hebrew texts was employed to support a variety of elements of Christian teaching—for example, Isaiah 7:14, originally applied to the restoration of Israel through the presence of God (Immanuel), was applied by Christian teachers like Matthew to the innovative doctrine that Jesus had been born of a virgin, despite the fact that the Hebrew text uses only the term for "young woman" (*almah*).

Christians were often driven to such interpretations out of apologetic necessity. Lacking the political power to control the Jesus movement, Jewish polemic insisted that following the burial of Jesus his followers stole his body after bribing guards at the tomb (Matt. 28:15), a story already persistent by the waning days of the first century. Jewish charges that Jesus was an absent savior, a charlatan who had deserted his misled followers, were answered by the doctrine of the mystical presence of Jesus in the community (Matt. 28:20), or, in a development derived from the Elijah-Passover tradition, that Jesus was present in the breaking of the bread (Mark 14:22f., pars.; Luke 24:30ff.) and concocted jesuine propoecies wherein Jesus himself becomes the legitimator of his own death (Mark 8:31, 9:30f., 10:45f.; Luke 24:6). The doctrine of the "Holy Spirit," which later becomes a feature of trinitarian Christianity from about the third century, seems to have begun as a way of defending against the Jewish charge that Jesus had abandoned his community following a humiliating and unexpected failure to win an audience in Jerusalem; remnants of this defensive posture are common to the New Testament itself (John 20:22; Luke 24:21, 24:49), especially in the inconsistent narratives known as the "departure stories" (Mark 16:19f.; Luke 24; Matt. 28:16; John 20:16–20).

Later Resistance: The Toldoth Yeshu. Jewish resistance to Christianity continued unabated throughout the first three centuries of the common era and informed Roman polemic (below) as well. With the dawn of Christianity as an imperial religion in the fourth century, public Jewish opposition was destined to abate. In the intervening period, random attacks on the Christian gospel gradually become a part of a folklore tradition, embodied partly in revisions of the Talmud, and partly in nonrabbinical legends known as the *Toldoth Yeshu*. In these traditions, Jesus (Yeshu, though the name may not be identical) is the son of a certain Miriam who is impregnated by a Roman soldier (or betrayer of Jewish law) known as Panthera. In the *Tosefta* references to Yeshu, the title ben-Pandera (son of Pandera) is added after the name. The Latin name, derived from Greek *pantheras*, literally meaning "panther," is unusual but not unknown.

The Yeshu of these sources is also known as "ben Stada," or "the son of one who has gone astray," presumably a reference to his mother's situation or to his own apostasy from Judaism. It is possible that this tradition is early and the gospel account of the virgin birth is an attempt to supplant it. Ben-Stada is also mentioned in the Jerusalem Talmud. In Shabbat 12:4 III he is mentioned as having learned magic by cutting marks in his flesh. In Sanhedrin 7:12 he is recalled as an example of someone caught doing magic by hidden observers and subsequently stoned (cf. Mark 2:23). The references to magic are in keeping with Jesus's reputation as a healer and magician, and it is sometimes suggested that rabbinical opinion was divided in the first century about whether Jesus should be revered for his ability to perform miracles and enact healings, an issue already implied in Mark 3:20–24.

While confused over time, elements of the *Toldoth Yeshu* seem very ancient. In 178 CE the pagan writer Celsus, in his polemic against Christianity, claimed that he had heard from a Jew that Mary had been divorced by her husband after having an affair with a Roman soldier named Pantheras who was the real father of Jesus. The main import of this tradition is that it indicates a *tranche* of Jewish thought which understood Jesus as a garden-variety magician and apostate from Jewish teaching. The dating of individual elements of the tradition make its use as a historical source—for example, as Jewish corroboration of the life of Jesus—impossible.

ROMAN RESISTANCE

It is common if not unproblematical to date the persecution of the Christians from the time of the great fire of Rome in July 64, during the reign of Nero. The source of this opinion is a single passage in the *Annals* of the historian Tacitus, written between 112 and 120 CE, some sixty years after the events he describes:

Therefore, to put an end to the rumor Nero created a diversion and subjected to the most extra-ordinary tortures those hated for their abominations by the common people called Christians. The originator of this name (was) Christ [Chrestus], who, during the reign of Tiberius had been executed by sentence of the procurator Pontinus Pilate. Repressed for the time being, the deadly superstition broke out again not only in Judea, the original source of the evil, but also in the city (Rome), where all things horrible or shameful in the world collect and become popular. So an arrest was made of all who confessed; then on the basis of their information, an immense multitude was convicted, not so much of the crime of arson as for hatred of the human race.

While the precise meaning of Tacitus's phrase "hatred of the human race" and the source of his opprobrium for Christianity remain uncertain—many scholars have suggested Jewish reports and intrigue—the passage is broadly expressive of the growing suspicion of Christians by pagan intellectuals. It is not certain however that the hostility Tacitus records can be dated from as early as the middle decades of the first century, before, indeed, the existence of any written gospel.

Political Resistance. Systematic resistance to Christianity in the form known as *persecutio* or *coercitio* does not arise before the early second century. Traditional scholarship names ten periods of persecution, dating from the time of Nero and including the reigns of Domitian, Trajan, Hadrian, Marcus Aurelius, Septimus Severus, Maximus the Thracian, Decius, Valerian, and Diocletian/Galerius. Of these, only the persecutions under Marcus Aurelius, Decius, and Diocletian seem to have been violent; it is clear that their effectiveness as a form of resistance was questionable from as early as the late second century, when the church father Tertullian boasts that Christians occupy positions of importance throughout the Roman world, and that without the support of the church "the emperor would find himself without an empire to rule." Trajan's policies are the earliest well-documented ones, being known from a letter written to him by the governor of Pontus, Pliny the Younger around 111, and answered by the emperor himself. In this correspondence, Pliny seems uncertain what to make of the new cult—one he does not recognize from the register of "licensed" practices—and is instructed by the emperor to be lenient with its adherents unless they persist in their mischief, whereupon the governor is given permission to punish the accused parties. Trajan's policy is remarkable in its leniency: Christians are not to be hunted down; their recantations are to be taken at face value; and anonymous pamphlets and accusations are to be disregarded in any case involving the new sect. With the passage of time and growing concern that the sect had begun to acquire members among the imperial classes, persecutions worsened. By the time of Decius the repression of Christianity became programmatic, though much of the evidence for this persecution comes not from secular but church history. Early in 250 Decius issued the edict for the suppression of Christianity. Measures were first taken demanding that the bishops and officers of the church sacrifice to the emperor, a matter of an oath of allegiance that was taken by Christians as profoundly offensive. Just at this time there was a second outbreak of the Antonine Plague, which at its height between 251 and 266 was taking the lives of five thousand a day in Rome. This outbreak is referred to as the Plague of Cyprian, who was the bishop of Carthage, where both the plague and the persecution of Christians were especially severe. Christians were blamed for the spread of the disease in much the same way Jews were used as scapegoats during the spread of the Black Death in the Middle Ages. The effect in this case, however, was to create a new class of martyrs which would serve as inspiration for the spread of the movement. The Diocletian persecution, the last before the legitimation of Christianity in 312–13, was severe largely because it represented a "sweep" of the empire.

Lactantius informs us that Diocletian acted under pressure from his advisors on the advice of a council of dignitaries in which Galerius played the principal part. Persecutions began in 303, the nineteenth year of his reign. This general outbreak had been preceded for three years at least by a more or less disguised persecution in the army. The Christian writer Eusebius says that a certain Veturius, in the sixteenth year of Diocletian, forced a number of high-ranking officers to prove their loyalty by the usual test of sacrificing to the gods of the empire, on penalty of losing their honors and privileges; in the process many officers were identified as Christians and executed. On February 23, 303, the Church of Nicomedia was torn down by order of the emperors. The next day a first edict was published throughout the empire ordering the churches to be destroyed, the sacred scriptures to be burned, and "inflicting degradation on those in high rank and slavery on their households." Two other edicts soon followed, one ordering the imprisonment of all church officials, the other commanding them to sacrifice to the gods. These edicts were repealed in the first year of Constantine's reign (312), which also marked an end of the official persecutions of the Christian Church.

The Literary Attacks on Christians. During the period of public persecution, and taking inspiration from it, a succession of philosophical and literary attacks against the Christian religion appeared. The earliest of these have not survived, but their substance can be known from the writings of the Christian apologists such as Tertullian, Justin Martyr, and Tatian, writing in the second and third centuries. Early views of the Christians included the opinion that they were poor citizens (they refused military service, avoided public events, and refused the sacrifices), were dangerous to public order, and had invented their religious ceremonies by taking bits and pieces from established customs and perverted their meanings. In the course of time, as Christianity and its potential for harm to the established order became widely recognized, these charges became more specific. Romans were especially suspicious of Christian ceremonies, and from the second century began to see similarities between the language used in the Christian eucharist and the love-feasts of the Bacchae, the cult of Dionysus that Rome had tried repeatedly to bring under control. The Latin writer Marcus Cornelius Fronto reported that the Christians were accustomed to sacrificing infants and to incestuous practices of various sorts. Among the other charges brought by early polemicists against the church, Tertullian mentions treason, cannibalism, murder, and, above all, ATHEISM—the last stemming from Christians' unwillingness to recognize the state gods of the empire. While some of the charges are transparently slanderous—the reference to incest seems to stem from the Christian habit of addressing fellow believers as "brother" and "sister"—other charges concerning the excesses of the movement are borne out in what is today known of the habits of fringe and extremist Christian communes.

By the middle decades of the second century, named opponents of the movement begin to proliferate. The cynic philosopher Crescens sees the Christians as "impious" troublemakers who revel in their "mischievoius atheism," while the rheorician Lucian of Samosata satirizes the cult's teachers as philosophical bumblers and the laity as simpletons who are prepared to believe anything they are told by their teachers. Christian martyrdom, used persistently by Christians as proof of their unwavering faith, is seen by the philosopher Epictetus as "sheer obstinancy," and by Marcus Aurelius as "mere suicide without moral value." The medical theorist Galen also took notice of the new religion, commenting that the followers of Christ "are unable to follow any demonstrative arguiment . . . and hence need parables and miracles" in order to lead a moral life. No pagan intellectual of the second or third century came to the defense of the new religious movement.

The Authors of Persecution. The faith of the Christians remains the focus of pagan poelmic from Galen's time onward, and is especially central to the works of the so-called authors of persecution (the name given the three by their Christian opponents): Celsus, Porphyry, and the emperor Julian (the "apostate"). Writing at the end of the first century, Celsus produced fifteen books against the Christians titled *The True Doctrine*, a pun intended to show that the Christian teaching was inferior to the true philosophy and religion of the Greeks. Lost to history after the fifth century, his work is only available from quotations in the writings of the church father Origen. Celsus regards Christianity as a danger to the Roman order, and cites as proof Christians' unwillingness to practice their rituals in the open. An unoriginal faith, it borrows, then subverts, the teachings of the Jews and adds to them the worship of a man "of recent date," condemned as a criminal, but thought by them to be the son of God. Celsus seems to know bits of the Jewish polemical tradition (most of his critique is delivered from the lips of a fictional dissenting Jew): Jesus's death had been unexpected; Christian scripture is contradictory ("if the story of Herod's slaughter of the newborns was designed to prevent you from becoming a king, why did you not become one?"); his life was lived in seclusion, and he was not even able to convince his disciples of his divine status. Celsus finds the resurrection of Jesus risible because it was not witnessed by anyone of repute; moreover, the Christians seem unaware that "multitudes have invented similar tales to lead simpleminded hearers astray." Perhaps the most renowned part of Celsus's critique is his view that the Christian themselves are drawn from the least intelligent caste of Roman society—a clutch of "wives, children, and beggars" who accept on faith what they cannot defend in reasoned debate.

The philosopher Porphyry, writing in the third century, was arguably more influential than Celsus. His books against the Christians (*Kata Christianon*) suffered the same fate as those of his predecessor, but are known from scattered quotations in patristic writings. Porphyry regards the Christians as a seditionist sect that hides behind acts of philanthropy to divert public attention from its true aim—political control of the empire. He shares with Celsus the belief that Christians come from the lowest and most gullible orders of Roman society, and is especially emphatic about the "absurd" nature of their stories. The gospels are full of preposterous tales, written in barbarous Greek, and not worth the attention of anyone seeking to know the truths of philosophy and religion. Much of his work was devoted to pointing out inconsistencies in the biblical accounts, contradictions in the writings of the evangelists concerning the birth and teachings of Jesus, and historical problems affecting their interpretation of prophecy. Porphyry is one of the first pagan observers to play close attention to the text of the New Testament, calling to attention discrepancies in the stories of the crucifixion and resurrection of Jesus. He seems to have been the first to suggest that the book of Daniel, a centerpiece in Christian apocalyptic thinking, had been written in the second century BCE, not in the sixth, and that Christian apocalypticism was disproved by the passage of time. Some of his most vicious language is reserved for the apostles Peter, a dullard, and Paul, a hypocrite by his own admission—vices Porphyry sees as especially typical of the cult's adherents. Toward the end of his work, he offers a scathing examination of the Christian belief in bodily resurrection, which he contrasts with the Greek understanding of immortality.

Following a period of Christian governance between 313 and 361, the pagan emperor Julian attempted a restoration of Roman religion before his death in 363. Julian's would be the last sustained attempt to rescue the Roman state from the advances of the Christian Church, a venture ultimately unsuccessful due to his premature death in the Persian campaign. Julian's energetic anti-Christian program is known to us through his correspondence, the work of his biographers, and a few remnants of his long treatise *Against the Galileans*, which was burned by imperial decree in the fifth century. Unlike his predecessors, Julian's tirade against the church comes from one who was probably raised a Christian, but was influenced by Greek teachers to embrace the old religion, the classical writers, and philosophical schools. Only after he became emperor did Julian reveal his agenda, which did not involve persecution but restraint of Christian teachers and infusions of money and energy into his program for reviving the temples and pagan priesthoods. Julian issued rescripts (bans) against Christian schoolmasters, personally intervened in theological disputes throughout the empire, encouraged the growth of Greek philosophy (an amateur philosopher himself), and offered, as a gesture of conciliation, to rebuild the Jewish temple in Jerusalem—an affront to the Christians who had seen its destruction as an irreversible prophetic sign. Julian's books against the Christians are less poignant and far more pedantic than those of Celsus and Porphyry, and he repeats many of their arguments. His purpose in *Against the Galileans* is to document the inferiority of Christian belief to ancient philosophy, while at the same time refuting the Christian claim that the church is the fulfillment of Hebrew prophecy. He is one of the first thinkers to insist that the real vice of Christianity is the intolerance of its believers, which he contrasts with the religious generosity of the Greeks. A consistent theme of the treatise is that Christianity is a "disease" which, left uncontrolled, would destroy the intellectual and spiritual life of the empire. On his death in 363, Julian was succeeded by the Christian emperor Jovian, who in concert with the rigorist orthodox bishop Athanasius initiated the process of restoring the prerogatives of the Christian Church throughout the empire. In an ironic twist that would not have escaped Julian, Jovian died a year later in February 364, asphyxiated by fumes from the fresh paint and plaster in the room prepared for him at Dadastana on his journey from Antioch and the East to Constantinople.

BIBLIOGRAPHY

The works of the "authors of persecution" have not survived. Reconstructions are those listed below.

Athanassiadi, P. *Pagan Monotheism in Late Antiquity.* Oxford: Oxford University Press, 1999.

Bowder, D. *The Age of Constantine and Julian.* London: Paul Elek, 1978.

Brown, P. *Power and Persuasion in Late Antiquity.* Madison: University of Wisconsin Press, 1992.

Chauvin, Pierre. *A Chronicle of the Last Pagans.* Cambridge, MA: Harvard University Press, 1990.

Croke, B., and J. Harries. *Religious Conflict in Fourth Century Rome.* Sydney: Macarthur Press, 1982.

Davies, W. D., and E. P. Sanders. "Jesus from the Jewish Point of View." In *Cambridge History of Judaism,* vol. 3. Cambridge: Cambridge University Press, 1999.

Ferguson, E. *Doctrinal Diversity: Varieties of Early Christianity.* New York: Garland, 1999.

Freeman, Charles. *The Closing of the Western Mind.* New York: Knopf, 2002.

Herrin, Judith. *The Formation of Christendom.* Oxford: Basil Blackwell, 1987.

Hoffmann, R. J. *Celsus: On True Doctrine.* New York: Oxford University Press, 1987.

———. *Julian's Against the Galileans.* Amherst, NY: Prometheus Books, 2004.

———. *Porphyry, Against the Christians: The Literary Remains.* Amherst, NY: Prometheus Books, 1996.

MacMullen, Ramsay. *Christianizing the Roman Empire.* New Haven, CT: Yale University Press, 1984.

Markus, R. *The End of Ancient Christianity.* Cambridge, MA: Cambridge University Press, 1990.

Ruether, Rosemary. *Faith and Fratricide. The Theological Roots of Antisemitism.* New York: Seabury, 1974.

Stark, Rodney. *The Rise of Christianity*. Princeton, NJ: Princeton University Press, 1996.

Taylor, Miriam. *Anti-Judaism and Early Christian Identity*. Leiden: Brill, 1995.

Wilken, R. L. *The Christians as the Romans Saw Them*. 2nd ed. New Haven, CT: Yale University Press, 2003.

R. JOSEPH HOFFMANN

CHRISTIANITY, UNBELIEF WITHIN. Unbelief—that is, the existence of doubt, of withholding belief or SKEPTICISM regarding certain religious practices and beliefs— has been present in the Christian religion since its beginnings. The early Christians were in doubt about numerous crucial issues in their religion: discipline, worship, authority, even contesting creedal statements. Moreover, the church established authoritative (canonical) scriptures that included many accounts of prophets and sages doubting and challenging long-held beliefs and practices. In the *locus classicus*, the book of Job, the hero steadfastly refuses to believe two ancient Hebraic theodicies: the Deuteronomic writers' insistence that suffering is the recompense for sin, and the claim that Job's excruciating suffering is God's test of his faith. For Job, God's purposes remain beyond understanding, transcendent and hidden "things too wonderful for me to know" (Job 42:3).

By the second century CE, Christianity was prompted to adapt its practices and the formulation of its beliefs to its new Greco-Roman Hellenistic environment (see CHRISTIANITY, RESISTANCE TO IN THE ANCIENT WORLD). Of particular importance was its engagement with Greek and Roman philosophy, in an effort both to adopt Stoic and neo-Platonic language and categories to better articulate its beliefs and emerging creedal statements (see STOICISM; PLATO), but also to challenge Hellenistic doctrines such as, for example, Manichean and Gnostic dualism and Greek and Roman academic skepticism (PYRRHONISM and the thought of CICERO) that appeared to challenge fundamental Christian beliefs. Thus began a philosophical dialogue that, with some lapses, remained vital to both parties to the present day. In this engagement we see that the question of unbelief and epistemological skepticism, and of religious belief or faith, were close to the center of both the philosophical and the theological enterprises.

While Pyrrhonism died out as a movement by 300 CE, its influence was briefly revived by Saint Augustine in his exploration of the skepticism of the Academy in his *Contra Academicos*. Augustine recognized that Pyrrhonism had to be engaged to overcome his own "despair of finding truth." Also, it could be used to undermine the dogmatic materialism (see MATERIALISM, PHILOSOPHICAL) of the Stoics and Epicurians (see EPICURUS). In his dialogue Augustine charges that while the Skeptics declare that wisdom entails the continuing withholding

of assent, they also give unqualified assent to their fundamental thesis—that wisdom entails the continuing withholding of assent—thus demonstrating that even the Skeptics are certain of some truths, as, for instance, that of two disjunctive propositions one is true and the other false. He then argues that because we human beings can doubt, we can be sure we exist, "for if you did not exist, you could not be deceived in anything." Here Augustine anticipates René DESCARTES. The bodily senses may deceive us, but we cannot deny the certain knowledge that the mind has of its own existence. But for Augustine, human understanding is not solely a matter of *intellect*. With Plotinus, he perceived the crucial relation between human knowledge and the moral life, thus the importance of the role of human sentiment and the will, or the faith factor, in all knowledge. Augustine declares that faith precedes REASON because *"nisi crediteritus, non intelligetis*: unless you believe, you will not understand." For Augustine, faith is understood as an act of intellectual assent, not simply trust.

The Augustinian view of the relation of reason and faith is crucial, for it largely dominated the debates on the subject throughout the Middle Ages. Augustine's Christian Platonism, with its confidence in reason, did prove to be a double-edged sword, since his doctrine of illumination gave such a dominant role to divine intervention. In later medieval nominalism—Duns Scotus and Occam and their followers—this resulted in skepticism regarding knowledge of God. To protect the *potentia Dei Absoluta*, the Occamists claimed that God could deceive—that is, that natural laws could be changed through divine intervention—hence the whole structure of natural knowledge was potentially shaken by this skepticism.

Early modern religious skepticism was also influenced by vestiges of Augustinianism, as well as by nominalism, but also by events that were to transform Western conceptions of the world. One event was the Renaissance recovery of the intellectual heritage of Greek and Roman literature and philosophy, including important Pyrrhonist texts; also, questions were raised regarding the Christian worldview, the result of the new discoveries of Asia and the Americas; and, finally, the skepticism engendered by the emerging scientific revolution profoundly threatened Ptolomaic cosmology and its theological worldview.

Especially significant for our subject was the rediscovery, by Christian humanists, of the texts of Sextus EMPIRICUS and Cicero which helped to cast doubts about the doctrines of medieval Catholic scholasticism. In similar fashion, the Christian humanists' investigations of textual variants in the Bible, provoked by new manuscript discoveries, ignited a theological revolution. Desiderius ERASMUS, a Catholic priest, was a central figure in this intra-Christian theological dispute. Erasmus's mind was a rather complex union of the pure classicism of Cicero and Plutarch and the moral spirit of biblical Christianity. He detested the logical hairsplitting and doctrinal disputes of the Scholastic theologians and, in *The Praise of Folly* (1509), his supreme humor, irony, and skepticism are directed at the sophistry and deceit of his Catholic Church. Ironically, while Martin Luther's reformation is considered a foundation of modern religious freedom, Erasmus abhorred Luther's own penchant for doctrinal doubt and contention as unnecessary, divisive, and destructive of the unity of the faith.

Erasmus's response to Luther, in *Diatribe concerning Free Choice* (1524), is essentially a skeptical indifference toward such theological enigmas as freedom and DETERMINISM. As he wrote, "So far am I from delighting in 'assertions' that I would readily take refuge in the opinion of the Skeptics. . . . We need only contemplate [God] himself in mystic silence." Luther, in turn, rejected Erasmus's simple moral piety, insisting that the Christian mind does, necessarily, make assertions. Yet Luther's own theological belief is, in fact, less one of intellectual assent (*assensus*) than it is *fiducia*, or the inclination of the heart and will in trust and confidence. Doctrine, for Luther, is but the attempt to express faith; it is not itself the object of faith.

The controversy between Erasmus and Luther over belief and skepticism epitomizes the broader struggle between the Protestant reformers more generally and the Catholic theologians. The issue between them was what are the proper criteria for determining the truth of theological assertions. A critical background to this dispute was the Christian humanists' rediscovery of the ancient texts of the Pyrrhonists. The Catholic apologists of the Counter-Reformation used these skeptical arguments against the Protestants, particularly against the Calvinists in France. The Protestant Reformers had insisted that the criterion of authority is the Bible alone. But, in turn, Catholic scholars pointed to the uncertainties regarding the reliability of the received text of the Bible when compared with earlier Hebrew and Greek manuscripts. Furthermore, the Protestants could not themselves agree on the interpretation of crucial biblical passages. Why should Luther's, or Calvin's, or Thomas Müntzer's interpretation be preferred to that of the wisdom of the universal church itself?

It was from these sixteenth-century *theological* disputes over belief and unbelief that the later controversies on this subject in the eighteenth-century Enlightenment (see ENLIGHTENMENT, UNBELIEF DURING THE) can be traced. This is perhaps best observed in the context of the writing of three key thinkers: Michel de Montaigne, Blaise Pascal (see PASCAL'S WAGER), and Pierre BAYLE. Montaigne ushered in *la crise Pyrrhonienne* of the seventeenth century and its aftermath. His *Apology for Raimond Sebond* (1580) became a famous Pyrrhonist text, and a key source not only of philosophical discussion but also in the Christian theological debates over skepticism and belief. Nominally the *Apology* is a defense of Raymond Sebond, a fifteenth-century Spanish defender of

Aristotelian natural theology (see ARISTOTLE), insisting that Sebond's theological arguments are as good as those of most other men. The essay is, in fact, the expression of Montaigne's own Pyrrhonian crisis of religious belief. The conclusions he draws from his profuse reiteration of skeptical arguments for a suspension of judgment are, surprisingly, the arguments of many of his contemporary religious apologists. Montaigne's conclusion is a conservative and conformist response of skepticism in the service of traditional religion. "Since I am not capable of choosing," he wrote, "I take the choice of other men and keep myself in the station in which God has placed me." This often is referred to as Catholic Pyrrhonism.

Some critics contend that Montaigne's religious conformism is a pretense that conceals his true, radically irreligious skepticism. Others argue, rather, that Montaigne's words are spoken in good faith, though they see his conformist religion as "thin soup." Pascal was one who saw Montaigne's skepticism as undermining faith, and offered his own apology for religious certitude.

Pascal, the great mathematician, scientist, and Christian apologist, grew up in a family circle of philosophers that included Marin Mersenne, Thomas HOBBES, and Descartes. He was introduced to Pyrrhonean skepticism through his deep reading of Montaigne. After a dramatic conversion experience, Pascal repudiated both the God of the philosophers—epitomized in Descartes's philosophy—and Montaigne's skepticism. But he used this Pyrrhonistic skepticism in what proved to be an influential critique of the limits of scientific and philosophic knowledge. He sought to demonstrate that scientific and philosophic truth claims are dependent on axioms which cannot, themselves, be demonstrated. Science can falsify hypotheses but not establish them.

In his uncompleted Christian apologetic—published after his death as *Pensées* (Thoughts)—Pascal offers a highly complex argument that explores the relation of skepticism, probabilism, faith, and certitude. His conclusion is often referred to as an exemplification of *fideism*, the view that religion is based on faith alone. Although passages in the *Pensées* can support this view, Pascal's understanding of the relation of faith and reason is rather more subtle. He first seeks to refute both the dogmatism of a Descartes and the skepticism of a Montaigne, and then seeks an alternative way that defends Christian faith without appeals to philosophy (*intellectus*) *alone*. He does this by showing how experience and knowledge can assist in facilitating belief.

First Pascal begins with lengthy demonstrations of the Pyrrhonist proof regarding the uncertainty of our reasoning and the fact that truth is unattainable. What then? Pascal proceeds to show that a full Pyrrhonism has never existed and can never exist. Sounding like the later David HUME, he suggests that "Nature backs up helpless reason and stops it going so wildly astray." Furthermore, to remain in a state of radical doubt, the Pyrrhonist's quietude risks a moral enervation. Since man is a self-transcendent creature, he is both an "imbecile worm . . . a sink of uncertainty and error," and a "prodigy," a "depository of all truth." This dual nature of human life—a strong Augustinian theme—is crucial to Pascal's argument. For the human heart, he insists, does not remain in a state of peaceful suspension of judgment. In man's search, he "strains to know what the true good is in order to pursue it."

This striving—natural to the human person—brings Pascal to his wager argument, an issue of considerable dispute. Reason's incapacity to either prove or to disprove the existence of God places a person in a position similar to one in a game of chance or the toss of a coin. Pascal argues that it is not irrational to bet on God's existence, since the odds are even, and "your reason is no more affronted by choosing one rather than the other." In Pascal's view, if one wagers that God does not exist, one gains little at best if one wins, but if one loses, one loses everything. These assumptions would not appear to be as self-evident to a modern unbeliever or agnostic facing the question of an afterlife.

But Pascal insists that, in such a circumstance wanting in proof, the wise and prudent man wagers that God exists, the reason being that the afterlife is, arguably, *not* the crux for Pascal: "Now what harm will come to you from choosing this course. . . . I tell you that you will gain even in this life, and that every step you take along this road . . . that in the end you will realize that you have wagered on something certain." Custom, sentiment (feelings), and reason are related here. "Our minds [*esprit*] and feelings [*sentiments*] are trained by the company we keep." For Pascal, all our reasoning comes down to surrendering to feeling (*sentiment*) by which he means the personal perception of first principles. How, then, does one distinguish sentiment from personal fancy? "Reason is available," he replies, "but can be bent in any direction. And so there is no [incorrigible] rule." Hence, "the will is *one* of the chief organs of belief, not because it *creates* belief, but because things are true or false according to the aspect by which we judge them." Faith, in this sense, is, for Pascal, not irrational, for it has justifying conditions. This is not proof, of course, for a demonstrable or justified knowledge is, itself, founded on a set of beliefs. As we will see, Pascal's views have some resonance with modern antifoundationalism.

In his *Historical and Critical Dictionary* (1697–1702), the Frenchman Pierre Bayle brought Pyrrhonian skepticism to its modern apex with his critique of all claims to knowledge in metaphysics, theology, and science. It is contested whether Bayle's skepticism ends in a radical fideism. But he clearly holds the belief that Christian claims cannot be known to be true by intellectual demonstration, but must be accepted by faith. Yet Bayle was not *simply* a skeptic; he was also a Christian philosopher deeply influenced by the reformer John Calvin and by his own travails as a minority Protestant Huguenot refugee who fled from persecution in his own

Catholic France. Later in life he rejected dogmatism of every stripe—but remained a heterodox Christian, endowed with a radical sense of God's absolute transcendence. This religious radicalism is the source of his attack on all idolatry, whether theological, clerical, or political—and is the root of his influential defense of toleration. In his own searchings, Bayle rarely found that the whole truth is on one side. Naturally, he was attacked by Christian rationalists on the Left and Christian dogmatists on the Right. But his ruling passion was that of a theologian, as can be seen in his radical monotheistic skepticism about finite claims; in his belief that the rule of judgment lies in the conscience, not the intellect; and in his final recourse to divine revelation.

Bayle's thoroughgoing skepticism had two significant legacies. The eighteenth-century philosophes, especially VOLTAIRE, drew upon Bayle's striking criticisms of the church, the Bible, and theodicy (see EVIL, PROBLEM OF) to discredit Christianity itself, which was not Bayle's aim. In the nineteenth and twentieth centuries, further emboldened by Immanuel KANT's *Critique of Pure Reason* (1781) some Germanic philosophers and theologians were to follow Bayle in his radical metaphysical skepticism and in his emphasis on conscience and the rule of moral judgment.

The influence of Kant's philosophy on Christian (particularly Protestant) theology in the modern era has been profound. Put succinctly, in the preface to his *Critique of Pure Reason*, Kant "found it necessary to deny [empirical] knowledge in order to make room for [moral] faith." Kant, importantly, contrasted faith with empirical knowledge, not faith with reason. However, the first *Critique* had a decisive influence on the origins of modern religious AGNOSTICISM, subjectivism, and PRAGMATISM. Also, taking their lead from Kant's *Critique of Practical Reason* (1788) in the nineteenth century, a number of neo-Kantian Protestant theologians opposed metaphysics and sought to free Christianity from both scientific and metaphysical knowledge and justification, as well as from confessional orthodoxy, and to ground Christianity in a faith-based moral freedom. In this it was a harbinger of twentieth-century Christian EXISTENTIALISM.

Between the 1780s and 1850s there also emerged a protest against the Enlightenment's trust in autonomous reason and its optimistic anthropology. This Counter-Enlightenment included thinkers such as J. G. Hamann and Søren Kierkegaard. Hamann, a friend and critic of Kant, had a considerable influence on Kierkegaard. Many of the latter's themes are found in Hamann in an embryonic form. Hamann perceived Christianity as profoundly opposed to Enlightenment RATIONALISM, and he called upon the skepticism of Socrates to oppose the philosophes' optimistic certainties—what he called their "philosophical idolatry." Hume played a large role in Hamann's appeal to "natural belief." In his *Socratic Memorabilia* (1759) he wrote: "Our own being and the existence of all things outside us must be believed and cannot be established in any other way." This opens the way to an active faith.

Faith, for Hamann, does not appear to be a "blind" faith, since experience and faith are dialectically related. One needs the other, since God cannot be known by discursive reason alone. For Hamann, God is perceived through our senses: in nature, in history, and in scripture. These senuous signs and images are particulars that deeply resonate in our experience. Hamann does, however, embrace a form of fideism, for while truth "must be dug out of the ground," only those illuminated by grace appear to have "the eyes to see and ears to hear." Hamann's eagerness to confound the rationalists with his skepticism may well have only darkened God's revelatory signs for others.

During the nineteenth century the encounter between Christianity and unbelief takes on a special significance, since much radical unbelief came from within Christianity itself in efforts to "demystify" the faith. David Friedrich STRAUSS, Ludwig FEUERBACH, and Friedrich NIETZSCHE—to note only a few—were either the sons of Lutheran pastors or began their careers as theological students. While their "hermeneutics of suspicion" was, for many, compelling, a number of modern Christian thinkers also recognized in their bold critiques a necessary corrective, a cleansing of a sterile orthodoxy or denunciation of the accommodation of Christianity to a bourgeois culture.

The Danish philosopher Søren Kierkegaard sought to disengage Christianity from its dependence on modern rationalism—in the forms of a Kantian and Hegelian attempt both cancel out and yet preserve Christian faith at a higher level. What Kierkegaard called his "project of thought" regarding reason and faith is undertaken in two of his pseudonymous philosophical works, the *Philosophical Fragments* (1844) and the *Concluding Unscientific Postscript* (1846).

The earlier work concludes that eternal happiness cannot be based on historical knowledge alone, for history is the realm of the relative and the probable. Hence, from the historical point of view, the Christian claim that the Eternal entered time is absurd. This "Christian paradox" can only be appropriated by faith, for religious truth is not acquired in the same way one obtains information; rather, only in "that infinite, personal, impassioned interestedness which is the condition of faith"— the central theme of the *Postscript*. Kierkegaard insists that Christian faith entails a double or absolute paradox, in that the learner is not only *given* the truth by the teacher but also the *capacity* to apprehend it.

Critics contend that Kierkegaard's "leap of faith" to the religious stage involves a renunciation of any intelligible choice; other scholars deny that he is an irrationalist. They contend that for Kierkegaard—as later for the Catholic theologian John Henry Newman—coming to faith or belief is analogous to a radical reenvisionment of the world, or to a moral transformation. These involve a convergence of factors which, together, reach a "critical threshold," one that results in a qualitative change in perspective. Such a process is experienced as both compelled and yet a free act.

In nineteenth-century Britain theological skepticism and unbelief proceeded from the rather tardy discovery of Kant's critical philosophy. A crucial source was the Scottish philosopher William Hamilton's *On the Philosophy of the Unconditioned* (1852). According to Hamilton's reading of Kant, the mind can only know the "conditionally limited," not the Infinite or Absolute, which "can be conceived by thinking away from, or an abstraction of, those very conditions under which thought is realized." "A God understood," he declared, "would be no God at all; to think that God is, as we can think him to be, is blasphemy." The idea of the Unconditioned or Infinite is, then, only negative. Hamilton's "learned ignorance" reintroduced into theology the idea of the *via negativa*, and what became popularly known in Britain as the Agnostic Controversy.

H. L. Mansel, professor of philosophy at Oxford and afterward dean of Saint Paul's in London, applied Hamilton's doctrine to the problems of a Christian knowledge of God in his *The Limits of Religious Thought* (1859). For Mansel, such a Christian philosophy "checks the pride of reason," reminding us "that there are truths which we cannot see." Mansel argued that our conceptions of God, for example, in the Bible, may be *speculatively* false and yet *regulatively* true, and that "regulative truth is our human guide to practice." Herbert SPENCER's *First Principles* (1862) carried further Hamilton's and Mansel's doctrine with his own concept of the Unknowable. Spencer's massive twelve-volume *Principles* became the "Bible of Agnosticism," and his incredible popularity attracted a group of clergy who adopted the name "Christian Agnostics." They praised Spencer for purifying the concept of God by removing all kinds of anthropomorphic encumbrances.

It was not only the liberal and heterodox Christian clerics and laity who spoke of the value of this agnostic temper of mind. The Jesuit theologian George Tyrrell was severe in his critique of theology's rash overconfidence. He urged that theology "be judged by a moral rather than an intellectual criterion." And the influential Roman Catholic writer Friedrich von Hügel confessed that we are all "such Agnostics in our better moments," since this quality of mind is "but a sense of mystery, the consciousness of how much greater is the world of reality . . . than is, can be, our clear, definable analysis and theory of it." What now was urged by noted philosophers, such as James Ward, Henry Sidgwick, and William James, was the moral right to "stake belief" on a live hypothesis and to test that belief in experience.

In the twentieth century a variety of philosophical critiques of religious belief prompted responses from Christian thinkers. In the first half of the century Existentialism attacked the then-influential scientific and philosophical POSITIVISM, associated, for example, with the Vienna Circle (see SCHLICK, MORITZ, AND THE VIENNA CIRCLE). Christian existentialist themes are prominent in the writings of the young Karl Barth, Paul Tillich, and Nikolai Berdyaev. Critical to these and other Christian writers of the time were Pascal, Kierkegaard, Nietzsche, and Dostoyevsky, all of whom were concerned with the depersonalization of the individual, human alienation, and inauthenticity. These writers emphasized human finitude and doubt and insisted that this element of human uncertainty cannot be removed, yet it demands the risk of courageous action. Tillich famously asserted that such an existential act of faith is the religious state of being "ultimately concerned," and that "doubt is a necessary element in it."

By 1950 the British school of linguistic analysis was philosophically dominant, and posed both new challenges to Christian faith and called forth new defenses of religious belief. There were numerous efforts to "demythologize" the antique language and worldview of the Bible. One response of Christian philosophers was to reject the older theological realism as not essential to Christianity's basic message, which is the moral resolution to live an "agapistic" way of life. This did not require foregoing certain traditional Christian spiritual practices, since they enhance this form of life. Other Christian thinkers, influenced by the later writings of the philosopher Ludwig WITTGENSTEIN, argue that the realist, or older supernatural, account of Christian faith is not the authentic account of that faith. An example is D. Z. Phillips, who cites certain New Testament texts describing belief in eternal life: "The immorality of the soul . . . refers to a person's relation to the self-effacement and love of others in dying to the self." This dying and life in Christ is itself the overcoming of the threat of death.

The challenge of analytical philosophy was also met by theological realists. One example is the work of the American philosopher Alvin Plantinga, whose aim is a critique of the assumptions of foundationalism. That is the doctrine that contends that for a belief to be rational, it must either be basic or be justified by other basic beliefs, such as self-evident propositions and incorrigible propositions that are recognized to be true by merely understanding them. While these may claim to be self-evident, Plantinga argues that such commitments are not capable of being proven incorrigible. Nor is the foundationalist justified in holding that other beliefs are not properly basic. Plantinga proceeds to argue that belief in God, that is to say biblical monotheism, is a proper basic belief: that is, it can offer reasonable warrants without basing the belief on other self-evident beliefs.

What is instructive about these recent and centuries-old dialogues over belief and unbelief is that they have not been simply intramural but, rather, have engaged secular thought from Greek skepticism to present currents in philosophy. And this, in large measure, is due to the fact that Christianity is itself a developing and multifarious historical phenomenon that resists efforts to define too simply what constitutes its essential features.

BIBLIOGRAPHY

Lightman, Bernard. *The Origins of Agnosticism: Victorian Unbelief and the Limits of Knowledge.* Baltimore and London: Johns Hopkins University Press, 1987.

Livingston, James C. *Modern Christian Thought: The Enlightenment and the Nineteenth Century*, vol. 1; *Modern Christian Thought: The Twentieth Century*, vol. 2. Upper Saddle River, NJ: Prentice Hall, 1997, 2000.

Penelhum, Terence. *God and Skepticism: A Study in Skepticism and Fideism.* Dordrecht: D. Reidel, 1983.

Popkin, Richard. *The History of Scepticism: From Savonarola to Bayle.* Oxford: Oxford University Press, 2003.

JAMES C. LIVINGSTON

CHUBB, THOMAS (1679–1747), influential English deist and rationalist. Thomas Chubb was born on September 29, 1679, in East Harnham, Wiltshire, England, the son of a humble tradesman. He worked as a glover until his eyesight became too poor, when he became a candle maker. Like many tradesmen who worked with their hands, Chubb's mind was free to ponder the questions of the day, and he devoted his life to the question of religion.

Chubb was not an original thinker, but his incisive mind and clear writing helped make deist thinking (see DEISM) accessible to others like him. He represented the rationalist wing of English Enlightenment thought (see RATIONALISM). Chubb believed that knowledge of God and Creation was open to all open-minded scholars, and that the consistent study of origins would help reveal deep truths. His first book, *The Supremacy of the Father Asserted* (1715), was a criticism of the Trinity. This endeared Chubb to the Unitarians (see UNITARIANISM TO 1961), and for several years he lived in London and associated with them. He eventually returned to Wiltshire, where he resumed work as a candle maker. He also wrote *The Previous Question with Regard to Religion* (1725), which won praise from VOLTAIRE, and *A Discourse concerning Reason* (1733), which argued that REASON is the only guide one should need in religious matters. Any religious urging not based in reason, Chubb argued, is bound to lead to superstition or fanaticism. In *The True Gospel of Jesus Christ Asserted* and *A Short Dissertation on Providence* (both 1738), Chubb reiterated the deist arguments against a personal, interventionist God. The testimony of revelation, upon which claims of intervention rely, cannot reasonably be expected to convince people not already part of that faith tradition, Chubb argued. And in *A Discourse on Miracles* (1741) Chubb anticipated the better-known arguments of Conyers MIDDLETON and David HUME. And Chubb also argued strongly that people are perfectly able to lead moral, responsible lives without the support of supposedly divine revelation.

Chubb escaped the persecution suffered by some of his contemporaries, Thomas WOOLSTON in particular. Instead, his orthodox opponents resorted mainly to ridicule to diminish his reputation. Because he was entirely self-taught, his works had some relatively minor weaknesses, which his enemies latched on to. But among the large number of skilled artisans among whom Chubb lived his life, his works were influential. Thomas Chubb died on February 8, 1747, in Salisbury, Wiltshire.

BIBLIOGRAPHY

Redwood, John. *Reason, Ridicule and Religion: The Age of Enlightenment in England 1660–1750*. London: Thames and Hudson, 1996.
Stephen, Leslie. *History of English Thought in the Eighteenth Century*. 2 vols. 1876. Reprint, New York: Harcourt Brace, 1962.

BILL COOKE

CHURCH, STATE, AND RELIGIOUS FREEDOM. Many religious believers and nonbelievers alike agree that separation of church and state—the idea that the government should not fund, promote, or advocate religion—is the only mechanism through which governments can maintain complete religious and philosophical freedom for diverse groups of citizens.

The separation of church and state in the United States came about thanks to the pioneering vision of a small band of Enlightenment thinkers, religious skeptics, and dissenting clergy. It was a radical idea when it was first proposed in colonial America and is not universally appreciated even today.

For centuries, the prevailing belief in the Western world was that neither church nor state could survive without mutual support. This idea was reinforced after pagan Rome became an officially Christian empire. It survived through the Byzantine era and into the Middle Ages, a period of state-established churches and often widespread religious persecution.

Even in the Middle Ages, when the all-consuming power of the Roman Catholic Church dominated religious life, some critics challenged conventional wisdom and asserted that government had no right to control religious affairs or vice versa. It wasn't until after the Protestant Reformation that the idea began to take hold—and even then, many advocates simply wanted Catholicism disestablished in favor of some other sect.

The experience of the American colonies led some forward thinkers to reassess the wisdom of merging religion and government. In Massachusetts, Puritans established a harsh theocracy that brooked no dissent over religious matters. Roger WILLIAMS, a Puritan preacher, challenged that view. Williams's views were deemed heretical, and he was forced to flee the region. He purchased land from the natives and founded his own settlement, Providence.

Williams was especially troubled by the persecution spawned by unions of church and state. Forced religious worship, he once wrote, "stinks in God's nostrils." In his book *The Bloudy Tenet of Persecution for Cause of Conscience*, Williams railed against state-sponsored religious persecution. Wrote Williams, "I must profess, while Heaven and Earth lasts, that no one Tenet that either London, England, or the World doth harbor, is so heretical, blasphemous, seditious, and dangerous to the corporal, to the spiritual, to the present, to the Eternal Good of Man, as the bloudy Tenet . . . of persecution for the cause of Conscience."

In *The Bloudy Tenet*, Williams spoke of the dangers of opening a "gap in the hedge, or wall of separation, between the garden of the church and the wilderness of the world." The use of the phrase is interesting, as it is very close to Thomas Jefferson's metaphor of a "wall of separation between church and state." However, there is no evidence that Jefferson knew of Williams's writings.

Williams's Rhode Island colony respected complete religious freedom. Even members of sects that Williams personally disliked, such as Quakers, found a haven there. But as other colonies were settled, different types of church-state arrangements emerged.

Generally speaking, northeastern colonies were the most repressive. The Puritan Church was established by law, and everyone had to pay taxes to support it—whether they were members of the church or not.

Middle colonies such as Pennsylvania and Maryland were a little more tolerant on religious liberty matters. William Penn allowed anyone who believed in one God to settle in Pennsylvania, although Sunday religious observances were mandated by law. Maryland was founded as a haven for Catholics. The colony's Toleration Act of 1649 extended religious freedom to all Christians. The concept of toleration at this time was not generally understood to include non-Christians or nonbelievers.

Southern colonies tended to be more repressive. Many of them officially established Anglicanism as the state faith and imposed church taxes on all citizens.

Virginia maintained strict laws concerning religious beliefs and worship. Failure to attend church was a crime. Parents who did not baptize their children could be imprisoned, and denying the existence of the Trinity was punishable by a three-year prison term.

Despite these harsh laws, it was the issue of church taxes that outraged many Virginians. Their protest over mandatory financial support for religion was to have national implications and help shape the separation of church and state and bring true religious freedom to the new nation.

The Virginia Protest. By the mid-1700s, Anglicanism was a minority faith in Virginia—yet all residents had to pay for its upkeep. Farmers were required to make in-kind contributions, in some cases being forced to donate crops and farm animals to the local Anglican minister.

In the 1760s, authorities cracked down on efforts by dissenting clergy to spread their views, going so far as to imprison some Baptists. In 1774 James MADISON noted that several Baptist clergy had been placed in jail for preaching on the streets. He was incensed, and, with great passion, wrote to a friend in Philadelphia about the incident. "That diabolical, hell-conceived principle of persecution rages among some and to their eternal infamy, the clergy can furnish their quota of imps for such business," wrote Madison. "This vexes me the worst of anything whatever."

During the Revolution, Madison worked to help shape Virginia's new government. Appointed to a Committee on Religion, he joined forces with Thomas JEFFERSON on a proposal to disestablish the Anglican Church in Virginia. The move turned out to be premature and garnered little support, but Madison and Jefferson had laid the groundwork for a battle they would eventually win.

After the Revolution, in 1784, Madison, then a member of the House of Delegates, led the opposition to a bill by Patrick Henry that would have imposed a tax on all Virginians to pay for "teachers of the Christian religion."

Henry's bill would have required all state residents to pay "a moderate tax or contribution annually for the support of the Christian religion, or of some Christian church, denomination or communion of Christians, or for some form of Christian worship."

In some respects, Henry's measure was less offensive than forced taxation for a state-established church. Under the Henry model, Virginia residents would have at least had the right to choose among competing Christian denominations.

But that made little difference to Madison. He was able to see that state-supported religion was wrong whether one church was favored or fifteen were. Madison called the Henry proposal "obnoxious" and began working with Baptist and other religious leaders to seal its fate.

To defeat the Henry bill, Madison penned one of the greatest statements of religious liberty ever crafted. The "Memorial and Remonstrance against Religious Assessments" is a list of fifteen reasons why no one should be forced to pay taxes to support religion. In language that still vibrates with relevance today, Madison demolished the assumption that religion needs the prop of the state to survive.

Copies of the "Memorial and Remonstrance" circulated throughout Virginia. When the general assembly reconvened in the fall of 1785, lawmakers were confronted with stacks of petitions against the Henry measure signed by Virginians throughout the state.

Henry himself had been elected governor, making it impossible for him to speak on behalf of the measure from the floor. The proposal was soundly defeated.

But Madison did not stop there. Seizing on the momentum generated by the defeat of the Henry bill, he pushed for passage of Jefferson's 1779 Bill for Establishing Religious Freedom. The measure stated bluntly, "[N]o man shall be compelled to frequent or support any religious worship, place or ministry whatsoever."

The bill also took a strong stand against church taxes, calling it "sinful and tyrannical to compel a man to furnish contributions for the propagation of opinions which he disbelieves and abhors."

Thanks in a large part to Madison's lobbying, the Virginia Assembly passed the bill by a vote of 60–27 in January 1786. Jefferson, who was in Paris at the time, rejoiced. He was especially pleased that efforts to confine the bill's scope to Christians only were defeated. This was proper, Jefferson later wrote, as he intended the bill to protect "the Jew and the Gentile, the Christian and Mahometan, the Hindoo, the infidel of every denomination."

Development of the First Amendment. The Virginia experience had a profound impact on the development of the First Amendment in 1789. Madison, chief author of the Constitution, played a key role in the development of the Bill of Rights.

The Constitution as originally written is mostly silent on religion—with one notable exception: Article VI bans "religious tests" for public office. This is significant because it says a lot about the mind-set of the framers. In colonial America, religious qualifications for public office were common. Those aspiring to hold public office, for example, usually had to be Trinitarian Protestants or state that they believed in a future state of rewards and punishments (i.e., heaven and hell). Thus, high office was limited not only to Christians but to certain types of Christians. That the US Constitution banned such religious qualifications for federal office marked an important step forward.

The Constitution is also notable for what it does *not* say about religion. Except for the pro forma usage of "in the year of our Lord" in the date, there is no mention of God, Jesus Christ, or Christianity in the body of the document. This omission was deliberate, and it did not sit well with some. During the Constitutional Convention, a minority faction argued in favor of recognizing Christianity in the document. Their views failed to carry the day.

After much debate, discussion, and revision, the First Amendment emerged in a form that encapsulates the separation of church and state in two ways: The religion clauses read, "Congress shall make no law respecting an establishment of religion, or prohibiting the free exercise thereof."

The first part of the provision is often called the Establishment Clause because it bars government from "establishing" a religion. By *establishment* the framers meant more than merely setting up an official church. Drafts of the First Amendment that would have done only that were considered and rejected as too weak. To the framers, laws funding, promoting, or furthering religion were "establishing" it.

The second half, which bars laws prohibiting the free exercise of religion, is often called the Free Exercise Clause. The wording here is broad, and the phrase has been interpreted to mean that government may not unduly interfere with the religious freedom rights of the people.

The religion clauses are only sixteen words long. Given their brevity, a certain amount of interpretation would be necessary over the years. In recent times, this has been the job of the Supreme Court.

What about the phrase "separation of church and state"? Where does it come from? What does it mean?

Jefferson's Famous Letter. Both Jefferson and Madison used the term "separation" to describe the proper relationship between church and state. Madison spoke of how the "total separation of the church from the state" had increased interest in religion in Virginia. He also observed that separation between religion and government is "strongly guarded" in the Bill of Rights.

But it was Jefferson's famous January 1, 1802, letter to the Danbury, Connecticut, Baptists that gave the metaphor of a wall of separation between church and state great currency.

Jefferson was not an orthodox Christian, but his advocacy of complete religious freedom was well known and admired by many Americans—especially those who had to live under state-sponsored religions. At the time the Bill of Rights was adopted, its provisions applied only to Congress. States were thus free to maintain established churches, and many did so.

Connecticut had established the old Puritan Church, Congregationalism. Although laws in Connecticut supposedly made it possible for dissenters to opt out of the church tax scheme, in reality this provision was ignored or interpreted in such a way that opt-outs were rarely granted. In other cases, the mechanism to get an opt-out—one had to appear before a government official and publicly declare his religion—was deemed offensive by dissenters.

Baptist leaders in Danbury wrote to Jefferson to express their dissatisfaction with this system. Though religiously conservative, the Baptists knew of Jefferson's support for religious liberty and hoped that his election as president in 1800 would free them from the oppressive Connecticut system.

The Baptists wrote to express their hope that Jefferson's view on religious freedom "like the radiant beams of the Sun, will shine and prevail through all these States and all the world till Hierarchy and Tyranny be destroyed from the Earth."

In his reply, Jefferson thanked the Baptists for their warm thoughts and went on to assert, "Believing with you that religion is a matter which lies solely between man and God, that he owes account to none other for his faith or his worship, that the legitimate powers of government reach actions only, and not opinions, I contemplate with sovereign reverence that act of the whole American people which declared that their legislature should 'make no law respecting an establishment of religion, or prohibiting the free exercise thereof,' thus building a wall of separation between Church & State."

As president Jefferson put his separationist philosophy into action. He even refused to issue proclamations calling for days of fasting and prayer. Madison, who followed Jefferson into the White House, was even firmer on maintaining the church-state wall. He vetoed bills giving surplus federal land to a church and granting a congressional incorporation to a church in Washington, DC, that would have charged it with the task of caring of the indigent.

Madison proclaimed days of prayer and fasting under pressure from Congress during the War of 1812, but later in his life wrote that he regretted having done so and even concluded that his actions had violated the First Amendment. Madison also opposed taxpayer-funded chaplains in Congress and in the military, and once blocked a proposed census that planned to classify Americans by occupation, asserting that questioning clergy would violate the First Amendment.

Because the Bill of Rights was originally limited to Congress, church-state cases were rare in the federal courts for many years. That changed after the Civil War, when Congress passed the Fourteenth Amendment. Among other things, this amendment was designed to impose portions of the Bill of Rights on the states, a process called incorporation.

Although the language of the Fourteenth Amendment is clear, extremely conservative Supreme Courts in the late nineteenth century refused to interpret the amendment in a manner that recognized incorporation. By 1920 the high court finally began adopting the incorporation doctrine with regard to free speech and press. In 1940 the Court more fully embraced incorporation in the landmark church-state case *Cantwell v. Connecticut*.

The Supreme Court's acceptance of incorporation led to a flood of cases in the federal courts. Many of these reached the Supreme Court, leading to a line of church-state cases that have shaped the law we know today.

Key Church-State Cases. Cases dealing with the Establishment Clause fall into several broad areas: religion in public education, taxpayer funding of religion, and government endorsement of religion. Leading church-state cases in Establishment Clause jurisprudence include:

- *Cochran v. Louisiana State Board of Education* (1930): Upheld a state textbook loan program that included religious schools.
- *Everson v. Board of Education* (1947): Upheld state law providing free bus transportation to private religious school students.

- *McCollum v. Board of Education* (1948): Banned voluntary religious instruction run by outside groups on public school grounds (see MCCOLLUM, VASHTI).
- *Zorach v. Clauson* (1952): Approved voluntary religious instruction off site during the public school day, a plan called "released time."
- *McGowan v. Maryland* (1961): Ruled constitutional state laws curbing commercial activity on Sundays, also known as blue laws.
- *Engel v. Vitale* (1962): Struck down mandatory school-sponsored prayer in public schools.
- *Abington Township School District v. Schempp* (1963): Banned mandatory school-sponsored Bible reading in public schools.
- *Epperson v. Arkansas* (1968): Struck down an Arkansas state law that banned the teaching of evolution in public schools.
- *Lemon v. Kurtzman* (1971): Struck down state laws that offered tax funding to pay for salaries at religious schools.
- *Torcaso v. Watkins* (1971): Struck down state provisions barring nonbelievers from holding public office.
- *Walz v. Tax Commission of the City of New York* (1971): Declared that laws giving tax exemption to religious groups are not a violation of church-state separation and that such exemptions are a right granted by statute, not the Constitution.
- *Mueller v. Allen* (1983): Upheld a Minnesota law giving tuition tax deductions for parochial- and private-school parents.
- *Marsh v. Chambers* (1983): Upheld use of taxpayer-funded legislative chaplains.
- *Lynch v. Donnelly* (1984): Upheld inclusion of religious symbols in a government display that also included secular symbols.
- *Wallace v. Jaffree* (1984): Declared state laws mandating "moments of silence" for prayer in public schools unconstitutional.
- *Edwards v. Aguillard* (1987): Struck down state laws requiring balanced treatment between evolution and creationism.
- *County of Allegheny v. ACLU* (1988): Struck down government display of religious symbols standing alone.
- *Board of Education of Westside Community Schools v. Mergens* (1990): Upheld voluntary "equal access" religious clubs run by students at public high schools.
- *Lee v. Weisman* (1992): Struck down public school-sponsored graduation prayer.
- *Santa Fe Independent School District v. Doe* (2000): Struck down school-sponsored prayers before public school sporting events.
- *Zelman v. Simmons-Harris* (2002): Upheld an Ohio law giving vouchers to private religious school students.

- *Locke v. Davey* (2004): Upheld a state constitutional provision barring tuition assistance to students studying to become pastors.

Leading Free Exercise Clause cases include:

- *Watson v. Jones* (1872): Held that secular courts have no right to meddle in internal church affairs to resolve conflicts.
- *Reynolds v. United States* (1879): Permitted states to ban polygamy, holding that its practice has always been illegal in Western societies.
- *Cantwell v. Connecticut* (1940): Struck down a state law requiring religious groups to gain permission from local authorities before proselytizing in public.
- *West Virginia State Board of Education v. Barnette* (1943): Struck down a state law allowing public schools to expel children for refusing to recite the Pledge of Allegiance.
- *United States v. Ballard* (1944): Stated that in cases of fraud allegations against religious groups, the only standard that may be applied is whether actual illegal forms of fraud occurred, not the content of the religious beliefs in question.
- *Prince v. Massachusetts* (1944): Held that state laws curbing child labor could be applied to religious groups that required children to distribute literature door to door.
- *Wisconsin v. Yoder* (1972): Upheld a state law permitting members of the Amish to withdraw their children from schools after the eighth grade.
- *Employment Division v. Smith* (1990): Held that the state is not required to show "compelling state interest" when passing laws that might infringe on religious liberty, only that such laws must be neutral and generally applicable and not intended to single out religion.
- *Church of the Lukumi Babalu Aye v. City of Hialeah* (1993): Struck down a Florida community's ordinance banning animal sacrifice, holding it was aimed at religion.

Current Threats to US Church-State Separation. Today church-state separation in the United States stands at a crossroads. In the 1980s President Ronald W. Reagan made a number of appointments to the US Supreme Court and lower federal courts who held views less favorable or even hostile to church-state separation. These appointments led to a reversal at the high court on the question of taxpayer funding of religion. The Court is moving close to adopting the view that government aid to religion is acceptable as long as it is offered in an evenhanded manner.

The 1980s also saw the rise of the Religious Right as a political force. Led by fundamentalist ministers like Jerry Falwell, Pat Robertson, and D. James Kennedy, the Religious Right is openly hostile to church-state separation. Its leaders often proclaim that separation of church and state is not in the US Constitution and insist that the country was founded to be a "Christian nation."

The Religious Right holds great power within the Republican Party in the United States. Some of its goals include banning all abortions, rolling back gay rights, restoring mandatory Christian worship to public schools, watering down or banning the teaching of evolution in public schools, censoring material in public libraries, curbing erotically tinged forms of entertainment, and erecting religious displays such as Ten Commandments markers and crosses in courthouses and other government buildings. As much as possible, the Religious Right would like the US government to embrace its theocratic vision and lower the church-state wall to the point where the First Amendment's religion clauses would be interpreted as banning only the creation of an official, state-run church.

Shortly after taking office in 2001, President George W. Bush unveiled a faith-based initiative that would funnel money to houses of worship to pay for various social service programs such as drug and alcohol addiction treatment, job training, soup kitchens, and homeless shelters.

Bush and his advisers have insisted that religious groups should be able to accept taxpayer funding and still include religious content in their programs and restrict hiring on religious grounds—even if those positions are paid for with public funds.

Many advocates of church-state separation believe the faith-based initiative is a form of church tax and note with irony that more than two hundred years after Madison wrote the "Memorial and Remonstrance against Religious Assessments," the nation seems prepared to debate the issue anew.

BIBLIOGRAPHY

Alley, Robert S. *James Madison on Religious Liberty*. Amherst, NY: Prometheus Books, 1985.

Cousins, Norman. *"In God We Trust": The Religious Beliefs and Ideas of the American Founding Fathers*. New York: Harper & Brothers, 1958.

Kramnick, Isaac, and R. Laurence Moore. *The Godless Constitution: The Case against Religious Correctness*. New York: Norton, 1996.

Miller, Robert T., and Ronald B. Flowers. *Toward Benevolent Neutrality: Church, State and the Supreme Court*. Waco, TX: Baylor University Press, 1992.

Pfeffer, Leo. *Church, State and Freedom*. Boston: Beacon, 1953.

ROBERT BOSTON

CICERO, MARCUS TULLIUS (106–43 BCE), Roman philosopher. Cicero was one of the great humanists of history (see HUMANISM). VOLTAIRE said that Cicero

"taught us to think." Pliny wrote that Julius Caesar, Cicero's adversary for much of his life, said that it was better to have pushed back the frontiers of the mind as Cicero did than to have pushed back the frontiers of the empire as he, Caesar, did. Cicero ranks as one of the great orators of history, and his correspondence and writings are keys to understanding the political, social, literary, and economic life of late Republican Rome.

Well educated in Rome and in Greece, Cicero was a dominant figure in Roman courts and politics. He was deeply involved in the conspiracies and struggles of the late Roman Republic; for a time he was exiled from Rome. During the civil war that led to the collapse of the Roman Republic, he was involved both for and against Julius Ceasar, Gnaeus Pompey, Marcus Crassus, Mark Antony, and Octavian (later known as Augustus) in his efforts to save the republic, an effort in which he was unsuccessful. He was executed by Octavian in Rome in December 43 BCE.

Cicero was a prolific writer, though much of his writing has been lost. Approximately nine hundred of his letters survive, fifty-eight of his *Orationes* (some incomplete), several of his rhetorical works, some of his poetry, and several of his dialogues on philosophy. He molded the Latin language and deeply influenced the Papal Chancery, for which Latin would remain a living language to the present day. So great was Cicero's influence on Latin that in the first part of the sixteenth century, ERASMUS felt a need to challenge some of his terms and substitute more up-to-date terms rather than to continue the use of pagan constructions.

In his younger days, Cicero studied under a variey of teachers, mainly in Greece: the Epicurean Phaedrus (see EPICURUS), the Stoic Diodatus (see STOICISM), and the Academic (follower of PLATO) Philo of Larissa, who held that certainity was unobtainable and that probability was the only guide. Cicero rejected the Epicurean viewpoint but was greatly influenced by the other two. He did not study with the Peripatetics (followers of ARISTOTLE), but he was influenced by them. He called himself an Academic since he preferred to be guided by probability rather than to allege certainty. In ethics, however, he was somewhat of a dogmatist because he tended to accept some presumptuous statements without a sufficient rational background, although even here he operated on Stoic principles where virtue alone is the only good. Still he tempered this with a Socratic ideal that the key was knowledge. In religion he was an agnostic through most of his life, although he apparently underwent a religious experience in connection with the death of his daughter. He wrote on such things as pleasure, virtue, death, evil, and similar topics, and much research has been devoted to finding his sources. He relied on the four schools of philosophy for his guide. He used the dialogue form but his model was more Aristotelian than Socratic. He usually started by stating an Epicurean view of a topic followed by a Stoic view, both of which were expounded and criticized.

He then concluded with views held in common by the Academics (Platonists) and the Peripatetics (Aristotelians).

Cicero is extremely important in the history of philosophy for his transmission of Greek ideas and thinking. In a sense he can be labeled a humanist no matter how one defines humanism. He is still worth reading for his own thinking which has had tremendous influence on Western thought.

BIBLIOGRAPHY

Hunt, H. A. K. *The Humanism of Cicero*. Melbourne: Melbourne University Press, 1954.

VERN L. BULLOUGH

CIORAN, EMIL M. (1911–1995), Romanian-born nihilist philosopher, essayist, and aphorist. Emil M. Cioran is undoubtedly the most consistent, comprehensive, and provocative philosophical nihilist of the twentieth century (see NIHILISM). For him, the world and human existence are without meaning, purpose, or value. In eight books, he maintains a sustained, withering negativity that is absolute and all-encompassing, condemning all belief systems, civilizations, religions, philosophies, art, reason, language, and himself.

Early Life. Cioran's father, Emilian, was a Greek Orthodox priest, and it is perhaps the potent influence of religion in his youth that led to his vehement condemnation of it later. Cioran studied philosophy at the University of Bucharest, graduating in 1928 with a thesis on Henri BERGSON. By the time he published *On the Heights of Despair* (1934), it is clear that he had rejected his father's religion and traditional philosophy, too. The strength of this first book allowed Cioran to study in Berlin from 1933 to 1935, and a French Institute fellowship in 1937 sent him to Paris, where he spent the rest of his life. After 1944 Cioran wrote exclusively in French.

Nihilist. Because of Cioran's nihilism, his aphoristic style, and his sometimes shrill tone, he is often inappropriately compared to the Friedrich NIETZSCHE of *The Will to Power*. However, whereas Nietzsche tried fiercely to overcome nihilism, Cioran's lifelong drive was focused on nurturing and declaiming nihilism. He offered no cure, no program, no hope; rather, he was adamantly committed to exposing all illusions that constitute the thin veneer of meaning to which the deluded cling. And he had a voracious appetite for hopelessness, endeavoring to leave readers fully disillusioned while confirming their worst existential fears. Accordingly, Cioran cannot be compared to the existentialists (see EXISTENTIALISM), whose ideas and methodologies represent a desperate effort to bring meaning to a world rendered meaningless by the corrosive effects of nihilism.

Cioran's first book in French, *A Short History of Decay* (1949), while critically celebrated, did not sell well. The book is useful for understanding Cioran's oeuvre because it not only reflects the existential issues expressed in earlier works but also sets the agenda for the five books that follow. Like all of his writings, this book is something between literature and philosophy. And like Cioran's other works, the prose is dense and sometimes paradoxical, zigzagging from one tersely phrased statement of opinion to another in an original and elegant style.

In *A Short History of Decay*, Cioran examines the history of nihilism's unfolding in Western civilization from its beginnings to the present, concludes that civilization is nearing its end, and expresses his relief. Cioran's essays also highlight his grimly pessimistic views on human existence. Any analysis of history, he writes, must begin with the equation that "existence equals suffering." The disaster of man begins at birth: "What sin have you committed to be born, what crime to exist?" History is a gloomy record of man's futile rage for order and the inexorable process of decay, a process that, he notes repeatedly, has been accelerated by the intolerance and absurdities of religion. At its core, human existence is endless suffering, grief, and depravation in a world where "everything conspires, elements and action alike, to harm you." Life, in short, is a "euphemism for Evil": "Of all that was attempted this side of nothingness, is anything more pathetic than this world, except for the idea which conceived it? Wherever something breathes there is one more infirmity: no palpitation which fails to confirm the disadvantage of being; the flesh horrifies me: these men, these women, offal that moans by the grace of certain spasms."

The catastrophe of existence, exacerbated by the nightmare of consciousness, requires human beings to hide from themselves, from others, and from reality. Regardless of the amassed evidence of history, then, most refuse to acknowledge that life is evil. And no wonder, declares Cioran; to admit to what *is*, is the equivalent of existential evisceration.

With this in mind, three options are available for coming to terms with our hideous existence: hope, resignation, or suicide. Cioran was obsessed with suicide most of his life, and he admired those who could kill themselves. For him, though, just the thought of suicide was a solace, he claimed, knowing that at any time he could escape to nothingness. Hope is a malicious lie, and those who wish for and expect fulfillment must be watched diligently because they are the source of fanaticism, insanity, and murderous violence. In his musings, Cioran seems to vacillate between resigning himself to nihilism in an epicurean debauch of "morphine, masturbation, or rum" or embracing a contemplative STOICISM: "Arm yourself in disdain, isolate yourself in a fortress of disgust." The danger of any form of resignation, however, is apathy because it produces ennui, which is the most unnerving experience of all.

Given Cioran's vituperative condemnation of nearly everything, his long life of eighty-three years seems contradictory, as does his aversion to absolutes of any form except his own. (This, of course, is the paradox of nihilism.) And in spite of his lifelong effort to appear indifferent to existential absurdity, it clearly must have disturbed him. He fought an ongoing struggle with depression; and an undertone of world-weariness, sadism, and masochism permeates his writings. Cioran's last book, *Anathemas and Admirations* (1987), is a revealing blend of "anathemas" that continues his bout with human folly and the horrors of the world juxtaposed with something new and positive, and "admirations," his warm recollections of Samuel Beckett, Jorge Luis Borges, F. Scott Fitzgerald, and others. Perhaps understanding even the futility of this, Cioran stopped writing completely after this book. During the 1990s he suffered from Alzheimer's disease, and he died in Paris in 1995.

Limited critical attention, both praise and blame, and the less-than-enthusiastic reception of his work by the reading public should not undermine Cioran's position as an important literary figure and thinker. Instead, these facts serve to underscore the caustic power of his penetrating but painful insights. And although the uninitiated and the life loving might be unsympathetic to Cioran's grim cynicism, fellow travelers and those with a well-developed sense of humor will find his ideas compelling in their sheer unmitigated negativity.

BIBLIOGRAPHY

Cahn, Zilla G. *Suicide in French Thought from Montesquieu to Cioran.* New York: Peter Lang, 1998.

Cioran, E. M. *On the Heights of Despair.* Translated by Ilinca Zarifopol-Johnston. Chicago: University of Chicago Press, 1992.

———. *A Short History of Decay.* Translated by Richard Howard. New York: Viking, 1975.

"Cioran, E. M." In *Contemporary Literary Criticism,* vol. 64, edited by Roger Matuz. Detroit: Gale Research, 1991.

Kluback, William, and Michael Finkenthal. *The Temptations of Emile Cioran.* New York: Peter Lang, 1997.

ALAN R. PRATT

CIRCUMCISION (AND ITS OPPOSITION) AS CAUSES. Circumcision and noncircumcision causes manifest themselves in widely varied forms, ranging from religious promotion, renunciation, and persecution to medicalization, spousal revenge, prohibition, and opposition to forced genital cutting in general. The continuum of pro- and anticircumcision activism can be viewed as a struggle between *evangelism* and *preservationism.* Evangelists for circumcision are very few in number, mostly clergy and physicians; these are unwittingly assisted by millions of followers who have chosen to accept evangelists' claims that circumcision is beneficial while ignoring the lack of supportive evidence to substantiate those claims. Preservationism, which aims to preserve the genitalia intact against surgical alteration, is a grassroots movement that believes all humans have a right to self-determination that includes a right to bodily integrity. Though circumcision is sometimes rationalized on religious grounds, FREETHOUGHT and humanist activists have not been conspicuous among its opponents, at least where male circumcision is concerned.

Ritual and cultural male infant circumcision has gone largely unchallenged by freethinkers, atheists (see ATHEISM), and humanists (see HUMANISM)—and also by most lawyers, physicians, and ethicists—despite evidence that circumcision is painful, traumatic, disadvantageous, and has serious lifelong consequences. This has remained the case even during an era when children's rights are increasingly advocated, at least until the rise of preservationism. In contrast, forced genital cutting of females has found few advocates and numerous opponents. It has not only been widely labeled a human rights violation, but is prohibited in many countries. In light of this, the freethought community's general failure to oppose forced male genital cutting seems peculiarly sexist if not misandrist.

Promotion. Promotion of genital cutting by evangelists for the practice is based on the belief that cutting, removing, or altering a child's genitalia will bestow upon the child certain negative or positive characteristics, including acceptance into a social group, conformity to a social norm, compliance with sexual norms, protection from disease, assurance of marriageability, control of sexuality through loss of function and decreased sexual pleasure, physical disfigurement, and more. What all of these diverse methodologies or rationales have in common is the primary goal: sexually altering the child.

Male circumcision is mistakenly regarded as a Jewish innovation, but the Jewish circumcision requirement was not original to the Bible. It had been previously used in Egypt and Africa to mark and sexually neutralize slaves. Jewish priests in Old Testament times seized upon the mutilation to cement their control over men through a required blood sacrifice, which could only be performed under the priests' auspices. Maimonides, a fifteenth-century Jewish scholar, reaffirmed religious circumcision as a physical reminder to men that by desensitizing their penis, they would focus on spiritual duties, adding that the procedure's pain was advantageous to accomplishing that task. In medieval times, Jews captured and circumcised non-Jewish boys as well as their non-Jewish servants, showing a markedly different understanding of the procedure.

The Christian Bible contradicts itself regarding circumcision, the Old and New Testaments taking opposite stands. Early Christianity took a strong stand against circumcision in the first century, forbidding the practice even though the first Christians were Jews. Infant circumcision has never been a religious requirement for Christians, yet many circumcise their boys, but not their girls. Although some Catholics circumcise their boys, the Catholic

Church rejected ritual circumcision as early as at the Council at Jerusalem (51 CE), a position reaffirmed at the Council of Vienna (1311) and in the papal bull of 1442.

As recently as 2003, the Malaysian government proposed using mass circumcision ceremonies to promote racial harmony. Meanwhile Egyptian fundamentalists consistently ignore their country's ban on female circumcision.

Forced religious conversion by circumcision occurs in many parts of the world, including in Indonesia, Sudan, and Pakistan (performed by Muslims); the United States (performed by Jews and Muslims); and in Kenya and South Africa (performed by traditional circumcisers). Such circumcision is most often performed on nonconsenting or coerced minors.

Medicalization. Many circumcision evangelists are physicians who gain financially from the practice. Members of this group have advocated circumcision as a cure-all since 1870. Throughout this period, evangelist physicians have invented new claims that circumcision is beneficial as quickly as previous false cures have been exposed. A cure looking for a disease, the latest in this long list of falsehoods is the claim that male circumcision is prophylactic against HIV/AIDS.

Renunciation. Jewish literature and tradition include several instances in which circumcision was renounced. Moses is believed to have abandoned the practice during the Jews' forty-year journey in the wilderness. Joshua is said to have reinstated circumcision at Gilgal after the death of Moses. Hellenistic Jews voluntarily restored their amputated foreskins in order to participate in Greek sporting events, which were usually performed in the nude. Jewish athletes would stretch their penile skin to cover their glans penis in order not to appear mutilated to the body-conscious Greeks. More recently German and American Jews participating in a Jewish reform movement (1843) proposed abolishing ritual circumcision, declaring that it was a cruel practice and not necessary for Jews.

Present-day nonobservant Jews increasingly reject ritual circumcision, *brit milah*, performed on the eighth day of life by a *mohel*, replacing it with a secular circumcision performed by a hospital physician shortly after birth. Some Jewish parents have replaced genital cutting with *brit shalom*, a noncutting birth ritual similar to the naming ceremony performed upon newborn Jewish girls. Other Jews simply forgo the practice altogether (see JUDAISM, UNBELIEF WITHIN). Christianity can be viewed as a former Jewish sect that renounced ritual circumcision of its males, eventually leading to a complete separation and the subsequent founding of a new religion in the beginning of the second century CE.

Revenge by Proxy. Divorced or separated parents may insist on cutting their sons' or daughters' genitals—using culture, religion, or hygiene as an excuse—to enrage their estranged spouse. The child may be secreted away to a circumciser in another state or country. This particular assault, even though illegal in some jurisdictions, is commonplace.

Persecution and Prohibition. Circumcision has been prohibited and its practitioners persecuted at various times in history. Classical Greeks and Romans placed a high value on the foreskin and the possession of a whole and unscarred body; they passed several laws to protect the prepuce (foreskin) by prohibiting circumcision. Circumcision was again prohibited during the French Revolution. The former Soviet Union abolished Jewish ritual circumcision in 1918. A counterexample is furnished by the Third Reich, which intentionally did not outlaw circumcision because the presence of a circumcision scar aided in identifying Jews. During the partitioning of India in 1947, a man's life—and his family's—depended on whether or not he was circumcised. If not, Muslims killed him; if so, Hindus and Sikhs killed him. Today traditional circumcisers in Kenya may be arrested if found forcibly circumcising males, yet they insist they will continue targeting uncircumcised boys since their tradition demands that all men be circumcised.

Sweden banned traditional circumcision in 2001, requiring circumcision of boys by physicians only. The child must receive pain relief administered by a physician or qualified nurse. The law has provoked strong opposition from the world's Jewish communities, which have accused the Swedish parliament of instituting the first law against Jewish religious practice since World War II. Meanwhile Denmark proposed a circumcision ban in 2004 on human rights grounds. Opponents painted this as a hostile initiative toward the country's Muslim minority.

Efforts to ban male genital cutting are sometimes labeled as anti-Semitic, even though religious circumcisions comprise a small fraction of the circumcisions performed. For example, in the present-day United States, less than one-tenth of 1 percent of all circumcisions are performed during a religious rite.

Defunding Circumcision Coverage. Since the middle of the twentieth century various countries, mostly Western, have experimented with removal of public funding for circumcision procedures. The United Kingdom was the first country to end national health plan coverage for infant circumcision in 1948. Canada has defunded coverage for circumcision in all of its provinces. In 2005 Denmark and Finland were discussing a ban of male circumcision or the elimination of coverage by national health plans. The Netherlands dropped coverage of infant circumcision from its national health plan in 2005. Sixteen American states have defunded routine male infant circumcision in their Medicaid programs as of 2005; more states are now considering the same step, all without sparking religious controversy. Opponents painted New Zealand's 2005 exclusion of circumcision from coverage under its national health plan as evidence that the New Zealand government is discriminatory and anti-Semitic. In this context, it is worth noting that since its founding in 1948, Israel has never covered infant circumcision in its national health plan.

Genital Integrity Movement. Physicians have published warnings about the harm of circumcision since 1890, and no medical society in the world recommends the procedure. At no time in its seventy-five years has the American Academy of Pediatrics ever recommended infant circumcision, and the American Medical Association goes even further, calling it "nontherapeutic." Yet even this criticism fell short of achieving real cultural momentum. A noteworthy contemporary development is anticircumcision activism based on emerging concepts of human rights. This opposition is not unconditional, as rare occasions are recognized when foreskin amputation is medically required—for example, to excise necrotic tissue following an accident, untreatable disease, or frostbite. This grassroots movement is opposed to cultural and ritual genital cutting, but not to life-saving medical treatment, hence, it is most accurately called the genital integrity movement. It opposes cultural and ritual genital modification from a stance based on humane bodily preservation and fundamental human rights.

The genital integrity movement began in earnest in 1985 with the formation of the educationally oriented National Organization of Circumcision Information Resource Centers (NOCIRC), an advocacy organization that now operates more than one hundred centers worldwide. Since then, other organizations have been founded around the world to oppose the practice.

Organizations that specifically oppose religious circumcision have been created in the past few years. Jews against Circumcision opposes Old Testament circumcision practice from a bodily integrity and children's rights perspective. Catholics against Circumcision opposes circumcision based on New Testament scripture and church teachings. In what may be a modern-day episode of Jewish renunciation, Jews tend to be overrepresented in the genital integrity movement relative to their numbers in a given country's population.

Various streams of anticircumcision activism are coalescing in the contemporary movement, encompassing not only opposition to male and female genital cutting but also opposition to the involuntary alteration of intersexed infants and children. At the same time the focus of the genital integrity movement is shifting from the immediate protection of individuals to a commitment to preserve future generations from a human rights violation through societal change.

In one example of this expanding activism, a 1996 US ban on female genital mutilation has come under attack as being unconstitutional because it does not provide fair and equal treatment. Efforts are under way to make the law's language gender neutral, which would continue protection for girls, and make nontherapeutic infant circumcision of boys and gender-norming surgeries upon intersexed children illegal without prior informed consent of the patient.

The International Coalition for Genital Integrity has proposed a moratorium on circumcision until such time as critical questions concerning physical and psychological health, as well as bioethical concerns for autonomy and nonmalificence are fully answered (see BIOETHICS AND UNBELIEF).

Regardless of the ignorance, good intentions, or superstitions of parents and circumcisers, genital cutting remains a generally unopposed and unprosecuted assault on defenseless, nonconsenting children.

BIBLIOGRAPHY

Fleiss, Paul, and Frederick Hodges. *What Your Doctor May NOT Tell You about Circumcision.* New York: Warner Books, 2002.

Glick, Leonard. *Marked in Your Flesh: Circumcision from Ancient Judea to Modern America.* New York: Oxford University Press, 2005.

Goldman, Ronald. *Questioning Circumcision: A Jewish Perspective.* Boston: Vanguard, 1998.

Gollaher, David. *Circumcision: A History of the World's Most Controversial Surgery.* New York: Basic Books, 2000.

DAN BOLLINGER

CLEAVER, ELDRIDGE (1935–1998), African American activist. Eldridge Cleaver was born Leroy Eldridge Cleaver in Wabbaseka, Arkansas, but raised in California. Incarcerated on a 1958 assault conviction, he spent much time reading and thinking about the oppression of blacks in the United States. He read FREETHOUGHT works by such luminaries as Robert Green INGERSOLL and embraced a secular Marxist/Leninist worldview.

Paroled in 1966, he joined the militant Black Panther Party, becoming its minister of information. In 1968 he wrote his best-known work, *Soul on Ice.* This collection of essays received great critical acclaim. Later that year, he ran for the US presidency on the Peace and Freedom Party ticket. In that same eventful year, he was involved in a shootout with police in Oakland, California, home of the Panthers' national headquarters. Cleaver and another Panther were injured. Cleaver was arrested and convicted. On November 24, 1968, three days before he was to be sentenced for his role in the shootout, he fled the country and eventually escaped to Algiers.

While in exile in Algeria, Cleaver continued to write and speak out, opposing male chauvinism among the Panthers and the bigoted cultural nationalism on the part of black activist Stokeley Carmichael, the Nation of Islam's (NOI) Elijah Muhammad, and others. He applauded Malcolm X for denouncing racism and breaking away from the NOI to form the secular Organization of Afro-American Unity.

In 1975 Cleaver returned to the United States; charges against him were dropped. He claimed to have had a religious awakening, and also reported abandoning many of his former political beliefs. He became an extremely conservative Christian, at one time flirting with the Unification Church of Reverend Sun Myung Moon. He was baptized in 1982 and was briefly a priest of the Church of Latter Day Saints, though he was listed as a church member until he died.

In 1986 Cleaver made an unsuccessful bid to be nominated as a Republican candidate for the United States Senate in California. He embraced American capitalism and conservative Christianity, yet continued to argue for women's rights. He remained opposed to the black cultural nationalism of Minister Louis Farrakhan and the NOI.

Like the Harlem Renaissance poets Claude MCKAY and Langston HUGHES, Cleaver became religious after his best years were behind him. However, his legacy as a leader of one of the most fascinating organizations in the history of black America is secure.

BIBLIOGRAPHY

Bringhurst, Newell G. "Eldridge Cleaver's Passage through Mormonism." *Journal of Mormon History* 28 (Spring 2002).

Bringhurst, Newell G., and Darron T. Smith, eds. *Black and Mormon*. Urbana and Chicago: University of Illinois Press, 2004.

Cleaver, Eldridge. *Soul on Ice*. New York: McGraw Hill, 1968.

Foner, Philip S., ed. *The Black Panthers Speak*. New York: Da Capo, 1995.

Newton, Huey P. *To Die for the People*. New York: Writers and Readers, 1973.

———. *Revolutionary Suicide*. New York: Writers and Readers, 1973.

Pearson, Hugh. *The Shadow of the Panther: Huey Newton and the Price of Black Power in America*. Reading, MA: Addison Wesley, 1994.

Scheer, Robert, ed. *Eldridge Cleaver: Post-Prison Writings and Speeches*. New York: Vintage, 1969.

NORM R. ALLEN JR.

CLEMENS, SAMUEL LANGHORNE (MARK TWAIN; 1835–1910), American author. America's most renowned author, Mark Twain lived an extraordinarily varied, productive, and complex life. He was born and raised in Missouri and subsequently spent significant parts of his life on the Mississippi River and in Nevada; California; Hawaii; Buffalo and Elmira, New York; and Hartford, Connecticut. He resided overseas for long periods of time in England, Italy, and Austria, and he traveled widely in the United States, Europe, the Holy Land, Australia, and India. By 1869 he had been a printer, a Mississippi River steamboat pilot, a gold and silver miner in Nevada, a journalist for Nevada and California newspapers, a lecturer, a nationally acclaimed

author, a personal secretary for a United States senator, a lobbyist in Washington, and a newspaper publisher. After 1871 he settled down to writing and spent most of the rest of his life composing the works that have since become famous, especially *Innocents Abroad* (1869), *Roughing It* (1872), *The Adventures of Tom Sawyer* (1876), *Life on the Mississippi* (1883), *The Adventures of Huckleberry Finn* (1884), *A Connecticut Yankee in King Arthur's Court* (1889), and "Letters from the Earth" (1909/1962). The importance to his thinking of his lifelong religious struggle is not commonly recognized, but the unorthodox religious ideas obvious in his late writings can be traced back in an unbroken line to his youth.

Religious Odyssey. The first exposure of Sam Clemens to religion lasted as an influence on him for his entire life. He attended a Presbyterian church in Hannibal, Missouri, that taught severe Calvinist doctrines. Chapter 5 of *Tom Sawyer* describes the sort of sermon that young Sam Clemens heard many times: a complicated argument about "limitless fire and brimstone" and a deity that predestined the great majority of humankind to damnation and elected only a minuscule number to salvation. As Sam grew older, he encountered Thomas PAINE's criticism of the Bible and conventional Christian theology and was intellectually converted to Paine's DEISM. Still later, after Clemens became Mark Twain and fell in love with Livy Langdon, whose family in Elmira were active adherents of liberal, evangelical Protestantism, he tried for some years to fit himself into that mold. The effort was unsuccessful; after imbibing Paine's deistic SKEPTICISM, he could no longer believe in the literal truth of the Bible or view all of its doctrines, and especially its deity, as benevolent. Despite this, the Calvinistic lessons of his youth retained a grip on him that he could never shake off. Twain mediated the conflict between his intellectual preferences and his emotional convictions with the use of irony. He attended a liberal Congregational church in Hartford, but often referred to himself in his writings and lectures as a Presbyterian and joked about Calvinist doctrines. In his later years, Twain continued his close friendship with his Congregational pastor Joseph Twichell, but was attracted to philosophical DETERMINISM and in 1906 published *What Is Man?* an extremely bleak argument that man is only a machine, programmed and totally controlled by such outside forces as heredity, training, and environment. Nevertheless, as "Letters from the Earth" shows, his mind was still profoundly preoccupied with religious issues concerning God and predestination.

Religious Convictions. Despite his public appearances and his intellectual preferences, Twain in effect remained a Calvinist his whole life, though a heretical one (see HERESY). His fundamental convictions can be inferred from an analysis of his literature, which early and late at its deepest levels reflects what in effect amounts to a "countertheology" to Calvinism. Indeed, the main works of his literature cannot be fully comprehended without appreciation of their theological foundations. Twain followed conventional Christianity in that he continued to believe in an omnipotent and omniscient God, but whereas Christianity maintains that God is benevolent, Twain's heresy was that he saw God as a malevolent trickster, whimsical and usually devious and cruel. In the published works of his early and middle periods, when he was still establishing his reputation and was apprehensive of alienating readers by his heretical beliefs, he concealed these positions very subtly, often under comic surfaces whose humor sugarcoated bitter cores. (Some posthumously published works from these periods display these core views more openly.) They could almost escape detection were they not the thematic elements that unify each of his important works and run through his oeuvre, constituting a common thematic signature. In his later period, after 1889, Twain was less concerned about disguising his beliefs. Accordingly, his heretical views are more easily seen—sometimes unavoidably—in works such as "The Man That Corrupted Hadleyburg" (1899), *What Is Man?* "Letters from the Earth," and the *Mysterious Stranger* fragments (1897–1908/1916).

Twain's central religious beliefs can be summarized as follows: (1) He believed in the existence of an inscrutably malevolent deity who is not a god of truth. Both testaments teach that he is infinitely loving and merciful but their records of his actions and commands expose him to be quite the opposite. (2) God immutably predestined all of creation. All events, and all details in individual lives—actions, words, thoughts, and feelings—are predestined. Nothing occurs by chance; there are no accidents. As a consequence, freedom and free will are illusions and impossibilities. (3) Human nature has been so (predestinedly) perverted by original sin that every individual deserves damnation. (4) Double damnation: so corrupt is human nature that even if humans had not already been predestined, the sins of even the most virtuous would infallibly damn them. (5) The overwhelming majority of the human race *is* reprobated to hell. Only a very small fraction of it has been elected for salvation, and not for any merit of its own but only because of God's mysterious and unearned grace.

All of these positions except the first are derived from Calvinism. Twain always hated them for being shockingly unfair and cruel, but he believed them because they accurately described the world he saw. Accordingly, tragedy in his works usually involves finite and fallible humans being cast as the unsuspecting playthings of a monstrous deity that deceives, tortures, and then defeats them.

BIBLIOGRAPHY

Baetzhold, Howard G., and Joseph B. McCullough, eds. *The Bible according to Mark Twain.* Athens: University of Georgia Press, 1995.

Berkove, Lawrence I. "Mark Twain's Hostility toward Joseph." *CEA Critic* 62, no. 3 (Summer 2000).

———. "Poe, Twain, and the Nature of Conscience." *ESQ* 46, no. 4 (2000).

———. "The 'Poor Players' of *Huckleberry Finn.*" *Papers of the Michigan Academy* 53 (1968).

———. "The Reality of the Dream: Structural and Thematic Unity in *A Connecticut Yankee.*" *Mark Twain Journal* 22, no. 1 (Spring 1984).

———. "The Trickster God in *Roughing It.*" *Thalia* 18, nos. 1 and 2 (1998).

Brodwin, Stanley. "Mark Twain's Theology: The Gods of a Brevet Presbyterian." In *The Cambridge Companion to Mark Twain,* edited by Forrest G. Robinson. New York: Cambridge University Press, 1995.

Cummings, Sherwood. *Mark Twain and Science: Adventures of a Mind.* Baton Rouge: Louisiana State University Press, 1988.

Wilson, James D. "Religion and Esthetic Vision in Mark Twain's Early Career." *Canadian Review of American Studies* 17, no. 2 (Summer 1986).

LAWRENCE I. BERKOVE

CLIFFORD, WILLIAM KINGDON

CLIFFORD, WILLIAM KINGDON (1845–1879), British mathematician, ethicist, and freethinker. William Kingdon Clifford is best remembered for his 1876 essay "The Ethics of Belief," in which he made the memorable assertion: "It is wrong always, everywhere, and for anyone, to believe anything upon insufficient evidence."

Clifford's Life. Clifford was born in Exeter, England. His father was a bookseller who dealt largely in devotional material and served for a time as a justice of the peace. Clifford's mother, whose maiden name was Kingdon, died when he was only nine. A precocious child, Clifford was educated at a small local school until the age of fifteen, when he was sent to King's College, London. Here, he began to reveal abilities not only in his chosen profession of mathematics, but also in the fields of literature and classics. In 1863 he won a scholarship to Trinity College, Cambridge.

Although slight in build, Clifford prided himself on his physical strength. His proudest feat, taken on a dare, was to hang by his toes from the crossbars of a church tower's weathercock—one of the last times he was to find himself near a church of any sort. In 1871, at the young age of twenty-six, Clifford was appointed to the professorship in applied mathematics at University College, London, where he would spend the remainder of his short career. It was a congenial place for a freethinker (see FREETHOUGHT) like himself, since it was founded in 1827 to be a strictly secular institution, where professors would be free from having to swear allegiance to any religious oath. In 1874 Clifford was elected as a Fellow of the Royal Society, one of the highest scholarly honors in the United Kingdom. He had previously turned down the offer, with the remark that he did not want to be respectable just yet.

In 1875 Clifford married Lucy Lane, by whom he had two daughters. Unfortunately, the marriage was to be a short one, as Clifford died at age thirty-three after a long battle with tuberculosis. His mathematical and philosophical papers were published posthumously by friends, including fellow freethinker Leslie STEPHENS (the father of Virginia Woolf). He is buried in London's Highgate Cemetery, with the following epitaph on his tombstone: "I was not, and was conceived; I loved, and did a little work; I am not, and grieve not."

Crisis of Faith. Clifford had been an Anglican in his early years, but came to lose his faith in the historical accuracy and present relevance of the teachings of Christianity. But unlike many others in his time—such as Matthew Arnold, who saw his own loss of faith as tragic—Clifford viewed this as a *positive* experience, not a cause of despair. He saw knowledge in terms of adaptability. As new information became available, humans could learn more about how the universe really works, as opposed to relying upon the patchwork beliefs which religious institutions offered as truth. Just as the Greek and Roman civilizations had overcome their reliance upon Zeus and Jupiter, so the modern world could overcome its reliance on Jehovah and Jesus.

Evolutionary Views. The impact of evolutionary theory (see EVOLUTION AND UNBELIEF), which had been hotly debated since the publication of Charles DARWIN's *On the Origin of Species* (1859), had a major impact on Clifford, as did his reading the moral writings of Herbert SPENCER. He came to believe that it was no longer necessary to explain scientific discoveries through the prism of existing religious dogmas. He came to view clerical institutions as the chief obstacles to scientific and moral advancement, and an impediment to human intellectual and social growth. He saw clearly that the chief opposition to Darwinian evolutionary theory was coming from the pulpits, and he allied himself with Thomas Henry HUXLEY, the biologist popularly known as "Darwin's Bulldog." His own writings on the possible biological basis of morality in many ways anticipated the field of evolutionary ethics (see ETHICS AND UNBELIEF).

Mathematical Contributions. Clifford was one of the first English mathematicians to become knowledgeable about the work being done on non-Euclidean geometry by Bernhard Riemann and Nikolay Lobachevski, going so far as to translate the former's work and publish it in the influential journal *Nature*. The introduction of non-Euclidean geometry was not only a challenge to mathematicians in particular—it was also a blow in general to those philosophers and theologians who held to the existence of necessary and universal truths. If even Euclid's axioms could be questioned, after thousands of years of being unquestioned, then what *else* might prove assailable? In addition, Clifford did work on the application of geometry to physics, and anticipated certain aspects of Albert Einstein's theory of gravitation.

Clifford's Materialism. One of the extracurricular activities Clifford became involved with was investigating psychical research. However, unlike many of his fellow professors, he was not taken in by so-called spirit mediums (see SPIRITUALISM AND UNBELIEF). In fact, he became a fierce advocate of the view that there was no such thing as disembodied consciousness (see SKEPTICISM), and he delighted in debunking paranormal claims. The field of psychology was just being formed, and it was still unclear what its limits would be. Clifford made it a special point to show how supposed psychics were guilty of using trickery of the basest sort to fool not only credulous believers but also learned professors. In addition, he argued that psychology's proper study was the physical brain and how it worked, *not* disembodied elements like ghosts. Not wishing to be considered a dualist, he devised a theory of "mind-stuff," which he held to be the basic unit of the universe. Although not all things possess mind or consciousness, they all possess some element of mind-stuff, and when such elements come together in a large enough unit, there is the beginning of sentience.

"The Ethics of Belief." In 1876 Clifford was elected to the famous debating group the Metaphysical Society, the youngest member so chosen. Members included his fellow freethinker T. H. Huxley, as well as such stalwarts as Catholic archbishop Henry Manning, Poet Laureate Alfred Lord Tennyson, and two British prime ministers, William Gladstone and Arthur Balfour. The society's discussions, which were primarily concerned with arguments for or against the rationality of religious belief, were of the highest caliber. For Clifford, the exercising of intellectual abilities in the company of fellow critical thinkers (whether they shared the same conclusions or not) was an opportunity not to be missed, and he attended as many sessions as he could. It was here that he delivered his most famous lecture, "The Ethics of Belief."

In this paper, Clifford argued that it was immoral to hold a belief for which one has no evidence. The method of science advocated treating all beliefs as provisional, and by advocating such a method society would free itself from the hold of false and pernicious beliefs. Not to test one's beliefs was not only a bad habit, it was a "sin" against general humanity. Many years later, the American philosopher William James, in his famed 1896 essay "The Will to Believe," was to chide Clifford for holding too stringent a view of belief formation and preservation. But Clifford had argued that it was permissible to act upon probabilities and inferences, provided one recognized them as such, rather than treating them as revealed truths or unassailable doctrines. Clifford's view has come to be called EVIDENTIALISM, and remains a controversial area in current epistemological debates.

Clifford as Freethought Activist. One of the last projects Clifford worked on was especially near and dear to his heart. After discussions with Huxley, he came to the conclusion that a gathering of freethinkers from across the world should be held, the aim of which would be to liberate the peoples of all classes from degrading dogmas. Combining his republican sentiments with his scientific advocacy, Clifford was the driving force behind the Congress of Liberal Thinkers, which was held on June 13–14, 1878, at the South Place Chapel in England (see SOUTH PLACE ETHICAL SOCIETY), just a few days after the commemoration of the centenary of VOLTAIRE'S death. More than four hundred delegates came from throughout the world. Unfortunately, his poor health prevented Clifford's attending. A fierce freethinker to the end, when made aware of a newspaper report which claimed that he was converting back to Christianity in his final days, he fired back a retort that, while his doctor had certified that he was ill, "'twas not mental derangement."

BIBLIOGRAPHY

Berman, David. *A History of Atheism in Great Britain: From Hobbes to Russell.* London: Routledge, 1988.

Chisholm, M. *Such Silver Currents: The Story of William and Lucy Clifford, 1845–1929.* Cambridge: Lutterworth, 2002.

Hollinger, David A. "James, Clifford, and the Scientific Conscience." In *The Cambridge Companion to William James,* edited by Ruth Anna Putnam. New York: Cambridge University Press, 1997.

Lightman, Bernard. *The Origins of Agnosticism: Victorian Unbelief and the Limits of Knowledge.* Baltimore: Johns Hopkins University Press, 1987.

Madigan, Timothy J., ed. *W. K. Clifford: "The Ethics of Belief" and Other Essays.* Amherst, NY: Prometheus Books, 1999.

Pyle, Andrew, ed. *Agnosticism: Contemporary Responses to Spencer and Huxley.* London: Thoemmes, 1995.

TIMOTHY J. MADIGAN

CLOUGH, ARTHUR HUGH (1819–1861), English poet and agnostic. Arthur Hugh Clough's AGNOSTICISM damaged his career and enhanced his poetry. The title of one of his poems, "The Questioning Spirit," sums up his life and work.

Clough was born in Liverpool in 1819, went with his family to the United States in 1822, and returned for an English education in 1829. He entered the renowned independent school Rugby, whose headmaster, Dr. Thomas Arnold, had a great influence on him. He was a prodigious youth, winning prizes and gaining prominence as head boy.

Clough entered Balliol College, Oxford, where he expected to continue his brilliant career. He saw it as a disaster when he gained a Second Class degree, not the expected First. He thus failed to gain a fellowship at Balliol, but gained a fellowship at the less prestigious Oriel College.

Religious discussion was rife at Oxford. Clough was expected to be ordained if he continued in his Oriel fellowship, but he felt that he could not subscribe to the Thirty-nine Articles of Faith of the Church of England, and left.

In 1848 he briefly took a position at a Unitarian hall of University College (see UNITARIANISM TO 1961), where religious affiliation was not insisted upon. He endeavored but failed to gain a position in the United States, where he had contact with Ralph Waldo EMERSON. Though he had published some admired poetry he felt his promise failing him, and was persuaded by his fiancée to take a post as examiner in the Education Office in London. Blanche (née Smith), now his wife, was cousin to Florence Nightingale, and Clough helped her in her writing and lobbying.

Clough traveled in Europe: to Paris at the time of the 1848 Revolution, to Rome at a time of conflict in 1850, and to Florence, where he died in 1861. His long poems, such as "Amours de Voyage" and "Dipsychus," have such places as their background and figures who are doubters and republicans, and have sexual feelings (which some Victorians denied). Two poems of particularly sceptical tenor are "Epi-Strauss-ium" and "Easter Day." The former refers to David Friedrich STRAUSS, whose 1835 *Leben Jesu* (Life of Jesus) portrays a Jesus who was human, not divine. The latter reiterates "Christ is not risen" throughout a resurrection-denying ode. Two of Clough's best-known lines are from "The Latest Decalogue," a sly satire on the Christian Ten Commandments:

Thou shalt not kill; but needst not strive
Officiously to keep alive.

These words are often quoted by supporters of voluntary euthanasia.

It was Clough's misfortune that he doubted not only religion but more importantly himself, which led to an unfulfilled life.

BIBLIOGRAPHY

Clough, Arthur Hugh. *Poems and Prose Remains, with a Selection from His Letters and a Memoir.* Edited by Blanche Clough. 2 vols. London: Macmillan, 1869.

Kenny, Anthony. *The Oxford Diaries of Arthur Hugh Clough.* Oxford: Clarendon, 1990.

Mulhauser, F. L., ed. *The Poems of Arthur Hugh Clough.* Oxford: Clarendon, 1974.

Thorpe, Michael, ed. *A Choice of Clough's Verse.* London: Faber and Faber, 1969.

JIM HERRICK

COGNITIVE SCIENCE AND UNBELIEF. The cognitive sciences are those that investigate the processes and constituents of thought. The range of phenomena that are studied is broad, including the subsecond processes of visual perception and the multigenerational processes of cultural change. The cognitive sciences include psychology, neuroscience, artificial intelligence, anthropology, philosophy, linguistics, and education. This interdisciplinary field often incorporates a view of cognition as a kind of information processing, leveraging insights from computer science and artificial intelligence in order to understand the structure of mental processes.

The recognition of supernatural entities, or the denial of the same, involves cognitive mechanisms. Thus, the cognitive sciences may shed light on the nature of belief and unbelief. In particular, studies of cognition have provided insights concerning (1) the nature of knowledge and beliefs, (2) how individuals draw inferences from their experiences, (3) why religious beliefs and practices are so common across cultures, and (4) what neural and cognitive mechanisms give rise to religious experiences (see RELIGIOUS AND MYSTICAL EXPERIENCES).

It is common to conceptualize a particular belief as a kind of proposition—a statement or sentence—that is marked with a "propositional attitude" that indicates that the statement is believed to be true. Under this view, the beliefs of an individual would simply be a collection of such propositions, represented in a way that allows them to generate consistent behavior. While beliefs are frequently communicated and contemplated in such a linguistic format, research in the cognitive sciences has increasingly found the knowledge that drives behavior to be much more fragmented, compartmentalized, graded, and situation specific. Rather than possessing a single pool of beliefs that are all consistently recalled and applied in any situation, it appears as if knowledge is largely fragmented across different cognitive skills and processes. Thus, knowledge regularly invoked and used in one situation may be completely ignored, or even contradicted, in another. It appears as if "beliefs" only describe the pattern of performance produced by various cognitive processes and skills, while different domain-specific cognitive processes within a single individual may reflect different contradicting "beliefs." This raises the question of whether it truly makes sense to ascribe "beliefs" to individuals, except as a kind of shorthand for coarse regularities in behavior. This domain-specific view of the organization of knowledge also helps to explain why inconsistent behaviors are so frequently overlooked by the true believer.

The domain specificity of knowledge and cognitive skills also provides some insight into why intellectually competent individuals can sometimes exhibit surprisingly poor reasoning in specific domains, such as religion. In general, people frequently exhibit essentially optimal reasoning performance in familiar domains that afford rich opportunities for practice, but fail miserably when those same reasoning skills are needed to deal with novel issues. Cognitive skills learned in one context often show dramatically little transfer to unfamiliar contexts. Since most people receive little practice reasoning about challenging issues of belief, it is not surprising that there are intellectual giants who reason like novices in this domain.

Even within a specific domain, the cognitive processes involved in drawing inferences from experience exhibit systematic patterns of error. It is tempting to imagine the process of learning about the world as one in which raw, uninterpreted experiences are analyzed in search of robust regularities that capture the causal structure of reality. This does not seem to be an accurate characterization of human learning processes. Cognitive learning mechanisms appear to be strongly "hypothesis driven," embodying "working hypotheses" about the nature of the world that can be incrementally modified by experience. Importantly, these "working hypotheses" color the very perception of our experiences, causing some aspects of our experiences to be attended and others ignored. Aspects of our experiences that are consistent with these "working hypotheses" are more easily retained in our memory, as well, with violations of expectations being lost unless they are particularly salient. This "hypothesis-driven" nature of learning also gives rise to a phenomenon known as "confirmation bias," in which evidence in favor of the current hypothesis is recognized and remembered much more reliably than evidence against that hypothesis. The result of these systematic biases is a kind of resistance to belief revision—a resistance that is particularly evident in domains in which complex experiences lend themselves to a multitude of interpretations, such as politics or religion.

In addition to uncovering general properties of knowledge and belief, some cognitive scientists have investigated questions that deal specifically with religion and religious experiences. One important question involves the cross-cultural prevalence of religious belief. Why is religion so common? Proposed answers to this question fall into two general categories: (1) religion is useful, and (2) religion is a side effect of other cognitive processes. Many researchers have identified positive contributions that religion makes to individuals and to communities, and they have argued that these positive effects have led to the cementing of religious propensities either in the human genome through natural selection or in various cultures through cultural evolution. Unfortunately, the cited positive contributions offer little in the way of explanation for the commonalities of religious belief across cultures. For example, some have argued that religion leads to community cohesion and cooperation, and has, therefore, led to cultural success. It is not clear, however, why frameworks for communal cohesion require the positing of the spirits and gods that are nearly universal constituents of religious belief. Other researchers argue that religion answers a deep individual need for answers concerning the nature of the universe, but this explanation seems to ignore the facts that (1) many people seem quite happy without such answers and (2) many religions offer little in the way of explanation, relishing mystery over knowledge. It is common in the West to see religion as a means to calm one's fear of death, but this cannot explain the ubiquity of religion, since many religions lack an afterlife or offer only a kind of afterlife that is "worse than death." In short, while it is difficult to deny that religion has served a variety of constructive purposes, these contributions generally fail to explain why religion is so common. An alternative to the "religion is useful" response to this question is to posit that religious belief is a side effect of other cognitive processes. Just as our experience of optical illusions is a side effect of how our visual system has evolved to deal with natural scenes, religious belief may be a side effect of how our brains have evolved to solve practical daily problems. In particular, humans are social primates whose evolutionary history is steeped in daily strife over issues of cooperation and conflict. Cognitive scientists have produced a growing body of evidence that the social nature of both our evolutionary past and our upbringing has shaped the cognitive mechanisms of our brains. For example, there appears to be a region in the temporal lobe of the brain that is particularly well-suited to process views of faces. Infants appear to distinguish between animate and inanimate objects early in development, suggesting that the brain is primed to learn this distinction. In some cases, people exhibit much better reasoning performance on social problems than on logically identical nonsocial reasoning problems. It may be the case that our social cognition capabilities have become so central to our success that they are automatically engaged and employed whenever a problem is to be solved. Thus, when lightning strikes a friend, our social cognition mechanisms immediately interpret the event in a social way, asking questions like "Who will benefit and who will suffer from this event?" "Who wanted this event to happen?" "Was this retribution for a violated social pact?" and so on. The constant autonomous functioning of social cognition systems could thus readily fabricate interpretations of events— "working hypotheses" concerning what happened—that involve unseen agents and "divine laws." In short, this view holds that coming up with social explanations for observed events is so important in our daily lives that our brains now produce such explanations automatically, even in situations in which a social explanation is inappropriate. This account explains the ubiquity of religion in terms of the universal importance of human social interaction, with the widespread appearance of spirits, gods, and magical action-at-distance arising from the reflex of social cognition systems to ascribe agent-based interpretations to situations in which no agents are visibly present. This hypothesis concerning the widespread nature of religious belief is consistent with a broad array of findings in the cognitive sciences, but it is still somewhat controversial. Research efforts are ongoing in search of additional supporting evidence for this account.

Most people acquire religious beliefs slowly, integrating the explicit education provided by their culture with their own daily experiences. Some individuals, however, have punctate experiences that substantially alter their religious beliefs and behavior. These experiences tend to be very emotional, filled with joy or dread, but they include other consistent properties, as well, such as a sense of the presence of an invisible "other" or a loss of the sense of self (see RELIGIOUS AND MYSTICAL EXPERIENCES). Cognitive neuroscience has begun to investigate the neural mechanisms that give rise to such experiences, offering a physical explanation for these phenomena to replace the standard explanation of spiritual revelation. Prompted by studies of temporal lobe epileptics, who sometimes report life-changing religious experiences during seizures, researchers have hypothesized that anomalous electrical activity in this part of the brain may give rise to such revelations. The temporal lobe contains a large variety of neural circuits, but the healthy function of some of these circuits appear to be particularly relevant to religious experiences. The outer cortical layers of the temporal lobe contain high-level portions of the visual system, embodying knowledge about the appearance and meaning of visual objects, including faces. This cortical tissue is also involved in the processing of linguistic meaning, suggesting that inappropriate stimulation may result in "hearing voices" or "receiving messages." Deep inside the temporal lobe are brain areas associated with emotional processing and structures involved in autobiographical memory. Stimulation of emotion areas may imbue religious experiences with a deep sense of personal significance, while anomalous electrical activity in memory areas might decouple current mental experiences from the "sense of self" constructed by our own personal memories, either disrupting this sense of self or making thoughts appear to stem from some other agent. Thus, it is quite possible that religious experiences are the natural result of inappropriate stimulation of temporal lobe brain areas. Indeed, magnetic fields can be used to induce electrical activity in the temporal lobe, and doing so can sometimes produce powerful hallucinations similar to religious experiences in healthy people. These experiments offer strong evidence for a physical, rather than supernatural, cause for religious experiences.

Researchers have also investigated the neural basis of experiences reported during meditation and prayer. Using modern brain-imaging techniques, changes in the activity of different brain areas can be detected while a subject is meditating. These studies have discovered a variety of interesting results, including an increase in frontal lobe activity and a decrease in activity at a particular locus in the parietal lobe. Frontal activation is often associated with effortful deliberation and purposeful focus of attention, which is likely to be present during meditation. The parietal lobe is involved in the representation of space around the body and active movement in that space, suggesting that the decrease in activity in this region may result in the "becoming one with the universe" feeling reported by some meditators. Once again, the cognitive sciences have offered hypotheses concerning the phenomenology of meditation and prayer that depend on the physical properties of the brain, rather than supernatural communication.

The cognitive sciences primarily focus on the fundamental processes of perception, thought, and action. This field has begun to paint a sufficiently elaborated portrait of human cognition, however, to begin the process of generating scientific hypotheses concerning the nature of belief and unbelief. As this line of inquiry continues, further efforts will be needed to test these hypotheses, providing additional supporting evidence for natural explanations of religious belief and religious experience.

BIBLIOGRAPHY

Anderson, J. R. *Cognitive Skills and Their Acquisition.* Hillsdale, NJ: Lawrence Erlbaum Associates, 1981.

Barkow, J., L. Cosmides, and J. Tooby, *The Adapted Mind: Evolutionary Psychology and the Generation of Culture.* Oxford: Oxford University Press, 1992.

Boyer, P. *Religion Explained: The Evolutionary Origins of Religious Throught.* New York: Basic Books, 2001.

Bransford, J., A. L. Brown, and R. R. Cocking, *How People Learn: Brain, Mind, Experience, and School.* Washington, DC: National Academy Press, 1999.

Cosmides, L. "The Logic of Social Exchange: Has Natural Selection Shaped How Humans Reason? Studies with the Wason Selection Task." *Cognition* 31 (1989).

Guthrie, S. *Faces in the Clouds: A New Theory of Religion.* Oxford: Oxford University Press, 1993.

Hill, D. R., and M. A. Persinger. "Application of Transcerebral, Weak (1 microT) Complex Magnetic Fields and Mystical Experiences: Are They Generated by Field-Induced Dimethyltryptamine Release from the Pineal Organ?" *Perceptual and Motor Skills* 97, no. 3 (2003).

Johnson-Laird, P. N., and R. M. J. Byrne. *Deduction.* Hove, UK: Lawrence Erlbaum Associates, 1991.

Kahneman, D., P. Slovic, and A. Tversky. *Judgment under Uncertainty: Heuristics and Biases.* Cambridge: Cambridge University Press, 1982.

Newberg, A. B., E. G. D'Aquili, and V. Rause. *Why God Won't Go Away: Brain Science and the Biology of Belief.* New York: Ballantine, 2002.

Persinger, M. A. "Experimental Simulation of the God Experience: Implications for Religious Beliefs and the Future of the Human Species." In *Neurotheology: Brain, Science, Spirituality, Religious Experience,* edited by R. Joseph. San Jose, CA: University Press, 2002.

Piattelli-Palmarini, M. *Inevitable Illusions: How Mistakes of Reason Rule Our Minds.* New York: Wiley, 1994.

Pinker, S. *How the Mind Works.* New York: Norton, 1997.

Wason, P. C., and P. N. Johnson-Laird. *Psychology of Reasoning: Structure and Content.* London: Batsford, 1972.

DAVID C. NOELLE

COHEN, CHAPMAN (1868–1954), English atheist journalist and campaigner. Chapman Cohen was born on September 1, 1868, to a Jewish family living in Leicester. Largely self-educated, Cohen had read many of the classic works of philosophy by the time he was seventeen. The two greatest influences on his thought were Baruch SPINOZA and Herbert SPENCER. Cohen came to FREETHOUGHT in 1889 after hearing a Christian Evidence Society speaker bullying and deriding an aged secularist. He immediately took the old man's side in the dispute, inquired into his beliefs and, soon after, joined the NATIONAL SECULAR SOCIETY (NSS). Cohen became a prominent member of the organization, and was one of its most popular and effective speakers for half a century. He was elected vice president of the NSS in 1895, and was widely seen as the person who would succeed G. W. FOOTE, the society's president. When Foote died in 1915, Cohen did indeed become president of the NSS and editor of its journal, the *FREETHINKER*. He remained a staunch defender of Foote's reputation for the rest of his life.

During these years Cohen was active in representing the NSS's interests in a lengthy legal struggle over a large bequest to the society, which had been challenged by aggrieved relatives on the grounds that bequests to organizations critical of religion were illegal. Such was the discrimination against freethinkers at the time that this objection commanded some legal validity. However, the NSS won the case in April 1915, the family's appeal was lost in July the same year, and the legality of the Bowman bequest was finally ratified by the House of Lords on May 14, 1917. This was a considerable victory in the struggle for the right of freethinkers to receive bequests.

Cohen's other lasting contribution was his steady stream of journalism. His editorship of the *Freethinker* lasted from 1915 to 1951, which makes him one of the longest-serving editors of any publication in freethought history, ranking alongside Charles Albert WATTS with the *Literary Guide*, Horace SEAVER with the *BOSTON INVESTIGATOR*, and James O. HANLON with the *New Zealand Rationalist*.

Much of Cohen's journalism was reprinted in pamphlet or book form. He had a strong preference for short works accessible to the general reader. His themes were dominated by classical freethought: the errors of the Bible (see BIBLICAL ERRANCY), the pagan origins of Christianity, free will and DETERMINISM, evolution over creation (see DARWINISM; EVOLUTION AND UNBELIEF; RELIGION IN CONFLICT WITH SCIENCE), and religion as a bar to progress. One of his most important contributions, and what set him apart from many of his contemporaries, was his fearless and consistent advocacy of ATHEISM rather than AGNOSTICISM. His were among the clearest expositions of popular atheism in the first half of the twentieth century. Cohen also put his excellent speaking skills to use in some memorable debates, most notably with Sir Arthur Eddington, a theistically inclined physicist, and Cyril Joad, a popular philosopher with leanings toward vitalism.

After World War II Cohen started to age rapidly. He eventually stepped down as president of the NSS in 1949, but retained, probably unwisely, the editorship of the *Freethinker* for two more years. He died on February 4, 1954. Cohen kept the details of his private life out of the public arena. We know little more than that he was happily married, and had a daughter, who died tragically at age twenty-nine, and a son, Raymond, who became a physician.

BIBLIOGRAPHY

Cohen, Chapman. *Almost an Autobiography*. London: Pioneer Press, 1941.
———. *The Grammar of Freethought*. London: Pioneer Press, 1921.
Herrick, Jim. *Vision and Realism: A Hundred Years of the* Freethinker. London: G. W. Foote and Company, 1982.

BILL COOKE

COLENSO, JOHN WILLIAM (1814–1883), English clergyman and African activist. John William Colenso was born in St. Austell, Cornwall, on January 24, 1814, and educated at St. John's College, Cambridge, thanks to the help of prosperous relatives. After several years teaching at Harrow, Colenso joined the Church of England. In 1853 he was appointed bishop of Natal. The conscientious churchman learned Zulu so that he could translate religious works into that language. When asked by a Zulu convert whether the story of the Flood was literally true, Colenso found himself at a loss to answer in the affirmative. This inspired him to write a book called *The Pentateuch and the Book of Joshua Critically Examined*, the first part of which appeared in 1862. Colenso denied that Moses was the true author of the Pentateuch (the first five books of the Old Testament) and pointed out many other historical absurdities in it. This was at the time a very controversial, even dangerous, claim to make. Only a century before Colenso, the English radical Peter ANNET had suffered imprisonment and two spells in the pillory for the same assertion. The first imprint of Colenso's book sold ten thousand copies, coming in the wake of the fractious debates over Charles DARWIN's *The Origin of Species* and *Essays and Reviews*, a collection of articles on BIBLICAL CRITICISM, which at the time was still more controversial. The Church of England was alarmed to face this new chal-

lenge, coming as it did from a bishop. Even normally tolerant religious liberals like Frederick Denison Maurice were moved to castigate what they saw as the historical and religious untruths of the work.

Colenso was subjected to a great deal of harassment as a result of his book. All but three English bishops signed a letter demanding that Colenso resign his office, which he refused to do. While he was defending himself in England, an Episcopal synod in South Africa condemned Colenso in his absence. In November 1863 Colenso was charged with denial of the doctrines of the divinity of Christ, the Atonement, endless punishment in hell, and the literal inspiration of scripture. Colenso appealed to the Privy Council, as the writers whose works appeared in *Essays and Reviews* had done shortly before. As it had with the earlier case, the Privy Council found in favor of Colenso and declared the South African decision null and void. However, the fanatical opposition, led by Bishop Gray of Cape Town, was not to be put off. Gray publicly excommunicated Colenso in 1864 and continued his campaign until 1869, when Colenso was finally stripped of his office.

Undaunted, Colenso remained in South Africa, where he extended his study of the Pentateuch to cover seven volumes, concluding in 1879. His work was influential among European biblical scholars, in particular the Dutchman Abraham Kuenen. The hostility of Gray and others toward Colenso was motivated as much by racism as by theological conservatism. After all, Colenso had taken seriously the question of his Zulu convert. He also had an honorable record championing the rights of Africans. During his time as bishop of Natal, Colenso had compiled a Zulu-English dictionary and, more controversially, permitted Zulu converts to retain their polygamous marriages. Colenso died in Durban on June 20, 1883.

BIBLIOGRAPHY

Hinchcliff, Peter. *John William Colenso, Bishop of Natal*. London: Thomas Nelson, 1964.
Robertson, J. M. *A History of Freethought in the Nineteenth Century*. London: Watts and Company, 1929.

BILL COOKE

COLLINS, ANTHONY (1676–1729), English freethinker. The "Goliath of freethinking," as Thomas Henry HUXLEY described him, Anthony Collins was educated at Eton and King's College, Cambridge, where his tutor was Francis Hare, author of the unorthodox *Difficulties and Discouragements* (1714), which Collins often quoted.

Scion of a wealthy legal family, Collins studied at the Middle Temple, one of the major legal societies in London, but was never called to the bar. His acquaintances included Lord SHAFTESBURY, Robert Molesworth, John TOLAND, Matthew TINDAL, Pierre Desmaizeaux,

John Trenchard, Thomas Gordon, Thomas CHUBB, and, most notably, John LOCKE, with whom he became intimate in 1703. Locke's letters to Collins, printed in 1720, express a high regard for his amiable character, love of truth, and grasp of Locke's philosophy. Collins, wrote Locke fondly, had "an estate in the country, a library in town, and friends everywhere."

Theoretical Writing. Collins's authorship falls into two periods of about a decade each. From 1707 to 1717 most of his writings are theoretical; from 1720 to 1729 they are mainly historical. All of his publications are anonymous. He was not, as was often claimed, the author of *Several of the London Cases* (1700), although he probably assisted Tindal in *The Rights of the Christian Church* (1706), with whose anticlerical opinions he was certainly in agreement. In 1707 he published *An Essay concerning the Use of Reason*, in which he champions RATIONALISM and cognitive language. His defense of minimal standards of reason against important theological qualifications (in this case mysteries supposedly above our understanding) is a prevailing feature of his works.

With *A Letter to Dodwell, Containing Some Remarks on a (Pretended) Demonstration of the Immateriality and Natural Immortality of the Soul*, also printed in 1707, Collins began a debate with Samuel Clarke, in which by 1708 each of the disputants had issued four pamphlets. Although Collins argues for the materiality of the soul and against its natural immortality, he says that he believes in its supernatural immortality, that is, an afterlife based not on philosophy or reason but on the gospel. Despite this appearance of orthodoxy, these pamphlets established Collins's reputation as a leading infidel; they also exerted a considerable influence later in the century on the French atheists, particularly Paul Henri HOLBACH and Jacques Andre Naigeon.

Less influential but hardly of less philosophical importance is the *Vindication of the Divine Attributes, in Some Remarks on Archbishop [King's] Sermon* (1710). Collins is generally taken to be a deist (see DEISM), and he does say that he believes in God. But there is no reasoned defense of natural theology in his writings, and his actual arguments are subversive of all religious belief. Thus in the *Vindication* he shows that literal knowledge of God is a necessary condition for theistic belief; and that Archbishop King's fideistic negative theology, which was designed to overcome apparent contradictions among the divine attributes by making those attributes literally inaccessible, cannot satisfy this necessary condition. Nor does Collins do anything to remove these contradictions, to which, as he says, Pierre BAYLE had called attention in his *Historical and Critical Dictionary* (1697–1702).

Moreover, in his last pamphlet against Clarke, *The Answer* (1708), Collins argues that as our thinking is material, it has an "intire and total Disagreement with Thinking, in that only Immaterial Being." From this it seems to follow that we can have no literal knowledge of God, and hence the necessary condition for theistic belief cannot be met. Again, in *The Answer*, Collins argues that in order to prove the existence of God it is necessary to have some idea of the creation of matter ex nihilo. But he suggests that there can be no such idea. Although he says that he wishes to defend theism, what he actually does here and elsewhere is to undermine it. Apart from such internal evidence for Collins's atheism, there is also important external evidence from George Berkeley, who claimed to have heard Collins say that he had found a proof for the nonexistence of God.

In 1713 Collins issued his best-known work, the *Discourse of Freethinking*, which continues his defense of reason by opposing restrictions on intellectual inquiry. The *Discourse* drew replies from Richard Steele, Jonathan Swift, William Whiston, Benjamin Hoadley, Berkeley, Francis Hare, and, most notably, Richard Bentley, who was said to have crushed Collins. There is some debate, however, about where the victory lies. In *Dynamics of Religion* John Mackinnon ROBERTSON vigorously champions Collins; more recently the older view has been endorsed by James O'Higgins in his informative study of Collins. However, Father O'Higgins—who dismisses the atheistic interpretation—tends to overrate Collins's opponents, particularly Bentley and Clarke. Soon after publication of the *Discourse*, Collins left England for his second visit to the Continent; rumor had it that he was forced to flee England by the threatening reception of his book.

Collins's next book, his classic defense of determinism, *Philosophical Inquiry concerning Human Liberty*, appeared in 1717. In this model of clarity and succinctness, Collins united the psychic determinism of Locke with the metaphysical determinism of Thomas HOBBES and Baruch SPINOZA. The *Philosophical Inquiry* was warmly praised by VOLTAIRE, Joseph Priestley (who reprinted it in 1790), Dugald Stewart, and the French atheists. This, *The Answer*, and *Vindication* are now the most readable and relevant of Collins's works.

Historical Work. After this, Collins's writing becomes more historical. Between 1720 and 1721 he collaborated with John Trenchard and Thomas Gordon on the periodical paper the *Independent Whig*, which Francis Squire described as "the most absurdly witty, profanely serious, fallaciously plausible, and rhetoricaly nonsensical [work] that was ever printed." Most of Collins's articles criticize some form of priestcraft.

The Grounds and Reasons of the Christian Religion (1724), directed against messianic prophecies, is Collins's most important historical work. As he noted in the sequel, *The Scheme of Literal Prophecy Considered* (1726), *The Grounds* elicited no less than thirty-five replying books and pamphlets. Here Collins opposed the prevailing view that theological doctrines could have the force of scientific statements without having to comply with the rigorous conditions of such statements.

Before Collins's critique, apologists tended to conflate

literal and symbolic fulfillment of the Old Testament prophecies. He argued that none of the prophecies concerning the Messiah could have been literally accomplished by Jesus, as described in the New Testament, since most of them could be shown to be about events that occurred many years before his birth. As there was no literal fulfillment of the messianic prophecies, and as the authenticity of the New Testament depends, Collins claims, on this literal fulfillment, the conclusion would seem to be that the New Testament is not authentic. However, this is not the conclusion Collins draws. He says that the New Testament is authentic because it contains symbolic fulfillment of the Old Testament prophecies. However, no commentator has taken him at his word. The works Collins published later—*Letter to the Author of the* Grounds (1726) and *Letter to Rogers* (1727)—are related to the prophecies debate.

Collins never articulated an original or well-rounded philosophy. His forte lay in developing, combining, and applying the radical doctrines of his predecessors, notably Locke, Spinoza, John Tillotson, Hobbes, and Bayle.

An obituary notice claimed that Collins said on his deathbed that he "was persuaded that he was going to that place which God had designed for those that love him." But it is hard to take such a statement seriously (see DEATHBED CLAIMS CONCERNING UNBELIEVERS). As we have seen, Collins did not believe (as deists are supposed to) that unaided reason could prove we were immortal. He said he believed in supernatural immortality; indeed, in the *Discourse of Freethinking* he asserts: "[T]he true Principles upon which immortality of the soul depends, are only to be fetched from the New Testament." But since it is generally agreed that he did not believe that the New Testament was divinely inspired, and that he had done much to undermine its authority in *The Grounds*, it does not appear that he had any basis for being "persuaded" of an afterlife.

While opinions differ concerning the extent of Collins's unbelief, there is universal agreement on his high moral character. Thus, the pious Lord Egmont, who "knew him and have eat with him," writes of Collins in an unpublished memoir: "In a word, his worst enemies could not charge him with immorality, nor his best friends acknowledge him a Christian." Egmont reports that Collins said, "I perceive myself the only man who believes nothing yet acts morally honest, while all my friends are by their scandalous lives a reproach to unbelief." Much of Collins's largely uneventful life was spent in rural Essex, either tending his ample estates (about twenty thousand acres) and his magnificent library (more than seven thousand volumes), or conscientiously discharging the duties of a county justice and treasurer.

Two essays by Collins appeared posthumously in the *Independent Whig* (1732): one on mystery, the other on religious authority. It is fairly certain that he was responsible, or largely responsible, for the 1741 annotated edition of CICERO's *Treatise on the Nature of the Gods*, which anticipates, in some measure, David HUME's argument against miracles. A work published in 1729, *Discourse concerning Ridicule and Irony*, has also been attributed to Collins.

BIBLIOGRAPHY

Berman, David. "Anthony Collins: Aspects of His Thought and Writings." *Hermathena* 69 (1975).

———. "Anthony Collins's Essays in the *Independent Whig*." *Journal of the History of Philosophy* (1975).

———. "Editor's Introduction." In *Atheism in Britain*. 5 vols. Bristol: Thoemmes Press, 1996.

———. *A History of Atheism in Britain*. London: Routledge, 1990.

———. "Hume and Collins on Miracles." *Hume Studies* (1980).

"Collins, Anthony." In *Biographia Britannica*. London, 1763.

"Collins, Anthony." In *Philosophical Inquiry*. London, 1890.

O'Higgins, James. *Anthony Collins: The Man and His Works*. The Hague: Martinus Nijhoff, 1970.

———. *Determinism and Freewill: Anthony Collins's* A Philosophical Inquiry concerning Human Liberty. The Hague: Martinus Nijhoff, 1976.

Robertson, J. M. *Dynamics of Religion*. London: Watts, 1927.

DAVID BERMAN

COLLINS, WILLIAM WHITEHOUSE (1853–1923), English-Australasian lecturer and editor. A prominent freethinker in three countries (see FREETHOUGHT), William Collins was exceptionally efficient, courteous, and popular.

Son of a well-to-do manufacturer, Collins was born on September 4, 1853, at Harbourne, Staffordshire, England, and educated in science and philosophy at Mason College, Birmingham. Intended for the Baptist ministry, he gravitated to commerce, worked in his father's office, and moved to London. At Science and Art Department classes in the NATIONAL SECULAR SOCIETY's Hall of Science under Edward Bibbins AVELING, he lost all religious beliefs and embraced the radical political and social program of Charles BRADLAUGH and Annie BESANT. Joining the society, he became an accredited lecturer in 1884 and lifetime vice president in 1885.

In 1885 the Australasian Secular Association invited him to Australia. After a Melbourne induction with Joseph SYMES, William Willis—the association's Sydney president—formally invited Collins to relocate there as resident lecturer. In 1886 Collins began a weekly, *Freethinker and New South Wales Reformer*, which soon merged with Symes's *LIBERATOR*. He also married the daughter of a leading freethinker, Ebenezer Skinner. In 1887 Collins lost his main source of income when Sunday lectures in theaters in New South Wales were banned, so he went on lecture tours round Queensland, New South Wales, Victoria, and Tasmania. For selling Besant's 1877 contraceptive booklet *The Law of Population* (see BIRTH CONTROL AND UNBELIEF) in 1888 he was fined five pounds, but was acquitted on appeal. In 1889 he launched a monthly, *Freedom: An Advocate of Social Political and Religious Liberty*, which ran a year. Then he left on a lecture tour of Tasmania and New Zealand.

His New Zealand tour began in Dunedin and ended in Christchurch, where the Canterbury Freethought Association (CFA) invited him to become secretary-lecturer. In 1893 he returned to Sydney to revive its ailing secularist movement, but soon returned to Christchurch to successfully contest a parliamentary election. He lost his seat in 1896, regained it in 1899, but lost again in 1902 and 1905. Throughout this period his debates on religion and morality and lectures on evolution (see EVOLUTION AND UNBELIEF) and astronomy continued uninterruptedly; and he published a monthly, *Tribune* (1894–95).

With his monthly *Examiner* (1907–17), conversion of the CFA into the New Zealand Rationalist Association (1909), and countrywide lecturing, he labored to establish a national movement. It slumped when he returned to Sydney in 1918, became president of the Rationalist Association of New South Wales, and died on April 12, 1923.

BIBLIOGRAPHY

Dakin, Jim. "New Zealand's Freethought Heritage." *New Zealand Rationalist and Humanist/Open Society* 74, no. 2, 3, 4; 75, no. 1, 2, 3 (2001–2002).

Tribe, David. *100 Years of Freethought.* London: Elek, 1967.

DAVID TRIBE

COLMAN, LUCY (1818–1906), American abolitionist and FREETHOUGHT activist. Lucy Colman was born at Sturbridge, Massachusetts. Opposed to slavery and skeptical of religion from her teens, she joined the Universalists (see UNIVERSALISM TO 1961). Twice married, through research she discovered that the legal rights of married women were scarcely broader than those of slaves and took as her cause the emancipation of slaves *and* women.

By 1852 she renounced Christianity, taking up Spiritualism (see SPIRITUALISM AND UNBELIEF). In that year her second husband died. Few jobs being open to women, she accepted employment as a teacher in a "colored school" in Rochester, New York. Repulsed by its segregation, she quietly lobbied parents to withdraw their children; the school closed within a year. A fellow teacher had been future suffrage leader Susan B. Anthony (see WOMAN SUFFRAGE MOVEMENT AND UNBELIEF), who arranged for Colman to address a state teacher's convention regarding her controversial opposition to corporal punishment. When a questioner objected

that the Bible endorsed corporal punishment, Colman replied that nineteenth-century civilization had outgrown the Bible. The resulting controversy built Colman's reputation; she became a full-time abolitionist and a speaker with a special gift for silencing Christian hecklers. Challenged by a minister for speaking in public with her head uncovered, both forbidden to women by the Bible, she demanded to know why he appeared in public clean-shaven, quoting a scriptural passage admonishing men not to trim their beards.

In 1862 Colman's only daughter died at seventeen. Refusing a Universalist service, Colman opted for a more secular funeral conducted by Frederick DOUGLASS. She moved to Washington, DC, where she orchestrated and attended an unsatisfactory meeting between Abraham Lincoln and the black evangelist-reformer Sojourner Truth. (A later meeting between Colman, Truth, and Lincoln's successor as president, Andrew Johnson, was more successful.)

Having broken with Spiritualism, Colman embraced freethought. She addressed numerous conventions and contributed regularly to movement papers including the *BOSTON INVESTIGATOR* and *THE TRUTH SEEKER*. She moved to Syracuse, New York.

She participated in the 1878 freethinkers' convention in Watkins (now Watkins Glen), New York, at which *Truth Seeker* publisher D. M. BENNETT and activists Josephine Tilton and W. S. Bell were arrested for selling the free-love pamphlet *Cupid's Yokes* (see SEX RADICALISM AND UNBELIEF; HEYWOOD, EZRA; COMSTOCK, ANTHONY, AND UNBELIEF). Colman paid Tilton's bail and campaigned for the trio's acquittal (the case expired without trial) while continuing her women's rights work. Also in 1878, at a meeting of the National Woman Suffrage Association, she offered a resolution indicting religion as the primary agent of woman's subjugation. Frederick Douglass rose to contend that self-sacrifice was good for women; according to a contemporary account, Colman cited Douglass's own principles to argue him into silence. Her proposition was adopted.

In 1891 Colman published her autobiography, *Reminiscences.* She died at Syracuse on January 18, 1906, aged eighty-eight.

BIBLIOGRAPHY

Colman, Lucy N. *Reminiscences.* Buffalo, NY: H. L. Green, 1891.

Gaylor, Annie Laurie. *Women without Superstition: "No Gods—No Masters."* Madison, WI: Freedom From Religion Foundation, 1997.

Gray, Carole. "I Love Lucy!" *American Atheist,* Spring 1997.

Macdonald, George E. *Fifty Years of Freethought.* New York: Truth Seeker Company, 1929.

New York Freethinkers Association. *The Proceedings*

and Addresses at the Freethinkers' Convention Held at Watkins, N. Y. New York: D. M. Bennett, 1878.

TOM FLYNN

COMSTOCK, ANTHONY, AND UNBELIEF (1844–1915),

American Protestant antivice crusader. This famous Christian fundamentalist, counted among the "monsters of creation" by critics of his moral crusades, was described as follows by his victim Ida CRADDOCK in her 1902 suicide note: "The man is a sex pervert: he is what physicians term a sadist—namely a person in whom the impulses of cruelty arise concurrently with the stirring of sex emotion. The sadist finds keen delight in inflicting either physical cruelty or mental humiliation upon the source of that emotion."

Born on March 7, 1844, at New Canaan, Connecticut, the son of Polly Lockwood and Thomas Anthony Comstock was of Puritan (Congregational) stock. This farm boy of sturdy health had six siblings. From his mother he learned religion, the obsession he would later impose upon millions of people. Comstock's life is simply a long list of crusades against evil, ranging from gambling to the discussion of sex, to abortion, or any criticism of Christianity. At age eighteen he shot rabid dogs and destroyed a whiskey still near Winnipauk, Connecticut. As an enlisted man serving in the Union Army for the last eighteen months of the Civil War, he found Protestant ministers who would preach to his regiment and organized countless prayer meetings. In St. Augustine, Florida, he was made the lay head of an Episcopal church, and he became unpopular for refusing to allow fellow soldiers to use the church for "singing and pleasure." His 1864 diaries describe his campmates wrecking his bed and gear in response to his strident piety.

After the war Comstock worked as a clerk in the dry goods business and became involved with the Young Men's Christian Association (YMCA) in New York. After a few years he settled in Brooklyn. The great cause of the YMCA was then the recreational behavior of young men during nonworking hours, which included gambling, drinking at saloons with "pretty waiter girls," not attending prayer meetings, and reading what was considered to be obscene literature. Comstsock believed that these erotic publications were "feeders of brothels," and that obscenity and drunkenness were "twin devils." He married Margaret Hamilton in 1871.

Not yet able to make arrests himself, Comstock arranged them, initially targeting the retail merchants of offending materials. He would buy a questionable item and take it to a police magistrate as evidence for a complaint. When the YMCA began financing his efforts as its Committee for the Suppression of Vice (which later became an independent society), he escalated his campaign by targeting publishers and the express drivers who transported the stock and printing plates. It is at this point that Comstock began to display the blind cruelty with which he practiced his Christianity. He would announce as achievements the deaths of his prey, by suicide or odd accident, in his public addresses.

Comstock arranged for the arrest of the spiritualist and feminist Victoria Woodhull and her sister, Tennessee Claflin, in 1872 for exposing a love affair between Reverend Henry Ward Beecher and Elizabeth Tilton, the wife of another preacher. The sisters spent a month in jail; while free on bail, they began slamming Comstock in yet another issue of their newspaper. Woodhull was rearrested, in an early example of countless cases in which the great moral crusader attacked people simply because they criticized his moral crusades, though also to protect the image of pious society. As Woodhull pointed out at the time, items in her newspaper that Comstock described as obscene had appeared in dozens of other newspapers, but Comstock attacked only hers. Woodhull's Spiritualism was another reason for her peculiar victimization by Comstock (see SPIRITUALISM AND UNBELIEF). It was partly because he failed to convict Woodhull that his case for a federal obscenity law was strengthened when he later brought his crusade to Washington.

In 1872 Comstock and wealthy backers from the YMCA founded the New York Society for the Suppression of Vice. There was a similar society based in Boston, and virtually all of the members of both were millionaires, in the social register, professionals, or businessmen. But Comstock's antivice movement was noticeably weaker in those US cities where it was unable to establish in the public mind that obscenity threatened the well-being of children, Philadelphia being one example. However, even in Philadelphia or in remote rural towns, Comstock did harm to people who expressed alternative opinions on women's rights, sexuality, contraception, abortion, marriage, and other topics of public interest (see BIRTH CONTROL AND UNBELIEF; SEX RADICALISM AND UNBELIEF; SOCIALISM AND UNBELIEF).

Comstock's actual authority as an arbiter of public morals originated with the Act for the Suppression of Trade in, and the Circulation of Obscene Literature and Articles of Immoral Use, which became known as the Comstock Act, passed by the US Congress on March 1, 1873. The law authorized him as a special agent of the US Post Office and gave him police powers to seize obscene or otherwise immoral materials and arrest those who sent them through the mail. This was the first federal obscenity law passed by the Congress, preceded by heavy lobbying by Comstock and a public exhibition of "obscene materials" such as dime novels and contraceptives. This exhibition, along with an unfavorable display of Spiritualist literature, was authorized by US vice president Schuyler Colfax.

In the preceding years, there had been a widespread public campaign against abortion, a common practice before the Civil War. Simultaneous with the lobbying and passage of the Comstock Act there unfolded an infamous corruption scandal involving the railroad financing company Credit Mobilier, which implicated many members of Congress as well as Vice President Colfax. In the wake of that scandal, Comstock took advantage of the outcry for morals in public life, but he redirected the finger of blame at ordinary citizens. There was an extremely serious economic depression at the time, and so the moment was perfect to create a law that improved the image of politicians. Also coinciding was the beginning of the modern era in Protestant revivalism, led by Dwight L. Moody and his singer, Ira D. Sankey. Moody bluntly indicated that his own message was God's message, and that all who "speak not according to this word, it is because there is no light in them." These extremely successful revivalists met in the very same YMCA that nurtured Anthony Comstock.

Two of Comstock's most famous arrests were made in November 1877. First was Ezra HEYWOOD, the free-love leader and anarchist (see ANARCHISM), for his birth control tract *Cupid's Yokes* and another piece called *Sexual Physiology*. Comstock physically seized Heywood during a convention, where he reported to have "looked over the audience of about 250 men and boys. I could see lust on every face." During the ensuing trial, the abject fraud of Comstockery, as his ideology was called, was brought to light. The court refused to allow the jury to see or hear any part of the offending texts. The defense was permitted neither to explain the publications nor to call any witnesses. The only admissible question was whether the texts had been mailed, while all of Comstock's assertions as to their obscenity were accepted without discussion. This routine would be repeated in countless cases throughout the vice hunter's long career. Heywood was sentenced to two years in prison and fined one hundred dollars. The Heywood family lost its home to foreclosure in the economic disaster of Ezra's conviction.

A week after Heywood's arrest, the editor of the leading freethought paper THE TRUTH SEEKER, D. M. Bennett, was arrested for sending two texts, including one by himself, "An Open Letter to Jesus Christ." A Comstock decoy letter had prompted the mailing. Bennett's case drew much attention and increased the circulation of his paper, which carried articles and letters attacking Comstock's tactics and motives. This first case ended in an acquittal, but Bennett was soon rearrested, fined three hundred dollars, and imprisoned for thirteen months for having distributed Heywood's book *Cupid's Yokes*. The ruling on this occasion by Judge Samuel Blatchford would serve as the standard in obscenity cases in the United States for fifty years. It relieved the court of any need to spell out on the record just what was obscene about the material in question.

Attacks upon Comstock and his crusade were numerous. In 1875 James Conroy, arrested for publishing obscene literature, drew a knife and slashed Comstock's face and head severely. On May 9, 1878, Comstock arrested a physician named Sarah Blakeslee Chase for a violation of the act. Chase was held for court, but after a grand jury found Comstock's case to be bogus, Chase had Comstock arrested at his office by sheriffs in New York on June 25, charging that he had arrested her "maliciously, and without proper cause." Her arrest had involved the ransacking of Chase's own and her tenants' apartments, and had caused her public disgrace as well as major financial losses. Comstock posted bail for twenty-five hundred dollars and was released.

In 1879 the pious Christian was charged with assault when he manhandled Fanny Hoffman in New York, demanding to know if she had written some intercepted letters and physically preventing her from summoning a policeman. Comstock and an assistant had cornered the woman in her home and refused to identify themselves, causing her to become alarmed. A magistrate named Pool humiliated Comstock in 1905, when the crusader arrested a dealer for allegedly obscene literature, but the magistrate was unable to find even the slightest suggestion of obscenity. When Comstock insisted that the issue was for him to decide, Pool shouted, "I don't want to hear it. Get out of this court."

Comstock received ridicule worldwide for his bizarre attacks against students and galleries of the fine arts. In one example, Comstock walked into the Art Students' League in New York and asked for a copy of *The American Student in Art*, then arrested the woman who had handed it to him and seized the entire stock of the journal. Art specialists everywhere were stunned, and students publicly jeered him. One student howled, "Why, if he were in Paris he would have been tossed in the Seine last night . . . that human moral mothball!" In other cases, only public amusement was the result, such as in 1888, when Comstock lectured at Princeton University and a statue on the campus called "The Gladiator" was provided with a red flannel garment, so as not to offend the famous prude's sensibilities. His raids on art dealerships in Philadelphia were dismal failures, with prosecutors flatly refusing to indict some of the defendants and all the cases resulting in acquittals.

It was a spectacle of corruption in public office that colored the banning of Lev TOLSTOY's newly translated novel *The Kreutzer Sonata* in July of 1890. The novel had been advance-ordered by the Philadelphia department store of John Wanamaker, but the publisher, anarchist Benjamin R. Tucker, replied that the store had missed the deadline for the early discount. It so happened that John Wanamaker was, at the time, US Postmaster General, and so he invoked the Comstock Act by declaring *The Kreutzer Sonata* unmailable on grounds of obscenity. In many American cities—though not in Philadelphia—Tucker humiliated Wanamaker in the daily papers. In Philadelphia, the postmaster general held far too much power over newspapers for his advertising revenue, for his standing as the leading lay Presbyterian, and quite a lot of raw political power as well. Editors of the *Boston Globe* (after pointing out that Tolstoy was perhaps the greatest living writer and a man of eminently religious life) wrote, "Postmaster General Wanamaker has made a burro of himself. He ought to be called upon to resign an office which he makes both harmful and ridiculous." Before the affair was over, Philadelphia police prosecuted six street peddlers for selling the classic novel and jailed them.

Moses HARMAN was another important victim of the Comstock's ruthlessness. Comstock arrested Harman in 1886 for publishing a letter from W. G. Markland concerning the case of a woman who, while recovering from surgery relating to a childbirth, had been raped by her own husband, tearing open her sutures and bringing her near death. The arrest took place eight months after the letter appeared in the paper Harman edited, *Lucifer, The Light-Bearer.* His fellow editors E. C. Walker and George Harman were arrested as well, jointly facing 270 counts of obscenity. After court battles lasting four years, they were acquitted. In 1890 Harman published a letter by the New York physician Richard V. O'Neill discussing sexual abuse he had seen within marriages that had resulted in injury or death. The letter included discussion of oral sex and sex between humans and farm animals. The trial and sentencing make a complicated tale, but with the new charge for the O'Neill letter and a resurrected charge regarding the Markland letter, Moses Harman was sentenced to five years in prison. The saga was repeated in 1905, when Harman was seventy-five years old. Articles from *Lucifer* were chosen at random (including Dora Foster's "Sex Radicalism"). He was sentenced to one year at hard labor.

While Harman moved in and out of prison in 1891–92, an anarchist writer named Lois WAISBROOKER served as the editor of *Lucifer*. It came to her attention that the US Department of Agriculture had released a book titled *Special Report on Diseases of the Horse.* While nothing in the book would surprise, much less offend, any farmer, Waisbrooker knew that if the same terms and interest were used in describing human organs, the Comstock Act would be invoked. So in an editorial, she quoted the government pamphlet verbatim, explaining that a horse's penis should be suspended in a sling if it is kicked by a mare or has been bruised by striking at the mare's thighs and failing to enter her. A postal inspector promptly charged *Lucifer* and the sixty-six-year-old Waisbrooker. It was the first of her three arrests under the Comstock Act.

Elizabeth ("Elmina") Drake SLENKER, a sex radical of the remote mountain village of Snowville, Virginia, was arrested in 1887 under the Comstock Act. After a long career as a feminist and free-love writer, she was contributing articles and advice in *Lucifer.* Slenker's opinions were not at all extreme (advocating sexual abstinence except for procreation and being involved in the Social Purity Movement). Her arrest for the possession of "ring letters" (soliciting opinions on sexual questions from people of all classes and walks of life) and other literature resulted in a dramatic trial. Defending herself

without a lawyer, she declared herself a materialist and refused to swear on the Bible, as she disbelieved in God and Christianity. By this time "Aunt Elmina" was a working grandmother who had a harelip, but she defended her work in sex education as a service to humanity and the so-called obscene literature as scientific material on medicine and surgery. She was acquitted.

A few campaigns were launched during Comstock's career to have him fired for taking bribes, but never with success. It is without doubt that by the beginning of the twentieth century this soldier of Christian decency had earned the reputation of a callous, brutal, and power-drunk religious extremist who was out of touch with the times. During the course of the trial of William Sanger for disseminating his wife Margaret SANGER's pamphlet *Family Limitation*, Comstock died September 21, 1915, of pneumonia. His cadaver was put into a hole at Brooklyn, New York.

BIBLIOGRAPHY

"Anthony Comstock Arrested." *New York Times*, June 26, 1878.

"Anthony Comstock Downed." *New York Times*, January 25, 1888.

"Art Students Jeer at Comstock's Raid." *New York Times*, August 4, 1906.

Bates, Anna Louise. *Weeder in the Garden of the Lord: Anthony Comstock's Life and Career.* New York: University Press of America, 1995.

Beisel, Nicola. *Imperiled Innocents: Anthony Comstock and Family Reproduction in Victorian America.* Princeton, NJ: Princeton University Press, 1997.

Blatt, Martin Henry. *Free Love and American Anarchism: The Biography of Ezra Heywood.* Urbana: University of Illinois Press, 1989.

Boyer, Paul S. *The Vice Society Movement and Book Censorship in America.* New York: Charles Scribner's Sons, 1968.

Broun, Heywood, and Margaret Leech. *Anthony Comstock, Roundsman of the Lord.* New York: Albert and Charles Boni, 1927.

"Cheap John's Nerve." *Boston Globe*, n.d. Reprinted in *Boston Liberty*, August 16, 1890.

"Comstock Charges Plot to Get His Job." *New York Times*, June 13, 1915.

"Get Out, Says Pool to Anthony Comstock." *New York Times*, October 7, 1905.

Haney, Robert W. *Comstockery in America: Patterns of Censorship and Control.* Boston: Beacon, 1960.

MacDonald, George E. *Fifty Years of Freethought: The Story of the* Truth Seeker *in the Form of a Biography, Vol. 1, Parts First and Second.* New York: Truth Seeker Company, 1929.

McGarry, Molly. "Spectral Sexualities: Nineteenth-Century Spiritualism, Moral Panics, and the Making of

U.S. Obscenity Law." *Journal of Women's History* (Summer 2000).

"Mister Comstock on Trial." *New York Times*, November 27, 1879.

Pivar, David J. *Purity Crusade: Sexual Morality and Social Control, 1868–1900.* Westport, CT: Greenwood, 1973.

Sears, Hal D. *The Sex Radicals: Free Love in High Victorian America.* Lawrence: Regents Press of Kansas, 1977.

ROBERT P. HELMS

COMTE, AUGUSTE (1798–1857), French philosopher. Auguste Comte is credited as the founder of sociology, and was a staunch proponent of POSITIVISM. In the fourth volume of his *Course of Positive Philosophy*, Comte proposed the word *sociology* (a hybrid term compounded of Latin and Greek parts) for his new positivist science. Comte believed that the reorganization of French society following the French Revolution would require intellectual reform. He hoped to replace religious dogma, especially Catholicism, with his positive philosophy, hence *positivism*. Comte's idea of positivism is based on the idea that everything in society is observable and subject to patterns or laws. Positivism was a way of explaining phenomena apart from supernatural (religious) or speculative causes.

Early Life. Isidore Auguste Marie Francois Xavier Comte was born January 19, 1798, in the southern French city of Montpellier during the most violent phase of the French Revolution. Long after his childhood and while living in Paris, Comte decided to call himself Auguste. His father, Louis-Auguste, was a humble employee of a tax office, and was well respected by his acquaintances. Louis-Auguste married Felicite Rosalie Boyer in 1797 in a secret Catholic ceremony. The revolutionary government had closed the churches of Montpellier, and consequently the Comtes had to hide their religious practices. Both Louis and Felicite were conservatives, which in that time and place meant Catholic and Royalist. The Comtes had three other children, Alix in 1800, Hernance (who died in infancy) in 1801, and Adolphe in 1802.

At age nine, Auguste entered lycée at Montpellier. Under Napoleon's rule, the lycées were boarding schools that served as training grounds for future soldiers and civil servants of the empire. Auguste excelled at academic pursuits and his photographic memory astounded his classmates and teachers alike. He could repeat hundreds of lines of verse after one hearing, and could recite backwards all the words on a page that he had read but once. A math teacher, a former Protestant pastor named Daniel Encontre, impressed Auguste the most. (His knowledge of mathematics would help him in his latter years when he attempted to establish the validity of the existence of "laws" in society.) At age sixteen, Auguste

entered the École Polytechnique, a school for the advanced sciences in Paris. In 1816 he led a protest of students against the teaching methods of a geometry instructor. The new conservative government ordered Comte and his whole class removed for their rebelliousness. This expulsion would have a lasting negative effect on Comte's academic career, as he never earned a college-level degree.

Claude Henri Saint-Simon. Comte insisted that his positivism developed naturally, but he was deeply influenced by the work of French utopian socialist Claude-Henri Saint-Simon. In 1817 Comte became Saint-Simon's secretary and developed a protégé-mentor relationship. At this time Saint-Simon was busy publishing the third volume of his work *L'Industrie*. Comte served as secretary and collaborator. Part 1 of this publication demonstrated how the idea of God, the explanation of nature, and morality, as proposed by the church, had been disproven by the critical ideas of the Enlightenment. Part 2 articulated a system of "positive ideas," including a philosophy without God, the "true" science of nature, and a world morality guided by liberal politics. The positivistic ideas of Saint-Simon and Comte were to be coordinated in a new *Encyclopedia of Positive Ideas*, but the financial backers of this project found the content too radical and withdrew their support. For seven years Comte and Saint-Simon collaborated on a number of projects until Comte broke from the master over a quarrel involving publication rights and intellectual issues.

The Law of Three Stages. Comte's Law of Three Stages was influenced by Saint-Simon, who had argued that changes in social organization take place (and are necessary) because of the development of human intelligence. He believed that there was a direct relation between ideas and social organization—the former influenced the latter. Thus, scientific study should be directed at the moral ideas of a society in a given point in time. Saint-Simon claimed that there were three distinct periods in western European history that were influenced by moral ideals (with each system being replaced by the next). These systems were: (1) Supernatural-Polytheistic (the belief of supernatural powers and multiple gods), established by the ancient Greeks and Romans; (2) Christian Theism (Socratic science, belief in one God), existing during the Middle Ages; and (3) Positivism (belief in science and rational thought), beginning with industrialization. Comte's evolutionary theory on societal development was centered on his belief that progress was a matter of the growth of the human mind. He reasoned that the human mind evolved through stages and so too, he proposed, must society. Like Saint-Simon, Comte stated that there were three different stages: (1) theological (reliance on supernatural or religious explanations to explain what man otherwise could not), a stage that hampered intellectual development; (2) metaphysical (the belief that mysterious forces control behavior), a transitory stage that witnessed the development of abstract thinking; and (3) positive (the belief that laws of human behavior exist and can be discovered through observation and the use of reason), the final stage of development highlighted by a reliance on science, rational thought, empirical laws, and observation. Comte's Law of Three Stages reflects his belief of social progress (an idea that had become quite popular in the eighteenth century) and the premise of human perfectibility—a term that refers to an ongoing process, not to some utopian ideal for individuals or for society.

Positive Philosophy. Comte believed that the object of all true philosophy is to frame a system that would comprehend human life under every aspect, social as well as individual. The role of the philosopher, then, is to understand the various elements of man's existence so that it may be conceived of theoretically as an integral whole. The key to understanding human behavior is to separate the subjective (e.g., beliefs) from the objective (facts). Comte insisted that the only reliable way of acquiring objective truth was through the methods of science. Knowledge based on scientific method was superior to metaphysical conjecture or theological assertion. Social positivists seek to discover social laws that will enable them to predict social behavior. Through observation of behavior a number of social relationships and arrangements should become identifiable as "facts" that can be separated from beliefs.

Comte was among the forerunners of the championing of positivism. Comte did not mean that human behavior was always subjected to these "laws"; rather, he saw positivism as a way of explaining phenomena apart from supernatural or speculative causes. Comte did believe that positivism would create theories based on factual information, evidence, and historical comparisons to predict future events. The discovery of basic laws of human behavior would allow for deliberate courses of action on the part of both individuals and society. Decision making, guided by science, would be positive. Positivism, then, would be superior to supernatural, philosophical, or religious explanations of human behavior. Comte viewed positivism as both a philosophy and a polity that must go hand in hand, the former being the basis of change and the latter as the comprehensive system to coordinate it. Morality forms the connecting link between philosophy and politics and at the same time draws the line of demarcation between them.

Positivism is grounded by a fundamental belief that there is an existing order of the universe and that the cause of every phenomenon is natural, not supernatural. Comte firmly believed that there are invariant laws of the social world and that the task of social thinkers is to discover those laws. His idea that social sciences should be grounded by empirical positivism remains a cornerstone of contemporary inquiry. Unfortunately, Comte's attempt in his later life to establish the "Religion of Humanity" (with a "positivistic church"), with himself as the "High Priest," clouded his otherwise lasting contribution to the search for scientific truth in the face of religious dogma.

BIBLIOGRAPHY

Comte, Auguste. *A General View of Positivism*. Translated by J. H. Bridges. New York: Robert Speller & Sons, 1957.

Delaney, Tim. "Auguste Comte: Proponent of Positivism and Evolutionary Thought," *Free Inquiry* 23, no. 4 (2003).

———. *Classical Social Theory*. Upper Saddle River, NJ: Prentice Hall, 2004.

Fletcher, Ronald. *Auguste Comte and the Making of Sociology*. London: Athlone, 1966.

Marvin, F. S. *Comte: The Founder of Sociology*. New York: Russell & Russell, 1965.

Pickering, Mary. *Auguste Comte: An Intellectual Biography*. Vol. 1. New York: Cambridge University Press, 1993.

Standley, Arline Reilein. *Auguste Comte*. Boston: Twayne, 1981.

TIM DELANEY

CONDORCET, MARIE JEAN ANTOINE NICOLAS CARITAT DE (1743–1794), French philosopher and politician. Marie Jean Antoine Nicolas Caritat de Condorcet was born on September 17, 1743, at Ribemont in Picardie (northern France), into a noble family of modest means. He was educated by his mother in a very strict Catholic tradition. He soon became sharply critical of the severe training he received in a Jesuit-run school whose entire program of studies was dominated by theological considerations. He complained of pedagogy under which "one learns by heart what one does not understand," guided by an absurd view of morality that "teaches the children that one cannot do good without divine grace." In his teens he became convinced that ATHEISM and science were the way he would follow.

In 1765 he published his first important essay on integral calculus, attracting the admiration of the famous mathematician d'Alembert, who is also (with Denis DIDEROT) the primary force behind the magisterial *Encyclopédie* (see ENCYCLOPÉDIE, L', AND UNBELIEF). At twenty-seven, Condorcet was elected to the French Academy of Sciences. Soon he formed acquaintances throughout learned society, including, of course, d'Alembert and all his many close friends: the economist Jacques Turgot, the famous socialite and hostess of salons Julie de Lespinasse, and of course the great encyclopedists, Denis Diderot, Étienne de Condillac, the jurist Chrétien Guillaume de Malesherbes, and others. Condorcet can thus be considered the last of the Encyclopedists. He met VOLTAIRE, whose battles for human rights impressed Condorcet indelibly after a few days spent with Voltaire at his home in Ferney.

Condorcet felt great revulsion at the widespread injustices of the Old Regime, and won regard for his natural benevolence, the purity of his enthusiasms, and his almost prophetic social views. He became close to the atheists Baron d'HOLBACH and HELVÉTIUS, and to the "Lodge of the Nine Sisters," a freethinking Masonic lodge in Paris (see FRANCE, UNBELIEF IN). He also befriended the Americans who at various times resided in Paris: Benjamin FRANKLIN, Thomas PAINE, and Thomas JEFFERSON. Under an assumed name he wrote the violently anticlerical *Letters of a Theologian*, and wrote the *Almanac against Superstitions* in which he charged that "[t]he Catholic religion is abominable, if only because it changes men into wild animals of whom priests orient the furor at their will." In 1773 Condorcet was named to the Secretariat of the Academy of Sciences (he would be named its perpetual secretary in 1776).

Condorcet was now a man of influence. His friend Turgot became minister of Louis XVI, a position of immense power. Condorcet became inspector of the Mint. For an interval he could imagine that the Enlightenment (see ENLIGHTENMENT, UNBELIEF DURING THE) stood victorious.

But his friend Turgot reached too far, issuing edicts in 1776 that dissolved the guild system, ended a tax of labor upon peasants, and instituted a single tax on land. Turgot's disgrace and dismissal would open a new phase in Condorcet's life. More and more disturbed at the state of public affairs, he argued openly with Jacques Necker, the new minister of finances, whom he hated. Meanwhile he continued to pursue his humanist activities. In 1781 he was elected to the Académie Française, the most prestigious academy of all. He embraced reform causes, fighting for the abolition of slavery, for the civil rights of Protestants and Jews, for women's right to vote, and against all sorts of then-popular obscurantisms.

In 1786 he married; his wife, Sophie, opened a salon frequented by Beccaria, Jefferson, Paine, La Fayette, and Beaumarchais. Concepts like revolutionary doctrine and the separation of church and state were freely discussed. Condorcet developed his ideas on democracy in an influential essay, "The Provincial Parliaments" (1787).

The French Revolution exploded in 1789. Condorcet befriended Emmanuel Joseph Sieyès, a revolutionary leader. Full of expectations, Condorcet became more active than ever. Entering politics, he drafted the Declaration of Human Rights (1789) and supported the 1791 (monarchic) constitution, though he found both insufficiently democratic in their final versions. Now a firm Republican, he was elected to the Legislative Assembly (of which he would become president in February 1792), then to the National Convention. At the same time he was indefatigable behind the scenes as a journalist and in drafting a vast number of reports and proposals.

At the beginning of 1792, he sided with the Girondins, a moderate Republican faction, but fought for unity among the then-dueling factions. He grew pessimistic in the face of the violent quarrels between the Girondins and their principal rivals, the Montagnards. Feeling isolated and lonely, he struggled in vain by means of many addresses and a notable journal, his *Chronique de Paris*, to convince other countries of the peaceful intentions of Revolutionary France—and to convince his colleagues to institute such economic measures as a minimum wage. He served on a nine-member committee charged with writing a draft (Republican) constitution; among the other members were Sieyès, Danton, and Paine. He often stood against majority sentiment; for example, during the trial of the king he openly opposed the death penalty. The proposed constitution, of which he had been the *rapporteur* or principal author, was not approved.

Condorcet then concentrated his energies on education reform. His splendid *Mémoires sur l'Instruction publique* of 1791 offered a prophetic plea for LAÏCITÉ, for coeducation, and generally for the democratization of education.

Meanwhile the Girondins were hurled from power; many were condemned and executed. Condorcet himself was accused of torpedoing the new constitution, so different from the one he had proposed. He escaped arrest and went into hiding from July 1793 to March 1794. At this time he wrote his most significant work, *A Sketch for an Historical Picture of the Progress of the Human Mind*. This was an enthusiastic, almost prophetic text, a rationalist manifesto that reflected the Enlightenment ideals of the Encyclopedists and which many could still endorse today. In it he denied any meaningful limits on human REASON and declared the perfectibility of humankind. Condemned to death in absentia, Condorcet was finally arrested on March 27, 1794, after an erratic manhunt. Two days later he was found dead in his cell. The manner of his death was never established; speculation ranged from suicide to a stroke to murder.

The last of the encyclopedists was also perhaps the first of the true democrats: firm in his rationalism, convincing in his atheism, and above all a devoted humanist.

JEAN-CLAUDE PECKER

CONFUCIANISM. It is impossible to reflect on any aspect of Chinese history, culture, or philosophy without reference to one of its oldest schools, Confucianism. Confucius, or K'ung-tzu (or K'ung-fu-tzu), lived from 551 to 479 BCE, and for centuries public life in China has reflected his teaching; in fact, his *Analects* still play a compulsory part in Chinese education. Some of the classical writings associated with him are known to be ascribed to him rather than actually his own, but they are consistent with his philosophy, which may be described as social HUMANISM.

The *Analects* were assembled by Confucius's students after his death, and in this work a number of key words emerge, reflecting the values which Confucianism has emphasized over twenty-five hundred years.

Fundamental to all is *jen*, loving kindness or (in Kantian terms) goodwill. This means treating people both with respect and as ends in themselves; (to quote the Golden Rule, which Confucius stated centuries before it appeared in the New Testament) not doing to others what one would not wish to have done to oneself.

Then follows *yi* (or *i*), righteousness, meaning that in certain situations one acts in a particular way simply because it is the right thing to do. Motives of an action are more important than the results, and intentions have intrinsic value (again one can identify a parallel with Immanuel KANT.)

Two ways of practicing *jen* are *zhong*, conscientiousness, and *shu*, altruism, both of which are immediately recognizable qualities in a *Chun-tzu*, a gentleman or superior man. Until Confucius's time this meant a person of superior birth, but Confucius spoke of it as a quality that any morally mature person might evince. It is the opposite of sourness, or small-mindedness, a feature which applies in politics and society as well as in personal and family life: in fact, it would be folly to look for it in the public domain if it were not first manifested in the private.

A quality that expresses the essence of Chinese values is *li*, propriety. Originally it related to rites and liturgy, but Confucius applied it to social sensitivity and etiquette. It is the basis of the Chinese concern not to cause others to "lose face," even where disagreement exists between parties. It is a means of ensuring that amid the conflicts which inevitably occur between people, society and its relationships continue to function in a civilized way.

Linked with *li* is *xiao*, filial piety. Confucius argued that the best way to honor one's ancestors is to honor and respect one's parents; even after their deaths one can honor them more by seeking to fulfill their aims than by offering sacrifices to their spirits.

We thus see that Confucius stamped his philosophy with common sense and practical wisdom. He believed that errors in the social order (and he identified many) could best be rectified through education, whereby people could and should be taught to do the right thing. Through education, he believed, anyone could become a *Chun-tzu*, making *xiao* (filial piety) the key to his actions. Confucius advocated this virtue more than one's duty to the state: a feature of his teaching which the legalist school, two centuries after his death, tried to undermine.

Confucius did not expressly reject any kind of spiritual dimension in the world, but ignored any discussion of it. His successor, Mencius (Meng-tzu), followed his teaching in most respects, but not this one. Mencius taught that one could align one's life with the spiritual forces in the world—a concept influenced by another major Chinese philosophical tradition, Taoism (see TAOISM, UNBELIEF WITHIN).

However, Mencius's main contribution to Confucianism was his assertion that human nature is essentially good, but that society warps it (a view not dissimilar to that of Jean-Jacques ROUSSEAU). It was, he said, as natural for man to show *jen* as for water to flow downhill. On this issue he was opposed by the third master in the Confucian hierarchy, Hsun-tzu, who argued the reverse: man was born selfish, and it was only through the guidelines and directions which society inevitably imposed, particularly through education, that the mold of morality could shape him. He would have agreed with both ARISTOTLE and Thomas HOBBES that it is the function of government to make the people good.

After suffering the effects of legalism for some centuries (that is, until around the beginning of the third century CE), Confucianism was infiltrated by the other two philosophies which have directly influenced Chinese thinking and behavior: Buddhism (see BUDDHISM, UNBELIEF WITHIN) and Taoism. This process of syncretization continued for about five centuries, and is generally described as neo-Confucianism. It saw the emergence of the *I Ching*, or *Book of Changes*, as an aid to meditation (and sometimes divination), used by many Chinese on a daily basis. An important later exponent of this new expression of Confucianism was Chu Hsi who laid great stress on *li* as the cosmic principle which, he believed, provided a metaphysical rationale for traditional ethics— a view which would have mortified Confucius.

There are thus two ethical strands in Confucianism. One, associated with Confucius and Hsun-tzu, is conventionalistic: we ought to follow the traditional codes of behavior for their own sake. The other, associated with Mencius and medieval neo-Confucianism, is intuistic: we ought to behave as our moral natures—or the heavenly order—dictate.

After the neo-Confucian period, philosophical concepts again became central in Confucian teachings, and the classical writings, including the *Analects*, became essential reading for all potential civil servants (this continued to be the case until 1905). The significance of Confucianism is still recognized in China and taught in schools: In fact, Mao Tse-tung ranked Confucius alongside Karl MARX, Friedrich Engels, and Vladimir LENIN (though whether Confucius would have appreciated the comparison or not is a moot point). Thus Confucianism remains, like Hinduism to Indians, quintessentially Chinese.

RAY BILLINGTON

CONJURING AND BELIEF IN THE SUPERNATURAL.

Conjuring, the stage magician's art, has frequently been employed by unscrupulous persons to foster belief in the supernatural. In return, conjurers like Harry Houdini have used their knowledge of trickery to uncover deceptions that often fool even scientists, since they are not trained to detect trickery.

Deception in the service of supernatural claims is

most ancient, early sorcerers not always having been as scrupulous as today's stage magicians to admit their wonders were accomplished by art rather than by occult powers. For example, the Westcar Papyrus in the British Museum (written circa 1500 BCE) tells of a wonder-worker named Dedi who could restore severed heads. He tactfully declined Pharaoh Cheops's offer of a prisoner for the decapitation, instead using, in turn, a goose, pelican, and ox. (With birds the head could be tucked beneath a wing and a dummy head brought into view, the magician reversing the process to resurrect the bird. Walter Gibson suspects the feat with the ox was merely a boast, although there are many ways such a trick could have been accomplished.)

Along similar lines, there is the biblical story of the duel between Moses's brother, Aaron, and the pharaoh's sorcerers. The account (Exod. 7:8–13) tells how Aaron cast down his rod, whereupon it became a serpent. When the Egyptian magicians duplicated the feat, Aaron's snake swallowed theirs. Although the events of the Exodus are not supported by external historical sources and the snake-swallowing detail smacks of pious legend making, the rod-to-serpent effect may well have been "a standard item among Egyptian sorcerers." According to Gibson, "[T]here are reliable reports of modern Egyptian wizards who have performed a similar trick." A suitable snake could be cleverly substituted for a staff of comparable form to work the pretended miracle.

Legend and magical deceptions were often interrelated, and it is typically impossible to sort out the exact relationship between them. For instance, there are stories involving magical vases, such as the miraculously refilling cruse of oil that accompanies the Jewish story of Hanukkah, the container with which Moses transformed Nile water into blood (Exod. 4.9), and, of course, the stone jars of Jesus's water-to-wine miracle at Cana (John 2:5–10)—among others. There were ancient conjurers's vases that were capable of producing just such effects, but it is difficult to know whether tricks with them prompted the legendary tales, or whether the stories instead inspired the creation of tricks to illustrate them (such as by today's "gospel magicians")—or whether the relationship between the tales and the vases is even more complex.

A stark example of magical deception is related in the fourteenth chapter of Daniel (in the Apocrypha), concerning a supernatural effigy. The Babylonian idol of Bel (or Baal) not only drank large quantities of water but also devoured vast amounts of food. By this seeming miracle the priests won over King Cyrus to the worship of Bel. Daniel, however, was skeptical, and so a test was arranged. Cyrus had the food and wine set forth as usual but sealed the door to prevent surreptitious entry.

The following morning the seals were intact yet the food and wine were gone. Cyrus believed a miracle had occurred, but Daniel called attention to the floor, which his servants had secretly covered with sifted ashes. Thus

were revealed "the footsteps of men and women and children"—those of the priests and their families—which led to "the secret doors through which they were accustomed to enter and devour what was on the table."

Although this story may be merely a pious legend, it could have been inspired by temple trickery that is known to have existed, and it no doubt helped to motivate Jews to resist idolatry. It can also be appreciated as a model of critical thinking—what the *New Catholic Encyclopedia* calls "clever detective work" from ancient times.

A milestone in skepticism was Reginald Scot's 1584 *The Discoverie of Witchcraft*. Scot set out to demonstrate that witchcraft was a fiction, and that the black arts—including soothsaying, astrology, exorcism, spell casting, and the like—depended not upon supernatural forces but rather on trickery or skill. His treatise explains many of the secrets of legerdemain, including, for instance, how "[t]o tell one without confederacie what card he thinketh." The implications of Scot's exposés were such that King James later branded them heretical and ordered that all copies of *The Discoverie of Witchcraft* be burned.

Concerning the biblical witch of Endor, who purportedly conjured up the ghost of Samuel at the request of Saul (1 Sam. 28:7–20), Scot was of the opinion that the endeavor was a sham. He concluded that the witch had not communicated with Samuel, that instead the effect was "contrived" by the "art and cunning" of the woman, without any "supernatural devices," probably, he theorized, by the use of ventriloquism.

Whereas the witch of Endor is described in the King James Bible as "a woman that hath a familiar spirit," in the revised standard version she is "a medium"—reflecting the present term for one who purportedly contacts spirits of the dead on behalf of the living. The modern wave of mediumship began in 1848 with the schoolgirl pranks of Maggie and Katie Fox at Hydesville, New York. Although four decades later the sisters confessed that the "spirit" rappings had been produced by trickery, in the meantime the phenomenon—eventually the religion—of spiritualism spread across America, Europe, and beyond. At séances held in darkened sitting rooms and auditoriums, mediums produced such physical phenomena as slate writing, spirit photography, and "materializations" of ghostly entities.

In time, however, mediums were repeatedly caught cheating. Magicians like John Nevil Maskelyne in England and later Harry Houdini in the United States attended séances and exposed deceptions. Maskelyne wrote a book, *Modern Spiritualism*, that exposed the methods of fake mediums. Later, after medium Henry Slade was arrested in London in 1876 for producing bogus "spirit" writing on slates, Maskelyne testified at his trial, enthralling those in attendance by performing each of Slade's tricks while standing in the witness box. Maskelyne also produced on stage a levitation inspired by the medium D. D. Home who, allegedly, in 1868 floated out an upstairs window of a house in Westminster and drifted in another. Although the witnesses have been discredited, and several simple means have been postulated to reproduce the effect by trickery, Maskelyne used Home's supposedly supernatural feat as the plot for a magician's illusion. Standing on stage at Egyptian Hall in London, he floated up to the top of the high-domed ceiling, in full view of the audience. Then, spotlighted, he turned and—as Home had done—floated horizontally back to the front of the stage.

Houdini (born Erich Weiss) crusaded against phony spiritualists during the latter part of his career. He befriended elderly mediums who, in return, taught the master deceiver the secrets of their own deceptions. Houdini also attended séances—occasionally in disguise—to learn secrets and uncover trickery. Sometimes during séances he would take advantage of the darkness to secretly place lampblack on a spirit trumpet, which would subsequently be found on the medium's hands and so prove it was not spirits who had "levitated" it. On some occasions, the magician would turn on a flashlight to catch a faker.

In the 1920s Houdini gave public demonstrations of spiritualist deceptions. "Do Spirits Return?" asked one of his posters. "Houdini Says No—and Proves It." On stage the nemesis of phony spiritualists sat at a draped table. While audience members held his hands and placed the toes of their shoes upon his, beneath the table a tambourine jangled, words were chalked on a slate, and a bell rang, signaling an end to the mock séance. An assistant then pulled the cloth aside, revealing that it was the magician's foot—slipped from its shoe and with the end of its stocking cut away—that had accomplished the effects.

Today, conjuring tricks are still being used to convince credulous folk of the reality of the supernatural. In the long tradition of Hindu holy men, for example, is Satha Sai Baba of India, the so-called man of miracles. Among his feats is the production of apports (objects allegedly materialized out of thin air or "teleported" from another place). His apports include *vibuti* (or "holy ash"), gold jewelry, religious statues, and other objects. Actually, films of Sai Baba's feats reveal that he is employing sleight of hand. Crusading against him and others of his ilk is the Indian conjurer B. Premanand, who differs from the Indian godmen only in his ready admission that he accomplishes his wonders by conjuring.

BIBLIOGRAPHY

Christopher, Milbourne. *Panorama of Magic*. New York: Dover, 1962.

Dawes, Edwin A. *The Great Illusionists*. Secaucus, NJ: Chartwell Books, 1979.

Gibson, Walter. *Secrets of Magic: Ancient and Modern*. New York: Grosset & Dunlap, 1967.

Houdini, Harry. *A Magician among the Spirits*. New York: Arno, 1972.

Nickell, Joe. *Looking for a Miracle*. Amherst, NY: Prometheus Books, 1998.

———. *Real-Life X-Files: Investigating the Paranormal*. Lexington: University Press of Kentucky, 2004.

Polidoro, Massimo. *The Final Séance: The Strange Friendship between Houdini and Conan Doyle*. Amherst, NY: Prometheus Books, 2001.

Scot, Reginald. *The Discoverie of Witchcraft*. 1584. Reprint, New York: Dover, 1972.

JOE NICKELL

CONSEQUENTIALISM. In its broadest formulation, consequentialism is the view that the morality of an action depends only on its *consequences*, and not on conditions that obtained prior to the action, such as intentions or circumstances. The most famous example of consequentialism in ethics is the theory of classical utilitarianism, which received its canonical formulation from Jeremy BENTHAM, John Stuart MILL, and Henry Sidgwick. Classical utilitarianism holds that an action is right when it maximizes happiness: that is, when the value of happiness for all minus the unhappiness for all resulting from the action is greater than the value of any other action available to the actor. However, as we will see, there are many consequentialist theories in normative ethics, and so the plausibility of consequentialism does not depend on the plausibility of classical utilitarianism. Consequentialist ethics are often considered radical alternatives to traditional religious ethics that evaluate action on the basis of obedience to divine commandment or conformity to divinely authored natural law. More generally, consequentialism contradicts the deontological (that is, duty-based) character of most traditional ethical systems which evaluate action on the basis of some intrinsic properties of an action itself—such as good intentions or virtue—rather than its effects. Thus, throughout history, consequentialism of various sorts has been particularly attractive to skeptics, nontheists, humanists, and philosophical naturalists.

To appreciate the general motivation for consequentialism, we must first distinguish two components that any reasonably comprehensive moral framework will include, if sometimes only implicitly: a theory of the good and a theory of the right. A theory of the good is a view about what kinds of things are morally valuable, what kinds of properties are desirable in our actions or in the world. For example, natural law doctrine asserts the value of our natural proper functions; Kantian deontology (see KANT, IMMANUEL) asserts the value of the goodwill; Bentham's utilitarianism insists that pleasure is the only intrinsic value. A theory of the right is a view about how we ought to behave so as to properly respond to such values. There are at least two ways one could respond to a moral value (if such a thing exists). One way is to protect it, or honor it; to keep it from being somehow violated or lost. Another way is to promote it, to act so as to bring about more of the value where possible. Another way to construe consequentialism is to say that whatever one's theory of the moral good, the proper response to that good is to promote it.

It can be argued that consequentialist theories have general advantages over nonconsequentialist theories in virtue of their superior theoretical simplicity and coherence with background knowledge. Everyone, including nonconsequentialists, would agree that there are at least *some* sorts of goods to which the proper response (if they are in fact goods) is to promote them: for instance, personal hygiene, health, or education. Consequentialism suggests that this single kind of appropriate response applies to goods of all sorts, including moral goods, whereas nonconsequentialism must maintain that there are some sorts of good for which promotion is not appropriate. But why should this be? Here the nonconsequentialist needs to present an account that distinguishes values to be protected from values to be promoted in some non–ad hoc way. This challenge is most clear in the case of deontological prohibitions on certain classes of action. Consider an action of type A, which some deontological theory classifies as wrong and prohibited. Suppose that by committing a single instance of A, an agent could bring about a situation in which far fewer instances of A take place. How is it, if there is some property of A that constitutes its wrongness, that a moral agent could be indifferent to whether there are more or fewer actions that have this property? If killing is wrong, what reason can be given why we must refrain to kill, say, a ruler bent on genocide, even when by so refraining we help to bring about a situation in which more killing takes place? Consquentialism's account of moral normativity also coheres well with the dominant view of rational or prudential normativity, or so-called instrumental rationality. This is noteworthy because many leading moral theories claim that there is some kind of intimate link between rationality and morality. According to instrumentalism about rationality, the prudent thing to do is choose the best means to one's ends; that is, efficiently to promote one's own good. Nonconsequentialist accounts must explain why this extremely attractive approach to prudential goods—promoting them—cannot be extended to moral goods.

Having considered an important source of motivation for consequentialism, let's turn to some of the major objections against it. First, there are well-known objections to utilitarianism. Classical utilitarianism holds that individual happiness is the only intrinsic good. Yet we can easily imagine situations in which people experience the greatest degree of happiness but still appear to be missing some things that make a life go well. The philosopher Robert Nozick illustrated this point in a famous thought experiment called the Experience Machine. Imagine a machine that creates totally comprehensive and convincing experiences. In this perfect virtual reality simulator, you can be made to experience composing a symphony, marrying the person of your dreams, winning the Tour de France, or just spending all your days relaxing and enjoying fine food and entertainment. And yet you would have done none of these things. Nozick asks whether, given the choice, you would choose life in the Experience Machine over an actual life, with its risks and unhappiness. The thought experiment suggests that the experience of happiness is not the only intrinsic good. We also care about actually accomplishing things in the world, entering into relationships with other people, and so on. Consequentialists respond by pointing out that even if classical utilitarianism is implausible as a theory of the good, that does not show that consequentialism is inadequate as a theory of the right. The idea that morality consists in promoting the good might be correct even if it turns out that happiness is not that good.

An objection that takes aim at consequentialism itself is the objection from fairness or justice. Consider a situation in which there are two possible actions, A and B, that are exactly equal in their potential to maximize the good, whatever it might be. But A involves causing a significant injustice, such as falsely accusing someone of a crime, or breaking a promise, or taking someone's property without compensation. Nevertheless, according to consequentialism, it seems, A and B are morally equivalent. This conclusion flies in the face of our considered moral judgments. Our considered moral judgments, and much of the accumulated moral teachings of humanity, suggest that certain things should not be done to people even if doing them would produce a greater good. That is to say, people have rights. Relatedly, duties to others, such as those generated by the promises we make, are not supposed to be weighed against other values that could be promoted were the duties violated. Indeed, duties are morally important insofar as they serve as constraints on the promotion of goods. A way to generalize this objection is that consequentialism seems to ignore backward-looking reasons, reasons for acting that arise out of past events like promise making. For the consequentialist, the only morally relevant facts are facts about the future, namely, facts about the good, bad, and indifferent states of affairs that may result from an agent's choices. Again, consequentialism fails to capture this aspect of our everyday moral experience.

Another objection against consequentialism is that it is impracticable. The consequences of our actions are often highly unpredictable, so how can they serve as the criterion by which we morally evaluate our options? More troubling is a problem Daniel Dennett has called the Three Mile Island effect. Events have causal repercussions extending indefinitely into the future, so whether they promote the consequentialist's favorite good may be depend on the future point at which one surveys those effects (consider the possibility that the Three Mile Island disaster eventually had the effect of improving the safety of America's energy supply and preventing similar disasters). How far into the future does consequentialism count, and why? Similarly, consequentialism has also been indicted as being too demanding. By treating everyone's good as equal, it asks the moral agents to overlook their special obligations to those with whom they have special relationships, such as children or spouses. Although one of two people caught in a burning building might be your daughter and the other might be a stranger to you, the consequentialist analysis appears incapable of accommodating the intuition that you have more reason to save your daughter than the stranger. Also, as philosophers such as Peter Singer, Peter Unger, and Tom Regan have argued, consequentialist ethics go much further than traditional ethics in obligating us to act on behalf of others' good, for example, by assisting faraway people suffering from famine or preventable disease, or forgoing the unnecessary consumption of animals for food or research. A common reaction to such suggestions is that morality simply cannot require that much of us.

Consequentialists have pursued two different general strategies in response to these objections. One strategy is to "bite the bullet" and insist that, in view of consequentialism's various theoretical advantages, the counterintuitive results it yields do not give us reasons to reject the theory but instead give us reasons to revise our conventional moral outlooks. If the most plausible moral theory on offer turns out to be "too demanding" or "unjust" by the lights of conventional ethics, so much the worse for conventional ethics. The other strategy is to distinguish between direct and indirect consequentialism, which can be appreciated by grasping the difference between a decision procedure and a criterion of rightness. A decision procedure is a pattern of reasoning or psychological disposition that tends to result in right action. A criterion of rightness states what makes it the case that an action is right. Consequentialisms contain an account of *what a right action consists in*—bringing about more good than any of the available options (or on "satisficing" versions, bringing about enough good). But consequentialisms can also contain accounts of *how to decide which action is right* (for a particular kind of agent in a particular situation). Given the cognitive and affective constraints of human nature and circumstance (such as highly imperfect knowledge of the probable results of our actions or certain kinds of emotional bias), there may be many situations in which we will be worse at promoting the good to the extent that we deliberately attempt to promote the good. By analogy, although the criterion for promoting a financial asset might be to maximize net investment returns over time, the best decision procedure might be to select an annuity with a

diverse portfolio. One of the remarkable things about consequentialism is its theoretical flexibility with respect to decision procedures, which, like everything else in a consequentialist universe, are subject to evaluation in terms of their overall effect. This flexibility is exploited in defenses against the above objections. For example, it can be argued that we can best promote certain goods indirectly by recognizing some constraining rights or according special weight to the interests of one's friends and relatives. Indirect consequentialism is not the same as so-called rule consequentialism. Rule consequentialism is an alternative criterion of rightness: it says that right actions are those that comply with general rules whose adoption promotes the good. Therefore, rule consequentialism generates conflicts with consequentialism as such, which looks at whether each action maximizes. Indirect consequentialism likewise evaluates any given action on whether it maximizes. It just denies that the action will be successful only by aiming at maximizing. Considerable work in ethics is now being devoted to articulating a defensible indirect consequentialism.

AUSTIN DACEY

CONTROVERSIES: ATHEISM, PANTHEISM, SPINOZISM.

The Atheism, Pantheism, and Spinozism controversies were a cluster of related religious and philosophical disputes that involved many of the most esteemed minds in late eighteenth- and early nineteenth-century Germany. The late eighteenth and early nineteenth centuries witnessed frequent disputes concerning faith and reason rooted in the German Enlightenment, or *Aufklärung* (see ENLIGHTENMENT, UNBELIEF DURING THE). The *Aufklärung* was characterized by an overweening confidence in reason. Its champions embraced critical thinking, individual autonomy, and religious tolerance. Although most agreed that enlightenment would foster human well-being manifest as unlimited intellectual, moral, and spiritual progress, many disagreed about how to promote this goal. Thus, unabashed fideism (reliance on individual faith as the ultimate criterion of truth) and romanticism flourished alongside detached SKEPTICISM, realism, and idealism. Perhaps inevitably, some children of the *Aufklärung* began to question the ultimate compatibility of human welfare and enlightenment and indeed, of human belief and knowledge.

The death of the *Aufklärer* Gotthold Ephraim LESSING initiated the *Spinozismusstreit*, or Spinozism Controversy, of 1783–87. Lessing's intimate of many years, the rational theist Moses Mendelssohn, had confided to their mutual friend, Elise Reimarus, that he intended to write a tribute to Lessing's character. Reimarus shared this information with the fideistic writer F. H. JACOBI, who revealed Lessing's "deathbed" confession that he had long followed Baruch SPINOZA's philosophy. This allegation wounded Mendelssohn insofar as it implied that Lessing had died a pantheist or even an atheist, that he had doubted his best friend's confidence, and that he had regarded Jacobi as his intellectual heir. Soon, Reimarus was playing intermediary in a quarrel between Jacobi and Mendelssohn wherein each behaved dishonorably. The resulting fray attracted Immanuel KANT, Johann Gottfried von HERDER, Wizenmann, and Johann Wolfgang von GOETHE, among others. Before it ended, the rigors of the public debate led to Jacobi's physical decline and to Mendelssohn's and Wizenmann's deaths.

Ostensibly, the Spinozism Controversy concerned the theological implications of Lessing's alleged Spinozism. Mendelssohn allowed that Lessing followed Spinoza, but he argued that Spinozism constituted refined or purified pantheism, which maintains a separation of God and world. Jacobi exaggerated Lessing's commitment to Spinozism, which he claimed led to pantheism, or the identification of God with nature, and thus, to materialistic ATHEISM.

Actually, the Spinozism Controversy involved the question of whether reason or faith should have priority. Whereas Mendelssohn insisted that reason—moderated by common sense—could justify moral and religious beliefs, Jacobi maintained that abstract knowledge undermined trust in external reality, freedom, and God, which required a *salto mortale*, or mortal leap of faith. Although Kant denied any knowledge of the objects of faith, he defended the possibility of rational belief in God, freedom, and immortality. Wizenmann clarified the issues at stake by exposing tensions within Mendelssohn's "common sense," Jacobi's "faith," and Kant's "rational belief." After Mendelssohn's death, interest in Kant's transcendental idealism eclipsed concern over Lessing's Spinozism. Nonetheless, the battle over faith and knowledge would reappear during the *Atheismusstreit*, or Atheism Controversy, of 1798–99.

The Atheism Controversy involved the social, moral, and religious implications of transcendental idealism. It began with the publication of two essays, "On the Basis of Our Belief in a Divine Governance of the World" (1798) by J. G. FICHTE, a popular young idealist at the University of Jena, and "Development of the Concept of Religion" (1798) by F. K. Forberg. In 1799, protests by concerned citizens led Friedrich-August, prince-elector of Saxony, to ban the essays and to coerce Duke Karl-August of Weimar to reprimand the authors. Fichte responded with a fiery self-defense that received a deluge of recriminations and justifications from every camp. His erstwhile allies Kant and Jacobi issued public repudiations of his philosophy. Eventually, Fichte resigned his position and sought refuge in Berlin.

Tradition holds that the Atheism Controversy concerned personal and theological issues. The firebrand Fichte had often found himself at odds with authorities, garnering a list of charges that included disrupting public worship and supplanting God with reason. Although he might have moderated his position, thus avoiding the entire dispute, he refused to compromise, insisting that

his critics were the true atheists. Kant suggested that if not necessarily atheistic, Fichte's theory lacked religious and philosophical significance, whereas Jacobi described it as a more thoroughgoing atheism than Spinozism.

In truth, the Atheism Controversy concerned more than Fichte's idiosyncratic personality and theology. It raised the question of whether idealism entailed social anarchy (see ANARCHISM AND UNBELIEF) and moral despair. Fichte's contempt for the Weimar Court threatened the tolerance that his moderate colleagues enjoyed under the enlightened Karl-August. Moreover, as a supporter of the French Revolution and self-proclaimed author of the "first philosophy of freedom," he tested the social and political order. Jacobi coined the term *NIHILISM* to describe the amoral egoism that he believed Fichte's "inverted Spinozism" implied (see also STIRNER, MAX). The Atheism Controversy opened fissures within post-Enlightenment thought that widened further during the *Pantheismusstreit*, or Pantheism Controversy, of 1811.

The Pantheism Controversy concerned issues raised by idealism, romanticism, and fideism. The sanctioned origin of the dispute was Jacobi's "Of Divine Things and Their Revelation" (1811), wherein he accused F. W. J. Schelling of pantheism, but his attack was motivated by Schelling's lecture "Concerning the Relation of the Fine Arts to Nature" (1807). Still earlier, Jacobi had quarreled with Schelling and G. W. F. Hegel over Hegel's *Faith and Knowledge* (1802), responding indignantly with letters to his young followers Köppen and Bouterwek. Eventually, the controversy alienated Jacobi from his former cohort, the romantic Goethe. More importantly, it demarcated boundaries between the older transcendental idealists, Kant and Fichte, and the younger absolute idealists, Schelling and his follower, Hegel.

Although Hegel wrote *Faith and Knowledge*, Schelling helped revise it before publication. Hegel and Schelling criticized Kant, Jacobi, and Fichte for failing to reconcile the dichotomies of God and nature, infinite and finite, and faith and knowledge. Hegel claimed that Kant opposed faith and knowledge, whereas Jacobi equated faith and knowledge, while Fichte tried to overcome the division between the objects of faith and finite knowledge by postulating an infinite striving to transform nature into an earthly "kingdom of God." He also disparaged Köppen, Friedrich Schleiermacher, and Johann Gottfried von Herder for their part in the Kantian-Protestant tradition of despair.

Although Schelling and Hegel thought that transcendental idealism neglected nature and religion, they rejected its romantic veneration of nature and its fideist elevation of faith as crassly sentimental and "unphilosophic." Despite their implicit critique of romanticism, Goethe supported Schelling and Hegel during the debate, describing himself as a polytheistic artist and a pantheistic scientist. Jacobi, for his part, regarded Goethe, Hegel, and particularly Schelling as pantheists, thereby guilty of the deification of nature they condemned. As Köppen, Bouterwek, and Fries rallied to his cause, Goethe argued that Schelling's philosophy of nature disguised Spinozism in appealing Platonic garments that would lead gullible youth into atheism and then nihilism.

Although the Pantheism Controversy destroyed neither lives nor careers, it ruptured the fragile bonds between the movements generated by the *Aufklärung*, shattering their vision of the concurrence of human happiness and enlightenment. So, the contest between the idealists, fideists, and romantics deadlocked over the priority of faith or knowledge. Nonetheless, the debate isolated rifts within enlightened thought, forcing theorists to clarify their positions and thereby to scrutinize the intricate relations between belief and reason in the post-Enlightenment world.

The Spinozism, Atheism, and Pantheism controversies profoundly affected European intellectual development. The Spinozism Controversy revived interest in Spinoza, arguably the most consistent and courageous modern philosopher. Moreover, it introduced the world to Kant's transcendental idealism, which influenced nearly every branch of the arts and sciences. By revealing the specter of nihilism, the Atheism Controversy compelled philosophers to examine the ethical implications of abstraction in general and of idealism in particular. As a result of the Pantheism Controversy, Hegel escaped Schelling's shadow and dominated the European universities for the next fifty years.

Fichte, Hegel, and Schelling influenced the pessimist Arthur SCHOPENHAUER and in turn, the protoexistentialists Friedrich NIETZSCHE, Søren Kierkegaard, and Fyodor Dostoyevsky. The theories that emerged during the controversial legacy of the Enlightenment generated contemporary EXISTENTIALISM, romanticism, and postmodernism. As the young Hegelians including Ludwig FEUERBACH and Karl MARX threshed out the social implications of Hegel's philosophy, initiating worldwide revolution, the proto-fascists misappropriated the idealist and romantic traditions, spawning international genocide. Thus, the reverberations of the Spinozism, Atheism, and Pantheism controversies extend well into the twentieth century.

BIBLIOGRAPHY

Beiser, Frederick. *The Fate of Reason: German Philosophy from Kant to Fichte*. Cambridge, MA: Harvard University Press, 1987.

Fichte, J. G. "On the Basis of Our Belief in a Divine Governance of the World" (1798). In *Introductions to the Wissenschaftslehre and Other Writings*, translated and edited by Daniel Breazeale. Indianapolis: Hackett, 1994.

Hegel, G. W. F. *Faith and Knowledge*. Translated and edited by Walter Cerf and H. S. Harris. Albany: State University of New York Press, 1977.

Jacobi, F. H. *The Main Philosophical Writings and the Novel* Allwill. Translated by George di Giovanni. Montreal: McGill-Queen's University Press, 1994.

Vallée, Gérard. *The Spinoza Conversations between Lessing and Jacobi*. New York: University Press of America, 1988.

YOLANDA ESTES

CONWAY, MONCURE DANIEL (1832–1907), American author, reformer, and minister. Moncure Daniel Conway developed through Methodism, Unitarianism (see UNITARIANISM TO 1961), and a generalized theism to a belief in humanity. He moved from the United States to London, where he became a dissenting ethical leader, a powerful lecturer, and a writer of some influence.

He was born in Stafford County, Virginia, to a Southern family of distinction. His father was a magistrate and planter with conservative views. His mother was an intelligent and feeling woman who was also a homeopathic healer.

At an early age he went to a Methodist college and underwent a conversion there. He felt unable to follow his father's legal career, being more attracted to the spiritual life. He moved to a Methodist ministry in a Maryland circuit in 1851, where he felt increasingly unhappy. He came into touch with a Quaker community whose tolerant antislavery views appealed to him. He decided to train as a Unitarian minister at Harvard. By this time he had abandoned a belief in the literalism of the Bible and was becoming doubtful about the nature of Jesus. In addition he was influenced by the writings of Ralph Waldo EMERSON.

Radical Developments. He became the Unitarian minister in Washington, DC, in 1854; his radical views rapidly became apparent, especially toward slavery. After an antislavery sermon and his increasingly skeptical views on religion led to a split in his congregation, he moved to Cincinnati, where again his views led to divisions.

He was increasingly exercised by abolition and the impending Civil War, which rent his family in two. He became coeditor of an abolitionist paper, the *Commonwealth*. Abolitionists funded a trip to London, where Conway was expected to rouse support for their cause. He decided to stay in London and brought his wife— Ellen, a sensitive, intelligent, and sensible life companion—and his children.

South Place Chapel. Among the many people of influence he met in London was Peter Alfred Taylor, MP, a member of the South Place Chapel, Finsbury, which was at that time without an effective leader. He invited Conway to give his first lecture at South Place on May 6, 1863, in what was to be a key moment in his career. In 1864 he was appointed leader on a trial basis and in 1866 he took a permanent appointment. He ceased the custom of wearing robes, abandoned prayer, and changed the Bible readings to readings from the world's religions— but liked hymns. His *The Sacred Anthology* (1874) was a valuable source of readings. He slowly moved from his generalized theist position to a belief in humanity, goodness, universal reason, immensity—fine sounding, but imprecise. Nevertheless, attendance grew and there was interest from such as Robert Browning, Thomas Henry HUXLEY, John Tyndall, and Friedrich Max Müller. Conway looked at comparative religion from an anthropological viewpoint as demonstrating the variety of the human response to the ultimate questions.

A creeping disillusion and pessimism led him to return to America in 1885. Journalism and writing preoccupied him. His two-volume *The Life of Thomas PAINE* (1892) was a great achievement of scholarship and the first major sympathetic account of Paine's life.

Conway returned to London in 1892 resuming his role at South Place, his successor Stanton Coit not having fit in. This time he was less happy and when in 1897 his wife became terminally ill, he left for America again. After the death of his wife he was outraged at the American war against Spain (he was an early peace campaigner) and was to become deeply opposed to England's Boer War. An earlier trip to India, where he was shocked at primitive religious rituals, led him to question the value of studying world religions. His overall outlook continued to become more pessimistic. He moved to Paris, where he died alone in 1907.

His was the remarkable career of someone pushing nonconformist religion beyond its limits. As a lecturer and writer his influence was wide. His legacy lives on in the activities of the South Place Ethical Society, which meets at Conway Hall in Red Lion Square, Holborn, London.

BIBLIOGRAPHY

Conway, Moncure. *Autobiography.* London: Cassell, 1904
———. *The Life of Thomas Paine.* Edited by Hypatia Bradlaugh Bonner. London: Watts and Company, 1909.
D'Entremont, John. *Moncure Conway (1832–1907) American Abolitionist, Spiritual Architect of "South Place," Author of the Life of Thomas Paine.* London: South Place Ethical Society, 1977.
Ratcliffe, S. K. *The Story of South Place.* London: Watts and Company, 1955.

JIM HERRICK

CRADDOCK, IDA C. (1857–1902), American freethinker, Spiritualist (see SPIRITUALISM AND UNBELIEF), sex radical, and martyr to FREETHOUGHT. Born at Philadelphia on August 1, 1857, Ida Craddock was raised by her mother, Elizabeth Decker, in affluent circumstances. Her ancestry included Quaker and French lineage. She was educated in history, literature, and several languages; a friend recalled that "her mental capacity and memory were astounding."

At twenty-five she had been teaching shorthand at Girard College and had self-published an impressive textbook. In 1882 she applied for admission to the University of Pennsylvania. After passing an exam "very satisfactorily," the Faculty of the Arts listed her for admission, but the Board of Trustees turned her away, explicitly because she was female. Ida was never enrolled.

Unable to obtain a formal degree in spite of her aptitude, Ida took on menial work. In 1889 she wrote to a friend, "Now that I have stood down in the ranks of the miserable workers whom I once despised as a race beneath me, I know how they feel when they have to face the daily prospect of starvation and misery; and, God helping, I mean to work for them one and all, as long as I live."

By invitation, Ida became the secretary of the AMERICAN SECULAR UNION in 1889. She held that office for about three years, handling the organization's mail, producing its journal, *THE TRUTH SEEKER,* hiring its speakers, and organizing its annual conventions.

In 1893 Craddock visited the World Columbian Exposition at Chicago, where she saw a young Egyptian woman perform the belly dance. The public fell in love with it, and in a pamphlet, Ida defended the tradition as a way for chaste and decent women to show their erotic personae. *Danse du Ventre* was declared unmailable under the Comstock Act (see COMSTOCK, ANTHONY, AND UNBELIEF), so she withdrew it from circulation. From around this time she lectured on the history of sexuality, and in 1894 she changed her title from "Miss" to "Mrs. Craddock." The change of titles was explained in a lecture entitled "Celestial Bridegrooms," in which she stated, "It has been my high privilege to have some practical experience as the earthly wife of an angel from the unseen world." In the lecture she quoted ancient texts where encounters took place between mortal women and deities, including the Virgin Mary. Meanwhile, Ida's mother began stalking her wherever she traveled, exposing her as an unmarried woman (not a real "Mrs.") who was not entitled to discuss marital affairs. For three months of 1898, Lizzie Decker had her daughter committed to an asylum in West Philadelphia.

She was again prosecuted in Chicago for writing an essay called "Right Marital Living" and for providing sex counseling. After three months in jail she relocated to New York City. Ida was arrested yet again when authorities seized her new pamphlet, *The Wedding Night,* which told newlyweds about having sex with a person for the first time. In that era, when sex was a completely taboo subject, many brides did not have a clear understanding of what would happen after the ceremony. Men understood the matter just as poorly and simply raped their wives when the opportunity came. Ida explained what was going to happen; how the man should be patient and no more aggressive than the woman wished. Doctors, ministers, and even "social purity" activists sent young people to Ida for this practical advice.

Sentenced to three months on state charges, Ida served the term in the spring of 1902. Upon her release, she was charged for the same offense under the federal statute and convicted again. Her attorney was not permitted to present arguments in her defense: the booklet was ruled obscene by the judge, and the jury was allowed only to decide whether she had mailed it. No person was alleged to have been harmed by anything she had written or taught.

Craddock was facing five years this time, and it was more than she could bear. On October 16, instead of appearing in court, she wrote suicide notes and took her own life. About Comstock, she wrote, "[T]he man is a sex pervert: he is what physicians term a sadist—namely a person in whom the impulses of cruelty arise concurrently with the stirring of sex emotion. The sadist finds keen delight in inflicting either physical cruelty or mental humiliation upon the source of that emotion."

Lizzie Decker wrote of her daughter, "[T]hat woman was as pure as God's snow and as chaste as His ice." An old friend wrote of Ida, "She was sacrificed to the monsters of creation, who kill what they cannot understand."

BIBLIOGRAPHY

The primary sources of Ida Craddock's life and work are the Theodore A. Schroeder Papers, Morris Library, University of Southern Illinois at Carbondale.

Craddock, Ida C. *The Heaven of the Bible.* Philadelphia: J. B. Lippincott, 1897.
———. *Letter to a Prospective Bride.* Philadelphia: Author, 1897.
———. *Primary Phonography.* Philadelphia: Author, 1882.
———. *Right Marital Living.* Chicago: Author, 1899.
———. *The Wedding Night.* Denver: Author, 1900.
Helms, Robert P. "Bride of the Angels." *Philadelphia Independent* 21 (Winter 2005).
Stoehr, Taylor. *Free Love in America: A Documentary History.* New York: AMS Press, 1979.

ROBERT P. HELMS

CREATIONISM. Creationism as a Cultural, Not Scientific, Issue.

In some sense, all religious people are creationists. If one believes in a supernatural entity of some sort, that entity is usually connected in one way or another with the origin of the universe, if nothing else. Moreover, the term *creationism* has had a long and complex history, beginning well before the modern creation-evolution controversy, and even predating the publication of Charles DARWIN's *The Origin of Species* in 1859. In pre-Darwinian times, *creationism* referred to the belief that the soul of each human fetus was specially created, in opposition to the theory of traducianism, according to which souls were inherited from one's parents. At the time of the debate on the inheritance of the soul, of course, essentially everybody was a creationist in the modern sense of the word.

However, the term *creationist* is relevant to today's cultural debate only in a sense that is both neither historically accurate nor as broad as the general belief in a creator God. Creationists, in the discussion that follows, are people who deny all or most of the modern theory of biological evolution, with the purpose of advancing a religious agenda. Accordingly, this article does not include under that label the occasional scientist outside the academic mainstream who may have genuine (if usually erroneous) concerns about evolutionary theory from a strictly scientific perspective (for example, the late cosmologist Fred Hoyle). It is assumed that the reader realizes that evolutionary theory has the same status in modern biology that quantum mechanics or relativity have in physics: While many issues remain open to further research (both fundamental physics and organismal biology are active fields of inquiry), few, if any, practitioners with the required expertise actually think any of these theories will be fundamentally challenged on scientific grounds any time soon. In other words, what follows is an analysis of creationism, not a defense of evolution.

To understand the controversy, one must first recognize the continuum of creationist positions. Creationism is by no means a single intellectual or cultural entity. Then the two most important classes of creationist approach can be understood: young-earth creationism, as embodied, for example, in the California-based Institute for Creation Research; and the intelligent design movement, orchestrated chiefly by the Discovery Institute in Seattle (see INTELLIGENT DESIGN THEORY). Finally, this article will examine the burden of science educators in the controversy, and conclude with some general thoughts about the future of the debate.

Basic Classification of Creationist Types. Eugenie Scott of the National Center for Science Education has proposed an interesting classification of beliefs about "origins" (i.e., the origins of humans, of life, and of the universe). While any attempted taxonomy of such a complex network of cultural practices and beliefs is, of course, a simplification, Scott managed to capture important features that help us to understand the debate. Her classification is based on the identification of a continuum of positions, which can, however, be clearly divided into two major classes: people who believe that the earth is very young, more or less in accord with a literal reading of the Judeo-Christian-Muslim Bible, and people who accept a major conclusion of modern science, that our planet is in fact billions of years old.

Within young-earth creationism, Scott identifies a progression of beliefs from people who think the earth is flat (yes, a few still exist), to those who are stuck in a pre-Copernican worldview (the earth is not flat, but it is the center of the universe), to more mainstream positions that accept science up to and including the findings of

Galileo GALILEI and Isaac Newton, but refuse to accommodate to nineteenth- and twentieth-century geology and biology. This is a progression in the important sense that these various positions can be aligned on a gradient of increasing acceptance of scientific findings. Indeed, we could classify these people according to the century in human history in which their worldview seems to be stuck. So, flat-earthism remains in the twelfth or thirteenth century (toward the end of the Middle Ages) and geocentrism in the sixteenth; young-earth creationism of the more common variety can be said to have "progressed" to the seventeenth century.

This trend continues across the divide identified by Scott which separates young- from old-earth creationists: so-called gap-theory and day-age creationists wish to retain some close reading of the Bible, but acknowledge nineteenth- and even some twentieth-century findings about an old earth. Consequently, they propose gaps in the biblical narrative or reinterpret biblical "days" as geological ages. However, they refuse to accept much of post-Darwinian biology, though some do grant a limited role to natural selection (but so do some young-earth creationists, admitting that natural selection can indeed eliminate maladaptive variants from within rather fuzzily described "kinds"—a biblical term—of plants and animals).

The final range of Scott's continuum of creationist positions includes more intellectually sophisticated (but still scientifically groundless) ideas, such as theistic evolution and, of course, intelligent design. Theistic evolution comes as close to a completely materialistic view of the universe as is possible for a religious person: God exists and he did create the universe, but afterward events unfold through the action of natural laws (put in place by the Creator, of course). Evolution by natural selection, therefore, is the way God decided to have things work in the biological realm. While this position has been criticized on philosophical and theological grounds all the way back to David HUME's *Dialogues concerning Natural Religion*, it is quite acceptable among scientists and science educators because it doesn't result in challenges to the way science is taught in public schools. The same cannot be said for the intelligent design movement, to be examined shortly.

Young-Earth Creationism: Emotion over Intellect. Young-earth creationists generally believe our planet is only a few thousand years old, and that human beings were created directly by God together with all "kinds" of living organisms. They also think God unleashed a worldwide flood about four thousand years ago (despite the total absence of geological evidence for this), and that a man named Noah single-handedly repopulated the earth with selected pairs of all animal and plant "kinds," a most radical exercise in genetic engineering. This author once pointed out to young-earth creationist Ken Hovind that to assume that the millions of species currently living on the planet are "derived" (that is,

evolved) from the few thousand kinds that were present immediately after the flood is actually to concede a rate of evolution that not even the most wildly optimistic evolutionary biologist would contemplate.

But of course that is precisely the point: logic and evidence have little to do with young-earth creationism. This is a belief system that is highly emotional and quite unsophisticated intellectually. While it is hard to imagine that people with the intellectual capacity to function in modern society can so fervently believe in self-contradictory fables written down thousands of years ago, that is a pretty accurate description of the young-earth position.

Young-earth creationists are often genuinely stunned when scientists refuse to yield to their "obvious" objections to evolution. How, they wonder, can anyone seriously think that a random process is capable of originating complex organisms adapted to their environment? (Answer: Evolution by natural selection is *not* a random process, because it relies on a combination of random mutations and nonrandom selection, the latter due to competition for resources among living organisms.) Or, the incredulous young-earther may ask, how can anyone believe in radioactive dating of rocks, when there are errors and discrepancies in the published measurements? (Answer: *Any* human measurement comes with a certain degree of error, which leads to discrepancies; the issue is not whether there are differences in the estimates of the age of the earth carried out with different methods or by different researchers, but *how large* those differences are. As it turns out, they are very small.) Young-earth creationism is a quintessential expression of anti-intellectualism, the preference for a folk understanding of the world over the one proposed by scientists and intellectuals.

Intelligent Design: The Intellectual Side of Creationism. Some creationists have acknowledged that modern, particularly Western, society is highly influenced by intellectual endeavors, science being the one that attracts both the most funding and the best media coverage. This insight underlies the intelligent design (ID) movement. ID proponents make strenuous efforts to distance themselves from the more overtly religious rhetoric typical of young-earth creationism, often denying that they are creationists at all. Their strategy (openly declared in an infamous planning document known as "The Wedge," which a leading ID organization unaccountably posted on its Web site for several months) is to make headway into academic circles and mainstream media by presenting themselves as defenders of a reasonable position that ought to have its day in the court of scientific and public opinion. Unspoken is the consequence that thereby a door would be opened for the teaching of religion in public schools.

The problem, of course, is that intelligent design already has had its heyday, culminating in the publication of William Paley's *Natural Theology* in 1831. Paley was taken very seriously by Darwin, and the debate between natural theology and a completely scientific view of the world raged throughout the eighteenth and nineteenth centuries (see EVOLUTION AND UNBELIEF; DARWINISM; HUXLEY, THOMAS HENRY). But intelligent design lost that battle on intellectual grounds: it is no longer either a scientific position or a philosophically viable one. This is why modern ID proponents such as Michael Behe (author of *Darwin's Black Box*), William Demsbki (*The Design Inference*, among several others), Jonathan Wells (*Icons of Evolution*), and Phillip Johnson (*Defeating Darwinism by Opening Minds*, among others) frankly embody a regression to the early nineteenth century—as far as any creationist view can hope to advance.

The important thing to understand about ID is that it is an entirely negative position: it begins (and ends) with the observations—denied by no serious scientist—that there are unexplained facts about biology, and that scientists have ongoing discussions regarding different mechanisms that may account for biological evolution. Both are certainly true (though ID proponents often misrepresent such debates), but the same holds in any viable science. The essence of scientific inquiry is that research is open ended; debate is continuous, and revisions of past positions are always possible (in sharp contrast, one might note, to any form of creationism proposed so far). To fault scientists for continuing their inquiries and disagreeing with each other is fundamentally to misunderstand (or actively to misrepresent) what science is about.

Moreover, what does ID propose as an alternative? Behe, Dembski, and their colleagues are characteristically vague about what they suspect their designer might actually be, or how it operates. And for good reason: were they to be more specific, they would have either to admit that ID is a thin veil for Judeo-Christianity or to propose testable statements that could actually be evaluated in the scientific process. But that latter is simply not possible. (Asked directly by this author what sort of experiments the Discovery Institute might undertake if it received federal funding to conduct research on ID, Dembski had no answer.)

Yet the intelligent design movement cannot be dismissed, as it appeals to conservative and even mainstream religious believers as a "reasonable compromise." What harm could there be in teaching our students that there is a controversy? Isn't the possibility of an intelligent designer at least conceivable? Indeed, the controversy could be taught, but in social studies classes in the context of the so-called culture wars, not in science classes—for the simple reason that ID is not science by any definition of the term. Yes, an intelligent designer is obviously conceivable, but science is not about conceivable possibilities, it is about empirical facts that can be subjected to observation, experimentation, and hypothesis testing. As for the portrayal of ID as a reasonable compromise, consider whether teaching both that the Holocaust happened and that it was a fabrication of Zionist propagandists (a position actually maintained by

some pseudohistorians) would be considered an acceptable compromise in history classes. It would not, unless there *actually were* a controversy raging among professional historians. But there is no such controversy, either among historians or among biologists.

Dealing with ID proponents requires more intellectual sophistication than dealing with their young-earth counterparts, partially because many defenders of ID have legitimate academic credentials and because their arguments are dense with jargon and quasi-genuine philosophical or mathematical points. That is why the most effective weapons against ID are probably improvements in science education for science teachers (which may also result in better science education for children), and tirelessly calling ID proponents' bluff by demanding details on the sort of testable hypotheses an ID research program might actually investigate.

The Sins of the Education Community. Despite all of the above, the current creation-evolution controversy cannot be blamed exclusively on the illiteracy or bigotry of a large part of the public. After all, that public is supposed to be getting an education from public schools and exposure to the media, so the educational and scientific communities are at least partly responsible for today's sorry state of affairs. Two important points should be kept in mind when discussing the role of science education in this or any other ideologically charged controversy: First, American culture has always been affected by different strands of anti-intellectualism whose causes are various and have been long studied by sociologists. It is therefore naive to expect that better science education alone will quickly eliminate the problem. Second, *science education* can have different meanings; simply having more of the kind of science education that is currently delivered is unlikely to affect the national level of understanding of science (and of evolution in particular) significantly.

While a discussion of science education is beyond the scope of this article, it is important to understand one crucial distinction: teaching factual knowledge of science with a minimal conceptual background is very different from teaching the conceptual foundations of science, peppered with enough factual information to ground the student's understanding in empirical reality. The first approach is by far the most common, but it is also the one that is arguably responsible for turning *off* many students to science, and it apparently does little to increase the level of critical thinking in our society, the real goal of liberal arts education.

The second approach is, however, slowly gaining ground, both at the college level and, more importantly, at high school and earlier levels. Online resources, teachers' conferences and workshops, and new textbooks are now available for educators seriously interested in turning the classical approach around: rather than hoping the foundational ideas of science will seep through an ocean of facts, one provides the students with the conceptual tools to seek and understand the relevant facts. Among many reasons why this is a positive trend is the obvious one: it is impossible to go on teaching "all the facts" in science because science keeps accumulating "facts" at a vertiginous pace. Consider, for example, that an introductory college textbook in biology is now more than a thousand pages long, typically devoting only a few of those pages to the methods by which scientists actually uncover those all-important "facts." Indeed, it is likely that the textbook industry will evolve toward offering separate reference and conceptual texts: just as one needs a dictionary to understand English literature, yet a sensible teacher wouldn't dream of having students memorize the dictionary in order to learn how to read or write, we need reference books for science facts accompanied by slimmer textbooks aimed at using selected parts of the "facts" database to teach how science actually works.

There are several reasons why this trend toward a more sensible science education will take a great deal of time to become mainstream. The principal obstacles in the United States are class size, excessive reliance on standardized tests, and teacher training practices that leave teachers ill equipped to master new conceptual approaches to science education. None of these obstacles is insuperable, but overcoming them may take a generation or more. Nonetheless, a different approach to science education, more focused on critical thinking and conceptual understanding, is a mandatory step not only in eventually overcoming the evolution-creation controversy, but more broadly in educating citizens better able to participate in a democratic society.

Will Creationism Ever Go Away? Will the creation-evolution debate ever be won? The resurgence of creationism during the 1990s and the early twenty-first century, especially in the guise of the intelligent design movement, appears not to justify optimism. Yet there are good reasons to hope for a better future. If we take the long view of human history, it is undeniable that vast progress has been made. Modern scientists no longer have to fear the sort of retaliation from religious bigots that Giordano BRUNO or Galileo GALELEI suffered only a few centuries ago. Moreover, once highly controversial notions (such as that the earth is not flat, or that it isn't the center of the universe) are now accepted by most people on the planet as a matter of fact.

Eventually, one can hope, the controversy over evolution will go away just as the controversy over Copernicanism did. But the uncanny ability of humans to believe in nonsense is never to be underestimated, and will always find new forms. It is conceivable, perhaps even likely, that a new frontier for irrationality will open when (or if) scientists produce a viable theory of how consciousness arises as a natural epiphenomenon of the brain, or when (or if) they succeed in producing genuine artificial intelligence (see COGNITIVE SCIENCE AND UNBELIEF). It is easy to imagine twenty-second-century religious fundamentalists who have accommodated to twen-

tieth-century science and accept the theory of evolution drawing a new line in the sand at the idea that a mere machine (or animal) can have consciousness: surely that must be the province of the soul. And so on.

There is also, of course, the very real danger that society might slip back, if not to the Dark Ages, at least to a point at which science illiteracy becomes so widespread as to endanger our capacity to flourish and to compete economically. Science and reason, as Carl SAGAN aptly put it, truly are "candles in the dark," and critical thinkers must be constantly on watch to make sure those candles stay lit. Fighting creationism and intelligent design in all their varying forms will be an important part of this ongoing battle.

BIBLIOGRAPHY

Altemeyer, B., and B. Hunsberger. *Amazing Conversions: Why Some Turn to Faith and Others Abandon Religion.* Amherst, NY: Prometheus Books, 1997.

Forrest, B., and P. R. Gross. *Creationism's Trojan Horse: The Wedge of Intelligent Design.* Oxford: Oxford University Press, 2004.

Hume, D. *Dialogues concerning Natural Religion.* Edinburgh: Gilbert Elliot, 1779.

Pigliucci, M. *Denying Evolution: Creationism, Scientism and the Nature of Science.* Sunderland, MA: Sinauer, 2002.

Rigney, D. "Three Kinds of Anti-intellectualism: Rethinking Hofstadter." *Sociological Inquiry* 61 (1991).

Sagan, C. *The Demon-Haunted World: Science as a Candle in the Dark.* New York: Random House, 1995.

Scott, E. C. "Antievolution and Creationism in the United States." *Annual Review of Anthropology* 26 (1997).

MASSIMO PIGLIUCCI

DANIELS, VIROQUA (1859–1942), American anarchist-Communist and poet. "A poor country girl, who has never had any advantages of education," this important anarchist writer has been forgotten, in part, because an injury forced her to lead a quiet life. Born December 4, 1859, at Tipton, Iowa, Viroqua Daniels arrived at age sixteen at her family's new homestead in northeastern California. Her very literate father, Sylvester Daniels, hunted and played violin to earn a living. At nineteen she caught her skirt in the brake handle of a wagon, hitting her head against the wheel, and the accident made her chronically ill. Between 1878 and 1895 she became interested in social questions. Living for some time with her brother Hubert, she educated herself, and was the "smartest" in her close-knit family. In 1898, when another health crisis brought her to San Francisco, she took a dietetic cure but was an invalid for some time. Around that time, she fell in love with Richard Daverkosen, a well-educated radical of German birth. They had one son, Hubert, in 1900 and remained together until death.

From 1895 Daniels wrote dozens of articles and fine poems, mostly for the *Firebrand* and *Free Society* until 1903, and occasional pieces for *Mother Earth* and *Why?* until 1914. She describes the rural poor who became paralyzed, crazed by anxiety and heartbreak, and killed by workplace accidents, starvation, or suicide. Her works, which were often reprinted, advocated strict anarchist-Communism to the exclusion of other theories, and held that "property, not morality, is the bulwark of the marriage institution." About Leon Czolgosz (who killed President William McKinley) Daniels wrote, "every rebellious act, whether great or small, wise or unwise, when done by a conscious slave, adds to the struggle for freedom." She wrote against religion (especially Catholicism) and for the practical education of children that encouraged individuality. Robbed of Richard's pension by the Catholic Church because their marriage was not "legal," Viroqua was looked after by her son until she died of breast cancer on November 5, 1942.

BIBIOGRAPHY

Daniels, Sylvester. *Frontier Times: The 1874–1875 Journals.* Edited by Tim Purdy. Susanville, CA: Author, 1885.

Daniels, Viroqua. "Diet vs. Drugs." *Free Society*, May 27, 1900.

———. "The Marriage Institution." *Firebrand*, June 9, 1895.

———. "Torture." *Firebrand*, January 19, 1896.

Gorzell, Jean E. (grand-niece of Viroqua Daniels). Telephone interview with the author. December 2, 2001.

ROBERT P. HELMS

DARROW, CLARENCE SEWARD (1857–1938), American lawyer and atheist. One of the best-known figures in twentieth-century American jurisprudence, Clarence Seward Darrow was not only one of the nation's top defense attorneys but also an orator, writer, and strong advocate for civil liberties causes. He was born in Farmdale, Ohio, one of eight children of Amirus, a furniture maker and undertaker, and Emily Darrow, who were intellectually curious and passed on their love of books and learning to their children.

Amirus Darrow had graduated from a theological seminary but soon afterward lost his faith, so he refused to preach. Despite their parents' antireligious views, the Darrow children were taken to church every Sunday, perhaps because the parents wanted to protect their children from disdain in their community. But young Clarence always felt the time he spent in church and Sunday school was wasted. The Darrows were scorned in the community for their atheistic views; however, they were also active abolitionists, allowing their home to serve as an Underground Railroad station.

Darrow attended Allegheny College for a year before dropping out to teach school in winter and work in a factory in the summer. After becoming interested in law he attended the University of Michigan Law School, but completed only one year. He gained practical experience in a law office in Youngstown, Ohio, while he prepared for the bar examination. At the age of twenty-one he gained admission to the bar. In that same year, 1878, he married Jessie Ohl. Five years later they had a son, Paul.

After moving to Chicago in 1888, Darrow befriended John P. Altgeld, a superior court judge and a man he had long admired for his liberal views on the penal system. Probably due to this association, Darrow was soon after appointed city attorney by Mayor DeWitt C. Cregier. Darrow assisted Altgeld in his successful bid for governor of Illinois, after which Altgeld pardoned the three remaining Haymarket martyrs, thus ruining his political career. After a few years, Darrow became general attorney for the Chicago and North Western Railroad, a large, corporate, antiunion company. It was Eugene Debs and his American Railway Union's involvement in the Pullman strike that spurred Darrow to change his allegiance, and he resigned his position at the railroad company. In 1894 he successfully defended Debs in a conspiracy case, then on a contempt of court charge a year later, turning the tables on the corporation. It was clear that Darrow's association with Debs had made a strong impression on him. Darrow and Jessie agreed to an amicable divorce in 1897. In 1903 Darrow married Ruby Hamerstrom, and she remained his devoted companion throughout his life.

Darrow became one of the top labor lawyers in the United States. At the same time he continued to work for corporations, defending himself against criticism by explaining that he had no interest in money but that he took cases that would pay him in order to use that money against the system. He funded his less lucrative cases from the money he earned from the corporate ones. His more radical and renowned cases included those of William D. (Big Bill) Haywood, charged with inciting to murder the governor of Idaho in 1907, and the McNamara brothers, accused of attempting to bomb the *Los Angeles Times* building in 1911. Darrow sympathized with anarchists and socialists, and was always willing to come to their defense. By this time famous for his skills as a trial lawyer, he was sought after in several high-profile cases, including the Leopold-Loeb murder trial in Chicago in 1924 and the Ossian Sweet murder case in Detroit in 1925, arising out of an angry white mob's attack upon an African American family's home.

As far as freethinkers are concerned, the most important legal case of Darrow's career was the evolution case, the 1925 Scopes Monkey trial. Although he often took cases for a drastically reduced fee, this was the only time Darrow ever offered to donate his services. In the early 1920s Tennessee and other states in the Bible Belt had, with the assistance of politician and religious fundamentalist William Jennings Bryan, passed a law against teaching evolution in the schools. As a result, John T. Scopes, a twenty-one-year-old high school teacher, was arrested in Dayton, Tennessee, for corrupting young minds with ideas that contradicted the creationist viewpoint. Darrow heard that Bryan had volunteered to serve as the prosecuting attorney, and knew that the case would be turned into a farce and a platform for Bryan's fundamentalist views. Public opinion was strongly against Scopes, and Darrow's plans for calling several expert witnesses in the field of science were dashed when presiding judge John T. Raulston refused to allow them to testify. Although Darrow was permitted to call Bryan as an expert witness on the question of religion, and was able for a time to expose Bryan's flimsy argument, Darrow was not allowed to proceed with his questioning, and Scopes was convicted. The decision was eventually overturned by the state supreme court, with Darrow receiving a long ovation after his closing argument.

In his autobiography, *The Story of My Life*, Darrow spends two chapters rationalizing logically and scientifically that there can be no god. Since childhood, he had studied science and reason, and had obviously given the topic a great deal of consideration. Realizing that human life was basically full of misery and fraught with pain and sorrow, he believed it is far better for people to treat each other with compassion in this life rather than hope for a better existence in the afterlife.

Clarence Darrow died in Chicago on March 13, 1938, after a long illness. Thousands of people from all walks of life attended his funeral. The undertaker kept the funeral parlor open for forty-eight hours in order to accommodate the crowds. After Darrow was cremated, his son scattered his ashes in Jackson Park.

Tennessee Williams dedicated his play *Not about Nightingales* to Darrow, whose "mental frontiers were the four corners of the sky."

BIBLIOGRAPHY

Darrow, Clarence. *The Story of My Life.* New York: Charles Scribner's Sons, 1932.

Lukas, J. Anthony. *Big Trouble.* New York: Touchstone, 1997.

Newfield, Jack, ed. *American Rebels.* New York: Nation Books, 2003.

Smith, Warren Allen, ed. *Who's Who in Hell: A Handbook and International Directory for Humanists, Freethinkers, Naturalists, Rationalists, and Non-Theists.* New York: Barricade, 2000.

Stein, Gordon, ed. *The Encyclopedia of Unbelief.* Amherst, NY: Prometheus Books, 1985.

JULIE HERRADA

DARWIN, CHARLES ROBERT (1809–1882), English naturalist. In an age when science and society were founded on creationist beliefs, Charles Darwin solved the "mystery of mysteries" of his day: namely, how living species originate. He abandoned the Bible as an authority on creation and explained the origin of species by divinely ordained natural laws. For his devotion to science and exemplary life, he received Britain's highest posthumous honor: scientists joined churchmen and politicians of all parties to inter his body in Westminster Abbey.

Early Life and Education. Charles Robert Darwin was born at Shrewsbury on February 12, 1809, the second son and second-youngest of six children. His father, a freethinking physician (see FREETHOUGHT), and his mother, a devout Unitarian (see UNITARIANISM TO 1961), had him christened in the parish church. As a boy, he attended chapel with his mother and was sent to the school run by the minister. He then sat under a future bishop at Shrewsbury School until 1825, when he went to Edinburgh to study medicine with his brother, Erasmus.

Edinburgh was freethinking and cosmopolitan, with strong cultural links to the Continent; its university had the best medical faculty in Britain. But a year later, after Erasmus left, Charles found it hard to concentrate. He preferred to explore the seashore with Dr. Robert Grant, an anatomy lecturer who gave him his first lessons in zoology. A Francophile materialist and evolutionist, Grant was dedicated to overthrowing the church and bringing about radical social change. He sponsored Charles's first scientific paper at a meeting of a student club, the Plinian Society. After the presentation, Charles saw a fellow student's remarks on the identity of mind and brain struck from the minutes. It was a lesson on the perils of unbelief.

He finally dropped out of medicine, unable to stomach surgery. To cure his indirection, his father prescribed a stint at Cambridge University to train for the Church of England. In a country parish, Charles would have a respectable social role, a guaranteed income, and above all the leisure to indulge his Edinburgh interest in natural history. After reading a few divinity books, Charles decided there was nothing in them he could not say he believed, and in early 1828 he went up to Christ's College to study for the BA and ordination.

Cambridge was a market town dominated by a medieval university—totally unlike Edinburgh. Here the professors were untainted by French radicalism: clergymen such as the botanist John Stevens Henslow and the geologist Adam Sedgwick, who agreed that species and society alike were kept stable by God's will. This was the reigning orthodoxy in Cambridge as taught from texts by Rev. William Paley. Everyone subscribed to it more or less. Unbelievers such as Rev. Robert TAYLOR, an apostate Cambridge ordinand who in 1829 attempted an "infidel mission" to the university, were ostracized.

Darwin never forgot the example of the man known as the "Devil's Chaplain."

At Cambridge, natural history became his passion. On his knees collecting beetles and on Henslow's botanical excursions, Charles took the parson-naturalist as his role model. After a geological field trip with Sedgwick in August 1831, Darwin received a letter from Henslow offering him a place as captain's companion on the HMS *Beagle*. This was the turning point of Darwin's life. His path to a country parish was now diverted by way of a voyage around the world.

The *Beagle* Voyage. For five years Darwin dreamed of a parson's life, seeing it as "a type of all that is respectable & happy." His religious beliefs and practices remained conventional. Like his Cambridge professors he rejected the book of Genesis as a literal account of creation, but quoted the Bible as a moral authority. A parting gift, the first volume of Charles Lyell's *Principles of Geology* (1830), convinced him that earth's crust had been laid down over countless ages according to fixed natural laws. He theorized about the formation of islands and continents and began to see himself as a geologist. The *Beagle*'s aristocratic captain, Robert FitzRoy, was a foil for his developing science and a reminder of Tory-Anglican prejudice. Soft on slavery, FitzRoy outraged Darwin's Whig abolitionist morals.

During the voyage, Darwin's view of nature and humanity was transformed by three unforgettable events. Wandering for the first time in a lush Brazilian forest, he had something like a religious experience. "No one can stand unmoved in these solitudes, without feeling that there is more in man than the mere breath of his body," he confessed, even while sensing that man and nature were one. At Concepcion in Chile, he survived a terrifying earthquake. Nature's power awed him; even the cathedral was not spared. Most moving was Darwin's first encounter with the aboriginal peoples of Tierra del Fuego. He wondered how these wild, naked nomads could have come from the same God who created Cambridge dons. The experience shook him to the core.

Before the voyage ended in 1836, Darwin began to suspect that species, like races of animals and plants and the races of mankind, had descended from one another. So much could be explained if the diversity and distribution of living things on continents and islands had come about through ordinary natural processes rather than creative miracles.

London and Marriage. Back in London, Charles stuck close to his brother. Erasmus was well connected—and a freethinker with radical ideas. His reforming friends believed in a God who ruled the world, not miraculously or directly, but through natural laws. God must have created living species by some progressive law, they speculated, but none of them knew what it was. Darwin, twenty-eight years old, determined to find out. He read voraciously—natural history, philosophy, theology, economics—and he made extensive notes.

In the first of a series of notebooks, he drew a branching tree to show how species had descended from one another. This was a family tree, full of the ancestors of today's species. After observing an adolescent ape in London's zoo, Darwin jotted excitedly: "Let man visit Ourang-outang . . . hear its expressive whine, see its intelligence when spoken [to] . . . see its affection . . . see its passion & rage, sulkiness, & very actions of despair; [then] let him look at the savage, roasting his parent, naked, artless, not improving yet improvable & then let him dare to boast of his proud preeminence." Darwin had seen humans in the raw; most naturalists and churchmen had not. They prided themselves in mankind's special creation, but for Darwin evolution explained the differences. It was "more humble" to have apes in the human family tree, to believe savages and civilized people alike were "created from animals."

Darwin's belief in creation by evolution was born of theological humility, though he admitted its heretical tendency: even our "love of the deity" is the "effect of [the brain's neural] organization," he jotted half-reproachfully; "oh you Materialist!" If one species changes, if one instinct can be acquired, he admitted, then the "whole fabric totters & falls"—the whole traditional fabric of creationist beliefs about nature, God, and humankind.

About this time Darwin became increasingly unwell, suffering headaches and stomach upsets. Insomnia and nightmares plagued him; once he even dreamt of public execution. He felt like a prisoner in London, tied down by his *Beagle* work, pondering evolution and dreading the consequences. In his notebooks he devised protective strategies against the day when he might publish. He would pitch his theory to traditional creationists, emphasizing its superior theology. A world populated by natural law was "far grander" than one in which the creator interferes with himself, "warring against those very laws he established in all organic nature." Imagine—Almighty God personally lavishing on earth the "long succession of vile *Molluscous* animals—How beneath the dignity of him, who is supposed to have said let there be light & there was light"!

In the spring of 1842, Darwin resumed the theme in a pencil sketch of his theory, which he now called "natural selection." It seemed so obvious: nature "selects" the best adapted organisms, as celebrated in Paley's old *Natural Theology* (1802). They survive the constant struggle for food, laid down as a law of nature in Rev. Thomas Malthus's famous *Essay on the Principle of Population* (1798), and pass on the adaptive advantage to their offspring. Thus, in Francis Darwin's words, through "death, famine, rapine, and the concealed war of nature" God's laws bring about "the highest good, which we can conceive, the creation of the higher animals. . . . [T]he existence of such laws should exalt our notion of the power of the omniscient Creator."

Darwin might have sounded like a parson, but the church was now the last thing on his mind. Harboring as he did a theory that subverted the "whole fabric" of traditional orthodoxy, he was plainly unfit for ordination, never mind his illness. With a generous legacy from his father, Darwin married his first cousin Emma Wedgwood in 1839. After two children were born they made plans to escape from London. In September 1842 they moved to the Kentish village of Downe, where Charles fulfilled his old dream to be a parish naturalist. Their new home, Down House, was the former parsonage.

Parish Naturalist. At Downe, Emma became his full-time nurse and the mother of ten. She was a sincere Christian like all Wedgwoods of her generation, Unitarian by conviction, Anglican in practice. Charles differed with her painfully. After he revealed his theory to her, she feared they would be separated in death and he would suffer eternal torments. Emma's anxiety remained a sad undercurrent in the marriage, her heartache and prayers increasing with his illness.

Outwardly respectable, Darwin continued to work privately on his theory, unwilling to publish. In his study, he wrote book after book on geology. He dissected almost every known barnacle, and in 1844 he transformed his pencil sketch of natural selection into a long essay. Revealing his belief in evolution was, he confided to a friend, "like confessing a murder"—a capital crime. He entrusted the essay to Emma, to be published "in case of my sudden death." Working obsessively, fearing his theory would make him an outcast, Darwin thought he might not survive to see natural selection in print.

Events came to a head when he had a serious breakdown after his father's death in 1848. For the first time Darwin felt that he himself was about to die. Four months at a spa worked wonders, but he returned home only to see his eldest daughter taken sick. When Annie died tragically over Easter 1851, aged ten, he found no comfort in Emma's faith. After years of backsliding, Darwin finally broke with Christianity. His father's death had spiked the faith; Annie's clinched the point. Eternal punishment was immoral. He would speak out and be damned.

Down House was now his pulpit, evolution his new "gospel." He pressed on, polishing his theory, extending it, finding illustrations everywhere. Finally in 1856, after receiving the Royal Medal of the Royal Society for his work on barnacles, Darwin was ready to write *On the Origin of Species*. As he started, a colleague remarked to him on the "indecency" of sexual relations in jellyfish. Darwin rejoined, "What a book a Devil's Chaplain might write on the clumsy, wasteful, blundering low & horridly cruel works of nature!" It was a book he feared he might be accused of writing, one that would cause him to be reviled as an unbeliever, like the first Devil's Chaplain, Rev. Robert Taylor.

In October 1859 Darwin fled to a spa on the Yorkshire moors to wait for the *Origin of Species* to be published.

To Henslow at Cambridge he wrote, "I fear you will not approve of your old pupil," and to another colleague he groaned: "Lord how savage you will be . . . how you will long to crucify me alive!" Those weeks of waiting, he said, were like "living in Hell." Fifty years old, at the pinnacle of his career, he had everything to lose. But his worst fears never came true.

The *Origin* and the Church. The *Origin of Species* (1859) was the last great work in the history of science in which theology was an active ingredient. The word *evolution* did not appear in the first edition, but Darwin used *creation* and its cognates more than one hundred times. Opposite the title stood a quotation from Francis Bacon about studying God's works as well as his word, and another by the Reverend Master of Trinity College, Cambridge, about "general laws" as God's way of working. On the last page, Darwin rhapsodized about the "grandeur" of viewing nature's "most beautiful and most wonderful" diversity as the product of "powers . . . originally breathed into a few forms or into one." This played to believers, but Darwin's tone and terminology—even the biblical "breathed"—were not insincere. From start to finish the *Origin of Species* was a pious work: "one long argument" against miraculous creation, but equally a reformer's case for creation by law.

There was doublethink in it, and a certain subterfuge. The book was the man after all—ambiguous, even contradictory. Darwin avoided the inflammatory subject of human origins, though it had been central to his theorizing from the start. The hints he dropped—"light will be thrown on the origin of man and his history," for example, or "some little light can apparently be thrown" on racial differences—pointed to a mass of research that would only be published twelve years later in *The Descent of Man*. Even then, he dreaded being thought "an outcast & a reprobate."

In the end the *Origin* held multiple meanings; it could become all things to everyone. Radicals loved it, the theology notwithstanding. Anglican diehards loathed it and muttered about Darwin's eternal destiny. Emma herself now worried more about her husband's suffering in this life as the *Origin* went into the world. Yet she prayed that his pains would make him "look forward . . . to a future state" where their love would go on forever.

Not all Anglicans damned Darwin. The "celebrated author and divine" quoted in later editions of the *Origin* was Rev. Charles Kingsley, a Cambridge professor. His plug for Darwin's theology—it seemed "just as noble" as miraculous creationism—was timely but timid, a "Yea" to the hearty "Amen" from Oxford's geometry professor Rev. Baden Powell. Writing in the liberal Anglican manifesto *Essays and Reviews*, he saw the *Origin* bringing about "an entire revolution of opinion in favour of the grand principle of the self-evolving powers of nature." For such remarks Powell and his fellow essayists were hounded for HERESY (see UNITED KINGDOM, UNBELIEF IN). When a private petition was got up in their defense,

Darwin rallied to the cause, adding his signature. He welcomed the efforts of these *septum contra Christum* (seven against Christ) to "establish religious teaching on a firmer and broader foundation."

Worse heretics embarrassed the church from without. In later years Darwin was asked again and again to support them. But although the *Origin* became all things to everyone, he himself found this impossible. He avoided public support for British heretics while quietly sending donations to the Free Religious Association in the United States. He agreed to "almost every word" of its creed, which augured "the extinction of faith in the Christian Confession" and the development of a humanistic "Free Religion" (see RELIGIOUS HUMANISM).

The *Descent* and Religion. In his long-awaited *Descent of Man* (1871), Darwin saw humans evolving physically by natural selection, and then intellectually and morally through the inherited effects of habit, education, and religious instruction: "With the more civilised races, the conviction of the existence of an all-seeing Deity has had a potent influence on the advance of morality," so much so that "the birth both of the species and of the individual are equally parts of that grand sequence of events, which our minds refuse to accept as the result of blind chance."

Two-thirds of the book was devoted to a knock-down argument for a theory barely discussed in the *Origin of Species*, "sexual selection." This was Darwin's prize solution to the central problem of nineteenth-century ethnology, the origin of racial diversity. Female choice among competing males according to local beauty standards gave rise to the physical and mental differentiation not only of the sexes, but also of the human races. Like fancy pigeons, the races are only varieties of a single species, members of one family. This traditional Christian belief in the unity of humankind, fortified by sexual selection, underwrote Darwin's lifelong hatred of slavery.

Given its subject matter, the *Descent* bore the imprimatur of Darwin's daughter Henrietta, an able stylist and fussy moralist. Parts he had feared would read like an infidel sermon—"Who w[oul]d ever have thought I sh[oul]d turn parson!"—he asked her to tone down. Emma herself jogged the editor, reminding her that however "interesting" the book's treatment of morals and religion might be, she would still "dislike it very much as again putting God further off." Henrietta tidied the proofs and the *Descent* caused few commotions. For her good work she was given a free hand in editing Charles's biographical sketch of his freethinking grandfather. *Erasmus Darwin* appeared in 1879 shorn of the religiously risqué. Beside her as she worked was her lawyer husband, who managed property for the Ecclesiastical Commission.

But Darwin could be more candid in his autobiography. It was written for the family, not publication, between 1876 and 1881, and contained his fullest statement on "religious belief." At first he had been unwilling to give up Christianity and had even tried to "invent evidence" to confirm the gospels, which prolonged his indecision. But just as his clerical career had died a slow "natural death," so his faith withered gradually. And there was no turning back once the deathblow fell. His dithering crystallized into a moral conviction so strict that he could not see how anyone—even Emma—"ought to wish Christianity to be true." If it were, "the plain language" of the New Testament "seems to show that the men who do not believe, and this would include my Father, Brother and almost all my best friends, will be everlastingly punished. And this is a damnable doctrine."

These words recalled the bitter months and years after his father's death. Since then Darwin's residual theism had been worn down by controversy. Now, as one with "no assured and ever present belief in the existence of a personal God or of a future existence with retribution and reward," he confessed, "I . . . must be content to remain an Agnostic" (see AGNOSTICISM)—an unbeliever, but no less an upright man, living without the threat of divine wrath. "I feel no remorse from having committed any great sin," he assured Emma and the family. "I believe that I have acted rightly in steadily following and devoting my life to science."

Discretion and Immortality. Darwin always avoided speaking publicly about religion. In private letters, he revealed that he no longer believed "in the Bible as a divine revelation, & therefore not in Jesus Christ as the Son of God." Yet, he admitted, his "belief in what is called a personal God" had been as strong as a prelate's when he wrote *The Origin of Species*; and three years before his death, he acknowledged that he had "never been an atheist, in the sense of denying the existence of a god . . . generally (& more & more as I grow older), but not always . . . agnostic would be the most correct description of my state of mind."

He believed "freedom of thought is best promoted," not by "direct arguments against christianity & theism," but "by the gradual illumination of men's minds, which follow[s] from the advance of science." He said so to Karl MARX's son-in-common-law, Edward Bibbins AVELING, in a letter marked conspicuously "Private." By a curious confusion, this letter was later thought to have been addressed to Marx himself, a myth now decisively exposed.

Shortly after receiving the letter, Aveling and Ludwig BÜCHNER, president of the International Federation of Freethinkers, lunched with Darwin at Down House. Aveling would later report Darwin's admission, "I never gave up Christianity until I was forty years of age." About this time, it appears, an evangelical temperance worker, Elizabeth Cotton, alias Lady Hope, also visited Darwin and, as she later claimed, found him reading the Bible. Her colorful account of their meeting, first published in 1915 in the United States, gave rise to rumors of a "deathbed conversion," now exposed as a legend (see DEATHBED CLAIMS CONCERNING UNBELIEVERS).

By keeping his religious beliefs and unbeliefs to himself, Darwin never knowingly gave offense except to radical freethinkers and atheists who wanted him publicly on their side. And for his reticence, his character, and his epoch-making science, he achieved immortality. On April 19, 1882, his remains were laid with religious pomp in Britain's most hallowed sanctuary, Westminster Abbey. Priests officiated at the graveside, politicians of all parties gathered around, and his agnostic allies joined them. Now called "scientists," they were paying their dues, for Darwin had delivered nature and human destiny into their hands.

Evolution had become respectable. No revolution took place, no pyrotechnics, just a quiet change at the top—a palace coup. Society would never be the same (see EVOLUTION AND UNBELIEF). A Devil's Chaplain had done his work.

BIBLIOGRAPHY

Barlow, Nora, ed. *The Autobiography of Charles Darwin, 1809–1882, with Original Omissions Restored*. London: Collins, 1958.

Barrett, Paul H., Peter J. Gautrey, Sandra Herbert, David Kohn, and Sydney Smith, eds. *Charles Darwin's Notebooks, 1836–1844: Geology, Transmutation of Species, Metaphysical Enquiries*. Cambridge: British Museum (Natural History) and Cambridge University Press, 1987.

Brooke, John Hedley. "The Relations between Darwin's Science and His Religion." In *Darwinism and Divinity: Essays on Evolution and Religious Belief*, edited by John R. Durant. Oxford: Blackwell, 1985.

Burkhardt, Frederick, et al., eds. *The Correspondence of Charles Darwin*. 15 vols. Cambridge: Cambridge University Press, 1985–2005.

Colp, Ralph, Jr. "The Myth of the Darwin-Marx Letter." *History of Political Economy* 14 (1982).

Darwin, Charles. *The Descent of Man, and Selection in Relation to Sex*. 2 vols. London: John Murray, 1871.

———. *On the Origin of Species by Means of Natural Selection, or the Preservation of Favoured Races in the Struggle for Life*. London: John Murray, 1859

———. *The Origin of Species by Charles Darwin: A Variorum Text*. Edited by Morse Peckham. Philadelphia: University of Pennsylvania Press, 1959.

Darwin, Francis. *The Foundations of the Origin of Species: Two Essays Written in 1842 and 1844*. Cambridge: Cambridge University Press, 1909.

Desmond, Adrian, and James Moore. *Darwin*. London: Michael Joseph, 1991.

Keynes, Richard Darwin, ed. *Charles Darwin's "Beagle" Diary*. Cambridge: Cambridge University Press, 1988.

Kohn, David. "Darwin's Ambiguity: The Secularization

of Biological Meaning." *British Journal for the History of Science* 22 (1989).

Moore, James. *The Darwin Legend*. Grand Rapids, MI: Baker, 1994.

———. "Darwin of Down: The Evolutionist as Squarson-Naturalist." In *The Darwinian Heritage*, edited by David Kohn. Princeton, NJ: Princeton University Press, 1985.

———. "Freethought, Secularism, Agnosticism: The Case of Charles Darwin." In *Religion in Victorian Britain*, vol. 1: *Traditions*, edited by Gerald Parsons. Manchester: Manchester University Press, 1988.

———. "Of Love and Death: Why Darwin 'Gave Up Christianity.'" In *History, Humanity and Evolution: Essays for John C. Greene*, edited by James Moore. Cambridge: Cambridge University Press, 1989.

Ospovat, Dov. *The Development of Darwin's Theory: Natural History, Natural Theology, and Natural Selection, 1838–1859*. Cambridge: Cambridge University Press, 1981.

Stecher, Robert M. "The Darwin-Innes Letters: The Correspondence of an Evolutionist with His Vicar, 1848–1884." *Annals of Science* 17 (1961).

JAMES MOORE

DARWINISM AND UNBELIEF. A fierce religious war is systematically being waged against the values of scientific truth, and the frontline trenches—by the enemy's choice—are in the field of biological education and specifically Darwinism. The reason is clear. Charles DARWIN comprehensively destroyed the biological version of the argument from design, always by far the most popular argument for belief in a deity (see EXISTENCE OF GOD, ARGUMENTS FOR AND AGAINST; EVOLUTION AND UNBELIEF). And the biological version of the argument is much more compelling than the physical or cosmological version, as William Paley, the author most readily associated with natural theology, recognized in 1802: "My opinion of Astronomy has always been, that it is *not* the best medium through which to prove the agency of an intelligent Creator . . . we deduce design from relation, aptitude, and correspondence of *parts*. Some degree therefore of *complexity* is necessary to render a subject fit for this species of argument. But the heavenly bodies do not, except perhaps in the instance of Saturn's ring, present themselves to our observation as compounded of parts at all."

Biology was a very different matter, and Paley milked it for all it was worth. The complexity of even the simplest living organism is prodigious, and the teleological delusion—the illusion of deliberate design for a purpose—ranges from impressive at one extreme to utterly stunning at the other. David HUME put it eloquently into the mouth of Cleanthes, his intelligent design spokesman: "All these various machines, and even their most minute parts, are adjusted to each other with an accuracy which ravishes into admiration all men who have ever contemplated them. The curious adapting of means to ends, throughout all nature, resembles exactly, though it much exceeds, the productions of human contrivance; of human design, thought, wisdom, and intelligence. . . . By this argument *a posteriori,* and by this argument alone, do we prove at once the existence of a Deity and his similarity to human mind and intelligence."

Hume's more intelligent protagonist, Philo, exposed logical flaws in Cleanthes' argument from design—it is indeed ultimately self-defeating—but the illusion of design in the living world remained bewitchingly potent. As long as there was no alternative explanation, merely exposing the logical fallacy seemed unsatisfying although (as Philo cogently showed) no more so than the design theory itself, properly thought through. Eighty years were to go by before Darwin came along with an idea so triumphantly fulfilling that it immediately overwhelmed all who understood it, and would have delighted Hume. Hume's *Dialogues concerning Natural Religion* could fairly be said to have uncovered a Darwin-shaped hole, gaping to be filled. The argument from design lost all right to life in 1859, although vestiges, born of misunderstanding, ignorance, and wishful thinking, are still kicking.

Teleonomy and the Impotence of Design. The problem that any theory of life has to solve—and which Darwinism uniquely solves—is the illusion of design: teleonomy. It is better not to call it teleology, because of the latter's unfortunate association with ARISTOTLE's final cause. The *Oxford Dictionary* defines *teleonomy* as "the property, common to all living systems, of being organized towards the attainment of ends." It is convenient to include all entities, whether living or manufactured, that look designed. An entity looks designed (and in some cases *is* designed) if it is composed of parts configured in a way that is statistically improbable, and efficient in some specified direction that an engineer might admire. Examples of teleonomic entities are birds and airplanes: both admirable flyers. If you shuffled the parts of either, a million random reconstitutions would not fly. The fact that birds and planes do fly in a sustained, directed, and controlled manner shows that each is the product of some very special process generating teleonomy. Only two such processes are known: design and natural selection. Humans understood design long before they understood natural selection, which is perhaps why many, to this day, can't understand natural selection. The prevalence of design in our human world acted as a smoke screen, retarding the discovery of natural selection.

Even among those who do understand natural selection, many mistakenly see design as a potential alternative that just happens to lack evidence. But design is ultimately no real alternative at all. It can serve only as a proximate explanation, never an ultimate or complete explanation of anything. A plane is designed by engineers, but the engineers themselves are teleonomic objects. Any attempt to explain a designer as designed by a higher designer inflates in an infinite regress. Darwin provides the only known escape from the regress: ultimately, engineers were "designed" by natural selection. Natural selection really can serve as an ultimate explanation for the heights of teleonomy, essentially because it creeps up on the problem from below. No other mechanism has ever been proposed that is even potentially an ultimate explanation.

To develop the point in another way, imagine, following a jeu d'esprit of Francis Crick and Leslie Orgel, that bacterial life on earth was deliberately seeded from elsewhere in the universe by an intelligent life form four billion years ago. If the bacteria used for this "directed panspermia" were themselves engineered (plausible, given that the technology to do this is less than a century ahead of ours), it would then be fair to say that life on earth originated by intelligent design. The point is that even in this hypothetical case, intelligent design would be only a proximate explanation. The designers on the distant planet must themselves have risen to their intelligent heights from somewhere. Maybe their life was seeded by yet another episode of directed panspermia from a yet older life-form? Fine, but the regress has to end somewhere. Eventually, complex and therefore improbable designers had to be bootstrapped from simpler beginnings by a stepwise incremental process: the kind of thing the philosopher Daniel Dennett calls a "crane" as opposed to a "skyhook."

If research in the well-financed Discovery Institute (see INTELLIGENT DESIGN THEORY) finally succeeded in uncovering convincing evidence that the bacterial flagellum was intelligently designed, which is highly unlikely, this would not—*could* not—be evidence for ultimate design by a primordial deity. It could only bespeak design by an extraterrestrial creature, who might well be so superior as to seem to us *godlike* but who must, originally, have been raised to those heights by a natural crane such as Darwinian natural selection.

Darwin's Powerful Idea. It makes sense to measure the power of a scientific theory as a ratio: how much it explains divided by how much it needs to assume in order to do the explaining. By this criterion, Darwin's theory of evolution by natural selection is arguably the most powerful idea ever to occur to a human mind. Think what it can explain (and that really means *explain,* in the fullest sense of the word): your existence and mine, as well as the form, diversity, and teleonomic elegance of all living things, not only on this planet but probably wherever in the universe organized complexity may be found. The explanatory work that the theory does, then—the numerator of the ratio—is immense. But the theory itself—the denominator—could hardly be smaller or simpler; you can write it out in a phrase: "nonrandom survival of randomly varying hereditary elements." That isn't quite how Darwin himself would have put it (see below), but it captures the essence of his idea in a way that he would recognize and surely enjoy.

And how does it solve the riddle of teleonomy? How does natural selection ultimately succeed where design only proximally succeeds? The key is gradualism. There is no infinite regress, for evolution starts simple and becomes more complex in a series of small steps, no single one of which is too improbable to credit, although the end product—if you ignore the intermediates—is far too improbable. Intelligent design necessarily *starts* complex, for simple entities cannot be intelligent. In reality, by contrast, intelligence, like all other manifestations of teleonomic complexity, must have arrived late in the universe as the end result of a process of gradual evolution. Any suggestion that intelligence predates evolution immediately falls foul of the argument from improbability—ironically often advanced *against* evolution!—and shoots itself in the foot.

Who Thought of It First? The Darwinian solution to the riddle of life's existence is so powerfully simple, so felicitous to the modern mind, it is hard to understand why no one thought of it until the mid-nineteenth century. It is further surprising—and probably telling—that this great inspiration, which looks so elegant from the modern armchair, eluded centuries of philosophers, mathematicians, and polymaths. PLATO and Aristotle never even got close, fooling about with "essences," "ideal forms," and the sublimely vacuous "final cause." Gottfried LEIBNIZ and Isaac Newton gave us calculus (which might seem a more exacting achievement), but not an inkling of the reason for our own existence. Hume would surely have recognized natural selection as a profoundly great idea if it had occurred to him, but it never did. Having eluded this galaxy of all-time talent, the answer finally came, almost simultaneously, to two English naturalists, Charles Darwin and Alfred Russel WALLACE.

We must not forget Wallace. He gets a poor deal at the hands of posterity, partly through his own generous nature. It was Wallace who coined the word *Darwinism*; he regularly called it "Darwin's theory," and he described himself as "more Darwinian than Darwin." But the main reason we know the name of Darwin more than Wallace is that a year after the Darwin/Wallace papers, Darwin went on to publish *The Origin of Species*. The *Origin* not only explained and advocated the Darwin/Wallace theory of natural selection, it also— and this really needed book-length treatment—set out the multifarious evidence for the *fact* of evolution itself.

Claims of priority are sometimes advanced on behalf of Patrick Matthew, Edward Blyth, and W. C. Wells, compatriots of Darwin and Wallace, and their near contemporaries. They independently proposed something like natural selection, in various restricted contexts, but only Darwin and Wallace grasped its huge significance as the driving force of all evolution and the ultimate answer to the riddle of life.

In any case, the priority we are talking about concerns only natural selection, not evolution itself, which is, of course, a much older idea. The distinction between the fact of evolution and the theory of natural selection is sometimes not clearly understood, and it will be explained in the next section.

The Fact and the Theory. The fact of evolution is the historical certainty that species are descended from other species, and that all species are cousins, tracing back along the branches of a family tree to a single remote ancestor. The French naturalist Jean Baptiste de LAMARCK, who is often touted as his predecessor, lacked Darwin's clear vision of a branching tree. Lamarck thought species were arranged on something more like a ladder than a tree, each one transforming itself into the species on the next rung up. Darwin had no use for ladders, whereas the image of the branching tree was so important to him that it constitutes the only illustration in *The Origin of Species*.

If the fact of evolution were limited to the existence of a branching family tree in which all species, no matter how different, are cousins, it would still need explaining, but something akin to random change would suffice. Plenty of physical processes branch, from river deltas to certain grown patterns in crystals. But random evolution is dramatically ruled out by teleonomy. Living organisms are "good" at doing things. Birds, bats, and insects are good at flying; fish, whales, dugongs, turtles, and squid are good at swimming; cheetahs and antelopes are good at running; moles and wombats are good at digging; trees are good at standing tall in all weather; and weeds are good at spreading.

Such obvious skills are tips of icebergs. All living creatures are "good" at the biochemical, cellular, and physiological processes that run their bodies, and at the embryological processes that originally built them. Despite revealing imperfections (of the kind that no intelligent designer would perpetrate), living creatures carry that overwhelmingly powerful impression of good design defined as "teleonomy."

The Origin of Species is a doubly important book, for it combines Darwin's encyclopedic mustering of the evidence for the fact of evolution with his explanation and advocacy of natural selection as the driving mechanism that generates teleonomy.

Classical Darwinism. Knowing nothing of genes beyond the folk wisdom that like begets like, Darwin treated natural selection at the level of organisms. He took the Malthusian point that in every generation there is overproduction. More offspring are born than are needed to replace the parental generation, in some cases grossly more. This inevitably generates competition, the "struggle for existence" in the famous phrase Darwin and Wallace independently coined. The individuals best fitted to survive the struggle in each generation contribute disproportionately to the next. Future generations inherit those attributes that fitted their parents to survive and pass them on. So more favored "varieties" (Wallace's word) or "races" (Darwin's) will tend to prevail, and this explains the improvement of evolutionary adaptation.

To Wallace and Darwin, in this context, "variety" and "race" meant not a local group of finches, say, but "that set of individual finches whose beaks were hereditarily stronger than usual." Darwin's use of "race" in the subtitle of *The Origin of Species* is sometimes dangerously misread: *The Preservation of Favored Races in the Struggle for Life.* As with Wallace's "variety," Darwin was using "race" to mean "that set of individuals who share a particular hereditary characteristic," such as sharp talons, *not* a geographically distinct race like the Hoodie Crow. By "variety" and "race" Wallace and Darwin meant what we would nowadays call "genetic type," even what a modern writer might mean by a gene (see "Neo-Darwinism," below).

Both Wallace and Darwin acknowledged the inspiration of Malthus for their powerful notion of the struggle for existence setting up the competition in which the fittest would survive and reproduce. Wallace's peroration could have been Darwin himself writing, and it will serve as our summation of classical Darwinism:

> The powerful retractile talons of the falcon and the cat-tribes have not been produced or increased by the volition of those animals; but among the different varieties which occurred in the earlier and less highly organized forms of these groups, those always survived longest which had the greatest facilities for seizing their prey. Neither did the giraffe acquire its long neck by desiring to reach the foliage of the more lofty shrubs, and constantly stretching its neck for the purpose, but because any varieties which occurred among its antitypes with a longer neck than usual at once secured a fresh range of pasture over the same ground as their shorter-necked companions, and on the first scarcity of food were thereby enabled to outlive them. Even the peculiar colors of many animals, especially insects, so closely resembling the soil or the leaves or the trunks on which they habitually reside, are explained on the same principle; for though in the course of ages varieties of many tints may have occurred, yet those races having colors best adapted to concealment from their enemies would inevitably survive the longest.

There is essentially no difference between Darwin's and Wallace's ways of expressing natural selection. Both clearly saw its huge importance. Neither saw it in the light of modern genetics, for the obvious reason that they didn't know modern genetics. This is where neo-Darwinism enters the story.

Neo-Darwinism. Genetics is the only subject in biology that Darwin got badly wrong. In other areas, he showed astonishing prescience, even down to fine details; his passages on ecology, on "entangled banks" and webs of inter-action, sound uncannily modern. But his genetics was the genetics of his time, and that means pre-Mendelian and pre-Weismannian genetics. Advances in genetics have spawned, in successive episodes, two neo-Darwinisms.

The first neo-Darwinism dates from the 1890s, and was mainly associated with the great German biologist August Weismann and his idea of the genetic material as an autonomous river flowing through time, with organisms as its temporary conduits. Weismannism is diametrically opposed to Lamarckism. Weismann's genetic river flows on inviolate, and acquired characteristics are never inherited. In slightly different language, Weismannism is orthodoxy today.

The second neo-Darwinism, the one to which the name is now normally applied, was initiated by the three fathers of population genetics in the 1920s and 1930s: R. A. Fisher, J. B. S. Haldane, and Sewall Wright. They substituted Mendelian *particulate* genetics for the blending inheritance accepted by Darwin and his contemporaries. After Mendel, genes do not blend in an individual when they come together from its father and its mother. Instead, each gene is a hard, discrete entity that is either present or absent in each individual, and is either passed on or not passed on to a given child. Mendelian genes are yes/no entities that you can *count.* Evolution, on the Neo-Darwinian view, is statistical change in gene *frequencies* in populations.

Sexual reproduction shuffles and reshuffles the discrete Mendelian genes in a population. We can, therefore, visualize a continually stirred "pool" of genes. Gene pools may be isolated from other gene pools, either because they belong to different species that can't or won't interbreed, or because they are separated by geographical barriers. The latter kind of isolation, as we shall see, is the usual prelude to the former in the origins of new species.

Some changes in gene frequencies are caused by nothing more than luck, that is, random genetic drift, and this is especially significant in small populations. Sampling error is one way to think of it. The gene pool of each generation is a reshuffled sample of the previous generation's pool. In a large population, the sample of children is large, and gene frequencies will resemble the parental generation's. But a small sample is not representative. It is subject to random sampling error. As the generations go by, random drift can lead to some alleles (alternative versions of a gene competing for the same chromosomal locus) disappearing from the gene pool by bad luck. When all the alleles at a locus but one have disappeared, the remaining one is said to be fixed. It has gone to fixation.

From a Darwinian point of view, such random fixations constitute a kind of null hypothesis, departures from which command our interest. Fixation is not always random. In adaptive evolution, an allele goes to fixation not because it is lucky, but because it has what it takes. That normally means it contributes to the embryonic development of a successful body, good at surviving and reproducing, or otherwise good at passing on copies of the same allele. That, in modern terms, is natural selection—neo-Darwinism. It is the nonrandom survival of alleles in gene pools by virtue of their phenotypic effects on organisms. Unless we are molecular geneticists, we notice it only through the consequent evolution of externally visible phenotypes.

Diversity and *The Origin of Species*. Although the illusion of design is the aspect of Darwinism that most acutely impinges on unbelief, it is not the only aspect Darwin explained. The diversity of life—the branching tree, which, as already mentioned, Darwin singled out for the only illustration in *The Origin of Species*—was one of his major preoccupations, as witnessed by the very title of that great book. And diversity powerfully affects believers, too, because the huge array of animals and plants, making their livings in such a dazzling plenitude of ways, seems to amplify the seductive illusion of design.

The number of species that have ever lived is estimated in the hundreds of millions or even billions, and all are descended from a single ancestor. A very large number of branching events have happened, therefore, and these are called—at least for the sexually reproducing organisms with which we are most familiar—speciation events. Speciation is the process whereby a new species comes into the world—the "origin of species"—by bifurcation of an existing species.

Sexual reproduction tends to oppose speciation. It continually recombines the genes in a gene pool, and this smothers any tendency for a subset of the gene pool to move off in its own evolutionary direction. Some kind of accidental separation is the normal prerequisite to speciation. Once split, two subpopulations are free to pursue separate evolutionary courses, following different selection pressures or even just drifting in different directions. The obvious accidental separation is geographical, and there are two ways in which this can happen. The geography can change, as when an earthquake raises a mountain range, a volcano makes a new island, or a drought shrinks a large lake down to a residue of smaller ones; or the organisms themselves can move, as when the ancestors of "Darwin's finches" were blown, by accident, from South America to the Galapagos Archipelago, or when a tree felled by a hurricane drifts, with a cargo of unwitting iguanas, to a distant shore.

Such events are rare, and it is crucial to the whole theory that they should be. If they were common, gene flow would not be interrupted and the incipient species would be genetically bound together and prevented from diverging. In those rare cases, successive incidents of gene flow are separated by intervals big enough to allow the budding species to separate from its origin species for long enough that, when the two do meet, they can no longer interbreed. When this condition obtains, speciation is complete and a new species, by definition, is born. The intermediate case is where separated populations are reunited sufficiently soon that interbreeding is still possible but hybrids are at a disadvantage, perhaps nearly infertile. This has prompted an additional, more controversial suggestion: natural selection, by penalizing any inclination to hybridize, accelerates speciation. Neat though it is, this reinforcement theory is not widely supported.

Speciation that results from geographical separation is called allopatric. Sympatric speciation is more controversial but it has been argued that insects, at least, may commonly speciate even if there is no geographical barrier to start the process. It seems, though, that there has to be some kind of initial barrier, even if it is only the separation between one food plant and another.

Species is the only rank in the taxonomic hierarchy with an objective definition. Once two populations can no longer interbreed, they are defined as different species. Speciation is the crucial step in evolutionary divergence. Every degree of separation above the species level—between apes and monkeys, between marsupial and placental mammals, between animals and plants—began as a single bifurcation: a speciation event, probably following an accidental geographic splitting of one breeding population. Recognizing this was one of Darwin's many great achievements.

Darwin's Other Theory. Perhaps from motives of prudence, Darwin omitted *Homo sapiens* almost totally from *The Origin of Species*. He was holding his fire for *The Descent of Man* (1871), which is really two books in one. Before launching his treatment of human evolution, Darwin expounded his "other theory," sexual selection, mentioned in *The Origin* but not fully developed. It is debatable whether sexual selection is as distinct from natural selection as Darwin's terminology suggested, but it can have conspicuously different results.

On any account of Darwinism, survival is only a means to the end of reproduction (or, in the neo-Darwinian formulation, gene survival). A penis is not an adaptation to individual survival; it is an adaptation to reproduction (or for propagating the genes that built the penis). For Darwin, however, a penis is (normally) shaped by natural, not sexual selection. Sexual selection produces adaptations whereby members of one sex compete with each other for members of the other. A penis would be shaped by sexual selection only if females choose males by comparing their penises, or if males fight other males for females by fencing with their penises. Iconic examples of sexually selected traits are the extravagantly beautiful tails of male birds of paradise (whereby they compete to be chosen by females) and the asymmetrically huge claws of fiddler crabs (organs for intimidating other males and indirectly competing for females). Sexually selected traits are typically larger, brighter, louder, and more wasteful than utilitarian adaptations to personal survival. The neo-Darwinian "gene's-eye view" sees both as adaptations to assist the survival of the genes that made them.

Only a Theory? Professional opponents of Darwinism (and the word *professional* is appropriate to these advocates and their richly financed, professionally spun campaigns) continually change the ground from which they snipe. In the United States today, they have discovered that the phrases "only a theory" and "never been proven" work readily to impress gullible audiences. The propagandists themselves know perfectly well (if their audiences do not) that *theory* and *proven* have technical meanings that, properly understood, nullify the propaganda point being made. Of course, they bank on their audiences *not* understanding this properly. Every scientific fact is, in this technical philosophic sense, a theory awaiting falsification (see FALSIFIABILITY). A well-established fact is a theory that has survived a bombardment of falsification attempts to the point where withholding the accolade "fact" becomes pedantic sophistry. Such is the current status of the fact of evolution.

Similarly, proof is something that mathematicians do when they deduce a conclusion as necessarily following from premises. Scientific theories about the real world, even "obvious" theories like the theory that the earth is round and orbits the sun, are not proved in this sense, although mathematical deduction often enters into their details.

Philosophical technicalities aside, evidence establishes the fact of evolution as strongly and securely as any fact in the whole of science. Since evolution mostly happened before we were born, a helpful simile is the detective who arrives at the scene of a crime after it is committed and solves it from the clues that remain. The difference is that the fact of evolution is a more secure "open-and-shut case" than any crime in the annals, and by a margin that exceeds all computation. The evidence for evolution is truly massive, and it piles on from all directions. As we detectives survey life, both extant and fossilized, we are overwhelmed by literally millions of observations that are exactly as they should be if evolution is, indeed, a fact, and natural selection did it. The distribution of DNA, of proteins, and of other molecules, is exactly as it should be if Darwinism is true. The distribution of animals and plants and fossils over the islands and continents of the world is exactly as it should be; the distribution of fossils in geological time is exactly as it should be; the distribution of bones, muscles, hearts, brains, and all other meticulously compared anatomical features is exactly as it should be if evolution is a fact. In the ordinary sense of the words *fact* and *proven*, evolution is a proven fact.

RICHARD DAWKINS

DEATHBED CLAIMS CONCERNING UNBELIEVERS.

One of the most long-lived pieces of popular evangelical apologetics is the story of the dying unbeliever, in a panic at the prospect of his imminent descent into hell, who wails out his last-minute repentance for having turned away from the Lord. For more than two hundred years all manner of freethinkers, be they atheists, deists, skeptics or humanists (see FREETHOUGHT; ATHEISM; DEISM; SKEPTICISM; HUMANISM), have been said to have died in pitiful remorse for their temerity in criticizing the truths of the Christian religion.

Stories of "infidel deathbeds," as they came to be known, were first gathered together in the book *Closing Scenes, or, Christianity and Infidelity Contrasted in the Last Hours of Remarkable Persons* by Rev. Erskine Neale, a rector of Kirton, Suffolk, England, and a sometime prison chaplain. This book was little more than a popular recycling of tales of dramatic deathbed cries of anguish by distraught freethinkers. The most popular, indeed ubiquitous, stories concerned Thomas PAINE and VOLTAIRE. Some of the stories Kirton gathered together were venerable even then. And their general theme is older still, reminiscent of the old stories of heretics confessing their sins as the flames licked around them.

The genuine, widespread bemusement over the calm death of David HUME helped to generate the later infidel deathbed tales. Hume's longtime friend James Boswell found it incomprehensible that Hume could die in such good humor. He asked Hume if it were at least possible that there was an afterlife. Hume replied that it was possible a piece of coal could be put on a fire and not burn, but it was "a most unreasonable fancy" that he should live forever. He quipped that the only positive aspect of immortality he could imagine would be living to see the "downfall of the prevailing system of superstition."

Whereas Hume attracted incredulity at the manner of his death, Voltaire was the target of many fabricated tales of his ranting for a priest in his death throes. The stories of Voltaire's deathbed agonies were largely the result of a need for vengeance on the part of those unable to get the better of him while he lived. The most reliable accounts of his death say that Voltaire refused absolution and thrust his hand against an importunate Curé, saying, "Let me die in peace." Voltaire's last words were spoken to his valet. He said simply, "Adieu, my dear Morand, I am gone."

In an interesting twist to the tradition of infidel deathbed stories, there has even been a long career of stories about Voltaire's house being used as a headquarters of the Geneva Bible Society. This story is as baseless as are the stories of his deathbed repentance.

The stories told of infidel deathbeds, popularized by people like Neale, had gained sufficient currency by the middle of the nineteenth century for freethinkers to feel the need for a response. Knowing that he had a chance of dying in the cholera epidemic then sweeping through London, the freethinking journalist Henry HETHERINGTON took the time to draw up a testament of his beliefs. As a leading opponent of church privilege and campaigner for press freedom, he knew he would probably be the subject of an infidel deathbed story. He wrote the testament two years before he died and signed it three days before his death in the presence of a friend, Robert Cooper, who left it at the office of their paper, the *Reasoner*. The testament began:

All life is uncertain, it behoves every one of us to make preparations for death; I deem it therefore a duty incumbent on me, ere I quit this life, to express in writing, for the satisfaction and guidance of esteemed friends, my feelings and opinions in reference to our common principles. I adopt this course that no mistake or misapprehension may arise through the false reports of those who officiously and obtrusively obtain access to the deathbeds of avowed infidels to priestcraft and superstition; and who, by their annoying importunities, labor to extort from an opponent, whose intellect is already worn out and subdued by protracted physical suffering, some trifling admission, that they may blazon it forth to the world as a Deathbed Confession, and a triumph of Christianity over infidelity.

Hetherington went on to reaffirm his rejection of any sort of transcendental temptation. Another nineteenth-century freethinker, Ernest RENAN, was sufficiently worried by the scenario of a deathbed conversion story that he wrote in his autobiography: "If such a fate is reserved for me, I protest in advance against the fatuities that a softened brain may make me say or sign. It is Renan sound in heart and head, such as I am now, and not Renan half destroyed by death, and no longer himself, as I shall be if I decompose gradually, that I wish people to listen to and believe."

Many prominent nineteenth-century freethinkers felt this need to insure their posthumous reputations against infidel deathbed stories. It was this need that motivated the English journalist and freethinker George W. FOOTE to compose *Infidel Deathbeds* in 1886. This work was little more than a collection of testimonies of prominent freethinkers, or of those who attended their dying moments, as to the freethinkers' beliefs immediately prior to death. To take one example, the section on the death of essayist and novelist Winwood Reade ends: "'From beside the grave opening to receive him,' said his life-long friend Moncure D. CONWAY, 'he warned these life-long victims that the only victory over death is to concentrate themselves on life.'" *Infidel Deathbeds* clearly satisfied a need, remaining in print for half a century, being revised, enlarged, and reissued many times until the 1930s.

But the popularity of these deathbed tales is not a historical oddity from the nineteenth century. To this day, many evangelicals recount tales of the dramatic last moments of Charles DARWIN—a particular favorite—Bertrand RUSSELL, Jean-Paul SARTRE, and even Gandhi, in the belief that such tales count as evidence against

them. Evangelical Web sites abound with tales of atheists crying out in their death throes. Even today Paine remains one of the favorite targets. One site quotes Paine as saying: "I would give worlds if I had them, that *The Age of Reason* had never been published. O Lord, help me! Christ, help me! . . . No, don't leave; stay with me! Send even a child to stay with me; for I am on the edge of Hell here alone. If ever the Devil had an agent, I have been that one." No source for this statement is given and there is no evidence whatever that Paine ever said this.

Stories of Paine's deathbed retraction can be traced back to the 1840s, when a newspaper article claimed to recount his deathbed wail of anguish. The article, appearing more than thirty years after Paine's death, was purported to have been written by Bishop Benedict J. Fenwick, who had himself only recently died. All the evidence suggests the article was bogus, not least because it perpetuated the old untruth that Paine was an atheist. Anybody who had actually attended Paine's death would presumably have known he was a deist who specifically and repeatedly repudiated atheism.

Another popular target of infidel deathbed tales is Charles Darwin. Many of these tales rely on the dubious testimony of an English evangelical and socialite, Elizabeth Cotton. After a career as a temperance campaigner, Cotton married into money and reinvented herself as a lady of leisure, going through the money of two husbands. Even after remarrying, she retained the title derived from her first husband: Lady Hope. In August 1915, four years after being declared bankrupt, Lady Hope sold a story to the Boston-based Baptist magazine the *Watchman-Examiner* concerning a visit she claimed to have made to Darwin as he lay dying in 1882. She recounted his last-minute conversion to Christianity and his declaration of admiration for the Bible. In fact, Lady Hope was not at Darwin's deathbed at all. It is possible she was granted a visit late in 1881, about six months before he died, but even that is uncertain. Henrietta Darwin, Charles's daughter, who *was* at his deathbed, repeatedly denied Lady Hope's story, but to little avail. And Henrietta could not recall Lady Hope ever visiting Down House. Assuming that the visit took place, no more can be read into it than Darwin graciously humoring a persistent caller.

Like most resilient myths, infidel deathbed stories can adapt to new times. The fashion for "near-death experiences" among popular New Age outlets has given the older infidel deathbed theme a new twist. The best illustration of this is the use made of A. J. AYER, who, in 1988, was technically dead for four minutes. A widely reported dream he had while returning to consciousness quickly took on a life of its own as evidence of a cocksure atheist having a brush with God. One source has Ayer admitting to his surgeon that he saw "the Supreme Being." When Ayer did in fact die, in June 1989, he died an atheist, remaining, according to those who were with him, "determinedly calm and cheerful."

The first point about the infidel deathbed stories is how primitive they are. It is a close relation of the prejudice that you don't find atheists in foxholes. The appeal of these stories rests on the core supposition that atheists could not face death with their convictions unchanged. It is a simplified version of PASCAL'S WAGER, which suggests that belief in God is the safest bet, in that if it is true one has secured immortality, while if it is false one has lost nothing. These prejudices only work if one's own religious belief is little more than a self-serving divine insurance policy. This unflattering understanding of religious faith is why the more sophisticated theologians and apologists have not resorted to the tales of infidel deathbeds.

But in a strange sort of way, the recipient of an infidel deathbed story is being paid a sideways compliment. It is, after all, recognition of that person's significance as a thinker and activist that those who disagree with him should seek to diminish his contribution with a story about a cowardly death. Many people whose works were placed on the Index of Forbidden Books were happy that the Roman Catholic Church had seen their work as sufficiently challenging to justify such a response. It was, in that sense, a badge of honor. The same can be said of recipients of infidel deathbed stories. Over the two centuries during which infidel deathbed stories have been popular, Paine remains the most frequent target, with Darwin a close second.

BIBLIOGRAPHY

Bradlaugh Bonner, Hypatia. *Did Charles Bradlaugh Die an Atheist?* London: A. & H. B. Bonner, 1898.

Foote, G. W. *Infidel Deathbeds*. London: Pioneer Press, [1933].

Moore, James. "Darwin—A Devil's Disciple?" British Humanist Association Darwin Day Lecture, February 11, 2005.

Rogers, Ben. *A. J. Ayer: A Life*. New York: Grove Press, 1999.

Ross, David. "Voltaire's House and the Bible Society." *Open Society* 77, no. 1 (Autumn 2004).

BILL COOKE

DEATH OF GOD THEOLOGY. Though it takes its name from the breathless proclamation of Friedrich NIET-ZSCHE's mad prophet in *The Gay Science*, Death of God theology—prominent in the 1960s but making a comeback—derives its inspiration from several sources. It began as one of several neoliberal reactions to the neo-Orthodox theology of Karl Barth, which dominated mainstream Protestantism through the 1950s. Barth, a revisionist Calvinist, had reaffirmed the traditional Reformed and Lutheran suspicion of pietistic subjectivism, since such dubiously claimed direct consciousness of the divine had led, starting with Friedrich

Schleiermacher, to subjective culture Protestantism, which for Barth blurred the line between divine revelation and human reason and culture. Barth had seen such liberal theology drift with shocking ease into the support of German imperialism in World War I, and this galvanized him to affirm the absolute transcendence of God as the Wholly Other, who had spoken definitively and objectively above the din of human voices in his living word, Jesus Christ. Barth affirmed the Weberian "disenchantment of the world" so as to make clear the difference between sinful man and the holy God who had bridged the gap between them in Jesus Christ alone.

But in the minds of many this left the world an airless moonscape, bereft of God. A few thinkers conceived a bleak but bracing vision. Drawing upon the prison writings of Dietrich Bonhoeffer, theologians including Harvey Cox, Anglican bishop John A.T. Robinson, and philosophical theologian Paul M. van Buren strove to forge a way in which contemporary Christians might learn to "speak in a secular fashion of God," or to "live without God before God," whence the alternate name for the movement, secular theology, arose. They urged that Christian ethical concerns be translated into secular terms, minus religious language, concepts, or warrant, and yet for religious reasons. This secularization of Christianity they saw as the consistent outworking of long-term trends begun in the scripture itself. In *The Secular City*, Cox sees the gradual disenchantment and rationalization of the world as a direct extension of the Israelite belief that God was freely active in ongoing history, not a divine embodiment of the cyclical forces of nature and therefore a prisoner to them. And when the apostle Paul teaches that Christ has freed humanity from the domination of the angelic principalities and powers who ruled us through religious regulations (a Gnostic motif), Cox claims it as a major step toward eventual secularization. God was already dying as humanity began to mature, but, as Nietzsche's prophet discovered, the light from that supernova would take many centuries to dawn on the run of mankind.

Cox urged upon Christians a moratorium on the use of the word *God* until it could be freed from the terrible and destructive associations it had gathered like barnacles over the millennia. Jewish thinker Martin Buber, in his *The Eclipse of God*, contemplated such a vow of theistic silence, but decided that faith cannot do without the word. Another Jewish theologian who did find himself a major voice of the Death of God movement was Richard L. Rubenstein, who saw the Holocaust as the definitive proof that Jews' belief in their role as God's chosen was not only false but pernicious. If Auschwitz could be considered compatible with the love or justice of God, then these terms are meaningless. And as long as Jews believe themselves, even in humility, to possess a special holiness, they are inevitably making themselves targets for rivals who will take that claim seriously enough to covet it and try to wrest it from Jews by destroying them, as witness the mimetic envy of both Christians and Nazis, self-perceived super-races that could not bear to share this honor with Jews.

William Hamilton saw Western culture in the 1960s as undergoing a collective dark night of the soul, suffering from the hiddenness of God. To Hamilton the only gleams amid the darkness were playful and optimistic developments in the secular arts, including the work of Michelangelo Antonioni and the Beatles. Some of Hamilton's essays seem embarrassingly facile in retrospect, and yet he was ahead of his time in recognizing that religious thought could never provide a comprehensive system of explanation. Nonetheless, Christians must and may take the historical Jesus, as Bonhoeffer understood him, as "the Man for Others," as their Lord and guide, the only token of divinity left us as we serve humanity in its suffering.

Paul M. van Buren did not relish his inclusion among the Death of God theologians, but the resemblance is undeniable. He approached modern theology from the perspective of analytical philosophy. Ultimately, he reasoned, Christianity in our time can retain no more than the distinctive *blik* or evaluative standpoint of Christianity, with no supernatural underpinnings. Secular Christianity is rather a way of seeing the world through the gospel. It is a vision of life, not a theory about the world, more of an agenda than a creed. It was not long, however, before van Buren, influenced by the thinking of William James, found his way back into a more traditional Christian identification, albeit one entirely colored by and tailored to the Jewish-Christian dialogue.

Thomas J. J. Altizer was by far the most radical of the Death of God theologians (or, as conservative Lutheran John Warwick Montgomery, who energetically debated Altizer, dubbed them, the Theothanatologists). Altizer called the bluff of traditional Christianity's claim to take history seriously (unlike, e.g., Buddhism). If Christians mean it, then in the modern world theologians must stop neutralizing and retreating from (secular) history into an interior fairyland of *Heilsgeschichte* or so-called salvation history. They must no longer ignore what has been revealed about reality by such thinkers and visionaries as Nietzsche, Sigmund FREUD, Ludwig FEUERBACH, and William Blake. Christian faith must take these insights into account. When it does, it realizes that it must stand against transcendence and must will the death of God. For Altizer it comes down to this radical negation instead of, say, some convenient redefinition of the God concept. This is because "God" is inseparable for us from what the word has come to mean in experience. And the experience we have of the transcendent God is one of alienation. What other "relation" could one possibly have to the Wholly Other? This God must die.

To proclaim and will the death of God is a Christian thing to do, Altizer proclaimed. In fact, those who do so are more entitled to the name "Christian" than most traditional and modern theologians, who have tried to reverse the apocalyptic thrust of Jesus's proclamation. What Jesus was getting at by proclaiming the imminent reversal of all things (including the God who once was far off, i.e., transcendent, but now is made near) is what we refer to in modern conceptuality as the self-emptying by God of his transcendence or spirit.

The myth of the Edenic Fall denotes the mutual alienation of God and humanity. Thus humanity as sinful and God as transcendent are both ipso facto *fallen*. We experience this God as the creator or divine ground of this world. The transcendent Creator transcends his creation. Thus if an eschatological reversal is to be truly *new* (as by definition it must be), and not a mere return to previous equilibrium—a homecoming to Eden—the final form of God must be immanent and not transcendent. How does this change occur? The incarnation of God in Christ occurs at the Resurrection, which is to be understood as a downward, not upward, motion. In Christ God became forever "enfleshed." The Resurrection is not an ascent into heaven (a reversal of the incarnation, a return to transcendence), but rather a descent into hell—where God stays, to be met in our experiences of the darkness and horror of the world.

Drawing on Buddhism (see BUDDHISM, UNBELIEF WITHIN), Altizer seems to make the Christian life that of a bodhisattva. The acceptance of the end of God's transcendence means also the yielding up of the autonomy of ego or self, as well as immersion in the world's darkness. The new "indifferent" (impartial) solidarity with all beings in that dark reality will issue in undiscriminating compassion (*karuna*), as in Buddhism.

Death of God theology enjoyed a brief but spectacular vogue in the 1960s, then died out soon after. In the 1980s and 1990s it staged a comeback; like Nietzsche's prophet, it seemed to have arrived before its time. But in the wake of the deconstructive antiphilosophy of Jacques Derrida and Paul de Man, Death of God theology seemed to make more sense than ever before. Philosophy had caught up with it. New theologians in this camp would include Mark C. Taylor, Charles E. Winquist, Carl A. Raschke, Robert L. Scharlemann, and the later Don Cupitt.

With Derrida, who banished any notion of a "transcendental signified," a logos-center or meaning-center external to language, deconstructive theology proclaims the Nietzschean Gospel of the death of God. But it also proclaims the death of man, of woman, of a transcendent consciousness as a mirror reflecting a pure vision of truth. Deconstruction sees all language as cross-referential, referring only to language. All reality is a textual field, a flat surface with much depth beneath it, a depth of unsuspected meanings, but no height, nothing above it to which it points.

To unpack this a bit, the death of God means, for the theology of deconstruction, that the divine has been poured out into the human, the profane, the secular, which henceforth is seen to glow with a kind of "trace," a witch-fire radiance of the lost sense of holiness. What once was there to be worshiped is now present only in its conspicuous absence. Religious worship must now be like the singing of the Lamentations of Jeremiah amid the ruins of the Temple of Solomon: over the debris one can make out the word *Ichabod* ("the Glory has departed"), and in that absence is the lingering trace of the holy—not a Holy Ghost, but a ghost of holiness. The rawness of the profane, which is all that is left to us in a world with no transcendent reference, somehow yet retains the hint, the echo, the trace of the holy that is gone.

With the death of any transcendent source of meaning or value outside language, with the revelation that every concept is only a metaphor, that even logical argument is only narrative, there can be no religious authority. No book can be more authoritative than any other, because there is no word of God. No particular reading of any book can be recovered as the true or binding one. All exists simply as text, a field of signifiers. We as readers break a path through the text as we read, but we can never be sure we are doing more than playing a word-search puzzle, imagining chains of signification where none were intended by the writer. Deconstructive theologians and critics thus have new respect for the subversive reading strategies of the Kabbalah, which did not hesitate to read the text backwards, and as acronyms, and as puzzles, and by means of puns.

Deconstruction abhors logocentrism, the abstraction of some element of the text and the idolatrous elevation of it as the key to the meaning of the text. The meaning of the text is the text itself. If Altizer proclaimed the death of God, today's deconstructive theologians proclaim the death of the logos, or word, of God.

BIBLIOGRAPHY

Altizer, Thomas J. J. *The Descent into Hell.* Philadelphia: Lippincott, 1970.

———. *The Gospel of Christian Atheism.* Philadelphia: Westminster, 1966.

Altizer, Thomas J. J., and William Hamilton. *Radical Theology and the Death of God.* New York: Bobbs-Merrill, 1966.

Altizer, Thomas J. J., and John Warwick Montgomery. *The Altizer-Montgomery Dialogue: A Chapter in the God Is Dead Controversy.* Chicago: Inter-Varsity, 1966.

Altizer, Thomas J. J., Max A. Myers, Carl A. Raschke, Robert P. Scharlemann, Mark C. Taylor, and Charles E. Winquist. *Deconstruction and Theology.* New York: Crossroad, 1982.

Bonhoeffer, Dietrich. *Letters and Papers from Prison.* Translated by Reginald H. Fuller. New York: Macmillan, 1953.

Buber, Martin. *The Eclipse of God.* New York: Harper & Brothers, 1957.

Cox, Harvey. *The Secular City: Secularization and Urbanization in Theological Perspective.* New York: Macmillan, 1966.

Cupitt, Don. *Creation out of Nothing.* London: SCM, 1990.

———. *Taking Leave of God.* New York: Crossroad, 1981.

Graham, Billy, Bernard Ramm, Vernon C. Grounds, and David Hubbard. *Is God "Dead"?* Grand Rapids, MI: Zondervan, 1966.

Hamilton, William. *The New Essence of Christianity.* New York: Association Press, 1966.

———. *On Taking God out of the Dictionary.* New York: McGraw-Hill, 1974.

Jackson Lee Ice, and John J. Carey, eds., *The Death of God Debate.* Philadelphia: Westminster, 1967.

Metz, Johannes. *Is God Dead?* Concilium: Theology in an Age of Renewal, Volume 16. New York: Paulist Press, 1966.

Ogletree, Thomas W. *The Death of God Controversy.* New York: Abingdon, 1966.

Raschke, Carl. *The Alchemy of the Word: Language and the End of Theology.* Missoula, MT: Scholars Press, 1979.

Robinson, John A. T. *Honest to God.* London: SCM, 1963.

Rubenstein, Richard L. *After Auschwitz: Radical Theology and Contemporary Judaism.* New York: Macmillan, 1966.

Scharlemann, Robert L. *The Reason of Following: Christology and the Ecstatic I.* Chicago: University of Chicago Press, 1991.

Taylor, Mark C. *Alterity.* Chicago: University of Chicago Press, 1987.

Vahanian, Gabriel. *The Death of God: The Culture of Our Post-Christian Era.* New York: George Braziller, 1957.

van Buren, Paul M. *The Secular Meaning of the Gospel: Based on an Analysis of Its Language.* New York: Macmillan, 1963.

Winquist, Charles. *Epiphanies of Darkness: Deconstruction in Theology.* Philadelphia: Fortress, 1986.

Woodyard, David D. *Living without God—Before God.* Philadelphia: Westminster, 1968.

ROBERT M. PRICE

DE CLEYRE, VOLTAIRINE (1866–1912), American anarchist, freethinker, and sex radical. Born November 17, 1866, in Leslie, Michigan, to a very poor family, Voltairine de Cleyre was the granddaughter of an abolitionist. Her father was a French-born socialist and freethinker (see SOCIALISM AND UNBELIEF; FREETHOUGHT). The strikingly intellectual child began a lifetime career as a poet at age six. Her education ended with three years in a convent school, where she was enrolled for practical reasons. Her training there was solid, but her opinion of Catholicism was that it turned bright young personalities into "prostrate nonentities." She declared herself a freethinker two years after graduating.

De Cleyre (her adopted spelling) wrote for freethought papers and lectured for the AMERICAN SECULAR UNION. From 1889 to 1910 she lived in Philadelphia, where she helped establish the city's anarchist-based secular clubs: the Ladies' Liberal League (1892), the Social Science Club (1899), and the Radical Library of Philadelphia (1905). Internationally acclaimed thinkers argued and taught at these clubs, including Pëtr KROPOTKIN, Emma GOLDMAN, and Edward Drinker Cope. Because of her charisma and intellectual prowess, de Cleyre was a key factor in the unusually favorable public persona earned by the anarchists of Philadelphia. She earned a meager living as a teacher of piano, French, and English to immigrants, especially Russian Jews. She learned Yiddish and invested much energy in understanding Jewish life and issues.

Though she contributed to dozens of periodicals, her main venues included the *Firebrand, Free Society, Freedom* (London), *Mother Earth*, and especially *Lucifer, The Light-Bearer*, to whose editor, Moses HARMAN, she was ideologically close. De Cleyre was a traveling lecturer from around 1886, making tours of the Midwest, the eastern United States, and Canada, and traveling also to Britain and Scandinavia in 1897 and 1903.

De Cleyre's anarchism was consistently predisposed toward the individualist school, but from 1897 she preached an anarchism explicitly "without adjectives." She held that general conceptions of world and universe do not inherently impede the struggle for human equality; that various atheistic or religious ideologies and different economic structures could be advantageously tried, so long as the spirit of individuality was encouraged and preserved. She held that both philosophical and revolutionary methods—ranging from Tolstoian nonresistance (see TOLSTOY, LEV NIKOLAYEVICH) to the assassination of heads of state—should be considered case by case as practical conditions were addressed. Considering marriage the sexual enslavement of women and an impediment to personal development for both sexes, she defended and practiced varietism (nonmonogamy) and criticized traditional domesticity and monogamy (see SEX RADICALISM AND UNBELIEF). She also defended the cause of labor, but opposed the concentration of power in the hands of either union officials or political parties. In this spirit she actively supported the most radical of unions, the Industrial Workers of the World, and the Mexican Revolution.

For most of her adult life, de Cleyre had health problems that punctuated her activities, including chronic sinusitis, complicated by one or more infectious diseases and aggravated by suicidal melancholia around 1894 and an abortion in 1897. She came near death after being shot by a deranged former pupil in 1902, and again from sickness in 1904. Her refusal to testify against her 1902 assailant and her efforts to defend him from prosecutors moved many hearts. She moved to Chicago in 1910, where she died from complications of infected sinuses on June 20, 1912.

BIBLIOGRAPHY

Avrich, Paul. *An American Anarchist: The Life of Voltairine de Cleyre.* Princeton, NJ: Princeton University Press, 1978.

De Cleyre, Voltairine. *Exquisite Rebel: The Essays of Voltairine de Cleyre—Anarchist, Feminist, Genius.* Albany: State University of New York Press, 2004.

———. *The First Mayday: Haymarket Speeches 1895–1910.* Orkney, UK: Cienfuegos Press, 1980

———. *Selected Works.* New York: Mother Earth, 1914.

De Lamotte, Eugenia. "Refashioning the Mind: The Revolutionary Rhetoric of Voltairine de Cleyre." *Legacy: A Journal of American Women Writers* (January–June 2003).

Marsh, Margaret S. *Anarchist Women, 1870–1920.* Philadelphia, PA: Temple University Press, 1981.

ROBERT P. HELMS

DEISM. A new understanding of the universe which rose to prominence in Europe during the seventeenth century in the wake of the progress of science, deism was pioneered especially by Copernicus through to Isaac Newton. Deism also owed much to the fracturing of Christian theology at the same time, particularly with respect to doctrines such as the Trinity. Deism is, in the main, a European movement, and relevant only to the Christian tradition against which it was reacting. Most of the influential leaders of the Enlightenment (see ENLIGHTENMENT, UNBELIEF DURING THE) were deists. The first known use of *deist* was in 1564, by the French Calvinist Pierre Viret, who used it to denote the person who believes in god in the abstract sense of being the creator of the universe, but who denies the divinity of Jesus Christ and other significant parts of Christian dogma. Viret castigated such people as wicked atheists (see ATHEISM). The word appeared in English for the first time in 1621 in Robert Burton's influential work *Anatomy of Melancholy*. Unlike Viret, Burton's use of the word was neutral. The first person to describe his own views as deist was the Englishman Charles Blount. It was not until 1682 that *deism* was used, and this was in John Dryden's preface to his poem *Religio Laici*.

The first important fact about the people now generally called deists is that they differed from each other as much as they agreed. It is easier to see a common program in deism when we examine what they rejected, rather than what they embraced. Generally speaking, the thinkers we now call deists rejected the mystical and revealed elements of Christianity such as miracles (see MIRACLES, UNBELIEF IN), original sin, the Virgin Birth, and the Trinity. In its place, deists advocated what they saw as a natural religion, which emphasized mathematical laws and natural harmony as had been uncovered by Newton, and which could be understood through the use of REASON. In most cases, deists advocated religious toleration, arguing that all religions were, to some extent at least, a representation of the divine truth in the universe. Deists tended to believe in a creator, but in most cases denied that the creator took any part in the day-to-day running of the universe. God was implicit in the universe but had no part in running it or in overseeing the moral lives of humans. And, in what now seems an odd anomaly to this package of ideas, most deists retained some belief in an afterlife (see IMMORTALITY, UNBELIEF IN).

Few of the principles of deism were original to those who adopted the label. Most deist ideas had been aired at some time by the Greeks and Romans. CICERO in particular articulated most of the views later taken up by deists in his work *De Natura deorum*. It is no coincidence that Cicero was an especially popular historical figure in the eighteenth century, when deism was at its height.

Two developments were significant in the rediscovery of these ideas and their reorganization into what became known as deism. One was the scientific breakthroughs of Galileo GALILEI and Newton, which opened up a universe infinitely larger and more complex than the simple, geocentric universe presented by Christian theology. The other factor was the growing disgust at the slaughter of heretics and schismatics in the name of religion in the century leading up to, and culminating in, the Thirty Years' War, which ended in 1648. The new scientific thinking and the wars of religion had both highlighted the difficulties in linking specific items of doctrine to religion. Deism was an attempt to retain what was seen as religion's core insight minus the doctrinal accretions.

One of the first statements of what is now called deism came in *De Veritate* (1624) by the Englishman Lord Edward Herbert of Cherbury. He did not speak of deism, but of "natural religion," which he said comprised five basic features: the existence of a supreme being; the requirement to worship this supreme being; worship being best manifested by personal virtue; the need for repentance when we fall from these standards; and being rewarded or punished in afterlife on the basis of the above points. The boldest overview of deist thought was John TOLAND's *Christianity Not Mysterious* (1696), which combined a blistering attack on the corruption of the churches and the bibliolatry of the Puritans with an attempted reconciliation of reason and religion. He also compared Christianity with Islam (see ISLAM, UNBELIEF WITHIN) and paganism, as if all three were of equal spiritual standing. Strictly speaking, Toland was a pantheist (see PANTHEISM AND UNBELIEF), which is the belief that when one speaks of God and the universe, one is speaking of the same thing. Another important deist was Lord SHAFTESBURY, who in his *Characteristics* (1711) gave a more Platonist rendering of deism, which concentrated on

the moral imperative for belief in a supreme being. His works were translated into French by Denis DIDEROT. Deism was expressed poetically by Alexander Pope in his *Essay on Man* (1733–34) and *Universal Prayer* (1738).

Deism reached its apogee with the publication in 1730 by Matthew TINDAL of *Christianity as Old as Creation*, a work that attracted 150 replies. Tindal extended the critique of scriptures by arguing that such texts, being human creations, are full of errors and inconsistencies and serve only to deflect our thoughts from the proper constitution of the universe. Anthony COLLINS, another influential thinker of the time, is usually considered a deist, but some recent scholarship has argued he should be thought of as an atheist. Other important deists include VOLTAIRE and, more problematically, Jean-Jacques ROUSSEAU, notwithstanding their significant differences of approach in most other respects. And in Germany, the closest approximation of deism can be found in Immanuel KANT's work *Religion within the Limits of Reason Alone* (1792–94). Here Kant argued that the limits of religion are set not by doctrine or scripture but by our own conscience and praxis.

A significant element of deism was its commitment to the idea of natural religion. This was most frequently explained in terms of the existence of a natural religious response to the world. This is not manifested in orthodoxy or doctrine, but in the evidence of our senses. Where we find common moral decencies, so the argument goes, there we find the natural religion inherent in us all. Though not normally considered a deist, David HUME articulated a form of this in his *Dialogues*, where he outlined the beliefs he thought were ubiquitous in human beings. The Hume scholar J. C. A. Gaskin has called Hume's philosophy of religion an "attenuated deism."

The more radical deists argued that religious orthodoxies and dogmas, far from encapsulating the core truth claims of any religion, are later corruptions from the simple purity that underlies true religion. They are superstitions and prejudices given an academic gloss. This was argued forcefully by Voltaire. Though describing himself as a theist, Voltaire was one of deism's better-known publicists.

Perhaps the most energetic and influential voice belonged to Thomas PAINE, whose *The Age of Reason* (1794–95) brought deist ideas to a wider audience than ever before. Paine wrote *The Age of Reason* with the specific intention of countering what he saw as harmful and incorrect atheism. But alongside this was a blistering attack on the corruption of the churches and the perversion of what he saw as the inherently simple and deist message of the Bible. The immorality of many Bible passages, the primitive notions of society that other passages assumed, and the anthropomorphic nature of still other passages all denoted human authorship, Paine argued. And in a brilliant volte-face of the conventional pejorative, Paine recast *infidelity* not as unorthodoxy, but as being untrue to oneself. In this way, it is the "infidel" who explains away the immoralities, absurdities, and contradictions of the Bible so as to retain belief in divine authorship, Paine argued. The true act of religion consists of discarding these all-too-human additions to allow freer access to the divine essence being forgotten.

The writings of Thomas Paine struck a nerve that went far beyond the polite disputes over the merits of deism. Shaftesbury, Collins, Tindal, and Thomas CHUBB had made many of the same points earlier in the century, but Paine's combination of these with radical politics and a critique of privilege was too much for the authorities. His influence also serves as a warning about the frequently made claim that deism was too patrician to gain widespread support. It is not that this claim is untrue, but there is a further element to it that is not usually observed. Most deists assumed their views were too sophisticated for the common people, who could be expected to prefer the anthropocentrism and emotionalism of revealed religion. But many of Paine's readers took to heart his condemnation of clerical corruption and bibliolatry and rejected *all* religion, even the deism Paine recommended. It seems the authorities were right to be worried by Paine's effect on "the vulgar."

Deism was seen by the established churches as a significant threat long before Paine. The first major attempt at a refutation came from Bishop Stillingfleet in 1677 in his *Letter to a Deist*. Indeed, Stillingfleet's letter marks something of a turning point in the history of Christianity, in that it was the first occasion when an established Christian authority figure was required to treat a rival theory seriously and not simply respond with physical coercion. From the middle of the eighteenth century, deism began to attract some powerful attacks from orthodox Christians. One of the most important was Joseph Butler's *Analogy of Religion* (1736), which argued that deism did not in fact break free from many of the philosophical problems said to trouble revealed religion so much. More interesting is that some of the most influential critiques of deism were from people who otherwise can be counted as deists. Rousseau spoke more positively about the emotions than any other deist, and Voltaire's classic satire *Candide* (1759) lampooned the sanguine confidence to which deism is susceptible with respect to the universe. Just as significant was Hume's posthumous work *Dialogues concerning Natural Religion* (1779), which fatally undermined any claim to the existence of a god, however conceived. And Percy Bysshe SHELLEY's essay *A Refutation of Deism* (1814) perceptively argued that deism was incapable of performing its task of providing a tenable refuge between Christianity and atheism. The problem that deism never effectively solved, and which Shelley understood, was its inability to demonstrate why the various shreds of religion it retained were any more intellectually sustainable than the doctrines that deists were happy to reject. This has been an ongoing problem for liberal religion to this day.

The true impact of deism is not to be found in the intellectual arena, but in politics. The deist denunciations of the corruption of clerical rule contributed to the secularization of politics. Nowhere was this more apparent than in the United States, where most of the Founding Fathers, including the first four presidents, subscribed to variations of deistic thinking. Susan Jacoby has outlined the general characteristics of the ideas of the Founding Fathers such as skepticism of the more rigid sects of the day; the conviction that if God exists, he created human rationality as the supreme instrument for understanding the world; and faith as an item of individual conscience rather than public duty. The Founding Fathers' deism was at the radical end of the spectrum, and was generally dismissive of the central tenets of Christian orthodoxy.

George Washington made no religious declaration on his deathbed (see DEATHBED CLAIMS CONCERNING UNBELIEVERS) and did not call for a clergyman to attend to his mortal demise. In true deistic fashion, Washington scorned most doctrinal contests. When petitioned by army chaplains not to appoint to their ranks a Universalist (see UNIVERSALISM TO 1961) who denied the existence of hell, he instead approved the appointment. He also oversaw a treaty with the Muslims of North Africa that declared that "the Government of the United States of America is not in any sense founded on the Christian religion" (see TRIPOLI, TREATY OF). This treaty was ratified during the presidency of his successor, John Adams.

Thomas JEFFERSON, the third president of the United States, expressed his deist principles in what has become known as *The Jefferson Bible*, which stripped Jesus of supernatural additions and presented him as a man of simple, unassuming wisdom. Jefferson was adamant that the United States should not repeat the mistakes of Europe in binding religion to the state. Echoing John LOCKE, Jefferson said that religion "is a matter which lies solely between man and his God."

James MADISON, the fourth president of the United States, was the least conventionally religious of them all, as when he declared that "[r]eligious bondage shackles and debilitates the mind and unfits it for every noble enterprise." One of the rare occasions when Madison used his veto was against a bill incorporating a church in the District of Columbia, on the grounds it infringed the separation of church and state. The separation of church and state is a logical consequence of deism and constitutes its most lasting and positive legacy.

In the first half of the nineteenth century, deism was overtaken among the uneducated by evangelical revivals, which pandered to the popular demand for transcendental consolations. Among the radical poor, the transition was toward atheism, led by Charles BRADLAUGH in Britain, and toward ANTICLERICALISM in France. In the United States, Robert Green INGERSOLL led people in the direction of AGNOSTICISM. However, deist ideas have remained influential among religious progressives, Unitarians, and religious humanists, have contributed in important ways to the ongoing division in contemporary Western religiosity between its liberal and evangelical wings.

BIBLIOGRAPHY

Berman, David. *A History of Atheism in Britain from Hobbes to Russell*. London: Croom & Helm, 1988.

Clark, David Lee, ed. *Shelley's Prose*. London: Fourth Estate, 1988.

Gaskin, J. C. A. *Hume's Philosophy of Religion*. New York: Macmillan, 1978.

Gay, Peter. *The Enlightenment: An Interpretation*. London: Wildwood House, 1973.

Jacoby, Susan. *Freethinkers: A History of American Secularism*. New York: Metropolitan, 2004.

Keane, John. *Tom Paine: A Political Life*. London: Bloomsbury, 1995.

Paine, Thomas. *Age of Reason*. London: Watts and Company, 1938.

Porter, Roy. *Enlightenment: Britain and the Creation of the Modern World*. London: Penguin, 2000.

Robertson, J. M. *A History of Freethought: Ancient and Modern*. London: Watts and Company, 1936.

Wollheim, Richard, ed. *Hume on Religion*. London: Collins, 1963.

BILL COOKE

DEMOGRAPHY OF UNBELIEF. Until the twentieth century all peoples were highly religious: supernatural belief was nearly universal and pervaded daily life. As late as 1900, AGNOSTICISM and absolute ATHEISM may have been held by only a few million persons, mainly intellectuals. Following the unprecedented growth in global communications and travel in the wake of the Industrial Revolution, many Western Christians presumed that their faith, then embraced by a third of the planet's population, would finally sweep the world in the twentieth century. This expectation inspired the evangelical Watchword movement. For their part, at the dawn of the twentieth century many nontheists thought the age of science would soon herald the end of mass faith. This expectation became known as the secularization hypothesis.

Which of these opposing visions has proven more accurate? The answer lies in a body of large-scale international surveys that recently sampled rates of belief and unbelief worldwide. During the 1990s, two massive studies, the International Social Survey Program—Religion I and II, measured religiosity in seventeen and thirty-three nations, respectively. The 2002 Pew Global Attitudes Project asked respondents in forty-four nations to rank religion's importance in their lives. The 2004 BBC/ICM survey of ten nations sought opinions on a number of issues bearing on religion. The results of these studies generally agree with polls conducted in single nations by Gallup and similar organizations. Another resource, the evangelical-authored *World Christian Encyclopedia*, tabulates national census data on religion, though faith communities' official membership statistics are sometimes contradicted by surveys designed to capture actual opinions among church members.

The twentieth century can be seen as a grand culture war, a vast, historically unique societal experiment in which agnostics, absolute atheists, and other nonreligious ballooned to about one billion, a sixth of the world's population. Driven largely by conversion of believers, this vast expansion in unbelief—a multi-hundredfold upsurge in absolute numbers, and a fiftyfold increase in percentage of population in one long life span—far outstrips the growth of any major faith in the twentieth century, and probably in history.

Current Situation. Believers in the supernatural belong to some ten thousand significant sects, most aligned within ten major organized religions. Christianity's percentage of the population has remained stagnant overall, at about one in three. Christians are divided among some thirty-four thousand denominations, one of which—Roman Catholicism—claims almost half of all Christians. Most demographic losses among Christians represent conversions to nontheism rather than to any of the other major religions. Among the ten major religions, only Islam has seen major relative growth, moving from about 12 percent of the global population in 1900 to nearly 20 percent today, largely due to population growth rather than conversion. The third-largest faith, Hinduism, claims about a seventh of the global population. Traditional animists, New Agers, and various pagans make up about a sixth of the world's people. In alarmed reaction to the fast growth of secularization, Abrahamic and Hindu fundamentalists mounted a resurgence in recent decades.

In general, rising levels of education and income correspond to higher rates of religious skepticism. For example, despite anomalously high religious belief in the United States (see below), most American scientists are nontheists; the degree of skepticism is highest among the most distinguished researchers. This pattern repeats at the level of nations: in most second and third world countries, rates of belief remain high and relatively little changed from the past. In these nations 80 to nearly 100 percent of survey respondents report remaining absolute believers and rate religion as very important in their lives. Even so, secularism has made gains. Among Latin American respondents, up to a third describe religion as only somewhat important. Fully a third of Turks are only somewhat religious, proof that a Muslim nation can experience significant secularization. Most interesting among the second world examples is South Korea, where only a quarter of respondents identify as strongly religious and a third report little interest, although few report none. Forty percent of South Korean respondents claimed to be agnostics and atheists.

Theism suffered severe losses under Communism. Contrary to Christian claims of a great post–Cold War revival, the percentage that reported considering religion very important remains in the mere teens in Russia, eastern Germany, Bulgaria, and the Czech Republic. Across this region half to three-quarters of respondents report limited or no interest in religion. In Russia some polls suggest high rates of religious interest and report that absolute belief in theism has doubled, but theists still constitute only a quarter of respondents and church attendance is low. A third of Russian respondents still identify as agnostics or absolute atheists. Meanwhile in eastern Germany, even after reunification fully half of respondents continue to express no interest in religion and profess to be agnostics and atheists. This is the highest reported incidence of unbelief in any democratic region. Still higher rates of disbelief may exist in China, which probably has the largest absolute number of non-theists, and in North Korea (though tempered by a bizarre superstitious aura surrounding the latter's fanatical leadership). In Vietnam just a quarter of the sample claim strong interest in religion, half report low or non-existent interest. In Islamic Uzbekistan, religious interest remains high among just a third of respondents; the same is true even in Poland, despite the cachet of Catholicism's role in helping to topple Communism.

Crisis in the West. Most striking is the crisis faced by organized religion in the west. During the last half of the twentieth century, all but one of the nineteen major prosperous developed democracies (the Western European nations, Canada, Australia, New Zealand, and Japan) experienced dramatic declines in religious belief and practice. Japan qualifies as among the most skeptical of first world democracies, with just 4 percent of respondents reporting "absolute" belief in God and fully a third self-identifying as agnostics and atheists. More than nine in ten Japanese respondents claim at most limited interest in religion; more than one in five report none whatever. In addition, rates of religious practice are low. No other democracy has so large a skeptical population in absolute terms. France exhibits even lower rates of religiosity, with a full third of respondents reporting no interest in religion, and four of ten identifying as agnostic or atheistic; the percentage reporting absolute belief in a creator is in the teens. Scandinavia, too, is a bastion of secularism, with absolute believers ranking in the teens, agnostics and atheists comprising a quarter to a third of respondents, and rates of religious practice at very low levels. Western Europe's Catholic nations are more theistic, yet even among Italians only a quarter report strong involvement in religion, while a third report little or none. Indeed half or more of Italians, Spaniards, and Irish hold no absolute belief in God. Taken as a bloc, only about one-quarter of the inhabitants of the secularized developed democracies describe themselves as absolute believers; an equal number report agnosticism or absolute atheism. In all of these countries, sizable majorities accept human descent from animals. In general, European Christianity is today generally liberal, with biblical literalists and "born-agains" comprising marginalized minorities.

It is difficult to overstate the dire condition of organized religion in the secularized democracies (that is, all of them except the United States). In none does a majority of the populace report ardent belief in a divine Christ. Meanwhile atheists are openly elected to high office and in some cases control state churches; believers in such evangelical staples as the Rapture are thought to be daft. Churches that lack state support are experiencing financial crises to the point that many churches are being converted to nonreligious uses or are renting space to commercial enterprises. So powerful is this secularizing tide that a commission of the Church of England has proposed dropping ill-attended Sabbath services and concluded that the advent of modern lifestyles "coincides with the demise of Christendom." No lesser authority than Pope John Paul II labeled Scotland "heathen." So beleaguered is European Christianity that second and third world churches are dispatching missionaries back to Europe. No significant grassroots revival appears to be in prospect in any of the secularized developed democracies. Instead, overall trends in faith point downward; for example, the number of nontheists in France has nearly doubled over the last quarter century. Although alternative modes of spirituality, including evangelicalism, Buddhism, and the New Age movement, have replaced mainstream Christian observance for some, they are by no means popular enough to offset Christianity's broad decay, especially as increasingly large numbers abandon any interest whatever in the supernatural. Likewise, though many report belief in varied paranormal claims, their level of interest is usually superficial and idle. All in all, nontheism has won the culture war in Europe, and has done so remarkably quietly and with little effort or cost.

The American Exception. The culture war still rages in the United States; alone among first world democracies, this nation displays primitive rates of religiosity otherwise seen only in the second and third worlds. Nearly two-thirds of Americans absolutely believe in God and consider religion important in their lives; nine in ten are favorable to the existence of a higher power. Not only is the United States the only nation to combine material prosperity with high levels of faith, American Christianity is exceptionally conservative by Western standards. Four in ten US respondents self-identify as born-again, about a third claim to believe that the Bible is literally true, and almost half deny human evolution. End-time novels are best-sellers and religious-themed films are blockbusters, while the media celebrates a mythical reconciliation of science and faith.

This has not always been the American norm. Many of the nation's revered founders were non-Christian deists, skeptics of a divine Christ who probably could not be elected today. Church membership has risen fairly steadily, climbing from less than one in five in revolu- tionary times to greater than three in five in the 1990s. In the latter third of the twentieth century, fundamentalism gained at the expense of less conservative Christian denominations. A Gallup analysis of multiple indicators concluded that US religiosity rose in the 1990s, reversing a long but modest decline during the 1950s and 1960s. Meanwhile, more than a third of Americans distrust unbelievers; 70 percent consider them unsuitable mates.

Yet US believers have a number of reasons for con- cern. Differing surveys place agnostics and atheists at 3 to 10 percent of the US population, making skeptics more numerous than American Jews or Mormons. American tolerance for unbelievers is growing. Lifestyles are increasingly secularized and liberalized: Sundays have largely become homogenized with the rest of the week, civil marriages are rising at the expense of religious ceremonies, and once-shocking "alternative" lifestyles and entertainment have become at least widely tolerated and frequently highly popular. Only a few percent of Americans live strict Bible-based lifestyles, and divorce rates remain high even among the born-again. Absolute God belief among Americans is already somewhat lower than typical in the third world—by inference, lower than it was in the American past. The percentage of those who absolutely believe in God, claim to be born-again, or accept literal descent from Adam and Eve has not risen for decades. A series of Gallup polls measured a consistent halving of claims of belief in the literal truth of the Bible, from nearly two-thirds in the 1960s to half that today. The most intriguing evidence comes from a growing body of sur- veys that consistently report declining rates of Bible reading, prayer, and church membership and atten- dance. Remarkably, Protestantism is quickly dropping from a significant majority down toward minority status, and Christianity as a whole is in proportional decline, from nearly 90 percent to about 75 percent. The surveys further indicate that the unchurched doubled during the 1990s, now comprising a quarter of the pop- ulation; over the same period those who express no reli- gious preference also doubled, in this case to a sixth of the total, having started from just a few percent a half century ago. Detachment from religioius indoctrination leaves people further inclined toward disbelief, so the churches face a retention crisis. Also, most nonreligious persons are men, and most children pick up their reli- gious beliefs from their fathers. That Southern Baptists are baptizing members at the same rate they did half a century ago when the population was half as large illus- trates the faith-based recruitment crisis. In the 1940s and 1950s between 1 and 2 percent of Gallup respon- dents said they did not believe in God, and up to 98 per- cent did. In two 2005 Gallup surveys, combined agnos- tics and atheists were more than 5 and 9 percent of the samples. There is no question that nontheism, including explicit atheism and agnosticism, is growing in America

at the expense of faith, despite the strenuous work of the world's wealthiest religious industry.

Although high rates of religiosity are found over much of the globe, they are specific to third and second world nations and the aberrant United States. Among the remaining developed democracies, secularism is increas- ingly the standard. If not for influxes of characteristically religious second and third world immigrants, all of the developed democracies, including the United States, would be undergoing greater secularization.

Geographic Distribution of Religiosity. Geographi- cally, devout Christianity is nearly extinct in its Middle Eastern home and has been largely abandoned in its his- torical European bastion; in the northern temperate zone, it is a strong majority phenomenon only in the United States. Christianity remains robust in much of Latin America, but is making major gains only in third world Africa, where it must compete with local animist beliefs. Two continents, Europe and Australia, can be considered wholly de-Christianized and secularized. Meanwhile, Islam continues to span the tropical Old World from the Atlantic to the Indian Oceans; mass Hinduism remains limited to the Indian subcontinent.

Demographics and the Secularization Hypothesis. Although modernity has by no means annihilated super- naturalism, for the first time religion has been dealt major blows, especially in advanced nations, partially fulfilling the secularist hypothesis and greatly disappointing evan- gelicals. Refuted is the widely debated chapter in Stark and Finke's *Acts of Faith* titled "Secularization, R. I. P.," in which the two pioneering sociologists of religion deri- sively deny Western secularization, arguing that faith is competitively superior to its alternative. Also contradicted is the widely held view that most people are strongly genetically, psychologically, or spiritually predisposed toward supernatural beliefs. Quite the contrary, religious opinion stands exposed by the data as brittle and readily subject to abandonment. The demographics of unbelief verify the argument that ardent mass faith requires evan- gelical promulgation by a conservative religious propa- ganda industry, consistently fading in the face of secular- ized liberal religion. In contrast, mass secularization is so potent that it occurs by spontaneous individual conversion even in the face of large-scale proselytizing and despite the absence of any comparably extensive—or expen- sive—secularist "missionary" movement.

Put simply, encouraging the inherently rational disbe- lief in supernatural deities is many times more cost effective than is promoting belief in what cannot be shown to exist. Were nontheism as evangelical and well organized as religion, then faith would be much worse off than it already is.

The Foundation of Belief. The factors behind the secular revolution's great potency are numerous and complicated, but one causal factor is clearly critical above others. Rather than being based upon unques- tioning faith as is often supposed, the belief of most religious individuals actually rests upon the notion that the universe and humanity must have been created by a greater intelligence. Until the early 1800s, science was seen as verifying natural theology, making denial of a creator difficult. Modern advances in geology, paleontology, cosmology, and evolutionary biology have largely eliminated the need for a creator in order to account for the state of the world. Deprived of its aura of physical necessity, supernatural belief can be recognized as mere unsubstantiated opinion and large numbers of people will simply abandon it. The better educated a person is in modern science, the more likely one is to make this rational decision (see DARWINISM).

The close negative correlation between the acceptance of human descent from animals and the existence of a creator in the developed democracies verifies the close inverse relationship between these factors. For instance, the Japanese report the strongest acceptance of evolution *and* the weakest belief in a creator; Americans display the opposite pattern. There is no documented case in which a prosperous democracy's population is both well-versed in evolutionary science and high in theistic belief and practice, or vice versa—and it is unlikely that any exists. Not well understood is whether acceptance of evolution leads to loss in faith, or the reverse, or—as seems most likely—that the two work together in a feedback system. The importance of advancing science in undermining faith cannot be overstated. Without it, the other contributing factors would be irrelevant.

Some of these other factors themselves depend upon science and technology. For example, the dramatic social changes of the industrial age have driven secularization. Two centuries ago, most people lived lives not much different from those of their ancient ancestors, with juvenile mortality rates of 50 percent, short adult life spans, and, by modern standards, almost ubiquitous poverty. Today, particularly in the first world, vast numbers of people travel the world almost at will, live in relative comfort and opulence, and enjoy abundant food and advanced medical care. Childhood death is rare and people regularly live into their seventies or eighties. Birth control and safe abortion allow sex to occur outside of sanctified marriage without the complication of pregnancy. The masses enjoy unprecedented access to a previously unimaginable variety of entertainment and information media. As the Church of England commission has acknowledged, living like pampered and protected demigods has undoubtedly emboldened millions to discard their beliefs in archaic myths.

The postwar collapse of religion in Europe's secular developed democracies has been associated with dramatic rises in both prosperity and education. Even Ireland threw off centuries of Catholic domination simultaneously with a technology-driven economic boom.

Historical Factors Influencing American Exceptionalism. While the collapse of ardent supernaturalism in virtually all prosperous democracies is readily explained, its survival—so far—in the United States is more puzzling. Historical patterns may play a role. Even after its Christianization, much of Europe, Scandinavia in particular, may not have been as devout as previously supposed. Disastrous events such as the Black Death, the Crusades, and extended religious wars combined with the impact of the Renaissance and Enlightenment to weaken faith further. Another possible factor may have been the steady export of religious zealots to North America, which in turn might explain why the young United States was markedly more theistic than Europe. The strongly theistic Scots-Irish who have greatly influenced southern and midwestern culture may be especially important. Stark and Finke support the hypothesis that separation of church and state created a religious free market in which American churches and clerics had to compete for adherents, in marked contrast to a Europe dominated by state churches whose clerics felt little need to work at retaining communicants. But this hypothesis does little to explain the thorough secularization of Australia and New Zealand, where relations between church and state resembled those in the United States. Thorough secularization has also occurred in democracies in which state and church were sundered long ago, such as Canada, in which religion was disestablished in the mid-1800s.

Historical Factors Influencing European Secularism. Vatican and clerical corruption, ranging from the "Irish Gulag" of juvenile slave laundry facilities to long-term ties with organized crime, has contributed to the collapse of European Catholicism. Likewise Catholic corruption may encourage declining piety in Mexico and other Latin American countries. Looking back, the shock of World War I severely damaged the concept of divine-right monarchy and encouraged the first major decline in European religion. The economic collapse of the 1930s, followed by the catastrophes of World War II and the Holocaust, delivered further blows to a Christianity that had signally failed to provide either the moral guidance or the divine intervention that might have been hopes to keep the historical stronghold of Christianity from descending into horrific chaos. Meanwhile atheism gained favor, in part because skeptics were conspicuous among opponents of fascism.

More recently, the continued failings of faith have continued to discourage belief in democracies more attuned to the international situation than America. For example, the most Christian African nations are strife-torn Rwanda and the Congo, where 80 to 95 percent are ardent believers. Violent Christian terrorist military organizations such as Zambia's Lumpa Church and Uganda's Lord's Resistance Army are committing mass atrocities of extreme brutality. When Baptist lay preacher Charles Taylor stepped down from his blood-drenched rule of Liberia, he cited God at length.

The Impact of World War II. The effect of World

War II on religious belief was most direct in Japan. In what may be history's single most effective blow against any faith, following the cataclysm an apologetic emperor admitted that he was not divine, instantly creating a nation of skeptics. Also affected by one person was post–World War I Turkey, were the antireligious Atatürk initiated a wave of secularism.

The American experience with the two world wars was quite different: they served as economic boosters, raising the country's global power and status while leaving it relatively unscathed, evidence to many of divine favor. Conservative America widely perceived the subsequent Cold War as an epic struggle between God-less communism and God-fearing democracy, an attitude that has now been transplanted more or less intact into rhetoric of a struggle between Christian righteousness and virulent Islam.

US Political and Religious Conservatism: A Vicious Cycle. The traditional historical, cultural, and political conservatism of the United States buttressed the popularity of conservative religions, which tended to exhibit the high levels of ardor needed to perpetuate their mythology. In turn, religious conservatism encouraged cultural-political conservatism in a classic feedback system. In particular, the common failure of US public and private school systems properly to teach evolutionary science is driven by the conservative religious community—nearly four in ten science teachers favor teaching creationism—which then benefits from the antievolutionism that favors conservative Christianity. It is no accident that the most conservative prosperous democracy is the most religious and vice versa, the one depending greatly on the other.

It is correspondingly ironic that the bulk of anti-Darwinist religious conservatives so ardently support free-market capitalism, which is strongly socially Darwinistic. High economic disparity results in higher US rates of poverty and maleducation than in Europe, perhaps encouraging more zealous faith (but see below). The fact that the more secular prosperous democracies enjoy lower rates of murder, incarceration, juvenile and adult mortality, STD infection, juvenile pregnancy, and abortion than in the United States may reduce their peoples' perceived need for the comfort of a benign deity. Contrary to the American conceit that the faith-based nation stands as a "shining city on a hill" to an increasingly skeptical world, the deep societal dysfunction of the sole prosperous Christian nation helps inspire growing skepticism in the rest of the West, aborting the very revival many Americans desire.

What Does the Future Hold? From the believer's perspective, then, the future of faith appears grim. S. Bruce observes that if the current trends continue, Christianity in England may soon be too small to be self-sustaining, in which case major denominations could go essentially extinct early in this century. With popular theism practically dead in Scandinavia and

Japan and showing no signs of revival in any other prosperous democracy, the United States is the last great Western hope of Christianity. But as D. G. Barrett et al. reluctantly acknowledge, the quickly rising number of the unchurched and those with no religion suggest that the United States is belatedly secularizing toward the Western norm. In fact, the level of nonreligiosity that Barrett et al. predicted for the year 2025 appears already to have been reached.

The options available to the defenders of faith are limited because most entail undesirable consequences. The current reactionary campaign to governmentalize faith by extending public funding to religious organizations in the United States risks assisting secularization in the way state churches arguably have done elsewhere. Although social conservatives have been successful in blaming liberalism for the materialistic, sex-focused, hedonistic mass culture that undermines faith-based lifestyles, the same conservative Christians lionize the corporate-driven social Darwinism that is by far the most powerful agent in defining culture away from traditional values. Evolutionary theory enjoys overwhelming scientific support, being a major contributor to the science and technology that remain central to the US economy and its place in the world. Evangelicals have little prospect of persuading more Americans to accept pseudoscientific creationism than already do so. Many liberal theists hold that faith can thrive in the face of widespread acceptance of evolutionary theory, but this view appears naive. J. Judis and R. Texeira predict a US sociopolitical liberalization that should encourage further declines in religiosity; the rapid growth of the unchurched and the nonreligious suggests that this process too is already under way.

Can Christianity compensate for an American decline by recruiting elsewhere in the world? Major Christian inroads are unlikely in formerly Communist Europe, in China, India, and the Islamic world, or among nontheists. The only rich sources of converts to Christianity are pagans and animists in the third and second worlds, particularly in Africa. Catholicism is poised to become a predominantly third world faith; meanwhile, if other Christians hoped that the low-grade war between political Islam and the secular/Christian West would spark a religious revival, they have few successes to point to. As for Islam, though it will continue to gain in numbers through population growth, the chronically poor economic performance of most Islamic nations will probably render it largely impotent. There is no reason to expect Hinduism to make major gains outside the Indian subcontinent. Nor are New Age or other alternative beliefs likely to sweep the globe.

Conclusion. The nineteenth-century expectation that advancing science and rationality would vanquish organized religion has not been disconfirmed after all. Unbelievers, particularly in the United States, may feel exasperation that religion has not collapsed more quickly and thoroughly, but the message of the demographic data is clear: it is believers in the supernatural, not skeptics, who have the most to fear in the twenty-first century.

BIBLIOGRAPHY

Barrett, D., G. Kurian, and T. Johnson, eds. *World Christian Encyclopedia*. Oxford: Oxford University Press, 2001.

Bishop, G. "What Americans Really Believe, and Why Faith Isn't as Universal as They Think." *Free Inquiry* 19, no. 3 (1999).

Bruce, S. "Christianity in Britain, R. I. P." *Sociology of Religion* 62 (2001).

De Tocqueville, A. *Democracy in America*. 1835.

Doughty, S. "Never on a Sunday: Church May Drop Sabbath Due to Lack of Interest." *Daily Mail*, January 20, 2004.

Duncan, O. D. "The Rise of the Nones, Parts 1 and 2." *Free Inquiry* 24, nos. 1, 2 (2004).

Frank, T. *What's the Matter with Kansas? How Conservatism Won the Heart of America*. New York: Metropolitan, 2004.

Gledhill, R. "Archbishops Back Guerrilla Tactics on War on Secularism." *Times* (London), January 20, 2004.

Grossman, C., and I. Yoo. "Civil Marriage on Rise Across USA." *USA Today*, October 7, 2003.

Larson, E., and L. Witham. "Scientists and Religion in America." *Scientific American* 281, no. 3 (1999).

Jenkins, P. *The Next Christendom: The Rise of Christianity in the 21st Century*. Oxford: Oxford University Press, 2002.

Jordan, M. "Inquiry Reignites Talk of Church's Drug Ties: Mexican Cardinal, a Recent Guest of Fox, Scrutinized in Money Laundering Probe." *Washington Post*, October 1, 2003.

Judis, J., and R. Texeira. *The Emerging Democratic Majority*. New York: Scribner, 2002.

Moore, R. "Educational Malpractice: Why Do So Many Biology Teachers Endorse Creationism?" *Skeptical Inquirer* 25 (2001).

Paul, G. "The Great Scandal: Christianity's Role in the Rise of the Nazis, Parts 1 and 2." *Free Inquiry* 23, no. 4 (2003); 24, no. 1 (2003).

———. "The Secular Revolution: It's Passed America By—So Far." *Free Inquiry* 22, no. 3 (2002).

Reid, T. "Hollow Halls in Europe's Churches." *Washington Post*, May 6, 2001.

———. *The United States of Europe*. New York: Penguin, 2004.

Stark, R., and R. Finke. *Acts of Faith*. Berkeley and Los Angeles: University of California Press, 2000.

Summerville, C. "Stark's Age of Faith Argument and the Secularization of Things: A Commentary." *Sociology of Religion* 63 (2002).

Thompson. B. "Fighting Indecency, One Bleep at a Time: Only Popular Culture and Big Media Stand in Parent Television Council's Way." *Washington Post*, December 9, 2004.

Williams, D. "Vatican Is Alarmed by Political Trend in Europe." *Washington Post*, October 20, 2004.

Williams, P. *The Vatican Exposed: Money, Murder, and the Mafia*. Amherst, NY: Prometheus Books, 2003.

Zuckerman, P. "Secularization: Europe—Yes, United States—No." *Skeptical Inquirer* 28, no. 2 (2004).

GREGORY S. PAUL

DENMARK, UNBELIEF IN. In 1999 Denmark had a population of 5.3 million and its official religion was Evangelical Lutheran. As of 1995 the religious affiliation of the population was distributed as follows: Evangelical Lutheran, 87 percent; other Christian, 1.7 percent; Muslim, 1.5 percent; and other/nonreligious, 9.8 percent (see DEMOGRAPHY OF UNBELIEF).

According to the *World Christian Encyclopedia*, the percentage of secularists (atheists and nonreligious) in Denmark was 6.6 percent in 1995, up sharply from 3.5 percent in 1980 and 0.2 percent in 1900. According to the same source, Sweden is the most secularized nation among Scandinavian countries, with 29.4 percent secularists, followed by Finland with 6.7 percent and then by Denmark with 6.6 percent. Norway trails with 2.4 percent.

A 1983 survey placed Denmark once more in the middle among Scandinavian countries on the question whether citizens believe in God. Only 52 percent of Swedes answered yes (35 percent no, 14 percent don't know), among Danes 58 percent said yes (27 percent no, 15 percent don't know), while in Norway 70 percent answered yes (23 percent no, and 7 percent don't know).

The first Dane to identify publicly as an atheist was probably Frederik Henrik Hennings Dreier. Dreier is best known as the first socialist in Denmark, but atheism was more important for him. This is expressed clearly in his *Aandetroen og den frie Tænkning* (Belief in Spirits and FREETHOUGHT, 1852). Dreier published a number of propaganda pamphlets in favor of socialism. As a medical student Dreier was well informed about the results of contemporary natural science, which strongly influenced him. Before Charles DARWIN, Dreier advocated a doctrine of evolution based on Lamarck. He died by suicide before his twenty-sixth birthday.

After Dreier's death, Georg Morris Cohen BRANDES praised his talents. Brandes was a writer and a leading critic and historian of literature. Influenced by Ludwig FEUERBACH, David Friedrich STRAUSS, and John Stuart MILL, Brandes introduced Friedrich NIETZSCHE to Scandinavia. In lectures at the University of Copenhagen he defended freethought and the theory of evolution (see EVOLUTION AND UNBELIEF). He attacked Christian ideology until the end of his life. Because of his atheism, he had to endure many years of delay before he was appointed a full professor at the University of Copenhagen.

Other early Danish atheists include the authors Jens Peter Jacobsen and Johannes V. Jensen. Jacobsen initially studied botany; he was an admirer of Darwin and translated his publications. In 1872 Jacobsen published the short story "Mogens," which attracted attention because of its distinctive style and psychology. In 1880 Jacobsen published his novel *Niels Lyhne*, which describes an atheist, dreamer, and romantic who cannot bear the heavy strain of real life. Even better known than Jacobsen is Johannes V. Jensen, one of the most gifted Danish authors of the twentieth century, who in 1944 won the Nobel Prize in Literature.

One of the philosophically most sophisticated Danish atheists of the twentieth century was Jørgen Jørgensen, professor of philosophy at Copenhagen between 1926 and 1964. Jørgensen contributed to studies in logic, psychology, and the scientific method. His basic views were close to those of members of the Vienna Circle with which he was associated (see SCHLICK, MORITZ, AND THE VIENNA CIRCLE). He is best known for his 1951 book *The Development of Logical Empiricism*.

As to organized unbelief in Denmark, the Humanistisk Forbund (Humanist Society) was established in 1960. It was quite active until about 1975, after which its level of activity was sharply reduced. At the end of the 1980s it changed its name to Humanistisk Debat (Humanist Debate), but no rise in activity resulted. In 1987 the society had about seven hundred members; by 2004 membership had fallen to about one hundred and the level of activity remained quite low.

In 2002 a new organization, the Dansk Ateistisk Selskab (Danish Atheistic Society), was established. As of early 2004, it had about forty members.

BIBLIOGRAPHY

Barrett, David B., et al., ed. *World Christian Encyclopedia: A Comparative Survey of Churches and Religions in the Modern World*. 2nd ed. Oxford: Oxford University Press, 2001.

Britannica Book of the Year 1998. London: Encyclopaedia Britannica, 1998.

Listhaug, Ola. *Norske verdier i et komparativt perspektiv*. Trondheim, 1983.

FINNGEIR HIORTH

DESCARTES, RENÉ (1596–1650), French mathematician and philosopher. René Descartes was a widely influential French philosopher who wrote on a broad range of other subjects in the sciences, including mathematics, astronomy, theories of motion, and human physiology. He spent most of his productive life in the liberal Netherlands, eschewing illiberal Catholic France. His most famous philosophical work, *Meditations on First Philosophy* (1641), sets out his philosophical method. In 1644 he published *Principles of Philosophy*, in which he linked his philosophical position to the sciences dealing with theories of matter, the universe, the earth, chemistry, and even the nature of sensations. Much of his philosophy was devoted to establishing an independent realm for the sciences and putting them on sure foundations of knowledge.

Descartes was not a philosophical skeptic; rather, he pushed SKEPTICISM to its limits hoping to show that it is a self-defeating doctrine. One aspect of Descartes's philosophical method (insofar as one can speak of this) is to subject all our ordinary beliefs and philosophical doctrines to radical and thoroughgoing doubt, and if they are open to doubt, to suspend both belief and disbelief in them. Only those doctrines that can survive such a radical critique were to be accepted as a firm basis for all other knowledge. By Descartes's time the growth of scientific knowledge had overturned what had previously been claimed to be knowledge (such as that the earth was stationary); so science is one source of doubt about received belief. But there are other sources of doubt. As had long been recognized, sensory belief can be open to error about how the world is (thus straight or bent sticks viewed in water appear bent). And on occasion it is difficult to tell whether something we remember really occurred or arose in a dream. Also, those who have lost limbs often think they can feel the presence of the limb. This last case illustrates Descartes's extreme form of doubt about the existence of the external world and even each person's material body. He imagines an evil genius who gives each of us impressions as if there were external objects like rocks and chairs, and impressions as if we have a hand, a leg, or a complete material body—but there are no such external objects or human body.

Descartes is one of the first to argue the logical possibility of the world being quite other than the way we experience it—including the possibility that, contrary to what we commonly believe, there is no external world of bodies at all. Finally he envisages the logical possibility of doubt in mathematics, say, 2 + 3 = 5. All of these radical doubts are raised in the *First* and *Second Meditations*. According to Descartes's method, if these claims are open to the least doubt, then we can accept none as certain knowledge. As a method it certainly seems quite corrosive of common belief, the extent of its corrosiveness being a matter of philosophical debate bequeathed to us by Descartes's very program.

Is there anything that is immune from all doubt? Here we come to one of the famous moments in philosophy with Descartes's claim that there is: *Cogito, ergo Sum* ("I think, therefore I am"). How is this to be understood? By "cogito" (which we can render, perhaps misleadingly, as "I think"), Descartes means any mental activity of doubting, perceiving, affirming, denying, willing, feeling, and so on. From the proposition "I think" (so understood) Descartes wishes to prove "I exist." In his various writings Descartes gives us two ways of understanding how this is done. The first is that Descartes's "cogito" is an argument: the conclusion "I exist" is meant to follow from the premise "I think" (note the first person character of the argument). One issue here is whether the premise "I think" is something that can be open to doubt; if so, then the conclusion cannot be certain. Another is whether the argument is valid, and whether we can be certain of it. On a second view we are invited to consider the logical impossibility of the proposition "I think but I do not exist." On either interpretation the intention is to show that radical skepticism fails in the case of "the cogito."

Just how radical is Cartesian doubt at this point? One matter that seems not to be open to doubt is the very meanings of the words that Descartes uses in "the cogito" and in other contexts. Another matter is whether we can be sure of the contents of our own minds, such as our knowledge of the mental operations we perform, given the various kinds of thing that fall under the broad notion of "cogito," or "think."

Next Descartes asks the question "What am I?" and answers "I am a thinking thing." I am not essentially a thing with a material body; this is only contingently so. What is essential to each of us is that not only do we have the property of thinking but also that we are a thing, a substance, that thinks. Here critics find that Descartes has assumed too much in claiming thing-hood for our essential selves. At best Descartes can only conclude from "the cogito" that thinking is going on, not that our essence is such that we are nonmaterial substances. This goes well beyond what his premises permit.

In the *Third Meditation* Descartes sets out to prove that God exists. So far the strategy of doubt allows that we may form ideas in our minds, but not that these ideas are about anything external to us. Thus we may form the idea of a mountain, hand, or unicorn; but there is nothing in these ideas that guarantee their existence or nonexistence. The exception for Descartes is the idea of God. The proof turns on the special feature of the very idea of God such that, once the idea is grasped, then the idea cannot be about a thing that does not exist. God, it is claimed, is a being whose essence is that it possesses all perfections; but not to exist is to lack a perfection; so, from the mere idea of the essence of God it follows that God must exist and cannot not exist. God is the unique case of a thing whose essence involves existence. Descartes's argument is a version of the Ontological Argument for the existence of God originally advanced by Saint Anselm in the eleventh century but rejected by Aquinas (see EXISTENCE OF GOD, ARGUMENTS FOR AND AGAINST). For various philosophical reasons, the argument has recently been subject to much critical examination, but has failed the most rigorous attempts at formulation.

Granted the above, the core premises of Descartes's attempt to refute skepticism and to put all knowledge on a firm footing are now in place. How can we show that there is an external world and that our perceptions are a true representation of it (i.e., that the very green we experience of leaves is a feature of the real world and not something we "project" on to it)? If God is perfect, then it will not be in his nature to deceive us as to how the world is, like the envisaged evil genius. So, in general, our ideas of the world are about something that exists; in other words, our perceptions of greenness and leafiness are genuinely of an external object, the leaf, which has the property of being green. If the underpinning of God is removed, then we have no such guarantee in Descartes's philosophical system. In this respect Descartes bequeathed to those who accept his starting point but reject any role for God the notorious problem of the existence of the external world, that our impressions and ideas do really correspond to how the world is, and that the external world is not radically "other" (e.g., lacks color). Descartes also bequeathed to us the problem of how two distinct substances, the mind (a thinking thing) and the physical matter of which our bodies and brains are composed, are related to one another (see COGNITIVE SCIENCE AND UNBELIEF). This is a crucial unsolved problem in any theory of the material basis of the mental at the heart of all psychology and of human understanding.

BIBLIOGRAPHY

Cottingham, J., ed. *The Cambridge Companion to Descartes*. Cambridge: Cambridge University Press. 1992.

Cottingham, J., R. Stoothof, and D. Murdoch, eds. *The Philosophical Writings of Descartes*. 3 vols. Cambridge: Cambridge University Press. 1984–91.

Gaukroger, S. *Descartes: An Intellectual Biography*. Oxford: Clarendon. 1995.

Williams, B. *Descartes: The Project of Pure Inquiry*. London: Penguin, 1978.

ROBERT NOLA

DETERMINISM. Determinism is the view that all events without exception are effects, or, a little more carefully, that every event is fully caused by its antecedent conditions or causal circumstances. The conditions or circumstances too are effects of prior sufficient causes, and so on. There are two sets of questions attending determinism. The first has to do with the proper characterization of determinism, and whether or not the thesis is true. The second concerns the implications of determinism for morality, religion, punishment, psychology, and other such things that seem to depend on or to presuppose the possibility of free choice or action. We will consider both sets of questions more or less together in what follows. They are not easy to keep separate.

Getting the thesis of determinism into clear view, putting flesh on the bare definition above, is not easy either. Determinism is sometimes explained by pointing to predictability. Marcus Pierre Simon de LAPLACE, for example, maintains that if a powerful enough intellect knew all the facts about the location and motion of every particle in the universe, and knew too the laws of nature and a little mathematics, then it could in principle predict the location and motion of every particle in the universe at any time in the future. It is a compelling thought, but not much help in clarifying the thesis of determinism—talk of predictability seems to depend on or presuppose the thesis rather than explain it.

Some try to cash the thesis out in terms of current scientific theory, and certainly Sir Isaac Newton's achievements led many to determinism. The clockwork picture of the universe, with all matter in motion in space obeying a set of causal laws, leads easily to the view that every event stands in a nomothetic (law-based) relation to certain others preceding it in the chain. Recently, interpretations of quantum theory and the uncertainty principle have persuaded some thinkers that determinism must be false. However, it is not obvious that micro-level events, about which quantum theory has something to say, have effects on macro-level events, about which the theory is largely silent and where determinism seems to matter. The things at the level of everyday observation seem bound up by causal laws, whether or not this is so for the particles of which they are composed. It is also true that freedom is not the same thing as indeterminism, uncertainty, or chance. Philosophers, anyway, tend to take the long view, noting that scientific theories come and go. Tying the truth or an understanding of determinism to our current scientific conception of the universe—some might unkindly say our best guess—seems to many a little short-sighted.

Philosophical Views of Determinism. What matters to us are not particles and quanta but beliefs, desires, hopes, and choices—and this point can be made without begging any questions concerning the metaphysics of things like beliefs and desires. Even if one is unwilling to embrace a thoroughgoing materialism about the mind (see MATERIALISM, PHILOSOPHICAL), it is at least a going proposition that mental events, whatever they are, stand in apparently causal relations to states of the brain. Brain states, it almost goes without saying, are as physical as anything (see COGNITIVE SCIENCE AND UNBELIEF). Even a dualist can be troubled by determinism.

On most readings of the truth of determinism, the upshot is that human freedom is at best problematic. If every event is an effect of prior causes and, say, your choosing to look up *determinism* in this book is an event, then your choosing appears as causal as anything which might happen on a billiard table. It might have felt, on the inside, that you looked up the term on a whim—or even for a good reason—but rewind the universe as far back into the past as you like and run it all forwards again, and causal forces will conspire to plant that whim or reason—even the feeling of your freedom in so choosing—in your head and move your hand toward the bookshelf as certainly as a billiard ball follows a precise trajectory when struck at a certain angle. The point can be pressed further by thinking not of searching for a definition, but of acts we condemn as morally wrong or acts we praise as heroic. Is there room at all for free will in, as William James puts it, "the iron block universe"? Philosophers have settled into two camps in response to this question.

Incompatibilism. Incompatibilists maintain that if determinism is true, there can be no freedom. Some, notably René DESCARTES, go on to deny the thesis of determinism outright, arguing instead for some doctrine of origination, an uncaused or self-caused act of will underlying free choice. Whether origination comes to much is uncertain. To wrench the will from the causal web entirely might result in freedom, but what help is an uncaused or random will? There might be other, empirical worries rooted in the study of human behavior and psychology for thinking that Descartes has to be wrong in characterizing the will as utterly undetermined. Other incompatibilists, so-called hard determinists, accept determinism and deny the existence of human freedom outright.

Compatibilism. Compatibilists such as Thomas HOBBES and John Stuart MILL take it that freedom and determinism are compatible, arguing for a view of freedom understood in terms of voluntary or uncompelled action, not origination. A person in prison or forced into a course of action at gunpoint is not free, but individuals not so compelled might be. Freedom, on this view, is not a matter of uncaused or undetermined action, but of voluntary action. The causal antecedents of free human actions are, as some put it, internal to the agent, consisting in his or her hopes, desires, and general character, as opposed to causal factors outside the agent, such as handcuffs, hypnotists, or prison walls. It is easy to feel a little shortchanged by compatibilism, as causal antecedents internal to an agent are still causal antecedents. Such an agent's action, though voluntary, is still determined.

Beyond Compatibilsm and Incompatibilism. Recently, Ted Honderich has argued that compatibilism and incompatibilism are both false, as each supposes that we have just one conception of freedom when in fact we have two. One conception involves origination and voluntary action; the other involves only voluntary action. The upshot, for Honderich, has to do with attitudes, the responses we give to the truth of determinism. On his view some positive or sustaining attitudes toward our life hopes, moral responsibilities, and so on, really are possible, once the two conceptions of freedom are recognized and thought through.

Arguments for Determinism. Most arguments for versions of determinism depend on the claim that the thesis of determinism is just part of the warp and weft of human thinking. It is only on the assumption that every event has a cause that we can come to an understanding of the physical universe. While David HUME argues that causal necessity is not, strictly speaking, in the world, he nevertheless concludes that seeing events as caused is part of the human factory specification. For Hume, thinking causally is not just the only way to understand the empirical world, it is something we cannot help, a natural custom or habit of mind. Immanuel KANT takes the so-called principle of universal causation as a fundamental category of the understanding, a part of the condition of the experience of an empirical world of objects. Without thinking causally, he argues, we could not have the experience we actually have. Seeing the world in terms of cause and effect is the only way to understand any object of knowledge. For both thinkers, determinism is not something we could give up; the question of determinism is not an open one.

Arguments for Free Will. No less forceful intuitions accompany the thinking in favor of free will. The world we experience includes ourselves, and from the inside we do have the experience of freedom. It seems to us that there are moments of choice, instances in which it is up to us to take one action as opposed to another. Determinism might not be something we can give up with respect to an understanding of objects, but it is something we can scarcely take seriously with respect to an understanding of ourselves. We have just as much difficulty trying to understand an uncaused car accident as we have in genuinely accepting that our inner experience of freedom is an illusion. Even the hardest of hard determinists does not simply wait to see what he or she chooses for dinner.

Although Kant argues that determinism is a precondition of an understanding of the empirical world, he maintains that freedom is no less a precondition of practical action. There is a distinction for Kant between thinking about objects and thinking about action, between theoretical as against practical reasoning. We have no choice but to think deterministically if we want to know something about the world, but when we *act* we cannot help but think of ourselves as free. Kant's line, it seems to many, underlines rather than resolves the difficulty.

Religious Controversies. Philosophical controversies concerning determinism are matched by those in theology, though the emphasis is clearly different. In Christian and other theologies, God is characterized as all-knowing, all-powerful, and all-good. Determinism can seem to follow quickly from these attributes. Reflection on the problem of evil (see EVIL, PROBLEM OF) and divine punishment and reward can tug in the opposite direction.

If God knows everything, this must include future facts, and the choices one has yet to make are among those facts. Presumably, God knows the choices we will make before we make them, and this suggests that our choices are not really choices at all. Either human beings are not free and God knows what we will do before we do it, or humans have a measure of freedom, compromising God's knowledge. If God's all-embracing knowledge is something the theist is not willing to dispense with, then human freedom has to give. There are obvious

questions concerning the coherence of divine reward and punishment, heaven and hell, if it turns out that no one really chooses to seek or avoid salvation or sin.

Saint Augustine, and later Aquinas, argue that there is a distinction between knowing what will happen and causing what will happen. God knows what we are going to do because we are going to do it; our doing it is not caused by his knowing. Both thinkers maintain that worries about determinism and God's knowledge depend on temporal categories that do not actually apply to God. God's eternity, a kind of existence outside of time, makes it possible for him to observe all events at once—or, better, independently of time. There is no real sense in which God knows about our choices before we choose them, as the very notion of "before" is not truly applicable to God's knowledge.

Similar motivations for determinism arise in connection with the consideration of God's omnipotence. If human beings really are free, then there is a clear sense in which humans might confound God's plans, might do something God did not intend. Worse, for Martin Luther and John Calvin, the thought that freely chosen human action could, in a sense, nudge a person toward salvation seems to restrict God's power intolerably. By acting in a certain way, it would seem, a person could force God's hand—that is, *make* God react appropriately by opening wide the pearly gates. For some religious thinkers, one could be saved from sin not by human choice, but only by being chosen by God. Again, if human freedom is limited in this way, no sense can be made of divine reward and punishment.

God's goodness, too, suggests a kind of determinism. The notion that a good creator could create only a good world, fixed on a settled path, was first scouted by the ancient Greeks. The Stoics (see STOICISM) contended that nature was both divine and cyclical, consisting in eternally repeating cycles of life and cataclysmic conflagration. The Stoics' famous steadfast indifference to the vagaries of life is partially explained by their view that whatever might happen in fact happens for the best, for the good aims of the universe itself. The view has echoes in Gottfried Wilhelm von LEIBNIZ, who argues that the goodness of God implies that this world is the only world God could have created, the best of all possible worlds.

The question of human freedom also arises in controversies concerning the problem of evil, which might pull the theist away from determinism. The problem of evil, roughly, is the claim that the following four propositions are incompatible, that is to say, they cannot all be true together: God is omniscient, God is omnipotent, God is omnibenevolent, and evil exists. As the last is undeniable, one of the other three must be false, which amounts to the claim that God as traditionally conceived does not exist.

In response, some theists distinguish between natural evil and human or moral evil. The former are "acts of

God," natural disasters like earthquakes and hurricanes. The latter is the evil that men do: war, murder, theft, and so on. Natural evil is then explained away with talk of soul building. The idea is that virtue requires a struggle against hardship, and natural evil is a kind of necessary test or midwife of the virtues. In any case, God is not responsible for human evil, it is argued, as this is the result of freely chosen human action. The gift of free will is itself good, it is claimed, and if we squander it on evil actions, the fault is our own.

The free will defense, as it is called, is found wanting by some thinkers, particularly following reflection on God's attributes. If God is all-knowing, it is argued, he would have known beforehand the disastrous consequences of creating human beings with the capacity to choose evil. Knowing this, and equipping us with free will anyway, God seems ultimately responsible for the evil we choose. If God is all-powerful, why did he not design us so as to freely choose the good? There are replies to these questions, and replies to those replies.

Nearby Conceptions and the Depth of the Problem. The general thesis of determinism pursued here is not the only conception in the neighborhood. Logical determinism, first noticed by the ancient Greeks but still under consideration today, begins with the innocent claim that every statement is either true or false. Propositions about future human decisions or courses of action are statements, and they too must be either true or false. Logical determinism settles the future as clearly as other determinisms do, but without talk of causation.

Doctrines of fatalism and predestination can also be distinguished from the general thesis of determinism. Fatalism is the view that no matter what one does, one's future or fate is settled. This implies that there is no point in planning, deliberating, or preparing for the future. The "idle argument," again first formulated by the Greeks, has it that if one is ill, there is no point in calling a doctor. If one is going to recover (or not), one will recover (or not) regardless of what the doctor or anyone else does. A determinist, though, is committed to the view that all events are effects, not that some events are fated to happen regardless of the preceding causal path. Talk of predestination or destiny implies a supernatural cause in the chain, either setting the lot in motion for a general aim, or fixing an individual's future for some particular end. Determinism as understood in most contemporary thinking has it that all causes are natural, not supernatural, and carries with it no commitment to the view that the causal sequence has some general aim or end.

Reflection on the long pedigree of determinism and nearby conceptions can lead one to the view that the question of human freedom is an unusually deep one. Even before philosophy got under way, humans had suspicions deterministic in flavor, and those suspicions have proved remarkably resilient. Perhaps the earliest suspicions resulted from the difficulties attending a difficult life, the experience of trying and failing regardless.

Some contemporary considerations of determinism retain something of this defeatism, a worry that what we do can make no difference, that the most human of concerns are based on an illusion, that our thoughts are not really our own. The ancient worries are still with us, because what is at issue is what matters most.

Controversies attending determinism, both philosophical and religious, exhibit a pattern that is suggestive of the depth of the problem too. Both philosophers and theologians have bumped into a set of conflicting intuitions. Both are drawn toward determinism in an effort to understand what each takes to be the fundamental nature of reality, as considered apart from human concerns. For the philosopher, this is a world of objects in causal relations, and for the theist, this is a creator or a created order. Both, too, are dragged away from determinism when the focus narrows to human interests. For the philosopher, there is the experience of freedom, and for the theist, there are the choices underpinning salvation and sin. The conflicting intuitions cannot both be right, but it is not clear that either set can be rejected.

BIBLIOGRAPHY

Aquinas, Thomas. *Summa Theologiae*, part 1. Edited by T. Gilby. 60 vols. London: McGraw-Hill, 1964–75.
Ekstrom, L. W. *Free Will: A Philosophical Study*. Boulder, CO: Westview, 2000.
Hobbes, Thomas. "Of Liberty and Necessity." In *The English Works of Thomas Hobbes*, vol. 5, edited by W. Molesworth. London: Scientia Aalen, 1962.
Honderich, Ted. *How Free Are You? The Determinism Problem*. Oxford: Oxford University Press, 2002.
———. *A Theory of Determinism: The Mind, Neuroscience and Life-Hopes*. Oxford: Oxford University Press, 1988.
Hume, David. *An Enquiry concerning Human Understanding*. Oxford: Oxford University Press, 1902.
Kane, R. *The Oxford Handbook of Free Will*. New York: Oxford University Press, 2002.
McFee, G. *Free Will*. Teddington, UK: Acumen, 2000.
Mill, John Stuart. *A System of Logic*. New York: Harper & Row, 1874.
Weatherford, R., *The Implications of Determinism*. London: Routledge, 1991.

JAMES GARVEY

DEVELOPING WORLD, UNBELIEF IN. In one sense ATHEISM and HUMANISM are ancient, and in another they are modern. The ideals of atheism, humanism, and the idea of the oneness of humanity date from time immemorial, and actually have their roots in the developing countries. Many of these countries are the cradles of ancient cultures and civilizations, with rich traditions of thought and belief that enthrall people even today. The lands of Asia, Africa, and South America were the birthplaces of the great religions, but also of philosophical thought that questioned the existence of god, promoting RATIONALISM, SKEPTICISM, and atheism. The Samkhya philosophy was an atheist strand of ancient Indian philosophical thought (see INDIAN MATERIALISM, ANCIENT). This broad-based mixture of the quest for truth, compassion for fellow humans, and a scientific temper produced many influential persons like the Buddha (see BUDDHISM, UNBELIEF WITHIN), the Mahavira, and Confucius (see CONFUCIANISM), who taught basic human values even as they reflected philosophical radicalism and skepticism.

Unlike in the West, where one religion tends to dominate any given country or region, in the East different philosophical, social, and religious systems coexist. The ancient, medieval, and modern streams of thought flow together, overlapping one another in a continuum.

In ancient India, the CARVAKAS and the Lokayatas kept the banner of atheism high, questioning the practices of religion and making clear the futility of belief in god and religion. Buddha's agnosticism, Mahavira's magnanimity, and Confucius's thoroughness continue to inspire many even as they do today. In the Middle Ages, while Europe groped, people in what we now call the developing countries already followed well-worn paths of tolerance, contentment, and compassion.

The twelfth-century revolutionary Basaveswara fought against the caste system and encouraged intercaste marriages. Brahmanayudu, a fourteenth-century minister to the king of Palnadu, advocated intercaste dining and socializing. The fifteenth-century poet Kabir opposed idolatry and preached Hindu-Muslim unity. The sixteenth-century Mughal emperor Akbar championed *Din-e-elahi*, or religious toleration. The late seventeenth- and early eighteenth-century philosopher, thinker, and campaigner Vemana condemned social evils and preached a universal outlook.

Europe's rediscovery of classical civilization led to its Renaissance, and eventually to the maritime powers' subjugation of colonies across what we now call the developing world.

The Colonial Era. The colonial era exposed the contradictions of Asian and African societies. Though their national liberation struggles in the twentieth century were meant to throw off the imperialism of the colonial powers, they were nonetheless strongly influenced by liberal Western traditions. Almost without exception the leaders of anticolonial independence movements were admirers of the modern rationalist and humanist traditions of the West. The ideals of the American and French revolutions inspired these leaders and through them, their countries' middle classes, kindling in them nationalism on the one hand and rationalism and humanism on the other. Western ideas of law, justice, equality, and fair play reinforced their own ideas for social reform in their respective countries. Hand in hand with resistance against the colonial powers, the secularization of these societies began.

Direct personal contact between the colonial and the developing countries brought a fresh breeze of ideas. Charles BRADLAUGH, the first atheist in the British Parliament, participated in the third conference of the Indian National Congress in Bombay and championed the cause of the Indians in Parliament. Western liberal and humanist ideals also inspired the anticolonial struggles in lands subjugated by the French, the Dutch (see MULTATULI), and others.

Nationalism and Humanism. Nationalism and humanism had a liberating influence, eroding the constricting shackles of religion and communalism as they did tribal loyalties. Even though some of the new national leaders might have believed personally in God and religion, they felt their newly independent states must have nothing to do with religion. When in the Constituent Assembly of India an amendment was moved to invoke the name of "God Almighty" in the preamble to India's constitution, it was defeated by an overwhelming vote. The secular stance taken in Turkey under Ata Turk Mustafa Kamal (who later took the name Atatürk) had a far-reaching impact on people. By the early to middle twentieth century, modernization and secularism were viewed as inseparable.

In many developing countries, law is an important instrument of social change. Not only does the preamble to India's constitution provide that India is a "SOVEREIGN, SOCIALIST, SECULAR DEMOCRATIC REPUBLIC" (capitalized in the original), Article 51A(h) of the India's Constitution states that it is the "FUNDAMENTAL DUTY" of every citizen "to promote scientific temper, spirit of inquiry, reform and humanism." Thus in India abortion, family planning, and many other progressive measures have constitutional as well as legislative sanction. Progressive legislation has resulted from continuous efforts by rationalists, humanists, atheists, and other progressive-minded people (see INDIA, UNBELIEF IN). Thus unbelief in the developing countries was not merely a system of philosophical thought, but also a ground for sociocultural action.

For the developing world's champions of unbelief, direct opposition to superstitions, blind beliefs, and obscurantism was integral to their programs, as were efforts to lessen social and economic inequalities, poverty, ill health, ignorance, and illiteracy. Secularism was not merely a cherished goal, but a practical necessity in view of religious strife and tribal feuds, including (in India) intercaste feuds. For Indian activists the eradication of untouchability and social reform in order to move toward a casteless society was central to their work.

The secularization of this period gave important social breathing space to unbelievers. Bradlaugh's case had a salutary effect on the developing countries. For example, the constitution of India provides for affirmation as a recognized alternative to swearing an oath in the name of one's god. India was formed without a state religion; freedom of expression and belief enjoy constitutional guarantee. The Special Marriage Act facilitates registration of marriages without reference to caste and religion.

Across the developing world, nationalist movements initially brought with them democratic socialist ideals, the rule of law, regular elections, and other liberalizing influences. With them came a scientific temper, a rational outlook, sex education, and other educational reforms.

Secular Nationalist Movements. The nationalist movements were inclusive, reflecting secularism and FREETHOUGHT. Nationalist leaders like India's Jawaharlal Nehru strongly emphasized science and the scientific temper. Mahatma Gandhi viewed religion as a personal matter which should be confined to the personal domain. "I do not want to bring my religion into the market place," he said. State education was liberal and secular minded. When Bangladesh emerged as a breakaway Muslim state, secularists viewed this as evidence that far from being a unifying bond that drew a country together, religion was inherently a centrifugal and divisive force.

Demands for gender equality in India continue gaining ground. One-third of the seats in every elected legislative body, from *Panchayat* (village) governments to parliament, are reserved for women. The active participation of female politicians has helped to prepare the ground for social justice and to establish a more liberal atmosphere.

Across India, regional governments encourage intercaste, casteless, and religionless marriages and protect them if need be. In some areas couples entering into such marriages qualify for monetary and employment incentives. At times police stations are employed as neutral venues for such weddings.

The influence of humane laws, social reforms, equality before the law, the sense of social justice, scientific discoveries, a rationalist approach, and liberal and progressive thinking have brought deep and abiding change. After a period during which the momentum of secularization seemed to have diminished in Indian society, the poor performance of fanatical religious parties in recent elections reveals that unbelief continues as an important force in the life of that nation.

Social Reform. South Asia has benefited from a long parade of reformers who uphold the banner of unbelief. Prominent names from the nineteenth and twentieth centuries include Raja Ram Mohan Roy, Eswar Chandra Vidya Sagar, Kesab Chandra Sen, Mahatma Phule, Maharshi Karve, Kandukuri Veeresalingam, Mahatma Gandhi, Dr. B. R. Ambedkar, PERIYAR E. V. Ramaswami, M. N. ROY, GORA, Abraham T. KOVOOR, V. M. TARKUNDE, Prof. H. Narasimhaiah, Dr. Indumati PARIKH, and Mrs. Saraswathi Gora. Because of them and others, unbelief continues growing, while orthodoxy faces unrelenting challenge.

Atheist, rationalist, humanist, and secularist organizations are playing significant roles in developing

countries. For instance, in India, the Andh Shraddha Nirmulan Samithi, the Atheist Centre, the Atheist Society, the Buddhivadi Samaj, the Dravidar Kazhgam, the Humanist Union, the Indian Rationalist Association, the Radical Humanist Association, the Taksheel Society, the Indian Secular Society, the Kerala Yukthivadi Sangham, the Indian Committee for the Scientific Investigation of Claims of the Paranormal, and many other organizations are striving for social change along secular lines. In Muslim countries persecution is strong, and hence people like Dr. Taslima NASRIN (Bangladesh) and Dr. Younus Shaikh (Pakistan) have been forced to seek asylum outside their countries.

In most countries across the region there is no social security program, and workers and peasants are largely unorganized. Progressive-minded unbelievers take up secular social work to aid women and children and those below the poverty line. Unbelievers are active in areas of social work including human rights, environmental awareness, and human resource development, as well as natural disaster relief.

A Constructive Approach. Unbelief does not confine itself merely to criticizing the traditional epics and religious beliefs, but is adopting a constructive agenda as well, building alternate structures in education and social service. By their work they seek to demonstrate by example that to do good, and to be good, the props of an imaginary god and religion are not necessary. Their message is that morality is a social necessity, and helping fellow humans is the responsibility of all. This social work expands beyond the frontiers of charity, laying groundwork for the positive empowerment of the people it serves. The result has been a growing democratic and egalitarian consciousness, especially among the impoverished, illiterate, and tribal groups. Education and awareness are the keys to social progress.

Resistance to religion also empowers the disadvantaged, because—especially in India—God and religion have become a multibillion-dollar industry whose profits are rooted in exploitation of the poor and gullible. Unbelieving activists have called attention to scandals in the temples and religious trusts, criticized the lavish lifestyles of many so-called *babas* and gurus, and focused scrutiny on their growing commercial ventures. Unmistakably, the god industry thrives with the connivance of politicians and administrators. Temples, churches, and mosques have begun establishing medical, engineering, and other colleges—even minting their own money while they enjoy tax exemptions based on their religious or minority status. Corruption is rampant. Unbelieving activists are working to catalyze a growing demand that religious institutions be taxed on par with commercial ventures— which is what so many of them now are.

Fighting Disparity in Resources. Unbelief in the developing world is contributing to liberalize and secularize the society. It strengthens secular ethics; strives for uniformity in civil codes; promotes gender equality;

inculcates humanistic and secular values; upholds science and the scientific outlook; organizes science exhibitions; exposes superstitions and the so-called miracles of exploitative god-men; and advocates alternatives to religious ways of life. The effort is silent but salient, exerting powerful social effects despite a paucity of resources.

While unbelieving organizations struggle to survive, religious organizations enjoy generous direct and indirect state support, including concessions, patronage, and resources for their educational institutions. Despite this disparity, unbelief is growing in a remarkable manner. Increasing numbers of people are moving away from religion. As understanding of science grows, confidence engenders disenchantment, and they come to see religion as superfluous. Religion is waging psychological counterwarfare, trying to maintain its stranglehold. But in many parts of the developing world, the march toward a postreligious society has begun.

A "Movement" Approach. In order to strengthen unbelief in the developing countries, education and awareness building require unswerving and persistent efforts. It is necessary to present atheism as an alternate way of life in which the human being, not a god, enjoys the preeminent position. Doing this will probably require that humanism, rationalism, atheism, and freethought should focus more on developing as movements than on developing membership organizations. The membership-organization model is suited to the West, where nonreligious organizations can organize themselves to some extent in parallel with the religious institutions that occupy in turn specified and delimited roles in society. Across Asia and Africa, religion functions as a part of culture. It is not organized as one institution among others, it rather is a way of life and pervades all of life. In that situation, humanism and atheism can best make strides as movements that address all aspects of life and provide a powerful counterexample to the life of religion. Hence, secular social work, the agitation for social reform, and rendering timely help to the needy are of utmost importance.

In the developing countries unbelief cannot be promoted in the abstract—it must be concrete. In the West the minimum needs of individuals may be guaranteed by the state through social security and other measures, but in the developing countries it falls to volunteers to render assistance to people. Unbelievers must be seen taking leadership roles in this work—and they are. Initiatives embodying this perspective included the late Indumati PARIKH's "Stree Hitakarini" work in reproductive health and hygiene among the slum dwellers of Bombay. Malladi Subbamma renders assistance to women in distress; Lavanam and Hemalata Lavanam work among the *jogins* (temple prostitutes) and criminals; M. V. Tarkunde strove for civil liberties; Dr. Samaram leads an untiring crusade for sex education and for dispelling superstitions. There are many others.

Distinctive Qualities of Unbelief. Today humanism, rationalism, freethought, atheism, and secularism are spreading in both villages and urban areas. The movement is growing horizontally rather than vertically. In the Indian context, it is not only the intelligentsia but also the common people who are enjoying the warmth of nonreligious ideas and supporting the movement. Each person may take small steps, but the cumulative effect is vast. Inspired by nonreligious ideals, an ordinary person may discontinue religious obervances. He or she may marry out of caste or religion; or a couple may champion the secular method of marriage. Similarly, while taking an oath, either in parliament or in a court of law, or at the time of assuming a public office, atheists, humanists, and rationalists may choose to affirm rather than swear an oath of office, which in India is enshrined in the constitution. These apparently small steps by ordinary citizens bring qualitative changes in their outlook, and distinguish them from the rest of the society as humanists and atheists. It is through such practices that humanism and atheism win credence and strength in the developing countries.

Unbelief in developing countries, in particular in India, is taken seriously by the people who champion it. It tends to be a way of life for them rather than merely an intellectual discourse. In child-rearing, secular moorings are visible; for example, they give their children secular rather than traditional names. One measure of the movement's impact is that today, even religious people look at atheists and rationalists as role models and expect them to live up to secular ideals.

BIBLIOGRAPHY

Gora. *An Atheist around the World*. Vijayawada, India: Atheist Centre, 1987.

Hiorth, Finngeir. *Atheism in India*. Mumbai: Indian Secular Society, 1998.

Suman, Oak, and S. V. Raju, ed. *14th World Congress of IHEU Commemorative Volume*. Mumbai, 1999.

Vijayam, G., et al., eds. *Atheism and Social Change: International Conference Souvenir*. Vijayawada: Atheist Centre, 1985.

———. *Atheist Centre Golden Jubilee (1940–90) International Conference Souvenir*. Vijayawada: Atheist Centre, 1990.

——— *Fifth World Atheist Conference, "Atheism and Social Progress," Souvenir*. Vijayawada: Atheist Centre, 2005.

———. *Fourth World Atheist Conference on Positive Atheism for a Positive Future Souvenir*. Vijayawada: Atheist Centre, 1996.

——— *Gora Birth Centenary International Conference Souvenir*. Vijayawada: Atheist Centre, 2002.

———. *International Conference on "Social Progress and Women" Souvenir*. Vijayawada: Atheist Centre, 1992.

————. *Second World Atheist Conference Souvenir.*
Vijayawada: Atheist Centre, 1980.

G. VIJAYAM

DEVIL, UNBELIEF IN THE. Monotheistic religions
(Judaism, Christianity, and Islam) identify "the devil," or
Satan, as the archenemy of God, and as a fallen or renegade angel who became evil by his own choice. This
concept, developed gradually during two millennia,
explains the presence of evil in a world overseen by a
single omnipotent, benevolent deity (see EVIL, PROBLEM
OF). The devil is not God's equal, but is extremely powerful. Although God could destroy him or defeat his evildoing, God prefers to allow the exercise of free will,
both to the devil and to the humans whose evildoing he
inspires. A world without evil would allow no possibility
of merit, so our imperfect world is actually superior to
one where no evil exists. Dualistic religions, which postulate an evil god almost as powerful as the good god,
explain the prevalence of evil more logically, but disparage creation (the cosmos defined as the work of a
god) by defining matter as intrinsically evil. The devil, a
spiritual or nonmaterial being ultimately responsible for
all evil, safeguards two ideas: that life in the material
world is good despite tragedy and injustice, and that God
himself is therefore fundamentally good.

Despite the coherence of this view, not all adherents of
monotheistic religions have accepted the premise that
Satan exists. Already in the time of Christ, the Sadducees, a Jewish sect, questioned the existence of spirits.
According to the Acts of the Apostles, "[T]he Sadducees
say that there is no resurrection, neither [is there any]
angel, nor spirit" (Acts 23:8; cf. 4:1–2; Matt. 22:23;
Mark 12:18; Luke 20:27). These Christian texts interpret
the Sadducees' doctrine as denying the essence and novelty of Christian teaching: the existence of suprahuman
spirits and the immortality of the human soul (1 Cor.
15:12–19). The story in Acts implies the Sadducees' fallacy: when Sadducee priests imprisoned Peter and
others, "an angel of the Lord" appeared to release them
(5:19). The Sadducees "were cut to the heart" by this
escape and "took counsel to slay" the apostles (5:33).

Through much of the Middle Ages, Sadducee doctrine
did not worry Christian commentators excessively; the
existence and influence of the devil seemed self-evident.
Questions about the reality of spirits began after 1100.
The reintroduction of Aristotelian philosophy into Latin
Europe in the twelfth and thirteenth centuries accelerated
discussion. Scholastic philosophy discussed the existence of "separate spirits" devoid of material bodies:
angels, demons, and the human soul after death. Thomas
Aquinas developed an elaborate philosophical system
that attempted to reconcile the "truths of faith" with the
evidence of reason and the senses as expounded by ARIS-
TOTLE, "the Philosopher" par excellence. Aquinas constructed systematic proofs of the existence of God, and

also scientific descriptions of angels, devils, and the
immortal human soul.

Although Aristotle's philosophy attracted Latin
churchmen for its rationality and empiricism, these qualities, far from automatically demonstrating the superiority
of Christian cosmology, ontology, and epistemology,
sometimes threatened their credibility. The Muslim
philosopher Ibn Rushd, or AVERROËS, worried Christians
by contending that Aristotle had not asserted the immortality of individual human souls; Averroës and others also
observed that Aristotle presumed the world was eternal—
and thus not created by God. Around 1225, Caesarius of
Heisterbach devoted an entire book of his *Dialogue on
Miracles* to proving that demons were not imaginary.

Aquinas's system did not require Satan's existence.
He admitted more than once that some Aristotelians did
not accept the reality of angels and devils, and once
asserted that neither Aristotle nor his disciples ever mentioned them. Aquinas countered that demonic possession
and necromancy refuted Aristotelian unbelief empirically. Aquinas's reservations, expressed in shorter, specialized treatises, received less attention than his major
works, which spoke more confidently of angels and
devils. But his reservations were not forgotten. In 1516
and again in 1520, the Aristotelian Pietro Pomponazzi
outraged theologians with systematic demonstrations
that Aristotle rejected angels, demons, human immortality—and witchcraft (see WITCHCRAFT AND UNBELIEF).
Not coincidentally, the Fifth Lateran Council (1513)
belatedly declared human immortality an article of faith.

Already by 1460 several early witchcraft treatises had
quoted Aquinas's reservations precisely, then announced
their authors' discovery that witchcraft proved empirically that angels, demons, and Satan's work in the world
were real. Investigating illiterate people's accusations
that certain people "bewitched" others, causing disease,
death, and the destruction of crops and livestock,
churchmen and magistrates argued that Satan and his
demons caused the damage in exchange for the witches'
souls. Aquinas's angelology and demonology were
invoked to explain how Satan and his demons, although
immaterial by nature (and thus imperceptible to human
senses), could create artificial or virtual bodies and
interact corporeally with witches through rites, dances,
and orgiastic sex. This verifiable physical interaction—
despite depending on *artificial* demonic bodies—was
elaborately analyzed as proof that demons were real. In
addition to the Sadducees, early witchcraft authors cited
ancient materialists or atomists such as Democritus and
EPICURUS among the opponents whose unbelief in the
spirit world they claimed to refute conclusively.

Its dependence on corporeality and physical interaction made witchcraft the preferred method for demonstrating the reality of spirit phenomena. From the beginning, theoretical writings on witchcraft stressed that
doubting the reality of the devil and demons, angels, or
human immortality was impious, and further that

doubting the reality of witchcraft led inevitably to Sadducism. This fear affected even opponents of witchhunting. When Johann Weyer wrote a long medical treatise to demonstrate the unreality of witchcraft and protest the barbarity of torturing and executing witches, he prefaced it thus: "I totally reject the maxims of Aristotle and the Peripatetics and also of the Sadducees, all of whom contend that demons do not exist in reality" and devoted another eighty-seven pages to scientific acceptance of the devil.

Jean Bodin replied that Weyer defended witches because he was a witch. Bodin argued as if Weyer doubted the devil and Aristotle did not: "There is an enemy of the human race . . . [who] was created right at the beginning, as is affirmed in Job. And not only Holy Scripture, but all [Platonists], [Aristotelians], Stoics, and Arab thinkers agree about the existence of spirits, so that to call it into doubt (as do the atheistic Epicureans) would be to deny the principles of all Metaphysics and the existence of God, as Aristotle has shown, and the movement of the celestial bodies, which he attributes to 'Spirits' and 'Intelligences,' for the word 'spirit' signifies angels and demons."

After Bodin's time, unbelievers in witchcraft were increasingly denounced as atheists rather than as Sadducees. The poet Torquato Tasso diagnosed himself as an unwilling atheist and unbeliever; perhaps influenced by Bodin, he imagined a long dialogue with an angelic being who attempted to demonstrate the real existence of his own species, but without notable success. Only the mention of witchcraft and spirit possession came close to convincing the skeptic. Christopher Marlowe's *Dr. Faustus* (1600) implies that Faustus becomes a necromancer in a similar personal crisis.

Perhaps owing to Satan's utility as an explanation of the origin of evil, his existence was not debated as early, explicitly, or frequently as that of an angelic/demonic species and a general spirit world. Yet the devil's existence was always implicit in these general discussions. When western European intellectuals began defending the reality of witchcraft in the 1400s, they opposed the longstanding consensus of the Latin church. For at least six hundred years, the church had taught that "bewitchment" and witches' supposed nocturnal activities were illusions caused by Satan, who made simple people imagine impossible feats. Defenders of witchcraft persecution aimed their treatises at refuting the main decree (Canon *Episcopi*, ca. 900) enshrining the church's unbelief in witchcraft. By declaring that Satan worked only in the human imagination, and predominantly in dreams, this decree left no means of proving that the devil interacted with waking, sane people, and thus that he was real.

As the debate over witchcraft wore on into the seventeenth and eighteenth centuries, the existence of the devil became more problematic: one defender wrote that "it is a policy of the Devil to persuade us that there is no Devil." The reality of the devil steadily receded in synchrony with the decline of witch persecution; a related aspect was the "decline of Hell" as an article of vivid belief among Christians. Puritan divines such as Increase and Cotton Mather of Massachusetts continually equated unbelief in demons with ATHEISM, as Bodin had done; after the 1692 Salem witch trials collapsed amid skepticism and scandal, both Mathers actively sought to encounter good angels, and Increase published a treatise, *Angelographia*, defending their existence. Non-Puritan contemporaries also continued to invoke witchcraft to defend the reality of spirits; Joseph Glanvill's *Saducismus Triumphatus* is emblematic. Citing Glanvill, John Wesley, the founder of Methodism, lamented that in the rationalistic climate of the mid-eighteenth century, proofs of spiritual reality were derided and scorned; Wesley warned that "the giving up of witchcraft is, in effect, the giving up of the Bible." Doubt further accelerated in the nineteenth century. In Fyodor Dostoyevski's *Brothers Karamazov* (1880), Ivan agonizes over the unjust suffering of the innocent, loses his faith, but encounters the devil one night. Aware of hallucinating, Ivan hears Satan ask why a proof of his existence should demonstrate the existence of God.

While belief in the devil continues to wane among modern Europeans, opinion surveys in the United States around 2000 indicated that a large majority claimed to believe in the devil's physical existence. Yet American fads indicated an ongoing hunger for proof that spirits—whether good or evil—really exist and interact with people: guardian angel worship, panics over "ritual child abuse" and other forms of "Satanic subversion," along with "alien abduction syndrome" and "realistic" evangelical novels about the coming apocalypse. Such movements uneasily intuit what seventeenth-century defenders of witch persecution made explicit: If there is no proof of the devil, there is no proof of God.

BIBLIOGRAPHY

Bodin, Jean. *De la démonomanie des sorciers.* 1580. Reprint, Paris, 1582. Translated as *On the Demon-Mania of Witches,* by Randy Scott, abridged and introduced by Jonathan L. Pearl. Toronto: Centre for Reformation and Renaissance Studies, 2001.

Glanvill, Joseph. *Saducismus Triumphatus: or, Full and Plain Evidence concerning Witches and Apparitions.* 3rd ed. 1689. Reprint, Gainesville, FL: Scholars' Facsimiles and Reprints, 1966.

Keck, David. *Angels and Angelology in the Middle Ages.* New York: Oxford University Press, 1996.

Mather, Increase. *Angelographia, or A Discourse concerning the Nature and Power of the Holy Angels, and the Great Benefit Which True Fearers of God Receive by Their Ministry. . .* Boston: B. Green and J. Allen, 1696.

Russell, Jeffrey Burton. *The Devil: Perceptions of Evil*

from Antiquity to Primitive Christianity. Ithaca, NY: Cornell University Press, 1977.

———. *Lucifer: The Devil in the Middle Ages*. Ithaca, NY: Cornell University Press, 1984.

———. *Mephistopheles: The Devil in the Modern World*. Ithaca, NY: Cornell University Press, 1986.

———. *Satan: The Early Christian Tradition*. Ithaca, NY: Cornell University Press, 1981.

Stephens, Walter. *Demon Lovers: Witchcraft, Sex, and the Crisis of Belief*. Chicago: University of Chicago Press, 2002.

———. "The Quest for Satan: Witch-Hunting and Religious Doubt, 1400–1700." In *Stregoneria e streghe nell'Europa moderna*. Convegno internazionale di studi (Pisa, 24–26 marzo 1994). Edited by Giovanna Bosco and Patrizia Castelli. Pisa: Pacini Editore, 1996.

———. "Tasso and the Witches." *Annali d'Italianistica* 12 (1994).

Thomas, Keith. *Religion and the Decline of Magic*. New York: Charles Scribner's Sons, 1971.

Walker, D. P. *The Decline of Hell: Seventeenth-Century Discussions of Eternal Torment*. Chicago: University of Chicago Press, 1964.

Weyer, Johann. *Witches, Devils, and Doctors in the Renaissance. Johann Weyer, De Praestigiis daemonum*. Translated by John Shea. Edited by George Mora, Benjamin Kohl, John Weber, Erik Midelfort, and Helen Bacon. Binghamton, NY: Medieval and Renaissance Texts and Studies, 1991.

WALTER STEPHENS

DEWEY, JOHN (1859–1952), American pragmatist philosopher. John Dewey was born on October 20, 1859, in Burlington, Vermont. He received his BA from the University of Vermont in 1879, and his PhD in philosophy from Johns Hopkins University in 1884. From 1884 to 1894 Dewey taught philosophy at the University of Michigan, interrupted by a year at the University of Minnesota in 1888–89. From 1894 to 1904, Dewey was professor and chair of the philosophy, psychology, and pedagogy department at the University of Chicago, and with his wife, Alice, he led his experimental Dewey School of primary education. Dewey joined the philosophy faculty of Columbia University in 1905, and he taught there until retiring in 1929. Until 1939 Dewey was active at Columbia as emeritus professor. During his final years, Dewey continued to promote liberal democratic causes and organizations, and published significant political and philosophical writings. Dewey died on June 1, 1952, in New York City. At his death, he was acclaimed as having been America's foremost philosopher and public intellectual for more than two generations.

From his early Hegelian idealism to his mature NATURALISM and humanistic ATHEISM (see also HUMANISM),

Dewey's philosophy remained committed to empiricism: the supreme importance of lived human experience in all its individuality, variety, and creativity. Dewey's early philosophy argued that experience supplies sufficient evidence of an all-encompassing absolute and divine mind. This absolute idealism healed the dualisms of the strict Calvinism of Dewey's upbringing, confirming his preference for universal salvation and an identification of religious faith with moral commitment, placing Dewey within the Social Gospel movement. By around 1895, Dewey decided that absolute idealism could not guide anyone toward moral progress, because the absolute's moral perfection condemns to failure all human experience and action. Religious ideals of moral conduct must be practical, Dewey decided, offering helpful guidance for the growth of moral character.

During the twentieth century, Dewey joined religious humanists (see RELIGIOUS HUMANISM) and naturalists in viewing any actual belief in the existence of a divine power to be incompatible with naturalism and quite irrelevant for a genuinely religious life. Since neither a supernatural authority giving unquestionable commandments nor a spiritual absolute offering inscrutable perfection could guide morality (and indeed these only obstruct morality), Dewey concluded that liberal Christianity must logically proceed to atheism. Dewey's atheism was philosophically sophisticated, naturally, as he continued to recommend "natural piety" toward the sources and supports of one's life. His understanding and sympathy for religious experience developed in the context of his social psychology and pragmatic theory of knowledge. Rejecting the Cartesian notion of private mental states and isolated rationality, Dewey's evolutionary social psychology instead held that the habits of intelligence are learned by education and modified by further experience in group practices.

Social Psychology and Functionalism. Three major dimensions of Dewey's social psychology shaped his mature philosophy. They are most explicitly developed in *Human Nature and Conduct* (1922) and *Experience and Nature* (1925). First, experience is not subjectively private. Second, people's beliefs and knowledge are not subjective, either, but instead are functions of purposive behavior that have socially shared significance for group practices. Third, all knowledge arises from experience, and thought increases the meaningfulness of experience, producing knowledge. Dewey's empiricism held that the techniques of inference that increase meaning that guide knowledge production (such as logic, mathematics, and scientific methodology) themselves gradually emerge from experience.

For Dewey, both experience and knowledge are thoroughly goal directed, social in nature, and cultural in significance. Dewey's philosophy could not take either the individual's "subjective" experience or science's "objective" knowledge to be more capable of revealing reality or somehow independent of all-embracing culture. Religion in Dewey's philosophy is similarly treated as an evolving social phenomenon that cannot be evaluated without considering its role in cultural development. The philosophical evaluation of any human practice must be pragmatic, according to Dewey (see PRAGMATISM).

Pragmatism. Dewey's functional psychology implies a pragmatist theory of knowledge. If all beliefs exist to serve the pursuit of practical goals (and not to match some idealized vision of "truth"), then the evaluation of beliefs is judged by finding in experiment how much they contribute to successful behavior. Older theories of knowledge assumed that meaningful mental entities can be easily identified (by the power of reflection?) and compared against the portion of reality to which they refer. Such theories must depict both mind and reality statically, implicitly presuming that an isolated internal mental entity has some magical power perfectly to select out the part or aspect of reality which it is trying to represent.

However, since 1900, scientific psychology has been dynamic, not static. No scientifically respectable psychology remains to endorse the possibility of the sort of comparison required by a correspondence theory of knowledge (leaving only skeptics and Thomists still attached to long-outdated psychologies). All that remains from medieval and Cartesian rationalism is the correspondence theory of truth, but its remaining defenders happily admit that their theory does nothing to actually assist increasing knowledge. Since pragmatism is primarily a theory of how we increase knowledge, its complaint against truth as correspondence amounts to pointing out its uselessness. In *The Quest for Certainty* (1929), Dewey explains the regrettable attractions of the notion of absolute truth and explains how modern science has replaced it. Pragmatists understand truth in accord with their theory of knowledge. Dewey's pragmatic theory of knowledge is fallibilistic, for it is possible to have knowledge now which later must be modified or replaced by new knowledge. Roughly, knowledge is scientifically justified belief. Truth is an irrelevant criterion, and therefore no Gettier-style problems arise for pragmatism because they all require scenarios in which current knowledge is compared unfavorably against some absolute truth. Dewey rarely used the term *truth* with approval, and was most comfortable instead labeling as "truths" everything currently known.

Dewey heard Charles Sanders Peirce's definition of truth as that ideal limit of communal scientific inquiry while a student at Johns Hopkins, and Dewey had no objection. The closest approach that a pragmatist can make to absolute truth is to assign such truth to propositions which are known by some inquirer, present or future, that would never be overturned if all possible inquiries were exhausted. The notion of truths (or some kinds of realities) existing forever beyond possible inquiry is not endorsed by pragmatism, although pragmatism offers no conclusive argument for their nonexistence.

Scientific Method. Pragmatism is a serious effort to understand and improve on scientific method, as the best way yet invented for increasing reliable knowledge. However, pragmatists, including Dewey, refused to assign science the unique responsibility of determining what really exists; reality, including experienceable reality, contains far more than what science could ever know about. Dewey's pragmatism and preference for science should not be interpreted as a commitment to scientific reductionism or materialism (see MATERIALISM, PHILOSOPHICAL). Dewey's naturalism thus amounts to a stern denial of supernaturalism and dualism. Scientific theories about entities and processes only instrumentally observable should be interpreted realistically, according to Dewey, although those entities postulated by science that are by definition forever inaccessible to even instrumentally aided observation should not. Dewey's pragmatism can hence be fallibly realistic about molecules and superclusters of galaxies, but not about forces of nature or subatomic particles (given the current state of scientific progress). Dewey's *Logic: The Theory of Inquiry* (1938) develops his theory of scientific method.

Unlike Peirce's narrow attention to the natural sciences, Dewey believed that scientific inquiry's fundamentally creative and experimental method could be applied to all human problems, including moral and political problems. Natural science's conclusions could not erect a new morality, but the scientific method of inquiry itself can be applied to any problematic situation in which current knowledge is unable to resolve doubt about what to do. Of course, our appreciation of our current situation is guided by a vast knowledge base, including principles that emphasize more relevant features of the situation and suggest the best course of action. Inquiry first tries to apply that knowledge base to a problem; failure indicates that further inquiry must experimentally modify the knowledge base. Dewey's *How We Think* (1933) provides his general account of the processes of learning through inquiry. In natural science, this learning eventually implies modifications to theories, while in morality or politics this implies modifications to moral or political norms.

Rejecting the Humean instrumentalist model of reasoning (see HUME, DAVID), Dewey understands the scientific method as capable of pragmatically evaluating both the means and the ends of actions in light of their further consequences; see his *Theory of Valuation* (1939). Consideration of the means necessary for an end, or of future consequences of achieving that end, is a reevaluation of that end's value and desirability. There is nothing that could be immune from such reasoned consideration, and therefore no end or good can be declared as supreme, final, or all-inclusive. The moral and political life instead requires the constant renegotiation of shifting priorities among innumerable goals, values, and norms.

Democracy. For Dewey, the scientific method applied to society is democracy. Like science, which proceeds through distributed intelligence among cooperating inquirers, democracy is the way of life in which mutually respectful citizens intelligently deliberate on their common social problems. *Democracy and Education* (1916) is Dewey's fullest statement of the essential role that scientific, moral, and civic education must play in a democracy. Dewey also sketched a theory of political democracy about the government that would best serve a democratic community. *The Public and Its Problems* (1927) and *Liberalism and Social Action* (1935) develop Dewey's theory of "publics": groups of people with common problems trying to modify social or political norms for remedies. These publics are educated in the skills of cooperative deliberation from schooling and past experience, and compete for attention from elected officials and from the whole community with the help of social scientists and other experts. Publics naturally dissolve when their problems are alleviated, and peoples' energies are redirected to other problems.

Against aristocratic theories of democracy that assign to the government and experts the responsibility for recognizing and solving social problems, Dewey expects greater citizenship skills from the masses so that they can do more than just vote periodically. Of course, if each person by oneself is expected to help with all of a country's problems, faith in democracy seems hopelessly utopian. However, Dewey explained how ordinary people can devote some measure of time, energy, and intelligence between voting to a few serious problems affecting them, and thus publics can be energized. Prominent examples include unions and civic organizations; national societies such the American Civil Liberties Union, the National Association for the Advancement of Colored People (Dewey was a cofounder of both), and the National Rifle Association; industry associations; and every sort of lobbying and special interest group imaginable. If a democracy can promote both the free formation of effective publics and the caring responsiveness from the whole body of citizens, then Dewey envisioned progress toward the ideal Great Community. Democracy is the form of community life and government which respects and peacefully promotes universal moral respect and empowers its citizens through education for the civic capacities of moral deliberation. As a regulative ideal, the notion of a Great Community helps to expose immorality and injustice and suggest remedies for transforming society.

Progressive Liberalism. Dewey departed further from traditional liberalism because he argued that people require more than John LOCKE's negative rights and liberties to be full citizens. The right to fair and safe employment (not just a right to individual property), to education in the skills of citizenship (not merely free speech), and to toleration and protection of ethnic heritage (not cultural assimilation and hegemony) are among the additional empowering rights justified in a healthy democracy. His *Ethics* (1932), written with James H. Tufts, provides a detailed theory of economic and social justice that owes much to both the liberal tradition and to utilitarianism, and especially to John Stuart MILL, although Dewey sometimes preferred the label of "social utilitarianism" since most goods are socially shared goods. Dewey was a democratic socialist, since he favored strong democratic intervention in the economic sphere to prevent injustice, but he was never a Communist since he rejected Communism's use of violence and preferred restrained capitalism to state ownership of all industry. Like many liberal progressives, Dewey instead expected strong unions and other types of effective publics to be able to peacefully negotiate for the things needed for greater social justice. For Dewey, the understanding of democracy as a moral community implies noncoercive deliberation to resolve conflicts. Dewey's demand that violence be only an absolute last resort linked him with pacifists such as Jane ADDAMS, who also demanded that governments should engage in international cooperation to actively prevent conditions provoking war. Dewey's other major concern was that wars are extremely hazardous to a democracy's civil liberties.

Dewey, like later communitarians, viewed people as deeply connected to a variety of social groups. He recommended an inclusive cultural pluralism in which people possess group membership while being free to enjoy and adopt other groups' ways. The morality that should be taught in public schools (private schooling encourages antidemocratic tendencies) consists of the civic virtues of respect for the equal dignity of all, cooperative group problem solving, and loyalty to the ideals and aims of democracy. The only intolerance innate to Dewey's democracy is the rejection of groups that claim to possess absolute moral norms and values that prevent their members from following democratic civic virtues and incapacitate them for cooperative public deliberation.

Democracy requires a somewhat flexible and experimental attitude toward even our most cherished moral norms and values, because a few may require modification during our lifetimes to permit the alleviation of serious social problems. Even Dewey's own specific formulations of the civic virtues and basic rights are advanced in a tentative manner, and he expected them to be gradually modified in the future. The principle that seems the most absolute in Dewey's philosophy, the standard by which he undertakes moral and political criticism, is the demand that all persons must have an equal opportunity to realize their capacities and enjoy life in a manner consistent with the greater social good. However, even this principle remains flexible for Dewey, since the practical meaning of "realizing capacities" will change into the future as the possibilities of human experience expand.

Religion. Dewey eloquently expresses his high valuation of religious experience (see RELIGIOUS AND MYS-TICAL EXPERIENCES), after being liberated from supernaturalism, in most of his major works. Unlike fellow pragmatist William James, whose mysticism found divinely inspiring powers present at the fringes of individual consciousness, Dewey required religious and moral experience and belief to have only social significance. Therefore, religious experience could only consist of one's communion with others in expressions of commitment (through group practices) to social values. What is Dewey's pragmatist alternative to a supernatural god? As early as 1892, Dewey concluded that a liberal, nonsupernatural Christianity was best for America. This liberal Christianity was still Christianity because the American community still holds Jesus to be an exemplary moral figure of love. For Dewey, the example of mutual love and respect for all people is simultaneously Christian and democratic, and democracy's progress is Christian progress. In the 1890s Dewey also asserted that Jesus offered no specific rules, doctrines, or creeds, and thus he left no church. The preferred alternative to churches and their religions of fixed truth is the "continual revelation" of new truths about how to fulfill the ideal of love which will arise from the process of democracy itself.

After these early pronouncements, Dewey was largely silent on the historical figure of Jesus (see JESUS, HISTORICITY OF), but he did remain hostile toward churches. In *A Common Faith* (1934), Dewey's distinction between *religions* (the churches' doctrines) and *the religious* (those liberated into pluralistic and progressive democracy) reemphasized his claim that the democratic experience is also religious experience. The religious are those who have escaped supernaturalism and sectarian creeds, and can join in the aesthetic appreciation of the pursuit of democracy. In *Art as Experience* (1934) Dewey found paradigms of aesthetic experience in communal practices devoted to ideals. In *A Common Faith* Dewey again appeals to the coextensive aesthetic/religious experience of pursuing ideals. The democratic commitment to moral respect for all people has the quality of a religious faith, and a democratic culture, like any culture, should possess a religion as a unifying social force diffused throughout all cultural activities. Dewey concluded that democracy is the form of life in which the shared aesthetic enjoyment of the democratic community life is collectively of great value, and that this communion is a kind of highly valuable religious experience.

In *A Common Faith* the notion of natural piety again plays a role. Dewey identified the object of natural piety as the organic unity of human strivings with cooperating natural forces. A democracy should likewise encourage this natural piety, and religious devotion is thus properly oriented toward human-environment relationships as well as human-human relationships. To the surprise of many, especially Dewey's humanist colleagues, he went farther, controversially offering the label of "God" for

the object of religious experience. Critics have pointed out that the name "God" at least implies a unified and purposive agency and perhaps a personality as well, signaling a retreat to older religious notions that Dewey himself rejected. Most philosophers and speculative theologians who have pursued Dewey's suggestions toward a naturalistic and humanistic religion remain quite wary of such labels as "God." However, the task remains to fully explain how the sort of intense religious devotion to ideals, still useful in any democracy, can be aroused and maintained without trespassing the boundaries set by naturalism.

BIBLIOGRAPHY

Campbell, James. *Understanding John Dewey.* Chicago: Open Court, 1995.

Dewey, John. *The Collected Works of John Dewey.* 37 vols. Edited by Jo Ann Boydston. Carbondale: Southern Illinois University Press, 1967–90.

Eldridge, Michael. *Transforming Experience: John Dewey's Cultural Instrumentalism.* Nashville, TN: Vanderbilt University Press, 1998.

Hickman, Larry A. *John Dewey's Pragmatic Technology.* Bloomington: Indiana University Press, 1990.

Rockefeller, Steven C. *John Dewey: Religious Faith and Democratic Humanism.* New York: Columbia University Press, 1991.

Ryan, Alan. *John Dewey and the High Tide of American Liberalism.* New York: Norton, 1995.

Schilpp, Paul A., ed. *The Philosophy of John Dewey.* 3rd ed. La Salle, IL: Open Court, 1989.

Shook, John R. *Dewey's Empirical Theory of Knowledge and Reality.* Nashville, TN: Vanderbilt University Press, 2000.

Westbrook, Robert B. *John Dewey and American Democracy.* Ithaca, NY: Cornell University Press, 1991.

JOHN R. SHOOK

DIDEROT, DENIS (1713–1784), French encyclopedist. Denis Diderot's relationship with religious thought and practice was complex and lifelong. This is because it was his habit as a writer to lay false trails in his works, often creating erroneous impressions of his ideas. It was also his custom to hide from his contemporaries some of his most original and daring writings, which remained unknown for many years. Consequently, the facts on which critics have had to base their judgments have changed substantially since his death, and the reassessment of his importance as an Enlightenment figure is still by no means complete.

Diderot was born into a devout family in Langres (Champagne), where his forebears had been cutlers for generations. He had a conventional religious education in the local Jesuit college, from which he received the tonsure (a step in preparation for the priesthood) in 1726. His younger brother Didier, with whom he would later quarrel violently over religion, became a priest, while a younger sister, Angélique, took the veil and died insane in a convent in 1748. His maternal uncle was a canon at the cathedral church of Langres, and if Diderot declined the opportunity to succeed him in this office, his interest in religion was still strong enough for him to enroll at the Jansenist Collège d'Harcourt in Paris in 1729. Having thus been a pupil of the two major religious sects of the time, he obtained his master's degree in 1732, the customary preliminary to preparing for the priesthood. Yet his faith (at least in the doctrines of the Catholic Church) was fast waning, and he never took this step. In the years between 1735 and 1745, his self-imposed program of studies in science, languages, and mathematics led him in quite other directions from the one he had first envisaged.

Diderot has often been assimilated into the great secular, atheistic movement of ideas that is central to the French Enlightenment, but this is to oversimplify the question. The earliest of his works to attest to his views on religion was a 1745 translation of Earl SHAFTESBURY's 1699 *Essay concerning Virtue and Merit*. This *Essai sur le mérite et la vertu* maintains that belief in God is necessary for the practice of virtue, which requires divine sanction, but that belief in Christianity is not. His independent outlook is further developed in the *Pensées philosophiques* (Philosophical Thoughts) of 1746. This short, portable book was quickly condemned as blasphemous, and always remained one of Diderot's most controversial writings. The *Pensées*, often described as atheistic, might better be thought of as an externalized dialogue on religion that Diderot conducts with himself. While he does not disguise his disillusionment with Christianity, he voices his preference for what he calls *naturalism*—a term left undefined but closely akin, it would seem, to deism. Diderot's belief in an omnipotent deity is more doubtful in *La Promenade du Sceptique* (The Skeptic's Walk), a dialogue written in 1747 but unpublished until 1830. In it Diderot casts doubt on the notion of God using the traditional weapons of the rationalist skeptic. Perhaps as a result of the death of his beloved younger sister Angélique, any lingering attachment he had to religious belief is absent from the materialistic *Lettre sur les Aveugles* (Letter on the Blind) of 1749; here, the blind mathematician Saunderson refuses to believe in God unless he can touch him. The *Lettre*, more than any of Diderot's other writings to date, finally exhausted the patience of the authorities, who jailed him for several months in 1749. This was despite the fact that he had by then become one of the editors of the great ENCYCLOPÉDIE, which was to occupy the next twenty or more years of his life. His imprisonment was not unduly harsh, but it marked his psyche and increased his tendency to ensure that any of his ideas that might be dangerous were not openly disseminated in print. Yet despite the *Lettre*, Diderot had not in reality abandoned all religious beliefs, though no consis-

tent expression of his views on religion (or on many other subjects) was readily forthcoming.

On the one hand, the labyrinthine complexities of the *Encyclopédie* allowed him to express skeptical ideas obliquely. Articles whose ostensible subjects have little to do with religion as such provided cover for criticisms of the church, or the Bible, or for the discussion of doctrinal issues. Hence, "Agnus scythicus" (1751) begins as the consideration of an obscure plant, whose remarkable properties, on closer examination, turn out to be wholly imaginary. This lesson in the critical evaluation of evidence was clearly intended to apply not only to such mundane reports, but to accounts of supernatural events such as miracles as well. In "Philosophy of the Chinese" (1753), he reports a seventeenth-century emperor asking Christian missionaries why their God had kept the Chinese so long in ignorance of his existence, a question to which no clear answer is forthcoming. In these and many other articles, Diderot and his collaborators made innumerable damaging forays against the edifice of official beliefs and doctrines enjoined by the Catholic Church. Theirs was a prolonged assault: the much-persecuted *Encyclopédie* was not finished until 1772, and the (indispensable) index to it did not appear until 1780.

On the other hand, whatever impression he contrived to give the public of his own robustly skeptical attitude toward religious belief, and particularly toward Christianity, Diderot was in private a more troubled man. A document has recently been published that must be set against the mockery of the *Encyclopédie*. This is *La Prière du Sceptique* (The Skeptic's Prayer) in his own handwriting, bound into a copy of his *Pensées sur l'Interprétation de la nature* (Thoughts on the Interpretation of Nature) of 1754. It opens with these words: "I began with Nature, which they called your handiwork, and I shall finish with you, whose name on Earth is God. O God, I do not know if you exist; but my thoughts shall be as though you saw into my soul, and I shall act as though I stood before you."

Though this prayer was published in a (rather unreliable) edition of Diderot's works in 1773, the publication of the holograph manuscript confirming his authorship puts many of his other utterances on religion in a different perspective. It seems clear that, although he began as an orthodox Christian believer who may even have had a religious vocation, he subsequently vacillated considerably in his beliefs, moving between deism, materialist atheism, and skepticism as his ideas changed. Yet if he later tried to reconcile himself with the idea of God, his disenchantment with Christianity, and his mockery of the Catholic Church for its repressive hold on the human mind remained constant. Indeed, these views are expressed in two more of his "secret" writings, the novel *La Religieuse* (The Nun, 1760) and the 1772 dialogue entitled *Supplément au voyage de Bougainville* (Supplement to Bougainville's Voyage). Both of these remained unpublished until 1796, a dozen years after his death. As they show unmistakably, his hatred of tyranny in all its forms was in later years an overriding preoccupation. In a short poem, "*Les Eleuthéromanes*" (The Zealots for Freedom, 1772), also published in 1796, he speaks of "weaving together the guts of a priest, to use as a rope for strangling kings." Diderot did not live to see the French Revolution, but he would not have been surprised at the course it took.

BIBLIOGRAPHY

Adams, D. J. *Diderot, Dialogue and Debate*. Liverpool: Francis Cairns, 1986.

Chouillet, Jacques. *La Formation des idées esthétiques de Diderot*. Paris: Armand Colin, 1973.

Israel, Jonathan I. *Radical Enlightenment. Philosophy and the Making of Modernity 1650–1750*. Oxford: Oxford University Press, 2001.

Strugnell, Anthony. *Diderot's Politics*. The Hague: Nijhoff, 1973.

Wilson, Arthur M. *Diderot*. New York: Oxford University Press, 1972.

DAVID ADAMS

DOUGLASS, FREDERICK (1818–1895), American orator and abolitionist. One of the most courageous abolitionists and greatest orators of the nineteenth century was born Frederick Augustus Washington Bailey. After this former slave gained his freedom as an adult, he changed his last name to Douglass following the advice of an associate.

Douglass was born into slavery to Harriet Bailey on Holmes Hill Farm in Easton, Maryland. He never met his white father. His grandmother Betsey Bailey raised him on the farm; he only saw his mother on a few occasions. In August 1824, when he was only six, his grandmother was forced to give him to new owners, and the painful separation from his loved ones was etched in his memory for the rest of his life.

In 1834 Douglass worked for Edward Covey, who had a reputation as being able to break any slave's will. The harsh, deeply religious slave driver brutalized Douglass. But one day Douglass rebelled, and the two fought for nearly two hours until Covey finally gave up. The sixteen-year-old Douglass felt enormously empowered, and the experience gave him great confidence.

In 1838 Douglass escaped slavery and fled to New Bedford, Massachusetts. On September 15, 1838, he married a free black woman named Ann Murray. (By 1845 they had four children.) It was also in that year that he changed his name to Douglass.

Not long after arriving in New Bedford, Douglass subscribed to the *Liberator*, the newspaper of the American Anti-Slavery Society, headed by the man who would become his idol, William Lloyd Garrison.

During the Civil War, Douglass served as an adviser to President Abraham Lincoln. He helped persuade Lincoln to use African American troops. On January 1, 1863, the president signed the Emancipation Proclamation, which was designed to free slaves in Confederate states, permitting them to join the Union army.

Douglass served as an army recruiter throughout the United States during the war. He recruited two of his sons, Charles and Frederick, who joined the renowned 54th Massachusetts Regiment. However, Douglass was not satisfied with the mere presence of African Americans in the Union army. On August 10, 1863, Douglass met with Lincoln to voice complaints about the shoddy treatment and low pay of African American soldiers.

Douglass respected and admired "the Great Agnostic," Robert Green INGERSOLL. Once, when Douglass was denied lodging because of his race when scheduled to speak in Illinois, Ingersoll welcomed him warmly into his home. Douglass was reported to have said that Lincoln—another freethinker—and Ingersoll were the only white men in whose company "he could be without feeling he was regarded as inferior to them."

Douglass was deeply humanistic (see HUMANISM). Indeed, he believed so firmly in SECULARISM that he once offered to debate a black preacher on whether organized prayers and Bible readings should be permitted in public schools. (Douglass was vigorously opposed.)

In 1870 Douglass spoke to a group in Philadelphia and another group in New York City. Though the black clergy and others had routinely thanked God, Douglass told the audiences he would not indulge in such "hackneyed" God talk. He preferred to thank the human beings who had clearly dedicated their lives to the abolition of slavery. He would express this view for the rest of his life.

In 1889 Douglass was appointed US minister to Haiti and chargé d'affaires of Santo Domingo. He noted the poor conditions in these countries, observing that Haiti was the first Caribbean nation to be taken over by Christianity. He believed it was better to give blacks political power than to give them faith in an afterlife.

Douglass was a committed humanist activist until the end. On February 20, 1895, he defended women's rights at the National Council of Women (see WOMAN SUFFRAGE MOVEMENT AND UNBELIEF). He died later that evening, ending the life of one of the most outstanding heroes in US history.

BIBLIOGRAPHY

Douglass, Frederick. *Narrative of the Life of Frederick Douglass: An American Slave*. Cambridge, MA: Harvard University Press, 1960.

Greeley, Roger, ed. *The Best of Robert Ingersoll: Selections from His Writings and Speeches*. Amherst, NY: Prometheus Books, 1983.

McFeely, William S. *Frederick Douglass*. New York: Norton, 1991.

Van Deburg. William L. "Frederick Douglass: Maryland Slave to Religious Liberal." In *By These Hands: A*

Documentary History of African American Humanism, edited by Anthony B. Pinn. New York: New York University Press, 2001.

NORM R. ALLEN JR.

DRAPER, JOHN WILLIAM (1811–1882), American chemist, physiologist, and historian. Unbelievers know John William Draper as creator of the so-called military metaphor of bitter struggle between science and religion (see RELIGION IN CONFLICT WITH SCIENCE). Rightly or wrongly, that view of relations between dogma and inquiry shaped much late nineteenth- and twentieth-century thinking in domains including evolution (see EVOLUTION AND UNBELIEF), cosmology, BIBLICAL CRITICISM, and sexual morality (see SEXUAL VALUES, IMPACT OF UNBELIEF ON). The writings of Draper and his successors were embraced by freethinkers and many humanists (see FREETHOUGHT; HUMANISM) as mainstream vindication for their views.

Draper was born on May 5, 1811, near Liverpool, England, the son of a Methodist minister. At the University of London he dabbled in POSITIVISM. Draper, his wife, and three sisters sailed for America in 1832; he appeared sufficiently orthodox to secure teaching appointments at Methodist colleges. In 1839 he assumed the chair in chemistry at the University of the City of New York.

Draper's religious views were conflicted. He was in some ways traditionally Methodist, in others a deist (see DEISM) who had accepted the principle of evolution well before the publication of Darwin's *Origin of Species*. Surely he had ceased to understand the Bible as divinely inspired. Draper's private life was touched by sectarian strife; he expelled from his household a sister who had converted to Catholicism.

In an ironic footnote to history, Draper addressed the British Association at Oxford on June 30, 1860, his extended remarks delaying the start of the celebrated evolution debate between Bishop Samuel Wilberforce and Thomas Henry HUXLEY. This debate emerged as a defining event of the Victorian era and likely spurred Draper's thinking on science and religion.

In an idiosyncratic *History of the Intellectual Development of Europe* (1864), Draper espoused a Comtean, positivist view of social development as bound by rigid laws (see COMTE, AUGUSTE), demonized the popes as enemies of science, and lauded Islamic civilization as friendlier toward discovery than the West. The book was well received; in 1873 Draper was approached by Edward Livingston Youmans, an American promoter of popular science books. Youmans envisioned a title by Draper on science and religion as the thirteenth volume in his successful "International Scientific Series." Pressed for time, Draper condensed large sections from his *History*, then added a preface and three concluding chapters reflecting recent events, particularly the Catholic Church's vigorous new campaign against modernity. In the Syllabus of Errors (1864) Pope Pius IX had denounced almost every fruit of science and scholarship; in 1870 the First Vatican Council had proclaimed him infallible. Draper responded with the *History of the Conflict between Religion and Science* (1874), an incendiary tract that indicted not Christianity but specifically Roman Catholicism for hobbling human progress.

Draper traced the origins of science to the fourth century BCE among Greeks stimulated by exposure to the Persian Empire. Religion's inherent incompatibility with science he dated to the fading days of the Roman Empire. A romanticized account introduced American readers to HYPATIA, a pagan woman scholar slaughtered by monks in Alexandria in 417 CE.

Draper famously observed, "A divine revelation must necessarily be intolerant of contradiction; it must repudiate all improvement in itself, and view with disdain that arising from the progressive intellectual development of man." In other words, conflict between science and religion is inevitable. His closing paragraph thundered: "As to the issue of the coming conflict, can any one doubt? . . . Faith must render an account of herself to Reason. Mysteries must give place to facts. Religion must relinquish that imperious, that domineering position which she has so long maintained against Science. There must be absolute freedom for thought. The ecclesiastic must learn to keep himself within the domain he has chosen, and cease to tyrannize over the philosopher . . . who will bear such interference no longer."

The book was spectacularly successful, both financially and in terms of its intellectual impact. It enjoyed fifty printings in the United States, twenty-one in Britain, and was translated into nine languages. The Spanish edition (1876) was placed on the Vatican's Index of Forbidden Books, setting Draper alongside such luminaries as Copernicus, Galileo GALILEI, John LOCKE, and John Stuart MILL.

Draper died on January 4, 1882, at Hastings-on-Hudson, New York. His *History of the Conflict between Religion and Science* would inspire a vigorous literature steeped in the military metaphor, most importantly Andrew Dickson WHITE's influential *History of the Warfare of Science with Theology in Christendom* (1896).

BIBLIOGRAPHY

Atschuler, Glenn C. *Andrew D. White: Educator, Historian, Diplomat.* Ithaca, NY: Cornell University Press, 1979.

Chadwick, Owen. *The Secularization of the European Mind in the Nineteenth Century.* Cambridge: Cambridge University Press, 1975.

Draper, John William. *History of the Conflict between Religion and Science.* New York: D. Appleton and Company, 1874.

———. *A History of the Intellectual Development of Europe.* 2 vols. New York: Harper & Brothers, 1864.

Fleming, Donald. *John William Draper and the Religion of Science.* Philadelphia: University of Pennsylvania Press, 1950.

Moore, James R. *The Post-Darwinian Controversies: A Study of the Protestant Struggle to Come to Terms with Darwin in Great Britain and America, 1870–1900.* Cambridge: Cambridge University Press, 1979.

TOM FLYNN

DREISER, THEODORE (1871–1945), American writer. As one of the most controversial and successful novelists of his day, Theodore Dreiser expressed its turbulent crosscurrents in a probing if ponderous style. Throughout a long, colorful life, he never forgot his poverty-blasted beginnings in Terre Haute, Indiana, as the son of a fervently Catholic father who was a skilled but unsuccessful woolen-mill operator. His mother had been a pietistic Mennonite who converted to Catholicism at her husband's demand. Growing up in a large family that frequently had to move one step ahead of the bill collectors and ill at ease with his looks and the family's chronic desperation, young Theodore yet maintained a rather dreamy nature. After a series of odd jobs and a year at Indiana University given him by a former teacher, Dreiser became a newspaper reporter and gravitated toward writing as a livelihood.

At an early age, Dreiser began to resist his religious upbringing. Ever restless and curious, he evolved a philosophy of DETERMINISM based on Herbert SPENCER. He adopted a naturalistic literary style. "We were taught persistently," he wrote, "to shun most human experience as either dangerous or degrading or destructive. The less you knew about life the better; the more you knew about the fictional heaven and hell ditto. People walked about in a kind of sanctified daze or dream, hypnotized or self-hypnotized by an erratic and impossible theory of human conduct which had grown up heaven knows where or how, and had finally cast its amethystine spell over all America, if not over all the world."

Dreiser's first novel, *Sister Carrie* (1900), was for all practical purposes repressed by its publisher, in part on grounds of immorality. A reviewer for the *Chicago Tribune* noted, "Not once does the name of the Deity appear in the book, except as it is implied in the suggestion of profanity," but went on to say that such a book had been long awaited. Eventually the novel was republished, and Dreiser was acknowledged to be a major figure in modern American literature. Despite such success, there was persistent opposition from "antivice" religious groups; H. L. MENCKEN remained Dreiser's constant friend and a champion of free expression.

In other novels Dreiser took up the theme of the "self-made man" in American society, exploring this type's need for sexual and political power. *An American Tragedy* (1926) tells the story of Clyde Griffiths, who rises from poverty in Kansas City and goes east to work in a relative's factory. There he is involved in a rich woman's drowning, for which he is convicted and sentenced to death. The early scenes on the streets of the metropolis, where a pitiful group of Clyde's family members sings and preaches the gospel, are clearly reminiscent of Dreiser's own pietistic youth. Their "virus of Evangelism" is no real cure for the "vast skepticism and apathy of life." The success of this novel made Dreiser wealthy at last.

In 1927 he journeyed to Soviet Russia, where his books had earned large amounts of royalties in rubles. Generally sympathetic to the great Communist experiment, Dreiser retained what he felt he needed, the freedom to observe conditions for himself and to criticize weaknesses. During the Great Depression, he journeyed to Harlan County, Kentucky, to write of the suffering and repression of coal miners for the radical magazine *New Masses*.

In his later years, Dreiser continued to write and publish fiction. Just before his death in 1945, he joined the Communist Party. At his funeral in Forest Lawn Cemetery, the presiding minister seemed ill at ease, at one point taking as his text "help thou my unbelief" (Mark 9:24).

BIBLIOGRAPHY

Lingeman, Richard. *Theodore Dreiser: An American Journey 1908–1945.* New York: Putnam, 1990.

———. *Theodore Dreiser: At the Gates of the City 1871–1907.* New York: Putnam, 1986.

FRED WHITEHEAD

DUBOIS, WILLIAM EDWARD BURGHARDT (1868–1963), Amrican scholar and activist. Widely regarded as the most important African American scholar of the twentieth century, W. E. B. DuBois attended what was then the all-black Fisk College (now Fisk University) in Nashville, Tennessee, between 1885 and 1888. He eventually graduated from Fisk and Harvard. He then studied history, sociology, and philosophy at the University of Berlin. In 1891 he received a master's degree from Harvard. In 1894 Harvard awarded him a doctorate in philosophy.

In 1896 DuBois was the recipient of a fellowship at the University of Pennsylvania. While there, he conducted a study of blacks in Philadelphia. The result was a classic called *The Philadelphia Negro*, leading some scholars to give him the title "the Father of Social Science."

Next DuBois worked at Atlanta University, where he studied African American life and culture. Moreover, he became deeply interested in the role of Africa in world history. While in Atlanta DuBois became involved in an ongoing debate with the black conservative Booker T. Washington, who believed that blacks should put emphasis upon vocational education, self-help, and the acquisition of skills. In 1903 DuBois published another classic work, *The*

Souls of Black Folk, in opposition to Washington's conservative program. DuBois argued that blacks should agitate for their rights. Moreover, he promoted the idea of "the Talented Tenth," an elite, educated class constituting 10 percent of the black population, which he believed would lead blacks into the twentieth century.

In 1906 DuBois and a small group of black men organized the Niagara movement in an effort to agitate for freedom, justice, and equality for blacks in the United States. Allegedly denied permission by racist whites to meet in Niagara Falls, New York, the group decided to meet on the Canadian side. No women were permitted to attend, because the men believed it would be too dangerous, considering the cause they were espousing. Out of the Niagara movement grew the National Association for the Advancement of the Colored People (NAACP) in 1909. Ironically, the organization's leadership was predominantly white. However, DuBois assumed the editorship of the group's magazine, *The Crisis*, and served in that position for twenty-four years.

In 1900 DuBois was the secretary of the first Pan-African Congress in London. The goal of these international congresses was to advocate self-determination for African and Caribbean nations and colonies. The early leaders of these congresses were DuBois, George Padmore, humanist C. L. R. JAMES, and Henry Sylvester Williams—the latter three from Trinidad.

In 1919 the second Pan-African Congress was held in Paris. The delegates presented the League of Nations with resolutions demanding independence from Western domination for African and Caribbean nations.

In 1923 a congress was held in London and Lisbon. In 1927 there was a congress in Harlem. DuBois chaired this congress, and there were 208 delegates and about 5,000 people in attendance. DuBois then wanted to hold a congress in Tunis, but the French government feared the possibility of a Tunisian rebellion. They granted DuBois permission to hold the congress in Paris. It was a moot point, however; the Great Depression arrived in 1929 and derailed the plans.

The Pan-African movement put DuBois in direct competition with Marcus Garvey, the charismatic and flamboyant leader of the Universal Negro Improvement Association (UNIA). Both leaders believed in African redemption, but had major differences in style and substance. Perhaps most importantly, Garvey advocated racial separation, while DuBois was willing to work with progressive whites to advance the cause. Many scholars believe that the debate between Garvey and DuBois far exceeded that between DuBois and Washington in intensity, hostility, and vitriol. Eventually, the US government deported Garvey and the UNIA was greatly weakened, losing members and financing. Meanwhile, DuBois would go on to lead another congress in 1945, in Manchester, England.

In 1933 DuBois left the NAACP over political differences, having also reached the conclusion that it was hard to effectively agitate for black advancement within the ranks of a protest organization headed primarily by whites. He returned to Atlanta University, and in 1935 he wrote another classic work about life after the Civil War, *Black Reconstruction*. He brilliantly demonstrated that blacks played highly influential roles in rebuilding the South after the war.

In 1940 DuBois wrote *Dusk of Dawn*, in which he examined the African American quest for freedom, justice, and equality. In 1946 he wrote *The World and Africa*, a major work showing that blacks in Africa made impressive contributions to world culture and human civilization.

Throughout his illustrious career, DuBois was an anticlerical agnostic (see AGNOSTICISM). He refused to lead prayers when asked to do so. He regarded the theology of the average black church as immature, dogmatic, and highly irrational. However, he believed that black churches had many redeeming qualities, though he believed the Christianity of whites had failed miserably.

In 1961 President Kwame Nkrumah of Ghana invited DuBois to the West African nation. DuBois accepted the offer, and died there, two years later. His remains are buried at the W. E. B. DuBois Memorial Centre for Pan African Culture in Accra.

BIBLIOGRAPHY

Aptheker, Herbert, ed. *Against Racism: Unpublished Essays, Papers, Addresses by W. E. B. DuBois, 1887–1961.* Amherst: University of Massachusetts Press, 1985.

DuBois, W. E. B. "On Christianity." From *Against Racism.* Reprinted in *African-American Humanism: An Anthology*, edited by Norm R. Allen Jr. Amherst, NY: Prometheus Books, 1991.

———. *The Souls of Black Folk: Essays and Sketches.* Chicago: A. C. McClurg, 1903.

Howard-Pitney, David. "W. E. B. DuBois: Black Scholar and Social Activist." In *African-American Humanism: An Anthology*, edited by Norm R. Allen Jr. Amherst, NY: Prometheus Books, 1991.

Martin, Tony. *Race First: The Ideological and Organization Struggles of Marcus Garvey and the Universal Negro Improvement Association.* Dover, MA: Majority Press, 1976.

NORM R. ALLEN JR.

EDELMANN, JOHANN CHRISTIAN (1698–1767), German theologian and agnostic. Son of a court musician at Sachsen-Weissenfels, Johann Christian Edelmann studied at Jena from 1720 to 1724 under the moderate philosopher-theologian Johann Franz Buddeus. Like many other intellectuals of this period in Germany, Edelmann began to work as a private tutor for nobility and clergy. After an intensive religious quest he broke with Lutheranism, influenced by the historian of HERESY Gottfried Arnold. From 1734, he followed a calling as a writer, publishing fifteen monthly pieces titled *Innocent Truths* on disputed theological questions. Settling in the liberal state of Sayn-Wittgenstein-Berleburg from 1736 to 1741, he engaged in discussions with various "pietist" and dissident circles, among them Herrnhuters and Mennonites, and read widely in European radical thought.

Fired by Baruch SPINOZA's *Tractatus Theologico-Politicus*, he published "The Revealed Face of Moses" (1740), in which he argued that the Bible is a purely human book and the teaching of Jesus contradicts the teaching of Christian churches. This publication provoked 172 published "refutations" through 1755, and was banned in most places. Edelmann himself had to flee repeatedly from Lutheran orthodox campaigns. After publishing an ironically titled "Confession of Faith" in which he averred that the use of REASON is the only true divine service, in 1746 he was forced to ask Frederick II of Prussia for protection. That protection was granted in 1749 on the condition that Edelmann henceforth keep public silence. In 1750 his books were burned by the "Imperial Book Commission." Now unable to publish, he was reduced to translating and extensively commenting on banned books for secret circulation in Masonic lodges. Moses Mendelssohn reports having met Edelmann living in Berlin, full of "fear of being recognized." Edelmann's autobiography (written 1749–1753) would only be published—and then in truncated form—in 1849.

Edelmann was the first to transmit radical Enlightenment ideas (see ENLIGHTENMENT, UNBELIEF DURING THE) in vernacular German, defying censorship. He brought about an irreversible shift toward DEISM in the German public, thus beginning the process his "freethinking" protector Frederick II had wanted to avoid: bringing enlightenment to the people.

BIBLIOGRAPHY

Anonymous [Johann Joachim Müller]. *De imposturis religionum (De tribus impostoribus). Von den Betrügereyen de Religionen.* Edited and annotated by Winfried Schröder. Stuttgart-Bad Cannstatt: Frommann-Holzboog, 1999.

Edelmann, J. C. *Sämtliche Schriften in Einzelausgaben.* 12 vols. Edited by Walter Grossmann. Stuttgart-Bad Cannstatt: Frommann-Holzboog, 1969–87.

Grossmann, Walter. *Johann Christian Edelmann.* The Hague: Mouton, 1976.

Israel, Jonathan I. *Radical Enlightenment: Philosophy and the Making of Modernity.* Oxford: Oxford University Press, 2001.

Otto, Rüdiger. "Johann Christian Edelmann's Criticism of the Bible and Its Relation to Spinoza." In *Disguised and Overt Spinozism around 1700*, edited by Wiep van Bunge and Wim Klever. Leiden: Brill, 1996.

Schaper, Annegret. *Ein langer Abschied vom Christentum.* Marburg: Tectum, 1996.

Schröder, Winfried. *Ursprünge des Atheismus.* Stuttgart-Bad Cannstatt: Frommann-Holzboog, 1998.

Ward, W. R. "Johann Christian Edelmann: A Rebel's Pilgrimage." In *Modern Religious Rebels*, edited by Stuart Mews. London: Epworth, 1993.

FRIEDER OTTO WOLF

EDWARDS, PAUL (1923–2004), American philosopher and encyclopedist. A member of the editorial board of *Free Inquiry* magazine and the International Academy of Humanism, Edwards was born in Vienna, Austria. A gifted student, he was admitted to the prestigious Akademische Gymnasium. After the Nazi annexation of Austria, his family sent him to stay with friends in Scotland. He later went to Melbourne, Australia, where he studied philosophy at the University of Melbourne and was influenced by the analytic tradition that held sway there. After the war he came to Columbia University, where he completed a doctorate in philosophy. He was to spend the rest of his life in New York City, teaching at such institutions as New York University, the New School for Social Research, and Brooklyn College.

Edwards is best known for editing the monumental *Encyclopedia of Philosophy*, which originally appeared in 1967 and has never since been out of print. It remains the essential reference work for the field of philosophy. Using his editorial prerogative, Edwards made sure that there were plentiful entries on ATHEISM, materialism (see MATERIALISM, PHILOSOPHICAL), and critiques of God's existence, and he himself cowrote the long entry on his own philosophical hero, Bertrand RUSSELL. In 1959 Edwards edited a collection of Russell's previously scattered writings dealing with religion, titled *Why I Am Not a Christian and Other Essays*, which became a seminal work in the promotion of unbelief.

Those who knew Edwards will always remember his erudition and his wicked sense of humor. An admirer of VOLTAIRE and Russell for their great wit, Edwards had a special fondness for the life and works of David HUME, the man he considered to be the best exemplar of a learned individual who lived life to the fullest and who remained to the day of his death a cheerful nonbeliever.

Shortly before his own death, Edwards published a collection of essays entitled *Heidegger's Confusions* (2004), dedicated to demolishing the legacy of the man whom Edwards considered to have done the greatest damage to the field of philosophy in the twentieth century. He particularly abhorred Heidegger's confusing writings on the nature of death and his cryptic comment that "[o]nly a God can save us now." For Edwards, such an expression was beneath contempt.

Edwards also wrote a biting critique of reincarnation, *Reincarnation: A Critical Examination* (1996). The volume he coedited with Arthur Pap, *A Modern Introduction to Philosophy*, was one of the most influential textbooks ever published in the field, and contained copious selections from such unbelievers as Paul Rée, John Stuart MILL, Clarence DARROW, Bertrand Russell, David Hume, Ernest NAGEL, and A. J. AYER, as well as Edwards's own insightful introductions and annotations. Never one to hide his own unbelief, Edwards often commented that his two main goals were to demolish the influence of Heidegger and keep alive the memory of Wilhelm REICH, the much-reviled psychoanalyst whose critiques of religion Edwards felt remained valid. Edwards's final book, *God and the Philosophers* (2007), a summation of the views of all the major Western philosophers on the subject of the deity, was published posthumously.

BIBLIOGRAPHY

Edwards, Paul. *Heidegger's Confusions*. Amherst, NY: Prometheus Books, 2004.
———. *Reincarnation: A Critical Examination*. Amherst, NY: Prometheus Books, 1996.
Edwards, Paul, and Arthur Pap, eds. *A Modern Introduction to Philosophy*, 3rd ed. New York: Free Press, 1973.

TIMOTHY J. MADIGAN

ELIOT, GEORGE. See EVANS, Marian.

EMERSON, RALPH WALDO (1803–1882), American author. Though Ralph Waldo Emerson no longer commands the Olympian deference accorded to him in the nineteenth century, some of his essays, such as "Nature," "Self-Reliance," "The American Scholar," and "Divinity School Address," remain popular in American classrooms. Even in circles where his transcendentalism is deprecated, he is sometimes hailed as a prophet of democratic idealism and individual autonomy. Because he insisted that institutional precepts be subordinated to the dictates of the "inner light," he can still ruffle guardians of tradition. In his day, he antagonized the orthodox clergy by denying the authority of biblical revelation and the efficacy of the Lord's Supper.

His Transcendentalism. Emerson believed true knowledge derives from intuitive flashes that transcend reason, logic, and sensation. At the heart of reality, he descried a friendly spirit, the Over-Soul, effusing benign ministrations to all sentient beings. The Over-Soul revealed to Emerson propositions he held dear: All division is mere appearance, God is omnipresent, the moral sense is innate and universal, evil is illusory, and truth will prevail.

Critique. Numerous seers, East and West, have registered their conviction that whatever the appearances, all is well. So long as seers do not try to validate their beliefs discursively, they do not invite criticism. But when they seek to persuade the world that their beliefs harmonize with external fact, their statements are liable to the rules of evidence.

Although Emerson maintained that ultimate reality lies beyond demonstration and verbal formulation, his rhetorical deeds belied the claim. In essays and letters, he habitually sought to demonstrate as well as provoke, exhort, and cajole. In the process he raided the arsenal of polemic device. He illustrated, exemplified, analogized, defined, classified, compared, and contrasted. He drew conclusions from premises, sought premises to support conclusions, and inferred causes from effects and effects from causes. When evidence to support his beliefs was available, he clasped it. When reason served, he embraced it. When evidence and reason palled, he tossed them into the trash bin of the lowly Understanding and appealed to Intuition, a higher mode of apprehension. He then adopted the venerable mystic precept that whatever one strongly feels must be cosmic truth: "Speak your latent conviction and it shall be the universal sense."

Emerson believed in a universal language of hearts: "To believe your own thought, to believe that what is true for you in your private heart is true for all men is genius." Had he eavesdropped on the hearts of Adolf Hitler, Joseph Stalin, Pol Pot, Ted Bundy, and kindred monsters, he might have qualified his belief—or at least had his hearing checked.

"The prized reality," wrote Emerson, "the Law, is apprehended, now and then, for a serene and profound moment amidst the hubhub of cares and works which have no direct bearing on it—is then lost for months or years, and again found for an interval to be lost again. In fifty years we may have half a dozen reasonable hours." Had Emerson recurred to impartial analysis, he might have suspected the "reasonable hours" were psychological aberrations, not revelations of eternal law.

BIBLIOGRAPHY

Allen, Gay Wilson. *Waldo Emerson: A Biography*. New York: Viking, 1981.
Michael, John. *Emerson and Skepticism: The Cipher of the World*. Baltimore, MD: Johns Hopkins University Press, 1988.
Miller, Perry. "From Edwards to Emerson." *New England Quarterly* 13 (1940).
Packer, B. L. *Emerson's Fall*. New York: Oxford University Press, 1979.
Sloan, Gary. "Emerson's Cosmic Sophistries." *RE:AL: The Journal of Liberal Arts* 25, no. 1 (2000).
van Leer, David. *Emerson's Epistemology: The Argument of the Essays*. Cambridge: Cambridge University Press, 1986.

GARY SLOAN

EMPIRICUS, SEXTUS (3rd century CE), Greek skeptical philosopher. Almost nothing is known about this late second- and early third-century CE physician and chronicler of ancient Greek SKEPTICISM. We do possess, however, his *Outlines of Pyrrhonism* (in three books) and his *Against the Mathematicians* (in eleven books). The first book of the former work sets out the basic Pyrrhonian position and way of life. It also explains the various skeptical strategies used against dogmatic assertions and distinguishes Pyrrhonism from other philosophical schools. The last two books of the work offer particular skeptical refutations of dogmatic positions in logic, physics, and ethics. The first six books of *Against the Mathematicians* examine the skeptical approach to the six arts of grammar, rhetoric, geometry, arithmetic, astronomy, and music. The remaining books contain a detailed examination of the material covered in *Outlines*.

The importance skeptics like Sextus placed on the refutation of dogmatic assertions about god or the gods is evident at the beginning of book nine of *Against the Mathematicians*. There Sextus reasons that dogmatists generally think that philosophy aims to cultivate wisdom of divine and human matters. If, however, it can be shown that the arguments for the existence of divine things are no more conclusive than the arguments against them, then it will have been shown that philosophy is no such thing.

Sextus sharply distinguishes the skeptical position from ATHEISM, which he thought was merely another form of dogmatism. The skeptic wants to show that no argument for the existence of a god or gods has any more probative force than its opposite. Recognizing this, one can thus eliminate from one's life all anxiety about "divine matters" and assume a benign attitude toward religious practices. With the rejection of arguments for the existence of gods, dogmatic assertions about such things as divine providence should come to an end since, as Sextus reasons, we can hardly know anything about the nature of the gods if we do not know of their existence.

Among the arguments that dogmatists use to establish the existence of the gods are (1) the argument based on universal agreement, (2) a design argument, (3) a reductio ad absurdum of the position that denies the existence of the gods, and (4) arguments specifically designed to refute atheist arguments.

In his *Outlines*, Sextus recounts the following skeptical argument: If we know of the existence of the gods, this is either because their existence is self-evident or not. It cannot be self-evident, since there is no agreement on this among people. If the gods' existence is nonevident, then *that* is known either on the basis of something self-evident or on the basis of something nonevident. In the former case, their existence would again be self-evident. In the latter, there would be an infinite regress of nonevident reasons adduced, none of which are conclusive without a self-evident foundation. Hence, no argument for the existence of the gods is conclusive; nor is any argument purporting to conclude the opposite. The only rational position to take regarding the gods is the suspension of belief. Although Sextus does not call this

position "AGNOSTICISM" (a modern term), it can be characterized as such.

As for the providence of the gods, Sextus reasons that either the gods are provident of everything or only of some things. If the gods are provident of everything, then either evil would not exist or the gods, supposed to be good, will themselves be responsible for it. If the gods are provident only of some things, then the gods are, counter to the view of theists, either weak or indifferent to the things over which they are not provident. In that case, they are malign. Hence, there is no reason to believe that even if the gods *did* exist, they would be provident; and with the rejection of providence goes fear of divine retribution.

BIBLIOGRAPHY

Barnes, Jonathan. *The Toils of Scepticism.* Cambridge: Cambridge University Press, 1990.
Burnyeat, Myles, ed. *The Skeptical Tradition.* Berkeley and Los Angeles: University of California Press, 1983.
Hallie, Philip, ed. *Sextus Empiricus. Selections from the Major Writings on Scepticism, Man, and God.* Indianapolis, IN: Hackett, 1985.
Hankinson, R. J. *The Skeptics.* London: Routledge, 1995.

LLOYD P. GERSON

ENCYCLOPÉDIE, L', AND UNBELIEF. A monumental and often heretical reference work, the *Encyclopédie, ou Dictionnaire raisonné des Sciences, des Arts et des Métiers* was published in Paris over some thirty years between 1751 and 1780. Almost from the outset, it met with vigorous opposition; its adversaries, both secular and ecclesiastical, succeeded for a time in preventing its publication, but the work eventually triumphed, not least of all because of the determination and commitment of its editor in chief, Denis DIDEROT. The *Encyclopédie* encountered hostility for many reasons, from its criticism of Cartesian philosophy (see DESCARTES, RENÉ) to its alleged plagiarism of the plates illustrating workshops and trades, as well as for alleged inaccuracies in articles dealing with a host of obscure and arcane subjects.

In looking at the role of religion in the *Encyclopédie*, two points should be noted. The first is that the work brought together dozens of contributors representing many shades of opinion on religion as on other matters, so that it is futile to seek any consistency of outlook even in the articles dealing with the same subject area. While a strong current of religious skepticism can often be discerned, religious belief per se was by no means excluded from the work. For one thing, it contained many articles written by pious authors who dealt in a wholly orthodox and unexceptionable way with aspects of Christian and Catholic doctrine. For another, several of the contributors might collectively be described as deists of one sort or another (see DEISM), that is, they believed in a divinity of some kind, usually envisaged as a supervisory entity whose intervention in human affairs was limited to ensuring that the laws of nature operated as they should.

The second point is that the editors used a system of cross-references (or *renvois*) to lead readers from innocuous articles to ones that were far more critical of the status quo, especially in political and religious matters. Consequently, those pursuing a particular train of thought or a series of intricate connections often had a choice of paths before them, and might not all reach the same destination. In this way, the editors managed to conceal the more audacious contributions behind a fig leaf of respectability, and perhaps threw at least some pursuers off the scent.

Yet even if the contributors were not united in their beliefs, and even if various readings of the articles on religion and other contentious matters were possible, one can discern in the *Encyclopédie* a fundamentally skeptical and often hostile attitude toward religion in general, and toward Catholicism in particular. In many respects, the presentation and discussion of religious questions exhibit the characteristics to be found in other areas of the work as well: an avowedly rational outlook, a wide knowledge of history, and a strong dislike of repressive authoritarianism.

The rational approach was apparent from the first volume, where the editors led the way; here, as in other articles, their ostensibly emollient tone scarcely disguised their skepticism. In the "Preliminary Discourse" (1751), Diderot's then coeditor, D'Alembert, claimed that Christianity had nothing to fear from rational investigation, for its truth was guaranteed by God. However ridiculous a religion might be, philosophers merely pointed out its absurdities; unlike priests, they did not force others to accept their point of view. Diderot (who in reality was more troubled by spiritual questions than he sometimes affected to be), likewise tried to pretend that he wanted to reconcile doctrine with reason. In his article "Adorer" (1751) he slyly promoted the rational over the spiritual when he wrote: "The way in which we worship the true God must never forsake reason, because God is the author of reason, and he wishes us to use it even when we judge what we should or should not do with regard to Him." This rational approach to religion emerged not simply as a matter of abstract principle, but of comparative sociology as well. If one attitude in particular characterized the work of the more overtly "philosophical" contributors, it was their awareness of the wide variations between human societies, and the concomitant range of religious doctrines attested by history. For this reason, many of them saw the story of Christianity and of the Catholic Church not as proof of divine intervention in human affairs, but simply as another example of a religious sect, of which many could be found through the ages. This relativist view led essentially to two consequences.

The first was that such authors denied any transcendent status to Christianity—or indeed to Mohammedanism (Islam), Hinduism, or any other creed—and hence they rejected entirely the church's claim to supreme spiritual authority. Nor was this approach surprising in the mid-eighteenth century. The doctrinal and historical claims made on biblical authority had been subjected for decades to rational, scholarly analysis along the lines pioneered by such notable figures as Richard Simon and Baruch SPINOZA, and had been found wanting. The *Encyclopédie* article "Bible" (1752) duly discussed in respectful tones and with much erudite detail the many conflicting versions of that work which had been modified or rejected over the centuries, while taking care to point out that it was nonetheless "inspired by the Holy Spirit."

In addition, literary figures like VOLTAIRE had long made good use of historical sources to argue that religions owed their power chiefly to their ability to exploit the credulity of the people. An oblique expression of this view can be seen in Diderot's article "Agnus Scythicus" (1751). This describes an obscure plant for which noted authorities had repeatedly vouched, but which turned out to be nonexistent. Using this example, Diderot drew more general conclusions as to the dangers of accepting authority without question, and explicitly warned against believing in unspecified "superstitions" allegedly based on facts. Again, if instances of priestly (mis)conduct discussed in the *Encyclopédie* (in articles such as "Consécration" in 1753) prudently referred to the distant past or to primitive societies, they were worded in ways that invited comparisons with the priesthood of contemporary France. By these and other means, therefore, some of the major contributors to the *Encyclopédie* set before the public the results of sustained scholarly investigation relating directly or indirectly to belief, allowing readers to infer the insubstantial basis for the claims made by religion in general and, by implication, the Catholic Church in particular.

The second consequence of relativism was that, having challenged the historical justification for the church's power in a number of important respects, some contributors argued that believers and unbelievers alike should allow those who did not share their views to live peacefully without interference. This extract from the article "Fanatisme" (1756) by Deleyre sums up these aspects of the work: "Punish if you will the libertines who attack religion only because they cannot bear to submit to a yoke of any kind. Prosecute them as enemies of good order and of society; but pity those who, to their regret, are not believers. Is their lack of faith in itself not already enough to bear, without their being insulted and hounded as well?"

Although a number of contributors positively advocated toleration in spiritual matters, others made the same point by emphasizing rather the harm fanaticism could cause. They dwelled at length on the havoc the wars of religion had wrought in France in the sixteenth century; they also emphasized the damage done to the country's economy by the expulsion of the Huguenots following the repeal in 1685 of the Edict of Nantes, which had put an end to those wars. Not least, they were keenly aware that, in contrast to France, the English did not allow religion to be all-powerful in the state; indeed, they knew that even if there were limits to her toleration, England's willingness to put commerce before creed had helped her to prosper, as Voltaire had so enthusiastically described in his *Letters concerning the English Nation* (1733).

Sentiments such as these were discernible in many articles, and at an early stage the authorities became suspicious of the *Encyclopédie*'s true intentions. Even some less outspoken contributions were anathema to a church whose place at the very center of French religious and political life was founded on its assertion that it alone possessed and taught the truth; any challenge to its authority was HERESY, and heresy must be extirpated by any means necessary. RATIONALISM, relativism, and toleration were ideas that threatened its very foundations, and those advocating such notions must, it urged, be punished severely.

All these entirely predictable reactions greeted the *Encyclopédie* as each new volume appeared, and they became increasingly vehement as its enemies leapt furiously upon every new outrage. The *Encyclopédie*'s skeptical attitude toward religion, more than anything else, accounts for the authorities' decision in 1759 to revoke its *privilege*, which allowed it to be published with official blessing. Thereafter, the *Encyclopédie* disappeared from public view for some years, although work on it continued clandestinely, with the connivance of the censor's office. While its enemies were by no means quiescent, growing demand for the *Encyclopédie* gradually rendered opposition ineffectual. The remaining volumes appeared, largely unimpeded, between 1765 and 1772; an index was added in 1780.

Suspecting that they had by this time effectively won the battle, some contributors now took matters to their logical conclusion, and denied with impunity that any notion of God was tenable. Perhaps the most forthright member of this group was the notoriously atheistic Jacques-André Naigeon, who wrote in "Unitaires" (1765): "[I]f we judge all religious doctrines in the court of reason, we thereby take a great step towards deism; but, what is more regrettable still, is that deism itself, whatever its apologists may say, is an inconsistent religion, and in trying to hold to it, we wander about without knowing where we are, and anchor ourselves in shifting sands."

As well as summarizing the state of human knowledge up to the middle of the eighteenth century, the *Encyclopédie* exhibits all the major conflicts that define the Enlightenment (ENLIGHTENMENT, THE, AND UNBELIEF): rationalism versus fanaticism; ATHEISM versus belief; informed, critical judgement versus dogma; and intellectual freedom versus intellectual stasis. Not all its contributors shared the same attitude toward religion, and many

were mutually antagonistic. Yet it proved possible to accommodate them all within this one work, thereby furnishing an example of the tolerance that the *Encyclopédie* so powerfully advocated and its enemies so deeply loathed.

DAVID ADAMS

ENGLISH LITERATURE, UNBELIEF IN. Early hints of unbelief may be found in the stoicism of Anglo-Saxon writing and the individualism and ANTICLERICALISM of some medieval writing. However, there is no clear unbelief until the Renaissance, in particular the towering HUMANISM of William Shakespeare (see SHAKESPEARE, RELIGIOUS SKEPTICISM IN), the atheistic antireligion of the playwright Christopher Marlowe, and the skepticism of Walter Raleigh. There was greater devoutness in the metaphysical poets and sermons of the seventeenth century, until Restoration plays and poetry ushered in a greater secular freedom of expression. The DEISM of the eighteenth century was reflected in the ordered poetry of Alexander Pope and the piety of novelists such as Henry Fielding and Samuel Richardson.

At the end of the eighteenth century, piety began to give way, the influence of science and philosophy began to play its part, and specifically unbelieving literature began to be written—particularly by the poets Percy Bysshe SHELLEY and Lord BYRON. The nineteenth century was the age of doubt, especially in the English novel, where unbelief was apparent in the major novelists George Eliot (see EVANS, MARIAN) and Thomas Hardy.

Renaissance and Restoration. Anglo-Saxon and Old English writings were written first with pagan influence and then in a largely Christian context. By the time of Geoffrey Chaucer there was greater human individuation, influence from the early European renaissance, and anticlerical tendencies (foreshadowing the Reformation). Chaucer was influenced by Boethius and translated the latter's *The Consolation of Philosophy*; Boethius was probably a Christian but was imbued with classical writings. *The Canterbury Tales* depicts pilgrim travelers telling stories as they move on. There was ribald humor in the Miller's Tale, and indication of sexual enjoyment in the Wife of Bath's account of her five husbands. Religious figures can tell tales of a greedy friar or of the sale of indulgences (religious trinkets)—the kind of behavior that was to lead to the Reformation. However, a learned and charitable parson provides balance.

Shakespeare was a dramatist who is one of the greatest writers in world literature. He has been described in the title of a critical work by Harold Bloom, *Shakespeare: The Invention of the Human*. It is hard to assess his personal views: he seemed to embrace the multifaceted nature of his numerous characters. He has been described as a Catholic or an agnostic—but the evidence is poor. He certainly read John Florio's translation of the fine and skeptical essayist Michel de MONTAIGNE. There is no sense of the divine in the plays, more a sense of the astonishing variety of human beings: "What a piece of work is a man! How noble in reason!" (*Hamlet*). Shakespeare is omnivorous in his working of human experience—all can claim him for their own. In the tragedies there are flaws or a sense of emptiness ("[A life] is a tale/Told by an idiot, full of sound and fury/Signifying nothing," *Macbeth*), of the cruelty of the gods (*King Lear*), but a culminating feeling that "ripeness is all."

Marlowe was a man of violence, a homosexual, a spy, and a superb dramatist. He was accused of being an atheist in the report of a government spy, suggesting that he "persuades men to ATHEISM willing them not to be afeard of bugbears and hobgoblins." A further allegation accused him of saying that "Christ was a bastard and his mother dishonest" and that "St. John the Evangelist was a bedfellow to Christ and leaned always to his bosome, that he used him as the sinners of Sodome." It is impossible to know the accuracy of these accusations, since they may have been part of an attempt to vilify him—but his plays suggest interest in both irreligion and homosexuality. Atheism during this period may have meant a belief that God played no part in human lives, rather than complete disbelief in a deity. Nevertheless there was fear that "the School of Epicure and the Atheists, is mightily increased in these days."

In Marlowe's first play, in two parts, *Tamburlaine the Great*, the mighty conqueror dies peacefully in his bed and is not brought low by his destruction as a Christian morality tale would have done. Two of his most famous lines come in *The Jew of Malta*:

I count religion but a childish toy
And hold there is no sin but ignorance,

The Massacre of Paris depicts the horrors of the conflict between religions and partakes both of his interest in violence and his presumed dislike of religion. His most famous play, *Dr. Faustus*, has the spiraling human desire to contain and control all, but a Christian conclusion with the overreacher ending in hell.

Raleigh, the explorer and poet, was accused of atheism—but the accusation may have been an attempt to discredit him. However, his essay "The Skeptick" summarizes the views of Sextus EMPIRICUS. Accusations and counteraccusations abounded in this period, suggesting that at the very least the ideas and writings played with ideas of unbelief.

The subsequent period of metaphysical poets and Miltonic epics shows a religious tenor in the writings, which was to some extent broken with the restoration to the throne of Charles II after the civil war and rule of Oliver Cromwell. Restoration comedy is renowned for its wit and bawdiness, and is entirely secular in nature.

The playwright and novelist Aphra Behn was probably the first British woman to earn her living by her writing. She wrote plays with all the wit and adventure of her colleagues. Her novel *Oroonoko, or the History of the Royal Slave* is based on her visit to Surinam, and contrasts the natural honor of the native Oroonoko with the faithlessness of the white Christians. The suggestion is that in this non-Christian country "religion would here but destroy that tranquillity they possess by ignorance."

A poet of the period, John Wilmot, Earl of Rochester, was an irreligious libertine. His poems were highly erotic and satiric. For instance his view of humanity was expressed:

Bless me! thought I, what thing is man, that thus
In all his shapes, he is ridiculous.

Wilmot did a poetic translation of some of the writings of LUCRETIUS. He returned to Christianity in the final months of his life.

In the eighteenth century, although it was said by Pope that "the proper study of mankind is man" and a civil urbanity characterized literature, the structure of thought was largely Christian. The development of the novel by Richardson and Fielding saw a Christian moralism struggling with moving accounts of amorous struggle. The influence of the Enlightenment (see ENLIGHTENMENT, UNBELIEF DURING THE) was felt more with the philosopher David HUME and the historian Edward GIBBON (see UNITED KINGDOM, UNBELIEF IN).

Toward the end of the century a few minor novelists wrote in a more rationalist style (see RATIONALISM). Thomas Holcroft was a radical and playwright who thought that "philosophy is a true enemy to religion" and that "benevolence and morality" were the essence of religion. *Anna St. Ives* (1792) puts forward a vision of human happiness and depicts a conflict between Anna and Frank, who follow "the claims of truth and reason," and the villainous Clifton who relies on authority and violence.

William GODWIN (1756–1836) was married to Mary WOLLSTONECRAFT, who died in giving birth to Mary Godwin, who was to marry Shelley. Godwin's anarchist views were expressed in *Enquiry concerning Political Justice* (1793); his best known novel was *The Adventures of Caleb Williams* (1794), in which Caleb's contact with an aristocrat leads him to believe in universal morals and integrity apart from religion.

Romantics and Victorians. The first generation of romantic poets, particularly Wordsworth and Coleridge, adhered to a form of Christianity, but the second generation, namely, Shelley, Byron, and Keats, were atheists or agnostics.

Percy Bysshe Shelley was expelled from Oxford for publishing a pamphlet entitled *The Necessity of Atheism* (1811). His conflict with his father, a conventional Whig MP, led to the indignation which he felt toward God: "Oh! I burn with impatience for the moment of Xtianity's dissolution." He believed that God cannot be deduced from reason. His atheistic views were enlarged in a note to his long poem *Queen Mab*, where he qualified his atheism with the view that the "hypothesis of a pervading Spirit coeternal with the universe remains unshaken." In this early poem he wrote of "the avenging God" as a "prototype of human misrule." His religious unorthodoxy was allied with a radical view of society—and a sympathy with working-class freethinkers and agitators. His poem *The Mask of Anarchy* presents a bitter, scathing view of the ruling class on the occasion of the Peterloo Massacre (an 1819 demonstration by radicals in favor of Parliamentary reform which was fired upon, resulting in several deaths). He modified the references to atheism, incest, revolution, and oppression in rewriting *Laon and Cynthia* as *The Revolt of Islam*. His works were published in pirated editions by working-class printers. His reputation as a radical in politics and religion was ironed out in the nineteenth century to leave a poet of prettiness, but his full reputation has been revived in the twentieth century.

His friend George Gordon, Lord Byron, was more of a skeptic than Shelley, finding that his beliefs wavered and constantly returned to the point of "not knowing." He scandalized upper-class Britain by his affair with his half sister Augusta and left England. His unfinished long poem *Don Juan* and his play *Cain* also shocked the literary world. *Don Juan* was at first condemned as "a filthy and impious poem," but its profuse seductions and satire slowly acquired an audience as it was published over the years. In the poetic drama *Cain: A Mystery,* Cain rages against his treatment by God and kills his brother Abel for sacrificing to God. The work was threatened with prosecution.

John Keats did not rage. His devotion to beauty, such as that of the Grecian urn and the richness of autumn, and his narrative sensitivity somehow made God irrelevant. Yet he was more realistic about human behavior than other romantics. He apparently refused religious assistance as he approached death from tuberculosis.

It was in the novel that the Victorian debate about religious belief was especially developed. The ever-popular Charles Dickens imbued his novels with a sentimental religiosity, despite some satirical portraits of men of the cloth, but the earnest AGNOSTICISM of George Eliot ran right through her fine novels.

George Eliot was a pen name for Marian EVANS. She went through an intense evangelical phase in her youth, but after acquaintance with the Unitarians Charles Bray and Caroline Hennell (see UNITARIANISM TO 1961) began to question her faith. She told her father she could no longer attend church regularly, which caused a rift resolved only by her agreement to attend and at the same time think what she wanted. She began to move in intellectual circles and translated D. F. STRAUSS's *Leben Jesu* (Life of Jesus), a work that undermined the theology of Jesus with a historical and skeptical approach. Later she translated Ludwig FEUERBACH's *The Essence of Christianity*, which gave a naturalistic account of

Christianity. She was effectively the editor of the leading *Westminster Review*.

Yet it is as a novelist that she is primarily remembered, her two most substantial works being *Middlemarch* and *Daniel Deronda*. *Middlemarch* portrays the complete community of a provincial town. The heroine, Dorothea Brooke, yearns for meaning in her life—meaning without traditional religious views. Two Christian figures are deeply flawed—Casaubon, who cannot complete his mighty work on mythology; and Bulstrode, a nonconformist hypocrite. The scientifically inclined Dr. Lydgate is portrayed more sympathetically. *Daniel Deronda* examines the Jewish religion, giving some support to the development of Zionism. Eliot believed that art should enhance human sympathies and had a duty to tell the truth about human nature and society.

Some lesser novelists also explored religious doubt. J. A. Froude, who became a very successful historian, wrote *The Nemesis of Faith* (1849) to depict those of high intellectual stature departing from religious faith. (The book was burned on a college fire, a disapprobation which only gave it more publicity. Froude's father was an archdeacon—one of the many active or renowned religious men who spawned a freethinking child.) The despairing author and apostate typically retained strong ethical principles. This was a common theme in life and literature and, for example, the protagonist of Mrs. Humphry Ward's *Robert Elsmere* also demonstrated strong ethical principles in working among the poor of the East End of London.

The poets of the period were less engaged with this debate, but Tennyson and Browning alluded to religious doubt, Tennyson in his *In Memoriam*, a lament for the loss of his friend Hallam, and Browning in poems such as *Bishop Blougram's Apology,* a monologue depicting an argument between the bishop and an unbeliever. Algernon Charles SWINBURNE, a disciple of Sade in theory and practice, allowed irreligion to streak through his poetry. Arthur Hugh CLOUGH was the very apogee of sincere doubt.

More to the heart of unbelieving Victorian poetry were the works of Matthew ARNOLD and James Thomson. Thomson was a secularist and friend of the atheist campaigner Charles BRADLAUGH. Thomson's poetical masterpiece is *City of Dreadful Night*, the portrait of a godless city of darkness, poverty, hopelessness, and depression. Matthew Arnold, a doubter who doubted even his own doubt, bequeathed some of the most famous lines on the decline of religion in *Dover Beach*: He described the Sea of Faith and its "Melancholy, long, withdrawing roar . . ."

A novelist who was also a poet was Thomas Hardy. There is no Christian comfort for the fated characters of his novels. In *Jude the Obscure* (1895) the central character, who was trying to study theology, takes all his books into the garden and burns them, a scene that shocked readers even at the end of the Victorian era.

Some of Hardy's poems have a distinctly anti-Christian tendency: In *The Wood Fire*, soldiers plan to make a fire of what has been the cross on which Jesus was crucified; in another he writes of *God's Funeral*.

Walter Pater was an art critic and novelist who knew Mrs. Humphrey Ward and Swinburne. He turned from his original plan of being ordained. He became well known for his *Studies in the History of the Renaissance* (1873), which was among those works of the time re-examining the Renaissance for its human and aesthetic brilliance. His novel *Marius the Epicurean* (1885) depicts a fictional character at the period of Marcus Aurelius and is influenced by the latter's stoic philosophy (see STOICISM). He influenced Oscar Wilde, whose brilliant drama overshadowed his serious work, *The Soul of Man under Socialism* (1891), written under the influence of George Bernard SHAW. Shaw was one of the major playwrights of the twentieth century, who rejected orthodox religious belief in favor of a belief in "the life force."

William Morris also broke from Christianity and developed his own version of socialism (see SOCIALISM AND UNBELIEF) that posited a value for all in the community and the importance of works of art for their function in daily life. His utopian novel *News from Nowhere* (1891) shows London and its environs turned into a socialist paradise. Another work of fantasy, *Erewhon* (1873), was composed by Samuel BUTLER, a person whose clerical family's intention that he pursue a life in the church was frustrated by Butler's unorthodox intellectual development. The Erewhonians appear to have little or no religious belief; academe is dominated by the Colleges of Unreason and ethics are based on the behavior of the "true gentlemen." *The Way of All Flesh* (published posthumously in 1903) satirizes Victorian religious practices more sharply. Butler was fascinated by Charles DARWIN's theory of evolution (see EVOLUTION AND UNBELIEF), but preferred an alternative Lamarckian explanation allowing for the hereditary transmission of acquired characteristics.

George Meredith was a nonbelieving Victorian novelist and poet who believed in the importance of rationality. Although he is now out of fashion as a novelist, two of his novels contain fine portraits of men and women in the search for a moral understanding of their lives and the world around. *The Ordeal of Richard Feverel* (1859) recounts the education of the eponymous hero as a "scientific Humanist" who finds life and love in the power of nature. *The Egoist* (1879) is "a combination of wit and humanity." Beyond the brittle ego there is a belief in the uniting of reason and instinct. Meredith's freethinking is demonstrated in his letter to the editor of the *FREETHINKER*, G. W. FOOTE, whose work he called "the best of causes."

The Twentieth Century. H. G. WELLS spanned the nineteenth and twentieth centuries, being essentially a scientist turned novelist and social commentator. Such a development tends to lead to rationalism. From lowly beginnings he was eventually educated at the Normal School of Science (London), where he came under the influence of T. H. HUXLEY.

A considerable amount of self-education took place with his reading of VOLTAIRE, Jonathan Swift, Thomas PAINE, and Gibbon. His early works were science fiction—a genre that enabled him to give the reader excitement and social comment at the same time. He wrote of one character's "innate skepticism"—a perspective that he maintained himself, occasionally giving way to vague theism.

His greatest novel was *Tono-Bungay*—a "condition of England" novel, which surveyed an entrepreneur's rise in English life by the sale of a patent medicine with the aid of advertising. Wells laced his novels with adventure and humor, which accounted for their success—but scientific and socialist ideas lay underneath.

Wells also wrote books popularizing knowledge. Two early volume's of the Thinker's Library published by the RATIONALIST PRESS ASSOCIATION were *First and Last Things* (1909) and *A Short History of the World* (1922). He became an honorary associate of the RPA in 1929. He offered a late work, *Mind at the End of Its Tether* (1945), to the RPA for publication—but it was not accepted, publisher C. A. WATTS being unhappy with its pessimism, a constant strand of Wells's thought, exacerbated by the World War II and his own declining health. Atheism and optimism need not go hand in hand.

Arnold Bennett, a chronicler in fiction of provincial life, knew Wells and was also an honorary associate of the RPA.

E. M. Forster, one of the most distinguished novelists of the twentieth century, was a certain unbeliever, who in later life had contact with humanist organizations such the Cambridge Humanist Society, the BRITISH HUMANIST ASSOCIATION, and the RPA.

His six novels have become classics, studied and filmed. *Howards End* (1910) is comparable to *Tono-Bungay* in attempting to exemplify the condition of England through characters and milieu. It pleads for people to "only connect"—between the world of heart and relationships and the milieu of business and finance. *A Passage to India* (1924) aims to break through colonial insensitivity to the complex world of the Indian people and Indian civilization.

In his later life Forster defended free speech and tolerance and in a famous essay, "What I Believe" (1938), he wrote: "I do not believe in belief . . . tolerance, good temper and sympathy—they are what matters really. . . . My law givers are ERASMUS and Montaigne. . . . My motto is 'Lord I disbelieve . . . help thou my unbelief.'"

Virginia Woolf, like Forster, embedded her ideas in her sensitive novels. Her father was Leslie STEPHEN, who wrote on agnosticism. She was a member of the Bloomsbury group (an extended artistic coterie of family and friends based in that part of London) and suffered from mental illness during many parts of her life, leading eventually to suicide.

Her novels show characters searching for meaning, some of whom are explicitly atheistic. In *Mrs. Dalloway*, "Clarissa Dalloway was 'one of the most thoroughgoing skeptics he [her husband] had ever met'; nevertheless she found life could be bleak and unhappy and needed to alleviate distress by decorating 'the dungeons with flowers and air-cushions.'" Later she thinks "love and religion! . . . how detestable, how detestable they are." Woolf uses a stream of consciousness technique in her later work and the idea of an epiphany—an ecstatic moment of all-pervading meaning. A character in *The Lighthouse*, on finishing a painting, declares, "Yes, I have had my vision"—but a secular vision.

James Joyce likewise uses stream of consciousness and the epiphany in a more original way. His autobiographical *Portrait of the Artist as a Young Man* (1914–16) shows the young man moving away from Irish nationalism, the Catholic Church, and his family. The hellfire sermon of Father Arnall gives an appalling picture of hell likely to deter people from belief in Christian dogmas. His masterpiece, *Ulysses* (1922), ranges over the day and life of a group of Dubliners in a totally secular vision of the richness and variety of life.

Later twentieth-century novelists demonstrate how unbelief had become the mainstream for English literature. This is demonstrated in, for instance, the works of George ORWELL, Aldous Huxley, C. P. Snow, Margaret Drabble, Iris Murdoch, Maureen Duffy, Angus Wilson, Brian Moore, and the plays of Arnold Wesker and Harold Pinter, as well as the plays and novels of Samuel Beckett.

The epitaph for this survey could be Forster's words. "Lord I Believe—Help thou my unbelief."

BIBLIOGRAPHY

Allen, Don Cameron. *Doubt's Boundless Sea: Skepticism and Faith in the Renaissance*. Baltimore, MD: John Hopkins University Press, 1964.

Bradbury, Malcolm. *The Modern World: Ten Great Writers*. London: Secker & Warburg, 1988.

Cockshut, A. O. G. *The Unbelievers: English Agnostic Thought, 1840–1890*. London: Collins, 1964.

Faulkner, Peter. *Humanism in the English Novel*. London: Elek/Pemberton, 1975.

Forster, E. M. *What I Believe and Other Essays*. Edited by Nicolas Walter. London: G. W. Foote, 1999.

JIM HERRICK

ENLIGHTENMENT, UNBELIEF DURING THE. Enlightenment unbelief was—or appears to have been—overwhelmingly deistic. Since DEISM is examined elsewhere in this work, I shall be concerned here with varieties of unbelief during the Enlightenment other than deism: that is, with the outright denial of the existence of God and of personal immortality. Complete unbelievers such as Paul Henri HOLBACH accepted the deistic critique of revealed religion, but rejected the two articles of natural religion that deists still retained, namely, God and an afterlife. Although not all those who denied the existence of an afterlife—the mortalists—were atheists, the history of ATHEISM and that of mortalism are closely connected.

Avowed atheism and mortalism emerged late in the Enlightenment—in 1770 on the continent and 1782 in Britain. Their comparative infancy has been obscured by, for instance, the tendency of scholars to confuse accusations of atheism and mortalism with professions of the same. Historians have assumed that with so much polemical smoke there must have been some atheistic fire. The Boyle lectures are prominent among the hundreds of eighteenth-century treatises written against atheists, and the *Guardian* essay of June 23, 1713, which castigates certain unnamed "dull and phlegmatic [men who] prefer the thought of annihilation . . . [and] endeavour to persuade mankind to [their] disbelief," is characteristic of the popular literature against mortalists.

Another way in which the smoke of religious apologists has tended to invent a history of atheism is that in order to cast doubts on the originality of their opponents, apologists presented even the most novel attacks on religion as rather old-fashioned. But there is nothing old-fashioned about professed atheism. The Enlightenment does show us something new. For the first time, a handful of people openly denied the existence of God and regarded themselves as atheists. To bring into focus this unprecedented event in the history of ideas and of unbelief, we must distinguish (1) avowed published atheism from (2) avowed posthumously published atheism from (3) reports of covert atheists from (4) covert implied atheism from (5) positions that tended toward atheism or could be exploited by atheists. Most historians have obscured the genesis of atheism in the Enlightenment in that they have conflated these different classes, especially (1) and (5); and the history of mortalism has fared similarly.

Avowed Published Atheism. Since this is the most straightforward type of atheism, it should provide the focus for a historical study. If a published work contains a denial of the existence of God—particularly if it is argued—or a profession of atheism, then it can be considered a work of atheism and the author regarded as an atheist. Of course, we assume in such cases that the author is using such key terms as *God*, *wisdom*, and *matter* in a literal and normal way, and that he is not, for example, speaking ironically or idiosyncratically. By such a standard we must see Baron d'Holbach's *La Système de la Nature* (1770) as a model of straightforward atheism, even though its title page falsely states that it was written by Mirabaud and was printed in London (in fact, it was printed in Amsterdam). Not only does it contain the first published denials of the existence of God and (probably) of an afterlife, but it also extensively argues the case for total unbelief.

The *Système* has two parts: in the first part d'Holbach outlines his empirically grounded MATERIALISM and DETERMINISM, in chapter 13 rejecting immortality as "an illusion of the brain." The second part is overtly atheistic; in chapters 2 and 3 he critically examines the most formidable arguments for the existence of God, which, he says, "have their origin in the false principle that matter is not self-existent or able to move itself."

D'Holbach's defense of atheism is, however, based not solely on his belief that matter is a necessary, uncreated substance eternally in motion, or on his detailed criticism of arguments for the existence of God, such as that given by Samuel Clarke. He also tried to show that there is a conflict within the theologian's conception of God. Moving hopelessly between the incomprehensible immaterial God of the philosopher and the affecting but all-too-human God of the ordinary worshiper, the theologian united the "metaphysical God" of natural theology with the anthropomorphic God of revealed religion (see ANTHROPOMORPHISM AND RELIGION). In short: How can "an immutable deity . . . cause those continual changes in the world?" and "How shall we attribute anger to a being who has neither blood nor bile?" The God of the theist and of the deist "is nothing but a mere fiction." D'Holbach also argued that materialistic atheism, with its naturalistic ideals of man's happiness and his survival, provides the only solid foundation for morality and social prosperity.

In 1772 d'Holbach published the *Bon Sens*—a work deeply indebted to the *Testament* of Jean MESLIER—which gave popular expression to the former's atheism. Four years later d'Holbach developed the moral aspect of his atheism in *La Morale Universelle*. D'Holbach was assisted in these classic atheistic works by his friend Jacques-Andre Naigeon, the "monk of atheism," who wrote the preliminary discourse to the *Système*. Naigeon's own atheistic position in the *Philosophie Ancienne et Modern* (1791–94), although in general agreement with d'Holbach's, emphasizes the life sciences as against the physical sciences. Denis DIDEROT, the third and most famous member of the atheistic triumvirate, helped d'Holbach, too, especially with the *Système* and the *Bon Sens*. Diderot was well known as an atheist—Samuel Romilly described his conversation in 1781 as "ostentations of total unbelief"—yet his celebrated radical writings, such as *Le Rêve de D'Alembert*, were not only less explicit than those of his two colleagues but were published posthumously.

Perhaps the most shocking French atheist was the Marquis de SADE. In literary works such as *La Philosophie dans le boudoir* (1795) he argued not only for speculative but also for "practical" atheism (immoralism).

The first avowedly atheistic publication in Britain was *An Answer to Dr. Priestley's Letters to a Philosophical Unbeliever* (1782). This little-known book purports to be the work of two men. The editor, who signed himself William Hammon, is responsible for the advertisement,

the prefatory address, and a postscript containing a letter to Joseph Priestley. The body of the work is supposed to be by a friend of the editor. This unnamed friend has been identified as Matthew Turner, a Liverpool physician, anatomist, classical scholar, and friend and helper of Josiah Wedgwood. Turner popularized the use of ether for medical purposes and lectured at Warrington Academy, where his lectures first interested Joseph Priestley in chemistry. The atheism of the *Answer to Priestley* is influenced most by d'Holbach's *Système*, which Turner quotes at length, and by David HUME's *Dialogues concerning Natural Religion* and his essay "Of Miracles."

The material world, Turner and Hammon urged, should be considered not as contingent, but as eternal and sufficient to explain any order or design in the world. They also argued against the orthodox claim that morality and social order require a religious foundation. Whereas Turner is at his best when pressing the argument from evil (see EVIL, PROBLEM OF), Hammon's most interesting comments are on the difficulties of being an atheist. Like d'Holbach, Hammon was aware that the possibility of atheism is widely disputed; like d'Holbach, he firmly resisted this repressive tendency: "[A]s to the question of whether there is such an Existent Being as an atheist, to put that out of all manner of doubt, I do declare upon my honor that I am one." Hammon also rejected (although more tentatively than d'Holbach) a future life. For nearly thirty years, until Percy Bysshe SHELLEY's *Necessity of Atheism* (1811), the *Answer to Priestley* was the only English work of avowed atheism.

Clandestine Atheism. The abbé Jean Meslier stands beside d'Holbach as the second giant of atheism. At his death in 1729 Meslier left three copies of his massive atheistic *Mon Testament*. Although not printed in its entirety until 1861–64, more than a hundred clandestine manuscript copies of the *Testament* were circulating in Paris alone by the middle of the eighteenth century, or so claimed VOLTAIRE, who in 1762 published a deistic *Extrait* of it. In some respects Meslier's achievement is even more extraordinary than that of d'Holbach. Not only did d'Holbach make extensive use of Meslier's work for *Bon Sens,* but Meslier seems to have worked out his all-embracing atheistic and mortalistic position in virtual isolation, whereas d'Holbach had the advantage of his brilliant coterie and their regular meetings at his Paris home, nicknamed the "Synagogue." Like d'Holbach, Meslier was a materialist and a determinist; just as d'Holbach argued at length against Clarke's 1704 *Demonstration of the Existence of God,* Meslier argued against Archbishop Fénelon's similarly themed *Demonstration* (1712). Meslier and d'Holbach are avowed, militant, and total unbelievers, who bring nearly every aspect of religion—natural as well as revealed, the soul as well as God—under unrelenting criticism. Of course, d'Holbach's atheism was openly avowed and published, whereas Meslier confided his avowed atheism only to his posthumously published manuscripts.

Although Meslier was the most outstanding clandestine atheist, he was not the only one. Other atheistic and mortalistic manuscripts—although none as explicit as the *Testament*—were circulating clandestinely in France, and to a lesser extent in Holland and in England, in the eighteenth century. Thus the *Dissertation sur la Formation du Monde*, an anonymous manuscript dated 1738, argues that God cannot have created the world because creation is inconceivable. And in the fourth chapter of the even more radical *Essais sur la Recherche de la Verite*, a manuscript dated around 1740, the author argues against the existence of God by showing that certain of his alleged attributes—for example, infinity and immateriality—are incompatible with one another.

Some of the clandestine manuscripts can be traced to the so-called Boulainvilliers coterie, among whom were Henry de Boulainvilliers, N. Fréret, César Chesneau Dumarsais, and Jean-Baptiste de Mirabaud. In 1743 a largely skeptical collection of five anonymous clandestine tracts was printed with the title *Nouvelles Libertés de Penser.*

Reports of Covert Atheists. While one must be cautious about accepting reports concerning Enlightenment atheists, one should not be entirely incredulous. We know that there were militant atheists who were prepared to avow their atheism verbally and in print (d'Holbach) and militant atheists who were not (Meslier). Clearly, autobiographical reports—such as William GODWIN's (in the Bodleian Library) that "I became in my 36th year [i.e., in 1792] an atheist"—are of the most compelling historical value; failing these, firsthand reports by atheistic friends must weigh more heavily than those by religious enemies. Among the more credible of such reports we find the names of Claude Adrien HELVÉTIUS and Augustin Roux of the Holbach coterie, and, in England, Erasmus DARWIN and Jeremy BENTHAM. However, in none of these cases is the evidence decisive, nor, more importantly, have any published or unpublished atheistic works been tied to these putative atheists. In the same way the evidence is unclear in Matthew TINDAL's case, for although the reports of his atheism are allegedly firsthand and contain interesting details, they are recorded by opponents rather than friends.

Covert Implied Atheism. Somewhat different is the case of Anthony COLLINS, who was reported by George Berkeley to have said that he had found a proof for the nonexistence of God. Although Berkeley was no friend of Collins, there is reason to believe that his firsthand testimony is reliable; it is also supported by secondhand reports. I have argued that some of Collins's published works are covertly atheistic, that his atheistic position was shared by his friend John TOLAND, and that their common position, which may be described as pantheistic materialism, was embraced by other so-called deists (see PANTHEISM AND UNBELIEF).

One of the most interesting pantheistic materialists was Albert Radicatti, count of Passeron. He lived for a time in England, where he published his radical philosophical works, the most important of which is *A Philosophical Dissertation upon Death* (1732). In the first ten or so pages Radicatti boldly sketched a materialistic version of pantheism, which clearly replaces theism or deism. "By the Universe," he wrote, "I comprehend the infinite space which contains the immense matter. . . ." Radicatti argued that matter and motion "are inseparable"; they are "of eternal co-existence" and they "exist necessarily." Because motion is essential to matter, and since both are necessary and eternal, no God was needed to add motion to matter or to create the world. But Radicatti made God not merely superfluous; he made him equivalent to the material world: "This Matter, modified by Motion into an infinite Number of various forms, is that which I call NATURE. Of this the qualities and attributes are, *Power, Wisdom, and Perfection,* all of which she possesses in the highest degree."

Neither Collins nor Radicatti denied the existence of God in his published works. Indeed, in *Twelve Discourses concerning Religion and Government* (1734), Radicatti goes out of his way to rebut the charge of atheism directed against Collins and others: "To say that Deists are Atheists is false; for they that are so-called by the Vulgar, and by those whose interest it is to descry them, admit a first cause under the names of God, Nature, Eternal Being, Matter, universal Motion or Soul. Such were Democritus, EPICURUS, Lucian, SOCRATES, Anaxagoras, Seneca, HOBBES, Blount, Spinosa [see SPINOZA, BARUCH], VANINI, St. Evremond, BAYLE, Collins and in general all that go under the name of Speculative Atheists; and none but fools or madmen can ever deny it. So that the word Atheist must signify Deist, or nothing, there being no such thing as an Atheist in the world."

By these standards it will be difficult, however, to imagine anyone who could be an atheist; and I have argued elsewhere that Radicatti's real aim was to encourage atheism by doing away with its negatively emotive name. For the pantheistic materialism of Radicatti, Collins, and Toland is not substantially different from the patently atheistic position of Meslier and d'Holbach. They all regarded the material world as an eternal, infinite, determined entity, which is self-caused, and believed it is possible to explain the order (and disorder) of the world without recourse to a transcendent immaterial being. The main difference is that whereas the position of Meslier and d'Holbach is overtly atheistic, that of Collins, Toland, and Radicatti is covert and implied.

Two late works of covert atheism which come close to being overt are: *Watson Refuted* (1796) by Samuel Francis and *An Investigation of the Essence of the Deity* (1797) by "Scepticus Britannicus." Francis not only rejected theism but went, as he tells us, "much further" than deism. Although he did not avow atheism or argue in its favor, he is plainly sympathetic toward it: "The world has too long been imposed upon by ridiculous attempts to vilify atheists and show their non-existence."

Scepticus's succinct *Investigation* is more important than *Watson Refuted*, however, in that it does argue for atheism by showing contradictions in the "theological Deity." God's alleged omnipotence, for example, is in conflict with his apparent inability to prevent Adam from sinning. God is supposed to be immutable, but he is also said to change his mind; and if he is immutable, "how truly ridiculous it is . . . to pray to him to alter His intentions." In the postscript, Scepticus's target shifts from theism to deism. Thus, deists such as Thomas PAINE claimed that God was omnipotent, but they also argued that he was incapable of producing the Bible. Nor could the deists explain "how an immaterial Being could create [i.e., from out of nothing] matter. . . ." Although Scepticus's atheism is not avowed, his pantheistic materialism is: "The Deity is material . . . in fine . . . the universe, or the whole material world is God."

Was Hume a covert atheist? My suspicion is that he was, although the scholarly consensus seems to be that he was not. One Hume scholar has recently described him as an "attenuated deist." There can be little doubt that Hume's arguments, especially in the *Dialogues*, bring him very close to atheism, even though it is not the sort of atheism of Scepticus or d'Holbach. Hume would have repudiated the metaphysical atheism of pantheistic materialism in favor of a more skeptical and epistemological variety. In the *Dialogues* he gradually but devastatingly stripped the concept of God of religious meaning, showing that the empirical evidence cannot warrant the inference to a creator of the world that is in any literal sense a wise person. At most Hume seemed prepared to allow that it is "probable that the principle which first arranged, and still maintains, order in this universe, bears . . . some remote inconceivable analogy to the other operations of nature, and among the rest the economy of human mind and thought."

Such an affirmation of God is, I would suggest, tantamount to a confession of atheism. Hume's attenuated conception of God and his statement that the "Atheist . . . is only nominally so, and can never be in earnest" should be interpreted along the same lines as I have interpreted Radicatti's statements.

While there seems to be little or no firsthand testimony that Hume considered himself an atheist, there is ample evidence from James Boswell's journals that he regarded himself as a mortalist. In 1776 Boswell recorded Hume as saying that "it was a most unreasonable fancy that we should exist forever." Thus Hume's essay "Of the Immortality of the Soul" must be seen as a case of covert implied mortalism. Here it is helpful to compare Collins and Hume, whose affirmations of conditional (gospel) immortality are remarkably similar. At the beginning of his essay Hume asserted that "in reality,

it is the gospel, and the gospel alone, that has brought life and immortality to light"; and in the *Discourse of Free-Thinking* Collins wrote that "the true Principles upon which the immortality of the Soul depends, are only to be fetched from the New Testament." The arguments of both men, however, are utterly subversive of the doctrine. Hence I am drawn to see Collins as a covert mortalist on the model of Hume, even though there was no Boswell present to chronicle his mortalistic profession. Similarly, I think we should see Hume as a covert atheist even though there was no Berkeley to record his denial of the existence of God.

Positions That Tend toward Atheism. In any case, there can be no doubt that Hume's works nurtured atheism, even if they did not imply it; and a similar judgment can be passed, a fortiori, on the works of Collins, Radicatti, and Toland. Enlightenment atheism was helped mainly by Thomas Hobbes, Baruch Spinoza, Charles Blount, Pierre Bayle, Lord SHAFTESBURY, and John LOCKE. Hobbes contributed materialism and empiricism; Spinoza, pantheism and militant RATIONALISM; and both a defense of determinism. Blount helped by translating and popularizing irreligious works—by Hobbes and Spinoza, among others—and also by writing some of the most provocative tracts of the seventeenth century, most of which are included in his *Miscellaneous Works* (1695). Bayle fostered atheism by the skepticism of his *Historical and Critical Dictionary* and, in his *Reflections of a Comet*, by severing religious belief from moral behavior and social order, a process that was continued by Shaftesbury. Locke's contribution was his epistemological approach, his empiricism and moderate rationalism. Although these thinkers rendered important services to atheism, and particularly to d'Holbach's 1770 synthesis, it seems unlikely that any of them, with the possible exceptions of Hobbes and Blount, was a covert atheist.

BIBLIOGRAPHY

Berman, David. *A History of Atheism in Britain.* London: Routledge, 1990.

———. *Ueberwegs Grundriss der Geschichte der Philosophie.* Basel: Schwabe, 1998.

Gaskin, John. *Hume's Philosophy of Religion.* London: Macmillan, 1978.

Kors, A. C. *The Coterie Holbachique.* Princeton, NJ: Princeton University Press, 1976.

Robertson, J. M. *Dynamics of Religion.* 2nd ed. London: Watts and Company, 1926.

———. *A History of Freethought, Ancient and Modern, to the Period of the French Revolution.* 2 vols. London: Watts and Company, 1936.

Spink, J. S. *French Free-Thought from Gassendi to Voltaire.* London: Athlone, 1960.

Wade, Ira O. *The Clandestine Organization and Diffusion of Philosophic Ideas in France from 1700 to 1750.* Princeton, NJ: Princeton University Press, 1938.

Weis, C., and F. Pottle, eds. *Boswell in Extremis: 1776–1778*. London: Yale University Press, 1971.

DAVID BERMAN

EPICURUS (341–270 BCE), Greek philosopher. Epicurus was the founder of the Epicurean school of philosophy, a leading intellectual movement of the Hellenistic era that began as an outgrowth of the atomism of Democritus and Lucippus. He was born in Samos, also the birthplace of Pythagoras. Along with several colleagues, Epicurus wrote numerous works that came to serve as the canon for the school. Epicurus alone authored about three hundred works, most notably his definitive treatise *On Nature*. The most important site of Epicurean scholarship and learning was located in a garden outside Athens, and yet Epicureans did not seek a garden of earthly delights of the sort that the modern term *epicurean* has come to invoke. For them happiness lay in the cultivation of the pleasures of knowledge, friendship (Epicurus's disciples were called simply the Friends), and simple and natural bodily experiences, which could be found in even the most modest everyday meal. More importantly, Epicurus taught that the key to achieving the good life was overcoming fear of pain and fear of gods. Epicureans sought to avoid the rigors of public life, but they accepted the legitimacy of civil law and justice as a prudent strategy for coordinating the interests of individuals. While Thomas JEFFERSON held up a Stoic philosopher, Epictetus, as a theorist of civic virtue (see STOICISM), in ethics Jefferson was much more Epicurean, as he once confided in a letter to a friend: "I consider the genuine (not the imputed) doctrines of Eipicurus as containing everything rational in moral philosophy which Greece and Rome have left us."

A radical empiricist about knowledge (see EMPIRICISM) and a materialist in metaphysics (see MATERIALISM, PHILOSOPHICAL), Epicurus envisioned an atomistic world composed of an infinite quantity of indissoluble particles moving in an infinite quantity of absolute void, governed by three natural laws of weight, collision, and an indeterministic factor, the "swerve." From the novel patterns initiated by the swerve, Epicurus generated a naturalistic model of human free will. In keeping with his metaphysics, Epicurus rejected the personal deities of traditional religion that interact meaningfully with the rest of nature. Epicurus gave a very clear statement of the theological problem of evil: "Either God want to abolish evil, and cannot; or he can, but does not want to. . . . If he wants to, but cannot, he is impotent. If he can, but does not want to, he is wicked. . . . If, as they say, God can abolish evil, and God really wants to do it, why is there evil in the world?" (see EVIL, PROBLEM OF). He cited the existence of crocodiles as part of the evidence against a benign creator. However, reasoning that the widespread belief in the gods required some explanation, he concluded that the gods have a real existence, but as images or shades of a peculiar kind composed of extremely fine atoms. These image-beings occupy the spaces between the universes, our universe being only one of an infinite number. There they do nothing but experience a kind of placid contentment, in an endless ideal representation of the Epicurean good life. The gods are not persons, nor creators of the world, and they are in no way concerned with human affairs. Accordingly, prayer is ineffectual because the gods are unresponsive. In any case, people are sufficient for their own happiness. Still, people should not entirely spurn the religious traditions of the culture in which they find themselves, since this would only create discord and confrontation with fellow community members. Furthermore, contemplation of the gods is a natural kind of meditation that can have salutary effects on the mind.

Famously, Epicurus argued that although death results in the annihilation of the self, we have nothing to fear from it: "Whatsoever causes no annoyance when it is present, causes only a groundless pain in the expectation. Death, therefore, the most awful of evils, is nothing to us, seeing that, when we are, death is not come, and when death is come, we are not. It is nothing, then, either to the living or to the dead, for with the living it is not and the dead exist no longer." The wise person, therefore, overcomes fear of pain, death, and gods and is freed to spend his days in peace, repose, friendship, intellectual study, and play: "The true understanding of the fact that death is nothing to us renders enjoyable the morality of existence, not by adding infinite time but by taking away the yearning for immortality."

AUSTIN DACEY

ERASMUS, DESIDERIUS (1466–1536), Dutch scholar and humanist. An early and internationally known Dutch humanist (see HUMANISM), Desiderius Erasmus was born in Holland at either Rotterdam or Gouda, the illegitimate son of a priest. Erasmus studied in Holland and was ordained a priest in 1492. Disliking monastic life, in 1494 he became Latin secretary to the bishop of Cambray. The next year he went to the University of Paris to study theology, but he did not like scholastic philosophy.

In 1499 Erasmus went to England, where he became a friend of the humanists John Colet and Thomas More. Erasmus increasingly devoted himself to the study of the classics and sacred literature. He combined the new humanism, based on the revival of interest in the classics, with Christian learning. In 1500 he returned to the Continent and devoted himself to the study of Greek.

Liberal and reformist theologians and classical scholars were inspired by Erasmus. He became important in the movement for reform of the Catholic Church. But when the reform movement developed into a radical direction, Erasmus tried to stay aloof from it. When Martin Luther became more aggressive and violent in his words, and when other reformers criticized Erasmus for his refusal to join them, he pointedly withdrew.

In 1524 Erasmus came out against Luther in his *On Free Will*, in which he argued against Luther's views on the free will. Luther replied sharply in his *De Servo Arbitrio* (1525). Luther could not stomach Erasmus's gentle SKEPTICISM and his willingness to accept Catholic teachings. As matters unfolded, Erasmus to a large extent broke with the reformers.

In his thinking Erasmus advocated a "philosophy of Christ" as different from various scholastic theories. The "philosophy of Christ" was to be reached by pious studies rather than by disputations. By this Erasmus intended to convey a simple form of Christianity, not a systematic theology but a message to be lived.

On the whole, Erasmus was a scholar. He seems to have been a moderate and cautious Christian, rather than an agnostic. It is not likely that he was ever an atheist (see AGNOSTICISM; ATHEISM).

BIBLIOGRAPHY

Hiorth, Finngeir. *Secularism in the Netherlands, in Belgium, and in Luxembourg*. Oslo: Human-Etisk Forbund, 2000.

Popkin, Richard H. "Erasmus." In *The Encyclopedia of Philosophy*, edited by Paul Edwards. New York: Macmillan Free Press, 1967.

FINNGEIR HIORTH

ETHICAL CULTURE. In some cases, yesterday's unbelief becomes today's commonplace. Unbeliefs are always contextual, shaped by time and place. The Ethical Culture movement provides a test of such generalizations. Ethical Culture, like many religious movements, stemmed from a prophetic individual who selected from and recast his inheritance.

Felix ADLER was born in Germany in 1851 and immigrated to the United States when his father became rabbi of New York City's Temple Emanu-El, the wealthiest Jewish congregation in the country. After graduating from Columbia University, he studied for the rabbinate in Berlin and Heidelberg. In 1873 in his first sermon at this temple he called for "[a] religion not confined to church and synagogue alone shall go forth. . . . A religion such as Judaism claimed to be—*not of the creed but of the deed*."

Although what would come to be known as Reform Judaism was already emerging within German American Jewry, this vision was too extreme, and young Adler left with a small group of enthused supporters. Three years later, in a rented hall, he expanded upon these themes, leading to the incorporation of a Society for Ethical Culture: "Judaism was not given to the Jews alone, but . . . its destiny is to embrace in one great moral state the whole family of men. . . . We propose to entirely exclude prayer and every form of ritual. . . . Freedom of thought is a sacred right of every individual man. . . . Diversity in the creed, unanimity in the deed."

Such statements evoked the wrath of orthodox Jews and Christians. Adler was processing his admiration for Ralph Waldo EMERSON's new "moral religion" and Immanuel KANT's rational morality, both highly controversial heresies in their time. In addition, the academic world was digesting Charles DARWIN's new theory of evolution that devastated design justifications for a god (see EVOLUTION AND UNBELIEF), which, for thoughtful theologians, had remained as the last intellectual defense of any kind of orthodoxy.

Critics perceived an actual ATHEISM in Adler's AGNOSTICISM, whereas a much smaller group of supporters viewed it as the only survival platform for any kind of religion.

Also influencing Adler was his participation in the Free Religious Association. Founded in 1871, mostly by Unitarians alarmed by a growing creedalism in their own denomination, ideas such as transcendentalism and scientific theism were surfacing here, along with explorations of religion beyond liberal Christianity and Judaism. In 1878 Adler was elected president of the Free Religious Association. Frustrated by discussions that did not lead to concrete action, he resigned in 1882—and this may have crystallized his decision to move ahead with the new organization and career.

Adler's new society based itself upon what he called the Supreme Ethical Rule: "Act So as to Elicit the Best in Others and Thereby Thy Self." Adler was able to assemble and hold the intense loyalty of a group of successful and wealthy New Yorkers, and to motivate them to focus upon needs of the community. For persons of Jewish background, this was a clear element of their heritage. Ethical Culture's absence of metaphysical discussions, religious identities, behavioral laws, and rituals helped maintain this focus and eliminate distractions. Adler's vision continually opened new areas of ethical advance. He was successful in stimulating societies in other cities and in recruiting and guiding the education of future leaders. Within a few years, additional societies were established in Chicago, Philadelphia, and St. Louis that still are strong.

At the same time, Adler was continually guiding the education of potential leaders. Most of these early leaders and would-be leaders had left the religions of their childhoods, as had Adler. The closest parallel was within the Unitarian ministry (see UNITARIAN UNIVERSALISM), and some came from it while others shifted into it.

What was emerging was a new form of religion, without rituals or creeds and operating with leaders rather than ministers. The sole commitment in this religion was to work for ethical change in society. Such change was the surest way to effect individual ethical growth. The rapid industrialization of the United States had left much of an earlier Protestantism in small towns, and had left cities populated with immigrants from oppressive countries abroad who were assimilating only slowly. Thus this was a time for social experimentation, however limited the scale. A "social gospel" was being explored in liberal Protestant circles, and a few Catholics were exploring what they termed an "Americanist" movement.

Although most members of Adler's supporting circles were economically well-off, their immigration memories kept them concerned about those less advantaged (some of their historians regarded this as noblesse oblige or even guilt)—but whatever the motivations alongside their ethical concerns, they were pioneers.

To serve poor children, the new society in 1877 created a District Nursing Department that set the pattern for visiting nursing movements. The first free kindergarten east of the Mississippi was created by Adler and the society a year later.

That same year a Workingman's School was created, extending the ethical concern to compensate for the limitations of the new public school movement. A women's group from the society turned to the study of child development and the "new psychology." Here was established a blend of academic education and practical skills that set the pattern for what would later be called "progressive" pedagogy and that was a forebear of PTA developments.

Another protégé, Stanton Coit, had discovered Adler's ideas while a student at Amherst. After sponsored study at Berlin and Columbia, he founded in 1886 the Neighborhood Guild in New York (later known as University Settlement). Patterned on London's Toynbee Hall, this was the first US settlement house. Here radical university students could live and work among "the masses," creating "the enlightenment of the people in social principles." Two years later, Jane ADDAMS founded Hull House in Chicago along similar lines of organizing and empowering the poor so that they could better control their own destinies.

Adler founded the Child Labor Society in 1904, and he and other society members were leaders in the development of the National Association for the Advancement of Colored People and the American Civil Liberties Union. Members played key roles in creating successful prison reforms, and as European turmoil brought refugees in the 1930s, members were in the forefront of resettlement efforts.

Adler never lost his vision that ethics depended upon education, and the experiments with schools that started with the children of the poor evolved into more integrated schools, both in class terms and in ethnic terms. In 1895 the original school was turned into the Ethical Culture School, with guaranteed scholarships for poor children and provision for "pay pupils."

In 1903 Anna Garlin Spencer, a Unitarian minister, joined as an associate leader. In 1908 she began directing a summer school in Madison, Wisconsin. Her work for women's rights, however, was not supported by Adler and she left in 1913 for an academic career.

By the 1920s the vision generated the Fieldston plan for a large school at Riverdale. What was needed was an alternative to the "mass schools" (public schools) and the "class schools" of the rich. John D. Rockefeller helped finance the venture, and V. T. Thayer was appointed director. The pragmatism of John DEWEY thereby entered Ethical Culture despite Adler's reservations.

In the 1940s Florence Klaber collaborated with the Unitarian Sophia Fahs to produce a new series of religious education materials for posttraditional schools. Students read various creation stories from around the world, for instance, climaxing the unit with views from modern science.

Adler held an appointment in Columbia University's philosophy department and taught an annual seminar. Over the years, many colleagues became involved with the society and were also involved in the academic training of leaders: among others, David Muzzey, John Herman Randall, Horace Friess, Herbert Schneider, and Joseph Blau. Leaders were also involved in creating a number of organizations, for example, Algernon Black with the Encampment for Citizenship and Jerome Nathanson with the Conference on Science and Democracy. These post-Adler leaders increasingly moved away from a Kantian idealism into a naturalistic instrumentalism reflecting Dewey's dominant role in American philosophy.

Leaders and members of societies might give varied responses to the question of whether Ethical Culture is a religion. In a recent Texas case, it was successfully argued that it deserved tax-exempt status on this basis. Perhaps more importantly, the movement has shown that a focus on ethics alone permits a very small number of persons to accomplish a great deal within their culture. The concentration of intellectual life in Manhattan has also helped, since the society is able to provide physical space and platform to many national causes.

Looking at the society today, it is clear that a majority of leaders would comfortably identify themselves as humanists who work within a postpatriarchal, transethnic, and postnationalistic worldview. On the international scene, they are well represented in the INTERNATIONAL HUMANIST AND ETHICAL UNION.

BIBLIOGRAPHY

Adler, Felix. *Creed and Deed.* New York: G. P. Putnam's Sons, 1877.

——— . *Creed and Deed: A Series of Discourses.* New York: Arno, 1972.

——— . *The Essentials of Spirituality.* New York: J. Pott, 1905.

——— . *The Reconstruction of the Spiritual Ideal.* New York: London: D. Appleton, 1924.

Radest, Howard. *Toward Common Ground: The Story of the Ethical Societies in the United States.* Garden City, NY: Fieldston, 1969.

ROBERT B. TAPP

ETHICS AND UNBELIEF. Introduction. This article critiques the very idea of there being a cosmic underpinning for morality. I put my argument principally in Christian terms by explicating and critiquing the Thomistic tradition of natural moral law and the Protestant Reformationist tradition of divine command morality. But the reference to the Christian tradition is completely inessential. Similar points could be made for Judaism or Islam with inessential changes. Moreover, a secular humanist critique could also be mounted of the attempts to give a cosmic grounding for morality by the other great world religions and by the so-called primitive religions of other cultures, though in both cases the specifics, of course, would have to be different. But the main thrust would remain against the need for, and indeed the very possibility of, a coherent cosmological grounding for morality or of the very attempt by such means to give our lives significance.

I should add, however, that a secular humanist critique of attempts at a religious grounding for morality could also be made of the other great world religions, but there the arguments would not be so very similar to the ones I shall make here, though again the main thrust would remain against the need for and indeed the very possibility of a cosmic underpinning for morality.

I

Thomas Aquinas argues that all human beings have at least the potential to attain objective knowledge of good and evil. Moral knowledge, for him, does not rest on divine revelation nor need we simply assume on *faith* that the ordinances of God are good. We all have, Aquinas would have us believe, at least the capacity to know that there are certain fundamental things that we should avoid and certain fundamental things that we should seek.

If we will only note and then dwell on our most basic inclinations and the inclinations—the strivings and avoidings—of our fellow humans, we will come to know what is good. Good is thus said to be an objective concept, and it is somehow a part of the very nature of things. But it is not in physical nature that one finds what is good. As a neo-Thomist philosopher, Father C. B. Daly, puts it: "The Catholic moralists . . . do not pronounce morally right whatever nature does; do not equate statistical averages of subhuman physical events with the moral good." The good, the moral law that we can at least dimly apprehend, is to be discovered in our own human natures. As "physico-spiritual" beings we find the rule of right within.

If we stopped at just this empirical strand in Aquinas's thinking—a strand that Jacques Maritain likes to stress when he is talking about relativism—Aquinas's theory would be a variety of ethical NATURALISM and his theory would be beset with the standard difficulties facing ethical naturalism. "X is good" does not mean "I approve of X," "My culture approves of X," "People generally seek X," "Humans desire X," or "Normal humans seek X," for people may desire, approve of, or seek something that is bad. Indeed something could be widely approved of and still be evil. Most people at some time desire to commit adultery, but that people have this desire does not by that very act establish that adultery is good.

The fact is equally true that my culture's approval of something does not establish that it is a good thing to do. The Greeks of Plato and Aristotle's time (like people in many other cultures) approved of infanticide. That this is so is established by anthropological investigation, but this does not establish the truth of the moral statement "Infanticide is sometimes a good thing." What makes the anthropological statement true does not make the ethical statement true. Plato would not be contradicting himself if he said, "My culture approves of infanticide but infanticide is evil"; and I would not be *contradicting* myself if I said, "People generally disapprove of engaged couples sleeping together before they marry, but in reality there is nothing wrong with it." I might in some way be mistaken if I were to assert that there is nothing wrong with it, but in the present context that is beside the point. What is to the point is that I do not *contradict* myself, or say anything incoherent or conceptually out of order, in making that statement. We do not by that very act establish that something is good by discovering that I or others approve of it, like it, desire it, strive for it, seek it, and the like. A cross-cultural examination of what people desire is no doubt very important to a full understanding of what is good and what ends are worth seeking, but it is not enough to establish which ends are good or what ought to be. Even when people desire something, after careful reflection it does not follow that what they so desire is desirable. They might in various ways be mistaken about what they desire or their moral thinking might in some way be defective. If we stress only this empirical strand of natural law morality, we will encounter all of the traditional difficulties connected with ethical naturalism.

II

Aquinas's theory, it should be noted, is not simply an empirical theory. It has a metaphysical-theological strand as well. Father F. C. Copleston correctly remarks that we can only properly understand Aquinas's conception of the natural moral law if we place it against his doctrine of man as a creature of God in a rational purposive universe. If we secularize the natural moral law we are, according to Maritain and Father Peter Kossel, cutting out its very heart. All men, whether they know it or not, are, Aquinas believes, seeking union with God. The *summum bonum* is in God's very essence. In this life we cannot know what that essence is, but God, in his mercy, enables us to understand *something* of his goodness. All lesser goods on this account derive their goodness from God. Without God, life could have no meaning or value, indeed nothing could have value, for in a godless world nothing could, in Aquinas's view, be genuinely good. God tells us what is good by giving us laws. Laws, for Aquinas, are "ordinances of reason" promulgated "for the common good, by him who has care of the community."

For Aquinas there are four basic kinds of law, though all laws must have the above-mentioned features. There is eternal law. This is God's blueprint for the universe. It is an expression of God's "divine subsisting reason." It springs from God; one of the ways it is promulgated is through divine law, which is that part of the eternal law that humans cannot grasp with their reason but is given to man by God through divine revelation. The natural law, by contrast, is that part of the eternal law that man can grasp by the use of his reason, if his natural inclinations have not been "corrupted by vicious habits" or "darkened by passions and habits of sin." The natural law is simply the specifically rational moral law in which rational beings conform their conduct to the eternal law.

In addition, there is what most people would ordinarily mean by *law*, namely, human law, which, according to Aquinas, must be a precept devised by human reason for the common good. The important thing to remember about Aquinas's conception of human law is that in order to be genuine human laws, the laws must *not* be incompatible with natural law. (Given this theory, one is committed to the paradoxical contention that what ordinarily would be called "an evil or vile law" is not a law at all.)

Natural law is the unwritten, and in its primary forms unalterable, law graspable by the reason of all normal adult human beings not corrupted by sin. It emanates from God's reason and is that part of his law knowable by human beings. There are, of course, different natural laws. There is the first primary (and what certainly seems to be the vacuous) first principle of the natural law. This primary precept—as it is called—is "Good is to be done and evil is to be avoided." There are other less fundamental but substantive secondary precepts of the natural law. "Life ought to be preserved," "Men ought to know the truth about God," and "Ignorance ought to be avoided" are examples of such natural moral laws.

While people can come to understand these natural laws through the use of their reason, it is important to understand, as Maritain in particular stresses, that man is not the measure of what are or are not natural laws. Man does not simply *resolve* to treat certain laws as crucial to his well-being and then correctly label them "natural laws." Rather he apprehends—though sometimes rather dimly—these unalterable natural laws. Human beings do not create them and they cannot alter them by their collective decisions. They are not always *self-evident to* an individual or even to a whole society, but they are indeed *self-evident in themselves*, serving as an absolute and unalterable foundation for correct moral decisions in our political, social, and personal lives.

III

The natural moral law has a long and varied history, and we understand very well the strong emotional support natural law conceptions have provided for many of the morally perplexed from the Greeks until the present. However, as emotionally comforting as these conceptions are, they do not constitute an adequate foundation for morality. I shall limit myself here to four general criticisms of the Thomistic conception of the natural moral law.

1. We are told that natural moral laws are self-evident, absolute, rational laws. They are certain and can be known without any doubt at all to be true. This sounds very reassuring, for it promises to give us the kind of objective knowledge of good and evil we desire. But there is here no genuine surcease from our perplexities about an objective justification of moral beliefs. It would be a mistake to believe that advocates of natural law are claiming that honest, nonevasive, intelligent reflection will necessarily make it clear to impartial and informed examiners that there are natural moral laws and that the laws generally claimed to be natural laws are indeed natural laws. Since the natural laws are only *self-evident in themselves* and not necessarily self-evident to us, what could it *mean* to say they are certain and that we can justifiably claim to be certain of them?

For such a certain knowledge of good and evil, we require moral principles that can be *seen* or somehow appreciated to be self-evident to us, or natural moral laws of whose truth we can be certain. But since natural moral laws are only self-evident *in themselves* (assuming we know what that means) and since it is God's reason and not man's that is the source of the moral law, we poor mortals can have no rational certitude that the precepts claimed to be natural laws are really natural laws. Beyond this it is surely a mistake to claim that laws or anything else are self-evident in themselves where it is impossible to know or have grounds for asserting that they are self-evident.

If a law or proposition *p* is such that we could never, even in principle, be in a position to justifiably claim that it either is or is not self-evident (since we mortals have and can have no grounds for claiming that it is self-evident), then it is senseless to assert or deny that *p* is self-evident in itself. If human beings can have no grounds for asserting that something is self-evident, they can have no grounds at all for asserting it is self-evident in itself. What we don't know we don't know is a significant tautology.

2. We find out what a human being *ought* to be, natural law theorists claim, by finding out what are the specific rational ways in which a person is to conform to the eternal law. We in turn find this out, by finding out what we are—by discovering our *essential nature*. As one natural law moralist put it, "Morality is man's knowledge that he ought to become what he is; that he ought to become a man by conduct becoming to a man."

In order to know how we humans should live and die, the natural law account goes, we must understand man's essential nature.

But to this it can be objected that, from the point of view of science, human beings have *no* essential human nature. We are not artifacts with an assigned function. It is both linguistically odd and cosmologically question begging to ask what human beings are for—assuming by this very question that a person is a divine artifact rather than a person in his own right. Science does not ask what humans are for; it does not know how to make such inquiry or even *what it is* to inquire into our essential nature. Science has no conception of this and philosophy has deconstructed it.

For the Thomist to speak of our essential nature requires the acquaintance and acceptance of the background assumption that a human being is a creature of God. But that human beings are creatures of God is not part of the corpus of any science. In fact, it is a completely unverifiable statement whose very *factual* intelligibility is seriously in question. But unless we can establish the factual significance of such an utterance, we have no grounds at all for saying we have, in the requisite sense, an essential nature. If we have no grounds for saying that human beings have an essential nature, then we have no grounds for claiming there are natural moral laws, at least as the Thomist tradition construes "natural laws."

3. The first principle of the natural moral law is a tautology (if you will, an empty truism) and is thus not a substantive moral proposition or principle. It is compatible with a completely relativistic or subjective view of morals, for it does not tell us what is good or what is evil, but it only makes explicit what is already implicit in the use of the words *good* and *evil*, namely, that if something is good it is, everything else being equal, to be sought; and if it is evil it is, everything else being equal, to be avoided. But it does not and cannot tell us *what* is to be sought and *what* is to be avoided.

To discover this we must turn to the substantive secondary precepts of the natural moral law. But some of these run afoul of the facts concerning cultural relativity, for some of them are not always assented to, much less are they always accepted as self-evident by all people. If we say (as Aquinas does) that all people whose natural inclinations are not "corrupted by vicious habits" and "darkened by passions and habits of sin" acknowledge these natural laws, we can ask in turn: Where do we get our criteria for deciding whose habits are vicious and sinful and whose are not? To rule out some natural inclinations as corrupt or sinful indicates that we are using a criterion in moral appraisal that is distinct from the natural law criterion of basing man's moral conceptions on his natural inclinations.

What actually happens is that those moral beliefs incompatible with Catholic doctrine (and as a result, called corrupt and sinful) are simply arbitrarily labeled *unnatural* and *abnormal*. But to do this is not to base morality squarely on natural law conceptions. We have here the application of moral criteria that are not based on natural law conceptions. Without such an application—an application drawn from religious doctrine and not from what we learn about human nature or from what we can derive from the first principle of the natural law—natural law conceptions could not overcome the cultural relativity they were designed to transcend.

If in defense of such natural-law conceptions it is replied, "We do not claim that all people and cultures always acknowledge these laws, but the crucial thing is that most of them do," we make another egregious error, for, if we argue in this way, we have presupposed that moral issues can be settled by statistics or by some cross-cultural poll. But Aquinas and his followers would surely not wish to say that moral issues are "vote issues." To argue that what most people value is valuable is to assume rather simple democratic standards, and by assuming them we again have a standard which is (a) *not* self-evident and which is (b) *independent* of the natural law. To avoid ethical relativism, the natural-law theorist must incorporate into his theory moral conceptions that are not based on the natural moral law and which are questionable in their own right.

4. Natural moral law theorists confuse talking about what is the case with talking about what ought to be the case. They confuse de jure statements with de facto statements. A statement about what normal people seek, strive for, or desire is a factual, nonnormative statement. From this statement or from any conjunction of such statements alone no normative (de jure) conclusions can be validly deduced except in such trivial cases as from "He wears black shoes" one can deduce "He wears black shoes or he ought to be a priest." But this simply follows from the conventions governing *or*.

Moreover, because the above compound sentence is a disjunction, it is not actually action-guiding; it is not actually normative. Moreover, to discover what our natural inclinations are is simply to discover a fact about ourselves; to discover what purposes we have is to discover another fact about ourselves, but that we ought to have these inclinations or purposes or that it is desirable that we have them does not follow from statements asserting that people have such and such inclinations or purposes. These statements could be true, but no moral or normative conclusions follow from them.

IV

Natural law theorists and religious moralists generally feel that without a belief in God and his moral order, an objective rational morality is impossible. This seems to me an utter mistake. The choice is not between NIHILISM and God.

Morality is a practical (that is, action-guiding, attitude-molding) rule-governed activity, whose central function it is to adjudicate the conflicting desires and interests of everyone involved in some human conflict in an impartial and fair manner. In morality, we are most fundamentally concerned with the reasoned pursuit of what is in everyone's best interests. How do we decide what is in anyone's best interest, let alone what are the best interests of everyone? In talking about a person's best interests we are talking about his or her most extensive welfare and well-being, and in talking about the best interests of everyone we are talking about the most extensive well-being possible for all in a given situation. This, of course, is not a pellucid notion, but it is also not the case that we cannot say anything reasonable about it. It is this, though not only this, that morality tries to further.

The concept of well-being is indeed vague, but it is not so vague that it is not evident that certain social practices could not be in our welfare. Drastically frustrating our normal needs for sleep, food, sex, drink, elimination, and the like could not be in our welfare. Moreover, it is not just these mundane matters that are a part of every conception of human well-being. Any way of life that denigrated personal affection, integrity, conscientiousness, knowledge, and the contemplation of beautiful things would be an impoverished way of life, for to stifle any of these things is to strike a blow at our very well-being. Similarly, a community could not be a community whose social practices served human welfare if those social practices pointlessly diminished self-respect, the appreciation and concern for others, creative employment, play and diversion. So while *welfare* and *well-being* are defeasible, context-dependent terms, they are *not* so vague as to not exclude at least some social systems both possible and actual—the Nazis, the Dobuans, or the Aztecs—as not furthering the welfare of all or even most of their members.

In morality we are concerned with the practical tasks of guiding conduct and altering behavior in such a way as to harmonize conflicting desires and interests so as to maximize to the greatest extent possible the welfare and well-being of each person involved. (One of the reasons why John Rawls's principles of justice as fairness are so important is that their stress is not just on maximizing well-being, or indeed maximizing welfare at all, but their stress is on a concern, as a crucial element of what it is to be fair, for the well-being of *everyone* alike.) We should judge our moral rules and social practices by this standard; and individual actions unambiguously governed by the moral practices that the agent or agents in question are so committed to are to be judged by whether or not they are in accordance with the moral practice in question. To act in accordance with them, when one sees that they are so related to such practices, is to act on principle: to act as a morally good person and not just as a person of good morals.

Using this general conception of the function of morality, or at least as a central function of morality, we can make appraisals of many practical issues. The natural law moralist can do this as well. But using my framework I can do it more reasonably and with greater objectivity and internal consistency that can advocates of the natural moral law. I can avoid the reified conceptions of the Thomistic conception of natural law.

V

I shall now illustrate how this is so by turning to some specific moral issues that often divide religious moralists and secular humanists. Consider the issue of miscegenation and the moral issues that have emerged around the use of contraceptives (see BIRTH CONTROL AND UNBELIEF). I could make similar points with reference to adultery, abortion, artificial insemination, same-sex marriage, and euthanasia; I pick these two issues because on the first I suspect that by now, between religious moralists and secularists, there is often practical agreement over what is right and what is wrong, while on the second there is no such agreement. By airing the respective grounds for making one claim rather than another, we can gain some idea of the differences—and, I hope, of the respective merits and deficiencies—of the contrasting orientations to morality.

Miscegenation is the mixture of races through marriage or other sexual contact. It was illegal in apartheid South Africa, and, until relatively recently, it was against the law in many southern states of the United States for whites and blacks to marry. Such a law and the moral attitude behind it is plainly immoral and should be strenuously opposed. But that is not the natural inclination or the considered judgment of everyone or even of the majority of people in all societies.

A natural law theorist might well argue that laws or rules forbidding marriage between people of different races is evil because it is contrary to the natural moral law. I think it would be difficult for him to make out such a case. It seems to me that it is, as a matter of fact, a quite natural inclination for many people. It is very natural for many human beings to make sharp and discriminatory distinctions between their own kind and those who have different pigmentation, physique, language, religion, or mores. It took a papal bull to make the conquistadors regard the Peruvian Indians as human beings with immortal souls. People who are very different from us are quite naturally (that is, typically) regarded with distrust and aversion. It seems to be natural for us to regard ourselves and our particular mores and physical traits as being intrinsically superior. We can only overcome these inclinations by a cosmopolitan education, including some *hard moral thinking*.

If, on the one hand, we turn to man's primitive, immediate, unrehearsed inclinations and strivings—the strivings and inclinations of "raw human nature"—we could hardly find a ground for the condemnation of the moral belief that there should be no mixture of the races. If, on the other hand, we take only the inclinations that withstand reflection and examination—careful moral and factual scrutiny—we have already imported into morality principles that are not simply derived from or based on human inclinations. Rather, we are speaking of considered judgments that would not be extinguished when they faced the tribunal of wide reflective equilibrium.

On the humanist view of morality we have, by contrast, a clear and unequivocal basis for opposing the belief that it is wrong for the races to intermarry. Biological and anthropological studies have made it abundantly clear that no one race is biologically inferior to another. They have also made it perfectly clear that no biological harm could come from such marriages. If anything, it might make for a certain hybrid vigor. But the serious point is that there are no rational grounds for being against intermarriage. This removes one supposed major impediment. Culturally speaking, it would cause distress to some people, but this distress has no basis in reason—in the use of our intelligence—and it could be slowly alleviated by proper education and time. This distress, in turn, is plainly outweighed by the continued feelings of inferiority or racial tension that such irrational and discriminatory laws engender. Similar things should be said about same-sex marriage. The gut feeling of many people that it is "unnatural" has no rational basis or biological warrant. Moreover, it runs against our deeply embedded principle of respect for human beings.

Moreover, it is not enough for morality to simply consider the welfare and well-being of the *majority*; it must consider the welfare and well-being of *everyone*. Sometimes, in tragic situations, an individual's interests must be sacrificed, but they can only be sacrificed on nonarbitrary grounds (say, in the protection of the interests of the vast majority of people in a war), but in miscegenation or same-sex unions nothing like this is even remotely at issue. What we have are prejudices, and nothing else, of a goodly number of people on the one hand, and the welfare and well-being of the people who love each other and wish to marry on the other. If people's prejudices are not catered to, their welfare is not being sacrificed, but rather the welfare of the people who wish to marry is being sacrificed by such laws and to such prejudices. Interests deserve protection but not prejudices, and the two are not the same.

Let us now consider the use of contraceptives as devices for birth control. I think contraceptives are something that people with normal sexual desires ought to use in many circumstances of their lives. The need and desire to make love is normal and natural. It should go without saying that it is one of the most intensely pleasurable experiences that we humans can have. When accompanied by deep affection and complete acceptance and understanding, it can help us to experience a feeling of oneness and union that is precious in a world where we human beings so often feel alienated and alone. These are precious and positive values of sex that have nothing to do with the reproductive function of intercourse, and there is no reason at all to inhibit their expression by forbidding all sexual activity not intended to function in the service of procreation.

The Roman Catholic version of the natural law position says that the use of artificial contraceptive methods is always wrong. It is unnatural, for in the words of Father Daly, it places an artificial substance between the lovers that obstructs the natural function of sex. It represents—we are told by Father Daly—both a psychological and a physical withdrawal, and hence is a variety of onanism. In his words: "Every contraceptive appliance or device is a 'hard wall of the ego' (or of two egos) refusing to be two-in-one-flesh."

This argument, if it can be so dignified, is utterly without merit. Few would deny that sexual experience without contraceptives was, until the age of the pill, usually a fuller, more enjoyable experience. But given modern oral contraceptives this very slight disadvantage of contraceptives completely disappears. And the positive values of contraception completely outweigh what is sometimes with some contraceptives their very slight disvalue. This is highlighted dramatically by the role of contraceptive devices such as condoms in AIDS prevention. The Catholic supposed "natural law" doctrine on this is deeply immoral.

More fundamentally still, if we are going to say "sexual intercourse under such circumstances is wrong because it is unnatural since it interrupts a natural function," we should also say that shaving, cutting one's toenails or hair, removing cancerous growths, wearing glasses, having an appendectomy, giving blood, or being circumcised (see CIRCUMCISION AND ITS OPPOSITION AS CAUSES) are also immoral because unnatural. Part of the human animal's glory and creativeness lies in the human ability to transform nature, including human nature, and not simply to be a frail reed completely at the mercy of one's animal ancestry. There are no good grounds at all for arguing that something is wrong because it is unnatural.

Further, it is the case that there are good reasons—urgently good reasons—for controlling population growth. Throughout the world approximately fifty thousand people die each day from malnutrition and other easily preventable disabilities. It *may* be that we are sufficiently inventive to prevent our world from becoming a "plundered planet" without the institution of artificial birth control techniques, but it is still a very grave risk to take, and overpopulation is at present causing severe misery in many parts of the world. It seems to me that a continued adherence to a dogmatic theology prevents us from adopting this humane and rational measure.

It is not only considerations of overpopulation that count in favor of the use of contraceptives, but also more personal considerations of human welfare and well-being. Where contraception is not practiced, children are frequently born to parents who do not want them or cannot really afford to have them. It is a deep and permanently wounding blow to a child who slowly realizes that he or she was not wanted. Mothers in families that do not practice contraception frequently have children in too rapid succession. Their physical and psychological health is often badly shaken; they suffer, and as a result their children and husbands suffer as well. Lastly, for various financial or medical reasons, some couples cannot risk having children. Under these circumstances it is irrational and immoral to deny these couples the pleasure and sense of oneness they would gain from sexual union.

By their very creativeness human beings have distinguished themselves from other primates. We have the distinctive capacity for culture and the correlative ability to transform our environment rather than being subject to it. The Catholic "natural moral law" doctrine on contraception in effect overrides and denies this distinctive human gift. It would in effect make man subject to blind forces that he could otherwise rationally control. It is certainly not "unnatural" to seek not to be in bondage to them.

VI

It is not unnatural to ask: Given the Decalogue, why the natural law? Natural law moralists reply, "Because what the Decalogue commands us to do is also discoverable by reason and not everyone has heard the Word." Indeed, as the Father Victor White puts it, "A Christian cannot and will not judge the Decalogue in the light of natural law; but he will find in the Decalogue the divine approbation of the intrinsic, though limited, rightness of natural law." Attractive as this claim is, if my argument in the previous sections has been even near to being correct, we can see that such a Thomistic conception of the natural law is thoroughly mythical and cannot serve as a sound foundation for our moral beliefs. But we still have the Decalogue and, what is called by religious people, the revealed word of God. Let us now look at those radical reformationist, and in effect voluntaristic, claims that contend that this is all we *have* and all that we *need* to give significance and direction to our moral lives.

The distinguished Protestant theologian Emil Brunner argues that we cannot discover any sound abstract principles of right action or good conduct under which we could subsume particular moral claims that concretely direct us to do this or that. *Genuine human good is found only in the unconditional, unquestioned obedience of man to God.* Human conduct is good—that is, we are doing what we ought to be doing—only when God himself acts in it, through the Holy Spirit.

The religious person's obedience is not, Brunner would have us understand, obedience to a law or a principle "but only to the free sovereign will of God." The will of God cannot be summed up under any principle. We do not know what God is or what love is by apprehending a principle. We do not even understand these conceptions unless, quite concretely—existentially, if you will—"we learn to know God in His action, in faith." All ethical thought and moral understanding is rooted in such an existential knowledge of God; and "really good Christian conduct" needs to have the whole of the revealed existential Christian knowledge of God behind it. This *Deus Absconditus*, the God that we should love and fear, is manifested only in his revelation.

We, Brunner recognizes, indeed long for something that goes beyond revelation. We long for something we can rationalize, for something that can give us a rationally justifiable standard in accordance with which we can live, but, natural law theorists notwithstanding, *we human beings have no natural knowledge of good and evil*. We have not been able, for all our Faustian drives, for all our intelligence and knowledge, to seize the tree of knowledge of good and evil. The truth of the Jewish-Christian-Islamic claim that God is the "perfect good" and obedience to God's command is the sole desirable ultimate end of human action is not "a truth of reason" or a truth that is objectively verifiable or in any way objectively establishable. Only the person of *faith* can know or even understand it. But it nonetheless remains true that this Christian ethic has universal validity. As Brunner puts it:

> But this does not mean that the Christian ethic makes no claim to universal validity. Whatever God demands can be universal, that is, valid for all men, even if those who do not hear this demand do not admit this validity and indeed do not even understand the claim to universal validity. The believer alone clearly perceives that the Good, as it is recognized in faith, is the sole Good, and that all that is otherwise called good cannot lay claim to this title, at least not in the ultimate sense of the word. It is precisely faith and faith alone which knows this: that alone is good which God does; and indeed, faith really consists in the fact that man knows this—and that he alone can be known, namely, in the recognition of faith. But once man does know this he also knows the unlimited unconditional validity of this conception and of the divine demand.

Since we cannot rely on abstract principles, we can never, as the natural law tradition claims, know beforehand what God requires. Rather God commands, and whatever it is he commands we must obey. Therein lies our sole good, for "the Good is simply what God wills that we should do on the basis of a principle of love." It is indeed true that God wills our true happiness; but *he* wills it, and he wills it in such a way that no one else knows what his will is. If we try to stick to the use of our own reason and a sense of our own most fundamental inclinations or considered judgments, we will "never know what is right for us, nor what is the best for the other person." Here, as children of faith, we must simply and humbly rely on God. Doing the right thing is simply obeying God's commands.

We go astray when we think that we can deduce our moral obligations "from some principle or another, or from some experience." This casuistry, this reasoning by cases and principles, Brunner contends, is legalistic thinking in the worst sense of that term. Our very conception of God and his divine love is distorted if we think that we can know what God ought to will for us in accordance with his love. What his love is, what he would judge to be for our own good, is too utterly far from us to allow us this judgment. "But of one thing we may be quite sure: his will is love, even when we do not understand it—when he commands as well as when he gives." But it is a complete mistake to think that we can take the measure of it by our ideas of love. God's love is beyond that.

Many people, including Kantians, have complained that a morally good man (as distinct from a man who is only a man of good morals) does what is good because it is good, not because of what he will get out of it or because he will be damned or punished if he doesn't. The truly moral person, Immanuel KANT argues, requires no such sanctions, no such pricks to his own intent. To require them is a perversion of moral endeavor. It is—in the Kantian phrase—to make morality *heteronymous*. We ought instead to do the good simply for the sake of the good.

Brunner rejects this Kantian approach. He argues that such a critique of the morality of divine commands fails to recognize "that the Good is done for the sake of the Good when it is done for the sake of God, in obedience to the Divine Command."

VII

Starkly contrasting with the traditional Thomistic conception of the natural moral law, we have in Brunner's exposition a powerful and classical expression of the morality of divine commands, a conception of morality that has been a central one in the Protestant tradition.

To start to look at it critically, let us first ask again this ancient question: "Is something good because God commands it or does God command it because it is good?" Let us consider the alternatives we can take here. If we say God commands it because it is good, this implies that something can be good *independently* of God. Why? Because "God commands it *because* it is good" implies that God apprehends it to be good or takes it to be good or in some way knows it to be good and then tells us to do it. But if God does this, then it is at least *logically* possible for us to see or in some way know or come to appreciate that it is good without God's telling us to do it or informing us that it is good—that is, without knowing anything of God.

This last point needs explanation and justification. The preceding clearly implies that good is not a creation of God—something is not *made* good by God's willing it—but rather is something apprehended by God or known by God. Since God apprehends something to be good, since it doesn't become good simply because he wills it or commands it, it is not unreasonable to believe that there can be this goodness even in a godless world. Translated into the concrete, this means that it would be correct to assert that even in a world without God, killing little children just for the fun of it is vile and caring for them is good.

Someone might grant that there is this *logical* independence of morality from religion, but still argue that, given human beings' corrupt and vicious nature (the "sin of the Old Adam"), they, as a matter of fact, need God's help to understand what is good and to know what they ought to do. Humans are pervasively sinful, and there is and always will be much corruption in the palace of justice.

Such a response is confused. With or without a belief in God we can recognize such corruption. In some concrete situations at least, we understand perfectly well what is good or what we ought to do. The "corruption" religious people have noted does not lie here. The corruption they are interested in comes not in our knowledge but in "our weakness of will." We find it in our inability to do what, in a "cool hour," we acknowledge to be good—"the good I would do that I do not." Religion—for some people at any rate—may be of value in putting their *hearts* into virtue. But that for some it is necessary in this way does not show us how it can provide us with a knowledge of good and evil by providing us with our ultimate standard of goodness.

Suppose we say instead—as Brunner surely would—that an action or attitude is right or good simply because God *wills* it or *commands* it. Its goodness arises from divine fiat. *God makes something good simply by commanding it.* (That is the course a consistent divine theorist should take. It goes well, as it did in the Middle Ages for William of Occam, with his voluntarism.)

Can *anything* be good or become good simply by being commanded or willed? Can a fiat, command, or ban create goodness or moral obligation? I do not think so. Suppose you are in a course and the professor tells you, "You must get a loose-leaf notebook for this class." His commanding it, his telling you to do it, does not by that very act make it something you *ought* to do or even make doing it good, though it might, given your circumstance, make it a prudent thing to do. But whether or not it is prudent for you to do it, given his position of authority, and your dependence on him, it is (if there are no reasons for getting that particular type of notebook or any notebook at all, other than those consequent on his telling you to do it) all the same a perfectly arbitrary injunction on his part and not something that could properly be said to be good or something morally speaking you ought to do. Commanding it doesn't make it either good or obligatory.

Suppose, to appeal to a similar consideration, a mother says to her college-age daughter, "You ought not to go to class dressed like that." Her telling her daughter that does not by that very act make it a bad thing, and her ordering her daughter not to go to class dressed in a particular way doesn't make it the case that her daughter ought not to go to class dressed like that. For the mother to be right, she must be able to give reasons, and indeed arguably cogent reasons, for her judgment.

More generally speaking, the following are all perfectly intelligible: (1) He wills *y* but should I do it? (2) *X* commands it, but is it good? (3) *X* told me to do it, but all the same I ought not to do it. (4) *X* proclaimed it but all the same what he proclaimed is evil. Items (3) and (4) are not contradictions and (1) and (2) are not senseless, self-answering questions like: Is a wife a married woman? (Think here of G. E. Moore's open question arguments.) This clearly indicates that the moral concepts "should," "good," and "ought" are, in their actual use, not identified with the willing of something, the commanding, the proclaiming of something, or even with simply telling someone to do something. Even if moral utterances characteristically tell us to do something, not all "tellings to" are moral utterances or even things we otherwise should do. Among other things, "moral tellings to" are "tellings to" that must be supportable by *reasons* and for which it is always logically in order to ask for reasons. But this is not true for simple commands or imperatives. As a mere inspection of usage reveals, moral utterances are not identifiable with commands.

To this it will be replied: "It is true that these moral concepts cannot be identified with any old commands but *divine* commands make all the difference. It is *God's* willing it, *God's* telling us to do it, that makes it good." It is indeed true that, for the believer, it's being *God* who commands it, who wills it, that makes all the difference. This is so because believers assume that God is good. But now, it should be asked, how does the believer *know*, or indeed does he know, that God is good, except by what is in the end his own quite fallible moral judgment that God is good? Must he not appeal to his own considered judgments, his own moral sense here? Is there any escaping that?

It would seem not. We must, to know that God is good, see or come to appreciate that his acts, his revelation, his commands, are good. It is through the majesty and the goodness of his revelation in the scriptures that we come to understand that God is good, that God is the ultimate criterion for all our moral actions and attitudes. But this, of course, itself rests on our own capacity to make moral assessments. It presupposes our own ability to make moral judgments and to recognize or appreciate the difference between right and wrong. It is we who acknowledge, or fail to acknowledge, that God's commands must be obeyed. There is no escaping this relying on our own moral capacities—our own need to appreciate what we are to do here. Whatever we decide our need for decision—our own decision—is inescapable.

Furthermore, it can be denied that *all* the commands,

all the attitudes exhibited in the Bible are of the highest moral quality. The behavior of Lot's daughters and the damnation of unbelievers are cases in point. But let us assume what in reality should not be so lightly assumed, that the moral insights revealed in our scriptures are of the very highest order and that through his acts God reveals his goodness to us. However, if believers so reason, they have by that very fact shown, by their own line of reasoning, that they think—inconsistently with what are taken to be God's own proclamations—that they have some knowledge of good and evil which has no logical dependence on its being willed by God.

We can see from the very structure of the argumentation here that we must use our own moral understanding to decide whether God's acts are good. We finally must judge the moral quality of the revelation; or, more accurately and less misleadingly, it is finally by what is no doubt fallible human understanding that we must judge that what *purports* to be revelation is *indeed* revelation. We must finally use our own moral understanding, if we are ever to know that God is good or, again more accurately, that there is a reality of such goodness that we should call that reality "God." Many believers do not think they think this way, but their very way of reasoning (their very use of discourse) reveals they are mistaken *about* their moral beliefs. (Our moral beliefs may be right while our beliefs *about* them—really metabeliefs—are mistaken.)

The believer should indeed concede that if we start to deliberate about the goodness of God, we cannot but end up saying something very similar to what I have just said. But our mistake, he could argue, is in ever starting this line of inquiry. Who are we to inquire into, to question, the goodness of God? That is utter blasphemy. No *genuine believer* thinks for one moment that we can question God's goodness. That was the mistake that Job made. That God is good, that indeed God is the Perfect Good, is *a given* for the believer. Given the believer's usage, it makes no sense to ask if what God commands is good or if God is good. Any being who was not good could not properly be called "God"; nor would we call anything that was not perfectly good God. A person who seriously queried, "Should I do what God ordains?" could not possibly be a believer. Indeed, Jews and Christians and Muslims do not mean by "He should do *X*" that "God ordains *X*"; and "One should do what God ordains" is not equivalent to "What God ordains God ordains." Still it is not only blasphemy; but it is, logically speaking, *senseless to question* the goodness of God.

Whence then, one might ask, the ancient problem of evil? But let us assume what it is reasonable to assume, namely, that in some way "God is good" and "God is the Perfect Good" are tautologies or "truths of reason." It still remains true that we can only come to know that anything is good or evil through our own moral insight. Let us see how this is so. First, it is important to see that "God is good" is not an identity statement: that is, "God" is not equivalent to "good." "God spoke to Moses" makes sense. "Good spoke to Moses" is not even English. But not all tautologies are statements of identity. "Wives are women" and "Triangles are three-sided" are not statements of identity, but they are clear cases of tautologies. Perhaps it is reasonable to argue "God is good" has the same status, but, even if it does, we still must independently understand what is meant by *good* and the fundamental criterion of goodness remains *independent* of God.

As we could not apply the predicate *women* to wives if we did not first understand what women are and the predicate *three-sided* to triangles if we did not understanding what it was for something to be three-sided, so we could not apply the predicate *good* to God unless we already understood what it meant to say that something is good, and had some criterion of goodness. Furthermore we can and do meaningfully apply the predicate *good* to many things and attitudes that can be understood by a person who knows nothing of God. Even in a Godless world, to relieve suffering would still be good.

But is not "God is the Perfect Good" an identity statement? Do not *God* and *the Perfect Good* refer to the same thing? The meaning of both of these terms is so indefinite that it is hard to be sure, but it is plain enough that a believer cannot, while remaining a believer, question that "God is the Perfect Good." But granting that, we still must have a more fundamental criterion for good that is independent of religion, that is independent of a belief in God, for clearly we could not judge anything to be *perfectly* good unless we could judge that it was good, and we have already seen that our more basic criterion for goodness must be independent of God.

Someone might still say: "Look, something must have gone wrong somewhere. No believer thinks he or she can question or presume to *judge* God. A devoutly religious person simply must use God as his ultimate criterion for moral behavior. If God wills it, as a "knight of faith" one must just do it!

Surely this is in a way so, but it is perfectly compatible with everything I have said. "God" by *definition* is "a being worthy of worship," "wholly good," "a being upon whom we are completely dependent." These phrases partially define the God of Judaism, Christianity, and Islam. This being so, it makes no sense at all to speak of *judging* God or deciding that God is good or worthy of worship. But the crucial point here is this: Before we can make any judgment at all that any conceivable being, force, ground of being, transcendent reality, or what not could be *worthy* of worship, could be properly called "good" and even "the Perfect Good," we must have a logically prior understanding of goodness. That we could call anything or any foundation of anything "God" presupposes we have a moral understanding, an ability to discern what would be *worthy* of worship, perfectly good. Morality does not presuppose religion; religion presupposes morality. Ludwig FEUERBACH was at least partially right: Our very concept of

God seems, in an essential part at least, a logical product of our moral categories.

In sum, then, we can say this: A radically reformationist ethic, divorcing itself from natural moral law conceptions, breaks down because something's being commanded cannot by that very act make something good. Jews, Christians, and Muslims think it can because they take God to be good and to be a being who always wills what is good. "God is good" no doubt has the status of a tautology in Christian thought, but if so, "God is good" still is not a statement of identity, and we must first understand what *good* means (including what criteria it has) before we can properly use "God is good" and "God is the perfect good." Finally we must judge concerning *any command* as to whether it ought to be obeyed; and we must use, whether we like it or not, our own moral insight and wisdom, defective though it undoubtedly is, to judge of *anything whatever whether* it is good, and finally as to whether anything could possibly be so perfectly good that it is *worthy* of worship.

If this be arrogance or hubris it is inescapable, for it is built into the logic of our language about God. We cannot base our morality on our conception of God. Rather, our very ability to have the concept of God we have presupposes a reasonably sophisticated and independent moral understanding on our part. Brunner, and the whole divine-command tradition, has the matter topsy-turvy.

VIII

Suppose someone argues, "It is a matter of faith with me that what God commands is what I ought to do; it is a matter of faith with me that God's willing it is my ultimate criterion for something's being good." Such a believer might say: "I see the force of your argument, but for me it remains a straight matter of faith that there can be no goodness without God. I do not *know* this is so; I cannot give *grounds* for believing that this is so; I simply humbly accept it on faith that something is good simply because God says that it is. I have no independent moral criterion."

Such believers surely exist. My answer to such fideists—to fix them with a label—is that in the very way they reason, in their very talk of God as the being *worthy* of worship, they show that in reality—their professions to the contrary notwithstanding—they *have* such an independent criterion. Their own generalizations *about* what they do notwithstanding, they show in their very behavior, including their linguistic behavior, that something's being willed or commanded does not by that very act make it good or make it something that they ought to do, but that its being willed by a being *they take to be* superlatively *worthy* of worship does make it good. But we should also note that it is by their own reflective decisions, by their own honest avowals, that they take some being or, if you will, some *x* to be so *worthy* of worship and thus they show in their behavior that they do not even take anything to be properly designatable as "God" unless they have made a moral judgment about that being: that they take that being to be superlatively worthy of worship. Moreover, it is their own moral judgment and understanding that enables them to take it that anything could be worthy of worship. They *say* that on faith they take God as their ultimate criterion for good, but their actions speak louder than their words, and they show by them that *even their God is in part a product of their moral sensibilities.* Only if they had a moral awareness could they use the word *God*, as a Jew or a Christian or a Muslim uses it, so that, their protestations notwithstanding, they clearly have a criterion for good and evil that is *logically* independent of their belief in God. Their talk of faith will not alter that.

If the fideists reply: "Look, we take it on faith that your argument here or any argument here is wrong. We will not trust you or any philosopher or even our own reason against our Church. We take our stand here on faith and we won't listen to anyone." If they take their stand here, we must shift our argument. We can and should point out that they are acting like blind, fanatical irrationalists— like persons suffering from a *total* ideology.

Suppose they reply: "So what? Then we are irrationalists!" We can then point out the painful consequences to themselves and others of their irrationalism. We can point out that even if for some unknown reason they are right in their claim that one ought to accept a religious morality, they are mistaken in accepting it on such irrationalist grounds. The consequences of irrationalism are such that anything goes, and this, if really followed, would be disastrous for them and others. It is like the fascist idea of "thinking with your blood."

If they say "So what?" they do not care even about this. It seems that if we were to continue to reason with them, we would now have to, perhaps like a psychoanalytic sleuth, question their *motives* for responding in such a way. They can no longer have any reasons for their claims, and indeed they do not care about reasons. So argument, deliberation, or discussion with them is out of place, though we can inquire into what *makes* them take this absurd stance. We look for *causes* here that are not *reasons*. We are a step beyond where we can ask for reasons.

There is another objection that I need to consider briefly. Someone might say: "I'm not so sure about all these fancy semantical arguments of yours. I confess I do not know what to say about them, but one thing is certain: If there is a God, then he is the author, the creator, and the sustainer of everything. He created everything other than himself. Nothing else could exist without God, and in this fundamental way everything else is totally dependent on God. Without God there could be nothing to which moral principles or moral claims could be applied. Thus, in one important respect, morality,

logic, and everything else is dependent on God, if such a reality exists."

I would first like to argue that there is a strict sense in which even this at least prima facie plausible claim of the religionist is not so. When we talk about what is morally good or morally right, we are not talking about what, except incidentally, *is* the case, but about what *ought* to be the case or about what *ought to exist*. Even if there was nothing at all—that is, if there were no objects, processes, relations, or sentient creatures—it would still be correct to say that *if* there were sentient creatures, a world in which there was less pain and suffering than the present world has would be a better world than a world like ours.

The truth of this is quite independent of the actual existence of either the world or of anything's existing, including God, though indeed we would, in reflecting on this possibility, still have to have an *idea* of what it would be like for there to be sentient life and thus a world. That its truth is independent obtains for the perfectly trivial reason that the "we" would denote a contingently empty class. Though no one could announce this truth, since if this hypothesis were true there would be no people, yet it still would be true that if there were a country like the United States and it had a president like President John F. Kennedy, then it would be wrong to have killed him. To talk about what exists is one thing, to talk about what is good or about what ought to exist is another. God could create the world, but he could not— that is, logically could not—create moral values. *Existence is one thing; value is another.*

If all this arcane argument of what ought to be as being something independent of what is strikes you as stuff of too heady a nature, consider this independent and supplementary argument against the theist's reply. To assert that nothing would be good or bad, right or wrong, if nothing existed is not to deny that we can come to understand, without reference to God, that it was wrong to kill Kennedy and that religious tolerance is a good thing. The religious moralist has not shown that such killing would not be good even if the atheist were right and God did not exist. But the religious person must show that in a godless world morality and moral values would be impossible if his or her position is to be made out. If there is no reason to believe that torturing little children would cease to be evil in a godless world, we have no reason to believe that, in any important sense, morality is dependent on religion.

We can see that we have independent criteria for what is right and wrong or good and bad. God or no God, religion or no religion, it is still evil pointlessly to inflict pain on helpless infants. This, of course, is an extreme case, but it makes vivid how our moral categories are not religion dependent. In more mundane situations this is also plainly the case. In a godless world, the practice of promise keeping would still have a rational point.

IX

There is still a further stage in the dialectic of the argument about religion and ethics. I have shown, if my arguments have been on the mark, that in a purely logical sense fundamental moral notions cannot rest on the doctrinal claims of religion. In fact, quite the reverse is the case, namely, that only if we have a religiously independent concept of good and evil can we even have the Jewish-Christian-Islamic conception of deity. In this very fundamental sense, it is not morality that rests on religion, but religion that rests on morality. Note that this argument could be made out even if we grant theists their metaphysical claims about what there is. That is to say, the claims I have hitherto made are quite independent of skeptical arguments about the reliability or even the intelligibility of claims to the effect that God exists.

Some defenders of the faith will grant that there is indeed such a fundamental claim, as independent of ethical belief as it is from religious belief, though very few, if any, would accept my last argument about the dependence of religious belief on human moral understanding. They could accept my basic claim and still argue that to develop a *fully human* and *adequate normative* ethic one must make it a religious ethic. Here, in the arguments for and against, the intellectual reliability of religious claims will become relevant.

The claim that such a religious person wishes to make is that only with a God-centered morality could we get a morality that would be adequate, that would go beyond the relativities and formalisms of a nonreligious ethic. Only a God-centered, and perhaps only a Christ-centered, morality could meet our most persistent moral demands. Human beings have certain desires and needs; they experience loneliness and despair; they create certain "images of excellence"; they seek happiness and love. If the human animal were not like this, if we were not this searching, anxiety-ridden creature with a thirst for happiness and with strong desires and aversions, there would be no good and evil, no morality at all. In short, our moralities are relative to our human nature. And, given the human nature that we in fact have, we cannot be satisfied with any purely secular ethic. We thirst for a divine father who will protect us, who will not let life be just one damn thing after another until we die and rot. We long for a God who can offer us the promise of a blissful everlasting life with him. We need to love and obey such a Father. Unless we can picture ourselves as creatures created by such a loving sovereign, and convince ourselves of the truth of our picture, our deepest moral expectations will be frustrated.

No purely secular ethic can offer such a hope. Whatever the irrationality of such a faith, our very human nature, the claim goes, makes us long for such assurances. Without it, many feel that their lives will be without significance, without moral sense; morality finds its *psychologically* realistic foundation in certain human purposes; a human life without God will be devoid of everything but trivial purposes. Thus without a belief in God, there could be no humanly satisfying morality. On this view SECULAR HUMANISM is in reality inhuman.

It is true that a secular morality can offer no hope for a blissful immortality (see IMMORTALITY, UNBELIEF IN); it is also true that secular morality does not provide for a protecting, loving father or some overarching purpose to life. But we have to balance this off against the fact that these religious concepts are myths. We human beings are helpless, utterly dependent creatures for years and years. Because of this there develops at least in many of us a deep psychological need for an all-protecting father or, depending on what culture we are in, some other cosmic assurances. It is natural enough for human beings to thirst for such security. But there *is* not the slightest reason to think that there is such security. That we have *feelings* of dependence does not mean that there is something, particularly some transcendent something, on which we can depend.

Furthermore, and more importantly, if there is no such architectonic purpose *to* life this does not at all mean there is no purpose *in* life—that there is no way of living that is ultimately satisfying and significant. It indeed appears to be true that all small purposes, if pursued too relentlessly and exclusively, leave us with a sense of emptiness. Even Mozart listened to endlessly becomes boring, but a varied life lived with verve and with a variety of conscious aims can survive the destruction of Valhalla.

We do not need a God to give meaning to our lives by making us creatures of his sovereign freedom. We, by our deliberate acts and commitments, our reflective endorsements, give meaning to our own lives. Here we have that "dreadful freedom" that yields human dignity; freedom will indeed bring anxiety, but we will be the *rider* and not the *ridden*, and by being able to choose, seek out, and sometimes realize the things we most deeply prize and admire, our lives will take on significance. A life lived without purpose is indeed a most dreadful life, but we do not need God or the gods to give purpose to our lives. We, without God, have many things we would do or be.

There are believers who would say that these purely human purposes, forged in freedom and anguish, are not sufficient to meet our deepest moral needs. We need very much to see ourselves as creatures with a purpose in a divinely ordered universe. We need to find some cosmic significance for our ideals and commitments; we want the protection and the certainty of having a function. As Dostoyevsky's Grand Inquisitor realized, and as some religionists argue, this is even more desirable than our freedom. We want and need to live and be guided by the *utterly sovereign will of God*. If that entails a sacrifice of our autonomy, so be it.

If religious moralists really want this and would continue to want it on careful reflection, after all the consequences of this view and the alternatives had been placed vividly before them, we *may* with them finally get back to an ultimate *disagreement in attitude*. But before we get there, there is a good bit that can be said. How could their purposes really be *their* own purposes, if they were creatures made for God's sovereign purpose and under the sovereign will of God? Their ends would not be something they had deliberately chosen, but would simply be something that they could not help realizing. Moreover, is it really compatible with human dignity to be *made for* something? To ask, "What are you *for*?" is an insult! Finally, is it not infantile to go on looking for some father, some order, that will lift all the burden of decision from you? Some children follow rules blindly, but do we want to be children all our lives?

It is hardly arrogance on our part to want a world where we can make our own decisions and live as we reflectively want in ways that do not harm others. We will want to follow the rules and have the practices we do, not simply because we have been enculturated into them, but because we see and accept their point. We want to have moral norms where we do not have to crucify our intellects in trying to belief these norms answer to some transcendent rationale whose very intelligibility is seriously in question. To charge secular humanists with hubris here is symptomatic of a dying religion suffering a failure of nerve in a world which in Max Weber's conception is becoming progressively disenchanted. The present task is not only to continue disenchanting and demystifying, but also to struggle to make our world a place that we would like to live in: that would answer to what we reflectively and nonevasively find desirable. Religion cannot achieve that for us, but as long as we by our own collective actions do not achieve it for ourselves, there will arise from the conditions of our social life pitiful phenomena like that of the Moral Majority or Christian Evangelicals for Bush.

BIBLIOGRAPHY

Baier, Kurt. "The Meaning of Life." In *The Meaning of Life*, edited by E. D. Klemke. Oxford: Oxford University Press, 1981.

Daniels, Norman. *Justice and Justification.* Cambridge: Cambridge University Press, 1996.

Donagan, Alan. *Reflections on Philosophy and Religion.* Oxford: Oxford University Press, 1999.

George, Robert P., ed. *Natural Law Theory.* Oxford: Clarendon, 1992.

Idziak, Janine Marie, ed. *Divine Command Morality: Historical and Contemporary Readings.* New York: Mellen, 1979.

Klemke, E. D., ed. *The Meaning of Life.* Oxford: Oxford University Press, 1981.

Nielsen, Kai. "Ethical Relativism and the Facts of Cultural Relativity." *Social Research* 33 (1966).

———. *Ethics without God.* Amherst, NY: Prometheus Books, 1990.

———. *God and the Grounding of Morality.* Ottawa, ON: University of Ottawa Press, 1991.

———. *Naturalism and Religion.* Amherst, NY: Prometheus Books, 2001.

———. *Naturalism without Foundations.* Amherst, NY: Prometheus Books, 1996.

KAI NIELSEN

EUGENICS. The term *eugenics* was originally coined by Francis Galton in 1893, under the influence of Charles DARWIN's work *The Origin of Species.* The word *eugenics* was intended to refer to attempts to improve the condition of the human race by means of what we would now call genetic policies. The term *genetics* itself was introduced only in 1905 by William Bateson to provide a name for the science of heredity, the study of how like normally begets like.

In the last quarter of the nineteenth century, a number of biological and social scientists came to believe that the quality of the populations of the Western nations was deteriorating. They thought this was happening because of a relaxation of natural selection, the process by which in every generation the unfit tend to be eliminated by the reduction of their fertility and/or by their relatively early deaths. They had in mind improvements in medicine and sanitation, and adaptive devices such as eyeglasses. Once natural selection becomes relaxed by such means, they argued, genetic deterioration becomes inevitable. They therefore concluded that this process of degeneration had already begun.

Some of these practically minded Victorians therefore began to ask themselves what could be done to counter such genetic degeneration. The obvious solution was to replace natural selection by a deliberately designed artificial selection by which human societies would become able to control and improve their own genetic quality. Such genetic policies would be of two kinds: positive, attempting to promote the birth of children to, and the raising of children by, parents perceived to be of a superior kind; and negative, attempting to prevent the birth to, and the raising of children by, parents perceived to be of an inferior kind.

Galton himself tried to promote positive eugenics in two ways. One was by establishing local eugenics associations to promote eugenic principles in their localities. The other was by trying to identify those families in those localities that had, by virtue of their qualities of health, ability, and character, made valuable social contributions over several generations, and to make them aware of their duty to have children, and thereby to increase, or at least maintain, their numbers in future generations. Galton's final contribution to this campaign was to announce, in a lecture to the Sociological Society at the London School of Economics in 1905, that he was funding a research fellowship at University College, London to undertake the task of compiling pedigrees of elite families. This research was then begun by Edgar Schuster. The first volume, which dealt with the pedigrees of eminent British scientists, was published in the following year.

Galton's negative eugenics was directed at curtailing the fertility of so-called undesirables. This social group roughly corresponds to what much later became known as the underclass. Subsequent debates might have been less politically confused had the word *set* been used here instead of the word *class*. (By Cantor's Axiom for Sets, the sole essential feature of a set is that its members have at least one common characteristic, any kind of characteristic.)

Galton had read and digested the American sociologist Richard Dugdale's account of the degenerate Jukes family, which had produced seven generations of criminals, alcoholics, unemployables, and prostitutes. That account was the first detailed study of what was later to be called "the intergenerational cycle of transmitted deprivation." Such families, Galton believed, were not confined to the United States. England too was "overstocked and overburdened by the listless and incapable." He considered that such persons "are exceptionally and unquestionably unfit to contribute offspring to the nation." He "believed that stern compulsion ought to be exerted to prevent the free propagation of stock of those who are seriously afflicted by lunacy, feeble-mindedness, habitual criminality, and pauperism." Galton himself was confident that democracies would ultimately refuse consent to that liberty of propagating that was then allowed to the undesirable classes.

Although the twentieth century is now some years behind us, British democracy has not yet shown any sign of justifying Galton's confidence. But well before the end of that century, sterilization laws had been adopted in several other countries. By 1913 such laws had been adopted by twelve US states, and by 1931 by thirty; these laws were implemented on a substantial scale. It was, for instance, estimated by Ludmerer that by 1935 about twenty thousand sterilizations had been performed in the United States, and that by 1970 this figure had risen to about sixty thousand, of whom about half were mentally retarded and half were both mentally retarded and criminal. From the early 1970s some sterilizations continued to be performed in the United States, but the number was greatly reduced as the result of legal challenges, changes in public sentiment, and pressure by civil liberties organizations.

Sterilization laws similar to those in the United States were introduced in 1920 in the Canadian province of Alberta, in Denmark, and in Switzerland; in 1933 in Germany; in 1934 in Norway and Sweden; and in 1935 in Finland. In 1977 it emerged that approximately 60,000 people had been sterilized in Sweden between 1934 and 1976, the year during which the sterilization law was repealed. That amounts to roughly the same proportion of the population as was sterilized in Nazi Germany between 1933 and 1939. Eugenic sterilization was introduced in Japan in 1948, allowing doctors to sterilize those

with gross mental or physical handicaps without their consent. It is estimated that 16,520 Japanese women were compulsorily sterilized between 1949 and 1995. The Japanese Sterilization Law was repealed in 1996.

Although the intellectual firepower exercised in support of eugenics in the United Kingdom seems to have been greater than that exercised in any other nation state, its actual effect on state policy has been negligible. Before the end of the nineteenth century the social philosopher Herbert SPENCER and the Fabian socialist Sidney Webb declared their support for Galton's views. Webb did research in the 1890s that showed "the improvident" had above-average numbers of children, and he wrote of the high fertility of the "degenerate hordes of a demoralized residuum." The leading exponent of eugenics in that pre–World War I period was Karl Pearson, a professor of applied mathematics at University College, London now mainly remembered for working out the statistical method of the Pearson correlation coefficient.

Until roughly two-thirds of the way through the twentieth century, eugenics continued to command the support of many, if not most, professional biologists. Thus Julian HUXLEY (grandson of the Thomas Henry HUXLEY, who became known as Darwin's bulldog, and brother of Aldous Huxley, who described a eugenic state in his novel *Brave New World*), who himself became the first director general of UNESCO, was always a member of the British Eugenics Society, was its president for the period between 1949 and 1968, and gave its annual Galton Lecture in 1936 and 1962.

But in the 1960s support for eugenics began to decline. All over the world eugenics societies put themselves into voluntary liquidation. A crucial year was 1969, when the American Eugenics Society ended publication of its journal *Eugenics Quarterly* and replaced it with *Social Biology*, and the British Eugenics Society ended publication of the *Eugenics Review* and replaced it with the *Journal of Biological Science*. In 1972 the American Eugenics Society changed its name to the Society for the Study of Social Biology. In 1974 the president of the new society explained that "[t]he society was groping for a wholly new definition of purpose. It was no longer thinking in terms of 'superior' individuals, 'superior' family stocks or even of social conditions that would bring about a 'better' distribution of births. It was thinking in terms of *diversity*" (italics added).

In France the Nobel Prize–winning physician and eugenicist Alexis Carrell had been honored by the medical faculty at the University of Lyons being named after him; streets were also named after him in Bordeaux, Strasbourg, and several other cities. In the 1970s and 1980s Carrell's name was removed from the Lyons medical faculty and from the streets.

In the United States, three people, Mark Haller, Kenneth Ludmerer, and Daniel Kevles, published polemical and abusive histories of the eugenics movement. Extracts from the third of these were serialized in the

New Yorker, while the *New York Times Book Review* described it as "a revealing study by a distinguished historian of science." For an alternative and better-informed view of this work of Kevles see pp. 15–17 of the first chapter of Richard Lynn's scholarly *Dysgenics: Genetic Deterioration in Modern Populations* (Westport, CT: Praeger, 1996).

ANTONY FLEW

EUPRAXSOPHY. The term *eupraxophy*, later modified to *eupraxsophy*, was introduced to characterize a way of life different from either religion or philosophy. It applies especially to SECULAR HUMANISM, which combines a method of inquiry, a cosmic worldview, a life stance, and a set of social values.

Fundamentalist religionists have attacked secular humanism as a "religion," which it is not. There has been no word in the English language adequate to describe secular humanism fully (though see LIFE STANCE). The Dutch, for example, have the word *levensbeschouwing*, which can be translated as "reflection on, consideration of, or view of life." Dutch also has the adjective *levensovertuiging*, which is stronger than *levensbeschouwing* because *overtuiging* means "conviction." Thus there are no religious overtones. *Religion* in Dutch is *godsdienst*, which means "service to God." English has no such terminology.

The term *eupraxsophy* is a term that can be used in many languages. Literally, *eupraxsophy* means "good practical wisdom." It is derived from the following Greek roots: *e*, *praxis*, and *-sophia*. *E* is a prefix that means "good," "well," "advantageous." It is combined in words such as *eudaimonia*, which means "well-being" or "happiness"; it is also used in *eulogy* (good speaking, as of the dead), *euphoria* (good feeling), *euthanasia* (good death), and so on. *Praxis* refers to "action, doing, or practice." *Eupraxia* means "right action" or "good conduct." The suffix *-sophia* is derived from *sophos* ("wise") and means "wisdom." This suffix appears in the term *philosophy*, combining *philos* ("loving") and *-sophia* ("wisdom") to mean "love of wisdom."

In its original sense, philosophy—as metaphysics or "the science of being"—investigated the general principles and categories by which we can understand nature and interpret reality. The classical philosophers attempted to work out a system of nature in which certain principles were considered to be basic. Metaphysics has suffered considerable disrepute in modern times, particularly at the hands of skeptical critics. At the very least, metaphysics analyzes and interprets the basic concepts of the sciences, attempts to make some sense out of them, and, if possible, to unify them. This is a very complex task today because of the continuing proliferation of new disciplines and fields of learning, and the enormous difficulty for any single mind to be able to master the expanding corpus of knowledge.

Philosophical inquiry also focuses on epistemology, the theory of knowledge. It is concerned with questions of meaning and truth and with the principles of valid inference: inductive and deductive logic. There are many other branches of philosophy, including logic, aesthetics, ethics, the philosophy of science, political and social philosophy, and the philosophy of religion; indeed, almost any field can be approached philosophically.

Synthetic philosophy attempts to offer universal or general principles and to develop an overall view, a cosmic perspective or *Weltanschauung*. This is sometimes called synoptic or speculative philosophy, but since the development of modern science in the sixteenth and seventeenth centuries, this approach has been seriously questioned on methodological grounds, for it cannot be done independently of science but only in relation to it. Nonetheless, philosophy, in this sense, is thinking about generalities; it is concerned with root questions and cosmic coherence. Analytic and critical philosophy, on the other hand, are far more modest in scope. Analytic philosophy is concerned with understanding the nature of meaning and truth, and in defining and analyzing the key concepts within any particular field of inquiry. Critical philosophy is evaluative; it strives for clarity, but it also seeks to appraise the validity of truth claims.

These activities are primarily intellectual in purpose, and they are neutral in regard to their practical consequences. The Greeks distinguished contemplative from practical wisdom. Philosophy, as the love of wisdom, begins primarily in the theoretical or contemplative mode. There is another branch of normative philosophy, however, that strives for practical wisdom in ethics and politics. Here, classical philosophy sought to provide some guidance for the good life and the just society. ARISTOTLE maintained in the *Nicomachean Ethics* that ethics has practical import and that we should study it in order to live well. He held that the development of character and virtue and the exercise of practical wisdom would contribute to the achievement of happiness. Many ethical philosophers, however, have focused primarily on the meta-analysis of concepts such as "good," "bad," "virtue," "value," "justice," and so on. This was expanded in latter-day Kantian philosophy (see KANT, IMMANUEL) to the definitions of "right," "wrong," "obligation," "responsibility," and the like. Whether or not these terms can be defined has been hotly debated down to the present; objectivists believe that they can be defined, but there is a skeptical tradition (see SKEPTICISM) that denies their definability. Be that as it may, classical ethics always had a normative purpose.

A basic distinction can be made between customary morality (see MORALITY FROM A HUMANIST POSITION), which refers to the moral conceptions that already prevail in a given cultural group, and *ethics*, which involves a reflective and critical component (see ETHICS AND UNBELIEF). Today, many philosophers concerned with ethics emphasize the need for ethical rationality—but virtually for its own sake; and many eschew making any concrete recommendations beyond this in dealing with problems that arise in customary morality. This is particularly true in universities and colleges, where philosophy is taught as an academic discipline, where philosophers do philosophical research and publish their disquisitions in scholarly journals, and where philosophy teachers have no clearly identifiable positions. They consider their primary pedagogical method to be the presentation of alternative philosophical theories and do not attempt to inculcate a set of beliefs or values; that is, they do not seek to persuade their students or the general public to accept their philosophical outlook. Since their task is pure inquiry, similar to that of other disciplines, such as history and the natural and social sciences, they can safely retreat into splendid isolation in an ivory tower—being philosophers qua philosophers—without any need to vindicate their personal positions. The virtue of this form of philosophy is that the professor imparts a love of wisdom and the skills of critical thinking without imposing his or her own biases on the student. The professor does not wish to indoctrinate or propagandize for a particular cosmic outlook. He or she wants to be objective, or may even fear reprisals from those who support the conventional wisdom of the day. Yet this kind of philosophy does not satisfy the deeper queries either of students, or of ordinary men and women. It presents no worldview; it does not defend a theory of meaning and truth; nor does it seek to persuade others of the comparative reasonableness of the philosopher's own considered normative or social ideology. Philosophy, as the love of wisdom, aside from being committed to fair-minded and objective critical analysis, most often is *neutral*. It can take no position; it can draw no normative conclusions from its formal analyses. It is largely a cognitive enterprise; it involves no attitudinal or emotive component. Nor does it seek to arouse conviction or inspire commitment.

How far this form of philosophy has come from the original Socratic vision of the good life! For SOCRATES, philosophy had direct relevance to how we should live. The unexamined life is not worth living, he averred, and he was even willing to die for his convictions. Baruch SPINOZA's *Ethics* seems to have expressed both a philosophy and a eupraxsophy, at least implicitly. We might even say that many or most philosophical systems implicitly had a pragmatic function and that their task was to provide an alternative to religion and a guide to ethics and politics. Contemplative wisdom was often a mask for deeper utilitarian purposes. Karl MARX clearly marked a break with the contemplative mode of philosophy, particularly when he said that the task of philosophy was not simply to interpret the world but to change it! Philosophy in this sense has momentous significance—as it did for Jeremy BENTHAM, John Stuart MILL, Friedrich NIETZSCHE, Arthur SCHOPENHAUER, Bertrand

RUSSELL, Jean-Paul SARTRE, John DEWEY, Sidney HOOK, and others. Thus many philosophers historically played analogous roles. Alas, philosophy today has all too often become wedded to the academy or corrupted by narrow specialization. Philosophy has lost out to religion and ideology, which in competition for the "souls" of men and women now rule the day.

Eupraxsophy differs from antiseptically neutral philosophy in that it enters consciously and forthrightly into the arena where ideas contend. It takes new directions and seeks to carve out a new approach. Unlike pure philosophy, it is not simply the love of wisdom, though this is surely implied by it, but also the *practice* of wisdom. This does not mean that ethicists should not be interested in developing the capacity for critical ethical judgment. That is an eminently worthwhile goal. But eupraxsophy goes further than that, for it provides a coherent, ethical life stance. Moreover, it presents a cosmic theory of reality that seems reasonable at a particular point in history in the light of the best knowledge of the day. Secular humanist eupraxsophy defends a set of criteria governing the testing of truth claims. It also advocates an ethical posture. Also it is committed, implicitly or explicitly, to a set of sociopolitical ideals. Eupraxsophy combines both a *Weltanschauung* and a philosophy of living. But it takes us one step further by means of commitment; based upon cognition, it is fused with passion. It involves the application of wisdom to the conduct of life.

Analytic and formalistic philosophies are unwilling to affirm this conviction. They examine all sides of a question, see the limits and pitfalls of each, but are unwilling to take a stand on any. This has some merit; the open mind must recognize that it may be mistaken and that views may have to be modified in the light of new arguments or evidence. For the *eupraxsopher*, a skeptical attitude is essential—but not at the price of forfeiting all convictions (see SKEPTICISM). The eupraxsopher does make choices—the most reasonable ones in light of the available evidence—and this enables him or her to act. After all, theologians, politicians, generals, engineers, businessmen, lawyers, doctors, artists, poets, and plain men and women have beliefs, and they act. Why deny this right to the informed philosopher-eupraxsopher? For the eupraxsopher, one's beliefs should be based upon reason, critical intelligence, and wisdom. This is what the suffix *-sophy* refers to. Wisdom in the broad sense includes not only philosophical and practical judgment, but also *scientific understanding*.

Merriam-Webster's Collegiate Dictionary defines *-sophia* or wisdom as follows: "1. The quality of being wise; ability to judge soundly and deal sagaciously with facts, especially as they relate to life and conduct; knowledge, with the capacity to make due use of it; perception of the best ends and the best means; discernment and judgment; discretion; sagacity. 2. Scientific or philosophical knowledge."

Explicit in this definition is a *scientific* component, for wisdom includes the best scientific knowledge drawn from research and scholarship in the various fields of inquiry. Unfortunately, expert practitioners in the various scientific specialties often feel qualified to judge only matters within their own areas of competence, failing to engage the broader questions that have direct bearing on life. There is a crisis in modern science, for the specialties are growing exponentially, with many specialists feeling that they can talk only to those within their own disciplines. Science thus has become fragmented. Who is able to cross the boundary lines and draw meta-inferences about nature, the human species, society, or life in general? The eupraxsopher deems it his mission to do so. E. O. Wilson characterizes the goal of this enterprise as *consilience*, an attempt to interpret and integrate scientific knowledge across many disciplines.

Theoretical scientific research is morally neutral. The scientist is interested in developing causal hypotheses and theories that can be verified by the evidence. Scientists describe or explain how the subject under study behaves without evaluating it normatively. There is, of course, a pragmatic element to science, particularly the applied sciences; for we constantly seek to apply our scientific know-how to practical technology. Moreover, scientists presuppose epistemological criteria that govern their process of inquiry. They are committed to a set of values including truth, clarity, consistency, rationality, and objectivity. But scientists qua scientists do not go beyond that, and restrict themselves in the quest for knowledge to their specialized domain of inquiry.

Secular humanist eupraxsophy, on the other hand, attempts to draw the philosophical implications of science to the life of human beings. It seeks to develop a cosmic perspective, based on the most reliable findings encountered on the frontiers of science. It recognizes the gaps in knowledge and the things we do not know that still need to be investigated. It is keenly aware of the need for fallibilism and AGNOSTICISM about what we do and do not know. Yet it boldly applies practical scientific wisdom to life.

Eupraxsophy, unlike philosophy or science, does not focus on one specialized field of knowledge; it seeks to understand the total impact of scientific knowledge on a person's life. Yet the areas of philosophy, science, and eupraxsophy are not rigid. Philosophers can assist scientists in interpreting their discoveries and relating them to other fields of inquiry, and in developing a broader point of view. Still, eupraxsophy moves beyond philosophy and science in seeking to present a coherent, naturalistic life view as the basis on which we are willing to act. It is the ground upon which we stand, the ultimate outlook that controls our view of reality.

Accordingly, the primary task of eupraxsophy is to understand nature and life and to draw concrete normative prescriptions from this knowledge. Eupraxsophy thus draws deeply from the wells of philosophy, ethics, and science. It involves at least a double focus: a cosmic perspective and a set of normative ideals by which we may live.

BIBLIOGRAPHY

Dewey, John. *Reconstruction in Philosophy.* New York: Holt, 1920.

Hook, Sidney. *Convictions.* Amherst, NY: Prometheus Books, 1990.

Kurtz, Paul. *Eupraxophy: Living without Religion.* Amherst, NY: Prometheus Books, 1989. Republished as *Living without Religion: Eupraxsophy.* Amherst, NY: Prometheus Books, 1994.

———. *Forbidden Fruit: The Ethics of Humanism.* Amherst, NY: Prometheus Books, 1988.

———. *The New Skepticism: Inquiry and Reliable Knowledge.* Amherst, NY: Prometheus Books, 1992.

Mill, John Stuart. *Utililarianism.* New York: Liberal Arts Press, 1957.

Nietzsche, Friedrich Wilhelm. *Thus Spake Zarathustra.* Translated by Walter Kaufmann. New York: Penguin, 1978.

Wilson, E. O. *Consilience: The Unity of Knowledge.* New York: Vintage, 1998.

PAUL KURTZ

EURIPIDES (485?–406 BCE), Greek playwright. Of the ninety plays Euripides is believed to have written, nineteen have come down to us—a far higher proportion than that of any other Greek playwright, but nevertheless a partial and perhaps unrepresentative selection.

Even in antiquity, Euripides developed a reputation for ATHEISM. The comic playwright Aristophanes has one of his characters remark: "But now that man [Euripides] by his tragic poetry has persuaded men that there are no gods at all." The classical scholar A. W. Verrall made Euripides' atheism the focus of his study *Euripides the Rationalist* (1913); but, granting that our knowledge of Euripides' work is imperfect (and granting further that, as with any playwright or novelist, it is highly problematic to attribute any given character's utterances to the author himself), it is the consensus of modern scholars that Euripides, while expressing skepticism and even scorn of the Greek pantheon and of the miraculous stories attributed to the gods, was not what one would today call an atheist.

The evidence for Euripides' religious skepticism is not easily interpretable. One fragment seems clear on the matter: "Who is it, anyway, that says the gods exist in starry heaven?/ They don't. They don't exist at all./Anyone still willing to talk in that old-fashioned way is a moron." But it is not clear how this utterance fits into the drama of which it is a part. Another fragment is less ambiguous: "If the gods do evil, they are not gods." This, in effect, is the thrust of Euripides' surviving play *Herakles*, in which the hero Herakles (believed to be the son of Zeus and a mortal, Alcmene) is maddened by Hera and kills his own wife and children. Theseus, attempting to console Herakles after his madness has subsided and he is consumed with guilt for his actions, notes that even the gods commit adultery and other acts that would be branded as sinful. To this Herakles replies: "I don't believe gods tolerate unlawful love./Those tales of chainings are unworthy; I never did/And never will accept them; nor that any god/Is tyrant of another. A god, if truly god,/Needs nothing. Those are poets' lamentable myths." The remarkable statement "[a] god . . . needs nothing," while probably derived from XENOPHANES, constitutes a radical repudiation of the basis of Greek religion, in which the gods were believed to be pleased with the animal sacrifices and other rituals that mortals made in their honor; it is also a striking anticipation of the theology of EPICURUS.

It would seem that Euripides, a generation younger than Aeschylus and a younger contemporary of Sophocles, and writing in the full flower of the radical skepticism engendered by the Sophists, was evolving a theology that repudiated the scandalous legends pertaining to the Greek gods as well as the notion, found in such writers as Hesiod, Pindar, and Aeschylus, that the gods were both powerful and just. Euripides has several characters express scorn of belief in oracles. The *Bacchae* has been thought to display the viciousness of some Greek religious rituals, as Pentheus is torn apart by women (including his own mother) maddened by Dionysus. But the exact degree of Euripides' religious skepticism will always remain a matter of doubt.

BIBLIOGRAPHY

Grube, G. M. A. *The Drama of Euripides.* London: Methuen, 1941.
Meagher, Robert Emmet. *Mortal Vision: The Wisdom of Euripides.* New York: St. Martin's, 1989.
Verrall, A. W. *Euripides the Rationalist.* Cambridge: Cambridge University Press, 1913.

S. T. JOSHI

EVANS, MARIAN (GEORGE ELIOT; 1819–1880), British writer. The SKEPTICISM of George Eliot is best summed up in words attributed to her in conversation with Fredrick William Henry Myers, a fellow of Trinity College, Cambridge, who also had lost his Christian faith. Myers "remembered how, at Cambridge, I walked with her once . . . on an evening of rainy May; and she, stirred somewhat beyond her wont, and taking as her text the three words which have been so often as the inspiring trumpet-calls of men,—the words *God, Immortality, Duty*—pronounced, with terrible earnestness, how inconceivable was the *first*, how unbelievable the *second*, and yet how peremptory and absolute the *third*."

Early Life. Mary Anne (later Marian) Evans, the youngest of three children from the second marriage of Robert Evans, the estate manager of the Newdigate

family of Arbury Hall in North Warwickshire, was born at South Farm on the Arbury Estate on November 22, 1819. Her mother, Christiana Pearson, was a farmer's daughter who had two other children, Christiana ("Chrissey") and Isaac, with whom Mary Anne had a complex lrelationship.

The family moved when she was only a few months old to nearby Griff, the family home until she was twenty-one. Between 1825 and 1835 she attended various local boarding schools, where she was subject to daily Bible readings and hymns. At home, as Eliot scholar G. S. Haight notes, John Bunyan's *The Pilgrim's Progress*, Daniel Defoe's *The Political History of the Devil*, and Jeremy Taylor's *Holy Living and Holy Dying* were among the few books allowed. At school she came under the influence of Maria Lewis, an Evangelical teacher. Their letters are replete with biblical citations, allusions, and religious piety. Between the ages of thirteen and sixteen she boarded at a school in Coventry run by the two daughters of a Baptist minister, where the daily diet of Bible readings and hymns continued.

Coventry: The 1840s. Her mother died in 1836, and Evans, in addition to looking after her brother and her father, continued to read widely and learn languages. Following Isaac's marriage in 1841, she and her father moved to Foleshill, a Coventry suburb. In August 1838 she made her first visit to London. Eliot scholar John Walter Cross notes: "[S]he was so much under the influence of religious and ascetic ideas that she would not go to any of the theaters with her brother, but spent all her evenings alone reading . . . the chief thing she wanted to buy was Josephus's *History of the Jews*." Such interest in life under the Romans at the time of Jesus and of Jewish Resistance to the Romans suggests a questioning of received notions of the life of Jesus. Her neighbors and close friends at Foleshill who remained lifelong friends included the wealthy Unitarians (see UNITARIAN UNIVERSALISM) Charles Bray, Caroline Bray, and Sara Sophia Hennell. The Brays' house, Rosehill, was a mecca for freethinkers and radicals. Eliot read Charles Christian Hennell's *Inquiry concerning the Origin of Christianity* (1838), which questioned the belief in miracles and Jesus's divinity. On January 2, 1842, she refused to attend church with her father. She wrote to him that she regarded the "Jewish and Christian Scriptures . . . as history consisting of mingling truth and fiction." At Rosehill during the 1840s she met many radical thinkers, including Ralph Waldo EMERSON, Herbert SPENCER, Harriet MARTINEAU, and the London radical publisher John Chapman, for whom she was to work.

Important translations questioning received religious opinion emerge from this period. She took over from her friend "Rufa" Brabant the task of translating into English David Friedrich STRAUSS's *Das Leben Jesu*, published in German in 1835. The translation was sponsored by the radical freethinking politician Joseph Parkes and published by Chapman in June 1846. The translator's name was absent from the title page of this reexamination of the events of Jesus's life, which found them without historical foundation and based on myth (see JESUS, HISTORICITY OF). During this period Evans wrote and reviewed for the *Coventry Herald*, and began a translation of the political writings of the great Dutch Jewish pantheist and radical Baruch SPINOZA.

London: The 1850s. In March 1850 Evans returned to England from Geneva, where she had gone following her father's death in May 1849. For a few years she lodged with her employer, John Chapman, and his family. She worked as an editor and contributor to his publications, mainly with the radical journal the *Westminster Review*. Chapman specialized in publications reflecting radical and skeptical perspectives. At Chapman's home she met many skeptics and freethinkers including Herbert SPENCER and George Henry Lewes. The former, a distinguished political philosopher, rejected her personal overtures. She formed a close relationship with Lewes, a journalist, editor, dramatist, physiologist, philosopher, novelist, and man of letters, which lasted from the mid-1850s until his death twenty-five years later. Lewes, married with children, was unable to obtain a divorce from his wife. Upon learning of the relationship, her beloved brother, Isaac, broke off all direct contact with his sister. He resumed it only in 1878, following Lewes's death. In addition to breaking totally with social convention in her personal life, she edited and wrote extensively on diverse subjects, including radical German thought.

In 1854 Chapman published under the name "Marian Evans" her translation of Ludwig FEUERBACH's free-thinking *Das Wesen des Christenthums*, first published in 1840. At the core of Feuerbach lies a belief found in her fiction: the importance of human relationships rather than the supernatural or reliance upon a deity or god. Evans had, however, the greatest respect for religious expression and belief. She wrote to Charles Bray on July 5, 1859: "I can't tell you how much melancholy it causes me that people are, for the most part, so incapable of comprehending the state of mind which cares for that which is essentially human in all forms of belief, and desires to exhibit it under all forms with loving truthfulness. Free-thinkers are scarcely wider than the orthodox in this matter,—they all want to see themselves and their own opinions held up to the true and the lovely."

During the 1850s Evans and Lewes were influenced by the Positivist writings of the French thinker Auguste COMTE (see POSITIVISM). The early writings, with their emphasis upon the importance of human relationships, rejection of the metaphysical, and belief in some kind of objective reality, had a considerable impact upon Evans's writings. His later creation of positive rituals she and Lewes found themselves less in sympathy with. Ironically, George Eliot's poem "O May I Join the Choir Invisible," written in 1867, was adopted by the positivists as a central hymn in their ceremonies.

The Priory and Success. Encouraged by Lewes to write fiction, her early *Scenes of Clerical Life* (1858) and *Adam Bede* (1859) achieved success. She adopted the pseudonym "George Eliot." *The Mill on the Floss* (1860), a thinly disguised autobiographical novel, and *Silas Marner* (1861) cemented her status as a best-selling novelist. Real financial security was secured by the publication of *Romola*, the rights for which were negotiated by Lewes with the London publisher George Smith. This was the only occasion on which Lewes and Eliot left Blackwood's, the Edinburgh publisher with whom she published her other fiction, because of an exceptionally generous prepublication advance offered by Smith. As it happened, Smith lost money when sales of the novel failed to make good the advance; nonetheless, from its proceeds Lewes and Eliot moved in November 1863 to the Priory near Regents Park, where they would live until Lewes's death of enteritis on November 30, 1878. In November 1876 Eliot and Lewes bought the Heights, in Witley, Surrey, as a country retreat. In addition to traveling frequently on the European continent with Lewes, she produced poems and essays in addition to fiction. Her last three published novels, *Felix Holt, the Radical* (1866); *Middlemarch, A Study of Provincial Life* (1871–72); and *Daniel Deronda* (1875–76), have contrasting settings: provincial England in the time of the Reform Act, and, in her last completed novel, aristocratic English settings, European gambling casinos, and impoverished London Jewish homes. A central preoccupation in them is the theme of the improbable becoming possible.

Final Years: After Life. Following Lewes's death, Eliot shut herself away from the world. Somewhat surprisingly, on May 6, 1880, she married the banker John Walter Cross, twenty years her junior. On December 22, 1880, she died of kidney disease. Burial in Westminster Abbey was denied, and on December 29, 1880, she was laid to rest alongside Lewes in the dissenters' section of Highgate Cemetery, North London.

Following a period of critical neglect in the earlier part of the twentieth century, George Eliot's work became recognized as among the very greatest productions of Victorian fiction. In the words of the radical writer William Hale White, "[S]he was really one of the most skeptical, unusual creatures I ever knew."

BIBLIOGRAPHY

Ashton, Rosemary. "Evans, Marian." *Oxford Dictionary of National Biography*, vol 18. Oxford: Oxford University Press, 2004.

Baker, William, and John C. Ross. *George Eliot: A Bibliographical History*. London: British Library; New Castle, DE: Oak Knoll, 2002.

Cross, John Walter. *George Eliot's Life as Related in Her Letters and Journals*. 3 vols. Edinburgh and London: William Blackwood, 1885.

Haight, Gordon S. *A Century of George Eliot Criticism.* London: Methuen, 1965.

———. *The George Eliot Letters.* 9 vols. New Haven and London: Yale University Press, 1954–1978.

Myers, Frederick William Henry. *Essays—Modern.* London: Macmillan, 1883.

White, William Hale [George Eliot]. *Athenaeum* (London), November 28, 1885.

Wright, T. R. *The Religion of Humanity: The Impact of Comtean Positivism in Victorian Britain.* Cambridge: Cambridge University Press, 1986.

WILLIAM BAKER

EVIDENTIALISM. Evidentialism is a theory of epistemic justification which claims that the only propositions that should be accepted as true are those for which one has sufficient evidence. Propositions that are not so supported should not be accepted. The best known expression of this view is found in William Kingdon CLIFFORD's 1876 essay "The Ethics of Belief," in which he writes: "It is wrong always, everywhere, and for any one, to believe anything upon insufficient evidence."

Clifford was not the first to propose evidentialism. John LOCKE had earlier issued an evidentialist challenge to religious believers. Locke was critical of those he called *enthusiasts*—individuals who claimed to have received private revelations from God but who could offer no evidence other than their own word to support their claims. Locke was not only troubled by the seeming irrationality of such claims; he also held that enthusiasm in this regard was antisocial. Locke argued that only religious beliefs that could be supported by evidence were worthy of being held. He was confident that the doctrines of Christianity could be so supported—a view which Clifford would later strongly oppose.

Unlike Locke, David HUME raised serious questions about whether it is possible to choose one's beliefs, or alter them at will, in which case evidentialism would have no empirical support. Hume made a distinction between the vulgar masses, who in general do not examine their beliefs, and the wise, who as a result of experience have formed the habit of developing their critical faculties. Clifford would make no such distinction. For him, the duty to examine one's beliefs is the same for the intellectual in the ivory tower as it is for the simple tradesman drinking a beer in the alehouse. "No simplicity of mind," he was to write in "The Ethics of Belief," "no obscurity of station, can escape the universal duty of questioning all that we believe."

Since the mid-1970s, especially with the rise of the so-called reformed epistemology school in philosophy, Clifford's epistemic position has become more of a focal point of criticism, especially by Christian philosophers Peter van Inwagen and Alvin Plantinga. The former notes that Clifford's evidentialism, although theoretically pertinent to *any* human belief, is almost always applied to *religious* beliefs rather than to philosophical, economic, social, or political beliefs. However, Clifford himself was careful to state that his admonition was indeed for all beliefs—it is just that religious beliefs tend to be the ones that are more likely to be shielded from criticism.

No doubt the most prominent contemporary Christian writer to criticize Clifford is the Notre Dame professor Alvin Plantinga. A self-professed reformed epistemologist, tracing his intellectual sympathies back to John Calvin, Plantinga has long argued that it is rational to believe in God despite not having any evidence whatsoever, and that evidentialists like Clifford fail to make a good counterargument. Plantinga argued that some beliefs are "basic"—it is not necessary to provide evidence for them, since they are a matter of trusting our very cognitive faculties. Asking for evidence is equivalent to demanding what the foundation is for one's belief, but if basic beliefs do not exist, then foundationalism itself is guilty of infinite regress.

Plantinga criticizes foundationalism for holding to the view that propositions obtain warrant in only one of two ways: either through being a basic belief, or else through acquiring warrant by virtue of being believed on the basis of some other proposition that already has warrant. But this being the case, a proposition like "I believe in God" can be treated in the same manner as a proposition like "I believe I had Rice Krispies for breakfast this morning." Why do foundationalists demand evidence for the former and not the latter? Furthermore, members of a given belief community need not justify their basic beliefs to others. While faulting Clifford for his strident and simplistic tone, Plantinga is equally guilty of presenting the evidentialist view in an overly simplistic manner. Plantinga treats Clifford as a "stock" or "paradigm" figure, without necessarily carefully examining what Clifford himself really meant. Utilizing the views of John Calvin with approval, Plantinga argues that God has so created us that we have a tendency or disposition to see his hand in the world about us. Those who deny this, like Clifford, are deliberately ignoring such dispositions implanted within us by the creator. Why do some people not accept such beliefs? Plantinga implies that the nonbelievers either have an improperly functioning intellectual system, or are guilty of committing willful sin.

Locke and Clifford present a formula by which knowledge may be advanced on an objective basis. Critics of Plantinga point out that abandoning evidentialism leads to a type of fideism, a justification of beliefs based solely upon one's faith. Plantinga and his fellow reform epistemologists, for all their erudition, come rather close to following the enthusiastic line which Locke had critiqued at the very beginning of the evidentialist debate.

In addition to the foundationalistic controversy, there are other questions raised by evidentialism. First of all, do we really have control over our beliefs? This volitionalist argument has led some to doubt that evidentialism is itself a tenable claim. If we cannot truly alter our beliefs in light of new evidence, then the very topic is moot. Others have given a more restrained volitional argument. William James, for instance, criticized Clifford in his 1896 essay "The Will to Believe" by claiming that Clifford's evidentialism was too rigid. There are cases where the evidence is itself inconclusive, such as when a person has climbed a mountain and found that the path down has become impassable. He or she needs to jump from one mountain peak to another in order to escape, but has no conclusive evidence as to whether this is possible or not. James argued that in such cases one has a *right* to believe, because the belief itself can aid in bringing about the very thing desired, reaching the opposite peak safely. Clifford would have responded that this was not a matter of believing in the truth of a proposition, but rather weighing probabilities, what he would call a "provisional belief." The difference between a Jamesian and Cliffordian evidentialism, therefore, revolves around whether, as James phrased it, "faith in a fact can help create the fact," and whether such faith can actually create its own verification (see VERIFICATIONISM). For James, religious beliefs tend to fall within this area, for by acting *as if* they are true, one can perhaps actually bring about the state of affairs—such as God's existence or an afterlife—to which they refer. Critics of James have pointed out that he confuses action itself with a disposition to act. The key point is that James actually agrees with Clifford's main assertion, that one should never believe anything upon insufficient evidence.

Another challenge to evidentialism is just what would constitute "sufficient evidence." As philosopher Mario Bunge has pointed out, evidence comes in degrees: strong, weak, and inconclusive. With strong evidence, nothing else but that evidence would confirm a claim or prediction. With weak or inconclusive evidence, however, that which tends to support a claim or prediction could be otherwise interpreted. For example, one person may hold that the existence of crop circles in an empty field is evidence of space aliens, whereas skeptics would argue that such circles have either a naturalistic explanation or are a hoax perpetrated by human beings. Advocates of evidentialism, therefore, are closely connected with adherents of the scientific method, and argue that proper evidence must be verifiable, testable, and replicable in order to count as strong or conclusive support. Religious claims based upon personal experience or strong emotions would be categorized as weak or inconclusive.

Finally, several contemporary writers have pointed out that a distinction needs to be made between ethical and epistemological evidentialism. Clifford conflates the two, but one can look upon them separately. For instance, there are bad epistemic habits, such as sloppy inquiry, jumping to conclusions, and wishful thinking, which, if unchecked, can have harmful effects upon one's forma-

tion of beliefs, but it is by no means evident that this is a moral issue. Lorraine Code, in her book *Epistemic Responsibility* (1987), has carefully distinguished these two categories, and Earl Conee and Richard Feldman, in their edited volume *Evidentialism* (2004), have given the strongest contemporary defense of epistemic evidentialism. Code herself, however, also provides a possible approach toward defending Clifford's overall strategy of combining ethical and epistemic evidentialism, by developing a model of what she calls "an intellectually virtuous character." This is a person, argues Code, who maintains "a matter of orientation toward the world and toward oneself as a knowledge-seeker in the world. . . . Intellectually virtuous persons value knowing and understanding how things really are. They resist the temptations to live with partial explanations where fuller ones are attainable; they resist the temptation to live in fantasy or in a world of dream or illusion, considering it better to know, despite the tempting comfort and complacency a life of fantasy or illusion (or one well tinged with fantasy or illusion) can offer."

BIBLIOGRAPHY

Bunge, Mario. *Philosophical Dictionary*. Amherst, NY: Prometheus Books, 2003.

Code, Lorraine. *Epistemic Responsibility*. Hanover, NH: University Press of New England, 1987.

Conee, Earl, and Richard Feldman. *Evidentialism*. Oxford: Oxford University Press, 2004.

Plantinga, Alvin. *Warrant: The Current Debate*. Oxford: Oxford University Press, 1993.

Van Inwagen, Peter. *God, Knowledge and Mystery: Essays in Philosophical Theology*. Ithaca, NY: Cornell University Press, 1995.

TIMOTHY J. MADIGAN

EVIL, PROBLEM OF. The idea that at least some of the evil present in the world constitutes a problem for belief in the existence of God is both an ancient idea—going back at least to Job, and presumably beyond—and a very natural one. Whether evil is, however, a decisive objection to the existence of God has remained unclear, as various formulations of the argument from evil that initially seemed plausible have proven problematic. This entry is concerned, accordingly, with how the argument from evil should be formulated, and with the various ways in which theists can respond to the argument.

Formulating the Argument from Evil. *Relevant Conceptions of God.* If a creator of the universe is conceived of in certain ways, the existence of evil in the world has no bearing at all upon the likelihood that such a creator exists. This is true, for example, if one thinks in terms of a deistic god who brought the world into existence, but who then had no concern at all about the events that subsequently took place, and so who would never intervene in the world in any way (see DEISM).

The argument from evil becomes relevant when one has a god whose moral character, in contrast to that of the god of deism, provides a ground for believing that fundamental human hopes—that death is not the end of an individual's existence, that evil will not triumph over good, and that, in the end, justice will be done—will be realized. To provide such a ground for hope, however, one needs a deity that is very powerful, very knowledgeable, and morally very good—and ideally, one who is unlimited in these respects.

A good starting point, accordingly, is with the question of whether the evils we find in the world provide good reason for concluding that the God of traditional monotheism—that is, an all-powerful, all-knowing, and perfectly good person who created the world—does not exist. As a result, formulations of the argument from evil typically focus upon precisely this conception of God. But this is not to say that the relevance of the argument from evil is limited to God, thus conceived: properly formulated, the argument from evil may also tell against a wide range of possible deities with finite knowledge and power who are less than perfectly good.

Logical versus Evidential Formulations of the Argument from Evil. The argument from evil starts from the fact that the world appears to contain states of affairs that are bad, or undesirable, or that should have been prevented by any being who could have done so; and it asks how the existence of such states of affairs is to be squared with the existence of God. But the argument can be formulated in two very different ways. First, it can be set out as a purely deductive argument that attempts to show that certain facts about the evil in the world are logically incompatible with the existence of God. One especially ambitious form of this first sort of argument attempts to establish the very strong claim that it is *logically impossible* for God to exist if there is *any* evil at all in the world.

So understood, the argument might be put as follows. If God exists, he will want to prevent evil, since he is by definition morally perfect. Being omniscient, he will know about any evil that is about to come into existence. And being omnipotent, he will have the power to prevent any such evil. So if God exists, he will be willing and able to prevent all evil. Therefore, if God exists, there will not be any evil. But the world does contain evil. Therefore, God does not exist.

This form of the argument initially has a striking and perhaps impressive quality. It seems very doubtful, however, that it is sound. The reason is that the claim that a morally perfect being would want to eliminate any evil that exists is not unproblematic, since what this claim can be seen to rest upon, when it is scrutinized, is the assumption that no evil is ever logically necessary for some good state of affairs that outweighs it. Is this claim true? Some people have argued that it is not. For example, some people have argued that the world is a

better place if people develop desirable traits of character—such as patience and courage—by struggling against obstacles, including suffering. But if this is right, then the elimination of *all* suffering would actually make the world a worse place, by depriving people of the chance to develop desirable traits of character by responding appropriately to suffering that they undergo.

The examples that are usually advanced of cases where some evil is logically necessary for a greater good that outweighs the evil are not, perhaps, convincing. But, on the other hand, they do seem to show that one cannot establish, without appealing to some substantive, and controversial, moral theory, that there cannot be cases where some evil is logically necessary for a greater good that outweighs it. Consequently, it would seem that the argument from evil should be formulated in a different way—not as a deductive argument for the very strong claim that it is logically impossible for both God and evil to exist (or for God and certain types, or a certain amount, of evil to exist), but as an inductive (or evidential or probabilistic) argument for the more modest claim that some evils that actually exist in the world make it very unlikely that God exists.

Responses to the Argument from Evil: Refutations, Defenses, and Theodicies. A successful version of the argument from evil involves two claims. The first is that there are facts about evil in the world that make it prima facie unlikely that God exists. The second is that the situation is not altered when information about such facts is conjoined with all the other things that one is justified in believing. The existence of God is, therefore, also unlikely relative to the totality of what one is justified in believing.

A theist can respond to the argument from evil, then, by questioning either of these claims. Thus, a theist might grant that there are facts about evil that, other things being equal, render it unlikely that God exists, but then argue that when those considerations are combined with everything else that one is justified in believing, it turns out that it is not unlikely that God exists, all things considered. Alternatively, a theist can attempt to defend the more radical thesis that there are no facts about evil in the world that make it even prima facie unlikely that God exists.

If the latter thesis is correct, the argument from evil does not even get started. So let us refer to such responses to the argument from evil as attempted *total refutations*.

The claim that relevant facts about evils in the world do not make it even prima facie unlikely that God exists probably strikes most people as rather implausible. A number of philosophical theists have, however, attempted to defend this type of response to the argument from evil.

The other alternative open to the theist is to grant that there are facts about evils in the world that make it prima facie unlikely that God exists, but then to argue that the existence of God is not unlikely, all things considered. But here there are two different possibilities. One involves offering a *theodicy*. For this, the theist must specify, for every actual evil found in the world, some state of affairs that it is reasonable to believe exists, and that constitutes a morally sufficient reason for an omnipotent and omniscient being's allowing the evil in question.

The second possibility open to the theist who grants that there are facts about evils in the world that render it prima facie unlikely that God exists is to offer a *defense*, where this involves attempting to show that it is *likely* that *there are* facts that would justify an omnipotent and omniscient being in not preventing the evils that we find in the world, even if we do not know what they are.

In short, a defense attempts to show only that some God-justifying reasons probably exist; a theodicy, by contrast, also attempts to specify what those God-justifying reasons are.

Total Refutations? How might one attempt to show that the evils found in the world are not even prima facie evidence against the existence of God? Three main ways have been advanced, involving, first, the ontological argument; second, the claim that there is no best of all possible worlds; and third, an appeal to human epistemological limitations.

An Appeal to the Ontological Argument. One way of attempting to show that facts about evil do not provide even prima facie evidence against the existence of God is by appealing to the ontological argument. For while relatively few philosophers have held that the ontological argument is sound, there have certainly been some who have—such as Anselm and René DESCARTES, and, more recently, Norman Malcolm, Charles Hartshorne, and Alvin Plantinga.

If the ontological argument were sound, it would certainly provide a completely decisive answer to all versions of the argument from evil, since if, as the ontological argument attempts to show, it is a logically necessary truth that an omnipotent, omniscient, and morally perfect being exists, then it follows that the proposition that God does not exist must have probability zero on any body of evidence whatever.

But is the ontological argument sound? The vast majority of present-day philosophers believe that it is not, and one way of arguing for that view is by appealing to variants on a type of objection that was directed against the ontological argument by Gaunilo, a contemporary of Anselm. What Gaunilo argued was that one can parallel Anselm's argument for the existence of a perfect being to arrive at the corresponding conclusions concerning perfect beings of any sort whatever—such as perfect islands, perfect unicorns, and so on. These conclusions, however, are surely very implausible. But, in addition, one can strengthen Gaunilo's objection by focusing on versions that lead to mutually incompatible conclusions, such as the conclusion that there is a perfect solvent, together with the conclusion that there is a perfectly insoluble sub-

stance. For if arguments with precisely the same logical form as the ontological argument and with equally acceptable premises generate contradictions, then the ontological argument must be unsound.

The "No Best of All Possible Worlds" Response. A second way of attempting to set out a total refutation of the argument from evil is by appealing to the claim that there is no best of all possible worlds, since if it is true, for *every* possible world, however good, that there is a better one, then the fact that this world is not the best of all possible worlds provides no reason for concluding that, if there is an omnipotent and omniscient being, that being cannot be morally perfect.

This response to the argument from evil has been strongly advocated by George Schlesinger and, more recently, by Peter Forrest—though Forrest, curiously, describes the defense as one that has been "neglected," and refers neither to Schlesinger's well-known discussions, nor to the very strong objections that have been directed against this response to the argument from evil.

The natural reply to this attempt to refute the argument from evil has been set out very clearly by Nicholas La Para and Haig Khatchadourian among others, and it has been developed in an especially forceful and detailed way by Keith Chrzan. The basic point is that the argument from evil, when properly formulated in a deontological fashion, does not involve the claim that this world could be improved upon, nor the claim that it is not the best of all possible worlds: it turns instead upon the claim that there are good reasons for holding that the world contains evils, including instances of suffering, that it would be morally wrong, all things considered, for an omnipotent and omniscient being to allow. As a consequence, the contention that there might be better and better worlds without limit is simply irrelevant to the argument from evil, properly formulated.

Human Epistemological Limitations. The most popular way of attempting to construct a total refutation of the argument from evil—and also one of the most common responses to the argument by present-day philosophical theists—involves an appeal to human cognitive limitations. The idea is this. Suppose that it is granted that there are apparent evils in the world that, judged in the light of the right-making and wrong-making, or goodmaking and badmaking, properties that we are aware of, it would be morally very wrong for an omnipotent and omniscient person to allow to exist. An omnipotent and omniscient being would surely be aware, however, of morally significant properties that we are not aware of. But, then, how can one be justified in concluding that apparent evils for which we can see no justification *have* no justification? How can one show that there are no God-justifying reasons for such evils that lie outside the scope of human knowledge?

This is a very important response to the argument from evil. The answer, as we shall see in section 6, is that an application of inductive logic enables one to show that while it is logically possible that such God-justifying reasons exist, the probability that they do is very, very low.

Defenses to the Argument from Evil. Let us now consider defenses to the argument from evil—where, as indicated earlier, a defense involves an attempt to show that it is likely that every apparently gratuitous evil is such that an omnipotent and omniscient person would have a morally sufficient reason for not preventing its existence, but where no attempt is made to specify what those morally sufficient reasons might be.

The Appeal to Positive Evidence for the Existence of God. Theists have often contended that there are a variety of arguments that, even if they do not prove that God exists, provide positive evidence to that effect. The question arises, then, whether such positive evidence might not outweigh the negative evidence of apparently unjustified evils.

This thought has led a number of philosophers to claim that in order to be justified in asserting that there are evils in the world that establish that it is unlikely that God exists, one would first have to examine all of the traditional arguments for the existence of God, and show that none of them is sound. Alvin Plantinga, for example, says that in order for the atheologian to show that the existence of God is improbable relative to one's total evidence, "he would be obliged to consider all the sorts of reasons natural theologians have invoked in favor of theistic belief—the traditional cosmological, teleological and ontological arguments, for example." And in a similar vein, Bruce Reichenbach remarks: "With respect to the atheologian's inductive argument from evil, the theist might reasonably contend that the atheologian's exclusion of the theistic arguments or proofs for God's existence advanced by the natural theologian has skewed the results."

If one is defending an evidential version of the argument from evil, one certainly needs to consider what sorts of positive reasons might be offered in support of the existence of God. But Plantinga and Reichenbach are advancing a much stronger claim here, for they are saying that one needs to look at *all* of the traditional theistic arguments. They are claiming, in short, that if one of those arguments turned out to be defensible, then it would serve to undercut the argument from evil.

To see that this view is mistaken, consider the cosmological argument. In some versions of the cosmological argument, the conclusion is that there is an unmoved mover; in others, the conclusion is that there is a first cause; in still others, it is that there is a necessary being, having its necessity of itself. The crucial point is that none of these conclusions involves any claim about the moral character of the object in question, let alone the claim that it is a morally perfect person. In the absence of such a claim, however, one does not have an argument that, even if it turned out to be sound, could undercut the argument from evil.

The situation is not substantially different in the case of arguments from order in the world, since while such arguments, if sound, might provide grounds for drawing some tentative conclusion concerning the moral character of the designer or creator of the universe, the conclusion would not be one that could be used to overthrow the argument from evil. The reason is that given the mixture of good and evil that one finds in the world, no argument from order could provide support for the existence of a designer or creator who was even very good, let alone one who was morally perfect (see INTELLIGENT DESIGN THEORY).

A similar conclusion holds for other arguments, such as those that appeal to purported miracles, or religious experiences (see RELIGIOUS AND MYSTICAL EXPERIENCES). Thus, although in the case of religious experiences it might be argued that personal contact with a being may provide additional evidence concerning the person's character, it is clear that the primary evidence concerning a person's character must consist of information concerning what the person does and does not do. So, contrary to the claim advanced by Robert Adams, even if there were veridical religious experiences, they would not provide one with a satisfactory defense against the argument from evil.

An effective way of seeing the basic point here is by noticing that an alternative way of setting out the argument from evil is by assuming, for the sake of argument, that there is an omnipotent and omniscient person, and then viewing the argument as showing something about the moral character of any such omnipotent and omniscient person, namely, that is it is very unlikely that such a person is even morally good, let alone morally perfect.

Given such a reformulation of the argument from evil, it is clear that the vast majority of considerations that have been offered as reasons for believing in the existence of God are of no help to the person who is trying to resist the argument from evil, since most of them provide, at best, very tenuous grounds for any conclusion concerning the moral character of any omnipotent and omniscient being who may happen to exist.

The ontological argument is, of course, a notable exception, and, consequently, the advocate of the argument from evil certainly needs to be able to show that it is unsound. But almost all of the other standard arguments for the existence of God are simply irrelevant.

Induction Based on Partial Success. A second type of defense has been mentioned by Richard Swinburne. In an article in which he argued in support of the conclusion that theists need to offer a theodicy, Swinburne noted one minor qualification—namely, that if one could show, for a sufficiently impressive range of evils that initially seemed problematic, that it was likely that an omnipotent and omniscient person would be morally justified in not having prevented them, then one might very well be justified in believing that the same would be true of other evils, even if one could not specify, in those other cases, what the morally sufficient reason for allowing them might be.

What Swinburne says here is surely reasonable, and there would not seem to be any objection in principle to a defense of this sort. The problem with it, however, is that no theodicy that has ever been proposed has been successful in the relevant way—that is, no theodicy has been able to point to an impressive range of apparent evils where, when people are confronted with some proposed theodicy, they come to believe that the apparent evils are not really evils, all things considered.

Theodicies. Let us turn now to theodicies. What are the prospects for a complete or nearly complete theodicy? Some philosophers, such as Swinburne, are optimistic, and believe that "the required theodicy can be provided." Others, including many theists, are much less hopeful. Plantinga, for example, remarks: ". . . we cannot see *why* our world, with all its ills, would be better than others we think we can imagine, or *what*, in any detail, is God's reason for permitting a given specific and appalling evil. Not only can we not see this, we can't think of any very good possibilities. And here I must say that most attempts to explain *why* God permits evil— *theodicies*, as we may call them—strike me as tepid, shallow and ultimately frivolous."

What types of theodicies have been proposed? An exhaustive survey will not be possible here. Four approaches, however, are especially important. These involve an appeal, first, to the value of a world that is governed by natural laws; second, to the value of libertarian free will; third, to the value of the freedom to inflict horrendous evil upon others; and fourth, to the value of acquiring desirable traits of character in response to suffering.

Natural Laws. One historically important approach to theodicy turns upon the idea that it is crucially important that the world be governed by natural laws. This type of theodicy involves the following four claims. First, it is essential that events in the world take place in a regular way, since otherwise effective action on the part of humans would be impossible. Second, events will exhibit regular patterns only if they are governed by natural laws. Third, however, if events are governed by natural laws, the operation of those laws will give rise to events that harm individuals. Hence, fourth, God's allowing natural evils is justified because the existence of natural evils is entailed by natural laws, and a world without natural laws would be a much worse world.

This type of theodicy is open to decisive objections. First, precisely what natural evils a world contains depends not just on the laws of that world, but also on the initial, or boundary conditions. For example, an omnipotent being could create ex nihilo a world containing human beings, and with the same laws of nature as our world, but without nonhuman carnivores. Such a world would have immensely less suffering than our world, where many animals die very painful deaths at the hands (or, rather, claws and teeth) of other animals.

Similarly, our world, rather than being a limited globe, could be an infinite plane, with unlimited room for populations to expand, along with ample natural resources to support such populations.

Second, many evils depend upon precisely what laws the world contains. An omnipotent being could, for example, easily create a world with the same laws of physics as our world, but with slightly different laws linking neurophysiological states with qualities of experiences, so that extremely intense pain either did not arise, or could be turned off when it served no purpose. Alternatively, additional physical laws of a rather specialized sort could be introduced that would cause very harmful viruses to self-destruct.

Third, this first approach to theodicy provides no account of moral evil—that is, the evil that results from immoral actions, unless it is held that human actions are also causally determined by natural laws. Of course, if other theodicies could provide a justification for God's allowing moral evil, that would not be a problem. But, as we shall, that does not appear to be the case.

Libertarian Free Will. A second important approach to theodicy, and one that focuses especially upon moral evil, involves the following ideas. First, while there are conceptions of free will that are compatible with one's behavior being completely determined, there is a type of free will—known as libertarian free will—that is incompatible with DETERMINISM, and it is precisely this type of freedom that is of great value. Second, because it is part of the definition of libertarian free will that an action that is free in that sense cannot be caused by anything outside of the agent, not even God can cause a person to freely do what is right. Third, in view of the great value of libertarian free will, it is better for God to create a world where agents possess libertarian free will—even though they may misuse it, and may do what is wrong—than for God to create a world where agents lack libertarian free will.

One problem with an appeal to libertarian free will is that no satisfactory account of the concept of libertarian free will is yet available. Thus, while the idea that, in order for an action to be free in the libertarian sense, it must not have any cause that lies outside the agent is unproblematic, this is not a sufficient condition, since that condition would be satisfied if the behavior in question were caused by random events within the agent. So one needs to add that the agent is, in some sense, the cause of the action.

But the problem with this is that present accounts of the metaphysics of causation typically treat causes as events, or states of affairs, and if one adopts such an approach, then it seems that all that one has when an action is freely done, in the libertarian sense, is that there is some uncaused mental state of the agent that causally gives rise to the relevant behavior, and the question is then why freedom, thus understood, should be thought to be valuable.

The alternative is to shift from event causation to what

is referred to as "agent causation." But then the problem is that there is no satisfactory account of agent causation.

But even if this initial difficulty concerning the nature of libertarian free will is set aside, there are still several very strong objections to any freewill approach to theodicy. In the first place, the fact that libertarian free will is valuable does not entail that one should never intervene when someone is performing an action that involves an exercise of libertarian free will, since very few people think, for example, that one should not intervene to prevent someone from committing rape or murder. On the contrary, almost everyone would hold that a failure to prevent heinously evil actions when one can do so would itself be seriously wrong.

Second, the claim that libertarian free will is valuable does not entail that it is a good thing for people to have the power to inflict great harm upon others. An omnipotent and omniscient being could, accordingly, create a world where individuals had libertarian free will, but did not have the power to torture and murder others.

Third, many evils are caused by natural processes, such as earthquakes, hurricanes, tsunamis, volcanoes, and so on, and by a wide variety of diseases. Such evils certainly do not appear to result from morally wrong actions, and if they do not, then no appeal to the value of libertarian free will can provide an answer to any version of the argument from evil that focuses upon such natural evils.

Some writers—such as C. S. Lewis and Alvin Plantinga—have suggested that what appear to be natural evils may ultimately be due instead to the immoral actions of supernatural beings. If that were so, then the result would be that the first two objections mentioned above would have increased force, since one would have many more cases where individuals were not only being given the power to inflict great harm on others, but also were being allowed by God to perform horrendously evil actions leading to enormous suffering and many deaths. But it can also be plausibly argued, in response to this Lewis/Plantinga move, that, although it is *possible* that earthquakes, hurricanes, cancer, and the predation of animals are all caused by malevolent supernatural beings, the probability that this is so is extremely low.

The Freedom to Do Great Evil. It was noted above that agents could be free in a libertarian sense even if they did not have the power to inflict great harm upon others. This point has led at least one theistic philosopher—namely, Richard Swinburne—to argue that, while free will is valuable, precisely how valuable it is depends upon the range of actions open to one. If possible actions vary enormously in moral worth, then, Swinburne claims, libertarian free will is very valuable indeed. But if the variation in the moral status of what one can do is very limited, then, Swinburne contends, libertarian free will adds much less to the world: one has, to his way of thinking, a "toy world," where one has very little responsibility for the well-being of others.

Swinburne's variant on the appeal to libertarian free will is also open to a number of objections. First, and as with freewill theodicies in general, this line of thought provides no justification for the existence of what appear to be natural evils.

Second, if what matters is simply the existence of alternative actions that differ greatly in moral value, such differences can exist even in a world where one lacks the power to inflict great *harm* on others, since there can be actions that would benefit others enormously, and which one may either perform or refrain from performing.

Third, what exactly is the underlying line of thought here? In the case of human actions, Swinburne surely holds that one should intervene to prevent someone from doing something that would be morally horrendous, if one can do so. Is the idea, then, that while occasional prevention of such evils does not significantly reduce the scope of the moral responsibility of others, if one's power were to increase, a point would be reached where one should sometimes refrain from preventing people from performing morally horrendous actions? But why should this be so? One answer might be that if one intervened too frequently, then people would come to believe that they did not have the ability to perform such actions. But, in the first place, it is not clear why that would be undesirable. People could still, for example, be thoroughly evil, for they could wish that they had the power to perform such terrible actions, and be disposed to perform such actions if they ever came to have the power. In the second place, prevention of deeply evil actions could take quite different forms. People could, for example, be given a conscience that led them, when they had decided to cause great injury to others, and were about to do so, to feel that what they were about to do was too terrible a thing, so that they would not carry out the action. In such a world, people could surely still feel that they themselves were capable of performing heinously evil actions, and so they would continue to attempt to perform such actions.

A Soul-Making Theodicy. A fourth and very important type of theodicy, championed especially by John Hick, involves the idea that the evils that the world contains can be seen to be justified if one views the world as designed by God as an environment in which people can, through the free decisions that they make, undergo spiritual growth that will ultimately fit them for communion with God:

> The value-judgment that is implicitly being invoked here is that one who has attained to goodness by meeting and eventually mastering temptation, and thus by rightly making responsibly choices in concrete situations, is good in a richer and more valuable sense than would be one created *ab initio* in a state either of innocence or of virtue. In the former case, which is that of the actual moral achievements of mankind, the individual's goodness has within it the strength of temptations over-

come, a stability based upon an accumulation of right choices, and a positive and responsible character that comes from the investment of costly personal effort.

Hick's basic suggestion, then, is, first, that soul making is a great good; second, that God is therefore justified in designing a world with that purpose in mind; third, that our world is very well designed in that respect; and thus, fourth, that if one views evil as a problem, it is because one mistakenly thinks that the world ought, instead, to be a hedonistic paradise.

Is this theodicy satisfactory? There are a number of reasons for holding that it is not. First, there is the horrendous suffering that people undergo, either at the hands of others—as in the Holocaust—or because of terminal illnesses such as cancer. What is one to say about such evils? One writer—Eleonore Stump—has suggested that the terrible suffering that many people undergo at the end of their lives, in cases where it cannot be alleviated, is to be viewed as suffering that has been ordained by God for the spiritual health of the individual in question. But given that it does not seem to be true that terrible terminal illnesses more commonly fall upon those in bad spiritual health than upon those of good character, let alone that they fall only upon the former, this "spiritual chemotherapy" view seems very implausible. More generally, there seems to be no reason at all why a world must contain *horrendous* suffering if it is to provide a good environment for the development of character in response to challenges and temptations.

Second, and as illustrated by the weakness of Hick's own discussion, a soul-making theodicy provides no justification for the existence of any animal pain, let alone for a world where predation is not only present but a major feature of nonhuman animal life. The world could perfectly well have contained only human persons, or only human persons plus herbivores.

Third, the soul-making theodicy provides no account either of the suffering that young, innocent children endure, either because of terrible diseases or at the hands of adults. For here, as in the case of animals, there is no soul-making purpose that is served.

Finally, if one's purpose were to create a world that would be a good place for soul making, would our earth count as a job well done? It is very hard to see that it would. Some people die young, before they have had any chance at all to master temptations, to respond to challenges, and to develop morally. Others endure suffering so great that it is virtually impossible for them to develop those moral traits that involve relationships with other people. Still others enjoy lives of ease and luxury where there is virtually nothing that challenges them to undergo moral growth.

Inductive Logic and the Evidential Argument from Evil. In his article "Ruminations about Evil," William Rowe focuses upon the case of a young girl who is bru-

tally beaten and murdered by her mother's boyfriend. If one knowingly allowed such an event to take place, one would be doing something that possessed a very serous wrong-making feature—that is, a property that would make one's failure to intervene morally wrong, and seriously so—unless there was some counterbalancing right-making property. When we humans contemplate such an occurrence, none of the right-making properties that we are familiar with are both present and sufficiently weighty to make it morally permissible for one not to have intervened, if one could have done so.

Consequently, the following claim is justified:

1. There are cases of allowing a young girl to be brutally beaten and murdered where the action of doing so has a serious wrong-making property that is not counterbalanced by any right-making property that we are aware of.

The crucial question is now whether we are justified in moving inductively from this claim to the conclusion that the following claim is *probably* true:

2. There are cases of allowing a young girl to be brutally beaten and murdered where the total wrong-making properties of allowing this, *both known and unknown*, are not counterbalanced by the total right-making properties, *both known and unknown*.

The reason that this inference is crucial is, first, that it can be shown, by a sound *deductive* argument, that (2) entails that God, defined as an omnipotent, omniscient, and morally perfect being, does not exist; and second, it then follows via postulates of inductive logic that, given (1), it is unlikely that God exists.

In the section "Human Epistemological Limitations," it was noted that one of the most common present-day responses to the evidential argument from evil involves the claim that probabilistic inferences of the sort involved in the move from (1) to (2) are rendered unsound by the fact that there may be any number of morally significant properties that lie outside the scope of human knowledge. Is this contention correct? The answer is that it is not.

To demonstrate this would require a rather technical argument in inductive logic. But one can gain an intuitive understanding of the basic idea in the following way. Suppose that there is some very significant right-making property of which we have no knowledge. If an action of allowing a child to be brutally killed possessed that property, then it might not be wrong to allow that action. But the existence of unknown right-making properties is no more likely, a priori, than of unknown wrong-making properties. So let us suppose, then, that there are two morally significant properties of which we humans have no knowledge—a right-making property, R, and a wrong-making property, W. Let us suppose, further, that these two properties are equally weighty, since, a priori, there is no reason for supposing that one is more significant than the other. Finally, let A be an action of knowingly allowing a child to be brutally killed. We can see that there are four possibilities:

1. Action A has both unknown properties, R and W. In this case, those two unknown properties cancel one another out, and action A will be morally wrong, all things considered.
2. Action A has the unknown right-making property, R, but not the unknown wrong-making property, W. In this case, action A may be morally permissible, all things considered, if property R is sufficiently strong to outweigh the known wrong-making property of allowing a child to be brutally killed.
3. Action A has the unknown wrong-making property, W, but not the unknown right-making property, R. In this case, action A is even more wrong, all things considered, than it initially appeared to be.
4. Action A does not have either of the unknown, morally significant properties, R and W. In this case action A is morally wrong to precisely the degree that it initially appeared to be.

The upshot is that in three of the four possibilities that we have considered, action A turns out to be morally wrong, all things considered. Accordingly, the idea that there may be moral properties that lie outside the scope of human knowledge does not undermine in any way the probabilistic inference that is involved in the move from statement (1) to statement (2): if an action of knowingly allowing a child to be brutally killed is morally wrong as judged by the moral knowledge that we humans possess, then it is more likely than not that it is morally wrong judged by the totality of moral knowledge, including any moral truths that lie outside our ken.

A full exposition of this argument requires a careful application of inductive logic. But if one undertakes that task, what is the result? The answer is that if one considers a *single* action that is morally wrong as judged by the moral knowledge that we possess—such as that of knowingly allowing a child to be brutally killed—then the probability that that action is not morally wrong, all things considered, can be shown to be less than one half. If one considers *two* actions that are morally wrong as judged by the moral knowledge that we possess, then the probability that neither action is morally wrong, all things considered, can be shown to be less than one-third, since it turns out that the general result that one can establish is this:

Suppose that there are n events, each of which, judged by *known* right-making and wrong-making properties, is such that it would be morally wrong to allow that event. Then, the probability that, judged in the light of *all* right-making and wrong-

making properties, *known and unknown*, it would not be morally wrong to allow *any* of those events, must be less than $\frac{1}{n+1}$.

The conclusion, accordingly, is that by considering n apparent evils, one can show that the probability that God exists must be less than $\frac{1}{n+1}$.

The probability that God exists depends, then, on the number, n, of apparent evils. But this number is surely very large, given, for example, that the present population of the world is about six billion, and that most of those people during their lifetimes will suffer evils that they do not deserve to undergo—including various diseases, aging, and death. If this is right, then a version of the evidential argument from evil that makes use of inductive logic can be seen to generate the result that the probability that God exists is very low.

BIBLIOGRAPHY

Adams, Robert M. "Plantinga on the Problem of Evil." In *Alvin Plantinga*, edited by James E. Tomberlin and Peter van Inwagen. Dordrecht: D. Reidel, 1985.

Chrzan, Keith. "The Irrelevance of the No Best Possible World Defense." *Philosophia* 17 (1987).

Draper, Paul. "Pain and Pleasure: An Evidential Problem for Theists." *Noûs* 23 (1989).

Forrest, Peter. "The Problem of Evil: Two Neglected Defenses." *Sophia* 20 (1981).

Hartshorne, Charles. *The Logic of Perfection*. La Salle, IL: Open Court, 1962.

Hasker, William. "Suffering, Soul-Making, and Salvation." *International Philosophical Quarterly* 28 (1988).

Hick, John. *Evil and the God of Love*. New York: Harper & Row, 1966.

Howard-Snyder, Daniel, ed. *The Evidential Argument from Evil*. Bloomington: Indiana University Press, 1996.

Hume, David. *Dialogues concerning Natural Religion*. Edited by Norman Kemp Smith. Indianapolis, IN: Bobbs-Merrill, 1947.

Kane, G. Stanley. "The Failure of Soul-Making Theodicy." *International Journal for Philosophy of Religion* 6 (1975).

Khatchadourian, Haig. "God, Happiness and Evil." *Religious Studies* 2 (1966).

La Para, Nicholas. "Suffering, Happiness, Evil." *Sophia* 4 (1965).

Lewis, C. S. *The Problem of Pain*. London: Fontana, 1957.

Malcolm, Norman. "Anselm's Ontological Arguments." *Philosophical Review* 69 (1960).

Martin, Michael. "Reichenbach on Natural Evil." *Religious Studies* 24 (1988).

McKim, Robert. "Worlds without Evil." *International Journal for Philosophy of Religion* 15 (1984).

O'Connor, David. "Swinburne on Natural Evil." *Religious Studies* 19 (1983).

Plantinga, Alvin. *God, Freedom, and Evil.* New York: Harper & Row, 1974.

———. *The Nature of Necessity.* Oxford: Clarendon, 1974.

———. "The Probabilistic Argument from Evil." *Philosophical Studies* 35 (1979).

———. "Self-Profile." In *Alvin Plantinga*, edited by James E. Tomberlin and Peter van Inwagen. Dordrecht: D. Reidel, 1985.

Reichenbach, Bruce R. "The Inductive Argument from Evil." *American Philosophical Quarterly* 17 (1980).

———. "Natural Evils and Natural Law: A Theodicy for Natural Evils." *International Philosophical Quarterly* 16 (1976).

Rowe, William L. "The Problem of Evil and Some Varieties of Atheism." *American Philosophical Quarterly* 16 (1979).

———. "Ruminations about Evil." In *Philosophical Perspectives, 5, Philosophy of Religion*, edited by James E. Tomberlin. Atascadera, CA: Ridgeview, 1991.

Schlesinger, George. "The Problem of Evil and the Problem of Suffering." *American Philosophical Quarterly* 1 (1964).

———. *Religion and Scientific Method.* Boston: D. Reidel, 1977.

Smith, Quentin. "An Atheological Argument from Evil Natural Laws." *International Journal for Philosophy of Religion* (1991).

Stump, Eleonore. "Aquinas on the Sufferings of Job." In *Reasoned Faith*, edited by Eleonore Stump. Ithaca, NY: Cornell University Press, 1993.

Swinburne, Richard. "Does Theism Need a Theodicy?" *Canadian Journal of Philosophy* 18 (1988).

———. *The Existence of God.* Oxford: Clarendon, 1979.

———."Some Major Strands of Theodicy." In *The Evidential Argument from Evil*, edited by Daniel Howard-Snyder. Bloomington: Indiana University Press, 1996.

Tomberlin, James E., ed. *Philosophical Perspectives, 5, Philosophy of Religion, 1991.* Atascadera, CA: Ridgeview, 1991.

Tomberlin, James E., and Peter van Inwagen, eds. *Alvin Plantinga.* Dordrecht: D. Reidel, 1985,

Tooley, Michael. "Plantinga's Defence of the Ontological Argument." *Mind* 90 (1981).

Wykstra, Stephen J. "The Humean Obstacle to Evidential Arguments from Suffering: On Avoiding the Evils of 'Appearance.'" *International Journal for Philosophy of Religion* 16 (1984).

MICHAEL TOOLEY

EVOLUTION AND UNBELIEF. See LIFE, ORIGIN OF, AND UNBELIEF.

EXISTENCE OF GOD, ARGUMENTS FOR AND AGAINST. Arguments for and against God's existence number in the hundreds. Only the "top ten" in each category will be presented and discussed here. The theistic arguments are numbered 1–10 and the atheistic arguments are numbered 11–20.

DEFINITIONS OF *GOD*

Before getting to the arguments, it is important to present the various definitions of *God* that they employ.

D1: God is the eternal, all-powerful, personal being who created and rules the universe. (Being eternal, God cannot come into or go out of existence. Being all-powerful, he can perform any action that is logically possible to perform. Being personal, he has some characteristics in common with humans, such as thinking, feeling emotions, and performing actions. The universe is understood to consist of all the space, time, matter, and energy that has ever existed.)

D2: God is the eternal, very powerful, personal being who rules the universe, loves humanity, and gave humanity its moral conscience.

D3: God is the eternal, very powerful, personal being who rules the universe, loves humanity, and strongly desires that that love be reciprocated.

D4: God is that being which is self-existent, that is, which contains the explanation for its own existence within itself.

D5: God is that being which is (objectively) perfect in every way. (The term "perfect" is here understood in an objective sense, as opposed to a subjective sense relative to individual values, so the term may be used in public reasoning.)

D6: God is the deity described in the Bible as interpreted by evangelical Christianity.

Each argument will be presented by means of a step-by-step formulation, followed by a consideration of possible objections to it. It will be indicated for each argument which of the above definitions of *God* it employs.

ARGUMENTS FOR GOD'S EXISTENCE

1. The Cosmological Argument (D1). (a) The entropy (or quantity of used-up energy) of the universe constantly increases. Also, the universe constantly expands and the hydrogen within each star is constantly being used up in the production of heat and light by atomic fusion. (b) Therefore, if the universe has always existed, then by now it would have reached a state of maximal entropy (with no usable energy remaining) and maximal expansion, and there would be no stars containing any hydrogen. (c) But the entropy level of the universe is not maximal. Usable energy still exists. Also, the universe is not in a state of maximal expansion and there are stars that contain hydrogen. (d) It follows that the universe has not always existed: it must have had a beginning of some sort. (e) But everything that begins to exist must have a cause. (f) Therefore, the universe must have a cause. (g) But the only possible cause would have been an act of creation by God as defined by D1. (h) So God must have created the universe at some time in the past, and, being eternal, he cannot have gone out of existence. (i) Hence, God as defined by D1 must presently exist.

Objections. 1. Scientists have no information as to whether the entropy of the universe has always (from the beginning of time) been increasing. For all they know, there may have been periods in the past (maybe prior to the Big Bang) when the entropy of the universe decreased. Perhaps it regularly increases and decreases, and presently happens to be in an increasing stage. That the process may be reversed is also true of the expansion of the universe and the atomic fusion that occurs within stars. Although this alternate "oscillating universe" model is not advocated by a majority of cosmologists at the present time, it has not been definitely refuted either. It follows that premise (a) of the Cosmological Argument cannot be regarded as an established fact. For all that scientists know, the universe (i.e., space, time, matter, and energy), in some form or other, may have always existed.

2. There is no good reason to claim that things never come into existence uncaused. The fact that we do not experience such events in everyday life is not a good reason. Quantum theory allows for it and there are cosmologists who theorize that that is precisely how the universe originated. Therefore, premise (e) of the Cosmological Argument can legitimately be doubted.

3. Even assuming that the universe was caused, the cause need not have had all the properties ascribed to God in definition D1. Therefore, premise (g) of the Cosmological Argument is false, which makes the argument unsound.

2. The Argument from Design (D2). (a) Scientists try to explain the complexity that we observe in nature by appeal to the theory of evolution (TE). (b) But if TE were true, then we would probably have found by now an orderly sequence of fossils showing intermediate forms between main groups of organisms. (c) Yet no such fossils have ever been found. (d) Also, if TE were true, then there must have occurred (within the evolutionary process) violations of the second law of thermodynamics. (e) But no such violations have ever occurred. (f) Furthermore, an implication of TE is that, both in the chemical evolution of the original life-form and in the later biological evolution of complex life-forms from simpler forms (by chance mutations), there must have occurred a series of events with a probability so small as to be negligible. (g) For each of these three reasons [(b,c), (d,e), & (f)] taken separately, TE is very likely

false. Taken jointly, they overwhelmingly establish the falsity of TE. (h) The only alternative to TE is to explain the complexity that we observe in nature by appeal to intelligent design. (i) The living organisms on earth exist in a physical environment that ideally suits them, or at least they did exist in such an environment in the past. (j) Hence, very probably, the earth's living organisms were created by some intelligent being who also designed their physical environment to ideally suit them [from (g)–(i)]. (k) But no being other than God as defined by D1 could have carried out such a creation. (l) So, it is highly likely that at some time in the past God, thus defined, created the earth's living organisms and designed their physical environment to ideally suit them, and thus exists.

Objections. 1. It is only under rare and unusual circumstances that dead bodies become fossilized, and it is only specially trained people who can recognize fossils. Hence, for any given organism that dies, it is highly unlikely that any part of its body would ever become fossilized and then discovered and recognized as being a fossil. Therefore, there is no reason whatsoever to regard premise (b) of the Argument from Design to be true.

2. Premises (c), (d), and (f) of the Argument from Design have all been refuted within the sciences. Thus, each of the three subarguments leading to step (g) of the argument contains at least one false premise, making each of them unsound. So, that step has not been established.

3. Even if TE were rejected, there are other alternatives to it than that mentioned in premise (h) of the Argument from Design, for example, the theory that the life-forms on our planet came to it from outer space. That refutes (h) and shows the argument to be unsound.

4. Living organisms on earth have always been subject to a hostile environment that has included severe storms, floods, droughts, earthquakes, volcanic eruptions, meteorite bombardments, disastrous weather patterns, disease, and predators. Therefore, their physical environment has never suited them ideally. It follows that premise (i) of the Argument from Design is false, which makes the argument unsound.

5. Even assuming that the life-forms on earth were created, there is no reason whatever to believe that their creator had all the particular defining properties of God given in definition D1. Therefore, there is no reason whatever to think that such a creator must have been God, thus defined. It follows that premise (k) of the Argument from Design is false, which makes the argument unsound.

Comment. The issues involved in objection 2 are enormously complex and the scientific literature relevant to them would fill a library. It is regrettable that space restrictions prohibit a fuller treatment and fuller bibliography on the topic here. This also applies to the objections to argument 1.

3. The Fine-Tuning Argument (D1). (a) The combination of physical constants that we observe in our universe is the only one capable of giving rise to, and sustaining, life as we know it. (b) Some explanation is needed as to why our universe has that particular combination of constants rather than some other conceivable combination. (c) One very good explanation of the given fact is the God hypothesis, according to which God, as defined by D1, designed our universe with the particular combination of physical constants that it has for the purpose of giving rise to, and sustaining, life as we know it. (d) No other explanation is as good as that one. (e) Hence, there is strong evidence that God, as defined by D1, exists.

Objections. 1. Definition D1 is unclear in various ways. For that reason, the hypothesis according to which God (as defined by D1) designed our universe fails to explain in a clear way what God is. It also fails to explain how God was supposed to have done the designing in question, why he made the universe so large in relation to life-forms, and why he permitted so much time (more than 10 billion years) to elapse for present-day life-forms to come about. Thus, the God hypothesis is unclear and incomplete, which makes it a poor explanation for the fact in question. It follows that premise (c) of the Fine-tuning Argument is false, which makes the argument unsound (see ANTHROPIC PRINCIPLE).

2. Physicists are trying to develop a "theory of everything" that would explain, among other things, why the universe has the particular combination of physical constants that it has. If successful, they would have a better explanation for the given facts than is the God hypothesis. There is no good reason to think that those physicists will eventually fail. Hence, there is no good reason to believe premise (d) of the Fine-Tuning Argument.

3. The fact that the universe has the particular combination of constants that it has can be regarded as simply a "brute fact" about it (i.e., a matter of sheer coincidence). It is possible that there are or have been in fact trillions of other universes with other combinations of constants. It is also possible that other combinations of constants would have produced universes at least as complex and interesting as ours. There is no reason to deny either of those possibilities and if either of them were true, then there would be nothing surprising about the fact that our universe has the particular combination of constants that it has, even if it were just a brute fact that it does so. But the brute-fact hypothesis does not have any of the defects of the God hypothesis. Hence, it is a better explanation for the given facts than is the God hypothesis. Therefore, premise (d) of the Fine-Tuning Argument is false, which makes the argument unsound.

4. Even given that our universe was designed to have the particular combination of physical constants that it has, the hypothesis that it was designed by some being or beings other than God, as defined by D1, is more likely true than the God hypothesis. Hence, premise (d) of the Fine-Tuning Argument is false, which makes the argument unsound.

4. The Argument from Mind (D1). (a) Mind (or consciousness or reason) exists. (b) One very good explanation for it is that God, as defined by D1, created it. (c) No other explanation is adequate. (d) Thus, there is strong evidence that God, as defined in the given way, exists.

Objections. 1. The God hypothesis can be severely attacked (objection 1 to argument 3, above, and objection 2 to argument 7, below). Hence, the God hypothesis is not a good explanation for anything. Therefore, premise (b) of the Argument from Mind is false, which makes the argument unsound.

2. Biology, psychology, and neuroscience together provide an adequate explanation for the existence of mind. Therefore, premise (c) of the Argument from Mind is false, which makes the argument unsound.

5. The Argument from Miracles (D1). (a) A miracle, by definition, is an event that violates some law of nature and is caused by a supernatural being. (b) Miracles, defined in that way, have occurred. An example is the raising of Jesus from the dead. Other examples are miraculous healings (unexplainable by science) that have occurred. (c) Those miracles (by definition) must have been performed by some supernatural being. (d) If any supernatural being exists, then God, as defined by D1, must also exist. (e) Hence, God, thus defined, exists.

Objections. 1. For every miracle ever alleged to have occurred, there is a body of eyewitness evidence (call it *M*) that supports the occurrence of the miracle and another body of evidence (call it *L*) against it, including all the evidence supporting the law violated by the alleged miracle. Since all laws of nature are supported by a body of evidence that is huge and vast, *L* must be huge and vast. There has never been a case, so far as we know, in which *M* outweighed *L*. For every alleged miracle, evidence *L* has always outweighed evidence *M* (see HUME, DAVID). Thus, for every alleged miracle, it is more likely that it did not actually occur than that it did. Hence, premise (b) of the Argument from Miracles is probably false (see MIRACLES, UNBELIEF IN).

2. Even if miracles occur, they may be brought about by supernatural beings other than God (as defined by D1) and God may not exist. Therefore, premise (d) of the Argument from Miracles is false, which makes the argument unsound.

Comment. A defect in the concept of omnipotence is pointed out in argument 13, below. Because of that, no argument for the existence of God as defined by D1 could possibly succeed. (This could be regarded as an additional objection to each of the arguments, above, that make use of D1.) In definitions D2 and D3, the expression "all-powerful" is replaced by "very powerful," so argument 13 is not applicable to those definitions.

6. The Moral Argument (D2). (a) There are certain actions that everybody agrees are morally right or morally wrong. (b) Given such agreement about morality, there must exist objective moral values. (c) Therefore, it is a fact that such values exist. (d) That fact is adequately explained by the hypothesis that God, as defined by D2, created moral values. (e) There is no other adequate explanation for the given fact. (f) Hence, God, thus defined, must exist.

Objections. 1. The fact that there is much agreement among people regarding moral values (assuming that is a fact) can be adequately explained without appeal to the idea that those values are objective, for example, within the fields of anthropology and sociobiology. Hence, the Moral Argument's premise (b) is false, which makes the argument unsound (see ETHICS AND UNBELIEF).

2. Even given that there are objective moral values, God could not have created them, for it is conceptually impossible for God to have made something morally right that we know is wrong, or vice versa. Therefore, premise (d) of the Moral Argument is false, which makes the argument unsound.

3. The existence of objective moral values (assuming they exist) could be adequately explained by various nontheistic ethical theories, such as CONSEQUENTIALISM and intuitionism. Therefore, premise (e) of the Moral Argument is false, which makes the argument unsound.

7. The Cumulative Case Argument (D2).

(a) There are many facts and events that need to be explained. The existence of the universe, complex living organisms and their sustaining environment, the conditions that made life possible, mind (or consciousness), the occurrence of alleged miracles, and the existence of objective moral values (mentioned in the arguments above) are just a few of them. Some others are the universality of religious belief, the occurrence of religious experiences in people, love, and the willingness of some people to die for their faith. (b) Theism and ATHEISM, understood in terms of definition D2, are the two great hypothetical frameworks within which explanations for all those facts and events might be constructed. (c) Theism is able to adequately explain all the phenomena. (d) Atheism is unable to do it. (e) There are also prudential factors which make the theistic hypothesis the preferable one: (1) It is being on the safe side, just in case God does exist. (2) It helps people to be moral because they think that would please God. (3) It provides people with a sense of meaningfulness (or purposefulness) in life, which is good to have, by causing them to see the world as a great system in which they and everyone and everything else has been assigned some significant role. Also, it gives people comfort and hope because they see the world as being providentially guided by a loving father and as containing the opportunity for eternal life. (f) For all of the reasons mentioned in (c), (d), and (e), taken cumulatively, theism must be declared the preferable hypothesis between the two explanatory frameworks. (g) It follows that theism is more likely true than atheism: God, as defined by D2, probably exists.

Objections. 1. There are many definitions of "God" other than D2, and many different explanatory frameworks for the various phenomena mentioned in premise (a) of the Cumulative Case Argument. It follows that premise (b) of the argument is unduly narrow and false, making the argument unsound.

2. The purpose of explanation is illumination and understanding. In order for the God hypothesis to provide those things, we need to know what God is, how and why God does things, and how God originated. But we do not know what God is. Definition D2, above, does not adequately provide that information. We need to know God's composition and in what respects, if any, God is like a human, and these things we do not know. Nor do we know how God does things; theists simply declare that to be a great mystery. Nor do we know why God does things. The motivations ascribed to him in the Bible conflict with the way we observe the world to be (as shown in the arguments from Evil, Nonbelief, and Confusion, below). Theists usually end up with the Unknown-Purpose Defense, thereby conceding that we do not know why God does things. Nor do we have any intelligible answer to the question of God's origin. (See arguments 8 and 17, below.) Hence, the God hypothesis provides no illumination or understanding, and so it does not satisfy the purpose of explanation. It follows that the God hypothesis does not really explain anything at all. Thus, premise (c) of the Cumulative Case Argument is false, which makes the argument unsound.

3. As argued by Richard Carrier and others, atheism in the form of metaphysical naturalism can adequately explain all the relevant phenomena. Therefore, premise (d) of the Cumulative Case Argument is false, which makes the argument unsound.

4. The practical or prudential factors appealed to in premise (e) of the Cumulative Case Argument do not make theism preferable to atheism in any sense of the term "preferable" that entails that theism is more likely true than atheism. Therefore, premise (e) of the argument lends no support whatever to its conclusion (g), and is irrelevant to the topic.

5. Some further objections to premise (e) are the following: (1) There is no reason whatsoever to think that theists are "on the safe side." For all we know, there may be unseen forces that make it very risky to be a theist. If one is going to believe in supernatural beings, one could as well believe that they are hostile toward theists as that they are friendly toward them. Therefore, there is no reason whatsoever to believe part (1) of premise (e), as given (see PASCAL'S WAGER). (2) Many atheists are moral and many theists are not moral. Therefore, part (2) of premise (e) applies, at most, to only some people. It is unclear how theism might help people to be moral. (Is it through an appeal to their selfish desire for future rewards? If so, then clearly more than theism is involved there, and furthermore, their motivation for being moral

is defective.) For these reasons, part (2) can be doubted. (3) There is no reason whatever to think that God, as defined, has assigned a purpose to everyone and everything, or is like a loving father, or has provided people with an opportunity for eternal life. Hence, anyone who has the sense of purposefulness or the sort of comfort or hope mentioned in part (3) has not obtained it from theism alone. Furthermore, not everyone wants to have a sense of purposefulness gained from the idea that God assigns purposes. Some people prefer feeling free to formulate their own purposes in life. And not everyone gains comfort or hope from ideas associated with theism. Some people are mentally disturbed by it all. For these reasons, part (3) of premise (e) of the Cumulative Case Argument lends no support whatever to the conclusion that theism, as a hypothesis, is preferable to atheism. We can see that not only is the whole appeal to practical or prudential reasons irrelevant to our topic, but the actual reasons which are given are in themselves exceedingly weak. The alleged "Cumulative Case" fails in every respect.

8. The Ultimate Explanation Argument (D4). (a) If everything were to depend for its existence on something else, then there would be an endless regress of things, without there being any ultimate explanation for anything. (b) But it is impossible that there should be no ultimate explanation for anything. (c) Thus, it is impossible that everything should depend for its existence on something else. (d) It follows that there must be something that exists totally independently and necessarily, which contains the explanation for its own existence within itself. (e) Hence, God, as defined by D4, must exist.

Objections. 1. The concept of necessary existence is unclear. (As Hume said, "[W]hatever can be conceived of as existing can also be conceived of as not existing.") Also, the concept of something "containing the explanation for its own existence within itself" and the concept of an "ultimate explanation" are both unclear. (See argument 17, below.) Therefore, the Ultimate Explanation Argument, which makes appeal to all those concepts, is unclear. It is hard to make any sense of it whatever. Hence, the argument is defective and needs to be rejected.

2. Even aside from the unclarity inherent in the Ultimate Explanation Argument, there is no reason whatever to accept its premise (b). Why not maintain that time, events, and explanations for things simply go back indefinitely, with no starting point, or alternatively, that it all began at some initial moment, uncaused, and thereby unexplained? (See objections 1 and 2 to argument 1, above.) Without any support for premise (b), the argument may be reasonably rejected.

Comments. A slightly different version of the Ultimate Explanation Argument appeals to the idea that God, by definition, is not a contingent being in the sense of something that may or may not exist, thus God's existence is either necessary or impossible. And since there is no contradiction inherent in the idea of God's existence, it follows that his existence is not impossible, and so he necessarily exists. (This is sometimes called the Modal Cosmological Argument, distinguishing it from argument 1, above, which is called the Temporal Cosmological Argument.) Aside from the unclarity inherent in the idea of necessary existence, there is the further objection that the argument can simply be turned around: "Since God's existence is either necessary or impossible, and since there is no contradiction inherent in the idea of God's nonexistence, it follows that his existence is not necessary, and so it is impossible for God to exist." With no good reason to prefer the theistic version of the argument over the atheistic version, both arguments should be dismissed as absurd.

It should be noted that definition D4 and the Ultimate Explanation Argument are not used in ordinary language or in the thinking of laymen or any clear-minded theists. They are sometimes encountered in the writings of philosophers or theologians, which is the only reason for including them here. The same is true of definition D5 and the Ontological Argument, below.

9. The Ontological Argument (D5). (a) God as defined by D5 is objectively perfect in every way. (b) For a being to exist is better than not to exist. (c) So, if a being were nonexistent, then it could not be objectively perfect in every way. (d) Thus, God cannot be nonexistent [from (a) & (c)]. (e) Hence, God, as defined by D5, must exist.

Objections. 1. Perfection is relative. What is perfect to one person may not be perfect to another, and there is no objective way to settle such disputes. Therefore, the concept of "objectively perfect," as a concept to be employed in public reasoning, makes no sense. It follows that definition D5 and premise (a) of the Ontological Argument, both of which make appeal to that concept, are incoherent. Hence, the argument is defective and must be rejected.

2. Even assuming that the Ontological Argument is intelligible, there is no good reason to accept its premise (b). There are some beings (e.g., demons) that practically everyone would regard to be better not to exist. Therefore, the argument has failed to establish its conclusion.

10. The Argument from the Bible (D6). (a) The Bible contains all of the following: remarkably fulfilled prophecies, an absence of unfulfilled prophecies, a convincing eyewitness account of the resurrection and subsequent appearances of Jesus, an absence of contradictions, amazing facts about the planet earth that were unknown to the general public in ancient times, an absence of factual errors, and a perfect moral system. (b) The only reasonable explanation for all of that is the hypothesis that the Bible, as interpreted by evangelical Christianity, is divinely inspired and totally true. (c) It follows that the deity described in the Bible, as interpreted by evangelical Christianity (which is God as defined by D6), must exist.

Objection. All the alleged facts appealed to in premise (a) have been discredited, so the argument is unsound; see argument 19, below.

ARGUMENTS AGAINST GOD'S EXISTENCE

11. The Anticreation Argument (D1, D6). (a) If X creates Y, then X must exist temporally prior to Y. (b) But nothing could possibly exist temporally prior to time itself (for that would involve existing at a time when there was no time, which is a contradiction). (c) Thus, it is impossible for time to have been created. (d) Time is an essential component of the universe. (e) Therefore, it is impossible for the universe to have been created. (f) It follows that God, as defined by D1 and D6, cannot exist.

Discussion. A similar argument might possibly be constructed with regard to the other components of the universe as well: space, matter, and energy. It is very hard to comprehend how a being could have created the universe without existing within space and without any involvement with matter or energy.

The God of evangelical Christianity (defined by D6) is included here (and for argument 12, below) because of the first sentence in the Bible, which evangelicals take to refer to the entire universe.

12. The Transcendent-Personal Argument (D1, D6). (a) In order for God to have created the universe, he must have been transcendent, that is, he must have existed outside space and time. (b) But to be personal implies (among other things) being within space and time. (c) Therefore, it is logically impossible for God, as defined by D1 or D6, to exist.

Discussion. It might be suggested that God has a part that is outside space and time and another part that is inside space and time and that it is the latter part, not the former part, which is personal in nature. But the idea of a being that is partly personal and partly transcendent is incomprehensible. Furthermore, definition D1 implies that God, as a personal being, existed prior to the universe, and it is incomprehensible how a personal being could do so.

Aside from conceptual considerations that have to do with the very concept of "being personal," there are empirical considerations relevant to premise (b). It might be argued that to be personal requires having thoughts, and that science has very strongly confirmed that having thoughts is dependent on having a physical brain. For example, since brain damage has always been found to delete, or at least disrupt, thoughts, it can be extrapolated that there can be no thoughts at all in the total absence of a brain (see COGNITIVE SCIENCE AND UNBELIEF).

Although the empirical support for premise (b) is very strong, that may not be a factor that would impress people who are not scientifically oriented to begin with.

13. The Incoherence of Omnipotence Argument (D1, D6). (a) If God as defined by D1 or D6 were to exist, then he would be omnipotent (i.e., able to do anything that is logically possible). (b) But the idea of such a being is incoherent. (c) Hence, such a being cannot possibly exist.

Discussion. Definition D6 is included here because evangelical Christians maintain that the biblical description of God as "Almighty" is accurate. The issue of whether or not premise (b) is true is complicated. Some writers claim that the idea of omnipotence in itself is inconsistent. Also, some writers claim that being omnipotent is incompatible with possessing certain other properties. (For example, an omnipotent being could commit suicide, since to do so is logically possible, but an eternal being, by definition, could not. Hence, the idea of the deity defined by D1 or D6 is incoherent.) Whether or not the given claim is true is here left open. See comments on the concept of "incoherence" made in connection with argument 17, below.

The divine attribute of omniscience gives rise to similar considerations, and there is an Incoherence of Omniscience Argument that could be raised. That argument, which is omitted here to save space, also has a premise (b) (worded as in argument 13), which introduces issues that are exceedingly complicated and controversial.

14. The Lack of Evidence Argument (D1, D2, D3, D6). (a) If God as defined by any of the four definitions in question were to exist, then he would have to be deeply involved in the affairs of humanity and there would be good objective evidence of his existence. (b) But there is no good objective evidence for the existence of a deity thus defined, seeing as arguments 1 through 7 and 10, above, have all been refuted. (c) Therefore, God, as defined by D1, D2, D3, or D6, does not exist.

Discussion. The rationale behind premise (a) is that the sort of deity in question, a personal being who rules the universe or who loves humanity (and perhaps wants that love reciprocated), would need to become involved in the affairs of humans and thereby reveal his existence overtly. It might be claimed that God has achieved such involvement just by means of subjective religious experiences, without providing humanity with any good objective evidence of his existence. This assertion could be attacked on the grounds that people who claim to have had such experiences are mistaken about the nature and cause of them. It might also be reasonably argued that religious experiences would be insufficient for the given divine purposes, and only good objective (publicly testable) evidence of some sort would do. Argument 14 is a versatile argument that can be widely used by atheists to attack God's existence, given many different definitions of "God."

Another argument similar to 14, sometimes put forward by scientifically oriented atheists, is the Argument from Metaphysical Naturalism, according to which all phenomena ever observed are best explained by appeal to natural causes. Since that premise is a reason to accept naturalism, it provides an evidential argument against God's existence. However, the given premise is an extremely sweeping one and for that reason alone argument 14 would be preferable.

15. The Argument from Evil (D2, D3, D6).

(a) If there were to exist a very powerful, personal being who rules the universe and loves humanity, then there would not occur as much evil (i.e., suffering and premature death) as there does. (b) But there does occur that much evil. (c) Therefore, there does not exist such a being. (d) Hence, God, as defined by D2, D3, or D6, does not exist.

Discussion. This formulation of the argument is a version of what is called "the Logical Argument from Evil" (see EVIL, PROBLEM OF). If the word "probably" were to be inserted into steps (a), (c), and (d), then it would be a version of what is called "the Evidential Argument from Evil." Similar considerations arise in connection with the different versions.

According to the Freewill Defense, premise (a) is false because God wants people to have free will and that requires that they be able to create evil. The evil that actually occurs in our world is mankind's fault, not God's. Thus, God can still love humanity and be perfectly good despite all the evil that occurs. There are many objections to this defense. One of them is that much of the suffering and premature death that occurs in our world is due to natural causes rather than human choices, and the Freewill Defense is totally irrelevant to that form of evil.

16. The Argument from Nonbelief (D3, D6).

(a) If there were to exist a very powerful, personal being who rules the universe, loves humanity, and who strongly desires that his love for humanity be reciprocated, then there would not exist as much nonbelief in the existence of such a being as there does. (b) But there does exist that much nonbelief. (c) Therefore, there does not exist such a being. (d) Hence, God, as defined by D3 or D6, does not exist.

Discussion. As with the Argument from Evil, an "evidential" version of this argument could be constructed by inserting the word "probably" into steps (a), (c), and (d). Similar considerations arise for all the various versions. The argument is directed against the deity defined by D6, as well as the one defined by D3, because evangelical Christians take God to have all the properties mentioned in D3. Possibly the argument might also be directed against the deity defined by D2, and something like that is attempted by J. L. Schellenberg, though there it would not be quite so forceful.

The rationale behind premise (a) is that nonbelief in God is an impediment to loving him, so a deity as described by definition D3 or D6 would remove that impediment if he were to exist (see UNBELIEF AS A PROBLEM FOR THEISM).

Defenses similar to those in the case of the Argument from Evil could be raised, and similar objections to them could be presented.

17. Arguments from Incoherence (D4, D5, D6).

(a) In order for X to explain Y, not only must Y be derivable from X, but the derivation needs to be in some way illuminating. (b) If X is derived from itself, then the derivation is in no way illuminating. (c) Thus, it is impossible for anything to explain itself. (d) God as defined by D4 is supposed to explain itself. (e) It follows that the idea of "God" as defined by D4 is incoherent. (f) Furthermore, as pointed out in connection with argument 9, perfection is relative, and so the concept of "objectively perfect," as a concept employed in public reasoning, makes no sense. (g) Hence, the idea of "God" as defined by D5 is also incoherent. (h) In addition, the Bible contains descriptions of God that are incoherent (e.g., implying both that Jesus is God and that Jesus is God's son, that God is spirit or a spirit and that God is love). (i) Evangelical Christians interpret those descriptions literally. (j) Therefore, it might be argued that the idea of "God" as defined by D6 is also incoherent.

Discussion. Unlike the other arguments in this section, these arguments do not aim to prove God's nonexistence, but rather, the incoherence of God talk when "God" is defined in certain ways. The point is not that theists who employ such God talk are mistaken about the world, but that they are confused in their language (see NONCOGNITIVISM).

The idea of "incoherence" is also sometimes applied to contradictions or other sorts of conceptual incompatibility. For example, arguments 12 and 13, above, could each be regarded as a kind of "argument from incoherence," for they appeal to conceptual incompatibilities between pairs of divine attributes. (This point might also be applicable to definition D5 if theists were to try to combine it with other definitions. For example, if a theist were to claim that God is both perfect [as given in D5] and the creator of the universe [as given in D1], then it might be argued that such a notion is incoherent, since a perfect being can have no wants, whereas a creator must have some wants. Or if a theist were to claim that God is perfect and also loves humanity [as given in D2 and D3], then it might be argued that such a notion is incoherent, since a perfect being can feel no disappointment, whereas a being who loves humanity must feel some disappointment.) However, this notion of "incoherence" is different from that appealed to in the Arguments from Incoherence, for if incompatible properties are ascribed, at least there is a conjunction of propositions there, even if it is a contradictory pair. In that case, it would still make sense to say that the sentence "God exists" expresses a (necessarily) false proposition. But with the sort of "incoherence" appealed to in the Arguments from Incoherence there is no proposition expressed at all, whether true or false. (For more on incompatible-properties arguments against God's existence, see Martin and Monnier, 2003.)

18. The Argument from Confusion (D6). (a) If the deity described in the Bible as interpreted by evangelical Christianity were to exist, then there would not exist as much confusion and conflictedness among Christians as there does, particularly with regard to important doctrinal issues such as God's laws and the requirements for salvation. (b) But there does exist that much; Christians disagree widely among themselves on such issues, as shown, among other things, by the great number of different Christian denominations and sects that exist. (c) Therefore, that deity does not exist. (d) Hence God as defined by D6 does not exist.

Discussion. The rationale behind premise (a) is that the God of evangelical Christianity is a deity who places great emphasis upon awareness of the truth, especially with regard to important doctrinal issues. It is expected, then, that if such a deity were to exist, he would place a high priority upon the elimination of confusion and conflictedness among his own followers with regard to important doctrinal issues. Because of the great abundance of Christian confusion of the relevant sort, this argument is a very forceful one.

19. The Argument from Biblical Defects (D6). (a) If the deity described in the Bible as interpreted by evangelical Christianity were to exist, then the Bible itself would not have the defects that it has. That is, it would not contain textual errors, interpolations, contradictions, factual errors (including false prophecies), and ethical defects. Also, the canon would have been assembled with less political involvement and would not have original manuscripts or parts missing. (b) But the Bible does contain those defects. (c) Therefore, that deity, which is God as defined by D6, does not exist.

Discussion. Premise (a) is based on the point that evangelical Christians regard the Bible to be God's main form of revelation to humanity. So, given that their God exists, it would be expected that the Bible would possess features implied by the motivations which they ascribe to him. Premise (a) follows quite naturally.

20. The Argument from Human Insignificance (D6). (a) If the deity described in the Bible as interpreted by evangelical Christianity were to exist, then it would be expected that humans occupy some significant place in the universe. (b) But, both from the standpoint of space (the size of the universe in relation to the size of the earth) and from the standpoint of time (the length of time in which the universe has existed in relation to the length of time in which humans have existed),

humans do not occupy any significant place in the universe. (c) Hence, God, as defined by D6, probably does not exist.

Discussion. The idea behind the first premise here is that the Bible describes God as having a very special interest in humans. Since humans are so important, they should naturally occupy some significant place in space and time. To reject that idea is to reject the evangelical Christian outlook on the nature of reality. (A slightly different version of this argument is referred to by Nicholas Everitt as "the Argument from Scale.")

There are many other arguments against God's existence. Some are inductive in form; some make appeal to cosmological assumptions. In this brief outline, just those regarded as the main ones were selected for coverage.

SUMMARY

The various arguments can be matched up with the six definitions of *God* as follows:

DEFINITION	ARGUMENTS FOR GOD	ARGUMENTS AGAINST GOD
D1	#1–5	#11–14
D2	#6, #7	#14, #15
		(+ possibly #16)
D3	–	#14–16
D4	#8	#17
D5	#9	#17
D6	#10	#11–20

All of the arguments for God's existence can be refuted by at least one objection, and all of the definitions of "God" considered here permit God's nonexistence to be established (or else God talk to be shown incoherent) by at least one argument. Other definitions of "God" are used in ordinary language, but all of them permit God's nonexistence to be established by appeal to similar or analogous considerations. There is much more to be said about the various arguments.

BIBLIOGRAPHY

Carrier, Richard. *Sense and Goodness without God: A Defense of Metaphysical Naturalism.* Bloomington, IN: AuthorHouse, 2005.

Craig, William Lane, and Walter Sinnott-Armstrong. *God? A Debate between a Christian and an Atheist.* Oxford: Oxford University Press, 2004.

Craig, William Lane, and Quentin Smith. *Theism, Atheism, and Big Bang Cosmology.* Oxford: Oxford University Press, 1993.

Drange, Theodore. "The Argument from Non-Belief." *Religious Studies* 29 (1993).

———. "The Fine-Tuning Argument Revisited." *Philo* 3, no. 2 (2000).

———. *Nonbelief & Evil: Two Arguments for the Nonexistence of God.* Amherst, NY: Prometheus Books, 1998.

Everitt, Nicholas. *The Non-existence of God.* London: Routledge, 2004.

Le Poidevin, Robin. *Arguing for Atheism: An Introduction to the Philosophy of Religion.* London and New York: Routledge, 1996.

Martin, Michael. *Atheism: A Philosophical Justification.* Philadelphia: Temple University Press, 1990.

Martin, Michael, and Ricki Monnier, eds. *The Impossibility of God.* Amherst, NY: Prometheus Books, 2003.

———. *The Improbability of God.* Amherst, NY: Prometheus Books, 2006.

Mattill, A. J., Jr. *The Seven Mighty Blows to Traditional Beliefs.* Gordo, AL: Flatwoods Free Press, 1995.

Schellenberg, J. L. *Divine Hiddenness and Human Reason.* Ithaca, NY: Cornell University Press, 1993.

Sobel, Jordan Howard. *Logic and Theism: Arguments For and Against Beliefs in God.* Cambridge: Cambridge University Press, 2004.

Stenger, Victor J. *Has Science Found God?* Amherst, NY: Prometheus Books, 2003.

THEODORE DRANGE

EXISTENTIALISM. Existentialism is the name given to the body of thought of a number of loosely linked, mainly French and German, thinkers. Like most such umbrella terms, it conceals a great deal of diversity; inevitably, attempting to characterize the main themes and views of the movement obscures a number of fundamental disagreements. For the most part, existentialists were unified by shared themes, rather than shared truth claims, as well as by a shared sense of the reality and the importance of freedom in human life. Existentialists stressed the limits of reason and the concomitant necessity of the individual committing oneself to a life plan justified only by one's resolute choice. A life chosen in this way is lived according to the master value of existentialism: authenticity.

Existentialism is essentially a twentieth-century movement, first emerging clearly in the early work of the German philosopher Martin Heidegger, especially in his masterpiece *Being and Time* (1927). However, it had its roots in the nineteenth century, in broad cultural movements like Romanticism, and more especially in the work of the two thinkers who deserve to be called its founding fathers, Søren KIERKEGAARD and Friedrich NIETZSCHE. Beginning from premises that were diametrically opposed, both men reached the characteristic existentialist conclusion that a free and ultimately unjustifiable choice was central to authentic human existence. For Kierkegaard, this choice was a leap of faith, an acceptance of God's existence and the truth of Christianity in the face of a lucid recognition that this leap goes beyond what is rationally demonstrable. Nietzsche, too, stresses the necessity of a choice that is unjustifiable, but for him the unjustifiability is the product of the "death of God," by which he means not only increasing religious SKEPTICISM, but also the growing recognition that values are not part of the fabric of nature. For Nietzsche, the death of God signifies the end of an era in which values were held to govern human life in much the same way as the laws of nature; now that we recognize that values are invented, not discovered, we can and must choose our own.

After the death of god *or* in the face of the inability to rationally justify our ultimate values, we are each forced back upon ourselves in choosing our life plan. For both Nietzsche and Kierkegaard, an authentic life requires each of us to choose without regard to the opinions of the masses of humanity. Each sees easy conformism as a constant temptation, and as a sure route to meaninglessness. The authentic individual makes his or her own way in the world, and answers for his or her own choices. In this affirmation of the importance of the individual against the threat of envelopment in the masses, it is hard not to see a response to the growth in anonymous cities, mass produced products, and regular working hours that characterized the Industrial Revolution.

The thinker with the best claim to being the ideal-type existentialist was the French philosopher Jean-Paul SARTRE. In Sartre's work, the themes of freedom, choice, and authenticity are developed into a unified system at once metaphysical and moral. Moreover, Sartre exemplified another aspect of existentialism which cannot be overlooked: its connection to everyday life. Existentialism is for its exponents, notoriously, not merely an academic movement but a way of life. With his lifelong relationship with the feminist thinker Simone de BEAUVOIR, his numerous affairs, his support for a range of radical political movements, and his involvement in theatre and literature (he was awarded, and declined, the 1964 Nobel Prize in Literature), Sartre exemplified the existentialist as bohemian.

Sartre did not coin the term *existentialism* and at first rejected it. However, he was himself responsible for giving it broad currency, by adopting it for the title of his famous 1946 lecture "Existentialism Is a HUMANISM." Here Sartre set out his influential justification for the centrality and unjustifiability of radical choice in human life. For human beings, and them alone, Sartre argued, "existence precedes essence." Human beings, uniquely among all the entities in the universe, *are*—that is, they exist—before they *are* anything in particular, and therefore what they shall be is up to them. We do not have essences or fixed psychological characteristics; instead, we must each choose how we are going to behave. Just as Nietzsche and Kierkegaard called upon us to commit ourselves to a life which we cannot rationally or morally justify, so Sartre called upon us to create ourselves according to a pattern of own making. By rejecting the notion of a human essence, Sartre completed the revolution begun by Nietzsche: Not only were values not to be found inscribed in nature or in the mind of a god, they were not to be found within ourselves either.

One of Sartre's most original contributions to existentialist thought was the notion of *bad faith*. Bad faith is a kind of self-deception, but it is self-deception with regard to a very specific topic: human freedom. Sartre claimed that every human being senses possession of the freedom to mold one's own life as one chooses, and that there are no values independent of one's choices, which could justify them. He argued that the sense of absolute freedom this knowledge brings is almost unbearably terrifying, and that we are all therefore tempted to deny our radical freedom. We deny our freedom by arguing either that we are not able to choose at all—by taking refuge in scientism and DETERMINISM, for instance—or by holding that our choices are uniquely justified by values independent of ourselves. When we deny our freedom, we are in bad faith. We do not simply assert or believe something that is false, but we try to convince ourselves of something we know to be false. Hence bad faith is a kind of self-deception, which is traditionally conceived as intentional self-deceit.

Religion in all its forms was, for Sartre, a paradigm of bad faith. The religious believer claims that his or her way of life is uniquely justified inasmuch as it conforms to God's plan for the universe. But bad faith can take many forms, and atheistic varieties can be found as well. The humanist who argues that human nature or the flourishing of the species (or whatever it may be) justifies humanism uniquely is equally in bad faith.

Whatever differences existed among them, existentialists were united in their stress on the individual. In postwar Europe, individualism was increasingly unfashionable as a variant of Marxism that stressed the power of social forces to determine ideas and took hold of the imaginations of intellectuals. Sartre and others struggled heroically to reconcile existentialism with Marxism, but their presuppositions were too different for the project to succeed.

When existentialism faded from the intellectual landscape, it was largely as a consequence of the vagaries of fashion. Nevertheless, and as Sartre himself came to see, the (broadly) Marxist focus on the social background of individual action exposed a genuine and seemingly intractable difficulty with existentialism: by making freedom so radical, existentialism actually made it impossible. No one is able to choose a way of life or a system of values from the ground up; this is not merely psychologically impossible, but genuinely incoherent. The very terms in which we make our choices, if they are not merely arbitrary flips of a coin, must be inherited from our social background (or innate in the human mind). A more modest freedom is the only freedom that is coherent.

Today, existentialism no longer occupies an important place in academic philosophy or elsewhere in intellectual life. Nevertheless, its central themes continue to exercise a powerful hold on the imagination of ordinary people. As Charles Taylor recently stressed, authenticity remains an unrepudiable value for us; we each believe that it is important to reject the forces of conformism and choose the life appropriate for ourselves. Existentialism, like Freudianism, has suffered defeats within academic life from which it looks unlikely to recover, yet it has triumphed more broadly by becoming absorbed into the fabric of our cultural commonplaces.

BIBLIOGRAPHY

Heidegger, Martin. *Being and Time.* Translated by John Macquarrie and Edward Robinson. New York: Harper & Row, 1962.

Kierkegaard, Søren. *Concluding Unscientific Postscript.* Translated by David F. Swenson and Walter Lowrie. Princeton, NJ: Princeton University Press, 1971.

Nietzsche, Friedrich. *The Gay Science.* Translated by Walter Kaufmann. New York: Vintage, 1974.

———. *Thus Spoke Zarathustra.* In *The Portable Nietzsche,* translated by Walter Kaufmann. New York: Viking, 1975.

Sartre, J. P. *Being and Nothingness.* Translated by Hazel Barnes. New York: Washington Square Press, 1955.

———. *Critique of Dialectical Reason I: Theory of Practical Ensembles.* Translated by Alan Sheridan-Smith. London: Verso, 1976.

———. "Existentialism Is a Humanism." In *Existentialism from Dostoevsky to Sartre,* edited by Walter Kaufmann. Cleveland: Meridian, 1968.

Taylor, Charles. *The Ethics of Authenticity.* Cambridge, MA: Harvard University Press, 1992.

NEIL LEVY

FAITH HEALING. Successes and Failures. Because learning comes by trial and error, the history of medication is one of both successes and failures. Some cultures have been more advanced than others in eliminating harmful potions. Contemporary medicine and pharmaceutical companies strive to speed the process of trial and error in laboratories in the hope of both detecting harmful side effects and generating more effective medications.

Over the centuries, desperate human beings tried whatever seemed promising in their battle against infirmities. Certain members of the community who were accepted as authorities in countering illness resorted to a variety of techniques, practices, formulas, and concoctions. Those seeking healing or relief from suffering often exercised faith in the sense of trusting in the guidance of the authorities. In some cases, the guidance proved more helpful than harmful. In other cases, its effect proved either harmful or negligible.

Having "Faith In." To have faith in someone implies believing that he or she can be relied on to do certain specific things or to be a certain kind of person under specified conditions. In ordinary discourse, the word *faith* may or may not have a religious context. A husband who has faith in his wife as a pilot or electrician might not have faith in her as a surgeon. In each case, his faith, trust, or confidence is either justified or unjustified. We can also have faith in inanimate objects such as chairs and benches, trusting that they will not collapse if we sit on them.

For clients to have faith in the counsel of their lawyers is to heed it. If the counsel proves repeatedly faulty, clients who persist in following it are indulging in blind faith. Both trust and distrust are essential to living. The opposite of blind faith is the inability to trust when trust would be appropriate and rational. No one can live without both faith and distrust, although people may differ regarding what they trust and distrust. Some Christians have faith in faith healers whereas other Christians distrust them.

Controversy among Conservative Christians. Theological conservatives among Protestants divide sharply over the issue of miraculous cures. The first camp claims that miraculous healings occurred during biblical times only. The second camp claims not only that miraculous healings continue to this day, but also that faith-healing revivals are special outpourings of the Holy Spirit. Furthermore, some individuals are believed to possess the special gift of healing. Evangelists who regard themselves as enjoying this special "healing ministry" tend to believe they are divine instruments for casting out demons. Many of them, including Oral Roberts, tend to think that demons contribute significantly to human illnesses and diseases.

The third camp includes Protestants (and many Catholics) who regard PRAYER as an effective part of the healing process. They trust the medical profession and see prayer in especially severe cases as complementary. They tend to regard so-called faith healers as either misguided zealots who do considerable harm or manipulative and arrogant frauds. Some faith healers are accused of spreading the false and harmful doctrine that *all who truly believe will be healed while those who are not healed did not truly believe*. Many Christians of the third camp look with disgust upon televangelists who peer at the TV camera and profess to mediate healing to people they neither see nor know.

Medicine and Faith Healers. Some faith healers in the twentieth century taught their followers to place no faith in doctors. Three factors were involved. First, many of those attending the "healing revivals" lacked the funds for doctors, medication, and hospital care. The second factor was a theological doctrine according to which bodily healing was a part of salvation. Faith healers of this school referred to biblical passages portraying Jesus as effecting forgiveness and healing simultaneously. The third factor was the faith healers' personality. Many of them looked upon doctors as rivals. If healing was a miracle and if being a healer was a gift of the Holy Spirit,

medical schools were institutions that propagated a rival view of healing that credited doctors, rather than God, with the healings. By implication, the doctors robbed the faith healers of their role and influence.

The Strange Case of Evangelist Jack Coe. Born in Oklahoma City in 1918, Jack Coe was perhaps the most flamboyant of the faith healers. In his vast tent, thousands arrived to witness his performances. He would lift people from wheelchairs, and if they fell, he would say they did not have faith. He relished inveighing against "the devil and his crowd." A brilliant exploiter of controversy, he found himself accused of practicing medicine without a license. In a two-day trial in a Miami courtroom, he called upon other faith healers to testify on his behalf. The case centered around the evangelist's failure to deliver the polio-stricken son of one Mrs. Clark from his affliction. Coe contended that God had explained to him that despite his faith and prayers, some people could not be healed because they did not know how to receive healing: "More people would be healed if only they knew how to accept and keep it." The judge ruled he could not "condemn the defendant or anyone who in good faith advocates and practices Divine Healing."

Ironically but not miraculously, ten months later, in December 1956, Coe fell critically ill while preaching in Hot Springs, Arkansas. Since he had been careless of his health and was severely overweight, he thought he had succumbed to exhaustion. In fact, he had fallen victim to polio. Despite his hostility toward the medical profession, he permitted his wife to satisfy her conscience by admitting him to a hospital. He died at the age of thirty-nine. A fellow evangelist complained of being prevented from praying for Coe and laying on hands, since Coe had been quarantined. Another evangelist scolded Coe's wife for not calling on him to come and raise Coe from the dead. Apparently, the latter evangelist, who claimed to have received several communiqués from the deity, had been unavailable to receive a divine message encouraging him to pray for Coe's resurrection.

Financial Healing. Within the charimatic and Pentecostal movement, some believers experimented with the gospel of prosperity. As prosperity for many in the middle class became a reality after World War II, Pentecostals could afford medical treatment, mortgage payments, automobiles, televisions, and other manifestations of affluence. As financial health emerged, a new theology developed to help believers feel comfortable with prosperity and with becoming concerned about maintaining their financial health.

Giving regular donations to "gospel ministers" became an important plank of the gospel of prosperity theology. One televangelist emphasized the "hundred-fold principle" based, he believed, on Mark 10:30. His wife explained," [G]ive $1000 and receive $100,000. . . . Give one car and the return would furnish you a lifetime of cars. In short, Mark 10:30 is a very good deal." Pat Robertson, writing of "miracles involving money," tells of a Texas oilman who contributed a sizable share of his business profits and personal income to "God's work." The man claimed to receive visions and "the word of knowledge," that is, supernatural drilling information.

Money, Medicine, and Faith Healing. Oral Roberts claimed to have heard God talk to him about building a hospital in Tulsa, Oklahoma, the city in which his organization was located. Historian David Harrell Jr., a student of the Pentecostal branch of Protestantism in America, explains, "Oral's vision, as always, was a coalescing of insights rather than a flash of revelation." Roberts appeared obsessed with building the hospital: "There's no hospital built on this earth that can do what I dream about." Against sound advice from friends with business experience, he persisted. He wanted his followers to believe in and support his vision. Some observers understood him to be driven by the need to legitimize faith healing by somehow blending it with the medical profession. Most of the middle class remained suspicious of both the motives and claims of faith healers; if Roberts could somehow bring the doctors and faith healers together in the same hospital, and if through prayer and research they could find a cure for cancer, then the skepticism about faith healers would miraculously vanish. The "primal self in the pit of his belly which he identified with the voice of God" drove him to build the hospital. The harder he drove himself, the more he became convinced that a satanic conspiracy had launched a "last-ditch move against God's work." When the inevitable financial crisis came, with its stack of debts growing taller each month, Roberts proclaimed that suddenly he felt a holy presence all around him. Upon opening his eyes, he saw standing before him none other than Jesus Christ, "a full 300 feet taller than the 600 foot tall City of Faith." Roberts needed a towering Jesus to deal with the tall stack of unpaid bills.

In his book *The Faith Healers*, James Randi, who systematically investigates faith healers, explains why the hospital venture was doomed from the start: Roberts had failed to engage in elementary marketing research. He could have learned from the business instructors at Oral Roberts University or from honest business friends in Tulsa. But he did not listen to the mere mortals because he believed he was listening to God.

Raising the Dead and Raising Money. Although Roberts more than once announced that he had frequently witnessed the dead rise at his healing services, he was unable to raise the money to keep the hospital afloat. Its financial condition had deteriorated and not even the gospel of prosperity could heal it. Eventually, the dream of the hospital died.

Another Interpretation of Faith. Among naturalists and many theists, faith is not a doorway leading into a world of magic and miracles. The human organism is physical and must constantly interact with a physical environment. Rational faith as a mode of daily living in a physical environment includes ordinary hope, trust, and commitment. In times of illness, faith and reason can combine to reinforce recovery. Faith is a way of keeping alert to practical and tested measures for maintaining health and countering sickness. Although they do not believe supernatural miracles happen, naturalists are often able to appreciate the goodwill behind one person's praying for another person's recovery. Naturalists and theists often recognize the crucial role of social reinforcers in maintaining good health. Get-well cards, kind words and deeds, caring gestures, gifts, and numerous other forms of social nurturing are aspects of both mental and physical health. Rational faith includes openness to the goodness and encouragement coming from friends and family.

In many cases, this trust or openness helps the afflicted to deal better with chronic illness. Biomedicine informs us of the laboratory aspects of illness, genetics and disease, medical ecology, the evolution of diseases, nutrition, demography, and paleopathology. Medical anthropology explores the social and cultural dimensions of illness, including the psychosocial sense of loss.

The Crisis of Loss. Illness brings loss of control over some aspect of one's body and environment. Loss of one's job or career because of illness can threaten an individual's self-identity and role in the community. Cultural anthropologists refer to the "loss of meaning" that sometimes comes with sickness. Each culture has a worldview that purports to offer some explanation of sickness. In highly anthropomorphic cultures, prolonged or severe illness often evokes the question "Why?" or even "Why *me*?" This can signify an emotional and intellectual crisis for both the afflicted and his or her family. Behind the "Why?" lies the assumption that a conscious, supernatural agent has chosen either to inflict the sufferer or to permit the illness to come about for reasons not clear to the sufferer.

With severe loss comes grief in varying degrees. Cultures and subcultures vary in their ways of dealing with grief and placing it in a wider context. In many cases, a community of family and friends helps share the grief, thus bringing needed comfort. Healing is control not only of disordered biological process, but also of psychological dysfunction and disturbing symptoms.

The Global South. Some students of religion contend that a branch of Pentecostalism, with its wild claims of healing miracles and the most cynical aspects of faith-healing ministries, will spread in the global south. Faith-healing claims will thrive where the benefits of medical research and medical technology are unavailable. Poverty and unchecked anthropomorphism are the seedbed of faith-healing revivals.

Fraud and Chicanery. In the 1980s James Randi and Joe Barnhart discovered that evangelist W. V. Grant Jr. supplied wheelchairs for individuals who came to his "healing services" an hour or so early under their own power. Seating themselves in the audience along the wall to the evangelist's left, they appeared bound to their wheelchairs by disabling illness. During the service, Grant hurried over to them and, with microphone in hand, pronounced some of them cured by "Dr. Jesus." He then urged one of the women to rise from her wheelchair and run up the aisle, giving the distinct impression that the evangelist had been the instrument of her miraculous, instant cure.

Later, in Fort Lauderdale, Randi exposed the Grant team's practice of using crib sheets by which to collect and use information about individuals and their illnesses. Grant used specific details in a public display to give the impression that the information had come to him by divine communiqué. Randi exposed the heartless cynicism behind the deceit. He also exposed faith healer Peter Popoff's use of a tiny listening device in his left ear to receive previously gathered information from his wife. Through this deception, Popoff gave the impression that he was receiving information from heaven rather than from his wife backstage. Thanks to the tenacious Randi and his assistants, some of the most blatant deceptions practiced by some faith healers have been well documented and carefully explained. For example, as Randi reported: "Before the end of our investigation, [undercover volunteer] Don Henvick would be healed by four different healers, in six different cities, of six different diseases, under four different names and two different sexes."

Austin Miles, a Pentecostalist preacher who briefly embraced HUMANISM before returning to the Christian ministry, showed during his humanist period how the "renowned Reverend William Branham, faith healer and prophet of God, had been using parlor tricks! He was deliberately staging his supposed messages from God in order to manipulate vulnerable people."

Culturally Induced Crises and Cures. In *Sensory Deception*, Peter Slade and Richard Bentall note that culturally induced expectations reinforced by social factors can sometimes generate psychological crises, including hallucinations of the dead, ghosts, spirits, demons, and hauntings. Sometimes hallucinations play a healing role by reducing induced anxiety. In turn, their anxiety-relieving property reinforces the acceptance and frequency of hallucinations. This is especially true in cases of bereavement and loss of a loved one or a highly significant object.

A similar self-fulfilling cycle can be observed in orthodox Christianity. The orthodox culture inculcates acceptance of original sin and its accompanying sense of guilt, which in some cases becomes pathological. To create a need for their professed healing or cure, theologians not only invented the notion of original sin, but also labeled it as a disease of the soul, heart, and mind. Having induced guilt as the cause, the same orthodox culture then offers a putative cure, which purports to restore the believer to a state of forensic guiltlessness, provided the believer acknowledges the vicarious atonement that is reputed to remove original sin.

BIBLIOGRAPHY

Barnhart, Joe E. *Jim and Tammy: Charismatic Intrigue Inside PTL.* Amherst, NY: Prometheus Books, 1988.

Cuneo, Michael W. *American Exorcism: Expelling Demons in the Land of Plenty.* New York: Doubleday, 2001.

Harrell, David Erwin, Jr. *All Things Are Possible: The Healing and Charismatic Revivals in Modern America.* Bloomington: Indiana University Press, 1975.

———. *Oral Roberts: An American Life.* Bloomington: Indiana University Press, 1985.

Hollenweger, Walter J. *The Pentecostals.* Peabody, MA: Hendrickson, 1972.

McConnell, D. R. *A Different Gospel: A Historical and Biblical Analysis of the Modern Faith Movement.* Peabody, MA: Hendrickson, 1988.

Miles, Austin. *Don't Call Me Brother: A Ringmaster's Escape from the Pentecostal Church.* Amherst, NY: Prometheus Books, 1989.

Pilch, John J. "Insights and Models for Understanding the Healing Activity of the Historical Jesus." In *Society of Biblical Literature 1993 Seminar Papers.* Atlanta: Scholars Press, 1993.

Poloma, Margaret, *The Charismatic Movement: Is There a New Pentecost?* Boston: Twayne, 1982.

Randi, James. *The Faith Healers.* Amherst, NY: Prometheus Books, 1987.

Robertson, Pat. *Beyond Reason: How Miracles Can Change Your Life.* New York: Bantam, 1984.

Sholes, Jerry. *Give Me That Prime-Time Religion: An Insider's Report on the Oral Roberts Evangelistic Association.* New York: Hawthorne, 1979.

Simson, Eve. *The Faith Healers: Deliverance Evangelism in North America.* St. Louis, MO: Concordia, 1977.

Slade, Peter, and Richard Bentall. *Sensory Deception: A Scientific Analysis of Hallucination:* Baltimore, MD: Johns Hopkins University Press, 1988.

JOE EDWARD BARNHART

FALSIFIABILITY. In *Objective Knowledge* Karl POPPER states, "Instead of discussing the 'probability' of a hypothesis we should try to assess what tests, what trials, it has withstood; that is, we should try to assess how far it has been able to prove its fitness to survive by standing up to tests."

Empirical Method. The empirical method characteristically exposes to falsification, in every conceivable way, the system to be tested. Since the same collection of data often appears to support rival theories or systems of theories, one task of science is not to protect this or that system, but to test the most promising ones rigorously and to conclude which is, by comparison, the fittest. If the *goal of science* is to create the best system of theories about the real world, then great theories need not only to be enriched with depth and scope of content, but also to be well artic- ulated. The better theoretical systems *say* more, and pre- dict with greater scope and precision. "It will rain or not rain tomorrow" is not refutable or falsifiable because it says nothing. Since it purports to offer no positive infor- mation, it cannot clash with what purport to be observation statements. Science generates bold hypotheses with deductive consequences that must be spelled out so that they can be subjected to thorough criticism.

Risking Refutation. All scientific theories risk trials. In the attempt to improve their theories or to replace them with better ones, scientists consciously search for errors and mistakes. Rigorous experiments are designed to make the investigation more critical and severe. The higher the theory's informative content, the greater its risk. A theory with rich content and scope that eventually becomes falsified can advance knowledge better than can a thin theory that has not risked refutation. By dis- covering where and how elements of a theory have been falsified, researchers sometimes discover ways to create a better theory.

A scientific theory does not purport to explain every- thing that could possibly happen. Rather, it rules out most of what could possibly happen. If what it rules out does happen, the theory, or some aspect of it, has been refuted. The more a theory says, the more it rules out. "Laws" of nature do not guarantee or enable; they prohibit.

A scientific theory's testability grows with its degree of universality and its degree of definiteness, or preci- sion. The larger the range of events about which the theory can venture predictions, the more falsifiable the theory becomes. That is, its testability increases. Great advances in science require, therefore, bold, risk-taking theories. A vague theory runs few risks of being either false or profound. While it might be trivially true, it will not open doors to new empirical discoveries or help resolve what Thomas Kuhn calls scientific "puzzles."

Explanation and Prediction. A new hypothesis is better than another if it explains all that the old hypoth- esis successfully explained and avoids some of the serious errors of the old hypothesis. It must do the latter not by retreating to vagueness but by submitting to and withstanding some of the most critical tests. Scientists give added weight to a new hypothesis that also makes definite, bold, and fruitful predictions that give promise of being refutable.

No theory exists in isolation. It gains meaning and sig- nificance within a network of other hypotheses (Quine's "web of belief"). Its explanatory power increases if it integrates with other fruitful, falsifiable theories. In the case of fecund scientific revolutions, a new coalition of bold new theories forms a new web of interconnection that provides greater explanatory power.

Intensifying the Testing Process. Awareness of falsi- fiability may generate fear of chaos in a society where there is little awareness of alternative views. In some respects, where falsifiability is openly tolerated, alterna-

tives are more likely to emerge. Science may be viewed as rational thinking that is intensified. Instead of waiting for events to come along that might challenge a hypoth- esis, science designs experiments to speed up the process. By creating new experimental situations, sci- ence runs ahead of the natural pace. Ideally, it becomes an institution that liquidates theories rather than the per- sons who articulate the new theories.

Simulated Falsification. Although not all rational discourse can be tested empirically, simulated falsifia- bility can apply in metaphysics. Behind falsifiability is the detection of *contradictory* statements and claims. In metaphysics, statements can be spelled out and com- pared with other carefully articulated statements. Even when empirical testing seems impossible or difficult to implement, rational discourse may nevertheless be pos- sible. Doctrines or theories may be articulated in the interest of making them say something definite that can be logically analyzed and compared with rival doctrines purporting to refer to some aspect of reality.

Everyday Testing. Falsifiability has a constructive function in therapy, engineering, plumbing, the applied sciences, and daily living. When beliefs are acted upon, the expected consequence may at times fail to materi- alize. All societies that survive for a long time have learned to make at least some crucial revisions, and in some cases replacement of some beliefs with others. Some beliefs prove lethal if acted upon. Others appear to belong to an imaginary realm where falsifiability can be safely ignored or handled with more purely imaginary adjustments. Yet even in an imaginary narrative, vast areas of possibilities are ruled out. That is, not every claim can be accepted as belonging to the story. Internal contradictions beyond a certain point will turn a story into disjointed episodes at best.

Religions have invented stories with claims that the gods require special kinds of sacrifice that rule out other kinds. These stories cannot be regarded as empirical claims, however, because no definite tests can be designed and enacted to determine the gods' preferences. In religious traditions, attempts have been made to con- nect divine preferences with publicly observable or nat- ural phenomena. When the consequences fail to materi- alize as predicted, the adjustments to account for the accumulated anomalies may not integrate coherently with its primary web of beliefs. In genuine scientific experiments, researchers must keep careful records of the predicted consequences and the adjustments made in either the experiment or the relevant theory. In short, when scientists design rigorous tests, they keep careful records for the purpose of determining the cognitive price paid in making theoretical adjustments when some aspect of the theory appears falsified.

Theology and Simulated Falsification. When a reli- gious tradition's storytelling generates mutants with new claims, the accompanying theology must produce revi- sions and, in the process, develop its own standards (canons) for determining which claims and theories to accept and which to rule out. Simulated falsification occurs as theologians detect internal conflicts and problems within the evolving story. When believers expand the story by attempting to make more or less precise contact (including predictions about) with the natural world, theologians are forced to deal with the religion's falsified claims by either revising the problematic doctrine/theory or generating new ad hoc doctrines. The history of Christian doctrines of the Trinity, for example, is the history of (1) theories that encountered simulated falsification and (2) the revisions or replacements purporting to overcome the contradictions. In *When Prophecy Failed*, Robert P. Carroll deals with (1) the problems encountered in reinterpreting falsified prophecies and (2) the practice of avoiding dissonance by shifting prophecy into highly metaphorical language. Among snake-handling fundamentalists, when a poisonous snake bites and kills an occasional believer, the surviving believers need not take the death as falsification of either Mark 16:18 or the insufficiency of the victim's faith. Rather, the believing survivors may make an ad hoc adjustment by reinterpreting the death as God's way of calling his servant home. This shifts the discourse to the realm of the metaphorical. Stated perhaps more simply, the believers *equivocate* regarding Mark 16:18's prediction that if they take up serpents, they will not be injured.

Narratives for Living. The human species lives partly by a variety of stories, narratives, or accounts of what people regard as aspects of reality relative to their lives. When some of the accounts do not correspond with the relevant facts, adjustments often become necessary. Therapists may deal with clients who either cannot make adjustments or make adjustments that do not work. Much of therapy includes teaching clients the skill of (1) admitting that some of the beliefs they are acting upon have been falsified and (2) generating revised or new beliefs that can be acted upon without the problematic consequences.

In *Bargains with Fate*, Bernard J. Paris draws from Shakespeare and Karen Horney's insights into the failure to acknowledge elementary falsifiability in certain critical expectations. Horney taught her clients to detect their *inconsistencies* and to deal with them. Great suffering and sometimes tragedy develops from the inability to change behaviors that proceed from expectations that cannot be fulfilled in the real world.

Human beliefs, hypotheses, theories, and expectations function as prophecies or predictions. Daily living operates by betting on them. The crucial role of falsifiability is that of acknowledging when, where, and how important predictions have failed. Learning comes partly through recognizing mistakes and creating new beliefs and actions that do not repeat the mistakes. Denial is one way of dealing with a prediction that has suffered refutation. Self-delusion is another way. When, in self-delusion, we more or less recognize that our belief prediction has failed, we may develop other beliefs that help us to avoid testing (and thus accountability) by giving way to an obscurantism that allows us to take refuge in haziness or concealment. Much of therapy (whether through professional counselors, friends, or reading material) is a process of reducing some of the haziness of thought and language. If the unconscious is the habit of thinking obscurely and, in some cases, cryptically (as in so-called schizophrenia), rational thinking is a process in which implicit beliefs become sufficiently explicit for our analyzing them. *Analysis* in this context is a conscious explication of beliefs by (1) specifying the predicted actions implicit in the beliefs and (2) becoming more accurate and precise in observing their impact on the actor, on others, and on the most relevant aspects of the environment. Sensitivity to falsifiability can become so well developed that it becomes second nature or subconscious, as when a driver quickly anticipates a mistake and corrects it without having to verbalize either the mistake or the correction. Much of what is called "intuition" is probably a quick detection and overriding of plans or theories that will not work (i.e., either would be falsified or would fail to develop sufficient precision for testing). The quick detection often frees the mind to focus on other plans or theories that exemplify a promising degree of definiteness and fruitfulness.

BIBLIOGRAPHY

Carroll, Robert P. *When Prophecy Failed: Cognitive Dissonance in the Prophetic Traditions of the Old Testament.* New York: Seabury, 1979.

Paris, Bernard J. *Bargains with Fate: Psychological Crises and Conflicts in Shakespeare and His Plays.* New York: Insight, 1991.

Popper, Karl R. *Objective Knowledge: An Evolutionary Approach.* Rev. ed. New York: Oxford University Press, 1989.

Smith, T. C. *Reading the Signs.* Macon, GA: Smyth and Helwys, 2002.

JOE EDWARD BARNHART

FARBER, MARVIN (1901–1980), American philosophical naturalist. Educated at the University of Buffalo and at Harvard, Marvin Farber studied in Germany with Edmund Husserl, Ernst Zermelo, Heinrich Richert, Karl Jaspers, and Martin Heidegger before completing his Harvard PhD in 1925 with a dissertation titled "Phenomenology as a Method and as a Philosophical Discipline." Committed to logic and radical social philosophy, he wished to combine the rigor of mathematics with the materialism (see MATERIALISM, PHILOSOPHICAL) of MARXISM. Although he became the preeminent American authority on Husserl, he rejected the idealism in Husserl's later work and was critical of many of Husserl's disciples, most vehemently of Heidegger. His classic study of Husserl, *The Foundation of Phenome-*

nology: *Edmund Husserl and the Quest for a Rigorous Science of Philosophy*, was published in 1943.

Farber taught almost his entire career at the University of Buffalo (after 1962 called the State University of New York at Buffalo). An atheistic Jew, he aided many European intellectuals in coming to America to escape Nazism.

Farber founded in 1940—and edited until his death forty years later—*Philosophy and Phenomenological Research* (PPR), a quarterly intended to foster the most scientifically descriptive, logically rigorous, and socially beneficial philosophy. PPR was also the most pluralistic and international philosophical journal of its time. During the Cold War Farber edited (with R. W. Sellars and V. J. McGill) *Philosophy for the Future: The Quest of Modern Materialism*, a book that made his sympathies with Marxism widely known. In 1959 he published his most important work of original philosophy, *Naturalism and Subjectivism*, in which he formulated a naturalism that sought to improve on the American tradition of NATURALISM (such as the philosophy of John DEWEY) by incorporating phenomenological method and elements of Marxism. These themes were further developed in a manuscript that he completed before his death, *The Search for an Alternative: Philosophical Perspectives of Subjectivism and Marxism*. Although in earlier publications he had used the words "naturalism" and "materialism" interchangeably, in this final work only "materialism" was used "to name a philosophy of man and natural existence which is science-oriented in the broadest possible way and includes in its scope the recognition of social conflicts and the motivation for change." He praised the materialism of "uncompromising honesty" found in the work of Vladimir Ilyich LENIN, but warned Marxists against the overextension of the dialectical method. He insisted that the transcendental method of phenomenology was equally important, though it, too, must not be overextended. Farber's continuing commitment to mathematical logic also found a place in his "materialistic phenomenology." He argued that mathematics and formal logic, like phenomenology, could lay bare structures and features of experience otherwise inaccessible.

BIBLIOGRAPHY

Cho, Kah Kyung, ed. *Philosophy and Science in Phenomenological Perspective*. The Hague: M. Nijhoff, 1984.

Farber, Marvin. *The Aims of Phenomenology: The Motives, Methods, and Impact of Husserl's Thought*. New York: Harper & Row, 1966.

———. *Basic Issues of Philosophy: Experience, Reality and Human Values*. New York: Harper & Row, 1968.

———. *The Foundation of Phenomenology: Edmund Husserl and the Quest for a Rigorous Science of Philosophy*. Cambridge, MA: Harvard University Press, 1943.

———. *Naturalism and Subjectivism*. Springfield, IL: C. C. Thomas, 1959.

———. *Phenomenology and Existence: Toward a Philosophy within Nature*. New York: Harper & Row, 1967.

———. *Phenomenology as a Method and as a Philosophical Discipline*. Buffalo: University of Buffalo Studies, 1928.

———. *The Search for an Alternative: Philosophical Perspectives of Subjectivism and Marxism*. Philadelphia: University of Pennsylvania Press, 1984.

Farber, Marvin, R. W. Sellars, and V. J. McGill. eds. *Philosophy for the Future: The Quest of Modern Materialism*. New York: Macmillan, 1949.

Hare, Peter H. "Marvin Farber." In *American National Biography*, edited by J. A. Garraty and M. C. Carnes. New York: Oxford University Press, 1999.

Riepe, Dale, ed. *Phenomenology and Natural Existence: Essays in Honor of Marvin Farber*. Festschrift for Farber, 1973.

Rosenthal, Sandra B. "Phenomenology and Naturalism: Marvin Farber's Attempted Rapproachement." *Transactions of the Charles S. Peirce Society* 18 (Spring 1982).

PETER H. HARE

FARMER, JAMES (1920–1999), American civil rights activist. Born in Marshall, Texas, on January 12, 1920, James Farmer was a cofounder of the Congress of Racial Equality (CORE) and spent much of his life as a civil rights activist, educator, and administrator. Raised in an environment in which education and religious faith were valued, Farmer was an outstanding student. At the age of fourteen he entered Wiley College in Marshall, Texas. Graduating in 1938, Farmer went on to Howard University's School of Religion, from which he graduated in 1941. Farmer opposed war in general; when the United States entered World War II later that year, he applied for conscientious objector status but found that he was deferred from the draft because he had a divinity degree. Farmer objected specifically to the prospect of serving in the segregated ranks of the US military in a fight against fascism.

Rather than become an ordained Methodist minister, Farmer chose instead to go to work for the Fellowship of Reconciliation (FOR), becoming that organization's secretary for race relations. In that position, Farmer helped the Quaker pacifist organization develop its responses to such social ills as racial prejudice, war, violence, and poverty. It was a job that left Farmer enough time to begin forming his own approach to these issues, one based less on FOR's Quaker pacifism than on the principle of nonviolent civil disobedience.

Farmer and several Christian pacifists founded CORE in 1942 with the express purpose of using Gandhian tactics of nonviolent civil disobedience in order to apply direct challenges to American racism. Farmer's religious beliefs resulted in his refusal to serve in the armed forces during World War II. In 1947 he participated in CORE's campaign of sit-ins, which successfully ended discriminatory service practices against African Americans at two Chicago restaurants. An articulate and charismatic figure, Farmer became CORE's national director in 1961, which enabled him to help organize student sit-ins and Freedom Rides across the Deep South.

In 1966 Farmer saw that CORE was drifting away from its Gandhian roots and decided to leave the pioneering civil rights organization. Always an active writer and speaker, he continued to direct a national adult literacy project lecture publicly on civil rights and eventually took a teaching position at Lincoln University in Pennsylvania. Running as a Republican, Farmer failed in an attempt to win a New York congressional seat in 1968, running against Shirley Chisholm. Shortly afterwards, the new president, Richard Nixon, appointed him assistant secretary of Health, Education and Welfare. After leaving Nixon's administration in 1971, Farmer worked for the Council on Minority Planning and Strategy, an African American think tank. In his final years Farmer completed his autobiography, *Lay Bare the Heart* (1985). James Farmer was awarded the Congressional Medal for Freedom by President Bill Clinton in 1998. He died a year later on July 9, 1999.

JUAN FLOYD-THOMAS

FERRER GUARDIA, FRANCISCO (1859–1909), Spanish anarchist educator. Francisco Ferrer Guardia's Barcelona Escuela Moderna (1901–1906) influenced many Spanish secularist and radical schools. His execution for allegedly instigating the July 1909 Barcelona riots inspired international liberal, rationalist, and socialist protests recalling the Dreyfus case.

Early Life. Ferrer was born on January 10, 1859, at Alella, near Barcelona. His parents were conservative Catholics, but Ferrer became a zealous atheist, anticlerical (see ANTICLERICALISM), and republican in his teens. He fled to France in 1886 after participating in several Spanish republican uprisings in the 1880s.

Paris Years. Ferrer lived in Paris from 1886 to 1901, teaching Spanish and meeting French and European liberals, rationalists, socialists, and anarchists. His republicanism deepened into socialism and eventually anarchism, becoming convinced of the need to educate the masses to achieve lasting social change. When a wealthy Spanish language student left him her fortune, he used it to establish the Escuela Moderna.

The Escuela Moderna. Ferrer opened the "Modern, Scientific, and Rational School" in Barcelona in September 1901. It was coeducational, antireligious, antimilitary, and antistate, without punishment, competition, or examinations. Ferrer also ran a publishing house, which published a monthly, *Boletín de la Escuela Moderna* (1901–1906, 1908–1909), on educational theory. He published cheap books on reading, grammar, science, history, ethics, and sociology, mostly translations of foreign secularist and anarchist works. Many Spanish secularist and workers' schools adopted Ferrer's methods and textbooks, inspiring rumors of Ferrer "endowing" them.

Similar schools using Ferrer's books also arose in Portugal, Latin America, and elsewhere.

The authorities closed the Escuela Moderna after Mateo Morral Roca, a former manager of Ferrer's publishing house, attempted to assassinate King Alfonso XIII on May 31, 1906. Morral committed suicide, but Ferrer was arrested on suspicion of complicity. He was tried a year later, in June 1907, but acquitted for lack of evidence. After his release, Ferrer was not permitted to reopen the Escuela Moderna.

Last Years. Ferrer returned to Paris in 1907, founding the International League for the Rational Education of Children. In 1908 he began an education journal, *L'École Renovée*, and also resumed his *Boletín de la Escuela Moderna*. Ferrer's old interest in Spanish anarcho-syndicalism also revived. In June 1909 he returned to Spain to visit sick relatives.

The Tragic Week. In July 1909, protests against a Spanish military expedition to Morocco led to the "Tragic Week" in Barcelona. Republican extremists escalated a Socialist general strike into anticlerical rioting. Blaming religious orders with an interest in Moroccan mines for the expedition, Barcelona mobs burned churches and convents from July 26 to July 30, before order was restored.

Ferrer's Execution. Ferrer was arrested on September 1 as the suspected organizer of the insurrection. On October 9 he was tried, convicted, and sentenced to death in a military trial. Violently revolutionary statements from his past writings were added to the testimony of witnesses claiming to have seen or heard him speaking with rioters and republican extremists. Ferrer was executed by a military firing squad at Barcelona on October 13.

International Protests. Ferrer's execution sparked worldwide protests by liberals, rationalists, socialists, and anarchists hailing him as a martyr for intellectual freedom. Liberal and socialist newspapers attacked the execution as a "judicial murder." European intellectuals signed manifestoes denouncing the execution. Protest meetings, processions, and strikes were held in cities throughout Europe and the Americas. Many European cities renamed streets for Ferrer. In Spain opposition leaders invoked the protests in the government crisis bringing down Antonio Maura's Conservative government. In the United States, Ferrer was commemorated by "modern schools" modeled on the Escuela Moderna, some surviving into the 1950s.

BIBLIOGRAPHY

Abbott, Leonard D. *Francisco Ferrer: His Life, Work, and Martyrdom.* New York: Francisco Ferrer Association, [1910].

Archer, William. *The Life, Trial, and Death of Francisco Ferrer.* London: Chapman & Hall, 1911.

Avrich, Paul. *The Modern School Movement: Anarchism and Education in the United States.* Princeton, NJ: Princeton University Press, 1980.

Ferrer, Sol. *La vie et l'oueuvre de Francisco Ferrer. Un Martyr au XXe Siècle.* Paris: Librairie Fischbacher, 1962.

———. *Le véritable Francisco Ferrer d'après des documents inédits.* Paris: Editions Les Deux Sirènes, 1948.

Ferrer Guardia, Francisco. *The Origin and Ideals of the Modern School.* Translated by Joseph McCabe. London: Watts and Company, 1913.

Park, T. Peter. "The European Reaction to the Execution of Francisco Ferrer." PhD diss., University of Virginia, 1970.

Ullman, Joan Connolly. *The Tragic Week: A Study of Anticlericalism in Spain, 1875–1912.* Cambridge, MA: Harvard University Press, 1968.

T. Peter Park

FEUERBACH, LUDWIG (1804–1872), German humanist and religion critic. Although Ludwig Feuerbach began his career as a metaphysical idealist, he became an aggressive critic of both it and Christianity and ended his career as a proponent of a humanism based on "sensuousness" and the solidarity of I and Thou. His best-known work was *The Essence of Christianity* (1841).

Life. Feuerbach was the fourth child in a distinguished German family. Originally intending to study theology in Heidelberg, he became enchanted by Hegelian idealism and switched to Berlin in order to study philosophy with Hegel. In his first academic position he quickly established a reputation as a rising young philosopher, but his career was prematurely aborted when it was discovered that he was the anonymous author of *Thoughts on Death and Immortality* (1830), which attacked the notions of a personal god and personal immortality. Unable to find employment in a German university, he retired to a small town near Ansbach, where his wife's father owned a porcelain factory.

His book *The Essence of Christianity* (1841) created a sensation, and he became one of the leaders of a group of radicals called the Young Hegelians, who were dedicated to democracy and the separation of church and state. Between 1842 and 1848 he drafted several documents enunciating the principles of a new HUMANISM. Regarded by the German students as a hero, he was invited to lecture at the University of Heidelberg in 1848 but was denied university facilities and forced to use the city hall. Disillusioned by the failure of the revolutions of 1848, he retreated back to his porcelain factory. When it went bankrupt in 1859, he was forced to move to a small town near Nürnberg, where, ill and virtually penniless, he lived out his life with the financial aid of friends.

The Critique of Religion. Feuerbach's earliest writings were in the tradition of German idealism, in which both nature and spirit are regarded as aspects of one infinite spirit. But in the 1830s he began rethinking his position, which culminated in a published attack on G. W. F. Hegel in 1837. The publication of *The Essence of Christianity* created a sensation not only because of its radical interpretation and repudiation of Christianity but because Hegelian categories were employed to accomplish it. Hegel's metaphysics was based on the notion that the Infinite Spirit perpetually pours out or objectifies its life in the finite and struggles with the resulting externality (self-alienation) until finally overcoming it in self-knowledge. Feuerbach, by contrast, argues that it is the human spirit that comes to self-consciousness in and through its objectification in the idea of God. In the process of differentiating itself from other selves, the self, or I, becomes aware that it is a member of the species with certain predicates. These predicates are naturally regarded as perfections, and the imagination seizes on them and under the pressure of wish converts the idea of the species into a perfect individual subject. The Christian idea of a deity possessing perfect reason, moral integrity, and love is simply the most advanced idea of humanity's essential nature.

In the first part of the book, Feuerbach took up the various doctrines of Christianity in order to show that they are really a mystified anthropology. His aims were to account for the form of the doctrine, to exhibit the contradictions that result when it is taken seriously as theology, and, finally, to exhibit what he called "the characteristic illusion of the religious consciousness," the illusion that attributes everything to God and nothing to humanity. In the second part Feuerbach attempted to show how the projection of human predicates onto the divine results in conceptual confusion and alienation.

As Feuerbach became critical of idealism and moved toward a naturalistic empiricism, he tended to drop the Hegelian emphasis on consciousness objectifying itself and argued that the origins of religion are rooted in the encounter with nature. In his *Lectures on the Essence of Religion* (1848), he wrote that the human person is an embodied sensuous being immersed in a field of forces that impinges on it from within and without and upon which it is absolutely dependent. In primitive times, these natural forces struck human beings with emotional force and the imagination seized on these qualities and personified them. The result was polytheism. As civilization developed and nature was conceived of as a unified whole, the result was monotheism. But in both cases, human dependency and the desire for happiness results in personifying nature into a being that can be propitiated and grant that desire.

Whereas in *The Essence of Christianity* Feuerbach had argued that the concept of a transcendent being alienates the human being from its own attributes, here he described Christianity as a disorder of the desires. Christians really want to exceed the limits that nature places on human life and which make it possible. Consequently, they identify their faith with belief in the miraculous and, above all, with belief in an eternal existence free of necessity.

The New Philosophy. Although Feuerbach was pre-occupied with religion, this was but the negative side of what he called his new philosophy. Unfortunately, he was never able to put this new philosophy into a fully developed and coherent work. Nevertheless, some major themes may be described. Against idealism, he argued that one cannot make the ego the basis of certainty. Rather, the new philosophy claims that certainty is only given through "sensuousness" and this, in turn, is mediated by the body. The human body is the way in which the human self is in the world and this body has its own unique constellation of senses for mediating that world. Each sense has its own special need for satisfaction. Nevertheless, the human organism is a "universal being," which is to say that any given sense is elevated by consciousness above its bondage to its particular need. Consequently, the philosopher must think in harmony with the senses and this requires dedication to the concrete rather than the abstract.

Feuerbach was never able to complete the ethics of his new philosophy and what he did write leaves many questions unanswered. Nevertheless, it seems founded upon two basic principles: (a) self-consciousness only emerges in relationship to another self-consciousness, so that only the social person is a person; and (b) every living organism is in the grip of a drive toward self-fulfillment. This drive is the aggregate of all human drives, needs, and predispositions, and the function of reason and will are to direct these drives in the interest of the entire organism. This drive to happiness is not itself subject to moral judgments but is, rather, the presupposition of any theory of morality. Morality arises only when one considers the effects of one's actions stemming from the drive to happiness upon others.

BIBLIOGRAPHY

Feuerbach, Ludwig. *The Essence of Christianity*. Translated by George Eliot. Amherst, NY: Prometheus Books, 1989.

———. *The Essence of Religion*. Translated by Alexander Loos. Amherst, NY: Prometheus Books, 2004.

———. *The Fiery Brook: Selected Writings of Ludwig Feuerbach*. Translated by Zawar Hanfi. Garden City, NY: Doubleday, 1972.

———. *Lectures on the Essence of Religion*. Translated by Ralph Manheim. New York: Harper & Row, 1967.

———. *Thoughts on Death and Immortality from the Papers of a Thinker, along with an Appendix of Theological-Satirical Epigrams, Edited by one of his Friends*. Translated by James A. Massey. Berkeley and Los Angeles: University of California Press, 1980.

Harvey, Van A. *Feuerbach and the Interpretation of Religion*. New York: Cambridge University Press, 1995.

Rawidowicz, S. *Ludwig Feuerbachs Philosophie:*
Ursprung und Schicksal. 2nd ed. Berlin: Walter de Gruyter, 1964.

Toews, John Edward. *Hegelianism: The Path toward Dialectical Humanism, 1805–1841*. Cambridge: Cambridge University Press, 1980.

Wartofsky, Marx. *Feuerbach*. New York: Cambridge University Press, 1977.

VAN A. HARVEY

FICHTE, JOHANN GOTTLIEB (1762–1814), German idealist philosopher. Johann Gottlieb Fichte was born in Rammenau, Saxony, on May 19, 1762. Although the son of poor ribbon weavers, he studied at several exclusive schools, including the Pforta preparatory school and the universities of Jena, Wittenburg, and Leipzig, due to the charity of the Baron Ernest Haubold von Miltitzs. After his patron's death, Fichte struggled as a tutor for privileged children. He would remain chary of unmerited authority: a quixotic, temperamental, but earnest soul. Originally a fatalist, Fichte converted to transcendental idealism after discovering that Immanuel KANT's philosophy reconciled the naturalism of his "head" with the moralism of his "heart." His philosophy, *Wissenschaftslehre* (Theory of Scientific Knowledge) or the "first philosophy of freedom," would reflect an abiding commitment to scientific rigor, moral responsibility, and social justice.

Fichte's first book, *Attempt at a Critique of All Revelation* (1792), helped him to gain a position at the University of Jena, which allowed him to marry his long-suffering fiancée, Johanna Rahn, who later bore his son, Immanuel Hermann. In Jena Fichte established himself as a beloved educator and luminous mind, but also a divisive personality. In crowded lectures, the dynamic professor incited talented youth such as Friedrich Hölderlin and F. W. J. Schelling to think independently. His predecessor, the celebrated K. L. Reinhold, lauded his original interpretation of transcendental philosophy. Nonetheless, conservative foes hounded Fichte with allegations, ranging from disrupting public worship to fomenting insurrection, based on misinterpretations of his lectures and writings. The enlightened Duke Karl-August of Weimar, who had authority over the University of Jena, usually disregarded these specious claims, but Fichte eventually lost his position as a result of accusations of ATHEISM, which initiated the Atheism Controversy of 1798–99 (see CONTROVERSIES: ATHEISM, PANTHEISM, SPINOZA).

In 1798 Fichte published "On the Basis of Our Belief in a Divine Governance of the World." In this essay he denied traditional arguments for a deity, defining *God* as the moral world order or law-governed spiritual realm. Fichte claimed that true religion is not concerned with venerating deities but rather with performing one's duty regardless of the consequences. Moreover, atheism consists in shirking one's duty for the sake of reward or punishment. Because "Divine Governance" was written for philosophers, it remained obscure until the appearance of a mawkish pamphlet wherein an anonymous author warned impressionable youth to eschew Fichte's atheism. This initiated a veritable pamphlet war between Fichte's friends and foes. The literary mêlée attracted the attention of Friedrich-August, prince-elector of Saxony, who banned "Divine Governance" and threatened to withdraw all Saxon students from Jena.

The Saxon ban scarcely concerned Duke Karl-August, but the threat required his delicate response, so he prepared an obligatory admonition to placate Saxony. Had Fichte suffered this rebuke in silence he might have weathered the Atheism Controversy, but he was truly offended because he was no atheist, by his own definition. In haste, he mailed a letter to Duke Karl-August at the Weimar Court, swearing to resign if censured. Equally affronted, the duke sent the prepared reprimand with a postscript accepting Fichte's resignation. Two student petitions containing hundreds of names were sent to Weimar on Fichte's behalf, but Karl-August held firm. Fichte fled to Berlin, where he published *Vocation of Man* (1800) and "Way Towards a Blessed Life" (1812).

In *Vocation* and "Blessed Life," Fichte developed the religious theory nascent in "Divine Governance." Particularly, he elucidated the moral world order, arguing that human consciousness transcended sensible awareness to include spiritual awareness evoked by free interaction between social beings. He remained true to his original idea that genuine religiosity involved steadfast pursuit of moral perfection rather than concern for worldly or otherworldly consequences. Fichte anticipated that readers would construe these works as signifying his reconciliation with orthodox religion, but he explicitly denied such an interpretation.

While nursing Prussian soldiers wounded in the war against Napoleon, Fichte's wife, Johanna, became ill and infected her husband. Johanna survived the fever, but Fichte died in 1814. Their son dedicated his life to editing and defending his father's work.

BIBLIOGRAPHY

Breazeale, Daniel. "Introduction: Fichte in Jena." In *Fichte: Early Philosophical Writings*, translated and edited by Daniel Breazeale. Ithaca, NY: Cornell University Press, 1988.

Fichte, J. G. *Attempt at a Critique of All Revelation.* Translated by Garrett Green. Cambridge: Cambridge University Press, 1978.

———. "On the Basis of Our Belief in a Divine Governance of the World." In *Introductions to the Wissenschaftslehre and Other Writings*, translated and edited by Daniel Breazeale. Indianapolis: Hackett, 1994.

———. *The Vocation of Man.* Translated by Peter Preuss. Indianapolis: Hackett, 1987.

———. "The Way towards a Blessed Life." In *The Popular Works of Johann Gottlieb Fichte*, translated by William Smith. London: Trübner, 1889.

La Vopa, Anthony. *Fichte: The Self and the Calling of Philosophy (1762–1799).* Cambridge: Cambridge University Press, 2001.

Solomon, Robert C. *Continental Philosophy Since 1750: The Rise and Fall of the Self.* Oxford: Oxford University Press, 1988.

YOLANDA ESTES

FIELDING, WILLIAM JOHN (1886–1973), FREETHOUGHT writer. William John Fielding was born in Port Oram (later renamed Wharton), New Jersey, on April 10, 1886. His mother died when he was six, and he was educated through the eighth grade before quitting to work as a blacksmith in his father's shop at age fourteen. His father moved the family, and Fielding found work for a time on a crew of "sandhogs," men cutting a railroad tunnel under the Hudson River in Jersey City.

Fielding decided that he needed to return to school and went to business school to learn typing and clerking. Eventually he applied and became a correspondent (clerk) for Tiffany and Company. Fielding worked at Tiffany's for fifty-four years, and worked his way up to the position of executive secretary. He also became secretary-treasurer of the Louis Comfort Tiffany Foundation.

Fielding had interests in writing and poetry, and began attending lectures on the various social sciences. His interest in socialism led him to meet Emanuel HALDEMAN-JULIUS, the socialist and freethinker who had founded a nationwide publishing empire. Fielding eventually wrote thirty pocket-sized Little Blue Books for Haldeman-Julius Publications, including titles on psychology and sexology. According to Haldeman-Julius, the books on sex were his best sellers, and Fielding became known as "Tiffany's Sexologist." As a result of his research in connection with these books, he became closely tied to the birth control movement (see BIRTH CONTROL AND UNBELIEF) and made the acquaintance of Margaret SANGER.

Fielding wrote a number of books, but his most famous work is *The Shackles of the Supernatural*. This work was originally published by Haldeman-Julius Publications as a Big Blue Book, but was enlarged and republished in 1969. In the introduction, atheist leader Joseph LEWIS describes the work as "one of the most vital and essential books of our time." The book shows the damaging effects organized religion has exerted on humanity, and it should be one of the cornerstones of any collection of books on unbelief.

Fielding also wrote and edited a number of periodicals during his life. Many from his early years were socialist works. He also edited or wrote for a number of freethought publications, including *PROGRESSIVE WORLD*, *Age of Reason* (published by the Freethinkers of

America), the *Freethinker* (London), and the *American Rationalist*.

Fielding was a tireless worker for a number of groups, including the Thomas Paine Foundation, the American Ethical Union, and the Freethinkers of America. He died on December 20, 1973.

BIBLIOGRAPHY

Fielding, William J. *All the Lives I Have Lived*. Philadelphia: Dorrance, 1972.
———. *The Shackles of the Supernatural*. New York: Vantage, 1969.
Richardson, Kenneth. "William J. Fielding." *American Rationalist* (January–February 1974).
Ryan, William F. "The Biblio-File: *All the Lives I Have Led* by Wm. J. Fielding." *American Rationalist* (January–February 1974).
———. "In Memoriam." *Progressive World* 27, no. 12 (February 1974).

Timothy Binga

FINE-TUNING ARGUMENT See **Anthropic Principle, The.**

FINLAND, UNBELIEF IN. Finland is not a part of Scandinavia; it lies between Scandinavia and Russia. It was a colony of Sweden between 1200 and 1809 and a part of Russia between 1809 and 1917. Since 1917 Finland has been independent. The first Finnish association to discuss the philosophy of the Enlightenment (see Enlightenment, The, and Unbelief) was the Valhalla Association (1781–86). At that time, Finland was a part of Sweden, and there was no freedom of belief. Foreign books on related topics were held at two locations. The Monrepo estate had books of Julien Offray de La Mettrie, Paul-Henri Thiry (Baron) d'Holbach, and Claude Adrien Helvétius. The Fagervik estate held books of Denis Diderot. The best-known atheist in Finland at this time was Johan Kellgren, who was a clear atheist and supported a hedonistic moral code.

In 1809 Finland became a part of Russia. The situation regarding religious freedom changed little. The official religion was Lutheran Christianity, but the Eastern Orthodox Church became the other accepted church. Anders Chydenius and Robert Lagerborg wrote on freedom of religion in 1863.

Shortly afterward, Darwinism reached Finland (see also Evolution and Unbelief), and Nils Nordenskiöld discussed the new theories in the *Literary Magazine*. The first attempt to acquaint the masses with Charles Darwin's ideas occurred in 1889 in the city of Jyväskylä, where the newspaper *Keski-Suomi* published popular articles on Darwinism written by well-known individuals such as Juhani Aho and Minna Canth. The editor of *Keski-Suomi* was Eero Erkko, whose grandson Aatos Erkko would become the richest man in Finland.

The Association for Freedom of Religion and Tolerance (*Föreningen för religionsfrihet och tolerans in Finland*) was founded by Viktor Heikel and Mathilda Asp in 1887–88 but quickly suppressed by the economic department of the senate. Some of the members of this association were religious. The first issue of its journal *Free Thoughts* (*Wapaita Aatteita*) was published in 1889 but czarist censorship put an end to it as it did almost everything else. Also notable was the Raketen Club (1896–1900), a forum where the ideas of Georg Morris Cohen Brandes and Friedrich Nietzsche had notable influence. One member of this club was Rolf Lagerborg, a philosopher and author who fought the church on questions concerning morality and equality between the sexes. The most rebellious of Edvard Westermarck's disciples, Lagerborg had a turbulent academic career. His two dissertations on moral philosophy were rejected in Finland, but French versions were subsequently approved at the Sorbonne. Lagerborg studied moral philosophy, epistemology, and psychology, and was the first exponent of behaviorism in Finland. Theologians vehemently opposed his professional advancement because of his opinions, and because of his participation in the Prometheus Student Association (*Ylioppilasyhdistys Prometheus*, 1905–1914), Lagerborg never attained a professorship. He was a contributor to the literary and art magazine *Euterpe* (1902–1905), which promoted secularist ideals.

The Prometheus Student Association was established in 1905. Its chairman was Edvard Westermarck, professor at the universities of London and Helsinki and the founder of Finnish sociology. His most important work is the gigantic *The Origin and Development of the Moral Ideas*, considered by Finnish philosopher Georg Henrik von Wright the most important philosophical work ever written by a Finn. Westermarck was a Finnish social anthropologist and scholar whose area of specialization was the history of marriage, morality, and religious institutions. Westermarck gained international fame with his doctoral thesis, "The History of Human Marriage," which was inspired by the ideas of Darwin. It argued that contrary to then widely held ideas, there was no matriarchal stage of human development and that early humans were not universally promiscuous. The study appeared first in 1891 and later in three volumes in 1922.

The school of social anthropology Westermarck created was the best known in the world in the early twentieth century. Westermarck's life was devoted to science and enlightened Freethought. His naturalistic criticism of religion became a guiding influence, especially among academic youth. Westermarck headed the Prometheus Association during the entire period of its activity, from 1905 to 1914.

Another member of the Prometheus Association was Rafael Karsten, who held the post of professor of practical philosophy at the University of Helsinki, from 1922 to 1948. Karsten wrote several books on anthropology and the science of religion, as well as many reports on his extensive travels.

The journal *Free Thought* (*Vapaa Ajatus*) was published by S. E. Kristiansson from 1909 until his disappearance during or after Finland's civil war. Alfred Bernhard Sarlin wrote many books under the pseudonym "Asa Jalas." Both Kristiansson and Sarlin spent time in jail for BLASPHEMY.

Finland's civil war, in the wake of the collapse of czarist Russia brought on by the Bolshevik Revolution, was a catastrophe for atheists in Finland. Most freethought leaders were murdered by the anti-Bolshevik White Guard, including perhaps Kristiansson, whose fate was never determined.

Finland's first law providing for freedom of religion was enacted in 1922, but it was no more than a compromise between the church and political parties. The first freethinkers' association after the civil war was organized in 1927; the oldest freethinkers' organization still existing was established in the city of Kotka in 1929. The Union of Freethinkers of Finland (originally called the Union of Civil Register Associations, *Suomen Siviilirekisteriyhdistysten keskusliitto*) was founded in 1937. The latter was sharply attacked by the church, and Interior Minister Urho Kekkonen (later prime minister and president of Finland) tried to stop it. At his order, the city court of Tampere suppressed the local freethinkers' association in 1937. But the union survived and became a member of the World Union of Freethinkers in 1946.

About twenty-five union associations still exist with about fifteen hundred dues-paying members. The union publishes the magazine *Free Thinker* and maintains seven cemeteries where secular burials take place. It receives financial support from the government of Finland. Several independent freethought, humanist, and atheist organizations also exist.

In spite of the adoption in 2000 of a new constitution, which formally guarantees the freedom of religion and conscience, there is no real freedom from religion in Finland. The human rights of atheists are violated in the schools, and in some areas of the country the situation is becoming worse.

ERKKI HARTIKAINEN

FREE-LOVE MOVEMENT AND UNBELIEF. See **SEX RADICALISM AND UNBELIEF.**

FOOTE, EDWARD BLISS (1829–1906), American birth control educator and sex radical (see BIRTH CONTROL AND UNBELIEF; SEXUAL VALUES, IMPACT OF UNBELIEF ON; SEX RADICALISM AND UNBELIEF). Edward Bliss Foote was the most important American writer on contraception in the last half of the nineteenth century. Born in a village near Cleveland and raised as a Presbyterian, as a young man Bliss was influenced by the radical Unitarians who founded the Free Religious Association. He

contributed money to *THE TRUTH SEEKER*, founded in 1873 by the freethinker D. M. BENNETT, and became a spokesman and advocate for FREETHOUGHT.

Foote started out as a printer's apprentice, became a compositor, and for a time edited a paper in New Britain, Connecticut. From there he moved to New York as associate editor of the *Brooklyn Morning General*. He then went on to study medicine, graduating from the University of Pennsylvania in 1860. After practicing briefly in Saratoga, New York, he moved back to New York City. Even before getting his medical degree, Bliss had written the book *Medical Commonsense*, in which he mentioned the best ways to control reproduction. He refused to discuss the methods, but told his "married" readers to write him, enclosing one dollar as well as information about their "temperaments," and he would send the information. Apparently emboldened by the replies he received, he revised the book and in his 1864 edition he added a long section on reproductive control and sexual physiology. He gave somewhat lengthy descriptions of four contraceptives that he claimed he had invented, including a "membranous envelope," a type of condom made from fish bladders; the "apex envelope," a penis cap of hard rubber; a "womb veil," a diaphragm made of rubber; and an electromagnetic preventive machine that Foote claimed prevented conception by altering the partner's electrical current during intercourse. The first three were probably somewhat effective, but the last one emphasizes just how much "quackery" was part of the practice of many physicians of the time. Bliss sold condoms for three to five dollars a dozen, while the womb veil cost six dollars. With the passage in 1873 of the Comstock Act (see COMSTOCK, ANTHONY, AND UNBELIEF) forbidding dissemination of information on contraception, Foote ceased publication of the book and instead published a new version titled *Plain Home Talk*, which was revised several times under a variety of titles before he died. This volume contained no contraceptive information but instead advised "married" readers that they could obtain an important pamphlet on the topic for ten cents, either by dropping by Foote's office or by writing him for a copy. The pamphlet, originally titled *Confidential Pamphlet for the Married*, and later simply *Words in Pearl* because it was printed in Pearl Type, included updated versions of his earlier pamphlet. In it he gives one of the earliest references to the newly developed latex rubber condoms.

Bliss was arrested in 1874 for violation of the Comstock Act, was convicted of distributing obscene material, and fined five thousand dollars. In spite of this he continued to publish his guides, but distributed them differently. He opened a Sanitary Bureau near his office that became a distibuting point for his publications. His wife, Dr. Mary Bond Foote, was also a lecturer and crusader for birth control, and one of his sons, Edward Bond FOOTE, continued in his father's footsteps and wrote his own booklet of contraceptive advice.

Foote was an ardent feminist, and felt a major mission

in his life was to encourage women to believe that they had a right to decide when and how they had families.

BIBLIOGRAPHY

Brodie, Janet Farrell. *Contraception and Abortion in Nineteenth-Century America.* Ithaca, NY: Cornell University Press, 1994.

VERN L. BULLOUGH

FOOTE, EDWARD BOND (1854–1912), American Malthusian, sex radical, and eugenist. The son of free-thinkers Edward Bliss FOOTE and Mary Bond Foote, Edward Bond Foote followed his parents' path to become active in the FREETHOUGHT movement and in medicine. He also followed in his father's footsteps by writing his own book on contraceptive advice, *The Radical Remedy in Social Science; or, Borning Better Babies through Regulating Reproduction by Controlling Contraception.* His brother Hubert managed the Sanitary Bureau established by their father for the distribution of his publications.

Foote was active in the Liberal Club of New York and was made its president in 1888. He described himself as an almost-practicing vegetarian who avoided tobacco and did not drink alcohol. He also said he was a neo-Malthusian who subscribed to EUGENICS and advocated woman suffrage, the sexual emancipation of women, reduced bondage in marriage, and greater freedom in divorce. He held that every child born should be as legit-imate in law as it was in nature. As far as religion was concerned, he said he was an AGNOSTIC and a freethinker who looked forward to being cremated when he died and who anticipated nothing further after that.

BIBLIOGRAPHY

Putnam, Samuel P. *Four Hundred Years of Free Thought.* New York: Truth Seeker Company, 1894.

VERN L. BULLOUGH

FOOTE, GEORGE WILLIAM (1850–1915), English free-thinker. George William Foote was born in Plymouth on January 11, 1850. His father, a customs officer, died when he was four. He was largely self-educated but became an Anglican, later moving to Unitarianism (see UNITARIANISM TO 1961) and SKEPTICISM. He took up work in a library in London in 1868, demonstrating his abiding love of literature—Percy Bysshe SHELLEY, Lord BYRON, George Meredith, and, above all, William Shakespeare (see SHAKESPEARE, RELIGIOUS SKEPTICISM IN). He started the Young Men's Secular Association to encourage young men to support the FREETHOUGHT cause and also became superintendent of the Hall of Science Sunday School (the hall was an institution for popular

education and freethought lectures). He met Charles BRADLAUGH, president of the NATIONAL SECULAR SOCIETY (NSS), and published an article on William Blake in his *National Reformer.* He was attracted to George Jacob HOLYOAKE's more moderate SECULARISM and critical of Bradlaugh's authoritarianism and support for the publication of the birth control pamphlet *The Fruits of Philosophy* by Charles KNOWLTON (see also BIRTH CONTROL AND UNBELIEF).

He joined the rival group the British Secular Union, which was not to demonstrate lasting strength. He launched numerous journals during his life, at this stage originating the *Secularist* (1876–77) and the *Liberal* (1879). In 1881 he started the journal that he would edit for the rest of his life, the *FREETHINKER.* He opened with the forthright statement: *"The Freethinker* is an anti-Christian organ, and must therefore be chiefly aggressive. It will wage relentless war against Superstition in general, and against Christian Superstition in particular." The *Freethinker* included such departments as "Profane Jokes," "Acid Drops" (sharp comments on freethought matters), and "Sugar Plums" (good news for freethinkers). With provocative intentions he published anti-Christian cartoons taken from Léo Taxil's *La Bible Amusante.* Asked why he had become more militant, he cited Charles Bradlaugh's protracted struggle to claim the seat in Parliament he was repeatedly denied because of his ATHEISM.

As he had anticipated, prosecutions came; he was found guilty of BLASPHEMY and imprisoned for a year.

Conditions in jail were hard and his reading matter at first was confined to the Bible. Even prominent Christians thought the sentence was excessive. This experience would fuel Foote's antireligious animus for the rest of his life. A reception awaited him when he left jail on February 25, 1884, and in a few days he was lecturing on the topic "How I Fell among Thieves." Foote promised the judiciary more cartoons—and published them—but there were no more prosecutions.

In 1891, when Bradlaugh was ailing, Foote was elected president of the National Secular Society, but the force of secularism as a cause was spent. Foote wrote: "The heroic period of Freethought is well-nigh over." Many secularists had shifted their energies to socialism. Foote was a Liberal, specifically a supporter of the Liberal Party, one of the main political institutions; in general, he wanted change brought about by individual efforts rather than communal actions, and believed that society operated by individual actions rather than communal ones. Still, he believed that freethought should be neutral in politics. He had debated freethinker and socialist Annie BESANT on the topic "Is Socialism Sound?" Foote found many other topics for the *Freethinker* to cover in the subsequent years: Christian logicality (the study of the illogical nature of arguments for Christianity), secular education (a cause he particularly espoused), Ireland, war, and the "God of Battles."

An important element of his legacy was the founding of the Secular Society Ltd., a charitable organization to which bequests might be given, thus putting the *Freethinker* on a sounder financial basis. Hitherto freethought organizations had been held unable to receive bequests because their aims—presumptively, to promote blasphemy—were illegal. The Bowman case (1915 and 1917) established the right of freethought organizations to receive bequests. Foote brought about other organizational changes, such as the establishment of the publishing firm G. W. Foote and Company. The role of the NSS was sustained by widening the scope of its campaigns, by promoting its public profile, and by gaining support from well-known freethinkers.

Foote also left behind fine writing, in books and pamphlets as well as the journal. It disappointed him that he never wrote the magnum opus on Shakespeare that he wanted to produce. Two series of *Flowers of Freethought* contained many impressive essays. An early essay, "Secularism, The True Philosophy of Life," sets forth the foundation of his whole perspective. He also wrote on the false accusations of deathbed conversions (see DEATHBED CLAIMS CONCERNING UNBELIEVERS), a favorite Foote theme. *The Bible Handbook* (coauthored with W. P. Ball) was a forensic dissection of the Bible, used for many decades until a time when no one in the UK knew enough about the Bible to dissect it.

Foote's friendship with the poet and novelist George Meredith was much valued: in a letter, Meredith told Foote, "You carry on a brave battle, for *the best of causes*," coining a phrase that endured in British freethought circles. Through his editing of the *Freethinker*, his writings, and in his public avowal of the freethought cause, Foote's leadership and literary power sustained freethought for half a century.

BIBLIOGRAPHY

Foote, G. W. *Flowers of Freethought*. 2 vols. London: G. W. Foote and Company, 1893–94.

———. *Secularism: The True Philosophy of Life*. London: G. W. Foote, 1879.

Herrick, Jim. *Vision and Realism: A Hundred Years of* The Freethinker. London: G. W. Foote and Company, 1982.

Royle, Edward. *Radicals, Secularists and Republicans: Popular Freethought in Britain, 1866–1915*. Manchester: Manchester University Press, 1980.

JIM HERRICK

FORMAN, JAMES (1928–2005), American civil rights leader and humanist. Born in Chicago, James Forman became interested in desegregation struggles in Little Rock, Arkansas. In 1958 he covered the story for the *Chicago Defender*, one of the most influential newspapers in black America. In 1960 he joined the secular Congress for Racial Equality (CORE). One of his first tasks was to help Tennessee sharecroppers who had been evicted for registering to vote.

In 1961 he joined the Student Nonviolent Coordinating Committee (SNCC), another secular organization. Within a week he became the group's executive secretary. He organized student protests against white supremacy, including dangerous Freedom Rides in order to desegregate buses in the American South. He organized voter registration drives and helped provide bail money for jailed civil rights workers. Forman himself was harassed, beaten, and jailed several times for his efforts.

In 1963 Forman helped organize the historic March on Washington. He and John Lewis—who later became a United States congressman—were primarily responsible for watering down the radical language of some of the civil rights leaders who spoke at the march. As a result, Malcolm X deemed the march "nothing but a circus, with clowns and all," in his famous "Message to the Grassroots" speech.

In 1964 Forman invited thousands of people to join a voter registration drive in Philadelphia, Arkansas. Among the invitees were Andrew Goodman, James Chaney, and Michael Schwerner. The three were murdered in one of the most sensational cases of the civil rights movement.

Though Forman was becoming increasingly militant, the most influential leaders of SNCC thought he was not forceful enough. Eventually, Stokely Carmichael, H. Rap Brown, and other militants had him replaced.

Since the early 1960s Forman had been formulating a plan to demand that white churches pay African Americans $500 million in reparations for their role in the slave trade and black oppression. Forman publicized his demand in 1968 at New York's Riverside Church. Though white churches did not embrace the plan, Riverside agreed to contribute a percentage of its annual income toward efforts to fight poverty.

In his book *The Making of Black Revolutionaries*, Forman discussed his personal path to humanism. While at college, he began to have doubts about God. He learned that matter could not be created or destroyed. He saw much injustice in the world—especially for blacks. He went to ministers with his questions, but they could not provide persuasive answers. Moreover, he grew weary of the calculating church politics to which he was exposed. Eventually, Forman took a philosophy course, and it was just a matter of time before he abandoned his belief in God altogether. He held that theism led to a quietism particularly harmful to black people.

In 1993 African Americans for Humanism presented Forman with an award, and during his acceptance address he reiterated his commitment to humanist ideals. In his later years, Forman led the Unemployment and Poverty Action Committee—yet another secular organization—headquartered in Washington, DC. He continued to fight for social justice until his death in 2005.

BIBLIOGRAPHY

"Forman Highlights Free Inquiry Conference." *AAH Examiner* (Fall 1993).

Forman, James. "Corrupt Black Preachers." In *By These Hands: A Documentary History of African American Humanism*, edited by Anthony B. Pinn. New York: New York University Press, 2001.

———. "God Is Dead: A Question of Power." In *By These Hands: A Documentary History of African American Humanism*, edited by Anthony B. Pinn. New York: New York University Press, 2001.

———. *The Making of Black Revolutionaries*. Seattle: Open Hand, 1985.

"James Forman, 1928–2005." *Free Inquiry* (April/May 2005).

NORM R. ALLEN JR.

FRANCE, UNBELIEF IN. Americans are often astonished at the deep secularization of French society. Whereas in the United States a large majority observes the rites of one church or another, fewer than 20 percent among the French do the same—even though Muslims now make up 4 million of France's roughly 60 million people.

But in France as elsewhere, there are different shades of "unbelief" ranging from simple SKEPTICISM of religious dogmas to DEISM, AGNOSTICISM, and outright ATHEISM. And in France the concept of *unbelief* principally connotes unbelief in Roman Catholic dogmas. Under the absolute monarchy, that is until the French Revolution of 1789, France was utterly dominated by the Roman Catholic Church, which controlled every aspect of life for common citizens, nobles, and even the king. The earliest French kings, going back to Clovis I, were crowned under authority of the church—originally in the basilica of Saint-Denis, then for centuries in the Cathedral of Reims. Because of Clovis I's early conversion, France has then and now borne the title of "eldest daughter of the Church."

The Lasting Influence of the Religious Wars. In order to understand the ubiquity of unbelief in France today, one must grasp how this attitude developed as a consequence of France's heritage of quarrels and warfare over religious dogmas—and as a consequence of the humanist reaction against that heritage of conflict.

By way of background, it should be noted that French clergy have long displayed reluctance to bow to the authority of Rome. Perhaps this reflects a nostalgia for the independence of the popes who reigned in Avignon from 1348 to 1417, at first unquestioned in their authority, later competing with the popes of Rome during the "Great Schism." In addition, the rise of Protestantism, especially the sixteenth-century Calvinist Reformation, was well received in several regions of France, principally in the southwest, in Bordeaux and La Rochelle and in the Cévennes in the southeastern part of the Massif Central. Such an avid embrace of Protestantism precipitated violent opposition during the Counter-Reformation. The wars of religion may have been waged more ferociously in France than anywhere else in Europe; they extended over several decades, encompassing the reigns of Charles IX, Henri III, and even Henri IV. One key date was the massacre of Protestants on Saint-Barthélemy (St. Bartholomew's) Day 1572. This was organized by the Italian-born queen mother Catherine de Medicis and her son, the weak king Charles IX. French Protestants, known as Huguenots, were forced into hiding. At the close of this turbulent period, Henri de Navarre, a Protestant, converted to Catholicism in order to reunify France and to affirm his power. Famously he declared *"Paris vaut bien une messe"* (Paris is well worth a mass), taking the throne under the name of Henri IV. Through his famous Edict of Nantes (1598), he returned to French Protestants substantial freedoms.

Throughout this period of conflict, writers and philosophers took skeptical positions with regard to religion. Even before the religious wars, and though he himself was a Catholic priest, François Rabelais sharply mocked religious dogmas and the priests' way of life in his famous *Pantagruel* (1546–64). A still better example is Michel de MONTAIGNE, a Catholic probably of Jewish origin, and definitely a deist. His famous *"Que sais-je?"* (What do I know?) became a motto for the humanists of that time. Often in his *Essais* (1580–95) he defends some "heretical" idea: for example, he offers a brash defense of Julianus the Apostate, the Byzantine emperor who persecuted the state Christianity installed by his predecessor as emperor, Constantine the Great (see CHRISTIANITY, RESISTANCE TO IN THE ANCIENT WORLD).

But Catholic France did not give up. After the death of Henri IV (under the knife of a Catholic fanatic), and under the queen mother Marie de Médicis, the Protestant town of Montauban was sacked; later, forces under the Cardinal de Richelieu, minister of Louis XIII, besieged and defeated the independent Protestant city of La Rochelle, which had formed an alliance with Charles I of England. During the seventeenth century, the Huguenots were but poorly tolerated, and even that tolerance even came to a stop after Louis XIV, the "Sun King," abolished the Edict of Nantes in 1685. He thereafter sought to reimpose Catholicism on all France. The ensuing persecution drove many French Protestants to emigrate to Germany, the Netherlands, or Britain. Some militants tried to resist, such as the Camisards in the Cévennes, but they were cruelly repressed.

Still, among the people something of the old Protestant spirit remained: the feeling that the French should not depend so strictly upon the Roman Catholic Church. There was mild revolt within the French church itself as in the minds of many individuals, most of them not Protestants but freethinkers of some stripe.

The so-called *libertins*—Théophile de Viau, Cyrano de Bergerac, Scarron, and others—expressed mild criticism of dogma, challenged clerical authority, and decried hypocritical intolerance among the priests (see ANTICLERICALISM). Their works were generally published pseudonymously in Holland, yet still they were sometimes punished for expressing these almost heretical ideas (see HERESY).

Gallicanism and Jansenism. Such conflicts also resonated within the church itself. The priest, mathematician, and natural philosopher Marin Mersenne assembled a circle of scholars and priests who began to think boldly about the world and humanity's place within it. Mersenne's friend René DESCARTES proposed a rationalistic, effectively godless philosophy; he was obliged to end his days outside France, dying at the court of Sweden's Queen Christine. Nicolas Malebranche tried to reconcile Cartesian RATIONALISM with church teaching. Even the French government sought some modus vivendi, hoping to coexist with the church rather than live under it. One appealing model was the pre-Reformation Concordat of 1616 between the papacy and the French throne, which had allowed the French church some independence from Rome. The Gallican movement began with a 1682 declaration by the bishop Jacques-Bénigne Bossuet at an extraordinary general assembly of the French clergy. Bossuet declared the king of France independent of Rome in secular matters, adding that even in matters of faith the opinion of the pope is not always infallible. This was accepted by the assembly and, without quite constituting open rebellion against Rome, gave France badly needed breathing room.

In France as elsewhere, Catholic scholars and theologians were divided into monastic or philosophical communities. The often bitter quarrels among them may have further promoted the rise of skepticism. Jansenism, rooted at the abbey of Port-Royal, looked back to the teachings of the church fathers as opposed to the teachings and practices of the powerful Jesuit order. Jansenism gave rise to popular literary works such as the *Provinciales* (1656–57) of Blaise Pascal, a witty but trenchant attack upon the Jesuits and upon what Pascal considered the hypocritical morality of Jesuit conduct in public life. Though Gallicanism and Jansenism had many differences, both movements aimed at securing greater independence of thought with regard to Rome. How much independence? It is worth noting that in his famed *Pensées*, published posthumously, Pascal said of the universe: *"Le silence éternel de ces espaces infinis m'effraie"* (The eternal silence of these infinite spaces frightens me)—hardly the words of someone believing blindly in the Holy Scriptures!

Pierre Bayle. Pierre BAYLE is probably the first French author to present systematic views leading to a reasoned atheism. He was born in 1647, near Toulouse, the son of a minister of the Reformed church. After a short stay at the Reformed academy of Puylaurens in 1669, he converted in 1681 to Catholicism, breaking all links with his family. But no thoughtful son of a Reformed church minister could long accept the authoritarian Jesuit understanding of Catholicism; his return to Protestantism made him a "relapsed heretic" subject to severe penalties, and he left France for Geneva, returning in 1674 under a pseudonym. He became a professor of philosophy at the Protestant academy in Sedan. As repression of Protestantism grew, the Sedan academy was closed in 1681. Bayle moved to Rotterdam, Holland, where he remained for the rest of his life. By then he knew of the writings of Malebranche and of Baruch SPINOZA, the Jewish-Dutch philosopher whose *Ethics Demonstrated in a Geometrical Order* (1677) expressed great skepticism.

Even before the Edict of Nantes was revoked in 1685, Holland hosted a vigorous Huguenot community that included several publishers. Bayle emerged early at the head of an expatriate virtual République des Lettres that forcefully critiqued French Catholicism. Bayle's 1683 attack upon Louis Maimbourg's highly critical history of Calvinism was condemned and burned in Paris in 1683. Together with Henri Desbordes, Bayle published an influential monthly journal, *Nouvelles de la République des Lettres* (News from the Republic of Humanities). Catholic retaliations followed; not until 1696 could Bayle begin publication of his major work, the *Dictionnaire Historique et Critique*, known in English as *Bayle's Dictionary*. This was in many ways a harbinger of the great *Encyclopédie* of Denis DIDEROT and Jean LeRond d'Alembert (see ENCYCLOPÉDIE, L', AND UNBELIEF). The *Dictionary* went through several editions, and it dragged Bayle once more into contention with the church. Bayle died in Rotterdam in 1706. Though his religious attitudes changed several times during his life, he always displayed a critical attitude. In his final years he was still a believer, but also a noncredulous humanist. Let us quote him: "One cannot say anymore that theology is a Queen, of whom philosophy would only be a servant. . . . Even the theologians recognize that any dogma which would not be justified, verified, registered at the supreme parliament of reason and of the light of Nature, cannot aspire to anything but a staggering authority, as fragile as glass."

Voltaire's Deism and Diderot's Atheism. By this time a critical attitude toward Roman influence, especially over French political life, had grown common among educated Frenchmen. This was true even inside the church. Jean MESLIER was a Catholic priest who lost his faith after concluding that the wretched life of French peasants should not be tolerated by a good God (see EVIL, PROBLEM OF). His writings, of which several are lost, presented critical examinations of Catholic dogmas, condemned Christianity's morality of resignation and submission, and defended a rationalist theory of knowledge. Meslier's works were known and much admired by the philosophers of the Enlightenment (see ENLIGHT-ENMENT, UNBELIEF DURING THE), but he died in poverty and despair.

The famous and prolific writer VOLTAIRE thought along similar lines, but enjoyed substantially greater influence. He considered Bayle as his spiritual guide:

> J'abandonne Platon, je rejette Epicure;
> Bayle en sait plus qu'eux tous; je vais le consulter.
> La balance à la main, Bayle enseigne le doute,
> Assez sage, assez grand, pour être sans système.

I leave alone PLATO, I discard EPICURUS;
Bayle knows more than all of them; I will consult him.
The scales in hand, Bayle teaches doubt
Wise enough, grand enough to be without any system.

Voltaire was certainly no Catholic; it was he who coined the famous motto *"Écrasons l'infâme"* (Let us crash the loathsome thing), speaking of Catholicism and especially its claims to royal power. (In Voltaire the Revolution lay already in sight.) In fact, he was a deist:

> L'univers m'embarrasse et je ne puis songer
> Que cette horloge existe et n'a point d'horloger.

The universe worries me, and I can't avoid to think
Of that clock existing without a clockmaker.

Denis Diderot, the main author of the *Grande Encyclopédie* (1751–72) and the writer who perhaps best typified the Century of Enlightenment, was definitely an atheist. Let us quote him also: "Nature is not God; . . . Man is not a machine; . . . one hypothesis is not a fact." Like Voltaire, Diderot was subject to judicial persecutions; while Voltaire spent the last part of his life in Ferney with the Swiss border at his back, Diderot languished for many years in the Bastille. Both were fighters for unbelief and for skepticism. But Voltaire, perhaps more than Diderot, was a man of action who compelled the rehabilitation of prominent Frenchmen censured or executed for various slights against the church. Among the best known were Jean Calas, a Protestant of Toulouse tortured to death under false charges that he murdered his son to prevent his converting to Catholicism; Count Lally Tollendal, executed for treason because he surrendered a French colony in India to the British; and the Chevalier de la Barre, condemned for having refused (or forgotten) to bow to a religious procession. Voltaire's personal war against Catholic intolerance made him a hero among the French people.

The French Revolution and the Bonapartist Compromises. Between Voltaire and the coming Revolution, there extends an intriguing historical bridge. As in the past, official France remained reluctant to accept control by Rome. Because of their intrigues on behalf of Roman influence, the Jesuits were partially barred from France in 1764 and wholly forbidden in 1773. In 1778, the atheists the Baron d'HOLBACH, Claude Adrien HELVÉTIUS, and Jérôme de Lalande, all Freemasons, founded at Paris the Lodge of the Nine Sisters (or Nine Muses), a Masonic outpost devoted to profound skepticism. Among its other members were Voltaire, inducted a few months before his death, and also Benjamin FRANKLIN, then American ambassador to France, recruited by Lalande. Lalande remained a popularizer of astronomical knowledge and a fighting atheist until his death in 1807.

Strongly infuenced by the skepticism of Voltaire, by the social romanticism of Jean-Jacques ROUSSEAU, and by the wise political theories of Montesquieu, the French Revolution exploded as a revolt against the absolute power of monarchy—but also, and simultaneously, against the not-so-occult political and social power of the Roman Church.

Before the Revolution, skepticism and atheism had been limited to private circles and generally denied public expression. The Revolution toppled the monarchy, whose fall dragged with it all the traditional institutions of French society. Into this new vacuum could be introduced such radical reforms as democratic structures rooted in the principles defined earlier by Montesquieu: a radical tripartite arrangement in which the executive, the legislature, and the judiciary checked one another's power. The Revolution opened a completely new era throughout society; countless ideas previously hidden and condemned suddenly roared into the light at full strength as though they had always been ruling French society.

The French priesthood suffered terribly from the first years of the Revolution, and much church infrastructure was dismantled. But the Revolution and its aftermath would last only a short time; the church and the papacy observed France patiently, waiting for change. In the event, after a bit more than a quarter century, Rome managed to reconstruct some of its power in France, though never the overwhelming dominance it had enjoyed before the Revolution.

The evolution of the Revolution and the empire is extremely complex. It is during this short period (1789–1815) that we find the roots of the present French fight for *LAÏCITÉ* (laicization, hereafter "laicity," a concept that has much in common with SECULARISM), a fight which in contemporary France is pressed not only by atheists and deists but by many thoughtful Catholics and Protestants as well. Still, broad outlines can be traced by reference to a few key events, notably those concerning religion.

July 14th, 1789: The Fall of the Bastille. This richly symbolic event heralds the launch of the new era.

July 14, 1789–August 10, 1792: The First Period. Constitutional monarchy is in the making. Many priests actually assume political roles. Religion is reenvisioned as a public service; taxes paid by the people are suspended, and the belongings of the religious are put at the disposal of the public. Priests are encouraged to quit the church and nuns to abandon their convents. Some bishops and many responsible Catholic laypersons favor these changes; remembering the Gallican movement, they see in the new order a promise of escape from the overburdening authority of Rome. Pope Pius VI officially condemns the Declaration of Human Rights in March 1790. Defiantly the Constituent Assembly votes to group all the recent decrees and laws into the "Civil Constitution of the Clergy," which takes effect in June 1790. This completely reorganizes the temporal situation of the church, redefining the relations between church and state and between church and papacy. Priests are no longer subjects of Rome, and must instead swear fidelity to the constitution. Several priests refuse; the king, emboldened by Rome's continuous opposition to the new laws, vetoes a decree against priests who refused to accept the constitution.

This period marks the divorce between the revolution and Catholicism, and sees the rise of a new, almost definitive dichotomy between clerical and anticlerical strains within public opinion.

August 10, 1792–July 27, 1794 (9 Thermidor, year III): The Second Period. The monarchy is abolished, the king is condemned; the hard times take hold. In northern France there is war against Austrian troops. The Terror roils Paris, Lyons, Nantes, and other cities. The Catholic teaching orders, which enjoyed exclusive control of education under absolute monarchy, are dissolved. There is widespread persecution of priests. The Jacobin dictatorship rises.

July 27, 1794–November 9, 1799 (18 Brumaire, year VIII): The Third Period. This is the so-called Thermidorian reaction, the "Directoire." Joseph Lakanal, a former teacher who rose to the National Convention's Committee of Public Instruction, institutes a very strict *laïque* (secularized) system of schooling under the Law of 27 Brumaire, year III (November 17, 1794).

November 9, 1799–1815: The Fourth Period. The "Consulate." Napoléon Bonaparte is named "First Consul" and in 1802 assumes the Consulate for Life. A law prepared by the chemist Antoine-Francois de Fourcroy creates the *lycées* (public high schools). There priests are reinstated as chaplains. Administrative responsibility for primary schooling passes to the towns.

Napoléon was personally indifferent to religion; he was even listed as sympathetic to atheism by Lalande in his first supplement to Sylvain MARÉCHAL's *Dictionary of Atheists* (1800). But in 1801 Napoléon decides it prudent to seek peace with Rome. He signs a new Concordat, which many faithful revolutionary atheists bitterly deplore. Retaliating for this criticism, Napoléon issues a letter that describes atheism as a menace to the

moral fiber of the nation and forbids Lalande to speak at the Academy of Sciences.

Napoléon crowns himself Emperor of France in the presence of Pope Pius VII in Paris on December 2, 1804. War follows, but also a normalization of the law and of the school system. The Law of 18 Germinal, year X (April 8, 1802) returns the ownership of religious buildings to the religious authorities. The First Restoration of the monarchy occurs in 1814, marked by the reestablishment of the Jesuits in France; Napoleon attempts to reclaim power (the "Hundred Days," ended at Waterloo), and in 1815 the former emperor is exiled at Saint-Helene. Restored yet again, the new French regime of Louis XVIII almost reclaims the absolutist splendor of the monarchy of Louis XVI.

The Nineteenth Century and through 1905. Though Napoléon had restored the authority of the church, the French people never forgot their former, now-traditional critical view of Roman power. The nineteenth century was marked by an oscillating balance between conservative Catholics and the heirs of the absolute monarchy on the one hand, and skeptical freethinkers of a Voltairean bent and surviving Republicans and revolutionaries on the other. Rightist princes or ministers sometimes held power, including Charles X, Villèle, Guizot, later Napoleon III, and later still Patrice MacMahon. They more or less alternated with more liberal personalities, including Alphonse de Lamartine and François Arago, prominent figures of the Second Republic (1848–52), and later, Léon Gambetta and the atheists Émile Combes and Jean Jaurès, heroes of the Third Republic (1871–1940).

A key event at the close of the nineteenth century put an end to this oscillation of influence. The Dreyfus affair (1894–99) showed the deep division between the two Frances more clearly than anything preceding it. As well, it demonstrated the dangers of such deep division in the face of a strong, victorious, and still quite aggressive Germany, now united after the crushing defeat of France in the Franco-Prussian War (1871).

Alfred Dreyfus, a modest captain of the French army and a Jew, was accused, on the basis of falsified documents, of having communicated secret information to the German government. He was condemned to deportation in a trial that electrified the nation. French society aligned along the fault lines of this controversy, divisions falling often within the same social circles or even within families. The *dreyfusards* coalesced as fighters for human rights; the Ligue des Droits de l'Homme (League for the Rights of Mankind) dates to this period. The *antidreyfusards* created such groups as Ligue de la Patrie Française (League of the French Nation) and the Comité de l'Action Française (Committee for French Action), led by such figures as the anti-Semitic journalist Édouard Drumont and the ardent monarchist and nationalist Charles Maurras. Polarized, France lay near collapse. But *dreyfusard* campaigners including Bernard Lazare, Émile Zola, and Lt. Col. Georges Picquart accumulated proof that the prosecution had been a plot of the dominant anti-Semitic wing of the army. The Dreyfus affair concluded in 1906 with the rehabilitation of Dreyfus and also of Zola, who had fled to England after being condemned for his violent antiarmy and antigovernment pamphlet *J'accuse* (1898). The Catholic right wing stood ashamed, and for many years was blocked from regaining significant power.

The nature of the dichotomy between the two Frances is reflected in their respective mottos. The ruling liberals claimed as their motto the revolutionary triplet *Liberté, Egalité, Fraternité* (Liberty, Equality, Fraternity), while the disgraced conservatives began to embrace the motto *Travail, Famille, Patrie* (Work, Family, Nation), which would be adopted in 1940 as the official motto of Marshal Pétain's collaborationist Vichy regime during the Nazi occupation of France. It is further noteworthy that the word *liberté* (freedom or liberty) was sufficiently ambiguous to be usable by both camps. The leftists associated it with solidarity, the freedom of some being duly limited by the need to protect the freedom of others. The rightists associated it with the freedom to introduce religion in the schools and to develop capitalism and "free" enterprise. This often meant "freedom" at the expense of others, but why should the powerful care?

The Third Republic and Laïcity. The year 1905 saw transforming change in the wake of the Dreyfus affair. The minister Jules Ferry had already managed to pass a law excluding religion from public schools; this is the most definite imposition of the concept of laïcity into French law. Some Catholic leftist movements already existed by 1905; Catholic thinkers who had recognized negative aspects of church power even before the Dreyfus affair included Marc Sangnier, whose *Sillon* (Furrow) movement of 1894 was condemned by Pope Pius X; and the Catholic *dreyfusard* writer Charles Péguy, who launched an influential magazine, *Cahiers de la Quinzaine* (Fortnightly Review), in 1899. These were the ancestors of France's modern "Christian Democrats." Their emergence marked the dawn of an era in which religious belief was no longer exclusively associated with the political right.

Yet divisions remain. In France religious private schools are famously termed *école libre* (free school) by the Catholics who use them, but *école confessionnelle* (confessional school) or, more generally, *école privée* (private school) by nonbelievers—though some private schools are nonreligious. Yet Catholics of the political left, firmly attached to the principle of laïcity, resolutely sent their children to public schools throughout the twentieth century. This tendency diminished with the dawn of the twenty-first century, and it is paradoxical that young Muslim girls who want to wear the veil, now forbidden in French public schools, are accepted by Catholic schools. Meanwhile the political right is by no means monolithically religious; many on the right are non-Catholics rooted in the anticlerical tradition.

The events of 1905 ushered in a reorganization that cemented a new view of the status of religion in French society, but more specifically—and quite precisely—redefined the status of religion in French schooling. It is during this period that the French philosophy of *laïcité* (laïcity, desacralization, or secularism) was frozen in. Out of this philosophy emerged the 2004 French law that bars the wearing of the Muslim veil, indeed any obvious trapping bespeaking religious commitment, in public schools.

Laïque, Laïc,* and *Laïcité. At this point it is imperative to define three French words whose meaning is often elusive in English: *laïque* and *laïc*—two quite different words, both of which can be used either as nouns or as adjectives—and the noun *laïcité.*

Laïc is a term of canon law, referring to persons who are faithful Catholics but have not received the sacrament of ordination. In other words, they are not members of the religious—priests or nuns—but rather belong to the laity. *Laïc* is the characteristic of belonging to the laity, of being a lay person.

Laïque—and the noun *laïcité*, which designates the status of being *laïque*—has a broader connotation. It labels an object or person that is independent from any religious doctrine. One can say that "*la France est une République laïque,*" that is, independent from any religion. Ideas that are thought of today as *laïques* were already mentioned as such by Montaigne in the sixteenth century.

Article 2 of the present French Constitution says clearly: "France is a indivisible, *laïque,* democratic and social Republic." The roots of this sentence are of course to be found in the Enlightenment and in the French Revolution. But over the years it has been formalized with progressively greater precision, especially as regards the schools. The reasons have to do with the principles that guide French public education. Laws dating to the 1880s state that schooling must be provided for all children free of charge, and make primary education compulsory for children aged six through fourteen regardless of gender or French citizenship. As the public school is free and open to all, it must in return insist that no sign of religious membership or distinction between children on grounds of belief be displayed. Two other laws of the 1880s bar priests from the teaching staff of public schools, specifically repealing an 1850 law that had given priests some powers to review public schools. It was further recognized that children are entitled to receive some religious education; a fifth law from the 1880s created a five-day school week, freeing up one day in addition to Sunday on which parents could obtain religious education for their children outside of public schools. Though the schools do not provide religious education, they can and do provide moral and civic education, and are in fact required to do so.

The idea of formal *laïcité* originated with the Third Republic, which began in 1871 and which applied *laïcité* to all domains of social life. In 1881 the religious character of cemeteries was abolished; nonreligious burials were authorized in 1887. Divorce was legalized in 1884. Public prayers at, for example, the opening of parliamentary sessions were abolished in 1884. Over many years the public hospitals, previously largely controlled by religious orders, became laïcized. Years later, a 1972 law did away with oaths sworn to God at the beginning of court proceedings. Any mention of God has been eliminated from official statements, laws, and rules.

Of greater importance than all of these is the Law of December 9, 1905, largely the work of the socialist Jean Jaurès, which mandates complete separation between church and state. It opens with a statement that the republic guarantees freedom of conscience and free exercise of religion. It states that all buildings used for the exercise of religion are the property of the state, and of local authorities (cities or departments), placed at the free disposal of religious authorities organized in legally recognized associations.

The *laïques* laws of the 1880s and especially the law of 1905 were unmistakably intended to institute permanent reform. Lawmaking ever since has generally moved in the direction of further clarifying and expanding the idea of *laïcité*. But the Catholic church remains ill-disposed toward laïcization, and has pressed for laws that strengthen its political position whenever public opinion leans toward greater conservatism. So in 1959 the Debré law was passed to create a class of private religious schools operating under contract with the state. The Lang-Cloupet agreements of 1993 extend public support for the education of private school teachers.

Unbelief in France at the Dawn of the Twenty-first Century. In its attitudes with respect to religion, contemporary French society of course fully reflects the rich and sometimes contradictory history that this article has briefly sketched. Present-day France is undoubtedly composed mostly of titular Catholics, who very rarely attend Sunday services, but still marry and baptize their children according to traditional rites. The smaller population of Protestants, mostly Calvinists, tends to be somewhat more observant than Catholics, perhaps reflecting its minority status. Among French Jews, very few observe the full strictness of Orthodox practice. Meanwhile French Muslims display the highest levels of ritual observance and ardent belief of any faith community in France. Cultural factors may be in play, including feelings of rejection or exclusion from French social life on the part of Muslims, who as a group constitute France's most recent immigrants.

But neither denominational affiliation nor the intensity of ritual observance tells the full story. If an opinion poll were conducted today to examine where the French stand regarding religious matters, a large majority—even among titular Catholics—would almost certainly identify themselves as deists or agnostics. A substantial number would admit to atheism, though only few partic-

ipate in any organized atheist association. Even among the strictly observant, a sharp dichotomy could be expected to appear between believers who nevertheless examine critically the dogmas of their own faith communities, and a smaller number who credulously accept any teaching, any "miracle" (see MIRACLES, UNBELIEF IN), or any holy manifestation. These are more than believers; we might describe them as "the credulous." In marked contrast to them are the "unbelievers," the "incredulous" (in French, *incroyants* or *incrédules*). They are outspokenly skeptical of written scripture and the dogmas taught by the various churches. In particular, they apply an anticlerical skepticism toward the teachings devised and proclaimed by the successive popes of the Roman Catholic Church.

This skepticism is based on a critical appraisal of religious dogmas, and upon the unbeliever's recognition of the genuine "impossibility" of believing in them. This is the basis of modern unbelief in France. Though its origins are essentially social and political in character (as shown above), its deeper justification lies with a critical, rational approach toward unproven and unprovable dogmas of every kind. In France today few indeed accept the virginity of Mary or the official Catholic position on the Eucharist, which still holds that God is literally transsubstantiated into bread and wine. Few fail to accept the evolution of species, or of the universe itself over eons of time. Few entertain any spirituality or anthropomorphism in their view of the cosmos. French society has indeed made the minds of the French generally rationalistic, and there seems no reason anymore to believe in the old dogmas.

Organizations of Unbelievers. In view of the great prevalence of what we might call *practical* unbelief, it is astonishing to recognize that unbelievers in France are but poorly organized, belonging in modest numbers to small, separate groups such as the LIBRE PENSÉE, the Union des Athées, and the UNION RATIONALISTE. As for Freemasonry, its popularity is declining and it is difficult to say to what degree it still attracts deists or atheists as once it did. Unbelievers are by nature independent thinkers, and the strong individualism encouraged by French society further disinclines them toward identifying with any "community," even a community of freethought. And so organized unbelief remains fragmented and weak, despite the pervasiveness of unbelief throughout French life. On the other hand, religious affiliation and participation are undergoing a revival. This can be seen in Catholic and Jewish circles as well as in the fast-growing number of mosques. Pandering to this trend, in 2004 some French politicians advocated "softening" the secularizing laws of the 1880s and 1905. This is considered a serious danger among French freethinkers. Another worrisome trend is the postmodern tendency to view the achievements of modern science and technology, biology in particular, with alarm or even revulsion. Such thinking necessarily implies a disaffection from rationalism which might modify popular attitudes—especially when the political strength of the church, at least in France, is strongly weakened, and no longer perceived by most as a danger.

JEAN-CLAUDE PECKER

FRANKLIN, BENJAMIN (1706–1790), American printer, editor, and author, was also a prolific inventor (of bifocals, lightning rod, a stove, and the water-harmonica), and scientist (studied electricity and the Gulf Stream). He was also a philosopher, ethicist, Freemason, politician, statesman, diplomat, abolitionist, opponent of dueling, defender of Indian rights, educator, educational reformer, and civil libertarian, and the founder of a subscription library, a fire company, a militia, and a philosophical society.

Among Benjamin Franklin's many signal accomplishments, he served as governor of Pennsylvania, founded the University of Pennsylvania, and influenced Thomas PAINE to move to America. He recruited the Marquis de Lafayette and Baron von Steuben to assist the American revolutionary cause. He was a leading delegate to the Continental Congress and helped to write the Articles of Confederation, the first US Constitution. As a diplomat he negotiated the all-important military treaty with France in 1778 and was the main architect of the final Treaty of Paris in 1783 that formally ended the American Revolution. He helped Thomas JEFFERSON produce the Declaration of Independence and helped draft the Constitution in 1787. The following year he wrote that at the age of twenty-five, he had come up with the idea of a "United Nations" organization.

Franklin and Religion. Though raised as a Presbyterian, at an early age Franklin became a deist (see DEISM) and freethinker (see FREETHOUGHT) after the eighteenth-century manner. He never joined a church and seldom attended "public worship." In the last year of his life Franklin defined his deism in this way in a letter to Dr. Ezra Stiles, president of Yale College: "I believe in one God, the creator of the universe; that he governs it by his Providence; that he ought to be worshipped; that the most acceptable service we can render to him is doing good to his other children; that the soul of man is immortal, and will be treated with justice in another life respecting its conduct in this. These I take to be the fundamental points of all sound religion, and I regard them as you do, in whatever sect I meet with them." These views are remarkably similar to those expressed a mere four years later by Paine in *The Age of Reason*.

Elsewhere Franklin implicitly criticized traditional religion this way: "I wish it [Christianity] were more productive of good works. . . . I mean real good works . . . not holy-day keeping, sermon hearing . . . or making long prayers, filled with flatteries and compliments despised by wise men, and much less capable of pleasing the Deity." He added in the same letter that "[a]s to Jesus of Nazareth, my opinion of whom you particularly desire, I think his system of morals and his religion, as he left them to us, the best the world ever saw, or is like to see; but I apprehend it has received various corrupting changes, and I have, with most of the present dissenters in England, some doubts as to his divinity; though it is a question I do not dogmatize upon, having never studied it." These views are quite similar to those of Jefferson.

On other occasions Franklin had this to say about religion: "Revelation, indeed, as such, had no influence on my mind." "Lighthouses are more helpful than churches." "The way to see by faith is to shut the eye of reason." "The [constitutional convention of 1787] except for three or four persons, thought that prayers [at the convention] unnecessary."

Clearly, Franklin was not an orthodox Christian. Consummate politician that he was, however, he went out of his way to get along with people of every variety of religion. In a 1772 letter to a British newspaper defending religious dissenters, he wrote: "If we look back into history for the character of present sects in Christianity, we shall find few have not in their turns been persecutors, and complainers of persecution. The primitive Christians thought persecution extremely wrong in the Pagans, but practiced it on one another. The first Protestants of the Church of England, blamed persecution in the Roman church, but practiced it against the Puritans: these found it wrong in the Bishops, but fell into the same practice themselves both here [England] and in New England." As Franklin put it, "every sect believing itself possessed of all truth, and that every tenet differing from theirs is error." Some believed it their "duty" to persecute "HERESY."

In this vein, as early as 1738 Franklin wrote that "I think vital religion has always suffered when orthodoxy is more regarded than virtue. The scriptures assure me that at the last day we shall not be examined on what we thought but on what we did."

Franklin went on to write that "[b]y degrees more moderate and more modest sentiments have taken place in the Christian world; and among Protestants particularly all disclaim persecution, none vindicate it, and few [practice] it. We should then cease to reproach each other with what was done by our ancestors, but judge the present character of sects or churches by their present conduct only." As historian Gregory Schaaf puts it, "This was easier said than done, but he deserves credit for attempting to moderate the situation."

Elsewhere Franklin wrote, "I respected [every religion], [though] with different degrees of respect, as I have found them more or less [mixed] with other articles, which, without any tendency to inspire, promote, or confirm morality, [served] principally to divide us, and make us unfriendly to one another. This respect to all, with the opinion that the worst had some good effects, [induced] me to avoid all discourse that might tend to lessen the good opinion another might have of his own religion; and as our province [increased] in people, and new places of worship were continually wanted, and generally erected by voluntary contributions, my mite for such purposes, whatever might be the sect, was never refused."

However, as Anson Phelps Stokes and Leo Pfeffer point out, Franklin had a high opinion of the Baptists because they had no formal creed. (Franklin would have to revise this view today in view of the fundamentalist takeover of the machinery of the Southern Baptist Convention.)

Finally, Franklin, who, like Jefferson and Paine, could be thought of as a sort of "proto-humanist" (see HUMANISM), articulated a view common among many religious progressives today: "Serving God is doing good to man, but praying is thought an easier service and therefore is more generally chosen."

Franklin and Church-State Issues. Though he had less to say about religious liberty and church-state separation than his colleagues Jefferson and James MADISON, Franklin was unquestionably in harmony with their views. In 1780 he wrote the following to a Quaker friend, Richard Price:

> I am fully of your opinion respecting religious tests [for public office]. . . if we consider what that people were 100 years ago, we must allow they have gone great lengths in liberality of sentiment on religious subjects. . . . If Christian preachers had continued to teach as Christ and his Apostles did, without salaries, and as the Quakers now do, I imagine tests would never have existed; for I think they were invented, not so much to secure religion itself, as the emoluments [profits] of it. When a religion is good, I conceive that it will support itself; and, when it cannot support itself, and God does not care to support [it], so that its professors are obliged to call for the help of the civil power, it is a sign, I apprehend, of its being a bad one.

Thus in one short paragraph Franklin anticipated the ban on religious tests in Article VI of the Constitution, the First Amendment principle of separation of church and state as Jefferson and Madison understood it, and the US Supreme Court's magnificent explanation of that principle in the 1947 *Everson* and subsequent rulings.

Norman Cousins ends his selection of Franklin quotes with this: "God grant that not only the Love of Liberty but a thorough knowledge of the rights of man [a book title used by Paine shortly after Franklin's death] may pervade all the nations of the earth, so that a philosopher might set his feet anywhere on its surface and say, 'This is my country.'"

BIBLIOGRAPHY

Cousins, Norman, ed. *The Republic of Reason: The Personal Philosophies of the Founding Fathers.* San Francisco: Harper & Row, 1988.

Cremins, Lawrence A. *American Education: The Colonial Experience 1607–1783.* New York: Harper & Row, 1970.

Franklin, Benjamin. *The Autobiography of Benjamin Franklin.* New York: Collier, 1962.

Gaustad, Edwin S. *Faith of Our Fathers: Religion and the New Nation.* San Francisco: Harper & Row, 1987.

Schaaf, Gregory. *Franklin, Jefferson and Madison on Religion and the State.* Santa Fe, NM: CIAC Press, 2004.

Seldes, George, ed. *The Great Quotations.* New York: Lyle Stuart, 1960.

Stokes, Anson Phelps, and Leo Pfeffer. *Church and State in the United States.* New York: Harper & Row, 1964.

EDD DOERR

FREE ENQUIRER, THE. A significant US FREETHOUGHT periodical of the early-to-middle nineteenth century, the *Free Enquirer* began as the *New-Harmony Gazette,* house organ of the utopian colony at New Harmony, Indiana, founded by British industrialist and social reformer Robert OWEN and led by his son, Robert Dale OWEN. Coedited by the younger Owen and Frances WRIGHT, prominent American abolitionist, feminist, atheist (see ATHEISM), and reformer, the *Gazette* was published from October 1, 1825, to October 22, 1828. Dissatisfied with the Indiana colony's performance and seeking greater prominence in American thought, Owen and Wright retitled the paper the *New-Harmony Gazette or Free Enquirer* until February 25, 1829. They then relocated to New York and adopted the title the *Free Enquirer.*

For three years Owen was the paper's leading force. The *Free Inquirer* focused not only on atheism or freethought (then often called "infidelity") but also labor and social reform. According to historian Albert Post, the paper gave voice to "the most radical demands of the politically conscious workingmen. . . . [I]n fact, the *Free Enquirer* was an important factor in the creation of the laboring class's ideology" (see LABOR MOVEMENT AND UNBELIEF). Also advocated were unfettered inquiry on all subjects, religion included; abolition of debtor's prisons and capital punishment; equality for women; and the right to testify in court without swearing an oath.

Owen's coeditors were Wright and briefly Robert L. Jennings, a former Universalist minister (see UNIVERSALISM TO 1961) turned atheist. At its peak the *Free Enquirer* had one thousand subscribers.

In October 1829 Wright left the paper, sailing with Owenite reformer William Phiquepal and a shipload of slaves, residents of her failed abolitionist colony of Nashoba, Tennessee, whom she intended to set free in Haiti. Wright and Phiquepal had a daughter together, subsequently entering into a doomed marriage that would remove Wright from public life. Owen edited the *Free Enquirer* until May 1832. After his unconventional marriage with Mary Jane Robinson (see RITUAL, CERE-

MONIAL, AND UNBELIEF), he returned briefly to Europe and put the *Free Enquirer* behind him.

Reluctantly succeeding Owen was Amos Gilbert, a radical Quaker who found criticism of religion unedifying. Circulation plummeted and Gilbert retired after five months. For two months the paper was published by Benjamin H. Day, who later founded the *New York Sun*; Day was succeeded by H. D. Robinson, a combative English printer who advocated strident atheism and a bellicose ANTICLERICALISM. This alienated freethinkers of a deistic bent (see DEISM), notably Gilbert VALE. The *Free Enquirer* declined steadily, publishing its final issue on June 28, 1835.

Though short-lived, the *Free Enquirer* was significant not only for its content during the Owen years, but also for publishing innovations that would become staples of the freethought press (see PERIODICALS OF UNBELIEF). As early as the New-Harmony period, Owen and Wright broke new ground by publishing extracts from then-classic freethought works. Later these extracts were gathered into books, arguably the first products of a dedicated US freethought press. Titles included works by Wright and Owen, Thomas PAINE, Baron d'HOLBACH, and Percy Bysshe SHELLEY. Augustus Matsell, an assistant to Owen at the *Free Enquirer*, later opened a pioneer "liberal bookstore" and published an even broader line of reprints. Even the incendiary H. D. Robinson translated several d'Holbach works into English and issued a series of freethought titles under the New York Philosophical Library imprint.

While Kneeland's *BOSTON INVESTIGATOR* enjoyed a longer life (1831–1904), the *Free Enquirer* enjoyed great influence during its heyday. In particular it helped forge ties with a spectrum of radical reform movements that would influence nineteenth- and early twentieth-century freethought (see WOMAN SUFFRAGE MOVEMENT AND UNBELIEF; SEX RADICALISM AND UNBELIEF; ANARCHISM AND UNBELIEF).

In 1980, when Paul Kurtz, Gordon STEIN, and others founded the Council for Democratic and Secular Humanism (now the Council for Secular Humanism), its magazine was named *Free Inquiry* in partial tribute to the heritage of the *Free Enquirer.*

BIBLIOGRAPHY

Brown, Marshall G., and Gordon Stein. *Freethought in the United States: A Descriptive Bibliography.* Westport, CT: Greenwood, 1978.
Post, Albert. *Popular Freethought in America, 1825–1850.* New York: Columbia University Press, 1943.

TOM FLYNN

FRENCH LITERATURE, UNBELIEF IN. See FRANCE, UNBELIEF IN.

FRENCH REVOLUTION. See FRANCE, UNBELIEF IN.

FREETHINKER, THE. The longest-running British freethought journal, the *Freethinker* was founded in 1881 and is still published monthly. G. W. FOOTE started the monthly journal in May 1881, and it became a weekly in September of that year (reverting to a monthly only in 1973 for economic reasons). It was avowedly anti-Christian from the start. Foote, whose instincts were literary and genteel, had been persuaded by the furor of Charles BRADLAUGH's struggle to enter Parliament to produce an aggressive organ of advocacy. It aimed to employ "any weapons of ridicule or sarcasm that may be borrowed from the armoury of Common Sense."

Satirical accounts of religious meetings, for instance, those of the evangelists Dwight Lyman Moody and Ira David Sankey, were accompanied by exposure of the contradictions of theological thought and biblical texts. Foote believed that a detailed knowledge of scripture was invaluable in the criticism of Christianity. Two regular features were "Acid Drops," sarcastic comments on religious matters, and "Sugar Plums," notes about advances of secularism.

Foote was determined to wage war with all the tools of journalism, including antireligious cartoons. A series of cartoons based on biblical stories was introduced, many of them coming from the Frenchman Léo Taxil's *La Bible Amusante.* Foote was provoking prosecution, and it came in 1882, in connection with two cartoons from the *Freethinker*'s Christmas issue of 1882. One, titled "Moses Getting a Back View," was a picture of the backside of the deity. Another, captioned "Divine Illumination," showed an old man lighting his pipe.

Foote; his manager W. J. Ramsey; and printer Henry Kemp were prosecuted and tried before Lord North, a bigoted Catholic judge. After an inconclusive outcome a retrial was held at which Foote, despite making a stirring speech in his defense, was found guilty. He was sentenced to twelve months' imprisonment; Ramsey was given six months and Kemp three months. Foote said in reaction to the harsh sentence: "I thank you, my lord, it is worthy of your creed."

Even opponents were shocked by the severity of the punishment, and a public outcry followed. Edward Bibbins AVELING took over editorship of the journal, bringing in more coverage of social injustice and women's rights.

A third trial took place while Foote was jailed. The new judge, Lord Coleridge, was a more reasonable man who had established precedents about BLASPHEMY law— for instance, that there was a difference between blasphemy and indecency. The case was withdrawn, but Foote continued in jail until his release to acclaim from his freethinking supporters. Foote promised more provocation but there were no more prosecutions.

Foote resumed the editorship, which he retained until his death in 1915. There were serious financial difficulties during this period and Foote had problems keeping the *Freethinker* going. He established the legal right for bequests to be made to irreligious organizations with a case upholding the legality of a bequest.

Chapman COHEN, who had assisted Foote in producing the *Freethinker* for many years, took over the editorship in 1915 and held the post until 1951. Cohen was particularly good at presenting philosophical ideas to readers, although the journal's emphasis upon countertheology did not weaken. Free speech, divorce reform, birth control (see BIRTH CONTROL AND UNBELIEF), blasphemy law, the powers of the BBC, and the ever-present contradictions of clerics and theologians continued through the twentieth century. During World War I, Bertrand RUSSELL wrote a long letter on the topic of conscientious objection. World War II brought objection to days of prayer and Bibles for the forces. The *Freethinker* offices were bombed during the Blitz—fortunately, an emergency issue had been prepared to prevent a gap in publication.

After Cohen's resignation a succession of editors included F. A. Ridley, David Tribe, Nigel Sinnott, Bill McIlroy, Jim Herrick, Peter Breary, and Barry Duke. The *Freethinker*'s robust criticism of religion remains forceful and heartfelt.

A publication by the same name was issued in the United States by atheist activist Joseph LEWIS from the middle of the 1940s until its name was changed in the 1950s.

BIBLIOGRAPHY

Cooke, Bill. *The Blasphemy Depot: A Hundred Years of the Rationalist Press Association.* London: Rationalist Press Association, 2003.

Herrick, Jim. *Vision and Realism: A Hundred Years of the* Freethinker. London: G. W. Foote, 1982.

Tribe, David. *100 Years of Freethought.* London: Elek, 1967.

Walter, Nicolas. *Blasphemy Ancient and Modern* London: Rationalist Press Association, 1990.

JIM HERRICK

FREETHOUGHT. Literally the questioning of received opinion and traditional customs, *freethought* has come to mean arrival at and acting upon heterodox views, especially in religious matters. The freethinking editor Gordon STEIN declared that simple unbelief should be called *free thought* and the term *freethought* applied only to the movement with a tradition and philosophical base embracing the use of reason and ethics and the elimination of superstition of all kinds. Obviously, heterodox views cannot be known unless expressed orally or in writing, or by actions such as abandoning churchgoing, but it takes some time for their exponents to be properly called a movement. In naming freethinkers in histories and biographical dictionaries, compilers usually adopt a relative

standard: that is, the degree of heterodoxy detected is inversely proportional to the power of orthodoxy in the freethinker's environment. As this judgment is largely subjective, such works may attract criticism from skeptical reviewers who question whether non-Christian theists, deists, and reverent agnostics should be included.

Deism. In fact, *freethought* was originally deemed synonymous with DEISM. Its evolution in Europe, including Britain, is outlined in James Mackinnon ROBERTSON's *History of Freethought Ancient and Modern to the Period of the French Revolution* (1936). According to Robertson, a pantheistic, antinomian sect called Brethren of the Free Spirit flourished in France and Italy between the thirteenth and fifteenth centuries. Following Saint Paul, antinomians asserted that Christ had freed them from the Mosaic law, including the moral law. They claimed to live virtuously without it, while enemies accused them of using their doctrine as an excuse for licentiousness. French names for a freethinker recorded in Pierre BAYLE's *Dictionnaire* (1697) and elsewhere were *bel esprit* (beautiful spirit), *esprit fort* (bold spirit), and *libertin* (libertine), with greater ambiguity then than today. In its sixth edition (1820), the *Encyclopedia Britannica* said that the name "freethinker... seems to have been first assumed as the denomination of a party about the middle of the sixteenth century, by some gentlemen in France and Italy" wishing to disguise their anti-Christianity. (The latest, fifteenth edition of 1974 curiously has no corresponding entry.) Robertson identified their label as "deist." Certainly by the late seventeenth century both terms were used interchangeably. Previously unbelievers had been called "atheists," "infidels," or "rationalists." The *Oxford English Dictionary* names the first recorded use of "freethinker" in England as the title of S. Smith's 1692 booklet *The Religious Impostor... dedicated to Doctor S-lm-n and the rest of the new Religious Fraternity of Freethinkers near Leather-Sellers-Hall... printed in the first year of Grace and Freethinking.* Ever controversial, Robertson said this sect was really the less heretical "Freeseekers," and that the first recorded use of "freethinker" in English occurred in 1695 when, in a letter of December 24 to the empiricist John LOCKE, William Molyneux called John TOLAND a "candid freethinker."

Though leading French Encyclopedists admitted to ATHEISM (see *ENCYCLOPÉDIE, L'*, AND UNBELIEF), the great bulk of Continental, British, and American freethinkers of the eighteenth and early nineteenth centuries called themselves deists. Thomas PAINE is believed to have wanted to set up deistic churches, and one or two were independently established. On March 28, 1823, however, one of Paine's publishers, the imprisoned editor of the influential English *Republican*, Richard CARLILE, announced that he had turned from deism to atheism. While there were few other public conversions, the label "deist" rapidly disappeared thereafter. This was not the case with "freethinker."

The distinction between deism and atheism is largely one of convention, as both reject theism. Yet both deists and theists have some pretensions to piety, since the words are derived respectively from the Latin and Greek for "god." By general usage, however, the deity of theism is the biblical creator and sustainer of the universe, the entity that watches sparrows fall to the ground and answers—or declines to answer—human prayers. With discovery of the laws of physics and chemistry (notably planetary motion, gravity, thermodynamics, and conservation of matter and energy) and theories of evolution and relativity, it was no longer possible to accept theism by other than blind faith. Yet for centuries it was unsafe, and even today in the United States and elsewhere unsavory, to declare oneself an atheist, even though the term literally means "without" and not "against" god. So unbelievers adopted the deist label. In England this was sourced to *De Veritate* (1624) by Edward Herbert of Cherbury. Originally the expression denoted rejection of revelation, biblical or personal, in favor of so-called natural religion, which posited that nature itself testified to the existence of a deity; it later came to signify belief in a god that had created the world then left it to its own devices. Essentially this was the god of Thomas Aquinas's "five proofs" in *Summa Theologiae* (1265–73) that was disproved by Immanuel KANT in *Critique of Pure Reason* (1781) (see EXISTENCE OF GOD, ARGUMENTS FOR AND AGAINST). Such a god involved logical absurdities including the notion of the "uncaused cause," needless complexity in defiance of Occam's razor, and hypotheses not amenable to the verification principle (see VERIFICATIONISM). Religious apologists asserted that if these assumptions could not be proved scientifically, they equally could not be disproved.

Beyond Deism. In a twentieth-century riposte, Karl POPPER conclusively showed that any proposition that can never be falsified is not true but meaningless (see LOGICAL POSITIVISM). Yet the real reason for abandoning deism was probably that it was, like Dean Arthur Stanley's Broad Church, "not worth believing in." Not everyone who abandoned deism turned to atheism. Some chose SKEPTICISM or AGNOSTICISM; others, more affirmatively, opted for SECULARISM, Liberalism, eclecticism, ETHICAL CULTURE, RATIONALISM, or HUMANISM. But underlying them all was freethought. Before those other labels became fashionable, "freethought" or "freethinkers" was included in the titles of sundry bodies of unbelievers round the world: in Amsterdam (1855); Dunedin, New Zealand (1878); France (1879); Canterbury, Wellington, and Auckland, New Zealand (1918); France and Germany (1919); Sydney University (1930); Poland (1934). It also featured in the name of the first international body of unbelievers, the International Federation (after 1936, World Union) of Freethinkers (1880).

The above account demonstrates how the movement was basically reactive, and opponents have thus branded it as negative. A frequent jibe leveled at freethinking speakers is, "You've spent all this time telling us what you don't believe in. Now tell us what you do believe in." Unfortunately, a few respond with "nothing." As will emerge, this is far from the truth. Robertson rightly dismissed as a "whimster" someone with no consistency, responding entirely to mood and "flighty nonconformity." This has a political counterpart in someone always "agin' the government," no matter what it is or does. Nevertheless, negativity is a necessary first step, especially when dealing with "religions of the book" (Judaism, Christianity, Islam). All progress is by incremental steps arising from criticism of the status quo. A caveman objects to the dark before seeking a means of introducing light. A farmer removes weeds before planting crops. A surgeon extracts pus before stitching up a wound. Religionists have followed the same route. Reformed churches arose through objections to Roman Catholicism; Islam, to Christianity; Christianity, to Judaism; Judaism, to idolatry. Until these objections had been voiced and acted upon, sweeping aside old presuppositions and "venerable" institutions, development was impossible. Some aspects of the old, seen as of abiding value, were retained, and some aspects of the new, seen as "jumping out of the frying pan into the fire," were censured in their turn and replaced by later generations.

Another criticism leveled at freethinkers is that they believe in inevitable progress—a neophilia that worships change for its own sake—and it is true that until World War I there was something like a facile cult of progress in the first world. But this was not confined to freethinkers, and it has all but vanished now. Even if it were still influential, it is surely better than a cult of Armageddon.

Harking back to freethought's French and Italian derivation, other critics have indicted it for profligacy. Whatever the original meaning of "libertine," it is certainly associated more with Casanova than with Kant. As Rector Kroll says in Henrik Ibsen's *Rosmersholm* (1886), "I have always believed that between freethought and free-love no great gulf is fixed." Yet while Robert OWEN, George ELIOT and G. H. Lewes, H. G. WELLS, C. E. M. Joad, and Bertrand RUSSELL regarded conventional marriage as mere priest-made law, freethinkers do not appear to lead more "abandoned" lives than others of their social class and occupation. Indeed, many could be called puritanical. Nor do they seem more prone to homosexual activity. But if sexual "perversion" be an issue, what is more perverse or "unnatural" than clerical celibacy?

A more recent and sophisticated criticism of freethought is that it is, by most freethinkers' own philosophy, an oxymoron in that they profess belief in DETERMINISM. This issue has been ignored by many writers on the subject, but Robertson and Chapman COHEN, long-serving president of the NATIONAL SECULAR SOCIETY, attempted to deal with it. Robertson argued that thought is a "basic instinct," where the idea of being "free" or "bound" should not apply. Freethought, on the other hand, points to a different degree of employment of the faculty of criticism: freethinkers are not terrorized by a veto on criticism, and they are not hampered, or are less so, by ignorant presuppositions. Cohen argued that "freethought" is a word used in sociology, analogous to phrases like "free man" or "free people," to denote the absence of restraint or foregone conclusion, and that it "says nothing as to the nature of thought, the origin of thought, or the laws of thought." According to him, "thought" applies to physical science, where freethought has no meaning.

In the light of modern knowledge we can say that thought is not only mediated by neurotransmitters and synapses (chemicals and connections between nerve cells) in the brain, but that thought strengthens and extends them. Thus, unless checked by self-censorship induced by external forces, thought leads to more thought in a deterministic fashion until eventually old ideas no longer relate to experience and so become incredible, while new ones with a better relation emerge to take their place. Following Lewes's emphasis on the "social medium" of language, in his *Grammar of Freethought* (1921) Cohen stressed that if freethought does not lead to free expression and social interaction, it is lost to both society and the individual. Indeed, without language thought itself is scarcely possible and, in odd cases, children brought up without it present as jibbering idiots. Since our early ancestors came down from the trees there has been relatively little biological evolution. Development has been psychosocial. Removal of barriers to thought and its transmission has thus been a major objective and achievement of freethought.

Essentials of Freethought. Giving a National Secular Society centenary lecture in 1966, the philosopher Paul Foulkes said freethought has five basic characteristics: (a) no party line, (b) no absolutes, (c) no censorship, (d) no sacred books, and (e) no sacred names. At first glance this catalog may seem to reinforce the perception of negativity at the heart of freethought, but scrutiny shows these apparent negatives have positive outcomes.

(a) In the nineteenth century it was quite common for freethinking literature to refer to "the freethought party." This was not meant in a party-political sense. There was no intention to endorse parliamentary candidates, though individual freethinkers who did contest elections were usually assured of strong support from their colleagues. From the 1860s to the 1880s, when Charles BRADLAUGH was chasing and eventually capturing a seat in Parliament, almost all British freethinkers supported the Liberal Party on its Radical, not Whig, flank. Since that time political views have been more polarized among English-speaking freethinkers. On the Continent there has long been a close association with socialism. But a feature of freethought organiza-

tions is that political and philosophical labels are left to individuals to adopt.

(b) In contrast with worldviews, mostly religious, that claim to be valid for all time, freethought does not acknowledge absolutes. Ideas and opinions fundamentally depend on knowledge, and as it changes so may they. But two false conclusions from this proposition must be corrected. First, freethinkers are not in a state of perpetual mental flux. The name for that is neurosis. Actions need the guidance of stable attitudes. All freethought proclaims is that these are provisional. Second, though some freethinkers may adhere to postmodernism, relativistic ethics, or other manifestations of deferment to any and every personal "judgment," most do not (see EUPRAXSOPHY; MORALITY FROM A HUMANIST PERSPECTIVE). While allowing that we do not always—and may never—know which scientific and social beliefs and practices are "right," we do know beyond reasonable doubt that some are "wrong." These include witch phenomena and persecution, flat-earthism, geocentrism, fortune telling, belief in demon possession, trial by ordeal, animal and human sacrifice, slavery, torture, exploitation, extortion, child abuse, and major felonies. And we have a duty to speak out against and try to eliminate them without causing greater harm through indiscriminate warfare.

(c) However well intentioned, curbs on free expression are usually wrong everywhere and every time. They deprive the engine of society of its essential fuel for advancement, oppress their victims, and corrupt their perpetrators. Thus freethinkers have been implacable foes of censorship operated through catchall laws against sedition, obscenity, BLASPHEMY, and defamation whose aim is to stifle legitimate criticism of tyranny, prudery, absurdity, and corruption. They have sought to rescue manuscripts from oblivion and books from burning, and to save authors, artists, publishers, printers, and booksellers from fines, jails, or gallows. Yet they recognize that, especially with the power and penetration of modern media, there are legitimate limits to free speech and publication when the well-being and safety of nations and individuals are threatened. These include curbs on the publication of military (not "official") secrets, child pornography, incitements to ethnic violence, and malicious libel.

(d) A particular feature of freethought is that it has no sacred books. Throughout the literature of unbelief one will find frequent references to seminal works that have liberated humankind from past errors and prejudices. Such titles include Paine's *Rights of Man* and *The Age of Reason*, Charles DARWIN's *Origin of Species*, Winwood Reade's *Martyrdom of Man*, Ernst HAECKEL's *Riddle of the Universe*, James Frazer's *The Golden Bough*, and *The Works of Robert G. INGERSOLL*. These are revered but not venerated. Freethinkers acknowledge that they are creations of their time, owing much to writers who went before them and containing errors and omissions corrected by writers who followed them. In this crucial way they are very different from the sacred books of "revealed" religion, which are generally believed by the faithful to be divinely inspired and free of error. If they contained only devotional and theological material, that would be bad enough for their stultifying effect on believers. Unfortunately, in most cases they also purport to be compendia of the physical sciences, textbooks of the social sciences, and manuals of morality. Protected from criticism by temporal powers and taught in both Sunday and secular schools, these "spiritual" texts enshrine the beliefs and customs of bygone ages. As there are some "eternal verities," not everything in them is valueless or pernicious, and their language has often enriched secular literature. But there is no religious yardstick to distinguish among the good, indifferent, and bad. However retranslated and reinterpreted, they retain an unyielding hold on society that each generation has to struggle against.

(e) Just as the writings of freethinkers have no special status placing them beyond criticism, so freethought's writers and organizers do not enjoy infallibility or special privileges. Yet in all fields there are acknowledged authorities whose range of scholarship and depth of thought entitle them to a position of influence and citation. Individuals do not rethink all knowledge for themselves. They assimilate a modicum, hopefully reflect on it, and perhaps modify it to become authorities themselves. If they become celebrated freethinkers they do not expect to be accorded sanctity by their fellows and assuredly will not achieve it.

Aspirations of Freethought. While freethinkers have usually outshouted religious reformers in their criticism of existing faiths and have been willing to face scorn, obloquy, or persecution for their heterodox opinions, they do not on the whole embrace negativity for its own sake. Indeed, as this author said in *Nucleoethics: Ethics in Modern Society* (1972), "Many of them would be inclined to say, with an indulgent smile, that if myths brought comfort and did no harm it would be churlish to denounce them." Of course they would still feel an obligation, in the interests of truth, to observe that myths are neither history nor philosophy, though some may encapsulate a useful symbolic or moral message. But they would feel no urge to unite with like-minded people to create organizations and publications to promote their views. There may be "many mansions" in a heavenly father's house; there are none within freethought.

Some freethinkers may be driven by an emotional cussedness, but most see positive benefit to society in VOLTAIRE's *ecrasez l'infame* (literally, "curse infamy") and David HUME's railing against "the whole train of monkish virtues" and faith that is impervious to reason and often to humanity. They recall Voltaire's aphorism that those who believe absurdities can commit atrocities, but always with the best will in the world. Apart from that, reliance on God or gods undermines self-reliance, and belief in an afterlife devalues this life. For if we were really spiritual beings with an immortal destiny, nothing would be more appropriate for us all than monasticism.

From the foregoing it can be seen that the two fields where freethinkers have been most active are education and law reform. Clearly they have been in the forefront of demands for secular education, but they have also campaigned for free, compulsory, and further education. While believing that it should be available to all children through state schools and that the process should be publicly fostered throughout life, they supplement government provisions with classes and lectures of their own. Generally, their exertions are intellectual; but they recognize the role of physical training and the arts. Special attention is also given to moral education.

Freethought's moral benefits come from exposing immoralities in religious beliefs (biblical crimes, substantial abandonment of individual responsibility, penalizing opinion, putting faith before works) and not from unbelief per se; actual behavior is influenced by the quality of parental care, education, pragmatism, technology, mass media, bureaucracy, and law. Thus freethinkers have been prominent in reform of the laws that restrict legitimate freedoms, obstruct science, and promote injustice, chauvinism, and inhumanity.

BIBLIOGRAPHY

Brown, Marshall G., and Gordon Stein. *Freethought in the United States: A Descriptive Bibliography*. Westport, CT: Greenwood, 1978,

Cohen, Chapman. *A Grammar of Freethought*. London: Pioneer, 1921.

Herrick, Jim. *Vision and Realism: A Hundred Years of the* Freethinker. London: G. W. Foote, 1982.

Robertson, J. M. *A History of Freethought Ancient and Modern to the Period of the French Revolution*. 4th rev. ed. London: Watts and Company, 1936.

———. *A History of Freethought in the Nineteenth Century*. London: Watts and Company, 1929.

Stein, Gordon. *Freethought in the United Kingdom and the Commonwealth*. Westport, CT: Greenwood, 1981.

Tribe, David. *100 Years of Freethought*. London: Elek, 1967.

Wheeler, J. M. *A Biographical Dictionary of Freethinkers of All Ages and Nations* London: G. W. Foote, 1889.

DAVID TRIBE

FREIE GEMEINDEN. The Freie Gemeinden (Free Congregation) movement had its origins in dissension within the established Evangelical (Lutheran) and Catholic churches in Germany in the early nineteenth century. The post-Napoleonic repression confirmed a conservative alliance between church and state, giving rise to a rationalist countermovement (see RATIONALISM). While this dissent sometimes produced congregations that remained Christian, others, influenced by radical

Hegelianism, moved toward a fully secular orientation. Religious holidays, scriptures, and authority were replaced with broader-based alternatives. Instead of pastors, there were "speakers" elected by local members. By the mid-1840s, these groups converged into an outright armed resistance to the government, erupting in the revolution of 1848–49.

With the defeat of the revolution, thousands of freethinkers (Forty-Eighters) immigrated to the United States, where they quickly established new Freie Gemeinden in cities like St. Louis and Milwaukee, and also in rural areas. A few similar groups already existed, such as those established by Friedrich Münch and Edward Mühl in rural Missouri. Some forty Free Congregations had been formed by the early 1850s; they featured lectures, debates, and the foundation of inexpensive schools. A competing organization, the Verein Freier Männer (Free Men's Society) criticized the practice of paying speakers on the grounds that it encouraged a priesthood. There was also political division; older rationalists had been drawn into the orbit of the Democratic Party, while more recent arrivals generally endorsed the new Republican Party and its more explicit opposition to slavery.

Anticipating armed conflict, freethinkers formed paramilitary groups whose hundreds of members engaged in regular military drills. At the outset of the Civil War, many such groups enlisted directly in the Union army. In Missouri they played a dramatic role in saving that state for the Union cause. Whole regiments from Indiana, Illinois, Wisconsin, and Missouri were made up of radical Germans. When required to designate a chaplain, one Indiana regiment selected one of its most militantly freethinking members and confirmed beer as the sacramental beverage. General August Willich, a Forty-Eighter who had been a Communist in the old-country revolution, led the successful charge up Missionary Ridge in the Battle of Chattanooga in 1864. Thus German immigrant freethinkers served decisively to defend the republic against the reactionary treason of the Christian Confederacy.

After the Civil War the Freie Gemeinden were reestablished, often constructing impressive new buildings. The St. Louis building, which still stands, bears the motto *Wahrheit Macht Frei* (Truth Makes Us Free). These premises supported extensive libraries, classrooms, and auditoriums. While the leadership tended to come from the intellectual or professional class, the rank and file was dominated by workers in various trades. A turn-of-the-century bulletin from the North St. Louis group promoted night courses "for such men as are eager to receive an industrial education and cannot afford either the time or the money required for colleges or universities." Hence, the buildings came to serve as community centers, with a wide range of activities including singing societies and the like. They sometimes cooperated with the *Turnverein* (athletic organizations later popularly known as Turners); at other times Turner groups gravitated to more mainstream nonpolitical activities, distancing themselves from the more radical ANTI-CLERICALISM of the freethinkers.

In social-democratic strongholds like Milwaukee, a working alliance developed among Turners, Socialists, and freethinkers (see SOCIALISM AND UNBELIEF), cemented by Socialist victory in local elections in 1910. From the time of Haymarket in the 1880s (see ANARCHISM AND UNBELIEF), Chicago had always had a militant tradition. But the advent of anti-German and anti-radical policies during World War I blunted its advance and precipitated a long, slow process of decline for the Freie Gemeinden. To be sure, local organizations persisted for decades, contributing to the formation of the AMERICAN RATIONALIST FEDERATION in 1955. In 1967 the Milwaukee group marked its centennial; Mayor Henry W. Maier sent greetings, stating: "That you have contributed to the cultural, the social and the literary life of Milwaukee is without question. You have also maintained for posterity those precious old-world customs which might otherwise have been forever lost." A commemorative book noted that "for a century now, these rationalist groups provided a much needed forum for unorthodox, and often very unpopular ideas. EMERSON spoke to them, and INGERSOLL, Clarence DARROW and Emma GOLDMAN. They provided a platform for those who advocated prison reform and woman suffrage; they discussed unemployment insurance and social security long before the days of the New Deal."

But elsewhere, dwindling membership led to dissolution. The St. Louis group ceased operation in 1970, donating its remaining funds to the Ethical Society (see ETHICAL CULTURE). Walter HOOPS, a mainstay of the group, continued to be active in the Rationalist Society, which still exists.

A 1966 study of the Sauk City, Wisconsin, group focused on the reasons for its decline, stating it was in a "death trance" and noting that it had affiliated with the Unitarian Universalists (see UNITARIAN UNIVERSALISM) in 1955. But gainsaying that dire analysis, in 2002 this last surviving Freie Gemeinden marked its 150th anniversary with a celebration, as "a Bavarian band played polkas, children danced among swirling leaves, adults sipped beer in the sunshine—and no one told anyone what to believe." Similarly, in rural Hermann, Missouri, Eduard Mühl's house has been incorporated into the complex of buildings maintained by the state to mark the permanent contributions Germans made to Missouri history. And in Austin, Texas, the original building of the German Free School, built in 1857, is now the headquarters of the German-Texan Heritage Society. In these ways, the Freie Gemeinden survive as a part of America's intellectual heritage.

BIBLIOGRAPHY

Cooper, Berenice. "Die Freie Gemeinde—Freethinkers on the Frontier." *Minnesota History* 41 (1968).

Demerath, N. J., III, and Victor Thiessen. "On Spitting against the Wind: Organizational Precariousness and American Irreligion." *American Journal of Sociology* 71 (1966).

Keil, Hartmut, ed. *German Workers' Culture in the United States 1850 to 1920.* Washington, DC: Smithsonian Institution Press, 1988.

Muehl, Siegmar. "Eduard Mühl: 1850–1854: Missouri Editor, Religious Free-Thinker and Fighter for Human Rights." *Missouri Historical Review* 81, no. 1 (1986).

Rowan, Steve, ed. *Germans for a Free Missouri: Translations from the St. Louis Radical Press, 1857–1862.* Columbia: University of Missouri Press, 1983.

Smith, Susan Lampert. "Freethinkers Liked to Have Fun." *Wisconsin State Journal,* October 7, 2002.

Whitehead, Fred, and Verle Muhrer, eds. *Freethought on the American Frontier.* Amherst, NY: Prometheus Books, 1992.

Zucker, A. E., ed. *The Forty-Eighters: Political Refugees of the German Revolution of 1848.* New York: Columbia University Press, 1950.

FRED WHITEHEAD

FREUD, SIGMUND (1856–1939), Austrian founder of psychoanalysis.

Early Life. Sigmund Freud was born in Freiberg, Moravia, in 1856, and his family moved to Vienna when he was four years old. He entered the science and medical faculty of the University of Vienna in 1873, specializing in anatomy and physiology. From 1876 he studied under Ernst Brücke, a member of the Helmholtz School, a group committed to applying the methods of the physical sciences to medicine. Freud's impressive research in Brücke's Institute of Physiology opened up the prospect of a promising academic career, but financial considerations led to his undertaking a course in medicine in 1882 with the aim of starting a private practice. Toward the end of his medical studies he spent some six months in Paris studying under Jean Martin Charcot, whose ideas on the nature of what was termed *hysteria* (symptomatology for which there was no apparent organic cause) were to have a considerable influence on his future.

Career. In 1886 Freud set up in private practice as a neuropathologist, and was soon to become effectively what we would now call a psychotherapist. In the period in the 1890s during which he developed his psychoanalytic techniques, he treated patients for a variety of mental and physical ailments which, under the influence of the ideas of Charcot and of Josef Breuer, he believed had their origins in mental disturbances, predominantly episodes of a sexual nature that the patient could no longer recall. (In Freudian terminology, the memories had been repressed into the unconscious.)

In the mid-1890s a combination of preconceived theory and his analytic technique for reconstructing unconscious memories (incorporating his belief that somatic symptoms were symbolic representations of traumatic events) led to Freud's claiming clinical confirmation for his postulate that repressed memories of sexual abuse in early childhood constituted an essential precondition for hysteria and obsessional neurosis. However, he soon lost faith in what psychoanalysts later called the seduction theory, eventually harnessing his dubious clinical claims (retrospectively modified) to support the notion of infants having a rich psychosexual fantasy life. These latter ideas, which to a large extent replaced the analytic search for early childhood traumas, became the bedrock of psychoanalysis. A detailed presentation of his psychoanalytic interpretative procedures was given in *The Interpretation of Dreams* (1900), and the first fruits of his new direction were described in *Three Essays on the Theory of Sexuality* (1905). Contrary to traditional accounts, Freud's early psychoanalytic writings were generally treated with respect, though several contemporary psychologists and psychiatrists expressed doubts about his clinical claims and his largely speculative theories in terms that present-day critics recognize as having considerable merit.

There followed a constant stream of writings over the next thirty years, during which Freud published a handful of case histories designed to illustrate his clinical methodology, as well as a great number of publications in which he developed his ideas further in a variety of directions, culminating in his (unfinished) final work in which he attempted to sum up his achievements, *An Outline of Psychoanalysis* (1940). Concurrently he inaugurated and led psychoanalytic organizations whose central purpose rapidly became that of disseminating his ideas to a wide public. They accomplished this purpose to such an extent that by the middle of the twentieth century, many of Freud's ideas achieved the status of received knowledge throughout the Western countries, most notably in the United States.

The last period of Freud's life was blighted by cancer of the mouth, diagnosed in 1923. Nevertheless, despite numerous operations, he remained a prolific writer throughout these years. Following the Nazi takeover of Austria in 1938 he emigrated to London, where he died in 1939.

Religious Beliefs and Writings. Born to nonpractising Jewish parents, Freud remained an atheist (see ATHEISM) to the end of his life. However he retained a strong sense of a Jewish identity, becoming conversant with the Old Testament in his early childhood, though his first writings on the origins of religious beliefs were of a general nature. As early as 1907, in his paper "Obsessive Actions and Religious Practices," he drew an analogy between the rituals of religion and those of obsessional neurosis. In his essay on Leonardo da Vinci (1910) he associated the belief in a personal God with a child's relation to a father figure, and developed this notion in *Totem and Taboo* (1913), in which he proposed that the origins of religion, among other social and cultural phenomena, were to be found in the Oedipus complex. He reiterated these propositions in *The Ego and the Id* (1923), in which he argued that religious and moral values originally arose in the very earliest stages of human history from the process of mastering the Oedipus complex, and that these had then become an inherited characteristic of humankind.

In his lengthy study of religion, *The Future of an Illusion* (1927), Freud brought all these themes together in an essay that combined an occasional astute analysis of the psychological sources of religious belief with more contentious propositions based on psychoanalytic concepts. Describing religion as comparable to a childhood neurosis, he ended by expressing his view that human beings will eventually overcome their dependence on such beliefs. He made use of these same themes in his final foray into religion, *Moses and Monotheism* (1939), in which he maintained that monotheism originated in Egypt and that Moses was an Egyptian prince who assumed the leadership of a Semitic tribe. This highly speculative essay was ill-received by Jewish and other biblical scholars.

Psychoanalysis as a Belief System. Many commentators have observed that the man who claimed to have unmasked religion as a neurotic belief system was himself the founder of a movement that had many characteristics in common with dogmatic religion. Freud saw himself as a man with a mission to spread the word about psychoanalysis, and his propensity to compare himself with Moses has frequently been noted. Some of his basic ideas he treated as obligatory articles of faith rather than as fallible scientific theory; he described both his dream theory and the Oedipus complex as "shibboleths" that separated believers from unbelievers. Dissenters from the true path, such as Adler, Stekel, and Jung, were forced out of the Vienna Psychoanalytic Society and denounced as heretics. In his public writings Freud's explanation for their supposed transgressions was that they had encountered within themselves resistances to "analytic knowledge" which resulted in their rejecting what they had previously learned. In similar fashion, he explained opposition from "the representatives of official science" as a "manifestation of the same resistance which I had to struggle against in individual patients"; in other words, intellectual opposition was of little account other than as an exemplification of his own theories. In such ways Freud ensured that, for the believer, classical psychoanalysis was impervious to criticism.

The cultlike nature of the fledgling psychoanalytic movement was exemplified by its exclusiveness and hostility toward critics, excessive reverence for the founder, evangelistic fervor, and propensity for the formation of schisms. From these beginnings it flourished like no other movement that claimed the status of science (though precedents can be found in religion). Both critics and converts have remarked on the capacity of Freud's psychoanalytic writings to be a source of inspiration and consolation comparable to religious literature. But influential as it has been, the failure of psychoanalysis as a discipline to provide plausible grounds for the truth of its more distinctive propositions resulted in its decline in the last decades of the twentieth century. Nevertheless, its intrinsic capacity to provide facile explanations for virtually any human psychosocial phenomenon is likely to ensure its survival in one form or another for the foreseeable future.

BIBLIOGRAPHY

Breger, Louis. *Freud: Darkness in the Midst of Vision*. New York: Wiley, 2000.

Cioffi, Frank. *Freud and the Question of Pseudoscience*. Chicago: Open Court, 1998.

Crews, Frederick C. *Unauthorized Freud: Doubters Confront a Legend*. New York: Viking, 1998.

Ellenberger, Henri. *The Discovery of the Unconscious*. New York: Basic Books, 1979.

Fancher, Robert E. *Psychoanalytic Psychology: The Development of Freud's Thought*. New York: Norton, 1973.

Freud, Sigmund. *The Standard Edition of the Complete Psychological Works of Sigmund Freud*. London: Hogarth, 1953–1974.

Gellner, Ernest. *The Psychoanalytic Movement*. Aylesbury, UK: Paladin, 1985.

Jones, Ernest. *Sigmund Freud: Life and Work*. 3 vols. London: Hogarth, 1953–1957.

MacIntyre, Alisdair. "Psychoanalysis: The Future of an Illusion?" *Encounter*, May 1968.

Macmillan, Malcolm. *Freud Evaluated: The Completed Arc*. Cambridge, MA: MIT Press, 1997.

Roazen, Paul. *Freud and His Followers*. New York: Knopf, 1975.

Sulloway, Frank J. *Freud: Biologist of the Mind*. New York: Basic Books, 1979.

ALLEN ESTERSON

FROMM, ERICH (1900–1980), German humanistic psychologist. Erich Fromm balanced a strong allegiance to his practice, which he termed "radical humanistic psychoanalysis," and his desire to write. A chronicle of his writings shows Fromm to be as much a moral philosopher and social critic as he was psychologist.

Born in Frankfurt, Germany, he grew up in a devout Jewish family. An intensive religious education provided models for his intellectual growth, some of which he would later modify and some reject, moving toward an ethics built on understanding of the human condition (see HUMANISM).

Crossing the Boundaries of Traditional Disciplines. Fromm trained in philosophy, sociology, and psychology, receiving a doctorate in philosophy at the University of Heidelberg at age twenty-two. It was this background that Fromm brought to his studies at the Berlin Psychoanalytic Institute, approaching the practice of psychoanalysis from the standpoint of philosophy rather than medicine. He lent a cultural and social perspective to psychoanalysis by contending that neurosis can result from culturally inspired needs rather than from frustration of biological drives. He held that psychoanalysts, like theologians, should waken the "voice of conscience" so as to appeal to a patient's morality.

Fromm began practicing psychoanalysis as a disciple of Sigmund Freud, but soon took issue with Freud's preoccupation with unconscious drives and his consequent neglect of the role of societal factors in human psychology. His career was under way when Fromm immigrated to the United States in 1934, shortly after the Nazis assumed power in Germany. Inspired by fellow neo-Freudians, among whom he is generally counted, by the writings of Karl MARX, and by the humanistic tradition, he explored new themes. Throughout his years on the faculty of Columbia University (1934–41) he came into conflict with orthodox Freudian psychoanalytic circles.

Increasingly Controversial Views. His name lights a fire of recognition: it was Fromm who spotlighted such concepts as alienation and self-awareness, now part of our vocabulary. His numerous writings on human nature, ethics, and love attracted the interest of social scientists and a wide general readership. In *The Art of Loving*, Fromm recognized that love is the only sane and satisfactory answer to the problems of human existence. He became known as the Apostle of Love. He also wrote books of criticism and analysis, on Freudian and Marxist thought, on psychoanalysis, and on religion—presenting views that were increasingly controversial (and surprising from a psychoanalyst), challenging, as he did, religions that have at their roots an authoritarian ethics, and rekindling the query, "If God is dead, is everything allowed?" He argued for a humanistic ethics as the rightful alternative both to authoritarianism and to moral relativism. He argued for the use of reason and he upheld the claim that ethics is objective, that some values are higher than others.

Fromm was a forerunner in broadening the viewpoint of the social sciences—recognizing their need to involve themselves with issues of immediate concern to society. A profound critic of materialistic values, he argued for a society that fosters productive and meaningful relations with others and responds to what he saw as each person's basic need to avoid loneliness. In the 1950s he warned against the dangers of a society dominated by technology, and in 1957 helped to found the National Committee for a Sane Nuclear Policy (SANE), the name taken from one of his widely read books, *The Sane Society*.

In the territory which he has made his own, "Frommi-

anism," he defined the need for a radical humanism. He called for a rebirth of enlightenment in a transformed society which would allow each person to fulfill his or her individual needs while maintaining a sense of belonging through bonds of social brotherhood. He believed that we could develop a sane, psychologically balanced society. His criticisms of our maladies ran deep, but his hopes ran high.

Relation to the Social and Intellectual Times. Because Fromm crossed so many disciplinary boundaries, including those of religion, sociology, history, and economics, many academics regarded him as a dilettante. Traditional psychoanalysts found his focus on social psychology of little value to their clinical practices. His widespread influence on the human potentials movement, however, is indisputable, as is the growing recognition of Fromm as a vital contributor to social thought in the modern era. He received the accolade of rare honorary Swiss citizenship, having moved to Switzerland four years before his death. Many of his (more than thirty) major works are considered classics. Erich Fromm's vision has not been abandoned.

BIBLIOGRAPHY

Fromm, Erich. *The Art of Loving*. New York: Harper & Row, 1956.
———. *Escape from Freedom*. New York: Avon, 1941.
———. *Man for Himself*. New York: Rinehart, 1947.
———. *Psychoanalysis and Religion*. New Haven, CT: Yale University Press, 1950.
———. *The Sane Society*. New York: Holt, Rinehart & Winston, 1955.

JEANNETTE LOWEN

FROUDE, JAMES ANTHONY (1818–1894), English historian, author, and agnostic (see AGNOSTICISM). James Anthony Froude's writings reflect the religious concerns and struggles of the mid-Victorian era. He was born at Darlington rectory, Devon, where his father, Robert Hurrell Froude, was rector. Formative influences on Froude were his father, a learned, cultivated man and talented artist; his brother, Richard Hurrell Froude, a man of considerable genius and dominant personality who joined with John Henry Newman in the Anglo-Catholic Oxford ("Tractarian") movement; and Newman himself, whose personality and striking sermons (Froude described them as "incisive," "never unreal," "subtle"), early drew the young Froude toward Catholicism.

A precocious and sensitive youth, Froude entered Westminster School in 1830, where he suffered brutal humiliations at the hands of schoolmasters and students. Froude relates this experience through his fictional alias, Edward Fowler, in *Shadows of the Clouds* (1847). Leaving Westminster, Froude was tutored privately before entering Oriel College, Oxford, in 1836, taking rooms immediately above Newman's. He was elected a fellow of Exeter College, Oxford in 1842. During these academic years, Froude was spiritually torn and anguished—divided between his devotion to Newman while increasingly repelled by his Catholic doctrines. The struggle is portrayed in his controversial book, *The Nemesis of Faith* (1849), which he called a "cry of pain." While emotionally moving, the story is sentimental and melodramatic, but something of an epitome of the crisis of the mid-Victorian "honest doubter."

While preparing for deacon's orders in the Church of England, Froude was concurrently reading Ralph Waldo EMERSON, Gotthold Ephraim LESSING, Friedrich Schleiermacher, Thomas Carlyle, and Baruch SPINOZA. The latter two proved especially powerful influences as Froude moved away from the dogmas and historical claims of orthodox Christianity. Another crucial event for Froude was Newman's invitation to write *Life of St. Neot* for Newman's *Lives of the English Saints* series. As Froude examined the sources on Saint Neot, he was struck by the unhistorical fables and the credulity revealed in these accounts. As Froude found, the *Lives* "were not so much strict biography, as myths, edifying stories . . . designed not to relate facts, as to produce a religious impression." Thereafter, Froude vehemently opposed miracle stories and the supernatural as historical categories.

Froude's fame rests primarily on his four-volume biography *Thomas Carlyle* (1882–84) and his numerous historical works, most notably the controversial twelve-volume *History of England from the Fall of Wolsey to the Defeat of the Armada* (1856–70). The latter can be read as a critique of both the Catholic Church and the Oxford movement, and a defense of the Protestant protest against what he saw as superstition and moral equivocation.

Through his life, Froude remained attracted to aspects of Newman's subtle mind and religious sentiments while wholly won over by the prophetic power and rectitude of Carlyle and the saintly virtue and rationalism of Spinoza. The religious skeptics of the next Victorian generation, including Leslie STEPHEN and William Kingdon CLIFFORD, did not suffer the same anguished choice; their agnostic essays breathe a sure, often fierce, confidence in positivist science (see POSITIVISM) and RATIONALISM.

BIBLIOGRAPHY

Chadwick, Owen. *The Secularization of the European Mind*. Cambridge: Cambridge University Press, 1975.

Dunn, Waldo Hilary. *James Anthony Froude: A Biography*. 2 vols. Oxford: Clarendon, 1961–63.

Livingston, James C. *The Ethics of Belief: An Essay on the Victorian Religious Conscience*. Tallahassee, FL: American Academy of Religion/Scholars Press, 1974.

Markus, Julia. *J. Anthony Froude: The Last Undiscovered Great Victorian*. New York: Scribners, 2005.

Paul, Herbert. *James Anthony Froude*. New York: C. Scribner's Sons, 1905.

Popkin, Richard H. *History of Scepticism from Erasmus to Spinoza*. Berkeley and Los Angeles: University of California Press, 1979.

Willey, Basil. *More Nineteenth Century Studies: A Group of Honest Doubters*. New York: Columbia University Press, 1956.

JAMES C. LIVINGSTON

GAGE, MATILDA JOSLYN (1826–1898), American suffragist and freethinker. The youngest member of the National Woman Suffrage Association (NWSA) leadership triumvirate with Elizabeth Cady STANTON and Susan B. Anthony, Matilda Joslyn Gage was born March 24, 1826, in Cicero, New York. The three women, editors of the first three volumes of the *History of Woman Suffrage*, "will ever hold a grateful place in the hearts of posterity," predicted the *Woman's Tribune* in 1888.

Gage dropped out of the suffrage cause after an unsuccessful move to prevent what she perceived as a conservative takeover of the women's movement in 1889. Believing that the attempt on the part of Christian fundamentalists to place God in the Constitution and prayer in the public schools represented the great "danger of the hour," Gage turned to what she believed was her "grandest, most courageous work." In 1890 she formed the Woman's National Liberal Union, an organization with a dual purpose: to challenge the drive by her time's Religious Right to merge church and state, and "to free woman from the bondage of the church," which was the "chief means of enslaving woman's conscience and reason." She published her magnum opus, *Woman Church and State*, in 1893. Anthony COMSTOCK, self-appointed censor of the US press and mail, immediately banned the book from public school libraries. A powerful indictment of the church's primary role in the oppression of women, the book documented the gynocidal witch burnings (9 million women, Gage estimated, murdered by the church and later the state) and the institutionalized sexual abuse of women and children by the priesthood.

The "theory that woman brought sin and death into the world" is the "foundation of the Christian Church," Gage charged at an 1878 FREETHOUGHT convention, and woman was placed in a "condition of subjection, of subordination" to man as punishment. Women's "political, legal, educational, industrial, and social disabilities of whatever character and nature" result from "this "prevailing religious idea," she argued.

Gage theorized that the early church accepted the equal feminine nature of the divine, citing evidence of women serving at the altar and administering the sacrament. Slowly forcing women out of the priesthood and removing the female in the godhead, the church "passed over to idolatry in a worship of the masculine." This transition marked the greatest depth of "the night of moral and spiritual degradation," she continued. "In place of truth, falsehood prevailed; in place of unity, division." Making marriage a sacrament, the church required women to pledge obedience to their husbands in the marriage ceremony. When canon law became the foundation for common law, married woman's subordinate position rendered her legally nonexistent. The idea that the "two shall become one and the one is the man" robbed wives not only of their rights, but even their legal identity.

The great underlying creative principle, Gage believed, is "solely and distinctively feminine." At the 1888 International Council of Women, Gage expressed "profound surprise and astonishment" at the "almost total ignoring of the Divine Motherhood of God by those who have in any way referred to the Supreme Power" during the council. Each session began with an invocation, and Gage had been hard-pressed to find a woman minister who would "evoke the divine motherhood" in the prayer opening Gage's session. "In all ancient nations we find goddesses seated everywhere with gods, in many instances regarded as superior to them," she told the audience. Critical to elevating the position of women was returning the motherhood of God to the place of sacredness from which she had been removed by the patriarchal/Christian overthrow.

Women were not the only victims of Christianity; the church had also been the "bulwark of slavery" and the authority of the Bible had been used to oppose "science, art, inventions, reforms of existing wrongs," resulting in "even the most enlightened nations" becoming stuck in the stage of "barbarism," Gage charged. "I look upon ordinary religious belief as almost death to the soul," she wrote to her son that year, fearing that he was "drifting into Churchianity." Gage embraced moral relativism, explaining that "no absolute standard exists, but morality is relative, depending upon the general condition of society, and what is looked upon as right in one age of the world is regarded as wrong in a preceding or succeeding one."

Gage moved to an interest in THEOSOPHY, joining the American Theosophical Society in 1885. Her investigation of the occult—she attended séances and psychic readings and had astrological charts cast for her family members—was based on the premise that paranormal events constituted simply another aspect of the natural world, which had been relegated to the world of female/evil in the patriarchal/Christian political takeover.

Contributing to *The Woman's Bible*, which Stanton edited, Gage moved to a new level of analysis, interpreting the Bible as "an occult work written in symbolic language." While recognizing that it could be read as history or mythology, Gage suggested the Bible might also be "[a] Book of the Adepts . . . a record of ancient mysteries hidden to all but initiates." The book of Revelation, she suggested, understood from this perspective, "is a purely esoteric work, largely referring to woman, her intuition, her spiritual powers, and all she represents."

A year before her death, Gage explained her theosophical belief in reincarnation to her ten-year-old grandson: "You are more alive than ever you were after what is called death. Death is only a journey, like going to another country . . . people . . . come back and live in another body, in another family and have another name."

Gage remained hopeful about the future of women in her religious tradition who were rising up "against the tyranny of Church and State," in the most important revolution the world had yet seen. It "will shake the foundations of religious belief, tear into fragments and scatter to the winds the old dogmas upon which all forms of Christianity are based," she predicted. The result "will be a regenerated world."

Gage died on March 18, 1898, and her cremated remains are buried in the Fayetteville, New York, cemetery under a tombstone emblazoned with her motto: "There is a word sweeter than mother, home or heaven. That word is Liberty."

BIBLIOGRAPHY

Brammer, Leila R. *Excluded from Suffrage History: Matilda Joslyn Gage.* Westport, CT: Greenwood, 2000.

Gage, Matilda Joslyn. "The Church, Science, and Woman." *Index*, April 29, 1886.

———. "The Foundation of Sovereignty." *Woman's Tribune* (April 1887).

———. *Woman, Church, and State.* Amherst, NY: Humanity Books, 2002.

———. "Woman in the Early Christian Church." In *Report of the International Council of Women.* Washington, DC: National Woman Suffrage Association, 1888.

Stanton, Elizabeth Cady, Susan B. Anthony, and Matilda Joslyn Gage, eds. *History of Woman Suffrage.* Vols. 1–3. 1881–1887. Reprint, Salem, NH: Ayer, 1985.

Wagner, Sally Roesch. *Matilda Joslyn Gage: She Who Holds the Sky.* Aberdeen, SD: Carrier Press, 2002.

SALLY ROESCH WAGNER

GALILEI, GALILEO (1564–1642), Italian physicist and astronomer. A founder of modern science—which is to say, of modern methods of investigating natural phenomena—Galileo Galilei strongly asserted the need for REASON and experimental verification as opposed to the acceptance of truths based on dogma and the authority of the scriptures or handed down from ancient philosophers and through tradition. This stance earned him the fierce opposition of the Catholic Church, which fought his ideas to the point of convicting him of HERESY. He is one of the most important figures in the history of modern thought, the first to promote mathematical RATIONALISM versus the millennia-old logico-verbal approach embraced by the followers of ARISTOTLE. Despite his formal displays of respect toward the church, he became a worldwide symbol of independence of thought and of the necessity for human beings to ground their beliefs in observed facts and in rational analysis of problems.

Early Life. Galileo was born in Pisa, Tuscany, on February 15, 1564, the son of musicologist Vincenzio Galilei and Giulia Ammannati. When he was ten, his family moved to Florence. At the age of seventeen his father sent him to the University of Pisa to study medicine, but he showed no interest in the discipline, devoting himself instead to mathematics and physical sciences under the tutelage of Ostilio Ricci. It is during this period that he established the isochronism of pendular oscillation—the fact that the period of a pendulum's swing is independent of the arc of its swing—giving rise to the legend that he had deduced it through careful observation of swinging lamps in Pisa cathedral. More plausibly, fine lute player that he was, he extended to pendulums a property observed in vibrating strings. The invention of the hydrostatic microbalance and a treatise on the center of gravity in solids led to him becoming known all over Italy. In 1589 Grand Duke Ferdinando I of Tuscany appointed him mathematics lecturer at the University of Pisa, where he began to study the motion and the fall of bodies (another legend is that to this end he dropped weights from the Leaning Tower of Pisa, that experiment being actually performed only years later by his pupil Renieri).

Teaching in Padua. In 1592 he moved to the University of Padua, where he was awarded the chair of mathematics, a more lucrative position in the lively cultural milieu of the Republic of Venice. While there he witnessed the tragic fate of philosopher Giordano BRUNO, denounced to the Inquisition for heresy and eventually burned at the stake in Rome for having claimed that the universe is infinite, an affair that left an indelible mark on Galileo and led to his cautious prudence toward the church. He remained in Padua for eighteen years, establishing the law of uniformly accelerated motion by means of an experiment using an inclined plane, which, by slowing down the fall of a sphere, allowed him to measure the time intervals involved. He also defined the principles of inertia and of relativity, disproving the Aristotelian misconception that the motion of a body is possible only under the action of a force (thrown bodies were supposed to carry along the force initially "impressed" on them).

Though Galileo became increasingly convinced of the validity of the Copernican heliocentric theory (as his private letters demonstrate), his charge in Padua was to teach the Ptolemaic system. Only after he learned in 1604 of the sudden appearance of a new star (actually a supernova) did he begin to speak publicly against the Aristotelian view of immutable skies and an immobile earth at the center of the universe.

Exploring the Skies. In 1609 Galileo learned about telescopes being made in Holland. Making basic improvements, he built a telescope with a linear magnification of about 30, a truly scientific instrument fit for exploring the skies. This enabled him to see the rugged and mountainous nature of the moon's surface, not the smooth reflecting sphere claimed by Aristotelians; to discover Jupiter's satellites (which he called *Sidera Medicea*, in honor of his former pupil and future employer Cosimo II de' Medici, Grand Duke of Tuscany); to describe the nature of the Milky Way as a cluster of separate stars; to perceive the unusual shape of planet Saturn; to observe the phases of Venus, similar to those of the moon; and to investigate the spots on the sun's surface. These astronomical discoveries led to the publication of his book *Sidereus Nuncius* (The Sidereal Messenger) written in Latin, as was customary at the time in the sciences. Despite widespread skepticism of the book's audacious claims, it publication made him famous throughout Europe, receiving the approval of Kepler and even of the Jesuit scholars in the Roman College.

During his years in Padua he lived with Marina Gamba, who bore him three illegitimate children, Virginia, Livia, and Vincenzio. The two daughters were later to become nuns, as was often the case when the father could not provide an adequate dowry for marriage.

Move to Florence. In 1610 he was appointed "Principal Mathematician and Philosopher" to the Grand Duke in Florence, with no teaching obligations and much more time for research. Between 1610 and 1616 he had an acrimonious dispute with Jesuit Christoph Scheiner over who had claimed priority in the discovery of sunspots. Aware that his Copernicanism was meeting with opposition from the church, he wrote the so-called Copernican letters, in which he tried to persuade ecclesiastics that the new scientific ideas were not at odds with the Bible if the Bible was interpreted correctly, and that it was in the interests of the church not to take a stand that in the face of evidence it would sooner or later have to recant. The letters represented, at the same time, a firm defense of the independence of science from faith. This resulted in a violent attack on Galileo by two Dominican friars, who accused him of heresy and unleashed what became a mounting tide of clerical opposition.

Conflict with the Church. In 1616 Galileo was warned by the authoritative theologian Robert Cardinal Bellarmine that while the Copernican model could be used as a mathematical tool in describing astronomical phenomena, it could not be considered true. This kept Galileo silent on the subject until 1623, when Cardinal Maffeo Barberini—an open-minded man of culture and an admirer of Galileo—became Pope Urban VIII. Full of hope, Galileo published *Il Saggiatore* (The Assayer), a brilliant lecture on the new scientific method and a pungent criticism of mediocre science (in particular meant to strike at Jesuit Father Orazio Grassi). It contains the famous pronouncement that "the Book of Nature is written in mathematical characters." For *Il Saggiatore* Galileo adopted the Italian language, as he would for all his subsequent works, with the intention of reaching a wider audience than just the savants. Galileo's writing style ranks him at the highest levels in Italian literature.

Reassured by the success of *Il Saggiatore*, in 1632 Galileo published his celebrated *Dialogo sopra i due massimi sistemi del mondo* (Dialogue concerning the Two Chief World Systems), presented as an objective comparison of the Ptolemaic and Copernican systems, but in reality an open defense of the latter and a devastating argument against traditional Aristotelian views. The book deals with a wide range of subjects—motion, inertia, relativity, the universal behavior of falling bodies in a vacuum, and the movements of the earth—all brilliantly debated by three interlocutors, Salviati (Galileo's alter ego), Sagredo (a referee), and Simplicio (Aristotle's advocate). The main argument in support of the earth's rotation was based on the occurrence of tides (a mistake prompted by Galileo's eagerness to find experimental evidence for his claim). In order to obtain the imprimatur or mark of approval by the church, Galileo was obliged to close the book with this statement of Urban VIII: "God in His infinite power and wisdom could have conferred upon the watery element its observed reciprocating motion using some other means . . . and He would have known how to do this in many ways which are unthinkable to our minds." However he committed the impudence of putting the statement in the mouth of simple-minded Simplicio, thereby incurring the pope's resentment. At the time, Urban VIII was in difficulty, as Spanish cardinals were accusing him of being solicitous toward heretics. He had Galileo urgently summoned to Rome to be questioned by the Inquisition; eventually the old scientist was to undergo formal prosecution.

Conviction and Abjuration. During the trial Galileo was shown the torture chamber, if not actually tortured. He was found guilty of heresy for having claimed in contradiction of scripture that the sun is immobile and the earth rotates around it. He signed a written abjuration, prepared by the judges, that helped him escape more drastic punishment: "[W]ith sincere heart and unfeigned faith I abjure, curse, and detest the aforesaid errors and heresies and generally every other error, heresy, and sect whatsoever contrary to the Holy Church, and I swear that in future I will never again say or assert, verbally or in writing, anything that might furnish occasion for a similar suspicion regarding me; but, should I know any heretic or person suspected of heresy, I will denounce him to this Holy Office." He was sentenced to prison and to recite penitential psalms for three years. His *Dialogue* was banned and remained in the church's Index of forbidden works until 1835.

Galileo is said to have whispered, immediately after his abjuration, "and yet it [the earth] moves." Although this is quite unlikely, it is a fact that, only a few days later, he set out upon the reaffirmation of his Copernican credo, beginning to write his scientific masterpiece, *Discorsi intorno a due nuove scienze* (Dialogues concerning Two New Sciences). In this book—published in 1638 by the Elseviers in Holland—he dealt in particular with the resistance of materials and "local motion" (kinematics). Many topics had already been discussed in earlier books, but in *Discorsi* they are treated more rigorously and with extensive use of mathematics, including early approaches to infinity and infinitesimals.

This work was possible because his imprisonment, by concession of the pope, had soon been commuted to confinement in his villa in Arcetri, near Florence. Here he was to live in great isolation, receiving assistance in his later years from his pupils Viviani and Torricelli, and occasional visits from friends, admirers (including the English poet John Milton), and protectors such as the grand duke of Tuscany. His health, which had never been particularly good, gradually worsened, and he eventually became totally blind. He died on January 9, 1642.

Galileo and Modern Science. Galileo's legacy consists of three main points: the value of experiment for the advancement of knowledge, the importance of the mathematical treatment of phenomena, and the introduction of the concept of a reference system. Some of his methods have become standard practice in modern science, for instance, his approach to problems by concentrating first on the basic mechanism underlying a phenomenon, and only later introducing secondary effects as perturbations; his way of studying an ideal process by a gradual variation of feasible situations (for example, predicting the free fall of bodies in a vacuum through the analysis of their fall in increasingly diluted gases); his attention to technology and to its interplay with fundamental science; his recognition of the greater value of "doing" than of "speaking"; and his effort to make scientific approaches known to a wider public, even outside science.

Galileo's Intellectual Revolution. Galileo's greatness lies not only in his discoveries, in his cultural battles, and in his scientific methodology, but also in the problems he raised and left to his successors. He symbolizes the need for science not to be enslaved by power or commitments to dogma.

"Rehabilitation." The Catholic Church recently promoted Galileo's rehabilitation. However, seeing that abjuration is a violent imposition, it is cause for shame and guilt on those who impose it: it is therefore the church that should have been rehabilitated. This should have consisted not so much in a condemnation of the judges of Galileo's time, as in a denunciation of the church itself, which continues to commit the same mistakes that led to the prosecution of the scientist and, in particular, persists in its determination to impose its truth upon others.

BIBLIOGRAPHY

Drake, Stillman. *Galileo at Work*. Chicago: University of Chicago Press, 1978.

———. *Galileo: Pioneer Scientist*. Toronto: University of Toronto Press, 1990.

Fantoli, Annibale. *Galileo*. Translated by George V. Coyne. Notre Dame, IN: University of Notre Dame Press, 2003.

Frova, Andrea, and Mariapiera Marenzana. *Thus Spoke Galileo*. Translated by Jim Mc Manus and the authors. Oxford: Oxford University Press, 2006.

Galilei, Galileo. *The Assayer*. Translated by Stillman Drake and C. D. O'Malley. In *Controversy on the Comets of 1618*. Philadelphia: University of Pennsylvania Press, 1960.

———. *Dialogue concerning the Two Chief World Systems*. Translated by Stillman Drake. Berkeley and Los Angeles: University of California Press, 1970.

———. *Dialogues concerning Two New Sciences*. Translated by Henry Crew and Alfonso de Salvio. New York: Dover, 1954.

———. *Sidereus Nuncius or The Sidereal Messenger*. Translated by Albert Van Helden. Chicago: University of Chicago Press, 1989.

Geymonat, Ludovico. *Galileo Galilei*. Translated by Stillman Drake. New York: McGraw-Hill, 1965.

Santillana de, Giorgio. *The Crime of Galileo*. Chicago: University of Chicago Press, 1955.

Sharratt, Michael. *Galileo Decisive Innovator*. Cambridge: Cambridge University Press, 1996.

ANDREA FROVA AND
MARIAPIERA MARENZANA

GARDENER, HELEN HAMILTON (1853–1925), American freethought activist. Helen Hamilton Gardener was born Alice Chenoweth on January 21, 1853, near Winchester, Virginia. Her father was a circuit-riding preacher who aided the Union during the Civil War and died soon after. Her mother was a lifelong Calvinist. Alice graduated in 1873 from the Cincinnati Normal School, taught school until marrying at age twenty-two, then studied biology at Columbia University in the early 1880s. She adopted the name Helen Hamilton Gardener in her thirties. While lecturing and writing for newspapers using a male pseudonym, she met the nineteenth century's most prominent proponent of FREETHOUGHT, Robert Green INGERSOLL, and his wife, Eva. They encouraged Gardener to undertake her much-admired 1884 lecture series, "Men, Women, and Gods." She was dubbed "Ingersoll done in soprano" by the *New York Sun* and "the pretty infidel" by the *Chicago Times*. THE TRUTH SEEKER published her elegant lectures in print form the following year. A friend of Elizabeth Cady STANTON, Gardener was a member of the committee contributing to Stanton's *Woman's Bible*. As an agnostic

in sympathy with Stanton's views, she was designated by Stanton to deliver her memorial address. Gardener quipped in that memorial statement that while most suffragists found *The Woman's Bible* too radical, she found it not radical enough.

Gardener incorporated her suffragist, freethinking views into several novels and wrote for an array of periodicals, from *Popular Science Monthly* to the *Arena* of Boston. After her first husband, Charles Selden Shaart, died, Gardener later married Col. Selden Allen Day. She was pressed into activism as a suffrage leader, at one time acting as chief liaison with President Woodrow Wilson's administration. Although Gardener believed in no miracles, she was credited by coworkers with making them on behalf of woman suffrage.

At age sixty-seven Gardener became the first woman appointed to the United States Civil Service Commission, serving five years with distinction. She died of heart disease at Walter Reed Army General Hospital in 1925. The *New York Times* not only covered her death as major news, but breathlessly reported on her will being carried out. Gardener had bequeathed her brain to Cornell University to set to rest the common bigotry of her day that women's brains were inferior.

In her eloquent, still timely *Men, Women, and Gods*, Gardener noted: "This religion and the Bible require of woman everything, and give her nothing. They ask her support and her love, and repay her with contempt and oppression. I do not know the needs of a god or of another world. . . . I do know that women make shirts for seventy cents a dozen in this one."

BIBLIOGRAPHY

Gardener, Helen. *Men, Women, and Gods: And Other Lectures*. New York: Belford, Clarke, 1885.

James, Edward D., ed. *Notable American Women: 1607–1950: A Biographical Dictionary*. Vol. 2. Cambridge, MA: Belknap Press, 1971.

Willard, Frances E., and Mary A. Livermore, eds. *A Woman of the Century*. Buffalo, NY: Charles Wells Moulton, 1893.

ANNIE LAURIE GAYLOR

GAUVIN, MARSHALL JEROME (1881–1978), Canadian rationalist lecturer and writer. Marshall Gauvin was born in Dover, New Brunswick, on May 3, 1881, the eighth of ten (some say eleven) children. He was baptized Marcel, but took on the anglicized Marshall as a young man, and added the middle name later on. His mother, Madeleine Dorion, was a devout Roman Catholic, but his father, Israel Gauvin, had converted to the Baptist faith. Gauvin's youth was spent in a climate of bitter religious acrimony.

During a visit to Boston in 1899, Gauvin became exposed to the FREETHOUGHT lectures of the Rev. J. F.

Bland, a former Unitarian minister and disciple of Robert Green INGERSOLL, whose name he had heard denounced from the pulpit. Influenced by Bland, Gauvin developed a lifelong admiration of Ingersoll and his works. For the next twelve years, he worked as a carpenter for the Intercolonial Railway in Moncton, New Brunswick. His leisure time was spent devouring the works of Thomas PAINE, Thomas Henry HUXLEY, Charles DARWIN, Herbert SPENCER, and others. He also became intimately familiar with the Bible. He would hold single pages of scripture in one hand while continuing to work with the other. In 1909 he wrote his first articles for the American freethought paper THE TRUTH SEEKER, a relationship which lasted seven decades.

In 1912 Gauvin left the railway and began his career as a full-time rationalist lecturer (see RATIONALISM). His opponents dubbed him "the Canadian antichrist." He lectured in Toronto and Indianapolis before moving to Pittsburgh in 1914 to lecture for the newly formed Pittsburgh Rationalist Society. Between 1918 and 1920 he toured North America lecturing on behalf of *The Truth Seeker* before taking up a position in Minneapolis for the Twin City Rationalist Society. In 1921 he married Martha L. Becker, herself the product of a German freethinking family. They had one daughter.

In 1926 Gauvin moved to Winnipeg, Manitoba, where he lived for the rest of his life. For fourteen years he was the full-time lecturer for the Winnipeg Rationalist Society, which in 1934 he renamed the Winnipeg Humanist Society. Gauvin finally retired from active lecturing in 1940, noting that the day of the lecturer was over as radio and the cinema were becoming more popular ways to spend leisure time. Between 1921 and 1940 Gauvin gave more than eight hundred lectures.

After spending the war working as a carpenter once again, Gauvin's freethought career seemed once again to come back to life, when he was elected president of the newly formed National Liberal League in 1946. This organization was apparently named in tribute to the nineteenth- and early twentieth-century NATIONAL LIBERAL LEAGUE, which had numbered Ingersoll and other luminaries among its presidents. For much of the next eight years, Gauvin lived in New York trying to build the league. His efforts, though considerable, came to nothing, falling victim to infighting and dissension. In 1954 he returned to Winnipeg. From then until shortly before his death he continued to write for *The Truth Seeker*, although he was increasingly alarmed by the racism and anti-Semitism that was characteristic of the paper at that time. Marshall Gauvin died on September 23, 1978, aged ninety-seven.

BIBLIOGRAPHY

Gauvin, Marshall. *The Fundamentals of Freethought.* New York: Peter Eckler, 1922.
———. *Where Is Hell?* New York: Peter Eckler, 1926.
Macdonald, George E. *Fifty Years of Freethought.* New York: Truth Seeker, 1929.

BILL COOKE

GAY HUMANISM. During the past two to three decades, various gay humanist and atheist groups have been set up in the UK, the United States, the Netherlands, Norway, and Sweden.

The Gay Atheist League of America (later renamed Gay and Lesbian Atheists, retaining the acronym GALA) was established in San Francisco in 1979. It had a national membership with chapters in several other US cities, and published *GALA Review* bimonthly. Also, at about this time, a gay group was set up under the auspices of the Humanistisch Verbond in the Netherlands (see NETHERLANDS, THE, HUMANISM IN). It published a regular newsletter and arranged some very successful weekend gatherings which were open to all Dutch gays. Later, another group, Gay and Lesbian Atheists and Humanists (GALAH), was established in the United States. This was based in Washington, DC. GALAH held meetings in Washington, San Francisco, and Los Angeles; it published a newsletter, set up a Web site, and engaged in campaigning. Sadly, both of these US groups and the Dutch group eventually folded. The Pink Group was set up in 1992 under the auspices of Human-Etisk Forbund in Norway to provide a forum for gay humanists (see NORWAY, UNBELIEF IN). Nordic Rainbow Humanists was set up in 2000 in Sweden (see SWEDEN, UNBELIEF IN) and has since arranged a number of seminars on humanism and gay rights at international conferences and cultural festivals in Sweden, Finland, Estonia, Latvia, Lithuania, Poland, Croatia, Russia, Macedonia, and elsewhere.

Still very much alive and kicking after twenty-seven years of hectic campaigning and other activities is the UK-based Gay and Lesbian Humanist Association (GALHA). GALHA is a democratically governed and autonomous national/international membership group. It enjoys close, friendly links with kindred UK humanist organizations and is affiliated to Amnesty International and the INTERNATIONAL HUMANIST AND ETHICAL UNION. In terms of longevity, it is an infant compared with the NATIONAL SECULAR SOCIETY and the SOUTH PLACE ETHICAL SOCIETY, both well over a century old, and the BRITISH HUMANIST ASSOCIATION, founded in the 1960s. However, by the standard of lesbian and gay groups, to have thrived for twenty-seven years is no mean achievement—all the more remarkable since, with no external funding, GALHA's administration is carried out and its activities organized on an entirely voluntary basis. It has been sustained financially by its loyal members and supporters.

GALHA was launched in 1979, two years after Mary Whitehouse, a self-appointed guardian of the nation's morals, brought a successful private prosecution for blasphemous libel against *Gay News*—then the UK's only gay newspaper (see BLASPHEMY). Whitehouse, a committed Christian, became the target of vociferous protest—not least from the National Secular Society, which had been campaigning for years for repeal of the blasphemy laws. She began declaring in public that "everything good and true" that "every decent person believes in" was being undermined by "the humanist gay lobby." This was enough to set a few gays in the humanist movement thinking: Although any such lobby was just a figment of Whitehouse's imagination, perhaps it would be a good idea to set one up.

An ad hoc committee of six met to discuss the possibility. They included Jim Herrick, now a very well-known figure in the international humanist movement and former editor of *New Humanist* magazine, and Barry Duke, the current editor of the *FREETHINKER*. A threefold agenda was settled on: to make gay people aware of the gay-friendly humanist ethical outlook; to further an awareness among heterosexual humanists of the widespread prejudice and discrimination suffered by gays while encouraging their support; and to play a part in the ongoing campaign for gay and humanist rights.

At the 1978 conference of the Campaign for Homosexual Equality (CHE, then the leading UK gay rights organization), the ad hoc committee set up a humanist information stall and held a meeting to assess possible interest in a gay humanist group. Having decided to go ahead, the committee had leaflets printed and a large number were distributed in London's Hyde Park at the start of the Gay Pride march in June 1979. This was exceptionally well attended (for that time) by eight thousand people. The march outreach generated sufficient publicity and interest that a formal launch meeting was held in August 1979 during CHE's conference in Brighton. The conference attracted about six hundred participants.

At the inaugural meeting, the decision was taken to form the Gay Humanist Group (GHG). The keynote speaker at this meeting was Bill McIlroy, a former general secretary of the National Secular Society, who had already served one term as editor of the *Freethinker*. He sounded a warning that the gay movement's small gains made within the previous ten years "could quite easily be wiped out as a result of the growing influence of evangelical Christians in the corridors of power." No doubt he had in mind the Nationwide Festival of Light—later to become Christian Action, Research and Education (CARE), which, together with the Christian Institute, is very active today lobbying against lesbian and gay rights.

Those attending the CHE conference had not long to wait before the sort of hostility Bill McIlroy referred to became evident. A half-page advertisement appeared in the *Brighton Evening Argus* sponsored by twenty-two local Christian clergymen, who stated their strong opposition to the town's hosting the conference. The founding members of GHG were in the vanguard of protest

against this hostility, taking part in a demonstration outside the church of one of the clergy responsible. This would be the first of many such "direct actions" taken by the group over the following years. Nowadays, such direct action is associated almost exclusively with the UK group OutRage! and such US organizations as Queer Nation; many younger lesbians and gay men in the UK remain unaware of the courageous demonstrations that took place (and in which GHG participated) years before OutRage! was founded.

In addition to the 1979 protest in Brighton, GHG demonstrated on the occasion of Pope John Paul II's visit to Britain in 1982, when it launched POPE (People Opposing Papal Edicts); the group organized or participated in protests throughout the 1980s in locales including Rugby; Nottingham; Wombourne, Staffordshire; and Manchester. GHG displayed a clear early commitment to direct action, and it can confidently claim to have played a part in helping to further the cause of lesbian and gay equality.

In 1987 the GHG was renamed the Gay and Lesbian Humanist Association (GALHA). About this time campaigns to organize letter writing on issues of gay and humanist concern, already in place during the GHG era, were more stringently organized. A postal action plan was launched involving a substantial number of GALHA members. This facilitated substantial lobbying of MPs, government ministers, commercial firms, and the media on dozens of issues relating to gay and humanist rights. Many submissions have been made to government bodies on such issues.

In 1987 a humanist "affirmation" ceremony of love and commitment was devised for same-sex couples as *the* alternative to the gay Christian "blessing" (a non-legally binding attachment ceremony performed for gay couples by a progressive-minded priest, often one who is gay himself). With the help of celebrants affiliated with the British Humanist Association and the Scottish Humanist Society, affirmations have been held in all parts of the country from Aberdeen in the north to the Channel Islands in the south. Part of the ceremony was depicted by a television program aimed at teenagers, which featured the first gay kiss on British television, provoking outrage from Whitehouse and other Christian morality campaigners. In 1992, with the voluntary assistance of gay lawyer Peter Ashman, GALHA set up a registered charity, the Pink Triangle Trust, which later took over the arrangement of the ceremonies.

GALHA has held regular public meetings in London since its founding. Thanks to the friendly welcome given by the South Place Ethical Society, which owns the Conway Hall Humanist Centre in central London, these meetings have invariably been held in the hall's library. They have been addressed by a wide range of speakers from the gay and humanist movements. Some very popular forum meetings have also been arranged, including several political forums preceding general elections.

From time to time over the past twenty-seven years, GALHA has provided speakers about its activities and the humanist outlook to other gay and lesbian groups, including university LGB societies, and on lesbian and gay rights to humanist groups in various parts of the country. It has also provided information on humanism and its stance on gay rights to many pupils and students doing projects.

The organization's publishing activity began with a six-page newsletter issued in November 1979 by the GHG. The publication continued as a newsletter until 1983, when it was upgraded to a small magazine featuring news, features, and reviews. Beginning in 1990, it became a full-size professionally printed magazine which is now entitled *Gay Humanist Quarterly*. It is issued free to GALHA members and has subscribers in the UK, other European countries, and the United States. In late 1993 GALHA turned over the publication to the Pink Triangle Trust. Titled *Gay & Lesbian Humanist* but now publishd again by GALHA with the title *Gay Humanist Quarterly*, it is issued free to GALHA members and has subscribers in the UK, the United States, and other countries.

As for the future, as the UK Labour government grants more and more privileges to religionists— granting them exemption from employing gays in its employment regulations, funding an increasing number of faith schools, failing to introduce gay marriage for fear of religious opposition, and kowtowing to homophobic Muslims—it seems that GALHA will still be providing a useful role as a campaigning group for LGBT and humanist rights for some years to come.

GEORGE BROADHEAD

GERMAN LITERATURE, UNBELIEF IN MODERN (1700–1900).

The term *unbelief* implies primarily the rejection of any supernatural being, and "modern German literature" refers to all writers and thinkers who wrote most of their major works in German between 1700 and 1900. Therefore writers like Thomas Mann, Robert Musil, Franz Kafka, Gottfried Benn, and Bertold BRECHT, who were born before 1900 but completed their major works after 1900, will not be dealt with.

Winckelmann. One of the central reasons for German writers and thinkers to doubt the existence of a supernatural world is the fact that ancient Greek culture was regarded as a cultural ideal in Germany. One person in particular helped to shape the German understanding of ancient Greek culture: Johann Joachim Winckelmann, who held: "The only way for us to become great or even inimitable if possible, is to imitate the Greeks." His two most important works were the *Geschichte der Kunst des Altertums* (History of Ancient Art, 1764), in which he gave a detailed description of specific works of ancient Greek art; and the *Gedanken über die Nachahmung der griechischen Werke in der Malerei und Bildhauerkunst* (Reflections on the Imitation of Greek Works in Painting and Sculpture, 1755), by means of which he provided the nineteenth century with a philosophical understanding of ancient Greek culture. According to Winckelmann, ancient Greek culture, in particular the sculptures, is based on "noble simplicity and quiet grandeur." The Greeks were supposed to have had an inborn sense and longing for beautiful Olympian forms.

Lichtenberg. The first significant modern German writer and thinker in whom one can directly find aspects of antireligious reflections is Georg Christoph LICHTENBERG. His most noteworthy writings are his *Sudelbuecher* (The Waste Books, 1765–99), which is a collection of his notes and aphorisms published directly after his death. Most of his theological remarks were directed against both the teachings of the church and the institution itself, for he thought that the expansion of reason was hindered by the church. However, one can also find ideas in his writings in which the existence of a supernatural being is doubted. He remarked that the phrase "God created human beings according to *his* image" most probably means that human beings created God according to their own image, and that he thought the world will one day be so refined that it will be as ridiculous to believe in God as it is to believe in ghosts. Although the cited phrases could imply that God is nothing but a human invention, other remarks in his work imply that Lichtenberg was never able to transcend his belief in the existence of God.

Goethe. Only seven years younger than Lichtenberg was the most influential German writer and one of the founders of German culture: Johann Wolfgang GOETHE. By some, he is seen as a modern Christian, by others as a pantheist or panentheist, and still others praise him as a defender of paganism. During the nineteenth century he was seen principally as a despiser of religion. Goethe was brought up in the Lutheran tradition, but as a student he severed his bonds with the church. Particularly dominant aspects of his work are his sympathy toward pagan antiquity and his focus on what it means for human beings to live a good life in this world. These topics play a particularly significant role within his *Iphigenie* (1786) and *Wilhelm Meisters Lehr- und Wanderjahre* (Wilhelm Meister's Apprenticeship and Travels, 1777–1829). Goethe declared himself a disciple of Baruch SPINOZA, who stressed the unity of the world and the divine aspect within the whole of nature. It must be noted that he rejected both materialism and the idea of a solely transcendent spiritual God. He also rejected an ethics that denies the polarity within human nature. Evil, according to him, is the privation of goodness, and in one of his letters he stresses that, like nature, he wishes to be good and evil. If nature is good and evil, then the universe and human beings are also bound to be both. Toward the end of his life, he seemed to develop a higher estimation of Christianity again, but even then he does not seem to abandon his belief that all it amounts to is a divine nature which is completely this-worldly.

Weimar and Jena. During Goethe's time was the golden age of German thinking and writing, with all the authors of Weimar classics like Johann Paul Friedrich Richter (known as JEAN PAUL), Johann Christian Friedrich Hölderlin, and Johann Christoph Friedrich von Schiller; the romantic writers like Georg Philipp Friedrich Freiherr von Hardenberg (known as Novalis); and idealist philosophers like Immanuel KANT, Friedrich Wilhelm Joseph von Schelling, Johann Gottlieb FICHTE, and Georg Wilhelm Friedrich HEGEL. Besides Kant, all of them were based in the region of Jena and Weimar at least during some period of their lives. Most of them can still be regarded as Christians. It is only the philosopher Johann Gottlieb Fichte and the writers Jean Paul and Johann Christian Friedrich Hölderlin who have to be mentioned in this survey. Fichte was accused of ATHEISM, and as a consequence was dismissed by the court of Weimar (see CONTROVERSIES: SPINOZISM, ATHEISM, PANTHEISM). Within his *Ueber den Grund unseres Glaubens an eine goettliche Weltregierung* (On the Grounding of our Belief in a Divine World Order, 1798), he referred to God as nothing but the active and living moral order of the world, without God being a specific thing or substance. Later in his life he altered this position and identified God with the infinite, absolute world ego. Another aspect of his philosophy can be seen as crucial, for he regarded philosophy as the result of one's own personality. According to him, which philosophy one chooses depends on one's personality. The idealist philosophers represent the intellectual background for both the Weimar classicists and the later romantics. Jean Paul's relationship toward Christianity cannot be described unambiguously, either. That there are significant skeptical elements in his belief system becomes apparent in one chapter of his novel *Siebenkaes* (1796–97), which bears the title "The Dead Christ Proclaims from the Top of the World Edifice That There Is No God." Here he deals with the problem of NIHILISM as a consequence of free subjectivity. Like Jean Paul, Hölderlin can be seen as belonging neither to the classicist nor the romantic tradition, although one can find elements of both traditions in his writing. Hölderlin's works mainly deal with the gods and myths of the ancient Greek religion, as he saw the Greek gods as true and living forces in this world. He had studied theology, but he could not see himself becoming a Lutheran pastor, for he was deeply embedded in this world. This becomes particularly clear in his ode *Die Heimat* (The Home, 1800), in which he writes the following lines: "For they who lend us the heavenly fire, the Gods, give us sacred sorrow too. Let it be so. A son of earth I seem; born to love and to suffer." He died after having spent the last thirty-six years of his life insane.

Kleist. Heinrich von Kleist died at the age of only thirty-four. His inner conflicts led him to commit suicide by shooting himself. In his farewell letter, he referred to his own life as the most painful a human being has ever had to endure. His life and work represent the ambiguity of the modern self and the awareness of a fragmented world. Originally, Kleist had a rationally worked-out plan for his life, which he tried to follow in an exaggerated manner. After reading Kant, he came to the conclusion that in this world it is impossible to grasp the truth as corresponding with the world, which brought about a significant crisis in spring 1801. It is this crisis that turned Kleist into a poet. As mysterious as Kleist's life were his works, in which disturbing figures like Penthesilea and Michael Kolhass turn up who are puzzled by God. Extreme personalities, raw passions ungovernable by reason, and a complex description of psychological states are significant elements of his writings.

Schopenhauer. The fundamental drives are of central relevance not only in the life of Kleist, but also in the philosophy of Arthur SCHOPENHAUER. The whole world is nothing but a blind and permanently striving will, and human beings are appearances of this will with individuated personal wills. As the wills strive all the time, each will always has to overcome other things. Overcoming is painful. Therefore, striving always implies the experience of pain. The prevailing presence of pain is one reason for Schopenhauer to reject the Judeo-Christian God, as he thought human beings experience so much pain on earth that this situation would have to be unbearable for a God who had created the world. In addition, he put forward more reasons why he regarded Christianity to be misleading. Christians hold that human beings have an immortal soul, but animals do not, and therefore are things, which is the reason why human beings are separated from the animal kingdom. According to Schopenhauer, human beings fundamentally belong to the animal kingdom. Religions in general come about due to ignorance, and Schopenhauer advocated not giving lessons in religion to children before the age of fifteen.

Heine. In contrast to Schopenhauer, who put forward an ascetic lifestyle, Heinrich HEINE did the opposite. He has to be seen as a herald of the emancipation of the flesh who identified revolution with a bacchanal, as he was significantly influenced by Saint-Simon. Consequently, it is unsurprising that he had a rather negative attitude toward Christianity. However, it cannot be said about him that he was indifferent to religion. He himself claimed that God was the beginning and end of all his thoughts. Even though he appeared to be sentimental, satirical, and frivolous, a nondogmatic religiosity was a significant part of his character. His origins were Jewish, but in 1825 he converted to Protestantism.

Feuerbach. Seven years younger than Heine was the philosopher Ludwig Andreas FEUERBACH. Feuerbach tried to reduce the content of religious faith to its psychological roots, so that all theology turns into anthropology. However, he did not regard religion to be a worthless illusion, rather holding that religion is the dream of the human spirit and the human consciousness of an infinite being. The divine being represents the nature of a human being, objectified as a separate being but without his limits as an individual person, and in particular without all their weaknesses and their repulsive elements. The qualities of God are constituted out of the wishes, emotions, and desires of human beings, and so are all the basic dogmas of Christianity. Faith contains what is holy for human beings. Though Feuerbach analyzed all aspects of religion as being reducible to anthropological elements, he recognized valuable elements within religion, such as the love of humanity and love toward the pure nature of human beings. Love is seen as the essential element for human salvation, as love enables the finite world to be dissolved in the infinite, and truth is essentially connected to love, too. It has to be stressed that Feuerbach did not want to get rid of religion, he merely separated it from the relationship with God. Religion does have the potential to heal the inner conflict of human beings. However, God should be replaced by the human race and the afterworld by the future of humanity.

Stirner. The philosopher Max STIRNER, pseudonym for Johann Kaspar Schmidt, regarded Feuerbach as his major opponent and criticized him for being too religious. Stirner was one of the most radical defenders of individualism, and according to him even Feuerbach's humanity is something fictitious, for anything abstract, ideal, and general does not exist. All these notions are mere inventions of human beings in order to promote themselves. The only real thing is the ego; others and things are only valuable if they serve or satisfy the ego. I am everything, and everything I need is my property and is there for me, Stirner held: "Divine things are God's concern, human things the concern of human beings. Neither what is divine, nor what is human, nor the truth, the good, the right, the free and so on, but only my things are my concern. . . . There is nothing more important than myself." Stirner regarded himself as the absolute, the perfect, and the only thing, with the world being his own creation and the society as nothing but a company of egoists. In contrast to Kant, who held that one should never treat any human being solely as a means to a further purpose, this is exactly what Stirner demanded. Not only did he regard human beings as means for his own purpose, but also all other things, and plants, and animals. Stirner can be seen as the defender of an extreme type of anarchy. According to him, even atheists are pious people, as they believe in the human, order, and the future.

Büchner. In contrast to Stirner, Georg BÜCHNER attributed far greater importance to other people. Like Schopenhauer's, his thinking was based on the fundamental insight that life means nothing but pain. It was Büchner's goal to transcend this pain and to help others to transcend it. He was particularly acquainted with all aspects of human suffering, as he was a medical doctor, as had been his father also. Within his novella *Lenz*

(1842), the hero is on his quest for a religious meaning for all the suffering and pain. In order to reduce suffering on a social level, Büchner cofounded a secret society for human rights in the spring of 1834, the goal of which was to establish a republican and egalitarian society. Even while a school pupil, Büchner was fascinated with the French Revolution. He was particularly keen on strengthening the interests of the working class compared with the interests of the liberal middle class.

Marx. Karl Heinrich MARX's goals concerning an ideal society were similar to Büchner's. However, his account was theoretically more detailed, and his actual influence more effective. His theory focused primarily on the economic well-being of citizens: "It is not the consciousness of men that determines their being but, on the contrary, their social being that determines their consciousness." By social being, he referred mainly to the economic class to which someone belongs. Analogous to Marx's understanding of society is his understanding of religion: "Just as religion does not create man, but man creates religion, so the constitution does not create the people but the people the constitution." Like Feuerbach, Marx held that the qualities attributed to God are a collection of human wishes and desires. In consequence, he came to the conclusion that "the abolition of religion as the illusory happiness of the people is a demand for their real happiness. The demand to give up the illusions about their condition is a demand to give up a condition that requires illusion. The criticism of religion is therefore the germ of the criticism of the valley of tears whose halo is religion."

Haeckel. Marx acknowledged the immense importance of Charles DARWIN, as did Ernst HAECKEL, who was the main defender of Darwinism (see DARWINISM AND UNBELIEF) in Germany. Besides Darwin, Haeckel held Goethe in high esteem, particularly concerning his understanding of the world. Haeckel's worldview was strictly monistic, whereby body, spirit, matter, and energy are all qualities of the one, universal substance (Hylozoism) which is also eternal, infinite, and unlimited. All atoms can perceive and strive. God, according to Haeckel, could only be described as the sum of all natural forces. Yet there is nothing outside of or additional to nature, and, therefore, there is no difference between pantheism and atheism (see PANTHEISM AND UNBELIEF). In one of his monographs, he described monism as the connection between religion and science. Haeckel also cofounded the German Monist Union. As a consequence of his conviction that everything which exists belongs solely to this world, he was a fierce opponent of dualism, theism, and spiritualism, and he held that the dogmas of all positive religions have to be rejected. However, human beings are social vertebrates, and both egoism and altruism are basic constituents of human nature. Morality, according to Haeckel, does have a bio-sociological basis.

Nietzsche. Another defender of monism was

Friedrich Wilhelm NIETZSCHE. According to him, the world is will to power, meaning that it is constituted out of quanta who are permanently trying to overcome themselves. However, his unbelief in any transcendent world, and in particular in a Christian God, not only becomes obvious in his own immanent worldview but rather in various types of complex, clever, and witty criticisms he put forward. One can distinguish at least three types of criticism: the genealogical, the perspectival, and the depth-psychological critique. By means of the genealogical approach, he tried to make Christianity unappealing by putting forward an account of how Christianity and Christian morality in particular came about. In this way, he could not prove the falsity of Christianity, but he was able to advertise a different morality and convince the reader that Christianity has to be associated with qualities that are unpopular among human beings. Nietzsche described how in late antiquity Christianity grew more and more influential among slaves. With the notion of "slaves," he referred not only to actual slaves, but also to weak, ill, and ugly people. The invention of Christianity can be traced back to the will to power of the slaves, and Christianity is the tool of the weak to gain power, according to Nietzsche. As no one wishes to be associated with the ugly, the weak, and the ill, and in Nietzsche's writings a strong case is put forward for associating these undesirable characteristics with Christianity, Christianity gradually becomes less popular. By means of the perspectival critique, Nietzsche provided us with alternatives to generally accepted positions, so that the contingency of widespread, popular positions becomes plausible. In this way, he laid open that the equality of human beings, which is connected to the assumption that all human beings have a soul, is not a theory which has to be taken for granted, for in ancient Greece it was common to distinguish between the moralities of slaves and noblemen. By means of his depth-psychological arguments, he tried to reveal hidden motives of types of human beings. He was particularly convincing in the case of priests, as well as that of common believers. By showing that their beliefs and actions can also be explained by egoistical motives, he convinced many readers that their motives actually are the egoistic ones, as egoistic motives often appear as more plausible than other more upright ones.

Further Writers. Some slightly less important authors who also belong to the history of unbelief in modern German literature are the following: Luis Charles Adélaïde de Chamisso de Boncourt (known as Adelbert von Chamisso), Christian Dietrich Grabbe, N. Franz Niembsch Edler von Strehlenau (known as Nikolaus Lanau), Karl Gutzkow, Wilhelm Richard Wagner, Georg Herwegh, Gottfried Keller, Gerhart Hauptmann, Benjamin Franklin Wedekind (known as Frank Wedekind), and Stefan George.

BIBLIOGRAPHY

Beutin, Wolfgang, Volker Meid, and Helmut Hoffacker, eds. *A History of German Literature.* London: Routledge, 1994.

Bubnerü, Rudiger. *Modern German Philosophy*, Translated by Eric Matthews. Cambridge: Cambridge University Press, 1981.

Galling, Kurt, ed. *Die Religion in Geschichte und Gegenwart: Handwörterbuch für Theologie und Religionswissenschaft.* 7 vols. Stuttgart: UTB, 1986.

Gorner, Paul. *Twentieth-Century German Philosophy.* Oxford: Oxford University Press, 2000.

Hahn, Hans J. *German Thought and Culture: From the Holy Roman Empire to the Present Day.* Manchester, UK: Manchester University Press, 1995.

Lutz, Bern, ed. *Metzler Philosophen Lexikon.* Stuttgart: Metzler, 2003.

O'Hear, Anthony. *German Philosophy Since Kant.* Cambridge: Cambridge University Press, 1999.

Ten, C. L., ed. *Routledge History of Philosophy: The Nineteenth Century.* London: Routledge, 1994.

Watanabe-O'Kelly, Helen, ed. *The Cambridge History of German Literature.* Cambridge: Cambridge University Press, 2000.

Williamson, George S. *The Longing for Myth in Germany: Religion and Aesthetic Culture from Romanticism to Nietzsche.* Chicago: University of Chicago Press, 2004.

STEFAN LORENZ SORGNER

GERMANY, UNBELIEF IN. The division of religious people for legal purposes according to different religious denominations reflects the incomplete separation of church and state typical of Germany. For example, church taxes are collected by Germany's Ministry of Finance according to the denomination to which each taxpayer claims to belong. Approximately 7.5 billion euros per year are paid to the churches by government each year.

Following World War II, Germany's religious and ideological diversity increased. Within a total population of 82.5 million inhabitants (*Statistical Yearbook of the Federal Republic*, 2003 figures) figures compiled by REMID (Religionswissenschaftlicher Medien-und Informationsdienst/Science of Religion Media and News Service) show that there are 26 million Protestants, 26 million Catholics, 3.2 million Muslims, 1 million Orthodox (Russian, Greek, Ukrainian, and other), 200,000 Jews, 150,000 Buddhists, and 100,000 Hindus. Another 500,000 to 850,000 claim affiliation with smaller religious communities (for example, 165,000 Jehovah's Witnesses).

The number of people who report belonging to none of the above-mentioned religious groups has grown quite large: approximately 25 million. This unaffiliated group, nearly the same size as the Protestant and Catholic groups, is frequently spoken of as a "third denomination." Although avowed atheists (see ATHEISM) do not form the majority among the unaffiliated, atheism is gaining in importance, especially in eastern Germany, where explicit atheists comprise 20 percent of the population. There, despite German unification, sociologists predict that atheism will be dominant nationwide in four generations. On every index the gap in religious identification between east and west is very sharp. In the west the unaffiliated form 12 to 15 percent of the population; in the east they amount to 65 to 75 percent. In western Germany 70 percent of the population claim membership in some church, compared to only 24 percent in the east. In the west approximately 15 percent of residents attend church weekly, in the east a mere 3 percent. In addition, the proportion of religious believers tends to decrease among younger age groups. A consensus public "civil religion" as is commonly expressed in the United States does not exist in Germany.

Humanism and Freethought in Germany. A recent study indicates that 7 percent of the population strongly supports a humanistic viewpoint (see HUMANISM) without being connected to any religion, and an additional 42 percent does so to a lesser extent. While the number of Germans affiliated with formal humanist and freethought groups has declined, the number of secular officiants able to perform humanist services such as weddings and memorial sevices has risen, tracking the increase in the unaffiliated population. Today, approximately twenty to fifty thousand people are members of various humanist or FREETHOUGHT associations, so-called LIFE STANCE organizations that are nonreligious but serve some of the same social needs as churches. This is about the same number of Germans who belonged to nonreligious organizations prior to World War I.

Unbelief in Modern Germany. The first democratic nonreligious life stance associations were founded five years before the revolution of 1848–49. Their members were dissidents or renegades who thought of themselves as free religious (*freireligiosen*), which is to say practicing free thought within the religious community. The spread of the ideas of Charles DARWIN and later Karl MARX in the second half of the nineteenth century led first to liberal, then to social democratic freethinking associations such as the Deutscher Freidenkerverband (German Association of Freethinkers), founded in 1881 (see EVOLUTION AND UNBELIEF; MARXISM; SOCIALISM AND UNBELIEF). Additionally there were numerous cultural and fraternal societies, many with connections to freethinking Germans who had emigrated to the United States, whose programs included a secular approach to spiritual welfare, moral instruction, and education. As noted, participation in nonreligious life stance organizations was strong before World War I, but grew rapidly thereafter. By the end of the 1920s nearly 1 million people were organized in nonreligious and freethinking associations. In 1933 most associations were forbidden by the Nazis and their property dispossessed. While a handful of nonreligious accepted racist fascism, it is widely understood that former freethinkers formed the majority of active resistance fighters. After the war ended all the freethought organizations that existed in the 1920s were reconstituted, but they failed to capture broad popular support and eventually collapsed. There were various social and political causes for this. In the west, a rapid expansion of individualism since the 1980s lessened the appeal of fraternal and social organizations. The close organizational connections that the traditional nonreligious organization had enjoyed with traditional worker's parties and political liberals lost relevance. In addition, as the Cold War had split Germany itself, all of the freethinking organizations suffered an east-west split. In the former East Germany, atheism was state policy and no autonomous freethought movement was permitted. By the time the Berlin wall fell, the remains of the freethinking movement had become insignificant.

German Humanism: A New Beginning. Since 1993 the Humanistischer Verband Deutschlands (HVD; Humanist Asssociation of Germany) has tried to spark a new beginning, offering a spectrum of human services including social work, nursery schools, ethics curricula for schools, coming-of-age celebrations, secular funerals, get-togethers for senior citizens, living wills, and support for voluntary euthanasia, among other projects. Furthermore, the association strives to link the theoretical and political content of atheism with the ideals of liberal and social democracy. In Berlin and other large cities in Germany, this has been successfully accomplished. At present, the HVD has approximately ten thousand members. Humanists view their life stance not as a "religious belief" but rather as a "scientific worldview." This point of view and its implications are summarized in the following list of concepts, all of which are vital to describing the way humanists see themselves:

- Indifference toward any god
- Trust in one's own cognition and empirical science
- Rejection of beliefs in redemption, rebirth, and resurrection
- Respect for individual uniqueness and human rights
- Self-determination as a primary value
- Secularity, insofar as is possible, of all matters regarding public life
- Solidarity, tolerance, and communication with fellow human beings
- Criticism instead of belief as a general principle

BIBLIOGRAPHY

Fincke, Andreas. *Freidenker—Freigeister—Freireligiöse. Kirchenkritische Organisationen in Deutschland seit 1989* [Freethinker—Free Mind—Free Religious; Church-Critical Organizations in Germany Since 1989]. Berlin: EZW-Texte, 2002.

Groschopp, Horst. *Dissidenten. Freidenkerei und Kultur*

in Deutschland [Dissidents, Freethinkers and Culture in Germany]. Berlin: Verlag J. H. W. Dietz Nachf, 1997.

Weir, Todd. "The Secularization of Religious Dissent: Anticlerical Politics and the Freethought Movement in Germany, 1844–1933." In *Religiosity in the Secularized World: Theoretical and Empirical Contributions to the Secularization Debate in the Sociology of Religion*, edited by Manuel Franzmann, Christel Gardner, and Nicole Koeck. Wiesbaden: VS Publishing, 2006.

HORST GROSCHOPP
TRANSLATED BY C. VELAZQUEZ

GIBBON, EDWARD (1737–1794), English historian. Edward Gibbon is best known for his seven-volume (in most editions) history *The Decline and Fall of the Roman Empire*, which treats the period from the second century to the fifteenth century CE. The work has two parts. The first covers the history of the empire in the west to its end in the last decades of the fifth century. The second part covers the one thousand years of what we now call the Byzantine Empire, the last vestiges of which were conquered by the Turks in the fifteenth century. Gibbon's theme was the decline of political and intellectual freedom that he found in classical literature of the past; he is particularly unsympathetic to the Byzantine Empire. Today his work is regarded as one more of literature than history, in light of two centuries of scholarship on the subject since his time. His sources were primarily the Latin and to a lesser extent the Greek works then known, and these have since been supplemented by archaeological findings, the use of inscriptions, writings in languages other than Latin or Greek, and thousands upon thousands of monographic studies on every aspect of the period on which he wrote. Even in his own time, the second section of the book had serious omissions in his narrative and often unsatisfactory summaries, perhaps because Gibbon was not as facile in Greek as he was in Latin. Though he says he wrote to vindicate intellectual freedom, he concluded toward the end of his work that he had ended up describing "the triumph of barbarism and religion." Historically, Gibbon is particularly important to rationalists (see RATIONALISM) and freethinkers (see FREETHOUGHT) because of his insistence that religion in the Roman Empire, particularly Christianity, be subject to the same kind of historical inquiry to which Roman history itself was.

Gibbon came from a wealthy background and always had an independent income. His problem was what to do with his time and energy, and he early on decided that history was "his proper food." Though sickly as a child, he seemed to recover at puberty and remained in more or less good health throughout his life. He entered Magdalen College, Oxford, on his fifteenth birthday, where he became interested in theology and, as one biographer said, "read himself" into Roman Catholicism, to which

he converted a year after going to Oxford. His father almost immediately removed him from the college and sent him to Switzerland to study with a Calvinist minister, Daniel Pavillard, under whose guidance he studied classical literature, French, mathematics, logic, and within a year had once again become a Protestant. He also fell in love, but his father opposed his engagement; he broke it off and never married.

While in Switzerland he made the acquaintance of VOLTAIRE and other figures of the French Enlightenment (see ENLIGHTENMENT, UNBELIEF DURING THE), and on his return to England upon the death of his father, he joined English intellectual society, including membership in the Club, the circle of friends around Dr. Samuel Johnson, where he became intimate with Joshua Reynolds and David Garrick. He also served briefly in Parliament and in the South Hampshire militia. He published the first volume of his history in 1776; it was both successful and controversial, as it dealt with the rise of Christianity. His fifteenth and sixteenth chapters were attacked by many pamphleteers and subjected to ridicule, most of which he ignored, except for those that accused him of falsifying his evidence; to these he felt it necessary to reply. He also served for a time as a commissioner of trade and plantations, and for a time debated with himself whether to finish his magnum opus or concentrate on a political career. When he lost his paid position as commissioner, he moved to Lausanne in Switzerland to economize, and there he finished his writing of the *Decline and Fall*, all volumes of which had been published by 1788. He also wrote a memoir of his life and many other works. He returned to England in 1793 and died in 1794.

His "exposure" of the crimes and futility of Christianity have led many freethinkers to call him one of their own. Certainly, his treatment of Christianity in his own lifetime led him to be attacked and ridiculed by many of his contemporaries, who feared that his skepticism would shake the existing church and government establishment. In the nineteenth century, agnostics (see AGNOSTICISM) seized upon him as one of their own. He himself was not a particularly militant nonbeliever, and regarded himself as a historian who treated religion as a phenomenon of human experience. He did not believe in divine revelation and had little sympathy for those who did. Joseph McCABE in his study *Free Thinkers* labeled him a deist on the way to agnosticism, and Gibbon's chapters on early Christianity are still worth reading today. In fact the whole book makes for a good read, and his insistence that early Christianity should be subject to the same critical studies as the secular classical literature makes him particularly important for freethinkers and rationalists everywhere.

BIBLIOGRAPHY

There are many editions of Gibbon's *Decline and Fall of the Roman Empire,* including the Modern Library edition. His other writings can be found in most major libraries.

Low, D. M. *Edward Gibbon*. New York: Random House, 1937.

Oliver, E. J. *Gibbon and Rome*. New York: Sheed & Ward, 1958.

VERN L. BULLOUGH

GIBSON, ELLA E. (1821–1901), American feminist, freethinker, and Bible critic. Ella E. Gibson was apparently the first freethinking woman to write a feminist analysis of the bible, *The Godly Women of the Bible, by an Ungodly Woman of the Nineteenth Century* (c. 1878). The Truth Seeker Company published *Godly Women* and apparently kept it in print for the next thirty years, but today it is a rare artifact.

Gibson was born in Winchendon, Massachusetts, taught public schools for twelve years in New England, and also wrote and lectured. She organized Soldiers' Ladies Aid Societies in Wisconsin at the start of the Civil War, then joined the Eighth Wisconsin Volunteers, where she was elected chaplain of the First Wisconsin Regiment, Heavy Artillery. Her appointment was apparently approved by President Abraham Lincoln on November 10, 1864, but the secretary of war refused to muster her because she was a woman. By an act of Congress on March 3, 1869, payment for her services as a chaplain was approved, but she did not receive a pension until 1876.

By that time, Gibson was an outspoken freethinker, and much of her government pension went into the freethought cause. Although a bout of malaria during the war reduced her to frequent invalidism, Gibson kept her pen active, often writing from her sickbed. Freethought biographer Samuel P. PUTNAM noted that Gibson wrote for nearly every "Liberal" (freethought) newspaper in the United States, as well as editing the *Moralist* in 1891. Gibson also wrote *The Holy Bible Abridged* and various pamphlets.

Gibson took a more outspoken and less euphemistic approach in describing the Bible's treatment of women than did Elizabeth Cady STANTON, whose classic look at the Bible, *The Woman's Bible*, was published in the late 1890s. In the conclusion of her work Gibson prophesied: "The time will come when King James's Bible (present version) will not be spoken of without a blush of shame tingling the cheek of modesty, or referred to except as a textbook obsolete, superannuated, blasphemous, false, pernicious, corrupt, immodest, obscene, and too immoral to be tolerated, even as a past nuisance, ancient, foreign, and worthless."

She wrote of the Bible: "Away with its false teachings, fables, pagan mythology, and abuse of woman, and assist her to free herself from these shackles and to overcome these vile aspersions descending down from the dark ages and settling like a pall over her existence and the existence of the race!"

Gibson died at age seventy-nine in Barre, Massachusetts.

BIBLIOGRAPHY

Gibson, Ella E. *The Godly Women of the Bible, by an Ungodly Woman of the Nineteenth Century*. New York: Truth Seeker Company, [1878].

MacDonald. E. M. *Fifty Years of Freethought: Story of the* Truth Seeker *from 1875*. 2 vols. New York: Truth Seeker Company, 1929–1931.

Putnam, Samuel P. *Four Hundred Years of Freethought*. New York: Truth Seeker Comapny, 1894.

ANNIE LAURIE GAYLOR

GILMAN, CHARLOTTE PERKINS (1860–1935), American feminist, evolutionist, and author. Charlotte Perkins Gilman, an internationally recognized humanist (see HUMANISM) and social critic, wrote dozens of books and hundreds of articles and gave thousands of lectures, all in an effort to understand the world in order to change it fundamentally.

The restructuring of relations between men and women was the central focus of her radical vision and the central theme of her most famous book, *Women and Economics: An Examination of the Relationship between Men and Women as a Factor in Social Evolution* (1898). The book had an immediate and enormous impact. The world is masculinist, she declared, and she wished to create an equitable balance between men and women. Only in the human species, unlike other animals, does the female depend on the male for food. Thus, the sex relationship is also an economic one. Women, narrowed by their subjugated position in society, must be freed from their domestic place in order to improve society as a whole. Gilman called for economic independence for women, which in her vision included kitchenless homes, professional child rearing, and communal dining (see SEX RADICALISM AND UNBELIEF). It is true, however, that Gilman did not challenge some of the major views prevalent in her lifetime, such as racism and xenophobia.

Important as *Women and Economics* was, and continues to be, it was only the first step in Gilman's ambitious project. In *Concerning Children* (1900), she asserted that damaging childrearing ideas resulted from treating children only as parts of a family instead of as members of society. *The Home: Its Work and Influence* (1903) followed soon thereafter. Gilman indicted "an institution owned by man, in which wife and children are forcibly held, forcibly by virtue of economic dependence and ideological pressure." In *The Man-Made World, or Our Androcentric Culture* (1909), a study of "excessive maleness," she analyzed the kind of mischief that occurs when one sex dominates the other. The best known of her works today, "The Yellow Wallpaper" (1892), protests the mistreatment of women suffering from depression subjected to the medical profession's "rest cure."

In *Our Brains and What Ails Them* (1912), she asked the question: With our vast knowledge, why are humans "the most vicious, the most unhappy, the sickest beast alive?" In her last book (except for her autobiography), *His Religion and Hers: A Study of the Faith of Our Fathers and the Work of Our Mothers* (1923), Gilman answered that question and the others she had posed throughout her life. The first book explored the economic relations between men and women. At the end of her life Gilman summed up her work with a study of the power of ideology—isolating religion as a central part of the human ideological system.

Gilman was a Beecher, and the Beechers were the most famous family in America. Lyman Beecher, her great-grandfather, still living when Gilman was born, was a zealot and evangelist, setting as his goal in life to regenerate society through his Christian teaching. All the Beecher men became ministers. The Beecher women, though banned from the ministry, created their own ministerial version, as educators, writers, or activists. Harriet Beecher Stowe, author of *Uncle Tom's Cabin*, was one of Charlotte's aunts. Another, perhaps more famous at the time, was Catherine, who effectively persuaded her generation that the home was the nation's moral center. She idealized the idea of domesticity with maternal self-sacrifice at the core. Gilman stood Aunt Catherine on her head by challenging the prevailing ideology of domesticity, as she did in *Women and Economics* and subsequent books. But she turned the entire Beecher clan on its collective head by asserting that religion, which defined the life of her prominent ancestors, has done more disservice to humanity than any other institution or any other ideology.

"Religion is the strongest modifying influence in our conscious behavior," she wrote, and it should serve our best interests, but it does not. It focuses on worrying about putting souls in heaven rather than concerning itself with this life. That we suffer so much on earth is not god's fault or the devil's fault, but our own. A life in heaven is appealing because it exists in the imagination as a fantasy about which we have no knowledge and feel no responsibility. The real future is the world we leave behind. Religions are concerned with the beyond for each individual after death, instead of human life as one generation is replaced by the next.

We are also burdened with another aspect of dominant masculinity, "the guileless habit of blaming women."

To believe and to obey are the chief demands of religion. What "the fathers" saw and thought was probably the best they could manage at the time, but to force their limited vision on those who come after is endlessly damaging. Such is "his" religion. In Gilman's view, women are oriented toward birth, not death, toward creation—creating agriculture, while men hunted—and nurturing the young. The human race lives immortally on earth, endlessly re-created through birth. Social improvement is our chief duty. What we call god is the life within us. Gilman took the nineteenth-century notion of maternal service and made it the foundation of a benevolent non-religious ethical system and guide to human conduct.

BIBLIOGRAPHY

Golden, Catherine J., and Joanne Schneider Zangrando, eds. *The Mixed Legacy of Charlotte Perkins Gilman.* Cranbury, NJ: University of Delaware Press, 2000.

Karpinski, Joanne B. *Critical Essays on Charlotte Perkins Gilman.* New York: G. K. Hall, 1992.

Kessler, Carol Farley. *Charlotte Perkins Gilman: Her Progress toward Utopia with Selected Writing.* Syracuse, NY: Syracuse University Press, 1995.

Knight, Denise D. *Charlotte Perkins Gilman: A Study of the Short Fiction.* New York: Twayne, 1997.

Lane, Ann J. *To "Herland" and Beyond: The Life and Work of Charlotte Perkins Gilman.* New York: Pantheon, 2000.

Scharnhorst, Gary. *Charlotte Perkins Gilman: A Bibliography.* Metuchen, NJ: Scarecrow, 1985.

ANN J. LANE

GODWIN, WILLIAM (1756–1836), British writer, philosopher, and novelist. William Godwin had a strongly religious childhood. His father was a Dissenting minister, belonging to a sect that refused subscribe to the Thirty-nine Articles of the Church of England. He underwent rigorous training for the ministry under a strict Sandemanian, a member of a hyper-intellectualist sect that damned the vast majority of those John Calvin deemed saved, followed by three years at the Hoxton Dissenting Academy and a brief spell as a minister (from which he published a collection of sermons). Despite it all Godwin came to abandon his religious beliefs in his late twenties, ascribing his DEISM and ultimate ATHEISM to the works of the philosophes, especially Baron d'HOLBACH, Claude Adrien HELVETIUS, and Jean-Jacques ROUSSEAU, and to conversations with friends. The only explicit attack on religion that he published was *The Genius of Christianity Unveiled*, his final work, left for posthumous publication, which provided a thoroughgoing critique of Christian belief. Yet his heterodox opinions were clear to his critics from the first publication of his major work, *An Enquiry concerning Political Justice* (1793), and from the later notoriety generated by his candid *Memoirs of the Author of the Vindication of the Rights of Woman* (1798), his heartfelt, if unwise, tribute to his wife, Mary WOLLSTONECRAFT. Yet for all that *Political Justice* espoused a secular mixture of utilitarianism and DETERMINISM, it retained a central emphasis on the right and duty of private judgment and advocated a highly intellectualized view of the nature of pleasure, both of which owe much to his background and friendships in rational Dissent. While later editions diminished his rationalism, confidence in truth, and repudiation of the private affections, private judgment remains central both to his moral philosophy and to his final denunciation of the imposture of Christianity.

Life. The seventh of thirteen children, Godwin was trained for the ministry at his own insistence from the age of eleven, and he stubbornly held to the extreme Calvinism and Tory politics he was taught by his schoolmaster until the 1780s. He had a number of brief and unsuccessful appointments as a minister, and he moved to London in the early 1780s to try his hand as a writer. He wrote a biography of William Pitt the Elder, first Earl of Chatham; various political pamphlets; and three rather weak novels before being taken on as a writer with the Whig news review the *New Annual Register. Political Justice* was written in part as a response to the Revolution Controversy sparked by Edmund Burke's *Reflections on the Revolution in France* (1790), but it expanded in its execution, becoming a founding work of philosophical anarchism and canvassing the possibility of human immortality. It was an immediate success, especially in literary and radical circles. In May 1794 Godwin's first major and most successful novel, *Things as They Are, or The Adventures of Caleb Williams*, was published, adding further to his literary reputation. Two further editions of *Political Justice* in 1796 and 1798 saw the removal of many of the more rationalist elements, suggesting the declining influence of Dissent on Godwin, although some have ascribed the changes also to his relationship with Wollstonecraft, whom he married in March 1797, six months before she died giving birth to their daughter, Mary.

At the end of the 1790s, in the wake of the French Revolution came a backlash against radicalism. Godwin found himself reviled in pamphlets and anti-Jacobin novels and reviews. He lived an increasingly penurious life, supporting Wollstonecraft's first child, Fanny; their daughter, Mary; and providing for his second wife, Mary Jane Clairmont, her two children by a previous relationship, and their own son, William Godwin Jr. He ran a children's publishing house under his wife's name, and continued to write a range of novels, memoirs, histories, and essays, using a pseudonym for his children's books. Percy Bysshe SHELLEY, fired by *Political Justice*, sought him out and offered to raise money on the contents of a sequestered inheritance to help. The relationship turned sour when Shelley wanted half the money raised to divorce his wife, Harriet, so he could marry Godwin's seventeen-year-old daughter, Mary. Shelley and Mary then eloped to France, taking Mary's stepsister, Jane, with them. A succession of tragic family events followed, ending with the deaths of Fanny, Shelley's first wife, and Shelley himself.

For the last thirty years of his life Godwin was plagued by debt and his health deteriorated (he suffered increas-

ingly from fits). He continued to publish widely, but was increasingly concerned to avoid the scandal that his *Memoirs . . .* had generated and which his links to the Shelley circle had revived. Accordingly, while he was determined to set down his position on the imposture of Christianity, he was unwilling to publish it in his own lifetime, and he left it with Mary Shelley with an injunction to publish it, which she effectively ignored—for similar reasons. When Godwin's trenchant attack on organized religion, the Bible, and belief in an afterlife was published in 1873, its time had passed and it aroused little hostility.

BIBLIOGRAPHY

Clark, John P. *The Philosophical Anarchism of William Godwin.* Princeton, NJ: Princeton University Press, 1977.

Locke, Don. *A Fantasy of Reason: The Life and Thought of William Godwin.* London: Routledge & Kegan Paul, 1980.

Marshall, Peter, H. *William Godwin.* New Haven, CT: Yale University Press, 1984.

Philp, Mark. *Godwin's* Political Justice. London: Duckworth, 1986.

———, ed. *Collected Novels and Memoirs of William Godwin,* 8 vols. London: Pickering and Chatto, 1992.

———, ed. *Political and Philosophical Writings of William Godwin,* 7 vols. London: Pickering and Chatto, 1993.

Pollin, Bruton R. *Education and Enlightenment in the Works of William Godwin.* New York: Las Americas, 1962.

St. Clair, William. *The Godwins and the Shelleys: The Biography of a Family.* London: Faber and Faber, 1989.

MARK PHILP

GOETHE, JOHANN WOLFGANG VON (1749–1832), German author. Much of Goethe's theorizing in biology reflected his view of the unity of nature. He did not explain underlying similarities between animals by alleging that they had common ancestors, for he held that evolution had played a quite insignificant role in the history of species. Rather he supposed that nature used a single archetype in constructing them, and that the task of the biologist is to form a clear idea of this archetype from comparison of a large number of animal forms. He was convinced that nature proceeds in this way, from ideas, just as a human artist creates works from ideas in his mind. For Goethe, "nature" making her plans was no other than God making his plans; and his reading of Baruch SPINOZA confirmed him in this pantheistic view.

In his autobiography Goethe maintained that natural religion of this kind has nothing to fear from rational inquiry, whereas revealed religion, depending as it does on traditions handed down over time, is vulnerable and so requires unquestioning acceptance, which he could not give. His skepticism toward central Christian beliefs was explicit, and more so in his letters and conversations than in his publications. Thus he wrote to the Swiss pastor J. C. Lavater on August 9, 1782, that a voice from heaven would not make him believe in a virgin birth or a resurrection. Nevertheless, his respect for the Bible was such that he claimed to have derived his own moral orientation almost exclusively from it, and deplored scoffing criticism of it. His standpoint was that valid criticisms do not involve the abandonment of its essentials; but just what these are is not altogether clear from his account of them.

The Efficacy of Faith. In his essay on Israel in the desert ("Israel in der Wüste," included in his notes to the poems of his "West-ostlicher Divan") Goethe declared: "The conflict of faith and unbelief remains the proper, the only, the deepest theme of the history of the world and of mankind. All epochs in which faith is dominant, no matter in what form, are magnificent, heart-warming and fruitful for contemporaries and for posterity; whereas all epochs in which unbelief in whatever form sustains its wretched triumph . . . vanish from the standpoint of posterity."

This would make the Renaissance and the eighteenth century of much less significance than the Dark Ages and the period of the Crusades. Goethe's appreciation of the value of received tradition for social stability (understandable in one who had lived through the upheavals of the French Revolution) seems to have led him here into unduly wide generalizations. The same high evaluation of social stability surely underlay his insistence that the Bible is not to be rejected, but can be reduced to acceptable essentials.

Goethe's views were sufficiently unorthodox to earn him, throughout Germany, the title "the great heathen." He deplored the doctrine that man, insofar as he lacks divine grace, is the helpless victim of sin and depravity; and he refused to supplement his Pelagian optimism concerning human nature with what he regarded as orthodox irrationalisms. "I believed in God and in nature and in the triumph of what is noble over what is base," he said to his secretary, Eckermann, on January 4, 1824. "But that was not enough for pious souls, who wanted me also to believe that three are one and one three. That went against my feeling for truth, and in any case I did not see how it would in the least have profited me." For clergy who promulgated such doctrine he had little respect. In the very last of these conversations recorded by Eckermann (dated March 11, 1832, shortly before Goethe's death), where he allows that the "eminence and moral culture of Christianity" as reflected in the gospels will never be surpassed, he complained that "the richly endowed clergy fear nothing more than the enlightenment of the lower masses" and "kept the Bible from them as long as that was possible."

BIBLIOGRAPHY

Eckermann, J. P. *Gespräche mit Goethe in den letzten Jahren seines Lebens.* Edited by H. H. Houben. Wiesbaden: Brockhaus, 1959.

Loewen, H. "Goethe's Pietism." In *Deutung und Bedeutung. Studies in German and Comparative Literature*, edited by Brigitte Schludermann et al. The Hague and Paris: Mouton, 1973.

Luke, David. "Vor deinem Jammerkreuz'. Goethe's Attitude to Christian Belief." *Publications of the English Goethe Society*, New Series 49 (1990).

Trunz, Erich, ed. *The Collected Works of Goethe*, 14 vols. Hamburg: Christian Wegner Verlag, 1949–.

Wells, G. A. *Goethe and the Development of Science, 1750–1900.* Edited by G. L. E. Turner. Alphen aan den Rijn: Sijthoff and Noordhoff, 1978.

———. "Goethe on Learning, Knowledge, and Faith." *Journal of English and Germanic Philology* 83 (1984).

GEORGE A. WELLS

GOLDMAN, EMMA (1869–1940), American anarchist activist. Emma Goldman was a poor teenaged immigrant working in a sweatshop in Rochester, New York, when she learned about the Haymarket tragedy. She had escaped the tyranny of a cold and orthodox father in Russia, and with her sister landed in Rochester. Finding herself trapped in a loveless marriage, Goldman left her husband and in 1889 moved to New York City, where she immersed herself in the cause of the Haymarket martyrs. She befriended and became lovers with the anarchists Alexander Berkman and Johann Most, who opened her mind to the ideas and possibilities of anarchism (see ANARCHISM AND UNBELIEF).

In New York Goldman earned her living in sweatshops, but her leisure time was spent reading anarchist literature and discussing and debating social and political issues with the people who congregated at Sach's café on Suffolk Street, "headquarters of the East Side radicals." She began speaking publicly, addressing meetings on such topics as the eight-hour workday, and soon found her niche as a stirring and persuasive orator as well as a tireless labor organizer. She plunged herself into these activities after Berkman's arrest and imprisonment for the attempted murder of Henry Clay Frick, the ruthless union-busting chairman of Carnegie Steel, which Goldman had helped plan. She was arrested for inciting to riot during one of her speeches, when she told the workers to "demand bread" and, if they were denied bread, to take it. For this crime, she served a year at Blackwell's Island Penitentiary, where, when asked by the matron about her religion, she proudly declared herself an atheist and refused to attend church.

While incarcerated at Blackwell's Island, Goldman worked in the prison hospital tending to the sick, and upon her release, attended nursing school in Vienna.

She returned to New York in 1896 and resumed her activities.

As a result of Goldman's public declarations and actions, she was arrested and jailed many times. When the anarchist Leon Czolgosz assassinated William McKinley in 1901, Goldman, who had never met Czolgosz but had publicly defended him, was arrested. Several times when she promoted birth control, free-love, and women's emancipation, she spent time in jail (see BIRTH CONTROL AND UNBELIEF; SEX RADICALISM AND UNBELIEF; WOMAN SUFFRAGE MOVEMENT AND UNBELIEF). Once, in Detroit, she was invited to speak at the Congregational church by a liberal-minded pastor, and told the parishioners. "I do not believe in God, because I believe in man. Whatever his mistakes, man has for thousands of years past been working to undo the botched job your God has made."

In 1906 Goldman began publishing a monthly magazine, *Mother Earth*, one of the most important anarchist magazines in US history. With the help of her comrades such as Berkman, Hippolyte Havel, and Max Baginski, *Mother Earth* lasted eleven years, and included editorials, poetry, news of labor struggles and radical movements throughout the world, and philosophical essays in support of anarchism and against religion. It ceased publication when Goldman and Berkman were arrested and deported.

The only war Goldman ever supported was the class war, so when the Wartime Espionage Act was passed in 1917, she and Berkman, along with hundreds of other radicals, were arrested for violating the act by speaking out against the war and by writing articles in *Mother Earth* that encouraged young men to refuse military service. She spent two years in prison, and afterward was stripped of her US citizenship and, with Berkman, deported to Russia.

Although both Berkman and Goldman were at first excited about the idea of joining the revolution in Russia, they soon awakened to the realities of the Bolshevik regime. Brokenhearted, they left Russia as quickly as possible. Afterward both wrote books and articles attacking Vladimir Ilyich Lenin and the Bolsheviks for destroying the Russian Revolution.

Goldman moved to England and married James Colton in order to obtain a British passport. She then set about writing her autobiography, which has been reprinted many times and translated into many languages. It remains one of the most popular autobiographies of all time. After completing it, Goldman toured Germany, which enabled her to foresee the danger of fascism. She promptly targeted the fascists and the Nazis, addressing large groups about the dangers facing Europe if the Nazis were not stopped.

After a final tour of the United States in 1934, Goldman spent time with Berkman in France, and then in Canada. He committed suicide in 1936. Goldman, devastated, immersed herself in the cause of the Spanish anarchists, spending two years supporting their fight against Franco's fascism. In 1938 she returned to Canada, and died in Toronto in 1940. US authorities allowed her to be buried in Chicago's Waldheim Cemetery next to the Haymarket Monument.

Goldman's ATHEISM was rooted in her belief that anarchism is the method to free all people from their economic and spiritual misery, and that a humane and beautiful world will be realized once theism is exposed as the oppressive sham that it is. "Mankind has been punished long and heavily for having created its gods; nothing but pain and persecution have been man's lot since gods began," she wrote. "There is but one way out of this blunder: Man must break his fetters which have chained him to the gates of heaven and hell, so that he can begin to fashion out of his reawakened and illumined consciousness a new world upon earth."

BIBLIOGRAPHY

Gaylor, A. L., ed. *Women without Superstition: "No Gods—No Masters."* Madison, WI: Freedom From Religion Foundation, 1997.

Madison, Charles A. *Emma Goldman: A Tribute.* New York: Libertarian Book Club, 1960.

Goldman, Emma. *Living My Life.* New York: Knopf, 1931.

———. "The Philosophy of Atheism." *Mother Earth* 10, no. 12 (February 1916).

JULIE HERRADA

GORA (1902–1975), Indian atheist activist and social reformer. Founder of the Atheist Centre in Vijayawada, India, the first institution of its type in the world, Gora championed ATHEISM as a positive way of life. Imprisoned in 1942 during India's struggle for freedom, he went on following Indian independence to lead numerous nonviolent campaigns for social change. In 1972 he organized the First World Atheist Conference at Vijayawada. In 2002, on the centenary of his birth, the government of India honored Gora with a commemorative postage stamp.

Consistent in Thought and Action. Born into an orthodox family, Gora lectured at the college level for fifteen years, once heading a department of botany. The rebel in him came to fore in 1926 when the American College in Madurai offered to send him to Yale for research, provided he become a Christian. He refused. After extensive study, he announced himself an atheist.

At Madurai he stayed in a "haunted house," challenging popular belief in ghosts. In 1928 he encouraged his wife, Saraswathi, to view a solar eclipse, taboo for pregnant women. Dispelling superstitions, he walked on fire; challenged local god-men, or *babas*; popularized science exhibitions; and promoted secular education and the scientific outlook.

Throughout his early life he suffered adversity because of his atheism. Because he refused to follow traditional religious practices, his parents demanded that he leave home. After writing an article titled "The Concept of God," he was dismissed from the faculty of Kakinada College in 1933. The Hindu College at Machilipatnam dismissed him again in 1938, citing his atheism.

With the concurrence of wife and family, Gora founded the Atheist Centre in the village of Mudunur in 1940, shifting it to Vijayawada in 1947. Renouncing private property, Gora operated the Centre on his own sacrifice and commitment and the goodwill of the public.

Campaigns for Equality and Dignity. Gora and the Atheist Centre campaigned for social equality and human dignity. In practice, this meant campaigning against the caste system and untouchability. Braving stiff orthodox opposition, Gora organized intercaste dining, opened public wells to so-called untouchables, and made a point of lodging among untouchables as he traveled in the course of his public engagements. All over the Indian state of Andhra Pradesh he performed casteless and secular marriages. He fought for equality of the sexes and women's liberation. He also initiated steps for social integration of the so-called criminal tribes and opposed their segregation. To break religious barriers, he organized friendship meals at which beef (forbidden to Hindus) and pork (forbidden to Muslims) were served.

Gora's zeal for reform extended to his family life. He gave each of his nine children a nontraditional, secular name. He raised his children on the progressive, atheistic, and democratic model that he advocated for others. He encouraged his children to marry across caste lines, and even to marry untouchables. He attended only weddings to which the local untouchables were also invited, including even the weddings of his close relatives.

Gora's zeal and tenacity of purpose attracted Mahatma Gandhi, who invited Gora and his coworkers to his Sevagram Ashram. *An Atheist with Gandhi* (1951) recounts their discussions.

On the political front, Gora opposed the rise of political parties, which he regarded as an obstacle to social progress. He campaigned for decentralized government and party-less democracy. From 1961 and 1962, he organized an eleven-hundred-mile, hundred-day foot march from Gandhi's Sevagram to New Delhi with the theme "Government Ministers are Servants, People are Masters."

Gora's Positive Atheism. Gora asserted that atheism was a positive stance, opposed to all forms of mental slavery. He said that the essence of atheism lies in the moral freedom of the individual coupled with social responsibility, thus releasing immense human potentialities for development. Atheism as Gora viewed it was not merely a theological position, it was as a way of life: "The spread of the atheist outlook is the hope of humanity to turn from war to peace, from slavery to freedom, from superstition to a sense of reality, from conflict to cooperation."

Gora wielded an indefatigable pen, created an extensive atheist literature, and edited the journals *Sangham* (Society) and *Atheist* for three decades. His advocacy of secular art and culture, his calls for atheists and humanists to cleanse theistic terminology from their language, and his continual pressure to move India toward a postreligious society guaranteed that he was never far from controversy. In 1970 and 1974 Gora toured the world, including the Soviet Union, to strengthen the worldwide atheist and humanist movement.

When Gora died in 1975, a so-called untouchable lit his funeral pyre in the presence of hundreds of admirers. Then–prime minister Indira Gandhi said, "Gora was a man who felt deeply about the evils in society and was dedicated to reform. The movement for the abolition of untouchability, in particular, owes much to him."

The Atheist Centre continues in the forefront of atheism and social reform in India. Mrs. Saraswathi Gora, its cofounder, has won national and international recognition as an outstanding social reformer. Under her guidance, the organization continues a broad agenda of secular social work and has hosted three additional world atheist conferences in 1980, 1996, and 2005.

BIBLIOGRAPHY

Bandiste, D. D. *Positive Atheism of Gora*. Vijayawada: Atheist Centre, 2002.

Gora. *An Atheist with Gandhi*. Ahmedabad: Navajivan Publishing House, 1951.

———. *Positive Atheism*. Vijayawada: Atheist Centre, 1972.

———. *We Become Atheists*. Vijayawada: Atheist Centre, 1975.

Gray, Hugh. "Gora, Gandhi's Atheist Follower." In *Rule, Protest, Identity—Aspects of Modern South Asia*, edited by Peter Robb and David Taylor. London: Centre for South Asian Studies, School of Oriental and African Studies, University of London, 1978.

Naess, Arne. *Gandhi and the Nuclear Age*. New York: Bedminster, 1965.

Shet, Sunanda. *Gora—His Life and Work, a Biographical Study*. Tamilnadu: B. Premanand, 2000.

G. VIJAYAM

GOTT, JOHN WILLIAM (1866–1923), secularist activist. John William Gott is best known for having been imprisoned several times for blasphemy between 1911 and 1922. A secularist and socialist from Bradford, West Yorkshire, England, in 1894 he commenced publication of a monthly titled the *Truthseeker* (not to be confused with the US freethought paper *THE TRUTH SEEKER*) devoted to "mental health and social freedom."

This was taken over by Chapman COHEN, who had met Gott during a speaking tour of the north of England during which Cohen revived branches of the NATIONAL SECULAR SOCIETY (NSS). Cohen attributed the success of his tour to Gott's organizational efforts. However, Cohen dropped the paper, because he objected to the combination of propaganda with advertisements for Gott's clothing business. Thereafter until its extinction in 1913, the paper was edited by Gott.

Gott was "a thorough Yorkshireman—strongly (though stockily) built, with a fresh complexion, golden hair and bright blue eyes," as biographer T. A. Jackson described him. Gott neither drank nor smoked. He ran a clothing business and was in the habit of including with the suits he sold samples of the "more vulgar and scurrilous types of anti-clerical propaganda."

In 1903 Gott helped found the British Secular League (BSL), of which he became treasurer. The secretary was Percy Ward, and the president was George Jacob HOLYOAKE. Within two years, they would be joined by William Stewart Ross, editor of the *Agnostic Journal*, who became the BSL's vice president. Gott represented the BSL at an international freethought congress in Rome in 1904.

Gott's modest success as a businessman enabled him to employ the victimized Birkenhead socialist Bert Killip as organizer of the BSL. Gott remained active as a member of the National Secular Society, and was a delegate from Bradford to its 1905 conference in Liverpool. Later, as the result of a free speech fight in Leeds, that town's Roman Catholic chief constable contemplated prosecuting Gott for blasphemy. However, the proceedings were quietly dropped. In 1908 Gott was expelled from the Social Democratic Federation (SDF) for refusing to stop selling his pamphlet *Socialism: Christ the Enemy of Mankind* at its conference. (SDF leadership viewed religion as a private matter that should be ignored, while Gott and others took the position that religion and socialism were antithetical and religion should be fought.)

In Dewsbury, *Socialism: Christ the Enemy of Mankind* was burned by Ben Turner, who had been secretary of the Huddersfield Secular Sunday School and belonged to the Independent Labour Party, whose leader Philip Snowden, influenced by nonconformist Christianity, had come under attack in Gott's pamphlet.

Undaunted, Gott set up the Freethought Socialist League, of which he was president. He was aided by T. A. Jackson, a victimized London compositor turned freelance Marxist lecturer who would conduct two meetings in the evenings and three on Sundays from the plinth of the statue of Queen Victoria in Leeds. Jackson was amazed at Gott's prowess as a seller of his own publications.

In 1911 Gott was imprisoned for four months for selling his pamphlet *Rib Ticklers, or Questions for Parsons*. Gott was again imprisoned for two weeks in 1916 in Birkenhead and for six weeks in 1917 in Birmingham. Having served another three months in Birmingham in 1921, he was rearrested in Stratford Broadway, East London. Although George William FOOTE had attacked Gott in articles in the *Freethinker*, this time the NSS rallied to his defense, taking his case to the Court of Crim-inal Appeal. However, the judge described Gott as an atheist and socialist of the worst sort and sentenced him to nine months hard labor, which he served in full. Suffering from acute diabetes, Gott died shortly after his release.

BIBLIOGRAPHY

Crick, Martin. *The History of the Social Democratic Federation*. Keele, UK: Keele University Press, 1994.
Jackson, T. A. *Solo Trumpet*. London: Lawrence and Wishart, 1953.
Royle, Edward. *Secularists, Radicals and Republicans*. Manchester, UK: Manchester University Press, 1980.

TERRY LIDDLE

GOULD, STEPHEN JAY (1941–2002), American zoologist and evolutionist. Stephen Jay Gould was unquestionably one of the most public, influential, and controversial biologists of the late twentieth century. A paleontologist by training, he was coauthor with Niles Eldredge of the controversial yet scientifically fruitful theory of punctuated equilibria, which proposed a new interpretation of the known fossil record. He wrote prolifically for the general public; his long-running column in *Natural History* magazine was anthologized in a series of books. The Harvard-based Gould aggressively attacked sociobiology and what he saw as the dangers of biological determinism, engaging in a lifelong intellectual struggle against British evolutionary biologist and popular author Richard Dawkins. Moreover, while fighting CREATIONISM in the public arena, he also wrote an essay (and then a book) maintaining that science and religion can peacefully coexist (see EVOLUTION AND UNBELIEF; RELIGION IN CONFLICT WITH SCIENCE). Gould was a brilliant speaker and writer, yet he was prone to childish behavior toward his audiences, such as shouting after people who left his lectures while he was speaking. His writing style could be extremely rococo, with page-long parenthetical statements and multipage footnotes.

Such a complex figure cannot satisfactorily be analyzed in a brief entry, but it is probably fair to take somewhat of a middle-ground view of Gould as indubitably brilliant, yet flawed; one not to be easily dismissed, yet one whose contribution to science will in the end be less important than he would have hoped.

The 1972 theory of punctuated equilibria maintains that species change on relatively rapid time scales and then undergo periods of stasis over millions of years of nonevolution. Arguably Gould's (and Niles Eldredge's) major scientific accomplishment, the theory had a large impact on paleontology and evolutionary biology. For all the attempts to dismiss it out of hand, it generated a controversy that lasted more than two decades and a string of technical papers reflecting copious research by leading paleontologists and evolutionary biologists. This is more influence than the overwhelming majority of scientists ever achieve during their careers. On the other hand, the theory was foreshadowed by the work of paleontologist George Gaylord Simpson in the 1940s, which Gould admitted only reluctantly. Moreover, Gould's initial claims as to the revolutionary status of his proposal and the imminent demise of the modern synthesis (see DARWINISM AND UNBELIEF) paradigm that it portended were bold overstatements. They not only sparked partially justified acrimony from the evolutionary community, but arguably gave unnecessary ammunition to the creationist cause by fostering an inaccurate perception that scientists were divided as to the fundamental soundness of evolutionary theory. A 1999 article in the *New Yorker* dubbed Gould "the accidental creationist."

Another of Gould's influential battles was that against sociobiology and biological determinism, which resulted in the publication of a highly influential paper co-authored with Harvard colleague Richard Lewontin in 1979, as well as his book *The Mismeasure of Man* (1981). Again, we see the same pattern of controversy, good but idiosyncratic scholarship, and plain exaggeration. Gould and Lewontin were right in criticizing the then common "adaptationist" assumption in evolutionary biology, which amounts to the proposition that almost anything in living organisms is the result of natural selection. On the other hand, it is also true that—contrary to some of Gould's later statements—natural selection is still the primary explanatory principle in evolution, for the simple reason that it is the only causal factor that we know of that can generate adaptations. In turn, explaining how adaptations come about is really what is most interesting about the Darwinian view of the world, despite Gould's repeated calls to focus on non-adaptive features of living organisms. Similarly, while *The Mismeasure of Man* is a highly readable book that offers much-needed counterpoint to the checkered history of racism in biology, it is ludicrous to dismiss—as Gould did on several occasions—the importance of biological (that is, genetic) factors in explaining some of the variation, not only in physical, but more importantly in cognitive, traits among human beings. Humans result from complex genotype-environment interactions that are reducible neither to simplistic forms of genetic or environmental determinism.

The same mixed pattern holds for Gould's less technical contributions to the intellectual debates of the late twentieth century. On the one hand, he was always adamant that creationism in all its forms is pure nonsense, publicly confronting it on numerous occasions, including a much-publicized 1981 Arkansas trial sometimes dubbed "Scopes II." Yet in his *Rocks of Ages* (1999), he took the fashionable and rather politically correct position that science and religion cannot contradict each other, as they are—to use his somewhat baroque language—two separate and nonoverlapping "magisteria." In this Gould explicitly agreed with Pope John Paul II's equally neat distinction between faith and reason. Of course this concept originated with neither Gould nor John Paul II; it can be traced at least to the mid-nineteenth century, for example, to the writings of John Henry Newman in 1873. More importantly, the soundness of Gould's contention is directly proportional to the vagueness of the concept of "God" that one is willing to espouse. If one's vision of "God" is sufficiently blurry, then it is essentially impossible to find any conflict with empirical evidence, and hence with science. But this is not characteristic of the ongoing debate over science and religion: people who believe that such a conflict exists usually embrace specific concepts of God, which usually include falsifiable (and false!) claims about the physical universe, such as the occurrence of a worldwide flood four thousand years ago. Gould's effort to separate the "magisteria" fails to convince.

Gould concluded his long writing career with additional anthologies of his essays, and most importantly with *The Structure of Evolutionary Theory* (2002), a technical treatise consciously intended as his scientific testament. Once again, and to the end, Gould's contradictions loom large. The book presents an important synthesis of a particular way to look at evolution. Professional biologists must reckon with Gould's vision for a long time to come, either as a reference for further research along the directions outlined by Gould, or as the starting point for criticism and rejection of Gould's view of science and the philosophy of science. However, at Gould's insistence the book was published almost without editorial input, and it shows: it is ponderously long, convoluted, and dotted with irrelevancies. Few would wish something so idiosyncratic and, to many readers, irritating as their permanent legacy. But Gould wanted it that way, and his wishes will inspire and frustrate generations of students and scientists to come.

MASSIMO PIGLIUCCI

GUIGNEBERT, CHARLES (1867–1939), French biblical scholar and critic. One of a "trinity" of French critics (see BIBLICAL CRITICISM) along with Alfred LOISY and Maurice Goguel, Charles Guignebert lectured at the Sorbonne and served as professor of the history of Christianity at the University of Paris. He wrote in the wake of David Friedrich STRAUSS, Rudolf Karl Bultmann, and Albert Schweitzer, assimilating their chief insights, adding many striking observations, and synthesizing the whole into a masterful portrait of Christian origins. Guignebert's arguments are both lucid and judicious, always on guard against premature judgment prompted by either dogmatic allegiance or intolerance for ambiguity.

Guignebert was born on June 18, 1867, at Villeneuve Saint Georges, near Paris. His parents were humble artisans. His father died while Charles was still an infant. His stepfather, a schoolteacher, saw to it that Charles received a good education. First attracted to music, he seriously considered a career as a tenor. But late-blooming research skills set his life in a different direction. His interest in church history first focused on the early 1400s but steadily crept backward to the study of Christian origins.

Though he could not accept either the Christ myth theory, which held that no historical Jesus existed, or the Dutch Radical denial that Paul authored any of the epistles, Guignebert took both quite seriously. Some of his suggestions are quite radical in their own right. He rejected the *Testimonium Flavianum* (Josephus's supposed paragraph about Jesus) as well as the Slavonic Josephus championed by Robert Eisler. Guignebert considered the gospels difficult to date, and thought they had reached us only in reedited form. He believed that they contain but rare scraps of historical truth, and those almost by accident since their authors were not historians but evangelists and propagandists. For Guignebert, the facts of Jesus's life were immediately lost behind the stained glass wall of Christological dogma.

Among Guignebert's contentions: Jesus's birthplace is unknown, Bethlehem being a function of fictive prophetic fulfillment, and "the Nazarene" being no reference to Nazareth but rather, most likely, an epithet equivalent to "the Holy One." "Jesus" itself was probably not the birth name (now lost) of the Galilean prophet, but rather a cultic title meaning "savior." The Virgin Birth doctrine is not even original to the texts of Matthew and Luke, but a later syncretistic import. "Son of God" denoted only "servant of God" in Palestine. It became a metaphysical designation only on Greek soil. Jesus may have been baptized by John, but the gospel account is probably a piece of liturgical fiction, setting the example for the baptized. Jesus's public ministry lasted but a few months or even weeks. The impression of Jesus thronged by crowds is artificial, secondary to the rival notion that he was mostly rejected by contemporaries. He probably had only a dozen or so followers, though "the Twelve" were consolidated as a group only after Jesus's death. The stories of the triumphal entry and cleansing of the temple are both pious fictions; had they occurred, Jesus would have perished then and there. The Passion reflects the bare fact of Jesus's crucifixion (which may not have occurred under Pilate or during Passover), and it has been filled out by scriptural details, drawing especially from Psalm 22. The Romans eliminated Jesus, but the gospels shift the blame gratuitously to the Jewish authorities: Mark to the Sanhedrin, Luke to Herod Antipas. The disciples returned to Galilee, the fishermen continuing together, and Peter's mounting sense that Jesus was alive with God issued in a vision of the living Jesus. They eventually returned to Jerusalem to quietly build a community of the like-minded. Jesus had (erroneously) heralded the imminent end of the age, and the disciples made him into the Messiah who would soon return to inaugurate the kingdom. Like Jesus, they were Torah-observant Jews. Hellenistic Jews with a more cosmopol-

itan outlook soon distanced themselves from Jewish law and particularism, fleeing Jerusalem and initiating the first real evangelism. Paul first opposed the Hellenists but then joined them. He, no doubt like his predecessors, interpreted Jesus as a resurrected savior in the categories of the mystery religions with their sacraments of union with a resurrected god.

Just before World War I Guignebert was active in the movement to separate church and state in France and to free public education from the grip of Catholic dogma. He died on August 27, 1939.

BIBLIOGRAPHY

Guignebert, Charles. *Ancient, Medieval and Modern Christianity: The Evolution of a Religion*. New York: University Books, 1961.
———. *The Christ*. New York: University Books, 1968.
———. *Christianity, Past and Present*. New York: Macmillan, 1927.
———. *The Early History of Christianity: Covering the Period from 33 BC to the Origins of the Papacy*. New York: Twayne, 1950.
———. *Jesus*. New York: University Books, 1956.
———. *The Jewish World in the Time of Jesus*. 2 vols. New York: University Books, 1959.

ROBERT M. PRICE

HACKER, JEREMIAH (1801–1895), American Spiritualist, anarchist, and pacifist. Born at Brunswick, Maine, on May 16, 1801, to American Quaker parents, Jeremiah Hacker received a common school education and worked as a schoolteacher. From 1837 he wandered Maine denouncing "government-craft" and "religious forms of any kind," treating injuries, and stressing the divine inspiration of Jesus within the individual. Widowed in 1839 with nine children, he married Submit Tobey in 1845 and moved with her to Portland, Maine, where he published his weekly *Pleasure Boat* under various titles until 1864. Nearly deaf and known for personal warmth, the "Owner, Master, and Crew" declared he had "launched our little boat upon the waters of love . . . ready to receive passengers on an excursion of pleasure." Militantly abolitionist, giving direct support for fugitive slaves, he opposed war as a solution. While dismissing the ballot as a method for an unjust majority to rule, he fought for women's equality, prison reform, and against land monopoly by developers (see ANARCHISM AND UNBELIEF). Before 1859 he toned down his Christianity and preached as a Spiritualist (see SPIRITUALISM AND UNBELIEF). In 1867 the Hackers moved to Berlin, New Jersey, from where he lectured and briefly resumed publishing his paper. His essays and poems sometimes appeared in *Lucifer* and the *Firebrand* until his death in Vineland, New Jersey, on August 30, 1895.

BIBLIOGRAPHY

Maine Historical Society holds the *Pleasure Boat* (Portland, ME, 1844–47), *Portland Pleasure Boat* (1847–62), and *Chariot of Wisdom and Love* (1864).

Streeter, Donald. "Journal of Jeremiah Hacker with a Biographical Sketch." *Vineland Historical Magazine* 17–19 (1932–1934).

ROBERT P. HELMS

HAECKEL, ERNST HEINRICH (1834–1919), German evolutionary philosopher. Ernst Haeckel was born in Potsdam, Prussia, on February 15, 1834, and died in Jena on August 9, 1919. As a scientist, he is best remembered for his work on radiolarians, his avocation of recapitulation, the idea that "ontogenesis is a brief and rapid recapitulation of phylogenesis, determined by the physiological functions of heredity (generation) and adaptation (maintenance)," and for his neologisms (for example, "phylum," "phylogeny," and "ecology" were all his coinages). It is as a vocal supporter of cosmic evolutionism, however, that he has received his greatest infamy (see EVOLUTION AND UNBELIEF).

Haeckel's reading of Charles DARWIN's *Origin of Species* in the spring of 1860 conclusively changed his life. Abandoning medicine, he became professor of zoology and comparative anatomy at the University of Jena, where he remained until his death. He saw Darwinian natural selection and common descent as a principle that would unify philosophy, politics, and science into a single monistic worldview. As he noted nearly forty years later in *Riddle of the Universe*, his most popular work, this monism "recognizes one sole substance in the universe, which is at once 'God and nature'; body and spirit (or matter and energy) it holds to be inseparable. The extra-mundane God of dualism leads necessarily to theism; and the intra-mundane God of the monist leads to pantheism." Such cosmic pantheism—which he admitted to be a polite form of ATHEISM—led him to deny the immortality of the soul, human free will (see DETERMINISM), and the existence of a personal God (see EXISTENCE OF GOD, ARGUMENTS FOR AND AGAINST). However, this pantheism too had obvious religious overtones, reflecting a certain longing of the Romanticism of the earlier part of the nineteenth century (for this, see the documentary *Proteus*). In his *The Riddle of the Universe*, Haeckel declared that "truth unadulterated is only to be found in the temple of the study of nature" and "the only available paths to it are critical observation and reflection—the empirical investigation of facts and the rational study of their efficient causes. . . . The goddess of truth dwells in the temple of nature, in the green woods, on the blue sea, and on the snowy summits of the hills—not in the gloom of the cloister . . . nor in the clouds of incense of our Christian churches." Anthropocentrism was to be eschewed: humans were as much a part of nature as any other organism, and human body and mind both arose through the inexorable action of natural forces. The continuity of nature was expressed in Haeckel's willingness to draw speculative phylogenies, something Darwin would never have done publicly. Most famously, it led him to predict the existence of a "missing link" between man and ape, which would, he claimed, be found in Southeast Asia. Astonishingly, such a specimen (which he named *Pithecanthropus alalus*, "ape without speech") was subsequently found in Java by Heackel's young disciple Eugene Dubois in 1891.

Haeckel's antipathy toward the Church was obvious. In his *Natural History of Creation*, he saw Christian morality as a distortion of nature. He noted: "If we contemplate the mutual relations between plants and animals (man included), we shall find everywhere and at all times, the very opposite of that kindly and peaceful social life which the goodness of the Creator ought to have prepared for his creatures—we shall rather find everywhere a pitiless, most embittered struggle of all against all." Unlike Darwin's other great popularizer, Thomas Henry HUXLEY, who argued against drawing moral lessons from the natural world, Haeckel felt that such natural struggle offered hope for the intellectual development of humankind. He continued: "The result of the struggle for life is that, in the long run, that which is better, more perfect, conquers that which is weaker and more imperfect. In human life, however, this struggle for life will ever become more and more an intellectual struggle, not a struggle with weapons of murder. . . . The man with the most perfect understanding, not the man with the best revolver, will in the long run be victorious; he will transmit to his descendants the qualities of the brain which assisted him in the victory." Paradoxically, while Haeckel saw struggle and selection all around, he felt that Darwin's mechanism, natural selection, was insufficiently strong to *generate* observed biological diversity. Instead, he believed, the environment acted directly on organisms resulting in new races, thus positing a form of Lamarckianism. Once formed, on Haeckel's view, the *survival* of these races depended on their interaction with the environment through a form of natural selection.

Haeckel's popular writings led to the development of a cult of personality that formalized itself around the Monist League, which he founded in 1906 with the goal of replacing Christianity with a "true religion" of science and reason. The league promoted a concept of society in which natural selection was seen as a natural social principle, and its members held that certain races were more fit than others and would necessarily triumph (see EUGENICS). Some (such as Gasman) have thus argued for Haeckel's influence on the development of National Socialism. This has been contested by others (such as Weikart) who are often more willing to posit (equally erroneously) a more direct lineage running from Darwin to the Nazis. While the origin of Nazi race theory has many factors, certainly Haeckel's rhetoric in many places foreshadows that of the Nazis: In *Freedom in Science and Teaching*, he noted that the "selection, the picking out of these 'chosen ones,' is inevitably connected with the arrest and destruction of the remaining majority." His philosophical support for eugenics and anti-Semitism, when coupled with his undoubted popularity, were perhaps crucial in providing a scientific legitimization for such ideas. It is perhaps notable that, while the Monist League was disbanded when Adolf Hitler became chancellor in 1933, its influence still lives on in the "cosmotheism" advocated by some white supremacists, in particular followers of William Pierce.

BIBLIOGRAPHY

Boelsche, W. *Haeckel: His Life and Work.* London: Fisher Unwin, 1906.

Di Gregorio, M. A. *From Here to Eternity: Ernst Haeckel and Scientific Faith.* Göttingen: Vandenhoeck & Ruprecht, 2005.

Gasman, D. *Haeckel's Monism and the Birth of Fascist Ideology.* New York: Peter Lang, 1998.

———. *The Scientific Origins of National Socialism: Social Darwinism in Ernst Haeckel and the German Monist League.* London: Macdonald, 1971.

Haeckel, E. *Freedom in Science and Teaching.* London: C. Kegan Paul, 1878.

———. *The Natural History of Creation.* 2 vols. New York: Appleton, 1868.

———. *The Riddle of the Universe: At the Close of the Nineteenth Century.* New York: Harper, 1899.

Proteus: A Nineteenth Century Vision, directed by David Lebrun. New York: First Run/Icarus Films, 2004.

Weikart, R. *From Darwin to Hitler: Evolutionary Ethics, Eugenics, and Racism in Germany.* London: Palgrave, 2004.

JOHN M. LYNCH

HALDEMAN-JULIUS, EMANUEL (1889–1951), American freethought publisher. David and Elizabeth Zolajefsky emigrated from Odessa to the United States in 1887, two years before the birth of their fifth child, Emanuel. They had lost one child to illness en route. David Zolajefsky, trained as a bookbinder, was able to find satisfactory work in the new country, though it was his first employer who, out of convenience, changed the name Zolajefsky to Julius. Although both their fathers were rabbis in Russia, neither David nor Elizabeth was particularly religious, but neither were they freethinkers. According to Emanuel, "they were indifferent, for which I thank them." Emanuel Julius was born on July 30, 1889, in Philadelphia.

At thirteen Julius left school to help his family as a wage earner, taking a series of odd jobs. It was during this time that Emanuel's education really started. Although he first began reading dime novels, he soon encountered the writings of Thomas PAINE and Robert Green INGERSOLL. The question of God was soon resolved for good as far as this young boy was concerned, and he became a freethinker. He continued to read voraciously, science and history as well as literature. In his teens Julius discovered the local Socialist Party headquarters in Philadelphia, which he referred to as a "citadel of social consciousness" and began listening to discussions of the older members.

Following his conversion to socialism, Julius moved to New York at age seventeen. In Tarrytown, New York, he worked as a bellboy at the Castle School for Girls, and won the friendship of the kindly librarian of the school, Lilian Parsons, who became a strong influence. She recommended readings and introduced him to the writings of Mark Twain (Samuel CLEMENS).

It was while working at the school that Julius began enthusiastically writing, submitting his articles to Socialist newspapers. Upon Twain's death, he wrote his first bylined article, "Mark Twain: Radical," for the *International Socialist Review*, which gained him some recognition. Soon after, he began working as a copy editor for the *New York Evening Call*, a Socialist newspaper in New York City, whose editor at the time was Louis Kopelin. He and Kopelin became the targets of anti-Semitic attacks from liberals and leftists, people whom Julius thought would have transcended such behavior. This caused a reaction in him that resulted in overwork and overachievement. He developed a level of stamina that would continue throughout his life.

In 1911 Julius was offered a job in Milwaukee with Victor Berger's new Socialist newspaper, the *Leader*. He earned a reputation as a hard worker; assigned work from morning to night, Julius enjoyed the work and was happy to have writing practice.

After gaining valuable writing experience at the *Leader*, Julius went to Chicago in 1913 to work on the *Chicago World*, but didn't stay long before moving to Los Angeles to work with a weekly labor newspaper, the *Citizen*. Shortly afterward he became associate editor of *Western Comrade*, a monthly owned by Stanley Wilson. The paper was not a commercial success, however, and Wilson soon turned its ownership over to Julius. Five months later, although true to his promise of making it a success, he gave up ownership to return to New York to take a position as editor of the Sunday magazine edition of the *Call*.

After a year, Julius was offered a position of staff correspondent of *Appeal to Reason* with his old associate, Louis Kopelin in Girard, Kansas. With a circulation of one million, the *Appeal* was the largest Socialist newspaper in the country. The *Appeal* was suffering as a result of founder J. A. Wayland's suicide in 1912. In addition, its vacillation over the issue of US entry into World War I had caused a drop in circulation. In 1915 Julius left the *Call* and went to Girard, Kansas, to work with Louis Kopelin on the *Appeal*.

In June of 1916 Julius married Marcet Haldeman, a former actress turned banker, heiress, feminist, and niece of Jane ADDAMS of Hull House fame. They were married in the Presbyterian Church, but here convention ceases. At the suggestion of Marcet's aunt Jane, the couple combined their last names to form a new surname: Haldeman-Julius. In addition, they kept their individual incomes separate and split evenly their common expenses. Under an agreement that was made prior to their marriage, Emanuel had no access to Marcet's money. Emanuel and Marcet had two children, Alice and Henry, and a foster child, Josephine.

World War I brought a split in the Socialist Party that affected the *Appeal*'s livelihood. Circulation suffered and, although the majority of members continued to oppose the war, it was only a two-thirds majority. The *Appeal* vacillated on its position for months, until, facing possible violation of the Espionage Act, the paper finally decided to express public support for the war. The name of the paper was changed to *New Appeal*. Haldeman-Julius continued to write for the new paper, eventually becoming part owner with Kopelin and Marcet.

In 1919 Haldeman-Julius began publishing a pocket series of small booklets that were sold for fifteen to twenty-five cents apiece. Covering everything from classic literature and poetry to socialism, FREETHOUGHT, and self-help, the so-called Little Blue Books became big sellers. Among his favorite authors to print were Paine, Ingersoll, and the former priest Joseph McCABE. Haldeman-Julius was a master at promoting these booklets, often changing the original, mundane titles of reprinted texts to more titillating ones. This tactic boosted sales dramatically.

By 1922, with the great success of the pocket series, and with his goal to make literature accessible to all Americans, the *Appeal* was renamed the *Haldeman-Julius Weekly*. It maintained some news reporting and included more book reviews, but essentially became an opinion paper and an advertising medium for the pocket series. Soon Haldeman-Julius introduced another publication, *Life and Letters*, a literary magazine devoting each issue to a particular literary figure. His *Haldeman-Julius Monthly*, begun in 1924, was dedicated to "the memory of that Great Liberator—that Mighty Gladiator in the War on Superstition and Intolerance—VOLTAIRE." One of the earliest issues of the *Monthly* contained an article written by Haldeman-Julius entitled "Religion—a Pile of Garbage." This was Haldeman-Julius's freethought paper, launched during the Scopes monkey trial in Tennessee. In the 1920s the matter of religion in American society was a divisive topic. In 1925 Emanuel and Marcet traveled to Dayton, Tennessee, to report on the Scopes trial, meeting Clarence DARROW there.

In 1925 the name of the pocket series was officially changed to Little Blue Books, and more attention was dedicated to the topic of sex, renaming the category "Social Hygiene." Kopelin sold his part of the business to Haldeman-Julius and returned to New York.

The American Freethinkers' League, founded by Haldeman-Julius in 1925, was an association of freethinkers, anticlericals, believers in free speech, protectors of the torch of reason and science, and warriors "against all forms of rampant Fundamentalism," as promoted in the *Haldeman-Julius Monthly*. Within the first month, membership was reported at 1,628.

In 1928 the *Haldeman-Julius Monthly* became the *Debunker*, and another publication, the *Haldeman-Julius Quarterly*, became the *American Parade*. After authoring a few novels, two of them (*Dust* and *Violence*) in collaboration with his wife, Haldeman-Julius wrote and published *The Outline of Bunk, including The Admirations of a Debunker*. Describing "bunk" as "all attempts to understand and explain life on the basis of subconscious mind, primitive personality, religious mysticism, romanticism, idealism, subjectivism, and other basically irrational isms," the book met with mixed reviews.

In April 1929 Haldeman-Julius launched the *American Freeman*, and even the marketing genius himself could not protect it from the severe grip of the Great Depression. Within a year it was operating at a deficit, but Haldeman-Julius persisted. He started a smear campaign against capitalism in general and against President Herbert Hoover and Vice President Charles Curtin in particular. Each issue and even some special issues of the *American Freeman* contained scathing attacks on them. In 1931, because of continuous financial losses, he combined the *Debunker* and *American Parade* with the *American Freeman*. With the paper's continued attacks on Hoover, circulation increased. The US Post Office deemed the *Freeman* unmailable, bringing more publicity to it than its publisher could have hoped for. After Hoover lost to Franklin D. Roosevelt in 1932 (and Haldeman-Julius lost his bid for the Senate), sales of the *Freeman* slid. Haldeman-Julius introduced yet another new publication, the *Militant Atheist*, which did not do well. A year later he suspended publication, transferred the subscriptions to the *Freeman*, and slowed that paper's frequency to a monthly. With unflinching dedication, the publishing company survived the Depression years, and the Little Blue Books and the *American Freeman* survived as well.

Marcet and Emanuel's relationship deteriorated over the years, mainly due to money and Emanuel's womanizing. Although they technically continued living under the same roof, Marcet spent a lot of her time at the family farm in Cedarville. Their financial statuses had reversed, Marcet having transferred most of her stock to the publishing company in the 1920s. Because of their agreement when they married always to keep their financial matters separate, she struggled constantly to make ends meet. Marcet suffered from a weak heart and died in 1941. There is no indication that Emanuel mourned her death.

Haldeman-Julius continued to advertise the Little Blue Books, offering special sales on the entire collection and discounts on individual titles. At the same time he attacked convention and religion, particularly the Catholic Church and the pope, in the pages of the *Freeman*. Joseph McCabe, one of Haldeman-Julius's most prolific sources for Blue Book titles, obliged him with ever more anti-Catholic works. Controversy over the advertising of these titles brought more and more publicity.

In 1950 Haldeman-Julius was indicted for tax fraud, and in 1951 he was found guilty on two counts of income tax evasion. He was awaiting appeal when he drowned in the swimming pool of his Girard estate.

The years of high energy, feverish writing, hectic publishing schedules, frequent title changes of his publications, and an action-packed lifestyle, countered by "long fits of depression," suggest that Haldeman-Julius might have suffered from bipolar disorder. His persistent and outspoken debunking was much appreciated by the freethinking public, which certainly benefited from the work of the "Henry Ford of literature."

BIBLIOGRAPHY

Cothran, Andrew Neilson. "The Little Blue Book Man and the Big American Parade: A Biography of Emanuel Haldeman-Julius." PhD diss., University of Maryland, 1966.
Stein, Gordon, ed. *The Encyclopedia of Unbelief.* Amherst, NY: Prometheus Books, 1985.
Whitehead, Fred, and Verle Muhrer, eds. *Freethought on the American Frontier.* Amherst, NY: Prometheus Books, 1992.

JULIE HERRADA

HALL, SHARLOT (1870–1943), American freethought lecturer. Born October 27, 1870, in frontier Kansas to a literate mother and an illiterate father, Sharlot Hall was given her Native American first name by her uncle. Her family moved near Prescott, then to Dewey, Arizona. Bright and talented, Sharlot chafed at the monotony and isolation of ranch life. To escape, she worked for room and board for a half year in order to attend Prescott High School. She also began writing, and received her first payment for a story early in her teens. Her mother's illness forced her return to the rigors of domestic duties and outdoor work. Observing the lot of her mother and most women she knew, Sharlot vowed never to marry. She became interested in photography and explored ancient Native American cliff dwellings with her brother.

Sharlot and her family attended lectures by freethinker Samuel Porter PUTNAM in Prescott in 1895. She joined Putnam on the platform in his final speech, speaking about Thomas PAINE. She was twenty-four to Putnam's fifty-six, but apparently fell in love. Putnam died from a gas leakage in 1896. His fully clothed body was found in a hotel room with that of a clothed young woman lecturer, Mary L. Collins. The hint of impropriety created scandalous national headlines. Although Putnam's death was a great shock to Hall, she commemorated his memory with poetry published in *THE TRUTH SEEKER.*

Hall wrote for many newspapers, and became the protégée of Charles F. Lummis, editor of *Land of Sunshine* in Los Angeles. Through Lummis, she met freethinking luminaries of her day, including Charlotte Perkins GILMAN. Two volumes of her poetry, including occasional irreverent verse, were published. Hall began a project of taking oral histories of Arizona pioneers. In 1909 territorial governor Judge Richard Sloan, her friend, made her territorial historian. She was granted an office in Phoenix and traveled throughout the state collecting history, supported by the Federation of Women's Clubs. After Arizona achieved statehood, the first governor dismissed her in 1912. Soon after, her mother died. Hall retired to a nearly reclusive lifestyle, caring for her father until his death in 1925. In 1927, when she was fifty-seven, the city of Prescott awarded Hall a life lease on the governor's mansion, to restore it as a museum of early Arizona history. She died of heart trouble on April 9, 1943. The mansion and the Sharlot Hall Museum remain open.

BIBLIOGRAPHY

Maxwell, Margaret F. *A Passion for Freedom: The Life of Sharlot Hall.* Tucson: University of Arizona Press, 1928.
Wright, Nancy Kirkpatrick, ed. *Sharlot Herself: Selected Writings of Sharlot Hall.* Prescott, AZ: Sharlot Hall Museum, 1992.

ANNIE LAURIE GAYLOR

HANLON, JAMES OGDEN (1899–1986), New Zealand rationalist and journalist. James Ogden Hanlon was born and lived most of his life in Auckland, New Zealand. His father had been Catholic but at some point became a rationalist, and brought up his son that way. Hanlon worked as a cub reporter before he enlisted for service in the First World War. After his demobilization he returned to journalism, working most of his life for Auckland's evening paper, the *Auckland Star.* As a young reporter for the *Star* in 1923, Hanlon covered the lectures given by Joseph MCCABE in Auckland. This was a defining moment in Hanlon's life.

After a ten-year stint in the United Kingdom working on provincial newspapers, Hanlon returned to New Zealand and his job with the *Star* in 1938. He also joined the Rationalist Association, and over the course of his half century of membership served as vice president three times between 1945 and 1961, and as president from 1955 until 1958 and again, briefly, between August 1958 and May 1959. But his main contribution was in his role as editor of the *New Zealand Rationalist*, which in October 1964 became the *New Zealand Rationalist and Humanist*. Hanlon served as editor from September 1939 to March 1942, late 1943 to May 1953, May 1955 to August 1958, October to December 1959, August 1961 to November 1973, and February 1974 until September 1975. During these twenty-nine years Hanlon wrote 218 editorials and a great many other articles, shorter contributions, and several pamphlets. Hanlon was one of the longest-serving editors of any publication in freethought history, ranking alongside Charles Albert WATTS with the *Literary Guide*, Horace SEAVER with the *BOSTON INVESTIGATOR*, and Chapman COHEN with the *FREETHINKER*.

In some ways Hanlon stayed on too long, becoming something of a liability in his later years. His rationalism was very strongly influenced by McCabe, Cohen, and the RATIONALIST PRESS ASSOCIATION. He became progressively less able to adapt as rationalism gave way to HUMANISM in the 1960s. Very appropriately, however, Hanlon was made a life member of the Rationalist Association in 1955.

Hanlon was also active in the Worker's Educational Association, the Howard League for Penal Reform, and the Voluntary Euthanasia Society of England. He married Alice Horspool in 1928. They had no children.

BIBLIOGRAPHY

Cooke, Bill. *Heathen in Godzone: Seventy Years of Rationalism in New Zealand*. Auckland, NZ: New Zealand Assoication of Rationalists and Humanists, 1998.

BILL COOKE

HANSBERRY, LORRAINE (1930–1965), American playwright, painter, and humanist. Lorraine Hansberry's *A Raisin in the Sun*, the first drama by a black woman to be produced on Broadway, won the New York Drama Critics' Circle Award for best play of 1959, chosen over plays by such celebrated figures as Tennessee Williams and Eugene O'Neill. With this success Hansberry became the first black woman intellectual to achieve national celebrity status.

Hansberry was born in Chicago. Her uncle was a leading African American scholar; her parents often hosted black celebrities at their home, including Joe Louis, Jesse Owens, Paul Robeson, Duke Ellington, and civil rights leader Walter White.

In 1950 Hansberry went to work for *Freedom*, a paper published by Robeson. She became actively involved in civil rights struggles. Her influence increased, and she became the associate editor of *Freedom*. The following year, she studied African culture and history under W. E. B. DuBois at the Jefferson School for Social Science. In that same year, she married songwriter Robert Nemiroff. The couple divorced in 1964.

A Raisin in the Sun was based on Hansberry's real-life experience. To challenge racist real estate practices, Hansberry's parents bought a house in a predominantly white neighborhood near the University of Chicago in 1938. A mob tried to run them out of the community. The family sued, eventually winning an important 1940 US Supreme Court decision (*Hansberry v. Lee*). The title *A Raisin in the Sun* was borrowed from a Langston HUGHES poem: "What happens to a dream deferred?/Does it dry up/like a raisin in the sun?/. . ./Or does it explode?"

Hansberry was outspoken about her SECULAR HUMANISM. In her works she never recognized God or transcendent morality. She believed human beings could conquer their problems with the use of reason, and that so long as there was suffering and injustice in the world, attempts to make the world a better place would give human beings all the meaning in life they would ever need.

Hansberry was a lesbian, feminist, and socialist, but her primary interest was in fighting against white supremacy and liberating black people. However, many black people—intellectuals included—have erroneously believed that Hansberry was sympathetic to the idea that Christianity could be a liberating force in the lives of black people. Hansberry said in an interview that people revert to religion when they are afraid, but she expressed confidence that rationality would triumph in the end.

On January 12, 1965, Hansberry succumbed to cancer at the age of thirty-four. However, *To Be Young, Gifted, and Black* was culled from her writings and produced off Broadway in 1969. *A Raisin in the Sun* continues to thrill audiences in numerous regional theater productions throughout the United States.

BIBLIOGRAPHY

Carter, Steven R. *Hansberry's Drama: Commitment amid Complexity*. Urbana and Chicago: University of Illinois Press, 1991.

Hansberry, Lorraine. *Les Blancs: The Collected Last Plays of Lorraine Hansberry*. New York: Viking, 1973.

———. *A Raisin in the Sun (Expanded Twenty-fifth Anniversary Edition) and The Sign in Sidney Brustein's Window*. Edited by Robert Nemiroff. New York: New American Library, 1987.

———. *To Be Young, Gifted, and Black: Lorraine Hansberry in Her Own Words*. Adapted by Robert Nemiroff. New York: New American Library, 1973.

NORM R. ALLEN JR.

HARMAN, LILLIAN (1869–1929), American sex radical and editor. At the age of sixteen, Lillian Harman challenged the marriage laws of Kansas by entering into a "free (nonchurch, nonstate) marriage" with thirty-seven-year-old Edwin C. Walker. Her subsequent role in the publication of *Lucifer, The Light-Bearer*; *Fair Play*; *Our New Humanity*; and the *American Journal of EUGENICS* brought her international recognition.

Childhood. The daughter of Moses and Susan (Scheuck) Harman, Lillian was born in Crawford County, Missouri, in December 1869. Her mother died when she was seven, and in 1879 her father moved Lillian and her brother, George, to the rural community of Valley Falls, Kansas. Immersing himself in the local chapter of the NATIONAL LIBERAL LEAGUE, he became coeditor of the league's paper, the *Valley Falls Liberal*, which in 1883, as sole editor, he renamed *Lucifer, The Light-Bearer*. As thirteen-year-old Lillian set type for her father's paper, she learned about such causes as women's sexual emancipation and the freedom of the press to address sexual topics.

The Free Marriage. Lillian Harman chose to protest church- and state-sanctioned marriage because of the power it gave a husband to control his wife's property, identity, and body (see SEX RADICALISM AND UNBELIEF). Arrested and convicted for violating the Kansas Marriage Act, she served time in jail for refusing to pay court costs. Publicity surrounding her free marriage transformed Harman into a national icon for women's sexual emancipation and prompted sex radical women and others to debate such feminist issues as age-of-consent legislation and marital rape, and to challenge authorities denying them access to sexual information. It also helped swell *Lucifer*'s subscription list, transforming the struggling regional weekly into the nation's leading voice for sex radicalism.

Sex Radical Activism. Upon her release from jail in 1887, Harman assumed a more active role in the publication of *Lucifer*, and in 1888 she and Walker established their own anarchist publication, *Fair Play*, which was published intermittently until its demise in 1908. In the 1890s and 1900s she aided her father in the publication of the short-lived *Our New Humanity* and *American Journal of Eugenics*, which ceased after Moses HARMAN's death in 1910. Her published works include *Some Problems of Social Freedom* (1898), *Marriage and Mortality* (1900), and *The Regeneration of Society* (1900).

Committed to the cause of free motherhood, in 1893 Harman chose to have a child with Walker (even though they lived separately for much of their married life). Before becoming a "free mother," she required him to sign a document stipulating that he would provide his share of support for the child, whom she named Virna Winifred Walker. Lillian Harman's commitment to sex radical activism earned her international recognition in 1897 when she became president of the Legitimation League, established in England in 1893 to advocate the legitimacy of nonmarital sexual relations and to ensure that partners and their offspring would have the same rights of property and inheritance. Writing numerous articles for *Adult* (the league's journal, published between 1897 and 1899), she campaigned against age-of-consent legislation because of the limits it placed on women's freedom. Harman regarded reformers like Frances Willard of the Woman's Christian Temperance Union as well-intentioned but misguided, because they promoted the image of women as sexually vulnerable.

Later Years. In the early 1900s Harman married a radical Chicago newspaper printer named George R. O'Brien and in 1910 he became president of the Chicago Typographical Union. Their son, George Harman O'Brien, studied law and Harman's daughter became a musician and dancer. Little else is known about Lillian Harman's life after the *American Journal of Eugenics* ceased publication in 1910. She died around 1929.

BIBLIOGRAPHY

Harman, John William. *Harman-Harmon Genealogy and Biography*. Parsons, WV: Author, 1928.

Passet, Joanne. *Sex Radicals and the Quest for Women's Equality*. Chicago and Urbana: University of Illinois Press, 2003.

Sears, Hal D. *The Sex Radicals: Free Love in High Victorian America*. Lawrence: Regents Press of Kansas, 1977.

JOANNE E. PASSET

HARMAN, MOSES (1830–1910), American free-love activist. One of the most fervent and dedicated male feminist activists in US history, Moses Harman was born in Virginia to Job and Nancy Harman, and grew up in the Ozarks of Missouri. His parents farmed, mined, and wove baskets: subsistence living, to be sure. Moses attended only a few months of school, but, partly due to an accident that left him lame, he was an avid reader. He began teaching school at the age of sixteen, and two years later started his formal studies.

An ordained Methodist minister by the age of twenty, at twenty-one he discovered the Universalists (see UNIVERSALISM TO 1961) and preferred their antislavery position. He continued to teach and study, traveling but eventually returning to Missouri. By that time he was an outspoken abolitionist, not a popular stand in Crawford County; his views nearly got him killed. He tried to enlist in the Union army, but was rejected twice because of his physical disability.

Following the Civil War, Harman married Susan Scheuck and had two children, George and Lillian HARMAN. Although it was a conventional marriage ceremony, the two entered into an agreement vowing a relationship based on love rather than obligation (see SEX RADICALISM AND UNBELIEF). Susan died in childbirth, along with their third child. Harman took George and Lillian to live on a farm with his cousin Noah Harman in Valley Falls, Kansas.

After participating in an exchange in the local Valley

Falls paper, the *New Era*, between religionists and free-thinkers (see FREETHOUGHT), Harman and some other freethinkers began publishing a paper under the auspices of the Valley Falls Liberal League, an organization devoted to the separation of church and state. In 1880 Harman began editing the *Valley Falls Liberal*. The named was later changed to the *Kansas Liberal*.

Two years later, the *Kansas Liberal* became *Lucifer, The Light Bearer*, a free-love periodical that advocated total equality between men and women and openly discussed the sexual aspects of their relationships. In addition to *Lucifer*, Harman also published a number of pamphlets on similar topics. An individualist anarchist (see ANARCHISM AND UNBELIEF) and proponent for absolute freedom of speech, Harman would not censor any articles or letters, resulting in continuous harassment by the authorities for violations of the Comstock Act (see COMSTOCK, ANTHONY, AND UNBELIEF). The first violation came in June 1886, when he published a letter depicting an incident of sexual abuse in a marriage, referring to it as "rape." Moses, George, and Edwin C. Walker were arrested and indicted on 270 counts of obscenity. Walker, incidentally, was already in jail, along with Lillian, for entering into a non-state-sanctioned marriage. The obscenity charges against George Harman and Walker were soon dropped, but Moses stood trial and was found guilty on four counts of obscenity. Although initially sentenced to five years' imprisonment, he served only four months. He was again tried for obscenity on a separate charge, and this time served eight months. To keep *Lucifer* going during this time, he appointed Lois WAISBROOKER as coeditor. She followed the house tradition by publishing an article over which *Lucifer* was banned from the mails. After his release, Harman was sentenced again on another charge, and served one year of hard labor.

Many supporters of Harman and *Lucifer* considered his actions unwise; he was criticized by some for creating his own problems with the law by printing articles sure to get him arrested, but most were sympathetic and felt he received excessive punishment. Thousands signed petitions criticizing the unjust treatment he received. Upon his release from prison in 1896, Harman moved to Chicago, taking *Lucifer* with him.

In 1905 Harman was again arrested on obscenity charges and at the age of seventy-five was sentenced to one year of hard labor at Joliet Prison. He spent eight months breaking rocks and became so ill that he was transferred to Leavenworth, to complete his sentence in the hospital there.

The constant government harassment against *Lucifer* began to wear thin, while at the same time Harman became increasingly interested in the topic of birth control and a woman's right to choose if, when, and with whom to bear children. In 1907 *Lucifer* became the *American Journal of EUGENICS*. Harman relocated to Los Angeles in 1908, continuing to publish the *Journal*. He died there in 1910, and Lillian published a final memorial issue.

Lucifer, The Light Bearer is still considered one of the most influential and compelling feminist newspapers in US history.

BIBLIOGRAPHY

McElroy, Wendy. "Moses Harman: The Paradigm of a Male Feminist." 2001. http://www.ifeminists.net/introduction/editorials/2001/0220.html.
Sears, Hal D. *The Sex Radicals: Free Love in High Victorian America*. Lawrence: Regents Press of Kansas, 1977.
Whitehead, Fred, and Verle Muhrer. *Freethought on the American Frontier*. Amherst, NY: Prometheus Books, 1992.

JULIE HERRADA

HARRISON, HUBERT HENRY (1883–1927), American humanist activist. One of the greatest intellectuals and orators of his day, Hubert Henry Harrison was born in Concordia, St. Croix, Danish West Indies, and arrived in New York City in 1900. Over the next seven years, he abandoned Christianity and embraced FREETHOUGHT.

In 1911 he became a leading proponent of socialism as a member of the Socialist Party (see SOCIALISM AND UNBELIEF). Later, he became disenchanted with and criticized the party's racism, and was subsequently suspended. Due in large part to his negative experiences with the socialists, Harrison developed his concepts of "Africa first" or "race first." Though he opposed racism in all its forms, he believed people of African descent had to put their interests as a people above all other interests, including class interests.

In 1917 he introduced activist Marcus Garvey to a large meeting of his own organization, the Liberty League, at a Harlem church. Garvey founded the Universal Negro Improvement Association (UNIA), one of the largest mass movements of black people in US history. In 1920 Harrison became the managing editor of the UNIA newspaper the *Negro World*. Though he later he became critical of Garvey and left the UNIA, he continued to contribute to the *Negro World*.

Harrison was perhaps first of a long line of Harlem street orators, or "street scholars," his oratorical skills enthralling as many as eleven thousand people at a time. In scathing attacks upon religion, he called attention to biblical contradictions and absurd biblical ideas. He urged audiences to read the lectures of Robert Green INGERSOLL, Thomas PAINE's *Age of Reason*, Andrew Dickson WHITE's *Warfare of Science with Theology*, and other classics of freethought. He critiqued the so-called myth of Ham, the claim that a curse placed upon Canaan (son of Ham) by his grandfather Noah doomed the black race to eternal subservience. He acidly noted that while God, Jesus, the Holy Ghost, and the angels were all depicted as whites, the only powerful black character in the Christian drama was the devil. Harrison said that freethought should be more widespread among African Americans, who were, after all, among the most oppressed victims of Christianity. He emphasized that despite lip service given to Christian love, blacks were not even allowed to pray in white churches.

Consistent in his commitment to universal human rights, Harrison also championed the white working class, fought for Irish home rule, and supported liberation struggles in China and India. He won admiration from Americans from all walks of life, and thousands paid homage at his funeral.

BIBLIOGRAPHY

Allen, Norm R. "Humanism in Political Action." In *By These Hands: A Documentary History of African American History*, edited by Anthony B. Pinn. New York: New York University Press, 2001.

Harrison, Henry H. *When Africa Awakes*. Baltimore: Black Classic Press, 1997.

———. "On a Certain Conservatism in Negroes." In *By These Hands: A Documentary History of African American History*, edited by Anthony B. Pinn. New York: New York University Press, 2001.

Inniss, Patrick. "Hubert Henry Harrison: Great African American Freethinker." *AAH Examiner* (Winter 1994–95).

Perry, Jeffrey B., ed. *A Hubert Harrison Reader*. Middletown, CT: Wesleyan University Press, 2001.

Ragland, John. "Atheists of a Different Color." *American Atheist* (February 1987).

Rogers, Joel A. "Hubert H. Harrison; Intellectual Giant and Freelance Educator." In *World's Great Men of Color*, Vol. 2. New York: Macmillan, 1947. Republished in *African-American Humanism: An Anthology*, ed. Norm R. Allen Jr. Amherst, NY: Prometheus Books, 1991.

NORM R. ALLEN JR.

HARTMANN, KARL ROBERT EDUARD VON (1842–1906), German philosopher and pessimist. Karl Robert Eduard von Hartmann was originally an artillery officer in the Prussian army; he turned to philosophy after an injury ended his military career. Returning to Berlin, where he would spend the rest of his life, he wrote most of his work while in bed, suffering great pain from his leg wound. Following in the footsteps of Arthur SCHOPENHAUER, he argued that the basis of ethics should be grounded in a realization of the utter futility of life. Combining Schopenhauer's pessimistic metaphysics with the ethical writings of Immanuel KANT and the process philosophy of George Hegel, von Hartmann published a series of books which received wide recognition and made him one of the best-known thinkers of his day.

Von Hartmann's first and most popular work, *Die Philosophie des Unbewussten* (The Philosophy of the Unconscious), was published in 1869, and became an immediate best seller. In it, he advocated what he called "Spiritual Monism," the view that matter is both idea and will. The opposition of these two forces accidentally created the existence of consciousness.

The existence of consciousness creates a problem, though, as conscious beings become increasingly aware of the misery of the world around them. The evolution of human beings, with their highly developed awareness of their world, led to three stages in the attempt to combat pessimism. The first stage claimed that happiness is possible in the here-and-now (and was identified with the rise of the Roman Empire and its claims to have pacified the world). When this was found untenable, the second stage arose, which claimed that happiness would be found in the next world (as found in the doctrines of PLATO, Christianity, and Islam). The third stage, identified with the rise of POSITIVISM and socialism (see SOCIALISM AND UNBELIEF), claimed that true happiness would be found in a future state of earthly utopia.

Yet, von Hartmann argued, increasingly consciousness shows that all three stages are mere wishful thinking. This is indeed the best of all possible worlds, but it would be much better if no world existed at all. The growing awareness of this fact will eventually lead to a cooperative effort among all conscious beings to bring about the end of existence. Suicide would not be sufficient, as this would merely eliminate individuals, not the entire human species. And even the complete destruction of human life would not suffice, as other life-forms would eventually become conscious and experience the same futility. Therefore, the proper goal would be for the total development of all particular wills to the point where consciousness would be developed to its fullest potential and where the final solution—the termination of all life itself—could be arrived upon through cooperative effort.

Von Hartmann thought this was the epitome of ethical thinking, as it gave a common end (teleology) that could truly unite all beings. Previous attempts to ground ethics upon formal principles, pursuit of pleasure, or transcendental wish-fulfillment were doomed to failure, because they are false and the evolving consciousness would see through such falsehoods eventually (see ETHICS AND UNBELIEF). Surprisingly enough, von Hartmann's advocacy of (eventual) mass destruction met with an enthusiastic audience, and his unique approach to pessimism made him a popular writer until his death in 1906. Among other things, von Hartmann was a strong critic of liberal Protestant Christianity, which he felt to be the last gasp of the Christian transcendental ethics. The Social Gospel movement, which tried to shift the emphasis of Christian teachings from the next world to bettering the present earthly condition, was merely a move from the second to the third stage of optimistic illusion.

A few reasons for von Hartmann's popularity include the clarity of his writing style, his usage of up-to-date scientific findings, and his rejection of the shallow religious and secular utopian movements of his time. In addition, the paradoxical view that human beings—and indeed all life-forms—could be united under one common project was appealing to those of a universalist point of view, even if that project was the end of all life itself. Still, after his own cessation of being, von Hartmann's writings fell into obscurity, and were superceded by more vehemently nihilistic movements of the twentieth century (see NIHILISM). Freethinkers can nonetheless benefit from his criticisms of transcendental escapism and reflect upon his objections to secular utopian visions.

BIBLIOGRAPHY

Darnoi, Dennis. *The Unconscious and Eduard von Hartmann: A Historico-Critical Monograph.* The Hague: Nijhoff, 1967.

Hall, G. Stanley. *Founders of Modern Psychology.* New York: Appleton, 1912.

Von Hartmann, Eduard. *Philosophy of the Unconscious: Speculative Results According to the Inductive Method of Physical Science.* London: Kegan Paul, 1931.

TIMOTHY J. MADIGAN

HAWTON, HECTOR (1901–1975), English humanist and author. One of the most significant humanists in postwar Britain (see HUMANISM), Hector Hawton was born on February 7, 1901, into an ardently Protestant family and raised on *Foxe's Book of Martyrs* and *Pilgrim's Progress.* His father worked as a railway engineer. Partly in rebellion against his upbringing, Hawton converted to Catholicism at the age of fifteen. He remained a Catholic until his early thirties, when study of science and philosophy led him briefly to MARXISM before he became a humanist.

Hawton's career was built around his prodigious capacity to write. He worked as a journalist on Fleet Street before moving to Hampshire to earn his living as a writer, turning his hand to romantic fiction (under the pseudonym "Virginia Curzon"), children's adventures (under the pseudonym "John Sylvester"), detective stories (under the pseudonym "Jack Lethaby"), and serials for magazines. A feature of his novels was his ability to create three-dimensional female characters. During World War II he worked for Bomber Command's Group Four at Heslington Hall in York. He wrote two books on aspects of the Royal Air Force's war effort.

After the war, Hawton became active in the humanist movement. He was secretary of the SOUTH PLACE ETHICAL SOCIETY from 1948 until 1954, and was an active participant in the establishment of the INTERNATIONAL HUMANIST AND ETHICAL UNION in 1952. But it was in his work with the RATIONALIST PRESS ASSOCIATION (RPA) that his biggest contribution was made. Between 1953 and 1960 Hawton oversaw a radical downsizing of the RPA that saved the organization from financial ruin. At the same time, he guided the RPA's journal through one of its finest periods. Hawton edited the *Humanist* (he had dropped the previous title, *Literary Guide*) from 1953 until 1971, and again from 1974 until his death in 1975. During his editorship the *Humanist* was a very good magazine indeed, with a wide range of good quality articles from capable authorities. Most of the main thinkers of postwar Britain had an article in the *Humanist* at some time or other. And under a series of pseudonyms, Hawton contributed mightily himself. His most important pseudonym was "R. J. Mostyn," though "Humphrey Skelton," "James Plender," "George Robinson," "Jonathan Yeo," and "W. B. Pengelly" also discharged frequent assignments.

Hawton's unusually wide reading and clarity of style made his humanist books the best then available. His major nonfiction works include *Men without Gods* (1948); *Philosophy for Pleasure* (1949), which had a long career on the American paperback market; *The Thinker's Handbook* (1950), thought by many to be his best; *The Feast of Unreason* (1952), a brilliant demolition of existentialism; *The Humanist Revolution* (1963); and *Controversy* (1971).

Hawton continued to write fiction through these years, now mostly under his own name. And in his spare time he ghostwrote most of the books attributed to popular psychologist and fellow humanist Eustace Chesser. Chesser titles written by Hawton include *Love without Fear*, *Unmarried Love*, and *Grammar of Marriage.*

Hector Hawton was loved by his friends as a raconteur, drinking companion, and friend. He died on December 14, 1975. He was survived by his second wife, Mary Hawton (née Ferretti), and two sons.

BIBLIOGRAPHY

Cooke, Bill. *The Gathering of Infidels: A Hundred Years of the Rationalist Press Association.* Amherst, NY: Prometheus Books, 2004.

"Hector Hawton." *New Humanist* 91, no. 10 (February 1976).

BILL COOKE

HEDENIUS, INGEMAR (1908–1982). See SWEDEN, UNBELIEF IN.

HEINE, HEINRICH (HARRY) (1797–1856), German writer.

Life. Heinrich (Harry) Heine was born in Düsseldorf to tradesman Samson Heine and his wife, Betty, both assimilated Jews. From 1815 to 1819 Heine studied law at the universities of Bonn, Göttingen, and Berlin. In order to evade discrimination on account of his Jewish heritage, he converted to Protestantism and changed his first name to Christian Johann Heinrich in 1825. In the same year he obtained his doctorate at Göttingen, but even armed with a baptismal certificate, he failed to find an employment as a civil servant. From 1825 to 1831 Heine lived as a writer in Lüneburg, Hamburg, Munich, and Berlin. Then he went into self-declared exile in Paris, where he worked as a correspondent for various German newspapers. After a physical collapse due to a still-unknown illness in 1848, Heine was confined to bed until his death in 1856. He is buried in Montmartre Cemetery.

Major Works. Heine's works deeply reflect the struggle between liberal and restorative forces of the *Vormärz*, the years between the German war of independence (1813–15) and the 1848 revolution. While his early publications, such as *Book of Songs* (*Buch der Lieder*, 1827), are characterized by romanticism, later texts display an increasingly ironic use of romantic style as well as a turn toward political subjects.

Heine gained fame with his *Pictures of Travel* (*Reisebilder*, 1826–31), in which he satirically criticized the contemporary German restoration, the government's attempt to shatter the achievements of Enlightenment and to restore pre-Napoleonic conditions.

French Affairs (*Französische Zustände*, 1833), an anthology of newspaper articles, describes the political and social conditions in post-revolutionary France. In it Heine also criticizes the German authorities' tightened censorship. Only two years later, the works of several liberal writers, among them Heine himself, were banned, accused of being destructive of morality and an assault on the Christian religion.

In later works, such as *Religion and Philosophy in Germany* (*Zur Geschichte der Religion und Philosophie in Deutschland*, 1835), Heine emerged as a leading opponent of the conservative alliance between clergy and nobility in Germany.

In the mid-1840s Heine wrote epic poems, especially "Germany: A Winter's Tale" (*Deutschland. Ein Wintermärchen*, 1844), attacking the authoritarian Prussian German state by contrasting it to an egalitarian earthly paradise. *The Gods in Exile* (*Die Götter im Exil*, 1852–53), one of his last works, compares pagan and Christian mythology. It can be regarded as a summary of Heine's conception of history, in which, just as Christianity replaced paganism, in its turn Christianity will be replaced by Communism.

BIBLIOGRAPHY

Heine, Heinrich. *The Poems of Heine, Complete.* New York: Gordon, 1977.

Höhn, Gerhard. *Heine-Handbuch. Zeit—Person—Werk.* Stuttgart: Metzler, 1997.

Kortländer, Bernd. *Heinrich Heine.* Stuttgart: Reclam, 2003.

Kruse, Joseph A., Martin Hollander, and Ulrike Renter,
eds. *Ich Narr des Glücks. Heinrich Heine 1797–1856. Bilder einer Ausstellung.* Stuttgart: Metzler, 1997.

Liedtke, Christian. *Heinrich Heine.* Reinbek: Rowohlt, 1997.

INGE HÜSGEN

HELL-FIRE CLUBS. "Hell-fire clubs" is the collective name for a style of underground club, established in the eighteenth century by members of the English aristocracy, that became notorious for black masses, orgies, and the consumption of inordinate quantities of alcohol. On occasions hell-fire club rampages ended up with people being killed, but the privileged social standing of the club members ensured that they escaped punishment.

The hell-fire clubs emerged alongside a movement of heretical Freemasons known as the Gomorgons, which parodied extravagant Masonic rituals. The first hell-fire club was founded in 1719 by two Freemasons, the duke of Wharton and the earl of Litchfield. Wharton was also a prominent member of the Gomorgons. The group, known as the "unholy twelve," met at the Greyhound Tavern in London before moving to the George and Vulture in 1746. Their tenure at the George and Vulture ended in 1749 when the pub burned down, probably after a club meeting got out of hand. This club went under a variety of satirical titles. At various times it was the Brotherhood of St. Francis of Wycombe, named after a leading personality, Sir Francis Dashwood, MP; later on it was known as the Monks of Medmenham, after the abandoned twelfth-century Cistercian abbey where the club met after 1755. One of the members had bought the site and rebuilt to it the fashionable gothic taste, whereupon it became a playground for the club. It disbanded in 1762 due to internal disputes and heavy outside pressure, but many new clubs, now openly called hell-fire clubs, formed in its place. At its peak it had included very senior British politicians including a prime minister and a chancellor of the exchequer, as well as the artist William Hogarth and the American diplomat Benjamin FRANKLIN.

A friend of Wharton's and possibly another Gomorgon was Richard Parsons, the first earl of Rosse, who created the first Irish hell-fire club in Dublin in 1735. The president of the club was called "the King of Hell" and the position of vice president was usually left vacant for Satan, to whom a toast was drunk. Other clubs were established in the United States. From this time on, the generic title "hell-fire club" was applied to aristocratic entertainments of this sort. Hell-fire clubs revived in popularity during the Regency period when, under the influence of the mercurial poet Lord BYRON, Dionysian excess became once again fashionable.

BIBLIOGRAPHY

Ashe, Geoffrey. *The Hell-Fire Clubs*. Lanham, MD: National Book Network, 2000.

BILL COOKE

HELVÉTIUS, CLAUDE-ADRIEN (1715–1771), French philosopher and Enlightenment figure. A tax collector by profession, Claude-Adrien Helvétius was the son of a physician to the queen of France, which did not stop him from becoming a strong critic of both the French government in general and the monarchy in particular. He was one of the best-known figures of the French Enlightenment, and was on personal terms with Jean-Jacques ROUSSEAU, Denis DIDEROT, Jean LeRond D'Alembert, and VOLTAIRE—all of whom, however, distanced themselves from his outspoken criticism of religion.

Called an "atheist" by his critics (see ATHEISM), Helvétius was in fact a thorough-going materialist (see MATERIALISM, PHILOSOPHICAL). His *De l'esprit* (On the Mind), published in 1758, was an exploration of the origins and influences of human intelligence. It was based in part on the sensation psychology of John LOCKE, and agreed with Locke that the human mind at birth is a tabula rasa, or blank slate, which becomes activated by the various sensations it experiences. The book also revised the ancient philosophy of Epicureanism (see EPICURUS), arguing that human beings are motivated primarily by pleasure and pain, and construct a world of ideas based upon this. Interesting enough, he was also a forerunner of chaos theory—he argued that trivial and chance events could have far-reaching and unanticipated consequences. Helvétius reduced all human behavior to pure self-interest, which not only scandalized many of his fellow philosophes but enraged the powers that be as well. The Sorbonne (the theological faculty of the University of Paris) and the Parlement of Paris issued condemnations of the book, which was then publicly burned. It was also denounced by Pope Clement XIII. Helvétius was forced to recant and found it prudent to leave France, traveling first to England and then to Prussia, where he was welcomed by the Enlightenment emperor Frederick the Great. Even Frederick had qualms about Helvétius's radical materialistic and hedonistic views, which were similar to the views of Julien LA METTRIE, author of *L'Homme machine* (Man, a Machine), a fellow exile in Frederick's Berlin.

Helvétius was elected a member of the Berlin Academy, and while in that city wrote his second major work, *De l'homme, de ses facultés intellectuelles et de son éducation* (On Man, on His Intellectual Faculties and His Education), one of the major works in the philosophy of education. In it, he strongly criticized the views of Rousseau as found in the book *Émile*. He held that Rousseau was too elitist, and argued contra *Émile* that all people—women as well as men—are capable of being educated, and that the hope for human progress depends upon this. The book was not published until after his death.

One reason for Helvétius's unpopularity was his biting wit. "A man who believes that he eats his God," he wrote, "we do not call mad; a man who says he is Jesus Christ, we call mad." His advocacy of women's equality was influenced by his formidable wife, Madame Anne Catherine DeLingville Helvétius—renowned for her great beauty—who presided over one of the most famed salons in all of Paris. After her husband's death she had many admirers, including Benjamin FRANKLIN, who frequented her scandalous freethinking salon, which she ran until her death in 1800.

BIBLIOGRAPHY

Cumming, Ian. *Helvétius*. New York: Routledge, 2003.
Goodman, Dena. *The Republic of Letters: A Cultural History of the French Enlightenment*. Ithaca, NY: Cornell University Press, 1996.
Horowitz, Irving Louis. *Claude Helvétius: Philosopher of Democracy and Enlightenment*. New York: Paine-Whitman, 1954.
Smith, David Warner. *Helvétius: A Study in Persecution*. New Haven: Greenwood, 1982.

TIMOTHY J. MADIGAN

HENRY, JOSEPHINE K. (1846–1928), American freethinker, sex radical, and suffragist. Josephine K. Henry is credited with mobilizing support for Kentucky's Married Women's Property Act (1894). Her active role as a member of the revising committee of Elizabeth Cady STANTON's *Woman's Bible*, however, led to censure by state and national organizations of suffragists who believed her desire to liberate women from religious oppression would detract from their cause (see WOMAN SUFFRAGE MOVEMENT AND UNBELIEF).

Early Years. Born in southwestern Ohio in 1846, Josephine Kirby Williamson married William Henry and by 1870 had settled in Versailles, Kentucky, where she resided the remainder of her life. The music teacher began corresponding with Elizabeth Cady Stanton in the 1880s. As a freethinker her interest in such topics as birth control, divorce, dress reform, and sex education led Henry to join with Laura Clay as cofounder of the Kentucky Equal Rights Association (KERA) in 1888. A powerful speaker and writer, she became increasingly politicized while agitating on behalf of women's rights, and in 1890 Henry became the first Kentucky woman to run for state office when she stood as the Prohibition Party's candidate for clerk of the Kentucky Court of Appeals. Four years later she received the nomination for state superintendent of public instruction.

Married Women's Property Act. In 1890 Kentucky was the only state in which married women had no property rights. They could not make wills, receive the wages they earned, or be the guardians of their children. Henry, convinced that women's economic independence must precede suffrage, campaigned tirelessly for the Married Women's Property Act, which passed in 1894.

The Woman's Bible. Stanton provoked significant controversy in 1895 with the publication of the collaboratively authored *The Woman's Bible*, a commentary on key biblical passages pertaining to women. One of Stanton's most vocal supporters, Henry condemned the church for demanding everything of woman while giving her little in return. As a result of her participation on this project, both the KERA and the North American Women's Suffrage Association (NAWSA) ostracized Henry.

Later Years. Undeterred by the criticism her work on *The Woman's Bible* engendered, Henry devoted herself to writing and published *The New Woman of the New South* (1895), *Woman and the Bible* (1905), *Marriage and Divorce* (c. 1905, dedicated to sex radical physician Edward Bliss FOOTE), hundreds of newspaper articles, and a work of poetry titled *Musings in Life's Evening*. In 1920 NAWSA awarded her a Pioneer Distinguished Service certificate. She died in Versailles in 1928.

BIBLIOGRAPHY

Kern, Kathi. *Mrs. Stanton's Bible*. Ithaca, NY: Cornell University Press, 2001.

Potter, Eugenia K. *Kentucky Women: Two Centuries of Indomitable Spirit and Vision*. Louisville, KY: Four Colour Imports, 1997.

JOANNE E. PASSET

HERDER, JOHANN GOTTFRIED VON (1744–1803), German historian, philosopher, and theologian. Johann Gottfried von Herder's first work (the *Fragmente* of 1767) is essentially a plea that works of literature should not be judged by absolute standards, but understood in the light of the historical conditions of their time. Better known are his views on language. After early arguing that it is a human invention, he repudiated, in a famous prize essay of 1772, both this view and the claim that language is of divine origin. This attempt to give it a natural foundation without invoking invention led him into quite unsustainable arguments.

Many of Herder's writings in the five years from 1771 to 1775 are marked by a strong religious enthusiasm, quite different from the more rationalistic cast of his earlier period and of his time in Weimar from 1776. Schweitzer (referring to the 1780–81 *Letters on the Study of Theology*) noted that Herder recognized that the first three of the canonical gospels are incompatible with the fourth. His writings on the Old Testament treat much of its material as oriental poetry, not to be taken seriously as science or philosophy. Cheyne noted that Herder, with J. G. Eichhorn, established "the custom of referring to the 'orientalism' of the Scriptures, which the traditional orthodoxy had been accustomed to regard as in all senses unique."

His *The Spirit of Hebrew Poetry* (1782) was still considered worth translating into English fifty years later.

The History of Civilization. For Herder, neither literature nor theology can be understood except in the light of history; and so it is not surprising that his greatest achievement lies in his work as historian. Whereas his *Another Philosophy of History as a Contribution to Human Culture* of 1774 is no more than a polemic against deists and rationalists (see DEISM; RATIONALISM), his *Ideas on the Philosophy of the History of Mankind* (published in four volumes between 1784 and 1791) is a history of civilization up to the time of the Crusades, embodying many years of historical and scientific research. The whole burden of its opening sections is to show by comparing human being, body and mind, with other animals that we are a natural species, and that human behavior must be understood in the same way as that of any other creature. Herder argued along these lines long before the theory of evolution was well established to support him (see EVOLUTION AND UNBELIEF). Indeed, he regarded species as immutable.

The final sections of the work include an orthodox account of the origin of Christianity but a very unorthodox account of its development, including the judgment that Edward GIBBON had treated the subject with "great mildness." It may well be that a planned fifth volume, covering world history from the Crusades to the French Revolution, was never written because as court preacher of Protestant Weimar, Herder could not afford to be as outspoken about the Reformation as he had been about the Catholic Church.

The four published volumes conclude with a confident assurance that the advance of reason is continuing and bodes well for the future of humankind. Such optimism seems strange today, but it was natural that Herder should be struck by the superiority of the eighteenth to earlier centuries; and it was easy for him to show that this superiority depended on an increase in knowledge.

In Herder's final years the increasing popularity of the Kantian philosophy, which he bitterly opposed, served to isolate him. In his view, reason cannot transcend experience, and this struck at the very roots of Immanuel KANT's doctrine of a priori knowledge. Kant himself was well aware that the kind of anthropology pursued by Herder would be dangerous to the new philosophy, and did his best to discredit him. In any case, Herder's attempt to explain human affairs in terms of natural laws could hardly find favor in an age when the laws underlying even geological phenomena had not been properly grasped, and when biology, and chemistry, too, were relatively backward.

BIBLIOGRAPHY

Cheyne, T. K. *Founders of Old Testament Criticism*. London: Methuen, 1893.

Herder, Johann Gottfried von. *Abhandlung über den Ursprung der Sprache*, 1772.

————. *Auch eine Philosophie der Geschichte zur Bildung der Menschheit*. 1774.

————. *Briefe, das Studium der Theologie betreffend*. 1780–81.

————. *Fragmente Uber die neuere deutsche Literatur*. 1767.

————. *Ideen zur Philosophie der Geschichte der Menschheit*. 1784–91.

————. *Sämtliche Werke*, edited by B. Suphan. 33 vols. Berlin: Weidmannsche Buchhandlung, 1877–1913.

————. *Vom Geist der ebräischen Poesie*. 1782.

Schweitzer, A. *The Quest of the Historical Jesus*. 3rd ed. London: Adam and Charles Black, 1954.

Wells, G. A. *Herder and After: A Study in the Development of Sociology*. The Hague: Mouton, 1959.

————. *The Origin of Language. Aspects of the Discussion from Condillac to Wundt*. La Salle, IL: Open Court, 1987.

GEORGE A. WELLS

HERESY. Defined as the crime of holding minority opinions in a closed society, heresy is not the same as BLASPHEMY, which traditionally involved reviling the name of God or outraging fundamental religious sensibilities. Heresy is the profession of unacceptable doctrines while accepting the fundamental tenets of the faith. This means that heresy is always relative to whatever orthodoxy is being defended. It also means that heresy is very largely a problem confined to cultures dominated by a monotheistic brand of religion or universalizing ideology that is not prepared to brook any rival interpretation of reality. In a free society where all manner of thought is encouraged, heresy is impossible. It is not accidental that the word is derived from the Greek *hairesis*, which means "choice" or "able to choose." In the Asian traditions of Hinduism (see HINDUISM AND UNBELIEF), Buddhism (see BUDDHISM, UNBELIEF WITHIN), CONFUCIANISM, and Taoism (see TAOISM, UNBELIEF WITHIN), it is well nigh impossible to find space for the concept of heresy, because these traditions do not revolve around notions of one god whose message is inscribed in scripture. Without these absolute pillars of belief, obedience to which constitutes the measure of one's orthodoxy, the holding of divergent opinions is, at worst, an occasion of disapproval.

But in the monotheistic religions, it matters a great deal what the scriptures say, and who has the power to enforce the prescribed interpretation. It was with this in mind that the philosopher Baruch SPINOZA observed: "No heretic without a text." Ironically, one of the earliest uses of the notion of heresy is in the New Testament itself, and against Christians. Acts 24:5, for example, which refers to the "sect of the Nazarenes," should, if translated accurately, read "the hairesis of the Nazarenes," which places the emphasis not on the sect but on the beliefs (*hairesis*) that characterized that sect. In the tolerant world of Roman polytheism, no opprobrium was attached to the term, a condition that would not last.

The persecution of heresy derived its scriptural warrant from passages such as John 15:6, which states: "If a man abide not in me, he is cast forth as a branch, and is withered; and men gather them, and cast them into the fire, and they are burned." And 2 Peter, one of the latest works included in the New Testament, warns against false prophets and damnable heresies. The author of Peter was anxious to hold together the infant Christian community in the light of Christ's failure to return in the lifetime of his hearers. Those who interpreted this failure in ways perceived to threaten church unity were, accordingly, labeled heretics. The church fathers set a tone of fanaticism. One of the first written condemnation of heretics was from Irenaeus of Lyons, who attacked the Gnostics in *Against Heretics*. Saint Jerome declared that anyone against the church was by default with Satan, and as such had relinquished the right to life. And Saint Augustine distinguished between unjust persecution, which the impious commit against the church, and just persecution, which the church commits against the impious. In a letter to the tribune Boniface in 417 CE, Augustine noted that the church "persecutes out of love and the impious out of cruelty."

Until the fourth century CE, the charge of heresy amounted to little more than a stratagem in factional quarrel, about which little could be done since neither party exercised coercive power. But when Christianity became the official religion of the Roman Empire, being labeled a heretic became a lot more dangerous. Constantine is usually counted as the first Roman emperor to publicly embrace the Christian religion. The Council of Nicaea, over which he presided, helped to solidify the officially sanctioned dogma of the church. This made it easier, and more deadly, to identify as heretics those whose views differed. It also meant that churches identified as heretical could lose the tax exemption enjoyed by their orthodox neighbors.

But while Constantine was credited as the first emperor who embraced Christianity, it was Theodosius who declared Christianity the official religion of the empire, on February 27, 380. Within five years the first known execution of a heretic Christian took place. In 385 Priscillian, a Spanish bishop, scholar, and ascetic, was executed with official sanction because of his views. Theodosius's declaration was followed by a succession of increasingly draconian decrees against all unorthodox variants of Christianity as well as non-Christian beliefs and practices. In the Theodosian Code of 438 it was decreed simply that all "heresies are forbidden by both divine and imperial laws and shall forever cease." Almost a century later, in 529, Justinian closed down PLATO's Academy and all other sources of learning where people might be able to choose what to believe about the world. The closing of the Academy is taken by many historians as an appropriate symbolic date for the start of the Dark Ages. By now there was a relatively coherent understanding of what constituted heresy. In the Gothic successor states to the western Roman Empire, it was Nicaean Christians who were the heretics, but in the eastern Roman Empire it was the Arians. In the end, the greater ability of the eastern empire to enforce its will ensured that its views as to who was the heretic would triumph.

There is no exact equivalent with the concept of heresy in Islam (see ISLAM, UNBELIEF WITHIN), although there are a couple of close parallels. The Arabic word *Bid'a* literally means "innovation" but, revealingly, has come to mean heresy. Technically, however, *Bid'a* does not denote heresy; not all innovation is inevitably seen as heretical, although conservatives have been happy to use the term in that context for centuries. The closest parallel is *Ilhad*, although this word can also be translated as "apostasy." *Ilhad* means a deviation from the correct path. Apostasy can also be translated as *Irtidad* and *Ridda*.

Part of the explanation of the lower prominence of the notion of heresy in Islam is that there are fewer core tenets of Muslim belief that can become a focus for dispute than is the case in Christianity. The Christian view of Jesus as God's son generated a large body of doctrine, culminating in the Trinity, the purpose of which was to clarify and explain this relationship. But inevitably, it also provided rich pickings for alternative interpretations. The losers of these struggles earned the title "heretic" and suffered accordingly. But within Muslim thought, any questioning of core tenets of belief meant the challenger was less able to be seen as a heretic, in the sense of questioning aspects while remaining loyal to the rest of the doctrine, and more of an apostate, one who rejects the entire Muslim corpus.

It is also interesting to see close parallels within the world of communism. The large body of doctrine, the changes over the years from Karl MARX, through Vladimir Ilyich LENIN and Joseph Stalin and on to Mao Tse-tung, allowed for a plethora of different interpretations. And this in turn allowed for the closest imaginable secular parallel to heresy. The labels used to brand opponents—"right-wing deviationist," "leftist adventurer," and, the ultimate crime, "Trotskyite"—all carried the same subtle shifts in emphasis and coded information as to the nature of the opinion being denounced. But in the end, it was simply the wish of the victors that counted.

These digressions notwithstanding, it remains that heresy is primarily a phenomenon of Christian history and practice, and so we will return to our historical survey of heresy in the Christian context. It was Pope Innocent III who set the extirpation of heresy onto a new footing. Many people had suffered for their opinions before, but Innocent raised the stakes when, on March 25, 1199, he declared heresy to be high treason against God, and that the children of heretics "are to be subjected to perpetual deprivation for the sins of their par-

ents." From the beginning there was a capricious element to this process. When faced with two reform movements espousing similar ideas of returning to Christlike simplicity and austerity, one group—the Waldensians—was declared heretical, while the other—the Franciscans—was accepted into the structure of the church. Half a century after the death of Saint Francis in 1226, this would change when his more puritanical followers, known as the Spirituals, fell foul of the church and were persecuted as heretics.

The persecution of heresy reached a new frenzy when Innocent III was faced with a popular French heretical movement known as the Cathars. Innocent reacted brutally, declaring in 1208 that the war against them was a Crusade. By this declaration, all the rewards of absolution for crimes committed while fighting that had traditionally been given to those who had slaughtered Muslims was now extended to those fighting fellow Christians. Over the next two decades, fighting of the utmost savagery reduced Provence to a wasteland. But the heretics were crushed.

Innocent oversaw harsh legislation against heretics at the Fourth Lateran Council in November 1215. Encouraged by Innocent's successor, Pope Honorius III, harsh penalties on heretics were enacted by Frederick II in 1220 and by Louis VIII six years later, while he was finishing off the last remnants of the heretical Cathars. Innocent III having reestablished the elimination of heresy as a papal priority, the scholars set to work to clarify once more what heresy consisted of. Thomas Aquinas spoke of heresy as "a species of infidelity in men who, having professed the faith of Christ, corrupt its dogmas." He went on to distinguish two types of heresy: refusing to believe in Christ himself (a failing he attributed to pagans and Jews), and retaining some items of Christian belief while rejecting others. During his struggles with the Spirituals, Pope John XXII issued a bull defining heresy as "any baptized person who, retaining the name Christian, pertinaciously denies or doubts one or another truth believed by divine and catholic faith." Most medieval heretics saw themselves as the true followers of Christ's teaching, which they usually interpreted as involving poverty, simplicity, and a distrust of things of the flesh and priestly hierarchies.

The papal concern with the extirpation of heresy fueled the development of what became the Inquisition. The first reference to the title of inquisitor was at the Council of Tours in 1163, which was preoccupied with the Cathars. On November 4, 1184, Pope Lucius III's *Ad abolendum* decretal spoke of the need to "make inquisition" for heresy. The work of the Inquisition was helped in May 15, 1252, when, in *Ad Extirpanda*, Innocent IV permitted the torture of heretics. Amended versions of this bull allowed the inquisitors themselves to be present at the torture. It was not until 1816 that the papacy finally condemned the practice of torture.

The papal initiative was followed with varying

degrees of enthusiasm around Europe. It was not until 1400 that official recognition of heresy was established in England. That year the English king, Henry IV, agreed to clerical demands for bishops to be granted harsh new powers of arrest and detention of anyone whom they accused of heresy. Church authorities moved so quickly that their first victim, William Sawtre, a follower of John Wycliffe, was burned on March 2, 1400, eight days before the Statute of Heretics was officially passed. Henry V strengthened the already generous clerical powers in 1414, and for the next two hundred years innumerable people went to the flames in the name of true religion. The last burning of a heretic in England took place in 1610, and the statute was finally abolished in 1677, although ecclesiastical courts retained the power to bring people to trial for heresy. Witches, who technically were not heretics, were burned for another century. And in 1698 a harsh statute was passed under which any person found guilty of criticizing Christianity was liable to face a wide range of penalties, including ineligibility to hold public office, purchase land, or take legal action. This statute only encouraged critics of Christianity to write their criticisms in oblique ways. A popular method was to criticize Roman Catholicism or Islam in the name of "true religion," while allowing readers to draw the conclusion that the criticisms applied to all Christianity.

The persecution of heresy reached its apogee in Europe in the century preceding the Treaty of Westphalia in 1648. Charles V enacted a comprehensive law against heresy in the Holy Roman Empire in 1523, and the Hapsburg monarch Philip II of Spain put renewed emphasis on the extirpation of heresy. France at this time suffered eight wars of religion between Catholics and Protestants, known as Huguenots. The hatred reached its peak on August 23 and 24, 1572, when twenty thousand Huguenots were massacred in Paris in what became known as the Massacre of Saint Bartholomew. Pope Gregory XIII celebrated the event with a solemn *Te Deum* and thanksgiving events. Philip II was said to have laughed when he was told of the slaughter. The religious bloodletting continued on to the Thirty Years' War (1618–1648), which had the dubious honor of being the bloodiest war in European history until the First World War. The war left Germany severely underpopulated and impoverished, and it took a century to recover fully.

The Reformation fatally undermined the ideological foundations upon which the idea of heresy rested. Once Protestantism was established as a credible alternative to the hierarchy of Rome, it was no longer possible to argue that all civil and moral order could be thought to rest on one mode of belief. On April 15, 1598, the Edict of Nantes gave French Huguenots a degree of religious freedom and served as an example of how people of different faiths could live together. The edict was revoked in 1685, leading to an exodus of Huguenots from France. This provided the next lesson: that religious toleration also allows for greater prosperity than coerced unifor-

mity. And during this century, the scientific revolution comprehensively undermined the limited, geocentric universe as understood by medieval Christians (see RELIGION IN CONFLICT WITH SCIENCE). This allowed more scope for divergent views as to how the Christian scriptures could be interpreted.

In the decades following the end of the Thirty Years' War, the growing disgust at slaughter in the name of religion—combined with the realization that there are many ways a Christian may worship—encouraged the search for a new way of interpreting scripture. Spinoza, himself branded a heretic by the Jews of Amsterdam, offered a radical solution. Writing in the 1670s, Spinoza said that it is not the purpose of government to "change men from rational beings into beasts or puppets, but to enable them to develop their minds and bodies in security, and to employ their reason unshackled; neither showing hatred, anger, or deceit, nor watched with the eyes of jealousy and injustice. In fact, the true aim of government is liberty." Spinoza articulated the principal political conclusion drawn from the terrible wars of religion: mixing religion and politics is dangerous. In the century following Spinoza, there arose a greater willingness to criticize openly the crimes of religion. VOLTAIRE began a study of heresy by noting that it "is not greatly to the honor of human reason that men should be hated, persecuted, massacred, or burned at the stake, on account of their chosen opinions."

The collapse of the worldview which gives rise to notions like heresy became apparent in the nineteenth century when the Englishman John Henry Newman, who converted to Catholicism and became a cardinal, claimed that it was better for the universe to expire than for one venial sin to be committed. Only in the closed world of nineteenth-century Catholicism could such a pronouncement be understandable. Pope Pius IX did what he could to give meaning to Newman's wish when he published, on December 8, 1864, the *Syllabus of Errors*, a comprehensive condemnation of all the thoughts that sustained the modern world.

The popes who followed Pius IX proved just as amenable to this hardline approach. Pius X oversaw the production of the *Institutes of Public Ecclesiastical Law* (1901), which supported the death penalty for "obstinate heretics and heresiarchs." While they were no longer in any position to give effect to this wish, the church was determined to operate with the harshest possible iron fist, as the biblical scholar Alfred Firmin LOISY discovered to his cost. Loisy devoted his scholarly life to defending Catholicism from Protestant claims that it distorted the teachings of the apostles. But doing so involved accepting some of the tenets of biblical scholarship, in particular jettisoning any dogmatism about biblical inerrancy (see BIBLICAL ERRANCY). In 1908 Loisy was excommunicated for his efforts.

Outside the Catholic Church, the idea of heresy was taking on newer, lighter meanings. By the beginning of the twentieth century, people felt able to describe themselves as heretics and expect to be applauded as rebels. The holding of unconventional opinions, self-described as heresy, became a badge of honor, a practice the conservative English journalist G. K. Chesterton lamented in a book he called *Heretics*. Such people, Chesterton wrote, have philosophies that are "quite solid, quite coherent, and quite wrong." Chesterton's bluster notwithstanding, it was apparent that heresy had ceased to be a crime of substance, because those making the charges no longer had the coercive power to back them up. At the Second Vatican Council, even the Catholic Church tried to acknowledge the new spirit of the times when it asserted, however dubiously, that "it has always been the teaching of the church that no one is to be coerced into believing."

For a while after World War II, it looked as if heresy could be consigned to the history books, at least in the Western world. Churches can still instigate heresy trials, and occasionally do. In 1906 the Episcopalian Church of America charged one of its clergymen, Algernon Sidney Crapsey, with heresy. He was found guilty and expelled from the church. Crapsey continued his career as a state parole officer and peace campaigner. And in New Zealand, the Presbyterian Church charged one of its prominent theologians, Lloyd Geering, with heresy in 1967. Geering was acquitted and went on to have a successful career as a public intellectual and religious humanist. During the pontificate of John Paul II, the Catholic Church moved away from many of the liberalizing moves of the Second Vatican Council. This was best illustrated when, in 1979, John Paul II revoked Hans Küng's authority to teach as an officially recognized Catholic scholar because he criticized papal infallibility. Like Crapsey and Geering, Küng went on to have a very successful career. But as many Christian denominations drift back to conservative positions, it would be premature to predict the end of heresy. But the closed, geocentric understanding of the universe that gave rise to the notion of heresy has gone forever.

BIBLIOGRAPHY

Bradlaugh Bonner, Hypatia. *Penalties upon Opinion*. London: Watts and Company, 1912.

Chesterton, G. K. *Heretics*. London: John Lane/Bodley Head, 1911.

Cooke, Bill. *A Rebel to His Last Breath: Joseph McCabe and Rationalism*. Amherst, NY: Prometheus Books, 2001.

George, Leonard. *Crimes of Perception: An Encyclopedia of Heresies and Heretics*. St. Paul, MN: Paragon House, 1995.

Herrin, Judith. *The Formation of Christendom*. London: Phoenix, 2001.

Spinoza, Baruch. *Tractatus Theologico-Politicus*. London: Routledge, [1885].

Zagorin, Perez. *How the Idea of Religious Toleration Came to the West*. Princeton, NJ: Princeton University Press, 2003.

BILL COOKE

HETHERINGTON, HENRY (1792–1849), English religious reformer and freethinker. Known as "the poor man's guardian," Henry Hetherington was born in Soho, London, and as a youth was apprenticed to Thomas Hansard, son of the printer of parliamentary reports that now bear his name. After release from his apprenticeship, Hetherington went to Belgium in search of work and was caught up in radical politics. He returned to London after two or three years, set up a printing business, and immersed himself in radical politics. His first important contribution was the publication in 1828 of the pamphlet *Principles and Practice Contrasted: or, A peep into the only true Church of God upon Earth, commonly called Freethinking Christians*. He accused Freethinking Christians of hypocrisy in their attempt to reconcile scientific knowledge with religious belief. Hetherington also published a lot of material for the emerging trade union movement.

Hetherington found his true vocation in opposing the Stamp Tax on newspapers. The Six Acts of 1819 had required publishers to deposit substantial bonds as guarantees of good behavior, and a four-penny duty was imposed on all regular newspapers. These restrictions became known as the taxes on knowledge and generated sustained opposition. Between 1830 and 1835 Hetherington led a nationwide opposition to the tax, going to prison several times in the process. In 1831, after his first spell in prison, Hetherington set up a weekly paper, the *Poor Man's Guardian*. It sold for one penny, with no extra charge to pay the Stamp Tax. During the course of the campaign against the taxes on knowledge, more than six hundred people were imprisoned for selling the *Poor Man's Guardian*. The campaign wound down after the stamp duty was reduced to one penny in 1836.

Hetherington then turned his attention to British blasphemy laws. In 1840 he was brought to trial for distributing pamphlets that some Church of England authorities had decided were blasphemous (see BLASPHEMY). Hetherington conducted his own defense with great vigor and skill, but there was never any doubt he would be found guilty. Once again he went to prison. After his release, he resumed publishing heretical tracts, including VOLTAIRE's *Questions of Zapota*; Atheos's *Atheism Justified*; and his own works, *Is Man a Free Agent?* and *A Few Hundred Bible Contradictions*. Hetherington was working actively for the Chartist movement when he died in the cholera epidemic that swept through London. The Chartists were working-class radicals seeking an extension of democratic rights to people of their class. Hetherington died on August 23, 1849, and in his will he declared himself an atheist (see ATHEISM; DEATHBED CLAIMS CONCERNING UNBELIEVERS).

BIBLIOGRAPHY

Collet, C. D. *History of the Taxes on Knowledge.* London: Watts and Company, 1933.
Hetherington, Brian. "Henry Hetherington: 'The Poor Man's Guardian.'" *Literary Guide* 54, no. 8 (August 1949).

BILL COOKE

HEYWOOD, EZRA H. (1829–1893), American atheist, pamphleteer, and editor. The son of Ezra and Dorcas (Roper) Hoar took the name Heywood several years after his father died in 1845. A Princeton, Massachusetts, native, he earned an undergraduate degree from Brown University in 1855 and a master's degree one year later. Heywood spent two additional years at Brown preparing for the Congregational ministry, but left the church in 1858 as a result of his exposure to the abolitionist involvement. A radical Garrisonite, he believed in the perfectibility of humankind and became an early advocate of women's rights; a pacifist; a free-lover (see SEX RADICALISM AND UNBELIEF); a freethinker (see FREETHOUGHT); and, after meeting Josiah Warren in 1863, an individualist anarchist (see ANARCHISM AND UNBELIEF). As editor of a radical reform newspaper titled the *Word* (1872–93), he shared his freethought and free speech convictions with a national readership and became a leader within the post–Civil War sex radical community.

An uncompromising reformer, Heywood married the like-minded Angela Fiducia Tilton, in Worcester, Massachusetts, in 1865, and they had four children: Hermes, Angelo, Vesta, and Psyche. The Heywoods moved to Princeton, Massachusetts, in 1871 and established "Mountain Home," a summer hotel that accommodated such sex radicals and freethinking spiritualists as Stephen Pearl Andrews and Josiah Warren. While ostracized by neighbors, Heywood nonetheless earned respect for his kindness, integrity, and devotion to his family. Working as partners, the Heywoods established the Co-Operative Publishing Company, and with only the help of their children published the *Word* and a host of radical pamphlets, including a condemnation of marriage titled *Cupid's Yokes* (1876), *Uncivil Liberty* (1870), and *The Great Strike* (1878).

Dedicated to reform, Ezra and Angela Heywood played key roles in founding the New England (1869) and American (1871) Labor Reform Leagues, the New England Free Love League (1873), the New England Anti-Death League (circa 1878), and the Union Reform League (1879), an organization that supported land reform, freethought, repeal of the Comstock laws (see COMSTOCK, ANTHONY, AND UNBELIEF), women's rights (see WOMAN SUFFRAGE MOVEMENT AND UNBELIEF), and dress reform. After founding the New England Free Love League, Heywood began dating his correspondence and issues of the *Word* with Y. L. (Year of Love) instead of A. D.

As a free-lover, freethinker, and advocate of free speech, Heywood endured prosecution five times under the Comstock Act for mailing obscene publications. He steadfastly refused to censor contributors like his wife, who freely used words like "fuck" and "cunt," and he defiantly published advertisements for contraceptive devices. Arrested and convicted in late 1877, he served six months in the Dedham, Massachusetts, jail before being pardoned by President Rutherford B. Hayes in mid-1878. Arrested again in 1882, 1883, and 1887 on obscenity charges, he successfully eluded conviction until 1890, when a judge sentenced him to a two-year term in the Charlestown, Massachusetts, state prison. Worn down from this prison sentence, Heywood nonetheless continued to participate in reform conventions until his death, which came one year after his release. Freethinking friends and family members honored his wish for a freethinker's funeral, commemorating his life with tributes rather than prayers and scripture readings.

BIBLIOGRAPHY

Blatt, Martin. *Free Love & Anarchism: The Biography of Ezra Heywood.* Urbana: University of Illinois Press, 1989.
Blatt, Martin, ed. *The Collected Works of Ezra H. Heywood.* Weston, MA: M and S, 1985.
"He Is Beyond Our Prayers," *Boston Herald*, May 28, 1893.

JOANNE E. PASSET

HIBBERT, JULIAN (1801–1834), English freethinker and philanthropist. Befitting his privileged background, Julian Hibbert was educated at Eton and Trinity College, Cambridge, England's two most prestigious educational institutions. Hibbert studied classics at Cambridge and was admitted to Lincoln's Inn to train for the law, although he never practiced.

His privileged background notwithstanding, Hibbert was a rebel with respect to matters of religion. At the age of only twenty-four, he began contributing to papers most of his associates would have considered dangerously radical. Chief among them was the *Republican*, run by Richard CARLILE, for which Hibbert wrote a series called *Theological Dialogues*. He was also a supporter of Robert TAYLOR, a former priest who was known as the "Devil's Chaplain," and of Robert OWEN. And perhaps most radical of all, he also wrote for Henry HETHERINGTON's *Poor Man's Guardian*. Hibbert was especially concerned to challenge the prejudice common among his peers that propagating freethought among the working classes some somehow seditious. One of his main essays was "On the Supposed Necessity of Deceiving the Vulgar."

In 1826 Hibbert set up a printing establishment with a view to publishing freethought material. He had plans for a range of reference and other works, most of which never began or were cut short by his untimely death. A biographical dictionary of freethinkers was never started and a *Dictionary of Modern Anti-Superstitionists* was published in 1826, but got only halfway through the letter *A*. Hibbert also put his classical education to good use in books like *Plutarchus and Theophrastus on Superstition* (1828).

Hibbert's other important contribution was his financial contributions to Richard Carlile during the latter's years of imprisonment for publishing Thomas PAINE's *The Age of Reason*. Carlile's courage would not have been sufficient without Hibbert's generous support to keep his publishing business afloat during his incarceration.

Hibbert worked staunchly for freethought throughout his last illness. In 1833 he was subpoenaed to a London court, where his ATHEISM was publicly condemned. The magistrates sat by while the sick man was led away amid hisses and abuse from the crowd. Julian Hibbert died in December 1834. He left generous bequests for his freethought comrades in his will.

BIBLIOGRAPHY

Cole, G. D. H. *Richard Carlile 1790–1843*. London: Victor Gollancz, 1943.

Robertson, J. M. *A History of Freethought in the Nineteenth Century*. London: Watts and Company, 1929.

BILL COOKE

HINDUISM AND UNBELIEF. Two qualifiers make this essay difficult. *Hinduism* is a Western concept imposed on a subcontinent whose classic languages have no useful word for *religion*. And those life views that Westerners have called *religions* in India have always been plural, and usually without central authorities who could define "right belief." We will here treat *unbelief* as the rejection of classical traditions in favor of modern, naturalistic, and scientific views (see NATURALISM; RATIONALISM).

Ancient Unbelief. Northern invaders imposed "Vedic" polytheisms upon local tribal beliefs in the second millennium BCE. Historical writings are skimpy in India, but several alternative ideologies and practices such as Buddhism (see BUDDHISM, UNBELIEF WITHIN) and Jainism emerged around 500 BCE. That will allow us to outline the dominant background of the continent.

These early innovators rejected a highly stratified caste system and an already sizable pantheon of gods. They also rejected a revelational treatment of certain memorized texts (said to have been "seen" whereas lesser texts were simply "heard"). But they continued the downgrading of ordinary realities in favor of a superior mental-spiritual realm being set forth in contemporary *Upanishads*. This bias included a downplaying of family, sexuality, and social order in favor of a solitary discipline that would lead individual men to enlightenment. However, the innovators retained the idea of sam-

sara, the expectation of many rebirths until release from earthly suffering had been achieved. That goal represented not an individual immortality, but an absorption into an "All" or an enlightenment that was a dissolution of all components of any "self." Finally, the innovators retained the idea of karma, the belief that a ledger of the accumulated effects of one's good and evil deeds is somehow retained to influence one's future lives.

The result was a potential Hindu agnosticism, as can be seen in a famous concluding stanza of the *Rig-Veda*:

This world-creation, whence it has arisen,
Or whether it has been produced or not,
He who surveys it in the highest heaven,
He only knows or ev'n he does not know it.

X.129

Later Religious Migrations. Small Jewish and Christian immigrations to India occurred without major impacts on existing worldviews. Later and larger Muslim invasions proved more disruptive. Zoroastrians fleeing Islam in Iran settled in western India (where they would become known as Parsis). Sikhism emerged, blending some Hindu and Muslim strands. French, Portuguese, and particularly British invaders later proved hostile to indigenous religious thought.

The twentieth-century scholar Dale Riepe traced the emergence of naturalism in Indian thought, using the term in its current philosophical sense. His treatment of the Ajivika, CARVAKA, and Samkhya schools of thought shows their relationship to Buddhism and Jainism and suggests Hellenistic parallels (without claiming any direct influences). Riepe's method is to compare theories of knowledge, metaphysics, and ethics. The still-standard treatments of Indian thought by Dasgupta and Radhakrishnan also made much of parallelisms, writing sympathetically of ways in which Western philosophical idealism could relate to Hindu schools of thought. As Riepe put it, that idealism "tried to make pleasant an imaginary life when the natural one was frequently intolerable."

On the ethical level, British (and therefore Christian) influences in the nineteenth century generated reform movements such as Brahmo Samaj, which rejected caste and widow immolation and welcomed Western science. Ramakrishna claimed to have reached the same goal of enlightenment by a variety of Hindu paths as well as those of Christianity and Islam, and his disciples created a movement that remains both social reformist at home and missionary throughout the world. These and other reform movements, while moving away from temple Hinduism and more polytheistic practices, have retained most of the classical Indian theories of knowledge and the distinctions between an apparent world and a more real spiritual one.

The British Christianity that impinged upon India had already learned to live with renaissances, reformations, and modern science. As Surendra Ajnat viewed it, "The so-called Dynamic Brahmanism which survived the onslaught of many alien conquests and religious conversions could not withstand the trend of westernization which is exerting an abiding and all round pressure for rationalistic regeneration even to-day."

Subhayu Dasgupta was similarly sharp in describing this impact: "The Hindu personality, that for long remained conformist, submissive and authoritarian, had his baptism in independent thinking and rationalism. The rejection of scholasticism and apriori knowledge inherited from the past in favour of the findings of science, rights of human dignity against the hierarchy of castes and the growth of an enquiring mind which asked for rational explanation for all events, social or natural and refused to be satisfied by the supernatural or the mystic marked the stages of social transition in India."

One response to the challenges of the West was the *Arya Samaj*, emphasizing the superiority of traditional Hindu practices. Sarvarkar's *hindutva* movement in the 1920s made the dividing line whether a group viewed India as "home." Islam was, and remains, the principal intractable "foreigner" in the view of this ideology.

Regional-linguistic differences, caste stratifications, interreligious tensions, and economic grievances formed the backdrop for the nationalist movements of the twentieth century. Whether Indians should support Britain became problematic for independence movements during both the world wars.

Religiously, independence leaders took different paths. Gandhi's education in the West led him to nonviolence, to a rejection of caste, and to a pluralistic view of religious equality. This is illustrated by the fact that his assassin was a Hindu nationalist. Nehru's education instead led him to a scientific humanism. As he put it: "The diversity and fulness of nature stir me and produce a harmony of spirit and I can imagine myself feeling at home in the old Indian or Greek pagan and pantheistic atmosphere, minus the conception of God or Gods that was attached to it."

M. N. ROY became a socialist and a member of the first Comintern. Eventually he broke with Joseph Stalin and moved toward a radical democratic view that allowed him to join the Indian Congress movement, which was then pressing for greater local autonomy under British rule. Roy was an uneasy member of Gandhi's Congress; during World War II his opposition to fascism led him to support the British, a stance many Indian activists found perverse. But Roy's confidence, eventually borne out by events, was that a socialist postwar British government would free India.

In 1940 Roy quit the Gandhi-Nehru Congress to form the Radical Democratic Party. By 1946 he had issued a manifesto stating: "[T]he quest for freedom is the continuation, on a higher level—of intelligence and emotion—of the biological struggle for existence. The search for truth is a corollary thereof. Increasing knowledge of nature enables man to be progressively free from the tyranny of natural phenomena and physical and social environments."

Finally, in 1948, having come to view parliamentary parties as inadequate, Roy created the Radical Humanist Movement.

Traditional Hinduism rooted morality in custom and dharma. Roy rejects that past, saying: "Reason is only sanction for morality, which is an appeal to conscience, and conscience, in its turn, is the instinctive awareness of, and reaction to, environments. . . . Humanism is cosmopolitan. It does not run after the utopia of internationalism, which presupposes the existence of autonomous National States."

Other important Indian pioneer unbelievers were PERIYAR, who founded a Dravidian organization in 1929, and GORA, who founded the Atheist Centre in 1940 (see INDIA, UNBELIEF IN). While many of their writings have appeared in English, their successes in building movements depended upon their use of regional languages. This is still the case.

Most of the present movements, regional and Indiawide, have affiliated with the INTERNATIONAL HUMANIST AND ETHICAL UNION now based in London. Their names and themes typically use words such as rationalist, secular (see SECULARISM), radical humanist (see HUMANISM), and atheist (see ATHEISM).

Typical activities of the unbeliever groups concern rejection of caste divisions and the encouragement of intercaste marriages; the social defense of *dalits* (untouchables); support for birth control; attacks upon traditional dowry killings of brides; and opposition toward child labor. There is also concern for equalizing the status of women (including critique of Muslim divorce customs). In addition, there is a recurrent "no-god" theme and persistent campaigns against "god-men" and gurus who claim magical powers. All of these concerns also revolve around pressing for educational access for both boys and girls.

Emphases such as those just listed remind us that unbelief always emerges within a particular context of beliefs. It should also remind us that human history is seldom a smooth advance from belief to unbelief in which reason and science and rational ethics supplant more "primitive" thinking. A more accurate accounting of history shows us that every success toward secularization stirs up strong resistances, and that the strengthening of religion A not only slows secularization within that context but stimulates strengthening within religions B , C, and the rest. In India, politicized Islam and politicized Hinduism feed on each other, while the officially "secular" constitutional society finds itself threatened by both. Whether unbeliefs within such religions will succeed is never assured—their survival and progress continue to depend upon fresh ideas and fresh leaders.

BIBLIOGRAPHY

Ajnat, Surendra. *Old Testament of Indian Atheism.* Jullundur: Bheem Patrika, 1978.

Almond, Gabriel Abraham, R. Scott Appleby, and Emmanuel Sivan. *Strong Religion: The Rise of Fundamentalisms around the World.* Chicago: University of Chicago Press, 2003.

Dasgupta, Subhayu. *Hindu Ethos and the Challenge of Change.* Calcutta: Minerva Associates, 1972.

Dasgupta, Surendranath. *A History of Indian Philosophy.* Cambridge: Cambrige University Press, 1922

Nehru, Jawaharlal. *The Discovery of India.* Calcutta: Signet, 1946.

Radhakrishnan, S. *Indian Philosophy.* London: Unwin Hyman, 1989.

Riepe, Dale. *The Naturalistic Tradition in Indian Thought.* Seattle: University of Washington Press, 1961.

Roy, M. N. *New Humanism: A Manifesto.* Calcutta: Renaissance, 1961.

ROBERT B. TAPP

HOBBES, THOMAS (1588–1679), English philosopher and political scientist. Born the second son of a wayward country vicar, Thomas Hobbes was sustained throughout a long life of many writings by the patronage of the great, mainly by William Cavendish, first earl of Devonshire. The only nearly complete edition of the works of Hobbes was by the philosophical radical Sir William Molesworth. It begins with a translation of Thucydides' *History of the Peloponnesian War* and ends, when Hobbes was in his late eighties, with translations into English verse of both the *Iliad* and the *Odyssey* of Homer.

Like John LOCKE and Immanuel KANT, but unlike George Berkeley and David HUME, Hobbes matured late. His friend John Aubrey tells in his *Brief Lives* how the intellectual awakening of Hobbes occurred in a gentleman's library, when he chanced upon the theorem of Pythagoras in Euclid. That, instantly sweeping him away by its irresistible deductive power, made him fall in love with geometry. This rationalist inspiration, mated with his theoretical concern with politics, enabled him to recognize Thucydides as "the most politic historiographer who ever writ."

The first birth of this union was "a little treatise in English" of which "though not printed, many gentlemen had copies." Since its immediate implications were royalist, in the assembly of the Long Parliament in 1640, "Mr. Hobbes, doubting how they would use him, went over into France, the first of all that fled." There philosopher-mathematician Marin Mersenne immediately persuaded him to write the *Third Set of Objections* to be published with the forthcoming *Meditations* of René DESCARTES. The third and most substantial offspring was

De Cive (Concerning the Citizen), a treatise Hobbes saw as expounding his new science of the state.

This was specifically not the mere political geography that, since Aristotle founded the subject, had passed as political science. Hobbes was, he believed, onto the real thing, a new science strictly on a par with the work of William Harvey and Galileo GALILEI. It was Galileo who "was the first that opened to us the gate of natural philosophy universal" while "the science of man's body . . . was first discovered by our countryman Dr. Harvey." However, "civil philosophy," the political equivalent of the natural philosophy which we now call physics, "is no older than my own book *De Cive*."

That putative new political science was represented, along with the best of what Hobbes had to say about everything else, in his *Leviathan*. That is, by common consent, his masterpiece. Like Descartes, Hobbes believed that the secret of success in investigations was to find out and to use the right methods. For him this was the method Galileo and Harvey learned in the University of Padua. In his preface to *De Cive* Hobbes wrote: "[E]verything is best understood by its constitutive causes. For as in a watch . . . the matter, figure and motion of the wheels cannot be well known, except when it is taken insunder [that is, apart] and viewed in parts; to make a more curious search into the rights of states and duties of subjects, it is necessary (I say, not to take them insunder, but yet that) they be so considered as if they were dissolved."

Hobbes therefore proceeded to consider what men are like and, more particularly, what they would be like if all the restraints of law and society were removed. From Galileo Hobbes had caught a vision of a universe in motion. Just as the restless atoms are the sole components of a through-and-through mechanical universe, so we ourselves are the turbulent creatures which alone compose every social machine.

To understand the nature and the function of the state we have to consider what our condition would be if there were no state; what sometimes indeed, when that machinery has collapsed, it actually is. This is the Hobbist state of nature and, Hobbes insisted, it would be "a war of every man, against every man." This often quoted purple passage ends: "And the life of man, solitary, poor, nasty, brutish and short."

Whereas for Locke the state of nature was a condition in which some of everyone's ancestors once lived, and from which they in fact escaped by making a social contract, for Hobbes the crux was not historical but hypothetical: this is what would happen if . . . and what will happen unless. . . . Security is to be achieved only by concentrating all the powers of a sovereign state into the hands of "one man or assembly of men"; though Hobbes expressed a personal preference for monarchy as opposed to any form of collective despotism.

What has been most studied and valued in Hobbes is his contribution to political thought. But he was also the founding father of modern metaphysical materialism: "the Universe, that is the whole mass of things that are, is corporeal, that is to say body." This metaphysical commitment Hobbes pursued right through to the end. Where every contemporary was careful to provide for incorporeal physical substances, exemplified in God and the human soul, Hobbes argued with a perhaps reckless but certainly characteristic audacity that all such talk is, quite simply, incoherent and absurd. God? God is a great corporeal spirit; yes, altogether corporeal, albeit of an exceptionally refined constitution. And people? Here Hobbes takes the Aristolean and Rylean line of saying that talk about souls or minds is just a special sort of talk about the flesh and blood creatures which we are. It is no better than absurd, "when a man is dead and buried," to say that "his soul [that is, his life] can walk separated from his body, and is seen by night amongst the graves."

Descartes—that "French cavalier who set forth with so bold a stride"—saw reason to maintain only that all inanimate nature, the brutes, and the human body, are or may be regarded as machines. Hobbes has no Catholic or Cartesian inhibitions. The whole universe is mechanical; not excluding, indeed particularly including, the state and human beings.

Two sets of suggestions in Hobbes are of especial interest. First, he maintained, both in a long controversy with Bishop Bramhall and elsewhere, a compatibilist position about free will: "Liberty and necessity are consistent: as in the water, that hath not only liberty but also the necessity of descending by the channel." Second, Hobbes had a general interest in the use and abuse of language. He believed that a deal of pretentious, technical-sounding talk could be utterly discredited by trying and failing to discover its cash value in the down to earth vernacular.

Particularly in his philosophy of religion—especially in the final anti-Catholic chapters of *Leviathan*—Hobbes attacked doctrines not as unscriptural or as *merely* false but as incoherent and absurd. To Hobbes, as a staunch secularist and an anticlerical materialist, the doctrine of transubstantiation was peculiarly offensive: "[T]hey say that the figure, and colour, and taste of a piece of bread has a being there, where they say there is no bread . . . , the Egyptian conjurers, that are said to have turned their rods to serpents, and the water into blood, are thought but to have deluded the senses of the spectators by a false show of things, yet are esteemed as enchanters. But what should we have thought of them, if there had appeared in their rods nothing like a serpent, and in the water enchanted nothing like blood, nor like anything else but water, but that they had faced down the King that they were serpents that looked like rods, and that it was blood that seemed water?"

Finally, it should not be overlooked that Hobbes must have devoted much of his time between the original publication of the King James Bible in 1611 and that of his own *Leviathan* in 1651 to what is now called biblical criticism. By far his most important finding was, in his own words, that "it is said besides in many places [that the wicked] shall go into everlasting fire: and that the worm of conscience never dieth; and all this is comprehended in the word everlasting death, which is ordinarily interpreted everlasting life in torments. *And yet I can find nowhere that any man shall live in torments everlastingly*" (emphasis added).

Antony Flew

HOLBACH, BARON PAUL HEINRICH DIETRICH D'

(1723–1789), French author and encyclopedist. Paul-Henri Thiry was born in January 1723 in Edesheim (Rhenish Palatinate), Germany. His uncle Franciscus Adam Holbach became a wealthy man in Paris and purchased a sinecure (an office without duties) and entered the nobility, adding the prefix *d'* to his name. The elder d'Holbach brought Paul to Paris after the demise of d'Holbach's sister (Paul's mother), and had Paul educated in the classics. Paul was eventually named heir to the family title and fortune. He studied law at the University of Leiden (Netherlands), one of the finest centers of learning of the day, where he developed his taste for a free exchange of ideas and for dinner parties.

In 1749 Thiry married his second cousin. After several years, she passed away and Thiry married her sister. After the death of Franciscus, Paul (now the baron d'Holbach) inherited a vast fortune, purchased his own sinecure, and acquired a home in Paris, with whose salon his famed dinner parties would become synonymous. Grandval, his family's traditional estate, was located a few miles outside Paris, and Holbach occasionally entertained here. But his Paris home became the center of France's social, philosophical, and literary elite.

The Salon. At Leiden Holbach had enjoyed the sociability and educational rigor of university life. When he returned to Paris, he began to host dinners for a few close friends in the salon of his home. They became an institution. Every Thursday and Sunday he hosted fabulous dinners that brought together many of the day's finest minds to share food and to share, refine, and discuss ideas on all subjects. The roster of participants evolved over time, but there were a few "core" guests, including Denis DIDEROT, Friedrich Grimm, Jean-François Marmontel, Augustin Roux, and Jacques André Naigeon. Others who visited at various times included Claude HELVÉTIUS, David HUME, Jean-Jacques ROUSSEAU, Joseph PRIESTLEY, Adam Smith, Benjamin FRANKLIN, Jean d'Alembert, and Edward GIBBON. There is some debate as to whether Thursdays were reserved for the *coterie holbachique* (as Rousseau dubbed it)—the core group—and Sundays for invited guests. Scholars now believe that this was not the case, but discussion continues.

There has also been much debate as to the true nature of these dinners. Some scholars have asserted that the core group was dominated by atheists (see ATHEISM) who pressed explicitly toward atheistic, materialistic, and rationalistic thought (see MATERIALISM, PHILOSOPH-ICAL; RATIONALISM). Others have argued that the salons featured a more free exchange of ideas. What is known is that clergy frequented the dinners, and attended regularly. Presumably clergy normally would not tolerate atheistic discussion for extended periods, so it must be assumed that discussion was substantially free. One of the rules of Holbach's salon was the willingness to listen respectfully to others' ideas, no matter how heretical they might become. Many salons were held in Paris during this period, but Holbach's was considered the finest, and it was considered quite an honor to attend.

Holbach's Writings. Holbach's primary interest in writing originated with his translations of German works on chemistry and mineralogy. Holbach's association with Diderot led to his writing some four hundred articles for the latter's *Encyclopédie* (see ENCYCLOPÉDIE, L' AND UNBELIEF), beginning with scientific articles on mineralogy and chemistry. Holbach also guaranteed the *Encyclopédie* financially, insuring its completion. From there, he moved toward translating philosophical works from the English, including works by John TOLAND, Anthony COLLINS, Thomas WOOLSTON, and David HUME. These works then led to the formulation and eventual publication of his own ideas.

In Holbach's day, controversial writers could seek anonymity in a number of ways. One was to write as another author, another was to publish outside of France, and yet another was to append misleading publishing information. In order to evade persecution for his writings, Holbach did all three. He had his works printed in Amsterdam by Marc-Michel Rey, with publishing information that falsely indicated they were printed in London. Books were then smuggled back into France. His anonymity was airtight enough that several regular members of his salon did not know him as their author. Naigeon knew, having transcribed the works and facilitated their printing, but others did not recognize the works as Holbach's, or chose not to point it out. There was much discussion between VOLTAIRE and Jean LeRond d'Alembert as to who the authors of these various writings might be. Voltaire had a reputation for publicly identifying the authors of anonymous works (whether correctly or not), but neither he nor anyone else was able to link Holbach directly to his writings during his life.

Holbach began writing his more controversial works against religion under the name of Nicholas Boulanger. Boulanger died in 1759, but Holbach edited a Boulanger manuscript, *L'Antiquité dévoilée par ses usages* (Antiquity Revealed) in 1766. Next Holbach wrote *Le Christianisme devoile* (Christianity Unveiled, 1767) himself but attributed it to Boulanger. Holbach then supposedly "translated" a few English works whose originals were never found. Those works are now considered original writings of Holbach.

Holbach continued to write original works attributed to others. *La Contagion sacrée* (The Holy Disease, 1768) was attributed to the Englishman John Trenchard. *Theologie portative* (Portable Theology, 1768) was attributed to Abbe Bernier. In 1770 he wrote two works without attribution to others, but also without acknowledging authorship: *Histoire critique de Jesus-Christ* (A Critical Enquiry into the History of Jesus Christ) and *Tableau des Saints* (Table of the Saints) examined the gospels critically.

Systeme de la Nature. Holbach reverted to his practice of attributing his writings to others with his most controversial work, *Systeme de la Nature* (1770). Jean-Baptiste Mirabaud was named as author of this work, which was almost as controversial as Charles DARWIN's *Origin of Species* when it appeared. The thesis of this "bible of materialism" (as it has been labeled) is that science, experience, and reason can explain all things in the universe. All things must conform to the laws of physics, and there are no supernatural causes for any phenomenon, including the existence of God. Religion is unnecessary, as human beings can exist morally with reason and experience as their sole guide. Holbach's "scientific materialism" follows his early education, his schooling, and his subsequent interests rooted in science.

This work was widely attacked; refutations were written by at least ten different authors, including even Voltaire and d'Alembert. Voltaire attacked its atheistic materialism, arguing that God was necessary as an intelligent designer. Others attacked it on ad hominem grounds, arguing that someone without belief in a deity could not be trusted. Despite the controversy and the attacks upon the work, more than eighty editions of *Systeme* have appeared in print since the 1770s.

A more concise version of *Systeme*, called *Le Bon-sens ou idees naturelles opposees aux idees surnaturelles* (Good Sense), appeared in 1772. Again, this work was unattributed; later editions (as early as 1791) were falsely attributed to Jean MESLIER. A subsequent translation from French to English by Anna Knoop changed the title to *Superstition in All Ages*, under which title it enjoyed some popularity among freethinkers (see FREETHOUGHT), further cementing the false attribution to Meslier.

Holbach's Later Life. Holbach translated Hobbes's *Human Nature*, followed by another anonymous religious work, *Recherches sur les Miracles* (Research on the Miracles, 1773). He wrote several treatises on politics, *La Politique Naturelle* (Natural Politics) and *Systeme Social* (The Social System, both 1773), and *Ethocratie* (Ethocracy, 1776), based upon ideas he first expressed in *Systeme*. His final works dealt with morals: *La Morale Universelle* (Universal Morality, 1776) and *Elements de la morale universelle* (Elements of Universal Morality, written in 1765 but published posthumously in 1790). Holbach died on January 21, 1789.

Although he didn't live to see it, some historians believe that Holbach, his salon, and his writings laid important groundwork for the French Revolution. Holbach's views struck many as extreme, but some of them—notably the reversal of special church privileges and separation of church and state—would be achieved (if but briefly) during the revolutionary period. Holbach's ideas regarding a moral society without the need for superstition contributed greatly to the divorce of morality from religion and the idea of separation of church and state. Although he never expressly endorsed revolution, he advocated for changing the *Ancien Régime*. Holbach's ideas can still be found in later SECULAR HUMANISM, rationalism, materialism, and related movements.

BIBLIOGRAPHY

Cussing, Max Pearson. *Baron d'Holbach: A Study of Eighteenth-Century Radicalism in France*. New York: M. P. Cushing, 1914.

Kors, Alan Charles. *D'Holbach's Coterie: An Enlightenment in Paris*. Princeton, NJ: Princeton University Press, 1976.

Pecharroman, Ovid. Nature and Moral Man in the Philosophy of Baron d'Holbach. PhD diss., Fordham University, 1974.

Wickwar, W. H. *Baron d'Holbach: A Prelude to the French Revolution*. London: Allen & Unwin, 1935.

TIMOTHY BINGA

HOLYOAKE, AUSTIN (1826–1874), English secularist publisher. Austin Holyoake was a quieter, younger brother of George Jacob HOLYOAKE, whose diligence and integrity were of value to the FREETHOUGHT movement.

Born in Birmingham, England, of devoutly religious parents, Holyoake became an Owenite (see OWEN, ROBERT) and freethinker as a young man. He assisted in printing the *Reasoner*, his brother's journal, having been trained in printing by his brother-in-law, J. G. Hornblower. He was active in public meetings of growing size in the north of England—though he was never really a public speaker.

In 1853 he took over James WATSON's publishing business, later transferring it to better premises in Fleet Street. This became the Fleet Street House, with a reading room, a meeting room, and a center for creating and distributing freethought literature; Holyoake became the secretary and general assistant until 1862. His own printing work continued from premises in Johnson's Court from 1864 to 1874.

He was on good terms with Charles BRADLAUGH, and for ten years printed and coedited Bradlaugh's journal, the *NATIONAL REFORMER*. In 1866 he was nominated a vice president of the NATIONAL SECULAR SOCIETY. He supported the publication of Charles KNOWLTON's birth control pamphlet *Fruits of Philosophy*, which divided the secular movement (see BESANT, ANNIE; BIRTH CONTROL AND UNBELIEF; BRADLAUGH, CHARLES; NATIONAL SECULAR SOCIETY). In addition he wrote a neo-Malthusian pamphlet of his own, *Large or Small Families* (1870).

He was a member of the Garibaldi Committee, the Association for the Repeal of Taxes on Knowledge, the Reform League, and the London Republican Club (republicans opposed continuation of Britain's hereditary monarchy). When participating in republican club meetings, he opposed the use of ostentatious flags and banners, true to his modest approach. (His wife was known as an accomplished actress.)

Two further works of his were *Would a Republican Form of Government Be Suitable to England?* (1873) and, together with Charles Albert Watts, *The Secular Manual of Songs and Ceremonies* (1871). The latter contained a burial service that was used at his own funeral in 1874. As he approached death from consumption, he wrote *Sick Room Thoughts Dictated Shortly before His Death* (1874). He was very anxious to make it widely known that the approach of death had not changed his freethought views. In a memorial article in the *National Reformer* of April 10, 1874, Bradlaugh wrote: "I have lost a friend, the movement has lost a worker."

BIBLIOGRAPHY

Holyoake, George Jacob. *Sixty Years of an Agitator's Life*. London: T. F. Unwin, 1892.

National Reformer, April 10, 1874.

Royle, Edward. *Radicals, Secularists and Republicans: Popular Freethought in Britain, 1866–1915*. Manchester, UK: Manchester University Press, 1980.

———. *Victorian Infidels: The Origins of the British Secularist Movement, 1791–1866*. Manchester, UK: Manchester University Press, 1974.

JIM HERRICK

HOLYOAKE, GEORGE JACOB (1817–1906), English freethough advocate. George Jacob Holyoake was a leading secularist (see SECULARISM) and supporter of the cooperative movement. Although less forceful than Charles BRADLAUGH, he was a pioneer in developing secularist groups and secularist ideas.

Holyoake was born in Birmingham, the second child of a large family. His father was a whitesmith and young George was taken at the age of nine to learn the whitesmith's trade. He gradually became interested in education and participated in the Birmingham Mechanics Institute. Here he met Owenite socialists (see OWEN, ROBERT) and Unitarians (see UNITARIANISM TO 1961). In 1840 he opened the Birmingham District Rational Schools and was elected president of the Birmingham Owenite Branch.

He was invited to lecture at Worcester and gained a post there. His first lecture, "An Enquiry into the Incentives Offered by Present Society in the Practice of Honour, Honesty, and Virtue," suggests a worthy rather than exciting style. He was not a powerful public speaker, and his high-pitched voice and dry material tempered his success as an orator throughout his life.

Holyoake moved to Sheffield, then visited Bristol in 1840, where he met Charles SOUTHWELL, who had been prosecuted for BLASPHEMY for a scurrilous description of the Bible in the *Oracle of Reason*. Holyoake was falling out with the Owenites over their unsuccessful attempts to create utopian communities. Swayed by Southwell toward a firmer ATHEISM, he took over editing the *Oracle of Reason* while Southwell was in prison.

In 1842 Holyoake walked from Sheffield to Bristol, and paused to lecture in Cheltenham en route. His subject was "Home Colonisation as a Means of Superseding Poor Laws and Emigration." This would not have caused controversy had he not been asked by a clergyman at the end what place there would be for God in his new community. He replied: "If I could have my way I would place the Deity on half-pay as the government did the subaltern officers." It was an untypical moment of defiance.

He was imprisoned for blasphemous libel in Gloucester Gaol. After protest that he was not given due legal procedure he was released until the trial, where he spoke for nearly eleven hours in his defense. This did not impress the jurors sufficiently to deem him not guilty, and he was given a six-month sentence. Prison conditions were hard, but he was sufficiently industrious to write two thousand letters and a few pamphlets. He was always bitter that poverty led to hardship for his family and death for his daughter. After release, he was in demand lecturing as the "Liberated Blasphemer." He traded on his martyrdom for the remainder of his life, without doing much more to justify the reputation.

After his release he founded a journal, the *Movement*, whose aim was to "maximise morals, minimise religion." He continued lecturing at the Glasgow Rational Society and at the Blackfriars Rotunda in London. Under the influence of the printer James WATSON, he then founded the *Reasoner*, which proposed to be "Communistic in Social Economy—Utilitarian in Morals—Republican in Politics—and Anti-Theological in Religion."

Secularism. After the failure in 1848 of the Chartists, who advocated political reforms friendly to the working class, radicals were depressed and in disarray. Holyoake founded the Society of Theological Utilitarians to oppose "the vast organized error of religion." In 1851 in London he gave a lecture at the London Hall of Science leading to the foundation of the Society of Reasoners, which shortly changed its name to the London Secular Society. Holyoake had developed the word *secularism* to create a more positive label for antireligious thought and activity. Influenced by Auguste COMTE, he liked to quote the latter's dictum that "[n]othing is destroyed until it is replaced."

Holyoake wanted to create a federation of secular groups around the country, but was not confident of success. By 1854 the London Secular Society became a leading group (there were also strong groups in the north of England). He became president of the federation in 1854. Secularism as developed at this time was influenced by Owenism and Chartism, and the movement flourished as a series of social groups. But Holyoake's leadership was weak, and it was not until Bradlaugh took over that a forceful movement developed.

The *Reasoner* was tame and pedagogic, but nevertheless Holyoake's pen was more effective than his voice. Like many FREETHOUGHT journals, it struggled to remain solvent and died in 1861, by which time the *NATIONAL REFORMER* had taken over. Holyoake was active in the movement to abolish the so-called taxes on knowledge, which acted as a brake on the publication of journals. Another campaign he espoused was national secular education. Holyoake thought that by this time, substantial social change had occurred: there was an improvement in the tone of controversy, the BLASPHEMY laws were discredited, and belief in sin, eternal punishment, and the infallibility of the Bible had declined.

When Bradlaugh took over the Secularist movement, Holyoake retained some respect but little influence. He irritated Bradlaugh by opposing the latter's struggle to take his Parliamentary oath. His opposition to Bradlaugh in the trial of the birth control pamphlet the *Fruits of Philosophy* (see BIRTH CONTROL AND UNBELIEF; BESANT, ANNIE) led him to join an alternative group, the British Secular Union. He still argued for abolition of church taxes, blasphemy law, and Christian oaths in courts. Criticism of the Crimean War and support of European revolutionaries such as Giuseppe Mazzini were part of his agenda. He became venerable but not influential. His books tended toward self-justification, but are of historical interest.

Holyoake's later life was particularly taken up with a defense of the cooperative movement. He wrote the *History of Co-operation* (1858) in Rochdale, and later became the historian of the movement. His monument was perhaps Holyoake House in Manchester, the headquarters of the cooperative movement.

Writing and publishing were important during the latter thirty years of his life. He had established Fleet House with his brother Austin HOLYOAKE as a freethought publishing center. Among his works his autobiography, *Sixty Years of an Agitator's Life* (1893), is important but inaccurate, unduly emphasizing the many important people he had known. *Bygones Worth Remembering* (1905) has a title that might be doubted by some. One of his best volumes, because it has within it the pulse of events, is *The Last Trial for Atheism in England: A Fragment of Autobiography* (1871). His interest in publishing is reflected in his becoming the first chairman of the RATIONALIST PRESS ASSOCIATION.

Holyoake was a significant campaigner and writer, hovering between activism and moderation, respected but not revered, keen to lead the working-class movement from which he originated but ever eager to be recognized by the higher classes with which he came in touch.

BIBLIOGRAPHY

Grugel, Lee E. *George Jacob Holyoake: A Study in the Evolution of a Victorian Radical.* Philadelphia: Porcupine, 1976.

Herrick, Jim. *Against the Faith.* London: Glover and Blair, 1985.

Holyoake, George Jacob. *The Last Trial for Atheism in England: A Fragment of Autobiography.* London: Trubner, 1871.

———. *Sixty Years of an Agitator's Life.* 2 vols. London: T. F. Unwin, 1893.

Royle Edward. *Radicals, Secularists and Republicans: Popular Freethought in Britain, 1866–1915.* Manchester, UK: Manchester University Press, 1980.

———. *Victorian Infidels: The Origins of the Secularist Movement 1791–1866.* Manchester, UK: Manchester University Press, 1974.

JIM HERRICK

HOOK, SIDNEY (1902–1989), American political philosopher and educator. Sidney Hook was a proponent of pragmatic NATURALISM (see also PRAGMATISM). A trenchant critic of totalitarianism, Hook defended democracy, the use of scientific methods, naturalistic ethics (see ETHICS AND UNBELIEF), and SECULAR HUMANISM. Hook was considered the leading advocate of the philosophy of John DEWEY. He held that philosophers should be concerned with the large problems of human affairs and should have something to say to their fellow citizens and not only to other philosophers.

Hook was born on December 20, 1902, in New York City. He studied under Morris R Cohen at City College of New York, where he took a BS in 1923, and under John Dewey at Columbia University (MA, 1926; PhD, 1927). He joined the faculty of New York University (1927–67), where he became chair of the philosophy department. Hook also taught at the New School for Social Research (from 1931), Harvard University (1961), the University of California at Santa Barbara (1966), and the University of California at San Diego (1975). He helped initiate many organizations, including the American Committee for Cultural Freedom, the Conference on Methods in Science and Philosophy, and the New York University Institute of Philosophy, and was a cofounder of University Centers for Rational Alternatives. He served on the National Endowment for the Humanities Council (1972–78) and was vice president of the League for Industrial Democracy. Hook was elected president of the Eastern Division of the American Philosophical Association (1959–60) and was president of the John Dewey Foundation and a Humanist Laureate of the International Academy of Humanism (1983). In the later part of his life, he was senior research fellow at the Hoover Institution at Stanford University. His awards included Guggenheim and Ford Foundation fellowships,

a Nicholas Murray Butler Medal from Columbia University, and a Presidential Medal of Freedom (1985). Hook was also a fellow of the American Academy of Arts and Sciences. He died in Stanford, California, on July 12, 1989.

Hook's main interests were normative. As a "Socratic gadfly" his focus invariably was on concrete ethical, social, and political issues. He was considered an outstanding polemicist, debating many of the leading thinkers of his day, including Bertrand RUSSELL, Max Eastman, Mortimer Adler, Jacques Maritain, Noam Chomsky, Albert Einstein, and Paul Tillich (see RELIGIOUS HUMANISM).

The young Hook was one of the first avowed Marxists on an American university faculty. In *Towards the Understanding of Karl Marx* (1933) and *From Hegel to Marx* (1936), he interpreted Marx in pragmatic terms, testing theoretical ideas by their consequences in praxis (see MARX, KARL; MARXISM). Later, disenchanted with Marxism-Leninism, he became one of the leading critics of communism. Although he was a critic of Leon Trotsky, Hook organized, along with John Dewey, an inquiry into Stalinist charges against Trotsky that was held in 1938 in Mexico City. (Though critical of Trotsky's ideology, the commission exonerated him of the charges.) Hook considered himself a democratic socialist (or social democrat), maintaining that the central issue of our time was not socialism versus capitalism but totalitarianism versus democracy. This conviction he spelled out in *Reason, Social Myths, and Democracy* (1940) and *The Hero in History* (1943).

Hook sought to justify democracy empirically by whether it led to a higher standard of living, lessened duplicity and cruelty, and enlarged the dimensions of human freedom, creativity, and growth. As a system of government, democracy was based on the freely given consent of the majority. It respected the rule of law, the legal right of opposition, and civil liberties. But it was grounded on the ethical principles of freedom and equality: individuals should be afforded the freedom and opportunity to realize their unique talents and needs and, where necessary and possible, be provided with the economic and cultural means to satisfy them.

Some critics have found a disparity between the early Hook, who was a revolutionary Marxist, and the later Hook, who emphasized democratic social change. He denied that he had ever become a "neoconservative." Philosopher Lewis S. Feuer considered him to be the political thinker of the twentieth century most responsive to the events of the day.

Hook was committed to a naturalistic value theory: ethical judgments should be tested by rational inquiry into the facts of the case and be evaluated according to the consequences of alternative courses of action in the actual "natural" world.

Hook defended some form of naturalistic ethics. It is here that Hook has made his major contribution, for unlike many of his fellow philosophers, who withdrew into the sanctuary of metaethics, he descended to the world of concrete moral and social problems and attempted to apply pragmatic intelligence to their solution. In this area he displayed a unique virtuosity in his moral perceptions and deliberations.

Hook held that the subject matter of ethics was autonomous, not deducible from prior metaphysical or theological premises, and that it is possible to use critical thinking to modify our values in the light of evidence.

The question often is raised, Where does the ethical naturalist begin? Are there first principles that govern human moral behavior? Hook expressed some skepticism. On his view, we cannot find first principles from which we can deduce moral imperatives. Rather, we must begin in the midst of life, embroiled in problematic situations that need resolution, and we make moral choices by appealing to various principles and norms that we accept; but we may evaluate and modify them if need be in the light of their factual and consequential effects. Hook applied the empirical method of pragmatic intelligence to a wide range of topics: euthanasia, academic freedom, affirmative action, the ethics of scientific research, the curriculum in the schools, US foreign policy, and so on.

Like Dewey, Hook was a strong defender of the public schools. In *Education for Modern Man* (1963), he maintained that the key role for education in a democratic society was to develop an appreciation for critical intelligence. He sought to defend the universities as institutions devoted to research and teaching, and he criticized efforts to politicize them or to replace the study of great ideas in history with a multicultural curriculum.

Hook took issue with both absolutist theological dogma and postmodern subjectivism. He did not think that there was sufficient evidence to prove the existence of God or personal immortality (*The Quest for Being*, 1961). Neither, he thought, could noncontradictory ethical principles be derived from theological premises.

Hook stands out as one of the leading philosophical defenders of secular humanism in the twentieth century against its neoconservative, orthodox, and fundamentalist critics.

Throughout his career, Hook considered himself a naturalistic humanist. He began to use the term *secular humanist* especially in the last decade of his life (he was a charter founder of *Free Inquiry* magazine and a signer of the Secular Humanist Declaration of 1980), no doubt in response to the many attacks that secular humanists had suffered at the hands of the US Religious Right.

The terms *secular humanism* and *naturalistic humanism* overlap and share a common agenda. They differ only in regard to focus and emphasis. *Secular humanism* came into vogue to differentiate it from *religious humanism*, a term bandied about by many dedicated humanists. In *A Common Faith*, John Dewey was willing to use the term *religious* to denote our commitment to ideal ends that move us. Indeed, Dewey, who was a nontheist, even used the term *God* in a metaphorical sense to refer to the "unification of our values."

Sidney Hook was critical of John Dewey's use of *religious*, which he thought was ambiguous and confusing. Thus the term secular was applied to HUMANISM to differentiate it from fuzzy-minded religious humanism.

The term SECULARISM thus gained popular recognition in American life, but only because of the need within the US political scene to defend it. The term *naturalism* is, however, the basic philosophical concept that underlies contemporary humanism.

The first premise of Hook's naturalism is methodological, for he considered the methods of science to be the most effective way of understanding nature and solving human problems. He interpreted the methods of science broadly as "the method of intelligence." This presupposes that science is continuous with common sense; and it endeavors to test ideas, hypotheses, and theories by their experimental consequences. Hook maintains in his essay "Naturalism and First Principles" that "there are working truths on the level of practical living . . . viz., the effective use of means to achieve ends."

Hook likewise defended a second form of naturalism, which may be called scientific naturalism. This is an endeavor to develop a generalized account of experience in nature as humans transact in the world; it draws its knowledge primarily from the various sciences, not from religion, tradition, or the arts. It also defends, at root, the primacy of "matter" rather than "spirit." But Hook's materialism was nonreductive. He defended a form of emergent evolution, because he held that each kind of phenomenon encountered should be described and accounted for on its own level and in its own terms. This was consonant with his earlier defense of Marxist dialectics, which dealt with social and cultural phenomena without attempting to reduce them to physics or chemistry.

What is crucial for Hook is that naturalism reject supernatural claims because they do not meet the test of public VERIFIABILITY. Hook did not think that there was sufficient evidence or reasons that would demonstrate the existence of God, let alone enable us to define it. There are many conceptions of God and the soul, Hook maintained, that are so unintelligible and vague that nothing significant can be said of them. Concepts such as God have no empirically discernible effects, and no publicly observable evidence that can be brought to support the claim that God exists. Hook questions the cognitive legitimacy of purely speculative metaphysics or ontology. The quest for being as such, "as an all-inclusive category," is not meaningful "for it does not seem to possess an intelligible opposite."

Hook was skeptical of classical Thomistic arguments for the existence of God (see EXISTENCE OF GOD, ARGUMENTS FOR AND AGAINST). He likewise questioned the famous queries posed by Heidegger, "Why is there something; why is there not nothing?" And he claimed that these are devoid of sense except as a "sign of emotional anxiety." Similarly for Paul Tillich's "shock of non-being or being not," which refers to unfulfilled or disappointed expectations, a "purely psychological category." Neither of the above have any ontological status. Hook's analysis is in accord with Immanuel KANT's critique of rational theology, for in talking about "Being as such" we are not referring to a predicate, attribute, or property. "There is no absurdity," paraphrasing Morris R. Cohen, "to which a philosopher will not resort to defend another absurdity!"

Although Hook articulated a nonreductive naturalism, he left a significant place for various aspects of human experience, including the arts, morality, and cultural creativity.

Expressing confidence in the ability of humans to solve their problems by means of intelligence and courage, Hook had little use for the "irremedial tragic dimensions" of human existence, the nihilistic desire to withdraw from the universe, or the illusory promises of utopian salvation in this world or the next (*Pragmatism and the Tragic Sense of Life*, 1974). In his last work, *Convictions* (1990), published posthumously, he defended the right to a dignified death, suicide, and voluntary euthanasia.

Hook identified with humanism as an ethical doctrine. "An ethical humanist," he affirmed, "is one who relies on the arts of intelligence to defend, enlarge, and enhance the areas of human freedom in the world" (*The Humanist Alternative*, edited by Paul Kurtz, 1973). *Out of Step: An Unquiet Life in the 20th Century* (1987), Hook's autobiography, presents a graphic memoir of his lifelong commitment to political freedom and social justice.

BIBLIOGRAPHY

Crowley, John D. *Sidney Hook: A Bibliography.* Saint Louis, MO: St. Louis University Press, 1967.

Hook, Sidney. *Education for Modern Man.* New York: Dial, 1946.

———. *From Hegel to Marx: Studies in the Intellectual Development of Karl Marx.* New York: Reynal and Hitchcock, 1935.

———. *The Hero in History: A Study of Limitation and Possibility.* New York: John Day, 1943.

———. *The Metaphysics of Pragmatism.* Chicago: Open Court, 1927.

———. *Out of Step: An Unquiet Life in the 20th Century.* New York: Carroll & Graf, 1988.

———. *Pragmatism and the Tragic Sense of Life.* New York: Basic Books, 1975.

———. *The Quest for Being and Other Studies in Naturalism and Humanism.* New York: St. Martin's, 1961.

———. *Reason, Social Myths, and Democracy.* New York: John Day, 1940.

———. *Sidney Hook: Philosopher of Democracy and Humanism.* Amherst, NY: Prometheus Books, 1983.

Hook, Sidney, et. al. *The Meaning of Marx.* New York: Farrar and Rinehart, 1934.

Kurtz, Paul W., ed. *Sidney Hook and the Contemporary World: Essays on the Pragmatic Intelligence.* New York: John Day, 1968.

Levine, Barbara, ed. *Sidney Hook: A Checklist of Writings.* Carbondale: Southern Illinois University Press, 1989.

Phelps, Christopher. *Young Sidney Hook: Marxist and Pragmatist.* Ithaca, NY: Cornell University Press, 1997.

Shapiro, Edward S., ed. *Letters of Sidney Hook: Democracy, Communism, and the Cold War.* Armonk, NY: M. E. Sharpe, 1995.

PAUL KURTZ

HOOPS, WALTER (1902–1999), German American freethought activist. Walter Hoops was born to a working-class family in Hanover, Germany, on April 2, 1902. His father was a mail carrier and a Social Democrat. He was not particularly politically active; young Walter was more influenced by an uncle who belonged to a union (see SOCIALISM AND UNBELIEF). German education was very good, and Walter was always interested in books and reading. At the age of sixteen he was sent to a farm near the Dutch border and received compulsory military training. He returned to school after World War I was over. He was able to attend the university as a "working student" but had to return home after a year to help his family.

Walter's older brother was killed in the war. His mother became angry with God for letting this happen, and the family never again attended church.

In 1922, after Nazis assassinated Walter Rathenau, a political leader Hoops much admired, he was enraged and went to Socialist headquarters to volunteer his services. Placed in charge of the youth movement, he developed sixteen groups in Hanover. When his company, which sold school and architectural supplies, transferred him to Frankfurt he continued this work.

The Socialist movement was an excellent resource for recruiting members for the *Freidenker* (freethinker) movement (see GERMANY, UNBELIEF IN). Germans were automatically enrolled in a church and had to pay a church tax unless they went before a judge and requested to leave. Hoops arranged for an attorney able to take such statements present at *Freidenker* meetings so recruited members could leave the church on the spot. Part of the success of the *Freidenkers* was due to the fact that they offered a free funeral, providing a horse and wagon and an orator to anyone who was a member for five years. This was an excellent recruiting tool, and the dues of these members (whether they attended meetings or not) provided financing for a magazine and other needs. The membership rose to eight hundred thousand, of which seven hundred thousand were "crematory" members.

Hoops's company transferred him to Vienna and then

to New York City in 1924. There he joined in Socialist protests and worked with Sidney HOOK. He likened Union Square to Hyde Park and recalls forming a cordon around Margaret SANGER to protect her from harassment. The new "talking" motion pictures helped him improve his English.

He sent for his sweetheart from Germany; they were married and they traveled together through much of the United States in connection with his work. They came to St. Louis in 1931.

With the rise of Adolf Hitler in Germany, the company employing Hoops folded. His wife got work as a modern dance instructor, and Hoops found whatever work he could, including driving a truck for a dry cleaner. The couple stayed in St. Louis, where they had one daughter.

After World War II Hoops worked with a Jewish committee helping Jews come into the United States. Each Jew seeking to immigrate had to have an affidavit; Hoops later recalled signing ninety-nine in one day. He also gathered donations of clothing and supplies to send to people in Germany who had lost their possessions in the war. He recalled that during a visit to Germany in 1991, people still thanked him for sending the packages.

In St. Louis, Hoops was a member of the FREIE GEMEINDEN (a German freethought group) and also of the Ethical Society (see ETHICAL CULTURE). He was one of the founding members of the Rationalist Society of St. Louis, of which he said, "They talk a lot, but they don't do much." He often gave talks on topics such as the French Revolution and Denis DIDEROT.

When the *AMERICAN RATIONALIST*, a freethought periodical, began publishing book reviews, subscribers asked for an easy way to purchase the books under review. Hoops started St. Clair Book Service, a direct-mail bookselling service he ran from his home. It carried each title reviewed in *American Rationalist* and many titles and pamphlets published by the Rationalist Association. He also offered Emanuel HALDEMAN-JULIUS's Little Blue Books. After Haldeman-Julius's death, his son contacted Hoops and sold him the books by the pound. The book service brought in thousands of dollars for *American Rationalist*.

Hoops died in 1999, a venerated figure in the rationalist and freethought movement. He maintained his socialist and freethought convictions all his life and will be remembered for his contributions.

BIBLIOGRAPHY

Hoops, Walter. Personal interviews with Fred Whitehead, 1990–91.

BARB STOCKER

HORN, KRISTIAN (1903–1981), Norwegian freethinker and humanist activist. Kristian Horn was in 1956 the main founder of Human-Etisk Forbund (Human-Ethical Society), the largest Norwegian organization of churchless persons (see NORWAY, UNBELIEF IN). Horn was also the society's first national leader from 1956 until 1976, when Levi Fragell succeeded him. Horn studied chemistry, botany, zoology, geology, and paleontology at the University of Oslo where he earned a master of science degree. Later, between 1947 and 1970, he was research assistant at the botanical laboratory of the University of Oslo. For many years Horn, who also studied philosophy, FREETHOUGHT, and the history of religions, was the main ideologist of Human-Etisk Forbund.

Horn's ideology has four main elements: (1) RATIONALISM, which for Horn primarily meant a positive attitude toward reason. (2) AGNOSTICISM, which for Horn meant the will to stick to what is known and not to go beyond it. In his agnosticism Horn emphasized what he called the "experience of honesty," that is, one should be honest and not maintain more than the evidence allows one to do. And he maintained that humans do not know anything about God, gods, or other so-called supernatural forces. (3) A third major element in Horn's SECULARISM was his view that ethics does not have its basis in any religion, but rather in human life and experience. (4) A fourth and final element of Horn's ideology was a strong emphasis on the Golden Rule as the main ethical rule to which he appealed. The Golden Rule has two versions, a positive one, "Do to others what you want them to do to yourself," and a negative one, "Do not do to others what you do not want them to do to yourself."

Under the leadership of Horn and afterward, Human-Etisk Forbund strongly promoted the practice of secular ceremonies at various stages of life (see RITUAL, CEREMONIAL, AND UNBELIEF). At first secular confirmations (coming-of-age ceremonies) were stressed as alternatives to traditional religious confirmations of youngsters aged about sixteen. Over the years secular confirmations have become very common. Secular funeral ceremonies followed, then secular name-giving ceremonies for infants, and, still later, secular marriage ceremonies.

For many years Horn was active in the area of secular ceremonies. He gave talks in various groups and wrote on the ideology of Human-Etisk Forbund. In his work he was primarily supported by his wife, Ester Horn, and a handful of other collaborators.

BIBLIOGRAPHY

Hiorth, Finngeir. *Secularism in Norway*. Oslo: Human-Etisk Forbund, 2002.

FINNGEIR HIORTH

HUBBARD, ELBERT (1856–1915), American writer and promoter. Elbert Hubbard was world renowned as a writer and homespun philosopher because of works like his most famous essay, "A Message to Garcia," and because of his flamboyant self-promotion. He founded an important organization of arts, crafts, printing, and publishing known as the Roycrofters, and helped to defend, publish, and promote the agnostic orator Robert Green INGERSOLL. Hubbard's timing was often lucky—he wrote and published "Message to Garcia," an essay he dashed off in an hour, in 1899. This moralistic homily about a soldier dutifully and resourcefully getting a message from President William McKinley through to a Cuban rebel leader appealed to residual patriotism from the 1898 Spanish-American War. It also won almost immediate approval of captains of industry and military leaders around the world, which generated eventually as many as forty-three million reprints—and quickly made Hubbard famous. Hubbard published a biographical piece on Ingersoll—an idiosyncratic appreciation that included pages of Ingersoll quotations skewering Christianity and fundamentalism—soon after Ingersoll's death in 1899. Hubbard's essay extolled and defended the Great Agnostic at a time when many were eager to bury Ingersoll's effective critique of religion along with the man. Hubbard also published some of Ingersoll's lectures as pamphlets. This promotion of Ingersoll came just as Hubbard's own fame and fortune were growing rapidly and helped keep Ingersoll world famous.

Hubbard was a contradictory figure. Sometimes conservative and moralistic, sometimes radical and egalitarian, a critic of orthodoxy and fundamentalism but a defender of spirituality, Hubbard built a career and fortune on selling. He first sold soap, then became chief marketer for the Larkin Soap Company of Buffalo, New York, where he introduced the idea of including premiums, such as dishes, for buyers. Tired of that success, Hubbard sold his interests and established the Roycrofters in East Aurora, New York. He gained fame both by writing sometimes sentimental, sometimes "spiritual," aphorisms and by publishing collections of others' wisdom.

With his second wife Hubbard sailed for Europe, reportedly traveling in hopes of visiting with Kaiser Wilhelm and urging him to end World War I. The couple died when the Germans sank the *Lusitania* in 1915.

BIBLIOGRAPHY

Champney, Freeman. *Art and Glory: The Story of Elbert Hubbard.* New York: Crown, 1968.

Elbert Hubbard's Scrapbook: Containing the Inspired and Inspiring Selections, Gathered During a Life Time of Discriminating Reading for His Own Use. East Aurora, NY: Roycrofters, 1923.

Hubbard, Elbert. *Little Journey to the Home of Robert G. Ingersoll.* East Aurora, NY: Roycrofters, 1902.

Larkin, Daniel Irving. *John D. Larkin: A Business Pioneer.* Amherst, NY: Author, 1998.

The Roycroft Books: A Catalog and Some Remarks without Prejudice concerning the Publications Issued from the Shop This Year. East Aurora, NY: Roycrofters, 1902.

ED BUCKNER

HUGHES, LANGSTON (1902–1967), American poet, author, and humanist (see HUMANISM). Born in Joplin, Missouri, on February 1, 1902, Langston Hughes was one of the twentieth century's most prolific and widely admired poets, regarded as black America's poet laureate. But poetry was not his only talent. He was also a playwright, a writer of short stories, a novelist, and an essayist. Following in the footsteps of the African American poet Paul Laurence Dunbar, Hughes became only the second African American to make his living as a writer.

Hughes's great-grandfather was a white planter from Virginia who risked alienation from his family by falling in love with and living with a black woman and their children. Three of their sons actively opposed slavery and racial segregation, one becoming a United States congressman and US representative in Haiti.

Another son—Hughes's grandfather, Lewis Sheridan Leary—fought alongside John Brown in his famous raid on Harpers Ferry. The following day he was shot, and he died two days later. Leary's widow, Mary—Langston's grandmother—received the shawl in which he died. She read to young Langston during his young boyhood, telling him stories of heroic black men and women who worked hard to uplift their people. She and her abolitionist husband had worked on the Underground Railroad, and she imparted their values to young Langston, who slept under the shawl in which his grandfather had died. Mary Leary would later marry Charles Howard Langston, another Virginia planter and defender of human rights.

Hughes lived in various places and with different guardians during his childhood: with his mother, Carrie; his grandmother; and his father, Jim. In the middle of April 1909 he left his mother and returned to live with his grandmother in Lawrence, Kansas. On August 31, 1910, he observed the dedication of the John Brown Memorial Battlefield in Osawatomie, Kansas. His grandmother occupied a special seat on the platform; former US president Theodore Roosevelt delivered a stirring speech.

Eventually, Hughes moved to Cleveland, Ohio, graduating from Central High School in 1920. In 1921 the *Crisis,* the magazine of the National Association for the Advancement of Colored People (NAACP), published his poem "The Negro Speaks of Rivers." In 1922 he briefly attended Columbia University, intending to earn an engineering degree to fulfill his father's wishes. However, he dropped out to travel and pursue his writing career.

In 1925 he won the first prize in poetry from *Opportunity* magazine. In 1926 he published his first volume of poetry, *The Weary Blues.* By 1929 he had earned a degree from the historically black Lincoln University. In 1930 he published his first novel, *Not without Laughter.*

For a brief time, Hughes worked in the office of leading black historian Carter G. Woodson, hailed in his day as the "Father of Negro History." Woodson was responsible for establishing Negro History Week in 1926. The celebration has since expanded into today's Black History Month.

Hughes wrote a regular column for the *Chicago Defender*, one of black America's leading newspapers. In 1930 he went on a tour throughout the South and wrote about the Scottsboro Boys in Alabama—a sensational case in which black men were accused of raping a white woman.

In his autobiography, *The Big Sea*, Hughes included a section titled "Salvation," in which he discussed a negative religious experience he had as an adolescent. Attending a revival at his aunt's church, he had asked Jesus to come into his life; when nothing happened, he was disillusioned. He then rejected theism and embraced a secular worldview (see ATHEISM; SECULARISM).

Later in life, Hughes would embrace Marxist/Leninist thought (see MARXISM; MARX, KARL; LENIN, VLADIMIR ILYICH). He wrote two poems widely considered blasphemous, "Christ in Alabama" and "Goodbye Christ." Many Christians were outraged.

In a letter to secular humanist Warren Allen Smith, Hughes said that he rejected theism, but did not particularly care for the term *humanist*.

Though he rejected theism, he continued to be attracted to black spirituality and black religious music. Near the end of his life, when his health began to fail him, he seemed to become increasingly religious.

Hughes's literary accomplishments were remarkable, some influential writings being published only after his death. His poems have influenced some of the most influential African Americans in history, including Martin Luther King Jr. On February 1, 1991, Maya Angelou, Amiri Baraka, and other famous writers gathered at the Schomburg Center for Research in Black Culture in Harlem to inter his cremated remains in the "I've Known Rivers" tile floor.

BIBLIOGRAPHY

Allen, Norm R. "Langston Hughes." In *Humanism Worldwide: An Introduction to Non-Western Humanists*, edited by Katja Beerman. Holland: Jong HV/Dutch Humanists League for the Project of Worldwide Humanism, 2004.

Hughes, Langston. "Christ in Alabama." *Contempo: A Review of Books and Personalities* (December 1931).

———. "Goodbye Christ." *Contempo: A Review of Books and Personalities* (December 1931).

———. "The Need for Heroes." *AAH Examiner* (Spring/Summer 2001).

———. "Salvation." In *The Big Sea*. New York: Hill and Wang, 1940. Reprinted in Norm R. Allen Jr., ed. *African-American Humanism: An Anthology*. Amherst, NY: Prometheus Books, 1991.

Rampersad, Arnold. *The Life of Langston Hughes*. 2 vols. New York: Oxford University Press, 1986–88.

NORM R. ALLEN JR.

HUMANISM. Humanism has had a long and significant history. Over some twenty-five hundred years it has acquired a number of different meanings. In Western thought, the concept of humanism can be traced back to the Greeks, who, in their efforts to develop a theoretical philosophical and scientific outlook on nature, placed foremost emphasis on human rationality, believing that the good life could be achieved by human power and the fulfillment of human nature.

The Anicent World. One of the early advocates of this view was PROTAGORAS in the fifth century BCE, who stated that "man is the measure of all things." For him each person must be his or her own authority. Protagoras was also one of the first Sophists, a term applied to itinerant teachers in Athens and elsewhere in Greece who gave instruction for a fee regarding how to cope with (or get ahead in) the world. The Sophists attacked conventional morality and sought to establish an ethic of REASON. Being a Sophist could be dangerous; Protagoras was impeached for not respecting the gods and was either banished from Athens or had his books burned, depending on which source one consults. The most famous Sophist, SOCRATES, was forced to commit suicide. Yet both thinkers achieved cultural immortality. In the fourth century BCE, ARISTOTLE expanded on this new humanism in his *Nichomachean Ethics*, which served as a model for a humanistic life devoted to practical wisdom and the fulfillment of virtue and excellence.

These concepts were picked up in the expanding Roman Empire, where they would inspire the formation of widely varied schools of thought. Epicurism as developed by EPICURUS held that sense perception was the one and only way to knowledge. The most complete rendition of this concept is given by LUCRETIUS. In his *De Rerum Natura* (On the Nature of Things), he held both that the world was governed by mechanical laws that could be known, and that the soul died with the body. A different interpretation was advanced by STOICISM, in its Roman form an ethical system holding that virtue was based on knowledge. Seneca, Epictetus, and the emperor Marcus Aurelius carried this message to the Roman world. A third school, the Skeptics, developed through the writings of Sextus EMPIRICUS and others, insisted on the need to suspend final judgment about dogmatic theory and knowledge (see SKEPTICISM). Probably the most important transmitter of these ideas into the post-Roman world was CICERO, whose highly eclectic works explained and borrowed from all who had gone before.

Humanism in Medieval and Early Modern Europe. As Rome's influence over western Europe declined, the class of educated laymen like Cicero disappeared. Education was slow to revive and usually centered in monastic and cathedral schools, which initially emphasized theology. As the dislocations attendant on the destruction of the western Roman Empire subsided, the schools' curricula gradually expanded. By the twelfth century, the first universities had appeared.

Christian theology, based mainly on the works of Saint Augustine, was now challenged by the rediscovery of Aristotle. The twofold result was that Aristotle was Christianized through the works of Thomas Aquinas and others, while Christianity became more Aristotelian in a movement known as Scholasticism. At first it was a selective Aristotelianism; but Aristotle's more humanistic works, too, eventually appeared in Latin. There was also a deliberate search for other classical manuscripts and a corresponding effort to disseminate the thinking expressed in them.

Cicero had been known previously, but he became an exemplar for the new humanism of the fourteenth and fifteenth centuries. Thinkers beginning with Petrarch sought to revive classical writing and concepts as a cultural model. In this context, humanism emphasized what we now call the humanities, but also included elements of the earlier humanism, including a sort of skepticism that promoted a willingness to challenge church doctrine. Nicholas of Cusa, for example, demonstrated that the so-called Donation of Constantine was an eighth-century forgery, not written in the fourth century as claimed. The popes had used this forged document to claim authority over all the churches in the West and to claim primacy for Rome over the other patriarchal centers at Antioch, Alexandria, Constantinople, and Jerusalem. If the Donation was a forgery, other church doctrines too could be challenged; there followed a widespread effort to bring the classical manuscripts preserved and copied in the monasteries to a wider readership.

Most important in spreading humanistic ideas was the development of printing in the fifteenth century. Pamphlets and books reached ever-larger audiences. Humanism began to outgrow its focus on reviving classical literature, emphasizing also classical views of the place of human beings in the universe. Philosophical humanists including Gianozzo Manetti, Marsiglio Ficino, and Giovanni Pico della Mirandola emphasized the dignity of humans, their capacity for freedom, and the need for tolerance. Desiderius ERASMUS, writing as struggle raged between Catholicism and the developing Protestant movement, is noteworthy for his defense of religious toleration.

As this new marketplace for ideas widened, some humanists and scientists grew more keen to challenge ecclesiastical and political censorship. Giordano BRUNO challenged the teachings of the Catholic church with caustic satire, for which he was burned at the stake. Galileo GALILEI enjoyed greater influence with the papal establishment and so escaped the stake, but was forced to recant and forbidden to teach. Despite his recantation, his books continued to be published, marking the beginning of modern science. Galileo's observation that the earth moved around the sun changed the whole nature of science and its view of the universe, which came to be seen as heliocentric rather than geocentric. What Galileo did for views of the solar system, William Harvey did for

understanding of the human body, both challenging traditional and long accepted concepts.

If such a radical change could take place in cosmic outlook, traditional ideas in other areas could be challenged as well. Individuals such as Michel MONTAIGNE felt free to express both skeptical and humanist values, while Baruch SPINOZA went so far as to defend what we would now recognize as FREETHOUGHT. He rejected biblical revelation as a source of ethics and paved the way for a new science of nature. The growing tendency to naturalize religion by identifying God with nature and reason underlay the writings of VOLTAIRE and Denis DIDEROT.

Confidence grew that through reason, science, and education, human beings could be liberated from superstition. New universities appeared, and new thinking diffused to places previously not known as centers of learning. The Enlightenment philosophers of the eighteenth century, such as René DESCARTES, Sir Francis Bacon, John LOCKE, and David HUME, turned to reason, experience, or both, rather than to religious authority, to account for natural causes and to discover causal laws (see ENLIGHTENMENT, UNBELIEF DURING THE). All these thinkers were humanists in that they emphasized the ability of humans to deal with the world's problems.

The utilitarians Jeremy BENTHAM, James Mill, and his son John Stuart MILL took up the cudgels in the early nineteenth century, defending freedom of thought against political and ecclesiastical repression. They insisted on tolerance of opposing viewpoints and championed the idea of freedom of conscience. By the end of the nineteenth century, increasing numbers viewed neither religious revelation nor long-held traditional belief as an authoritative source of knowledge. A few went so far as to deny that either was a source of reliable knowledge at all.

Humanism as an Alternative to Religion. The beginnings of organized humanism as an explicitly nontheistic alternative to religion can also be traced to the nineteenth century. Auguste COMTE described three ages of religion in humans. The first, he said, was the *theological*, in which humans ascribed to the supernatural whatever they did not understand. This was succeeded by the *metaphysical*, in which ideas were thought to be the key to natural phenomena; and finally by the *positive*, in which phenomena were understood using the scientific method. Positive clubs were formed in Europe and in the Americas with the goal of launching this third stage of religion. There was even a Church of POSITIVISM established in Brazil in 1881.

Humanistic organizations began to form more rapidly. Though conceived more or less explicitly as alternatives to traditional religion, most patterned themselves after the congregational life of the churches. A group calling itself the Humanistic Religious Association was formed in London in 1853. Its members proclaimed themselves free from the compulsory dogmas, myths, and ceremonies of the ancient past. They met regularly for cultural and social meetings, provided education for their children, and furnished assistance to members in need. In Germany, a new liberal Christian denomination, the Bund Friereligose Gemeinden Deutschlands (German Federation of Free Religious Congregations), was established in 1859. In the United States dissenters from creedalism within the Unitarian Church (see UNITARIANISM TO 1961) founded the Free Religious Association under the leadership of Ralph Waldo EMERSON. A similar movement occured in American Judaism with the formation of ETHICAL CULTURE in 1876. It focused on social service and concentrated on issues of life in this world. The ideas of Ethical Culture founder Felix ADLER were picked up by others in Chicago, Philadelphia, and St. Louis. Moncure CONWAY, an American minister at a Unitarian chapel in London, began guiding his congregation in a specifically ethical nontheistic direction; his church became the SOUTH PLACE ETHICAL SOCIETY.

Other initiatives were less closely modeled on the churches. Avowed atheist Charles BRADLAUGH brought together other English freethinkers to form the NATIONAL SECULAR SOCIETY, an activist organization, in 1866. In the United States a growing freethought movement was energized by the oratorical powers of the agnostic Robert Green INGERSOLL, the most popular—and controversial—public speaker in nineteenth-century America.

Though only one of these movements employed the term *humanism*, all were nontheistic, and forerunners of what in the twentieth century would become organized humanism.

Supportive Social Trends. Though churches remained powerful, their grasp on what people could or could not do was being challenged by the rise of SECULARISM: the conviction that conduct and action should be judged by worldly and temporal standards, rather than spiritual and sacred ones. Morality could be freed from religious authority. Once that occurred, the secular values and ideals of reason, freedom, happiness, and justice could be substitued for the Christian virtues of faith, hope, and charity—and the exaggerated sense of sin inherent in the faith. This engendered a challenge to ecclesiastical control over various institutions of society from marriage and divorce (see SEX RADICALISM AND UNBELIEF) to birth control (see BIRTH CONTROL AND UNBELIEF), Sunday closing laws, and other economic and educational issues.

This humanistic and secularizing impulse was enshrined in the US Constitution with its separation of church and state. Thomas PAINE, Benjamin FRANKLIN, and James MADISON, among other founders, were strongly influenced by the humanist and secular values of the Enlightenment. Many figures of the nineteenth and twentieth centuries reflect a humanistic heritage, among them Karl MARX, Sigmund FREUD, Bertrand RUSSELL, John DEWEY, and many others included in this volume. Movements such as MARXISM, EXISTENTIALISM, PRAGMATISM, NATURALISM, Positivism, behaviorism, libertarianism, social construction, and many others have claimed humanist credentials.

Indeed, so influential did humanism become that some religious leaders have felt it important to proclaim themselves humanists. Pope John Paul II called himself a humanist; the Roman Catholic philosopher Jacques Maritain claimed that Christian humanism is the only authentic humanism. Maritain saw Christianity as concerned with ameliorating the human condition on earth, one of the major goals of humanism as well.

Secular and Religious Humanism. Certainly, the modern movements of SECULAR HUMANISM and RELIGIOUS HUMANISM have shared roots in Christianity and Judaism. A large number of self-identifying humanists refer to themselves as religious. In the United States many members of the Unitarian Universalist Church, as well as other churches, identify themselves as religious humanists (see UNITARIAN UNIVERSALISM). To be sure, in the first part of the twentieth century the American humanist movement was dominated by those who viewed humanism as their religion. Many such humanists observed a distinction between a "religion" and "the religious"; they rejected theism but emphasized the spiritual qualities of experience. Some were willing even to consider such ideas as God, though only if they define the terms. John Dewey considered the term *God* to signify the highest human ideals, sounding very much like the Christian theologian Paul Tillich, who defined God as the "ultimate concern." Such interpretations give a nontheistic meaning even to the term *God*.

Only in the mid-twentieth century did organizations develop that explicitly called themselves humanist (the mid-nineteenth-century Humanistic Religious Association having disappeared long before). The first humanist groups formed in the United States, starting with the AMERICAN HUMANIST ASSOCIATION in 1947. Humanist organizations began forming or adopting the humanist label in many Western countries starting in the 1960s. By the turn of the twenty-first century, humanism had become a truly international movement with explicitly humanist organizations active in eastern Europe, Latin America, Asia, and Africa.

Conclusion. Over its twenty-five-hundred-year history, humanism has had many meanings. At least one meaning of humanism—perhaps the most salient today— is as follows: Humanism is the worldview of the nontheistic individual who is committed to the scientific method of inquiry; who considers all human knowledge fallible and even well-established principles and hypotheses subject to modification; who nonetheless believes that nature is intelligible to scientific reasoning and explainable by causal hypotheses; and who believes that through experience over time, human beings have developed a body of moral values which can serve as guideposts for living. Humanists believe that the good life is attainable by human beings, and that the challenge for humanists is to discover the conditions that best lead to happiness.

BIBLIOGRAPHY

Blackham, H. J. *Humanism*. London: Penguin, 1968.

Bullough, Vern L. *The Scientific Revolution*. New York: Holt, Rinehart, and Winston, 1969.

Hook, Sidney. *The Quest for Being*. New York: St. Martin's, 1961.

Kurtz, Paul, ed. *The Humanist Alternative*. Amherst, NY: Prometheus Books, 1973.

Lamont, Corliss. *The Philosophy of Humanism*. New York: Philosophical Library, 1957.

VERN L. BULLOUGH

HUME, DAVID (1711–1776), English philosopher and skeptic. David Hume was one of the first philosophers to produce an autobiography: "My Own Life" is brief and by any standard extraordinary. After a few details about his family, Hume says he "passed through the ordinary Course of Education with Success." In fact, he attended the University of Edinburgh without taking a degree, but no doubt having learned a lot. He then tells us literature "has been the ruling Passion of my Life," and that his favorite authors were CICERO and Virgil. More than anything else, Hume was a writer, a creative artist working in words, and his written work is best read as a whole.

His Great Work. Hume produced mainly essays and history, some important letters, and what is by some considered the greatest philosophical treatise ever written in English, his *Treatise of Human Nature*, composed chiefly at La Fleche in Anjou (France) under a self-imposed resolution "to maintain unimpaired my Independency, and to regard every object as contemptible, except the Improvement of my Talents in Literature." The first two volumes of the *Treatise* were published in 1738. Hume expected the public to be shocked by his account of human nature, but they merely ignored it. Hume tells us, "It fell *dead-born from the Press*; without reaching such distinction as even to excite a Murmur among the Zealots." In December of 1737 Hume had written to Henry Home about a plan to submit the *Treatise* to Joseph Butler for his opinion. Butler, not yet a bishop but well known for his *Sermons* (1726) and very recently published *Analogy of Religion* (1736), is, along with John LOCKE, Earl SHAFTESBURY, Bernard MANDEVILLE, and Hutcheson, on the short list of what Hume describes, in the introduction to the *Treatise*, as "late philosophers in England, who have begun to put the science of man on a new footing." Hume tells Home, "I am at present castrating my work, that is, cutting off its nobler parts; that is, endeavouring it shall give as little offence as possible, before which, I could not pretend to put it into the Doctor's hands. This is a piece of cowardice, for which I blame myself, though I believe none of my friends will blame me. But I was resolved not to be an enthusiast in philosophy, while I was blaming other enthusiasms." The context indicates that what Hume took out of the *Treatise* was what eventually became his essay "Of Miracles." Hume had clearly made a close study of Butler, and with regard to both moral and general metaphysical questions seems almost a close colleague of Butler's, but on specifically religious questions not only do they differ, but the issue never seems properly joined. Once Butler became a bishop, Hume abandoned the idea of approaching him and there never was any exchange, which is a great pity. It is said that Butler later praised Hume's essays, and many critics have felt that the Cleanthes character in Hume's *Dialogues concerning Natural Religion* is based on Butler. This last point is especially important for the interpretation of Hume, since Hume makes Cleanthes the nominal winner of the debate, and describes the *Dialogues* as his most artful work. Most readers feel the Hume character, Philo, actually gets the better of the argument. It may be that Hume was more a writer than an advocate for anything and was encouraging readers to draw their own conclusions, just as Butler had suggested in the preface added to the second edition of his *Sermons* (1729). Hume tells Home he wants Butler's opinion because "my own I dare not trust to," a sentiment that may follow from Butler's sermon on the dangers of self-deception. The posthumous careers of Butler and Hume are also of interest. In his life, Hume eventually became known, indeed well known, not for his philosophical works but for his *History of England*. Butler's *Analogy* became one of the most successful works of Christian apologetics and was extraordinarily well known throughout the UK, Ireland, and the United States during the nineteenth century. By the 1920s the *Analogy* was almost forgotten, but Hume's philosophical work, and especially the *Treatise,* was well on its way to the recognition it had so long deserved. By the 1950s students of philosophy and theology were routinely told that the reason natural theology was no longer practiced seriously was because of the criticisms of Hume and Immanuel KANT. Kant, of course, acknowledged that Hume had awoken him.

Hume continued to rewrite his philosophy, and eventually met with some success, but not the sensation he had hoped for. Having finished the first volume of his history, he returned to the topic of religion and published his *History of Religion*, a very important and very sadly neglected work. Hume's final illness began in the spring of 1775, but he insisted on keeping his spirits up, telling us "I possess the same Ardor as ever in Study, and the same Gaiety in Company." By the end of this short autobiography, the ruling passion is not just literature but "my Love of literary Fame." Hume did not marry, but tells us he took "particular Pleasure" in the company of women.

Foundations of His View. What was Hume trying to do in his first and monumental work, the *Treatise of Human Nature,* a title taken from Hobbes and signaling his affiliation with the younger writers (Butler, Hutcheson, and Mandeville) who looked back to Shaftesbury and Locke, and even to Francis Bacon? Of course, one theme is that our reasonings ought to be based on experience, our own experience, rather than traditional authority; but fully explicated, this becomes the bolder and more revolutionary theme, some would say what we mean by "Enlightenment," such as the notion that the resources of human nature are sufficient for all we need or want, without any God and without a godlike Reason (see ENLIGHTENMENT, UNBELIEF DURING THE). The great question, then as now, is whether one can toss out all that can be attributed to enthusiasm and superstition and still retain a system of godless virtue sufficient to maintain the life of the community. Thus stated, the stakes are high, so one needs to be motivated by recognition of the harm religion does.

Hume on Religion. Religion was, of course, a major topic of discussion in Scotland and England during the eighteenth century. The disputants felt justly proud they had learned—for the most part—to argue with words, however polemic, rather than fight to the death. Hume's texts on religion are absolutely fundamental for modern agnostic HUMANISM first, because it is in these texts that the position was first developed, second because the religious views are embedded in both a theory of knowledge and a philosophy of life, and third because Hume had good knowledge of and respect for his more important opponents.

"Of Miracles" and "Of a Particular Providence and of a Future State" were published in 1748, a decade after the first two volumes of the *Treatise*; "The Natural History of Religion" finally appeared in 1757, but the *Dialogues concerning Natural Religion*, one of Hume's greatest works both as philosophy and as literature, became available to the public only in 1779, three years after Hume's death.

"Of Miracles" is perhaps Hume's best-known single essay, a standard in beginning courses in philosophy, but the value and quality of his argument remains controversial even among those who strongly disbelieve in miracles and generally support the Humean position on religion. Technically, Hume is not arguing against the occurrence of miracles, but rather against our having good reason to believe that such have occurred. If miracles are, by definition, violations of a law of nature, then no matter what evidence, say from testimony, we have in favor of the miracle, all the evidence of whatever sort collected in support of the law of nature is necessarily evidence against the occurrence of the miracle, or of any event that violates that law. When Hume first proposed the argument, a Jesuit attempted to rebut it by saying it could not be valid, since if it defeated belief in latter-day miracles it would operate just as well against the gospel. Hume merely smiled at this reply, but it was many years before he dared to publish the essay. Some otherwise friendly critics, C. D. Broad, for example, have dismissed Hume's piece as nothing but sophistry, and clearly theologians have learned to define "miracle" so

as to escape Hume's trap. Hume concludes the essay by pointing out that what he has said of miracles applies equally to prophecy. In Hume's time, and for more than a century after, apologists for religion presented miracles and prophecy as the "Christian evidences." Hume then ends with one of his most famous lines, "whoever is moved by Faith to assent to [the Christian Religion], is conscious of a continued miracle in his own person, which subverts all the principles of his understanding, and gives him a determination to believe what is most contrary to custom and experience." Humanists tend to hear only the sarcasm here, but there are still today sincere fideists who celebrate this conclusion.

"Of a Particular Providence and of a Future State" first appeared along with the essay on miracles, but it was the essay on miracles that caused the most excitement, and, as he had hoped, earned Hume notoriety as a controversialist. Even as the replies piled up in the 1750s, Hume generally ignored them. Much of Hume's work on religion is important just as a matter of fact in intellectual history, but all of it is significant as an unfolding in detail of the opinions of one of the great modern skeptics. "Particular Providence" is cast as a dialogue, but lacks the great literary quality of the *Dialogues concerning Natural Religion*. The "divinity," Hume says, may have attributes we have never seen manifested and may be governed by principles of action which we cannot discern, such may be the case but to us it is all "mere possibility and hypothesis." We cannot infer from what we have not observed, and we have not observed the consequences one would expect of the divinity according to religionists. What follows, and what most alarmed the religionists, is that even if some religious teachings are true and useful, such teachings can never take us beyond that which we could infer just by attending to the course of nature as experienced in ordinary life. Thus Hume, especially in his *Treatise*, finds common cause with the rational theologians and religious moralists who opposed, for example, the egoism attributed to Hobbes. But he insisted that the religious hypothesis at best did no good beyond what we could get from our human nature and experience, and at worst could do harm by appearing to support irrational beliefs and actions.

"Of Suicide" is of significance primarily because it raises the logical question of what it can mean to violate the divine will, since if the divinity is all-powerful it ought to be impossible to violate his will. Appreciation of the "Natural History of Religion" is hindered by its being a work of now quaint scholarship, an early study of the psychosocial origins of religion. Hume's project, remember, is to give an account of human nature that is free of any appeal to reason or to the supernatural, self-knowledge based entirely on experience. Such knowledge, Hume thought, would be most reliable and as such most useful. Since religion is a prominent part of life, it is necessary to account for the history of religion in accord with Hume's general philosophy. To his credit, Hume does this himself rather than leaving the task to others.

Having expressed his skepticism regarding the justification of religion and having given a detailed account of its origins, Hume weaves his deepest thoughts on the subject into a superb work of art, *The Dialogues concerning Natural Religion*. Everything about this work is controversial and deeply puzzling, but that only adds to its philosophical value. Just as the last line of the essay on miracles can be taken in a way favorable to faith beyond reason rather than doubt within reason, the end of the *Dialogues*, in which the character who propounds the argument from design is pronounced the winner, can be taken as sympathetic to religion in the end; but such an interpretation is supported only by a small minority of critics. Most of those who know Hume best recognize he is here being ironic, as he often is elsewhere. But Hume's irony is an especially clever and thoughtful irony, and the main conclusion seems to be that one must think for oneself. Hume is confident those who do examine the matter de novo will, if they maintain a clear and open mind, come to reject all the pretensions of religion, but in the *Dialogues*, at least, he presents his (Philo's) opponents (Cleanthes = Bishop Butler, Demea = Samuel Clarke) in their best possible light. The argument tilts back and forth, with the relations among the characters constantly in flux.

Later Life and Influence. James Boswell visited Hume shortly before his death and recorded an entirely agreeable account of his final thoughts on religion and a future life. At one point, Boswell described him as "indecently and impolitely positive in his incredulity," a character we can see in his writings if only less explicitly. In his magnificent little essay "My Own Life," Hume repeatedly insists that he died pleased with the reception of his work in his own time, even if he had hoped for greater acclaim. Certainly he was widely appreciated for his *History of England*. After his death, he was ill treated by many philosophers far less talented, but his strongest early opponent was another Scot, and a very great philosopher, Thomas Reid. Kant's acknowledgment that it was Hume who woke him from "slumber" is well known, but it does not appear that Kant made any close study of Hume's own writing. So, it was only in the early twentieth century that serious philosophical interest in Hume began to build, but that momentum eventually brought him to the very highest ranks of esteem by a nearly unanimous vote. Those with even the slightest interest in philosophy or religion can only be urged not to read too much *about* Hume but to make a careful and close study of his own words. The arguments, even when dated or sophistical, are always entertaining and have a marked tendency to induce enlightenment.

BIBLIOGRAPHY

Flew, Antony. *Hume's Philosophy of Belief.* New York: Humanities, 1961.

Greig, J. Y. T. *The Letters of David Hume.* 2 vols. Oxford: Clarendon, 1932.

Hendel, C. W. *Studies in the Philosophy of David Hume.* Princeton, NJ: Princeton University Press, 1925.

Hume, David. *Enquiries concerning Human Understanding and concerning the Principles of Morals.* Edited by L. A. Selby-Bigge, revised by P. H. Nidditch. Oxford: Oxford University Press, 1975.

———. *A Treatise of Human Nature.* Edited by E. C. Mossner. London: Penguin, 1985.

Klibansky, R., and Ernest C. Mossner, eds. *New Letters of David Hume.* Oxford: Clarendon, 1954.

Mossner, Ernest Campbell. *The Life of David Hume.* 2nd ed. Oxford: Clarendon, 1980.

Wollheim, Richard, ed. *Hume on Religion.* Cleveland: World, 1964.

Yandell, Keith E. *Hume's "Inexplicable Mystery": His Views on Religion.* Philadelphia: Temple University Press, 1990.

DAVID WHITE

HUMPHREY, JOHN PETERS (1905–1995), Canadian diplomat and principal author of the United Nations Universal Declaration of Human Rights. John Humphrey was born in Hampton, New Brunswick. After high school he trained as a lawyer, being called to the bar in 1929. He practiced law privately for six years before joining the law faculty at McGill University in Montréal, where he lectured for ten years. In 1946 he was appointed as the first director of the Human Rights Division of the United Nations. Within two years, the United Nations ratified and adopted the Universal Declaration of Human Rights (UDHR), of which Humphrey was the principal author. Eleanor Roosevelt was a member of the executive group that ratified Humphrey's draft with only slight modifications.

He continued to work as a diplomat for the UN for about twenty years, during which period he oversaw the implementation of sixty-seven international conventions, in addition to assisting in the drafting of new constitutions consistent with the UDHR for literally dozens of countries. In 1963 Humphrey first proposed the establishment of a UN High Commissioner for Human Rights; thirty years later, that position was ratified by then–secretary general Boutros Boutros-Ghali.

In 1966 he returned to McGill University and resumed his teaching career. Concurrently, he was a Director of the International League for Human Rights and served on the Royal Commission on the Status of Women. Along with others, he participated in the creation of Amnesty International Canada as well as the Canadian Human Rights Foundation. In addition, he served on several international inquiries into human rights violations, such as in the Philippines under Marcos and abuses of Korean women by the Japanese, as well as securing reparations for Canadians who had suffered in captivity during World War II.

Among the thirty articles of the UDHR, two are of special interest to freethinkers. Article 18 asserts, "Everyone has the right to freedom of thought, conscience and religion; this right includes freedom to change religion or belief and to manifest such religion or belief," and Article 19 asserts, "Everyone has the right to freedom of opinion and expression; this right includes freedom to hold opinions without interference."

In 1974 Humphrey was made an Officer of the Order of Canada "in recognition of his contributions to legal scholarship and his world-wide reputation in the field of human rights." In 1988, on the fortieth anniversary of the UDHR, he was granted the Human Rights Award by the UN. He died in Ottawa in March 1995.

GLENN HARDIE

HURSTON, ZORA NEALE (1891?–1960), American author and humanist. One of the most complex, contradictory, and fascinating figures of the twentieth century, Zora Neale Hurston was an essayist, anthropologist, novelist, storyteller, and journalist. Moreover, she wrote, directed, produced, and starred in plays and musicals. Hurston often distorted the truth even concerning some of the most important details of her life. For example, she claimed that she was born in Eatonville, Florida, the first incorporated black community in the United States. However, some researchers believe she might have been born in the less historically resonant town of Notasulga, Alabama.

Hurston graduated from Baltimore's Morgan Academy, a high school affiliated with historically black Morgan College, now Morgan State University. She went to historically black Howard University, eventually receiving a BA in anthropology from Barnard College and Columbia University.

Hurston was a major figure during the Harlem Renaissance, widely regarded as the top expert on black culture of the day. In 1928 she wrote her best-known essay, "How It Feels to Be Colored Me." In 1934 her first novel, *Jonah's Gourd Vine*, was published. In 1935 she wrote *Mules and Men*, in which she examined voodoo practices among African Americans in Florida and New Orleans. In 1937 her most important novel, *Their Eyes Were Watching God*, was published. In 1938 she wrote *Tell My Horse*, about her travels and the practice of voodoo in the Caribbean. The following year she wrote another novel, *Moses, Man of the Mountain*.

In 1942 Hurston wrote her autobiography, *Dust Tracks on a Road*. Most scholars doubt its veracity; others believe it contains so many errors, omissions, fantasies, and outright lies that it can hardly be said to be a genuine autobiography. In the book, Hurston said that her father was a Baptist preacher. However, she raised difficult theological questions throughout her childhood, especially when she overheard other church members laughing about some of the testimony at the services her father conducted. Despite her doubts, she did not reject religion as a child.

In college, Hurston studied the history of religion and concluded that the "great" religions were anthropocentric creations of the human imagination (see ANTHROPOMORPHISM AND RELIGION). She came to believe that religion and prayer are rooted in fear and insecurity. After rejecting religion she seemed to have found the inner peace that most religionists seem to believe only comes from God. However, like the unbelievers Langston HUGHES and writer James Weldon Johnson, she continued to be fascinated with religious themes and the drama of religion.

Hurston was the target of many attacks by secular humanists. Though many women now regard her as a groundbreaking feminist, she supported reactionary politicians of her day. While her work expressed themes consistent with black nationalism, she wrote that slavery was beneficial because it gave blacks civilization. She went so far as to oppose *Brown v. Board of Education*, the 1954 Supreme Court decision that made segregation illegal.

Hurston died on January 28, 1960, broke and forgotten. The 1970s ushered in a rediscovery of the woman and her work. Today publishers are reissuing her once-forgotten works. Numerous Web sites are dedicated to her life and work. She has been the subject of significant essays, and her plays have been produced. Many festivals that bear her name—particularly the Zora Neale Hurston Festival held every year in Eatonville, her probable nonhometown—are held annually. Journals, foundations, literary societies, and awards have been launched in her name, and she is the subject of numerous biographies. In 2005, a new Broadway musical called *Eatonville* was under development, with music written by the Grammy Award–winning jazz trumpeter Wynton Marsalis. Her niece, Dr. Lucy Hurston, signed a contract with Doubleday to author a book on the Hurston family titled *Now You Cookin' with Gas*.

Perhaps the ultimate proof of Hurston's enduring popularity occurred on Sunday, March 6, 2005. On that day, Oprah Winfrey presented a major network television adaptation of the novel *Their Eyes Were Watching God*. The program starred Academy Award–winning actress Halle Berry as Janie.

BIBLIOGRAPHY

Boyd, Valerie. *Wrapped in Rainbows: The Life of Zora Neale Hurston.* New York: Lisa Drew Books/Scribner, 2003.

Hurston. Zora N. *Dust Tracks on a Road.* New York: HarperCollins, 1942.

———. "Religion." From *Dust Tracks on a Road.* Reprinted in Norm R. Allen Jr., ed. *African-American Humanism: An Anthology.* Amherst, NY: Prometheus Books, 1991.

Kaplan, Carla. *Zora Neale Hurston: A Life in Letters.* New York: Doubleday, 2002.

NORM R. ALLEN JR.

HUXLEY, JULIAN (1887–1975), English humanist scientist and philosopher. Julian Huxley was a major shaper of neo-Darwinism, but we will focus on his contributions in philosophy and religion. In 1946 he became the first director general of the United Nations Educational, Scientific and Cultural Organization (UNESCO) but resigned when it became clear that most nations were not ready for his kind of scientific humanism (the United States played a central role in this rejection).

Thomas H. HUXLEY, his grandfather, had been Charles DARWIN's great defender, but focused on a view of nature as, in Tennyson's phrase, "red in tooth and claw." In his 1893 Romanes Lecture he had argued that human ethics must combat the "gladiatorial" life of prehuman animals. Julian's 1943 Romanes Lecture, however, saw human social evolution as producing the many kinds of human ethics, and saw modern science as helping choose among them.

In the 1920s he was already hailing a new religion "without revelation" (and of course without supernatural entities), and in his 1952 founding presidential address to the INTERNATIONAL HUMANIST AND ETHICAL UNION he reiterated his argument that once we humans understood evolutionary processes, both biological and social, we became responsible for them. He even argued there that we should study yoga and mystical belief systems scientifically, so that we could utilize any of their good features without relying upon improbable beliefs.

In his commemoration address at Chicago's 1959 Darwin celebration, broadcast internationally, the stress he laid upon human responsibilities in an evolving but designless universe shocked many hearers as he outlined "the Humanist view of the three great activities of man in which he transcends the material business of making a living—art, science and religion. . . . Art opens the doors of that other world in which matter and quantity are transcended by mind and quality. . . . [Science is] the process of discovering, establishing, and organizing knowledge."

As for religion—now was the time to "to replace the multiplicity of conflicting and incompatible religious systems" with a "scientific theology." We should view religion as "applied spiritual ecology" whereby men and women come to understand the world around them, themselves, and all other humans more effectively.

Huxley came down hard here on those positivist philosophers who regarded human values as subjective nonsense, and on those Marxists (see MARXISM) who absolutized Trofim Lysenko instead of subjecting his pseudoscience to normal verification.

Huxley chose to include this Chicago speech in his 1962 volume including essays by twenty-five distinguished scholars who were willing to allow him to label them as "humanist." They come from a wide range of disciplines; many had met during two post-UNESCO years in an Idea-Systems Group that he had assembled. The assumption was that "the knowledge-explosion of the last hundred years was providing man with a new revelation, a new vision of his destiny." The first critical event in the past of evolution came when the process "transcended itself," passing from the inorganic to organic life; the second was the transition to the "psychosocial." We are now, he argued, at the threshold of "a consciously purposive phase." The best label for this is "evolutionary humanism."

Huxley is clearly the type of humanist who redefines concepts rather than rejecting them. His own scientific writings ranged from the very technical to the quite popular, and he stretched his own expertise with a lifelong commitment to birdwatching. He befriended the Jesuit and evolutionary paleontologist Pierre Teilhard de Chardin (whose own church had forbidden him to publish), and wrote the preface for *The Phenomenon of Man*, one of Teilhard's posthumous publications. Huxley could appreciate Bishop John Robinson's radical rethinking of Christianity (in the best-seller *Honest to God*) but still say that this, like Paul Tillich's parallel efforts, was trying "to keep his cake and eat it" in retaining the ambiguous god concept.

"Today the god hypothesis has ceased to be scientifically tenable, has lost its explanatory value and is becoming an intellectual and moral burden to our thought," he declared. Nevertheless some "outer" events (hurricanes, death) and some "inner" events (inspiration, possession, insanity) are "awe-inspiring" and "divinity-suggesting," and can seem "transnatural" (although, of course, not supernatural): "The new religion of evolutionary humanism will explore these, but always within the new centrality: promote further evolutionary improvement and to realize new possibilities; and this means greater fulfilment by more human individuals and fuller achievement by more human societies."

Huxley retained many traditional terminologies to make contact with his readers (divinity, theology, religion, inspiration) and also used descriptive terms from anthropology such as *possession*. But these were continually recast into his radical evolutionism. That basically naturalistic framework, coupled with his high visibility, made him one of the paramount unbelievers of the twentieth century. The need of the world is, as he put it, "not merely a rationalist denial of the old but a religious affirmation of something new."

Understandably, speculation continues about the possible role of genetics in this very accomplished family, which also produced his brother Aldous and his sons Francis (prolific anthropologist) and Anthony (prolific biologist). Gavin de Beer, in his preface to Ronald Clark's *The Huxleys*, said, "There can be few men more religious, in the proper sense of the word, than T. H., Julian, and Aldous, devoting all their energies and gifts to improving the sorry lot of men, without mummery, petitionary prayer, or superstition."

BIBLIOGRAPHY

Huxley, Julian. *Essays of a Humanist*. Harmondsworth: Penguin, in association with Chatto & Windus, 1966. Reprinted as *Evolutionary Humanism*. Amherst, NY: Prometheus Books, 1992.

―――. *Evolution, the Modern Synthesis*. New York and London: Harper & Brothers, 1943.

―――. *The Humanist Frame*. New York: Harper, 1962.

―――. *Religion without Revelation*. London: E. Benn, 1927.

―――. *UNESCO, Its Purpose and Its Philosophy*. London: Preparatory Commission of the United Nations Educational, Scientific and Cultural Organisation, 1946.

ROBERT B. TAPP

HUXLEY, THOMAS HENRY (1825–1895), English naturalist and essayist. Thomas Huxley was born on May 4, 1825, in the country village of Ealing, the youngest of seven children of George and Rachel Withers Huxley. His schooling was irregular, but even as a young boy he was interested in a staggering array of subjects. From James Hutton he learned about geology. From Sir William Hamilton's "The Philosophy of the Unconditioned" he embraced the skepticism that typified his mature thought. From Thomas Carlyle he developed sympathy for the poor that was later reinforced by his exposure to the squalor and poverty he saw in the East End of London. He taught himself German to read Goethe and Kant in the original. This would serve him well in later years, allowing him to become acquainted with the tremendous biological advances being made in Germany that few English men of science were able to follow. He began studying medicine at quite a young age and received a scholarship to the medical school attached to Charing Cross Hospital. Except for physiology, most of the medical curriculum bored him although he did extremely well. Between 1846 and 1850 Huxley traveled around the world as assistant surgeon on the HMS *Rattlesnake*, resulting in some of his most important scientific work. He met his future wife, Henrietta Anne Heathorn, while visiting Australia. They married in 1855 and had a long and happy marriage and seven children.

Huxley's life was one of incessant activity. He lectured at the School of Mines and was also a professor at the Royal College of Surgeons. Evenings were often spent speaking before working men or learned societies. He was president of numerous societies, including the British Association for Advancement of Science (BAAS), the Geological Society, and the Ethnological Society. He authored several hundred scientific monographs as well as countless popular essays. Huxley's early work from the *Rattlesnake* voyage established his reputation within the scientific community, but it was his defense of DARWINISM that brought him into the public

spotlight. His famous encounter with Bishop Samuel Wilberforce at the 1860 meeting of the BAAS was an important milestone in his career (see EVOLUTION AND UNBELIEF; DRAPER, JOHN WILLIAM). Not only did it ensure that Charles DARWIN's theory received a fair hearing, but it let the public know that that he was a force to be reckoned with in the world of science and religion.

Huxley's interests were not confined to science. He loved music, art, and literature, and was a member of two famous London clubs: the X Club and the Metaphysical Society. The X Club was founded in 1864 at his suggestion in order for his scientific friends to keep in touch with one another. The Metaphysical Society's members represented the intellectual elite of London society. It provided the perfect forum for Huxley to present his views on theological and metaphysical questions, religion, and the nature of knowledge.

It was Huxley's membership in the Metaphysical Society that caused him to coin the word AGNOSTIC to describe his own belief system and to distinguish it from other –isms, such as POSITIVISM, MATERIALISM, ATHEISM, and even empiricism. It was meant to be antithetic to the "gnostics" of church history, who claimed to know so much about the very things of which he was ignorant. Typically agnosticism is thought to be concerned with religious belief. However, this was not Huxley's original meaning. Rather, agnosticism represented an epistemological claim about the limits to knowledge. Building on the Kantian principle that the human mind had inherent limitations and further elaborated by David HUME, Huxley maintained that our knowledge of reality was restricted to the world of phenomena as revealed by experience.

Huxley was often called a materialist, which he firmly denied. However, it is easy to understand why people labeled him one. On the tree of knowledge his idiosyncratic definition of materialism placed materialistic terminology on the branch of physics while materialist philosophy went on the twig of metaphysics. Materialist methodology had led to tremendous advances in physiology and psychology. However, for Huxley materialist philosophy involved "grave philosophical error," because we know the material world only by the forms of the ideal world. The fundamental doctrines of philosophical materialism, like those of spiritualism, lay outside the limits of philosophical inquiry.

Agnosticism is perceived as having an antireligious bias, in part because Huxley was well known for his polemics against theology. While agnosticism certainly challenged orthodox Christianity, it also placed limits on the kinds of phenomena science could explain as well. Theological and metaphysical questions interested Huxley, but he regarded science and philosophy as occupying distinct domains. On questions that were not amenable to the scientific method, those that went beyond the cognizance of the five senses, he declared himself an agnostic. He had no reason for believing in immortality (see IMMORTALITY, UNBELIEF IN), but he also had no means of disproving it. He drew distinctions between religion, theology, and science. Religion belonged to the realm of feeling, and he claimed that a deep sense of religion was compatible with the entire absence of theology. Science and theology, while distinct, belonged to the realm of the intellect as they both made empirical claims about the nature of the world. Therefore, theological claims must be subject to the same standards of proof as scientific ones. Theology would become "scientific" when the scriptures were treated as a collection of ordinary historical documents and analyzed using the research methods of philology, archaeology, and natural history. Huxley had tremendous antagonism toward natural theology, often attributed to his belief in Darwinism. However, his enthusiasm for evolution was in part due to the absence of theology in Darwin's theory. He used Darwin's theory to promulgate his antitheological and anticlerical views (see ANTICLER-ICALISM), and as a vehicle to gain power in intellectual, institutional, and political arenas.

More than anyone else, Huxley was responsible for disseminating Darwin's theory to the Western world. However, Huxley had a research program established long before he went to battle against the enemies of evolution. In spite of dubbing himself "Darwin's bulldog," he was skeptical of the two basic tenets of Darwin's theory—natural selection and gradualism. Pre-*Origin*, Huxley did not believe in transmutation because the work of Karl Ernst von Baer and Georges Cuvier as well as his own research suggested that organisms could be grouped into discrete types and that no transitional organisms existed between them. While his early work from the *Rattlesnake* superficially appears to be merely a series of detailed monographs on various invertebrates, he had a much more ambitious agenda. He wanted to provide a theoretical foundation for taxonomy in order to understand how form came to be generated. The concept of type was crucial to this enterprise. With the publication of *Origin of Species* in 1859, Huxley recognized that the unity of type he was observing was the result of descent from a common ancestor. Darwin also claimed that species gradually change. But Huxley argued that saltation or evolution by "jumps" better described the geological record with its abrupt appearance of most forms. Saltation allowed Huxley to explain the gaps in the fossil record, accept evolution, and maintain a belief in the concept of type. Huxley eventually converted to gradualism as more and more transitional organisms were found. *Archaeopteryx* and the birdlike dinosaurs led Huxley to argue that dinosaurs were the connecting link between reptiles and birds. Natural selection was not relevant to the kinds of questions that interested Huxley. Although he thought it would eventually be proved, he remained skeptical about the power of natural selection to cause new species, rather than just well-marked varieties. However, this difference with Darwin was not so much over natural selection or even the interpretation of experimental results, but rather over what constituted proof of a hypothesis.

Man's Place in Nature is Huxley's most famous work. Published in 1863, eight years before Darwin published *Descent of Man*, Huxley provided compelling evidence that humans were no exception to the theory of evolution. Claiming that the classification of humans should be determined independent of any theories of origination of species, Huxley removed the question of human ancestry from theological concerns. This allowed him to promote his larger agenda of keeping theology and science distinct domains.

Huxley oversimplified the conflicts surrounding Darwinism; they cannot be reduced simply to an analysis that describes science as at war with religion (see RELIGION IN CONFLICT WITH SCIENCE). However, Huxley correctly recognized that the battle for the acceptance of evolution had to be fought on theological grounds not only in the public arena, but also within the scientific community. While Huxley's philosophical views provided the framework for his scientific views, his experience as a scientist provided the framework for his philosophy. René DESCARTES's "consecrated doubt" underlay his agnosticism and resulted in his belief that science was the path to knowledge. Thus, in spite of coining the word *agnostic*, Huxley was not deeply involved with the many agnostic societies that sprung up. It was only at the end of his life that he wrote a series of essays that were specifically a defense of agnosticism.

BIBLIOGRAPHY

Desmond, Adrian. *Huxley: From Devil's Disciple to Evolution's High Priest*. Reading, MA: Addison-Wesley, 1994.

Huxley, Thomas. *Collected Essays*. 9 vols. London: Macmillan, 1893–98.

———. "The Hypothesis of Evolution: The Neutral and the Favorable Evidence." In *American Addresses with a Lecture on the Study of Biology*. London: Macmillan, 1877.

———. *Lay Sermons, Addresses, and Reviews*. London: Macmillan, 1871.

———. *Life and Letters of Thomas H. Huxley*. 2 vols. Edited by L. Huxley. New York: D. Appleton, 1900.

———. *Scientific Memoirs of Thomas Henry Huxley*. 4 vols. Edited by Michael Foster and E. Ray Lancaster. London: Macmillan, 1898–1902.

Lightman, Bernard. *The Origins of Agnosticism: Victorian Unbelief and the Limits of Knowledge*. Baltimore, MD: John Hopkins University Press, 1987.

Lyons, Sherrie. *Thomas Henry Huxley: The Evolution of a Scientist*. Amherst, NY: Prometheus Books, 1999.

SHERRIE LYONS

HYPATIA OF ALEXANDRIA (355–417 CE), philosopher and mathematician. Hypatia is the first well-known woman philosopher, mathematician, and professor. Her birth year was once considered to be 370 CE, but scholars have placed it earlier, at around 355. Her father was Theon, the noted Alexandrian mathematician and leader of the Museum (what we would today call a university). Hypatia was educated by her father in mathematics, astronomy, and some philosophy. Theon wrote about Ptolemy and Euclid, and Hypatia shared his interest in these men and their body of work. Hypatia had a further interest in philosophy, and according to some sources traveled to Italy and Greece to further her education in the philosophy her father couldn't teach her.

Upon her return to Alexandria, Hypatia became the leader of the Neoplatonic School of Alexandria. She became a revered teacher, who pursued varied scholarly interests, including the invention of the astrolabe, her work in philosophy, and teaching. Hypatia was also a confidante of Orestes, the governor of Alexandria. As a woman, a pagan, a scholar, community leader, and friend of the governor, she became the focal point for the clash between the old world (paganism) and the new (Christianity).

In 415 Hypatia was set upon by an angry mob of Christians and brutally murdered. Her body was hacked apart and her remains burned by the mob. Cyril, the patriarch of Alexandria, may or may not have been directly involved in her demise. Cyril's motives for either instigating or directly ordering the murder can be attributed to his religious fervor to rid Alexandria of pagans. There may also have been political overtones, as Cyril had been trying to consolidate his power in the city.

It is important to note that Hypatia, while a pagan in the strict sense of the word, really did not practice paganism. She was lumped into the group because she was a mathematician, scientist, and astronomer—and because she was not a Christian. Astronomers and mathematicians were placed into the same category as numerologists and astrologers, and scholarship was an enemy to Christians at this time as well.

Hypatia's death is seen by many as marking the end of the classical world. The great Museum and libraries were systematically being destroyed and replaced by churches. Scholars began to flee Alexandria, perhaps the greatest learning center of the time; the slow decent to the Dark Ages had begun.

There is a romantic notion among unbelievers that Hypatia was a martyr. Christian apologists have tried to show Hypatia as a villain, a witch, or a magician (all tied to her mathematics), while unbelievers portray her as making a stand against the Christians. Hypatia's death was only loosely associated to her religious attitudes; her death was more a product of her era rather than the result of any conscious stand against Christianity.

BIBLIOGRAPHY

Deakin, Michael. "Hypatia and Her Mathematics." *American Mathematical Monthly* 101, no. 3 (March 1994).

Dzielska, Maria. *Hypatia of Alexandria.* Cambridge, MA: Harvard University Press, 1995.

Fideler, David. *Alexandria 2: Cosmology, Philosophy, Myth, and Culture.* Grand Rapids, MI: Phanes, 1993.

Mohar, Ronald E. "The Murder of Hypatia of Alexandria." *Free Inquiry* 3, no. 2 (Spring 1983).

TIMOTHY BINGA

IAROSLAVSKII, EMEL'IAN MIKHAILOVICH (Minei Izrailevich Gubel'man; 1878–1943), Soviet atheist leader. A key party ideologist, Emel'ian Iaroslavskii served the Communist Party of the Soviet Union as an administrator, antireligious activist, party historian, and prolific author (see PROPAGANDA, ANTIRELIGIOUS [SOVIET]).

Early Life. Iaroslavskii was born to poor Jewish exiles in the eastern Siberian city of Chita in 1878. Despite only three years of formal schooling, Iaroslavskii developed a passion for self-education and was drawn to the writings of populist and Marxist revolutionaries. In 1898 he became a Social Democrat. Until 1917 he promoted revolution in cities across Russia, enduring arrests, imprisonment, and exile.

Political Work. Part of the Stalin faction, Iaroslavskii was a longtime member of the Party Central Committee. From 1933 he was a member of the Central Purge Commission, later the Party Control Commission. Iaroslavskii also held posts in the Soviet government as a member of the Central Executive Committee from 1923 to 1937 and from 1938 until 1943 as a deputy of the Supreme Soviet.

Historical Activity. Iaroslavskii was a founder of the field of party history and participated in the bitter struggles within the historical profession in the 1920s and 1930s. He was the author of textbooks and numerous propagandistic works, including biographies of Lenin and Stalin. He was elected to the Academy of Sciences of the USSR in 1939.

Antireligious Activity. One of the leading architects of Soviet antireligious policy, Iaroslavskii chaired the Central Committee's Antireligious Commission from 1923 to 1929. He founded the League of the Militant Godless in 1925 and served as its president until its demise in 1941. Under his guidance, the league sponsored antireligious campaigns and an active publishing program aimed at creating a new atheistic culture. Iaroslavskii was founder, editor, and frequent contributor of the league's weekly newspaper, *Bezbozhnik* (Godless). He authored some 440 articles and books on antireligious subjects. The most famous was his *Bibliia dlia veruiushchikh i neveruiushchikh* (The Bible for Believers and Nonbelievers, 1923–25), a detailed study of the Old Testament in which he sought to popularize the findings of biblical criticism. It went through many editions up to the late 1970s and was translated into several languages.

BIBLIOGRAPHY

Enteen, George M. *The Soviet Scholar-Bureaucrat: M. N. Pokrovskii and the Society of Marxist Historians.* University Park: Pennsylvania State University Press, 1978.

Iaroslavskii, Em. *Bibliia dlia veruiushchikh i neveruiushchikh* [The Bible for Believers and Nonbelievers]. Moscow: Gosudarstvennoe izdatel'stvo politicheskoi literatury, 1958.

Peris, Daniel. *Storming the Heavens: The Soviet League of the Militant Godless.* Ithaca, NY: Cornell University Press, 1998.

Savel'ev, S. N. *Emel'ian Iaroslavskii–Propagandist marksistskogo ateizma* [Emel'ian Iaroslavskii: Propagandist of Marxist Atheism]. Leningrad: Izdatel'stvo Leningradskogo universiteta, 1976.

HEATHER J. COLEMAN

IKHNATON (Akh-en-ton; 1372–1354 BCE), Egyptian monotheist pharaoh. The son of Amenhotep III and husband of Nefertiti, Ikhnaton became pharaoh of Egypt as Amenhotep IV. Once on the throne he changed his name to Ikhnaton (some spell it as Akh-en-ton, often translated as "he who is serviceable to Aton"). The name change is indicative of a change in religion in which he installed Aton, symbolized by the sun disk, as the sole god. He also moved the capital from Thebes to Tel-el-Amarna. His attitude toward his god is expressed in a hymn to Aton that shows the universality and beneficence of Aton. James Breasted, the early twentieth-century historian of Egypt, was struck with the semblance of the hymn to the 104th Psalm and believed there was a direct relationship between the two. Because Ikhnaton was devoted to this God alone, the Amarna religion has been called monotheistic by Breasted and others, and he has been regarded as sort of a founder of monotheism. This assumption has since become debatable. Though it is clear that Ikhnaton and his family worshiped Aton, his courtiers worshiped Ikhnaton himself, while the great majority of Egyptians were either ignorant of or hostile to the new faith.

Though the light of Aton was supposed to benefit all races of mankind, Ikhnaton was a disaster as a ruler. In pursuing his mystical dream he ignored his governmental functions, and his empire crumbled away, the government more or less disintegrating as his own representatives betrayed him. Still, the so-called Amarna period saw remarkable stylistic changes in art, if only briefly. Differences between the sexes appear to be almost obliterated. Men and women of the upper circles imitated the royal couple in wearing identical loose garments, so thin and diaphanous that they revealed that the ideal image of the body underneath was virtually the same. Some have argued that the reason for this is that the king regarded himself as having the male and female principles united in his own person. Whatever the reasons, the changes were short lived. His successors reverted to the worship of the old gods, and restored old customs and traditions. The "new center" of the kingdom at Amarna was abandoned.

BIBLIOGRAPHY

A standard translation of the Hymn to the Aton is by John A. Wilson who also points out the similarity to verses in the 104th Psalm. It was printed in volume 1 of James B. Pritchard, *The Ancient Near East, An Anthology of Texts and Pictures,* a collection often reprinted.

VERN L. BULLOUGH

IMMORTALITY, UNBELIEF IN.

Who would fardels bear,
To grunt and sweat under a weary life,
But that the dread of something after death,
The undiscover'd country, from whose bourn
No traveller returns, puzzles the will,
And makes us rather bear those ills we have
Than fly to others that we know not of?
Thus conscience doth make cowards of us all . . .

Shakespeare, *Hamlet,* I, iii

Shakespeare's Hamlet, as he mused in this way, was assuming that as a flesh-and-blood human being, a person, he was really and essentially an incorporeal spirit enjoying (in the context of eternity) strictly temporary control of his human body. It was to conscience, in this present sense of consciousness, that Albert Einstein was referring when he remarked during a conversation with Herbert Feigl that "[i]f there were not this internal illumination, then the Universe would be a mere rubbish heap."

In discussing the present subject we must never forget that until the beginnings of modern science, absolutely everyone believed that the universe was full of incorporeal spirits endowed with active powers. But such spirits were ill equipped to serve as the hypothetical entities of an explanatory theory, for no one was able to propose any way in which such spirits could be identified without reference to the very movements they were being introduced to explain. Nor, once such a hypothesis had been adopted, were there any fresh and testable inferences that could be drawn from it.

It is worth quoting here an illuminating comment made by Herbert Butterfield in his classic work on *The Origins of Modern Science*: "The modern law of inertia, the modern theory of motion, is the great factor which in the seventeenth century helped to drive the spirits out of the world. . . . Not only so—but the very first men who in the middle ages launched the great attack on the Aristotelian theory were conscious of the fact that this colossal issue was involved in the question. . . . Jean Buridan in the fourteenth century pointed out that his first alternative would eliminate the need for the Intelligences that turned the celestial spheres. He even noted that the Bible provided no authority for these agencies."

But it appears to have been several centuries before this elimination from classical mechanics of the conception, or misconception, of incorporeal agent spirits began—at least in the English-speaking philosophical world—to have any effect on either the philosophy of mind or the philosophy of religion. Indeed, until the publication of Gilbert Ryle's *The Concept of Mind*, the standard work on the philosophy of mind, to which beginning philosophy students were routinely referred, was C. D. Broad's *The Mind and Its Place in Nature*.

Broad himself was much interested in, and published a volume of his own essays about, what was then called psychical research. That discipline has since been developed and extended into parapsychology. Psychical research was mainly, although not quite exclusively, concerned with putative communications between living people and the supposedly surviving spirits of their deceased friends and relatives. These putative communications were usually mediated by professional mediums, who were almost exclusively females.

To achieve any firm and relevant findings about—and from—the putative mediumistic performances of any supposed medium, it is necessary first somehow to establish that at last some of her utterances during some particular sitting were really expressed by a spirit who had survived his or her own death. To achieve this ambition it would be necessary first to identify the putative communicator as being a disembodied spirit, and then to reidentify him or her as the disembodied spirit of some particular person now deceased. This achievement is much more easily described than actually compassed. For when supposed spirits of one particular deceased person provide information about their alleged prior lives on earth, or even speak in a manner that is peculiar to and characteristic of the persons whose putative spirits are supposedly communicating through the mouth of the medium, it is still very difficult to rule out the possibility that that medium acquired that information in some perfectly normal way, and is making use of it quite innocently.

It is only when we come to consider the eschatological teachings of the two great revealed religions, Christianity and Islam, that we are forced to recognize that the notices that were at one time to be seen outside US Army Air Force bases—"Drive carefully, death is so final!"—were not expressions of an undiscussably obvious known truth. For both of the two great monotheistic religions claim to reveal that, after our merely earthly deaths, all of us human beings will, whether immediately or ultimately, become occupants of an eternal heaven or—more likely—an eternal hell.

The question of a future life is one that, although it is not specifically mentioned in Adam Lord Gifford's will, one might expect to see discussed fairly frequently in a series of lectures that famously included William James's *The Varieties of Religious Experience*. But in fact there was no series of Gifford lectures on immortality—what, for Immanuel KANT, was the third of the three great questions of philosophy—between those of A. S. Pringle-Pattison, published in 1922, and those of Richard Swinburne and those of Antony Flew, both published in 1986.

The crucial stimulus to one if not to both of these two latter writers was the publication in 1948 of Gilbert Ryle's *The Concept of Mind*. In that work Ryle's fundamental contention was that the word *mind* is not a word for an entity that could significantly be said to survive the death and dissolution of the flesh-and-blood person whose mind it had been. For—and Ryle himself would have enjoyed putting the matter in this way—to construe the question whether she has a mind of her own as a question about a hypothesized incorporeal substance would be like taking the loss of the Red Queen's dog's temper as it if was on all fours with the loss of its bone, or like looking for the grin remaining after the Cheshire Cat itself had disappeared.

Ryle, probably for very good political reasons, neither attempted nor encouraged others to attempt to apply a similar critique to the concept of soul. But Richard Swinburne, in a recent paper titled "The Possibility of Life after Death," begins by claiming "that a human on Earth consists of two interconnected parts (two substances in philosophical terminology)—body and soul. The body is material, the soul is immaterial. The soul is the essential part of the person; it is the continuing of my soul which constitutes the continuing of me." He concludes this initial paragraph by expressing the hope that he can, in his paper, "prove to you that there is a soul for something to happen to." What is so very remarkable is that Swinburne should have hoped to establish this conclusion without attempting to explain either how individual spiritual substances are to be identified in the first place or later reidentified as the same individual spiritual substances. Instead, after first disposing of "hard materialism," as he terms it, he attempts to dispose of "soft materialism." Soft materialism, for Swinburne, says that you have told the whole story of the world when you have said what material objects exist and which properties (mental and physical) they have. However, full information of this kind would still leave one ignorant of whether some person continued to exist or not; knowledge of what happens to bodies and their parts will not show you for certain what happens to persons.

It is hard to understand how Swinburne could have persuaded himself that this is a compellingly powerful argument. For surely no one, not even one of Swinburne's misbegotten hard materialists, would ever want to deny that there is a very real and enormously important difference between living and dead human beings. Surely, too, full knowledge of all the properties, both mental and physical, of a human being has to include knowledge of whether he or she was alive and conscious or already dead at the time in question.

At this point Swinburne tries to make much of the facts that the human brain consists of two hemispheres and brain stem, and that human beings can survive and behave as conscious beings even if much of one hemisphere is destroyed. He then asks the reader to suppose that his own brain (hemispheres plus brain stem) was divided into two, and each half brain was then taken out of Swinburne's skull and then transplanted into the empty skull of another body from which the brain has just been removed; and there to be added to each the half brain from some other person—along with whatever other parts are necessary for there to be two living persons with lives of conscious experiences. Swinburne then asks: "Which of the two resulting persons would be me?"

The important thing to be said about this question is that it is a question with no antecedently correct answer. If such a question came before the courts for a decision, the case would be one of those in which a predicament has arisen the possibility of which had not been foreseen by the original legislators. It therefore requires later lawyers to decide what in future correct legal usage is to be. A previous discussant of a similar problem referred to an actual twentieth-century case in which a court had had to decide whether, under a law introduced in a much earlier century, a flying boat was or was not a ship.

Something must be said here about the difficult and controversial subject of ARISTOTLE. For it was upon suggestions he found in what Thomas HOBBES described as "the vain philosophy of Aristotle" that Thomas Aquinas developed his own teaching that the separable but separated and still-surviving form or essence of an individual person would maintain the identity of that individual person over the time gap between his or her death and his or her resurrection. Aquinas appreciated that, without some such maintenance of identity, God would have been punishing or rewarding not the actual whoever-it-was, but only a no-doubt-perfect replica of that former person.

Aristotle's most characteristic and fundamental thesis is that the life or soul is the form, or essence, the what-it-is-to-be (the "quiddity") of any particular organism. This Aristotelean notion of a form or a quiddity—that last a barbarous term derived from Scholastic Latin—is tricky and must be firmly and with special care distinguished from that of PLATO's Forms or Ideas. Certainly an Aristotelean form is no more a corporeal thing than a Platonic Form would be. But then it is not a spiritual one either. It is not, in the crucial philosophical sense, a substance at all. The soul as an Aristotelean form stands to the stuff of a body as the configuration of a statue stands to the materials of which it is made, as vision stands to

the eye capable of seeing, as cutting power stands to the serviceable axe (these illustrative examples all come from Aristotle himself). So it is obvious that the Aristotelean soul is not separable from the body and, furthermore, that this inseparability must be a matter not of physical but of logical impossibility. It is upon this insistence that we must rest Aristotle's claim to be regarded as the patron of all monistic and materialistic views of the nature of man.

Against this there was a hermeneutic tradition, descending from Alexander of Aphrodisias through AVERROËS (respected by the Scholastics as the Commentator), that attributed to Aristotle a belief in some sort of eternal intellect. But whatever this does amount to, it quite clearly is not a doctrine of the immortality of individual human souls. That was fully appreciated by Aquinas, who was moved to compose, with unwonted heat, a polemical pamphlet *de unitate intellectus contra Averroistas Parisienses* (On the Unity of the Intellect against the Parisian Averroists).

One kind of reason that might be proffered for saying that the abstract intellect (or, for that matter, any other putative abstract reality) is essentially eternal is, really, no sort of reason for saying that anything at all goes on forever. Certainly it is, in a way, correct to say that such things as logically necessary truths and logical relations between concepts are somehow timeless and eternal. Yet this is equally certainly not a matter of anything eternal actually existing, but rather of its just not making sense to ask temporal questions about the periods during which these truths and these relations obtain. For eternity, in this sense, we can have nothing either to hope or to fear.

Third, supposing Aristotle really had wanted to suggest that individual intellects could and would survive, then presumably a large part of his reason would have lain in his belief that ratiocination, unlike sight or hearing, is not localized in any organ. Even if that belief had turned out to have been erroneous, it would still have been necessary to insist that the absence of any specialist (corporeal) organ provides no justification for assuming that our intellectual attributes must, or even might, be those of incorporeal substances. The lack of specialist organs of volition is surely not to be construed as providing grounds for seeking invisible and immaterial sources to which to attribute people's feeling happy or feeling depressed. These and other more intellectual characteristics are, simply and obviously, attributes of the flesh-and-blood people concerned.

Aristotle himself never employed any such easily disposable argument. What he actually argued about the intellect was that, "since it thinks all things, it must [in the words of Anaxagoras] be unmixed with any if it is to rule, that is, to know." This idiosyncratic saying has sometimes been construed as an expression of a belief that our intellects are both incorporeal and yet (in the philosophical sense) substances: a belief which might seem to mesh in well with Aristotle's undoubted conviction that to know abstract truths is something rather grand, divine even—an essential characteristic of the most superior sort of person.

Certainly, as he makes very clear in the *Nicomachean Ethics*, Aristotle did believe that both the highest style of life and the happiest is the life of the intellect; and that anyone who attains this lifestyle attains it "in virtue of something within him that is divine." But the cherishing and attaining of an ideal of this kind is entirely consistent with a rejection of any belief in the reality of individual immortality.

The nearest Aristotle came to deploying formal argument in support of his doctrine of the soul, whatever it may be, is in the first chapter of book 1 of the *Metaphysics*. He began: "Doubtless it would be better not to say that the soul pities or learns or thinks, but that the man does so with the soul; and this too not in the sense that the motion occurs in the soul, but in the sense that the motion sometimes starts from and sometimes reaches to the soul."

That was not a good start. It would have been better not to say that either the mind or the soul either pities or learns or thinks, or indeed that it does anything else. But the preferable alternative is to say that it is the person who pities or learns or thinks or what have you. For if you insist on saying that either the man or the woman—or even, politically correctly, the sexually indeterminate person—does this or that with his or her soul, then you may be tempted, especially in the prestigious context of a treatise on the soul, to construe your chosen idiom in an instrumental rather than an adverbial way. Yet, to read any Greek analogues of such phrases as "with my whole mind" as referring to the instrumentality of some personal portion of not-matter, instead of as referring to the manner in which some activity was performed, would be as grossly, as grotesquely, wrong as to look for a dog's lost temper or for a grin detached from a grinning face.

Aristotle's argument proceeds: "But intellect would seem to be developed in us as a self-existing substance and to be imperishable. For, if anything could destroy it, it would be the feebleness of old age. But, as things are, no doubt what occurs is the same as with the sense organs. If an aged man could procure an eye of the right sort, he would see just as well as a young man. Hence old age must be due to an affection or state not of the soul as such, but of that in which the soul resides, just as is the case in intoxication and disease. In like manner, then, thought and the exercise of knowledge are enfeebled through the loss of something else within but are themselves impassive."

This—as Wittgenstein so often said—is a terrible argument, just terrible. Of course old age, like intoxication and disease, afflicts some but only creatures of flesh and blood—specifically old people, drunks, and the sick. And maybe if the transplant surgeons could give some old person two young eyes, that person would see much better. Maybe, too, if the brains of the senile demented could be replaced by younger, more vigorous, and well-stocked substitutes, they would think better. But even granting all this, it simply does not begin to look like showing that intellect is "developed in us as a self-existing substance" that is "impassive" and hence "imperishable."

All in all, the correct conclusion seems to be that Aristotle's treatment of the possible separability and consequent immortality of the intellect was an aberration. Certainly any attempt to recruit these tentative probings to support what has been labeled "the logically unique expectation" has to be stopped short by noticing the abrupt contempt with which in the *Nicomachean Ethics* he inhibits any such immortal fears or longings: "Choice cannot have for its object impossibilities: if a man were to say he chose something impossible he would be thought a fool: but we can wish for things that are impossible, for instance immortality."

There was, during the late fifteenth and early sixteenth centuries, much discussion of both the interpretation of Aristotle and the substantive issue of the nature of the soul. It is said that in those days—days remarkably different from our own!—students often interrupted lectures with impatient cries of "What about the soul?" In the long and frequently furious controversies of that period, the effective last word was said by Pietro Pompenazzi—the Peter of Montua often hailed as "the last of the Schoolmen and the first of the Aristoteleans." Book 4 of his great polemic *De immortalitate animae* (On the Immortality of the Soul) concluded first, on his own account and on the substantive issue, that the soul, including the intellect, is in no way truly itself an individual. "And so it is truly a form beginning with and ceasing to be with the body, and then, second, and on the issue of interpretation, that any other view is totally un-Aristotelean."

Having said so much about the fundamental difficulty, indeed the sheer impossibility, of identifying a hypothesized individual incorporeal spirit as present at one particular time and in one particular place, it is now necessary to proceed to point out the further difficulty, indeed again the sheer impossibility, of reidentifying a spirit identified as present at a later time in the same or another place as the same spirit as had been identified as present at the earlier time.

It has sometimes been suggested that these hypothesized incorporeal spirits might be endowed with a capacity to remember their own past conscious experience, and thus reveal to themselves that they were at time two the same individual spirits as they had been at time one. The truly devastating objection to this suggestion is one which, by anyone tolerably familiar with the classical philosophical literature, is always credited to Joseph Butler. Bishop Butler—he held the senior English see of Durham—wrote: "And one should really think it self-evident, that consciousness of personal identity presupposes personal identity, and therefore cannot constitute personal identity, any more than knowledge, in any other case, can constitute truth, which it presupposes." People just are, despite all the positive and negative implications, creatures of flesh and blood and bones.

In a nutshell the conclusion is that there will be no empirically meaningful doctrine of human immortality until and unless someone's incorporeal spirit has been shown to be identifiable at an earlier time, time one, and reidentified as the incorporeal spirit of the same individual person at a later time, time two.

ANTONY FLEW

INDIA, UNBELIEF IN. Introduction. Unbelief in religion has never been strong in India. In about the third century BCE materialist thought briefly prevailed under the names CARVAKA and Lokayata. Religious fundamentalists soon suppressed the Carvaka movement and destroyed most of its writings. During subsequent periods Buddhist philosophies held sway (see BUDDHISM, UNBELIEF WITHIN), but these endured only as long as they enjoyed the favor of local rulers. Eventually Buddhism became nearly extinct in India even as it transformed into a religion and spread to other parts of Asia.

Centuries passed before India saw new agitation toward organized unbelief. When the opportunity arose, it was a consequence of Great Britain's occupation and subsequent rule of India. A small number of Indians who had traveled abroad brought back Western ideas about the Renaissance, the Industrial Revolution, and the scientific worldview.

Throughout the nineteenth century there were nearly continual efforts at religious reform, but most were unsuccessful in bringing about radical or deep-rooted social change. Harmful institutions such as India's strong caste system, untouchability, the practice of *Sati* (burning the widow alive on her husband's pyre), and a demoralizing conviction regarding Karma or irresistible fate were rooted directly in ancient Hindu scriptures. While some nineteenth-century reform movements— including the Arya Samaj, Brahmo Samaj, Prarthana Samaj, and even THEOSOPHY in its reformist aspects— brought about some social change, their impact was short lived because none of them questioned the prevailing belief system in a fundamental way. So long as no reform movement dared to confront messages of India's so-called holy scriptures, the social evils opposed by reformers would always endure in some form, enjoying popular support on the false grounds that they embodied India's tradition and heritage.

Indian Unbelief in the Early to Mid-Twentieth Century. Only with the beginning of the twentieth century did a more resilient and dynamic form of unbelief emerge. Not surprisingly, it arose in southern India, a region then at the forefront of efforts to force drastic changes in India's social structure.

E. V. Ramaswami, better known as PERIYAR, launched an anti-Brahmin movement in what is now the state of Tamil Nadu in 1925; Tripuraneni Ramaswami (no relation) simultaneously launched a similar movement in Andhra Pradesh. Periyar and Ramaswami independently published literature in Tamil and Telugu, spreading iconoclastic ideas in opposition to long-established oppression by upper-caste Brahmins. By publishing in local languages, the two activists challenged the supremacy of the Sanskrit language, whose privileged status as the official language of the scriptures and the priesthood helped perpetuate social differentiation. In addition Periyar and Ramaswami urged the replacement of Brahmin priests with non-Brahmins.

Never mincing words, Periyar and Ramaswami used strong language to express their atheistic ideas and to challenge prevailing Hindu rituals, taboos, and customs such as child marriages. Ramaswami organized charitable institutions, including nursing homes to aid the downtrodden. Periyar and Ramaswami challenged Hindu holy scriptures and organized training camps that introduced a small number of middle-class people to the rational outlook. They performed intercaste marriages, which raised eyebrows in the early twentieth century. Ramaswami organized sensational processions against the Hindu god Rama in which he would strike a poster-sized image of Rama with shoes, a supreme gesture of disrespect. Ramaswami moved the masses with his speeches and organized rallies that attracted large crowds.

This movement had deep influence among the state's intelligentsia. S. Ramanathan, a prominent politician and a minister in Tamil Nadu's government, carried Periyar's mantle until the early 1980s. Periyar's Dravida Khazagam (Self-Respect) movement attracted charismatic leaders such as Annadurai Conjeevaram Nataraja and Karunanidhi Muthuvel, both of whom would later become chief ministers of the state. But they ended up by taking the organization into politics, effectively ending the movement Periyar had begun.

Other second-generation leaders stayed closer to the rationalist vision. Veeramani tried to continue the Dravida Khazagam movement and later joined India's humanist movement (see HUMANISM). Others, such as Ravipudi Venkatadri, carried the rationalist flame in Andhra Pradesh.

One of the shining lights of southern India's unbelief movement was GORA, or Goparaju Ramachandrarao. Gora was a Brahmin who stood against Brahmin supremacy, for which he was excommunicated from the caste. He hailed from Andhra Pradesh and was closely associated with Mohandas K. Gandhi in the freedom fight against the British.

Gora never compromised on the principles of ATHEISM, including resistance to the caste system. In 1940 he famously moved into the hamlet of Mudunur, a village for untouchables only, and lived among them. His wife, Saraswathi, also from an orthodox Brahmin family, soon became actively involved. Together they led the atheist movement.

Also in 1940, Gora established the Atheist Centre in Vijayawada, a coastal town in Andhra Pradesh, from which he spread his ideas through magazines, literature, and meetings. Gora toured many countries of the world and contacted world atheist leaders such as Madalyn Murray O'HAIR. To make a point, Gora organized beef and pork dinners targeting both Hindus and Muslims, who respectively considered those meats sacred or unclean. Gora championed democracy without political parties, simple living, and the spread of a positive atheism centered upon ethical living. His family continues promoting his ideas: his sons, Lavanam, Vijayam, and Samaram; his daughter, Chennupati Vidya; his daughter-in-law, Hemalatha; and his grandson, Vikas Gora.

Gora officiated at several intercaste and interreligious marriages; also, his daughter and one of his sons married untouchables, practicing by example what their father preached. The Atheist Centre established by Gora and managed by his family is known for its trailblazing activity throughout India, and admired in rationalist circles worldwide.

Andhra Pradesh's atheist movement spawned several splinter groups, several of which publish their own magazines and literature. Jayagopal, Katti Padmarao, B. Sambasivarao, Ramakrishna, Gutta Radhakrishna Murthy, Saraiah, M. Subbarao, I. Muralidhar, C. L. N. Gandhi, Siddarth Baksh, M. Basavapunnarao, M. Sharif, Pasala Bhimanna, Vikram, and others continue to fly the flag of atheism, however small or localized their efforts might be.

Other southern and western Indian states, including Kerala, Karnataka, and Maharastra, also saw an early twentieth-century surge in rationalist activity. Abraham KOVOOR, originally of Kerala, electrified the skeptics' movement with his speeches and demonstrations, touring several states in India as well as Sri Lanka, where he settled. His books debunking astrologers and wonder-working "god-men" remain popular today. Another active rationalist in Kerala is Govindan, who edits the magazine *Sameeksha*. The father-and-son duo of Joseph and Sanal Edamaruku was also instrumental in challenging god-men and exposing fraudulent "miracles." They toured extensively to demonstrate the falsehood of miracle claims that figure so prominently in rural Indian life. In 1980 Sanal Edamaruku moved to Delhi, where he launched an international rationalist organization with a Web site, journals, books, and an active campaign.

In 1954–55 B. R. Ambedkar led a large campaign in Maharastra state to convert Hindus into Buddhists so that they could discard inequality, end caste, and attain human rights with dignity. Unfortunately this movement met with little success.

Skeptics groups focused on science and the critical examination of paranormal and supernatural claims began working in states including West Bengal, Orissa, Bihar, Punjab, Gujarat, Andhra Pradesh, Karnataka, Maharashtra, and Tamil Nadu. Master magician and debunker B. Premanand arranged a federation of these groups and conducted several meetings at the national level. Premenand personally instructed several activists in magic for the purpose of exposing fraudulent faith healers and god-men and -women. In Andhra Pradesh the Federation of Atheist, Rationalist, and Humanist Associations (FARAH), a state-level federation of skeptical groups, campaigned against fraudulent claims involving god-men, alternative medicine, and the supernatural under its coordinator, Innaiah Narisetti.

The Rationalist Association was launched in Mumbai (then Bombay) during the 1930s and slowly gained momentum. Among its active participants and advocates were Abraham SOLOMON, Lokhandawala, M. N. ROY, M. V. Ramamurhty, R.Venkatadri, Avula Gopalakrishna Murthy, and Innaiah Narisetti.

M. N. Roy was distinctive in that he promoted a particularly philosophical and scientific outlook among unbelievers across India. In the 1940s he organized camps for intellectuals, teachers, youths, and activists. There he taught them the scientific method and methods of applying it to study politics, economics, and social problems. This was a unique experiment among whose several hundred participants were future humanist leaders including V. M. TARKUNDE and Indumati PARIKH. Roy also established radical humanist, renaissance, and rationalist organizations at the national and international levels. Often he challenged the Gandhian spiritual ideology prevalent among Indian intellectuals.

Unbelief in Independent India. Despite its impact among the intelligentsia, unbelief had limited impact on India at the policy level. As the first prime minister of an independent India, Jawaharlal Nehru established a secular framework for the country, but he was forced to compromise his secularism on several occasions due to religious and political pressures. In particular he had to give up on the idea of a uniform civil code applicable to all Indians, instead allowing the various religious communities to regulate marriage, divorce, inheritance, and other family law issues in accord with their religions. Today the Congress Party, which is by far the most liberal and secular in its stated outlook, continues to make compromises with all religious groups. The BJP, a Hindu fundamentalist party recently in power, sharply reversed trends toward greater rationalism in public life and education. Meanwhile, communist parties won power in three states—in Kerala during the 1960s, in West Bengal during the 1970s, and twice in Tripura during the 1970s and 1980s—in each case raising hopes of greater rationalism and commitment to a scientific thought. Instead, communists repeatedly compromised with popular religious sentiment and never encouraged the efforts of rationalists, humanists, or skeptics. For example, communist leaders continue to encourage popular religious festivals such as West Bengal's Durga Puja and Kerala's Ayyappa festival in order to attract pilgrims, tourist revenue, and voter support. The Marxian principle that "[r]eligion is the opium of the people" has been little recognized whenever India's communists have held regional power.

After the death of M. N. Roy in 1955, several intellectuals carried on his spirit of inquiry through study camps, training classes, publications, seminars, and magazines. They diversified the activism of Roy's movement into such fields as human rights (V. M. Tarkunde), equality of women (Indumati Parikh, Malladi Subbamma, and Gauri Malik), publications (Shib Narayan Ray, Prem Nath Bazaz, Philip Sprat, Ram Singh, R. M. Pal, R. L. Nigam, C. R. M. Rao, Balraj Puri, and Niranjan Dhar, author of *Vedanta and Bengal Renaissance*), civil liberties (N. D. Pancholi, C. T. Daru, Jayant Patel), international organizations (G. R. R. Babu), and secularizing activities (Avula Gopalakrishna Murthy).

V. B. Karnik and Maniben Kara concentrated their efforts among the labor and humanist movements. A. B. Shah founded the Indian Secular Society and tried to educate Muslims with the help of Hamid Dalwai. He also established Satya Shodak Mandal (Search for Truth) in hopes of bringing Muslim youth into the mainstream of secular society. His book *Muslim Politics* provoked much discussion. Shah enraged Hindus by questioning the ban on killing cows, but he is best known for championing the scientific method as a solution to India's problems. His book *Scientific Method* achieved a rare breakthrough into Indian academe when it was accepted as a textbook by Bangalore University during the vice chancellorship of outspoken activist H. Narasimhaiah. Shah launched several publications, including the magazines *Humanist Review*, *New Quest*, and the *Secularist*, as well as educational reform campaigns advocating humanism and secularism.

Unbelief in the Late Twentieth Century. Much of the effort to promote unbelief in India has become a regional effort marked by pockets of resistance to the country's fundamentalism and continued distaste for scientific thinking.

In West Bengal, for instance, local humanists and rationalists Prafulla Kumar, Manoj Dutta, Samaren Roy, and Sushil Mukherjee have questioned the claims of miracles attributed to the late Mother Teresa. In Andhra Pradesh and Kerala, the focus of activism has been against god-men and god-women who claim to perform miracle cures. In Andhra Pradesh, rationalists opposed the unscientific alternative medicine of homeopathy; exposed the psychic surgery claims of Alex Orbito; and campaigned against the swallowing of live fish for asthma cures, the hugging of regional holy woman Matha Amrithananda Mayi in order to obtain prosperity, and *Vaastu*, the Indian form of geomancy or feng shui.

Rationalist groups have published several well-documented books about fraudulent god-men such as Satha Sai Baba (*Murders in Sai Baba Ashram* by Premanand) and Jillellamudi Amma (by M. V. Ramamurthy). Other well-received titles include N. V. Brahmam's *The Truth about the Bible*, R. Venkatadri's *The Falsehood of Geomancy*, N. Innaiah's *Lie Hunting*, Narasimhaiah's *The Unscientific Nature of Astrology*, Ramendra's *Why I Am Not a Hindu*, Justice R. A. Jahagirdar's *Secularism Revised*, and Abraham Kovoor's *Be Gone Godmen*. Books exposing the holy scriptures include Laxman Sastri Joshi's *Critique of Hinduism*, V. R. Narla's *The Truth about the Gita*, Premnath Bazaz's *Gita*, P. H. Gupta's *Critique on Ramayana*, and Agehananda Bharati's *Ochre Robe*. The writings of Kushwant Singh also helped to spread the skeptical viewpoint.

Basava Premanand, Sanal Edamaruku, Innaiah Narisetti, Ramanamurthy, and G. R. R. Babu continue to question the authenticity of holy persons and have taken their message to an international level, drawing considerable media attention to Indian affairs. *Charvaka*, a Vijayawada-based magazine in Telugu edited by Thotakura Venkateswarlu, had great impact on Indian youth in early 1970s.

Increasingly, humanist, skeptical, and rationalist groups received support from Indians living abroad, people such as Aramalla Purnachandra, Nirmal Mishra, and Jyothi Sankar.

Despite activists' best efforts, miracle cures and other dubious religious and paranormal claims continue to draw thousands of believers, many of whom are enticed into making large financial contributions in the hope of restoring health or achieving some supernatural reward.

Unbelief in the Twenty-first Century. India entered the twenty-first century having failed to achieve the scientific society of which the past century's secularizing reformers dreamed. While small groups in various Indian states continue the fight against fundamentalism and traditional practices that affront human rights, India's skeptical, rationalist, secularist, atheist, and humanist groups face an uphill struggle toward their goal of modernizing Indian society.

Functioning in various regions are the Indian Secular Society, whose journal, the *Secularist*, is edited by V. K. Sinha; the Indian Radical Humanist Association, led by Sangeeta Mall, the managing editor of the *Radical Humanist*; the Indian Humanist Union, led by Prakash Narain; the Bihar Buddhiwadi Samaj, led by Ramendra; the Satya Shodhak Sabha in Surat and Babubhai Desai in Gujarat; the Andha Viswas Nirmula, an antisuperstition organization based in Maharastra and led by Narendra Dhabolkar; a humanist group in Rajastan led by Mohanot Ugamraji; rationalist groups led by Srini Pattathanam and T. Oomen; the Manavata Vadi Viswa Samstha in Haryana, led by the activist Manavatavadi; the Indian Skeptic Society (FIRA) in Mangalore, led by Narendra Naik; and Subhankar, a humanist group in West Bengal. Each of these organizations has a small membership; taken together, they comprise an almost insignificant minority among India's more than one billion people. But they continue to express their views and raise their voices, often making clever use of local media to fight back against the power of tradition, religious fundamentalism, and dogmatic thinking.

Over time, India's humanist, rationalist, atheist, and skeptical organizations in India have established numerous connections with like-minded foreign and international organizations. Several international atheist, humanist, and skeptical conferences have been organized in India and attended by leading foreign experts and thinkers. Organizations important in this regard include the INTERNATIONAL HUMANIST AND ETHICAL UNION, the Center for Inquiry, the Committee for the Scientific Investigation of Claims of the Paranormal, and the humanist and rationalist associations of various Western countries. At the same time, key Indian leaders have participated in numerous overseas conferences and congresses. Also important has been the translation of key books and articles by Indian and international authors into India's myriad languages. Skeptics in India have also benefited greatly from the populist writings of James Randi, who offers a $1 million challenge for scientific verification of any paranormal claim. Despite repeated offers of this challenge to Indian god-men, none has yet come forward to perform "wonders" under controlled conditions.

BIBLIOGRAPHY

Acharya, N. K., ed. *Rationalist Essays*. Chivala, India: Hema Publications, 1993.

Innaiah, N., and G. R. R. Babu. *The Humanist Way*. Mumbai: Indian Radical Humanist Association, 1994.

INNAIAH NARISETTI

INDIAN MATERIALISM, ANCIENT. India has an ancient tradition of RATIONALISM, FREETHOUGHT, and ATHEISM whose roots extend deeper than recorded history. Materialism (see MATERIALISM, PHILOSOPHICAL) is the basic concept that underlies ancient atheism. It is as ancient as Indian philosophy itself, and deeply rooted in speculative philosophy. According to Hindu tradition, an atheist is not just one who denies the existence of god but also one who defies the authority of the Vedas (scriptures).

Samkhya, an early system of rationalistic philosophy, had its roots in pure philosophic speculation concerning *prakruti*, a complex primal substance, and *purusha*, a sentient principle that was held to have disturbed *prakruti*, thus triggering the evolution of the contemporary universe. This process was described without any reference to *iswara*, that is, God. Kapila, revered as the founder of Indian philosophy (c. 800 BCE), is considered the founder of *Samkhya* (sometimes termed *Nireswara Samkhya*—"Nireswara" meaning "godless.") *Samkhya* proceeds from the ideas of *swabhava* (physical reality, or the laws of nature) and *parinama* (an active principle best summarized as "evolution").The *Samkhya* system was originally atheistic, but over generations the-

ists succeeded in smuggling God into it, presented as a supreme spirit ruling over both *prakruti* and *purusha*.

The followers of the *Mimamsa* school—which had established the authority of the Vedas (classical Hindu scriptures)—set such stock by Vedic ritual that they felt no need for a god. They believed that merely chanting mantras would produce certain effects directly. So for them the *devas*, or nature spirits described in the Vedas, had only verbal significance and did not actually exist. The *Nyaya* school, believed founded by Gautama (variously dated between the third century BCE and the first century CE), was also rationalistic, stressing above all rigorous logic in argumentation. The philosopher Kanada (dates unknown), who founded the rationalistic *Vaiseshika* school, believed in the existence of atoms. But the later advocates of the *Nyaya* and *Vaiseshika* systems imported God into them, rendering them theistic.

The *Carvaka* and *Lokayata* schools of philosophy (see CARVAKA) also flatly denied the existence of gods and belittled God's importance in shaping human affairs. The Lokayata system, which believed only in the four classical elements and the world of experience, is considered the foremost materialistic philosophy of ancient India. Krishna Mishra, a contemporary of Gautama Buddha, summarized *Lokayata Darshana* (Lokoyata teaching) in these words: "only perceptual evidence is authority. The elements are earth, water, fire and air. Matter can think. There is no other world. Death is the end of all."

The Jaina and Buddhist schools of thought developed around 500 BCE, independently of the Vedic tradition. Their greatest exponents, the Jaina commentator Gunaratna and his Buddhist counterpart Santarakshita (both c. fourteenth century CE), put forward convincing arguments against the existence of any god.

Thus ancient India is not only a cradle land of religion, but also of atheism. History demonstrates there unbelievers were numerous in ancient India, even in the times during which the Upanishads were compiled. Long before the advent of the Buddha, there were atheists known as *Nasthiks* (no-sayers) or *sangaya* (nihilists or agnostics). Revered philosophers including Purana Kashyapa, Maskarin Gosala, and Ajia Kasakamblin were unbelievers. Even that central Hindu epic, the *Ramayana*, depicts Satyakama Jabali—a teacher of humble birth who was openly skeptical about the existence of God. The later Upanishads and the oldest Buddhist books alike name numerous heretics who denied the existence of God; the Hindu sage Brihaspathi was an icon of this school of thought. The previously mentioned Caravakas and Lokayatas condemned superstitions and Hindu orthodoxy. They challenged the concept of rebirth, the idea of the soul, and diverse religious practices. These ancient atheists challenged the authority of the Vedas and the Upanishads. They spread the *Nasthika* movement far and wide, challenging the supremacy of the Brahmins whose prestige rested in part on those scriptures.

The Jain teacher Mahavira and the Buddha also advocated unbelief, though in a refined manner. Buddha's teachings essentially made god unnecessary; he claimed "enlightenment" but never inspiration, and never pretended that a god was speaking through him. He founded Buddhism without making any reference to God. The positive materialistic content of Buddhism was very popular in India for nearly a thousand years.

Unlike Jainism and Buddhism the *Nireswara Samkhya*, Caravaka, and Lokayata schools never enjoyed royal patronage. They were simply rationalistic, materialistic, and atheistic. Their followers were vilified, excommunicated, and hounded out. The legendary Indian lawgiver Manu is said to have given an injunction (c. 1500 BCE) that a *nasthika* (atheist) should be driven out of good society. Over the centuries, this dictate was frequently obeyed. The manuscripts of the early atheistic thinkers were destroyed. For example, the Carvaka school died out shortly after 1400 CE; its principal works survive only as fragments cited in the works of Hindu and Buddhist opponents. But even those fragments reveal that the early atheists were bold freethinkers. Theists could not ignore them, as atheistic freethought enjoyed strong support, and its ideas had to be taken seriously and faced rigorously.

Atheism had strong roots in traditional Indian wisdom. According to Debiprasad Chattopadhyaya, the leading researcher on ancient Indian atheism, the overwhelming majority of the accredited exponents of major philosophical views were committed atheists. He reiterates: "[T]hey were not simply indifferent to the question of God, as some of the early Greek philosophers perhaps were. The Indian philosophers, on the contrary, faced the problem of God with all the seriousness they were capable of and they reached the reasoned conviction that His existence could be admitted only at the cost of clear logic. Such a situation is really unique. It has hardly any parallel in the history of world-philosophy."

Traditional Indian atheism is, then, truly ancient. It represented an extensive area of clear agreement among the traditional Indian philosophers. In spite of their commitment to atheism, these philosophers represented diverse worldviews; thus atheism in India had to develop with a peculiar self-sufficiency all its own. Philosophers had to defend atheism as such, without allowing its admixture with their other preoccupations. For the Lokayatas, atheism formed part of a clear and consistent materialistic outlook. They denied god in order to make room for the doctrine of the exclusive reality of the material elements. It was more or less true, as well, in the case of *Sankhya* philosophers.

Ancient Indian philosophers did their best to prove that, logically speaking, God was only an illusion; and they were greatly successful in their efforts. Theism and atheism represented for them clear-cut and diametrically opposed philosophical positions. They concluded firmly that God is a simple superstition, an empty assumption, and an object of misdirected reverence.

Let us close with the words of Debiprasad Chattopad-hyaya, who, summing up the status of God in Indian philosophy, declared, "Of all our major philosophies, only the Vedanta (with some reservation) and specifically the later version of the *Nyaya-vaisesika* were theistic. By contrast, Buddhism, Jainism, Purva-mimamsa, Samkhya, Lokayata and Nyaya-vaisesika in its original form were philosophies of committed atheism. Thus, the stupendous importance of atheism in Indian wisdom can be questioned only by disallowing the largest majority of the significant Indian philosophers representing it."

BIBLIOGRAPHY

Chattopadhyaya, Debiprasad. *Indian Atheism: A Marxist Analysis*. Mumbai: People's Publishing House, 1983.
———. *Lokayata, a Study in Ancient Indian Materialism*. Mumbai: People's Publishing House, 1973.
Kashinath. *The Need to Revive Atheism in India*. New Delhi: Ajanta, 1992.
Rao, Avula Sambasiva. "The Materialistic Thought in India." In *Atheist Centre Golden Jubilee Souvenir*. Vijayawada, India: Atheist Centre, 1990.

LAVANAM

INDONESIA AND SOME OTHER ISLAMIC COUNTRIES, UNBELIEF IN. Indonesia: An Overview. In 2000 Indonesia had a population of 212 million. Its official religion has been described as monotheism. The national ideology, *Pancasila* (Five Principles), presupposes the existence of one supreme God. As of 1999, religious affiliation was distributed as follows: Muslim, 83 percent; Protestant, 9 percent; Roman Catholic, 4 percent; Hindu, 2 percent; Buddhist, 1 percent; and other (comprising religious persons and atheists), 1 percent. As these figures indicate, Indonesia is a predominantly Islamic society. Religious people other than the Muslims are found mostly in cities and in some eastern parts of the country. Indonesia is the world's most populous Islamic country. Religious fanaticism is not common among Indonesians, but for decades strong tensions have existed between Christians and Muslims, resulting in occasional clashes.

As regards freedom of religion, the situation in Indonesia is complex. After several centuries as a Dutch colony, Indonesia became independent in 1949. Its first president was Sukarno, who was extremely popular. In 1966 General Suharto became the second president; he ruled until May 1998. During this period Indonesia had five recognized religions: Islam, Roman Catholicism, Protestantism, Hinduism, and Buddhism. People were encouraged or forced to join one of these religions, and discouraged or disallowed from joining other religions. Thus ATHEISM, SECULAR HUMANISM, and irreligion were possible only in private.

Atheism has often been confused with Communism in Indonesia. Communism was allowed as a political option from 1945 until October 1965, but from October

1965 until the end of the Suharto regime in May 1998, Communists were harshly persecuted.

Indonesia Compared with Some Other Islamic countries. According to the *World Christian Encyclopedia*, in 1995, 2.1 percent of the Indonesian population consisted of secularists, that is, either atheists or the nonreligious. In 1980 the corresponding figure was 1.6 percent; in 1900, 0 percent. According to the same source, Islamic countries never incorporated into the Soviet Union generally have low percentages of secularists. In 1980 Jordan had the highest percentage of secularists (2 percent) among seventeen such Islamic countries. By 1995 Algeria was the Islamic country with the highest percentage of secularists (3 percent), followed by Syria (2.9 percent), Indonesia and Turkey (2.1 percent each), Jordan (1.9 percent), Sudan (1.1 percent), and Morocco (1 percent). In the other Islamic countries never incorporated into the Soviet Union, secularists made up less than 1 percent of the population.

Islamic countries that have been a part of the Soviet Union and therefore touched by aggressive atheism (see PROPAGANDA, ANTIRELIGIOUS [SOVIET]) have higher levels of secularism (atheism or agnosticism). The *World Christian Encyclopedia* reports that in 1995 Azerbaijan contained 11.7 percent secularists; Kazakhstan (with a partly Christian background), 43 percent secularists; Kirghizia, 29.6 percent secularists; Tajikistan, 15 percent secularists; Turkmenistan, 11.7 percent secularists; and Uzbekistan, 23.2 percent secularists. In sum, in those Islamic countries once part of the Soviet Union, no less than 11.7 percent of any country's population was made up of secularists. Because this rate is so much higher than is seen in Islamic countries never a part of the Soviet Union, it may be assumed that the heightened level of secularism seen in formerly Soviet Islamic countries is at least partly due to the influence of Soviet atheism.

Albania. The Muslim parts of the Soviet Union are not the only areas of the world in which Islam and other religions underwent fierce attacks in the twentieth century. In Albania both Christians and Muslims were subjected to harsh persecutions by Albanian communists under the leadership of Enver Hoxha from 1944 on. In 1967 all churches and mosques were closed and Albanians were forbidden to possess religious literature. After 1990, when the communist regime broke down, efforts were made to introduce religious and political freedom in Albania.

Turning again to the *World Christian Encyclopedia*, we find the following snapshots of religious affiliation in Albania at the beginning and near the end of the twentieth century:

Muslims	1900	68.5%	1995	36.3%
Christians	1900	31.3%	1995	33.4%
Nonreligious	1900	0.1%	1995	20.2%
Atheists	1900	0%	1995	10.1%

Presumably, between 1944 and 1995 Islam had been sharply weakened—although to the degree these figures are reliable, in 1995 Islam remained the largest religious community in Albania. Yet by that year Christianity was only marginally weaker than Islam. The true novelty in the 1995 figures is an almost entirely new secularist group, comprising 30.3 percent of the population. This means that in 1995 the religious landscape in Albania was almost evenly divided among Muslims, Christians, and secularists.

Atheism in the Islamic World. Explicit atheism remains rare in the Islamic world. This seems to be the case even in some of the Islamic countries exposed to Soviet atheism. Though Soviet atheism was aggressive, it was able to eradicate religious beliefs only to a limited extent in its areas of influence. Some fifty countries around the world have majority Muslim populations. Few scholars appear to have explored the phenomenon of atheism in Islamic countries, to the degree it exists.

Marxism and Communism in Indonesia. In the twentieth century MARXISM and communism were powerful vehicles for the spread of atheism. Marxism comprises the ideas advocated by Karl MARX, Friedrich Engels, Vladimir I. LENIN, and other thinkers and activists. Communism, of which several forms exist, was often a radical and intransigent kind of political Marxism.

Marxism was the first atheistic philosophy presented to parts of the Indonesian population in any systematic way. In fact it has been the only atheistic philosophy to wield significant influence in Indonesia, even if often in distorted or watered-down versions.

Marxism was first brought to Indonesia by Dutchmen. Hendricus Sneevliet disembarked at Semarang, Java, in 1913, and a year later started a socialist club in Surabaya. Sneevliet's eagerness to propagate socialism was frustrated by other members of the club, who preferred for it to function only as a study group. Another socialist group was established by Adolf Baars in Surabaya in 1917. Both this group and the earlier group founded by Sneevliet were able to attract some Indonesian members.

More important for Marxism than these early Dutch-founded groups was the Sarekat Islam, founded in 1911 as a society of Muslim merchants. Its aim was to offer Javanese and Arab traders protection against encroachments by Chinese traders. Although Sarekat Islam was a Muslim organization, some of its members were Muslims in name only; some were influenced by Marxist thought. In 1920, Marxists established what later came to be the Indonesian Communist Party (PKI). The most important of these early communists were Semaun, Alimin Prawirodirjo, Musso, Darsono, and Tan Malaka. Of these, Tan Malaka is ordinarily considered the most important theorist. Darsono, too, reportedly made a serious study of Marxism.

Early Indonesian communists were not antireligious; to the contrary, they were cautious in their public stance toward religion. Most were nominal Muslims, only too aware of Islam's importance in Indonesia. Little is known regarding their personal religious views.

Although opponents constantly stressed the atheism of Indonesian communists, Indonesian communists rarely propagated atheism. On the road to Indonesia, the thought of Marx, Engels, and Lenin was in practice deprived of explicit atheism. Where atheism was not avoided outright, it was never emphasized. In Indonesia religion remained broadly popular, and atheism did not serve the purposes of the left. Atheism as an ideology was quite foreign to a large part of the Indonesian population.

Later Communism in Indonesia. The earliest phase of communism in Indonesia was short lived, being suppressed in 1927. In this early period the Indonesian Communist Party never had more than three thousand members. Probably only a fraction of these were atheists or agnostics. A new and more auspicious period for Indonesian communism began in 1951, ending in a catastrophe of historic dimensions in 1965–66. The leader and main theorist during this period was Aidit. Available biographical information says nothing about his personal religious beliefs, if any.

Some leading communists from this period were presumably atheists, including Lukman, Nyoto, Sudisman, and Nyono. On the whole, very little is known about their personal religious views. Most were nominally Muslim, whereas some were nominal Christians or without known religion. Among leading socialists, a few had privately declared themselves to be atheists, though they did not admit it in public. In fact, no well-known twentieth-century Indonesian offered a public statement of his atheism, if he was an atheist. Atheism was always a private view.

Indonesian communists ordinarily presented themselves as nationalistic, as being opposed to the use of violence in the pursuit of political objectives, as defenders of democracy, and as sympathetic to religion. In November 1954, communist leaders for the first time announced their adherence to Sukarno's *Pancasila* ideology, which included "belief in one God" as one of its tenets. Although communist leaders would later retract their positive commitment to *Pancasila*, *Pancasila* nonetheless became an element of Indonesian communist ideology, culminating in *Pancasila*'s inclusion in the Communist Party constitution in 1962.

Atheists in Islamic Countries. An interesting feature of the *World Christian Encyclopedia* is that it presents precise numbers of atheists for almost every country in the world—though it is not always clear how these figures were arrived at. For example, the *Encyclopedia* informs us that there are no known atheists in Vatican City. As to Islamic countries, the *Encyclopedia* lists the following atheist populations, as of 1995:

Afghanistan	400
Indonesia	460,000
Iran	7,600
Iraq	31,000
Libya	90
Mauritania	180
Saudi Arabia	4,400
Senegal	3,600
Syria	30,000
Tunisia	3,400
Turkey	62,000

It is difficult to gauge the accuracy of these numbers; it is also difficult to identify and contact atheists, even in Muslim countries that supposedly contain many of them. Across the Islamic world, as elsewhere, atheism has largely remained "invisible."

BIBLIOGRAPHY

Barrett, David, George Kurian, and Todd Johnson, eds. *World Christian Encyclopedia: A Comparative Study of Churches and Religions in the Modern World.* 2nd ed. Oxford: Oxford University Press, 2001.

Hiorth, Finngeir. *Atheism in the World.* Oslo: Human-Etisk Forbund, 2003.

FINNGEIR HIORTH

INGERSOLL, ROBERT GREEN (1833–1899), American orator, secularist, agnostic, lawyer, and freethinker. In the course of a thirty-year speaking career, Robert Green Ingersoll—"the Great Agnostic"—was seen and heard by more Americans than any human being prior to the advent of motion pictures and radio. In his day the best-known representative of ATHEISM, AGNOSTICISM, SECULARISM, and FREETHOUGHT, he unfortunately built no organization to perpetuate his influence.

Early Life. Ingersoll was born on August 11, 1833, the third and youngest child of John and Mary Livingston Ingersoll. His birthplace, a modest two-story frame house in Dresden, New York, has been fully restored and now greets the public as America's only freethought museum (see SHRINES AND MONUMENTS TO UNBELIEF). Ingersoll's father was an itinerant Presbyterian minister who was said to have but two sermons to give. The first was on abolitionism, then a contentious minority position even in the North; the second concerned hell's temperature. Reverend Ingersoll changed congregations frequently.

Ingersoll's middle name reflects his parents' abolitionist sentiments; it honors the Congregational minister Beriah Green, who delivered the first series of abolitionist sermons preached in America at a small Ohio college. In the summer of 1833, Green journeyed east to assume the presidency of the Oneida Institute, a pioneering racially integrated boarding school near Utica,

New York. Green may have visited the Ingersolls enroute about a month before Robert's birth.

Characteristically, Reverend Ingersoll wore out his welcome at this church, leaving Dresden with his family when Robert was but four months old. Mary Ingersoll died at Cazenovia, New York, in 1835. Reverend Ingersoll and the children hopped from one church posting to another, following the frontier west. Ingersoll's formal education ended with high school. He was, however, a voracious reader and he possessed a photographic memory. He formed a passionate appreciation for the writings of William Shakespeare (see SHAKESPEARE, RELIGIOUS SKEPTICISM IN) and Robert Burns. Ingersoll became a lawyer by completing his "apprenticeship" at age twenty-six. He and his brother Ebon practiced law together in southern Illinois, later moving to Peoria. There, the prominent judge and freethinker Benjamin W. Parker, impressed with Ingersoll's histrionics in his courtroom, invited Ingersoll to his home for dinner. On that occasion Ingersoll met the judge's daughter, Eva Amelia Parker. It was love at first sight for both of them. They married in 1862 and would later have two daughters. Shortly after his wedding, Ingersoll raised a cavalry regiment, was commissioned a colonel, and went off to the Civil War. In its first battle, Ingersoll's 11th Illinois Cavalry was completely surrounded. He surrendered his entire command. Paroled and repatriated to Peoria, he resumed the practice of law. He achieved regional prominence as a speechmaker in support of the Union cause. In 1867 Ingersoll was appointed attorney general of Illinois, the only public office he would hold.

Emergence as a Public Speaker. Ingersoll's career as a public speaker and an open agnostic was prompted by Eva and her father. They urged him to use his oratorical skills to attack the evils of organized religion. He was unequivocal, unsparing, and unrelenting in his attacks on traditionalist Christianity and especially its doctrine of eternal punishment, which he considered uniquely pernicious.

Ingersoll delivered his first major lecture in 1869, his last in 1899, the year of his death. During those thirty years he toured the nation almost continuously, delivering six or seven lectures each week to sold-out houses. A ticket to hear Ingersoll cost fifty cents (about seven dollars in today's money), sometimes as high as a dollar; yet wherever he traveled he consistently outdrew area revivalists who preached for free. Ingersoll commanded a large repertoire of two-, three-, and four-hour orations, all delivered from memory. His rhetoric brimmed with wit, deep feeling, and poetic expression. Titles of his principal freethought orations include "The Gods," "Heretics and Heresies," "The Ghosts," "About the Holy Bible," and "Some Mistakes of Moses." His repertoire also included orations on literature, science, women's rights, and the political affairs of the day. His complete lectures and interviews would fill twelve volumes.

On several occasions Ingersoll applied his legal skills in the service of freethought. In 1887 he defended liberal religionist Charles B. REYNOLDS against charges of BLASPHEMY in Boonton, New Jersey. When Ingersoll lost the case, he waived his fee and even paid the defendant's fine! But so thoroughly had Ingersoll ridiculed the idea of blasphemy laws in a free society that no state brought another blasphemy prosecution; the Reynolds case stands to blasphemy law in much the same way that the Scopes trial stands to evolution (see EVOLUTION AND UNBELIEF).

In another famous freethought case, Ingersoll defended D. M. BENNETT, convicted under the infamous Comstock Act for having sent "obscene" literature through the US mails (see TRUTH SEEKER, THE; COMSTOCK, ANTHONY, AND UNBELIEF; SEX RADICALISM AND UNBELIEF; TILTON, JOSEPHINE). Bennett, a freethinker, had publicly opposed traditional religion through his national newspaper The Truth Seeker, and had previously tangled with agents of Comstock when arrested for selling a birth control tract at a freethought convention in Watkins Glen, New York. Ingersoll personally interceded with President Rutherford B. Hayes, but failed to secure a pardon for Bennett in a case whose verdict would supply the legal definition of obscenity that ruled American law for about three-quarters of a century.

Political Oratory. Despite his agnosticism—and despite the fact that none of the successful political candidates for whom he campaigned dared appoint him to public office—Ingersoll was the foremost speechmaker of the post–Civil War Republican Party. (It should be remembered that the GOP was then the party of Abraham Lincoln, having taken a stronger line than the Democrats against the Southern secession and slavery.) Ingersoll's career as a political speaker of national stature began in June 1876, when the Republican National Convention was held in Cincinnati. Ingersoll agreed to nominate Maine senator James G. Blaine for president. When Ingersoll was introduced, the applause was so great that ten minutes elapsed before he could begin his remarks. Praising Blaine in florid, poetic language, Ingersoll described his nominee as a "plumed knight." Blaine would be known ever after as the Plumed Knight, and Ingersoll's "Plumed Knight" speech would be reprinted and studied as an exemplar of political rhetoric for decades. As it happened, the convention nominated not Blaine, but Hayes—for whom Ingersoll campaigned, and who won the White House. Indeed, during Ingersoll's public life every Republican presidential candidate for whom he campaigned, from Grant to McKinley, was elected; the sole GOP candidate for whom he refused to campaign—ironically, James G. Blaine—failed to attain the White House.

Also in 1876 Ingersoll gave a sentimental Decoration Day speech in Indianapolis about the sufferings of Union soldiers and their families in the Civil War. An evocative excerpt was widely reprinted as "A Vision of War." Contemporaries regarded it as the noblest statement on the war, save only Lincoln's Gettysburg Address. Ingersoll became a sought-after Decoration Day speaker and often addressed units of the Grand Army of the Republic, the Civil War veterans' group.

Combining his roles as GOP campaign firebrand and bard of the Union veterans, Ingersoll is said to have invented "waving the bloody shirt"—a Republican campaign technique that centered on tarring Democratic candidates as former supporters of slavery and Southern secession who bear personal responsibility for the innumerable scars borne by the nation during war.

High Points of Ingersoll's Oratorical Career. On October 20, 1876, months after his "Vision of War" and "Plumed Knight" speeches, a crowd estimated to exceed fifty thousand gathered at Chicago—*indoors*—to hear Ingersoll speak. The venue was the Interstate Industrial Arts Exposition Building. Designed by W. W. Boyington, whose Chicago Water Tower still stands, the "Expo" was a giant web of steel and glass panels, nine hundred feet long and two hundred feet wide, its interior unobstructed by supporting columns. It occupied the site where the Chicago Art Institute stands today. Ingersoll would speak on behalf of the Republican candidate for president, Rutherford B. Hayes. People began to fill the cavernous building two full hours before Ingersoll was to speak—of course, without benefit of any public address system. Such was Ingersoll's reputation that more than fifty thousand people would crowd together knowing that most of them could only *hope* to hear his voice.

On January 25, 1893, Ingersoll gave the dedicatory remarks for a new theater in tiny Dowagiac, Michigan. The town's economy was sustained by the Round Oak Stove Company, founded by millionaire atheist and onetime Dowagiac mayor Philo D. Beckwith. Beckwith had dreamed of building a theater and bringing culture to Dowagiac. Following his sudden death, his wife and children had fulfilled his dream by building the splendid Beckwith Theater as his memorial. Its exterior was decorated with large stone medallions carved in the likenesses of persons Beckwith had admired, such as VOLTAIRE and Thomas PAINE. Six of the medallions depicted women, among them the suffragist Susan B. Anthony (see WOMAN SUFFRAGE MOVEMENT AND UNBELIEF). One of the medallions depicted Ingersoll. It now rests in the Ingersoll Birthplace Museum in Dresden.

On the evening that Ingersoll dedicated the new facility, a New York theater critic who happened to be present wrote, "The Beckwith is the finest theater in America." In future years the Beckwith would host such national-level performers as actress-singer Lillian Russell and "march king" John Philip Sousa. The theater was demolished in 1968. But January 25, 1893, was the night of the theater's dedication. Ingersoll gave a rousing memorial tribute to Philo Beckwith followed by a three-hour lecture on Shakespeare. The next evening Ingersoll delivered a three-hour lecture on Robert Burns in Chicago. To deliver two such lectures plus the memorial tribute in a space of twenty-four hours, all without notes, suggests the scope of Ingersoll's extraordinary gifts.

Ingersoll also became a sought-after provider of eulogies, speaking at the gravesides of Walt WHITMAN and Henry Ward Beecher, among many others.

Ingersoll on Religion. Was Ingersoll an atheist or an agnostic? On one occasion, Ingersoll observed that "an agnostic is an atheist, an atheist is an agnostic"—thoughtful people wearing either label know that they lack any knowledge that a god exists. Ultimately, whether one labels Ingersoll atheist or agnostic *is secondary to his identity as a secularist.* Ingersoll's secularism became the basis for his affirmative philosophy of living. He was a man of substantial beliefs—beliefs devoid of supernatural content but rather having profoundly to do with justice, REASON, the Enlightenment (see ENLIGHTENMENT, UNBELIEF DURING THE), and the fruits of science.

Ingersoll's own definition of secularism spells out the essence of his worldview, excerpted from a much longer definition that he gave extemporaneously in response to a reporter's question:

> Secularism is the religion of humanity. It embraces the affairs of this world. It is interested in everything that touches the welfare of a sentient being; it advocates attention to the planet on which we happen to live; it means that each individual counts for something; it is a declaration of intellectual independence, it means the pew is superior to the pulpit, that those who bear the burdens shall have the profits and they who fill the purse shall hold the strings. It is a protest against being the serf, subject or slave of any phantom or of the priest of any phantom. It is a protest against wasting this life for the sake of one we know not of. It proposes to let the gods take care of themselves. . . . It is living for ourselves and each other, for the present instead of the past, for this world in instead of another. . . . It is striving to do away with violence and vice, ignorance, poverty and disease. . . .
>
> It does not believe in praying and receiving but in earning and deserving. . . . It says to the whole world, Work that you may eat, drink and be clothed; work that you may enjoy; work that you may not want; work that you may give and never need.

Early in his public speaking career, Ingersoll would occasionally debate clergymen. He gave it up, declaring, "Debating the clergy is like giving medicine to the dead."

Ingersoll spoke for social justice and equality of opportunity, and against racism, anti-Semitism, sexism, and the abuse of children. He proclaimed that suicide was not a sin. Far ahead of his time, he called for an international court of justice to adjudicate disputes between nations. He proclaimed: "While I am opposed to all orthodox creeds, I have a creed of my own, and my creed is this. Reason is the only torch; justice the only worship, humanity the only religion, love the only priest. The time to be happy is now. The place to be happy is here. The way to be happy is to help make others so."

Ingersoll brought a ready wit to his attacks on traditional Christianity, as two brief examples will attest. Dining alone prior to an evening lecture, Ingersoll was spotted by a Catholic priest. The priest approached him and demanded, "How dare you disagree with Sir Issac Newton? He believed in God!" Ingersoll smiled and replied, "How dare you, sir, disagree with Sir Issac Newton, he was a Unitarian!" On another occasion, a young man timidly approached Ingersoll on a train. Summoning up his courage, he introduced himself as a cigar maker and asked Ingersoll's permission to attach his name to a new cigar. Smiling, Ingersoll replied, "Certainly—and what's more, I'll give you a slogan for the Ingersoll Cigar. 'Smoke in this world—not the next!'"

Ingersoll profoundly frustrated his religious critics; though he lacked the religious beliefs that they believed necessary for moral living, his conduct was irreproachable. No Ingersoll critic documented a single irregularity in Ingersoll's business dealings or in his personal life, notwithstanding prodigious efforts. By all accounts Ingersoll's family life was idyllic. Mocking his Christian attackers, Ingersoll once recounted an effort to spread the malicious rumor that his son was a hopeless drunkard. He spun out the story, pausing for effect until he smiled and reminded his listeners: "I have no son."

Preservation of Ingersoll's Lectures. As previously mentioned, Ingersoll carried his entire repertoire in memory. Texts of a few popular lectures were published during his life by his son-in-law, Clinton P. Farrell; others were published independently by enterprising local publishers who would be regarded today as bootleggers. (Frequently they retained stenographers to attend an Ingersoll lecture and write down every word, a task performed with varying accuracy.) Though Ingersoll's wife, Eva, had filled one hundred scrapbooks with newspaper accounts of his speeches and interviews, no authoritative text existed for most of his lectures. Goaded by his son-in-law, Ingersoll spent the last two summers of his life reviewing and correcting the newspaper accounts, then writing out the final versions in longhand. This task had but lately been completed when he died on July 21, 1899.

The recovered lectures filled the first four volumes of the twelve-volume *Works of Robert G. Ingersoll*. Farrell first published this collection in 1900 under the imprint of the Dresden Publishing Company, named for the village of Ingersoll's birth. The Dresden Edition, as the collection became known, went through many printings. Printings after 1911 included an Ingersoll biography by Herman Kittredge as a thirteenth volume. The last sizable printing was struck in 1929.

Ingersoll's Death. Ingersoll died of a heart attack on July 21, 1899, in Dobbs Ferry, New York. He was buried with full military honors in Arlington National Cemetery. The religious establishment rejoiced; its prayers had been answered! A number of libraries discarded or destroyed Ingersoll's books. Prelates who had struggled unsuccessfully to uncover a single immoral act by this "Godless infidel" assumed that, following his death, Ingersoll's secularism would no longer pose a threat to organized religion.

They were almost right. Ingersoll established no organization to promote his secularism. He twice served as president of the leading unbeliever organization of the day, the NATIONAL LIBERAL LEAGUE, but split with it repeatedly over its policy regarding birth control information. Some league activists wanted to distribute birth control information through the mail (see BIRTH CONTROL AND UNBELIEF); Ingersoll regarded that as indecent.

Organized HUMANISM, atheism, ETHICAL CULTURE, and RATIONALISM would emerge later, without direct succession from Ingersoll or the organizations of his day. And they would never enjoy the popularity Ingersoll knew.

America's so-called Golden Age of Freethought began at the end of the Civil War, when the impact of Charles DARWIN's *Origin of Species* began to be felt. It ended with Ingersoll's death just before the turn of the twentieth century. The last significant public figure who had actually heard Ingersoll and publicly embraced secularism as a result was Clarence DARROW: fittingly, the lawyer who defended evolution in the Scopes trial. Darrow died in 1938.

Ingersoll's Disappearance from History. Robert Green Ingersoll is the best-known American of the past who is so largely unknown today. During his life he was known to all—orthodox Christians who reviled him (though thousands paid to hear him) as well as numberless freethinkers who credited his words with liberating them from the cruelty and fears fostered by religion. How is it, then, that in one short century this towering figure has become a footnote to history? In 1912 journalist Michael Monahan gave the best explanation for Ingersoll's "disappearance" from the mind of the American public: "The circle of the man's philanthropy was complete. He filled the measure of patriotism, civic duty, of the sacred relations of husband and father, of generosity and kindness towards his fellowman. But he had committed treason against the Unknown, and this, in spite of the fame and success his talents commanded, made of him a social Pariah. The herd admired and envied his freedom, but for the most part, they gave him the road and went by on the other side."

We shall never see the likes of Robert Ingersoll again. Truly, his only fear was the fear of doing wrong. Fortunately he has not been totally erased from history. He was the subject of thirteen biographies, the most recent, Frank Smith's excellent biography, appearing in 1990. The Dresden Edition remains available online, on CD-ROM, and on the antiquarian book market. The Council for Secular Humanism operates a freethought museum at Ingersoll's birthplace and a variety of online freethought history resources. Ingersoll once said, "The hands that help are better far than the lips that pray." Today a handful of hands are seeing to it that the memory of this remarkable American will not be wholly lost.

BIBLIOGRAPHY

Anderson, David D. *Robert Ingersoll.* New York: Twayne, 1972.

Baker, Newton. *Robert G. Ingersoll: An Intimate View.* New York: C. P. Farrell, 1920.

Cramer, C. H. *Royal Bob: The Life of Robert G. Ingersoll.* Indianapolis: Bobbs-Merrill, 1952.

Greeley, Roger E. *The Best of Robert Ingersoll: Selections from His Writings and Speeches.* Amherst, NY: Prometheus Books, 1983.

Ingersoll, Robert G. *The Works of Robert G. Ingersoll.* 12 vols. New York: Dresden, 1900.

Jacoby, Susan. *Freethinkers: A History of American Secularism.* New York: Metropolitan, 2004.

Kittredge, Herman E. *Ingersoll: A Biographical Appreciation.* New York: Dresden, 1911.

Larson, Orvin. *American Infidel: Robert G. Ingersoll.* New York: Citadel, 1962.

Page, Tim. *What's God Got to Do with It? Robert Ingersoll on Free Thought, Honest Talk, and the Separation of Church and State.* Hanover, NH: Steerforth, 2005.

Rogers, Cameron. *Colonel Bob Ingersoll: A Biographical Narrative of the Great American Orator and Agnostic.* Garden City, NJ: Doubleday Page, 1927.

Smith, Frank. *Robert G. Ingersoll: A Life.* Amherst, NY: Prometheus Books, 1990.

Stein, Gordon. *Robert G. Ingersoll: A Checklist.* Kent, OH: Kent State University Press, 1969.

Wakefield, Eva Ingersoll, ed. *The Letters of Robert G. Ingersoll.* New York: Philosophical Library, 1951.

TOM FLYNN
AND ROGER E. GREELEY

INTELLIGENT DESIGN THEORY. A modern version of creationism (see CREATIONISM AND UNBELIEF; EVOLUTION AND UNBELIEF), intelligent design theory is based on the assumption that the universe in general and biological life in particular are too complex and too highly specified to have come into existence by chance and therefore must be products of purposeful action by an intelligent designer.

Despite its religious roots, intelligent design "theorists" present it as a "scientific" theory.

In its most recent rendition, intelligent design theory entered the discourse in the early 1990s as a version of creationism more sophisticated than its precursors (such as creation science or young-earth creationism). Creation science had suffered legal defeats, including the 1987 US Supreme Court ruling in *Edwards v. Aguillard.* This and other court decisions (notably the landmark decision of

December 2005 in *Kitzmiller v. Dover School Board*) determined that creation science is not science but religion, and therefore cannot be taught in public school science classes because doing so would violate the Establishment Clause of the First Amendment to the US Constitution.

Intelligent design theorists have largely abandoned the most egregious absurdities of the earlier creation science movement (such as the assertion that the Second Law of Thermodynamics makes evolution impossible). The key figures of intelligent design theory are well educated, sport advanced degrees from prestigious universities, and use argumentation that is suffused with mathematical symbolism, accompanied by references to real scientific sources, and often impressive looking on its face. Nevertheless, the scientific community has overwhelmingly rejected intelligent design theory, viewing it as just a better-packaged version of creationism ("creationism in a cheap tuxedo").

Intelligent design theory is essentially a more elaborate and refined version of the argument from design, which has a long tradition (see EXISTENCE OF GOD, ARGUMENTS FOR AND AGAINST). A famous rendition of the argument from design was offered by William Paley in 1802. According to Paley, nobody would assume that such a complex contraption as, say, a watch, whose multiple parts are well matched and perform a specific function, could have emerged spontaneously ("by chance"). A watch displays unmistakable features of design. Paley's argument concluded that "if there is a watch, there must be a watchmaker." Since the universe is more complex than a watch and features an intricate clocklike order, thus displaying the signs of design, Paley's idea extends to the universe the assertion that "if there is design, there must be a designer."

For Paley and many of his followers, the designer was unequivocally identified as the God of the Christian Bible. However, in modern versions of argument from design such as intelligent design theory, the identity of the designer is often deliberately left undefined, or sometimes is assumed to be some entity of an extraterrestrial origin, as in the Raëlian cult.

The argument from design was shown to be philosophically deficient by the British philosopher David HUME in 1777, but nevertheless has recrudesced time and time again since the publication of Paley's book.

Essentially, the argument from design is tantamount to the argument from improbability: the spontaneous emergence of a complex contraption such as a watch has an exceedingly small probability, therefore its existence leads to a design inference.

The estimation of probability depends on our knowledge about the situation. The reverse side of the coin is that probability reflects the level of ignorance about a situation. Therefore the argument from design is in fact a version of the argument from ignorance (also known as the God-of-the-gaps argument).

One fatal weakness of the argument from design is the

problem of infinite regress. If the universe and/or biological life are products of a purposeful design, the inevitable question is: Who designed the designer? If the probability of the universe's existence by chance is extremely small, so must be the probability of the existence of its creator, as well as that of the creator's creator, and so on ad infinitum. Applying Occam's razor, the preferable conclusion is that there is no reason to hypothesize the existence of a supernatural creator.

Emergence of the Intelligent Design Movement: Phillip Johnson. The recent vigorous activity of intelligent design theorists began with the publication of the book *Darwin on Trial* by Phillip Johnson, a professor of law at the University of California, Berkeley. Its main content was an assault on evolution theory that, according to Johnson, is grounded in materialistic philosophy while not supported by genuine scientific data.

In *Darwin on Trial* and in a series of subsequent publications, Johnson covered numerous points, rejecting essentially all the tenets of Darwinism (see DARWINISM AND UNBELIEF). One such point is the alleged unbridgeable chasm between microevolution and macroevolution. The term *macroevolution* as a part of the parlance of evolutionary biology in the usage of intelligent design advocates refers to changes that biological organisms undergo without producing new species— and hence also no taxonomic groups above the species level. Most intelligent design advocates accept microevolution as an observed fact (for example, the development of strains of bacteria resistant to antibiotics, or creating various breeds of dogs). What intelligent design advocates including Johnson deny is macroevolution (or, more properly, speciation), in which new species or even larger taxonomic categories develop as a result of descent with modification. Evolutionary biology denies any substantive difference between microevolution and macroevolution. Random mutations in the genome accompanied by natural selection (and/or by a number of other mechanisms studied by evolutionary biology) have no limits that would prevent the emergence of new species. When enough differences accumulate in the genome and the novel forms of organisms happen to be geographically separated from their progenitor form, the new offspring may become incapable of interbreeding with the progenitor species and so a new species emerges. The fact of speciation has been well established.

Another point Johnson construes as an argument against Darwinism is the Cambrian explosion, the emergence of new groups of organisms in the course of *relatively* short period of time (a few million years) some 540 million years ago. In fact, evolutionary biology can account for the Cambrian explosion quite comfortably.

Johnson also offers a series of purely philosophical arguments, suggesting that the theory of natural selection is pure tautology and that Charles DARWIN's theory is nothing more than circular reasoning. These points in Johnson's output have been repudiated from within his own camp as philosophically invalid.

Professional biologists have overwhelmingly rejected Johnson's arguments. In particular, a critique of Johnson's book reflecting a consensus of biologists was published by the prominent expert in evolution theory Stephen Jay GOULD in 1992. It was followed by other critical reviews of Johnson's literary output from various standpoints. Nevertheless Johnson's book, with its lawyerly style of argument delivered with considerable eloquence, has gained wide popularity among religiously inclined audiences. This audience finds in Johnson's book what they consider a well-substantiated repudiation of evolution theory, which they view as being at odds with their religious beliefs.

As Johnson has claimed himself, and as was acknowledged more than once by his followers, he "assumed the leading role" in an enterprise which soon became known as the intelligent design movement.

In the early 1990s Johnson was instrumental in establishing the Center for Renewal of Science and Culture (later renamed Center for Science and Culture; CSC) at the Discovery Institute in Seattle, Washington. The Discovery Institute is a conservative think tank funded by large grants from various sources, among which ultra-conservative religious foundations hold a prominent place.

In a few years a group of intelligent design theorists coalesced at the Discovery Institute. Most of the known intelligent design theorists are fellows of the Discovery Institute.

Since Johnson possesses no scientific background, he soon became a figurehead of the intelligent design movement, leaving the detailed discussions to his better-educated younger colleagues.

Behe: Irreducible Complexity. A milestone in the intelligent design movement was the publication of the book *Darwin's Black Box* (1996) by Michael J. Behe, a professor of biochemistry at Lehigh University. Behe is one of the few intelligent design advocates who is a genuine scientist with a record of publications in peer-reviewed journals. The book in question, however, is no scientific monograph, but rather a popular tale addressed to a general audience, and has little relation to Behe's biochemical research. This book has gained considerable popularity and has been widely reviewed.

In his book Behe introduced the concept of irreducible complexity of molecular assemblies in biological cells. According to Behe, a system is irreducibly complex if it performs a certain function (for example, clots blood) and consists of such well-matched and indispensable parts that the removal of even a single part renders the system dysfunctional.

Behe maintained that an irreducibly complex system could not have evolved by a Darwinian path (which entails random mutations and natural selection). Indeed, Darwinian evolution works only on existing, already functioning systems. Since a system that has even only one part of the irreducibly complex system missing, is, by Behe's definition, dysfunctional, it could not have served as an evolutionary precursor to the irreducibly complex system. Hence, stated Behe, irreducibly complex systems must have been created rather than evolved from precursor systems.

Behe's concept of irreducible complexity was not really new. To start with, long before Behe, advocates of argument from design had suggested similar ideas but applied them not to the molecular assemblies in the cell, but to, say, the eye, or to the venom-injecting system of snakes. When arguing that an eye could not have evolved by a Darwinian path because "half an eye is of no use," the antievolutionists had in fact used the same reasoning Behe did for protein systems in a cell. Moreover, even the concept of irreducible complexity in molecular systems had been suggested some ten years prior to Behe's book.

Most biologists rejected Behe's concept and indicated that irreducibly complex systems, as Behe defined them, could have evolved by a Darwinian path indirectly, utilizing what metaphorically has been called a scaffold approach. This term has been borrowed from the practice of building various structures, for example, arches. The arch cannot stand unless its lateral halves are locked together by a keystone. On the other hand, the keystone cannot stay in place unless supported by the rest of the arch. However, the problem is easily solved by using scaffolds which are removed after all parts of the arch are in place. Similarly, precursors to an irreducibly complex system could have existed but could have had functions different from the present functions (such examples abound in the biological literature); after the irreducibly complex system evolved from a precursor, some of the precursor's parts become unnecessary and, like a scaffold, are disassembled by the evolutionary process.

In his book and in several papers, Behe disputed critiques of his work. However, he ignored the extensive literature wherein biologists provided many examples of realistic Darwinian paths that could have led to the evolution of irreducibly complex systems.

Although Behe's book has been subjected to a strong critique from various standpoints, both within and without biology, and was almost unanimously rejected by mainstream biology, intelligent design theorists adopted Behe's idea of irreducible complexity of protein systems in the cell as one of the main tools in defense of their theory.

Intelligent Design Theory Goes Mathematical: William Dembski. The next milestone in the development of intelligent design theory was the publication of *The Design Inference* (1998) by William A. Dembski, followed in the next few years by several other books by the same author. Dembski possesses advanced degrees in mathematics, philosophy, and theology. He brought to intelligent design theory a new level of seeming sophis-

tication. In fact, however, his numerous publications cannot conceal that Dembski has neither performed any real scientific research nor made any innovative contribution to mathematics. Dembski has introduced into intelligent design theory several concepts that, along with Behe's idea of irreducible complexity, have become pillars of the theory. These concepts are: (a) the explanatory filter (EF); (b) the law of small probability and the associated concept of the universal probability bound (UPB); (c) complex specified information (CSI), also referred to as specified complexity; (d) the law of conservation of information (LCI), acclaimed by intelligent design advocates as a revolutionary breakthrough on a par with Newton's discoveries; (e) the calculation of the probability of a spontaneous emergence of complex biological structures such as the bacterial flagellum, and some others. Dembski's ideas have not only been largely ignored by mainstream science, they have also been repudiated by a number of experts in pertinent fields (such as information theory and molecular biology).

Dembski's explanatory filter is a flow chart that supposedly can serve as a reliable tool for discriminating between necessity (regularity, law), chance, and design as the causes of an event. Although the explanatory filter has been vigorously promoted by Dembski and praised by his cohorts, it has so far never been used to solve any specific problem. As critics have pointed out, the procedure prescribed by the explanatory filter is unrealistic. The artificial demarcation between three distinctive causes—necessity, chance, and design—does not reflect reality because more than one cause is often instrumental in causing an event. The fatal shortcoming of the EF is that it produces both false negatives and false positives, thus making it an unreliable tool.

Dembski's law of small probability states: "Specified events of low probability do not occur by chance." He suggests the threshold of the sufficiently small probability named the universal probability bound (UPB), which is about 10^{-150}. Dembski obtained this number by multiplying three quantities: (1) the estimated number of particles in the known universe (10^{80}); (2) the maximum number of interactions between particles (i.e., the number of state changes) per second (10^{45}); and (3) the age of the known universe (less than 10^{25} seconds). As can be shown, the value of UPB suggested by Dembski is based on poorly substantiated assumptions. For example, the number of particles in the universe may in fact be immensely larger than 10^{80} if we account for the actual (unknown) size of the entire universe (rather than only for the known, observable part of it).

Moreover, regardless of the value of UPB, adding specification does not save the design inference from being a purely probabilistic exercise. Analysis of CSI shows that its three components (information, complexity, and specification) in Dembski's rendition all represent, either directly or indirectly, the probability of an event. Therefore arguments in favor of intelligent design based on CSI essentially boil down to the worn-out argument from improbability. This type of argument states that the universe (or biological life) is so complex that its spontaneous emergence is too improbable to be considered seriously. The argument from improbability has no evidentiary power and science has successfully explained how extremely complex objects could have spontaneously emerged without a supernatural guiding hand (as, for example, in studies of self-organization).

The argument from improbability (especially in its form of a God-of-the-gaps argument) has been rejected as unreliable even by some philosophers among intelligent design advocates.

Dembski's law of conservation of information (2002), for which he claims the status of a Fourth Law of Thermodynamics, was acclaimed by intelligent design advocates as a revolutionary breakthrough in science. It was, however, shown to contradict the Second Law of Thermodynamics. It has not been accepted in either information theory or in thermodynamics, but is nevertheless persistently promoted by intelligent design advocates as an allegedly great scientific achievement.

Dembski's calculations of the probability of a spontaneous emergence of complex biological structures (such as a bacterial flagellum) are based on a multiplication of partial probabilities of imaginary sequential steps, each requiring coincidences of a very low probability (for example, a coincidental gathering of numerous proteins which are constituents of the emerging flagellum, all in the same location at the same time). No biologist has suggested a process like that imagined by Dembski, wherein the improbable coincidences are assumed to be the steps of biological evolution. His approach is analogous to the example of the "tornado in a junkyard" creating by chance an airplane. This scheme of many coinciding improbable events has nothing to do with biological science, which has developed many ideas regarding the pathways of evolution, in particular for the flagellum, wherein no assumptions of such improbable coincidences need be suggested. Dembski's calculations are irrelevant for biology.

Likewise certain other parts of Dembski's conceptual conglomerate are either plainly erroneous or irrelevant. A telling example is Dembski's misuse of certain theorems of optimization theory—the no free lunch (NFL) theorems. As one of the originators of these theorems, David Wolpert, wrote, "Dembski's treatment of the No Free Lunch Theorems is written in jello." Dembski's attempt to assert that the NFL theorems make evolution via a Darwinian path impossible was based on a misinterpretation of these theorems. The NFL theorems show that no search algorithm (including an evolutionary algorithm) is better than any other algorithm if its performance is averaged over all possible fitness landscapes. Dembski interpreted this result as a proof that evolutionary algorithms cannot outperform blind search. Since blind search is too slow for evolution to

have happened during the earth's existence, evolution must be not feasible as the mechanism of appearance of the variety of species—or so says Dembski. However, Dembski ignores the crucial feature of the NFL theorems: they refer only to the *average* performance of various algorithms. They say nothing about relative performance of various algorithms on particular fitness landscapes. In fact, evolutionary algorithms are known to immensely outperform blind search on relevant landscapes, and therefore the NFL theorems in no way prohibit evolution.

One more concept promoted by Dembski is the displacement problem, rendered by Dembski in two versions, incompatible with each other. Its essence is that the evolution process (which Dembski equates to a "search") allegedly requires a preceding search over the "information-resource" space in order to find either the pertinent fitness function (in the original version of the problem) or the search algorithm suitable for the particular search (in the second version). The information-resource space, according to Dembski, is supposedly much larger than the original search space, so the problem becomes much harder to solve, thus, again, allegedly making evolution improbable.

This schema is unsubstantiated in both versions. In real-life problems both search algorithms and fitness functions are given and therefore there is no need to search some information-resource space (the concept of which is absent in the context of the NFL theorems).

In 2004 Dembski announced that he is working on a set of papers under the overall title "Mathematical Foundation of Intelligent Design." As of April 2006 he had posted on the Internet the first three installments of the planned set. In the first installment Dembski claimed to have developed a new measure of information he labeled "variational information." However, as was immediately pointed out on the Internet by experts in the matter, this article did not offer any new mathematics. In fact Dembski's allegedly novel concept of variational information was identical with a quantity well known for more than forty years, Rényi's divergence of the second order. Additionally, some of Dembski's derivations in that article were shown to be in error. Dembski hastily amended his article, adding a reference to Rényi, but the amendments contained imprecise notions. More important, though, the article in question, regardless of its quality and contrary to Dembski's announced goal, contained no notions relevant to intelligent design.

As the second installment in the announced set, Dembski resurrected his article about uniform probability, which was published fourteen years earlier. Like the first installment, it had practically no relevance to intelligent design, for which it supposedly provides a mathematical foundation. In the third installment (where Dembski introduced the second version of the displacement problem), he suggested to construe evolution as a search for a small target in a large search space.

According to Dembski, such a search is hardly capable of locating the target unless it is "assisted" by input from some intelligent source, hence natural evolution must be impossible. This argument is false because evolution is not a search for a target; it is not directed to a predetermined outcome and therefore all Dembski's mathematical exercises based on his schema are irrelevant both to evolution theory and to the intelligent design concept. There is no reason to expect that the entire set of promised articles will provide a foundation for intelligent design, mathematical or otherwise.

Other Proponents of Intelligent Design. Besides Johnson, Behe, and Dembski, there are among the prominent members of the pro–intelligent design task force the philosophers Stephen C. Meyer, Jay W. Richards, and John M. Reynolds; the biologist/theologian Jonathan C. Wells; the astronomer Guillermo Gonzalez; and others.

Intelligent design advocates have often been criticized for their failure to publish papers in peer-reviewed scientific journals, which reflects the absence of scientific content in their theory. Apparently this critique caused discomfort in intelligent design circles, so intelligent design advocates began striving to break into peer-reviewed media. Meyer was apparently one of the intelligent design advocates who succeeded. He found a crack in the wall of the reviewing procedure when the editor of *Proceedings of the Biological Society of Washington* was temporarily an apparent sympathizer of intelligent design. Meyer's review paper arguing in favor of intelligent design appeared in that journal in 2004. The publication of Meyer's paper caused loud jubilation in intelligent design circles. The leadership of the Biological Society of Washington promptly disavowed Meyer's paper and stated that the editor, Richard von Sternberg, violated the policies of the journal. Biologists who criticized Meyer's paper pointed out that Meyer's review contained no original research results, that Meyer made some unsubstantiated claims, ignored many of the relevant sources that contradict his thesis, and that overall his paper was "substandard."

Jonathan C. Wells is perhaps the foremost biologist (besides Behe) in the intelligent design movement. As Wells himself revealed, he was chosen to get a PhD degree in biology by his "spiritual father," Unification Church leader Sun Myung Moon, with the explicit goal "to destroy Darwinism." Obviously such an intention adopted before having studied the subject points to Wells's preconceived bias. Wells published a popular book titled *Icons of Evolution* (2002), wherein he pounced on a number of features found in the textbooks on biology. Among these features are the famous Miller-Urey experiment, which demonstrated spontaneous production of amino acids in a simulated primeval atmosphere subjected to electric discharge; observations of industrial melanism in the peppered moth; Ernst Heinrich HAECKEL's drawings of embryos

of various species; and the like. Wells maintained that all these "icons" of evolutionary theory are at best in error and at worst fraudulent. Like the rest of the antievolution arguments, Wells's assertions were overwhelmingly rejected by mainstream biologists, who pointed to multiple distortions and misrepresentations of facts in Wells's book.

Another aspect of intelligent design was presented in Guillermo Gonzalez and Jay W. Richards's *Privileged Planet* (2004). These authors argue in favor of intelligent design, pointing to the alleged unique properties of the earth, which, they maintain, combines highly improbable "habitability" and "measurability." Most of the authors' arguments are based on correlations. Such an approach, as is known from mathematical statistics, should be used with caution as it often leads to arbitrary conclusions. This seems to be the case with Gonzalez and Richards's assertions, which at best allow for various interpretations, often contradicting those drawn by the authors.

Conclusion. In March 1999 a paper from the Discovery Institute that became known as the Wedge Document surfaced on the Internet. Its principal author is believed to be Phillip E. Johnson. It contained a detailed plan for achieving a complete overhaul of science based on intelligent design theory. This victory would be achieved in stages. While in the initial stages of the "Intelligent Design revolution" its religious motivation would be kept under wraps for tactical reasons, ultimately it would result in "nothing less than the overthrow of materialism and its cultural legacies."

The Wedge Document was a five-year action plan for the intelligent design movement covering the period between 1999 and 2003. In fact, however, the Wedge Document was supposedly laying foundation for an "Intelligent Design revolution" over a much longer period of time. The details of the Wedge Document and the progress in the implementation of its staged strategy are described by Barbara Forrest and Paul R. Gross in *Creationism's Trojan Horse* (2004). The plan envisioned activities in several directions, including publication of books and papers promoting intelligent design theory, public relations campaigns, organizing conferences, interviews, lobbying politicians and governmental agencies, and working with school boards all over the country with the aim of introducing the intelligent design theory into school curricula, first under the slogan "teach the controversy" but ultimately as a legitimate alternative to "naturalistic" science.

At the end of the initially envisioned five-year period, it was clear that the intelligent design movement had achieved substantial success in those aspects of its actions that related to public relations, recruiting politicians to their cause, and gaining considerable publicity. President George W. Bush spoke in favor of intelligent design, as did Democratic presidential candidates. Language supportive of intelligent design has found its way into resolutions of the US Senate (although it failed to become law). A number of school boards in several states included intelligent design theory in the curricula of a few local schools (although such cases are so far rare, and have been subject to lawsuits from parents and organizations defending scientific education). Intelligent design advocates also published dozens of books and many papers, as well as a great many Web postings promoting intelligent design theory. However, the other part of the Wedge strategy, which envisioned intelligent design theory breaking into mainstream science, had failed. There were no papers in mainstream scientific media where results of genuine research based on intelligent design concepts were presented. Intelligent design advocates had not suggested a single testable scientific hypothesis relevant to intelligent design theory in any field of science. They had suggested no research program based on intelligent design theory. From this, it was clear that intelligent design theory is scientifically futile and that its quasi-scientific mantle barely conceals its religious roots and motivations.

BIBLIOGRAPHY

Behe, Michael J. *Darwin's Black Box*. New York: Touchstone, 1996.

Cairns-Smith, A. G. *Seven Clues to the Origin of Life*. Cambridge: Cambridge University Press, 1986.

Dembski, William A. *The Design Inference*. Cambridge: Cambridge University Press, 1998.

———. *No Free Lunch*. Lanham, MD: Rowman & Littlefield, 2002.

Forrest, Barbara, and Paul R. Gross. *Creationism's Trojan Horse*. New York: Oxford University Press, 2004.

Gonzalez, Guillermo, and Jay W. Richards. *Privileged Planet*. Washington, DC: Regnery, 2004

Gould, Stephen J. "Review of Phillip Johnson's *Darwin on Trial*." *Scientific American*, July 1992.

Hume, David. *An Enquiry concerning Human Understanding and concerning the Principles of Morals*. Oxford: Clarendon, 1975.

Johnson, Phillip E. *Darwin on Trial*. Downers Grove, IL: InterVarsity, 1991.

Meyer, Stephen C. "The Origin of Biological Information and the Higher Taxonomic Categories." *Proceedings of the Biological Society of Washington* 117, no. 2 (2004).

Miller, Kenneth R. *Finding Darwin's God*. New York: HarperCollins, 1999.

Musgrave, Ian. "Evolution of the Bacterial Flagellum." In *Why Intelligent Design Fails*, edited by Matt Young and Taner Edis. Brunswick, NJ: Rutgers University Press, 2004.

Paley, William. *Natural Theology*. London: Faulder, 1802.

Pennock, Robert T. *Tower of Babel*. Cambridge, MA: MIT Press, 2000.

Perakh Mark. "There Is a Free Lunch After All." In *Why Intelligent Design Fails*, edited by Matt Young and Taner Edis. Brunswick, NJ: Rutgers University Press, 2004.

———. *Unintelligent Design*. Amherst, NY: Prometheus Books, 2004.

Plantinga, Alvin. "Evolution, Neutrality, and Antecedent Probability." In *Intelligent Design Creationism and Its Critics*, edited by Robert T. Pennock. Cambridge, MA: MIT Press, 2001.

Raël [Claude Vorilhon]. "The Book Which Tells the Truth." In *The Message Given to Me by Extraterrestrials*. Tokyo: AOM, 1986.

Ratzsch, Del. *Nature, Design, and Science*. New York: State University of New York Press, 2001.

Shanks, Niall. *God, the Devil, and Darwin*. New York: Oxford University Press, 2004.

Wells, Jonathan. *Icons of Evolution*. Washington, DC: Regnery, 2002.

Wolpert, David H. "Review of Dembski's *No Free Lunch*." *Mathematical Reviews* (February 2003).

Wolpert, David H., and William G. Macready. "No Free Lunch Theorems for Optimization." *IEEE Transactions on Evolutionary Computation* 1, no. 1 (1997).

Young, Matt, and Ian Musgrave. "Moonshine: Why the Peppered Moth Remains an Icon of Evolution." *Skeptical Inquirer* 29, no. 2 (2005).

MARK PERAKH

INTERNATIONAL HUMANIST AND ETHICAL UNION (IHEU). The International Humanist and Ethical Union is an international federation of humanist organizations. It unites a hundred member organizations from thirty-seven countries worldwide. Member organizations represent a diversity of movements: humanists, atheists, rationalists, secularists, ETHICAL CULTURE groups, religious humanists, agnostics, skeptics, and freethinkers (see ATHEISM; RATIONALISM; SECULARISM; RELIGIOUS HUMANISM; AGNOSTICISM; SKEPTICISM; FREETHOUGHT). However, the IHEU stresses what binds all of these together—in the words of former IHEU president Levi Fragell, "the eight letters," that is, HUMANISM without qualifying adjectives.

The IHEU's mission is threefold. First, it wants to stimulate international contact between humanists worldwide, and serve as "a clearing-house for [humanist] information and inspiration." Humanists can meet at world congresses, held every two to five years, and more frequent regional conferences. In between congresses, the IHEU's quarterly newsletter, *International Humanist News*, and its Web site keep humanists informed about relevant developments worldwide.

Second, the IHEU strives to promote humanism as a LIFE STANCE and as an authentic ethical alternative for religion (see EUPRAXSOPHY), and to work out a humanist identity. The voice of the IHEU has been condensed in hundreds of public statements issued by IHEU congresses or by its board. These vary from limited comments in specific affairs to comprehensive declarations of principle, such as the Amsterdam Declarations of 1952 and 2002, which aimed to define basic features of humanism, or an appeal for a new global ethics based on the 1988 statement "Planetary Humanism."

The IHEU also supports humanist organization building in countries where humanism is still feeble. In the 1950s such an initiative in Norway was very successful, but later, similar attempts in the third world and in the former Soviet states were often handicapped by communication problems, insufficient knowledge of the local situation, and other causes. Only since 1988, when the IHEU launched a momentous partnership with the Dutch Humanist Institute for Development Cooperation (HIVOS), have results improved, both in the form of wholesome developmental projects and in the form of regional and local humanist networks.

The IHEU's third major task is to represent the humanist voice in international bodies. Since its founding congress, the IHEU has voiced its close engagement with the United Nations and with issues of global importance, such as the nuclear arms race, the world population explosion, and third world underdevelopment. The IHEU now has representatives at the United Nations in New York, Geneva, and Vienna, at UNICEF and UNESCO, and at the Council of Europe.

History. The IHEU was founded August 26, 1952, at an international humanist congress in Amsterdam presided over by Sir Julian HUXLEY. The founding members were seven organizations from Europe, the United States, and India. The initiative was prepared by Jaap VAN PRAAG of the Dutch Humanist League HV and the Englishman Harold J. BLACKHAM. Both intended to create an alternative to the already existing World Union of Freethinkers (WUFT), which they had found to be too rigidly antireligious and anticlerical (see ANTICLERICALISM).

IHEU headquarters was set up within the office of the Dutch Humanist League at Utrecht. Practical difficulties were formidable. The IHEU was a tiny organization with worldwide pretensions, a small budget, unreliable communication with its members, and heavy dependence on volunteers. It was not until the 1960s that substantive projects could be started. These included working parties that brought together humanists from several countries who were interested in the same subject, a separate humanist youth organization (IHEYO), and a series of dialogues with representatives of other life stances, including Roman Catholics and Marxists.

In 1997 IHEU headquarters moved from the Netherlands to London. There, under a new executive director and through wider use of the Internet and other modern media, communication was revolutionized, resulting in more efficient decision-making processes, rapid response to vital developments worldwide, and increased publicity. Successful campaigns were launched in support of victims of blasphemy legislation, such as Bangladeshi writer Taslima NASRIN and Pakistani professor Younus Shaikh. Activities focused on issues such as bioethics, women's rights, and further

development of the youth movement. Much attention was also given to supporting humanist initiatives in South Asia, Latin America, and Africa.

BIBLIOGRAPHY

Gasenbeek, Bert, and Babu Gogineni, eds. *International Humanist and Ethical Union 1952–2002. Past, Present and Future*. Utrecht: De Tijdstroom, 2002.

HANS VAN DEUKEREN

ISLAM, UNBELIEF WITHIN. We know from the Qur'an itself that there were Arab skeptics in Mecca who did not accept the "fables" recounted by Muhammad; they scoffed at his notion of the resurrection of the body, they doubted the divine origins of his "revelation," and they even accused him of plagiarizing pagan Arab poets. Pagan Arabs were seldom wont to thank superior powers for their worldly successes, and we should not be surprised that these pagan attitudes prevailed in the early years of Islam. Arabs converted out of cupidity and hope of booty and success in this world. Thus many outwardly confessed their belief but in fact had no inclination toward Islam and its dogma and ritual. At the death of Muhammad, the number genuinely converted to his creed did not exceed a thousand. If things went wrong, the Bedouins were ready to drop Islam— that is, to apostasize—as quickly as they had adopted it. The fact that Islam restricted wine drinking and sexual intercourse, "the two delicious things," did not endear Muhammad's religion to them, either.

The Arabs also resisted the institution of Muslim prayers, in particular ridiculing their associated body movements. There is much evidence for the indifference of the desert Arabs to prayer, for their ignorance of the elements of Muslim rites, and even for their indifference toward the Qur'an itself, including their ignorance of its most important parts. The Arabs always preferred to hear the songs of the heroes of paganism rather than holy utterances from the Qur'an. Al-Jahiz, himself gently skeptical and a Mu'tazilite, recounts how the Arabs mocked and derided the Qur'an. A Muslim leader of the early days is reputed to have said: "If there were a God, I would swear by his name that I did not believe in him."

The general ignorance of Islamic doctrine and ritual continued well into the first Islamic century under the first ruling dynasty, the Umayyads. Indeed, Islam cannot properly be said to have existed in the sense of a fixed body of dogma until significantly later on. We glimpse the atmosphere in which the caliph al-Walid II grew up by these verses he addressed to the Qur'an, referring to Qur'anic threats against "stubborn opponents": "You hurl threats against the stubborn opponent, well then, I am a/stubborn opponent myself./When you appear before God at the day of resurrection just say:/My Lord, Al-Walid has torn me up."

Al-Walid II is said to have stuck the Qur'an onto a lance and shot it to pieces with arrows while repeating the above verses. He certainly did not abide by its inter-dictions: an intensely cultivated man, he surrounded himself with poets, dancing girls, and musicians, living the merry life of the libertine with no interest in religion.

***Kafir, Mulhid, Murtadd*, and *Zindiq*.** The terms *Kafir* and its cognate *kufr*, *Mulhid* and its cognate *Ilhad*, *Murtad*, and *Zindiq* and its cognate *zandaqa* all have precise meanings. But in fact they were used synony-mously in a very loose way to mean deviator, apostate, heretic, renegade, unbeliever, atheist, materialist, and skeptic. To complicate matters further, even the precise meaning of each term changed over the centuries. Thus, for example, *Mulhid* was used during the Umayyad period as a synonym for "rebel" and "splitter of the ranks of the faithful." Soon after the Abbasids took power as the ruling dynasty in 750, *Ilhad* came to signify materi-alist skepticism and atheism.

Strictly speaking, *Zindiqs* were the adherents of Manichaeism, a dualistic doctrine of primeval conflict between God and matter, light and darkness, truth and error. Yet the term *Zindiq* came to be applied indiscrim-inately to heretics (see HERESY), atheists (see ATHEISM), and freethinkers (see FREETHOUGHT). Fear of persecution made it difficult for writers and thinkers to express their views openly, and so we are often left wondering what any particular *Zindiq* really thought.

Djad ibn Dirham was said to be a materialist (see MATERIALISM); his followers are said to have accused the Prophet Muhammad of lying and to have denied the resurrection. Serious persecutions of *Zindiqs* began under the Abbasid caliph al-Mansur. Many *Zindiqs* were put to death under his reign, the most famous being Ibn al-Muqaffa, who was the intellectual heir to the ratio-nalist tradition that flourished at the time of the Sassanid king Chosroes Anusharwan. The latter is said by the scholar Gabrieli to have fostered a "veritable Hellenistic *Aufklarung* (Enlightenment)." At any rate, Ibn al-Muqaffa attacked Islam, its Prophet, its theology and theodicy, and its concept of God from the perspective of the Manichaean faith. How do we reconcile Ibn al-Muqaffa's rational skepticism and his adherence to Manichaean dualism? Some scholars point out that intellectuals like Ibn al-Muqaffa had already given an allegorical interpretation to the Manichaean mythology, interpreting the universe and man's place in it in gnostic, even Hellenistic and rational, terms.

Under Mansur's successors caliph al-Mahdi and al-Hadi, repression, persecution, and executions were applied with even greater ferocity. Special magistrates were appointed to pursue heretics, the whole inquisition being masterminded by the Grand Inquisitor, called the *Sahih al-Zanadiqa*.

Ibn Abi-l-Awja was one of the more interesting *Zindiqs*. He believed that light had created good, while darkness had created evil; he also taught metempsychosis (the transmigration of souls after death) and the freedom of the will. Before his death, Ibn Abi-l-Awja confessed that he had fabricated more than four thousand traditions (hadith) in which he forbade Muslims from doing what was in fact permitted, and vice versa—that is, he made Muslims break the fast when they should have been fasting and so on. He is supposed to have posed the problem of human suffering (see EVIL, PROBLEM OF), asking: "[W]hy . . . are there catastrophes, epidemics, if God is good?" A recorded discussion with the imam Jafar al-Sadiq reveals the full extent of his unorthodoxy: according to the record, he believed in the eternity of the world and denied the existence of a creator. One day he asked Jafar to justify the institution of pilgrimage, and refused to accept the answer that it was ordered by God, since this reply merely pushed the question further back to someone who was not present. He also cast doubt on the justice of some of the punishments described in the Qur'an. Ibn Abi-l-Awja was also said to accuse some of the prophets mentioned in the Qur'an of lying, in partic-ular Abraham and Joseph. Like so many *Zindiqs* of the period, he doubted the official dogma of the inimitability of the Qur'an. Even if we cannot specifically link the above dialogue with the historical figure of Ibn Abi-l-Awja, it gives a true picture of *Zindiq* beliefs of that time. He was taken prisoner and put to death in 772.

One of the charges often leveled at *Zindiqs* such as Bashshar bin Burd was that they continually undermined the orthodox view of the miraculous nature of the Qur'an, whose text the orthodox considered inimitable. On the orthodox view, no mortal writer was capable of matching the perfection of the Qur'an. Bashshar bin Burd, a poet, seems to have denied the resurrection and the last judgment in some of his verses. He may well have believed in metempsychosis as well. In celebrated verses Bashshar defended Iblis (the devil), being made of fire, for refusing to prostrate himself before Adam, who was made of ordinary clay. In another verse Bashshar prayed to the Prophet Muhammad to join with him in an attack upon the deity. He also seems to have held Manichaean beliefs laced with Zoroastrianism. But, in the words of the scholar Régis Blachère, "along with these beliefs there would seem always to have been a profound skepticism mingled with a fatalistic outlook leading Bashshar to pessimism and hedonism." Still pru-dence obliged him to pay lip service to orthodoxy. This view of Bashshar as a skeptic is endorsed by the scholar Vadja, who argues that it seems totally out of character for someone as dissolute as he to adhere to a religion as ascetic as Manichaeism.

Basra produced a conspicuous but little-documented group of freethinkers. In our sources certain names keep cropping up, but seldom accompanied by details about their views or works. Thus we are told that Qays bin Zubayr was a notorious atheist, that al-Baqili denied the resurrection, that Ibrahim bin Sayyaba was a *Zindiq,* even that he claimed that pederasty was the first law of *zandaqa.*

We know a little more about Muti bin Iyas, who gives every sign of being a *Zindiq.* But the details we have of his life point rather to someone with a skeptical turn of mind but no deep interest in religion. Beginning his career under the Umayyads, he was devoted to the caliph Walid bin Yazid, who found in Muti a fellow after his own heart, "accomplished, dissolute, an agreeable companion and excellent wit, reckless in his effrontery and suspected in his religion." When the Abbasids came to power, Muti attached himself to the caliph Mansur. Many stories are told of the debauched life, which he led in the company of *Zindiqs* or freethinkers. As scholar R. A. Nicholson observed, "His songs of love and wine are distinguished by their lightness and elegance."

Abu Isa Muhammad bin Harun Al-Warraq was accused of *zandaqa* and is important for, among other reasons, being the teacher of the Great Infidel himself, Al-Rawandi. Unfortunately none of his literary work survives; we have only tantalizing glimpses of it in quotations by other Arab scholars. Some of his works are also known from refutations which have survived. Al-Warraq began as a Mu'tazilite theologian, but seems to have been excommunicated for holding heterodox opinions. He wrote a remarkable history of religions in which his objectivity, rationalism, and skepticism enjoyed free rein. His critical examination of the three branches of Christianity of his time again reveal his dispassionate tone and rationalism, free from any hint of dependence on revelation.

Al-Warraq's political sympathies may have lain with the Shia party, and it is uncertain whether he was really a Manichaean. However, he does seem to have believed in the two principles of good and evil, and very certainly in the eternity of the world. The scholar Massignon correctly summed him up as an independent thinker and skeptic who embraced no fixed system of thought. A victim of the Abbasid persecution, Al-Warraq died in exile in Ahwaz in 909.

Al-Mutanabbi is considered by many Arabs as the greatest poet in the Arabic language. According to Blachère, Al-Mutanabbi was influenced in his religious and philosophical development by a certain Abu l-Fadl of Kufa, the town of his birth. Abu l-Fadl was a "complete agnostic" and an early patron of Al-Mutanabbi's works. Under l-Fadl's influence, Al-Mutanabbi cast off Muslim religious dogmas which he regarded as spiritual instruments of oppression. He then adopted a stoic and pessimistic philosophy (see STOICISM), holding that the world is made up of seductions which death destroys; stupidity and evil alone triumph. Out of social and political frustration, Mutanabbi led a rebellion of a politico-religious character, claiming to be a prophet with a new Qur'an. He was defeated, captured, and imprisoned for two years.

Al-Mutanabbi wrote a vast number of odes, sometimes praising second-rate patrons and at other times lauding the great Sayf al-Dawla, leader of the Aleppo (Syria) branch of the Hamdanid dynasty. Some of the odes are full of bombast, some are sublime; beneath them all we can discern a certain skeptical disillusionment with a world kept in chains by ignorance, stupidity, and superstition from which only death can liberate us. But, as the scholar Daniel Margoliouth points out, for many Muslims Al-Mutanabbi's odes are "defaced by utterances which imply disrespect for the prophets and revealed religion."

The spirit of philosophical inquiry did eventually lead to a questioning of the fundamental tenets of Islamic belief late in the ninth century, leading people like al-Kindi's pupil Ahmad bin al-Tayyib Al-Sarakhsi into deep trouble. Al-Sarakhsi, tutor to the caliph al-Mutadid, took an interest in Greek philosophy. He incurred the wrath of the caliph for discussing heretical ideas rather openly, obliging the caliph to order his execution in 899. According to the ninth-century historian al-Biruni, al-Sarakhsi wrote numerous treatises in which he attacked the prophets as charlatans. Al-Sarakhsi was led into his religious skepticism by the rationalism of the Mu'-tazilites, with whom he sympathized, and by his own philosophical inquiries.

Often the historian of atheism wthin Islam is forced to rely on the works of Islamic scholars who made it their duty to refute thinkers and writers they considered atheist. The writings they attack often are not extant, and we should be thankful for these refutations, which often contain extensive quotes from the lost originals. This is the case, for example with both Ibn Rawandi and AL-RAZI.

From the early tenth century onward—the early Abbasid period—survive many refutations of the *mulhidun* or atheists. Thus, for example, the scholar Mulhid observes that the *"Kitab al-Radd ala'l-mulhid"* by the Zaydi imam al-Kasim bin Ibrahim al-Rassi (died 860) clearly portrays the anonymous *mulhid* as a religious sceptic inclining to atheism." Other refutations were written by the grammarian Kutrub and the theologians al-Jahiz and al-Zabidi. Many of these refutations were written by Mu'tazilite theologians to whom we shall now turn.

The Mu'tazilites and Rationalism. There was great excitement in liberal circles in Europe in 1865, when Heinrich Steiner of Zurich published a study devoted to the ideas of the Mu'tazilites, whom he praised as the "freethinkers of Islam." Writing in 1906, the freethought historian John Mackinnon ROBERTSON still describes them as freethinkers. However, it is now clear that the Mu'tazilites were first and foremost Muslims, living in the circle of Islamic ideas and motivated by religious concerns. There was no sign of truly liberated thinking or of a desire, as Goldhizer puts it, "to throw off chafing shackles, to the detriment of the rigorously orthodox view of life." Furthermore, far from being "liberal," they turned out to be exceedingly intolerant and were involved in the *Mihna,* the Muslim Inquisition under the Abbasids.

However, the Mu'tazilites are important to a discussion of Islam and unbelief because they introduced Greek philosophical ideas into the discussion of Islamic dogmas. These in turn brought with them skepticism, rationalism, and liberating doubt that could only lead to opposition to current orthodoxy. They were, Goldziher reminds us, "the first to expand the sources of religious cognition in Islam so as to include a valuable but previously—in such connection—rigorously avoided element: reason ('aql)." Some of them even said "the first, necessary condition of knowledge is doubt," and others that "fifty doubts are better than one certainty." For them, there was a sixth sense besides the usual five, namely, 'aql, reason. They raised reason to a touchstone in matters of belief. One of their early representatives, Bishr ibn al-Mu'tamir of Baghdad, wrote a veritable paean to reason as part of a didactic poem of natural history: "How excellent is reason as a pilot and companion in good fortune and evil,/As a judge who can pass judgment over the invisible as if he saw it with his own eyes./One of its actions is that it distinguishes good and evil,/Through a possessor of powers whom God has singled out/With utter sanctification and purity."

The Mu'tazilites ruthlessly criticized popular superstitions, especially the mythological elements of eschatology, which they no longer considered a part of Muslim belief. They gave an allegorical explanation of the bridge Sirat, which one had to cross to get to the next world. They excised the Balance or scales in which the acts of man are weighed, and eliminated many other childish fantasies. But Muslims they remained.

Conclusion. Was Islam tolerant of heresy and unbelief? Certainly it was intolerant of unbelief. As T. P. Hughes's *Dictionary of Islam* tells us under the article "Sin," Muslim scholars held that there were seventeen great sins; at the top of the list, the number one sin was *Kufr*, or infidelity (in the sense of unbelief). Murder appeared well down the list in fifteenth place.

The situation undoubtedly varied from country to country, ruler to ruler, and period to period. In general, the Umayyads are seen as more tolerant than the later Abbasids, precisely because the Umayyads had not yet defined themselves as Muslims.

So long as one had royal patronage and protection in addition to talent, one could often get away with blasphemy, heresy, and even unbelief, at least for a time. For instance, the Barmakids, a Persian family, served several Abbasid caliphs as advisers though they were often accused of unbelief, or at least of secretly harboring anti-Islamic sentiments. When royal favor was withdrawn, this influential family fell from grace. An indication that heresy was otherwise little tolerated under Islam is the fact that plotters seeking to eliminate a rival often resorted to accusing their target of heresy. The fear of being labeled a heretic was pervasive. We might mention the constant persecution of the Ismailis, one hundred thousand of whom are said to have been exter-minated by Abbas, lord of the city of al Rai, in the eleventh century.

Thus we have the spectacle of periodic persecution of various groups (Kharijites, Shiites, Ismailis, and so on) considered either doctrinally suspect or politically subversive. We see individual philosophers, poets, theologians, scientists, rationalists, dualists, freethinkers, and mystics imprisoned, tortured, crucified, mutilated, and hanged. Time after time their writings were burned, including those of AVERRÖES, Ibn Hazm, Al Ghazali, Al Haitham, and Al Kindi. Surely it is significant that none of the heretical works of Ibn Rawandi, Ibn Warraq, Ibn Al Muqaffa or Ar Razi has survived. Accused heretics were often forced to flee from one ruler to the domain of another, more tolerant ruler. Some were exiled or banished (for example, Averröes). Many were forced to disguise their true views and opinions by difficult or ambiguous language. Those who managed to get away with blasphemy were those who enjoyed the protection of the powerful and influential.

BIBLIOGRAPHY

Al-Jahiz. *Al-Bayan wa'l-tabyin.* 2 vols. Cairo, 1893–95.
Encyclopedia of Islam. 2nd ed. Leiden: E. J. Brill, 1960–.
Goldziher, I. *Introduction to Islamic Theology and Law.* Princeton, NJ: Princeton University Press, 1981.
———. *Muslim Studies.* 2 vols. Translated by C. R. Barber and S. M. Stern. London: George Allen & Unwin, 1967–71.
Hughes, T. P. "Sin." In *Dictionary of Islam.* Delhi: Rupa, 1999.
Margoliouth, D. "Atheism (Muhammadan)." In *Encyclopaedia of Religion and Ethics*, edited by J. Hastings. Edinburgh: T. & T. Clark, 1910.
Nicholson, R. A. *A Literary History of the Arabs.* Cambridge: Cambridge University Press, 1930.
Stroumsa, Sarah. *Freethinkers of Medieval Islam: Ibn Al-Rawandi, Abu Bakr Al-Razi and Their Impact on Islamic Thought.* Islamic Philosophy, Theology, and Science, Vol. 35. Leiden: E. J. Brill, 1999.
Urvoy, D. *Les Penseurs libres dans l'islam classique* [Freethinkers in Classical Islam]. Paris: Albin Michel, 1996.
Vadja, G. "*Les Zindiqs en pays d'Islam au début de la période Abbasside*" [Zindiqs in Islam at the Beginning of the Abbasid Period]. *Rivista degli studi orientali* 17 (1938).

IBN WARRAQ

ITALY, UNBELIEF IN. The Middle Ages. With the collapse of the Roman Empire, the Italian provinces underwent a series of occupations and wars. Despite economic breakdown and what amounted to foreign control over the country, the region's system of written law and its Catholic religion survived, adopted by ruling classes essentially foreign to the Roman culture. At the beginning of the second millennium, Italy joined in a general European process of economic and demographic growth; there, the flourishing of local communal polities and the rise of new and vital social groups was peculiar to Italy, at least to its northern and central regions. Southern Italy, conversely, remained a feudal society for a longer period; there, Emperor Frederick II Hohenstaufen headed an empire comprising Swabia and Sicily. Frederick's court was an island of unsurpassed freedom of thought where science and learning were protected. Therefore, Frederick was praised as the "wonder of the world" by his admirers and reviled by his critics as the Antichrist.

Criticism of papal temporal power and of the moral corruption of the clergy was a constant refrain of Italian heretical preachers, including the reformer Arnold of Brescia, who developed a religious doctrine of poverty in contrast with the opulence of the church; Brother Dolcino, who condemned clergy corruption and marked the Donation of Constantine as the moment when the church was handed over to Satan; and the Dominican monk Girolamo Savonarola. In literature, criticism of religion is evident in Giovanni Boccaccio, author of the *Decameron*, who also went so far as to write a rationalistic *Genealogy of the Pagan Gods*. Poggio Bracciolini's skeptical and sarcastic *Facetiae* (Witty Tales) presents both anticlerical and materialistic arguments. Centuries later, both were accused of having authored *De tribus impostoribus*, the anonymous atheist attack on Moses, Jesus, and Muhammad.

On the side of natural sciences, physician and philosopher Pietro d'Abano of the University of Padua was a pioneer in the study of anatomy, physiopathology, astronomy, and astrology. His heretical views included unbelief in divine providence and in miracles (he even denied physical resurrection, alleged cases of which he explained as merely apparent death followed by return to consciousness). He was sentenced to death but died in prison before execution. In 1327 Francesco Stabili (better known as Cecco d'Ascoli, from his native town) was burned at the stake in Florence for his research, notably about astrology.

The Renaissance. Italy is undoubtedly the country where Renaissance HUMANISM was born. Its celebration of human dignity, freedom, and reason arose primarily from the interest in ARISTOTLE—not in the corrupted version used by Thomas Aquinas to serve his theology, but rather the Aristotle of AVERRÖES, stressing the eternity of the world, a concept of the celestial spheres influencing earthly events that somehow displaced divine intervention, and the notion of a rational soul that downgraded theology in favor of rational inquiry. In the fourteenth and fifteenth centuries, this humanistic vision developed in two main ways, both of which were to challenge Christendom: the analytical and antimetaphysical study of nature as the "reign of humanity" (e.g., Marsilio

Ficino's activity in the Platonic Academy in Florence), and the investigation into moral issues centered on a more humanistic view (see, for instance, Pico della Mirandola's *De hominis dignitate oratio*, dated 1486). Aside from these, ANTICLERICALISM continued to be a defining Italian trait—perhaps more so than the cultivation of heretical theological views—in particular since the time of Dante Alighieri.

The most inspired eulogy for the joy of living, as opposed to sacrifice and asceticism, was published in 1432 by the humanist Lorenzo Valla as *De voluptate* (On Pleasure). Valla had no later troubles with the Inquisition, in spite of his treatise *De libero arbitrio* (On Free Will) of 1439, which presented a rather agnostic longing for nature. This work would later influence Martin Luther and also Gottfried Wilhelm von LEIBNIZ in his *Theodicy*. On the other hand, Valla's debunking *De falso credita et ementita Constantini donatione declamatio* (Discourse on the Falsely Believed and Forged Donation of Constantine), published in 1444, caused him to be accused of heresy. The *Discourse* demonstrated that the emperor Constantine's supposed donation of the central Italian territories to the papacy was a medieval forgery. General acceptance of such a view would sap the foundation of the papacy's temporal power. Valla's action moved along other lines as well: historical and philological studies and religious and social criticism. In Renaissance literature, materialistic and antireligious stances are also shown in Pietro Aretino's comedies and in several of Niccolò Machiavelli's plays. Machiavelli went so far as to contend that church domination over society was the cause of the spread of irreligion through Italy.

Pietro Pomponazzi, a quintessential Renaissance scholar, studied medicine in Padua and later held the chair of moral philosophy at that university. Pomponazzi was skeptical of the immortality of the soul, a position based upon the more materialistic interpretations of Aristotle's writings. For his *Tractatus de immortalitate animae* (Treatise on the Immortality of the Soul) of 1516, and for having denounced the ignorance and superstition of the clergy, he was indicted and compelled to retract. His important treatise *De naturalium effectuum admirandorum causis sive de incantationibus* (On the Causes of Amazing Natural Effects, or on Incantations)—in which he criticized the belief in magic and miracles, though admitting astrology as a study of purely natural effects—was published in 1556, after his death. He has been considered an atheist by many, as has been Girolamo Cardano. Cardano, who also studied medicine in Padua, epitomizes the ideal of the Renaissance man: his writings deal with such diverse topics as algebra, astrology, medicine, and ethics, with a naturalistic and deterministic view of nature, and an unconventional new spirit in ethical and political matters; see, for instance, his 1562 *Encomium Neronis* (Encomium for Nero), praising the Roman emperor who had been the bête noire of Christianity. The lawyer and historian Francesco Guicciardini held high political positions in the Florentine administration and even under Pope Clemens VII, a Medici. However, Guicciardini's skepticism (unlike that of Machiavelli and Vico) extended to any general body of rules that could govern politics and civil life, and this led him to a disenchanted view of political ethics: in his memoirs, he admitted to having been at the service of the papacy although hating the "wicked tyranny of the clerics."

The Counter-Reformation was a dark period in Italy, as it was everywhere else in Europe, despite the fact that few organized challenges to Catholic orthodoxy had emerged in Italy. Lutheranism initially found favor in Venice (where it was espoused by Pietro Carnesecchi), Ferrara and Mantua, Tuscany (espoused by Bernardino Ochino), then Naples and Sicily. Usually, dissidents such as Ochino, who disbelieved in the Trinity and in the divinity of Christ, were described as atheists. Aonio Paleario was prosecuted in Siena, but later lectured in Lucca and Milan. His *Indictment against the Popes of Rome* was found only years after his death at the stake.

Repression of heresy during this period was violent and uncompromising: The first edition of the church's Index of Prohibited Books (1564) condemned such masterpieces of Italian literature as Boccaccio's *Decameron* and Ludovico Ariosto's *Orlando Furioso*. In 1557 the philosopher Iacopo Aconcio had to flee to England after expressing sympathy toward the Lutheran and Waldensian reformations. Later, in 1565, he would write the *Satanae stratagemata* (The Stratagems of Satan) in defense of religious tolerance and against dogmatism.

The Averröistic school of the Padua University and the interest in natural sciences were to develop and spread through France through the influence of Giordano BRUNO, Giulio Cesare VANINI, and Campanella. To a certain extent their FREETHOUGHT can be considered less hesitant and cautious than that of the early seventeenth-century libertinism; even so, the history of Italian Renaissance humanism is strewn with censorship, indictment, and torture. Bernardino Telesio's *De rerum natura iuxta propria principia* (On the Nature of Things according to Its Own Principles; 1586) was condemned, albeit only ten years after publication. Telesio's disciple Tommaso Campanella, who championed a secular government in the utopian *La Città del Sole* (The City of the Sun) and a purely rational religion in his thirty-volume *Theology*—and who authored an *Apology of Galileo*—underwent unspeakable tortures during nearly thirty years of imprisonment and escaped a death sentence only by pretending insanity. Although not a declared atheist, Campanella promoted many naturalistic and rationalist concepts in his *Atheismus triumphatus* (Atheism Defeated) of 1631, though it was formally a defense of the Catholic faith. Even Bruno was condemned for a combination of reasons: his philosophy, though centered on the then-new Copernican cosmology, treated a wide range of subjects. Inherently blasphemous as his ideas on the deity, the Trinity, and

the universe collided with fundamentals of Christian dogma, and defiant of the cosmological beliefs of the time, he also was an ill-tempered person who missed no occasion to denounce ignorance and authoritarianism. He well understood his divergence from the mainstream thought of the day: "that which others see from a distance, I leave behind" (from a sonnet in *On the Infinite Universe and Worlds*). A few years after Bruno's death, the former Carmelite Lucilio Vanini was tortured and put to death in Toulouse for having claimed unbelief in the immortal soul and in the divine origin of humanity, and for having praised Queen Nature in his naturalistic account of the world. However, executing precursors and heroes of a new world vision could not weaken progress: in 1609, the Copernican theory of 1543 having been condemned by Luther and John Calvin but not yet by the pope, Galileo GALILEI began to point his new telescope skyward.

The Seventeenth Century. Although a renowned group of French thinkers is commonly taken as the prime example of early seventeenth-century libertinism and religious skepticism, some notable Italian thinkers followed similar paths. Both Cartesianism (see DESCARTES, RÉNE) and the atomist thought of Pierre Gassendi spread through the peninsula, not only because of exceptional supporters like Campanella and Galileo, but also because Cartesianism and atomism suggested a criticism of authority more clearly than they did a threat to religious belief. Yet proponents of antiauthoritarianism, too, risked heavy sanctions: in 1634, one year after Galileo's censure, Campanella had to seek refuge in France, with the assistance of Gassendi himself. In the Republic of Venice, historian Paolo Sarpi, a friend of Galileo, championed religious independence against the papal interdict imposed on Venice in 1606. To a certain extent Sarpi expressed hostility toward dogmatic religion in general. Unsurprisingly, he was excommunicated. Cesare Cremonini, a commentator upon Aristotle's writings and a lecturer at Padua perhaps best known for his refusal to view Jupiter's satellites through Galileo's telescope, nonetheless supported separation between science and religion and believed in the mortality of the soul. He thus incurred an investigation by the Holy Office; fortunately the University of Padua was under Venetian rule at that time. French *libertine érudit* (learned libertine) Gabriel Naudé, who had attended Cremonini's teachings in Padua, wrote reports upon details of Italian unbelief, highlighting a notable distinction between those who could safely declare their skepticism or unbelief—even in Rome—by complying with exterior devotional requirements, and those who criticized the papacy in any way and were repressed. Naudé names the poets Boccaccio, Pietro Aretino, Nicolò Franco, and Marcello Palingenio; thinkers including Cardano and Bruno; and even the pope's physician, as Italians who were open unbelievers.

Two main historical upheavals distinguish seventeenth-century freethought from that of the preceding century: the growing challenge of the Reformation and the impact of the great geographical explorations. In the Italian peninsula, as in Spain, the Reformation's influence was minimal (see, for instance, the anti-Catholic libels of Calvinist Gregorio Leti); on the other hand, the study of distant civilizations and cultures enjoyed immense popularity among scholars. The first part of the seventeenth century saw the spreading of anti-Trinitarian and rationalistic literature, a flourishing of atomism, and the decay of scholastic Aristotelianism in the light of advances in biology, medicine, and astronomy. Adding to these the "discovery" of Far Eastern civilizations, notably that of China as described by Italian Jesuit scholars, offered a vivid example of an advanced and very ancient civilization devoid of any concept of salvation or of a personal deity.

Even the more mature learned libertinism of the second half of this century (that of Pierre BAYLE and Bernard Fontenelle) is rooted in the Italian humanist tradition, as depicted on the heading page of the Viennese edition of the *Theophrastus Redivivus* (1659): this anonymous text of almost certain French origin clearly shows the author to be indebted to Cardano, Pomponazzi, Giulio Cesare VANINI, and Jean Bodin.

The Eighteenth Century and the Enlightenment. Despite relatively wide circulation in manuscript, the Italian version of LUCRETIUS's *De Rerum Natura* by Alessandro Marchetti could only be printed in London, in 1717. Before that date, an attempt to publish it in Naples was blocked by the Inquisition, showing that educated Italians participated in the general cultural trends of Europe in the seventeenth and the eighteenth centuries, notably the process of transition from libertinism to Enlightenment (see ENLIGHTENMENT, UNBELIEF DURING THE). Thanks to more liberal administrations, Italian science flourished in several towns, with important contributions to astronomy, mathematics, and life sciences. Lorenzo Magalotti met British, Dutch, and French freethinkers in his travels through Europe. His *Lettere familiari contro l'ateismo* (Family Letters against Atheism), which circulated in manuscript at the beginning of the century, offers a formal defense of religion but actually champions science and atomism. Freethinker, Freemason, and former pastor Antonio Conti traveled through Europe, meeting Fréret, Boulainvilliers, Malebranche, Newton, and Leibniz. Again, Italian dissidents were more concerned with criticism of the church and attention to church-state relationships than with philosophical speculation. Historian Pietro Giannone was excommunicated in 1723 for his rationalistic religious ideas and for claiming that the church had always been a force for regression and obscurantism. After exile in Vienna and Geneva, he was lured into a trap in Italy, then jailed for the last twelve years of his life. His works, translated into many languages, were notably studied and appreciated by Montesquieu. Adalberto Radicati di

Passerano had to flee to London because of his criticisms of the church, but after publishing antireligious libels there, he was expelled from England and repaired to the Netherlands. Economist and philosopher Antonio Genovesi, lecturer in ethics at the University of Naples, was censored by the Inquisition for his critical positions and had to resign. In 1766 the Holy Office put onto the Index Cesare Beccaria's *Of Crimes and Punishments*, a masterpiece that advanced an Enlightenment vision of a more humane judicial system and for the abolition of the death penalty and torture. Together with Beccaria, philosopher and economist Pietro Verri animated Milanese society in favor of Enlightenment ideas.

The *Risorgimento* and Italian Unity. The Kingdom of Italy's efforts to annex the papal states provoked fiery reaction from the church, indeed a genuine war against the whole of civil society. In 1864 Pius IX published his *Syllabus* of the errors of his time: naturalism, rationalism, liberalism, and any aggression against his temporal power were condemned. On the opposite side, the kingdom had enacted laws to secularize the country. Much credit goes to Camillo Cavour, who coined the famous separationist motto "a free Church in a free State." Eventually Piedmontese troops occupied what was left of the Papal States in Rome (1870) and put an end to the pope's temporal power. It is therefore not surprising that most of the leaders of the *Risorgimento* were anticlerical. Giuseppe Garibaldi, the "hero of two worlds," was a Freemason and the honorary president of freethought and atheist societies. His follower Alberto Mario also published anticlerical writings on ecclesiastical politics, as did economist Carlo Cattaneo, the most eminent follower of the Enlightenment in Italy. Patriot Aurelio Saffi, an associate of Mazzini and Carlo Pisacane, wrote polemical books espousing RATIONALISM and anti-Catholicism. The "Roman question" about what the status of the church would be in the new Italy was a central theme of the *Risorgimento*. For many, patriotic feelings virtually implied anticlericalism.

Other influences on freethought in this period included the politicians and writers Francesco Domenico Guerrazzi and Luigi Settembrini, anticlerical journalist Aurelio Bianchi Giovini, and the former priest Bertrando Spaventa, who published anti-Jesuit writings and championed secular public education. As a philosopher Spaventa opposed POSITIVISM, but he tried to demonstrate a secularist inclination in Italian philosophy. Pedagogue Pietro Siciliani proposed a humanistic model of education, open to science and free from religious indoctrination. Materialism and unbelief advanced thanks to Dutch physiologist and freethinker Jakob Moleschott, who taught in Italy for more than thirty years, and to radical politician and positivist historian Giuseppe Ferrari. In literature, materialistic and essentially atheistic traits can be seen in Giacomo Leopardi, one of the greatest authors of the time, from his juvenile but learned *Saggio sopra gli errori popolari degli antichi* (1815) to the pessimistic meditations of the *Operette Morali* (Minor Works on Morality), which was placed on the Index in 1860. Caustic anticlerical poems appear in the works of Olindo Guerrini (known as Lorenzo Stecchetti), Cesare Pascarella, and Nobel laureate Giosué Carducci, a Freemason since 1865 and a prominent anticlerical; his *Hymn to Satan*, in which revolt against Christianity is seen as the essence of progress, earned him excommunication.

Among the political parties, an anticlerical inclination was mostly seen in the extreme left: in the Italian Republican Party with Arcangelo Ghisleri, Eugenio Chiesa, and positivist philosopher Giovanni Bovio; in the nineteenth-century Radical Party with Felice Cavallotti; and later in the Socialist Party with Andrea Costa. On the side of anarchism, Mikhail BAKUNIN lived in Italy between 1864 and 1867 and influenced Italian libertarian unbelief (see ANARCHISM AND UNBELIEF).

Organized unbelief in Italy was more political than philosophical in nature. Former priest Cristoforo Bonavino, known as Ausonio Franchi, founded the periodical *La Ragione* in 1854 and helped to form an early organized freethought movement, together with Mauro Macchi and Luigi Stefanoni. Stefanoni translated Ludwig BÜCHNER, founded the periodical *Il Libero Pensiero*, and published atheistic and virulently anticlerical writings as well as an imposing *Storia critica della superstizione* (Critical History of Superstition) in 1869. Other local freethought groups were headed by such leaders as Garibaldi, Bovio, and Cavallotti. Ghisleri and Moleschott were the first to contact the International Freethought Federation (IFF) in 1880. Italian representatives to that body later included such renowned personalities as Roberto Ardigò, the leading figure in Italian positivism; politician and sociologist Napoleone Colajanni; renowned psychiatrist and criminologist Cesare Lombroso; and poet and playwright Mario Rapisardi, translator into Italian of Lucretius and Percy Bysshe SHELLEY.

Anticlerical propaganda culminated in Italy in the second half of the century. In 1869 the deputy Giuseppe Ricciardi organized an "Anti-Council" in Naples, which openly opposed the First Vatican Council and summoned all "freethinkers of the civil world." More than sixty Italian members of the parliament, Freemasons, and freethinkers from twenty foreign countries contributed to this atheistic and anticlerical initiative. Starting in 1885, several Italian personalities (in addition to Ludwig Büchner, Charles BRADLAUGH, Ernst HAECKEL, Victor Hugo, Henrik Ibsen, Robert Green INGERSOLL, Ernest RENAN, Herbert SPENCER, Algernon Charles SWINBURNE, and many others) joined a fund-raising initiative to erect a statue in Rome's Campo de'Fiori, where Bruno had been burned. Other supporters included Ghisleri, Lombroso, Ardigò, Carducci, and the politicians Aurelio Saffi, Giuseppe Zanardelli, and Antonio Labriola. In 1889 this monument was dedicated. Bovio delivered an inauguration speech to a huge crowd, and Bruno became

the symbol of Italian freethought that he remains today. Even so, the nineteenth century would end with a period of censorship and repression.

The Twentieth Century. At the beginning of the twentieth century, freethinkers' activities blossomed into the formation of cultural and social charities. The international freethought congress of 1904 was organized in Rome, chaired by Ghisleri and anthropologist Giuseppe Sergi, a supporter and translator into Italian of Ludwig Büchner, Haeckel, and Spencer. Among the foreign personalities who participated were Haeckel, Moncure CONWAY, and Francisco FERRER. In those years the anticlericalist and Masonic Grand Master Ernesto Nathan was mayor of Rome; the satirical magazine *L'Asino*, published by freethinker Guido Podrecca, reached a circulation of one hundred thousand. Even the early futurist movement had particular anticlerical leanings, stemming from its antitraditionalist stance. But organized rationalism and democracy at large would fall under fascist guns and batons. Soon after establishing his regime, Benito Mussolini, a former socialist leader and rationalist activist who had written an atheistic pamphlet, "*L'uomo e la divinità*" (Man and God), came to an agreement with the papacy and largely restored the fortunes of the church. On the opposite side, idealist philosopher and liberal senator Benedetto Croce headed the spare parliamentary opposition to Mussolini's 1929 Concordat, or pact, with the Vatican. His small 1945 essay in response to Bertrand RUSSELL's *Why I Am Not a Christian*, "*Perché non possiamo non dirci cristiani*" (Why We Cannot But Define Ourselves Christians) of 1945 has been a milestone on the subject of combining disbelief in Christian theology with an embrace of the "cultural values" of Christianity.

In 1931, only twelve university professors refused to pledge allegiance to the fascist regime; among them were Ernesto Buonaiuti, the excommunicated modernist historian of Christianity; philosopher Piero Martinetti, deeply religious but a critic of Catholicism; and Francesco Ruffini, lecturer on ecclesiastical law but an unsurpassed champion of separation of church and state and of freedom of thought. An isolated case is that of philosopher Giuseppe Rensi, whose criticism of the idea of God (*Apologia dell'ateismo*; 1925) conveyed a sort of "religious" ATHEISM reminiscent of Lucretius, Leopardi, and Shelley. Many other antifascist activists and authors were anticlerical or openly irreligious and denounced the Concordat regime, including historian Gaetano Salvemini, jurist Piero Calamandrei, and Antonio Gramsci, one of the leading personalities in the birth of the Italian Communist Party. In addition, several secularist authors and activists were part of the antifascist movement Giustizia e Libertà (Justice and Liberty), including Riccardo Bauer, Alessandro Galante Garrone, and, notably, Ernesto Rossi, who published many anticlerical books and articles.

After World War II. The 1929 pacts with the Vatican

were sanctioned in the Italian republican constitution of 1948. Movements to repeal the Concordat never achieved great popularity. Still, despite the persistent clerical privileges the Concordat engendered and a solidly pro-Catholic political majority, the secularization of Italian civil society proceeded rapidly, culminating in the 1970s with a vote in favor of abortion rights and divorce.

Religious arguments in contemporary Italy are viewed less as theological matters and more with regard to their political implications for the church, large political parties, ethnic minorities, and the like, and with regard to their significance in terms of basic social principles and human rights. Therefore, outside of the relatively minor anarchist and freethought movements, the key question of belief often remains a personal issue, even for many academics who openly declare their atheism. The controversial dismissal of philosopher Emanuele Severino from the Catholic University of Milan in 1969 and the later, analogous case of Luigi Lombardi Vallauri in 1997, turned on their unorthodox views about religion rather than on plain unbelief. A classical Enlightenment and Marxist critique of theism and of religions was proposed by Arturo Labriola, but only a few other philosophers challenged religious belief. Conspicuous among them are Franco Lombardi, who advanced an antimetaphysical view devoid of any theological vestiges; Guido Calogero, who in the 1950s revolted against Christianity's monopoly over the so-called values of our civilization; and Nicola Abbagnano, a liberal philosopher who promoted a "New Enlightenment" movement together with Ludovico Geymonat. Geymonat was a communist partisan, rationalist, and Marxist philosopher who held the first Italian chair of philosophy of science and made logical EMPIRICISM known in Italy. Giulio Preti offered an analysis of the relationships between religion, philosophical trends, and science in which he labeled AGNOSTICISM as inconsistent and instead advocated outright atheism.

In other areas, speculation on religious unbelief was often mixed with considerations of political, moral, or historical issues. Historian of Christianity Ambrogio Donini was a Communist senator and an illustrious freethinker. Cesare Musatti, father of the Italian psychoanalytical school, was openly atheistic and anticlerical; Marcello Craveri, author of a much translated *Life of Jesus* (1966), and philosopher Norberto Bobbio also deserve mention in this regard.

The profession of explicit unbelief is unusual in contemporary Italian society: public persons often dare only to define themselves as skeptical, as did the liberal intellectual Giuseppe Prezzolini, or to confess a sense of inferiority with regards to believers, as did writer and film director Pier Paolo Pasolini. It is therefore not atypical that playwright and Nobel laureate Dario Fo, though his works are strongly anticlerical and blasphemous, was married in Milan by the archbishop. Other renowned unbelievers were the writers Primo Levi and Italo Calvino. On the academic side, anthropologist Ida

Magli, Nobel laureate neurobiologist Rita Levi-Montalcini, and, notably, astrophysicist Margherita Hack made public statements of their secularism and unbelief.

The Church of Rome has given Italian society little conceptual room for organized dissent, but has also given it a religion without passion—superficial, increasingly superstitious, and more preoccupied with pleasing the hierarchy than with clinging to dogmas. Today indifference and incredulity are widespread, but open profession of atheism is rare. It might be said that conformity matters more than convictions.

BIBLIOGRAPHY

Capizzi, Antonio. *Dall'Ateismo all'umanismo. Correnti incredule del dopoguerra e loro prospettive dialogiche*. Roma: Edizioni dell'Ateneo, 1967.

Craveri, Marcello. *L'eresia*. Milano: Mondadori, 1996.

Franzinelli, Mimmo. *Ateismo laicismo anticlericalismo. Guida bibliografica ragionata al libero pensiero e alla concezione materialistica della storia*. Ragusa: La Fiaccola, 1990–94.

Hunter, Michael, and David Wootton, eds. *Atheism from the Reformation to the Enlightenment*. Oxford: Clarendon, 1992.

Minois, Georges. *Histoire de l'athéisme*. Paris: Fayard, 1988.

Mola, Aldo A., ed. *Anticlericali e laici all'avvento del fascismo*. Foggia: Bastogi, 1986.

———. *Stato, Chiesa e società in Italia, Francia, Belgio e Spagna nei secoli XIX–XX*. Foggia: Bastogi, 1993.

Pepe, Gabriele, and Mario Themelly, eds. *L'anticlericalismo nel Risorgimento 1830–1870*. Manduria: Lacaita 1966.

Verucci, Guido. *L'Italia laica prima e dopo l'Unità—1848–1876. Anticlericalismo, libero pensiero e ateismo nella società italiana*. Roma-Bari: Laterza, 1981 (1), 1996 (2).

Zoli, Sergio: *Dall'Europa Libertina all'Europa Illuminista. Alle origini del laicismo e dell'Illuminismo*. Firenze: Nardini, 1997.

ROBERTO LA FERLA

JACOBI, FRIEDRICH HEINRICH (1743–1819), German philosophical writer. Friedrich Heinrich Jacobi was born in 1743 in Düsseldorf, Germany. Science, art, and religion enticed the reserved youngster. Jacobi's merchant father apprenticed him with a business at Frankfurt-am-Main in hope that he would devote his life to commerce, but also permitted him to study philosophy in Geneva, where he read Lesage, Jean-Jacques ROUSSEAU, and Bonnet. Abandoning hopes of a medical career, Jacobi returned to Düsseldorf and helped maintain the family business. Throughout his life, he remained concerned with the possibility of discovering theoretical and practical truth without compromising personal freedom.

After a surreptitious relationship with Anna Katharina Müller (a household servant who bore his illegitimate son), Jacobi married Elisabeth (Betty) von Clermont. Intellectual interests united the young couple. They established a cultural haven with Jacobi's brother, the poet Georg, and his half-sisters, Charlotte and Helene, at the family's country home in Pempelfort, which enjoyed visits by GOETHE, Denis DIDEROT, Friedrich von Humboldt, and Johann Gottfried von HERDER. The Spinozism Controversy (see CONTROVERSIES: SPINOZISM, ATHEISM, PANTHEISM) and the loss of a son undermined his health. In 1794 the French invasion forced the family to flee to Wandsbeck and later, to settle in Eutin. After brief forays into local politics, Jacobi devoted himself to philosophical study and writing.

Jacobi's novels and essays influenced many different members of the intellectual community, earning respect from fideists, idealists, and romantics. He questioned the adequacy of philosophy as a means of articulating human and divine existence, calling for a return to common sense and faith. Jacobi claimed that abstract speculation generated either SKEPTICISM or DETERMINISM, which led to ethical despair that could only be averted by belief in a personal, creative God.

As a writer, Jacobi developed primarily through his critiques of other thinkers. After examining Baruch SPINOZA's philosophy, he concluded that it threatened religion and freedom by promoting both the Enlightened "tyranny of understanding" (see ENLIGHTENMENT, UNBELIEF DURING THE) and the romantic "cult of nature." During the Spinozism Controversy, Jacobi criticized pantheism, ATHEISM, and rationalist metaphysics in the *Spinoza Letters* (1785), attacking Moses Mendelssohn as a representative of the Enlightenment and Herder as a representative of romanticism.

After studying David HUME and Immanuel KANT, Jacobi explained more precisely his rejection of abstract analysis in favor of common sense and belief. In *David Hume on Faith or Idealism and Realism* (1787), he addressed Hume's skepticism. Hume had claimed that external reality lacked objective justification and thus, that human activity depended on belief or custom. Jacobi replied that individual self-awareness provided subjective evidence for the coexistence of external things, other people, and a personal creator, thus revealing an immediate knowledge.

In his *David Hume*, Jacobi also considered Kant's transcendental idealism. Kant distinguished between sensibility and reason, claiming that the nonsensible objects of rational faith (God, freedom, and immortality) transcended knowledge. Jacobi thought Kant had produced a new skepticism, because the sensible objects of knowledge never compared to the ideals of reason. He rejected Kant's attempt to derive the content of rational faith from individual moral experience rather than from communal, historical religious experience.

For Jacobi, J. G. FICHTE's idealism exceeded Spinoza's materialism, Hume's skepticism, and Kant's transcendental idealism. During the Atheism Controversy he accused Fichte of egoistic NIHILISM in *Jacobi to Fichte* (1799), claiming that idealism reduced individual subjectivity to a formal ego and faith in a personal God to belief in an abstract moral principle. Later, he attacked Fichte's follower F. W. J. Schelling, thus instigating the Pantheism Controversy.

Jacobi communicated his nascent philosophy through hints, symbols, and allegories. His idiosyncratic use of terms such as REASON, faith, and knowledge was perplexing. According to Jacobi, two species of knowledge derived from two types of sensibility, or feeling. Sensation, which was mediated by conceptual analysis, generated discursive knowledge of nature. Reason provided immediate, nondiscursive knowledge of God, freedom, and spirit. Rational knowledge involved intuition of the primordial ideals: the True, the Good, and the Beautiful.

Jacobi's final years were quiet. After retiring in 1812, he supervised the publication of his collected works. Although he never recovered from the financial, physical, and emotional damage suffered during the Spinozism Controversy and the French invasion, he enjoyed relative comfort surrounded by a wide circle of family and admirers. In 1819 he died in Munich.

BIBLIOGRAPHY

Beiser, Frederick C. *The Fate of Reason: German Philosophy from Kant to Fichte*. Cambridge, MA: Harvard University Press, 1987.

Jacobi, F. H. *The Main Philosophical Writings and the Novel* Allwill. Translated and edited by George di Giovanni. Montreal: McGill-Queen's University Press, 1994.

Vallée, Gérard. *The Spinoza Conversations between Lessing and Jacobi*. New York: University Press of America, 1988.

YOLANDA ESTES

JAMES, CHARLES LEIGH (1846–1911), scholar and anarchist. Considered the most profound scholar among American anarchists (see ANARCHISM AND UNBELIEF), Charles Leigh James was born October 23, 1846, at Baden-Baden, Germany. The son of an English novelist and diplomat, he traveled extensively and met noted intellectuals through his family. Raised an evangelical Anglican and sometimes privately tutored, he attended Cheltenham College from 1861 to 1863; in 1865 he moved permanently to Eau Claire, Wisconsin, where he became a journalist. In 1866 he and Ohio-born Maria Hoyt opened a grocery store. James was very active in the Free Religious Society of Eau Claire and lectured on temperance. Leading an 1885 laborers' strike, he raised funds for the destitute families, urging them to "avoid violence above all things." He compared marriage to chattel slavery at age twenty-four, but we know little about Hoyt (see SEX RADICALISM AND UNBELIEF). The couple had three daughters by 1880, and in 1893 they married with a religious ceremony. James believed that not only Christians, but Hindus, Buddhists, or free-thinkers could endeavor to become the "ideal self." Though he wrote a full-length world history covering the earliest known civilizations through his own day, only one part (on the French Revolution) became a book. His Shakespeare criticism was said to be of the highest quality, and his countless articles, letters, and poems appeared in leading anarchist journals.

James held that "possession is natural; that property, as distinguished from possession, is robbery; and that robbery is artificial, made possible only by government." He insisted that anarchism rests "on Induction, whose evidences are alike for all men, whatever dogmas they were taught to believe." He viewed the belief in govern-ment as a superstition that would become, "like the belief in witchcraft, an object of general ridicule." His inductive method examined the problems of war, reli-gion, morals, and aesthetics. In scientific debates, he defended vivisection and vaccination.

"Eau Claire's only anarchist" seems not to have traveled outside of the Midwest once he'd settled down. He died June 3, 1911, of heart disease and was warmly eulogized.

BIBLIOGRAPHY

James, C. L. *The Law of Marriage: An Exposition of Its Uselessness and Injustice.* Chicago: Author, 1870.
———. *The Vindication of Anarchism.* Partly serialized in *Free Society* in 1903.
"The Strike." *Eau Claire Daily Leader.* May 13–30 and June 2–18, 1885.
Jaxon, Honoré J. "A Reminiscence of Charlie James." *Mother Earth* 5 (July 1911).
Reichert, William O. *Partisans of Freedom: A Study in American Anarchism.* Bowling Green, OH: Popular Press, 1976.

ROBERT P. HELMS

JAMES, C. L. R. (1901–1989), political theorist and humanist. Cyril Lionel Robert James was one of the most brilliant and original Marxist theorists of the twen-tieth century (see MARXISM). Moreover, he excelled in other areas, including sports writing, literary criticism, cultural criticism, and history.

James was born in Port of Spain, Trinidad. When he was a young boy, he loved cricket, watching and playing the game. His study of cricket enabled him to make pro-found observations on race, class, power, culture, the relationship between the individual and society, and life in general.

James also studied the works of Aeschylus, Shake-speare (see SHAKESPEARE, RELIGIOUS SKEPTICISM IN),

William Thackeray, Fyodor Dostoyevsky, Lev TOLSTOY, and other great writers. Furthermore, his father, a teacher, often welcomed Hubert Alfonso Nurse as a houseguest; Nurse was the father of Malcolm Nurse, who, as George Padmore, would become a leader of the Pan-Africanist movement, which held that people of African descent are united by ancestry, culture, history, and destiny. James's father and the elder Nurse often dis-cussed Pan-Africanism, influencing the younger James.

James's parents were devout Anglicans, and James embraced religion during his youth. When he was about twenty-one, however, he started reading books by ratio-nalists (see RATIONALISM). By about age twenty-three, he was highly skeptical of Christianity and placed a high value upon reason instead of faith.

James spoke to a Roman Catholic friend about his doubts. The friend suggested that James share his views with a priest. James did so, but the priest essentially told him that he had to accept theism on faith. James was unimpressed with the priest's answer and shared his doubts with a Protestant minister. James was surprised when the Protestant minister gave him a similar response.

At twenty-four, teaching in Queen's Royal College, James rejected Christianity completely. He came to the conclusion that God is a concept created by human beings. Rejecting theism, he embraced a non-religious worldview, became an agnostic (see AGNOSTICISM), and never looked back.

At age thirty-one James sailed to England. He wrote newspaper articles on cricket, embraced Marxism, and thought profoundly about politics and culture. He became a member of the Independent Labour Party and eventually joined the Trotskyist movement.

James's most popular book is *The Black Jacobins: Toussaint L'Overture and the San Domingo Revolution.* In this work, James examined the Haitian rebellion from a Marxist perspective. Some of his critics believed he focused on class while giving short shrift to the subject of race. However, *Black Jacobins* is considered to be a classic among Marxists and Afrocentrists alike.

In 1935, with the blessing of the pope, Italy invaded Ethiopia. As a result, James began to focus more sharply on trying to meld Marxism and Pan-Africanism into a unified theory of human liberation. He saw no contradic-tion between the two, though many black nationalists thought Marxism could not adequately address the needs of people of African descent. On the other hand, many Marxists saw African nationalism as shortsighted and a threat to working-class unity.

In 1938 James focused on economic developments in the United States. He believed the American people were waking up to the need for government action in improving the lives of citizens. On the other hand, after Adolf Hitler and Joseph Stalin signed a 1940 unity agree-ment, James became increasingly critical of Trotskyism.

By 1941 he had left the Socialist Workers Party and

formed the Johnson-Forest Tendency. James and the other members of this group drew upon Marxism and Hegel's dialectical materialism in an effort to formulate a progressive vision for society.

James spent fifteen years in the United States, during which time he produced what he and others considered some of the most intellectually stimulating work of his life. Offering penetrating insights into popular US culture, he demonstrated great respect for the cultural contributions of ordinary people.

James's American wife, the writer and political activist Constance Webb, had a great impact upon his thinking. He credited her with bringing about much of his intellectual creativity. She was one of the most influential members of the Johnson-Forest Tendency. The couple had a son together. However, the US government eventually planned to have James deported, and he returned to England alone.

Today the James legacy is kept alive in New York City at the C. L. R James Institute. Its web site features articles, essays, speeches, books, photos, and other information on the life and thought of C. L. R. James.

BIBLIOGRAPHY

Buhle, Paul. *C. L. R. James: The Artist as Revolutionary.* London: Verso, 1986.

Farred, Grant, ed. *Rethinking C. L. R. James.* Oxford: Blackwell, 1996.

Grimshaw, Anna. *C. L. R. James: A Revolutionary Vision for the Twentieth Century.* New York: Smyrna, 1991.

———, ed. *The C. L. R. James Reader.* Oxford: Blackwell, 1992.

James, C. L. R. *Beyond a Boundary.* New York: Pantheon, 1983.

———. *The Black Jacobins: Toussaint L'Ouverture and the San Domingo Revolution.* London: Allison and Busby, 1980.

———. *The Case for West Indian Self Government.* London: Hogarth, 1933.

NORM R. ALLEN JR.

JEFFERSON, THOMAS (1743–1826), American statesman. Our certain knowledge concerning Thomas Jefferson's opinions on religion is limited by our awareness of three constraints: (1) He was a man of extreme reticence and reserve, with many good (and some less admirable) reasons for safeguarding his privacy. (2) He lived in a period during which the natural sciences were in the ascendant, but also at a time when the revelation (if that should be the right term) of Darwinism (see DARWINISM AND UNBELIEF) was still a few decades in the future. (Charles DARWIN was born on the very same day as Abraham Lincoln: history may well judge which of the two men was the greatest emancipator, but both of them had to attend to important business which Mr. Jefferson had left unfinished.) (3) He was a man of very strongly marked contradiction, both in his public and his private life.

With these limitations to our inquiry fully admitted, it is nonetheless permissible to infer that the third President of the United States and author of its Declaration of Independence had at least conducted a flirtation with ATHEISM, had a strong dislike of organized religion if not for religion itself (see ANTICLERICALISM), and believed that wherever the truth might lie, it did not lie with any religious establishment and could only be properly explored in a society that observed a strict boundary between church and state.

The likeliest and most logical explanation of all these opinions and contradictions may be the simplest one: Jefferson was a "deist" (see DEISM). In other words, and like many thoughtful men of his day, he believed that the observable order of nature and of the universe argued for an author or "designer," but he could not be persuaded that (a) this author or designer's wishes could be known, still less made known, to his creatures or (b) that any divine wishes or further interventions were necessarily involved. On one point we can be certain: at no stage of his life does Jefferson appear to have believed that any priesthood could hold the key to this mystery.

Not unlike William Paley, founder of the simplistic "Natural Theology" (see EVOLUTION AND UNBELIEF), Jefferson was fond of the analogy of the timepiece: a work that not even a primitive human, ignorant of its purpose, could confuse with a rock or a vegetable. He compared his own body to a watch, and indeed observed dryly in old age that its springs and wheels appeared to be wearing out. But how can "design" encompass the idea of innate breakdown and failure? The same paradox is evident in Jefferson's own reflections on evil and injustice: in discussing the great stain of slavery he observed: "I tremble for my country when I reflect that God is just," and, less famously, commented on the one-vote defeat of an antislavery resolution that "Heaven was silent in that awful moment." Biblically derived rhetoric was universal in that period, and Jefferson was not exempt from the requirement to address an audience which often knew only one book, so that his resort to such tropes is no great wonder. (The two uses of the word "creator" and "created," in the preamble to the Declaration of Independence, are an obvious example. Though the meaning of "equality" and "rights" would be unaffected by the absence of any such references, the new nation was clearly not going to begin by addressing a divided American people in secular, let alone in agnostic or atheist tones.)

However, he was not of a mind to be content with any idea of god taking any side, let alone the just one. Or else what would be the need for the Enlightenment and the science of which he was such a student? (see ENLIGHTENMENT, UNBELIEF DURING THE). In a letter to his nephew Peter Carr, written from Paris 1787 and suggesting a course of education, he wrote: "Fix reason firmly in her seat, and call to her tribunal every fact, every opinion. Question with boldness even the existence of a God; because, if there be one, he must more approve of the homage of reason, than of blindfolded fear. . . . Do not be frightened from this inquiry by any fear of its consequences. If it ends in a belief that there is no God, you will find incitements to virtue in the comforts and pleasantness you feel in its exercise, and the love of others it will procure you. If you find reason to believe there is a God, a consciousness that you are acting under his eye, and that he approves you, will be a vast additional incitement; if that there be a future state, the hope of a happy existence in that increases the appetite to deserve it; if that Jesus was also a God, you will be comforted by a belief of his aid and love."

This letter is of considerable interest, because it is one that Jefferson can never have expected anyone else to read, and because it both demonstrates his own open-mindedness and proves that he had, at least for a time, steadily contemplated the idea of a godless world. In many ways, and in other paragraphs, it also anticipates his own much later edition of the New Testament (commonly called "The Jefferson Bible," and a manual for Unitarians (see UNITARIANISM TO 1961) in which he firmly repudiated the idea of the divinity of Jesus. But that text, too, was never intended to be read by others in the course of Jefferson's lifetime.

However ambivalently we may have to "read" Jefferson on the numinous and the supernatural, we are freed from this encumbrance when it comes to the church, or the churches. It is rare indeed to find him using the word "priest" or "monk" without some terse allusion to "superstition" or "witchcraft." Of the only three achievements that he thought worthy of mention on his memorial obelisk (which was uninscribed with any devotional words about faith or the hereafter) the two besides his authorship of the Declaration of Independence were the foundation of the University of Virginia and the sponsorship of the Virginia Statute on Religious Freedom. The university was the first secular campus in America and the only one not to endow a chair of theology, and the Statute is, in all its essentials, the cornerstone of the First Amendment to the United States Constitution.

Jefferson was much attacked for his laconic but deliberate remark that "it does me no injury for my neighbor to say that there are twenty gods, or no god. It neither picks my pocket nor breaks my leg." But more important was the legal "rider" that he attached to this seemingly uncontroversial proposition: Injury could indeed by done by those who expected their belief to enjoy the sanction and protection of law. Jefferson's Virginia Statute on Religious Freedom set out to ensure that no faith or congregation could expect any means of support beyond itself. It is important to bear in mind that, at the time, the constitution of Massachusetts extended "equal protection," and the right to hold office, only to "Chris-

tians" and only to those Christians who had abjured the pope. In New York, equality was likewise denied to Catholics but permitted to Jews. In Maryland, the position was the exact obverse. Delaware demanded that its officeholders bear witness to their belief in the Trinity, while in South Carolina it was declared that the official religion was simply "Protestantism." Only in Virginia, at first, was it suggested that the state's tithes and taxes underwrite no sect or faith.

In order for this bill to pass, it may not be too fanciful to imagine, its 1779 preamble had to contain some ostensibly devotional rhetoric: "Well aware that Almighty God hath created the mind free; that all attempts to influence it by temporal punishments or burdens, or by civil incapacitations, tend only to beget habits of hypocrisy and meanness, and are a departure from the plan of the Holy Author of our religion, who being Lord both of body and mind, yet chose not to propagate it by coercions on either, as it was in his Almighty power to do; that the impious presumptions of legislators and rulers, civil as well as ecclesiastical, who, being themselves but fallible and uninspired men have assumed dominion over the faith of others, setting up their own opinions and modes of thinking as the only true and infallible, and as such endeavoring to impose them on others, hath established and maintained false religions over the greater part of the world and through all time."

The stress, here, may be laid on the fourth and fifth words "Almighty God," which perform something of the same function that the two words "their Creator" fulfill in the Declaration of Independence. A general reference to a higher power may sometimes have the effect of irritating true believers, who insist on something more specific to their own creed. It was proposed that the words "Almighty God" be removed and replaced with "Jesus Christ." This crude tactic, which was defeated by a surprisingly large majority, allowed Jefferson to claim "proof that they meant to comprehend, within the mantle of its protection, the Jew and the Gentile, the Christian and Mahomedan, the Hindoo, and infidel of every denomination." In that sense, it might be argued, he had subtly employed the zeal of the faithful, as well as their rhetoric, against the faithful themselves. And, since he showed tactical genius and skill at compromise throughout his political life, there is no reason for us to suppose that he was not playing the same hand on this occasion, too.

It needs to be added that Jefferson, in defending his Bill, laid stress on the ways in which the state could corrupt the churches (by means of pelf and preferment) as well as the other way around. But his private conviction may be better illustrated by his view that "our civil rights have no dependence on our religious opinions, any more than our opinions in physics or geometry." The latter two instances are perhaps significant. Jefferson was a friend to science and a believer in the Enlightenment, and he helped advance the idea of vaccination against smallpox, for example, at a time when that leading Yale divine Dr.

Timothy Dwight was denouncing injection as a profane interference with god's design. However, there were other men of science and enlightenment, such as Dr. Benjamin Rush, whose Christianity was unshakeable. (Rush even dropped his friendship with Thomas PAINE after the latter published *The Age of Reason*: it may or may not be suggestive that Jefferson never disowned Paine, even in adversity.)

His later time in office, as successively minister to Paris, Secretary of State, Vice President and (twice) President does not allow a very minute insight into his private opinions. We know that Jefferson made a point of attending divine service as occasion required, just as we know that when his daughter wanted to become a nun, he drove straight to the school in Paris where she had acquired the idea and removed her from the establishment that very day. It was, however, while he was in his first term as President, on New Year's Day, 1802, that he took the opportunity of replying to an address from the Baptist Association of Danbury, Connecticut. After some opening courtesies, he wrote: "Believing with you that religion is a matter which lies solely between man and his God, that he owes account to none other for his faith or his worship, that the legislative powers of government reach actions only, and not opinions, I contemplate with sovereign reverence that act of the whole American people which declared that their legislature should 'make no law respecting an establishment of religion, or prohibiting the free exercise thereof,' thus building a wall of separation between Church and State."

There seems no reason to doubt that this wall also enclosed, in his mind at least, the rights of those who professed no religion of any kind. Nor can the Framers of a constitution that deliberately eschewed all mention of a deity have intended any other outcome.

When, in retirement at Monticello, Jefferson took up a task that he had actually begun while in the White House, and decided to revise the New Testament by purging it of all magical and absurd and superstitious accretions, he seems to have felt a sense of mission that was part secular and part devotional. To renew attention to the teachings and precepts of a good man was, he felt, to define himself as a true "Christian" in the sense that one might now call oneself a Spinozist (see SPINOZA, BARUCH) or Darwinian: in other words, to affirm the teachings of a teacher without having to worship him in any extravagant manner. This—the repudiation of Trinitarian casuistry and the focus on the individual human— had in his mind the additional advantage of putting the priests out of a job, because what could be plainly understood "would not answer their purpose," since "their security is in their faculty of shedding darkness." This form of Unitarianism, he wrongly believed, would soon win a majority simply by its appeal to reason.

As death approached, and as he continued to suffer at the thought of his wife and two of his daughters having predeceased him, Jefferson may have allowed himself

and his surviving daughter a few moments of emotion on their behalves, and even the yearning for a reunion beyond the grave. But his last public letter was a blast against "monkish ignorance and superstition," and he repeatedly confronted the inevitable by telling friends that he did so with neither "fear" nor "hope." In words that might have appealed to any freethinker, he informed one of the many who tried to coax him into confession or allegiance that: "I am of a sect by myself." This statement may not allow him to be annexed by the materialist camp, but it keeps him from the clutches of all who prefer faith to reason.

CHRISTOPHER HITCHENS

JESUS, HISTORICITY OF. Denying Jesus's historicity means asserting that Christianity is based on a founder figure who is wholly mythical. This was the position argued by Bruno BAUER in in 1850 and later; he was supported at the turn of the century by Arthur Drews in Germany, William Benjamin Smith in America, and John M. ROBERTSON in England, among others, in a fierce debate on the subject that was not without some impact even on Christian scholars. Thus in chapters added to the second (1913) German edition of his famous history of life-of-Jesus research, Albert Schweitzer allowed that Christianity must reckon with the possibility that it will have to surrender the historicity of Jesus altogether, and must have, in readiness for such a contingency, a metaphysical basis for its beliefs.

However, Robertson and the others of that time made the mistakes of setting aside as interpolations all New Testament passages they found inconvenient, and of trying to explain Jesus away in terms of pagan parallels (as simply another Osiris or Hercules), when the Jewish background is clearly of greater importance. As a result, by around 1920 nearly all scholars had come to regard the case against Jesus's historicity as totally discredited; since then, attempts to reopen the discussion have met with the response that *that* battle has been fought and won by the apologists, and that it would be otiose to fight it all again.

Today, most secular scholars accept Jesus as a historical, although unimpressive, figure. They are aware that much that is said of him, and by him, in the New Testament is no longer taken at face value even by scholars within the mainstream churches, who either discount much of its material as inauthentic, or justify it by more novel interpretations. However, from about 1960 an increasing number of skeptics have come forward with denials of Jesus's historicity. In my first books on Christian origins, I myself denied it, but in works published since 1995 I am not quite as radical, although I still go further than critical Christian scholars in that I regard even the Jerusalem Passion and execution under Pilate as non historical, and am concerned to argue that case here. The more radical view that there was no historical Jesus at all is still vigorously defended by a few scholars, notably Earl Doherty and Robert M. Price.

The starting point for any questioning of Jesus's historicity must be the observation that the earliest extant Christian documents do not confirm the portraits of him given in the canonical gospels. These latter, widely agreed to have been written between 70 and 100 CE, and not by eyewitnesses of the events portrayed in them, depict Jesus as a teacher and miracle worker in Galilee early in the first century who died in Jerusalem at the behest of the Roman governor Pontius Pilate. But none of these supposedly historical events are mentioned in extant Christian documents that are either earlier than the gospels or are early enough to have been written independently of the gospels—that is, before the gospels, or the traditions underlying them, had become generally known in Christian circles.

The discrepancy is particularly striking when behavior or teaching recorded in the gospels has obvious relevance to the concerns of the earlier authors. Some scholars have frankly called it baffling that Paul, writing substantial epistles in the 50s—they include Romans, 1 and 2 Corinthians, Galatians, and Philippians—fails to refer to the teachings and actions of Jesus, particularly at points where he could have clinched his arguments by doing so. For instance, one of the major issues confronting him was: Should Christians be required to keep the Jewish law? One would never suppose, from what Paul says, that Jesus had views on this matter—as, according to the gospels, he had. Again, is Jesus's second coming, which will bring the world to an end, imminent? And will it be preceded by obvious catastrophes, or occur without warning? On these points, 2 Thessalonians (probably a little later than Paul, although it claims to be his writing) contradicts the genuinely Pauline 1 Thessalonians, but neither appeals to any teachings such as those detailed in the gospels. This is very hard to understand if Jesus had in fact spoken of these things only a decade or two earlier.

Paul tells his readers to "bless those that persecute you," bids them "judge not," and urges them to "pay taxes." Surely in such instances he might reasonably be expected to have invoked Jesuine authority, *had he known* that Jesus had taught the very same doctrines. It seems likely that certain precepts concerning forgiveness and civil obedience were originally urged independently of Jesus, and only later put into his mouth and thereby stamped with his supreme authority. This is more probable than that Jesus really gave such rulings but was not credited with having done so by Paul, nor indeed by Christian epistle writers of the following generation, for they write of his earthly life in much the same vague way.

This early post-Pauline material is substantial, comprising three of the letters falsely ascribed to Paul in the canon (2 Thessalonians, Colossians and Ephesians) and also the letter to the Hebrews, the epistle of James, the first epistle of Peter, the three epistles of John, and the book of Revelation. These writings are dated between 70 and 95 CE (that is, within the period when the gospels were being written). Nevertheless, although most of them stress one or more of Jesus's supernatural aspects (his existence before his life on earth, his resurrection, and second coming), they do not ascribe to him the teachings or miracles attributed to him in the gospels; most strangely, they give no historical setting to the crucifixion, the only episode Jesus's incarnate life which they see fit to mention at all. This suggests that there was an interval before the biographical material of the gospels became generally known and widely accepted in Christian circles. That older Christologies should have persisted in some quarters while newer ones were emerging in others is hardly a matter for surprise.

There is, then, a disparity between all these documents and the gospels which cannot readily be discounted. It is perverse when many scholars reduce the whole problem—if indeed they acknowledge it at all—to the silences of Paul, when so many others are equally silent about matters which, had they known of them, they could not but have regarded as important.

General Characteristics of the Early Material. The most striking feature of the early documents is that they do not set Jesus's life in a specific historical situation. Not only are there no parables nor miracles, but also no Galilean ministry, nor Passion in Jerusalem, indeed no indication of time, place, or attendant circumstances at all. The words Calvary, Bethlehem, Nazareth, and Galilee never appear, and the word Jerusalem is never used in connection with Jesus, who figures as a basically supernatural personage who took human form, "emptied" then of his supernatural powers (Phil. 2:7)—certainly he is not portrayed as the gospel figure who worked wonders that made him famous throughout "all Syria" (Matt. 4:24). He was indeed crucified for our redemption, yet the Passion is not as in the gospels. In Paul, for instance, there is no cleansing of the temple (which, according to Mark and Luke, was the event that triggered the resolve of the chief priests and scribes to kill Jesus), no conflict with the authorities, no Gethsemane scene, no thieves crucified with Jesus, no weeping women, no word about the place or time, and no mention of Judas or Pilate.

Paul's colorless references to the crucifixion might be accepted as unproblematic if it were unimportant for him. But he himself declares it to be the very substance of his preaching (1 Cor. 1:23 and 2:2). Yet he lived as a Christian for three years before even briefly visiting Jerusalem (Gal. 1:17f.), and says nothing that would indicate that he took interest in, or even had awareness of, holy places there.

Assuming human form brought Christ into the domain of the *archontes*, the "rulers" of this world, the evil angelical powers variously designated in the early documents as the world's "elements" (Gal. 4:3, 9) and as authorities, powers, thrones, dominions, principalities (Rom. 8:38;

Cols. 1:16; 2:10, 15). It was these "rulers" who, according to Paul (1 Cor. 2:8), effected the Lord's crucifixion. Kittel's standard *Theological Dictionary of the New Testament* observes that Paul is not here referring to earthly authorities—and so certainly not to Caiaphas and Pilate—and that arguments to the contrary are "not convincing." Colossians (2:15) likewise seems to place the event in a supernatural milieu. Ephesians mentions (2:2) "the prince [*archon*] of the power of the air" to whom the recipients of the epistle used to be beholden, and declares that "our wrestling is not against flesh and blood, but against the principalities, against the powers, against the world-rulers of this darkness, against the spiritual hosts of wickedness in the heavenly places" (6:12). Such passages betray that early Christians conceived the present world order to be under the control of supernatural beings whose power Christ was bringing to an end (1 Cor. 2:6).

Jesus's resurrection was of course as important as his crucifixion. Paul describes himself as "called to be an apostle" (Rom. 1:1) since he had seen the risen Lord and on this basis had entered into his service (1 Cor. 9:1). No one in these letters is called a "disciple" (a personal acquaintance of the earthly Jesus). The word used is "apostle," and it here means no more than Christian missionary.

Paul does not even commit himself unambiguously to designating Jesus's death, burial, and resurrection as recent events. He specifies eyewitnesses of the appearances of the risen Lord (including himself), and stresses that most of these persons are still alive, thus stamping the appearances as recent, but not the death, burial, and prompt resurrection (three days after the death), which he merely says occurred "in accordance with the scriptures" (1 Cor. 15:3–8). This does not mean the gospels, which did not then exist, but the sacred books of the Jews. These appearances of the risen Lord convinced him that the general resurrection of the dead, already heralded by Christ's resurrection (1 Cor. 15:20), and the final judgment of both living and dead, were imminent. Now that Christ was not only risen, but had also begun to manifest himself from heaven, these final events could not be long delayed.

There are admittedly a few statements in Paul's letters which, if read in the light of prior knowledge of the gospels, can be taken to imply that he knew of Jesus's ministry as depicted there. For instance, on one occasion Paul uncharacteristically appeals to the authority of "the Lord" to support an ethical teaching (on divorce: 1 Cor. 7:10). It is, however, not necessary to suppose that he believed the doctrine to have been taught by the historical (as opposed to the risen) Lord; for, as M. E. Boring and others have shown, in Paul's day Christian prophets gave directives in the name of the risen one as the obvious way of supporting rulings of their own that they wished to inculcate. At a later stage it would naturally be supposed that Jesus must have said in his lifetime what the risen Lord had said through his prophets; and so the doctrine came to be put into the mouth of the earthly Jesus and recorded as such by evangelists.

That Paul received communications from the risen Lord is beyond doubt. He expressly records (2 Cor. 12:9) what the Lord had said personally to him in answer to a prayer; and the speaker can only have been the risen Lord, for Paul did not know Jesus before his resurrection, and as a Pharisaic persecutor of Christians, certainly did not then pray to him. The early documents reiterate the importance at that time of Christian prophets as spokesmen of the Spirit. In church, says Paul, "two or three prophets" may speak, while others "weigh what is said"; and "if a revelation is made to another sitting by," then the first should be silent, "for you can all prophesy, one by one" (1 Cor. 14:28–31). He repeatedly speaks of "revelations" which he himself felt impelled to pass on to the community (1 Cor. 2:13; 7:40; 14:37). Other early documents show how widespread the phenomenon was. Ephesians tells of what "has now been revealed to Christ's holy apostles and prophets by the Spirit" (3:5). The book of Revelation refers to prophets as integral to the church (22:9), and delivers *logia*, sayings of the risen Lord, through his spokesman, the author (22:16 and 20).

The first Christian epistles that depict Jesus in a way that significantly resembles to gospel portrayals are some of those which are agreed to have been written circa 90–110 CE; namely the three so-called pastoral epistles (1 and 2 Timothy and Titus, ascribed to Paul in the canon but generally admitted to be from a later hand), 2 Peter (widely regarded as the very latest book in the canonical collection), and, outside the canon, the anonymous letter known as 1 Clement and the seven letters of Ignatius of Antioch. Since, then, all these do give biographical references to Jesus, it cannot be argued that epistle writers generally were disinterested in them, and it becomes necessary to account for the fact that only the earlier ones give the historical Jesus such short shrift.

Jewish Wisdom Literature. The religion of one day is often largely a reshuffling of ideas of a yesterday, and since Christianity emerged from Judaism, it is there that we must look for its most significant antecedents. Jewish Wisdom traditions are here relevant. Wisdom is a primordial feminine being who (in the book of the Wis. 9:4) sits beside God's throne as his consort and participates with him in the creation of the world (Prov. 3:19 and 8:22–31). When she sought an abode on earth, mankind refused to accept her, whereupon she returned in despair to heaven (1 Enoch 42:1f.). This figure of Wisdom, though feminine, greatly influenced Christian thinking about Jesus. The "Christology of pre-existence and incarnation" (according to which Christ existed in heaven before his birth on earth) is—in the wording of Metzger and Coogan's handbook—generally agreed to have "developed from the identification of Jesus with the wisdom of God."

The gender problem already exercised pre-Christian Jews. For Philo, the Jewish sage of Alexandria who died circa 50 CE, although Wisdom's Greek name is feminine her nature is masculine, and she is called feminine only to indicate her inferiority to the masculine maker of the universe. Philo made her almost synonymous with the "Word," the masculine Logos, the highest of God's "powers," which function sometimes as aspects of him and sometimes independently of him. By the time we reach the prologue of the fourth gospel, the masculine Logos had come to be established as a designation of the supernatural figure so close to God. Nevertheless, virtually everything said of the Logos here had already been predicated of Wisdom in Judaism.

That Jewish Wisdom ideas influenced early Christian writings is undeniable, for Jewish statements made about Wisdom are there made of Jesus. Christ is called "the power of God and the wisdom of God" (1 Cor. 1:24); in him are "hidden all the treasures of wisdom and knowledge" (Cols. 2:3). Like Wisdom, Christ assisted God in the creation of all things (1 Cor. 8:6)—an idea spelled out in the Christological hymn of Colossians 1:15–20. And like the Jewish Wisdom figure, Jesus sought acceptance on earth but was rejected and returned to heaven. Furthermore, in the Wisdom of Solomon, the righteous man, Wisdom's ideal representative (no particular person is meant), is persecuted but vindicated post mortem. His enemies have condemned him to "a shameful death" (2:20), but he then confronts them as their judge in heaven, where he is "counted among the sons of God" (5:5). Cognate is the martyrological book 2 Maccabees, with its belief in the resurrection of the faithful; also, 4 Maccabees adds to this the idea that someone steadfast in the faith can benefit others, because God will regard his death as a "ransom" for their lives, as an expiation for their sins (6:28f.; 17:21f.). That a martyr's death could function as an atoning sacrifice, to be followed by his immortality, was, then, an idea not unfamiliar in the Hellenistic environment of early Christianity.

Transition to the Gospels. It is, however, difficult to believe that the gospel Jesus is no more than an expansion and elaboration of the obscure Jesus of the early Christian documents. The gospel traditions are too complex and too specific in their references to time and place to have developed within a short time from no other basis. Accordingly, some elements in the Galilean ministry can be better understood as traceable to the activity of a Galilean preacher of the early first century, who figures in what is known as Q (an abbreviation for *Quelle*, German for "source") which can be reconstructed from what is common to the Gospels of Matthew and Luke, yet does not derive from Mark's gospel (from which they also, again independently of each other, drew). Q consists mainly of Jesus's sayings. Doherty and Price have (quite impressively) argued that these were originally anonymous, Jesus being introduced as their speaker only at a relatively late stage in the development of the material. But most scholars regard them as deriving from a single historical figure—a view which I myself accept.

As Tuckett observes, Q is widely held to have originated in northern Galilee or nearby, circa 40–70 CE. It assigns Galilean localities to Jesus's activities and links him with John the Baptist, known from the Jewish historian Josephus to have been executed before 39 CE. It never calls Jesus "Christ," nor does it identify him with Wisdom, but represents both him and the Baptist as human messengers sent by Wisdom to preach the need for repentance before the imminent arrival of a supernatural figure, "the Son of man," who will effect a terrible and final judgment. Q has no Passion narrative, and does no more than hint that the hostility Jesus met with—in the Deuteronomic tradition of rejection of prophets—may have led to his being killed. His death is certainly not regarded as redemptive, nor is there mention of his resurrection. This human Jesus is, then, in so many respects different from the redeeming Pauline Christ of no specified time and place that the two must surely have separate origins.

Already in Mark, the oldest extant gospel, there are Q-type traditions; and in all four gospels the two Jesus figures have been to a large extent fused into one. The Galilean preacher of Q has been given a salvific death and resurrection, and these have been set in a historical context consonant with the Galilean preaching. As Bultmann observed, Mark's purpose was "the *union of the Hellenistic kerygma* [preaching] *about* Christ, whose essential content consists of the Christ-myth as we learn it in Paul, . . . with the *tradition of the story of Jesus*."

This novel synthesis may well not have immediately appealed to all Christian communities, even if we assume that communication between them was such that they all knew of it. Hence it is not surprising that some of the epistles written circa 90 CE continued, as we have seen, to proclaim the earlier, Pauline view of Jesus.

Other factors apart from Q will have prompted the assigning of Jesus's life to the early first century. The evangelists will have known that Paul and his fellow apostles experienced their visions of the risen Jesus about the year 30; and so they naturally assumed that the crucifixion and resurrection had occurred shortly before. This would seem plausible enough to evangelists writing outside Palestine, after earlier events there had been obscured from view by that country's devastating war with Rome from 66 CE. It was also easier to cope with gnostic Christologies, which described Jesus's redemptive work in mystical terms, if he could confidently be placed in definite historical circumstances. It was in order to confute such deviationists that Ignatius of Antioch—the earliest Christian writer outside the canon to link Jesus with Pilate—insisted that Jesus was truly born from a human mother, the virgin Mary; that he was dependent on food and drink like any other man; and was truly "nailed to the cross" in the days of "Pontius Pilate and Herod the Tetrarch."

Once Pilate had been introduced to give the crucifixion a historical setting, the rest of the gospels' Passion narrative was prompted by musing on what was taken for prophecy in the Old Testament. As Helmut Koester puts it, "the details and individual scenes of the narrative do not rest on historical memory, but were developed on the basis of allegorical interpretation of Scripture."

None of this implies conscious fraud. Only those who lack understanding of the processes whereby myths are formed can suppose that either a tradition is true or else it was maliciously invented by cynics who knew the facts to be otherwise. In ancient times just as now, people constructed situations in their minds in accordance with their convictions about what "must" be (or have been) the case, and so had no hesitation in affirming that the relevant events had actually occurred.

In sum, the Jesus of the early epistles is not the Jesus of the gospels. The ministry of the latter may well be modeled (with considerable mythological embellishment) on the career of an itinerant Galilean preacher who lived during the early first century; whereas the Jesus of the early documents derives largely from Christian interpretation of Jewish Wisdom figures. Hence it is not unreasonable to suggest that not only the Virgin Birth in the reign of Herod the Great (documented only in two gospels, and in narratives that are mutually exclusive) and the resurrection from the dead some thirty years later (which many Christian scholars themselves now reject as unhistorical), but also the crucifixion in the time of Pilate, can be set aside as legendary.

Pagan and Jewish Comments. Christian apologists make much of the fact that, as far as we know, no one in antiquity denied that Jesus had existed. But this is readily explicable. Since Christianity long remained insignificant, its major pagan critics all wrote only after the gospels had become established, and gathered from them that Jesus was a teacher and wonder worker of a perfectly familiar kind. Hence they had no reason to doubt the main outlines of the life there ascribed to him. It is clear from what Arnobius records of pagans' criticisms of the early fourth century that, like most people today, they assessed Jesus from what is said of him in the gospels, from which they gathered that Christians were foolish enough to worship a being who was born a man, behaved as an ordinary magician, and died a death which would have shamed the lowest of humankind. Here was substance enough for their rejection of him, and it is unrealistic to expect them to have pursued their investigations into what for them was obvious rubbish to the extent of discriminating the documents and recognizing the problems which thereby emerge—something which has been only slowly and painfully achieved in modern times (see BIBLICAL CRITICISM). Indeed, it was not until the early twentieth century that some theologians both recognized a gulf between the Jesus of the gospels and the Pauline Christ, and showed some awareness of its importance for theories of Christian origins. Even today, such recognition is far from universal. The Toronto theologian S. G. Wilson admits, with

characteristic frankness, that "it sometimes seems that the topic is instinctively avoided because to pursue it too far leads to profound and disturbing questions about the origin and nature of Christianity."

Appeal is still sometimes made to Tacitus as having confirmed that Jesus suffered under Pilate. But even his testimony is too late to serve as such confirmation. The Catholic scholar J. P. Meier allows that Tacitus, and Pliny too, both writing circa 112 CE, "reflect what they heard Christians of their own day say" and so are not "independent extracanonical sources." As for Jewish testimony, "no rabbinic early text . . . contains information about Jesus," and later ones "simply reflect knowledge of, and mocking midrash on, Christian texts and preaching." Meier does accept Flavius Josephus—who in one passage seems to treat Jesus's resurrection as historical fact—as an independent confirmatory source. But in fact Josephus too was writing the relevant book, *Antiquities of the Jews*, at a time (circa 94 CE) when at least some of the gospels were available, and at a place (Rome) where he could well have heard about Jesus from Christians. In any case, few allow that the obviously Christian words in that paragraph flowed from the pen of this orthodox Jewish historian. Had he believed what is here ascribed to him, he would not have confined his remarks on Jesus and Christianity to a few lines.

The theological world is now engaged in what is called "the third quest for the historical Jesus," the first (starting in the nineteenth century) and second (starting in the 1950s) having ended in failure. Meier concedes that "all too often the first two quests were theological projects masquerading as historical projects."

BIBLIOGRAPHY

Boring, M. E. *The Continuing Voice of Jesus. Christian Prophecy and the Gospel Tradition.* Louisville: Westminster/John Knox, 1991.

Bultmann, R. *The History of the Synoptic Tradition.* Oxford: Blackwell, 1963.

Doherty, E. *The Jesus Puzzle. Did Christianity Begin with a Mythical Christ?* Ottawa: Canadian Humanist Publications, 1999.

Kittel, O. "Archon." In *Theological Dictionary of the New Testament,* Vol. 1. Grand Rapids: Eerdmans, 1964.

Koester, H. *Ancient Christian Gospels.* Philadelphia: Trinity Press International, 1990.

Macgregor, G. H. C. "Principalities and Powers. The Cosmic Background of Paul's Thought." *New Testament Studies* 1 (1954).

Meier, J. P. "The Present State of the 'Third Quest' for the Historical Jesus." *Biblica* 80 (1999).

Metzger, B. M., and M. D. Coogan. "Jesus Christ." In *The Oxford Companion to the Bible.* New York and Oxford: Oxford University Press, 1993.

Price, R. M. *Deconstructing Jesus.* Amherst, NY: Prometheus Books, 2000.

Tuckett, C. M. *Q and the History of Early Christianity.* Peabody, MA: Hendrickson, 1996.

Wells, G. A. *Can We Trust the New Testament?* La Salle, IL: Open Court, 2004.

———. *The Jesus Myth.* La Salle, IL: Open Court, 1999.

Wilson, S. G. "From Jesus to Paul: The Contours and Consequences of a Debate." In *From Jesus to Paul*, edited by P. Richardson and J. C. Hurd. Waterloo, ON: Wilfrid Laurier University Press, 1984.

GEORGE A. WELLS

JOHNSON, JAMES HERVEY (1901–1988), American editor and philanthropist. James Hervey Johnson was born on August 2, 1901, in Bakersfield, California. Raised a Methodist, particularly under the influence of his minister grandfather, Johnson regularly attended Sunday school until he was fourteen. But his discovery of Thomas PAINE's *The Age of Reason* in his father's desk changed his life. He soon became a freethinker (see FREETHOUGHT) and developed a commitment to help liberate others from religion. He also became committed to lifelong bachelorhood when his freethought came into conflict with the devout Roman Catholicism of the only woman he ever loved.

At age twenty-nine, in 1930, Johnson was elected assessor for San Diego County, California. Once in office he took a get-tough policy with tax delinquents. In flamboyant raids eagerly covered by the local press, he seized and auctioned off cars, equipment, boats, and houses—reducing the average San Diegan's tax burden by about 25 percent. Moreover, in an age before the codification of exemption laws, he taxed the churches, ignoring vociferous complaints against the practice.

But his most outlandish action occurred on August 30, 1932, when he tried to auction off the San Diego Zoo for unpaid taxes. Standing at the front gate, banging his gavel before an amused crowd, he called for bids on the individual animals. The police, however, had earlier given warning that anyone who tried to remove an animal would be arrested. So no bids were made. Johnson then tried to auction the park as a whole. When that also received no bids, he rapped his gavel a final time, declaring, "Sold to the State of California for delinquent and unpaid taxes." After that, the episode was thrown into the courts, where it took weeks before a resolution was reached, one that worked out largely in the zoo's favor—though Johnson did eventually collect the tax money.

His political career ended when he received a felony conviction on an unrelated technicality. By now nicknamed "Scurvy" Johnson, he was removed from office in February 1936.

In 1942 Johnson ran for Congress, protesting, among other things, the US government's internment of Japanese Americans. Though not elected, he actively helped preserve the possessions of some of the internment victims—until he was drafted into the military at the age of forty-two.

Throughout his life, Johnson secured personal wealth through real estate and the stock market. In 1949 he self-published *Superior Men*, his freethought book, sold both through his own bookselling operation, Superior Books, and the Truth Seeker Company, publisher of THE TRUTH SEEKER. Johnson wrote occasionally for that publication, which was owned and edited by Charles Lee SMITH. Eventually, by 1963, Johnson had bought control of the company, merging it with his own Superior Books. Then, upon Smith's death late the next year, Johnson assumed *The Truth Seeker* editorship, promptly moving the whole operation from New York to San Diego.

Now the intellectualized racism and anti-Semitism that had become an important part of *The Truth Seeker* under Smith became more vitriolic under Johnson. Health food extremism and animal rights advocacy were given more space. Quality typography disappeared. As a result, paid subscriptions rapidly declined. When *The Truth Seeker* celebrated its hundredth anniversary in 1973, its paid circulation had fallen from the roughly two thousand Smith had bequeathed to Johnson to below eight hundred.

At the time Johnson took over the Truth Seeker Company he also secured control of Smith's AMERICAN ASSOCIATION FOR THE ADVANCEMENT OF ATHEISM (publisher of the *Atheist*) and Smith's National Liberal League (not to be confused with the NATIONAL LIBERAL LEAGUE, a prominent nineteenth-century freethought organization of the same name, later renamed the National League for the Separation of Church and State). Johnson was already running at least three other groups, the Set You Thinking Club, the Tax Relief League, and the Freethinkers Society of San Diego. In these his racism and health advocacy were conspicuously absent. Outside the pages of *The Truth Seeker*, Johnson was conscientious about keeping his freethought separate from his other causes—so much so that many of his fellow freethinkers never knew he held these other opinions.

In his writings on religion, however, Johnson did propound a genetic theory intended to account for the observed prevalence of religious belief and the scarcity of atheism. Citing scriptural references to stonings and religious genocide, he concluded that atheists had been "systematically exterminated" by religious leaders.

Overall Johnson's views were a unique mix of the pernicious and the noble, expressed with both hostility and humanity. For example, on eugenic grounds (see EUGENICS), he favored the extermination of "all criminals." But he also expressed support for the Bill of Rights, the rights of homosexuals (albeit condescendingly), general sexual freedom, and the decriminalization of prostitution. He supported abortion rights, nursing home reform, and senior citizens' rights. A strict vegetarian, he also opposed the use of leg-hold traps on animals long before animal rights grew fashionable.

But increasingly Johnson became better known for his

bigotries, which most likely led to the apparent arson of the Truth Seeker Company on October 3, 1981. All of Johnson's stock, records, and archives were completely destroyed in the blaze. Because he lived in the top floor of the building, he barely escaped with his life, suffering minor burns. And eleven days later, while crossing the street in front of the building's remains, he was struck by a car in an accident. Johnson was hospitalized for weeks afterward in a Roman Catholic hospital, during which time several of his properties were looted. The driver's insurance company eventually paid Johnson $50,000.

After that, when Johnson resumed his publishing of *The Truth Seeker*, a change in content began to emerge. Most of the material on race and health disappeared. The tone softened. Freethought concerns dominated. Added were a number of detailed and illustrated articles critical of routine infant male circumcision. Also added were positive articles suggesting solutions (albeit naive and simplistic) to domestic and world problems and pointing out select positive aspects of some religions. Nonetheless, the publication's decline continued unabated, dropping to around three hundred subscribers by the end of 1984.

In his personal life, because Johnson distrusted doctors and rejected the germ theory in favor of the "toxemia theory" of disease, he self-treated various ailments that were probably symptomatic of cancer and diabetes. So it was that on August 6, 1988, while in his bath trying to soak away pain, Johnson died of a heart attack. He was eighty-seven. At his request, no memorial service was held. And in his will he bequeathed his entire estate of roughly $17 million toward the continuance of *The Truth Seeker* and the establishment of a trust to "expose religion as against reason and to publicize my views on religion and health."

That trust was subsequently established: the James Hervey Johnson Charitable Educational Trust. But the story didn't end there. Over a decade of litigation and controversy followed. Madalyn Murray O'Hair, president of American Atheists, sued unsuccessfully to secure the estate. After *The Truth Seeker* was relaunched as a glossy magazine partially devoted to eccentric reform topics, James W. Prescott—for a time its editor—sued unsuccessfully to secure alleged unpaid compensation. He also reported to California authorities alleged breaches of the trust; during the early 1990s grants were often made to San Diego community groups such as the local Boy Scouts organization instead of deserving freethought organizations. After a state investigation, grants to freethought organizations increased. Then, by a stratagem where all grants were made to a single organization set up for the purpose of receiving them, which then distributed the monies in various ways, freethought organizations ceased to benefit. But in 2005, apparently due to pressure from the state of California, significant grants to freethought organizations resumed. The *Truth Seeker* ended publication in 1997, though the company itself still exists.

BIBLIOGRAPHY

Edwords, Frederick. "Bucking the Currents: The Life and Legacy of James Hervey Johnson." *Humanism Today* (1993).

Johnson, James Hervey. *Superior Men*. San Diego: Superior, 1947.

Sheehan, Margot. "He Auctioned the Zoo in '32." *San Diego Reader*, November 27, 1991.

FRED EDWORDS

JUDAISM, UNBELIEF WITHIN. There are two kinds of secular Jews. The first group includes Jews who value their Jewish identity and seek to preserve it in a nonreligious way. The second group includes Jews who are freethinkers and who find no value in their Jewish connection. Only the first group is of interest to this study. The second group belongs to the general history of SECULARISM.

Discovering the Jewish secular tradition is sometimes difficult. Outside of Israel, Jews have given up the unique languages—like Hebrew, Yiddish, and Ladino—that defined their ethnic separation. Diaspora communities generally present themselves to the Gentile world as religious fraternities. Except in Israel, secular Jews remain isolated from the Jewish establishment. When they have chosen to organize, they have combined their secular agenda with a socialist (see SOCIALISM AND UNBELIEF) or Zionist one. Frequently the socialist or Zionist commitment pushes the secular strategy into the background. Further, the absence of a professional class of secular Jewish leaders—a counterpart of the rabbis—has deprived the secular community of visibility and power.

The secular tradition, as a literature, is comparatively new. But the secular tradition as an experience has deep roots in Jewish history. No written anticlerical traditions survive from the ancient past. We know about them only through denunciation.

Arguments with God about morality of his behavior are also part of the secular roots. When Yahweh became an all-powerful and all-good God, the problem of theodicy emerged. If God has the power to prevent evil, why does he not choose to do so? The outcry of the pious Berdichever Rebbe, who put God on trial, is a discreet manifestation of the challenge. Given the suffering of the Jewish people, SKEPTICISM was inevitable, even though it was not safe to articulate it publicly (see EVIL, PROBLEM OF).

The economic experience of the Jews laid the foundation of secularism. As the Jews turned from farming to commerce, peasant piety was replaced by the entrepreneurial skills of merchants and bankers. Literacy came with urbanization and trade, and affluence produced the leisure for secular studies. In Arab Spain, Jewish poetry often abandoned the subject of God for reflections on love and nature.

In modern times the admission of Jews to secular professions such as medicine and law produced secular intellectual rivals to the rabbis. Secular universities replaced yeshivas as the vehicles of social advancement. Secular education was the quickest way for Jews to climb the ladder of success.

Philosophically, part of the rabbinic establishment was also "corrupted" by exposure to Greek philosophy. Under the influence of the ideas of PLATO and ARISTOTLE, medieval Jewish philosophers turned Yahweh into a God atheists would be comfortable with. Saadia's God was a Platonic abstraction. And the God of Maimonides, who could be described only in terms of what he was not about, was as interesting as Aristotle's first mover. Both prayer to and passion for such a deity were moving apart. RATIONALISM became one of the rabbinic modes and threatened to undermine religious fervor.

DEVELOPMENT

Jewish secularism became an open and clear option with the emergence of the ENLIGHTENMENT in western Europe. The Age of Reason undermined Jewish segregation and the authority of the rabbinic establishment. From the middle of the eighteenth century, Jewish HUMANISM was no longer an underground movement. It produced leaders and literature.

The *Haskalah*, the Jewish Enlightenment. The *Haskalah* found its first center in Berlin. It was there that Moses Mendelssohn denied that Judaism compelled theological belief. It was there that Naphtali Herz Wessely opened the Jewish Free School in 1788. The Free School was the first Jewish school in which secular studies were the primary focus of Jewish education. It produced a secular Jewish elite who were to transform German Jewish life. Both Reform Judaism and humanism were creations of this conversion to reason.

The use of Hebrew as a secular language became the vehicle of the *Haskalah*. Pious Jews regarded Hebrew as a sacred language, appropriate only to religious devotion and study. Yiddish was the popular tongue, available for profane use. The use of Hebrew by the *Maskilim* (the devotees of the *Haskalah*) for secular purposes demonstrated the elitist and snobbish side of the rationalist pioneer, and it segregated them from the Jewish masses. But it gave them a unique and prestigious symbol with which to assault the religious establishment. The Hebrew periodical *Ha-Messef* became the voice of the new Jewish Enlightenment.

The exaltation of reason over traditional faith led to public declarations of radical belief. While ATHEISM was still too dangerous to embrace, the God of DEISM became fashionable. Imprisoned by his own irreversible decrees, God could do nothing to change the laws of nature. The universe was guided by inexorable laws that were indifferent to prayer. The God of Mendelssohn and his Enlightenment cohorts logically required neither praise nor ritual. It was only a hop, skip, and jump to SECULAR HUMANISM.

The Enlightenment ultimately led to the secular fervor of the French Revolution. The consequence of this upheaval was the emergence of the secular state and the political emancipation of the Jews. The new National Assembly created in 1789 separated religion and ethnic origin from the new concept of French citizenship. All native-born residents of territorial France were eligible to be Frenchmen. Jews were granted the status of French citizens. They were no longer to function as a distinct nationality.

The emancipation produced a major crisis in Jewish life. Until modern times the Jews had viewed themselves and were viewed by others as an ethnic group, a "nation" without a country. This awareness was reinforced by a unique language, by a unique national religion, and by the alien status of the ghettoized community. But liberation brought with it the tyranny of the centralized secular state. No dual political loyalty was allowed, and cultural conformity was the order of the day.

Political safety demanded that the Jews redefine themselves as a religious denomination. With the disappearance of Yiddish among the Ashkenazic Jews of western Europe, such a deception could be maintained. Jewish leaders confessed to Napoleon that they were only Frenchmen of the Mosaic faith. The Age of Reason had become unreasonable.

The reform movement assumed the burden of this political strategy. Secularized Jews who valued their Jewish identity or who were prevented from assimilation by anti-Semitism now found themselves with the need to be religious. But the ideology they embraced was not always friendly to genuine religious commitment. The result was a religious movement with a secular heart and a religious body. Jews who were openly nonreligious were denied "Jewish" status by this odd turn of events.

Political emancipation retarded the development of Jewish secularism in western Europe. Ethnic Jewishness could not fit into the available social categories respectably open to Jews. The thrust of religious reform drove honest secular Jews out of the Jewish community.

Two developments ultimately rescued Jewish secularism. The rise of racial anti-Semitism in France, Germany, and Austria around 1880 forced assimilated Jewish freethinkers to confront their Jewish identity. Moses Hess, Theodore Herzl, and Max Nordau are leading examples of prominent intellectuals who decided to rescue Jews. For Edouard Drumont and William Stewart Chamberlain, the most prominent propagandists of the new anti-Semitism, religious belief was irrelevant to Jewish identity; birth and racial connection were primary. With such adversaries, pleading atheism was useless.

The *Haskalah* in Eastern Europe. The arrival of the *Haskalah* in eastern Europe transformed the Jewish communities of Poland and Russia. In a world of millions of Yiddish-speaking Jews who enjoyed no political emancipation and who suffered government persecution, a secular Jewish nationalism was bound to be successful.

As the assault of secular education dissolved old religious beliefs, many Jews refined their Jewish identity without any reference to theology. Yiddish culture became the secular criterion for Jewishness.

Despite its revival of secular Hebrew, the *Haskalah* in western Europe ultimately yielded cultural assimilation. Cultural pluralism was not a viable option in the urban centers of France, Germany, and England. But the *Haskalah* in eastern Europe stimulated an intense secular nationalism, which thrived on political persecution and ethnic segregation.

In Poland and Russia the economic and political hardships of Jews were so enormous that no successful secular movement could focus on secularism alone. Two proposed solutions to the Jewish problem emerged. The first was socialism; the second was Zionism. All socialists were secularists, whether they were of the populist or Marxist variety. But not all Zionists were, even though the leadership of the movement was in secular hands.

Adolf Hitler and the Holocaust ultimately destroyed the home bases of *Haskalah* assimilation and *Haskalah* nationalism. They were also assisted, in eastern Europe, by the hostility of the new Communist authorities to Zionism and Jewish socialism. The drama of Jewish history moved elsewhere. The western European setting of cultural assimilation moved to America. The eastern European setting of secular nationalism moved to Israel.

VARIETIES

It is possible to distinguish five varieties of Jewish secular humanism, each producing its own style and literature. Some are assimilationist, some are intensely nationalistic, while still others are a combination of both.

Ethical Culture. The ETHICAL CULTURE movement does not identify itself as a Jewish movement, but many outsiders have. For many years the overwhelming majority of its members were Jews. Bourgeois Jewish secularists who were neither nationalistic nor Zionist found a home there. While the movement did nothing positive to develop Jewish self-awareness, the organization enabled Jews, especially intellectual and social-activist Jews, to spend time with like-minded Jews. It was a haven for many Jews who could find no comfortable place in establishment institutions.

Founded in 1876 in New York City by Felix ADLER, the son of a radical Reform rabbi, Ethical Culture was dominated for many years by the culture and the style of the German Jewish elite. Although Adler denied that Judaism was anything more than a religion and maintained that Jewish identity was a religious identity distinct from Ethical Culture, some felt that he functioned as an agnostic rabbi who served the cultural community with which he was familiar. Although Adler insisted that this ethical philosophy was a religion, God and prayer were omitted from the Sunday meetings. It was the kind of setting that a secularist, agnostic, or atheist would feel comfortable in.

The Ethical Culture movement was partly the result of the need of assimilated Western Jews to define themselves religiously for reasons of political safety. Cultural pluralism was anathema to the German Jewish bourgeoisie. Conversion to Christianity was intellectually unacceptable and emotionally guilt producing. Ethical Culture was a suitable compromise granting philosophic integrity and Jewish association. In New York it became an important presence in Jewish life. In recent years the Jewish membership has declined, and in certain communities, such as the St. Louis Ethical Culture Society, there has never been a large number of Jewish members.

Jewish Socialism. For many Jews secularism was an aspect of their socialist commitment. While some romantic socialists, such as A. D. Gordon, were mystical and religious—hoping to turn the Jews into a nature-loving peasantry—the so-called scientific socialists followed Karl MARX and found in atheism a personal liberation.

Jewish socialists could not separate secularism from egalitarian politics. Dismissing God went hand in hand with elevating the proletariat. Atheistic fervor was tied to revolutionary passion. Since Yiddish was the language of the Jewish masses, it too could not be separated from the atheist enterprise. The negative attitudes of the social-climbing Jewish bourgeoisie to the use of Yiddish made this commitment especially important to Jewish socialists. Promoting a secular Yiddish literature was added to MARXISM and humanism.

Jewish socialists were never united. They were divided by controversies over many issues. The Russian Revolution and the policies of the Soviet government sparked endless debate. The rise of Zionism posed the question of where the socialist paradise should be created. And chronic anti-Semitism undermined the radical hope that proletarian self-awareness would replace Jewish identity. Jewish socialist atheism became a carnival of internal arguments.

The strongest socialist group was the Bund. Founded in 1897 in the Russian Empire (one year before the establishment of the Russian Social Democratic Party), it was committed to Marxism and Yiddish nationalism. Standing in opposition to the Zionists and the Communists, the Bund mobilized thousands of Jewish radicals. After the Bolshevik Revolution made Russia hostile territory, it flourished in Poland. As a political and cultural force between the wars, it spoke for a large part of the Jewish community.

Immigrants brought the Bund to North America. Named the Arbeiter Ring (Workman's Circle), it created its own system of schools and cultural institutions. But America was not an environment conducive to the survival of either Yiddish or socialism. While the Holocaust destroyed the Bund in Poland, the power of Anglo-Saxon capitalism undermined it in the New World.

Today Jewish socialism encompasses only a diminishing group of aged radicals who have only enough energy for nostalgia. The formerly powerful Yiddish socialist newspapers like the *Vorwaerts* and the *Morgan Fruheit* have lost their readers.

Secular Zionism. The modern movement to establish an independent Jewish homeland has been the most large-scale Jewish enterprise in the twentieth century. No other Jewish project has claimed the support of so many people, Jews and non-Jews alike. The state of Israel has become the single most important institution in Jewish life, uniting divided communities and giving reality to Jewish identity.

The founders of modern Zionism were secular Jews who believed that the homeless condition of the Jewish masses could only be alleviated with the establishment of a Jewish culture in a Jewish state. Pinsker, Herzl, and Nordau—and the Jews who followed them—found in Zionism an alternative to religion. Some of the early Zionists were religious, but the overwhelming majority was searching for a secular way to save Jews and Jewish identity.

Secular Zionists came in three varieties. Bourgeois Zionists like Herzl and Brandeis wanted a Jewish state that resembled a European capitalist democracy. Nationalist Zionists like Jabotinsky preferred a militant state that was defended by proud and fearless warriors. Socialist Zionists dreamed of a model egalitarian state where clerical, bourgeois, and military domination would cease to exist. As time went on, the bourgeois and nationalist Zionists discovered that opposition to religion subverted their political ambitions. Only the socialist Zionists remained fiercely secular.

The kibbutz commune became a dramatic example of secular socialism. Most kibbutzim rejected religious behavior and religious authority. They sought to secularize Jewish holidays and life-cycle ceremonies. Because they were self-contained communities united by a strong ideology, they succeeded in fashioning a secular ceremonial alternative to traditional ritual. They stood in sharp contrast to urban humanists, who were never able to establish a support system that would enable them to go beyond the negative rejection of religion to a positive secular identity.

Today in Israel the secular position is weaker than it was at the inception of the Jewish state. Oriental Jewish immigration, the disillusionment with the Left, and the obvious political advantages of religious nationalism have undetermined the secular majority. The collapse of the kibbutz movement has removed the strongest source of secular idealism and energy from the political scene. The old secular political party Yahad, begun by Shulamit Aloni, still lingers on the periphery of power. A new secular political party, SHINUI, founded by television star Tommy Lapid, has a problematic future. The Orthodox religious parties offer a large, volatile constituency that both liberals and conservatives cannot ignore when they

form coalitions. Outside the political framework, urban secularists are striving to serve the domestic needs of secular Jews. Secular ceremonialists are offering alternative ceremonies to those of the Orthodox rabbis who hold a state monopoly on marriage and divorce rites. Secular rabbis, who have been trained at the Jerusalem campus of the International Institute for Secular Humanistic Judaism, the educational arm of the growing humanistic Jewish movement, are now available as teachers, counselors, and ceremonialists. Strong attempts are being made to supplement hostility to Orthodox power with a deeper awareness of a more positive humanism.

Jewish Secularism. In North America many secular Jews who were wary of socialist and Zionist controversies established schools for Jewish children that had no political agenda. They took names like the Sholem Aleichem Institute, Jewish Peoples Institute, Jewish Parents Institute, the Secular Jewish Association, and many others. However, their failure to create viable adult communities and to train professional leaders limited their growth. Today, the Congress of Secular Jewish Organizations has become their federation.

The ideas of philosopher Horace Kallen have been used to define the program of this nonpolitical secularism. In the North American setting where ethnic groups retain self-awareness within a context of dispersion and linguistic assimilation, Kallen recommended the value of democratic, cultural pluralism. He rejected the goal of turning America into a "melting pot" and upheld dual cultural loyalties. A good citizen could participate in both American and Jewish cultures.

The periodical *Jewish Currents*, originally established as a public voice for anti-Bundist and anti-Zionist Jewish Communists, has now abandoned its old format and become a useful periodical for more moderate secularists.

Humanistic Judaism. In 1963 the Birmingham Temple was established in the Detroit area. Led by Sherwin T. Wine, who was trained as a Reform rabbi, it embraced a Jewish secularism it labeled "humanistic Judaism." The uniqueness of this new institution lay in its willingness to borrow from the religious sector the idea of organized, nonpolitical adult communities and the idea of trained professional leaders. Wine maintained that without these structures a secular Jewish identity could not be successfully maintained in a Western urban setting.

In 1969 the Society for Humanistic Judaism was established to organize new secular Jewish congregations and communities. At present forty Humanist Jewish communities exist in North America. The journal of the Society, *Humanistic Judaism*, has become an important secular Jewish voice for English-speaking Jews. In 1986, at the initiative of the Society for Humanistic Judaism, an International Federation of Secular Humanistic Jews was created in Detroit. Fifteen national federations and schools from seventy-two countries are presently members, with an estimated population of fifty thousand. Given the fact that close to 50 percent of the world's Jewish people (some six million) identify themselves as secular or cultural Jews, the task of organization has just begun.

The future of Jewish secular humanism will be determined by the following realities: (1) Jewish professional education will continue to undermine traditional religious beliefs. (2) Increasing intermarriage between Jews and non-Jews will enable many Jews who have intermarried to deal with their Jewishness as a cultural rather than a religious identity. (3) The affirmation of ethnic roots will enable many alienated Jews to cope more effectively with the experience of urban rootlessness. (4) The national culture of the state of Israel, its literature, arts, and celebrations, will provide a modern secular alternative to the religious culture of the past.

BIBLIOGRAPHY

Cook, Harry, ed. *A Life of Courage*. Detroit: Milan Press, 2003.

Dubnow, Simon. *Nationalism and History*. Philadelphia: Jewish Publication Society, 1958.

Ginsberg, Asher. *Selected Essays by Ahad Haam*. Philadelphia: Jewish Publication Society, 1944.

Goodman, Saul. *The Faith of a Secular Jew*. New York: Ktav, 1976.

Hertzberg, Arthur, ed. *The Zionist Idea*. New York: Athenaeum, 1959.

Kogel, Renee, ed. *Judaism in a Secular Age*. Detroit: Milan Press, 1995.

Levin, Nora. *While Messiah Tarried: Jewish Socialist Movements*. New York: Schocken, 1977.

Wine, Sherwin. *Humanistic Judaism*. Amherst, NY: Prometheus Books, 1978.

———. *Judaism beyond God*, Detroit: Milan Press, 1995.

———. *Staying Sane in a Crazy World*. Detroit: Milan Press, 1995.

SHERWIN T. WINE

KANT, IMMANUEL (1724–1804), German philosopher. Immanuel Kant is generally recognized as one of the greatest philosophers of the Western world. His reputation is based mainly on his contributions to the theory of knowledge and to moral philosophy, although he also has contributed to other parts of philosophy, including the philosophy of religion. The general admiration for Kant is perhaps somewhat exaggerated. Much of what he had to say was wrong or badly founded, and stylistically, Kant is a catastrophe. Though there are German philosophers who have an even more opaque style, Kant's style is obscure enough to have produced numerous academic headaches and an extensive "Kant industry."

Still, Kant is an original philosopher and his historical importance is beyond any reasonable doubt. Many professional philosophers view Kant's impact on subsequent philosophy as rivaled by few other thinkers. And although few contemporary humanists agree with the whole of Kant's philosophy, to some extent he remains important for modern HUMANISM.

Philosopher of the Protestants? Kant is sometimes regarded as a philosopher of the Protestants in the same way that Thomas Aquinas is considered *the* philosopher of the Catholics. One might think a philosopher so important for Protestantism an unlikely candidate for a similar position among secular humanists (see SECULAR HUMANISM). But this is not so, for various reasons.

First, secular humanists (unbelievers concerned with humane living and values) share some ideals with the best of Christianity. It is mainly in the *justification* of these ideals that secular humanists part company with Christians.

Second, and more important, Kant is in no way an official philosopher of the Protestants. Many Protestants ignore philosophy of any kind, or hold fragmented philosophical beliefs drawn from various sources and seldom integrated into a unified system. (A similar situation prevails among some secular humanists, some of whom do not even know that they are humanists.) Even Protestants with a philosophical education do not always look to Kant to justify their faith. Some look to the religious existentialists for support, whereas others look to one or more medieval philosophers, including a major source of them all: Augustine. But it is characteristic of many thinking Christians that they look to philosophers for support of their faith: the Bible simply is not enough.

Proofs of the Existence of God. Kant, like secular humanists, rejected the Bible as a reliable source of truth. He did not do this in any straightforward way, but this conclusion is implied throughout his writings. So in his celebrated *Critique of Pure Reason* (1781) he rejected traditional "proofs" of the existence of God. Although elements of these proofs can be found in antiquity, the proofs were developed in their classical form during the Middle Ages, not the least by Thomas Aquinas.

Kant undertook a new classification of the proofs or arguments. He distinguished between the ontological, the cosmological, and the physico-theological arguments (see EXISTENCE OF GOD, ARGUMENTS FOR AND AGAINST). We do not need to go into the details of these arguments. What is important here is that Kant rejected them all. Although he does not say it in so many words, Kant further believed that there were no other arguments of importance, and that the arguments he had considered and rejected were singly and jointly without force for any belief in God. Thus, for the Kant of the *Critique of Pure Reason*, it was impossible to prove the existence of God.

God's position in Kant's philosophy was not improved in Kant's next important publication, *Foundation of the Metaphysics of Morals* (1785). In this slim book (about seventy pages), Kant gives an analysis of the foundation of ethics. What is remarkable from a secular point of view is that God is ignored in the *Meta-physics of Morals*. The word "God" occurs only in unimportant passages, and it is abundantly clear that for the Kant of 1785, ethics finds its basis in man, not God. Thus, here we find another feature common to Kant and secular humanism: ethics has its foundation in the human world. True, in his attempts to find a basis for ethics Kant presents a curious and unconvincing view of humanity. But at least God is considered irrelevant to this process.

God: The Moral Argument. On the whole, Kant's view remains the same in his next publication, the *Critique of Practical Reason* (1788). This book follows the same main lines of the *Metaphysics of Morals*, but it is less concise. God makes an unexpected appearance in book 2, chapter 2 of the *Critique of Practical Reason*, and this passage has had the effect of endearing Kant to many religious believers. Having rejected that the existence of God can be established within the framework of theoretical reason, Kant here argued that the reality of God was a postulate of practical or moral reason.

The background of this new way of thinking was the following. According to the Kant of 1788, the highest good, which is the aim of the moral will, often cannot be reached on this earth. The highest good includes both virtue and happiness. And this cannot always be reached in this life. If this life were all there is, then moral behavior would become meaningless. As moral behavior is not meaningless, we are forced to postulate a life after this one. In this way Kant postulates both immortality and God. Having thrown God out through the front door in the *Critique of Pure Reason*, the Kant of the *Critique of Practical Reason* readmits God through the back door.

Still, it remains unclear what Kant means when he defines God as a postulate of practical reason. He continues to maintain that the existence of God cannot be proven. But he clearly states that it is "morally necessary to assume the existence of God." Kant has been widely interpreted as introducing a new argument for the existence of God, the so-called moral argument. But at the same time Kant writes as if he has no new argument to offer after having demolished the former arguments for the existence of God. In any case it is important to notice that Kant's new contention in no way makes God the basis of ethics. It is rather that ethics is made the basis of God.

Thus, Kant continues to agree with secular humanism. God is not the basis of ethics; ethics still finds its foundation in humanity. But the secular humanist cannot agree that ethical behavior can provide any basis for postulating the existence of God. Ethical behavior is largely identical with customs and habits, inculcated in children from a very tender age, and which adults either accept without reflection or may justify by referring to the importance of ethical behavior if families and societies are to function successfully. In this way ethical behavior is justified by referring to something greater than the individual—but the object held greater than the individual is the family or society. Neither ethical behavior nor anything else provides any convincing evidence for the existence of God or the existence of an afterlife.

In his ethical theory Kant emphasized the good will, the only good that is good without qualification, and which is manifested in acting for the sake of duty. Duty means acting out of reverence for the moral law that is prescribed by reason. Kant's emphasis on reason makes him a child of the Age of Enlightenment to which many humanists hearken (see ENLIGHTENMENT, UNBELIEF DURING THE).

Secular humanists do not commonly stress duty to the same extent as Kant. In fact, secular humanists often tend to downplay duty in their ethical accounts. But it is fully possible to be a secular humanist and emphasize duty to almost the same extent as Kant. But it is not convincing to base duty on pure reason. It is doubtful whether anything like "pure reason" exists, and we cannot base our duties on something of doubtful existence. Our duties must be based on our relations to other human beings.

Human Beings as Ends in Themselves. One of the two or three main versions of Kant's celebrated categorical imperative makes a reference to human beings. Kant postulates that the human, and in fact any rational being, is an end in itself. We should always treat any other person as an end, and never merely as a means. Even though this version of the categorical imperative refers to rational beings only and contains no element of compassion, it is of great ethical significance.

This is not the first time in the history of Western ethical philosophy that our relation to fellow beings is stressed. The Golden Rule, which states that we should treat other persons as we would be liked to be treated ourselves, makes its appearance already in PLATO, and for ARISTOTLE friendship was an important value. But as a whole, historically important ethical philosophers did not stress relations to other persons. It is only with Kant and the utilitarians that such relations become a major theme in ethical philosophy. Here the secular humanist can again find common ground with Kant.

Conclusion. There are some similarities but also many differences between Kant's philosophy and secular humanism. For secular humanism, Kant's criticism of the arguments for the existence of God, and his effort to base ethics upon human beings rather than God, remain viable elements of his philosophy. Secular humanists will, of course, dissociate themselves from Kant's attempts to reintroduce God and immortality in his later philosophy. Secular humanists might also learn from Kant by emphasizing duty more than is commonly done, if not to precisely the same extent.

Secular humanists may also agree with Kant when he states that we should treat our fellow beings as ends and not only as means. Kant's attitude toward metaphysics is also of interest to secular humanists, who might benefit from abandoning a one-sidedly negative view of metaphysics in favor of developing and defending some kind of explicitly materialistic metaphysical position.

Kant, in spite of many doubtful features in his philosophy, remains a predecessor of secular humanism. Kant's philosophy as a whole is rather remote from contemporary secular humanism; surely he was no secular humanist, and it may be misleading to call him a humanist at all. Still, Kant's thought constitutes one of the many intellectual roots of secular humanism.

BIBLIOGRAPHY

Hiorth, Finngeir. "Kant and Humanism." In *Introduction to Humanism*. Mumbai: Indian Secular Society, 1996.

FINNGEIR HIORTH

KAUFMANN, WALTER (1918–1980), American philosopher and translator. Although raised in his native Germany as a Lutheran, Walter Kaufmann converted to Judaism, the faith of his ancestors, at the age of twelve, since he could not believe in the reality of Jesus. Before his formal conversion to Judaism, Adolf Hitler came to power and Kaufmann was warned that it would be best to remain nominally a Christian. Demonstrating his lifelong commitment to intellectual honesty, he refused to change his mind. While he initially planned on becoming a rabbi, Kaufmann came to doubt the existence of a supreme being (in part due to the absence of divine intervention to prevent the Holocaust, in which several of his relatives were killed). He came to refer to himself as a "heretic" (see HERESY). In 1939 he left Nazi Germany for America, graduating from Williams College with honors in 1941. Kaufmann served in the US military during World War II. Afterward, he completed a PhD from Harvard University in the philosophy of religion and became a professor of philosophy at Princeton University, where he would remain until his death.

Kaufmann is best known for his translations and introductions to the works of Friedrich NIETZSCHE. During Hitler's regime Nietzsche became known as the "Nazi Philosopher," and after the war no one did more to clear his name than Kaufmann. In 1950 he wrote the popular book *Nietzsche: Philosopher, Psychologist, Antichrist*, which took pains to separate Nietzsche's advocacy of individualism and FREETHOUGHT from the heinous usage made of his teachings by the Nazis. Kaufmann would later edit for Penguin Books the best-selling volume *The Portable Nietzsche*.

His collections *Existentialism from Dostoevsky to Sartre* (1956) and *From Shakespeare to Existentialism* (1959) did much to popularize the philosophy of existentialism in the English-speaking world (see SARTRE, JEAN-PAUL; EXISTENTIALISM; SHAKESPEARE, RELIGIOUS SKEPTICISM IN). In addition, Kaufmann wrote two major works discussing his own views on religion and belief: *Critique of Religion and Philosophy* (1958) and *The Faith of a Heretic* (1961). In these books, he extols the virtue of living a freethinking existence, and castigates theology in all its flavors. "Theology" means literally the study of God, and yet no one knows for sure if such a being exists. How, then, can there be a science based upon a being who remains at best a hypothesis? Kaufmann had a passion for truth and for courage, and shared with the existentialists (most of whom he strongly criticized for not living up to their own ideals) an advocacy for authenticity. His chief complaint against theology was that it is neither a science nor a philosophy, but rather a type of doublespeak, wherein texts are made to communicate contradictory views to different readers.

In *The Portable Nietzsche*, Kaufmann states that the history of modern philosophy, from René DESCARTES to the present, is the story of emancipation from religion. He was especially caustic in his critique of the view that morality cannot exist without religion. In *Faith of a Heretic*, he writes that "this odd retort is in a way irrelevant, but often gives expression to a heartfelt worry. Why irrelevant? The same retort might well be made when Santa Claus is questioned. In that case, one answers: You have to grow up and face the facts; honesty is important, too; and parents can still reward the well-behaved child while withholding presents from the naughty one, without invoking Santa Claus. In the case of God and organized religion, the same answer will do: secular authorities remain to discourage evil."

Kaufmann was also a noted translator of the works of GOETHE, and a poet in his own right. He was a strong advocate of clarity in writing, and argued that the obscure writing style of Immanuel KANT, G. W. F. Hegel, and Martin Heidegger, among others, was perhaps due to their own fear of discovering truths they were not prepared to deal with. He felt it a scandal that so many philosophers hid behind abstruse and confusing language, and took it as a mark of pride to be as precise and clear as possible in his meanings.

Kaufmann signed *A Secular Humanist Declaration* shortly before his untimely death in 1980.

BIBLIOGRAPHY

Kaufmann, Walter. *Critique of Religion and Philosophy*. New York: Harper and Brothers, 1958.
———. *The Faith of a Heretic*. Garden City, NY: Doubleday, 1961.
———, ed. and trans. *The Portable Nietzsche*. New York: Viking, 1959.

TIMOTHY J. MADIGAN

KELLGREN, JOHAN HENRIC. See SWEDEN, UNBELIEF IN.

KHAYYÁM, OMAR (c. 1048–1123 CE), Persian poet and mathematician. The name of Omar Khayyám was mentioned in Basel in 1583, but the first that the West encountered his poetry was probably in 1700, when Thomas Hyde in his *Veterum Persarum . . . religionis historia* gave a Latin translation of one of Khayyám's quatrains. In 1771 Sir William Jones in his *A Grammar of the Persian Language* quoted without attribution a complete quatrain and part of another, generally ascribed to Khayyám. Several Persian quatrains were published in a Persian grammar compiled by F. Dombay in Vienna in 1804. In 1816 H. G. Keene produced further translations into English. Edward Fitzgerald's inspired translation/paraphrase relied largely on a manuscript discovered in the Bodleian Library at Oxford in 1856 by the man who had taught Fitzgerald Persian, E. B. Cowell.

Khayyám's quatrains, or *rubai*, are independent epigrammatic stanzas—in other words, short, spontaneous, self-contained poems. Each *rubai* stands on its own. Fitzgerald, however, makes them a continuous sequence, saying that the stanzas "here selected are strung into something of an Eclogue." In addition, he sometimes combined fragments of once-distinct quatrains into new ones. Thus, far from being a close translation, in the words of scholar V. Minorsky, Fitzgerald's version is a paraphrase of "exceptional poetical merits."

But who was Omar Khayyám? Very little is known for certain of his life and writings, particularly his poetry. He was probably born in 1048 in Nishapur, Persia, and died there in 1123. Khayyám was, according to George Sarton, "one of the greatest mathematicians of mediaeval times." He also wrote on physics (the specific weight of gold and silver), astronomy, geography, music, metaphysics, and history. While in Samarkand (now Uzbekistan) Khayyám worked at the newly built astronomical observatory, and helped draw up a new calendar that was in many ways far superior to the Julian calendar—certainly comparable in accuracy with the Gregorian one.

Khayyam also wrote five philosophical treatises, much influenced by the renowed Ibn Sina (Avicenna). They stand in direct contrast to the SKEPTICISM and AGNOSTICISM of his verse, arguing, for example, for the necessity of God as the final cause of all causes. In another treatise, Khayyám explained the stability and permanence of phenomena by the will of God. In his last philosophical work, Khayyám defended Ibn Sina's theory of a "chain of order," and in a classification of "men who strive to know truth" he accorded Sufis the highest place.

In one of our early sources of his life and poetry, *Mirsad al-'Ibad* (The Watchtower of the Faithful), Khayyám is described as an atheist (see ATHEISM), philosopher, and naturalist: "Observation (of the world) leads to faith, the quest (for the Eternal) to gnosis. The philosopher, atheist, and naturalist are denied this spiritual level; they have been led astray and are lost." Omar Khayyám is considered by the blind as a sage, an intelligent man. However he is so lost in doubt and shadows that he says in quatrains:

This circle within which we come and go
Has neither origin nor final end.
Will no one ever tell us truthfully
Whence we have come, and whither do we go?

*

Our elements were merged at His command
Why then did He disperse them once again?
For if the blend was good, why break it up?
If it was bad, whose was the fault but His?

There is no consensus as to what constitutes Khayyám's poetic corpus, each generation casting doubt on the authenticity of this or that quatrain. But from an early period, various writers ascribed to him the melancholic philosophy that we have come to associate with him. For instance, Farid al-Din Attar summed up Khayyám's thinking thus: "Since neither the beginning nor the end of life is clear, no one will find in this inferior world either head or tail. The sky is a ball without beginning or end, the earth is a foul valley where all men lose their way, the world is misery, the Wheel [of fate] plays with us." Writing in the late twelfth century CE, Zahiri-i Samarkandi described Khayyám's poems as adding to the "theme of the precariousness of a world devoid of reason, that of the consequences of withdrawing from it; since no one will return to the world below to reveal the secrets of other places, it is imperative that all enjoy their share of good living, in particular the pleasures of wine and romance. Not to do so would be a mistake. [Khayyám's] poems also evoke the theme of the earth as dust; the cup and the pitcher are made from remains of humans who were proud."

The constant themes of Khayyám's poetry are the certainty of death, the denial of an afterlife, the pointlessness of asking unanswerable questions, the mysteriousness of the universe, and the necessity of living for and enjoying the present:

*

No one has ever pierced this veil of secrets;
No one will ever understand the world.
Deep in the earth's our only resting place;
Cry out, 'This is a story without end!'

*

The heavenly bodies that circle round the skies
Are full of mystery even to learned men;
Hold firm the thread of wisdom in your hand,
For those who plan their lives will be confused.

*

A drop of water fell into the sea,
A speck of dust came floating down to earth.

What signifies your passage through this world?
A tiny gnat appears—and disappears.

*

Long will the world last after we are gone,
When every sign and trace of us are lost.
We were not here before, and no one knew;
Though we are gone, the world will be the same.

*

Of all the travellers on this endless road
Not one returns to tell us where it leads.
There's little in this world but greed and need;
Leave nothing here, for you will not return.

*

I am not here for ever in this world;
How sinful then to forfeit wine and love!
The world may be eternal or created;
Once I am gone, it matters not a scrap.

*

When once you hear the roses are in bloom,
Then is the time, my love, to pour the wine;
Houris and palaces and Heaven and Hell—
These are but fairy-tales. Forget them all.

The above quatrains are not from Fitzgerald's translation, but from translations compiled by Ali Dashti in his *In Search of Omar Khayyam* and translated into English by Elwell Sutton.

Fitzgerald himself, in his prefaces to his many editions, would have no truck with squeamish or puritanical scholars who pretended to see something spiritual in Khayyám's verses, and who interpreted every appearance of the word "wine" mystically. For Fitzgerald the burden of Khayyám's song, if not "let us eat," is assuredly "[l]et us drink, for tomorrow we die!" Some may see Khayyám as a Sufi, but "on the other hand, as there is far more historical certainty of his being a philosopher, of scientific insight and ability far beyond that of the age and country he lived in, of such moderate worldly ambition as becomes a philosopher, and such moderate wants as rarely satisfy a debauchee; other readers may be content to believe with me that while the wine Omar celebrates is simply the juice of the grape, he bragg'd more than he drank of it, in very defiance perhaps of that spiritual wine which left its votaries sunk in hypocrisy or disgust."

Here are some examples of Fitzgerald's paraphrase of Khayyám, from his first edition:

*

Dreaming when Dawn's Left Hand was in the Sky
I heard a Voice within the Tavern cry:
"Awake, my Little ones, and fill the Cup
Before Life's Liquor in its Cup be dry."

*

And, as the Cock crew, those who stood before
The Tavern shouted: "Open then the Door!
You know how little we have to stay,
And, once departed, may return no more."

The Worldly Hope men set their Hearts upon
Turns Ashes—or it prospers; and anon,
Like Snow upon the Desert's dusty Face
Lighting a little hour or two is gone.

BIBLIOGRAPHY

Dashti, Ali. *In Search of Omar Khayyam.* Translated by L. P. Elwell-Sutton. New York: Columbia University Press, 1971.
Minorsky, V. "Omar Khaiyam." In *Encyclopedia of Islam*, 1st ed. Leiden: E. J. Brill, 1913–1938.
Sarton, G. *Introduction to the History of Science.* Washington, DC: Williams & Wilkins, 1927
Tirtha, Swami Govinda Tirtha. *The Nectar of Grace. Omar Khayyam's Life and Works.* Allahbad, 1941.
"Umar Khayyam." In *Encyclopaedia of Islam*, 2nd ed. Leiden: E. J. Brill, 1960–.

IBN WARRAQ

KIRKENDALL, LESTER A. (1903–1991), American sex educator and humanist. A professor at Oregon State University, Lester A. Kirkendall laid claim to having taught the first course on human sexuality on a university campus in the United States, and he is best known as a sex educator. With Mary CALDERONE, he founded the Sex Information and Education Council of the United States (SIECUS) in 1964, and traveled across the country speaking about sex education. He wrote extensively on sexual matters, writing or editing some of the foundational books of the sexual revolution of the 1960s.

Kirkendall signed *Humanist Manifesto II* (1976) and was recognized as Humanist of the Year by the AMERICAN HUMANIST ASSOCIATION in 1983.

BIBLIOGRAPHY

Kirdendall, Lester A. *A New Bill of Sexual Rights and Responsibilities.* Amherst, NY: Prometheus Books, 1976.
———. *Premarital Intercourse and Interpersonal Relationships.* New York: Julian Press, 1961.
———. *Sex Education and Human Relations.* New York: Inor, 1950.
Kirdendall, Lester A., and Arthur E. Gravett, eds. *Mar-

riage and Family in the Year 2020. Amherst, NY: Prometheus Books, 1984.

Kirkendall, Lester A., and Robert N. Whitehurst, eds. *The New Sexual Revolution.* New York: Donald Brown, 1971.

VERN L. BULLOUGH

KNEELAND, ABNER (1774–1844), American freethinker. Born in Gardner, Massachusetts, on April 6, 1774, Abner Kneeland was one of ten children of Timothy and Moriah Stone Kneeland. With little formal education, Abner was expected to enter the carpentry trade like his father. He also worked as a teacher and an author of spelling books, but he found his first calling in the Baptist Church.

After serving briefly as a Baptist preacher in Vermont, Kneeland met Hosea BALLOU, the prominent Universalist minister (see UNIVERSALISM TO 1961), and was influenced by Ballou's theology. Kneeland's conversion to Universalism led to his becoming ordained in 1804. He served for seven years as minister at a church in Langdon, New Hampshire. During this time, he and Ballou compiled a new Universalist hymnal, and several of the provocative hymns contributed by Kneeland were rejected by the New England Universalist General Convention.

In 1811 Kneeland transferred to a new church in Charlestown, Massachusetts. Three years later he abruptly resigned and went into business with his wife. He stayed in touch with Ballou; their letters were later published as *A Series of Letters, in Defence of Divine Revelation; in Reply to Rev. Abner Kneeland's Serious Inquiry into the Authenticity of the Same.* At the urging of the general convention, he returned to the ministry in 1816, this time in Whitestown, New York. His reservations about religion surfacing again, Kneeland continued voraciously reading skeptical writings. He was transferred to Philadelphia in 1818.

After more than twenty-five years as a Baptist, then Universalist, minister, Kneeland's growing RATIONALISM led him to become a frequent contributor to Robert Dale OWEN and Frances WRIGHT's paper, the *FREE ENQUIRER*, and to edit the *Olive Branch and Christian Inquirer*, a newspaper devoted to "free inquiry, pure morality and rational Christianity." In 1829, after inviting Wright, a noted freethinker and labor and women's rights advocate, to speak to his congregation, he requested, and was granted, permission to withdraw himself from the fellowship of Universalists.

Kneeland went to Boston and began lecturing on rationalism, leading a group called the First Society of Free Inquirers, and founded the *BOSTON INVESTIGATOR*, the first rationalist journal in the United States. In its December 20, 1833, issue, he printed a letter stating among other things that "Universalists believe in a god which I do not; but believe that their god, with all his moral attributes, aside from nature itself, is nothing more

than a chimera of their own imagination." In addition, he also printed two other articles, for which he did not claim authorship but for which he bore legal responsibility as editor. One had to do with the Virgin Birth and was considered profane in its language; the other was a mocking criticism of prayer.

He was summarily charged with violation of the 1782 Act against BLASPHEMY for publishing "a certain scandalous, impious, obscene, blasphemous and profane libel of and concerning God." He was convicted in the municipal court and appealed the conviction. After two mistrials with two different lawyers in the Massachusetts Supreme Court, Kneeland represented himself, successfully arguing his case regarding the two articles not penned by him. However, the jury determined his letter about the Universalists had indeed denied the existence of God, thus breaking the law. Despite Kneeland's claim that he was not an atheist but a pantheist, the original conviction was upheld. He again appealed, and four years after the original indictment the case was heard by the full state supreme court. Chief Justice Lemuel Shaw presided and handed down the guilty verdict, with Justice Marcus Morton dissenting. Kneeland served sixty days in the Suffolk County jail. One hundred seventy people signed a petition calling for a pardon, including Theodore Parker, Ralph Waldo EMERSON, and William Lloyd Garrison. No action was taken, however, and despite public outcry Kneeland served his time. While in jail, he wrote and published a review of his own trial, conviction, and imprisonment.

After his release, Kneeland resigned as editor of the *Boston Investigator* and, in the spirit of his friend and utopian founder Robert Dale Owen, moved west to Salubria, Iowa, on the banks of the Des Moines River, to join a colony planned by the First Society of Free Enquirers. The colony project never came to fruition, but Kneeland stayed on the farm, running for the legislature on his Free Thought ticket (he lost) and teaching school (his schoolhouse blew down in a storm) until his death in 1840 at the age of seventy-one.

BIBLIOGRAPHY

Commager, Henry Steele. "The Blasphemy of Abner Kneeland." *New England Quarterly*, March 1935.

JULIE HERRADA

KNIGHT, MARGARET (1903–1983), English rationalist whose broadcasts on humanism were notorious. Margaret Knight spent the greater part of her professional life as an academic psychologist at the University of Aberdeen, where her husband, Rex Knight, led the psychology department.

She "had the moral courage to throw off my beliefs" while in her third year at Cambridge University, under the influence of the philosophers Bertrand RUSSELL, J. M. E.

McTAGGART, and C. D. Broad. She came to believe deeply that she should speak out to support those many people who held covert humanist beliefs. The public media was then deferential to the waning Christianity of the time.

She approached the BBC in 1953 with a script setting out her "affirmations of unbelief," and was immediately rejected. She was "prepared to make a nuisance of herself" and persisted in her approach. Eventually it was agreed that she would talk about moral education for children of unbelievers. These became what were the infamous two talks on "Morals without Religion" in 1955. They sparked an uproar in the press and vociferous letters to the BBC. Headlines brayed about "The Unholy Mrs. Knight" and journalists wrote of her as a menace. More thoughtful Anglicans conceded that she should be argued with rather than denigrated. A third broadcast in the series featured a discussion between Margaret Knight and Mrs. Jenny Morton, a former missionary, on the upbringing of children.

Morals without Religion and Other Essays contained the texts of her talks and a description of the reaction they engendered, together with essays on other subjects which interested her such as evil, telepathy, intuition, and statistics.

Throughout the remainder of her career she lectured on humanism at almost all the British universities. She became an Honorary Associate of the RATIONALIST PRESS ASSOCIATION and contributed to the *Humanist*.

In response to Bishop J. A. T. Robinson's *Honest to God* (1960), a description of God as "the ground of our being" which gained wide attention in the UK, she wrote a rejoinder volume, *Honest to Man*. In 1961 she produced a *Humanist Anthology from Confucius to Bertrand Russell*, prompted by discussions of humanism with students that led her to realize that there was a need for much more knowledge of the historical humanist tradition. A new edition extensively revised by this author was published in 1995 and remains in print.

BIBLIOGRAPHY

Cooke, Bill. *The Blasphemy Depot*. London: Rationalist Press Association, 2003.

Knight, Margaret. *Honest to Man: Christian Ethics Re-Examined*. London: Elek, 1974.

————. *Humanist Anthology, from Confucius to Bertrand Russell*. London: Barrie & Rockliff, 1961.

————. *Morals without Religion and Other Essays*. London: Dennis Dobson, 1955.

JIM HERRICK

KNOWLTON, CHARLES (1800–1850), American birth control pioneer. The first person in the history of the birth control movement (see BIRTH CONTROL AND UNBELIEF) to be imprisoned for advocating and writing a booklet on birth control, Charles Knowlton was a freethinker (see FREETHOUGHT) who did some unusual and unrespectable things in his younger years. Born in rural Worcester County, Massachusetts, to a moderately well-off family, the youthful Knowlton studied medicine with various area physicians. Unhappy over his lack of knowledge of anatomy, he broke into the local graveyard, removed a recently deceased corpse, and dissected it. He apparently continued to rob graves, because he later spent two months in jail for performing illegal dissections. After his father paid more than $250 to secure his release from jail, he went on to attend lectures at Dartmouth Medical School, from which he received a medical degree in 1824.

Extremely ambitious, Knowlton wanted to be regarded as a new John LOCKE, and to this end he wrote and self-published a book, *Elements of Modern Materialism*. When it did not sell anywhere near the one thousand copies he had ordered, he had to sell his household goods to satisfy his creditors and return to the practice of medicine. He opened up an office in Ashfield, Massachusetts, a town of about eighteen hundred people. Ever the nonconformist, he delighted in scandalizing local churchgoers by playing his violin on Sunday mornings as they passed his house.

Knowlton found his cause in birth control. Concerned that young couples often suffered financial burdens because of too-frequent births, and recognizing that numerous pregnancies led to ill health among mothers as well, he decided in 1832 to publish a booklet titled *Fruits of Philosophy, or the Private Companion of Young Married People, by a Physician*. Apparently it sold well, since a second edition was published in 1833. Knowlton recommended douching immediately after intercourse with, among other things, a solution of alum with infusions of almost any available astringent herb, such as raspberry leaf or hemlock bark. Since alum has spermicidal effects, this formula was probably somewhat effective. He also recommended a douching solution of zinc sulfate, as well as formulas incorporating other compounds, which would not have been particularly effective.

Knowlton gave lectures in various towns in order to sell his book. He was fined in 1832 in Tautnon, Massachusetts, and in 1833 he was jailed at Cambridge for three months. A third attempt to convict him in Greenfield, Massachusetts, failed. One of the effects of his legal troubles was to further publicize his book, which by 1839 had sold ten thousand copies. *Fruits of Philosophy* continued to be published throughout the nineteenth century, mostly by various freethought presses. Knowlton or those publishing his book added supplementary information to later editions. The last authorized US edition was published in 1877, but it continued to be published in England with somewhat revised content after that. It was in England that *Fruits of Philosophy* was involved in the famous Bradshaw-Besant trial (see BIRTH CONTROL AND UNBELIEF; BRADLAUGH, CHARLES; BESANT, ANNIE).

Knowlton's many critics accused that following his recipes would encourage people to engage in illicit intercourse, but he argued that if a woman's chastity could be overcome with the knowledge his book imparted, it could also be overcome without it. Others claimed that birth control was against nature, but Knowlton answered that civilized life was one continuous battle against nature, and that birth control methods would not change that. Rather *conception* control, he said, would prevent overpopulation; mitigate the evil of prostitution; reduce poverty, ignorance, and crime; help prevent hereditary diseases; preserve and improve the species; and prevent ill health among women who would otherwise suffer from excessive childbearing or habitual abortions.

Knowlton himself largely retired from the battle over birth control in the early 1840s. Some measure of his standing among his fellow physicians can be seen with his election in 1844 as a fellow of the Massachusetts Medical Society. He continued to write articles on a variety of medical topics until his death.

BIBLIOGRAPHY

Fryer, Peter. *The Birth Controllers*. London: Secker and Warburg, 1965.

Knowlton, Charles. *Fruits of Philosophy*, with commentary by Norman E. Himes and Robert Latou Dickinson. Reprinted from the tenth edition. Mount Vernon, NY: Peter Pauper Press, 1936.

VERN L. BULLOUGH

KNUTZEN, MATHIAS (1646–?), German atheist pamphleteer. Born in Holstein, Mathias Knutzen studied theology and caused controversy by his sermons. He came to the university town of Jena in 1674 after traveling extensively throughout Germany. After distributing several handwritten pamphlets, he fled to Altdorf and is said to have died in Italy. His pamphlets explained that some people all over Europe took their knowledge and conscience as the sole criterion for rightness and goodness. He declared that there was no God, that he despised authority, and that he rejected the church and its priests. There was only one life, and neither reward nor punishment was to be expected after death. If there was a God, Knutzen asked in his pamphlets, where had he come from? Knutzen contended that the Bible was not holy but a contemptible scripture, confused and dark, without coherence and sense, just a fable.

BIBLIOGRAPHY

Becker, Karl. "Unbelief in Germany." In *The Encyclopedia of Unbelief*, edited by Gordon Stein. Amherst, NY: Prometheus Books, 1985.

Smith, Warren Allen. *Who's Who in Hell*. New York: Barricade, 2000.

FINNGEIR HIORTH

KOTARBINSKI, TADEUSZ (1886–1981), Polish philosopher. Tadeusz Kotarbinski was a leading representative of the Lvov-Warsaw school in philosophy, which was related in spirit to the Vienna Circle (see SCHLICK, MORITZ, AND THE VIENNA CIRCLE). For many years, Kotarbinski was the chairman of the Department of Logic at Warsaw University, then the president of the Polish Academy of Science (1957–62) and of the Institut International de Philosopie (1960–63). He was a member extraordinary of the British Academy, and received honorary doctorates from several universities in Poland and abroad. His main domains of scientific research were ontology, in which he developed his own version of nominalism, called reism; epistemology, in which field he defended EMPIRICISM and RATIONALISM; praxiology or general methodology, of which he was a pioneer; philosophical logic, which was his main subject of teaching and the subject of his most comprehensive book, the so-called *Elementy*; and ethics, in which he developed the concept of independent ethics, that is, secular ethics free of any religious assumptions. But Kotarbinski always considered teaching to be his principal calling. He had numerous disciples of different generations, strongly influencing the way of thinking of large group of people who owe to him their strict intellectual standards and moral values.

As the best attitude toward other people, he suggested the attitude of reliable carer, one who is ready to help when help is needed and to protect others (including animals) against suffering. He himself could be the personal model of this attitude, being unusually sympathetic toward people and sensitive to all forms of harm and injustice. Prior to World War II he strongly protested against racism, especially anti-Semitism, and religious intolerance in Poland. As a member of the Freethinkers' Society, he published many articles in its journal, the *Rationalist*, demanding separation between the church and the state, condemning racial and religious discrimination at Polish universities, and arguing for the right to free expression of opinions in public life. He was hated by Catholic militants and conservatives, who derided him as a representative of Bolshevism.

In spite of his materialist and leftist views, he never accepted Marxism, which became the officially promoted philosophy in Poland after World War II. Kotarbinski considered this philosophy to be much akin to religious doctrines. So he was classified by Marxist authorities as an idealist bourgeois philosopher. For some years he was allowed to teach only logic, not philosophy. Political liberalization after Joseph Stalin's death made it possible for him to teach freely and to publish his philosophical works, even to hold the highest academic office. Nevertheless, he remained sharply critical of the limitations on freedom under the Soviet system.

After the change of political system in Poland in 1989, the Catholic Church regained its dominant role in public life. As a result, recent efforts have been made to cause Kotarbinski to be forgotten, or at least to diminish recognition of his contribution to Polish intellectual culture.

BIBLIOGRAPHY

Kotarbinski, Tadeusz. *Elementy teorii poznania, logiki formalnej i metodolgii nauk* [Elements of the Theory of Knowledge, Formal Logic and the Methodology of Science]. Warsaw, 1929.

———. "Ethical Evaluation." *International Philosophical Quarterly* 11, no. 3 (1971).

———. "The Importance of Free Expression." *Pacific Philosophy Forum* 2 (1963).

———. "Mastery and Humanism." *Dialectics and Humanism* 4, no. 1 (1977).

———. *Medytacje o zyciu godziwym* [Meditations on the Good Life]. Warsaw, 1966.

BARBARA STANOSZ

KOVOOR, ABRAHAM (1898–1978), Indian rationalist and debunker of god-men. Abraham Thomas Kovoor represents a colorful era in the history of the Asian rationalist movement (see RATIONALISM). His direct and trenchant criticism of all kinds of spiritual frauds and organized religions excited audiences wherever he appeared and initiated a new dynamism in the rationalist movement, especially in India (see INDIA, UNBELIEF IN).

Born at Tiruvalla in Kerala, India, on April 10, 1898, Abraham was the son of Reverend Kovoor Eipe Thomma Katthanar, the vicar general of the Mar Thomma Syrian Church of Malabar. He was educated at Serambur Bengabasi Colleges at Calcutta. After working briefly as a junior professor in Kerala, he migrated to Sri Lanka, where he spent the rest of his life. He taught botany in several colleges and retired as a professor at Thurston College, Colombo, in 1959. After retirement Kovoor devoted his life to the rationalist movement. He spent most of his time building up the Ceylon Rationalist Association and was elected its president in 1960—an office he retained until his death. He edited an annual journal, the *Ceylon Rationalist Ambassador*. In 1961 he traveled in Europe and established contact with the World Union of Freethinkers there (see FREETHOUGHT). Kovoor wrote articles in newspapers and magazines in Ceylon about his encounters with the paranormal under the pseudonym "Narcissus"; these became popular. These articles were translated and published in India, first in Malayalam by Joseph Edamaruku (using Kovoor's actual name

instead of the pseudonym "Narcissus") and later in other Indian languages.

In the 1960s and 1970s Kovoor traveled in India several times and addressed hundreds of meetings. His brilliant oratory enlivened with his scientific approach and the spirit of critical thinking had an almost magical effect on audiences in Indian villages and towns. Kovoor led four "miracle exposure" lecture tours in India, all organized by the Indian Rationalist Association, and challenged and exposed the "miracles" performed by so-called god-men. During his last journey to India in 1976, Kovoor visited the ashram of India's most prominent god-man, Sai Baba, and famously challenged him to face a test of Kovoor's devising, an offer the god-man refused.

Kovoor died on September 18, 1978. "I am not afraid of death and life after death," he wrote in his will. "To set an example, I don't want a burial." He donated his eyes to an eye bank and his cadaver to a medical college for anatomy studies. He wanted his skeleton to be given to the science laboratory of Thurston College. Everything was done according to his last wishes.

SANAL EDAMARUKU

KREKEL, MATTIE (1840–1921), American freethought-liberal lecturer and author. Mattie Krekel began her career as a Spiritualist trance speaker and traveling lecturer for liberal reform. She was a speaker for the New York Freethinkers Association and was appointed vice president of the AMERICAN SECULAR UNION in 1885, drawing the admiration of Robert Green INGERSOLL.

Spiritualist Beginnings. The child of liberal parents, to whom she was grateful for discouraging her from religious orthodoxy, Mattie Hulett was born in Indiana on April 13, 1840. Her earliest connections to liberal reform came through Spiritualism, closely connected in the nineteenth century to freethought. Her first lecture on the liberal platform took place in Rockford, Illinois, at the age of fifteen. Her advent as an adolescent female speaker was typical of Spiritualist lecturers following the Fox sisters' popularization of the movement in 1848. Young women were considered more open to spirit communication, and trance speaking empowered women like Mattie to more freely address controversial topics in an era in which "spirits" were more likely to receive polite attention than women.

After her marriage to T. W. Parry in 1862 and the births of her six children, she continued working as a traveling lecturer through the 1870s appearing as a delegate from Illinois to the 10th Annual Convention of the American Association of Spiritualists in Chicago in 1873, and as a speaker at the Spiritualist Camp Meeting in Dubuque, Iowa, in 1876.

Freethought and Secularism. Her work continued in the 1880s after her marriage to her second husband, Austrian-born US District Court Judge Arnold Krekel, himself also an agnostic lecturer. She shared with him the honor of addressing the New York Freethinkers Association, a group that first met in Watkins Glen, New York, to advocate scientific inquiry, civil rights, and liberal reform, and that hosted such notable speakers as Amy Post, Ingersoll, D. M. BENNETT, and Matilda Joslyn GAGE.

In 1885 she was appointed vice president of the American Secular Union. In his opening speech at the American Secular Union convention in Albany, Ingersoll commended Mattie Krekel for her courage of self-expression both as a woman and as a freethinker. Following her husband's death in 1888, she continued to ably express her courageous unconventional opinions in an article appearing on February 15, 1890, in THE TRUTH SEEKER in which she equated freethought with self-assertion.

BIBLIOGRAPHY

Gaylor, Annie Laurie. *Women without Superstition.* Madison, WI: Freedom From Religion Foundation, 1997.
Patrick, Lucia. "Religion and Revolution in the Thought of Matilda Joslyn Gage (1826–1898)." PhD diss., Florida State University, 1996.

MELINDA E. GRUBE

KROPOTKIN, PËTR (1842–1921), Russian anarchist-evolutionist activist. Pëtr Kropotkin was born in Moscow on December 9, 1842, the son of a wealthy prince. His childhood was typical of the Russian nobility, with the exception that his mother died when he was three. At age fifteen, he became a page at the court of Nicholas I at Saint Petersburg and attended a prestigious school attached to the court. The education he received was somewhat liberal; for example, he was able to study the French Encyclopedists (see ENCYCLOPÉDIE, L', AND UNBELIEF). He excelled in the study of science.

After completing his education at Saint Petersburg, Kropotkin fulfilled his military duties. His interest in geographic science led him to join or lead several survey expeditions into Manchuria, Siberia, and Finland. These expeditions would be instrumental both in Kropotkin's development as a scientist and in his later embrace of anarchism (see ANARCHISM AND UNBELIEF). Kropotkin's reports on these expeditions were well received by the scientific community, so much so that Kropotkin was offered a position with the Imperial Geographical Society. But during his years in Siberia he had lost faith in government; he turned down the appointment, opting instead to pursue helping humankind through anarchism.

Kropotkin's Ideas. During his time in Siberia, Kropotkin had realized that a web of small, almost autonomous towns and villages offered a more commodious way of life than large states ruled by impersonal, bureaucratic governments. In large part his anarchist philosophy developed from this realization. But he also came to understand as central to village life the process by which independent persons come together for mutual benefit. He also visited a group of village watchmakers in Switzerland, confirming what he had learned in Siberia. After his return from Switzerland, he stated he had become an anarchist from that point forward.

He then began applying this insight to other areas, including evolutionary theory. During this time frame, many "social Darwinists" (actually far removed from Charles DARWIN) had made a fetish of "survival of the fittest" (see DARWINISM AND UNBELIEF; SPENCER, HERBERT), depicting competition between species as the only force driving evolution. Kropotkin's experiences showed him that on the contrary, cooperation played a significant role. From this began his work on the theories that would later be published in his best-known book, *Mutual Aid* (1902).

In opposition to social Darwinist views, Kropotkin believed that all creatures were basically cooperative, and that when it was possible to do so, one creature would generally help another. He found this to be true among animals as well as human beings. For Kropotkin, Darwinian natural selection was the leading factor in individuals' competition to survive and reproduce, but cooperation became the dominant factor at the species level. The emphasis Kropotkin placed on cooperation offered a significant counterweight to the ruling social Darwinism of the day, and helped to guide the development of evolutionary theory into a more reasonable direction.

Kropotkin was also an optimist regarding human nature. It was his opinion that when small autonomous collectives had replaced the state, everyone would be eager to work because competition would be inoperative and people would want to be busy.

Kropotkin's Activism. Following his refusal of the geographical post, Kropotkin devoted his full energies to the international anarchist movement. He participated in the founding of numerous anarchist journals, was imprisoned several times, and spent forty years in exile, much of it in England. In 1892 he published his seminal anarchist work, *The Conquest of Bread*. Published ten years before *Mutual Aid*, it reflected many of the same ideas. In plain language that could be understood by all he described his ideal of "anarchist communism," essentially the sharing of all, by all, and for the benefit of all. His anarchism, his belief in human goodness, and his theory of mutual cooperation were all blended in this work.

Kropotkin's exile ended with the February Revolution. He returned to Russia in June 1917. After he returned to Russia, he was not treated kindly by the Bolsheviks. He was forced to move several times before settling in a small village called Dmitrov, where he lived basically in exile, cut off from information about the outside world. He died in poverty on February 8, 1921.

BIBLIOGRAPHY

Avrich, Paul. *Anarchist Portraits.* Princeton, NJ: Princeton University Press, 1988.

Nettlau, Max. *A Short History of Anarchism*. Translated by Ida Pilat Isca, edited by Heiner M. Becker. London: Freedom Press, 1996.

Read, Herbery, ed. *Kropotkin: Selections from His Writings*. London: Freedom Press, 1942.

TIMOTHY BINGA

KWANZAA. Noted Afrocentrist and nontheist Maulana Karenga created the Kwanzaa celebration in 1966, during the heyday of the Black Power movement in the United States. The purpose of the celebration—held from December 26 to January 1—is to promote black pride, unity, and respect for African culture, values, and traditions.

Kwanza means "first fruits" in Swahili. Karenga added an extra *a* to the end of the word to distinguish it from *kwanza* celebrations held throughout Africa. Various first fruit celebrations have been held in ancient Egypt and Nubia, Ashanti land, Yoruba land, South Africa, southeastern Africa, and Central Africa.

Karenga, who speaks fluent Swahili, laid out the *Nguzu Saba*, or "Seven Principles of Blackness," in the seven days of Kwanzaa:

- Umoja (Unity): For the family, community, nation, and the black race.
- Kujichagulia (Self-Determination): For determining the collective future and destiny of black people.
- Ujima (Collective Work and Responsibility): For the building of the black community and striving for solutions to the problems that afflict black people.
- Ujamaa (Cooperative Economics): For pulling together the economic resources of the black community for collective empowerment.
- Nia (Purpose): For the building of a black community that will be conducive to black greatness.
- Kuumba (Creativity): For finding creative ways to build a better black community.
- Imani (Faith): For believing in ourselves and our parents, our teachers, our leaders, and our ancestors.

Notably, faith is celebrated on the seventh and final day. Though celebrants may define faith in their own way, Karenga has secular ideas in mind. Indeed, he is always careful to point out that Kwanzaa is a cultural celebration rather than a religious observation. He believes the celebration could help combat some of the divisiveness of organized religion.

Some of the objects used during Kwanzaa include the following:

- The *kinara* candleholder, which holds seven candles (one black, three green, and three red). The colors represent black people (the black), the blood shed by African people (the red), and the color of the

motherland (green). Marcus Garvey popularized the colors with the African liberation flag during his heyday.
- The *mbeka*, or placemat, which is preferably made from straw.
- The *mazao*, or crops, particularly fruits and vegetables.
- The *vibunzi/muhindi*, ears of corn that represent each child in the household.
- The *kombe cha umoja* or *kikombe cha umoja*, the communal unity cup.
- The *mishumaa*, the actual candles used throughout the celebration.

Celebrants pour libations (*tambik*) to the ancestors and decorate their houses in African motifs, using red, black, and green. The kwanzaa *karamu*, or feast, is traditionally held on December 31. Those celebrating New Year's Eve are advised to hold the feast earlier in the day.

Karenga and other Kwanzaa celebrants bristle at the charge that it is simply a "black Christmas." Most celebrants are against the commercialization of Kwanzaa. Gifts are supposed to be inexpensive and homemade, as opposed to expensive and store-bought. However, many businesses still manage to make a lot of money by selling Kwanzaa cards and other gifts; and many businesses use the holiday to advertise their products and services.

Kwanzaa has had other critics as well. For example, the African American scholar Gerald Early believes that African Americans have no genuine connection to African culture as promoted by Kwanzaa. Furthermore, some conservatives have said that the celebration is merely a racket to promote Afrocentric scholars. Others have charged that whites have been prevented from attending some Kwanzaa gatherings.

Despite what its detractors say, Kwanzaa is celebrated by millions of people throughout the world, and has gained mainstream acceptance. In 1997 the US Postal Service issued a 32-cent postage stamp in honor of the celebration, and its popularity continues to grow.

BIBLIOGRAPHY

Allen, Norman R. "The Role of Humanism in Promoting African Unity and Identity in the World." Excerpted in *A Commemorative Issue of the First Humanist Week in Uganda (Africa), 20th–28th May 2004*. Kampala: Uganda Humanists Association. 2004.

Karenga, Maulana. *Kwanzaa: Origin, Concept and Practice*. Los Angeles: University of Sankore Press, 1978.

NORM R. ALLEN JR.

LABOR AND UNBELIEF. Throughout history churches and other religious institutions have relied on the financial support of their constituents. Clerics are paid more or less directly by those to whom they provide spiritual guidance. So it is natural that religious institutions become a microcosm of society as a whole, with all its class structures. The poorer a given institution's congregants, the less money it has. Conversely, customs arise by which the rich can buy their way into the institution's good graces, leaving the poor and working class to wait their turn. Common practices such as the sale of pews reserve access to the best seats for the wealthy, relegating the poor to "back of the bus" status. Moreover, the rich can simply build a new church or synagogue in order to have a place of worship separate from the undesirables.

Though the labor movement has pronounced connections to ATHEISM, FREETHOUGHT, and ANTICLERICALISM, in fact well-known champions of labor hail from both sides of the religious divide. From Karl MARX to Dorothy Day, those who seek to abolish capitalism or simply to reform existing labor laws to bring about a more equitable society have come to their convictions from various perspectives. Regardless of their approach, their motives are the same.

Welsh atheist and labor reformer Robert OWEN published controversial pamphlets critical of religion and the church. He founded an industrial partnership in a mill town called New Lanark, near Glasgow, Scotland. There he set his ideals for labor reform into practice, reducing the hours in the workday, establishing strict sanitation habits, and opening a school for workers' children that included dancing as part of its curriculum. Eventually Owen found his way to the United States, where he established the community of New Harmony, Indiana (see WRIGHT, FRANCES). There he invoked a nonreligious set of principles, including the substitution of ethical lectures for religious worship, public care of children, and cooperative labor practices. Owen also published a freethought newspaper, the *New Harmony Gazette*.

New Harmony ultimately failed and Owen returned to Great Britain, but he did not cease his activities. He founded the London Cooperative Society and the Equitable Labor Exchange, which issued labor notes in exchange for hours of work, and continued to be openly critical of religion, although he managed to escape BLASPHEMY charges. Many of his progressive ideas were eventually realized. Child labor laws, the establishment of bureaus of labor statistics, and the eight-hour workday are significant labor reforms that can be traced to Owen.

German philosopher and socialist Karl Marx did not argue about the existence of God, but distinguished the unachievable pie-in-the-sky promises offered by religion from what he viewed as the achievable objectives of materialism as a means to end capitalism and the oppression of the working class. His oft-paraphrased dictum "Religion is the opium of the people" has a deeper meaning when quoted at fuller length. In the introduction to his *Contribution to the Critique of Hegel's Philosophy of Right* (1844) he wrote: "Religion is the sigh of the oppressed creature, the heart of a heartless world, just as it is the spirit of a spiritless situation. It is the opium of the people."

In 1905 Vladimir Ilyich LENIN characterized the oppression of the working class as both social and spiritual slavery, asserting that a class-conscious worker "leaves heaven to the priests and bourgeois hypocrites." Lenin believed that all socialists are atheists. Though he was not opposed to freedom of religion, he thought the state should regard religion as a private matter, insisting that the Russian Revolution enforce separation of church and state in order to prevent coercion in matters of religion. He believed this was imperative if political freedom were to be achieved.

Lenin urged workers to demand that corrupt clergy abandon their privileges and join in their struggle in response to their ultimatum that "the class-conscious Russian workers will declare ruthless war on you." He felt it necessary, however, to relegate the issue of religion to the background, and to deal with economic and political struggles first. Once the workers were emancipated, in his view, atheistic consciousness would follow, although not automatically. There should still be an organized fight against religious doctrine; at the same time, care should be taken not to offend believers unduly, since this could backfire and result in fortification of religious fanaticism.

The trade unions that emerged in Europe during the nineteenth and early twentieth centuries were Marxist-dominated and conspicuously antireligious. Christian workers tended to avoid these unions, a tradition that continues to the present day. To protect their constituencies European churches established their own trade union federations. These were largely impotent in terms of achieving labor reform, but they separated the believing workers from the unbelievers. According to Christian labor historian George Higgins, the Dutch Catholic Church established a mandate that "decreed that Catholics should belong to Catholic unions and no others." The dichotomy between believing and unbelieving workers was essentially complete and enduring.

For their part, activists of the militant labor movement consistently regarded religion as an oppressive tool of the ruling class. This reflected a long tradition of corruption within the churches of Europe at the expense of peasants and workers. In revolutionary times, labor activists generally pursued a zero tolerance policy toward religious institutions and their patrons. When mass uprisings of workers and peasants occurred, clergy were often among their first targets.

In Spain anarchists and labor revolutionaries directed their attacks at crooked clergy and the Catholic Church, which, with the help of fascist governments, exerted an irresistible stranglehold on the peasants (see ANARCHISM AND UNBELIEF; FERRER, FRANCISCO). In 1923 the Spanish anarchists Francisco Ascaso and Torrès Escartin opened fire on a car carrying Don Juan Soldevila Romero, the cardinal-archbishop of Saragossa, mortally wounding him. Soldevila was widely known as a corrupt and powerful cleric, responsible for a violent and repressive crackdown against the Spanish people in the decade leading up to the Spanish Revolution. During the Spanish Civil War (1936–39) anarchists burned churches and ran out the clergy in retaliation for their collusion with the fascists.

American trade unions were not nearly as antireligious as their European counterparts. One of the first union federations in the United States was the late nineteenth-century Knights of Labor, which welcomed nearly every kind of worker except "bankers and bartenders." Although Catholics elsewhere were forbidden to join the Knights, American bishops saw the union as a way to win the favor of Catholic workers. This avoided a split in the labor movement between Catholics and other workers, as had occurred in Europe and Canada. A few decades later, as anti-Communist sentiment began to burgeon in the United States, the church came to the forefront of efforts to run Communists, real and imagined, out of organized labor.

If even Lenin had been cautious about criticizing religion for fear of scaring away the faithful masses, one important union displayed no such caution. Even before its official formation in Chicago in 1905, the Industrial Workers of the World (IWW) was open and unabashed in denouncing not only religion, but the clergy as well. As a labor union, the IWW was (and still is) unsurpassed in militancy and radical political methods, including direct action. One of its founding members and a principal author of the IWW Preamble was a radically antireligious former priest named Thomas J. Hagerty, who was not the least bit timid about his views. Without attacking religion itself, he and others were quick to point out the antilabor activities of the church and were successful in attracting many atheist workers.

The line "Pie in the sky—that's a lie!" won national popularity in the song "The Preacher and the Slave" (1911) by Joe Hill. Perhaps the most famous Wobbly (IWW activist) and a proud atheist, Hill was executed on dubious charges by the state of Utah. "The Preacher and the Slave" is now thought to be the most popular antireligious song in US history. The IWW's unofficial atheistic position was threatening enough that the church struck back, attacking the union for supposedly being immoral and sinful. However, while the union was vehemently antireligious, its attacks were usually aimed at greedy and duplicitous clergy and not so much at the teachings of the Bible. Although IWW propaganda often depicted Christ as the "hobo agitator of Nazareth," the union's stand was that the church was a tool of the capitalist class and therefore an enemy of the worker. No other union condemned the church so openly and persistently, in the pages of its newspapers as well as in the lines of its songs and poetry. The union's *Little Red Songbook* ("Songs for the Workers to Fan the Flames of Discontent") was rife with such lyrical and inventive creations.

Any discussion of the labor movement and atheism must include such progressive believers as the Catholic Workers and the Liberation Theologists. Despite their ties to the church, their political ideals were extremely radical. The larger conservative wing of the church tried to distance itself from these groups, but was unable to ignore them completely.

Peter Maurin, a French anarchist and former cleric, left France in 1909 and lived and worked in Canada and the United States before settling in New York City in the late 1920s, where he became "an agitator for Christ." His anarchist principles kept him leery of trade unions, but Maurin believed the capitalist system was inherently unethical and corrupting, and he was particularly influenced by the Communist anarchism of Pëtr KROPOTKIN.

Despite receiving her political education from the socialists, anarchists, and the IWW, Dorothy Day converted to Catholicism in 1927. Day met Maurin in 1933 and together they founded the Catholic Worker movement. Under Day's editorship, the movement's newspaper, the *Catholic Worker*, was ardently pro-labor; established Catholic Worker groups aided strikes by picketing and by providing meals to strikers and by giving publicity and moral support. Off the picket line, its activities centered on voluntary poverty, pacifism, and social justice activism. Its anarchist style—autonomous communities with no central authority, no board of directors, no salaries, and no federal tax-exempt status—continues to be practiced today in more than 130 communities.

Day and others, such as the monsignors Charles Owen Rice and George W. Higgins and Father John Corridan, are only a few of the radical Catholics who have devoted their lives to labor reform. Their faith somehow led them to understand that the economic system lay at the root of society's problems.

Succeeding the Catholic Workers by several decades, the aim of the Liberation Theologists was similar to that of the Marxists: to bring about economic equality and help establish a better life for the poor and working classes. Rooted in the Christian Left, it gained influence in Latin America in the late 1960s; several influential congresses were held in the early 1970s.

Apart from the IWW, the American labor movement today remains deeply rooted in Christianity, although labor struggles in general seem to have been abandoned by left-wing religious activists. Unions continue to lose clout and membership, representing less than 8 percent of the private-sector work force.

BIBLIOGRAPHY

Betten, Neil. *Catholic Activism and the Industrial Worker.* Gainesville: University Presses of Florida, 1976.

Foner, Philip S. "The Industrial Workers of the World, 1905–1917." In *The History of the Labor Movement in the United States*, vol. 4. New York: International Publishers, 1965.

Gaskin, J. C. A., ed. *Varieties of Unbelief from Epicurus to Sartre*. New York: Macmillan, 1989.

Higgins, George G. *Organized Labor and the Church: Reflections of a "Labor Priest."* New York: Paulist Press, 1993.

Paz, Abel. *Durruti: The People Armed*. Translated by Nancy MacDonald. New York: Free Life Editions, 1977.

Rosemont, Franklin. *Joe Hill: The IWW and the Making of a Revolutionary Workingclass Counterculture*. Chicago: Charles H. Kerr, 2003.

Thompson, C. Bertrand. *The Churches and the Wage Earners: A Study of the Cause and Cure of Their Separation*. New York: Charles Scribner's Sons, 1909.

JULIE HERRADA

LAÏCITÉ. The term *laïcité* is used primarily in Romance-language countries with a strong Catholic tradition. In English the word *secularism* is often substituted, but that word does not completely translate *laïcité*, as *laïcité* connotes a form of organization of society itself and also of public venues. *Laïcité* comes from the Greek word *laos*, meaning the people who compose society. It refers to a way of organizing society which achieves a real separation between the public space and its institutions (which are common property) on the one hand and the churches with their different religious or philosophical convictions (which pertain to sphere of citizens' private concerns) on the other.

Only when the state is *laïque*—that is, when it successfully implements *laïcité*—can it guarantee impartial treatment of and true equality for all citizens, whatever their convictions. On this view, only *laïcité* can guarantee total freedom of conscience, freedom of thought, and of religion.

Laïcité in France. Near the end of the eighteenth century, both France and Belgium witnessed the earliest steps in the "laïcization" of civic institutions. Responsibility for the administration of so-called civil register certificates (acknowledging births, marriages, and deaths) passed from the clergy to public authorities. Public authorities also began to recognize the right to divorce (forbidden by the church) and to extend equality for all, to the great advantage of Protestants and Jews.

In the nineteenth century France stood divided between two ideological camps. The liberal, *laïque* France supported human rights; it confronted a conservative Catholic France that opposed what it called the "pernicious freedoms"—freedom of thought, of religion, of the press—and human rights. Catholic France was particularly outspoken in supporting Pope Pius IX's reactionary encyclical "Quanta Cura" with its infamous Syllabus of Errors (1864). Moreover the French Catholic Church had openly opposed the ideals of the French Revolution and was intensely antirepublican. Because of this historical confrontation, *laïcité* has often been seen as antireligious. In fact, *laïcité* is not antireligious, though it is anticlerical insofar as it has sought to put an end to the social power of the clergy (see ANTICLERICALISM).

By the progressive separation of church from state, *laïque* activists sought to preserve and expand religious freedom. Among its earliest propagandists were well-known individuals including Benjamin Constant, Jules Michelet, Edgar Quinet, Lamennais, and the poet Lamartine. In the second half of the nineteenth century, FREETHOUGHT organizations and the Masonic lodges of the Grand Orient of France, among others, emerged as defenders of separation.

In 1905 France passed a historic law known as the Law on Separation of Churches and State. It states in part: "The Republic ensures freedom of conscience. It guarantees the free exercise of religion. . . . The Republic does not recognize, remunerate nor subsidize any religion." Yet even this law allows the state to pay the salaries of chaplains and to subsidize the maintenance of (predominantly Catholic) places of worship. Today the implementation of this law poses problems because Islam (now France's second most important religion) remains excluded from it.

Laïcité in Belgium. Since the nineteenth century Belgium developed legislation concerning "recognized religions" which is also based upon the principle of separation of churches and state. In contrast to France, the ministers of six "recognized religions" (Roman Catholicism, Reformed Protestantism, Anglicanism, Judaism, Islam, and Orthodoxy) are paid by the state. In the early 1970s, so-called nonconfessional organizations serving nonbelievers and humanists (see HUMANISM) federated, demanding—on grounds of the *laïque* principle of equality of citizens—treatment equal to that given to religious organizations. Advocates argued that humanism is also a LIFE STANCE, nonreligious and no less respectable than any religious conviction. This activism culminated in a 2002 law that also provides state-funded salaries for the delegates of nonconfessional organizations, including humanist counselors and celebrants.

Laïcité in Civil Society. The claim for a *laïque* society and the defense of a nonconfessional, humanistic personal ethics complement one another. *Laïcité* is thus seen a twofold concept, on the one hand implying a neutral and impartial state, on the other hand calling for humanistic citizens who will defend the principle of *laïcité*.

In countries with a strong *laïque* tradition, then, *laïcité* operates in effect as a life stance in its own right. This life stance is neither a new religion nor a mere rejection of religion. Far from being limited to a simple atheism or agnosticism, it encompasses a full commitment to humanism with an explicit ethical dimension. As a humanist life stance, it holds that men and women should not seek for some preexisting and abstract understanding of the meaning of life, such as one handed down by a god; rather men and women must undertake the labor of constructing their own meanings for human existence and human actions.

Contrary to theocratic or authoritarian regimes that invariably seek to interfere in the private sphere of conscience, the secular (laïque) state guarantees freedom of religion and of conviction. Moreover it is the only one to do so. Political secularism is the patrimony common to all democrats, whether religious or not; thus it is in no way the monopoly of agnostics, atheists, and humanists.

In fact, it is fortunate that the democratic will to secularize the State is not the preserve of "heathens" alone, but is rather the common aim of all democrats. By the same token, all citizens should welcome the recognition that the search for meaning in life—for "spirituality," if one will—is neither the exclusive preserve of religions.

Pluralism of conviction must be guaranteed in part so that dialogue is possible—not just predictable interactions between experts or high dignitaries, but a true grassroots dialogue among citizens of differing life stances, conducted in a setting of equality. On the laïque view, this can only be guaranteed if the state and public authorities observe a true impartiality between citizens of every philosophical and religious conviction, allowing each to blossom in the private sphere.

PHILIPPE GROLLET AND GEORGES C. LIÉNARD
TRANSLATED BY EDITH NAGANT

LA METTRIE, JULIEN OFFRAY DE (1709–1751), French atheist philosopher. Julien Offray de La Mettrie, a medical doctor, was one of the most outspoken materialistic writers of the eighteenth century. His uncompromising description of humans as material beings and denial of an immaterial and immortal soul made him famous all over Europe as "Mr. Machine."

Life and Principal Works. La Mettrie was born in the port of Saint-Malo in Britanny, where he practiced as a doctor after his medical studies and his degree from Reims University. In 1733 and 1734 he stayed in Leyden to attend the lectures of the renowned Hermann Boerhaave. He afterward presented himself as Boerhaave's pupil and translated the great teacher's works, as well as publishing his own medical observations. He went to Paris in 1742, became doctor to the French Guards, and took part in military campaigns, as well as mixing in philosophical and libertine circles.

His first openly irreligious work, *Histoire naturelle de l'âme* (Natural History of the Soul), was published clandestinely in Paris in 1745 and was immediately seized by the police and burned by the Paris Parlement. In 1746 La Mettrie left France for the more tolerant Holland, and

published his notorious *Homme machine* (Machine Man) in Leyden in 1747. It caused such a scandal that he had to leave the country rapidly for fear of being arrested and found refuge at the court of King Frederick II of Prussia. Here he published *L'Homme-plante* (Man a Plant; 1748) and a translation of Seneca's *De vita beata*, with an introduction that was reworked in 1750 and 1751 as *Anti-Sénèque* (Anti-Seneca), posthumously retitled *Discours sur le bonheur* (Discourse on Happiness). In 1750 he published *Système d'Epicure* (System of Epicurus).

Philosophy. These works contained a gradually more outspoken materialistic explanation of humans in terms of sensitive living matter that, when properly organised in the brain, can produce thought. He came to deny the existence of any human soul or divine providence, claiming that the whole world was the result of natural configurations of living matter. He thus, despite the deliberately provocative title of his most famous work, rejects Cartesian dualism and combines mechanistic explanations with various medical theories concerning vital matter. He also draws on the Epicurean tradition and takes arguments from the irreligious works which circulated clandestinely in eighteenth-century France. He denies the existence of any absolute moral values and insists that humans are determined by their physical makeup; his claims that education cannot produce social behavior and that only coercion can ensure social peace led to his rejection by other atheistic philosophers, despite the influence of his works on their own materialism.

BIBLIOGRAPHY

La Mettrie, Julien Offray de. *Machine Man and Other Writings*. Edited by Ann Thomson. Cambridge: Cambridge University Press, 1996.

Thomson, Ann. *Materialism and Society in the Mid-Eighteenth Century: La Mettrie's "Discours préliminaire."* Geneva: Droz, 1981.

Vartanian, Aram. *La Mettrie's l'Homme machine, a Study in the Origins of an Idea*. Princeton, NJ: Princeton University Press, 1960.

Wellman, Kathleen. *La Mettrie. Medicine, Philosophy, and Enlightenment*. Durham, NC: Duke University Press, 1992.

ANN THOMSON

LAMONT, CORLISS (1902–1995), American humanist activist. Corliss Lamont was an active member of the humanist movement (see HUMANISM), especially the AMERICAN HUMANIST ASSOCIATION, which he supported financially over many years. Lamont was a lecturer in the Department of Philosophy of Columbia University and served on the board of the *Journal of Philosophy*. The son of Thomas Lamont, a business partner of J. P. Morgan, Corliss supported many left-wing causes.

Among Lamont's many interests were his belief in civil

liberties and democracy. He publicly battled Sen. Joe McCarthy and later the US State Department, which had denied him a passport. But according to Sidney Hook and others, Lamont was also an apologist for some of the worst excesses of Communist totalitarianism (see LENIN, VLADIMIR ILYICH; MARXISM; SOCIALISM AND UNBELIEF). Hook registered this objection in a 1981 letter to the editor in *Free Inquiry* magazine, sparking a passionate exchange of views between Hook and Lamont in subsequent issues. Although never a member of the Communist Party, Lamont was accused of being a "fellow traveler." Clearly he did not recognize the totalitarian character of Stalinism and Leninism until late in life. As head of the American-Soviet Friendship Committee, Lamont maintained that Stalin's Moscow purge trials were unreal.

In his 1974 book *Voice in the Wilderness*, Lamont penned a statement in which he withdrew his earlier views about the Moscow purge trials and criticized the Soviet Stalinist dictatorship for its denial of civil liberties and democracy.

Lamont was a defender of the philosophy of naturalistic humanism (see NATURALISM; SECULAR HUMANISM). He was a secular rather than a religious humanist (see RELIGIOUS HUMANISM) and he criticized John DEWEY for using the term *God* in his book *A Common Faith*. Lamont believed that one could live an authentic life here and now without any reliance upon a deity, and that this was possible through the application of reason and science.

Corliss Lamont's important humanist books were *The Philosophy of Humanism* (1957), which outlined the main principles of humanism; and *The Illusion of Immortality* (1935), which criticized the concepts of the soul and the afterlife.

BIBLIOGRAPHY

Lamont, Corliss. *The Illusion of Immortality.* New York: G. P. Putnam's Sons, 1935.

———. *The Philosophy of Humanism.* New York: Philosophical Library, 1957.

———. *Voice in the Wilderness.* Amherst, NY: Prometheus Books, 1974.

PAUL KURTZ

LATIN AMERICA, UNBELIEF IN. Background. With the arrival of the Spaniards and Portuguese in the sixteenth century in what is now known as Latin America, Ibero-America, Indian-America, or *America Mestiza*, the predominant and official religion of the aboriginal peoples became Roman Catholicism. Previously they had lived in advanced civilizations, worshiping their sovereigns and the forces of nature, but now Catholicism was imposed and made mandatory by the conquistadores through blood, sword, and fire. In addition, native peoples were heavily evangelized, even as they were ruthlessly dominated and exploited. Catholicism remained as the only legal religion until the end of the nineteenth century.

The Counter-Reformation, Catholicism's response to the Protestant Reformation centered in Europe, made its influence strongly felt in Latin America. From the sixteenth to the eighteenth centuries, the Tribunal of Holy Inquisition pursued, tortured, and killed not only aboriginal practitioners of idolatries but also heretics (see HERESY), unbelievers, and Jews, the latter with special ferocity.

The nineteenth century saw the rise of fighters for independence, including Venezuela's Francisco de Miranda and Simón Bolívar, Argentina's José San Martin, and Cuba's José Martí. These were liberal Freemasons and presumably deists (see DEISM); they generally favored a limited religious tolerance, especially toward Protestant evangelicals, and put into place some secularizing laws. Other prominent figures were open freethinkers (see FREETHOUGHT) and highly critical of the Catholic clergy (see ANTICLERICALISM), including the Peruvian anarchist writer Manuel González Prada, the Peruvian liberal writer Ricardo Palma, the Colombian author José María Vargas Vila, the Argentinean educator Domingo Faustino Sarmiento, and the Mexican lawyer Benito Juárez. The latter two rose to govern their countries; Mexico's Juárez even instituted reforms that confiscated church lands.

Successful, generally populist political activists including Argentina's Juan Domingo Perón, Mexico's Lázaro Cárdenas, Peru's Victor Raúl Haya de la Torre, and Brazil's Getulio Vargas confronted clerical power at least one time in the twentieth century.

Liberal movements, especially POSITIVISM, played an important role in the secularization and consolidation of the nascent Latin American countries during the second half of the nineteenth century and the first half of the twentieth. In Brazil, for example, with the installation of the republican system in 1889, the motto of Auguste COMTE, "Order and Progress," was placed on the national flag. At the same time, a law separating church from state was put into effect. Reform went so far that the prescribed closing greeting used in official state correspondence was changed from "God save you" to "health and fraternity." A Positivist Church was founded with the motto "Love the Principle and Order the Basis, Progress the Aim." It meets on Sundays to the present day. In Uruguay, under the liberal President José Batlle y Ordóñez, the names of religious holidays were secularized. Christmas became the "day of the family," Easter the "week of tourism," and so on. Political institutions were declared autonomous from military and ecclesiastical control and a secular public school system was instituted. The 1857 Mexican constitution prohibited ecclesiastical entities to have real estate and abolished any ecclesiastical privileges. That year President Juárez confiscated church properties, canceled all religious orders, and gave power to the state governors to choose what buildings could be for religious services. Mexico's first religious civil war was between 1857 and 1860 in reaction to the secular laws. The constitution of 1917 institutionalized many of the nineteenth-century secular reforms and had the most extensive restrictions on the Roman Catholic Church. In the middle 1920s and until the late 1930s, various federal and state administrations enforced the constitutional edicts and related law against the church. That produced the second Mexican religioius war, the Cristero Rebellion of 1926–29. So the Vatican and Mexico broke relations, which were not restored until 1992. And only in 2003 was abortion made partially legal in Mexico.

In Peru in the second half of the nineteenth century, liberal legislators succeeded in passing laws to establish secular cemeteries, civil marriages, religious tolerance, and lay education, as had already been done in Brazil, Uruguay, and Chile. But by 1979, Peruvian affairs had moved in the opposite direction: in that year the military government and an apostolic nuncio signed a concordat by which Peru exempted Catholic Church properties from taxation, exempted priests from income taxes, and pays salaries to clergy and schoolteachers who lead Catholic religion courses in the public schools. Such courses were made obligatory in the constitution of 1979. The most recent Peruvian constitution, adopted in 1993, again privileged the relations between Peru and the Vatican. In 2004 there was a failed effort to modify the constitution and declare a real separation between the Catholic Church and the Peruvian state. Among those fighting for separation are homosexual and feminist groups, and even some Christian groups, Catholic and otherwise.

In 2004 Argentina's capital, Buenos Aires, recognized same-sex civil unions. In 2005 Chile became the last country in the Americas to legalize divorce.

As for anarchist and socialist ideas, while these were already widespread across the region in the first decades of twentieth century, it was with the Cuban revolution of 1959—soon declared socialist and Marxist by its leader, Fidel Castro—that Marxist political ideology and atheistic philosophy gained numerous followers in Latin America and the third world—even Communist parties included many believers as members. But after the fall of European Communism, Castro's dictatorship favored relationships with official Catholicism. And several anarchist organizations across the rest of Latin America have enjoyed a more or less mild resurgence, as they have in other parts of the world; some of these movements continue in a minimal way to spread the historic ATHEISM and anticlericalism of their founders. There are even some Christian anarchist groups. The Marxist rebel groups of the late twentieth century met diverse fates. Those that could survive civil war, persecution, and slaughter were variously able to hide inside their countries, to abandon them, to surrender or sign a peace treaty, to be formalized, or simply to become social-democratic or environmentalist parties.

The nations of Latin America remain numerically Roman Catholic, despite rapid recent increases of interest in other religions, especially Protestant evangelicalism, Eastern religions, and indigenous cults. Catholicism retains its exclusive privileged relationship with most governments and armed forces across the region. On the other hand, some Catholic practice takes a syncretic form, blending elements drawn from American or even African aboriginal religion.

The Rationalistic Groups: Humanist and Skeptical. Even as other non-Catholic minorities have expanded, national censuses and opinion surveys reveal a significant increase in the number of citizens who declare themselves unbelievers in religion or skeptical of paranormal claims. As in the rest of the world, this increase seems related to disillusionment among serious students of Bible, and to growing exposure to critical thought and scientific knowledge, in educational systems and especially in cyberspace.

Among the earliest Latin American rationalistic groups were the Humanist Association of Argentina, active in the late 1960s and 1970s, and the Argentinean Center for the Investigation and Rebuttal of Pseudoscience, which published the newspaper *El Ojo Escéptico* (Skeptical Eye), active during the 1990s. Following on the Humanist Ethical International Conference in Costa Rica in 1995 and the Thirteenth Humanist World Congress in Mexico in 1996, there has been an explosion in the formation of organized rationalistic groups. At the same time a diverse group of individuals has emerged through mass media and the Internet who foment secularism, criticism of religious beliefs, the popularization of science, or criticism of paranormalist beliefs. Some have committed to the full range of these agendas.

These groups and individuals vary widely in their level of activity. The most active publish articles in print, via electronic bulletins, or on the World Wide Web; some also publish books, organize public meetings, and offer distinctive merchandise. Others exist formally or virtually, that is, they have ceased to publish and organize meetings some time ago, while their Web sites remain available to visit.

It must be underlined that not all groups and activists use the adjectives *humanist* or *skeptical* in their names. In addition, even more so than in other regions, in Latin America *humanist* doesn't always mean "secular humanist" or "unbeliever." As is the case worldwide, academicians and experts in humanities or human or social sciences describe themselves as humanists, though many are religious. Other sources of lexical confusion with regard to the word *humanist* are more idiosyncratic to Latin America. For example, Brazil's Humanist Party of Solidarity and the Peruvian humanist movement both have social-Christian tendencies. A so-called humanist movement was founded by Silo, an Argentinian once called "the Messiah from the Andes," and spawned humanist parties following his ideas. Siloism advances an eclectic collectivist philosophy with no relation to rationalistic secular humanism.

A few Latin American humanist associations are already members of the INTERNATIONAL HUMANIST ETHICAL UNION (IHEU) and the Center for Inquiry (CFI), but a majority of the Ibero-American skeptical organizations remain independent. Humanist organizations vary in their offerings—for example, only some offer humanist ceremonies like name giving or marriage (see RITUAL, CEREMONIAL, AND UNBELIEF). They need to increase their memberships substantially in order to enjoy fully developed democratic organizations like the humanist, rationalist, and atheist groups of India, and to expand their financial bases in order to enjoy economic independence like the European and North American organizations. Of course the developed countries have a very different economic, social, and political history.

The table below provides current information from online sources regarding Latin American rationalistic groups and associations.

Members' country	Group	Year founded	Official periodical
SEVERAL	ASIBEHU (Ibero-American Ethical-Humanist Association)	1995	Bulletin (d)
	Sin Dioses (Without Gods)	2002	Bulletin (e)
	Hispanic Chapter, Atheists of Florida, Inc.	2002	Bulletin (p)
	Pensar. Latin American Magazine for Reason and Science (from CSICOP, Inc.)	2004	*Pensar* (p) (To Think)
	MAHF (Hispanic Nonreligious Movement of Florida)	2005	
	Federación Iberoamericana Humanista (Ibero-American Humanist Federation)	2006	
ARGENTINA	AHEA Argentinian Ethical-Humanist Association) Association *Deodoro Roca*	1997	*El Desorden* (d)
	ASALUP (Argentinian Association for Fighting against Pseudosciences)	2001	Bulletin (e)
	Dios! (God!)	2002	
	Argentina Skeptics	2003	*Argentina Skeptics Report, Evolution Report* (e)
	Center for Inquiry/ Argentina	2005	
BRAZIL	Sociedade da Terra Redondo (Flat Earth Society)	1999	
	Sociedade Brasileira de Céticos e Racionalistas (Brazilian Society of Skeptics and Rationalists)		
	Projeto Ockham (Ockham Project)	2002	
COLOMBIA	Escépticos de Colombia (Colombian Skeptics)	2001	
COSTA RICA	ASEHUCO (Costa Rican Ethical-Humanist Association)	1989	*El Iconoclasta* (d) (Iconoclast)
	IPPC (Initiative for Promotion of Critical Thinking)	2000	
CUBA	MHEC (Cuban Humanist Evolutionist Movement)	1996	
CHILE	ILEC (Secular Institute of Contemporary Studies)	2000	
	La Nave de los Locos (Crazies' Ship)	2000	*La Nave de los Locos* (Crazies' Ship)
	Chilean Atheist and Freethinking Society	2004	
	Humanismolaico Chili	2006	
	Librepensamien Chili	2006	
ECUADOR	*Prociencia*	2003	*Prociencia* (p) (Pro-Science)
MEXICO	SOMIE (Mexican Society of Skeptical Research)	1989	
	AMER (Mexican Ethical-Rationalist Association)	1991	*Razona-mientos* (e) (Thinkings)
PERU	AERPFA (Peruvian Journal of Applied Philosophy Publishing Association)	1995	*RPFA* (p) (Peruvian Journal of Applied Philosophy)
	MPHA (Peruvian Humanist Non-religious Movement)	1998	*Eupraxofia* (d)
	CIPSI–PERU (Center of	1998	*Neo-Skepsis* (d)

	Investigations of Paranormal Claims, Pseudosciences, and Irrationality in Peru)		
	MASA–PERU (Anti-Cult Movement from Arequipa-Peru)	2000	Bulletin (e)
	Centro de Cuestiona-miento del Perú (Center for Inquiry/ Peru)	2002	Bulletin (e)
	APER (Peruvian Ethical-Rationalist Association)	2005	
PUERTO RICO	Peurto Rican Skeptical Society	2003	
VENEZUELA	AREV (Venezuelan and Skeptical Association)	2001	*El Lúcido* (e)

d = discontinued, e = electronic version, p = printed version

BIBLIOGRAPHY

Estrella, Hugo. "Humanism in Latin America—A Less-Than-Easy Choice." *International Humanist News* 10, no. 1 (2003).

Gasenbeek, B., and Babu Gogineni. *International Humanist and Ethical Union, 1952–2002: Past, Present and Future.* Leusden, the Netherlands: De Tijdstroom, 2002.

Paz-y-Miño, Manuel A. *Católicos, evangélicos, otros creyentes e incrédulos* (Catholic, evangelicals, other believers and nonbelievers). Lima: FEPSM, 2005.

MANUEL A. PAZ Y MIÑO

LATINO LITERATURE, UNBELIEF IN. "Latino literature" refers to literary works, mostly in English, produced by people living in the United States who trace their ancestry to the Spanish-speaking countries of Latin America. With a current estimated population of more than forty million, Latinos, also called Hispanics, constitute the largest "minority" in America and they are providing new expressions of unbelief in American literature. The Latino population can be subdivided into four major subgroups: Mexican Americans (20.6 million), Puerto Ricans (3.4 million), Cuban Americans (1.2 million), and Dominicans (765,000). (Population figures are rounded and derived from the 2000 US Census.) The term *Chicano* is not as relevant in this context, being a self-identification used by some Mexican Americans particularly during the 1960s and 1970s.

The Latino religious experience has its roots in the Latin American religious experience, whose distinctive character resides in the particular, triadic mixture of religious traditions that have interacted only during the last five hundred years. Prior to 1492, Native Americans had never mixed with either Europeans or Africans. US Latinos have transferred and adapted that Latin American religious experience to the United States. In addition, US Latinos are undergoing a rapid shift from Catholicism to Protestantism.

Mexican American Literature. Mexican American history itself begins in 1848, when a large section of Mexico became part of the United States. For much of the nineteenth century and most of the twentieth century, authors such as Fray Angélico Chávez either expressed outright adoration of Catholicism or did not criticize religion or Catholicism directly. Antonio Villarreal's *Pocho* (1959), sometimes hailed as the first Chicano novel, marks the first significant espousal of ATHEISM by a Latino or Latina literary protagonist. In that story a young boy, Richard Rubio, experiences a journey from belief to unbelief as he enters adolescence. His questioning of Catholic dogma is intertwined with his emerging sexual awareness.

In the 1960s and early 1970s, a number of Mexican American authors began vociferous critiques of the Catholic Church and of organized religion in general. One of the most vocal was Oscar "Zeta" Acosta, who disappeared mysteriously in 1974. Once a Protestant, Acosta eventually left Christianity altogether. In *The Revolt of the Cockroach People* (1973), Acosta assailed the Catholic church for its oppression of Chicanos. Tomás Rivera centered his work . . . *And the Earth Did Not Swallow Him* (1971) on a young boy's growing suspicion that neither the devil nor God exist, especially in light of the evil that existed in a Chicano migrant farmer's world. In 1972 Rudolfo Anaya published *Bless Me, Ultima*, which quickly became a classic of Mexican American literature. Opting for a sort of pantheistic eclecticism, Anaya includes a scathing critique of organized religion, particularly Catholicism. Anaya also includes a strong and sympathetic atheist character who is persecuted for his unbelief.

Happy Birthday, Jesús (1994) by lawyer Ronald L. Ruiz is one of the most caustic attacks on Catholicism ever published in American literature. Ruiz has stated that he does not practice Catholicism or any kind of religion. *Happy Birthday, Jesús* presents the story of a young man named Jesús Olivas, who kills his sexually abusive priest in Fresno, California. Jesús also has a deep hatred for his grandmother, who abuses him with strict interpretations of Catholicism. The story suggests that the very theology of the Catholic church does not help society, but rather creates violent sociopaths. The fact that one can be forgiven easily, through confession and penitence, is an incentive to sin.

Unbelief has strong representation in feminist authors, who although not atheists, are skeptical of organized religion. Gloria Anzaldúa is perhaps the best-known Mexican American feminist writer. Her book *Borderlands/La*

Frontera: The New Mestiza (1987) outlines a strong rejection of Christianity in favor of indigenous Mesoamerican traditions. Ana Castillo penned a strong indictment of an androcentric Catholicism in *So Far from God* (1993), premised on the idea that all religious traditions should be judged by how they serve the needs of women.

Puerto Rican Literature. Puerto Rico became a territory of the United States in 1898, but Puerto Rican literature on the mainland came into full force in the aftermath of great migrations (mostly to New York City) after World War II. Some of the earliest expressions of unbelief in religion may be found in the work of Jesus Colón, an avowed Communist, who wrote *A Puerto Rican in New York and Other Sketches* (1961). Piri Thomas, who grew up in New York City, wrote some gritty works, including *Down These Mean Streets* (1967) and *Savior, Savior, Hold My Hand* (1972), that outline his dissatisfaction with the racist nature of Christianity. Ed Vega critiques many religious traditions in *The Comeback* (1985), a farcical expression of Ludwig FEUERBACH's thesis that God is a human creation.

Cuban American and Dominican Literature. The direct literary expression of unbelief among Cuban Americans and Dominicans has been negligible. Cuban American literature is best dated from 1959, when many Cubans came to the United States in the aftermath of the Communist takeover of the island by Fidel Castro. The reluctance to express unbelief is perhaps due to the fact that many Cuban Americans see themselves as fleeing an atheistic Communist government. Dominicans have not yet produced nearly the volume of work of the other subgroups in America. However, in *How the Garcia Girls Lost Their Accents* (1991) Julia Alvarez, the best-known Dominican American writer, portrays a growing secularization of characters after their immigration to America. Consumerism becomes the new religion. A similar secularization theme is found in *Dreaming in Cuban* (1992) by Cristina Garcia, a Cuban American whose alter ego in that book becomes disdainful of religion.

Conclusion. Despite the fact that most Latinos and Latinas describe themselves as religious, there is a small but notable group of Latino/Latina literati who openly espouse atheism or manifest SKEPTICISM toward organized religion. Otherwise, many Latino writers often resemble Anglo-American writers who have constructed eclectic and individualized forms of religion. Overall, Hispanics have already provided new expressions of unbelief that are only expected to increase as the Latino/Latina population grows even larger.

BIBLIOGRAPHY

Avalos, Hector, ed. *Introduction to the U.S. Latina and Latino Religious Experience*. Boston: Brill, 2004.

———. *Strangers in Our Own Land: Religion in U.S. Latina/Latino Literature*. Nashville: Abingdon, 2005.

Gordon, David J. *Literary Atheism*. New York: Peter Lang, 2002.

HECTOR AVALOS

LAW, THE, AND UNBELIEF. Since ancient Greece, at the very least, atheists, agnostics, and other freethinkers (see ATHEISM; AGNOSTICISM; FREETHOUGHT) have suffered legal prosecution as "infidels." The famous trial of SOCRATES was conducted to correct the wrongs he committed by "corrupting" the youth of Athens in teaching them to think and question even the religious dogma of their parents. Strange, then, that PLATO (who chronicled the trial of Socrates) thought that infidels ought to be executed. In his *Republic*, Plato makes "impiety" a criminal offense, subject to punishment by imprisonment of five years for the first offense, and by death if convicted twice.

In the second century of the common era, Christians were grouped with atheists as infidels under Roman law. The legal status of infidels is apt to shift over time as one religion becomes dominant and others fade. Turning the table, Saint Thomas Aquinas suggests that non-Christian infidels should be "exterminated from the world by death," but due to his Christian mercy, he thinks that should not occur until the third offense. As long as polities and churches were commingled either directly (as with the Holy Roman Empire and other theocracies) or less directly through monarchs whose authority stemmed from divine right, disbelief amounted to treason. BLASPHEMY and infidelity were offenses against the state itself, and atheists as well as members of minority religions were equally liable to legal action. During the Inquisition, this legal action meant swift and terrible justice by execution of atheists and other heretics, but it is arguable that modern law, as divorced from action by or on behalf of a state church, is an entirely different sort of creature.

Legal institutions, created separate and apart from churches, are meant to dole out justice and offer some minimum form of what we call "due process." These secular institutions have for some time nonetheless been the instruments of persecution via prosecution of atheists and agnostics. When embarked upon under the auspices of due process, the legal persecution of nonbelievers is especially odious; even so, it continues throughout the world to this day. The most remarkable forms of legal prosecutions for atheists and other infidels are for blasphemy, which crime is defined as some sort of direct challenge to religious dogma which warrants legal action. What is noteworthy about such prosecutions is that trials for blasphemy have been conducted outside of the church, by jurists, and under the color of the common law, even relatively recently.

Blasphemers. Of course, blasphemers have been tried and executed by religious authorities throughout the ages. Churches acting in various instances as judicial authorities either with the support of the state, or in the state's stead, have meted out such punishments since the dawn of religion. Christianity has been adept at carrying out such prosecutions, notably under the auspices of the Spanish Inquisition. Only the most liberal interpretation of the term *judicial* could make these proceedings part of a legal institution in the most modern sense. Appellate procedures were lacking or laughable, rules of evidence capricious. But blasphemy as a crime reared its ugly head even under modern legal systems at various times.

In 1676 Chief Justice Sir Matthew Hale in Britain developed the common law rule of blasphemy in a prosecution of a man for declaring the Bible to be a "cheat." Hale opined that "Christianity was part and parcel of the law of the land," and so one issuing blasphemous statements violated the common law and could be legally punished. By the close of the seventeenth century, numerous challenges to traditional notions of the Trinity encouraged passage of a British law making such blasphemers legally accountable. That act was partially repealed in 1813. Notable blasphemers subjected to legal action as well as social and professional stigma included Thomas WOOLSTON and John LOCKE. John Stuart MILL made himself liable to prosecution for his lectures calling into question the divine authority of the Bible in 1851.

Prosecutions under English common law and blasphemy statutes continued in the American colonies as well. The original law of the Connecticut colony, for instance, punished blasphemers with death. Under Maryland law, it was a crime even in the early twentieth century "to blaspheme or curse God or write or utter profane words about our Saviour Jesus Christ or of or concerning the Trinity or any of the persons thereof" (Md. Ann. Code [Bagby, 1924] art. 27, sec. 24). In the United States, however, which instituted a facially secular constitution whose authority stemmed from the people rather than God, blasphemy was usually not itself illegal, with the notable exceptions of Maryland, Maine, and Massachusetts. (In this connection, however, it is worth noting that a Massachusetts court went out of its way in *Commonwealth v. Kneeland*, 20 pick 206 [Mass. 1838] to hold that orthodox Christian belief was true, and other faiths mere "chimera" and products of "imagination" (see KNEELAND, ABNER). Even when not being specifically punished for blasphemy, "blasphemous contracts and associations" have suffered under the law. In the United States, a contract for leasing rooms as a forum for lectures concerning the potential untruth of Christ's teachings was held to be illegal as late as 1867 (*Cowan v. Milbourn*, L.R. 2 Ex. 230). In 1870 a Pennsylvania court held that the "Infidel Society" of Philadelphia was not entitled to receive a bequest because it was illegal, despite the legal incorporation of the society, and the technically correct manner of the bequest's language and execution" (*Zeisweiss v. James*, 63 Pa. 465). Prosecutions for blasphemy were for some time supplanted by prosecutions for "obscenity." Notably, Charles C. MOORE of Lexington, Kentucky, edited the freethought journal the *Blue Grass Blade*, and was prose-

cuted under the state's obscenity laws and subsequently served jail time in 1899. His crime was to publish speculation as to the divine nature of Jesus. In 1891 Moses HARMAN, the editor of an anarchist and free-love publication named *Lucifer, The Light Bearer*, published in Topeka, Kansas, also served jail time for publishing obscene materials speculating about established religious dogmas (see SEX RADICALISM AND UNBELIEF).

The applicability of the First Amendment's Establishment Clause took some time to be settled with regard to the states, even after the passage of the Fourteenth Amendment, and so disestablishment in the States is still not settled according to some stalwart theocratic Justices. (In his written opinion in the *Newdow* decision regarding the use of "under God" in the pledge, US Supreme Court Justice Clarence Thomas went out of his way to make his legal case that somehow the First Amendment's Establishment Clause is not applicable to the states even though the rest of the First Amendment apparently is.) As early as 1811, Chancellor Kent of New York offered an explanation for disparate treatment of non-Christians, arguing that members of religious minorities and other infidels were "imposters" (specifically discussing Muslims who at the time outnumbered Christians worldwide), and infidels had no rights before a court in a Christian nation such as the United States (*People v. Ruggles*, 8 Johns 291 [N.Y. 1811]).

Moreover, atheists, agnostics, and other infidels have been subject to legal action and discrimination under the law in subtler, though not less harmful, ways.

Oaths and Impeachment. Atheists, agnostics, and others who profess no belief in a god of vengeance or in an afterlife system of rewards or punishments had long been legally prevented from giving testimony under oath. The rule was derived from English common law and survived until rather recently in US federal and state law, either by practice, common law, or by statute. Even when an atheist was permitted to testify, his or her lack of religious faith could be used to impeach the credibility of the witness. Thus, in a Tennessee case in which a civil judgment was awarded to an atheist, the defendant appealed on the basis that he was not allowed to inquire as to the plaintiff's disbelief in "God or a future state of rewards and punishments." The cause was remanded for a new trial, and the plaintiff lost after receiving the condemnation of the Supreme Court of Tennessee, which added insult to injury, stating, "The man who has the hardihood to avow that he does not believe in a God, shows a recklessness of moral character and utter want of moral sensibility, such as very little entitles him to be heard or believed in a court of justice in a country designated as Christian" (*Odell v. Koppee*, 5 Heisk. 88). New Hampshire's appellate court said similarly: "He who openly and deliberately avows that he has no belief in the existence of a God, . . . is unworthy of any credit in a court of justice" (*Norton v. Ladd*, 4 N.H. 444).

As recently as 1929 this rule was used in at least two

cases in North Carolina to discredit the testimony of self-professed communist strikers who were also not so coincidentally atheists. In the 1920s and 1930s, this rule was almost exclusively used in prosecutions of reputed communists and other liberal "agitators." As of 1938, seven states explicitly prohibited testimony from anyone professing disbelief. Eight others allowed impeachment of the witness on the basis of his or her disbelief. In other words, a witness's atheism or status as an "infidel" could be used to suggest to a jury that his or her testimony was questionable. This author knows of at least one case in New York State, involving a defendant on trial for manslaughter who had named himself "Calvin of Oakknoll," whose atheism was used to show that he supposedly lacked regard for human life. He lost the last of his many appeals via writs of *habeas corpus* and died in prison. This happened in the 1990s. The author's knowledge is based on his work for the New York State attorney general's office in countering the appeal.

This principle has also been used to justify the exclusion even of jurors who will not swear on a Bible. Again, a Tennessee court held that the atheist juror could "not hold any office . . . because he could not take an oath—he cannot be trusted" and that he was "an evil genius in a sacred place" (*McClure v. State*, 1 Yerger [9 Tenn.] 207).

The theory of excluding the testimony of atheists, or preventing them from sitting in judgment on a jury, has been that their disbelief in a God of vengeance who metes out punishment in an afterlife fails to act as a deterrent to lying to disbelievers. Absent from this analysis is an examination of how a forgiving God might excuse worldly lying for the faithful, who by all accounts lie on the stand just as frequently, if not more so, than do atheists.

Other, more egregious, fates than being prohibited from testifying or having testimony discredited have been met by atheists under US law. One legal rule that effectively encouraged the assassination of atheists and other infidels is a judicially carved exception to the rule of dying declarations.

Dying Declarations. One particularly odious legal rule which treated the atheist, agnostic, or infidel differently under the law was the rule regarding "dying declarations." Typically, the unsworn, out-of-court statements of another are inadmissible by quotation in court. This is the age-old rule of hearsay. The justification for the rule is that the person who is alleged to have made a statement is not available in court to verify it, and there is no way to probe its truth. There are a number of exceptions to the rule, one of which is that of "dying declarations." A dying declaration may be admissible for the truth of the matters asserted in it because of the presumption that one who is dying has no reason to lie; he or she has nothing to gain by it. Another part of the assumption is that deathbed declarations are presumptively true because of the imminence of death, and the dying person's fear of the salvation of his or her everlasting soul . . . so again, merely having nothing to gain by lying is apparently not enough—rather fear of the consequences of lying is what makes such statements presumptively valid under the rule as it long stood (see also DEATHBED CLAIMS CONCERNING UNBELIEVERS).

Naturally, given the religious explanation for the validity of deathbed statements, it is clear how the rule might be challenged for nonbelievers. The net effect of the challenge, and of exclusion of such declarations, is what is truly frightening. The United States Supreme Court stated (*Carver v. U.S.*, 164 U.S. 694): "[Dying declarations] . . . may be discredited by proof that [the deceased] did not believe in a future state of rewards or punishments." The rule has been used in far too many cases to protect Christians accused of the murders of infidels.

In a Missouri case from 1920, two men were found by a jury to be guilty of murder. They shot an allegedly peaceable, elderly, and ill man. His sons found him dying from several bullet wounds, and he told his sons the manner and cause of his fatal injuries, as well as who exactly the assailants were. The trial court did not permit the defendant's attorney to inquire into the dead man's alleged atheism. The Supreme Court of Missouri held that the trial court's exclusion of evidence of the dead man's atheism was a reversible error (grounds for reversing the prior verdict), and remanded the case back to the trial court with instructions that the evidence of atheism should be admitted and could be used to help undermine the dead man's credibility (*State v. Rozell*, 225 S.W. 931).

The Court of Appeal of California held that the dying declarations of nonbelievers must never be admitted without a specific admonition by the court that the jury *must* view such statements "with great caution" (*People v. Lim Foon*, 155 Pac. 477). In New York the medieval reasoning behind this rule was upheld by a court stating that "no testimony is entitled to credit, unless delivered under the solemnity of an oath, which comes home to the conscience of the witness, and will create a tie arising from his belief that false swearing would expose him to punishment in the life to come" (*Jackson v. Gridley*, 18 Johns. 98).

The rule is clearly derived from that regarding the giving of testimony and swearing of oaths, but when applied to the exception of dying declarations, unmistakably makes it open season on atheists. Ironically, this rule contradicts the oft-stated myth that "there are no atheists in foxholes," which rests on the assumption that, seeing death as imminent, atheists almost invariably repent and become believers. If that were so, wouldn't all deathbed declarations be presumptively believable, as even atheists would be, at least at that moment, as trustworthy as any believer?

Instead, dying atheists are treated under the rule of dying declarations as presumptively evil. As a Mississippi court noted, "the law presumes, not that they will be converted, that being a remote possibility, for between them, as with the devil, whose subjects they be, and the Christians, there is perpetual hostility, and can be no peace" (*Heirn v. Bridalut*, 37 Miss. 209, 226).

The logic of this exception to the hearsay exception holds for all infidels, agnostics included, as well as Unitarians (see UNITARIANISM TO 1961; UNITARIAN UNIVERSALISM) and others who do not share a belief in a vengeful God and a future state of rewards and punishments. This is the explicit language and reasoning of the US Supreme Court in the *Carver* decision cited above.

A West Virginia court made plain the net result of the dying declaration exception as applied to nonbelievers, stating: "His goods may be stolen, his dwelling broken into by the midnight robber, or burned by the incendiary; his child may be beaten, or his wife murdered before his face, and the offender escape because of the incapacity of the injured man to give evidence against him" (*State v. Hood*, 59 S.E. 971).

Holding Public Office. Even in enlightened times, it has been the law in several states that atheists, agnostics, and other infidels could not be sworn in to hold public office. Once again, the practice originates in the inability or unwillingness of atheists to swear oaths, but in a number of cases the principle has been extended to amount to explicit prohibition. As late as 1953, prior to the *Torcaso* decision (*Torcaso v. Watkins*, 223 Md. 49, 162 A.2d 438, 364 U.S. 877 [1960]), eight state constitutions required belief in God in order to hold public office. By extension, the prohibition would act to prevent even civil service by atheists in those states. This was so despite the US Constitution's provision in Article VI declaring that "no religious test shall ever be required as a Qualification to any Office or public Trust under the United States."

As with other discriminatory practices against atheists, this rule would apply even to certain Christians. For instance, in Maryland, the law required belief in "either a present or future divine punishment" as well as a belief in God (Md. Const. art. 37. Other state laws as of 1960 included: Ark. Const. art. 19, sec. 1; Miss. Const. art. 14, sec. 265; N.C. Const. art. VI, sec. 8; PA Const. art. I, sec. 4; S.C. Const. art. XVII, sec 4; Tenn. Const. art. IX, sec 2; Tex. Const. art I, sec. 4.) Obviously deists, Unitarians, Universalists (see UNIVERSALISM TO 1961), Quakers, and other liberal Christians who reject a notion of hell or of a vengeful God, would be technically disqualified from holding office under the Maryland rule.

In some states, the belief in God and of a future state of rewards and punishments was required simply to *vote* (S.C. Const. of 1778, Art. XIII). South Carolina was one of those states that, even as late as 1895, maintained that "[n]o person who denie[d] the existence of a Supreme Being shall hold any office under this Constitution" (S.C. Const. of 1778, Art. I sec. 4). Massachusetts and Maryland denied the office of governor to all except Christians, and in New Hampshire, North Carolina, New Jersey, and South Carolina, only Protestants could be governor.

These restrictions and similar legal iniquities directed against atheists were effectively declared unconstitutional under the *Torcaso* decision, by which the Supreme Court held that state constitutions' provisions requiring a belief in God were unconstitutional deprivations of liberty. The enforceability of these provisions in the present day is at least doubtful, but certainly may be apt to change with the resurgence of fundamentalism.

Conclusion. The laws of theocratic states existing today methodically discriminate against both unbelievers and "infidels," but, as discussed above, theocratic systems of law by which the church and state are the same entity do not amount to what we would consider as justice in a modern state. Law as a social institution, with a system of courts and a principle of "rule of law," has nonetheless been used as an instrument of persecution by *religious people* even where it has not been under the direct authority of any particular *religion*. This possibility, as described in the instances and examples above, is worth noting. That secular legal systems such as that of the United States and those of the various American states have been used to persecute unbelievers even until modern times challenges the notion that somehow atheism is not a civil rights issue. It clearly is.

In sum, a number of common law and statutory forms of outright discrimination have existed in the laws of both England and the United States. The spirit behind them continues to motivate fundamentalists to enact new laws—or to seek enforcement of existing laws—in ways designed to abrogate the civil rights of unbelievers. The history of such discrimination teaches us that we ignore those motivations at our peril.

BIBLIOGRAPHY

American Civil Liberties Union. "Legal Discrimination against Religious Disbelievers." December 1938.
"The First Amendment and Civil Disabilities." *Duke Bar Journal* 3, no. 2 (Spring 1953).
Royle, Edward, ed. *The Infidel Tradition: From Paine to Bradlaugh.* London: Macmillan, 1976.
Smith, George H. *Atheism: The Case against God.* Amherst, NY: Prometheus Books, 1979.
Swancara, Frank. "Judicial Aspersions on the Non-Religious." *Journal of Criminal Law and Criminology* 23, no. 2 (July–August 1932).
Wright, Herbert. "Religious Liberty under the Constitution of the United States." *Virginia Law Review* 27, no. 1 (1940).

DAVID KOEPSELL

LAW, HARRIET (1831–1897), English feminist and freethought lecturer. Born Harriet Teresa Frost in Ongar, Essex, her early experience was as a strict Baptist. When her father's farm failed, the family moved to London, where she ran a school and Sunday school. At the Philpott Street Secular Hall, she met freethinkers such as Charles BRADLAUGH, Charles SOUTHWELL, and George Jacob HOLYOAKE. By the time she married secularist Edward Law in 1855, she too held secularist beliefs. In 1859 she began to lecture in her own right.

She lectured throughout the country for over twenty years. She was said to have great command of an audience, a quick memory, and a powerful ability to deal with hostile audience members. Her polemical skills were assisted by her deep knowledge of the Bible. Compared with the educated and polished Annie BESANT, Law was sturdy and steadfast, having, according to George W. FOOTE, "a powerful common-sense kind of eloquence."

She was based in Birmingham, and from 1876 to 1878 took over the running of the *Secular Chronicle*, which had been begun by Birmingham printer George Reddalls in 1872. According to Foote she made a mess of it, but the *Chronicle* was sustained and its scope was widened to include republicanism, cooperative ideas, the International Working Men's Association, and women's rights. Freethought publishing was not a route to financial success, and it is thought she lost one thousand pounds through the venture. She was the first freethought publisher to give space to Karl MARX. She and the journal remained impartial during the dispute within the NATIONAL SECULAR SOCIETY (NSS) over the defense of the birth control pamphlet *The Fruits of Philosophy* (see BIRTH CONTROL AND UNBELIEF), and was neutral regarding the resistance to the authoritarianism of Bradlaugh.

Harriet Law was active in the national movement and was offered, but refused, the vice presidency of the NSS in 1867 and 1876. She was elected to the general council of the International Working Men's Association in 1867. In 1878 her health began to decline, and she was inactive in the movement for the rest of her life. While not an intellectual, she was according to Bradlaugh, "earnest [and] brusquely honest."

BIBLIOGRAPHY

Foote, G. W. "Harriet Law." *Freethinker*, July 4, 1915.
Moss, Arthur B. "Famous Freethinkers I Have Known—Mrs Harriet Law." *Freethinker*, June 6, 1915.
Royle, Edward. *Radicals, Secularists and Republicans: Popular Freethought in Britain, 1866–1915.* Manchester, UK: Manchester University Press, 1980.
Wheeler, J. M. "Death of Harriet Law." *Freethinker*, August 1, 1897.

JIM HERRICK

LEA, HENRY CHARLES (1825–1909), American historian, publisher, and philanthropist. Henry Lea was born into a Philadelphia book-publishing dynasty begun in colonial times by his maternal grandfather, Matthew Carey. He was privately tutored and did not attend college. During adolescence, and as a young man beginning his responsibilities at the publishing firm, Lea pursued varied literary and scientific interests as an autodidact. He published poetry, translations from ancient and modern languages, and empirical scientific papers.

At twenty-two, while convalescing from illness brought on by overwork, Lea read French court memoirs and was fascinated. He set out to write the history of the coercive aspects of the medieval church using an objective scientific methodology. Understanding the jurisprudence, economics, and geopolitics behind the events would benefit his study of that history, much as understanding physics and chemistry benefits the study of life sciences.

Lea developed a worldwide network of correspondents and booksellers for procuring all pertinent research materials. He bought or borrowed when possible, and when necessary had archival materials copied out by paid copyists. From those resources grew Lea's massive fifty-year output of books and articles on such topics as the Inquisition (*A History of the Inquisition of the Middle Ages*, 1887; *Chapters from the Religious History of Spain Connected with the Inquisition*, 1890), priestly celibacy (*An Historical Sketch of Sacerdotal Celibacy in the Christian Church*, 1867), priests as unpunished sex offenders (*Studies in Church History*, 1883), and the prosecution of witches, demon exorcism, and the marketing of indulgences (*A History of Auricular Confession and Indulgences in the Latin Church*, 1896). They were groundbreaking works in their day and most are still a pleasure to read.

For Lea, rule by a monolithic prelacy exemplified the harm arising from religion. His writings reflected his apprehensions about an ascendant Roman Catholic Church in the United States.

Lea was a pillar of the Republican Party and the Union League. He took charge of local recruitment—including African Americans—for the Union army. "The Bible View of Slavery," a pamphlet by Bishop John Henry Hopkins, was seriously touted as justification for the Confederate cause: in 1863 Lea published a pseudonymous, albeit scripturally accurate, satire, "The Bible View of Polygamy," in response.

Lea's publishing interests—specializing increasingly in medical and scientific books—and his real estate holdings flourished. He was among the largest benefactors of institutions of learning, libraries, and hospitals in southeastern Pennsylvania. He was a high-profile opinion leader, exerting influence on a wide range of public policy matters.

Lea declared no religious stance of his own. No personal religious crisis shaped him. Among his forebears, diverse religious traditions—including Roman Catholicism—were represented. He did contribute financially to the First Unitarian Church in Philadelphia, and its emeritus pastor gave his eulogy. Lea's library, papers, research materials, and the reassembled oak-paneled library room from his Walnut Street mansion are housed in the Van Pelt Library of the University of Pennsylvania.

BIBLIOGRAPHY

Bradley, Edward Sculley. *Henry Charles Lea: A Biography.* Philadelphia: University of Pennsylvania Press, 1931.
Cheney, Edward Potts. "On the Life and Works of Henry Charles Lea." *Proceedings of the American Philosophical Society* 50, no. 194 (January–April 1911).

EDMUND D. COHEN

LEIBNIZ, GOTTFRIED WILHELM VON (1646–1716), French philosopher, mathematician, and Enlightenment figure. Gottfried Wilhelm von Leibniz was referred to by his contemporaries as the last man who knew everything. While not true, it was also not much of an exaggeration. A genuine polymath, in addition to making important contributions to philosophy and mathematics he was also a historian, librarian, diplomat, physicist, legal advisor, linguist, and scholar; he exemplified the Enlightenment thirst for knowledge.

The son of a professor of moral philosophy at the University of Leipzig, Leibniz was extremely well educated. Eschewing a career in academia, he spent most of his life as a diplomat, serving the dukes of Hanover in various professional capacities which entailed his traveling throughout most of Europe. This both broadened his knowledge of the world and increased his concern to find a solution to the growing religious warfare that was raging at the time.

Leibniz was a critic of much of the religious thinking of his time, but was by no means an unbeliever. In fact, he is perhaps best known—other than for codiscovering the differential and integral calculus—for his defense of the deity in light of the problem of evil (see EVIL, PROBLEM OF), in his famous work from 1710, *Essais de Théodicée sur a bonté de Dieu, la liberté de l'homme et l'origne du mal* (Essays of Theodicy on the Goodness of God, the Liberty of Humankind and the Origin of Evil). In it, he made the claim that God could have created the world any way he wished, and since he is all good, it must be the case that this is the best of all possible worlds. The cause of suffering is due to the gift of free will, which allows humans to perform heinous acts but also prevents them from being mere puppets. This answer to the problem of evil proved wanting, and was mercilessly parodied in VOLTAIRE's classic work *Candide*, where Leibniz's views are expressed by the ridiculous character Doctor Pangloss (which means "All Tongue").

Hoping to develop a comprehensive system of knowl-edge based upon logical principles, Leibniz was wary of the materialistic philosophy of René DESCARTES. However, partly because of his myriad activities and partly because of an inability to focus his attentions, he was never able to produce the grand unifying work of philosophy he hoped would overcome the growing influence of ATHEISM and religious differences.

In his quest for international peace, Leibniz devised a scheme to unite Protestantism and Catholicism by focusing on their areas of agreement; when this came to naught, he focused his attentions on bridging the gaps between Western and Eastern thought. He was fascinated by the information Christian missionaries were sending back to Europe about China and the Far East, and speculated as to why these countries seemed to have such moral citizens even without knowing the message of the Holy Bible. He jocularly wrote that the Chinese should send missionaries to civilize the Europeans. Leibniz's follower Christian Wolff, a pious Christian, was deprived of his chair in philosophy in 1721 because of his praise for CONFUCIUS. He had argued that Confucian ethics and Christian ethics were compatible. Immanuel KANT, another great Enlightenment figure, was trained in the Leibniz-Wolff tradition, and his own influential work "Toward a Perpetual Peace" (1796), which postulated a prototype for the United Nations, was based in part on Leibniz's dream of a world united by rational principles, where religious and national differences would be overridden through the common pursuit of truth.

BIBLIOGRAPHY

Adams, Robert Merrihew. *Leibniz: Determinist, Theist, Idealist.* New York: Oxford University Press, 1998.
Jolley, Nicholas. *Leibniz.* New York: Routledge, 2005.
Mates, Benson. *The Philosophy of Leibniz: Metaphysics and Language.* New York: Oxford University Press, 1989.

TIMOTHY J. MADIGAN

LEICESTER SECULAR SOCIETY, THE. The Leicester Secular Society was a leading British regional secularist group in the second half of the nineteenth century; its Secular Hall is the only building erected by an English secularist or freethought group of that period still under its original ownership.

Leicester, a town in England's East Midlands, had a radical tradition of Owenites (see OWEN, ROBERT) and secularists in the 1840s and 1850s. Engineer Josiah Gimson and tailor William Holyoak (no relation to freethought leader George Jacob HOLYOAKE) were prominent in this movement. It is claimed that the Leicester Secular Society was founded in 1851, but although the group existed intermittently from that date, it was not fully established until 1867.

In the 1870s the division within the NATIONAL SECular SOCIETY (NSS) affected the Leicester Secular Society. The conflict between the Bradlaughites (followers of Charles BRADLAUGH) and the dissenting group was partly personal, and partly a difference over strategy, whether to espouse forthright atheism or a more positive approach. The Leicester Secular Society supported the anti-Bradlaugh British Secular Union, and Gimson refused to let the Society's premises for NSS events. The division was healed by the end of the decade.

In 1869 the Society acquired premises with a reading room at 43 Humberstone Gate. (Reading was greatly important to nineteenth-century secularists.) In 1873 they moved to 77 Humberstone Gate with the hope of building a new hall. The Secular Hall Company was launched in 1872 with John Sladen of Sladen's Indigo Works as president, Josiah Gimson of Gimson's Engineering Works as treasurer, and W. H. Holyoak as secretary. The Secular Hall held its opening ceremony in 1881 with a lineup of luminaries in attendance that included Bradlaugh, George Jacob Holyoake, G. W. FOOTE, Charles WATTS, and Harriet LAW.

A renowned feature of the Hall was the sculptures decorating the front of the structure: busts of SOCRATES, VOLTAIRE, Thomas PAINE, Robert Owen, and—Jesus. Local Christians were outraged at the inclusion of Jesus in a secular pantheon, but the secularists considered that like the others, Jesus was a freethinker who had challenged the established religious orthodoxy of his day.

The Leicester Secular Society prospered better than most such groups in the latter part of the century. Their "positive" secularism compared favorably in the eyes of many with the purely negative atheism of the NSS. The hall was used for lectures, reading, a Sunday school, and social activities.

Two notables among the society's organizing secretaries were the former Franciscan Joseph McCABE (1898), a famous FREETHOUGHT writer and lecturer, and F. J. Gould (1899), who was well known for his espousal of moral education, that is, to encourage and promote the idea and practice of moral behavior in schools.

The society continued with rather varied success during the twentieth century, but the centenary of the hall was feted in 1981 with the well-known Labour politician Michael Foot on the platform. Today most of the building is rented out to other users, but it is still owned by the Leicester Secular Society which continues its existence in a modest way.

BIBLIOGRAPHY

Gould, F. J. *History of the Leicester Secular Society.* Leicester: Leicester Secular Society, 1900.
Royle, Edward. *Radicals, Secularists and Republicans: Popular Freethought in Britain, 1866–1915.* Manchester: Manchester University Press, 1980.

JIM HERRICK

LENIN, VLADIMIR ILYICH (1870–1924), Russsian socialist revolutionary. Given the focus of the *New Encyclopedia of Unbelief*, this article will stress Lenin's positions regarding religion and to a much lesser extent his positions regarding empiricism and POSITIVISM. None of these makes Lenin an important historical figure; his importance lies is his role as a political and revolutionary leader. What Lenin had to say about religion and philosophy was always subservient to his political and revolutionary agenda, and takes what importance it has from that.

Vladimir Lenin was the principal figure in the development of MARXISM in the early twentieth century, the first and a deeply influential leader of the Soviet Union, and the architect and developer of the Bolshevik Revolution. Still, the struggle against religion and to develop and to propagate ATHEISM so that it would become an integral part of popular consciousness in Communist societies—eventually in a Communist world—and to develop as a first step an atheist society free of religion, was a key aim of both Lenin and the Soviet Union (see PROPAGANDA, ANTIRELIGIOUS [SOVIET]). As Lenin and most others understood it, Marxism is materialist (see MATERIALISM, PHILOSOPHICAL), and as such left no room for belief in God or belief in immortality.

Capitalist democracies display a commitment to the independence of state from religion. The state must be neutral vis-à-vis religion; our societies must remain pluralist, and there must be neither an insistent state religion (demanding strict adherence by all its citizens and/or forming the official agenda of the state) nor state antireligion. Religion, nonreligion, or irreligion are seen as a private matter exempt from state demand, a need for official authorization, or even expressions of state preference or orientation. Indeed, one of the key functions of the state, on standard liberal preconceptions, is to protect us from these things. Lenin's position was importantly different from this liberal ideal. It is important to understand that position and its rationale.

Formation of Lenin's Views on Religion. Lenin was brought up in a religious but unbigoted atmosphere. At age fifteen or sixteen he lost his faith; this occurred long before he had any contact with or knowledge of Marxism, and took a typical rationalistic, Enlightenment-based, and anticlerical form, much more in the tradition of Baron d'HOLBACH than Ludwig FEUERBACH (see RATIONALISM; ENLIGHTENMENT, UNBELIEF DURING THE; ANTICLERICALISM). He thought, and would continue to think throughout his life, that the development of science had made atheism obvious (see RELIGION IN CONFLICT WITH SCIENCE). For Lenin, the beliefs in God and immortality and their associated doctrines had been shown decisively to be illusions, and often dangerous illusions. A scientific education revealed that religion was little better than a nest of superstitions.

It was only later, after studying Karl MARX and Friedrich Engels, that he came to see something of the extent of the class content of religion and the harmful social functions of religion. Lenin maintained that the very idea of God "has always lulled to sleep and dulled 'social sentiments' substituting dead for living things, always being an idea of slavery . . . [that] *tied down* the oppressed *classes* with a faith in 'the divine character of the oppressors.' The real content of the idea of God consists of 'filth, prejudices, sanctification of stupor. Religion was in the service of autocracy; churches were means of keeping the masses submissive and humble, an "ideological knot" used to keep the exploiters in power and the masses in a state of misery, on the one hand, and of serfdom and monarchy on the other.'"

This is strong stuff, but Lenin's hatred of and opposition to religion was very strong. He had no interest in inquiring into or discussing religion in order to see whether it has any justification or a raison d'être. That it had neither, he believed, except as an ideological instrument of suppression by the ruling classes, was so obvious that it was not worth discussing. The merits, or lack thereof, of religion were not something to be discussed; rather, our energies should be devoted to eradicating religion whenever and wherever possible. Any deviation from that aim was merely temporary and tactical. He was interested in ascertaining how and under what conditions religion could be brought to an end and be replaced by a thoroughly materialist and revolutionary outlook.

Lenin's interest in religion, to repeat, was tactical and political. He saw religion as an ideological weapon of the exploiting classes; what was required was to struggle effectively against it, not to prattle on concerning whether it could have any justification. Enlightenment philosophers and scientists had already conclusively established the case for atheism.

Lenin's Tactics toward Religion. We should distinguish three periods during which Lenin, always taking his tactical approach to religion, faced sharply different situations with regard to it. The first period was slightly before and around the revolution of 1905. During that period Lenin's tactical consideration of religion centered mainly on opportunities to expand political agitation. The second stage peaked around 1917, in the context of the second and successful Bolshevik Revolution. At this time, in his struggle with certain tendencies and factions within the revolutionary party, he set forth a Bolshevik program and tactics on religion. The third stage came when, as the leader of the newly formed Soviet Union, he was charged with leading its governance in very difficult circumstances. In the latter situation he was faced with a massively religiously orthodox population hostile to the aspirations of the Soviet Union. Against this background, he had to make policy for the new society in accordance with his (and the party's) antireligious social program: a social program for a thoroughly secular socialist society.

During the first phase Lenin stressed presenting the Orthodox Church as a servant of czarist aristocracy: an oppressor of the people, keeping them ignorant and superstitious, leading them into slavish obedience and subservience, and promising that if they obeyed church doctrine and the established order, they would in their "next life" be rewarded with a glorious heavenly kingdom and with perpetual bliss. The clergy—"gendarmes in cassocks"—perpetuated this heavenly swindle along with a host of other superstitions. The clergy aimed to keep the masses docile in their ignorance and fear. (The fear of hell was particularly driven into them.) Lenin lay stress on exposing these things, and in an anticlericalism that demanded complete separation of the church from the state and of the church from the schools, as well as freedom of conscience. Here he supported the cause of sectarian religious opposition to the established church, hoping to bring the sectarian faithful over to supporting the revolution.

During the second phase, which peaked in 1917 but began with the 1905 revolution, Lenin turned his attention to setting a Communist Party program toward religion. In his *Socialism and Religion*, written in 1905 and probably his most important general statement concerning religion, Lenin wrote:

We demand that religion be regarded as a private matter in relations to the state, but under no circumstances can we consider religion to be a private matter with regard to our own party. The state must not concern itself with religion; religious societies must not be connected with the state power. Everyone should be absolutely free to profess whatever religion he prefers or to recognize no religion. . . . There must be no discrimination whatever in the rights of citizens on religious grounds. . . . No subsidies must be paid to the state church, and no state grants must be made to ecclesiastical and religious societies, which must be absolutely free, voluntary associations of like-minded citizens independent of the state. . . . As for the party of the socialist proletariat, religion is not a private matter. Our party is a league of conscious, leading fighters for the liberation of the working class. Such a league cannot and must not be indifferent to lack of consciousness, ignorance or obscurantism in the shape of religious beliefs. We demand a complete separation of church from state in order to fight against religious fog with purely ideological and only with ideological weapons—our press, our word. We created our league, the RSDWP [Russian Social Democratic Workers Party], among other things, precisely for such a struggle against all kinds of religious deception of the workers.

However, Lenin quickly qualified his stern stance by remarking that the party should not forbid the admission of believers who are committed to the proletarian revolution and to socialism. With a good tactical sense, he remarked that the enemies of socialism would like to split the socialist movement by playing off its believers against its atheists. The party should for the time being tone down its antireligious propaganda (discursive agitation and indoctrination). As far as its platform was concerned, the party should remain firmly atheistic, but would not strike committed comrades from its ranks because of their religion. Lenin's hope and belief was that by participating in the class struggle, believing comrades would come to see the reactionary, obfuscating, and thoroughly instrumental role religion plays in supporting and furthering the interests of capitalism.

Lenin is again tactical here. He is "softening" neither his atheism nor his belief in the need for a Marxist socialism to display explicit atheism and a firm antireligious orientation. This can be clearly seen by his intense negative reaction to the so-called god builders, a faction of party intellectuals that included Anatoly V. Lunacharsky and Maxim Gorky. Lenin did not call for their expulsion from the party, but his criticism of their position was unqualifiedly hostile. The god builders argued for a humanist religion without God or any other "spookish" substitutes. They called for a completely secularized religion of humanity in the tradition of Auguste COMTE and Feuerbach, a religion of humanity and of love and respect for the "new proletarian man" who would come slowly into existence with the struggle for and finally the achievement of socialism.

One might have thought Lenin would have been mildly amused by the prospect of attaching such harmless decorations to the cause. Instead he reacted explosively. He saw god building as a subtle bit of illusory irrealism and antimaterialism, dangerous because in effect, though not in intent, it served as propaganda to revive religion among the masses. For Lenin, it was all the more dangerous because it was cleverly disguised, though not by conscious subterfuge on the part of the god builders. He recognized that they were not aware of the ideological content of what they were setting forth. The god builders saw their program as a sanitized method by which a Communist should bring enlightenment to workers and peasants. Lenin believed it would have an entirely different effect. The problem with a refined secular religion without God, as Lenin saw it— again in tactical terms—was that (as he wrote to Gorky):

The crowd is much more able to see through a million *physical* sins, dirty tricks, violences and *physical* infections which are therefore much less dangerous than is the *subtle* spiritual idea of dear little god [*bozhen'ka*] arrayed in the smartest of ideological costumes. A Catholic priest who violates young girls (about whom I happened to read just now in a German newspaper) is *much less* dangerous . . . than are priests who do not wear cassocks, priests without vulgar religion, ideological and democratic priests who preach the creation and making of dear little gods. . . .

There was a time in history when . . . the struggle of democracy and the proletariat took the form of the struggle of *one religious* idea against the other. But this time had passed long ago. Now, both in Europe and in Russia, *every*, even the most refined, most well-intentioned, defence or justification of the idea of god is a justification of reaction.

Both "god-building" and "god-seeking" are essentially one and the same exercise in "ideological necrophilia." Regardless of the subjective intentions of their advocates, *objectively*, under the present relationship of class forces, they help to adorn and sweeten the political and economic oppression of the people.

According to Lenin, the party must oppose all forms of religion and religious consciousness, both Russian Orthodoxy and a Feuerbachian religion of humanity, with the firmly materialist and scientific worldview of the Marxism of Marx and Engels.

From where we stand now, this sounds more like Marxist fundamentalism, like a Communist church, than a scientific orientation. Moreover, there is little evidence that such humanistic religious talk ever seduced the masses. Where the masses noticed it at all, if they did, it would surely have seemed to them a perversion of their faith and of all the promises that religion held out for them. Atheism and Marxism had nothing to fear from those god builders. This dispute was purely an exercise in point-counterpoint among the chattering classes, with little ideological or practical effect.

The third phase of Lenin's treatment of religion began after the successful Bolshevik Revolution. It centered around the problem of leading the newly emergent Soviet Union in the face of an implacable and openly hostile Russian Orthodox Church, which had soaked the masses of the peasantry in the crudest form of religion. It was one thing to claim that the state must be religiously neutral while the party must not when the Bolsheviks were not in power—but it was quite another thing when the Bolsheviks were in power, when they, with their atheistic commitments and atheistic worldview, governed, and in some functional sense *were*, the state. In such a situation, how could the party's nonneutrality toward religion fit with state neutrality toward religion? It did not and could not.

By decree, the Bolshevik vanguard party nationalized all ecclesiastical and monastic lands, separating the church from the state and schools from the church. The church was no longer a juridical person and had no right to own property. This in effect made the church dependent on the state. It was also the case that antireligious propaganda was intensified. Freedom of conscience came in effect to mean freedom from "religious opium"; private religious instruction was forbidden for people under the age of eighteen; most monastic institutions were disbanded; the Soviet Commissariat of Justice carried out a campaign of opening Orthodox religious relics to expose religious frauds; churches were deprived by government decree of all facilities for the training of clergy or the publication of religious literature.

Lenin remained zealously committed. He even wrote a new section for the party program adopted at the Eighth Congress in 1919 and reaffirmed in 1923 by the Comintern's executive committee, and declared obligatory for all its member parties. In this section Lenin wrote: "The party strives for the complete dissolution of the ties between the exploiting classes and the organization of religious propaganda, as well as for the real emancipation of the toiling masses from religious prejudices; to this end, the party organizes the widest possible scientific, educational and anti-religious propaganda."

Immediately afterward Lenin, always the astute tactician, added, "At the same time it is necessary carefully to avoid giving offence to the religious sentiments of believers as that only leads to that strengthening of religious fanaticism."

Lenin believed he must engage in the strategies and tactics necessary for the achievement and consolidation of socialism. With this aim in mind, Lenin pressed relentlessly for action on the antireligious front. But he still remained carefully tactical. In his last public statement concerning religion, "On the Significance of Militant Materialism" (1922), he acknowledged the need for flexibility as well as moderation in carrying a long-range approach to atheistic indoctrination. He recognized that this was often ignored in the practices of the party cadres, and he called for more intelligent defenses of atheism. In this, cadres should take instruction from the eighteenth-century materialists.

Despite his conviction that tactics should change with context, from the age of sixteen until the end of his life Lenin maintained his Enlightenment trust that science and reason would bring liberation from the mystifications and illusions of religion. Like Lenin himself, the party, even in the governing of the state, "could not be philosophically neutral: it was materialistic, therefore atheistic and anti-clerical, and this world-outlook could not be a matter of political indifference." What was needed, he thought, was a committed government led by a vanguard party for an atheist state.

Leninism, Justice, and Unbelief. Many secular humanists (including many who are firm atheists) are first shocked by Lenin, and then, on reflection, led to reject much of Lenin's stance concerning religion. Even some of those who are firm socialists as well as atheists are reluctant to embrace a view that commits socialism, even a Marxist socialism, to a militant atheism in matters of governing policy. They are reluctant, that is, to commit socialism to atheism (militant or nonmilitant) as a matter of state or even party policy. They have no wish to be the mirror image of the Vatican nation-state. To them, religious belief or unbelief should be purely a matter of private conviction. (Lenin, of course, would

view this as liberal shilly-shallying.) They recognize that there exist committed socialists (Simone Weil and David McLellan, for example) who also are firm religious believers—as attuned to the pervasive ills and ugliness of religion as socialist atheists, yet holding religious beliefs and commitments that form a central part of their lives and about which they have thought deeply.

Some socialist atheists (though not necessarily for the same reasons) may be as convinced as Lenin was of the unjustifiability, unreasonableness, and even the irrationality of religious belief. Some are as convinced as he that there is no God. Indeed some even think there *can* be no God as God has come to be construed in medieval and modern Judeo-Christian-Islamic tradition. But they will also recognize (as Lenin *seems* not to) that there exist some religious believers, even believers in the more orthodox conceptions of religion, who think otherwise—and that some of these are reasonable and informed persons, as intelligent as any atheist, and possessing as much integrity and thoughtfulness as even the most reflective atheists. Here, such atheists will feel to the full what John Rawls calls the burdens of judgment. Further, they recognize that in a pluralist society (indeed, a pluralist world), many divergent conceptions of the good life and many different worldviews are arguably reasonably held. The social glue that binds us, at least in modern societies—a thin though not insignificant adhesive—is a common family of general conceptions of social justice consistent with what Rawls would term a reasonable pluralism. Only the recognition and acceptance of these conceptions makes living together tolerable. In short, these atheists have bought into the Jeffersonian-Rawlsian compromise, and recognize as well that in the very weak (but practically acceptable) Rawlsian sense that some of these reasonable pluralisms are religious ones. Moreover, standing in back of this is a principle that is less normative, more of a modus vivendi. It is rooted (wittingly or unwittingly) in a recognition of the importance of the Treaty of Westphalia, which brought an end to Europe's religious wars. It is a pragmatic recognition, available to all who are not fanatics, that religious wars or deep religious civil strife are to be avoided, including wars or civil strife between belief and unbelief. And this conviction may remain, no matter how unreasonable, fantastic, and frequently ideological they may take religions, religious doctrines, and religious belief and practices to be. Such convictions incline atheists of this flavor to an almost knee-jerk rejection of Lenin's stance on religion.

I too (though with some ambivalence) accept that Jeffersonian-Rawlsian compromise, particularly in its Rawlsian form. Moreover, I believe that we need something like the peace of Westphalia both between one religious belief and another, and between religious belief and unbelief. Most of the decrees and practices concerning religion carried out by the Soviet Union under Lenin's leadership were far too draconian, offering a mirror image of the tendencies we deplore in the Vatican and reflecting a similar mind set.

However, in his general program for secular commitment on the part of a socialist party and its cadres, Lenin was committed to achieving class emancipation, and (with classlessness secured) to moving beyond that toward a general human emancipation. This, he thought, would require a secularist turn. It is not so clear to me that Lenin was wrong over such basics; it is not clear to me that we should instead embrace the Jeffersonian-Rawlsian compromise and insist on state neutrality concerning religion. To be sure, the state should remain neutral toward *liberal* religions, all of which are compatible with both socialism and a reasonable pluralism. In contrast to the liberal religions, the great orthodox faiths, including those Lenin set his face against—the Roman Catholic Church, Russian Orthodoxy, Calvinism, Orthodox Judaism, Orthodox Islam, and the various fundamentalist Jewish, Christian, and Islamic doctrinal stances—engage in practices that severely harm millions of people, causing grave injustices to women and children, to the lower classes, and sometimes to anyone whose religious or nonreligious orientation differs from their own. These orthodox creeds frequently breed hatred, intolerance, and repression. These are severe injustices in the very terms of the conception of justice that Rawls articulates. It is understandable that Lenin was so exercised about religion. *These* religious beliefs and belief systems are (to put it mildly) not compatible with a Rawlsian reasonable pluralism. To the extent that liberals and socialists tolerate them, it is *only* for modus vivendi reasons—for example, they will crush us if we don't; firmly opposing them will set in motion once again the horrors of religious wars; or we have no overlapping consensus from which we might develop a successful practical action program.

Given considerations such as these, we secularists (socialist and nonsocialist), if we are reasonable, will slog on through the slow processes of sober reasoning together with religious people, all the while hoping that increasing and more equally distributed wealth, increasing democracy, and increasing education (say, on the model of contemporary Scandinavian societies) will gradually lead them out of the religious and moral wilderness of their beliefs. Still, some of the most powerful of these religions (though not all of them to the same extent, nor over the same things) give rise to terrific injustices. Intransigent Catholic policy on the use of condoms condemns millions of very young children to parentless lives in poverty and neglect. Islamic sharia law and Orthodox Jewish law on divorce allow men to brutally dominate women. Many orthodox traditions exclude—and sometimes, as when the Taliban held power in Afghanistan, even murder—homosexuals. Many allow extreme wealth to accrue to religious hierarchs while the poor starve, or seek to undermine women's knowledge of and access to abortion and even contraception. The injustices surge on owing to the commitment of these religions to obscurantist, utterly unjustifiable beliefs, and to their propagation and protection by a religious aristocracy. Faced with injustices as great as these, and recognizing their intractability, must we think Lenin so wrong in his militant atheism—so far afield in his demand that atheism form part of the platform of a political party devoted to the good of human beings? There is sense, even wisdom, in the Jeffersonian-Rawlsian compromise. But I think the question about Lenin's wrongness needs a sober second reconsideration.

BIBLIOGRAPHY

Bociurkiw, Bohdan R. "Lenin and Religion." In *Lenin: The Man, the Theorist, the Leader*, edited by Leonard Schapiro and Peter Reddaway. London: Pall Mall, 1967.

Katkov, George. "Lenin as Philosopher." In *Lenin: The Man, the Theorist, the Leader*, edited by Leonard Schapiro and Peter Reddaway. London: Pall Mall, 1967.

Kline, G. L. *Religious and Anti-religious Thought in Russia*. Chicago: University of Chicago Press, 1968.

Kolakowski, Leszek. *Main Currents of Marxism*. Vol. 2. Oxford: Clarendon, 1978.

Lenin, V. I. "On the Attitude of the Workers' Party Towards Religion." In *Collected Works*. Vol. 15.

———. "On the Significance of Militant Atheism." In *Collected Works*. Vol. 33.

———. "Programme on Religion to Eighth Congress." In *Collected Works*. Vol. 28.

———. "Socialism and Religion." In *Collected Works*. Vol. 28.

———. "To the Village Poor." In *Collected Works*. Vol. 19.

———. "Two Tactics of Social Democracy in the Democratic Revolution." In *Collected Works*. Vol. 9.

KAI NIELSEN

LENNSTRAND, VICTOR EMANUEL (1861–1895), Swedish teacher, lecturer, and publicist. Founder of the Utilistiska Samfundet (Utilitarian Society) in 1888, the first and only Swedish atheist organization at the time, numbering two thousand members (see SWEDEN, UNBELIEF IN), Victor Emanuel Lennstrand edited two periodical publications between 1890 and 1894, *Tänk Sjelv!* (Think for Yourself!) and *Fritänkaren* (Freethinker), the latter of which attained a circulation of thirty-five hundred copies. Elected a member of Sweden's first Convention for Popular Vote, Lennstrand delivered speeches in front of thousands of people and started a massive movement against the church and religion. He translated works by Robert Green INGERSOLL, Charles BRADLAUGH, John Stuart MILL, and others. In addition he published many of his own essays and lectures: "What We Believe and What We Want" (1888), "Jehovah Is Dead," "The Republic, the Popular Vote and Freethinking" (1891), "What I Said and What I Did Not Say" (c. 1890), and others.

Born in a family with strong Christian beliefs, at the age of twenty Lennstrand entered Upsala University to study theology. In 1883 he published a selection of sentences and maxims favoring the Christian religion. Ingve Sahlin, professor at Upsala University, convinced him to read John LOCKE, Mill, Auguste COMTE and others. Once acquainted with rationalist literature, Lennstrand's clear and penetrating mind led him to abandon his parents' faith. On September 27, 1887, he gave a lecture titled "Is Christianity a Religion for Our Time?" that marked the beginning of his battle against church, religion, and monarchy, and exasperated Upsala's police chief.

Between 1888 and 1893 Lennstrand was prosecuted seven times, condemned four, and imprisoned for fourteen months in squalid conditions. He was forced to leave the university and became an outcast to his family. Nevertheless, he devoted his short life to the ideal of utilitarianism, which he called Utilism—the doctrine of the English philosophers Jeremy BENTHAM and Mill that consists in the attainment of the highest amount of happiness or profit for humanity as the moral purpose, the establishing of human reason as the only judge in moral questions and the rejecting of the existence of God (see CONSEQUENTIALISM).

Lennstrand kept in contact with the principal representatives of nonbelief of the late nineteenth century, including freethinkers of France, Germany, Belgium, and Spain. In 1892 he promoted a motion addressed to the Swedish Parliament abolishing Sweden's BLASPHEMY law, but it came to nothing. He was invited to the International Congress of Freethinkers, held in Chicago in 1893 and sponsored by the Unitarians of the United States. He was compelled to postpone and ultimately cancel the trip due to his deteriorating health.

In December 1894 he was forced to give up all his activities due to a painful, mysteriously contracted illness that provoked his death on November 1, 1895. The disease—"possibly tuberculosis," wrote one of his friends—was never clearly identified.

BIBLIOGRAPHY

Björklund, C. J. *En fritänkares levnadssaga, Viktor Lennstrand, banbrytare för den fria tanken bland Sveriges folk*. Stockholm: Brandes förlag, 1926.

———. *Sanningar om Lennstrand*. Stockholm: Frihetsförbundets förlag, 1908.

Ljungdals, Oscar. *Viktor Lennstrands minne*. Stockholm: O. Ljungdals förlag, 1895.

Svenska Biografisk Lexikon. Stockholm: Statens Arkivstyrelse, 1979.

JOSÉ MANUEL FERNÁNDEZ SANTANA

LESSING, GOTTHOLD EPHRAIM (1729–1781), German dramatist and critic. The son of a scholarly Lutheran pastor, Gotthold Ephraim Lessing was sent to study theology at Leipzig University. There he was influenced by the popular RATIONALISM of the Enlightenment (see ENLIGHTENMENT, UNBELIEF DURING THE), whose leading contemporary exponent was Christian Wolff. Lessing was influenced in the same direction by friends from Berlin, Friedrich Nicolai and Moses Mendelssohn, and by various writings of English deists (see DEISM), many of which had been translated into German. Although literature and especially drama became Lessing's supreme interest, he was to return to theology in the last decade of his life.

Lessing was above all a critic of literature. His nonconformity made him appear perennially restless. He was never permanently satisfied to adopt the conventional opinions of society, always preferring to be in a "minority of one." He moved beyond his parents' theological beliefs and the commonplace deism of his youth until he, influenced by Baruch SPINOZA, prepared the way for the romantic reaction against the Enlightenment.

Lessing's best-known work of criticism is his *Laokoon* (1766), a study of art, paintings, and poetry. Lessing's writings on art and literature do not constitute a serious analysis and critique of aesthetic experience, but aim at liberating the artist from limiting rules and conventions. Lessing was not a romantic writer, but because of his demand for the free expression of natural feelings and his interest in antiquity, he occupies an important place among the forces that made German romanticism possible.

In 1773 Lessing began to publish essays on historical theology. Lessing had met the deist Hermann Samuel Reimarus, whose daughter lent him the manuscript of an unpublished book by her father, *Apology for Rational Worshippers of God*. In 1774 and in 1777–78, Lessing printed extracts from this work as fragments of the writings of an anonymous deist. Reimarus was a believer in natural religion and skeptical about revelation. His objections to traditional Christianity presuppose that biblical inerrancy is essential to faith (see BIBLICAL ERRANCY). Lessing sometimes wrote as if he shared this assumption, and sometimes as if he did not.

Prevented by his superior from indulging in theological controversies, Lessing put his theology into a play, *Nathan the Wise* (1779). It has been read as a plea for religious indifference, on the ground that what is required of man is not an assent to the propositions of a creed but sincerity, brotherly love, and tolerance. It is not known precisely what Lessing's positive beliefs were, but he probably accepted a common thesis of the Enlightenment that the essence of Christianity, hidden beneath the accretions of theology, consists in universal brotherhood and a basic moral code. Henry Chadwick has said that "Lessing spent his life hoping that Christianity was true and arguing that it was not. But his basic attitude toward religious belief was neither one of affirmation nor of denial; it took the form of an impassioned question."

BIBLIOGRAPHY

Chadwick, Henry. "Lessing, Gotthold Ephraim." In *The Encyclopedia of Philosophy*, edited by Paul Edwards. New York: Macmillan/Free Press, 1967.
Dürr, Volker. "Lessing, Gotthold Ephraim." In *The Encyclopedia of Unbelief*, edited by Gordon Stein. Amherst, NY: Prometheus Books, 1985.

FINNGEIR HIORTH

LeSUEUR, MERIDEL (1900–1996), American author and radical. From her origins in Murray, Iowa, at the dawning of the twentieth century, Meridel LeSueur was shaped by and intimately connected to the rural Midwest throughout her long and productive life. Her mother, Marian, graduated from Drake University, where she showed intellectual promise, but was unhappily married to a preacher. The young family moved to Texas, but Marian escaped with her children to Oklahoma, where the laws were fairer to women in such circumstances. At the People's College in Fort Scott, Kansas, Marian became a teacher, and she is credited by some with the original idea of the Little Blue Books so successfully developed by Emanuel HALDEMAN-JULIUS. At the college she met and married Arthur LeSueur, the head of the law school, beginning a long and fruitful alliance in radical causes of all kinds.

Meridel LeSueur had left high school before graduating, and went on to Chicago and then to New York, where she lived in Emma GOLDMAN's anarchist commune. This Bohemian milieu of free spirits nurtured LeSueur's rebellious and lyrical tendencies, and soon she began writing of her experiences and feelings in notebooks. Inspired by the general atmosphere of radicalism, LeSueur joined the Communist Party in 1924. She began her formal writing with a story, "Annunciation," in 1927. She witnessed the dramatic Teamster's strike in Milwaukee in 1934, and described it in "I Was Marching," published in the proletarian magazine *New Masses*.

She participated in the American Writers Congress of 1935 and contributed a short essay to the volume of its proceedings, emphasizing the continuity of the midwestern radicals with the earlier Industrial Workers of the World, a group not exactly in favor with the Communist Party at that time. A first volume of stories, *Salute to Spring*, was issued in 1940. During a period of catastrophic social, economic, and environmental upheaval, LeSueur lamented "the dreary villages, the frail wooden houses, the prairies ravished, everything impermanent as if it were not meant to last the span of one man's life, a husk through which human life poured." This volume,

along with LeSueur's avowedly revolutionary politics, confirmed her place as a brave yet lyrical literary voice.

During the early 1940s LeSueur worked on *North Star Country*, a folk history of the upper Midwest. Published in 1945, its success was blunted by LeSueur's blacklisting during the McCarthy repression. While she continued to publish a few children's books through the publisher Knopf, for the most part she was driven out of mainstream publishing. Indeed, she could not even keep a menial job such as waitressing without being harassed by the FBI. In spite of this she managed to travel the country, preserving on tape the life histories of veteran radicals. She also wrote stories about the impact of the blacklist and Korean War on grassroots American people.

With the rise of the modern feminist movement in the mid-1970s, LeSueur was "rediscovered," though she protested, "I never was lost." West End Press began to collect her stories from obscure left-wing magazines, and in 1977 issued two small but richly textured volumes, *Harvest* and *Song for My Time*. The next year, West End published a short novel, *The Girl*, a chronicle of the Great Depression LeSueur started in the 1930s but later reworked and expanded. *Ripening*, a volume of selected works, appeared in 1982.

LeSueur's maternal grandmother was a devout member of the Disciples of Christ in Oklahoma, and some ethical aspects of popular Christianity appealed to her. Even so, LeSueur became a resolute foe of Puritanism in all its forms, viewing it as a profound capitalist threat to "the body" and to humanity. And while she was friendly to FREETHOUGHT, she also counseled "not to forget the Tao of physics," as, she believed, earlier societies had contributed much of value to our store of culture. LeSueur's personal library is now at Augsburg College in Minneapolis, and her notebooks are in the collections of the Minnesota Historical Society.

BIBLIOGRAPHY

My People Are My Home. Minneapolis: Twin Cities Women's Film Collective, 1976.
"The Sybil of Socialism." *People's Culture* 34 (1996).

FRED WHITEHEAD

LEUBA, JAMES H. (1868–1946), American psychologist. James H. Leuba was born in Neuchatel, Switzerland, where early skeptical reaction to Calvinist doctrine and behavior prompted a lifelong interest in understanding religious experience. After receiving a bachelor's degree from the University of Neuchatel, Leuba moved with his family to the United States. He earned a doctorate in psychology at Clark University under G. Stanley Hall, with a dissertation on the psychology of religious conversion. He spent his entire academic career as professor and, for a time, chairman of the department of psychology at Bryn Mawr College.

Body of Work. Leuba's approach to the study of religious experience was resolutely naturalistic and empirical, carefully reasoned and forthright. This earned him intermittent critical reactions from religious colleagues and apologists throughout his career. While his lasting reputation rests upon seminal studies of beliefs in a personal God and immortality in the United States, the balance of his work deserves equal, if not greater, attention. In *The Psychological Origin and the Nature of Religion* (1909) and *A Psychological Study of Religion* (1912), Leuba sounds several themes that frame his lifelong view of religious experience. To maintain clarity about the subject, religion is delimited to "that part of human experience in which man feels himself in relation with powers" of a "psychic," divine, or supernatural nature. He rejected the utility of definitions of "religion" that encompass "anything that is of considerable value to man." Religious experience is viewed as a complex, natural, functional, and in certain forms dysfunctional means of meeting basic human needs. Leuba was critical of attempts to reduce religion to a single dimension. In its internal aspect, religion involves "willing, feeling, and thinking" aimed at the gratification of human "needs, desires, and yearnings." In its external aspect, it involves practices, rites, ceremonies, and institutions.

Leuba vigorously combated the view that, due to its claimed supernatural content, religious experience falls outside the purview of science. He insisted that since religious consciousness is a psychological process, it is accessible to empirical inquiry: "*[T]he gods of religion are inductions from experience*, and are therefore proper objects of science." Leuba could not be persuaded "that divine personal beings . . . have more than a subjective existence." At the same time, religion arose from natural psychological processes to meet human needs. It should be "looked upon as a functional part of life, as that mode of behavior in the struggle for life in which use is made of powers characterized . . . as psychic, superhuman, and usually personal."

Leuba offers compelling, if speculative, accounts of the likely origins of religious beliefs. Ideas of ghosts, nature-beings, and gods emerge from a wide range of psychological processes, including altered states of consciousness (such as trances, dreams, apparitions, and hallucinations), prescientific perceptions of striking natural phenomena, and the human penchant for attributing purposive agency to "explain" natural events. Throughout his work, Leuba was critical of religious ideas at odds with scientific knowledge and moral progress. In this connection, he was consistently critical of selected aspects of Christian monotheism (such as a personal relationship with God). The closing chapter of *The Belief in God and Immortality: A Psychological, Anthropological, and Statistical Study* (1916) is an eloquent essay on the independence of moral knowledge from religious belief and the threats to moral progress posed by certain religious forms (see ETHICS AND UNBELIEF).

In *The Belief in God and Immortality*, Leuba reported on the first of his statistical surveys of (un)belief in a personal God and immortality among American scientists, historians, college students, and others (see SCIENCE, UNBELIEF WITHIN). Thanks in part to a general replication of his surveys of scientists in the 1990s by Edward J. Larson and Larry Witham, Leuba's findings remain in the public eye. He found, for example, that fewer scientists overall were believers than "doubters" or "disbelievers" in a personal God (42 percent in 1914, declining to 30 percent in a subsequent survey in 1933). Belief in immortality was slightly more prevalent, but also showed a decline from 49 percent in 1914 to 33 percent in 1933. Also, believers in both a personal God and immortality were substantially rarer among "elite" compared with "lesser" scientists, and among social scientists compared with physical or biological scientists.

In *The Psychology of Religious Mysticism* (1925), Leuba provided an extensive and detailed analysis of the varied forms, causes, and perennial allure of altered and ecstatic states (see RELIGIOUS AND MYSTICAL EXPERIENCES). Drawing from extensive historical source materials, his unflinching naturalistic analysis drew critical reaction. His view that associations of God or the divine with the "immediate" content of mystical experience result from post hoc cognition, rather than direct "knowledge" of such realities, contrasted with William James's greater propensity to allow that the apparent immediacy of such associations may offer evidence of their referent truth. The fact that Leuba's work has remained obscured in the shadow of James's "The Will to Believe" and *The Varieties of Religious Experience* is noteworthy and regrettable.

In *God or Man? A Study of the Value of God to Man* (1933) and *The Reformation of the Churches* (1950; published posthumously), Leuba recapitulated his main themes and looked to the future of religion, human needs, and moral progress. Throughout his career, he held that religious ideas and forms at odds with scientific knowledge or moral progress would gradually be supplanted (the secularization hypothesis). Rather than a complete eclipse of religious by scientific or secular worldviews, Leuba foresaw forms of experience and behavior that preserve some of the functional benefits of religion in harmony with scientific knowledge. He repeatedly cited Felix ADLER's ETHICAL CULTURE as one possible model for such future "religion"—retaining a sense of the "spiritual," a natural and consequence-based moral approach, and due regard for scientific inquiry and knowledge. He spoke hopefully about the early promise of philosophical HUMANISM. However, he held "no expectation . . . of a rapid transformation of all the churches," noting that "fundamentalist churches are far from having been outgrown by all the people," a "religious rear guard will remain with us for a long while," and that "intellectual and moral progress is distressingly slow." The whole of Leuba's body of work and its central messages deserve renewed attention and reappraisal.

BIBLIOGRAPHY

Brown, C. Mackenzie. "The Conflict between Religion and Science in Light of the Patterns of Religious Belief among Scientists." *Zygon* 38 (September 2003).

James, William. *The Varieties of Religious Experience: A Study in Human Nature*. Mineola, NY: Dover, 2002.

———. "The Will to Believe." In *The Will to Believe and Other Essays in Popular Philosophy*. New York: Dover, 1960.

Larson, Edward J., and Larry Witham. "Leading Scientists Still Reject God." *Nature* 394 (1998).

———. "Scientists and Religion in America." *Scientific American* 281 (September 1999).

———. "Scientists Are Still Keeping the Faith." *Nature* 386 (1997).

Leuba, James H. *The Belief in God and Immortality: A Psychological, Anthropological, and Statistical Study*. Boston: Sherman, French, 1916.

———. *God or Man? A Study of the Value of God to Man*. New York: Henry Holt, 1933.

———. "The Making of a Psychologist of Religion." In *Religion in Transition*, edited by Vergilius T. Ferm. London: Allen & Unwin, 1937.

———. *The Psychological Origin and the Nature of Religion*. London: Archibald Constable, 1909.

———. *A Psychological Study of Religion: Its Origin, Function, and Future*. New York: Macmillan, 1912.

———. *The Psychology of Religious Mysticism*. New York: Harcourt, Brace, 1925.

———. *The Reformation of the Churches*. Boston: Beacon, 1950.

———. "Religious Beliefs of American Scientists." *Harper's*, August 1934.

FRANK L. PASQUALE

LEWIS, DAVID (1941–2001), American atheist philosopher. A professor at Princeton University for most of this academic career, David Lewis was a towering figure in philosophy in the second half of the twentieth century. He made important and original contributions to a wide range of philosophical fields, including metaphysics, epistemology, philosophy of mind, philosophy of language, philosophical logic, ethics, political philosophy, and philosophy of religion.

Lewis was born into a nonreligious household and initially seemed destined for a career in chemistry. When he reverted to philosophy, he brought with him a firm attachment to both atheism and reductive materialism (see NATURALISM; MATERIALISM, PHILOSOPHICAL). He played a central role in the development of contemporary materialistic philosophies of mind, where he defended a version of the doctrine that mental states are merely certain kinds of states of the brain and central nervous system (see COGNITIVE SCIENCE AND UNBELIEF). More generally, he defended the view that there is a sense in which everything is physical: at least roughly speaking, he held that there are no objects or properties that are not ultimately, in principle, analyzable in terms of microphysical objects and microphysical properties (see PHYSICALISM).

Lewis's ATHEISM is visible in much of his writing. His analysis of ontological arguments in "Anselm and Actuality" (1970) is one of the most penetrating articles on that topic. His take on problems of evil and, in particular, on free-will theodicies in "Evil for Freedom's Sake?" (1993) is subtle and persuasive. His discussion of the Christian doctrine of atonement in "Do We Believe in Penal Substitution?" (1997) is an interesting addition to a small literature.

Lewis is perhaps most notorious for his "modal realism," that is, for his view that all possible worlds exist, though no other possible world has any connection to our own space and time. On Lewis's view, there are talking donkeys, even though there are no talking donkeys in the part of reality that we inhabit. Lewis's modal realism led him to the view that there are both gods and unembodied minds—but only in possible worlds other than the one that we actually inhabit. Setting aside Lewis's modal realism, this means that he accepted that the existence of gods and unembodied minds are unrealized logical possibilities. While Lewis's rejection of the claim that it is logically necessary that there are no gods and no unembodied minds finds widespread support, there are many atheists and materialists who prefer to disagree with Lewis on this matter.

BIBLIOGRAPHY

Lewis, D. K. "Anselm and Actuality." *Noûs* 4 (1970).

———. "Do We Believe in Penal Substitution?" *Philosophical Papers* 26 (1997).

———. "Evil for Freedom's Sake." *Philosophical Papers* 22 (1993).

———. *Papers in Ethics and Social Philosophy*. Cambridge: Cambridge University Press, 2000.

GRAHAM OPPY

LEWIS, JOSEPH (1889–1968), American atheist activist. Joseph Lewis was arguably one of the two most prominent atheists in the United States during the first half of the twentieth century, the other being Emannuel HALDEMAN-JULIUS; however, Lewis never achieved the recognition in the international freethought movement that he deserved. Lewis was born into a Jewish family in Montgomery, Alabama, the youngest son of Samuel and Ray Lewis. In 1898, strained financial circumstances forced him to leave school to seek employment. He continued his education by reading avariciously in his limited spare time, later describing himself as self-educated. In the course of his reading, he encountered a work by Robert Green INGERSOLL that drew his attention to Thomas PAINE's *Age of Reason*, and this, he told a meeting of the Thomas Paine Society in London in 1964, was instrumental in converting him to atheism.

On May 12, 1914, Lewis married Fay Jacobs. There were two children: a son born in 1916, who died in the influenza epidemic of 1920, and a daughter born in 1916. His first wife predeceased him, and in 1952 he married Ruth Stoller Grubman. No children resulted from this second marriage.

In 1920 Lewis moved to New York, where he established a mail-order clothing business. His unbelief led him into contact with the Freethinkers of America, founded in 1915. In 1925 Lewis arranged for its legal incorporation and was elected as its president. He held that office for the rest of his life, at times, it has been claimed, using underhanded methods to retain the post. Very much an individual, Lewis demanded his own way and resented any opposition, which on one occasion led to several distinguished honorary vice presidents resigning in protest. His control of the Freethinkers was strengthened because he personally met its annual deficit; it became in effect his private fiefdom. He used its journal, first published in January 1937 as the *Bulletin of the Freethinkers of America*, later as *Freethinker*, and finally as *The Age of Reason*, primarily to publicize his ideas and promote his various campaigns. The journal, like the Freethinkers, was never a financial success and was, according to his close friend William J. Fielding, Lewis's "hobby," though he qualified this by adding, "if it may be said he had one."

Lewis was able to subsidize the Freethinkers of America from the considerable profits he made from two publishing firms he established. The first was the Freethought Press Association, which he set up in 1921 to publish his first book, *The Tyranny of God* (1921). His policy was to sell books at low prices through the mail, and his advertising usually prominently displayed his own portrait. He was the author of several other freethought works, notably *The Bible Unmasked* (1926), thought by many to be his best work. He also printed the texts of several of his freethought lectures under the title *Atheism and Other Addresses*, which first appeared in 1930 and was subsequently updated and added to during the course of its several editions. The book he considered his finest atheist propagandist work was a massive treatise called *The Ten Commandments* (1946). His most courageous work was *An Atheist Manifesto*, published in 1954 at the height of the Cold War, when US public opinion viewed atheism as un-American.

Lewis's second publishing concern was the Eugenics Publishing Company, set up in 1930 and unquestionably his most profitable business venture. Lewis used the same methods he employed in freethought publishing, offering low-priced editions by mail covering birth control and related themes. He marketed his books to the general public rather than the medical profession.

From an early date, Lewis initiated a series of lawsuits to curb what he saw as the attempts by religious groups to circumvent the United States' constitutional separation of church and state.

As a consequence of his publishing activities, Lewis became a wealthy man, living in some comfort on a large estate in Westchester County, New York. He also owned a house in Miami Beach, Florida, where he usually spent the winter months, and an apartment on Park Avenue in Manhattan. According to Fielding, he enjoyed the company of "libertarians, iconoclasts, and exponents of various unorthodox philosophies." He corresponded with and entertained many leading figures in the worlds of art, science, and literature. He became a life member of American Association for the Advancement of Science.

Lewis lionized freethought icons such as Paine and Robert Green Ingersoll, and he sought to promote interest in them and defend their reputations against critics. He established two private organizations, the Robert G. Ingersoll Memorial Association and the Thomas Paine Foundation. In 1954 he succeeded in restoring Ingersoll's birthplace at Dresden, New York, for the second time and having it officially recognized as a public memorial (see MONUMENTS TO UNBELIEF). Lewis also raised substantial sums to erect statues of Paine in Paris; Morristown, New Jersey; and Thetford, England, Paine's birthplace. His lengthy agitation for a US postage stamp to commemorate Paine ultimately succeeded, although he stormed out of its unveiling ceremony at Philadelphia in January 1968 in protest because prayers were said. In addition, Lewis had a bust of Paine placed in New York University's Hall of Fame, though he failed to win Ingersoll a place there. Lewis also authored several short works on people such as Thomas JEFFERSON, George Washington, and Benjamin Franklin, in which he stressed their unorthodox religious opinions.

Convinced that Paine was the real author of the Declaration of Independence, Lewis presented his arguments in his book *Thomas Paine, Author of the Declaration of Independence* (1947). Although this work has been described as more polemical than historically convincing, some of the facts noted by Lewis would suggest that Paine had some input into the famous document.

Lewis died in New York on November 4, 1968. Attempts to continue the Freethinkers of America failed. It had become too much an extension of Lewis himself; moreover, his antagonism to any perceived threat to his leadership had ensured that there was no one in a position to take over effectively.

BIBLIOGRAPHY

Fielding, William J. *All the Lives I Have Lived*. Philadelphia: Dorrance, 1972.

Howland, Arthur H. *Joseph Lewis—Enemy of God.* Boston: Stratford, 1932.

Melton, J. Gordon. *Biographical Dictionary of American Cult and Sect Leaders.* New York: Garland, 1986.

Ryan, William F. "Joseph Lewis." In *The Encyclopedia of Unbelief,* edited by Gordon Stein. Amherst, NY: Prometheus Books, 1985.

ROBERT W. MORRELL

LEWIS, SINCLAIR (1885–1951), American novelist. From obscure origins in the small town of Sauk Center, Minnesota, Sinclair Lewis rocketed to fame in the 1920s as the author of a series of satirical novels about Puritanism, power, and corruption in American life. The son of a physician and a mother who died of tuberculosis at a young age, Lewis had a difficult childhood and youth. Tall, gangly, and red-headed, he was not popular because of his eccentricities, among them a pronounced love of reading. While taking college preparatory courses at Oberlin, he was converted to Christianity, but soon began to have doubts. At Yale, he grew skeptical of the conservative secret-society culture that prevailed there. Eventually he gravitated to magazine writing in New York City, which enabled him to develop his craft but confirmed his dour view of commercialism.

His novel *Main Street*, published in 1920, is a pungent portrait of a remote Minnesota town called Gopher Prairie, obviously modeled after Sauk Center. It was largely autobiographical. The main character, Carol Kennicott, "an uneasy and dodging agnostic," finds fitting in to local society deadening, with its dull routine of gossip and oblivion concerning any form of modern or progressive culture. In spite of its biting satire (never a very popular art form in America), *Main Street* sold very well. It represented one of the most eloquent documents in what came to be known as the "Revolt from the Village," a literary trend to attack and expose the Puritanism and intellectual narrowness of rural life.

Even among those disposed to dislike Lewis's critical stance, his skill in language and realistic detail was widely applauded. In quick succession, he exposed the small businessman in *Babbitt* (1922) and medical research in *Arrowsmith* (1925). Then, in 1926, Lewis turned to the subject of religion, just at the time of the Scopes trial in Tennessee (see DARROW, CLARENCE; EVOLUTION AND UNBELIEF). He journeyed to Kansas City, where he took a hotel room and gathered ministers around him who were curiously eager to share their views and experiences, both virtuous and scandalous. While there, Lewis took a turn at a church pulpit, daring God to strike him down, if he existed. When the allotted minutes passed and Lewis still lived, his stunt made headlines across the country. *Elmer Gantry*, the novel resulting from his Kansas City research, caused a sensation upon its publication in 1927. Lewis described the novel as "a blast of protest against all organized religion. It is blasphemous, it is in bad taste, it is violent, it is—however humorous it may be in its minor details—in essence unhumorous; it is simply a roar of protest."

Paradoxically, Lewis's success as an outspoken critic of trends in American culture introduced him to high life. He fully participated in the excesses of the Roaring Twenties, becoming, like F. Scott Fitzgerald, an alcoholic of epic proportions. He frequently had to go into hospitals and clinics to "dry out." After refusing the Pulitzer Prize in 1927 on the grounds it was under the control of conservatives on the board of trustees at Columbia University, he accepted the Nobel Prize for Literature in 1930.

As a longtime rebel, Lewis supported labor unions, and was a good friend of the prominent socialist Eugene Debs. In the 1930s Lewis tried to write a novel about labor leader Debs, but abandoned the effort. *It Can't Happen Here*, published in 1935, was an exposé of fascist trends in America, but Lewis had difficulties relating to the various forms of Marxist rhetoric and organizations that arose during that period.

By the late 1940s Lewis was spending most of his time in Europe. Always restless, he traveled almost aimlessly from place to place. He continued to write and to publish novels, but with much less success than he enjoyed in the 1920s. Suffering from advanced alcoholism, he died in a Rome clinic, almost alone. His ashes were returned to Sauk Center for burial; he specified in his will that there be no religious ceremony.

BIBLIOGRAPHY

Lingeman, Richard. *Sinclair Lewis: Rebel from Main Street.* New York: Random House, 2002.

FRED WHITEHEAD

LIBERAL, MISSOURI. The short-lived experiment of a churchless town in the Bible Belt of southwestern Missouri, Liberal was the brainchild of George Henry Walser, a poet, Civil War veteran, and lawyer who had moved to Lamar in Barton County, Missouri, in 1866 and established a successful law practice there. He became well known in the area and was elected twice as state legislator on the Republican ticket beginning in 1868.

In 1880 Walser bought two thousand acres of arable farmland with rich underlying coal deposits, seventeen miles to the west of Lamar at the crossing of the Missouri Pacific and Frisco railroads, six miles from the Kansas border. In defiance of the notorious Comstock Act of 1876 (see COMSTOCK, ANTHONY, AND UNBELIEF), Walser advertised his city on the hill as a place where "we could enjoy the full benefits of American citizens without having some self-appointed bigot dictate to us what we should think, speak, write, print or send through the mails."

On the original plat for Liberal, he wrote: "It is the only town in the United States set apart for Liberalism alone, and the only town of its size in the WORLD without a *priest, preacher, saloon, God or hell.*"

The population of Liberal grew to three hundred within three years of its inception, and may even have topped one thousand by the end of the century. Newcomers had to sign an agreement with Walser not to hold religious services on their properties. To curry favor with readers of THE TRUTH SEEKER, the largest FREETHOUGHT newspaper in circulation at the time, he deeded a lot to its editor, D. M. BENNETT, in 1881.

Liberal's institutions included a National Liberal Orphans Home, a Freethought University with a faculty of seven, a normal day school, a secular Sunday school, and Walser's own Universal Mental Liberty Hall, where public debates were held. Walser also founded an Odd Fellows fraternity he called the Brotherhood, whose particular purpose was to "visit the sick, relieve the distressed, bury the dead and educate the orphan."

For the public enjoyment and to promote a healthy lifestyle, Walser constructed and maintained a twenty-acre park that he filled with catalpa trees. In addition to being the site of his own house, the park sported a large lake for bathing and boating, open air band concerts, and picnic areas where at night, lit by kerosene lamps and the stars, the people of Liberal could join together for a merry evening of square dancing. At Walser's invitation Catalpa Park became a regular venue for American Spiritualist camp meetings (see SPIRITUALISM AND UNBELIEF).

Trouble was not long in coming. This hotbed of heathenism proved an easy target for a troublemaking Disciple of Christ preacher, Rev. Carl Braden, described in *Fifty Years of Freethought* as a "vituperative polecat" who "distributed lies by pamphlet." After a short visit Braden wrote one of his most virulent pamphlets on Liberal's sinful lifestyle, which was widely publicized by columnist Samuel Keller in the *St. Louis Globe-Dispatch* in May 1885.

Liberal fought back. One of the town innkeepers filed a libel suit against Braden for ruining his business (he had been accused of running a house of ill repute); Braden was arrested on criminal libel charges in addition to a separate embezzlement charge that had followed him from Nebraska. Both charges were later dropped.

Liberal might have managed to survive as a freethought town despite the bad press if the railroads had not raised their transportation rates, making coal mining unprofitable. With substantial holdings in the local mines, Walser got into financial trouble and sold his beloved Universal Mental Liberty Hall (UMLH) to the Methodists, who built a church on the site. Walser had invested most of his money in Liberal; Catalpa Park alone had cost him $40,000, an enormous sum in those days. Many of the original wooden buildings including Walser's own house had to be rebuilt due to a spate of fires in 1895, which demolished most of the town's businesses.

There were also serious splits among the townspeople themselves. Always the autocrat, with Walser it was a case of "either his way or the highway," so when Henry Replogle, coeditor with Walser of the *Liberal News*,

asked if he could publish a second newspaper, *Equity*, to espouse free-love (see SEX RADICALISM AND UNBELIEF) and his own peculiar philosophy of Egoism, Walser saw this request as unwelcome competition. After a particularly rowdy debate at UMLH in which the free-lovers had to defend their position against the other townspeople, Replogle's house was attacked. Henry Repogle and his wife, Georgia, were literally run out of town by an angry gun-wielding mob. The couple ended up in San Francisco, where *The Truth Seeker* management was only too happy to share its presses with them.

Walser became deeply involved in Spiritualism due to his friendship with a self-styled medium, Dr. J. B. Bouton. Unfortunately Bouton was revealed as a complete fraud when his house caught fire and the firefighters revealed an assortment of trap doors, wires and pulleys, and table rapping equipment. The exposure of Bouton's shenanigans caused great amusement in the town at the time, but made Walser look rather foolish. Dating from this period there still exists in Liberal a curious wheel-shaped cemetery where, the story goes, Walser had planned to be buried in the center, so that if there was to be a resurrection all the people buried there would see him first.

Local farmers began to buy land close to the Liberal boundary and started small communities apart from the freethinkers. One was named Pedro, after a popular card game; there a saloon was established, much to Walser's disgust as he was a temperance man. The infidels turned out in force, and under Walser's instruction installed a high barbed wire fence to separate the two communities. A "Get thee out of Sodom" sign was placed close to the fence on the insurgent side, and Walser dispatched friends to the railway station to try and prevent more Christians coming to the area.

Toward the end of his life, Walser turned to religion and gave up the fight to preserve Liberal as a purely freethought town, though he stayed in the area until his death in 1910. The funeral was held at his home in Catalpa Park; he was buried together with his books, not in the Liberal cemetery, but in a mausoleum in Lake Cemetery in Lamar. The tomb bears the intertwined symbols of his Odd Fellows affiliation: *F L T* (Friendship, Love, Truth).

The Freethought University moved its operation in 1897 to Silverton, Oregon, home of an active freethinkers' group (see WAKEMAN, THADDEUS BURR).

Liberal still bears evidence of its early history, though it is now home to seven different church fellowships—one for every one hundred residents. The original street names have been preserved, named after freethought heroes such as Robert Green INGERSOLL, Charles DARWIN, and Thomas PAINE. There is also a Slenker Street, named after Elmina SLENKER, whose trial for sending sex and marriage information through the mail rocked Virginia in the 1880s and was a cause célèbre for freethinkers of the time.

Of historic note: Lamar is the birthplace of Harry S. Truman, thirty-third president of the United States, and the town where Wyatt Earp, the famous US Marshal, began his career in law enforcement in 1869 at age twenty-two. There is another town named Liberal in southwest Kansas, which got its name from its founder who gave water "liberally" to passing travelers.

BIBLIOGRAPHY

Macdonald, George E. *Fifty Years of Freethought.* New York: Truth Seeker, 1972.

Moore, J. P. *This Strange Town, Liberal.* Liberal, MO: Liberal News, 1963.

Sears, Hal D. *The Sex Radicals: Free Love in High Victorian America.* Lawrence: Regents Press of Kansas, 1977.

Whitehead, Fred, and Verle Muhrer. *Freethought on the American Frontier.* Amherst, NY: Prometheus Books, 1992.

ELIZABETH M. GERBER

LIBERATOR, THE. For twenty years one of the most effective FREETHOUGHT newspapers in the world, the *Liberator* was founded in 1884 by Joseph SYMES as a vehicle for Australian freethinkers. Symes conceived that the *Liberator* would do for Australian readers what the *NATIONAL REFORMER* and *FREETHINKER* offered their British cousins. In the tighter colonial market, the *Liberator* would need to provide both the lengthy analysis and political commentary of the *National Reformer* and the shorter, more polemical journalism of the *Freethinker*. The first issue of the *Liberator* was released on June 1, 1884. Symes summarized the paper's outlook as republican and atheist (see ATHEISM) and open to all forms of freethought. Religious opponents were assured of a standing invitation to rebut such claims as they felt moved to.

Reaction to the *Liberator* was splenetic, with Symes being vilified as a "leprous-tongued reptile" and the journal described as "bristling with bathos and blasphemy." The cause of offense lay as much with the cartoons Symes chose to feature as with the articles. Following the example of the *Freethinker*, the cartoons in the *Liberator* satirized some of the more absurd stories of the Old Testament. Symes's articles were trenchant and combative, but never intentionally offensive.

At its heyday the *Liberator* ran as a weekly newspaper of anything up to twenty pages an issue, though it was usually between twelve and eighteen pages. Circulation ran as high as twenty thousand. The *Liberator* experienced hard times in the 1890s as an economic depression sapped the paper's readership. It was a tribute to Symes's energy and that of his courageous wife, Agnes, that the paper continued through that decade, surmounting ongoing financial hardship and harassment. The paper enjoyed a brief revival in 1897 as funds flowed in his direction following a favorable turn in factional politics of the freethought movement. But this did not last, and the last four years of the *Liberator* were as hard as any in the depressed 1890s. The *Liberator* finally suspended publication on March 12, 1904, after twenty years. Symes cited "mad legislation, wholesale sport, gambling, and Socialism in its most insane form" as the reasons for the demise of the paper. Another aspect of the problem was that Symes was not a team player and had not groomed a successor who could have carried on his work.

BIBLIOGRAPHY

Dahlitz, Ray. "Secularism Down Under." *Free Inquiry* 14, no. 4 (Fall 1994).

Sinnott, Nigel. *Joseph Symes, the "Flower of Atheism."* Melbourne: Atheist Society of Australia, 1977.

BILL COOKE

LIBERTARIAN MOVEMENT AND UNBELIEF. Libertarianism is politically revolutionary, affirming the primacy of individual rights over those of any groups, notably the state, throughout public affairs. Libertarianism is advanced on various philosophical grounds. Most are secular, though some Christians and other believers hold that since faith must be a matter of free choice, a libertarian society is required for bona fide faith to blossom. Though often associated with the political Right in the United States and the United Kingdom, and thus with religiously based politics, libertarianism draws its philosophical fuel mostly from nonreligious or at most mildly religious thinkers in the classical liberal tradition, such as Baruch SPINOZA, John LOCKE, Adam Smith, Thomas JEFFERSON, James MADISON, Gustav de Molinari, John Stuart MILL, Herbert SPENCER, and others.

Ancient Libertarian Intimations. In ancient China, Lao Tzu (see CHINA, UNBELIEF IN) proposed an early libertarianism by noting:

Why are people starving?
Because the rulers eat up the money in taxes.
Therefore the people are starving.
Why are the people rebellious?
Because the rulers interfere too much.
Therefore they are rebellious. . . .

Lao Tzu reportedly believed that all religions were superstitious and nonsensical.

An early Western inkling of libertarianism comes from a dialogue between Alcibiades and Pericles, recounted by the Greek historian and philosophical essayist Xenophon. Alcibiades argued that law rightly understood is the absence of the initiation of physical force, so that only where liberty reigns can there be genuine lawfulness. Thus, if law uses coercive force, it is not law but aggression. If it does not use coercive force, then it is law proper. There is little evidence that Alcibiades was pious or religious.

From ARISTOTLE we learn about Lykophron and Hippodamus of Miletus, two Greek sophists (see SOPHISM) who advanced reasonably mature notions of liberty. Lykophron defended minimal government as the "guarantor of mutual rights." Hippodamus thought government should be limited to adjudicating disputes. Neither of these sophists is linked with supernaturalism.

Aristotle is often viewed as opposing classical liberalism because for him the polis must foster virtue. However, in Aristotle "the polis" can mean either the government or the community (as Fred D. Miller maintains). If it is the latter, then there need be no statism implicit in Aristotle. This is compatible with the polity of liberty, which does not conflict with the fostering of moral virtues by small, voluntary communities such as kibbutzim, the Rotary Club, or Disneyland. Aristotle's theology is minimalist—he believed there must be an unmoved mover, an idea close to DEISM.

Around the twelfth century we find a growing concern for natural rights to liberty and property. William of Occam has written that "natural [divine] right is nothing other than a power to conform to right reason, without an agreement or pact." Occam's line of analysis could be read to mean that in order for one to be able to make and act on sound moral judgments, one must also be recognized to possess basic rights, implying a necessary sphere of personal jurisdiction. Generalized, this view is comparable with Robert Nozick's modern libertarian idea of "moral space."

A radical individualism was developed by Thomas HOBBES. An absolute monarchist in his political science, Hobbes laid the crucial philosophical foundations for the *homo economicus* approach to human social life. His politics have come to be recognized as the basis for much of classical political economy. This is acknowledged by both critics and supporters of the free society, including Ian Shapiro and James Buchanan. (Shapiro notes that "[Hobbes's] negative libertarianism survived and achieved the preeminent status it did in the dominant ideology because of its affinity with these emerging economic and social relations.")

Spinoza argued that a good government will provide the people with as much liberty as possible, especially as regards the expression of political views. Spinoza's limited liberalism never quite amounted to a doctrine of the individual's right to liberty, but it would influence the development of liberal public policy.

Modern Libertarianism. The first modern philosopher with a full-blown (classical) liberal political theory is John Locke. He held that each person is by birth a sovereign with no natural rulers or natural subjects (though this sovereignty takes full effect only in adulthood). Government is established to protect individual rights, and the consent of the governed is required so as to legitimize government and to limit its powers. Locke gives a prominent place to the right to private property as an extension of the right to life and liberty. His famous exception, "the Lockean Proviso," does nothing to dampen Locke's enthusiasm for the free society, since when Locke says that we can acquire property "at least where there is enough, and as good left in common for others," all this need be construed to mean is that no legal monopolies may be established.

Locke professed Christianity, but his piety was doubted, especially by Leo Strauss and his followers, a group of scholars who link Locke to Hobbes's materialist philosophy.

Adam Smith, like David HUME, rested his defense of the liberal society first on inborn moral sentiments, and second on the public utility of having people pursue their private goals. Smith, too, appears to have eschewed supernaturalism.

J. S. Mill rested his defense of liberty on the two main ideas, first that happiness can be best pursued by free men and women, and second that happiness actually includes personal autonomy as an essential ingredient. Mill was most probably an unbeliever as well.

Herbert Spencer believed in essence that the human species is growing up—rather as Karl MARX did—and that in its fully grown state it will exhibit far-reaching individuation. In other words, the highest form of humanity is the most diversified form, which requires the scope for free action afforded only by laissez-faire capitalism. Spencer was an explicit atheist.

Carl Menger and the Austrian school—economists who stress the discovery process and entrepreneurship in market transactions and champion pure laissez-faire—drew initially on Aristotelian and individualist ethics, with the realization that the fulfillment of (even proper) individual goals is best accomplished in a free market and that economic affairs are best understood as the interplay of such diverse values by the agents who must pursue them. There is no evidence of any religious inclination on the part of Menger.

Also deserving of mention are the nineteenth-century individualist anarchists Josiah Warren, Benjamin Tucker, and Lysander Spooner, the precursors of contemporary anarcho-libertarianism (see ANARCHISM AND UNBELIEF), none of whom is closely linked with any religious thought.

Recent and Contemporary Libertarians. Recent Austrian economists who have exerted great influence on libertarian thought include the school's founding scholar, Ludwig von Mises, and his most famous student, Nobel laureate Friedrich August von Hayek; they were both explicit unbelievers. Prominent among the well-known Chicago school advocates of the free market are the Nobel laureates Milton Friedman, George Stigler, Gary S. Becker, and James M. Buchanan, none of whom is associated with any theological system.

Among philosophical champions of libertarian politics there is the intellectually influential and quite controversial atheist Ayn RAND and several neo-Randians, including David Kelley, Eric Mack, Douglas Den J. Uyl, and Douglas B. Rasmussen, none of them theists. Rand, a Russian-born novelist and nonacademic philosopher, advocated among many challenging philosophical positions the pure libertarian (or, as she called it, capitalist) society, insisting that its foundations cannot rest on faith. Murray N. Rothbard, who led the anarchist strain of classical liberalism in the twentieth century, was also an unbeliever. So have been John Hospers, Robert Nozick (the most prominent academic libertarian in the contemporary era), Jan Narveson, and Loren Lomasky.

The classical liberal tradition out of which libertarianism developed has not been espoused solely by the nonreligious. Lord Acton may be the earliest classical liberal who was importantly religious. Later examples include, in our own time, the Acton Institute cleric Robert Sirico and lay theologian Michael Novak of the American Enterprise Institute.

Still, the majority of champions of a fully free, libertarian, laissez-faire capitalist political and economic order have been unbelievers.

BIBLIOGRAPHY

Bandow, Doug. "Irreconcilable Differences?" *Liberty*, July 1992.

Boaz, David. *The Libertarian Reader.* New York: Free Press, 1997.

Den Uyl, Douglas J. *Power, State and Freedom: An Interpretation of Spinoza's Political Thought.* Assen, The Netherlands: Van Gorcum, 1983

Den Uyl, Douglas J., and Douglas B. Rasmussen. *Liberty and Nature.* Chicago: Open Court, 1991.

Hospers, John. *Libertarianism.* Los Angeles: Nash, 1972.

Lomasky, Loren. *Persons, Rights, and the Moral Community.* New York: Oxford University Press, 1990.

Machan, Tibor, ed., *Individuals and Their Rights.* Chicago: Open Court, 1989.

———. *The Libertarian Alternative.* Chicago: Nelson-Hall, 1974.

———. *The Libertarian Reader.* Lanham, MD: Rowman & Littlefield, 1982.

Miller, Fred D., Jr. "The State and Community in Aristotle's *Politics.*" *Reason Papers* 1 (1974).

Narveson, Jan. *The Libertarian Idea.* Philadelphia: Temple University Press, 2001.

Nozick, Robert. *Anarchy, State, and Utopia.* New York: Basic Books, 1974.

Rommen, Heinrich A. "The Genealogy of Natural Rights." *Thought* 29 (1984).

Rothbard, Murray N. *Man, Economy and State.* Princeton, NJ: Van Nostrand, 1962.

Sell, Ala P. F. *Mill on God.* Burlington, VT: Ashgate, 2004.

Shapiro, Ian. *The Evolution of Rights in Liberal Theory.* Cambridge: Cambridge University Press, 1986.

Sprague, Rosamond Kent, ed. *The Older Sophists.* Columbia: University of South Carolina Press, 1972.

Xenophon. *Memorabilia.* Translated and annotated by Amy L. Bonnette. Ithaca, NY: Cornell University Press, 1994.

TIBOR R. MACHAN

LIBRARY COLLECTIONS ON UNBELIEF. As Gordon STEIN, editor of the original *Encyclopedia of Unbelief,* noted in 1985, books, periodicals, and other media expressing unbelief are often difficult to locate. Most such works were—and still are—published by small publishers in short press runs (see PERIODICALS OF UNBELIEF). The population of unbelievers who actively participate in "unbelief activities" (who purchase unbelief books and periodicals or belong to an unbelief advocacy group) is very small, as is the community of believers who study unbelief. Together they may constitute less than one tenth of 1 percent of the population of the United States, or roughly 250,000 persons (see DEMOGRAPHY OF UNBELIEF). This is not a large enough population to support widespread publication of—hence easy access to—its literature. While the rise of the Internet has made it easier for contemporary atheists, agnostics, freethinkers, and humanists to share their ideas, it remains difficult to find and use collections of older unbelief items. A number of older FREETHOUGHT works whose copyrights have expired (and hence have entered the public domain) have been made available through the Kentucky-based Bank of Wisdom project, originally as scanned text files and more recently as PDF-format image files distributed on CD-ROM. Another selection of public-domain freethought works has been made available online by Project Gutenberg. Even so, a number of historic freethought works, including many of the rarest works, remain unavailable in electronic form.

Even in physical libraries access to works expressing unbelief may be made unnecessarily difficult because the material is controversial. In *Libraries in the Age of Mediocrity*, Earl Lee, librarian of the HALDEMAN-JULIUS freethought collection at Pittsburg State University in Kansas, accuses librarians of systematically misfiling freethought works. This gives the libraries that hold them a false impression that they receive little usage; the books are not being used because patrons and researchers cannot find them while browsing library shelves. This causes those works to be prematurely deaccessioned. Believing that no one is interested in these materials, librarians give over the shelf space to other works that might be better utilized. Lee points out several specific items that are frequently classified incorrectly or incompletely, thus making it unlikely that a browser walking through a library's stacks could find them. For example, consider a work whose subject matter is the evidence for or against the existence of Jesus (see JESUS, HISTORICITY OF; BIBLICAL CRITICISM). Such a work should be cataloged under the Library of Congress subject *Jesus Christ—Historicity* (BT 303.2) or the Dewey equivalent (232.908), rather than under *Atheism, Freethought or Christianity—Controversial Literature*, where it can be found in many libraries. Today's cataloging methods make these works easier to find; cross-referencing is especially powerful in today's electronic cataloges. While this aids knowledgeable researchers in locating the works in question, especially if they know in advance that the works exist, the would-be reader browsing physical stacks remains unlikely to encounter them.

Lee points out that the reason for miscataloging could be that these works are cataloged by librarians who are subject specialists on religion and philosophy, rather than on topics of unbelief. These librarians have limited or no experience with cataloging unbelief or are "uninterested" in these works, and subsequently give works of unbelief little attention and exert little effort to catalog them properly. Exacerbating this problem is the fact that there are very few librarians who are subject specialists in the areas relating to unbelief.

Libraries as a group are conservative in nature, and tend to present ideas seen as controversial by the general public in, at best, a limited way. Therefore, few public libraries carry these materials in any more than a superficial way; those that do so have specific reasons for doing so. Such libraries have often been given the papers and books of someone who was interested in unbelief under a bequest whose terms require the recipient libraries to hold and catalog them. It is likely that only a fraction of the personal collections willed to public libraries reach their intended destinations. In some cases libraries refuse the bequest because of the controversial nature of the collection; in many other instances, believing family members of a deceased unbeliever destroy the willed materials before the bequest can be implemented.

Genesis of an Unbelief Library. Libraries of unbelief come into existence most often as an outgrowth of the archiving function of an organization associated with a publisher active in unbelief. The best-known libraries of unbelief in the United States all result from this type of association: the Elizabeth Elliott Library, the library of the Freedom From Religion Foundation; the Charles E. Stevens American Atheist Library and Archives (CESAALA), the library of American Atheists; the library of the AMERICAN HUMANIST ASSOCIATION; and the Center for Inquiry Libraries (CFI Libraries), which contains the library of the Council for Secular Humanism.

As mentioned before, another method in which collections of unbelief materials are gathered is through donations by individuals, the core of many of the unbelief collections held by public and university libraries. The New York Public Library (NYPL) acquired a significant portion of its freethought holdings when it received the Irving Levy Collection, which consists of mostly British but also some American freethought; the NYPL has one of the richest collections of freethought of any public library in the world.

Unbelief materials are also gathered through libraries that actively acquire them through purchase; most libraries engaging in such acquisitions already hold a core of such materials to begin with. Many of the libraries in this category, perhaps surprisingly, are theology school libraries, including the Princeton Theological Seminary, Union Theological Seminary, and Andover-Harvard Theological Library. These libraries continue actively to acquire materials in support of their collections of unbelief materials.

Unbelief Libraries of Asia, Australia, and New Zealand. India is the only Asian country with a significant indigenous tradition of unbelief (see INDIA, UNBELIEF IN) and, therefore, significant library collections of unbelief. In Chennai (formerly Madras), the Theosophical Society holds a large collection of Indian freethought journals (see THEOSOPHY; BESANT, ANNIE), and the Indian Rationalist Society holds both Indian and British Freethought items. The Periyar Centre in New Delhi also has library facilities. The Atheist Centre in Vijayawada experienced a serious loss in 1977, when some ten thousand of the fifteen thousand volumes in its library were lost to a catastrophic cyclone and tidal wave. Over the years since, this loss has been only partially made up.

Australia and New Zealand have a rich freethought history (see AUSTRALIA, UNBELIEF IN; NEW ZEALAND, UNBELIEF IN). An as yet unpublished survey by US bibliographer Bruce Cathey reports that in each country the national library has fewer unbelief-related holdings than the various state libraries. The Mitchell Library (the State Library of Sydney) contains a good collection of freethought materials of Australian origin. The National Library of Australia (Canberra) holds the Pearce Collection of freethought from both Australia and New Zealand. The Dr. Robert STOUT Collection, in the Beaglehole Room at the University of Wellington, Victoria, New Zealand, is a collection of rationalist and related materials including books and bound pamphlets, comprising items of American, British, and Australian origin.

New Zealand is home to two special libraries with freethought holdings, operated by the Humanist Society of New Zealand in Turnbull House, Wellington, and by the New Zealand Association of Rationalists and Humanists (NZARH), also publisher of the magazine *Open Society*, based in Rationalist House in Auckland. According to Cathey, these libraries hold fine collections of British and American freethought materials but are not as rich in materials from Australia and New Zealand as some of the libraries noted above.

British and Canadian Libraries. Canada is not nearly as rich in unbelief holdings as New Zealand or

Australia. The National Library of Canada in Ottawa is a repository library, so most items that have been published in Canada are held there. Also in Ottawa, the University of Ottawa holds some unbelief titles. The University of Toronto holds some Russian-language unbelief items as well.

The three best collections of unbelief in Canada reside in university libraries. York University in Toronto has a very good collection of British freethought. The Elizabeth Dafoe Library at the University of Manitoba (Winnipeg) holds the Marshall GAUVIN Collection, comprising about four thousand books plus papers and manuscripts, part of a collection donated in 1980 by the family of this prominent Canadian freethought activist. There is little Canadian unbelief here; the collection consists of most American freethought. McMaster University in Hamilton, Ontario, purchased the Bertrand RUSSELL papers and has created an archive of Russell materials.

In Great Britain, many of the libraries with significant unbelief holdings are associated with publishers of unbelief. The following are all located in London: the SOUTH PLACE ETHICAL SOCIETY has a good collection of British freethought; materials relating to Annie Besant can be located at the Theosophical Society (originally a close colleague of atheist politician Charles BRADLAUGH, Besant later turned from nontheist to Theosophist, and her unbelief items can be located along with her Theosophical writings here); the NATIONAL SECULAR SOCIETY and the RATIONALIST PRESS ASSOCIATION have significant collections on unbelief as well; the Bishopsgate Institute holds in its archives the papers of Charles Bradlaugh and George Jacob HOLYOAKE.

One of the next most significant unbelief collections in Britain is located in Norfolk. The Norfolk Public Library (Thetford branch) holds the Ambrose G. Barker Collection and Thomas Paine Society Collection. Both are very good collections of materials on Thomas PAINE—not surprisingly, as Thetford is the birthplace of Paine. Ambrose G. Barker also gave a collection of Charles Bradlaugh materials to the Northampton Public Library (Northampton was Bradlaugh's riding, or district, when he served as a Member of Parliament). In Manchester, the Co-Operative Union Institute holds additional papers of George Jacob Holyoake as well as the papers of Robert OWEN. Oxford, Cambridge, and Bristol all have collections including some unbelief materials, and can all be accessed via British online union catalogs, as can the British (National) Library.

United States Libraries of Unbelief. Since the Library of Congress (LC) functions as the de facto national library, two copies of each book published in the United States must be deposited there, in keeping with its function as a copyright library. As such, the LC holds a far greater collection of unbelief materials than any other library. The LC also holds most of the papers of nineteenth-century freethought orator Robert Green INGER-

SOLL. In addition, the LC is responsible for the majority of all the cataloging incorporated in the various bibliographic databases that libraries use to "copy catalog" and create their own catalogues. Most academic libraries also use the classification system created by the LC in their libraries. The familiar Dewey Decimal System is adequate for general-interest libraries, but libraries holding numerous works on closely related topics would have decimal numbers going out eight to ten places, making it much harder to use than LC Classification, which employs subject headings and corresponding classification letters and numbers.

Several US colleges and universities have significant collections on unbelief. The University of Texas (Austin), Columbia (New York City), Ohio State (Columbus), Northwestern (Evanston, Illinois), the University of Chicago, UCLA, Princeton, Rutgers (New Brunswick, New Jersey), and the University of Maryland (College Park) all have good collections in such areas as freethought, DEISM, and similar topics. The University of Wisconsin (Madison) and Yale (New Haven, Connecticut) hold collections of British freethought materials. The theology schools mentioned above have good collections, as does the Duke University Divinity School (Durham, North Carolina).

But three university collections stand out above all others. Southern Illinois University (Carbondale, Illinois) holds a large collection of Ingersoll materials and houses the Center for Dewey Studies, devoted to the work of American naturalist philosopher John DEWEY. The University of Michigan (Ann Arbor) is home to the Labadie Collection on Social Protest Movements; holdings include unbelief and such closely related topics as socialism, anarchism, and the labor movement (see ANARCHISM AND UNBELIEF; LABOR AND UNBELIEF). The Leonard H. Axe Library of Kansas State College (at Pittsburg) contains the publications and archives of Emmanuel Haldeman-Julius, publisher of the Little Blue Books and other influential mid-twentieth-century publications.

Two notable collections reside off university campuses. The Illinois State Historical Society (Springfield) contains a large volume of papers from Robert G. Ingersoll. The American Philosophical Society in Philadelphia holds the Richard Gimbel Collection on Thomas Paine, which has many handwritten items from Thomas Paine, including a manuscript for *Common Sense* (see also MONUMENTS TO UNBELIEF).

Private US Collections of Unbelief. As stated earlier, four major collections of unbelief materials are held by publishers of unbelief. The Freedom From Religion Foundation (FFRF) in Madison, Wisconsin, has the Elizabeth Elliott library, containing more than two thousand freethought books. FFRF members may borrow books, and the collection is available to researchers by appointment.

The Charles E. Stevens American Atheist Library and Archives (CESAALA), the library of American Atheists (see O'HAIR, MADALYN MURRAY), is located at the new American Atheist Center in Cranford, New Jersey. According to spokesperson Conrad Goeringer, as this is written the library is still undergoing some reorganization within the new facility, but the fifty to sixty thousand books originally held by Madalyn Murray O'Hair in Austin, Texas, have been received and are being placed into the Center in a climate-controlled room fitted with "dry" fire suppression equipment. Goeringer estimates the additional holdings at five hundred thousand periodicals and ephemera, plus audiovisual materials, archival materials, and papers and publications of early freethought groups such as the UNITED SECULARISTS OF AMERICA. The library does not have public hours, but it does accommodate serious researchers; those wishing to use the facilities should contact American Atheists.

The American Humanist Association (AHA) moved from Amherst, New York, to Washington, DC, several years ago. Their collections (formerly known as the Dewey-Muller Library and Wilson Archives) include thousands of books, audiovisual materials, microforms, periodicals, and electronic media. The library contains items on freethought and humanism, but also materials on philosophy, politics, and other items that relate to their broad humanistic worldview. Again, this is a research library; workers desiring to access the collection should make an advance appointment.

The Center for Inquiry (CFI) Libraries at Amherst, New York, hold approximately fifty thousand books in addition to thousands of periodicals, newsletters, microforms, archival materials, and other items. These include the collections for the Committee for the Scientific Investigation of Claims of the Paranormal (CSICOP) and the Council for Secular Humanism. The facilities are available for serious researchers by appointment during normal business hours. The CFI Libraries employ two professional librarians, among whose priorities is cataloging rare materials collected there that are not held or cataloged anywhere else in the world. Many of the rare items were acquired from the estate of Gordon Stein, well-known freethought bibliographer and founding director of the CFI Libraries. Holdings cover such topics as freethought and SECULAR HUMANISM, philosophy, church-state separation, history of religions, comparative religion, and items critical of religion. There are also holdings on general topics that touch tangentially on all areas of unbelief.

Conclusion. Since the first *Encyclopedia of Unbelief* was published, the general trend has been to create privately owned libraries associated with the various causes of unbelief. The Library of Congress must by law continue to add to its collections, and the various theology schools have been acquiring some unbelief materials. Personal collections have been moving out of private hands, usually upon the death of the collector, either being destroyed by believing family members or bequeathed to the libraries of the various unbelief organ-

izations. Readers who own an unbelief collection can ensure its future availability for use by future scholars by making advance arrangements to donate materials to one of the unbelief libraries named in this entry.

BIBLIOGRAPHY

Brown, Marshall G., and Gordon Stein. *Freethought in the United States: A Descriptive Bibliography.* Westport, CT: Greenwood, 1978.
Cathey, Bruce E. *Bibliography of Australian and New Zealand Non-serial Rationalist/Secularist/Humanist and Related Publications, 1850–1999.* Unpublished manuscript, 2000.
Lee, Earl. *Libraries in the Age of Mediocrity.* Jefferson, NC: McFarland, 1998.
Stein, Gordon. *Freethought in the United Kingdom and the Commonwealth: A Descriptive Bibliography.* Westport, CT: Greenwood, 1981.

TIMOTHY BINGA

LIBRE PENSÉE, FÉDÉRATION FRANÇAISE DE LA.

Libre pensée in French means "freethought." France is a country whose freethinkers can be counted in the millions, but where the need to belong to an association is not strongly felt. France's tradition of anticlericalism is also a tradition against the formation of mass associations, excepting trade unions. Nevertheless, the organization known as La Fédération Française de la Libre Pensée has a long history and has had a very strong influence despite its relatively small membership, which has allowed it to take often rather radical positions with regard to the problems of the nation, even on subjects far removed from the fight for secularism and for the right to unbelief, narrowly defined.

The Libre Pensée traces its intellectual and ideological heritage to Ancient Greece (EPICURUS) through the Middle Ages (François Villon) and the Renaissance (François Rabelais), to the triumphs of the eighteenth-century ENLIGHTENMENT and the French Revolution. The proud label of "freethinker" can be applied to all those who rejected revealed truths imposed by authorities and who dared to stand up and say "no" to obscurantism and oppression. A crucial period was the time of the Reformation, at the beginning of the sixteenth century. The Reformation was both a social rebellion and a rebellion against dogma. Religious sects proliferated, and alongside them pioneering thinkers such as Desiderius ERASMUS proposed systems of free inquiry that acknowledged no revealed religion.

The Libre Pensée was founded in 1847 at a meeting of militants from the dawning republican and labor movements. Initial goals included secularism, the strict separation of religion from school and state, and an uncompromising struggle against religious oppression. The Libre Pensée included in its ranks the most famous personalities of the nineteenth and twentieth centuries: François-Vincent Raspail, Auguste Blanqui, Victor Hugo, Maximillien LITTRÉ, Paul Bert, Ferdinand Buisson, Aristide Briand, Georges Clémenceau, Emile Zola, Romain Rolland, Victor Basch, Edouard Herriot, Anatole FRANCE, Jean Jaurès, Bertrand RUSSELL, and Jean Rostand were among its members. As of 2004 the Fédération Française de la Libre Pensée numbered about two thousand active members. In each of the *départements* (subregional governments) of metropolitan France, the Libre Pensée maintains a departmental federation of militants. It is represented in the parliament by an informal intercameral group comprising members drawn from the three chambers of the French Republic. There is an association of local politicians (mayors, and *départemental* and regional elected representatives) known as the Amis de la Libre pensée (Friends of Freethought). In addition, the Libre Pensée publishes a review, *La Raison* (Reason), with a circulation of about ten thousand. It is available wherever quality magazines are sold. The Libre Pensée publishes also a quarterly review, *L'Idée Libre* (The Free Idea). The Libre Pensée is directed by a national administrative council composed of fifteen members. The Libre Pensée is affiliated with the INTERNATIONAL HUMANIST AND ETHICAL UNION (IHEU) as full member; Christian Eyschen, in 2005 its general secretary, is a member of the IHEU's delegation to UNESCO; and Roger Lepeix is, since 2005, the treasurer of the IHEU.

The Libre Pensée is devoted to five basic principles typical of freethought activism throughout French history:

1. It is anticlerical, opposing any meddling by religion in the operation of secular society and republican institutions. It campaigns for a return to strict implementation of the landmark December 9, 1905, law requiring strict separation of church and state, which was passed on as the result of a Libre Pensée campaign. The Libre Pensée stands for an established secularism and the withdrawal of all public funds from private schools.
2. The Libre Pensée is antireligious, regarding religion as one of the main sources of obscurantism and human oppression. It believes that men and women must seize their happiness in this life, not in an extraterrestrial pseudoparadise. It rejects any claims of revealed truth, challenges all dogma, and campaigns for complete liberty of thought.
3. The Libre Pensée is antimilitarist, staunchly opposing the doctrine that people should make war and slaughter each other for interests which are not their own. It campaigns for unilateral disarmament.
4. The Libre Pensée is internationalist, valuing the interests of all people over those of any national group. In light of its antimilitarism and internationalism, the Libre Pensée has adopted a clearly pacifist orientation.
5. The Libre Pensée is anticapitalist, opposed to any economic exploitation that, like political and religious oppression, violates the legitimate rights of individuals. On the social level, the Libre Pensée campaigns for the complete emancipation of the individual.

Members of the Libre Pensée commit themselves not to take part in religious ceremonies, either for themselves and for their underage children, and to have secular funerals.

Thanks to the officers of the Libre Pensée, Roger Lepeix and Christian Eyschen, for their assistance.

JEAN-CLAUDE PECKER

LICHTENBERG, GEORG CHRISTOPH (1742–1799), German polymath, satirist, and aphorist. Like many of the "critical spirits" of the eighteenth century, Georg Christoph Lichtenberg came from a middle-class family. Disfigured by a hunchback, his professional choices were limited; he entered university academics at Göttingen, where he became professor of physics.

Lichtenberg's life was eventful, including distinguished work in applied science, travel to England (resulting in an influential book explaining the English painter/engraver William Hogarth to his fellow Germans), satirical confrontations with his academic contemporaries, and coediting a literary journal with the naturalist and revolutionary Georg Forster, known by his participation in Cook's travels. Especially in his scrapbooks, Lichtenberg developed self-reflective modernity to an impressive depth, based on his stance of "materialist Spinozism" (see MATERIALISM, PHILOSOPHICAL). He formulated the main argument against the ego-based RATIONALISM of René DESCARTES, namely, that it offers no ground for inferring a personal ego as a specific entity. He anticipated a central thesis of the later Ludwig FEUERBACH: "God created man after his image, which probably means that man created God after his own image." This should not be seen as mere witticism, but rather as the application of a more general insight into his own age, which was still struggling toward enlightenment (see ENLIGHTENMENT, UNBELIEF DURING THE) and as yet little able to frame concepts of explicit unbelief. Like most of his contemporaries, Lichtenberg found it difficult to conceive of a society entirely liberated from religion—and yet he could declare: "Our world is going to be so sophisticated one day that it will be as ridiculous to believe in God as it is nowadays to believe in ghosts."

Lichtenberg is one of the radical thinkers largely forgotten in German culture after the failed democratic revolution of 1848.

BIBLIOGRAPHY

Brinitzer, Carl. *A Reasonable Rebel: Georg Christoph Lichtenberg.* Translated by Bernard Smith. London: Allen & Unwin, 1960.

Buechler, Ralph W. *Science, Satire, and Wit: The Essays of Georg Christoph Lichtenberg*. New York: Lang, 1991.

Craig, Charlotte M., ed. *Lichtenberg: Essays Commemorating the 250th Anniversary of His Birth*. New York: Lang, 1992.

Knopper, Françoise. "A Virtuous Agnostic? Belief and Superstition in the Work of Georg Christoph Lichtenberg." In *Le Spectateur européen/The European Spectator*, vols. 3 and 4. Montpellier: Presses Universitaires, 2002.

Lichtenberg, Georg Christoph. *Gesammelte Schriften: Historisch-kritische und kommentierte Ausgabe*. Göttingen: Wallstein, 2005ff.

———. *Hogarth on High Life: The Marriage à la Mode series from Georg Christoph Lichtenberg's Commentaries*. Translated and edited by Arthur S. Wensinger with W. B. Coley. Middletown, CT: Wesleyan University Press, 1970.

———. *The World of Hogarth; Lichtenberg's Commentaries on Hogarth's Engravings*. Translated and with an introduction by Innes and Gustav Herdan. Boston: Houghton Mifflin, 1966.

Lichtenberg, Ludwig Christian, ed. *Georg Christoph Lichtenbergs vermischte Schriften*. Wien: Kaulfuß and Armbruster, 1800–1806.

Mautner, Franz H., and Henry Hatfield, ed. and trans. *The Lichtenberg Reader: Selected Writings of Georg Christoph Lichtenberg*. Boston: Beacon, 1959.

FRIEDER OTTO WOLF

LIFE, ORIGINS OF, AND UNBELIEF. Origin problems occupy a unique place in science. Everyday scientific explanation involves the formulation of general laws and principles that are meant to be tested against observable facts. Origin problems, in contrast, refer to unique events in the past, beyond the reach of direct observation. They are historical, even forensic in nature, but the attempt to resolve them casts light on deep and at times unrecognized issues in the study of the phenomenon whose origin is to be explored. For life on Earth, we are dealing with an event that took place some 3.5 to 4 billion years ago. We know (from the spectra of distant stars) that the laws of physics, and hence those of chemistry, were the same as today, but conditions on the planet were very different from now, no direct traces remain, and the mechanisms of biology had (by definition) not yet come into operation. Indeed, it is precisely the origin of these mechanisms that needs to be explained. Thus one of the major benefits of the search for the origins of life is a deepened understanding of life itself. Since the work of Benoît de Maillet and George-Louis Leclerc, Comte de BUFFON in the mid-eighteenth century, biological science has been concerned with tracing the origin and common ancestry of living things through the operation of purely natural causes. This program has been stunningly suc-cessful in explaining everything from the fossil record to the engineering strengths and weaknesses of human anatomy to the unity of biochemistry. Our current attempt to understand the origins of life on Earth represents the latest stage in this process. It has been made possible by advances in molecular biology, complexity theory, planetary science, and geology, in the past few decades. This program makes no reference to supernatural or divine agencies, and to invoke such agencies in this context would be to abandon the domain of science altogether (see EVOLUTION AND UNBELIEF; RELIGION IN CONFLICT WITH SCIENCE).

Much has changed since H. James Birx's article on this subject in the original *Encyclopedia of Unbelief*, to which we refer the reader for the older historical background. It is now possible to distinguish between the "easy question" of how the so-called molecules of life could have originated, and the much more difficult (and interesting) question of how these molecules came to be organized in a way that gives life its distinctive nature. We have much more precise information about the antiquity of life, and about the environment in which it would appear to have arisen. NASA has set up and devoted considerable resources to an umbrella institution for the study of "astrobiology," the study of the place of life in the universe, of which the study of the origin of life is an integral part. Stimulated in part by this development, astrobiology has gained recognition as an academic discipline, with useful textbooks being written at both the general and the more specialized scientific level. At the same time, the intervening decades have seen a resurgence of antiscientific, or worse, pseudoscientific, discussions of the development of living things, challenging the very notion that the origin and variety of life on Earth is amenable to naturalistic explanation. Deplorable as they may be, such challenges need to be answered.

For reasons of space, I will not provide detailed references to every point raised in this article, but have assembled a representative list of relevant texts in the bibliography; in addition, NASA and the online *Astrobiology Magazine* maintain excellent Web sites. For the same reason, I will have little to say about the possibility of life on other planets, or of life-forms not based on chemistry, or what would qualify as "artificial life." Finally, I would emphasize that many of the topics I discuss are still, in their details, matters of active scientific controversy, and that what follows should be regarded as one individual's perspective.

How is life possible? And, while we are on the subject, what about advanced life, life that can sit around a dinner table and discuss its own existence? What about life elsewhere in the universe? This last is the central question of the area of *exobiology*, a branch of science which shares with theology the distinction of having a subject matter that has not been shown to exist.

In other words, what are the things that have to happen

before you can have life as we know it, and how likely is it that all these things should happen? And, by implication, how probable was it that life would arise on Earth? Or, indeed, elsewhere? Is life a monstrous freak, a cosmic commonplace, or somewhere in between? We have no idea.

The Nature of Life. From our present perspective, the defining qualities of life are the ability to impose an extremely high degree of organization on matter in a defined region at the molecular level, and the ability to reproduce itself. Both of these seem to defy the Second Law of Thermodynamics, but the conflict is apparent only. Living systems are open systems, open to both the flow of energy and the flow of matter. The local increase in order associated with the activities of life is purchased at the expense of increased disorder, or, more technically, the exploitation of sources of free energy, from somewhere outside. In the case of life on Earth, this somewhere can be sunlight (photosynthesis), chemical disequilibria in geological systems, especially hot spots (lithotrophic and chemotrophic bacteria), or (as in the case of all animals) the degradation of living or once living tissue consumed as food. This process of imposing local order is what we call metabolism, and in terrestrial life is conducted by the catalytic action of enzymes, which are mainly protein.

If the products of this local order are not to simply diffuse away, they need to be physically confined. Thus all living things have a boundary that separates inside from outside. The vast majority of living things consist of a single cell with a cell wall. More complex organisms, including ourselves, are of course organized communities of cells. The cell wall, a basic component of all living things, is produced by the processes of metabolism.

The final essential component of life as we know it is a central information store, the genetic material (for life on earth, the DNA), which performs two subtly different functions, those of inheritance and control. For the information to be inherited, it must be copied from one generation to another. For the information to be used, it is translated through a complicated molecular machinery into instructions for making proteins, which carry out the work of metabolism. Put simply, the metabolic system carries out the operations of life, while the genetic system tells it what to do. The entire process is further complicated by feedback loops, at present poorly understood, which control the expression of genes and their response to the external (and, for multicellular organisms, the internal) environment.

Metabolic and informational activities both depend, at every stage, on the process of molecular recognition, by which chemical groups of different kinds attract or repel each other. At its simplest, molecular recognition explains why sugar dissolves in water but not in gasoline. At its most complex, it governs the way in which proteins stick to each other and in which DNA is replicated.

Thus life possesses three essential components: a metabolism, a boundary surface, and an information store. It is difficult to see how any one of these could function without the others. That is why the origin of life is such a difficult and fascinating problem.

The Antiquity of Life: Evidence from Geology. It has been seriously suggested that life evolved elsewhere in the universe, and that somehow it traversed space to arrive on, and inoculate, the early Earth. This suggestion vastly increases the space and time available, but requires incredible resilience in an organism that would have had to survive—most probably for many millions of years—the cold, vacuum, and unfiltered radiation of deep space.

The alternative, which is certainly the working hypothesis of most scientists in the field, is that life arose from nonliving matter here on Earth by the operation of natural processes. If so, we can specify the time interval involved with reasonable accuracy.

We know from extensive radioactive dating using several different isotopes that the solar system formed some 4.5 billion years ago, and the Earth-moon system some 4.2 billion years ago. This occurred by the accretion of dust to make larger particles, coalescing under the influence of gravity to form progressively larger bodies; just such processes have been seen in action around young stars. At the time when the inner planets emerged from this process, our part of the solar system would still have been full of rocky accretions, similar to those that now form the asteroid belt. In addition, icy material would have been abundant in the region of the outer planets, where the gravitational effects of chance encounters would have led to episodes of cometary infall. It seems likely that this cometary infall provided a major part of the water of our oceans, and of volatile elements such as carbon that are essential to life. Thanks to the action of plate tectonics, no part of Earth's crust survives from that period, but we have terraines on the moon that are known to be 4.2 billion years old, and the surface of Mercury and much of that of Mars is generally assumed to stem from the same period. These surfaces are heavily cratered, and radioactive dating of lunar samples indicates that this bombardment was still going strong some 3.8 billion years ago. Impacts of such magnitude on the young Earth would have boiled the oceans, although it is conceivable that life could have survived at depth and recolonized the earth. There is indeed some evidence that this is exactly what happened.

The oldest proven microfossils are around 3.65 billion years old, and so life was definitely in existence by then. However, there is geochemical evidence that life is even older. The oldest known sedimentary rocks, comprising the Isua formation of Greenland, contain granules of carbon whose isotopic composition is powerful evidence for biological processing. If so, there was life on Earth when these rocks were formed, some 3.85 billion years ago.

Thus, while the details are still uncertain, it would

seem that life appeared on Earth almost as soon as it possibly could, in geological terms. This suggests (although of course it does not prove) that the process was perhaps not all that difficult.

Evidence from Molecular Biology. Molecular biology enables us to compare genetic material from different organisms; from how widely they differ and what we know about the rate of genetic change, we can estimate how long ago they diverged. (It was actually the surrealist painter Salvador Dali who first proposed the use of this biological "soft clock.") In this way, we can construct a tree of life by extrapolating backwards from all the different surviving branches. We then find that the simplest organisms, the bacteria, which do not possess a distinct nucleus within the cell, actually comprise two distinct domains which separated some billions of years ago. (Viruses, once regarded as distinct primitive life-forms, are now seen as detached fragments of material from higher organisms.) These domains, now called Eubacteria and Archaebacteria or Archaea, differ profoundly in chemistry and most especially in the composition of their cell walls. The third and most recent domain, the Eukaryotes, includes all plants and animals. It consists of those cells with distinct intracellular scaffolding and a separate nucleus, and is essentially an early branch off from the Archaea, with major borrowing of material from Eubacteria that took up their homes inside it and became so well adapted as to fuse into a single organism. Green plants also contain material contributed from a later fusion episode, in which cyanobacteria (blue-green algae) contributed the chloroplasts that perform photosynthesis. The oldest branches, those most similar to the inferred *cenancestor* (the last common ancestor from which all organisms are descended) on both the Archaea and the Eubacteria side, all turn out to be *chemautotrophs* and *hyperthermophiles*, making their own constituent organic molecules from available simple components, getting the energy needed to do this from chemical reactions, not sunlight, and living in ocean vents or hot springs at temperatures from 70° to 100°C or more (150° to upwards of 212°F; temperatures above 100°C are possible in liquid water at ocean depths because of the pressure). One can understand that in the absence of other life to feed on, the cenancestor had to synthesize its own component molecules, and that it used chemical energy rather than sunlight to do so, since photosynthesis requires an elaborate apparatus. It was, however, totally unexpected that the last common ancestor should have been a hyperthermophile, since there are plenty of organisms that use chemical energy at temperatures in between 0° and 40°C (freezing and 100°F), the normal range for life.

There are two possible interpretations. First, life could have originated at these elevated temperatures. This appears unlikely for several reasons. Higher temperature means more random molecular motion, hampering control and making it more difficult to discriminate between wanted and unwanted reaction pathways; conditions in hot spots are unstable; and individual hot spots probably don't last that long, on the geological timescale. The second alternative is that the last common ancestor was a survivor of catastrophe. We have at hand a possible candidate, in the form of the tail end of the crater-forming bombardment. Imagine an impact not quite energetic enough to totally sterilize the earth, but large enough to raise its ocean's surface temperature to boiling. Such a near-sterilizing impact would have wiped out all life-forms except hyperthermophiles. This suggests that in the narrow time window—perhaps a mere 100 million years—between the last fully sterilizing impact and the last near-sterilizing impact, life had evolved, diversified, and filled even such difficult niches (for they are difficult) as those now resided in by the hyperthermophiles. On this interpretation, the time window becomes very narrow indeed, and the occurrence of life on other warm, wet planets seems more and more likely.

If the process occurred so readily, why do we not see life repeatedly reemerging? Charles Darwin's speculative answer was that if it did, it would promptly be eaten. A more plausible generalization is that it would be unable to compete. The very first life-forms could go about their business slowly and inefficiently, provided only that they managed to replace themselves. It might also be suggested that life could not emerge today because of changed chemical conditions, but this is too glib an answer. The earth's surface has certainly changed from chemically reducing (i.e., richer in hydrogen and carbon than in oxygen) to oxidizing, but reducing conditions persist near midocean ridges, and everywhere at depth, much as they did 4 billion years ago.

The Nature of the Last Common Ancestor. The process of working backwards takes us to an organism (or population) from which all organisms are descended, the cenancestor. This organism was itself already highly involved in structure, with DNA, the present-day genetic code, RNA in its various functions, the same kind of translation machinery, and enzymes constructed from the same set of amino acids, as in modern life-forms. It had already experienced several gene doubling events, and comparisons between different copies of these doubled genes in the three different domains of life, while not in complete agreement, point to the conclusion that the cenancestor belongs somewhere in between Eubacteria and Archaea.

Even this may be too definite a conclusion. We have already mentioned horizontal gene transfer, all too familiar in present-day hospitals as drug resistance spreads from one strain of bacterium to another. This, presumably, occurred even more readily in the earliest stages of evolution, when organisms would have been less different from each other, and have had less sophisticated cell walls and other means of distinguishing self from nonself. In addition, the genetic repair apparatus (which in present-day organisms is highly elaborate) would have been much cruder or totally absent. Thus, one might speculate, perhaps we should speak of a last common ancestry rather than a last common ancestor, and this may have resembled a cooperative colony, rather than a single self-sufficient individualist.

However this debate turns out, it is clear that any kind of account of the origins of life would have to explain the occurrence of organic building blocks, their assembly into molecules such as proteins and nucleic acids (highly specific nonrepeating polymers), and the development within the system of a degree of complexity far surpassing anything now seen outside of biological systems and their artifacts.

The Molecules of Life. The modern study of the origins of life is generally traced to the work of J. B. S. Haldane and, independently and at much greater length, A. I. Oparin, starting in the 1930s. Both of these suggested that surfactant (soaplike) molecules on the early Earth could have given rise to cell-like structures, precursors of the earliest organisms. The subject received an enormous boost in 1953, with the demonstration by Stanley Miller, working with the geochemist Harold Urey as adviser, that the action of light, or indeed almost any form of energy, on a mixture containing methane, ammonia, and water, would give rise to amino acids and other biologically interesting molecules. This was a breakthrough, psychologically as much a scientifically, moving the subject from the realm of speculation to that of experiment. However, its importance is all too often exaggerated. To this day, biology texts often give the impression, in their opening chapters, that these discoveries essentially solved the problem of the origin of life, and that all that remains is to fill in the details. Such claims deserve to be met with total unbelief.

First of all, Urey-Miller chemistry requires an extremely hydrogen-rich atmosphere, one in which carbon is present in the form of methane rather than carbon dioxide or even carbon monoxide. Such an atmosphere was consistent with Urey's "cold accretion" theory of planetary formation, but not with present knowledge. Second, yields are poor, and do not improve with time, as the products are transformed into intractable tar. Third, the products are not biologically signficant polymers like proteins, but rather their simpler components, and the conversion of these components to polymer in the presence of water is a process that needs an input of energy. Finally, and most important, the problem of how a disorganized mixture can be converted to the highly organized system required for life is not even touched on.

If Urey-Miller chemistry is rejected as a source for the original building blocks of life, what possibilities remain? We have at least four to choose from, and these are not mutually exclusive. I have already mentioned cometary input as a probable major contributor to the oceans. Comets are dirty snowballs, and the dirt is a rich collection of organic molecules. Second, ultraviolet light hitting the atmosphere, even in the presence of very small amounts of organic material, would generate formaldehyde and hydrogen cyanide, highly reactive molecules which are now known to be key intermediates in the original Urey-Miller experiments. Third, clays (of which more later) or other minerals could have acted as traps for solar energy, and used it to convert carbon dioxide to more interesting and useful materials. Finally, sulfur-rich minerals, such as those generated under conditions of high temperature and pressure in submarine hotspots, have been shown to react with carbon dioxide to give hydrogen-rich molecules. Very interestingly, these molecules often contain carbon-sulfur bonds, which have been postulated by de Duve (1991) and others as important in prebiotic chemistry, and which do in fact play a very active role in all living systems.

All of these mechanisms would have been available on the early Earth. We know (see above) that the process of sweeping up cometary debris had barely come to an end when life emerged; Earth's atmosphere, being devoid of oxygen and ozone, would have been far less shielded from the sun's high-energy ultraviolet light than it is today; and submarine volcanic activity would have been far more intense than it is today, when the heat-releasing radioactive decay processes that drive it have decayed to a fraction of their original power.

We are still left with the underlying problem of organization.

The Accumulation of Complexity. If the origin of organic chemicals does not present a major problem, we still need to explain the origin of organization. Organization can be accumulated with great efficiency by the processes of evolution, since incremental advantages are preserved and since the difficulties of a multistep task are added rather than multiplied. Thus, in a simple thought experiment, we can correctly assemble a correct sequence of fifty amino acids, each chosen at random from the twenty or so different kinds available, in about one hundred random trials, if we are allowed to save each correct choice. But if we had to start from fresh each time, we could expect to have to conduct around 20^{50} trials, a number with sixty-five zeros. And this corresponds to one rather small protein molecule.

In addition to the direct accumulation of advantages, there are two other extremely powerful ways in which evolution generates novel information. The first of these is accidental doubling. If a sequence is copied twice, the second copy is free to vary until it finds a new function, sometimes totally different, sometimes complementary. Thus the photosynthetic apparatus of plants contains two separate related systems, Photosystem I and Photosystem II, related by this genetic doubling mechanism, and each of these is itself the product of genetic doubling.

The second mechanism is transmission of genetic information between different organisms. Whole chunks of information can be carried by viral vectors between one species and another. The most important and dramatic examples of such transfer appear to have taken place between very distantly related single-celled organisms, the Archaea and the Eubacteria, whose fusion gave rise to the Eukaryotes.

The Central Problem. If there is no difficulty in accounting for the organic chemicals of which life is constructed, why do I not regard the problem of life's origins as solved?

Life as we know it requires a metabolism (based on enzymes, which are mainly proteins), and a heredity mechanism (principally based on DNA). Without enzymatic activity, DNA could not be replicated; without recourse to the information stored in the DNA, specific enzymes could not be synthesized. This is a chicken and egg problem of some severity.

The situation is even more puzzling than this suggests. Regardless of details and division of labor, the apparatus of any replicating cell must be of great complexity. As we have seen, the mechanism by which living forms have in diverse ways generated such complexity is by evolution and selection. This process works by continual tinkering. Incremental advantages in one generation of species are built upon in subsequent generations. What was once incremental can then become essential, being built into systems of ever greater elaborateness. The backbone of vertebrates, for instance, would at first have arisen as incrementally useful stiffening, but is now the essential centerpiece of a highly elaborate internal skeleton. Contrary to the claims of the promoters of intelligent design (see CREATIONISM; INTELLIGENT DESIGN THEORY), there is no such thing as "irreducible complexity" in biology. There is, however, one critical constraint on what can be generated by descent with variation. Whatever is generated by this mechanism cannot be essential to the organisms in which it first arises. For if it were, their immediate ancestors would not have been viable.

Now apply this principle to the actual process of duplicating genetic information. If this is essential for the operation of descent with variation and selection, it could not have been brought into being by this mechanism. We appear to be faced with a paradox.

Logically, there are only two escape routes available. We can say that the original genetic apparatus was readily accessible on the early Earth, and thus antedates evolution; this gives us what Dyson (1985) refers to as "genes first" theories. Or we can say that a distinct genetic apparatus was not necessary for the first evolving organisms, but represents a subsequent specialization; this gives us "metabolism first" theories. Both "genes first" and "metabolism first" theories presuppose the existence of some satisfactory enclosure, or adhesion to a surface, providing a defining boundary. Mirroring the three components essential to life, we have three separate emphases regarding its origins, as will be evident in the next section.

Some Current Approaches. At a high level of abstraction, the emergence of life can be seen as a special case of the spontaneous emergence of order far from equilibrium. This is a common enough phenomenon, visible in mottled cloud patterns, much studied in "chemical waves" of reactivity that spread through systems which create their own catalysts, and invoked, with uncertain success, as one agent in embryonic development.

Generating complexity is one thing; generating complexity that contains instructions for its own replication is quite another. The key factor here would be molecular recognition. Imagine, for instance, a network of molecules each of which, by such a process, catalyzed with some degree of specificity the formation of other molecules within the network. It can be shown, as, for instance, in Dyson's treatment, that such a system would become spontaneously self-refining once a critical degree of accuracy had been reached. This is a "metabolism first" scenario; catalysis precedes information storage.

Speculation of this kind will carry much more conviction if it becomes possible to point to real systems that catalyze each other's production in the required manner. Such systems are being approached from several different directions, using molecules with specific binding patterns to trap and orient complementary fragments. The binding motifs used are commonly inspired by those found in actual biological systems. This could represent a shortfall of imagination, or it could be regarded as deep wisdom, building one's machinery like any good engineer from components that are known to work.

Ribozymes, discovered in 1982, are pieces of ribonucleic acid that can function as enzymes. This gives us the liberating idea that the same material might at the origins of life have had both genetic and metabolic functions. Even before ribozymes were discovered, it was known that many catalytic processes require coenzymes incorporating nucleotides, as the building blocks of nucleic acids are called. Enthusiasts for ribozymes even speak of an "RNA world" as a distinct stage in the emergence of life. RNA is chemically simpler to produce than DNA, and single chains of RNA are somewhat more flexible. For these reasons, DNA is thought to be more recent than RNA, to be purely informational in function, and to have developed because it can be copied between generations with greater accuracy.

Between the "RNA world," if such a thing ever existed, and the most complex products of abiotic chemistry, there is still a huge gap to be bridged. RNA is a polymer, in which the information containing components are strung out along a chain made out of sugar (ribose) molecules and phosphate groups. Sugars are easy enough to build from simpler components, but the reaction is messy and gives rise to literally hundreds of different products. The sugar-phosphate bond is unstable in water, and a dehydrating agent is needed for its formation. Finally, the number of possible different RNA molecules that would perform any useful function, however poorly, is a small fraction of the total possibilities, just as the strings of letters that convey a message, however brief or banal, form a small fraction of all those that could arise by chance. Even a single functional RNA molecule represents such an enormous improbability, relative to non-living matter, that from the present point of view it is closer to the winning post than the starting line. Inspired by such reasoning, much recent research is based on simplified alternatives to nucleic acid, and on substances that could have done double duty as building blocks for nucleic acid–like or for proteinlike molecules.

Before life there were minerals, and minerals are highly structured. This structure could have contributed to the emergence of life in a number of ways. Minerals most certainly possess the ability to concentrate organic molecules, catalyze their reactions, and impose specificity on otherwise messy processes. Indeed, much of the modern chemical industry relies on these facts. This gives them a minimal role, as substrates on which critical reactions could have taken place. Or, as mentioned earlier, the minerals themselves could have been critical reagents, converting even such unpromising materials as carbon dioxide into useful building blocks, possibly even activated by the presence of carbon-sulfur bonds. In one variant of this scenario, minerals could have acted as photosensitizers, traps for the energy of sunlight. The boldest claim made on behalf of minerals is that they could themselves have been the first replicating systems undergoing selection pressures. Clay minerals show huge richness of structure, and it is easy to envisage them being selected for catalytic properties, especially if (as certainly seems possible) the products of such catalysis would in turn promote the production of more clay, for instance by reacting chemically with igneous rocks. Earlier claims of replication in clays have unfortunately not been substantiated, but reexamination of this possibility seems timely.

As for the origin of the membrane, this is the least of our problems. If the critical stages in the origin of life took place on the surface of minerals, or in their internal space, the minerals themselves would have fulfilled the original membrane function. If not, almost any organic molecule with a water-attracting and water-repelling region (in structural terms, oxygen-rich and hydrogen-rich region) could have formed part of a cell wall, with the water-attracting parts facing outward, and the water-repelling parts tucked inward. Such rough and ready cell walls would certainly have been leaky, but this could actually have been an advantage, since such leaky walls have been shown to admit simple monomers, while preventing the escape of bulkier and more complex products built up from them.

At an origins of life conference, you will find devotees of all these approaches, and others I have not mentioned, hotly discussing the advantages of their own scenario at the implied (or even explicit) expense of all the others. But standing back a little, it seems clear that the emergence of life was a multistage process, with different kinds of mechanisms operating at different stages.

Practical Applications of Origins-of-Life Research. Advances in several commercially or medically important areas have been directly inspired by origins-of-life research. Models of the "RNA world" spurred the development of antisense RNA-binding drugs, which inhibit the replication of retroviruses (including HIV). Studies of hyperthermophiles have led to the isolation of heat-resistant enzymes, with uses ranging from biotechnology to the domestic washtub. Close scrutiny of molecular interaction has given us methods for creating new enzymes, and, more generally, fresh insights into molecular self-assembly. There are numerous foreseeable applications in catalysis and nanofabrication, and doubtless even more important applications that have not yet been foreseen.

Conclusions. The problem of the origins of life is still unsolved. Or, more accurately, it is incompletely solved. We have fragmentary and partial solutions, but do not know how they connect. It is a little like having fragments of a proposed travel plan, which cannot be evaluated until the complete route is in our hands.

We should also frankly face the fact that our knowledge of the remote past is uncertain, and the implication that when surveying the specific alternatives, we may be unable to choose between them. Nonetheless, we are much closer than a generation ago to identifying the general processes involved. Consider as an analogy trying to reconstruct the journey of Lewis and Clark from a current road map of the northwestern United States. A seemingly impossible task! However, we would notice that there were very few roads across central Idaho, and infer the existence of obstacles, which we would identify with mountains. We would notice that these mountains were most easily crossed through valleys associated with rivers, and hypothesize that the rivers had worn these valleys away. We would do model experiments to show that flowing water does indeed wear away soil, and speculate that Lewis and Clark had crossed the mountains by following a great river. We could not say exactly which fork of which river they used, but despite this we would have shown what the correct solution to our problem should look like, and learned a great deal about other matters in the process.

BIBLIOGRAPHY

Bennett, Jeffrey, Seth Shostak, and Bruce Jakosky. *Life in the Universe*. San Francisco: Addison-Wesley, 2003.

Birx, H. James. "Life, Origin of, and Unbelief." In *The Encyclopedia of Unbelief*, edited by Gordon Stein. Amherst, NY: Prometheus Books, 1985.

Cairns-Smith, A. Graham. *Genetic Takeover and the Mineral Origins of Life*. New York: Cambridge University Press, 1982.

De Duve, Christian, *Blueprint for a Cell: The Nature and Origin of Life*. Burlington, NC: N. Patterson, 1991.

Dyson, Freeman J. *Origins of Life*. New York: Cambridge University Press, 1985.

Fry, Iris. *The Emergence of Life on Earth*. New Brunswick, NJ: Rutgers University Press, 2000.

Kauffman, Stuart A. *The Origins of Order*. New York: Oxford University Press, 1993.

Keller, Evelyn Fox. *Making Sense of Life*. Cambridge, MA: Harvard University Press, 2002.

Lunine, Jonathan I. *Astrobiology, a Multidisciplinary Approach*. San Francisco: Pearson/Addison-Wesley, 2005.

Miller, Stanley L., and Leslie E. Orgel. *The Origins of Life on the Earth*. Englewood Cliffs, NJ: Prentice-Hall, 1974.

Scott, Eugenie C. *Evolution vs Creationism: An Introduction*. Westport, CT: Greenwood, 2004.

PAUL S. BRATERMAN

LIFE STANCE. Life stance denotes an individual's or a community's relationship with what he, she, or it finds to be of ultimate importance; the commitments and presuppositions of this; and the theory and practice of working this out in living. The term refers both to the style and to the content of that undertaking.

One's "stance" should be the secure base for one's action. A good "stance" is basic to success in almost any sport. One's "life stance" is the dynamic base for one's life.

The definition of the term is explicitly designed to be impartial between the different foundations on which people base their life stances. Humanists find the happiness and suffering of individual sentient beings to be of ultimate importance (see HUMANISM), and the human qualities that enable us to ameliorate the happiness and suffering in the world (see MORALITY FROM A HUMANIST POSITION). Religions find a superpurposive reality to be ultimately important, typically a God (for more on the basic divide between naturalistic and superpurposive, see RELIGION; NATURALISM). The concept of life stance is inclusive, and not itself "judgmental." It also includes commercial materialism: the acceptance that money and the possession of goods is ultimately important.

The relation of life stance to religion on the one hand, and to science on the other, is critical, and humanism furnishes a critical example. These relations involve two dichotomies: that between a naturalistic claim and one that is superpurposive; and that between a factual claim and one that is evaluative.

	Factual	**Evaluative**
Naturalistic	Science A naturalistic life stance is both factual and evaluative	A naturalistic morality
Superpurposive	Theology	A religious morality A religion is both factual and evaluative

Many religions (including Christianity) also imply factual statements that are naturalistic. Their claims therefore interact with science.

It is perverse to contrast religion and science (see RELIGION IN CONFLICT WITH SCIENCE), and then suppose (as many religious people do) that as humanism is based on science it will not give values. Humanism is *based on* science, but has fundamental values as well. It is equally perverse to run humanism and atheism together (as many religious people do). ATHEISM clears the ground, but humanism is a life stance, and therefore it sets positive beliefs and values in the empty space.

Any understanding of morality must be founded on claims about the world and what is important in it. (One cannot get morality a priori; a real morality must refer to something.) One finds these claims in one's life stance, if one is interested in foundations.

Many people lead their lives without thought of any life stance. Most such people live according to the way they have been brought up and the culture in which they live. This opens a serious question. The quality of life in a society is very much dependent on the quality of the life stance or life stances that are implicit in it. What is the quality of *your* culture? Many humanists find commercial materialism on the one hand, and religion on the other, much too influential in Western societies. It is, then, up to them to make humanism influential in their own society.

Can there be a life stance which will be generally accepted all over the world? Not in the foreseeable future. The fact that human nature is universal does not mean that humanism could be this life stance. All life stances do indeed share a range of important moral values, because we all are of the same human nature. But human nature is not so rational that evidence will lead everyone to accept one answer on these matters. The general rejection of gods is far over the horizon! This will lead to life stances with vitally different moral theories. Most religious life stances call upon their God to condemn certain things—homosexuality, the equal rights of women (the *majority* of Christians worldwide reject the equality of women in the priesthood), and so on.

It is interesting to note how Christians, and god-religious people in general, do not want to open up the idea of "religion" in this way. Perhaps they instinctively recognize that this opening up is a vital threat to them and their authority. Religion can do good: it inspires commitment and a morality, and it can support people in leading good lives. But the religious element in most religions distorts their moral theories, and can make them damaging. Once people see that the good in religion does not necessarily presuppose a God, then the authority of Christianity and its privileged status are both lost. Then humanism must be admitted on equal terms.

"Life stance" is the genus that includes humanism, Christianity, Islam, and so on ad infinitum as species (see also EUPRAXSOPHY). To distinguish a particular life stance from any other mental phenomenon such as philosophy, culture, ideology, a religion, or science will specify the genus, life stance; and the particular claims it makes, and the particular values and principles that inform and guide its activity. This is how the INTERNATIONAL HUMANIST AND ETHICAL UNION sets out its "Minimum Statement of Humanism," which is accepted by all its member organizations.

BIBLIOGRAPHY

Stopes-Roe, Harry. "The Concept of a 'Life Stance' in Education." *Learning for Living* 16 (Autumn 1976).
———. "Humanism as a Life Stance." In *Building a World Community*, edited by Paul Kurtz. Amherst, NY: Prometheus Books, 1989.

HARRY STOPES-ROE

LINDSEY, BEN (1869–1943), American sex radical (see SEX RADICALISM AND UNBELIEF). Benjamin B. Lindsey was born in 1869 in Jackson, Tennessee, to Landy Tunstall Lindsey and Letitia Barr Lindsey. Landy, a Civil War veteran and an alcoholic, caused a family rift when he converted to Catholicism. In 1879 he moved the family to Denver. A year later, Ben and his younger brother, Chal, were sent to Catholic boarding school in Indiana. Ben's experiences there were fairly agreeable. He was exposed to the positive side of the church and made a lifelong friend of one of the nuns there; however, he later attributed his lack of trust in organized religion to that early family conflict.

Two years later Landy lost his job, and Ben and Chal were removed from the boarding school and sent back to Tennessee to live with their grandfather. Ben attended Southwestern Baptist University, a preparatory school, for three years, after which he returned to his parents in Denver. Rather than finishing his education there, he was forced into full-time employment, along with his brother, as a result of his father's ill health. Distraught over his illness and economic circumstances, Landy committed suicide; it was Ben who discovered his father's body in the cellar. As the new head of the family, Ben Lindsey worked two jobs, including one as a clerk in a law office, but the family remained in poverty. Exhausted and utterly discouraged at his inability to improve his family's situation, Lindsey attempted suicide by placing a gun to his head and pulling the trigger, but the gun did not go off.

Lindsey used this fortunate event to sink himself into the study of law, and in 1894, at the age of twenty-five, he was admitted to the bar in Colorado, and was soon assigned as public defender. After a series of political appointments, at the age of thirty-one he was asked to fill a vacancy in a county judgeship.

Early on, Lindsey developed an effective and innovative method of dealing with juvenile delinquents. Over the course of his judicial career, Lindsey became the most active and successful advocate of child law reform in United States history, and he pioneered the juvenile court system.

Lindsey was convinced that many of society's ills rested on its puritanical and repressive ideas about sex. Authors Havelock Ellis and Walter Lippmann had a strong influence over Lindsey's intellectual development. He wrote several books and articles on the topic, including *The Doughboy's Religion* (1920), *The Revolt of Modern Youth* (1925), *The Companionate Marriage* (1927), and his autobiography, *The Dangerous Life* (1931). His books advocated sex education for young people; accessible birth control for women, including unmarried women (see BIRTH CONTROL AND UNBELIEF); and uncomplicated divorce for childless couples.

Well known for his compassion and idealism, Lindsay remained active in liberal causes throughout his life, although in 1927 a political feud resulted in his removal from the bench, and he was disbarred in Colorado. He was eventually elected to the Superior Court of Los Angeles County. He died at the Good Samaritan Hospital in Los Angeles on March 26, 1943.

BIBLIOGRAPHY

Larsen, Charles. *The Good Fight: The Life and Times of Ben B. Lindsey*. Chicago: Quadrangle, 1972.
Lindsey, Ben B., and Rube Borough. *The Dangerous Life*. New York: Horace Liveright, 1931.

JULIE HERRADA

LITTLE BLUE BOOKS. See HALDEMAN-JULIUS, EMANUEL.

LITTRÉ, ÉMILE (1801–1881), French philologist and positivist. Maximilien Paul Émile Littré is chiefly remembered for his contributions to French philology and lexicography and his research into ancient medicine. Especially noteworthy is his monumental *Etymological, Historical, and Grammatical Dictionary of the French Language* (1863–77). Less well known but equally important is his role as spokesperson for POSITIVISM.

His positivist involvement began in 1840 when he first read Auguste COMTE's *Course in Positive Philosophy* (1830–42). Four articles by Littré in *Le National* in 1844 were the first writings to present Comte's theories to the general public. Basic Comtean ideas popularized by Littré then and subsequently included the assertions that all religions are destined for extinction, that objective observation and scientific method are the only valid means of arriving at truth, and that all religious claims amount to unverifiable hypotheses.

Littré broke with his mentor in 1852, rejecting the mysticism of Comte's "second career." An ardent republican, he was further repelled by Comte's support of the Second Empire of Napoleon III. Henceforth Littré would continue to disseminate the tenets of the *Course* while dismissing Comte's second phase as an aberration.

Littréist positivism gained a forum in 1867 when Littré and the Russian scientist Grégoire Wyrouboff founded the bimonthly review *La Philosophie positive* (Positive Philosophy). The periodical survived until 1883, with Littré contributing some sixty articles.

For much of his life Littré was vilified as the embodiment of antireligion and atheism. (In his 1855 *Dictionary of Medicine*, he provoked a scandal by defining man as "a mammalian primate with opposable thumbs.") When he applied for admission to the French Academy in 1863, the powerful prelate Bishop Félix-Antoine Dupanloup, himself an academician, denounced Littré as an archmaterialist and successfully thwarted his election. When Littré's second application was accepted in 1871, Dupanloup resigned his own chair in protest.

Following Littré's death, a rumor circulated that he had undergone a deathbed conversion (see DEATHBED CLAIMS CONCERNING UNBELIEVERS). This alleged reversion to Catholicism was refuted by Wyrouboff, who dismissed the claim as sensationalism fabricated by *Le Figaro* in an effort to boost sales. The *Catholic Encyclopedia* maintains the truth of this fabricated story to this day.

BIBLIOGRAPHY

Charlton, Donald G. *Positivist Thought in France during the Second Empire*. Oxford: Clarendon, 1959.

Hamburger, Jean. *Monsieur Littré*. Paris: Flammarion, 1988.

Manuel, Frank E. *The Prophets of Paris*. Cambridge, MA: Harvard University Press, 1962.

Simon, Walter M. *European Positivism in the 19th Century: An Essay in Intellectual History*. Ithaca, NY: Cornell University Press, 1963.

WILLIAM RAYMOND CLARK

LOCKE, JOHN (1632–1704), English political philosopher and empiricist. John Locke is a key figure in the history of British empiricism and liberal democratic theory. His works on religion and on education are less read today, but were significant in the history of those subjects. Locke's father was a Puritan, on the side of Parliament in the Civil War. Locke was a student and teacher at Oxford University. He was a fellow of the Royal Society and a friend of Robert Boyle; he trained as a physician. His early career developed in association with the first earl of SHAFTESBURY, who rose to become Lord Chancellor. Shaftesbury fell from power in 1673, and Locke was twice forced to leave England for reasons of security. His famous *Two Treatises of Government* were not published until after the Glorious Revolution of 1688.

Locke returned to England in the entourage of William and Mary in 1689, and within a year published not only the *Two Treatises of Government* (1689) and the first *Letter on Toleration*, but also *An Essay concerning Human Understanding* (1690), now universally regarded as a foundational text of empiricism. Locke served as an advisor to the Whigs, and his later writings include works on religion, on money, and on education. During his last years he was a commissioner on the board of trade.

Locke's Importance. Locke is one of the most important figures in the history of English philosophy. His *Essay* served as a basic textbook to several generations; the influence of his political ideas is so pervasive that scholars have stopped trying to uncover it. The writings on religious tolerance and in defense of religion place religion within the limits of REASON. Locke's idea of tolerance did not extend to Roman Catholics or to unbelievers, and although his religious theories led to accusations of his being an opponent of religion, these same works served as an inspiration to liberal elements (the latitudinarians) in the Church of England. Locke's political theory, while undoubtedly of the highest importance, also has an ambiguous element.

The Political Philosophy. Locke agreed with Thomas HOBBES about the dangers to life in the state of nature, but he thought the solution was to transfer to government only limited authority, not full sovereignty as Hobbes urged; and whereas Hobbes allowed revolt only when the government directly threatened one's life, Locke set the conditions of revolution much lower. His favorable reception in the American colonies therefore comes as no surprise.

Locke's doctrine of property is central to his political work. Locke was no armchair philosopher; he had considerable practical experience with political issues. In the first *Treatise of Government*, Locke argues against Robert Filmer, who followed the biblical account of property, namely, that God had given dominion to Adam and his heirs. This treatise is of particular interest since Locke proposes an interpretation of scripture that is the result of original thought and not just the conventional citing of proof texts. Still, it is in the second treatise that we get the well-known and classic doctrines that originally the earth was common to all, but every man had a property in his own person and in what was produced by the labor of that body. By eating I made part of what was common literally part of me, and by mixing my labor with parts of what is common I remove those parts from the common.

The Theory of Knowledge. The great *Essay concerning Human Understanding* cannot be considered an easy read, and its contents have been analyzed and evaluated from every conceivable angle. Locke is to English philosophy what René DESCARTES was to French and Gottfried Wilhelm von LEIBNIZ to German, and should be read in that context. Leibniz wrote an extended commentary on Locke, and Locke's introduction of the concept of an *idea* into English brings him closer to Descartes than one might expect, given his association with the empiricism conventionally opposed to Cartesian RATIONALISM. Another difficulty is caused by the understandable habit of students not to read large treatises in their entirety but to be content with digests or abridgements.

What makes the *Essay*, though seriously dated, still breathtaking is the boldness of its conception. Right at the time so many empirical discoveries were being announced and so many scientific theories were under revision, Locke proposed to review the entire "compass" of human knowledge, and to examine critically the whole field from sense perception to language to morals, in all cases carefully distinguishing between that which is certain and that which is merely probable. In one important section he classifies the logical fallacies according to a scheme still widely taught today. His analysis of memory is still useful, and Locke's theory of personal identity is a classic and still discussed at length. Even though the *Essay* is a carefully organized and systematic treatise, it is not easy to place Locke in any one philosophical camp. For example, he is called an empiricist because he traces all our ideas to experience, there are no innate ideas for him; but he does not construct knowledge directly from the observations. Knowledge, for Locke, is the perception of the connection and agreement or disagreement of our ideas.

Continuing Relevance in Religion. Locke's treatment of religion reaches some conclusions that force us to classify him as a believer. He gives a proof of God's existence and defends the possibility of revelation. He believed in a future life and affirmed that Jesus was the Messiah. Most orthodox religionists were nevertheless unhappy with Locke, since he always gives reason the upper hand. The clear implication of his writing on religion, and what makes it important for skeptics and unbelievers, is that while he endorses some religious beliefs he does so only because he thinks there are rational grounds for them. Locke's theory has come to be called "EVIDENTIALISM" and is often severely criticized by conservative philosophers of religion today. Religionists, especially those committed to religious dogma come what may, have good reason to stay clear of Locke. Skeptics are perhaps in a more comfortable position. On the one hand, Locke's evidentialism and his general empirical ethics of belief is acceptable to them, and on the other, if Locke or one of his followers is able to demonstrate or present convincing evidence for a religious claim, then there is no reason for the rational skeptic not to accept that claim. Presumably, the skeptic's commitment to reason and free inquiry takes precedent over dissent from any particular religious article of faith. If one insists on some form of evidentialism as a standard of belief, then fairness requires one put one's own beliefs on the table to be subjected to scrutiny. Dogmatic unbelievers, on the other hand, even

if they turn out to be right, have nothing over dogmatic religionists, at least from the point of view of knowledge. John Locke is one of the great founders of the liberal school of religion, which dominated in the Church of England, at least among the bishops, during the Whig period of the eighteenth century. Locke's theological heirs are a diverse lot; while some merely emphasized the value of experience and probable reasoning, others challenged the more severe Christian doctrines such as the Trinity and the Incarnation. This legacy includes many deists (see DEISM) and those who reduced Christianity to a system of moral teachings that could easily be accepted by a compassionate atheist (see RELIGIOUS HUMANISM).

BIBLIOGRAPHY

Cranston, Maurice. *John Locke: A Biography*. London: Longmans, 1957.

Locke, John. *An Essay concerning Human Understanding*. Edited by Peter H. Nidditch. Oxford: Oxford University Press, 1979.

———. *Two Treatises of Government*. Edited by Peter Lassett. Cambridge: Cambridge University Press, 1960.

Yolton, John W. *A Locke Dictionary*. Oxford: Blackwell, 1993.

DAVID WHITE

LOGICAL POSITIVISM. Also known as logical empiricism or logical neopositivism, logical positivism is a philosophical movement that originated in Austria and Germany in the 1920s. Concerned primarily with the logical analysis of scientific knowledge, it held that statements about metaphysics, religion, and ethics are devoid of cognitive meaning and thus nothing but expressions of feelings or desires; only statements about mathematics, logic, and the natural sciences have definite meanings. Principal exponents included Rudolf Carnap, considered the leading figure of logical positivism; Herbert Feigl; Philipp Frank; Kurt Grelling; Hans Hahn; Carl Gustav Hempel; Victor Kraft; Otto Neurath; Hans Reichenbach; Moritz SCHLICK; and Friedrich Waismann.

History. Albert Einstein's theory of relativity exerted great influence over the origin of logical positivism, its founders seeking to clarify the theory's philosophical significance. Schlick wrote two essays on relativity in 1915 and 1917; Reichenbach attended Einstein's lectures on relativity theory at Berlin University in 1917 and wrote four books on the topic in the 1920s; Carnap's first work was an essay about the theory of space published in 1922. Quantum mechanics was also a major subject for philosophical investigations; works in this area were published by Schlick and Reichenbach. Another influence upon logical positivism was the development of formal logic. Carnap attended three courses on logic under the direction of Gottlob Frege, the father of modern logic. In addition, the logical positivists had extensive contacts with a group of Polish logicians (mainly Jan Lukasiewicz, Kazimierz Ajdukiewicz, and Alfred Tarski) who developed several branches of contemporary logic including the algebra of logic, many-valued propositional calculus, and semantics for logic.

By the 1930s logical positivism was a prominent philosophical movement actively promoting its new ideas in Europe and the United States. Meetings on epistemology and the philosophy of science were organized at Prague (1929 and 1934) and Konigsberg (1930), where Kurt Gödel presented his influential theorems asserting the completeness of first-order predicate calculus and the incompleteness of formal arithmetic. The First Congress of Scientific Philosophy was held in Paris (1935) and subsequent congresses were held in Copenhagen (1936); Paris (1937); Cambridge, UK (1938); and Cambridge, Massachusetts (1939).

The political attitudes of logical positivists were progressive, democratic, and sometimes socialist; this aroused hostility from the Nazis. After Adolf Hitler seized power in 1933, many logical positivists were persecuted and forced to emigrate from Austria and Germany; Schlick and Grelling were murdered. Neurath and Waismann sought refuge in England. The United States became the new home for most of the others: Carnap taught at the University of Chicago and UCLA; Feigl at the universities of Iowa and Minnesota; Frank at Harvard; Hempel at Yale, Princeton, and the University of Pittsburgh; and Reichenbach at UCLA.

Meaning. According to logical positivism, all meaningful statements can be divided into two classes. One class contains statements that are true or false by virtue of their logical forms or their meaning; these statements are called analytic a priori. The other class contains statements whose truth or falsity can be ascertained only by means of experience (called synthetic a posteriori). Logic and mathematics belong to the class of analytic a priori statements, since they are true by virtue of the meaning ascribed to the logical constants (the words *and*, *or*, *not*, and *if*) and to mathematical terms. The class of synthetic a posteriori statements includes all genuine scientific statements, such as those of physics, biology, and psychology. A statement is meaningful if and only if it can be proved true or false, at least in principle, by virtue of its meaning or by means of experience. Moreover, the meaning of a statement is its method of verification: that is, we know the meaning of a statement only if we know the conditions under which the statement is true or false. This assertion is called the verifiability principle (see VERIFICATIONISM). Thus statements about metaphysics, religion, and ethics are meaningless and must be rejected as nonsensical. Much of traditional philosophy is meaningless as well. Many alleged philosophical problems, such as the controversy between realists and instrumentalists, are actually pseudoproblems, the outcome of a misuse of language. They concern not matters of fact but rather the choice between different linguistic frameworks. Thus the logical analysis of language was regarded by logical positivism as a major instrument for resolving philosophical problems. Characteristic of this was the intense analysis of scientific language performed by Carnap and Hempel.

Scientific Language. According to logical positivism, a scientific theory is an axiomatic system that acquires an empirical interpretation by means of suitable statements—called coordinative definitions or axioms of coordination—that establish a correlation between real objects or processes and the abstract concepts of the theory. The language of a scientific theory includes three kinds of terms: logical, observational, and theoretical. Logical terms denote logical constants and mathematical objects; observational terms denote objects or properties that can be directly observed or measured; and theoretical terms denote objects or properties we cannot observe or measure but can only infer from direct observation. Examples of theoretical terms are *electron*, *atom*, and *magnetic field*. Early logical positivism believed that all theoretical terms were definable with the help of observational terms. Further research by Carnap and Hempel showed that theoretical terms cannot be defined by observational ones; therefore, theoretical terms are indispensable to any scientific theory.

Logical positivism did not consider the pragmatic aspects of scientific research; it was concerned not with the real process of discovery but with the rational reconstruction of scientific knowledge—that is, the study of the logical (formal) relationships between statements, hypotheses, and empirical evidence.

Ethics. The logical positivist most interested in ethics was Schlick. He endeavored to give an account of ethics in agreement with logical positivist philosophical principles. Schlick maintained that ethics is a descriptive scientific theory: statements about ethics are not normative statements prescribing how people ought to behave, in which case they would be meaningless according to the verifiability principle. Schlick understood statements about ethics as descriptive statements relating to the origin and the evolution of the ethical principles in human society. He asserted that human beings naturally prefer conditions that do not produce pain and do produce pleasure; thus, in the first instance, the good is simply that which gives pleasure and no pain. The very first ethical principle is therefore egoistic, but human behavior is subject to the evolutionary processes that sometimes select an altruistic or cooperative way of action as better adapted than a purely egoistic one. This is particularly true in a complex human society, where we can find a struggle between egoistic behaviors arising from human nature and social behaviors generated by the evolutionary process.

BIBLIOGRAPHY

Barone, Francesco. *Il neopositivismo logico* [Logical Neopositivism]. Bari: Laterza, 1977.

Beckwith, Burnham Putnam. *Religion, Philosophy, and Science; an Introduction to Logical Positivism.* New York: Philosophical Library, 1957.

Carnap, Rudolf. *An Introduction to the Philosophy of Science.* New York: Basic Books, 1974.

Friedman, Michael. *Reconsidering Logical Positivism.* Cambridge: Cambridge University Press, 1999.

Nagel, Ernest. *The Structure of Science.* New York: Harcourt, Brace & World, 1961.

Parrini, Paolo, Wesley C. Salmon, and Merrilee H. Salmon, eds. *Logical Empiricism—Historical and Contemporary Perspectives.* Pittsburgh: University of Pittsburgh Press, 2003.

Reichenbach, Hans. *Philosophical Foundations of Quantum Mechanics.* Berkeley and Los Angeles: University of California Press, 1944.

———. *The Philosophy of Space and Time.* New York: Dover, 1958.

Salmon, Wesley C., and Gereon Wolters, eds. *Logic, Language, and the Structure of Scientific Theories: Proceedings of the Carnap-Reichenbach Centennial, University of Konstanz, 21–24 May 1991.* Pittsburgh: University of Pittsburgh Press, 1991.

Spohn, Wolfgang, ed. *Erkenntnis Orientated: A Centennial Volume for Rudolf Carnap and Hans Reichenbach.* Dordrecht: Kluwer, 1991.

MAURO MURZI

LOISY, ALFRED FIRMIN (1857–1919), French scholar and philosopher. The great spearhead of Catholic Modernism, Alfred Firmin Loisy was born in 1857 to a farming family in the village of Ambrières, France. At age seventeen he undertook studies for the priesthood. A pious and gifted student, he went on to study at the Institut Catholique in Paris in 1878 and was ordained the following year. Though scientific biblical criticism was rare in France at the time, Loisy imbibed it from the lectures of Abbé Vigouroux—an orthodox apologist who explained critical views in order to refute them, but whose rationalizations Loisy could not accept—and Ernest RENAN. His doctoral dissertation, which remains unpublished, was prescient in arguing that any modern doctrine of biblical inspiration must be corrected and informed by the results of criticism and could not limit them.

Loisy's teaching of the Hebrew Bible at the Institut piqued the suspicions of his superiors, who fired him in 1893. His subsequent teaching as chaplain at a Dominican convent school awakened in him a desire to help midwife Catholicism into the modern world. In 1899 he moved on to a post at the École Practique des Hautes Études where he could work free of inquisitorial scrutiny. In 1902 Loisy composed *The Gospel and the Church*, a rejoinder to the newly translated manifesto of liberal Protestantism, *What Is Christianity?* by Adolph von Harnack. Harnack argued that Jesus had propounded a threefold gospel of the fatherhood of God, the coming of the kingdom of God, and the infinite value of the human soul, all of which reduced to pious devotion to God the Father (not to Jesus himself) as the very essence of Christianity. This was the kernel of Jesus's preaching, from which theology must separate the husk of contemporary apocalyptic and other Jewish thought-forms. Harnack viewed all subsequent Christian history as distortion and betrayal of the kernel of Jesus's filial piety.

Loisy saw here an opportunity to float his approach to modernizing the Catholic tradition. Loisy was inspired by John Henry Cardinal Newman's theory that Catholic theology had indeed developed (in contrast to the traditional position that the Church had never changed), but under the guidance of the Holy Spirit and in harmony with its inner logic. Even so, Loisy urged that what Harnack had called the kernel was really the *seed* of the gospel. What Harnack dismissed as the husk was rightly to be understood as the mature and still-growing *oak*. He also argued that Harnack had no business as a historian in trying to distill some abstraction of an ancient set of beliefs. (Today he would rightly have accused Harnack of "logocentrism.") No, argued Loisy, Christianity began as a social movement and continued to survive by adapting to a changing world. And so must Catholicism adapt today, for example, by accepting biblical criticism. Loisy was excommunicated in 1908. He was ahead of his time, as history would reveal. For instance, in the late twentieth century, Raymond E. Brown, also a Catholic priest, easily obtained the imprimatur, or mark of church approval, for critical work reminiscent not only of Loisy but of David Friedrich STRAUSS.

In his 1902 *The Religion of Israel*, Loisy outlined the current positions of Old Testament criticism after the seminal Old Testament scholar Julius Wellhausen. Chief points in which biblical science has since surpassed Loisy include his belief that Yahwism had always been monolatrous, repelling the syncretistic addition of foreign gods (today's scholars view ancient Israel as simply one more native Canaanite group, sharing the regnant polytheism except with different, local divine names) and his post-Exilic dating of the Psalms (which form-criticism since Sigmund Mowinkel places firmly, for the most part, in the Jerusalem Temple liturgy during the Monarchy). Loisy's neglected original insights include the notion that Jeremiah's accusation of scribal falsification of the Torah (Jer. 7:22; 8:8) had in mind the seventh-century fabrication of Deuteronomy, and that Ezekiel's rich mythic allusions attest a secret priestly "gnostic" syncretism in Judah stemming from the reign of Manasseh.

Loisy's major New Testament work may be found in his posthumously published *The Birth of the Christian Religion* (1948) and *The Origins of the New Testament*

(1950). He was a radical critic, dismissing by far most of the gospel narrative as liturgical drama and legend, though he rejected the Christ myth theory, preferring to see Jesus as a rebel prophet like Theudas the Magician or the Egyptian messiah, both mentioned by Josephus. Loisy understood Romans and both Corinthian epistles as compilations of materials from various sources, and questioned the authenticity of Galatians. Among his numerous sadly neglected observations are that 2 Peter 1:16–18 refers not to the Synoptic transfiguration story, but to an episode in the noncanonical Apocalypse of Peter; that the Field of Blood (Matt. 27:8; Acts 1:18–19) was originally the burial place of Jesus, not the site of Judas's death; that the story of Peter's cowardly denial is unhistorical smear propaganda put about by Paulinists; that Matthew's beatitude upon Peter (16:17) was a later Petrinist counterclaim to Galatians (1:11–12, 15–16); that the empty tomb of Jesus was a rechristening of a grotto believed sacred to the resurrected Adonis; that Pilate's verification of Jesus's quick death (Mark 15:44–45) is an apologetical fiction to rebut the suspicion that Jesus had been rescued alive from the cross; that the "report" of Jesus being the risen John the Baptist (Mark 6:14) was a Christian attempt to undercut John's sect's own resurrection preaching. At a number of other points, Loisy anticipated the theories of later scholars who got credit for them instead.

All in all, Loisy was the ideal scholar of Christian origins by Renan's standard: one who had once believed in the religion (and hence was able to understand it from the inside) and who no longer believed in it (and hence was able to understand it from the outside). He died in 1919.

BIBLIOGRAPHY

Loisy, Alfred Firmin. *The Birth of the Christian Religion*. Translated by L. P. Jacks. London: Allen and Unwin, 1948.

———. *The Gospel and the Church*. Translated by Christopher Home. London: Ibister, 1903.

———. *The Origins of the New Testament*. Translated by L. P. Jacks. London: Allen and Unwin, 1950.

———. *The Religion of Israel*. Translated by Arthur Galton. New York: G. P. Putnam's Sons, 1910.

Scott, Bernard Brandon. Introduction to Alfred Loisy. In *The Gospel and the Church*, translated by Christopher Home. Lives of Jesus series. Philadelphia: Fortress, 1976.

Vidler, Alec. *A Variety of Catholic Modernists*. Cambridge: Cambridge University Press, 1970.

ROBERT M. PRICE

LOKOYATA. See CARVAKA.

LORULOT, ANDRÉ (1885–1963), French freethinker, anticlerical, and anarchist. André Lorulot was born

October 23, 1885. During much of his anarchist career he was known as André Georges Roulot. While still a young man, Lorulot turned to anarchism (see ANARCHISM AND UNBELIEF). He was influenced in particular by the charismatic one-legged revolutionary Albert Joseph, who was known as Libertad. In 1905 Lorulot began writing in Libertad's journal *L'anarchie* (Anarchy). The following year, along with his girlfriend, Emilie Lamotte, Lorulot joined the libertarian commune at St. Germain en Laye. While living there Lorulot wrote the pamphlet *L'idole, patrie at conséquence*, which provoked a charge of inciting soldiers to disobedience. When he emerged from his fifteen-month prison sentence, the St. Germain en Laye commune had folded and Libertad was dead. Lorulot took over control of *L'anarchie* paper and also began *L'idée libre*, a review.

Lorulot spent much of World War I in prison as a pacifist. After the Bolshevik revolution he moved from anarchism to communism. It was at this point that he became an active freethinker. During his imprisonment Lorulot wrote lengthy memoirs, among which appeared the observation: "Man: a species of ape who believes in the gods and who imitates them without ceasing to be an animal."

Lorulot's FREETHOUGHT was peppered with a strong strain of ANTICLERICALISM. During the 1956 Hungarian uprising he wrote, "A criterion (that has never yet failed me!) is 'Distrust everything that comes from Rome.'" Taking the Soviet side, Lorulot saw the uprising as a Catholic-inspired white reactionary movement, and condemned it accordingly. He was at this time vice president of the World Union of Freethinkers. In 1958 he became the organization's president, continuing the pro-Communist stance the WUF had taken since the mid-1930s. Lorulot died on March 11, 1963.

BILL COOKE

LUCRETIUS, TITUS CARUS (99–55 BCE), Roman philosopher and poet. Aside from his authorship of *De Rerum Natura* (On the Nature of Things), little is known of Lucretius. He apparently came from an obscure branch of an ancient family and was well educated. *De Rerum Natura* is an exposition in Latin hexameters of the metaphysical system of EPICURUS, only a miniscule portion of whose work survives. Lucretius transformed the workaday prose of the Greek philosopher into sterling poetry.

The Epicurean Gods. The Epicurean gods dwelled between worlds, ensconced in a Shangri-la of blissful stasis. They did not create the universe, stage-manage events, answer prayers, reward virtue, punish vice, inspire sacred texts, impregnate mortals, or traverse the cosmos. They were limited in knowledge, power, and inventiveness. Whether Lucretius believed these gods existed or was merely deferring to Epicurus is problematic.

Misconceptions about the Gods. Lucretius scoffed at

the notion that the gods created the earth for humans. The terrain and climate were inhospitable to creatures of our kind, much of the land barred to mortals by scorching heat and biting cold. Moreover, the gods had no incentive to create humans: "What largess of beneficence could our gratitude bestow upon beings immortal and blessed that they should do anything for our sake?" Nor would the gods necessarily confer a benefice by creating us: "He who has never tasted the love of life, never been enrolled in the lists, how does it hurt him never to have been made?"

For Lucretius, fear of the gods was held irrational. Nature is a law unto herself. Humans need not worry that capricious gods will undo the orderly motions of the heavens. Nor should we fear that the gods will punish us either here or hereafter. Such beliefs generate needless fear of death and natural phenomena. The underworld is a fiendish projection of earthly travails. Fear of death also results from misapprehensions about eternal oblivion. When people picture themselves dead, they imagine they will retain bodily sensations. They think they will miss life's pleasures, forgetting that "no longer will any desires possess them."

Materialism. Lucretius embraced a mechanistic universe. Everything in it, including events called mental, is a manifestation of the interaction of particles (see MATERIALISM, PHILOSOPHICAL). Ultimately, nothing exists but atoms and the void (*corpora et inane*). There is no ghost in the machine. Just as the letters of an alphabet can be variously ordered to create an infinite number of words, so diverse combinations of atoms produce an inexhaustible supply of entities. The movement of the atoms is fortuitous, undirected, without behest. Creator or designer gods are an unnecessary hypothesis.

Lucretius held that belief in providential deities stems from ignorance and indolence. By treating gods as the causal agents of natural processes, people avoid the labor of seeking the real causes. The ascription of causal efficacy to the gods is a mistake for which humans pay dearly: "What groans did we create for ourselves, what wounds, what tears for generations to come!" True piety, according to Lucretius, consists in the ability "to survey all things with tranquil mind." Observe closely and reason carefully, he advised. Be prepared to abandon entrenched suppositions and to adopt new premises: "Ponder everything with keen judgment; and if it seems true, own yourself vanquished, but, if it is false, gird up your loins to fight."

Legacy. Lucretius has inspired many writers. Echoes of *De Rerum Natura* can be found in Virgil, Ovid, William Shakespeare (see SHAKESPEARE, RELIGIOUS SKEPTICISM IN), John Milton, William Wordsworth, Matthew ARNOLD, Alfred, Lord Tennyson, and other luminous legatees. Lucretius's conviction that the cosmos can be understood without appeal to supernatural agencies led to the suppression of *De Rerum* in the Middle Ages.

BIBLIOGRAPHY

Sloan, Gary. "Lucretius: The Roman Poet of Freethought." *Free Inquiry* 22, no. 1 (2001–02).

Smith, Martin Ferguson, ed. Introduction to *De Rerum Natura*. Translated by W. H. D. Rouse. Loeb Classical Library. Cambridge, MA: Harvard University Press, 1982.

Winspear, Alban Dewes. *Lucretius and Scientific Thought*. Montreal: Harvard House, 1963.

GARY SLOAN

MACDONALD, GEORGE EVERETT HUSSEY (1857–1937), American freethinker and journalist. George Macdonald was born in modest circumstances in Gardiner, Maine. Macdonald's father was killed at the age of thirty-six in the second battle of Bull Run in August 1861. His mother, Asenath (*née* Hussey), was from a Maine Quaker family. Later in life Macdonald dropped his third initial, not because of any discord with his mother, but rather because of his horror at the tedium of Quaker lives, which he recalled as "so dreary that I have been under the depression of it ever since."

Macdonald began his working life as a farm hand, but soon moved to New York City, where he took up work as a printer's devil for the newly established freethought paper THE TRUTH SEEKER. This paper was to determine his life and shape his attitudes. Macdonald had not been in New York long when *The Truth Seeker*'s founder and editor, D. M. BENNETT, went to prison for thirteen months for supposedly sending "obscene" material through the mail. Bennett was prosecuted under the notorious Comstock Laws (see COMSTOCK, ANTHONY, AND UNBELIEF). A petition bearing two hundred thousand signatures was insufficient to secure Bennett's release.

Macdonald stepped in as editor, and *The Truth Seeker* survived Bennett's imprisonment. Macdonald continued to work for the paper until 1888, when, with his friend Samuel Porter PUTNAM, he went to San Francisco and founded the journal *Freethought*. In that year he also married Grace Leland, daughter of the radical Mary Chilton. The couple had two sons, Eugene Leland and Putnam Foote Macdonald. After *Freethought* folded in 1891, Macdonald went north to Snohomish, Washington, where he worked for the town's paper, the *Eye*. In 1893 Macdonald returned to New York and resumed his connection with *The Truth Seeker*. He remained with the paper for the rest of his life.

In 1909 he took over the editorship of *The Truth Seeker* after his brother, Eugene Montague Macdonald, who had edited the paper since 1883, died of tuberculosis. Macdonald remained the editor of *The Truth Seeker* until his death in 1937. Macdonald shares with Chapman COHEN of Great Britain and James O. HANLON of New Zealand the distinction of being one of the longest-standing editors of a freethought magazine.

As well as his prodigious writing load for *The Truth Seeker*, Macdonald wrote a history of the Inquisition titled *Thumbscrew and Rack: Torture Implements Employed in the XVth and XVIth Centuries* (1904). Beginning in 1923, he set himself the task of writing a history of the American freethought movement over the half century of his involvement. *Fifty Years of Freethought* came out in two volumes, the first in 1929 and the second in 1931. He had a delightful writing style: candid and self-deprecatory, but also principled. *Fifty Years of Freethought* remains an invaluable history of freethought and an incisive memoir of American life in the nineteenth century. Macdonald was also instrumental in gathering together the material and compiling the index for the Dresden Edition of the works of Robert G. INGERSOLL, published by C. P. FARRELL.

Taking the lead from Putnam, Macdonald's FREETHOUGHT was liberal, with a high level of confidence in progress. Macdonald took a phrase from the *First Principles* (1862) of Herbert SPENCER, his favorite philosopher, and used it almost as a creed: "Not adventitious therefore will the wise man regard the faith which is in him. The highest truth he sees he will fearlessly utter; knowing that, let what may come of it, he is thus playing his right part in the world."

BIBLIOGRAPHY

Macdonald, George E. *Fifty Years of Freethought*. New York: Truth Seeker Company, 1972.

Putnam, Samuel P. *Four Hundred Years of Freethought*. New York: Truth Seeker Company, 1894.

BILL COOKE

MACKIE, J. L. (1917–1981), English philosopher. John Leslie Mackie is one of the best-known atheistic philosophers of the second half of the twentieth century. Mackie hailed from Sydney, Australia, but spent the last—and most productive—part of his career as a fellow of University College, Oxford.

Mackie's reputation in philosophy of religion derives mainly from two works: "Evil and Omnipotence" (1955), an early article defending a logical argument from evil (see EVIL, PROBLEM OF; EXISTENCE OF GOD, ARGUMENTS FOR AND AGAINST), and *The Miracle of Theism* (1982), a posthumous book that provides a systematic defense of atheism. Both of these works provoked extensive subsequent discussion.

While many theistic philosophers now claim that Mackie's logical argument from evil has been demolished, principally by the work of Alvin PLANTINGA, many atheistic philosophers view matters in a different light. In Mackie's view, if there were an omnipotent, omniscient, and perfectly good creator of the universe, such a being would have made a universe in which there is no moral evil, that is, a universe in which everyone always freely chooses the good. Since it is plain that

there is moral evil—it is plain that not everyone always freely chooses the good—it follows that there is no omnipotent, omniscient, and perfectly good creator of the universe. The main difficulty with this argument is that it is not clear that it is possible for beings to be made such that they all always freely choose the good. If beings are made such that they all always choose in a certain way, how can it be that the choices of those beings are genuinely free? Mackie assumed—and believed—that freedom is compatible with DETERMINISM; not all philosophers agree with him on this point.

On the other hand, there is much nearer to universal agreement—among theistic and atheistic philosophers alike—that *The Miracle of Theism* is among the very best works that have been produced by atheistic philosophers of religion. It contains penetrating discussions of ontological arguments, cosmological arguments, arguments from design, moral arguments, arguments from consciousness, arguments from miracles and testimony (see MIRACLES, UNBELIEF IN), arguments from religious experience, arguments from evil, arguments from natural histories of religion, PASCAL'S WAGER, and the relationship between belief and reason. Mackie's conclusion is that "the balance of probabilities comes out strongly against the existence of a god," that is, against the existence of a supernatural creator of our universe.

Mackie made important contributions to other areas of philosophy that bear on his views in philosophy of religion. Most famously, Mackie defended the metaethical view that there are no objective moral values. This defense is recorded in his book *Ethics: Inventing Right and Wrong* (1977). Mackie also wrote extensively about the analysis of causation—see, for example, *The Cement of the Universe: A Study of Causation* (1974)—and about significant figures in the history of philosophy, as in *Problems from Locke* (1974) and *Hume's Moral Theory* (1980).

BIBLIOGRAPHY

Mackie, J. L. *Ethics: Inventing Right and Wrong*. Harmondsworth, UK: Penguin, 1977.

———. "Evil and Omnipotence." *Mind* 64 (1955).

———. *The Miracle of Theism*. Oxford: Oxford University Press, 1982.

GRAHAM OPPY

MADISON, JAMES (1751–1836), American politician, political philosopher, civil libertarian, and champion of religious liberty and church-state separation. After completing his studies at Princeton, James Madison spent the rest of his life involved in politics. He served in the Virginia General Assembly, the Virginia Revolutionary Convention, the United States Congress, as a delegate to the Constitutional Convention in 1787, as an adviser to President George Washington, as secretary of state under President Thomas JEFFERSON, and president for two terms, from 1809 to 1817. He was also coauthor of the Federalist Papers with Alexander Hamilton and John Jay.

Madison is regarded as the most important figure in the development of religious liberty and church-state separation, as the chief architect of the Constitution and Bill of Rights, and as the cofounder, with Jefferson, of what is now the Democratic Party.

Madison, Religion, and Religious Liberty. Very little is known about Madison's personal views on religion, though he was at least a nominal Episcopalian all his life. Indeed, his cousin and friend of the same name was an Episcopal bishop. He did his university work at Princeton (then the College of New Jersey), a Presbyterian institution, where he was greatly influenced by Scottish professor John Witherspoon, later one of the signers of the Declaration of Independence. Princeton's goal then was "to cherish the spirit of liberty and free enquiry."

Madison, who studied theology at Princeton, was possibly a Deist like Benjamin FRANKLIN, Jefferson, and Thomas PAINE. He wrote at one point that belief in an all-powerful, all-wise deity "is essential to the moral order of the world and the happiness of man," but declined to express any opinion about the nature of the deity. He kept his religious opinions to himself, perhaps because he knew well of the negative reactions to Ethan ALLEN's *Reason, the Only Oracle of Man* and Paine's *Age of Reason*, and the bitter attacks on Jefferson in the 1800 election campaign. Probably, like Franklin, he knew that involvement in religious disputes would interfere with his goal of promoting religious liberty and church-state separation.

As early as 1774, at the age of only twenty-two, Madison wrote to his Philadelphia college friend William Bradford Jr., complaining of his Virginia neighbors indulging in the "diabolical, hell-conceived principle of persecution." As historian Edwin Gaustad points out, "By jailing half a dozen well-meaning men [Baptist preachers] for merely proclaiming their religious positions, Madison's neighbors unwittingly launched a career committed to liberty in religion. It was his very first libertarian concern; it was to be his last."

Madison wrote to Bradford again in 1774 comparing "the liberality of Pennsylvania with the intolerance of Virginia." He wrote, "Religious bondage shackles and debilitates the mind and unfits it for every noble enterprise, every expanded prospect."

At the Virginia Revolutionary Convention in 1778, Madison and George Mason succeeded in injecting the following provision into the state constitution: "That religion, or the duty which we owe to our Creator, and the manner of discharging it, can be directed only by reason and conviction, not by force or violence; and therefore, all men are equally entitled to the free exercise of religion according to the dictates of conscience." Mason's original bill had provided for "the fullest Toleration in the Exercise of Religion," but Madison

improved it by changing "toleration" to "free exercise," a phrase that turned up later in the First Amendment. Thus began the years-long struggle to completely separate church and state. The next item of business was to eliminate compulsory support of churches in Virginia, which was temporarily halted in 1779. In 1784, however, the legislature called up a bill to provide tax support for "Teachers of the Christian Religion." Madison led the opposition to the bill, which had considerable support from the Episcopal clergy, though opposed by Baptists, Presbyterians, and others.

As historian Robert Alley shows, Madison, fearing that the "general assessment" bill might be passed, developed a shrewd strategy for its defeat. First he arranged that the legislature would postpone action until late 1785. Then he supported the election of Patrick Henry to the governorship, removing Henry from the legislature, where his eloquence had exerted a powerful influence in favor of tax aid to religion. Finally he wrote and widely circulated his "Memorial and Remonstrance against Religious Assessments." This document has been heralded by historian Elwyn Smith as "the premier public document of American church-state thought" and by the twentieth-century church-state activist lawyer Leo PFEFFER as "one of the great documents in the history of human liberty" which "should be required reading in every American school." Madison biographer Irving Brant writes, "The remonstrance against religious assessments continues to stand, not merely through the years but through the centuries, as the most powerful defense of religious liberty ever written in America," while Canon Anson Phelps Stokes considered it "one of the truly epoch-making documents in the history of American church-state separation; as impressive and convincing today as it was over a century and a half ago."

The Memorial and Remonstrance (readily available from many sources) eloquently spells out fifteen reasons why any tax aid (even "three pence only") for the support of religion would be harmful to religion, government, and individual rights. The Memorial was persuasive; the religious assessments bill was defeated. This in turn paved the way for passage of Jefferson's Statute for Establishing Religious Freedom in 1786.

In 1787 the Constitutional Convention met in Philadelphia to produce the framework of government that continues to serve. Unlike the Declaration of Independence, it contains no reference to a deity. The Declaration stated that "all Men are created equal [and] are endowed by their Creator with certain unalienable Rights, . . . That to secure these Rights, Governments are instituted among Men, deriving their just Powers from the Consent of the Governed." In 1776 this country was more or less evenly divided among those supportive of, opposed to, or indifferent about the Revolution. The rather disorganized Americans were up against the nation with the best army and navy in the world, a nation, like most in Europe, that supported the notion of the "divine right of kings." How better to counter the "divine right of kings" than with the "divine rights of the people"—though as frequently noted, in its invocation of the creator and "nature's God" the Declaration uses language more characteristic of DEISM than Christianity.

By 1787, however, the Revolution was receding into the past and the outdated Articles of Confederation had to be completely revised. Reference to a deity in the new Constitution was no longer considered necessary. Following the lead of the Declaration, the new document began/begins: "We the People of the United States, in Order to . . . do ordain and establish this Constitution for the United States of America."

Madison, justly regarded as the "Father of the Constitution," guided the process through to completion. The only references to religion in the charter, found in Article VI, were/are the bans on mandatory oaths of office and religious tests for public office.

Once completed, the Constitution had to be ratified by the states, a process that threatened to stall because of the absence of a bill of rights. Jefferson, in Paris as American ambassador, made this point in a communication to Madison. At the end of the day Madison and other leaders promised to add a bill of rights. The Constitution was ratified and the first Congress set to work on twelve, later reduced to ten, amendments, which in turn were ratified.

Again, Madison was the main architect of the Bill of Rights. The First Amendment, which is of paramount importance in America today, stipulates that "Congress shall make no law respecting an establishment of religion, or prohibiting the free exercise thereof." In 1802 President Jefferson, in a letter to the Baptists of Danbury, Connecticut—a letter cleared through his attorney general, Levi Lincoln—declared that the amendment built "a wall of separation between church and state." In 1879 in *Reynolds v. United States* (98 U.S. 145) the Supreme Court cited Madison's Memorial and Remonstrance and Jefferson's letter to the Danbury Baptists, traced the history of church-state relations, and concluded that Jefferson's "wall" metaphor "may be accepted almost as an authoritative declaration of the scope and effect of the amendment." This view in turn was accepted, developed, and amplified by a unanimous Supreme Court in 1947 in *Everson v. Board of Education.*

Parenthetically it might be noted that Madison wanted the Bill of Rights to apply to the states as well. This view was rejected because of the belief, which proved mistaken, that the state governments offered adequate protection. It was not until after the Civil War that the Fourteenth Amendment was added to the Constitution to make the Bill of Rights applicable to state and local government, a view the Supreme Court began to apply piecemeal only after World War I.

The significance of the pioneering work of Madison, Jefferson, and their colleagues is of great importance today, given the Supreme Court's drift away from the separationist position of the *Everson* Court in 1947 and its rulings for a third of a century thereafter. This drift is well focused in Chief Justice William Rehnquist's long dissent in *Wallace v. Jaffree* (1985), in which he wrote that Jefferson's "wall of separation between church and state" is "a metaphor based in bad history, a metaphor which has proved useless as a guide to judging." (An examination of the three dozen Supreme Court rulings on religious liberty, church-state issues, and reproductive freedom of conscience in which Rehnquist participated through June 4, 2005, shows that he came down on the side opposed to separation and freedom of conscience 90 percent of the time.)

Who is right, then, about the meaning or "original intent" of the First Amendment: "accommodationists" from Patrick Henry to justices William Rehnquist, Antonin Scalia, and Clarence Thomas, or the "separationists" from Madison and Jefferson to majorities of the Supreme Court justices from 1947 to about 1990? The historical record favors the separationists.

Between June 7 and September 25, 1789, Congress deliberated over how to shape the religious freedom clause of the First Amendment, considering no fewer than ten different versions before arriving at the one agreed upon by the House-Senate conference committee and then approved by both houses of Congress. One thing is clear: The framers of the First Amendment were not concerned about preventing a single national religious establishment, as in Britain, but about whether to have "accommodationist" language that would permit multiple establishments. By 1789 there was no single religious establishment in any state and multiple establishments in only a few.

The story of the separation legacy of Madison, Jefferson, and the other Founders is still evolving in ways whose end cannot be predicted.

Religious liberty and church-state separation remained among Madison's central concerns. In 1785 he opposed a proposal that Congress set aside one section of each township in the Northwest Territory for the support of religion; by 1787 the Northwest Ordinance was passed, stripped of any mention of aid to religion. In 1790 Madison successfully opposed using questions about religion in the first United States census.

As president from 1809—the year in which both Abraham Lincoln and Charles DARWIN were born—to 1817, Madison continued to defend the separation principle, vetoing bills to incorporate the Episcopal Church in Alexandria, Virginia, and the District of Columbia (he feared that incorporation would stimulate a dangerous accumulation of land and wealth by churches) and a bill to grant a small parcel of land to a Baptist church in the Mississippi Territory. Of course the War of 1812 kept Madison busy for several years, but its conclusion guaranteed the young country's survival.

The Virginian's interest in religious liberty continued after he left the White House. In a letter to Robert Walsh in 1819 he declared that "the number, the industry, and the morality of the Priesthood, & the devotion of the people have been manifestly increased by the total separation of the Church from the State." In 1822 he wrote to Edward Livingston that governments "do better without Kings & Nobles" and that "Religion flourishes in greater purity, without than with the aid of Gov[ernmen]t."

Between 1817 and 1832 Madison wrote a series of observations on various topics. These notes were only discovered in 1946 among the papers of Madison biographer William Cabell Rives. They were published by Elizabeth Fleet in the *William and Mary Quarterly* that same year as the "Detached Memoranda." The "Memoranda" clearly show the strong positions he continued to hold until the end of his life. He elaborated on "The danger of silent accumulations & encroachments by Ecclesiastical Bodies [not having] sufficiently engaged attention in the U.S. . . . are the U.S. duly awake to the tendency of the precedents they are establishing, in the multiplied incorporations of Religious Congregations with the faculty of acquiring & holding property real as well as personal?" He went on to oppose grants of public land to churches, tax exemption of religious entities, mention of the deity in government documents, congressional chaplaincies ("a palpable violation of equal rights, as well as of Constitutional principles"), and religious proclamations by government.

Madison was not hostile to religion, though often critical of abuses by religion. His consuming lifetime interest was in defending freedom of *and* from religion to the maximum extent possible through total separation of church and state.

Though of small stature—Washington and Jefferson towered over him—and with a soft speaking voice, Madison made himself into one of the most important figures in the development of democracy and human rights. As historian William Lee Miller put it: "John Marshall, the future chief justice, who was usually an opponent of Madison's, nevertheless said of him that if eloquence included 'persuasion by convincing, Mr. Madison was the most eloquent man I ever heard.' He persuaded by his thorough preparation, his layers of reading, his logical powers; he made his mark not by his tongue or his throat, or by his presence, but by his pen and his brain and his diligence."

BIBLIOGRAPHY

Alley, Robert S., ed. *The Constitution & Religion: Leading Supreme Court Cases on Church and State*. Amherst, NY: Prometheus Books, 1999.

———. *James Madison and Religious Liberty*. Amherst, NY: Prometheus Books, 1985.

———. *Public Education and the Public Good*. Silver Spring, MD: Americans for Religious Liberty, 1996.

Brant, Irving. *The Bill of Rights: Its Origins and Meaning*. Indianapolis: Bobbs-Merrill, 1965.

Fisher, Louis. *Religious Liberty in America: Political Safeguards*. Lawrence: University Press of Kansas, 2002.

Gaustad, Edwin S. *Faith of Our Fathers: Religion and the New Nation*. San Francisco: Harper & Row, 1987.

———. *Neither King nor Prelate: Religion and the New Nation, 1776–1826*. Grand Rapids, MI: Eerdmans, 1993.

Madison, James. "Advice to My Country." Charlottesville: University Press of Virginia, 1997.

———. *Debates in the Federal Convention of 1787*. 2 vols. Amherst, NY: Prometheus Books, 1987.

Menendez, Albert J., and Edd Doerr, eds. *Great Quotations on Religious Freedom*. Amherst, NY: Prometheus Books, 2002.

Miller, William Lee. *The First Liberty: Religion and the American Republic*. New York: Knopf, 1986.

Pfeffer, Leo. *Church, State and Freedom*. Boston: Beacon, 1967.

Schaaf, Gregory. *Franklin, Jefferson & Madison on Religion and the State*. Santa Fe, NM: CIAC, 2004.

Smith, Elwyn A. *Religious Liberty in the United States: The Development of Church-State Thought Since the Revolutionary Era*. Philadelphia: Fortress, 1972.

Stokes, Anson Phelps, and Leo Pfeffer. *Church and State in the United States*. New York: Harper & Row, 1964.

Wilson, John E., and Donald L. Drakeman. *Church and State in American History*. Boston: Beacon, 1987.

EDD DOERR

MALRAUX, ANDRÉ (1901–1976), French novelist and activist. A man of many talents and indefatigable energy, André Malraux distinguished himself first and foremost as a writer, but also as a soldier, art critic, and eventually minister of culture under Charles de Gaulle. He was born into a modest family that had been established for generations in the port town of Dunkirk on the north coast of France. He challenged convention from the outset; though obviously gifted intellectually, he decided to abandon formal schooling at the age of seventeen, and the restless spirit of the autodidact was to mark his work thereafter. While still a teenager he persuaded a seller of rare books and prints to recruit him as an employee. Malraux's prodigious intellectual appetites and boundless self-confidence ignited his passion for art, and he soon propelled himself into the orbit of figures at the cutting edge of modern art. Becoming friends and not just clients, artists like Georges Braque and Fernand Léger even agreed to provide illustrations for Malraux's first foray as a published author.

Malraux was already an established author by the time he reached his late twenties and his greatest novelistic achievements appeared within the space of a decade: *Les Conquérants* (The Conquerors, 1928), *La Condition Humaine* (Man's Fate, 1933), and *L'Espoir* (Days of Hope, 1937). His description by some critics as a "pre-existentialist" stems from the fact that one of the themes running through all his novels is the challenge faced by the individual attempting to leave his or her mark on a world apparently devoid of enduring values. In the imaginary exchange of philosophical letters between a European and an Oriental, which he published in 1926 under the title *La Tentation de l'Occident* (The Temptation of the West), the French correspondent argues that the West has burned its old gods only to find itself facing the abyss of an existence without meaning. What the chief protagonists attempt to establish in his subsequent novels are ways of asserting those fraternal values that defend the dignity of humanity in an indifferent world often convulsed by conflict and pointless brutality. Malraux's reputation as a defender of humanist values was further enhanced by his support of the democratic cause during the civil war in Spain, where he served as a fighter pilot and helped organize the aerial battle against Gen. Francisco Franco and his fascist allies. After France was pulled into the global conflict against fascism, Malraux served with distinction in the Free French Forces that had rallied around Charles de Gaulle, and he eventually played an active part in the campaign by those forces, following the successful Allied landing on D-day, that succeeded in expelling German troops from eastern France, thereby finally liberating the country.

In common with many intellectuals during the 1930s, Malraux sympathized with the humanist ideals of MARXISM and supported the Soviet Union as a necessary counterweight to the manifest inhumanity of Nazism. But disillusionment soon set in after the end of World War II, when the truth concerning the systematic brutality of Joseph Stalin's Communist regime in the Soviet Union began to emerge. Drawing ferocious criticism from former left-wing allies, Malraux decided to offer his political allegiance to de Gaulle and ultimately became a very high-profile minister of culture in his administration following the establishment of the Fifth Republic in France in 1958. Malraux's novel writing came to an end in the 1950s; his intellectual energies were increasingly invested in art. Works such as *Les Voix du Silence* (The Voice of Silence, 1951) and *Le Miroir des Limbes* (Anti-memoirs, 1976) expressed a sensibility that was turning away from political engagement in pursuit of humanist values, toward a belief in the redemptive possibilities offered by artistic creation and in particular the potential for art to communicate, from one generation to the next, the enduring vision that allows us to humanize the world. Malraux's writing on art was not without its critics, but there was more positive agreement concerning his efforts as a government minister to democratize the enjoyment of culture during the 1960s by initiating the creation of a regional network of *Maisons de la culture*. Malraux's reputation was revived in the 1990s, and in 1996 his remains were transferred to the Pantheon in Paris, to rest alongside the other illustrious proponents of the French Republic's humanist values.

BIBLIOGRAPHY

Bevan, David. *André Malraux: Towards the Expression of Transcendence*. Montreal: McGill University Press, 1986.

Blend, Charles. *André Malraux, Tragic Humanist*. Columbus: Ohio State University Press, 1963.

Harris, Geoffrey. *André Malraux: A Reassessment*. Basingstoke, UK: Macmillan, 1996.

Jenkins, Cecil. *André Malraux*. New York: Twayne, 1972.

Lacouture, Jean. *A. Malraux, une vie dans le siècle*. Paris: Seuil, 1973.

Raymond, Gino. *André Malraux: Politics and the Temptation of Myth*. Aldershot, UK: Avebury, 1995.

Todd, Olivier. *André Malraux: une vie*. Paris: Gallimard, 2002.

GINO RAYMOND

MANDEVILLE, BERNARD DE (1670–1733), Dutch philosopher. Born in Holland, Bernard de Mandeville was educated at the Erasmian school in Rotterdam and at the University of Leiden, where he studied medicine and philosophy. He specialized in nervous disorders but showed an early literary bent, being well read in French skeptical literature by the time he was at university.

His family were respectable bourgeois folk, many of whom had been medical doctors. But it is possible that the young Mandeville was involved in the Costerman Riots in Rotterdam in 1690. At any rate, he emigrated to England in the following year, settling down into a good practice with well-to-do clients and marrying an English lady, Ruth Elizabeth Laurence.

The successful doctor (who counted the eminent Sir Hans Sloane among his friends, and who met Benjamin FRANKLIN while the latter was in London) turned his attention to literary matters, producing "The Grumbling Hive or Knaves Turned Honest," a doggerel poem that formed the kernel of his magnum opus, *The Fable of the Bees*. This was published in two parts, first in 1714 and then in 1729. Mandeville's *Fable* is an extended essay of a philosophical, sociological, economic, and political character that advances a Hobbesian theory of human nature and an economic theory of social mechanism which anticipates Adam Smith's "Invisible Hand." In a paradoxical flourish, Mandeville defends luxury, whatever its moral effect, as an agent of prosperity and employment in modern commercial society. The book became notorious in 1723 when Mandeville appended an essay on charity schools attacking the usefulness of educating the "labouring poor." To its author's delight, the *Fable* was condemned by the Grand Jury of Middlesex and burned at Tyburn by the public hangman, ensuring wide publicity for several generations.

Mandeville wrote a number of other works, on prostitution, women's rights, hanging, and (adding to his reputation as an unbeliever) a book suggesting that Christianity did good when harnessed to war. But *The Fable of the Bees*, with its paradoxical subtitle, "Private Vices, Public Benefits," remained his most celebrated work and attracted the attention of generations of clerics and philosophers (Bishop Joseph Butler, Bishop George

Berkeley, David HUME, Smith, and VOLTAIRE, to name only some) who held him to be a true unbeliever.

BIBLIOGRAPHY

Jack, Malcolm. *Corruption and Progress: The Eighteenth-Century Debate*. New York: AMS, 1989.

Mandeville, Bernard. *The Fable of the Bees or Private Vices Publick Benefits*. 2 vols. Edited by F. B. Kaye. Oxford: Oxford University Press, 1924.

Primer, Irwin, ed. *Mandeville Studies: New Explorations in the Art and Thought of Bernard Mandeville*. The Hague: Martinus Nyhof, 1975.

Prior, Charles, ed *Mandeville and Augustan Ideas: New Essays*. English Literary Studies 83. Victoria, BC: University of Victoria, 2000.

MALCOLM JACK

MARÉCHAL, PIERRE-SYLVAIN (1750–1803), French revolutionary and atheist. Sylvain Maréchal, as he is often called, was one of the most prominent of the militant atheists who flourished in France during the eighteenth century. While he is perhaps less celebrated than figures such as Julien Offray de LA METTRIE and Baron d'HOLBACH, his ferocious hostility to religious belief of any kind is as intense as anything to be found in their writings. Yet he was not content simply to oppose the church, for he combined his atheism with a strong commitment to social change and eventually became not so much an atheist as an anarchist. These uncompromising views were not, however, instinctive. Born the son of a wine merchant in Paris, he trained as a lawyer. His earliest publications were poems of a conventional, pastoral kind, which impressed contemporaries enough to earn him a position in 1770 as sublibrarian at the Bibliothèque Mazarine in his native city, a post which he held for some fifteen years. His position gave him the leisure and the opportunity to read widely, and he rapidly became a disciple of writers such as Jean-Jacques ROUSSEAU and Etienne-Garbriel Morelly, who deplored the gross inequalities created by the pursuit of wealth. Like Morelly in particular, Maréchal advocated as a remedy for these ills a return to a form of simple agrarian communism, a doctrine which he set out in *Le Livre de tous les âges* (The Book of All the Ages, 1779). He then concluded that social revolution could not be effective without the abolition of organized religion, a case argued in two anonymous works, the *Fragmens d'un poème moral sur Dieu* (Fragments of a Moral Poem on God, 1780) and the *Livre échappé au déluge* (The Book Which Escaped the Flood, 1784), the second of which he apparently printed himself. Having been dismissed from his post for his views, Maréchal was by now notorious enough to be regarded (perhaps wrongly) as the author of an *Almanach des honnêtes gens* (The Good People's Almanack, 1788), a sort of humanist calendar in which the names of saints were replaced by those of the "benefactors of humanity." Imprisoned for three months in Saint-Lazare for his alleged audacity, Maréchal published most of his later writings anonymously. During the French Revolution, he lived by producing potboilers of various kinds, including a history of costume. His main role, however, was to use his position as editor of the widely read periodical *Révolutions de Paris* to advocate his increasingly ferocious antiroyalist and antireligious opinions. His experience of the factional infighting into which the Revolution descended disillusioned him with all organized political structures, as he showed in his *Manifeste des Egaux* (Manifesto of the Equals, 1794), which advocated a wholly egalitarian society. The views to which he clung for much of his life were encapsulated in his last significant work, the *Dictionnaire des Athées* (Dictionary of Atheists) of 1800. While he wrote copiously on a variety of subjects, Maréchal is perhaps best remembered today for his play *Le Jugement dernier des rois* (The Final Judgment of Kings, 1793), a striking (not to say murderous) one-act "prophecy" in which the crowned heads of Europe, deposed by popular uprisings, are taken to a tropical island; having reluctantly confessed their crimes, they are left to perish in a spectacular volcanic eruption.

BIBLIOGRAPHY

Apostolidès, Jean-Marie. "Theater and Terror: *Le Jugement dernier des rois*." In *Terror and Consensus: Vicissitudes of French Thought*, edited by Jean-Joseph Goux and Philip R. Wood. Stanford, CA: Stanford University Press, 1998.

Aubert, Francoise. *Sylvain Maréchal: Passion et faillite d'un eqalitaire*. Paris: Nizet, 1976.

Mannucci, Erica Jay. "The Anti-Patriarch: Utopianism in Sylvain Maréchal." *History of European Ideas* 16 (January 1993).

DAVID ADAMS

MARTIN, EMMA (1812–1851), English FREETHOUGHT pioneer. Brought up in a strict Baptist family from Bristol, Emma Martin quickly revealed unusual intellect. At the age of twenty-four, she was editor of the *Bristol Magazine*. Initially a fervent Christian, Martin began her career as a critic of infidelity, denouncing it as an effusion of weak minds and the resource of guilty ones. She lost her faith after a long period of study and thought, brought on by the trials for BLASPHEMY of George Jacob HOLYOAKE and Charles SOUTHWELL. She also had to struggle with a desperately unhappy marriage, eventually having to maintain her children on her own, something nineteenth-century England made formidably difficult for women.

Martin became a prominent exponent of women's rights (see WOMAN SUFFRAGE MOVEMENT AND UNBE-

LIEF) and of freethought. Fluent in Italian, she also translated the *Maxims* of Guicciardini into English. Martin also penned several short tracts, including *Baptism a Pagan Rite* (1843), *Religion Superseded, Prayer, A Conversation on the Being of God*, and a protest against capital punishment. She also wrote a novel called *The Exiles of Piedmont*. And in order to make a living for herself and her children, Martin trained as a "physician for women."

Emma Martin was struck down in her prime, dying of consumption at her home in London in October 1851, aged only thirty-nine. George Jacob Holyoake, who spoke at her funeral, described Emma Martin as "a handsome woman, of brilliant talent and courage."

BIBLIOGRAPHY

Underwood, Sara A. *Heroines of Freethought*. New York: Charles P. Somerby, 1876.
Wheeler, J. M. *A Biographical Dictionary of Freethinkers*. London: Progressive, 1889.

BILL COOKE

MARTINEAU, HARRIET (1802–1876), English author and freethinker. Harriet Martineau, one of the first practitioners of sociology, was a significant role model as a nineteenth-century female author who supported herself with her writings, signing her own name. Martineau was born a Unitarian but noted in her autobiography, "I disclaim their theology *in toto*." Sixth of eight children of a silk manufacturer in Norwich, England, Martineau was a sensitive child whose first inner rebellion was at chapel. She grew quite deaf by the age of twelve, and became devoutly religious. Martineau's first book was *Devotions for Young People* (1823). Her monthly tracts on political and economic issues made her sought after as a writer. She toured America for two years in her early thirties, writing the two-volume *Society in America* (1837), as acclaimed a work in its day as Alexis de Tocqueville's study. She felt American women had an unhealthy obsession with religion. After Martineau endorsed freethinking abolitionist William Lloyd Garrison, she spent the final three months of her tour being mobbed by opponents.

Among her series of essays and books is *The Hour and the Man* (1841), a tribute to Haitian revolutionary Toussaint L'Ouverture. After overcoming a period of invalidism, Martineau visited Egypt, Palestine, and Arabia in 1846, writing *Eastern Life, Past and Present* (1848), which examined the genealogy of the various faiths. A collection of letters she exchanged with H. G. Atkinson, *On the Laws of Man's Nature and Development* (1849), made clear her freethought views: "There is no theory of a God, of an author of Nature, of an origin of the Universe, which is not utterly repugnant to my faculties; which is not (to my feelings) so irrelevant as to make me blush; so misleading as to make me mourn."

Wanting to write a book for "the Secularist order of parents," she produced *Household Education* (1848). Martineau translated and condensed the six volumes of French atheist and philosopher Auguste COMTE into two volumes, with his approval, in 1853. She wrote fifty books, nearly all nonfiction, and more than sixteen hundred articles.

Mistakenly diagnosed with fatal heart disease in 1855, Martineau wrote her autobiography, but lived until 1876. In this two-volume work she candidly recorded her rejection of "the superstitions of the Christian mythology." After her death Garrison praised her service to abolition. On September 29, 1867, Florence Nightingale wrote that Harriet Martineau "was born to be a destroyer of slavery, in whatever form, in whatever place."

BIBLIOGRAPHY

Martineau, Harriet. *Autobiography*. 2 vols. Edited by Maria Weston Chapman. Boston: James R. Osgood, 1877.
Rossi, Alice S., ed. *The Feminist Papers: From Adams to de Beauvoir*. New York: Columbia University Press, 1973.
Underwood, Sara A. *Heroines of Freethought*. New York: Charles P. Somerby, 1876.

ANNIE LAURIE GAYLOR

MARXISM. Early Marxism, or "scientific socialism," held a number of characteristic positions on religion: (1) religion, usually equated with the Abrahamic faiths, has been shown to be false by the advances of science; (2) religion, like all false ideas, is a distorted reflection of reality in the human mind; (3) religion is an imaginary compensation and solace for people's dissatisfaction with existing conditions; (4) religion changes as social conditions change (the rise of Protestantism, for example, corresponding to the rise of bourgeois social relations of market exchange); (5) the state should regard each person's religion as "a private matter," and not discriminate on grounds of religious practice or affiliation; (6) religion is generally an instrument of class oppression, but some past episodes, such as the rise of the early Christian church and medieval peasant revolts, show religion at the service of oppressed classes; and (7) with the coming of socialism, but not before, religion will spontaneously disappear.

These positions have continued to characterize most Marxist thought, though they have been qualified and emphasized in a variety of ways and occasionally called into question. They are related to the Marxist theory of historical materialism, which declares that the social relations of production are the "base" of society, on which rests a dependent "superstructure" that includes religion as well as philosophy and law. The claims of historical materialism are famously ambiguous—and, contrary to a widespread supposition, historical materialism, as a theory about social processes, is independent of the question of theism or any other religious tenet (see ATHEISM). The materialist claim that mental or "spiritual" activities exist as a by-product of particular arrangements of matter (see MATERIALISM, PHILOSOPHICAL) neither implies nor is implied by the twin historical-materialist contentions (1) that the general character of a whole society is determined by its social relations of production and (2) that changes in the social relations of production occur in response to changes in the forces of production (roughly, technology).

Marxism embraces materialism in both senses; its opposition to religion is an aspect of its opposition to philosophical idealism. Dialectical materialism ("diamat") is a narrower doctrine, possibly not held by Karl MARX, but derived from Friedrich Engels, Plekhanov, and Vladimir Ilyich LENIN. It maintains that various processes of thought (most famously the negation of the negation, the transformation of quantity into quality, and the Fichtean triad of thesis-antithesis-synthesis) identified by idealists like G. W. FICHTE and G. W. F. Hegel as processes in the world of thought should properly be attributed to events in the physical world. Dialectical materialism, like Lysenkoist biology but unlike historical materialism, has drawn virtually no respect from scholars other than committed Marxists.

In the fin de siècle and the early twentieth century, there was much discussion of the attitude Marxist parties should take to workers who sympathized politically with socialism while believing in Christianity. The predominant view, with many variations of detail, was that scientific socialists should seek the political support of religious proletarians while continuing to promulgate materialism and atheism. The opinion, held by the French socialist leader Jean Jaurès and the Austro-Marxist Max Adler, that religious belief is fully compatible with scientific socialism, has always remained extremely rare.

Pre-Bolshevik Marxism was open to new ideas from non-Marxist thinkers about the origin and social function of religion. The theories of writers like Herbert SPENCER, Ernest HAECKEL, Tylor, and Max Müller were readily absorbed. Heinrich Cunow's 1913 work drew upon such theoretical developments to criticize the earlier Marxist view that religion arose from ignorance of natural forces, advancing instead the theory, evidently more compatible with historical materialism, that the origin of religion lay in the social structure.

Before 1914 the world center of Marxism was Germany, where the leading Socialist Party theoretician, Karl Kautsky, was dubbed "the Pope of Marxism." Kautsky contended that early Christianity had not been primarily a slave movement, as Engels had maintained, but a proletarian movement, and that Jesus was crucified for violent rebellion against the ruling class. (Strong interest in the early Christian church, and awareness of similarities between that phase of history and modern socialism, has been a recurring feature of Marxism, uniting such diverse figures as Sorel and Antonio Gramsci.) Although, in line with Engels, Kautsky tried to show the derivation of religious developments from economic causes, his thinking became gradually more subtle, and in his *The Materialist Conception of History* (1927) he depicted religious belief as social morality objectified in the form of "collective representation."

With the formation of the Comintern in 1920, Moscow became the recognized center of Marxism. The Russians had been among the more zealously antireligious Marxists (see PROPAGANDA, ANTIRELIGIOUS [SOVIET]). The Soviet government pursued a strongly antireligious policy, with occasional vacillations and concessions. This policy had three components: persecution of religious activities (denial of civil rights to active theists), propaganda for atheism, and the attempted creation of a puppet church under government control. The official theory was that there was freedom of religion in the Soviet Union, because the antireligious activities were carried out by the Communist Party, not the state. But this distinction was inconsequential in practice because the Party was merely an instrument of the state. The traditional Marxist positions, that the state should not curtail religious freedom and that the Marxist party should vigorously oppose religion, took on a different complexion when the Marxist party was the sole legal political movement—something that Marxists before 1917 had not anticipated.

In January 1918 Patriarch Tikhon denounced the Bolshevik government for its brutality, and the Bolsheviks reacted by killing thousands of Orthodox clergy and laypeople, arresting thousands more, seizing all church assets, and forbidding churches to own property or educate children. Christian intellectuals and church activists were denied membership in the Communist Party, while Christian workers or peasants were admitted subject to "reeducation."

The League of the Godless, later renamed the League of the Militant Godless, was instituted in 1925. After some relaxation in the late 1920s, a fierce assault was launched on religion in 1929. There was a big push to recruit schoolchildren to the "Young Godless." Over the next decade, the number of openly functioning churches in the Soviet Union was reduced from forty thousand to fewer than one thousand.

Leading up to World War II there was a change to a more tolerant tone. It became official doctrine that the conversion of Russia to Christianity had been historically progressive. Following the German invasion of Russia in 1941, in which the Germans permitted churches to open in the occupied territories, atheistic activities in Russia, including periodicals, were shut down. The League of the Militant Godless was quietly liquidated. Christian elements in traditional Russian culture were treated more favorably, for example, the permissible valuation of the novelist Dostoevsky was greatly enhanced.

Beginning in 1947, the relaxation of antireligious state policy began to be reversed. Churches, seminaries, and monasteries permitted to open during the war were pressured to close down. The old and crude Militant Godless was replaced with a new "Knowledge Society," which preached atheism intermingled with popular science education. Denial of elementary civil rights to active religionists was expanded and intensified in the Khrushchev period.

The Soviet era was characterized by monstrous intolerance, showing once again that any doctrinal system, supernatural or not, if made a state religion or "established church" can become a fount of bigotry, injustice, and brutality. To a large extent, the civil rights of active Orthodox Christians were restored under Mikhail Gorbachev's perestroika policies, beginning in 1986, though comparatively minor harassment of "new" sects and cults continues in the post-Soviet era. With the downfall of Communism, there was a great gain in global religious freedom. Persecution persists in mainland China (see CHINA, UNBELIEF IN), though the official line is no longer obtrusively atheistic. Instead, the government has a concept of "normal religion," which it uses to justify persecution of supposedly abnormal sects such as the Falun Gong movement.

Following the events of 1956 (Nikita Khrushchev's "secret" denunciation of Stalin and the suppression of the Hungarian uprising), there was an accelerated exodus of intellectuals from Communist parties and their affiliates in the non-Communist world. This New Left did not develop any major new ideas on materialism or religion, but some of its adherents were more favorable than the Communists to collaboration with religious organizations. This was followed by the Sino-Soviet split and the growth of "Eurocommunism"—greater diversity of thinking within the Western Communist parties themselves, which no longer were required to toe the Moscow line on every detailed issue.

In this new climate there developed both the Christian-Marxist Dialogue and Liberation Theology. The dialogue arose out of the recognition by Communists, especially in Italy and France, that any political gains for Communism would require the support of Catholics. While the Italian Communist Party went to great lengths to court Catholics, the French party cracked down on Roger Garaudy and others, and partly under the influence of Louis Althusser, reverted to a more traditional line of uncompromising hostility to religion. Garaudy himself eventually ceased to be a Marxist.

Liberation Theology, a term first used in 1973 by the Peruvian priest Gustavo Gutierrez, is primarily a movement among Catholic theologians and priests concerned about the plight of the poor and the repressions of dictatorial right-wing regimes, and to some extent admiring the Castro regime in Cuba. The writings of Gutierrez and of Juan Segundo and Jose Miranda clearly exhibit and acknowledge the influence of Marxist language and thinking. Sympathetic to the plight of poor people in these countries and to the Communist guerrilla movements, the priests absorbed much of simplified Marxism into an essentially Catholic outlook. Two priests were part of the Sandinista government in Nicaragua, and Jean-Bertrand Aristide, president of Haiti, adhered to Liberation Theology.

Liberation Theology drew inspiration from the Second Vatican Council and numbers bishops among its adherents, but approval from the hierarchy was damped down by the late Pope John Paul II, who publicly rejected the conception of Christ as a political revolutionary while acknowledging a "kernel of truth" in Marxism. Pope Benedict XVI is even more firmly opposed to Liberation Theology than his predecessor. Some Protestant religious thinkers, such as Rubem Alves and Jose Miguez Bonino, have also adopted a form of Liberation Theology.

With the fall of the Soviet Union, the collapse of intellectual credibility of Marxism, and the end of effective insurrectionary movements in the third world, both the Christian-Marxist Dialogue and Liberation Theology have declined steeply. Liberation Theology retains much support among left-leaning Catholic theologians but no longer has political significance.

BIBLIOGRAPHY

Bukharin, Nikolai. *Historical Materialism: A System of Sociology*. Ann Arbor: University of Michigan Press, 1969.

Cohen, G. A. *Karl Marx's Theory of History: A Defence*. Princeton, NJ: Princeton University Press, 2000.

Cunow, Heinrich. *Die Ursprung der Religion und des Gottesglaubens*. Berlin, 1913.

Garaudy, Roger. *From Anathema to Dialogue*. New York: Herder and Herder, 1966.

Kautsky, Karl. *Foundations of Christianity: A Study in Christian Origins*. New York: Monthly Review Press, 1972.

———. *The Materialist Conception of History*. New Haven, CT: Yale University Press, 1988.

Kolakowski, Leszek. *Main Currents of Marxism*. 3 vols. Oxford: Clarendon, 1978.

Marx, Karl, and Frederick Engels. *Karl Marx and Frederick Engels, Collected Works*. Vol. 25. New York: International, 1987.

McLellan, David. *Marxism and Religion*. New York: Harper & Row, 1987.

DAVID RAMSAY STEELE

MARX, KARL HEINRICH (1818–1883), German revolutionary thinker. Karl Marx was born in Trier, in the

Rhineland, recently part of Napoleon's empire. He studied law, philosophy, and history, and was awarded a doctoral degree in 1841. Marx became known as an outspoken atheist, which made an academic career inaccessible. He moved to Paris, where he met Friedrich Engels, heir to a Lancashire textiles firm, who became his literary collaborator and patron. Expelled from France for political reasons, Marx moved to Brussels, where he and Engels wrote and published anonymously the widely read *Manifesto of the Communist Party* (1848). From 1849 until his death, Marx lived in London. He got some income from his writing, but depended on gifts from Engels. Aiming to write a definitive four-volume critique of economic theory, Marx read everything he could find on this subject, becoming the most knowledgeable person in the history of economic thought up to that time. Only the first volume of this monumental work, *Capital*, appeared in his lifetime.

The intellectual climate of Marx's youth was heavily influenced by G. W. F. Hegel, by consciousness of German political and economic backwardness, by the presumption that the most advanced political ideas came from France, and by a dominant Christian orthodoxy under intellectual challenge from higher biblical criticism. In 1842 there appeared *The Socialism and Communism of Present-Day France* by Lorenz von Stein, which identified socialism and Communism as middle-class and working-class doctrines, respectively. Marx became a Communist and a self-appointed spokesman for the proletariat, the new, expanding class of industrial wage-workers.

Ludwig FEUERBACH's *The Essence of Christianity* (1841) had a profound and permanent impact on Marx's thinking. The atheist Feuerbach tried to show that theology could be dissolved into anthropology: statements about God are mystified statements about human beings. Marx did not think it worthwhile to write further refutations of religious belief. Instead, he took Feuerbach one step further: since human talk about God is really mystified talk about the human community, religion is a symptom of inadequacy in the human condition and can therefore ultimately only be exorcized by changing the actual human condition through Communist revolution, so that human potential comes to be realized. Marx also came to see social institutions other than the nominally religious, such as the authority of the state and the power of capital, as being essentially akin to religion in that they represent a kind of mystification, in which the activities of humans are perceived by those humans as oppressive external powers. For example, "capital" is the accumulated labor of the workers, yet the workers see capital as an enemy and feel compelled to struggle against its demands upon their time and energies.

In his graveside eulogy for Marx, Engels cited the materialist conception of history and the theory of surplus value as his two greatest achievements. Marx's historical materialism is independent of philosophical materialism: The theory that human thoughts are physical processes in the brain is logically compatible with the theory that human development is mainly governed by ideas, while the theory that the driving force of social evolution is economic is logically compatible with the existence of supernatural entities (see MATERIALISM, PHILOSOPHICAL).

Historical materialism was not elaborated in detail, and its precise specification remains controversial. Marx sees the "social relations of production," such as the relation of master and slave or capitalist and wage worker, as the base on which rests a superstructure of ideas, including religion and law. This slippery metaphor has never been satisfactorily unpacked: if the claim is that autonomous developments in the superstructure can never modify the base, then it is obviously false, while if it means that "the economy is important" in social evolution, then it is far from distinctive to Marx.

Surplus value is the theme of Marx's economic theories. Marx developed a new, strict form of the labor theory of value in which value, defined as abstract, socially necessary labor time, is sharply distinguished from empirically observable prices, the former being considered essential to an adequate explanation of the latter. Marx's economic theories were a blind alley, rendered irrelevant by the 1870s marginalist revolution, which Marx failed to address. In the last years of his life, Marx did virtually no work on *Capital*, apparently because he had reached an impasse in his analysis.

Marx's contention that workers are necessarily exploited by capital requires the assumption that accumulated means of production do not add to the value of output, an assumption requiring an arbitrary defintion of *value*.

Marx predicted that industrial concentration, tending to eliminate competition, would lead to the disappearance of all small firms. He expected the class struggle to grow more intense, and to precipitate a Communist revolution in the industrially most advanced countries. The new Communist society, without markets or money or any coercive state apparatus, would plan the whole of industry as a single enterprise, and this would be more efficient than capitalism. Marx's view that a nonmarket organization of industry could surpass or even match the output of a market organization was criticized by Ludwig von Mises, F. A. Hayek, Michael Polanyi, and others.

BIBLIOGRAPHY

Hunt, Richard N. *The Political Ideas of Marx and Engels*. 2 vols. Pittsburgh: University of Pittsburgh Press, 1974, 1984.

Marx, Karl, and Friedrich Engels. *Marx and Engels: Collected Works*. 50 vols. New York: International Publishers, 1975–2004.

McLellan, David. *Karl Marx: His Life and Thought*. New York: Harper & Row, 1973.

————. *The Young Hegelians and Karl Marx.* New York: Praeger, 1969.

Rubel, Maximilen, and Margaret Manale. *Marx without Myth: A Chronology of His Life and Work.* New York: Harper & Row, 1976.

Sweezy, Paul M., ed. *Karl Marx and the Close of His System by Eugen von Böhm-Bawerk, and Böhm-Bawerk's Criticism of Marx by Rudolf Hilferding.* Clifton: Kelley, 1973.

————. *The Theory of Capitalist Development.* New York: Monthly Review Press, 1968.

DAVID RAMSAY STEELE

MASTERS, EDGAR LEE

MASTERS, EDGAR LEE (1868–1950), American poet and critic. Edgar Lee Masters received religious instruction in the Methodist and Episcopalian churches in his boyhood hometown of Petersburg, Illinois, and occasionally attended the Cumberland Presbyterian Church with his paternal grandparents. Both of Masters's parents had been raised as Methodists, but they enjoyed little happiness in their marriage, and Masters regarded their Methodism as a divisive force.

Early Education. The family's move to Lewistown, Illinois, in 1880 provided Masters with a better public school education that was augmented by after-school readings in various authors. His disenchantment with Lewistown's Presbyterian Church and his discovery of Robert Green INGERSOLL's *Some Mistakes of Moses* helped turn Masters into an atheist (see ATHEISM). One year in the preparatory unit of nearby Knox College brought Masters two college nicknames, "Old Soph," for Sophocles, and "the Atheist." Unable to afford a second year at Knox, Masters studied for the law and read on his own such independent thinkers as Johann Wolfgang von GOETHE, Percy Bysshe SHELLEY, Ralph Waldo EMERSON, and Walt WHITMAN, as well as evolutionists Thomas Henry HUXLEY and Herbert SPENCER.

Spoon River Anthology. By the time Masters published *Spoon River Anthology,* the book for which he is chiefly remembered, in 1915, he had both the reading and life experiences to universalize his creations. Masters's 214 free-verse epitaphs telling of the lives and deaths of villagers in a small midwestern town became a literary sensation and gave widespread circulation to his unhappiness with religion. He attacked both Christianity and churchgoers through his epitaphs, the owners of which casually violate most of the Ten Commandments. Ministers and church officers come in for special contempt: Deacon Taylor is an alcoholic; Deacon Rhodes and Sunday School Superintendent Henry Phipps are greedy hypocrites; Reverend Sibley is untruthful; Reverend Lemuel Wiley is gullible; Reverend Peet is vain; community moralist A. D. Blood is ineffective—and the list could be extended.

The epitaph reflecting Masters's own view of religion belongs to "The Village Atheist." He explains that he spent much time debating the immortality of the soul, but with his final illness upon him, he contemplates his reading and paraphrases Baruch SPINOZA in his final words: "Immortality is not a gift," he says, but "an achievement;/And only those who strive mightily/Shall possess it."

Near the end of his life, Masters said that he had long considered Spinoza's writings and had decided that God and mind are the same thing: "As to God, after thinking it over all my life, I have come to the conclusion that there is a mind as large as the universe that is in everything"; "all we see in the heavens and in the earth is Mind."

Like his friend H. L. MENCKEN, Masters enjoyed belittling the stodginess of the Bible Belt, the religiosity of the middle class, and conservative values generally. Such behavior helped make Masters famous, first through the poems in *Spoon River Anthology,* and then infamous—for he exemplified in his personal life the iconoclastic values he articulated in his books. In the end, however, Masters equated God with nature, not exactly rejecting God so much as embracing Spinoza's idea of an afterlife involving some form of intellectual knowing. "I have been called an atheist," he said, "but my atheism is that of Spinoza . . . , and he was an all-God man, not an atheist."

BIBLIOGRAPHY

Masters, Edgar Lee. *Spoon River Anthology.* New York: Macmillan, 1915.

————. *Spoon River Anthology: An Annotated Edition.* Edited with introduction by John E. Hallwas. Urbana: University of Illinois Press, 1992.

Primeau, Ronald. *Beyond Spoon River: The Legacy of Edgar Lee Masters.* Austin: University of Texas Press, 1981.

Russell, Herbert K. *Edgar Lee Masters: A Biography.* Urbana: University of Illinois Press, 2001.

HERBERT K. RUSSELL

MATERIALISM, PHILOSOPHICAL

MATERIALISM, PHILOSOPHICAL. Philosophical materialism is a critical philosophical position that considers matter as the beginning, origin, and cause of whatever exists. The term was first used by Robert Boyle in *The Excellence and Grounds of the Mechanical Philosophy* (1674), and adopted by the eighteenth-century Enlightenment philosophes (M. J. A. de Caritat de CONDORCET, Condillac, Denis DIDEROT, Claude Adrien HELVÉTIUS, VOLTAIRE, and others) to designate their naturalistic positions in physics and physiology, their radical critiques against religion, their hedonistic moral codes, and their opposition to the educational and moral conventions of the *Ancien Regime* (see ENLIGHTENMENT, UNBELIEF DURING THE). Classical philosophical materialism suffered from Immanuel KANT's criticism and the effects of idealism during the nineteenth century. The so-called materialism dispute (*Materialismusstreit*) in Germany led to the consolidation of different varieties of materialism: physicalist, moral, historical, dialectical, and so on (see CONTROVERSIES: ATHEISM, PANTHEISM, SPINOZA). Materialism's theoretical varieties have multiplied throughout the twentieth and twenty-first centuries as our scientific knowledge of matter and the universe has become more refined.

The original understanding of matter was associated since classical times with the *cosmological atomism* of Democritus, EPICURUS, LUCRETIUS, and others, which held that atoms were the smallest units of matter and could not be divided. This was a purely theoretical concept which could not be tested until the scientific revolution of the sixteenth century. Since atoms have proven to be divisible and no longer appear as the ultimate components of reality, later materialism takes a more *methodological* aspect, and all its varieties, including the Positivist or Marxist views (see POSITIVISM; MARXISM), stress the ontological primacy of matter over spirit and the priority of experimental and theoretical scientific knowledge over other types of knowledge: religious, mystical, or extrasensory.

Ontic Varieties of Materialism. The different conceptions of "matter" gave rise to a great variety of materialist systems. *Materialism* means different things depending on the context. We distinguish three principal contexts, which relate the idea of matter to *the world*, with the *idea of God*, or with *knowledge*.

In the most immediate context, the ontic one, which considers the relationships of the general idea of matter with the different realities that filled the "world" just as they appeared to us, we underlined four major types of materialism.

Cosmological materialism considers matter to be the basis of the universe and postulates it as the substratum or foundation of all reality. Its "mechanist" variant adds to matter the distribution of parts in the universe (substances, atoms, masses, and the like) and the existence of forces capable of moving and combining them, without appealing to final causes or spiritual powers. This relates to the ancient materialism of Democritus and Epicurus, nineteenth-century classical materialism, and nineteenth-century Positivism. The energistic tradition in physics, nevertheless, led G. Ostwald to proclaim in 1895 that the concept of matter was futile and that scientific materialism had been superseded. When the equivalence between mass and energy was recognized by Einstein in the twentieth century, the cosmological idea of matter, associated through the idea of a "force field" or cosmological constant, seemed to revive. But in 1932 the astronomer Jan Oort detected a type of matter that exerts gravitational force but does not emit or absorb light. Before 1980 people thought that this "dark matter" was ordinary matter in some undetectable form such as gas, low-mass stars, and star corpses like white dwarfs or black holes. Then astrophysical calculations established first that dark matter comprises 90 percent of the mass of the universe, and second that it is made up of neutrinos or some more exotic form of particle still undiscovered by high-energy laboratories. Today's cosmological view of dark matter spread throughout the universe corresponds in some ways to the ancient cosmological materialism.

Anthropological materialism centers on explaining human nature by its physical and physiological components. By distinguishing categorically the *res cogitans* (or soul) from the *res extensa* (or body), René DESCARTES contributed to the spreading of anthropological materialism in the modern age. The thesis of the materiality of the soul unified the clandestine writings of the Libertines and served as a spearhead for the Enlightenment challenge to Christian tradition. Medical and physiological discoveries demonstrating the dependence of supposedly spiritual functions upon anatomic and organic conditions allowed Julien de LA METTRIE to devise a natural history of the soul and to formulate his famous thesis "man a machine" (1748). Along similar lines David Hartley defended the indivisibility of thought and sensation (1749). Following them, Baron d'HOLBACH stressed the natural character of human capacities: "A man of genius produces a good work, in the same manner as a tree of a good species, placed in a prolific soil, cultivated with care, grafted with judgment, produces excellent fruit" (1770). In addition Holbach offered a critique of religion and proposed an ethics of pleasure and a policy of solidarity through common interest. Along the same lines Claude A. Helvétius developed an ethical program based on self-esteem and perceived usefulness, relying on education to reconcile state and private interests. In this ideological context the French Revolution took place, which for Kant's "enlightened" generation meant the definitive progress for humankind (see FRANCE, UNBELIEF IN). After the conservative reaction that followed, a reductionist and physiological materialism took form in Germany with Carl Vogt, who famously observed that "thought is to the brain the same as bile is to the liver" (1854). This materialism consolidated in the wake of Charles DARWIN's theory of evolution (1859) (see EVOLUTION AND UNBELIEF) and matured in the works of Thomas Henry HUXLEY (1863) and Ernst HAECKEL. The latter added to scientific materialism a practical moral component, setting as life's aim human corporeal welfare, pleasure, and health: "moral and ethical materialism, in the proper sense of the word, is a practical direction of life which has no other purpose than the most refined sensitive pleasure" (1868). This version of materialism was branded "vulgar" and "dogmatic" by critics, but it played an important role in the refutation of popular beliefs in spirits and abstract or transcendent realities. Albert Lange (1866) criticized it for its false aim of expanding human knowledge beyond its limits; by giving objective value to its imaginative constructs,

Lange argued that this anthropological materialism has turned into a "metaphysics." Against this criticism Paul Kurtz has reformulated, in his *Eupraxsophy* (1988), an anthropological materialism more resistant to "the transcendental temptation" (1986), reconciling HUMANISM with twentieth-century scientific progress (1991).

Historical materialism is the name Friedrich Engels applied to the historical and economic view of human social development expressed in Karl MARX's 1859 preface to *The Critique of Political Economy*. It is a perspective concerned not only with understanding the world but also with changing it. Marx's analysis distinguishes between the economic *basis* of society (the "means of production" and "relations of production") and the *superstructure* (law, science, religion, art, philosophy, and other disciplines), which he saw as being determined in the final analysis by economic factors. But antagonistic relationships obtain between the *forces* and the *relations* of production within each "mode of production" (slavery, feudalism, capitalism, and so on), which eventually cause each mode of production to break down. Marx argued in *Capital* (1867) that knowledge of the natural sciences becomes the central productive force in an industrial society. Marx expected that this contradiction, linked with the fact that man is treated as a commodity, would lead to the final crisis of capitalism.

Marx and Engels imbued the concept of matter with a *real complexity* and an *objective plurality*, separating it from subjectivism, while at the same time they underlined its dynamic and evolutionary nature. In this sense, for historical materialism, conscience is not the determining principle of human history but a result of that history which merits no special privilege. This "turning upside down" (*ümstulpen*) of Hegel's history of philosophy definitely separates philosophical materialism from idealism. Nevertheless, within the Marxist orthodoxy historical materialism was an application of dialectical materialism, polemically defined by Engels (1878) as a general science of the dialectical laws of movement (the law of the transformation of quantity into quality, the law of the interpenetration of opposites, and the law of the negation of the negation). Marxist materialism scientifically studied the origins and functioning of different historical societies in their own context. Works such as *The Class Struggle in France* (1850) and *The Eighteenth Brumaire of Louis Bonaparte* (1851) illustrate the distance between contextual and historical scientific practice and the economic determinism or the vulgar historicism usually attributed to Marx. Historical materialism was one of the most intensely debated aspects of Marxist thought during the twentieth century, not only on the part of Marxist authors who favored the materialistic view—including Lukás, Korsch, Arturo Labriola, Antonio Gramsci, the early Sidney Hook (1936), and Louis Althusser—but also among nonmaterialist sociologists, anthropologists, and historians including Max Weber, Mannheim, Merton, Gouldner, and others. A North American version, which closely follows historical materialism but adds ecological elements, is the *cultural materialism* defended by Leslie A. White (1959) and Marvin Harris (1982).

Under the heading of *formalist materialism*, I embrace the heterodox position of those who have explained the abstract entities of "ideal" or "essential" nature from matter alone without reducing them to the subjective. In the philosophy of ARISTOTLE, matter was already viewed as an intrinsic *active cause*. It also exerted *operative power*, so that "things which have in themselves the principle of their genesis, would exist by themselves when anything external would prevent it." This view regarding matter's self-sufficiency to develop leads to a heterodox tradition. The expression "intelligible matter" was coined by Plotinus, and was developed through Scotus Eriugena's "divisions of Nature" and Avicebron's "fountain of life," culminating in Nicholas of Cusa, for whom matter is the "undetermined possibility" in which the earth, the sun, and the rest of the universe are *contracted*. Against the concept of passive and inert matter, Giordano BRUNO, that follower of Copernicus and Galileo GALILEI, identifies matter with form. This tradition tends to meander beyond the ontic context, verging into matters of ontology and the theory of science. Manifesting this form of materialism in the twentieth century is the Russian Formalism of Bakhtin and Voloshinov (1929).

Materialism and Atheism. It was traditionally considered that "materialism" entailed the negation of God or ATHEISM, as under Soviet Communism (see PROPAGANDA, ANTIELIGIOUS [SOVIET]). However, there are two ways of getting around the incompatibility between theism and materialism. The former entails conceiving of the gods as corporeal entities, after the practice of Epicurus and Thomas HOBBES, who did not deny God's existence but were *practical atheists*. Another, more subtle, method involves adding a rational divine principle which operates causally in the world, either *dissolved inside* (stoic pantheism), or *from outside* by creating atoms (as in Tertulianus or Pierre Gassendi), or arranging it (enlightened deism), or transmitting to it force and movement in the style of Ralph Cudworth and the Cambridge Platonists, for whom matter was of a *plastic nature*, a living force which directly derives from God (1678). Newton and his disciples took advantage of scientific progress to support their religious beliefs on this basis.

Their atheist rivals, rationalists as well, did the same. Baruch SPINOZA (1677) accepted the equivalence between God, Substance, and Nature at the level of *general ontology* to turn atheism into an impregnable position. Identifying God with *everything which exists* denies meaning to the traditional distinctions between *matter* and *spirit* as different realities. For Spinoza there is only one substance, which is however not one, but multiple or even *infinite*, composed of an infinity of attributes of which we know but two: *thinking* and *exten-*

sion. Spinoza refutes the ghost-in-the-machine myth (Descartes) and also Gottfried Wilhelm von LEIBNIZ's monistic psychophysical parallelism, because neither body nor soul are independent substances. On the contrary, "the order and connection of ideas is the same as the order and connection of things." Thus, "I am my body" and "by body I mean a mode which expresses in a certain determinate manner the essence of God, in so far as he is considered as an extended thing." Atheism was never so subtle and daring; Spinoza's *Ethics* should be a Bible for every unbeliever.

In this line Gustavo Bueno formulates an ontological materialism (1972) which also distinguishes between a general level (*Natura naturans*) and another special level (*Natura naturata*). Materialism is the exercise of philosophical reason in decoding the *symploké* or puzzle of ideas that defines our present experience. Philosophical reason is different from the scientific, political, and technological modes of reasoning because it is applied to ideas. Yet it is not idealistic, because ideas are functions whose values are determined in each historical moment according to the objects in which they become incarnated. This general-ontological materialism is opposed to the metaphysical idea of "universe" as *omnitudo realitatis* ("everything real is rational"—Hegel) that culminates in monism or in harmonic holism; but it does not accept a limitless multiplicity. In the regression from what is a given process (the objects themselves), the idea of radical plurality or general-ontological matter is reached as a limit. Nevertheless, materialism is an alternative to NIHILISM, which dissolves reality; so it doesn't get stranded with an abstract and indeterminate "matter," but progresses from it toward worldly realities. In this progression worldly beings are organized in three special-ontological genres of materiality (M_1, or the group of physical objects, or extensive bodies; M_2, or the collection of subjective realities—headaches, experiences, etc.; and M_3, or the set of "essences"—numbers, theories, etc.—which are not exactly subjective nor physical but rather are materially objective). The reduction of any genre of materiality into another is criticized, because the three are "incommensurate."

This ontological materialism supports a militant atheism against the new wave of fundamentalisms. For this neither the Enlightenment theory about religion beginning with priestly deception nor the Marxist idea about religion as "the opium of the people" is enough. According to Bueno (1985), throughout their evolution human beings were accompanied by religion not because they had a divine gene or some sacred faculty inside, but because they had arisen in contact with the large predatory animals of the Pleistocene Age, which humans could hunt but to which they could also become prey. Gods are not anthropomorphic projections of consciousness (as in Ludwig FEUERBACH), but material *Numens* shaped by humans in the image of wild beasts. Ethology, the study of animal behavior, is the new theology. It is essential to atheistic materialism to claim that many cultural facts, usually relegated to the domains of spiritualism and idealism (zodiacal signs, sacrifices), are in fact materialistic events.

Finally, scientific materialism involves denying that matter remains constrained within the conscious or epistemological sphere of the world. Its opposite is "immaterialism," the assertion that the domain of ideas and knowledge subsists independently of matter. Scientific materialism furnished a third context whose action we can recognize when we review the process by which methodological materialism has built up from Hobbes to Rudolf Carnap. For Hobbes, to know something is to understand its *genesis*. That is why the sole possible objects of human knowledge are bodies and their movements, and philosophy is divided in two: *natural* philosophy studies organic bodies, and *civil* philosophy studies the social body (*De Corpore*, 1655). Diametrically opposed to this naturalism is Ernst Mach's *Empiriocriticsm* or phenomenalism. For Mach (1900), scientific knowledge entails the study of phenomenal relationships, so that matter is reduced to "a certain relation of the sensitive elements in accordance with a law." Vladimir Ilyich Lenin (1909) criticized this "immaterialist" position, but his materialistic theory of science could not counteract the enormous success enjoyed by "objective idealistic" theories of science expressed by PLATO and more recent neo-Kantians such as Windelband, Cohen, and Cassirer.

The twentieth century also saw the failure of the "materialist" efforts of LOGICAL POSITIVISM due to its extreme linguistic reductionism. Carnap's "physicalism" got bogged down in the "statements of protocol" which supposedly describe the data transmitted by senses. The "unified science" thesis (Otto Neurath) could not halt Carl Gustav Hempel's theoreticism and the "idealist" bloom of the "new post-Popperian philosophy of science" as represented by Thomas Kuhn, Paul Feyerabend, Imre Lakatos, and others.

The so-called categorical closure theory (1976/1994) of Bueno, which studies the connection between the level of facts and theories as the essence of the process by which scientific truths are constructed—these are not analytic but "synthetic identities"—provides a materialistic theory of science. In this sort of materialism, the sciences have no formal object, but rather are fields of heterogeneous objects; for example, biology does not deal with life, but with tissues, organs, cells, nucleic acids, and so on. The multiple material objects of a scientific field do not exist apart from the productive activities that scientists carry out when they form investigative teams or found scientific research institutions.

BIBLIOGRAPHY

Berkeley, G. *A Treatise concerning Principles of Human Knowledge*. London: Fontana, 1736.

Bueno, Gustavo. *El animal divino*. Oviedo: Pentalfa, 1985.
———. *Ensayos materialistas*. Madrid: Taurus, 1972.
———. *Teoría del cierre categorial*. 5 vols. Oviedo: Pentalfa, 1992–94.
Cornforth, M. *Dialectical Materialism*. 3 vols. London: Lawrence & Wishart, 1952–54.
Churchland, Paul. *Matter and Consciousness*. Cambridge, MA: MIT Press, 1984.
Darwin, Charles. *The Origin of Species or the Preservation of Favoured Races*. London: Murray, 1859.
d'Holbach, Paul Heinrich Dietrich. *The System of Nature*. Translated by Wilkinson. London, 1820.
Einstein, Albert, and Leopold-Infeld. *The Evolution of Physics: The Growth of Ideas from Early Concepts to Relativity and Quanta*. New York: Simon & Schuster, 1938.
Engels, F. *Anti-Dühring*, 1878; *Dialektik der Natur*, 1872–86 (ed. Berstein in Berlin, 1924).
Haeckel, E. *Natürliche Schöpfungsgeschichte*, 1868; *Die Welträtsel*, 1899; Stuttgart: Neve Zeit, 1899.
Harris, M. *Cultural Materialism*. Madrid: Alianza, 1982.
Hook, Sidney. *From Hegel to Marx: Studies in the Intellectual Development of Karl Marx*. Ann Arbor: University of Michigan Press, 1962.
Huxley, Thomas H. *Man's Place in Nature*. London: Williams and Norgate, 1863.
Kurtz, Paul. *Living without Religion: Eupraxophy*. Amherst, NY: Prometheus Books, 1988.
———. *Philosophical Essays in Pragmatic Naturalism*. Amherst, NY: Prometheus Books, 1991.
———. *The Transcendental Temptation: A Critique of Religion and the Paranormal*. Amherst, NY: Prometheus Books, 1986.
La Mettrie, O. de. *L' Homme machine*. Leyden: Elie Lizac, 1748.
Lange, Albert. *Geschichte des Materialismus*. Berlin: J. Baedeker, 1866.
Lenin, Vladimir I. *Materializm i empiriokriticizm*. Moscow, 1908.
Ostwald, G. *Die überwindung des wissenschaftlichen Materialismus*. Berlin, 1895.
Peña, Vidal. *El materialismo de Spinoza*. Madrid: Revista de Occidente, 1974.
Spinoza, B. *Ethica more geometrico demonstrata*. Amsterdam, 1677.
Stalin, Josef. *Materialismo dialéctico y materialismo histórico*. Moscow: Progreso, 1938.
White, Leslie A. *The Evolution of Culture: The Development of Civilization to the Fall of Rome*. New York: McGraw-Hill, 1959.

ALBERTO HIDALGO DE TUÑON

McCABE, JOSEPH MARTIN (1867–1955), English atheist scholar. One of the most remarkable—and neglected—polymaths of the twentieth century, Joseph McCabe was a difficult personality with few friends among his contemporaries. He was a gifted popularizer long before that was recognized as an honorable vocation. What is more, McCabe was ready to identify himself as an atheist (see ATHEISM), materialist (see MATERIALISM, PHILOSOPHICAL), and feminist (see WOMEN AND UNBELIEF; WOMAN SUFFRAGE MOVEMENT AND UNBELIEF) long before these terms were academically respectable.

Joseph Martin McCabe was born on November 11, 1867, into an English family of modest means. As the second-born, Joseph was earmarked for the church, which he duly entered at sixteen to study for the priesthood, despite an occasion of sexual abuse that even someone as emancipated as McCabe did not feel able to disclose until he was seventy-four years of age. From early on in his church career, McCabe suffered doubts, which were not alleviated by the official response to them, which was known as the blush technique: "How dare I, an ignorant boy, doubt what such legions of great men believed!"

Father Antony, as he became, rallied repeatedly, expelled his doubts, and rose through the ranks. He did so well in his studies that he was appointed professor of philosophy and ecclesiastical history at a seminary in London in 1890, at the age of only twenty-three. But from 1893 onward, Father Antony's doubts became, in his words, dark and permanent, and he spiraled into a crisis of faith at the end of 1895. On Ash Wednesday 1896, he left the church to begin a new life in the wide world. McCabe was twenty-eight when he emerged into the world, completely untutored in its ways. His first purchase was a book on etiquette.

McCabe soon found a new life in London, becoming associated with the fledgling RATIONALIST PRESS ASSOCIATION (RPA). As he had done in the Catholic Church, McCabe rose quickly through the ranks of the RPA. By 1914 a Christian opponent described him as the RPA's "leading spirit." For more than half a century McCabe made his living from his pen, writing an extraordinary range of books, monographs, pamphlets, magazine and newspaper articles, and encyclopedia entries—and indeed, entire encyclopedias.

As well as his written output, McCabe gave more than four thousand lectures around the world, from Melbourne to the Rhineland, and from the Harvard Club in the United States to coal mines in New Zealand. McCabe also took part in at least a dozen major debates with religionists, creationists (see CREATIONISM), and Spiritualists (see SPIRITUALISM AND UNBELIEF). The most notable of them was with the eminent Spiritualist Sir Arthur Conan Doyle in 1920. The research McCabe undertook for that debate alone generated two books.

But as with his experience in the Roman Catholic Church, McCabe's time in organized FREETHOUGHT was not without conflict. McCabe never came to terms with the fact that people leave religion in many different ways. He had taken the passionate route of the betrayed believer, one whose belief had stolen twelve years from his life and exacted a great toll in suffering and isolation. McCabe always found it difficult to accept that others, whose path to freethought had been less fraught with suffering, were equally sincere.

Over the course of a quarter of a century, McCabe managed to offend just about everyone in rationalist circles (see RATIONALISM). McCabe broke with the RPA in 1928, although a partial rapprochement was effected in 1934. Most of his later works were published by the eclectic American publisher Emmanuel HALDEMAN-JULIUS. McCabe died on January 10, 1955, aged eighty-seven. He expressed the wish (which went unfulfilled) to have as his epitaph, "He was a rebel to his last breath."

McCabe was deeply interested in popularizing evolution (see EVOLUTION AND UNBELIEF; DARWINISM AND UNBELIEF; RELIGION IN CONFLICT WITH SCIENCE) for nonspecialist readers. The outstanding feature of his understanding of evolution is its breadth and accuracy. He had an admirable ability to distinguish a genuine intellectual development from a passing fad. And on most occasions when he departed from the conventional wisdom of the time, it was to assert a strictly Darwinian reading of the issue at hand. In these instances, of course, events have largely proved him correct.

More often than not it was the very same academics who scorned McCabe as a popularizer who succumbed to the fads he was able to see through. For example, McCabe was intelligently skeptical of social Darwinism, which he denounced in 1914 as a "pseudo-scientific application of evolutionary views to social problems," insisting that there is no scientific justification for a doctrine of eternal struggle. He was also scornful of the fad among some evolutionists between the wars known as "emergent evolution," which sought to emphasize a vitalist creativity in each new evolutionary development. McCabe dismissed emergence as nothing more than "mystic machinery." He noted that it was this variety of evolutionary thinking that the Church of England had in mind when it decried the conflict between religion and science. And he dismissed EUGENICS as "secular Calvinism."

Neither was McCabe guilty of scientism, or placing faith in science as an agency of salvation. Rather than giving "laws of nature" a cosmic inevitability, McCabe wrote of them straightforwardly as trustworthy "only insofar as [the scientist] knows it to have been based on extensive observations. He keeps an open mind until repeated observations all the world over have brought the same result." McCabe made the simple observation that we "do not want to substitute the word science for the word God."

With respect to the Catholic Church, McCabe wrote both as an original scholar and as a popularizer. Fluent in Latin, Greek, French, German, Spanish, and Italian, McCabe was able to use original documents not available to others in the course of his work. *Crises in the History of the Papacy* (1916) remains a sound work of historical writing and was many decades ahead of what Catholic writers were able to say about their church. McCabe also wrote some autobiographical studies of living in the church, in particular *Twelve Years in a Monastery* (1897). In this moving work, McCabe writes movingly of fellow priests driven mad by sexual frustration, ruined by drink, or sunk into triviality as the only means of surviving the unnatural regime under which they lived. His autobiographical works avoided the tabloid sensationalism that so many others writing this sort of work indulged in.

Only later in his life did some of McCabe's writing on the Catholic Church become polemical. He never got used to the level of abuse he received from lesser apologists; the misdeeds of Pius XII's pontificate further contributed to this trend. Even in this work he rarely lapsed into anti-Catholic ranting, as so many of his contemporaries were wont to do. The best of his later works on the Catholic Church is *A History of the Popes* (1939).

Perhaps most remarkable was McCabe's record as a feminist. His three main publications in this area, *The Religion of Woman* (1905), *Woman in Political Evolution* (1909), and *Key to Love and Sex* (1928), remain the most unjustly neglected examples of rationalist feminism in the twentieth century. Once again McCabe avoided the errors of many of his contemporaries of indulging in the stereotyping of women as wives and mothers, the bearers of the next generation, while appearing to be ardent feminists. McCabe frequently criticized males who advocated female liberation merely so that they could have a freer access to problem-free sex. He patiently refuted all the prejudices of the day about women being more emotional, more religious, and less capable of sustained action than men. He even devoted time to defending blondes from the usual accusations.

McCabe wrote widely in other areas, including some well-received biographies of Saint Augustine, Pierre Abelard, Johann Wolfgang von GOETHE, Charles-Maurice de Talleyrand, and Cardinal Richelieu. He also wrote an underappreciated critique of George Bernard SHAW and a history of divorce laws. He even wrote two novels, *In the Shadow of the Cloister* (1908, under the pseudonym Arnold Wright) and *The Pope's Favorite* (1917).

Even where he was wrong, McCabe set a good example. For instance, he defended the notion of the ether far longer than was seemly, which also made it difficult for him to accept Albert Einstein's theory of relativity. But when, by the mid-1920s, he did finally accept that he had been wrong, he launched into explaining the theory of relativity to his readers. In other words, when the evidence became overwhelming, he was prepared to change his opinion and adopt new views.

Joseph McCabe was a gifted and responsible popularizer of contemporary thinking to nonspecialist readers. Despite being largely self-taught, he avoided all the fashionable errors of his day and gave his readers sensible, balanced, and reliable overviews on a staggering variety of subjects. His books, whether on evolution, the Catholic Church, feminism, or a host of other subjects, anticipated current ideas by two generations. McCabe deserves to be linked with Isaac ASIMOV and Carl SAGAN as among the most intelligent, acute, and lucid popularizers of the twentieth century.

BIBLIOGRAPHY

Cooke, Bill. *A Rebel to His Last Breath: Joseph McCabe and Rationalism*. Amherst, NY: Prometheus Books, 2001.

Goldberg, Isaac. *Joseph McCabe: Fighter for Freethought*. Girard, KS: Haldeman-Julius, 1936.

McCabe, Joseph. *Eighty Years a Rebel*. Girard, KS: Haldeman-Julius, 1947.

———. *A Rationalist Encyclopedia*. London: Watts and Company, 1948.

BILL COOKE

McCOLLUM, VASHTI CROMWELL (1912–2006), American church-state litigant. Vashti Ruth Cromwell, named for the queen in the first book of Esther, who was one of few biblical women to stand up for women's rights, was born in Lyons, New York, to the freethinkers Arthur G. and Ruth C. Cromwell. She was raised in Rochester, New York, and after graduation from a public high school attended Cornell University on scholarship until the stock market crash of 1929. After transferring to the University of Illinois Champaign-Urbana, she met and married Dr. John P. McCollum, had three sons, and earned two degrees.

Vashti McCollum was to live up to her namesake when she was pressured to enroll her eldest son, Jim, in a Christian religious education class that was offered during school hours in the Champaign public schools. Resisting the pressure at first, she and her husband eventually relented and allowed Jim to attend the classes for the balance of his fourth-grade year. However, the following year, the McCollums, feeling that such a program was inappropriate in the public schools, refused further participation.

After unsuccessful attempts to get the program discontinued, McCollum filed suit in the Champaign County Circuit Court in the late summer of 1945. This became a challenging period for the McCollums, marked by physical confrontations between Jim and his peers, vandalism of the McCollum home, and unsuccessful efforts to end Dr. McCollum's employment at the university. He was protected by tenure, but her employment as an adjunct instructor in the women's physical education program was not, and she was terminated.

A three-judge circuit court panel decided that, in spite of the Illinois constitution's clear language to the contrary, Champaign's religious education program vio-

lated neither the state constitution nor the establishment clause of the First Amendment to the US Constitution. The Illinois Supreme Court agreed, and the case was appealed to the US Supreme Court, which granted certiorari in the fall of 1947. On March 9, 1948, the Supreme Court handed down its landmark decision in *McCollum v. Board of Education* (333 U.S. 203 [1948]), finding for McCollum and against the schools in an 8–1 verdict.

Written by Justice Hugo L. Black, the *McCollum* decision was a landmark case in US constitutional law. Its significance was that it was the first decision to hold the several states accountable to the strictures of the establishment clause under the due process clause of the Fourteenth Amendment, which makes provisions of the US Constitution binding upon the states. All subsequent church-state decisions involving school prayer, aid to parochial schools, sectarian religious displays on public property, and other such incursions into Thomas Jefferson's "wall of separation between Church & State" by states and municipalities descend from the *McCollum* case.

For several years after the conclusion of her landmark legal battle, McCollum became active in the humanist movement, serving on the board of the American Humanist Association and as its president. Among the awards and recognition accorded her in subsequent years were the prestigious Johns Haynes Holmes Award (now the Holmes-Weatherly Award) from the Unitarian Fellowship for Social Justice. She also has received recognition from the Illinois ACLU; the Champaign County chapter of the Illinois ACLU; the Roger Baldwin Foundation; Americans United for the Separation of Church and State; the Rochester, New York, chapter of Americans United; and the American Humanist Association.

Vashti McCollum wrote a book about the circumstances of her case, *One Woman's Fight*, which remains in print. She died in August 2006.

BIBLIOGRAPHY

McCollum, Vashti. *One Woman's Fight*. Garden City, NY: Doubleday, 1951.

JAMES McCOLLUM

McGEE, LEWIS (1893–1979), African American Unitarian leader. Lewis McGee was the first minister of an experimental interracial congregation in Chicago. He was born on November 11, 1893, in Scranton, Pennsylvania. Much like his father, who became an African Methodist Episcopal (AME) minister, Lewis McGee felt he was called to the ordained ministry. The family moved frequently due to his father's status as an itinerant preacher. In 1912 McGee graduated from high school and then attended the University of Pittsburgh for a year before going to Payne Theological School at Wilberforce

University, where he received a Bachelor of Divinity (BD) in 1916. The following year he was ordained as an elder in the AME church.

In 1918 McGee joined the army as a chaplain, and later served as minister for a number of AME churches in Ohio and West Virginia. In 1927 he moved to Chicago where he became a social worker with Illinois Children's and Home Aid Society. While there McGee took college courses and subsequently received a Bachelor of Arts degree from Carthage College. He returned to parish ministry briefly in Gary, Indiana, before leaving to join the US Army once again as a chaplain in 1943. He remained in the military until after World War II was over and was discharged with the rank of captain. That autumn, he married his wife, Marcella.

McGee's interest in Unitarianism (see UNITARIANISM TO 1961) evolved gradually. He later commented that he had encountered Unitarianism many years before attending seminary, when he stumbled across a copy of the *Christian Register* while delivering mail. He later met Curtis Reese, a Unitarian minister, and read Reese's book of humanist sermons in 1928 (see HUMANISM; RELIGIOUS HUMANISM). Reese told him then that the Unitarian church offered no opportunities for African Americans. After the war, McGee felt like the time for integration had arrived, and he decided he wanted to be part of an interracial church. He enrolled at Meadville Lombard Theological School in the spring of 1946, where he studied for a year, after which he received Unitarian fellowship. Meadville Lombard president Wallace Robbins tried to help McGee find a position, but a new opportunity opened in Chicago.

By conducting a survey of African Americans in Chicago's South Side neighborhood on behalf of the American Unitarian Association (AUA), McGee was charged with inquiring about the potential for starting a Unitarian church in the African American community. Ultimately, McGee was able to convince the AUA that there was room as well as interest for an interracial church in Chicago. This racially integrated fellowship was organized on April 25, 1948, and McGee was installed as minister in June of that year. Although this fellowship grew to nearly one hundred members, it never met with the overwhelming success that either he or the AUA had hoped for. After he left the fellowship, he worked for a time at the AMERICAN HUMANIST ASSOCIATION. Meanwhile, he served as senior minister of several predominantly white churches in southern California, the first African American to do so in the United States. He died on October 10, 1979, in Pullman, Washington, leaving his wife and two children, Ruth Harris and Charles McGee.

JUAN FLOYD-THOMAS

McKAY, CLAUDE (1890–1948), American poet and humanist. One of the leading poets of the humanistic arts

movement known as the Harlem Renaissance, Claude McKay was born in Jamaica in 1890 and immigrated to the United States in 1912. He wrote poetry and read FREETHOUGHT literature by the age of ten.

His parents were deeply religious. However, McKay was an agnostic throughout most of his life. His older brother, U. Theo, was one of the most important influences in his life. U. Theo taught him about great freethinkers such as Thomas Henry HUXLEY and Charles BRADLAUGH. McKay eventually adopted a secular worldview (see SECULARISM) informed by FREETHOUGHT.

In his early teens, McKay joined London's RATIONALIST PRESS ASSOCIATION and accepted Fabian socialism. Later, he lived with U. Theo and his wife. Feeling alienated, McKay discussed his AGNOSTICISM with other boys his age. He was successful in bringing some of his new friends into the freethought fold by founding a young agnostics group.

Embracing his older brother's worldview, McKay later fought against police brutality and opposed cruelty to animals. He was deeply influenced by Fabian feminists and the literature of British Victorian women writers, especially George ELIOT. He was very sympathetic toward prostitutes and their plight.

After racial violence erupted across the United States in 1919, McKay wrote perhaps his most famous poem, "If We Must Die." The poem called for blacks to defend themselves against violent attacks by white supremacists. Winston Churchill would later quote from the poem to rally the British against the Nazis during World War II.

In 1929 McKay wrote a novel titled *Banjo: A Story without a Plot*. This story about an African musician in Paris deeply influenced leaders of the Negritude movement, including the Academy of Humanism laureate Léopold Senghor.

On October 11, 1944, suffering from hypertension, heart disease, and worsening health, and disillusioned with his secular worldview, McKay accepted baptism in the Roman Catholic Church. He moved from New York to Chicago to work for the Catholic Youth Organization. However, his contributions as a secular humanist continue to enlighten people throughout the world.

BIBLIOGRAPHY

Allen, Norm. "A Poet for Humanism." Review of *A Fierce Hatred of Injustice*, by Winston James. *Free Inquiry* (Summer 2002).

James, Winston. *A Fierce Hatred of Injustice*. London: Verso, 2000.

NORM R. ALLEN JR.

McQUEEN, BUTTERFLY (1911–1995), American atheist actress. Best known as the memorable character Prissy in *Gone With the Wind*, who spoke the immortal line, "Oh, Miss Scarlet, I don't know nuthin' 'bout birthin' babies," Butterfly McQueen hated her given name, Thelma. The name "Butterfly" came from the way she waved her arms in a 1935 Harlem Theater group production of *A Midsummer Night's Dream*; she later had the name legalized.

McQueen was born an only child in Tampa, Florida. She attended public school in Augusta, Georgia, and graduated high school in Long Island, New York. In 1975, at the age of sixty-four, she earned a bachelor's degree in political science from the City College of New York.

McQueen played a maid in many of her roles, and worked as a maid in real life. From 1947 to 1951 she had a regular role on the controversial radio show *Beulah*, whose stereotypical portrayal of blacks as dim-witted, subservient, and inarticulate was criticized by activists, including the NAACP. She later starred on the television version of *Beulah*, also known as *The Beulah Show* (1950–52).

McQueen lamented the fact that she had to assume stereotypical roles. However, blacks simply were not respected as complete human beings by the Hollywood establishment throughout most of her career. Indeed, she could not attend the premiere of *Gone With the Wind* in 1939 because it was held at a whites-only theater.

Many of McQueen's roles, particularly her role as Prissy, have been the source of much black embarrassment and anger. The NAACP and other civil rights organizations boycotted *The Beulah Show*, and criticized McQueen and other black actors and actresses for taking demeaning roles.

McQueen had roles in other memorable productions, such as television productions of *The Adventures of Huckleberry Finn* in 1981 and 1985, and a television production of *The Green Pastures* in 1957. In 1980 she won an Emmy for her role in a children's production called *The Seven Wishes of a Rich Kid*.

McQueen was a lifelong atheist (see ATHEISM) and was a member of the Freedom From Religion Foundation from 1981 until her death in 1995. In 1989 the foundation awarded her a Freethought Heroine Award. In the same year, African Americans for Humanism contacted her to ask if she would be interested in working with the group to promote humanism among African Americans. She declined, saying that her hero, Booker T. Washington, was not listed as a great African American humanist in a partial list of black humanists in one of the group's brochures. (In fact, Washington was not a humanist—he was strongly religious.)

McQueen was highly critical of religion—particularly Christianity. She said that black slaves were attracted to Christianity because church attendance on Sundays was the only time they were permitted to dress up.

McQueen died in an accident caused by a fire. Her body was donated to medical science and she left the balance of her personal bank account to the Freedom From Religion Foundation.

BIBLIOGRAPHY

"Butterfly McQueen Remembered." *Freethought Today* (January/February 1996).

Hine, Darlene Clark. ed. *Black Women in America: An Historical Encyclopedia*. Brooklyn: Carlson Publishing, 1993.

NORM R. ALLEN JR.

McTAGGART, JOHN McTAGGART ELLIS (1866–1925),

English philosopher. A Hegelian philosopher, John McTaggart Ellis McTaggart achieved the rare feat of combining a commitment to ATHEISM with an equally serious commitment to personal immortality. McTaggart's contribution to the development of twentieth-century atheism is more substantial than he is given credit for, although the fault for this omission lies with McTaggart himself.

McTaggart was the son of Francis and Caroline Ellis, the surname McTaggart being added by his father in order to fulfill a condition for an inheritance. The now-prosperous family sent young McTaggart to the prestigious Clifton School and to Trinity College, Cambridge. While visiting his widowed mother in New Zealand in 1892, McTaggart met Margaret Elizabeth Bird. The two married on his next visit to New Zealand in 1899. McTaggart's entire academic career (1897–1923) unfolded at Cambridge, where he developed his brilliant though idiosyncratic blend of Hegelian idealism and atheism. He died suddenly and unexpectedly in January 1925.

McTaggart presented his philosophy of religion primarily in his work *Some Dogmas of Religion* (1906) and *The Nature of Existence* (1921). He and G. E. Moore were good friends, despite the latter's role as the most influential critic of British Hegelianism. Along with Moore and Bertrand RUSSELL, McTaggart belonged to the irreverent Cambridge club known as the Apostles. And like Russell, he was happy for some of his speeches to be published by the RATIONALIST PRESS ASSOCIATION.

In *Some Dogmas of Religion*, McTaggart's justification for religion was dauntingly rigorous. Any religious belief, he argued, requires the prior belief that the universe is good. But there is no reliable method by which one can believe this other than dogmatically. And dogmas in turn require a metaphysical investigation for which most people lack the time or inclination. Therefore, regardless of whether any religion is actually true, the vast majority of people accept their religions on false grounds. This in turn leads to a larger number of people living without religion, but also without its consolations, and who will therefore be unhappy. Having said this, McTaggart was equally unconvinced of any link between religious belief and happiness.

Running counter to the naturalistic trend of this line of argument, McTaggart advocated a mitigated version of personal immortality. After criticizing most arguments against, as well as many of those for, personal immortality, McTaggart advocated a concept of a disembodied mind linked with a universal spirit composed principally of love.

Among professional philosophers McTaggart is best remembered for his work in logic, which remains influential to this day. Outside of logic, McTaggart's thinking suffered from his almost complete ignorance of science and his inability to see its value. For instance, while his arguments against the existence of God were very powerful, they were predicated on his conviction of the unreality of time, which has not achieved general acceptance.

BIBLIOGRAPHY

Berman, David. *A History of Atheism in Britain.* London: Routledge, 1990.

McTaggart, John McTaggart Ellis. *Some Dogmas of Religion.* New York: Kraus Reprint, 1969.

Passmore, John. *A Hundred Years of Philosophy.* London: Penguin, 1967.

BILL COOKE

MECHANISM. Mechanism is the view that human beings are machines in a mechanical world. The idea that the whole universe is a vast machine was encouraged by the work of René DESCARTES and, especially, Sir Isaac Newton. Influential in the development of Enlightenment attitudes, it now has mainly historical interest.

Mechanism and Materialism. What is to count as a machine? If only systems powered by water, springs, steam, or oil are machines, mechanism is obviously false. If you count sophisticated computer-controlled robots as machines, mechanism may strike you as possibly true. If you count anything as a machine provided only that it works in accordance with the laws of physics, you may regard mechanism as scarcely open to serious challenge, since by that definition everything in the world is a machine—unless, as some maintain, consciousness or other aspects of the mind resist explanation on that basis. The view that all aspects of mentality are explicable in physical terms is materialism (see MATERIALISM, PHILOSOPHICAL; PHYSICALISM). Understood in the broad sense just noted, therefore, mechanism adds nothing to materialism.

Descartes thought that although all animal behavior and much human behavior was explicable mechanically, the most characteristic features of human behavior were not. If a machine were constructed to resemble a human being, two things would betray it. One is that it could not produce utterances suitable for the expression of thoughts appropriate to its situation. The other is more general: all its behavior would be seen to spring from built-in responses rather than from reason. (The behavior of computers does not generally consist of built-in responses; but there were no computers in the seventeenth century). On other grounds, too, he argued that human behavior could only be explained in terms of something utterly different from anything mechanical or, indeed, physical: an immaterial mind, interacting with the brain.

Gottfried Wilhelm Von LEIBNIZ argued that if thoughts and feelings could be explained "mechanically, that is, by means of shapes and movements," then we could imagine a suitable machine enlarged so as to allow us to enter it, just as we can enter a mill. But inside there would only be pieces of machinery turning or pushing against one another, and nothing—according to Leibniz—that could explain thoughts, feelings, or perceptions. In one form or another that reasoning remains influential, but it is hardly compelling. Leibniz seems just to have assumed that machines could not think. Why otherwise should he have expected that gazing at the machinery would reveal whether or not thinking and feeling were going on?

Turing Machines. It has become clear that the brain does not have the structure of a computer; so if mechanism implies we are just like computer-controlled robots, it is false. However, more general ways of defining machines were devised by Alan Turing. One type of "Turing machine" is a *finite deterministic automaton.* This has a finite number of possible states, a finite number of possible inputs, and a finite number of possible outputs. At any moment it is in one of those possible states and may be receiving one of those possible inputs. For each pair consisting of a state and an input, the system's next state and output are thereby determined. Although all systems of this kind are realizable by programmed computers, some might also be realized by very different structures, including human bodies.

Arguments Against. Two famous arguments have been thought to refute any variety of mechanism based on such ideas.

John Searle's "Chinese Room" argument attacks the view that a suitably programmed computer would be intelligent. If a certain program were supposed to make a computer understand Chinese, for example, then when he himself played the part of the computer, following instructions in English equivalent to the original program, that ought to make *him* understand Chinese. But it would not, since he would simply be shuffling what were, for him, meaningless squiggles. He concludes there could be no such program. His opponents object that it is beside the point that *he* does not understand Chinese; what matters is whether the whole system, of which he is only a part, understands Chinese. After all, none of his brain cells understands English, but the system of which they are components does.

Kurt Gödel proved it was impossible to devise a consistent set of axioms and rules (a "formal system") for generating all and only the truths of arithmetic. Some have attempted to use this result against mechanism, arguing that if we were machines of the sort in question, none of us would be able to do what any competent logician, by following Gödel's methods, could do. The argument depends on several problematic assumptions. One is that if we instantiated formal systems, they would be consistent. Another is that if a certain formal system successfully models the workings of a human body whose activities include doing arithmetic, then that formal system must itself be adequate for arithmetic. This may seem reasonable, especially when combined with another assumption popular in the early days of artificial intelligence (it no doubt influenced the Chinese Room argument): that human cognition can be appropriately modeled in terms of the processing of formulas resembling sentences or sentence parts. But the behavior of human bodies can be described and explained at different levels, including the atomic, the molecular, and the psychological. Conceivably, a formal system that was not itself adequate for arithmetic could successfully model the workings of a human body that, as a whole, engaged in sophisticated mathematics.

Conclusion. If you are convinced the world is purely physical, then you are a physicalist (materialist). Physicalism does not commit you to anything but the uninteresting version of mechanism noted in the second paragraph above. Good reasons for going beyond that are hard to find.

BIBLIOGRAPHY

Copeland, Jack. *Artificial Intelligence: A Philosophical Introduction.* Oxford: Blackwell, 1993.

Dennett, Daniel C. *Brainstorms.* Cambridge, MA: MIT Press, 1978.

———. *Consciousness Explained.* Boston: Little, Brown, 1991.

Descartes, René. *Discourse on Method and the Meditations.* Translated by F. E. Sutcliffe. London: Penguin, 1968.

Hofstadter, Douglas R., and Daniel C. Dennett, eds. *The Mind's I.* New York: Basic Books, 1981.

Lucas, John R. "Minds, Machines and Gödel." *Philosophy* 36 (1961). Reprinted in A. R. Anderson, ed. *Minds and Machines.* Englewood Cliffs, NJ: Prentice-Hall, 1964.

Parkinson, G. H. R., ed. *Gottfried Wilhelm Leibniz: Philosophical Writings.* London: Dent, 1973.

Putnam, Hilary. "Minds and Machines." In *Dimensions of Mind*, edited by Sidney Hook. New York: New York University Press, 1960. Reprinted in his *Mind, Language and Reality: Philosophical Papers*, Vol. 2. Cambridge: Cambridge University Press, 1975.

Searle, John R. "Minds, Brains, and Programs." *Behavioral and Brain Sciences* 3. Reprinted in Douglas R. Hofstadter and Daniel C. Dennett, eds., *The Mind's I.* New York: Basic Books, 1981.

Turing, Alan M. "Computing Machinery and Intelligence." *Mind* 59 (1950). Reprinted in Douglas R. Hofstadter and Daniel C. Dennett, eds., *The Mind's I.* New York: Basic Books, 1981.

ROBERT KIRK

MENCKEN, HENRY LOUIS (1880–1956), American journalist and cultural critic. Best known for his scathing reports of the Scopes trial of 1925 (see EVOLUTION AND UNBELIEF), H. L. Mencken referred to himself as a "theological moron": he had "no sense whatever of the divine presence or of a divine personality," although he was quick to note that he was "anything but a militant atheist." In his youth, he and his brother were sent to a Sunday school by his father, although he claimed that this was only because his father wished to have some peace and quiet for afternoon naps. Mencken states that his father was "what Christendom abhors as an infidel," and it was no doubt from him that Mencken first derived his ANTICLERICALISM, later augmented by his study of Friedrich NIETZSCHE. He would later translate Nietzsche's *The Antichrist* (1920).

It is a vexing question whether Mencken was an actual atheist, "militant" or otherwise. In the late essay "What I Believe" (1930), he stated only that "I believe that religion, generally speaking, has been a curse to mankind—that its modest and greatly overestimated services on the ethical side have been more than overborne by the damage it has done to clear and honest thinking." He went on to declare flatly that "the evidence for immortality is no better than the evidence for witches, and deserves no more respect."

For the majority of his career, Mencken—as a columnist for the *Baltimore Evening Sun* (1906–48), coeditor of the *Smart Set* (1914–23), and founder and editor of the *American Mercury* (1924–33)—devoted his energies to attacking religion for the social, cultural, and political harm it causes. Much of his writing lampoons religion and religious figures with pungent satire and ridicule. He took particular aim at flamboyant religious figures such as the evangelist Billy Sunday (whose several revival meetings in Baltimore in 1916 Mencken attended), Aimée Semple McPherson (whom he saw during a visit to Los Angeles in 1926), and the "radio priest" Charles Coughlin. These individuals regaled him because they embodied, in the religious sphere, the entertaining buffoonery he found so richly prevalent in American politics.

Because his prime political concern was absolute freedom of speech, Mencken made no attempt to silence religious discourse or practice, even at its most preposterous and dangerous. He even condemned a Maryland law making it a misdemeanor for Christian Science "healers" to accept a fee for their services. He expressed little concern that such healers' "bungling" might cause grave injury or death to the persons they treated, since he felt that the prohibition of Christian Science teaching might lead to other and worse suppressions. Conversely, he spoke out strongly when Christian Scientists attempted to suppress the sale of a biography critical of its founder, Mary Baker Eddy, in 1929.

Early in his career Mencken waged incessant battle against local and national religious figures for their attempts to legislate morality, specifically with regard to

Sunday laws. Maryland was laboring under a particularly harsh statute of 1723 (extended in 1874) prohibiting a wide variety of activities on Sunday, ranging from playing golf to orchestra concerts. The onset of Prohibition in 1920 did nothing to assuage Mencken's fears that religion was becoming dangerously linked with government. He came to believe that the passage of the Eighteenth Amendment was largely a product of heavy lobbying by the Anti-Saloon League, itself the creature of the Baptist and Methodist churches. More controversially, Mencken also maintained that the rise of the Ku Klux Klan (whose objects of attack included not only African Americans but also Catholics, Jews, and secularists) was also largely a function of the Methodist and Baptist churches—a claim that has a nucleus of truth but which Mencken exaggerated considerably.

Mencken gained his greatest celebrity by his coverage of the Scopes trial in 1925. It is, however, not widely known that he remained in Dayton, Tennessee, only for the first week of the trial, missing Clarence DARROW's spectacular cross-examination of William Jennings Bryan in the trial's second week. Nevertheless, Mencken's numerous and extraordinarily mordant reports, widely syndicated, permanently affected the American people's perception of the trial and its ramifications. In these articles Mencken emphatically repeated his long-held position that religion was a kind of security blanket embraced by the ignorant and the timid as a shield against intellectual and social advances they could neither understand nor welcome. His famously vicious obituary of Bryan—first published as "Bryan" in the *Baltimore Evening Sun* in July 1925 revised as "William Jennings Bryan" in the *American Mercury* in October 1925, and revised again as "In Memoriam: W. J. B." in *Prejudices: Fifth Series* (1926)—has been criticized as an uncharitable attack on the dead, but Mencken was well aware of the dangers that Bryan's brand of fundamentalism posed to freedom of thought and expression.

Mencken's most exhaustive treatment of religion is found in *Treatise on the Gods* (1930), but this is an unwontedly sober and rather dry chronicle of the evolution of religion (specifically Christianity) from primitive thought, and its anthropology is now somewhat outdated. But Mencken remained a fierce battler of religion to the end: In "What Is to Be Done about Divorce" (1930), he asserted that the liberalization of divorce laws would not occur "until the discussion is purged of religious consideration." He also claimed that African Americans must free themselves from the influence of evangelical Christianity—which he identified as a holdover from the era of slavery—if they were to attain the civil and political rights they deserved.

BIBLIOGRAPHY

Fecher, Charles A. *Mencken: A Study of His Thought.* New York: Knopf, 1978.

Hobson, Fred. *Mencken: A Life.* New York: Random House, 1994.
Mencken, H. L. *H. L. Mencken on Religion.* Edited by S. T. Joshi. Amherst, NY: Prometheus Books, 2002.
Teachout, Terry. *The Skeptic: A Life of H. L. Mencken.* New York: HarperCollins, 2002.

S.T. JOSHI

MENDUM, JOSIAH P. (1811–1891), American FREETHOUGHT editor and publisher. Josiah P. Mendum was born in Kennebunk, Maine, on July 7, 1811. He was brought up in the tolerant Universalist tradition (see UNIVERSALISM TO 1961), but while still a young man was radicalized by the persecution of Abner KNEELAND, the editor of the rationalist newspaper the *BOSTON INVESTIGATOR* (see RATIONALISM). Kneeland was prosecuted for BLASPHEMY in 1834 and abruptly left Boston in 1838. The *Investigator* was saved from closure that year when Mendum became its publisher. Two years later he became sole owner.

Along with Horace SEAVER, Kneeland's successor as editor, Mendum oversaw a new look for the *Investigator*, broadening its scope to appeal in particular to working-class readers interested in questions of labor relations and social reform (see LABOR MOVEMENT AND UNBELIEF; SOCIALISM AND UNBELIEF). Mendum also improved the *Investigator*'s publishing arm by publishing new editions of the works of great freethinkers like VOLTAIRE, Baron d'HOLBACH, Thomas PAINE, Robert TAYLOR, and Constantin Volney.

Mendum was particularly enamored of Paine, and was the main force behind building the Paine Memorial Hall on Appleton Street in Boston. Mendum raised most of the money for the project and was its guiding spirit (see MONUMENTS TO UNBELIEF). He eventually passed the property on to his son, Ernest, who went on to sell his interest in the property to Ralph Chainey. Ernest, who was named after the pioneering feminist and freethinker Ernestine L. ROSE, also inherited the *Investigator* from his father. Ernest maintained it until it was consolidated with *THE TRUTH SEEKER* in 1904.

A slightly built man who usually sported a neat, brown beard, Mendum married Elizabeth Munn in New York in 1847. In addition to Ernest, the couple had three daughters. Elizabeth Mendum died on April 13, 1872, and Josiah on December 10, 1891.

BIBLIOGRAPHY

Macdonald, George E. *Fifty Years of Freethought.* New York: Truth Seeker Company, 1972.
Putnam, Samuel P. *Four Hundred Years of Freethought.* New York: Truth Seeker Company, 1894.

BILL COOKE

MESLIER, JEAN (1664–1733), French atheist and apostate. Jean Meslier was born in Mazerny, the Ardennes region of France. (Some early sources place this date as late as 1678, but later scholarship has found the 1664 date to be correct). Meslier's father, Gerard, was a wool merchant, and the family was somewhat prosperous. As such, and despite his misgivings, Meslier's parents convinced him to become a priest. In 1688 he was appointed to a parish in Etrépigny, in the Champagne district.

Meslier was the typical country priest of the time, supported financially both by his family (as was the custom) and by a small tithe from his parishioners. He was known for his honorable ways and his charity toward his parishioners. He had some difficulty with Antoine de Touly, the noble of the village where Meslier's church was located. This seems to have started as a personal quarrel over noble privileges, and eventually became a dispute of the nobility versus peasants generally. In caring for the members of his "flock" in this manner, Meslier demonstrated what might be considered a political concern for their general welfare; some scholars have seen in his attitude a harbinger of the French Revolution, which would occur sixty years after Meslier's death. Others have viewed him as a possible precursor to the writings of Karl MARX.

Meslier became "notorious" after his death, with the discovery of three handwritten copies of a book he titled *Mon Testament* (My Testament). In it he described his lack of faith and asked for forgiveness from his parishioners for not being more forthcoming about his views. Meslier explained that he was not strong enough to reveal his apostasy during his lifetime, and feared retribution. He discussed various aspects of Christian dogma, showing them to be invalid under scrutiny.

Apologist scholars have characterized this work as possible revenge upon the church, which sided with Touly during Meslier's various disputes with him. Others have sought to marginalize Meslier by showing that he had little (if any) impact on the church itself.

Meslier's name is attached to other works, adding to confusion as to what he actually wrote. A book appearing in 1774 and titled *Le bon sense* was linked to Meslier. This work was eventually attributed to the Baron Paul Henri Thiry d'HOLBACH, who had in fact written it, but by then a publisher had already retitled the work *Le Bon Sense du Curé Meslier*. A later translation of d'Holbach's work titled *Superstition in All Ages* also misattributed it to Meslier. This is probably the best-known work attributed to Meslier, though his only actual written work remains *Mon Testament*.

Others have made use of his ideas and portrayed them in different ways. In 1762 VOLTAIRE wrote *Extrait des sentiments de Jean Meslier*, which admixed extracts of Meslier's thought with Volatire's own deistic thought (see DEISM). Not until 1864, with *Le Testament de Jean Meslier* edited by Rudolf Charles, did the full text of Meslier's *Testament* see publication.

BIBLIOGRAPHY

Meslier, Jean. *Le Testament de Jean Meslier.* 3 vols. Edited by Rudolf Charles. Amsterdam: La Librarie Etrangère, 1864.
"Meslier, Jean." *Superstition in All Ages.* Translated by Anna Knoop. New York: Eckler, 1890.
Morehouse, Andrew R. *Voltaire and Jean Meslier.* New Haven, CT: Yale University Press, 1936.
Stein, Gordon. "So You Think You Own a Copy of Meslier's Work? A Bibliographic Confusion between d'Holbach and Meslier." *Freethought History* 3 (1992).

TIMOTHY BINGA

MIDDLETON, CONYERS (1683–1750), English deist author. Conyers Middleton was born December 27, 1683, and educated at Trinity College, Cambridge. He was a curate near Cambridge for a while before serving as rector of Coveney. In 1721 he was appointed librarian of Trinity College, and from 1731 until 1734 he was Woodwardian professor there.

Middleton spent his career trying to find a theology of rational belief that was entirely free of supernaturalism and "enthusiasm," the term then used to mean excitable evangelicalism. His career is a prime example of what is called theological lying. This is David Berman's term for the sort of dissimulation forced upon heterodox writers in the ages before freedom of the press. In order to escape censure, ostracism, and even torture and death, heterodox writers resorted to different forms of subterfuge to disguise their real thoughts while hoping to insinuate themselves to the discerning reader. This could be done by beginning one's work with some conventional piety, then criticizing the foundations of that same piety. It could also be done by criticizing some other faith tradition and leaving it to the reader to see that the criticisms applied to Christianity as well.

Suspicions about Middleton's orthodoxy began as a result of his *Letter from Rome* (1729), which outlined the significant debt Christianity owed to paganism. These suspicions were confirmed by Middleton's next important written work, the *Letter to Dr. Waterland* (1738). Waterland had written a conventional reply to Matthew TINDAL's *Christianity as Old as Creation* (1730). *Letter to Dr. Waterland* is ostensibly a rebuke of Waterland for not having argued against DEISM with sufficient thoroughness and vigor. And yet Middleton's arguments are far tighter and penetrating against Waterland's orthodoxy than against the deism both men feigned to oppose.

Middleton's best-known and least controversial work was an adulatory two-volume *History of the Life of M. Tullius CICERO* (1741). While not being particularly original, the work sold well, as Cicero was something of a hero to educated people of the eighteenth century.

Middleton's last and most substantial work had the revealing title *Free Inquiry into the Miraculous Powers which are Supposed to Have Subsisted in the Christian Church from the Earliest Ages* (1749). Middleton was careful not to express his views openly, but his SKEPTICISM of most elements of supernaturalism, miracles in particular (see MIRACLES, UNBELIEF IN), caused a sensation. The ostensible target of this book was the Roman Catholic Church, but few failed to notice that Middleton's criticisms of Rome were just as relevant to Christianity in general. David HUME's work on miracles had appeared in the previous year, so Middleton's work reignited a significant controversy. Middleton died on July 28, 1750, just as controversy over his latest work was building.

BIBLIOGRAPHY

Hunter, Michael, and David Wootton, eds. *Atheism from the Reformation to the Enlightenment*. Oxford: Clarendon, 1992.

Robertson, J. M. *A History of Freethought: Ancient and Modern*. London: Watts and Company, 1936.

BILL COOKE

MILL, JOHN STUART (1806–1873), English utilitarian philosopher. Born in Pentonville, London, John Stuart Mill was the eldest son of the Scot immigrant James Mill, who was chief examiner of the East India Company. James Mill was a member of a radical school of thinkers that included Jeremy BENTHAM, the father of utilitarian moral philosophy. J. S. Mill was a child prodigy, educated by his father beginning at a very early age. His father's stated goal was to mold the young Mill into a genius capable of carrying on the utilitarian tradition after his and Bentham's demise. By the age of thirteen, Mill was reading Greek and Latin so that he could master the classics in their original languages. By fourteen, he had mastered much of history, the classics, economic theory, and had completed significant work in logic and mathematics. At eighteen he edited major manuscripts of the Benthamites at the direction of his father; steeped in their works, he began his own literary career. In 1823 his father helped him get a junior position in the East India Company. He was eventually promoted to his father's position of chief examiner. He visited France in 1820 and became fluent in French, which influenced him in becoming a student of French philosophy and history. In 1826 Mill became suddenly and seriously depressed. His depression continued for a number of months, although he continued his work. He began to believe that the strict training his father had given him had repressed his capacity for emotion, educating his mind at the neglect of his emotional life. Mill found that reading Wordsworth helped cure his depression and encouraged his developing internal emotional life. He is most noted for his contributions to utilitarian moral philosophy, specifically in his work *Utilitarianism*, and for his

defense of free inquiry and free speech in *On Liberty*, which is still a staple for most students of philosophy and political science.

Mill was a product of the British Enlightenment (see ENLIGHTENMENT, UNBELIEF DURING THE), and was heavily influenced by his personal relationship with Bentham and his readings of Auguste COMTE and Claude-Henri Saint-Simon. The influence of Saint-Simon and Comte are evident in Mill's *On Liberty*. Among Saint-Simon's historical theories is the notion of "critical" and "organic" phases of history. During "critical" phases, society is in the process of breaking down old structures and institutions, and during "organic" phases, societies undergo a process of rebirth, building upon new thoughts, philosophies, ways of life, and the like. It is clear that Mill believed that he lived on the cusp of one of those "organic" phases, and that his life and works were part of the process of rebirth. He devoted much of his work following his breakdown to an apparent attempt to reconcile the works of the world of REASON he was raised in with the world of emotion he found in poetry, and in his long friendship and marriage to Harriet Taylor. His relationship with Taylor was considered scandalous, given that it began while she was married, was extremely close for twenty years, and concluded in marriage after the death of her husband. Mill's and Taylor's response was to flaunt it and ignore criticism. Their free and open relationship clearly stoked and inspired his creative process.

As with much of his thought, Mill was influenced by his father in his views on religion. Mill wrote in his autobiography: "Growing Up without God. Those who admit an omnipotent as well as perfectly just and benevolent maker and ruler of such a world as this, can say little against Christianity but what can, with at least equal force, be retorted against themselves. Finding, therefore, no halting place in Deism, he [Mill's father] remained in a state of perplexity, until, doubtless after many struggles, he yielded to the conviction that, concerning the origin of things nothing whatever can be known [see DEISM]."

Mill was almost certainly an atheist or agnostic, though he took great care to hide his own views, perhaps out of a very real concern that they would undermine his other philosophical works in the court of public opinion (see ATHEISM; AGNOSTICISM). In fact, his publicly stated opinions did at one time indict him in a very real court (see LAW, THE, AND UNBELIEF). Nonetheless, Mill's views were clearly a bit more tolerant toward religious belief than were those of his father, of whom he writes further, stating: "As it was, his aversion to religion, in the sense usually attached to the term, was of the same kind as that of LUCRETIUS; he regarded it with the feeling due not a mere mental delusion, but to a great moral evil. He looked upon it as the greatest enemy of morality; first by setting up factitious excellencies, belief in creeds, devotional feelings, and ceremonies, not connected with the good of human kind and causing these to be accepted as substitutes for genuine virtues; but above all, by radically vitiating the standard of morals, making it consist in doing the will of a being, on whom it lavishes indeed all the phrases of adulation, but whom in sober truth it depicts as eminently hateful."

Mill's own view of religion was that it might be saved for utilitarian ends. As with American Enlightenment deists, he viewed the proper role of religion as molding people into better citizens and encouraging moral behavior. Despite his indictment for engaging in public speculation as to the meaning of the Trinity, he saw Christianity as, at its base, a force for good moral teaching, though in practice something else entirely. Again, writing about his father in his *Autobiography*:

I have a hundred times heard him say that all ages and nations have represented their gods as wicked, in a constantly increasing progression, that mankind have gone on adding trait after trait till they reached the most perfect conception of wickedness which the human mind can devise, and have called this God, and prostrated themselves before it. This *ne plus ultra* of wickedness he considered to be embodied in what is commonly presented to mankind as the creed of Christianity. Think (he used to say) of a being who would make a hell—who would create the human race with the infallible foreknowledge, and therefore with the intention—that the great majority of them were to be consigned to horrible and everlasting torment.

The time, I believe, is drawing near when this dreadful conception of an object of worship will no longer be identified with Christianity; and when all persons, with any sense of moral good and evil, will look upon it with the same indignation with which my father regarded it. . . . The world would be astonished if it knew how great a proportion of its brightest ornaments—of those most distinguished even in popular estimation for wisdom and virtue— are complete skeptics in religion.

While rejecting the dogma of Christianity, he promotes a cultivation of the best parts of its moral code in his essay "The Utility of Religion." He further argues that belief in a supernatural power may have at one time been useful in maintaining such a moral code, but that it is now no longer necessary and indeed harmful.

Influenced as he was by his breakdown and subsequent emotional and poetic reawakening, Mill also writes of an aesthetic role of religion, writing in "The Utility of Religion": "Religion and poetry address themselves, at least in one of their aspects, to the same part of the human constitution; they both supply the same want, that of ideal conceptions grander and more beautiful than we see realized in the prose of human life." But his first two essays in "The Utility of Religion" argue further that the aesthetic and moral role of supernatural religion

should be replaced with a religion of "humanity." The final essay in this work argues less stringently against the existence of God per se, in order to press the point of his positive humanistic goals (see HUMANISM). Mill argues that there is room for divine creation of the present imperfect world, and that this creation leaves room for the work of human beings to improve both the world and themselves. "If man had not the power by the exercise of his own energies for the improvement both of himself and of his outward circumstances, to do for himself and other creatures vastly more than god had in the first instance done, the Being who called them into existence would deserve something very different from thanks at his hands."

He concludes that faith is not rational in light of the lack of evidence of the supernatural, but he leaves open the role of religion in fostering "hope." Mill criticizes appeals to the alleged evidence of miracles, arguing that there is absolutely no evidence to support these claims. He admits only that a benevolent deity might have indicated its intent to award a life after death to those who aspire to it, but that if no evidence supports that, then one might still hope. He allows then that Jesus was Christ, and that He brought such a message of "glad tidings" for the hopeful.

Despite Mill's argument that the proper rational attitude toward supernatural religion is neither atheism nor agnosticism, he concludes in the last essay of "The Utility of Religion" that "the whole domain of the supernatural is thus removed from the region of Belief into that of simple Hope." In this light, Mill is best characterized as a humanist with, at most, deistic leanings.

BIBLIOGRAPHY

J. S. Mill. *Autobiography.* New York: P. F. Collier & Son, 2001.
———. *On Liberty.* Suffolk, UK: Penguin, 1984.
———. *Three Essays on Religion.* Amherst, NY: Prometheus Books, 1988.
———. *Utilitarianism.* New York: Liberal Arts Press, 1957.

DAVID KOEPSELL

MIRACLES, UNBELIEF IN. Two Theistic Approaches to Miracles. Traditionally, theism has moved in two seemingly opposite directions regarding miracles. One branch emphasizes local miracles as divine intervention for someone's benefit or punishment; miracles are heaven's wonderworks and revelations brought to earth. The other branch of theism views nature with its dependable regularities as the creator's perpetual revelation of cosmos over chaos; the *orderly* universe itself is the one great miracle of grace that makes life and daily existence possible. Local miracles, therefore, threaten the designed stability and predictability.

A Dilemma. A miracle requires supportive miracles that require still more miracles, with no conspicuous end to the proliferation. But if the proliferation does not end, the value of miracles declines and perhaps the very definition of *miracle* collapses. In the early eighteenth century Anglican bishop George Berkeley, doubtless seeing the problem generated by Roman Catholic miracle claims, advanced the following thesis: While God gave all human mortals experiences, including sensations, directly, they *arrived fundamentally in an orderly, coherent manner*. To this orderly input operating with regularity he gave the name *Nature*. Learning from Berkeley and the deists (see DEISM), the founder of Boston Personalism, Borden Parker Bowne, contended that if miracles broke with all law, they would be nothing intelligible. Furthermore, if the regular connections between human actions and their consequences were suspended by the proliferation of miraculous interventions, moral responsibility would go on a permanent holiday. Not even the most dedicated believer in miracles would find meaning in such unpredictable chaos.

For Bowne, miracles were more like signs guiding the mind to find meanings and connections it might otherwise miss: "[W]e cannot suppose them wrought at random and without reference to antecedents and environments." Whereas the deists conceived of nature as something of a vast and complex watch or machine operating more or less on its own and with its own laws, Personalists like Bowne, Peter Bertocci, and E. S. Brightman viewed God as operating *perpetually* through the laws and the regularities he designed. Scientists, evolutionists, and naturalists were, therefore, welcomed as investigators of the continuity of law and rational connection: "Even admitting a miraculous factor, we should not expect any such magical departure from all the psychological and historical uniformities and continuities." Just as the human senses must be tested by critical inquiry, so reports of miracles must be critically tested. Sound religion is not advanced by uncritically embracing claims of a speaking ass, a talking serpent, a floating ax head, a male's rib becoming a woman, or a prophet's riding a flaming chariot from earth to heaven. Supernatural causality works through natural means and method.

A Question of Definition. Theists like C. S. Lewis and Richard Swinburne believed that if an omnipotent creator could create the entire universe, he could surely perform local miracles. Much of this argument seems to be a definition that goes something like this: Omnipotent God is by definition a miracle-working being. Therefore, if he exists, he performs miracles. Since creation out of nothing is among the earliest miracles, all other miracles on earth follow as needed. But does it follow that this deity could perform miracles once he sets up his program? Could he, for example, create a Savior who was also a rapist? If by *Savior* is meant, among other things, a supremely moral being, then the answer is that he could not. Not all things are possible. Even for an omnipotent

creator, any program always rules out numerous options. After creating and programming a being to be a donkey, could omnipotence make that being converse rationally in Hebrew with a human prophet? Is there a point beyond which the putative modifications render the original being no longer the same being?

Many Jews and Christians have learned to view supposed miracles in the Bible as literary devices for expressing insights—some profound, others mundane, and still others entertaining. Some scholars believe the miracles of the book of Acts, for example, function as ingredients of an entertaining novel like those found in ancient Jewish and Greek novels.

In many ways, Fyodor Dostoyevsky's treatment of miracles is more profoundly telling than is David HUME's. Examining miracles as a general category tends to generate entanglements and elusiveness, whereas focusing on specific miracle claims proves more fruitful. The narrator of *The Brothers Karamazov* notes that the youngest brother, Alyosha, believed not only in the elder Zosima's power to work miracles, but also that a coffin flew out of the church. By making it clear that Alyosha's expectation of miracles to follow upon Zosima's death was falsified, the narrator raises the question of whether Zosima's healings were really a supernatural cure "or merely a natural remission." There can be little doubt that Dostoyevsky, a member of the Russian Orthodox Church, was personally troubled about the miracle question. In March 1854, when he was thirty-three, he wrote the following to the wife of a fellow prisoner: "I am a child of this century, a child of doubt and disbelief, I have always been and shall ever be (that I know), until they close the lid of my coffin."

One Miracle Usually Requires Others. As is often the case, to support one miracle, others have to be brought in as support. Miracles proliferate with surprising quickness. According to Acts 7 (possibly written also by the author of the Gospel of Luke), Stephen the deacon was on the verge of being attacked because of a long, religiously incorrect sermon he had just delivered: "Being full of the Holy Spirit, [Stephen] looked up to heaven and saw (*eiden*) God's glory, and Jesus standing at God's right hand. Look [or Behold](*idou*), I see heaven open and the Son of Man standing at God's right hand" (7:55–56).

This interesting story raises some crucial questions. Did Luke himself think that if others present had looked up, they would have seen the Son of Man? In short, for Luke, was the Son of Man's standing at God's right hand publicly observable at that particular time and place, or was it a case of "faces in the clouds?" Did Luke mean to imply that he, Luke, personally believed that Stephen literally saw the heavens part, and saw the Son of Man standing literally at God's literal right hand? Or was he merely reporting, or at least telling a story, about a man named Stephen who only *thought* he was looking at Jesus (and possibly God) in heaven? In this putative account, is Stephen's "seeing" the resurrected Jesus the same kind of "seeing" as those reported in the Gospel of Luke? According to Acts 10:9–13, while Peter was hungry and waiting for the meal to be prepared, he fell into a trance and "saw" heaven open. From it descended a large sheet (or perhaps a tablecloth) containing all kinds of four-footed animals as well as reptiles and birds. A voice then told him to get up, kill, and eat.

Did Luke mean to suggest that Stephen, too, had fallen into a trance or perhaps hallucinated, thinking he saw heaven open and Jesus standing at God's right hand? According to Acts 16:9–10, Paul had a "vision" during the night of a Macedonian begging him to come to Macedonia. The question naturally emerges: did Luke make any distinctions between visions, actual public appearances of someone, dreams, hallucinations, and trances? Can the words for "see" be used in all these cases? If so, how do they functionally differ? Of course, we are faced with Thomas HOBBES's question: *What is the difference between saying God spoke to someone in a dream and saying he dreamed God spoke to him*?

According to Acts 16:10, "After Paul had seen the vision, we got ready at once to leave for Macedonia, concluding that God had called us to preach the gospel to them." This is truly a revealing passage. Is it perhaps an ordinary dream *interpreted* to be a divine revelation? Furthermore, whereas only one person had the dream, *more than one* interpreted it to be a deity's specific instructions. Moreover, readers must make their own interpretations of what actually happened or did not happen, but their interpretations depend partly on Luke's interpretation of what he believed did or did not happen. Who told him about Paul's vision? Was it a secondhand report? Firsthand? Fourthhand? Did he believe it? Or was he writing with a specific agenda that gave him a storyteller's license?

Luke goes out of his way to give the resurrected Jesus a body of flesh and bone. But the flesh cannot be ordinary flesh, otherwise it could not travel through the stratosphere en route to heaven. Temperatures far below freezing would turn the fleshly body into a frozen block. So several supplemental miracles are required to prevent freezing. At the same time, the oxygen above three miles would become too thin for him to breathe; hence, suitable lungs and blood cells would become necessary to keep the brain reasonably intact.

All these adjustments can be made in the world of miracles, just as necessary adjustments occur in the world of Harry Potter. For the sake of the story, however, authors must draw the line on adding the supplemental miracles or works of magic. Every wonderwork requires an expanding network of supplemental wonderworks to make it possible within the story. The stopping point is somewhat arbitrary.

Auxiliary Hypotheses. Theories cannot be absolutely falsified *if* we are willing to pay the price of making numerous revisions and calling on numerous auxiliary hypotheses for reinforcement. Reinforcements, however, can sometimes become so heavy as to sink our home theory or revise it beyond recognition. Some aspects of our theories do sometimes appear to be falsified unless we make drastic revisions and corrections. The job is to keep track of the revisions and to keep a record of *the severe prices paid to keep them*. Sometimes, as we work from two or more models, we begin somewhere along the way to think that one model is more fruitful and intellectually promising. The other model seems less credible. Once believers step into the arena of miracles, they face the problem of their proliferation and thus the proliferation of hypotheses not only to account for each of them, but also to expose the presumed miracles in rival religions as pseudomiracles.

The Problem of Containment. B. B. Warfield hoped to persuade his fellow evangelicals that miracles had ceased during the Apostolic Age, that is, roughly the first century. For him, miracles after that century were merely counterfeit. Challenging Warfield, in 1993 Protestant author Jon Ruthven wrote a defense of the perpetuity of miracles. He did not intend to wrestle profoundly with the question of where to draw the line determining what is a genuine miracle and what is not, nor does he seriously address the proliferation problem.

Two Apostles Who Failed to Recognize Jesus. One of the most puzzling aspects of the resurrected Jesus narratives can be found in Luke 24:13–32. Although two apostles on the road to Emmaus meet the resurrected Jesus and converse and dine with him, they do not recognize him. This is a strange little story. Did its author mean to suggest that despite having only recently been two of Jesus's followers, they neither recognized his body with their eyes nor recognized his voice with their ears? If he did not look like Jesus or sound like him, how could they be sure he was not someone else? If Jesus had undergone a radical facelift, the story might at least have some internal plausibility. According to Matthew 28:9, however, two women, each named Mary, *recognize him instantly* and worship him, holding him by the feet. (On the other hand, according to John 20:14–16, Mary of Magdala did not recognize him at first but thought she was talking with the gardener.) Of course, Luke had a point to make, namely, that those two Emmaus apostles, one of them named Cleopas, were so "foolish" and "slow of heart" that they could not recognize him. They would have had to be also dull mentally.

Luke wanted to impress on his readers that Jesus's resurrected body was flesh and bones. The Greek word is *sarx* (flesh), not *soma* (body): "I am myself. Feel me and see. A ghost does not have flesh and bones, as you see I have" (24:39). Luke has Jesus eating fish to prove he is no ghost. The ancient Greeks faced the question of their gods' bodily fluid. In the *Iliad*, the gods, lacking mortal blood (*anaimones, haima*), possess a different humor (*ikhor*). Since the fluid passing so copiously through the veins of the gods was produced by what they ate, the

Greek gods had their special diet, namely, ambrosia. It is noteworthy that the Gospel of Luke in particular, while emphasizing Jesus's flesh and bones, says nothing about retrieving his blood, which was presumably spilled earlier.

Luke's flesh-and-bones Jesus can suddenly disappear from the Emmaus apostles' sight after breaking bread at their table and handing it to them (24:30–31). A similar disappearance might be affirmed in Luke 4:30, but the passage can be interpreted differently.

The Gospel of John tells the story of Mary of Magdala, who, upon eventually recognizing the resurrected Jesus, apparently grabs his feet or is about to. "Do not hold on to me," Jesus says, "for I have not yet returned to the Father" (20:16–17). After that, Jesus makes a quick trip to the Heavenly Father and then returns to perform the miraculous sign of appearing to the disciples, who are behind locked doors (20:19, 30).

Prayers and Sacrifices. Some theists and polytheists have believed their prayers carried something akin to lobbying influence that increased the controlling power's propensity to bestow miraculous interventions. PLATO regarded this aspect of prayer as a lack of real piety. Ironically, some cultures have ritualized or instituted sacrifices and prayers on a regular basis in the hope of securing the *order* of the universe. Conversely, in times of war, conflicting prayers for soliciting miraculous advantages for one's side and disadvantages for the enemy would seem to contribute to chaos rather than cosmos.

BIBLIOGRAPHY

Bowne, Borden Parker. *Studies in Christianity*. Boston: Houghton Mifflin, 1909.

Frank, Joseph, and David I. Goldstein, eds. *Selected Letters of Fyodor Dostoevsky*. Translated by Andrew MacAndrew. New Brunswick, NJ: Rutgers University Press, 1989.

Guthrie, Stewart Elliot. *Faces in the Clouds: A New Theory of Religion*. New York: Oxford University Press, 1993.

Pervo, Richard I. *Profit with Delight: The Literary Genre of the Acts of the Apostles*. Philadelphia: Fortress, 1987.

Price, Robert M., and Jeffery Jay Lowder. *The Empty Tomb: Jesus beyond the Grave*. Amherst, NY: Prometheus Books, 2005.

Ruthven, Jon. *On the Cessation of the Charismata: The Protestant Polemic on Postbiblical Miracles*. Sheffield, UK: Sheffield Academic, 1993.

Sissa, Giula, and Marcel Detienne. *The Daily Life of the Greek Gods*. Stanford, CA: Stanford University Press, 2000.

Wells, G. A. *Religious Postures: Essays in Modern Christian Apologetics and Religious Problems*. Chicago: Open Court, 1988.

JOE EDWARD BARNHART

MIRACULOUS PHENOMENA. The Anglican writer C. S. Lewis defined a miracle succinctly as "an interference with Nature by supernatural power." Supposed miracles have been reported since the most ancient times, and ironically—even in our own relatively enlightened culture—they continue to be touted, especially among Catholics and evangelical Protestants.

Many claims involve supposedly miraculous relics—objects associated with a saint or martyr. So prevalent had relic veneration become in Saint Augustine's time (about 400 CE) that he deplored "hypocrites in the garb of monks" for hawking the bones of martyrs, adding with due skepticism, "if indeed of martyrs." His contemporary Vigilantius of Toulouse condemned the veneration of relics as being nothing more than a form of idolatry, but Saint Jerome defended the practice on the basis that God works miracles through them.

Among the "miraculous" relics of Catholicism is the much publicized "blood" of San Gennaro—Saint Januarius—in Naples. Januarius was supposedly martyred during the persecution of Christians by Diocletian, although the church has never been able to verify his existence as an actual historical person. In any case, since the fourteenth century what is represented as the martyred saint's congealed blood periodically liquefies, in apparent contravention of nature's laws.

While outside researchers have never been permitted to conduct definitive tests on the material in the sealed vial, two modern investigative teams have nevertheless proposed solutions to the mystery. One, by three Italian chemists, involves a thixotropic gel (made by mixing chalk and hydrated iron chloride with a small amount of salt water) that liquefies when agitated and resolidifies when allowed to stand. The other, proposed by forensic analyst John F. Fischer and Joe Nickell, uses an oil-wax-pigment mixture that liquefies at even a slight increase in temperature. Although the actual formula may never be uncovered, it is important to note that the "blood" has occasionally liquefied on its own, without the usual prayerful entreaties and under circumstances (such as repair of its casket) that would seem unlikely for the working of a miracle. Also, since the fourteenth century there have been several additional saints' bloods that liquefy—all in the Naples area and thus suggestive of some regional secret.

Even more macabre relics exist—among them the allegedly "incorruptible" bodies of saints, that is, corpses that have "miraculously" failed to succumb to decay. Actually, however, in many cases artificial means, such as wax masks, have been employed to conceal their poor condition. Some appear merely to have become mummified (fostered by tomb rather than earthen burial), or otherwise preserved (as by burial in lime-impregnated soil, which converts the body fat into a hard, soaplike substance that resists putrefaction). It should also be noted that many instances of alleged incorruptibility cannot be verified—or, more importantly, are disproved by the facts, the bodies eventually being reduced to bones or requiring extensive restoration in order to be placed on view.

Another important category of miracle claims involves images that are said either to be supernatural in origin or to exude some magical power. Among the former are simulacra—images seen, Rorschach-like, in random patterns. A classic of the genre is an image of Jesus discovered in the skillet burns of a tortilla in 1978 (as still preserved at the New Mexico home of Maria Rubio). This was followed by similar "miraculous" images that appeared in such unlikely locations as the foliage of a vine-covered tree (West Virginia, 1982), rust stains on a forty-foot-high soybean oil tank (Ohio, 1986), and a forkful of spaghetti illustrated on a billboard (Georgia, 1991). As well, portraits of the Virgin Mary have been seen in such diverse places as the stains on the bathroom floor of a Texas auto parts store (1990) and in the grime on a window in an Italian village (1987). These appeared not to be anything more than the result of what one priest termed "a pious imagination."

Other notorious effigies are the "weeping," "bleeding," and otherwise animated icons that surface from time to time and raise troubling questions even for religious believers. For in shifting from the view that a statue is only a *representation* to the belief that it is truly *animated* is to seemingly cross a line from veneration to idolatry. Invariably, however, these are either investigated and found to be pious frauds or they are withheld from scrutiny. An example of the former was the statue of Our Lady of Fatima at a Catholic church in Thornton, California, in 1981. The sculpted virgin not only changed the angle of her eyes and tilt of her chin, reported churchgoers, but also wept, and even moved about the church at night. A bishop's investigation, however, found that the movement of the eyes and chin were apparently only variations in photographic images, while the weeping and perambulations were branded a probable hoax.

As the Thornton case indicates, allegedly miraculous photographs are quite common. A few of these are blatant hoaxes, while most are photographic "glitches" of one sort or another. As "Investigative Files" columnist for the *Skeptical Inquirer* magazine, this author received in 1995 some "miracle" photos from the popular TV series *Unsolved Mysteries*. My subsequent investigation showed that one was a "Golden Door" photo common to Marian apparition sites and thought by pilgrims to be proof of the doorway to heaven mentioned in Revelation 4:1; in fact, the effect was caused by the lens aperture of the Polaroid One-Step camera. Another photograph's "angel wings" were caused by light leakage into the film pack, and so on.

Some Christian fundamentalists place special emphasis on what are called "charismatic gifts of the Spirit" which include, notably, speaking in tongues, prophesying, and even (among a distinct minority) demonstrating imperviousness to fire and poisons, including poisonous snakes.

Speaking in tongues—known as *glossolalia*—is an ancient practice, mentioned in the New Testament (Acts 2:1–4) and recurring in Christian revivals through the ages. Modern analysis, however shows that it is actually "linguistic nonsense." William T. Samarin, professor of anthropology and linguistics at the University of Toronto, conducted an exhaustive five-year study of the phenomenon on several continents and concluded: "Glossolalia consists of strings of meaningless syllables made up of sounds taken from those familiar to the speaker and put together more or less haphazardly. The speaker controls the rhythm, volume, speed and inflection of his speech so that the sounds emerge as pseudolanguage—in the form of words and sentences."

Another charismatic gift of the spirit is prophecy. Early Christians mined the richly metaphorical ore of the Old Testament to "discover" therein supposedly prophetic passages of Jesus Christ as the Messiah. For example, Isaac Asimov points to a passage in Matthew—one absent from the other gospels—"[w]hich may well have arisen merely out of Matthew's penchant for interpreting and describing everything in accordance with Old Testament prophecy, ritual, and idiom."

Among modern prophecies, the most attention-getting ones are those that predict the biblical apocalypse or other doomsday scenarios. For instance, consider the prophecy made by the founder of the Church Universal and Triumphant, Elizabeth Clare Prophet. She predicted that the world would end in a nuclear holocaust, and her followers located themselves on a Montana ranch where they busily built nuclear shelters and stockpiled weapons. She frequently postponed the date of Armaggedon and explained each change as the result of fervent church prayers. Countless such cases have occurred throughout history, not only attesting to the failure of prophecy but also bearing witness to the credulity of religious zealots.

Taking up serpents is a practice of certain fundamentalist Christians (who read literally the passage from Mark 16:16–18, "they will pick up snakes in their hands") that is too extreme even for many ardent Pentecostals. The practice is actually part of a regular church worship that includes fervent preaching, singing, "witnessing," and speaking in tongues. While poisonous snakes are indeed dangerous and must be handled carefully, the knowledge the rural folk bring to the practice can be most helpful. For example, unless snakes are hot, hungry, or frightened, they move little and are relatively nonaggressive. Snakes raised from hatchlings can become accustomed to handling. Large snakes grasped behind the head will be unable to bite, and whenever they are lifted from the ground they usually will not bite.

In the event a participant is bitten, it is attributed to lack of faith. The devout forgo any medical help for snakebite, but that does not mean they forgo all treatment, which may consist of rest, the use of ice packs, and elevation of the wound to slow the spread of the poison and thus lessen the shock to the body. Even so, some who are bitten do succumb, including, ironically, "the original prophet of snake handling," George Went Hensley, who died in 1955 of a snakebite sustained during a religious service.

The same biblical passage that refers to taking up serpents also promises, "if they drink any deadly thing, it shall not hurt them." This informs the custom among certain independent "Holy Roller" churches of drinking strychnine. This often precedes snake handling, which is interesting in light of the fact that strychnine has been advocated to treat certain physiological effects resulting from snakebite. It would appear that a healthy person could sip a little dilute strychnine without serious harm and that, in the event of snakebite, its presence could actually be beneficial.

"Fire immunity" is sometimes practiced by members of the Free Pentecostal Holiness Church, and it usually takes the form of holding kerosene lamps improvised from bottles to their hands or feet, or even their chests and faces. Credulous writer Scott Rogo was impressed by this "type of 'miracle,'" but in fact the fire handlers invariably place their flesh *beside* rather than *above* the flames, keep their hands moving when they pass through the fire, and otherwise apply well-known principles of physics—just like firewalkers and fire eaters throughout history have done.

Among Catholics, an impressive variety of phenomena are held to be miraculous, including stigmata and visionary experiences. Stigmata, the supposedly miraculous duplication of Christ's wounds upon the body of a Christian, typically take the form of wounds in the hands—less commonly the feet, side, and brow (as from the nail and lance wounds and punctures from the crown of thorns). Some writers believe the explanation for stigmata is an autosuggested effect, although experimental attempts to duplicate the phenomenon, as with hypnosis, have been ultimately unsuccessful. The most likely explanation for most cases is pious hoaxing.

Catholicism has a long tradition of visionary experiences, including that of a Mexican peasant named Juan Diego. In 1531 he was allegedly visited by the Virgin Mary, who caused her self-portrait to appear miraculously upon his cloak. Miraculists claim that beneath the paint on the obviously traditional portrait is the divine image.

Among the Marian apparitions in the twentieth century, only the visions at Fatima, Portugal, in 1917 were declared authentic. They were reported by three shepherd children, only one of whom—ten-year-old Lucia de Jesus dos Santos, a fantasy-prone child who frequently claimed to see angels and other apparitions and whose own mother described her as "nothing but a fake who is leading half the world astray"—talked with the Virgin. The events culminated on a rainy October 13 with an estimated seventy thousand pilgrims in attendance. Suddenly, Lucia directed everyone's gaze upward as the sun appeared from behind clouds, whereupon many experienced what is known in the terminology of Marian apparitions as a "sun miracle." The effects are varyingly described, but many say the sun performed strange gyrations—none of which actually occurred, as astronomers know. The effects were surely optical ones; for example, because one cannot focus on an object so bright, the eyes may dart back and forth, thus creating, by the effect of image and afterimage, the appearance that the sun is "dancing," or the eyes may attempt to focus, retreat, again attempt, and so on, thereby giving the illusion that the sun is "pulsating." Sun miracles are still reported at modern-day sites such as those which began at Medjugorje, in the former Yugoslavia, in 1981, and in Conyers, Georgia, in 1990.

Other reported phenomena include rosaries that reportedly turn to gold. Examinations of many of these show them to have acquired a yellowish tarnish or to have their silver plating worn off so that the underlying brass showed through. An even more remarkable claim came from Conyers, where statues with heartbeats were alleged. Asked to investigate these (and other effects) by an Atlanta television station, I found that there were no heartbeats detectable by stethoscope. Apparently people reaching up to experience the pulsations were feeling the pulse in their own thumbs.

One of the most significant of the Marian apparitions was that allegedly seen in 1858 by fourteen-year-old Bernadette Soubirous (now Saint Bernadette) at a grotto near Lourdes, a town in the foothills of the Pyrenees. Although the parish curé branded the affair a hoax, Bernadette's several visions culminated in her being directed to a hidden spring in the cave that had "healing" waters. Despite "multitudinous failures" over the intervening years (one such failure being Bernadette herself, who suffered for many years from tuberculosis of the bone and died at age thirty-five), a few cases have been certified as miraculous. Independent medical investigators have found otherwise, however, observing that virtually all of the diseases that were supposedly cured were those that were susceptible to psychosomatic influences and/or were known to show spontaneous remissions. Emphasizing the uncertain nature of Lourdes's power, French writer Anatole France visited the site in the late nineteenth century and said, surveying all the discarded crutches, "What, what, no wooden legs?"

Uncertainty is characteristic of faith-healing cases in general. Healing occurs naturally in the body and as many as an estimated 75 percent of patients would get better even if they had no medical treatment. That fact—together with spontaneous remissions, illnesses that have been misdiagnosed or simply misreported, and other factors, including psychosomatic illnesses and even outright fraud—helps to explain the apparent success of so many faith healings. Quite often, the apparent success is short lived and follow-ups often reveal that the old condition has resurfaced. So-called faith healing can even be deadly if it causes people to reject medical treatment. This has happened in all too many instances, notably among adherents of Christian Science.

Of course one cannot prove miracles do *not* exist, but—apart from the well-known difficulty of proving a negative—one does not have that burden, which actually lies upon the claimant. Invariably, when we subtract the cases which have been clearly disproved, or that have plausible counter-explanations, or that are inadmissible because they cannot be substantiated, there seems insufficient grounds for invoking a miracle. Instead we see how easily people are deceived—not only by pious frauds but also by their own wish-fulfilling natures.

BIBLIOGRAPHY

Asimov, Isaac. *Asimov's Guide to the Bible*. Vol. 2, *The New Testament*. New York: Equinox, 1969.

Lewis, C. S. *Miracles: A Preliminary Study*. Glasgow: Fontana, 1974.

Nickell, Joe. *Looking for a Miracle: Weeping Icons, Relics, Stigmata, Visions, and Healing Cures*. Amherst, NY: Prometheus Books, 1998.

———. *Real-Life X-Files: Investigating the Paranormal*. Lexington: University Press of Kentucky, 2001.

Nickell, Joe, with John F. Fischer. *Mysterious Realms*. Amherst, NY: Prometheus Books, 1992.

Rogo, D. Scott. *Miracles: A Parscientific Inquiry into Wondrous Phenomena*. New York: Dial, 1982.

JOE NICKELL

MONUMENTS TO UNBELIEF. Across the United States and the world, varied statues, graves, and historic sites—marked and unmarked—attest to the colorful histories of ATHEISM, AGNOSTICISM, SECULARISM, FREETHOUGHT, and related movements of unbelief.

No freethought figure is more lavishly memorialized than Thomas PAINE. At Paine's birthplace in Thetford, Norfolk, England, stands a statue erected in 1964 by the mid-twentieth-century US atheist leader Joseph LEWIS. The site of Paine's birth bears a plaque donated by the Thomas Paine Society. Thetford's public library contains a large collection of Paine items. At New Rochelle, New Jersey, where Paine long resided, a bust of Paine by Wilson MacDonald stands atop a marble monument owned by the city. Also at New Rochelle is Paine's cottage, site of a troubled museum. The cottage is owned and administered by the adjacent Huguenot Historical Society; the museum is operated by the Thomas Paine National Historical Association. At this writing, the museum is in poor repair, much of the association's board has resigned, and an effort by management to sell key Paine artifacts is under investigation by the attorney

general of the state of New York. At Burnham Park, Morristown, New Jersey, stands a full-length Paine statue by Georg Lober, a 1950 gift of Joseph Lewis. (Lewis also prevailed on the socialist government of France in 1936 to accept a statue of Paine sculpted by Gutzon Borglum, sculptor of Mount Rushmore; the statue was not dedicated until 1948, and stands today in Montsouris Park, Paris.) The site of the house where Paine died in New York City's Greenwich Village is marked by a plaque. A bust of Paine adorns the Hall of Fame at New York University. Another, by sculptor Samuel H. Morse, is displayed in the library of the American Philosophical Society in Philadelphia. This bust was commissioned by a freethought organization, the NATIONAL LIBERAL LEAGUE, in 1876; sponsors hoped to place it in Philadelphia's Independence Hall in conjunction with that year's national centennial celebration. Religious opposition caused the bust's rejection. Remarkably, it languished in obscurity until the late 1960s, when it was acquired by the Philosophical Society. In 1997, a new Paine statue sculpted by Lawrence Holofcener was dedicated at Bordentown, New Jersey. In October 1992 the US Congress authorized the erection of a Paine memorial statue on the National Mall; private fundraising is ongoing.

The subject of the next largest number of memorials is doubtless Robert Green INGERSOLL. While he lived, a small town in Bowie County, Texas (near Texarkana), was briefly named for him. Ingersoll, Texas, grew up in the mid-1870s around a sawmill apparently operated by freethinkers who chose the community's name. After a Christian revival converted most of the residents in 1886, renaming was urgently sought. A newly dug well was yielding red water, so the townspeople dubbed their community Redwater. The Redwater, Texas, post office was officially renamed in 1894, five years before Robert Ingersoll died. More substantive memorials include Ingersoll's grave, Site Number 1620 in Arlington National Cemetery, Arlington, Virginia. Ingersoll began his law career in Peoria, Illinois; in that city's Glen Oak Park stands a full-length statue by Fritz Triebel mounted on a stone plinth. Ingersoll's widow and other family members attended its dedication on October 28, 1911. Two memorial plaques have adorned the Gramercy Park Hotel, constructed in 1924 on the site of Ingersoll's former New York brownstone residence. The original plaque was vandalized; it was replaced in 1988 but removed during a 2006 renovation. The mansion where Ingersoll died stands at Dobbs Ferry, New York. Originally the residence of Ingersoll's daughter Eva and her husband, the building bears no historical marker. At Chico Springs, New Mexico, an eccentric desert compound built by picaresque politician Stephen W. Dorsey still stands. Dorsey was one of two plaintiffs whom Ingersoll defended in the Star Route trials (1882), among the most sensational corruption cases of the late nineteenth century. Dorsey "paid" for Ingersoll's services by making Ingersoll a partner in a cattle company and building for him a log cabin mansion of eccentric design on one hundred twenty acres of desert rangeland. Ingersoll lived there for two months in the fall of 1884, just long enough to decide that either the rancher's life—or having Dorsey for a neighbor—did not agree with him. In the next year Ingersoll was forced to sell out his position in the cattle company at a loss. The site now operates as a Dorsey museum. Once part of the Museum of New Mexico, since 1987 the Dorsey Mansion State Monument has been privately operated.

The best-known Ingersoll memorial is his birthplace, a small two-story frame house at Dresden in New York's Finger Lakes district. Ingersoll lived there only for the first four months of his life. Twice the birthplace was restored—in 1921, and again in 1954 by Joseph Lewis—only to fall into disrepair. Near collapse in 1986, the house was purchased by the Council for Democratic and SECULAR HUMANISM, which raised $250,000 to rehabilitate the structure. On Memorial Day weekend in 1993, the Robert Green Ingersoll Birthplace Museum opened to the public as America's only freethought museum; it has been open each summer and fall weekend since. The museum's holdings include numerous Ingersoll artifacts and what is believed to be the most complete collection of printed works by and about Ingersoll.

In the nineteenth century, west-central New York State was a cauldron of social, political, and religious ferment—the Southern California of its age. The US woman suffrage movement (see WOMAN SUFFRAGE MOVEMENT AND UNBELIEF), Spiritualism (see SPIRITUALISM AND UNBELIEF), and the Mormon and Seventh-Day Adventist churches all originated there. The region is so rich with freethought sites that the Council for Secular Humanism (as the Ingersoll Museum's operator has been known since 1996) established an informal Freethought Trail of marked and unmarked sites within two hours' drive of Dresden.

Suffrage landmarks include the site of the 1848 Women's Rights Convention, wellspring of the suffrage movement. Part of the Wesleyan chapel in which the event was held still stands in downtown Seneca Falls; it is now a National Historic Park with an impressive adjacent museum established by the US Park Service. Most leaders of the women's rights movement were freethinkers, including Elizabeth Cady STANTON, Susan B. Anthony, and Matilda Joslyn GAGE. Stanton's Seneca Falls home has been lavishly restored by the Park Service. Anthony's home in Rochester is a privately owned museum. The Gage home in Fayetteville is being restored by a foundation under the leadership of feminist historian Sally Roesch Wagner. It intermittently displays its holdings and hopes to establish a museum.

Other Freethought Trail sites include Elmira, where a statue of Mark Twain (see CLEMENS, SAMUEL LANGHORNE) and the octagon study in which he wrote many of his novels stand on the campus of Elmira College.

Twain's grave lies in Elmira's Woodlawn Cemetery. The Syracuse home of abolitionist and regional freethought leader C. D. B. Mills, father of prominent suffragist Harriet May Mills, is undergoing restoration. The mansion of Andrew Dickson WHITE—first president of the first secular university in the United States, Cornell, and the accidental immortalizer of the "military metaphor" of warfare between science and theology—stands on Cornell's Ithaca campus. It houses academic offices.

One of the richest locations along the Freethought Trail, though it contains no marked sites, is the village of Watkins Glen. Watkins, as the village was then known, was the site of the New York Freethinkers Convention of 1878, despite its name a national gathering. There D. M. BENNETT, publisher of the influential freethought paper THE TRUTH SEEKER, was arrested with two others for selling Ezra HEYWOOD's sex manual Cupid's Yokes (see also SEX RADICALISM AND UNBELIEF; COMSTOCK, ANTHONY, AND UNBELIEF). The arrest became a national cause célèbre that would come to involve figures including Ingersoll and US president Rutherford B. Hayes. Outdoor portions of the convention were held at the village park, which still exists along Fourth Street; indoor portions were held in a meeting hall that stands on the southeast corner of Fourth and Franklin streets. This was the site of Bennett's arrest. The impressive stone building is in fairly good repair. The upper floor, site of the meeting hall, is unoccupied; the ground floor houses several busy local restaurants. Indeed, the entire village center retains strong echoes of its nineteenth-century appearance. Armed with Bennett's Truth Seeker account of his arrival at Watkins by train, one can walk the eleven blocks down Franklin Street from the lakeside rail station (now also a restaurant) and past the meeting hall to Watkins Glen State Park. Many of the landmarks Bennett described remain recognizable, particularly the town's spectacular, eponymous gorge, which remains substantially as it was when Bennett toured it; his account is as good a guide to its uncommon rock formations and waterfalls as anything one might purchase at the park's gift shop.

Sites across the country memorialize the so-called Forty-Eighters, liberals and freidenkers (freethinkers) who fled Germany after the failed democratic revolution of 1848. Thousands settled in Wisconsin, Minnesota, Kansas, Missouri, and Texas, then undergoing rapid settlement. Opposed to slavery, freidenkers leapt into the controversies preceding the US Civil War; some historians believe freidenker agitation was critical in ensuring that Kansas entered the Union as a free rather than a slave state in 1861.

Thomas Cemetery, near Fergus Falls, Minnesota, is a rare freethinkers' cemetery, containing mostly remains of German freidenkers. Wisconsin sites include a Freethought Hall at Sauk City, now a Unitarian meeting hall, and a disused FREIE GEMEINDEN (Free Congregation) hall on Jefferson Avenue in Milwaukee. A Freie Gemeinden hall at Dodier Street and Florissant Avenue in

St. Louis now serves as a community center. At Herrmann, a German-American town in central Missouri, journalists Charles Strehly and Eduard Mühl published the German-language newspapers the *Hermanner Volksblatt* and the freethought paper *Licht Freund* (Friend of Light). Both were regionally influential voices of abolition and ANTICLERICALISM. Strehly's house stands and bears a historical marker. In 1880 poet-lawyer George Henry Walser established the "freethought town" of LIBERAL, MISSOURI, whose charter forbade the erection of churches or saloons. Though the town's nonreligious character did not survive the turn of the twentieth century, Liberal endures complete with streets named for Ingersoll, Paine, Charles DARWIN, and other freethought heroes. One educational institution from Liberal's heyday, the wholly secular Liberal University, survived into the twentieth century. In 1897 it moved to Silverton, Oregon, where it operated for a few years under the leadership of Thaddeus Burr WAKEMAN, also publishing the newspaper the *Torch of Reason*. At some point the institution moved to Kansas City, apparently expiring in 1903. At Silverton, one of the buildings used by the university survives, a large brick structure in the central business district.

Freidenkers also settled the Texas hill country, establishing Utopian socialist communities at Sisterdale, Boerne, and Comfort. A *freidenker* memorial at Comfort became a local bone of contention. In August 1998 a fifteen-foot stone monument or cenotaph acknowledging the *freidenkers* as Comfort's founders was installed in the town park. The monument had the approval of civic and public authorities, complete with a marker furnished by the Texas Historical Commission. Outraged Christian fundamentalists forced the town's chamber of commerce and its heritage foundation to reverse their previous support. The cenotaph was removed from the town park by a private contractor in December 2000 and dumped a few miles outside Comfort. After an interval it was installed on private property in the town's historic district.

Gravesites of freethinkers include the grave of D. M. BENNETT in Brooklyn's Green Wood Cemetery. *Boston Investigator* founder and birth control activist Abner KNEELAND (see BIRTH CONTROL AND UNBELIEF) was buried on his Iowa farm; in 1881 his grave was moved to a cemetery in nearby Farmington, its current location. The grave of Frances WRIGHT in Cincinnati's Spring Grove Cemetery bears an impressive monument that was restored in 1997 by the Feminist Caucus of the American Humanist Association, the Freedom From Religion Foundation, and the Free Inquiry Group of Cincinnati and Northern Kentucky. The ashes of Moncure CONWAY are interred in Kensico Cemetery at Kensico, New York.

Visitable graves of British freethinkers include those of Richard CARLILE and Henry HETHERINGTON in Kensal Green Cemetery, London; Carlile's grave is ill marked. Highgate Cemetery, London, contains the graves of numerous freethinkers including George Jacob and Austin HOLYOAKE, William Kingdon CLIFFORD, and Charles WATTS, as well as the grave of Karl MARX. Charles BRADLAUGH and William Stewart ROSS (Saladin) lie in the Nonconformists' section of the Brookwood Necropolis southwest of London. Thomas H. HUXLEY is buried in Marylebone Cemetery, Finchley.

Perhaps the best-known London building associated with unbelief is Conway Hall in Red Lion Square. It was built in 1929 to replace the South Place Chapel, whose facade was preserved in its construction. A handsome bust of Bertrand RUSSELL adorns Red Lion Square, the publicly owned courtyard outside. Conway Hall remains home to the SOUTH PLACE ETHICAL SOCIETY and the headquarters of the NATIONAL SECULAR SOCIETY.

Several unmarked locations near Fleet Street have freethought associations. The west corner of Fleet Street with Bouverie Street was the location of Carlile's shop, where he printed the books and magazines that sparked his various arrests. Carlile and Robert TAYLOR lectured at the Rotunda, which stood on Blackfriars Road at the corner of Stamford Street. Johnson's Court, a small street running between Fleet Street and the Samuel Johnson house, was for many years the site of the RATIONALIST PRESS ASSOCIATION's offices. George W. FOOTE's Progressive Publishing Company, at which the *FREETHINKER* magazine was founded, stood at 28 Stonecutter Street, another tiny lane off of Fleet. All these sites are occupied by newer buildings.

Two London sites of freethinker imprisonments can be visited. Off of Holloway Road stands the Holloway Gaol, where Foote served a year for BLASPHEMY. The Giltspur Street Compter (jail) at the corner of Giltspur and Newgate streets, where Carlile served several years, has been demolished; the site is marked by a plaque.

A life-size statue of Bradlaugh stands in the public square in Northampton, which he long represented in Parliament.

Though much diminished, the historically significant LEICESTER SECULAR SOCIETY continues to occupy its own building at Humberstone Gate, Leicester. Most of the building is rented out to non-freethought tenants.

In Australia, Joseph SYMES's Hall of Science in Melbourne remains almost wholly intact; now called Brenan Hall, it is an annex of Saint Vincent's Hospital. Ironically its survival is due to Melbourne's early twentieth-century Roman Catholic archbishop, who acquired the building circa 1913 and incorporated it into the expanding hospital. In Sydney, the former Freethought Hall or Lyceum still stands, now housing law offices.

The New Zealand Association of Rationalists and Humanists continues to operate from Rationalist House at 64 Symonds Street in Auckland. The 1912 building, originally a doctor's residence and surgery, was acquired by the association in 1960. In 1997 the building was named a Heritage Site by the Auckland City Council. The nearby Symonds Street Cemetery contains the grave of Charles SOUTHWELL.

Also noteworthy are a statue of Giordano BRUNO in

Rome's Piazza del Flora, where he was burned at the stake in 1600; and a very large statue of David HUME (for some reason portrayed wearing a Greco-Roman toga) unveiled in Edinburgh, Scotland, in 1997.

The author acknowledges Gordon Stein's entry "Shrines and Monuments of Unbelief" in his 1985 Encyclopedia of Unbelief, *from which this entry was in part derived. Also gratefully acknowledged is the extraordinary assistance of Rod Bradford, Ken Burchell, Ray Dahlitz, Clinton Estell, Annie Laurie Gaylor, Jim Herrick, Carolyn Hutton, Nigel Sinnott, and Fred Whitehead.*

BIBLIOGRAPHY

Brandt, Patricia. "Organized Free Thought in Oregon: The Oregon State Secular Union." *Oregon Historical Quarterly*, Summer 1986.

Caperton, Thomas S. *Rogue! Being an Account of the Life and High Times of Stephen W. Dorsey.* Santa Fe: Museum of New Mexico Press, 1978.

Larson, Orvin. *American Infidel: Robert G. Ingersoll.* New York: Citadel, 1962.

Whitehead, Fred, and Verle Muhrer, eds. *Freethought on the American Frontier.* Amherst, NY: Prometheus Books, 1992.

TOM FLYNN

MOORE, CHARLES CHILTON (1837–1906), American atheist publisher. Charles Chilton Moore received his early education at small schools in Kentucky, and from tutors. Eventually he attended Bethany College in Virginia, where upon graduation he was ordained to the ministry by Alexander Campbell, founder of the Disciples of Christ sect. Moore then began a two-and-a-half-year itinerant ministry in the mountains of eastern Kentucky, finally returning home to his widowed mother.

He met William J. Hatch, a Confederate soldier who was a distant kinsman. Hatch was scholarly and skeptical about religion (see SKEPTICISM), so Moore proposed that they make a study of the evidences for and against Christianity, which they did for six weeks, ten or twelve hours a day. The intense study caused Moore to become gravely ill of a fever, bedridden, unable to walk or sleep. As a result of his studies, Moore lost his faith in the Old Testament, and resolved to preach only from the New Testament.

He accepted a pastorate at the Christian church in Versailles, Kentucky, but eventually had to resign when further study caused him to discard the New Testament as well. At this time Moore was a deist; he later became an agnostic and finally an atheist, which he considered to represent the most advanced thought of the age (see DEISM; AGNOSTICISM; ATHEISM). Moore worked on the farm for a while, and then at various jobs in mills and banks, and even sold coffee for a year and a half.

He became a newspaper reporter, but was repeatedly dismissed by editors for his outspoken views against liquor and religion.

One night while walking home from Lexington, Moore decided to start his own paper so that he could say just what he wanted to. Thus was born the *Blue Grass Blade*. Early issues focused largely on alcohol prohibition with some FREETHOUGHT material; later issues were more centered on freethought with some prohibition articles. Moore's first book (1890) was *The Rational View*, a scholarly refutation of the Bible and theism in general.

In 1899 Moore was indicted for sending obscene material through the mails because of articles on marriage published in the *Blade*. He was accused of promoting free-love, which he abhorred (see SEX RADICALISM AND UNBELIEF); after a farcical trial, he was sentenced to two years in the federal prison in Columbus, Ohio. The real and unspoken reason he had been prosecuted was his atheism. After hundreds of petitions were sent to President William McKinley, Moore was pardoned after serving only five months. He came home to a hero's welcome; more than five hundred persons greeted him. While in prison, Moore wrote *Behind the Bars: 31498*, (1899—"31498" was his prisoner number), which is largely autobiographical and rich in Kentucky history.

In 1903 Moore embarked on a trip to the so-called Holy Land, his goal being to write a detailed exposé of the locales at which Bible stories had supposedly occurred, from the spot on which Lot's wife purportedly still stood to Jesus's tomb and the site of his alleged ascension. Moore felt that Mark Twain had made some exaggerations in his best-selling *Innocents Abroad* and wished to set the record straight. Moore also had much to say concerning the Muslims then in control of all the Christian artifacts and sites. The result was his final book, *Dog Fennel in the Orient* (1903).

In the fall of 1905, Moore developed congestive heart failure, from which he suffered greatly, dying on February 7, 1906. Well over a thousand people attended his funeral, at which the prominent freethinkers Josephine K. HENRY and J. B. Wilson delivered addresses.

BIBLIOGRAPHY

Moore, Charles C. *Behind the Bars: 31498.* Lexington, KY: Blue Grass Printing, 1899.

———. *Dog Fennel in the Orient.* Lexington, KY: James E. Hughes, 1903.

———. *The Rational View.* Louisville, KY: Courier-Journal, 1890.

MICHAEL ADCOCK

MORALITY FROM A HUMANIST POSITION. John Stuart MILL had a deep understanding of morality, in particular the centrality to it of consequence, of happiness, and of (broadly speaking) "virtue." But he could not solve two basic problems. First, happiness cannot be the goal of moral action, because happiness is not always morally good: consider the successful confidence trickster. Second, the happiness of one individual is often incompatible with that of another; who should get the happiness? Mill acknowledged that pleasures can be graded as "higher" or "lower." But he provided no acceptable criterion for this evaluation; in the end, only total quantity counted in the utilitarian standard "the greatest amount of happiness altogether." This cannot be accepted for two reasons: first, there is no adequate basis for the quantification of happiness, or for its summation over many individuals; second, it allows the imposition of iniquitous suffering on one individual if sufficiently many benefit.

But Mill's basic idea was right: "Happiness is desirable, and the only thing desirable, as an end." Aristotle was looking in the same direction. He described *eudaimonia* as the "best, noblest, and most pleasant thing in the world." *Eudaimonia* was translated "happiness," now more usually "well-being." It is clear that the words *happiness*, *pleasure*, *satisfaction*, *well-being*, and *eudaimonia* point in various ways to the "good state." This is complex and ambiguous in human beings.

There are two problems. First, there is a fundamental ambiguity in the idea of "good": does it mean "good according to the person who enjoys it," or "good according to some external standard, such as morality"? No fundamental analysis of morality can simply assume an external standard; any standard must be justified. Thus, if "the good state" (for a person) is assumed as basic, it must be taken in the sense "good as self-evaluated." "The good state" in the sense "good as moral" requires further definition and justification. The second problem is that all the words that might be used here suffer pejorative overtones of superficiality or "mere hedonism." This is unfair, and corrosive of moral understanding. An individual's "happiness" may be critically dependent on the happiness of another person, and it may be guided by ideals and moral values. The concept is vital to us, but there is no "clean" term to express it.

The first of these problems can be resolved by stipulative definition: I use *happiness* to refer to whatever the individual feels as happiness. "Morally acceptable happiness" has a *moral* quality, whatever that is. Human good lies in *morally acceptable* happiness. As to the second, I just ask the reader to reject pejorative overtones.

Morality is the expression of concern for the good of other people. It is an amazing thing: How can it be that human beings find such odd ideas *important*? The only possible answer is that human beings have certain powers and propensities that led them to construct *ideas about* morality, and to feel the importance of these ideas. But these powers and propensities develop very differently in different communities. Has any community got "moral sensibility" right? I will show that there are

objective criteria defining moral sensibility; and that proper deployment of these powers and propensities will lead us to *true* moral sensibility.

What Is Morality? No explicit definition is possible. Morality is, rather, defined implicitly by the moral aspiration, which characterizes the ideal of moral action:

> The **Moral Aspiration**: That my actions should be guided by principles and supported by adequate understanding of the situation. The principles should express a concern for individuals that excludes no individual, and treats each fairly, insofar as this is possible in the situation. The criterion for the "fair" treatment of individuals should carry compelling importance. (This departs considerably from Rachels, but was inspired by him.)

My object is to pick out premises that are manifestly valid, and to construct a theory of morality that will affirm the principles of morality.

> *I here consider the morality of an action in abstraction from the morality of the agent in acting thus. Both are determined by the way things are, including the evaluations and agent-centered prerogatives of those involved. Neither is constrained by limitations to human knowledge.*

What Is Humanism? I here require only three key points.

Humanism claims: (1) The universe is naturalistic. (2) The principles of moral action derive from certain attributes (including evaluations) carried in human nature. (3) The importance of moral action derives from, on the one hand, the importance of individuals and of their happiness and suffering; and on the other, the significance of the human ability to respond meaningfully to this importance.

The universe is **naturalistic**: Values, purposes, and meanings derive only from evaluations by, and intentions of, natural beings.

A **natural being** is a being capable of consciousness and limited by a material body.

This definition of *naturalistic* does not limit value to things actually evaluated by a natural being: It includes values that "derive from" the evaluations of natural beings. If one thing is valuable, and there is something that protects or secures that thing, then the second thing acquires value from the value of the first, whether the original evaluator recognizes it or not.

All meaningful ideas of God see him as not limited by a material body, and they also see him as valuing us and our actions. Therefore, if the universe is naturalistic, then there is no meaningful "god." This premise also excludes an ontologically independent realm of values, such as the Platonic "the Good."

Human beings have a propensity to develop a moral sensibility, not because it gave our forebears selective advantage, but because evolution gave us certain attributes each of which confers selective advantage. These together, if developed properly with intellectual and emotional effort, will lead us to the beliefs, evaluations, and propensities that constitute moral sensibility.

Developing Moral Theory: The Basis. People have beliefs and evaluations, mental capacities and dispositions; I will refer to these collectively as their "attributes."

"Morality" is a meaningful idea for normal human beings only because they have certain attributes. These lead people to a concern for other people's happiness and a concern for fairness, and these attributes also lead people to develop understanding of how people feel happiness, and of the logical and practical difficulties in this. And further, normal human beings have a tendency to develop their concern for people according to their understanding. This much is obvious. The following argument develops these points. It seems to me obvious that the general achievement of happiness will be enhanced if the level of understanding, and the degree of concern, increase. Therefore, *very broadly speaking*, it would be a good thing to increase understanding and concern: it is *morally* good to do so. To turn this idea into a fundamental theory of morality requires some further very general premises, and in particular an assumption concerning the sources of evaluation in the universe.

My analysis will follow an idealized moralist who is engaged in developing moral theory. I assign her the female gender, and give her the proper name **Moralist**. At the start of her theorizing she has the moral aspiration, and she has the attributes, *to perfection*, which will enable her to understand the facts and evaluations which are relevant, and to draw valid inferences. So the judgments she will develop will fulfill the moral aspiration. They will be valid moral judgments. Further, Moralist has the evaluations implicit in the above, and no other evaluations. Unlike actual human beings, she has no personal values. Therefore her evaluations will express evaluations that are purely moral. This theoretical "perfect person" is an abstract aid to inquiry, rather like the physicist's idealized "frictionless pulley," or the Carnot Cycle. She does not exist in the real world.

The development of Moralist's theory expresses the development of her moral understanding. First she discovers the fundamental moral principles; then she applies them to particular situations. The fundamental principles depend on how things are in certain very general respects: in particular, the character of human nature, and the reality or otherwise of a god. We ordinary human beings can reproduce Moralist's derivation of the fundamental principles. We cannot follow her analysis of particular situations; but her theory illuminates practical morality for us, and we can apply it, subject to our limitations.

The structure of Moralist's theorizing is determined by the fact that the principles of morality are defined by conditions they must fulfill, stated by the moral aspiration, and not defined in any explicit sense. Moralist must find an explicit identification. Her analysis may be compared with an algebraist finding a number defined by an equation that must be solved. The algebraist uses x to represent the unknown number that fulfills the equation. Moralist uses "moral concern" as her unknown:

Moral concern: A concern that values the happiness and suffering of every individual as important, guided by principles of action that fulfill the criteria of the moral aspiration.

The algebraist and Moralist use these terms (x and *moral concern*) without knowing what they refer to. At the end of their analyses, the algebraist will have identified the number that fulfils the equation and Moralist the principles of action that satisfy the moral aspiration.

The critical point about Moral Concern is that it includes the principles of action that satisfy the Moral Aspiration. But Moralist introduces it as a hypothesis, without the principles of action being specified. She must identify them.

The first step in Moralist's analysis is to recognize that there are certain attributes any individual must have if those of his or her enterprises which do not involve moral considerations are to be effective:

The **Basic Attributes** are those of the mental attributes established in the species nature of human beings that an individual must have if he or she is to achieve any of his or her desires that do not involve moral considerations.

It is not relevant for me to list the Basic Attributes, but these are clearly essential:

The **Basic Attributes** include: (a) a drive to achieve knowledge; (b) a capacity to interact with reality, and to describe aspects of it and to recognize the significance of those aspects which are relevant to the fulfillment of one's desires (as I am here assuming humanism, Moralist will not discover any nonnaturalistic reality); (c) a capacity for understanding people's feelings (sympathy is here excluded); (d) a capacity to understand general principles; (e) a capacity to draw inferences from factual and evaluative statements; and (f) a drive to achieve coherence between one's knowledge, one's values, and one's life.

Each of these is necessary if one is to be successful in enterprises involving other people. But they are not sufficient to realize morality. A *concern* for other people's feelings is also essential. An understanding of another person may equally be used to exploit them and to benefit them. Normal human beings are born with a propensity to develop realizations of the basic attributes: Attributes (a) and (f) drive the development of human understanding and values, while (b), (c), and (d) guide it. Attributes (a) to (e) give knowledge. Attribute (f) leads one to internalize one's cognitive understanding of moral values. Internalization is critical; it is lacking in burglars. Burglars may know that theft is wrong, but they have not internalized the evaluation. Moralist therefore has a double development—of knowledge and of evaluations "internalized."

Ordinary people develop their beliefs and evaluations informally; often they "feel" things, and often they introduce false premises and invalid inferences. Thus they generate their personal "moral" values. Moralist is an ideal: She possesses the basic attributes to perfection, and also a concern for people, not merely understanding. Further, as she is a theoretical concept, I can give her the capacity to acquire knowledge of the particular facts and evaluations relevant to a particular situation. Thus her evaluations truly are *moral* evaluations, general and particular.

Developing Moral Theory: Argument. *The argument is based on five moves, which introduce matters of moral and factual substance.* These give the premises for Moralist's argument. She numbers conclusions that express knowledge gained; and she adds a star to conclusions, which express her evaluations, for example, (5*).

Moralist first considers moral sensibility. Its definition is:

Moral Sensibility: Those attributes that lead a person to act morally.

Moralist must identify the attributes that constitute moral sensibility. The concept may be taken in two ways: referring to the attributes that a normal human being has, well or ill developed, which lead him or her to behave more or less morally; and referring to the ideal.

Moralist defines these as *Ideal Moral Sensibility* and *Personal Moral Sensibility*, respectively.

The first move: Moralist identifies Ideal Moral Sensibility in terms of moral concern (as yet unidentified) and the basic attributes.

Moralist first defines a concept that brings together the basic attributes and concern. This is a theoretical concept that applies only to ideal individuals who have the power to acquire perfect knowledge of particular facts and evaluations.

The *Perfected X Attributes*: (1) moral concern; (2) the basic attributes extended by the ability to acquire perfect knowledge of particular facts and of the evaluations made by ordinary individuals; and (3) attributes this ideal individual develops by his application of (1) and (2). This process also leads to the rejection of some attributes.

"X" reminds us that the concept carries moral concern, as yet unidentified.

An action that satisfies moral concern is a moral action. Then (1) below *follows tautologically from* these definitions.

(1): An individual with the perfected X attributes would know the facts appropriate to his or her situation, and evaluate them morally. Basic attribute (f) would then lead him or her to act morally.

The attributes that constitute the perfected X attributes constitute the attributes that constitute perfect moral sensibility. Because the latter attributes are defined as the attributes which lead an individual to act morally; and (1) establishes that possession of the former attributes would lead an individual to act thus.

(2): The perfected X attributes constitute *Ideal Moral Sensibility*.

The second move: Moralist defines Personal Moral Sensibility.

Ordinary human beings are endowed with the Basic Attributes, and also an unsophisticated concern for other people, as against Moral Concern. All too often, people develop their basic attributes with improper assumptions and muddled thinking. But people usually learn some sort of "personal moral sensibility" Moralist therefore establishes a weaker form of (1).

(3): Insofar as the evaluations and beliefs of an individual are *compatible with* Ideal Moral Sensibility perfectly developed for his or her situation, and include feeling the importance of satisfaction and suffering, and no other attributes cancel them, he or she will *tend to* act morally.

(4): Insofar as an individual's attributes fulfill the conditions specified in (3), those of them that contribute to this constitute his *Personal Moral Sensibility*. I will omit "personal" where the context makes the qualification clear.

The third move: Moralist derives an evaluation. She first derives a cognitive conclusion from (3) and (4), using an implication of the definition of a "morally good" action: "It is morally good for a person to have attributes that lead him or her to moral action."

(5): It is morally good that an individual should have well-developed personal moral sensibility.

Such an individual will be more likely to act morally. Moralist's basic attribute (f) then leads her to accept this evaluation into her own evaluations:

(5*): It is good [i.e., moralist feels it to be good] that an individual should have well-developed personal moral sensibility.

(5*) suggests that it would be good to enhance the development of an individual's moral sensibility; but this does not follow. Such an action would have good consequences for other individuals; but would it be *fair* to the individual who suffers education? The Moral Aspiration requires that discrimination be justified by a *fair* criterion. A standard for discrimination is *fair* if and only if:

(1) the necessary attributes can be acquired by a normal individual; (2) the standard is of adequate significance; (3) it can be recognized as such by normal individuals; and (4) it is impartial between individuals. Further, the criteria must be applied with sensitivity to human limitations.

The fourth move: Moralist recognizes that the attributes that constitute moral sensibility have the necessary significance to be the standard for *fairness*:

(6*): The human capacity to develop an effective personal moral sensibility can enable the general enhancement of human and animal flourishing. It therefore has an all-inclusive importance. These attributes when developed are the supreme expression of our humanity.

Therefore:

The degree of development of an individual's moral Sensibility, compared against ideal moral sensibility, is a ***morally fair*** criterion for discrimination in respect to him because: (1) Normal human beings can develop a degree of moral sensibility; (2) (6*) establishes the all-inclusive importance of moral sensibility as a human attribute; (3) normal human beings are born with a propensity to recognize its special importance; and (3) the ideal of moral sensibility does not involve the particularities of any individual.

The morality of an action depends on its outcome. Moralist can now define two categories of morally acceptable outcome. There are two ways in which one may benefit a group of individuals: by giving satisfaction to one of them, without damaging any of the others; by making one individual a better person (without being unfair to him or her), for then he or she will be more likely to benefit the others. (I simplify by supposing that only one individual is directly affected.) These alternative outcomes may be expressed more accurately:

(7*): If an individual's having a certain satisfaction is not implicated in prejudice to the moral sensibility of any individual (the given individual or any other), then it is in itself good.

(8*): If enhancing the moral sensibility of an individual does not involve denying him or her satisfaction disproportionate to the inadequacy of his or her moral sensibility, then it is in itself good.

Moral Satisfaction: A satisfaction that fulfills (7*).

Each of these outcomes expresses concern for members of the group. Each benefits one or more of the group without disbenefiting the others unfairly (insofar as the situation allows): each therefore is in itself good. But each excludes the other individuals, giving them no benefit. Fair application of both over time would not exclude any.

Moralist now poses the question: *Are (7*) and (8*), together, adequate?*

The fifth move: Humanism: The Sufficiency of the Natural World. *Moralist* employs a premise of the life stance within which the moral theory lives. In this article, humanism is assumed and Moralist therefore accepts that the universe is naturalistic. Therefore, moral evaluations derive from the evaluations and the attributes of natural beings, they are discovered by our ordinary faculties, and there is no God to give us knowledge or practical support. Therefore human beings do not require a specific faculty to discover moral evaluations. Further, it seems that moral sensibility is the only human attribute of such importance that achieving its enhancement or preventing its prejudice justifies discrimination. Finally, it is generally accepted that no individual human being or collection of human beings has the authority to establish moral evaluations. Therefore:

(9): (a) The Basic Attributes ideally strengthened, with a concern for all individuals, are sufficient for developing the principles of action for guiding moral judgments. **(b)** (7*) and (8*) are valid moral principles; for moral sensibility is the only ground which is adequate for rejecting an individual's happiness. **(c)** There are no further fundamental moral principles; for there are no other attributes independent of moral sensibility that could be relevant.

Therefore:

(10): (7*) and (8*) are the ***fundamental principles of morality***. They constitute the evaluative principles called for by the moral aspiration.

Moral concern can now be set out explicitly in terms of (7*) and (8*).

Moral concern: A concern which values the happiness and suffering of every individual as important, guided by (7*) and (8*).

Moral sensibility: Moral concern supported by the Basic Attributes developed for the particular situation.

(7*) and (8*) are defined without appeal to any undefined moral concept, for moral sensibility is defined in nonmoral terms, as above. These principles require one to evaluate an outcome according to the way it has affected the moral sensibilities of the individuals affected: An individual's moral sensibility is enhanced or prejudiced by enhancing or prejudicing any of his basic attributes, or his feeling for the importance of the happiness and suffering of individuals, or his concern for (7*) and (8*).

The recurrence of (7*) and (8*) expresses the fact that moral concern calls on one to follow out the consequences of one's actions, reiterating the same tests at each point, for each individual affected. The iteration of moral sensibility establishes that one must consider the impact of one's action on the moral sensibility of each of the individuals affected in the sequence of consequences, repeating the same tests. It does not allow that moral sensibility may involve some further concepts. Subject to the humanist claims, there are no concepts independent of the above that could be relevant to a fundamental theory of morality.

Moralist does not find criteria to decide which of two acceptable outcomes to seek, or which of two unacceptable outcomes; nor does she find criteria for "proportionate" in (8*). Further, actions normally lead to a number of outcomes, and Moralist does not find criteria to balance the significance of different outcomes. I do not believe there are general objective criteria for these decisions. I feel, however, that John Rawls's "veil of ignorance" provides a serviceable substitute.

Moral action will lead to an outcome that fulfills (7*) or (8*) and avoids bad outcomes, insofar as such an outcome can be achieved in the circumstances.

It is particularly appropriate to enhance one's own moral sensibility. People can *enjoy* this. People also require their personal values and ideals.

Application. Moralist derives the fundamental principles of morality without needing ideal knowledge, so we can follow her. Indeed, we have just done so.

We cannot follow Moralist in analyzing the particularity of actual situations. Working out likely consequences for moral decisions is most difficult. But real situations demand action, and we must do the best we can, in morality

as elsewhere. It is doubtful if consequences are determinate beyond a limited range. Moral argument beyond this point becomes absurd, for there is nothing there!

Few people think in terms of fundamentals. They use maxims such as "Do not lie." But fundamental principles are important, because principles justify and limit the maxims, and they may open unexpected possibilities. Whether abortion is murder or not depends on one's ontological assumptions. If a hearer accepts a lie, his or her actions are likely to turn out badly; if the hearer does not, his or her sense of reciprocity and trust are damaged. Either way, the lie prejudices his or her ability to act well. Thus lying is morally wrong, *unless* by lying one achieves a greater outcome, like hiding a Jew from the Gestapo.

The analysis shows why morality is authoritative: Moral sensibility is the supreme expression of our humanity, because it allows us to enhance the achievement of happiness in the world. This carries duty and motivation: one debases one's humanity by lying; unless by lying one achieves a greater outcome.

All conscious beings have rights, because they enjoy and suffer. Only beings with moral sensibility have responsibilities. We are responsible for lions; lions are not responsible for us.

BIBLIOGRAPHY

Kukathas, Chandran, and Philip Pettit. *Rawls: A Theory of Justice*. Cambridge: Polity, 1990.

Mill, John Stuart. *Utilitarianism*. Edited by Mary Warnock. Glasgow: Fontana, 1962.

Rachels, James. *The Elements of Moral Philosophy*. 2nd ed. New York: McGraw-Hill, 1993.

Sen, Amartya, and Bernard Williams, eds. *Utilitarianism and Beyond*. Cambridge: Cambridge University Press, 1982.

HARRY STOPES-ROE

MULTATULI (Eduard Douwes Dekker; 1820–1887), Dutch polemic novelist, author, and freethinker. Eduard Douwes Dekker was born on March 2, 1820, in Amsterdam. He died on February 19, 1887, in Germany. Dekker is one of the most important writers—if not the most important—the Netherlands has produced. He is known under the pseudonym Multatuli ("I suffered greatly").

He grew up in a middle-class family marked by the liberal tolerance of his Mennonite father, a ship captain. In secondary school he underachieved, failing his final exams. In 1838 he boarded his father's ship for the Dutch East Indies, seeking work in the colonial civil service. He secured a position in Natal (Sumatra) and began to rise through the ranks.

In 1846 he married Baroness Everdine (Tine) van Wijnbergen. Now holding a post in Mid-Java, he developed an abiding concern about the situation of the natives. By 1851 Dekker's letters to friends in Holland suggest that he had moved from Christianity to AGNOSTI-CISM or ATHEISM.

By 1855 Dekker was assistant commissioner of Lebak, Western Java. He discovered that the native governor was corrupt and harshly exploiting the native population. Dekker accused the governor and his son-in-law of bribery and exploitation. Far from supporting Dekker, his superiors discharged him.

What next? Dekker could seek another civil service position, or he could write about colonial abuses in the Indies. He chose the latter. In Brussels, in a single month near the end of 1859, he wrote *Max Havelaar*, a fierce and satirical critique of the colonial system, under the pseudonym Multatuli. Multatuli sent copies of the manuscript to several acquaintances, some of whom promised him lucrative jobs if he would leave the novel unpublished; he refused because of his "passion for truth." *Max Havelaar* appeared in 1860. In its polemics and stylistic vigor it was unprecedented, creating an immediate sensation in Dutch letters, life, and politics.

Multatuli continued to write, again criticizing colonial abuses, arguing for womens' rights, and championing the working class. But his stance was neoliberal, and he never sympathized with Karl MARX or the socialist parties.

Through his brother Jan he made contact with the Dutch freethinkers society De Dageraad (Dawn). In its periodical he published "Het Gebed van den Onwetende" (Prayer of the Ignorant) in March 1861, inspiring generations of Dutch agnostics and atheists. Multatuli felt kinship with the freethinkers and their distaste for dogmatic thinking, Christian dogmatic thinking in particular. For the rest of his life Multatuli remained associated with De Dageraad.

In 1866 Multatuli went to Germany, where he wrote for Dutch journals and edited books. *Max Havelaar*, the semiautobiographical *Woutertje Pieterse*, and the play *De Vorstenschool* (Monarch's School) are his most admired writings.

Multatuli produced little during his final decade because of failing health. Upon his death in 1887 he was the first Dutchman to be cremated.

BIBLIOGRAPHY

Ett, Henri A. *De beteekenis van Multatuli voor onzen tijd* [The Meaning of Multatuli for Our Time]. Amsterdam: Breughel, 1947.

Maas, Nop. *Multatuli voor iedereen (maar niemand voor Multatuli)* [Everyman's Multatuli, but No One for Multatuli]. Nijmegen: Vantilt, 2000.

Meulen, Dik van der. *Multatuli. Leven en werk van Eduard Douwes Dekker* [Multatuli, Life and Work of Eduard Douwes Dekker]. Nijmegen: Sun, 2002.

Multatuli. *Volledige Werken* [Complete Works]. 25 vols. Amsterdam: Van Oorschot, 1950–95.

Spigt, P. *Keurig in de kontramine. Over Multatuli* [Exquisitely Argumentative: On Multatuli]. Amsterdam: Athenaeum-Polak & Van Gennep, 1975.

Straten, Hans van. *Multatuli. Van blanke radja tot bedelman: een schrijversleven* [Multatuli, from *White Raja* to *Beggarman*: A Writer's Life]. Amsterdam: Lubberhuizen, 1995.

Veer, Paul van 't. *Het leven van Multatuli* [Multatuli's Life]. Amsterdam: Arbeiderspers, 1979.

JO NABUURS

MURRAY, JON GARTH. See O'HAIR, MADALYN MURRAY.

NAGEL, ERNEST (1901–1985), American philosopher. Ernest Nagel was born on November 16, 1901, in Bohemia in the Austro-Hungarian Empire (now in the Czech Republic). He emigrated with his family to the United States in 1911, becoming an American citizen in 1919. He studied with Morris R. Cohen at the City College of New York, receiving a BS in 1923. Nagel then received his MA in 1925 and PhD in philosophy in 1930 from Columbia University, where his teachers included John DEWEY. Nagel was professor of philosophy at Columbia from 1931 until 1970; in 1955 his title became John Dewey Professor of Philosophy. He was president of the American Philosophical Association Eastern Division, and elected to the National Academy of Sciences. Nagel died on September 20, 1985, in New York City.

Nagel made major contributions to understanding the methodology of natural and social science, formal logic, and philosophy of logic and mathematics. He applied his views to problems such as realism versus idealism, free will versus DETERMINISM, and mechanism versus teleology. His admiration for Charles Peirce's logic of science, Dewey's atheistic NATURALISM (see also ATHEISM; HUMANISM), and the logical positivists' vision of the unity of science (see LOGICAL POSITIVISM) is central to several of his major writings. For a generation Nagel was the most prominent American philosopher of science and logic, and for several decades he was among the foremost representatives of naturalism.

With Cohen, Nagel wrote *Introduction to Logic and Scientific Method* (1934), an early and influential logic textbook notable for including symbolic deductive logic and inductive logic. Like Cohen, Nagel initially was a logical realist who held that logical axioms are a priori necessities which correspond to universal and unchanging structures of the world. By the mid-1940s Nagel had been converted by Dewey and logical positivism to the view that logical principles are instrumental rules of inference having no direct ontological implications. In essays such as "Logic without Ontology" (1944) and "Sovereign Reason" (1947) and in two books, *Sovereign Reason* (1954) and *Logic without Metaphysics* (1956), Nagel explored the pragmatist alternative of justifying logical principles by science itself. If the rules of inference used by science cannot be independently justified by pure reason or metaphysics, they can still be justified by the empirical progress of scientific explanation. Nagel soon followed out a consequence of this scientific basis for logic, concluding that logical principles are revisable in the course of scientific progress and hence are more like a posteriori propositions.

Nagel's reunification of empiricism with naturalism, long delayed by empiricism's capture by subjective idealism, permitted him to reformulate naturalism in a striking way. By the early 1950s C. I. Lewis had already taken a pragmatic view of supposedly a priori principles, and W. V. Quine had rejected the analytic-synthetic dichotomy, but at that time both philosophers still believed that phenomenalism was a viable option. It was Nagel who forged ahead with a Deweyan confidence in scientific method in his "Naturalism Reconsidered" (1955), defining naturalism as a philosophy that declares reality as broad as the potential reach of scientific evidence and theory.

Nagel's greatest work, *The Structure of Science* (1961), attempts to describe the scientific methodology of hypothesis formulation and testing, often labeled the "deductive-nomological model," that must be common to every natural and social science. *The Structure of Science* also proposes how to accomplish the "reduction" of the entities and laws of one science to those of another by using "bridge laws." Although reductive materialists (like the later Quine) have confidently taken physics as definitive of reality, expecting that all other sciences will be reduced to physics, Nagel disavowed this restricted sort of naturalism. Naturalism should only require a common scientific methodology and not any specific results, and should accept the diverse plurality of contingent natural things without seeking any ultimate rational unity behind nature.

Nagel only sought a "contextual naturalism." This broad naturalism, which remains a widely attractive option in Anglo-American philosophy, would be strong enough to obstruct dualism and supernaturalism, yet flexible enough to permit the many interconnected empirical sciences to postulate explanatory natural processes without worrying whether they can be "reduced" to the terms of physics. The liberty of the sciences is not unlimited, however. Naturalism is violated whenever explanations appeal to powers or forces other than the properties of objects in space-time and their causally deterministic relations. For the sciences of biology and psychology, Nagel was especially concerned to forbid dangerous routes away from naturalism. In biology, he argued that teleological and functional explanations can be replaced by causal explanations; see *Teleology Revisited and Other Essays* (1979). In psychology, he argued that key mental properties (though not necessarily all) can be reduced to physical properties of the brain.

In accord with his naturalism, Nagel believed that most, if not all, religious beliefs are unwarranted and unnecessary. In "Philosophical Concepts of Atheism" (1976), Nagel held that empirical science will explain any alleged religious phenomena and never accept disembodied spirits.

BIBLIOGRAPHY

Nagel, Ernest. *Logic without Metaphysics.* New York: Free Press, 1956.

———. "Philosophical Concepts of Atheism." In *Critiques of God*, edited by Peter Angeles. Amherst, NY: Prometheus Books, 1976.

———. *Sovereign Reason.* New York: Free Press, 1954.

———. *The Structure of Science: Problems in the Logic of Scientific Explanation.* New York: Harcourt, Brace & World, 1961.

———. *Teleology Revisited and Other Essays in the Philosophy and History of Science.* New York: Columbia University Press, 1979.

Nagel, Ernest, and Morris R. Cohen. *Introduction to Logic and Scientific Method.* New York: Harcourt, Brace, 1934.

JOHN R. SHOOK

NANSEN, FRIDTJOF (1861–1930), Norwegian scientist, explorer, diplomat, and author. Fridtjof Nansen was a zoologist who worked at the Bergen Museum and wrote scientific works including "The Structure and Combination of the Histological Elements of the Central Nervous System" (1827) and "A Protandric Hermaphrodite (*Myxine glutinosa*) among the Vertebrates" (1888). In 1895 Nansen explored the northernmost point at the North Pole aboard the research vessel *Fram* and wrote another book describing the adventure: Fram *across the Polar Sea* (1897).

At the end of World War I, Nansen was commissioned by the League of Nations to repatriate five hundred thousand prisoners and to assist the Red Cross in Russia. He gave a special passport—"Nansen's pass"—to thousands of refugees without nationality. In 1922 he received the Nobel Prize for Peace.

In matters of religion, Nansen was a humanist: "The religion of one age is, as a rule, the literary entertainment of the next," he once declared. Nansen maintained that whatever the citizens' religious views might be, everyone should, if possible, be given sound ethical ideas fitted to make him or her a useful and skillful member of the community—such ethical views necessarily being based on a scientific outlook.

JOSÉ MANUEL FERNÁNDEZ SANTANA

NATIONAL LIBERAL LEAGUE. An American FREETHOUGHT organization whose brief career encapsulates many of the ongoing challenges faced by such groups, the National Liberal League was organized by a group of secularists (see SECULARISM) who met in the Concert Hall, Chestnut Street, Philadelphia, on July 1–4, 1876. The group adopted the Nine Demands of Liberalism, which were composed by the Unitarian Francis Ellingwood ABBOT in 1872. Taken collectively, the Nine Demands articulated a comprehensive separation of church and state and served for many years as a clarion call for American secularists.

The first annual congress of the league met at Rochester, New York, on October 26, 1877, and heard Henry Ward Beecher deliver what would become a famous sermon repudiating the doctrine of hell. Abbot served as the league's first president and restricted its activities to advocacy of the Nine Demands, which he interpreted relatively narrowly. Under Abbot, the league was reluctant to associate itself openly with freethought or to condemn all of the Comstock laws, a series of punitive regulations on moral issues whose noisiest champion was Anthony COMSTOCK, the longtime secretary of the New York Society for the Suppression of Vice. The league was vocal in its support of abolition and, to a lesser extent, women's rights (see WOMAN SUFFRAGE MOVEMENT AND UNBELIEF).

Its careful approach notwithstanding, the league was castigated by the religious press and caricatured as a nest of unbelievers and immoralists. The stridency of this opposition tended to encourage the very process of radicalization that Abbot was anxious to avoid. Within three years the league adopted a more radical secular stance, condemning the Comstock laws and sending D. M. BENNETT, editor of THE TRUTH SEEKER, as its delegate to the World Freethinkers' Congress in Brussels in August 1880. The vote against the Comstock laws was strongly opposed by Robert Green INGERSOLL, who thought the Comstock laws merited amendment rather than abolition. Ingersoll withdrew from active support of the organization after this. The league went on to gather between fifty and seventy thousand signatures calling for the repeal of the Comstock laws. Congress ignored the petition.

By 1885 it was clear that the league was not going to attract the middle ground. If much of its leadership consisted of Unitarians with patrician leanings, many of its members were German Americans with a strong tradition of freethought tinged with radical politics. The question of labor relations proved as divisive as the tensions between the materialist and the spiritualist wings of the movement (see LABOR MOVEMENT AND UNBELIEF). At the league's congress of October 9–11, 1885, in Cleveland, the National Liberal League renamed itself the AMERICAN SECULAR UNION. Ingersoll returned to become president, and the freethinking journalist Samuel Porter PUTNAM was named secretary. A rump group opposed to the name change lingered on until the turn of the twentieth century, but the initiative now lay with the American Secular Union.

In 1945 another attempt was made to form an organization called the National Liberal League under the presidency of the veteran Canadian freethinker Marshall GAUVIN. The reformed group never achieved the profile needed to attract significant funding and was weakened by factional dissension. It lasted about fifteen years.

BIBLIOGRAPHY

Jacoby, Susan. *Freethinkers: A History of American Secularism*. New York: Metropolitan, 2004.
Macdonald, George E. *Fifty Years of Freethought*. New York: Truth Seeker Company, 1972.
Putnam, Samuel P. *Four Hundred Years of Freethought*. New York: Truth Seeker Company, 1894.
Rinaldo, Peter. *Atheists, Agnostics, and Deists in America: A Brief History*. New York: DorPete, 2000.

BILL COOKE

NATIONAL REFORMER, THE. The *National Reformer* was the major atheist paper during the second half of the nineteenth century in Britain. It was closely associated with Charles BRADLAUGH and the NATIONAL SECULAR SOCIETY (NSS).

A group of secularists in the north of England founded a company to establish a secularist paper in February 1860. The first issue came out in April 1860 as a demifolio of eight pages priced at two pence. The coeditors were the young Bradlaugh and Joseph Barker, a former Methodist preacher and Chartist. Success led to weekly publication and a circulation of over five thousand after the first year. Barker left in 1861 after a disagreement with Bradlaugh over the publication of discussions of neo-Malthusianism (birth control: see BIRTH CONTROL AND UNBELIEF).

George Jacob HOLYOAKE became a chief contributor and John WATTS the subeditor. At a time of illness for Bradlaugh, John Watts took over and Charles WATTS became subeditor; John Watts subsequently died of consumption. The paper declined during this interregnum before Bradlaugh resumed the editorship in 1866, the year in which the NSS was founded with him as the first president. Bradlaugh edited the *National Reformer* until his death in 1891. It chronicled his radical FREETHOUGHT and political career, taking much of his energy and being "a sort of personal diary." John M. ROBERTSON took over from Bradlaugh and revived the paper for a while, but publication was discontinued for economic reasons in 1893.

Important contributors over the years included the economist and philosopher J. H. Levy; Edward Bibbins AVELING, a scientist with a particular interest in Darwin's ideas; and Bradlaugh protégée Annie BESANT, who became coeditor in 1881. There was much discussion as to what degree the *National Reformer* should be a freethought paper that debated religion or a general political journal. Bradlaugh wrote that it should be "an *avant-courier* on political, social and sociological questions, but that it should never deal with one to the exclusion of others."

The peak of the *National Reformer*'s success was in the early 1880s, the time of Bradlaugh's struggle to enter Parliament. The critique of religion was always important and done on a more philosophical and counter-theological level than the *Freethinker* with its reliance on biblical arguments. In its early years the Reform Bill to enlarge the suffrage for parliamentary elections, and republicanism to abolish the monarchy, were hotly debated. Later in the century Home Rule, to give self-rule to Ireland, and independence for India became important issues to Liberals such as Bradlaugh. Literature was not neglected; to the *National Reformer* belongs the honor of being first to publish James Thomson's "The City of Dreadful Night" (see ENGLISH LITERATURE, UNBELIEF IN). Also noteworthy is a perceptive article by G. W. FOOTE on William Blake.

A vigorous debate on socialism versus liberalism occupied the paper's columns—this issue divided Bradlaugh and Besant. The readership was largely working class until the later part of the century, when J. M. Robertson lamented the dumbing-down from the improving self-education of the Mutual Improvement Society to the light entertainment of the music halls. The heavy seriousness of the paper is a demonstration of the diligence and thoughtfulness of the self-taught free-thinker of the time.

BIBLIOGRAPHY

Herrick, Jim. *Against the Faith*. London: Glover & Blair, 1985.

Royle, Edward. *Radicals, Secularists and Republicans: Popular Freethought in Britain, 1860–1915*. Manchester, UK: Manchester University Press, 1980.

JIM HERRICK

NATIONAL SECULAR SOCIETY. Founded in 1866, the National Secular Society (NSS) became the major organization campaigning for secularism in England in the second half of the nineteenth century. Its principles assert that this is the only life we have, and that we should work for its improvement. Morality, it is claimed, is social in origin, and secularists call for the complete separation of church and state. There is an overriding ambition to develop the freedom and dignity of humankind.

The coinage of SECULARISM came from G. J. HOLYOAKE, and the earliest secularist groups around the country developed out of "progressive" Owenite groups (see OWEN, ROBERT). Holyoake thought that ATHEISM came across as narrow and bigoted, and wanted to add affirmative aims. The failure of the Chartist movement left radical campaigners in disarray. By the 1860s there

was a climate of greater radical action. Charles BRADLAUGH and Charles WATTS moved to create a national secular movement in 1866. Bradlaugh became the first president and Watts the first secretary of the NSS. Though it was primarily an organization for individuals, secularist groups and their members round the country also affiliated with it.

There was early success, but the impetus was not maintained. Ill health and political activities forced Bradlaugh to withdraw, leaving the society inactive in 1872. There was also some criticism of Bradlaugh's authoritarian style and his vigorous promotion of Annie BESANT as a secularist leader.

Bradlaugh's Struggle. In 1877 Bradlaugh and Besant were brought to trial for publishing *The Fruits of Philosophy*, a birth control booklet by the American doctor Charles KNOWLTON (see BIRTH CONTROL AND UNBELIEF). Besant and Bradlaugh were found guilty and sentenced to prison, but acquitted on appeal. This case caused division within the NSS, birth control being controversial even among secularists. A breakaway group led by Charles Watts became the British Secular Union. But there was inadequate support for two national secular groups, and the British Secular Union petered out.

The NSS became very concerned with Bradlaugh's struggle to enter Parliament. He was elected for Northampton in 1880 and was not allowed to take his seat because he could not be sworn in. Asked to swear on the Bible, Bradlaugh said this would have no meaning for him as an atheist. He asked to affirm rather than swear his oath of office, but was refused. It took six years of struggle until a new Parliament finally allowed him in. During this struggle secularism became a recognized social force: this period marked the peak of the society's action and influence. It was claimed that the NSS had six thousand members, including affiliated supporters. Secularist ideals were discussed in the national press and public debates.

In 1890 Bradlaugh resigned as president due to overwork and poor health. G. W. FOOTE took over, but the society had by now passed its peak. Individual membership declined from a peak of 3,792 in 1884 to 735 in 1900. Foote stated that the heroic period of freethought in England had come to an end. The development among young radicals of support for socialism (see SOCIALISM AND UNBELIEF), to which secularists were neutral or in some cases unsympathetic, lessened the remaining secularists' impact. Foote remained as NSS president, combining it with his long-standing role as editor of the *Freethinker* until his death in 1915. Agitation about the BLASPHEMY law, secular education, and the right to leave bequests to secular organizations were then among the NSS's principal concerns.

Chapman Cohen's Role. Chapman COHEN took over from Foote as editor of the *Freethinker* and president of the NSS, holding the former role until 1951 and the latter until 1949. He was a tireless lecturer and prolific writer, particularly good at presenting philosophical ideas to the general public.

Two prominent presidents in the second half of the twentieth century were David Tribe and Barbara Smoker. During their terms the NSS shifted to more aggressive use of the media to gain publicity, for example, pressing complaints that the British Broadcasting Company was biased in favor of religion. The reforms of the 1960s in areas such as abortion, divorce, and homosexuality were supported, especially in the face of clerical opposition to those reforms. Under NSS executive director Keith Porteous Wood there was emphasis on parliamentary and legal issues together with an increased presence in the media. New areas of importance included the expansion of faith (denominational) schools and the increasing impact of religions other than Christianity. By the beginning of the twenty-first century, the NSS had experienced a revival of membership and activity.

BIBLIOGRAPHY

Herrick, Jim. *Vision and Realism: A Hundred Years of the Freethinker.* London: G. W. Foote, 1982.
Royle, Edward. *Radicals, Secularists and Republicans: Popular Freethought in Britain, 1866–1915.* Manchester, UK: Manchester University Press, 1980.
Tribe, David. *100 Years of Freethought.* London: Elek, 1967.

JIM HERRICK

NATURALISM. Introduction. In its most familiar and general meaning, *naturalism* is the view that only natural entities and processes exist. Thus, naturalists repudiate all supernatural entities, powers, spirits, and occult forces such as ghosts, gods, devils, and demons. Let us call such a view ontological naturalism. Ontological naturalism can be contrasted with ethical naturalism, the view that ethical properties are either reducible to natural properties or dependent on them; epistemological naturalism, the view that epistemology is either a branch of psychology or is committed to no nonnatural properties; and methodological naturalism, the view that for the purposes of science, supernatural entities should not be assumed to exist. Because of space limitations, only ontological naturalism and methodological naturalism will be discussed here.

Characterizing Ontological Naturalism. *The Scientifically Explicable Account.* One standard approach to ontological naturalism is to characterize it in terms of what is in principle scientifically explicable. However, one problem with the thesis that the only entities that exist are those that are in principle explicable by science—let us call this the scientifically explicable account (SEA)—is that it is uncertain what will be explicable scientifically in the future. Phenomena that are now unexplained by science may be explained in the next several hundred years.

How serious a problem is this for SEA? Although it does not mean that SEA is useless as a test of the natural, it does mean that one must know how to use it. For if phenomenon P is not explainable at time t, it does not follow that P is not natural, since at time $t + 1$, P might be explainable. One will have to make a judgment based on the available evidence as to how likely it will be that P will become explainable in the future. Sometimes such judgments can easily be made. For example, the prospects are good that future science will explain out-of-body experiences (OBEs); indeed some investigators think that we already have the beginnings of an explanation of OBEs. So it is likely that OBEs are natural. Moreover, at present the prospects are very bad that future science will be able to explain the bodily resurrection of billions of persons in the Second Coming of Jesus Christ. Thus, one can say that if the bodily resurrections associated with the Second Coming were to occur, they would not be natural. Fortunately for naturalism, there is no reason to suppose that such bodily resurrections will occur and good inductive grounds to suppose that they will not.

A more serious problem with SEA is that many philosophers maintain that there is a realm of abstract objects consisting of numbers, sets, propositions, and so forth that cannot be explained in terms of science, although their existence must be presupposed in doing science. Does the existence of such a realm mean that ontological naturalism is not true? It might be supposed that one way to handle this problem is to show that the realm of abstract objects can be reduced to something else that is in principle explainable by science, but the prospects of such a reduction seem remote. A more plausible approach to the problem is to give a less expansive definition of ontological naturalism. It has been suggested that ontological naturalism is the view that everything with causal powers in the natural world can in principle be explained by science. Since abstract entities, unlike theological entities, have no causal powers, they pose no problem for ontological naturalism.

The Physical Dependency Account. Some naturalists have preferred to define ontological naturalism metaphysically, rather than in terms of scientific explicability. What may be called the physical dependency account (PDA) is that natural events are purely physical events, objects, or entities whose properties are completely dependent on physical events or objects. Thus, for example, even if thoughts, desires, and the like are not identical with physical objects or events, they may well be dependent on physical objects and events.

However, PDA also seems to have problems relative to the future. First, given our present understanding of the physical, it is uncertain whether certain phenomena such as near-death experiences will in the future be considered physical or not. Moreover, the present understanding of the physical might change, so that in a future science, some entities that are not now thought to be physical, although they are probably considered dependent on the physical, will be considered physical in some broadened account of the physical.

As in the case of SEA, one has to know how to apply PDA. If phenomenon *P* is discovered to be purely a physical phenomenon or completely determined by the physical, then it is natural. But suppose our evidence is inconclusive, and at time *t*, *P* is not established as physical or as dependent on the physical. It would not follow that *P* is nonnatural, for at time *t + 1* the evidence might establish *P* as physical. Again a judgment based on the available evidence would have to be made about the likelihood of *P* being considered physical or dependent on the physical in the future development of science. For example, suppose parapsychology confirms that some genuine psychic phenomena exist (something it has not done so far). It seems that this would more likely be someday assimilated to PDA than would Jesus's alleged walking on water.

The abstract entity problem affects PDA as well. But again, one might say that ontological naturalism is the view that everything with causal powers in the natural world can in principle be explained in terms of physical entities or what is dependent on physical entities. Since abstract entities have no causal powers, they pose no problem.

The Spatial-Temporal Account. Other naturalists have opted for still a different account of ontological naturalism, namely, that the natural should be characterized in terms of being in space and in time. Thus, the spatial-temporal account (STA) holds that a natural event or object is one that is a spatial-temporal event or object. It might be thought that this adds nothing new to PDA, because all spatial-temporal objects are physical or dependent on the physical. But this criticism seems mistaken. An incarnated god such as Jesus Christ would presumably be a spatial-temporal object, but it would not meet the requirement of PDA at least in terms of our present understanding of the physical. The Jesus of the gospels was neither just a physical object nor completely dependent on the physical. He was more than this, for as the Son of God he was also a supernatural being. So the Incarnation would likely be a counterexample to ontological naturalism construed in terms of PDA, but it would not be a counterexample to it interpreted in terms of STA. This consequence shows however that there is something basically wrong with STA; for surely if anything is a supernatural event, it is the Incarnation. Again, fortunately for ontological naturalism, there is no reason to suppose that the Incarnation took place.

Ontological Naturalism and the Nature of Mind. Ontological naturalism is compatible with a variety of positions on the relationship between the mind and body (see COGNITIVE SCIENCE AND UNBELIEF). Ontological naturalism is certainly compatible with mind-body

reductionism, according to which the mental is reducible to the physical. For example, it is compatible with analytical behaviorism, a conceptual reduction of the mental to the physical where statements about mental states are analyzed into and thus have the same meaning as statements about actual and hypothetical behavior. It is also compatible with the identity theory, in which mental states and brain states are contingently identical. On this view mental state terms do not have the same meaning as brain state terms, but they refer to the same thing.

Ontological naturalism is also compatible with eliminative MATERIALISM. On this view the mental is not reducible to the physical; rather, it is maintained that there are no such things as mental states, just as there are no such things as ghosts and Santa Claus. In a future science, talk of mental states will simply drop out and will presumably be replaced by a nonmental vocabulary. Eliminative materialism should not be confused with nonreductive naturalism, a position on the mind-body relationship that is also compatible with ontological naturalism. On this view it is maintained that mental properties supervene on physical ones; that is, all mental properties and truths are determined by physical properties and truths.

Atheism and Ontological Naturalism. Most religious thinkers today suppose that God is a supernatural being transcending the natural order, yet it is possible to hold a naturalistic view of god—in other words, to believe that there is a god and that this entity belongs to the natural order. In the twentieth century John DEWEY, for example, defined "God" as "the unity of all ideal ends arousing us to desire and action." In his eyes such a unity was explainable by scientific method and was part of the natural order. In the nineteenth century Auguste COMTE in his turn developed an organized religion completely within a naturalistic framework whose object of worship was humanity (see POSITIVISM). Comte sometimes referred to humanity as the supreme being, and this is compatible with ontological naturalism. Other philosophers, for example, Baruch SPINOZA in the seventeenth century, identified God with nature itself. Pantheistic views like his may well be compatible with ontological naturalism characterized in some of the ways specified above.

The acceptance of ontological naturalism does not exclude belief in god or gods interpreted in a nonsupernatural way. Nevertheless, such an interpretation tends to be misleading. By "God" most people mean a supernatural being, and by "atheism" most people mean a view that rejects God. If God only means what Dewey meant by this term, the famous atheists of history could well believe that God exists.

In any case, atheism does not entail ontological naturalism. Certain Eastern religions, such as Jainism, are atheistic in the sense that they do not assume the existence of an all-knowing, all-powerful, and all-good god, and yet the worldview presented in these religions is not obviously naturalistic. In Jainism the law of karma plays an important role, and it is unlikely that such a law, if it did exist, could be explainable by present or future science.

Defending Ontological Naturalism. How can the truth of ontological naturalism be defended? One powerful argument is to point to the success of science in various realms such as medicine, psychology, meteorology, geology, and astronomy. As science improves, fewer and fewer supernatural explanations are taken seriously by educated people and more and more natural explanations are accepted. Extrapolating from this data, one can inductively infer that there is reason to suppose that there are no sound supernatural explanations, and that eventually all supernatural explanations will be replaced by natural ones.

Keith Augustine has developed an interesting argument along these lines:

1. If after an intensive search of the natural world, scientists and historians have found no uncontroversial evidence for likely candidates for a supernatural event, then naturalism is probably true.
2. After an intensive search of the natural world, scientists and historians have found no uncontroversial evidence for likely candidates for a supernatural event.

3. Therefore, naturalism is probably true.

By "uncontroversial evidence," Augustine means evidence that is accepted by a consensus of experts doing research within the relevant empirical subject areas. Some may wonder if that requirement is too strong. Augustine maintains, however, that extraordinary claims require extraordinary evidence. This heuristic principle applies to the evaluation of claims about natural events that radically conflict with well-established scientific theories, and also to claims about supernatural events that in the light of our scientific background knowledge are initially very improbable. Augustine points out that they remain improbable even given eyewitness testimony, because empirical studies have shown time and again that such testimony is unreliable in accidents, robberies, and other ordinary events. Surely, then, there is no reason to suppose that it would be any more reliable in the case of eyewitness reports of supernatural events.

In addition to the argument from the success of science, there are atheological arguments that show that the existence of God is improbable and even impossible (see ATHEISM; EXISTENCE OF GOD, ARGUMENTS FOR AND AGAINST). But then the most common basis of supernaturalism, namely, that supernaturalism is based on belief in a theistic God, is false. To be sure, supernaturalism does not have to be based on theism, but the falsehood of theism removes a major support for supernaturalism.

In addition, there is reason to believe that the concept of the supernatural is incoherent. Thus, Gilbert Fulmer

has examined the concept of a God who possesses the single attribute of being the creator of the universe, which includes being the creator of all natural laws. Fulmer argues that God's creation of the universe, including all natural laws, depends on the fact that what God wills is put into effect; in particular, it presupposes the natural law that provides that what God wills to be created is created. However, since God's creation of this natural law presupposes its prior existence, the attribute of creator of the universe is self-contradictory, and therefore a God who is creator of the universe does not and cannot exist. But since God's being creator of the universe is one of the major doctrines of the supernatural worldview, one of the major bases of supernaturalism is defeated.

Methodological Naturalism. It has sometimes been argued that science is committed to methodological rather than ontological naturalism. Methodological naturalism is a much weaker position than ontological naturalism, for it does not deny the existence of supernatural entities per se. It simply assumes for the purpose of inquiry that supernatural beings do not exist; that in the context of inquiry, only natural processes and events exist. Thus, it is compatible with theism and does not presume atheism.

The question arises: If one rejects ontological naturalism, how can methodological naturalism be justified? Methodological naturalism (MN) can be understood as the methodological rule:

MN = In the context of science use only natural explanations!

Because it is a rule, methodological naturalism is neither true nor false. It can, however, be evaluated by pragmatic criteria. Thus one may ask what the consequences would be of following methodological naturalism in contrast to an alternative rule such as:

MS = In the context of science assume that God is the direct or indirect explanation of everything!

There are at least five rationales for methodological naturalism: testability, the use of laws in explanations, fruitfulness, the promotion of agreement and cooperation, and the avoidance of blocked inquiry. However, the most plausible reason for adopting methodological naturalism is that supernatural explanations are "science stoppers," in that they block inquiry. This idea can be stated by the methodological rule:

MR_1 = Do not use explanations in science that cut off further inquiry!

What is the justification for this rule? One might be inclined to argue for MR_1 on inductive grounds. However, the main argument for MR_1 is based not on induction but on vindication. Quite simply, one can never rule out the logical possibility that there is a scientific explanation of a phenomenon. Following MR_1 would not assure us that such an explanation would be discovered even in the long run, but operating with alternative rules could result in the loss of potential scientific explanations if they exist.

For example, suppose one adopted this alternative rule:

MR_2 = Do not use explanations in science that cut off further inquiry unless inquiry-blocking explanations are the only plausible ones that can be thought of after twenty years of deliberation and research!

Following MR_2 would be unacceptable. Suppose there were an explanation that could be discovered only after more than twenty years of deliberation and research. Following MR_2 would prevent one from finding it. Other restricted methodological rules would have similar implications.

Despite the promise of MR_1 in providing a rationale for methodological naturalism, one problem remains—namely, we must make the assumption that naturalism in the context of science does not itself block inquiry. As it happens, this is not obvious. Certainly methodological naturalism does not entail MR_1. Indeed, there could be naturalistic explanations that are supposed to be brute facts, ultimate principles, and the like. Would not these block inquiry just as much as appealing to God's direct action? They would if they were allowed, but good scientific methodology should never permit anything to be more than a tentative brute fact or a provisional ultimate principle, since we can never be sure that what we think is an ultimate naturalistic explanation really is not.

Thus MR_1 can be understood as an independent constraint on MN, or MN can be revised to include this constraint. Thus we could characterize MN by the methodological rule:

MN' = In the context of science assume that explanations can be explained naturalistically at least in the long run!

MN' is compatible with scientists acting for long periods of time as if certain explanations are ultimate, relative to their evidence and background theories. But such practice would not block inquiry, because in contrast to supernatural explanations, it would be possible for these explanations themselves to be explained as science progresses.

Conclusion. Ontological naturalism can be explicated in different ways: the scientifically explicable account (SEA), the physical dependency account (PDA), and the spatial-temporal account (STA). Although these explications raise important issues, none of them shows that ontological naturalism is untenable. Three rationales provide a strong case for ontological naturalism: the suc-

cess of science, the case for atheism, and the incoherence of supernaturalism. Ontological naturalism is compatible with several positions on the mind-body problem, including analytical behaviorism, the identity theory, eliminative materialism, and nonreductive materialism. Although ontological naturalism is compatible with some pantheistic and humanistic views of God, it is incompatible with traditional theistic notions. There are several rationales for methodological naturalism, but the most plausible is that properly construed, it does not block inquiry.

BIBLIOGRAPHY

Alston, William. "Natural Reconstructions of Religion." In *Encyclopedia of Philosophy*, edited by Paul Edwards. New York: Macmillan/Free Press, 1967.

Audi, Robert. "Naturalism." In *Encyclopedia of Philosophy Supplement*, edited by Donald M. Borchert. New York: Macmillan Reference, 1996.

Augustine, Keith. "A Defense of Naturalism." Master's thesis, University of Maryland–College Park, 2001.

Danto, Arthur. "Naturalism." In *Encyclopedia of Philosophy*, edited by Paul Edwards. New York: Macmillan/Free Press, 1967.

Dewey, John. *A Common Faith*. New Haven, CT: Yale University Press, 1934.

Fulmer, Gilbert. "The Concept of the Supernatural." *Analysis* 37 (1976/77). Reprinted in Michael Martin and Ricki Monnier, eds. *The Impossibility of God*. Amherst, NY: Prometheus Books, 2003.

Pennock, Robert T. *Tower of Babel*. Cambridge, MA: MIT Press, 1999.

MICHAEL MARTIN

NATURALISTIC FALLACY. G. E. Moore and David Hume. According to English philosopher G. E. MOORE, the naturalistic fallacy is the mistake of identifying *good* with any such naturalistic characteristic as well-being, freedom, survival, pleasure, or self-realization. In attacking subjectivism in ethics, Moore contended that neither divine commands nor any of the other reputed candidates qualify as *good*. To open the door for one contender at the exclusion of any or all of the others would be an arbitrary selection. Furthermore, it could not be an open question as to which natural properties suffice, since good is its own unique property. The sphere of ethics, Moore argued, must then define itself by reference to this simple, unanalyzable, indefinable property.

David HUME had earlier denied that moral duties could be derived from a description of natural facts. No moral *ought* can be deduced from what *is*, no ethical conclusion from factual premises. Moore's so-called Common Sense philosophy regards facts as objective by their existing independently of any private consciousness. Good, too, he argued, has objective status and must be directly intuited, which means its reality does not derive from individual private, subjective attitudes. Good is unique and is not a composite of other qualities. As an intuitionist, Moore regarded as self-evident that it is morally wrong to knowingly commit an act that would make the world on the whole truly worse.

Intrinsic Value. In seeking to rise above moral subjectivism, Moore concluded that good is intrinsic and not instrumental to something else. Intrinsic value or intrinsic worth refers to the unique object or property *good*. Consequently, in asserting that an action is *the* best thing to do, we assert, said Moore, that it together with its consequences presents a sum of intrinsic value greater than any possible alternative.

Ordinary Language. While Moore helped to birth ordinary language analysis, especially in England, his analysis of ethics seems ironically to pay insufficient attention to the richness and subtlety of everyday language. He failed to grasp that the objective good as a distinct, unanalyzable property is a fiction. He did not see clearly that human morality must involve both the subjective and the objective. Without individual desires, wants and needs, morality and ethics would be both impossible and pointless. Moore asked us to imagine two worlds: one is filled with beauty; the other is a heap of filth. Which world is the better? The question makes no sense unless it presupposes the existence of an experiencing subject to experience it. Without at least the possibility of an experiencer, the choice between the alternative worlds would make no difference. For whom would it make a difference? At the same time, the physical conditions and social environment are the objective pole of morality. When we speak of a good community, good climate, good food, good colleagues, and even a good question to advance an argument, we involve both subjective and objective factors. A killer distinguishes a good rifle from a bad one. A good killer might prove to be a bad citizen. The careful study of ordinary language can throw far more light on ethics than Moore apparently realized.

Darwin and Natural History. Charles DARWIN devoted considerable thought to human morality, including love and the sense of oughtness. In chapter 4 of *The Descent of Man* he wrote that the moral sense or conscience is the major difference between our species and other species. In particular, this refers to the philosopher Immanuel KANT, who drew a sharp line between our sense of oughtness on the one side, and our desires and appetites on the other side. Darwin set out to understand moral consciousness by probing what he called natural history, raising the question of whether the study of other animals could cast light on the human conscience. Moore raised doubts about any attempt to become informed of the content of goodness by studying other species. He granted that Darwin had written profoundly of social instincts and sociability among various

species. From such descriptions, no matter how accurate, however, no moral duties for humans can be derived, Moore argued. Many species engage also in aggressive conflict, demonstrating considerable hostility toward outsiders. From that fact, can we derive the conclusion that human beings, too, *ought* to engage in hostilities toward outsiders?

Herbert Spencer's Naturalistic Hedonism. Moore discussed at length the evolutionary theory of Darwin's friend Herbert SPENCER, who recognized two critical facts about a great variety of species: (1) the members of a species tend to form small groups that provide mutual support and reinforcement, and (2) the groups tend to develop hostility toward members of other groups of the same species. Given the two facts, which of them provides our species with information about the content of the good? Assuming that Spencer's *description* of other animals' behavior is reasonably accurate, we still face the *ought* question. Ought we as human beings take what Spencer regarded as the amity-enmity complex and cultivate it as a moral principle for ourselves?

Moore charged that in assuming the ethic of naturalistic hedonism (maximizing pleasure) to be self-evident, Spencer commited the naturalistic fallacy. While acknowledging that his fellow Englishman's descriptions may make a valuable contribution to the field of ethics, Moore insisted that what is needed is a clear discussion of the "fundamental principles of Ethics." He replaced naturalistic hedonism with "good" and then insisted that it denotes a unique, indefinable quality that is self-evident.

Some philosophers in the tradition of ARISTOTLE regard self-realization as the self-evident base of ethics. Other thinkers advance different candidates. John Hospers in *Human Conduct* defends a version of utilitarian hedonism, which is greatly different from the Cyrenaic school, which emphasizes maximum pleasure in the present without regard for tomorrow. A hedonist might ask Moore, Aristotle, Kant, and others the following two questions: Would you want or approve of a world filled with goodness, self-realization, goodwill, divine commands, or rational freedom if that world were devoid of all pleasure and all hope of pleasure? Could such a world exist?

Fruitful Inquiry. Karl POPPER suggested that the quest for the manifest truth or self-evident truth of this or that claim has much in common with the quest for the infallible source of truth. While no self-evident principle or source in ethics has materialized, the quest and its accompanying criticism have nevertheless stimulated new directions of inquiry and generated fruitful ideas that have thrown light on the course of human commitments and values. A study of the natural history of our own species suggests that at any moment in time, our institutions and traditions have generated both horror and values. Popper noted that they imposed limitations on our creative freedom and on our powers of rational criticism. The same institutions and traditions have provided us numerous values we might not choose to abandon—including that of criticizing and modifying our institutions and traditions, not by the dictates of an infallible source or criterion, but by the accumulation of wisdom and insights that comes through free exchanges in an open society.

BIBLIOGRAPHY

Barnhart, J. E. "Egoism and Altruism." *Southwest Journal of Philosophy* 7, no. 1 (Winter 1976).

Darwin, Charles. *The Descent of Man.* Amherst, NY: Prometheus Books, 2000.

Hospers, John. *Human Conduct: Problems of Ethics.* New York: Harcourt Brace, 1996.

Kurtz, Paul. "Naturalistic Ethics and the Open Question." In *Philosophical Essays in Pragmatic Naturalism*, edited by Paul Kurtz. Amherst, NY: Prometheus Books, 1990.

Moore, Barrington, Jr. *Moral Purity and Persecution in History.* Princeton, NJ: Princeton University Press, 2000.

Moore, G. E. *Principia Ethica.* New York: Cambridge University Press, 1903.

Perry, David L. *The Concept of Pleasure.* The Hague: Mouton, 1967.

Popper, Karl. *Conjectures and Refutation: The Growth of Scientific Knowledge.* New York: Harper & Row, 1989.

JOE EDWARD BARNHART

NEPAL, UNBELIEF IN. Nepal is centrally located on the southern slope of the Great Himalayan Range in south central Asia, commonly known as the Hindu Kush. Bound by China to the north and India to the east, west, and south, it is the location of Mount Everest and Kathmandu. Before characterizing unbelief in Nepal, which comprises both explicit humanist activism (see HUMANISM) and a broader social resistance against traditional social structures often mediated by religion, we must explore the existing social and religious context of this complex society.

The social fabric of Nepali society is based on the caste system and a fatalism for which Hindu religion provides the ideological superstructure. Until very recently, orthodox Hinduism was the traditional basis of state polity and of interethnic relations, and the various caste and ethnic groups exist in a hierarchical structure with the Hindu high-caste groups at its apex. The two highest Hindu caste groups of *Brahmin* and *Chhetri* have traditionally exercised economic and political dominance in the society, and this advantage is also shared by one Tibeto-Burman ethnic group, the *Newar*, who mostly come from the agriculturally fertile valley of Kathmandu and have traditionally benefited from its commercial and political significance.

Peoples. The cultural landscape of Nepal is characterized by a north-south horizontal divide consisting of the Tibetan cultural tradition in the north, a spillover of the Indo-Gangetic (Indian) civilization in the southern plains, and an admixture of the two in the middle hills. Similarly, the society is also characterized by a vertical divide between Hindu caste groups on one hand and various Tibeto-Burman ethnic groups on the other, the latter traditionally identified with specific geographic subregions of the country. There are sixty recognized ethnic/caste groups in Nepal, though the method of characterizing them is inconsistent. Most of the settlements in the country are ethnically mixed; they are generally shared by various Hindu high-caste groups, Tibeto-Burman ethnic groups, and the traditionally untouchable Hindu low-caste occupational groups, now generically known as *Dalits*, who mostly earn their livelihood by rendering specialized services and unskilled labor to other households in an age-old patron-client relationship.

Religion and Society. Religion occupies an integral position in Nepali life and society. Until very recently, Nepal was the only constitutionally declared Hindu state in the world; there is, however, a great deal of intermingling of Hindu and Buddhist beliefs. The constitution of 1990 provided for freedom of religion and permitted the practice of all religions with some restrictions, though the government generally has not interfered with the practice of other religions. The constitution described the country as a "Hindu Kingdom," which meant that the state did not treat all religions on an equal footing, but this scenario has changed with the proclamation of Nepal as a secular state by its House of Representatives following the historic democratic movement of 2006. The Nepali government formed after the democratic movement of 2006 is in the process of holding an election for Constituent Assembly which will draft a new constitution presumably institutionalizing all proclamations of the House of Representatives, including that concerning secular statehood. Nepal has begun its journey toward secular democracy, but it has not yet reached its destination.

Those who convert to other religions from Hinduism may face isolated incidents of violence or some social ostracism, but generally do not fear admitting their affiliations in public. The US government discusses religious freedom issues with the government of Nepal in the context of its overall dialogue and policy of promoting human rights. The US Embassy maintains regular contact with Hindu, Christian, Buddhist, Jewish, Baha'i, and other religious groups.

For decades, dozens of Christian missionary hospitals, welfare organizations, and schools have operated in the country. These organizations have been criticized for proselytizing the poor hill ethnic groups. Yet missionary schools are among the most respected institutions of secondary education in the country; many of the country's governing and business elite, including the top rebel Maoist leader, graduated from Jesuit high schools.

Societal Attitudes. The adherents of the country's many religions generally coexist peacefully and respect all places of worship. Most Hindus respect Buddhist shrines located throughout the country; Buddhists accord Hindu shrines the same respect. Buddha's birthplace in Nepal is an important pilgrimage site for Hindus, and Buddha's birthday is a national holiday.

Some Christian groups report that Hindu extremism has increased in recent years. Of particular concern are the Nepali affiliates of the India-based Hindu political party Shiv Sena, locally known as Pashupati Sena, Shiv Sena Nepal, and Nepal Shivsena. During late 2001, Muslim leaders complained that Hindu fundamentalists increased their campaigns of anti-Islamic pamphleteering and graffiti. Government policy apparently does not support Hindu extremism, although some political figures have made public statements critical of Christian missionary activities.

Although discrimination is prohibited by the constitution, the caste system strongly influences society. Societal discrimination and government inaction against members of higher castes remains widespread and persistent. Hindu religious tradition long prohibited members of the lower caste from entering certain temples. Due to the persistent pressure of HUMAN, Nepal's national humanist group (see below), and the Center for Inquiry/Nepal, the government was forced to announce that caste-based discrimination is illegal. This has to some extent facilitated temple access for members of the lower castes.

Social Reform and Religious Opposition. Hindu religion has not only provided the metaphysical base for perpetuating the social oppression of the *Dalit* castes but also has seriously hindered the social reform movement attempted in the past to socially integrate these castes. Even after the advent of democracy in 1990, the conditions and the fate of untouchable castes have not changed. Realizing the need for a strong organizational base to effectively carry out the progressive interventions in every aspect of social life, *Dalits* and other low-caste groups have formed many organizations with a view to create greater space for their participation in political and social process. They have initiated and provided some leadership toward a progressive social reform movement. Organized humanism has significantly contributed to the rise of this reform movement, particularly by campaigning against oppression of untouchables.

Ethnic activism can be seen as another important and potentially powerful movement for social change. Ethnic activism arose in Nepal in the aftermath of the 1990 people's movement, prior to which it was widely assumed that the subjugated people had previously accepted the inevitability of their fate, perhaps generations ago. As a platform for the common cause, a federation of ethnic groups was formed (Janajati Mahasangh). It includes twenty-two mostly non-Hindu ethnic groups, many of which were represented at the National Convention of Nepali Indigenous People in April 1993.

The 1990 constitution declared Nepal as a multiethnic and multilingual state despite retaining the holdover title of "Hindu Kingdom." The freedom whereby subjects have become citizens has unleashed new political pressures.

Organized Humanism. Because Hindu beliefs and tradition so strongly anchor Nepalis in ancient and abusive structures such as the caste system, it is reasonable that only a strong humanist and social reform movement could rupture the traditional bondage of Hindu casteism and push Nepali society toward progressive transformation. The Humanist Association of Nepal (HUMAN) was established in 1997 with the objective of disseminating humanist values, principles, and ideals through secular humanist education campaign activities. Its founding president was Gopi Upreti, a professor at Tribhuvan University, Nepal, a teacher of ecological agriculture and horticulture at Institute of Agriculture and Animal Sciences (IAAS), and principal founder of the Nepal Institute of Health Sciences (NIHS) at Purbanchal University, Nepal.

The Center for Inquiry/Nepal (CFI/Nepal) was formed as an affiliate organization of the Center for Inquiry/Transnational in 2004. Since its formation CFI/Nepal has been very active in its campaign for secular democracy, the use of science and reason to guide human behavior, tolerance and social harmony, and the elimination of religion and caste-based discrimination in Nepal. HUMAN and CFI/Nepal share fundamentally the same humanist philosophy, values, and principles, and operate collaboratively.

HUMAN and CFI/Nepal each came into existence with the objectives of upholding and promoting scientific rationality, human dignity, and freedom through humanist education and secular democracy. They have become the frontline organizations in fighting against superstitions, paranormal practices, fatalism, the caste system and untouchability, the dowry system for marriage, and religious and political fundamentalisms. Calling for unqualified respect for the fundamental human rights of all citizens, they have spearheaded a campaign for the secularization and democratization of Nepali society. This is evident from the significant roles they have played in the democratic movement of 2006, particularly in nurturing the concept of secular democracy and statehood. This is, indeed, a matter of great pride.

HUMAN and CFI/Nepal have contributed significantly to the drafting of legislation to protect untouchables and other innocents from varied social malpractices induced by religious and superstitious worldviews. In conjunction with human rights activists, *Dalit* organizations, women's organizations, political parties, and the young, HUMAN and CFI/Nepal have initiated a movement of secular democratization of Nepali society that deserves the continuing support of the world humanist movement.

HUMAN and CFI/Nepal are increasingly concerned about an emerging phenomenon of religious proselytizing by well-organized and funded religious missionary organizations following the historic proclamation of secular statehood. A number of Muslim and Christian missionary organizations, long present in Nepal, have now become very active. The proclamation that Nepal is a secular state has also given an excellent pretext for Hindu fundamentalists and erstwhile royalists to organize and protest against the realization of secular democracy. The task of HUMAN and CFI/Nepal will become even more challenging in the days to come, both in helping to continue the secularization and democratization of Nepali society, and in creating an environment that can promote social harmony and tolerance among different religious and ethnic communities.

BIBLIOGRAPHY

Bista, D.B. *People of Nepal.* Kathmandu: Ratna Pustak Bhandar, 1967.

Burghart, R. "The Formation of the Concept of Nation-state in Nepal." *Journal of Asian Studies* 44 (1984).

Fischer, Claude, et al. *Inequality by Design: Cracking the Bell Curve Myth.* Princeton, NJ: Princeton University Press, 1996.

Gellner, David, Joanna Pfaff-Czarnecka, and John Whelpton, eds. *Nationalism and Ethnicity in a Hindu State: The Politics and Culture of Contemporary Nepal.* Amsterdam: Harwood, 1997.

Gurung, Harka. *Nepal Social Demography and Expressions.* Kathmandu: New Era, 1998.

Upreti, Gopi. *Humanism: Fighting against Superstition and Para-normal Practices.* Kathmandu: HUMAN, 2000.

———. *A Research Report on the Cult of Kumari in Nepal.* Kathmandu: HUMAN, 2001.

Upreti, Gopi, and Ganga Subedi. *A Report on the Victims of Alleged Witchcraft Practices in Mahottari District of Nepal.* Kathmandu: HUMAN, 2002.

GOPI UPRETI

NETHERLANDS, THE, HUMANISM IN. "The capacity to give meaning to and shape one's own existence characterizes the Netherlands from the past to the present, and from bottom to top. Reclaiming land from the sea, building up an international trading network, establishing freedom and tolerance in a world of violence and religious fanaticism: in other words, making a paradise from a swamp." This is how Rob Tielman, a sociologist and former chairman of both the Dutch Humanist Association and the INTERNATIONAL HUMANIST AND ETHICAL UNION (IHEU), described the Netherlands back in 1994. This image of paradise has taken a few knocks between then and 2005. The nation's more than sixteen million inhabitants live in a society that is characterized by "abundance and unease" or "[t]he embarrassment of riches." In a financial, economic, and social sense, there is considerable abundance, albeit distributed less than perfectly among the population. In a cultural, political, and moral sense, the unease can be observed in problems of integrating immigrants into society, fundamentalism from Left to Right and from believer to unbeliever, a loss of confidence in politics, declining tolerance, as well as in a quest for new or different ways of giving meaning to life.

In the Netherlands, no fixed frameworks for the meaning of life have existed for some decades. Whereas in 1966 some 64 percent of the population were church-goers, in 2005 only 37 percent of the Dutch population belonged to a church, and of these, 60 percent were marginal members, attending church only a couple of times a year and believing in the church's positions on matters such as the existence of heaven and hell only to a very limited extent. Of the population born after 1960, no more than 27 percent belonged to a church. Conversely, 39 percent of the population had a system of values that was largely consistent with the core values of HUMANISM—self-determination, equality, responsibility, tolerance, and the like—and also feel affinity with organized humanism. More specifically, approximately one million people eighteen years of age and over living in the Netherlands can be said to show tangible evidence of active affinity with the humanist movement. This makes humanism the third-largest LIFE STANCE movement in the Netherlands, after Protestantism and Catholicism. However, the official number of organized humanists (registered members of one of the two large humanist organizations) is far lower, and is even declining: approximately twenty-eight thousand members. Nevertheless, organized humanism offers a broad and comprehensive package of services, which, although largely paid for by the government, is completely independent of the government in terms of content. Understanding this paradoxical situation requires some knowledge of the history of the Netherlands.

Religion and Secularization. The Dutch have a long tradition of religious tolerance and pluralism, and especially of religious freedom, from the Napoleonic period in the early nineteenth century. The preceding two centuries were dominated by the Dutch Reformed Church, although other religious traditions were tolerated. More to the point, the Dutch have a strong humanist tradition drawn from Desiderius ERASMUS, Dirck Volckertszoon Coornhert, and Baruch SPINOZA; the first Dutch constitution of 1798 incorporated several essential principles for building a secular democratic constitutional state. The most important of these were: "Every citizen has the freedom to serve his god in accordance with the conviction of his heart," and a radical separation of church and state. The Calvinists, who separated from the Reformed Church in the nineteenth century, and the Catholics felt that they were being treated as second-class citizens in the second half of the nineteenth century, and started to organize themselves separately. They can be viewed as social movements based on religion. Their aim for emancipation was based on the principle of equal rights. These emancipation processes resulted in a typically Dutch solution: "the ideological separation of society," which is also referred to as the "pillarized society." Society was divided into different religious "pillars," a metaphor for pillars standing side by side, without contact except by way of the roof that they are supporting. Each pillar had its own institutions including political parties, trade unions, newspapers, hospitals, broadcasting stations, and social work institutions. The social life of citizens was often restricted to their own community. At the end of the nineteenth century there were two large communities, or pillars, based on worldview: the Catholics and the Protestants. A third pillar consisted of nonreligious groups, such as liberals, socialists, and freethinkers (see FREETHOUGHT), or humanists; this was called the neutral pillar. This social constellation was possible because of two simultaneously acting principles: on the one hand, pacification and nonintervention in one another's spheres of influence; and on the other hand, the principle of equal entitlements, which meant that the different communities would receive identical rights and services. One reason this could work is that the pillars were numerically roughly equal. Until approximately 1960, the pillarized system worked well, but then disintegrated rapidly as a consequence of the all-embracing modernization process in society, which was characterized by rationalization, individualization, and SECULARIZATION. The traditional communities fell apart and lost influence. The pillars and the related institutions were dismantled at a rapid pace by this process, with the exception of parts of the healthcare, education, and broadcasting sectors.

An essential point for the current position of organized humanism is that between 1945 and about 1989, it had been able to benefit from the equal entitlement principle mentioned above by setting up a variety of organizations for practical activities, from social work and education to broadcasting, which were largely paid for by the government. This happened despite the fact that humanists were and are opposed in principle to dividing society into pillarized blocs.

Organized Humanism. The founding in 1856 of the freethinkers association De Dageraad, currently De Vrije Gedachte (see NETHERLANDS, THE, UNBELIEF IN), marked the beginning of the modern organized humanist movement in the Netherlands. Shortly after the end of World War II in May 1945, two humanist organizations were founded independently of each other: in May 1945 Humanitas, and in February 1946 the Humanistisch Verbond (HV).

Humanitas is an organization for social services on a humanist basis. Its founders, predominantly social democrats, wanted to provide churchless people with an alternative for the social assistance traditionally provided by the churches. They mainly offered practical help to people in need. For them, *humanism* was translated as seeing the person as an individual, but at the same time as a part of society. The focus was on both personal responsibility and care for other people, which was substantially different from church-based charity. Humanitas expanded considerably in a short time and organized itself into local departments. A characteristic feature of Humanitas was, and still is, that a substantial part of its work is carried out by self-trained volunteers. Over the years, this work evolved from providing individual social services more toward community development. The number of members declined between 1980 and 1994, while many subsidies have stopped, and Humanitas is in search of new ways forward. These ways are being found in the promotion of community development, especially that based on "empowerment": supporting people in marginal positions to acquire a substantive place in society through their own efforts and with their own, possibly limited, resources. In 2005 the work was carried out by approximately ten thousand volunteers in five districts and eighty local departments. Humanitas has approximately fifteen thousand paying members, and the volunteers are supported by approximately two hundred paid executive staff. In addition, Humanitas itself is spawning several large independent humanist organizations in the fields of child daycare and care for the elderly, with more than three thousand workers and eight hundred volunteers. The Humanitas motto is "Do what you have to do," which is a good example of an extremely practical form of humanism.

The Humanistisch Verbond (HV, Dutch Humanist Association), founded on February 17, 1946, gave both substantial and organizational direction to organized humanism in the Netherlands between 1946 and 2000. The two most important motives for founding the *Verbond* were described by Jaap van PRAGG, the undisputed "father of modern Dutch humanism," as "the major and the minor struggle." The "major struggle" was concerned with supporting and providing a life stance "roof" for the large group of people that the church had abandoned and who had a mainly implicit humanist worldview, if any: they were at risk of sliding into futility and nihilism (moral indifference), partly in response to memories of the horrors of World War II. The minor struggle was for the emancipation of churchless people seeking a full-fledged position in society. The minor struggle in particular was conducted with verve, and made grateful use of the same weapons that its opponents, especially the Catholics and Protestants, had developed in their own emancipation struggles. These weapons included pacification and nonintervention in one another's spheres of influence and the principle of equal rights for separate ideological groups. Despite the Verbond's small membership, because of considerable hard work, effective lobbying on the part of a strategically formed board, and by keeping in step with Dutch civil society without causing offense, the Verbond's struggle had delivered many successes by around 1970. Conspicuous were equal state-funded entitlements in humanist counseling, broadcasting, development aid, and education. A milestone was reached in 1965 with a government declaration that explicitly recognized both the Judeo-Christian tradition and humanism as the basis of society.

The secularization of society also had a direct influence on the course of the Verbond. From 1966, the HV had considerable difficulty in finding a new mission and a new humanist program that could command enthusiasm in what was becoming an increasingly humanist society. Under the chairmanship of Rob Tielman, the HV had a clear identity as an organization that favored a worldview based on the principle of self-determination of individuals, worked for legalizing abortion and euthanasia, opposed discrimination against homosexuals, and promoted the emancipation of women. After this period came a long episode in which the HV searched for form and content. This coincided with the loss of subsidies and a considerable fall in the number of members. In 2005 the HV was concentrating on the association itself (forty-three departments); providing services, such as speeches at funerals, humanist counseling, and relationship celebrations; and propagating a humanism centered on individual freedom of choice and responsibility. The motto of the Humanistisch Verbond is "Think independently, live in fellowship."

It is possible to defend the assertion that what van Praag called the "major struggle"—against nihilism and for the moral resilience of the public—never really took off, but is actually where a great need exists in the current time of abundance and unease. The HV is now trying to satisfy this need in the Humanistische Alliantie (Humanist Alliance), which was founded in 2001 and is reviewed below.

For the HV, humanist counseling (a sort of secular chaplaincy) was an important practical form of humanism. It became established after 1950 in the army, prisons, and the healthcare sector. In the 1970s army, prison, and hospital counseling were spun off into separate organizations still under the supervision of the HV. Since 1989 counselors have been trained at the University for Humanistics in Utrecht, which is fully state-financed as an accredited university, like the Roman Catholic and Protestant theological universities (see NETHERLANDS, THE, HUMANIST EDUCATION IN). As of 2005 some 250 humanist counselors work on a professional basis.

Other Organizations. Hivos (Humanist Institute for Development Aid), founded by the HV and De Vrije Gedachte in 1968, is a humanist development organization that stands for emancipation, democratization, and poverty reduction in developing countries. The reason for founding Hivos was the complete absence of a state-supported development organization that worked from a non-Christian ideology and explicitly used non-Christian

channels to deliver aid. As an official nongovernmental organization, Hivos spends more than 70 million yearly in support of local organizations and initiatives in developing countries: currently in more than thirty countries in Africa, Asia, and Latin America. Among the priority areas are human rights and AIDS, the environment and development, gender, and women. The IHEU is an important link for Hivos in supporting humanist-oriented organizations in developing countries.

From around 1946, the sound of humanism has been heard on national radio and later on national television. In 2005 the Humanistische Omroep (Humanist Radio and TV) operates an independent foundation under the Verbond, with approximately twenty paid staff providing 208 hours of radio and 39 hours of television a year. Characteristically programming focuses on topics such as world citizenship, culture, autonomy, and social engagement. In addition, the humanist movement has two explicitly humanist periodicals that are independent of the direct influence of any organization. The *Humanist* is a bimonthly magazine aimed at a general public, with articles on the broad areas of giving of meaning to life and worldview. The *Journal for Humanistics* can be considered an academic journal. Published four times a year, it focuses on the interface between social developments, cultural issues, and existential themes.

A fairly recent branch of the humanist organizations' family tree is the Humanist Archives, founded in 1996 as a center for the archiving and documentation of history with respect to humanism in the Netherlands from 1850 to the present. In addition to managing archives such as the IHEU archive, the Humanist Archives collect publications and maintain a heavily used Web site.

All the explicitly humanist organizations, mentioned above or otherwise, form a complex weave of theoretical and practical orientations that cover a large number of social fields including healthcare, education, mass media, human rights, development aid, social work, and dealing with the existential concerns of individuals. The roots of this family tree are formed by De Vrije Gedachte, Humanitas, and the Humanistisch Verbond.

Renewal of Organized Humanism. A renewal effort for organized humanism was urgently called for. Because the core values of humanism had been widely accepted and a high level of individual emancipation had been achieved in Dutch society, organized humanism needed to redefine its mission. In addition, there had been a sharp decline in the number of organized humanists and an almost total disappearance of state subsidies. This renewal effort is currently proceeding along two lines.

The Humanistische Alliantie (Humanist Alliance, a federation of humanist organizations), founded in 2001, aims to act as a "network organization" to strengthen humanism and the humanist movement, among other things by jointly developing humanist-inspired visions and practices, promoting common interests in the world of politics and society, conducting joint communication activities, and coordinating fundraising activities. Above all, they aim to give humanism in the Netherlands a voice in societal debates. All large humanist organizations and others belong to the Alliantie, comprising (as of 2004) seventeen member organizations and about twenty-five partner organizations, encompassing some 12,870 volunteers, 57,550 members/donors, and 6,410 paid staff.

The second line of innovation is related to the content of humanism as a worldview. "The" humanism is no longer a clearly defined entity in the Netherlands, having splintered in recent decades into substantially different "humanisms." Besides the traditional humanism as a life stance and worldview, oriented toward giving meaning to life, there is "political" humanism, which sets out to achieve the humanization of society from moral and political motives and is rapidly gaining ground. Nor have atheistic humanism or RELIGIOUS HUMANISM disappeared. At the same time, humanism has spread far and wide in society. Although the number belonging to humanist organizations has declined, humanism as a social principle is clearly on the rise.

Though a relatively small percentage of the population counts itself part of the humanist movement, a far larger percentage feels affinity with humanist ideals, while the values shared by an even larger fraction of the population reflect such humanist core values as self-determination, equality, responsibility, tolerance, and the like.

BIBLIOGRAPHY

Boelaars, Bert. *De kostbare mens. Inleiding tot het humanisme* [The Precious Human: Introduction to Humanism]. Amsterdam: De Arbeiderspers, 1997.

Derkx, Peter. "Modern Humanism in the Netherlands." In *Empowering Humanity: State of the Art in Humanistics*, edited by A. Halsema, and D. van Houten. Utrecht: De Tijdstroom, 2002.

Gasenbeek, Bert. "An Analytical Framework for Describing and Analysing Humanist Organizations." In *Humanism and Laicity in Europe*. Berchem: European Humanist Federation, 2002.

Lammerts, Rob, and Susan Hakvoort. *Humanisme in beeld: een onderzoek naar de daadwerkelijke affiniteit met het humanisme* [Humanism in View: A Survey on Affinity with Humanism]. Utrecht: Verwey-Jonker Instituut, 2004.

Tielman, Rob. "Is Nederland van God los?" [Are the Netherlands Separated from God?] *Civis Mundi* 33, no. 4 (1994).

Van Houten, Douwe. "Humanist Counseling in the Netherlands." In *Empowering Humanity: State of the Art in Humanistics*, edited by A. Halsema and D. van Houten. Utrecht: De Tijdstroom, 2002.

Van Praag, J. P. *Foundations of Humanism*. Amherst, NY: Prometheus Books, 1982.

BERT GASENBEEK

NETHERLANDS, THE, HUMANIST EDUCATION IN.

The Netherlands is one of the most secular societies in the Western world. Half of the Dutch are atheists or agnostics (see NETHERLANDS, THE, UNBELIEF IN). Humanism is accepted constitutionally as an alternative LIFE STANCE with equal status to any of the theistic religions, including the right to found state-funded humanist schools. The humanist movement in the Netherlands is one of the strongest in the world: 40 percent of all Dutch adults identify themselves as humanists, and 17 percent of all Dutch pupils attend humanist education (see below) in pluralist (public) schools (see NETHERLANDS, THE, HUMANISM IN).

The Dutch humanist movement has always been in favor of pluralist schools attended by pupils of different life stances. No religion is imposed upon others, and information about various life stances is taught as objectively as possible. Pluralist education is not value neutral, because it recognizes that values play an important role in daily life. Students are encouraged to give meaning and shape to their lives in a nondogmatic and tolerant way.

Though the Dutch humanist movement was legally able to found humanist schools, it chose not to do so out of concern that life stance–based schools might become dogmatic and indoctrinate children in their parents' philosophy of life. From a humanist perspective, children are not the possession of their parents but only of themselves. This implies that parents and educators have to guide children in such a way that they are increasingly empowered to create their own lifestyles. This human right to self-determination is so fundamental that children should understand it at an early age. Humanists support this process by offering optional humanist education classes as an alternative to the similarly optional religious education classes already offered in a pluralist school system.

The Dutch school system implements the separation of church and state, but does offer parents and children the choice of optional humanist or religion education during set hours in pluralist schools. Humanist educators conduct humanist education classes under the jurisdiction of Dutch humanist organizations. Optional religious education is taught under the jurisdiction of the various churches, mosques, and synagogues. All life stance education is supervised by school inspectors. Mandatory education in factual knowledge on all important life stances is the responsibility of the pluralist schools in the Netherlands. By this division of jurisdictions, the Dutch state can guarantee the separation of church and state and at the same time offer an opportunity to give life stance–based education within constitutional limits to those who want it.

In the past, many humanists assumed that education in itself guaranteed the development of an ethically responsible world. Their assumption was that spreading knowledge was equivalent to spreading ethical awareness. In reality, what happened instead is that theocracy tended to be replaced by technocracy. Democracy is more than spreading information freely. It demands the concrete training of individuals' capacity to give meaning and shape to life. In the battle between theocracy and technocracy, humanists defend democracy. Ethical education is therefore essential.

Science is a necessary but insufficient condition for humanist education. Most Dutch humanist educators do not believe in the dogma of scientific and economic "progress" as a natural law, though this does not mean that they oppose progress as such. While many Dutch humanist educators would describe themselves as postmodern in their viewpoints, postmodernism is not monolithic. We must distinguish between at least two types: antimodernism and neomodernism. Antimodernism assumes that all science is bad; its clarion call of "back to nature" means the elimination of human values as basic principles. In contrast, neomodernism incorporates nature without making it sacred, recognizing that we are free and responsible to give meaning to our existence. Neomodernism embraces the best of the Renaissance and Enlightenment (see ENLIGHTENMENT, UNBELIEF DURING THE) with their humanistic traditions of self-determination.

In Dutch humanist education, the ideals of the French and American revolutions play an important role. Freedom is not considered to be the absence of rules but rather the presence of self-determination. Equality does not mean uniformity but rather equal access to human rights by all people. Solidarity is not imposed but rather seen as the consequence of implementing self-determination: the concept of enlightened self-interest. Freedom is frequently misinterpreted as the right to discriminate against others, whereas equality implies the right not to be discriminated against. This dilemma can only be solved by a principle higher than freedom or equality. That higher principle is self-determination.

Self-determination means the right to give meaning and shape to one's own life as long as others are not prohibited from exercising their own rights to self-determination. More practical than the concepts of freedom and equality, the principle of self-determination is able to settle tensions among individuals and between minorities. It is very understandable why the Dutch people chose to incorporate this principle as the leading concept guiding their constitution. The Netherlands has a long tradition of dealing with religious, ethnic, and other minorities, and most Dutch are aware of the fact that they themselves belong to various minorities. When all citizens recognize their minority status and their need for minority rights, they will become more sensitive in defending minority rights for everyone else so long as others are not harmed. This awareness can help to guarantee a true pluralist democracy.

This tolerant perspective has faced a new challenge with the rise of Islamic fundamentalism in the Netherlands. Should democracies be so tolerant as to allow intolerant activities? Democracy is not the dictatorship of the majority, but the implementation of the right to self-determination. Fundamentalist parties that seek to take over power in order to end democracy should therefore not be tolerated in democratic elections. But it is a mistake to think that all Muslims are fundamentalists. Most Dutch Muslims are not; indeed, the Netherlands has a long liberal Islamic past in its former colony, Indonesia (see INDONESIA AND SOME OTHER ISLAMIC COUNTRIES, UNBELIEF IN). By excluding Islamic religious education from neutral public schools, as in France, one creates a vacuum that fundamentalists can easily exploit. By allowing optional Islamic religious education under the same human rights–based democratic conditions in pluralist schools, we support the integration of minorities in society.

We could speak of an integration paradox. By excluding religious education from neutral public schools we create a vacuum that supports segregating fundamentalist tendencies. By including religious education in public schools without making it optional, we violate the rights of nonbelievers such as humanists. By integrating both religious and humanist education in an optional way in pluralist schools we prevent both theocratic and technocratic tendencies and strengthen democracy. In fact, many pupils of Islamic background make a free choice for humanist education in Dutch pluralist schools. Comparing the Netherlands with Northern Ireland, Iraq, and the former Yugoslavia, one can understand the importance of life stance–pluralist education for human rights–based democracy.

The Dutch humanist movement implements these principles in daily life in a practical and pragmatic way. Practical humanism assumes that people act according to their own life stance based upon self-determination. The task of the humanist movement is not to attack religions but to create a positive alternative to theism. Humanists try to guide people in such a way that they will be as free and as responsible as possible. In the Netherlands about 400 humanists are educating young people in humanist life stance and life styles. Over 250 humanist professionals are counseling people in hospitals, prisons, and the army in finding solutions to their existential problems. Some twenty journalists present humanist ideas to the general public through humanist media, including the Humanist Broadcasting Company. More than ten professors are now employed full time in humanist studies, taking responsibility for the training of humanist professionals in various universities all over the country. In addition, the state-funded University for Humanistics in Utrecht has eight professors and more than three hundred students who are trained as humanist professionals in counseling, education, research, and related fields. And the *Journal for Humanistics* gives the necessary professional information and guidance.

ROB TIELMAN

NETHERLANDS, THE, UNBELIEF IN. In the Netherlands, native country of the internationally famous humanist Desiderius ERASMUS, the first real freethinker probably was Herman van Rijswijk, who in 1512 was burned at the stake because of his liberal ideas. Other forerunners of the FREETHOUGHT movement were the humanist Dirck Volckertszoon Coornhert, an advocate of religious tolerance; and the philosopher Baruch SPINOZA.

Nineteenth-century Dutch freethought history begins with a book—and ever since, Dutch freethinkers have been prodigious writers and readers. In 1854 Franz Junghuhn published *Licht- en schaduwbeelden uit de binnenlanden van Java* (Images of Light and Shadow from Inner Java). In this moving and influential study, the author expressed his indignation at the way missionaries in the Dutch Indies propagated their ideas. Junghuhn rated the native religions, based on nature and reason, at least on a par with Christianity and saw the Christian faith as destructive.

In October 1855 Junghuhn and publisher Frans Christiaan Günst launched the freethinker periodical *De Dageraad* (Dawn). One year later, on October 4, 1856, a society of the same name was founded by Günst and some fellow members of the unorthodox Amsterdam masonic lodge *Post Nubila Lux* (After Darkness the Light). The ubiquitous light-and-dark metaphor refers to the contrast between the obscurity of the Christian revelation and the enlightenment associated with human reason, science, and the autonomy of mankind.

The "heroes" of De Dageraad were Spinoza, the polemical author MULTATULI, Jacob Moleschott, and Johannes van Vloten, as well as the German materialists Ludwig FEUERBACH and Ludwig BÜCHNER.

The theoretical base of the freethought movement in the Netherlands was twofold. The majority adhered to the materialist monism of philosophers like Feuerbach, Büchner, and Moleschott. A small minority supported the spiritual monism of Spinoza, Felix Ortt, and Bart de Ligt, for whom not only the organic world but also the inorganic realm was "animated": even, as Gustav Fechner asserted, the whole cosmos.

In the first decade after 1856 most members of De Dageraad were deists (see DEISM) and socially conservative. In the latter part of the century, ATHEISM spread. A considerable minority inclined toward social revolution, while others, such as Adrien Henri Gerhard, became social democrats. In 1883–84 the tension between the followers of a more social approach and the so-called hard atheists came to a head. The radicals, among them the anarcho-socialist Ferdinand Domela Nieuwenhuis, left De Dageraad. Among the more moderate stay-behinds were men like Gerhard, who would in 1894 be prominent among the founding fathers of the Dutch Labour Party SDAP.

Prior to the gradual introduction of a national social security system (starting in about 1900), De Dageraad founded its own life insurance company, Aurora, in 1887; a relief fund for poor freethinker families in 1888; and an orphans' fund to place orphans of freethinkers into freethinkers' families or in a free orphans' house in 1896.

By the early 1900s De Dageraad membership had declined to around five hundred members, though this number included many celebrities. The group's fiftieth anniversary in 1906 marked a revival, and by 1908 a new and independent freethought periodical, once again called *De Dageraad*, had joined the existing *De Vrije Gedachte* (Freethought). In 1909 De Dageraad organized protest meetings against the murder of the Spanish anarchist and secular school reformer Fernando FERRER. In 1911 a permanent Commission for Separation from the Church was instituted, whose members gave free legal support to people who wanted to leave their church. Pieter Frowein and Domela Nieuwenhuis were very active at international freethought congresses.

When the freethinker C. J. Vaillant died in 1914, he had himself illegally cremated. The executors of his will, fellow members of De Dageraad, were prosecuted, but in the end the high court acquitted them. From then on, anyone in the Netherlands could demand to be cremated.

From about 1912 De Dageraad mounted growing protests against growing militarism, nationalism, and colonialism across Europe. After the outbreak of war, freethinkers such as the clergymen de Ligt and N. J. C. Schermerhorn and feminist Wilhelmina Drucker vehemently denounced war atrocities. After 1918 this pacifist and antimilitarist movement remained strong among freethinkers, and many became active in the International Anti-Militarist Union.

The postwar years were a boom period for De Dageraad, with increasing membership and new programs including Sunday morning lectures, public debates, brochures, and extensive propaganda tours. Half a dozen printing houses published a steady stream of freethought books. In 1928, a Freethinkers' Broadcasting Society was organized. Among the radio speakers were De Dageraad celebrities such as Gerhard, the jurist and philosopher Leo Polak, and Jan Hoving, the inspiring president of De Dageraad from 1917 until 1938.

As the activities of De Dageraad increased, this prompted opposition from the religious. Confessional groups launched specialized periodicals to fight De Dageraad, such as *De Middaghoogte* (Mid-day Zenith). De Dageraad tried to penetrate the homogenously Catholic southern province of Limburg, where Catholic bishops and priests controlled trade unions, political parties, schools, and the press—a very inhospitable setting for freethinkers and social democrats. The "atheists" from the north were often met with aggressive, sometimes violent counterprotests led by priests.

Major targets of Dageraad protests in the 1920s included the imprisonment of conscientious objectors in the army, the execution of the anarchists Nicola Sacco and Bartolomeo Vanzetti in the United States, Benito Mussolini's fascism, and the pope, because of his 1929 "concordat" with Mussolini. In the 1930s De Dageraad spearheaded the attack on anti-Semitism in Europe. It organized meetings, issued pamphlets, and broadcast radio speeches denouncing all sorts of nationalism and fascism in Germany, Italy, and Spain. Politically and intellectually, 1933 was De Dageraad's "finest hour," and its membership in that year—twenty-seven hundred—has never been equaled. However, in that same year the government forbade all civil servants to belong to "subversive organizations," and De Dageraad was number one on the red list. Repression came not only from Catholics but also from the National Socialist Party. By 1936 the freethinkers' radio broadcasts, always subject to censorship, were prohibited altogether.

However, De Dageraad members remained active, campaigning for the right to say a solemn pledge instead of swearing an oath on the Bible; advocating human-centered morality and education ("humanity first"), a more enlightened approach to sexual morality, and nondiscriminatory marriage legislation; promoting birth control, cremation, the antivivisection movement, and vegetarianism; and pursuing the humanization of criminal law.

After the German invasion of the Netherlands in May 1940, De Dageraad, with its anti-Nazi record, instantly dissolved itself. After the war De Dageraad resurfaced, its periodical *De Vrijdenker* resumed publication, and program activities recommenced. However, two kindred humanist organizations were soon founded: Humanitas (Social Work) in May 1945 and the Humanistisch Verbond (Humanist League) in February 1946. Both appealed explicitly to people outside the churches, but without identifying their position with atheism (see NETHERLANDS, THE, HUMANISM IN). Both humanist organizations soon grew larger than De Dageraad, which today has some twelve hundred members. Relations between humanists and freethinkers, though mutually benevolently critical, can be described as cooperative.

In 1958 De Dageraad changed its name to De Vrije Gedachte (Freethought), and the name of its main periodical into *Bevrijdend Denken* (Liberating Thought). Since 1978 its periodical has been called *De Vrije Gedachte*.

Freethinkers and unbelievers in the Netherlands stand for a nondogmatic, independent, rational, and human way of thinking. Their ideal was and is a combination of freethought and solidarity.

BIBLIOGRAPHY

Bokkel, Jan G. A. ten. *Gidsen en Genieën. De Dageraad en het vrije denken in Nederland 1855–1898* [Guides and Geniuses: De Dageraad and Freethought in the Netherlands 1855–1898]. Dieren: FAMA, 2003.

Constandse, A. L. *Geschiedenis van het Humanisme in Nederland* [History of Humanism in the Netherlands]. Den Haag: Kruseman, 1967.

Nabuurs, Jo. *Vrijdenkers in verzuild Nederland. De Dageraad 1900–1940. Een bronnenstudie* [Freethinkers in the Pillarized Netherlands: De Dageraad 1900–1940, an Original Study]. Utrecht: Humanistisch Archief, 2002.

Noordenbos, O., and P. Spigt. *Atheïsme en vrijdenken in Nederland in de negentiende eeuw, een kritisch overzicht* [Atheism and Freethought in the Netherlands in the Nineteenth Century, a Critical Survey]. Nijmegen: SUN, 1976.

Thissen, Siebe. *De Spinozisten, wijsgerige beweging in Nederland (1850–1907)* [The Spinozists, a Philosophical Movement in the Netherlands (1850–1907)]. Den Haag: Sdu, 2000.

JO NABUURS

NEW ZEALAND, UNBELIEF IN. New Zealand is one of the most secular societies on earth (see SECULARISM). The nationwide census of 2001 revealed a post-Christian society in the making. Of the 3,737,277 census responses to the question of religious affiliation, 1,028,052 described themselves as having no religion and a further 239,241 exercised their right to object to the question. And the vast majority of those who acknowledged some religious affiliation do so in a purely nominal way. At the end of the twentieth century, regular churchgoers accounted for little more than about 15 percent of the population, and those who attended monthly or more frequently are fewer still. Regular churchgoers are usually in the older age cohorts, with those in their twenties being only half as likely to attend church as those over sixty.

While 67 percent of New Zealanders believe in some sort of god, only 47 percent believe in a soul and 43 percent in life after death (see IMMORTALITY, UNBELIEF IN). Sin, hell, and the devil all register much lower levels of adherence. And of those who make some profession of belief in god, a significant proportion attend church never or very rarely.

Most mainline denominations are experiencing consistent decline in membership. The Church of England, once the heavyweight on the New Zealand religious scene, has shrunk the most noticeably. In 1926, 575,731—40 percent of census respondents—claimed adherence to the Church of England, but in 2001, despite a fourfold increase in the country's population, Anglican numbers were just 584,793, or about 21 percent.

The secular nature of New Zealand society is also apparent in the country's politics. Of the twenty-four cabinet ministers who took their posts in 1999, only two swore their oaths on the Bible, and one of those subsequently lost his job over a scandal involving sex with an underage girl. At the time of writing, neither the country's prime minister nor the leader of the opposition is religious. The prime minister's AGNOSTICISM is public knowledge and has never been a relevant issue for the vast majority of voters.

Since the late 1980s there has been an attempt to construct an American-style Religious Right in New Zealand politics, but it has failed to make significant headway. In 1996 an alliance of two right-wing Christian parties formed a coalition to exploit the new proportional representation system New Zealand had adopted, but failed to get the required 5 percent threshold to be represented in parliament. The coalition soon broke up amid acrimony; the Christian Heritage party, its more uncompromising component, rarely rose above 2 percent approval ratings. In 2005 Graham Capill, its leader from 1989 until 2003, was found guilty of the sexual exploitation of underage girls.

By contrast, the United Future Party took pains to describe itself as a secular party of the political center. On this platform it did well in the 2002 election, securing 6.9 percent of the vote and ensuring a place in parliament. But the party soon squandered its election night vote with a series of muddles and scandals, and its voter rating dropped to levels as low as that of the Christian Heritage Party. In July 2003 a still more radical fundamentalist party, called Destiny New Zealand, was formed. It seized attention with a march through Wellington in October 2004 in which its male marchers wore black shirts.

New Zealand has no established church. Among the intellectually oriented of the mostly English and Scottish immigrants who created the modern state in the nineteenth century, the two most influential thinkers were John Stuart MILL and Herbert SPENCER, both staunch agnostics. The influence of these thinkers, and the ascendancy at the time of agnosticism and SECULARISM, were well timed to have a formative influence on the developing national psyche. Some of the most eminent of the early prime ministers of New Zealand were freethinkers. Perhaps the earliest premier whose views were unorthodox was Alfred Domett, who played a formative role in developing New Zealand's secular education system. Domett served as premier between 1862 and 1863. Later in the century rose John BALLANCE and Sir Robert STOUT. Ballance was influential, even after his death, in the long-lived Liberal government of 1890–1906, which did much to shape the growing sense of New Zealand identity. And into the twentieth century, two of the country's most significant prime ministers, Michael Joseph Savage and Peter Fraser, were rationalists (see RATIONALISM). Savage led the Labor Party to a landslide victory in 1935 and enacted a series of sweeping economic and social reforms that helped to drag the country out of the Depression and to construct a comprehensive welfare state. Following Savage, Fraser solidified these reforms and led the country through World War II. Fraser also helped found the New Zealand Symphony Orchestra.

By contrast, very few of the country's prime ministers had been known to be overtly religious. One of the most religious of the country's leaders was Bill Massey, who had links to the bitterly anti-Catholic Protestant Political Association.

The longest-lasting issue that divides religious from secular-minded New Zealanders is the role of religion in schools. The notion of free, secular, and compulsory education is as old as government in New Zealand. The formula was introduced into the province of Nelson in the 1840s, and was developed by Domett into a model the rest of the country would follow in 1877, when, after the demise of the provincial form of government, New Zealand developed a national education policy. The 1877 Education Act was passed by a coalition that represented a wide range of viewpoints. As well as the small groups of agnostics and Jews, a large number of nominally religious people were anxious to create conditions whereby no one religion would exercise unchallenged control in the nation's schools. The safest solution, they reasoned, was that no religion should enter the schools.

Church groups have remained unreconciled to this legislation since its enactment. In 1897 they managed to insert a half-hour slot of religious instruction, during which time the school was deemed to be closed. The questionable legality of this stratagem was in dispute until it was finally legitimized in the 1964 Education Act. Religious instruction is theoretically required to avoid any form of indoctrination and disparagement of other religions, but in practice both of these go on. Bible in Schools, as this program is commonly known, is offered only in primary schools, which teach children up to ten years of age, and only at schools that choose to offer it—it is not compulsory for all New Zealand schools. Parents have the option to withdraw their children from the program, and many do.

The secular nature of New Zealand has posed a tricky set of problems for the country's humanist movement (see HUMANISM). The first problem is how to arouse any interest in the sort of questions that have traditionally motivated humanists. In a society as secular as New Zealand, very few people feel the need to belong to an organization catering to them as nonreligious people. The movement has responded in various ways. The five principal FREETHOUGHT organizations are divided by their respective attitudes toward religion, in particular the degree to which they believe it should be subjected to criticism.

The Skeptics organization is based in Christchurch and focuses on pseudoscience in medicine, the media, and politics. It generally says little about religion. The Skeptics has the best media presence of all the freethought groups in the country. Criticism of religion, promoting the humanist alternative, and defending the secular state have become the main preserve of the Auckland-based New Zealand Association of Rationalists and Humanists. This is the oldest and most well-funded of all the New Zealand freethought organizations. The smaller Humanist Society, restricted to the Wellington region, deals with similar issues. The main organization catering for religious humanism is the Sea of Faith. This movement was founded by the heterodox English churchman Don Cupitt in 1984 on the strength of a book by that title. It was transplanted into New Zealand shortly afterward by Lloyd Geering, the country's best-known theologian, a radical religious humanist (see RELIGIOUS HUMANISM). There are also small Unitarian communities (see UNITARIAN UNIVERSALISM) that cater to a similar constituency. There is a significant crossover of members between these organizations. Other issues in which humanists have played a part include the debate over voluntary euthanasia, capital punishment, BLASPHEMY laws, and religious pluralism.

BIBLIOGRAPHY

Cooke, Bill. *Heathen in Godzone: Seventy Years of Rationalism in New Zealand.* Auckland: NZ Association of Rationalists and Humanists, 1998.

———. "Humanism in New Zealand." *Tijdschrift voor Humanistiek* 10, no. 3 (June 2002).

Dakin, Jim. "New Zealand's Freethought Heritage." *New Zealand Rationalist & Humanist/The Open Society.* Eight-part series from Summer 2000/2001– Autumn 2002.

Mackey, John. *The Making of a State Education System.* London: Geoffrey Chapman, 1967.

Webster, Alan, and Paul Perry. *The Religious Factor in New Zealand Society.* Palmerston North: Alpha/New Zealand Study of Values, 1989.

BILL COOKE

NEWTON, HUEY P. (1942–1989), African American activist. Huey P. Newton led an erratic and maddeningly inconsistent life in which he constantly vacillated between criminality and heroism. Newton was born in Louisiana, moving with his family to Oakland, California, at age three. He was arrested many times for petty crimes beginning at age fourteen. At twenty-two he was convicted of assault with a deadly weapon and spent most of his six-month sentence in solitary confinement.

Newton eventually taught himself how to read well and attended several Bay Area colleges, earning two associates degrees and helping to found Oakland City College's first black history course. He studied Malcolm X, Mao Tse-tung, Che Guevara, Frantz Fanon, and other revolutionary thinkers.

In 1966 Newton helped found the Black Panther Party (BPP), becoming the group's minister of defense. At its peak, the Panthers had more than two thousand members in chapters in several cities throughout the United States. Though primarily known for its militancy and engaging in shootouts with the police, the BPP also operated valuable social services. Panther ideology was based on Marxist-Leninist ideals, a theory that Newton called revolutionary HUMANISM. It included a wholly secular ten-point program of self-determination, full employment, decent housing, education, healthcare, and the like. Newton detested the reactionary bigotry of cultural nationalist groups such as the Nation of Islam, believing that black-led revolutionary organizations must work with poor and progressive whites, Latinos, Native Americans, and other groups.

Newton argued that while people might feel the need for religion in the beginning, science and reason would eventually fill the void created when the folly of religion became manifest. Nonetheless the BPP sometimes formed uneasy tactical alliances with black churches. In his book *Revolutionary Suicide* (1973), Newton eulogized fellow Panther George Jackson, murdered in San Quentin, writing that a person's spirit lives after his physical death, but not "in the superstitious sense." Rather, the person's ideas can be carried forward and others can emulate his or her actions.

Achievement and criminality continued to alternate in Newton's life. In 1968 he was found guilty of killing an Oakland police officer in a shootout, but the case was dropped on a technicality. In 1974 Newton was arrested several times, once on charges of murdering a prostitute. He fled to Cuba, returning in 1977 when he believed a fair trial was possible. Two trials ended in hung juries and he was freed. In 1980 Newton received a PhD in social philosophy from the University of California. The title of his dissertation was "War against the Panthers: A Study in Repression in America." In the 1980s he twice faced charges of embezzling from Panther community programs and was convicted in 1989. Later that year a drug dealer shot him to death in Oakland.

Newton's legacy is kept alive by various Web sites and the Commemoration Committee for the Black Panther Party in Oakland. Despite the sad state of his later life, the photograph of a confident, defiant, and courageous revolutionary Huey P. Newton posing with a gun in his right hand and a spear in his left continues to leave a lasting impression on the minds of millions.

BIBLIOGRAPHY

Anthony, Earl. *Spitting in the Wind: The True Story behind the Violent Legacy of the Black Panther Party.* Malibu, CA: Roundtable, 1990.

Foner, Philip S., ed. *The Black Panthers Speak.* New York: De Capo, 1995.

Newton, Huey P. "On the Relevance of the Church." In *By These Hands Alone: A Documentary History of African American Humanism,* edited by Anthony B. Pinn. New York: New York University Press, 2001.

———. *Revolutionary Suicide.* New York: Writers and Readers, 1973.

———. *To Die for the People.* New York: Writers and Readers,

Pearson, Hugh. *The Shadow of the Panther: Huey*

Newton and the Price of Black Power in America. Reading, MA: Addison Wesley, 1994.

NORM R. ALLEN JR.

NIETZSCHE, FRIEDRICH WILHELM (1844–1900),

German philosopher. In 1882 Friedrich Nietzsche wrote, "God is dead." Nietzsche was an enemy of all religions, but particularly of the religion that surrounded him in nineteenth-century Europe, Christianity. His engagement with Christianity goes far beyond the vitriolic attacks for which he is known, however. It is a theme he returned to again and again throughout his published works: in his criticism of Christian morality, in his analysis of the psychological and cultural impact of Christianity, and in his creation of a compelling portrait of a life without Christianity.

Life. Nietzsche was born near Leipzig, Germany, on October 15, 1844. His family was solidly Protestant—his father and both grandfathers were employed as ministers in the Lutheran Church—but the family was not fanatically religious. When Nietzsche was four years old his father died, an event that left a deep impression on the young boy. In keeping with his passionate and sensitive nature, Nietzsche had been an earnestly pious boy, but by age eighteen he was already an unbeliever.

Nietzsche achieved early recognition as a brilliant scholar of the Latin and Greek classics, being appointed to the chair in classical philology at the University of Basel when he was only twenty-four. As his interests shifted toward philosophy and the analysis of culture, however, his professional colleagues were increasingly baffled by his writing. At first he was able to find an audience among people who shared his admiration for the philosopher Arthur SCHOPENHAUER and the composer Richard Wagner. After his philosophy diverged from these influences, however, he became increasingly intellectually isolated, until eventually there was almost no one among his contemporaries who sympathized with his work.

During his adult life Nietzsche suffered from frequent, debilitating migraine headaches and other illnesses that forced him to resign his professorship at Basel in 1879. After that he lived a seminomadic and largely solitary existence, staying in boarding houses in the Swiss Alps during the summer and in southern France or Italy during the winter. Once he had distanced himself from the academic community and from Wagner's sphere of influence, the elements of his mature philosophy emerged quickly. In between bouts of illness he wrote continually, existing in an almost constant fever of creativity for ten years. His major works were all written during this period.

In January 1889 he suffered a mental breakdown from which he never recovered. From periods of lucidity punctuated by violent outbursts, his condition gradually deteriorated until he was entirely unresponsive, apparently capable of neither thought nor emotion. He died on August 25, 1900. Nietzsche's madness accomplished what his brilliant writing had not: it brought his ideas to the attention of the reading public. In 1888 an influential critic had begun to comment on his work, and, aided by the romantic image of their author in the grip of insanity, his books quickly rose in popularity.

Critique of Christianity. Nietzsche's scathing criticism of Christianity is directed toward precisely that element of Christianity that people usually find the most appealing, namely, its moral code. Nietzsche saw Christian morality as based on two fundamental principles, both of which he condemned. First, Christianity values altruism: sacrificing one's own good for the good of others is praised. Second, Christianity defends the weak against the strong: dominating people weaker than oneself is condemned.

Nietzsche's objection to altruism is based on his analysis of its psychological consequences for the person acting altruistically. The Christian demand that people ignore their own needs and selfish desires in favor of helping others ends up destroying the altruist's independence and individuality, Nietzsche believed. The result is what he calls "herd men" or "last men": people so alienated from their own desires that they are unable to set goals for themselves. They are dependent on the authority of God or society to tell them what to do, and incapable of the sort of productive selfishness that leads to great art or new ideas.

Nietzsche's objection to Christianity's defense of the weak is based on his theory of the will to power. In his view, the defining characteristic of the living human being is the desire to make the world around oneself reflect one's unique personality. Nietzsche called this desire to exert influence on the world the "will to power." Christians are expected to suppress their own desire for power; in Nietzsche's view, this amounts to a form of self-mutilation. The weak, whose will to power is exhausted, are already mutilated in this way, and Nietzsche seemed to have little hope that they could regain their human potential.

Nietzsche's perception that Christianity favors people who are half-destroyed over people who still contain the possibility for greatness gave rise to his most fundamental criticism of Christianity: that it is permeated by contempt for the life we really have here on earth. Christians view life on earth as an inferior prelude to an ideal afterlife in which they will dwell in eternal bliss, freed from the sufferings and unruly desires of their mortal bodies. Nietzsche's concept of the "eternal recurrence" is meant as a counterideal to this concept of a heavenly afterlife. Someone who truly loved life, Nietzsche contended, would not desire the eternity promised by Christianity, but would rather desire the life he or she actually experienced, with all the suffering and unfairness that accompany any human life, repeated over and over again eternally. The first edition of *The Gay Science* ends with this question: "How well disposed would you have to become to yourself and to life *to crave nothing more fervently* than this ultimate eternal confirmation and seal?"

Values without Christianity. Nietzsche's rejection of the Christian life immediately raises the question of what sort of life would be better. In *Thus Spoke Zarathustra*, Nietzsche borrowed the messianic rhetoric of the Bible to describe the sort of person who represents his ideal, the *Übermensch*, or superhuman (often rendered in English as "Overman"). One characteristic of the *Übermensch* has already been mentioned, namely, the ability to confront the suffering in one's life honestly and yet joyfully embrace that life as a whole. In addition, the *Übermensch* is able to choose independently what values will guide his or her life rather than living in accordance with a moral code dictated by an outside authority. These two characteristics are deeply intertwined, since one's values are the standard by which one judges whether or not one's life has been good. Nietzsche conceived the *Übermensch* as an individualist whose life goals are the result of a complex interplay between an honest assessment of the unique person he or she is and a vision of the person he or she could be.

The picture of life without Christianity embodied in the *Übermensch* concept provides only a formal criterion by which to assess whether one has led a good life: one's personality, one's values, and the events in one's life must form a coherent whole. However, this criterion seems to permit some sorts of life that most people would find reprehensible, for example, a life dedicated to the enjoyment of other people's pain. This possibility is particularly worrying in light of Nietzsche's rejection of Christian morality, which had placed strict limits on the acceptable treatment of other people. Nietzsche's motivation for holding this disturbing position is best understood by examining his claim that God is dead.

In proclaiming the death of God, Nietzsche was not only celebrating the independence of the unbeliever, but also responding to the cultural circumstances of modernity. He thought that an intellectually honest belief in God is no longer possible, and his philosophy is in part an attempt to come to terms with the implications of this fact. The significance of the death of God is twofold. First, it means that there is no one with the authority to demand conformity to any particular set of values. The individual's free commitment to them is the only real ground for the principles that guide his or her choices. This commitment must be responsive to the peculiarities of the individual's situation and personality, so there can be no universally applicable rules about what sorts of life are permissible. Second, Nietzsche believed that an authentic commitment to the altruistic moral code of Christianity is impossible because this code requires the individual to reject the needs and desires that form the basis of his or her unique identity. To accept the Christian ideal as the model of a good life is to will one's own death.

The nineteenth-century atheists who were Nietzsche's contemporaries believed that they could renounce belief in God without giving up the moral framework that gave meaningful structure to their lives. Nietzsche predicted that this moral framework would crumble without God at its center. His ultimate message to his reader is this: If your life is to be meaningful, you must create that meaning yourself.

BIBLIOGRAPHY

Higgins, Kathleen, and Bernd Magnus, eds. *The Cambridge Companion to Nietzsche*. Cambridge: Cambridge University Press, 1996.

Hollingdale, R. J. *Nietzsche: The Man and His Philosophy*. Rev. ed. Cambridge: Cambridge University Press, 1999.

Nietzsche, Friedrich. *Beyond Good and Evil* [1886]. Translated by Walter Kaufmann. New York: Vintage, 1989.

———. *Ecce Homo* [1888]. Translated by R. J. Hollingdale. New York: Penguin, 1993.

———. *The Gay Science* [1882]. Translated by Walter Kaufmann. New York: Vintage, 1974.

———. *On the Genealogy of Morality* [1887]. Translated by Maudmarie Clark and Alan J. Swensen. Indianapolis: Hackett, 1998.

———. *Thus Spoke Zarathustra* [1883–85]. Translated by Walter Kaufmann. New York: Penguin, 1978.

Tanner, Michael. *Nietzsche*. Oxford: Oxford University Press, 1995.

SARAH DARBY

NIHILISM. In his poem "McDougal Street Blues," Jack Kerouac wrote, "Nobody believes that there's nothing to believe in." But there actually have been people over the eons who have literally believed in nothing. Called Nihilists, they give new meaning to the word *unbelief*. *Nihilism* (from the Latin *nihilo*, meaning "nothing") has been an important worldview for several centuries and has been a central concern to philosophers, theologians, novelists, poets, and psychologists since at least the late nineteenth century, when Friedrich NIETZSCHE wrote: "God is dead and we have killed Him."

There are various types of nihilism that must be differentiated, including the following: (1) epistemological nihilism, the denial that there are any objective or reliable grounds of determining what is true; (2) ethical nihilism, the denial that there are any objective moral norms or systems that one must accept; (3) political nihilism, the denial that there are any political structures or laws to which one must pay allegiance; (4) metaphysical nihilism, the theory that the universe is meaningless; (5) axiological nihilism, the theory that nothing has any value; (6) praxiological nihilism, the theory that nothing is worth doing; and (7) semantic nihilism, the theory that language is so imprecise that all statements are ultimately meaningless. What all of these have in common is the view that, as the rock group Queen put it in their song "Bohemian Rhapsody," nothing really matters.

One of the earliest discussions of nihilism is found in PLATO's dialogue *The Gorgias*. In it, the Sophist Gorgias (see SOPHISM), famed for his rhetorical skills and his ability to make the most absurd position seem plausible, declares that human beings cannot know if anything exists at all, and even if we could, we would not be able to communicate this knowledge, due to the inadequacy of human language. While Gorgias seems not to take his own argument seriously, other Ancient Greek philosophers, especially the Skeptics (see SKEPTICISM), were apparently in earnest when they made similar claims. Cratylus, for instance, was said to have refused to answer any questions, since he could not be certain of their meaning, and would only wiggle his finger to indicate that he did acknowledge receiving some sort of stimuli in the air. Even this concession was too much for the most extreme Skeptics.

Such discussions remained purely theoretical until the rise of modern philosophy in the seventeenth century. René DESCARTES's methodological skepticism called into question all beliefs about the external world, including God's existence. While Descartes thought he could restore such beliefs on a step-by-step basis through logical argumentation built upon a foundation of certain knowledge, there were those who found his philosophy a liberating approach to all dogmatic thinking (which is one reason why his works were placed on the Vatican's Index of Forbidden Books). Cartesianism thereby made epistemological nihilism one of the most troubling puzzles for students of cognition ever since. As Senator Howard Baker would phrase it during the Watergate trials, What do we know and when do we know it? And how can we know if what we know is true?

It was Nietzsche who made ethical nihilism a major concern for moralists. If God is dead, he argued (meaning not a literal supreme being but rather the belief in such a being), then any moral system sanctioned by God must also be dead. Or, as Fyodor Dostoyevsky (the most famous novelist to grapple with nihilism) put it in his masterpiece *The Brothers Karamazov*, "If God is dead, everything is permitted." Such a nihilistic view of morality has been attributed to Nietzsche himself, but it is important to note that Nietzsche was an opponent of nihilism, which he felt to be ultimately a worldview that led only to despair and inaction. For him, the will to power and the desire to bring about a life-form superior to present-day humans (the *Übermensch* or Overman) were inspirational moral codes based upon the natural laws of the universe. These would replace the Christian concepts of compassion and the role model of a suffering Christ. Nietzsche was sympathetic to the Buddhist notion of nothingness, but found it too anemic and too pacifistic for his own taste. But he recognized that

without some belief system to guide them, humans would necessarily come face to face with the void, and the likely outcome would be horrifying. To replace the Christian concept of an afterlife, he proposed the idea of eternal return, the view that one leads the exact same life over and over, and thus is never really dead. Nietzsche scholars have debated ever since whether he was sincere (which is to say, did he *really* believe this?) or whether he was offering up one myth to replace another.

Political nihilism was a force identified with the Russian radical Mikhail BAKUNIN, who extolled the virtue of violence and the need to overthrow all political systems. The Russian novelist Ivan Turgenev captured this attitude in the character of Bazarov in his 1862 book *Fathers and Sons*, thereby creating the most noted fictional nihilist. There were close connections between nihilism and the anarchist movement of the nineteenth and early twentieth centuries (see ANARCHISM AND UNBELIEF), several of whose members assassinated such world political leaders as Czar Alexander II of Russia, US president William McKinley, French president Sadi Carnot, and the Empress Elizabeth of Austria. But not all anarchists were necessarily nihilists—most believed in the natural goodness of human beings and eschewed violence. And not all political nihilists were necessarily anarchists—if all political systems are corrupt, what is the use of overthrowing them, just to have them replaced by ones equally untenable? No government can be just as bad as any government. Cynicism is also compatible with political nihilism, as is passivity. What difference would it make to change political regimes if nothing really matters at all?

The German philosopher Martin Heidegger gave perhaps the strongest arguments for metaphysical nihilism, in his 1927 work *Being and Time* (which directly influenced the Existentialist philosophers, particularly Jean-Paul SARTRE, who furthered the discussion in his 1943 work *Being and Nothingness*). Heidegger followed from Nietzsche's lead, but claimed that Nietzsche himself had not worked out the full implications of what it means to look into the abyss, that is, to try to grapple with the very meaning of "Nothingness." Nietzsche's will to power is a metaphysical dodge, an attempt to replace God with an equally Unconditioned Force whose origin remains mysterious. Philosophy must confront the meaninglessness of the world, and try to understand what existence itself means. Existentialists like Sartre and Albert CAMUS took up the challenge by advocating living authentic lives in defiance of an absurd universe (see EXISTENTIALISM), but Heidegger himself retreated into mysticism, noting in an interview (significantly, published posthumously) that "[o]nly a God can save us now." Although he spoke often of death as a person's final project, philosopher Paul EDWARDS, in his book *Heidegger's Confusions*, shows that he left open the possibility of survival after death. Thus, Heidegger was guilty of the same offense he accused Nietzsche of committing—not having the courage of his own convictions.

Axiological and praxiological nihilism are interconnected—if there is no value in the universe, it follows that there is nothing worth doing. Camus, who said that the only real philosophical question remains "Why not commit suicide?" offered up the myth of Sisyphus in response—while we may be doomed to perform actions that outwardly have no meaning or significance, we still inwardly feel that such actions have worth. We authenticate ourselves through freely choosing our own identities. To avoid doing so, to try to take on social roles just to please others, is, Sartre further argued, to be guilty of bad faith. Still, even the existentialists were found wanting by more hard-core nihilists, such as the punk rock group the Sex Pistols, who announced the end of hope and sang, "There's no future for you." But, pragmatically speaking, such a literal dead-end was not sincerely embraced by many, who preferred to sing about rather than jump into the void. Even Sex Pistol Sid Vicious seems to have died of an accidental drug overdose, not by deliberate suicide. If nothing matters, then why write songs about it? Surprisingly enough, nihilism was one of the main motivating forces for artists of the late twentieth century. In the words of the Nobel Prize winner Samuel Beckett—the premier absurdist writer of that period—"I Can't Go On . . . I'll Go On."

As for semantic nihilism, philosophy in the twentieth century was dominated by the analysis of language (what Richard Rorty called "the Linguistic Turn"). But it soon became clear—as Plato had understood many centuries earlier—that the correspondence between words and things is tenuous at best. Perhaps the best example of semantic nihilism was found in Ludwig WITTGENSTEIN's 1922 *Tractatus Logico-Philosophicus*, which argued that the limit of our language is the limit of our world, and that the most important matters of life cannot be put into words. A nihilist could well take this to mark the death of all writing, yet somehow the publishing industry did not come to a halt, and in fact the number of books written about Wittgenstein and language is sufficiently large to fill a good-sized library.

When all is said and done, nihilism in its many versions remains a conundrum. Like the Cyclops blinded in Homer's *Odyssey*, who cries out loudly that "Nobody" blinded him, all thoughtful truth seekers must admit, when asked what most troubles them, that the answer is "nothing at all."

BIBLIOGRAPHY

Carr, Karen Leslie. *The Banalization of Nihilism.* Albany: State University of New York Press, 1992.

Edwards, Paul. *Heidegger's Confusions.* Amherst, NY: Prometheus Books, 2004.

Morrison, Robert G. *Nietzsche and Buddhism: A Study in Nihilism and Ironic Affinities.* Oxford: Oxford University Press, 1999.

Pratt. Alan. *The Dark Side: Thoughts on the Futility of Life from the Ancient Greeks to the Present.* New York: Citadel, 1994.

TIMOTHY J. MADIGAN

NOAH'S FLOOD AND UNBELIEF. Noah's Flood refers to an event described principally in Genesis 6–8 of the Bible. According to Genesis 6:1–4, divine beings seduced or raped human women who consequently produced a mutant race called the *Nephilim*. The biblical god, Yahweh, thereafter decided to destroy all life, except the righteous Noah and his family.

Late Antiquity and the Middle Ages. Perhaps the earliest recorded instance of unbelief in Noah's Flood is found, albeit opaquely, in the Bible itself (e.g., Matt. 24:37–39). But it is in *Against Celsus*, the famous pro-Christian manual written by Origen, that we find the earliest report of substantive attacks on the biblical Flood story. According to Origen, the anti-Christian polemicist Celsus made at least three arguments: (1) Its monstrous size renders the Ark unseaworthy; (2) the Ark could not contain so many animals; and (3) the story seems borrowed from the Greek story of Deucalion.

The influential theologian Augustine also recorded skeptical comments in his *City of God*, including the improbability that rain could fall on the highest mountains given that clouds are too light to hold together at such a height. Augustine himself argued that not every animal needed to be on the Ark, especially those that can be produced by spontaneous generation. The existence of animals on distant islands also troubled Augustine; he suggested the possibility that angels transported those animals.

Meanwhile, Jewish writers also recorded bothersome questions about the Flood. In *Antiquities of the Jews* (first century), the Jewish historian Flavius Josephus cites a number of Babylonian sources including Berossus, a Babylonian priest of the fourth century BCE, in an apparent attempt to confirm the authenticity of the biblical account. The great medieval Jewish commentator Rashi asked why God would ask Noah to build an ark when there were so many other ways to save him.

The Renaissance and the Enlightenment. The discovery of the New World during the Renaissance produced a new set of problems for belief in Noah's Flood. Skepticism originated less in antibiblical writers than in writers who attempted to harmonize biblical accounts with Europeans' encounters with animal species and peoples in the New World and in Australia. Some asked why these animals weren't found in the Old World. How did animals manage to arrive at Noah's Ark from isolated and distant areas such as Australia? One response to such questions is elaborate mathematical calculations designed to defend the feasibility of Noah's Flood. Thus, Johannes Buteo in *De Arca Noe* calculated that the interior of the Ark contained 350,000 cubic cubits of usable space, and so could accommodate any species known. A local flood, rather than a worldwide inundation, began to be envisioned in order to suppress questions about the amount of water that would have been required for water to rise fifteen cubits above the tallest mountains.

The Nineteenth Century. By the early nineteenth century, the science of geology had matured sufficiently to pose a direct challenge to belief in Noah's Flood. It was becoming obvious that most extinct species represented by fossils, many of which had been conceived as remnants of Noah's Flood, were never accompanied by traces of human presence. Thus, some scholars reasoned that there were prehuman extinctions, as well as a lengthy history of the earth prior to human habitation.

One early pioneer of geology, the Frenchman Georges Cuvier, synthesized scientific evidence showing that the earth had sustained a series of catastrophic events that had extinguished some forms of life, and that these were followed by the appearance of unprecedented forms. Though Cuvier would still identify the latest of these catastrophes with Noah's Flood, he diminished the privileged position of the Flood in explaining extinctions. By 1831 Adam Segdwick, the influential president of the Geological Society (England) had openly decried the folly of giving credence to Mosaic accounts at the expense of what is observed in nature.

"Christian Geology." The revolution in geology in the nineteenth century resulted in the vigorous promotion of a pro-Christian version of geology in the twentieth century, especially in the United States. One of the most famous proponents was George McCready Price, a Seventh-Day Adventist who wrote *The New Geology* (1923) and founded the Deluge Geology Society. His most prominent successors were John C. Whitcomb and Henry Morris, authors of *The Genesis Flood* (1961), which became the standard statement of what is sometimes known as "Flood Geology," itself part of a broader response to evolution. Many creationists argue that Noah's Flood can explain the order of all fossils in the stratigraphic record.

Modern Archaeology. Archaeology confirms that there exists no global discontinuity in human habitation at the time to which most believers date the Flood (10,000–5000 BCE). A single archaeological stratum should be correlated around the globe recording such an interruption in human habitation. The famous British archaeologist Sir Leonard Woolley did claim to find evidence of Noah's Flood at Ur in Mesopotamia. But this announcement was soon reversed when it became obvious that even other parts of that city had not suffered flooding. Nonetheless, Woolley's premature claim is cited in many Christian apologetic books.

Modern Biblical Scholarship. Detecting the multiple and contradictory sources behind the biblical account of Noah's Flood is probably the main contribution of modern biblical scholarship, which had crystallized by the late nineteenth century. For example, in Genesis 6:19, Noah is commanded to bring aboard the Ark one male and one female member of every kind of animal. In 6:22 the author informs us that Noah completed this task ("Noah did this"), but Genesis 7:2 introduces a new command to bring aboard *seven* pairs of clean and one pair of unclean animals, which is nonsensical if there was already one pair of every kind aboard. For these and other reasons, the consensus of modern scholarship is that variant flood stories have been combined.

The discovery of Mesopotamian flood stories, beginning in the nineteenth century, confirmed that biblical accounts were variants of earlier nonbiblical flood stories reaching back to the third millennium BCE. The most famous of these is found in the epic of Gilgamesh, a copy of which was found in the library of the Assyrian king Ashurbanipal at Niniveh. That story also features a hero, Utnapishtim, who is told to build a boat to save himself from a flood about to be sent by hostile gods. After the flood subsides, Utnapishtim sends out three birds (Noah sends two), and the boat comes to rest on a mountain. As in the case of Noah, Utnapishtim offers sacrifices after his exit from the boat.

The Mass Media and Unbelief in Noah's Flood. The mass media has become another venue for debate about Noah's Flood. One interesting example is the television "documentary" *The Incredible Discovery of Noah's Ark* (1993), produced by Sun Pictures under the aegis of David Balsiger, author of other dubious efforts to support biblical beliefs. Soon after the program's broadcast on CBS, skeptic George Jammal announced that he had manufactured some of the items that were touted as relics of Noah's Ark in that program. Jammal helped to expose the fact that many Christian apologists, including the noted creationist John Morris (who, at one point, apparently accepted Jammal's artifacts as authentic), were uncritical in evaluating data.

Otherwise, there have been many sensationalized reports of sightings or visits to the Ark. In the 1950s French businessman Fernand Navarra, author of *Noah's Ark: I Touched It* (1974), claimed to have visited the Ark and brought back wood from it. The American astronaut James Irwin, who walked on the moon as part of the Apollo 15 mission in 1971, mounted a few expeditions to Mount Ararat in the 1980s and wrote *More Than an Ark on Ararat* (1985).

Recent Developments. In 1998 two oceanographers, William Ryan and Walter Pitman, published *Noah's Flood: The New Scientific Discoveries about the Event That Changed History*, which argued that a real inundation that created the Black Sea around 5600 BCE underlies both the Mesopotamian and the biblical accounts. Ryan and Pitman claim that most people survived this flood because there was enough time to flee to safer areas. However, among other problems, Ryan and Pitman provide no scientific criteria to distinguish a genuinely preserved memory from a subsequent literary creation. For example, why is there a "memory" about a boat on top of a mountain if thousands of people had no need to escape in a boat at all?

Conclusion. The tsunami of 2004 shows that catastrophes involving water are a recurrent part of the human experience. Therefore, it is not surprising to find flood stories all over the world. Insofar as Noah's Flood is concerned, the fact remains that there has never been found either a single layer of flood destruction that can be correlated around the globe, or definitive evidence of an ark on a mountain. In short, there is no evidence for the occurrence of Noah's Flood, while a veritable flood of evidence points to its legendary character.

BIBLIOGRAPHY

Cohn, Norman. *Noah's Flood: The Genesis Story in Western Thought*. New Haven, CT: Yale University Press, 1996.

Dundes, Alan, ed. *The Flood Myth*. Berkeley and Los Angeles: University of California Press, 1988.

Numbers, Ronald L. *The Creationists: The Evolution of Scientific Creationism*. Berkeley and Los Angeles: University of California Press, 1992.

HECTOR AVALOS

NONCOGNITIVISM. Noncognitivism is the philosophical view that certain classes of sentences are not cognitive (or cognitively meaningful). For a sentence to be cognitive, it needs to be the kind that can express knowledge, which implies expressing a proposition. (A proposition is any set of ideas that is true or false, can be believed or disbelieved, asserted, and employed in reasoning, and which can be regarded as the meaning of a declarative sentence. An example would be the proposition that snow is white.) When noncognitivism claims that certain classes of sentences are not cognitive in that sense, it is saying that their declarative form is misleading, concealing their true import. Instead of stating something true or false, as they appear to do, such sentences actually fail to convey any literal meaning. The main candidates for the classes of sentences deemed to be noncognitive are value judgments and religious utterances. When dealing with unbelief, the focus is on declarative sentences that contain the word *God* (sometimes referred to as God-talk). Noncognitivism in this context (theological noncognitivism) is the view that God-talk is noncognitive; in other words, it fails to express any proposition or anything that is true or false.

Noncognitivism needs to be distinguished from ATHEISM, taken as the view that God does not exist (sometimes called positive atheism). According to atheism in that sense, the sentence "God exists" does express a proposition but a false one. In contrast, noncognitivism says that the sentence "God exists" expresses no proposition whatever. Whereas atheists maintain that people's concept of God does not match anything in reality, noncognitivists maintain that there is no such thing as a concept of God, the word "God" itself

being literally meaningless. On the other hand, if atheism were instead simply defined as the absence of theistic belief (sometimes referred to as negative atheism), then it would include noncognitivism (along with AGNOSTICISM and positive atheism). The earliest defense of noncognitivism was by Charles BRADLAUGH, though he referred to it as atheism. The earliest use of the term *noncognitivist* was by Rudolf Carnap.

The view most closely associated with noncognitivism is LOGICAL POSITIVISM, which advocates the principle that a statement is literally meaningful (i.e., cognitive) if and only if it is either analytic or empirically testable, as stated by Sir Alfred Jules AYER. This principle is objectionable for many reasons. First, it is unclear what a statement is supposed to be. If it is a proposition, then it is not the sort of thing that could be called meaningful or meaningless (since it is already a meaning of a certain sort). And if it is a sentence, then it is not the sort of thing that could be said to be testable (or verifiable), those terms being applicable only to propositions. Second, since only propositions could correctly be said to be untestable, the untestability of something cannot be used to show that it fails to express a proposition. In other words, if there is no proposition there, then there is nothing there that could be said to be untestable, so testability/untestability cannot be a criterion of cognitivity/noncognitivity. A third objection often raised is that, for various reasons, it is unclear just what it is for something to be empirically testable. A good critique of logical positivism is given by Paul Edwards.

The question might be raised whether contradictions are cognitive. As *cognitive* is defined above (requiring merely that there be a proposition expressed), contradictions are indeed cognitive, for they do express propositions and are usually regarded as false. (Every contradiction is a conjunction of two propositions, and every conjunction of two propositions is itself a proposition.) The logical positivists regarded analytic sentences to be cognitive. If *analytic* includes analytically false as well as analytically true, then contradictions would be included, for they are analytically false. On the other hand, the term *cognitive* might be taken to mean "expressing a thinkable (or conceivable) proposition," in which case contradictions would be excluded. This alternate usage of cognitive is discussed elsewhere; let us disregard it here, as it is not the most common usage and it would take us too far afield.

A Transcendent God. Whether or not God-talk is cognitive (expressive of propositions) depends on how God is defined. Consider the following definition (call it D1):

D1: God is the omnipotent, omniscient, transcendent, nonphysical, personal being who created the universe out of nothing and currently sustains and rules it.

Is the sentence "God exists" cognitive when God is defined as in D1? In other words, does the sentence express a proposition? It might be argued that some of the given properties are incompatible with each other. For example, being omnipotent might be incompatible with being omniscient, since an omnipotent being can make himself ignorant, whereas an omniscient being cannot do that. Consider also the property of being transcendent, that is, existing outside (or independent of) space and time. It might be argued that a personal being cannot possibly be transcendent since a personal being needs to be a particular entity that is able to perform physical actions within space and time, whereas something that is transcendent cannot be or do such things. (Similar considerations could be raised with regard to the property of being nonphysical.)

The issue of whether the properties in definition D1 are compatible with one another will not be pursued here. Even if they are incompatible, the sentence "God exists" would still express a proposition (albeit a necessarily false one). It need not be a contradiction (or analytically false), as there are other kinds of incompatibilities between properties, but there would definitely be a false proposition there, indeed one which could be proven false. Hence, the sentence "God exists," taking God as in D1, would still be cognitive (or literally or cognitively meaningful) even if the properties in the definition were incompatible with one another.

In order to prove that the given sentence fails to express any proposition whatever, one would need to show that at least one of the individual terms within D1 is itself incomprehensible. Some have argued that *omnipotent* or *omniscient* is meaningless. However, if that just means that the given term is self-contradictory, then we are back to the situation of incompatible properties. For example, suppose it is argued that "omnipotent" is meaningless because an omnipotent being would need to be able to make himself weak, but for an omnipotent being to be weak would be a contradiction. Even if this were a good argument, all it would show is that "omnipotent" is a self-contradictory concept, which would make "God exists," as understood in terms of D1, a self-contradictory statement. As seen above, that is not enough to make the sentence noncognitive.

A more likely target would be the term *transcendent*. What possible sense could be attached to "being outside (or independent of) space and time"? Even physicists who speak of other forms of time do not go so far as to speak of something being totally outside (or independent of) space and time. Maybe a sense could be attached to the term if it is applied to abstractions. Might it be said of numbers, for example, that they are independent of space and time? It is a controversial issue, but let us be charitable and say that there are things (abstract entities such as numbers) that are transcendent. At least that would allow the term "transcendent" to have some meaning or use and would make a sentence of the form "X is transcendent" cognitive, for there would then be some proposition expressed by it. Of course, there would remain the

problem of whether "X is transcendent" is compatible with "X is a personal being," but that is a separate issue, and, as shown above, not relevant to the cognitivity of "God exists," as understood in terms of definition D1. The verdict is still out, but there is reason to maintain the cognitivity of "God exists," understood in the given way.

Other Definitions. Consider the following three alternate definitions of God:

D2: God is that being which is absolutely perfect in every way.

D3: God is that being which is self-existent, that is, which contains the explanation for its own existence within itself.

D4: God is the ultimate ground of Being, which cannot be positively characterized in any way.

Each of these presents additional problems. The question for each definition is whether or not it would allow the sentence "God exists" to express a proposition. If "being perfect" is a subjective predicate, as seems reasonable, then it appears that definition D2 would fail in that regard. The sentence "God exists," taken in that way, would turn out to be noncognitive.

Similarly, definition D3 would be a failure if no literal meaning could be assigned to "X contains the explanation for its own existence within itself." Philosophers and theologians have made some effort toward clarifying that clause, but their work remains dubious and controversial. If they fail, then "God exists," taking God as in D3, would also need to be regarded as noncognitive.

As for definition D4, several problems arise. There is, first, the problem of comprehending what Being is supposed to be. Then there is the problem of understanding the idea of an ultimate ground and, in particular, the expression "the ultimate ground of Being." Finally, there is the question whether any concept is defined when no positive characteristics are assigned to it. If all we are told is that God is not this and not that, and so on, running through every predicate in the language, then what are we left with? Philosophers have complained that the so-called *via negativa* necessarily fails to define any concept, and the complaint seems legitimate. In that case, no proposition is expressed by "God exists" when God is defined by D4, and the sentence is properly characterized as noncognitive.

Each of these issues is complex and ongoing, but there certainly is point to the charge that "God exists" is sometimes noncognitive. There is merit to the hypothesis that although the anthropomorphic God-talk of everyday people in ordinary language is cognitive, at least some of the arcane God-talk of theologians (and some philosophers) is noncognitive. In any event, the issue of the cognitivity of God-talk needs to be addressed on a case-by-case basis, with very close attention given to the exact definition of God supplied.

We are left with a question of statistics: What proportion of the uses of the word "God" by people speaking or writing English would allow the sentence "God exists" to express a proposition and thereby be cognitive? In other words, what proportion of God-talk are cognitivists right about, and what proportion of it are noncognitivists right about? There have been no specific studies directed at these questions, but the proportion in each case seems to be significantly greater than 0 percent and significantly less than 100 percent. My own rough guess is that about half of all God-talk that actually occurs is cognitive and another half (mainly in the speech and writings of theologians and philosophers) is noncognitive.

BIBLIOGRAPHY

Ayer, A. J. *Language, Truth and Logic*. London: Victor Gollancz, 1936.

———, ed. *Logical Positivism*. Glencoe, IL: Free Press, 1959.

Bradlaugh, Charles. "A Plea for Atheism." In *Charles Bradlaugh: Champion of Liberty*, edited by J. P. Gilmour. London: Watts, 1933.

Carnap, Rudolf. "The Elimination of Metaphysics through Logical Analysis of Language." Translated by Arthur Pap. *Erkenntnis* 2 (1932). Reprinted in A. J. Ayer, ed., *Logical Positivism*. Glencoe, IL: Free Press, 1959.

Drange, Theodore. "Is 'God Exists' Cognitive?" *Philo* 8, no. 2 (2005).

———. *Nonbelief & Evil: Two Arguments for the Nonexistence of God*. Amherst, NY: Prometheus Books, 1998.

———. *Type Crossings: Sentential Meaninglessness in the Border Area of Linguistics and Philosophy*. The Hague: Mouton, 1966.

Edwards, Paul. "Logical Positivism and Unbelief." In *The Encyclopedia of Unbelief*, edited by Gordon Stein. Amherst, NY: Prometheus Books, 1985.

THEODORE DRANGE

NORWAY, UNBELIEF IN. In 2000 Norway had a population of about 4.5 million. The official religion is Evangelical Lutheranism, to which 86.2 percent of the population belonged in 1999. Other Protestant and Catholic groups had 3.8 percent; other religious groups, 5.2 percent; and "none," 4.8 percent.

ATHEISM was slow in coming to Norway. Jo Gjende, an early freethinker (see FREETHOUGHT), seems to have been a deist (see DEISM) from about 1830 on. Marcus M. Thrane, "the first Norwegian socialist" and another early freethinker, claimed to believe in God, but his concept of God was so devoid of content that Thrane undoubtedly was very close to atheism. Søren Jaabæk, a well-known peasant politician, was a sharp critic of organized religion, but he continued to believe in God.

The famous playwright Henrik Ibsen seems to have been an atheist as an adolescent, but later seemingly became a deist. Another famous author, Knut Hamsun, seems to have been an atheist as a young man, and perhaps also later in life, but in old age he seemingly returned to his childhood religious faith.

A few stable forms of atheism established themselves in Norway from around 1870 on. The biologist Gerhard Henrik Armauer Hansen seems to have been an atheist from around 1870 to the end of his life. He was influenced by Charles DARWIN, as was the zoologist, explorer, and humanitarian Fritjof NANSEN, an atheist most of his life.

The author Arne Garborg seems to have been a reluctant atheist from about 1873 on. He arrived at his basic beliefs through religious thinking and religious doubt. The author Alexander Kielland was a sharp critic of organized religion and seems to have been an atheist from the 1880s on. Another radical author, Hans Jæger, seems to have been an atheist from about 1878 on.

The shipowner and politician Christian Michelsen, prime minister of Norway between 1905 and 1907, can probably be best described as an agnostic for most of his adult life.

Throughout most of the nineteenth century, there was very limited freedom of expression and no real freedom of religion in Norway. Everyone was expected to be Lutheran. Widespread suspicion was directed against everyone who was not, particularly against Jews, Catholics (especially Jesuits), and of course freethinkers and atheists. Until sometime between 1850 and 1870, atheism was commonly considered unthinkable and popularly linked with immoral behavior. For the rest of the century atheism remained a rare phenomenon. Even in the first decades of the twentieth century, atheism was rarely advocated openly and continued to be associated by its adversaries with immoral behavior.

The growth of atheism was stimulated by Darwinism, by religious doubts for which no satisfactory answers could be found, by a growing awareness of the multiplicity of religions all claiming to represent the truth, and by internal and external criticism of religion, including Marxist criticism (see MARXISM). Friedrich Nietzsche's atheism, known in Norway since about 1890, stimulated the growth of Norwegian atheism only to a very limited extent.

Beginning in or just before the 1920s, atheism came to be taken for granted in some circles, often stimulated by Marxism, growing knowledge of the natural sciences, astronomical discoveries, common sense, and rising awareness of the existence of moral systems without any religious foundation.

Apart from some freethought clubs that sprung up between 1911 and 1915, nonpolitical atheism generally remained unorganized in Norway until the Human-Etisk Forbund (Human-Ethical Society) was established in

1956. Then, in 1974, Det Norske Hedning-Samfunn (Norwegian Society of Heathens) was established. Both organizations still exist. Human-Etisk Forbund, with about sixty thousand current members, may be the largest freethought society in the world, whereas there are about three hundred registered Heathens.

According to Norway's Central Bureau of Statistics, in 1999, 86.2 percent of Norwegians belonged to the Norwegian Lutheran State Church, as noted above. This means that in that year, 13.8 percent of the Norwegian population did not belong to the state church. These nonmembers belonged either to another religious organization, or organizations such as Human-Etisk Forbund and Hedningsamfunnet, or did not belong at all. (As recently as 1970, as much as 95.1 percent of the population belonged to the Norwegian Lutheran State Church.)

Survey studies of the Norwegian population suggest that in the 1990s about 70 percent of the population had a religious belief of some kind, believing in a personal god, spirit, or life force, whereas about 30 percent did not have such a belief. About 30 percent of the population believed in a personal god, that is, a god who cares about the fate of each individual. Also, up to 30 percent of the population did not believe in any god, and thus were atheists in the broad sense of the word.

Survey studies indicate that in 1997, 16.9 percent of the members of the state church were atheists in the sense of not believing in any god.

BIBLIOGRAPHY

Hiorth, Finngeir. *Secularism in Norway*. Oslo: Human-Etisk Forbund, 2002.

FINNGEIR HIORTH

NYSTRÖM, ANTON (1842–1931). See SWEDEN, UNBELIEF IN.

OFFEN, BENJAMIN (1772–1848), American freethought activist, lecturer, and author. Benjamin Offen was born in Sussex, England, to a farming family on December 30, 1772. He was self-educated and worked on his family's farm until the age of nineteen, when he then began training as a shoemaker. At the age of twenty-two he completed his training and eventually moved to London to ply his new trade. After opening a shop and trying several religions (he was unsatisfied with those he experienced) he and his family immigrated to West Point, New York, and later moved to New York City in 1824.

Upon his arrival in New York City, Offen began his vocation as a freethinker. In 1827 he helped create the Freethought Press Association (FPA) and became its president. He began to lecture and debate on various freethought topics, but his specialty seemed to be BIBLICAL CRITICISM. The FPA disappeared in 1829, and

Offen reappeared as a contributor and lecturer for the Society of Moral Philanthropists.

The Society of Moral Philanthropists conducted lectures and debates on Sundays in Tammany Hall, and Offen was a regular lecturer for over ten years. Offen also went on speaking tours, mostly in upstate New York, and continued these "missions" until the early 1840s. During these tours he lectured, debated clergy, and sold freethought books and subscriptions to the various freethought publications published in New York and Boston. His own book on biblical criticism, *A Legacy to the Friends of Free Discussion* (1846), wasn't available until after he ended his speaking tours. Offen was a regular contributor to such freethought publications as the *BOSTON INVESTIGATOR, Correspondent*, and the *Beacon*.

Offen worked tirelessly to promote freethought, to the detriment of his shoemaking business, which he seemingly ignored for great stretches of time as a result of his freethought activities. Some of his freethought colleagues (including Gilbert VALE and Frances WRIGHT) held a benefit for him in 1839 to raise funds for him to live on. Despite this lack of funds, Offen retired from shoemaking at the age of seventy. Offen was the impetus for Vale's purchase of sixty acres of Thomas PAINE's farm as a haven for destitute freethinkers.

BIBLIOGRAPHY

Allen, William H. "Funeral Oration, Eagle Hall, New York. May 21st, 1848." *Boston Investigator*, June 7, 1848.

Bennett, D. M. *World's Sages, Infidels and Thinkers*. New York: Bennett, 1876.

Post, Albert. *Popular Freethought in America, 1825–1850*. New York: Octagon, 1974.

TIMOTHY BINGA

O'HAIR, MADALYN MURRAY (1919–1995), American atheist activist. Courageous, intelligent, and good company on the right day, Madalyn Murray O'Hair was also abusive, divisive, and a source of strength for the enemies of ATHEISM. Born Madalyn Evalyn Mays on April 13, 1919, in Pittsburgh, Pennsylvania, she was the second child of John Irvin and Lena Christina Mays. The family was quarrelsome and forever short of money, forcing it to move often, either in search of work or to dodge creditors.

World War II opened up a new range of opportunities for people like Madalyn Mays. After a brief marriage to John Henry Roths in 1941, Madalyn enlisted with the Women's Auxiliary Army Corps in January 1943 and found her war service liberating and exhilarating. She returned to the United States in 1945, pregnant following an affair with William Murray, a Catholic officer who then disowned her. The baby, William Joseph Murray III, was born on May 25, 1946. After a while Madalyn started calling herself Madalyn Murray.

Far too intelligent and restless for the narrow range of choices available to women of her generation and background, Murray moved around—physically, emotionally, and intellectually. Having inherited her feisty intelligence from her mother, she graduated with a BA from Ashland College in Ohio in 1948 and a law degree from South Texas College of Law in 1952. Madalyn's second child, Jon Garth Murray, was born on November 16, 1954, the product of a brief liaison with a work colleague after she moved to Baltimore. In 1965 Murray married Richard O'Hair, a shady character with an excessive love of drink. Like all of her relationships, her marriage to Richard O'Hair was turbulent and had long broken down when Richard was diagnosed with cancer in 1977. In the final act of their love-hate relationship, Madalyn nursed Richard right up until his death in 1978.

It was in the mid-1950s, after flirting with communism and trade unionism (see SOCIALISM AND UNBELIEF; LABOR MOVEMENT AND UNBELIEF), that Madalyn Murray found her vocation in atheism. She had concluded that organized Christianity was behind much of the hypocrisy, shallowness, and conformism of American life. The rest of her life was concerned with an idiosyncratic blend of self-promotion and dedication to an unpopular cause.

Madalyn Murray O'Hair, as she came to be known, claimed to be the most significant legal figure of the twentieth century. While this is far from being the case, nothing can diminish her courage during the long struggle that led to the June 17, 1963, Supreme Court decision in *Murray v. Curlett*, which ruled that school prayer was indeed unconstitutional. This decision was hugely important for American education, law, and politics. It helped reshape the American cultural landscape, but was achieved at a high personal cost. O'Hair and her family were the target of ongoing harassment and abuse. Characteristically, though, O'Hair squandered her moral authority as a victim of persecution for her beliefs by advancing a selective account of the legal battle, in particular an unseemly squabble for priority with a concurrent case, *Abington Township v. Schempp*, in which the plaintiffs were practicing Unitarians (see UNITARIAN UNIVERSALISM). O'Hair later claimed that the Supreme Court decision, which responded to both cases together, was an attempt to deny O'Hair and atheism the kudos for the victory.

On the strength of the *Murray v. Curlett* decision, O'Hair founded American Atheists, although a predecessor organization had been founded in 1959. Over the next thirty years O'Hair became one of the best-known opponents of Christianity in American history. In contrast to most other significant non-Christian leaders, O'Hair attracted quite a lot of media attention. This was a double-edged sword for the movement. If all publicity is indeed good publicity, O'Hair's exposure could only be a good thing. But viewed from the perspective of combating old prejudices about atheism, O'Hair's media exposure was to say the least unhelpful.

O'Hair was not reticent in advancing her claims for priority. The O'Hairs were frequently referred to in their own literature as the First Family of Atheism. More specifically, O'Hair described herself as the best-educated, most widely known atheist leader in the United States. Elsewhere, she described herself not simply as *an* atheist, but as *the* Atheist. Declarations such as this were backed up by regular purges of members who were thought to have forgotten that fact. These histrionics notwithstanding, O'Hair did occasionally get it right, as with *O'Hair v. Hill* (1984), where she successfully overturned the discriminatory practice in Texas of requiring state employees and potential jurors to vow a belief in God.

The most serious reversal for O'Hair was the defection of Bill Murray, her son and the person in whose interest *Murray v. Curlett* was originally brought. Bill had never been able to find his feet. He drank heavily and drifted from job to job and woman to woman. Occasionally he returned to O'Hair and American Atheists, only to argue once again with his mother and storm off. He fathered a daughter, Robin, whom O'Hair filed to adopt in 1967, raising her as Robin Murray-O'Hair. Bill "found God" in 1980 and set about forging a career that revolved around trading on his past. With that in mind, in 1982 he published a self-serving tell-all account of his years as an atheist. There were some famous arguments within the ranks of atheism as well. George H. Smith, author of the Objectivist-inclined *Atheism: The Case against God*, was an early casualty. Others came and went, not infrequently people who had won awards at American Atheists conventions only the year before.

Perhaps the most ill-judged, expensive, and counterproductive of O'Hair's legal battles was over the fate of THE TRUTH SEEKER. Once the United States' greatest freethought paper, *The Truth Seeker* was a shadow of its former self in 1981 when O'Hair suggested to James Hervey JOHNSON that she take the paper over and inherit its substantial capital assets. Johnson turned the offer down. O'Hair ruminated on this for several years before engineering a takeover of the paper in 1987 that provoked a squalid contest that was still under way when the O'Hairs disappeared in 1995. O'Hair made every possible error of judgment during this case and the only winners were the lawyers.

By the early 1990s it was apparent that American Atheists was in serious trouble. In October 1991 O'Hair had a serious heart attack; she never recovered her former health and vitality. Her weakened condition exacerbated growing tensions and quarrels. This was brought to a head early in 1992, when O'Hair dissolved the regional chapters and centralized the organization. The main reasons for this were chronic infighting in the chapters and their tendency to challenge O'Hair's primacy. Problems also grew for *American Atheist* magazine, which had improved considerably between 1988 and 1992. Under growing financial and health pressures, the journal staggered and in 1992 collapsed. It was replaced by an expanded newsletter.

By the time Madalyn, Jon Garth, and Robin Murray-O'Hair disappeared in September 1995, the organization was in severe difficulty. Not least of its woes was the ever-dwindling number and quality of people prepared to work for it. Everyone else had left, bitterly estranged by the time David Waters, a career criminal with convictions for a range of brutal crimes, was employed as typesetter and office manager. It was Waters, along with two accomplices, who bore responsibility for the abduction and murder of the O'Hairs. The most likely date of their death is September 29, 1995, although it is possible that Robin died four days previously.

Madalyn Murray O'Hair's legacy is mixed. *American Atheist* had its ups and downs, but in its day was a good magazine. One strength was its historical awareness, particularly with respect to freethought history. But such an orientation serves to give a journal a backward-looking emphasis, which contributes in turn to the generally hostile and uncomprehending attitude to the world as it actually is. Less successful were the books American Atheists chose to publish, which pursued eccentric theses or were poorly written. More valuable were the pamphlets, which were concise and well designed for their target market.

O'Hair made three great contributions to the progress of atheism: two of them marked by what she did, the other by what she didn't do. The first of the positive contributions was the *Murray v. Curlett* case, which helped change cultural conditions in America forever. The second positive contribution was to advance the cause of atheism in a way nonspecialists could appreciate. For all the valid criticisms made of American Atheists during her lifetime, that organization was a refuge for many people who had seen the discriminatory side of religion and who wanted a full-bodied rejection of religion. O'Hair was one of the greatest promoters of popular atheism since Joseph MCCABE and Chapman COHEN.

O'Hair's other major contribution was in what she didn't do. At no time did she give any comfort to the fundamentalists who sought to portray atheism or HUMANISM as a religion. If O'Hair's rejection of religion was often unhelpfully expressed and easily used by opponents to portray atheism as extreme negativity, it never fell into the trap of painting atheism as a "me too" substitute to religion.

Balanced against these positive contributions are the negatives. O'Hair's legendary vulgarity served only to confirm the prejudices of those who would equate atheism with a breakdown in morality. It also drove away many who might otherwise have been worthwhile allies. Her high media profile was as much due her ability to single-handedly damage the atheist position as to any recognition of her eminence. More damaging still

was her destructive bunker mentality, which also served to alienate friends and strengthen enemies.

These personal flaws may well have been surmountable, but they were exacerbated by intellectual flaws of similar magnitude. The greatest of these was in not seeing the intellectual limitations of atheism. Atheism is not enough of a foundation on which a viable nonreligious system can be built. Atheism states only what one does not believe in; the next step is to move forward and determine what one does believe in. Exploring the realms of NATURALISM and humanism are essential to giving atheism a positive orientation. Organizations united only by what they hate or fear rarely prosper long without feuding and dissension. But more important than mere organizational tension, such an approach misunderstands and fatally undersells humanism as a viable way of living without religion. Humanism is much more than mere rejection of religion, and here Madalyn Murray O'Hair made no positive contribution whatever.

BIBLIOGRAPHY

Cooke, Bill. "Atheist in a Bunker." *Free Inquiry* 23, no. 2 (Spring 2003).

LeBeau, Bryan. *The Atheist: Madalyn Murray O'Hair*. New York: New York University Press, 2003.

O'Hair, Madalyn. *An Atheist Epic*. Austin, TX: American Atheist Press, 1989.

Seaman, Ann Rowe. *America's Most Hated Woman: The Life and Gruesome Death of Madalyn Murray O'Hair*. New York: Continuum, 2005.

Zindler, Frank. "Madalyn Murray O'Hair." *American Atheist*, Spring 2002.

BILL COOKE

O'HAIR, ROBIN MURRAY. See **O'HAIR, MADALYN MURRAY.**

ORWELL, GEORGE (ERIC ARTHUR BLAIR; 1903–1950), English author. Eric Arthur Blair, who later adopted the pseudonym "George Orwell," was born in India as the son of a civil servant. In 1904 his mother took him and his sister to England for their education. He later described his childhood loneliness and said he felt "isolated and undervalued." The misery of his life in preparatory school is described in "Such, Such Were the Joys" (1953), which was so scathing it could not be published even overseas until after his death. Young Eric qualified as a King's Scholar at Eton, but seems to have done little during the next four years except to read whatever he pleased. He did not apply for university, but in 1922 went to Burma to join the Indian Imperial Police. In his introduction to the French edition of *Down and Out in Paris and London* (1935), he describes himself as "totally unsuited" for police work. In that same introduction, he makes the point, so important for interpretation of his whole work, that although his theme, the misery of the human condition, is unpleasant, and although he writes directly and honestly, it does not follow that his memories of his own life are necessarily unpleasant. He seems to have found his place as a writer early in life, and although commercial success was slow in coming, there is every indication that he relished his life as a writer.

In England on leave in 1928, he resigned to devote himself to writing, a career he pursued with mixed success to the end of his life. Orwell's works include novels, documentary books, journalism, and poetry, but he is today most widely known for the concepts presented in *Animal Farm* (1945) and in *Nineteen Eighty-Four* (1949), specifically the way that language can and has been used to control thought, a process Walter Lippmann had earlier called the "manufacture of consent" and that has since become universally known as Orwellian abuse of language, through such techniques as insisting on the use of Newspeak as opposed to the ordinary traditional speech and engaging in doublethink, the ability to maintain contradictory ideas simultaneously.

Nineteen Eighty-Four is a warning, if not a prediction, with regard to the future, but it is also a satire on the England of the year it was finished—1948—with the last two digits reversed, as is documented in W. J. West's *The Larger Evils*. It also reflects Orwell's concern for the disregard for objective truth going back at least to his experiences in the Spanish Civil War.

Orwell's View of Religion. Orwell wrote a good deal about religion, but his remarks are scattered about in his writings. More importantly, almost all his work bears on aspects of the human condition that must be of concern to anyone interested in religion and the critique of religion. The state of the church as portrayed in *A Clergyman's Daughter* (1935) and the state of the poor as presented in *Down and Out in Paris and London* (1933) and in *The Road to Wigan Pier* (1937) are essential background to any theology or antitheology.

Orwell was an atheist (see ATHEISM), but because of his knowledge of, sympathy for, and fairness toward the religion of his native England, some commentators have presented him as at least a partial believer. A more accurate view is that Orwell was a tough-minded atheist who saw the difficulty inherent in all positions on the religious question and who had a profound understanding of what it is about human life that has made traditional religion so appealing to so many for so long.

Proof of Orwell's Atheism. According to biographer Bernard Crick, Orwell was "a clear Humanist, even a Rationalist with a pronounced anti-Catholicism, even though one with an ironic attachment to the liturgy, the humane political compromises and the traditions of the Church of England" (see HUMANISM; RATIONALISM; ANTICLERICALISM). The depth of Orwell's atheism is evidenced by his remark to David Astor that anyone who claimed to believe in life after death was being dis-

honest. Orwell was assigned to write the 1947 volume *The English People* in the popular *Britain in Pictures* series. He began the second chapter by pointing out that since about 1800, religion for almost all of the English people had been little more than the formalities of marriage and burial and acceptance of an ethic of loving one's neighbor, all of which applied to him personally. He went on to say English people "do not know the Bible stories even as *stories.*"

His "Religious" Belief. Orwell referred to an *unspoken* doctrine of the church, which he said was held by the bulk of the common people and by himself, but not by the upper classes. That doctrine is that might is not necessarily right. "If there is hope, it lies with the proles," he wrote in *Nineteen Eighty-Four.* The proles are "uneducated" and so they still assume that truth is one thing and what is said by those in power is another. The modern, educated classes know otherwise. Fear of punishment after death sustained this belief in objective reality in the past, but the great problem of the modern world is that we have lost that hope and that fear. As Orwell wrote in 1944, "Life on earth, as [our ancestors] saw it, was simply a short period of preparation for an infinitely more important life beyond the grave. But that notion has disappeared, or is disappearing, and the consequences have not really been faced." These are the opinions of a thoughtful atheist, nothing more.

The Modern Quandary. Orwell's view of the impossible situation of humanity in modern times is best illustrated in chapter 5 of *Keep the Aspidistra Flying* (1936). There, a character describes our situation as rather like that of Buridan's donkey, except that there are three alternatives: socialism (see SOCIALISM AND UNBELIEF), suicide, and the Catholic Church. More generally, the "Catholic Church" stands for traditional religion. Modern people who are serious and take the doctrines literally, as intended, understand those doctrines are factually false, but this is not to say that they would not be effective for the good of society if we were able to believe them. The problems with socialism are illustrated in *Animal Farm* and are argued at length in many of Orwell's essays. Orwell found all substitutes for religion unsatisfactory. What he discovered in Spain during the civil war and in his wartime work for the BBC was that the defense of democracy against totalitarianism may require resort to techniques of thought control that end up undermining democracy. So without hope of divine intervention there is no hope at all, except perhaps with the proles. The third alternative, suicide, correlates with the "nihilistic quietism" Orwell attributed to Henry Miller. Here again he shows nuanced feelings of attraction and repulsion. Orwell eventually considered a fourth alternative, the reconstruction of Christian doctrine as being true in some sense, but not literally so. Here his criticism is almost unmitigated.

BIBLIOGRAPHY

Crick, Bernard. *Orwell: The First Complete Biography.* Boston: Little, Brown, 1980.

Orwell, George. *The Complete Works of George Orwell.* Edited by Peter Davison. 20 vols. London: Secker, 1998.

Rodden, John. *The Politics of Literary Reputation: The Making and Claiming of "St. George" Orwell.* New York: Oxford University Press, 1989.

Spiller, Leroy. "George Orwell's Anti-Catholicism." *Logos: A Journal of Catholic Thought and Culture* 6, no. 4 (2003).

Taylor, D. J. *Orwell: The Life.* New York: Holt, 2003.

Thiemann, Ronald F. "The Public Intellectual as Connected Critic: George Orwell and Religion." In *George Orwell: Into the Twenty-first Century*, edited by Thomas Cushman and John Rodden. Boulder: Paradigm, 2004.

West, W. J. *The Larger Evils.* Edinburgh: Canongate, 1992.

DAVID WHITE

OUIDA (MARIE LOUISE DE LA RAMÉE; 1839–1908), English novelist and long-closeted freethinker. Ouida was born Louise Ramé at Bury St. Edmunds, Suffolk, England, to a middle-class Englishwoman and a French rake. Before he vanished Louis Ramé managed to give young Ouida (as she childishly mispronounced "Louise") an above-average education, also filling her head with romantic notions of intrigue and elite culture. In time he stole to Paris to vanish during the 1871 Commune. By then, Ouida—now her chosen pseudonym—was a household name.

At eighteen, Ouida had persuaded her mother and grandmother to move to London so she could become a novelist. In short order she sold a story to W. Harrison Ainsworth, editor of a popular literary review. He would publish eighteen more in the next three years. Ouida's characters were larger than life, her plots melodramatic, her stories "naughty" but free of Victorian moralizing. She became a sensation; at age twenty-six her novels sold as briskly as those of Charles Dickens. Some theorized she was actually George ELIOT. Her *Strathmore* (1865), *Chandos* (1866), and *Under Two Flags* (1867) were hugely successful; in the lattermost, Ouida invented the troubled character who joins the Foreign Legion in order to forget. Unsurprisingly, Edward George Bulwer-Lytton praised her work; but so did Henry James. As late as 1891, freethought orator Robert Green INGERSOLL told the Chicago *Inter-Ocean* that "Ouida is probably the greatest living novelist, man or woman." She is best known today for her 1872 children's story, the oft-filmed *A Dog of Flanders.*

Ouida moved to Europe and lived beyond her eventually dwindling means. Alternately she fled from creditors (sometimes accompanied by as many as thirty dogs) and campaigned for animal rights, helping to found the Italian Society or Prevention of Cruelty to Animals. She died in poverty in Italy.

Ouida's fiction dealt but little with religion; she revealed freethought views in an 1895 nonfiction book, *Views and Opinions.* Her essay titled "The Failure of Christianity" demonstrated an understanding that all religions, Christianity included, are human inventions; she accused Christianity in particular of moral hypocrisy and of fomenting the very hostilities that its ethic of love claims to prevent. The essay had some minor impact in view of Ouida's prior fame; it was cited approvingly by anarchist Emma Goldman (see ANARCHISM AND UNBELIEF) as late as 1917.

BIBLIOGRAPHY

Gaylor, Annie Laurie. *Women without Superstition.* Madison, WI: Freedom From Religion Foundation, 1997.

Goldman, Emma. "Anarchism: What It Really Stands For." In *Anarchism and Other Essays*, 3rd ed. New York: Mother Earth, 1917.

Sutherland, John. *The Stanford Companion to Victorian Fiction.* Stanford, CA: Stanford University Press, 1989.

TOM FLYNN

OWEN, ROBERT (1771–1858), British industrialist, philanthropist, polemicist, and social reformer. Robert Owen is primarily remembered as a crusader for communitarian socialism, early childhood education, and the cooperative movement. Most of his life was dedicated to attempts to improve the working conditions, education, and environment of impoverished factory workers and the development of cooperative utopian communities. Convinced that character was the product of the interaction between human nature and the environment, Owen argued that education was the key to improving human society. Education would lead to a universal revolution in human thought and behavior that would replace irrationality with rationality. Owen presented his vision of a new rational society with the certainty of a prophet in his many lectures, debates, pamphlets, journals, and books. His ideas and goals, however, were regarded with suspicion among his more conservative peers because of his outspoken criticism of capitalism and traditional religious beliefs.

Challenging prevailing social and religious doctrines, Owen publicly admitted that he believed all religions contained gross errors that caused human beings to become bigots, fanatics, and hypocrites. In particular, Owen thought that the religious doctrines held by his contemporaries were detrimental to the advance and implementation of social reform. Critical of many aspects of religion and capitalism, Owen predicted the eventual emergence of a "new moral world." Marxist critics such as Friedrich Engels called him a "utopian socialist," while even his admirers considered him rather naive and overly optimistic in his assessment of human nature.

Early Life and Career. Owen was born on May 14, 1771, in Newtown, a small town in North Wales, to Anne Williams Owen, the daughter of a farmer, and Robert Owen, an ironmonger and saddler. Although Owen was an excellent student and remained a prodigious reader throughout his life, his formal education ended when he was nine. After serving as an apprentice in a draper's shop in Manchester, he established a firm that manufactured cotton-spinning machinery and became manager and part owner of several different cotton mills. During this period, Owen became a member of the Manchester Literary and Philosophical Society and a member of the Manchester Board of Health.

In 1799 Owen and his partners purchased David Dale's cotton mills in New Lanark, Scotland. That same year, Owen married Dale's daughter, Anne Caroline Dale, and became a member of one of England's leading industrial families. Dale's factories employed more than one thousand men, women, and children. While continuing to make respectable profits, Owen instituted a series of programs that improved living and working conditions for all workers, establishing schools and stores, and refusing to hire children under the age of ten.

Although the New Lanark mills continued to provide respectable profits, Owen's partners objected to his expanding reform efforts, forcing him to enlist more enlightened individuals to buy out his original partners. Convinced that industrialists would not voluntarily support labor reforms, Owen campaigned for laws that would protect workers. Parliament passed a Factory Act in 1819, but it was far weaker than the legislation Owen had proposed.

By 1816, having accumulated a considerable fortune, Owen was able to relinquish routine management of the mills and devote himself to pursuing his social and educational theories. Owen disseminated his ideas through lectures, publications, and the creation of organizations such as the Institute for the Formation of Character and the Home Colonization Society.

Communitarian Villages. To create a better society and solve the social and economic problems of workers, Owen suggested the establishment of self-sustaining cooperative villages. Communitarian villages would offer decent housing, communal kitchens, nurseries, and schools, as well as farm and factory work. Unfortunately, the model villages inspired by Owen's theories were generally short-lived.

Hoping to find a more receptive environment in America, Owen purchased land in Indiana. His New Harmony venture consumed much of Owen's wealth, but his plans for a new utopia were thwarted by disagree-

ments about property rights and opposition to his outspoken views on religion. Leaving New Harmony to his sons, William and Robert Dale OWEN, he returned to London, where he devoted himself to publicizing his causes in a series of generally short-lived newspapers, including the *Crisis*, the *Rational Quarterly*, and the *Millennial Gazette*. In 1832 he announced the establishment of a "labor exchange" in London. Although this venture was unsuccessful, the concept of allowing workers to exchange "labor notes" for consumer goods provided a model for consumer cooperatives and labor exchanges. In 1858 Owen published his autobiography, *The Life of Robert Owen, Written by Himself*. He died on November 17 in the same year, in Newtown, the town of his birth, and was buried next to his parents.

BIBLIOGRAPHY

Bestor, Arthur. *Backwoods Utopias: The Sectarian Origins and the Owenite Phase of Communitarian Socialism in America, 1663–1829*. Philadelphia: University of Pennsylvania Press, 1970.

Cole, George Douglas Howard. *The Life of Robert Owen*. Hamden, CT: Archon, 1966.

Cole, Margaret. *Robert Owen: Industrialist, Reformer, Visionary, 1771–1858*. London: Robert Owen Bicentenary Association, 1971.

Harrison, John F. C. *Quest for the New Moral World: Robert Owen and the Owenites in Britain and America*. New York: Scribner's, 1969.

Owen, Robert. *The Life of Robert Owen, Written by Himself: With Selections from His Writings and Correspondence*. 2 vols. New York: Augustus M. Kelley, 1967.

———. *A New View of Society or Essays on the Formation of the Human Character*. New York: Augustus M. Kelley, 1972.

Pollard, Sidney, and John Salt, eds. *Robert Owen, Prophet of the Poor*. London: Macmillan, 1971.

Royle, Edward, *Robert Owen and the Commencement of the Millennium: A Study of the Harmony Community*. Manchester, UK: Manchester University Press, 1998.

LOIS N. MAGNER

OWEN, ROBERT DALE (1801–1877), American writer, educator, reformer, legislator, diplomat, and statesman. Although Robert Dale Owen held beliefs that many of his contemporaries regarded as radical, he became a respected member of the Indiana General Assembly and the US House of Representatives. Owen supported progressive social legislation and was instrumental in the establishment of the Smithsonian Institution. Considered an advocate of FREETHOUGHT, Owen campaigned for causes ranging from the abolition of slavery to birth control, rights for women and workers, free public schools, and better roads. Owen's writings included books and pamphlets on architecture, education, birth control, theology, and spiritualism.

Early Life. Robert Dale Owen, the eldest son of the British industrialist and social reformer Robert OWEN and Caroline Dale Owen, was born in Glasgow, Scotland, on November 7, 1801. Young Robert and his siblings absorbed the traditional religious beliefs of their mother, but their father introduced them to the world of skepticism, freethought, and comparative theology. Robert was educated at his father's model school in New Lanark and Emmanuel von Fellenberg's progressive school in Switzerland. Returning to New Lanark in 1823, he assumed much of the burden of managing the family's factories and supervising the school.

In 1825 the elder Robert Owen purchased property in Indiana in order to establish a communitarian village called New Harmony. Two years later, discouraged by the apparent failure of his Indiana venture, Robert Owen returned to England. Robert Dale Owen and four of his siblings remained in New Harmony and became distinguished American reformers, scientists, and educators. As editor of the *New Harmony Gazette*, Owen became closely associated with the abolitionist, feminist, social reformer, and atheist Frances WRIGHT. Owen accompanied Wright on a trip to her experimental community at Nashoba, Tennessee; Europe; and New York, where Owen became editor of the freethought journal the *Free Enquirer*.

Perhaps the most controversial work that Owen undertook was the publication of *Moral Physiology: or A Brief and Plain Treatise on the Population Question* (1830), the first American book to advocate birth control (see BIRTH CONTROL AND UNBELIEF). Although clergymen condemned Owen's book, it went through many editions and sold more than seventy-five thousand copies before Owen's death in 1877. Owen argued that women should not be burdened with ignorance and unwanted pregnancies. By recommending coitus interruptus (also known as onanism), however, he placed the burden for limiting pregnancies on men. According to Owen, French physicians had told him that this method was widely and successfully used in France. Owen discussed the barrier sponge method and partial withdrawal, which had been recommended by Richard CARLILE in *Every Woman's Book: or, What Is Love?* (1826), but dismissed these methods as ineffective. The adoption of birth control, Owen believed, was part of the inevitable progress of human improvement. In 1832 Charles KNOWLTON, an American physician, published a similar book, *The Fruits of Philosophy: or The Private Companion of Young Married People*, which was famously denounced as an "indecent, lewd, filthy, bawdy, and obscene book."

Marriage Protest and Political Career. On April 12, 1832, Owen married Mary Jane Robinson in a simple ceremony performed by a notary public. The Owens explained that their decision to contract a legal marriage was not because they thought marriage necessary or useful, but because they did not want to be subjected to the petty "annoyances" that would occur if they simply became companions. Owen and his wife signed a declaration in which Owen forfeited the unfair rights granted to husbands over wives by law and religious dogma. Although Owen acknowledged that their declaration was not legally binding, he publicly declared that he considered himself "utterly divested" of the unjust rights that were "the barbarous relics of a feudal, despotic system." The newlyweds then visited England, where Owen helped his father edit the *Crisis* and organize a labor exchange in London before the couple returned to settle in New Harmony.

On returning to Indiana, the former radical successfully confronted the need to support his own family through farming and land speculation. Owen became interested in politics, actively pursued public office, and focused his reform activities on education, the abolition of slavery, and women's rights. In 1838 he was elected to the first of three terms in the Indiana General Assembly. Before becoming a candidate for the US House of Representatives, Owen acknowledged that his youthful enthusiasm had led him to support causes that might seem radical, but he argued that these activities had provided a foundation for his commitment to pragmatic social reforms. This concession might have caused Owen's estrangement from former associates in the freethought movement. Conservative critics, however, continued to view Owen as a radical. For example, when Owen was invited by the Union Literary Society of Hanover College to deliver an address, the president of the college and some of the trustees refused to allow an "infidel" to speak on campus.

After two unsuccessful campaigns, Owen was elected to his first term in the House of Representatives, where he served from 1843 to 1847. As a member of Congress, he introduced the bill that established the Smithsonian Institution. Owen's attempt to win a third term in Congress was unsuccessful. In 1850 Owen was elected to Indiana's Constitutional Convention, where he was instrumental in securing property rights for widows and married women, tax support for public schools, and the reform of divorce laws.

To reward Owen's party loyalty, President Franklin Pierce appointed him charge d'affairs and resident minister to Italy, where he served from 1853 to 1858. On his return to the United States, Owen became an outspoken opponent of slavery, authoring *The Policy of Emancipation* (1863) and *The Wrong of Slavery* (1864). On September 17, 1862, Owen wrote a letter to President Abraham Lincoln urging him to issue a proclamation emancipating the slaves. Owen argued that the nation could never enjoy peace and prosperity if the "blighting curse" of slavery continued to exist. Lincoln said that Owen's letter struck him "like a trumpet call." Five days later, Lincoln issued the Emancipation Proclamation.

Spiritualism. Historians called Owen a radical who

believed in the inevitability of progress and a skeptical attitude toward ancient dogmas. Contemporaries, however, were struck by the fact that he began his public life as an "infidel" and ended his career as a believer in spiritualism (see SPIRITUALISM AND UNBELIEF). Owen's conversion to spiritualism became widely known in 1859 when he published *Footfalls on the Boundary of Another World*. In 1871, after the death of his first wife, Owen published *The Debatable Land between This World and the Next*. These books were highly regarded by members of the spiritualist community, but condemned by American freethinkers and evangelical Christians. In 1876 Owen married Lottie Walton Kellogg. He devoted his last years to writing about social problems and an autobiography, *Threading My Way* (1874). On June 24, 1877, he died at his summer cottage on Lake George, New York.

BIBLIOGRAPHY

Bestor, Arthur. *Backwoods Utopias: The Sectarian Origins and the Owenite Phase of Communitarian Socialism in America, 1663–1829*. Philadelphia: University of Pennsylvania Press, 1970.

Kesten, Seymour R. *Utopian Episodes: Daily Life in Experimental Colonies Dedicated to Changing the World*. Syracuse, NY: Syracuse University Press, 1993.

Kolmerten, Carol A. *Women in Utopia: The Ideology of Gender in the American Owenite Communities*. Bloomington: Indiana University Press, 1990.

Leopold, Richard William. *Robert Dale Owen: A Biography*. Cambridge, MA: Harvard University Press, 1940.

Owen, Robert Dale. *Robert Dale Owen's Travel Journal, 1827*. Edited by Josephine M. Elliott. New Harmony: Indiana Historical Society, 1978.

———. *Threading My Way: Twenty-seven Years of Autobiography,* New York: A. M. Kelley, 1967.

———. *The Wrong of Slavery, the Right of Emancipation, and the Future of the African Race in the United States*. New York: Kraus, 1969.

Owen, Robert Dale, and Charles Knowlton. *Birth Control and Morality in Nineteenth-Century America; Two Discussions*. New York: Arno, 1972.

Pancoast, Elinor, and Anne E. Lincoln. *The Incorrigible Idealist: Robert Dale Owen in America*. Bloomington: Principia, 1940.

Zellner, W. W., and William M. Kephart. *Extraordinary Groups: An Examination of Unconventional Lifestyles*. New York: Worth, 2001.

LOIS N. MAGNER

PAINE, THOMAS (1737–1809), American author, revolutionary, freethinker, and reformer. Thomas Paine's life as archetype and the works of his pen as ideology continue to inspire and animate almost every social and political movement for equal rights, democracy, and liberty of conscience. The history of unbelief would be incomplete without reference to Paine's *Age of Reason,* an analysis and critique of the Bible and superstition, and the greatest attack on established religion and Christian doctrine ever written. No other figure from the late eighteenth century exerted a greater continued influence upon leaders and movements for reform, FREETHOUGHT, and democracy than Thomas Paine.

Early Life. Paine was born in Thetford, England, on January 29, 1737. His father, Joseph Paine, was a Quaker and his mother, Frances Cocke, a member of the Church of England. Paine's childhood in a mixed-religion household doubtless provided the foundation for his at once unorthodox and tolerant views on religion. He followed his father's trade and became a staymaker, but Paine was always yearning for something more than manual labor. He left home at sixteen years and later, "heated with the false heroism" of an admired schoolmaster, joined the crew of the privateer *Terrible,* whose skipper sported the audacious moniker Captain William Death. Paine's affection and admiration for his father may be felt in his recollection that "[f]rom this adventure I was happily prevented by the affectionate and moral remonstrance of a good father who, from his own habits of life, being of the Quaker profession, must have begun to look upon me as lost." The *Terrible* lost 90 percent of its crew, including Captain Death. The impression left by his father's remonstrance and the fate of the *Terrible* must have suffered the short half-life of youth, because the following year Paine went to sea on the *King of Prussia*. The voyage was successful and Paine received for his portion of the prize what seemed a handsome sum to a young man of humble means.

Paine stayed in London about a year subsequent to his return from sea. As Paine recounted, "[T]he natural bent of my mind was to science. . . . As soon as I was able I purchased a pair of globes, and attended the philosophical lectures of Martin and Ferguson, and became afterward acquainted with Dr. Bevis, of the society called the Royal Society, then living in the Temple, and an excellent astronomer." Later he moved to Dover, Sandwich, and Margate, where he practiced his father's trade, probably dabbled with Methodism, and married a young woman of whom he became enamored, Mary Lambert. His wife and infant died in childbirth. Historians speculate to what degree his young wife's death affected Paine; he left not a word on the subject.

Paine first gained prominence, ironically enough, while an officer of the Crown in the excise or tax service. His first appointment was in the market town of Alford, center of a region then known for smugglers. Paine was afterward dismissed and rehired in a series of events still debated among historians. Paine's new post was in the village of Lewes, Sussex, where he met and married his second wife, Elizabeth Ollive, in 1771. Here Paine wrote his first published work, a twenty-one-page request for better pay and working conditions known as *The Case of the Officers of the Excise* (1772). Paine was sacked for his efforts while he lobbied in London, and not long afterward he and Elizabeth agreed to an amicable separation. Paine never remarried, and he was never again credibly linked with another woman in other than a platonic friendship.

The world owes Thomas Paine's epic revolutionary career to Benjamin FRANKLIN. While in London, Paine had a copy of his excise pamphlet delivered to Irish playwright Oliver Goldsmith along with the request of "his company for an hour or two." Goldsmith agreed and the two quickly became friends. Paine arranged an introduction through Goldsmith to Franklin, who would become his lifelong mentor and friend. Franklin encouraged Paine to emigrate to America in 1774. He was thirty-seven years old.

American Works. Franklin's letter of recommendation gained Paine a position as editor of the *Pennsylvania Magazine*, where he improved his already considerable skills in writing and polemic. Unable to resist the climate of change and reform that infused American life, Paine plunged into the issues of the day and launched a career that would make his name renowned.

A good deal of confusion exists concerning the authorship of early essays credited to Paine, thanks to the near-universal reliance on pseudonym in that period. Historian Frank Smith long ago proved that Paine did not write *An Occasional Letter on the Female Sex* (1775), an early plea on behalf of women. Paine gets credit for its publication, but did not author it. The case is somewhat stronger for *African Slavery in America* (1775), but while every biographer and editor since Moncure CONWAY has accepted Paine's authorship, historian Alfred Owen Aldridge believed "there is no good reason" to ascribe the work to Paine. Regardless of the authorship of that essay, Paine was throughout life an outspoken critic of slavery and inhumanity of all forms. While at the *Pennsylvania Magazine*, Paine advanced his lifelong interest in poetry and wrote essays against cruelty to animals, dueling, aristocratic titles, and in support of Quakers who found pacifism inadequate in the face of British attacks.

Thomas Paine's *Common Sense* (1776), caused Joel BARLOW (see TREATY OF TRIPOLI), not John Adams, to write that "the great American cause owed as much to the pen of Paine as to the sword of Washington." From the wealthiest landowner to the humblest shoemaker, colonists were won over to the idea of independence by Paine's pamphlet. Widespread acceptance of its arguments prepared the way for the signing of the Declaration of Independence six months later. So universally acclaimed was his earliest important work that Paine himself was known as "Common Sense" and was so addressed by many throughout his life. Paine appreciated the importance of his seminal work. Thirty-three

years later his last wish was that his gravestone simply say, "Thomas Paine—Author of *Common Sense*."

Paine's first major work united the colonists for independence. His second, a series of essays titled *The American Crisis* (1776–83), preserved Washington's army and inspired the populace in one of the revolution's darkest hours. By December of 1776, defeat, retreat, desertion, and short enlistment expirations had reduced Washington's original army by more than half. They camped half frozen, poorly equipped, sullen, and bloodied while Congress abandoned Philadelphia and patriotic citizens evacuated in droves. Those who had never wholly supported the rebellion infected others with their discontent. The infant republic appeared stillborn, and Washington wondered if he might be hanged, drawn, and quartered for treason. Paine's "These are the times that try men's souls . . ." is a phrase still almost universally invoked in times of great urgency. If *Common Sense* may be said to have inspired the Revolution, *The American Crisis* preserved and sustained it. Washington ordered it read to his troops on Christmas Eve 1776, the night before the colonials' first victory in the Battle of Trenton. Printing presses leaped into action and Paine's fame soared, but this was just the beginning.

Paine's reputation for letters now widespread, the Continental Congress called upon him to serve as the secretary to the Committee for Foreign Affairs. His exposure of an early defense procurement scam caused a scandal and made enemies that would shadow him the rest of his life. Paine went to France with John Laurens in order to secure desperately needed arms, ammunition, and supplies. They returned with funding and equipment that enabled the colonies' first major victory, the Battle of Saratoga. Paine also served for a time as secretary to the Pennsylvania General Assembly, where he had a hand in writing the first law in the world governing the abolition of slavery.

Paine was an inventor who remained deeply interested in the sciences throughout his life. He secured a position in the history of engineering with his invention of the first single-span iron bridge. He also developed a smokeless candle and discussed ideas for a planing machine, steam navigation, a crane, and a theory that gunpowder might serve to drive a motor. The desire to promote his iron bridge took Paine back to England not long after the cessation of revolutionary hostilities.

Return to Britain. While in England, Paine authored *Rights of Man* (1771–92), his two-part reply to Edmund Burke's attack on the French Revolution and still the foundational text on democratic government. He was then fifty-four years of age. The storm of controversy it sparked in England and its subsequent sales were even greater than those of *Common Sense*. Historian John Keane calls it "the best selling book in the history of publishing." Paine's list of enemies within the elite swelled.

During a 1791 visit to Paris, Paine joined Brissot de

Warville, the Marquis de CONDORCET, Etienne Chaviére, and Achille Francois Châtelet to found the Société des republicains, which opposed the restoration of Louis XVI. With Lanthenas and Paine's lifelong friend, publisher Nicolas de Bonneville, he started the journal *Le Républicain.* Paine and Châtelet plastered the streets of Paris with a manifesto against monarchy and in favor of a new French Republic. Said Paine, "[A]gainst the *whole hell* of monarchy . . . I have declared war." When Bonneville was later put under arrest and denied exit from France, Paine sheltered his friend's wife and children in America.

By the time Paine returned to Britain, a political storm had broken out, with his *Rights of Man* at the center of the cyclone. A judicial summons was issued and the jaws of the law closed upon him. Forewarned by William Blake of his imminent arrest and likely execution, Paine rode to Dover, a government spy in close pursuit, and sailed for the French coast.

France. Received as a revolutionary hero in France, Paine was elected to the French Assembly from four *départements*, the French equivalent of states. He co-authored the first French constitution and spoke eloquently against Louis XVI's execution, a performance that enraged the Jacobins and put his life in danger. Paine was trapped. He could return neither to England nor to America without risk of capture and execution.

The guillotine rose and fell with the breath of the doomed as Paine's friends went one by one to the scaffold. Paine expected his own arrest daily. He had already written his political testaments. Now he hoped to live long enough to address the most dangerous and volatile issues of all: theology and established religion. The first part of his *Age of Reason* (1794) was completed six hours before his arrest and passed to Barlow as Paine was led to prison. He wrote the greater portion of the second part in jail, despite grave illness. Saved from the guillotine by a jailer's chalk mark on the wrong side of a door, Paine lived to again attend the French Convention and receive a young admirer, Napoleon, who said he slept with *Rights of Man* under his pillow and that a "statue of gold should be erected to you in every city of the universe."

The Age of Reason was another runaway best-seller in America and Europe. But as its circulation grew, religious fundamentalists reacted with alarm and Paine's political enemies gloated. In perhaps the most successful smear campaign in history, Federalists flogged Paine with his religious views in order to discredit his democratic radicalism, while religious conservatives called down anathema and invective on the great "Agent of Lucifer." Though *Age of Reason* was written to forestall a headlong descent into ATHEISM by the French Revolution, it was called the work of an atheist. Though Paine wrote movingly in praise of the God of Nature (see DEISM), his enemies painted him as a godless man.

Agrarian Justice (1795) is another important contribution to social justice written in this time. Less well known than many of Paine's works, it contains the earliest proposal for a funded social security system. The US Social Security Administration considers it a formative text, and it is posted in the history section of its Web site today.

Last Days in America. Paine returned to America in 1802 when treaties opened a brief window of opportunity to travel without risking arrest. Popular reaction to the Federalist administrations of Washington and Adams had placed Paine's friend Thomas JEFFERSON in the presidency. When Jefferson welcomed Paine to the White House, a firestorm of protest erupted in the Federalist press. Paine was hounded and castigated at least as much as he was honored and feted upon his return. He continued to write essays on religious subjects, many of which appeared in Elihu PALMER's *Prospect* and are generally cataloged as *The Prospect Papers* (1804). Paine also wrote on political and economic subjects, including *Constitutions, Governments, and Charters* (1805), and a a December 25, 1802, letter to Jefferson that may be the earliest proposal for the Louisiana Purchase.

Thomas Paine died peacefully on June 8, 1809. Undiscerning biographers still repeat the slanders published by Paine's enemies, despite the efforts of FREETHOUGHT and reform publisher Gilbert VALE to systematically disprove them in his *Life of Thomas Paine*, written more than 160 years ago. Paine never was the impoverished, broken-down mess that his enemies described after his death. He was a moderate drinker who consumed less than the standard for his day. His estate was valued at twelve thousand dollars at his death, a substantial sum for that period. Paine bequeathed most of it to Madame Bonneville and her children, one of whom became Captain Benjamin Bonneville of western exploratory fame. Paine lived abstemiously in later life, but he was far from impoverished or ungenerous. Nor did he recant his religious views, another fraudulent litany still chanted by religionists today.

In 1839 Vale erected a marble monument over Paine's gravesite in New Rochelle, New York. The grave itself had been robbed of its contents in 1819 by William Cobbett, who took the bones back to England, where they subsequently disappeared after Cobbett's death.

Paine's Legacy. Thomas Paine lives on through his life and works. Paine has been admired and invoked by individuals as diverse as Ronald Reagan, Emma GOLDMAN, Walt WHITMAN, Barry Goldwater, Thomas Edison, and Abraham Lincoln. All of Paine's major writings and many lesser-known works are still in print. His ideas are discussed in schools and universities, historical societies, political parties, freethought associations, and even in churches. His works formed the nexus around which the struggle for press freedom was waged in Great Britain. Paine's early practical proposal for arms reduction and a League of Nations is a dream still in progress at the United Nations.

The history of unbelief is inextricably intertwined with Thomas Paine and his *Age of Reason*, the foundation text of American and British SECULARISM. Thomas Paine birthday celebrations, first held in 1818 in England

and 1825 in the United States, are occasions when the leaders of freethought, equal rights, labor, secularism, and cooperation may meet, recharge their enthusiasm, and organize around the words and life of the "father of modern reform," Thomas Paine.

BIBLIOGRAPHY

Claeys, Gregory. *Thomas Paine: Social and Political Thought.* Boston: Unwin Hyman, 1989.

Conway, Moncure Daniel. *The Life of Thomas Paine.* New York: G. P. Putnam's Sons, 1908.

———. *The Writings of Thomas Paine.* New York: G. P. Putnam's Sons, 1906.

Foner, Philip S., ed. *The Complete Writings of Thomas Paine.* New York: Citadel, 1945.

Fructman, Jack. *Thomas Paine: Apostle of Freedom.* New York: Four Walls Eight Windows, 1994.

Kaye, Harvey J. *Thomas Paine: Firebrand of the Revolution.* New York: Oxford University Press, 2000.

Keane, John. *Tom Paine: A Political Life.* Boston: Little, Brown, 1995.

Vale, Gilbert. *The Life of Thomas Paine.* New York: G. Vale, 1841.

Williamson, Audrey. *Thomas Paine: His Life, Work, and Times.* New York: St. Martin's, 1973.

KENNETH W. BURCHELL

PALMER, ELIHU (1764–1806), American freethinker and militant deist. Elihu Palmer, who began his public life in 1787 as a Presbyterian minister in what is now the New York City borough of Queens, metamorphosed into one of the most radical freethinkers in the young American republic. A local historian with whom Palmer apparently stayed while recovering from a smallpox inoculation witnessed the early stages of the minister's transformation. One evening Palmer's host overheard him reciting a well-known couplet embodying Calvinist orthodoxy: "Lord, I am vile, conceived in sin,/And born unholy and unclean." Palmer turned to another guest and declared that he did not believe a word of this sentiment. The guest advised him to be cautious about such remarks, given that they would not sit well with local parishioners.

The warning proved prophetic; Palmer was dismissed from his pulpit less than a year later, moved to Philadelphia, and joined the more liberal Baptist Church in 1789. The Baptists dismissed him, too, and Palmer then announced his allegiance to the new Universalist Church and his rejection of the divinity of Christ (see UNIVERSALISM TO 1961). There was only one problem: Universalists believed in the divinity of Jesus, and Palmer and his small group of followers were soon banned in Philadelphia. Palmer then placed an advertisement in a local publication of his intention to preach a sermon challenging the divinity of Jesus. His biographer later reported that "the society of Universalists were in an uproar; and being joined by people of other denominations, instigated probably by their priests, an immense mob assembled at an early hour before the Universalist Church, which Palmer was unable to enter. In fact, it is stated, he was in personal danger, and was induced to quite [quit] the city, somewhat in the stile of the ancient apostles on similar occasions."

Deciding that his prospects in any ministry were nil, Palmer took up the study of law and passed the bar in 1793. A few months later, the nation's first epidemic of yellow fever took more than five thousand lives in Philadelphia. Palmer's wife was among the dead, and although he survived, his sight was destroyed. His enemies saw his blindness as God's punishment for heresy, notwithstanding the thousands of fresh graves housing the corpses of pious Christian believers.

Since blindness had put an end to his prospects as a lawyer, Palmer then took to the road as an itinerant lecturer on deism. His first stop was Augusta, Georgia—Georgia had modeled its law separating church and state on Virginia's pioneer 1784 statute establishing religious freedom—where he delivered a series of lectures from the steps of the courthouse. In contrast to his treatment in Philadelphia, Palmer's reception in Georgia reflected a religious liberalism that still prevailed in a region where Thomas JEFFERSON and James MADISON were revered. Then Palmer swung north to New York City, where he received a decidedly cooler reception when he attacked the doctrine of the Virgin Birth on Christmas Day. He even delivered a scathing attack on Christianity's most sacred doctrine—the redemption of man by Christ's death on the cross.

For all his abrasiveness, Elihu Palmer is an important figure in the history of American SECULARISM because, like the much better known Thomas PAINE, he attempted to carry the message of DEISM beyond its original audience of educated upper-class intelllectuals. Between 1804 and his death in 1806, Palmer published two deist newspapers in New York—the *Temple of Reason* and *Prospect, or View of the Moral World.* He organized deist societies in New York City; Newburgh, New York; Philadelphia; and Baltimore; their membership was drawn not from prominent citizens but from artisans and shopkeepers.

Palmer's only full-length book, his 1801 *Principles of Nature; or, a Development of the Moral Causes of Happiness and Misery among the Human Species,* sold out three editions before 1806. In Palmer's view, all nonreligious advances in human thought began with the invention of the printing press and proceeded toward the day when philosophical assaults on church and state despotism produced both the American and French revolutions. "This philosophy," he declared, "has already destroyed innumerable errors; it has disclosed all the fundamental principles which have been employed in the construction of machines, mathematical instruments, and the arrangements of those moral and political systems which have softened the savage and ferocious heart of man, and raised the ignorant slave from the dust, into the elevated character of an enlightened citizen."

Elihu Palmer died destitute in 1806. His widow (he had remarried after his first wife died of yellow fever) was supported by Thomas Paine, a man of great personal charity in spite of his own reduced financial circumstances.

BIBLIOGRAPHY

Fellows, John. "Memoir of Mr. Palmer" In *Elihu Palmer's "Principles of Nature,"* edited by Kerry S. Walters. Wolfboro, NH: Longwood, 1990.

Koch, G. Adolph. *Republican Religion: The American Revolution and the Cult of Reason.* New York: Henry Holt, 1933.

Riker, James. *The Annals of Newtown, in Queens County, New-York.* New York: D. Fanshaw, 1852.

SUSAN JACOBY

PARANORMAL, BELIEF IN THE. Though there are many definitions of *paranormal* (literally, *para-* "beyond" the normal), the term often refers to phenomena or events that seem to defy naturalistic explanations. Typical paranormal topics include astrology, psychic powers, UFOs, fortune telling, homeopathy, ghosts, and auras. Strictly speaking, a paranormal event is not simply one beyond the ordinary, since remarkable, odd, and unusual occurrences happen all the time. (As one statistician noted, in a country with three hundred million people, a one-in-a-million chance happens three hundred times a day.) Nor is a paranormal phenomenon merely one for which there is no ready explanation at hand, since *unknown* is not the same as *unknowable.* Information unknown one day may be common knowledge the next; diseases once thought to be caused by curses are now known to be the result of germs and genes.

Belief lies at the core of the paranormal, since truly paranormal events, like supernatural beings, have never been proven to exist. Evidence, on the other hand, lies at the core of science. Botanists are not asked if they "believe in" photosynthesis, and physicists are not asked if they "believe in" gravity. Yet skeptics are often asked if they "believe in" astrology or phrenology, and atheists or agnostics may be asked if they believe in God. For skeptics, as for unbelievers, the issue is not belief but evidence.

Belief in the paranormal is widespread; surveys show consistently that significant numbers of Americans believe in ghosts, psychic powers, astrology, UFOs as extraterrestrial spacecraft, and so on. Expanding the definition of *paranormal* to include belief in God moves that number into the majority. Many paranormal claims touch upon issues of religion and unbelief; those interested in atheism, humanism, and unbelief will find much in common with those skeptical of the supernatural and the paranormal.

Philosopher Paul Kurtz has discussed a "transcendental temptation," the tendency in human nature to accept a paranormal or occult universe. The inherent human desire to look outside ourselves for meaning leads some to religion, some to paranormal belief, and many to both. Unbelief can be viewed as the logical conclusion of skepticism, and surveys of top scientists have found that a vast majority of them hold no religious belief. While many skeptics are humanists or unbelievers, others quite comfortably hold beliefs in deities and find no contradiction between these beliefs and their skepticism.

Paranormal and Religious Belief. Nearly all religions are based on a belief in paranormal gods or a single god (see RELIGION). Lesser paranormal entities (such as angels, demons, djinn, etc.) may also be invoked as messengers or agents of the supernatural deities. Many religions have miracles and paranormal beliefs unique to them. Christianity, for example, has an entire subset of explicitly Catholic paranormal claims, such as Marian apparitions, simulacra (appearance of holy personages in random patterns such as stains on cloth, in windows, clouds, etc.), and miraculous statues that bleed or weep (see MIRACULOUS PHENOMENA). These are often the result of proven fraud or perceptual errors, such as pareidolia (in which the mind creates specific images in response to ambiguous stimuli).

Those who claim to miraculously bear the wounds of Jesus are referred to as suffering from stigmata. Stigmatics will sometimes exhibit blood on their hands and feet, as well as on their side (as from a spear wound) and head (as from a crown of thorns). Stigmata appear only among devout Catholics, and the wounds are such that fraud and trickery cannot be ruled out. Many cases of religious-paranormal hoaxing are committed not for financial or personal gain, but instead to draw adherents and reinforce faith among believers.

Exorcism and demonic possession are also explicitly religious paranormal phenomena. The Bible cites several examples of Jesus exorcising demons (e.g., Matt. 17:18, Luke 9:42, Luke 11:1), though exorcisms have become somewhat secularized by mass-market pop-culture treatments (films and books such as *The Exorcist* and *The Amityville Horror*, for example).

Because both religion and the paranormal presume the supernatural, adherents share many common attributes. Indeed, the line between religion and the paranormal can be porous. Many cults combine Christian endtimes prophecy with belief in extraterrestrial aliens and UFOs. The most famous example in recent years was the Heaven's Gate cult, whose leaders believed they were special messengers from God. The group, thirty-nine of whose members committed suicide in 1997, believed that the comet Hale-Bopp was a sign to exit the earth for their heavenly rewards.

Like religion, the paranormal often separates believers from nonbelievers. Though believers claim plentiful evidence for their ideas, most also recognize that the issues fundamentally rest on faith. Thus the question "Do you believe in UFOs?" (or Bigfoot, or psychics) is parallel to "Do you believe in Catholicism?" Skeptics and unbelievers, in contrast, distinguish themselves by questioning the very premises of belief. A platitude often heard in paranormal circles is that "for those who don't believe, no evidence will suffice. For those who believe, no evidence is necessary."

Though there is some debate about the appropriate breadth of scientific and skeptical inquiry regarding religion, traditionally the skeptical movement has restricted itself to examining testable claims. For example, the issue of whether humans have souls is not a testable (or falsifiable) question (see FALSIFIABILITY), though a claim that the soul can be measured is appropriate and verifiable through scientific inquiry. (At one point the weight of the human soul was believed to be twenty-one grams, the amount of weight a body lost at death as mismeasured by a doctor.) Similarly, a stigmatic either does or does not have actual wounds that open up spontaneously and miraculously; a clairvoyant or dowser either can or cannot perform feats under controlled conditions. Other paranormal religious claims said to have been validated by science include creationism, the existence and location of Noah's Ark (see NOAH'S FLOOD AND UNBELIEF), and faith healing.

Whether the issue is unseen ghosts, unseen aliens, or unseen deities, the underlying question in both paranormal and religious claims is why people believe as they do. Belief in the paranormal is in this respect a psychological issue at its core. The human mind is designed to seek patterns, and is so successful that it often sees patterns where none exist. Thus gamblers may believe they are on a lucky streak when in fact random chance has just caught up with them, or a devout pilgrim may see a "miraculous" religious image in tree bark or a coffee stain. Neither belief is inherently silly—instead, both result from natural and common human errors in thinking.

Paranormal Belief through the Ages. Belief in the paranormal has apparently remained a constant in human history. Early societies held animistic beliefs, imbuing natural objects such as trees, water, and earth with spirits that could be petitioned or controlled through rituals. Stories of miracles and monsters date to before biblical times. As the Enlightenment flourished and science provided naturalistic explanations for previously mysterious phenomena, the paranormal took on new forms. Paranormal ideas mutate and are periodically repackaged and translated into a new context for each new generation. Bigfoot and the Loch Ness monster have replaced unicorns and mermaids; claims of talking to the dead have replaced claims of raising them.

For example, many trace the modern UFO or flying saucer era back to 1947, but fanciful stories of crashed spacecraft and their dead alien occupants date back to the late nineteenth century and earlier, when such ideas were expressed in fiction before being adapted to the modern UFO lore. Even a phenomenon as apparently timeless as communicating with the dead has changed dramatically over the past century. As longtime paranormal investigator Joe Nickell has pointed out, messages from beyond the grave were florid and profuse at the turn of the twentieth century, yet "[b]y contrast, today's spirits—whom [modern] mediums supposedly contact—seem to have poor memories and difficulty communicating. . . . Gone is the clear-speaking eloquence of yore; the dead now seem to mumble."

Strictly speaking, the paranormal involves supernatural or magical elements, powers, or deities. Magical thinking and superstition are common to both religious belief and the paranormal. Unseen and unknowable forces more powerful than ourselves are believed to influence our lives, whether through astrology, divine intervention, psychic powers, the spirit world, and so on. These forces suggest a personal involvement with the supernatural. Instead of an impersonal God uninterested in human lives and affairs, deities offer paternalistic, individualized attention. Similarly, witnesses to supposedly paranormal events often speak of having been specially chosen to receive the experiences. Thus ghosts and aliens, for example, are seen as messengers from beyond the grave or beyond the stars, imparting personally relevant warnings and wisdom.

Both paranormal and religious belief systems contain an underlying (and often implicit) dissatisfaction with humanity and its potential. We are not happy with ourselves or our abilities, and so we seek soothsayers in robes or collars to reassure us of the future and impart the specialized wisdom they claim to access. Astrologers and psychics hold the same relation to the unseen world as priests and rabbis do.

The paranormal, like religion, often elevates certain people above others. It suggests that a select few have access to special abilities and powers. The paranormal field teems with authors, gurus, self-appointed experts, and spirit guides who claim to have esoteric connections and powers others don't. A fundamental tenet of skepticism and unbelief, in contrast, is that we are all the same deep down: no one has magical psychic powers or divination tools unavailable to the rest of us; none of us is any "better" than other people, except in how we conduct and improve ourselves.

Skepticism, like unbelief, suggests that the answers to our problems and questions lie not in the stars, nor in mystical books or unseen gods, but in ourselves. It is our very human capacities that unite us; skepticism shows us that we should measure ourselves against our fallible, uniquely human qualities, not our wishful notions of mystical powers.

Recognizing and Avoiding Paranormal Beliefs. Like any belief based upon insufficient evidence, paranormal beliefs can be dangerous, especially when they influence important life decisions. People who believe that their bad luck is caused by a curse or black magic sometimes take lethal revenge on the person they believe cast the curse; disease victims have shunned traditional medical treatment in favor of prayer or unproven "alternative" medicines. The skeptical literature is rife with such examples.

Though perceptual mistakes and the logical pitfalls of magical thinking may be hard-wired in the brain, paranormal beliefs themselves are cultural phenomena, learned by children from their friends and family. Being aware of some of the most common and most important skeptical principles can help weed superstition from the garden of the mind. In his book *The Demon-Haunted World* (1996), Carl Sagan suggested some guidelines for "baloney detection," including requiring independent confirmation of the facts of a case, suggesting more than one hypothesis to explain a given phenomenon, being willing to abandon a hypothesis if it is not useful, ensuring that all links in a chain of argument are valid, and using only hypotheses and propositions that are falsifiable.

Conclusion. It has been said that skeptics take hope away, while the paranormal and religion give hope. After all, there's something wonderful and hopeful about the idea that we all have (or could develop) psychic powers, or that we are being watched by peaceful, all-knowing aliens or gods, or that we will be reunited with long-dead loved ones someday. Most people prefer a world in which coincidences are part of a cosmic plan and not simply random chance, a world in which we are individually chosen instead of "genetic blends with uncertain ends." Yet we cannot bend the world to suit our wishes; we must accept it with all its limitations and randomness and unfairness. And if our self-esteem is not too terribly fragile, we might adopt a measure of humility about our beautiful and ultimately insignificant place in the universe.

BIBLIOGRAPHY

Gilovich, Tom. *How We Know What Isn't So: The Fallibility of Human Reason in Everyday Life*. New York: Free Press, 1991.

Kurtz, Paul. *The Transcendental Temptation: A Critique of Religion and the Paranormal*. Amherst, NY: Prometheus Books, 1991.

Nickell, Joe. *The Mystery Chronicles*. Lexington: University Press of Kentucky, 2004.

Sagan, Carl. *The Demon-Haunted World: Science as a Candle in the Dark*. New York: Ballantine, 1996.

Whittle, Christopher H. "Development of Beliefs in Paranormal and Supernatural Phenomena." *Skeptical Inquirer* 28, no. 2 (March/April, 2004).

BENJAMIN RADFORD

PARIKH, INDUMATI (1918–2004), Indian humanist and reformer. Known as "India's humanist heroine," Indumati Parikh was one of the pillars of Radical Humanist movement in India (see INDIA, UNBELIEF IN). A medical doctor, she devoted herself both to organized humanism and to caring for the downtrodden in the slums of Bombay (now Mumbai), India. She created an organization called Strihitakarini (Helper of Women), which rendered noteworthy service to poor women, particularly the prostitutes of Bombay. She was instrumental in starting the Third World Humanist Center in Bombay, the M. N. Roy Memorial Humanist Development Campus. That facility now houses the headquarters of the Indian Radical Humanist Association, the Indian Renaissance Institute, Strihitakarini, the Center for the Study of Social Change, the monthly publication *Radical Humanist*, and the bimonthly publication *Secularist*. The campus is named for the famed rationalist activist M. N. ROY.

Parikh came into contact with the Indian humanist movement in the early 1930s. Her husband, Professor G. D. Parikh, was rector of Bombay University, a great orator, and a follower of M. N. Roy; she served the humanist cause silently while her husband was alive, devoting herself to her medical work. She recruited her own group of devoted workers who served the needs slum dwellers. Edd Doerr, former president of the AMERICAN HUMANIST ASSOCIATION, said emphatically that her work during this time was far greater than that of Mother Teresa.

After the death of her husband, Parikh took a direct, active role in humanist organizing, injecting new dynamism as she addressed numerous humanist conferences, study camps, and training classes for youth and women. She was twice honored by the INTERNATIONAL HUMANIST AND ETHICAL UNION for her activism.

Among her achievements, she authored articles in English and Marathi on HUMANISM, SECULARISM, and the rights of women. She advocated for population control and women's liberation (see BIRTH CONTROL AND UNBELIEF). She actively participated in India's Renaissance movement, founded by Roy to spread the scientific spirit among the Indian public and recast Indian history from a scientific point of view. She recruited experts to produce scientific studies on the gynecological problems and sexual diseases faced by poor Indian women. She overcame opposition by fundamentalist Hindu groups in Bombay while serving as president of the Radical Humanist Association and building the Humanist Center in India. In addition, she vehemently opposed the nuclear tests conducted by India and warned of the dangers such tests posed for the subcontinent and for world peace. In 1999 she conducted the World Congress of International Humanists in Bombay, where she expressed her concern regarding population growth, and an International Rationalist conference in Trivendrum, Kerala. Devoted to humanism, she continued working for the cause until her death in 2004.

INNAIAH NARISETTI

PASCAL'S WAGER. Pascal's Wager is an argument that claims it would be prudent for those who do not believe that the Christian God exists to do things to try to make themselves believe that proposition. It was expressed by (and named after) the mathematician Blaise Pascal in a collection of notes entitled *Pensées* (Thoughts) published posthumously in 1670. Let us label it PW.

Using GC to mean "the God of Christianity," PW could be formulated in a precise way as follows:

(a) The probability that GC exists is greater than zero.

(b) If GC were to exist, then probably whoever believes that would gain eternal happiness in an afterlife, whereas whoever does not believe that would end up being eternally tormented.

(c) If GC were not to exist, then it would matter very little to people whether or not they believe that GC exists.

(d) Hence, people who do not believe that GC exists are at a great disadvantage. The expected utility of their belief situation is infinitely worse than that of the believers [from (a)–(c)].

(e) But the unbelievers are able to do things to try to make themselves believe that GC exists.

(f) Therefore, it would be prudent for them to try to do those things [from (d) & (e)].

This version of PW comes very close to Pascal's own formulation, though the argument is sometimes expressed in terms of God in general rather than the God of Christianity. (The "general God" version is considered below.) Step (d) makes reference to the concept of expected utility. The expected utility of an action, given two possible outcomes O1 and O2, is the payoff for O1 times the probability of O1 added to the payoff for O2 times the probability of O2. Let us assume that believing is an action and take O1 and O2 as the situations of GC existing and GC not existing. Even if the probability that GC exists is quite small, say, only 1 percent, the expected utility of believing that GC exists would turn out to be infinite because of the infinite positive payoff for such belief. In contrast, the alternate action of not believing that GC exists would have an expected utility of minus infinity. It follows that to be an unbeliever is prudentially irrational.

Objections to PW. 1. Premise (a) can be attacked on the grounds that GC, as described by Christians, has incompatible properties. It would follow that GC's existence has a probability of zero.

2. In addition, there are powerful arguments that the existence of an afterlife, even if it were conceptually possible, is nevertheless shown to be physically impossible by the findings of brain science (see COGNITIVE SCIENCE AND UNBELIEF). Such arguments render moot PW's premise (b), which makes appeal to the concept of an afterlife.

3. Even if an afterlife were possible, the ideas of eternal happiness and eternal torment in an afterlife are incoherent. Happiness and torment are so bound up with earthly bodies and adaptation to the experience (perhaps even eventual boredom) that the idea of them continuing forever apart from earthly bodies is incomprehensible. This is further reason to reject premise (b).

4. According to the Bible, more is required for salvation (eternal happiness) than mere belief that GC exists. One also needs to repent (Luke 13:3), be born again (John 3:3), be born of the water and of the Spirit (John 3:5), believe everything in the gospel (Mark 16:16), eat the flesh of Jesus and drink his blood (John 6:53), be like a child (Mark 10:15), and do good deeds, especially for needy people (Matt. 25:41–46; Rom. 2:5–10; John 5:28–29; James 2:14–26). Other biblical passages (Rom. 8:28–30, 9:18; Eph. 1:4–5, 11; 2 Thess. 2:13; Rev. 13:8, 17:8) support the idea that there is nothing we can do to be saved, since it is all predestined beforehand. Therefore, premise (b) of PW, according to which mere belief that GC exists is probably sufficient for salvation, can be attacked by appeal to the Bible.

5. There are many Christians, such as universalists who believe that eventually everyone will be saved, who would deny PW's premise (b). So the issue of the truth of that premise is far from settled even within Christianity. Furthermore, if the latter part of premise (b) were true, then that in itself could be the basis for a strong argument against the existence of GC. Thus, the given premise is conceptually problematic.

6. There are several reasons to deny PW's premise (c). Most people who believe that GC exists devote significant time to prayer and to church activities. Such people presumably also contribute money, perhaps a tithe (10 percent of their income). In addition, many such people go through life with inhibitions (some of them quite extreme) on both thought and behavior—inhibitions regarding sexual practices, divorce, birth control, abortion, reading material, and association with other people. In some Christian communities, women have historically been oppressed. Some Christians have persecuted and even killed others (as in inquisitions, religious wars, attacks on homosexuals, abortionists, etc.) because they believed this was what GC wanted them to do. Some people, such as members of the clergy, devote their entire lives to GC. For these various reasons as well as others, if GC does not exist, it would indeed matter a great deal whether or not one believes that GC exists, at least for most such believers. Therefore, premise (c) of PW is false.

7. As another attack on premise (c), it may be that GC does not exist and, instead, some other being (e.g., the God of Islam) rules the universe. That being may dislike intensely (and may inflict infinite punishment on) anyone who believes that GC exists or who tries to self-induce such belief. A person who comes to believe that GC exists on the basis of PW would in that case be in "a heap of trouble." The expected utility of the Christian's belief situation would then be infinitely worse than that

of the non-Christian. It follows that premise (c) of PW can be doubted and is in need of some independent support, which has not been provided.

It should be noted that this objection, unlike objection 6, would still attack premise (c) even if that premise were revised to read as follows: "If GC were not to exist, then whether or not a person believes that GC exists would matter considerably less than in the situation where GC does exist." This revised premise, though it could perhaps withstand objection 6 and though it would suffice for the derivation of step (d), nevertheless succumbs to the possibility described in objection 7 in which it is the Christians who are at a great disadvantage.

8. Moving on to premise (e), it might be argued that to believe that GC exists, one must believe, not only the contradictions mentioned in objection 1, above, but also the doctrine of the Incarnation (or Trinity), according to which Jesus Christ is God (John 1:1; Col. 2:9) and the creator of the universe (John 1:3,10; Col. 1:16) as well as the Son of God (Matt. 3:17), also that Jesus was with God (John 1:1–2) and had a God (Mark 15:34; John 20:17), was created by God (Col. 1:15; Heb. 1:6) and begotten on a specific day (Acts 13:33, Heb. 1:5–6), that Jesus was both equal to his father (John 10:30) and inferior to his father (John 14:28) and presently sits at the right hand of God (Rom. 8:34; Col. 3:1). But all those things are a hodgepodge of contradictions, which it is impossible to genuinely believe. (Similar absurdities may be derivable from other Christian doctrines such as the doctrine of the Atonement.) Hence, it is impossible to genuinely believe that GC exists, which makes PW's premise (e) false. People cannot try to make themselves believe that which does not make logical sense.

9. One final consideration is that belief is not directly subject to the will, at least not in psychologically normal people. So even if such people were to comprehend something they did not believe, it would still not be possible for them to try to self-induce belief in it. Even the indirect methods of self-inducing belief advocated by Pascal (associating with people who hold the belief, etc.) are arguably irrational. Thus, premise (e) of PW is false, at least with regard to normal people.

Other objections to PW might be raised, especially ones that point toward the unethical character of GC as depicted in the argument, but (for space considerations) they are omitted here.

The General God Version. To avoid many of the above objections, PW could be applied only to God in general (i.e., God defined merely as the creator and ruler of the universe) rather than to the God of Christianity. Its second premise would then read:

(b)' If God (in general) were to exist, then probably whoever believes that would gain eternal happiness in the afterlife, whereas whoever does not believe that would end up being eternally tormented.

The big problem here is that it is hard to find any reason whatever to accept the premise. That was not the case with regard to the previous (Christian) version. Although doubt could be expressed regarding premise (b), as shown in objections 2 through 5, above, there is nevertheless some significant biblical support for it. However, premise (b)' is a mere assertion lacking any support whatsoever. Assuming that God (in general) exists, there is no more reason to believe that he would reward all and only believers than that he would not do that. Without any backing for its second premise, this version of PW does not even get off the ground.

Perhaps the first three premises of the argument could be reconstructed as follows:

(a)" There is some nonzero probability that God (in general) exists, that whoever believes that proposition would gain eternal happiness in an afterlife, and that whoever does not believe that proposition would end up being eternally tormented.

(b)" Other situations, such as God not existing or God existing but there being no positive or negative payoff for people who do or do not believe that proposition, also have some nonzero probability.

(c)" The mere truth of premise (a)" provides believers with an infinite expected utility.

The rest of the argument would proceed in a way similar to the original version. However, at least objections 2, 3, and 9, above, would still apply against this version of the argument. And even a version of objection 7 could be put forward. One of the premise-(b)" situations having a nonzero probability is that in which the world is ruled by a being who would inflict infinite punishment on anyone who believes that God (in general) exists or who would try to self-induce such belief. When that factor is entered into the expected-utility computations, it turns out that premise (c)" is false. The chance of the infinite positive payoff involved in the situation appealed to in (a)" would be canceled out by the risk of the infinite negative payoff involved in one of the situations appealed to in (b)". The result is that step (d)" cannot be derived. That is, there would be no way to show that the unbelievers are running a greater risk than the believers.

In the end we are led to the result, accepted by almost all philosophers, that PW is a failure. However it is formulated, it does not show any prudential irrationality whatever in being an unbeliever.

BIBLIOGRAPHY

Drange, Theodore. *Nonbelief & Evil: Two Arguments for the Nonexistence of God.* Amherst, NY: Prometheus, Books, 1998.

Geivett, R. Douglas, and Brendan Sweetman, eds. *Con-*

temporary Perspectives on Religious Epistemology. New York: Oxford University Press, 1992.

Jordan, Jeff, ed. *Gambling on God: Essays on Pascal's Wager.* Lanham, MD: Rowman & Littlefield, 1994.

Martin, Michael, and Ricki Monnier, eds. *The Impossibility of God.* Amherst, NY: Prometheus Books, 2003.

Rescher, Nicholas. *Pascal's Wager: A Study of Practical Reasoning in Philosophical Theology.* Notre Dame, IN: University of Notre Dame Press, 1985.

THEODORE DRANGE

PENTECOST, HUGH OWEN (1848–1907), American radical orator. Hugh O. Pentecost was born on September 30, 1848, at New Harmony, Indiana, moving at two to nearby Albion, Illinois, where he learned utopian social ideas as family traditions. He was a printer's apprentice for seven years, then in seminary for one. Preaching at twenty-three, he pastored at seven churches, including Baptist and Congregational churches and his own nonsectarian Church of the People. By 1887 he was also speaking for Henry George's single-tax movement. He married his second wife, Ida Gatling, daughter of the wealthy gun inventor, in 1880. In November 1887 at Newark, New Jersey, in a bold sermon titled "Four More Murdered Men," Pentecost denounced the execution of the Haymarket anarchists (see ANARCHISM AND UNBELIEF) from his pulpit. One month later, he resigned from Christianity altogether and began delivering lectures to his new Unity Congregation. With titles like "The Sins of Government," his talks appeared in early issues of his weekly *Twentieth Century* (started in 1888), defending both the single tax and philosophical anarchism. Though he always supported the rights of working people, he had distanced himself from organized labor by 1889 (see LABOR MOVEMENT AND UNBELIEF). As his family lost its fortune, Pentecost became a lawyer to secure an income. At the end of 1893, he was appointed as assistant district attorney through his wife's influence, but a storm of public outrage against the "anarchist attorney" prevented his being sworn in. In a public letter that the Democratic Party ordered him to write, he renounced the single tax as "utopian imaginings," stated that the Haymarket executions had been just, and swore loyalty to Tammany Hall. His otherwise stellar record for defending human freedom was permanently fouled. One anarchist labeled him a "blackmailed harlot"; another named him as an example of one's higher nature being degraded through marriage. Ruined in politics, Pentecost practiced law and resumed lecturing, focusing on FREETHOUGHT. When he died on February 2, 1907, he was warmly eulogized.

BIBLIOGRAPHY

De Cleyre, Voltairine. "Hugh O. Pentecost." *Mother Earth* 1 (1907).

———. "They Who Marry Do Ill." *Mother Earth* 2 (1908).

"Hugh Owen Pentecost: The Famous Preacher and Where He Came From." *Manitoba Daily Free Press*, September 14, 1889.

"The Pentecost Blunder," *New York Daily Tribune*, January 1, 1894.

Stephenson, E. Frank, Jr. *Gatling: A Photographic Remembrance.* Murfreesboro, NC: Meherrin River Press, 1993.

T[ucker, Benjamin R.]. "A False Confession." *New York Liberty*, February 24, 1894.

ROBERT P. HELMS

PERIODICALS OF UNBELIEF. A moderate number of freethinkers have come to and maintained unbelief by reading influential books including the Bible or the collected writings and speeches of such notables as Thomas PAINE, Robert Green INGERSOLL, the British socialist Robert Blatchford, and the like. From the mid-nineteenth century on, however, the reading habits and cultural assumptions of unbelievers were increasingly formed more from periodicals than from books. Over the past two centuries, the periodical has become a dominant medium of print publication used by large numbers of freethinkers on a regular basis, and periodicals of unbelief have been associated with all major movements of FREETHOUGHT during this period. Indeed, to read the literature of unbelief of the nineteenth and later centuries in an informed way, one needs to read through the lens of contemporaneous periodical readers.

Many hundreds of periodicals espousing worldviews of unbelief have been published in the last two centuries. These periodicals, issued at the local, regional, and national levels, have served varied special interests such as ATHEISM, RATIONALISM, SECULARISM, and HUMANISM, and have been published in dozens of countries. Despite the importance of these serials to an understanding of unbelief in general, they have been subjected to little scholarly analysis. No systematic survey of these publications has ever been issued. There are no reliable estimates of total world circulation, or even tentative estimates of the number of subscribers, to say nothing of readers, these periodicals may have reached even in the more developed countries. Still it is reasonable to assume a worldwide circulation today of at least several million.

Those who subscribe to a freethought—atheist, rationalist, or secularist—magazine or journal are rarely familiar with the range of periodicals that claim to interpret the world in terms of their own perspective of unbelief. And the larger public outside the freethought movements has little knowledge of such publications, or of the amount and type of influence such periodicals may exert.

This article deals with serial freethought works having

a publication frequency less than daily (*periodicals of unbelief* or *freethought periodicals*). Closely related terms such as *serials, journals, magazines,* or terms denoting frequency of publication (*monthlies, quarterlies, annuals,* etc.) will occasionally be used. Coverage will be restricted to publications of national or international scope, even though there have been hundreds more such publications of a relatively local, state/provincial, or regional focus in numerous countries. Only a few major titles will be cited. Titles, place(s), or frequency of publication may vary from time to time. The article will undertake (1) to provide some historical perspective for the different streams of periodical journalism of unbelief, (2) to specify the audience for such publications, (3) to indicate the special interests and presuppositions of that journalism and that audience, (4) to indicate the nature and diversity of periodicals of unbelief, and (5) to define how good a job this press has been, and is, doing.

Historical Perspective. A full-fledged historical treatment would require a history of the beginnings and early development of periodical publishing among unbelievers, discussing the major individuals and institutions responsible for the magazines and suggesting the circumstances in national history and culture that helped shape this press. However, because most studies have concentrated on the historical situation in England or the United States, the available information is primarily applicable to periodicals of these two major English-speaking countries.

Although freethought owed much to Enlightenment thought (see ENLIGHTENMENT, UNBELIEF DURING THE), the freethought movement emerged more or less full-fledged in the numerous radical democratic movements spawned first by the French Revolution (see FRANCE, UNBELIEF IN) and more fully in England, across much of Europe, and in the United States after the end of the Napoleonic wars (1815). After 1815, in England especially, a growing flood of pamphlets and periodicals attacked a wide range of political and social institutions, increasingly including organized religion. The British antireligious press was early intermixed with other secular forms of radicalism. Some such writings were less specifically focused, attacking Christianity (institutionalized and generally); many British writings attacked the Church of England (and its wealth) in particular. Ideological standpoints varied from an increasingly obsolescent DEISM to eccentric HERESY to explicit atheism. In periodical publications, the relative proportions of social, political, or religious attacks fluctuated over time; thus, the extent to which a given publication was strictly an organ of unbelief in the modern sense (as opposed to a more generically radical organ) is often difficult to specify.

Increasingly, the more influential among these writings were periodical in nature—whether issued regularly or irregularly with periodicities varying from daily to annual. Periodicals were well suited to publish the genre of the short essay focused on a single topic, and could offer the promise of periodic return to, and repeated emphasis upon, common enduring themes, in comparison to the definitive but lengthy one-time treatments usually presented in books or pamphlets. Also, short essays were typically seen as more suitable for those with little leisure time to read, and perhaps for those readers having little experience of following an extended argument.

Freethought periodicals gradually came to be sold, erratically, in a variety of news distribution centers beyond the traditional bookshop (which many purchasers would seldom or never visit), and their advertisements tended to reach a wider market than ads inserted in late nineteenth-century monographs and pamphlets. Further, the consumer of the product—the reader—was stimulated to buy succeeding numbers of the product at more or less regular intervals.

There were various social and legal hazards and stumbling blocks presented to the regular issuance of such publications. A major hazard in many countries was the legal concept of BLASPHEMY (an offense against the dominant national religion, being in England, for example, a crime under English common law); the upholders of the established order in church and state relied on blasphemy prosecutions in their attempts to muzzle the radical opposition's attacks on Christianity. In England in the eighteenth and nineteenth centuries, a local, perhaps idiosyncratic, barrier was the stamp tax on *newspapers* (which term over time seems to have come to denote publications produced with a frequency greater than every twenty-six days) imposed by statutory law. This tax was raised in 1815 to fourpence, at the time a rather high price that in effect priced legal newspapers out of the reach of the lower classes. Radical and freethought newspapers that refused to pay the stamp tax constituted an illegal underground press. As such, publishers, printers, and distributors were potentially subject to fine and imprisonment.

There consequently arose in both the radical and antireligious press an agitation against the stamp tax (sometimes called *taxes on knowledge*); freethought journals were caught up in this controversy. Writers and publishers of anti-Christian pamphlets and journals were frequently prosecuted in England, and some early nineteenth-century freethinkers—notably, Richard CARLILE and several of his associates and shopmen (and women)—were imprisoned for nonpayment of the stamp tax and/or for blasphemy, usually with success until 1842. Not surprisingly, religious periodicals that likewise failed to pay the tax (but that were not publishing blasphemy) were rarely prosecuted. (The stamp tax was reduced to a penny in 1836, and after 1842 successful prosecutions for blasphemy declined markedly.)

After 1840 in England (and somewhat later in Europe and the United States), freethought—atheism, AGNOSTICISM, secularism, and the like—developed as organized movements, thus facilitating outreach to diverse markets including the large urban centers. In freethought as in many other movements, the inauguration of a journal has often served as a rite of passage indicating that a particular interest or faction within the movement has now come of age. Indeed, the journal has come to represent a formal or informal claim by a freethought group for public status. This trend was clear in England, Europe, and America, and in later years has been seen across the developing world. It has become increasingly common for a freethought periodical to be not a freestanding publication but the official organ of particular organizations, including book and pamphlet publishers. Although none may be said to be the sole or official journal of any particular secularist (etc.) movement, some periodicals having a particularly extensive circulation or influence may be perceived by the general public as representing a sort of quasi-official voice of freethought.

English Freethought. The emergence of organized English freethought largely reflected the efforts of one man, George Jacob HOLYOAKE, whose career, spanning most of the nineteenth century, combined freethought activities with social and political radicalism. Holyoake became a publisher of various periodicals in succession and was associated in these ventures at various times with other notable freethinkers. In the latter two-thirds of the nineteenth century, a number of other major freethinkers in Britain were associated with organizing efforts and with periodicals of unbelief. These include Annie BESANT, Charles BRADLAUGH, Robert Cooper, George William FOOTE, Robert OWEN, and Charles WATTS. Some major figures were associated primarily with organizing efforts, others such as W. Stewart ROSS and Charles SOUTHWELL more with publishing. One major stream, following Holyoake's lead and at various times associated briefly with him in one or another venture, was agnostic and somewhat politely secularist in orientation; the other, following Bradlaugh's lead, was more radically atheistic and aggressively secularist. The one stream later gave rise to the RATIONALIST PRESS ASSOCIATION (RPA), the other gave rise earlier to the NATIONAL SECULAR SOCIETY, both major publishers of books, pamphlets, and periodicals of unbelief in the twentieth century.

In the last decades of the nineteenth century, the most significant figure in the British freethought periodical press was Charles Albert WATTS, the son of Charles Watts, a leading figure in earlier organizational and publishing movements of unbelief. The younger Watts succeeded Holyoake at the *Secular Review* (later *Agnostic Journal*) and in general inherited the Holyoake tradition. In 1884 he assumed control of Charles Watts's printing, publishing, and bookselling concern, the principal London outlet for the freethought press. Watts primarily acted as a clearinghouse for freethought periodicals, although he did publish journals of his own including the monthly *Agnostic* (1885) and *Watts' Literary Guide* (1885–94, which became suc-

cessively the *Literary Guide*, 1894–1956; then the *Humanist*, 1956–72; since 1972 *New Humanist*). The *Literary Guide* began as an advertiser for "liberal and advanced publications" (including freethought and nonfreethought radical publications) offered for sale by Watts and Company, and later also became the official organ of the Rationalist Press Association (1899–). Also associated with Watts and Company and the RPA was a distinguished annual issued under variant titles: *Agnostic Annual* (1884–93), *Agnostic Annual and Ethical Review* (1894–1907), *Rationalist Annual and Ethical Review* (1908–19), *R.P.A. Annual and Ethical Review* (1920–26), and *Rationalist Annual* (1927–66); this was succeeded by the annual *Question* (1967–80). From 1884 on, this annual consisted principally of focused essays or reviews upon major topics, initially primarily agnostic, then more generally rationalist, then secularist and even secular. The Watts/RPA books, pamphlets, and periodicals, generally high in quality, came to be dominant in the global British Empire market of unbelief for several decades after 1884. The *New Humanist* is even today England's most prestigious freethought journal (see UNITED KINGDOM, UNBELIEF IN).

Leading periodicals associated with the National Secular Society and/or its major figures included the *National Reformer* (1860–1993) and the *Freethinker* (1881–), both radical freethought publications of international as well as domestic stature.

The United Kingdom has produced dozens of other periodicals of unbelief in the nineteenth and twentieth centuries, several lasting well beyond a decade or two; this country is perhaps second only to the United States in the range and substantive scope of the periodicals of unbelief that it has produced. Until the twentieth century, British freethought periodicals were dominant worldwide; then for much of the twentieth century the United Kingdom shared this dominance with the United States. By the final quarter of the twentieth century, US periodicals of unbelief had become dominant in the world market of freethought. Particularly outstanding examples today include *Free Inquiry* and the *Secular Humanist Bulletin* (both originally published at Buffalo, now Amherst, New York).

In the United States hundreds of periodicals of unbelief were published in the nineteenth and twentieth centuries, including newspapers, newsletters, bulletins, journals, reviews, and other types. The list of fugitive, short-lived publications is extensive. However, a number of other periodicals have been relatively long-lived (e.g., *Age of Reason*; AMERICAN RATIONALIST; BOSTON INVESTIGATOR; the *Crucible* [Seattle]; *Ethical Outlook*; *Freethinker's* magazine, later *Free Thought* magazine; *Freethought Today* [Wisconsin]; *Humanistic Judaism* [Michigan]; the *Independent Pulpit* [Texas]; the *Index* [Toledo, Ohio, and Boston]; *Progressive World*; and THE TRUTH SEEKER), and many have been distributed worldwide (e.g., *American Atheist* and the *Humanist*). A few

US periodicals of unbelief, short- or long-lived, have been issued in languages other than English (e.g., *Freidenker* [Minnesota; German]; *Forskaren* [Minnesota; Swedish]; and others in Czech, French, German, Swedish, and other languages, to target major US ethnic groups with a substantial freethought heritage (see UNITED STATES, UNBELIEF IN).

Outside Europe and America during the nineteenth century, there was substantial competition from overseas publications, particularly from Britain. As with books and pamphlets, foreign periodicals, particularly British (and by the late nineteenth century and continuing today, American), have always found a ready audience generally throughout the British Empire, now the Commonwealth of Nations. British and American freethought periodicals could be relatively rapidly and cheaply imported, and often sold for less than their local imitators or competitors. The British and American publications had the advantage of well-known contributors, and in the nineteenth century the British periodicals in particular in many colonies could also draw on the nostalgia of a predominantly British émigré population. In non-British colonies, antireligious periodicals of the respective colonial power likewise competed with local products for readership. In numerous smaller English-speaking countries today (see INDIA, UNBELIEF IN), one continues to see this predominance of periodicals of unbelief distributed from the major publishing countries of North America and Europe, especially the United States and United Kingdom.

In colonies of the nineteenth-century British Empire, and in the United States through the first half of the nineteenth century, homegrown freethought journals faced various difficulties especially endemic to countries with relatively small populations: high production costs, failure to attract advertising, limited circulation, limited mass distribution beyond urban centers (until the development of railroads), and the like. Such factors continue to operate today against such journals in developing countries, within and outside the commonwealth.

In Australia, New Zealand, Canada, and probably other British colonies, early freethought periodicals tended to be largely derivative in both format and content from British and American models or competitors. Several freethought periodicals appeared in the latter half of the nineteenth century in Australia, mostly short-lived. The twentieth-century periodicals of unbelief in Australia have had longer runs, several today having continued in various forms for decades (e.g., *Australian Humanist, Australian Rationalist* [under various titles]; see AUSTRALIA, UNBELIEF IN). In the nineteenth century, New Zealand's need for freethought journals was apparently satisfied largely by British periodicals; the local products were all short-lived until well into the twentieth century, when the more long-lived *Open Society* (1927–; formerly *Truthseeker*, later *New Zealand Rationalist*, later *New Zealand Rationalist and Humanist*) and the

New Zealand Humanist (ca. 1970–; see NEW ZEALAND, UNBELIEF IN) were published. Canada had few such publications in the nineteenth century, but *Avenir* (Montreal; French) ran from 1847 to 1857, and *Secular Thought* (Toronto), begun by Charles Watts during his Canadian sojourn, ran from 1885 to 1911. Since the mid-twentieth century, Canadian freethought journals have had much longer runs—for example, *Humanist in Canada*; now *Humanist Perspectives* (1967–) (see CANADA [ANGLO-PHONE], UNBELIEF IN; CANADA [FRANCOPHONE], UNBELIEF IN). Periodicals of unbelief in India appeared mostly from the twentieth century on, but many of these persisted for extended periods of time (e.g., *Atheist* [Vijayawada], *Humanist Outlook* [Lucknow], *Radical Humanist* [various places], *Secularist* [Bombay, now Mumbai]), and a number are published today; major languages of publication have included English, Tamil, and Telegu.

The Anglo-American periodicals influenced periodicals of unbelief elsewhere in the nineteenth and twentieth centuries. In the twentieth century, the number of both Anglo-American and non-Anglo-American freethought periodicals exploded.

In continental Europe, periodicals attacking religion reached full force many decades later than in England, apparently not becoming a major publishing focus even in the leading capitals until about the 1880s or later. In Catholic countries (e.g., Western Mediterranean), periodicals of unbelief from their beginnings generally maintained a vigorous multidimensional thrust against the institutionalized basis of Roman Catholicism (anti-Papal, antihierarchical, anticlerical, antibiblical, etc.) and, often, to a lesser extent against Christianity more generally; in countries with major pluralist traditions (e.g., Germany and Switzerland), this thrust would be reversed. Leading twentieth-century European periodicals of unbelief include *Cahiers du Cercle Ernest-Renan, Cahiers Rationalistes, Libre Pensée* (France); *Freidenker, Wege ohne Dogma* (Germany); *Ragione* (Italy); *Vrijdenker* (successor to *De Dageraad*, the Netherlands); *Human-Etikk* (Norway); *Argumenty* (Poland); *Nauka i Religiya* (successor to *Antireligioznik*), *Voprosy Nauchnogo Ateizma* (Russia); and *Freidenker* (Switzerland). Many journals of this sort are also markedly radical politically (socialist or even anarchist), economically, and culturally, though they emphasize church-state issues most particularly. Hundreds of periodicals of unbelief have been published throughout Europe, mostly in the twentieth century and later (see FRANCE, UNBELIEF IN; GERMANY, UNBELIEF IN; ITALY, UNBELIEF IN; NETHERLANDS, THE, UNBELIEF IN; NETHERLANDS, THE, HUMANISM IN; NORWAY, UNBELIEF IN; SWITZERLAND, UNBELIEF IN).

Non-English-speaking European countries with substantial traditions of publishing periodicals of unbelief include, but are not limited to, Belgium, France, Germany, the Netherlands, Poland, the Soviet Union, and

Sweden (see BELGIUM, UNBELIEF IN). Italian twentieth-century ventures, mostly sputtering, in this domain were published mostly in Rome. Spain's limited record of publishing periodicals of unbelief was clearly exceeded in several former Latin American colonies (most notably, Argentina, Mexico, Uruguay; see LATIN AMERICA, UNBELIEF IN; LATIN AMERICAN LITERATURE, UNBELIEF IN). Little information was found for periodicals of unbelief in most Asian and African countries other than India (see AFRICA, UNBELIEF IN; INDONESIA AND SOME OTHER ISLAMIC COUNTRIES, UNBELIEF IN; NEPAL, UNBELIEF IN).

The leading international-scope periodical of unbelief is *International Humanist News*, published quarterly by the INTERNATIONAL HUMANIST AND ETHICAL UNION under this and similar titles since 1952 (see UNBELIEF AROUND THE WORLD).

The Control of, and Audience for, the Publications. Since their heyday in the nineteenth century, periodicals have exhibited many characteristics that have been fruitfully investigated as social aspects of journalism. For example, the publishers of periodicals, and also their contributors, become dominant within the ideology by virtue of their control of the material means of its propagation. The owners, editors, and contributors, of course, have more power to define their world and make their meanings stick than have their readers. Not unexpectedly, the dominant voices in freethought have generally controlled freethought periodicals, though usually leaving gaps for oppositional voices and oppositional discourse. A given publication thus exhibits an ideological center of unbelief; correspondingly, there are less obvious, more marginal, even subversive or liberal or orthodox-oriented views, pressuring the ideological center of unbelief represented by the proprietary and editorial interests of the periodical.

Accordingly, in the world of freethought, periodicals of unbelief are not merely a mirror of the culture of unbelief, or merely a secondary and derivative aspect of that culture, or merely a means of expressing that culture, rather these periodicals must be seen as a central component of that culture—part of the context within which freethinkers live and work and think, and from which they derive their perceptions of and reactions toward the larger world. From the early days of the nineteenth century, periodicals have been very much an interactive component of the world of unbelief, by both reporting the culture of unbelief and by driving its development.

That press likewise contributes to the construction of freethought and humanist opinion and identity. For subscribers themselves, a periodical of unbelief serves as a symbol of affiliation and "communication membership" with others of like mind.

Special Interests and Presuppositions of the Periodical Press. The earliest journals promoting unbelief—often organs of generically radical rather than merely antireligious thought—were intended to stir up the lower and middle classes, and aroused in the dominant classes and in the religious establishment anxieties of revolution. In the Anglo-American world and in the Western world more generally today, the goals of periodicals of unbelief are diverse and multifocal, but generally include those articulated by the RPA:

- To promote the study of rational thinking
- To encourage the spread of rational thinking in human conduct
- To fight irrationality and superstition wherever they affect human conduct
- To defend freedom of thought and inquiry, particularly where a rational approach to human affairs may conflict with traditional creeds and beliefs
- To advance a secular system of education, the main object of which shall be to cultivate in the young moral and intellectual fitness for social life

Today most of the leading periodicals of unbelief are multifocal in both their content and their intended audiences. Some such periodicals have expanded from an earlier niche and become more universal in scope: dozens of major topics of concern regularly recur between the covers of such publications as *Free Inquiry*, the *Freethinker*, the *New Humanist*, and dozens of other major periodicals. Indeed, one might characterize modern freethought periodicals as periodical supermarkets of unbelief. Meanwhile the book and pamphlet literature of unbelief has tended to focus upon elaborating major concerns and issues to an extent that cannot be addressed in the more facile and time-limited medium of the periodical journal essay.

Nature and Diversity of Periodicals of Unbelief. Over the course of the nineteenth and twentieth centuries, periodicals of unbelief have shown extreme diversity, even miscellaneity, of:

Frequency. The publication schedule may be weekly, biweekly or semimonthly, monthly, bimonthly, quarterly, semiannually, or annually. In the ealier days of the radical press, the newspaper tended to be preferred because of its frequency and cheapness. However, freethought matters generally lack the sense of urgency or timeliness that would typically fuel the publication schedule of a daily or weekly newspaper. Further, high-frequency publication might require a paid editor or staff and therefore a larger supporting circulation than a lesser-frequency publication schedule requires. Because of the economic limitations of their likely markets (the middle and lower classes), and perhaps because of the more ephemeral nature of the content of daily newspapers in a freethought milieu concerned with occasional repetition of issues of a more enduring character, the medium of choice for freethought periodical publishing became products of biweekly, monthly, quarterly, or lesser frequency. Because of the frequency of issue, in contrast with books, periodicals of unbelief until recent decades were generally printed on relatively cheap paper, and with paper rather than board covers; indeed, they have been designed for speed of production and cheapness rather than durability. Some of the more prestigious such journals, especially in the Western world, are now printed on more durable paper, but still with paper covers. The typical periodical format, usually double- or multiple-column like that of the newspaper, has tended to encourage the use of small type and to fill up most of the space on all pages, by plugging empty portions with news items, poetry, or other filler material, in order to conserve paper, because the cost of paper became one of the most important components of the price.

Genre and Format. As in general with periodicals, content may include editorials; signed articles and/or reviews; current news announcements; notes and short notices; correspondence, especially to the editor; book reviews; advertisements; and perhaps other material such as poetry or cartoons may be included; some of these items may appear only occasionally in a given periodical.

Editorials and letters to the editor are generally developed or selected in accordance with some explicit or implicit (perhaps fluctuating) editorial policy.

Particular to freethought periodicals, signed articles and reviews tend to be philosophical, scientific, or anti-Christian, or at least opposed to revelation. Articles tend to be highly partisan, often tendentious.

News reports or announcements followed over time may be of distinct value in evaluating the waxing and waning success of a periodical or the organization or movement which it represents. One must be alert to possible bias in these reports, inasmuch as the periodical may represent a sort of party organ: during the nineteenth century the owners and editors of periodicals and/or sponsoring organizations participated in many of the events which they reported; further, the freethought press has admittedly often tended to exaggerate the importance of the freethought movement in the larger public scheme of things.

Book reviews may discuss a variety of major works in science, philosophy, theology, and the religion of the time. Emphasis tends to be on books published by the affiliated/sponsoring publisher, if any.

There is a major tendency to evaluate issues, books, and noteworthy individuals from the standpoint of how they further or impede the progress of rationalism/secularism/humanism. Reviews of eminent authors tend to put an emphasis on rationalistic or humanistic rebelliousness or commitment. It is of definite interest to note the names most often referred to with rational or deferential reverence by the magazine's less well-known contributors.

Topical notes may suggest much about the character of the magazine, its contributors, and the intellectual and social milieu of which they are a part; notes on the affiliated

or sponsoring association's social functions—in the nineteenth century usually part of the principal periodical—now more often appear in a separate bulletin or newsletter, especially in the larger movements or organizations.

Advertisements suggest, by their number and the range of products offered, something about the nature of the readership, or, in some cases, perhaps what the advertisers *opine* about the nature of the readership.

Content. Although some freethought periodicals are clearly house organs, the periodical press of unbelief contains mostly serials of a different character. Like most material products, of course, the periodical is not only a product to be consumed; it also enters into the processes of signification or meaning making. The periodical is usually at least somewhat anticlerical (see ANTICLERICALISM), being generally opposed to religion and religious institutions; its characteristic topics are in opposition to religious traditions rather than being suffused with them. However, the culture of unbelief dominating these journals may serve as arenas of struggle over issues and techniques of dissent to be expressed, which secular domains to explore as battlegrounds for unbelief, and the like. Periodicals of unbelief typically offer contention and debate on a wide range of issues, some of which are largely secular in origin, such as models of religion as a whole, aspects of religion (especially Christianity), and secular domains where the emphasis is on the divorce from religious ideological or indoctrinational dominance. However, one must recognize the de facto plurality and diversity of voices between the covers; indeed, some such journals are notable for what has been called a "repressive tolerance," with gaps left for oppositional views. (Many freethought periodicals invite—sometimes urbanely, but often tauntingly—replies from believers to be published in subsequent issues with, of course, well-crafted editorial or other replies.)

Within a given periodical or individual issues, one may see various "conventional" expectations as to what to disbelieve, how or how much, contingency issues ("If _____ were found, would you continue to disbelieve x, or would you resume belief in x?"). Issues crucial to the history of the movement—including aesthetic standards, historical context, the crystallization and packaging of themes of unbelief, and the construction of identity of the unbeliever, among others—have shaped the movement itself and, accordingly, the fortunes of the periodicals and their sponsoring organizations, if any.

In some countries, especially Anglo-American countries, many periodicals of unbelief have been distinguished by contributions by leading secular authorities on culture, civilization, and historical and scientific topics; in other countries, especially in the third world, the press may comprise primarily organs of anticlericalism or at least polemical antireligion. In radical freethought periodicals associated with anarchist leaders (see ANARCHISM AND UNBELIEF), the art of invective has particularly flowered; terms used by European radicals against the Catholic Church may be hurled against fundamentalist or evangelical leaders.

In periodicals associated with a publishing house, many contributors will be authors of books published by that publishing house. Indeed, many freethought/ humanist writers have published works of unbelief initially in installments or initial trial essays in periodicals of unbelief, particularly periodicals associated with the subsequent book publisher. This was especially true of freethought novels in nineteenth-century England and America. Of course, major or more established freethinkers have often published freethought items in major elite magazines or other serials in the mainstream literature (such as the eminent "quarterly reviews" of Victorian England and, in the United States, the *North American Review* to which Robert Green INGERSOLL was a recurring contributor), especially in countries with traditionally strong general subcultures of unbelief.

Periodicals of unbelief are useful to identify not only the leading figures in a given organization or stream of freethought, but also many of the lesser members of a freethought movement. In periodicals of the nineteenth century in England, Europe, and the United States—and even well into the twentieth century in developing countries—contributed articles are often unsigned or pseudonymous. Over the years, however, the tendency has been for contributors to be specifically identified, perhaps with a brief note suggesting the interests or expertise of the writer in producing a focused essay on the topic at hand. Other features that yield important information about the lesser members of the movement include letters to the editor, reports of local activities from and about local activists, lists of names (for example, listings of subsidy contributors), obituary notices, and sometimes other items.

How Good a Job Is This Press Doing? Through most of the nineteenth century in countries other than England, the power of periodicals of unbelief to influence public opinion was largely confined to publishers in major urban centers; the expansion of means of mass distribution (especially railways) to effect shipment to remote locations boosted circulation and hence influence well beyond the major publishing centers.

Although in part intended to win converts to freethought, periodicals of unbelief have for the most part constituted variegated preachments to the already deconverted. The mid- and late Victorian freethought periodical press not only defended unbelief aggressively against Christianity, but, in the form of secularism (and in the twentieth century to the present time, in the form of humanism), this press increasingly defended unbelief for its own sake. The longer life span of freethought periodicals in the later Victorian and twentieth-century eras suggests that such psychological reinforcement has a definite and continuing function in the maintenance of unbelief. Also, by buying or subscribing to such periodicals, adherents of unbelief proclaimed their freethinking status more clearly than by formal membership in a freethought organization. Often, however, the two have gone hand in hand, the periodicals being a subscription benefit of membership in the organization.

For the larger secular world, the secularist press has to inform the public of the relevance of various freethought and secularist traditions to the problems we share in common; the scope of secularism's impact on society; and the associated need to show how secularist emphases promote better understanding of the economic, political, social, and cultural complexities of today's world. Secularist editors should always bear in mind that they should perform such tasks in the light of the same high standards that they invoke in commenting on the ideologies or performance of the religious community.

A small number of periodicals of unbelief fully recognize a mission much beyond their immediate constituency: to bring the messages of freethought to the forefront of the larger community; to convert the larger community in general to the policies, if not the doctrine, of freethought or secularism; to attempt to identify the universal relevance of freethought or secularism; or to endeavor to place contemporary political, social, and economic issues within a secularist context.

At their best, serials of unbelief enable open-minded outsiders in the community to perceive grave public issues in a framework more specifically focused than that of the ordinary secular magazine. A freethought organ moves beyond special pleading for unbelievers when it connects its views on education or some other domain with a conception of human nature and human objectives that can engage the adherents of both religious and secularist traditions.

The larger cultural community in general can benefit in understanding, even when it does not accept, either the sources or the content of the conclusions that are reached. Outsiders are necessarily faced with the problem of how to respond to the often disturbing ideologies of irreligion or secularism found in periodicals of unbelief.

BIBLIOGRAPHY

A partial and very preliminary list of periodicals of unbelief was published in an appendix to Stein, Gordon, ed. The Encyclopedia of Unbelief. *Amherst, NY: Prometheus Books, 1985.*

Altholz, Josef L. *The Religious Press in Britain, 1760–1900.* Contributions to the Study of Religion, no. 22. New York: Greenwood, 1989.

Brake, Laurel, et al., eds. *Investigating Victorian Journalism.* Houndsmills, UK: Macmillan; New York: St. Martins, [1990].

Don Vann, J., and Rosemary T. VanArsdel, eds. *Victorian Periodicals: A Guide to Research.* Vol. 2. New York: Modern Language Association of America, 1989.

BRUCE E. CATHEY

PERIYAR (ERODE V. RAMASWAMI NAICKER; 1879–1973), Indian atheist, organizer, businessman, and political activist. *Periyar* in Tamil means "great one," a title he acquired in 1938 at a conference of women in appreciation of his leadership and anti-Hindi agitation.

Periyar was born on September 17, 1879, as the second son of a well-to-do merchant in Erode, a city in Tamil Nadu, South India. *Naicker* indicates the caste to which he belonged. For most of his long life, Periyar was a convinced and active atheist (see ATHEISM). He may have been an atheist from the age of twelve, but it may be that he only became a convinced atheist after a visit to the holy city of Varanasi in 1904. It was, he discovered, no holier than any other city. The brahmins there, people belonging to the caste of priests, ate meat and drank toddy. Having become an atheist, he rarely wavered in his atheism. Periyar was also a strict teetotaler throughout his life.

As early as 1926, Periyar had warned against adopting Hindi as a national language. As Periyar saw it, the adoption of Hindi as a national language would strengthen the hand of the brahmins and weaken the influence of the Tamils and their language and culture. For many years Periyar also hoped to create a united front of Dravidians (south Indians) against the north Indians, but his influence remained restricted to Tamil Nadu, and even there it remained limited. On the other side, many in Tamil Nadu agreed with his Tamil nationalism, with its emphasis on the ancient roots and importance of Tamil language and culture.

The Self-Respect movement, with which Periyar identified himself during most of his life, is one of India's most interesting reform movements. The Self-Respect movement is often traced back to 1925, but it has also been claimed that it goes back to the Self-Respect League, which was founded by S. Ramanathan in 1926. Periyar was active in the Self-Respect movement at least from 1929.

To Periyar religion was the root of evil and injustice in society. In Periyar's opinion the brahmins used religion to dominate the people, and it should be replaced by RATIONALISM, in which Periyar put his trust. Periyar attacked the brahmins for their caste superiority. He was strongly opposed to the caste system and he fought untouchability (see INDIA, UNBELIEF IN).

As Periyar saw it, since religion was the main impediment to progress toward a just and equal society, it had to be eradicated and replaced by rationalism. Periyar thought highly of human reasoning capacities and saw a clear contrast between belief and reason. Rationalism for him stood for reason, development, and equality, whereas religion represented superstition, fear, exploitation, and irrationalism. For Periyar rationalism and religion were diametrically opposed to each other and excluded each other. For him rationalism also implied materialism (see MATERIALISM, PHILOSOPHICAL). In the booklet "Prakriti or Materialism," Periyar advocated a scientific alternative to religion. Only human reason can further true progress, but it is only in the last 150 years that reason really has started to play an important role. Rationalism also includes education, and Periyar firmly stressed the importance of education.

In his ethical views, Periyar emphasized social concern for equality and justice. As Periyar firmly rejected any transcendent power, he held that ethics is limited to and determined by life in this world. Among his rules of wisdom may be mentioned: "Accept what appears to be right and throw away the rest"; "What we expect from others we shall give to them" (a variant of the Golden Rule); "Man must think of others, make his own sacrifice, help others"; and "Rationalism must improve morality." In thinking of humans as rational beings, Periyar optimistically ascribed to them both goodwill and dignity. He emphasized social duty, equality, and justice. Three virtues or ideals were often repeated by Periyar: *Olukkam*, good behavior; *nanayam*, honesty; and *unmai*, truth.

Periyar's propaganda was organized through local groups supported from a central office, first at Erode, later at Tiruchirapalli and Madras (Chennai). In Tiruchirapalli, where Periyar mostly lived during his later years, he had his office and some of his archives. He ran a grade school and a teacher-training school, and he also invested money in other educational institutions. Periyar's speeches were extensively reported in daily papers and often reprinted. He wrote many propagandistic booklets. For his publications Periyar secured his own press facilities as the daily publications in Tamil Nadu, in his opinion, were controlled by brahmins or people sympathizing with brahmins.

Periyar died on December 24, 1973, at Vellore Christian Hospital in Tamil Nadu. His body was brought to Madras (Chennai), some 150 kilometers away, where he was buried on December 25 in a simple wooden coffin in a distinctly un-Hindu ceremony. Periyar was active until a few weeks before his death.

The vehemence of his attacks on theism can be gauged by the following words on his memorial in Chennai: "There is no God. There is no God. There is no God at all. He who invented God is a Fool. He who propagates God is a Scoundrel. He who worships God is a 'Barbarian.'"

BIBLIOGRAPHY

Diehl, Anita. E. V. *Ramaswami Naicker–Periyar, a Study of the Influence of a Personality in Contemporary South India*. Lund, Sweden: B. I. Publications, 1977.

Hiorth, Finngeir. *Atheism in India*. Oslo: Human-Etisk Forbund, 1999.

FINNGEIR HIORTH

PFEFFER, LEO (1909–1993), American church-state activist. Born to an Orthodox Jewish rabbi in Hungary,

Leo Pfeffer came with his family to New York when he was two. He became the foremost church-state lawyer of the twentieth century. He was admired or scorned, depending on how strongly one believed in the separation of church and state.

Pfeffer attended public elementary and Jewish secondary schools. He graduated from City College of New York in 1930 and New York University Law School in 1933. In 1945 he joined the American Jewish Congress as staff attorney, the beginning of a career during which he became the principal church-state strategist for the American Jewish community. During the next four decades he wrote a multitude of amicus curiae (friend of the court) briefs and argued many cases before the US Supreme Court. He was so successful that many credit him for forging the Court's church-state doctrine during the 1960s and 1970s.

He also became a prolific scholar in the field, his *Church, State, and Freedom* (1953) becoming a classic. He also wrote on constitutional law generally and on the history of the Supreme Court. He taught at several universities, notably serving as professor and chair of political science at Long Island University, where he taught until 1985, all the while writing and arguing cases for the American Jewish Congress.

Although religious freedom was his forte, he also worked in the area of race relations. He recruited lawyers to represent civil rights workers in the South. In 1989 Leo and Freda Pfeffer endowed the International Pfeffer Peace Prize, awarded annually through the Fellowship of Reconciliation.

He was honored by many. Among these were the LHD degree from Hebrew Union College; the Trustee Award for Scholarly Achievement, Long Island University; the Thomas Jefferson Religious Freedom Award, Unitarian Universalist Association; Religious Freedom Award, Americans United for Separation of Church and State; Certificate of Merit, Council of Jewish Federations; Citation for Contributions to Public Education, Horace Mann League. The AMERICAN HUMANIST ASSOCIATION named him "Humanist of the Year" for 1988.

His Thought. A man of faith, Pfeffer was an observant Jew and regularly attended synagogue. But he was a strict separationist in his church-state philosophy. He believed that religion was an absolutely private matter. Civil government ought to have nothing to do with one's religious faith or practice, neither should it aid nor hinder religious groups in any way. He thought the authors of the Constitution believed as he did, that strict separation was best for the state and best for religious institutions. A self-described "absolutist" on the matter, he said: "Absolutists serve an important function in church-state law; any compromise becomes too often the starting point for further compromises." The practical implication of strict separationism was that prayer or religious instruction in public schools, government aid to church-related schools, religious requirements for public

office, or property and income tax exemptions for religions were all unconstitutional. He was vigorously opposed by the Catholic leadership because he won so many cases opposing government aid to parochial schools and by some in the Jewish community who were afraid he would alienate so many Christians it would result in anti-Semitism. Toward the end of his life he began to see his separationist philosophy being eroded, both in Supreme Court decisions and among scholars.

He is widely credited with inventing the phrase "secular humanism" in his *Creeds in Competition* (1958). By this he did not mean antireligion, as the phrase was later used, but simply those unaffiliated with organized religion and concerned with human values.

His personal papers are in the George Arents Research Library at Syracuse University and the J. M. Dawson Institute of Church-State Studies at Baylor University. His library is at the Middletown, New York, Thrall Library.

BIBLIOGRAPHY

Ivers, Gregg. *To Build a Wall: American Jews and the Separation of Church and State*. Charlottesville: University of Virginia Press, 1995.

Pfeffer, Leo. "An Autobiographical Sketch." In *Religion and the State: Essays in Honor of Leo Pfeffer*, edited by James E. Wood Jr. Waco, TX: Baylor University Press, 1985.

———. *Church, State, and Freedom*. Boston: Beacon, 1958.

———. *God, Caesar, and the Constitution: The Court as Referee of Church-State Confrontation*. Boston: Beacon, 1975.

———. "The 'Religion' of Secular Humanism." *Journal of Church and State* 29 (Autumn 1987).

Preville, Joseph R. "Leo Pfeffer and the American Church-State Debate: A Confrontation with Catholicism." *Journal of Church and State* 33 (Winter 1991).

RONALD B. FLOWERS

PHYSICALISM. Physicalism is a claim about what the mind is. It seeks to understand what it is; it does not deny its reality.

Physicalism is not a claim about how we know about the mind or about how we can describe it. The idea that psychological statements can be translated into physical statements is not a valid interpretation of physicalism. That is absurd. Human thought involves meanings and evaluations, whereas physics excludes meanings and evaluations from its subject matter. Further, psychological theory would be impossible if it referred only to atoms and molecules of the brain.

I will, in the next three sections, present some basic points about mental activity. They are not normally considered by common thinking, but they flow from its intelligent application. This gives them a presumptive status, and I will not discuss objections to them by philosophers. These are crucial mental processes which must be accommodated by any deep theory of the mind.

Responsibility for what one does is central to the life of human beings. This requires continuity of the mental qualities and processes that make me what I am as a person. I must continue to be me. Any deep theory of the mind must come to terms with personal responsibility, and therefore with the continuity of the person. This requires:

The mental continuant: Whatever carries an individual's mental qualities and processes.

The idea of responsibility is essential to human living, but it is in tension with another essential quality: free will. Freedom requires that one could have done something different. But the idea of responsibility requires that what one is determines what one does; that is, given what one is, one would not choose otherwise (see DETERMINISM). This is a conundrum, whatever theory of mind one may hold. The outline of an answer is (I suggest) that my free will lies in my ability to determine what I do, on the basis of surveying what I know; deliberating; and reaching a conclusion according to my values. If my understanding of the world were different, or if my values were different, then my action would be different.

Intentionality: One knows about things in the external world by interacting with things in the external world. Consider seeing a British letter box. The letter box is red because its surface has a structure which reflects only red light. But no part of my mind reflects red light. I know the redness of the letter box because some aspect of my mental state represents it (the redness) as something I am seeing. This "aspect of my mental state" is a sensation. If I stop and think about it, I can think "I am having a sensation of redness" or "a sensation representing redness."

If you and I and a blind person have interacted with the external world, and in particular each other, you and the blind person can infer that I am having a sensation with the abstract quality "representing redness." We all can know this abstract quality, but the sensation as I feel it, its felt-quality, is private to me. I know the character of my sensation because I have it; other people infer an abstract description of its character as "representing redness." The blind person knows that I am having a sensation such as normal people have when confronted by a red object. (My vision is normal.)

Other manifestations of intentionality are language, and theories about the world.

The setting up of these mental states and processes take place at particular times. This historical basis is essential for the formation of the human mind.

Consciousness: The human mind spends much of its time being conscious. It also manifests unconscious thoughts, beliefs, and evaluations; and blindsight; and the representation of the environment that guides routine activities like driving to work; and split-brain phenomena; and ambiguous mental states like dreaming. All these are mental states and processes.

Being conscious is a system of mental states and processes being active. The range of mental states and processes which may constitute an individual's consciousness is to be discovered by empirical inquiry, interpreting current usage of the term.

Physicalism (in a wide sense) does not presuppose any particular identification of the mental states which constitute consciousness. Peter Carruthers discusses many aspects of consciousness.

A key feature of human consciousness is a unified representation of the environment, of the individual, and of his or her thoughts, ideas, feelings, and values; with the individual able to attend severally to elements of the world and of his or her mental state, to focus on one of them and to perceive it in more detail (to some extent), and to think about them, form theories about them, and evaluate them. This sets human beings apart from all other animals; for human beings can come, progressively, toward understanding the world and basing their ideas, theories, and values on the way it really is. This gives them enormous advantages.

Consciousness normally includes representations of "things" set, where appropriate, in the space of the shared world, and with a time. This is an identity: there is no causal relation; there is no separation. Seeing a thing is having a representation of it. "Seeing a letter box" is seeing a letter box, not seeing a representation of a letter box. When one is conscious, one is conscious of "things," not of their representations, with the suggestion that we are like viewers in a cinema. I have my sensation with its felt-quality, and I am conscious of the quality in the world it represents.

NATURALISM. *Physicalism* provides an appropriate name for this deep theory of the mind, but "physics" can not be the basis for analysis until we have defined the scope of "physics." *Materialism* is not appropriate, because physics has already established that matter is not enough. The key concept is:

A theory or phenomenon is *naturalistic* if that theory or phenomenon does not involve values, purposes, or meanings which do not derive from evaluations by, or the intentionality of, beings limited by material bodies of moderate size.

In a naturalistic universe, "the physical sciences" can be defined: "The sciences of those processes which do not depend on biological or psychological processes." Biology is not "a physical science," but it and physics are naturalistic, for they do not involve values, purposes, or meanings. Psychology and physicalism are concerned with evaluations, purposes, and meanings; but these are attributed to persons limited by material bodies.

Definition of Physicalism. I first define a more general concept of physicalism, then the specific form which I will defend.

Physicalism presupposes that the universe is naturalistic: in particular, all parts of a person's body are governed by naturalistic laws, and the human species evolved by naturalistic processes. It claims:

(1) The *mental continuant* consists of certain parts of the functioning body of an individual who is of an appropriately evolved species.
(2) The identification of the relevant parts of the body is a matter for empirical inquiry, about which physicalism makes no particular claims. However, neurons are obviously the major component, and I will use neurons as representative of the mental continuant.

The defining characteristics of *biographical physicalism* make clear that it does not deny the reality of mind. The point lies elsewhere.

Biographical physicalism claims:

(1) A *person* is constituted of a moderate-sized material body with a mind.
(2) A *mind* is constituted of mental states and processes, and these only, these being carried by neurons.
(3) The mental state *carried* by a neuronal state of an individual is the mental attributes given to the neuronal state by the processes which generated it. First, interactions with the environment experienced by the individual's ancestors established the individual's species-nature; this gives each individual of the species a system of neuronal states that serves functions characteristic of mind, and propensities to generate further mental attributes. Second, the individual's interactions with the external world, and his or her responses to them, generate the particular mental states carried by particular neuronal states. (Some mental states involve other bodily processes: for example, fear involves adrenaline. I can not here consider these other processes.)

The identification of the neuronal or other structures that carry given kinds of mental processes is a matter for empirical inquiry.

Evolution is the prehistory of the human mind. At an individual's birth one's mental qualities are largely latent; but one quickly develops understanding and the ability to discriminate, deliberate, and choose. One's mind is then created in the course of one's interactions with the world, largely according to one's own decisions.

The evolution of one's species, with one's personal biography, determine the way one's consciousness works out—"What it is like to be me." The evolution of the bat mind, and the biography of a bat, determine what it is like to be a bat (cf. Thomas Nagel). Bats and humans each have their sensations. These have their respective felt-qualities, and they represent "things" set in the shared three-dimensional space of the real world.

In a sense, the process of constructing a mind is like programming a computer. But there is no programmer, for a "programmer" is an agent external to the "computer." First, during the evolution of the species and some of the early stages after birth of the individual, one might say that the programmer is reality. But reality is not an "agent." Second, as the individual matures, and one's processes of consideration and decision become effective, we might say that the individual oneself is the programmer. But one's self is not "external."

Biographical Physicalism Is a Scientific Theory. The broad concept of physicalism goes no further than to identify the mental continuant. The theory would have been impossible if the contents of the skull had been different—a reservoir of fat against bad times, perhaps. Therefore it is refutable in Karl POPPER's sense, though not refuted. Therefore physicalism is a scientific theory. Physicalism enters as a plausible theory because the human body includes a structure (the neuronal system) of an order of complexity such that it could carry mental processes as we know them.

Biographical physicalism adds the claim that mental attributes are carried by neuronal systems, and specifies how the relations are set up. It is a scientific theory because it would be rendered untenable if continued effort on some mental attribute sharpened the problems rather than clarifying the solution. It would fade into absurdity. Scientists will establish the balance of the evidence here for and against biographical physicalism.

There is no question of a clear-cut proof or refutation for the identification of the mind. It is in the same logical position as the identification of the causes of lung cancer. Each theory is claiming that its analysis has caught the key factors, subject to adjustment of detail. Nothing can prove or refute such claims; for they amount to the claim that there is nothing more of comparable significance in the phenomenon in question. But if the progress of brain science and evolutionary psychology continues well, those who refuse the evidence could become like the tobacco companies who refused to accept the "proofs" that smoking causes lung cancer.

The processes of the mental continuant are not introspectable. One "sees the red patch," one does not see what is going on when one "sees the red patch." One knows what "being conscious" feels like, not what is going on when one is conscious. Even Harry has no authority in determining what constitutes "Harry seeing a red patch" or "Harry being conscious"; and no one else is better placed. It requires empirical investigation by psychologists and physiologists, and scientific theorizing. I believe the analysis I am outlining implements contemporary thinking by these scientists.

An individual is "seeing a red patch" because his or her neuronal system representing "red" is linked to his or her "external world" neuronal system. These neuronal systems represent color, and the space of the external world, because primitive forms of them, used as such, did indeed represent the color and space of the external world, and gave his or her ancestors survival advantage. Consider a bee. It has a visual system because this enables it to find a flower and get honey from it. Semir Zeki describes the complexities of human vision. The innate structures of human beings represent reality, in their complex ways, and allow us to theorize about it and value bits of it, because this has enabled individuals to survive and (in recent times) to live better lives. Morality is a particular development. It is of unique importance because its criteria are uniquely important (see MORALITY FROM A HUMANIST POSITION; ETHICS AND UNBELIEF).

Some scientists and philosophers argue that the very idea of a physicalist account of consciousness is "absurd" or "impossible." But the existence of such charges against a fundamental scientific theory by no means establishes that the theory is wrong. The theory of relativity is a classic example of a scientific theory thus attacked. The critics simply had not come to terms with the radical novelty in the theory. Biographical physicalism does not identify mind or mental processes with physiological objects or physiological processes. Biography is essential to the identity of a mind. And this makes all the difference.

BIBLIOGRAPHY

Carruthers, Peter. *Phenomenal Consciousness: A Naturalistic Theory.* Cambridge: Cambridge University Press, 2000.

Nagel, Thomas. "What Is It Like to Be a Bat?" *Philosophical Review* 83, no. 4 (1974). Reprinted in Block, Ned, Owen J. Flanagan, and Güven Güzeldere, eds. *The Nature of Consciousness.* Cambridge, MA: MIT Press, 1997.

Zeki, Semir. *A Vision of the Brain.* Oxford: Blackwell, 1993.

HARRY STOPES-ROE

POPPER, KARL RAIMUND (1902–1994), English philosopher. Born in Vienna, Popper became a Marxist in his early and middle teens (see MARX, KARL; MARXISM), aligning himself with communists for two or three months. Near the age of seventeen, he became an anti-Marxist. The Marxists' intellectual presumption, dogmatism, and unwillingness to fight against the fascists in Austria revolted him. "Scientific socialism" seemed not to exemplify the scientific attitude he discovered in Albert Einstein, who exposed his own theory to criticism and critical testing. The years between the two world wars were both grim and exhilarating for Popper. While serving in Austria as a social worker and teacher, he continued to read ravenously and to study music. He chose the history of music as a second subject for his PhD examination. He conjectured that musical and scientific creation had much in common. A kind of preliminary dogmatism (e.g., the canonization of the Gregorian melodies) provided the necessary scaffolding or frame of coordinates needed for exploring the possible order of the new unknown. He argued that science, beginning with myth (and later metaphysics), developed the critical method, speeding up and intensifying the process of trial and error. Against the background of old coordinates, the bold imagination of the great scientists and musicians imposed new possibilities and models that could be subjected to correction and improvement. Popper argued that in both creative music and creative science, problems surfaced and sometimes became articulated. His study of Ludwig von Beethoven's notebooks disclosed a creative composer hard at work, trying version after version of an idea to clarify and simplify it.

Though Popper was never a positivist (see POSITIVISM) or a member of the esteemed Vienna Circle of philosophers (see SCHLICK, MORITZ, AND THE VIENNA CIRCLE), one member nicknamed him "the Official Opposition." His criticisms of VERIFICATIONISM took their toll on positivism, eventually bringing about its demise. Aware of Adolf Hitler's expanding anti-Semitism and knowing that an individual of Jewish origin stood little chance of becoming a university professor in Austria, Popper accepted an invitation to teach at the University of New Zealand. There he worked closely with neurophysiologist John Eccles, who later won the Nobel Prize and recommended Popper's teachings on philosophy of science and scientific investigation.

During World War II, Popper worked on *The Open Society and Its Enemies* (1945), an unprecedented two-volume defense of liberty. This work, along with *The Poverty of Historicism* (1936), helped initiate his international reputation. His first book in philosophy of science, *Logik der Forschung* (1934–35), was translated into English under the title *The Logic of Scientific Discovery* (1959). After sailing around Cape Horn to begin teaching logic and philosophy of science at the London School of Economics in 1946, he encountered many of England's most influential philosophers and scientists, among them Bertrand RUSSELL and Ludwig WITTGENSTEIN. The latter had gained a reputation by contending that philosophy had only puzzles (mostly linguistic) rather than genuine problems to solve. Popper never succeeded in drawing Wittgenstein out in an unemotional, rational discussion of this issue.

While still in Austria, Popper had developed the thesis that far from needing the induction myth, science operated by deducing consequences from content-rich theories that could be severely tested. The process of articulating in-depth theories and falsifying at least aspects of them, Popper argued, offered the possibility of creating better theories. His postwar lectures, articles, and books spelled out his "critical rationalism" for physics, psychology, and biology. His wrestling with the views of such physicists as Erwin Schrödinger, Niels Bohr, Ludwig Boltzmann, Einstein, Ernst Mach, and Werner Heisenberg proved fruitful. His discussions with Schrödinger and Einstein in particular challenged him to clarify his theories of indeterminism, objectivism, and realism. The last two views served as instruments for opposing the rising subjectivism in physics and essentialism in philosophy.

Like all great philosophers, Popper learned from scholars and specialists who were not philosophers by profession. In England, Ernst H. Gombrich (author of *Art and Illusion*), Friedrich August von Hayek, Peter Medawar, and L. Robbins profoundly influenced him. In 1950 he gave the Harvard University William James Lectures. This first visit to America made a tremendous difference to his life. He renewed old friendships from Europe and made new friends, including the great physicist Percy Bridgman. Both Einstein and Bohr attended his lecture at Princeton. Einstein insisted that Popper meet with him to discuss indeterminism. Against Einstein's determinism, which amounted to a four-dimensional Parmenidean block universe, Popper argued for the reality of time and change: In an "open" universe, "the future was in no sense contained in the past or present, even though they do impose severe restrictions on it." Earlier, Popper had argued that the evolution of physics was likely to be an endless process of correction and better approximation to truth about the cosmos.

Ironically, Popper's spreading international fame helped increase the number of readers who seemed content to read extracted passages from his books without reading any of them as a whole. His highly influential *The Open Society and Its Enemies* attracted many readers, some evidentially unwilling to appraise its arguments. By contrast, the British writer, philosopher, and member of Parliament Bryan Magee accustomed himself to Popper's terminology. He concluded that all of Popper's work "is super-abundantly rich in argument." He placed Popper among the four philosophers who would more likely appear to future generations as the most interesting of the twentieth century.

Popper's *Conjectures and Refutations: The Growth of Scientific Knowledge*, a truly remarkable book of scope and depth, was published in 1963; the fifth edition (revised) appeared in 1989. This book alone, strewn with stunning insights and clear argument, would have placed any writer among the luminaries of philosophy. His highly sophisticated theories are for the most part written in commonsense language and with a down-to-earthness that has earned him well-deserved praise. His decades of fascination with "Darwinism as a metaphysical Research Programme" led to his giving the 1961 Herbert Spencer Memorial Lectures in Oxford under the title "Evolution and the Tree of Knowledge." His 1972 *Objective Knowledge: An Evolutionary Approach* gave him the opportunity to reply to his critics by indicating either how he learned from them or how some failed to read him carefully. In both this work and *The Self and Its Brain* (1977, coauthored with John Eccles), important similarities (and differences) with process philosophy in the United States become apparent. He had often expressed his admiration of the work of Charles Sanders Peirce and his notion of "objective chance." In Popper's words, "the first emergence of a novelty such as life may change the possibilities or propensities in the universe.... [T]he newly emergent entities, both micro and macro, change the propensities, micro and macro, in their neighborhood. . . . [T]hey create *new fields of propensities*, as a new star creates a new field of gravitation."

BIBLIOGRAPHY

Magee, Bryan. *Philosophy and the Real World: An Introduction to Karl Popper.* Chiacgo: Open Court, 1990.
———. *The Philosophy of Schopenhauer.* Rev. ed. New York: Oxford University Press, 1997.
Miller, David. *Critical Rationalism: A Restatement and Defense.* Chicago: Open Court, 1994.
Munz, Peter. *Beyond Wittgenstein's Poker: New Light on Popper and Wittgenstein.* Williston, VT: Ashgate, 2004.
Popper, Karl R. *Conjectures and Refutations: The Growth of Scientific Knowledge.* 5th ed., rev. New York: Routledge, 1989.
———. *In Search of a Better World: Lectures and Essays from Thirty Years.* Translated by Laura J. Bennett. New York: Routledge, 1992.
———. *Objective Knowledge: An Evolutionary Approach.* New York: Oxford University Press, 1972.
———. *The Open Society and Its Enemies.* 2 vols. New York: Harper & Row, 1962.
———. *The Poverty of Historicism.* ARK ed. New York: Routledge, 1986.
Popper, Karl R., and John Eccles. *The Self and Its Brain: An Argument for Interactionism.* New York: Routledge, 1983.
Schlipp, Paul Arthur, ed. *The Philosophy of Karl Popper.* 2 vols. Library of Living Philosophers. Chicago: Open Court, 1974.

JOE EDWARD BARNHART

PORTUGUESE LITERATURE, UNBELIEF IN. Although the word *unbelief* has a wider meaning, we shall restrict ourselves to consideration of religious disbelief in Portuguese literature. Religious feeling in Portugal is strong and of long standing (reflected in general adherence to the Catholic Church). Since this piety has been reflected in Portuguese literature since its inception, this article will briefly discuss the way in which unbelief appeared and how it found a place in the Portuguese literature during the nineteenth and twentieth centuries.

In the nineteenth century, Romanticism—in Portugal as throughout Europe—was characterized by a return to religiosity in a reaction to the RATIONALISM that had characterized the century of the Enlightenment (see ENLIGHTENMENT, UNBELIEF DURING THE). Some romantic authors exalted the moral values of Christianity, while others preferred the aesthetic and sentimental side of the faith. However this religious fever did not hinder the first and greatest Portuguese Romantic writers, Almeida Garrett and Alexander Herculano, from breaking free of Catholic institutional teaching and disputing the power of the church. Both liberal catholics, Garrett and Herculano contributed to the secularization of Portuguese culture and pressed for the separation of state and church. Garrett, the more worldly of the two, celebrated the modernization of behavioral norms, rejected any form of Catholic conservatism, and openly denounced the clergy for its corruption and its alliance with the powerful (see his historical novel *O Arco de Sant'Ana* [The Arch of Saint Ann]). For his part, Herculano defended public civil marriage and questioned the historical veracity of some elements of official doctrine. In particular he questioned the dogma of the Immaculate Conception and allegations of a miracle of the Battle of Ourique (1139), in which the fledgling Portuguese nation had won a critical battle against the Moors, supposedly through divine intervention. In his novel *Eurico, o Presbítero* (Eurico the Minister), a genuine best seller of its day, he criticized celibacy as a requirement for the priesthood. Another well-known Romantic writer was Camilo Castelo Branco, author of *Amor de Perdição* (Disgraceful Love). Branco lived his life with little regard for Catholic teachings and he engaged in polemics against the church.

The literature of the second half of the nineteenth century was deeply influenced by the emerging positivist philosophies (see POSITIVISM) and therefore leaned toward scientific reason with an iconoclastic and even a Jacobin flavor. The main figures of this period, known as the "Generation of '70," were engaged in a remarkable polemic against Romanticism published in Coimbra in 1865. They mounted an intense campaign of ANTICLERICALISM spread across a remarkable range of genres. These include some realistic novels of the author who is probably the greatest prose stylist in the Portuguese language, Eça de Queirós, *O Crime do Padre Amado* (The Crime of Father Amado) and *A Relíquia* (The Relic); the satirical poems of Guerra Junqueiro, such as *A Velhice do Padre Eterno* (The Oldness of the Perpetual Priest); and the chronicles of Ramalho Ortigão and of Fialho de Almeida. But there were others, as well: poet and philosopher Antero de Quental, who indicted the church and its influence in his *Causas da Decadéncia dos Povos*

Peninsulares (Causes of Decadence of Iberian People), and historian Oliveira Martins, who is remembered for his *Portugal Contemporâneo* (Contemporary Portugal). All of these writers defended the ideal of a secular and progressive society in which reason, science, and social morality should completely replace dogmas and religious pedagogy. They did not dispute the historicity of Jesus Christ or the evangelical thrust of the gospels, but they considered Catholicism in general—and the influence of the clergy in social life and politics in particular—obsolete and alienating.

The strong positivist movement ushered in its own dialectical reaction in later years: the fin-de-siècle Neo-Romantic movement displayed some return to religious values, a revival of mystical spirituality, and a return to the traditions of national culture.

The twentieth century would bring modernity. In 1910 the republic was established and in 1911 the state was officially separated from the church. The poets of the so-called First Modernism in the teens and twenties included great Portuguese poets like Fernando Pessoa, who published but a single book-length work during his life, the esoteric-patriotic poem *Mensagem* (Message); and Mário de Sá-Carneiro, author of *Confissões de Lúcio* (Lúcio's Confessions). Both were personally relatively indifferent in matters of religion. Fernando Pessoa was a believer in esotericism, astrology in particular. However, the "Second Modernism" of the thirties and forties—which included writers and poets such as José Régio, author of *Poemas de Deus e do Diabo* (Poems of God and Devil), and Miguel Torga, author of *Contos da Montanha* (Tales from the Mountains)—ushered in a Christian humanism marked once again by some anticlericalism, though not so pronounced as it was among some realists at the end of the nineteenth century.

Given his originality and his worldwide fame, Fernando Pessoa deserves special mention. Pessoa wrote in his own name and as a series of heteronyms, or literary alter egos: Alberto Caeiro, Álvaro de Campos, Ricardo Reis, Alexander Search, and others, each with a completely distinct personality, background, and style. For example, Alberto Caeiro was a keeper of sheep, contemplative and sensual, while Álvaro de Campos was a naval engineer, worldly and a futurist. Both expressed SKEPTICISM regarding God and religion. Caeiro admired nature instead of God, while Campos admired the power and diversity of technology. Wrote Caeiro:

To think of God is to disobey God
Because God wanted us not to know him,
And therefore did not show himself to us . . .

Campos wrote:

And in each corner of my soul there's an altar to a different god.

Of the many writers who followed, in regard to religious unbelief, two names deserve particular attention: Vergílio Ferreira and José Saramago.

Vergílio Ferreira, not well known outside of Portugal (his works have been translated only into Spanish and French), is the author of *Manhã Sumersa* (Submerged Morning), *Aparição* (Appearance), and *Para Sempre* (Forever). He was a philosophical writer, sympathetic with the existentialism of Jean-Paul SARTRE. He declared himself an atheist after a somewhat traumatic experience during his infancy at a Catholic seminary (this is told in his book *Manhã Submersa*). His characters, faithful to their author, declare the death of God: only the man remains, with all his anguishes, in particular the anguish of death. Ferreira wrote: "Nobody can be instead of us—not even God." The only substitute for God—inadequate as it may be—would be art.

On the other hand, José Saramago, Nobel laureate in literature in 1998—to date, the only Portuguese so honored—wrote *Memorial do Convento* (Baltazar and Blimunda), regarding the construction of a great baroque monastery. The retitling of the English version refers to the two main characters: Baltazar, who has a single hand, and Blimunda, who possesses paranormal powers. In a magical scene these two representatives of the common people fly in a primitive balloon together with a priest who is being pursued by the Inquisition. Saramago's other works include *O Ano da Morte de Ricardo Reis* (The Year of the Death of Ricardo Reis), concerning the return of Ricardo Reis to Lisbon after his death; *Evangelho Segundo Jesus Cristo* (The gospel according to Jesus Christ, a story of Jesus told in the first person, contravening tradition); and *Ensaio sobre a Cegueira* (Blindness). Saramago is a declared unbeliever in God but its incredulity extends far beyond the religious domain. It can even be said that he is a radical pessimist, since he thinks that humankind is its own worst enemy. He is also known for his skeptical positions regarding progress and the contribution of science and technology to social well-being. His SECULARISM is clear in *Evangelho Segundo Jesus Cristo*, which caused a scandal in Portugal when it appeared. His atheistic position is evident in his essay "The God Factor," which he published in the press shortly after the attacks on the Twin Towers on September 11, 2001: "Nietzsche said that all was permissible if God did not exist, and I reply that it is precisely because of God and in God's name that everything has been permitted and justified, principally the worst of things, principally the most cruel and horrendous." For Saramago, belief in God may be the source of the greatest evil.

BIBLIOGRAPHY

Pessoa, Fernando. *The Keeper of Sheep*. Translated by Edwin Honig and Susan M. Brown. New York: Sheep Meadow, 1986.
———. *Selected Poems*. Edited and translated by Peter Rickard. Austin: University of Texas Press, 1972.
———. *Selected Poems by Fernando Pessoa, Including Poems by His Heteronyms: Alberto Caeiro, Ricardo Reis [and] Alvaro de Campos, as Well as Some of His English Sonnets and Selections from His Letters*. Translated by Edwin Honig. Chicago: Swallow, 1971.
Queirós, Eça de. *Crime of Father Amaro: Scenes from the Religious Life*. Translated and with an introduction by Margaret Jull Costa. New York: New Directions, 2003.
Saramago, José. *Baltasar and Blimunda*. Translated by Giovanni Pontiero. San Diego, CA: Harcourt Brace, 1998.
———. *Blindness: A Novel*. Translated by Giovanni Pontiero. London: Harvill, 1997.
———. "The God Factor." Translated by George Monteiro. Available at http://www.plcs.umassd.edu/plc57 texts/monteiro.doc.
———. *The Gospel according to Jesus Christ*. Translated by Giovanni Pontiero. New York: Harcourt Brace, 1994.
———. *The Year of the Death of Ricardo Reis*. Translated by Giovanni Pontiero. San Diego CA: Harcourt, 1991.
Torga, Miguel. *Tales from the Mountains*. Translated by Ivana Carlsen. Fort Bragg, CA: QED, 1991.

CARLOS FIOLHAIS

POSITIVISM. Positivism is a philosophical current akin to empiricism and NATURALISM. In the literature one can find a distinction between legal positivism, moral positivism, and positivist philosophy. Legal positivism is the theory that the law of the state is based on the will of the holder of sovereign power in the state, whereas moral positivism, also known as theological voluntarism or the divine command theory, is the theory that God's commands in themselves make certain actions right and others wrong.

Positivist philosophy, *positive philosophy*, and *positivism* are terms used to designate a worldview that is conceived of as being in tune with modern science, and which accordingly rejects superstition, religion, and metaphysics as prescientific forms of thought which will cede to positive science as humankind continues its progress. This usage is derived from Auguste COMTE who established it in his writings, especially from the 1830s on.

The Frenchman Comte invented the term *sociology*, and has often been considered to be the founder of sociology. What is distinctive about Comte's positivism in its first form is its attempt to describe the history of human thought as evolving through certain definite stages, which he called the religious, the metaphysical, and the scientific. Of these, the last was the most productive and valuable, though the earlier ones had their value too and were not to be simply dismissed as primitive and useless. Indeed, toward the end of his life Comte himself thought it necessary to introduce a religion of humanity, a religion that still survives in France, Brazil, and Chile.

According to positivist theories of knowledge, *all* knowledge, or at least all empirical knowledge, is ultimately based on sense experience. There cannot be different kinds of knowledge. Positivist theories of knowledge do not always recognize a sharp distinction between the formal sciences (logic and mathematics) and the empirical sciences (all other sciences). All genuine inquiry is said to be concerned with the description and explanation of empirical facts. There is no difference in principle between the methods of the physical and the social sciences, for example.

Nonpositivist theories of knowledge often emphasize the difference between formal sciences and empirical sciences. This distinction is often neglected in positivist theories of knowledge.

Empiricist philosophers like Francis Bacon and David HUME can be regarded as precursors of positivism. In the nineteenth century important representatives of positivism, apart from Comte, were Herbert SPENCER, Ernst HAECKEL, Richard Avenarius, and Ernst Mach. These four thinkers have not always been called positivists, but they have all been close to positivism in a broad sense of the word.

Positivist ideas gained a foothold in the public mind and were accepted by many radical philosophers and progressive intellectuals. In England, for instance, there were the authors George Henry Lewes and George ELIOT and the philosopher John Stuart MILL. Lewes published the book *Comte's Philosophy of the Sciences* (1853), which contributed greatly to making Comte's ideas known in the English-speaking world.

As to Mill, it seems that he first was attracted to Comte's positivism. But later, in his 1865 *Auguste Comte and Positivism*, Mill was quite critical of Comte's philosophy.

From the 1850s onward, Comtean positivism gained a marked influence in France and came to expression in anticlerical and anticonservative politics (see ANTICLERICALISM). This was even more the case in some countries in Latin America. The ideas behind the revolution in Brazil in 1889 were positivist (see LATIN AMERICA, UNBELIEF IN), and the Brazilian flag carries the positivist motto "Order and Progress."

In sharp contrast to positivism in the nineteenth century, there is no comparable political dimension in the predominant variety of twentieth-century positivism, that is, the philosophical outlook advocated by members of the Vienna Circle. This circle was particularly active during the years 1924 to 1936 and its members included Moritz SCHLICK, Rudolf Carnap, and Otto Neurath.

The British philosopher Alfred Jules AYER was in his youth deeply influenced by the ideas of the Vienna Circle. These ideas became known as *LOGICAL POSITIVISM*, a label first given to the movement in articles by Eino Kaila and Åke Petzäll, two Nordic sympathizers, around 1930. Logical positivism, also known as logical empiricism, differed from earlier versions of positivism in its

approach to the formal sciences (logic and mathematics), but agreed with the earlier varieties in its empiricism and its emphatic rejection of metaphysics.

Between 1924 and 1936, the main center of logical positivism was the Vienna Circle. The Vienna Circle evolved in 1923 out of a seminar led by Schlick and attended, among other students, by Friedrich Waismann and Herbert Feigl. Schlick began teaching in 1922, and in 1925 out of this nucleus a Thursday evening discussion group was formed. Many of the participants were not professional philosophers. Even if some of them taught philosophy, their original fields of study lay in other fields. Schlick, for example, had specialized in physics, and his doctor's thesis, written under the guidance of Max Planck in Berlin, concerned a problem in theoretical optics.

Active members of the Vienna Circle during its first years were, in addition to Schlick, Feigl, and Waismann, the mathematician Hans J. Hahn, the sociologist Neurath, the historian Victor Kraft, the lawyer Felix Kaufmann, and the mathematician Kurt Reidemeister. An occasional but important visitor was the physicist Philipp Frank, based in Prague at that time.

In 1927 and again in 1932, the Finnish psychologist and philosopher Eino Kaila was present as an active and important member. Another visitor from Scandinavia was the Swede Åke Petzäll. Among the younger participants was the mathematician and logician Kurt Gödel and the philosopher Gustav Bergmann. Other visitors were Carl G. Hempel of Berlin, A. E. Blumberg of Baltimore, and Alfred Jules Ayer of Oxford. Among those more loosely affiliated with the group were Karl Menger, E. Zilsel, Karl POPPER, Hans Kelsen, Ludwig von Bertalanffy, Heinrich Gomperz, and B. von Juhos.

The most decisive and rapid development of ideas began in 1926 when Rudolf Carnap was called to the University of Vienna. His contributions to axiomatics and his theory of the constitution of empirical concepts (as published in *Der logische Aufbau der Welt*, 1928) proved a source of very stimulating discussions.

Also in 1926, Ludwig WITTGENSTEIN's *Tractatus Logico-Philosophicus* was studied in the circle. The philosophical position of logical positivism at the end of the 1920s was the outcome of these incisive influences. Though a number of the basic ideas had already been enunciated in a general manner by Schlick, they were formulated more fully and more radically by Carnap. Schlick was deeply influenced by Carnap, but perhaps even more by Wittgenstein, who at that time lived in Austria.

In contrast to Carnap, who between 1926 and 1930 was a regular and most influential participant in the Vienna Circle, Wittgenstein associated only occasionally with some members of the circle. It seems that Wittgenstein never attended any meetings of the Vienna Circle. Even so, participants obtained some information about obscure passages of his extremely condensed (and to some extent also profound) *Tractatus*.

An exposition of the work and worldview of the Vienna Circle was given in 1929 in a pamphlet titled *Wissenschaftliche Weltauffassung: Der Wiener Kreis* (Scientific Worldview: The Vienna Circle) written by Hahn, Neurath, and Carnap. Here, the aim of the Vienna Circle was said to be to form a unified science comprising all knowledge of reality accessible to humanity without dividing it into separate, unconnected special disciplines such as physics and psychology, natural science and letters, philosophy, and the special sciences. The way to attain this aim was by the use of the logical method of analysis, a method said to have been worked out by Peano, Frege, Whitehead, and Russell, a method that could serve to eliminate metaphysical problems and assertions as meaningless, as well as to clarify the meaning of concepts and sentences of empirical science by showing their immediately observable content: *the given* (das Gegebene).

In 1936 the English philosopher Alfred J. Ayer published his book *Language, Truth and Logic*. The book was a sensation and soon became an important manifesto of logical positivism. The book was written with much greater fervor than is common with philosophical books.

In his argumentation, Ayer among other things states that "if 'god' is a metaphysical term, then it cannot even be probable that a god exists. For to say that 'God exists' is to make a metaphysical utterance which cannot be either true or false. And by the same criterion, no sentence which purports to describe the nature of a transcendent god can possess any literal significance."

As seen by Ayer in 1936, and in 1946 when the revised edition of his *Language, Truth and Logic* appeared, both ATHEISM and AGNOSTICISM were "nonsensical," a quite remarkable view.

Since the end of the 1930s logical positivism has no longer existed as a distinctive movement, but many individuals have been inspired by the ideas of the logical positivists and have hearkened back to these sources for further inspiration.

Comte's rejection of traditional religion and metaphysics, his faith in science and progress, his theory of history, and his pioneering work in sociology have all had a strong and persistent influence on subsequent thought. Logical positivism can be seen as a movement which continued some of Comte's ideas in a more radical form. Comte's theory of history has fascinated many intellectuals but several of its elements have always remained disputed.

BIBLIOGRAPHY

Ayer, Alfred J. *Language, Truth and Logic*. London: Victor Gollancz, 1936.
———. *Logical Positivism*. Glencoe, IL: Free Press, 1959.
Hiorth, Finngeir. *Positivism*. Oslo: Human-Etisk Forbund, 2004.
Jörgensen, Jörgen. *The Development of Logical Empiricism*. Chicago: University of Chicago Press.

FINNGEIR HIORTH

PRAGMATISM. In contemporary philosophy, *pragmatism* is used to characterize an array of positions and attitudes ranging from the hard-nosed naturalism of W. V. O. Quine to the economic reductionism of Richard Posner to the postmodernist relativism of Richard Rorty to the commonsense empiricism of Susan Haack. Rather than try to sort out the various senses of the term as it is employed in contemporary debates, I shall focus on the doctrines associated with the American philosophers most commonly credited with founding the pragmatist tradition: Charles Sanders Peirce, William James, and John DEWEY. The philosophical difference among these original pragmatists partly accounts for the variety of ways the term is understood today.

Peirce and the Pragmatic Maxim. The essence of Peirce's pragmatism lies in the principle of meaning, known as the pragmatic maxim, first expressed in his most famous essay, "How to Make Our Ideas Clear" (1878). However, this principle is itself derived from the theory of belief launched in his earlier article, "The Fixation of Belief" (1877). It is with this that we begin.

On traditional accounts, to have a belief is to be in a certain psychological state with regard to a given idea. That is, to believe that *snow is white* is to adopt a certain psychological attitude—one of affirmation—toward the statement "Snow is white." On this kind of analysis, belief is essentially a psychological phenomenon; beliefs are inner, mental, and private. Peirce sought to rid philosophy of the notion of an "inner" consciousness that it inherited from René DESCARTES. Wanting to set philosophy on more scientific ground, Peirce proposed a theory according to which beliefs are not essentially mental states, but rather *rules for action*, or as Peirce would say, "habits." On the Peircean analysis, to believe that *this knife is sharp* is to be disposed to *behave* in certain ways when presented with the knife. Put more generally, to have a belief is simply to have acquired a habit of acting in certain ways under certain conditions. As beliefs are, in essence, habits, they are not inner and private, but publicly observable.

How a particular belief will lead us to act is a function of the *meaning* of the idea or statement to which the belief refers. That is, the belief that *this knife is sharp* will generate certain behavior depending upon the meaning of the idea "This knife is sharp." Therefore, Peirce's theory of belief entails a theory of meaning. In "How to Make Our Ideas Clear," Peirce formulates his theory of meaning, which is often called the pragmatic maxim: "Consider what effects, that might conceivably have practical bearings, we conceive the object of our conception to have . . . our conception of these effects is the whole of our conception of the object."

The concept of meaning also has been traditionally understood to be primarily a psychological property. Here, again, we find Peirce resisting the traditional tendency; on Peirce's view, the meaning of an idea is to be analyzed in terms of the effects of its object in a person's experience. Accordingly, to say that some object X is hard is to say that it will scratch other objects. Meaning is therefore brought down to "what is tangible and conceivably practical"; the meaning of a term consists in the "sensible effects" it predicates of an object, and the meaning of a statement is essentially a proposal, or a prediction, regarding the functioning of its object. For any idea, then, one may extract its complete meaning by drawing out the proposals for action that it suggests. Meaning is thus taken out of the realm of private consciousness and placed into the world of action and behavior.

According to Peirce, the primary function of this conception of meaning is to help philosophers "dismiss" the "make-believes" of previous philosophizing. That is, the pragmatic maxim is to be used as a weapon against the imprecise and vague vocabulary of traditional philosophy, especially metaphysical philosophy. Peirce writes: "[Pragmatism] will serve to show that almost every proposition of ontological metaphysics is either meaningless gibberish—one word being defined by other words, and they by still others, without any real conception ever being reached—or else downright absurd."

Peirce imagined a time at which, through the application of his maxim, philosophy would be purged of all nonsense. At this time, all that would remain is "a series of problems capable of investigation by the observational methods of the true sciences."

James's Pragmatism. Unlike Peirce, who thought that pragmatism would expose the meaninglessness of metaphysics, James claims that pragmatism is "primarily a method of settling metaphysical disputes that otherwise might be interminable." Following Peirce, James locates the meaning of an idea within its practical consequences for behavior. However, whereas Peirce limits the practical consequences of an idea to those functional proposals which it predicates of its object, James designs his pragmatism to include within a given idea's pragmatic meaning its implications for the entirety of the believing subject's experience. That is, James realizes that belief in certain philosophical doctrines can be *paralyzing*, that certain philosophical doctrines can induce attitudes that *obstruct* action and literally stifle the flow of life. Such consequences, which may be characterized as "psychological," are certainly *practical*—they most definitely affect our behavior—and James thought that a practical philosophy must account for them. That is, Jamesian pragmatism "plunges forward into the river of experience" and attempts to confront it whole.

Accordingly, James does not follow Peirce in dismissing traditional philosophy's metaphysical disputes as only so much nonsense. The Jamesian strategy is to translate the competing metaphysical claims into propositions about our own attitudes and behavioral dispositions toward the world. Once cast in Jamesian-pragmatic terms, we shall find that either the competing claims mean the same thing (which is to say that they result in attitudes leading to the same kind of action), or that one frustrates while the other assists action. James argues that as ours is, for better or worse, a world that demands that we *act*; we should adopt those metaphysical propositions which facilitate action, support our efforts, and underwrite our deepest hopes. Hence one finds James *defending* a range of metaphysical doctrines—including certain religious claims—on pragmatic grounds.

Yet pragmatism is for James not only a method of dealing with metaphysics, but also "a certain theory of truth." James's pragmatic conception of truth is notoriously complex, and it has received more than its share of critical comment. I can offer only a sketch here.

Philosophers have long defended the intuitive idea that a statement is true just if it *corresponds* to reality. Decidedly philosophical difficulties arise once one is asked to specify precisely what the relation of "correspondence to reality" is. James's pragmatic theory of truth attempts to answer this question by applying the pragmatic maxim to the notion of correspondence. On James's analysis, the essential thing about truth "is the process of being guided" in action; "correspondence to the way the world is" and "agreement with reality" is "essentially an affair of leading." Hence to say that a statement is true is to say that, were one to believe it, one would be successfully led in action. A statement is true, then, insofar as it is a reliable (James often says "useful") guide for action. Thus the oft-cited but infrequently understood motto, "truth is what works."

Critics have charged James with making the truth of a statement depend upon our wishes, purposes, and desires. Although in some writings James invites this charge, the pragmatist theory of truth is not quite so crude. James retains Peirce's functionalist account of belief: The meaning of a belief is the habit of action it produces, and every meaningful belief thus has a *purpose* insofar as it is adopted for the sake of successful action. But action is not to be understood simply as an individual event, an isolated *doing*. Action occurs within a complex network of experience. For example, the act of taking a sip of coffee involves the coordination within experience of a wide variety of factors: My beliefs about the location of the cup and how it is to be grasped, the commonsense trust in the existence and general stability of medium-sized physical objects, and the workings of gravity and other physical forces, among others. Given that actions occur within the manifold of experience, it is perhaps more correct to think of a belief as a guide for *activity*. Now, the pragmatic conception of truth says that beliefs are to be evaluated according to their ability to guide activity; accordingly, beliefs "become true just in so far as they help us to get into satisfactory relation with other parts of our experience." Hence the "usefulness" James associates with truth has to do with a belief's ability to guide action successfully *within* the whole of experience. Wish as I may that I had millions of dollars in my bank account, this belief could not reliably guide my action, and is therefore false. The "working" and "usefulness" that James associates with truth are not reducible to human whim or desire.

Dewey's Pragmatism. Dewey articulates a version of pragmatism that he called experimental naturalism. Dewey's philosophy is naturalist in that it takes as its fundamental category the Darwinian creature (see DARWINISM), a biological agent interacting with an environment. It is experimentalist in that it offers a conception of experience based in its naturalism. On Dewey's view, experience is not to be analyzed on the model offered by the traditional empiricisms of John LOCKE and David HUME, according to which experience is the passive receiving of impressions. For Dewey, experience is an "active affair primarily of doing," an "affair of the intercourse of a living being with its physical and social environment." As the relationship between a creature and its environment is a dynamic one of simultaneous and mutual doings and undergoings, experimentation is built into the very fabric of nature.

From this fundamental holism of agent and world, or of experience and nature, Dewey launches a devastating critique of traditional philosophies from PLATO to KANT and beyond. According to Dewey, all traditional philosophies presume a "spectator theory of knowledge"; that is, traditional philosophies presume that there is a *metaphysical* difference in kind between the knowing subject and the object known. Typically, this difference is analyzed in terms of an "inner" mind and an "external" reality. From this assumption, all the standard epistemological and metaphysical puzzles of philosophy grow. The familiar problems of skepticism, the existence of the external world, the validity of induction, and the relation of mind and body all arise from this fundamental dualism. On Dewey's view, the idea that the knowing subject is essentially a passive "spectator" looking on an external world of objects is exploded by the holistic Darwinian paradigm. According to Dewey, "[T]he interaction of organism and environment, resulting in some adaptation which secures utilization of the latter, is the primary fact." Once this is recognized, we see that knowledge is essentially a kind of *activity*; it is the activity of developing experimental hypotheses and testing and revising them in the course of experience.

Dewey is perhaps best known for drawing the implication from his experimentalist epistemology to a distinctive conception of politics. Dewey reasons that, as experience itself is bound up with processes of experimentation, and since knowledge itself is to be analyzed in terms of experimental confirmation and success, the most human and most just political order is that which best enables and supports human experience. Dewey

held that democracy, understood as collective and participatory self-government, is the only political order in which the full potential of human experience can be realized. In this way, Dewey held that all social institutions, including schools, households, and workplaces, should be democratically ordered.

Dewey's rejection of the spectator theory of knowledge and his experimentalist alternative provides the core of a comprehensive philosophical system that ranges from epistemology and metaphysics to aesthetics, ethics, and political philosophy. We have here only scratched the surface of Dewey's pragmatism. Suffice it to say that Dewey's pragmatism is driven by an abiding insight that philosophical theorizing must begin from a fundamentally scientific understanding of life and experience, and must be directed toward the resolution of human problems.

Conclusion. To conclude, let us identify four broad themes prevalent in the pragmatist tradition. First, pragmatism is a kind of NATURALISM; that is, pragmatists reject philosophical appeals to supernatural entities or forces, and aspire to keep philosophical speculation within the bounds of respectable science. Second, pragmatism is a kind of *empiricism*; that is, pragmatists insist that philosophical concepts must be understood in terms of human experience. Third, pragmatism is a kind of *functionalism*; that is, pragmatists tend to emphasize *action* or *activity* in their philosophizing—they hold that to understand something is to understand *what it can do*. Finally, pragmatism is a kind of HUMANISM; that is, pragmatists insist upon the powers of free human intelligence and open inquiry to resolve the moral, political, and material problems we confront today.

BIBLIOGRAPHY

Dewey, John. *The Collected Works of John Dewey.* 37 vols. Edited by Jo Ann Boydston. Carbondale: Southern Illinois University Press, 1967–90.

Hartshorne, Charles, Paul Weiss, and Arthur Burks, eds. *Collected Papers of Charles Sanders Peirce.* 8 vols. Cambridge, MA: Harvard University Press, 1931–58.

McDermott, John J., ed. *The Writings of William James.* Chicago: University of Chicago Press, 1977.

ROBERT BASIL TALISSE

PRAYER. Prayer is an aspect of religion that many unbelievers secretly regret abandoning, but most stories of its rediscovery on their deathbeds are clerical inventions (see DEATHBED CLAIMS CONCERNING UNBELIEVERS).

Befitting its paradoxical status, prayer is variously classified. The *Encyclopedia of Religion* (1987) identifies petition, invocation, thanksgiving (praise or adoration), dedication, supplication, intercession, confession, penitence, and benediction; the *New Encyclopaedia Britannica Macropaedia* (1974) identifies petition, confession, intercession, praise and thanksgiving, adoration, and unitative prayer (mystical union or ecstasy). Apart from the last, the Britannica's classification is more logical. While theologians endlessly romanticize about the psychological importance and lofty aspirations of prayer, the *Encyclopedia of Religion* concedes that addresses to the deity on personal and material matters, which it defines as petition, are "thought to be the most widespread and hence oldest type." "Supplication" is similar to "petition" in its essentially anthropocentric and selfish implications, but may be less material and usually seeks to advance the interests of a wider group—family, tribe, nation, or all humanity—of which the individual is a part.

The loosest definitions apply to "intercession." Strictly, it involves the use of mediators with a *locus standi* (official status) to put the cause of humankind before the deity. In Trinitarian Christianity, this means God the Son interceding with God the Father, as spelled out in 1 Timothy 2:5: "For there is one God, and one mediator between God and men, the man Christ Jesus." Jesus himself reportedly endorsed this role in "Father, forgive them; for they know not what they do" (Luke 23:34). The practice of invoking Jesus is commonly followed by evangelical Protestants, though the Holy Ghost or Spirit (Rom. 8:26) may also be called upon. Roman Catholics, on the other hand, usually seek the intercession of a particular saint associated with the desired boon and/or the Virgin Mary. Hence the rosary: "Holy Mary, Mother of God, pray for us sinners now and at the hour of our death." Bodhisattvas function similarly within Mahayana Buddhism. By extension, "intercession" has come to mean prayers by individuals or groups on behalf of other people and is even, as the *Oxford English Dictionary* concedes, "loosely used for a petition or pleading on one's own behalf." To combine petition, supplication, and intercession under "petitionary prayer" would seem logical.

However defined, this is what most concerns unbelievers in religious controversies; though freethinking moral philosophers are equally critical of the way confession and penitence are employed to advance clericalism (see ANTICLERICALISM) and undermine personal responsibility and reparation. All the other forms of prayer are generally deemed beyond polemics.

Public prayers are often a jumbled blend of categories. The following analysis may be made of the famous Lord's Prayer (Matt. 6:9–13) of Christians:

Our Father, which art in heaven [*invocation*] hallowed be thy name [*praise*]. Thy kingdom come; thy will be done in earth, as it is in heaven [*invocation*]. Give us this day our daily bread [*petition*] and forgive us our trespasses [*confession/penitence*] as we forgive those who trespass against us [*intercession*]. Lead us not into temptation, but deliver us from evil [*supplication*]. For thine is the kingdom,

and the power, and the glory, for ever and ever [*adoration*]. Amen [*dedication*].

Religious and philosophical objections to the concept of prayer, especially petitionary prayer, were well stated by clerics or former clerics in the nineteenth century. In *The Religion of the Universe* (1864) Robert Fellowes bluntly stated, "We anthropomorphize the Deity: we make a man, a frail, mutable, vacillating man of the Eternal." Christian Socialist F. D. Maurice said that while Trinitarianism "makes prayer possible" by invoking Jesus as a mediator, the idea of a Sole God in Unitarianism (see UNITARIANISM TO 1961) is inconsistent with the concept. "Is God's Will good? then why attempt to move it by petitions and intercessions? Is it not good? then how hopeless the effort must be, seeing that he is omnipotent." More diplomatically, *The Bible Reader's Encyclopedia and Concordance* (n.d.) admits, "One of the gravest obstacles in the way of believing that God answers prayer is that to do so would be to alter His own natural and moral laws, and hence to 'change His mind.'" Then in a bold sleight of hand it asserts that, according to Jesus, God's mind involves fellowship with humankind, whose real need is to find God, and that, as prayer satisfies both expectations, it is always answered.

Less ingenious but equally specious arguments claim to establish the same proposition. It is argued, for example, that through prayer the faithful discover what God's will for their lives really is and that, even though it may be different from what they originally sought, they come to terms with it, revise their expectations, and so find their prayers answered. Clearly this is not what average petitioners expect when they get down on their knees to pray for rain, a miracle cure of disease, or their nation's victory in warfare. Warfare in particular is a time when the deity is notably ear-bashed and put in an impossible position. For even if Yahweh, Allah, and the rest are not different names for the same supreme being, the Holy Trinity itself has often been enlisted in the cause of each rival Christian nation. As freethinking historian John Mackinnon ROBERTSON put it in his *History of Freethought in the Nineteenth Century* (1929), "Prayer implicates all the self-contradictions of theism."

Amid the various conceptions of prayer there are two characteristics that all authorities agree on. The communion of humankind with God (or other sacred entities) has already been considered. Universality is its other feature. Anthropologists dispute whether prayer is a simple evolution from the magical incantations found in animism, or represents an entirely separate phenomenon. In tribal cultures, prayer to the disembodied spirits of ancestors or spirits inherent in sacred objects like amulets or talismans may involve bribery or blackmail (offering or withholding sacrifices) or even intimidation (beating objects that fail to perform as expected). While all believers have always been considered capable of praying on their own behalf, in ancient pagan and later religions priestly castes have arisen with formalized and formularized praying functions, though their sacramental role is more important. In Islam dervishes, or mystics, are deemed to have special nonpriestly powers.

In Orthodox Judaism, following the Torah and lives of the patriarchs, demonstrable piety, as in public praying, is held to bring material benefits. In the Judaism of the prophets and in early Christianity, this supposed benefit of religion is subordinated to otherworldly considerations. But religious materialism could not be easily eradicated, and particularly in Christian Science, Mormonism, and latter-day cults, prosperity in this life is advertised as a benefit of prayer.

If prayer brought only so-called spiritual benefits, unbelievers would have no means of explaining, measuring, or refuting them. It is a different story when psychological and/or material consequences are said to flow. Here one may apply both the verification and the falsification principles (see FALSIFIABILITY; VERIFICATIONISM; LOGICAL POSITIVISM). With private prayer, only believers know the objective and outcome of their prayers. If they claim their prayers are answered, surely that is verification. Maybe; yet it must be recognized they may well have a vested interest, professional or emotional, in making such a claim. But not only is it impossible to deny—as distinct from explaining—particular veridical (anecdotal) experiences, the sophisticated apologetics outlined above makes clear there is never a way to deny *any* claim for answered private prayer. Whatever results can be said to be God's will. Thus the claim fails the falsification principle's test and is either false or meaningless.

Sometimes a distraught petitioner does seem to display psychological improvement after praying. Is this a manifestation of divine intervention or any other type of supernatural force? That might be the case only if no other procedure were capable of producing the same effect. In fact, many such procedures exist. In the late nineteenth and early twentieth centuries, great store was placed on autosuggestion, associated with Émile Coué. By simply encouraging his patients to frequently repeat "Every day, and in every way, I am becoming better and better," this French pharmacist-turned-psychotherapist claimed, perhaps justifiably, to have effected improvements and even cures.

Not only may such widespread and imperfectly understood mental conditions as depression and anxiety states respond to psychological stimuli, but so may a number of physical diseases called psychosomatic. These displays of "mind over matter" perhaps associated with physical factors include hypertension (high blood pressure), respiratory and gastrointestinal disorders like asthma and chronic gastritis, migraine, impotence, frigidity, and dermatitis. Even certain cancers and diabetes are said to have a psychosomatic element. Today Coué is virtually replaced by a cocktail of drugs and cognitive behavioral therapy.

Not surprisingly, apart from wars and natural disasters, petitionary prayer flourishes in times of sickness and bereavement. Shamans who lead prayers are also called witch doctors or medicine men, and priests in many old religions were said to have healing powers (see FAITH HEALING). Apart from the psychosomatic illnesses listed above, there are a number of progressive conditions, such as multiple sclerosis and rheumatoid arthritis, that from time to time display spontaneous remissions that kindle hope in their victims. When these remissions occur during times of prayer or the laying on of hands by faith healers, messages transmitted by Spiritualist mediums, blessings by gypsies, immersion in healing springs, taking orthodox or quack medicines, hypnosis, acupuncture, aromatherapy—the list is all but endless—the lucky intervention is hailed as a miracle cure. But never is there an incontestable demonstration of prayer's power—say, the regrowth of an amputated limb. Remissions of this sort are part of the broader phenomenon of coincidence on which not only proponents of healing prayer, but astrologers, tarot card and teacup readers, stock market and racing tipsters, parapsychologists and fortune-tellers, depend. Some of their forecasts are bound to come true, be paraded by their givers, and remembered by their receivers. The rest are quietly buried. Nobody does a statistical analysis.

Even less often than with claims for the paranormal can scientific researchers persuade the faithful to submit the purported efficacy of prayer to rigorous investigation (see PARANORMAL, BELIEF IN THE). Where investigations do occur, they are often conducted by believers in the phenomenon being studied. While such people may be consciously honest, they have an unconscious urge to turn a blind eye to dishonesty in their subjects or irregularities in the procedure, and to select favorable results as valid and reject unfavorable ones as flawed.

If the investigators are dishonest they will try to bamboozle any observers present or, if they find this impossible, excuse unfavorable results or truncate the experiment on the grounds of disabling "negativity" or "bad vibes" produced by SKEPTICISM.

Even when properly conducted, at best such investigations turn out not to provide a 100 percent occurrence of answered prayers, telepathy, precognition, or whatever, but a result "beyond chance expectation." But every research finding has a standard deviation about the mean, and an unusual result need not be significant unless found in a sufficient number of similar experiments. A one-off trial, however impressive, has no statistical value.

All the above reservations apply to a much-touted and, at first glance, imposing investigation conducted at prestigious Columbia University Medical Center and critically reported on by Bruce Flamm. The Columbia study purported to show that "infertile women who were prayed for by Christian prayer groups became pregnant twice as often as those who did not have people praying for them." The study was published in the (normally peer-reviewed) *Journal of Reproductive Medicine* in 2001, and was immediately reported on around the world. Not only was the sponsoring institution highly reputable, but the lead author was chairman of its Department of Obstetrics and Gynecology. The study involved 199 infertility patients in Seoul, South Korea, 100 of whom received in vitro fertilization (IVF) plus prayer from Christian prayer groups in the United States, Canada, and Australia, and the control group of 99 patients received just IVF. Neither group knew of the experiment. The pregnancy rate for the first was 50 percent, for the second, 26.

Perusal of the findings revealed a complex and unsatisfactory operation of the groups of persons performing the praying, who were divided into tiers, blocks, and units. Some prayed for fertilization, some "that God's will or desire be fulfilled in the life of the patient," and some for other praying blocks. No reason was given for this complexity. Further, "[t]he authors made no attempt to discover how much prayer was being conducted outside the study protocol, perhaps to other gods, since only one-third of Koreans are Christians." Equally unsatisfactory was reportage of the findings.

One of the study's three authors at the time was director of the Columbia Infertility Medical Center, "but apparently severed his relationship with Columbia soon after the study was published." Subsequently, the ostensible lead author claimed he first learned of the study six to twelve months after it was completed, and "primarily provided editorial review and assistance with publication." The third author, previously unknown at Columbia, turned out on investigation to have a checkered past and a number of aliases. Known as a doctor and head of an organization called Healing Sciences Research International, he has no medical qualifications and his previous research involved "studies on mysterious supernatural or paranormal phenomena, mainly dealing with alternative and spiritual healing." His specialty has been noncontact therapeutic touch, where the healer "scans" and "rebalances" the "human energy fields" of patients; but he has also evaluated patients of a spiritual healer trained in the Philippines *Espiritista* system of faith healing, which includes "psychic surgery," laying on of hands, and distant prayer healing. Apparently these professional engagements were insufficiently lucrative for the Columbia researcher, for in 2004 he was convicted of conspiracy to commit mail fraud and bank fraud involving "more than $3.4 million in income and property obtained by using false identities."

Flamm reminds us: "It must be emphasized that, in the entire history of modern science, no claim of any type of supernatural phenomena has ever been replicated under strictly controlled conditions." Faced with the above exposé, the *Journal of Reproductive Medicine* removed the Columbia prayer study from its Web site, but the damage had been done. Faith healers across America continued to quote it as vindicating intercessory prayer. While some may consider such ministrations harmless and possibly helpful to the gullible, the real danger is that while these charades are proceeding, any underlying pathology is left untreated by proper medical intervention.

BIBLIOGRAPHY

Flamm, Bruce. "The Columbia University 'Miracle' Study: Flawed and Fraud." *Skeptical Inquirer* (September/October 2004).

James, William. *The Varieties of Religious Experience.* London: Longmans, Green, 1902.

"Prayer." *Encyclopedia of Religion.* Vol. 11. New York: Macmillan, 1987.

"Rites and Ceremonies, Sacred." *New Encyclopaedia Britannica Macropaedia.* Vol. 26. Chicago: Encyclopaedia Britannica, 1974.

Robertson, John Mackinnon. *A History of Freethought in the Nineteenth Century.* London: Watts and Company, 1929.

DAVID TRIBE

PROGRESSIVE WORLD. See UNITED SECULARISTS OF AMERICA.

PROJECTION THEORY. In psychoanalytical literature, projection theory attempts to explain how and why the phenomenon occurs in which a person attributes to (projects onto) another object or person attitudes or characteristics of oneself. In theories of religion, it is an attempt to explain how and why the gods are the objectification of some aspect of human nature or human nature as a whole. Although the idea goes back to ancient times, it was not until the nineteenth century that Ludwig FEUERBACH constructed a theory of religion based on projection. He argued that gods arise when, in the process of the self-differentiation of the I from the thou, the I realizes it is a member of a species. The imagination then seizes upon the ideal predicates of the species, strips them of their limitations, and unifies them in the notion of a divine individual subject for whom human beings are objects. In the last century, the intellectual disciplines of anthropology, psychology, and sociology have cast up a variety of influential theories of religion in which the concept of projection is at the core: in anthropology, Weston La Barre, Ernest Becker, Melford Spiro, and Anthony Wallace; in psychology, Sigmund FREUD, Carl Jung, Erich FROMM, and Ana-Marie Rizzuto; in sociology, Peter Berger, Emile Durkheim, and Guy Swanson, to mention a few.

The sheer variety of such theories should caution us against easy generalization. Not only is projection conceived differently in the various theories, but it yields quite different interpretations of religion. Insofar as "projection" is a technical term, it acquires its meaning from the theoretical context in which it occurs.

The phenomenon of projection tends to be conceived in two different ways. In the first, projection is conceived as an objectification of the self or one of its aspects. In the second, projection refers more broadly to the framework used to interpret experience. The first conception lends itself to metaphors taken from the cinema or, as in the nineteenth century, from the magic lantern. Images taken from the self are said to be projected onto the screen of nature; hence the shorthand reference to "beam" theory. The second conception lends itself to metaphors taken from templates, schemata, and grids; hence the shorthand reference to "grid" theories.

Beam theories of religion tend to contain four closely related ideas. (1) An essential aspect of religion is belief in supernatural, anthropomorphic beings. (2) The projections must themselves be explained by psychic processes of some kind—the relationships between the instincts, as in the case of Freud, or the archetypes in the collective unconscious, as in the case of Carl Jung. (3) There is a close conceptual relationship between the theory of the psychic processes and the principles used to interpret the religious symbolism. Thus, Jung interprets the idea of God in terms of the functions of the archetype of the Self. (4) The theory of the self which informs the theory of projection provides the criteria for the judgment whether the religious projection is an illusion and whether or not it should be considered pathological or healthy. It is an interesting aspect of some object-relations psychological theory that it regards some religious projections as "transitional objects" similar to teddy bears and hence as equally healthy. For Freud, by contrast, the religious illusion is infantile, whereas Jung argued that the psychologist has no competence to judge the truth of the religious projection. Jung's concern was whether the religious archetype integrates the self or not.

The second (grid) type of projection theory is based on the view that human beings construct conceptual and symbolic frameworks by means of which they categorize and coordinate their ordinary experience. These frameworks mold the consciousness of individuals and provide the basis for self-identity. The use of the term *projection* in this extended sense makes use of linguistic associations inherent in the verb *to project*, such as *to cast* or *to throw*. Some philosophers have argued that since these frameworks reflect instrumental purposes, they may be viewed as projections. Insofar as a religion provides a worldview or symbolic framework by means of which people orient themselves, then it may be conceived of as a projection in this sense.

When the term *projection* is used in this fashion, we can understand why grid theorists do not necessarily define religion as a type of anthropomorphism, and hence necessarily false. They tend to view religion as a sacred worldview whether there are anthropomorphic deities involved or not. Moreover, grid theorists tend to distrust appeals to theories of the self that are characteristic of beam theorists. The grid theorist is primarily interested in the social and cultural institutions over which religion has thrown a "sacred canopy."

Grid theories may be conceived of in many different ways: perceptual, categorical, cultural, and metaphysical. The Dutch anthropologist Fokke Sierksma, for example, has argued that religious projection needs to be seen in the context of perception itself, which he regards as a type of projection. All perception, he argues, is species specific. Every species relates to the world through a unique noetic apparatus that is necessarily selective. Any given species responds to only a few of the stimuli emanating from the world. Consequently, there is much that escapes the human perceptual grid. The human creature that possesses self-consciousness is dimly aware that that there is a reverse side of things, so to speak, that escapes what we perceive. Although not everyone subjectivizes this unknown surplus, there are others who become preoccupied with it, because it is this ungraspable reality that gives humans the feeling that they are no longer at home in their stabilized world. The distinctiveness of Buddhism, Sierksma argues, is that it relates projection to perception and has developed a religious practice devoted to revoking projection and perception. It criticizes all forms of objectification (projection) and even the notion of the self.

BIBLIOGRAPHY

Becker, Ernest. *The Denial of Death*. New York: Free Press, 1973.

Berger, Peter. *The Sacred Canopy: Elements of a Sociological Theory of Religion*. Garden City, NY: Doubleday, 1967.

Feuerbach, Ludwig. *The Essence of Christianity*. Translated by George Eliot. Amherst, NY; Prometheus Books, 1989.

Freud, Sigmund. *The Future of an Illusion*. Translated by W. D. Robson-Scott, revised and newly edited by James Strachey. Garden City, NY: Doubleday, 1964.

Harvey, Van A. *Feuerbach and the Interpretation of Religion*. New York: Cambridge University Press, 1995.

Jung, C. G. *The Archetypes and the Collective Unconscious*. Translated by R. F. C. Hull. Princeton, NJ: Princeton University Press, 1959.

LeBarre, Weston. *The Ghost Dance: Origins of Religion*. New York: Dell, 1970.

Rizzuto, Ana-Marie. *The Birth of the Living God: A Psychoanalytic Study*. Chicago: University of Chicago Press, 1979.

Sierksma, Fokke. *Projection and Religion: An Anthropological and Psychological Study of the Phenomena of Projection in the Various Religions*. Translated by Jacob Faber. Ann Arbor: University of Michigan Books on Demand, 1990.

Spiro, Melford E. *Culture and Human Nature: Theoretical Papers*. Chicago: University of Chicago Press, 1987.

VAN A. HARVEY

PROPAGANDA, ANTIRELIGIOUS (CUBAN). Shortly after the 1959 Cuban Revolution, all those opposed to the new Marxist regime, whether Catholic or Protestant, faced expulsion. While they remained in Cuba, they were denied the opportunity to run schools, which cut deeply into the churches' financial resources. Also, church properties were nationalized and the religious bodies' private media (including newspapers, radio, and television programs) were discontinued. Church members were routinely watched by the government. Many bishops, priests, and ministers were placed under house arrest. Christians were denied membership in the Communist Party, an important channel for economic advancement, and were declined admittance to high-level government and university positions. Many, mostly in the white middle class, chose to flee to Miami rather than stay and fight the regime. This exodus drained the island of educated entrepreneurial talent and further weakened the churches' power base. From 1965 through 1968, thousands of artists, hippies, university students, intellectuals, and homosexuals were abducted by the State Secret Police and interned without trial in the Military Units for Assistance to Production (UMAP) reeducation labor camps. Also interned were Jehovah's Witnesses, Gideonists, and Catholic or Protestant activists. An era of "internal exile" began.

After several decades, tension between the church and government subsided. The church ceased to challenge Fidel Castro's authority, gaining some governmental tolerance for religion. The Catholic Church in particular began to reconcile with Castro's regime under the leadership of Cesare Zacchi, the Vatican emissary appointed in 1962. He praised Castro's social reforms, criticized prerevolutionary Cuba, and admonished clergy who had abandoned the island after the revolution. On April 10, 1969, a decisive break with the past occurred when the Catholic Church published a letter authored by Cuba's bishops denouncing the US embargo of the island. For the first time, the Catholic Church had committed itself to work for the development of Cuba without condemning the ideology of the regime.

Protestants also sought a rapprochement with the Cuban government. In 1977 the Confession of Faith of the Presbyterian-Reformed church in Cuba declared, "The Church lives joyfully in the midst of the socialist revolution." Castro reciprocated by giving a televised speech from the pulpit of a Protestant church flanked by church leaders during the 1984 visit to Cuba by US Baptist minister and political figure Jesse Jackson. Additionally, the 1985 publication of Castro's best seller, *Fidel y la religión* (Fidel and Religion), began a public dialogue concerning areas of cooperation between Marxists and what Castro called "honest" Christians.

Castro sought this strategic alliance by establishing Christian-Marxist dialogues. He was influenced by priests such as Camilio Torres, who had in 1966 ceased to celebrate Mass in Columbia so as to promote its revolution. The 1979 success of the Sandinista revolution in Nicaragua furthered affected Castro's attitudes toward religion. Several Catholic priests and Protestant leaders, motivated by their religious convictions, had distinguished themselves in Castro's eyes by taking part in the struggle against Nicaragua's corrupt president Anastasio Somoza and by assuming important governmental positions in the new Nicaraguan regime.

Because the Cuban Revolution had preceded the liberalizing reforms of the Second Vatican Council, the theological trajectory followed by Catholicism in Cuba differed from that taken elsewhere in Latin America. Although Cuban representatives participated in Vatican II and in the 1968 Medellín reunion of Latin American bishops, Cuba developed its own form of theological thought. "Theology in revolution" became a homegrown means by which some Cubans began to understand their faith. Unlike the liberation theologians of Latin America who read their experience through the lens of the biblical book of Exodus—in which a liberating God guides God's people toward the promised land—Cuban theologians such as Israel Batista maintained that Cubans are liberated and already live in the promised land. Consequently, the task facing Cubans is not liberation, but constructing and building society. Such a pragmatic interpretation required a "prophetic reading," providing the people with the necessary praxis (practical application of theory to real life) to develop a revolutionary society. "Prophetic" in this case implied not the right to criticize the revolution, but rather the obligation to break open the sacred space occupied by theologians so that they can come into step with the people. Other Cuban theologians such as Sergio Arce Martínez made it clear that when Christians reflect theologically on the revolution, they do not do it for the benefit of revolutionaries, or to provide a service to the revolution. Rather, reflection is done for Christians and the church so that they can render a service to both revolutionaries and the revolution. He insists that Christians do not speak for the revolution, which is not Christian; instead they speak for the Christian revolutionary who plays an active part in Christ's church located within a socialist country, as well as for their socialist homeland, in where a Christian church exists.

Yet liberation theologians such as Gustavo Gutiérrez expressed concern that theologies steeped in revolution have the tendency to "baptize" the revolution by placing it beyond criticism. Castro's well-known phrase, "Everything within the revolution, nothing outside of the revolution," fixes limits of acceptability upon all discourse, including Christianity. Gutiérrez accuses the theologies of revolution of "reductionism," of reducing the gospel to sociology, economics, or politics. Faith becomes a justification for Christians to participate as actors in achieving the goals of the revolution. Similarly, Clodovias Boff states that the overall process of revolution tends to be confused with just one of its moments, the moment of breakage, of rebellion. Revolutionary immediatism fails to recognize that the ultimate goal of social change is a long-term historical process, not an immediate call to arms. Fulfilling basic needs is not the end, but the means to a full realization of humanity.

Antireligious propaganda is no longer seen in Cuba. In Cuba today there is the freedom to proclaim one's faith, but there is still no freedom to question or challenge governmental authorities based on the tenets of that faith.

BIBLIOGRAPHY

Castro, Fidel. *Fidel and Religion: Castro Talks on Revolution and Religion with Frei Betto*. Translated by the Cuban Center for Translation and Interpretation. New York: Simon & Schuster, 1987.

De La Torre, Miguel A. *La Lucha for Cuba: Religion and Politics on the Street of Miami*. Berkeley and Los Angeles: University of California Press, 2003.

———. *The Quest for the Cuban Christ: A Historical Search*. Gainesville: University Press of Florida, 2002.

Gutiérrez, Benjamin F., and Dennis A. Smith, eds. *In the Power of the Spirit: The Pentecostal Challenge to Historical Churches in Latin America*. Louisville, KY: Presbyterian Church, 1996

Kirk, John M. *Between God and the Party: Religion and Politics in Revolutionary Cuba*. Tampa: University Presses of Florida, 1988.

Masó y Vazquez, Calixto C. *Historia de Cuba: La lucha de un pueblo por cumplir su destino histórico y su vocación de libertad*. Miami: Ediciones Universal, 1998.

Moore, Carlos. *Castro, the Blacks, and Africa*. Los Angeles: Center for Afro-American Studies, University of California, 1988.

Ramos, Marcos Antonio. *Panorama del Protestantismo en Cuba*. San José, Costa Rica: Editorial Caribe, 1986.

———. *Protestantism and Revolution in Cuba*. Coral Gables, FL: University of Miami, 1989.

Stevens-Arroryo, Anthony M. *Papal Overtures in a Cuban Key: The Pope's Visit and Civic Space for Cuban Religion*. Scranton, PA: University of Scranton Press, 2002.

MIGUEL A. DE LA TORRE

PROPAGANDA, ANTIRELIGIOUS (SOVIET). From the 1917 revolution until its fall from power in late 1991, the Communist Party of the Soviet Union promoted the longest sustained antireligious campaign in history. It developed a wide range of antireligious propaganda techniques, many of which were later emulated by other socialist regimes.

Antireligious Legislation and the Need for Propa-
ganda Campaigns. As Marxists (see MARXISM), the Soviet Communists viewed religion as a product of the socioeconomic system of feudal and capitalist exploitation, doomed to "wither away" as socialism built a nonexploitative, classless society. Initially, then, many believed religion would simply die out after the 1917 revolution. In January 1918 a decree "On the Separation of Church and State" expropriated all ecclesiastical land and property without compensation, stripped religious organizations of their juridical status, and banned religious instruction in schools. Later in the summer, the Constitution of 1918 formally provided for religious freedom and established the "right to conduct religious and atheist propaganda." But religion did not crumble, even though its economic base had been removed. And the state was not neutral to religion, for the Communists' goal was to achieve a society that was not merely secular, but enthusiastically atheist. They soon realized that more concerted measures would be needed to replace the worship of God with devotion to the revolutionary state and its ideals. Thus, from the first years of Soviet power, a campaign to promote the rejection of religion and the adoption of an atheist worldview accompanied legal strictures on religious activity. The main target was the Russian Orthodox Church, the former state religion, but policies also addressed minority faiths such as Islam, Judaism, Catholicism, Protestantism, Buddhism, and the various religious sects.

Antireligious policy throughout the Soviet period had both propaganda and police-administrative, at times violent, components. Tension between these two approaches arose, since Communist policymakers recognized both a need to consolidate political power among ordinary people who might be offended by antireligious measures, and the goal of eliminating competing centers of social and ideological power in Soviet society.

Early Antireligious Propaganda. The Communist Party program for 1919 called for broad antireligious propaganda, but provided little guidance about what that propaganda would look like. As a result, early Soviet antireligious measures were rather haphazard. Certain policies aimed at scientifically debunking particular cherished beliefs. The most controversial of these was the opening of the coffins of saints in order to show that, contrary to the belief of the Orthodox faithful, the bodies of the saints had decomposed. Among the most popular measures were antireligious debates, in which Communist lecturers challenged members of the clergy. These were discontinued in the mid-1920s, however, for fear of providing as much of a platform for religious as for antireligious voices. Also attention getting were the Young Communist League's anti-Christmas and anti-Easter carnivals, which involved often rowdy parades and stunts such as mock trials of gods.

The League of the Godless. The year 1923 saw a shift to a systematic program of antireligious agitation as part of the campaign to build a socialist society and the perceived need to be more vigilant about ideological matters in the context of the New Economic Policy's relaxation of economic controls. This new attention was symbolized by the founding in late 1922 of the Party Central Committee's Commission for Implementing the Separation of Church and State, charged with formulating and overseeing policies to destroy religious organizations and promote ATHEISM. One of its first moves was to ask the party's Agitation and Propaganda department to create an antireligious newspaper, *Bezbozhnik* (Godless). In 1924 its editor, Emel'ian IAROSLAVSKII, organized a Society of Friends of the Newspaper *Bezbozhnik*. At a congress in April 1925, that group became the All-Union League of the Godless. The league was a mass voluntary organization dedicated to promoting antireligious views. Under the leadership of the party, its local cells sold *Bezbozhnik* and other league publications and organized lectures, discussions, reading circles, museum tours, demonstrations, and other activities. In 1929, during the Cultural Revolution that accompanied the onset of Stalinist industrialization, it was renamed the League of the Militant Godless. By 1932 it boasted 5.5 million members. Although not formally disbanded until 1947, in practice the league disappeared in mid-1941 after the German attack on the Soviet Union. During the war, antireligious propaganda was largely muted and the Orthodox Church's public position was partly restored.

Propaganda Techniques. The regime employed a variety of means to convey its atheist message. The most important was print propaganda. The weekly newspaper, *Bezbozhnik*, was joined, in the 1920s and 1930s, by other Russian-language periodicals, such as *Antireligioznik* (Antireligious Activist), *Derevenskii bezbozhnik* (Village Godless), *Bezbozhnik u stanka* (Godless at the Workbench), and a wide array of similar journals in the languages of the various national minorities of the USSR. The league also published numerous pamphlets and mass-circulation textbooks for antireligious activists and the general population. Materials aimed at a general audience featured articles on science, on religious history, and on the benefits of the new Communist life the regime was building, alongside a lively variety of verse, fiction, cartoons, and reports from local correspondents ridiculing the clergy and various religious practices.

In the face of still-high levels of illiteracy in the 1920s, visual and audio forms of propaganda also played an important role. Posters depicted religion standing in the way of education, women's liberation, industrialization, and an enlightened new Soviet lifestyle. Films, newsreels, and league-sponsored radio broadcasts mocked religious activities and reported the arrest of religious leaders and activists for various counterrevolutionary activities. A central antireligious museum opened in Moscow, and local league councils created similar museums in former churches, synagogues, and mosques, or installed antireligious displays at local his-

tory museums. Where once religious icons had adorned corners in public places such as factory workshops and dormitories, activists sought to replace them with godless or Lenin corners.

Antireligious propaganda also focused on debunking religious holidays and substituting Soviet holidays and rituals for them. At Christmas or Easter—or Passover or Ramadan—the number of antireligious events spiked, with lectures and demonstrations organized to conflict with religious observances. Articles in the press debunked the basis for the holidays and reported on the decline of observance of them. Simultaneously, citizens were encouraged to celebrate a range of revolutionary festivals, from May Day (close to Orthodox Easter) to a new Harvest Day designed to replace the traditional Orthodox *Pokrov* holiday in October. In the 1930s New Year's emerged as the great family winter holiday, complete with decorated trees and visits from Grandfather Frost. *Bezbozhnik* printed numerous stories about new Soviet secular rituals, including "Octobering" ceremonies to name a new baby and "red" weddings and funerals.

Scientific Atheism. The successor to the League of the Militant Godless was the All-Union Society for the Dissemination of Political and Scientific Knowledge (known after 1963 simply as the Knowledge Society). It was founded in 1947 as a mass scientific and educational voluntary organization. At first, it showed little interest in antireligious propaganda, although most branches of the society had a section dealing with scientific atheism. Only in 1959, when the party under Nikita Khrushchev launched a fierce new attack on religion, did it begin vigorous work in this field. Eschewing much of the ridicule and carnival aspects of the prewar period, the society's approach emphasized the intellectual component of antireligious work, in particular refuting religious beliefs and replacing them with an atheist, scientific worldview and Communist morality. In 1960 it launched the journal *Nauka i religiia* (Science and Religion).

This intellectual emphasis prompted the creation of a new field of scholarly activity, scientific atheism. In 1964 an Institute of Scientific Atheism was established in the Academy of Social Sciences of the Party Central Committee. It concentrated on concrete, mostly sociological, research and on assisting atheist activists rather than conducting propaganda itself. Around the same time, a required course on scientific atheism was introduced for all students in universities, as well as in medical, agricultural, and pedagogical institutes.

On the more popular level, in the late 1950s "atheism clubs" and "houses of atheism" were established. Working under the guidance of the party and in cooperation with the Knowledge Society, they organized libraries and reading rooms, held lectures, showed films, and provided training programs. Schools and other groups toured the Museum of the History of Religion and Atheism in the former Kazan Cathedral in Leningrad, which welcomed half a million visitors in 1960 alone.

Effectiveness and Challenges Faced. For seventy years, Soviet antireligious propagandists consistently faced the same difficulty: it was one thing to challenge religious belief and practice but quite another to get people excited about atheism. By the 1980s, nine out of ten Russians were not raised in the Orthodox Church and three-quarters did not believe in God. The Soviet population thus exhibited high levels of passive irreligiousness, but this did not necessarily translate into militant atheism. Indeed, it was not clear to what extent the Party's propaganda efforts were responsible for this situation, or whether they reflected the broader secularizing effects of the modernization and social displacement that the Soviet era witnessed. Moreover, in the late Soviet period, a revival of interest in religion suggested that this irreligiousness was reversible. A survey of religious views taken in 1991 as the USSR was collapsing found that half the population professed belief in God and 22 percent reported that they had once been atheists but now believed.

BIBLIOGRAPHY

Bryan, Fanny E. "Anti-religious Propaganda in the Soviet Union: Attacks against Islam during the 1920s and 1930s." *Modern Greek Studies Yearbook* 9 (1993).

Greeley, Andrew. "A Religious Revival in Russia?" *Journal for the Scientific Study of Religion* 33, no. 3 (1994).

Husband, William. *"Godless Communists": Atheism and Society in Soviet Russia, 1917–1932.* DeKalb: Northern Illinois University Press, 2000.

Luukkanen, Arto. *The Party of Unbelief: The Religious Policy of the Bolshevik Party, 1917–1929.* Helsinki: Suomen Historiallinen Seura, 1994.

———. *The Religious Policy of the Stalinist State. A Case Study: The Central Standing Commission on Religious Questions, 1929–1938.* Helsinki: Suomen Historiallinen Seura, 1997.

Peris, Daniel. *Storming the Heavens: The Soviet League of the Militant Godless.* Ithaca, NY: Cornell University Press, 1998.

Pospielovsky, Dimitry V. *A History of Soviet Atheism in Theory and Practice, and the Believer.* 3 vols. Houndmills, UK: Macmillan, 1987–88.

Powell, David E. *Antireligious Propaganda in the Soviet Union: A Study of Mass Persuasion.* Cambridge, MA: MIT Press, 1975.

Young, Glennys. *Power and the Sacred in Revolutionary Russia: Religious Activists in the Village.* University Park: Pennsylvania State University Press, 1997.

HEATHER J. COLEMAN

PROTAGORAS (5th century BCE). Greek Sophist. The Sophists were professional teachers who trained students for life in a democratic and litigious society. Protagoras of Abdera, one of the earliest and most influential sophists, is known primarily for his subjectivism and for his AGNOSTICISM. The precise years of his birth and death are unclear, with estimates ranging from 490 to 481 BCE for his birth and from 420 to 411 BCE for his death. He traveled widely and observed a variety of cultures, and by the middle of the fifth century had established himself as a professional teacher in Athens. His status as a rhetorician and teacher was such that Plato named a dialogue after him, and he either appears or is referenced in a number of other Platonic dialogues as well. Despite fundamental differences in philosophy, Plato treats him and his doctrines with sufficient respect to serve as a significant and reliable source of information on Protagoras. Unfortunately, very little of his own work survives, and much of what is known about him comes from the writings of Plato, Diogenes Laertius, Sextus EMPIRICUS, and others.

Subjectivism. "Man is the measure of all things, of the things that are that they are, and of the things that are not that they are not." Protagoras is probably most famous for this quotation and the subjectivism it reveals. According to this doctrine truth is relative to the observer, and what is true or useful or good to me may be very different from what is true or useful or good to you. He also seems to have defended the claim that, as any claim of truth is necessarily a claim about appearances, it is impossible to speak falsely, and that it is possible for an opinion to be true and false at the same time. He is credited with being the first to teach that there are two sides to every argument, and claimed to be able to make the weaker argument defeat the stronger. This concern for what was persuasive rather than for what was "true" served him well in his preparation of students for trial, but it also helped generate the suspicion that increasingly surrounded the sophists.

Agnosticism. In light of his subjectivism concerning truth, it should come as no surprise that Protagoras thought suspension of judgment to be the appropriate course regarding the gods. Plato's *Thaetetus* attributes to Protagoras a refusal to even discuss the question of the existence of the gods. Protagoras's own work *On the Gods* begins with the claim that the obscurity of the subject and the shortness of human life prevents him from being able to discover anything about the form of the gods, or even if they exist. Protagoras's subjectivism was based on the idea that that which appears to me to be true is true, and thus "truth" lies only in appearances. Agnosticism would come naturally to those that live only by appearances. As a central component of Protagoras's view is a denial of the possibility of objective knowledge regarding even those objects that present themselves to our senses, it is easy to understand why he would refuse to make dogmatic claims about those matters for which we had not even the suspect evidence of our senses. A disputed account by Diogenes Laertius contends that it was Protagoras's commitment to agnosticism that eventually led to the seizure and burning of his works and his banishment from Athens.

BIBLIOGRAPHY

Diogenes Laertius. *Lives of Eminent Philosophers.* Vol. 2. Translated by R. D. Hicks. Cambridge, MA: Harvard University Press, 1942.

Guthrie, W. K. C. *The Sophists.* Cambridge: Cambridge University Press, 1971.

Mates, Benson. *The Skeptic Way. Sextus Empiricus's Outlines of Pyrrhonism.* New York: Oxford University Press, 1996.

Plato. *Protagoras.* Translated by C. C. W. Taylor. New York: Oxford University Press, 1991.

———. *Theaetetus.* Translated by John McDowell. Oxford: Clarendon, 1973.

JASON GRINNELL

PROUDHON, PIERRE-JOSEPH (1809–1865), French philosopher and anarchist. Pierre-Joseph Proudhon was born on January 15, 1809, in Mouillère, a suburb of Besançon in eastern France. Pierre's father, Claude-François, was a journeyman brewer and his mother, Catharine, a servant. He was the eldest of five children.

Pierre's mother taught him to read at a very early age; however, as the family was fairly religious the only books available to him were Bibles and almanacs. When Pierre was eleven, his mother insisted that he study more broadly. The family had no money for books, so Pierre spent all his free time in the library.

As a boy Proudhon had little use for the religious rituals his family practiced, and he began to question the religious dogma of his teachers in his midteens.

Although forced to leave school and choose a trade, Proudhon continued his studies on his own and secured employment in a printing office in Besançon. In 1829, while working as a proofreader for the publisher Antoine Gautier, he was given the task of proofreading a new edition of *Lives of the Saints* in Latin. He so impressed the editor, Gustave Fallot, with his Latin skills that Fallot insisted on meeting Proudhon. Fallot wrote Proudhon a long letter in 1831, predicting his future success as a great philosopher. The two became close friends.

Dedicated to helping Proudhon find a way to continue his studies, Fallot offered him a place to live and study in Paris, which Proudhon accepted until Fallot contracted cholera and was no longer able to provide such luxuries. When Proudhon's younger brother Jean-Etienne was conscripted, Pierre was obliged to return to Besançon to help his family. He took a job as editor of *L'Impartial*, but upon being told that the censor would have to authorize his articles before they were printed, he quit. In 1833 Jean-Etienne died during military training, and this event radicalized Proudhon even more, instilling in him a profound disdain for the state.

In the mid-1830s Proudhon became foreman of the church history and theology publisher Gautier & Co., correcting the proofs of religious texts. He taught himself Hebrew in order to be able to compare the original texts with the Latin. This experience led him to the study of comparative philology. He later used the skills gained as a printer and editor of religious texts in arguments against the church and on the nature of belief. Authority in any form became the main target of his criticism.

Proudhon's first book, *Qu'est-ce que le propriété* (What Is Property? 1840), was critically acclaimed by many, including his ideological adversary Karl MARX. In his *Système de contradicions économique ou philosophie de la misère* (The System of Economic Contradictions), published in two volumes in 1846, Proudhon explored the entire economic basis of contemporary society, including Providence, in which he refuted both VOLTAIRE's and Jean-Jacques ROUSSEAU's arguments about the existence of God as illogical. Although his denunciation of God and religion was quite severe, he suffered neither censorship nor prosecution until the publication of several newspapers critical of Bonaparte during the 1848 revolution. Proudhon served three years in prison.

In 1849 Proudhon married Euphrasie Piégard in a civil ceremony, although she was a devout Catholic and remained so throughout her life. They had four daughters, two of whom did not survive their father. On his deathbed, Proudhon refused the visit of a priest and instead said to his wife, "I shall confess to you."

BIBLIOGRAPHY

Proudhon, Pierre-Joseph. *Selected Writings of Pierre-Joseph Proudhon.* Edited by Stewart Edwards. London: Macmillan, 1970.

———. *System of Economical Contradiction or the Philosophy of Misery.* Translated by Benjamin R. Tucker. Boston: Proudhon Library, 1888.

———. *What Is Property?* Translated by Benjamin R. Tucker. New York: Humboldt, n.d.

Woodcock, George. *Pierre-Joseph Proudhon: A Biography.* London: Routledge & Kegan Paul, 1956.

JULIE HERRADA

PUTNAM, SAMUEL PORTER (1838–1896), American freethinker. Born in Chichester, New Hampshire, on July 23, 1838, the son of a Congregational minister, Samuel Porter Putnam entered Dartmouth College in 1858. Three years later he enlisted in the Union army as a private and saw Civil War action in the Shenandoah Valley and several theaters along the Gulf of Mexico. In 1864 Putnam, by now the captain of a company of black soldiers, had a religious conversion and resigned from the army to pursue a career as a minister. After three years of study at the Chicago Theological Seminary, Putnam worked as a Congregationalist preacher. But his stay with religious orthodoxy was brief. In 1871 Putnam joined the Unitarians (see UNITARIANISM TO 1961), but even this move could not keep pace with his ever more radical religious views. Within a few years he left the Unitarians and turned to organized FREETHOUGHT. Putnam's radicalization also helped destroy his eighteen-year marriage to Louise Howell, which ended in 1885 on the ground of "religious and temperamental differences."

Putnam's link to organized Freethought was cemented during a celebrated case in 1879 when D. M. BENNETT, editor of THE TRUTH SEEKER, was imprisoned for thirteen months under the infamous Comstock laws for supposedly passing blasphemous material through the postal system (see COMSTOCK, ANTHONY, AND UNBELIEF). After securing a position as a clerk in the New York Custom House in July 1880, Putnam began his career as a freethought lecturer. For the next sixteen years, Putnam traveled throughout the United States, lecturing in all but four states of the union. He estimated that he traveled one hundred thousand miles during his lecturing career. In the summer of 1895 Putnam made a successful lecture tour of Great Britain.

In 1888 Putnam went with his friend George E. MACDONALD to San Francisco, where they founded the journal *Freethought*. It was funded largely by Putnam's tireless traveling and lecturing. The Depression of the 1890s caught up with *Freethought*, which folded in 1891. Back in New York in 1892, Putnam turned to the question of freethought organization. At a meeting he called in Chicago on September 4, 1892, Putnam formed the Freethought Federation of America, with himself as president. It was Putnam's goal to create an effective political voice for freethought. Putnam remained president of this organization until his death.

In 1895 the Freethought Federation combined with the AMERICAN SECULAR UNION to form the American Secular Union and Freethought Federation. Putnam's greatest political success was his efforts to defeat a proposal in 1896 to alter the US Constitution by inserting mention of God. Putnam's speech before the Joint Judiciary Committee of the US House of Representatives on March 11 helped kill the bill, a fact acknowledged by his Christian opponents.

Putnam also found time to write poetry and articles, but his most sustained work was *Four Hundred Years of Freethought* (1894), a massive work published to coincide with the four hundredth anniversary of the discovery of America. The title notwithstanding, the book was really a celebration of freethought as it stood at that time.

Putnam died on December 11, 1896, in mysterious circumstances. He, along with an attractive twenty-year-old protégé, May Collins, were both found dead in her hotel room in Boston. Putnam had been waiting for Collins in order to accompany her out to the theater when they were "poisoned by illuminating gas." Putnam's friend George Macdonald hastened to add that the "bodies of both, dressed for the street, were found on the floor."

BIBLIOGRAPHY

Macdonald, George E. *Fifty Years of Freethought*. New York: Truth Seeker Company, 1972.
Putnam, Samuel P. *Four Hundred Years of Freethought*. New York: Truth Seeker Company, 1894.

BILL COOKE

PYTHAGORAS (ca. 582–ca. 507 BCE), Greek mathematician and philosopher. An Ionian Greek said to have been born on the island of Samos, Pythagoras fell foul of Polycrates, the tyrant who ruled the Samians, and fled to Crotona in Southern Italy, where he founded a secret society. Not much is known about the real Pythagoras, famous for the Pythagorean theorem in geometry and credited with coining the word *philosopher* (meaning "a lover of wisdom"). Legend states that his friends were so amazed by his intellectual talents that they spread the rumor that he must be a god disguised as a human. No doubt flattered by such a claim, he reassured them of his humanity through strict logic: The gods, by definition, know everything; he, Pythagoras, was always seeking knowledge. Therefore, he could not be a god. He was, instead, a lover of wisdom.

The earliest known references to Pythagoras date to the time of PLATO, two hundred years later, and he remains a mysterious figure in the history of thought. A movement grew up dedicated to his teachings, which included the view that numbers constitute true reality (which influenced Plato's conception of the forms). Connected with this was the doctrine of the transmigration of souls; followers of Pythagoras apparently believed that souls, before attaching themselves to a corporeal form, resided inside beans, waiting to be consumed by a pregnant woman in order to enter the fetus within. Thus, one of the strongest admonitions of the Pythagoreans was that men not eat beans, one of the stranger dietary laws associated with an organized religion. Consumption of meat was also frowned upon, as such carcasses might once have held the souls of one's friends or ancestors.

For freethinkers Pythagoras has also come to symbolize one who questioned the existence of the gods, at least as generally understood at the time, and also one who explored the relationship of human beings to the cosmos. For the Pythagoreans, philosophy involved using reason and observation to gain understanding of the universe. The order of the cosmos should be mirrored in the order of the human soul. The search for underlying principles led Pythagoreans to believe that numbers, unchanging and perfect, must be the basic reality of the universe. Related to this, Pythagoreans discovered that musical harmony is based upon mathematical proportions (the credit for this being given to Pythagoras himself, who was enchanted by the clanging of a blacksmith's hammer). From this interest in harmony related theories developed, such as the view that health involves a proper harmony of bodily fluids; the notion that moral excellence is a kind of harmonious relationship with nature; and most notably the idea of "the music of the spheres," wherein the heavenly bodies themselves move in such a way as to produce beautiful music, which most people do not hear because they are not themselves living in proper harmony with the universe.

A neo-Pythagorean movement, consisting of elements from Plato, ARISTOTLE, and the Stoics (see STOICISM), became influential in the first century BCE. Pythagorean mystical beliefs rose to prominence again during the Renaissance. For most freethinkers, though, the movement was too fraught with esoteric religious mysteries to be of much use in the search for truth.

BIBLIOGRAPHY

Arieti, James A. *Philosophy in the Ancient World: An Introduction.* New York: Rowman & Littlefield, 2005.
Hadot, Pierre. *What Is Ancient Philosophy?* Cambridge, MA: Harvard University Press, 2002.
Nussbaum, Martha. *The Therapy of Desire: Theory and Practice in Hellenistic Ethics.* Princeton, NJ: Princeton University Press, 1994.

TIMOTHY J. MADIGAN

RAND, AYN (1905–1982), American novelist, founder of Objectivism. Ayn Rand was born in Saint Petersburg, Russia, where as a youth she witnessed the Bolshevik revolution. She studied philosophy and history at Petrograd University with the aim of becoming a novelist. By this time, Rand had also reached some of the philosophical conclusions she would maintain for the rest of her life, including ATHEISM and anticommunism.

Novels. In 1925 she fled the Soviet Union for America, where she worked in Hollywood as a screenwriter. Her first novel, *We the Living* (1934), was a semiautobiographical work intended to show the crushing effect of totalitarianism on people of independent spirit.

Rand's next major work, *The Fountainhead* (1943), told the story of Howard Roark, an innovative architect who fights to live and work by his own standards in the face of social pressures to conform. As a novel of ideas, it dramatized Rand's distinctive form of individualism that opposed self-sacrifice in any form—both the Christian altruism of most conservatives and the collectivist morality of the socialist Left. *The Fountainhead* became a best seller and was made into a movie starring Gary Cooper in 1949.

Rand's magnum opus, *Atlas Shrugged*, was published with great fanfare in 1957. It translated her ethic of individualism into a vast political epic about what happens when "the men of the mind," the producers who carry the world on their shoulders, go on strike against the expropriation of their wealth by a society that demands they serve others. While critics denounced the work for what they saw as its strident advocacy of selfishness and laissez-faire capitalism, it earned Rand a large following.

In the remaining years of her career, she wrote essays articulating her philosophical ideas, commenting on political and cultural issues of the 1960s and 1970s, and giving public lectures and interviews on her ideas. Much of her work was published in *The Objectivist*, a magazine she founded with her associate Nathaniel Branden; the most important of her essays were republished in a series of books on epistemology, ethics, politics, and aesthetics.

Humanism. Rand held that religion is a primitive effort to serve a genuine human need for a comprehensive worldview and moral code, but that it is based on an irrational belief in the supernatural. Similarly, she held that religious notions of reverence and worship reflect the idealism of moral aspiration but are misdirected toward the suprahuman. "It is this highest level of man's emotions," she wrote, "that has to be redeemed from the murk of mysticism and redirected at its proper object: man. . . . The man-worshipers, in my sense of the term, are those who see man's highest potential and strive to actualize it."

In this respect, Rand was clearly a humanist. Like other humanists, she believed that morality must be based on human nature rather than divine commands; she admired classical civilization as well as the modern Enlightenment, and regarded the medieval era as a dark interlude. She did not describe herself as a humanist, however, believing that the term was too general to be useful in describing a philosophical standpoint. She would have rejected many of the points in such humanist manifestos as the Council for Secular Humanism's "Affirmations of Humanism." Instead, she coined the term *Objectivism* as the name of her philosophy.

Objectivism. Objectivism subscribes to a broadly Aristotelian view of nature as a realm of entities operating in accordance with causal laws, knowable through observation and reasoning. Rejecting the claims of faith on the one hand and skepticism on the other, it holds that reason is the only means of acquiring knowledge, including knowledge of values. It also holds that the capacity to think must be exercised by choice. Reason is thus a faculty of the individual, no matter how much one may learn from others or gain from cooperation with them.

Independence in thought and action was one element in Rand's individualism. The other was ethical egoism— *The Virtue of Selfishness*, as she titled one of her books. If one is to act independently, she argued, then one cannot make service to others one's primary aim in life.

The foundation of the Objectivist ethics is the thesis that values arise from the conditional nature of life. Any organism must act to maintain its existence in the face of the possibility of death. In relation to that ultimate end, certain things are good for it while others are destructive. For human beings, whose primary tool of survival is reason, a conscious, principled code of values plays the role that reflex and instinct play for other animals, guiding action to promote successful life and happiness (which Rand saw as the inner emotional barometer of meeting life's needs).

In line with her naturalistic ethics, Rand argued that productive work is the central value in human life, providing for the physical needs of survival as well as psychological needs for autonomy, creativity, and self-esteem. In line with her view of reason, she held that rationality is a cardinal virtue, with such virtues as integrity and justice as corollaries. In this respect, she believed in the selfishness of virtue: To achieve success and happiness in life, we should act on principle in pursuit of long-range goals, rather than indulge the whims of the moment or pursue short-term expediency.

Like Friedrich NIETZSCHE, Rand criticized altruism as a moral code that sacrifices the best in man—and the best *of* men—to the worst. But she rejected Nietzsche's belief in the right of "Supermen" to subordinate and exploit their inferiors. The basic principle of Objectivism's social ethic is that every individual is an end in himself and needs the freedom to act on the basis of his independent judgment. People should interact by voluntary means to mutual benefit. The role of government should be limited to protecting individual rights to life, liberty, and property, leaving people free in both the personal, spiritual realm (freedom of speech, conviction, lifestyle, sexual activity, etc.) and in the economic realm (freedom to work, trade, acquire and dispose of property). Thus the Objectivist political philosophy is libertarian: individual rights, limited government, and capitalism—free markets as well as free minds. Rand was and remains one of the chief influences on the libertarian movement today (see LIBERTARIAN MOVEMENT AND UNBELIEF).

Rand also wrote extensively about aesthetics. She held that art served a vital human need to keep abstract principles, values, worldviews, and ideals tied to the concrete reality in which we live and act, and to give such abstractions the immediacy of sensory experience. In effect, the artist re-creates reality in accordance with his or her (implicit) philosophy, through the selection and portrayal of subject matter; viewers respond in accordance with their own implicit worldviews. In *The Romantic Manifesto* (1971), she applied this theory to the major forms of literary, visual, and musical art. As an artist herself, Rand identified with Romantic novelists like Victor Hugo for their emphasis on human beings' power to choose and pursue values.

Reactions. Rand's ideas placed her outside the mainstream of opinion. As an advocate of capitalism, she was attacked by liberals for rejecting the welfare state and by conservatives for rejecting religion. At the same time, she was widely admired for offering a bold and inspiring alternative to conventional thought: bold in challenging common assumptions and pursuing her analysis to its logical conclusions; inspiring in its vision of human achievement and liberation. In the years since her death in 1982, a small but growing number of scholars have sought to understand and evaluate her work on its own terms. Her novels are increasingly read in courses on American literature, and she has entered the canon of major twentieth-century American writers and thinkers.

BIBLIOGRAPHY

Branden, Barbara. *The Passion of Ayn Rand*. Garden City, NY: Doubleday, 1986.

Gladstein, Mimi Reisel. *The New Ayn Rand Companion*. Westport, CT: Greenwood, 1999.

Rand, Ayn. *Atlas Shrugged*. New York: Random House, 1957.

———. *Capitalism: The Unknown Ideal*. New York: New American Library, 1966.

———. *The Fountainhead*. New York: Bobbs-Merrill, 1943.

———. *Introduction to Objectivist Epistemology*. New York: New American Library, 1979.

———. *The Romantic Manifesto*. New York: New American Library, 1971.

———. *The Virtue of Selfishness*. New York: New American Library, 1964.

———. *We the Living*. New York: Macmillan, 1936.

DAVID KELLEY

RANDOLPH, A. PHILIP (1889–1979), American labor organizer and humanist. Asa Philip Randolph is widely regarded as the "grandfather" of the US civil rights movement. He was born to a Methodist preacher but became an atheist (see ATHEISM). In 1917, he founded the *Messenger*, a radical publication advocating workers' rights and FREETHOUGHT. Like Randolph, the magazine's coeditor, Chandler Owen, was a freethinker. Both men were deeply influenced by the radical black freethinker Hubert H. HARRISON.

Randolph advocated socialism (see SOCIALISM AND UNBELIEF), pacifism, and atheism—three positions that most blacks could not accept. Randolph therefore downplayed many of his ideas, and even held an honorary membership in a black church in his later years.

Randolph organized black workers in many different areas of employment. In 1929 he became president of the Brotherhood of Sleeping Car Porters. Within three years, he built that black union into one of the most important and influential labor unions in the United States.

In June 1941 Randolph threatened a march on Washington to protest against segregation in businesses that received government contracts. In response to the threat, President Franklin D. Roosevelt signed the Fair Employment Act, making discrimination illegal in defense industries and in national government departments. Randolph kept the pressure on, even after the war ended. Due largely to his efforts, on July 26, 1948, President Harry S. Truman signed Executive Order 9981, making racial segregation in the United States armed forces illegal. In 1955 Randolph was selected to serve on the executive council of the AFL-CIO. Three years later, he led a march of ten thousand students to desegregate public schools in Washington, DC.

Randolph was regarded as one of the "Big Six" civil rights leaders, and helped to organize and lead the 1963 March on Washington.

In his later years, Randolph abandoned socialism, but his worldview remained progressive. He signed the *Humanist Manifesto II* and supported progressive causes throughout the remainder of his life. He died on May 16, 1979. His funeral was attended by dignitaries including President Jimmy Carter. The US Postal Service issued a twenty-five-cent postage stamp bearing his portrait. Today the A. Philip Randolph Institute keeps the leader's legacy alive.

BIBLIOGRAPHY

Allen, Norm, ed. "Interview with Norman Hill." *African-American Humanism: An Anthology.* Amherst, NY: Prometheus Books, 1991.

Pfeffer, Paula. *A. Philip Randolph: Pioneer of the Civil Rights Movement.* Baton Rouge: Louisiana State University Press, 1990.

NORM R. ALLEN JR.

RATIONALISM. The term *rationalism* refers to two quite different intellectual traditions and has two very different meanings. On the one hand, rationalism refers to a particular mode of mainly Western philosophy that emphasizes the order and rationality of the universe and the ability of human beings to understand this order by the use of human REASON. The philosophers most commonly associated with this tradition are PLATO, René DESCARTES, Baruch SPINOZA, and Gottfried Wilhelm von LEIBNIZ. On the other hand, rationalism also refers to a strand of contemporary nonreligious thinking and activism whose intellectual roots owe more to empiricism than to rationalism. We will consider each in turn.

Philosophical rationalism is as old as Western philosophy itself. A principal characteristic of traditional rationalism is the belief that true knowledge of the universe exists, and that humans can, if with difficulty, grasp this true knowledge. The nature of this knowledge was conceived differently, as was the means by which people could grasp it, but its existence was essential. For Plato, this knowledge existed in the Forms, which only specially trained philosophers could hope to understand fully. For Spinoza, the laws of nature/laws of God—the two being the same thing—performed that function. Those laws could be grasped by anyone of sound heart

and mind who eschewed dogmatism and embraced charity and practical kindness.

Spinoza gives a good example of traditional rationalism in action when he posited what he called the divine law, the characteristics of which include: it is innate in human nature and is therefore common to all people; it does not depend on the truth of any specific historical situation; it cannot be understood through the performance of rituals or ceremonies; and, knowledge of nature/God constitutes the highest reward of the divine law. Plato outlined his variation of the divine law when he had SOCRATES declare: "Then of our laws laying down the principles which those who write or speak about the gods must follow, one would be this: *God is the cause, not of all things, but only of good.*"

The other defining feature of traditional rationalist philosophy was the exalted role given to reason as the premier means by which this essential knowledge of the universe could be grasped. For Spinoza, the key to understanding the divine law is our "natural reason," which "consists in deducing and proving the unknown from the known." For Plato it was a more mystical "capacity to grasp the eternal and immutable," which was his definition of a philosopher. Plato insisted we must "strive to reach ultimate realities by the exercise of pure reason without any aid from the senses."

It was in the light of this philosophical tradition that the agnostics at the end of the nineteenth century (see AGNOSTICISM) looked at the word *rationalism* to encapsulate their cause. Like their philosophical antecedents, the agnostics believed there was an understandable order in the universe, although they attributed it to laws of nature as evinced by evolution and physics rather than imponderable laws of God (see EVOLUTION AND UNBELIEF). And, just as important, the agnostics believed that reason was a sure means to arrive at reliable knowledge of the world, a means that could elevate itself above the hurly-burly of sectarian argument and counterargument. The agnostics also had a more recent usage of rationalists to draw from: the German Higher Critics of the Bible (see BIBLICAL CRITICISM). These scholars were often described by their evangelical opponents as rationalists, in the sense of overemphasizing the role of reason in understanding the Bible at the expense of faith.

This, then, was the context in which the RATIONALIST PRESS ASSOCIATION (RPA) was established in Britain in 1899. The RPA's adoption of the word *rationalist* was deeply influential on FREETHOUGHT movements throughout the British Empire. Australia, India, and New Zealand all have rationalist organizations to this day. The RPA defined rationalism as "the mental attitude which unreservedly accepts the supremacy of reason and aims at establishing a system of philosophy and ethics verifiable by experience and independent of all arbitrary assumptions of authority."

On the face of it, the RPA's definition carried on the rationalist tradition, particularly when it spoke of "unreservedly accepting the supremacy of reason." But other aspects of this definition worked along a completely different trajectory. In eschewing arbitrary assumptions of authority and locating the basis of a system of philosophy and ethics in experience, this understanding of rationalism amounted to a comprehensive rejection of the traditional understandings of rationalism. The RPA's understanding of rationalism had as much in common with traditional empiricism as it did with rationalism. What is more, the definition was internally unstable, and it was not long before some of the tensions within this definition became apparent. There was the problem of accepting *unreservedly* the supremacy of reason when reason seems to work best precisely when it questions arbitrary assumptions of authority. Then there was the discontinuity between seeing reason as an attitude of mind and, at the same time, a philosophical system.

The 1899 definition of rationalism was a compromise between three divergent understandings of the term among nonreligious people. There was rationalism in the sense of being a cerebral corrective to irrational religious fervor. People who spoke of rationalism in this sense frequently saw a positive core to the religious impulse that was trivialized by popular zeal and superstition. They were the people most likely to speak of "rational religion" or the "religion of humanity." The utopian schemes of Auguste COMTE appealed to people who understood rationalism in these terms. This element within rationalism was moribund by the beginning of World War I. The true descendants of this line of thinking are today's religious humanists (see RELIGIOUS HUMANISM).

Other rationalists viewed their rationalism as being in fundamental opposition to religion. These were the people who traced their intellectual lineage from courageous rebels like Thomas PAINE, Richard CARLILE, and Charles BRADLAUGH. Paine's inclusion here is paradoxical, in that by virtue of the arguments he made in his principal works, he deserved to be considered as belonging to the strand of rationalism discussed above. But Paine's memory was preserved by people more at home in rationalism of this second sort. This militant understanding was expressed most fully by John M. ROBERTSON, who described rationalism as standing "first and last for the habit and tendency to challenge the doctrines which claim 'religious' or sacrosanct authority." The people who prefer to describe themselves solely as atheists (see ATHEISM) and who eschew other nonreligious titles as evasions are the descendants of this strand of thinking.

The third understanding of rationalism at the turn of the twentieth century was the one that took longest to find its natural constituency. It was best expressed by Adam Gowans Whyte in an unjustly neglected book called *The Religion of the Open Mind* (1913). Whyte was more sympathetic to the diversity of opinion among people, rationalists included. "A direct principle of rationalism," Whyte wrote, "is that every man must make his own religion." After noting the old ideal of the saints and apostles that we shall all one day profess the same faith, Whyte added that "it will, happily, never be realized."

Whyte's understanding of the open-endedness of rationality turned out to be the longest lasting of the three variations of rationalism that were apparent at the beginning of the twentieth century. His religion of the open mind is what developed into contemporary HUMANISM, which has come to speak less of rationalism and more of rationality as part of an integrated personality. When the British philosopher A. E. Heath was asked about rationalism in 1947, he spoke in terms of what it cannot do. Rationalism, Heath wrote, "cannot give us the glittering prizes of final certitude, which resplendent dogmatisms hold out for our attention. Nor can it provide us with the assurances and comfort of intellectual safety." It was with this in mind that the Rationalist Press Association changed the name of its annual publication in 1968 from the *Rationalist Annual* to *Question*. In justifying the change, Hector HAWTON wrote that commitment to "rational inquiry means that nothing at the outset is taken for granted, everything is open to question."

So, the contemporary understanding of rationalism has moved progressively away from the traditional understandings of philosophical rationalism—so much so that "rationalism" as a label for the movement has generally given way to "humanism."

Probably the finest rhetorical affirmation of rationalism was given by the great popularizer and controversialist Joseph MCCABE. Speaking in 1920 to a packed audience at Queen's Hall, London, during his famous debate on spiritualism with Sir Arthur Conan Doyle (see SPIRITUALISM AND UNBELIEF), McCabe declared: "I represent Rationalism. That is to say, I want the whole world to use its reason, every man and woman in the world. I will respect any man or any woman, no matter what their conclusions may be, if they have used their own personality, their own mind, and their own judgment, rigorously and conscientiously." We can quibble with this or that aspect of McCabe's formulation, but it captures the spirit of free inquiry which has always been the core principle of rationalism as understood by freethinkers.

BIBLIOGRAPHY

Cooke, Bill. *The Gathering of Infidels: A Hundred Years of the Rationalist Press Association.* Amherst, NY: Prometheus Books, 2004.

Hawton, Hector. *The Thinker's Handbook.* London: Watts and Company, 1950.

Herrick Jim, ed. *Rationalism in the Twenty-first Century.* London: RPA, 2001.

McCabe, Joseph. *Modern Rationalism.* London: Watts and Company, 1909.

Plato. *The Republic.* London: Penguin, 1987.

Robertson, J. M. *Rationalism.* London: Constable, 1912.

Spinoza, Benedict. *Tractatus Theologico-Politicus.* London: George Routledge, [1885].

Whyte, Adam Gowans. *The Religion of the Open Mind.* London: Watts and Company, 1913.

BILL COOKE

RATIONALIST PRESS ASSOCIATION. The Rationalist Press Association (RPA) was one of the most significant FREETHOUGHT organizations of the twentieth century. Prior to its founding in 1899, freethought organizations usually had brief lives that revolved around one or two towering individuals. Once they departed, the organization quickly withered. It was the genius of Charles Albert WATTS to see the need for a new type of organization, and to succeed in creating one. In 1882 Watts inherited a tiny publishing firm from his father, Charles WATTS. Young Charles Albert developed Watts and Company into a profitable business, unlike most previous freethought publishing operations, which had brief, cash-strapped lives before becoming insolvent. Watts was an unassuming man who worked best outside the public glare, but he was brilliant at attracting lifelong loyalty from people wealthier and more outgoing than himself. His transparent honesty and willingness to take only a minimal wage from his publishing ventures helped boost that confidence.

The RPA grew out of a small committee that met in London on July 2, 1890, to discuss legal constraints against the expression of freethought. This group called itself the Propagandist Press Committee. In March 1893 it renamed itself the Rationalist Press Committee. By this time it was becoming clear to Watts and his allies that there was considerable support waiting to be tapped by an organization that avoided overly controversial or vulgar forms of freethought advocacy. In 1898 Watts rallied his many allies to transform the Rationalist Press Committee into a more ambitious form of organization. Taking advantage of the discovery by George W. FOOTE that formally constituted freethought bodies were legally entitled to receive donations and bequests, the Rationalist Press Association received its certificate of registration on May 26, 1899, and on September 18 of that year held its first public meeting.

The RPA was established as an educational organization and book club, with members receiving Watts and Company titles in proportion to the annual fee they paid. The *Literary Guide,* the principal RPA publication, served as an advertising organ for forthcoming Watts and Company titles and authors, additionally providing news and opinion on the current state of religion, and pieces on the history and nature of freethought. As an organization, the RPA rarely took direct part in political agitation, though it was happy to support various reform movements, and Watts and Company frequently published material advocating one reform or another.

The RPA's golden age included the years from its inception in 1899 until the onset of World War I. During that time it made some significant contributions to the secularization of Great Britain. It did this with a series called the Cheap Reprints, which proved to rival publishing houses that there was a large market for low-cost reprints of serious nonfiction. Light fiction had been published in this form before, but nobody believed that the poor, who could not afford the price of a hardcover book, would want to buy weightier material in cheap form.

Watts had to borrow money to launch the series, and it is testimony to his character that his friends were prepared to invest in such an apparently risky venture. The first Cheap Reprint was a collection of *Lectures and Essays* by Thomas H. HUXLEY, a hero of Watts's. Against all expectations, the Cheap Reprints sold very well. The first impression of *Lectures and Essays* sold more than 30,000 copies and the five titles released in 1902 sold more than 155,000 copies. Hardcovers sold for a shilling, and paperbacks at what Watts called the "wastepaper price" of sixpence. The series went on for ten years (with one title added as an afterthought in 1918) and sold more than 4 million copies. In the process, the RPA had rewritten the rules about publishing. Other publishers now saw that inexpensive nonfiction was economically viable. The road was open for the paperback and for works of popular science geared toward the general reader.

Established religion was alarmed by these developments. A flurry of pamphlets and articles lamented the poisoning of the working-class mind with so much ATHEISM and unbelief. In fact, not one of the Cheap Reprints advanced atheism. Most ranged from a liberal Christianity, through what would now be called RELIGIOUS HUMANISM, to a genial AGNOSTICISM. The Cheap Reprints series was gradually starved into submission after a protracted campaign by churchmen to prevent titles being sold at railway stalls and being stocked in libraries.

Watts and Company suffered from its own success. Its Cheap Reprints series attracted a host of competitors, chief among them Penguin, which began issuing cheap paperbacks in 1935. In 1929 Watts and Company tried to recapture the initiative with the Thinker's Library series. Altogether there were 140 titles in the Thinker's Library series, covering a wide range of topics and from a wide range of perspectives. Like the Cheap Reprints, the Thinker's Library was designed to make the works of leading thinkers available to people of modest means. The inexpensive hardbound volumes were originally sold at one shilling each, though prices soon rose in the wake of the Great Depression. Viewpoints expressed in the series ranged from those of nineteenth-century liberals and agnostics to firebrand Marxists (see MARXISM) radicalized by the Spanish Civil War. Subjects discussed were similarly broad: from sober histories to essays and light relief, from complicated works of science to undemanding novels, from Charles DARWIN to the rationalist journalist Charles Gorham, from Samuel BUTLER to the gothic novelist Marjorie Bowen. For several decades people spoke of coming across a Thinker's Library title as being the turning point on their road to freethought. About 5 million Thinker's Library titles were sold over the life of the imprint.

Another important publication of the RPA was its *Annual*. It began in 1884 as the *Agnostic Annual*, becoming the *RPA Annual* in 1907, the *Rationalist Annual* in 1927, and *Question* in 1968. The series finally came to an end in 1980. During those years some of the best minds of the century were published in the annual: Bertrand RUSSELL, Karl POPPER, A. J. AYER, Antony Flew, Subrahmanyan Chandrasekhar, J. B. S. Haldane, H. G. WELLS, and many others. Throughout its run the *Annual* was one of the most important vehicles for rationalist scholarship and criticism.

And then there were the stand-alone titles published by Watts and Company. Without doubt its most successful from a commercial point of view was *The Riddle of the Universe*, written by Ernst HAECKEL and translated by Joseph McCABE. The RPA's edition of this work, published in 1900, sold more than a quarter million copies and contributed mightily to the young organization's financial well-being. *The Riddle of the Universe* was one of the most influential books of the first decade of the twentieth century, attracting more than a hundred reviews and several book-length replies. Other important Watts and Company publications include the still-unsurpassed histories of freethought by J. M. ROBERTSON, McCabe's *Biographical Dictionary of Modern Rationalists* (1920), and some fine examples of popular science, including *Man Makes Himself* (1936) by V. Gordon Childe and *Science and History* (1954) by J. D. Bernal.

Conditions after World War II were not kind to the RPA or to Watts and Company. Charles Albert Watts retired from active participation in 1930 and died in 1946. His son Fred died in 1953, having worked himself into an early grave for the company. The Thinker's Library ground to a halt in 1951 and sales of stand-alone works plummeted while costs soared. The RPA took Watts and Company over in 1954 and sold it in 1960. The RPA then established a more modest publishing venture, Pemberton Books, which published a worthwhile series called the Humanist Library. Some generous bequests funded a short-lived revival of Pemberton titles in the 1980s before fading out later in that decade. Since then the RPA has published a few works under its own name, but the true successor to Watts and Company has become Prometheus Books in the United States. The outstanding individual at the RPA through these years was Hector Hawton, a journalist, author, and polymath.

After Hawton's death in 1975, questions about the future of the RPA have periodically been raised, especially as it has effectively left the publishing scene. To date no firm conclusion has arisen. The only wing of the original RPA to survive is its magazine. Originally *Watts's Literary Guide*, then between 1894 and 1956 the *Literary Guide*, then the *Humanist*, and since 1972 the *New Humanist*, the RPA's magazine is a remarkable record of intellectual and social thought since the 1880s. As with the *Rationalist Annual/Question*, some of the finest minds of the past century have contributed to the *New Humanist* and its predecessors. From the days of Gladstone to those of Tony Blair, the *New Humanist* has been giving a humanist perspective on the issues of the day.

BIBLIOGRAPHY

Cooke, Bill. *The Gathering of Infidels: A Hundred Years of the Rationalist Press Association*. Amherst, NY: Prometheus Books, 2004.

Gould, F. J. *The Pioneers of Johnson's Court*. London: Watts and Company, 1929.

Whyte, Adam Gowans. *The Story of the RPA 1899–1949*. London: Watts and Company, 1949.

BILL COOKE

REASON. Talk of reason—of rationality and of being reasonable—has come under considerable pressure in (if you will) our postmodern times (really a form of modernity), and from philosophers and other intellectuals who have felt—perhaps with a kind of misinterpretation—the force of Ludwig WITTGENSTEIN's, Thomas Kuhn's, Michel Foucault's, and Richard Rorty's thought. Even when sensitively employed, it is not evident that there is anything like objective and crosscultural criteria or norms of rationality and reasonableness with sufficient substance to enable impartial, well-informed people capable of careful reasoning to achieve a reflective consensus concerning the comparative rationality or irrationality—or the reasonableness or unreasonableness—of our various social institutions and social practices, or indeed of whole ways of life or views of the world. I am skeptical, though not extensively so, of this extensive SKEPTICISM about reason. I shall give here some of the reasons for doubting that reason is so wanton, while remaining acutely conscious that we do not sometimes speak of "wanton reason" for nothing.

Often we are not able to make fine enough discriminations and, in such circumstances, we have no basis for rankings or judgments in terms of the rationality or reasonableness of the various practices, institutions, or ways of life we are reflecting upon. But in some other circumstances it is plain enough what should be said. Before we judge reason to be wanton, we should be careful not to assimilate certain difficult cases to the more general run of things where the rational or reasonable thing to do is often not that problematic. That reason cannot always tell us what we ought to do does not mean that it never can, or even that it cannot often give us guidance in important areas of our lives.

I shall first set out a characterization of what is ordinarily meant by *rationality*, followed by a characterization of criteria of rationality both instrumental and noninstrumental. I shall then show how the important concept of reasonability cannot be assimilated to rationality and how it is also an important conception in our social life. That will be followed by what might be taken as a crucial test case: namely, whether Jewish, Christian, or Islamic belief for an educated twenty-first-century person is a rational or reasonable option. I shall attempt to show something of what must be done to answer this question, and I shall end with an examination of a Wittgensteinian challenge which claims that to attempt to make such global assessments of the rationality or reasonability of whole belief-systems is to give reason a *rationalistic* task that is not genuinely its own.

I

To understand rationality it might be well to start with a dictionary. If we look up *rational* and *reasonable* in the *Oxford English Dictionary* (OED), we find such things as the following. To be rational is to be endowed with reason: to have, that is, the faculty of reason. It is also to exercise one's reason in a proper manner and to have sound judgment and to be sensible and sane. Rational beliefs or rational principles of action are those which pertain to or relate to reason or are based on or derived from reasoning. They are beliefs and principles which are "agreeable to reason" and thus are "reasonable, sensible, not foolish, absurd or extravagant."

If we turn to the closely related term *reasonable*, we are told that to be reasonable is to have sound judgment, to be sensible, sane. We are also told that it sometimes means, curiously enough, "not to ask for too much." Moreover, something that is reasonable—say, a consideration, claim, or argument—is something that is agreeable to reason, not irrational, absurd, or ridiculous. And there is in the OED, as well, the somewhat surprising claim that being reasonable is "not going beyond the limit assigned."

I think philosophers would be ill-advised to make sport of these notions. They give us a sense of the terrain we are concerned with, and we might indeed even be somewhat skeptical whether in such a specification we philosophers have done much better. But all the same, if we are perplexed about rationality or reasonability, these dictionary definitions are not going to do much to help us. We surely are going to be puzzled about this "faculty of reason" or about being "endowed with reason." And we are going to be suspicious, as Charles Saunders Peirce was, about talk of "being agreeable to reason." What is this reason that we are or may be endowed with? If it is only the faculty of speech and the ability to think and argue that is being talked about, then it should be remarked that irrational people have that ability too, and also that thoroughly irrational claims have been

expressed in nondeviant English, French, German, and so on. Moreover, extravagant and irrational claims have had valid arguments as their vehicles. Validity is but a crucial necessary condition for sound and rational argumentation. So, if being "endowed with reason" is only understood as being able to speak, to think, and to be able to form valid arguments, it will not be sufficient to give us an understanding of rationality.

Alternatively, we need to ask whether being endowed with reason or being agreeable to reason is simply its being the case that what is agreeable to reason is established or establishable by sound arguments, namely, valid arguments with true premises. If it is, then we are at least on familiar terrain. The problem then becomes the familiar one of determining when arguments are valid and of determining when statements are true or probably true. While this is surely part of the task of determining what is meant by rationality, it is not all of it, for there are principles of action which are said to be rational and attitudes of which the same thing is said. Yet concerning both such principles and such attitudes, it is not clear that the notions of truth or falsity have any determinate and/or unproblematic meaning. Moreover, we do not, in some instances at least, seem to be talking about knowledge claims here. But why should the lack of that rule out rationality? Finally, in this context, and to make a quite different point, it is also perhaps the case that not everything that is reasonably believed is believed for a reason or (arguably) because it is known to be true or probably true. So, while reason is perhaps not wanton, it is, on such a characterization, still perplexing.

We are, if we are perplexed by rationality, also going to have trouble with the OED's characterizations of rationality in terms of "exercising one's reason in a *proper* manner" and "being *sensible, sane* and of *sound* judgment," "not *foolish, absurd,* or *extravagant*." And having trouble with those, we are going to have still more trouble with such at least seemingly conservative and perhaps ideological notions as that to be rational is "not to ask for too much" or "not going beyond the limits assigned." The various notions cited only have a determinate meaning in a culture-specific environment. Some of them at least are definitely ideological; some of them are normative terms with a definite emotive force (*foolish, absurd, extravagant*); and (*proper, sensible, sound*). Even if some uses of these terms are not always emotive in their force, they are still normative and, as well or at least, are terms with criteria which are in many circumstances contestable. (Normative judgments about *the past*, such as "Greek slavery was wrong" or "Chinese foot-binding was evil," are characteristically not emotive utterances.)

Manifestly rational and reasonable human beings—or at least intelligent and well-informed human beings capable of cool judgment—often disagree about their criteria and about who is or is not of sound judgment, sensible, reasonable, and the like. When a diplomat with a powerful agenda announces that such and such is a reasonable policy or that the parties in question are not being reasonable, I suspect—given my different orientation—that a rather ideological *persuasive* definition has been utilized; I realize that he or she and I do not, in some very important ways, agree about the criteria for rationality and reasonability.

II

Let us now look at some criteria that philosophers have set out for *rational belief* and *rational principles* of action to see if they are an improvement. Presumably, a rational human being will have rational *principles of action* and *rational beliefs*. Moreover, such a person will have rational attitudes that square with these principles and beliefs, and to be irrational—though this perhaps is not all that it is—is to not act in accordance with these principles and beliefs. But what are they? And are they as contested and as indeterminate as the conceptions expressed in the dictionary entries?

Rational beliefs are typically beliefs that can withstand the scrutiny of people who are critical of their beliefs: that is to say, they are beliefs that are typically held open to refutation or modification by experience including in some contexts experimental investigation and/or reflective examination; rational beliefs—to spell out a little of what is involved in the notion of reflective examination—are beliefs that must be capable of being held in such a way, all other things being equal, so as not to block or resist reflective inspection—namely, attempts to consider their assumptions, implications, and relations to other beliefs. Rational beliefs also are typically beliefs for which there is good evidence or good reasons or at least they are, all other things being equal, beliefs for which such evidence or reasons, where justification is needed, will be conscientiously and intelligently sought and evidence or reasons (when available and utilizable) will not in most circumstances be ignored by people who hold such beliefs. Finally, rational beliefs are beliefs that do not involve inconsistencies, contradictions, or incoherencies.

A rational person will also have rational principles of action. Moreover, he or she, at least habitually and unwittingly, will act in accordance with those principles, and it will be irrational of him or her not to act in accordance with these principles. The following are at least plausible candidates:

1. The most efficient and effective means are to be taken, all other things being equal, to achieve one's ends.
2. If one has several compatible ends, one, all other things being equal, should take the means that will, as far as one can ascertain, most likely enable one to realize the greatest number of one's ends.
3. Of two ends, equally desired and equal in all other relevant respects, one is, all other things being equal, to choose the end with the higher probability of being achievable.
4. If there are the same probabilities for two plans of action, which secure entirely different ends, all other things being equal, that plan of action is to be chosen that secures ends at least one of which is preferred to one of those secured by the other plan. (If none is, it is quite problematic which plan of action to prefer.)
5. If one is unclear about what one's ends are or what they involve or how they are to be achieved, then it is usually wise to postpone making a choice among plans of action to secure those ends.
6. Those ends that, from a dispassionate and informed point of view, a person values higher than his other ends, are the ends that, all other things being equal, he or she should try to realize. A rational agent will, all other things being equal, seek plans of action which will satisfy his other ends, but they should be adopted only insofar as they are compatible with the satisfaction of those ends he or she values most highly. (Is this to say that what is *valued* in certain circumstances must be *valuable*?)
7. A rational person will have rational beliefs, that is, beliefs that satisfy the preceding criteria of rationality, and rational principles of action; and he or she will in almost all circumstances act in accordance with them. (This does not mean a person will constantly be calculating what is the rational thing to do. To act rationally will be in accordance with those principles, but that does not mean that to be rational one must be consciously following those principles. We need a *dispositional* account here.)

With these principles of rationality, as with the dictionary definitions as well, there are areas of indeterminateness. Indeed they were quite self-consciously introduced in their statement. The clause *all other things being equal* is essential, as are such qualifiers as *typically* or *usually*, for without them the principles will surely fall to counterexamples: that is to say, there will be situations, real or plausibly imaginable, when it will be at least arguable that the rational or reasonable thing to do in those situations will not be to act in accordance with one or another of those principles.

However, even *if* something tighter is possible and is ultimately to be desired, a strong consideration in favor of the principles of rationality I set out is that they are at least a good subset of the principles of rationality operative in our lives and that these principles, like prima facie duties, usually always hold. That is to say—so as to make clear that I am not unsaying what I say here—it is always the case that these principles, where applicable, usually hold—there is a presumption in all instances that they hold—in a way quite analogous to the way that for everyone all of the time it is the case that promises, generally speaking, are to be kept.

III

The preceding characterization of rationality is a rather minimal one that might with some plausibility be thought to apply cross-culturally and to hold for everyone. Jürgen Habermas, developing a conception of rationality following in the tradition of the Frankfurt School, has in his early writings given us a much richer but very normatively freighted conception of rationality. It would, no doubt, contain the principles of rationality already specified and it, like those principles, goes beyond what is specified in the ordinary use of *rational* and *reasonable* and their German equivalences; but it is still, I believe, in the spirit of those uses. At least it is plainly not in conflict with them. It will be well, in trying to gain an understanding of rationality, to set alongside the principles of rationality I have articulated, those conceptions of Habermas that are distinctively different. Then the ensemble should be up for critical examination.

Habermas in his earlier writings (including *Toward a Rational Society*) in a very considerable measure cashes in the concept of rationality in terms of an articulation of the concepts of enlightenment and emancipation. A fully rational human being will be an emancipated, enlightened human being. Such people will have critical insight and an enlightened consciousness, that is, a holistically coherent consciousness. They will have a firm sense of self-identity, and will have achieved adult autonomy, an understanding of human needs, and a liberation from the various illusions and dogmatisms that fetter humankind. Rationality, of course, admits of degrees, and this conception is trying to capture that heuristic ideal—*a fully rational person*—but it is also an attempt to specify what we put into our conceptualization of and indeed our ideal of full rationality or, perhaps, more in accordance with ordinary usage, full reasonability. This full reasonability will be coextensive with what it is to be enlightened and emancipated. Where enlightened and emancipated conditions obtain, and thus fully rational conditions (reasonable circumstances) obtain, people generally will be informed, perceptive, liberated, autonomous, self-directed agents committed to developing their own distinctive powers and capable of fairness, impartiality, and objectivity. They will typically be reflective about their ends, knowledgeable about the means for their efficient attainment, and they will be critical people not under the bondage of any ideology. Indeed, free from all self-imposed tutelage and indoctrination, they will see the world rightly. They will have identified the major evils of the world, and they will understand the conditions for surcease or amelioration of these evils and for the achievement of human community, to the extent that that community can be achieved at all.

Since then Habermas, worried about the indeterminateness of talk of "enlightenment," "emancipation," and the like, developed a much more theoretical conceptualization of rationality, namely, his account of what he calls *communicative rationality* that, while not in conflict with the above, goes in an importantly different direction and indeed meets an important lacuna in our thinking about rationality.

Habermas noted that ordinary language plays a distinctive coordinating role in human interaction. Language is used not simply *strategically* to achieve our ends but more fundamentally *communicatively* as well. I say "more fundamentally," for without these communicative uses, the strategic uses would be impossible. There are certain speech acts (a doing things with words) such as stating, deliberating together, arguing with each other, asserting, questioning, denying, proclaiming, doubting, interrogating, and the like which are *speech acts oriented toward public understanding and cooperation*. They are ways toward consensus building and trust-gaining between human beings. These are distinctive forms of rationality that cannot be reduced to instrumental rationality and without this communicative rationality, human interaction, including purposive rationality, would be impossible. Communicative rationality is typically procedural, but this procedural rationality would vindicate at least in ideal speech situations the substantive norms of rationality I have taken from Habermas's pre-1970 work.

IV

What I have said about rationality and reasonableness so far, with the exception of my last remarks about Habermas and communicative rationality, are equally compatible with foundationalism or antifoundationalism. Foundationalism has come on bad days, and I do not for a moment wish to suggest that this is just a fashion in philosophy, though only (and then not decisively) time will tell. But I do want to say something about wide reflective equilibrium which is a major *nonfoundationalist* and *coherentist* method of explaining and justifying, and with this showing the rationality and justifiability of beliefs. This is most clearly exemplified in rationalizing moral and political beliefs, though I have elsewhere as well extended it to critically examining the claimed justification of religious beliefs.

Arguably it is the dominant and most persuasive method for both explaining and justifying moral and normative political beliefs, commitments, and whole accounts of morality. Shuttling back and forth between our specific considered judgments, principles, well-embedded and reflectively acceptable practices, well-established empirical considerations, and similarly established theoretical conceptions, it attempts to get our various considered judgments or convictions, uncontroversially accepted empirical beliefs, and uncontroversial theoretical scientific theories, plus beliefs of critical and reflective commonsense, into a coherent pattern of consistently held beliefs and judgments. This is a coherentist method but not a *purely* coherentist method for it takes our considered judgments, uncontroversial empirical, scientific, and commonsense beliefs to have some *initial* credibility. It seeks to forge these varied beliefs into a consistent and coherent pattern, perspicuously displayed, showing how they are not just a jumble. In the processes of winnowing some of them out, some of our considered judgments will be revised or sometimes even abandoned. We are certainly not sticking with "received opinions." In this way it is a *self-correcting method*. To achieve this is to achieve for a time a wide reflective equilibrium. It will only be for a time, for as inquiry and reflection go on any reflective equilibrium will eventually be upset and hopefully and reasonably expected to be replaced by another and more adequate reflective equilibrium.

Some *initial* credibility obtains for those of our considered judgments that we reflectively endorse and take as our starting points. Those that do not get winnowed out as we proceed in equilibrating, and continue to be reflectively endorsed, have considerable weight with us. Indeed, contrary to the proclivities of rationalistic ethical theorists, they have the strongest weight that any considerations can have. They are our beginning points and ending points in moral reflection. There is, of course, a strong urge on the part of many people to "get behind," to "find a securer foundation" for such a coherent cluster of considered convictions: to put more "trust in reason" than I am prepared to do. There is nothing like that to be had. To think there is, is a rationalist delusion. When there is such a coherence among our particular considered beliefs, the principles and practices that govern them, and the well-confirmed factual considerations that back them up, where they provide support or explanation for each other and they are optimally acceptable to us as evidenced by our disinclination to revise them further, we have the best justification of our beliefs that for a time it is possible to have.

If we say by way of criticism of the method of wide reflective equilibrium that we should appeal, instead of to considered judgments, to the *desires* that would remain (would not be extinguished) after thorough consideration of (1) the facts available to us and (2) logic, the proper response is that these desires are shaped by the same acculturating influences as are our considered judgments and convictions. We do not get anything more objective here, anything that is "closer to reality," more truth-tracking, or more rationally vindicated.

I have in the above sections treated "rationality" and "reasonableness" as if they meant much the same thing; and while they both come from the same Latin root *ratio* (reason), they are actually importantly different, and in moral and normative political thought "reasonableness" is the more salient notion. Moreover, though philosophers from PLATO to Thomas HOBBES to David Gauthier have tried to derive reasonableness from rationality, these efforts have turned out to be failures. A reasonable person will be fair and impartial in his or her dealings with other persons. A rational person might not. A reasonable person generally will not just press his or her advantage against others without considering their interests and without trying to consider them impartially. In other words, being reasonable in one of its central uses is something more directly linked with being moral than is being rational. Reasonability is linked with mutuality and reciprocity in a way that rationality need not be (except perhaps communicative rationality, which is best seen as a centerpiece of reasonability). We live in pluralistic societies where people have, in a way that cannot be overcome by careful reasoning, deeply different and sometimes conflicting conceptions of the good; but it is possible, where people can and will be reasonable, to agree not on conceptions of the good, but on conceptions of justice rooted in fairness or impartiality. Reasonable people will see they need a socially operative common conception of justice as one crucial thing which helps in keeping life from becoming nasty, brutish, and short. If reasonable people will reflect carefully, such a conception of justice will be regulative for them. Moreover, at least in liberal societies, to be justifiable to citizens of such a society, the conception of justice must be something that can reasonably be accepted by everyone where citizens are to be respected as free and equal and where everyone accepts that. This basic Rawlsian insight gives reasonableness a central role in moral and political thought and a priority over rationality in such thought. Both are, of course, central; but where a rational egoist or amoralist offends against reasonableness, as they must to be consistently either, *from a moral point of view their views are justifiably overridden.* From such a point of view and rooted in what it is to be reasonable there is no room for the question "Why should we be moral?" or "Why should I be moral?" But for a purely rational person with no more than at best an instrumental concern for reasonability (if such a being could exist), it is not so evident that such questions are closed.

VI

I turn now to a consideration of the rationality and reasonableness of religious belief. Consider a specific religion such as Judaism or Christianity. Can we both understand it and believe it? Are our criteria of rationality and intelligibility such that it can be established that the core beliefs of Judaism or Christianity are irrational? Most fundamentally what we—or at least many of us—want to know is whether Jewish or Christian belief in God is a rational or a reasonable belief, or at least not an irrational belief. Not that this is perfectly parallel to a question pursued by E. E. Evans-Pritchard, Peter Winch, Alasdair MacIntyre, Steven Lukes, Martin Hollis, Charles Taylor, Jürgen Habermas, and others: Is the Zande belief in witches a rational belief? (The Azande are an indigenous Sudanese people, the rationality of whose supernatural beliefs has become the object of frequent philosophical examination.)

What we are trying to ascertain, both in the Zande case and in the Jewish or Christian case, is whether in terms of a common notion of rationality such as we have articulated in the previous sections, such beliefs can and indeed should be said to be rational, or at least not irrational. On the basis of what we said earlier about rationality, we are now assuming that it is *not* the case that one standard of rationality applies to the Azande and another to us; or in a more familiar context, that one standard of intelligibility applies to the Christian and another to the secularist. I will, that is, start by assuming a unitary conception, in certain ways indeterminate though it may be, of rationality, and see where it leads us.

In asking about the rationality of the Jewish and Christian belief in God, as well as in asking about the rationality of Zande belief in witchcraft, it is wise, I believe, to break down the question in the following way. (I shall do it first for the Zande.) Is the Zande belief in witches a rational belief? can be taken as either (a) Can we members of twenty-first-century Western culture with the rather full information and learning available to an educated member of our culture rationally believe in witches as the Azande do? or (b) Are the Azande rational in believing in witches? Have they acted reasonably and not disregarded evidence, reasoning, and information readily available to them in believing in witches?

In talking about the Azande it is plainly evident that it is important to distinguish between these two questions because what we have learned from social anthropology concerning other cultures should make us extremely loath (or at least wary) of claiming that an average Azande or the average member of any other tribe is irrational. But, given the pervasiveness and centrality to their way of living of Zande belief in witchcraft, this is exactly what we should conclude if we answer (b) by claiming that the Azande are irrational in believing as they do. But that seems very implausible. It would mean saying of a normal and average member of a culture that he or she is irrational. That very much sounds like ethnocentric hubris. Yet, on the other hand, we do not want, in acknowledging that the Azande are not behaving irrationally in believing in witches, to give to understand that if we Westerners do not believe in witches we are being irrational or ethnocentric or just pushing our lib-

eral culture? Hence the importance of distinguishing between (a) and (b).

I will maintain that it is important to make a parallel distinction in talking about the rationality of Christian and Jewish belief in God. However, since in speaking of Christian and Jewish belief we are talking intraculturally and not cross-culturally between radically different cultures, the importance of drawing that distinction is not so evident to us. (It may be perfectly evident to someone coming from another culture.)

Let me first draw this distinction with greater exactitude, and then I shall try to show the importance of drawing it. Is the Judeo-Christian belief in God a rational belief? can be understood as either (c) Can we members of twenty-first-century Western culture with the rather full information and learning available to an educated member of our culture rationally believe in the God of the mainstream Jewish and Christian traditions? or (d) Are Christians and Jews rational in believing in God? Have they acted reasonably and not disregarded evidence, reasoning, and information readily available to them in believing in God?

There is an important disanalogy between (a) and (b) on the one hand, and (c) and (d) on the other, which we should note. There is no overlap in the class of persons referred to in (a) and (b), but there is in (c) and (d). There are plenty of Christians and Jews who are manifestly rational and reasonable and are members of the class of twenty-first-century persons who are highly educated and reflective. This is a sociological fact that we should not allow any ideological or philosophical convictions to obscure or distort. If anyone is to answer (c) in the negative, as one presumably would answer (a) in the negative, one will need to make out a very good case for the claim that while there are some Christians and Jews who are reflective, well educated, and manifestly rational, nonetheless their belief in God is irrational and that, in living in accordance with that belief, they—though perhaps understandably enough—are being irrational. (This, of course, does not mean that in other respects they are being irrational.)

This is a strong and indeed an embarrassing claim to make in our tolerant and (in many respects) liberal ethos. However, it is just the claim that anyone who consistently supports (c) must make, and it is a claim, radical as it is, that I shall make. (It is because of things like this that some people have accused me of "evangelical ATHEISM.") The important thing to see is whether it can be given a reasonable explication and a sound defense. There are many who believe that any such claim is thoroughly wrongheaded. T. M. Penelhum, for example, believes that while the claims of natural theology to give sound reasons for believing in God do not succeed, neither do the allegedly clinching arguments against religious belief, so that vis-à-vis Judaism and Christianity we are left in a stalemate. Reason—that is, human ratiocination and rationality—cannot, he and many others believe, settle the matter one way or another.

What we are asking (assuming we are members of the class of reasonably educated twenty-first-century Westerners or are people who have gained a participant's understanding of that cultural background) is whether it is rational to believe in the God of the Jews and the Christians. We want to know whether such a belief is irrational for such people, that is, educated Westerners or people who have gained a firm participant's grasp of Western culture. Just as there are Azande who reasonably believe in witches, given what they can readily know, so there are plenty of Jews and Christians who are neither scientifically nor philosophically nor in any other very extensive way educated, who, given what they know and what is readily available to them, reasonably believe in God. This is not at all a patronizing remark, for we all stand—and unavoidably so—in that position vis-à-vis some beliefs.

Hegel is right in asserting that we cannot overleap history. (This note is not a form of relativism or skepticism, though it is a historicism.) But unless a certain relativism or skepticism about rationality is true (and indeed sufficiently coherent so that it could be true), there is no obvious reason, and perhaps no sound reason at all, for thinking that it could not correctly be claimed that reasonable people can have *some* irrational beliefs and indeed some very fundamental ones at that. In recognizing that we are all in the same boat, that we all may very well have some irrational beliefs, I show that I am not being patronizing to Jews or Christians.

VII

What synoptically should be said about the rationality/irrationality of beliefs is this: a belief (religious or otherwise) is in most circumstances irrational for the person who holds it if the person holding it is being either (a) inconsistent, (b) unintelligible (does not make sense), (c) incoherent, or (d) claims things that he or she could readily come to know are false or very probably false. It is also something which is irrational for him or her to believe if (e) it is held by that person in such a way that no attention is given to considerations of evidence that might be relevant (directly or indirectly) to the holding of that belief, or (f) the belief is held in such a way that the holder of the belief will not countenance the reflective inspection of its implications for his or her other beliefs or practices.

Centrally in asking whether the Judeo-Christian belief in God is rational, or at least not irrational, we are asking: (a) Is belief in such a God free of inconsistencies or contradictions? (b) Is belief in such a God intelligible? (Does such a belief make sense?) (c) Is belief in such a God a coherent conception? and (d) Is belief in such a God a belief in something which we have very good grounds to believe not to be the case?

If a belief in God is inconsistent, unintelligible, inco-

herent, or a belief which the person has very good grounds for believing that it is not the case, then belief in such a God is, all other things being equal, irrational for a person who recognizes any of these things or for a person who is in a position where he could, but for self-deception, recognize these things. (I say "all other things being equal" because if *only* the last condition holds, there is space for being a reasonable fideist.) We can say derivatively, if this is so, that the beliefs are irrational beliefs for that person.

The first and fourth questions, at least on the surface, are fairly straightforward, and only careful examination of the appropriate strands of religious discourse would give us good grounds for answering one way or another. But (b) and (c) are more troublesome. What are we claiming when we claim that such a religious belief is unintelligible or incoherent? What counts as "being unintelligible" or "being incoherent" here, and how can we (or can we) ascertain when this condition obtains? It would seem, from the above, that we are saying such beliefs are irrational because they are unintelligible or incoherent. But it has also been suggested that to say "a belief is irrational" is to say (among other things) that it is inconsistent, incoherent, or unintelligible. But then the *because* loses much of its force. Plainly, to make any headway here we must gain some clarity concerning what we are talking about when we claim that a religious belief is incoherent or unintelligible.

VIII

However, here, with the issues posed as they were in the previous section, we have a characteristic way of posing philosophical questions. There will be those who will feel that in posing them in that way we have unwittingly steered things in the wrong direction. There are, some will claim, no substantive norms or principles of rationality or criteria of reasonableness that afford us an Archimedean point in accordance with which we can make such sweeping judgments. The conception of rationality is too thin to give us such a skyhook. We need to take to heart Wittgenstein's penetrating and unsettling realization that there are just a diverse, sometimes incompatible, number of language games and forms of life with their attendant world pictures, with no possible objective ground (if that isn't redundant) for ranking them or choosing between them. We simply are taught (that is, socialized into) some world picture; we are unreflectively and matter-of-factly drilled in or indoctrinated in or, if you will, socialized into one such world picture. With that we have a number of beliefs—indeed, a system of beliefs—that stand fast for us, that we, at least in our practice and actual judgments, typically feel certain of and *assume* in investigating, doubting, knowing, or rationally believing. They are, if you will, our *vor Wissen* that we take as a matter of course in our diverse activities. They are the grounds, or at least the essential background, for what we rationally believe; but they themselves are ungrounded—and necessarily so. Or so Wittgenstein claims.

Christians—say, of the Middle Ages—had one such world picture with its related language games and forms of life, and Zande at the time Evans-Pritchard visited them, and contemporary Western secularists (to take two very different cases), have other importantly dissimilar world pictures. It is in accordance with these world pictures that we can say what rational/irrational or reasonable/unreasonable beliefs, practices, and institutions are. But we have no vantage point—and indeed can have no such vantage point—for making assessments of these diverse and sometimes incompatible world-pictures themselves.

If this is so, then the questions I tried to ask—or so at least it seems—are in reality questions that cannot sensibly be asked. We, it will be claimed, have no possible way of answering them that would not involve the question-begging procedure of simply, in accordance with the norms of rationality of one world picture, criticizing and judging the beliefs distinctive of a different world-picture. We use—or so it seems—one world picture as a club to beat the other world picture down. There is no way, the claim goes, of sensibly asking whether Christian belief is irrational because incoherent or inconsistent or whatever. This can no more be made out than it can be made out that English is inconsistent or German is incoherent or ordinary language is inconsistent. Such remarks are not sufficiently intelligible for the engine even to be idling.

So, at least some Wittgensteinians would say, we should not try straightforwardly to answer my questions, but we should first examine Wittgenstein's account—an account which, if near the mark, shows the senselessness or at least pointlessness of asking what I am trying to ask. However, it is also important to note that, whatever the results of that endeavor, Wittgenstein's account not only presents a challenge for arguments with a skeptical thrust such as my own, but it is also a challenge for a variety of theistic accounts as well. If one argues, as has been argued, that (a) the ontological argument, if sound, provides a rational ground for worship, and (b) argues that, as Norman Malcolm has, the ontological argument is sound, one runs afoul of the preceding Wittgensteinian questions about "rational ground."

One faces a similar difficulty if one claims that we should believe in God because the theistic interpretation is the most rational or reasonable explanation of human religious experience (see RELIGIOUS AND MYSTICAL EXPERIENCES). And finally, if Wittgenstein's remarks about rationality and world-pictures are right, it is impossible to establish in any significant way that, as John Hicks puts it, "faith-awareness of God is a mode of cognition which can properly be trusted and in terms of which it is rational to live." Even if we do not balk at "faith-awareness" and a "mode of cognition," whether it

is rational to place our trust here and so to live is trivially "answered," if we accept Wittgenstein's account, in terms of the world picture we were taught. If you were brought up with a Christian, Jewish, or Islamic world picture and the instruction and indoctrination took, it is rational for you to trust the truth of that "faith-awareness." If you were brought up with a secular or Buddhist or Zande world picture, it is not. And that is the end of it. There is, and indeed can be, no superior vantage point of reason or cross-cultural criteria of reasonableness, our *wishes* to the contrary notwithstanding.

There is, in short, if Wittgenstein is right, no vantage point from which we could make progress with the "question" that many of us—who have no taste for metaphysics at all, in certain moods at least—very much want answered: to wit, and most centrally, which vantage point or world picture is the more reasonable one to accept and to live in accordance with? These are not—and cannot be—genuine questions if Wittgenstein's account is on the mark. But that very much cuts back our human expectations and hopes. It is hard to live with that. But if Wittgenstein is right, we should reconcile ourselves to it.

IX

We should, however, be cautious about drawing such severe relativistic or skeptical conclusions. Language games and forms of life are not *compartmentalized*. The criteria of rational appraisal I have described cut across them. Very basic things like asserting, inquiring, questioning, hoping, concluding, and remonstrating are distinct language games, but these we can engage in either in a rational or a not-so-rational way. Even if we think of larger activities such as the particular forms that science, religion, and law take in a particular society at a given time, there is no good reason to think they are in a class of their own and uncriticizable. At the very least, questions can be raised about how the various practices and forms of life of a society fit together. Could we get them into wide reflective equilibrium? If elements of the law or of religion conflict with well-grounded scientific claims, or with plain and careful empirical observations of what is the case, then given these conflicts, there is plainly a need to make adjustments somewhere in the belief system of the society and, given the strong way in which the scientific claims in question and the common-sense empirical claims in question are warranted, there are good reasons in such a circumstance to abandon or radically modify at least certain elements of the religious or legal claims. *If* this is scientism, then so be it. Am I just (unwarrantedly) using modernist enlightenment criteria to batter religious points of view?

Similarly, since the language games in a given culture are not insulated from each other (they are not self-contained units), there is good reason to believe that the criteria of what it makes sense to say and believe are not utterly idiosyncratic to a particular language game. And to talk of incommensurability here assumes what Donald Davidson and others have made very questionable, namely, that that notion makes sense. Our conceptions of consistency, coherence, and evidence are not utterly language-game dependent. The words *not* and *or* do not function differently in religious, scientific, and legal discourse.

Coherence criteria are more difficult, but if, in one domain, we are forced to use conceptions that are very different from our other conceptions and that are conflicting or at least are apparently conflicting with conceptions in other domains of what it makes sense to say—conceptions we are indeed very confident of—we have good reason to be skeptical of the idiosyncratic conceptions: they are the odd person out. This is exactly the position that certain key religious conceptions appear at least to be heir to.

Jews and Christians, for example, must believe that there is an infinite individual (indeed a person) who is transcendent to the world, yet standing in a personal relation of caring for and loving the world and its creatures. Yet it is anything but evident that such talk makes any coherent sense at all. How can we give to understand that an individual is both transcendent to the world and that, at the very same time, that very same individual stands in some personal relation to it? Here the theist surely seems at least to be unsaying what he or she has just said. It is only a thinly veiled way of saying that at time *t*, *S* has property *p* and property not-*p*. Furthermore, it is anything but evident that we can understand talk of "a being transcendent to the world." If we are honest with ourselves, we should be very skeptical about whether such a conception has any coherent sense at all. And it is doubly impossible for an individual to have such a characteristic. Moreover, an "infinite individual" certainly appears to be self-contradictory. (If we say all these terms are used metaphorically, then we still must—at least in principle—be able to say in nonmetaphorical terms what they are metaphors of.)

Considerations concerning evidence are also not *that* language-game or form-of-life eccentric. It is true that theories are underdetermined by the evidence or data. We know, for example, from the archeological evidence that agricultural tools of a certain sort spread gradually into Europe over a certain period of time. But the theory that they arrived with new invading peoples who pushed out or killed the hunters and gatherers, and the opposing theory that the hunters and gatherers themselves, through cultural borrowing, gradually took up their use, are both plausible and they are both (or so it is plausible to believe) equally compatible with the evidence. The evidence does not determine which, if either, theory to accept. We cannot simply read off our theories or overall accounts from the evidence. When we have some well-elaborated and systematically coherent theories for which there is considerable evidence, the rational thing to do, again, all other things being equal, is to accept the theories for which there is the best evidence. (Stated in just the way I have, Galileo's theory is not a disconfirming instance.) Where, for all we can ascertain, the evidence is equally good, we should appeal to considerations such as fruitfulness, simplicity, elegance, or fit with accounts in adjacent fields.

While there *may* be some groundless beliefs for which nothing like evidence is in order, yet which are still rationally believed (for example, "Every event has a cause"), it is still the case that reasonable people will in most situations assume, in situations where evidence is relevant, that if their beliefs are justified there is evidence for them, and when their beliefs are not in accord with the evidence and others come up with a plausible set of beliefs that are in accord with the evidence, reasonable people will, all other things being equal, alter their beliefs in accordance with the evidence. Such remarks are not scientist remarks reflecting the hegemony of "the scientific attitude" but cut across the various forms of life and, in that crucial sense, are not the property of one particular language game or cluster of language games.

So, if my argument is near to the mark, reason is not so wanton as some have alleged it to be. Principles of rationality and reasonableness exist that are universal and there are general ways in which we can appraise practices, institutions, traditions, and forms of life—though not all of them at once—with respect to their rationality or reasonableness without being entrapped in ethnocentrism or in some tendentious doctrinal or ideological stance. Judaism, Christianity, and Islam are such forms of life, and they can be so appraised in the light of experience and reason. The consistency, coherence, and evidential warrant of Jewish, Christian, and Islamic belief is of a very low order. I have articulated a tolerably unproblematic conception of rationality, and on that conception such doctrinal belief systems are not rational or reasonably adhered to by a twenty-first-century person with a good understanding of Western scientific and philosophical culture. It is neither reasonable for such a person to believe in Azande witchcraft nor is it reasonable for such a person to believe in any of the doctrinal systems of Judaism, Christianity, and Islam. Familiarity, for those whose lives are immersed in them, typically breeds acceptance, but that is all: not reasonable or rational acceptability, given a good knowledge of the world.

BIBLIOGRAPHY

Benn, S. I., and G. W. Mortimer, eds. *Rationality and the Social Sciences*. London: Routledge and Kegan Paul, 1976.

Deardon, R. F., et al., eds. *Education and the Development of Reason*. London: Routledge and Kegan Paul, 1972.

Geraets, Theodore, ed. *Rationality Today*. Ottawa, ON: University of Ottawa Press, 1979.

Habermas, Jürgen. *The Theory of Communicative Action.* Vols. 1 and 2. Boston: Beacon, 1981.

———. *Toward a Rational Society.* Boston: Beacon, 1970.

Nielsen, Kai. "Moral Point of View." In *Encyclopedia of Ethics,* 2nd ed., edited by Laurence C. Becker and Charlotte B. Becker, New York: Routledge, 2001.

———. *Naturalism and Religion.* Amherst, NY: Prometheus Books, 2001.

———. *Naturalism without Foundations.* Amherst, NY: Prometheus Books, 1996.

———. "Philosophy as Wide Reflective Equilibrium." *Iyyun* 64 (1994).

———. *Reason and Practice.* New York: Harper & Row, 1971.

Nielsen, Kai, and D. Z. Phillips. *Wittgensteinian Fideism?* London: SCM, 2006.

Penelhum, Terence. *Religion and Rationality.* New York: Random House, 1971.

Richards, David A. *A Theory of Reasons for Action.* Oxford: Clarendon, 1971.

Wilson, Bryan R., ed. *Rationality.* Oxford: Basil Blackwell, 1970.

KAI NIELSEN

REICH, WILHELM (1897–1957), Austrian psychiatrist and sexual revolutionary. One of the most controversial writers of the twentieth century, Wilhelm Reich remains difficult to categorize. For some he was a genius whose writings on the function of the orgasm, the biological basis for neuroses, and the connection between the rise of fascism and sexual repression remain classics. For others he was an unstable eccentric whose writings on orgone energy, UFO attacks, and cancer cures were pseudoscientific at best and sheer madness at worse. Whatever one thinks about him, Reich was a true freethinker whose radical views upset all the existing power structures of his time, from the Nazis in Germany to the Communists in the Soviet Union to the members of the Eisenhower administration in the United States. As was once said of President Grover Cleveland, we should love him for the enemies he made!

Reich began his career as a member of Sigmund FREUD's circle, but was excommunicated when he questioned the efficacy of talk therapy. He developed his own approach to the mind-body problem by postulating a direct connection between repression and what he called "body armoring," holding that muscular rigidity was often caused by sexual frustration. This thoroughly materialistic view (see MATERIALISM, PHILOSOPHICAL) was perhaps his greatest contribution to the field of psychoanalysis, and for many years he was a successful practitioner in various parts of the world. He usually ended up leaving the countries where he lived (such as Austria, Germany, Denmark, and Norway), finding himself unwelcome for his advocacy of sexual liberation (he argued, for instance, that teenagers should be provided with private homes in which to experiment with sex partners) and his unorthodox political views. He was for a time a strong proponent of communism, but left the movement when he came to the conclusion that most of its advocates were essentially puritanical when it came to sexual matters. After coming to the United States he embraced the strong anticommunist views of the American conservative movement, and was therefore astonished when the US Food and Drug Administration prosecuted him for peddling false cancer cures through his production of so-called Orgone Accumulators. He had claimed to have discovered the basic force of life, "orgone," which could be harnessed for health purposes. Reich was sentenced to five years and died in prison.

One of the most moving works discussing Reich's life and career is his son Peter's *A Book of Dreams* (1989), which details from a child's viewpoint his father's iconoclasm and paranoia. It later inspired a popular song by the British singer/songwriter Kate Bush. One of Reich's strongest supporters was the philosopher Paul EDWARDS, a patient of Reich's in New York, who argued that for all of Reich's bizarre views much remained salvageable in his theories. In particular, Edwards felt that Reich's therapeutic innovations and his theory of "character armor" were still tenable, as were Reich's strong criticisms of organized religion as basically a perpetuation of patriarchal control.

Reich never wavered in his assertions that the basis for most religions was the sexual repression of believers. Religions tend to despise hedonistic enjoyment of any type, and control their members by making them ashamed of natural desires, which become perverted into desires for unachievable afterworldly bliss. All mystical and religious experiences, Reich held, are essentially antisexual and indeed substitutes for sexuality. He argued that if human beings were allowed to fulfill their sexual natures unhindered, most religions would die out and humans would for the first time in history be basically satisfied.

BIBLIOGRAPHY

Corrington, Robert S. *Wilhelm Reich: Psychoanalyst and Radical Naturalist.* New York: Farrar, Straus and Giroux, 2003.

Edwards, Paul. "Wilhelm Reich." In *The Encyclopedia of Unbelief,* edited by Gordon Stein. Amherst, NY: Prometheus Books, 1985.

Reich, Peter. *A Book of Dreams: A Memoir of Wilhelm Reich.* New York: Dutton, 1989.

Sharaf, Myron. *Fury on Earth: An Biography of Wilhelm Reich.* New York: Da Capo, 1994.

TIMOTHY J. MADIGAN

REINCARNATION. The idea of reincarnation—the view of life as a repetition of cycles and the physical world as an illusion or test—presents itself in the history of philosophy and religion in a variety of contexts. At the most basic level, the belief involves speculation about a non-material essence or "soul" which survives the body at death and which may be reincarnated or reborn in plant or animal life, or in the form of other human beings. Many ancient religions held loosely connected ideas about spiritual and physical changes after death (for example, Proteus, who could change his form at will); these seem to be derived from crude understandings of reincarnation. Similarly, although reincarnation does not normally entail belief in resurrection of the body as it has been understood in Christian theology, many scholars feel that both Judaism and early Christianity, in formulating their ideas of the afterlife, came under the influence of Greek reincarnational thought. The following article deals with the theory under the following headings: (a) Egyptian and later Near Eastern thought, (b) Eastern and Indian philosophy, (c) Greek thought, and (d) Early Christian theology.

Egyptian and Later Near Eastern Thought. It is often suggested that the origins of speculation about reincarnation can be traced to the ancient Near East (ANE) and to Egypt in particular. References to the underworld in ancient epics, such as that of Gilgamesh (second millennium BCE) seem to suggest that early inhabitants of the fertile crescent taught psychic survival as part of their religious tradition. The evidence for belief in reincarnation, however, is absent in Mesopotamian civilizations and must be read back into the literature from the religious theories of later periods. Similarly, there is no unambiguous reference to the preexistence or "transmigration of souls" (metempsychosis) in Egyptian literature, and a majority of scholars now feel that the cultures of the region, including ancient Hebrew civilization in Palestine, were generally pessimistic about after-death survival. The claim that the ancient Egyptians taught reincarnation is not based on references found in Egyptian texts, but on comments about the transmigration of the soul made by ancient Greek writers like Herodotus. The Egyptian Book of the Dead, for example, speaks of the soul being able to change itself into various life-forms after death. But this change is best understood as a sort of spiritual evolution in the heavenly realms, not a bodily return to this earth. As such, the belief seems to anticipate the later Christian and Gnostic idea that in ascending to heavenly realms to become "conformed" to life beyond the world, the soul undergoes a divestiture of physical substances. James Breasted, a noted professor of Egyptology at the University of Chicago, summarized the opinion of most Egyptologists when he said, "It was this notion [divestiture] which led Herodotus to conclude that the Egyptians believed in what we now call transmigration of souls, but this was a mistaken impression on his part." While it is true the ancient Egyptians believed both in an afterlife and in a "spiritual" realm beyond the world, the practice of mummification and the filling of burial

chambers with practical items and symbolic trinkets was intended to prepare the deceased for the next world, not a return to this one or for survival as some other life-form.

It is equally clear that the Egyptian understanding of afterlife was based on an ancient caste system: members of the royal family and perhaps adopted members of the household were considered privileged to enjoy the benefits of the afterlife as reward for their high social standing. Ordinary persons were not included in the number of the elect, and were not considered able to transcend the limits of physical existence. In Egypt this belief remained fundamentally a hierarchical one: Eternal life is available to the few, forbidden to the many, and was a matter of class rather than moral status. This theme persists in the Gnostic religions of Upper Egypt until at least the fifth century CE.

The Near East beyond Egypt. Some references to reincarnation can be found in Zoroastrianism (Persian dualism), which flourished as early as the seventh century BCE; and in Mithraism, a mystery religion which survived into late antiquity and which preserves significant elements of the Persian cosmology. Mithraism was typical of the many salvation cults which emerged from the social and political upheavals that followed in the wake of Alexander the Great's colonization of the eastern Mediterranean. As the Middle East became more cosmopolitan, many ethnic and religious groups were uprooted and brought into contact with others in the mixing process known as religious syncretism. The resulting amalgamation of religious ideas and practices acted as a crucible which forged new religious movements with occult overtones, and these in turn were blended with Greek and Persian philosophy. In many respects these cults were expanded versions of more ancient expressions of pantheistic shamanism—the "witch doctor" religions of spirit worship common to all cultures. A crude form of reincarnation or rebirth remains a fairly common belief in shamanistic systems, with examples still to be found in Africa, the South Pacific, rural Asia, and even Alaska. These survivals encourage many scholars to conclude that the early roots of the doctrine lay in ancestor worship, fear of the dead, and other spectral practices rooted in tribal society.

Islam. Of the major world religions, only Islam persists as a dominant force in the contemporary Middle East. Arising some six centuries after the time of Jesus, Islamic belief is derived largely from biblical thought and history, though claiming its immediate derivation from its prophet, Muhammad. As a result of its grounding in biblical eschatology, the orthodox mainstream of Islam has disavowed reincarnation, adhering to the orthodox Judeo-Christian concept of resurrection of the dead and a Day of Judgment. It is sometimes maintained that the mystical wing of Islam, the Sufis, whose beliefs incorporate considerable oriental teaching and practice, have been believers in reincarnation since their inception. Showing traces of both Asian and

Gnostic influence, Sufism emphasizes the theme of the "journey" of the soul to life and spiritual rebirth. Scholars of the Sufi tradition however point out that the most prominent Sufi teacher, the imam al-Ghazali, insisted on the fashioning of individual souls and their "infusion" into human bodies at the moment of creation. Since the preexistence of the soul and its multiple rebirth is a defining feature of reincarnational belief, it is difficult to see Sufism as an exemplar of the tradition.

Eastern and Indian Philosophy. The precise historical origins of reincarnation doctrines in the East are difficult to trace, largely because Eastern philosophy is less concerned with the history and dating of events than the West. Nevertheless, most historians of religion would agree that the idea of reincarnation had its origin in the ancient speculative philosophies of India. A few Hindu scholars insist that the oldest of the Hindu scriptures, the Samhitas (not before 1200 BCE), teach reincarnation; but in fact no clear statement of the doctrine can be found in this very early literature. The majority of experts concur that the pervasive teaching of the Vedas is that of resurrection and immortality with the gods, similar to that found in other polytheistic religions of the time. The absence of early references to reincarnation in the Vedic literature suggests that the idea was not taught by the Aryans, who recorded these first Hindu scriptures. The first agreed mention, though very brief, comes in the Brihadaranyaka Upanishad, dating from the sixth century BCE. More elaborate discussion comes in the so-called Puranic age, at the time that the Puranas were composed, then cross-fertilized with Buddhist ideas. Many would date common acceptance of reincarnation in Hinduism from about 300 BCE, by which time the theme had been substantially explored by the Greeks.

R. C. Zaehner, an Oxford orientalist, was one of the first to argue that it is only when we come to the Upanishads that we first meet with the doctrine that was to become central to all Hindu thought. Zaehner maintained that in the Rig (earliest) Veda "the soul of the dead is carried aloft by the fire god, Agni, who consumes the material body at cremation, to the heavenly worlds where it disports itself with the gods in perfect, carefree bliss. There will be eating and drinking of heavenly food and drink, reunion with father, mother, wife and sons." In the Brihadaranyaka Upanishad (6.2. 15–16), however, a distinction is made. Purified by the fire that has consumed their bodies, the dead pass on into the flame, the day, the world of the gods, and hence into the lightning. A spiritual person conducts them into the worlds of Brahman. Of these there is no return; they have achieved eternal bliss. The followers of the sacrificial cult, however, pass on into smoke, the night, the world of the fathers, and finally into the moon. There they become the food of the gods: "but when that passes away from them, they descend into space, from space into the air, from air into the rain, and from rain into the earth. When they reach the earth, they become food. Once again they are offered as an oblation in the fire of a man, and thence they are born in the fire of a woman. Rising up into the worlds, they circle round within them. But those who do not know these two ways, become worms, moths, and biting serpents." Here, Zaehner thought, for the first time we meet the fully-fledged doctrine of rebirth.

While unarticulated ideas of postdeath survival predate belief in reincarnation, a popular doctrine of rebirth seems to have flourished from about 300 BCE. It is more apparent in the later scriptures, such as the late Upanishads and especially the Bhagavad-Gita. This semicanonical text, rewritten and edited well into the common era, refers pointedly to reincarnation in a number of passages, as when Krishna says to Arjuna: "Just as a person casts off worn-out garments and puts on others that are new, even so does the embodied soul cast off worn-out bodies and take on others that are new."

Buddhism. Belief in spiritual rebirth has been an integral part of Buddhism as well, although the imagery and vocabulary used in the Buddhist tradition differs somewhat from the Hindu system. The Sanskrit word *Samsara* or "wandering" is usually employed when speaking of the cycle of karma (justice) and rebirth. In ordinary use today among Buddhists and Hindus, it is taught as a law rather than as a doctrine subject to debate. Nonetheless, debate seems to have been fairly common among philosophers and sages in the Buddha's day (see BUDDHISM, UNBELIEF WITHIN). Whether the Buddha himself actually believed in its physical reality, taught it as an ethical concept, or as the continuance of the life force in some abstract sense is unclear. Classical Buddhist doctrine postulates the existence of *skandhas*, which are usually imagined as unrelated psychic energies or "causes" that are dissolved upon death and reactivated at birth. However, this notion is impersonal and hence different from the Hindu concept of an individual soul being reborn. In Buddhist speculation, each individual is born with characteristics from a variety of past lives and other karmic sources, in the same way a new house might be assembled from the wreckage of many houses. The characteristic ambiguity of Buddhism on this point is evident in this quotation from the Majjhima Nikaya, attributed to the Buddha himself upon being asked whether the world is eternal: "I have not elucidated that the world is eternal, and I have not elucidated that the world is not eternal. I have not elucidated that the saint exists after death, I have not elucidated that the saint does not exist after death. I have not elucidated that the saint both exists and does not exist after death."

The influence of reincarnational thought can be seen in early Chinese religion and philosophy as well. While such speculation is generally accepted in Taoism, for instance, its founder, the philosopher Lao-tse, did not explicitly teach reincarnation (see TAOISM, UNBELIEF WITHIN). Lao-tse's disciple Chuang-tzu, on the other hand, did teach the doctrine. Plausibly, therefore, reincarnational thought developed in China at about the same time it was being accepted in India.

Greek Thought. PLATO knew and employed a concept of reincarnation as a literary device in his dialogues, most famously in the tenth book of the *Republic* ("The Myth of Er"). It is not absolutely certain how literally one should take his references, since they are tied to his larger understanding of the immortality of the soul, the form of justice and the good, and the soul's inevitable separation from the body. Plato's laconic reference to the doctrine is attributed to SOCRATES, who speaks of it as an "ancient belief"—perhaps an allusion to the teaching of the mathematician-philosopher PYTHAGORAS, who held to a belief in metempsychosis, or successive reincarnation of the soul in different species until its eventual purification (particularly through the intellectual life of the ethically rigorous Pythagoreans). In both the Platonic and Pythagorean forms of the belief, the soul's preexistence and survival is contrasted with the imperfection and mutability of the physical body. The presence of the soul accounts for life, mind, and the potential for knowledge; its absence for death and decay. As with the presocratic idea of *nous* and *logos*, especially among the followers of Heraclitus, the mind-principle is conceived as an energy which "inhabits" material (the *soma* or body) but is not coextensive with it.

While Greek influence in the West faded with the demise of Alexander the Great's empire the doctrine of reincarnation survives in Roman philosophy, chiefly among the Stoics, and in the neo-Platonism of Plotinus and others. Both STOICISM and Neoplatonism possessed theosophical traits which mixed philosophical speculation with the teachings of the mystery religions, influences from Persia and India, and elements of traditional religion from the Greek and Roman pantheon. The "perfecting" of the soul for a higher existence through a series of rebirths was incorporated in both systems, which tended to see "salvation" as the solution of the body-soul dichotomy. A religious movement with an inconsistent teaching of reincarnation was Christian (and other) "Gnosticism," not a single religious phenomenon but a salad of beliefs which incorporated theological, mystagogic, and philosophical ideas about the origin and destiny of the soul. In its developed form in Egypt, North Africa, and the Middle East, gnosticism taught a division of humanity into elect, struggling, and "earthly" castes, determined on the basis of their spirituality and the soul's capacity for knowledge (*gnosis*) of revealed truth. Gnosticism taught the transmigration of souls among the spiritual class without, apparently, regard for moral evaluation or karmic law. The capacity for knowledge and hence for "salvation" from the entropy of the material world was denied to the *hylics* or "earthly," in much the same way ancient Egyptian speculation denied the benefits of the afterlife to the lower classes of society. Typically, where the doctrine is present, the speculation of late antiquity stressed that the goal of reincarnation is not the enjoyment of successive mortal life but the cessation of the pain of rebirth, often imagined as the regathering of the "fullness of the godhead" to primordial unity (*Pleroma*). Individual (pyschic) survival is not the goal of stoic discipline or gnosis, and in this respect reincarnational thought found itself at odds with rapidly evolving Christian ideas about the afterlife and personal immortality.

Pre-Christian and Christian Europe. The settlers of northern and central Europe, such as the Teutons, Celts, and Druids, had fairly sophisticated religious systems which were probably influenced by the thought of Greece and its colonies. Germanic and Celtic thought seems to have had points of contact with some forms of Eastern thought. Life was considered a time of trial: if its initiation was successfully passed, the spirit rested after death until the moment came for another return to earth. This continued until, after many lives, some attained to the state of spiritual perfection. These connections to the speculation of Greece, Rome, and the East were quickly obscured by the triumph of biblical religion after the fourth century CE.

The mainstream of Jewish tradition prior to the Hellenization of Palestine after the fourth century BCE shows a deficit in regard to speculation about reincarnation and resurrection, the latter becoming the core doctrine of the early Christian movement. Early Judaism possessed no dogma of resurrection and was silent on the subject of the soul's rebirth, preferring instead to emphasize a monism of body and soul.

Early Christian Theology. As a textual matter, the Bible does not teach the rebirth of souls. Nevertheless, at various times in the history of the church, particular passages have been interpreted by some theologians and movements to support a belief in reincarnation. Chief among these are John 6:4–5, words directed at the "seeker" Nicodemus ("One who has not been born again cannot inherit the kingdom of God") and a tradition relating to John the Baptist as the reincarnation of the prophet Elijah (Matt. 11:14: "If you are willing to accept it, he [John] is Elijah who is to come"; cf. 2 Kings 2:11). In general however, it is best to conclude with Geddes Macgregor that "[r]eincarnation was certainly not part of the principal ideological furniture of the Bible as it was of the literature of India that was the heritage of Buddha."

Reincarnation and the Early Church. Reincarnation was not officially condemned as heretical by the church until the sixth century. Prior to that time, individual Christian writers explored the doctrine with greater or less enthusiasm for its theological usefulness, most finding it, however, irreconcilable with a belief in personal immortality and a literal day of "final" judgement or eschaton. Of these, the most significant are the second-century writer Justin Martyr and the third-century theologian Origen, whose views concerning the preexistence of the soul were belatedly condemned at the Council of Constantinople in 553. In his "Dialogue" with Trypho,

Justin speaks of the soul inhabiting more than one human body, and mentions a belief that souls which fail in their duty pass into grosser forms." Justin does not embrace the idea, however, and agrees with his Jewish opponent Trypho that "souls neither see God nor migrate into other bodies."

The greatest controversy on the subject of reincarnation in the early church has raged around Origen, who is sometimes put forward as the most prominent proponent of the doctrine among the church fathers. Origen's views, however, were based on his radical insistence that the immortality of the soul entails its preexistence, in the same way the birth of the human person in time entailed the fact of his death. In his later writings, Origen explicitly denies a belief in reincarnation: "Let others who are strangers to the doctrine of the Church, assume that souls pass from the bodies of men into the bodies of dogs. We do not find this at all in the Divine Scriptures." Similar reviews of the belief, which was well attested in the opinions of the early writers up to the sixth century, are found in the writings of Tertullian, Jerome, and Irenaeus. Jerome's "Letter to Avitus" criticizes Origen for his Platonic ideas, and in a "Letter to Demetrius" he refutes Origen's teaching on preexistence, calling the latter's literary ramblings "a fountainhead of gross impiety." Jerome completes a succession of Middle Eastern and North African Christian writers who saw belief in reincarnation as fundamentally damaging to a belief in personal immortality as dogmatic accompaniment to the doctrine of the resurrection. Irenaeus devoted the entirety of chapter 33 of his polemic "Against Heresies" ("Of the Absurdity of the Doctrine of Transmigration of Souls") to refuting heretical appraisals of orthodox belief in resurrection, and Tertullian of Carthage lambasted the teaching of Pythagoras, concluding that "the doctrine of transmigration is a falsehood which is not only shameful, but also hazardous. It is indeed manifest that dead men are formed from living ones; but it does not follow from that, that living men are formed from dead ones." Among Christian scholars who studied the writings of pagan antiquity, Gregory of Nyssa was the most critical of the theory of transmigration: "They tell us that one of their sages said that he, being one and the same person, was born a man, and afterwards assumed the form of a woman, and flew about with the birds, and grew as a bush, and obtained the life of an aquatic creature. And he who said these things of himself did not, so far as I can judge, go far from the truth: for such doctrines as this, saying that one soul passed through so many changes, are really fitting for the chatter of frogs and jackdaws, the stupidity of fishes, or the insensibility of trees."

The nearly univocal view of the Christian West as it came more and more to be associated with the concept of "orthodoxy" (concurrence with the dogmatic pronouncements of bishops and councils) was that any attempt to accommodate reincarnational thought detracted from the doctrine of personal moral responsibility and the belief in individual immortality—especially the doctrine of future reward and punishment. Augustine, himself trained in the Platonic tradition and a Manichaean for a decade before his conversion, rejects the idea that souls can be "imprisoned" in the body for the deeds of past lives.

R. JOSEPH HOFFMANN

RELIGION. A word of many uses, in the past *religion* was an honorable word. One might reject the ideas it carried, but one could respect the integrity of the word itself. Today its meaning has largely disintegrated. This has caused considerable confusion, not least in the world of HUMANISM, RATIONALISM, SECULARISM, and FREETHOUGHT. In response to this confusion, the Board of Directors of the INTERNATIONAL HUMANIST AND ETHICAL UNION passed the following resolution in 1989:

Use of the word "religion"

Being concerned about the confusion and contention sometimes caused by the words "religion" and "religious":

This Board wishes to place on record the following points which can be agreed by all Humanists:

a. Some Humanists use the word "religion" as roughly equivalent to "LIFE STANCE"; others take it to imply some theistic or non-naturalistic reality.
b. Those Humanists who use the word "religious" to describe themselves or their organizations do not imply that their Humanism accepts any theistic or non-naturalistic realities.
c. In the sense of the word "religion" which implies "accepting a god," Humanism is not a religion; in the sense of "religion" meaning "life stance," Humanism is a religion.
d. There is disagreement among Humanists about which is the "true" or "appropriate" meaning of the word "religion."

Religion and God. *God* and his works are key problems for religion. As *God* is indefinable, I base my analysis on a *necessary condition* for the reality of any god. This is based on the concept *naturalistic*:

The universe is *naturalistic*: Values, purposes, meanings, and symbols derive only from evaluations by, and intentions of, natural beings.

A *natural being*: a being capable of consciousness and limited by a material body.

This is an abbreviated definition of *naturalistic*. Ideals are not excluded, nor are extraterrestrial conscious beings, if they are limited by material bodies.

I introduce the word *superpurposive* for use in discussions of religion because *supernatural* has prejudicial associations with such dubious concepts as fairies, magic, and witch doctors:

> A *superpurposive being*: a being that evaluates and is not limited by a material body.

> The universe is *superpurposive*: There are values etc. which do not derive from evaluations etc. by natural beings. (Typically, they are the evaluations of a superpurposive being, but the Platonic Good [see PLATO] also is superpurposive.)

It seems plausible to accept that any meaningful god is superpurposive. Gods are seen as not limited by a material body, and also as evaluating things. For example, the Christian God loves us. The incarnation of the Christian God, like those claimed for the Hindu gods (see HINDUISM AND UNBELIEF), do not deny their transcendence of body. *Superpurposive*, thus defined, can replace the slippery and uncertain words *transcendent* and *spiritual* when these words are used in nonnaturalistic senses.

Religion is wider than God, but traditional concepts of religion appeal to a superpurposive reality. Thus the basis of the *Oxford English Dictionary* definition of *religion* is: "Recognition on the part of man of some higher unseen power as having control of his destiny, and as being entitled to his obedience, reverence, and worship." This "higher unseen power" must be superpurposive. Further, "life after death" also implies a superpurposive state, unless combined with resurrection of the body and the absence of consciousness until then. A "spiritual" existence for human beings after death would seem to imply a life with values but without a material body; again, this is superpurposive. Spiritualism (see SPIRITUALISM AND UNBELIEF) and communication with the dead through a medium are superpurposive. The idea of REINCARNATION as in Eastern religions presupposes a continuity of the person. This will include his or her evaluations, until nirvana has been reached. Primitive religions manifestly appeal to superpurposive powers. But a significantly different category of *naturalistic religion* has emerged over the last few centuries.

I will look at the ways "religion" has developed in response to new understanding. I will first look at those who have sought to keep a superpurposive reality in their religion. I will then look at those who have rejected the idea of *God*. Both these parts fall into two parts.

Maintaining a Meaningful God. People who have sought to keep God in their religion have responded in two ways: a conservative or full-blooded approach, and a liberal approach. Conservatives have countered attacks on belief by making claims that, if true, would allow a positive understanding of God to survive. Liberals have attenuated and obfuscated the idea of God in ways that conceal the term's degeneration. Christianity and Judaism are the principal homes of the latter approach, Islam of the former; Christianity, however, has a very strong conservative wing. Numerically, liberals are in decline, conservatives expanding. It is doubtful whether Anglicanism can avoid a schism between conservatives and liberals as here defined.

Full-blooded, doctrinally conservative Christianity may be summed up as *fundamentalism*, a term introduced in 1909 to refer to the inerrancy of the Bible, including in particular God's creation of the world, Christ's virgin birth, physical resurrection and future return in glory, and original sin, with Jesus's death as sacrifice for mankind. In all of this, Roman Catholicism is traditionally fundamentalist in substance; but fundamentalism in its proper sense also rejects any authority other than the Bible, so it rejects the Catholic acceptance of an authoritative tradition. Further, Rome has yielded more to science than has fundamentalism, for instance, accepting some elements of DARWINISM.

God's creation of the world has always been fundamental to Christian thought. *Evolution as such* does not exclude intelligent design (see INTELLIGENT DESIGN THEORY), for evolution might depend on a designer at certain key points. On the other hand, *naturalistic evolution* poses a fundamental threat, for random variation plus natural selection excludes God from the process *by definition*. Intelligent design is excluded only if naturalistic processes are sufficient at all key points.

The claim of biblical inerrancy (see BIBLICAL ERRANCY) still leaves open a wide range of ways for interpreting the text. For example, the six "days" of the Genesis creation story can be interpreted as "periods," and "begat" as "ancestor of." Creation extending over a long period is not inconsistent with a superpurposive creator; God might have employed the naturalistic processes accepted by geologists for the evolution of most features of the world. Different religious traditions reject different naturalistic claims, generating different interpretations of "religion," with the doctrine that the world was created from nothing in 4004 BCE at one extreme. The Roman Catholic church now seems to accept biological evolution. Some fundamentalist claims about evolution have a "flat Earth" quality, and they can be rejected as such. But if intelligent design is necessary for the evolution of humanity, God is necessary for creation. Thus naturalism, which rejects these assertions, requires PHYSICALISM and an effective naturalistic account of morality (see MORALITY FROM A HUMANIST POSITION).

Personal experience also is important, and not only for fundamentalists. Extreme manifestations—for example, those who have come to "know Jesus" at an evangelical meeting, or find their PRAYER answered, or seem to witness a miracle (see MIRACLES, UNBELIEF IN)—may come to an unshakable belief, however well argued the alternative interpretation. This is *evangelical religion*.

Keeping an Attenuated God. The pressures of liberal

thought lead to the abandonment of religious values, the abandonment often being justified by absurd interpretations of Scripture. For example, the Bible very clearly condemns homosexuality, as in Romans 1:24–27. Therefore Christian liberals who take inclusive positions toward homosexuality indulge in manifestly absurd manipulations of the text. Likewise, Muslim leaders point to the Qur'an's sura 5:32 to prove that Islam condemns killing people; but if one reads on one realizes that this passage forbids only the killing of those friendly to Islam, whereas (as demonstrated in the verse immediately following) nothing is too bad for those who attack Islam (see ISLAM AND UNBELIEF).

Another cause of religious decay is the widespread rejection of ethnocentrism: We no longer consider ourselves entitled to say that our culture is better than any other. Then must all the major religions be true? John Hick, a leading exponent of this view, solves the apparent contradictions by saying that no claim about the Real (his term that replaces "God") is either true or false. This would make acceptance of the Real literally useless. But Hick's basic claim is that no categories in human thought can describe the Real. So he saves religion by making an exception: *the Real is good from our point of view*. Thus he is able to draw positive conclusions.

The liberal wing of Christianity often expresses contempt for a "God of the gaps," that is, a conception of God postulated to fill gaps in our scientific explanations of reality. But rejecting a "God of the gaps" ultimately destroys God. For the only reasons to accept a superpurposive reality involve explaining those aspects of reality inexplicable on naturalistic, that is to say scientific, grounds. So, if a supposed God *explains no gaps*, there is *no reason* to accept his reality. Belief in god would be arbitrary, or based on a tradition based on nothing.

Finally, we come to Paul Tillich, whose radically inclusive definition of God drives much liberal religious thinking. Tillich opens an argument, "The name of this infinite and inexhaustible depth and ground of all being is *God*." He then allows "if that word has not much meaning for you, translate it, and speak of the depths of your life, of the source of your being, of your ultimate concern, of what you take seriously without any reservation." From this he concludes: "You cannot then call yourself an atheist or unbeliever." This is the ultimate degradation of religion: so to interpret god, that belief in God is the same as atheism.

No God. One may well conclude that there is no superpurposive reality. But this does not mean that there is no "ultimate reality." The happiness and suffering of individuals is ultimately important, and that (with the other elements identified in MORALITY FROM A HUMANIST POSITION) constitutes a *naturalistic* "ultimate reality." I now turn to the life stance of humanism. How is the word *religion* to be used?

Traditionally, *religion* has connoted not only God, but also ideas of commitment, community, morality, and much more. This does not make these concerns depend on "God"; they are essential human concerns which belong to all human beings. God believers have embezzled them. How then does a humanist interpret the word *religion*? One may recover these essential human concerns from the god believers in two ways.

People who have suffered the moral distortions introduced by appeal to "God" may *maintain* the superpurposive implications of "religion," and condemn it.

People who have experienced the good in their religion may keep the word to mark these human concerns. They are religious humanists (see RELIGIOUS HUMANISM). They explicitly *exclude* superpurposive implications from their definition of the word *religion*.

This sets up the two uses of *religion* noted in the IHEU resolution quoted above. No fair-minded person will impose his meaning of *religion* when he interprets a statement by the other group.

Religious humanists maintain the sufficiency of human foundations, in particular for ethics. ETHICAL CULTURE founder Felix ADLER also preached tolerance: on his view the supremacy of ethics and its independence of theology are essential; rejection of theism is not. Adler therefore left an element of inadequacy. *If there really is* a "God," "his" judgments could be vital: suppose that abortion *is* murder because God implants a human soul at conception. The independence of ethics from theology *requires* a key theological claim: the *rejection* of the "God" of the so-called major world religions. This premise was left implicit. Was Adler wrong not to impose such a philosophy on all his followers?

The difference between the first and the second group among those humanists who reject God is one of temperament, not of doctrine. Therefore the addition by the first group of the adjective *secular* (see SECULAR HUMANISM), *which declared secular humanists then use as a basis for attacking the second group*, is divisive and damaging to the humanist movement. Each group should respect the temperamental differences of the other. I also argue that the addition of "religious" by declared religious humanists is unhelpful.

Names are important. Humanists have made Humanism (I and others choose to capitalize the *H*) the name of their life stance, and they should fight for it, and against Christians who have recently recognized that "humanism" is an attractive idea. But the addition of an adjective is not the only response. The initial capital "H" can mark "Humanism" as the Humanist life stance.

Condemning Religion. Finally, I note that the word *religion* may also be used to refer to the undesirable aspects of religion. The Roman philosopher LUCRETIUS interpreted religion as *being bound by superstition*. Many modern users define religion as fanatical. Modern theists also reject *religion*. Thus Dietrich Bonhoeffer rejected religion as institutionalized, a special department of life. Christians sometimes call atheism a religion, in a way that seems to be abusive.

BIBLIOGRAPHY

Stopes-Roe, Harry. "Understanding the History of Humanism." *New Humanist* 112 (December 1997).

HARRY STOPES-ROE

RELIGION IN CONFLICT WITH SCIENCE. Science and religion are modes of thought whose relationship with each other depends on viewpoint. Here we present a brief historical survey of how the relationship has been viewed in Western cultures. In general, two opposed positions may be identified. The first is a compatibilist view, which holds that science and religion are complementary and harmonious modes of knowledge.

Many historians of science would argue that the incompatibilist view is exemplified definitively in Andrew Dickson WHITE's *A History of the Warfare of Science with Theology in Christendom* (1896), which argues that theology has been a main opponent of science. However, White made a distinction, even if inconsistent, between religion and theology, which he saw as a dogmatic and arbitrary endeavor practiced by major organized religions such as the Catholic church. "Religion," which White viewed as the recognition of an "eternal law" that provided harmony for the universe, was compatible with science. A better example of an incompatibilist today might be Richard Dawkins.

A more recent trend is the so-called complexity thesis, usually attributed to John H. Brooke, which emphasizes that religion can both help and hinder science. One example is how many of the great scientists (for instance, Copernicus and Sir Isaac Newton) believed that it was their religious duty to study the universe, and also claimed that their discoveries validated their religious convictions. Complexity advocates would also argue that the very categories called "religion" and "science" did not exist in much of Western history, and so there could not have been any animosity between categories that were not recognized as such.

Part of the problem in determining the relationship between science and religion is how one defines those main terms. For our purposes, religion is a mode of life and thought premised on the existence of, and relationship with, supernatural forces and/or beings. Science relies only on one or more of the five natural senses and/or logic in order to verify any conclusions about the universe and its components. Under this definition of science, the term *supernatural* is meaningless, as it does not refer to anything that can be detected or inferred by any of the five senses and/or logic.

Ancient Times to Late Antiquity. Before the rise of Greek civilization, it is difficult to find any coherent use of nonsupernatural explanations for the universe and human experience. The eminent American Egyptologist James Henry Breasted identified the Edwin Smith Surgical Papyrus (approx. 1550 BCE) as the earliest known scientific document. This Egyptian medical manual lists physical conditions based on observation, presents diagnoses devoid of supernaturalistic language, and suggests treatment with natural substances or procedures. More contested are claims that certain healthcare consultants in ancient Mesopotamia used nonsupernatural means of healing.

The claim that the Bible contains "scientific" descriptions is found mostly in "creationist" Christian authors. For example, Isaiah 40:22, which refers to "the circle of the earth," is often used to argue that the author had supernatural knowledge of the true shape of the earth. However, the Hebrew word translated as "circle" can refer to the horizon or to the disk-shaped earth known from Babylonian sources. Other supposed instances of scientific thinking in the Bible are similarly the result of poor exegetical and linguistic analysis.

The tension between naturalistic and supernaturalistic approaches first clearly occurs in ancient Greece. In the work titled *The Sacred Disease*, Hippocrates argued that the condition often identified as epilepsy "is no more divine than any other; it has the same nature as other diseases." Hippocrates in fact argued that the disease process responsible for epilepsy was located in the human brain.

De Rerum Natura (On the Nature of Things; first century BCE) by the Roman philosopher LUCRETIUS strives to explain all of nature on the basis of naturalistic assumptions. Lucretius saw science as a tool of ethics, insofar as the purpose of the former was to help us determine how best to live a happy and productive life. Nonetheless, *De Rerum Natura* has many of the elements that are standard in modern scientific explanations, including the idea that the earth is not designed for the benefit of human beings but is the result of random processes.

Christianity in late antiquity was already seeking ways to harmonize scriptural teachings with empirical observations. The church father Tertullian is sometimes credited with the idea that nature and scripture are two complementary revelations of God's workings. This idea can be traced in one form or another to the present. Augustine, the famous church theologian, opined that God could accommodate revelation to the simpler understanding of human beings, with the result that not everything in the Bible needs be taken literally. At other times, however, Augustine proposed divine miracles to explain scriptural statements (e.g., angels ferrying animals to Noah's Ark from distant islands).

The Middle Ages. The history of science has been marked by a tendency to identify pre-Renaissance precursors for modern science. This effort is part of a broader conflict about whether the Renaissance is as innovative as thought by some scholars. Another historiographical shift has been away from viewing any medieval scientific achievement as part of a unilineal descent from ancient Greco-Roman civilization to a view that emphasizes an Islamic synthesis of Syriac, Persian, Indian, and Greco-Roman traditions. Also important was the rise of universities, which collected learned scholars and important books.

Among the compatibilists or exponents of the complexity thesis for the Middle Ages, we find David C. Lindberg, who argues that "there was no warfare between science and the church" because there was nothing close to modern science in medieval times. Nonetheless, even Lindberg grants that the reintroduction of ARISTOTLE into the West raised some serious concerns for the church's cosmology. Aristotle posited that the universe, including its basic structure and modes of operation, was eternal; this challenged the biblical notion of a divine plan with a definitive beginning and ending.

At least three responses to Aristotle were outlined: (1) The eternity of the universe could be demonstrated rationally, as argued by AVERRÖES; (2) the noneternity of the world was rationally demonstrable, as held by Saint Bonaventure; (3) reason could not decide the matter, a mediating position championed by Saint Thomas Aquinas. Nonetheless, the Aristotelian doctrine of the world's eternity was formally condemned by Catholic theologians in 1270 and 1277. The problem of causation, which can be traced to at least Aristotle and Plato, also concerned medieval theologians. Thomas Aquinas has been classified as a "concurrentist" in arguing that God and natural causes act together, in contrast to "occasionalists" who attributed all causation to God.

Similar conflicts can be seen in Islam. Averröes wrote *The Decisive Treatise on the Harmony between Religion and Philosophy*, which argued that there was no conflict between philosophy and religion. Averröes was writing in response to al-Ghazali, who believed that science must be judged by its utility for religion. In addition, al-Ghazali was an occasionalist who denied the existence of natural causes. However, some compatibilist scholars (e.g., Alnoor Dhanani in *Science and Religion: A Historical Introduction*) argue that the conflict between al-Ghazali and Averröes was untypical of medieval Islam.

The Renaissance. The Renaissance saw the beginnings of some of the most heated conflicts between religion and science, especially because new instruments such as the telescope and more careful observations of the universe found results incompatible with biblical statements about cosmology. Galileo GALILEI took one of the first steps leading toward the death of biblical cosmology by mounting a systematic challenge to the biblical notion that Earth was the center of the universe.

Ptolemy, inspired by Aristotle, held that an immovable Earth was orbited by concentric spheres in which the various planets and stars were embedded; this view was adopted as the official teaching of the Catholic Church. In contrast, Galileo sought to confirm the theory developed by the Polish astronomer Copernicus in his *De Revolutionibus Orbium Coelestium* (On the Revolutions of the Celestial Spheres, 1543) that the sun was the center of the universe. The church placed Copernicus's *De Revolutionibus* on the Index of Prohibited Books in 1616. In 1633 Galileo was tried and found guilty of teaching the Copernican system. His sentence included imprisonment, which was commuted to house arrest at his home near Florence for the remaining years of his life.

Some important historians of science argue that most of Galileo's arguments were no better empirically than those of Ptolemy, and that definitive confirmation of the Copernican system was not found until long after Galileo's death. Galileo's certainty seems to have rested on the assumption that mathematical simplicity is a guide to truth. Nonetheless, the Galileo episode shows that stark conflicts between religious and scientific conclusions were beginning to appear by the late Renaissance.

The Enlightenment through the Twentieth Century. The definitive rise of modern science is usually placed in the Enlightenment (see ENLIGHTENMENT, THE, AND UNBELIEF), a period during which we can see the compatibilist and incompatibilist positions emerge quite vigorously. Sometimes one can see incompatibilism as a natural outgrowth of the older idea that nature and revelation were two complementary books for understanding the universe. Francis Bacon, in his *Novum Organum* (1620), criticized Paracelsus, the Swiss physician and philosopher, for using the Bible to make conclusions about nature. For Bacon, the Bible often spoke metaphorically and was not a reliable source for understanding the workings of the physical universe. It was however a source for moral guidance and higher truths. In effect, Bacon, who favored empirical observation and experimentation, inspired others to make a sharp distinction between the domains of religion and science.

Isaac Newton provides a curious example of how religion and science could coexist in the same mind. Newton developed a form of calculus and outlined the law of gravitation in his brilliant *Principia Mathematica* (1687). Yet Newton was also heavily involved in the study of biblical chronology and prophecy, for instance, calculating that Jesus would return by 1948. Modern compatibilists use Newton to argue that religion and science need not be at odds. Compartmentalization of religious and scientific pursuits may also be another explanation, especially since none of Newton's scientific conclusions regarding gravity, calculus, or the spectral distribution of visible light depended directly on any supernaturalist supposition. When Newton erred, as in predicting the return of Jesus, it is when he did not use scientific rigor.

By the late eighteenth century, one finds naturalists whose work makes no reference to the supernatural. James Hutton's *Theory of the Earth* (1795), for example, lacks any reference to the Bible to draw its conclusions about the history of the earth. Charles Lyell, one of the founders of modern geology, joined other scientists of his day in beginning to blame reliance on the Bible for the retardation of scientific progress.

The first half of the twentieth century saw the meteoric rise of physics, marked by the near-total absence of any reference to supernatural premises. In the twentieth century the theories of Albert Einstein and the maturation of quantum mechanics under Erwin Schrödinger, Werner Heisenberg, and others, showed how difficult it is to speak of "cause" at the subatomic level, a fact that both compatibilists and incompatibilists have tried to cite to their advantage.

Whereas cosmology dominated the conflicts of the Renaissance and Enlightenment, biology—in particular, evolution—gained prominence in the twentieth century. The prime trigger was Charles DARWIN's *On the Origin of Species* (1859), which outlined what came to be known as the theory of evolution. For many Christians, Darwin's theories threatened the trustworthiness of the Bible, as both a scientific and a moral guide to truth (see LIFE, ORIGIN OF, AND UNBELIEF).

One hallmark of the twentieth century, particularly in America, was reliance on the legal system to define science and religion. The Scopes monkey trial (1925), wherein a Tennessee schoolteacher was prosecuted for teaching evolution, was an American highlight of this use of the legal system. Mid-twentieth-century US Supreme Court decisions urging a stronger separation of church and state led to the development of "scientific creationism," which purported to show without any recourse to biblical statements that the universe was the work of a (presumedly divine) creator. By 1987, in *Edwards v. Aguillard*, the US Supreme Court reaffirmed that evolution was "science," while scientific creationism was not. The latter, therefore, could not be taught in school as science.

Such Supreme Court decisions have prompted new refinements of creationism. INTELLIGENT DESIGN THEORY purports to show without recourse to any religious text that the universe, and particularly the earth, is intelligently designed for human habitation. However, critics argue that since the earth possesses millions of unique and infelicitous features such as viruses and cerebral palsy, intelligent design does not explain why we must conclude that the earth was especially designed for life, but not for any other unique feature, especially one deemed evil, such as cerebral palsy.

Equally significant is the globalization of the conflict between religion and science. The popular contemporary Turkish writer Harun Yahya (pen name of Adnan Oktar) promotes an Islamic version of creationism in books such as *The Creation of the Universe* (1999) and *The Disasters Darwinism Brought to Humanity* (2001). In his *Vedic Physics: Scientific Origins of Hinduism* (1999), Raja Ram Mohan Roy argues that the Hindu Vedas contain accurate descriptions of cosmology and physics, among other sciences. Usually, such non-Western harmonizations of science and religion follow indigenous as well as Euro-American models.

Another important development was the maturation of the field of the history of science itself. Thomas Kuhn's *The Structure of Scientific Revolutions* (1962) inspired many historians to argue that science is not an objective enterprise but rather a social and politically constructed endeavor. Thereafter, many Christian apologists began to use Kuhnian language to argue that science was no more objective than religion.

By the mid-twentieth century, improved technologies cured diseases previously attributed to supernatural causes. Yet the late twentieth century saw renewed efforts to integrate faith and medicine. In other ways, changing scientific definitions confronted some religious beliefs, as when the authoritative manuals of psychiatry moved away from seeing homosexuality as an illness to seeing it as part of the normal human spectrum of sexual expression. Technological changes introduced new ethical conflicts related to the prolongation of life, abortion, the increasing efficacy of contraception, and the medical utilization of biological resources such as stem cells (see BIOETHICS AND UNBELIEF). Old possibilities became realities: for example, cloning and the use of frozen embryos make it possible to be born years after the death of one's genetic parents.

Conclusion. A 1996 survey concluded that about 60 percent of scientists expressed "personal disbelief" or "doubt or agnosticism" about a personal god (see SCIENTISTS, UNBELIEF AMONG; LEUBA, JAMES). "Compartmentalization" rather than "complexity" may best explain why some scientists such as Newton could combine religious belief and scientific rationales in the same mind. Despite postmodernist academic movements that deny the existence of objective truth, universities continue to be the main exponents of nonsupernaturalistic approaches to knowledge. And if history is an indication, the relationship between religion and science will continue to center as much on sociopolitical developments as it does on epistemological issues. What is often at issue is not only epistemology but ethics, because scientific and religious moral systems can have vastly different consequences. In any case, compatibilists and advocates of complexity have yet to show where any scientific fact is directly derived, or needs to be derived, from supernatural premises.

BIBLIOGRAPHY

Avalos, Hector. "Heavenly Conflicts: The Bible and Astronomy." *Mercury* 27, no. 2 (1998).

Breasted, James Henry. *The Edwin Smith Surgical Papyrus.* 2 vols. Chicago: University of Chicago Press, 1930.

Brooke, John H. *Science and Religion: Some Historical Perspectives.* Cambridge: Cambridge University Press, 1991.

Dawkins, Richard. *A Devil's Chaplain: Reflections on Hope, Lies, Science, and Love.* Boston: Houghton-Mifflin, 2003.

Ferngren, Gary, ed. *Science and Religion: A Historical*

Introduction. Baltimore, MD: Johns Hopkins University Press, 2002.

Kurtz, Paul, ed. *Science and Religion: Are They Compatible?* Amherst, NY: Prometheus Books, 2003.

Lindberg, David C. *Science in the Middle Ages.* Chicago: University of Chicago Press, 1978.

Lloyd, Geoffrey, and Nathan Sivin. *The Way and the Word: Science and Medicine in Early China and Greece.* New Haven, CT: Yale University Press, 2002.

Numbers, Ronald, and David C. Lindberg, eds. *God and Nature: Historical Essays on the Encounter between Christianity and Science.* Berkeley and Los Angeles: University of California, 1986.

Pennock, Robert T. *Intelligent Design Creationism and Its Critics: Philosophical, Theological and Scientific Perspectives.* Cambridge, MA: MIT Press, 2001.

HECTOR AVALOS

RELIGIOUS AND MYSTICAL EXPERIENCES.

The word *religion* seems to come from the Latin *religio*, meaning a joining or yoking, which is also exactly the meaning of *yoga*. Religious experience, then, would be experience that seems to join one with the divine or the cosmos. "Mysticism" stems from the Greek root *my-* and Sanskrit *maun* or *mun*, denoting silence and secrecy. In Greek, a *mystes* was an "initiate," one who had been introduced into the secrets of the cult, concerning which one must henceforth be silent, either so as not to cast one's pearls before swine (Matt. 7:6), or because they are "unutterable utterances" (2 Cor. 12:4). Thus mystical experience would be that of which those who say don't know, while those who know don't say.

Is There a Distinctively Religious Experience? Rudolf Otto agreed with Friedrich Schleiermacher that in the absence of revealed knowledge, we must try to show that religion is still something more than morality, lest religion be reduced to morality. So he argued, based on extensive research, that there is a uniquely religious type of experience. He called it the "numinous" experience, the encounter with the Holy. We usually think of *holy* as a moral term, denoting a morally blameless character. But that is a later, rationalizing redefinition. Originally no one sought to confine God within human categories of "good" and "evil." Instead, *Holy* meant "Wholly Other." Our experience with the uncanny other is twofold. First, we experience holy terror before the *Mysterium Tremendum* because it is overpowering, full of awe, and urgent with living energy. Second, we experience the lure of the *Mysterium Fascinans*, since the Holy is experienced as inherently august or worthy of worship and praise, as well as subjectively fascinating to us. Thus we are simultaneously attracted and repelled, enthralled and afraid. We feel keenly our own unworthiness and insignificance, not moral shame but ontological deficiency. This humility is "creature feeling" (something not too different from Schleiermacher's proposed

"feeling of absolute dependence" as the essence of piety). Despite such abashment, we linger and dare to approach the Holy because, in its greatness, it is precisely what we need in order that our meager existences may be fulfilled. (Otto did not imagine that all or most religious believers actually experience the numinous. But the great religious founders must have, and the rest follow in their wake.)

Otto's theory has been widely accepted, but not by all. William James, for example, denied that there was any one specifically religious feeling. "Religious experiences" are instead constituted by the religious object and occasion of feelings that are as easily, in other contexts, moved by and directed to other things: fear, love, joy, and so forth. René Girard dismisses Otto's schema as ideological mystification of the fear inculcated by the higher classes, whose privileges all caste taboos exist to protect. There is nothing inherently "sacred" about it, unless one equates the sacred with priestcraft.

Conversion. James explains that in conversion a divided and unhappy person becomes happy and integrated as the result of a firmer grasp of religious reality. This may happen gradually or suddenly. Ordinarily we have various interests that take precedence at various times. Or we may have two parallel sets of aspirations, one of which always lies unattainable at the periphery of consciousness. But if one interest permanently takes precedence, and if this change is religious, we call it conversion—all the more if it happens suddenly. (Eric Hoffer, however, notes the same dynamics in play with conversion to any mass social movement, secular or religious.) The new commitment to religion channels and focuses all attention and emotional energy on religious subjects, providing a blessed sense of purpose and direction, though perhaps at the cost of repression and narrowness. The transformation may be effected by emotional shocks setting in motion great subconscious forces unknown to the convert and which he or she then considers to result from divine intervention, the grace of the Holy Spirit.

Conversions are a typical on-schedule puberty rite of passage, occasioned by the anxious awakening of hormones and new urges, of which the young person (likely already a churchgoer) is afraid and for which an inherited religious code makes him or her feel guilty. Conversion is a way of sublimating these libidinal energies into constructive religious channels. But, at least according to James, such conversions are a kind of imitation of the turnabouts of grown adults, who convert from irreligion to religion in a time of crisis. These latter are therefore normative for our understanding of conversion and yield two types: voluntarily wrestling oneself into repentance, and passive self-surrender. In the first case we can speak of "subconsciously maturing processes," the growth of religious attitudes, "eventuating in results of which we suddenly grow conscious." With the other type, after all agonizing seems fruitless one gives up, only to find the desired change appearing *apparently* without effort. Actually, one's strivings, now abandoned, have unleashed subconscious processes which, left alone at the point of surrender, do their work unaided. Thus the conversion is achieved, apparently, from without.

Nondualism. The obliteration of all distinction between the self, the world, and the divine is the only experience to which the adjective *mystic* may be aptly applied. Agehananda Bharati says, "[I]t is the person's *intuition of numerical oneness with the cosmic absolute, with the universal matrix, or with any essence stipulated by the various theological and speculative systems of the world.* This alone is the mystical effort; a person who pursues it, and pursues it as his overwhelmingly central avocation—doing everything else marginally, so to speak—and who at the same time *states* that he has embarked on this quest, is a mystic."

This experience appears to be available in all religions, even those with which it would not seem readily compatible theologically. We find it described in very similar terms in Vedanta Hinduism (see HINDUISM AND UNBELIEF), Mahayana Buddhism (see BUDDHISM, UNBELIEF WITHIN), Sufism, and Christianity, as in the case of Meister Eckhardt. As Gershom G. Scholem, the great authority on Jewish mysticism, says, the mystics of any tradition are perfectly willing, not to say compelled, to reinterpret the scriptures and doctrines of their tradition to accommodate their experiences. While it is not uncommon for mystics henceforth to believe that their experiences have verified the ontological truth of their faith's doctrines, such assertions are both gratuitous (since they cancel one another out) and highly relativized by the demythologizing they themselves undertake on inherited orthodoxies. Richard Jeffries, Walt WHITMAN, and others have shared nondual mystical experiences without assuming any religious beliefs at all. Nor do nondual states of consciousness presuppose or cultivate any particular moral concomitant. They are neither reserved only for the righteous nor productive of righteousness. Bharati, himself both a Hindu monk and an anthropologist, readily admits that the experience is hedonistic in character, for all its shaking profundity. In this he differs from Huston Smith, who disdains Western religion for its supposed definition of the greatest good as heavenly pleasure, preferring Eastern mysticism with its supposed desire for the greatest degree of reality.

(Jewish mysticism alone seems to shy away from nondualism, retaining some fine line between the contemplating creature and the contemplated creator. Merkabah mysticism centers upon scripture meditation leading to visionary journeys to the heavenly throne, while most Hasidic mysticism is an almost Pentecostal rejoicing in the Torah and the presence of God.)

Brain science (see COGNITIVE SCIENCE AND UNBELIEF) has to a great extent accounted for the mechanisms underlying the nondual experience, suggesting that it is occasioned by an induced stymieing in the temporal parietal lobe of that function that enables the infant to begin differentiating himself from the world around him. This, of course, is exactly what Sigmund Freud had theorized without knowing the neurology of the matter. He understood mysticism as a return to the oceanic feeling of the womb. It is important to note, however, that the ancient yogis themselves understood the chakras, the kundalini, or even the deity as imaginary constructions focusing consciousness to bring about an altogether immanent psychological transformation. They described the "gods" as resident in the chakras, thus as functions of the human psycho-organism.

Bhakti Devotion. A major rival to nondualist mysticism in Hinduism and Buddhism is the yoga of devotion, bhakti. It is the fervent, heartfelt worship of a chosen patron deity. One seeks not the apprehension of static oneness with the god, but rather a thrilling love relationship with a savior who will provide salvation for his bhaktas, symbolized in Krishna worship as the Gopis: milkmaids ("groupies," as we should say) of playful Krishna. The rapturous Hare Krishna sectarians one sees dancing and chanting to drums and flutes represent a venerable bhakti sect stemming from the fourteenth-century guru Lord Chaitanya, whom they esteem a historical avatar (incarnation) of Krishna. But one need not abandon secular life to engage in bhakti devotion. In the signal text of this tradition, the Bhagavad Gita, Krishna tells the general Arjuna that he must obey the dictates of his socially (and divinely) prescribed dharma (destiny understood as assigned caste duty) of slaughtering his foes. This emphasis is sometimes called karma yoga, in which the devotee renounces worldly motives and rewards for ordinary tasks, performing them instead as an offering to one's patron god. Other objects of bhakti devotion include the fearsome "Mommy Dearest," Kali; her husband, Siva; and Ram, the heroic avatar of Vishnu whose exploits are recorded in the *Ramayana*.

Perhaps the largest Buddhist denomination in the world, the Pure Land school of Shinran, is a bhakti faith as well. In this case, the divine patron is Amitabha (Amida) Buddha, the subject of the Sukhavati (Pure Land) Sutras. This great being is thought to have lived as a king in ancient India, where he heard the preaching of one of the previous Buddhas and vowed on the spot to bend his pious efforts toward the creation of a pure land free of worldly distractions, into which all might be reborn who devoted themselves to him by calling upon his name in faith. Many millions have taken him up on his offer since the fourth century CE, when this form of Buddhism seems to have begun. Innumerable other Buddhists are devoted with loving fervor to Avalokitesvara, "the Lord Who Looks Down" in compassionate providence. Though technically a Bodhisattva (one on the way toward Buddha-hood), this savior, who even delivers sinners from hellfire, is thought to contain and embody all Buddhas and Bodhisattvas within himself.

Christianity has its own forms of bhakti devotion-alism, including both the Roman Catholic cult of patron saints and the Evangelical Protestant "personal relationship with Jesus Christ" as one's "personal savior." This sort of Evangelical devotion seems to have originated in the late-sixteenth-century German Lutheran Pietist movement, from there spreading through Methodist revivalism, nineteenth-century Protestant world missions, and the twentieth-century Pentecostal movement—until it is now the predominant form of Christianity in the world. It might be described as a set of practices, especially daily prayer and introspection, in which Jesus functions rather like a child's "imaginary playmate."

Possession. Throughout history individuals have both sought and feared possession by alien entities, in the first case gods, in the second, demons. What is going on psychologically when people fall into trance states, believing themselves to have yielded to powerful discarnate spirits? William Sargent employed abreactive therapy with neurotic war veterans: If they could be induced to imaginatively relive their war traumas, Sargent thought, they would emerge free of them. Then Sargent discovered it was not so much the reliving of an actual past experience that did the trick as the cathartic emotional frenzy itself. Any story would do, even imaginary, so long as sufficient anger and fear were generated. The result would be calm and relief. Demonic possession, then, would be an effective imaginary experience generating the therapeutic frenzy, as well as the subsequent relief.

Structural anthropologist Claude Lévi-Strauss observed that the mythical dramas involved in primitive healing rites enable the afflicted person to give a name to what is bothering him or her and to join in the fight against it. A woman in the midst of a difficult childbirth may believe that demons are holding back the baby, and so she (or the shaman) summons Grandfather Alligator and his spiritual hosts to the fight, and she gives birth. It is required of the mythic drama only that it be analogous to the actual distress, for then it allows the sufferer to "get a handle on it" and participate in the struggle.

Both Sargent and Lévi-Strauss acknowledge that psychotherapy is a secular and naturalistic version of the very same abreactive technique. Exorcism, then, is a matter of self-fulfilling prophecy. In gaining recognition of oneself as "possessed," one is adopting a well-defined role in a game with strict rules, one of which stipulates that, after a suitable struggle with the one playing the exorcist role, one must retire from the field.

Speaking in Tongues (Glossolalia). This ancient practice of ecstatic or automatic "nonsense" speech has sometimes been understood as speaking a foreign language unknown to the speaker, thus inspired by God. Others, especially those who call it "speaking with the tongues of angels" (1 Cor. 13:1), have understood it as a metaphor, representing no literal language. Certainly the latter are correct, based on twentieth-century linguistic studies of glossolalia. For one thing, in long glossolalic utterances, "sentence melodies" (think of the formulaic singsong of news reporters or ad pitchmen) tend to be monotonously repeated, indicating artificially stylized speech. For another, each glossolalist manifests a distinct consonantal pattern (more or fewer dentals, diphthongs, etc.) which does not vary in that person's utterances, implying no foreign language, where patterns would vary, but that he or she is spontaneously "winging it," utilizing familiar speech patterns. Then there are too many "vowel rhymes" (*handalashondai*) for a genuine language. Nor is there apparent any syntactical structure, something discernable even without knowledge of a language's vocabulary. One's glossolalic utterances tend to sound more like those of one's initiator than the tongues spoken in another congregation or by a different "coach." Similarly, a congregation's glossolalic pattern is often temporarily influenced by the tongues-speech of visiting preachers. Additionally, glossolalic "sentences" or "bars" tend to be shorter and more emphatic earlier in the speech, itself rather long. Later on, the speeches as a whole tend to shrink in length, while the individual utterances become less intense run-on sentences. As time goes by, sentences become flatter, more monotone, made of fewer and easier vowels. These are not the marks of a language.

Psychological estimates of glossolalia differ widely. William James and George Barton Cutten, two of the earliest scientific investigators, viewed tongues as uncontrollable, senseless speech erupting from the subconscious like a "vocal hallucination." More recently, Felicitas D. Goodman has described it as the speech of "hyperarousal dissociation," a genuine but hardly pathological "altered state of consciousness." Julius Laffal wrote off glossolalia as a disguised or coded expression of repressed wishes on analogy with the verbal salad of schizophrenics; however, application of the Minnesota Multiphasic Personality Inventory indicates that even snake-handling Pentecostals are by no means psychologically abnormal and may even test as somewhat *less* neurotic than outsiders! John Kildahl found that glossolalists seemed more submissive, suggestible, and leader dependent than most, but other surveys by Vivier, Gerlach and Hine, and Alland found tongues-speakers to be *less* suggestible than the general population.

Carl Jung characterized speaking in tongues as the intrusion of the Collective Unconscious directly into consciousness, causing emotional instability in those who are unable to assimilate it. The Jungian Morton Kelsey, an Episcopalian priest and counselor, sees nothing aberrant in the practice: it is an entirely appropriate sign of an experience of the Collective Unconscious, which he pretty much equates with the Holy Spirit. Wayne Oates, also a pastoral counselor, and anthropologist Peter Worsley see glossolalia as a regression to infantile babbling, expressing childish megalomania and feelings of omnipotence. Worsley views this as quite natural when glossolalia occurs among oppressed peoples.

Linguist William J. Samarin describes speaking in tongues as a "pseudolanguage function" possessed by most people but seldom used, except occasionally to fake foreign languages as a joke. Religiously, it functions much like the Latin Mass before Vatican II dumbed down the liturgy into Hallmark-card English. That is, glossolalia invokes a sense of numinous mystery for those gathered for worship. It is an "audial sacrament" of the "real presence" of God. Furthermore, insofar as all members of the group are urged to practice tongues-speech at one time or another, glossolalia functions as a "sign of election" as well as a shibboleth for group solidarity.

BIBLIOGRAPHY

Bharati, Agehananda. *The Light at the Center: Context and Pretext of Modern Mysticism.* Santa Barbara, CA: Ross-Erikson, 1976.

Cutten, George Barton. *Speaking with Tongues, Historically and Psychologically Considered.* New Haven, CT: Yale University Press, 1927.

Dasgupta, S. N. *Hindu Mysticism.* New York: Frederick Ungar, 1959.

Eliade, Mircea. *Yoga: Immortality and Freedom.* Translated by Willard R. Trask. Bollingen Series 56. Princeton, NJ: Princeton University, 1970.

Erb, Peter C., ed. *Pietists: Selected Writings.* Classics of Western Spirituality. New York: Paulist, 1983.

Girard, René. *Violence and the Sacred.* Translated by Patrick Gregory. Baltimore, MD: Johns Hopkins University Press, 1977.

Goodman, Felicitas D. *Speaking in Tongues: A Cross-Cultural Study of Glossolalia.* Chicago: University of Chicago Press, 1972.

Hoffer, Eric. *The True Believer: Thoughts on the Nature of Mass Movements.* New York: Harper & Row, 1951.

James, William. *The Varieties of Religious Experience: A Study in Human Nature, Being the Gifford Lectures on Natural Religion Delivered at Edinburgh in 1901–1902.* New York: New American Library, 1958.

Kildahl, John P. *The Psychology of Speaking in Tongues.* New York: Harper & Row, 1972.

Lévi-Strauss, Claude. *Structural Anthropology.* Translated by Claire Jacobson and Brooke Grundfest Schoepf. Garden City, NY: Doubleday Anchor, 1967.

Nicholson, Reynold A. *The Mystics of Islam.* London: Routledge and Kegan Paul, 1963.

Otto, Rudolf. *The Idea of the Holy: An Inquiry into the Non-rational Factor in the Idea of the Divine and Its Relation to the Rational.* Translated by John W. Harvey. London: Oxford University Press, 1924.

———. *Mysticism East and West: A Comparative Analysis of the Nature of Mysticism.* Translated by Bertha L. Bracey and Richenda C. Payne. New York: Macmillan, 1932.

Sargent, William. *The Mind Possessed: A Study of Possession, Mysticism and Faith Healing.* Baltimore, MD: Penguin, 1975.

Scholem, Gershom G. *Major Trends in Jewish Mysticism.* New York: Schocken, 1961.

Smith, Huston. *Forgotten Truth: The Primordial Tradition.* New York: Harper & Row, 1976.

ROBERT M. PRICE

RELIGIOUS HUMANISM. Most contemporaries will understand HUMANISM as meaning "without God." The academic discipline of comparative religion could, however, have reminded us that several major religious traditions have long had variants that are "without god or gods"—Buddhism (see BUDDHISM, UNBELIEF WITHIN), Hinduism (see HINDUISM AND UNBELIEF), Jainism, CONFUCIANISM, Taoism (see TAOISM, UNBELIEF WITHIN). This article, nevertheless, will operate within the current Western meaning and treat "religious humanism" as a very recent movement holding that, to remain viable, religion must outgrow previous god-concepts and related practices.

While some Protestant and Roman Catholic Christians have called themselves humanist, this article will restrict itself to that considerably smaller group of persons recognized in academic circles and Internet circles as religious humanists in our time.

This modern religious humanism is much more than ATHEISM or AGNOSTICISM—although for most adherents it may well have begun with and remained grounded in some form of nontheism. Humanists, religious as well as secular, are strongly monistic and naturalistic (see NATURALISM)—there is but one world and one life, and the search for optimal values in the here and now is the supreme human quest.

Contemporary religious humanism has emerged largely from Unitarian circles (see UNITARIANISM TO 1961). In turn, those Unitarians who became religious humanists had in almost all cases first moved into or through a "liberal Protestant" position. In that intermediate orientation they had probably already discovered that religions change over time.

At the end of the eighteenth century, modern science combined with the thought of David HUME and Immanuel KANT had made it almost impossible for thoughtful persons to retain most of the classical arguments for theism (see EXISTENCE OF GOD, ARGUMENTS FOR AND AGAINST). Charles DARWIN demolished the last argument based upon alleged design in the universe (see EVOLUTION AND UNBELIEF). This left only newer arguments from moral values, intuition, and feelings—variously developed by Friedrich Schleiermacher, Albrecht Ritschl, the rise of a "social gospel," and several putative reconstructions of a "historical Jesus."

In the United States, the same freedom that allowed hundreds of denominations to be created allowed radical religious experimentations and freethinking (see FREETHOUGHT). The Civil War had shown that it was impossible to speak meaningfully of a "Christian ethic" (since slavery had polarized most denominations). The emerging industrialism—with the immigration, racism, and imperialism it spawned—led to workers' unrest and suffragist movements (see ANARCHISM AND UNBELIEF; LABOR MOVEMENT AND UNBELIEF; WOMAN SUFFRAGE MOVEMENT AND UNBELIEF). For some Christians, arrogant triumphalism had been transcended by means of interreligious conferences and movements. But World War I again exposed the impotence of any alleged "Christian ethic."

In this same period, individual Unitarians, Universalists (see UNIVERSALISM TO 1961), Quakers, and Reform Jews had created organizations such as the Free Religious Association to develop posttraditional formulations (see UNITARIAN UNIVERSALISM; ETHICAL CULTURE). In some university-affiliated Protestant seminaries such as Harvard, Boston, and Chicago, frustrated theologians were exploring the viabilities of such modernisms as naturalistic theism, finite theism, process theism, naturalistic mysticism, and scientific theism. The most adventurous were even wrestling with Søren KIERKEGAARD's "infinite qualitative distance" (between the biblical God and us) and with Friedrich NIETZSCHE's Zarathustra proclaiming that "God is dead."

Religious humanism as such emerges from the efforts of several Unitarian ministers and several philosophers who mostly had Unitarian sympathies. John Dietrich, Curtis Reese, and Charles Francis Potter, the ministers, interestingly enough, had all grown up in quite conservative Protestant denominations. And the Unitarianism into which they settled was outside of the established New England conservative small-town variety. The American West had been developed by more adventurous ministers, including women (who were not likely to be called to congregations on the Eastern Seaboard).

Potter began as a Baptist minister, converted to Unitarianism, served a Universalist church, and finally in 1929 moved beyond churches to found the First Humanist Society of New York City. His books, many related to biblical scholarship, were widely read, and Mason Olds lists him as one of the main leaders of early humanism. His later interests in parapsychological issues distanced him from most other humanists.

Dietrich began as a Reform minister but was ousted for HERESY. He then took a Unitarian pulpit in Spokane, Washington, and soon attracted crowds so large that a theater auditorium was rented. He began using the term "humanism" there, and in 1916 was called to the First Unitarian Society of Minneapolis, a group with a liberal history. Reese began as a Southern Baptist minister, and shifted to the Unitarians in 1913. From his Iowa pulpit he worked on a number of social causes and then became secretary of the Western Unitarian Conference, based in Chicago. Reese had been using the term "democratic

religion," but after a 1917 meeting with Dietrich began calling it "humanism."

Both were influenced by a University of Michigan professor, Roy Wood Sellars, whose books were proclaiming that the next step for religious people would be humanistic religion. When his ideas were also published by the Unitarians, the full-scale "humanist-theist" controversy emerged. In 1928 a Humanist Fellowship emerged among Chicago students, and in 1932 Sellars drafted a "Humanist Manifesto." Despite the economic depression gripping the country, this heavily optimistic document was published the following year. Signers included the professors John DEWEY, Edwin A. Burtt, A. Eustace Haydon, and J. A. C. Fagginer Auer. Jacob Weinstein (a Reform rabbi) and several ministers, mostly Unitarian, also signed.

The manifesto asserted that all supernaturalisms must be abandoned in order for human creativity to flourish, and for the "complete realization of human personality to occur." The new humanistic religion would extend to all human activities ("labor, art, science, philosophy, love, friendship, recreation") and will include cooperative social commitments, with the recognition "that existing acquisitive and profit-motivated society has shown itself to be inadequate and that a radical change in methods, controls, and motives must be instituted."

The signatories concluded: "Though we consider the religious forms and ideas of our fathers no longer adequate, the quest for the good life is still the central task for mankind. Man is at last becoming aware that he alone is responsible for the realization of the world of his dreams, that he has within himself the power for its achievement. He must set intelligence and will to the task."

The American Unitarian Association (AUA), distraught over its slow growth, appointed a Commission of Appraisal whose report in 1937 supported religious pluralism (and therefore kept conservative forces from suppressing humanism). Its chair, Frederick May Eliot, then served as AUA president until his death in 1958.

In 1941 the AMERICAN HUMANIST ASSOCIATION (AHA) was formed with Curtis Reese as president. As it grew, more secular liberals joined and the Unitarian dominance weakened. Corliss LAMONT, for instance, a major contributor and author, had little interest in, and few expectations for, a "religious" humanism.

To preserve the option for a humanism within a religious context, within the AHA and elsewhere, Edwin Wilson, along with other Unitarian ministers, founded the Fellowship of Religious Humanists in 1963. The name was later gender-corrected to "Friends of" and currently is HUUmanists. With Wilson as editor, the journal *Religious Humanism* began in 1967.

Within the ETHICAL CULTURE movement there was a development paralleling the humanistic emergence within Unitarian and Universalist circles. With this acceptance of a "humanist" labeling often went a willingness to see their movement as "religious." The movement had historically focused on the "ethical" rather than the "religious" (Deed before Creed). Felix ADLER's underlying philosophical idealism was being replaced by a naturalistic PRAGMATISM. The initial aversion to supplanting any former religions that members might have chosen to retain privately had also been lessening. Thus closer cooperation and interchange occurred.

The Massachusetts Convention of Universalists, in 1948, underwrote the Charles Street Meeting House as a radical experiment. Kenneth Patton explored the world's religions naturalistically and produced a large body of humanistic poetry, prose, and hymnody. For instance, Luther's Reformation tocsin "A Mighty Fortress" was rewritten as "Man is the Earth Upright and Proud."

Leaders and ministers moved back and forth within these movements, and common educational programs were emerging for young people. Some of the unfulfilled dreams of the Free Religious Association were being realized.

In 1961 the Unitarians and Universalists effected a merger, using such adjectives as "free" and "liberal" to describe themselves. A 1966 survey indicated that a majority of members no longer saw themselves in either a Christian or a traditionally theistic orientation. Knowledge was held to come via science, and values were human constructions. An attempt to build the sciences, central in modern humanism, into the curriculum of Meadville/Lombard Theological School, however, failed. The journal *Zygon*, created during that attempt, is now managed by a Lutheran seminary.

Sherwin Wine, a Reform rabbi, created the Society for Humanistic Judaism in 1963, supporting a nontheistic form of Judaism that has spread internationally and created a training seminary (see JUDAISM, UNBELIEF WITHIN). The membership largely consists of persons wanting to affirm a Jewish identity and to maintain certain ritual practices without beliefs and laws that they view as no longer relevant.

In 1982 individual humanists from the major competing organizations formed the North American Committee for Humanism. Sherwin Wine was the founding president. The Humanist Institute, with Howard Radest as founding dean, was started with a three-year curriculum for leaders that would involve intensive study and coming together three times each year. More than a hundred students had graduated by 2005. The assumption was that recapturing common heritages would increase cooperation. Since then, Humanistic Judaism, Ethical Culture, and the Center for Inquiry have all instituted programs that draw from the same student pool. The Institute's journal, *Humanism Today*, reflects this across-the-board humanism in the writings of the Institute's adjunct faculty.

In 1980 Paul Kurtz founded an alternative organization, the Council for Secular and Democratic Humanism ("democratic" was included to avoid any confusions

with Marxist "humanisms" in Stalinist countries). A major rationale was to combat the new strategy of the Religious Right in the United States that argued that "since humanism was a religion, it could be kept out of schools," an argument being used in opposition to the teaching of evolution (see EVOLUTION AND UNBELIEF).

If initial debates had revolved around whether humanism could be considered a religion, more recent discussions have concerned whether humanism should be regarded as secular and therefore not religious (see SECULAR HUMANISM). Humanists of all kinds are committed to church-state separation, so that kind of SECULARISM is not at issue.

Certainly, religious humanists exist. Most who would so self-identify are in Unitarian Universalist churches. Their practice generally involves sermons, hymns, Sunday schools for the young, and rites of passage (such as child dedications, marriages, and funerals). Their lessons are usually drawn from many religions and cultures. Many members of ethical societies would not employ most of these rituals, but might nevertheless define their group and activities as religious.

BIBLIOGRAPHY

Olds, Mason. *American Religious Humanism*. Rev. ed. Minneapolis: Fellowship of Religious Humanists, 1996.

Schulz, William F. *Making the Manifesto: The Birth of Religious Humanism*. Boston: Skinner House, 2002.

Wilson, Edwin H., and Teresa Maciocha. *The Genesis of a Humanist Manifesto*. Amherst, NY: Humanist Press, 1995.

ROBERT B. TAPP

REMSBURG, JOHN ELEAZER. (1848–1919), American FREETHOUGHT lecturer and biblical critic. John Eleazer Remsburg was born on January 7, 1848, in Fremont, Ohio. He had little formal education early in his life, but was taught by his mother until he attended a few years of public school. On the whole he was largely self-taught. At the age of sixteen, he enlisted in the Union army and fought late in the Civil War in and near Washington, DC, and Maryland. After the war, he became a teacher and later superintendent of public instruction for Atchison County, Kansas. While there, Remsburg and his wife, Nora, had seven children. Remsburg continued his career in education until 1880.

After his career in education ended, Remsburg devoted his time to freethought lecturing and writing. He was involved with the AMERICAN SECULAR UNION (ASU), and was its president for several years. Strongly interested in United States history, Remsburg lectured on American historical figures and their religious beliefs. He published these lectures in books such as *The Life of Thomas Paine* (1880), *The Fathers of the Republic*

(1886), and works challenging the Christianity of Lincoln and Washington.

One of Remsburg's most famous works was *Six Historic Americans* (1906), an expanded version of *The Fathers of the Republic*, which was based on the lecture Remsburg delivered to the ASU Congress in 1886. Robert Green INGERSOLL, then president of the ASU, endorsed the *Fathers* publication, and this endorsement appears at the beginning of *Six Historic Americans*. Remsburg added the second part of the book, which dealt with Lincoln and Grant, to create this longer study.

Remsburg also had great interest in biblical criticism. Some of his published works in this area are *False Claims* (1883), *Bible Morals* (1884), *The Bible* (1903), and his other famous work, *The Christ* (1909). Remsburg's criticism dealt mostly with the morality of the Bible, showing conflicts between the various scriptures, but also with the morality of his time.

Remsburg was considered by many of his contemporaries as one of the great freethought lecturers, evidenced by his thousands of lectures delivered and his service to the freethought movement. Remsburg died in Porterville, California, on September 24, 1919.

BIBLIOGRAPHY

"Freethought Leader Dead." *New York Times*, September 25, 1919.

McCabe, Joseph. *A Bibliographical Dictionary of Modern Rationalists*. London: Watts and Company, 1920.

Putnam, Samuel P. *Four Hundred Years of Freethought*. New York: Truth Seeker Company, 1894.

TIMOTHY BINGA

RENAN, ERNEST (1823–1892), French biblical scholar. Ernest Renan cut short his Roman Catholic seminary studies to pursue a career as a private teacher and writer. He once commented that in order to write the history of a religion, one must both have believed in it once and believe in it no longer. From this standpoint Renan did go on to write a string of books on Christian origins and church history. The first of them was by far the most famous: *The Life of Jesus*, published in 1864. It triggered explosive controversy in Catholic France.

As he makes plain in his introduction, Renan had deeply imbibed German Higher Criticism, especially that of David Friedrich STRAUSS, whose *The Life of Jesus Critically Examined* (1835–36) shattered the supposed historical basis for drawing up a biography of Jesus from the gospels. And yet from Strauss Renan drew a surprising lesson, recalling Friedrich NIETZSCHE's dictum that when truth is seen to be a fiction, we have no alternative to creating our own fictions, all the while remembering that our fictions remain fiction, never allowing them to slip surreptitiously over into the vacant category of truth. Renan seemed to imagine that after Strauss, the biographer of Jesus was entitled to say what he pleased with no inconvenient facts to limit his performance.

Renan penned his *Life of Jesus* while vacationing in Palestine, the very scene of the gospel stories. It is plain that he allowed the gentle rusticity of the place to inspire him far more than whatever he might have read in Strauss. Essentially Renan composed a novel, full of romantic sentimentality. He drew upon the gospels interchangeably, troubling himself scarcely at all over either their historical authenticity or their original narrative order. Strauss had shown him that John's Gospel was itself fiction, but Renan took what he liked of it to embellish his portrait, leaving aside only the divinity of the Johannine Jesus. He equivocated on the question of miracles, finally coming down on the side of the rationalists, with their fanciful explanations of staged and misunderstood events.

The career of Jesus as Renan chronicled it had much in common with other early liberal lives of Jesus, envisioning an initial "Galilean Spring" of gentle teaching about a gospel of love and of the Kingdom of Heaven found in happy human fellowship in the summer twilight. After this, thanks to an insidious whispering campaign mounted by interloping Jerusalem Pharisees, the crowds begin to turn against Jesus, whereupon he headed south to Judea and Jerusalem, where he confronted his intransigent enemies with tragic results. In Renan's version, Jesus turned from his initial "Summer of Love" as he fell under the spell of messianic revolutionism. He began to rely upon miracle mongering (possibly chicanery) to reinforce the loyalties of the crowd as he made his way to the Holy City. But he soon realized this course was hopeless, and so he turned his thoughts to the doom which must surely overtake him. Renan speculated whether, during the agony of Gethsemane, Jesus might regretfully have contemplated the forfeited pleasures of an idyllic Galilean existence as a simple carpenter, enjoying the charms of one of the women who followed him with dreamy eyes.

The Life of Jesus, a pitiful piece of historical criticism, was nonetheless such an enjoyable piece of literature that it went through printing after printing, translation after translation. And it brought forth a plethora of rejoinders and rebuttals from traditionalists. But today's readers may be familiar with two modern life-of-Jesus fictions that are very much in the spirit of Renan and were very likely directly inspired by his *Life of Jesus*. These are Kahlil Gibran's *Jesus the Son of Man* (1928) and Nikos Kanantzakis's *The Last Temptation of Christ* (1960). Both partake of Renan's love for local color and natural splendor. And Kazantzakis appears to incorporate Renan's schema of stages: His Jesus first preaches love, then revolution, the fervor for which is quickly extinguished by the realization that he must die, prompting a reflection on the wholesome, mundane life he had sacrificed.

BIBLIOGRAPHY

Renan, Ernest. *The Antichrist*. Translated by Joseph Henry Allen. Boston: Roberts Brothers, 1897
————. *The Apostles*. Boston: Roberts Brothers, 1889.
————. *The Gospels*. London: Mathieson, n.d.
————. *Letters from the Holy Land*. Translated by Lorenzo O'Rourke. New York: Doubleday, Page, 1904.
————. *The Life of Jesus*. Translated by Charles Edwin Wilbour. New York: Carleton, 1875.
————. *Marcus Aurelius*. London: Mathieson, n.d.
————. *Saint Paul*. Translated by Ingersoll Lockwood. New York: Carleton, 1869.
Schweitzer, Albert. *The Quest of the Historical Jesus: From Reimarus to Wrede*. Translated by W. Montgomery. New York: Macmillan, 1961.

ROBERT M. PRICE

RESURRECTION. Resurrection refers to the supposed miraculous return to life of Jesus, the founder of Christianity, after his crucifixion and burial. The stories of the resurrection appear in the gospels at Matthew 28, Mark 16, Luke 24, and John 20. This article will treat the history of unbelief in the resurrection and also offer some reasons that justify that unbelief.

New Testament to Late Antiquity. The resurrection accounts themselves contain some of the earliest expressions of unbelief from both Christian and non-Christian sources. Matthew 28:13, for example, indicates that a story about Jesus's body being stolen was circulating among Jews within days of the supposed event. A disciple named Thomas is portrayed as initially incredulous about the resurrection (John 20:25ff.). In Luke 24:34–43, Jesus eats food in order to combat skepticism about his bodily resurrection.

Some self-described followers of Christ were ideologically opposed to belief in a resurrection. Of particular importance were Gnostic Christians, who believed that matter is evil and that God, who is pure spirit, cannot mix with flesh. Thus, the true God cannot die or be resurrected. Important Gnostic gospels (dating to around the fourth century and written in Coptic, a late form of Egyptian) were discovered in 1945 in Nag Hammadi, Egypt. In one of those Gnostic gospels, *The Second Treatise of the Great Seth*, Christ says: "For my death which they think happened, (happened) to them in their error. . . . It was another upon whom they placed the crown of thorns." Overall, the Great Seth deems the orthodox version of the life of Christ a fiction meant to obscure the life of the real Christ, who is completely spirit. The Gospel of Thomas, a copy of which was also found at Nag Hammadi, shows no awareness of the resurrection of Jesus.

Nonetheless, the resurrection became a central tenet of orthodox Christianity, which often appealed to 1 Corinthians 15:14 for support: "If Christ has not been raised, then our proclamation has been in vain and your faith has been in vain." However even in that chapter the author seems to be arguing for a spiritual, rather than a bodily, resurrection of Jesus.

Among non-Christians, the first substantive attack on the resurrection is found in *Contra Celsum* (Against Celsus), the apologetic handbook attributed to Origen. Ascribed to Celsus are various arguments that recur, in some form, to the present day: (1) the disciples lied or hallucinated; (2) some of the witnesses were women, and so could not be trusted; (3) the Christian story imitates pagan stories; and (4) Jesus may not have been as gravely wounded as the gospels make it appear. Celsus also wonders why Jesus did not show himself to everyone after the resurrection, something that would have put any doubts to rest.

Middle Ages and the Renaissance. By the Middle Ages, belief in the resurrection of Jesus was the orthodox position. A main rationale for belief was summarized in the dictum of Vincent of Lerins, who, in his "Commonitorium" (434 CE), defined truth as something "believed everywhere, always, and by everyone" (*quod ubique, quod semper, quod ab omnibus creditum est*). This dictum became easier to accept once the church had destroyed dissenting traditions, including most varieties of Gnosticism. Pope Leo I, for example, writes about the destruction of gospels that differed substantially from the canonical ones. At the same time, some medieval Christian figures such as Saint George were said to have been resurrected.

In medieval and Renaissance Europe, Judaism continued to be the main source of non-Christian unbelief in the resurrection. However, a new major strand of skepticism came from Islam, which according to orthodox Islamic historiography was a religion born in the seventh century in Arabia under God's last prophet, Muhammad. Its principal scripture, the Qur'an, explicitly denies that Jesus was crucified or killed (Sura 4:157) and repeats apparently Gnostic ideas that Jesus merely appeared to have experienced death.

During the Renaissance, the European encounter with groups of people in the Americas eroded confidence in the standards of truth outlined by Vincent of Lerins. It became clear, for example, that the Christian resurrection story was not believed everywhere or by everyone. Missionaries often struggled to explain why the Christian resurrection story merited more credence than many of the stories found in the New World, some of which, like the Mayan *Popol Vuh*, also included gods who returned from the underworld.

Enlightenment and the Nineteenth Century. During the Enlightenment there was a definitive shift away from the reliance on authority and toward privileging reason and the five natural senses in any determination of truth. Within Christianity, John TOLAND (*Christianity Not Mysterious*, 1696) argued that nothing contrary to reason or above reason should be part of Christianity. René

DESCARTES penned a famous dictum (*dubito ut intelligam*; "I doubt so that I may know") emphasizing the use of skepticism as an instrument of truth. For Descartes, only those propositions that can survive the fiercest of skeptical attacks are worthy of the label "true."

Yet reticence to question the resurrection publicly, especially among non-Christians, is illustrated by Baruch SPINOZA, the famous Jewish philosopher. His views on the resurrection were most clearly detailed in private correspondence rather than in his celebrated *Theologico-Political Treatise* (1670), which otherwise acutely critiqued biblical miracle stories. Spinoza understood the resurrection of Jesus to be allegorical and spiritual rather than an actual historical event. Among other critical observations, Spinoza noted (á la Celsus) that the resurrected Jesus could have shown himself to everyone but did not.

Hermann Samuel Reimarus, a Christian scholar from Hamburg, Germany, is often credited with producing the first modern critical inquiry into the "historical Jesus" in an anonymous work called the *Wolfenbüttel Fragments*, which appeared in 1774–78. Reimarus set out systematically to examine critically three types of Christian arguments for the resurrection: (1) the evidence of the Roman guard, (2) Christian testimony, and (3) Old Testament prophecies. For Reimarus, nothing contrary to reason should be held as historically established, and he placed special emphasis on internal contradictions in evaluating historicity.

Specifically, Reimarus noted that Matthew is the only gospel that includes an account of the Roman guard, while the women in Mark seem to not know of any guards posted. Reimarus also notes that Mary Magdalene certainly thought it was possible for the body to have been removed (John 20:13). He added that if some of Jesus's own followers were skeptical, then modern readers, who are farther removed from the events, have even more right to be skeptical. Reimarus theorized that Jesus was a failed revolutionary killed by the Romans: Jesus's disciples, unwilling to accept his death, created the fiction that he had been resurrected.

Another German scholar, David Friedrich STRAUSS, brilliantly extended the work of Reimarus. Finished in about a year, the fifteen-hundred-page manuscript of Strauss's *Das Leben Jesu* (The Life of Jesus) was published in 1835 when the author was only twenty-seven years old. Strauss deemed it philosophically untenable to use acts of God to explain anything in history. Therefore, he held that there were only two reasonable explanations for the resurrection stories: (1) Jesus did not really die in the manner depicted, and (2) Jesus did not really rise from the dead.

The section on the resurrection in *The Life of Jesus* focused on internal contradictions among the gospel accounts. Strauss was particularly interested in inconsistencies regarding the locations at which Jesus was first sighted after the resurrection. In Matthew 28:7 an angel instructs the women to tell the disciples to go to Galilee, where Jesus will be seen. But then Jesus himself appears near the tomb and gives the same instruction in verse 10. For Strauss, incompetent editing could explain why many contradictions were not removed from the gospel accounts.

Twentieth Century. The twentieth century is marked by important textual and archaeological discoveries related to the Bible, the most famous being that of the Dead Sea Scrolls, first identified in 1947. The Dead Sea Scrolls also helped to overturn the notion that a homogeneous Judaism with only a single idea of a Messiah existed in the first century. Otherwise, twentieth-century skeptics continued to espouse variants of arguments made standard by Celsus, Reimarus, and Strauss.

The later twentieth century also saw dominance in biblical studies shift from Europe to the United States. Some of the most skeptical scholars were those belonging to the Jesus Seminar, initiated by Robert Funk, who served as president of the Society of Biblical Literature in 1975. The Jesus Seminar attempted a systematic ranking of historical probability for individual verses in the gospels, and, in true American democratic fashion, determined those rankings by a vote. Most Jesus Seminar scholars, John Dominic Crossan conspicuous among them, had in fact accepted the idea of "demythologization" popularized by the influential German scholar Rudolf Bultmann. "Demythologization" emphasized that the "truth" of Christianity did not reside in the literal historicity of key events. The story of the resurrection, for example, could convey "higher truths," such as hope in the face of despair.

The new media that matured in the twentieth century—motion pictures, radio, television, and the Internet—played an unprecedented role in debates about the resurrection. *The Last Temptation of Christ* (1988), the controversial film based on a book of the same name by Nikos Kazantzakis, ends with a crucifixion, not a resurrection. On a more humorous level, *Monty Python's Life of Brian* (1979) raised the possibility of an invented Messiah. Even Mel Gibson's *The Passion of the Christ* (2004), though a clear reaction against secularism, did not focus on the Resurrection as the main event of Jesus's life. Dan Brown's *The Da Vinci Code* (2003) challenged orthodox Christianity by suggesting that non-canonical gospels are more accurate in depicting Jesus as living a relatively normal and married life that included neither crucifixion nor resurrection.

Media attention is also largely responsible for maintaining interest in objects that, despite repeated refutation of their authenticity, continue to be advanced as supporting evidence for the resurrection. For example, radiocarbon dating indicates that the Shroud of Turin, which believers claim is the actual burial shroud of Jesus complete with the latter's image, is a creation of the Middle Ages (see SHROUD OF TURIN, UNBELIEF IN). But numerous books still labor to show that it is authentic.

In 2002, sensational claims about the so-called James Ossuary began to be promoted by the popular magazine *Biblical Archaeology Review*. The ossuary, a container used to store human bones, bears an Aramaic inscription that translates as, "James, son of Joseph, brother of Jesus." Defenders assume that this James is the brother of the biblical Jesus, and argue that the ossuary constitutes the oldest extant evidence for Jesus's existence. However, the Israel Antiquities Authority has declared the ossuary inscription to be a forgery. Even if authentic, the James Ossuary would not show that Jesus resurrected, though believers often argue fallaciously that if one biblical claim is proven, then all biblical claims are presumed to be proven (e.g., if we can prove there was a Jesus, then we can presume that there was a resurrection).

Current Apologetic Trends. Academic defenses of the bodily resurrection of Jesus now emanate mostly from so-called evangelical/fundamentalist streams of Protestant Christianity; most combine older arguments with postmodernistic attacks on the "scientism" and "naturalism" of historians who disbelieve in the resurrection. In actuality, many of these apologists employ antinaturalism inconsistently. For example, the apparitions of the Virgin Mary at Medjugorje and elsewhere have supposedly been witnessed by thousands of people and exhibit many other parallels to the Jesus resurrection traditions, including witnesses of low status, the persistence of testimony despite threats, and the development of written traditions within the lifetime of the witnesses. Yet most Protestant apologists will use naturalistic explanations to discredit Marian apparition accounts while using antinaturalistic explanations to explain the Jesus resurrection accounts. Usually, defenses of the resurrection such N. T. Wright's massive *The Resurrection of the Son of God* (2003) do not even address seriously the parallels posed by Marian apparition stories.

William Lane Craig, perhaps the best-known apologist in Protestant evangelical circles, is typical in using a small set of supposed historical "facts" to support the historicity of the resurrection. Craig's inconsistent definition of a "fact" becomes apparent when one compares his view of Matthew 27:52–53, which relates that scores of resurrected people walked around Jerusalem at the time of Jesus's crucifixion. In that case, Craig believes that story not to be a "fact" because it occurs within an "apocalyptic" genre. Aside from not defining clearly why that passage is "apocalyptic" in genre, Craig leaves unexplained why he does not regard claims reported in an apocalyptic genre as facts. Nor does Craig explain why all of Matthew or Mark cannot be seen as apocalyptic, thereby rendering the story of Christ's resurrection no more a "fact" than what is found in Matthew 27:52–53. A more likely reason that Craig does not regard that story as a "fact" is simply that scores of resurrected people walking all over Jerusalem should have left some notice in non-Christian records.

We may briefly respond to some of the other common arguments for the resurrection as follows:

1. *We cannot otherwise explain the empty tomb.* As the Elvis phenomenon demonstrates, occupied tombs don't always prevent stories of empty tombs (or at least stories that the supposed occupant is not there at all). Moreover, the empty-tomb story cannot be verified by any independent source outside of the Bible.

2. *The disciples were willing to die for their testimony in the resurrection, which presumes that their testimony is true.* We actually do not know whether the disciples were willing to die for anything. Besides, a willingness to die for one's beliefs does not make those beliefs true.

3. *There was no preexisting resurrection tradition, so the Resurrection can be presumed to be linked to an authentically new event.* False. Mark 6:16 portrays Herod as invoking a resurrection belief in order to explain supposed sightings of John the Baptist, who had been beheaded. Besides, all traditions are, by definition, not preexisting traditions at their inception.

4. *Five hundred witnesses cannot be wrong or refuted.* Empirical evidence shows that large groups of people can report seeing nonoccurring events. Marian apparitions have been reportedly witnessed simultaneously by thousands of people, but most evangelical apologists do not see that as proof that Mary is alive. Besides, the claim of five hundred witnesses is found in a letter to the Corinthians (1 Cor. 15:6), who lived more than seven hundred miles from the supposed events, and so could not easily verify the truth of the claim in the first place.

5. *The time between the claimed event and the stories is too short for legendary development.* Usually, such a claim is based on dubious statistics about how long it takes for legends to develop, as well as very biased views of what constitutes a "legend." We know that highly developed stories can be promulgated and disseminated within hours or days of the supposed events (as was the case with Elvis stories).

6. *The gospels have otherwise been proven reliable.* Not true, or it depends on how one interprets certain passages. Luke, who is often regarded as the author of Acts, has a particular habit of mislocating burial places. Acts 7:15–16 indicates that the tomb of Abraham is in Shechem, while Genesis 25:9–10 (see also Gen. 23:19–20) places Abraham's tomb near Hebron. Moreover, Acts 13:27–29 indicates that it was the residents of Jerusalem, not the disciples, who placed Jesus in a tomb, something that contradicts other gospels that insist

that Jesus was buried by his own disciples (e.g., Matthew 27:57–61).

7. *The social disregard for women's testimony renders it unlikely that biblical authors would have chosen women as witnesses, and so we can presume the women's testimony to be an authentic tradition.* The use of supposedly unreliable witnesses in stories of extraordinary events is one of the most persistent literary devices in the world. Thus, in Virgin of Guadalupe apparition traditions, an Indian peasant is the primary witness in events dated to 1531 in Mexico. In the movie *Independence Day* (1996) an alcoholic character serves as a primary initial witness to the arrival of aliens.

8. *Secular historians don't apply the same critical standards to non-Christian figures such as Augustus Caesar.* No secular historian argues for the historicity of any supernatural claim made for Augustus Caesar (who was also called "son of god") or any other figure, Christian or otherwise. But contemporary government documents and many inscriptions attest to the existence of Augustus Caesar in the first century, whereas not a single item for Jesus can be securely dated to the first century.

Conclusion. Stories of resurrections or their variants are generated more frequently than most people might believe: consider the resurrection stories associated with Saint George, the Virgin Mary, and Elvis. Apologies for Jesus's resurrection are still largely based on naive views about how quickly traditions of extraordinary events can originate and develop substantive followings. The idea that Jesus would resurrect is no more extraordinary than the development of the idea that Saint George was resurrected, or that Elvis is still alive. These traditions fulfill varying psychological, social, and political needs. Otherwise, we cannot trace the story of Jesus's resurrection any earlier than New Testament manuscripts of the third century BCE, notwithstanding adherents' great desire to believe that those manuscripts represent traditions of the first century.

BIBLIOGRAPHY

Copan, Paul, and Ronald K. Tacelli, eds. *Jesus' Resurrection: Fact or Figment? A Debate between William Lane Craig and Gerd Lüdemann.* Downers Grove, IL: InterVarsity, 2000.

Craig, William L. *Assessing the New Testament Evidence for the Historicity of the Resurrection of Jesus.* Rev. ed. Lewiston, NY: Edwin Mellen, 2002.

Crossan, John Dominic. *The Historical Jesus: The Life of a Mediterranean Jewish Peasant.* New York: HarperCollins, 1992.

Lüdemann, Gerd. *The Resurrection of Jesus: History, Experience, Theology.* Minneapolis: Fortress, 1994.

Nickell, Joe. *Inquest on the Shroud of Turin: Latest Scientific Findings.* Amherst, NY: Prometheus Books, 1998.

Robinson, James M., ed. *The Nag Hammadi Library in English.* San Francisco: Harper & Row, 1977.

Wright, N. T. *The Resurrection of the Son of God.* Minneapolis: Fortress, 2003.

HECTOR AVALOS

REVELATION, UNBELIEF IN. The claim that the gods had revealed their will and their plans for the future to human beings is ancient, and was part and parcel of the claimed divine right of kings to rule unquestioned. At the same time, the belief has also functioned since time immemorial as a source of balm to sooth the anxieties of societies, serving a purpose analogous to psychotherapy in our own. Given the fundamentally social nature of revelation, prophecy, and divination, it took major social dislocations and evolution to make disbelief in revelation thinkable at all. When a belief is as fully presupposed as the air we breathe, the air has to start smelling of pollution before anyone questions it.

In the most primitive societies, belief in revelation took the form of divination, a version of sympathetic magic based on the notion of the microcosm reflecting the macrocosm. If the one mirrored the other, one might discern the direction of one's fortunes by learning to anticipate certain stars coordinated with one's birth. Or one might be able to "read" the entrails of sacrifices, or the tea leaves from a cup one has drunk. People still read horoscopes today for the same reason: a dose of imagined security to help one face tomorrow. Shamans the world over went a step further than this, inducing trances so they might consult one's departed ancestors to see if they were causing one's troubles as a rebuke or to send a message. People still visit spirit mediums for the same reason (see SPIRITUALISM AND UNBELIEF). Shamans served as prophetic ombudsmen to resolve "small claims." But as societies became polytheistic, then monotheistic, divination was frowned on—albeit replaced by analogous means of revelation, namely, the oracles of the gods/God. The Urim and Thummim of early Israel and the mysterious ephod of the Old Testament were licit, as were the Delphic and other oracles in Olympian Greece.

As just anticipated, governments had their own forms of "official" revelation. Thus "unbelief" in the earlier, popular forms was often the function of competition between official and popular divination, especially since both could be lucrative. Hence Isaiah the prophet (Isa. 8:19; 47:13), himself attached to the regime in Jerusalem, rebukes people for consulting mediums and astrologers when they ought to be seeking guidance from God (which is to say, the priests of Yahweh).

Ancient societies drew no distinction between the various departments that we call "government," "religion," "culture," and so on. All values, beliefs, and mores cohered in the "sacred canopy" of a worldview whose linchpin was the gods, an ultraworldly peg from which the whole complex might be hung. As Émile Durkheim explained, individual conscience was imbibed from the society as a whole, as each one internalized the group's beliefs. These included the notion that disobedience to the laws, while it might escape the watchful eyes of human authorities, could not escape divine notice. Such fear would serve to keep people in line. At the same time, ascribing society's laws to a divine source signaled how fundamentally important they were considered, just as even secularists in our society tend to treat the Constitution with the reverence of a revealed scripture because it is fundamental to our national life. Thus it is no surprise that all countries believed and taught that their laws were mandated by the gods. Hammurabi received his code from Shamash, Moses from Yahweh, and so on.

The concept of a heavenly book whose pages might be glimpsed on occasion by a seer or visionary goes back to ancient Babylon. As part of the yearly festival of creation and monarchy renewal, the newly recrowned king would retreat into the temple behind closed doors and there ascend to heaven, where he would be vouchsafed a glimpse of Marduk's Tablets of Destiny. He would thus return to the throne forewarned and forearmed for another year. The people would be fools to question the policies of such a person. He was privy to the divine plan; they were not. For "unbelief" to arise in such a context required the overthrow of the government and its replacement by a new regime backed by foreign gods, who would henceforth do their own revealing to their own earthly vicars. Once monarchies fell to greater empires, the native traditions of periodic heavenly journeys of revelation fell to scribes, prophets, and priests, who assumed the pen names of ancient scribes like Baruch and Enoch, prophets like Elijah and Zechariah, and priests like Levi. That the belief in revealed books continues to shake the world today is evident from the crucial role still played in political extremism by both the New Testament book of Revelation and the Qur'an.

In ancient Israel, dissidents did not doubt the divine character of the legal order, but only that certain elites were entitled to mediate the official revelation as in the cautionary tales of Miriam, Aaron, Dathan, Abihu, and Korah. In Athens, SOCRATES' contemporaries, the Sophists (see SOPHISM), had learned an important lesson of cultural relativism and taught that no country's laws were god given. Though they did not mean to challenge the status quo their teaching was considered seditious, undermining public confidence in the government. In the mid-second century CE, Plutarch had his hands full arguing in *The Obsolescence of Oracles* against sophisticated skeptics who at least implicitly doubted the truth of the Delphic and other oracles—asking, for instance, why oracles were so much more rare than in past years, if they really constituted a divine phenomenon. And why

did they speak so enigmatically? As RATIONALISM grew in the ancient world, social mediation increasingly took the form of court systems and arbitration. Laws were authored by governments in their own names. And even some who disbelieved in the gods altogether still thought it best to uphold the old religion publicly for the sake of the social order (see Cicero, *On the Nature of the Gods*).

It was only with the dawning of the Enlightenment that the twin movements of SECULARISM and the denial of revelation emerged powerfully (see ENLIGHTENMENT, UNBELIEF DURING THE). Each made the other possible. Doubting the rights of monarchs to rule entailed rejecting their claims to revelation, while losing confidence in revelation made it possible to doubt the king's divine authority. All fields of knowledge had been disengaging themselves from the church's apron strings since the Renaissance; and this meant, sooner or later, the setting aside of the myth and obsolete natural philosophy of the biblical writers as merely that, and not revelation. As the eighteenth and nineteenth centuries rolled on, developments both in philosophy and in biblical criticism shattered belief in revelation for many intellectuals. Immanuel KANT, himself the product of a German Pietist upbringing, established an epistemology according to which no knowledge was available that did not result from the processing of sense data by our mental categories of perception and logical functions of judgment. He had learned from David HUME the futility of the attempts of Gottfried LEIBNIZ, René DESCARTES, and others to find the truth by sheer speculation. And alleged revelation fell prey to the same objection as speculation: it did not rest on sense data, and thus could yield no certainty. With his famous set of antinomies, Kant showed how all questions about God, eternity, and the like which are beyond the proper scope of the senses and of rational processing, result in self-contradictions. Revelation thus proved philosophically untenable. Subsequent liberal theology, especially that of Friedrich Schleiermacher and Albrecht Ritschl, took Kant for granted and sought to rebuild Christian theology based on subjective religious experience or moral values, not on the bankrupt notion of propositional revelation—that is, information conveyed by God.

The higher criticism of the Bible (see BIBLICAL CRITICISM) revealed the book's many contradictions, myths, false authorship ascriptions, theological disagreements, and factual errors (see BIBLICAL ERRANCY). The upshot was that even if the idea of revelation were philosophically tenable, this book did not appear to be a revelation. Fundamentalists rejected these results of criticism, retreating into a ghetto-mentality hostile to all new knowledge (especially that of biology and evolution; see EVOLUTION AND UNBELIEF). Liberal Protestants shifted the meaning of revelation and redefined their view of the Bible. As the liberal Protestant Harry Emerson Fosdick would say, the Bible is a record of the spiritual evolution of ancient Jews and Christians, hence the unadorned humanness of the book; but it was an unfolding experience of encounter with God—and this means that the Bible is a disclosure of the divine person, chiefly and definitively in the personality of Jesus. Neo-Orthodox theologians like John Baillie would say that what God reveals—primarily in the ancient events of biblical history, but also as we read of them in scripture—is not information about himself, but simply *himself*. The Bible, then, becomes revelatory as a catalyst for religious experience (see RELIGIOUS AND MYSTICAL EXPERIENCES). Theology is then the articulation of that experience (as Schleiermacher had already said). Scientific modernists and religious humanists such as the Unitarian John H. Dietrich simply rejected all belief in revelation rather than redefining it to death.

Nonetheless, it would be a grievous error to imagine that belief in divine revelation is passing from the world any time soon. It may be that resurgent Islamic and Christian fundamentalisms are revitalization movements dedicated to locking the barn door of their culture after the horse has escaped. Their very vehemence may betray their deep awareness that the jig is up and their fairy-tale world has passed. But, like Nietzsche's mad prophet proclaiming the death of God, we may have to recognize that this news has come to us too soon, and that the struggle with antirational revelation belief will yet be long and hard. For the time being we find ourselves like Queen Penelope, repelling a thousand suitors for our faith in their various "revealed" screeds. Walter KAUFMANN aptly sums up the position of the reasonable man or woman, and the inevitable necessity for unbelief in revelation:

Those who pit commitment against reason and advise us to blind and destroy our reason before making the most crucial choice of our life are apologists for one specific set of doctrines which, to use Paul's word, are "foolishness" to those who have not taken leave of reason. They say their doctrine is infallible and true, but ignore the fact that there is no dearth whatsoever of pretenders to infallibility and truth. They may think [we ought to choose] their doctrine because it is offered to us as infallible and true; but this is plainly no sufficient reason: scores of other doctrines, scriptures and apostles, sects and parties, cranks and sages make the same claim. Those who claim to know which of the lot is justified in making such a bold claim, those who tell us that this faith or that is *really* infallible and true, are presupposing, in effect, whether they realize this or not, that they themselves happen to be infallible. Those who have no such exalted notion of themselves have no way of deciding between dozens of pretenders if reason is proscribed. Those who are asking us to spurn reason are in effect counseling us to trust to luck. But luck in such cases is unusual.

BIBLIOGRAPHY

Baillie, John. *The Idea of Revelation in Recent Thought*. New York: Columbia University Press, 1956.

Berger, Peter L., and Thomas Luckmann. *The Sacred Canopy: Elements of a Sociological Theory of Religion*. Garden City, NY: Doubleday Anchor, 1969.

Dietrich, John H. "Who Are These Fundamentaliists?" In *The Humanist Pulpit: A Volume of Addresses*. Minneapolis: First Unitarian Society, 1927.

Durkheim, Émile. *The Elementary Forms of the Religious Life*. Translated by Joseph Ward Swain. New York: Macmillan, 1965.

Eliade, Mircea. *Shamanism: Archaic Techniques of Ecstasy*. Bollingen Series 76. Translated by Willard R. Trask. Princeton, NJ: Princeton University Press, 1972.

Fosdick, Harry Emerson. *The Modern Use of the Bible. Lyman Beecher Lectures on Preaching at Yale, 1924*. New York: Macmillan, 1924.

Huxley, Julian. *Religion without Revelation*. New York: New American Library, 1958.

Kant, Immanuel. *Religion within the Limits of Reason Alone*. Translated by Theodore M. Greene and Hoyt H. Hudson. New York: Harper & Row, 1960.

Kaufmann, Walter. *The Faith of a Heretic*. Garden City, NY: Doubleday Anchor, 1963,

Niebuhr, H. Richard. *The Meaning of Revelation*. New York: Macmillan, 1941.

Watt, William Montgomery. *Islamic Revelation in the Modern World*. Edinburgh: Edinburgh University Press, 1969.

ROBERT M. PRICE

REVOLUTION, FRENCH. See FRANCE, UNBELIEF IN.

REYNOLDS, CHARLES B. (1832–1896), American FREETHOUGHT lecturer. Charles B. Reynolds was born in New York on August 5, 1832. His mother died giving birth to him; his father died before Charles was five. By 1868 he was an Adventist preacher. Historical inconsistencies in the Bible undermined his faith. The "ex-Reverend" Reynolds addressed his first freethought conference in 1883. Inside two years he was chair of the executive committee of the AMERICAN SECULAR UNION, a successful itinerant "liberal lecturer," and a regular contributor to the freethought papers THE TRUTH SEEKER and the BOSTON INVESTIGATOR.

Reynolds expounded a "Gospel of Humanity" whose principles were to "Do Justice, Love Mercy, Promote the Happiness of Others and thus Promote Our Own." He held "liberal tent revivals" in towns lacking halls to rent. He pitched his tent at Boonton, New Jersey, on July 26, 1886. Local churches whipped up opposition; Reynolds was arrested for BLASPHEMY, later rushed by a mob. He fled for his life, the tent a total loss. On October 13, 1886, he lectured, tentless, at Morristown, New Jersey, and was indicted on blasphemy charges. Reynolds selected as his defender the agnostic orator and prominent attorney Robert Green INGERSOLL.

The trial was held at Morristown on May 19, 1887, amid great excitement. Ingersoll called no defense witnesses, hanging the case on his summation, a florid oration several hours long. The next day the jury returned a guilty verdict, but the judge—perhaps chastened by Ingersoll's arguments—imposed a token sentence totaling seventy-five dollars in fines and costs. Ingersoll paid this from his pocket, also forgoing any fees. The summation became a popular freethought publication.

Like the Scopes "monkey trial" argued by Clarence DARROW in 1925 (see EVOLUTION AND UNBELIEF), the Reynolds trial featured a renowned defense attorney and ended in conviction, but changed the climate of opinion so as to preclude further prosecutions of the same type.

Reynolds and his wife moved to Washington in 1889; he lectured in Walla Walla, Tacoma, and Seattle before dying in a fall at his home on July 3, 1896.

BIBLIOGRAPHY

Ingersoll, Robert Green. "Trial of C. B. Reynolds for Blasphemy: Address to the Jury." In *The Works of Ingersoll*, edited by C. P. Farrell. Vol. 11. New York: Dresden, 1900.

Kittredge, Herman E. *Ingersoll: A Biographical Appreciation.* New York: Dresden, 1911.

Macdonald, George E. *Fifty Years of Freethought.* New York: Truth Seeker Company, 1929.

O'Hair, Madalyn Murray. "Blasphemy!" *American Atheist*, October/November/December 1986.

Putnam, Samuel Porter. *Four Hundred Years of Freethought.* New York: Truth Seeker Company, 1894.

Reynolds, Charles B. Poster for a lecture by ex-Rev. and Mrs. Reynolds, March 20 and 21, 1886. Collection of the Robert Green Ingersoll Birthplace Museum.

TOM FLYNN

RICKER, MARILLA MARKS YOUNG (1840–1920), American freethinker, abolitionist, suffragist, and attorney. The second of four children, Marilla Marks Young was born into a farming community in Durham, New Hampshire. Her father, Jonathan Young, was a freethinker (see FREETHOUGHT), her mother a Free Will Baptist whose religion Marilla hated even as a child. Widowed after five years of childless marriage to a rich farmer, John Ricker, she became independently wealthy at the age of twenty-eight. After four years of European travel, she settled in Washington, DC, to study law. She was admitted to the bar of the Supreme Court of the District of Columbia in 1882 and to the bar of the US Supreme Court in 1891. A notary public, in 1884 she was the first woman to be appointed a United States commissioner and examiner in chancery by the judges of the District's Supreme Court,

becoming the first woman in the District of Columbia to perform quasi-judicial functions. Known as the "prisoner's friend," her wide and distinguished law practice consistently favored the poor and unfortunate. She worked hard and successfully for many prison reforms. She was the first woman to vote in the United States, fifty years before woman suffrage was legalized. As a widow of large property, Marilla Ricker, using the Fourteenth Amendment to support her cause, registered to vote in Dover, New Hampshire, in 1870 in a state election. Her vote was refused that year, but in the 1871 state election her vote received no opposition. She was Suffrage candidate for governor of New Hampshire in 1910, but the state's attorney general disallowed her candidacy. An active suffragist, she served as an officer of the National Woman Suffrage Association for many years.

A major contributor to *THE TRUTH SEEKER*, she wrote an outstanding collection of freethought essays, widely circulated in pamphlets she entitled: "*I Don't Know. Do You?*" and "*I Am Not Afraid. Are You?*" which were full of witty, down-to-earth one-liners such as: "Resolved: A steeple is no more exempt from taxation than a smoke stack" and "The presence of a hypocrite is a sure indication that there is a Bible and a prayer-book not very far away." She also wrote a book, *The Four Gospels* (1911).

Responding to anarchist Emma GOLDMAN's assertion that suffragists were too religious for the vote to do them any good, Ricker stoutly maintained that all pioneer suffragists were freethinkers. She thought it politic, however, that at suffrage conventions, parsons be allowed to "lead in prayer" ("they never lead in anything else") because they might possibly "absorb some knowledge."

Ricker died of a stroke at age eighty in 1920, the year universal suffrage was finally introduced in the United States.

BIBLIOGRAPHY

"Pioneer Suffragists Were Freethinkers." *Truth Seeker*, February 19, 1910.

Stanton, Elizabeth Cady, Susan B. Anthony, and Matilda Joselyn Gage, eds. *The History of Woman Suffrage.* Vol. 2. New York: Fowler & Wells, 1881.

ELIZABETH GERBER

RITUAL, CEREMONIAL, AND UNBELIEF. One dictionary defines *ceremony* as "a formal act or set of acts performed as prescribed by ritual or custom," but also as "a formal act without intrinsic purpose; an empty form." The tension between these conceptions is reflected among unbelievers. Some reject all ritual as a vestige of the churches or as an obstacle to freedom; others eagerly innovate to replace the rites and ceremonies cast aside when transcendental beliefs were abandoned. Reflecting that diversity of views, this entry is divided into three sections, each contributed by one or more advocates of a particular viewpoint.

OPPOSITION TO RITUAL AND CEREMONY

Prominent unbelievers have often defied what aboli-tionist Beriah Green called the "factitious distinctions and artificial arrangements of society," rejecting the institution of marriage; rites of passage, including baby-namings, coming-of-age observances, and end-of-life or memorial ceremonies; and holidays of the orthodox cal-endar. Space permits listing only a few. Ethan ALLEN, US revolutionary hero and first American author of a freethought book, was buried without religious cere-mony. In 1832 reformer Robert Dale OWEN married Mary Jane Robinson in a secular ceremony adminis-tered by a notary public. Owen famously foreswore the statutory privileges of husbands over wives, stating that he and Robinson would have cohabited had the legal environment permitted it. In 1853 the first freethought association known to call itself "humanist" formed in London; members of the Humanistic Religious Associ-ation renounced the dogmas, myths, and *ceremonies* that they associated with the ancient past (see HUMANISM). Horace SEAVER, second editor of the freethought paper the *BOSTON INVESTIGATOR*, is credited by Samuel PUTNAM with being the first to cast aside a formal, ritualized funeral when his wife died in middle age, substituting a "social funeral" marked by the informal exchange of fond memories. Free-love activist Ezra H. HEYWOOD and novelist Sinclair LEWIS were among several nineteenth- and twentieth-century unbe-lievers whose wills forbade a religious memorial cere-mony. Like many freethinkers of their generation, *TRUTH SEEKER* associate editor Woolsey TELLER, *Truth Seeker* editor James Hervey JOHNSON, and German-born US rationalist activist Walter HOOPS directed that no memorial service be held after their deaths, an appeal Hoops's Missouri admirers disregarded.

Unbelievers who scorned the ceremonial seldom wrote about their decisions, leaving us to guess at their motives. No doubt some acted from reflex, rebuffing social conventions associated with rejected religious tra-ditions. Others gave signs of more sophisticated ratio-nales, rooted in the French Enlightenment (see ENLIGHT-ENMENT, THE, AND UNBELIEF) and individualist anarchism (see ANARCHISM AND UNBELIEF).

French Enlightenment thought cultivated an unprece-dented individualism that sought to burst fetters of reli-gion, state, and social convention. The sex radicals of the later nineteenth century (see SEX RADICALISM AND UNBELIEF) built upon this, reinterpreting traditional con-cepts regarding sexual relations, marriage, the family, and their associated rituals in light of their own personal judgments.

Still more radical individualism was expressed by the transcendental idealist Johann Gottlieb FICHTE. Fichte vested supreme value in the "I," the individual exer-cising will; the "I" enjoys maximal freedom only by releasing itself from all constraints, including those implied by ceremonial. Anarchist philosopher Max STIRNER went further, asserting in *The Ego and Its Own* (1845) that no one is free so long as "there still exists even one institution which the individual may not dis-solve." On this view, individual development consists primarily in emancipating oneself from the nested tyran-nies of family, village, state, and church, necessarily rejecting the rites and ceremonies through which those institutions customarily mediated or constrained individ-uals' life choices.

Late nineteenth- and early twentieth-century anar-chists embraced these principles passionately and articu-lately, leaving some of the most coherent accounts of lives deliberately purged of ritual. Unconventional living arrangements and the avoidance of matrimony were common among them. US anarchist and freethinker Emma GOLDMAN lived communally or with lovers during her most active years. Her anarchist colleague Voltairine DE CLEYRE forswore not only matrimony but even committed relationships; rejecting lover Samuel Gordon in 1897, she wrote to him that she would rather be alone than "be the slave of my own affection for you." Regarding the disposition of her body after her death she wrote, "I want no ceremonies nor speeches over it. I die, as I have lived, . . . owing no allegiance to rulers, heav-enly or earthly." For De Cleyre, a memorial rite would unacceptably affirm the power of society, state, or church to determine *for the individuals who mourned her* what her life had meant.

Through the years, some unbelievers have consis-tently rejected ritual and ceremonial not simply as ves-tiges of religion, but as vestiges of a pre-Enlightenment, authoritarian social order that is inimical to individual autonomy and self-actualization.

Opposition to Holiday Observances. Unbelievers also vary in their attitudes toward observance of tradi-tional holidays, particularly those of religious origin. Philosopher George SANTAYANA and playwright George Bernard SHAW conspicuously refused to celebrate Christmas. Others, including atheist campaigners Madalyn Murray O'HAIR (US) and Barbara Smoker (UK), defended the holiday, arguing that its pagan and secular heritage outweighs its religious cargo. This author dissented in 1993, arguing that while much about Christmas observance is nonreligious, the holiday is so deeply associated with Christianity that unbelievers risk being perceived as hypocrites when they observe Christmas, or even an alternative holiday like the Winter Solstice or HumanLight. Additionally, if unbelievers can benefit socially and politically when their true numbers are acknowledged, refusing to celebrate Christmas enhances unbelievers' social visibility. In contrast, con-ventional holiday observance reduces that visibility, per-versely supporting the myth that Christianity is ubiqui-tous at holiday time.

In the view of some unbelievers, a thoroughgoing individualism requires the firm rejection of any ritual, ceremonial, or holiday observance that might affirm arbitrary limits on individual autonomy.

BIBLIOGRAPHY

Avrich, Paul. *An American Anarchist: The Life of Voltairine de Cleyre.* Princeton, NJ: Princeton University Press, 1978.

Flynn, Tom. "Humanist Ceremonies? Over My Dead Body." *Secular Humanist Bulletin* 9, no. 1 (1994).

———. "Legitimize Bastardy!" *Secular Humanist Bulletin* 12, no. 1 (1997).

———. *The Trouble with Christmas.* Amherst, NY: Prometheus Books, 1993.

Gillespie, Michael A. *Nihilism before Nietzsche.* Chicago: University of Chicago Press, 1995.

Putnam, Samuel Porter. *Four Hundred Years of Freethought.* New York: Truth Seeker Company, 1894.

Sears, Hal. *The Sex Radicals: Free Love in High Victorian America.* Lawrence: Regents Press of Kansas, 1977.

Tom Flynn

EMBRACE OF RITUAL AND CEREMONIAL

Though some nineteenth- and early twentieth-century freethinkers rejected the practice of ceremony in their lives, many others assuredly did not. Today's celebrants, such as those affiliated with the ETHICAL CULTURE movement, the AMERICAN HUMANIST ASSOCIATION, and the Celebrant USA Foundation and Institute, trace their influences to earlier thinkers who looked for ways to express their exuberance and their sense of solidarity after having been released from the stultifying traditions of conventional religions.

In the 1850s in France, for example, August COMTE, who had developed the science of sociology in order to bring progress to humankind through the application of reason, founded the Positivist Church, a "religion" energized by a celebration of humanity, but divested of anything metaphysical (see POSITIVISM). The idea spread to other European countries including Holland, Norway, Great Britain, and Germany, where the best known of the new organizations was named the Free Religious Society. Though they had not freed themselves from ecclesiastical terminology, these movements sought to provide the human benefits of close-knit community, ceremony, and celebration without the trappings of theism.

In 1876, very much from this tradition, Felix ADLER founded the Ethical Culture Society in New York as an agnostic religion. Adler saw ethics as replacing theology and superstition, but nonetheless retained an acceptance of "spirituality" in the sense of acknowledging some unknowable force for good in the universe. Today, this view has been replaced by naturalistic HUMANISM, although the structure of the society remains congregational, with ceremonies conducted by the society's trained leaders.

The American Humanist Association, founded in 1941, first began certifying celebrants in 1964 under what was then the Division of Humanist Counseling (now the Humanist Society). Much influenced by humanist psychologists at the time, the celebrants still see ceremony as a response to human needs, but also as a way to make manifest and strengthen the bonds of the human community.

To protect the ceremonial rights of secular people, in 1973 Australian humanist and rationalist attorney general Lionel Murphy initiated the world's first program for independent civil celebrants appointed by the state. The International College of Celebrancy, based in Australia, certified its first US celebrants in 2001. The Celebrant USA Foundation and Institute has continued this work, certifying students for careers as civil celebrants. Their mission is to provide students with extensive training in the theory and practice of ceremony, so that they might work closely with clients to create beautiful and highly personalized ceremonies that reflect the clients' values, traditions, and tastes.

The Purposes and Benefits of Ceremony. Practicing celebrants see many practical benefits to ceremony. For the unbeliever, ceremony is seen as a human contrivance, though one with the potential to boost the health and enrich the lives of individuals while increasing the strength and cohesiveness of community. It is a chance for people to draw together in order to communicate what is meaningful; to express thoughts and emotions through the arts; to state, transmit, and reinforce values; to recognize milestones that mark personal histories; to measure progress; to acknowledge achievements; to honor the distinctiveness and worth of each individual; to proclaim love or admiration; to face transitions with courage; to share happiness and grief, laughter and tears; and to party with those closest.

Today's celebrants are asked to perform ceremonies that fall into three general categories, recognizing common patterns of life experience—rites of passage (baby welcomings, coming of age, weddings/commitments, end of life), seasonal or annual (HumanLight, anniversaries), and event-specific (graduations, recovery from illness, divorce, opening of a new business). The structure of ceremony allows participants to focus in on their lives at the present moment, review the past, and approach the future with renewed determination and the support of family and friends. Ceremony reduces isolation and alienation by allowing participants to see their lives as part of the story of all humankind.

The best ceremonies appeal to all aspects of human nature—the senses, the imagination, the emotions, and the intellect. Putting together a ceremony can be seen as a rational process, which brings clarity, order, and self-reflection to our busy, scattered lives. And ceremony serves the humanist ideals as expressed in the Council for Secular Humanism's "Affirmations of Humanism" (to strive for "the fullest realization of the best and noblest that we are capable of as human beings") and the American Humanist Association's "Humanism and its Aspirations" ("the joining of individuality with interdependence" in creating "lives of personal fulfillment").

However, ceremonies need not appeal to everyone. Contemporary celebrants agree there should be no established orthodoxy of belief or practice, but rather an open set of choices. Unbelievers should be wary if ceremony replaces the rightful function of rational inquiry or settles into some rigid form of required participation. Rather, to contribute to the vitality of each humanist community, ceremony has to be constantly rethought and reinvented, personalized for each individual, family, generation, and nationality.

INTERVIEWED FOR THIS ENTRY

Khoren Arisian, Senior Leader, New York Society for Ethical Culture

Joseph Chuman, Leader, Ethical Culture Society of Bergen County

Fred Edwords, Editorial Director, American Humanist Association

Arthur M. Jackson, President, Humanist Community in Silicon Valley

Terri Mandell-Campfield, National Board Member, American Humanist Association

Dally Messenger III, Principal, International College of Celebrancy

Gaile Sarma, Executive Director, The Celebrant USA Foundation

BARRY KLASSEL AND CHARLOTTE EULETTE

EMBRACE OF HOLIDAY OBSERVANCE

Humanism is much more than just a rejection of supernatural beliefs and the practices based on those beliefs. It is a framework for a good life and a path to peace and justice. Public humanist celebrations, including a recently developed holiday called HumanLight, hold great potential to further these psychological, moral, and practical ideals of humanism.

As Aristotle noted, we humans are social animals. We thrive when we participate in community and relationships. However unfortunately or unjustly, in most of the world today community and family life are structured to a great extent around theistic religious traditions. Participation is limited or forbidden for those who are unwilling to act as if they share predominant religious beliefs.

So long as unbelievers are unwelcome as full participants in many community and family gatherings, aspects of their psychological needs for social connectedness can only be satisfied by specifically humanist social events. Although most humanist organizations provide regular occasions for people to get together to educate themselves and to discuss intellectual issues of importance, these cannot suffice. Any human community will consist of those who are too young to participate and those who are not attracted to these types of intellectual activities.

Periodic gatherings to celebrate and commemorate humanism create opportunities for the entire community to come together. Relationships among individuals and families can be established, maintained, and strengthened in an open, welcoming, and relaxed atmosphere. The HumanLight holiday in particular is a promising candidate for a humanist celebration that can grow to be highly popular and well known. The first HumanLight event occurred in 2001 in the New York metropolitan area, and in the few years since has been conducted in dozens of locations around the United States.

HumanLight is December 23, and is celebrated on or near that date. Although some object to the proximity of HumanLight to Christmas and other religious holidays, the reality in many societies is that the culture carves out this period of time both structurally and psychologically as an occasion for celebration and contemplation of life's deeper meanings. It is, from a pragmatic point of view, an excellent opportunity to hold a large social gathering. Furthermore, a major event at this time of year can alleviate feelings of alienation and isolation from society.

By bringing our children to gatherings that celebrate humanism, we convey to them our commitment to its ethical principles. These social events can impress upon young minds the importance of humanist principles in unique and influential ways, and can help create the emotional foundation for a lifelong commitment to humanism.

Humanists also want to provide a public hearing for our ideas so that they may be considered in social and political decisions, and we want to reach out to those people who are humanists at heart but do not know that humanist groups exist. Celebrations such as HumanLight, when publicized, are an excellent positive way to let the public know that humanist organizations exist and provide an important alternative approach to confronting life's critical questions.

There are dangers associated with ritualized celebrations, and these must be acknowledged. But we can weave this awareness into the fabric of the celebration itself to minimize these risks. Likewise, it must be understood that the idea of holiday celebrations does not appeal to all humanists. Nonetheless, given the great value that many humanists have already found in HumanLight and the potential of such events for raising public awareness of humanism, all humanists should be able to support HumanLight and other such celebrations.

GARY BRILL AND JOE FOX

ROALFE, MATILDA (1813–1880), English activist and bookseller. After working with George Jacob HOLYOAKE and the London Anti-Persecution Union in the 1840s, Matilda Roalfe decided dramatically and personally to challenge British blasphemy laws. Her colleague Thomas Paterson had opened up a bookshop to sell banned books in Edinburgh in 1843, for which he was arrested, tried, and imprisoned. Thomas Finley next took over the shop, and was likewise arrested, convicted, and jailed. In 1844, Roalfe traveled to Edinburgh, where she reopened the Atheistical Depot at 105 Nicolson Street to offer for sale a list of persecuted books, such as those by Thomas PAINE. Roalfe publicized her crime in a sixteen-page tract, "Law Breaking Justified" (1844). She wrote that "to resist bad laws, is no less duty than to respect good ones." She pledged to "publish irreligious opinions," regardless of the consequences. She was arrested, convicted, and spent sixty days in jail. True to her word, she continued her blasphemous bookselling upon release from prison. She later married and settled in Scotland.

BIBLIOGRAPHY

McCoy, Ralph E. *Freedom of the Press, an Annotated Bibliography.* Carbondale: Southern Illinois University, 1995.
McCabe, Joseph. *A Biographical Dictionary of Modern Rationalists.* London: Watts and Company, 1920.

ANNIE LAURIE GAYLOR

ROBERTSON, JOHN MACKINNON (1856–1933), English freethought historian. John Mackinnon Robertson was one of the major rationalist writers of the late nineteenth and early twentieth centuries (see RATIONALISM). As well as being active in the FREETHOUGHT movement, he was a successful Liberal politician and a prodigiously industrious researcher and writer.

Robertson was born on the Isle of Arran in Scotland. Having left school at thirteen, he was largely self-educated—he continued a process of study until his death. As a young man he moved to Edinburgh, where he became a journalist and then assistant editor of the Edinburgh *Evening News*. He was active in the Edinburgh Secularist Society and was inspired when he heard Charles BRADLAUGH speak. Annie BESANT persuaded him to move to London and work for Bradlaugh's *National Reformer*, of which he became assistant editor.

On the death of Bradlaugh in 1891, Robertson took over the editorship, but the publication survived only until 1893. He next founded the progressive and literary journal *Free Review*, which he edited until 1897. Some thought him likely to take over leadership of the NATIONAL SECULAR SOCIETY, but the majority favored the more populist G. W. FOOTE. He shared many secularist views, describing himself as "Republican, Atheist and Malthusian." He also opposed compulsory vaccination and favored free speech, being a member of the Free Defense Committee that defended the publication of Zola's *La Terre* and Havelock Ellis's pioneering book on homosexuality, *Sexual Inversion.*

He sought election to Parliament, succeeding in 1906, and stood as a Liberal for the constituency of Tyneside. He had already been active in politics, having visited South Africa at the time of Boer War; at that time he criticized British imperialism and the institution of concentration camps. He later argued for self-government in India and Egypt. He was made parliamentary secretary to the Board of Trade in Asquith's government in 1911 and became a member of the Privy Council in 1915. He failed to win reelection in 1918.

Robertson wrote more than one hundred books and numerous articles, not all of which have been documented. Two works may be considered his masterpieces: *A Short History of Freethought* (1899), two substantial volumes published throughout his working life in many reprints and revisions; and *A History of Freethought in the Nineteenth Century* (1929; also two substantial volumes and frequently reprinted). He was interested not only in individual freethinkers but in the process whereby freethought developed historically. His style is dense and dry, but it is hard to imagine this topic better covered. He saw the development of freethought ideas as a constant contest, an ebb and flow, but ultimately showing "a law of evolving reason."

Other areas of great importance in his writing were Shakespeare studies, the historicity of Jesus (see JESUS, HISTORICITY OF), and the development of Christianity. He argued that Shakespeare's plays contained many insertions by other writers, a thesis that dented his admiration for Shakespeare's plays not in the least.

It was of a piece that he doubted the existence of Jesus, in particular thinking that some of the New Testament contained insertions from a morality play. His belief in the power of myth reinforced these views. The morality play theory is not now accepted, but the possibility that Jesus had no actual existence is still put forward by scholars such as G. A. Wells.

Robertson wrote about the development of Christianity, believing its success to be due to good organization and—once it had become a ruling religion—the power of the state. The development of all religions in his view followed a pattern, which he explored in his book *The Dynamics of Religion*. He was one of the earlier figures to bring a sociological approach to much of his writing.

His reputation has not been sustained except among specialists. His lack of academic qualifications and his position as a secularist activist probably told against him. However no one who played such a large part in the rationalist cause also had such a prominent political career. When he died he possessed more than twenty thousand books; given his extraordinary industry it could be believed he benefited from them all.

BIBLIOGRAPHY

Cooke, Bill. *The Blasphemy Depot: A Hundred Years of the Rationalist Press Association.* London: Rationalist Press Association, 2003.

The Literary Guide (70th Birthday Tribute). London: Rationalist Press Association, 1927.

Wells, G. A., ed. *J. M. Robertson (1856–1933): Liberal, Rationalist & Scholar.* London: Pemberton, 1987.

Whyte, A. Gowans. *The Story of the RPA.* London: Watts and Company, 1949

JIM HERRICK

ROBINSON, CHARLES (1818–1894), American politician and freethinker. Passing his childhood and early years in rural Massachusetts, Charles Robinson graduated from the Berkshire Medical School and practiced medicine for a few years before joining the gold rush to California in 1849. Passing through what would become Kansas Territory, Robinson would remember its promise for future settlement. After the passage of the Kansas-Nebraska Act that opened the territory, Robinson became active in the New England Emigrant Aid Society, "an organization with a moral mission that intended to make a profit through real estate speculation." The city of Lawrence was established by the society as a center of the Free State movement, which opposed the expansion of slavery. Robinson served as president of the town company, and became a founder of the Free State Party in 1855.

During the conflict that ensued, Robinson was arrested on the charge of treason in May 1856, and was jailed for four months. Pro-slavery forces from Missouri burned and sacked Lawrence on May 21, which in turn led to armed resistance led by Captain John Brown. Robinson participated in the foundation of the town of Quindaro, on the Kansas side of the Missouri River, in what is now Kansas City, Kansas. Quindaro became a "station" on the Underground Railroad, but after an economic depression began in 1857, the town's growth faltered.

When Kansas was admitted to the Union as a free state in 1861, Robinson served as the first governor, but served just one term due to controversies concerning the alleged improper sale of bonds. The flamboyant Gen. James H. Lane was a determined adversary of Robinson's in the turmoil of Republican Party politics at the outset of the Civil War. Robinson was impeached in the Kansas legislature in connection with the bond sale charges, but was acquitted at trial. Later he participated in the establishment of the University of Kansas in Lawrence and served as its chancellor.

Robinson was active in opposing the movement to declare the United States to be a Christian nation that arose in the 1870s. The NATIONAL LIBERAL LEAGUE, of which Robinson was a state leader, claimed to have more than two hundred local groups in Kansas by 1879. The Liberal League opposed "the use of the Bible in public schools, the public support of sectarian schools and charitable institutions, the official recognition of religious holidays, and the judicial oath." Robinson promoted liberal encampments and spoke at these, saying in 1879 that "the old time theological barricades erected around the most ignoble of superstitions is fast crumbling into dust. A decade more and they will all have vanished from before the advancing footsteps of enlightened civilization, and in place of the altar of sacrifices to unknown Gods or a triumvirate of Gods and deities, will be erected a monument to the most beautiful of all faculties, Reason!" But by the early 1890s, the Liberal League in Kansas "ceased to function as anything more than a loosely knit intellectual society with exchanges of correspondence between a few members."

To mark the 150th anniversary of the founding of the city of Lawrence, the Free State brewery there produced Governor Robinson's Lager.

BIBLIOGRAPHY

Wilson, Don W. *Governor Charles Robinson of Kansas.* Lawrence: University Press of Kansas, 1975.

FRED WHITEHEAD

RODDENBERRY, GENE (1921–1991), American television producer, creator of *Star Trek*. The "father" of the television phenomenon *Star Trek*, Eugene Wesley (Gene) Roddenberry was born in El Paso, Texas, to a cavalry officer, Eugene Roddenberry, and a housewife, Carolyn (Golemon) Roddenberry. His mother insisted on a religious upbringing for young Gene, with church and Bible studies very much a part of his daily life (although his father generally ignored religion). As a young teen, however, Gene gradually realized that most of religion, and Christianity in particular, with its rituals, "thou shalts," and "thou shalt nots," was alien to him. "I've been set down here among cannibals!" he protested after realizing the literal implications of eating Christ's "body" and drinking Christ's "blood."

Early Life. Gene Roddenberry was the oldest of three children. When Gene was only two, his father moved the family to Los Angeles, where he became a policeman. A decorated World War II fighter pilot, Gene joined Pan American Airways after the war. By the early 1950s he quit being a "bus driver in the sky," and with his wife and two young daughters relocated to Los Angeles, pursuing the family tradition of police work. Walking a beat by day, moonlighting as a speech writer for Police Chief William H. Parker, Gene still found time to write scripts for the new medium of television. Soon he was earning considerably more as a writer than as a police officer, and he resigned from the LAPD.

***Star Trek* Is Born.** After many years of writing for top TV series like *Dragnet* and *Have Gun Will Travel*, he created his first series, *The Lieutenant* (1963–64). This was followed by *Star Trek* (1964). *Star Trek* wasn't an easy sell; studios thought it "too cerebral," but eventually Desilu took a chance on the fledgling series. The show aired on NBC for three years, from 1966 to 1969, and was a critical failure. It was only during syndication that it became a phenomenon. In 1979 Roddenberry produced *Star Trek: The Motion Picture*. During his lifetime, there were several more films and a spin-off series, *Star Trek: The Next Generation*.

Roddenberry's Humanism. An agnostic most of his life, Roddenberry insisted that *Star Trek* be free of religion's "petty superstitions," refusing to put a chaplain onboard the starship *Enterprise* in both the original series and *Next Generation*. When fellow science fiction writer Isaac Asimov (then honorary president of the American Humanist Association) sent Roddenberry some literature in 1988, he became an avid humanist, realizing this had been his personal philosophy most of his life.

Roddenberry died on October 24, 1991, at the age of seventy. He was survived by two daughters; his first wife, Eileen; his second wife, *Star Trek* actress Majel (Barrett) Roddenberry; and their son.

Following his death, *Star Trek*'s producers chose to ignore his unbelief and humanism in favor of more mysticism, especially evident in the spin-off series *Star Trek: Deep Space Nine*.

BIBLIOGRAPHY

Roddenberry, Gene. *Star Trek: The Motion Picture, A Novel*. New York: Pocket Books, 1979.
Roddenberry, Gene, with Susan Sackett. *The Making of Star Trek: The Motion Picture*. New York: Pocket Books, 1980.
Roddenberry, Gene, with Stephen E. Whitfield. *The Making of Star Trek*. New York: Ballantine, 1968.
Sackett, Susan. *Inside Trek: My Secret Life with Gene Roddenberry*. Tulsa, OK: Hawk, 2002.

SUSAN SACKETT

ROGERS, J. A. (1883–1966), American anthropologist and humanist. Joel Augustus Rogers was born in Negril, Jamaica, in 1883. He immigrated to the United States in 1906 and became a naturalized citizen in 1917, the year he self-published his first book, *From Superman to Man*. He spent more than fifty years researching black history throughout the world. He was an anthropologist, historian, and journalist, visiting some sixty countries without institutional funding or support of any kind. He was largely self-taught, teaching himself French, German, Spanish, and Italian.

During his childhood, Rogers learned about the so-called myth of Ham, the belief that in Old Testament times blacks were cursed by God to be servants of whites. He was taught that blacks had produced no

worthwhile civilization, and that they were in almost every way inferior to whites.

Rogers delved into ancient history to prove otherwise. He collected rare photos of statues and paintings of African pharaohs, black gods and goddesses, and so forth. He argued that "there is but one race, the human race," and showed that the various peoples of the world have been mixing since antiquity.

Rogers was an atheist (see ATHEISM) and he was especially critical of the Church of Latter Day Saints (Mormons), considering their religion to be especially racist. He wrote that the LDS Church taught that God had cursed blacks, doomed them from birth, and would never allow them to enter heaven.

Rogers was sympathetic toward Islam, but he thought Christianity in general was harmful to blacks. While blacks were praying for pie in the sky, many whites were enjoying heaven on earth. He thought Christianity made many blacks apathetic to their plight. He believed that people of African descent would do well to pay less attention to the teachings of Christ and more attention to Friedrich NIETZSCHE.

Rogers published many more books, including the three-volume *Sex and Race*, *Nature Knows No Color Line*, *One Hundred Amazing Facts about the Negro*, and *Africa's Gift to America*. His writings influenced some of the most influential blacks of the twentieth century, including Hubert H. HARRISON, W. E. B. Du BOIS, Malcolm X, and Haile Salassie.

BIBLIOGRAPHY

McBryde, Mike. "Joel Augustus Rogers: A Leading Scholar, Thinker and Motivator." In *African-American Humanism: An Anthology*, edited by Norm R. Allen Jr. Amherst, NY: Prometheus Books. 1991.
Rogers, J. A. *As Nature Leads*. Baltimore, MD: Black Classic Press, 1987.

NORM R. ALLEN JR.

ROJAS, FERNANDO DE (1473?–1541), Spanish writer and playwright. Fernando de Rojas was probably born in La Puebla de Montalban, province of Toledo. He was of Jewish descent; presumably his great grandfather had converted to Christianity to avoid deportation. Fernando thus belonged to a converted family, so he was among the so-called new Christians—ancestrally Islamic or Jewish Christians whose sincerity of conversion was often doubted.

Around 1488 Rojas journeyed to Salamanca, site of the most prestigious Spanish university. There he studied Latin, philosophy, and other subjects for at least six years, aiming to earn his Bachelor of Law degree. At the time he wrote the last fifteen "acts" of his only known play—which was published in 1499 as *The Comedy of Calixto and Melibea*. However, many scholars attribute the first act of this work to Juan de Mena or Rodrigo de

Cota. Some years later, he added five further acts to the sixteen of the original play, titling the revised work *Tragicomedy of Calixto and Melibea*. Calixto and Melibea were star-crossed lovers brought together by La Celestina, a wicked and callous matchmaker who was not above employing black magic. La Celestina dies, stabbed, near the end of the play; Calixto and Melibea die also, in a way much like William Shakespeare's Romeo and Juliet.

What Rojas called "acts" in his play would later be known as "scenes." Many caused scandal, because he openly treated physical love and lust. Calixto even exalts his love for Melibea as being greater than any love he can feel toward God, going so far as to call Melibea his goddess. This was dangerous in a Spain that hunted down and killed former Jews regarded as less than true converts. (As recently as the 1950s, the play was banned as "immoral" in Mexico City.)

In 1507, following costly litigation brought against him by one of his neighbors, he settled in Talavera de la Reina, where he worked as a lawyer until the end of his days. There he married Leonor Álvarez de Montalbán, also a descendant of Jewish converts. She gave him seven sons and daughters who survived to adulthood. His first son chose his father's career at law. About 1538 Rojas became the mayor of Talavera.

Rojas died in 1541, never suspecting that his play—soon to be known as *La Celestina*—would became one of the great masterpieces of Spanish literature. The play ushered in the so-called Golden Century, during which few if any topics were too sensitive or controversial for literary treatment, paving the way for works such as Cervantes's *Don Quixote*, written more than a century after *La Celestina*.

Scholars have debated whether Rojas was truly a conspicuous convert scorned by an intolerant society. His last will and testament portrays him as a respected and vastly wealthy man, apparently well accepted in society. Though many suspected that he was never a true Catholic, he was careful enough never to give away any sign that might have compromised him with the Spanish Inquisition.

MARIO MENDEZ ACOSTA

ROSE, ERNESTINE L.

ROSE, ERNESTINE L. (1810–1891), American freethinker and women's rights activist. Blasted by ministers and newspaper editors as a "female devil" for speaking in public on freethought and women's rights, Ernestine L. Rose was one of the major intellectual forces behind the women's rights movement in nineteenth-century America. Yet today virtually no one knows her name.

Ernestine Potowski was born in Poland on January 13, 1810, of Jewish parents. By all accounts, she was a precocious child who learned Hebrew scriptures at an early age and chafed at her father's strict religion. Leaving home at seventeen, Ernestine ended up in London, where she became a disciple of Robert OWEN in the early 1830s and met her husband, William Rose, also an Owenite reformer.

In May of 1836 Ernestine Rose and her husband sailed to New York City to begin their married life in a country that promised equality to all under a Declaration of Independence. Within only a few months of her arrival, Ernestine was speaking to groups of New Yorkers about "Mr. Owen's system" while William opened a jewelry repair shop to help support her efforts. She spent her first decade in the United States lecturing on traditional Owenite concerns: the harm of private property, the evils of organized religion, the importance of education and freethought, and the significance of women's rights. Rose's first cause was the Married Women's Property Act: she spent her first winter in New York gathering signatures to support legislation that would allow married women to retain their own property after marriage.

By the 1840s Rose was increasingly dedicated to the intertwined issues of women's rights and FREETHOUGHT. She believed, as Robert Owen had before her—until he converted to Christian mysticism in his old age—that organized religion and the capitalist economic system were the root causes of women's inequality with men. Multilingual in a variety of ways, Rose was equally at home on the stage with "infidels" such as Robert Owen and Benjamin OFFEN, with woman's rights activists such as Elizabeth Cady STANTON and Susan B. Anthony, or with abolitionists such as William Lloyd Garrison.

Beginning in 1850, Rose helped organize the woman's rights conventions—both national and local—that were held throughout the 1850s and some of the 1860s, until the war intervened. An experienced speaker, unlike many other women in the movement, Rose was often a president or vice president of these conventions, and, as the movement grew, Rose became known as one of its greatest orators. As Susan B. Anthony reminisced, when Ernestine Rose was on the stage, "we all felt safe."

At the end of the Civil War, Rose joined her friends Susan B. Anthony and Elizabeth Cady Stanton to create the National Woman's Suffrage Association, an association dedicated to obtaining the franchise for women. Though the women's rights movement would splinter in 1869 over just who (women or black men) would get the right to vote, Rose's position never faltered, just as she never used the racist rationales that plagued the efforts of speakers like Anthony and Stanton. To Rose, the Declaration of Independence said it best: "We desire," wrote Rose in 1863, "to promote human rights and human freedom. In a republic based upon freedom, woman, as well as the Negro, should be recognized as an equal with the whole human race."

Ernestine and William returned to England in 1869, when the women's rights movement split apart. They spent the rest of their life in England, watching their expenses, as they had both devoted themselves to furthering an idea of individual freedom, not to making fortunes. Despite her importance to the women's rights movement, Ernestine Rose, who died in 1891, is perhaps the most forgotten of the women's rights activists. Her disappearance from history is telling. Not only was she scorned by newspaper editors and ministers, she was also isolated from and sometimes ignored by the very women and men with whom she shared reform platforms. Rose was outspoken, ironic, and, perhaps the most important, a freethinker who was born Jewish in Poland. In a movement that drew much of its moral and intellectual energy from appeals to Christian piety, Rose's atheism, her foreign accent, and her outspoken ways rendered her an "other" in a movement of others.

CAROL KOLMERTEN

ROSS, WILLIAM STEWART (SALADIN; 1844–1906), Scottish freethought journalist and poet. William Stewart Ross was born on March 20, 1844, in the Scottish county of Dumfries, the son of a farmhand. Coming from such modest beginnings, he was fortunate to receive any education at all, much less a university education. After going to New Abbey Parish School, Ross was sent to Hutton Hall Academy, where he studied and worked as an usher. His abilities were apparent by this time and he was able to go to Glasgow University, where he studied theology with a view to becoming a clergyman. But during the course of his studies he lost his Christian belief and became a convinced freethinker (see FREETHOUGHT).

Ross began earning his living as a journalist. In the fashion of the day, he wrote a novel which ran in serial form in the *Glasgow Weekly Mail*. He soon moved down to London, where in 1872 he set up a publishing business, specializing in educational books and magazines. But against the run of his business interests, Ross also became increasingly involved in the freethought movement.

While Ross had rejected religion, he was strongly opposed to taking up a hostile position against religion on all matters. He was also opposed to identifying the movement with ATHEISM. This put him on a collision course with Charles BRADLAUGH, who championed atheism as a moral rejection of the transcendental temptation. Also Ross was not a man willing to share the limelight, which ensured a further poisoning of relations with the better-known Bradlaugh. In 1880 Ross collaborated with Charles WATTS to coedit the *Secular Review*. Watts and Bradlaugh had parted ways in 1877 over disagreements as to the best course of action in a widely publicized legal action over their publication of a pamphlet in favor of birth control (see BIRTH CONTROL AND UNBELIEF). In 1884 Ross took ownership of the journal, which in 1889 he renamed the *Agnostic Journal and Secular Review*. Ross's own contributions were under the pseudonym of "Saladin," the great Muslim nemesis of the Christians.

Ross also collaborated in the short-lived British Secular Union (BSU), a freethought movement set up in 1878 largely by Charles Watts as an anti-Bradlaugh freethought vehicle. The figurehead of the BSU was the quixotic Marquis of Queensbury, who is better known for his virulent hatred of Oscar Wilde and his development of what are now known as the Queensbury rules of boxing. The BSU was already moribund when Charles Watts left for Canada in 1886 (see CANADA [ANGLOPHONE], UNBELIEF IN).

Ross allowed his intense dislike of Bradlaugh to cloud his judgment when in 1888 he collaborated in the publication of a scandalously libelous biography of his enemy. In subsequent lawsuits it was determined that Ross had assisted the nominal author, Charles McKay, with an unpublished manuscript he had already prepared, and with other material. Ross and McKay subsequently fell out and a costly legal battle ensued between them as well as between Ross and a justly aggrieved Bradlaugh.

Throughout his turbulent career, Ross kept up a steady stream of freethought writing, much of which began life in his *Agnostic Journal* and ended up published in book form. Notable titles include *God and His Book* (1887), *Roses and Rue* (1891), and *Woman: Her Glory and Her Shame* (1894). He was awarded a gold medal for the best poem on Robert Burns at the unveiling of a statue to him in 1879. Ross's contribution to freethought is enigmatic. He was fiercely opposed to Bradlaugh's atheism, though his own writing was far more incendiary than Bradlaugh's. But at his best, Ross produced some of the finest writing, both prose and poetry, in the service of freethought. He died on November 30, 1906.

BIBLIOGRAPHY

Bonner, Hypatia Bradlaugh. *Charles Bradlaugh: A Record of His Life and Work*. London: T. Fisher Unwin, 1908.

Columbine, W. B. "The Passing of Saladin." *Literary Guide*, January 1 1907.

Tribe, David. *President Charles Bradlaugh, MP*. London: Elek, 1971.

BILL COOKE

ROUSSEAU, JEAN-JACQUES (1712–1778), Swiss writer, musician, philosopher, and romantic. Jean-Jacques Rousseau's writings on religion offended both the Catholic authorities of Paris and the Protestant leaders of his native Geneva, forcing him to flee from both cities. However, he also quarreled bitterly with his fellow Encyclopedists VOLTAIRE, Jean le Rond D'Alembert and Denis DIDEROT (see also *ENCYCLOPÉDIE, L'*, AND UNBELIEF) over the proper role which religion should play in human affairs. He thus cannot be considered an unbeliever, but his works did much to help break the hegemony of Christianity over Western thought; also, his advocacy of a simple life was a precursor to the modern environmental movement.

Life. Rousseau was born in Geneva, Switzerland. His father was an itinerant watchmaker, his mother the child of a Calvinist cleric. She died a few days after giving birth to him, and as Rousseau puts it in his infamous *Confessions* (in which he goes into excruciating detail about the private facets of his life), "So my birth was the first of my misfortunes." There would be many more to come. He was to lead an erratic existence: orphaned at the age of ten, brutalized as an apprentice to an engraver in his teens, and finally wandering away from Geneva after discovering the city gates were closed to him when he returned from one of his frequent nature rambles. Rousseau found protection in the home and bed of Mme. De Warens in Turin, Italy. He became so attached to her that he abjured his Protestant religion and converted to Catholicism in her honor, although he was later to reconvert back to Calvinism in 1754 during a futile attempt to settle down in Geneva once more. For the rest of his life he would wander from one European city to another, usually living off the largesse of aristocrats who agreed theoretically with his denunciations of inherited wealth, and attempting to provide for his common-law wife Thérèse Le Vasseur, an illiterate serving girl with whom he had five illegitimate children. While himself a philosopher of education, Rousseau never put into practice any of his pedagogical views on his own children, as he sent them all to foundling homes upon their birth. He initially hoped to have a career as a composer and music theorist, and his opera *Le Devin du village* (The Village Soothsayer) was successfully performed before King Louis XV. He was invited to write articles on music for the *Encyclopédie*, the great compendium of human knowledge being edited by Diderot and D'Alembert. In 1750 he won an essay contest sponsored by the Academy of Dijon which helped to make him a well-known figure in France. However, his subsequent writings were denounced by the Catholic Church, causing him to return to Geneva, where he quickly offended the Swiss ecclesiastics. He then fled to London, and was for a time the guest of the noted freethinker David HUME, but his increasing paranoia led to a public break between the two. Rousseau eventually came back to Paris, where he was protected by the powerful marquis de Girandin, at whose estate he died in 1778. One of his visitors there was a young lawyer named Maximilien Robespierre, who would later credit his revolutionary political views to Rousseau's influence, and who would make it a point to extol the need to believe in a Supreme Being, sharing Rousseau's dislike of the materialism (see MATERIALISM, PHILOSOPHICAL) of the Encyclopedists.

Writings. Rousseau's award-winning essay of 1750 set the tone for his later writings. The question asked by the Dijon committee was whether the increasing role of the arts and sciences in human affairs had contributed to the betterment of society. Rousseau was the only one not to answer in the affirmative, marking his break from the Enlightenment RATIONALISM of his peers and demon-

strating his advocacy of what came to be called Romanticism—the view that human affairs should be connected with emotional rather than rational support systems. His brilliant writing style nonetheless won him the prize, even though his conclusion was diametrically opposed to the views of both the Academy of Dijon and his fellow Encyclopedists. However, his defense of the natural goodness of human beings was also in direct opposition to the Christian concepts of original sin and the fall from grace. In his later works, Rousseau postulated an original primitive state of existence, where humans lived together in harmony, their happy way of life based upon innate feelings of compassion for their fellow creatures. This idyllic world (which he admitted was purely hypothetical) came to an end with the rise of a settled agricultural society and an emphasis upon property rights, which divided people into haves and have-nots. Social inequalities arose, and civilization—rather than taming savages, as the common view would have it—was the means by which the masses were trained to accept their lots in life, respect the landowners and aristocrats who kept them from having sufficient food or shelter, and worship a God who presided over the despotic situation. "Man is born free," he wrote, "but everywhere is in chains." Modern society has taught humans to despise themselves and find their self-worth through adhering to artificial customs, rather than to appreciate their true natures.

Education. Given his strong condemnation of existing social structures, it is not surprising that Rousseau developed a prescription for the woes of humanity. It would not be possible to return to the Golden Age of the past, when all lived together simply and in peace, but one can try to avoid the corruptions of modern-day cultures by proper educational techniques. He delineated these in his much-debated books *La nouvelle Héloise* (1761) and *Émile* (1762), the latter becoming one of the most influential works in the philosophy of education. Children should be raised alone, rather than in common schools, and their emotional development should be the primary concern. Books should be eschewed, as these interfere with the direct contact with nature. Even the Bible should be avoided until at least the teenage years. The only exception Rousseau allowed was Daniel Defoe's *Robinson Crusoe*, since this book taught the importance of self-reliance and human resourcefulness. While critical of current educational practices, he still adhered to the rigid separation of the sexes, arguing that woman's nature was different from that of man's, and she should be trained to be a helpmate, not an equal. Mary WOLLSTONECRAFT, although deeply influenced by *Émile*, was to take Rousseau to task for not being radical enough in his social views. In her 1792 *A Vindication of the Rights of Women* she argued forcefully for coeducation and equal opportunity for women.

Perhaps the most controversial part of *Émile* was a long section titled *Profession de foi du vicaire savoyard* (The

Profession of Faith of a Savoyard Priest). It is an account of a cleric who in old age pens his memoirs, which describe how he never really believed in the austere and antierotic Catholic worldview. The work extols the virtue of nature, and argues that traditional orthodox beliefs—both Catholic and Protestant—are an affront to the name of the Deity, who has provided a world where all creatures have room to roam and plenty to eat. It was this section of *Émile* that particularly enraged the religious authorities of the time.

Religion. While criticizing the supernatural aspects of Christianity, Rousseau made it quite clear that he did not consider himself to be either an atheist or a materialist. In his 1762 *Contrat social* (The Social Contract) he went so far as to advocate a "Civil Religion" which would unite all members of a society under one belief system. He always expressed great respect for the moral teachings of Jesus, but could not accept the idea of the incarnation and original sin. And while he agreed with many of the Encyclopedists that the ancient philosophy of Epicureanism, with its emphasis on pleasure as the highest goal for human beings, needed to be revived, he nonetheless distanced himself from the view that hedonism meant the satisfaction of mere physical desires. For Rousseau, humans have a spiritual nature as well, which likewise needs to be satisfied. The organized religions of Christianity have perverted this by directing their attentions to dogmatic rivalries and through despising the natural world, but a true religion of humanity, he felt, was a real possibility once human beings finally broke away from artificial constructs. Finally, again unlike many of the freethinkers of his own time, Rousseau refused to give up a belief in an afterlife.

The study of Rousseau's philosophy can be frustrating, as he frequently seems to contradict himself, at times appearing to be almost an anarchist, at other times appearing to advocate a totalitarian system of government. But he himself claimed that he would rather be a man of paradoxes than a man of prejudices. His rich body of work and his personal example as a seeker of truth and iconoclastic shatterer of orthodoxies made him a major figure in the history of ideas.

BIBLIOGRAPHY

Bloom, Harold, ed. *Jean-Jacques Rousseau.* New York: Chelsea House, 1988.

Damrosch, Leo. *Jean-Jacques Rousseau: Restless Genius.* New York: Houghton Mifflin, 2005.

Melzer, Arthur M. *The Natural Goodness of Man: On the System of Rousseau's Thought.* Chicago: University of Chicago Press, 1990.

Reisert, Joseph R. *Jean-Jacques Rousseau: A Friend of Virtue.* Ithaca, NY: Cornell University Press, 2003.

Swenson, James. *On Jean-Jacques Rousseau.* Palo Alto, CA: Stanford University Press, 2000.

TIMOTHY J. MADIGAN

ROY, MANAVENDRA NATH (1887–1954), campaigner for social justice, international revolutionary, freedom fighter, and a major leader of the Indian humanist movement (see INDIA, UNBELIEF IN), M. N. Roy was one of the most extraordinary figures of the twentieth century. He was born Bhattacharyadranath Bhattacharya on March 21, 1887, in the village of Arbalia in the province of West Bengal.

A Time of Ferment. During Bhattacharya's childhood India lay under British colonial rule, a poor nation increasingly animated by nationalist sentiment. In the closing years of the nineteenth century figures destined for major roles in the saga of Indian independence were active across the world. Mohandas Karamchand Gandhi was in South Africa, where he battled racial discrimination against ethnic Indians there and campaigned for their rights. The Indian religious activist Swami Vivekananda, having turned from the aggressive skepticism of his youth to become the disciple of Hindu mystic Ramakrishna Paramahamsa, introduced the West to Hinduism at the first World Congress of Religions in Chicago (1893), then toured the United States, expressing an aggressive nationalism that inspired many leaders in India to fight against the British rule. Bankim Chandra Chatterjee's novel *Ananda Mutt* was published in 1904, provoking several leaders and sparking the revolutionary scheme known as *Bhavani Mandir.* The poet, political activist, educator, and later mystic Aurobindo Ghosh returned to India after withdrawing from civil service examinations in England. He founded a national school to educate students participating in the nationalist movement.

In 1898 young Bhattacharya's parents moved to the village of Kodalia. Bhattacharya studied in Harinabhi Anglo-Sanskrit School from 1899 to 1905 and caught the nationalist fervor. When the British government took the wholly unpopular decision to divide the province of Bengal, Bhattacharya expressed opposition and was expelled from school for doing so. He came into contact with local revolutionary groups. A turning point in the life of Bhattacharya came in 1905 with the death of his father. The following year, Bhattacharya entered the Bengal National College (the school Aurobindo Ghosh had founded) and studied at the Bengal Technical Institute for two years. By 1907 he was active with revolutionary terrorist groups opposed to British rule. That December he participated in the robbery of a railway station at Chingripota village in Bengal. In 1908 Bhattacharya was arrested in connection with the robbery, but the authorities could not establish sufficient evidence and he was released. His mother also died in that year.

Bhattacharya became very active in local revolutionary movements inspired by Aurobindo and discontinued his formal education, which he would never resume. In 1909 he participated in a *dacoity* (armed robbery) at Netra. He was arrested in January 1910, but again released due to lack of evidence. Between 1911 and 1914 he battled against British rule under the leadership of the prominent Bengali revolutionary Jatin Mukherjee. As part of a scheme to contact the Germans for help against the British, Bhattacharya sailed to Batavia (now Jakarta, Indonesia) under a pseudonym in April 1915. He returned to India that June, only to go again to Batavia for the purpose of acquiring arms, ammunition, and money from the Germans. In September 1915 Jatin Mukherjee was shot dead by British police. Dismayed at news of this, Bhattacharya resolved not to return to India until he could strike a telling blow against British rule. For nine months he wandered about Asia, seeking help from leaders including Chinese nationalist leader Sun Yat-Sen. Then German agents advised him to come to Germany for help.

Thus began the adventurous journey of the Indian revolutionary abroad. Bhattacharya posed as a Catholic priest from Pondicherry, the French colony in India. He grew a beard and carried a Bible. He also acquired a false passport and traveled from Japan to the United States by ship. By the time he landed in San Francisco in June 1916, the local press had published news about him; he did not linger in San Francisco but rushed to Stanford University, where Bengali writer Dhan Gopal Mukherjee was a student. He presented introductory letters to Dhan Gopal, who suggested that Bhattacharya adopt a new name. The identity of Manavendra Nath Roy was created in the United States in 1916.

Roy was still in the United States when Gandhi returned to India from South Africa, and so could not participate in what many considered the Indian nationalist movement's most glorious period. Instead, during this time he began to build an international reputation as a communist (see SOCIALISM AND UNBELIEF) and a rationalist (see RATIONALISM). Roy met Evelyn Trent, a Stanford University graduate who fell in love with him. Despite bitter opposition from her family, the two married in New York in 1917. Roy tasted the cosmopolitan life and Bohemian culture in New York. He met writer and politician Lajpat Rai, the "lion of Punjab," living in exile in New York. Engaged by Roy's sincerity and devotion to the cause of Indian freedom, Rai assisted him with paying work.

The British police continued tracking Roy in the United States in conjunction with their search for German agents of Indian nationality. Arrested in 1917, he was released after a warning. The Roys traveled to Mexico to escape the British police. While in Mexico, Roy began his embrace of socialism. To that point Roy's major commitment had been to nationalism.

Surprisingly, the financial help the Germans had promised reached him in Mexico. That enabled Roy to lead a comfortable life as he worked for the dual causes of India and his emerging socialist ideas. Roy was also in a position to offer hospitality and financial assistance to Mikhail Markovich Borodin, a Russian communist who was in desperate straits, having lost all his money.

Borodin acquainted Roy with the theory and practice of communism.

Roy played an important role in Mexican politics and moved in higher circles of power. He became friends with the first president of the new Mexican Republic, Venustiano Carranza. Quick in learning languages, Roy mastered Spanish and contributed articles to *El Pueblo*, a Mexico City daily, and *El Heraldo de Mexico*, for which he wrote in Spanish and English. He also published several theoretical articles in Spanish. But he never forgot his own country, writing articles and books on the cause of Indian freedom.

Roy organized the Socialist Party of Mexico and became its general secretary, organizing the party's National Congress in the fall of 1919. Influenced by Borodin, the party later was converted into the Communist Party of Mexico, the first such party outside Russia. This brought Roy to the attention of Vladimir Ilyich Lenin. At this time the Russian Communist Party was establishing contacts with revolutionaries throughout the world. Lenin invited Roy to attend the Second Congress of the Communist International in Moscow.

Roy and Evelyn traveled to Moscow by way of Cuba, Spain, and Germany, forging contacts with several revolutionaries along the way. He befriended August Thalheimer in Germany and met with some Indian revolutionaries already working there; he befriended Hendricus Sneevliet in Holland. In May 1920 Roy reached Moscow. Roy's first meeting with Lenin was a surprise for both. Lenin was under the impression that Roy was elderly; instead he found a bubbling youth with intellectual flash. Roy was surprised at Lenin's short stature and his friendliness in conversation. Roy quickly forged friendships with top communist leaders including Leon Trotsky, Joseph Stalin, and Nikolay Bukharin, and met the famous writer Maxim Gorky.

At the Second Congress of the Communist International, Roy submitted an alternative thesis on national and colonial affairs. Lenin saw its point and allowed the proposal to come before the congress; it was discussed and accepted. Buoyed by this victory, Roy at once started work to establish the Communist Party in India. He was elected chairman of the Central Asiatic Bureau of the Comintern. Accompanied by Evelyn, he traveled to by train to Tashkent in present-day Uzbekistan, bearing a full load of arms and ammunition. Roy and Evelyn established an Indian military school in Tashkent and trained some *Mujahirs*—Islamic warriors against the British—who had journeyed from India.

On October 17, 1920, Roy, Evelyn, and others created the first Communist Party of India in exile at Tashkent. At great risk they sent money, literature, and advice to Indian communists. In India, British colonial rulers scented Roy's involvement and resumed their hunt for him. Meanwhile Roy established direct contact with top leaders of the Indian National Congress Party, addressing letters to Chitta Ranjan Das, the Congress president. In 1921, Roy and Stalin established the Communist University of the Toilers of the East. Future presidents and prime ministers of colonial countries, including future Vietnamese leader Ho Chi Minh, received training in this institute; Roy and Evelyn served on its faculty. Between 1921 and 1929 Roy enjoyed a meteoric rise in the international communist movement, brushing aside opposition from Indian revolutionaries such as Virendranath Chattopadhaya and Avani Mukherjee then living in Russia and Germany.

Roy proved his ability through writings like *India in Transition*, a penetrating analysis. He launched a fortnightly magazine from Berlin, *The Vanguard of Indian Independence*. Evelyn assisted with the editing and wrote numerous articles under the name of Shanti Devi. When British rulers in India proscribed the journal, Roy launched another, *The Advance Guard*. Expelled from Berlin and France for his communist activities, Roy strove to continue to aid the Indian communist movement as he moved constantly around Europe. Even so, he played key roles in the international communist movement, holding many posts including top positions in the Comintern's Executive Committee, Politburo, Presidium, and Colonial Commission.

Roy edited yet another magazine, *The Masses of India*, which was dispatched into India clandestinely. In 1925 Roy and his wife, Evelyn, separated; she moved permanently to the United States, where she would die in 1970.

Conspiracy charges were lodged against Roy in India by the British police. But by 1927 Roy was in China aiding the Communist Party there. He met Mao Tsetung, Chou Enlai, and other top leaders. Also present, representing Moscow, was Borodin, whom Roy had aided in Mexico. In China they clashed over policy matters. When China's Kuomintang government attacked the communists, Roy escaped across the Gobi Desert to Russia. The only Indian leader whom Roy met during his stay in Moscow was Jawaharlal Nehru, who appreciated Roy's intellectual brilliance. Leadership quarrels in Russia kept Roy out of the communist mainstream. Falling sick, Roy went to Germany for treatment. There he wrote articles in Thalheimer's journal, so angering the Stalin group that Roy was expelled from the party.

Eventually Roy decided to return to India. Traveling incognito, he arrived in 1930, joining Nehru's camp and working secretly under the name of Mahmood. Still, the British police discerned his presence after the Congress Party passed a resolution concerning fundamental rights that bore Roy's stamp.

In 1930, Indian communists following the Stalinist line exposed Roy to the British. He was arrested, tried, and sentenced to twelve years' imprisonment, which was reduced to six on appeal. No lesser figure than Albert Einstein appealed to the British to treat Roy humanely while in prison. Roy made productive use of his jail days, writing copious amounts of political, philosoph-ical, and social criticism including his monumental work *The Philosophical Consequences of Modern Science*, portions of which would be published as *Heresies of the Twentieth Century*, *Materialism*, and *Science and Philosophy*. He corresponded extensively with political leaders and intellectuals worldwide, and with his girlfriend Ellen Gottschalk, then living in Germany. His letters to Ellen were hailed within India as literary masterpieces.

In November 1936 Roy was released from prison. His ideas had changed significantly, as they would continue to do; in particular, his reflections on MARXISM and communism had led him to emphasize critical thinking. Roy and Ellen married in 1937. In that year he joined the Indian National Congress, and briefly played an important role. Roy made enemies, among them Gandhi; dissatisfied with Gandhi's mystical obscurantism, Roy had backed the more nationalistic Subhas Chandra Bose against Gandhi in the 1938 presidential campaign. Ultimately he recoiled from national politics in that year, declaring nationalism an antiquated cult.

During World War II, Roy understood the dangers of fascism. He opposed the Indian communists, who had made a temporary pact with Adolf Hitler, going so far as to support the British. Roy predicted that if the British won the war they would soon leave India, a prediction that would come true. Yet at this time Roy was a voice in the wilderness, at odds with both communists and nationalists. In 1940 he started his own party, the Radical Democratic Party, India's first political party with an explicitly scientific orientation. His thinking continued its development; after eight years he recognized the defects of the party system and abandoned the Radical Democrats. Roy began touring throughout India, lecturing and recruiting intellectuals to join his Indian Renaissance movement, which was designed to spread the scientific spirit among the Indian public and recast Indian history from a scientific point of view. Roy launched journals including *Independent India*, *Marxian Way*, *Humanist Way*, and *Radical Humanist*.

India attained independence in 1947, validating Roy's earlier prediction. He grew yet more critical of Marxism and communism. By now Roy had turned all of his intellect and experience toward the evolution of humanist thought in India (see HUMANISM). He wrote extensively about scientific politics and the need to study history scientifically. In 1948 he published his definitive statement of humanist theory, *Principles of Radical Democracy*, comprising twenty-two theses.

When representatives of US and European humanist organizations founded the INTERNATIONAL HUMANIST AND ETHICAL UNION in Amsterdam in 1952, they elected Roy as vice chairman (in absentia). By then Roy had met with an accident in which he suffered brain damage. In his last days, Roy began dictating an autobiography, serialized in *Radical Humanist*; he would live only to cover the period to 1925. He also wrote a two-volume work titled *Reason, Romanticism and Revolution* (1952, 1955), which would be praised by eminent humanists including Erich FROMM.

Roy died in Dehra Dun, India, on January 25, 1954. Several of his writings were published posthumously. Oxford University Press released a four-volume set of his works edited by the radical humanist Sib Narayan Ray, who also published a biography of Roy.

BIBLIOGRAPHY

Narisetti, Innaiah. *M. N. Roy: Radical Humanist.* Amherst, NY: Prometheus Books, 2004.

Roy, M. N. *Reason, Romanticism and Revolution.* 2 vols. Calcutta: Indian Renaissance Publishers, 1952, 1955.

Sib Narayan Ray, ed. *Selected works of M. N. Roy.* 4 vols. Oxford: Oxford University Press, 1987–98.

INNAIAH NARISETTI

ROYALL, ANNE NEWPORT (1769–1854), American church/state activist and newspaper editor. Champion of the separation of church and state, Anne Newport Royall fought corruption and religious influence in American politics as a travel author and as editor of the newspapers *Paul Pry* and the *Huntress.* Her blunt honesty so annoyed her adversaries that she became the first American to be tried and convicted as a "common scold."

Frontier Beginnings. Anne was born in Baltimore, Maryland, in 1769, but was reared on the frontier of western Pennsylvania. At eighteen she moved to West Virginia and served as housekeeper for Revolutionary War veteran Maj. William Royall, who saw to her education in natural rights theory. They married when she was twenty-eight.

Following Major Royall's death in 1812, the Royall family contested Anne's inheritance of his estate. In 1819 a jury annulled William Royall's will, forcing Anne into an impoverished widowhood. Not undone, the resourceful Mrs. Royall began life as a travel writer. The resulting nine books documented sometimes embarrassing information about influential people she met in her travels from Louisiana to Maine.

Washington Lobbyist. After petitioning unsuccessfully to Congress for her husband's pension, she remained in Washington to put the principles she learned in Major Royall's humanist library to work. Though opposed to slavery and the use of alcohol, she disliked the religious positions of abolitionists and prohibitionists. She opposed religious influence in public schools and was known to destroy religious tracts by dumping them off steamboats and to chase evangelicals out of the congressional building with an old green umbrella.

In 1829 a conflict with a Presbyterian congregation resulted in a charge against her as a "common scold." On June 31 she became the first American found guilty of such a crime punishable by dunking. While the US Marines constructed a dunking stool, her attorney convinced the judge to change the punishment to a ten-dollar fine.

Following this humiliating event, she dedicated herself to the publication of two successive newspapers, *Paul Pry* and the *Huntress.* She spent the remainder of her eighty-five years exposing corruption and interviewing every president from James Monroe to Franklin Pierce with only the assistance of her friend Sally Stack and a handful of orphan boys. In 1854 the nearly penniless and unpopular editor died, a stalwart defender of eighteenth-century rationalism against the growing tide of nineteenth-century evangelism.

BIBLIOGRAPHY

Earman, Cynthia. "An Uncommon Scold." *Library of Congress Information Bulletin* 59, no. 1 (2000).

Jackson, George Stuyvesant. *Uncommon Scold: The Story of Anne Newport Royall.* Boston: Bruce Humphries, 1938.

MELINDA GRUBE

RUSSELL, BERTRAND (1872–1970), Welsh-born English philosopher and mathematician. Bertrand Russell is remembered for theoretical work in philosophy and mathematics, for practical work as a reformer of such institutions as marriage and education, and for antiwar activism, but for many he is most noted for his mastery of English prose, for which he was awarded the Nobel Prize in Literature in 1950. Throughout his long life, Russell was an outspoken advocate of skepticism and a severe and effective critic of religion. In 1957 he prepared a preface for a new edition of his *Why I Am Not a Christian*, including a definitive statement of his AGNOSTICISM: "There has been a rumor in recent years to the effect that I have become less opposed to religious orthodoxy than I formerly was. This rumor is totally without foundation. I think all the great religions of the world— Buddhism, Hinduism, Christianity, Islam, and Communism—both untrue and harmful."

Russell's Scrutiny of Religion. Russell examined the alleged proofs of the truth of religion with the philosophical acumen for which he is famous. His most scholarly examination of proofs of God's existence was in relation to his study of the philosophy of Gottfried Wilhelm von LEIBNIZ, but perhaps his best known is his debate with Father F. C. Copleston. Sexual teachings of the Catholic Church were a special target because they did "definite harm." As a young man, Russell was attracted to the writings of William Kingdon CLIFFORD, a mathematician known for his statement of the ethics of belief, that belief must always be based on sufficient evidence; in 1946 he wrote that he saw in Clifford every ground for regarding the old virtues of tolerance and enlightenment as the basis for the hopes that are possible after two world wars.

Foundations of His View. The story of Russell's own life was by no means so simple. His parents intended that he be brought up without religion, in stark contrast to the community, but when they both died prematurely, the young Russell was turned over to his grandparents by court order. His grandfather, Lord John Russell, twice prime minister, died when Russell was still quite young, so the entire supervision of his introduction to religion and morality was left in the hands of his grandmother, Lady John Russell, and his aunt. As a child, Bertie had some exposure to enlightened thinking from contact with this older brother, Frank, and from some tutors hired to educate him at home, but his grandmother's austere and dogmatic religion prevailed, and Bertie found his brilliant mind was not allowed any outlet at home. Lady Russell was, as Russell tells it, the sort of Scotch Presbyterian liberal who demanded that everyone be well housed but at the same time opposed the construction of new houses on the grounds they were an eyesore. Lady Russell's religious opinions were sufficiently broad that she became a Unitarian when she was age seventy, but Russell's dominant impression was that she never understood "the claims of animal spirits and exuberant vitality." Russell loved his grandmother for the care and affection she showed him, but did not mind when she died. Many years later, he came to appreciate how much her character had shaped his own: fearlessness, public spirit, and contempt for convention. One of her favorite texts became a leading one in his later life, "Thou shalt not follow a multitude to do evil."

At Cambridge Russell could at last say what he thought without fear of derision, and he enjoyed university greatly even before he met G. E. Moore, a freshman in Russell's third year. Russell's particular joy at Cambridge was a small discussion society known to outsiders as The Apostles. While still a freshman, Moore read a paper to the society that began: "In the beginning was matter, and matter begat the devil, and the devil begat God." Russell tells us the paper ended with the death of God, then the death of the devil, and finally with only matter left. Russell often described himself as a disciple of Lucretius in the manner of Moore, and Moore as one who fulfilled his idea of genius, but admits he derived no benefit from the official lectures at Cambridge.

His first marriage, to Alys Pearsall Smith in 1894, resulted in a number of complex conflicts over religion. Alys was a believing member of the Society of Friends. Russell supported her in the campaign for votes for women, and became a pledged teetotaler to please her. She had to modify her view that "sex was beastly" to please him. In letters from almost a year before their marriage, Russell made clear to Alys that he was utterly out of sympathy with Christianity and was at best some sort of metaphysical pantheist. Using arguments he would continue to deploy against believers for the rest of his life, he tried both to convince Alys and to reach a state of mutual toleration. Russell pointed out that when

with her, her religion seemed right, but when he thought about it he realized her religious beliefs were not based on any evidence but only on her wishes, "which thee would not accept as sufficient ground for an opinion about anything else." In this context, Russell mentioned John Stuart Mill's *Autobiography* as one of the deep roots of his own unbelief.

His Growth as a Writer. At about the time of his first marriage, Russell decided not to pursue a professional career but to become a writer. Ever since he was a child, Russell had dismissed organized religion, but he took religious experience, mysticism, and humanitarian impulses that transcended the individual ego very seriously, and throughout his life he read deeply in Christian classics. More importantly, he attributed his own style to his knowledge of the *Book of Common Prayer* and the King James version of the Bible.

By the turn of the century, Russell and Alfred North Whitehead had both produced mathematical books for which they planned second volumes. They decided to write a joint work, which eventually took over a decade to complete in three volumes and was titled *Principia Mathematica*. In the winter of 1900–1901, the same winter that Russell began to plan his great work, he had one of his most profound experiences, an experience which he claims changed his life forever, turning him from an imperialist into a pro-Boer and a pacifist. Russell went on to say that the mystic insight "largely faded," and his habit of analysis reasserted itself. Russell began an essay inspired by this experience while on a visit to Italy, and "The Free Man's Worship" was published in December of 1903. Although Russell rewrote part of the essay and repudiated some of its stoicism, it remains one of his most frequently reprinted, discussed, and appreciated short works, and serves well to document the nature of his unbelief at that time.

While still married to Alys, Russell became romantically involved with another, married woman with deep and complex religious convictions, one a year younger than himself but who had considerable experience in extramarital relationships. His liaison with Lady Ottoline Morrell, begun in 1911, resulted in a huge correspondence, much of it on religion. Nicholas Griffin has advanced the theory that were it not for the complexity and sincerity of her religious convictions, Lady Ottoline would not have been so attractive to Russell.

Russell first met Ludwig Wittgenstein in 1911, at about the same time his relationship with Ottoline reached a crisis over her inability to understand Russell's unbelief and his inability to impress upon her the importance of basing all one's beliefs on evidence. Nicholas Griffin argues a desire to collaborate more with Ottoline was a major reason for his decision at this time to concentrate more on popular writing and less on technical work. During World War I, Russell worked vigorously in the antiwar movement. After the war, he resumed his work with Wittgenstein. Russell's main association with

Wittgenstein had to do, of course, with logic, but Russell took great interest in the mysticism of Wittgenstein's *Tractatus* and in the religious works Wittgenstein was reading during the war.

In the summer of 1920, while preparing for a long trip to China with Dora Black, who was later to become his second wife, Russell decided that he must obtain a divorce from Alys. To meet the legal requirements of the day, he staged an "official adultery" for the benefit of the lawyers in a London hotel.

Second Marriage. Russell's relationship with Dora Black shows his complete break with conventional social mores. From the late 1920s and into the 1930s his sincere opposition to religion and his need to raise funds for the Beacon Hill School corresponded. His lecture "Why I Am Not a Christian" (1927) was recognized as a classic, and was soon followed by *Sceptical Essays* (1928) and *Marriage and Morals* (1929). This last work caused great controversy, and the Episcopal bishop of New York was especially distressed. He had to wait more than a decade to get revenge. In 1940 he and other religionists were successful in preventing Russell from being appointed to teach at the City College of New York (CCNY).

After losing the CCNY job, Russell worked for the Barnes Foundation in Philadelphia. This, too, eventually ended in a dispute. Nevertheless, out of it came one of his best-selling books, *A History of Western Philosophy* (1945).

Later Life and Influence. In 1948, after World War II, Russell engaged Father Copleston in a radio debate on the existence of God as a BBC Third Program. The transcript has been reprinted many times and continues to be discussed in introductory classes in philosophy. Copleston was then unknown, but is now well known for his celebrated history of philosophy. Also in 1948 Russell wrote, "I hobnob with the Archbishop of York." Here the attraction was shared views on control of atomic energy. In 1954 Russell offered only mild objection when his daughter embraced Christianity. In 2004 the archbishop of Canterbury urged study of Russell's works as part of a program of religious education. The archbishop maintained that consideration of views like Russell's "protest atheism," that religion is morally bad, both in its practice and in its requirement that we worship a God who appears to be ultimately responsible for evil in the world, form a necessary part of teaching religion and that no good is served by ignoring one's critics.

Russell did not object to being called an atheist, an agnostic, a humanist, a skeptic, or a rationalist, but neither did he embrace any of these terms with enthusiasm. His writings are filled with nuanced discussions of the meaning of these terms. In particular, we may note his denial of ATHEISM on the grounds that there is some very small possibility that God does exist; his denial of skepticism such as that adopted by David HUME, which denies that any knowledge is possible; and his denial of HUMANISM on the grounds that on the whole the non-human part of the cosmos is much more interesting and satisfactory than the human part.

BIBLIOGRAPHY

Monk, Ray. *Bertrand Russell.* Vol. 1. New York: Free Press, 1996.

———. *Bertrand Russell.* Vol. 2. London: Jonathan Cape, 2000.

Russell, Bertrand. *The Autobiography of Bertrand Russell.* Vols. 1 and 2. Boston: Little Brown, 1967, 1968.

———. *The Autobiography of Bertrand Russell.* Vol. 3. New York: Simon & Schuster, 1969.

———. *Bertrand Russell on God and Religion.* Edited by Al Seckel. Amherst, NY: Prometheus Books, 1986.

———. *A History of Western Philosophy.* New York: Simon & Schuster, 1945.

———. *Russell on Religion.* Edited by Louis Greenspan and Stefan Andersson. London: Routledge, 1999.

———. *The Selected Letters of Bertrand Russell.* Edited by Nicholas Griffin. Vol. 1. London: Penguin, 1992.

———. *The Selected Letters of Bertrand Russell.* Edited by Nicholas Griffin. Vol. 2. London: Routledge, 2001.

Weidlich, Thom. *Appointment Denied: The Inquisition of Bertrand Russell.* Amherst, NY: Prometheus Books, 2000.

DAVID WHITE

RUSSELL, DORA (1894–1986), English sex radical and progressive activist. Born Dora Black, she became the second wife of Bertrand RUSSELL. A tireless proponent of peace, progressive education, and enlightened sexual policies, she was an effective organizer, a successful author, and one of the most important English feminists of the period between the world wars.

Early Experience. Well educated (Girton College, Cambridge), serious, and practical on political and social issues, Russell was primarily a sexual idealist. In 1917 during a dangerous crossing of the Atlantic, she was attracted to a naval officer, "a kind of daredevil who could have been a pirate." He was on a secret mission while still recovering from having his ship blown up by a submarine, but had never met the likes of Dora. One night, she wrote, minus the mandatory lifejackets, "in mid-Atlantic, on the top deck and a folded heap of sailcloth, under a bright moon and scudding clouds, he took my virginity."

With Bertrand Russell. Dora had a long and important career in progressive politics with and without help from Bertrand Russell. They both believed in sexual freedom, but understood it differently. Dora's writings on behalf of all women and all children are more detailed, more profound, and more inspiring than the philosopher's contributions. Dora first admired Bertie, as she always called him, for his public opposition to World War

I, and always credited him with teaching her to stand up and speak out for unpopular ideas. She would have been happy to continue as his partner in love, in the progressive school they ran together, and in movement for greater human freedom. Bertrand insisted they marry to provide an heir to his title. Neither demanded a monogamous relationship. Dora's analysis of their relationship, their life together, and especially of Bertrand's character is one of the most penetrating to appear in print: she understood she had to be both wife and mother to him.

Main Message. Dora was unimpressed with "external devices for the preservation of virtue." She considered marriage laws, police, and the military indications of human incompetence. She described European life as "treading the path of corset civilization," with laws and customs guided by an a priori religious ethic rather than considerations of needs and creative desires. The publication of her most important work, *Religion of the Machine Age* (1983), was long delayed. Ever since her visit to Russia in 1920, Russell understood that democracy could be defeated by the totalitarian tendencies of capitalism and of communism as industrialization became the organizing principle of society. She died at her home in Cornwall, where she had lived much of her life.

BIBLIOGRAPHY

Russell, Dora. *The Dora Russell Reader.* London: Pandora Press, 1983.

———. *The Religion of the Machine Age.* London: Routledge & Kegan Paul, 1983.

———. *The Right to Be Happy.* Garden City, NY: Garden City Publishing, 1927.

———. *The Tamarisk Tree.* 3 vols. London: Virago, 1977, 1981, 1985.

DAVID WHITE

RUSSIA, THE SOVIET UNION, AND UNBELIEF: See PROPAGANDA, ANTIRELIGIOUS (SOVIET).

SADE, DONATIEN ALPHONSE FRANÇOIS, MARQUIS DE (1740–1814), French writer, philosopher, and libertine. Virtually unknown during his own lifetime, the Marquis de Sade's writings have since become almost sacred texts for generations of individuals fascinated by his extremism, his outrageousness, and his provocativeness. For with his unflinching honesty and his dogged effort to describe nature as it really is, Sade is the ultimate un-Romantic, the Dark Knight of the Enlightenment (see ENLIGHTENMENT, UNBELIEF DURING THE). His advocacy of strength as the ultimate moral virtue precedes that of Friedrich NIETZSCHE, and his atheistic avowal that life has no ultimate meaning anticipates the EXISTENTIALISM and postmodernism of the twentieth and twenty-first centuries.

Born in Paris to an aristocratic family, Sade was raised by his uncle, the Abbe de Sade, whose notorious sexual habits had a profound impact on his nephew, among other things inculcating his lifelong ANTICLERICALISM. Sade was to spend most of his life in prison for sexual deviancy, and it was there that he wrote most of the works for which he is now known. These erotic books—which include *Justine, Juliette, Philosophy in the Boudoir,* and *The 120 Days of Sodom*—are overly long, repetitious, and ultimately soporific. The saving grace of Sade's writings is not the sexual passages, which are more likely to nauseate than titillate, but rather the witty and incisive philosophical passages (often put into the mouths of the most monstrous of characters), which all too briefly pop up when one least expects them. It is these nuggets that have been of more influence than the endless descriptions of human degradation that consume so many of his pages.

Sade's first published work was the 1782 "Dialogue between a Priest and a Dying Man," in which the dying man convinces the priest through ruthless argumentation that there is no god or afterlife, and that hedonism is the only logical ethical system. The priest joins him in an orgy with three prostitutes as the man expires. This hilarious work was later issued as a pamphlet by the FREETHOUGHT publisher Emanuel HALDEMAN-JULIUS. It demonstrates Sade's affinity with the materialist philosophers of his day (see MATERIALISM, PHILOSOPHICAL), as well as his delight in shocking the sensibilities of his contemporaries.

Sade despised religious figures, and indeed all authority figures—not surprisingly, as he was imprisoned by the royal court of Louis XVI, the revolutionary government of Robespierre, and the regime of Emperor Napoleon I. He extolled the virtue of BLASPHEMY and argued that if God did exist He was the worst mass murderer and tyrant of all time.

In his last will and testament, Sade demanded that his body be buried in an unmarked grave with acorns planted within, so that a tree would grow upon the spot, completely obliterating his memory. In 1990 the respected French series *Bibliotheque de la Pleiade* issued a scholarly edition of Sade's complete work, encased in leather binding (being bound in leather, by the way, adding a nice if unanticipated Sadeian touch). The Marquis' scabrous writings now share space with the works of Balzac, Hugo, and other French "Immortals." After centuries of opprobrium, Sade seems to have finally become respectable.

BIBLIOGRAPHY

Airaksinen, Timo. *The Philosophy of the Marquis de Sade.* New York: Routledge, 1995.

Bongie, Lawrence L. *Sade: A Biographical Essay.* Chicago: University of Chicago Press, 1998.

Gray, Francine du Plessix. *At Home with the Marquis de Sade.* New York: Simon & Schuster, 1998.

Sawhney, Deepak Narang, ed. *Must We Burn Sade?* Amherst, NY: Humanity Books, 1999.

Schaeffer, Neil. *The Marquis de Sade: A Life.* Cambridge, MA: Harvard University Press, 2001.

TIMOTHY J. MADIGAN

SAGAN, CARL (1934–1996), American astronomer and popularizer. Carl Sagan was the world's leading planetary astronomer during the golden age of planetary exploration, a gifted teacher, the author of best-selling science books for the public, cocreator and host of the thirteen-part *Cosmos* television series, and outspoken spokesman for the excitement of scientific discovery and the highest values of science. He was also a prominent humanist and skeptic, always advocating open-minded skepticism toward questionable claims.

Sagan was the David Duncan Professor of Astronomy and Space Sciences and director of the Laboratory for Planetary Sciences at Cornell University throughout most of his career, where he played leading roles in the Mariner, Viking, Voyager, and Galileo unmanned spacecraft expeditions to the planets. Born in New York City, Sagan was educated at the University of Chicago, receiving his AB, BS, MS, and PhD degrees there from 1954 to 1960. He then taught at Harvard before moving to Cornell in 1968. In his scientific work he published widely on planetary science, especially planetary atmospheres. He had special interests in what led other planets' atmospheres to differ so vastly from that of the Earth and whether some might contain the building blocks of life. In addition to his deep interests in astronomy, he early on developed an interest in biology and the origins of life. During summers at Chicago he apprenticed to the Nobel laureate geneticist H. J. Muller. This combination of interests led to his first notable book, *Intelligent Life in the Universe* (1966), a unique collaboration with the Russian astronomer I. S. Shklovskii. Sagan arranged a translation of the Russian's book on the subject and with Shklovskii's encouragement extensively added to it, carefully marking with triangular symbols where his emendations began and ended. The result was a highly readable excursion through the science and best-informed scientific speculation about the possibilities of life elsewhere.

The book showed that the young Sagan had not only immense curiosity and broad and deep scientific knowledge, but also a wonderful talent for expressing serious scientific ideas in highly readable form. Over the coming decades this talent rocketed him to the forefront of the world's science popularizers and made him virtually a household name.

His 1973 book *The Cosmic Connection* brought him to the attention of a wide public. He revealed a fresh, lyrical, at times even poetic, style of expression and popularized the notion that we are star-stuff, composed of elements created inside of stars and spewed out over space in supernova explosions. His interests in the evolution of human intelligence led to his next book, *The Dragons of Eden* (1977). It won a Pulitzer Prize. Now Sagan was a superstar of science. That year he made the cover of *Newsweek*, and in 1980, the cover of *Time*.

His next two books, a collection of essays titled *Broca's Brain: Reflections on the Romance of Science* and *Murmurs of Earth*, were preludes to his most ambitious project yet, the thirteen-part public broadcasting television series *Cosmos* (1980). Here all of his eclectic interests, talents, and aesthetics came brilliantly together in a series of one-hour programs that, beyond their informative content, had a powerful inspirational quality. *Cosmos* was a huge hit. It was seen by half a billion people in sixty countries. It won Emmy and Peabody awards. Sagan's simultaneously published, handsomely illustrated book of the same title became the best-selling science book ever published in the English language.

Unlike many scientists, Sagan had no qualms about speaking and writing directly for the general public. He considered it an obligation and a privilege. He appeared nearly thirty times on NBC's *Tonight Show* with Johnny Carson and later became a regular contributor to *Parade*, the national newspaper magazine supplement. He always spoke entertainingly but eloquently about science, and of how the processes of science are uniquely able to determine truths about nature.

While Sagan saw science as an ennobling aspect of the human spirit to know and explore, he also recognized the tempting appeal of pseudoscience and the dangers of public misunderstanding or ignorance of science. Often against opposition, he encouraged his fellow scientists to openly examine rather than ignore controversial and unscientific claims on the fringes of science. In 1969 he and astronomer Thornton Page organized a symposium at the annual meeting of the American Association for the Advancement of Science (AAAS) applying the scientific method to UFOs, and they later edited a book based on it, *UFO's: A Scientific Debate* (1972). In 1974 Sagan and Immanuel Velikovsky squared off in another AAAS symposium, this one examining Velikovsky's bizarre planetary-pinballs ideas. This famous encounter is still debated today.

When the Committee for the Scientific Investigation of Claims of the Paranormal (CSICOP) was created in 1976, Sagan was a Founding Fellow. He remained an active supporter throughout his life, twice delivering keynote addresses at CSICOP conferences and receiving CSICOP's two highest awards. He also was a member of the Council for Secular Humanism's International Academy of Humanism. His writings and public appearances frequently addressed these issues. *Broca's Brain* contained a large section called "The Paradoxers," including a revised version of his Velikovsky paper and a lead chapter "Night Walkers and Mystery Mongers: Sense and Nonsense on the Edges of Science."

Major Sagan books exemplifying the power and beauty

of science continued coming. He wrote two with his wife, Ann Druyan (cocreator of the *Cosmos* series), *Comet* (1985) and *Shadows of Forgotten Ancestors* (1992), followed by *Pale Blue Dot: A Vision of the Human Future in Space* (1995). In between was his big science fiction novel, *Contact* (1985), eventually made into a thoughtful 1997 motion picture starring Jodie Foster.

In 1996 Sagan organized his thoughts and writings over the previous ten years about pseudoscience, superstition, and irrationality into a single book, *The Demon-Haunted World: Science as a Candle in the Dark*. He critically examined "alien abductions," "channelers," faith-healing fraud, the "face" on Mars, "past lives," hypnosis-based pseudotherapies, and crashed-saucer claims. He worried whether we might be on the brink of a new Dark Age, "the siren song of unreason more sonorous and attractive." He argued that scientific thinking and skepticism are our best way to safeguard democratic institutions. The book combined his uncanny knack for scientifically skewering questionable claims with compassion for those who sincerely believe in them. He reenunciated how creative thinking and skeptical thinking work together to provide powerful insights: "At the heart of science is an essential balance between two seemingly contradictory attitudes—an openness to new ideas, no matter how bizarre or counterintuitive, and the most ruthless skeptical scrutiny of all ideas, old and new. This is how deep truths are winnowed from deep nonsense."

Since late 1994 Sagan had been battling a rare disease, myelodysplasia, requiring a move with his family to Seattle for his treatments. He died on December 20, 1996, at the age of sixty-two. He had completed his final book, *Billions and Billions*, only two months earlier. It was a tragically premature death for a brilliant proponent of science and reason, a foe of all forms of superstition and irrationality, and an inspiring chronicler of humanity's fledging steps toward exploring and understanding the universe.

KENDRICK FRAZIER

SANGER, MARGARET HIGGINS (1879–1966), American birth control activist and feminist. Margaret Higgins was born in Corning, New York, one of eleven children. In *An Autobigraphy* (1938), Sanger recorded her childhood introduction to FREETHOUGHT and the power of the Roman Catholic Church to turn back social progress. Her freethinking father invited famous agnostic Robert Green INGERSOLL to speak in Corning, renting the town's only hall, which was owned by the local priest. Just before the address, the priest learned the speaker's identity and locked the doors. Sanger's father led the speaker and the audience through a mob and into the woods, where Margaret and others sat spellbound as Ingersoll orated. Her father's stalwart advice to his family was to be chained to no dogma, to depend not on a church but on oneself, and to "leave the world better because you, my child, have dwelt in it."

Spending three comparatively carefree years in Claverack, a coeducational school in the Catskills, Sanger returned home to nurse her dying mother in 1896. Weakened by multiple pregnancies, Anne Purcell Higgins died at age forty-eight of tuberculosis. Sanger, infected herself by the disease, attended nursing school in White Plains, New York, specializing in obstetrics. She married architect William Sanger in 1902 and had three children, Stuart (1903), Grant (1908), and Peggy (1910). Sanger nearly died of tuberculosis after Stuart's birth.

Sanger's Activism Begins. Sanger moved with her family to the heady atmosphere of New York City in 1912, rubbing shoulders with Emma GOLDMAN, Bill Haywood, and other radicals at Mabel Dodge's radical salons. That year Sanger, working as a nurse, helped supervise the relocation of children during the "Bread and Roses" textile workers' strike in Lawrence, Massachusetts. Sanger made national headlines when she testified before an investigating Congress. Sanger began a weekly column, "What Every Mother Should Know," for the *Call*, published by the Socialist Party. She turned her columns into a pamphlet, along with a second series, "What Every Girl Should Know," which was censored because Sanger used the words *syphillis* and *gonorrhea*.

Sanger's turning point was witnessing the death of patient Sadie Sachs from her second illegal abortion. When the twenty-eight-year-old mother had pleaded with her doctor for birth control, he had responded, in Sanger's presence: "Tell Jake [Sadie's husband] to sleep on the roof." Sanger took off her nurse's uniform and resolved to learn the secrets of fertility control and to share them with women. Sanger researched contraception, coining the term *birth control* (see BIRTH CONTROL AND UNBELIEF) while editing a monthly newspaper, the *Woman Rebel*. Its motto was "No Gods, No Masters," and its purpose was to challenge the 1873 Comstock Act, which classified contraceptives as "indecent articles" and prevented dissemination of contraceptive information through the mails (see COMSTOCK, ANTHONY, AND UNBELIEF; SEXUAL VALUES, IMPACT OF UNBELIEF ON). Facing forty-five years in prison when indicted under the Comstock Act, Sanger fled the country in 1914, leaving behind a book, *Family Limitation*. It sold ten million copies while Sanger continued her research in England and the Netherlands.

Sanger returned to the United States after her estranged husband was personally arrested by Comstock and jailed for a month. Her daughter, Peggy, died of pneumonia in November 1915. Devastated, Sanger went on a headline-making speaking tour to challenge the charges against her. Sanger announced that, like earlier English birth control advocate Annie BESANT, she would defend herself. Famous names petitioned the president on her behalf as news coverage built, and the charges were dropped in 1916.

A Practical Activist. Sanger opened the first birth control clinic that year, in Brooklyn, New York; it was raided ten days later. Although Sanger's conviction and thirty-day sentence were upheld by the New York State Supreme Court in 1917, the court ruled that contraceptive advice could be given to cure and prevent disease. By 1923 Sanger had recruited Dr. Hannah Stone to staff the Birth Control Clinical Research Bureau, which scrupulously documented birth control efficacy and trained physicians.

Sanger financed a gynecologist to lecture physicians on birth control techniques, signing up twenty thousand physicians to take referrals. She personally recruited two doctors to design a contraceptive jelly to use with diaphragms. She provided her Brooklyn clinic with up to one thousand diaphragms a week, bootlegged through Canada by her second husband, oil tycoon Noah Slee, whom she had married in 1922. Slee loaned money to birth control supporters to open America's first diaphragm factory. Continually beseeched by women seeking help, Sanger was believed to have received the highest volume of mail of nearly any contemporary private citizen. She excerpted these poignant letters in *Motherhood in Bondage* (1928).

Sanger wrote *My Fight for Birth Control* in 1931, when fifty birth control clinics were open in United States. When Japanese diaphragms she had ordered were destroyed by US Customs under the Comstock law, Sanger sued. In 1934 a federal judge ruled in *United States v. One Package* that the Comstockian Revenue Act did not apply to contraceptives. The Circuit Court of Appeals agreed in 1937, ending the sixty-three-year reign of Comstockian censorship over the mails.

By the late 1930s, the United States had more than three hundred birth control centers, but World War II put the movement on hold. Marginalized for a while in her movement, Sanger, seventy-three, planned a world conference in 1952, cosponsored by Albert Einstein, Eleanor Roosevelt, and others. It resulted in the International Planned Parenthood Federation and Sanger became its first president. With financial help from a woman benefactor, Sanger next commissioned a study on steroid hormones and other laboratory studies, which resulted in "the pill," released in 1960. Sanger lived to witness the US Supreme Court decision *Griswold v. Connecticut* (1965), declaring a constitutional "right to privacy" in striking down a Comstockian law denying married couples contraception.

A Secular Visionary. *Woman and the New Race*, published in 1920, promoted erotic fulfillment for women and named Christianity as the principal enemy of women's progress. It sold a quarter of a million copies. Sanger accused Christianity of having turned the clock back two thousand years for women. Wherever she spoke, in the United States and around the globe, Sanger was dogged by Roman Catholic censors. The most celebrated episode involved Catholic Archbishop Patrick J.

Hayes, who canceled her talk on "Birth Control—Is It Moral?" at Town Hall in New York City and had her arrested. After World War II, Gen. Douglas MacArthur barred her from entering Japan at Roman Catholic behest.

Sanger wrote and published extensively, including two long-lived journals on birth control and fertility. Her books make freethought references, such as her autobiographical comment: "I wanted each woman to be a rebellious Vashti, not an Esther." Although she spoke and wrote with great effectiveness, her greatest contributions were deeds, not words. Though a streak of mysticism surfaced in the emotional Sanger during some crises, she was without religion. Not content with simply being "a rebellious Vashti" herself (she was jailed eight times), Sanger was determined to deliver birth control information and devices worldwide during her lifetime. Willing to confront the power of the churches and their dogma head-on, Sanger succeeded in her quest, becoming the twentieth century's most effective feminist activist.

BIBLIOGRAPHY

Baskin, Alex, ed. *Margaret Sanger, The Woman Rebel, and the Rise of the Birth Control Movement in the United States.* Stony Brook: State University of New York at Stony Brook Press, 1976.

Douglas, Emily Taft. *Margaret Sanger: Pioneer of the Future.* New York: Holt, Rinehart & Winston, 1970.

Sanger, Margaret. *An Autobiography.* New York:. Norton, 1938.

———. *My Fight for Birth Control.* New York: Farrar & Rinehart, 1931.

———. *Woman and the New Race.* New York: Brentano's, 1920.

Sicherman, Barbara, and Carol Hurd Green, eds. *Notable American Women: The Modern Period.* Cambridge, MA: Belknap Press of Harvard University Press, 1980.

ANNIE LAURIE GAYLOR

SANTAYANA, GEORGE (1863–1952), American philosopher. George Santayana was born Jorge Austin Nicolas de Santayana on December 16, 1863, in Madrid, Spain. His mother brought him to the United States in 1872 and deposited him in Boston. He attended Boston Latin School and Harvard University, reading voraciously in several languages and writing poetry and philosophy. Upon graduation from Harvard, he shared a fellowship to Germany, where he studied philosophy and worked on his dissertation.

Upon his return to the United States, Santayana started teaching at Harvard, where he was eventually promoted to professor. He taught with passion and was greatly admired by his students. Nevertheless, he retired as soon as he could afford it, sailing for Europe in 1912.

He spent the next forty years of his life traveling from city to city, writing almost until his last days. He died in Rome in 1952 at the age of eighty-nine.

Santayana's father was a freethinker (see FREETHOUGHT), meaning that he refused to accept beliefs merely because they were orthodox. His son followed in his footsteps and in the process developed a philosophical system uniquely his own. At the center of his convictions is the insistence that human theories and practices must not be at odds with each other. His call for honesty in philosophy makes it impossible for hungry skeptics to claim, for example, that they can't know if anything exists, so long as they can find their way to the refrigerator.

Santayana is, by native tendency, a materialist (see MATERIALISM, PHILOSOPHICAL), seeking the natural or biological foundations of our hopes and values, and refusing the cheap consolation offered by imagining a rational and just world operating under divine guidance. But he is in love with the symbolic life of religion and with the higher reaches of spirituality it sometimes fosters. His system of thought can be seen as an attempt to graft the insights of religion onto a naturalistic view of life. He writes as if his central question were: What role can religion play in a world without God, immortality, and a reassuringly stable human nature? His thought offers a constructive and systematic answer to this question, an answer attractive to religious and secular people alike.

He maintains that it would be in vain to deny the obvious: human beings are animals whose power and lives are limited by nature. The world is pretty much as we experience it, offering no evidence of divine regulation or of a glorious destiny for any of us. We are psyches—intelligent material organisms—engaged in a constant struggle for survival. Our home is the world of substance in which everything preys on everything else, for "matter is essentially food." A vision of the future, along with self-control, enable us—under favorable circumstances—to live a life of reason. This requires limiting our desires to those that do not get in each other's way and thereby allow us a modest maximization of our satisfactions.

A life of reason offers harmony of our natural impulses. It involves realistic assessments of our situation, intelligence, hard work, and a spirit of compromise. But its values are neither absolute nor unconditional; reason is a good only to those who embrace it. There are, in fact, no universal values. What we prize depends on who we are, and human natures are indefinitely various. The right moral stance, therefore, is toleration of others so long as their satisfactions do not interfere with ours, along with fierce allegiance to our chosen way of life. Santayana has no difficulty in reconciling universal sympathy for life in all its forms with personal preference for a limited set of values; the good is relative when we try to understand people and absolute when we enact our own.

Spirituality consists in consciousness—"intuition" in Santayana's language—of essences, which are features of existence and themes of thought. The specific essence intuited matters little; everything hangs on the stance with which mind approaches its object. The spiritual attitude is one that forswears use and practical interest, permitting absorbed contemplation or enjoyment of what is presented. This occurs in our experience whenever we take delight in the appearance of things without concern for their promise or fate. A world of beauty opens when, forgetting past and future, mind sheds its cares. The unhurried exploration of pure form completes life by making each of its moments satisfying and significant. This is "religion" in its purer, spiritual form. It provides no consolation for the fragility and passage of biological existence, but serves as the capstone of human life.

Santayana was raised a Catholic and never officially relinquished his religion. He made a careful study of the Bible, the results of which are well demonstrated in his *The Idea of Christ in the Gospels or God in Man*. He is thoroughly familiar with the classics of Christian and Jewish theology, and he often refers to Hindu, Buddhist, and Muslim religious notions and texts. He was as concerned with the truth of religious ideas as he was with the role of religion in a full and satisfying life.

His first attempt to understand the nature of religion, *Interpretations of Poetry and Religion* (1900), set the tone and established the main theses of his view. Religion, he argues, is poetry when it becomes a guide to life. Its truth is symbolic: it offers a description of the human condition in imaginative terms, with consequent prescriptions for how to lead it. What look like factual claims in sacred texts need to be reinterpreted as symbolic insights into human life and destiny. "The fear of the Lord is the beginning of wisdom," for example, is best understood if we drop reference to a mighty person who may arbitrarily punish us and substitute for it the source of fear with which we are all familiar, namely, nature in its uncontrolled manifestations.

The imagination is a vital human faculty, expressing the deepest concerns and keenest insights of the psyche. For this reason, calling religion a work of the imagination is no insult: it is an authentic and relevant response pressing circumstances wring from the animal soul. To take such poetry literally is to lose its meaning or to demean it by converting it into fairy tales. Such "dreaming in words" is not uncommon among childlike or superstitious people, but cooler heads have always thought that stories of the exploits of gods need interpretation.

There are two major tendencies in religion. The first leads to religions of piety toward the source, the second to what he calls "ultimate religion." The central object of piety is the power of nature; on it depend our precarious lives. The association of religious values with hearth and home, with land, with the seasons, and with the productivity and destructiveness of nature all point to faith focused on human flourishing. Beliefs in immortality and heaven are extensions of this concern for abundant life.

Ultimate religion faces in the other direction, seeking spirituality rather than well-being. It accepts whatever nature may provide, but does not lay up its treasures on earth. In Santayana's view of the spiritual life, it makes no demands and asserts no preferences. Its attitude is one of humility or even indifference toward worldly matters, as it celebrates the glory of the moment. This drunkenness with the immediate obliterates concern with animal life and opens the door to eternal rapture or contemplative absorption.

When it comes to God, Santayana is uncompromising: he denies the existence of a deity conceived as "the creator of the world and the dispenser of fortune." For him, the question of God's existence boils down to the issue of whether the power we call by that name deserves a designation suggesting providential care. Santayana thinks that, considering the way of the world, it does not; it is more accurate to call that power *matter*, a force that is indifferent to human welfare. Yet the notion of the triune Godhead is useful for identifying the similarities and differences between Santayana's ontology and ordinary religious consciousness.

At the culmination of his monumental *Realms of Being*, Santayana examines the conception of the Trinity, comparing it to his four-realm ontology. He finds that the Nicene Creed and subsequent theology have the makings of a sound account of reality but, unfortunately, lose their way when they dissolve necessary distinctions in the unity of the divine individual. Persons are ontological hybrids, combining matter, form, consciousness, and, because they have a history, even truth. The point of ontological analysis is to differentiate categories; it does not help the cause of understanding to conflate them by assigning all of them to a primordial, generative person. Santayana reverses the process by reducing Christian theology to its "secret interior source." He does so by showing how the Trinity can be interpreted in terms of the distinctions of his naturalistic four-realm ontology.

God the Father, the all-powerful maker of heaven and earth, is the religious name for the realm of matter. The Nicene Creed specifies that all things are created through the Son, and this suggests to Santayana the necessary role that essence plays as an element in all existence. Matter and essence are equi-primordial, and together constitute the Logos, the truth or formal structure of the world. The Holy Ghost that speaks by the prophets proceeds from both the Father and the Son; this is a good description of spirit, a product of matter and form united in living animals that enjoys primacy as the locus of all knowledge and communication.

Santayana's elegant style makes his works a pleasure to read. His grand project of reconciling a naturalistic worldview with the positive achievements of art, religion, and morality may not succeed in every particular, but it sets a high standard. His views resonate deeply with individuals who value religion but find theology not very plausible, and also with those admirers of science who hunger for a worldview that acknowledges more than the movement of matter in space. Santayana has now emerged from the usual obscurity that attends death and appears to be on his way to new levels of appreciation. Thoughtful people will always find his works tough minded but full of light.

BIBLIOGRAPHY

Arnett, Willard. *George Santayana*. New York: Washington Square, 1968.

Lachs, John. *George Santayana*. Boston: Twayne, 1988.

———. *On Santayana*. Belmont, CA: Wadsworth, 2005.

Levinson, Henry Samuel. *Santayana, Pragmatism, and the Spiritual Life*. Chapel Hill: University of North Carolina Press, 1992.

McCormick, John. *George Santayana: A Biography*. New York: Knopf, 1987.

Singer, Beth. *The Rational Society: A Critical Study of Santayana's Thought*. Cleveland, OH: Press of Case Western Reserve University, 1970.

Sprigge, Timothy. *Santayana: An Examination of His Philosophy*. London and Boston: Routledge, 1995.

Woodward, Anthony. *Living in the Eternal: A Study of George Santayana*. Nashville, TN: Vanderbilt University Press, 1988.

JOHN LACHS

SARTRE, JEAN-PAUL (1905–1980), French philosopher and author. After his father died, when he was only four years old, Jean-Paul Sartre grew up in the home of his grandfather, Crétien-Charles Schweitzer, uncle of the more famous Albert Schweitzer. In his autobiography *Words* (*Les Mots*, 1963) Sartre gives an amusing account of the hothouse atmosphere of this household, in which he felt as though his mother was his elder sister, and in which he was treated in every way as a boy genius. The idyll came abruptly to an end with his mother's remarriage to an engineer from La Rochelle, and the move to this town introduced Sartre to an environment that was tougher and more realistic than his grandfather's library. In 1924 he gained entrance into the École Normale Supérieure. He failed in his first attempt to pass the *aggregation*, the French teaching qualification, in 1928, but in 1929 topped the year, followed by Simone de Beauvoir, who had become his lover. During the 1930s he taught philosophy in a lycée in Rouen and spent some time in Berlin studying the phenomenology of Edmund Husserl and Martin Heidegger, whose philosophy had been introduced to him in a book by Emmanuel Levinas. When war broke out he was called up, and for a short time made a prisoner of war, but he returned to Paris in 1941. It was during World War II that he first published the work which made him famous as a philosopher, *Being and Nothingness* (*L'Être et le néant*, 1943).

A number of fundamental ideas developed in *Being*

and Nothingness were first set out in works published by Sartre during the 1930s. Sartre's first and most famous novel, *Nausea* (*La Nausée*, 1938), gives expression to his belief in the contingency and meaninglessness of material things considered in themselves. On the last pages of the novel, the "hero" Roquetin's relief at hearing a jazz melody hints that the origin of all value lies in human creativity. The claim that values are grounded in human freedom would remain a central proposition of Sartre's philosophy, both early and late. In the *Imaaginary* (*L'Inaginaire*, 1940) Sartre developed a rejection of idealism, and anticipated his theory of our experience of the image as a nonexistent being, which was to play an important part in *Being and Nothingness*. His "Transcendence of the Ego" (*La Transcendance de l'Ego*), which appeared in *Recherches Philosophiques* in 1936–37, argued that the ego is outside consciousness and "is a being of the world, like the ego of another." In order to argue for this he made consciousness a transcendental field, contrasting it with the I, the empirical ego. These two ideas combine in *Being and Nothingness* to form a picture of consciousness as a pure relation to being in itself, which it is not, and so as ultimately the origin of nothingness. Many features of the philosophy of *Being and Nothingness* show evidence of the influence of Heidegger. In particular, Sartre's belief that phenomenology can illuminate ontology derives from Heidegger. Notoriously, he also shares Heidegger's tendency to speak of nothingness as having a kind of being that cannot be reduced to the subjective act of negation. But unlike Heidegger he thinks of the nothing not as something extramundane that is the ground of being, but as a relation "coiled in the heart of being—like a worm" that separates consciousness from the being that it is conscious of. This separation is the source of our radical freedom.

It is the implicit awareness of our radical freedom and responsibility for the values that we promote that Sartre says we experience as anguish, and which we attempt to flee when we fall into bad faith. Lying to oneself requires a paradoxical capacity to both know the truth and to hide it from oneself. Sartre rejects attempts to explain the phenomenon of self-deception as residing in the unconscious, for it seems to him that there must always be some element of the system, the censor, which both knows the truth to be hidden and hides it. Sartre concludes from this that in order for bad faith to be possible people must ambiguously be what they are not and not be what they are. This lack of self-coincidence is something that humans attempt to flee when they strive to be a Godlike in itself/for itself. This attempt is a useless and unachievable passion. Nevertheless, Sartre hints at the possibility of the achievement of good faith, or authenticity, when an embodied consciousness does not attempt to deny its lack of self-coincidence, nor the freedom and responsibility that results from it.

Since freedom is for Sartre a fundamental feature of consciousness, no social constraint could rob a conscious being of its freedom. This led him to his notorious claim that a slave in chains is as free as his master, a claim which he himself later gave up, and of which he said that he found it incredible that he could ever have expressed it. After the war Sartre became convinced that Marxism had captured a good deal of the truth of history, but he never accepted a deterministic dialectic. In works such as *Search for a Method* (*Question de Méthode*), the first version of which appeared in 1957, he outlined his view that without consciousness and intentionality history would be meaningless. He summed up his mature attitude to man's relation to history in the first volume of *Critique of Dialectical Reason* (*Critique de la raison dialectique*, 1960), where he says that man makes history to the extent that history makes man. This complex attempt to acknowledge how the congealed praxis of past generations, the concrete and ideological constraints that have been built up over time, limit the freedom of the human individual, without negating the responsibility for transcending the past, has been far less read than Sartre's early work. Consequently he is often characterized as the philosopher of a rather naive radical freedom.

Despite a philosophy that superficially looks like an ethical nihilism, and which grounds ethical values in human freedom, Sartre was in fact a philosopher who took ethical and political issues extremely seriously. His novels constitute an attempt to write an engaged literature, which makes relevant to a readership beyond the philosophical community important political and ethical issues. Although Sartre sometimes wrote as though all values could be questioned, there is a sense in which honesty remained for him an unquestioned value. Implicitly, he demonstrated a faith that an honest acceptance that ethical mores are our collective responsibility and that they rest on nothing more than our decision to endorse them would, if universally adopted, lead to the rejection of oppression, inequality, dogmatism, and the self-delusion that allows people to accept situations in which some individuals tyrannize over others.

BIBLIOGRAPHY

Sartre, Jean-Paul. *Critique de la raison dialectique*. Vol. 1. Paris: Gallimard, 1960.
———. *L'être et le néant*. Paris: Gallimard, 1943.
———. *L'Imaginaire: Psychologie phénoménologique de l'imagination*. Paris: Gallimard, 1940.
———. *La Nausée*. Paris: Gallimard, 1938.
———. *La Transcendance de l'Ego*. Paris: Vrin, 1937.
———. *Les Mots*. Paris: Gallimard, 1963.

KAREN GREEN

SCANDINAVIA, UNBELIEF IN; SCANDINAVIAN LITERATURE, UNBELIEF IN. See **DENMARK; FINLAND; NORWAY; SWEDEN.**

SCHILLER, FERDINAND CANNING SCOTT (1864–

1937), pragmatist and commentator. An important philosopher in his day, now largely forgotten, Ferdinand Schiller championed a version of PRAGMATISM he called HUMANISM. Schiller was born in Denmark to a German family living in England that had made its money in India. He was educated at Rugby and Balliol College, Oxford. In 1897, after a short but significant stint at Cornell University in the United States, he returned to Corpus Christi College, Oxford, where he taught until 1926. While in the United States, Schiller had been exposed to the emerging philosophy of pragmatism, especially as articulated by William James. Schiller spent his career arguing for his version of pragmatism, which he called humanism. From 1926 onward Schiller spent part of each year lecturing at the University of Southern California. In 1935 he moved there permanently. He died on August 9, 1937.

While acknowledging James's importance, Schiller took pragmatism in a more subjectivist direction than his mentor. While remaining a theist, Schiller resolutely opposed any form of foundationalism, or claim of objectivity. All truths are human creations, he argued. In speaking of humanism, Schiller wanted to anthropomorphize pragmatism. He often returned to the saying attributed to the pre-Socratic philosopher PROTAGORAS that the human being is the measure of all things. Where NATURALISM spoke of humanity's accommodation with nature, humanism spoke of its control of nature. It is now apparent that Schiller's understanding of humanism suffers from an element of anthropocentric conceit, although, in his defense, he did criticize this aspect of human nature, which he called "yahoo-manity." Schiller's understanding of humanism did not survive him.

Schiller was a prolific and facile writer. His main works were *The Riddle of the Sphinx* (1891), *Humanism: Philosophical Essays* (1903), *Studies in Humanism* (1907), and *Our Human Truths* (1939). Unusually for philosophers, Schiller was famous for his sense of humor. In 1901 he wrote *Mind! A Unique Review of Ancient and Modern Philosophy, Edited by A. Troglodyte, with the Cooperation of The Absolute and Others.* This spoof of the prestigious philosophical journal *Mind* included articles titled "The Critique of Pure Rot," by I. Cant. Later in his life Schiller penned an essay called "Must Philosophy Be Dull?"

BIBLIOGRAPHY

Abel, Reuben. *Humanistic Pragmatism: The Philosophy of F. C. S. Schiller.* New York: Free Press, 1966.
Winetrout, Kenneth. *F. C. S. Schiller and the Dimension of Pragmatism.* Columbus: Ohio State University Press, 1967.

BILL COOKE

SCHLICK, MORITZ, AND THE VIENNA CIRCLE. Moritz

Schlick (1882–1936) studied physics in Berlin under Max Planck. He was professor of philosophy at the University of Vienna from 1922 until he was shot dead by an insane student. Schlick was the initiator and leader of the Vienna Circle, a group of philosophers, scientists, and mathematicians who met regularly for intense discussions from 1923 until 1936.

Schlick was deeply influenced by Ludwig WITTGENSTEIN, who lived in Austria but never was a member of the Vienna Circle. Schlick was also deeply influenced by Rudolf Carnap, who was a leading member of the Vienna Circle. Other important members of the Vienna Circle were the sociologist and philosopher Otto Neurath, the philosophers Friedrich Waismann and Herbert Feigl, the mathematician Hans Hahn, the historian and philosopher Victor Kraft, the lawyer Felix Kaufmann, and the logician and mathematician Kurt Gödel. In addition the Vienna Circle received a number of visitors from abroad, including the Prague physicist Philipp Frank, the Finnish philosopher Eino Kaila, the Danish philosopher Jörgen Jörgensen, Carl G. Hempel from Berlin, Alfred Jules AYER from Oxford, and the Norwegian philosopher Arne Næss.

Many members of the Vienna Circle and its visitors subscribed to a philosophy called LOGICAL POSITIVISM or logical empiricism. The logical positivists were sharply critical of metaphysics. Their aim was a unity of science expressed in common language, to be achieved by logically analyzing and clarifying the statements of various sciences. In this clarification a verifiability principle of meaning was introduced (see VERIFICATIONISM), according to which only the analytic statements of logic and mathematics and verifiable statements of the empirical sciences were said to be meaningful. Other statements were metaphysical and meaningless. This implied that the concept of god and other metaphysical concepts were by definition meaningless. Explicitly or implicitly, the logical positivists were atheists (see ATHEISM) and rejected religion. In general, the logical positivists took small interest in ethics, but Schlick wrote *Fragen der Ethik* in 1930. It was published in English as *Problems of Ethics* in 1939.

BIBLIOGRAPHY

Ayer, Alfred J. *Language, Truth and Knowledge.* 2nd. ed. New York: Dover, 1946.
———, ed. *Logical Positivism.* Glencoe, IL: Free Press, 1959.
Jörgen Jörgensen. *The Development of Logical Empiricism.* Chicago: University of Chicago Press, 1951.

FINNGEIR HIORTH

SCHROEDER, THEODORE (1864–1953), American lib-

ertarian activist. The child of progressive German immigrants, Albert Theodore Schroeder was born near Horicon, Wisconsin, on September 17, 1864. His father was an agnostic, his mother, a Protestant. Theodore left home at fifteen to travel, taking brief odd jobs and eventually visiting every state. He called this time period his "wanderlust years." He attended school during the winter months. He was an avid reader of authors such as Ludwig FEUERBACH, Robert Green INGERSOLL, John Stuart MILL, Herbert SPENCER, VOLTAIRE, and Thomas PAINE. In college at the University of Wisconsin, he was also active in the Sigma Chi fraternity, and earned degrees in civil engineering and law.

Schroeder opened a law office in Salt Lake City, Utah, in 1889. At first he sympathized with the Mormons for what he thought was unfair persecution based on their religious practices, but soon he saw trouble in the close relationship between church and state in Utah and became increasingly anti-Mormon. He wrote several pamphlets challenging the Mormon Church. By the time he left Utah in 1900, he had successfully prosecuted Mormon church leader and politician Brigham H. Roberts, ensuring his ouster from the US House of Representatives. Schroeder's wife of five years, Mary Parkinson, died in 1896; he also lost a young daughter.

In 1900 Schroeder moved to New York City. He still practiced law, but became more interested in research and writing. In New York he met many socialists and anarchists and worked to defend their civil liberties (see SOCIALISM AND UNBELIEF; ANARCHISM AND UNBELIEF). The Free Speech League was formed in 1911 by Leonard D. Abbot, Lincoln Steffens, Bolton Hall, Gilbert E. Roe, and E. B. FOOTE, with Schroeder serving as secretary, as well as writing publications and providing legal assistance. The league was a precursor to the American Civil Liberties Bureau, now the American Civil Liberties Union. Other radicals such as Emma GOLDMAN later became involved. Schroeder also aided in the defense of Moses HARMAN during his 1905 obscenity trial (see SEX RADICALISM AND UNBELIEF). He continued to write and publish articles and books on free speech cases and obscenity laws, such as Free Speech for Radicals (1912, 1916) and Free Speech Bibliography (1922). He was associate editor of the periodical Arena and also wrote for THE TRUTH SEEKER and the American Journal of Eugenics.

Schroeder had long been interested in psychology, and by 1901 started to develop a theory that promoted a connection between emotional and intellectual maturity, applying a psychological approach to society's ills. His attacks against religion increased, and in the 1920s he assisted Bishop William Montgomery Brown in a HERESY case brought by the Protestant Episcopal Church. Brown's radical views had increasingly come into conflict with his church, and four years after he published an essay titled "Communism and Christianity," heresy charges were brought against him.

Nancy Sankey-Jones, a libertarian feminist, married Schroeder in 1908, and they moved to Connecticut, where he died in his sleep on February 10, 1953. After his death, two relatives were successful in preventing the publication of the remainder of his unpublished writings. The case went to court, where the judge ruled that Schroeder's writings "offend religion and extol antisocial ideas."

BIBLIOGRAPHY

Domayer, Dennis L. "Theodore Schroeder: A Biographical Sketch." In Theodore Schroeder, A Cold Enthusiast: A Bibliography, compiled by Ralph E. McCoy. Carbondale: Southern Illinois University Press, 1973.
Maddaloni, Arnold. Schroeder—The Public Excuser: A Biographical Outline to Which Are Added Some Published Opinions concerning His Personal Traits. Stamford, CT: n.p., 1936.
Stein, Gordon, ed. The Encyclopedia of Unbelief. Amherst, NY: Prometheus Books, 1985.
Schroeder, Theodore. Free Speech for Radicals. Enlarged edition. Riverside, CT: Hillacre Bookhouse, 1916.

JULIE HERRADA

SCIENTISTS, UNBELIEF AMONG. Science and religion are not necessarily at loggerheads, and the results of scientific inquiry do not necessarily controvert religious belief; nevertheless, there are clear tensions between scientific and religious knowledge systems (see RELIGION IN CONFLICT WITH SCIENCE). Scientists employ "methodological NATURALISM," the normative concept that scientific investigations use only natural law and its consequences, and deal only with objects or claims that have testable consequences in the natural world. Methodological naturalism is different from "philosophical naturalism," the ontological conviction that nothing exists beyond natural law and effect. While scientists are necessarily methodological naturalists, they are not necessarily philosophical naturalists and therefore not necessarily unbelievers.

The theologian Ian Barbour has developed several models to describe the interaction between (naturalistic) science and (supernaturalistic) religion. Adopting one of these models, Stephen Jay GOULD prominently argued that science and religion are not incompatible, that they occupy what he termed "nonoverlapping magisteria," or separate teaching authorities; his claim received largely negative attention from scientists and theologians alike. For example, as John Lynch has noted, Gould defined religion precisely to ensure the success of his proposal. He thus presented a theology with jurisdiction solely over ethics and morals, and stripped religion of most of its traditional meaning and power: in Gould's religion, there is no discussion of origins, design, progress, purpose, guided process, or a personal deity. By so defining religion, Gould could easily claim no overlap or conflict—science retains its power and prestige, while religion is redefined so as not to distress the scientific mind.

Two Conflicts between Science and Religion. While Gould may be right in principle, science has made claims about matters religious and religion about matters scientific since before the dawn of modern science. Two scientific theories in particular, heliocentrism and EVOLUTION, have caused significant conflict. The heliocentric theory of Nicolaus Copernicus presented a profound challenge to the church, which believed that the earth was the center of the universe. A generation or so after Copernicus, Giordano BRUNO speculated that the universe was infinite and the stars were suns like ours. Bruno subscribed to a theory of nonoverlapping magisteria and maintained that the Bible should be read for its moral but not scientific value; partly for this HERESY he was burned at the stake in 1600. For his support of Copernicus's ideas, Galileo GALILEI ran into trouble with the church and spent his last decade under house arrest. The trials of Galileo and Bruno set the stage, at least within the popular imagination, for the clash between modern science and certain doctrinaire religious beliefs. Nowhere did this clash become more apparent than in the rise of evolutionary thought (see DARWINISM AND UNBELIEF).

Evolution was in the air when Charles DARWIN and Alfred Russel WALLACE independently developed their theory of natural selection. Darwin's grandfather, Erasmus DARWIN, had proposed a vague teleological theory of evolution, and Jean-Baptiste de LAMARCK in the early 1800s devised a theory of inheritance of acquired characteristics. The explanatory power of geologist Charles Lyell's actualism—the principle that only forces operating today can be used to explain occurrences in the past—and his uniformitarianism—the principle that geological forces have operated at a constant rate and strength throughout time—proved great enough to finally unseat the biblical account. However, as evidence for an earth much older than the age calculated from biblical genealogies was accumulating, a number of "scriptural geologists" denounced the emerging discipline of professional geology, which they rightly saw as undermining literalist beliefs. Many Victorian geologists, however, remained believers and maintained strong evangelical credentials when faced with scientific findings.

Darwin himself may have postponed publishing *On the Origin of Species* (1859) for fear of the religious establishment. Later in life he became an agnostic (see AGNOSTICISM), partly because of the death of his ten-year-old daughter, Annie. Darwin's eventual lack of belief was thus ultimately for moral (rather than scientific) reasons, and indeed the theory of evolution does not necessarily militate against belief. Asa Gray, a scientist contemporary with Darwin, for example, accepted evolution while remaining a devout Christian. But Darwin's ferocious popularizer, the skeptic Thomas H. HUXLEY, perceived Darwin's naturalistic theory as a way to separate science from the old order. His famous debate with Bishop Samuel Wilberforce, in which he is said to have trounced Wilberforce, helped foster the perception that science and religion are antagonists. This view was promulgated in the United States by the writings of both John W. DRAPER and Andrew Dickson WHITE, and later by Richard Dawkins and Daniel Dennett.

War between Science and Religion in the United States. The tensions between science and religion are stronger in the United States than in Europe and are strongest among Protestants. These tensions may have begun in their modern form during the furor that followed after Ezra Cornell and White in 1865 founded Cornell University as a nonsectarian university that put the sciences on an equal footing with other studies. Draper thought the fight was between science and religion in general, whereas White came to believe that it was between science and dogmatic religion.

The Scopes trial, wherein John T. Scopes was convicted of teaching evolution in 1925, was a skirmish in the war, but its repercussions are felt to this day as biblical literalists oppose teaching evolution and support a "scientific creationism" that denies the great age of the earth and the common ancestry of living things. Modern opponents of evolution see themselves as oppressed by a scientific, naturalistic hegemony. A few of these opponents hold scientific credentials but refuse to allow their science to influence their (often literalist) religious beliefs. When scientific creationism was literally thrown out of court in the Supreme Court's 1987 decision *Edwards v. Aguillard*, it was replaced by intelligent design creationism (see INTELLIGENT DESIGN THEORY). This variation of the argument from design claims that living organisms are too complex to have evolved by natural mechanisms; therefore, an intelligence must have guided evolution. Though it tries to appear scientific, intelligent design creationism undermines science, for example, by ruling naturalistic explanations out of bounds for certain phenomena such as the origin of complex molecular systems. Indeed, Phillip Johnson, a retired Berkeley law professor and a leader of the movement, erases the critical distinction between methodological and philosophical naturalism and admits that his intention is to defeat naturalism. Intelligent design creationism, like scientific creationism, is a frontal attack on science in the service of a religious agenda. It thus profits from the public image of scientists as disbelievers, and helps to maintain that image. But is that image borne out by the data?

Measuring Unbelief among Scientists (1914 and 1933). In the years surrounding the Scopes trial, the psychologist James H. LEUBA surveyed a large number of US scientists in order to learn their beliefs about God and immortality. In both polls, disbelievers (not including doubters or agnostics) represented a plurality over believers and doubters (see table 1). Further, the least likely to be believers were psychologists, followed by sociologists, biologists, and physicists, in that order. The order stood firm across the years. Distinguished scientists (as identified by *American Men of Science*) exhibited a substantially greater rate of disbelief than "lesser" scientists.

Table 1. Rates of disbelief among scientists, percent.

Survey	All Scientists		Greater Scientists	
	God	Immortality	God	Immortality
Leuba, 1914	42	20	53	25
Leuba, 1933	56	41	68	53
Larson, 1996–98	45	47	73	73

Leuba's poll was, however, not without problems. First, because the United States was almost monolithically Christian, Leuba formulated two questions that asked, in essence, whether respondents believed in a particular Christian conception of God. Asking his questions in that way militated against getting positive responses from, for example, pantheists such as Robert Millikan and Albert Einstein, who associated God with the universe and its laws and thus did not revere, in Leuba's words, "the God of our Churches." Leuba asked respondents whether they believed in "a God to whom one may pray in the expectation of receiving an answer" (a question specifically defined to exclude psychological or subjective consequences of prayer), disbelieved in such a God, or had no definite belief. Second, several questionnaires were returned with remarks intended to justify the respondents' refusals to answer the questions. According to Leuba, most of these were from disbelievers; hence, he concluded, the percentage of disbelievers may have been understated in his poll.

Scientists are more educated than the general population, and Leuba, a religious humanist, thought that increasing education would decrease rates of belief in God. To test his hypothesis, he surveyed college students at two unidentified colleges: a high-ranking college that was divided among the major Protestant denominations and a college that was "radical" in its leanings. In both colleges, the number of believers in both God and immortality decreased with age or academic advancement (freshman through senior years). Leuba also cited a decrease in belief at one of the colleges between 1914 and 1933, as well as similar results found at Syracuse University in 1926. Leuba, a professor at Bryn Mawr College outside Philadelphia, did not identify the two colleges in his study, but they were probably in the northeast, if not the Philadelphia area. If the major Protestant denominations means the mainline Protestant churches, then Leuba's studies of college students may not be representative, inasmuch as they omitted students affiliated with churches not heavily represented in the northeast. Oddly, Leuba did not mention the Roman Catholic Church.

Measuring Unbelief among Scientists (1990s). In 1996 and 1998, Edward J. Larson and Larry Witham replicated Leuba's surveys. For consistency, they did not edit Leuba's questions, despite the cultural changes that had occurred in eighty years. Additionally, *American Men and Women of Science* no longer highlights eminent scientists, so Larson and Witham derived their "greater" scientists from the membership of the National Academy of Sciences; comparison with Leuba's "greater" scientists is therefore problematic, because the NAS probably contains substantially more-eminent scientists than the highlighted scientists of the earlier surveys.

Larson and Witham found that nearly 50 percent of the scientists and nearly 75 percent of the "greater" scientists surveyed disbelieve in both God and immortality. An additional 15 to 20 percent are doubters. It is hard to make much of a series of three numbers, but during the century the percentage of disbelievers increased monotonically in every category, except for a peak in the percent of scientists who disbelieved in 1933. Disbelief in immortality more than doubled among scientists in general and nearly tripled among "greater" scientists. It is thus hard to credit Larson and Witham's claim that belief among scientists has remained more or less steady for eighty years.

C. Mackenzie Brown has analyzed Leuba's data and also suggested that demographics may make comparison between Leuba's and Larson and Witham's surveys difficult. For example, more scientists now are women, and women (though not necessarily women scientists) are statistically more likely to be religious than men. This factor could reduce the number of disbelievers in the later surveys and possibly disconfirms Larson and Witham's conclusion that scientists' religious beliefs have not changed much since 1914. Brown has similarly noted that applied scientists are underrepresented among the greater scientists and adds dryly that their underrepresentation may be relevant to any discussion of the beliefs of eminent scientists.

In 1998 Laurence Iannaconne and his colleagues examined existing data gathered between 1972 and 1990, and tried to assess the prevalence of scientists' belief in God. They found that 19 percent of "professors/scientists" have "no religion" and 11 to 21 percent "oppose religion" (see table 2). It is hard to compare these figures with those of Leuba and Larson, but arguably between 27 and 40 percent of professors/scientists may be doubters or disbelievers. The study broke the data down further by discipline and found a hierarchy similar to that found by Leuba: Social scientists, at 36 percent, were most likely to have no religion, followed by physical scientists and mathematicians (27 percent) and life scientists (25 percent). Among the social scientists, sociologists (35 percent), psychologists (48 percent), and anthropologists (57 percent) were most likely to have no religion. According to a 2003 Harris poll, by contrast, 90 percent of all adults believe in God and 84 percent in survival of the soul after death; that is, 10 percent disbelieve in God or are doubters, and 16 percent disbelieve in immortality or are doubters.

Table 2. Rates of disbelief or doubt among professor/scientists, percent

Survey	Has no religion	Opposes religion	Immortality
Iannaconne, 1972–90	19	[a]	34[b]
Math, Physics, Life Sciences	~25	11	
Social Sciences	36	13	
Psychology	48	21	
Anthropology	57	19	

[a] Not given.

[b] That is, 66 percent believe in afterlife.

Interpreting the Data. Leuba speculated whether scientists become disbelievers or whether independent thinkers willing to confront reigning orthodoxies become scientists. The greater scientists are presumably on average more-independent thinkers than the lesser; the fact could account for the increase of disbelief among greater scientists. That conclusion is supported by a study by Fred Thalheimer, who concluded that religious beliefs are frequently set during high school or college and that nonreligious students may choose more intellectual or theoretical endeavors.

Scientists who study biology, psychology, and sociology and anthropology are more likely to disbelieve in God and immortality than physical and applied scientists. Leuba speculated that physicists and engineers see a creator in the lawfulness of the physical and engineering worlds. Social and biological scientists may be less likely to see lawfulness in their studies, and Brown asks, further, whether social and biological scientists are perhaps influenced by the suffering that they see and physical scientists do not see. Thus, the question may be why biological and social scientists are more likely to disbelieve, rather than why physical scientists and engineers are less likely. Arguably, then, science leads to disbelief, at least among those already inclined to be independent thinkers.

Leuba predicted that increasing scientific knowledge would lead to increasing disbelief. That prediction is apparently (at least partly) correct. He further predicted that the religions would adapt to the best scientific insights and "replace their specific method of seeking the welfare of humanity by appeal to, and reliance upon, divine Beings, by methods free from a discredited supernaturalism." That prediction, at least so far, is largely incorrect.

BIBLIOGRAPHY

Barbour, Ian G. *Religion in an Age of Science.* San Francisco: HarperSanFrancisco, 1990.

Brown, C. Mackenzie. "The Conflict between Religion and Science in Light of the Patterns of Religious Beliefs among Scientists." *Zygon* 38, no. 3 (2003).

Bruce, Steve. *God Is Dead: Secularization in the West.* Malden, MA: Blackwell, 2002.

Forrest, Barbara. "Methodological Naturalism and Philosophical Naturalism: Clarifying the Connection." *Philo* 3, no. 2 (2000).

Gould, Stephen Jay. *Rocks of Ages: Science and Religion in the Fullness of Life.* New York: Ballantine, 1999.

"Harris Poll: The Religious and Other Beliefs of Americans 2003." *Skeptical Inquirer,* July–August 2003.

Iannaconne, Laurence, Rodney Stark, and Roger Finke. "Rationality and the 'Religious Mind.'" *Economic Inquiry* 36, no. 3 (1998).

Keynes, Randal. *Darwin, His Daughter and Human Evolution.* New York: Riverhead, 2001.

Larson, Edward J., and Larry Witham. "Leading Scientists Still Reject God." *Nature* 394 (1998).

———. "Scientists Are Still Keeping the Faith." *Nature* 386 (1997).

———. "Scientists and Religion in America." *Scientific American* 281, no. 3 (September 1999).

Leuba, James H. *Belief in God and Immortality.* Boston: Sherman, French, 1916.

———. "Religious Beliefs of American Scientists." *Harper's Monthly,* August 1934.

Lynch, John M. "Review: Gould, Rocks of Ages." *Journal of the History of Biology* 33 (2000).

———. "'Scriptural Geology,' Vestiges of the Natural History of Creation and Contested Authority in Nineteenth-Century British Science." In *Repositioning Victorian Sciences?* edited by D. Clifford, E. Wadge, A. Warwick, and M. Willis. London: Anthem, 2006.

Stenger, Victor. *Has Science Found God?* Amherst, NY: Prometheus Books, 2003.

Thalheimer, Fred. "Religiosity and Secularization in the Academic Professions." *Sociology of Education* 46 (1973).

Young, Matt. *No Sense of Obligation: Science and Religion in an Impersonal Universe.* Bloomington, IN: First Books Library, 2001.

MATT YOUNG AND JOHN LYNCH

SCOTT, THOMAS (1808–1878), English freethought pamphleteer. Thomas Scott was born into a wealthy family. His early life is rather obscure, but it is known that he was a page in the court of Charles X, a noted fisherman and hunter, and a world traveler. He is also known to have spent some time with Native Americans.

Between the years of 1850 and 1860, Scott became a rationalist (see RATIONALISM) and began publishing what we know today as the Scott Pamphlets. Scott used his own fortune to publish works that were heterodox in thought. Beginning in 1862, Scott published well over 250 of these tracts from his home in Ramsgate (about thirty kilometers southeast of London).

The authors of these works included rationalists, atheists (see ATHEISM), freethinkers (see FREETHOUGHT), and also Anglican clergy, Unitarians, and others as well.

Scott himself wrote about various aspects of Christianity. Some of the more prolific authors of Scott's tracts included Moncure CONWAY, Charles Voysey, Charles Bray, James Cranbrook, George Jacob HOLYOAKE, Francis Newman, and George G. Zerffi.

Another of Scott's writers was Annie BESANT, who—after having lost her faith and before she met atheist activist and member of Parliament Charles BRADLAUGH—became acquainted with Scott and his wife. The Scotts helped to support Besant after her Anglican husband kicked her out of their home. Scott paid her for writing a number of tracts, mostly about Christianity, but also on euthanasia, prayer, and natural religion. In her autobiography, she stated that "[t]o no living man—save one—do I owe a debt of gratitude that I owe to Thomas Scott."

During this time, Scott played host to a salon of thinkers, similar to Baron d'HOLBACH's coterie. At its gatherings the ideas of the day were discussed and argued over. Scott himself remained a theist, actually becoming a patron of Charles Voysey, who was removed as a Church of England vicar and subsequently founded the Theistic Church of London. But Scott was a freethinker in the sense that he allowed all types of thought, including heretical, atheistic, and religious, to be written about in his pamphlets and spoken of in his home. Scott died in December 1878.

BIBLIOGRAPHY

Besant, Annie. *Annie Besant: An Autobiography.* London: T. Fisher Unwin, [1920].

Besterman, Theodore. *Mrs Annie Besant: A Modern Prophet.* London: Kegan Paul, 1934.

Wheeler, J. M. "Scott, Thomas (1808–1878)." *Oxford Dictionary of National Biography.* Oxford: Oxford University Press, 2004.

TIMOTHY BINGA

SEAVER, HORACE (1810–1889), American writer and editor. Though in early life he desired to become an actor against his parents' hope that he would become a minister, Horace Seaver instead became a dedicated editor and speaker in the cause of FREETHOUGHT. As a result of working as a printer for the freethought paper BOSTON INVESTIGATOR while its editor and publisher Abner KNEELAND faced trials for blasphemy in Boston in the 1830s, Seaver was won over to "the cause." After Kneeland left for Iowa in 1838, Seaver became a coeditor of the *Investigator*, where he remained for the rest of his long career.

Seaver served as president of the Infidel Association of the United States, founded in 1858, the year of the *Dred Scott* decision, and he became identified with the abolitionist cause at that time. Like William Lloyd Garrison, he vigorously protested the support of slavery by various Christian churches.

At one point during the Civil War, Gen. Ulysses S. Grant issued an order expelling Jews from territory under his command on grounds they were profiteering from the conflict. Though the order was soon rescinded, it marked a low point in anti-Jewish prejudice in the Union ranks. Similarly, in 1863 Seaver commenced a series of articles about the backwardness of the Jews, published in the *Investigator*. The noted atheist activist Ernestine ROSE replied indignantly. The ensuing exchange, which continued for three months in the pages of the *Investigator*, probed the difficult problem of the parameters of criticism of an ethnic group and its religious views. Seaver weakly protested that his criticism of the Jews was of their religion, and not of them as a people. Rose was sensitive to the long, sordid past of anti-Semitism by Christians, but neither did she defend conservative Judaism. Modern scholars have suggested that the debate reflects the persistence of nativist views among the ranks of some nineteenth-century freethought leaders.

Upon the death of his wife, Seaver introduced a bold innovation at her funeral, where instead of having a minister or priest presiding, "he addressed the mourning circle of friends, and the address was printed in pamphlet form, and is admired as a model of eloquence, pathos, and noble sentiment."

In his latter years, Seaver attended freethought conventions and also took an interest in Spiritualism (see SPIRITUALISM AND UNBELIEF). Upon Seaver's death in 1889, Robert Green INGERSOLL delivered a tribute in Boston's Paine Hall, saying that "reared amidst the cruel superstitions of his age and time, he had the manhood and courage to investigate, and he had the goodness and the courage to tell his honest thoughts. . . . He attacked the creed of New England—a creed that had within it the ferocity of Knox, the malice of a Calvin, the cruelty of a Jonathan Edwards—a religion that had a monster for a God—a religion whose dogmas would have shocked cannibals feasting upon babes."

BIBLIOGRAPHY

Berkowitz, Sandra J., and Amy C. Lewis. "Debating Anti-Semitism: Ernestine Rose vs. Horace Seaver in the *Boston Investigator*, 1863–1864." *Communication Quarterly* 46 (1998).

Putnam, Samuel Porter. *Four Hundred Years of Freethought.* New York: Truth Seeker Company, 1894.

Seaver, Horace. *Occasional Thoughts.* Boston: J. P. Mendum, 1888.

FRED WHITEHEAD

SECULAR HUMANISM. In a time when many have forsaken otherworldly religions, what does human life mean? What is its significance? Are there any ethical values and principles that nonreligious individuals can live by? Secular humanism attempts to answer these questions in a way that resonates with human aspirations and the findings of science. It provides a scientific, philosophical, and ethical outlook that exerts a profound influence on civilization: one which may be traced back to the ancient world, through the modern world, down to the present. Today many schools of thought broadly identify with humanist ideas and values. By conjoining the term *secular* with *humanism*, we may narrow its focus and meaning, enabling us to distinguish secular humanism from other forms of humanism, particularly RELIGIOUS HUMANISM.

Succinctly, secular humanism rejects supernatural accounts of reality; but it seeks to optimize the fullness of human life in a naturalistic universe. Secular humanism and modernism have often been considered as synonymous, for secular humanism finds meaning in this life here and now and expresses confidence in the power of human beings to solve their problems and conquer uncharted frontiers, the theme of the modern world of exploration and discovery. In the contemporary world, however, secular humanism affirms a bold *new paradigm* that weaves together many historical threads, but adds much more that is relevant to our rapidly emerging planetary civilization.

History. *Classical Roots.* Secular humanism traces its heritage back to Confucian China (see CONFUCIANISM), to the CARVAKA materialist movement in ancient India (see INDIAN MATERIALISM, ANCIENT), and to the writers, artists, and poets of ancient Greece and Rome (see ANCIENT WORLD, UNBELIEF IN). Its origins can be glimpsed in early Greek philosophy, especially in its efforts to develop a theoretical philosophical and scientific outlook on nature, in its emphasis on human rationality, and in its conviction that the good life can be achieved through the exercise of human powers and the fulfillment of human nature. PROTAGORAS stands out as a humanist in view of his statement that "man is the measure of all things." However, humanistic strains can be seen in other Greek philosophers: the Sophists (see SOPHISM), who attacked conventional morality and sought new ethical standards; and also SOCRATES and Plato, who rejected the Homeric myths and sought to base ethics on rational inquiry.

ARISTOTLE's *Nicomachean Ethics* has been taken as a model of humanistic ethics as it champions the life of practical wisdom and the fulfillment of virtue and excellence. Roman philosophy also expressed humanistic values: this was especially true of Epicureanism (Epicurus and LUCRETIUS), STOICISM (Epictetus and Marcus Aurelius), and SKEPTICISM (Carneades, Pyrrho, and Sextus EMPIRICUS).

Humanism was eclipsed during the Dark Ages, during which faith dominated Western culture and humans looked vainly outside of themselves to a deity for salvation. Humanism began to reappear with the rediscovery and translation by the Islamic philosopher AVERRÖES of the works of Aristotle in the twelfth century, and their transmission to Europe during the Middle Ages.

Modern Secular Humanism. It was during the Renaissance, beginning in the fourteenth century—when there was a turning away from the Bible back to classical pagan virtues, and an effort to secularize morality—that humanism began to flourish again as a literary and philosophical movement. Writers emphasized that the good life and happiness were possible and that earthly pleasures were to be cultivated, not condemned. Gianozzo Manetti, Marsilio Ficino, and Giovanni Pico della Mirandola were philosophical humanists. They highlighted the dignity of human beings, their capacity for freedom, and the need for tolerance (see ITALY, UNBELIEF IN). Desiderius ERASMUS of Holland was especially noted as a humanist because of his defense of religious tolerance.

The emergence of modern science in the sixteenth and seventeenth centuries enabled secular humanism to assume a recognizable form. Many thinkers helped to bring this outlook into being. For example, Michel de Montaigne expressed both skeptical and humanistic values. Baruch SPINOZA, a bridge between the medieval and modern outlook, defended FREETHOUGHT, rejected biblical revelation as a source of ethics, paved the way for a new science of nature, and attempted to naturalize RELIGION by identifying God with nature.

The first major protest by what we may recognize as modern secular humanists was their defense of freedom of inquiry against ecclesiastical and political censorship. In part because of this, secular humanism and freethought are closely identified in the modern world. The fates of Giordano BRUNO, burned at the stake, and Galileo GALILEI, shamed and sentenced to house arrest, for challenging traditional views of the cosmos are central to the humanist call for freedom.

It was the development of the scientific method and its application to nature that brought a decisive intellectual influence to bear on humanist thought. Humanists wished to use reason (as with René DESCARTES) or experience (as with Sir Francis Bacon, John LOCKE, and David HUME) to account for natural processes and discover causal laws. This meant that appeals to the authority of religious revelation and tradition were held illegitimate as a source of knowledge.

The scientific revolution began with the impressive development of physics, astronomy, and natural philosophy. The Enlightenment or Age of Reason (see ENLIGHTENMENT, UNBELIEF DURING THE) is testimony to humanist efforts to extend the methods of reason and science to the study of society and the human being. In the eighteenth and nineteenth centuries there was widespread confidence that with the spread of reason, science, and education, human beings could be liberated from superstition and build a better world. Thinkers like M. J. A. de Caritat de CONDORCET set forth a progressive prospectus for humanity. Deists (see DEISM) were critical of clericalism (see ANTICLERICALISM), rejected appeals to biblical revelation, and sought to develop a religion of nature and reason. Significant figures include VOLTAIRE, Denis DIDEROT, and the Baron d'HOLBACH. Also in the modern period, democratic revolutions proclaimed "liberty," "equality," and "fraternity," and heralded "life, liberty, and the pursuit of happiness." (For the French Revolution see FRANCE, UNBELIEF IN; see also FRANKLIN, BENJAMIN; JEFFERSON, THOMAS; MADISON, JAMES; PAINE, THOMAS.) Humanists defended the ideals of freedom against a repressive government or church, insisted on tolerance for opposing viewpoints, and championed a belief in the right of free conscience and dissent. Utilitarians including Jeremy BENTHAM, James Mill, and John Stuart MILL continued these trends in the nineteenth century, judging legislation by its effect on the common good.

Secularism. Along with the growth of humanism has come the growth of secularist ideals (see SECULARISM). The modern world has witnessed the widespread secularization of life. This means first that morality could be freed from religious authorities. The values and ideals of REASON, freedom, happiness, and social justice would be substituted for the virtues of faith, hope, and charity—and for an exaggerated sense of sin. Second, secularization involved an effort to limit ecclesiastical control over the various institutions of society, especially the state, the schools, and the economy. Fear of an established church led to the principle of the separation of church and state, embodied in the First Amendment to the US Constitution, a document that explicitly derives its authority not from God but from "We the People." Thomas Jefferson, Thomas Paine, Benjamin Franklin, James Madison, and other leaders of the American Revolution were deeply influenced by secular and humanist ideals.

Contemporary Secular Humanism. In the nineteenth and twentieth centuries a growing number of thinkers (Karl MARX, Sigmund FREUD, Albert CAMUS, Bertrand RUSSELL, John DEWEY, George SANTAYANA, Alfred J. AYER, and Sidney HOOK) and movements (MARXISM, EXISTENTIALISM, PRAGMATISM, NATURALISM, positivism, behaviorism, libertarianism, and others) have claimed humanist credentials. Forms of humanism that claim to be religious also proliferated, especially in the twentieth century. The term *humanism* is considered so ennobling that few thinkers are willing to reject it outright. Thus, the Roman Catholic philosopher Jacques Maritain referred to "Christian humanism" as a concern for the amelioration of the human condition on earth, and maintained that Christian humanism is the most authentic form of humanism. Liberal UNITARIAN UNIVERSALISM also fits under this rubric. Religious humanists introduced a distinction between a "religion" and the supposed "religious" qualities of experience, choosing to emphasize the latter. They considered "God" not as an independently existing entity but as a human expression of the highest ideals (Dewey) or of our "ultimate con-

cern" (Paul Tillich). Such attempts at redefinition are generally nontheistic.

In contemporary society secular humanism has been singled out by critics and proponents alike as a position sharply distinguishable from any religious formulation. Religious fundamentalists in the United States have waged a campaign against secular humanism, claiming that it is a rival "religion" and seeking to root it out from American public life. Secular humanism is avowedly *nonreligious*. It is a EUPRAXSOPHY (good practical wisdom), which draws its basic principles and ethical values from science, ethics, and philosophy.

In the late twentieth century the papacy of John Paul II had abandoned the reformist agenda of the Second Vatican Council (Vatican II, 1962–65), which had expressed many humanist values. In the early twenty-first century, Pope Benedict XVI rejected "secularism" and "relativism," which he considered to be purely subjective. Islam has likewise vigorously opposed secularism, many adherents insisting that Muslim law (sharia) is rooted in the Qur'an. Muslim extremists have defended theocracy rather than democracy, and they have even threatened jihad against those who espouse the secular outlook and champion freedom of conscience. Following Heidegger, many French postmodernist philosophers have likewise rejected humanism, along with any notion that science can be objective or that science and technology can provide the basis for a philosophy or ideology of emancipation. It should be noted, however, that other French thinkers held dissenting positions. Jean-Paul SARTRE argued that existentialism *was* a humanism; Simone de BEAUVOIR constructed an emancipatory defense of the rights of women rooted firmly in humanist principles. Contemporary secular humanists have been highly critical of postmodernism for its rejection of modernism, its pessimism, and its NIHILISM about the human prospect.

A New Paradigm. Secular humanism provides a comprehensive synthesis of several key intellectual and ethical trends in world civilization. This new paradigm draws from freethought and RATIONALISM, ATHEISM and AGNOSTICISM, skepticism and unbelief. Yet it goes beyond these historic movements by crafting a new outlook relevant to contemporary times. It has sometimes been taken as negative because it criticizes the sacred cows of society; but it actually delivers a positive ethical message that has significant pragmatic consequences for human culture. It presents affirmative alternatives to the reigning orthodoxies.

The secular humanist paradigm has six main characteristics: (1) it is a method of inquiry; (2) it provides a naturalistic cosmic outlook; (3) it is nontheistic; (4) it is committed to humanistic ethics; (5) it offers a perspective that is democratic; and (6) it is planetary in scope. I should point out that many allies within the freethought or rationalist movement may accept one or more of these characteristics without accepting them all. Some mistakenly consider secular humanism to be equivalent with atheism, others with methodological naturalism, and still others with humanistic ethics. Secular humanism, however, is broader than any of these views; for it provides an integrated scientific-philosophical synthesis that encompasses all of these and more. This is sometimes called naturalistic humanism.

Ultimately, secular humanism proposes nothing less than the complete implementation of the agenda of modernism. This agenda in fact has yet to be fully implemented; what is necessary for it to occur is a *post-post-modernist* New Enlightenment.

Method of Inquiry. Secular humanism relies on the methods of science to test claims to truth. This is known as methodological naturalism, the cornerstone of modern science. Broadly conceived, it is the hypothetical-deductive method, in which hypotheses are tested by their experimental effects and predictive power, integrated into theories, and validated by their comprehensive character and mathematical elegance. The grounds of a hypothesis are open to anyone who can examine the evidence and the reasons for its support. These can be objectively corroborated by independent inquirers. On this interpretation, the scientific method is no esoteric arcane art available only to a narrow coterie of disciples; nor does it lay down fixed rules of investigation. Rather, it is continuous with ordinary common sense or critical intelligence, and it involves the controlled use of the methods of inquiry that are successful in other areas of life as well.

All human knowledge is fallible and all claims to ultimate or absolute truth questionable. Hypotheses should be taken as tentative, for even well-established principles may later be modified in the light of new evidence or more comprehensive explanations. Thus the scientific method entails some degree of skepticism, but this is not of a negative character, denying any meaningful possibility of knowledge. Quite the contrary, humanists believe that a significant body of reliable knowledge can be arrived at by scientific inquiry, and that thoughtful applications of science and technology can enhance the human condition. Secular humanists wish to extend the methods of science to all areas of human endeavor, in marked contrast to conservative believers who have often campaigned to block scientific research (see RELIGION IN CONFLICT WITH SCIENCE).

Secular humanism is receptive to a wide range of human experiences, including art, morality, poetry, and feeling. Indeed, it is inspired by the arts no less than the sciences. But it is unwilling to declare any belief as validated by private intuitive, mystical, or subjective appeals. Rather validation comes only through the tests of intersubjective confirmation. If intersubjective confirmation is not achievable, then the only reasonable position is to suspend judgment about the hypothesis until such time as we can marshal decisive evidence for or against it. Karl POPPER's nonfalsifiability principle (that

a theory is admissible only if there are conditions under which it can be falsified) has been used against those who propose nontestable claims, particularly in the areas of the paranormal or religion (see FALSIFIABILITY; LOGICAL POSITIVISM); though others deny that such a line of demarcation can be so easily drawn.

Naturalistic Cosmic Outlook. Naturalists maintain that the universe is intelligible to human reason and explainable by reference to natural causes. This may be called scientific naturalism. The modern secular humanist outlook has been profoundly influenced by naturalism. It looks to the sciences in order to understand nature. What do today's sciences tell us? They describe a world in which physical-chemical processes, matter and energy and their interactions, and the regularities discovered by the natural sciences are primary in the executive order of nature. But nature cannot be reduced simply to its material components; a full account also must deal with the various emergent levels at which matter is organized and functions. Explanations are derived from various contexts under observation. We may approach this on the macro level by reference to our planet and solar system, or to the expanding universe or galaxies (or multiverses) discovered by astronomy, or on the micro level of subatomic particles observed by physics and chemistry, or by reference to organic matter in the biosphere explored by the biological sciences. This is sometimes known as "systems theory."

Ever since Charles DARWIN in the nineteenth century, evolutionary concepts have become central to our understanding of nature (see DARWINISM AND UNBELIEF). The theory of evolution seeks to explain the change of species through time in terms of chance mutations, differential reproduction, adaptation, natural selection, and other natural causes. This may very well be called evolutionary naturalism. Human behavior is thus understood by drawing from many sciences, including biology, genetics, psychology, anthropology, sociology, economics, and other behavioral sciences (see COGNITIVE SCIENCES AND UNBELIEF). The historical sciences help us to interpret the functioning of social institutions and human culture. Any "theories of reality" are thus derived from the tested hypotheses and from theories rooted in scientific inquiry, rather than from poetic, literary, or theological narrations, interesting as these might be.

Naturalists believe that we need to develop, if we can, interdisciplinary integrative generalizations drawn from across the sciences. The concept of "coduction" aptly applies. Contrasted with *induction* and *deduction*, this means that we *coduce* explanations that cut across scientific disciplines in order to develop a more comprehensive cosmic outlook. E. O. Wilson has used the term *consilience*, which he borrowed from the nineteenth-century philosopher of science William Whewell. In any case secular humanists need to make every effort to develop a "synoptic perspective," a summing-up, as it were, drawing from many sciences. Secular humanists believe that it is important to convey to the public some understanding of what the sciences tell us about the universe and the place of the human species within it.

This generalized naturalistic theory avoids materialistic reductionism—the insistence that all phenomena can be explained by reference to first principles, as in the attempt to explain psychological or biological phenomena purely by reference to chemistry or physics. Rather, it encompasses two system-theoretical insights: that emergent phenomena appear at successive levels of complexity that cannot be explained simply in terms of lower-level phenomena, *and* that these nested systems of phenomena themselves constitute a natural phenomenon requiring new hypotheses and new theories appropriate to that level of complexity. A graphic illustration of this of course is the emergence of countless new species that Darwin discovered on the Galapagos Islands. Such an outlook does not threaten a naturalistic worldview because it supplements reductive explanations with higher-order explanations, while it does *not* make room for spiritual or mystical explanations. This insight also undergirds the capacity of secular humanism to respond to the living world in all its plurality, diversity, and richness, and it leaves room in human culture for science and social institutions, moral justice, and the arts. It also allows us to draw upon human intentions as telenomic explanations of complex psychological behaviors. This approach encompasses both consilience and systems theory. On this interpretation, coduction does not just stretch "horizontally" across disciplinary boundaries, as consilience does; it also stretches "vertically," encompassing the layers of emergent phenomena, from the micro level to the macro level. It is thus both interdisciplinary and intrasystematic.

This naturalistic perspective of the universe competes with the traditional theological outlook that postulates a supernatural realm, a doctrine of salvation, and an immortal soul, all concepts that scientific naturalists reject.

Nontheism. Secular humanists are dubious of any effort to divide nature into two realms: the natural and the supernatural. They find the classical definition of an omnipotent, omniscient, and beneficent God to be unintelligible, the alleged proofs for God's existence inconclusive (see EXISTENCE OF GOD, ARGUMENTS FOR AND AGAINST), and the problem of reconciling evil with presumptions of divine justice insurmountable (see EVIL, PROBLEM OF). Arguments from a first cause or unmoved mover are fallacious, for we can always ask, "Who caused God?" If that question is unanswerable, so also is the question: "Why should there be something rather than nothing?" Highly suspect are the postulations of "fine-tuning," "intelligent design" (see INTELLIGENT DESIGN THEORY) and the "ANTHROPIC PRINCIPLE." In any case, the theistic belief that God is a "person" represents an anthropomorphic leap of faith that cannot be justified (see ANTHROPOMORPHISM AND RELIGION). All such explanations as these are suspect because they transcend nature and hence pose immense, probably insurmountable problems of verification; perhaps the best posture about such questions is that of the agnostic. At the very least we should suspend judgment about the surmised transcendental origins of the universe until such time as such theories can be responsibly and evidentially confirmed or disconfirmed.

Appeals to alleged revelations from God or his emissaries as the basis of religious truths are uncorroborated by competent observers and also highly questionable. The historic claims of revelation on the part of the Abrahamic religions encoded in the Hebrew Bible, the Christian New Testament, and the Muslim Qur'an are not attested to by sufficiently reliable eyewitnesses. Biblical and Qur'anic criticism (see BIBLICAL CRITICISM; ISLAM AND UNBELIEF) have shown that these books are not inscribed by God, but are written by fallible human beings; they are the products of apologists for competing faiths. Moreover, if their claimed revelations are taken at face value, they contradict each other. The historical existence of the prophets of the Old Testament such as Moses, Abraham, Isaac, Joseph, and others is dubious. None of the supposed authors of the New Testament— Mark, Mathew, Luke, John, or even Paul—knew Jesus directly. Nor, with the exception of Paul, were their books even written by the men whose names have become attached to them through tradition. These scriptural accounts are second- and thirdhand testimony based on an oral tradition that was often contradictory, and in any case merits suspicion because it was conveyed to posterity by propagandists for a new faith. Similarly, the historical accuracy of the Qur'an and hadith concerning the life of Muhammad is highly suspect, for contrary to Muslim claims that the Qur'an was dictated to Muhammad in a single miraculous event, there is ample historical and textual evidence that there were many different versions of the Qur'an, implying that the Muslim scripture underwent a process of historical development not unlike that of the New Testament.

Basically, secular humanists are *nontheists*; that is, they find insufficient evidence for belief in God, particularly in the monotheistic sense of God as a person. Some secular humanists have declared that they are outright atheists and have no wish to deny that fact. The difference between nontheists and atheists is that atheists usually define themselves primarily by what they are against, whereas nontheists consider their unbelief to be only part of a broader scientific-philosophical-ethical outlook.

Contemporary secular humanists are also not deists in the eighteenth-century sense, for they do not believe that a divine being created or designed the universe and then left it alone. Still, some secular humanists are not unsympathetic to a Spinozistic conception of the universe in which the regularities or laws of nature inspire an appreciation for its vast magnificence; this may even elicit a thoroughly naturalistic form of "natural piety."

Secular humanists reject any belief in the efficacy of PRAYER, in the existence of human immortality (see IMMORTALITY, UNBELIEF IN), or in any hope of receiving salvation from a personal deity. On their view there is insufficient evidence for the claim that the "soul" is separable from the body, that there is a mind-body duality or any "ghost in the machine." All attempts to document an immaterial component to human consciousness, such as the soul, by means of psychical or parapsychological research have thus far been inconclusive (see SPIRITUALISM AND UNBELIEF). According to neurological science, "consciousness" is most likely a function of the brain and nervous system (see COGNITIVE SCIENCE AND UNBELIEF).

Humanist Ethics. Secular humanism expresses an affirmative set of ethical principles and values. Indeed, some humanists even consider humanist ethics to be its most important characteristic of their worldview, which should be emphasized in response to religionists who egregiously maintain that "you cannot be good without belief in God" (see ETHICS AND UNBELIEF). Humanists hold that ethical values are relative to human experience and need not be derived from theological or metaphysical foundations. Implicit in this is the idea that ethics (like science) is an autonomous field of inquiry. Humanist ethics does not begin or end with metaethics—the epistemological analysis of the language of ethical discourse—important as that inquiry is. It focuses instead on concrete conduct in order to make actual normative judgments and recommendations.

The good life is attainable by human beings; the task of reason is to discover the conditions that enable us to realize happiness. There is some controversy among humanists as to whether happiness involves hedonic pleasure primarily or need-satisfaction, creative growth, and a more elevated contentment such as self-actualization. Hedonism historically drew from Epicureanism, self-actualization theories from Aristotle. Modern hedonism is influenced by utilitarianism, while modern theories of self-realization draw upon humanistic psychology as described by Abraham H. Maslow, Carl Rogers, and Erich FROMM. Humanistic psychologists tend to view human beings as potentially good. They argue that each human's development of moral tendencies depends in part on the nurturing care received by the individual and the satisfaction of biogenic and sociogenic needs (including homeostatic and growth needs, self-respect, love, the experience of belonging to some community, creativity, and the capacity for peak experiences). Many humanists have argued that happiness involves a combination of hedonism *and* creative moral development; that an *exuberant* life fuses excellence and enjoyment, meaning and enrichment, emotion and cognition.

Lawrence Kohlberg and Jean Piaget maintained that there are stages of moral growth and development in children and adolescents. Humanists wish to promote such growth in matters of ethics, seeking to elevate the level of taste and appreciation in society. They believe that secular moral education is essential in order to develop the capacity for moral, intellectual, and aesthetic experiences. Moral tendencies have developed in the human species over a long period of evolutionary time; and they are expressed in the development of character and cognition.

Philosophers from Aristotle through Spinoza, Mill, Dewey, Hook, and John Rawls have argued that ethical choices, at least in part, are amenable to reflective wisdom. Some secular humanists were earlier in the twentieth century sympathetic to emotivism—the view that ethical terms and sentences are subjective and cannot be objectively warranted (see LOGICAL POSITIVISM). This position is now largely discredited because many ethical judgments are considered to be objectively justifiable. For those who recognize the role of cognition in ethics, deliberation is an essential part of decision making. During this process value judgments may be appraised in the light of various criteria including our preexisting values and principles, which may be modified; the causes operative in a problematic situation; the facts of the case before us; means-end considerations; the costs of alternative courses of action; and their consequences.

There is some disagreement between those who maintain that the main test of moral principles should be teleological—that is, judging moral rules by whether they fulfill our long-range ends—or deontological, following Immanuel KANT, who maintained that prima facie, general moral principles have some independent moral status. Most humanists argue that we should take into account both sets of data—values and ethical principles—though the most important test is consequential and involves an examination of competing claims within a given situation (see CONSEQUENTIALISM). Moral absolutism is rejected as dogmatic and repressive. This position has been labeled "situation ethics" by Joseph Fletcher (see BIOETHICS AND UNBELIEF), and has been attacked as "relativistic" by critics who claim that it implies a breakdown of all moral standards. Secular humanists deny this, demonstrating that they believe in moral standards but insisting that these grow out of reflective inquiry. Thus secular humanists would consider themselves to be *objective* rather than subjective relativists. They also defend naturalistic ethics, the view that moral problems can best be solved by reference to factual knowledge and human experience.

Clearly, naturalists in ethics reject supernatural morality. They maintain that although the classical religious literature may express moral insights, it is often inadequate to the contemporary situation, for it is based upon an earlier (prescientific, nomadic, and agricultural) level of cultural and moral development. A few examples will suffice to demonstrate this inadequacy. (1) Given belief in the fatherhood of God, any number of moral injunctions may follow concerning the role of women, monogamy, divorce, abortion, war or peace, and the like. It is thus clear that such belief creates no particular moral obligations. (2) Moral obligations do not depend upon divine sanctions or rewards. To do something because of God's commandments, fear of punishment, or hope for reward in the afterlife, is hardly moral; rather, it may impede the development of a mature inner sense of empathy. (3) A whole series of modern critics— Friedrich NIETZSCHE, Marx, Sigmund Freud, and others—have shown that religion may seek to censor truth, repress sexuality, oppose progress, exacerbate human impotence, and offer solace instead of striving to ameliorate the human condition. "No deity will save us, we must save ourselves," declares *Humanist Manifesto II* (1973). We are responsible for our own destiny; we cannot look outside ourselves and our society for succor or salvation.

Three key humanist virtues are courage, cognition, and caring—not dependence, ignorance, or insensitivity to the needs of others. Humanistic ethics therefore focuses on human freedom. It encourages individual growth and development. It focuses on the need of humanists to control their own destinies; to take individual and collective responsibility for their own plans and projects; to enter into the world not simply in order to understand or adore it, but with the intent to use it with prudence to satisfy our needs and desires. Humanistic ethics emphasizes independence, audacity, and resourcefulness. Prometheus can be recognized as the mythical "saint" of humanism, because he is said to have challenged the gods on high, stealing fire and endowing humans with the arts of civilization.

Life presents us with possibilities and opportunities. The meaning of life grows out of what we discover in our own mortal existence; it emerges in our acts of free choice, our goals and aspirations. Insofar as human beings exist for themselves, they are able to define their own realities; they are always in their individual processes of becoming. The salient virtue here is autonomy. Concomitant with this, however, is the recognition that no person can live in total isolation, for humans are social animals. Among the most enduring of human goods are those that we share with others. Some form of altruistic caring is essential to our very being. Developing an appreciation for the common moral decencies (or virtues) and cultivating a general sense of goodwill toward others helps human beings to restrain purely ego-centered interests.

The conflict between self-interest and the social good represents the classical moral paradox. For secular humanists, there may be no easy solutions for some of the dilemmas and tragedies that we encounter in life. Only a reflective decision can best balance competing values and principles, or balance self-interest with the needs and demands of others. Although there are some prima facie general guidelines, what we do depends in the last analysis upon the context in which we decide.

Humanist ethics expresses a concern for equality and social justice. Humanists agree with the religious tradition insofar as it supports the idea of the siblinghood of humankind—though not because God commands it, but rather because moral reflection recognizes that we have responsibilities to other human beings. Each individual is to count as equal in dignity and value, an end in himself or herself, entitled to moral consideration; that is the basis of our conception of democracy and human rights, particularly on the global level. We also have some obligation to other forms of sentient life and to other species on the planet Earth.

Sociopolitical Perspective: Democratic Humanism. Secular humanism has had a variety of sociopolitical outlooks during various historical periods. It is concerned throughout with justice and the common good. In the modern world it has emphasized the civic virtues of democracy. There are many sources of the democratic philosophy. John Locke defended human rights, tolerance, and the right of revolution, and John Stuart Mill the right of dissent. In the twentieth century, Sir Karl Popper indicted totalitarian regimes from Plato to Marx and defended pluralistic open democratic societies. John Dewey characterized liberal democracy as a "method of inquiry" engaged in by the public in order to develop sensible policies and elect the officials to carry them out. Dewey wished to rely on education to cultivate an intelligent citizenry able to make informed judgments. Sidney Hook sought to justify democracy on empirical grounds, in the light of its consequences: democratic societies provide more freedom and equality of concern, less duplicity and cruelty, more opportunities for cultural enrichment, creativity, and shared experiences, and higher standards of living. Secular humanists maintain that *political democracy* is essential for a democratic society. The laws and policies of a just government are derived from the "freely given consent" of a majority of the adults voting in elections, with the legal right of opposition, minority rights, due process of law, and civil liberties guaranteed. This is dependent also upon voluntary civic associations and a free press. It presupposes that there is some measure of social equality and free access without racial, ethnic, class, religious, or gender discrimination. It also believes in some measure of economic democracy, in the sense at least that the working population can share in the goods produced by the economy, and that it can through government exercise some democratic control by such means as regulation and taxation.

There has been considerable controversy in the twentieth century between the advocates of economic libertarianism and the proponents of social democracy. Disciples of laissez-faire such as Ayn RAND wish to limit governmental intrusion in the economy, and maintain that free-market economies are better able than planned economies to achieve growth. Social democrats and liberals believe that the government has an obligation to step in when the private sector is unable to satisfy public needs or the general welfare, and when it violates what they consider to be social justice and the "principles of fairness." Secular humanists recognize that although they may rightly disagree among themselves about any number of specific economic policies, what they share in common is a commitment to the democratic process and the application of reason and science to the solution of social and political problems.

A central controversy that engaged secular humanists throughout the twentieth century was the dispute between liberal democratic humanists and Marxist-Leninists. Western liberal humanists such as Sir Isaiah Berlin and Sidney Hook emphasized the vital importance of civil liberties and political democracy, asserting that totalitarian Marxist regimes had betrayed the principles of humanism. Some Eastern European Marxist humanists pointed to Marx's youthful *Economic and Philosophical Manuscripts* (1844) with its emphasis on freedom. The vigorous opposition to Stalinism by such thinkers and activists as Svetozar Stojanović, Ljubomir Tadić, and others helped to blunt the force of totalitarian communism in Eastern Europe.

During the historic battles within democratic societies for equal rights, humanists and secularists, often in alliance with liberal religionists, have generally supported an agenda of liberation. In the nineteenth century they opposed slavery (see DOUGLASS, FREDERICK; INGERSOLL, ROBERT GREEN; WRIGHT, ELIZUR) and campaigned for woman suffrage (see WOMAN SUFFRAGE MOVEMENT AND UNBELIEF). In the twentieth century they supported the battle for feminism and advocated the rights of minorities, blacks (see FARMER, JAMES), gays and lesbians, the disadvantaged, and the handicapped.

The continuing battle for democracy has been accompanied by a call for the separation of church and state. The Religious Right in the United States has insisted on making the voice of religion inappropriately prominent in the public square, and it has attempted to secure governmental funding for religious schools and charities (see CHURCH, STATE, AND RELIGIOUS FREEDOM). It has sought to mandate the teaching of creationism or intelligent design alongside of evolution in the public schools and has tried to limit the rights of unbelievers. All such measures were opposed by secular humanists. They believe that religion should be a private matter, that the integrity of science should be defended so that students can be exposed to the best of science, and that the rights of nonbelievers should be given equal status with believers.

Secular humanists have been especially strong proponents of the *right to privacy*. In questions of medical ethics, this entails support for the right to confidentiality, and to informed consent on the part of patients (see BIOETHICS AND UNBELIEF). Secular humanism has also stood in favor of reproductive freedom, including access to contraception, abortion, and in vitro fertilization (see BIRTH CONTROL AND UNBELIEF; SEXUAL VALUES, IMPACT OF UNBELIEF ON). It has also defended the right to die with dignity through such causes as beneficent euthanasia, assisted suicide, and living wills. The right to privacy has been extended to sexual freedom: freedom from undue censorship (entailing the right of adults to publish or read pornographic literature), and of consenting adults to pursue their own sexual proclivities (including for example adultery, consensual sodomy, and same-sex relationships) without repression by the state.

The right of privacy, however, is not defended in isolation from other rights, nor is the relationship of the individual to the social fabric ignored. Although secular humanists emphasize tolerance of competing lifestyles in a pluralistic society, they are not defenders of unbridled libertinism. They advocate the development of excellence and creativity, moderation and self-restraint, and prudence and rationality in an individual's personal life, and some sensitivity for the needs of others. They do not wish to legislate private morality, but rather seek by persuasion to develop moral character and ethical rationality.

The secular humanist movement has not confined itself simply to abstract theoretical ideas, but has sought to put its ideas and values into practice. It has endeavored to develop grassroots support by building centers and communities worldwide for nonreligious people who are committed to reason, science, free inquiry, secularism, humanist ethics, and democracy. It has focused on education as the best means of developing an appreciation for critical thinking, the naturalistic cosmic outlook, and humanist values.

Planetary Humanism and the New Paradigm. Secular humanists recognize that it is no longer possible for any one nation to solve its problems in isolation from the rest of the world. Interdependence is clearly evident in the areas of trade and commerce, communications and travel, education, culture, and science. Unfortunately, severe political, economic, and military competition has often led to war. Religious hatred has likewise engendered violence.

The underlying and unresolved issue the world faces is the use of force by independent nation-states to settle disputes among themselves. The failure of the League of Nations led to the founding of the United Nations in 1945 at the end of World War II. The problem confronting an exhausted world was how to develop principles of collective security, enabling nations to resolve disputes peacefully without the resort to war. Secular humanists have played an important role in attempting to work out methods of negotiation and compromise on the global scale.

Many humanists were involved during the early days of the United Nations, including Sir Julian HUXLEY (first head of UNESCO), Lord John Boyd-Orr (head of the World Food Organization), and Brock CHISHOLM (first director general of the World Health Organization). Both the INTERNATIONAL HUMANIST AND ETHICAL UNION and the Center for Inquiry/Transnational have special consultative advisory status within the UN as nongovernmental organizations. *Humanist Manifesto II*, published in 1973 at the height of the Cold War, deplored the division of humankind on nationalistic grounds.

Humanist Manifesto 2000 (HM2000), endorsed by the International Academy of Humanism, provides a "new global agenda" to implement humanist values. It states that the overriding need is "to develop a new Planetary Humanism" that will seek to preserve human rights and enhance human freedom and dignity and will emphasize our commitment "to humanity as a whole." The underlying ethical principle "is the need to respect the dignity and worth of all persons in the world community." Thinkers as diverse as Peter Singer and Hans Küng also emphasize the need for a new global ethic beyond nationalistic, racial, religious, and ethnic chauvinism. HM2000 sets forth a new "Planetary Bill of Rights and Responsibilities." This includes the recognition that the planetary community has an obligation to do what it can to preserve the global environment and end world hunger, disease, and poverty. National programs of health, welfare, education, ecology, and prosperity now have to be transformed to the transnational level. HM2000 recommends a set of measures that would strengthen existing UN institutions. But it goes further by calling for an effective new World Parliament elected by the people of the world, not by nation-states; a worldwide security system to resolve military conflicts; an effective world court with enforcement powers; and a transnational environmental protection agency able to preserve the natural ecology and protect other species from extinction. It also recommends an international system of taxation to assist the underdeveloped regions of the world; universal education and healthcare for every person on the planet; some procedures for regulating multinational corporations; a free market of ideas through universal access to the media of communications, which would be under the control neither of nation-states nor global corporations; and some respect for multicultural differences, notwithstanding the need to find common ground for the new planetary civilization that is emerging.

HM2000 concludes with a note of optimism about the human prospect. It rejects theologies or ideologies of despair that look outside of nature for salvation. It affirms that life on planet earth can be continually improved and enhanced, provided that human beings are willing to assume responsibility for their own destinies and are willing to undertake cooperative efforts with other men and women of goodwill to achieve a better future for all.

Conclusion. Secular humanism emphasizes the use of reason and critical intelligence to solve human problems. It has confidence in the ability of the human species to apply science and technology for the betterment of human life; it is skeptical of the existence of occult, paranormal, or transcendent realities. Although it is the modern-day version of classical atheism in what it

rejects, it also expresses a positive normative concern for developing constructive ethical values relevant to the present conditions of humankind on this planet. It is uncompromising in its commitment to democracy and planetary humanism, and it considers human freedom and fulfillment to be the highest human values. In all of these ways it offers a new paradigm for guiding human life in what might be termed the post-postmodern era.

BIBLIOGRAPHY

Ayer, A. J., ed. *The Humanist Outlook*. London: Pemberton, 1968.

Blackham, H. J. *The Future of Our Past: From Ancient Rome to Global Village*. Amherst, NY: Prometheus Books, 1996.

———. *Humanism*. London: Penguin, 1968.

Blackham, H. J., et al. *Objections to Humanism*. London: Penguin, 1974.

Bullock, A. *The Humanist Tradition in the West*. London: Thames & Hudson, 1985.

Davies, T. *Humanism*. London: Routledge, 1997.

Dewey, John. *A Common Faith*. New Haven, CT: Yale University Press, 1934.

———. *The Quest for Certainty*. New York: Minton, Balch, 1929.

Firth, R. *Religion: A Humanist Interpretation*. London: Routledge, 1996.

Flew, Antony. *Atheistic Humanism*. Amherst, NY: Prometheus Books, 1994.

Frolov, I. *Man, Science, Humanism: A New Synthesis*. Amherst, NY: Prometheus Books, 1990.

Goodman, A., and Angus MacKay, eds. *The Impact of Humanism on Western Europe*. London: Longman, 1990.

Hawton, Hector. *The Humanist Revolution*. London: Barre and Rockliff, 1963.

Herrick, Jim. *Humanism: An Introduction*. Amherst, NY: Prometheus Books, 2004.

Hook, Sidney. *The Quest for Being*. New York: St. Martin's, 1961.

Humanist Society of Scotland. *The Challenge of Secular Humanism*. Glasgow: Humanist Society of Scotland, 1991.

Huxley, J. *Evolutionary Humanism*. Amherst, NY: Prometheus Books, 1992.

———. *The Humanist Frame*. London: George Allen and Unwin, 1961.

Knight, Margaret. *Humanist Anthology: From Conscious to David Attenborough*. London: Rationalist Press Association, 1961.

Krikorian, Yervant H. *Naturalism and the Human Spirit*. New York: Columbia University Press, 1944.

Kurtz, Paul. *Eupraxsophy: Living without Religion*. Amherst, NY: Prometheus Books, 1994.

———, ed. *The Humanist Alternative*. Amherst, NY: Prometheus Books, 1973.

————. *Humanist Manifestos I and II*. Amherst, NY: Prometheus Books, 1973.

————. *Humanist Manifesto 2000*. Amherst, NY: Prometheus Books, 2000.

————. *In Defense of Secular Humanism*. Amherst, NY: Prometheus Books, 1984.

————. *Philosophical Essays in Pragmatic Naturalism*. Amherst, NY: Prometheus Books, 1990.

————. *A Secular Humanist Declaration*. Amherst, NY: Prometheus Books, 1980.

————. *Skepticism and Humanism: The New Paradigm*. New Brunswick, NJ: Transaction, 2001.

————. *The Transcendental Temptation: A Critique of Religion and the Paranormal*. Amherst, NY: Prometheus Books, 1991.

Lamont, Corliss. *The Philosophy of Humanism*. New York: Ungar, 1982.

Popper, Karl. *The Open Society and Its Enemies*. Princeton, NJ: Princeton University Press, 1971.

Santayana, George. *The Life of Reason*. 5 vols. New York: Scribners, 1905–1906.

Sartre, Jean-Paul. *Existentialism and Humanism*. London: Methuen, 1948.

————. *L'Existentialism est un humanisme*. Paris, 1948.

Smith, J. E. *Quasi Religions: Humanism, Marxism, and Naturalism*. Hampshire, UK: Macmillan, 1994.

Smoker, Barbara. *Humanism*. London: National Secular Society, 1984.

Soper, K. *Humanism and Anti-Humanism (Problems of Modern European Thought)*. London: Hutchinson, 1986.

Storer, M. *Humanist Ethics: A Dialogue on Basics*. Amherst, NY: Prometheus Books, 1980.

Van Praag, J. P. *Foundations of Humanism*. Amherst, NY: Prometheus Books, 1982.

PAUL KURTZ

SECULARISM. *Secularism* is one of three nouns (the others being *secularity* and *secularization*) derived from the adjective *secular*, but is used in most general encyclopedias to encompass all three. Thus *Britannica* defines it simply as "a movement in society directed away from otherworldliness to life on earth." This dichotomy has always been more pronounced in Christendom than among other religious communities, which have tended to associate sacred and secular concerns more intimately. *Secular* comes from the Latin, as in *ludi saeculares* (Secular Games), held by Etruscans and ancient Romans every *saeculum* (generation or century)—ironically, as a dedication to the gods.

Early in the Common Era, Christians were often persecuted and so tended to go underground, literally and metaphorically, in Rome, or into the desert as hermits or members of small communities, where they looked to the Second Coming of Jesus for deliverance. After Christianity became the established religion of the Roman Empire, these communities persisted in monas-

teries, convents, and, later, friaries. Because each followed a "rule" devised by the order's founder that regulated members' entire existence, they became known as "regular clergy." Some remained completely cloistered, while others ventured outside to preach, teach, or minister. Though a few secular orders were recognized, the term "secular clergy" referred principally to parish priests who belonged to no order and were responsible solely to their diocesan bishop.

During the Renaissance and the Reformation, the systematic study of ancient languages in order to standardize variant manuscript versions of scripture and facilitate translation into the vernacular unearthed a number of nonreligious texts. These revealed advanced philosophical and protoscientific ideas that unsettled scholars among the faithful and caused some to become religious humanists (see RELIGIOUS HUMANISM), others to become atheists. During the religious wars of the seventeenth century, open profession of ATHEISM became too dangerous. Unbelievers who could not accept the creator-sustainer god of theism opted instead for the First Cause god of DEISM or a noncommittal FREETHOUGHT. By the nineteenth century it was safe to return to ATHEISM or to embrace the new Unitarianism, Universalism (see UNITARIANISM TO 1961; UNIVERSALISM TO 1961; POSITIVISM, AGNOSTICISM, ETHICAL CULTURE, or RATIONALISM). In the twentieth century a more ambiguous HUMANISM emerged.

Secularity. The nineteenth century also saw the rise in the first world of democracy and civil liberties, together with the concept of secularity, or the separation of church and state. It was the beginning of what is now called multiculturalism. This was a demand for the removal of, first, civil disabilities experienced by religious minorities and unbelievers; and second, special privileges enjoyed by the religious majority. The latter demand took many forms: where there was an established church, its disestablishment and disendowment; removal of state funding for all religions, majority or minority, and an end to the special status of chaplains in state institutions like prisons, hospitals, and the armed forces, and to the automatic right of religious leaders to sit in legislatures; abolition of BLASPHEMY laws that protected one or some religions from public criticism, and of penalties and taxes that disadvantaged heterodox publications; and the introduction of free, compulsory, and secular education. This meant the absence of prayers, acts of worship, and tendentious religious instruction in state schools, and the end of public funding for religious schools. Usually there was no complaint against objective teaching about religion in history, social studies, and similar lessons. Especially in the United States, lobbies today have partly succeeded in undermining secularity by getting "creation science" or creationism onto some syllabi as an alternative to evolution (see CREATIONISM AND UNBELIEF; INTELLIGENT DESIGN THEORY). But occasionally the implementation of secular education has been taken to extremes. Examples are the bowdlerization of popular poems in the state schools of Victoria, Australia, early in the twentieth century to exclude the Persons of the Trinity, and the recent banning in French state schools of "religious attire" like large crucifixes, Jewish skullcaps, and Muslim head scarves.

The secular principle defends the basic rights of freedom of conscience, worship, speech, publication, and assembly, and equality of opportunity. A country's government is for all its people, regardless of the ideology of individuals. Each person has a right to all the benefits of the state, and the state has a duty of evenhandedness. Religious privileges encourage hypocrisy and timeserving among those who affect a belief to gain a benefit, while undermining the independence, sincerity, and vigor of religious institutions themselves. Thus a minority of religionists, especially among Protestant Christians, supports secularity. Believing that the spiritual and temporal worlds should remain apart, they invoke injunctions attributed to the gospel Jesus— "Render to Caesar the things that are Caesar's, and to God the things that are God's" (Mark 12:17)—and the Apostle Paul—"And be not conformed to this world" (Rom. 12:2). Such Christians may speak of being "in the world but not of it." In the United States they have made common cause with unbelievers in such organizations as Americans United for the Separation of Church and State. There is no similarly powerful body in other countries, but secular societies commonly have some religious, even clerical, members or supporters.

Separation, including secular education, has been achieved in a minority of countries. Among them are the United States (1791), France (1795, 1871, and 1905), Mexico (1859), New Zealand (1877), Victoria and New South Wales, Australia (1872 and 1880), the Commonwealth of Australia (1901), Portugal (1911), the Soviet Union (1918), Turkey (1928), and India (1947). A paradox is that some of these countries, notably the United States, have a high proportion of churchgoers and display much public religiosity. Their secular constitutions are rarely attacked openly but are undermined by outsourcing public services to "faith-based" institutions and trying to sabotage secular education. This takes a dual form: increased public funding of church schools, and the introduction of prayers, bible readings, and creation science to state schools.

Contrary to popular opinion, for much of Islam's classical period (seventh to fourteenth century CE) separation of mosque and state existed, if controversially, in the Islamic world; only later were religion and politics seen as inextricably interwoven. Yet Turkey has demonstrated that secularity is still possible in twenty-first-century Muslim countries when there is tolerance on both sides.

Secularism. *Secularism* is the term by which unbelief was generally known in the English-speaking world for most of the second half of the nineteenth century. It persists today in the name of a few societies and in the description SECULAR HUMANISM.

On March 21, 1849, a prominent but disillusioned English Owenite and Chartist, George Jacob HOLYOAKE, recorded in his diary: "Issued the first 'Secular' number of the *Reasoner*," his freethinking weekly journal. In its December 3, 1851, issue he wrote: "Giving an account of ourselves in the whole extent of opinion, we should use the word 'Secularist' as best indicating that province of human duty which belongs to this life." He had rejected ATHEISM, *nethism*, and *limitationism* as too narrow, and *cosmism*, *realism*, and NATURALISM as too ambiguous. Though he attributed inspiration for his chosen label to George Henry Lewes, the life partner of George ELIOT, the freethinking solicitor and publisher W. H. Ashurst has been named instead by the historian Edward Royle. In subsequent lectures, newspaper articles, encyclopedia entries, and books, Holyoake elaborated the themes of "service of others a duty of life" and "the secular is sacred," so that the historian Rev. W. N. Molesworth called secularism "a system of ethics." Robert Green INGERSOLL, the prominent agnostic orator and president of the AMERICAN SECULAR UNION, called secularism "a religion of humanity."

In 1851, however, under Holyoake's auspices a Central Secular Society was formed in London with a broader and nonreligious statement of principles: (1) science is the true guide of man; (2) morality is secular, not religious, in origin; (3) reason is the only authority; (4) freedom of thought and speech are basic rights; (5) owing to the "uncertainty of survival" man should direct his efforts to this life only.

Up and down England, but chiefly in the industrial counties of Lancashire and Yorkshire where Owenism began (see OWEN, ROBERT), existing Owenite groups adopted the new name and new secular societies were formed. As the above principles show, their function was principally educational and propagandist. Many of their members, and indeed their leaders, had left school before their teens at a time when even the privileged and well-educated were faced with an explosion of new knowledge in the sciences, technology, and biblical criticism. Often they had been brought up in church or chapel and on leaving it became aware of its aesthetic, social, and emotional role, which they tried to reproduce with secular "hymns," rite-of-passage ceremonies, and wholesome entertainment.

Though he had once edited an atheist journal, the *Oracle of Reason*, and been imprisoned for blasphemy, Holyoake came to believe, like PROTAGORAS, that the gods—if they existed—could take care of themselves and "the Secularist deals only with what is provable by experience." When Thomas Henry HUXLEY coined the word *agnostic* in 1869, Holyoake adopted that label (see AGNOSTICISM). This was one of the views that, together with a series of personal disputes, brought him into conflict with a rising star in the secularist firmament.

Charles BRADLAUGH, mindful of how his local vicar's intervention had caused him to lose home and employment as a teenager, was militantly anticlerical, though he was to form friendly relations with more liberal clergymen. While he always said "I do not deny God, because that word conveys to me no idea," his view was: "Mr. Holyoake says truly that Secularism should be 'independent of theology,' but as theology demands universal empire, independence can only be achieved by Secularistic resistance to Theistic teachings—that is, by the promulgation of Atheistic views."

Though he had earlier been associated with revolutionary organizations and public demonstrations, Holyoake had come to dissociate himself from both. Above all, he declared that "freethought literature should be kept free from the suspicion of immorality." This taboo included contraceptive tracts, especially when—as in George Drysdale's *Elements of Social Science* (1854) and Charles KNOWLTON's *Fruits of Philosophy* (1832)—there was a hint that they could be used for more than family planning. Holyoake had in fact republished the latter volume himself but, when Bradlaugh and Annie BESANT were prosecuted in 1877 for the same "offense," Holyoake claimed never to have read it.

In 1860 Bradlaugh became a founding coeditor, and subsequently sole editor and proprietor, of the NATIONAL REFORMER. He described it as atheist, republican, and (neo-)Malthusian, though he did at one point assert that "Secularism is, in fact, humanitarianism." When all but four of Britain's secular societies united in 1866 to form the NATIONAL SECULAR SOCIETY, of which Bradlaugh became president, only this humanitarian goal was explicit. In addition to the aspirations of secularity outlined above, the society's principles did however declare that "the religious teachings of the world have been, and are, obstacles to the proper attainment of human happiness." From that point the influence of Holyoake and his views declined and that of Bradlaugh rose. The *Fruits* trial led to a split in the National Secular Society and formation of a British Secular Union in 1877, but the union attracted only those who were malcontents for a variety of reasons and folded in 1884.

With many motivations, notable secularists emigrated from Britain for a period or for life, most of them taking Bradlaugh's message with them. Some had been vice presidents and accredited lecturers of the National Secular Society and were sent out with his blessing at the request of freethinkers in the British colonies. Charles SOUTHWELL, Joseph SYMES, William Whitehouse COLLINS, Robert STOUT, John BALLANCE, William Willis, and others went to Australia and/or New Zealand, and Charles WATTS to Canada (see also WATTS, KATE EUNICE). In her role as a Theosophist, Besant took some of Bradlaugh's spirit to India (see THEOSOPHY). Organizations were formed, and have continued to be formed, with "secular" in their names at Auckland (1854); Toronto (1877); Melbourne (1882); Wellington, New Zealand (ca. 1885); New York (ca. 1885); Sydney (1966); Melbourne (1978); Amherst, New York (1980); and Sydney (2005). With the exception of the Council for Secular Humanism, which is still flourishing under Paul Kurtz, and the recent Sydney body, these bodies were transient; but their essentials continued under rationalist or humanist banners. And in Britain the National Secular Society is also flourishing, if with hiccups along the way.

The positive ethical, libertarian, and humanitarian message of secularism is enduring, but its "negative," or critical, objectives have changed with circumstances over the years. In Bradlaugh's lifetime the "religious teachings of the world" that attracted its chief criticism in Britain, and to some extent in the colonies, were those of the Church of England because of its political, educational, economic, and social power. While these criticisms have persisted into the twentieth and twenty-first centuries, increasingly the main sectarian target has been the Roman Catholic Church. This has brought the concerns of the Anglo-American world into harmony with those of the world outside. Not only the Vatican's involvement in the rise of Fascism, Nazism, and other repressive regimes around the world, but—strengthened by Protestant fundamentalism—its impact in every country on attitudes to abortion, artificial contraception, homosexual activity, embryonic stem cell research, and other issues of bioethics (see BIOETHICS AND UNBELIEF) is seen as a major impediment to civil liberties, health, and population control.

Secularist censure has also extended to fundamentalist Islam and beyond "religion," narrowly understood, to "supernaturalism" when it became clear that many who left mainstream churches were turning to bizarre cults, spiritualism, parapsychology, tarot cards, astrology, and other forms of fortune-telling. Political ideologies like Stalinism and Maoism that operated as quasi-religions were also repudiated.

Secularization. The documented departure of growing numbers from the churches in most Christian countries, and apparently from synagogues and temples if not from mosques, represents a global trend, though one which experiences reversals along the way at times of family, national, or international crisis. Without thinking about, let alone formulating specific views on, the truth or falsity of religion, people have been drifting away; at first fearfully lest the heavens open, then confidently as nothing untoward happens. Partly this arises from an explosion of alternative activities, sporting, recreational, and artistic, in which they can engage. Partly it has to do with the explosion of scientific and technical knowledge which has given humans greater control over human destiny. This development has advanced slowly since the Renaissance and the Industrial Revolution, but accelerated in the past fifty years (see DEMOGRAPHY OF UNBELIEF).

For knowledge of the natural world people turn to scientific literature, not Genesis 1. Instead of divine providence they rely on lightning rods, smoke detectors, and insurance policies. For personal advice they turn to doctors, therapists, social workers, accountants, and lawyers rather than priests. In brief, they conduct their lives on the pragmatic principle that "the Lord helps those who help themselves." Sociologists and theologians call it "secularization."

BIBLIOGRAPHY

Bradlaugh, C., and G. J. Holyoake. *Secularism, Scepticism, and Atheism.* London: Holyoake, 1870.

Chadwick, Owen. *The Secularization of the European Mind in the Nineteenth Century.* Cambridge: Cambridge University Press, 1975.

Holyoake, George Jacob. *The Principles of Secularism Illustrated.* 3rd rev. ed. London: Holyoake, 1871.

Tribe, David. *100 Years of Freethought.* London: Elek, 1967.

———. *President Charles Bradlaugh, M. P.* London: Elek, 1971.

DAVID TRIBE

SECULARIZATION HYPOTHESIS. See **DEMOGRAPHY OF UNBELIEF.**

SEMPLE, ETTA MARTHA DONALDSON KILMER (1855–1914), American freethinker and women's activist. Founder and president of the Kansas Freethought Association and vice president of the AMERICAN SECULAR UNION, Etta Semple edited and published a widely circulated FREETHOUGHT newspaper, first titled the *Freethought Vindicator,* then the *Freethought Ideal,* from 1895 to 1901. Through her paper she attacked racial bigotry, opposed capital punishment, strongly supported separation of church and state, and was a fearless champion of the working class. She wrote two novels on labor themes, *The Strike* and *Society,* and ran twice for public office on a Socialist Labor ticket, losing each time, but still ahead of others in the party (see LABOR MOVEMENT AND UNBELIEF).

In her "Demands of Liberalism" (1898) she demanded an end to church tax exemptions, the public employment of chaplains, public appropriations to sectarian charities, Bible reading in public schools, religious oaths, Sabbath blue laws, and national religious festivals.

Blazoned across each issue of the *Ideal* was this offer: "A Reward of $1,000 will be given to the Man, Woman or Child who will Furnish Positive Proof of A God, the Holy Ghost, Jesus Christ (as a savior), the Soul, the Devil, Heaven or Hell, or the Truth of the Bible."

A resident of Ottawa, Kansas, for twenty-seven years, she ran an osteopathic sanitarium in her own home, a rambling thirty-one-room house that, although now derelict, still exists. For many years it was the only hospital in Ottawa, and under her humanitarian charge no patient was ever turned away for inability to pay. She put her life and what little worldly goods she had to the service of her community. Despite her freethought views, which alienated many and even resulted in an assassination attempt, upon her death from pneumonia at age fifty-nine the whole town closed down in order that everyone could attend her funeral.

Her grave lay unmarked for eighty-seven years until the Franklin County Historical Society and local freethinkers raised sufficient funds to erect a headstone, which was dedicated May 1, 2002. The stone bears her own epitaph, which she wrote a few years before she died: "Here lies a woman that through her peculiar disposition lived a life of turmoil as did all who knew her."

BIBLIOGRAPHY

Lambertson, John Mark, "Atheist's Samaritan Bent Won Over Ottawa." *Ottawa Herald,* September 26, 1987.

———. "An Ottawa Pioneer with a Touch of Infamy." *Ottawa Herald,* September 27, 1987.

Whitehead, Fred, and Verle Muhrer, eds. *Freethought on the American Frontier.* Amherst, NY: Prometheus Books, 1992.

ELIZABETH M. GERBER

SEVERANCE, JULIET H. STILLMAN (1833–1919), American sex radical and physician. As a youth in the "Burned-over District" of upstate New York, Juliet H. Severance embraced antislavery, dress reform, temperance, water cure, and women's rights. She began to have doubts about her religious convictions in the late 1850s after encountering a Spiritualist medium and reading Thomas PAINE's *Age of Reason.* Becoming a staunch advocate of individual freedom, she devoted the remainder of her life to radical reform and gained recognition for her ideas among anarchists (see ANARCHISM AND UNBELIEF), freethinkers, and third-party politicians.

Early Years. Born in DeRuyter, New York, on July 1, 1833, to Walter F. and Catharine Stillman Worth, Severance was raised a Quaker but converted to the Seventh-Day Baptist faith while attending the DeRuyter Seminary. Socially conscious from an early age, she had by 1847 begun giving lectures on women's rights, dress reform, antislavery, and temperance. In 1852 she married John Dwight Stillman and moved with him to DeWitt, Iowa. The mother of two sons, she nonetheless traveled to New York City in 1857 to matriculate in Russell Trall's Hygeio-Therapeutic College, from which she graduated with an MD degree in May 1858. While there, exposure to Spiritualism and liberal literature led Severance to deliver her first speech against marriage (see SEX RADICALISM AND UNBELIEF).

Reform Career. Writing and speaking about evolution (see EVOLUTION AND UNBELIEF), marriage, and health reform, Severance practiced medicine in Iowa before moving to Whitewater, Wisconsin. Undeterred by the stigma of her 1862 divorce and her friendship with free-love advocate Victoria C. WOODHULL, she married freethinker Anson B. Severance in 1869. In addition to serving in state associations of Spiritualists in Illinois, Wisconsin, and Minnesota, she played a prominent role in the NATIONAL LIBERAL LEAGUE. Elected vice president in 1880, she represented a faction of freethinkers who wanted the League to demand repeal of the Comstock Law (1873; see COMSTOCK, ANTHONY, AND UNBELIEF). Angered by Severance's efforts to dominate the league's agenda, Robert Green INGERSOLL resigned and with other disaffected league members established the AMERICAN SECULAR UNION.

Final years. Disillusioned by the political ineffectiveness of American liberals, Severance turned to the Knights of Labor and the Union Labor Party. Following Milwaukee's Bay View Massacre in 1886, she increasingly aligned herself with anarchists, and in 1898 she moved to Chicago, where she practiced medicine, lectured at freethought and anarchist meetings, and supported the work of sex radical publisher Moses HARMAN. She retired from practice in 1908 and moved to New York City to live with her daughter. To the end, she had no fear of public opinion, and freely criticized church and state for their oppression of individual freedom.

BIBLIOGRAPHY

Freeman, Mattie A. "Juliet H. Severance, M.D." *New Thought* 1 (1892).
"Juliet H. Severance, M.D." *Truth Seeker* 46 (1919).
"Mrs. Juliet H. Severance." In *A Woman of the Century*, edited by Frances Willard and Mary Livermore. Buffalo, NY: Moulton, 1893.

JOANNE PASSET

SEX RADICALISM AND UNBELIEF. The free-love movement of the mid-nineteenth century was made up of atheists and agnostics as well as Spiritualists (see SPIRITUALISM AND UNBELIEF), sentimentalists who believed in spiritual connections between people rather than utilitarian marriages aimed at procreation. By the 1870s, however, a split occurred, with the more conservative (Spiritualist) faction of the free-love movement attempting to disassociate itself from the freethinkers, who emerged at the forefront of controversy and influence.

Sex radicals, as those involved in the nineteenth-century free-love movement are called, were not simply a promiscuous lot. Many of them, both males and females, were feminists who believed that woman's emancipation could never be achieved until she possessed complete dominion over her body. They advocated that one should be able to choose his or her sexual partners without interference or sanction by the church or state. In fact, Moses HARMAN maintained that, in the interest of improving the human race (see EUGENICS), every woman should have the right to freely choose her sex partners, because any

child born of such a union would be superior to one born of a coerced and loveless marriage where the woman was legally viewed as property. This ideal was in direct contradiction with many religious teachings, especially those of Christianity. Therefore, many sex radicals were rationalists, agnostics, or freethinkers, and a large number were former Christians.

Female free-love advocates like Dora Forster scorned the "double standard of morality" that Puritans imposed on unmarried women who were forced to live celibate lives while men (married or single) could hire prostitutes, who were also then degraded by society. Feminists especially envisioned the possibilities of a better society where both women and men were free to express themselves sexually (see SEXUAL VALUES, IMPACT OF UNBELIEF ON).

In addition to unorthodox ideas about sexuality and equality between men and women, other liberal ideas tended to prevail among the sex radicals. Most were social reformers. Abolitionism was a high priority for many; their belief in equality did not stop at gender, but expanded to race as well. They likened the status of women in society, especially married women, to that of slaves. Many free-lovers were anarchists (see ANARCHISM AND UNBELIEF) whose belief in the sovereignty of individuals necessarily extended to the abolition of the church and state, which exerted an unacceptable spiritual and economic hold on humanity.

One of these freethinkers was abolitionist and individualist anarchist Stephen Pearl Andrews, an attorney, author of *Science of Society*, philosopher, and a tireless proponent of Josiah Warren's equitable commerce theory. In 1851 Andrews and Warren founded Modern Times, a utopian community east of New York City where they could put their theories into practice. "Cost the limit of price" was the standard for commerce at Modern Times, and a Time Store was opened where members of the community could purchase goods on this basis. Labor notes were traded instead of money, and the cost of women's labor equaled that of men's. Modern Times briefly thrived under this style of economic self-government.

Andrews's belief in the sovereignty of the individual extended to personal relationships between men and women, and although he had legally married twice, philosophically he rejected traditional marriage, believing it constituted slavery for women. Hence, marriage arrangements at Modern Times were left up to the individuals involved. Word of this free-love commune spread, and along with it misunderstanding. Soon there was a barrage of various undesirables who all but ran the town into the ground, and Modern Times died a notorious death. Undaunted, Andrews packed up and moved his ideals and his family to New York and in the late 1850s founded the Unitary Home.

Andrews met Victoria WOODHULL in New York in 1870, just as she and her sister Tennessee Claflin were about to begin publishing *Woodhull & Claflin's Weekly*. His view that it is a woman's right to freely choose her sex partners so impressed the two sisters that they immediately gave him the post of editor. In 1872 Andrews endorsed Woodhull's candidacy for president on the newly formed Equal Rights Party platform. On Election Day in 1872, Woodhull was sitting in jail on charges of violating the Comstock Act (see COMSTOCK, ANTHONY, AND UNBELIEF) for her article exposing the extramarital affair of Elizabeth Tilton and the Reverend Henry Ward Beecher. The *Weekly* lasted until 1876. Andrews later became involved in the Manhattan Liberal Club, made up mostly of freethinkers, where he lectured regularly, and the more militant Uniform Reform League. He died in 1886.

The printed evidence of these sex and marriage reform movements was manifested in other papers as well, such as the *Word*, published by Ezra and Angela HEYWOOD of Princeton, Massachusetts; and *Lucifer, The Light Bearer*, published by Moses Harman of Valley Falls, Kansas. Ezra Heywood, an abolitionist and former student of the ministry, was influenced by the individualist anarchist Josiah Warren. Heywood became an anarchist and pacifist and openly criticized the Civil War, although most of his abolitionist comrades supported it. Begun in 1872 as a journal devoted to women's equality and labor and monetary reform, the *Word* followed some earlier tracts written by the Heywoods that promoted sexual liberation. After the formation of the New England Free Love League in 1873, the *Word* became a free-love newspaper. Ezra Heywood's pamphlet *Cupid's Yokes*, published in 1876, was a critique of marriage and promoted birth control. It was widely distributed, and it was Heywood's intent to "promote discretion and purity of love by bringing sexuality within the domain of reason and moral obligation."

Lucifer, The Light Bearer was by no means the first publication of the free-love movement, however, it was the most influential and longest running journal of them all. Initially published under the title the *Kansas Liberal*, it took on the most burning and controversial sexual issues of the day, and publisher Harman's no-censorship policy allowed these issues to be fully debated in print. He promoted "free marriage" between consenting adults and without religious or governmental interference. Harman's daughter Lillian HARMAN and her partner, Edwin C. Walker, were jailed for such a relationship.

Other free-love periodicals, such as *Hulls' Crucible*, published in Boston by Moses Hull; *Foundation Principles*, published in Kansas and California by Lois WAISBROOKER; and *Fair Play*, published in Kansas and Iowa by Edwin C. Walker and Lillian Harman, were also available to women who did not otherwise have access to information on sexual matters. Their common mission was in direct conflict with the puritan morals of Victorian society, but it was the Comstock Postal Act of 1873, which criminalized mailing or receiving "obscene, lewd

or lascivious material," that cost many people stiff fines and harsh jail sentences. Although the act failed to define those vague terms, any discussion of sex, abortion, or birth control was criminalized, even if it was reprinted from another text such as the Holy Bible or a government publication. The law also targeted freethinkers by outlawing criticism of Christianity. The First Amendment notwithstanding, all that was needed was for the local postmaster to decide a publication or even a postcard was in violation to prevent it from being delivered, and to have the perpetrators arrested and tried.

Anthony Comstock, a young, militant crusader of Puritan values, believed he was called upon by God. He was first hired by the New England Society for the Suppression of Vice, a private organization headed by soap magnate Samuel Colgate, to enforce the existing obscenity laws. Soon after, he was sent to Washington to lobby for a stronger law, and succeeded. The new act provided for prison terms of up to ten years for violation of the act. Comstock was given so much autonomy that he was able to relentlessly harass violators, ruining their lives and livelihoods, driving some to suicide (see CRADDOCK, IDA), about which he later boasted.

It was not only publishers of obscene materials who were targeted by Comstock. Those who sold, advertised, or distributed such materials were also on his hit list. Such was the case of D. M. BENNETT, editor of *THE TRUTH SEEKER*, a prominent freethought newspaper. Bennett had been arrested before on obscenity charges through Comstock's famous modus operandi, decoy letters. Bennett was fined three hundred dollars and given thirteen months in prison for selling copies of Heywood's *Cupid's Yokes*. While the National Defense Association, a group of reformers who joined forces to fight against obscenity laws in general and Comstock in particular, was able to procure President Rutherford B. Hayes's pardon of Heywood, Bennett was not so fortunate; he served his entire sentence. Even with the able agnostic Robert Green INGERSOLL taking Bennett's side, Comstock intervened and put pressure on Hayes to refuse to pardon Bennett. But while Bennett's sentence had a beginning and an end, Heywood would never be free from Comstock. Determined to continue his struggle to preserve his freedom of speech, Heywood was arrested three more times on obscenity charges, once for publishing an edition of Walt WHITMAN's *Leaves of Grass*. Other charges were based on advocating and selling contraceptive devices for women. Most indictments against Heywood were dropped, although finally, at the age of sixty-one, he served a sentence of two years (minus two months) at hard labor. He died a year after his release. Although Angela Heywood had committed the same crimes as her husband, and was at least as vocal and vehement in her ideas of women's sexual emancipation, she was never arrested.

Comstock continued his relentless vice hunting until his death. Although his health had deteriorated substantially due to his constant vigilance in the battle to protect society's morals, he rarely allowed himself a rest from his calling. Comstock died in 1915 of pneumonia, which he contracted shortly after his return from the International Purity Congress, to which he was appointed as a delegate by President Woodrow Wilson. Despite many attempts by his enemies to turn the tables on him and find some scandal that would vindicate them, Comstock seemed to have no vices.

Regardless of the blatant constitutional violations, as well as the efforts of many to repeal it, the obscenity law was not changed until the 1930s, but the free-lovers had made their mark. They were decades ahead of their time, and many of their radical ideals are common practice today.

BIBLIOGRAPHY

Beisel, Nicola. *Imperiled Innocents: Anthony Comstock and Family Reproduction in Victorian America.* Princeton, NJ: Princeton University Press, 1997.

Blatt, Martin Henry. *Free Love & Anarchism: The Biography of Ezra Heywood.* Urbana: University of Illinois Press, 1989.

Broun, Heywood, and Margaret Leech. *Anthony Comstock: Roundsman of the Lord.* New York: Literary Guild of America, 1927.

Forster, Dora. *Sex Radicalism as Seen by an Emancipated Woman of the New Time.* Chicago: M. Harman, 1905.

Passet, Joanne E. *Sex Radicals and the Quest for Women's Equality.* Urbana: University of Illinois Press, 2003.

Sears, Hal D. *The Sex Radicals: Free Love in High Victorian America.* Lawrence: Regents Press of Kansas, 1977.

Stern, Madeleine B. *The Pantarch: A Biography of Stephen Pearl Andrews.* Austin: University of Texas Press, 1968.

JULIE HERRADA

SEXUAL VALUES, IMPACT OF UNBELIEF ON. Sexual values in Western culture were heavily influenced by Christian culture, particularly the writings of Saint Augustine. Augustine's views combined neo-Platonism (see PLATO), neo-Pythagoreanism (see PYTHAGORAS), Gnosticism, and Manichaean dualism. These views he cobbled together to emphasize that sex was a weakness of the flesh and that continence was the most desirable lifestyle. He was particularly offended by the act of coitus, which he held brought the "manly" mind "down from the heights." Augustine was particularly upset that propagation of the human species could not be accomplished without what he felt were bestial movements and violent lustful desires. Sexual lust was, for him, the inevitable result of the expulsion of Adam and Eve from the Garden of Eden.

Augustine recognized that the Bible had commanded humans to be fruitful and multiply, and that he had to accept this as a Christian, but he was unhappy about it. He compromised enough to allow that sexual intercourse could be justified only within marriage and only for purposes of procreation. Marriage, he held, transformed coitus from a mere satisfaction of lust to a necessary duty, but it was only the employment of the sex act for human generation that ultimately allowed it to shed some of its inherent sinfulness. Augustine ended up condemning all sexual activity between unmarried persons, limiting sex within marriage to the sole purpose of procreation and then only in the male-superior position. Though Christians undoubtedly found these teachings about sex difficult if not impossible to accept in practice, they were reinforced by successive "doctors of the church" including Saint Thomas Aquinas.

Though Protestants in general objected to the imposition of clerical celibacy by law, seeing no special virtue in being celibate and considering celibacy unattainable for most, they continued to regard it as an ideal. But sex was still to be limited to those who were married; Martin Luther felt so strongly about this that he in at least one case condoned bigamy in order to keep sex within marriage. The most positive of the religious reformers in the area of sex was John Calvin. Calvin held that coitus was undefiled, honorable, and holy because it was an institution of God, though he remained uneasy about its pleasurable aspects. It should be added here that Judaism had a much more positive view of sex than Christianity, one attuned to the Talmud, which regarded sexuality as a normal aspect of life.

Enter the Unbelievers. Though a significant portion of the Christian population failed to live up to the Christian sexual ideal—and though even Augustine ended up accepting prostitution as a necessary evil—it was not until the seventeenth and eighteenth centuries that a serious challenge was raised against some of the basic Christian assumptions regarding sex. In England one of the main factors was a reaction by those segments of the population who opposed Puritan attempts to enforce conformity to their ideals. After the fall of the Puritans, the sexual licentiousness of the Restoration court of Charles II created an opening for wider public discussion of sexual matters.

But public discussion of sexuality was not limited to England; it was taking place across much of Europe, fueled in part by growing awareness that other peoples and cultures had quite different sexual customs and ideas. Travelers, explorers, and settlers reported on the way things were done in India, China, the Americas, and elsewhere, further encouraging a new examination of traditional beliefs. The growth of the secular state led to increasing control by the state rather than the church, making possible new challenges to church domination over the regulation of sexual behavior. The growing willingness of many to challenge existing beliefs about the world in general is exemplified by the new scientific discoveries of GALILEO, Sir Isaac Newton, and others, discoveries that forced religious authorities to reexamine some of their basic assumptions.

One result of this ferment was a growing sense that men and women should follow their natural instincts, not just do what church authorities told them. Nature, it was believed, prescribed a reason and a place for everything, and this could be determined by REASON and observation. The most prominent advocates of these new ideas were the French philosophes, who sought to apply reason to every phase of life, even sexuality, in order to undermine superstitious religious beliefs. Denis DIDEROT, for example, complained that religious institutions had "attached the labels of 'vice' and 'virtue' to actions that were completely independent of morality." He called for a return to the "natural man."

The difficulty faced by such challenges to traditional religious beliefs about sexuality was that the advocates of change had no evidence to disprove traditional ideas except their own logical thinking. They could question traditional sexual values and beliefs, but they were not certain what should replace them. VOLTAIRE in his *Philosophical Dictionary* (1764) challenged traditional Christian ideas about "Socratic Love" (homosexual love). He wondered how it was possible that it could be such an evil vice that threatened to destroy the human race, if when generally practiced it appeared to be such a natural act, as Plato and others had declared it. Though Voltaire ended up opposed to laws against morals, the philosophes were very much people of their own time. Jean-Jacques ROUSSEAU, in his *Confessions* (1781-88) wrote that he had masturbated, but never managed to eliminate his guilt feelings: "Even after the marriageable age, this odd taste, always increasing, carried even to depravity, even to folly, preserved my morals well, the very reverse of what might have been expected."

The critics achieved a major victory with the enactment in 1804 of the Napoleonic Code, which removed many sexual activities (including same-sex partnerships) from the roster of crimes. This action by France served as a model for many other countries. Sexual attitudes, however, have not only been influenced by religion, philosophy, and law, but also by medicine. The eighteenth-century attack on Christian sexual beliefs by unbelievers would be undermined by those who claimed scientific backing for maintaining a more restrictive stance. The source of this attack was a growing fear of the "dangers" of masturbation. In the minds of many these dangers extended to all forms of nonprocreative sex. The attack originated with an anonymous Grub Street publisher in London who, at the very time the French philosophes were at their height, published *Onanism*, a book on masturbation that became an international best seller. (Onan was an Old Testament character whom God struck dead not because he masturbated, but because he practiced withdrawal during sex so as to avoid impreg-

nating his late brother's wife, as tribal law required of him. His violation was his refusal to get his sister-in-law pregnant.)

Though Onan's action was not masturbation, his spilling of his seed was so interpreted by the Grub Street author, who proceeded to attribute all kinds of diseases to the practice. In a day when medicine could offer few causal explanations for any disease, masturbation came to be viewed as a major causal factor of disease and was seized upon by a large variety of writers, including physicians, as the base cause of many of the ills of the time. The fear of masturbation only began to ease at the end of the nineteenth century when the germ theory developed. Nonetheless, his name became enduringly associated with masturbation.

The physician who seized upon the anonymous booklet and gave it "scientific" justification was the distinguished Swiss doctor S. A. D. Tissot. Concerned with the "rising tide" of sexual immortality, Tissot published a 1758 book, also titled *Onanism*, that transformed the idea of masturbation as a cause of disease from a questionable folk supposition to one that enjoyed the backing of medicine as a whole. Tissot's book was based upon the ideas of the Dutch physician and chemist Hermann Boerhaave, who taught that physical bodies suffered from incessant wastage and this continuing loss was ultimately a cause of death. Tissot accepted Boerhaave's belief that this wastage included diarrhea, loss of blood, perspiration, and similar factors, but he added another class of wastage which he felt superseded all: the waste of semen through masturbation. Tissot held that waste of semen (or its equivalent in women) would lead to (1) cloudiness of ideas, sometimes even madness; (2) a decay of bodily powers, resulting in coughs, fevers, and consumption; (3) acute pains in the head, rheumatic pains, and an aching numbness; (4) pimples on the face, suppurating blisters on the nose, breast, and thighs, and painful itching; (5) eventual weakness of the power of generation as demonstrated by such things as impotence, premature ejaculation, gonorrhea, priapism, and tumors in the bladders; and (6) disordering of the intestines, resulting in constipation, hemorrhoids, and other ailments.

Tissot's critics were hard put to disprove his argument, which was extended by many to include all nonprocreative sex. Numerous other writers (both medical authorities and moral crusaders) added to Tissot's litany of the sequellae of masturbation. All kinds of devices were patented to prevent masturbation in children, held to be its most likely victims, although women were considered particularly vulnerable as well.

The whole edifice built upon assumptions that masturbation caused disease eventually came crashing down—due to the discovery of bacteria and germs by Louis Pasteur and others, the acceptance of the concept of infection, the development of asceptic techniques, and the rise of twentieth-century medicine. But it would take time to reverse the effects of more than a hundred years of negative campaigning. Throughout the nineteenth century there had been dissenters from the general belief in the dangers of masturbation, but until the rise of germ theory they had no way to prove their opponents wrong. Still, freethinkers such as Jeremy BENTHAM, John Stuart MILL, and Henry Sidgwick had argued for, among other things, tolerance of homosexuality. Giving impetus to the challenge was a newly developing field of sexual research that itself involved a large number of freethinkers. Havelock Ellis, Magnus Hirschfeld, Sigmund FREUD, and, later, Alfred Kinsey, all freethinkers if not atheists, led the battle. Carrying the message of the researchers to a wider public were freethinkers such as publisher Emanuel HALDEMAN-JULIUS, whose Little Blue Books were the main source of sex information for vast numbers of Americans in the 1920s and 1930s. Later, humanists (see HUMANISM) such as Lester Kirkendall and Mary Calderone led the struggle for better sex education in the schools. Margaret SANGER, the daughter of a freethinking father and herself an early humanist and a founder of the Planned Parenthood movement, carried on the struggle to impart accurate sex information (see BIRTH CONTROL AND UNBELIEF). One of the most receptive audiences for new ideas about sexuality was the readership of the AMERICAN HUMANIST ASSOCIATION magazine the *Humanist*, edited by Ed Wilson and later by Paul Kurtz, who also founded *Free Inquiry*. In fact it was, in part, the perceived leadership of humanists in the sexual revolution of the late 1960s and early 1970s that led the Moral Majority and its allies to look upon SECULAR HUMANISM as the causal factor in changing American morals. Unbelievers were never alone in their efforts, and they were often joined by indviduals and groups representing organized religion. Their battle, however, is far from over.

BIBLIOGRAPHY

Bullough, Vern L. *Sex, Society and History.* New York: Neale Watson, 1976.

———. *Sexual Variance in Society and History.* New York: Wiley Interscience, 1978.

Bullough, Vern L., and James Brundage. *Sexual Practices and the Medieval Catholic Church.* Amherst, NY: Prometheus Books, 1982.

Bullough, Vern L., and Bonnie Bullough. *Science in the Bedroom.* New York: Basic Books, 1994.

———. *Sexual Attitudes, Myths, and Realities.* Amherst, NY: Prometheus Books, 1995.

VERN L. BULLOUGH

SHAFTESBURY, ANTHONY ASHLEY COOPER, THIRD EARL OF (1671–1713), British writer and deist. Brought up by his politician grandfather, the first Earl of Shaftes-
bury, and tutored by John LOCKE, whom he greatly respected without uncritically following him, Anthony Ashley Cooper, third Earl of Shaftesbury, was kept from active political life by crippling and finally fatal asthma. He disliked abstract metaphysics, though occasionally making telling points, for example, that hard as it was to see how matter could generate mind, it was equally hard to see how mind could generate matter. Rejecting both the materialism and the egoism of Thomas HOBBES, he considered philosophy useless unless it told us how to live, and he emphasized the role of feeling and sensitivity, often appealing to emotions to supplement rational argument.

Ethics. Shaftesbury is most famous for introducing the moral sense theory whereby we detect good and evil, right and wrong, much as we detect beauty—recognizing them directly rather than by deducing them from premises, whether theological or other. But systematic development only came later, and he was so keen to stress the objectivity of values, both moral and aesthetic, and the need for taste to be trained, that this "sense" often verges on rational intuition, and it is unclear just what is intuited. A tension also seems to arise when Shaftesbury insists both that virtue and self-interest ultimately coincide, and that virtue must be chosen for its own sake. But this is only apparent: virtue will indeed benefit us—but only if not chosen for that reason.

Religion. Shaftesbury's religious position is not entirely clear, partly perhaps because of then-current social and indeed legal constraints, though he deplored censorship as counterproductive. He certainly believed in a creative God, mainly because of the empirical evidence of design in the universe, but in interpreting this he relied heavily on a moral principle that the good of the whole must always supersede that of a part, so that the evil we see around us becomes merely apparent if it is needed for a greater good—as he rather optimistically assumed it was. Emphasizing order and reason, he decried appeal to miracles and argued that revelation presupposed rational proof of God for its own authenticity. His virtual silence on specifically Christian doctrines means that Shaftesbury is often called a deist (see DEISM), though some doubt this because of his ambiguous attitude toward nature, which he sometimes seems to equate to God.

BIBLIOGRAPHY

Brett, R. L. *The Third Earl of Shaftesbury.* London: Hutchinson's University Library, 1951.

Cooper, A. A. *Characteristics of Men, Manners, Opinions, Times.* Edited by L. E. Klein. Cambridge: Cambridge University Press, 1999.

Grean, S. *Shaftesbury's Philosophy of Religion and Ethics.* Athens: Ohio University Press, 1967.

ALAN LACEY

SHAKESPEARE, RELIGIOUS SKEPTICISM IN. Born in 1564, William Shakespeare belonged to a generation that had never known an undivided Christendom: the biblical promise that there would always be an "eternal" and "visible" church had failed. The 1590s, when young Shakespeare matured as a dramatist, were marked (or disfigured) by extreme religious intolerance, in England and across Europe. For reasons that were more obviously political than religious, each of the confessions set about "unchurching" its rivals, insisting that it alone was the necessary instrument of individual salvation, and denying that any devout Christian was in a position to determine privately which was the "true" church, or "Bride of Christ." John Donne's blistering "Satyre III: Of Religion," which was written in the mid-1590s but for obvious reasons circulated only privately, characterized these rival confessions as whores pretending to be the promised "Bride of Christ." Donne's anger followed from his (Christian) conviction that the whorish pretenders' mutual intolerance would drive men into disbelief. In this respect Donne's poem provides an excellent introduction not only to the oppressive religious climate of the 1590s but to *Hamlet*, with its peculiarly troubling Ghost. "Remember me," says the Ghost, but nineteenth- and early twentieth-century critics who speculated about Hamlet's reasons for "delay" kept forgetting the most important reason. Hamlet is intermittently shaken by the thought that the Ghost may be a "damned goblin" or instrument of damnation, sent to take advantage of Hamlet's melancholy; if, on the other hand, the Ghost really is the ghost of Hamlet's father then Purgatory exists, which Protestants denied. If Hamlet is right to appeal to "Saint Patrick"—the patron saint of Purgatory—Protestant England, as well as Protestant Denmark, was in deep trouble.

Several modern scholarly studies have shown how thoroughly Shakespeare knew his (Genevan) Bible; as Tom Bishop shows in an excellent survey, this has been a fertile area of investigation in which much work remains to be done on how such knowledge fueled Shakespeare's creative imagination. But discussions regarding what religious beliefs, if any, Shakespeare may or may not have held have always been unconvincing or inconclusive, for two quite different reasons.

First, the surviving documentary and historical evidence that is assembled and examined at length in Samuel Schoenbaum's *Shakespeare's Lives* is too woefully sparse to yield any firm conclusions, although determined speculators have used this "evidence" as drunks use lampposts, for support rather than illumination. Here it should be noted that even if Shakespeare was *once* a Lancastrian Catholic (a popular speculation, at present), this would not establish whatever the later author of *Hamlet* and *King Lear* believed. Ben Jonson's and John Donne's overlapping circles of friends included many so-called "double converts." Just as our modern notions of "ATHEISM" can be misleading if we forget that

Renaissance science offered no alternative account of creation, our modern notion that religious "conversion" involves changing one's beliefs can be misleading, if we forget how many Christians changed their minds about which of the changing institutions could best accommodate their unchanged religious beliefs.

Second, Shakespeare's plays provide little evidence of his own beliefs because they are so markedly and (even by the standards of his own time) peculiarly perspectival. It is not so difficult to establish what Ben Jonson—or Bernard SHAW and Henrik Ibsen, or Gotthold LESSING and Bertolt BRECHT—think about the issues their plays explore. But Shakespeare habitually shows how differently his different characters see, and think or feel about, their different situations, or about issues like honor, the divine right of kings, or religion itself. Once again, countless determined critics and interpreters have made light of this difficulty by supposing that they somehow just know when Shakespeare is ventriloquizing through one character rather than another, and know whether their "Shakespeare" agrees with the mutually exclusive points of view of, say, Prospero and Caliban, or Shylock and Portia. Shakespeare is now the world's most performed dramatist; neither the history of Shakespeare criticism nor the history of the plays in performance vindicates, or even encourages, any confidently priestly or authoritarian claim to know whether Henry V or Michael Williams speaks with His Master's Voice. Moreover, because such claims are always striving to settle disputes by privileging one voice rather than another, in the distinctively Shakespearean plenitude of different, clamoring voices and views, such claims always work against the plays' power to excite or disturb audiences.

Shakespeare's SKEPTICISM, like Michel de MONTAIGNE's, was almost always radical, not terminal or dogmatic. True, young Shakespeare seems to have tried, to the best of his ability, to defend (or at least not to oppose) the Tudor myth of the divine right of kings in his first historical tetralogy; but he gave up. *King John*, which so few critics discuss, may provide some indirect record of the loss of an illusion not worth having, since it is fiercely and, for Shakespeare, unusually anti-Catholic. The second tetralogy is radically skeptical and perspectival, like the tragedies and "problem" comedies that followed *Hamlet*. *Troilus and Cressida* makes a comedy out of the intellectually demanding proposition that there are no objective values, and that, as Hamlet puts it, "There is nothing either good or bad, but thinking makes it so." In *Measure for Measure*, which followed a little later, Shakespeare was more concerned with the incompatibility of different absolute values, like those of the perfectly matched Isabella and Angelo: there is no possible way of reconciling the different claims of legal, moral, and divine "justice."

Atheistic sentiments are difficult to track in this period, since atheism was so severely punished: as David Berman shows, anti-atheistic tracts precede *published* professions of atheism by more than two centuries. Indirect evidence is to be found in the Public Records Office, where there are letters from priests complaining that they are spat upon or stoned in their villages; or in edifying, officially approved narratives of conversion, when writers like John Bunyan or Richard Baxter describe the climate of unbelief from which they (God be praised) emerged; or in drama, when villains like Shakespeare's Iago or Edmund can profess their unbelief because they are villains. But *Measure for Measure* includes an unforgettable portrayal of a decent, casual atheist in Isabella's condemned brother Claudio, who believes that when we die, we go "we know not where."

BIBLIOGRAPHY

Berman, David. *A History of Atheism in Britain: From Hobbes to Russell.* London: Routledge, 1988.
Bishop, Tom. "Shakespeare and Religion." In *Shakespearean International Yearbook.* Vol. 3. Brookfield, UT: Ashgate, 2003.
Bradshaw, Graham. *Shakespeare's Scepticism.* Ithaca, NY: Cornell University Press, 1987.

GRAHAM BRADSHAW

SHAW, GEORGE BERNARD (1856–1950), Anglo-Irish playwright and critic. With such plays as *Man and Superman*, *Major Barbara*, *Caesar and Cleopatra*, *Arms and the Man*, *Saint Joan*, and *Pygmalion*, the expatriate Irishman George Bernard Shaw forged a grand repertoire in English second only to William Shakespeare's (see SHAKESPEARE, RELIGIOUS SKEPTICISM IN). He was awarded the Nobel Prize in Literature in 1923.

ATHEISM. Until he was thirty or so, Shaw called himself an atheist. He adjudged the doctrines of the Church of Ireland, which he attended in childhood, unintelligible. Since the first of its thirty-nine articles describes God as "without body, parts, or passion," Shaw waggishly inferred that the church was atheistic; an incomprehensible God was tantamount to no God. In 1875 he blazoned his atheism abroad in a letter to *Public Opinion*, a Dublin newspaper. To save Shaw from hellfire, a friend prevailed on a Roman Catholic priest to catechize the upstart atheist. When the priest contended someone must have created the universe, since it exists, Shaw replied: "It is as easy for me to believe that the universe made itself as that the maker of the universe made himself, in fact much easier; for the universe visibly exists and makes itself as it goes along, whereas a maker for it is a hypothesis."

Shaw scoffed at superstition, churches, ecclesiastics, rituals, ceremonies, and creeds. In *The Adventures of the Black Girl in Her Search for God*, he derided the myopic sectarianism that strews dissension among Christians.

He depicted the God of Abraham and Moses as a boastful, imperious, and sanguinary fiend. While Jesus fared better than Yahweh, Shaw impugned the doctrines of atonement and universal love. Atonement he described as "a means by which we cheat our consciences, evade our moral responsibilities, and turn our shame into self-congratulation by loading all our infamies on to the scourged shoulders of Christ." Shaw deemed it psychologically impossible to love everyone.

Mysticism and the Life Force. In the 1890s Shaw renounced atheism and repackaged himself as a mystic. He now characterized atheists as "superficial and light-minded." His renunciation of atheism was accompanied by sallies against scientific MATERIALISM, especially DARWINISM, which he believed to hold "that every act of pity or loyalty is a vain and mischievous attempt to preserve inferior varieties from the efforts of nature to weed them out."

To combat Darwinism, Shaw preached "the Gospel of Shawianity." He evangelized for an idiosyncratic version of Henri BERGSON's emergent evolution. From the first decade of the twentieth century to the end of his life, in speeches, essays, stories, letters, and plays, Shaw expatiated on the "life force" —a mysterious power immanent in living matter that supposedly drove evolution. Shaw reified the power as an inchoate deity struggling to actualize itself in organisms. Every species had been an instrument of its effort to acquire power, knowledge, understanding, and empathy. In its odyssey to achieve fruition, the life force would create ever-higher forms of humanity—supermen, super-supermen, supermen to the third power. By evolving into omniscient, omnipotent, and omnibenevolent beings, humans would create God.

Critique. Shaw adduced no evidence in favor of the life force, other than an extraneous insistence that Darwinism was incompatible with hope, aspiration, and altruism. He merely postulated the existence of the force and described its modus operandi. When Shaw invoked the life force to explain the course of evolution up to the present, he violated Occam's razor, the principle of parsimony in hypotheses, since what the life force purports to illuminate can be illuminated without it. When he described the future course of evolution, he revved up his propensity for wild surmise.

Shaw's motive for believing in the life force was more emotional than intellectual. The conviction that virtue and wisdom will ultimately vanquish wickedness and ignorance justified his humanitarian zeal, bulwarked his native optimism, and quieted his inner demons. Shaw was a mixture of Mephistopheles and Jesus Christ. Though he ridiculed churches, clerics, and anthropomorphic gods, he retained the moral fervor of his Protestant heritage. When hawking the life force, he was a holy prophet pitching the Kingdom of Heaven.

BIBLIOGRAPHY

Pearson, Hesketh. *George Bernard Shaw: His Life and Personality*. New York: Atheneum, 1963.

Sloan, Gary. "The Religion of George Bernard Shaw: When Is an Atheist?" *American Atheist* 42, no. 4 (2004).

Smith, Warren Sylvester. *Shaw on Religion*. New York: Dodd, Mead, 1967.

GARY SLOAN

SHELLEY, PERCY BYSSHE (1792–1822), English poet. Percy Bysshe Shelley was born on August 4, 1792, the oldest son of Timothy Shelley, a Whig member of Parliament. In 1804 he was sent to Eton; in 1810 he went to University College, Oxford. He was expelled on March 25, 1811, for his coauthorship of the pamphlet *The Necessity of Atheism*. In August he eloped with and married Harriet Westbrook. In 1812 he began to correspond with William GODWIN, author of *An Enquiry concerning Political Justice* (1793), and to pamphleteer in Ireland and England for religious and political reform. In 1812 he printed and distributed *Queen Mab*, "A Philosophical Poem," a denunciation of tyranny and religion. In June 1812 Harriet gave birth to a daughter, Ianthe (named after the heroine of *Queen Mab*). In 1814 Shelley privately published *A Refutation of Deism*. He began a relationship with Mary Wollstonecraft Godwin, the daughter of Godwin and of Mary WOLLSTONECRAFT, author of *A Vindication of the Rights of Women* (1792), eloping with her on July 28, 1814. In November, Harriet and Shelley's second child, Charles, was born. In February 1815 Mary gave birth prematurely to a daughter who died unnamed; and in January 1816 she gave birth to a son, William. In May 1816 Shelley and Mary traveled to Lake Geneva, where Shelley began his relationship of reciprocal influence and uneasy but profound friendship with Lord BYRON. In June Mary began writing *Frankenstein*. Shelley wrote the poems "Hymn to Intellectual Beauty" and "Mont Blanc"; in hotel registers in Chamonix he signed himself in Greek as "democrat, philanthropist and atheist." Shelley and Mary returned to England in September. On December 10, Harriet committed suicide by drowning herself. Shelley married Mary on December 30, and attempted without success to gain custody of his and Harriet's children. Shelley and Mary became close friends of Leigh Hunt and acquainted with John Keats. In September Mary gave birth to a daughter, Clara. Shelley wrote, among other political pamphlets and philosophical essays, the unfinished "Essay on Christianity," which distinguishes Christ from the ignorance and fanaticism of his followers. Shelley's epic poem, *Laon and Cythna*, was published in December 1817; censored, it was republished as *The Revolt of Islam* in January 1818.

On March 11, 1818, Shelley left England for Italy. This was a period of unsettled traveling and of further personal suffering. The Shelleys' children died: Clara in May 1818, and William in June 1819. Shelley, however, remained very active creatively, depicting his renewed friendship with Byron in *Julian and Maddalo*, and expressing his radical views on religion, morality, and politics in a variety of essays and poems, including the "Lyrical Drama" *Prometheus Unbound*, the blank-verse play *The Cenci*, the balladic invocation *The Mask of Anarchy*, the sonnet "England in 1819," "Ode to the West Wind," the unfinished treatise "A Philosophical View of Reform," and the "Essay on the Devil, and Devils," satirizing Christian mythology, all written in 1819. Percy Florence (the only one of Mary and Shelley's children to survive him) was born in November 1819. Between 1819 and 1822 Shelley wrote several of his most significant and substantial works, including "Ode to Liberty"; *Epipsychidion*; his poetic credo *A Defence of Poetry*; *Adonais*, an elegy for Keats who had died in Rome in February 1821; his final major published poem *Hellas*; and his last-written poem, *The Triumph of Life*, unfinished when he died. At the end of April 1822, the Shelleys moved to near Lerici in the Bay of Spezia. In June Leigh Hunt arrived in Italy to join Byron and Shelley in the production of an antiestablishment journal, the *Liberal*; and on July 1, Shelley sailed to Leghorn in his own boat to meet with Hunt. On the return voyage, the boat sank in a sudden storm and Shelley drowned. His body, washed ashore on July 18, was exhumed and burned on a pyre on August 16. His ashes were placed in the Protestant Cemetery in Rome in 1823.

It is only since the latter half of the twentieth century that the range of Shelley's writings has become widely accessible. Despite recognition of his heterodoxy, there has been reluctance to acknowledge his ATHEISM. Although other terms can, with discrimination, be applied appropriately to Shelley's beliefs, David Berman has persuasively argued that *The Necessity of Atheism* and *A Refutation of Deism*, at least, are atheistic works; and that Shelley is of major importance as only the fourth-published speculative atheist in British intellectual history. In both texts, Shelley's position is primarily epistemological, derived from the empiricism of John LOCKE, the skepticism of David HUME, and from both Classical philosophers and Enlightenment philosophes (see ENLIGHTENMENT, UNBELIEF DURING THE). *The Necessity of Atheism* argues "that there is no proof of the existence of a Deity," and *A Refutation of Deism* presents in dialogue the arguments of a deist and a Christian that are mutually confounding. In many of Shelley's writings in prose and verse, his epistemological position compounds with an ethical and political stance: not only berating Christian belief as irrational and ignorant superstition, but also indicting Christianity as practiced deception, in service to despotic power.

An early letter allows one to savor Shelley's libertarian viewpoint at its most vehement and lively: "And

Liberty! Poor liberty, even the religionists who cry so much for thee, use thy name but as a mask, that they also may seize the torch, & shew their gratitude by burning their deliverer. *I* should doubt the existence of *a* God, who if he cannot command our reverence by *Love*, *surely* can have no demand upon it from Virtue on the score of terror. It is this empire of terror which is established by Religion."

BIBLIOGRAPHY

Berman, David. *A History of Atheism in Britain from Hobbes to Russell*. London: Croom Helm, 1988.

Cameron, Kenneth Neill. *Shelley: The Golden Years*. Cambridge, MA: Harvard University Press, 1974.

———. *The Young Shelley: Genesis of a Radical*. London: Macmillan, 1950.

Clark, David Lee, ed. *Shelley's Prose, or The Trumpet of a Prophecy*. Albuquerque: University of New Mexico Press, 1966.

Everest, Kelvin, and G. M. Matthews, eds. *The Poems of Shelley, 1804–1819*. 2 vols. Harlow: Longman, 1989, 2000.

Holmes, Richard, *Shelley: The Pursuit*. London: Quartet, 1976.

Jones, Frederick L., ed. *The Letters of Percy Bysshe Shelley*. 2 vols. Oxford: Clarendon, 1964.

Leader, Zachary, and Michael O'Neill, eds. *Percy Bysshe Shelley: The Major Works*. Oxford: Oxford University Press, 2003.

Murray, E. B., ed. *The Prose Works of Percy Bysshe Shelley*. Vol. 1. Oxford: Clarendon, 1993.

Reiman, Donald H., and Neil Fraistat, eds. *Shelley's Poetry and Prose*. New York: Norton, 2002.

Shelley, Percy Bysshe. *The Necessity of Atheism and Other Essays*. Amherst, NY: Prometheus Books, 1993.

GEORGE EDWARD DONALDSON

SHROUD OF TURIN, BELIEF IN. Of some forty alleged shrouds of Jesus that have appeared over the centuries, the most seriously promoted is a fourteen-foot length of linen kept in Turin, Italy, in the Roman Catholic Cathedral of Saint John the Baptist. Uniquely, it bears the front and back images of a bearded and apparently crucified man. Believers insist it is the actual burial wrapping of Jesus, stained with his blood.

The supposed relic first surfaced at a little church in the village of Lirey, in north-central France, ca. CE 1355. It was in the possession of one Geoffroy de Charny, who never explained how he, a man of relatively modest means, had acquired the most holy relic in Christendom. At that time, it was being used as part of a faith-healing scheme to bilk credulous pilgrims. Subsequently, however, the local bishop, Henri de Poitiers, "discovered the fraud and how the said cloth had been cunningly painted, the truth being attested by the artist

who had painted it," as stated in a later bishop's report to Pope Clement VII, dated 1389. (Clement was the Avignon Pope, the first of the antipopes in the Great Western Schism.)

In 1532 the shroud had to be rescued from a fire that consumed its chapel in Chambéry. A blob of molten silver from the reliquary penetrated the cloth's multiple folds, resulting in the burn marks. Eventually, in 1578, in a shrewd political move to relocate the capital of the Savoy duchy, the shroud was transfered to Turin.

The modern history of the shroud began in 1898 when its shadowy image was first photographed by Secondo Pia. The negatives returned an image that looked more realistic in its distribution of highlights and shadows, indicating that they were approximately reversed on the cloth. How, shroud proponents began to ask, could a mere medieval forger have produced a perfect photographic *negative* long before the invention of photography?

In fact, the image is a *quasi*-negative, the darks and lights being only *approximately* reversed. For instance, in the "positive" image shown on a photo negative, the figure's hair and beard are white—the opposite of what would be expected for a Palestinian Jew of Jesus's age. The effect would be consistent with an *imprint*.

However, experiments demonstrated that simple contact imprinting could not have produced such a harmonious image. A genuine body imprint would have had severe wraparound distortions—an inevitable fact of geometry—and other flaws.

Other "theories" about the image-forming process ranged from the discredited to the fantastic. For instance, a concept called vaporography was disproved when the postulated vapors produced only a blur. One scientist opined that the image was caused by "flash photolysis"—that is, a burst of radiant energy, supposedly yielded by Christ's body at the moment of resurrection.

Better photographs made available in the 1930s prompted shroud enthusiasts, like the French Catholic surgeon Pierre Barbet, to insist that certain anatomical elements and realistic "blood" flows represented details beyond the knowledge and abilities of a medieval forger. Skeptics countered that a bloody footprint on the cloth was anatomically incompatible with the image of the leg belonging to it; that the features were unnaturally elongated (like figures depicted in Gothic art); that the hair falls as for a standing rather than recumbent figure; that the blood had failed to mat the hair and was unnaturally picture-like; and that the blood had remained red, unlike old blood, which blackens with age.

Physical tests of the shroud were first carried out by an official, originally secret commission between 1969 and 1976. Two of the experts specifically questioned the provenance of the cloth and suggested it was an artwork made by some imprinting technique. Also, a pair of internationally known forensic serologists extensively tested "blood"-stained threads, but the red substance failed all of them: standard preliminary analyses, additional tests for hemoglobin, microscopic examination for blood corpuscles, and sophisticated instrumental analyses. Another expert, Professor Silvio Curto, discovered traces of what he believed was paint.

In 1978 a further examination was conducted by the Shroud of Turin Research Project (STURP) whose leaders, unfortunately, served on the executive council of the proauthenticity Catholic organization, the Holy Shroud Guild. Many STURP scientists indicated their proshroud bias before examining the cloth.

An exception was a world-famous microanalyst, Walter C. McCrone. He performed a "blind" microscopic study of samples that had been lifted from the cloth by sticky tape and placed on microscopic slides. McCrone found significant amounts of the pigment red ocher (red iron oxide) on image areas, but not on off-image ones. He first thought the pigment was applied as a dry powder but later concluded it was a component of a diluted paint applied in the medieval grisaille (monochromatic) technique.

He identified the "blood" as tempera paint, composed of red ocher and vermilion pigments in a collagen binding. He performed the identification by microchemical and instrumental analyses. For his efforts, McCrone stated, he was "drummed out" of STURP.

McCrone was replaced by two scientists, John Heller and Alan Adler, who soon challenged McCrone's findings as well as those of the commission's forensic experts. The pair claimed to have "identified" the presence of blood on the shroud. Unfortunately, neither was a forensic serologist, nor a pigment expert, raising the serious question of why they were selected to perform the analyses.

Forensic analyst John F. Fischer reviewed Heller and Adler's claims and observed that none of their tests was specific for blood, that their approach (an attempt to add together individual aspects, such as the presence of iron and protein) was not a forensically acceptable method of identifying blood, and that similar results might be obtained from tempera paint.

Skeptics of the shroud's authenticity were vindicated in 1988 after three laboratories (at Oxford, Zurich, and the University of Arizona) carbon-dated samples of the cloth. Using accelerator mass spectrometry, the labs obtained dates in very close agreement: The age span was circa CE 1260–1390, and it was given added credibility by correct dates obtained from a variety of control swatches.

Shroud proponents responded to the devastating carbon-14 test results with a variety of rationalizations. Some claimed the cloth samples had been taken from a patch, or that the imagined burst of radiation at Jesus's resurrection had altered the carbon ratio. Some accused the scientists of deliberate fraud. Another researcher offered a seemingly more scientific explanation when he claimed a microbial "varnish" had contaminated the cloth and skewed the radiocarbon date; however, for the date to have been altered by thirteen centuries, there would have to be twice as much contamination, by weight, as the cloth itself.

The accuracy of the radiocarbon dating is supported by other, corroborative evidence for the shroud's medieval origin. This includes a study of iconographic elements. By the eleventh century, artists had begun to depict the shroud as a single double-length cloth, although actual Jewish burial practice (as related in John 20:5–7) utilized multiple cloths. And by the thirteenth century we find ceremonial shrouds bearing full-length images of Jesus's body in death. In these, as in the Turin image, the hands are discreetly folded over the loins, an artist's motif that itself dates from the eleventh century. Found together in the Shroud of Turin, these traditions suggest it is the work of an artist of the thirteenth century or later. And, in fact, the long, thin forms of the figure are typical of French gothic art of the fourteenth century.

Among post–radiocarbon test claims about the Shroud of Turin is the allegation that human DNA was found in a shroud "blood" sample. Actually the scientist cited, Victor Tryon of the University of Texas, stated, "All that I can tell you is that DNA contamination is present and that the DNA belonged either to a human or another higher primate. I have no idea who or where the DNA signal came from, nor how long it's been there." He does not say it came from blood. As he observed, "Everyone who has ever touched the shroud or cried over the shroud has left a potential DNA signal there." Tryon resigned from a shroud project in the wake of exaggerations about his findings, disparaging "zealotry in science."

Still other claims concerned floral evidence. It was alleged that pollen on the shroud proved it came from Palestine, but the source for the pollen claim was a freelance criminologist, Max Frei, who once pronounced the forged "Hitler diaries" genuine. Frei's tape-lifted samples from the shroud were controversial from the outset, since similar samples taken by the Shroud of Turin Research Project in 1978 had comparatively little pollen. As it turned out, when Frei's tapes were examined following his death in 1983, they also had very little pollen—although one bore a suspicious cluster on the "lead" (or end), rather than on the portion that had been applied to the shroud. Accompanying the unscientific pollen evidence were claims that faint plant images have been "tentatively" identified on the shroud. These follow previous "discoveries" of "Roman coins" over the eyes and even Latin and Greek words, such as "Jesus" and "Nazareth," that some researchers see—Rorschach-like—in the shroud's mottled stains.

In recent years, the Shroud of Turin has been linked to another notorious cloth, the Sudarium of Oviedo, which some believe was the "napkin" that covered Jesus's face. However, the Sudarium lacks a facial image, and its presence would have prevented such an image from forming on the shroud. Also, the supposed matching of the bloodstains on the Turin and Oviedo cloths is but another exercise in wishful thinking. As to the alleged matchup of pollens, once again the evidence comes from the questionable tapes of Max Frei.

A desire to believe the Shroud of Turin is authentic—supported by rationalizations and questionable evidence—propels shroud enthusiasts' agenda. They offer one explanation for the contrary gospel evidence (*maybe* certain passages require clarification), another for the lack of historical record (*maybe* the cloth was hidden away), still another for the artist's admission (*maybe* the reporting bishop misstated the case), yet another for the paint pigments (*maybe* an artist who made a copy of the shroud ritualistically pressed it to the image), and so on. This should be called the "maybe" defense. It is all too characteristic of shroud advocacy, which has failed to produce any scientifically viable hypothesis for the image formation.

In contrast, the scientific approach is to allow the preponderance of prima facie evidence to lead to a conclusion: The shroud is the handiwork of a medieval artisan. The various pieces of the puzzle effectively interlock and corroborate each other. For example, the artist's admission is supported by the lack of prior record, as well as by the revealingly red and picturelike "blood" that, in turn, has been identified as tempera paint. And the radiocarbon date is consistent with the time the artist was discovered.

Given this powerful, convincing evidence, it is well to recall the words of Canon Ulysse Chevalier, the Catholic historian who brought to light the documentary evidence of the shroud's medieval origin. As he lamented, "The history of the shroud constitutes a protracted violation of the two virtues so often commended by our holy books: justice and truth."

BIBLIOGRAPHY

Antonacci, Mark. *The Resurrection of the Shroud.* New York: M. Evan, 2000.

Damon, P. E., et al. "Radiocarbon Dating of the Shroud of Turin." *Nature* 337 (1989).

McCrone, Walter C. *Judgement Day for the Turin Shroud.* Chicago: Microscope, 1966.

———. "Light Microscopical Study of the Turin Shroud." *Microscope* 28 (1980), 29 (1981).

Nickell, Joe. *Inquest on the Shroud of Turin: Latest Scientific Findings.* Amherst, NY: Prometheus Books, 1998.

———. "The Sacred Cloth of Oviedo." *Skeptical Briefs* 11, no. 3 (September/October 2001).

———. "Scandals and Follies of the Holy Shroud." *Skeptical Inquirer* 25, no. 5 (September/October 2001).

"Shroud of Christ?" *Secrets of the Dead* series, PBS, aired April 7, 2004.

Sox, H. David. *The Image on the Shroud: Is the Turin Shroud a Forgery?* London: Unwin Paperbacks, 1981.

Van Biema, David. "Science and the Shroud." *Time,* April 20, 1998.

Wilson, Ian. *The Blood and the Shroud.* New York: Free Press, 1998.

———. *The Shroud of Turin.* Rev. ed. Garden City, NY: Image, 1979.

JOE NICKELL

SILVER, QUEEN (1910–1998), American freethinker, feminist, and labor radical. Queen Silver was born on December 13, 1910, in Portland, Oregon. Her fame as a prominent advocate for atheism began during her childhood. Indeed, the legendary film producer Cecil B. DeMille called her "the Godless Girl" in a 1929 Hollywood movie of that same title whose main character was modeled after Queen and her organization, the AMERICAN ASSOCIATION FOR THE ADVANCEMENT OF ATHEISM.

Queen attended her first political rally at six days old. Her mother and fellow atheist Grace Verne Silver had interrupted a lecture tour on labor laws only long enough to give birth. Political agitation was a tradition for the Silver women. Queen's grandmother, Azuba, had been a vocal opponent of child labor. Thus, Queen delighted in introducing herself as "a second generation freethinker, a third generation feminist, and directly descended from framers of the Constitution."

At eight years old—and already a veteran soapbox speaker at the Free Speech Zone on Los Angeles Street in Los Angeles—the diminutive Queen stunned Los Angeles crowds by delivering a series of six lectures sponsored by the London Society of Science. The subjects ranged from Darwinian evolution to Einstein's new theory of relativity. In announcing one 1919 lecture, the *Los Angeles Recorder* wrote, "A good share will be extemporaneously delivered. She has already traveled 50,000 miles in work on the stage and lecture platform." Queen's lectures drew hundreds of people; hundreds more were turned away at the door.

Her most famous lecture and pamphlet, titled "Evolution, From Monkey to Bryan" (1923), was addressed to William Jennings Bryan, the prosecutor in the Scopes monkey trial (see DARROW, CLARENCE; EVOLUTION AND UNBELIEF). *Queen Silver's Magazine*, a freethought periodical she both published and edited, showcased the teenager's lectures and attracted more than five thousand subscribers worldwide.

Queen was also an activist. Late in 1925, Grace physically attacked an aggressive evangelist and was arrested for assault and battery. Queen acted as her mother's lawyer. Headlines in the *Los Angeles Evening Express* declared, "Modern Portia of 14 Fights for Mother Before Court." Queen won.

Queen and Grace were also active in the labor organization Industrial Workers of the World. As a result, Queen witnessed considerable police violence against dissidents. She also witnessed the destruction of Grace's bookstore—the first socialist and freethought bookstore in Los Angeles—which was raided three times by the

American Legion while the police stood by.

When Grace's health deteriorated badly in the mid-1930s, Queen withdrew from radicalism to become a clerk at the Department of Motor Vehicles. She eventually became one of the first woman court reporters in California.

When Grace died in 1972, Queen returned to a political advocacy that revolved around freethought, women's rights, and defending the First Amendment. She remained active in atheist circles in Los Angeles, often performing low-glamour work such as taking records or stuffing envelopes. She died on January 7, 1998.

BIBLIOGRAPHY

McElroy, Wendy. *Queen Silver: The Godless Girl.* Amherst, NY: Prometheus Books, 2003.

WENDY MCELROY

SINCLAIR, UPTON (1878–1968), American novelist. Upton Sinclair was born in Baltimore, Maryland, to Upton Beall Sinclair and Priscilla Sinclair. Upton Sr. was an alcoholic and died in 1907. Owing to his mother's piety, Upton Jr. had a deeply religious upbringing and was confirmed in the Episcopal Church at age twelve. Christian morality remained strong in Sinclair all his life, and he believed that true Christianity would eventually prevail, although he rejected organized religion. Sinclair's three main influences were Jesus, *Hamlet*, and the poet Percy Bysshe SHELLEY.

Sinclair enrolled in City College of New York when he was fourteen. After graduating in 1897, he spent three years at Columbia University, taking social science and humanities courses. He began writing small items such as jokes and captions for newspapers and magazines.

Introduced to socialism in 1902 by Leonard Abbott, Sinclair cofounded with Abbott the Intercollegiate Socialist Society (later the League for Industrial Democracy). He ran for congress as a Socialist three times and lost. In California he founded a political action group, End Poverty in California (EPIC), and ran on the Democratic Party ticket for governor in 1934, losing to the Republican candidate by a narrow margin.

In 1915 Emanuel HALDEMAN-JULIUS gave a favorable review in the *New York Call* of one of Sinclair's books, after which Sinclair became a regular contributor to Haldeman-Julius's *Appeal to Reason*, the *Haldeman-Julius Weekly*, *Monthly*, and *Quarterly*, as well as many of the Little Blue Books.

In Sinclair's *The Profits of Religion* (1918) he denounced established religious institutions for their corruption and their exploitation of the poor, especially targeting the Catholic Church. But Sinclair was no rationalist; he took his belief in the occult very seriously. In this book he also espoused "mental healing," claiming to have the psychic ability to heal by placing his hands on people.

An unhappy marriage to Meta Fuller resulted in a son, David. During this time, he was commissioned to write *The Jungle*, and spent two months in Chicago at the stockyards. The book, first published serially in *Appeal to Reason*, prompted Theodore Roosevelt to call upon Congress to pass the Pure Food and Drug Act and the Meat Inspection Act.

Sinclair won the Pulitzer Prize in 1943 for his *Dragon's Teeth*, the third novel in his Lanny Budd series. His many novels, such as *The Moneychangers* (1908), *King Coal* (1917), and *Oil!* (1927), remained true to his socialist ideals. A year before his death, Sinclair moved to Bound Brook, New Jersey, to be near his son.

BIBLIOGRAPHY

Buhle, Mari Jo, Paul Buhle, and Dan Georgakas, eds. *Encyclopedia of the American Left.* 2nd ed. New York: Oxford University Press, 1998.

Mordell, Albert, *Haldeman-Julius and Upton Sinclair: The Amazing Record of a Long Collaboration.* Girard, KA: Haldeman-Julius, 1950.

Upton Sinclair: Biographical and Critical Opinions. Long Beach, CA: Upton Sinclair, 1928.

Whitman, Alden, ed. *American Reformers.* New York: H. W. Wilson, 1985.

JULIE HERRADA

SKEPTICISM. Various forms of skepticism have emerged through history. The term derived originally from the Greek word *skeptikos*, which means "to consider, examine." It is akin to the word *skepsis*, which means "inquiry" and "doubt." According to *Merriam-Webster's Collegiate Dictionary*, *skepticism* denotes "an attitude of doubt or a disposition to incredulity, either in general or toward a particular object." There are various shades of skepticism, from NIHILISM, which denies that any knowledge is possible, to the careful use of skepticism in the process of scientific inquiry. In the latter case, new forms of skepticism provide powerful analytic tools of criticism in science, philosophy, religion and the paranormal, morality, and politics.

Ancient Skepticism. Two explicit forms of philosophical skepticism appeared in the ancient world of Greece and Rome: Pyrrhonism and Academic Skepticism.

Pyrrhonism is a school of skepticism that took its name from Pyrrho of Elis (360–270 BCE) and influenced subsequent thinkers in the Greco-Roman world. Sextus EMPIRICUS, who lived in the third century CE, was the leading proponent of Pyrrhonism. His book *Outlines of Pyrrhonism* made a considerable impact on modern philosophy. In 1880 the historian Edward Zeller summed up Pyrrhonic skepticism as follows: "We can know nothing as to the nature of things. Hence, the right attitude toward them is to withhold judgment. The necessary result of suspending judgment is imperturbability." Sextus, a medical doctor in his day, characterized Pyrrhonic skepticism as follows: It is *zetetic* (it is searching and examining) and it is *ephectic* (it involves a state of doubting). According to Sextus, the problem that we encounter in evaluating knowledge claims is that for every appearance (i.e., argument), we can find a contrary appearance or judgment. The only sensible solution is to suspend judgment, to neither affirm nor deny anything. Pyrrhonists do not seek to refute the claims of others; they are only saying that they neither believe nor disbelieve them. Thus Pyrrhonistic skepticism is excessive in its degree of doubt and is difficult to defend seriously today. It is impossible to live as a neutral person, for we need to make choices. Moreover, to deny the very possibility of knowledge is to ignore the considerable body of common sense and scientific knowledge that we possess. Many critics of Pyrrhonism find it to be dogmatic; it can easily lead to extreme negativism and nihilism.

A second school of skepticism that goes by the name Academic Skepticism emerged from PLATO's Academy in the third century BCE. Since we do not possess any of the writings of the Academic Skeptics, we must rely on secondhand sources. The Academic Skeptics attacked the metaphysical doctrines then prevalent, especially Platonism and STOICISM. According to CICERO, Arcesilaus used the term *epoché* to refer to the suspension of judgment in philosophical arguments. Arcesilaus introduced the doctrine of *eulogon*, which is to say the probable or reasonable, which provides us with some basis on which to make practical judgments, even though these are inconclusive and do not reveal to us the nature of reality. The views of Carneades are especially important, for he provided a constructive form of skepticism. He did not assume the neutralist suspension of judgment, but formed probabilistic judgments upon which we could act. Carneades did not think we could have knowledge about the nature of things, nor ultimate certitude. Nevertheless, some judgments are more probable than others. These are based upon empirical observations and inductive inferences, and the testing of beliefs in practice. It has been pointed out that Carneades could argue both sides of a question and illustrate the contradictory nature of judgmental claims; therefore the need for the suspension of judgment in such cases is prudent. Yet many of the scholars in the Academy argued for a *pithanon* approach, that is, a positive application of the skeptical method. These views are not unlike the *mitigated skepticism* of David HUME, which emerged in the modern world, and the use of skeptical inquiry by latter-day American Pragmatists (see PRAGMATISM).

Modern Skepticism. Skepticism became a major intellectual force in modern thought. The rediscovery of the writings of the ancient skeptics was important in the battle with dogmatic theology and speculative meta-physics. The use of skepticism led to the quest for a new method for understanding nature, and this paved the way for the birth of modern science. Writers such as Pierre BAYLE expressed the most thoroughgoing skepticism of the time. His influential *Dictionnaire Historique et Critique* presented scathing indictments of philosophical and religious theories. Many skeptics resorted to unlimited doubt, whether real or feigned. Thus RENÉ DESCARTES, often called the father of modern philosophy because of his search for a method, employed the technique of universal doubt, which was called "Cartesian doubt." This was not unlike the extreme form of ancient Pyrrhonistic skepticism. Descartes believed, however, that we could reach certainty by using the method of mathematics, wielding clear and distinct ideas and drawing deductive inferences from them in order to establish universal propositions. His RATIONALISM was rejected by empiricists, however, who thought that our knowledge of matters of fact was based on sense perceptions and empirical observations. John LOCKE, George Berkeley, and Hume attempted to resolve the central problem of modern epistemology: how ideas and/or minds could know external objects. In a sense the entire history of modern philosophy focused on the problem raised by the ancient skeptics: How was knowledge possible? What was the extent and limit of knowledge? What did this tell us about ultimate reality? This epistemological problem was exacerbated by the rapid development of Newtonian mechanistic and materialistic science, and its seeming conflict with our commonsense views of the world.

David Hume is no doubt the most influential skeptical philosopher of the modern world. He developed a form of *mitigated skepticism*. Wrestling with the challenge of Pyrrhonistic doubt, he argued that we develop knowledge about matters of fact based on sense impression. Our knowledge of causality is drawn from present observation, past experience, and the habit of expectation or custom, which allows us to make causal inferences. For Hume, although we cannot know ultimate reality, we do develop probabilities that can guide our conduct. Hume was a skeptic about the existence of God (see EXISTENCE OF GOD, ARGUMENTS FOR AND AGAINST), which he could not reconcile with the problem of evil (see EVIL, PROBLEM OF). His argument against miracles (see MIRACLES, UNBELIEF IN) rejected miracles on probabilistic grounds. It was reasonable to be skeptical of a miraculous claim because it conflicted with the regularities observable in nature.

Many other modern philosophers have been influenced by skepticism. Immanuel KANT attempted to combine both rationalism and empiricism. On Kant's view all knowledge has its origin in direct experience (phenomena), but this is structured or ordered by the forms of intuition and the categories of the understanding. Although knowledge of the phenomenal world was secure, Kant said, we cannot know the "thing in itself," in the noumenal world, nor could we prove the existence of God, freedom, or immortality.

The scientific revolution that began in the sixteenth and seventeenth centuries in the natural sciences was extended to the biological and the behavioral sciences and to technology in the nineteenth and twentieth centuries. It is widely conceded today that skepticism has an essential role to play in the course of scientific inquiry.

Pragmatic Doubt. Charles Sanders Peirce, an American Pragmatist philosopher, argued that inquiry begins where there is a state of real and living doubt. This is contextual. The quest for a belief to resolve doubt thus initiates inquiry. Scientific hypotheses need to be tested by means of a process of experimental confirmation and rational inference within an intersubjective community of inquirers. Such knowledge is fallible and open to modification in the light of new data and/or theories. This implies that any claims to knowledge need to be replicated before they are accepted. John DEWEY argued that the quest for certainty is elusive and illusive, but he thought that we could develop a progressive body of warranted assertions in the sciences. The methods of scientific inquiry, moreover, he said, were continuous with critical thinking in ordinary life and in making ethical judgments where we attempt to solve problems. Many skeptics have been influenced by Karl POPPER's nonfalsifiability principle (see FALSIFIABILITY). Popper suggested a demarcation line between science and pseudoscience. He said that a theory or hypothesis needs in principle to be falsifiable if it is to be considered scientific. He stated: "The criterion of the scientific status of a theory is its falsifiability, or refutability, or testability."

For contemporary skeptics there is thus an intrinsic relationship between inquiry and doubt. The process of investigation enables us to overcome doubt and develop a body of reliably tested hypotheses. Scientists need to be open to the possibility that new hypotheses may overthrow previously held theories. Science needs to test these hypotheses by rigorous standards of objectivity. Although modern skeptics believe that we can develop reliable knowledge in the sciences, they are unwilling to assert that we have reached any final formulation, and they are prepared to admit that any theory in time may be revised.

Skepticism has been used in all fields of human inquiry, especially in science and philosophy. In the area of religion skeptics tend to embrace either AGNOSTICISM, denying that there is sufficient evidence or proof for the existence of God, or ATHEISM, declaring that the existence of God has not been demonstrated by either argument or evidence. Even atheism connotes only the position that the existence of God is highly improbable, without foreclosing further inquiry. In ethics and politics, where practical judgments are at issue, some nihilistic skeptics take the position that there are no basic objective criteria and all ethical judgments are emotive (see LOGICAL POSITIVISM). Other skeptical inquirers have maintained, however, that there do exist rational considerations that are relevant, and that we can apply a "logic of judgments of practice" in evaluating their adequacy—though such skeptics likewise resist making absolute assertions.

The New Skepticism. Of considerable interest to classical and modern skepticism is the reemergence of a new skeptical movement in the twentieth century, which has focused on the scientific examination of "claims of the paranormal." The investigation of anomalous phenomena goes back to the examination of Franz Anton Mesmer and hypnotism at the end of the eighteenth century in France and England and Spiritualism and the Fox sisters in the United States in the nineteenth century (see SPIRITUALISM AND UNBELIEF). The founding of the British and American Societies for Psychical Research extended these studies to manifestations of mediumship, ghostly apparitions, claims for survivorship after death, and later parapsychological phenomena.

The establishment of the Committee for the Scientific Investigation of Claims of the Paranormal (CSICOP) in 1976 and its journal, *Skeptical Inquirer*, greatly expanded the skeptical movement in the United States and worldwide. This form of skepticism began with the recognition that skeptical inquiry was intrinsic to scientific discovery and to the process of corroborating scientific hypotheses, and further that there was a considerable body of reliable scientific knowledge that provided a benchmark for testing truth claims scientifically. CSICOP attempted to find empirical and causal explanations for so-called paranormal phenomena such as alleged extrasensory perception (ESP), telepathy, precognition, faith healing, astrology, the Shroud of Turin (see SHROUD OF TURIN, UNBELIEF IN), miracles, alternative medicine, and even UFOlogical visitations and abductions.

These methods have been also employed by the Committee for the Scientific Examination of Religion (CSER), founded by the Council for Secular Humanism and its journal, *Free Inquiry*, and now operating under the auspices of the Center for Inquiry. CSER is interested in applying the best methods of skeptical scientific inquiry to the vigorous examination of the Old and New Testaments, the Qur'an, and other so-called sacred documents (see BIBLICAL CRITICISM; JESUS, HISTORICITY OF; BIBLICAL ERRANCY; ISLAM, UNBELIEF IN). It endeavors to use linguistics and to seek archeological, anthropological, evolutionary, genetic, biological, psychological, and sociological explanations throughout all aspects of inquiry into religion. Skepticism is thus brought directly to bear on *paranatural* phenomena, such as revelation, mysticism, PRAYER, faith healing, and alleged miracles, which heretofore had been considered beyond the range of naturalistic explanations.

BIBLIOGRAPHY

Brandon, Ruth. *The Spiritualists: The Passion for the Occult in the Nineteenth and Twentieth Centuries.* New York: Knopf, 1983.

Descartes, René. *Discourse on Method.* Translated by Laurence J. Lafleur. Indianapolis: Bobbs-Merrill, 1980.

Dewey, John. *The Quest for Certainty.* New York: Minton Balch, 1929.

Empiricus, Sextus. *Outlines of Pyrrhonism.* Amherst, NY: Prometheus Books, 1990.

Finucane, R. C. *Appearances of the Dead: A Cultural History of Ghosts.* Amherst, NY: Prometheus Books, 1984.

Hoffmann, R. Joseph, and Gerald Larue, eds. *Jesus in History and Myth.* Amherst, NY: Prometheus Books, 1986.

Hume, David. *Enquiries concerning Human Understanding and concerning the Principles of Morals.* Edited by L. A. Selby-Bigge, revised by P. H. Nidditch. Oxford: Oxford University Press, 1975.

———. *A Treatise of Human Nature.* Edited by E. C. Mossner. London: Penguin, 1985.

Kant, Immanuel. *Critique of Pure Reason.* Translated by F. Max Muller. Garden City, NY: Doubleday, 1966.

Kurtz, Paul. *The New Skepticism.* Amherst, NY: Prometheus Books, 1992.

———. *Skepticism and Humanism: The New Paradigm.* New Brunswick, NJ: Transaction, 2001.

———, ed. *A Skeptic's Handbook of Parapsychology.* Amherst, NY: Prometheus Books, 1985.

Nickell, Joe. *Inquest on the Shroud of Turin.* Amherst, NY: Prometheus Books, 1983.

Peirce, Charles. *The Collected Papers of Charles Sanders Peirce.* Edited by Charles Hartshorne and Paul Weiss. Cambridge, MA: Harvard University Press, 1934.

Popper, Karl. *Conjectures and Refutations.* New York: Harper & Row, 1968.

———. *The Logic of Scientific Discovery.* New York: Harper & Row, 1968.

Zeller, Edward. *The Stoics, Epicureans, and Skeptics.* London: Longmans Green, 1880.

PAUL KURTZ

SLENKER, ELIZABETH "ELMINA" DRAKE (1827–1908),

American freethought writer and birth control advocate. Elizabeth "Elmina" Drake was born the oldest of six girls in LaGrange, New York. Her father had been expelled as a Shaker preacher for becoming a "Liberal." Elmina's skeptical awakening occurred when her mother offered her a dollar to read the Bible. "I became a sceptic, doubter, and unbeliever, long ere the 'Good Book' was ended," she wrote in *Studying the Bible* (1870). She married Isaac Slenker, who answered her ad for an egalitarian husband in the *Water-Cure Journal.* In the early 1880s they moved to Snowville, Virginia, where he operated woolen mills.

Slenker adopted Dianaism, a philosophy preaching sexual sublimation and other practices that offended the guardians of the Comstock Act (see COMSTOCK, ANTHONY, AND UNBELIEF) and helped avoid unwanted pregnancies. She advocated use of "contraceptics" in Moses HARMAN's *Lucifer, The Light Bearer.* When Slenker was arrested at age sixty in April 1887 for mailing private, sealed letters of advice on sex and marriage, it made national news. Bail was set at two thousand dollars. She was ushered into a cold cell and given a blanket to spread on the floor, she reported in THE TRUTH SEEKER, and was, she wrote, arrested simply "for speaking plain truths in plain words."

The *New York Times* and other press vilified Slenker for refusing to swear on a Bible, and for testifying that she did not believe in God, ghosts, heaven, hell, the Bible, or Christianity. Unable to raise bail, Slenker spent six months in jail awaiting trial. Readers of *The Truth Seeker* contributed to a defense fund, and freethinking attorney Edward W. Chamberlain represented her during the October 1887 trial before the United States District Court for the Western District of Virginia at Abington. Although a jury found her guilty, Slenker was set free by the judge on November 4, 1887, after Chamberlain argued that Slenker had not knowingly mailed obscene material.

Slenker wrote for nearly all the freethought journals, edited *Little Freethinker* (1892–98), and wrote novels including *The Clergyman's Victims*; *Mary Jones, the Infidel School-Teacher* (both 1885); and *The Darwins* (1879). Her 153-page book *Studying the Bible* was made up of columns originally published in the BOSTON INVESTIGATOR. Slenker died in Snowville, Virginia, in 1908.

BIBLIOGRAPHY

Chamberlain, Edward W. "The Trial of Mrs. Slenker." *Truth Seeker*, November 12, 1887.

Sears, Hal D. *The Sex Radicals: Free Love in High Victorian America.* Lawrence: Regents Press of Kansas, 1977.

Slenker, Elmina D. "Mrs. Slenker in Her Own Defense." *Truth Seeker*, May 14, 1887.

"The Trial of Mrs. Slenker." *Truth Seeker*, November 19, 1887.

ANNIE LAURIE GAYLOR

SMITH, CHARLES LEE (1887–1964), American atheist

activist and editor. Born near Fort Smith, Arkansas, Charles Lee Smith considered a career in the ministry, clerked in a law office, and passed the Oklahoma bar. Around 1912 he discovered *The Jefferson Bible*, Thomas JEFFERSON's redaction of the New Testament stripped of its miracles (see MIRACLES, UNBELIEF IN). Thus led him to FREETHOUGHT literature and eventually ATHEISM. After World War I Smith moved to New York, where he sold and wrote for the nation's leading freethought paper, THE TRUTH SEEKER, then edited by George E. MACDONALD.

In 1925 Smith and associate Freeman Hopwood

founded the AMERICAN ASSOCIATION FOR THE ADVANCE-MENT OF ATHEISM (the 4As), which won broad publicity for an ultimately barren scheme to organize student atheist groups. Among Smith's coups was a debate against the prominent evangelist Aimee Semple McPherson.

In 1928 Arkansas mulled an antievolution law (see EVO-LUTION AND UNBELIEF). Smith's quixotic protests demonstrated his combative style. Attempting to lobby in Little Rock, he challenged legislators for singing a hymn; the lower house barred Smith from its chambers. He rented a storefront "atheistic headquarters" where he gave away evolution tracts and antireligious brochures. A window sign read, "Evolution is True. The Bible's a Lie. God's a Ghost." Smith was arrested, then barred from speaking at his arraignment because he was an atheist. Rejecting a fine, Smith demanded jail time and launched a hunger strike. National publicity painted Arkansas as an ignorant backwater; charges were dropped. Smith reopened his store and was again arrested, this time for BLASPHEMY. After a conviction, years of appeals followed before the case was dismissed. The antievolution law passed.

Hurt by the Depression, the 4As became a paper operation after 1933. In 1937 the aged George Macdonald transferred *The Truth Seeker* to Smith. Influenced by its associate editor Woolsey TELLER, by 1950 Smith openly reshaped the magazine as the organ of socially conservative freethought: anti-communist, eugenicist (see EUGENICS), anti-Semitic, and racist. Circulation plummeted.

In 1956 Smith published a comprehensive statement of his philosophy. Almost unreadable, the two-volume *Sensism* sold poorly. In 1961 he gave five thousand dollars to Madalyn Murray O'HAIR, then beginning her school prayer lawsuit against the Baltimore public schools; so toxic was Smith's reputation by then that the attorney preparing O'Hair's first petition dropped the case. In 1964 San Diego atheist James Hervey JOHNSON purchased what remained of the Truth Seeker organization and the vestigial 4As. Moving to San Diego, Smith edited *The Truth Seeker* for six months before dying of a heart attack on October 26. He was cremated.

BIBLIOGRAPHY

Croy, Homer. "Atheism Rampant in Our Schools." *World's Work* 54 (1927).

Edwords, Fred. "Bucking the Currents: The Life and Legacy of James Hervey Johnson." *Humanism Today* 8 (1993).

Pankhurst, Jerry G. "Propaganda, Antireligious." In *The Encyclopedia of Unbelief*, edited by Gordon Stein. Amherst, NY: Prometheus Books, 1985.

Seaman, Ann Rowe. *America's Most Hated Woman: The Life and Gruesome Death of Madalyn Murray O'Hair.* New York: Continuum, 2005.

Smith, Charles Lee. *Sensism: The Philosophy of the West.* 2 vols. New York: Truth Seeker Company, 1956.

Stein, Gordon. "Charles Lee Smith: 1887–1964." *American Rationalist*, May/June 1984.

———. "Smith, Charles Lee." In *The Encyclopedia of Unbelief*, edited by Gordon Stein. Amherst, NY: Prometheus Books, 1985.

TOM FLYNN

SMITH, KATIE KEHM (1868–1895), American FREETHOUGHT lecturer and organizer. Born in Warsaw, Illinois, Katie Kehm graduated from high school in Ottumwa, Iowa, and took up teaching as a profession. As early as seventeen, she began to speak publicly on freethought and soon became well known in freethought circles as an eloquent lecturer.

Freethought groups were being formed in Oregon during the 1880s with encouragement from visiting lecturers including Robert Green INGERSOLL, Samuel Porter PUTNAM, B. F. UNDERWOOD, Mattie KREKEL, and others. In 1889 a state convention was held to form the Oregon State Secular Union. When Katie Kehm spoke before the union the following year, she made such an impression that she was appointed secretary, a position she would hold until her death five years later.

In 1891 she married David W. Smith, a Port Townsend, Washington, judge who was also a freethinker. In 1893 she started the First Secular Church and Sunday School in Portland, and her regular Sunday lectures soon attracted a congregation of hundreds, certainly as large as any of the other orthodox churches in Portland. Due to her energetic organizing, many more secular schools were soon set up throughout the states of Oregon and Washington.

Using her training as a teacher, she wrote and circulated lessons and training manuals so that the schools could all follow the same curriculum, writing as a guideline that "[a] Secular Sunday school must be founded on knowledge, not theories; upon facts, not fictions; upon things known not believed; upon that which pertains to men, women and children, and not to gods, angels or devils; in short, all that pertains to this world and the here and now, and not to some other world 'in the sweet by and by.'"

Basic to her secular philosophy was encouraging people to celebrate natural events such as the Winter Solstice rather than religious holidays. Besides the programs for young children, she also wrote comparative religion lessons for adults, and shortly before she died was making plans to set up a Liberal University at Silverton, Oregon (see WAKEMAN, THADDEUS BURR).

After her untimely death from a fever at age twenty-seven, the network of secular Sunday schools continued for a time under the leadership of Nettie A. Olds.

BIBLIOGRAPHY

Gaylor, Annie Laurie. *Women without Superstition.* Madison, WI: Freedom From Religion Foundation, 1997.

Gray, Carole. *Nineteenth Century Women of Freethought*. 2 vols. In *Woman: Her History* [CD-ROM], edited by Emmett Fields. Louisville, KY: Bank of Wisdom, 2004.

Macdonald, George E. *Fifty Years of Freethought*. New York: Truth Seeker Company, 1972.

Putnam, Samuel P. *Four Hundred Years of Freethought*. New York: Truth Seeker Company, 1894.

ELIZABETH M. GERBER

SOCRATES (469–399 BCE), Greek philosopher. A leading Athenian philosopher, Socrates wrote nothing, preferring to engage in argumentative conversations with his fellow citizens. Of the main sources concerning Socrates, PLATO's dialogues are the most important. It is a contested matter just how much of Plato's Socrates is a record of the philosophy and method of a man with whom the young Plato was acquainted, and how much is due to the literary and philosophical genius of Plato, who created Socrates the philosopher in his dialogues.

Plato's early dialogue *Apologia* purports to be Socrates' defense at the trial at which he was condemned to death. Socrates says that his role as a gadfly stinging the rump of the Athenian state was his God-appointed duty. His role as critic had never been opposed by his *daimonion*, his personal divine sign or "voice which whenever I hear it always turns me back from something I was going to do, but never urges me to act." The *daimonion* never prohibited his philosophical activity. His extraordinary affect on his contemporaries culminated in his enemies bringing two charges against him. The first was that he had corrupted the young (a matter the court normally did not hear); the second was that he did not obey the city's official gods and created his own. Surprisingly Socrates does not address the second charge directly, arguing instead that he is not an atheist (see ATHEISM) and does believe that there are divinities. These matters suggest that there was an irrational side to Socrates, who believed that he had direct access to divine forces.

But there is also a relentlessly rational side to Socrates. He would not expect anyone to base their beliefs, including religious beliefs, on any authority but reason: "the unexamined life is not worth living." He speculates that one reason for his trial was because he thought of himself as a superior "know-it-all" tripping people up with his clever sophistries with which the weaker argument could always defeat the stronger. Once the Delphic Oracle was asked: "Is there any person wiser than Socrates?" The answer was "No." On Socrates' understanding of the answer, he was wiser than others in only one respect. They claimed to know answers to his questions, but Socrates could show, time and again, that they did not. But nor did Socrates know the answers. His only wisdom was in the fact that whereas others claim to know but did not, Socrates knew that he did not know.

What were the kinds of questions that Socrates asked? Often they were of the form: What is X? where X could be love, friendship, beauty, piety, temperance, courage, virtue, justice, knowledge, and the like. Standardly a Socratic dialogue begins with some person suggesting an answer to one of these questions. By critically examining this initial definition using the method of question and answer (*eristic*), Socrates was able to drive them into a contradiction. This is the Socratic *elenchus*, cross-examination leading to contradiction or refutation. To escape the contradiction a revised definition was proposed which overcame the difficulties raised. But once more, by applying his eristic technique of cross-examination, Socrates drove the person into contradiction. And the process was repeated until the person ran out of further ideas, and no other interlocutor had any further ideas. At this point all are in a state of *aporia*, that is, there is no way forward and the disputants are in a state of perplexity. Often Plato's "Socratic" dialogues end at this point.

In such encounters it is clear that Socrates has no final answer to the "What is X?" question. As he put it in the *Theaetetus*, he is merely the midwife assisting at the birth of an idea had by someone else. As midwife, it is not Socrates giving birth to ideas; his role is to assist and then examine the birthchild of others for its intellectual health. But Socrates at least knows something. Even if he does not know the answer to a substantive question, he does know how to subject people's beliefs to critical evaluation. A person subject to critique by Socrates may have two reactions to the state of *aporia* in which he leaves them. Either they are pleased with Socrates for subjecting their ideas to critical examination, so that they know that their former claims to knowledge were defective and they are open to improvement; or they are resentful for being tricked yet again by Socrates and are not able to defend themselves.

Socratic dialogues move at two levels. The first is to seek answers to the substantive questions posed. The second is more methodological or philosophical in that questions are raised about the following: What is an adequate definition? Can we ever know that we have arrived at the correct definition? Does the question-answer method enable one to arrive at correct answers (this being the aim of *dialectic* as opposed to *eristic*)? What are the correct arguments we ought to employ? These and other questions take us to the heart of philosophical method and lie at the core of the critical approach championed by Socrates, in which dogmatism is to be resisted and the examined life becomes a worthy life to lead, even if there are no definitive answers as to what is right but several as to what is wrong.

BIBLIOGRAPHY

Guthrie, W. K. C. *Socrates*. Cambridge: Cambridge University Press, 1971.

Kahn, Charles. *Plato and the Socratic Dialogue*. New York: Cambridge University Press, 1996.

Vlastos, G. *Socrates: Ironist and Moral Philosopher*. Cambridge: Cambridge University Press, 1991.

———. *Socratic Studies*. New York: Cambridge University Press, 1994.

ROBERT NOLA

SOLARIN, TAI (1922–1994), Nigerian educator and pro-democracy activist. As a child Tai Solarin received his education in a Methodist missionary school in Nigeria. As an adult, he performed duty with the British Royal Air Force during World War II. He later studied at the University of London, and he was awarded a degree in history and geography from the University of Manchester.

In 1956 Solarin founded the Mayflower School, the first secular school in Nigeria. The school was unique in that it brought Christians and Muslims together without arguments or violence. Solarin placed strong emphases on self-reliance and critical thinking. He placed secular, human-centered messages on the buildings and in the classrooms throughout the campus. He often wore a white cap with bold yellow letters bearing the message "Knowledge Is Light" (a favorite saying of one of Solarin's heroes, Robert Green INGERSOLL).

Solarin believed that missionary schools could not be used effectively to educate African students. Furthermore, he challenged the notion that there were causal factors or a correlation between religious instruction and morality. Moreover, he believed that mission schools were basically tools to force Africans to carry out the will of the British government. He was especially critical of Roman Catholicism, believing that it was the religion most inimical to development of critical-thinking skills.

Solarin charged that the mission schools practically brainwashed Africans in denigrating efforts to "civilize" them by imposing Christianity. In this way, Africans were acquiring Western ways while learning to disrespect their own culture and customs.

Solarin was a fierce critic of government corruption and military leaders. In 1966 the civilian government of Nigeria attempted to have him assassinated. However, there was a military coup in the nation, and the assassination attempt was thwarted.

In 1976 Solarin gave the government control of Mayflower, even though he continued to lead the school. He wrote for many of Nigeria's leading newspapers, including the *Guardian*. He wrote several books, including his autobiography.

Solarin believed he was the only outspoken atheist in Nigeria—and he relished the role. He would courageously critique religion in the newspapers. He asserted that there is no evidence for the existence of God, and that if God exists, he owes the world an apology, especially the black race. He said that the world needs human leadership, and that all of the men supposedly sent by God had ultimately come up short. He contended that not prayer but hard work is chiefly to be valued, and he argued that Nigerian Christians and Muslims posed the greatest threat to the nation's security.

Solarin strongly criticized his country's military government and was often imprisoned for expressing his views. At the age of seventy-two, on the day before he died, Solarin participated in a march against the rule of Nigerian dictator Sani Abacha. Abacha's soldiers drove Solarin and his wife, Sheila, in separate vehicles to separate police stations. Crowds of people successfully clamored for their release, and Tai continued the march. He died the next morning.

The *New York Times* reported Solarin's death; humanist and Nobel laureate Wole Soyinka dedicated his book *The Open Sore of a Continent* to him. Before his death in 1994, Solarin served as a proud role model for the Nigerian group Action for Humanism and offered support to the Nigerian Humanist Movement.

In 2001 the Council for Secular Humanism and the Nigerian Humanist Movement held the first major international humanist conference in sub-Saharan Africa. Sheila Solarin, Tai's widow and the group's matriarch, read a paper, and students from the Mayflower choral group sang for those in attendance.

In June 2004 the INTERNATIONAL HUMANIST AND ETHICAL UNION (IHEU) and the Nigerian Humanist Movement hosted the Tai Solarin International Humanist Conference at the Mayflower School. Participants from Africa, Europe, and the United States were in attendance.

Solarin's legacy lives on in numerous books, papers, newsletters, and on numerous Web sites. But most importantly, Mayflower (now a junior and senior high school) continues to turn out some of Nigeria's best and brightest students.

BIBLIOGRAPHY

Allen, Norm R. "Humanism in Political Action." In *By These Hands: A Documentary History of African American Humanism*, edited by Anthony B. Pinn. New York: New York University Press, 2001.

———. "An Interview with Tai Solarin." *Free Inquiry*, Winter 1993/94.

Babalola, Dele. *Ògá Táséré: The Celebration of a Colossus Called Tai Solarin*. Black Rock, St. Michael, Barbados: Africana Ventures, 2004.

"Tai Solarin, 72, Nigeria Educator and Critic, Dies." *New York Times*, August 7, 1994.

NORM R. ALLEN JR.

SOLOMON, ABRAHAM (1914–2004), Indian humanist activist. Awarded the Distinguished Service Award by the INTERNATIONAL HUMANIST AND ETHICAL UNION (IHEU) in 1999, Abe Solomon initiated the formulation of the Universal Declaration of Human Values in 1988.

Solomon was born into Bombay's (now Mumbai) small Bene Israel community, a Jewish enclave whose members were descended from Galilean Jews shipwrecked on the Indian subcontinent circa 150 BCE. Brought up by his uncle, Solomon developed as a rationalist (see RATIONALISM). Solomon edited *Reason*, a Mumbai-based rationalist journal, starting in the early 1930s.

In 1933 Solomon was subjected to India's first BLASPHEMY prosecution. The case attracted wide notice and helped to establish Solomon's stature in India's rationalist movement. In 1934 he founded the rationalist Youth League in Mumbai. He and Nissim Ezekiel, also of the Bene Israel community, worked together in radical humanist student associations and movements. Solomon converted Nissim Ezekiel to ATHEISM, rationalism, and humanism. Ezekiel would gain fame as India's foremost English-language poet.

Solomon worked with various humanist and secularist associations in India, and collaborated with rationalist stalwarts like R. D. Karve, R. P. Paranjape, Erulkar, George Coheo, and Lotwala Ranchhoddas in India. He established Modern Age Publications, which brought out rationalist literature and published the English version of the influential *Critique of Hinduism and Other Religions* by Laxman Sastri Joshi. Joshi was a Marathi scholar and former adviser to Mohandas K. Gandhi who later came close to M. N. ROY. Modern Age also published Roy's controversial 1945 booklet on Nehru.

Solomon joined the International Confederation of Free Trade Unions, a worldwide association of labor unions. In 1936 he moved to Brussels, Belgium, where he resided until 1978. He was a board member of the IHEU from 1971 to 1978. During this time he represented the interests of Indian humanists within the IHEU. Solomon was active in the Indian Secular Society (see INDIA, UNBELIEF IN) as its vice president and, later, its president (following the death of founder A. B. Shah), and edited the society's journal, the *Secularist*. For a short period he also worked for the magazine *Quest*, based in Kolkatta. As a radical humanist, he collaborated with humanist leaders like Shib Narayan Ray, V. M. Tarkunde, Indumati PARIKH, R. A. Jahgirdar, Indian Humanist Association leader Prakash Narain, and G. R. R. Babu, who became executive director of the IHEU. Solomon's eleven articles were published in the US journals *Free Inquiry* and the *Humanist*, and in the Indian journal *Radical Humanist*. In these writings he traced the source of values in the dignity of human person, moving on to discuss such qualities as reason, critical intelligence, truth, tolerance, creativity, freedom, equality, justice, man and nature, and universal culture—a future culture rooted in freedom, truth, reason, and compassion that he spent his long life striving to help bring closer to reality.

BIBLIOGRAPHY

"Three Humanists." *Secularist* (2006).

INNAIAH NARISETTI

SOPHISM. A movement of itinerant philosophers that thrived in fifth-century BCE Greece, especially in Athens; members of Sophism were the first professional teachers. The Sophists were important figures in the history of FREETHOUGHT and unbelief. They were among the first to question the existence of supernatural beings, and to raise the question as to whether morality comes from the gods or is instead a human construct. Unfortunately, most of what is known about them is contained in the writings of the philosopher PLATO, who was decidedly opposed to them, particularly for their eschewal of metaphysical speculation.

The word *sophist* itself comes from the Greek *sophia*, and essentially means "the wise men." The Sophists claimed not only to possess wisdom, but to be able to impart it to others, for a fee. This is why they are called the first professional teachers. They taught the art of successful living (the word *sophisticated* describes the type of existence they advocated). It was important, they claimed, to dress well, speak persuasively on all matters, know the most up-to-date information on current affairs, and generally impress one's friends and neighbors. All of this, the Sophists held, could be learned and mastered. However, metaphysics—the search for ultimate knowledge—was, they argued, a futile pursuit. No human beings truly knew the answers to such questions as whether there is life after death, whether the gods exist and, if so, what their natures might be, and whether human beings possess an immortal soul. Such topics could be argued over endlessly but ultimately had no resolution. Therefore, for the Sophists, such speculation was off-limits.

The best-known Sophist was PROTAGORAS (for whom Plato dedicated a dialogue). He thrived in the city of Athens, where he helped to prepare many of the young men there for careers in politics (Athens being unique for having a democratic form of government, where leaders were elected and thus had to appeal to the populace for support). Like all the other Sophists in Athens, he was not a native, and could not vote himself, but he was a strong proponent of democracy, arguing that it was a form of government that had the blessings of Zeus himself. SOCRATES, or at least Socrates' chronicler Plato, was to call him to task for such an assertion, since first of all Protagoras did not apparently believe in the existence of Zeus, and could not therefore base his defense of democracy on supernatural support, and second, since he was what today we would call a cultural relativist, he could not claim that democracy per se was the best form of government, but only that it was the form that worked best in Athens. Protagoras would have replied that as a

Sophist, all he need do was teach his pupils to appeal to the beliefs that the Athenians themselves held in order to prepare them for successful careers. It was not necessary to further pursue the actual underpinnings of metaphysical beliefs, since this was immaterial to winning popular support, and indeed would be likely to infuriate the populace, who would not appreciate having their religious beliefs so questioned. This insouciant attitude toward the divine not only troubled Plato, it led to Protagoras's own banishment from Athens on the charge of impiety (the same charge for which Socrates himself would later be found guilty and executed).

The word *sophist* has come to be a derogatory term, implying one who gives facile answers, and is concerned only with surface meanings. But this is unfair to the Sophist movement, which thrived for several centuries and which has strong connections with later philosophical movements such as PRAGMATISM, relativism, and postmodernism. It is perhaps unfortunate that so much of what is known about influential Sophists such as Protagoras, Thrasymachus, Lysias, and Gorgias is found primarily in the unsympathetic writings of Plato. As James Arieti puts it, learning about the Sophists from Plato "would be like learning about Franklin Roosevelt from what Barry Goldwater wrote or about Ronald Reagan from what George McGovern wrote." It is important to note that the Sophists were considered influential public figures of their day (perhaps the first "celebrities"), and their development of the art of rhetoric made major contributions to this field. Some consider them to be the first professional attorneys as well (which might not be a mark in their favor!), as they also coached their students in the skills of presenting a good case in the courts of ancient Greece. Plato was critical of them for charging a fee for their services, but surely most professional philosophers today cannot look down upon them for that. In their own defense the Sophists would have asserted that they worked hard to develop their talents, through years of study and through traveling much of the known world to learn about different customs and beliefs. Their training was based upon rigorous methodology, time-tested and constantly evaluated. Why should they not receive proper compensation for imparting such knowledge to others?

The Sophists played a major role in delineating one of the most argued-about topics which still concerns us, namely, the "nature/nurture" debate. As Protagoras famously declared, "Man is the measure of all things." This sentence has been much debated, but the most accepted understanding is that all knowledge is determined by human standards. There is no "God's-eye view" allowing us to transcend our earthly existence and see the "big picture" in its entirety. While this may be called a relativistic viewpoint, the Sophists would ask what alternatives there are. In addition, the Sophists did claim that, while most human customs are peculiar to specific times and places, there are some constants that transcend these, such as human biology. Antiphon,

for instance, argued that Greeks and so-called barbarians (i.e., non-Greeks) have the same natural needs, breathe the same air, and eat with their hands in the same way. Thus, a code of ethics based upon common traits was certainly a possibility, but in point of fact most ethical systems were grounded upon cultural conventions, regardless of how universal their adherents might claim them to be. Since the Sophists actually traveled throughout the ancient world, as opposed to most people of the time who seldom left their native cities (including Socrates himself), they could claim to speak from experience.

For freethinkers, the Sophists are controversial ancestors, though clearly pioneers in bracketing metaphysical concerns and focusing on what could be reasonably achieved in the here and now. As Protagoras so eloquently put it: "As to the gods, I have no means of knowing either that they exist or that they do not exist. For many are the obstacles that impede knowledge, both the obscurity of the question and the shortness of human life." Most contemporary unbelievers would concur with these wise words.

BIBLIOGRAPHY

Arieti, James A. *Philosophy in the Ancient World: An Introduction.* New York: Rowman & Littlefield, 2005.
Dillon, John, and Tania Gergel, trans. *The Greek Sophists.* New York: Penguin Classics, 2003.
Hadot, Pierre. *What Is Ancient Philosophy?* Cambridge, MA: Harvard University Press, 2002.
Jarratt, Susan. C. *Rereading the Sophists: Classical Rhetoric Refigured.* Carbondale: Southern Illinois University Press, 1998.
Kerferd, J. B. *The Sophistical Movement.* New York: Cambridge University Press, 1981.

TIMOTHY J. MADIGAN

SOUTH PLACE ETHICAL SOCIETY. The London-based South Place Ethical Society has, over more than two hundred years, moved from Universalism and Unitarianism to rational religion and then ethical thought.

In 1793 a group of dissident nonconformists in Bishopsgate, London, at Parliament Court, were taken over by the American preacher Elhanan Winchester. Winchester and his congregation were Universalists; they believed there would be universal mercy and no descent to hell (see UNIVERSALISM TO 1961). He continued his ministry for eighteen months before returning to America. He was succeeded by the Sussex preacher William Vidler, who became convinced of the Unitarian belief that God was one entity and the Trinity was a fiction (see UNITARIANISM TO 1961). Vidler stopped preaching in 1814 because of illness and disability.

William James Fox. After a leadership gap, William James Fox became the group's most important leader during the first half of the nineteenth century. Born in Suffolk in 1786, he mixed with radical weavers. He began his ministry in Fareham, in Hampshire. He became an effective Unitarian preacher and in due course succeeded to the vacancy at the South Place Chapel in Parliament Court.

The chapel flourished under Fox. He was a brilliant speaker, writer, and pastor. His radical views were seen in his support for Richard CARLILE, who had been imprisoned for republishing Thomas PAINE's *The Age of Reason*. Fox spoke out for the rights of Catholics and Jews, who lacked legal parity. He was active in the Unitarian Association and edited its journal, the *Monthly Repository*.

He attracted an educated and well-to-do congregation. He met the young Harriet MARTINEAU and encouraged her writing. The young Robert Browning attended and was published by Fox. The chapel became known as a center of progressive religion and radical politics.

After he separated from his wife, his secretary and a prominent member of the chapel, Elizabeth Flowers, moved in to his house to assist him. This caused controversy. Fox slowly moved away from the chapel. He was very active in the campaign to repeal the Corn Laws. He became a Liberal MP for Oldham from 1847 to 1862. As he relinquished the South Place Chapel he became a leading figure in public life.

Moncure Conway. Three succeeding preachers—Philip Harwood, Henry Jerson, and H. H. Barnett—were found unsuitable and the society faced closure. However, the society was to survive and to flourish again under Moncure CONWAY.

Conway was an American from the South who moved from Methodism to Unitarianism and was influenced by Ralph Waldo EMERSON. He was forcefully antislavery and visited England in 1863 to speak on the antislavery platform. After an engagement at South Place, he was offered a six-month trial period that left the congregation in no doubt about accepting him as a permanent leader, after which the declining congregation revived and its financial position improved.

Conway brought changes; for instance, he declined to wear the black silk gown that had been Fox's uniform. He introduced alternative readings—in particular from Eastern religions. Prayers gave way to meditative readings. Ethical ideals were replacing theistic ones. He became friends with many of London's intellectual leaders, scientists and poets alike. He decided to leave and departed for America in 1884.

Conway suggested a pupil of the American Felix ADLER, founder of ETHICAL CULTURE, as a successor. But Stanton Coit was not, in the long run, a success. He introduced the word *ethical* into the society's title but was too domineering for the congregation's taste. He left to found the Ethical Church in Bayswater.

Conway returned from 1892 to 1897, after which he finally departed for good. His great task in his later years was to research and write the first full and unbiased life of Thomas PAINE.

After Conway's departure no single leader was found and a system was established under which several "appointed lecturers" took over the platform. Five people who took this role very successfully were: J. M. ROBERTSON, the freethinking scholar and Liberal politician; Herbert Burrows, a genial socialist and Theosophist; J. A. Hobson, a distinguished economist and historian indicting the empire; Cecil Delisle Burns, an ex-Catholic who lectured at the London School of Economics; and Joseph MCCABE, who trained as a priest and spent the rest of his life debating as a rationalist (see RATIONALISM).

The chapel was becoming old and difficult to maintain, so a move was agreed upon in 1913. World War I intervened, but land in London's Red Lion Square was bought in 1922, the foundation stone laid in 1927, and the building opened in 1929.

The society has remained to this day as an organization with Sunday morning meetings of lectures and discussions, with further talk in the afternoon. The musical concerts on Sunday evening have remained very successful. The building is of great value to London's myriad organizations looking for meeting rooms to debate and discuss the meaning of life: perhaps it is in this way that the spirit of Fox and Conway best lives on, as well as the continuing Sunday meetings of the South Place Ethical Society.

BIBLIOGRAPHY

Conway, Moncure. *Autobiography. Memories and Experiences of Moncure Daniel Conway*. 2 vols. London: Cassell, 1904.

Ratcliffe, S. K. *The Story of South Place*. London: Watts and Company, 1955.

Royle, Edward. *Radicals, Secularists and Republicans, 1866–1915*. Manchester: Manchester University Press, 1980.

JIM HERRICK

SOUTHWELL, CHARLES (1814–1860), English freethought activist. Charles Southwell was born in London into a large, poverty-stricken family. His unruliness led to his departure from education at the age of twelve. A colleague persuaded him to read Timothy Dwight's sermons, which began to develop his counter-theological tendencies.

He became an ultraradical bookseller in Westminster. Joining a lecture group, he discovered his powerful oratorical abilities. He spent a period fighting for the Spanish Legion as a mercenary.

On his return he joined the Owenite movement (see OWEN, ROBERT) as a socialist missionary (see SOCIALISM AND UNBELIEF). His dramatic powers led to his popularity as a speaker, but in due course he fell out with

Owen, not sharing the latter's Utopian ideals. Southwell preferred lectures and education as a means of change rather than the direct action favored by Owen. He was sent as a "missionary" to Bristol, where he resigned from Owen's network and started a paper with William Chilton in 1841: the *Oracle of Reason*, the first openly atheist journal in Britain (see ATHEISM).

In the fourth issue, an article on the Bible was titled "The Jew Book"; it contained the words "This revoltingly odious Jew production. . . . It is a history of lust, sodomies, wholesale slaughtering and horrible depravity." Southwell was arrested for blasphemous libel (see BLASPHEMY) and was sentenced to prison for one year and given a fine of one hundred pounds. After leaving prison he founded the *Investigator*, which lasted seven months. Moving north to reopen the Manchester Hall of Science in 1849, he established the *Lancashire Beacon*, which sold well, but lost money and closed in 1850.

In 1855 Southwell left for Australia—ever a fortune hunter. He sought election to the Victoria Legislature, but his chances were ruined when it became known that he was an atheist who had been imprisoned for blasphemy. He joined a troupe of Shakespearean actors who traveled to New Zealand. There, he started the *Auckland Examiner*, which concentrated on corruption, until he was forced to close it after three years because of ill health. He died in New Zealand, probably of tuberculosis, in 1860.

BIBLIOGRAPHY

Southwell, Charles. *Confessions of a Freethinker*. London, ca. 1845.
———, ed. *The Oracle of Reason*. Bristol, 1841–42.
Watts, John, and Iconoclast [Charles Bradlaugh]. "Charles Southwell." *Half Hours with Freethinkers*. 2nd series, no. 24. London: Austin, 1865.

JIM HERRICK

SPAIN, UNBELIEF IN. Since the fifteenth century, Spain has maintained religious uniformity by eliminating dissidents. This accounts for the absence of visible unbelievers until recent times. Earlier, between the eighth and fifteenth centuries, the Iberian Peninsula had been inhabited by Christianized Visigoths, Arabian Muslims, and exiled Jews. In order to preserve Catholic unity, during the late fifteenth and early sixteenth centuries the Spanish kings expelled all non-Christians. The honesty of those who converted to avoid exile was closely scrutinized. The Inquisition was created to suppress religious and political dissent; it prosecuted unbelievers as unpatriotic. Not surprisingly, anticlericalism (if not unbelief) spread widely. As Nobel laureate C. J. Cela commented, "Spaniards always follow priests, some to support them, some others to beat them." Yet only in the second half of

the twentieth century has Spain enjoyed sufficient freedom for nontheistic ideas to be aired widely in public discourse.

Medieval and Modern Periods. Spanish Muslims developed a refined civilization at Córdoba marked by high achievements in science, literature, and philosophy. Learning flourished also at the School of Translators in Toledo, where scholars from Spain's three cultures strove together helping to preserve ancient works. The "enlightened" society that prevailed there paved the way for an incipient unbelief. In his famed *Dictionary*, Pierre BAYLE quoted the Spanish writer Alonso de Madrigal's claim that learned Muslims faked their obedience to the Qur'an, inwardly rejecting many of its teachings as opposed to reason. In his *Critical History of Religious Ideas* (ca. 1028), Ibn H'azm offered refutations of those who denied the immortality of human soul or espoused a materialist philosophy. The identities of these skeptics are unknown, but they undoubtedly existed or Ibn H'azm would not have tried to refute them. Heterodoxies were reinforced by the philosopher of Córdoba, AVERRÖES, and his theory of double truth, which posited a split between the truth of reason and the truth of faith.

Confronted by Protestantism, Catholic Spain gave birth to *la Contrarreforma* (the Counter-Reformation). Erasmists (see ERASMUS, DESIDERIUS) and Protestants emigrated in haste. Miguel Servet was one of those obliged to run away. He moved to Switzerland, where, as Michael Servetus, he was burned alive by John Calvin at Champel, Switzerland, in 1553. Arias Montano was a biblical scholar who authored the Trilingual Bible of Antwerp and urged Christians to follow the Bible instead of church dogma. He much preferred research into the Hebrew language and biblical studies to the vacuous scholastic disputations then in vogue. In time he was banned from teaching; some of his disciples suffered more severe penalties.

In Spain there has been a long tradition of physician-philosophers, naturalists inspired by the atomism of Democritus, the Stoicism of LUCRETIUS, and the ideas of the later rationalists Pierre Gassendi and René DESCARTES. One of them was Juan de Prado, a *judaizante*, a Jew the sincerity of whose conversion to Christianity came into question. Going into exile in Amsterdam, Prado would exert a strong influence on the thought of Baruch SPINOZA.

By the late 1500s the mass expulsion, conversion, or execution of Muslims and Jews was largely complete, and the Inquisition turned to attack unbelief. Even the mention of unbelief in published works was forbidden. Gerónimo Gracián wrote *Diez lamentaciones del miserable estado de los ateístas en nuestro tiempos* (Ten Laments on the Miserable Status of Contemporary Atheists) but could not publish it in Spain; it was published in Brussels in 1611. In 1654 Francisco de Vega Vinero was probably the first Spaniard to be executed for the crime of ATHEISM.

Enlightenment ideas did make some headway in Spanish society, but they were expressed only in calls for incremental social and clerical reforms. No home-dwelling Spaniard dared challenge theism itself. In one sense this benefited the Spanish society of this period, as people holding Enlightenment ideals could attain high positions in politics or the clergy. On the other hand, only Spaniards living abroad could follow Enlightenment thinking to what was often its logical conclusion: unbelief.

Notable Spanish expatriate unbelievers of this period included the abbot José Marchena, whose sympathy with the French Revolution was so extreme that he traveled to Paris to join it; in his articles, essays, and translations he espoused open atheism as well as revolutionary politics. The priest José María White, of Irish descent and known as Blanco White (*blanco* being Spanish for "white"), fled to England, where he joined the Anglican Church. He read Francis Bacon, the iconoclastic Spanish monk Benito Feijóo (see SPANISH LITERATURE, UNBELIEF IN), Baron d'HOLBACH, and others, eventually becoming a skeptic and finally an atheist. Juan Antonio Llorente was a priest who joined Napoleon's army and settled in France, where he wrote a bitterly critical history of the Inquisition.

Nineteenth Century. After the turn of the nineteenth century, religious and political resistance to Enlightenment influences of every type became more pronounced. The aristocracy feared revolutionary uprisings, while citizens rebelled against Napoleon's invasion. Intellectuals who embraced the new values were disparaged as unpatriotic and labeled *afrancesados* ("Frenchified"). Unstable governments oscillated between clericalism and anticlericalism. Frequent revolts and riots attacked the priesthood as an author of miseries. No fewer than three civil wars erupted between liberals and conservatives. To weaken church power, liberals pushed reforms such as the expropriation of church-owned lands, the dissolution or expulsion of religious orders, and governmental rather than ecclesiastical control of education. In 1840 the cabinet of regent Joaquín Baldomero Fernández Espartero attempted to appoint Spain's bishops; as late as 1955, the regime broke diplomatic relations with Rome. The most radical project to separate church from state was the 1868 revolution and the short-lived First Republic, headed by secularists including Francisco Pi y Margall and Nicholás Salmerón.

On the intellectual front, unorthodox thought could be expressed again after the Inquisition was suppressed in 1834. Around 1860, Julián Sanz del Río launched a lively movement based on the rationalistic and humanist philosophy of Karl Krause (see PANTHEISM AND UNBELIEF). The *krausismo* movement advocated for laicism or secularism, and proposed a spirituality variously described as panentheist and AGNOSTIC. Its influence lasted into the twentieth century. In 1887 R. H. Ibarreta wrote *La Religión al alcance de todos* (Religion Explained to Everyone), the first best seller promoting unbelief. In it, he explained in popular language the errors, lies, and wrongdoings of religions and the churches.

Twentieth Century. Although most leading unbelievers did not formally ally themselves with any particular organized ideology, anarchism and MARXISM were widely held among twentieth-century unbelievers. The anarchist leader Francisco FERRER Guardia founded La escuela moderna (The Modern School) in Barcelona, where he pioneered secularizing educational reforms and pedagogic advancements. Ferrer was infamously executed in 1909 as part of a repression directed at violent anarchist mobs that had burned churches and killed priests.

During the Second Republic, President Manuel Azaña enacted varied reforms, secularizing education, declaring religious freedom, and instituting civil marriage and divorce. Controversially he declared that "Spain is no longer Catholic." Krausist ideals inspired the *Residencia de Estudiantes* (Students' Residence), which aimed to boost foreign exchanges of both students and professors from 1910 to the start of the Civil War in 1936. During those years it housed such outstanding artists and world-renowned figures as Federico García Lorca, Salvador Dalí, Luis Buñuel, and others. Twentieth-century Spain produced a number of outstanding unbelievers, especially among scientists, philosophers, critics of religions, and filmmakers.

Two Spanish scientists who have received the Nobel Prize defended a rational outlook. Santiago Ramón y Cajal espoused a philosophy of materialistic reductionism (see MATERIALISM, PHILOSOPHICAL); based on his neurological discoveries, he rejected any idea of the soul. He called for tantalizing ancient creeds to be overcome as a precondition for genuine social improvement. Severo Ochoa, a national celebrity after receiving one-half of 1959's Nobel Prize in Medicine, wrote only on scientific matters, but made public his denial of a spiritualist outlook upon the death of his wife in 1986. In spite of deeply felt abandonment and loneliness, he firmly rejected the consolation offered by belief in an afterlife.

Miguel de Unamuno was a forerunner of European EXISTENTIALISM. He wrote novels, poetry, drama, and philosophical essays. His thought is an agonized reflection upon the conflict between the impossibility of finding a rational proof of faith, and the impossibility of renouncing his longing for immortality. Enrique Tierno Galván, professor of law, politician, and first democratically elected mayor of Madrid, wrote a 1975 pocket book, *¿Qué es ser agnóstico?* (What Does It Mean to Be an Agnostic?). Gustavo Bueno merges radical anticlericalism with a completely systematized materialist philosophy that covers every field, from an original theory of science to an anthropological explanation of religion's origins, which he traces to the animal totems of ancient tribal societies. Bueno is arguably Spain's most profound twentieth-century philosopher. Fernando Savater has written drama, novels, essays, and newspaper articles. He explains ethics as a commitment of self-love that focuses not upon how to use one's body, but how to use one's mind. He portrays this commitment as a heroic task, using Friedrich NIETZSCHE's meaning. Savater is also a committed thinker who came out as an early opponent of Franco's dictatorship and remains active on the antiterrorist barricades today.

Diplomat Gonzalo Puente Ojea has written highly scholarly books focused on atheism, biblical criticism, Christianity as ideology, and the history of the Catholic Church. His thought draws on G. W. F. HEGEL's theory of alienation and Karl MARX's materialistic theory of consciousness, mixed with his own vast erudition. His works address a learned readership, and he is undoubtedly the leading contemporary champion of laicism in Spain. Less specialized books have been published by the ex-Jesuit Salvador Freixedo, the journalist Pepe Rodríguez, the physicist López Campillo, and others.

Luis Buñuel directed innovative surrealist films, realistic social commentaries, and satiric critiques on bourgeois manners. He received a US Academy Award in 1972. He was a lifelong iconoclast, freethinker, and a satiric exemplar of individualist anarchism. In his autobiography he portrayed himself as a proud unbeliever. Other Oscar-winning Spanish directors who are open unbelievers are Pedro Almodóvar and Fernando Trueba. Trueba directs comedies; accepting his 1994 Academy Award for his film *La Belle Epoque*, he said, "I cannot thank God because I do not believe in him, therefore I thank Billy Wilder."

Since the early 1960s, when the Second Vatican Council affirmed for the first time in Catholic history the right of every person to his or her own religion, Spanish life has been marked by a degree of religious freedom not seen since the fifteenth century. Non-Catholic denominations are permitted, and unbelievers can express themselves relatively freely. Freedom of religion was further strengthened in the 1978 Constitution. Nevertheless, the Roman Catholic Church retains a legally privileged position, receiving financial support from the state and holding a de facto monopoly on religious teaching. Many Spaniards, including most unbelievers, oppose the church's prerogatives. Spain's two main political parties hold conflicting positions on church prerogatives, but fortunately both sides contend nowadays in a nonviolent manner.

BIBLIOGRAPHY

Caro Baroja, Julio. *De la superstición al ateísmo.* Madrid: Taurus, 1981.

Ibarreta, R. H. *La religión al alcance de todos.* Gijón: Ediciones Júcar, 1978.

López Campillo, Antonio, and Juan Ignacio Ferreras. *Curso acelerado de ateísmo.* Madrid: Ediciones Vosa, 2000.

Puente Ojea, Gonzalo. *Fe cristiana, Iglesia, poder.* Madrid: Siglo XXI, 1991.

———. *Ideología e Historia. La formación del cristianismo como fenómeno ideológico.* Madrid: Siglo XXI, 1974.

Tierno Galvín, Enrique. *¿Qué es ser agnóstico?* Madrid: Tecnos, 1975.

JESÚS PUERTAS

SPANISH LITERATURE, UNBELIEF IN. Aside from short lapses during the nineteenth and twentieth centuries, unbelieving writers have not enjoyed freedom of expression until 1978, when the constitution now in force was passed. Prior to 1978 Spanish society still bore the imprint of the Catholic Inquisition and the reactions it had engendered. Established in 1480, the Inquisition was intended not to save heretic souls, but to maintain orthodoxy by frightening the people, as stated in the *Manual del Inquisidor* (Manual for the Inquisitor). The manual also stated that any means is allowable to achieve this goal, including secrecy, lies, threats, or blackmail. Under such oppressive conditions, most critical authors did not espouse ATHEISM or AGNOSTICISM, strictly defined; instead they focused upon demolishing the political, economical, and social power of the church. This attitude gave birth to a prevailing trait of Spanish character known as anticlericalism. Anticlericalism rejects clerical power while it denounces church crimes and immoralities. When it does not deny God's existence, it portrays Catholicism as but one of many possible ways to interrelate with God.

Before the Eighteenth Century. The first writers in the Spanish language expressed some anticlerical criticisms directly, and others through satire. *El Libro de Buen Amor* (The Book of Good Love) was written in jail by the poet and archpriest of Hita, Juan Ruiz, about 1335. Written in rhymed quatrains, the book justifies its sensuous and sinful content as a mode of instructing the reader about the love of God. To do this, he portrays himself in dialogue with Love personified, giving examples of the evil loves that must be avoided and telling humorous and irreverent stories of clerical misbehavior and abuse.

In 1499 Fernando de ROJAS wrote *La Celestina*, a novel in dialogue that treats human passions and ignores godly matters, which was most uncommon at that time. *La Celestina* tells the crude story of Calisto, who requests the aid of Celestina, a retired whore who makes her living by pimping. The old woman casts spells for Calisto so that he can win the love of Melibea. In one scene Calisto is questioned whether he believes in God; his answer is: "I am Melibean, I believe in Melibea." The novel ends tragically, as a warning to readers that they will face God's punishment should they persist in sin. This moral excuses the salacious content of the novel.

Protestant ideas first entered Spain with the works of Desiderius ERASMUS. At first the Erasmian preference for inner religious consciousness over public rituals was welcomed, even by the inquisitor general and the king. Before long, however, the church understood that allowing an unmediated relation with God would imply the end of the Catholic authority. The *erasmistas* were always under scrutiny and some were penalized; this happened to the author of the first Spanish grammar, Antonio de Nebrija. Concerned at the spread of what it considered dangerous novelties, the Inquisition intensified its scrutiny of unorthodox ideas, to the point that it proscribed the books of, and sometimes jailed, clerics who would later become towering figures in Catholic mysticism, including Saint Teresa of Avila, Saint John of the Cross, and Fray Luis de León.

The sixteenth and seventeenth centuries saw the golden age of Spanish literature. Most important writers were clerics, but anticlerical features can nonetheless be discerned in some works, for instance, in the anonymous novel *El Lazarillo de Tormes* (Lazarillo: Blind Man's Guide), or in Francisco de Quevedo's masterpiece *El Buscón*. These picaresque novels depict low-born characters who disregard any moral constraint as they struggle to survive in a poor, uneducated, and superstitious society. Picaresque style generally satirizes clerics as the abusive social class responsible for most of the people's misery. The popularity of the picaresque reflects a widespread pessimism; this may seem paradoxical, given that Spain was the most powerful country of that time, but it reflects the ineluctable decadence of a theocracy ruled by idle classes.

From the Enlightenment to the Present Day. Although the rationalistic outlook is present in some progressive writers, the Inquisition was still doing its best to lessen philosophical influences, but it couldn't avoid them entirely. Between 1726 and 1739 the monk Benito Feijóo published *Teatro Crítico Universal* (Universal Theater of Criticism), an encyclopedia of critical essays on numerous issues. Jovellanos, a statesman, focused on achieving economic and cultural progress through agrarian reform and educational development; his writings helped to instill doubt in Spain's theocratic system. Leandro Fernández de Moratín stood out in the realm of drama and comedy, satirizing the uses and moral values of higher classes. Félix de Samaniego and Tomás de Iriarte wrote irreverent and lubricious fables for which they were imprisoned by the Inquisition. José Cadalso, in his 1793 *Cartas Marruecas* (Letters from Morocco), used the epistolary style to debunk various superstitions. Mariano de Larra wrote critical articles and a literature of manners; in his poems, José de Espronceda depicted deeply romantic characters whose unfulfilled wishes lead them to blame God for their unhappiness.

Nineteenth-century Spain was riven by continual fights between conservatives and liberals; politics was unstable throughout this century which saw many constitutions, tens of governments, and three civil wars. The Inquisition disappeared, allowing unbelief to begin to flourish anew. Clarín, pen name of Leopoldo Alas, absorbed Krausist ideals (see SPAIN, UNBELIEF IN) and crusaded against the usurpation of power by the church. In 1884–85 he published *La Regenta* (The Regent's Wife), a masterpiece of world literature about an ambitious priest whose main goal is to increase his social influence as confessor of *La Regenta* (the wife of the local authority). Then he falls in love with her, which leads him to become to some extent both skeptical and hypocritical. Benito Pérez Galdós was an excellent and popular realistic writer. Through his novels he exposed how divisive and damaging religious dogmatism could become. Blasco Ibáñez criticized the power of Jesuits on the rich penitents and Pérez de Ayala in AMDG (for *Ad Majorem Dei Gloriam*, motto of the Society of Jesus) described the stifling education in Jesuit boarding schools. The loss of Spain's last colonies in 1898 convulsed the nation and inspired the Silver Age of Spanish literature. The Basque Pío Baroja was an individualist thinker whose confessed agnosticism pervades his novels and articles. The world-renowned Miguel de Unamuno adopted from Søren Kierkegaard the concept of anguish to express his recurrent oscillations between rational thinking and his emotional needs for immortality and justice. The novel *San Manuel Bueno, mártir* (Saint Manuel Bueno: Martyr) tells the story of a parish priest who is secretly agnostic but decides to stay in office pretending to believe, and acts so as not to disappoint his parishioners' longing for an afterlife. All his life long he keeps his agony hidden out of such altruistic devotion that people would later honor him as a saint and miracle man.

In the first half of the twentieth century, polarization between believers and unbelievers was one of the causes of the civil war. During Franciso Franco's regime, his policy of *nacionalcatolicismo* (national Catholicism) permeated public and private life, burdening Spaniards with yet heavier loads of sin and guilt. Yet at the same time, economic and educational improvements and the influence of millions of tourists from elsewhere in Europe led Spanish society in a more secular direction.

Today there are many unbelieving writers, although many act from motives that are more political than philosophical or anticlerical. The communist poet Rafael Alberti rejected the anti-Marxism of the church. Ramón J. Sender expatriated to the United States, where he taught and published his novels. Anarchist professor Agustín García Calvo opposed every form of social hierarchy, that of the clerics included. Antonio Buero Vallejo wrote dramas that displayed a crude and pessimistic social reality and debunked superstitions. Others, like Luis Martín Santos, Gabriel Celaya, Fernando Savater, Antonio Muñoz Molina, Luis Antonio de Villena, Lucía Etxeberria, Terenci Moix, and Antonio Gala, are only a few of the many writers who adopt an irreligious life stance.

BIBLIOGRAPHY

Alcalá, Angel. *Literatura y ciencia ante la inquisición española*. Madrid: Laberinto, 2001.

Brenan, Gerald. *The Spanish Laberynth*. London: Cambridge University Press, 1925.

Devlin, John. *Spanish Anticlericalism: A Study in Modern Alienation*. New York: Las Americas, 1966.

Esteban, José. *Refranero anticlerical*. Madrid: Ediciones Vosa, 1994.

Garcia-Calvo, Agustín. *De Dios*. Zamora: Ediciones Lucina, 1996.

Unamuno y Jugo, Miguel de. *La agonía del cristianismo* [The Agony of Christianity]. Madrid: Planeta, 1934.

———. *Del sentimiento trágico de la vida* [The Tragic Sense of Life]. Madrid: Planeta, 1934.

Vilar, Juan B. *Intolerancia y libertad en la España contemporánea*. Madrid: Istmo, 1994.

JESÚS PUERTAS

SPENCER, HERBERT (1820–1903), English sociologist, evolutionary theorist, and philosopher. Herbert Spencer was born in Derby, England, on April 27, 1820. Spencer's family were Methodist "Dissenters" with Quaker sympathies. From an early age, young Herbert was strongly influenced by the antiestablishment and anticlerical views of his father, a schoolteacher, as well as the Benthamite radical views of his uncle Thomas (see ANTICLERICALISM; BENTHAM, JEREMY). His early education was largely informal, though he eventually trained as a civil engineer for railways. He soon turned to political journalism and worked for the *Economist* financial weekly, where he came into contact with such controversialists as Thomas Carlyle, George Eliot (Marian EVANS)—with whom he had had a lengthy (though purely intellectual) association—and Thomas Henry HUXLEY. Despite the diversity of opinions to which he was exposed, Spencer's confidence in his own views was coupled with a stubbornness and a refusal to read authors with whom he disagreed.

Spencer's early writings reveal a sympathy with many of the causes of the "philosophic radicals" such as Jeremy Bentham. Some of his ideas (e.g., the definition of "good" and "bad" in terms of their pleasurable or painful consequences) show similarities to utilitarianism, and he held radical views on land nationalization, laissez-faire economics, and the role of women in society—though he came to abandon most of these stands later in life.

Spencer's first book, *Social Statics, or the Conditions Essential to Human Happiness*, appeared in 1851. Influenced by the POSITIVISM and empiricism of Auguste COMTE—the term *social statics* itself was borrowed from Comte—Spencer focused on the conditions of social order, preliminary to a study of human progress and evolution (i.e., "social dynamics"). Here, one finds an account of the development of freedom and a defense of individual liberties, based on a (Lamarckian-style) evolutionary theory. His principal targets were Bentham and John Stuart MILL.

Following the death of his uncle Thomas in 1853, Spencer received an inheritance that allowed him to devote himself to writing. In 1855 *The Principles of Psychology* was published. Again, Bentham and Mill were major targets, and Mill later came to accept some of Spencer's arguments. *The Principles of Psychology* was much less successful than *Social Statics*, however, and about this time Spencer began to experience serious (predominantly mental) health problems that affected him for the rest of his life.

Despite his ill health and his inability to write for more than a few hours each day, Spencer embarked upon the nine-volume *A System of Synthetic Philosophy* (1862–93), which sought to provide a systematic account of biology, sociology, ethics, and politics. This "synthetic philosophy" brought together data from the various natural and social sciences and organized them according to evolutionary theory.

In the first volume of the *System*, *First Principles* (1862), Spencer outlines his argument that all phenomena can be explained in terms of a process of material evolution (see EVOLUTION AND UNBELIEF). Specifically, Spencer held that homogeneous organisms are unstable, that organisms develop from simple to more complex forms, and that evolution constitutes a norm of progress. Spencer referred to this process as "survival of the fittest"—an expression that his contemporary, Charles DARWIN, later employed. Although critics have pointed out that this notion is both ambiguous—for it was not clear whether one was referring to the "fittest" individual or species—and far from universal, it provided a concise statement for the kind of process described by Darwin. Moreover, while Spencer's evolutionary theory was distinct from Darwin's, Darwin's respect for Spencer was significant.

In *Principles of Biology* (1864–67), Spencer argued that there is a gradual specialization in things toward self-sufficiency and individuation. The "tendency to individuation" was coupled with a natural inclination to self-preservation; in human beings, this was reflected in rational self-interest. Spencer also insisted that, over time, human nature has improved and changed, and so scientific—including moral and political—views that rested on the assumption of a stable human nature (presupposed by many utilitarians) were rejected. Nevertheless, Spencer recognized that individuals needed to be understood in terms of the "whole" of which they were "parts," and held an "organic" view of society. But he saw no inconsistency in holding both individualism and organicism, for individuals were mutually dependent, not subordinate to the organism as a whole.

Starting with the characteristics of individual human beings, Spencer believed that one could deduce, using the laws of nature, the character of social life. For example, since they reflect the same evolutionary principles as biological organisms do, society—and even social institutions such as the economy—can function without external control, just as the digestive system of a lower organism does. (In claiming this, Spencer arguably failed to see the fundamental differences between "higher" and "lower" levels of social organization.)

Spencer's ethics and political philosophy follow from this account of human nature. Beginning with the "laws of life," the conditions of social existence, and the recognition of life as a fundamental value, we can infer what will produce happiness. While progress was an inevitable characteristic of evolution, it could be achieved only through the free exercise of human faculties. Since individuals are "primary," individual behavior was fundamentally "egoistic."

The natural growth of an organism, then, required "liberty"—but Spencer held that, as individuals become increasingly aware of their individuality, they also become aware of the individuality of others and, thereby, of the *law of equal freedom*—that "[e]very man has freedom to do all that he wills, provided he infringes not the equal freedom of any other man" (*Social Statics*). Once this law is acknowledged, we have a moral basis for individual rights, and one can identify strains of a rights-based ethic in Spencer's writings. (This feature is evident, not only in his first major contribution to political philosophy, *Social Statics*, but in his later essays— several of which appear in *The Man versus the State* [1884].) Spencer saw associations with others as largely instrumental and contractual. He also followed earlier liberalism in maintaining that law is a restriction of liberty, and that this restriction, in itself, is evil and justified only where necessary to the preservation of a greater liberty. Not surprisingly, Spencer maintained that the arguments of the early utilitarians on the justification of law and authority and on the origin of rights were fallacious. He also insisted on an extensive policy of laissez-faire in economics and government.

Spencer's empirical method and his naturalistic account of knowledge are outlined in *First Principles*. He acknowledges that there are limits to human knowledge, and that the methods of the positive sciences are unable to explain all of reality. Specifically, we cannot know the nature of reality in itself (including complete knowledge of the nature of space, time, force, motion, and substance), and there was, therefore, something that was fundamentally "the Unknowable." While theists might regard this Unknowable as God, Spencer argued that we cannot know anything nonempirical—and so we cannot know whether there is a God or what its character might be.

Theism, he argued, cannot be adopted because there would be no way of determining whether there was any knowledge of "the Unknowable," such knowledge could not be acquired, and there would be no way of testing it. To this extent, his position on religion was agnostic (see AGNOSTICISM). Particular religious doctrines and practices could, however, be the appropriate objects of empirical investigation and assessment—and Spencer was a severe critic of them.

Spencer counted among his admirers both radical thinkers and prominent scientists. In the 1860s and 1870s the influence of his evolutionary theory was on a par with that of Darwin, and it has been said that, in 1896, "three justices of the Supreme Court were avowed 'Spencerians.'" His reputation was at its peak in the 1870s and early 1880s, and he was nominated for the Nobel Prize for Literature in 1902. In the last two decades of his life Spencer's health deteriorated significantly, and he died following a lengthy illness on December 8, 1903.

Though Spencer was a major figure in the intellectual life of the Victorian era, today he is remembered principally for his political thought, primarily for his defense of natural rights and for his criticisms of utilitarian positivism. His views are sometimes invoked by libertarians on issues concerning the function of government and the fundamental character of individual rights.

BIBLIOGRAPHY

Duncan, David, ed. *The Life and Letters of Herbert Spencer*. London: Methuen, 1908.

Fitzgerald, Timothy, "Herbert Spencer's Agnosticism," *Religious Studies* 23 (1987).

Kennedy, James G. *Herbert Spencer*. Boston: Twayne, 1978.

Peel, J. D. Y. *Herbert Spencer: The Evolution of a Sociologist*. London: Heinemann, 1971.

Spencer, Herbert. *An Autobiography*. 2 vols. London: Williams and Norgate, 1904.

———. *The Factors of Organic Evolution*. London: Williams and Norgate, 1887.

———. *First Principles*. London: Williams and Norgate, 1862.

———. *The Man versus the State*. London: Williams and Norgate, 1884.

———. *Principles of Biology*. 2 vols. London: Williams and Norgate, 1864, 1867.

———. *The Principles of Ethics*. 2 vols. London: Williams and Northgate, 1892.

———. *The Principles of Psychology*. London: Longmans, 1855.

———. *The Principles of Sociology*. 3 vols. London: Williams and Norgate, 1882–98.

———. *Social Statics*. London: Chapman, 1851.

———. *The Study of Sociology*. New York: D. Appleton, 1873.

Taylor, M. W. *Men versus the State: Herbert Spencer and Late Victorian Liberalism*. Oxford: Oxford University Press, 1992.

Weinstein, David. *Equal Freedom and Utility: Herbert Spencer's Liberal Utilitarianism*. New York: Cambridge University Press, 1998.

WILLIAM SWEET

SPINOZA, BARUCH or BENEDICT (1632–1677), Dutch philosopher. In 1656, at age twenty-three, Spinoza was excommunicated from the Amsterdam Jewish community, where he had been born and raised. The excommunication document mentions "the horrible heresies he practiced and taught," but refrains from spelling them out. Spinoza never returned to Jewish orthodoxy by repenting of his heresies. Nor did he convert to Christianity. Instead he reportedly wrote a defense of those heresies. It was not published or preserved, however, and we can only surmise how, if at all, it may have germinated into his subsequent writings. Around 1665 he announced in a private letter that he was writing a treatise about the Bible. It aimed, he said, at removing theological prejudices from potential philosophers, clearing his name of the charge of atheism, and vindicating the freedom of philosophizing in the face of overbearing preachers (Letter #30). These aims fit his *Theologico-Political Treatise* (1670) except in that, anticipating its notoriety, Spinoza published it anonymously. Nevertheless he soon became both execrated and celebrated throughout Europe as its author.

The *Treatise* is the philosophical founding-document of both scientific biblical criticism and modern liberal democracy—and so of modern liberal religion. Spinoza addresses Christians "who would philosophize more freely if this one thing did not stand in the way: they deem that reason has to serve as handmaid to theology." By loosening their attachment to biblical theology, Spinoza's *Treatise* would draw potential philosophers who are Christians to the theological and political benefits of a philosophy or science emancipated from traditional theological (and political) constraints.

Spinoza understood his project to be as pressing as it was far-reaching. Christians and other adherents of biblical religion were divided into competing, mutually persecuting sects. Despite widespread lip service to it, then, the Bible could hardly function effectively as Europe's social bond, that is, its common moral authority. Originally, the *Treatise* argues, Christianity taught simply "love, gladness, peace, continence, and faith toward all." It became a sectarian, persecuting religion only after it began defending its teachings by means of imported—Platonic and Aristotelian—philosophical arguments. These, being inherently dubious and controversial, led adherents into insoluble theological disagreements among themselves as well as with outsiders. Could the Bible be made to speak to adherents with a single voice again, Spinoza wondered, if both biblical theology and political society were refashioned on some new, scientifically validated basis? Spinoza's *Treatise* is a thought-experiment designed to answer this question philosophically and, at the same time, pave the way theologically and politically.

Of the *Treatise*'s twenty chapters, the first fifteen treat theological matters: redefining theological terms, establishing a scientific biblical philology modeled on modern natural science, and supplying a nonsectarian theology based on the new philology. These chapters culminate in a civil religion consisting of seven dogmas meant to be acceptable to all sectarians: (1) a supremely just and merciful God exists; (2) God alone requires our highest admiration, devotion, and love; (3) God is everywhere, and (4) all-powerful; (5) worshiping God consists solely in justice and charitableness; (6) such worship alone brings salvation, whereas hedonistic self-indulgence brings undoing; (7) God forgives the penitent. Such dogmas need not be true, the *Treatise* intimates, so long as they promote just and charitable behavior. Spinoza seems to have formulated them scientifically, by counting the frequency of occurrence of biblical "tenets" (*sententiae*), that is, opinions articulated at least once in the biblical text and isolable as sound bites. The seven listed, being in effect the most frequent, are least likely to foment controversy and are inherently compatible with the new philology, which identifies the Bible's most basic teachings with its most frequently repeated teachings.

The *Treatise*'s last five chapters consider the democratic basis of all political society, the pros and cons of the biblical theocracy, and the respective limits of religious and political authority. Political society, Spinoza argues, originates in a compact among self-interested individuals, each of whom transfers all his right or power to other self-interested individuals charged with making and enforcing laws for everyone's self-protection and self-enhancement. Individuals are apt to rebel, however, if they suspect rulers of abusing their delegated power. Practically speaking, the best society will be the most stable one consistent with individuals' enlightened self-satisfaction. It will not be a theocracy (ruled by religious authorities), nor a monarchy or aristocracy, but a democracy, since politically informed democratic majorities tend to restrict individuals' freedom least. More exactly, it will be a liberal democracy, where each remains free to think what he likes and say what he thinks. Even so, Spinoza places organized religion under the thumb of the political, to safeguard that freedom.

As Spinoza's *Treatise* deconstructs biblical theology to win philosophically inclined Christians to theological and political liberalism in general, so his posthumous *Ethics Demonstrated in a Geometrical Order* (1677) deconstructs natural (Platonic-Aristotelian) theology to win them to modern philosophy or science in particular. Its rhetorical structure imitates Euclid's *Elements*. It purports to derive pantheistic conclusions about God, mind, and the emotions "geometrically," that is, from antecedent definitions and axioms. Yet these, being merely stipulated rather than proved or even fully explained, appear rigged to favor conclusions resting as well, or instead, on independent empirical claims. The *Ethics*, then, is no homogeneous "system." Rather, its pantheistic façade houses strictly naturalistic arguments disjoined from anything theological. Among other things, Spinoza identifies God with the inexhaustible laws of nature, arranges mind and body in a strict parallelism (whereby thoughts always correlate with whatever outside bodies affect the thinker's own body), and conceives emotions behaviorally so as to allow their scientific management by minds trained into shape by the *Ethics*. In sum, the *Ethics* is not exactly pantheistic nor simply atheistic but, oddly, both. It leads its addressee partly by deductive steps, partly by inductive leaps, to the introspective insight that our bodies and emotions are entirely subject to God's or nature's law-abiding necessities except while, and insofar as, we contemplate them "geometrically" on the premises of modern mathematical physics.

BIBLIOGRAPHY

Spinoza, Benedict. *Ethics*. Translated by W. H. White. Rev. ed. New York: Hafner, 1949.
———. *The Letters*. Translated by Samuel Shirley. Indianapolis: Hackett, 1995.
———. *Opera*. Edited by Carl Gebhardt. 4 vols. Heidelberg: Carl Winters Universitätsbuchhandlung, 1925.
———. *Theologico-Political Treatise*. Translated by Martin D. Yaffe. Newburyport, MA: Focus Philosophical Library, 2004.

MARTIN D. YAFFE

SPIRITUALISM AND UNBELIEF. Spiritualism and unbelief have long had an ambiguous relationship. For some unbelievers, claims of contact with the afterlife threatened to confirm traditional religious beliefs; for others Spiritualism represented an application of scientific principles to offer logical explanations for phenomena previously viewed as the domain of faith alone. Briefly defined, *Spiritualism* is the belief that living persons can have contact with the dead or other beings in a spiritual realm. While elements of spiritualism have existed in many times, places, and cultures, Spiritualism as a philosophy had its heyday in nineteenth-century America and Europe.

Modern Spiritualism began with Emmanuel Swedenborg, "the father of modern Spiritualism." Swedenborg trained as an engineer, published Sweden's first scientific journal, and was a well-known and respected man of science. Visiting London in 1745, he saw an apparition, and began to concentrate his energies on a reinterpretation of the Bible and works of theology based on conversations with angels and spirits of the dead. He did not start the sect known as Swedenborgianism (or the "New Church" or "New Jerusalem Church"); rather, it was launched after his death by followers in the United States. Among Swedenborg's doctrines: God created humanity so as to exist simultaneously in the physical world and in the spirit world—both of which have societal structures and governments. Heaven is a normal society where souls continue as they might have on earth. Hell (where there is no Satan) is chosen by selfish, materialistic people who are free to commit any misdeeds they please, but they are punished (beaten by other souls) only if they become morally worse than they were when they were alive. Swedenborg's ideas influenced the "animal magnetism" movement of Franz Anton Mesmer, and writers such as William Blake, Samuel Taylor Coleridge, and Henry James.

Andrew Jackson Davis, "the Poughkeepsie Seer," is credited with providing a philosophical basis for Spiritualism more substantial than just the desire to communicate with the dead. In 1844, under the influence of mesmerism, he had a vision of Emmanuel Swedenborg and the Greek physician Galen. He published *The Principles of Nature* in 1845, based on his spiritualist experiences; the ideas expressed in this work combined Swedenborgianism with socialism in the vein of Charles Fourier. He believed he had a gift for spiritual healing, and practiced that art in New York for many years. His best-selling writings were considered heretical by many (see HERESY); he wrote, for example, that sin does not exist. In what would become a common theme among Spiritualists, he also lectured on women's rights and believed in equality of the sexes. His work is thought to have in turn influenced the development of Christian Science.

The Fox sisters were the first "professional" Spiritualists. Margaret "Maggie" and Katie Fox became associated with "rapping" noises in their home in Hydesville, New York, during the winter of 1847–48. The sounds were said to be communication from the spirit of a murdered peddler buried under the house. The rappings, later confessed to have started as a joke by the teenage Maggie and her younger sister, first became public when their mother called in neighbors to experience them. Rumors spread, and soon the family farmhouse was the destination of scores of curious visitors. The minister of their Methodist Episcopal church asked them to leave the congregation, believing them to be practicing witchcraft (see WITCHCRAFT AND UNBELIEF). Eventually the story of the mysterious haunting and the two young "mediums" reached attorney E. E. Lewis in nearby Canandaigua, New York, who came to investigate. In May of 1848 he published his findings in a pamphlet titled "A Report of the Mysterious Noises Heard in the House of John D. Fox, in Hydesville, Arcadia, Wayne County."

Lewis's pamphlet was read by the Fox sisters' elder sibling, Leah Fox Fish, a divorced single mother living in Rochester. Leah had previously read Davis's *The Principles of Nature* and was surprised to learn that her own family might be crossing the boundary between the worlds of the living and the dead. Leah paid her family a visit, and then invited her younger sisters to join her in Rochester. Leah was aware that Maggie and Katie were creating the rapping noises themselves (by cracking the bones in their toes), and shrewdly saw that the interest generated by her sisters' performances could be profitable. She began to promote them, starting with small private séances and moving to larger public meetings. Meanwhile a growing group of followers began to collect around them, drawn largely from the ranks of the progressive and religiously disaffected, who saw Spiritualism as a new, universalist religion free of the prejudices and intolerance of traditional Christianity. Controversy continued to surround the sisters, but they eventually became national celebrities and the focus of a movement that engaged more than one million followers in America.

Nineteenth-century technology played a major role in the debates between Spiritualists and their many critics. In an age when photography was still new and a telegraph message was viewed by many as a miracle, technological means were used by both mediums and skeptics to prove or disprove the presence of spirits. Some methods of the Spiritualists, such as spirit photography, are regarded as obviously fake today. Photographs typically showed a double exposure of a sitter and an image of one or more spirits floating in space. Others showed ectoplasm, a white, fluid substance that emerged from the medium, shaped by spirits into physical forms such as "pseudopods," phantom hands that extend from the earthly stomach.

Other methods used by Spiritualists included communication via table tapping, slate writing, and automatic writing; trance mediumship; and physical manifestations such as levitation, movement of objects by unseen forces, and apparitions of supposed spirit beings. Public interest in and outcry about Spiritualism encouraged many scientific minds of the day to test and explain these various phenomena. The medical scientists William Alexander Martin and R. Frederick Martin of New York even named mediumship or "mediomania" as forms or symptoms of specifically female insanity during the 1870s. While many remained skeptical or developed rational explanations for these occurrences, some men and women of science were persuaded into the Spiritualist camp, including Henri Bergson, Carl Gustav Jung, and Juliet H. Stillman SEVERANCE. Other leading figures who became enticed to some degree by Spiritualism included Harry Houdini, Arthur Conan Doyle, and J. W. Dunne.

Spiritualists included countless activists within radical social movements. Nonresistants, or antiauthoritarian abolitionists, denounced large Christian denominations as collaborators in slavery. Many of that movement's members, including Sarah Grimké, Adin Ballou, and Henry C. Wright, became ardent Spiritualists because that philosophy complimented the profound individualism that had led them to feminism and antislavery. As one scholar wrote, "while not all feminists were spiritualists, all spiritualists advocated women's rights." Elizabeth Cady STANTON, Matilda Joslyn GAGE, Susan B. ANTHONY, Lucy Stone, and Lucretia Mott were all Spiritualists.

The most famous group devoted to the scientific study of Spiritualist phenomena was the Society for Psychical Research, founded in London in 1882 by Sir William Barrett and Edmund Dawson Rogers. They were joined by the so-called Sidgwick Group, the circle of friends surrounding Henry Sidgwick, a professor of philosophy at Cambridge. All were wealthy and had copious leisure time to devote to their investigation of psychical matters, which they tried to approach with scientific rigor. The original group's high social standing attracted the interest of other luminaries of the day, including Sigmund FREUD and William James. The work was of such interest that an American branch of the society was established in 1885; both societies still exist.

One of the most controversial episodes associated with the Society for Psychical Research involved Sir William Crookes, a noted physicist, chemist, and inventor, member of the Royal Society, and later president of the Society for Psychical Research. Crookes began investigating Spiritualists in 1871, possibly as a result of his grief over his brother's early death. His efforts to report on British Spiritualist D. D. Home were rebuffed by the Royal Society, but he later had them published in the *Quarterly Journal of Science*. Further studies on Home and Katie Fox were published in 1874. However, it was his dealings with the young medium Florence "Florrie" Cook and her materialized spirit of Katie King in 1873–74 that caused the greatest controversy. Cook would go into a trance and Katie would manifest bodily; sometimes Cook would be conscious and both would converse. Crookes and others saw and spoke with Katie, and Crookes's descriptions of her often lapsed into the rhapsodic, recounting her "perfect beauty . . . the brilliant purity of her complexion." Forty-four photographs documented the encounters, including one of Crookes arm in arm with Katie.

Crookes gave up his efforts to prove the truth of psychical phenomena after another medium he had reported favorably upon was exposed as a fraud. Serious allegations also arose concerning Cook, namely, that Katie King was actually a human imposter, and that Crookes was in collusion with Cook in order to cover up an illicit affair. To the end of his life, Crookes never renounced his belief in Spiritualism, and it seems more likely that his was a case of scientific instincts being overcome by feminine wiles.

Although Spiritualism is no longer the major social movement it was in the nineteenth century, it still exists and was one of the major influences on the development of the so-called New Age movement in the twentieth century.

BIBLIOGRAPHY

Brandon, Ruth. *The Spiritualists: The Passion for the Occult in the Nineteenth and Twentieth Centuries.* New York: Knopf, 1983.

Braude, Ann. *Radical Spirits: Spiritualism and Women's Rights in Nineteenth-Century America.* Boston: Beacon, 1989.

Guiley, Rosemary Ellen. *Harper's Encyclopedia of Mystical & Paranormal Experience*. New York: Harper-Collins, 1991.

Stuart, Nancy Rubin. *The Reluctant Spiritualist: The Life of Maggie Fox*. New York: Harcourt, 2005.

ALISON M. LEWIS AND ROBERT P. HELMS

STANTON, ELIZABETH CADY (1815–1902), American women's rights activist and freethinker. One of the principal theoreticians for the American women's rights movement, Elizabeth Cady Stanton's genius supported the activism of nineteenth-century suffragists (see WOMAN SUFFRAGE MOVEMENT AND UNBELIEF), though her longtime friend Susan B. Anthony overshadowed her in popularity. Stanton's expansive, intellectual HUMANISM at once provided the theoretical backbone of the women's movement and made her anathema to the conservative Christian women who came to lead that movement in the post–Civil War era.

Early Education. The daughter of Margaret Livingston and Judge Daniel Cady, young Elizabeth informally studied law in her father's office in Johnstown, New York. In later years as she challenged legal inequities for women, this early education in jurisprudence served her well. Judge Cady desperately wanted a son but none of his male children survived. When Elizabeth's last surviving brother died, she informed her grieving father that she would endeavor to be like a son to him. Her academic success, first in Johnstown Academy then in Emma Willard's Troy Female Seminary, followed by a lifetime of political and intellectual achievements, failed to satisfy her father.

Marriage and Abolition. In 1840 Elizabeth Cady married the abolitionist Henry Stanton and accompanied him to London to an international meeting of antislavery agitators. It was there that she met the already noteworthy Lucretia Mott, with whom she shared her disgust at the convention's exclusion of female delegates. Mott, a liberal Quaker minister, encouraged the younger woman to read the writings of such freethinkers as Mary WOLLSTONECRAFT, Robert OWEN, and Frances WRIGHT, and to challenge the authority of the church and the Bible. Following her honeymoon in London, Stanton lived in Boston. There she and her husband moved in Garrisonian abolitionist circles, further radicalizing the young wife and mother and providing her with a wealth of intellectual and social stimulation. All of this would change when the growing Stanton family moved to the little central New York mill town of Seneca Falls in 1847.

Seneca Falls. Moving into a home purchased for her by her father, Elizabeth Cady Stanton set up housekeeping in Seneca Falls at the age of thirty-one. The novelty of domesticity was very soon replaced by a feeling of isolation, drudgery, and injustice, as she was left alone with her young children for lengthy periods while Henry pursued his political ambitions. Feeling women's limita-

tions keenly, Stanton joined a group of liberal Friends, including Lucretia Mott, to plan the first women's rights convention that would be held in Seneca Falls in 1848. There Stanton, Mott, and others presented their Declaration of Sentiments, modeled after the Declaration of Independence. Stanton's decision to include a demand for the right of suffrage in the Seneca Falls declaration was first considered too radical, even by Mott herself. However suffrage soon became the central focus of the nineteenth-century women's movement. Stanton became arguably its most influential theoretician for the next half century.

Woman Suffrage. As the mother of seven children, family life somewhat circumscribed Stanton's ability to take on a public a role as a traveling lecturer. But her partnership with the never-married Susan B. Anthony, which began in 1851, allowed her to put forward her deeply intelligent strategy and rhetoric through Anthony's skilled political agency. Following the ratification of the Fourteenth Amendment protecting citizenship for black males, the women's rights movement split over issues of strategy. While the National Woman Suffrage Association (NWSA), which Stanton served as president from 1869 to 1889, insisted that suffrage must be achieved and protected by an amendment to the US Constitution, the more socially conservative American Woman Suffrage Association (AWSA) favored a state-by-state approach. (The two organizations merged in 1889.) Stanton contributed significantly to the suffrage cause as writer, speaker, activist, and editor. Joining forces with Matilda Joslyn GAGE and Susan B. Anthony to produce the monumental *History of Woman Suffrage* (1881–86), Stanton sought to preserve the story of women's struggle for suffrage for future generations.

Beyond Suffrage. During these years of leadership, Stanton refused to accept suffrage as a panacea for women's liberation. With Susan B. Anthony and Parker Pillsbury, Stanton edited the *Revolution*, which investigated a multiplicity of feminist concerns. Her intelligent insight into the complexity of women's degradation caused her to venture from the suffrage agenda on numerous occasions to treat more dangerous issues such as sexuality and divorce (see SEX RADICALISM AND UNBELIEF). Increasingly, she believed that religion played a primary role in maintaining women's inferior status. With other humanists in the women's movement, Stanton consistently challenged religious authority. Her condemnations of the illiberal dogmatism of organized religion and its followers led to ongoing controversy among rank-and-file suffragists.

After the Civil War, suffragists courted the support of wealthy, well-connected Christian women who believed the vote would give them political power to enforce their religious morality. To such women, Stanton seemed dangerously radical. Following the NWSA's merger with the AWSA in 1898, Stanton seemed all the more out of step with the sentiments of the evangelical leadership of a new generation of suffragists. Even her longtime partnership with Anthony suffered, as Anthony found political need to divorce herself from Stanton's uncompromising humanist positions.

Marginalization. Finding suffrage too narrow for her great intellect, Stanton spent more and more time engaged in the intellectual conversations circulating among freethinkers. Throughout her later years, she maintained active correspondence with FREETHOUGHT leaders including the agnostic orator Robert Green INGERSOLL, for whom she felt an especial respect. Her growing disgust with the fundamentalist tenor of both the nation and the women's movement itself culminated in the publication of *The Woman's Bible* in 1895. Stanton was the primary contributor to this controversial biblical commentary, but she benefited from the skills of a team of authors, most of whom supported suffrage and all of whom would be marginalized by the mainstream women's movement (see WOMEN AND UNBELIEF). The National American Woman Suffrage Association (formed by the merger of NWSA and AWSA) was quick to distance itself officially from *The Woman's Bible* and its heterodox editor, despite protests by a minority of its members.

As a humanist, Stanton was dismayed by evangelical Christian usurpation of the suffrage cause. With the influence of such groups as the Women's Christian Temperance Union, the suffrage movement abandoned natural rights theory to promote women as social housekeepers in roles that merely expanded their domestic service as wives and mothers to the world at large. Such limited visions of women's potential led Stanton to reject her earlier populist idealism to declare that she would rather that women fail to achieve the right to vote than that they should enforce their religious morality on the nation. The poignant essay "The Solitude of Self," delivered in 1892 when she resigned the presidency of the National American Woman Suffrage Association, epitomizes her humanist ideals as a women's rights theorist. Unlike Susan B. Anthony, she never gained the approval of the new generation of suffragists like Carrie Chapman Catt and Anna Howard Shaw, who found her radicalism distasteful and dangerous. Decades after her death in 1902, Elizabeth Cady Stanton remained virtually ignored by the very movement she had been instrumental in creating.

BIBLIOGRAPHY

Dubois, Ellen Carol, ed. *The Elizabeth Cady Stanton–Susan B. Anthony Reader: Correspondence, Writing, Speeches.* Boston: Northeastern University Press, 1992.

Griffith, Elisabeth. *In Her Own Right: The Life of Elizabeth Cady Stanton.* New York: Oxford University Press, 1985.

Kern, Kathi. *Mrs. Stanton's Bible.* Ithaca, NY: Cornell University Press, 2002.

Stanton, Elizabeth Cady. *Eighty Years and More: Reminiscences, 1815–1897.* Boston: Northeastern University Press, 1992.

MELINDA GRUBE

STEIN, GORDON (1941–1996), American freethought bibliographer, librarian, historian, and editor. Well known among atheists, freethinkers, and humanists worldwide (see ATHEISM; HUMANISM; SECULAR HUMANISM), Gordon Stein was a familiar contributor to both American and foreign "movement" publications. He made the celebration of secular humanism and the exposure of hoaxes of all kinds—religious, paranormal, and otherwise—his life's work. Much of his production was written with religious skepticism as his filter.

Stein was almost universally recognized as the foremost collector and historian of FREETHOUGHT materials of his generation, contributing an estimated six hundred book reviews to various publications. At his death his suburban house was filled with an estimated twenty thousand books. He was the longtime editor of the *AMERICAN RATIONALIST*, a small-circulation bimonthly devoted to analyzing and combating the irrationalities of religion. As its editor, his philosophy was to publish solely materials directly relating to freethought and irreligion—he felt there were more than enough other magazines to handle such related but tangential issues as the environment, feminism, and politics.

Stein's last professional position seemed the one he was destined for: assembling the libraries of atheism, humanism, and skepticism at the Center for Inquiry in Amherst, New York, from 1993 to his death in 1996. In addition he was a senior editor at *Free Inquiry*, the secular humanist magazine published out of the Center for Inquiry, and a technical consultant of the Committee for the Scientific Investigation of Claims of the Paranormal (CSICOP), whose journal *Skeptical Inquirer* was also published from the center.

Stein was intensely private, so few knew the scope of his academic achievements. He held a bachelor's degree in psychology from the University of Rochester; three master's degrees, one from Adelphi in zoology and two from UCLA in management and library science; and a doctorate in physiology from Ohio State.

His publications included two influential anthologies; three significant encyclopedias, one the predecessor to the present work; and a number of bibliographies and other works.

In *The Encyclopedia of the Paranormal* (1996), Stein took a skeptical approach to all aspects of the paranormal. Still, his approach was fair-minded, with proponents of paranormal claims included among contributors with expert skeptical credentials. In *The Encyclopedia of Hoaxes* (1993) he brought together examinations of many of history's most intriguing deceptions. These included not only paranormal and religious claims but also hoaxes in politics, science, and history. His master-work was *The Encyclopedia of Unbelief* (1985), which provided unbiased and hard-to-find information about the nonreligious point of view, and was added to the reference shelves by libraries worldwide.

His two anthologies, *The Anthology of Atheism and RATIONALISM* (1980) and *A Second Anthology of Atheism and Rationalism* (1987), brought together important but obscure atheist and freethought texts of interest to historians, students, and humanist or atheist activists.

Stein's most academically significant work might be his four freethought bibliographies, the only such guides to a specialty literature that is otherwise almost destitute of formal scholarly apparatus: *God Pro and Con: A Bibliography of Atheism* (1990), *Freethought in the United Kingdom and the Commonwealth: A Descriptive Bibliography* (1981), *Freethought in the United States: A Descriptive Bibliography* (with Marshall Brown, 1978), and *Robert Green INGERSOLL: A Checklist* (1969).

Stein lectured widely, frequently debated believers on topics such as the existence of God, and in the age before online book buying traveled the country to search antiquarian booksellers for rare and obscure works for the Center for Inquiry collection or his own personal library.

Stein was twice married and divorced: his first wife, Barbara, bore him a daughter, Karen; his second wife was attorney Eve Triffo.

He expressed his philosophy in a 1985 work, "What Is Rationalism?" in which he wrote: "We should always keep an open mind about any new phenomenon in nature. To merely say, 'That's impossible, therefore it doesn't exist,' is to commit a severe error. A much better approach would be to say, 'That's quite unlikely, but show me the evidence you have that say that it may be so.'"

BIBLIOGRAPHY

Stein, Gordon. *The Anthology of Atheism and Rationalism.* Amherst, NY: Prometheus Books, 1980.

———. *The Encyclopedia of Hoaxes.* Detroit: Gale Research, 1993.

———. *The Encyclopedia of the Paranormal.* Amherst, NY: Prometheus Books, 1996.

———. *The Encyclopedia of Unbelief.* Amherst, NY: Prometheus Books, 1985.

———. *Freethought in the United Kingdom and the Commonwealth: A Descriptive Bibliography.* Westport, CT: Greenwood, 1981.

———. *Freethought in the United States: A Descriptive Bibliography.* Westport, CT: Greenwood, 1978.

———. *God Pro and Con: A Bibliography of Atheism.* New York: Garland, 1990.

———. *Robert Ingersoll: A Checklist.* Kent, OH: Kent State University Press, 1969.

———. *A Second Anthology of Atheism and Rationalism.* Amherst NY: Prometheus Books, 1987.

———. *The Sorcerer of Kings: The Case of Daniel Dun-*

glas Home and William Crookes. Amherst, NY: Prometheus Books, 1993.

BERNARD KATZ

STEPHEN, SIR LESLIE (1832–1904), English editor and scholar. While he regretted not having devoted more time to "creative" writing in moral philosophy, Sir Leslie Stephen's terse historical and biographical surveys represent an outstanding achievement and an exemplar in English literature. He was largely responsible for popularizing AGNOSTICISM among England's liberal intelligentsia.

Stephen was born in Kensington on November 28, 1832, into a cultivated and well-connected family. His father, Sir James, was an abolitionist politician; his mother, Jane, daughter of the evangelical rector of Clapham. Deemed a sickly child with a "precociously active brain," Leslie went to private schools, Eton, and King's College, London, but flourished only at Trinity Hall, Cambridge, where he was an outstanding endurance athlete and mathematics scholar. There in 1854 he gained a fellowship and assistant tutorship which obliged him to take holy orders within a year. He became a deacon in 1855 and a priest in 1859.

Reading the controversial *Essays and Reviews* (1860) and works by John Stuart MILL, Auguste COMTE, Herbert SPENCER, Charles DARWIN, and Immanuel KANT led Stephen to religious SKEPTICISM "without mental perturbation." He avoided chapel services, resigned his tutorship, but retained his fellowship. In America (1863) he met US literati. Back in Britain, in 1864 he left Cambridge for London and contributed to prestigious journals like the *Saturday Review*, *Fraser's Magazine*, and *Cornhill Magazine*, whose bland editor he was from 1871 to 1882, encouraging writers like Thomas Hardy, Henry James, and Robert Louis Stevenson, who would later become famous. On marrying Harriet Thackeray, daughter of William Makepeace Thackeray, in 1867, he resigned his fellowship and joined Thackeray's household. He also started taking bar dinners, a social prerequisite to a legal career, in case his "potboiling" literary journalism failed.

Keen on mountaineering, he became president of the Alpine Club (1865) and editor of its journal (1868). His first book was an English translation of *Die Alpen* (1861) in 1871. The seventies also saw his most important agnostic works: *Essays on Free Thinking and Plain Speaking* (1873); *History of English Thought in the Eighteenth Century* (1876), featuring deist and utilitarian writers (see DEISM); and four essays in John Morley's *Fortnightly Review*, including "An Agnostic's Apology" (June 1876). In 1875 his wife died. He relinquished holy orders, left the Thackeray household, and married Julia Duckworth, widow of Gerald, in 1877. After writing numerous acclaimed biographies for Macmillan's *English Men of Letters* and other series, he published *The Science of Ethics* (1882) to disappointing reviews. That year saw the launch of the *Dictionary of National Biography*, with Stephen as editor until 1890–91, and Sidney Lee as subeditor and future editor. Stephen himself contributed 283 signed entries.

During the 1880s, Stephen lectured at Moncure CONWAY's liberal religious chapel and was associated with the (London) Ethical Society (1886). In 1892 he became president of the London Library and West London Ethical Society. He drafted the (unsatisfactory) definition of RATIONALISM for the RATIONALIST PRESS ASSOCIATION and became its first honorary associate in 1899. Among numerous honors, he was knighted in 1902. He died on February 22, 1904.

BIBLIOGRAPHY

Annan, Noel Gilroy. *Leslie Stephen: The Godless Victorian.* London: Weidenfeld & Nicolson, 1984.
Stephen, Leslie. *Sir Leslie Stephen's Mausoleum Book.* Oxford: Clarendon, 1977.

DAVID TRIBE

STIRNER, MAX (1806–1856). German philosopher and nihilist. Born Johann Kaspar Schmidt in Bayreuth, Bavaria, Max Stirner derived his pen name from a childhood nickname (*Stirn* refers to his high forehead). He initially lived a double life: by day, a mild-mannered schoolteacher at an academy for young ladies in Berlin; by night, a fierce and unrelenting critic of organized religion, public education, and all forms of government. Hence the need for a nom de plume.

Largely a forgotten figure today, Stirner had a major influence on several philosophical movements, including anarchism (see ANARCHISM AND UNBELIEF), egoism, libertarianism, MARXISM, and EXISTENTIALISM, and his ideas can be found in the works of such disparate—indeed antithetical—writers as Friedrich NIETZSCHE, Mikhail BAKUNIN, Karl MARX, and Ayn RAND. Stirner was in fact initially a friend and colleague of Marx, who published Stirner's essay "The False Principle of Our Education" in 1842. But the two later had a bitter break, and Marx's *The German Ideology* has a large section attacking Stirner.

Stirner's best-known work was his 1844 *Der Einzige und sein Eigentum* (The Ego and Its Own), in which he argued for an extreme form of egoism. The only truth one can know is that one exists. All existing beings seek what is in their own interest. The human individual will is constantly besieged by the "ought"—relational bonds from without which attempt to conform the will and subject it. Worst of all are "fixed ideas," concepts that one is taught never to analyze or criticize. Stirner was a strong critic of all systematic belief systems. Every human being is completely and utterly unique, yet abstract belief systems deny this basic fact and attempt to fit humans into preex-

isting categories or formulas. For Stirner, a belief should be voluntary, and the best way to test this is to see whether or not one can choose *not* to believe it. Any thought which cannot be so overturned is, in his phrase, a "wheel in the head." Likewise, the society in which an individual lives inculcates certain rules and regulations which became a part of that person's very self—a "gendarme in the breast." A true egoist is one who can exorcise such wheels and gendarmes. The two most powerful and pernicious beliefs implanted into individuals at an early stage are religion and patriotism, which encourage one to make one's very existence subservient to the needs of church and state. The church encourages one to sacrifice in the name of God, the state encourages one to sacrifice in the name of the law, and optimistic liberals like George Hegel and Ludwig FEUERBACH encourage one to sacrifice for the good of humanity. All such causes are mere abstractions, ideals, with the shared purpose of robbing individuals of their freedom, or even of their awareness that they are free.

Following the logic of this argument, every belief is merely provisional, which leads to a type of nihilism. Most of Stirner's contemporaries, including Nietzsche (whose own debt to Stirner's work remains controversial), wished to steer clear of so radical a conclusion, but Stirner was fearless (at least in his writings). Anticipating Jean Genet, he advocated committing criminal acts that assert the ego and reject the sacred. If enough such free acts occur, the state itself will collapse, bringing about an initial (quoting Thomas HOBBES) "war of all against all." But after such a war, there will be a union of egoists—a true anarchist society where all decisions will be made on the basis of shared human needs, with real consensus. There would be a kind of dynamic balance among free individuals.

Stirner's later works did not receive the same attention as *The Ego and His Own*. His wife left him in 1847, and he died in poverty and obscurity in 1856. But his extreme defense of egoism remains much discussed in libertarian and anarchist circles.

BIBLIOGRAPHY

Calasso, Roberto. *The Forty-nine Steps.* Translated by John Shepley. Minneapolis: University of Minnesota Press, 2001.
Hook, Sidney. *From Hegel to Marx: Studies in the Intellectual Development of Karl Marx.* New York: Columbia University Press, 1994.
Paterson, Ronald William Keith. *The Nihilist Egoist: Max Stirner.* Oxford: Oxford University Press, 1971.
Stirner, Max. *The Ego and His Own.* Translated by David Leopold. New York: Cambridge University Press, 1995.

TIMOTHY J. MADIGAN

STOICISM. Stoicism was the dominant philosophical movement of the Hellenistic age. It was founded by Zeno of Citium around 300 BCE and developed by Cleanthes of Assos and most importantly Chrysippus of Soli, who is credited with developing early Stoicism into a comprehensive system. Stoicism takes its name from a decorated porch in the Agora at Athens where the members of the school would gather for lectures. Early Stoics engaged in protracted epistemological disputes with the skeptical philosophers of the Academy. The Stoics of the middle period (second to first century BCE), whose most notable representatives were Panaetius of Rhodes and Posidonius of Apamea, introduced the philosophy to the Roman world, and the writings of Seneca, Epictetus, and the great Stoic emperor Marcus Aurelius mark the latter, "Roman" period (first to second century CE), which was for the most part concerned with ethical subjects. Stoicism was rediscovered in the Renaissance and later came to influence Enlightenment thought and American transcendentalism. Ralph Waldo EMERSON's library contains numerous volumes by Epictetus, Marcus Aurelius, and other Stoics whom he apparently had been reading at least since his studies at Harvard. The core transcendentalist notion of finding ultimate reality and truth in a universal rational Nature is an echo of Stoic themes.

Although no formal writings of early Stoicism survive in complete form, reconstructions have been undertaken based on fragmentary quotations and more substantive accounts by others, often critics of the movement. Such reconstructions present us with a picture of a coherent, rigorously constructed system encompassing physics, logic, and ethics. In the physical theory of the Stoics, the fundamental ontology of the universe is made up of two coextensive principles: matter, thought of as entirely passive and inert, and an organizing principle of eternal reason, logos, or "god." Matter and reason are combined into the four elements of earth, water, air, and fire, which are the basic phenomena at the observable level. Reason is immanent in the universe in the same way that the rational souls of human beings are immanent in them. Indeed, the universe is conceived as an organism with an optimal arrangement of its parts. Any appearance of imperfection is an illusion resulting from the failure to see the proper place of some phenomenon in the larger design. The rational soul structures and directs the world in every detail in accordance with a predetermined plan. The plan is a sequence leading from an intial state of fire, followed by the generation of the other elements, the creation of the phenomenal world, and an eventual return to a fiery conflagration. This preordained cosmic cycle recurs endlessly. While there was a diversity of opinion among Stoics, it is fair to say that their concept of the divine was at most a form of universal DEISM.

Air and fire in combination form the ubiquitous life force of pnuema ("breath"), which interpenetrates all bodies. Its outward motion determines objects' observable external qualities; its inward motion maintains them as integrated wholes. Pneuma exists in different gradations. The kind of pneuma that gives form to an inanimate object is called a "tenor." The kind of pneuma found in plants is "physique," literally, "nature." The pnuema of animals is soul (*psychê*); in rational animals, it is further described as the faculty in command of thought and decision, the *hĺgemonikon*. Human beings also depend on physique for purely physiological and autonomic actitivies. Thus, Stoicism has no place for an immaterial soul or mind. The soul of a person is pnuema, and pneuma is a kind of matter, subject to generation and destruction like other matter. At the same time, the theory of an independently existing pnuema makes physically possible the survival of the soul after biological death. Some Stoics, such as Chrysippus, maintained that the souls of the wise exist after death until the next cosmic cycle.

In ethics, Stoics defended a kind of natural law theory which was strictly speaking nontheistic and nonreligious, but predicated on the premise of a perfectly fine-tuned rational nature. The goal of the good life is living in agreement with nature. One's choices are virtuous when they follow their proper functions. The root of vice is false value judgments, which result when the passions overrun rational evaluation and invest value in things that are actually morally indifferent in the final analysis (food, drink, sex, shelter, and so on). For those who find themselves playing a part in the grand, inevitable, and perpetually recurring drama of Stoic cosmology, wisdom consists in accepting fate with calm fortitude and welcoming the eventual universal conflagration.

Many early Christians from Paul onwards sought to draw connections between their fledgling faith and the ascendent Stoicism of the empire, even co-opting elements of the philosophy; for instance, the cosmopolitanism of Epictetus. Many early Christian texts were addressed to Roman rulers, attempting to persuade them to end their persecution. Because such rulers, like Marcus Aurelius, were schooled in Hellenic philosophy, Christians found it necessary to justify their religion in Stoic and Epicurean terms. In Acts 17, when in Athens Paul encounters Epicurean and Stoic philosophers curious about Christianity, he characterizes it to them in a way that would appeal to Hellenistic ears: "[God] hath made of one blood all nations of men for to dwell on all the face of the earth, and hath determined the times before appointed, and the bounds of their habitation. . . . For in him we live, and move, and have our being; as certain also of your own poets have said." When Paul came to the story of the resurrection and the promise of the eternal afterlife, however, the this-worldly Athenians began to mock him. As Marcus Aurelius wrote in his *Meditations*: "fail not to note how short-lived are all mortal things, and how paltry—yesterday a little [semen], tomorrow a mummy or burnt ash. Pass then through this tiny space of time in accordance with nature, and come to thy journey's end with a good grace, just as an olive falls when it is fully ripe, praising the earth that bare it and grateful to the tree that gave it growth."

AUSTIN DACEY

STOUT, SIR ROBERT (1844–1930), New Zealand jurist, politician, and educator. Sir Robert Stout served as premier and chief justice of New Zealand and chancellor of the University of New Zealand. He supported the RATIO-NALIST cause throughout his life and was also a leading Unitarian (see UNITARIANISM TO 1961). Stout has been described as being to New Zealand what Robert Green INGERSOLL was to America and Charles BRADLAUGH was to Britain.

Born on September 28, 1844, at Lerwick in the Shetland Islands, Scotland, from an early age he attended Sunday afternoon family discussions on scientific, religious, and political topics. He later said that "theological disputation was part of social life." These experiences led him to reject sectarianism and religious dogma.

In 1864 Stout emigrated to New Zealand, where he qualified as a lawyer. While at Otago University he became a friend of Professor Duncan Macgregor, a rationalist and advocate of the English philosopher Herbert SPENCER. Stout also adopted Spencer's philosophy. In 1876 Stout married Anna Paterson Logan, who descended from a prominent family of Dunedin freethinkers.

Stout was elected to parliament in 1876, where he took an important role in debates over the 1877 Education Bill, which provided for "free, secular and compulsory" primary education. He opposed denominational influence in university education and voted against the introduction of divinity degrees. He also worked to remove the influence of the Presbyterian Church over appointments to chairs at Otago University.

Stout was also active in FREETHOUGHT work. In his inaugural address to the Dunedin Freethought Association in 1880 he said, "Recognize no authority competent to dictate to us. Each must believe what he considers to be true and act up to his belief, granting the same right to everyone else."

Stout's political career reached its height between 1884 and 1887, when he was premier, attorney general, and minister of education. A year later he was out of politics and returned to his law practice. In 1893 he returned to parliament but had little political influence during his remaining five years. Upon resigning from the House he was appointed chief justice in 1899, a position he held until 1926.

Upon his retirement in 1926 he was appointed to the Legislative Council, New Zealand's Upper House, where he defended secular education and opposed the introduction of Bible reading and prayer in schools.

Stout played a significant role in the development of the New Zealand university system; from 1885 to 1930 he was a member of the Senate of the University of New Zealand and between 1903 to 1923 its chancellor. He received honorary doctorates from Manchester and Edinburgh universities and from Oxford.

Stout espoused a humanist approach in his writing and speeches during the last ten years of his life. In his time Stout was one of only three New Zealanders who were honorary associates of the RATIONALIST PRESS ASSOCIATION. In an address to the Wellington Unitarian Church he said: "If only we could get us a Humanist religion we would be able to solve many problems yet unsolved. But now Humanism has developed and we can hope for better days."

BIBLIOGRAPHY

Dakin, Jim. "New Zealand's Freethought Heritage, Chapter 3: The Rise and Decline of Freethought in Dunedin, 1880–90." *New Zealand Rationalist and Humanist* 74, no. 2 (2001).

———. "New Zealand's Freethought Heritage, Chapter 5: Early Freethought in Wellington and Other Centres." *New Zealand Rationalist and Humanist* 74, no. 4 (2001).

———. "Sir Robert Stout and Freethought." *New Zealand Rationalist and Humanist* (1995).

Hamer, D. "Stout, Robert: 1844–1930." In *The Dictionary of New Zealand Biography*. Vol. 2. Wellington: Bridget Williams, 1993.

WAYNE FACER

STRAUSS, DAVID FRIEDRICH (1808–1874), German biblical scholar. David Friedrich Strauss's *Life of Jesus Critically Examined* (1835), published when he was a mere twenty-seven years old, remains perhaps the greatest book on the gospels ever penned. After a brief pastoral tenure in southwestern Germany, Strauss went to Berlin to study with G. W. F. Hegel, who died just after Strauss's arrival. Two years later, Strauss himself obtained a teaching post at Tübingen University, where the great F. C. Baur also taught. Three years following, upon the explosive appearance of *The Life of Jesus Critically Examined*, Strauss was dismissed from his post over his heresies (see HERESY).

In his scrutiny of the gospels, Strauss fought a two-front war, refuting both the orthodox apologists who defended the text as inerrant scripture, and the religious rationalists who denied supernatural causation yet tried to save the appearances, arguing that the gospel events took place as described but with natural causes. For them, Jesus walked *by* the sea, not on it. He fed the multitude with supplies passed to him from Essenes in the cave behind him, and so on. Strauss mercilessly exposed the contrived harmonizations of both groups, demonstrating in case after case that each gospel episode had to be understood as neither hoax nor history but rather as *myth*, fanciful tales, sometimes told to make a religious point and often modeled upon Old Testament tales of Elijah, Elisha, and Moses.

Strauss adduced many examples of legends from Judaism and other religions, demanding to know why these ought to be dismissed as legends when their gospel counterparts were soberly accepted as history. Frequently he exposed the inaccuracies and anachronisms of the gospels by showing how no amount of ingenuity had proven able to reconcile their notices of, for example, Quirinius's census—Luke's occasion for Mary and Joseph going to Bethlehem—with extrabiblical documentation. But perhaps the greatest of Strauss's contributions to the study of the gospels is his countless juxtapositions of contradictory accounts between the gospels, or even within a single gospel.

John the Baptist provides an excellent set of examples of Strauss's eagle-eye scrutiny of the gospel texts. In Mark's and Luke's Jordan baptism scenes, there is nothing to suggest that John even knew who Jesus was. In Matthew and John, John the Baptist recognizes Jesus and, in John, publicly endorses him. But in Matthew, the Baptist defers to Jesus as soon as he sees him, before the descent of the Spirit, while in John's version, the Baptist says he recognized Jesus as the messiah only when he saw the Spirit descend upon him. According to Matthew 11:2ff. and Luke 7:18ff., John sent a pair of disciples to inquire of Jesus whether he might be the Coming One. How does this uncertainty square with the earlier recognition/endorsement in Matthew? Had John's previous faith begun to waver? No, we get the opposite impression: John sends his messengers because he has heard a report of Jesus's miracles. Miracles would hardly cause a former believer to doubt, but they might well light the spark of hope in one who had not heretofore believed. Here as elsewhere Strauss insists that, when faced with two versions of a story, the historian must reject the more spectacular in favor of the less spectacular. If John were known to have believed in Jesus, who would ever construct a story in which he only wondered? But if John had never done more than wonder, it is natural to suppose Christians would later tell a "better" story in which the famous saint endorsed their own hero.

Likewise with the Transfiguration scene, where the contradictions occur within a single gospel, Mark. In Mark 9:2–8, the disciples see Elijah, the messianic forerunner, with Jesus and Moses atop a mountain. But afterward, in verses 11–13, they ask, "Why then do the scribes say Elijah must come first?" as if this expectation has so far been disappointed. And Jesus answers that the fulfillment was figurative: "Elijah" was actually John the Baptist. Here are two mutually exclusive Christian devices aimed at solving the same problem: why no Elijah if Jesus is the true Messiah? One answer is the figurative one: John the Baptist. The other is the literal one: he came but few saw him. It may be that neither is historical, but we can be sure the Transfiguration vision is secondary. If Christians knew of Elijah's glorious epiphany, who would ever resort to the strained John the Baptist business?

Having demolished the credibility of the gospel narrative, Strauss took for granted the authenticity of much of the "sayings material" (verses recounting the sayings of Jesus), to the extent that he imagined the historical Jesus had (reluctantly) accepted acclamation as the Jewish Messiah. Others, like Bruno BAUER and Rudolf Bultmann, would later apply Strauss's magnifying glass to the sayings of Jesus with equally devastating results.

BIBLIOGRAPHY

Cromwell, Richard S. *David Friedrich Strauss and His Place in Modern Thought*. Fair Lawn, NJ: R. E. Burdick, 1974.

Harris, Horton. *David Friedrich Strauss and His Theology*. Monograph Supplements to the *Scottish Journal of Theology*. Cambridge: Cambridge University Press, 1973.

Schweitzer, Albert. *The Quest of the Historical Jesus: From Reimarus to Wrede*. Translated by W. Montgomery. New York: Macmillan, 1961.

Strauss, David Fridrich. *The Christ of Faith and the Jesus of History: A Critique of Schleiermacher's* The Life of Jesus. Translated by Leander E. Keck. Philadelphia: Fortress, 1977.

———. *The Life of Jesus Critically Examined*. Translated by George Eliot. New York: Macmillan, 1892.

———. *The Life of Jesus for the People*. London: Williams and Norgate, 1879.

———. *In Defense of My Life of Jesus against the Hegelians*. Translated by Marilyn Chapin Massey. Hamden, CT: Archon, 1983.

———. *The Old Faith and the New*. Translated by Mathilde Blind. Amherst, NY: Prometheus Books, 1997.

Zeller, Edward. *David Friedrich Strauss: His Life and Writings* London: Freethought, 1879.

ROBERT M. PRICE

SWEDEN, UNBELIEF IN. Statistically, unbelief (ATHEISM, AGNOSTICISM, SECULAR HUMANISM, RATIONALISM, and FREETHOUGHT) seems quite strong in Sweden. As of 1999, Sweden's population was 8.9 million and the official religion was the Lutheran Church of Sweden. Yet according to the 2001 *World Christian Encyclopedia*, 29.4 percent of the population in 1995 was without religious belief, up from 28.7 percent in 1980 and just 1.1 percent in 1900. According to this source, Sweden was the most secularized of twenty-one Western countries in 1980 and again in 1995. According to the 1998 *Britannica Book of the Year*, as of 1995 religious affiliation in Sweden was as follows: Church of Sweden, 86.1 percent (nominally; about 30 percent are nonpracticing); Roman Catholic, 1.9 percent; Pentecostal, 1 percent; others, 11 percent. These figures are approximately compatible with the figures of the *World Christian Encyclopedia*. Yet in *Religious*

Freedom in the World, editor Paul Marshall presents the following church membership breakdown for 1999: Evangelical Lutheran, 90 percent; Roman Catholic, 1.5 percent; Pentecostal, 1 percent; Muslim, 4 percent; and other religious groups, 3.5 percent. Marshall does not mention unbelievers, as if there were no unbelievers at all in Sweden in 1999!

Organized unbelief in contemporary Sweden goes back to 1979 when the Human-Etiska Förbundet (The Human-Ethical Society) was founded. Its first chair was José Santana. At its foundation, the aims of Human-Etiska Förbundet were said to be "to combat and destroy the obstacles standing in the way of complete freedom of thought . . . to work for a true non-confessional education in the schools . . . to support and make known the right to a concept of life without faith in gods or religions . . . to establish cultural contacts with nonbelievers of other countries."

Before long, the leadership was taken over by the art dealer Anders Aspegren, who was the leader for about ten years and then withdrew for reasons of health. Santana withdrew from the organization a few years after its founding. Other leaders have included lawyer Johan Rudolf Engström, police officer Per Claesson, and organist Ebon Stranneby, the only woman among the first leaders. In 1994 Gunnar Ståldal was elected chair. He had an education in theology and was for many years a teacher of religion at a secondary school. He was followed by Mikael Göransson, a businessman, who served as chair until 1999 when Professor Carl-Johan Kleberg became chair. In 2004 Ludvig Grahn succeeded Kleberg as chair.

In 1999 Human-Etiska Förbundet changed its name to Humanisterna (The Humanists). In 2004 Humanisterna had thirteen hundred members.

Whereas Humanisterna remains a relatively weak organization, Sweden can take pride in quite a number of individual unbelievers of impressive stature. As in other countries, unbelief in Sweden began with unorganized individuals. One of the first was Olof von Dalin, an eighteenth-century historian, poet, and author of parodies and satires, some of them anticlerical (see ANTICLERICALISM). Dalin was the foremost Swedish writer of his time.

More important than Dalin was Johan Henric Kellgren, an author, librarian, and secretary to King Gustav III. Kellgren was influenced by John LOCKE and thinkers of the French Enlightenment including Julien Offray de LA METTRIE and VOLTAIRE. He became a devoted advocate of freedom and a critic of religion; he praised the French Revolution. Some of his satires were considered to be blasphemous (see BLASPHEMY). Kellgren is probably the foremost representative of the Swedish Enlightenment (see ENLIGHTENMENT, UNBELIEF DURING THE).

After Kellgren, Fredrik Wilhelm Christian Areschoug was one of those who moved in a secular direction. He was a botanist and an admirer of Charles DARWIN, whose ideas he introduced at Lund University. Another interesting early figure was the publisher and writer Gustav Joachim Leufsted. Around 1870 he gave a lecture in which he criticized the church and dogmatic Christianity. This created quite a stir; critics branded Leufstedt the Antichrist.

Though these individuals moved in a secular direction, they were apparently not atheists. The first Swede who can be reliably identified as an atheist is Anton (Kristen) Nyström, a physician, writer, and political and social activist. He is one of the great names of Swedish SECULARISM. In and after 1873, Nyström came under the influence of Auguste COMTE. By the 1860s he had abandoned any belief in a personal god. During these years he continued to recognize only the existence of a supreme being, which he interpreted as a "summing-up of the eternal laws, the physical as well as the intellectual and moral laws." Comte's slogan "To Live for Other People" strongly appealed to Nyström, and for him this meant work for the underprivileged in society.

If Nyström was probably the first known Swedish atheist, another significant one was Viktor (Emanuel) LENNSTRAND. He was an atheist during the final years of his life, beginning in 1887.

Another early Swedish atheist, (Johan Gustav) Knut Wicksell, was for a few years a good friend and collaborator of Lennstrand. He was the first in Sweden to discuss birth control (see BIRTH CONTROL AND UNBELIEF). Beginning in 1880, Wicksell acquired a reputation as a dangerous champion of radical ideas. A "defense nihilist," he doubted the utility of the Swedish armed forces. He opposed teachings of the church that he believed contrary to historical facts, and in this way acquired the reputation of being antireligious. Apart from his roles as a social reformer, lecturer, and journalist, Wicksell also became a professor of economics at the University of Lund. Wicksell's radical past pursued him also during his time as a professor and in 1908 he was prosecuted for BLASPHEMY and sentenced to two months in prison for his lecture "The Throne, the Altar, the Sword, and the Pocketbook."

A further interesting Swedish atheist was Bengt Lidforss. He was a botanist, a writer, and a politician. Lidforss carried out thorough studies in cytology, physiology, and heredity; he became a professor at Uppsala in 1910 and at Lund in 1911. He was a capable popularizer with strong political and social interests. He wrote in the social democratic press on literature, religion, and politics. His articles have a dazzling style and are sharply polemical, but also full of humor.

A final great atheist to be mentioned here is Ingemar Hedenius. From 1947 until his retirement in 1973, Hedenius was professor of philosophy at Uppsala, specializing in moral philosophy. During the 1940s Hedenius had also acquired a reputation as a dangerous radical. Apart from his more technical and difficult writings, he also published more popular writings and in 1948 declared himself a freethinker. His reputation as a religious radical was significantly strengthened with the publication of his 1949 book *Tro och vetande* (Faith and Knowledge). The book created a sensation, becoming the focus of prolonged attention in newspapers, journals, and in other books. The attention particularly focused on Hedenius's essays dealing with religion, in which Christianity was sharply criticized.

BIBLIOGRAPHY

Barrett, David B., et al., eds. *World Christian Encyclopedia.* 2 vols. Oxford: Oxford University Press 2001.

Britannica Book of the Year, 1998.

Hiorth, Finngeir. *Atheism in the World.* Oslo: Human-Etisk Forbund, 2003.

———. *Secularism in Sweden.* Oslo: Human-Etisk Forbund, 1995.

Marshall, Paul, ed. *Religious Freedom in the World.* Nashville: Broadman & Holman, 2000.

FINNGEIR HIORTH

SWINBURNE, ALGERNON CHARLES (1837–1909), English poet, dramatist, and critic. Algernon Charles Swinburne was born in London on April 5, 1837, to a distinguished Northumbrian family. His mother brought him up in High Church Anglicanism, while his grandfather, Sir John Edward Swinburne, a devotee of FREETHOUGHT and republicanism, opened to young Algernon his sizable library.

Swinburne attended Eton and Oxford, but graduated from neither institution. At Oxford, Swinburne befriended not only members of the Pre-Raphaelite group, but also Old Mortality Society leader John Nichol, who is credited with effecting Swinburne's final break from Anglo-Catholicism. While Swinburne's religious thinking changed over time—assailing organized religion, exploring pantheism (see PANTHEISM AND UNBELIEF) and HUMANISM, and propounding a concept of art-as-religion transmitted by the poet-priest—AGNOSTICISM remained at its core.

From 1860 to 1879 Swinburne lived in London, actively writing but also drinking excessively, ruining his already delicate health. His first important work was *Atalanta in Calydon* (1865), modeled after Greek tragedy. In it, he called God "the supreme evil." The publication of *Poems and Ballads* in 1866 caused a scandal with its antitheisitic, erotic, and even sexually pathological themes. The year 1871 saw the volume of republican poems, *Songs before Sunrise*. Swinburne was also a brilliant parodist, as seen not just in parodies like *The Heptalogia* (1880) but in parodic elements of his serious verse, usually the appropriation of Christian symbols for other purposes including attacks on religion.

In 1879 Swinburne was taken under care by Theodore Watts-Dunton, and remained with his friend in Putney, a London suburb, for the final thirty years of his life. Watts-Dunton weaned Swinburne from alcohol and shielded him (some say overly so) from outside influences. One of the finest poems of this period is the erotic and anti-Christian epic *Tristram of Lyonesse* (1882).

Swinburne died of influenza on April 10, 1909. Friends who knew of Swinburne's longstanding hostility to religion were incensed when Anglican rites were read at the funeral.

From the mid-twentieth century on, there has been not only a critical reappraisal of Swinburne's later work—previously dismissed—but also a general rediscovery of the poet's intellectual complexity and lyrical beauty.

BIBLIOGRAPHY

Fuller, Jean Overton. *Swinburne: A Biography.* New York: Schocken, 1971.

Louis, Margot K. *Swinburne and His Gods: The Roots and Growth of an Agnostic Poetry.* Montreal and Kingston: McGill-Queen's University Press, 1990.

Rooksby, Rikky, and Nicholas Shrimpton, eds. *The Whole Music of Passion: New Essays on Swinburne.* Aldershot, UK: Scolar, 1993.

REBECCA BIZONET

SWITZERLAND, UNBELIEF IN. Switzerland, or, more precisely, the Swiss Confederation, exists as a democratic organization of small territories—later named Cantons—which have united against outside powers (princes, monarchs, and emperors) to maintain their freedom since approximately 1291. Over the centuries a modern republic developed with a tradition of freedom, four national languages, and a federal structure that was very progressive when it was established in 1874. The following articles of the 1874 constitution are very significant for women and men who no longer wish to be part of a religion (translation is approximate):

Art. 49. The freedom of belief and conscience is immutable. No one may be forced to take part in a religious community, religious instruction or religious ceremony or be punished in any manner for their religious views. The religious education of children up to and including their sixteenth year is the competence of the holder of parental authority. The exercise of civic or political rights can under no condition be restricted by conditions of a religious or confessional nature. Religious belief does not release from observance of civic duties. No one is required to pay taxes that are specially intended for cultic or religious purposes that they are not party to.

Art. 50. The Cantons and the Confederation retain the right to take appropriate measures in order to maintain order and peace in public life between the members of different confessions, as well as against the intervention of religious authorities in the rights of citizens and the state. . . . The establishment of bishoprics on Swiss territory must be approved by the Confederation.

Art. 51. The Jesuit Order and the affiliated societies are not permitted in any part of Switzerland, and their members are forbidden to exercise any activity in churches or schools. This restriction can be extended by a decree of the Confederation to other religious orders whose activities are deemed to be dangerous to the state or disturb the peace between the confessions.

Art. 52. The establishment of new or revival of dissolved religious houses or orders is not permitted.

The same spirit infuses the federal civil law code: "Art. 277 . . . If children have reached their sixteen year, their right to decide for themselves over their religious confession are inalienable."

Owing to this spirit of freedom under the law, freethinkers (see FREETHOUGHT) could publicly organize and participate in public life. Some of the more famous freethinkers of this period were Gottfried Keller, author and atheist; August Forel, psychiatrist and natural scientist whose portrait adorns the Swiss 1000 Franc note; Ernst Brauchlin, educator, author, and former president of the Swiss Freethinkers movement; Arnold Heim, geologist and author of the book *Reason Instead of Religion*; Jakob Stebler, popular author and president of the Swiss Freethinkers Association; Max Frisch, author, atheist (see ATHEISM), and freethinker; and Friedrich Duerrenmatt, author, atheist, and son of a pastor.

The first formal freethinkers' group in Switzerland was formed in Zurich in 1870, followed a few years later by organizations dedicated to propagating freethought in French-speaking Switzerland and the Canton of Tessin. But it was with the founding of the Swiss-German League of Freethinkers on April 12, 1908, in Zurich, under the chairmanship of the engineer August Richter, that an organization first arose with the financial and personal prerequisites to develop a national freethinkers' movement.

Two months after the foundation of the league, intolerant church authorities demonstrated their continuing willingness—and capacity—to persecute freethinkers. A lecture titled "Monism [approximately similar to Unitarianism (see UNITARIANISM TO 1961)] and Christianity" held by August Richter in Lucerne caused such enthusiasm that local freethinkers announced their intention to form a local association. The inaugural meeting was scheduled for one week later. Richter was arrested as he traveled to Lucerne to attend, and was imprisoned for two weeks on a charge of BLASPHEMY, followed by an exile from the Canton of Lucerne for eight years. The judgment was overturned by the Federal Supreme Court on April 3, 1909.

The financial situation of the freethinkers did not permit them at first to print their own paper, and they collaborated with a German Monist group on a joint publication. On April 1, 1915, the first issue of *Swiss Freethinker* was published. This periodical has continued uninterrupted to the present day under various names, except during the war years of 1919 to 1921.

Repression of freethought by the churches continued unabated until approximately World War II. Every conceivable means was brought to bear. This reached a peak in 1933, following the repression of the freethinkers in Germany by the National Socialists (see GERMANY, UNBELIEF IN). Mueller, the member of the Swiss parliament for Grosshoechstettern (Bern), introduced a motion demanding similar measures against the activities of freethinkers in Switzerland. The blatant sympathy of the Swiss Reformed and Catholic churches for this repression of alternative worldviews is very informative in this context. The *Reformed Swiss News* (*Reformierte Schweizer Zeitung*) of April 28, 1933, offered the opinion that the new government in Germany was correct to repress anti-Christian organizations. The Catholic *Lucerne Daily News* (*Lucerner Tagblatt*) congratulated Chancellor Engelbert Dollfuss of Austria for the repression of freethinkers there on June 23, 1933 (see AUSTRIA, UNBELIEF IN).

Swiss freethinker meetings were continually interrupted by violent means during this period. It was often necessary to cancel advertised freethought lectures at the last minute because those responsible for the lecture venues were placed under such massive pressure that they preferred to commit breach of contract than face the consequences of allowing the scheduled freethought event to go ahead. During this period, even membership in a freethinker organization could be reason enough for a household breadwinner to be fired. Hence it was necessary in 1931, for example, to dissolve one growing freethought group, the Toggenburg (Saint Gall) Association, in the face of united pressure by the church and employers. The churches also demanded an absolute monopoly over matters of religion and worldview in the radio.

Since this period, and in particular since World War II, some progress is apparent regarding tolerance. In part this was due to the increasing tempo of secularization in society, but not least also to the steadfastness of the freethinkers in this period. Increasingly few people are content with an antiquated ideology that offers inadequate solutions to contemporary problems because it originated in another epoch and under another social order. In a spiritual and moral sense, the state churches currently have a weak hold over the population: only 20 percent of those registered as members are actively involved in the churches; in the towns this can sink to as low as 2 percent.

Out of a population of seven million, eight hundred thousand registered as nonmembers of any confession (church) in the last census. This fragile demographic situation could not stand in more transparent contrast to the enormous financial means still available to the churches because of their historical symbiosis with the state, which allows religious bodies to maintain a bureaucratic apparatus far beyond their actual importance in society. Only in the Cantons of Geneva and Neuchatel, which maintain separation of church and state, are the churches obliged to keep their workforce to realistic levels as they do not receive tax revenue.

Irrespective of economic perceptions, the Christian churches still maintain that they are custodians of an absolute truth—just as members of other religions insist that this lies with *them*—and that they must fulfill a higher purpose (albeit one that they have given themselves). This anachronistic and monopolistic attitude, common to Christian state churches, free church groups, and fundamentalist groups of various religions, continues to manifest itself in the form of religious-political activities. It is particularly visible in special interest lobbying in public affairs. Examples include recent debates on tax reform, during which religious bodies lobbied for state support of particular denominations based on their "historical entitlement"; constitutional reform, in connection with which churches lobbied to protect the role of a state church and the formal acknowledgment of God in the constitution; and in educational issues including state control of religious education, church access to schools, and influence over curricula.

The Swiss Freethinkers (Freidenker-Vereinigung der Schweiz, FVS) offer an alternative for those who want nothing to do with organized religion and prefer to embrace the values of HUMANISM and SECULARISM. A science-based empirical worldview replaces religious speculation. The criteria for truth are held to be insight, experience, and common sense. But the FVS is fully aware that there are still people who believe they require the crutches of religion and a belief in an all-powerful, benevolent mentor. For this reason, the FVS demands that its interventions in public life display a tolerance for all worldviews, whether founded on a religious or on a scientific basis. Naturally the FVS aims beyond this—article 2 of its statutes defines the following goals: "The FVS promotes free and critical thinking on the basis of a humanistic and science-oriented worldview and ethics—not bound to any articles of religion or to political ideology. It strives to assert these values in state and society. It intervenes for the freedom of faith, of opinion, and of expression. It strives towards the equality of all scientific groups and their independence from the state (separation of church and state). It offers, in accordance with the current needs, social and cultural services, in particular, alternatives to religious services. It advocates humane living conditions and supports effective measures to protect the environment."

To realize this article, the Swiss Freethinkers work toward a strict separation of churches from all state institutions, including schools and the army. They intervene in the mass media for an appropriate consideration of freethought concerns, equality of men and women in economic and legal matters, the reform and extension of educational establishments from preschool to the universities, and meaningful support for countries in need of aid. The FVS intervenes nationally and internationally in matters that concern humanists or on behalf of humanists or sister organizations. However FVS membership is aging demographically, and is underrepresented in the Swiss population. In 2005 the FVS hired a general secretary to combat these problems, to increase its profile within Switzerland and the effectiveness of its interventions.

The work of the Enlightenment continues (see ENLIGHTENMENT, UNBELIEF DURING THE) for the freethinkers in Switzerland and in the rest of the world, against forms of superstition and against religious and irrational perceptions. Opposition to freethought has however diffused with the development of a free market for salvation, from state churches to diverse orthodox, fundamentalist, or state church groups, and even New Age esoteric groups. Recent changes in the FVS should help it regain lost momentum as an alternative to such groups, to become again an energetic movement for secularism and humanism.

JEAN KAECH,
TRANSLATED BY MARK FURNER

SYMES, JOSEPH (1841–1906), Australian lecturer, journalist, pamphleteer, and controversialist. Joseph Symes was born in Portland, Dorset, England, on January 29, 1841, a birthday he was proud to share with one of his heroes, Thomas PAINE. Symes's childhood was happy; he grew up a pious Wesleyan. At twenty-three he entered the Wesleyan College in Richmond, Surrey, to train as a minister. But he veered increasingly away from religion, stimulated by the reports of death and suffering during the Franco-Prussian War, the pope's declaration of infallibility, and the condition of the poor in England. Symes's passage away from religion was tortuous and exhausting, but by 1875 he was a convinced freethinker (see FREETHOUGHT).

In 1876 Symes began contributing to the *NATIONAL REFORMER*, the paper run by Charles BRADLAUGH. In the same year he was appointed the NATIONAL SECULAR SOCIETY's official lecturer at Tyneside. Symes took an active role in the National Secular Society for the next seven years, most notably in 1877, when he was an important figure in securing Bradlaugh's reelection as president of the society against a major challenge to Bradlaugh's leadership by opponents of his favorable views on birth control.

Symes worked tirelessly for the freethought movement, although he was disappointed not to be offered the editorship of the *FREETHINKER* during G. W. FOOTE's imprisonment for BLASPHEMY in 1883. It may have been with some relief that Bradlaugh passed on to Symes the request from Australian freethinkers that a lecturer be sent out to help their budding movement. Symes left England on the *Lusitania* on December 23, 1883, arriving in Melbourne in the middle of the following February, whereupon he launched immediately into a career of freethought activism.

During the next twenty years, Symes established himself as the leading personality in Australian freethought through the Australian Secular Association (ASA), serving for many years as president of its Victoria branch. Symes excelled as a lecturer, journalist, pamphleteer, and controversialist. His main vehicle was the newspaper the *LIBERATOR*, which he was instrumental in founding in 1884 and which ran until 1904. Symes was also more than competent as an astronomer and zoologist, although the Melbourne clubs dedicated to the advance of those disciplines took care to reject his applications for membership.

As a leading figure in Australian freethought, it was inevitable that Symes would attract opposition from within the movement as from without. In 1888 the ASA underwent a damaging split. Ostensibly the split was between pro- and anti-Symes factions, though the historical research of Nigel Sinnott reveals that deeper splits underlay and predated Symes's arrival in Australia. Prominent among Symes's opponents were radical anarchists (see ANARCHISM AND UNBELIEF) who thought their brand of revolution had outgrown SECULARISM. The next few years were taken up with feuding between the estranged factions of the freethought movement. As if this was not enough, in 1892 Matilda Symes, his wife of twenty-one years, died. The following year Symes married his publisher, Agnes T. Wilson.

Most disastrous for the freethought movement was the depression of the 1890s, which had the effect of scattering workingmen around the country in search of employment. Symes courageously continued lecturing and publishing the *Liberator*. In December 1899, he was attacked in broad daylight shortly before he was to give a lecture denouncing the Catholic Church's anti-Semitism, which had reached a toxic peak during the trial of Alfred Dreyfus in France. Symes's hearing was permanently impaired after the beating he received.

In 1906 the Symes family journeyed back to England, which Joseph had not seen for twenty years. The National Secular Society gave him a hero's welcome, with a series of dinners and presentations. Energized by his return to England, Symes undertook a grueling lecture tour of the country, despite the heart disease from which he had suffered for several years. While lecturing in his youthful stamping ground of Tyneside, he caught pneumonia and died suddenly on December 29, 1906, aged sixty-five. Among Symes's pamphlets included titles such as *Philosophic Atheism*, *Christianity and Slavery*, and *If Jesus Came to Melbourne*.

BIBLIOGRAPHY

Sinnott, Nigel. "1882: The Australian Secular Association." *New Zealand Rationalist & Humanist*, December 1982.

———. *Joseph Symes, the "Flower of Atheism."* Melbourne: Atheist Society of Australia, 1977.

———. "Joseph Symes and 1984." *New Zealand Rationalist & Humanist*, April 1984.

BILL COOKE

TAOISM, UNBELIEF WITHIN. See CHINA, UNBELIEF IN.

TAYLOR, ROBERT (1784–1844), English FREETHOUGHT pioneer, writer, and eccentric. Robert Taylor was born on August 18, 1784, in Edmonton, now a northern suburb of London. He was the second son of John Taylor, a wealthy ironmonger, and Elizabeth Jasper. Though Robert's father died when he was only seven years old, the family was well provided for and he received a good education. Notwithstanding his clear poetic ability, he learned medicine, eventually becoming a surgeon.

During his medical training, Taylor was converted to a zealous form of evangelical religion on behalf of which he abandoned his medical career. In January 1813 he graduated and took holy orders. While serving as a curate in Midhurst, Sussex, in 1818, Taylor befriended Henry Ayling, a local tradesman whose fine library included some of the works of Thomas PAINE. Taylor soon plunged into a period of doubt, which led to his being shunned by his parishioners. Though he formally recanted his heresies (see HERESY), Taylor was ostracized by his family. Also the church hierarchy made clear that he had no future as a clergyman. Taylor's recantation was short-lived; for the next ten years, he drifted around the British Isles, usually penniless, in search of employment. In 1824, after escaping violent persecution in Dublin, Taylor returned to London, where he set up the Christian Evidence Society, with the aim of proving that that was no evidence for the Christian truth claims. Ironically, there remains a Christian Evidence Society to this day, but with opposite aims.

The eloquence of Taylor's heretical lectures—and his habit of giving them in full clerical regalia—was an increasing scandal for the church authorities, which determined to bring him down. On trumped up charges of BLASPHEMY, Taylor was imprisoned twice: for a year in February 1828, and for eighteen months during 1831–32. During his first imprisonment, Taylor wrote *The Diegesis* (1829), which explored the origins, evidences, and early history of Christianity.

Taylor's intellectual legacy is mixed. He was an early advocate of the "myth theory" of Jesus (see JESUS, HISTORICITY OF), which is of interest only to historians of ideas, but significant strands of his BIBLICAL CRITICISM remain valid today. He argued forcefully, for instance, that the apostolic authorship of the gospels makes no historical sense. Few serious biblical historians would question that today.

Taylor also wrote a weekly letter to the *Lion*, a periodical his friend Richard CARLILE began on his behalf. These letters were later published as *The Devil's Pulpit* (1830). By this time, Taylor had been branded "the Devil's Chaplain" by his religious persecutors. Taylor's second term of imprisonment was harsher than the first. His health broke down under the strain, and he wrote nothing. Soon after his release he married a wealthy supporter, moved to France, and practiced medicine, taking no further part in organized freethought. He died on June 5, 1844.

BIBLIOGRAPHY

Cutner, Herbert. *Robert Taylor*. London: Pioneer Press, [1950].
Taylor, Robert. *The Diegesis*. London: E. Truelove, [1870s].

BILL COOKE

TELLER, WOOLSEY (1890–1954), American atheist writer, lecturer, and debater. Born on March 22, 1890, in Brooklyn, New York, Woolsey Teller was attracted to FREETHOUGHT in his teens by its flagship journal, *THE TRUTH SEEKER*. In the 1920s he joined the AMERICAN ASSOCIATION FOR THE ADVANCEMENT OF ATHEISM, founded by future *Truth Seeker* editor Charles L. SMITH and others. This organization, often referred to as "the 4As," received broad press coverage for an ambitious, ultimately sterile plan to organize student atheist groups. Teller was an officer of the organization for the rest of his life, editing its newsletter the *4A Bulletin* (after 1947, the *Atheist*). In 1936 Teller took up freethought work full-time, joining *The Truth Seeker* as associate editor.

Reputedly a fearless lecturer and debater, Teller specialized in confronting hostile religious audiences. In his regular *Truth Seeker* column, "Rougher Notes," he revealed a flinty, idiosyncratic RATIONALISM. For him, both evolution and the profligate wastefulness of the cosmos proved that God does not exist, a cosmological view not unlike Bertrand RUSSELL's. More controversially, Teller held that advances in science and technology made philosophy, psychology, the social sciences, and even mathematics irrelevant. Since evolution is a ruthless struggle for survival, altruism cannot have arisen among human beings; people who believe they act selflessly are deluded, unaware that they act only to satisfy themselves. Finally, Teller espoused EUGENICS and a toxic "scientific" racism. (Teller is considered partly responsible for *The Truth Seeker*'s sharp racist turn under Smith's editorship, which began in 1937; Smith and successor James Hervey JOHNSON championed racism and a venomous anti-Semitism largely absent in Teller.)

Teller wrote one book, *The Atheism of Astronomy* (1938), a refutation of the Design Argument for the existence of God (see EXISTENCE OF GOD, ARGUMENTS FOR AND AGAINST). A 1945 anthology of Teller's *Truth Seeker* columns, *Essays of an Atheist*, is better known.

Little is known of Teller's personal life. The dedication of *Essays of an Atheist* suggests that he had three children. Woolsey Teller died of a stroke in New York on March 11, 1954, aged sixty-three.

BIBLIOGRAPHY

Manners, John L., Marshall L. Gauvin, Charles L. Smith, Herbert Cutner, Irving Levy, Peter Biginelli, Arthur G. Cromwell, Frank C. Hughes, Charles Bradlaugh Bonner, Walter B. Stevens, Ira Cardiff, and Charles Francis Potter. "The Passing of an Atheist Leader: Woolsey Teller." *Truth Seeker*, April 1954.
Teller, Woolsey. *The Atheism of Astronomy*. New York: Truth Seeker Company, 1938.
———. *Essays of an Atheist*. New York: Truth Seeker Company, 1945.

TOM FLYNN

THEOSOPHY. Theosophy is a mystical movement teaching that the universe evolves through countless cycles. The present world is one of several manifestations that hosted thousands of cyclic revolutions of life, from the least to most advanced. Human beings are souls that undergo numerous reincarnations through various stages of evolution. Certain advanced souls with godlike qualities, called "masters," watch over and assist humanity. Theosophy teaches that matter and spirit are variations of the same reality. It posits an ethic of care for the world and for fellow human beings. Theosophy was rooted in late nineteenth-century religious and cultural life in Europe and the United States, and provided inspiration and intellectual grounding for many of the popular mystical movements that followed it.

Theosophy, which means "divine wisdom," was the term adopted by a small group of middle-class professionals and intellectuals who met in New York City in the 1870s to describe their search for commonalities in all world religions, for explanations of Spiritualism and paranormal phenomena, and for an ethical formula to unite all people. Their Theosophical Society was founded in 1875 by Helena Petrovna Blavatsky, a Russian immigrant, and Henry Steel Olcott, an American journalist. Blavatsky claimed to communicate with masters through paranormal means. Her acquaintances claimed to have witnessed her performing supernatural feats like precipitating objects out of thin air. Blavatsky traveled extensively in Europe and Asia before she came to New York. She read widely in the literature, religion, and philosophies of many cultures. In 1879 she and Olcott moved to southern India, where they established a headquarters at Adyar, near Chennai (formerly Madras). They cultivated a network of Anglo-British writers and Indians influenced by the Hindu renaissance of the era. They encouraged the founding of local Theosophical lodges, mirroring a social form found in

Freemasonry. Many early Theosophists were Freemasons who saw no contradiction between the symbols and secret teachings of Freemasonry and those of Theosophy. Blavatsky and Olcott fostered publishing projects that included periodicals and books. Blavatsky borrowed heavily from Hindu, Buddhist, and other Asian sources to support her philosophy of evolutionary advance. Theosophy was one of the first Western philosophical/religious movements to embrace Asian perspectives.

In 1885 Blavatsky became embroiled in a controversy. Critics accused her of forging letters supposedly from the masters, then claiming they had appeared through paranormal means. Because of the negative publicity that resulted, Blavatsky moved to Europe. She died in London.

One prominent British Theosophist influenced by Blavatsky was Annie Wood BESANT, a well-known writer, social reformer, and one of the leading freethinkers of the era. After converting to Theosophy, Besant quickly rose in Theosophical leadership. Eventually she led the Theosophical Society in Europe, and later from India, advocating Indian independence. Irish immigrant and attorney William Q. Judge led American Theosophists to declare their independence from the rest of the Theosophical Society in 1895 due to disagreements between Judge and Besant. Judge's successor, Katherine Tingley, established a Theosophical community at Point Loma, near San Diego, California. The organization descended from this community, the Theosophical Society (Pasadena), is now headquartered in Altadena, California. Theosophists in the United States loyal to Besant, the Theosophical Society in America, are headquartered in Wheaton, Illinois. Much of the disagreement between these two branches of Theosophy centers on the question of authority: Which tradition preserved Blavatsky's teachings most authentically and continued to receive guidance from the masters? The Theosophical Society (Pasadena) claims that it remained true to Blavatsky, through Judge and his successors, charging that the tradition of Besant had added doctrines supplementary to Blavatsky's teachings. The Theosophical Society in America looks to the extensions of Theosophical doctrine that Besant and others in her line advocated as being true to Blavatsky, if not always articulated exactly in Blavatsky's writings. Both of these major branches, and several smaller ones, publish Theosophical magazines and books.

Theosophists' numbers in Europe, India, the United States, and Australasia are greatly diminished from their heyday between 1890 and 1930, but many spiritual seekers who eventually gravitated to the New Age and other twentieth-century new religious movements read Theosophical literature during their spiritual pilgrimages.

BIBLIOGRAPHY

Besant, Annie. *The Ancient Wisdom: An Outline of Theosophical Teachings*. Adyar, India: Theosophical Publishing House, 1966.

Blavatsky, Helena. *The Key to Theosophy*. Wheaton, IL: Theosophical Publishing House, 1972.

———. *The Secret Doctrine*. 2 vols. Pasadena, CA: Theosophical University Press, 1988.

Campbell, Bruce F. *Ancient Wisdom Revived: A History of the Theosophical Movement*. Berkeley and Los Angeles: University of California Press, 1980.

Cranston, Sylvia. *HPB: The Extraordinary Life and Influence of Helena Blavatsky, Founder of the Modern Theosophical Movement*. New York: Tarcher/Putnam, 1993.

Judge, William Q. *The Ocean of Theosophy*. Covina, CA: Theosophical University Press, 1948.

Ransom, Josephine. *A Short History of the Theosophical Society*. Adyar, India: Theosophical Publishing House, 1938.

Ryan, Charles J. *H. P. Blavatsky and the Theosophical Movement: A Brief Historical Sketch*. San Diego, CA: Point Loma Publications, 1975.

W. MICHAEL ASHCRAFT

THUCYDIDES (460/455–ca. 400 BCE). Ancient Greek historian and humanist. Born between 460 and 455 BCE, Thucydides served as general in the Athenian forces against Sparta in 424, and died in the early fourth century. Exiled from Athens after a defeat in 424, he spent the rest of his life working on his *History of the Peloponnesian War*. After an overview of prehistory, this book tells the story of the war between Athens and Sparta and their respective allies through 411, covering the causes of war, the plague years in Athens, the effects of civil war, and a number of debates that set ethical points of view against pragmatic ones.

Thucydides was not an avowed atheist (see ATHEISM), but by comparison with his contemporaries his writing is strikingly godless. Before his time, the great writers about human events were poets such as Homer, whose epics are laced with episodes in which the gods take a hand in directing or undermining human action. Throughout his works Thucydides draws attention to the difference between his work and the poets: they told pleasant stories, he tells the truth. His older contemporary Herodotus, who wrote up the Persian Wars, included many tales involving divine intervention, and expresses none of the SKEPTICISM we find in Thucydides. Thucydides worked from an empirical theory of human behavior that furnishes explanations for the sorts of events that pious people attributed to the gods. He was the first European to write of human events making no reference to divine intervention. His is thus a kind of atheism by displacement; naturalistic explanation (see NATURALISM) leaves no role for the gods, who quietly drop altogether out of the human story.

Thucydides' prehistory (known as his "Archaeology") explains the origins of society in human terms, based on traditional reports, analogies with primitive peoples, and inferences from buried artifacts. His explanation of war distinguishes between the official explanation—that the Athenian empire violated justice—and the true one—that the Spartans were frightened by the growth of Athenian power. His account of the plague points out that religious observance made no difference to survival and makes light of oracles and prophecies. He displayed a rationalist contempt for oracles, though he once grudgingly agreed that one oracle turned out right.

Thucydides was not alone in his RATIONALISM. Others challenged the oracles and proposed naturalistic explanations for the origins of culture. Thucydides, however, is unique for the scope of his work and the pointed clarity with which he rejects the supernatural.

In addition to being a rationalist, Thucydides was a realist in holding that human actions are rarely motivated by religious or ethical concerns. Instead, he offered an account of human action in which fear, ambition (or love of glory), and greed are dominant. Religious concerns do not bring people to war or to peace, or even strengthen people's willingness to abide by their oaths.

His theory of human nature is flexible, however, since Thucydides believes that people's behavior is affected by circumstance; extreme conditions such as the plague undermine the veneer of ethical civilization that is celebrated by Pericles, a point Thucydides underlines by reporting Pericles' encomium to the virtues of Athens just before he tells how Athenian behavior declined during the plague. But as Thucydides sees it, the nastiest side of human behavior is brought out by civil war: "War is a violent teacher . . . it gives most people impulses that are as bad as their situation when it takes away the easy supply of what they need for daily life." The implication is clear: peace, health, and prosperity bring out the best in us, while religion is irrelevant.

PAUL WOODRUFF

TINDAL, MATTHEW (1657–1733), English deist writer. Matthew Tindal, who came from a High Church background, attended Lincoln College, Oxford, where he studied under George Hickes, who was to become one of his most hostile opponents. Moving to Exeter College, where he received his BA in 1676, Tindal became a law fellow of All Souls in 1678 and a doctor of law in 1685. The lawyer's approach is apparent in his writings, and he retained his law fellowship for the rest of his long and mostly uneventful life.

One major event was Tindal's conversion to Roman Catholicism. This was brought about, around 1685, by a "popish emissary" employed by James II at Oxford. Tindal's detractors have accused him of opportunism—he hoped, it was said, to become head of his college—but this seems unlikely since he publicly renounced Catholicism in 1687 or early in 1688 while James was still in power. His conversion to, and then away from, Catholicism was no doubt a factor in his move to FREETHOUGHT. Another, more general factor was the social disorders of the time, for which religious intolerance was largely responsible.

Early Freethought. Opposition to religious intolerance and sympathy for freethought and for social order are evident in Tindal's two anti-Trinitarian pamphlets, *A Letter to the Reverend the Clergy of Both Universities* (1694) and *Reflections on the Trinity* (1695), as well as in his *Essay concerning the Power of the Magistrate, and the Rights of Mankind, in Matters of Religion* (1697), which was approved by John LOCKE and advocated toleration along Lockean lines. Tindal also wrote *A Letter to a Member of Parliament, Shewing That a Restraint of the Press Is Inconsistent with the Protestant Religion, and Dangerous to the Liberties of the Nation* (1698), which was republished in shortened form six years later as *Reasons against Restraining the Press.*

In 1706 Tindal issued his first major work, *The Rights of the Christian Church Asserted, against the Romish and All Other Priests Who Claim an Independent Power over It*, which, he is supposed to have said, would make the clergy "mad." It did, provoking about two dozen replies and drawing strong criticism from Jonathan Swift and George Berkeley, among others. A more accurate but less strategic title would have been "The Rights of the Christian Laity," for the book defends liberty of conscience and worship against clerical claims to authority in these areas. The clergy, Tindal argues, can have no powers independent of the civil authority, which is obliged to protect the religious freedom of the laity, "so long as they do nothing prejudicial to the Civil Society." Tindal issued a *Defence of the Rights* in 1707, which, together with the *Rights*, was burned in 1710 by the common hangman by order of the House of Commons.

Between 1708 and 1713 Tindal published pamphlets relating to the *Rights* and the controversy about Sacheverell's Jacobitism (loyalty to the exiled Stuarts). The most entertaining is *A New Catechism* (1710) and the most substantial is *The Nation Vindicated*, part 2 (1712); here he defended previous freethinking works and lashed out at such enemies as Jonathan Swift, "this Reverend Buffoon"; Henry Dodwell, "this muddy-headed Irishman"; and his old teacher, "the Godly Dr. Hickes." Like Anthony COLLINS, Charles Blount, John TOLAND, John Trenchard, and Peter ANNET, he defended DETERMINISM—a position, according to Leslie STEPHEN and Ernest Mossner, that English freethinkers were supposed to oppose.

From 1713 to 1729 Tindal wrote fifteen more pamphlets, almost all of them on political topics. His next freethought work, *An Address to the Inhabitants of London and Westminster; In Relation to a Pastoral Letter . . . by the Bishop of London, Occasion'd by Some Late Writings in Favour of Infidelity* (1729), is also a defense of fellow freethinkers, notably Collins and Thomas WOOLSTON.

The Deist's Bible. The "grand work" upon which Tindal's fame mainly rests was issued in 1730 when he was more than seventy-two years old. This is *Christianity* *as Old as Creation: or, the Gospel, a Republication of the Religion of Nature*, the classic statement of constructive DEISM, often described as "the deist's Bible." The last part of his title was borrowed from a sermon by Bishop Sherlock, a practice that nicely illustrates his exploitation of the liberal or unguarded pronouncements of clergymen. Tindal drew out and synthesized the tendency toward natural and moral religion among liberal and Low Church writers such as Tillotson and Clarke. The book made the clergy even angrier than his first major work, eliciting well over a hundred replies. Although separated by almost twenty-five years, Tindal's two major works are closely connected. As the *Rights* opposed the clergy's having power independent of civil authority, so *Christianity as Old as Creation* denies to revealed religion any authority independent of reason; and as the first pretension leads to social and religious disorder, so, Tindal argued, the second will "weaken the force of the Religion of Reason and Nature, strike at all religion; and [he adds] there can't be Two Independent Rules for the Government of human Actions."

As with the *Rights*, Tindal intended to issue a second volume of *Christianity*. However, none appeared, although he published a *Second Address* (1730) which contains a defense of *Christianity* against an attack by Daniel Waterland; and in the British Library there is a fragment of the introduction to volume two, which contains answers to "Mr. Jackson, Mr. Foster, and Dr. Conybeare; the First a Low Churchman, the other a Dissenter, and the Third a High Churchman." It is often said that Edmund Gibson, bishop of London, suppressed the second volume, but there is good reason to doubt this.

Tindal was accused of being an immoral man, "a noted Debauchee and a man of very pernicious Principles," as Thomas Hearne put it. No doubt criticism of his moral character was designed partly to bring his principles into disrepute; for showing that the man who virtually reduced religion to morality was himself immoral would certainly help the enemies of deism. However, there is probably some truth in the accusations, for in a private memoir of Collins, Lord Egmont says that Collins "used to say my friend Tyndal [*sic*] is a rogue and a disgrace to us, for he is not honest or virtuous. . . ."

Deist or Atheist? Even more difficult is the question of Tindal's actual theoretical position. Was he a deist, as most commentators hold, or an atheist, as some of his critics claimed? Although there is little suggestion of ATHEISM in his writings, we have two similar but apparently independent stories about how Tindal argued against the existence of God: one is in the *Religious, Rational and Moral Conduct of Matthew Tindal* (1735), and the other, more circumstantial account is given by Lord Egmont in his diary (November 1735). In brief, Tindal argued "that space was infinite and eternal, and these were attributes commonly given to God; either therefore space is the Christian's God, or there are two Gods infinite and eternal, which at the bottom is as good as to say there is no God at all."

Tindal's assertion appears to be a garbled and materialistic version of the (Spinozistic) argument for pantheistic monism, which, in short, is this: there can be only one, most perfect, necessary being; for if there were two, they would cancel each other's perfection and necessity. Hence the one perfect and necessary being must embrace everything within itself, including extension. It is likely that Collins and Tindal—and perhaps also Toland's pantheistic societies—grounded their pantheistic MATERIALISM in this way. As the writer of the *Religious . . . Conduct of Tindal* put it: "Their God is at last the Universe; or, as they sometime express themselves, one only extended or material Substance differently modified." However, without additional evidence, it is difficult to decide whether Tindal accepted this atheistic line of argument (a line of argument that contains resonances of his opposition to two independent powers in the *Rights* and *Christianity*).

Tindal died on August 16, 1733, uttering blasphemies "scarce fit to be repeated," according to a witness, and "as proud of dying hard as ever he was to be reputed a Top Free Thinker."

BIBLIOGRAPHY

Berman, David, and Stephen Lalor. "The Suppression of Tindal's *Christianity as Old as Creation*, Volume 2." *Notes and Queries* 229 (March 1984).

Gawlick, Günter. "Introduction" to his edition of *Christianity as Old as Creation*. Stuttgart: Friedrich Frommann Verlag, 1967.

Lalor, Stephen. "Matthew Tindal and the Eighteenth-Century Assault on Religion." Unpublished thesis, Trinity College, Dublin, 1979.

Stephen, Leslie. *History of English Thought in the Eighteenth Century*. 2 vols. New York: Harcourt Brace, 1962.

"Tindal, Matthew." *Biographia Britannica*. London, 1766.

DAVID BERMAN

TOLAND, JOHN (1670–1722), Irish freethinker. Originally named Janus Junius Toland, John Toland was born in County Donegal in the north of Ireland. "Educated from the cradle in the grossest superstition and idolatry," he says in the preface to his *Christianity Not Mysterious* (1696), he threw off Roman Catholicism at age fifteen by "his own reason and such as made use of theirs." From his conversion away from the faith in 1685—a most imprudent time, given the known religious predilections of James II—Toland's life is marked by considerable travel and intellectual development.

Education. Toland attended the University of Glasgow from 1687 to 1690, and aligned himself with the Presbyterians. His original conversion was probably to Presbyterianism and not to Anglicanism as some claim, since in his 1697 *Apology* he speaks of "the Dissenter's worship [gaining] extraordinarily upon his affections, just as he was newly delivered from [popery]." From Glasgow he went to Edinburgh, and received an MA in 1690. He then moved to London, where he so impressed the Dissenters that they sent him to the University of Leyden to "perfect his education," as his biographer Pierre Desmaizeaux puts it. In Holland he studied under Spanheim and Leclerc and became a Latitudinarian—that is, a tolerant, rationalistic, liberal Christian.

Benjamin Furley, John LOCKE's Dutch correspondent, described Toland in 1693 as "a freespirited, ingenious man." This characteristic freespiritedness brought with it the besetting practical problem of his life; for, continues Furley, "having cast off the yoke of spiritual authority . . . has rendered it somewhat difficult for him to find a way of subsistence in the world." Having neither family fortune, as had Lord SHAFTESBURY and Anthony COLLINS, nor an Oxford fellowship, as Matthew TINDAL had, Toland was thrown upon the generosity of aristocratic patrons, such as the Duke of Newcastle, Prince Eugene of Savoy, Lords Shaftesbury and Molesworth, and the Earl of Oxford, who employed him as an editor, political pamphleteer, biographer, and probably a "general" spy. As his background was obscure, his prospects were generally uncertain, and he was forced to live by his pen. That he was an incessant writer and controversialist is amply shown in Giancarlo Carabelli's two-volume bibliography of his writings and replies to them; it runs to more than five hundred pages and lists nearly two hundred works by or attributed to him.

Toland is perhaps the first professional freethinker. Eliminating prejudice and religious intolerance was, by his own account, one of the main aims of his life. Most of his writings, and the best of them, are directed against established religion—not, of course, that he ever avowed this. Officially, he claimed, as in *Vindicius Liberius* (1702), to be a loyal member of the Church of England, anxious only to eliminate abuses of religion. However, critics such as Samuel Clarke saw him, rightly, as one of Christianity's most powerful enemies.

Christianity Not Mysterious. After leaving Holland, Toland spent some time in Oxford using its library facilities. From there he moved to London, where early in 1696 he published his most influential work, *Christianity Not Mysterious*. This short and forceful book made him notorious: according to some, it also began the so-called deist debate (see DEISM). Like nearly all of Toland's books, its subtitle is informative: *A Treatise Shewing, That There Is Nothing in the Gospel Contrary to Reason, Nor Above It: and That No Christian Doctrine Can Be Properly Called a Mystery*. Drawing especially on Locke's theories of meaning and nominal essence, Toland argued that since mysteries such as the Holy Trinity do not stand for clear ideas, Christianity must either employ meaningless doctrines or else be nonmysterious; for assenting to doctrines of which we have no clear ideas is like trying to believe in Blictri, a traditional nonsense word.

Early in 1697 Toland revisited Ireland, where in a short time he had "raised against him the clamour of all parties," as we are told by Locke's Dublin friend, William Molyneux; the clergy, especially, were "alarmed to a mighty degree against him." *Christianity Not Mysterious* was burned by the common hangman, and it was even moved by one member of the Irish House of Commons "that Mr. Toland himself should be burnt." Yet for all that, his book initiated the one great flowering of Irish philosophy, drawing creative replies from Peter Browne (whom Toland claimed to have made a bishop), Edward Synge, William King, and George Berkeley.

It is not clear why Toland returned to Ireland. There is some evidence that he expected a political appointment. Possibly he also wished (notwithstanding his protests in the *Apology*) to encourage a return to the tolerant religion of the ancient Irish, the "Western Latitudinarians," as he described them in *Nazarenus* (1718). He boasted, according to Browne, that he would become "the head of a sect." In any case, he was forced to flee to England, where he published the *Apology*, which deals with his reception in Dublin and contains most of the meager information we have on his early life.

Toland's concern for civil liberty, another professed aim, begins to appear in his editions of John Milton (1698), James Harrington (1700), and in his *Anglia Libera* (1701), a book that encouraged the British government to send him with a delegation to Hanover, where he is said to have gained the esteem of the future ruling family of England. In 1702 he revisited Hanover and also traveled to Berlin, where he engaged in philosophical discussions with the queen of Prussia, to whom he addressed his *Letters to Serena* (1704).

The RATIONALISM of *Christianity Not Mysterious* is continued in the *Letters*; but whereas the first may be described as deistic, the *Letters* are pantheistic (see PANTHEISM AND UNBELIEF). Once again this is not Toland's avowed view. In fact, in the penultimate section of Letter 5, "Motion Essential to Matter," he expressly repudiates Baruch SPINOZA's pantheism and affirms that there exists an immaterial presiding intelligence responsible for the formation of plants and animals. But, as F. A. Lange has suggested, this caveat should be seen as an application of the esoteric/exoteric (private/public) distinction, a subject Toland discusses at length in *Tetradymus* (1720), where he claims that the distinction is "as much now in use as ever; tho' the distinction is not so openly and professedly approved as among the Ancients."

That Toland was a pantheist in 1704, and hence that the penultimate section was designed for exoteric use, is borne out by the following considerations: (1) In *Socinianism Truly Stated*, a pamphlet printed in 1705, Toland signs himself "a Pantheist" (the first recorded use of the term in English). (2) The logical tendency of Letter 5 is toward pantheistic materialism, since allowing motion to be essential to matter undermines the most compelling reason for positing a transcendent cause of the world. (3) In the exuberant poem *Clito*, first printed in 1700, Toland explicitly develops and takes seriously a pantheistic theory. Moreover, his statements on key doctrines in the *Letters to Serena* are basically the same as those in the poem and in his 1720 *Pantheisticon*.

Letter 3 is a "History of the Soul's Immortality," in which Toland argues that the doctrine was invented by Egyptian priests for their own selfish interests. The drift of the letter is clearly irreligious, but once again in the penultimate section Toland issues a religious caveat. His strategy here bears comparing with that of David HUME, who, in the final paragraph of his essays "The Immortality of the Soul" and "Of Miracles," issues a similarly crude religious caveat. A "Bouncing compliment," as Toland observes in *Tetradymus*, "saves all."

In 1707–1709 Toland visited Prague and then the Hague, where he published his *Adeisidaemon* (directed against superstition) and *Origines Judaicae*, in which he suggests that Strabo was a sounder historian of the Jews than Moses. Gottfried LEIBNIZ commented critically on these works in letters to Toland, later to be printed in volume two of *A Collection of Several Pieces of Toland* (1726). In addition to writing numerous political pamphlets, such as "Reasons for Naturalizing the Jews" (1714) and "Political Anatomy of Great Britain" (1717), which continue his plea for religious toleration, Toland projected a number of "grand works." Among them was a history of the Druids, which appeared in a modest form in his posthumous *Collection*.

Later Work. *Nazarenus* is Toland's most significant contribution to biblical scholarship. It looks back to a controversy started by his *Life of Milton* (1698), wherein he defended Milton's view that *Eikon Basilike* was not written by Charles I, as claimed, but was a pious fraud composed by Bishop John Gauden. Toland then suggested that this recent forgery helped to explain the acceptance in earlier times of "suppositious pieces under the name of Christ and his apostles," a thesis he defended in *Amyntor* (1699), in which he lists more than seventy spurious gospels, Epistles, Acts, and so on. Toland said that he was not calling into question the canon of the New Testament; but few if any took this seriously. In *Nazarenus* he anticipates the so-called higher criticism in placing early Christianity firmly in a Jewish context. He argues that the first Christians—the Nazarenes, Ebionites—or, as he calls them, Jewish Christians—were obliged to keep the Levitical law, and that although true Christianity was perverted by the heathenism of the Gentile Christians (who were not meant to keep the law), it can be extensively reconstructed from the Gospel of Barnabas.

In 1720 Toland had *Pantheisticon*, his most exotic work, printed. It contains an explicit statement of pantheism and a liturgy that was taken to be a burlesque of the Christian liturgy. Whether there existed pantheistic societies that used this liturgy, as he suggests, is not known. It is generally agreed that his pantheism is closer to that of Giordano BRUNO (whose works he translated) than to that of Spinoza, who is criticized in the fourth essay in the *Letters to Serena*. In 1720 Toland also published *Tetradymas*, which, apart from the study of the esoteric/exoteric distinction, contains an essay on the murder of HYPATIA, a naturalistic account of the pillar of cloud and fire mentioned in Exodus, and a defense of *Nazarenus*.

Toland's impact on his generation was widespread and varied: few prominent writers of the time were not goaded by him. Many of his contemporaries affected a condescending attitude toward him, which was continued, unjustly, by Leslie STEPHEN in his influential *History of English Thought in the Eighteenth Century*. Other commentators rightly feel that, given Toland's undoubted powers, his intellectual contribution might have been more solid and sustained than it was. There is something swashbuckling about Toland's work: he is, as it were, an Irish adventurer in scholarship. His last years were bedeviled by financial worries; he lost money in the South Sea scheme, whose secret history he helped write. Yet he died on March 11, 1722, Desmaizeaux says, "without the least perturbation of mind," having a few days earlier written an epitaph that concludes: "If you would know more of him Search his Writings."

BIBLIOGRAPHY

Berman, David, ed. *Atheism in Britain*. 5 Vols. Bristol, UK: Thoemmes Press, 1996.

———. "Enlightenment and Counter-Enlightenment in Irish Philosophy." *Archiv für Geschichte der Phiosophie* 64 (1982).

Carabelli, Giancarlo. *Tolandiana: Materiali bibliografici per lo studio dell'opera a della fortuna di John Toland (1670–1722). La Nuova Italia 1975. Errata, Addenda e Indici*. 1978.

Heinemann, F. H. "John Toland and the Age of Enlightenment." *Review of English Studies* 20 (1944).

Lange, F. A. *The History of Materialism*. 3 vols. Boston: James Osgood, 1877–81.

McGuinness, P., A. Harrison, and R. Kearney, eds. *Toland's* Christianity Not Mysterious: *Text, Associated Works and Critical Essays*. Dublin: Lilliput, 1997.

Nicholl, H. F. "John Toland: Religion without Mystery." *Hermathena* 100 (1965).

———. "The Life and Work of John Toland." Unpublished thesis, Trinity College, Dublin.

Simms, J. G. "John Toland (1670–1722), a Donegal Heretic." *Irish Historical Studies* 16 (1969).

Stephen, Leslie. *History of English Thought in the Eighteenth Century*. 2 vols. London, 1876.

Sullivan, Robert E. *John Toland and the Deist Controversy*. Cambridge, MA: Harvard University Press, 1982.

Toland, John. *A Collection of Several Pieces of Mr. John Toland, with Some Memoirs* [by Pierre Desmaizeaux] *of His Life and Writings*. 2 vols. 1726.

DAVID BERMAN

TOLSTOY, LEV NIKOLAYEVICH (1828–1910), Russian novelist. Lev Tolstoy is celebrated primarily for his two great novels, *War and Peace* (1866–69) and *Anna Karenina* (1873–76), both of which contain serious speculation about how a human life should be led and whether religion has any useful part in the process. But he also wrote a number of works dealing directly with this subject.

Tolstoy's religious education began in the orthodox, or, more accurately, Orthodox way. He attended church with his family and absorbed all the practices and attitudes of the Russian Orthodox Church. All went smoothly enough until one day, when he was ten, an older boy announced to Tolstoy and his brothers that at school the older boy and his friends had made a discovery: God did not exist and everything they were being taught was untrue. It took Tolstoy a year or two to absorb this revelation, but he gradually shook off the trammels of the church, and by the time he left Kazan University (in midcourse) at the age of eighteen, he had abandoned every last vestige of the religious message that had been implanted in him during those early years.

We know these details because they are set down at the beginning of his most important religious text, *A Confession* (1879–81), written immediately after *Anna Karenina*, the closing pages of which show him (in the person of Dmitry Levin) to be entering a period of spiritual crisis. This climacteric, which occurred when he had just attained the age of fifty, was a renewal of the spiritual despair that had swept over him one night in 1869, just after he turned forty, when a vision of death had murdered sleep for him, filling him with dread and an agonizing sense of mortality.

A Confession is a cyclic work, starting and ending in religious acceptance, though its end is very different from its beginning. The autobiographical story goes as follows: Having renounced all thoughts of God and the Church, the young Tolstoy launched himself into several careers—soldier, writer, estate manager,—finding success in all of them but lasting contentment in none. On the contrary, he plunged ever deeper into despair. Turning to the great thinkers and prophets, he found their ideas riddled with inconsistencies and fallacies. No one could provide him with an answer to his questions that would justify his continued existence or dispel his fear of death, and for months on end he contemplated suicide. From this nadir of human experience he struggled back to an acceptance of life, and eventually discovered a plan for living that would suffice, though without bringing him any kind of happiness, for his remaining three decades. It was essentially religious, but not mystical or ecclesiastical. In a sense this was the fulfillment of a dream he had had as a young cadet: nothing less than the creation of a new, practical Christianity that would preserve the old morality and preach love as the only basis for human behavior, without retaining the dogma, mystery, and hypocrisy that bedeviled religious observance in the modern world.

The religious code of Tolstoy's last years was a severe form of asceticism based on a theory of love and non-resistance to evil which had its origin in Christ's Sermon on the Mount (Matt. 5–7). His writings on pacifism became known to a wide international audience, of which Mahatma Ghandi was but the most celebrated member; his famous estate became a focus of pilgrimage. (Tolstoy's inability, in his personal life, to show indulgence toward those nearest to him—especially poor Sonya, his wife, who had to put up with idiosyncrasy, depression, bad temper, and intransigence—remains as a dark stain on his reputation, undermining his right to instruct humanity on how to live a good life).

In this last period Tolstoy no longer considered all religious teaching to be a lie, though he thought there was more truth among the Russian peasantry than in the whole of the Orthodox Church. (For disseminating ideas like this he was excommunicated in 1901.) He made a profound study of theology culminating in a series of long religious essays and even a retranslation of the gospels from the Greek in an abbreviated and harmonized form (1881–82). His religious pronouncements are solidly based on years of study, comparison, and contemplation.

One of the most important is the little-known *What Is Religion, and What Does Its Essence Consist Of?* (1902), a succinct statement (in fewer than twenty thousand words) of all that Tolstoy saw as good and bad on the subject. While acknowledging that preachers and officials have debased religion, he deplored the modern spirit of secularism, and rejected the idea that religion has been rendered obsolete. It has always figured in human thinking, he asserted, and remains as relevant now as it has always been. All the great religions contain an essential truth that explains life and directs human conduct. That truth can be simply stated. We inhabit infinity—anything less than infinity is unimaginable—and yet we are ourselves finite in our short lives and limited powers of comprehension. The link between the two states is provided by religion (*religare* means "to bind"), the function of which is defined with acuity: "True religion is that relationship, in accordance with reason and knowledge, which man establishes with the infinite world around him, and which binds his life to that infinity and guides his actions" (see RELIGION). After a lifetime of struggling with these ideas, and many years of study, thinking, worry, and vacillation, this concept remained Tolstoy's final pronouncement on the subject.

A. D. P. BRIGGS

TONGUES, SPEAKING IN. *Speaking in tongues* refers to vocalizations attributed to supernatural or natural causes, and usually unintelligible to the speaker or listener(s). The general phenomenon is usually denominated as *glossolalia*, while the speaking of known languages otherwise foreign to the speaker (*xenoglossia*) may be considered a subcategory. Unbelief in the supernatural character of glossolalia is found in both Christian and non-Christian sources.

Ancient Times. Although some have claimed to find glossolalia described in documents from Mari, a kingdom on the Euphrates River (ca. 2000 and 1500 BCE) in what is now Syria, there are no unequivocal references to glossolalia before Christianity. According to Acts 1–2, after the ascension of Christ the disciples in Jerusalem awaited the arrival of Holy Spirit Baptism, a miracle that endowed them with special powers that included the ability to speak in previously unknown foreign languages (*xenoglossia*), in order to carry out their Christian mission. Acts 2:13–15 notes that some people mistook this event for drunkenness, suggesting that at least some witnesses tried to offer a naturalistic explanation. But it is also said that many foreigners in the crowd recognized their own languages being spoken. According to 1 Corinthians 13:1, there are also angelic tongues that human beings may speak, though an interpreter is needed if such tongues are spoken in a congregation (1 Cor. 14:2–5, 27).

Between the New Testament and modern times, we encounter very few instances of glossolalia in Christianity. One example is attributed to Montanus, a second-century figure whom Eusebius, the famous church historian, describes as a heretic. Eusebius suggests that Montanus's glossolalia was not authentic, at least by orthodox standards. Augustine, the influential Christian theologian, argued that glossolalia was no longer part of the Christian experience. In his *Homily on the First Epistle of St. John*, Augustine even appeals to empirical evidence insofar as he notes that the laying on of hands does not result in glossolalia, and that, therefore, Christians must presume that it no longer occurs.

Modern Times. Aside from reported sporadic glossolalia among Mormons and Shakers, as well as other groups, the most prominent sustained glossolalists are found in Pentecostalism, a complex of movements that first developed in America beginning in the late nineteenth and early twentieth centuries. Pentecostalism in its classical form holds that speaking in tongues is the only or main evidence of Holy Spirit Baptism. For Pentecostals, the spiritual gifts or powers mentioned in the New Testament, including healing and prophecy, still exist and should be actively cultivated by modern Christians. In general Pentecostalism now is a major force in Christianity, and it includes famous evangelists such as Jimmy Swaggart and Benny Hinn.

Naturalistic explanations for modern glossolalia can be found already in the late nineteenth century, in the work of the famed Harvard psychologist William James, who commented on cases that the speakers attributed to spiritual phenomena. However, James concluded that the language being spoken was in fact some sort of garbled English. A professor of psychology at the University of Geneva, Théodore Flournoy, was probably the first to outline a naturalistic categorization of glossolalia, which he divided into (1) incoherent random utterances; (2) neologisms created by psychosis, among other conditions; and (3) foreign idioms otherwise claimed to be unknown to the speaker. Flournoy based part of his work on the famous case of Hélène Smith, who believed herself to be speaking in Martian. The psychologist Carl Jung also examined at least two cases of glossolalia, and concluded that speakers distorted and repeated certain phrases that were otherwise meaningless.

In general, naturalistic explanations for glossolalia offered prior to the 1960s were variants of a "pathological" model, which portrayed glossolalists as suffering from some dysfunction, individually or as part of an inferior social group. For example, the French psychologist Emíle Lombard posited a type of automatism induced by hypnosis. Dr. George Cutten, a Baptist minister and president of Colgate University, suggests in *Speaking with Tongues* (1927) that glossolalists generally had lower mental abilities. Other naturalistic theories came from ethnographic accounts, such as those claiming that some Asian shamans were actually imitating animal sounds.

Beginning in the 1960s there was a dramatic shift to sociolinguistic and functionalist explanations for glossolalia. The medical anthropologist E. Mansell Pattison, for instance, concluded that the Pentecostals he studied actually functioned well in society. William Samarin has shown in great detail that his sample of Pentecostal glossolalists were not speaking any sort of meaningful language, natural or supernatural. He noted, in particular, that there were regionalisms in glossolalia, something that would not be expected of angelic tongues. Samarin stressed both the learned and the creative aspects of speaking in tongues.

Although pathological naturalistic evaluations of glossolalia have been found among social scientists, it is among non-Pentecostal Christians that one finds the most hostile evaluations of glossolalia. Thus, Robert G. Gromacki, an ordained Baptist minister, says that "[s]atanic power must be regarded as a live option as to the source of the modern tongues movement." Gromacki also believes that natural processes can account for some glossolalia.

Conclusion. Glossolalia probably has many explanations, and it is useful to distinguish different types of unintelligible utterances. The majority of Pentecostal glossolalia that I have observed, as a former Pentecostal preacher and trained anthropologist, is probably due to sociolinguistic causes and is not otherwise a meaningful language. Glossolalists imitate practices that are valued within the Pentecostal group to which they are committed, and sometimes exhibit creativity as well as imitation. Since the tongue is a muscle susceptible to involuntary spasms, it is also reasonable to posit that some states of excitement, especially when accompanied by music, can result in the involuntary generation of sounds that may be experienced as "possession." Otherwise, there is no evidence that glossolalia has any supernatural basis.

BIBLIOGRAPHY

Gromacki, Robert G. *The Modern Tongues Movement.* Grand Rapids, MI: Eerdmans, 1967.

Hovenden, Gerald. *Speaking in Tongues: The New Testament Evidence in Context.* London: Continuum, 2002.

Mills, Watson E., ed. *Speaking in Tongues: A Guide to Research on Glossolalia.* Grand Rapids, MI: Eerdmans, 1986.

Samarin, William. *Tongues of Men and Angels: The Religious Language of Pentecostalism.* New York: Macmillan, 1972.

HECTOR AVALOS

TREATY OF TRIPOLI. This treaty of 1796–97 is officially entitled "Treaty of peace and friendship between the United States of America and the Bey and Subjects of Tripoli of Barbary." (Tripoli is part of what later became known as Libya.) It is of little importance as a treaty or legal document, having been superseded by another treaty only nine years later. It has, however, been cited frequently, sometimes carelessly, as evidence against the claim that the United States was founded as "a Christian nation." The relevant language in the treaty, written in 1796, probably by diplomat Joel BARLOW, is to be found in the eleventh article of the treaty, which reads in its entirety:

> **Article 11.** As the government of the United States of America is not in any sense founded on the Christian Religion,—as it has in itself no character of enmity against the laws, religion or tranquility of Musselmen,—and as the said States never have entered into any war or act of hostility against any Mehomitan nation, it is declared by the parties that no pretext arising from religious opinions shall ever produce an interruption of the harmony existing between the two countries.

Musselmen was a term of the time for Muslims; *Mehomitan* was similarly a term for Mohammedan or Muslim. The treaty was brokered between Tripoli and the United States in late 1796 (initially signed and agreed to by both sides on November 4) at the end of the second presidential term of George Washington. There is no evidence that Washington was personally involved with or aware of the famous article, and it is therefore not wise to attribute the key words to Washington, as some FREETHOUGHT activists have done—though those words were indeed a product of Washington's administration. Yet there is no reason to believe that he would not have agreed with the idea. One Washington biogra-

pher, Paul Boller, wrote that "[v]ery likely Washington shared Barlow's view, though there is no record of his opinion about the treaty."

Purpose. The treaty grew out of negotiations between the Bey, or ruler, of Tripoli and Barlow, who either wrote the text or was its translator into English. The treaty was intended by the Americans to protect American shipping interests and American seamen, then under serious attacks and threats of more from "Barbary pirates." The treaty specified that the United States was paying to the Bey money, watches, rings, cloth, and brocade, and would add specific future items such as "twelve thousand Spanish dollars" and "twenty five barrels tar," to secure the peace. The treaty was somewhat successful in the short term, but in the end US Navy and Marine forces had instead to win the peace through force. The reference to Tripoli in the famous first line of the US Marine Hymn, "From the Halls of Montezuma to the shores of Tripoli," refers to Marine participation in the war against the pirates of the Barbary States (1801–1805) during Thomas JEFFERSON's administration.

Controversy. There has been great controversy about the treaty, probably because of its explicit rejection of Christianity as the basis for the government of the United States. Though such controversy is not groundless, there is no serious basis for rejecting the treaty as solid, though secondary, evidence of the framers' intent to establish a secular, non-Christian government. The US Constitution, lacking as it does any affirmative reference to religion, is both necessary and sufficient evidence of that secular intent, but the treaty provides weighty additional evidence of it less than a decade after ratification of the Constitution.

Among the objections to the treaty as evidence of the non-Christian nature of the American government is the possible fact that the Arabic version of the treaty, the one that the Bey and his representatives agreed to, did not include Article 11. The surviving Arabic version has in place of Article 11 a page of what can be best described as a diplomatic cover letter with some flamboyant Arabic gibberish, and no one seems to know why. Someone other than Barlow could well have substituted an Arabic page, perhaps even by accident at the time, or at some later time between the date it was written and the date the nontreaty page was discovered (in 1930). Barlow was very likely by 1796 a deist (see DEISM), though he had served earlier as a military chaplain, so one other possible (but unlikely) explanation is that Barlow wrote Article 11 and included it only in the English version—and therefore only for domestic consumption. If so, his motives may be suspect, but the Barlow translation with its famous clause is the one sent to the US Senate for ratification by President John Adams (the process of getting the treaty language approved and the documents back to America took several months). And it is the Barlow translation that is and always has been recorded as the official version of the treaty in American diplomatic archives and publications.

Another occasional objection is that the treaty was later superseded, after Jefferson's war with the Barbary pirates, by a new treaty that contained no such language. Indeed, some later treaties with nations such as Russia or Great Britain included flowery ceremonial language about the Christian Trinity. But it must be noted that the later treaties with such language were with nations that were at the time officially Christian nations—and none of the later treaties reversed, or even implied a reversal of, the declaration in the 1796–97 treaty that the US government is not founded on the Christian religion. The current importance of the treaty with its famous Article 11 language is neither formal nor legal but historical. The "not in any sense founded on the Christian Religion" wording merely reinforces what the US Constitution had recently established—a secular basis for government.

Adams, inaugurated in March, sent the treaty to the Senate in late May 1797. Copies were printed for the Senate and the committee considering it. The committee reported favorably to the Senate a week later and on June 7, 1797, the Senate voted to ratify, with all twenty-three senators present recorded in favor: "Bingham, Bloodworth, Blount, Bradford, Brown, Cocke, Foster, Goodhue, Hillhouse, Howard, Langdon, Latimer, Laurance, Livermore, Martin, Paine [not Thomas PAINE], Read, Rutherfurd, Sedgwick, Stockton, Tattnall, Tichenor, and Tracy." (The Senate, like the nation, was smaller then; also a few senators were not present.) For only the third time in the history of the Senate, a recorded vote was requested and approved despite unanimity, which is why we know the names of every senator voting in favor. There were up to that point 339 recorded Senate votes (out of thousands of votes in Senate history by then), but 336 were on matters where the Senate was divided and where, presumably, those in the minority wanted their own or their opponents' votes shown on the historical record. There is no record of any debate or dissension in the Senate on the treaty.

President Adams signed the treaty and proclaimed it to the nation on June 10, 1797. His message of transmission was a bit unusual:

Now be it known, That I John Adams, President of the United States of America, having seen and considered the said Treaty do, by and with the advice and consent of the Senate, accept, ratify, and confirm the same, and every clause and article thereof. And to the End that the said Treaty may be observed and performed with good Faith on the part of the United States, I have ordered the premises to be made public; And I do hereby enjoin and require all persons bearing office civil or military within the United States, and all other citizens or inhabitants thereof, faithfully to observe and fulfil [sic] the said Treaty and every clause and article thereof.

The wording of the treaty, including its now famous Article 11, as well as Adams's proclamation, was printed in newspapers of the day. Originals of some of those newspapers survive (for example, the Philadelphia *Gazette and Universal Daily Advertiser* for Saturday, June 17, 1797); microform copies of others can be read at the Library of Congress.

The treaty was short—only three or four pages long in most texts, even including the ceremonial signature section—so the famous Article 11 was not likely to have been overlooked. Searches of the newspapers for the days and weeks after the treaty language was published reveal no record of any public dispute or protest over Article 11.

Also of possible interest is the fate of the senators who voted that day that the US "government is not in any sense founded on the Christian Religion." None seems to have paid a political price for his vote; among the twenty-three were many who were reelected as senators. One senator, Theodore Sedgewick of Massachusetts, went on to become Speaker of the House (Henry Clay is the only other American in history to be first a senator, then Speaker). Another, Isaac Tichenor, became governor of Vermont, and then returned to the Senate for many years. A Georgia senator, Josiah Tattnall, did not return to the Senate, but he did serve thereafter as one of the youngest governors in Georgia's history and has a county in Georgia and a number of streets, squares, and the like named after him. Any who might be tempted to recommend the senators or Adams as freethought heroes for their actions with regard to the Treaty of Tripoli should instead reflect with satisfaction that this secular declaration was apparently considered ordinary and was broadly known and accepted at the time. There seems to have been no confusion then about whether the American government was or should be secular.

BIBLIOGRAPHY

Boller, Paul F. *George Washington and Religion*. Dallas: Southern Methodist University Press, 1963.

Boston, Rob. "A Tangled Tale of Pirates, a Poet and the True Meaning of the First Amendment." *Church & State* 50, no. 6 (1997).

Buckner, Edward M., and Michael E. Buckner, eds. *Quotations That Support the Separation of State and Church*. 2nd ed. Atlanta: Atlanta Freethought Society, 1995.

Claussen, Martin P., ed. *The Journal of the Senate, including The Journal of the Executive Proceedings of the Senate, John Adams Administration, 1797–1801, Vol. 1: Fifth Congress, First Session; March-July, 1797*. Wilmington, DE: Michael Glazier, 1977.

Miller, Hunter, ed. "Treaty of Peace and Friendship between The United States and the Bey and Subjects of Tripoli of Barbary." In *Treaties and Other International Acts of the United States of America. Vol. 2. Documents 1–40: 1776–1818*. Washington, DC: US Government Printing Office, 1931.

Walker, Jim. "Little-Known US Document Signed by President Adams Proclaims America's Government Is Secular." *Early America Review* 2, no. 1 (Summer 1997).

ED BUCKNER

THE TRUTH SEEKER. The world's oldest FREETHOUGHT publication, *The Truth Seeker* was founded in 1873 by DeRobigne Mortimer BENNETT and his wife, Mary Wicks Bennett, in Paris, Illinois. D. M. Bennett was a former Shaker and successful businessman who made and lost several small fortunes before trying his hand at publishing. Inspired by Thomas PAINE, the Revolutionary hero and author of *The Age of Reason*, Bennett promoted freethought (and himself) like no one before or since. "We embrace, as in one brotherhood Liberals, Free Religionists, Rationalists [see RATIONALISM], Spiritualists [see SPIRITUALISM AND UNBELIEF], Unitarians [see UNITARIANISM TO 1961], Friends, Infidels, Freethinkers and in short all who care to think and judge for themselves," Bennett declared in *The Truth Seeker*.

The following year Bennett relocated the publication to New York City, where it continued to thrive and provide a forum for freethinkers for nearly a century. With the financial assistance of Morris Altman, a wealthy New York merchant, Bennett transformed *The Truth Seeker* into the best-known reform journal in America. In 1875 he began a widespread distribution of liberal books, tracts, and pamphlets. The enterprising editor reprinted Viscount Amberly's controversial *Analysis of Religious Belief* and sold *The Elements of Social Science*, an important birth control book by George Drysdale (see BIRTH CONTROL AND UNBELIEF). Bennett was one of the first booksellers in America to furnish readers with the Bhagavad Gita and Theosophist Helena P. Blavatsky's *Isis Unveiled* (see THEOSOPHY). The editor popularized the Darwinian discoveries by serializing Ernest HAECKEL'S *The Doctrine of Filtration, or Descent Theory* in *The Truth Seeker* for three years (see DARWIN, CHARLES; DARWINISM AND UNBELIEF).

By the 1880s *The Truth Seeker* was practically an organization in itself with several thousand subscribers and fiercely loyal partisans. A prolific and provocative writer, Bennett published articles that dramatically chronicled his arrests, trial, imprisonment, and travels around the world. Bennett's "blasphemous" *An Open Letter to Jesus Christ* and *Sinful Saints and Sensual Shepherds*, exposing the immoral and criminal behavior or "black collar crimes" of Christian clergymen, amused freethinkers and infuriated religionists (see BLASPHEMY). "His journalism was of the sort called personal," one of his successors observed. "*The Truth Seeker* was Bennett, and in advertising himself he advertised the paper."

Eugene M. Macdonald became editor after Bennett's death in 1882. The following year *The Truth Seeker* faced a series of crises that nearly caused it to be discontinued. Among freethinkers there existed a broad divergence of opinions as to economic, political, and social questions. Even a letter printed in *The Truth Seeker* by Robert Green INGERSOLL explaining his Republican opinion on political matters caused readers to cancel subscriptions. Macdonald learned early in his career as editor that he had to tread lightly around politics.

During Macdonald's tenure, *The Truth Seeker* remained moderate on economic and political issues, avoiding populism and socialism (see SOCIALISM AND UNBELIEF). It remained steadfast and radical in maintaining separation of church and state. As editor of New York's most outspoken freethought and reform journal, Macdonald learned firsthand the effects of the alliance between church and state. In 1888 the editor was denied the right to vote because of his refusal to swear on the Bible. Eugene Macdonald's tenure as editor coincided with the birth of the militant labor movement in the United States (see LABOR MOVEMENT AND UNBELIEF). *The Truth Seeker* never hesitated in its attack on monopoly capitalists and supported labor reform and workers' rights. As early as 1877, D. M. Bennett saw a conflict on the horizon between capital and labor and castigated the "designing monopolists" and the "monied aristocracy" who, like Vanderbilt, were "rolling in affluence while the masses are stung with poverty and hunger." Like his mentor, Macdonald recognized the inequities of American society and continued to promote labor reform, and recognized and spoke out against the glaring disparity that he witnessed daily in the city of "magnificence and squalor," as he characterized New York.

In 1886 the Haymarket tragedy attracted widespread newspaper coverage and became a cause célèbre for the nation's freethinkers (see ANARCHISM AND UNBELIEF). During a peaceful gathering of striking workers at Haymarket Square in Chicago, a bomb was thrown, killing several civilians and eight police officers. Although the bomb thrower was never apprehended, the social revolutionaries or "anarchists" who organized the protest were arrested and later hanged. When it was learned that one of the anarchists was a member of the Chicago Liberal League, the religious press began associating anarchism with ATHEISM. The tragedy caused antagonism toward anarchists and freethinkers—dividing the country and creating America's first "Red Scare." It took courage to defend the convicted anarchists whose trial was one of the most unfair in the annals of American jurisprudence. Macdonald, who wrote passionately in defense of Bennett years earlier, maintained that the Haymarket defendants were convicted for their "opinions" and asserted: "The police by perjury connected the defendants with some wretch who threw a bomb, the lower court by partiality secured their conviction, and the higher court by sophistry sustains the verdict."

Macdonald's philosophy of life was formulated from the teachings of Stephen Pearl Andrews, one of

America's most prominent individualist anarchists and a close friend of Bennett and the Macdonald family. Although Eugene was a lifelong disciple of Andrews's doctrine of individual sovereignty, he had no sympathy for violent extremists. His initial response to the Haymarket tragedy exposed his naïveté when he wrote, "Even in war, no nation would use such horribly murderous weapons as dynamite bombs."

During Macdonald's watch, *The Truth Seeker* aggressively campaigned against church-sponsored laws that restricted citizens from enjoying social activities on Sunday, their only day off from work. Macdonald believed that Sunday laws were some of the most restrictive and menacing laws ever enacted. In 1891 *The Truth Seeker* played a pivotal role in securing the opening of New York museums on Sunday (a major triumph for freethinkers during the late nineteenth century, when religionists had a stranglehold on American society). "We have too much liberty," a clergyman with whom Macdonald debated the archaic Sunday laws declared in a newspaper. But when Macdonald asked the clergyman what "liberty" he would be willing to give up, he had no reply.

It was due to Macdonald's level-headed methods that *The Truth Seeker* kept afloat during the latter part of the nineteenth century. Assessing Macdonald's important contribution to *The Truth Seeker*, his brother George Everett Hussey MACDONALD wrote: "Institutions have their founders, and generally their saviors. Bennett and E. M. Macdonald played those parts. He always kept his balance, never leaning either way to get the favor of radical or conservative, nor committing *The Truth Seeker* to any advocacy but that of Free Thought, Free Speech, and Free Press." Eugene Macdonald died at the age of fifty-four on February 26, 1909. It is fitting that the man who devoted his life to promoting individual sovereignty and fighting for civil liberties for his fellow Americans died in a small village in upstate New York called Liberty.

George E. Macdonald succeeded his brother as editor of *The Truth Seeker*, the only significant freethought publication left in America (the *BOSTON INVESTIGATOR*, the oldest and most influential freethought journal in the nation, had suspended publication in 1904 and merged with *The Truth Seeker*). Freethought was still an unpopular cause and the twentieth century posed a new series of complicated challenges for the movement. In 1909, the year George Macdonald became editor, the centenary of Thomas Paine's death was celebrated. Serving as the primary organ to keep enthusiasm for the author-hero alive, *The Truth Seeker* proudly reported that Paine's influence was "steadily growing." That year also marked the one hundredth anniversary of Charles Darwin's birth. The evolutionist's influence, however, was still being debated and would not come into prominence in America for another decade and a half.

One of the most shocking events to confront the world's freethinkers and reminiscent of the Spanish Inquisition was the execution in 1909 of Francisco FERRER, the freethinking Spanish educator. Ferrer's rationalistic approach to teaching that excluded religious dogma infuriated Spain's powerful and pious government officials. *The Truth Seeker* was in the vanguard in recognizing Ferrer's "modern" philosophy of education and in exposing the injustice suffered by the educator, that Macdonald reported was "instigated by the church." The periodical began publicizing Ferrer's persecution during his trial in 1906; the case became a cause célèbre for intellectuals, scholars, and humanitarians. While the world's leading newspapers and magazines remained mute or indifferent during Ferrer's trial and execution by firing squad, Macdonald aggressively defended the educator and was relentless in his condemnation of the persecutors. *The Truth Seeker* gave voice to the world's freethinkers who were outraged at Ferrer's execution by church and state.

During World War I, free speech was fiercely suppressed in America. Despite difficulties, *The Truth Seeker* refused to let truth become a casualty during the war years. As they did during the Haymarket tragedy and in response to the McKinley assassination, some religious leaders denounced freethought. Outrageous statements by prominent priests and pastors such as "Darwin caused the war" and "atheists will be the first to be shot in the back when forced to go to war by conscription" were reported in *The Truth Seeker*. (George Macdonald's sons volunteered and served honorably.) *The Truth Seeker* remained patriotic, fiercely loyal, and above reproach; nevertheless, it was repeatedly suppressed for advocating SECULARISM. *The Truth Seeker* consistently reported the religious rhetoric of political leaders who claimed to have God on their side. George Macdonald's hard-hitting editorials exposing church graft and his unwavering attacks on the unethical actions of the YMCA and the Salvation Army earned the publication intense scrutiny. After an associate editor took issue with an Illinois governor over a religious argument, the solicitor of the post office in Washington pronounced *The Truth Seeker* "unmailable under the Espionage Act." When the editor of the magazine the *Nation* came to *The Truth Seeker*'s defense, it was also excluded from the United States mail.

The birth of "fundamentalism" in 1922 was initially thought by many freethinkers to be just another innocuous denominational religious movement within the church. But when the "curious phenomenon," as Macdonald described it, declared war on science and began aggressively campaigning against evolution, the editor fought back. Charles Darwin's scientifically established facts of evolution were promoted in *The Truth Seeker* since its inception. "*The Truth Seeker*," Macdonald wrote, "has been in the thick of the fight," and had dealt many effective blows against the champions of obscurantism." Not since D. M. Bennett's 1879 trial had the periodical gone to such an extent as it did while covering the Scopes Trial in Tennessee. Clarence DARROW (a second-generation subscriber) staged a brilliant cross-examination of William Jennings Bryan that filled six columns in *The Truth Seeker*. Some of the nation's newspapers called the trial a "tragedy," others a "comedy." One dubbed it a "comical tragedy." George Macdonald characterized it as "an inquisition" and predicted from the outset that the teacher would be convicted.

By the 1920s *The Truth Seeker* was no longer self-supporting and George Macdonald depended on donations to continue publishing. The stock market crash in 1929 and the subsequent economic collapse forced the editor to curtail production; the weekly became a monthly in 1930. Another dilemma faced by the elderly editor was whom to leave in charge of the publication, a concern neither D. M. Bennett nor Eugene Macdonald had needed to confront. The fact that the periodical was no longer a moneymaking endeavor limited the possibilities of finding a worthy candidate to sit in the editor's chair of what had become the world's oldest freethought publication. "There is admonition against crossing a bridge until you come to it," Macdonald wrote, "but there is a bridge not far ahead, and it may be down."

A militant group of freethinkers emerged in the 1920s. Stifled by Draconian laws restricting free speech during the war, these unremitting atheists lashed out against Roman Catholicism, fundamentalism, and other religious revivals that threatened progress. Their public street speaking and confrontational manner terrified religionists. One of these radicals was Charles Lee SMITH, who began contributing articles to *The Truth Seeker* in 1923 and selling the journal on the streets of New York, where he was arrested three times in 1924. In 1925 Smith, along with two other contributors, Freeman Hopwood and Woolsey TELLER, organized the AMERICAN ASSOCIATION FOR THE ADVANCEMENT OF ATHEISM, or the 4As, as it was known.

In 1937 the eighty-year-old Grand Old Man of Freethought—as George Macdonald is fondly remembered—reluctantly turned the monthly over to Charles Smith. Macdonald did not share Smith's militancy, but he admired his fortitude and determination. "He has lectured and been hissed, debated and lost the decision, taken the aggressive and been repulsed, agitated and landed in jail, talked Atheism and been convicted of blasphemy, attempted the enlightenment of a prophet of God [Aimee Semple McPherson] and been fined for his pains. And he thinks the Four-A's will win the world," the veteran editor wrote. Although George Macdonald did not describe himself as an atheist, he also never denied the accusation. "That means without God," he was quoted as saying by the *New York Times*. "Why should I say I am without a God any more than I would say I am without a devil, a spook or without whatever you can think of?"

George Macdonald continued as editor emeritus and contributed his "Observations" column until his death at the age of eighty-seven on July 13, 1944. "He [Macdonald] was the central and abiding factor in American Freethought for half a century," Smith declared.

"The world owes an enormous debt to the fighters for human freedom," Clarence Darrow wrote about George Macdonald and his fellow freethinkers. "And we cannot suffer their names to be forgotten now that we are reaping the fruits of their intelligence."

Charles Smith was publisher of *The Truth Seeker* from 1937 until 1964. Although Smith was one of America's most courageous atheists, he was also a racist; the once venerable publication became a soapbox for Smith's narrow-minded ideology. In 1964 James Hervey JOHNSON, a San Diego bookstore owner and former county tax assessor who shared Smith's bigotry, bought *The Truth Seeker* and moved it to San Diego. During Johnson's stewardship, *The Truth Seeker* deteriorated into a shoddy, semiliterate sheet filled with his racist rants. Johnson died in 1988, leaving a sizable estate that was placed in trust to finance *The Truth Seeker*, to expose religion against reason, and to publicize his views on religion and health. (Madalyn Murray O'HAIR, America's most notorious atheist, challenged Johnson's will in probate court without success.) Subsequently, Johnson's estate and *The Truth Seeker* have been controlled by lawyers, trustees, and editors with various visions.

Soon after Johnson's death, *The Truth Seeker* was acquired by Bonnie Lange, known as a New Age enthusiast. Lange published a slick periodical that recognized the historical importance of freethought and often paid tribute to Thomas Paine, Robert Green Ingersoll, and D. M. Bennett. Her journal, however, contained more metaphysical speculation than Bennett or the Macdonald brothers would have seen fit to print. After Lange published an informative 125th Anniversary historical issue in 1998, *The Truth Seeker* lapsed into obscurity.

Like most nineteenth- and early twentieth-century freethinkers, D. M. Bennett was inspired by Thomas Paine and believed that religious faith would fade in time under the light of scientific truth. Nevertheless, Bennett knew that superstition was resilient and that his religious opponents were a formidable force. "He asks that we continue the work he left unfinished" is engraved on the Bennett Monument in Green-Wood Cemetery, in Brooklyn, New York (see MONUMENTS TO UNBELIEF). Freethinkers can only hope that someday a rational publisher who shares Thomas Paine's humanitarian ideals will continue D. M. Bennett's work and recommit *The Truth Seeker* to "Free Thought, Free Speech, and Free Press."

BIBLIOGRAPHY

The Truth Seeker: A Journal of Freethought and Reform. 1873–1911. Library of Congress microfilm.

Macdonald, George Everett Hussey. *Fifty Years of Freethought: Story of* The Truth Seeker *from 1875.* 2 vols. New York: Truth Seeker Company, 1929, 1931.

Stein, Gordon. "Charles Lee Smith, One of Freethought's Forgotten Heroes." *Truth Seeker* 125 (1998).

Warren, Sidney. *American Freethought, 1860–1914.* New York: Gordian, 1966.

ROD BRADFORD

TSUN TZU (XUN ZI; ca. 291–238 BCE), Chinese atheist scholar. Also known by his personal name, Kuang, Tsun Tzu is regarded, after Confucius and Mencius, as the third sage in the Confucianist hierarchy (see CONFUCIANISM). By no means as renowned in the West as his predecessors, he never received a Latinized name. His dates are uncertain, but ca. 298–238 BCE has been generally accepted. He seems to have been an educational official in the Shandung province, but spent much of his time in teaching and research. His main writings, which are basically the only source of our knowledge of him, are in the book of which his name is the title, which is a series of essays on a variety of themes. Some of the themes, such as his emphasis on logic, his belief in progress, and his critical analysis of other philosophical schools, have made him more attractive to modern Chinese students than he seems to have been either to his contemporaries or to their successors over the ensuing two millennia. His essays have in fact a much more analytical structure than either the *Analects* of Confucius or Mencius. There is less of the pithiness of these writings, with none of the *Analects*' sometimes cryptic style; Tsun Tzu develops his arguments in a way not dissimilar to Western philosophical writings, pursuing issues logically and consistently.

Because two of his students, Han Fei and Li Ssu, became leading figures in the Legalistic School, Tsun Tzu has sometimes mistakenly been linked with that school, a viewpoint encouraged by the authoritarianism manifested in his teaching and writing. However, his emphasis on *li,* propriety, is essentially that of Confucius. Equally Confucian is his rejection of the word "supernatural" to describe occurrences of an unusual, inexplicable or spectacular nature. He is pre-Humean (see HUME, DAVID) in his rejection of the belief in miracles or ghosts: only if accepting the reality of these phenomena were more rational than rejecting them would he concur. "Ghosts," he wrote, "are imagined by confused people."

Like Confucius, he wrote about *T'ien,* or heaven, and at times used phrases such as "the will of heaven" or even "God's will." It is clear, however, that by these phrases he did not mean a dynamic spiritual entity but rather the world of nature, to which all people belonged and which helped them to live with a steady and unwavering purpose. In order to serve human beings, he said, it was necessary to follow natural laws. In his essay "On Heaven," he wrote: "It is better for us to conquer heaven than to overestimate it. It is better for us to control and use heaven's will than to praise it." The belief that a divine being, God, controlled the world, including human destinies, seemed to him absurd. Those who argued that they had (for example) prayed for rain and it had then rained were treated with bemusement on Tsun Tzu's part: it proved nothing, he said, for it would have rained anyway, even if nobody had prayed for it.

His main area of contention grew out of the question of whether human nature is naturally good or bad. His predecessor a century earlier, Mencius, had presented a forceful case for natural goodness, arguing that it was only society which modified or eroded the goodness with which everyone is born. It was, he argued, as natural to be good as it is for water to flow downhill rather than up. Tsun Tzu held precisely the opposite view. In his essay "The Nature of Man Is Evil," he affirmed: "Men are born with the love of gain. . . . They are filled from birth with the envy and hatred of others." Only by the strict observance of propriety could any person overcome this inherent selfishness. He did not deny that benevolence (Confucius's *jen*) was desirable, but asserted: "One cannot be brought up without propriety, a business cannot be done without propriety." Linked with this idea, he taught in another essay that morality should be the product of education, since schools existed to shape character. He thus establishes himself as a forerunner of Dr. Thomas Arnold, groundbreaking headmaster of Rugby School, England, in the nineteenth century. It is an idea based on ARISTOTLE's view that one of the chief functions of the state is to make the people good. Because of this view, he has often been compared to Thomas HOBBES, in contrast with Mencius's Jean-Jacques ROUSSEAU.

Until the twentieth century, Tsun Tzu held a secondary role in Chinese esteem, but his humanistic views have enhanced his reputation greatly in modern China. His stress on the need for self-reliance, together with his view that everything which is of value is the result of human effort, have in fact raised him today to a position of considerable eminence.

RAY BILLINGTON

TURMEL, JOSEPH (1859–1943), French ex-priest and FREETHOUGHT writer. Born into a poor and pious family in Rennes, France, Joseph Turmel was selected at school by a priest to pursue religious studies at the Rennes Great Seminary. He received higher education at the Angers Catholic Faculty, was ordained in June 1882, and in August of that year appointed professor of theology at the Rennes Great Seminary. He was then as fervent a believer as he was a clever and meticulous scholar.

In 1886, having made numerous translations from Hebrew, Greek, Latin, and German theological texts, he suffered a crisis of faith that definitively placed any belief in any religious dogma beyond his reach. He succeeded in hiding his new SKEPTICISM until 1892, when he was denounced by a student. After eighteen months in what amounted to ecclesiastical prison, he was dismissed from his professorial position but—at this time—still permitted to remain within the Catholic Church.

By 1898 he had begun to publish in the *Revue d'Histoire et de Littérature Religieuse* (RHLR). Directed clandestinely by the scholar and philosopher Alfred Firmin LOISY, RHLR provided a forum in which Catholic modernists could challenge—often defy—conservative theologians of the Roman church.

Until 1908 Turmel split his output between publishing under his own name in official reviews and under a series of pseudonyms, mainly in RHLR. Among his early pseudonyms were Herzog for his writings about the Virgin, and Dupin for his writings on the Trinity. In 1908 Pope Pius X condemned all forms of modernism in an encyclical; Loisy was excommunicated and Turmel was severely admonished. Until 1931 he would publish exclusively under pseudonyms (some fifteen), principally Coulange, Lagarde, Delafosse, Perrin, and Galerand.

In 1930 he was caught up in the conflict between Pius XI and Action Française, a political movement stressing nationalism and French sovereignty in the face of papal authority. Among those conspicuous in this group was Charost, archbishop of Rennes, who had secretly been protecting Turmel against further sanctions. Unprotected, Turmel was excommunicated *vitandus*—that is, by name, publicly and by judicial sentence, the most severe form of excommunication—and defrocked. Defying the pope, Turmel continued to affect priestly vestments until his death.

He published a series of works for the publisher Rieder, and for the review *L'Idée Libre* founded by Andre LORULOT. He affiliated with the National Federation of Freethinkers (see FRANCE, UNBELIEF IN) in 1935 and also served as honorary president of the Rennes Freethinkers Association. His most important work was *Histoire des dogmes* in six volumes, published by Rieder in 1935–37.

Turmel's motto was "Having been martyred for the truth, I shall be its apostle." A good summary of his materialist philosophy is given in his *Dieu*: "If a God exists, that's to say, a person endowed with intelligence and will, to whom belongs world government, this God has produced knowingly and deliberately all the evil which we are so harshly afflicted with; he is entirely responsible for this evil: God is a monster, he fills us with horror. But God does not exist. The world runs governed by mechanical laws of universal energy which exclude any outside intervention."

Turmel is well remembered. A colloquium was organized in Rennes to mark the sixtieth anniversary of his death. In addition to publishing the colloquium proceedings, several of his main books were reissued, including his *Autobiographie*, *Les Religions*, *Apocalypse et Quatrième Evangile*, and *La Sainte Vierge dans l'Histoire*. Contemporary study of his works reveals Turmel as a true materialist without any faith, a continuous defender of French institutional ANTICLERICALISM (*LAÏCITÉ*) as realized in the French state and its schools since 1905.

MICHEL LE NORMAND

UNBELIEF AND IRRELIGION, EMPIRICAL STUDY AND NEGLECT OF. There have been countless conceptual, theoretical, historical, apologetic, critical, and philosophical treatments of unbelief, irreligion, and related topics. Direct empirical studies, however, are comparatively few. There are numerous reviews of empirical research on religion, the religious, and religiosity, but there is no comprehensive summary of what available data do and do not reveal about the nature, antecedents, and correlates of affirmative unbelief and irreligion.

In his 1985 *Encyclopedia of Unbelief* entry "The Geography of Unbelief," William M. Newman observed that "unbelief has rarely been the direct focus of empirical studies in the social sciences" and that "information [on unbelief] typically is gleaned as a residual from studies of religious belief, identity, and affiliation." This remains true to the present. Findings can be culled from research on religiosity, the "unchurched," "nones" (those who declare no religious preference), "apostates," and religious doubt, among others. But what these tell us about the affirmatively irreligious varies greatly and must be carefully qualified. The aim here is to provide a map of the terrain where pertinent data may be found. Following this, some reasons for the general absence of direct research on irreligion and directions for future research are considered.

"Unbelief" and "Irreligion." Imprecise and inconsistent use of terminology is an obstacle to meaningful accumulation of knowledge on these topics. Reflecting a substantive definition of "religion," primary interest here lies with individuals who substantially or affirmatively (1) eschew theistic, transcendent, or supernatural worldviews; (2) consider such matters unknown, unknowable, or meaningless; and (3) do not identify with "traditions" or affiliate with institutions that embrace such worldviews. "Unbelief" and "unbelievers" reflect the first two of these criteria; "irreligion" and "irreligious" reflect all three (see EUPRAXSOPHY).

As in these definitions, language and long intellectual tradition in the West frame these subjects in terms of "religion" and its negation. It is useful to bear in mind, however, that what we wish to understand is not merely the absence or rejection of something called religion. We also wish to understand ways of conceptualizing and approaching human life that represent positive *alternatives* to those that involve theism, transcendentalism, or supernaturalism.

Religion Research. The fact that "religion" represents both a general field of inquiry concerning existential worldviews, and also very particular *kinds* of worldviews, has long been problematic. Empirical research bearing on alternatives to substantively religious approaches is largely to be found in religion research, the scientific study of religion, and the anthropology, sociology, or psychology of religion, among others. Since the primary focus in these fields is religion—variously defined—unbelief, irreligion, and related topics receive limited attention as direct subjects of inquiry. For example, the first twenty-year index (1961–81) of the *Journal for the Scientific Study of Religion* listed only 9 of 562 titles relevant to the affirmatively irreligious, such as "apostates" or "religious defectors," "nones" or "non-affiliates," the "unchurched" and "secularists." Apart from "secularization," no summary categories on irreligion or related concepts appeared. Rather, most of these studies appeared under categories such as "religiosity," "religious behavior," and "socioeconomic status and religion."

There has been some increase in attention to topics such as "the unchurched," "apostates" (or religious "defection," "disaffiliation, and "switching"), "nones," and religious doubt in the past two decades. But there is still little direct focus on the affirmatively irreligious, whether "unlabeled" or "labeled" (as atheists, agnostics, religious skeptics, rationalists, humanists, freethinkers, and so on). For example, of some 150 articles that appeared from 1989 to 2004 in the annual publication, *Research in the Social Scientific Study of Religion*, one title referred to "religious doubt" and another to "belief and unbelief." Additionally, one longitudinal study, five articles on secularization, and twelve on religiosity provided data of widely varying relevance to irreligion. Among the latter were articles on religiosity and secularization in Europe that indicate greater attention to atheist, agnostic, scientific, and other nonreligious worldviews among European social scientists. Yet in two articles concerning future directions for religion research, no mention is made of irreligion or any related topic.

The Unchurched and Apostates. The "unchurched" include all who report that they do not affiliate with religious institutions or have not regularly attended formal services for a period of time (such as six months or a year), regardless of beliefs. The category is therefore quite broad, including both religious believers and unbelievers. Depending upon definitions, year of study, and sampling techniques, estimates of the unchurched range from 35 to 50 percent of the US population.

Typologies of the unchurched may reflect constituent unbelievers, as in J. Russell Hale's "true unbelievers" category (subdivided into "atheists/agnostics," "deists/rationalists," and "humanists/secularists"). But little attention is typically devoted to the irreligious subset. Aggregate data on the unchurched provide general indications about those who are relatively less religious (for example, with respect to geographical distribution or population changes in general religiosity over time). But they do not provide an accurate picture of the irreligious. A substantial majority of the unchurched in the United

States, for example, pray, believe that Jesus Christ was the son of God, and desire religious training for their children.

Apostasy (or "religious defection" or "disaffiliation") refers to the abandonment of prior religious beliefs, affiliation, or identity at some point in life. Loss of apostates' religious participation is of concern to the churches they have left regardless of the stances they have adopted. With respect to understanding the irreligious, however, the relevance of data on apostates depends upon the orientation they have adopted by the time they are studied (such as unaffiliated religious belief, no stated religious preference, or affirmative irreligion). Among apostates who simply report no religious preference, several types have been identified that vary widely in religious beliefs and behavior, moral views, and lifestyles. In general, such individuals tend to be more often male than female, young, unmarried, well educated, and morally or politically liberal.

Psychologist Bruce Hunsberger and his colleagues have provided more relevant data in a series of studies of Canadian high school and college students who adopt substantially irreligious stances. They tend to measure low in authoritarianism, high in complexity of thinking, and they exhibit a more gradual process of attitude change that begins earlier in life than among religious converts. Weak or inconsistent findings emerge concerning psychological and social adjustment (such as reported happiness, optimism, or self-esteem). Earlier findings that suggested poor relations between young apostates with no religious preference and parents or other authority figures are not borne out by Hunsberger's data on irreligious apostates.

Survey Research—of "Nones" and "Nots." Survey research has become a valuable tool for mapping the nature, prevalence, temporal shifts, and geographical or cultural distribution of religious beliefs, affiliation, and related variables. Data on unbelief and irreligion are residuals of this work. Further, in survey research, findings follow form (of the questions put to respondents). For example, a widely cited Gallup "yes-no" measure has pegged US believers in God (or a higher power) in the mid–90 percent range for decades. But as George Bishop has illustrated, more detailed questions produce very different results.

When Gallup offered more options in three separate surveys, 8 to 10 percent of respondents said, "Don't really think there is a God," "Don't really know what to think," or "Don't know." When the Barna Group put even more nuanced questions to respondents about "God" in 1994, 67 percent subscribed to a traditional theistic conception (with an additional 3 percent endorsing polytheism), 10 percent thought of God as "a state of higher consciousness that people can reach," 8 percent endorsed "the total realization of personal human potential" (with an additional 3 percent feeling that "everyone is God"), 8 percent professed ignorance on the matter, and 2 percent said "no such thing." Religiosity and irreligiosity are better viewed as complex and continuous rather than as unidimensional or categorical variables. This said, finer-grained methods, analysis, *and* reporting are required to more meaningfully ascertain the prevalence of substantially nonreligious worldviews.

The most prevalent survey category relevant to the irreligious is known as "nones," a term that indicates that this is a function of survey method rather than a self-description. It refers to respondents who do not choose or volunteer a specific religious affiliation or identification, or who state "no religious preference" or "no religion." Included are the unaffiliated religious or "unchurched believers," atheists, and many gradations of belief and behavior in between. Data from sources such as the National Opinion Research Center's General Social Survey indicate that substantial percentages of "nones" hold religious beliefs, pray, or express confidence in the value of organized religion despite their lack of religious preference. As with the unchurched, data on "nones" supply suggestive findings about the relatively less religious, but not a detailed picture of the attitudes or behavior of those who are affirmatively irreligious. In other words, "nones" include, but are not equivalent to, "nots" (the affirmatively irreligious).

In a review of research from the 1950s to 1984, Norvall Glenn found that "nones" gradually increased from roughly 2 to 7 or 8 percent of the US population. In the 1990s a more rapid rise was observed from 7–8 to 14–15 percent in several sources, such as the 2001 American Religious Identification Survey (ARIS) and the General Social Survey (GSS). Michael Hout and Claude Fischer have offered evidence that the more recent increase may be attributable, in part, to a political alienation effect: as religious conservatism has grown in public prominence and political activity in the United States, some religious liberals may be distancing themselves from the phenomenon by relinquishing public religious identity or affiliation.

With respect to the incidence of "nots," analysis of specific survey items on religious beliefs, behavior, and identification yields useful but inconclusive results. Based on ARIS data, Keysar, Mayer, and Kosmin found that 3 percent of Americans profess "no religion," disagree that "God exists," and consider themselves secular rather than religious. GSS data indicate that from 1988 to 2002, an average of 6.5 percent of Americans said that they either "don't believe in God" or "don't know . . . and don't believe there is any way to find out." The Barna Group found that in annual surveys from 1995 to 2004, 7 to 13 percent of respondents were "atheist," "agnostic," or held "no religious faith." However, as many as 2 percent of these attended churches, 13 percent believed in the accuracy of the Bible, and 19 percent prayed. Work is clearly needed to consistently differentiate and accurately map the incidence of distinguishable forms of irreligion with respect to beliefs, behavior, and self-descriptions.

National surveys are perhaps not the most efficient method for studying the irreligious in depth, particularly in the United States. It is equally true, however, that organized irreligious populations (e.g., atheists, agnostics, religious skeptics, and secular humanists, among others) remain notably underresearched.

Direct studies of affirmatively irreligious populations in the United States are so rare that one of the most frequently cited is a report on members of an atheist organization—published in 1932. The finding for which this study is most often cited is that an unreported number of respondents under twenty years of age indicated a greater incidence of parental loss than in the general population at that time. Whether this is representative of other atheist or irreligious populations is unknown. It is not supported by Altemeyer and Hunsberger's data on young irreligious apostates. (It should be noted, too, that Vetter and Green's young atheist cohort would have spent their formative years in the World War I era—a time of pervasive cultural doubt and family loss in the West. Historical and cultural factors have powerful generational effects on religious and irreligious beliefs.)

One of the most valuable populations may be American scientists (especially behavioral and social scientists). James H. LEUBA's pioneering surveys of belief and disbelief in a personal God and immortality among US scientists suggested that the scientific community holds one of the largest concentrations of substantially irreligious individuals (see SCIENTISTS, UNBELIEF AMONG). Leuba's findings in 1914 and 1933 that a majority of the American scientists he surveyed did not affirm beliefs in a personal God or immortality, and that such beliefs were substantially rarer among "elite" than "lesser" scientists, were generally replicated in the 1990s. The methodology employed, however, was admittedly narrow in scope.

Subsequent research has addressed some aspects of academicians' (ir)religiosity. In general, academicians tend to be less religious than the general American population. Those who are more eminent or productive, committed to critical thought, intellectualism, or a "scholarly perspective" of open-ended inquiry, tend to be less religious. Consonant with Leuba's findings, disciplines in which religion is studied as a natural phenomenon (e.g., the behavioral and social sciences) tend more to attract and reinforce irreligious individuals (than the natural sciences).

Many questions remain, however, about the variety, content, correlates, and consequences of scientists' worldviews. In most of this research, (ir)religiosity is narrowly defined as the presence or absence of "Judeo-Christian" beliefs and behaviors (such as ideology, experience, ritual observance, and doctrinal knowledge). There has been limited differentiation of scientists' worldviews—religious, spiritual, or irreligious. Also, beyond general assessments of scientists' (Judeo-Christian) religiosity and selected antecedents, this population has not been closely scrutinized with respect to health, mental health, and other correlates of religious or irreligious worldviews.

International survey research suggests that culture may play a part in shaping social scientific approaches to religion and irreligion. Sources such as the World Values Survey, International Social Survey, and Pew Global Attitudes Survey consistently place the United States highest among economically developed and Western nations on measures of religious belief, behavior, and importance (with Ireland and Poland close by). Belgium, the Czech Republic, England, France, Germany, the Netherlands and Scandinavian countries are among the lowest. This may account for a greater willingness among European researchers to speak of atheist, agnostic, or "scientific" alternatives to religious worldviews.

Sociology of Religion and Irreligion. Given the theoretical importance of the concept of secularization, more direct attention to the irreligious might be expected in sociology. This has, however, proven to be the case only to a limited extent. This may be attributable to three central sociological preoccupations: functionalism, institutionality, and—paradoxically—secularization.

There has been intermittent theoretical and empirical attention to irreligion in sociology, particularly in the mid- to late twentieth century, when the secularization of "modernizing" societies seemed inevitable and well on its way (see DEMOGRAPHY OF UNBELIEF). Despite several promising starts, however, this never developed into a continuing line of sociological inquiry. Perhaps most notable was the work of Colin Campbell and N. J. Demerath III. Both sought to frame a sociology of irreligion and offered organizational analyses of irreligious movements. The substance of Campbell's *Toward a Sociology of Irreligion* was an analysis of secularist, humanist, and rationalist movements in the United States and England in the nineteenth and twentieth centuries. Contemporary empirical analyses of irreligion "on the ground" have been more rare. Demerath and Thiessen analyzed philosophical and organizational challenges contributing to the demise of a Wisconsin freethought community, for example.

Campbell's greater contribution was his analysis of possible reasons for sociological neglect of irreligion, which he attributed largely to the dominance of a functionalist view of religion as a universal feature of societies. Under the functionalist view "the religious" or "the sacred" are defined so broadly that substantially nonreligious worldviews tend to be overlooked or reconceptualized in such terms. This finds expression in such concepts as "invisible religion," "implicit religion," or "*homo religiosus*." Such expansion of the scope of *religion* tends to deny the epistemological legitimacy of unbelief or irreligion. In turn, this fosters a selective focus on "secular" features of society that lend themselves to analysis as though they were substantively religious (e.g., Marxism, psychoanalysis, environmentalism, or sporting events as "civil religious ceremonies"). This approach produces valuable insights, but it also tends to ignore alternative worldviews, social behavior, and affiliative patterns that are nonreligious or irreligious in meaningful senses. This tendency continues to be evident.

Paradoxically, the sociological view of the secular may discourage research on the irreligious by blurring distinctions between the mere absence of religion (as in purely economic or political activity) and deliberate avoidance or rejection of the religious, sacred, or transcendental. Concern has been, on a grand theoretical scale, with whether modernizing societies inexorably become less religious. In this context, the irreligious become a "deviant" minority footnote among many secular aspects of society.

At present, while European sociologists unavoidably attend to signs of "secularization" in their midst, resumption of an American sociology of irreligion is uncertain. Attention has been drawn to signs of religious resurgence and the challenges this presents to secularization theory. "Rational choice" and economic or market theories of religion stress the prevalence and benefits of religious belief and affiliation. While there are intermittent signs of scholarly attention to secularism, atheists, and related topics, increased focus on the "sacred" or "spiritual" has generally tended to push the "profane" into the background.

The societal and institutional focus of sociology may also work against substantial attention to the irreligious. The minority status and limited, shifting organization of the irreligious may render them too dispersed to be picked up by sociological radar. As a result, research on the irreligious tends to be displaced toward the study of individuals—in psychology. Even there, however, this tends to be more a residual aspect of the "psychology of religion" than a direct subject of empirical inquiry.

Psychology of Religion, Religiosity, Doubt, and Unbelief. Inadequate conceptualization and empirical study of unbelief or irreligion in psychology has repeatedly been acknowledged. For example, Paul Pruyser suggested that framing the field in terms of unbelief or irreligion tends toward exclusion rather than recognition of "describable alternatives to a religious point of view." David Wulff questioned the belief/unbelief dichotomy, suggesting that this masks a rich range of belief systems and associated behavior. He also noted that prevalent use of fixed-item questionnaires tends to mask the range of individual differences and types, suggesting greater use of idiographic techniques. This is found in Altemeyer and Hunsberger's study of young apostates or European work on atheists and other unbelievers. These are, however, exceptions rather than the norm. Major texts in psychology and the psychology of religion typically provide few, if any, references or index entries pertaining to unbelief or the irreligious.

"Religious doubt" figured prominently in the early history of the field. However, this reflected a prevalent view of such doubt as a natural, but transient, aspect of human development that, in normal circumstances, gives way to more mature religious commitment. This perspective continues to be evident today. Indeed, most psychological research on religious doubt or apostasy has focused on adolescents and young adults. Longitudinal research provides evidence of both stability and change in religious and irreligious orientations. And yet virtually no in-depth research with substantial samples of stable, long-term irreligious adults has been done.

The greatest vein of relevant information may be found in the large and rapidly growing literature on antecedents, correlates, and consequences of religiosity. This is, however, as much a minefield as a mine for data on the irreligious. Religiosity (assessed in various ways) has been correlated with measures of mental and physical health, coping styles, social behavior, life satisfaction, altruism, authoritarianism, prejudice, and so on. Findings present a positive-trending, but complex and inconsistent, picture of the relationship between varying forms or levels of religiosity and such variables.

As in survey research on "nones," while suggestive data about the relatively less religious can be culled from this work, relevance to the affirmatively irreligious is variable. Samples typically represent the general population, religious affiliates, college students, or special classes of individuals (e.g., medical patients). "Nonreligious" samples or control groups are frequently tantamount to "nones," with limited representation of substantially or affirmatively irreligious individuals. "Low religiosity" is a relative measure based on self-reports or scalar assessments of religious beliefs, behavior, and affiliation. Its meaning shifts with the nature of the underlying sample: low religiosity among religious affiliates is something apart from affirmative irreligion. Here as elsewhere, substantial samples of self-described atheists, agnostics, religious skeptics, secular humanists, or philosophical naturalists are rare. What is required is a painstaking analysis of studies and findings that are and are not pertinent to the irreligious.

The study of "mature" religion is pertinent. Gordon Allport provided an impetus for research on the topic by contrasting mature with immature forms of religiosity. These were further developed as "intrinsic" ("ends") and "extrinsic" ("means") religion. Batson added a third— "quest"—form of religiosity that is more searching and skeptical in nature. It is notable, however, that a parallel notion of "mature" unbelief or irreligion has never emerged. In fact, there is a noticeable tendency in some quarters to characterize secular, skeptical, scientific, naturalistic, or irreligious worldviews as puerile, myopic, pathological, or intrinsically inferior to the religious. Frank Barron suggested a distinction between "fundamentalist" and "enlightened" belief *and* unbelief. He offered a self-report scale and limited data employing it, but this has never been developed further.

Explaining the Neglect. The comparative size and cultural or political significance of the irreligious population may provide part of the explanation for empirical neglect (particularly in the United States). However, as Campbell observed, in absolute terms, the numbers of the irreligious are not negligible, whether in the United States or in countries with less religious populations.

Relatively weak organization of the irreligious may play a part. However, while specific irreligious movements and organizations have shifted over time, some have always existed since the emergence of the behavioral and social sciences (e.g., atheist, humanist, rationalist, secularist groups and organizations). They have been notably under-researched. Further, one of the largest accessible populations, that of irreligious scientists, has been studied only superficially.

Methodological lethargy may play a part. College students are quite possibly the most researched population, in part because they are conveniently at hand in the academy. Fieldwork is more demanding, especially with dispersed target populations. Yet researchers in many disciplines do go into the field or collaborate with a variety of institutions outside the academy (e.g., hospitals, clinics, churches) to study religiosity, religious organizations, and even small-scale sects, "cults," and new religious movements. There is more involved.

Campbell has suggested that the irreligiosity of many scientists may have rendered the phenomenon "too close to see." There are signs that naturalistic or other nonreligious worldviews are diminished or trivialized by some scholars—even "secular" ones. Boredom may be involved: newly emerging religious sects or "cults" are perhaps more novel and intriguing than "Enlightenment-style" worldviews, widely considered passé in "postmodern" intellectual circles. However, it has been in both periods of apparent secularization and religious resurgence that we find little direct empirical focus on the irreligious.

Cultural factors may be at work. A noticeable propensity for European researchers to focus more theoretical and empirical attention on irreligious individuals and worldviews may reflect differences in the prevalence and historical salience of such views. However, the volume and nature of empirical attention to the irreligious on both sides of the Atlantic has been limited.

Linguistic convention and intellectual heritage in the West concerning religion may tend to skew thinking about substantively nonreligious alternatives. As previously noted, there is a tendency in some quarters to define religiosity in such broad functional terms that to be human is unavoidably to be "religious." There is a need for a revised framework and lexicon that accords *positive* epistemological legitimacy to forms of substantive irreligion and allows for finer, yet consistent, discrimination among types of worldviews and associated behavior.

What Is to Be Learned? Whatever the explanations, limited research attention to the irreligious cannot be attributed to the possession of sufficient knowledge. Innumerable questions remain wholly or partially unanswered, such as:

- Why, when religiosity is so prevalent and the psychological rewards are widely promoted, do many individuals adopt and remain committed to irreligious worldviews?
- What distinguishable nonreligious or irreligious worldviews can be identified? What are their shared and differentiating attributes? How widely is each held?
- Is it meaningful to distinguish between "mature" or "immature," "positive" or "negative," "enlightened" or "fundamentalist" forms of unbelief or irreligion? If so, what are the antecedents, correlates, and consequences of such orientations (such as family background, prior religious experience, physical and mental health, personality characteristics, life satisfaction, social adjustment, or moral/ethical ideas and behavior)?
- What are the types, contents, antecedents, and correlates of scientists' worldviews?
- What are the patterns of social behavior and organizational affiliation among the irreligious? To what extent is there evidence of reduced social need among such individuals? Alternatively, to what extent do patterns of affiliation reflect philosophy, with social needs met by involvement in groups, organizations, or affiliative formats other than explicitly religious or irreligious ones?
- Are there identifiable differences between unbelievers who affiliate with organizations pertinent to their worldviews and those who do not?

Conclusion. There is need for change in the ways we conceptualize, categorize, and study those who hold positive alternatives to religious worldviews, or who affirmatively eschew worldviews and associated institutions concerned with the sacred, divine, transcendent, or supernatural. This call has been made repeatedly since the emergence of the behavioral and social sciences. It will continue to be made given the persistence of such alternatives, the people who affirm them, and the value of better understanding both.

BIBLIOGRAPHY

Allport, Gordon. *The Individual and His Religion*. New York: MacMillan, 1950.

Altemeyer, Bob, and Bruce Hunsberger. *Amazing Conversions: Why Some Turn to Faith and Others Abandon Religion*. Amherst, NY: Prometheus Books, 1997.

Barron, Frank. *Creativity and Psychological Health: Origins of Personal Vitality and Creative Freedom*. New York: D. Van Norstrand, 1963.

Batson, C. Daniel, Patricia Schoenrade, and W. Larry Ventis. *Religion and the Individual: A Social-Psychological Perspective*. Oxford: Oxford University Press, 1993.

Billiet, Jaak, Karel Dobbelaere, Ole Riis, Helena Vilaça, Liliane Voyé, and Jerry Welkenhuysen-Gybels. "Church Commitment and Some Consequences in Western and Central Europe." *Research in the Social Scientific Study of Religion* 14 (2003).

Bishop, George. "The Polls—Trends: Americans' Belief in God." *Public Opinion Quarterly* 63 (1999).

Campbell, Colin. "Analysing the Rejection of Religion." *Social Compass* 24 (1977).

———. *Toward a Sociology of Irreligion*. New York: Herder and Herder, 1972.

Corveleyn, Josef, and Dirk Hutsebaut, eds. *Belief and Unbelief: Psychological Perspectives*. Amsterdam: Rodopi, 1994.

Demerath, Nicholas J., III. "Program and Prolegomena for a Sociology of Irreligion." In *Actes de la X Conference Internationale: Types, Dimensions, et Mesure de la Religiosité*. Rome: Conference Internationale de Sociologie Religieuse, 1969.

Demerath, Nicholas J., III, and Victor Thiessen. "On Spitting against the Wind: Organizational Precariousness and American Irreligion." *American Journal of Sociology* 71 (1966).

Glenn, Norvall D. "The Trend in 'No Religion' Respondents to U. S. National Surveys: Late 1950s to Early 1980s." *Public Opinion Quarterly* 51 (1987).

Hadaway, C. Kirk, and Wade Clark Roof. "Apostasy in American Churches: Evidence from National Survey Data." In *Falling from the Faith: Causes and Consequences of Religious Apostasy*, edited by David G. Bromley. Newbury Park, CA: Sage, 1988.

Hale, J. Russell. *The Unchurched: Who They Are and Why They Stay That Way*. San Francisco: Harper & Row, 1980.

Hoge, Dean R., and Larry G. Keeter. "Determinants of College Teachers' Religious Beliefs and Participation." *Journal for the Scientific Study of Religion* 15, no. 3 (1976).

Hout, Michael, and Claude S. Fischer. "Why More Americans Have No Religious Preference: Politics and Generations." *American Sociological Review* 67 (April 2002).

Hunsberger, Bruce, and Bob Altemeyer. *Atheists*. Amherst, NY: Prometheus Books, 2006.

Hunsberger, Bruce, Barbara Mckenzie, Michael Pratt, and S. Mark Pancer. "Religious Doubt: A Social Psychological Analysis." *Research in the Social Scientific Study of Religion* 5 (1993).

Keysar, Ariela, Egon Mayer, and Barry A. Kosmin. "No Religion: A Profile of America's Unchurched." *Public Perspective* 14 (2003).

Kosmin, Barry A., and Ariela Keysar. *Relgion in a Free Market: Religious and Non-religious Americans*. Ithaca, NY: Paramount Market Publishing, 2006.

Larson, Edward J., and Larry Witham. "Scientists and Religion in America." *Scientific American* 281 (September 1999).

Lehman, Edward C., Jr., and Donald W. Shriver Jr. "Academic Discipline as Predictive of Faculty Religiosity." *Social Forces* 47 (1968).

Newman, William M. "The Social Geography of Unbelief." In *The Encyclopedia of Unbelief*, edited by Gordon Stein. Amherst, NY: Prometheus Books, 1985.

Pruyser, Paul W. "Problems of Definition and Conception in the Psychological Study of Religious Unbelief." In *Changing Perspectives in the Scientific Study of Religion*, edited by Allan W. Eister. New York: John Wiley & Sons, 1992.

Schumaker, John F. *Religion and Mental Health*. Oxford: Oxford University Press, 1992.

Swatos, William H., Jr., and Kevin J. Christianos. "Secularization Theory: The Course of a Concept." *Sociology of Religion* 60, no. 3 (1999).

The Unchurched American . . . 10 Years Later. Princeton, NJ: Princeton Religious Research Center, 1988.

Vetter, George V., and Martin Green. "Personality and Group Factors in the Making of Atheists." *Journal of Abnormal and Social Psychology* 27 (1932).

Wulff, David M. "Beyond Belief and Unbelief." *Research in the Social Scientific Study of Religion* 10 (1999).

FRANK L. PASQUALE

UNBELIEF AROUND THE WORLD. In *Atheism in the World* (2003), this author mapped the prevalence of ATHEISM in the world, accompanied by sketches about the history of atheism. *Atheism* as used in that book is more or less identical with *unbelief* as used in this encyclopedia, and encompasses AGNOSTICISM, FREETHOUGHT, NATURALISM, SECULAR HUMANISM, and SECULARISM. These terms are to some degree synonymous. In fact, the word *HUMANISM* alone, without any preceding adjective, is also often used to imply atheism.

Roots of Atheism. Atheism is in no way limited to the twentieth and twenty-first centuries. Material regarding atheism is easily found in the eighteenth and nineteenth centuries. But when we come to centuries before that, clear evidence of atheism is much scarcer. This does not mean that atheism only emerges in, say, the seventeenth century. But there is no good reason to assume that there have, throughout the history of humankind, always been sizable numbers of atheists. Available evidence around the globe indicates that atheism was rare in the eighteenth century, and even rarer before that.

In ancient Greek the word *atheos* (atheist) was mostly used as a word of abuse. A number of persons were called *atheoi*, "atheists" or "impious persons." In the period before SOCRATES, these persons included XENOPHANES and Anaxagoras, who were accused of impiety. By contrast, such figures as Diogenes of Apollonia, Hippo of Rhegium, PROTAGORAS, Prodicus, Critias, and Diagoras of Melos were accused of atheism.

Most of these persons were not atheists in the sense that they did not believe in God or gods. They believed in God or gods, but not always the "right" god(s). About a number of the preceding persons not much is known, and much of what is known about them is of limited interest for the history of atheism.

One of the persons mentioned above, Protagoras of Abdera, may have been an agnostic rather than a theoretical atheist. According to PLATO, Protagoras attacked the dogmatism of contemporary religion and philosophy. About the gods he reportedly said: "I am unable to know about the gods either that they exist or that they do not, and what form they have. For there are many things that prevent knowledge—both the obscurity of the subject and the shortness of human life."

In saying this, does Protagoras exemplify agnosticism? He claims that he does not know whether gods exist or not. This may be interpreted as saying that Protagoras is neutral with regard to theism and atheism. But it may also be interpreted as saying that Protagoras did not believe in any god, and hence was an atheist.

The best-known philosophers in Greek antiquity, Socrates, Plato, and ARISTOTLE, were not atheists. They believed in a god or in gods. Also, as different from most modern materialists, materialists in Greek antiquity believed in gods (see MATERIALISM, PHILOSOPHICAL).

In our search for the roots of atheism, we next turn to India (see INDIA AND UNBELIEF). India has often been assumed to have a long tradition of atheism. There is hardly any doubt that there have been some atheists in ancient India. In ancient India, atheism, naturalism (the view that nature is the ultimate cause), and materialism are intimately connected.

The author of the Indian atheistic school is believed to be CARVAKA, of whom little is known. The main work supposed to represent his views is the *Brhaspati Sutra* (ca. 500 BCE), which is lost. But it has been assumed that Carvaka's views can be reconstructed from contemporary Jaina and Buddhist texts and also from Hindu sources of the eighth century CE.

Summarizing the preceding, we can say that in ancient India there have been some atheists, but except for Carvaka their names are not known and their oldest writings have been lost. In ancient Greece we have been able to point to the agnostic Protagoras, who may also be called an atheist. But apart from Protagoras, atheists in ancient Greece, if any, have left few clear traces testifying to their existence.

In ancient China, some thinkers seem to have been close to atheism (see James Thrower's *The Alternative Tradition* for evidence for and against; see CHINA, UNBELIEF IN).

An early European atheist was the Italian Giulio Cesare VANINI. He questioned whether an immaterial God can create a material world, and was executed in a cruel way. Another early European atheist was the Pole Kazimierz Lyczynski, who published *De non existentia Dei* (About the Nonexistence of God). Lyczynski, too, was executed.

A third early European atheist is Jean MESLIER. It has been known for many years that Meslier was an atheist. He lived his whole life in the Ardennes in northern France; from 1689 until his death he was a parson (*curé*) in the village of Estrépigny. The importance of Meslier for the French Enlightenment seems to have been limited (see ENLIGHTENMENT, UNBELIEF DURING THE).

After Meslier, atheism and/or materialism (or closely related views) were advocated in France by writers like Julien Offray de LA METTRIE, Denis DIDEROT, Claude Adrien HELVÉTIUS, Baron d'HOLBACH, Jacques André Naigeon, and Pierre John George Cabanis.

Of these, Diderot and Holbach are particularly important. Holbach in 1770 published his important book *Système de la nature* (System of Nature) using the pseudonym Mirabaud. The book was a sensation in France and was sharply criticized by representatives of the church. The book is very clearly atheistic and materialistic and for many years was regarded as the Bible of materialism.

From the nineteenth century many atheists are known, for example, Karl MARX, Friedrich Engels, and Friedrich NIETZSCHE. These names suggest that atheism can be combined with many different basic views, a tendency that has been strengthened in the twentieth century.

Contemporary Atheism. As a whole, until about 1850 atheists qua atheists remained unorganized. To the degree that they were organized at all, they tended to be organized in religious, social, or political groups, not in atheist groups as such. Statistics on atheism prior to 1900 are rare. Even after 1900, statistics giving information about the prevalence of atheism in various countries in the world are either lacking or very uncertain.

The book *Atheism in the World* presents statistics about religion and atheists in 190 countries drawn from the best available sources. Sadly, the "best available" sources are not of high quality. Their treatment of atheism is scanty, in many cases conflicting, and often unreliable. What in this article is called "atheism" in the preceding statistics in a number of cases is called "no religion," "none," or "nonreligious." Often the term "other" occurs, a term that may lump together atheists and agnostics with nontraditional religious believers.

Not all nonreligious persons are atheists or agnostics. Some simply have no opinion about atheism or agnosticism. On the other side, many persons who are counted statistically as religious believers in fact may be atheists or agnostics. There are, therefore, many uncertainties hidden in statistics on religion and atheism.

From these general remarks on contemporary atheism, we turn to some countries which seem to be interesting in accounting for the phenomena of atheism today.

North Korea. According to the available sources, North Korea is the country with the highest percentage of atheists in the world: 68 percent.

This estimate is based on official figures given by a regime which harshly persecutes adherents of traditional religions and, for that matter, many other people. Marshall's *Religious Freedom* does not indicate what "atheism" stands for in North Korea. There is no reason to believe that "atheist" in North Korean statistics stands

for "convinced atheist." Atheism in that country was until the beginning of 2004 and many years earlier embedded in a political system that exerted tight control and largely barred independent public thinking on basic questions. Although there probably have been liberal atheists in North Korea, their voices have not been heard. The practice of human rights was almost nonexistent in North Korea during the 1990s. Traditional religions were repressed, but freethought was too.

China. From North Korea we turn to China, also a closed country, but not as tightly closed as North Korea. Here Marshall places the proportion of atheists at greater than 10 percent. According to other statistical sources, as early as 1980 religious affiliation among Chinese was distributed as follows: nonreligious, 51.9 percent; Chinese folk religion, 20.1 percent; atheist, 12 percent; Buddhist, 8.5 percent; Muslim, 1.4 percent; Christian, 0.1 percent; and other, 6 percent. These statistics suggest a total of 63.9 percent of agnostics or atheists. Barrett et al. count 50.7 percent of Chinese as nonreligious or atheists in 1995, also a high figure.

According to Marshall's *Religious Freedom*, China has to a greater or lesser extent repressed religion throughout the more than fifty years of Communist Party rule. Its aim is said to have been to make religion serve the interests of the communist state until religion disappears from Chinese society. This, according to Marshall, has remained the dominant view. State religious policy, as explained by Chinese president Jiang Zemin in March 1996, was "to actively guide religion so that it can be adapted to socialist society." Ye Xiaowen, head of the Religious Affairs Bureau, in 1996 urged the "handling" of religious matters according to the dictates of Vladimir Ilyich LENIN, and declared that "we will gradually weaken the influence of religion."

Taiwan. Marshall suggests the following statistics for Taiwan: a population of 22.3 million, of whom adherents of "Chinese religion" (Buddhist, Taoist, Confucian) comprise 80 percent; Christians, 4 percent; Muslims, 0.2 percent; atheists, 14 percent; and other, 1.8 percent.

Marshall offers no explanation why the percentage of atheists is so high in this noncommunist country (14 percent). One possibility is that atheism is more compatible with traditional Chinese culture than with traditional Western culture. In spite of tendencies toward secularization in Western countries, Western culture remains strongly influenced by Christianity, with its fear of and hostility toward atheism. We should not forget, however, that Barrett lists a mere 4.3 percent of "secularists" (atheists plus the nonreligious) in Taiwan for 1995. There is, thus, a serious discrepancy between 14 percent atheists in one source and 4.3 percent secularists in another one. They cannot both be right, and in fact, they can both be wrong.

South Korea. Whereas North Koreans remain under strict political surveillance, South Korea developed in a democratic direction beginning in 1987. Prior to 1987,

South Korea also had an authoritarian regime, but in marked contrast to North Korea's, the South Korean regime had a positive attitude toward religion. In 2000, South Korea had a population of 47.3 million. Marshall presents the population breakdown as follows: Christians, 48 percent; Buddhists, 40 percent; Confucians, 3 percent; and Shamanists, adherents of *Ch'ondogyo*, and others, 9 percent. These statistics suggest that at the end of the 1990s, the percentage of atheists in South Korea was less than 9 percent.

But a breakdown in *Britannica Book of the Year* paints a quite different picture: "religious," 51.1 percent (Buddhist, 23.3 percent; Protestant, 19.8 percent; Roman Catholic, 6.7 percent; Confucian, 0.4 percent; and traditional and other religions, 0.9 percent), with the "nonreligious" making up 48.9 percent. If these figures are correct, then South Korea is almost equally divided between the "religious" and the "nonreligious."

Meanwhile Barrett, an explicitly Christian source, shows only 1.6 percent secularists in South Korea in 1995. The discrepancy between these three figures (or sets of figures) is extreme.

Japan. The situation is similar in Japan. In 2000 its population was 126.9 million, with no official religion. Marshall gives the following breakdown: Buddhist, 49 percent; Shinto, 45 percent; Christian, 1 percent; and other, 5 percent. *Britannica Book of the Year* claims Shinto and related religions, 51.3 percent; Buddhism, 38.3 percent; Christian, 1.2 percent; and other, 9.2 percent. Meanwhile Barrett et al. find 12.9 percent secularists in Japan for 1995.

Japan is a country strongly influenced by Chinese culture with a high level of religious freedom. Despite vigorous missionary activity, Christianity has not been able to convert more than about 1 percent of the population. The percentage of atheists is quite uncertain. Atheists are generally lumped together with "other" groups credited with making up 5 to 9.2 percent of the population. Yet as noted above, Barrett et al. give a 12.9 percent figure as either atheistic or nonreligious. For his part, Marshall notes that "in Japan many people adhere to more than one religion: the total number of adherents is about twice the population." Thus, the percentage of atheists in Japan is quite uncertain, at the end of the 1990s comprising anywhere between 5 and 13 percent of the population.

As Buddhism has a central place in traditional Japanese culture, it may be noted that Buddhism in its traditional tenets does not presuppose any almighty god. Buddhism has sometimes been called an atheistic religion. Though this is misleading, Buddhism is in theory less negative toward atheism than Western religions like Christianity, Islam, and Judaism. Many atheists may feel at home in Buddhism, especially if they agree with traditional Buddhist tenets. So it is quite possible that some, even many, of the claimed 49 percent of Japanese who are Buddhists may also be atheists.

Similarly, many of the 40 percent Buddhists in South Korea may be atheists. The low percentage of Buddhists in North Korea, only 2 percent, may be due to the limited freedom of religion and belief in that country.

Percentages of Atheists. The same lack of freedom of religion and belief in North Korea may lead us to look at the figure of 68 percent atheists given for that country with suspicion. If we disregard the dubious case of North Korea and try to assess the percentages of atheists in the remaining countries, Marshall's *Religious Freedom in the World* suggests the following order:

1.	Latvia	43.7 percent
2.	Cuba	40 percent
3.	Estonia	39 percent
4.	Russia	32.1 percent
5.	Netherlands	30 percent
6.	Moldova	28.1 percent
7.	Belarus	27.7 percent
8.	Germany	27 percent
9.	Uzbekistan	25.5 percent
10.	Ukraine	25.3 percent
11.	Kazakhstan	23 percent
12.	Belgium	20 percent
13.	Armenia	17.7 percent
14.	Georgia	15 percent
15.	Singapore	14.3 percent
16.	Romania	14 percent
17.	Taiwan	14 percent
18.	Lithuania	13.1 percent
19.	Spain	13 percent
20.	Hungary	12.5 percent
21.	Finland	12 percent
22.	United States	11 percent
23.	China	10+ percent
24.	Vietnam	10 percent
25.	Austria	9 percent
26.	France	9 percent
27.	United Kingdom	5 percent
28.	Norway	3.2 percent
29.	Brazil	3 percent

Even among these figures, many are probably erroneous, as Marshall does not maintain any consistent definition of "atheist" from country to country. For example, his statistics for Hungary (12.5 percent) actually reflect a 12.5 percent minority categorized as "nonreligious/other." This category may include religious believers as well as atheists and agnostics.

It will be apparent that many of the countries with large percentages of atheists have been under the influence of Soviet communism: Latvia, Cuba, Estonia, Russia, Moldova, Belarus, Uzbekistan, Ukraine, Kazakhstan, Armenia, Georgia, Romania, Lithuania, and Hungary. Countries like China and Vietnam nowadays exhibit a mixture of communism and capitalism. Still, the high (or fairly high) percentages of atheists in these countries can perhaps partly be explained by communist influence.

But note that according to Marshall, Bulgaria, for many years within the Soviet sphere of influence, had few atheists, perhaps less than 1 percent (classified under the category "other"). Poland, too, seems to have few atheists, the category "other" comprising just 1.7 percent of the population.

As for the former Soviet Union, Armenia is an interesting case. In the year 301, Armenia was the first state in history to adopt Christianity as its official religion. The Armenian Apostolic Church (78.5 percent) is still the largest religious community in Armenia. The second largest group in Armenia is the group of atheists and agnostics (17.7 percent).

Yet it will be seen that other countries with high percentages of atheists belong to the liberal Western sphere: the Netherlands, Germany, Belgium, Spain, Finland, and Austria. Though East Germany was strongly influenced by Soviet communism, the other countries in this group have no such background.

As far as evidence is available, there generally seem to be few atheists (less than 2 percent) in Islamic countries and in sub-Saharan Africa. An exception is Uzbekistan, with 68.2 percent Muslims and 25.5 percent "nonreligious/other." The human rights situation in Uzbekistan was in 1999 and for many years previously quite bad; Marshall gives the country a low religious freedom rating.

Another former Soviet republic, Kazakhstan, has a mixed population, with 47 percent Muslim, 25 percent Russian Orthodox, and 23 percent "other." As a result of Stalinist purges and enforced Slavic immigration during the Soviet era, ethnic Kazakhs constitute only about 45 percent of the population. Russians and Ukrainians constitute 35 percent. Approximately 80 percent of the Kazakhs self-identify as Muslims, for many a mainly nominal affiliation. About 60 percent of the Russians and Ukrainians identify themselves with the dominant Orthodox Church, also generally a nominal affiliation. Marshall gives no information about the 23 percent who are classified as "other," but probably many of them are atheists. The human rights situation in Kazakhstan in 1999 was not good, but somewhat better than Uzbekistan.

Soviet atheism may have had limited influence in Azerbaijan. In this country 95 percent are nominally Muslim, whereas according to Marshall less than 1 percent seem to be atheists. Yet Barrett et al. put the figure of atheists and nonreligious in Azerbaijan in 1995 at 11.7 percent, which is quite high for a Muslim country.

A similar situation prevails in Turkmenistan, with a putative 89 percent Muslims and 9 percent Eastern Orthodox. Apparently there are few atheists in this country. But again, Barrett et al. put the figure of atheists or nonreligious in 1995 at 11.7 percent. Freedom of religion in this country has for many years been very limited. In terms of human rights, Turkmenistan has for

many years been one of the most repressive of the former Soviet republics.

Still another former Soviet republic, the Kyrgyz Republic, is said by Marshall to house few atheists. The statistics mention 75 percent Muslim, 20 percent Russian Orthodox, and 5 percent other religious groups. There is no separate category of atheists who are counted as members of religious groups. But again, Barrett et al. put the atheist or nonreligious population in this former Soviet republic in 1995 at 29.6 percent, thus quite high.

Atheism has undoubtedly made an impact in the Islamic parts of the Soviet Union. Kazakhstan, with a religiously mixed population, and Uzbekistan, with a more purely Muslim population, seem to show this. But what about atheism in Muslim countries which have not been under Soviet influence? Let us have a look at some of these Muslim countries.

Available statistics (subject to all of the usual caveats) suggest that Bangladesh is 86.6 percent Muslim, with apparently very few atheists. Egypt is 87.5 percent Muslim, apparently with few atheists. Indonesia is 83 percent Muslim, and has a category of "other" of 1 percent, which probably accomodates atheists but also religious believers (see INDONESIA AND SOME OTHER ISLAMIC COUNTRIES, UNBELIEF IN). Iran has 99 percent Muslims and not more than a handful of other religious believers or atheists. Malaysia, with 58 percent Muslims, has a category "Sikh, animist, other" of 5 percent, and apparently few atheists.

Mauritania is more than 99 percent Muslim, with apparently at most a handful of atheists. Similarly, Morocco is 99.75 percent Muslim, with at most a handful of atheists. Nigeria is 45 percent Muslim, 40 percent Christian, and has a category of "other" of 6 percent. Pakistan is 93 percent Muslim, 7 percent other religious groups, and very few atheists. Saudi Arabia is 97 percent Muslim, about 3 percent other religious groups, and apparently very few atheists. Sudan is 70 percent Muslim, 19 percent Christian, 10 percent traditional religionist, and 1 percent "other or none." Turkey is 99 percent Muslim, with 1 percent other religious groups. Turkey often is claimed to defend a "secular" state which apparently does not include freethought.

Thus, in countries in which Islam is the predominant religion, there generally seem to be few atheists. As a whole, Islam has shown itself to be very resistant not only to atheism, but to all competing religions, including Christianity.

A remarkable exception, however, is Albania, a country not treated by Marshall. This country was predominantly Muslim (about 70 percent) until 1944. In the following years, after communists had taken power, religious believers were persecuted in savage ways. In 1967 all mosques and churches were closed for divine services, and during the period from 1967 until the end of 1990 it was prohibited to import and own religious literature.

The evidence relating to Mongolia is conflicting. Using Marshall as a source, it might seem that Soviet atheism has not had much influence. The population apparently has continued to be Tibetan Buddhist (95.5 percent). Tibetan Buddhism to a large extent represents Buddhist theory and practice as it had developed in India over the first fifteen hundred years of its existence. But according to Barrett et al., in 1995 Mongolia had 40.3 percent atheists or nonreligious. Whom are we to believe?

Although Buddhism is a religion which may be accomodating to atheism, this apparently is not always the case. So Burma (Myanmar), with 87.5 percent Buddhists, seems to have few atheists. Religious groups comprise 99 percent of all Burmese in official statistics, with a category of "other" comprising only 1 percent. Burma was in 2003 (and for many years before) ranked as one of the most repressive countries in the world.

In most Latin American countries, with Cuba and Uruguay as apparent exceptions, there seem to be few atheists (see LATIN AMERICA, UNBELIEF IN). Statistics present Argentina with a category of "other" numbering 2.5 percent; Brazil has a category of "none" with 3 percent. In Chile the category "none" accounts for 6 percent. In the case of Colombia, the "nonreligious" are lumped together with Mormons, Orthodox, and Jehovah's Witnesses, together comprising 2.1 percent. El Salvador has the category "none," 2 percent. Guatemala has the categories "other" and "none," each 1.5 percent. Mexico has the category "none," 3.5 percent. Yet Barrett et al. suggest that Uruguay in 1995 may have had 32.6 percent atheist or nonreligious.

Even though Marshall's *Religious Freedom* is in general not obviously erroneous, there are exceptions. A strange case is Sweden. If we are to believe Marshall's information, there would almost be no atheists in that country. However, according to studies of secularization this author carried out in the 1990s, in 1980 Sweden was already the most secularized of twenty-one Western countries, with 28.7 percent atheists or agnostics.

Another case is Norway. In a recent study of secularism in Norway, this author arrived at the result that at the end of the 1990s at least 10 percent of the population were atheists. The figure may be higher, but it hardly exceeds 30 percent. Yet according to Marshall, at the end of the 1990s only 3.2 percent of the Norwegians did not have any religion. This should be considered, however, in light of statistical studies of members of the Norwegian Lutheran State Church, which indicate that about 17 percent of church members are atheists.

On the whole, it is quite possible that persons who in various countries are counted as, say, Christian, Muslim, Jew, Hindu, or Buddhist, in fact are atheists. But it seems likely that North Korea, which according to official sources has 68 percent atheists, in fact has a much lower percentage of atheists.

Global trends. According to Barrett et al., in 1980 the global percentage of secularists was estimated at 20.8 percent. This was a significant rise from an estimated 0.2 percent in 1900. In the 2001 edition, the proportion of secularists worldwide as of 1995 was given as 15.6 percent. This represents a decline of 5.2 percent as compared to 1980. In 2000, according to Barrett et al., the global percentage further declined to 15.2 percent.

The decline of global atheism (in a wide sense) from 1980 to 1995 and 2000, if real, can perhaps partly be related to the breakdown of the Soviet Union in 1991. From 1988 on, the situation for religious believers in the Soviet Union improved after about seven decades of oppression or harassment. The same happened in a number of other countries which had been within the sphere of Soviet influence.

BIBLIOGRAPHY

Barrett, David B., et al., eds. *World Christian Encyclopedia*. 2 vols. Oxford: Oxford University Press 2001.

Britannica Book of the Year, 1998.

Hiorth, Finngeir, *Atheism in the World*. Oslo: Human-Etisk Forbund, 2003.

———. *Secularism in Norway*. Oslo: Human-Etisk Forbund, 2005.

———. *Secularism in Sweden*. Oslo: Human-Etisk Forbund, 1995.

Karatnycky, Adrian, ed. *Freedom House: Freedom in the World*. Piscataway, NJ: Transaction, 2000, 2001.

Marshall, Paul, ed., *Religious Freedom in the World*. Nashville, TN: Broadman & Holman, 2000.

FINNGEIR HIORTH

UNBELIEF AS A PROBLEM FOR THEISM. As a recent line of argument against the existence of God (see EXISTENCE OF GOD, ARGUMENTS FOR AND AGAINST) developed during the 1990s by J. L. Schellenberg and Theodore Drange, "unbelief as a probelem of theism" is closely related to what has been called "the problem of divine hiddenness" explored by, among others, Daniel Howard-Snyder and Paul K. Moser. If God exists and is perfectly loving, then why has he remained hidden from so many people, and why are there so many unbelievers? It would be expected that God would reveal himself clearly to people because it is in their best interest that he do so, and a perfectly loving deity would want what is in people's best interest. The problem is analogous to the problem of evil (see EVIL, PROBLEM OF). Just as a loving God, were he to exist, would probably prevent (or reduce) as much evil (i.e., suffering) as there is, so also he would prevent as much unbelief as there is. And so arise twin problems for theism: how to explain why there is so much evil (suffering) and why there is so much unbelief.

The problem can be pressed even more forcefully by way of an argument: Since a loving God would prevent unbelief, the fact that there are so many unbelievers constitutes good evidence that such a deity does not exist.

This is sometimes called the argument from nonbelief. This argument is especially strong when applied to the God of Christianity, who is supposed not only to love everyone, but also to want everyone to come to a knowledge of the truth (1 Tim. 2:4). The best explanation for the fact that so many people have not been made aware of (what Christians regard as) the truth is that the deity who is supposed to be all-powerful and to want that to happen simply does not exist.

Theists might make various attempts to solve (or get around) the problem of unbelief. Just three of them will be considered here: the free will defense, the afterlife defense, and the unknown-purpose defense.

The Free Will Defense (see DETERMINISM). The claim is made that God wants people to come to believe in him freely and not as the result of any sort of coercion. He knows that people who do not believe that he exists would indeed come to have that belief if he were to perform spectacular miracles. But for him to do that would overwhelm them and thereby interfere with their free will, which he does not want to happen. God's desire that humans retain their free will outweighs his desire to bring about universal belief, and that explains why he has not done things to make everyone a believer, which in turn solves the problem of unbelief.

One main objection to this is that people's free will is not affected by them being shown the truth, even by God. For one thing, people do not normally use their wills in the process of belief acquisition, but rather rely on the available evidence. For another thing, they want to know the truth, and therefore would not be forced against their will to acquire it if they were to be shown something. Assuming that God exists, for unbelievers to become aware of that truth would actually make them more free, for it would open up options to them that were not available before. There are a great variety of ways by which God might impart knowledge about himself, from performing miracles to inspiring humans to write scripture indicative of divine inspiration and then helping to disseminate knowledge of such scripture worldwide. It is counterintuitive to claim that God cannot do any of these things without interfering with people's free will.

It should be pointed out that in the Bible God is often described as performing miracles to get people to believe certain things, for example, before the Israelites and the Egyptians in order to demonstrate to them that he is the true God. Many other examples could be cited. Since God is supposed to have done those things, it seems that, contrary to the given defense, either such actions do not actually interfere with free will, or else God is not more concerned about free will than he is with people's unbelief.

Even if there were a conflict between God getting people to be aware of his existence and the preservation of their free will, God ought to prefer awareness to free will, because people would greatly benefit by coming to know how things really are. That would be especially true if one needs to have the right beliefs in order to get

saved, a view supported elsewhere in the Bible (Mark 16:15–16; John 3:18, 36, 14:6; Acts 4:12). Even if it means interfering with unbelievers' free will, it would be far better for God to enlighten them, allowing them to be saved, than to permit them to remain unenlightened and thereby eventually damned. Furthermore, even if exclusivism were false and one need not be a believer in order to get saved, there would still be great benefits both to God (assuming he exists) and to the unbelievers if they were to become theists. They would get into a proper relationship with God, and, at least from a theistic perspective, they would come to see meaning in life and lose their depression and sense of alienation. They would be more likely to come to love and worship God, which would benefit him, since he is supposed to desire that greatly. According to most theists, it would also probably help people to be more moral and loving toward their fellow human beings. Thus, it might plausibly be argued from the theists' own viewpoint that there is greater value in people becoming aware of God's existence than in their completely retaining free will, assuming that it is not possible for both to obtain. Therefore, an all-loving God should want to enlighten the unbelievers even if that were to interfere with their free will, which further refutes the free will defense.

Still another objection is that there are well over a billion people on the planet who lack belief in God. Assuming that God wants all of them to come to have such belief, how does he expect them to do that if he is unwilling to provide the evidence they need? Does he expect them to come to have belief in some irrational manner? Theists may reply that there is evidence for the existence of God and thus theistic belief is in no way irrational. Advocates of the free will defense would add that there is just the right amount of evidence: enough to make theistic belief rational but not so much as to interfere with free will. If God were to provide still more evidence of his existence, no matter how slight, then that would cross the line and start interfering. However, the fact is that there really is no good evidence for God's existence and, furthermore, even if there were such evidence, apparently billions of people would be unaware of it and would be in need of something more. Presumably for God to provide that little extra would in fact not interfere with those people's free will, for it would only bring their level of awareness up to that of the theists who (with no interference with their free will) already are aware of the given evidence. Thus, there would be no good reason for God to permit unbelievers to remain that way. If there is a level of evidence sufficient for belief but less than that which would interfere with free will, then God should see to it that everyone is made aware of evidence for his existence at that level.

Many other objections could be raised, but from what has already been said it is clear that the free will defense will not work.

The Afterlife Defense. The claim here is that God plans

to enlighten unbelievers about his existence in the afterlife. If that were so, it would certainly get around the problem of unbelief. But what about salvation? Although most theists do not accept the idea that people can gain a second chance at salvation in the afterlife, some of them (e.g., Jehovah's Witnesses) do. Does the idea have any merit? There are of course excellent reasons to deny that an afterlife is physically possible (see IMMORTALITY, UNBELIEF IN; REINCARNATION), but let us disregard that here.

One objection, at least for some theists, is that the Bible conflicts with the implication that some people will meet the criteria for salvation only in the afterlife. The Bible says, "Now is the day of salvation" (2 Cor. 6:2) and "It is appointed for men to die once, and after that comes judgment" (Heb. 9:27). This requires that the criteria for salvation be satisfied in this life. Still other incompatibilities with the Bible and with doctrines of the Western church could be cited. At the very least, it seems that the afterlife defense conflicts with the religious views of most theists in the United States.

Another objection to the afterlife defense is that it would make many matters inexplicable. Why should God set up the world in such a way that there is a prior period when people are pretty much left on their own, followed by an afterlife period in which God reigns? What is the purpose of it all, especially if people can attain the most important goals of their existence, including satisfying the criteria for salvation, during the second period? Why even bother with the earlier period? If the earlier period has some significance, then it would seem that people who are in it ought to be able to attain whatever self-fulfillment is possible for them. But that would require that they become aware of the truth about God. Those who live their entire earthly lives ignorant of that truth would have missed out on something beneficial. The question is why God would permit that benefit (knowing the truth) to be withheld from so many people in this earthly life. The afterlife defense leaves all that not only unexplained, but inexplicable, and that is still another reason to regard it as unsatisfactory.

The Unknown-Purpose Defense. The last-resort defense is that God does have some purpose for permitting all the unbelief that there is, but it is unknown to humanity. Contrary to the afterlife defense, God does want to eliminate the unbelief here on earth, but there is something else that conflicts with that desire, something which he wants even more. If we were to learn what that "something else" is, then we would understand why God has permitted so many people to live their earthly lives without any awareness of his existence.

Whoever claims that a divine purpose exists which would explain why there are so many unbelievers in the world has a certain burden of proof to support that claim. If God exists, even if he does not want to tell us what his unknown purpose is, it would behoove him at least to tell us that he has such a purpose. But there is nothing whatever in scripture or elsewhere that would support such a

notion. In contrast, there is excellent biblical support for the idea that God wants what is best for people and wants them to be aware of the truth, including the truth of his own existence. Thus, the unknown-purpose defense fails to meet its burden of proof.

Furthermore, an appeal to an unknown purpose is simply an appeal to mystery, which is antithetical to most theists' desire to explain the way things are. An appeal to mystery can never explain anything whatever, so it runs counter to any evangelical spirit or desire to spread the truth to others. That in itself is reason for theists to steer clear of it.

Another objection is that almost all theists take God to want his love for humanity to be reciprocated. But if God were to want people to love him, then it would be counterproductive (perhaps even irrational) for him to stay hidden from them. Although it is logically possible for God to have some (unknown) purpose which overrides his desire for people's love, the idea is nevertheless counterintuitive. Combine that with the earlier point that a loving God presumably wants whatever would benefit people in the long run, which would include knowing the truth. If God loves people greatly, then presumably he could not permit them to be so deprived. The appeal to the unknown-purpose defense again becomes increasingly far-fetched. There is intrinsic value to wisdom and to knowing the ultimate nature of reality. If God loves us, then he must want us to have that. Such considerations refute the unknown-purpose defense. There are other objections to it in addition to these.

Other defenses, in addition to the three considered here, could be constructed, but they too have been refuted, as by Drange. The overall conclusion on this topic seems inescapable: despite some efforts made, theists have not successfully solved or circumvented the problem of unbelief.

BIBLIOGRAPHY

Drange, Theodore. "The Argument from Non-Belief." *Religious Studies* 29 (1993).

———. *Nonbelief & Evil: Two Arguments for the Nonexistence of God.* Amherst, NY: Prometheus Books, 1998.

Howard-Snyder, Daniel, and Paul K. Moser, eds. *Divine Hiddenness: New Essays.* Cambridge: Cambridge University Press, 2002.

Schellenberg, J. L. *Divine Hiddenness and Human Reason.* Ithaca, NY: Cornell University Press, 1993.

THEODORE DRANGE

UNBELIEF AS A WAY OF LIFE. Discussing the notion of unbelief as a way of life inevitably draws attention to what is meant by the word *unbelief*, not least because of the difficulties arising from how something defined negatively can also be a way of life. The first task is to understand who is—and who is not—being spoken of when we speak of unbelief. In particular we need to distinguish between those who reject revealed religion in the name of some constructive, naturalistic worldview from those who are simply indifferent to all organized systems of belief, be they naturalist or supernaturalist. In the sense used here, *unbeliever* will refer only to the former group, while *indifferentist* will refer to the second group. Having made this distinction, the main problem with the idea of being an unbeliever becomes apparent, because this group, in contrast to the indifferentist, builds its identity around what it believes as much as what it does not believe. This, in turn, highlights the injustice of reducing *belief* to mere *religious belief*. This reduction is absurd and offensive, so for the purposes of this article, we shall now speak of unbelief as FREETHOUGHT and unbeliever as freethinker.

In the conclusion to *The Varieties of Religious Experience*, William James wrote: "The pivot round which the religious life, as we have traced it, revolves, is the interest of the individual in his private personal destiny. Religion, in short is a monumental chapter of human egotism." Paul Kurtz drew our attention to the same phenomenon when he spoke of the transcendental temptation, by which he meant the temptation to arrogate to ourselves a cosmic significance to which we are not entitled. Kurtz's public career has been about empowering people to reject the transcendental temptation in favor of his vision of an exuberant, dynamic HUMANISM. The core of freethought, then, lies in its willingness to reject the transcendental temptation. In making this rejection, freethinkers are rejecting what they see as a presumptuous belief that we, as individuals, are sufficiently deserving of a special corner of the universe to act as repository for one's immortal soul. The distinctiveness of freethought as a way of life arises from this rejection.

The first important consequence of freethought, in the sense of rejection of supernatural verities, is humility. If the motivating principle of religious life, as William James said, is human egotism, then the motivating principle of the freethinker's life is cosmic modesty. Bertrand RUSSELL gave classic expression of this understanding when he asked: "Is there not something a trifle absurd in the spectacle of human beings holding a mirror before themselves, and thinking what they behold so excellent as to prove that a Cosmic Purpose must have been aiming at it all along?" Russell was following in the tradition of Baruch de SPINOZA, who extolled the virtue of being able to acquire the perspective of *sub specie aeternitatis*, or "under the aspect of eternity." Similar sentiments can be found in the Taoist writings of China (see TAOISM, UNBELIEF WITHIN) and in some Indian philosophy (see INDIAN MATERIALISM, ANCIENT).

The achievement of a proper sense of cosmic modesty is a major part of the life journey for the conscientious freethinker. The more comprehensively this sense has been incorporated, the more firmly the transcendental temptation has been rejected. On this firm foundation freethinkers can then erect the framework of their lives. This framework will consist of three major qualities: altruism, toleration, and joie de vivre.

We have one life to live, and it is beholden on us to live that life to the fullest. And it is at this point that the freethinker parts company with the indifferentist. The indifferentist is likely to agree that we have only one life to live, but may then conclude that a life of hedonism is the only sensible conclusion to draw from that. Freethinkers, by contrast, recognize that in order to be consistent the egotism of hedonism needs to be rejected on much the same grounds as the egotism of personal immortality.

From this, the freethinker arrives at the value of altruism. This virtue is given its best voice in the notion of AGATHONISM, a refinement of the Golden Rule devised by the philosopher Mario Bunge, which says, "Live well and help others live well." One lives well by being the best person one is possibly capable of being; by loving as openly and disinterestedly as one is able, and being able to receive love in the same spirit. Affirmed in the love of a few people close to us, we can help others achieve satisfaction in their lives. This can be undertaken in any number of ways. As the Buddha said, right livelihood is an important component of right living. So the minimum requirement to helping others live well is to avoid noxious employments which add to the worldwide bankroll of suffering. More positive ways to help others live well may involve devoting time to the alleviation of suffering or to promoting excellence in others. The ways this can be done are limited only by one's imagination.

If freethought is defined first by cosmic modesty and next by altruism, the third consequence is toleration. In the absence of universalizing absolutes, and without the benefit of a supposedly infallible scripture to determine good from evil, freethinkers are faced with the challenge of working these values out for themselves. And with this human activity comes the possibility of error and the recognition that we can learn from others. In this way, toleration of others—other people and other ways and thoughts—is a necessary condition of freethought. Many humanist theorists have taken the next step by replacing the word *toleration* with *celebration*. Sometimes this can seem trite, but the thought behind it is valid. The existence of different people with different values, aspirations, and ways really is something to celebrate, not merely to put up with.

An important point about this is that the so-called unbelievers share some important features with believers. Both would agree that the life spent fashioning a coherent view of the world and seeking to live according to a set of principles is a worthwhile use of one's time. In this the freethinker and the believer have more in common with one another than with the indifferentist, who would be more likely to see such activity as a waste of time.

This does not mean, however, that freethought is some sort of substitute religion. To claim that reflects a presumption that only religion can provide the basis for a comprehensive worldview, clearly a false assertion. If the freethinker and the believer share the same priority given to the examined life, they part with respect to the conclusions they draw as to how this life should best be lived. At issue is the type of evidence each party gives weight to. Where the believer, particularly from the monotheist religions, gives primacy to faith, the freethinker is more impressed by REASON. It is not accidental that faith should have such an important role for the believer. The believer's focus is with the supernatural, however conceived, and no way to relate to the supernatural has yet been conceived that does not require the abandonment of reason. The freethinker's focus is with the natural world (see NATURALISM), and the principles of the natural world are best understood by our reasoning processes. The success of science is testimony to this truth. In the language of Daniel C. Dennett, it is the difference between cranes and skyhooks. Cranes are rooted firmly in the soil of naturalism while skyhooks hang precariously from some metaphysical trick with mirrors.

But the life of the freethinker is not defined solely by these rather somber virtues of humility, altruism, and toleration. Whereas the monotheist faiths are predicated on the suspicion that something is wrong with the world and with human beings, among those who have rejected the transcendental temptation the feeling is quite different. Life has its joys and sorrows, and each is doubly sweet because of the knowledge that our life will come to an end, and that end is permanent, final, and irrevocable. For the followers of the monotheist faiths, life is a vale of tears where they are tested, with the usual proviso that they will be found wanting in some basic way. Everything is a preparation for death, and what is supposed to happen after it. The contrast with the freethinker can hardly be more stark. The freethinker's attitude to life is joyful and exuberant. From Democritus, known as laughing philosopher, to *Monty Python's Flying Circus*, the freethought tradition has cherished the humor in life. In refusing to take ourselves too seriously, freethinkers leave room for the simple everyday joy of living.

So far we have distinguished the ways of life between believers and freethinkers as well as between freethinkers and indifferentists. But useful distinctions can also be drawn within the various branches of freethought. The English sociologist Colin Campbell has discerned two contrasting styles. On the one hand are abolitionists, who generally have a more combative relationship with religion. Abolitionists see the error and exploitation in religion and see religion as a something that needs to be struggled against. The substitutionist, by contrast, has a more benign attitude toward religion and is more concerned to re-create in freethought some of the pleasanter features of religion: a sense of belonging and shared purpose. People whose transition from religion to freethought has been traumatic are more likely to be abolitionist in approach, whereas people whose transition from religion was less painful, or who have never been religious, are often more inclined to take the substitutionist path. Whichever of these orientations one prefers helps determine which freethought organization one chooses to belong to. It has been an ongoing challenge for freethought organizations to successfully represent both strands within their membership. Substitutionists are inclined to become impatient with what they see as endless discussions about the nonexistence of God or scriptural contradictions, while abolitionists can be equally unwilling to indulge in what they see as playing at wannabe religion.

We can see, then, that the freethinker shares important traits with the religious believer, most notably a commitment to finding answers to questions many see as unanswerable or even irrelevant to the enjoyment of life. But if they agree that the questions are worth asking, freethinkers and religious believers disagree on the answers they reach. The freethinker's rejection of the transcendental temptation leads to an enhanced love of life.

The value of the freethinkers' way of life can be inferred by looking at their constructive role in society. It has been a staple of the more reactionary brands of religious apologetics that freethinkers cannot be, or, at least find it difficult to be, moral citizens. The truth, of course, is quite the opposite. The people who have traditionally been deemed unbelievers are among the best educated, most productive members of society. The percentage of freethinkers (as opposed to indifferentists) in prisons is minuscule. And freethinkers frequently show up in psychological studies as being less encumbered by dispositions to an authoritarian personality than is usual. Freethinkers, as a general rule, have above-average levels of education, hold down responsible jobs, and are active, productive members of society. The way of life of the freethinker is characterized by cosmic modesty, love of life, altruism, toleration, and joie de vivre. These characteristics help make freethinkers valuable members of society.

BIBLIOGRAPHY

Altemeyer, Bob, and Bruce Hunsberger. *Amazing Conversions: Why Some People Turn to Faith and Others Abandon Religion*. Amherst, NY: Prometheus Books, 1997.

Bunge, Mario. *Philosophy in Crisis: The Need for Reconstruction*. Amherst, NY: Prometheus Books, 2001.

Campbell, Colin. *Toward a Sociology of Irreligion*. London: Macmillan, 1971.

Cooke, Bill. *Dictionary of Atheism, Skepticism, and Humanism*. Amherst, NY: Prometheus Books, 2006.

Dennett, Daniel C. *Darwin's Dangerous Idea*. London: Allen Lane Penguin, 1995.

James, William. *Varieties of Religious Experience*. London: Longmans, Green, 1908.

Kurtz, Paul. *Affirmations*. Amherst, NY: Prometheus Books, 2004.

———. *The Transcendental Temptation*. Amherst, NY: Prometheus Books, 1986.

Russell, Bertrand. *Religion and Science*. London: Oxford University Press, 1960 [1935].

BILL COOKE

UNDERWOOD, BENJAMIN FRANKLIN (1839–1914), American freethought lecturer, author, and editor. The second of seven children, Benjamin Franklin Underwood grew up in Westerly, Rhode Island. He received a modest education, but read voraciously in science and philosophy. In 1862 he married Sara A. Francis, later a prominent suffragist (see WOMAN SUFFRAGE MOVEMENT AND UNBELIEF), while convalescing from a wound suffered in the US Civil War. His journalism career began in 1863, when he served while on active duty as war correspondent for the *Newport (RI) Daily News*.

After the war Underwood worked as a librarian, lecturer, essayist, and medical doctor. He was the official surgeon of the John Wood Post, Department of Illinois, Grand Army of the Republic, and authored an 1882 medical book on childhood diseases.

By the early 1870s, Underwood's reading and experience had led him to an unflinching materialism (see MATERIALISM, PHILOSOPHICAL) and a fervent embrace of Charles DARWIN's theory of evolution (see EVOLUTION AND UNBELIEF). He won prominence as a pamphleteer and debater, challenging clergymen across the eastern United States. He toured extensively, visiting most large cities in the American East and Midwest. Unlike his contemporary Robert Green INGERSOLL, the "Great Agnostic" (see AGNOSTICISM), Underwood's philosophy began with a no-holds-barred scientific account of the natural world, from which ATHEISM inevitably followed. In this, Underwood's philosophy resembled the atheism of England's Charles BRADLAUGH.

Underwood published numerous lectures and tracts, mostly through the Truth Seeker Company (see *THE TRUTH SEEKER*), founded by DeRobigne M. BENNETT. In 1880 Boston's Free Religious Association (see HUMANISM) invited Underwood to coedit what would become a noteworthy freethought paper, the *Index*, which he did for seven years. In 1887 Underwood moved to Chicago, briefly editing another long-lived freethought journal, *Open Court*.

Underwood's interests then turned away from freethought, toward mainstream journalism and toward spiritualism (see SPIRITUALISM AND UNBELIEF). He became secretary of Chicago's Psychical Science Congress; in 1896 he and his wife published a spiritualist book, *Automatic or Spirit Writing*. Despite these excursions from his erstwhile materialism, Underwood chaired the Congress of Evolution at Chicago's Columbian Exposition of 1893.

In 1897 Underwood moved to Quincy, Illinois, where he joined the *Quincy Daily Journal*, soon becoming its editor. He held that position until 1913, retiring to his childhood home of Westerly, Rhode Island, where he died on November 10, 1914.

BIBLIOGRAPHY

Ryan, William F. "Underwood, Benjamin Franklin." In *The Encyclopedia of Unbelief*, edited by Gordon Stein. Amherst, NY: Prometheus Books, 1985.

TOM FLYNN

UNION RATIONALISTE. The Union Rationaliste (UR) was founded in France on March 30, 1930. It aims at the defense and promotion of the spirit and the methods of science among the public at large. At once it was recognized as serving a real need, attracting the involvement of scientists of high stature, intellectuals, and citizens of diverse interests. Its first president was Henri Roger, MD. Paul Langevin, the well-known physicist, was founding vice president, and Albert Bayet the general secretary. The director of publications was the surrealist poet Philippe Soupault.

The UR's activities quickly multiplied. Public lectures were offered (already in 1930, notable lectures by Paul Langevin on science and determinism). In January 1931, the first issue of the UR journal *Les Cahiers Rationalistes* (*CR*) appeared. By April 1937 the UR had 1,260 members, including several outside France. Regional sections were created in France and abroad, including one in Mexico. A publishing company, Éditions Rationalistes (ER), was launched in 1936.

Until 1940 the UR was concerned primarily with the relations between science and moral values. Noteworthy publications include Albert Bayet's *La morale de la science* and Henri Roger's *Religion et Rationalisme*. Paul Langevin, elected UR president in 1939, published a lucid if somewhat pessimistic analysis in a paper titled *Science as a Factor of Moral and Social Evolution* published in *CR*. But then the war exploded. The Nazis arrested Langevin in October 1940. The UR became dormant until 1944. After French liberation, Langevin returned as leading officer of the UR, looking forward now to better prospects for the UR and for humankind. One token of his recovered optimism is the conclusion of his introduction to a talk by Fréderic Joliot-Curie: "A reason for us to be confident in the future is the extreme youth of mankind."

The presidents of the UR after Langevin were the aforementioned Joliot-Curie, physicist and Nobel laureate (1946–55); historian of religion Prosper Alfaric (1955); mathematician Albert Châtelet (1955–60); chemist Charles Sadron (1960–68); biochemist Ernest Kahane (1968–70); astrophysicist Evry Schatzman (1968–2001); then (after a change in the UR's bylaws), mathematician Jean-Pierre Kahane (2001–2004) and physicist Hélène Langevin (2004–).

The UR's activities developed in various directions during the fifties and sixties. To the *CR* was added in 1953 the *Courrier Rationaliste*. The UR then had 5,690 members and fifty-one regional sections organizing local meetings and lectures. *CR* had come into its own as a rich journal of ideas. ER was transformed into NER (Nouvelles Éditions Rationalistes).

Several lines of thought are easy to distinguish in UR activism during this period.

The first line concerned the problems of *LAÏCITÉ*, and of probing the history of religions. Alfaric's *De la foi à la raison* (From Faith to Reason) was published in 1959. Several other books along this line (including books aimed at children) were published by G. Fau, J. Rennes, E. Kahane, and Jacqueline Marchand.

The second line concerned the paranormal and the fight against false science and pseudoscience. In 1965 a pernicious movement was blooming in France: Planète was a strange and murky but very powerful organization that published several journals in the wake of the best-selling book that launched the movement, *Le Matin des Magiciens* (The Morning of the Magicians), by Bergier and Pauwels. The UR reacted vigorously by publishing several papers and books critical of paranormal phenomena, extraterrestrial fantasies, astrology, and other forms of irrationality. In particular, its journal *Crépuscule des Magiciens* (The Dusk of the Magicians), presented in the same format as the Planète movement's flagship journal, became a popular success.

The third line, the presentation of science and scientific methodology, remains the axis of the UR's activity. Books offering a scientific view of the origin of life were published beginning in 1955. ER published some fifteen books along this line, in particular the comprehensive five-hundred-page *Dictionnaire Rationaliste* in 1964, whose stated purpose was "to show on some well-chosen topics the scientific method in action."

In order to develop its ideas in a deeper way than in the mass-audience *CR* or in the *Courrier*, which was gradually disappearing, in 1967 Victor Leduc created a new journal, *Raison Présente* (Reason Today), published by NER. In later years the *Courrier* would be replaced by an Internet Web site.

The period between 1970 and 2000 is marked by the strong personality of UR president Evry Schatzman, who extended the range of the UR's activities by steering greater concern to social sciences and the humanities. This was also necessary because new media had emerged that were doing a good job of popularizing the sciences on a level beyond the capacity of the nonprofit UR. More prominence was given in UR publications to philosophical reflection.

But this period also saw the rise of new forms of irrationalism, in particular the New Age movement. Increasingly the UR responded to the need to fight against that

and other new forms of pseudosciences that hid behind spiritual pretenses. The CFIPP (French Committee for the Study of Paranormal Phenomena) was created by the UR under the leadership of physicist and Nobel Laureate Alfred Kastler and astronomer Jean-Claude Pecker. As a newborn brother to the Belgian Comité para and to the American CSICOP, it had engaged in a small number of strong protests before it was eclipsed by AFIS (French Association for Scientific Information), a sibling association of UR. AFIS published the journal *Science and Pseudo-Sciences*, led by journalist and UR activist Michel Rouzé, its first president, followed by J.-C. Pecker (2001–2002) and Jean Bricmont (2002–2004).

The UR developed its international connection early, starting at the creation in 1948 of the INTERNATIONAL HUMANIST AND ETHICAL UNION (IHEU). The IHEU was launched by the very founders of UNESCO, Bertrand RUSSELL and Thomas H. HUXLEY. Given that the UR is based in Paris, UR members often take the lead in representing the IHEU at the UNESCO General Assemblée. In addition, they often act as representatives and spokespersons of other international bodies.

The UR boasts a proud tradition. It continues to pursue the goal first defined by Paul Langevin, to model its actions on the example of scientific inquiry, to illustrate the role of scientific research in confronting the great challenges facing humankind, and to keep permanently in view the human march toward a conscious maturity.

JEAN-CLAUDE PECKER

UNITARIANISM to 1961. Closely defined, Unitarianism means belief in one God and in Jesus as his human prophet. However, other unorthodox positions on the nature of God and the relationship between God and Christ, such as anti-Trinitarianism, Arianism, Adoptionism, and Sabellianism contributed to Unitarianism's development and are often included with it. According to church historian Earl Morse Wilber, Unitarianism was characterized by freedom, reason, and tolerance; it stressed ethics over doctrine. Additionally, Unitarians displayed strong interest in science and education. By 1961 the American Unitarian Association tended toward humanism. In that year it merged with the Universalist Church (see UNIVERSALISM TO 1961) to form the Unitarian Universalist Association (see UNITARIAN UNIVERSALISM).

One major figure in the rise of Unitarianism was the Spaniard Michael Servetus, martyred in 1553 in Geneva, Switzerland. His writings against the Trinity influenced the Unitarian movement, which would emerge in Renaissance and Reformation Italy. Italian refugees settled in Poland and Transylvania. After the Polish Brethren, a sect holding Unitarian beliefs, was destroyed during the Counter-Reformation, refugees fled to the Netherlands and Transylvania. Unitarian churches remain to the present day in Romania and Hungary. Publications from Unitarians in the Netherlands influenced dissenters in the British Isles.

North American Unitarianism developed more or less independently out of Puritan Congregationalism, which stressed learned study and permitted diversity of doctrine. The oldest Puritan congregations became Unitarian, as well as the Separatist Pilgrim Congregation at Plymouth. The first New England Episcopal church, King's Chapel, also became Unitarian by affirming one God and a humanitarian Christology. King's Chapel and some other churches had contact with the British movement, whose "trust deed" chapels similarly were not required to embrace specific doctrines. Philosopher John LOCKE, who wrote the much-admired 1685 *Letter concerning Toleration* and whose theological views after his death would be revealed as anti-Trinitarian, influenced groups in North America and the UK. Among the founders of the United States, Thomas JEFFERSON and John Adams embraced Unitarian theology. There is evidence that James MADISON held similar beliefs. Other noteworthy figures influencing Unitarian thought include Jeremy BENTHAM and John Stuart MILL, who collaborated with his Unitarian wife, Harriet Taylor Mill, on most of his works.

In America and the UK, groups holding Unitarian beliefs were reluctant to tie themselves to the sectarian name. North American Congregationalists held an Arian theology, viewing Christ as superhuman but not equal with God. Their leader, William Ellery Channing, eventually developed a humanitarian Christology, viewing Jesus as less an angelic mediator than a remarkable human teacher. Human dignity was one of Channing's key concepts. In the United Kingdom, many holding Unitarian views were reluctant to name congregations for a doctrine, preferring to be known as Presbyterian, a label that described only their form of governance.

Later in the nineteenth century, the Higher BIBLICAL CRITICISM and German Idealism influenced Unitarians in North America and the UK. Ralph Waldo EMERSON was the primary American philosophical leader; James Martineau played this role in the UK. While congregations in Hungary and Romania remained close to their Protestant origins, in the United States the Western Unitarian Conference (organized in 1852) and the Free Religious Association (FRA, 1867) widened the scope of the movement after the US Civil War. In addition to Unitarians, the FRA embraced Reform Judaism's Isaac Mayer Wise and also Felix ADLER, the founder of ETHICAL CULTURE. There was also an interest in Eastern religion: Unitarians played a significant role in the 1893 World Parliament of Religions at the Columbian Exposition. The FRA's journal the *Index* was finally absorbed by Open Court, a significant philosophical publisher.

In both the United States and the UK, Unitarians made many contributions to social reform. Among these were woman suffrage; civil service reform; care for the poor, the blind, and the mentally ill; and humane treatment of animals. Unitarians supported the abolition of slavery, although not unanimously. After the American Civil War, they contributed financial help to freed slaves and Southerners. Significant Unitarian reformers included Harvard's Francis Greenwood Peabody, a major voice for the Social gospel, as was John Haynes Holmes during the first half of the twentieth century. Jenkin Lloyd Jones, from a Welsh Unitarian family, founded Chicago's Abraham Lincoln Center, a Unitarian contribution to the institutional church and social settlement movement. In the UK, Charles Dickens, whose novels stirred interest in the poor and efforts at reform, attended a Unitarian congregation when one was available where he lived.

In 1940 a Unitarian Service Committee was founded in the United States. It aided refugees from Nazi-occupied Europe including the non-Unitarians Franz Werfel, Heinrich Mann (Thomas Mann's brother), and Arthur Koestler; it also supported Albert Schweitzer's African jungle hospital. Schweitzer had long-term connections with Unitarians and sympathized with humanism; later—in 1961, the year when the Unitarians and the Universalists merged—Schweitzer joined the Church of the Larger Fellowship, a "church by mail" for Unitarians far from established congregations.

Unitarianism's lack of a creed and its stress on the humanity of Jesus and human dignity led eventually in a humanist direction in the United States. The 1933 Humanist Manifesto continued this inclusive trend. The first draft was written by prominent philosopher Roy Wood Sellars. Other important influences included PRAGMATISM, two of whose principal exponents, William James and John DEWEY, were involved with Unitarian congregations. Among other trends were Process Theology, the philosophy of Alfred North Whitehead (1861–1947) and others that stressed becoming over being and equated God with the cosmic Process; and the social ethics of James Luther Adams, interpreter of Paul Tillich, who saw Christ as the ideal human. Nevertheless, humanism became the predominant theological position.

BIBLIOGRAPHY

Ahlstrom, Sydney E., and Jonathan S. Carey. *An American Reformation: A Documentary History of Unitarian Christianity.* Middletown, CT: Wesleyan University Press, 1985.

Bumbaugh, David E. *Unitarian Universalism: A Narrative History.* Chicago: Meadville Lombard, 2000.

Cooke, George Willis. *Unitarianism in America.* Boston: American Unitarian Association, 1902.

Frothingham, Octavius Brooks. *Transcendentalism in New England.* New York: G. P. Putnam's Sons, 1876.

Gordon, Alexander. *Heads of English Unitarian History.* Portway, Bath, UK: Cedric Chivers, 1970.

Holt, Raymond V. *The Unitarian Contribution to Social Progress in England.* London: Lindsey, 1952.

Lyttle, Charles H. *Freedom Moves West: A History of the Western Unitarian Conference (1852–1952)* Boston: Beacon, 1952.

Marshall, George. *The Church of the Pilgrim Fathers.* Boston: Beacon, 1950.

Olds, Mason. *American Religious Humanism.* Minneapolis: Fellowship of Religious Humanists, 1996.

Persons, Stow. *Free Religion.* Boston: Beacon, 1963.

Robinson, David. *The Unitarians and the Universalists.* Westport, CT: Greenwood, 1985.

Schulz, William F. *Making the Manifesto: The Birth of Religious Humanism.* Boston: Skinner House, 2002.

Tapp, Robert B. *Religion among the Unitarian Universalists: Converts in the Stepfather's House.* New York: Seminar, 1973.

Wilber, Earl Morse. *A History of Unitarianism.* 2 vols. Boston: Beacon, 1945.

Wright, Conrad. *The Beginnings of Unitarianism in America.* Boston: Beacon, 1955.

WESLEY V. HROMATKO

UNITARIAN UNIVERSALISM.

By 1750 the forebears of Unitarians and Universalists were agreed on several things—human reason was the best way to reach truth, God's goodness precluded eternal punishment, and the dogma of Trinity was neither reasonable nor biblical. Their denominations came to dominate Harvard, founded St. Lawrence and Tufts, and ordained women ministers. In terms of contemporary Western culture, even in the experimentalist United States, these constituted major unbeliefs. Influenced by comparative religion, adventurous members founded the Free Religious Association, the World Parliament of Religions, the International Association for Religious Freedom—all respectful ways of becoming involved with liberals from other traditions.

Continuing shifts away from the religious mainstream created naturalistic and humanistic theologies, and Unitarians and Universalists predominated among the drafters and signers of the Humanist Manifesto of 1933 (see HUMANISM). Full merger came in 1961 as the Unitarian Universalist Association (UUA), and a 1966 survey showed that the majority of members were clearly post-Christian and posttraditional, as well as highly educated and economically strong. The new denomination pioneered in welcoming members of diverse sexual orientations, in funding movements of black empowerment, and in involving women in all structural levels. Participation in civil liberties and other liberal causes remained high. Innovative educational materials for youth were a high priority.

Historically, neither group had used creeds, but most of their members had grown up elsewhere and had therefore consciously chosen this distinct form of post-Christian, posttraditional new religiosity. The rightward shift of US culture after the 1960s was bound to affect all religions. Evangelical Protestants used the politicians' "Southern strategy" to advance their own claims to dominance; mainstream Protestantism and Catholicism lost members; and many Americans, including new immigrants, were drawn into Pentecostal or charismatic movements and megachurches. As it became clear that membership growth was lagging, UUA denominational priorities shifted toward a pluralism and inclusiveness that stressed that all beliefs were welcome. The UUA adopted and still highlights seven principles that are liberal, general, and quite inclusive.

The onetime humanist trajectory is now challenged by new caucuses—Buddhist, Christian, feminist, and pagan. This new diversity has been strengthened by a steady supply of clergy who have been trained in other denominations and who may have selected Unitarian Universalism for other-than-theological reasons, not to identify with this particular religious history. If unbelief means "believing differently," Unitarian Universalists may be losing their distinctiveness. Their new competition now consists of broadly spiritual movements, Eastern spiritualities, Unity, and Science of Mind. A 2005 banner from UUA headquarters puts this clearly: "Room for different beliefs. Yours."

BIBLIOGRAPHY

Howe, Charles A. *The Larger Faith: A Short History of American Universalism.* Boston: Skinner House, 1993.

Parke, David B. *The Epic of Unitarianism; Original Writings from the History of Liberal Religion.* Boston: Starr King Press, 1957.

Ross, Warren. *The Premise and the Promise: The Story of the Unitarian Universalist Association.* Boston: Skinner House, 2001.

Tapp, Robert B. *Religion among the Unitarian Universalists; Converts in the Stepfathers' House, Quantitative Studies in Social Relations.* New York: Seminar, 1973.

Unitarian Universalist Association. *The Free Church in a Changing World.* Boston: Author, 1963.

———. *Report of the Committee on Goals.* Boston: Author, 1967.

Wilbur, Earl Morse. *A History of Unitarianism.* Boston: Beacon, 1965.

ROBERT B. TAPP

UNITED KINGDOM, UNBELIEF IN.

Early unbelief in the UK was characterized by suppression and oppression. It was prudent for unbelievers to keep their views covert or to cloak them in moderating ideas, such as DEISM. Overt ATHEISM does not appear in print until the late eighteenth century, but there were earlier skeptical sallies during the English Renaissance and a ferment of confused but doubting ideas in the period of the Restoration of the monarchy after the Civil War and Cromwell's rule.

Early Skepticism. Sir Walter Raleigh was accused of atheism, but it was never substantiated. His book based on the work of Sextus EMPIRICUS, *The Skeptick*, at least suggests acquaintance with questioning ideas. Christopher Marlowe's plays (see ENGLISH LITERATURE, UNBELIEF IN) indicate strong antireligious views. The essayist Francis Bacon, in his essay *Of Atheism*, attacks atheism but confirms that such ideas were around to be criticized; his discussion of the extension of knowledge and the method of science were important forerunners for the development of science and the *encyclopedists* (see ENLIGHTENMENT, UNBELIEF DURING THE).

Two major thinkers in the seventeenth century were Thomas HOBBES and John LOCKE. Hobbes was reputed to be an atheist but never said so, although his major work of political thought, the *Leviathan*, contained hostility to church power and some clergy claimed that God's wrath at Hobbes's unbelief had caused the Great Plague and the Great Fire. Covert atheism was obviously in the air, given the need felt by the government to draft two acts against irreligion in 1666–67 and 1677–78.

The title of John Locke's classic work *A Letter concerning Toleration* (1689), which influenced VOLTAIRE, speaks for itself as an important precursor of FREETHOUGHT; but he did not extend toleration to those "who deny God" particularly because their bond or oath on the Bible could not be trusted. He was friendly with scientists such as Boyle and concerned with the scope of reason.

A pupil of Locke's was the third Earl of SHAFTESBURY, a benign man who believed in human and universal beneficence. Shaftesbury was a leading influence on the English deists who were so important in the first half of the eighteenth century. They displayed the constant denial of unorthodoxy alongside a constant iteration of deistic and non-Christian beliefs. J. M. ROBERTSON wrote of the "distribution of heretical views among the nominally orthodox, and of orthodox views among the heretics." Deists believed in a God who did not intervene in human life; theists lay more emphasis on God as a force of nature (see also PANTHEISM AND UNBELIEF).

Deistic Thought. Bishop Berkeley wrote of an "execrable fraternity of blasphemers in Dublin." John TOLAND was one of them. He was influenced by his study and sojourn in Holland—an important source of ideas of tolerance and skepticism. His *Christianity Not Mysterious* (1696) examined the truth of the Bible and offered a naturalistic view of religious mysteries. The book was ordered to be publicly burned in Dublin. It may be thought that some deism was a prudent move toward godlessness. But for others it was a legitimate philosophic approach to God.

Anthony COLLINS is thought by David Berman to be a speculative atheist, perhaps the first "strong-minded atheist." His most famous book, the *Discourse of Freethinking*, created an uproar after which he fled to Holland. Later works by him doubted the reliability of prophecy. Thomas WOOLSTON, a sober and earnest man like most of the deists, speculated that biblical stories were myths. Matthew TINDAL, who wrote *Christianity as Old as Creation* (1730), was fully theistic but anticlerical (see ANTICLERICALISM). Conyers MIDDLETON remained as a clergyman and academic: he withdrew from early skepticism, but toward the end of his life produced *A Free Inquiry into Miraculous Powers* (1748).

The politician and Tory Lord BOLINGBROKE in retirement wrote skeptical works that influenced the deist poet Alexander Pope (See ENGLISH LITERATURE, UNBELIEF IN). Bolingbroke's skeptical works were not published until after his death, which led the devout Dr. Johnson to say that Bolingbroke had charged the blunderbuss against religion and morality but "had no resolution to fire it off himself." The English deists let forth many shots against orthodox religion, provoked a wide public debate, and took an important step toward later full-blown freethought.

Philosophic and Historical Atheism. David HUME and Edward GIBBON—respectively, a philosopher and a historian—were two major skeptics of the eighteenth century. Hume was a Scotsman and part of the brilliant efflorescence of thought that was the Scottish Enlightenment. His writings did much to undermine the idea of God as First Cause (a deist position), his writing *On Miracles* demolished the idea that events contrary to nature took place, and his posthumous work *Dialogues concerning Natural Religion* presented an ironic view of the arguments against the existence of God. Hume was amazed, on an occasion when he visited France and dined with a group of philosophes, to be told that he was supping with atheists.

Gibbon's masterpiece *The History of the Decline and Fall of the Roman Empire* (1776–87) was a history from which the role of God had been removed. Gibbon's chapters on the rise of Christianity outraged clerics because they accounted for the religion's growth purely as a historical phenomenon without invoking the divine power of God. He wrote in his *Autobiography*: "The present is a fleeting moment, the past is no more, and our prospect of futurity is dark and doubtful." Gibbon also thought the consequences of the French Revolution would be dark and doubtful. Atheism at the upper echelons of society was found in that stern opponent of French post-Revolutionary hostility, Pitt the Younger. The poet from aristocratic origins, Percy Bysshe SHELLEY (see ENGLISH LITERATURE, UNBELIEF IN), wrote and published one of the earliest completely atheist pamphlets, *The Necessity of Atheism*.

Freethought became divided between growing working-class radicalism and higher-class intellectual debate. Joseph PRIESTLEY and Erasmus Darwin were Unitarian deists (see UNITARIANISM TO 1961) whose participation in scientific and cultural discussion clubs marked an important development. Meanwhile the working classes suffered for their freedom of thought and expression. Peter ANNET, for instance, attacked theology in a fiery tone and considered the problem of why God favored the immoral David of the Old Testament. He published nine issues of the *Free Inquirer* in 1761, which especially attacked the authenticity of biblical history. He was tried for BLASPHEMY in 1763, when he was in his seventies, convicted and pilloried twice, imprisoned for one year, and forced to endure one year's hard labor.

Thomas PAINE was a thinker and activist who took part in the American and French revolutions. His *Rights of Man* (1791–92) was one of the first major defenses of the right of all people to just government, legal justice, and fair distribution of wealth—such ideals were often linked with radical freethought. His *Age of Reason* (1793–94) was written largely while he was living in revolutionary France (barely escaping the guillotine). By the end of the eighteenth century his deism was rather old-fashioned, but his attack on Christianity was devastating. Paine took the Bible to pieces—and it was never really put together again. Paine's influence on radical freethinkers was enormous. He opposed censorship, but his work suffered from it.

Richard CARLILE was a self-educated publisher imprisoned for publishing *The Age of Reason*. He developed his ideas while in prison, and wrote in a pamphlet, *Address to the Reformers:* "I advocate the abolition of all religions, without setting up anything new of the kind." This became the task of the nineteenth-century thinkers and activists. Carlile was important for the completeness of his atheism, for his struggle against censorship, and for his attempt to develop organizations such as Free Inquiry and the Zetetic Societies—a crucial innovation for the nineteenth century. His partnership with Eliza SHARPLES strengthened their activities.

Jeremy BENTHAM was a key philosopher, as was John Stuart MILL, the son of Bentham's friend James Mill. Bentham's utilitarianism, with its catchphrase "the greatest happiness of the greatest number," was part of the process of separating ethics from theology that would be pursued through to such twentieth-century thinkers as G. E. MOORE and A. J. AYER. Bentham was never overtly atheistic, but was very critical of religion, especially in *Analysis of the Influence of Natural Religion on the Temporal Happiness of Mankind* (1822), which was published under the pseudonym of "Philip Beauchamps." It attacked the "Jug" (juggernaut) of the church. John Stuart Mill modified some utilitarian principles; he displayed no animosity toward religious thinking but rather a tendency toward a "religion of humanity." His *Three Essays on Religion* were published posthumously; they considered the "utility" of religion rather than its truth. A friend of Bentham and of James and John Stuart Mill was George Grote, the distinguished historian of ancient Greece. His atheism was covert but, as indicated by his personal notebooks, distinct. He was a founder of University College, London,

an institution which declined to sustain the religious requirements of other English universities.

Countertheology. The criticism of theology and the Bible moved apace through the nineteenth century. A new translation of the Bible in 1793 by Alexander Geddes, a Scottish Catholic, dated the Pentateuch (the first five books of the Bible, traditionally held to have been written by Moses) from the time of King Solomon. Further study was to throw the biblical chronology out of kilter, from internal deduction and later from historical research. German scholars pioneered the study of the New Testament, suggesting that authorship and dating were doubtful. E. B. Pusey's *An Historical Enquiry into the Probable Causes of the Rationalist Character of Germany* (1826–30) transmitted questioning of the Bible to Britain. H. H. Milman's *History of the Jews,* published anonymously in 1829, shocked readers by its insertion of historical factors into the study of a religious group.

A major German influence was the *Leben Jesu* (Life of Christ, 1835) by David Friedrich STRAUSS. It was intended as a work of history, not hagiography, and the gospel was to be "tried by the tests of science and consistency, in which all miracle was to be regarded as unhistorical and all vital contradiction as decisive against credibility" (J. M. Robertson). An English work published a little later, but without knowledge of *Leben Jesu*, was Charles Hennell's *An Inquiry concerning the Origin of Christianity* (1838), which was the first study of the religious works as historical documents. Wider knowledge of Strauss's seminal work came with the translation by Marian EVANS, later George Eliot (see ENGLISH LITERATURE, UNBELIEF IN).

A major work of countertheology was *Essays and Reviews* (1860), a collection of essays by seven clerics, all demonstrating the cumulative effect of critical religious studies in the first half of the nineteenth century.

Science. It was not just the many new scientific discoveries and theories that changed nineteenth-century thought, but the increasing understanding of the scientific process. The mathematician and freethinker William Kingdon CLIFFORD wrote in his lecture "On the Aims and Instruments of Scientific Thought": "The subject of science is the human universe, that is, everything that is, or has been, or may be related to man."

Charles DARWIN is the giant whose theory of evolution changed all thinking about the development of the earth and its species—in such a way that it was impossible to believe in the divine creation of Genesis (see EVOLUTION AND UNBELIEF). Before him came the geologist Charles Lyell, whose geological studies changed the understanding of the age and development of the earth. Darwin's theory as presented in *On the Origin of Species* (1859) was especially influential in suggesting that the development of species was continuous from primitive life through mammals and primates to man. This was heatedly challenged. Charles Kingsley wrote in 1863 that "Darwin is conquering everywhere, and rushing in like a flood, by the mere force of truth and fact." Darwin never rushed to conclusions and held quiet agnostic views (see AGNOSTICISM).

The man who coined the word *agnostic* was Thomas H. HUXLEY, known as "Darwin's Bulldog"; he did much to spread a detailed understanding of evolutionary theory. He was combative and part of that fiercely fought battle between science and religion (see RELIGION IN CONFLICT WITH SCIENCE)—despite the fact that some of the religious were beginning to embrace scientific discoveries. The title of John William DRAPER's book, *History of the Conflict between Religion and Science* (1874), sums up one aspect of the debate. Some followers of Darwin, such as Herbert SPENCER and Ernst HAECKEL, though not Darwin himself, developed a kind of social Darwinism which saw humanity evolving ever forward. This was attractive to those many freethinkers who anticipated the inevitable progress of humankind as religion withered away.

The literary and philosophic output of the nineteenth century pointed to the slow acceptance of a secular approach. Literature (see ENGLISH LITERATURE, UNBELIEF IN) showed the fine novelist George Eliot giving a picture of the way in which people find meaning and morality in their lives, while Thackeray shows how the hedonistic and moralistic sit side by side in a secular world. The poets Matthew ARNOLD and Robert Browning showed the struggle with belief in their poetry. Algernon Charles SWINBURNE and James Thomson wrote poetry in which pessimism and perversion were given play as part of human experience.

In a period that in Britain was not strong on philosophy, British philosophers were very concerned with ethics. Henry Sidgwick wavered in all directions, but never abandoned his concern with secular ethics. He renounced his academic post—something that many "without believing more than he did" refrained from doing. Spenser adopted the sociological approach. The influence of Auguste COMTE was passing, but his misty view of an agnostic social religion had some influence. That an eminent judge, Sir Justice James Stephen, should offer overt atheism was a sign of the times. He ridiculed the Comtist view of a social religion—"we can get on very well without religion." His brother, the literary figure Leslie STEPHEN, wrote *An Agnostic's Apology* (1876); in addition, he and Francis Newman (the agnostic brother of Cardinal Newman) conducted a vigorous campaign for secular education. A less well-known figure, whose writing survived among a readership of working-class freethinkers, was Winwood Reade. His *The Martyrdom of Man* combined anthropological and historical research in an account of Africa, which shifted the perceived center of civilization away from Europe. Reade was perhaps expressing a view held at the intellectual and popular level of unbelief: "To develop to the utmost our genius and our love—that is the only true religion."

Popular Freethought. Robert OWEN held utopian socialist views, and is best known for his contribution to the Co-Operative movement. He "abandoned all belief in religion" and replaced it with a sense of "universal charity." Early secularists (see SECULARISM) such as George Jacob HOLYOAKE were influenced by the Owenite movement, but moved away from its attempt to set up ideal communities. Owen believed that upbringing and environment could change people and society. Some followers believed that rejecting religion could equally bring improvements to society as a whole.

The founding of the NATIONAL SECULAR SOCIETY (NSS) in 1866 was a key moment in the development of overt and largely working-class freethought. Charles BRADLAUGH was its first president, and dominated the society until the 1890s. Bradlaugh struggled to take the oath to enter Parliament but was not allowed to do so, since he could not swear on a Bible he did not believe in. In this process he was rejected from Parliament on several occasions. His struggle to enter Parliament enhanced his reputation among unbelievers at all levels of society. The journals the *NATIONAL REFORMER* and the *FREETHINKER* chronicled the events and ideas of the movement. Both George Jacob Holyoake and George W. FOOTE were tried and imprisoned for blasphemy—and abolition of the blasphemy law remained an ambition of the movement. Republicanism, the campaign against the hereditary monarchy, was espoused by many secularists—particularly during the 1870s, when Queen Victoria was so unpopular. Support of neo-Malthusianism, or birth control (see BIRTH CONTROL AND UNBELIEF), was a cause of conflict among secularists. The need to develop secular education and the need for self-education were constant themes. Later in the nineteenth century there developed differences between those who espoused the new doctrine of socialism (see SOCIALISM AND UNBELIEF) and those who preferred to remain with liberal individualism.

The SOUTH PLACE ETHICAL SOCIETY held regular Sunday meetings, and in W. J. Fox had one effective intellectual leader, followed by another: Moncure CONWAY. Debates on DARWINISM, Comtism, philosophy, and literature were the lifeblood of the society. Ethical movements (see ETHICAL CULTURE) developed later in the century, partly in direct influence from the United States. It was a constant theme that ethical values were not lost when religion was discarded.

Toward the end of the century the RATIONALIST PRESS ASSOCIATION (RPA) was founded (1899) with the intent of publishing books on rationalist themes at a price which could be afforded by all. The RPA thus bridged the intellectual and popular levels of nineteenth- and twentieth-century unbelief.

Twentieth Century. The philosophical climate of Britain in the twentieth century was set by three atheistic/agnostic thinkers: G. E. Moore, John MCTAGGART and Bertrand RUSSELL. Moore, who importantly grounded ethics in the nonreligious world, wrote an essay "The Value of Religion" in which he rejected arguments for the existence of God. McTaggart in *Some Dogma of Religion* (1906) and *The Nature of Existence* (1921 and 1927) proffered a more assertive atheism: but his belief in immortality and defense of Anglicanism—though he was simultaneously a member of the RPA—made his atheism less well known. Bertrand Russell wrote two popular essays, *Why I Am Not a Christian* (1927) and *What I Believe* (1925), which exerted enormous influence. His pacifism, defense of nuclear disarmament, and popular essays made him a humanist favorite and a president of the RPA.

Unbelief had become more confident, and as the century progressed became the major undercurrent of thought in many spheres. Anthropology was used to give a rational explanation of religious practices (with James Frazer a respected, if now outdated, figure). Sigmund FREUD proposed the importance of the unconscious mind to our beliefs and the position of an internalized father figure as a reason for belief in God. His *The Future of an Illusion* (1927) aptly describes the unbeliever's twentieth-century attitude to religion.

Organized humanism did not entirely thrive now that it faced mostly indifferentism rather than hostility. The publications of the RPA had an impact, showing some decline in the 1920s but a revival in the 1930s with the very popular Thinker's Library series. Science was very important to the RPA: J. B. S. Haldane, Karl POPPER, and Albert Einstein were among those thinkers with connections with the RPA. The RPA's publishing program was overtaken by left-wing books in the thirties and the paperback revolution after World War II. The RPA's magazine, the *Literary Guide*, became the *Humanist* in the 1956 and the *New Humanist* in 1972 and continues today as a bimonthly.

The National Secular Society persisted with determination, with Chapman COHEN succeeding G. W. Foote as president, being more of a philosopher with a particular interest in materialism (see MATERIALISM, PHILOSOPHICAL). The NSS journal the *Freethinker* became a monthly in the later part of the century, and survives to this day as a lively polemical paper. Its supporters claim that its "negative" attitude is a positive call for change. It particularly argues for the rights of the nonreligious, for free speech, for separation of church and state, for the removal of state support for religious schools, and for the abolition of blasphemy laws. A blasphemy case created a stir in 1977, when Mary Whitehouse, a Christian morals campaigner, brought a prosecution against the newspaper *Gay News* for publishing a poem in which Jesus was depicted as a homosexual (see GAY HUMANISM). The editor was found guilty, fined, and given a suspended sentence. The blasphemy law remains on the statute books. The Gay and Lesbian Humanist Group began soon after the prosecution, energized with a particular case to argue and a particular constituency to support.

The BRITISH HUMANIST ASSOCIATION (BHA) emerged out of the ethical movement and was launched in 1963 in the House of Commons with the philosopher A. J. Ayer and Sir Julian HUXLEY as speakers. Ayer's "linguistic analysis" analyzed God out of the language (see LOGICAL POSITIVISM); Julian Huxley's *Religion without Revelation* (1927) indicated the softer line some humanists were taking. The BHA developed a network of local groups and offered nonreligious ceremonies (which today provide a major window to humanism for the general public). H. J. Blackham was a leader in founding and developing the BHA. Abortion, homosexuality, censorship, disarmament, race relations—all became matters of great concern to humanists.

The British Broadcasting Corporation (BBC) was first led by John Reith, a religious man with a believing agenda to push. Humanists have argued ever since for a fair place on the airwaves. Meanwhile non-Christian religions have become more important, Islam especially, and unbelievers' critical searchlight no longer focuses entirely on Christianity. In any case, Christianity had become a fuzzier target as Christian liberals abandoned metaphysics, increasingly defining their faith in such terms as "the ground of our being" and "ultimate concerns": Bishop John Robinson brought such theories (from Paul Tillich in particular) to the public.

There has been much discussion about the secularization of society: in two senses there can be no doubt of this—first, churchgoing in Britain has declined considerably; second, people and institutions no longer take religious "truths" as their guides in making decisions or creating their attitude toward life (see LIFE STANCE; MORALITY FROM A HUMANIST POSITION). This may be partly due to intellectual changes, partly to a preference for enjoying life without the hindrance of religion.

The nineteenth-century optimism upon which unbelief floated found itself in the twentieth century, despite its considerable advances, facing the pessimism that world wars and genocide engendered. Whether unbelief can replace religious belief remains an open question.

BIBLIOGRAPHY

Berman, David. *A History of Atheism in Britain: From Hobbes to Russell.* Beckenham, Kent, UK: Croom Helm, 1988.

Brown, Callum G. *The Death of Christian Britain.* London: Routledge, 2001.

Budd, Susan. *Varieties of Unbelief: Atheists and Agnostics in English Society 1850–1960.* London: Heinemann Educational, 1977.

Campbell, Colin. "A Rational Approach to Secularization." In *Rationalism in the 1970s.* London: Rationalist Press Association, 1973.

Cooke, Bill. *The Blasphemy Depot: A Hundred Years of the Rationalist Press Association.* London: Rationalist Press Association, 2003.

Herrick, Jim. *Against the Faith: Some Deists, Skeptics and Atheists.* London: Glover and Blair, 1985.

Robertson, J. M. *A History of Freethought in the Nineteenth Century.* London: Watts and Company, 1929.

JIM HERRICK

UNITED SECULARISTS OF AMERICA. This twentieth-century US organization began in March 1947 with the publication of the first issue of the monthly *Progressive World. Progressive World* in turn represented the amalgamation of five different publications: the *Orr Publications,* edited by Hugh Robert Orr; the *Humanist World,* edited by Lowell H. Coate; *Action for Human Welfare,* edited by Ray S. Kellogg; the *Comet,* edited by Gus Horack; and the *Hornet,* edited by W. Henry Davis. William McCarthy was also listed as a consulting editor, though he was not affiliated with any of the founding publications. These editors combined to form the American Progressive Association.

The first issue of *Progressive World* described the publication as intended to be governed by its subscribers. The founding editors stated that they wanted to promote freethought without money collected for subscriptions and donations going into private hands. It was their belief that the FREETHOUGHT movement itself had failed for this reason, causing there to be no truly national organization that spoke for freethinkers, rationalists, humanists, and the like, as at that time there was not. The editors wished to unite the many "freethinkers, humanists, progressives and liberals." The premier issue also included a "Purpose and Policy" statement, with strong similarity to the mission statements of many freethought-related groups today. Separation of church and state, elimination of superstition, promoting the taxation of church property, and keeping religion out of the public schools were all mentioned in this policy statement.

Progressive World held its first convention in August 1947 in Los Angeles. There began the project of organizing subscribers into the governing body of the magazine. The "owner-subscribers" named themselves the Progressive World Associates (PWA), and worked out how this publication would be run. Lowell H. Coate was named editor in chief, and the board of trustees was expanded.

The next organizational step occurred in the following year. The second convention was held in August at Chicago. This convention brought various regional freethought-related organizations together to create a national "union," which had not existed since the days of the old NATIONAL LIBERAL LEAGUE. Twelve groups were represented at the convention, including the FREIE GEMEINDEN of Milwaukee, the Friendship Liberal League, several humanist Unitarian churches, and the PWA. Under the union's constitution, each group would retain its individual status, but also be a part of the national organization. It was decided to change the orga-

nization's name so that the PWA would not be confused with the new national union of which it was a part. The name chosen for the new union was United Secularists of America, or USA. As for PWA, it became a local group based in Clifton, New Jersey, where *Progressive World* had been founded.

The editorial staff changed at this time as well. Lowell H. Coate being unable to continue as editor, Sherman Wakefield, formerly managing editor, was promoted to executive editor. Wakefield was married to Eva Ingersoll Brown, granddaughter of Robert Green INGERSOLL. Eva Ingersoll Brown Wakefield was a contributing editor, and wrote many times for *Progressive World.*

Progressive World and the USA continued to flourish. McCarthy, generally regarded as the USA's founder, became its business manager in late 1955. *Progressive World* moved its headquarters briefly to Chicago, then back to Clifton. A joint headquarters building for *Progressive World* and USA in Clifton was planned and funds raised toward its construction. Culbert L. Olson, freethought activist and former governor of California, was named chair of the building fund committee.

Scandal broke out in late 1957 when McCarthy was accused of filing false financial reports. A new treasurer and business manager were named and the editorial office was moved from Clifton to Los Angeles. The move occurred because Orr had been renamed as *Progressive World*'s editor and he refused to move to New Jersey. McCarthy lobbied the board to fire Orr, but he was unsuccessful. McCarthy resigned but refused to release the organization's papers to the new managers. A legal battle ensued. McCarthy died in November 1958 without surrendering the papers. The USA was eventually incorporated in California, with an East Coast branch in Clifton.

The USA continued to publish *Progressive World* but gradually declined. By 1981, the all-but-moribund USA suspended publication of *Progressive World.* Shortly afterward, Walter F. Kennon transferred ownership of the USA to the Madalyn Murray O'HAIR's American Atheists (AA). O'Hair listed the USA as an affiliated organization under American Atheists. It began to operate as a depository for AA's trust fund in 1988.

The USA became newsworthy again in 1995 in connection with the disappearance of Madalyn O'Hair, her son Jon Garth Murray, and daughter Robin Murray O'Hair. The three atheist activists were later found to have been kidnapped and murdered. According to reports, between $500,000 and $650,000 from the USA trust also disappeared. As is now known, the kidnappers had extorted the funds prior to killing them.

BIBLIOGRAPHY

American Atheists Member's Inside Newsletter 11, no. 1–4 (1976); 25, no. 5–7 (1986); 27, no. 6–9 (1988); 37, no. 8–12 (1998); 38, no.1 (January 1999).

Goeringer, Conrad F. "A Certain Closure." *American Atheist*, Spring 2001.

Progressive World 1, no. 1–9 (1947); 2, no. 1, 6–8 (1948); 3, no. 7 (September 1949); 4, no. 9 (November 1950); 11, no. 10 (November 1957); 12, no. 1–4 (1958); 38, no. 1, 2 and 4 (1981).

TIMOTHY BINGA

UNITED STATES, UNBELIEF IN. Contemporary Americans often assume that orthodox Christianity always dominated national life. In fact, surprising numbers of Americans simply ignored or rejected religious belief. No less underestimated may be the number and sophistication of organizations expressing ATHEISM, AGNOSTICISM, HUMANISM, SKEPTICISM, FREETHOUGHT, RATIONALISM, infidelity, or other forms of unbelief. This article will trace the history of unbelief in the United States.

The Revolutionary Era and Deism. On the eve of the American Revolution, a mere 17 percent of Colonials belonged to any Christian congregation. Sociologists Roger Finke and Rodney Stark maintain that this did not reflect external causes such as difficulty in reaching a church under frontier conditions, but rather (by modern standards) a very low level of participation in orthodox congregational life. Many among the more wealthy, educated, and politically active embraced some form of DEISM. Deism holds that a creator god exists, but cares nothing for human welfare and ordains nothing as to how men and women should live. As David Berman and others have noted, until the work of Charles DARWIN and Gregor Mendel furnished an intellectually satisfying model of how living things might have come to exist without miraculous intervention—an innovation of the nineteenth century—deism was about as far in the direction of unbelief as most educated people could stretch their minds. As an index of their boldness of thought, we may think of Revolutionary-era deists as the atheists or agnostics of their day. Surely they disbelieved in conventional Christianity.

Deism was widespread among the new nation's Founding Fathers. Thomas JEFFERSON, George Washington, John Adams, Thomas PAINE, Benjamin FRANKLIN, and James MADISON are positively known as deists. Nor was deism restricted to the highest ranks: Ethan ALLEN, homespun hero of Ticonderoga, made his deism conspicuous only because he published a book about it.

Deist literature was widely distributed, much of it imported from the mother country. In 1787 Ethan Allen released the first openly deistic and anti-Christian book published in North America: his own *Reason, the Only Oracle of Man*, published at Bennington, Vermont. Allen presented a rambling but reasonably sound rationalist critique of Christian doctrine. A fire at the publisher's offices destroyed much of the original edition, making copies extremely rare.

American deism peaked between 1795 and 1810 in the wake of the US appearance of Thomas Paine's *The Age of Reason* (1795). Though critics derided it as atheistic, *The Age of Reason* was in fact steeped in deism; Paine's text made clear that his aim was to protect reasonable and salutary religion (that is, deism) against the danger that conventional Christianity's gross absurdities might induce thinking people to discredit religion altogether. Nonetheless, by providing a powerful and most of all accessible debunking of core Christian beliefs, *The Age of Reason* arguably did more than any other single work to encourage abandonment of Christianity in favor of unbelief. The only book cited by more post-Revolutionary freethinkers as the cause for their renunciation of faith is, ironically enough, the Bible.

The first explicitly unbelieving organizations in the United States were deistic societies founded in New York, Philadelphia, Baltimore, and Newburgh, New York, by Elihu PALMER, a blind lawyer who became the new nation's leading deist preacher. Palmer published two deistic magazines at New York, *Temple of Reason* and *Prospect, or View of the Moral World*. His 1801 book *Principles of Nature* sold out three editions within five years.

Early Freethought. With Palmer's death in 1806 and Paine's in 1809, activity related to unbelief briefly vanished from the record. When it reappeared it would display a different social character, appealing to the working classes as much as to the educated elites who had largely sustained earlier deism. Unbelief reappears with a Thomas Paine birthday celebration organized in New York by Paine admirers on January 29, 1825. Out of this event eventually sprang a group called the Free Press Association, cofounded in 1827 by activist Benjamin OFFEN, apparently the first American to make his living as a freethought lecturer. In addition to his weekly lectures, Offen supported a radical magazine, the *Correspondent* (1827–29), edited by George Houston. Interest in unbelief was again on the upswing; in 1829 Robert Dale OWEN and Frances WRIGHT abandoned their utopian colony at New Harmony, Indiana, to establish their freethought paper the *FREE ENQUIRER* in New York. Aligned with it would be two organizations, the Society of Moral Philanthropists and its successor, the Society of Free Enquirers.

Self-taught Universalist minister (see UNIVERSALISM TO 1961) Abner KNEELAND arrived in Boston in 1830 to lecture to an existing group, the Society of Free Enquirers, not related to the New York group of the same name. Thereafter Kneeland launched a rationalist and atheist newspaper, the *BOSTON INVESTIGATOR*, for some time the nation's dominant freethought paper. Between 1834 and 1836 Kneeland faced multiple prosecutions for BLASPHEMY. Gilbert VALE edited the monthly freethought publication titled the *Beacon* from New York (1836–46).

At a regional freethought convention at Saratoga Springs, New York, in 1836, Kneeland and Offen urged creation of a national organization. The result was the United Moral and Philosophical Society for the Diffusion of Useful Knowledge. Despite its ungainly name, the group held annual conventions from 1836 to 1841 and enrolled members from several eastern states. In 1845 the Infidel Society for the Promotion of Mental Liberty was founded at New York; it would operate for three years. The proceedings of its inaugural meeting were published by J. P. MENDUM, second publisher of the *Boston Investigator*, under the title *Meteor of Light*. In 1857 another national organization, the Infidel Association of the United States, was founded at Philadelphia; its officers included *Boston Investigator* principals Horace SEAVER and J. P. Mendum, and feminist radical Ernestine ROSE. It met annually until at least 1860.

While unbelievers continued to use labels like "deist" and "infidel," a consensus was emerging as to the dominant term connoting religious skepticism. *Freethought* had emerged as a one-word term of art, suggesting the result of open inquiry and unfettered thought applied to the teachings of religion, particularly Christianity. The subtext was, of course, that the doctrines taught by the churches were obviously false, demonstrably contradictory, ill-defined, or perverse, so that any sincere, extended contemplation upon them must necessarily result in their abandonment.

The "Forty-Eighters." With the failure of the 1848 democratic revolution in Germany, thousands of politically and religiously liberal Germans fled to the United States. They accumulated where settlement was then most vigorous, a broad arc extending from Minnesota and Wisconsin through Kansas and Missouri into the Texas hill country. The "Forty-Eighters" founded numerous freethought papers and fraternal organizations. At Hermann, Missouri, Charles Strehly and Eduard Mühl published the *Licht Freund* (Friend of Light), which advocated abolition and ANTICLERICALISM. Every sizable German American community had a FREIE GEMEINDEN (Free Mind) society; their legacy included substantial halls in cities from Milwaukee to Saint Louis. *Turnvereins* or Turners' Clubs appeared wherever German Americans settled, promoting physical development and mutual defense through gymnastics and military drill, alongside an often strong component of freethought rhetoric (see MONUMENTS TO UNBELIEF). Nor was German American freethought activism limited to the Midwest. The *Blätter für Freies Religiöses Leben* (Paper for Free Religious Life) was edited by F. Schueneman-Pott in San Francisco and later Philadelphia. Nor was German the only language in which such freethought was expressed: the Swedish-language freethought paper *Forskaren* (The Scholar) was published in Minneapolis from 1893 to 1924.

The Golden Age of Freethought. The period between 1860 and 1900 is known as the Golden Age of Freethought. It marked a high point for unbelief in the United States as it did in England. In the United States,

the most conspicuous personalities were Benjamin Franklin UNDERWOOD, Robert Green INGERSOLL, DeRobigne Mortimer BENNETT, Samuel Porter PUTNAM, H. L. Green, Charles B. REYNOLDS, John E. REMSBURG, Thaddeus Burr WAKEMAN, and E. M. MACDONALD. This was the great age of American oratory, when public lectures on every subject were a dominant form of entertainment as well as education. Freethought lecturers moved about the country, inveighing against religion and debating clergy. For most it was an economically marginal enterprise of coach-class travel and home hospitality, but not for Ingersoll, the "Great Agnostic."

Ingersoll was not merely the most popular freethought orator, he was the most popular—if controversial—lecturer on the American "chautauqua" circuit. From the late 1860s until just before his death in 1899, he traveled the country lecturing to packed houses and was ubiquitous in newspapers and magazines. He considered God's existence unknowable, Christian doctrines ridiculous, and eternal punishment morally reprehensible. Ahead of his time, he advocated genuine equality for blacks and women, compassionate treatment of prisoners, economic justice for laborers and farmers, and other progressive causes. Despite his outspoken unbelief Ingersoll was the Republican Party's highest-profile political speechmaker; during his public life, no GOP presidential candidate whom he declined to endorse attained the White House.

Ingersoll also served unbelief as an attorney and as an officer of freethought organizations. When D. M. Bennett was arrested in Watkins (now Watkins Glen), New York, in 1878 for selling a birth control pamphlet (see BIRTH CONTROL AND UNBELIEF; MONUMENTS TO UNBELIEF), Ingersoll interceded with President Rutherford B. Hayes in an effort to deflect prosecution under the Comstock Act (see COMSTOCK, ANTHONY, AND UNBELIEF). When Charles Reynolds was tried for BLASPHEMY in New Jersey in 1887, Ingersoll defended him pro bono. When Reynolds was convicted, Ingersoll paid the fines and court costs. Along the way he had heaped such ridicule on the idea of state blasphemy prosecutions that no other such case ever reached trial. Ingersoll was repeatedly an officer of the NATIONAL LIBERAL LEAGUE, the largest freethought organization of the time, though he resigned in 1880 when it pressed for repeal of the Comstock Laws (see WAKEMAN, THADDEUS BURR). Ever the family man, Ingersoll feared creating the impression that freethinkers favored distribution of obscene materials through the mails.

The Golden Age was also distinguished by a cornucopia of freethought publications and organizations. Peter Eckler founded the company that bore his name in the 1840s; it published the semimonthly *Age of Reason* between 1848 and 1851, but published freethought books and pamphlets for almost eighty years. The Eckler Company also did printing for other freethought publishers, notably Clinton P. Farrell, Ingersoll's son-in-law and official publisher. Another important publisher was the Truth Seeker Company, which produced numerous books and pamphlets as well as the magazine of the same name. Principal freethought publications of the early Golden Age included *The Truth Seeker*; *Freethought*, edited from San Francisco by Samuel Porter Putnam and George Macdonald; *Iron-Clad Age*, a weekly edited from Indianapolis by J. R. Monroe between 1891 and 1898; and the *Boston Investigator*, still active from the preceding period.

The *Truth Seeker* was founded by D. M. Bennett in Paris, Illinois, in 1873, originally because Bennett despaired of inducing other papers to print his letters rebutting local ministers. After a year Bennett moved the paper to New York, expanded its circulation, and made it a weekly. He became a notorious adversary of decency crusader Anthony Comstock, and was repeatedly prosecuted by him, dying in 1882 as a result of an imprisonment Comstock had engineered. Editorship of *The Truth Seeker* passed to Eugene Macdonald, and in 1909 to Eugene's brother George E. Macdonald. By 1937 *The Truth Seeker* was no longer of national significance; in that year the aged Macdonald transferred the editorship to the eccentric Charles Lee SMITH.

Other significant publications included *Freethinker's* magazine (later *Freethought* magazine), published in Buffalo and Chicago by H. L. Green; the *Index*, published in Toledo and later Boston by Francis E. ABBOT and Benjamin F. Underwood; and the *Blue Grass Blade*, published weekly in Kentucky by Charles C. MOORE between 1884 and about 1905.

Some important freethought publishers have already been mentioned. The Truth Seeker Company was probably the most active during the nineteenth century. A close second was the J. P. Mendum Company of Boston, which grew out of the *Boston Investigator* after Mendum succeeded *Investigator* founder Abner Kneeland as the paper's publisher. Mendum was later succeeded by his son Ernest. Horace Seaver, who had succeeded Kneeland as the *Investigator*'s editor, was succeeded in turn by Lemuel K. WASHBURN. Also significant was Freidenker Publishing of Milwaukee, the largest supplier of German-language freethought materials.

The Golden Age also saw the birth of several prominent freethought organizations. Among the most important was the NATIONAL LIBERAL LEAGUE; this became the AMERICAN SECULAR UNION, which merged with the Freethought Federation of America circa 1919. Also noteworthy was the New York Freethinkers' Association (1877–late 1880s) whose annual conventions attracted unbelievers nationwide; D. M. Bennett's 1878 arrest at Watkins occurred at a New York Freethinkers Association convention.

Even in the Golden Age, freethought carried a tang of radicalism and appealed only to minorities. Still, it had sufficient mainstream appeal that some broadly influential progressives were willing to identify themselves as freethinkers, if not to become deeply involved in organized freethought. Among these were Thomas Alva Edison, Andrew Carnegie, Stephen Girard, Luther Burbank, and Charles Steinmetz. Also noteworthy is Mark Twain (see CLEMENS, SAMUEL LANGHORNE), whose posthumously published *Letters from the Earth* excoriated traditional Christianity. An authoritative edition of this long-closeted work did not appear until 1962.

Women in Freethought. The nineteenth-century woman's rights and woman suffrage movement meshed closely with freethought (see WOMAN SUFFRAGE MOVEMENT AND UNBELIEF). Amy Post was active in the New York Freethinkers Association and a variety of liberal religious causes as well as early feminism. Susan B. Anthony, born to a Quaker family in Adams, Massachusetts, and active in antislavery and temperance before the Civil War, devoted herself almost entirely to suffrage after 1854. In 1872 she was arrested and fined one hundred dollars for contriving to cast a vote at Rochester, New York. Her personal views were agnostic, though on pragmatic grounds she championed alliances between the suffrage movement and Christian temperance groups. In so doing she betrayed two more explicit freethinkers who had been conspicuous comrades in the suffrage movement, Elizabeth Cady STANTON and Matilda Joslyn GAGE. Stanton was a longtime member of the American Secular Union and an occasional contributor to *The Truth Seeker*; among her best-known works, *The Woman's Bible* (1895), an exposé of biblical misogyny, aroused sharp protest. Stanton had built her reputation in the woman's rights movement before revealing the scope of her unbelief, so that her memory was not wholly marginalized; Matilda Joslyn Gage was less fortunate. Coauthor with Stanton and Ida H. Harper of the authoritative four-volume *History of Woman Suffrage* (1881), Gage advocated for freethought throughout her career, and was until recently neglected in women's studies. Her 1893 *Woman, Church and State* unflinchingly attacked religion, particularly Christianity, for legitimating women's oppression through the ages. Gage also influenced the thinking of her son-in-law, L. Frank BAUM, author of the *Oz* children's books. One views the "Pay no attention to the man behind the curtain!" climax of *The Wizard of Oz* (filmed 1939) through fresh eyes after learning how profoundly Baum's thinking had been shaped by Gage's freethinking. Still, Baum himself was a Spiritualist as much as he was a freethinker (see SPIRITUALISM AND UNBELIEF).

Radical Social Reform and Freethought. Organized freethought interpenetrated with several American radical and reform movements, even Spiritualism. This is not so contradictory as it might appear; early on, before Spiritualism's empty paranormalism was well understood, noted scientists and freethinkers seriously imagined that it might offer evidence for an afterlife independent of Christian beliefs. Among freethought leaders who embraced—or defected to—Spiritualism, the best known is England's Annie BESANT, the close colleague of Charles BRADLAUGH who in the 1890s abandoned freethought for THEOSOPHY. Americans who followed similar trajectories include George Henry Walser, founder of the freethought town LIBERAL, MISSOURI; and freethought lecturer Benjamin Franklin Underwood.

Anarchism was a mostly European movement with an explicit anti-Christian or post-Christian stance. Anarchism attracted American adherents also, though its scope and power were often exaggerated by frightened cultural conservatives. American anarchists and freethinkers include activist-poet Voltairine DE CLEYRE, Emma GOLDMAN, and labor radicals including the Wobbly protest songwriter Joe Hill, whose "The Preacher and the Slave" is the most popular explicitly antireligious song in US history (see LABOR AND UNBELIEF).

Unlike anarchism with its European roots, sex radicalism and the free-love movement were largely American originals. Among the earliest sex radicals were birth control advocates (see BIRTH CONTROL AND UNBELIEF; SEXUAL VALUES, IMPACT OF UNBELIEF ON), many of whom were freethinkers. Charles KNOWLTON of Massachusetts self-published a pioneering birth control booklet, *Fruits of Philosophy*, around 1830. Though his religious views are not clearly known, his book became a staple of freethought publishers; in England, the atheist Bradlaugh and then-freethinker Besant faced an 1877 trial for publishing *Fruits of Philosophy* there. Another American freethinker, Edward Bliss FOOTE, published an 1864 book *Medical Common Sense* containing what may be the first modern description of condoms and diaphragms. Margaret SANGER, a freethinker's daughter, eventually won social acceptance for birth control in the United States and founded Planned Parenthood. Toward the end of her career she cosponsored research that led to the development of the 1960s birth control pill by freethinker Gregory Pincus.

As opponents of conventional structures for ordering the family, marriage, and sexual expression, sex radicals necessarily stood in tension to Christianity. Many were explicit atheists or freethinkers, also active in abolitionism or anarchism. The anarchists de Cleyre and Goldman were sex radicals in their writings and in their personal lives; Goldman promoted birth control. Stephen Pearl Andrews was a freethinker and socialist who cofounded Modern Times, a short-lived utopian free-love community east of New York City. Among the more extreme sex radicals were Ezra HEYWOOD, whose 1876 attack upon marriage and birth control handbook titled *Cupid's Yokes* precipitated D. M. Bennett's 1878 arrest. In Kansas, Moses HARMAN published the free-love paper *Lucifer, The Light Bearer*, which also ran freethought items. While Harman was imprisoned under the Comstock Act, freethinker Lois WAISBROOKER took over *Lucifer*, publishing even more outspoken free-love and birth control articles; her writings often blamed religion for the oppression of women. Ben LINDSEY, a free-

thinking twentieth-century reformer, argued for sex education, availability of birth control to unmarried women, and easier divorce. His best-known work was *The Companionate Marriage* (1927), in which he argued that matrimony should endure no longer than the partners' passion for one another.

Science, Religion, and Unbelief. The Golden Age of Freethought drew further momentum from the spread of BIBLICAL CRITICISM, which undercut the perceived authority of Jewish and Christian scripture. A flurry of scientific works challenged traditional Christian views to similar effect. As early as 1830, geologist Charles Lyell refuted Genesis chronology with his *Principles of Geology* (1830–33), marshaling rock-strata evidence for an ancient earth. Lyell's work influenced Charles DARWIN, whose 1859 *On the Origin of Species by Means of Natural Selection* precipitated enormous controversy (see EVOLUTION AND UNBELIEF). In 1863 Darwin's outspoken defender Thomas Henry HUXLEY published *Man's Place in Nature*, arguing that humans had been shaped by evolutionary forces no less than lower animals and anticipating arguments Darwin would offer eight years later in his *Descent of Man*. In 1874 American chemist and historian John William DRAPER published his bombastic *History of the Conflict between Science and Religion*, introducing the "military metaphor" of RELIGION IN CONFLICT WITH SCIENCE. In 1896 Cornell University cofounder Andrew Dickson WHITE (a believing Unitarian) completed the popularization of this metaphor with his *History of the Warfare of Science with Theology in Christendom*. Where Draper had traced Christian hostility toward science largely to Catholicism, White was more ecumenical, demonstrating that Protestant Christianity was no less guilty of hobbling discovery.

The Twentieth Century. Ingersoll died in 1899, never having translated his immense fame into an enduring freethought organization or periodical. (A twelve-volume edition of his collected *Works* remained in print from 1900 to 1929; editions after 1916 contained thirteen volumes, including an adulatory 1911 biography of Ingersoll by Herman Kittredge.) Ingersoll's death heralded the end of the Golden Age. In part, freethought was a casualty of its own success; much of the freethought critique had entered mainstream opinion and was no longer radical. Educated early twentieth-century moderns knew the earth was ancient, living things had evolved, and the Bible had developed over time. Many among them took irreligion for granted.

Still, organized freethought (which began to refer to *itself* as "atheism," rather than having the word hurled at it by enemies) did not want for advocates. Among the leading names in this period were Clarence DARROW, Emanuel HALDEMAN-JULIUS, Joseph MCCABE, Charles Lee Smith, Joseph LEWIS, Marshall Jerome GAUVIN, James Hervey JOHNSON, Madalyn Murray O'HAIR, Gordon STEIN, and Paul Kurtz. Also noteworthy were humanist and religious humanist movements whose thrust leaned toward unbelief (see HUMANISM; SECULAR HUMANISM; RELIGIOUS HUMANISM; UNITARIAN UNIVERSALISM). Religious humanist groups included ETHICAL CULTURE and the AMERICAN HUMANIST ASSOCIATION.

Darrow is well known for his lawyerly work, especially during the Scopes monkey trial of 1925 (see EVOLUTION AND UNBELIEF). An outspoken atheist, his 1932 autobiography offered an extended disproof of God's existence (see EXISTENCE OF GOD, ARGUMENTS FOR AND AGAINST). Emanuel Haldeman-Julius was the most astute businessman and promoter to emerge from the American Socialist movement (see SOCIALISM AND UNBELIEF). He turned a marginal Girard, Kansas, socialist tabloid into a publishing empire, along the way substantially inventing direct-mail marketing and the paperback book. He sold more than three hundred million of his Little Blue Books and Big Blue Books: compact, low-priced booklets, often on radical topics, that working people could afford and understand. Through the UNITED SECULARISTS OF AMERICA he published the periodical *American Freeman* (launched 1941), which continued until 1982 as *Progressive World*. The ex-priest Joseph McCabe supported himself by his pen for half a century, prolifically producing historical, philosophical, and freethought works, many of them published by Haldeman-Julius.

Charles Lee Smith was an Arkansas-born lawyer who moved to New York and in 1925 founded the AMERICAN ASSOCIATION FOR THE ADVANCEMENT OF ATHEISM ("the 4As"). Perpetually undercapitalized, the 4As achieved some impact through skillful media manipulation, especially with regard to the organization's largely vaporous plan to found atheist groups at vast numbers of American high schools. The 4As influenced legendary filmmaker Cecil B. DeMille, who based his last silent picture, *The Godless Girl* (1929), on one of the most charismatic 4As promoters, the Los Angeles–based child "atheist evangelist" Queen SILVER. Smith also debated and conducted bombastic campaigns against creationism. In 1937 he acquired the faded *Truth Seeker* from its aged second editor, George Macdonald. Influenced by associate editor Woolsey TELLER, Smith elbowed the paper toward social conservatism, anti-Semitism, racism, advocacy of EUGENICS, and ultimately obscurity. Smith died in 1964, passing the failing paper's editorship to James Hervey Johnson.

Joseph Lewis was the most prominent exponent of American atheism prior to Madalyn Murray O'Hair. He led the Freethinkers of America from 1925 until his death in 1968. Lewis instituted numerous church-state lawsuits and made many media appearances on behalf of atheism. He authored several books and edited a newsletter that ran under various titles for more than thirty years. He donated several statues of Thomas Paine still on view in the United States, England, and France, and engineered a successful drive for a US postage stamp memorializing Paine. He masterminded the

second restoration (1954) of the Robert Green Ingersoll birthplace in Dresden, New York (see MONUMENTS TO UNBELIEF). Marshall Gauvin was a Canadian who gave hundreds of rationalist lectures in the United States and Canada, wrote for *The Truth Seeker*, and in 1926 moved to Winnipeg, Mantioba, where he led a rationalist group. Between 1946 and 1954 he returned to New York to serve as president of a new and ultimately unsuccessful National Liberal League, named for the illustrious nineteenth-century freethought organization. In 1954 he returned to Winnipeg, remaining active in freethought until his death at age ninety-seven in 1978.

James Hervey Johnson succeeded Charles Lee Smith as editor of *The Truth Seeker* in 1964. He continued Smith's racism, anti-Semitism, and enthusiasm for eugenics, adding fringe medicine and arcane financial theories to the mix. Under his editorship *The Truth Seeker* became a crudely printed, typewritten hate sheet whose circulation descended to merely hundreds. Yet his investment principles had proven effective, abetted by his miserly lifestyle; at his death in 1988 Johnson left an estate of more than $16 million, part of which funded a charitable trust which has since the early 1990s functioned as the largest single source of charitable support for American unbelief. An ill-advised attempt by Madalyn Murray O'Hair to seize control of Johnson's estate shortly before his death led indirectly to the kidnapping of O'Hair and her children and their 1995 murder.

Madalyn Murray O'Hair. Madalyn Murray O'Hair was the most conspicuous US atheist in the second half of the twentieth century. Whether atheism benefited is subject to debate. A free-floating radical with casual communist ties, Madalyn Murray brought a lawsuit (*Murray v. Curlett*) against the Baltimore, Maryland, public schools over compulsory school prayer on behalf of her son William. Combined by the US Supreme Court with a similar case (*Abington School District v. Schempp*, brought by a Unitarian), it yielded the historic June 17, 1963, high court ruling ending teacher-led school prayer. On the plus side, this victory put atheism back on the cultural map after its near-suppression during the Cold War and created a momentum toward increasing secularization in American life that persisted for more than thirty years. On the minus side, it inspired decades of retrenchment and reorganization by US religious conservatives, paving the way for a fundamentalist resurgence that began in the late 1970s. Claiming more than her share of credit for the 1963 Supreme Court decision, the abrasive O'Hair (as she was known after marriage to Richard O'Hair) built American Atheists, until her death the country's largest atheist organization. Her tirade against a Bible reading by *Apollo* 8 astronauts circling the moon further swelled the roster of her enemies—but also ensured that when *Apollo* 11 landed on the moon in 1969, humanity's greatest technological achievement was wholly secular in character. O'Hair's numerous lawsuits ranged from quixotic efforts to remove "In God We Trust" from US currency and coins to the more significant *O'Hair v. Hill* (1984), which invalidated state laws barring atheists from public office, state employment, and jury service. Her son William, the former Supreme Court plaintiff, led a difficult life; Madalyn adopted William's illegitimate daughter, Robin, whom she raised thereafter as her own daughter. William later embraced fundamentalist Christianity and became a fixture on the evangelical lecture circuit. O'Hair ran American Atheists in mercurial fashion, purging members at whim. She also attracted millions of dollars in donations, which she sometimes treated as personal funds. In 1987 she launched a groundless effort to seize control of the Truth Seeker Company, key to the estate of the then terminally ill James Hervey Johnson. The effort quickly collapsed, sparking countersuits by Johnson estate trustees, Johnson himself having died in the interim. Most observers expected O'Hair to lose those suits to devastating effect; O'Hair apparently agreed. Evidence suggests that O'Hair, her son John Garth Murray, and now-daughter Robin Murray O'Hair arranged to transfer hundreds of thousands of dollars in American Atheist funds to New Zealand with plans to abscond there. Instead David Waters, a felon caught stealing while employed by American Atheists whom O'Hair had excoriated in the organization's newsletter, led a conspiracy that kidnapped the trio, extorted most of their liquid funds, and murdered Madalyn, Jon, and Robin in 1995. In a bizarre twist, police made little effort to track these high-profile missing persons until estranged evangelist son William Murray exerted political pressure. Not until 2000 was a conspirator, Gary Karr, convicted—not of murder, but merely of conspiracy.

Gordon Stein was the foremost collector and bibliographer of freethought materials in the second half of the twentieth century. He was longtime editor of the *AMERICAN RATIONALIST*, a bimonthly founded in 1956 by the AMERICAN RATIONALIST FEDERATION. Stein also compiled numerous bibliographies and encyclopedias, including the original *Encyclopedia of Unbelief* (1985). He was founding director of the Center for Inquiry Libraries, now the world's largest repository of English-language atheist, humanist, freethought, and skeptical materials. He died in 1996.

Several atheist organizations formed during the second half of the twentieth century, most remaining active today. American Atheists still operates, though on a smaller scale than in O'Hair's heyday. Based in New Jersey, it is led by Ellen Johnson, who attained control during the confusion following the O'Hair kidnappings. Perhaps the most active organization is the Freedom From Religion Foundation (FFRF), founded in Madison, Wisconsin, in 1976 by former O'Hair colleague Anne Nicol Gaylor. Aided by her daughter Annie Laurie Gaylor (a prolific contributor to this encyclopedia) and Annie's husband, evangelist-turned-atheist Dan Barker, FFRF publishes the monthly newspaper *Freethought Today* and varied freethought books and tracts. It has won significant church-state legal victories, especially in the Midwest. Atheists United, based in Los Angeles, was formed in 1982 from a group of American Atheists chapters cut adrift after Madalyn O'Hair ended the American Atheists chapter network. The group is active in various metropolitan areas and conducts an annual convention.

The Rise of Humanism. During the second and third quarters of the twentieth century, there occurred a "passing of the torch" as intellectual prestige and organizational energy passed from traditional atheism and freethought to the movement known as humanism. Where atheism and freethought traced their roots to the Enlightenment, the French Revolution, anticlericalism, and radical social reform movements, humanism sprang from Jewish and Christian liberalism. As early as 1876 Felix Adler had founded Ethical Culture as a naturalistic, secularizing offshoot of Judaism. Liberal Christianity gave rise to varied movements that responded to such causes as Darwinism and biblical criticism by reinterpreting Christianity in more secular terms. This trend was especially influential in the Unitarian Church (see UNITARIANISM TO 1961; UNITARIAN UNIVERSALISM). In 1933 the *Humanist Manifesto* presented a ringing statement of naturalistic moral ideals. It was drafted by one philosopher, Roy Wood Sellars, and signed by another, the influential John DEWEY, as well as several liberal Unitarian ministers. The *Manifesto* became a gathering point for a broad-based movement known as RELIGIOUS HUMANISM. Some religious humanists were supernaturalists who had chosen to attach primary value to this life rather than the next; others were naturalists who rejected beliefs in eternity or any spirit realm but adapted the vocabulary of religion to express the emotional and aesthetic aspects of their LIFE STANCE. In 1941 Unitarian minister Ed Wilson founded the American Humanist Association (AHA). Recognized by the US Internal Revenue Service (IRS) as an educational nonprofit organization in 1946, AHA enjoyed early vigor, winning the allegiance of international leaders of thought. In the 1960s and early 1970s AHA's magazine, the *Humanist*, achieved relatively large circulation and cultural influence under the editorship of Paul Kurtz. Kurtz drafted a successor to *Humanist Manifesto*, the 1976 *Humanist Manifesto II*, which attracted substantial attention.

One of the AHA's initiatives during the 1960s was a Division of Humanist Counseling, whose members sought privileges of clergy including the power to perform legally binding marriages. In 1968 the AHA applied to the IRS for recognition as a religious organization, which would buttress the Humanist Counselors' clerical standing. This had the effect, apparently unforeseen, of replacing the AHA's educational exemption with a religious one, making the AHA legally equivalent to a church. This made the group—and by extension, humanism itself—easy prey for Christian Right activists eager to portray humanism as a religion. In 1989 the

AHA undertook a reorganization, absorbing a liberal Quaker organization with a plan that this entity would maintain the clergy status of Humanist Counselors while the AHA reassumed an educational exemption. The effort was abandoned with little fanfare, perhaps upon discovery that the 1948 educational exemption no longer existed. A 2002 effort to redefine itself as an educational organization belatedly succeeded in 2007. The AHA still remains the most prominent organizational home for US religious humanists.

The Rise of Secular Humanism. Today the principal vehicle for activist unbelief is the secular humanist movement founded by Paul Kurtz and others. Secular humanism is a comprehensive nonreligious life stance that incorporates a naturalistic philosophy, a cosmic outlook rooted in science, and a consequentialist ethical system (see ETHICS AND UNBELIEF). Secular humanism hybridizes elements from religious humanism with elements from atheism, freethought, and SECULARISM. In sharp contrast to religious humanism, secular humanism is explicitly nonreligious. Yet the label has an ironic history, having achieved currency among religious believers decades before unbelievers took it up. Secular humanism was apparently spoken of as early as the late 1950s as a fuzzy label for a range of modernist initiatives that religious conservatives deplored: everything from EXISTENTIALISM, Freudian psychology (see FREUD, SIGMUND), and humanistic psychology to traditional freethought. In the US Supreme Court decision *Torcaso v. Watkins* (1961), which ended some states' practices of barring atheists from serving as notaries, Justice Hugo L. Black added an ill-informed footnote that listed "secular humanism" among nontraditional religions deserving legal recognition. Though Christian activists have made much of this, such dicta by individual justices carry no legal weight.

By the late 1970s secular humanism had become a favorite target of Religious Right activists. Only in 1980 was the first explicitly secular humanist organization formed: the Council for Democratic and Secular Humanism (CODESH), founded by a group including Gordon Stein and led by philosopher Paul Kurtz. With this event, secular humanism broke away from both religious humanism and socialist intellectualism and set out upon its own ideological path. Kurtz, a professor of philosophy at the State University of New York at Buffalo and former editor of the *Humanist*, drafted a follow-up to his *Humanist Manifesto II* titled "A Secular Humanist Declaration." Signed by scores of prominent intellectuals and activists, it drew wide attention. Also founded in 1980 was the council's journal, *Free Inquiry.* In short order the council established itself as the largest and most vigorous organization of unbelief in the United States. *Free Inquiry*'s circulation regularly exceeded the combined circulations of all other US humanist, atheist, and freethought publications. The council and its sister organization, the Committee for the Scientific Investiga-

tion of Claims of the Paranormal (CSICOP), jointly founded the Center for Inquiry in 1995. With its declared mission to promote and defend reason, science, freedom of inquiry, and ethical alternatives in every area of human endeavor, the Center for Inquiry emerged as a principal exponent of naturalism and humanistic ideals and created a network of national and worldwide branches. By 1996 the need to distinguish humanism from communist totalitarianism had passed, and so CODESH renamed itself the Council for Secular Humanism. In 1999 Kurtz drafted a new successor to the *Humanist Manifestos*; *Humanist Manifesto 2000* was signed by more than a hundred leaders of thought and attracted attention worldwide. In 2000 the *American Rationalist* passed from its original Saint Louis–based publishers to the Center for Inquiry.

The Prospects for Unbelief. Unbelief in the United States faces an uncertain future. The nation's idiosyncratic embrace of popular piety remains without precedent: the US since about 1980 is the only first world country in which rates of church membership, belief in religious doctrines, and the like remain at third world levels. Yet even while this trend continues, other indicators suggest new strength for unbelief. Between 1990 and 2000 the fraction of Americans who tell pollsters they have "no religious preference" doubled; so-called nones now constitute 16 percent of the population, more than forty-seven million adults and children (see DEMOGRAPHY OF UNBELIEF). Some late twentieth- and early twenty-firstcentury figures have succeeded in combining outspoken atheism with mainstream prestige, including the scientist-authors E. O. Wilson, Daniel C. Dennett, and Richard Dawkins (a British scientist with a strong independent American following), and social critic Wendy Kaminer. Certain initiatives of the Council for Secular Humanism, notably the International Academy of Humanism and the Committee for the Scientific Examination of Religion, have achieved significant stature in their fields. And new voices have continued to arise in defense of unbelief, among them *New York Times* science reporter Natalie Angier, historian Susan Jacoby, and perhaps most conspicuously Sam Harris, a graduate student whose 2004 antireligious polemic *The End of Faith: Religion, Terror, and the Future of Reason* became a surprise best seller for mainstream publisher W. W. Norton. The chronicle of unbelief in the United States continues to unfold.

BIBLIOGRAPHY

Brown, Marshall G., and Gordon Stein. *Freethought in the United States.* Westport, CT: Greenwood, 1978.

Finke, Roger, and Rodney Stark. *The Churching of America, 1776–1990: Winners and Losers in Our Religious Economy.* New Brunswick, NJ: Rutgers University Press, 1992.

Flynn, Tom. "A Secular Humanist Definition: Setting the

Record Straight." *Free Inquiry* (Fall 2002).

———. *The Trouble with Christmas.* Amherst, NY: Prometheus Books, 1993.

Gaylor, Annie Laurie. *Women without Superstition.* Madison, WI: Freedom From Religion Foundation, 1997.

Hecht, Jennifer Michael. *Doubt: A History.* New York: HarperSanFrancisco, 2003.

Jacoby, Susan. *Freethinkers: A History of American Secularism.* New York: Henry Holt, 2004.

Macdonald, George E. *Fifty Years of Freethought.* 2 vols. New York: Truth Seeker Company, 1929.

Moore, James R. *The Post-Darwinian Controversies: A Study of the Protestant Struggle to Come to Terms with Darwin in Great Britain and America, 1870–1900.* Cambridge: Cambridge University Press, 1979.

Morais, Herbert M. *Deism in Eighteenth Century America.* New York: Columbia University Press, 1934.

Post, Albert. *Popular Freethought in America, 1825–1850.* New York: Columbia University Press, 1943.

Putnam, Samuel Porter. *Four Hundred Years of Freethought.* New York: Truth Seeker Company, 1894.

Seaman, Ann Rowe. *America's Most Hated Woman: The Life and Gruesome Death of Madalyn Murray O'Hair.* New York: Continuum, 2005.

Whitehead, Fred, and Verle Muhrer, eds. *Freethought on the American Frontier.* Amherst, NY: Prometheus Books, 1992.

The author gratefully acknowledges Gordon Stein's entry "United States, Unbelief in the" in his 1985 Encyclopedia of Unbelief, from which this entry was in part derived.

TOM FLYNN

UNIVERSALISM TO 1961. Universalism is a religious position that affirms a common ultimate destiny for all humanity, and thus denies the existence of eternal punishment as part of the divine plan.

Universalism in the North America has two distinct roots. One is found in post-Reformation pietism, which held that God's basic attribute was love and that this love could not be thwarted; therefore, in the end, all of creation would be restored to harmony with the divine. The other root is in the Enlightenment (see ENLIGHTENMENT, UNBELIEF DURING THE), which applied REASON and logic to religious claims and found the doctrine of endless punishment to be unreasonable and illogical.

At the outset, Universalism offered a Bible-centered corrective to the hellfire teachings of mainstream Christianity. But early on, Universalists insisted that reason is the tool to be used in understanding the Bible, and that where biblical teachings contradicted reason, there was probably some fault in the transmission of the biblical tradition.

Organized as a movement in New England in the late eighteenth century, Universalism expanded into neighboring states and moved west with the frontier. In 1832 the *American Almanac* listed Universalism as the sixth-largest denomination in the country, and the following year the *Boston Recorder* proclaimed Universalism "the reigning heresy of the day."

By 1850 Universalism had stopped growing faster than the population, and by 1900 had begun a serious and steep decline. Some attributed the decline to the diversion of the movement's energies into social concerns. Universalists were champions of separation of church and state; struggled for decades for prison reform and the end of capital punishment; were the first to ordain women with full denominational authority; and spoke out early against slavery and for peace. Others believed that having won the struggle with the orthodox on the question of eternal hell, the movement had lost its central focus and had begun to drift toward formlessness.

As a creedless movement, Universalism attracted a broad spectrum of people—from those who reaffirmed the Christian core of the movement, to those who embraced Charles DARWIN's theory of evolution (see EVOLUTION AND UNBELIEF) and BIBLICAL CRITICISM, to those who, in the years after the Civil War, were entranced with the prospects of Mesmerism, phrenology, and Spiritualism. This provided a rich and heady mix of opinion, but little focus in the effort to halt denominational decline. The demographic shift that occurred in the years after World War I deepened the decline of Universalism, which had been centered in small towns.

Responding to this decline, leaders of the movement began to talk about a "new Universalism"—one larger in focus than Christianity. While only three signers of the *Humanist Manifesto* (see HUMANISM) were affiliated with Universalism, Universalists, with roots in the enlightenment and a historic commitment to the role of reason in religion, could not escape the influence of the emerging humanist movement.

In 1943, addressing the Universalist General Assembly, General Superintendent Robert Cummins said: "Universalism cannot be limited to Protestantism or to Christianity, not without denying its very name. Ours is a world fellowship, not just a Christian sect." Brainerd Gibbons, who would serve as president and general superintendent of the Universalist Church of America, insisted that Universalism and Christianity were simply irreconcilable.

In 1949 the Massachusetts Universalist Convention established the Charles Street Meeting House in Boston and hired Kenneth Patton as its minister. His charge was to create worship forms appropriate to a naturalistic, humanistic religion that had emerged from Christianity but was no longer defined by it. Patton's output was remarkable in quality and quantity. In a few years, he transformed the Universalist and also the Unitarian movements by providing them with a richly poetic, deeply spiritual language that reverenced the natural world and honored reason and moral compassion.

Unitarians (see UNITARIANISM TO 1961) and Universalists had already toyed with the idea of a merger for nearly a century when a commission on merger was appointed in 1955. The result was the consolidation of the Universalist Church of America and the American Unitarian Association into the Unitarian Universalist Association in 1961 (see UNITARIAN UNIVERSALISM). Universalism, which had begun with a concern for the afterlife, came to the merger focused on the world of here and now. The historic concern for a heavenly reconciliation of all people with God had been transformed into a concern for earthly reconciliation of human beings with each other.

BIBLIOGRAPHY

Bumbaugh, David E. *Unitarian Universalism: A Narrative History*. Chicago: Meadville Lombard, 2000.
Cassaro, Ernest. *Universalism in America*. Boston: Beacon, 1971.
Miller, Russell E. *The Larger Hope*. 2 vols. Boston: Unitarian Universalist Association, 1979.

DAVID E. BUMBAUGH

UNIVERSE, ORIGIN OF THE, AND UNBELIEF. Since religions usually claim that our universe was supernaturally created, denying that the universe has divine origins has been an important part of unbelief. The universe, unbelievers think, does not depend on any personal being outside of the natural order.

Philosophical discussions about the origin of the universe center on the classical cosmological argument for the existence of a God, expressing the intuition that everything contingent requires a cause, and that therefore the universe as a whole must be caused by something beyond the natural causes operating within the universe (see EXISTENCE OF GOD, ARGUMENTS FOR AND AGAINST). As with most philosophical arguments, varieties of the cosmological argument are never absolutely conclusive. It is not strictly necessary that the universe have any cause, divine or otherwise. Nevertheless, to many philosophers a divine cause for the natural universe has seemed more plausible than the option left to unbelievers, which is to provide no explanation at all.

Recently, however, the debate over the origins of the universe has shifted away from traditional philosophical territory. With the maturing of physical science, the universe as a whole has become subject to investigation within physics. Indeed, modern physics has changed the very concepts involved in discussing origins, such as causality, or a universe. So currently, though the philosophical tradition continues to influence the debate, the question of how the universe came about is primarily addressed by physical cosmology.

Early Ideas. Ideas about the origins of the universe took shape long before modern science. In antiquity, the alternative to stories of divine creation was to present the world as eternal, perhaps self-existing. The Greek philosophical tradition particularly encouraged belief in an eternal universe. Aristotle, for example, argued that some sort of God was necessary as a First Cause, but he also presented arguments that the world was eternal.

As Greek philosophy developed further, the notion of an eternal universe became more closely tied to philosophical ideas about divinity. The God of the philosophers had to be perfect: beyond time, beyond human passions, beyond anything subject to change. This meant that any direct involvement with the changeable realm of material objects would be an imperfection. Especially within Platonic philosophy, the highest divinity did not get its hands dirty with acts of creation. Instead, God "emanated," out of necessity, slightly less perfect intermediate beings such as Reason or Wisdom. These intermediates then did the actual work of shaping the material world. The universe depended on God—it derived its very reality from the God which was ultimately the only truly real being—but it was also eternal. And with a universe eternally emanating from the divine layers of reality, there was less change that even intermediaries had to be responsible for.

The Hellenistic period following Alexander's conquests, and the Roman Empire that followed, brought Greek speculative philosophy together with Near Eastern religious beliefs about creation. The version of Christianity that became the state religion of the Roman Empire tried to integrate philosophy and revealed beliefs in its theology; later, medieval Islam faced a similar challenge. Reason and revelation agreed on many things such as the existence of a supreme being, but there were also points of friction. Pagan philosophy favored an eternal universe, but the guardians of revelation were reluctant to allow other eternal entities alongside their creator God. The God of monotheism was much more personal, much more free to act, compared to the God of the philosophers who could seem too much in the grip of impersonal necessities. So monotheists developed a doctrine of creation ex nihilo. Creation from nothing went further than Near Eastern myths about divine forces shaping primeval chaos; not even raw material could be eternal like God.

Well into the Middle Ages, discussions of origins were framed by the contrast between the pagan option of a universe that was eternal, though dependent on God, and the monotheistic doctrine of creation out of nothing. Conceptually, the notion of creation from nothing was a potent source of headaches, but on the other hand, pagan concepts of eternity could also seem to harbor contradictions. Without the modern apparatus of transfinite mathematics to keep them straight, philosophers had plenty of opportunity to tie themselves into knots when thinking about infinities. Still, since an eternal universe was a pagan idea, it was attractive to the heterodox. Educated dissenters from officially sanctioned religion could embrace an eternal universe as an intellectually respectable alternative. Both in Christendom and the lands of Islam, belief in the eternity of the universe became a marker of infidelity.

The scientific revolution radically changed the accepted picture of the universe. The heavens no longer revolved around the earth; in fact, the heavens no longer embodied divine perfection in contrast with the sublunar realms of change and decay. Copernican astronomy and Newtonian physics presented a world where the same laws of physics applied everywhere, all the time. They joined the heavens and the earth, and removed some of the old philosophical motivations to think that the universe might be eternal. However, in the Newtonian clockwork universe, it was also hard to see how there could be a beginning in time. To reveal the presence of God, early modern science emphasized the classical design argument. Newtonian physics could not, it seemed, explain functional complexity. If the planets had stable orbits rather than undergoing haphazard motion, this must have been because a divine hand adjusted their orbits just so. Moreover, the complex structures of living things were clearly designed by an awesome intelligence. At the start of modern science, it remained easy to think that the history of the universe was as told in Genesis.

Eventually, however, Newtonian physics made it easier to conceive of a universe infinite in space and time. Problems such as the stability of orbits were solved within physics. Geologists found that our planet was much older than a few thousands of years. And finally, biological evolution showed that that complexity did not have to be due to intelligent design. At the end of the nineteenth century, it had become clear that the literal Genesis story was wrong.

Still, there remained one prominent physical argument that the universe was a divine creation in the distant past. This came from the second law of thermodynamics, which suggested that the universe would always change to become more disordered over time. The fate of the universe was regarded to be a "heat death" in which everything became a featureless soup in a state of maximum entropy, able to sustain no life nor any order of any interest. The religious implications of such a view were ambiguous; the notion of a heat death could just as easily feed into an ATHEISM of a cosmic-pessimist style. But believers looked toward the origins of the universe. If the clockwork universe was winding down, there had to be a beginning where an outside force wound everything up. The initial order could not be provided by physics, and there had to be a beginning in time. Once again, the design and cosmological arguments reinforced one another.

Modern Physical Cosmology. In the first half of the twentieth century, modern physical cosmology once again changed the debate over the origin of the universe. The most important theoretical development for cosmology was Albert Einstein's general theory of relativity. Now physicists could treat space and time as a single geometric entity shaped by the distribution of matter/energy throughout the universe. Gravity was due to energy bending space-time.

As it turned out, general relativity made it hard to construct static models of the universe, where the largest-scale structure of the universe looked more or less the same all the time. Einstein realized that his equations could include a "cosmological constant" term which led to a peculiar long-range repulsive force alongside ordinary gravity. A stable universe required a nonzero cosmological constant. Soon, however, the issue was settled by observational evidence: astronomers discovered that our universe was expanding and an expanding universe could be described without a cosmological constant.

Other new observations would also advance cosmology. Indeed, in the twentieth century, cosmology began to enjoy the mutual interaction between theory and observation that characterizes any successful science. Ideas about the origins of the universe could now be subjected to reality tests, becoming more than philosophical speculation. Aside from the expansion of the universe, other observations such as the cosmic microwave background radiation also supported the claim that our universe had started out, billions of years ago, from a much hotter and denser initial state. The Big Bang theory came to dominate cosmology in the second half of the twentieth century. In an expanding universe like ours, general relativity demanded that a singularity should exist back in time—not only was the universe once extremely hot and dense, it was infinitely so at the Big Bang. The Big Bang was, in fact, when the universe began.

It took no great leap of the religious imagination to equate the Big Bang, as the beginning of time, with a moment of creation. And so unbelievers, who have typically identified with the philosophical tradition of an eternal universe, have often been drawn to alternatives to Big Bang cosmology. The problem was that the alternatives were full of arbitrary assumptions, they failed to match the predictive success of the Big Bang, and they did not make sense of multiple independent lines of evidence as did the Big Bang.

One early rival to the Big Bang was the steady-state universe, in which the universe was eternal and looked the same at all times. This required the continual creation of new matter as the universe expanded. Fred Hoyle and collaborators continue working on a "quasi-steady-state cosmology" even today, but this has become a marginal effort, considered a failure by the vast majority of cosmologists. Another alternative that preserved an eternal universe was the notion that the universe oscillated. The expansion of each phase of the universe would be followed by a contraction to a "big crunch," followed by a new big bang and another cycle of the universe. This too has numerous difficulties, from failure to fit observations to arbitrary theoretical assumptions needed to make the universe rebound after the big crunch and to overcome the problems due to increasing entropy throughout the cycles. "Plasma cosmology" is the most recent attempt to construct a serious physical alternative to the Big Bang, though it also suffers from numerous defects and thus has not found acceptance in mainstream cosmology.

The standard model of the Big Bang had, besides the beginning, another feature attractive to religious thinkers who were willing to let go of a literally interpreted Genesis. The natural outcome of the Big Bang was a universe that almost immediately collapsed on itself. Our universe has been around for about fourteen billion years. It also looks very similar in all directions, even when areas of the universe farther than fourteen billion light-years apart are observed. But since no physical signal can travel faster than light, such areas could not have interacted with each other to become so similar. Our universe fit the standard Big Bang model, but nothing like our universe could come about unless the parameters that went into the model were adjusted with uncanny precision. This suggested that not only was the Big Bang a moment of creation, but that the creator was a designer who fine-tuned the physics just so the universe could support intelligent life (see ANTHROPIC PRINCIPLE; INTELLIGENT DESIGN THEORY).

So early physical cosmology had ambiguous consequences for unbelief. On one hand, cosmology became an ordinary branch of physics, addressed in the typically naturalistic fashion that dominates modern physics. This development could only demystify the origins of the universe, supporting the view that we live in a natural world that can be understood without gods and demons. On the other hand, in the context of the long-standing philosophical dispute about the eternity of the universe, physical cosmology came down on the side of a universe with a beginning.

Even now, thinkers who argue that science supports theism typically make cosmology a centerpiece of their case. The "kalam cosmological argument" has become popular; it asserts that the universe has a beginning, that everything that begins has a cause, and that the only cause that can act to create a universe is outside of nature—the free choice of a personal agent. Proponents of such updated cosmological arguments usually also bring up cosmic fine-tuning, saying it proves the universe is a result of intelligent design.

Quantum Cosmology. Cosmology today, however, is not so full of signs of God. Much of the current debate over cosmic origins and divine creation barely updates the traditional philosophical dispute; it continues to rely on commonsense understandings of time and causality which have been superseded by modern physics.

In relativity, time is tied to physical events such as the periodic ticking of a clock; time is not external to the physical universe. In general relativity, space-time as a whole is curved by matter/energy; there is nothing especially odd if the geometry of space-time turns out to be curved and finite rather than extending to infinity. It becomes easy to think of space-time as self-contained, regardless of its overall shape. The standard Big Bang is not the beginning of the universe *in* some point of time external to the universe. Physically, time cannot be extended back before the Big Bang. In fact, in the standard picture, time before the Big Bang is a meaningless concept, just like it makes no sense to talk about a location north of the North Pole. A year before the Big Bang is like a place with a latitude of 500°. So thinking of a cause preceding the Big Bang becomes difficult.

The standard Big Bang could still allow an echo of a conventionally conceived cause of the universe, however. This is because the Big Bang is a singularity—a boundary of space-time and hence a very special point. Attaching a God to the singularity can therefore seem attractive. Nevertheless, this is an arbitrary metaphysical exercise unless divine creation also succeeds in explaining some nontrivial features of the resulting universe. Hence a design argument, such as that for cosmic fine-tuning, has to do all the real work.

Even then, there is a fundamental problem. General relativity, and hence the standard Big Bang, is not a quantum theory. Therefore it cannot be entirely correct. It should break down particularly where very high energies and very small distances are concerned—precisely the conditions immediately after the Big Bang. No adequate account of the origins of the universe will be possible without a quantum theory of gravity.

If general relativity warps commonsensical notions of time and causality, quantum mechanics forces an even more radical rethinking. Even in Newtonian mechanics, the laws of physics do not distinguish between forward and backward directions of time; the "arrow of time," or the direction in which entropy increases, emerges only in many-particle systems. Quantum mechanics retains this time reversibility and introduces true randomness in the behavior of particles. The quantum universe is not a place of definite causes and effects, with clockwork motion proceeding in deterministic fashion. Instead, it is a sea of random, uncaused events, where even a "virtual" particle popping into being or vanishing in a vacuum is not a miracle but just the routine way of things. Everyday causes and effects emerge in the macroscopic world, from a substrate of random interactions. In other words, the intuitions about causality and time that go into the classical cosmological argument and the traditional debate about the origins of the universe are not applicable to a quantum universe.

Unfortunately, physicists have not yet been able to combine gravity and quantum mechanics to obtain a full-blown theory of quantum gravity. Still, physicists have *some* idea about what an eventual theory of quantum gravity should imply, and have been applying approximate quantum approaches to cosmology for some time. A common feature of quantum cosmologies is that they get rid of the singularity as it stands in the standard Big Bang. This removes the last hint, weak though that was, that the physical universe might depend on something external to itself.

For example, the boundary-free cosmology of Hartle and Hawking, though somewhat outdated now, illustrates how the universe can be finite in time and yet entirely self-contained. Their model smears out the singularity, removing the boundary of space-time that existed in the standard Big Bang. No point in the universe can be identified to which to attach a nonphysical cause.

Another approach is inflationary cosmology. Originally, inflation was developed to account for some of the puzzles raised by the standard Big Bang, such as certain kinds of apparent fine-tuning and the fact that the universe looked the same even for areas separated by more than fourteen billion light-years. Cosmology that includes quantum theories of elementary particles allows for a brief episode of "inflation" after the Big Bang, where a small bubble of space-time expanded much faster than the speed of light. Inflation solved the problems it was supposed to address, and was also developed further. Notably, the notion of inflating universes into being naturally brings up the notion of multiple universe-bubbles, perhaps inflating into existence randomly, somewhat like virtual particles in a quantum vacuum. Naturally, without a full theory of quantum gravity, none of these ideas can be worked out in a completely consistent fashion. Still, today, scenarios like chaotic eternal inflation, or infinite sets of universes linked together by what appear as singularities in general relativity (such as black holes), are commonly discussed in physical cosmology. Multiple universes have even been an impetus to think of populations of reproducing universes, and to speculate on whether a Darwinian-style mechanism ensures that large universes that create lots of black of holes, like ours, might be the most common variety.

A leading current approach to quantum gravity centers on the idea that the fundamental particles of physics are not extensionless points but strings or "m-branes." An immediate consequence of such theories is that there is a length scale beyond which objects cannot be compressed—the singularity disappears. String theory–inspired cosmological scenarios typically have an eternal universe, in that time can be extended back before the Big Bang. Still, the physics involved is alien to commonsense conceptions of time, so that thinking of such cosmological scenarios in terms of an eternal universe versus a universe with a beginning is misleading. Neither of the traditional options is really in play anymore.

Physical cosmology today is a rapidly changing field, with few settled conclusions. Large theoretical questions remain, from uniting gravity with quantum mechanics to figuring out problems with the cosmological constant. And improving observations continually produce surprises, such as the recent discovery that the expansion of the universe is accelerating. With better space-based telescopes to come, and further refinements to physical theories, cosmology will continue to change. So today's models of the origin of the universe are all highly uncertain. Nevertheless, some conclusions can be drawn.

Most important, physical cosmology has no need for the supernatural. The universe seems self-contained regardless of whether time can be extended back indefinitely. Any intervention by a supernatural creator would be a strange imposition on the structure of physics. The universe need not be eternal to be uncreated; the traditional debate is simply not relevant anymore. It is not a problem if there is no ultimate explanation for the universe, so that the universe appears uncaused. Modern physics heavily relies on randomness, finding that much in the universe appears to be fundamentally without cause, and that there is no good prospect to find a cause for such events. Physical science has been enormously successful in explaining the world in terms of combinations of chance and necessity—in terms of blind, purposeless, starkly physical processes. Cosmology has progressed in the same direction.

Attempts to provide a theistic explanation for the universe continue. At present, however, it is notable how bringing in God as an ultimate cause does not actually explain anything. Cosmology does not lack for unknowns and surprising discoveries, so any genuine explanation for the universe should be able to predict some new things. But current theistic ideas, including fine-tuning arguments, do not lead physicists to expect anything new; they produce only the dead silence of divine inscrutability. The classical cosmological argument has become irrelevant, and the design argument has become relegated to such fringes of science as the "intelligent design" movement.

BIBLIOGRAPHY

Craig, William Lane, and Quentin Smith. *Theism, Atheism and Big Bang Cosmology.* Oxford: Clarendon, 1993.

Edis, Taner. *The Ghost in the Universe: God in Light of Modern Science.* Amherst, NY: Prometheus Books, 2002.

———. *Science and Nonbelief.* Westport, CT: Greenwood, 2006.

Grant, Edward. *Science and Religion, 400 BC–AD 1550: From Aristotle to Copernicus.* Westport, CT: Greenwood, 2004.

Guth, Alan H. *The Inflationary Universe: The Quest for a New Theory of Cosmic Origins.* Reading, MA: Addison-Wesley, 1997.

Hawking, Stephen W. *The Universe in a Nutshell.* New York: Bantam, 2001.

Price, Huw. *Time's Arrow and Archimedes' Point: New*

Directions for the Physics of Time. New York: Oxford University Press, 1996.

Smolin, Lee. *The Life of the Cosmos.* New York: Oxford University Press, 1997.

———. *Three Roads to Quantum Gravity.* New York: Basic Books, 2001.

Stenger, Victor J. *Has Science Found God? The Latest Results in the Search for Purpose in the Universe.* Amherst, NY: Prometheus Books, 2003.

TANER EDIS

VALE, GILBERT (1788–1866), Anglo-American free-thinker and activist. Gilbert Vale was born in England and in the late 1820s moved to New York, where he taught navigation and higher mathematics. Vale used his income from teaching to finance his passion for FREETHOUGHT.

Vale was a DEIST and an academic in the physical sciences. He published works on astronomy and geology, and this worldview readily explains his devotion to Thomas PAINE. Vale originally wrote his *Compendium of the Life of Thomas Paine* in 1837, and later expanded it to his *Life of Thomas Paine* in 1841. *Life of Thomas Paine* was the first work to publish the correspondences between Paine and George Washington that had been purposefully excluded from earlier biographies of Paine. Vale's work was also the first to embrace Paine as a hero rather than assassinate his character, as the earlier major biographies had done. Vale's devotion to Paine extended to raising the money for a down payment to purchase sixty acres of Paine's original farm in New Rochelle, New York, and he helped to raise the funds necessary to place a memorial on Paine's farm as well (see MONUMENTS TO UNBELIEF).

Vale's other notable work was freethought publishing. He was an editor of several newspapers, including *Citizen of the World* (thought to be the first Sunday paper) and the *Sunday Reporter*. In 1836 he was asked to take possession of the *Beacon* from the United States Moral and Philosophical Society and became its publisher. Vale continued the *Beacon* until 1846, when it changed titles as the frequency of publication changed, and it eventually became the *Independent Beacon* in 1849, and subsequently disappeared. During this time, Vale also published a number of liberal tracts and pamphlets, including Mary WOLLSTONECRAFT's *A Vindication of the Rights of Women.*

Vale was a contemporary of Benjamin OFFEN, Abner KNEELAND, Peter Eckler, Robert Dale OWEN, and Frances WRIGHT, and was heavily involved with their attempts to found a national freethought society. Vale, according to his contemporaries, was rather "irritable" and had numerous conflicts with them. Despite all their efforts, a true national society of freethinkers did not come about.

BIBLIOGRAPHY

Bennett, D. M. *World's Sages, Infidels and Thinkers.* New York: D. M. Bennett, 1876.

Post, Albert. *Popular Freethought in America, 1825–1850.* New York: Octagon, 1974.

Putnam, Samuel P. *Four Hundred Years of Freethought.* New York: Truth Seeker Company, 1894.

TIMOTHY BINGA

VANINI, GIULIO CESARE (1585–1619), Italian freethought martyr. Giulio Cesare Vanini led a brief, picaresque life. His courage facing death at the hands of the church made him a FREETHOUGHT martyr second only to Giordano BRUNO.

Born at Taurisano, Italy, Vanini studied theology and philosophy at Naples and Padua, becoming a Carmelite monk and gaining his doctorate at twenty-one in 1606. Influenced by the writings of John Baconthorp, a fourteenth-century English Carmelite Averroist (see AVERRÖES), Vanini leapt into a European intellectual culture rife with Aristotelian heterodoxy. He studied and taught in a succession of European university towns.

By 1612 Vanini's growing naturalism (see NATURALISM, PHILOSOPHICAL) attracted suspicion. Voyaging to England, he insincerely converted to Anglicanism. Jailed on an unrecorded charge, he contrived to transmit to Rome an offer to return to the Catholic fold. After diplomatic intrigues spanning Italy, France, and England, the Vatican brokered his repatriation in 1614.

In 1615 Vanini published his first surviving work, *Amphitheatrum Æternæ Providentiæ,* or the *Amphitheater.* Superficially an orthodox attack on pagan philosophy, its oblique language actually defended pantheism, SKEPTICISM toward miracle claims (see MIRACLES, UNBELIEF IN), a libertine view of morality, and a challenge to God's existence based on the argument from evil (see EVIL, PROBLEM OF; EXISTENCE OF GOD, ARGUMENTS FOR AND AGAINST). Vanini's major work, *De Admirandis Naturæ Arcanis,* or the *Dialogues* (1616), continued this attack.

In 1617 Vanini withdrew to Toulouse under the pseudonym Pompeo Ugilio. On August 2, 1618, he was arrested on charges of ATHEISM and BLASPHEMY based on an associate's recounting of a private conversation. Historians differ whether the authorities at Toulouse recognized that they were trying Vanini, author of the *Amphitheater* and the *Dialogues.* At his trial Vanini/Ugilio eloquently maintained his theism. But his arguments emphasizing signs of design in nature could have been made by any deist or pantheist; the judges condemned him.

Vanini's comportment facing death cemented his fame. Immediately after sentencing on February 9, 1619, he was drawn through the streets of Toulouse wearing a placard reading "Atheist and blasphemer." Disarmingly calm before the executioner, he resolved "to die as becomes a philosopher." His tongue was cut out and he was strangled, his body burned, and the ashes scattered. He was thirty-three.

After his execution the church burned multiple copies of the *Amphiteater* and *Dialogues*; other works may have been lost utterly.

Together, Bruno and Vanini mark medieval ecclesiasticism's last opportunities to resist philosophical and scientific naturalism by taking human life. On September 24, 1868, a bust of Vanini was installed in a district hall near his birthplace. His rehabilitation was complete.

BIBLIOGRAPHY

Putnam, Samuel Porter. *Four Hundred Years of Freethought.* New York: Truth Seeker Company, 1894.

Robertson, John Mackinnon. *A Short History of Freethought, Ancient and Modern.* London: Watts and Company, 1915.

Papuli, Giovanni. "Vanini, Giulio Cesare." In *The Encyclopedia of Unbelief*, edited by Gordon Stein. Amherst, NY: Prometheus Books, 1985.

TOM FLYNN

VAN PRAAG, JAAP (1911–1981), Dutch humanist organizer. Jaap van Praag was born on May 11, 1911, in Amsterdam. He grew up in a secular Jewish and socialist family. Mainly through his mother and by much reading he acquired considerable knowledge of the Bible. He studied Dutch literature, philosophy, and history, and became a teacher in a secondary school. Until World War II he was extremely active in pacifist and socialist associations, concentrating mainly on peace-related issues and nonviolent resistance. In these associations he met many people who were later also to become active in the humanist movement (see HUMANISM). As a Jew, he was obliged to go into hiding during the German occupation of the Netherlands, which he did from 1943. The horrors of the war were essential to forming his later militancy and worldview. He went back to teaching from 1946 to 1954. From 1954 to 1974 he was on the executive board of the provincial government of South Holland.

Organizer. Immediately after the occupation, he was the most important initiator in founding the Humanistisch Verbond (HV, Dutch Humanist Association) in 1946. He was its chairman from 1946 to 1969; through his charisma, strategic insight, and diplomatic approach he succeeded in building up the Verbond. He was widely considered to be the "father," the "architect," and the "master builder" of organized humanism in the Netherlands. He had two motives for founding the Verbond. First and principally, he wanted to create a LIFE STANCE shelter for the large group of churchless people who were seeking meaning in life as religion declined and wanted to make people morally resilient. He also wanted to work for equality for humanists and other churchless people in a society that legally privileged Catholicism

and Protestantism. Mainly thanks to Van Praag's organizational capacity, this endeavor was ultimately extremely successful (see NETHERLANDS, THE, HUMANISM IN). Van Praag also played a crucial role in bringing together humanist people and organizations from all parts of the world, especially in terms of content. He was one of those responsible for founding the INTERNATIONAL HUMANIST AND ETHICAL UNION (IHEU) in 1952. He chaired the IHEU for twenty-three years, from its start until 1975, during which time his main efforts focused upon keeping the IHEU alive, often with great difficulty, and upon extending it. He enthusiastically established contacts with others, for example, the Vatican, and the Marxists in Yugoslavia.

The Foundations of Humanism. Even during the occupation, he started work on his theory of humanism. His *Modern humanisme: Een renaissance?* (Modern Humanism: A Renaissance?) was written in that period, and published in 1947. In this book he argues for a radical renewal of moral life in the Netherlands, in particular among the unchurched. For the practice of humanist moral counseling, he developed a theoretical underpinning and a methodology as early as 1953, which long served as a basis for this work. Van Praag's importance for the theory of humanism has been great. He was responsible for naming the theory of humanist counseling in the Netherlands "humanistics." Humanistics has become a profession or discipline dealing with the basic phenomena of humanism (see NETHERLANDS, THE, HUMANIST EDUCATION IN). Van Praag himself was professor of humanistics at Leiden University from 1964 to 1979. The book *Grondslagen van humanisme; inleiding tot een humanistische levens—en denkwereld* (Foundations of Humanism: Introduction to a World of Humanist Living and Thinking), published in 1978 (published in English by Prometheus Books in 1982), can be considered a worthy conclusion to a lifelong devotion to the organization and theory of humanism. The book states clearly what Van Praag considered the core of humanism, namely, to oppose indifference and moral emptiness and to encourage solidarity and human resilience as fundamentals for a democratic constitutional state. Jaap van Praag died on April 12, 1981.

BIBLIOGRAPHY

Derkx, Peter, and Bert Gasenbeek, eds. *J.P. van Praag, vader van het moderne Nederlandse humanisme* [J. P. Van Praag, Father of Modern Dutch Humanism]. Utrecht: De Tijdstroom, 1997.

Van Praag, J. P. *Foundations of Humanism.* Amherst, NY: Prometheus Books, 1982.

BERT GASENBEEK

VERIFICATIONISM. The philosophical movement verificationism claimed that for any proposition to have substantive content, it must be *verifiable*: that is, either confirmable or disconfirmable by at least some conceivable experience. In this way, to be intelligibly substantive, propositions must stand up to the tribunal of experience. If nothing either directly or indirectly empirically discernible counted either for or against them, the alleged positions in question were taken to be unintelligible: not genuine propositions at all.

I

Verificationism has had—and is still having—its ups and downs. With David HUME it had its first clear articulation; again, it found clear expression in the late nineteenth century in the writings of the German physicist Ernest Mach. Hume and Mach were important precursors of the movement variously called logical empiricism, LOGICAL POSITIVISM, or scientific empiricism. It had its earliest articulation in Scandinavia among social scientists, legal theorists, and philosophers in the circle around the Swedish philosopher Axel Hägerström, and then somewhat later among the so-called Vienna Circle and the Berlin Circle (see SCHLICK, MORITZ, AND THE VIENNA CIRCLE). It flourished principally under the influence of Rudolf Carnap, Moritz Schlick, Otto Neurath, Hans Reichenbach, and Carl Hempel; it was exported to the United Kingdom chiefly by A. J. Ayer. In North America, mostly in the United States, verificationism followed a somewhat different path, initially as an independent development by the pragmatists, principally Charles Sanders Peirce. With the onset of World War II, most of Europe's logical positivists moved to the United States, where they became a powerful philosophical force, joining with the pragmatists whom they regarded as their well-meaning but rather fuzzy colleagues. Ernest NAGEL and Sidney HOOK, two of John DEWEY's most talented students, were also influenced by logical positivism and developed distinctive accounts of verificationism.

With all these philosophers and the philosophical movements developing around them, verificationism flourished—most notably among the logical positivists who were at the cutting edge of the development of analytic philosophy from the 1930s to the 1960s. But it is also important to note in their actual practice, though not in programmatic articulation, verificationism was extensively employed in the work of Ludwig Wittgenstein and the philosophers under his influence, and by Gilbert Ryle and the so-called ordinary language philosophy practiced mainly at Oxford, though with considerable importance in the United States. All of those philosophers would disdain calling themselves verificationists, or for that matter disdain any labeling. But they deployed verificationist arguments repeatedly and at crucial junctures in their thought.

For all the logical positivists from Hägerström to Carnap (as with Hume and Mach as well), their verificationism carried with it a thorough rejection of religion and metaphysics. These were regarded as illusions to be firmly set aside—indeed, their key propositions were regarded as cognitively unintelligible pseudo-propositions.

II

So with logical positivism and Wittgensteinianism dominating the first stage of analytic philosophy, verificationism was in the ascendancy. However, in the mid-1950s verificationism, ordinary-language philosophy, and even Wittgenstein began to lose favor. By around 1960 verificationism was no longer in the ascendancy. Its decline was thought to have occurred principally through criticism from within. The logical positivists themselves, ever committed to clear articulation and rigor, realized that they were not able to articulate satisfactorily the verifiability (testability) principle central to their thought. When they attempted to do so, they came up with formulations (as we shall see) that were either too strict—ruling out plainly meaningful scientific and commonsense propositions as unverifiable—or too liberal, letting in the very metaphysical propositions the criterion was constructed to exclude.

It was also the case that philosophers such as Martin White, W. V. O. Quine, Frederick Waismann, and Stephen Toulmin showed that the allegedly firm distinction between the analytic and the empirical was little more than a dogma. In this onslaught on a distinction much heralded by positivists, Quine's attack was by far the most thorough and distinctive. But the others contributed also, in different ways. Third, a form of "scientific realism" or metaphysical realism was coming into favor, receiving careful articulation by analytical philosophers who were often naturalists (David Armstrong, C. B. Martin, J. J. C. Smart, David Lewis) but sometimes theists (Richard Swinburne, Saul Kripke, Robert Adams).

These realists believed that many kinds of things that exist, and what they are like, are independent of us and sometimes even of the ways by which we find out about them or characterize them. These things are there for us to discover, and are what they are independently of how we happen to view them—or even exist so we can view them—for example, trees, lakes, chimpanzees, or Halley's comet. It is either true or false that Mars exists. How we can find out about Mars, or *whether* we can find out, was thought to be another matter entirely. Most—though not all—objects are independent of our thought. We do not bring them into existence or sustain their existence. Verification procedures do not create the objects or states of affairs that they verify—or at least, not most of them. "God exists" (as most other things) cannot be identified with the method of its verification. The *meaning*, or the use, of "God exists" cannot be identified with how or whether we can confirm or disconfirm it. It has a use in the language, and the proposition "God exists" is either true or false in good realist fashion, whether we can know that God exists or not. How we determine whether or not God exists is another matter entirely. What reality is actually like and how we are to conceive it are typically separate questions. What is real is generally independent of our conceptions of it.

This is what a realist maintains and this, realists claim, verificationists *must* deny. But its denial is too implausible to be credible. This realist view has gained ascendancy, and together with the first two problems mentioned concerning verificationism, has put verificationism on the back burner.

III

We will now examine whether verificationists can adequately respond to these and related criticisms. Both Michael Martin and Kai Nielsen have made detailed and careful responses in defense of both verificationism and of atheism, and Martin as well has made an accurate explication of Nielsen's verificationist account.

We will seek an adequate formulation of the verifiability (testability) principle, moving from the simplest (though still prima facie plausible) articulations to increasingly (at least putatively) more adequate formulations. Remember that all of these formulations begin with the acceptance of something that is broadly an empiricist preanalytic conviction, namely, the conviction that experience is the sole legitimate source of information about the world. Any rationalist or supernaturalist attempt to go around this or beyond this, and say that the world just must be so-and-so or that reality must be such-and-such no matter what we experience, is to say something incoherent. It is to try to gain a kind of knowledge that cannot be had. Our challenge is to articulate verificationism *with* the realist intuitions described above intact (or nearly so), and to show how verificationists do not have to deny those realist intuitions as realists believe they do.

A verificationist starts with the above-stated idea about informativeness and experience, and seeks to set out, in that nonrationalist spirit, a verifiability principle that will serve as a kind of litmus test to sort out what it does and what it does not make sense to say: for example, "Lightning started the forest fire" as distinct from "An unknowable, indescribable ineffable cause started the forest fire." It seeks a general criterion to pick out sense from nonsense. In that spirit our first try at formulating the verifiability principle is this:

1. A proposition is meaningful if and only if it is empirically verifiable.

But this won't work for "2 + 2 = 4" or "all biological sisters are siblings." Both are plainly meaningful, and indeed are true, yet they do not even purport to be verifiable. Moreover, on this articulation of the verifiability principle, certain statements about the past—which, trivial though they be, are plainly meaningful—also become unverifiable under formulation number 1. Consider "Napoleon yawned just twenty times while on

Saint Helena's" or "There were only fifteen wild turkeys on Block Island in 1292."

So in the spirit of practically all the logical positivists, we amend formulation 1 to 2:

2. A proposition is meaningful if and only if it is at least in principle verifiable, that is, if it is logically possible to verify it.

Assuming problematically that we have some reasonably clear idea of what it is logically possible to verify and what is not, formulation 2 enables us to say that those truisms about Napoleon and the wild turkeys are each verifiable—for if there had been someone there in the past (and there could have been) concerned to record such trivia, and who had indeed recorded them, and had the record remained intact, we could confirm or disconfirm such propositions. But we are still left with the problem of so-called a priori propositions, so we amend 2 to 3, thereby in effect dropping any claim to having a *general* criterion of what it makes sense to say:

3. A nonanalytic proposition is meaningful if and only if it is at least empirically verifiable in principle.

But we still have problems with plainly intelligible normative propositions such as "Torture is always completely unacceptable" or "Due process must always be adhered to." They at least appear to be unverifiable. The move taken by most of the logical positivists was to amend 3 to 4:

4. A nonanalytic proposition is *cognitively* meaningful if and only if it is at least verifiable in principle.

But this in turn rests on a probably arbitrary or at least very controversial conception of *cognitive*, a conception rooted in a noncognitivist or nondescriptivist understanding of normative utterances that treats them as emotive or prescriptive, or otherwise nondescriptive, utterances without cognitive meaning. But this is very questionable for many moral and otherwise normative utterances, including the two given above. As with mathematical propositions, they are true or false without any concern for such obscurities as mathematical or normative objects or talk of correspondence.

This leads us to 5, something which better captures the underlying intent of the logical positivists:

5. A proposition is factually meaningful if and only if it is at least in principle verifiable.

Point 5 captures their underlying intent, for most crucially they wanted a criterion that would enable us to decide which of the many propositions or sentences embedded in our cultural space made genuine claims about the physical and social world—that is, claims that could give us empirical information about what that world is like. They wanted a criterion to distinguish factual propositions from pseudo-factual propositions such as the metaphysical and theological monsters of speculative philosophy and of metaphysical religiosity (which just seem to go with Judaism, Christianity, and Islam).

However, as it stands 5 will not quite work; for if we accept 5 as our criterion, all scientific laws and generalizations become unverifiable. Indeed this would be true generally of universal generalizations. If it is said that "All robins in Quebec migrate south in the fall," no amount of observation will verify the truth of that statement—will, that is, establish conclusively its truth—though some possible observations would count for its truth and some against it. But we cannot *conclusively* establish its truth, or that of any other empirical generalization. A nonmigrating robin might turn up in Quebec in the middle of winter that would falsify it. Such a proposition is *falsifiable* but not *verifiable*. This suggests turning the verifiability criterion into a *falsifiability* criterion:

6. A proposition is factually meaningful if and only if it is at least in principle falsifiable.

That may well work for general statements (laws of nature and the like), but clearly it does not work for existential propositions such as "There is at least one rattlesnake in Quebec." We can verify this proposition by, say, seeing a rattlesnake in the woods. But no amount of observation will definitely establish the proposition to be false. Some things will count toward its falsity, but no amount of observation will *conclusively establish* its falsity. An extraordinarily scrupulous and systematic search for rattlesnakes might be undertaken and none might be found, yet a rattlesnake still might turn up in Quebec.

Trying to avoid these difficulties it might seem plausible to propose:

7. A proposition is factually meaningful if and only if it is either at least in principle verifiable or at least in principle falsifiable.

Yet that won't work either, as Hempel pointed out, for the very same reasons as were given concerning the verifiability and the falsifiability criterion. Propositions like "Every substance has some solvent" or "Every democracy has some fascists" are neither conclusively verifiable nor conclusively falsifiable, even in principle.

So strong verificationism will not work. Moreover, the attempt to establish strong verificationism runs contrary to the *fallibilistic* spirit of science. In scientific inquiry—or anywhere else where significant matters of substance are at issue—we simply are not going to achieve conclusive certainty. The most we can reasonably hope for is that we can go on gaining ever more adequate scientific

accounts, better philosophical explications, and better accounts of science. This realization led in the first instance to a *liberalization* of the so-called verifiability or falsifiability criterion. The talk now centered on testability—confirmability or infirmability in principle. We can capture this idea in a formulation such as:

8. A proposition is factually meaningful if and only if it is either at least in principle confirmable or infirmable.

The problem here is not that 8 excludes too much—namely, established scientific propositions or well-established commonsense empirical beliefs—as nonsense under that criterion, but that 8 *lets back in* the metaphysical and theological monsters that the logical positivists had set out to exclude. All that is now being asked is that there be *some empirical observations* that are at least logically possible for us to make which could count either for or against a proposition taken to be genuinely factual. But that standard excludes very little. "God is our loving Father" or "God created the heavens and the earth" could be taken to be confirmable or infirmable by 8, and thus to have factual meaning. Human suffering counts against "God is our loving Father," and human well-being counts for it. The great age of the earth and its seeming eternity counts against "God created the heavens and the earth," and the Big Bang counts for it. But nothing counts even *nearly* decisively for or against either proposition. But exactly that is to be expected for 8. On that criterion, some religious and metaphysical propositions become empirically confirmable or infirmable—and *in that* way testable—and thus come to be seen to have empirical and factual meaning. (This has led *some* atheists to conclude that "God created the heavens and the earth" is false, rather than factually meaningless.)

With this chain of formulations we have watched logical positivism develop toward greater logical and empirical adequacy, at the same time losing much of its old antimetaphysical bite. As an exacting program to free the world of metaphysical and religious illusions (and the kind of moral and political illusions that go with them), it seems to have lost its way. This will be returned to in the next section.

But all that aside, it is important to recognize a different kind of difficulty that many have thought to be attached to even the liberalized, testability-in-principle version of verificationism. By 8 "It is not the case that all crows are black" plainly has empirical meaning; but then, it is claimed, so does "Either it is not the case that all crows are black or God is ersatz," on the grounds that it is reasonable to suppose that any logical consequence of a confirmable compound proposition is itself confirmable. Given that, "Either it is not the case that all crows are black or God is ersatz" is confirmable. And if "All crows are black," then "God is ersatz" can be deductively inferred from it, given the above. Since "God is ersatz" follows from confirmable statements, and thus from factually meaningful statements, "God is ersatz" on this account is confirmable and factually meaningful. But we could substitute any proposition at all for "God is ersatz" in the above argument and get a factually meaningful proposition. But this is a reductio. It looks like the verifiability, falsifiability, and testability criteria are incoherent. Plainly something has gone wrong.

It is difficult not to react by thinking that this is all very artificial and silly word play. But taking it and similar turns at face value, Wesley Salmon has produced a telling response to this. Salmon argues (against the standard interpretation of the propositional calculus) that a factually meaningful compound sentence can have factually meaningless components. Standardly, the propositional calculus tells us that compound sentences must be such that all of their components are either true or false. But whatever is the case in a formal system with its stipulated rules, in natural languages we have compound sentences where that does not follow. "The door is open and close the door" is a compound sentence; but the second component, being an imperative, couldn't possibly be either truth or false. And "Either it is not the case that all crows are black or wrinkler dinkler big" is either not a compound sentence at all (since the second component is meaningless) or it is a compound sentence with a meaningless component. Moreover (and independently of the above) a meaningless component cannot follow from anything, since it is meaningless; being meaningless, we could not even in principle ascertain whether it does or does not follow from anything. Some nonsense is so extreme that we cannot tell whether we even have a sentence rather than a meaningless concoction of words, that is, "Right melancholy equilateral." The standardly accepted moves to show that verificationism leads to absurdities because meaningless strings of words can follow from factually meaningful sentences (for example, those of Alonzo Church) are just so much love's labor lost. But what is important, once we arrive at the liberalized testability criterion of factual meaning, is that we have a metaphysical religious statement "God is our loving Father" which *on that criterion* is confirmable or infirmable and thus has factual meaning. With this, the logical positivist programmatic stance is undermined, for we have shown that at least some religious propositions are factually and empirically meaningful.

IV

Are things really so bleak for verificationism? It could be argued they are not, for the following reasons: (1) Though some religious utterances, embedded as they are in our ordinary language (say, "God is our loving Father"), may be weakly confirmable or infirmable, many less anthropomorphic ones characteristic of what Hägerström called "metaphysical religiosity" are much less evidently factu-

ally meaningful. Consider such propositions as "God is the ineffable Other," "God is the sole universe-transcending infinite individual," "God is the foundation of being and meaning," "God is being itself." With such sentences allegedly forming propositions, we *at least* arguably have no understanding of what counts (if anything) for or against them, even weakly. We simply do not understand what they mean or what they are trying to assert. (2) Propositions like "God is our loving Father" are weakly confirmable/infirmable in the way we have indicated. But the above religious propositions and propositions like them do not *follow* from the evidential ones. Moreover, we shouldn't even call them "propositions," for in reality they are meaningless strings of words. The evidential propositions, we should also note, are equally compatible with atheistic or agnostic views and the propositions that express them. Moreover, these secular views are articulated more economically, with fewer problematic assumptions, and arguably answer more fully to reflective human interests than the religious ones. In both common life and in science, it is not infrequently the case (as far as we can ascertain) that the empirical evidence is compatible, even equally compatible (again as far as we can tell), with different claims made in the light of the evidence. But there could be all sorts of other reasons for favoring one account over another: simplicity, fit with other theories, clarity, perspicuous representation, and the like. We are not just stuck with the religious interpretation. (3) To get a firmer grasp on the claims being made by religious utterances, we need something of a sense of what in our experience could count for them or against them. This is why we are not as totally lost with "God is our loving Father" or "We live with God's providential care" as we are with "God is the ineffable Other" or "God is the ultimate ground of being and meaning." But the last two are taken by most theologians to be central claims of (say) the Christian religion and what is shared ground between Judaism, Christianity, and Islam. (4) It is when we articulate a combination of verificationist and nonverificationist arguments that we get the most effective critique of religion. We are told by Jews, Christians, and Muslims that God is a person: an infinite individual who is also a pure spirit utterly without a body and transcendent to the world. In claiming that this is incoherent, it is not verificationist arguments that do the work, for we have no understanding of what verification (or testability) could come to concerning it. God is said to be an infinite individual; but if something is infinite, that reality could not be an individual or a person. And how could a person be "out of the world" but still somehow be acting in it? And how could a person act without a body and even be a person? What would it be for any of these things to obtain? All this (to put it mildly) is utterly mysterious. Words cannot intelligibly be put together in these ways. Finally, we have no understanding of what it would mean to be transcendent to the world: to be beyond space and time. It is not verificationist (or testability) considerations that tell us that such talk is meaningless—indeed, pure gibberish—but rather attention to the logic of our language. But verificationist (or testability) considerations enter this discussion in other ways. Someone says he has apprehended God, or experienced God in his life, or that he lives in the presence of God, or that God loves him. Here we can relevantly ask what (if anything) counts for or against such claims and, if anything does, how strongly?

Finally we should look at a consideration that is a favorite among the traditionalist critics of the verifiability (testability) criterion of meaning (such as F. J. Copelston or A. C. Ewing). It is said by them (and not only by them) that this criterion is self-refuting. The verifiability (testability) principle is neither analytic nor a factual empirical proposition, so it is on its own account meaningless or at least cognitively meaningless. But it is not. It neither purports to be analytic, nor in any other way (if there is another way) a priori, nor an empirical assertion, nor any other kind of assertion. It is rather set forth as a proposal as to how to take or construe our language, and as to how to decide what makes sense and what does not. It is not a principle making an assertion which is true or false either analytically or empirically, but as a pragmatic proposal for how to decide which of those myriad noises or marks we make in speaking or writing make sense. Of that great jumble of sentences that we are faced with and deploy, which of them should we take as making sense and in what ways, and which ones are to be rejected as incoherent or meaningless? We are looking for a criterion (perhaps more than one) which we judge in terms of its utility, economy, and perspicuousness, and do not regard as something that can be either true or false any more than we regard "Let's go to Ireland in October" as true or false. Proposals do not have truth conditions or assertability conditions, but are still intelligible.

Others, of course, can make their proposals too, but they, logical positivists plausibly claim, will lose out to the verificationists, when their aim is to gain criteria for what it is to come to understand what it is to make intelligible and sound claims about the world, where the only source of information about the world is experiential in the broad Deweyian understanding of "experiential." And that last claim—a core claim of any empiricist and naturalist—is either true or false. Verificationists place their bets on its being true. It is a point they make for which there is a lot of indirect empirical evidence. It is, to put it mildly, hard to understand what it is to have a nonexperiential grasp of the world.

BIBLIOGRAPHY

Bjanup, Jes. "Scandinavian Legal Realism." In *The Philosophy of Law: An Encyclopedia*, edited by Christopher Berry Gray. Vol. 2. New York: Garland, 1999.

Carnap, Rudolf. "Testability and Meaning." *Philosophy of Science* 3 (1936) and 4 (1937).

Diamond, Malcolm L., and Thomas V. Litzenburg Jr.,

eds. *The Logic of God: Theology and Verification.* Indianapolis: Bobbs-Merrill, 1975.

Hempel, Carl G. "The Concept of Cognitive Significance." *Proceedings of the American Academy of Arts and Sciences* 80, no. 1 (1951).

———. "The Empiricist Criterion of Meaning." In *Logical Positivism*, edited by A. J. Ayer. Glencoe, IL: Free Press, 1959.

———. *Selected Philosophical Essays.* Edited by Richard Jeffrey. Cambridge: Cambridge University Press, 2000.

Martin, Michael. *Atheism, Morality and Meaning.* Amherst, NY: Prometheus Books, 2002.

———. "The Verificationist Challenge." In *A Companion to Philosophy of Religion*, edited by Philip L. Quinn and Charles Taliaferro. Cambridge, MA: Blackwell, 1997.

Misak, C. J. *Verificationism: Its History and Prospects.* London: Routledge, 1995.

Nielsen, Kai. *Naturalism and Religion.* Amherst, NY: Prometheus Books, 2001.

———. *Naturalism without Foundations.* Amherst, NY: Prometheus Books, 1996.

Putnam, Hilary. *Ethics without Ontology.* Cambridge, MA: Harvard University Press, 2004.

Salmon, C. Wesley. "Verifiability and Logic." In *The Logic of God: Theology and Verification*, edited by Malcolm L. Diamond and Thomas V. Litzenburg Jr. Indianapolis: Bobbs-Merrill, 1975.

KAI NIELSEN

VOLTAIRE (FRANÇOIS MARIE AROUET; 1694–1778), French philosopher, historian, poet, and satirist. A pioneer in the development of a largely secular vision of human existence, Voltaire strongly criticized religion and religious fanaticism, waging a particularly vigorous campaign on behalf of religious toleration.

In assessing the course of Voltaire's life, it must be kept constantly in mind that he was living at a time when France was dominated by two overwhelmingly powerful forces—the monarchy and the church—which, both separately and in unison, held a stranglehold on all literary and political expression. In spite of his early success as an author (chiefly as a tragic playwright) and the large sums of money he made from his bewilderingly vast array of writings, Voltaire was in constant danger of imprisonment for perceived political and religious offenses in what today seem quite harmless literary works. His nearly sixty years as an engaged public intellectual were repeatedly filled with bold and, at times, reckless attacks upon the establishment.

Life and Work. Born in Paris, Voltaire was educated at a private school, Louis-le-Grand, which, although run by Jesuits, nonetheless produced several leading freethinkers of the period (see FREETHOUGHT), including Denis DIDEROT and Claude Adrien HELVÉTIUS. At the age of seventeen he began attending informal meetings of a group of freethinkers led by Philippe de Vendôme, at the same time developing his early interest in verse satire. An early poem, "*Le Vrai Dieu*" (The True God, 1715), points out the paradoxes involved in the Christian conception of a god immolating himself for the sake of sinners. Voltaire gained celebrity with the verse drama *Oedipe* (1718), a treatment of the Oedipus legend that indirectly expressed impatience with the stifling political and moral authority exercised by the church. Another early poem, *Epître à Uranie* (Epistle to Urania), written in 1722, presented an exhaustive condemnation of Christianity as both unjust and unreasonable—two dominant themes in Voltaire's later religious criticism. It was published surreptitiously in 1732. Another celebrated early work, the epic poem *La Henriade* (1723), although ostensibly a patriotic poem about Henri IV, presented a warning on the dangers of religious fanaticism, especially in its depiction of the bloody massacre of Saint Bartholomew in 1572.

Because he had offended a nobleman, Voltaire was forced to spend the years 1726–29 in England. There he was befriended by Lord BOLINGBROKE and other leading British intellectuals, and he came into first contact with the philosophy of John LOCKE and the science of Sir Isaac Newton. Tremendously influenced by the greater religious toleration found in the British Isles, Voltaire wrote the *Letters concerning the English Nation* in English (1733); a French version, *Lettres philosophiques*, appeared the next year, in which Voltaire's searing criticism of Pascal's religious dogmatism and obscurantism was added as an appendix. The French edition created an uproar and was publicly burned—a fate that would overtake a number of Voltaire's later works. It was also in England that Voltaire commenced his first major historical work, *Histoire du Charles XII* (1731).

Much of the period between 1734 and 1750 was spent at various country estates of wealthy aristocrats around Paris: Voltaire's work had already become so controversial, and had so offended the new king, Louis XV, that he could not enter Paris without the threat of imprisonment. In spite of his prodigious literary output, Voltaire did not neglect his personal life: aside from various short-term affairs with married noblewomen, he established two long-term romantic involvements, first with Madame du Châtelet (at whose estate at Cirey he spent most of the years between 1734 and 1744), and then with his own niece, Madame du Denis. He continued the writing of verse tragedies, including *Mahomet* (1741) and *Mérope* (1743), both of which continue to hammer home the horrors of religious fanaticism. *Mahomet* suggests that Islam (and, by implication, Christianity) is founded upon credulous belief in false miracles.

In 1750 Voltaire accepted an invitation by Frederick the Great of Prussia to stay at his court; previous correspondence with Frederick had led Voltaire to believe that he may have found his ideal of a philosopher-king, but the three years spent with Frederick convinced him otherwise, and he came to regard this royal dabbler in poetry and music as merely a duplicitous hypocrite. Although Voltaire published the flattering *Le Siècle de Louis XIV* (The Century of Louis XIV, 1751), a landmark work of historiography, Louis XV was so offended by Voltaire's abandoning France to go to Prussia that he forbade him to return to his native country. By 1755 Voltaire had settled in Geneva, thinking he had found a haven of religious and political toleration; but once again his hopes were dashed, and his continual offending of the Calvinist sensibilities of the Genevan ruling class forced him to purchase the estate of Ferney just across the Swiss border in France. This became Voltaire's home from 1758 to the end of his life; it also became a place of pilgrimage for numerous intellectuals from around Europe, and Voltaire would receive his guests as if he were himself a philosopher-king.

The year 1755 was traumatic for Voltaire on several counts. In November the Lisbon earthquake occurred, and its horrific death toll, numbering in the tens of thousands, was augmented by the fact that it had taken place on a Sunday, so that many people had died while in church. Voltaire, among many others, was shaken to the core: how could a benevolent and all-powerful god have allowed such a thing to happen? His searing poem, *Poème sur la désastre de Lisbonne* (Poem on the Disaster of Lisbon, 1755), contains some of his most plangent queries on the problem of evil. It was in 1755, also, that his scandalous poem *La Pucelle*, usually translated as *The Maid of Orleans,* was published in an unauthorized version: this mock-epic in which Joan of Arc spends all her time desperately protecting her virginity took aim at one of the sainted figures of French history, and it could not have helped Voltaire's attempts to ingratiate himself into the good graces of the king. His popularity, however, continued to increase, and he gained many new readers with a new literary genre he virtually created out of whole cloth, the *conte philosophique* (philosophical tale), the most celebrated example of which is the short novel *Candide* (1759), which pungently destroys Gottfried Wilhelm von LEIBNIZ's abstract arguments that, given an omnipotent and benevolent god, the earth as it exists must be the "best of all possible worlds."

In 1762 the case of Jean Calas broke. This hapless Protestant was accused of murdering his son because he had suspected him of secretly converting to Roman Catholicism. Calas was subsequently tortured and executed. Voltaire immediately turned his attention to the case, quickly discovering that Calas had been unjustly accused; he ultimately prevailed to the extent of securing a posthumous clearing of Calas's name in 1765. Another case involved Elizabeth Sirven, a young Catholic woman who was found dead in a well, leading to the accusation of her Huguenot family for her murder. This case occupied much of Voltaire's time all the way up to

1775, leading again to the family's exoneration. The chief result of all this work, however, was the imperishable *Traité sur la tolérance* (Treatise on Toleration, 1763), a pioneering work whose effects were immediate and pronounced.

The 1760s marked a period of unexampled productivity for Voltaire: among the major works produced at this time were the *Dictionnaire philosophique* (Philosophical Dictionary, 1764), later placed upon the church's Index of forbidden works; the *Philosophie de l'histoire* (Philosophy of History, 1765); *Questions sur les miracles* (Questions on Miracles, 1767); *Examen important de milord Bolingbroke* (Lord Bolingbroke's Important Examination, 1767), his broadest attack upon Christianity; and *Dieu et les hommes* (God and Men, 1769), an exhaustive and acerbic survey of religion from India to the Middle East to Judaism and Christianity. Although continuing to write, Voltaire found his health increasingly failing. He expressed a longing to return to the Paris that he had not seen in decades, and in early 1778 he surreptitiously crept back into the city. But his presence could not long be kept secret, and he was received with enthusiasm by populace and intelligentsia alike—by all, in short, except the court and the church. Voltaire died in Paris on May 30, 1778.

Fundamentals of His Thought. Voltaire called himself a deist (see DEISM); on occasion he would actually use the word *theist* as a synonym. In the *Dictionnaire philosophique* he defines a "theist" as "a man firmly convinced of the existence of a supreme being as good as he is powerful, who has created all extended, vegetating, sentient and thinking beings, who perpetuates their species, who punishes crimes without cruelty, and benevolently rewards virtuous behavior." In spite of the skepticism of Voltaire's leading scholar, Theodore Besterman, who maintained that Voltaire was for all practical purposes an atheist, there is little reason to doubt that he adhered sincerely to this conception of deity. Elsewhere in the same work, in the entry "Faith," Voltaire states: "It is evident to me that there is a necessary, eternal, supreme, intelligent being. This is not a matter of faith, but of reason." From the sum total of Voltaire's remarks, it appears that he was driven to postulate a "necessary" supreme being because he could see no way around the adoption of the argument from design: as he states in the entry "God, Gods" in the *Dictionnaire philosophique:* "Every construction which displays means and an end announces an artisan; therefore this universe, composed of mechanisms, of means, each of which has its end, reveals a very powerful, very intelligent artisan." Voltaire's repeated criticism of the more forthright atheism of Baron d'HOLBACH, Helvétius, Julien Offray de LA METTRIE, and others makes it abundantly clear that he did not wish to be considered in their camp.

Voltaire also considered belief in a supreme being, especially one who rewards virtue and punishes sin, as necessary to the maintenance of the social order. In this stance there was a certain cynicism, for Voltaire often stressed that this belief, even if false, was nonetheless *useful.* This is the basis for his celebrated statement (embodied in a letter of November 1, 1770): "If God did not exist, it would be necessary to invent him."

The distinction between deism and atheism is most clearly expressed in the short story "L'Histoire de Jenni, ou l'athée et le sage" (The History of Johnny, or the Atheist and the Sage, 1769; see ATHEISM). In this *conte philosophique*, the "sage," Mr. Freind, presents what are manifestly Voltaire's arguments in support of a deity, specifically the argument from design and the need to preserve good morals. When his opponent, the atheist Birton, responds that the universe appears to have come about of its own accord and that the existence of natural and human evils mitigates against the notion of a benevolent deity, Freind replies with the standard argument that human beings have brought evil upon themselves through an abuse of free will. Freind wins the argument with surprising ease, and Birton is converted to deism. The entire story portrays atheists as unprincipled libertines interested only in their own pleasure, who commit crimes with insouciance because they fear no retribution from God.

At the same time that Voltaire defended deism, he ruthlessly condemned the very foundations of the Christian religion. The belief that Voltaire was merely criticizing the excesses of Christianity—its persecution of heretics and infidels, its exercise of secular power—cannot be maintained in the light of such works as *Examen important de milord Bolingbroke* and *La Bible enfin expliquée* (The Bible Finally Explained, 1776), both of which are merciless in their examination of the errors, paradoxes, and inconsistencies in both the Old and New Testaments. The *Dictionnaire philosophique* entry on "Genesis" exhibits the contradictions to known laws of entity found in the creation story in Genesis, while the entry on "Julian" presents a sympathetic portrayal of the Roman emperor who tried to stop the spread of Christianity. Other works, such as the *Essai sur les moeurs* (Essay on Customs, 1756), were radical in their refusal to single out Christianity for privileged treatment, instead regarding the Christian religion as just one component in the universal history of humankind.

In Voltaire's eyes, other religions such as Judaism and Islam were just as irrational and absurd. His celebrated cry, "Écrasez l'infâme" (Crush the infamy), which he uttered hundreds of times in letters and public documents from the late 1750s onward, appears to refer specifically to religious superstition, but can be taken broadly as a condemnation of all fanaticism, whether political or religious. Voltaire was one of the first to adopt the anthropological method of accounting for the existence of religious belief: in the *Philosophie de l'histoire* he makes plain his belief that religion emerged in primitive times as a means of explaining and placating natural phenomena.

But Voltaire is perhaps best remembered for his unfailingly witty lampooning of the absurdities of religion, specifically of Christianity. Far more than Democritus, he deserves the appellation of "the laughing philosopher." While it is evident that Voltaire's raillery was strongly supported by learning and conviction, there is no denying the entertainment value of such works as *Le Taureau blanc* (The White Bull, 1774), in which the Witch of Endor comes to Egypt with a motley crew of animals—the serpent that tempted Eve, Balaam's ass, the fish that swallowed Jonah, Tobit's dog, and the like—in tow. The serpent presents a valiant defense of his urging Adam and Eve to eat of the fruit of the tree of knowledge ("Would the Supreme Being have wished to have been served by fools and idiots?"), while a raven tells of how Noah accomplished the prodigious feat of feeding all the animals on the ark for ten months. Voltaire's universalist perspective on religion is exemplified in the philosophical tale *Micromégas* (1752), in which an inhabitant of the star Sirius comes to Earth and notes with bemusement an array of human follies, many of them inspired by religious dogma and intolerance.

Voltaire's most immediate influence upon social, political, and intellectual history was in his fiery pleas for religious toleration. His involvement in the Calas and Servin cases in the 1760s and 1770s made it clear to him that the power of religious authority to enforce its dogmas by the use of deadly force was an unmitigated evil and must be curbed. And yet the *Traité sur la tolérance* presents some unexpected arguments for religious toleration. Unlike John Locke (*Epistola de tolerantia*, 1689), Voltaire places no particular emphasis on the need to preserve the separation of church and state; nor, like Pierre BAYLE, does he defend tolerance on the grounds of individual liberty of conscience. Following contemporary British example, which gradually removed civil disabilities from dissenters but still prohibited individuals not members of the Church of England from holding public office or even from practicing their religion openly, Voltaire presented the case for toleration as a means of maintaining social order: an established church is not in itself an evil, so long as it is not fanatical, superstitious, or intolerant. Far from recommending a strict separation of church and state, Voltaire maintained that the government should be used to restrain individual churches when they sought to inflict harm upon individuals for mere violations of religious dogma.

Although the core of Voltaire's views on religion can be found in the *Dictionnaire philosophique*, the *Philosophie de l'histoire*, the *Traité sur la tolérance*, and other well-known writings, the full scope of his criticism of religion in general, and Christianity in particular, cannot be grasped by English-speaking readers because many of his most substantial works—the *Examen important de milord Bolingbroke*, *Dieu et les hommes*, and *La Bible enfin expliquée*—have either never appeared in an Eng-

lish translation or have not been translated for well over a century. With the slow but steady publication of Voltaire's works in sound editions by the Voltaire Foundation, it is hoped that new translations of these and other works will be made available so that the dynamic, controversial, and pungently witty work of the eighteenth century's most celebrated public intellectual can be fully appreciated.

BIBLIOGRAPHY

Besterman, Theodore. *Voltaire*. London: Longmans, 1969.

Gargett, Graham. *Voltaire and Protestantism*. Studies on Voltaire and the Eighteenth Century, 188. Oxford: Voltaire Foundation, 1980.

Pomeau, René. *La Religion de Voltaire*. Paris: Nizet, 1956.

Voltaire. *Treatise on Tolerance and Other Writings*. Edited by Simon Harvey. Cambridge: Cambridge University Press, 2000.

S. T. JOSHI

WAISBROOKER, LOIS (1826–1909), American suffragist and sex radical. Little is known about Lois Waisbrooker's early life. She was born Adeline Eliza Nichols in Caroline, New York, to Grandison and Caroline (Reed) Nichols. The Nichols family moved to Dover Township in Cuyahoga County, Ohio, around 1839. Adeline's mother died and her father remarried. Adeline married George Fuller and had two children, Pauline and Abner. Fuller died in 1846. Adeline worked constantly as a domestic servant and was often ill, and because of this was forced to give up her children. In 1856 she married Isaac Snell, about whom nothing more is known. Sometime after 1860 Adeline changed her name to Lois Waisbrooker, but it is not clear why.

Averse to the life of a servant, Waisbrooker began formal education in 1852 and taught African American children in country schools. One Sunday she had a "revelation" in church while listening to a sermon. She realized she could do a better job of teaching than the minister could, and questioned why being a woman should stop her from doing so.

Waisbrooker began lecturing and writing on women's rights in the late 1860s, and continued to radicalize. By 1892, while Moses HARMAN was preoccupied with trials and jail sentences as a result of violating the Comstock Act (see COMSTOCK, ANTHONY, AND UNBELIEF), Waisbrooker took over as publisher of Harman's journal *Lucifer, The Light Bearer* (see SEX RADICALISM AND UNBELIEF), to which she was already a regular contributor. She defiantly took up where Harman left off, writing about sex, sexual servitude, rape, prostitution, and similar topics. She printed a graphic excerpt from a Department of Agriculture report on horse breeding and the care of horse penises. That issue of *Lucifer* was banned by the Post Office. Two years later, she was arrested and charged with publishing obscenity in connection with an article printed in her own journal *Foundation Principles.* The charges were dropped after two years. Afterward, she moved to an anarchist colony in Home, Washington, and published *Clothed with the Sun,* an anarchist-feminist journal. She was again charged with obscenity for publishing an article called "The Awful Fate of Fallen Women," and was found guilty and fined a hundred dollars.

Audaciously freethinking, Waisbrooker wrote several pamphlets and articles against God and the church, including "The Curse of Godism" (*Foundation Principles,* 1884), "The Folly of Worship" (speech before the 1891 Liberal Convention, Ottawa, Kansas, 1891), and "The Curse of Christian Morality" (published after her death in the *American Journal of Eugenics,* 1910). Much of her writing about women and sex included attacks against God, and her novels also included such principles.

Waisbrooker moved to Denver in 1904 and, although her health deteriorated, she continued to write prolifically. She died at the home of her son, Abner, in Antioch, California, on October 3, 1909.

BIBLIOGRAPHY

Gaylor, A. L., ed. *Women without Superstition: "No Gods—No Masters."* Madison, WI: Freedom From Religion Foundation, 1997.

Waisbrooker, Lois. *Lois Waisbrooker's A Sex Revolution with an Introduction by Pam McAllister.* New Philadelphia, OH: Society Publishers, 1985.

Whitehead, Fred, and Verle Muhrer. *Freethought on the American Frontier.* Amherst, NY: Prometheus Books, 1992.

JULIE HERRADA

WAKEMAN, THADDEUS BURR (1834–1913), American freethought activist and scholar. Thaddeus Wakeman was born on December 23, 1894, at Greenfield Hill, Connecticut. Calamity compelled the family's removal to a hardscrabble life in central New York when Wakeman was seven. In his late teens he moved to New York, later enrolling at Princeton to study for the ministry. He graduated with honors at age twenty, convinced by what he had learned that Christianity was untrue. He turned to the law, gaining admission to the bar in 1856.

Wakeman first won attention as an abolitionist. After the Civil War his interests turned to FREETHOUGHT. He was a leader in New York's Humanity Society, served as president of the influential New York State Freethinkers' Association, and succeeded Elizur WRIGHT as president of the NATIONAL LIBERAL LEAGUE, then America's foremost freethought organization. He was *TRUTH SEEKER* founder D. M. BENNETT's attorney during his prosecu-

tion under the Comstock Act for selling the birth control pamphlet *Cupid's Yokes* (see COMSTOCK, ANTHONY, AND UNBELIEF). Wakeman organized a national petition drive entreating Congress to repeal the Comstock Act. Wakeman's activism against Comstockery—which suggested to some that freethinkers favored distributing obscene matter through the mails—and his efforts to build a freethinking political party around such issues prompted Robert Green INGERSOLL to resign as vice president of the National Liberal League in 1880.

As an independent scholar, Wakeman distinguished himself by translating many of the works of Johann Wolfgang von GOETHE and writing a naturalistic account of the origins of Christianity influential among freethinkers of his time. He also wrote interpretive works designed to reconcile the European POSITIVISM of Auguste COMTE with the emerging American Socialist movement (see SOCIALISM AND UNBELIEF). From 1899 to 1904 Wakeman served as president of Liberal University at Silverton, Oregon, and later Kansas City (see LIBERAL, KANSAS), and assumed editorship of its paper, the *Torch of Reason.* Thereafter he edited a Chicago-based publication called the *Liberal Review* from 1904 to 1906.

A perennial convention speaker, Wakeman delivered funeral addresses for numerous deceased freethought leaders. He died on April 23, 1913.

BIBLIOGRAPHY

Brown, Marshall G., and Gordon Stein. *Freethought in the United States.* Westport, CT: Greenwood, 1978.

Larson, Orvin M. *American Infidel: Robert G. Ingersoll.* New York: Citadel, 1962.

Macdonald, George E. *Fifty Years of Freethought.* New York: Truth Seeker Company, 1929.

McCabe, Joseph. *A Biographical Dictionary of Modern Rationalists.* London: Watts and Company, 1920.

Putnam, Samuel Porter. *Four Hundred Years of Freethought.* New York: Truth Seeker Company, 1894.

TOM FLYNN

WALKER, THOMAS (1858–1932), Australian lecturer and reforming politician. Thomas Walker's mercurial and initially controversial career paralleled the fortunes of organized freethought in Australia.

Born in Preston, Lancashire, England, to Thomas and Ellen Walker on February 5, 1858, in his teens Walker was a Wesleyan lay preacher in England, and by 1872 a farm laborer and Spiritualist medium in Canada (see SPIRITUALISM AND UNBELIEF). He was assisting during an 1874 séance when some phosphorus used for "materializations" ignited and killed his employer. About to be charged with manslaughter, he hastily crossed into the United States, and in 1876 joined the entourage of leading Spiritualist Dr. James Peebles, who went to

Sydney, Australia, as a lecturer in 1877. Walker gave trance lectures there "controlled" by an unusual selection of spirit guides including geologist Sir Charles Lyell, VOLTAIRE, and Giordano BRUNO. From Sydney, Walker moved to the wealthier Melbourne, Britain (1879), and South Africa (1880). He married in Cape Colony in 1881, at which time he was invited to lecture by Australia's Victorian Society of Spiritualists.

In 1882 Walker disavowed mediumistic "phenomena" and broke with the Spiritualists to form the Australasian Secular Association (ASA), of which he became president and lecturer. In retaliation, in 1883 Spiritualist editor W. H. Terry revealed the Canadian episode; Walker decamped to Sydney, where he served as ASA branch president. Two years later he was convicted of exhibiting obscene pictures to promote birth control (see BIRTH CONTROL AND UNBELIEF), resigned as Sydney president, and was expelled from the ASA. He won an appeal against the conviction and affiliated with the Australasian Freethought Union as president, lecturer, and editor of its publication, the *Reflector*. In 1887 he was elected a member of the New South Wales Legislative Assembly and supported trade protection, easier divorce, and other social reforms.

In 1892 Walker accidentally shot a clergyman. He was acquitted of criminal negligence, but convicted of being drunk and disorderly; thereafter he became a florid temperance lecturer. He did not run for parliament in 1894. After a stint in New Zealand as temperance lecturer and elocutionist, in 1899 he went to Western Australia as a journalist covering the Kalgoorlie goldfields. In 1903 he edited a Perth Sunday newspaper, and from 1905 to his death was a member of the Legislative Assembly on the Labor Party ticket. He was also president of the Western Australia Rationalist Association (1918), farmed, and studied law. He held several high government posts, serving as minister for justice and education from 1909 to 1911; attorney general from 1911 to 1916, in which capacity he outlawed capital punishment and cruelty to animals; and Speaker from 1924 to 1930. He died in Perth on May 10, 1932.

BIBLIOGRAPHY

"Thomas Walker." *Australian Dictionary of Biography.* Vol. 6. Melbourne, 1979.
Walker, Thomas. *A Letter to My Constituents.* Sydney: Author, n.d.

DAVID TRIBE

WALLACE, ALFRED RUSSEL (1823–1913), English naturalist, biogeographer. Alfred Russel Wallace was born on January 8, 1823, in the Welsh border village of Usk, the eighth of nine children of Thomas Vere Wallace and Mary Anne Greenell. He described his formal education as worthless, learning far more from his own readings. In 1837 Alfred was sent to London to live with his older brother John. Although he spent only a few months there, this time profoundly influenced him. Attending evening meetings at the Hall of Science, he imbibed the social and political philosophy espoused by Robert OWEN. This was the beginning of the radical and egalitarian ideas that characterized his mature political and social thought. He attended lectures on AGNOSTICISM and SECULARISM and abandoned orthodox religion. That summer Wallace joined his brother William in Bedfordshire to learn surveying and mapping. As he wandered the hills he discovered his passion for nature.

In 1844 he moved to Leicester to teach. After reading Alexander von Humboldt's *Personal Narrative of Travels*—and having previously read Charles DARWIN's *Voyage of the Beagle*—he became determined to find a way to visit South America. He also attended lectures and demonstrations on mesmerism and soon became convinced of its legitimacy. George Combe's *The Constitution of Man*, with its mixture of phrenology and progressive ideas, resonated with his own political views and tapped into his growing interest in psychical phenomena. Robert Chamber's anonymously published *Vestiges of the Natural History of Creation* convinced Wallace that the doctrine of special creation could not possibly be true; thereafter he believed that the problems of natural history would be solved by natural laws, not natural theology.

In Leicester Wallace met the entomologist Henry Walter Bates, and in 1848 the two men went to the tropics of South America. He collected more than 125,000 specimens from the Amazon Basin. Although he lost most of his specimens and almost his life on the return voyage when the ship caught fire, in 1854 he embarked on another major expedition to the Malay Archipelago. In organizing his specimens, he pioneered the study of the geographical distribution of plants and animals that later provided crucial evidence to advance his theory of evolution by natural selection. Wallace noticed a division within the flora and fauna of the Australasian islands that followed a line of demarcation, which today is still known as the Wallace Line. His massive two-volume *The Geographical Distribution of Animals* (1876) entitles him to be considered the founder of the science of zoogeography. His book *The Malay Archipelago* (1869) remains one of the finest scientific travel books ever written. He was also the first prominent anthropologist to live for an extended period among the native peoples whom he studied. He seemed remarkably free of the racism and stereotyping of indigenous peoples that characterized the thinking of the time.

While in the Malay Archipelago Wallace, working independently of Darwin, came up with virtually the identical theory of natural selection. In 1858 he sent Darwin his paper titled "On the Tendency of Varieties to Depart Indefinitely from the Original Type." Not wanting Darwin's priority to be scooped, Charles Lyell and Joseph

Hooker arranged for Darwin's unpublished writings and Wallace's paper to be read jointly before the Linnaean Society. In 1864 Wallace suggested that humans had experienced two distinct stages in evolution. The first stage was just like that of any other organism. But once the human brain had evolved to a certain point and the moral and intellectual capabilities were fairly well developed, natural selection would no longer act on the human physical form, which would remain essentially unchanged. However, in 1869 Wallace claimed that neither natural selection nor a general theory of evolution could account for the origin of consciousness or the higher moral faculties along with various other physical traits.

It has been argued that Wallace changed his mind as a result of his involvement with spiritualism, which began in the mid-1860s, but that is too simplistic an analysis. Wallace insisted his new views were not a negation of the principle of natural selection. Instead, he grounded his argument on the principle of utility alone, maintaining that human beings had a variety of unique traits such as mathematical ability and various aesthetic and moral qualities that would not have been useful in the lowest state of civilization. Some power was guiding evolution in definite directions for future use. Wallace was developing an evolutionary model that was much broader than just explaining change within the physical/biological realm. For Wallace a belief in spiritualism was not incompatible with science. Rather, he wanted the boundaries of science to be extended to include phenomena that could not be explained in strictly materialistic terms.

Spiritualism provided Wallace with a practical morality that resonated with his egalitarian views, his sense of justice, and his unequivocal idealism and optimism regarding the future of the human race. Along with spiritualism, his involvement with various movements including land nationalism, women's rights (see WOMAN SUFFRAGE MOVEMENT AND UNBELIEF), and socialism (see SOCIALISM AND UNBELIEF) diminished his stature as a scientist. However, Wallace continued to publish first-rate work in biogeography that made no reference to his spiritualist beliefs. Few naturalists have made greater contributions than he in understanding the natural world.

BIBLIOGRAPHY

Fichman, Martin. *An Elusive Victorian: The Evolution of Alfred Russel Wallace.* Chicago: University of Chicago Press, 2004.

Kottler, Malcolm Jay. "Alfred Russel Wallace, the Origin of Man, and Spiritualism." *ISIS* 65 (1974).

Marchant, James. *Alfred Russel Wallace, Letters and Reminiscences.* 1916. Reprint, New York: Arno, 1975.

McKinney, H. Lewis. *Wallace and Natural Selection.* New Haven, CT: Yale University Press, 1972.

Shermer, Michael. *In Darwin's Shadow: The Life and Science of Alfred Russel Wallace: A Biographical*

Study in the Psychology of History. New York: Oxford University Press, 2002.

Wallace, Alfred Wallace. *Contributions to the Theory of Natural Selection.* London: MacMillan & Sons, 1875.

———. *The Malay Archipelago.* 1869. Reprint, New York: Dover, 1962.

———. *My Life: A Record of Events and Opinions.* 2 vols. London: Chapman and Hall, 1905.

———. *Natural Selection and Tropical Nature: Essays on Descriptive and Theoretical Biology.* 1898. Reprint, Westmead: Gregg International, 1969.

———. *The World of Life.* New York: Moffat, Yard, 1911.

SHERRIE LYONS

WANG CH'UNG (c. 27–100 CE), Chinese philosopher. Wang Ch'ung has become considerably better known in China since the revolution than at any other time since his death. He was one of the earliest opponents of any kind of superstition, and, conversely, one of the foremost exponents of rationality anywhere in the world in his time.

An orphan, he attended the national university after school and then became a civil servant, working mainly in the educational field. He became assistant to an inspecting censor, but then returned home to write and teach. He was known to be a quiet scholar and a devoted teacher. His main work, *Lun-heng*, contains eighty-four chapters in thirty books. It is usually translated as *Critical Essays*, but *Balanced Inquiries* is a title more in keeping with Wang's declared intention, which was to provide a balanced (or fair) discussion.

His criticisms were essentially of the developments in CONFUCIANISM during the 100 to 150 years prior to his birth. These changes seemed to him to be intellectually arid and therefore academically unacceptable. In particular, he wrote strongly against the belief that heaven was more than just the symbol of perfection described by Confucius. It was being endowed by later Confucians with purposiveness, imagined as possessing a will of its own that it displayed through miracles, portents, and prodigies. Wang rejected all these concepts as irrational, arguing that it was a pathetic fallacy to attribute teleology to the impersonal universe. He rejected the view of many of his contemporaries that Confucius was not merely a supreme sage, but worthy of deification. Wang insisted that Confucius's teaching should be judged by the *Analects*—compiled soon after the Master's death—not by the apocryphal literature written during the two centuries before Wang's birth. Thus fortune and misfortune are to be accepted as the consequence of chance, so that no "meaning" should be read into events nor lessons drawn from them. He argued further that nobody possesses an immortal soul (and therefore nobody becomes a "ghost" after death): the many around him who thought otherwise, he criticized for indulging in nothing less than wishful thinking.

Wang thus emerges as the Chinese CARVAKA or perhaps the Chinese LUCRETIUS. He stands out as a thoroughly independent thinker, borrowing frequently from the Confucian, Taoist (see TAOISM, UNBELIEF WITHIN), and Yin-Yang schools, but writing of them critically, and showing an interest in human institutions rather than metaphysics.

His basic contribution to Chinese thought, therefore, was to clear away the superstitions, beliefs, and dogmas that had developed over two centuries, and to enhance critical and rational thinking—seeds of which were being sown during his lifetime—by espousing an attitude of SKEPTICISM and NATURALISM that was to develop further among his successors during subsequent centuries. Thus he fostered a new ethos of inquiry rather than any specific field of research. For this he was known as one of the three geniuses of his time.

RAY BILLINGTON

WASHBURN, LEMUEL KELLY (1846–1927), American freethought editor and lecturer. Born in Wareham, Massachusetts, the youthful L. K. Washburn failed in his plan to become a lawyer; a few months in a Unitarian seminary convinced him he could never be a Christian minister. Yet in 1870 he successfully pastored a Unitarian congregation for one summer (see UNITARIANISM TO 1961), then began preaching at a hall in Ipswich, at whose pulpit he was ordained without joining any denomination. He preached in a controversial, socially radical vein for ten years, abandoned the ministry and took up bookkeeping, then surfaced as a freethought lecturer. Beginning in 1886 he delivered more than one hundred FREETHOUGHT lectures in Boston's Paine Hall, which had been erected by officers of the important freethought paper, the BOSTON INVESTIGATOR.

Upon the death in 1899 of Horace Seaver, second editor of the *Investigator*, Washburn was invited to succeed Seaver as editor, and oversaw the aging paper's final issues and its 1904 absorption by the still-vital national freethought paper, THE TRUTH SEEKER.

Washburn was a moderately successful freethought lecturer with liberal affinities to social reform causes. Oddly, his social rhetoric sometimes echoed proponents of the social gospel movement. In 1911 he published his only book, a collection of essays and aphorisms titled *Is The Bible Worth Reading?*

Washburn moved to Revere, Massachusetts, where he remained active as a freethought lecturer and a real estate agent until about 1920. He died in 1927, already largely forgotten; his newspaper obituary amounted only to a few lines.

BIBLIOGRAPHY

Forrey, Robert. "The Architecture of Americanism: The Revere Town Hall." *Essex Institute Historical Collections*, July 1990.

Putnam, Samuel Porter. *Four Hundred Years of Freethought*. New York: Truth Seeker Company, 1894.

TOM FLYNN

WATSON, JAMES (1799–1874), English publisher and reformer. Though he wrote little himself, James Watson was a fearless publisher of radical FREETHOUGHT books and magazines, serving as the bridge in an "apostolic succession" from pioneer publisher Richard CARLILE to the RATIONALIST PRESS ASSOCIATION. While writers of controversial works might escape detection and punishment, printers and booksellers like Watson had premises and were thus sitting ducks.

Watson was born in Malton, Yorkshire, on September 21, 1799. Educated by his mother, a Sunday school teacher, and in charity schools, at age twelve he briefly entered domestic service with a clergyman. After five years as an agricultural laborer he became a warehouseman in Leeds and met artisans studying works by Thomas PAINE and other deists (see DEISM). In 1822, while Carlile was in jail, he went to London as one of many shopmen carrying on the business and was prosecuted in turn for issuing Elihu PALMER's *Principles of Nature* (1801) in 1823. During his year in jail for "blasphemous libel" (see BLASPHEMY), he turned to "heavy" reading like the philosophy of David HUME and the histories of Edward GIBBON.

On his release, Watson studied printing and became compositor for Carlile's *Republican* and *Lion*. In 1826, he narrowly survived cholera, joined the Owenites (see OWEN, ROBERT), and was a storeman in the First Co-operative Trading Association. From 1827 he was wealthy freethinker Julian Hibbert's printer, and was active in agitation for female suffrage (see WOMAN SUFFRAGE MOVEMENT AND UNBELIEF), trade union formation, and abolition of the 1819 "taxes on knowledge" (duties on advertising and paper and a newspaper stamp). In 1831 he narrowly escaped jail for ordering a feast on a fast day. Hibbert gave him type and presses to issue Comte de Volney's *Lectures in History*. He continued releasing other heterodox literature and his own paper, the *Working Man's Friend* (1832–33). In 1833 he served six months' jail time for publishing Henry HETHERINGTON's unstamped *Poor Man's Guardian* (1831–35). With a 450-guinea bequest from Hibbert, he launched a "Cabinet of Reason" series in 1834.

Meeting William Lovett, he became an active Chartist. He also met George Jacob HOLYOAKE and printed the *Reasoner* from 1846 to 1854, when, helped by a 250-pound subscription, Holyoake bought his business. Still committed to reform and press freedom, Watson was the first president of the London Secular Society in 1853, treasurer of the Truelove Defense Fund in 1858, and supporter of the Charles BRADLAUGH

Defense Fund in 1868. He died in Norwood on November 29, 1874.

BIBLIOGRAPHY

Linton, W. J. *James Watson: A Memoir.* Hamden, CT: n.p., 1879; Manchester: Abel Heywood, 1880.
Thompson, E. P. *The Making of the English Working Class.* London: Gollancz, 1963.

DAVID TRIBE

WATTS, CHARLES (1836–1906), English writer and lecturer. Linking SECULARISM to RATIONALISM, possessing many talents, and establishing what amounted to a dynasty, Charles Watts would undoubtedly enjoy a higher reputation had he not fallen out with Charles BRADLAUGH in the middle of his career and been eclipsed by his son, Charles Albert WATTS, at the end.

Charles Watts was born in Bristol on February 27, 1836, the son of a cobbler and Wesleyan lay preacher. He showed an early interest in debating, temperance lecturing, and amateur theatricals. In his midteens he heard George Jacob HOLYOAKE lecture, went to London, met Charles SOUTHWELL and Robert Cooper, became a secularist, and brought his older brother, John WATTS, into the movement. John became its printer, first under the imprint of Holyoake at a Fleet Street House "collective" and then under that of Austin HOLYOAKE, Holyoake's younger brother, at Bradlaugh's *NATIONAL REFORMER*. In 1864 Charles joined as assistant printer and subeditor.

When the NATIONAL SECULAR SOCIETY (NSS) was formed in 1866, Watts became its secretary. At the 1868 parliamentary election he spoke on Bradlaugh's Northampton platform. Favoring the concept of a substitute church within the society, Watts established a secular Sunday school, devised a ceremony for the naming of infants (1868), and with Austin Holyoake wrote the *Secularist's Manual of Songs and Ceremonies* (1871). In 1872 a Hall of Science Club and Institute was formed to stage intimate musical and dramatic evenings free from "the blackguardism of a London music hall." Watts and his second wife, Kate Eunice WATTS, daughter of leading Nottingham freethinkers, were prominent performers.

Meanwhile, in a flurry of Republicanism, Watts became vice president of the London Republican Club in 1871 and in 1872 was nominated for the council of the National Republican Brotherhood, which the secularists soon repudiated. In 1874, while Bradlaugh was lecturing in America, Watts spoke on his behalf in Northampton. He supported Bradlaugh again in connection with an 1874 by-election. In that year Austin Holyoake died; Bradlaugh raised 650 pounds to purchase Austin's printing and publishing business, which Bradlaugh handed over to Watts—privately admitting that he trusted the business sense of Kate rather than Charles. At the same time Annie BESANT joined the NSS, became a

Reformer contributor at a guinea a week—the same pay Watts was getting as subeditor—and wrote a new *Secular Song and Hymn Book* (1875), eclipsing Watts's earlier work in this genre. But Watts, not Besant, edited the paper during another American lecture tour by Bradlaugh. Also demoted in the secularist hierarchy in consequence of Besant's advent was George W. FOOTE. At the 1876 NSS conference Watts resigned his secretaryship to concentrate on lecturing, debating, and writing, including *The History of Freethought* (1877), part 3 of *The Freethinker's Text-Book*.

In 1877 Watts was prosecuted for publishing Charles KNOWLTON's contraceptive manual *Fruits of Philosophy* (1832). He pleaded "in point of law guilty" and incurred twenty-five pounds in costs. Having expected Watts to mount a defense instead of offering a guilty plea, Bradlaugh dismissed Watts as *Reformer* subeditor and cancelled his printing and publishing engagement. Watts struggled until he printed for William Stewart ROSS, resigned from the NSS, bought Holyoake's *Secular Review*, merged it with Foote's *Secularist*, and with them formed the British Secular Union. When that organization collapsed in 1884, Watts went to Canada as a lecturer of the Toronto Secular Society and founded *Secular Thought* (1885–1911). On Bradlaugh's death in 1891, he returned to England, rejoined the NSS, and briefly led the Birmingham Secular Society. In 1899 he became a principal lecturer of the RATIONALIST PRESS ASSOCIATION, which was run by his son Charles Albert, resigned again from the NSS in 1902 after quarreling with Foote, and died on February 16, 1906.

BIBLIOGRAPHY

Royle, Edward. *Radicals, Secularists, and Republicans: Popular Freethought in Britain, 1866–1915.* Manchester: Manchester University Press, 1980.
Tribe, David. *President Charles Bradlaugh, M.P.* London: Elek, 1971.

DAVID TRIBE

WATTS, CHARLES ALBERT (1858–1946), English publishing pioneer. Charles Albert Watts was born on May 27, 1858, the firstborn of Charles WATTS, one of the most important freethought leaders of the nineteenth century. His mother, Mary Ann Watts, died in 1870, aged thirty-one, when he was twelve. That same year, young Charles Albert Watts joined his father as an apprentice in their small printing and publishing business. Watts learned the trade from the bottom up, which gave him valuable insights for the future. An unassuming man, Watts built up Watts and Company to a position of strength not equaled by any freethought publishing house until the advent of Prometheus Books a century later.

Along with Watts and Company, Watts was instrumental in establishing several other important organizations and periodicals, some of which are still with us today, most conspicuously the RATIONALIST PRESS ASSOCIATION (RPA). In 1884 Watts established the *Agnostic Annual*, which in 1907 became the *RPA Annual*, and in 1927 the *Rationalist Annual*. This publication, which Watts edited until 1943, brought together some of the best writing from the previous year. The annual continued publication until 1980 and was a respected vehicle for humanist scholarship throughout its life. Watts's other important creation was the *Literary Guide*, which began in 1885 and served as a vehicle for promoting Watts and Company books; it went on to become one of the premier humanist journals in the world, today published as the *New Humanist*.

Watts's genius was in understanding how the publishing trade actually worked, and in being able to inspire confidence in men richer than himself to finance his innovative publishing ventures. The most daring of these was his plan to reprint substantial works of FREETHOUGHT, history, science, and BIBLICAL CRITICISM in paperback form for only sixpence or hardback for a shilling. These prices made such works accessible to working-class readers. Conventional wisdom was that poorer people lacked the inclination or ability to read works of this sort, but Watts proved them wrong. Between 1902 and 1912 Watts and Company produced the Cheap Reprints series, which made works by Thomas H. HUXLEY, Ernst HAECKEL, and others available to readers of modest means. Many titles in this series sold in the tens of thousands, often to the alarm of church leaders, who were incensed at the prospect of poor people having access to this sort of material. Eventually changes to copyright laws and pressure against railway vendors forced the Cheap Reprints series to come to an end. But in the meantime publishing history had been made. Watts repeated this success with the Thinker's Library, which ran from 1929 until 1951.

Things became more difficult for Watts after World War I, and even his skills weren't sufficient to prevent Watts and Company from suffering at the hands of aggressive new competition that imitated his earlier successes, in the form of the cheap Penguin paperbacks and rival popular-science series. Watts retired from active involvement in the RPA and Watts and Company in March 1930, though he retained the editorship of the *Rationalist Annual* until 1943 and of the *Literary Guide* until his death. He was succeeded by his hardworking and loyal son Frederick C. C. Watts. A surge of book buying during World War II masked Watts and Company's problems until after Watts's death on May 15, 1946. That Fred Watts failed to save the firm was through no lack of effort on his behalf. In 1954 the RPA took over direct ownership of Watts and Company, and in 1960 they sold the firm to Sir Isaac Pitman & Sons. The Rationalist Press Association and the *New Humanist* remain Charles Albert Watts's longest-lasting legacies.

BIBLIOGRAPHY

Cooke, Bill. *The Gathering of the Infidels: A Hundred Years of the Rationalist Press Association*. Amherst, NY: Prometheus Books, 2004.

Gould, F. J. *The Pioneers of Johnson's Court*. London: Watts and Company, 1929.

Whyte, Adam Gowans. "Charles Albert Watts." *Literary Guide*, July 1946.

———. *The Story of the RPA 1899–1949*. London: Watts and Company, 1949.

BILL COOKE

WATTS, KATE EUNICE (1849–1924), English freethought pamphleteer and orator. "Kate Eunice" Watts, as she called herself and signed her publications, was registered as Eunice Kate Nowlan upon her birth, on February 8, 1849, and upon her marriage in 1870 to Charles (known as Charlie) WATTS. By the time of her death, she was registered as Kate Eunice.

She was the elder of two daughters of leading Nottingham freethinkers (see FREETHOUGHT), William and Eunice Nowlan, with whom Watts, the secularist printer, generally stayed during his lecture tours to the north of England; Kate grew up without ever having entered a church.

Charlie Watts's first wife, Mary Ann, died on April 6, 1870, aged thirty-one, and his two-year-old son, Wallace George, died less than two months later, leaving Watts with five surviving children aged between four and thirteen—the eldest son (aged twelve) being Charles Albert WATTS, who would later found the *Literary Guide* (now *New Humanist*), the *Rationalist Annual*, and the RATIONALIST PRESS ASSOCIATION (RPA). When Charlie married Kate on November 19, 1870, she must have come as, so to speak, a "godsend" to that doubly bereaved household.

Still young and pretty, she became the belle of the London freethought movement and a sort of hostess at the Hall of Science—though soon to be rivaled by the Charles BRADLAUGH protegée Annie BESANT. Kate's elocution, wit, and histrionic talent were much admired as she gave lectures, chaired meetings, and took part in social entertainments. She also wrote polemical essays for the *NATIONAL REFORMER* and later the *Secular Review*, sometimes reprinted as pamphlets.

She bore Charlie one daughter, Kate Eunice, in May 1875. Being a supporter of the neo-Malthusians (as family-planning advocates were then called), Kate probably thought this one addition to the family enough.

When Charles Watts broke with Bradlaugh and Besant over the *Fruits of Philosophy* controversy, Kate spoke and wrote in her husband's defense. The dispute arose when Watts, arraigned for trial in 1877 as the printer of that allegedly obscene booklet advocating birth control (written in the 1830s by the American doctor Charles

KNOWLTON), changed his original plea of "Not Guilty" to "Guilty in Law." He did this because Kate, having actually read the booklet, decided that the style of writing was too coarse to be defended—certainly if it were to result in several years' imprisonment at hard labor for her husband. The Bradlaugh faction saw this withdrawal as a cowardly betrayal and cancelled its contract with Watts to print the *National Reformer* and other secularist work—a serious financial blow.

Watts then acquired the *Secular Review* from George Jacob HOLYOAKE, including in it a series of three feminist articles on women's education and social status by Kate. However, it was a struggle to carry on. So, handing over the printing business to son Charles Albert—who had been working in it from the age of twelve—Charles and Kate left Britain in 1886 for Toronto to work on behalf of SECULARISM. They continued their lecturing and writing in Canada and founded the important Canadian freethought journal *Secular Thought* (1887–1909).

In a ten-cent pamphlet, *Christianity Defective and Unnecessary*, Kate commented that the fact that the Garden of Eden serpent was male proved that "the greater amount of wickedness was even at that early stage possessed by those of the masculine gender, and they have firmly and undeniably maintained their right to its possession ever since."

The Wattses returned to London in 1891. Charlie joined George William FOOTE on the *Freethinker*, while Kate developed her career as an actress under her stage name of Kate Carlyon, appearing in eleven successful plays in London and the United States. These included Jerome K. Jerome's *The Passing of the Third Floor Back* (1908), with 180 London performances. Her final recorded role was that of Mrs. Gilbey in George Bernard SHAW's *Fanny's First Play* (1915).

After a short illness, Kate Eunice Watts died on February 25, 1924. She bequeathed to the RPA letters from US agnostic orator Robert Green INGERSOLL and a large oil portrait of him, inscribed by him to Charles Watts.

The funeral oration at Golders Green Crematorium was given by F. J. Gould, and Kate's ashes were buried in Highgate Cemetery beside those of Charles Watts and next to the grave of G. J. Holyoake.

BIBLIOGRAPHY

"Death of Mrs. Charles Watts." *Literary Guide*, April 1924.

Executor's report, untitled. *Literary Guide*, December 1924.

Royle, Edward. *Radicals Secularists and Republicans.* Manchester: Manchester University Press, 1980.

———. "Watts, Charles." In *Oxford Dictionary of National Biography*. Oxford: Oxford University Press, 2004.

Watts, Kate Eunice. *Christianity Defective and Unneces-*
sary. Toronto: Secular Thought Office, 1900.

———. "The Education and Position of Women." *Secular Review*, September 27, October 4 and 18, 1879. Reprinted, London: Watts and Company, [1880].

———. *Mrs. Watts's Reply to Mr. Bradlaugh's Misrepresentations.* London: London Co-operative Printing and Stationery, 1877.

———. *Reasons for Not Accepting Christianity.* London: Watts and Company, [1877].

Wearing, J. P. *The London Stage.* Metuchen, NJ: Scarecrow, 1976.

BARBARA SMOKER AND VIRGINIA CLARK

WATTS, JOHN (1834–1866), English editor and writer. A good "all-arounder" and trusted lieutenant of Charles BRADLAUGH, he would be much better known were it not for his tragic early death.

John was born in Bedminster, Bristol, England, on October 2, 1834. He was the son of a cobbler and Wesleyan lay preacher and became a Sunday school teacher himself, but was converted to freethought by his younger brother, CHARLES. Following Charles to London, he learned the printing trade and from 1855 managed the printing agency at the Fleet Street House, a secularist "collective" directed by George Jacob HOLYOAKE. He also became subeditor of Holyoake's weekly *Reasoner* (1846–61). After Holyoake's younger brother, Austin, another printer and subeditor, entered the business, Watts was dismissed and threw in his lot with Bradlaugh, then coeditor of the NATIONAL REFORMER, in 1860, and became its subeditor. He also collaborated with Bradlaugh in a popular series of biographical sketches, *Half-hours with Freethinkers* (1858), and in radical political causes. In 1862 he was secretary of the Garibaldi Demonstration Committee, protesting against French occupation of Rome before Italian unification.

Bradlaugh, always struggling against poor health and increasingly involved in political and private financial affairs, handed over the *Reformer* editorship to Watts from March 7, 1863, to April 22, 1866. Though Watts wrote well here and in several pamphlets on religion and philosophy, he lacked Bradlaugh's unique capacity to identify newsworthy issues and attract outstanding contributors, and the paper's circulation declined. But what prompted Bradlaugh to resume the editorship was Watts's grave illness with tuberculosis. Nevertheless, Watts was one of four candidates for presidency of the NATIONAL SECULAR SOCIETY in September 1866. He died on October 31 of that year.

BIBLIOGRAPHY

McCabe, Joseph. *A Biographical Dictionary of Modern Rationalists.* London: Watts and Company, 1920.

Tribe, David. *President Charles Bradlaugh, M.P.* London: Elek, 1971.

DAVID TRIBE

WEINBERG, CHAIM LEIB (1861–1939), Born in Ciechanowiec in the Russian Empire (now Poland), Chaim Leb Weinberg was part of a family of well-to-do landowners who intended him to become a rabbi. Instead he emigrated to London, where he heard an atheistic speech by Charles BRADLAUGH. Finally, at age twenty-one, he arrived in the United States, where he worked rolling cigarettes, first in New York and then briefly in Durham, North Carolina, where sometime around 1884 he first discovered his oratorical talents during a union organizing drive.

From this period he became a follower of the Russian anarchist and atheist Johann Most, and for the rest of his life, Weinberg preached revolutionary anarchist-communism, always paired with intense atheism (see ANARCHISM AND UNBELIEF). In Philadelphia he was a member of the Knights of Liberty, which sponsored an elaborate and very public Yom Kippur Ball in 1889, enraging pious Jews. In 1891 the event was prevented by a police raid, which resulted in four men serving eight-month jail terms. His major activity was to give public orations in Yiddish on atheism, anarchism, and the labor struggle. Weinberg inspired striking Jewish workers with fiery speeches during countless strikes from 1889 through World War I, sometimes as a paid organizer for a bakers' and then a garment workers' union. Though he never put pen to paper, his skills as a storyteller, comic, and debater were legendary. Remembered as conspicuously ugly, sloppily dressed, and badly lame, he was sometimes laughed at as he approached the podium, only to hold the audience spellbound when he opened his mouth. Weinberg toured the United States, Canada, and England during his career, and was a stalwart of the anarchist movement at Philadelphia, especially forming cooperative businesses and communities. In 1900 he initiated the Jewish Workers' Cooperative Association, which had some nine hundred members and two retail stores at its peak. Arrested in 1908 for inciting a riot between police and unemployed workers, he was later acquitted. In old age he lived on a small farm in Willow Grove, Pennsylvania, where his memoirs were recorded in the form of oral testimony by Marcus Graham in 1930, and where fundraiser picnics were held to benefit anarchist projects. He died of heart disease.

BIBLIOGRAPHY

Avrich, Paul. *An American Anarchist: The Life of Voltairine de Cleyre.* Princeton: Princeton University Press, 1978.

Cohen, Joseph J. *The Jewish Anarchist Movement in the United States: A Historical Review and Personal Reminiscence.* Translated by Esther Dolgoff. Uunpublished, 1980.

Weinberg, Chaim Leib. *Forty Years in the Struggle for Social Revolution: Memoirs of a Libertarian Fighter among Jews in the United States.* Translated by Naomi Cohen. Philadelphia: Wooden Shoe Books, forthcoming.

ROBERT P. HELMS

WELLS, HERBERT GEORGE (1866–1946), English author and reformer. Although H. G. Wells was neither a deep nor a systematic thinker, his career-long humanist-socialist effort to challenge and revise orthodox religious beliefs received considerable attention. By age twenty-two, he spoke of religion as a collapsible cardboard structure that only a foolish child would depend on for support. Curious about religion's wide appeal, Wells read Christian writings including the Pauline epistles. His response ranged from an imagined future without anthropomorphic theology and religious denominations in *A Modern Utopia* (1905) to a vitriolic attack on the "evil institution" of Roman Catholicism in *Crux Ansata* (1943). Influenced by Fabian Society socialism and Darwinian biology, he channeled his own vestigial religious sentiment into societal programs designed to improve the human condition. He would become an honorary member of the RATIONALIST PRESS ASSOCIATION.

Evolutionary chance was a fact for Wells, but in the tradition of Ralph Waldo EMERSON and other Transcendentalists he also elevated the role of human will in responding to accident. In what he termed a confession of faith in *First and Last Things* (1908), Wells referred to this will as a Collective Mind. In a way reminiscent of Romantic pantheism, this Collective Mind emerges from and operates throughout human experience. In Hegelian fashion, this power destines humanity to increasingly evolved states of scientific advancement, rational insight, and social harmony.

Shocked by the horrors of World War I, Wells briefly reconfigured the Collective Mind in *God the Invisible King* (1917), a highly controversial publication he would eventually regret because it clouded rather than clarified his essentially positivist position concerning human destiny. This book seemed to acknowledge a supreme deity. In a risky maneuver designed to give hope during the war, Wells sought to accommodate popular belief in a higher being while also reiterating his notion of God as the Collective Mind or Mind of the Race. Again considering the allure of religion, especially during dark times, he affirmed that humanity's survival must be the biological purpose behind religious belief.

In Wells's followup novel, *The Soul of a Bishop* (1917), God again confusingly seems to be outside yet also within human experience. The protagonist rejects Christianity, espouses universal brotherhood, and preaches a heaven only on earth. The book concludes: "Faith is a sort of *tour de force*. A feat of the imagination. For such things as we are. Naturally." Emphasized here is the thorough grounding of faith in humanity's physical nature and limited mind (imagination). For Wells, faith is biological, not supernatural, in origin. A feature of our survival instinct, it serves the "Mind of the Race" that propels humanity toward ever-greater achievements in the material world.

After the war, Wells continued to recast revealed religion. Revising the biblical account of Job, *The Undying Fire* (1919) suggests that God is actually the collective human spirit struggling toward "the unity and release and triumph of mankind." In such books Wells meant to tap into the appeal of biblical stories, which he acknowledged in *The Salvaging of Civilization* (1921) to be fictional but nonetheless powerful in conveying humanity's dramatic relationship to the scheme of things. His *Outline of History* (1920), apparently a reworking of an unacknowledged manuscript by Florence Deeks, offered a new Bible-like story—a sweeping narrative of the human spirit undergoing conversion-like awakenings as it breaks free from one framework after another in the course of its steady evolution toward a rational collective consciousness on earth. This human-derived force is what people really mean by God, Wells explained in *Experiment in Autobiography* (1934); it is the spirit of human wills uniting to "master our world and release its imprisoned promise."

BIBLIOGRAPHY

Haynes, Roslynn D. *H. G. Wells: Discoverer of the Future*. New York: New York University Press, 1980.
Reed, John R. *The Natural History of H. G. Wells*. Athens: Ohio University Press. 1982.
Wells, H. G. *Crux Ansata*. New York: Agora, 1944.
———. *Experiment in Autobiography*. New York: Macmillan, 1934.
———. *First and Last Things*. New York: Putnam, 1908.
———. *God the Invisible King*. New York: Macmillan, 1917.
———. *A Modern Utopia*. New York: Scribner's Sons, 1905.
———. *The Outline of History*. New York: Macmillan, 1921.
———. *The Salvaging of Civilization*. New York: Macmillan, 1921.
———. *The Soul of a Bishop*. New York: Macmillan, 1917.
———. *The Undying Fire*. New York: Macmillan, 1919.

WILLIAM J. SCHEICK

WESTBROOK, RICHARD BRODHEAD (1820–1899),
American freethinker and educator. Born in Pike County, Pennsylvania, the son of a congressman, he was educated in common schools and became a traveling teacher. He earned a doctorate in divinity and was ordained in 1844 as a Methodist Episcopal minister. He switched to Presbyterianism in 1852 and served as secretary of missions for the American Sunday School Union between 1854 and 1861, establishing thousands of rural schools. He left the ministry and took an LL.D. at New York University, practicing law from 1863 to 1869, when he became a counselor in the US Supreme Court. During the 1870s he abandoned the law to invest in coal lands in western Pennsylvania, which he sold in 1882, retiring with considerable wealth to Philadelphia. An active member for many years in the Universal Peace Union, in 1884 he led the opposition to surrounding Philadelphia's City Hall with military statues, saying that they were better suited to cemeteries or prisons. The same year he became director of the Wagner Free Institute of Science, where he made a secular education and library available to the adult public, involved many leading scientists, and commissioned research expeditions. Westbrook served as president of the AMERICAN SECULAR UNION between 1888 and 1891. He authored five books and at least seven pamphlets, most of which were devoted to debunking the Bible and exposing church interference in education and marriage. Westbrook's active SECULARISM coincided with the death of his wife, Sarah Hall, in 1882. His second wife was Henrietta Payne, a physician and freethinker with whom he was an active member and lecturer of the Ladies' Liberal League from 1892. From 1888 he led a public campaign to enforce the secularist terms of Stephen Girard's will, which had established Girard College to educate orphan boys. The trustees of that institution had introduced religion into the curriculum. Westbrook died at his summer home in Rhode Island. He was remembered both for his religious and for his anticlerical periods, but always with warmth and respect.

BIBLIOGRAPHY

"Passed Away." Unidentified newspaper clipping of Rhode Island. Archives of Wagner Free Institute, Philadelphia.
"Richard B. Westbrook, D.D., LL.D." *Peacemaker*, June 1900.
Wagner Free Institute of Science. *In Memoriam Richard Brodhead Westbrook: proceedings on the occasion of a memorial meeting ... October 25, 1899*. Philadelphia, 1899.
Westbrook, Richard Brodhead. *The Bible, Whence and What?* Philadelphia: Author, 1882.
———. *The Eliminator; or Skeleton Keys to Sacerdotal Secrets*. Philadelphia: Author, 1894.
———. *Girard's Will and Girard College Theology*. Philadelphia: Author, 1888.
———. *Marriage and Divorce*. New York: Author, 1870.

ROBERT P. HELMS

WETTSTEIN, OTTO (1838–?), American freethought writer and lecturer. Otto Wettsetin was born April 7, 1838, in Prussia. His father, Theodore Wettstein, moved to Milwaukee,Wisconsin, in 1848. At age twelve Otto was sent to Chicago by his father to learn the jeweler's trade. From his mother's influence he became a Lutheran during this time. In 1857 he moved to Rochelle, Illinois, where he began business with a kit of tools, a trunk full of books, and four dollars. Later a friend gave him a copy of the freethought paper the *Boston Investigator*, which sparked his interest in science and poetry.

Through further studies Wettstein became a convinced materialist (see MATERIALISM, PHILOSOPHICAL). He began to express his views in articles published in the Rochelle and Chicago papers, which resulted in Christians boycotting his business. He countered by turning to the freethought community for patronage. He ran ads in many FREETHOUGHT journals advertising his "Wettstein Watches," for which he became famous.

In 1882 Wettstein began writing for the leading freethought paper in the nation, *The Truth Seeker*. In 1885 he designed and introduced his famous freethought badge, which represented the evolution of the world from the darkness of superstition to the light of reason and science. It came to serve as the de facto emblem of the nineteenth-century American freethought movement. Among Wettstein's later designs was the Robert Green INGERSOLL silver spoon, much prized by later collectors, and other trinkets.

His brother Herman was also a freethought writer. In 1897 Wettstein was elected treasurer of the AMERICAN SECULAR UNION, a major national freethought organization, and in 1908 was unanimously elected president of a group called the Materialist Association at its convention in Canal Dover, Ohio. Here he gave the address for which he would be best remembered, "The Ax to the Root, or a God Impossible in Nature."

Among the many articles he wrote for *The Truth Seeker* are "The Vagaries of Spiritism" (1890), "Is Theology Progressive?" (1886), "The Giant Delusion" (1893), "Which First, Mind or Matter?" (1883), and "What Caused a 'First Cause' to Create the Universe Six Thousand, but Not Six Quadrillion Years Ago?" (1888).

The date, place, and circumstances of Wettstein's death are unknown, but he had survived to age seventy when a short biography of him appeared in the freethought paper the *Blue Grass Blade* in 1908.

BIBLIOGRAPHY

Putnam, Samuel Porter. *Four Hundred Years of Freethought.* New York: Truth Seeker Company, 1894.

Macdonald, George E. *Fifty Years of Freethought.* New York: Truth Seeker Company, 1929.

Moore, Charles C., ed. *Blue Grass Blade.* [Lexington, KY], 1908.

MICHAEL ADCOCK

WHEELER, JOSEPH MAZZINI (1850–1898), English freethinker, editor, and scholar. Joseph Mazzini Wheeler was born in London of a radical father (hence the Mazzini, a tribute to Italian democratic reformer Giuseppe Mazzini). As a young man he spent time in Edinburgh as a lithographer. He met G. W. FOOTE in 1868 and they became lifelong friends. When Foote started the *Freethinker* in 1881, Wheeler became the subeditor, which he remained, apart from absences due to mental illness, until his death.

On Foote's imprisonment for BLASPHEMY in 1883, Wheeler became editor, but his oversensitive and manic behavior led to a breakdown at a period when he felt deeply for the suffering of Foote. He recovered, but instability dogged him until he died in an asylum in 1898. He himself contributed to the journal's forcefully anti-Christian material with a hilarious "Trial for Blasphemy" (1882) in which Matthew, Mark, Luke, and John appear before a Court of Common Sense accused of vilifying Almighty God.

He wrote numerous articles for the freethought press and a number of books, his considerable scholarship being bolstered by hours spent in the British Museum Reading Room. His greatest achievement was *A Biographical Dictionary of Freethinkers of All Ages* (1889), which comprehensively detailed figures across centuries and nations. His aim was to show "how many of the world's worthiest men and women have been Freethinkers."

Two other books were *Bible Studies and Phallic Worship* (1892) and *Footsteps of the Past* (1895). He was particularly interested in the anthropological approach, being an admirer of James Frazer. He produced in collaboration with G. W. Foote *Crimes of Christianity* (1885) and a pamphlet on VOLTAIRE (1894), one of many pamphlets he produced. Together with Foote he translated *Sepher Toldoth Jeschu* as *The Jewish Life of Christ.* His failure to complete a *History of Freethought in England* was a great loss, though some valuable parts remain.

Wheeler favored general secular education, to be paid for by disestablishment of the churches. His gentleness and sensitivity and his painstaking and accurate scholarship were admired by all, especially Foote, who said he was "true to others and true to himself." Even a member of the Christian Evidence Society sent a letter of condolence on his death.

BIBLIOGRAPHY

Herrick, Jim. *Vision and Realism: A Hundred Years of the Freethinker.* London: G. W. Foote, 1982.

Moss, A. B. "Famous Freethinkers I Have Known: Joseph Mazzini Wheeler." *Freethinker*, October 21, 1915.

Neuberg, Victor E. "Joseph Mazzini Wheeler." *Freethinker*, May 18, 1956.

Royle, Edward. *Radicals, Secularists and Republicans: Popular Freethought in Britain, 1866–1915.* Manchester, UK: Manchester University Press, 1980.

Unsigned obituary. *Freethinker*, May 15, 1898.

Wheeler, J. M. "'Sixty Years of Freethought,' from *Freethinker*." In *An Anthology of Atheism and Rationalism*, edited by Gordon Stein. Amherst, NY: Prometheus Books, 1980.

JIM HERRICK

WHITE, ANDREW DICKSON (1832–1918), American educational reformer, diplomat, and Christian liberal. Andrew Dickson White did more than any other American to impress upon late nineteenth- and twentieth-century thought the idea that science and religion are bitter enemies (see RELIGION IN CONFLICT WITH SCIENCE; EVOLUTION AND UNBELIEF)—though that was never his intent.

Early Life. Born into a wealthy Episcopalian family on November 7, 1832, at Homer, New York, White received a sound primary education and showed a flair for scholarship. In 1849 he entered Geneva (now Hobart) College, a small Episcopal academy selected by his father. Conditions were dismal, the curriculum irrelevant, the teaching pedantic, his classmates intolerably unruly—or so it seemed to young Andrew, who prevailed upon his father to enroll him in Yale the next year. Even Yale fell short of his hopes; after graduating in 1853 he undertook three years of work and study in Europe. Impressed by the University of Berlin, he dreamed of creating a "true university" along German lines in the United States.

At some point in his education White broke with orthodoxy. This process began when he recognized the dissimilarities between the genealogies of Jesus in the Gospels of Matthew and Luke. Influenced by the liberal Congregationalist minister Theodore Parker and Unitarian William Ellery Channing (see UNITARIANISM TO 1961), White settled into a poised DEISM that rejected belief in miracles and eternal punishment. Yet White always called himself a Christian, never embracing ATHEISM, AGNOSTICISM, or FREETHOUGHT. "I have never had any tendency to scoffing," he later wrote. This capacity to embrace radical and traditional positions simultaneously without regard for their mutual contradiction would prove characteristic.

Returning to America, White joined the newly formed University of Michigan. He won repute as a lecturer in history and an abolitionist, bringing Frederick DOUGLASS to speak at Ann Arbor. During the Civil War White undertook an informal diplomatic mission to bolster British support for the Union cause. Afterward he returned to New York and won election to the state senate. There he met fellow senator Ezra Cornell, who had made a fortune wiring the nation for telegraphy.

A Shared Vision. New York was pondering how to manage its windfall under the Morrill Act of 1862, which gave states tracts of western land the proceeds of whose sale must fund higher education. White and Cornell found they entertained compatible visions for New York's land-grant university. In Cornell's words, it would be "an institution where any person can find instruction in any study," from scientific and technical subjects to the humanities. More controversially, it would be nonsectarian. Both men's experiences had fostered antipathy toward denominationalism: Cornell had been ejected from the Society of Friends for marrying a non-Quaker, while White had his distasteful memories of Geneva College. Cornell having pledged land at Ithaca, New York, and a portion of his large fortune—and White having pledged a portion of his own more modest fortune—additional to land-grant proceeds, the two achieved control over the project. After political controversy, Cornell University was chartered in 1865. White would be its first president.

Cornell would be the first American university of stature unaffiliated with a religious body. Sectarian papers libeled it as a den of infidelity and perversity, accusing "indifferentism" (insufficient attention to fine points of doctrine) or outright godlessness. So wounding was this criticism that in October 1868, Governor Reuben E. Fenton made a last-minute decision to boycott Cornell's opening ceremonies, even though he had already journeyed to Ithaca for the sole purpose of attending them.

Retaliation. Frustrated, White fired back. On December 18, 1869, he delivered a pugnacious lecture indicting religion as the greatest enemy of scientific discovery. Widely reprinted, the lecture was soon expanded into a series of articles in *Popular Science Monthly*. (That journal's editor, Edward Livingston Youmans, would soon solicit historian John William DRAPER to write *A History of the Conflict between Science and Religion*, which in 1874 popularized the "military metaphor" of science and religion as adversaries.) In 1876 White published a small book based on his lecture. He had sharpened its focus, now indicting "ecclesiasticism" rather than religion as the chief impediment to scientific discovery. Nor was science the only victim: "Both Religion and Science have suffered fearfully from unlimited clerical sway," he wrote, "but of the two, Religion has suffered most."

Cornell University thrived despite controversy. Among other things it was the first US university to institute coeducational study, erect a nondenominational chapel, or offer a degree in electrical engineering. Pastors across America discouraged young people from enrolling, though with little effect on admissions. White erected a mansion on campus in which his family resided from 1874 (see MONUMENTS TO UNBELIEF). He frequently attended Unitarian services in Ithaca.

Despite his reform rhetoric, White never ceased to emphasize Cornell's embrace of generic Christianity, and on several occasions conceded to sectarian pressure. For example, having courageously recruited a Jewish instructor—ETHICAL CULTURE founder Felix ADLER—White stood by when conservative trustees forced Adler's dismissal following a controversial lecture on Christianity's intellectual debt to Judaism.

White held various diplomatic posts during and after his presidency of Cornell. As US minister to Germany he participated in establishing the international tribunal at The Hague. On an 1878 transatlantic voyage, White met agnostic orator Robert Green INGERSOLL; they talked about art. (White and Ingersoll would also share a posthumous maritime connection, both having their names attached to US "Liberty Ships" during World War II.) White continued to develop his ideas on science and religion.

White's *History*. Posted to Saint Petersburg as US minister to Russia in 1892–93, White began to assemble his magnum opus, a two-volume work published in 1896 as *A History of the Warfare of Science with Theology in Christendom*. In correspondence he wrote that he intended the work to stake out a position between "such gush as [Catholic apologist John Henry] Newman's on one side and such scoffing as Ingersoll's on the other."

As before, White distinguished between religion, which he reduced to the pure love of God and one's neighbor, and theology, which used the Bible as though a scientific text to make unprovable claims about the cosmos. White wrote to defend religion, "to keep the faith . . . in a Power in the universe good enough to make truth-seeking wise and strong enough to make truth-telling effective." He warned "against basing religious systems on miraculous claims which are constantly becoming more and more discredited and therefore more and more dangerous to any system which persists in using them."

Given White's intent, his method was curious. He wrote that "theological views of science" have "forced mankind away from the truth, and have caused Christendom to stumble for centuries into abysses of error and sorrow." Commitment to free inquiry made a scientist, he argued, dogmatism a theologian. This standard was not without problems: in different passages White placed Saint Augustine in both camps. White described how the medieval church's condemnation of usury had hobbled economic development. He offered a romanticized account of Galileo GALILEI's travails at the hands of the church. A similar treatment was accorded Copernicus. Where Draper's *History of the Conflict between Science and Religion* had been anti-Catholic in tone, White profiled Protestant failures as well, including belief in witches, the construal of earthquakes and comets as divine portents, and resistance to vaccination. White concluded that Christian theology had "arrested the normal development of the physical sciences for over fifteen hundred years"; moreover, beliefs concerning eternal punishment had emboldened European states to engage in increasingly brazen tortures and inhumane punishments.

The World Reacts. Though Draper's earlier volume outsold it, White's *History of the Warfare of Science with Theology in Christendom* enjoyed commercial success, including numerous printings over twenty-five years and translation into four languages. Its impact on scholarly and popular thinking regarding science and religion was greater still.

White was broadly misunderstood. A few clerics who grasped his intentions praised the book. But most who lauded it—among them Alexander Graham Bell, Lord Acton, and Andrew Carnegie—agreed with critics that the work constituted a devastating blow against Christianity. Freethinkers embraced it; atheist booksellers added it to their lists. Even Ingersoll wrote White a letter of praise, though he chided White for his deism, quipping: "The only power in the universe strong enough to make truth-seeking safe is man." Ultimately White's gift for incongruity undid him; most readers registered his surface radicalism yet failed to recognize the more traditional viewpoint hidden beneath the florid prose.

White continued in public life. In 1905 he published a two-volume autobiography, partly devoted to explaining once more what he had meant his *History* to achieve. In later years he worked for German-American friendship and other peace causes. He died on November 4, 1918, a week before the Armistice ended World War I. He was interred in Cornell's nondenominational chapel.

Writing in 1971, historian Paul Carter declared that White's *A History of the Warfare of Science with Theology in Christendom* did as much as any published work "toward routing orthodoxy in the name of science." *Rocks of Ages* (1999), zoologist Stephen Jay GOULD's eccentric plea for harmony between science and religion, made the same point. Insofar as science and religion came widely to be viewed as enemies, with science holding the moral high ground—and insofar as that conviction contributed to the growth of RATIONALISM, NATURALISM, and SECULARISM across the West during the twentieth century—Andrew Dickson White stands, however inadvertently, as one of the most effective and influential advocates for unbelief.

BIBLIOGRAPHY

Atschuler, Glenn C. *Andrew D. White: Educator, Historian, Diplomat.* Ithaca, NY: Cornell University Press, 1979.

Becker, Carl L. *Cornell University: Founders and the Founding.* Ithaca, NY: Cornell University Press, 1943.

Draper, John William. *History of the Conflict between Religion and Science.* New York: D. Appleton, 1874.

Gould, Stephen Jay. *Rocks of Ages: Science and Religion in the Fullness of Life.* New York: Ballantine, 1999.

Lindberg, David C., and Ronald L. Numbers. "Beyond War and Peace: A Reappraisal of the Encounter between Christianity and Science," *Perspectives on Science and Christian Faith* 39, no. 3 (1987).

Moore, James R. *The Post-Darwinian Controversies: A Study of the Protestant Struggle to Come to Terms with Darwin in Great Britain and America, 1870–1900.* Cambridge: Cambridge University Press, 1979.

White, Andrew D. *Autobiography of Andrew Dickson White.* New York: Century, 1905.

———. *A History of the Warfare of Science with Theology in Christendom.* New York: D. Appleton, 1896.

Tom Flynn

WHITMAN, WALT (1819–1892), American poet. Walt Whitman's *Leaves of Grass*, which went through nine editions, each containing new material, was an epochal volume. It gave legitimacy to free verse, enlarged the thematic domain of poetry, and signaled the arrival of an indigenous American poetry.

Science and Poetry. In 1855, when the first edition of *Leaves of Grass* was published, the Romantic aversion to science still chafed poetic sensibilities. Through its invasive procedures, the standard indictment read, science violated nature's pristine wholeness, disfiguring the beauty of natural forms. With its voracious appetite for analysis, it eviscerated myth, wonder, spontaneity, reverie, and awe. Whitman dismissed the charges: "Hurrah for positive science. Long live exact demonstration!" *Leaves of Grass* bristles with allusions to meteorology, conservation of energy, stellar life cycles, evolution, and other matters of science.

Science and the Church. When *The Origin of Species* became a cause célèbre, Whitman plumped for Darwinism (see DARWINISM AND UNBELIEF), desirable "as a counterpoise to widely prevailing and unspeakably tenacious, enfeebling superstitions." These superstitions were purveyed by ecclesiastical institutions for which the poet had little respect. From his father, an admirer of Thomas PAINE, Whitman had imbibed anticlerical sentiments (see ANTICLERICALISM). He scoffed at the disparate creeds of religion, each claiming to see the truth through the colored lenses of its own dogmatism. Though hardly an agnostic (see AGNOSTICISM), Whitman liked the brash way Robert Green INGERSOLL and Thomas Henry HUXLEY twitted the religious establishment: "It does seem," he remarked, "as if Ingersoll and Huxley without any others could unhorse the whole Christian giant." Whitman believed science could clear the way for spiritual regeneration by softening hidebound creeds, fables, and traditions.

Science and Mysticism. While science was a useful antidote to superstition, it could not penetrate the spiritual substratum of reality. Hence, Whitman relegated science to the role of data collector for a higher muse. Scientific facts had esoteric ramifications best elucidated by sages, seers, and poets. Properly illuminated, the lore of science corroborated Whitman's eclectic mysticism, a mishmash of moral and epistemological tenets derived directly or indirectly from Platonic and Kantian ide-

alism, Eastern mysticism, Quakerism (his mother was a Quaker), and American transcendentalism.

Like Ralph Waldo EMERSON, his proximate mentor, Whitman regarded material phenomena as cryptic symbols for spiritual truths: "The kernel of every object that can be seen, felt, or thought of has its relations to the soul, and is significant of something there." Everywhere Whitman turned, he found "letters from God" waiting to be deciphered. Decoded by the intuition, the letters revealed a suprasensible realm infused with forces, purposes, designs, and patterns emancipated from the laws of causality, logic, and probability. Whitman announced that life is indestructible, death is illusory, God is in everything, love binds all, evil is good, truth must be intuited, and truth is ineffable.

Criticism. For the empirically minded reader, Whitman's mysticism poses insuperable barriers. Since he treats intuition as a higher mode of cognition than reason, logic, and science, his claims cannot be evaluated by his own criterion for truth. When reason must defer to feeling and desire, anything goes. Subjected to mundane analysis, Whitman's claims emerge as semantic vacuums. Their import is largely psychological, metaphorical, and emotional.

Whitman denied metaphysical clout to pessimism. He insisted on a universe suffused with love, goodness, joy, equality, and justice, not one governed by what Robert Frost called "design of darkness to appall." Notwithstanding his hurrahs for science, Whitman was imbued with a romantic mentality. Earnest feelings were an entree to cosmic truths. Like Pascal, he thought everyone has an innate truth detector, the heart, which knows more than the head. All hearts spoke a common tongue because they had been instructed by the same cosmic tutor. So what seemed true to Whitman must be true for everyone. Had his mind been of an analytical cast, his reading of Ingersoll and Huxley might have raised a suspicion that hearts are multilingual. Fortunately for Whitman and the world, poetic truth need not be literally true.

BIBLIOGRAPHY

Asselineau, Roger. *The Evolution of Walt Whitman.* Iowa City: University of Iowa Press, 1999.

Beaver, Joseph. *Walt Whitman: Poet of Science.* New York: King's Crown, 1951.

Sloan, Gary. "Walt Whitman: When Science and Mysticism Collide." *Skeptical Inquirer* 27 (2003).

Woodress, James Leslie, ed. *Critical Essays on Walt Whitman.* Boston: G. K. Hall, 1983.

Gary Sloan

WHITTICK, WILLIAM A. (1847–1897), English anarchist, economist, and poet. Born at Devizes in Wiltshire, England, William Whittick passed through his Christian phase trying to save the souls of the poor at a Saint Giles Church (probably in London). He moved to the United States in 1868, first living in Newark, New Jersey, and finally settling in Philadelphia around 1890. By 1887 he declared himself an anarchist (see ANARCHISM AND UNBELIEF) and atheist, believing that "when God dies, Man shall live," since the deity was "the apotheosis of ignorance." His conception of free-love held that monogamous marriage has a "deplorable effect on the mind," and that government intervention in morals and sex relations bungled what people could regulate infinitely better themselves, and that it led to cruelty and debauchery (see SEX RADICALISM AND UNBELIEF). His theory that money should have an "invariable unit of value" was widely reviewed, and another economist, Arthur Kitson, was accused of having plagiarized it. He championed a system of mutual banking under which government would be unable to interfere in money matters, and where "the ideal dollar" would act only as an equivalent for complex exchange, with all commodities having monetary capacity. He opposed the tariff on moral and economic grounds, closing one essay with the slogan "Free Trade is Anarchy!"

Not confining himself to theory, Whittick attacked injustices like unprovoked police violence and censorship, writing on contemporary cases. Likewise his FREETHOUGHT did not alienate him completely from Christianity, but found him frequently eulogizing the "ideal Jesus," even defending Mormonism when it was under attack. He agreed with Henry Drummond that science and religion do not conflict (see RELIGION IN CONFLICT WITH SCIENCE). He would argue more contrary to his opponent than his beliefs took him, enjoying the intensity of debate. When he had hurt the feelings of an opponent, he would earnestly apologize. His poems and essays appeared in the *Alarm* (Chicago), *Twentieth Century* (New York), *Liberty* (Boston), the *Individualist* (Denver), *Justice* (Philadelphia), the *Conservator* (Philadelphia), and the *Firebrand* (Portland, Oregon). After dragging his very sick body to freethought meetings, Whittick died of cirrhosis of the kidneys on July 12, 1897, at his home, survived by his wife and son.

BIBLIOGRAPHY

Elwell, Mary. "In Memoriam." *Firebrand* [Portland, OR], August 1, 1897.

Whittick, William A. *Bombs: The Poetry and Philosophy of Anarchy.* Philadelphia: A. R. Saylor, 1894.

———. Letter to Henry Bool, May 16, 1897. Labadie Collection, University of Michigan.

———. *Value and an Invariable Unit of Value: An Important Discovery in Economics.* Philadelphia: J. B. Lippincott, 1896.

ROBERT P. HELMS

WICKSELL, KNUT (1851–1926). See SWEDEN, UNBELIEF IN.

WILLIAMS, ROGER (1603?–1683), colonial American church-state separation advocate. A colonial-era minister, Roger Williams founded Rhode Island after being forced to leave Massachusetts by Puritan authorities there. His 1644 book, *The Bloudy Tenet of Persecution, for Cause of Conscience,* took the bold stand that a union between church and state was blasphemous and dangerous.

Early Life. Williams is believed to have been born in England in 1603. Williams was among the Puritans who fled persecution and came to North America. In 1635 he was appointed pastor of the Puritan church in Salem, Massachusetts.

Oath Controversy. Williams grew angry over a policy of the Massachusetts General Court that required all males over the age of sixteen to swear an oath of allegiance ending in "so help me, God." Williams argued that forcing a person to swear a religious oath against his will was wrong, as it required that person "to take the name of God in vain."

On July 8, 1635, Williams was summoned before the General Court, warned that his views were "erroneous and very dangerous," and told to stop spreading them. He did the opposite, writing a series of letters to church officials complaining about his treatment. On October 9, the General Court found Williams guilty of spreading "diverse new & dangerous opinions" and ordered that he be expelled from the colony within six weeks. This deadline passed without incident, but upon learning that he was about to be forcibly deported to England, in January of 1636 he fled into the wilderness and lived among the Native Americans until spring. He purchased from them a plot of land and proclaimed a new settlement called Providence.

Growth of Providence. Providence became a haven for those fleeing the Puritans' oppressive theocracy. True to his principles, Williams allowed anyone who agreed to keep the peace to settle there, even Quakers, a sect Williams personally detested. By 1640 about forty families were living in Providence. The settlement's governing charter promised to "hold forth Liberty of Conscience."

From the safety of his settlement, Williams continued to argue with Puritan ministers. In one letter to John Cotton, Williams spoke of the need for a "hedge or wall of Separation between the Garden of the Church and the Wilderness of the world." The phrase is striking because of its similarity to Thomas Jefferson's famous metaphor of a "wall of separation between church and state," but there is no evidence that Jefferson knew of Williams's phrase.

In 1644 Williams penned *The Bloudy Tenet.* The book raises arguments for church-state separation that are still used today. Williams argued that government officials are not competent judges of theology, asserted that state-compelled worship harmed religion, and insisted that "soul liberty"—his term for religious freedom—was a gift from God, not the government.

Williams asserted that religious freedom was the birthright of everyone, "paganish, Jewish, Turkish, or anti-christian." He argued that the Christian church went astray when it accepted favored status from the Roman emperor Constantine the Great. He wrote in detail of the centuries of bloodshed sparked by Europe's religious wars.

In 1655 Williams wrote a famous letter appealing for religious toleration. He compared Rhode Island to a ship at sea. The voyage, Williams said, included "Papists and Protestants, Jews and Turks." The trip would go smoother, Williams insisted, if "none of the Papists, Protestants, Jews or Turks be forced to come to the Ship's Prayers or Worship; nor, secondly, compelled from their own particular Prayers or Worship, if they practice any." The commander of the ship, he wrote, like a government official, should stick to running the vessel and stay out of religious affairs.

Williams's Religious Views. Williams left the Puritan church in 1638 after deciding that he no longer believed in infant baptism. He became a Baptist but stayed with that faith less than a year. After that, Williams never formally joined another church. He came to believe that the true church would not be revealed until Jesus's second coming.

Williams died in 1683; the exact date is unknown. He was buried in a hillside near his home in Providence. The site is now a national park.

BIBLIOGRAPHY

Gaustad, Edwin S. *Liberty of Conscience: Roger Williams in America*. Grand Rapids, MI: Eerdmans, 1991.

————. *Roger Williams: Prophet of Liberty*. New York: Oxford University Press, 2001.

Morgan, Edmund S. *Roger Williams: The Church and the State*. New York: Harcourt, Brace and World, 1967.

ROBERT BOSTON

WITCHCRAFT AND UNBELIEF. "Thou shalt not suffer a witch to live." This single sentence (Exod. 22:18) provided the ultimate theological justification for the trial and persecution of hundreds of thousands of witches in early modern Europe, extending from the twelfth to the eighteenth centuries. Belief in witches is, however, an immensely complex phenomenon, and the widely varying levels of witch hunting from one country to the next, and from one era to the next, can be explicated not only by varying religious doctrines but also differences in social, legal, and political conditions. Nevertheless, there is no reason to doubt Jeffrey Burton Russell's formulation that "European witchcraft is best considered a form of HERESY."

The ancient Hebrews appear to have regarded a "witch" as a seer, diviner, or necromancer—something on the order of the witch of En-dor, who purportedly raised the spirit of Samuel (1 Sam. 28:1–25). The ancient Romans conceived of witches who could harness supernatural powers for the purpose of causing harmful acts (*maleficia*), but they lacked any sense of the heretical nature of such acts, and therefore their pursuit of witches was sporadic at best. It was only in Christian times, when the notion of *maleficia* was fused with heresy (specifically the belief that witches made pacts with demons or with the devil himself to gain their powers), that the European witch hunt could gain traction.

The first known witch trial in Christendom occurred in 373 CE, but during the first several centuries of Christian political dominance of Europe (roughly, the fourth through the eighth centuries) more attention was given to organizing the church hierarchy, stamping out doctrinal heresies, and suppressing pagan (Greco-Roman) belief than to persecuting witches. It was, however, in the early medieval period that the chief powers of witches (casting spells to harm individuals, livestock, or crops; sexual orgies with demons or with other witches; cannibalism, specifically involving the killing and eating of infants; the ability to fly through the air) were gradually fashioned, derived from primitive folklore and the remaining vestiges of paganism. Surprisingly, religious authorities exhibited some skepticism regarding such powers. The *Canon Episcopi*—written by Regino of Prüm around 906 and serving as a foundation of canon law for the next five hundred years—condemned those who believed that witches ride through the air. Such a belief, Regino argued, would be heretical because it infringed upon the powers of God. But such skepticism decreased as the Middle Ages proceeded.

The power of Satan and demons was increasingly felt in the twelfth and thirteenth centuries, a result of rapid social changes and the emergence of several heretical cults that Christian leaders saw as threats to orthodoxy. The Catharists (who repudiated the world of matter as the creation of the devil) and the Waldensians (a group that practiced extreme asceticism) were ruthlessly persecuted, and many of their beliefs were misinterpreted and later applied to witches. Punishments against witchcraft became increasingly harsh from the eleventh to the thirteenth centuries. Torture (first attested in a witch trial in 805) began to be widespread. The establishment of the Inquisition in the 1230s gave an added impetus to witch trials, although the belief of older historians that the Inquisition actually caused the later European witch hunt is plainly false. Not only did the Inquisition not hold all or even a majority of witch trials in Europe (episcopal and secular courts were also involved), but the Inquisition declined at the very time when the witch hunt attained its highest levels, in the fifteenth through the seventeenth centuries.

By the fourteenth century, witchcraft definitively came to be regarded as the worst kind of Christian heresy, as it signified actual repudiation of God and affiliation with the devil. The next century saw a vast expansion of both witch trials and witch literature, as the notion of the pact with the devil (a belief of the intellectual elite) fused with the popular notion of *maleficia*. There will always be a debate as to whether any of those accused of witchcraft actually practiced it in some fashion. Probably a small minority did so, but the great majority were accused not because of any actual satanic activities but merely because they were female (women were thought to be morally and intellectually weaker than men, and therefore more susceptible to temptation by the devil), elderly, practitioners of herbal magic or midwifery, and otherwise vulnerable and marginal members of society. (Margaret A. Murray's belief, in *The Witch-Cult in Western Europe* [1921], that European witchcraft was a holdover of an ancient fertility cult, has been thoroughly refuted.)

It is no paradox that the witch hunt was most virulent at the time of the Renaissance. Witch belief was a product of the generally magical worldview of medieval Christianity, and the leading intellectuals of the Renaissance not only failed to challenge this view but themselves endorsed it, although their "high" magic (astrology, alchemy, and so on) was very different from the "low" magic (spells, potions, and the like) accepted by the common people. Moreover, even those Renaissance thinkers such as Desiderius ERASMUS and Michel de MONTAIGNE who doubted the reality of witchcraft failed to overthrow the widespread belief in the power of demons or of the devil, and so were incapable of uprooting witchcraft belief at its source.

Pope Innocent VIII's bull *Summis desiderantes* (1484) confirmed papal approval of the Inquisition's witch hunts. The work he commissioned, the *Malleus Maleficarum* (The Hammer of Witches, 1486) by Heinrich Kramer and Jakob Sprenger, was only the culmination of witch treatises in the fifteenth century. Relatively few voices were heard on the other side. One of them was Johann Weyer, who in *De Prestigiis Daemonum* (On the Prodigies of Demons, 1563) and *De Lamiis* (On Witches, 1582) maintained that women who believed themselves witches were merely deluded; but he attributed these delusions to the devil, thereby indirectly endorsing witch belief. Even more bold was Reginald Scot, whose *Discoverie of Witchcraft* (1584) was the first English treatise devoted to witchcraft—a skeptical and mocking account that attributes "spiritual manifestations" to "artful impostures or illusions due to mental disturbance in the observers." The book was ridiculed by James VI of Scotland (later James I of England), who wrote his *Demonologie* (1597) as an explicit attempt to refute Scot.

The Protestant Reformation of the sixteenth century both enhanced the witch hunt—by emphasizing a close and literal reading of the Bible (including the notorious passage in Exodus) and by stressing the ever-present power of the devil in human affairs—and ultimately led to its decline. The idea gradually arose among philosophers and theologians that the sovereignty of God made it impossible for witches to perform their *maleficia* in defiance of God's wishes. By the seventeenth century, as thinkers and public officials came to realize that many individuals were being unjustly accused of, and executed for, witchcraft—through confessions extorted by torture, accusations from suspect sources, and the excessive zeal of prosecutors—a backlash finally began. Francis Hutchinson, in *An Historical Essay concerning Witchcraft* (1718), delivered perhaps the final intellectual blow to witchcraft belief, excoriating the unfairness and viciousness of witchcraft trials. In addition, scientific and philosophical advances led to the notion that the universe worked in an orderly manner, thereby making the supernatural machinations of witches (and of the devil himself) implausible. From this point onward, both witch trials and intellectuals' belief in witchcraft became increasingly rare. The Salem witchcraft trials of 1692 were an aberration in the American colonies, but Cotton Mather did not distinguish himself by confirming belief in witches in *Wonders of the Invisible World* (1693). As late as 1760, John Wesley, the founder of Methodism, declared in his journal that disbelief in witchcraft meant disbelief in the Bible.

BIBLIOGRAPHY

Burns, William E. *Witch Hunts in Europe and America: An Encyclopedia.* Westport, CT: Greenwood, 2003.

Clark, Stuart. *Thinking with Demons: The Idea of Witchcraft in Early Modern Europe.* Oxford: Clarendon, 1997.

Levack, Brian P. *The Witch-Hunt in Early Modern Europe.* London: Longman, 1987.

Robbins, Rossell Hope. *The Encyclopedia of Witchcraft and Demonology.* New York: Crown, 1959.

Russell, Jeffrey Burton. *Witchcraft in the Middle Ages.* Ithaca, NY: Cornell University Press, 1972.

Zika, Charles. *Exorcising Our Demons: Magic, Witchcraft, and Visual Culture in Early Modern Europe.* Leiden: Brill, 2003.

S.T. JOSHI

WITTGENSTEIN, LUDWIG (1889–1951), Austrian philosopher. Scion of one of the wealthiest families in Austria, Ludwig Wittgenstein came to England specifically to study with Bertrand RUSSELL, the best-known logician of the time. At first a protégé of Russell's, he later broke with him over the claim that mathematics can be firmly grounded in logic. The two for a time shared an interest in mysticism, but Russell seemed to ignore the underlying mystical nature of Wittgenstein's first book (and the only one published in his lifetime), the *Tractatus Logico-Philosophicus* (1922), for which he wrote an introduction. Russell was not the only one so fooled. The so-called Vienna Circle movement (see SCHLICK, MORITZ, AND THE VIENNA CIRCLE) likewise interpreted Wittgenstein's work to be saying that all of nature could be reduced to propositions. "A proposition," he wrote, "is a picture of reality. A proposition is a model of reality as we think it to be." They interpreted this to mean that all metaphysical statements were, strictly speaking, nonsense, since they were nonpropositional. If a claim could not be expressed in terms that were verifiable, then such a claim should be ignored. Followers of this view became known as Logical Positivists (see LOGICAL POSITIVISM), and credited their origin to Wittgenstein's writings. A. J. AYER, one of the circle's most prominent members, used this verification argument (see VERIFICATIONISM) to show that all claims about God were meaningless, and could thus be ignored. After all, Wittgenstein himself had written: "The limits of my language means the limits of my world."

Wittgenstein, who had disappeared shortly after publishing the *Tractatus* (he felt he had solved all the problems of philosophy in this short work, and could move on to other pursuits such as teaching elementary school, designing buildings, and working as a gardener for a monastery), was horrified upon learning that his book was being used to justify a materialistic, even atheistic, philosophical movement. Just because you could not express a concept did not mean the concept itself was nonsensical, he objected. It could simply be ineffable. He therefore left his unworldly pursuits to return to philosophy, teaching for a time at Cambridge and repudiating much of what he had written. Russell was to say of him that he resembled Blaise Pascal, who had likewise abandoned mathematics for piety.

There was a distinctive mystical air around Wittgenstein, and many of his students treated him like a guru. He spent the remainder of his life pursuing the question of the role played by language in human affairs and the limitations it places on the expression of ideas. These observations were published posthumously as the *Philosophical Investigations* (1953). Later, several of his students' notebooks and other uncollected and miscellaneous writings were published as well, which would have infuriated a man so careful with his views that he agonized over every word.

The question of Wittgenstein's own religious beliefs remains, like so much else about him, a mystery. His paternal grandfather (the founder of the vast Wittgenstein fortune) was a convert from Judaism to Protestantism, a fact that did not protect the Wittgenstein family in Vienna when the Nazis came to power. Wittgenstein's brother Paul paid a huge sum of money to the Hitler regime to arrange for the safe escape of his sisters from Austria. Wittgenstein's mother was Roman Catholic, and he himself was baptized in that faith. He manifested a strong ascetic streak throughout his life, as well as a proneness toward depression. Three of his brothers committed suicide, and when Ludwig several times expressed the desire to end his life, his family took it seriously. Russell once remarked that, upon seeing Wittgenstein pacing the room in apparent agony, he jocularly asked, "Are you thinking about logic or your sins?" to which Wittgenstein replied, "Both."

While Wittgenstein seemed to have no conventional religious views and was considered an atheist by some, he often expressed great sympathy for religious figures, particularly those of a contemplative nature. Although he was always loath to admit any influence upon him from previous philosophers, he did admit a fondness for certain aspects of Saint Augustine's writings. It also seems clear that he was familiar with Arthur SCHOPENHAUER's *The World as Will and Representation*, and seemed to agree with that atheist's claim that human beings are metaphysical by nature.

Perhaps what most marked Wittgenstein was his often-professed desire to be perfect. This high—indeed impossible—standard had a major impact upon all who came to know him. His tormented nature, his unceasing search for truth, his inability to suffer fools gladly, and his apparent lack of humor all attest to a modern-day mystic. Surprisingly enough, given how unsatisfied he seemed with the mundane world around him, his last words, according to his friend Norman Malcolm, were: "Tell them I've had a wonderful life!"

BIBLIOGRAPHY

Hacker, P. M. S. *Wittgenstein's Place in Twentieth Century Analytic Philosophy.* New York: Blackwell, 1996.

Monk, Ray. *Ludwig Wittgenstein: The Duty of Genius.* New York: Penguin, 1991.

Wittgenstein, Ludwig. *Wittgenstein Lectures and Conversations on Aesthetics, Psychology, and Religious Belief.* Berkeley and Los Angeles: University of California Press, 1967.

TIMOTHY J. MADIGAN

WIXON, SUSAN H. (ca. late 1840s–1912), American freethought writer and feminist. The daughter of Bethia Smith Wixon and Captain James Wixon of Dennis, Massachusetts, Susan H. Wixon was "born a Liberal," according to FREETHOUGHT editor Samuel Porter PUTNAM. In an early contretemps with an orthodox Sunday school teacher, Wixon suggested that anyone who would make a lake of fire and brimstone in which to incinerate his children ought to be the first one burned in it.

At the top of her public school class, Wixon began teaching school at age thirteen, placing first in a teacher's examination. Her father denied her a college education, but Wixon attended a seminary for one year before continuing her career as a teacher in Massachusetts and Rhode Island.

A radical freethinker, Wixon was the first woman to lecture at Paine Hall in Boston. She represented Massachusetts and spoke at the 1890 convention of the Woman's National Liberal League founded by Matilda Joslyn GAGE. She was honored by a local newspaper for her "thrilling eloquence" in successfully arguing as a stockholder against corporate funding of sectarian activities.

Wixon persuaded the governor of Massachusetts to appoint women factory inspectors in 1891. She traveled abroad in 1892, collecting statistics for lectures on women's work and wages. Wixon was elected to the woman's industrial advancement committee in the inventor's department of the World's Columbian Exposition. She wrote prose and verse for the freethought press, serving as editor of "The Children's Corner" for THE TRUTH SEEKER for at least a decade. Wixon's The Story Hour (1885) was advertised as the only illustrated freethought storybook for children. Her books include All in a Lifetime, Apples of God (1876, short stories), Sunday Observance; or, How to Spend Sunday (1883), and Summer Days at Onset (1887).

Her lecture "Woman: Four Centuries of Progress," delivered at the Freethinkers' International Congress in Chicago, Illinois, in October 1893 and reprinted as a pamphlet by the Truth Seeker Company in December 1893, traced the fall of woman under Christianity, listed the tenets of the canon law degrading to women, and argued, "Freethought has always been the best friend woman had."

BIBLIOGRAPHY

Putnam, Samuel P. Four Hundred Years of Freethought. New York: Truth Seeker Company, 1894.
Willard, Frances E., and Mary A. Livermore, eds. A Woman of the Century: Fourteen Hundred-Seventy Biographical Sketches Accompanied by Portraits of Leading American Women In All Walks of Life. Buffalo, NY: Charles Wells Moulton, 1893.

ANNIE LAURIE GAYLOR

WOLLSTONECRAFT, MARY (1759–1797), English deist and feminist. Mary Wollstonecraft is best known for her work A Vindication of the Rights of Woman. Written in 1792, it is considered the first book calling for equality of the sexes. Earlier she wrote A Vindication of the Rights of Men and was throughout her life an advocate of the rights of all human beings, including children. She was a DEIST and independent thinker.

Her father, Edward, was domineering and abusive. Wollstonecraft never forgot her mother's submissive attitude toward her husband and determined that women must be properly educated so as not to be dependent on the goodwill or whim of men. At age twenty-four, she and a friend established a day school. She also worked as a governess and wrote a pamphlet titled Thoughts on the Education of Daughters. The pamphlet was published by Joseph Johnson, who became her friend and benefactor.

When Wollstonecraft moved to London in 1787, Johnson welcomed her into his circle of friends. The circle included many of the influential thinkers of the time, including Thomas PAINE. Johnson gave Wollstonecraft work translating French and German books and writing short reviews for the Analytical Review which he published with Thomas Christie.

In 1790 Edmund Burke's Reflections on the Revolution in France, expressing his strong sentiments against the revolt, produced much dissent in the Johnson circle. In answer the Analytical Review carried "Replies to Mr. Burke." Wollstonecraft's Vindication of the Rights of Men was among the first to be published. In it, among other things, she bitterly attacked the institution of the Catholic Church. The piece, published anonymously, was a huge success. A second edition followed quickly, this time with her byline. Written in 1791, it was one of the earliest serious political polemics by a woman and made her known beyond the Johnson circle.

Less than two years later Wollstonecraft wrote A Vindication of the Rights of Woman. Here she clearly put forth her belief that the nature of humans, male or female, and their capability for happiness rested on reason, virtue, and knowledge. In it she wrote, "In fact it is a farce to call any being virtuous whose virtues do not result from the exercise of its own reason."

A Vindication of the Rights of Woman was also an elaboration on her earlier work on the education of women. Wollstonecaft advocated drastic changes in the education of boys as well as girls through a national system of free coeducational elementary schools. The curriculum she proposed for children aged five through nine included botany, mechanics, astronomy, reading, writing, arithmetic, and natural history. A Vindication of the Rights of Woman was a sensation. It made her famous, and in some circles infamous.

Wollstonecraft married the writer William GODWIN early in 1797. In September of that year she died of a massive infection following the birth of their child. She was thirty-eight years old. The baby, named Mary, is famous as the author of the novel Frankenstein.

BIBLIOGRAPHY

Flexner, Eleanor. Mary Wollstonecraft, A Biography. New York: Coward, McCann and Geoghegan, 1972.
Godwin, William. Memoirs of Mary Wollstonecraft. New York: Richard R. Smith, 1930.
Wollstonecraft, Mary. A Vindication of the Rights of Woman. Everyman's Library. New York: Knopf, 1992.

LOIS PORTER

WOMAN SUFFRAGE MOVEMENT AND UNBELIEF. For much of US history, the elective franchise was denied to its female citizens. The Constitution's separation of church and state notwithstanding, much of the argument against female suffrage was motivated by religious doctrine that seriously circumscribed the roles women were permitted to play in the public sphere. Therefore, those women who initially challenged the state's limitation of the elective franchise to (white) male voters were also directly confronting centuries-old religious tenets. Of all their demands, suffrage was initially the most radical. In time, however, suffrage would become the sole focus of the powerful evangelical branch of the women's movement, effectively marginalizing all other feminist demands and the freethinkers who espoused them.

Freethinking Foremothers. Christian belief based on an interpretation of the Pauline epistles forbade women from speaking publicly to mixed-sex audiences. The first American woman to break significantly with this tradition was Frances WRIGHT, a Scottish immigrant and humanist who began a lecture tour in 1828 in which she criticized religion and advocated women's education. To many, she was a model of courage. For most others in the highly charged Protestant atmosphere of the fledgling United States, she was simply monstrous. In 1836 another immigrant, the Polish atheist Ernestine L. ROSE, shocked American sensibilities when she drew up a petition for the Married Women's Property Act in New York, a bill that would not pass until 1848. In 1837 Sarah Grimke, who with her sister, Angelina, gave public lectures on abolition and women's rights, published *Letters on the Equality of the Sexes and the Condition of Woman.* The exclusively male clergy of the nation exploded in anger, decrying the women as unsexed and sinful. Women joined men in their disapproval of these freethinking women, believing that women did not need any more rights. That belief was about to change.

Zealots and Ultraists. Ironically, it was the religious enthusiasm that so characterized the first half of the nineteenth century that provided a nursery for the development of humanistic reform. Evangelical Protestantism, partaking of the Jacksonian spirit of individualism and enterprise, encouraged its adherents, male and female, toward the salvation of the world. As women became involved in activism, particularly on behalf of temperance and abolition, they became increasingly aware of their limitations both within the reform societies and within Christianity itself. Despite their tireless efforts and deep enthusiasm for reform work and regardless of their skill, they were not welcome in leadership positions and were relegated to segregated auxiliary groups.

Many women rebelled against these limitations by rejecting their churches' teaching of female inferiority, turning to alternative perspectives of less orthodox denominations such as the Universalists and the Unitarians. Many admired the Quaker belief in the equality of the sexes that had led that denomination to recognize women in the ministry. Others would reject Christianity altogether, choosing instead a nontheistic approach (see WOMEN AND UNBELIEF) as atheists, agnostics, humanists, spiritualists, and, later, Theosophists (see THEOSOPHY). These "ultraist" women, always a minority even among reform-minded women, embraced FREETHOUGHT as they challenged the very foundations of their society. As authors, lecturers, and agitators, they sacrificed propriety for the sake of a suffering humanity they believed only human agency could save. While history gives examples of individual women who made this assertion, never before did so many women join together with such undaunted persistence. Their actions on their own behalf would be revolutionary.

The Seneca Falls Convention. History recognizes 1848 as the year of revolutions. Margaret Fuller, freethinking editor of the Transcendentalist *Dial* and author of *Woman in the Nineteenth Century* (1845), was in Italy engaged in the Italian revolution in 1848. Because she died in a shipwreck off the shores of Fire Island two years later, the women's rights movement could not fully benefit from her feminist genius. But in the small upstate New York town of Seneca Falls another genius was engaged in her own revolutionary impulse, and she did not act alone. Elizabeth Cady STANTON was mentored and supported by Lucretia Mott, a Hicksite Quaker already well known as an accomplished public speaker and women's rights advocate. Joining Mott and Stanton were two liberal Quakers, Jane Hunt and Mary Ann M'Clintock. Together these women would organize the Seneca Falls convention at which they put forth the Declaration of Sentiments, a document following the language patterns and ideals of the Declaration of Independence. Relying on a republican theory of natural rights, among other things, they assailed the power of the church, called for equal access to colleges and the professions, for control of their property and children, and most shockingly, they demanded suffrage.

Lucretia Mott, whose mentorship was instrumental in formulating Stanton's growing religious heterodoxy, thought the younger woman's inclusion of the demand for the vote in the Declaration of Sentiments was unwise. It would never be accepted. Indeed, of all the resolutions, it was the only one that was very nearly rejected by the participants. Only the impassioned support of Frederick DOUGLASS convinced the participants to include it, and then only marginally. None of those present could have guessed that the call to suffrage would so soon become the focus for women's rights activism.

Spiritualism. Simultaneous with the birth of the organized women's rights movement in the United States was the advent of popular Spiritualism. Beginning with the activities of the Fox sisters in Hydesville, New York, a town only a short distance from Seneca Falls, the Spiritualist movement spread rapidly to all parts of the nation. Spiritualists were associated with freethought due to their disavowal of traditional religious claims in favor of a more egalitarian, human-centered spirituality. A spirituality dominated by women who broke with the Christian prohibition against women preaching in public through mediumship and trance speaking on reform lecture circuits, Spiritualists had a strong tendency toward women's rights activism, typically populating its most liberal wing. In 1848, the Quaker women who formed the nucleus of support for the nascent women's rights movement were also directly involved in the newborn Spiritualist experimentation that would soon overwhelm the nation.

Antebellum Radicals. In the years leading up to the Civil War, the women leading the suffrage cause moved among the most radical thinkers of the nation. Those people associated with the demand for suffrage were also likely to support the immediate freedom of slaves, prison reform, dress and dietary reform, and rights for children, indigenous peoples, and laborers. They were more likely to experiment with alternative expressions of spirituality, most notably as Unitarians, Universalists, and Spiritualists, or to eschew religious sentiment altogether in favor of rationalism and science. They joined communes, spoke on lecture circuits, and everywhere challenged organized religion's admonition that women learn quietly from their husbands at home.

Of these freethinking women, Matilda Joslyn GAGE, Elizabeth Cady Stanton, Susan B. Anthony, and Lucy Stone became the most prominent in the movement. They operated amid the support and genius of a generation of reformers who challenged the status quo of a slaveholding, sexist, and class-stratified society. As suffrage leaders, they all recognized organized religion's primary role in silencing the oppressed and in circumscribing women's roles. Freethinkers denounced the Christian view of women as primarily sinful sexual creatures, designed since the days of Eve to serve men. Susan B. Anthony, reared a Quaker, was an agnostic, as was Lucy Stone, but Gage and Stanton were the most radical of the suffragist leadership. While the other women saw the need to publicly soften their freethought positions, Stanton and Gage grew increasingly more intolerant of what they understood to be the underlying religious foundation of sexism.

Postwar Schism. The suffrage movement was all but suspended during the years of the Civil War, although many suffrage leaders, particularly Stanton and Anthony, continued to publicly advocate universal suffrage. Suffragists believed their service to the Union cause during the war would be rewarded. They were bitterly disappointed when following the war, the constitutional amendment to enfranchise black men included, for the first time, the use of the word "male" to qualify citizenship in the United States. This issue drove a wedge between suffragists with many, most notably Lucy Stone, opting to belay emphasis on white woman suffrage in favor of the fight for the rights of freed blacks. Susan B. Anthony and Elizabeth Cady Stanton, enraged and impa-

tient, even descended to racist rhetoric in their increasingly strident demand for women's enfranchisement.

But the split between the suffragists was about far more than racial politics. The two groups that formed in 1869 differed considerably in approach and theory. The National Woman Suffrage Association (NWSA), led primarily by Anthony, Gage, and Stanton, was the more liberal of the two. Focusing on the assumption that suffrage should be gained through federal acknowledgement of women's constitutional rights as citizens, its membership was more diverse, its platform broad enough to include a wide range of often dissenting theoretical and religious opinions. On the other hand, Lucy Stone's American Woman Suffrage Association (AWSA) adopted a strategy to achieve the vote state by state, and was a far more socially conservative organization appealing to white middle-class respectability.

Freethinkers Purged. Following the Civil War, an increasing number of women joined benevolent and reform societies. Unlike the radical reformers of the antebellum period, many of these women were religious conservatives who used their evangelical faith to expand their traditional roles as caregivers to social housekeeping in the public sphere. These participants in the social gospel were characterized by Frances Willard, leader of the Women's Christian Temperance Union (WCTU), who embraced the promise of suffrage to forward her agenda to promote Christian influence and morality into American life and politics.

While Stanton and Gage grew increasingly concerned with such controversial topics as matriarchal religion and the sexual exploitation of women and children, Susan B. Anthony became more singularly focused on suffrage as a panacea for all women's concerns. Despite the indignant opposition of Gage, Stanton, and their supporters, she and Lucy Stone orchestrated a merger between the more conservative AWSA and the NWSA in 1889 in an effort to pull in the support of socially conservative suffragists.

The growing dominance of religious fundamentalism in the newly formed National American Woman Suffrage Association (NAWSA) demanded the marginalization of freethinkers as dangerous to the respectability of the suffrage cause among Christian conservatives. Anna Howard Shaw and Carrie Chapman Catt disliked Stanton, fearing that her freethought positions would be dangerously unpopular with the Christian membership of the suffrage movement. After the publication of Stanton's *Woman's Bible* in 1895, the NAWSA passed a resolution disavowing any connection to it. Stanton had supporters in freethinkers Charlotte Perkins Stetson (GILMAN), Lillie Devereaux BLAKE, and Clara Colby. Additionally, the agnostic Susan B. Anthony temporarily turned from her evangelical allies to rally to her old friend's support. Nonetheless the resolution passed easily. Stanton, already discouraged by the narrow focus on suffrage at the expense of other women's rights concerns, distanced herself from the movement, preferring to write and think independently.

Matilda Joslyn Gage fared no better than Stanton in her attempt to challenge the religious right wing. She left the increasingly conservative NAWSA and began the Women's National Liberal Union, an organization that attracted freethought suffragists, prison reformers, anarchists, socialists, and other freethinkers. This organization drew sharp criticism from Anthony, who was offended by Gage's uncompromising radicalism. Her monumental work, *Woman, Church, and State*, though widely acclaimed by freethinkers, was spurned by the suffragist organization. Gage, like many other feminist freethinkers, would be effectively expunged from suffrage history.

A Singular Focus. From the 1880s to the ratification of the Nineteenth Amendment in 1920, women's rights activists had a singular focus. Except in token numbers, their doors were closed to women who might offend powerful Christian suffragists. Black women and women of alternative spiritual or philosophical traditions were an embarrassment to a movement that courted the support of well-to-do Protestant evangelical women.

Susan B. Anthony and her successor, Carrie Chapman Catt, eventually won the vote with this focused, conservative approach, but at a significant cost. With the elimination of diversity and serious theoretical women's rights scholarship from the suffrage movement, women were left with a mere shell of the thriving intellectual tradition they had begun in the early nineteenth century. As freethinkers, they had challenged not only their limitations as citizens, but had called into question the very religious foundation of bigotry in the United States. It would take several decades for women to reclaim their earlier work to liberate women from their multiple and complex bonds of sexual, familial, economic, and religious degradation. In their rejection of the freethinkers' leadership, evangelical Christian suffragists and their supporters declared that the vote alone would solve "the woman question." Following ratification of the Nineteenth Amendment, women remained oppressed by an increasingly muscular Christianity that continues to undermine full sexual equality. The vote was not enough.

BIBLIOGRAPHY

Braude, Ann. *Radical Spirits: Spiritualism and Women's Rights in Nineteenth Century America*. Boston: Beacon, 1989.

Dubois, Ellen Carol, ed. *The Elizabeth Cady Stanton-Susan B. Anthony Reader: Correspondence, Writing, Speeches*. Boston: Northwestern University Press, 1992.

Gage, Matilda Joslyn. *Woman, Church and State*. 1893. Reprint, Aberdeen, SD: Sky Carrier, 1998.

Kern, Kathi. *Mrs. Stanton's Bible*. Ithaca, NY: Cornell University Press, 2002.

Wagner, Sally Roesch. *She Who Holds the Sky*. Aberdeen, SD: Sky Carrier, 1998.

MELINDA GRUBE

WOMEN AND ISLAM. It cannot be denied that Islam is deeply, irreparably antiwoman. Islam stands as the fundamental cause of the repression of Muslim women, and it remains the major obstacle to the evolution of their position in Islamic societies. Islam has always considered women as creatures inferior in every way—physically, intellectually, and morally. This negative vision is divinely sanctioned in the Qur'an, corroborated by the hadiths, and perpetuated by the commentaries of the theologians (see ISLAM, UNBELIEF IN).

In the Beginning. Islam took the legend of Adam and Eve from the Old Testament and adapted it in its own fashion. The creation of humankind from one person is mentioned in the following suras (Qur'anic verses):

IV.1. O Mankind! Be careful of your duty to your Lord who created you from a single soul and from it created its mate and from them twain hath spread abroad a multiple of men and women.

XXXIX.6. He created you from one being, then from that (being) He made its mate.

VII.189. He it is who did create you from a single soul and therefrom did make his mate that he might take rest in her.

From these slender sources, Muslim theologians have concluded that man was the original creation—womankind was created secondarily for the pleasure and repose of man. The legend was further developed to reinforce the supposed inferiority of women.

In the Qur'an as in Genesis, God punishes Adam and Eve for disobeying his orders. But there is nothing in the Qur'anic verses to illustrate, as Genesis does, that it was Eve who led Adam astray. At this level Islam appears to offers more meager fuel for misogyny. Yet Muslim exegetes and jurists have created, as though from whole cloth, a myth of Eve the temptress that has become an integral part of Muslim tradition. Muhammad himself is reputed to have said: "If it had not been for Eve, no woman would have been unfaithful to her husband."

Berating the Goddesses. In attacking the female deities of the polytheists, the Qur'an maligns the female sex yet further.

IV.117. They invoke in His stead only females; they pray to none else than Satan, a rebel.

LIII.21–22. Are yours the males and His the females? That indeed were an unfair division!

LIII.27. Lo! it is those who disbelieve in the Hereafter who name the angels with the names of females.

Other Qur'anic verses also reflect misogyny:

II.282. But if he who oweth the debt is of low understanding, or weak or unable himself to dictate, then let the guardian of his interests dictate in (terms of) equity. And call to witness, from among your men, two witnesses. And if two men be not (at hand) then a man and two women, of such as ye approve as witnesses, so that if the one erreth (through forgetfulness) the other will remember.

IV.11. Allah chargeth you concerning (the provision for) your children: to the male the equivalent of the portion of two females.

IV.34. Men are in charge of women, because Allah hath made the one of them to excel the other, and because they spend of their property (for the support of women). So good women are the obedient, guarding in secret that which Allah hath guarded. As for those from whom ye fear rebellion, admonish them and banish them to beds apart; and scourge (beat) them. Then if they obey you, seek not a way against them Lo! Allah is ever High Exalted, Great.

Equally, in many of the hadiths upon which Islamic law is based, we learn that the woman's role is to stay at home, to be at the beck and call of man, to obey him (as a religious duty), and to assure man a tranquil existence. Muhammad compared women to domestic animals and gave men permission to beat them (as does the Qur'an: see sura IV.34 above). Muhammad said in the Hadith that a wife must never refuse a husband his conjugal rights, even if it is on the saddle of a camel or even on a scorching oven. Muhammad is said to stand at the gates of hell, where he sees to it that the majority of those who enter it are women. Why? Because of women's ungratefulness to men.

Misogyny after Muhammad. It will be appropriate to include a quote on the subject of women from the famous and much-revered philosopher al-Ghazali (1058–1111), whom scholar Montgomery Watt described as the greatest Muslim after Muhammad. In his "The Revival of the Religious Sciences," Ghazali defines the woman's role thusly:

She should stay at home and get on with her spinning, she should not go out often, she must not be well-informed, nor must she be communicative with her neighbours and only visit them when absolutely necessary; she should take care of her husband and respect him in his presence and his absence and seek to satisfy him in everything; she must not cheat on him nor extort money from him; she must not leave her house without his permission and if given his permission she must leave surreptitiously. She should put on old clothes and take deserted streets and alleys, avoid markets, and make sure that a stranger does not hear her voice or recognize her; she must not speak to a friend of her husband even in need. . . . Her sole worry should be her virtue, her home as well as her prayers and her fast. If a friend of her husband calls when the latter is absent she must not open the door nor reply to him in order to safeguard her and her husband's honour. She should accept what her husband gives her as sufficient. . . . She should be clean and ready to satisfy her husband's sexual needs at any moment.

The Sexes at the Bar of Justice. The inequality between men and women in matters of giving testimony or evidence or bearing witness in court is also enshrined in the Qur'an (sura II.282, quoted above). By taking the testimony of two beings whose reasoning faculties are faulty, we do not obtain the testimony of one complete person with a perfectly functioning rational faculty—such is Islamic arithmetic! By this logic, if the testimony of two women is worth that of one man, then the testimony of four women must be worth that of two men, in which case we can dispense with the testimony of the men. But no! In Islam the rule is not to accept the testimony of women alone in matters to which men theoretically have access. It is said that the Prophet did not accept the testimony of women in matters of marriage, divorce, and *hudud. Hudud* are the punishments set down by Muhammad in the Qur'an and the hadith for (1) adultery—stoning to death; (2) fornication—a hundred stripes; (3) false accusation of adultery against a married person—eighty stripes; (4) apostasy—death; (5) drinking wine—eighty stripes; (6) theft—the cutting off of the right hand; (7) simple robbery on the highway—the loss of hands and feet; robbery with murder—death, either by the sword or by crucifixion.

On adultery, the Qur'an says (sura XXIV.4): "Those that defame honourable women [that is, have sex with them] and cannot produce four witnesses shall be given eighty lashes." Of course, Muslim jurists will only accept four male witnesses. These witnesses must declare that they have "seen the parties in the very act of carnal conjunction." Once an accusation of fornication and adultery has been made, the accuser himself or herself risks punishment if he or she does not furnish the necessary legal proofs. Witnesses are in the same situation. If a man were to break into a woman's dormitory and rape half a dozen women he would risk nothing, since there would be no male witnesses. Indeed the victim of a rape would hesitate before going in front of the law, since she would risk being condemned herself and have little chance of obtaining justice. "If the woman's words were sufficient in such cases," explains Judge Zharoor ul Haq of Pakistan, "then no man would be safe." This iniquitous situation is truly revolting, and yet for Islamic law it is a way of avoiding social scandal concerning the all-important sexual taboo concerning rape: in Islamic society the concepts of honor and shame predominate, and a woman who is raped brings shame upon her family, even though having been raped is not her fault. It is lawful for a man to kill his wife and her lover if he catches them in the act. Women found guilty of fornication were literally immured, at first; the Qur'an ordains: "Shut them up within their houses till death release them, or God make some way for them" (sura IV.15). This harsh doctrine was later canceled; mere stoning was substituted for adultery, and one hundred lashes for fornication. But even stoning is a very different affair when directed at a woman. When a man is to be stoned to death, he is taken to some barren place, where he is stoned first by the witnesses, then the judge, and then the public. When a woman is stoned, a hole to receive her is dug as deep as her waist—the Prophet himself seems to have ordered such procedure.

In the case where a man suspects his wife of adultery or denies the legitimacy of her offspring, his testimony is worth that of four other men. Sura XXIV.6 proclaims: "If a man accuses his wife but has no witnesses except himself, he shall swear four times by God that his charge is true, calling down upon himself the curse of God if he is lying. But if his wife swears four times by God that his charge is false and calls down His curse upon herself if it be true, she shall receive no punishment." Appearances to the contrary, this is not an example of Qur'anic justice or equality between the sexes. The woman indeed escapes being stoned to death, but she remains rejected by her husband and loses her right to her dowry and her right to maintenance, whatever the outcome of the trial. Further, no woman may accuse her husband in a similar manner. Finally, for a Muslim marriage to be valid, there must be a multiplicity of witnesses; Muslim jurists tell us that two men form a multiplicity, but not two, or three, or even a thousand women.

In questions of inheritance, the Qur'an tells us that male children should inherit twice the portion of female children:

IV.11–12. A male shall inherit twice as much as a female. If there be more than two girls, they shall have two-thirds of the inheritance, but if there be one only, she shall inherit the half. Parents shall inherit a sixth each, if the deceased have a child; but if he leave no child and his parents be his heirs, his mother shall have a third. If he have brothers, his mother shall have a sixth after payment of any legacy he may have bequeathed or any debt he may have owed.

To justify this inequality Muslim authors lean heavily on the fact that a woman receives a dowry and has the right to maintenance from her husband. It is also true that according to Muslim law, no mother is obliged to provide for her children. To quote Bousquet, a twentieth-century Algerian expert in Islamic law, if a mother does spend money on her children, it is, "recoverable by her from her husband if he is returned to a better fortune as in the case of any other charitable person. Therefore there is no point in the husband and wife sharing in the taking charge of the household; this weighs upon the husband alone. There is no longer any financial interest between them."

This latter point simply emphasizes the negative aspect of Islamic marriage—that is to say, the total absence of any idea of "association" between "couples" as in Christianity. As to dowry, it is, of course, simply a reconfirmation of the man's claims over the woman in matters of sex and divorce. In any case, the dowry benefits the woman little as she is never able to use it for herself. The custom is either to use the dowry to furnish the house of the newly married couple, or for the wife to offer it to her father. According to the Malekites, one of the four orthodox Sunni schools of Islamic law, a woman can be obliged by law to expend her dowry in order to furnish the house. Muslim law also gives a woman's father or other guardian the right to cancel a marriage—even that of a woman of legal age—if he thinks the dowry is not sufficient. Thus the dowry, instead of being a sign of woman's independence, turns out once more to be a symbol of her servitude.

True, the married woman has the right to maintenance (that is, support), but this simply emphasizes her total dependence on her husband and the sense of insecurity which attends that. Muslim jurists have ruled that the husband is not obliged under Islamic law to pay for his wife's medical expenses in case of illness. Of course, financial independence for women would constitute a first step in the liberation of Muslim women; thus it is not surprising that it has been seen as a threat to male dominance.

Economic equality can sometimes be imposed if it imposes an equal *responsibility* on both sexes. Under Article 158 of Syrian law, Muslim women are now obliged to take equal responsibility for looking after their parents: "The child—male or female—having the necessary means is obliged to take responsibility for his or her poor parents."

The birth of a girl is still seen as a catastrophe in Islamic societies. The system of inheritance just adds to her misery and her dependence on some man. If she is an only child, she receives only half of her father's estate; the other half goes to the male members of the father's family, however remote these may be. If there are two or more daughters, they share between them two-thirds. This pushes fathers and mothers to prefer male children to female, so that they can leave the entirety of their effects or possessions to their own descendants. "Yet when a new-born girl is announced to one of them his countenance darkens and he is filled with gloom," intones sura XLIII.17. The situation is even worse when a woman loses her husband—she receives only a quarter of the legacy. If the deceased leaves more than one wife, all the wives are still obliged to share among themselves a quarter or even, is some cases, one eighth of the legacy.

Male Superiority: A Matter of Muslim Law. Muslim jurists are unanimous in their view that men are superior to women in virtue of their reasoning abilities, their knowledge, and their supervisory powers. And since it is the man who assumes financial responsibility for the family, it is argued, it is natural that he should have total power over the woman. These same jurists, of course, totally neglect changing social conditions under which a woman may contribute her salary to the upkeep of her family—even here, power over women remains a divine command and is seen as "natural" or "in the nature of things." Muslim thinkers continue to confine Muslim women to the home—to leave the house is against the will of God and against the principles of Islam. Confined to their houses, women are then reproached for not having any experience of the outside world!

While Islamic scripture, law, and tradition stand unchallenged, women stand at the back of every line.

BIBLIOGRAPHY

Al-Tabari. *The History of al-Tabari*. Vol. 9. *The Last Years of the Prophet*. Translated by Ismail Poonawala. Albany: State University of New York Press, 1990.

Ascha, Ghassan. *Du Statut Inferieur de la Femme en Islam*. Paris: l'Harmattan, 1989.

Aynu, *Umdad al-qari sharhal—Bukhari*. Cairo: n.p., 1308 AH/1890 CE.

Bousquet, G. H. *L'Ethique sexuelle de L'Islam*. Paris: Desclée de Brouwer, 1966.

Bukhari. *Sahih*. Translated by M. Muhsin Khan. New Delhi: Kitab Bhavan, 1987.

IBN WARRAQ

WOMEN AND UNBELIEF. Women in the Western world emerged as major players in the FREETHOUGHT movement by the end of the Enlightenment (see ENLIGHTENMENT, UNBELIEF DURING THE). Eighteenth-century freethinkers who ventured to publish unorthodox views gambled with loss of liberty, wealth, and sometimes life. Women heretics had even more to fear. The last witchcraft trials and executions took place in the early 1790s. Against this backdrop—at a time when women were still at the mercy of the New Testament injunction, "Keep silence"—the strong activism of female freethinkers is impressive.

Early Women Freethinkers. One of the earliest female deists (see DEISM) on record was Caroline, queen of England, who was exempted at her request from taking the oath by an act of Parliament when acting as regent, and refused deathbed sacraments. Catherine the Great, empress of Russia, was a deist who corresponded with VOLTAIRE. Marquise du Châtelet, a scientist and Voltaire's companion of thirteen years, was likewise a deist whose essay "Doubts on Revealed Religions," dedicated to Voltaire, was published posthumously in 1792.

By the time the common woman began to proclaim unbelief two hundred years ago, women's legal status was still "civil death": they could not vote, speak in public, make contracts, sue or be sued, sit on juries, attend colleges or universities, enter most trades or professions, control their own property or earnings, or be legal guardians of their own children. Despite onerous religious, domestic, and legal handicaps, women unbelievers found their voices by the early nineteenth century, and began lecturing, leafleting, writing, founding freethinking societies, editing publications, and agitating to remove religious control from civil laws.

The history of female unbelief runs parallel with the history of woman's rights advocacy. The earliest women freethinkers were also the trailblazers for feminism, since it took unorthodox women to challenge the religious status quo. Women freethinkers were the first women to call for woman suffrage, legal equality, marriage and divorce reform, dress reform, sexual equality, birth control, and educational rights (see BIRTH CONTROL AND UNBELIEF; WOMAN SUFFRAGE MOVEMENT AND UNBELIEF; SEX RADICALISM AND UNBELIEF).

Mary WOLLSTONECRAFT published the first influential book advancing women's rights, *A Vindication of the Rights of Woman* (1792). The British Wollstonecraft was a child of the Enlightenment, a deist who espoused reason in everything she wrote. A prototype of the women who would follow in her footsteps, Wollstonecraft not only repudiated orthodoxy and espoused feminism, but was a reformer as well.

Freethinking Scottish-born Frances WRIGHT was the first woman to speak publicly from the podium before men and women in the United States; her stated purpose was to "destroy the slavery of the mind." On a historic lecture tour in 1828, she became the first woman in America to call publicly for women's equality. Wright termed churches the most formidable enemy of world progress. Advocating that people "turn their churches into halls of science," she herself purchased a church for seven thousand dollars in the Bowery district of New York, renamed it the "Hall of Science," and inspired others to do likewise. She and Robert Dale OWEN published the *FREE ENQUIRER* in 1829, making her the first female freethought editor in the United States.

American Women Freethinkers. Polish immigrant Ernestine L. ROSE became the first publicly declared female atheist in the United States and also the first woman to canvass for women's rights. In 1836 she began lobbying for the Married Woman's Property Act, introduced in the New York state legislature by freethinking Judge Thomas Hertell, which passed in 1848.

Rose lectured in at least twenty-three states, helping women obtain property rights. As an open atheist, she was often shunned, not only by clergy but sometimes by women's rights advocates, such as some participants at the Philadelphia woman's rights convention of 1854 who unsuccessfully tried to bar her from presiding because of her atheism. Rose was active in "infidel" and early freethought organizations. Her classic lecture "A Defense of ATHEISM" was delivered in Boston in 1861, and reprinted as a pamphlet by Josiah P. MENDUM of the *BOSTON INVESTIGATOR*.

Freethinker Elizabeth Cady STANTON launched the women's rights movement. With four Quaker women, Stanton, a harried young mother, organized the first women's rights convention in Seneca Falls, New York, in 1848, shocking friends and the world with her public call for woman suffrage. Stanton later recalled in *The History of Woman Suffrage* "that the greatest obstacle we had to overcome was the Bible. It was hurled at us on every side." Stanton devoted her life to freeing women from "the fountain of all tyranny, religious superstition, priestly power, and the canon law." It was a rare speech or article by the "fearless, serene agnostic" that did not contain a trenchant criticism of religion. Stanton founded and served as first president of the National Woman Suffrage Association. She was editor of the irreverent the *Revolution* (1868–70), and was much published in the freethought press, lecturing before many Liberal groups. Stanton was friendly with the freethinkers of her day, including Robert Green INGERSOLL and Charles BRADLAUGH of England. She edited *The Woman's Bible* (1895, 1896), a best seller at the time, which, though repudiated by vote of the suffrage association in 1898, has endured. Stanton outspokenly called the Bible the most degrading book ever written about women. Stanton's colleague Susan B. ANTHONY, a Quaker-turned-agnostic, defended Ernestine L. Rose and *The Woman's Bible*. Anthony pronounced her creed as "the perfect equality of women."

Matilda Joslyn GAGE, a nonreligious national suffrage leader, shared Stanton's passionate conviction that women needed to be freed from superstition. Gage authored *Woman, Church, and State* (1893) to refute the myth that women's status was improved under Christianity.

Freethinking rank-and-file activists in the suffrage movement included Lillie Devereux BLAKE, a freethinker who directed the New York State Suffrage Association, winning many "firsts" for women. Marilla M. RICKER was a trailblazing attorney who worked with Robert Green Ingersoll on his Star Route mail fraud cases and promoted suffrage and legal equality. Her two decades of pithy columns for the freethought newspaper *THE TRUTH SEEKER* were published in two books. Fifty years after Ernestine L. Rose helped pass the first property reform for women, Josephine K. Henry became the main force behind the tardy adoption of the 1894 Woman's Property Act in Kentucky. Henry was declared an undesirable member of the state suffrage association she founded when her two letters critical of the Bible appeared in *The Woman's Bible*.

Helen H. GARDENER, a writer and suffragist, wrote the eloquent *Men, Women and Gods* (1885). She had been dubbed "Ingersoll in soprano" while delivering a lecture series based on her book. This still-timely work critiques not only the Bible's treatment of women but such theological doctrines as vicarious atonement.

Voltairine DE CLEYRE, a freethinker, writer, poet, and anarchist (see ANARCHISM AND UNBELIEF), believed that it is better to have a religion of deeds than a religion of creeds. She believed that it is better to work for humanity than for a god. A strikingly modern thinker, de Cleyre was a radical on sex questions, as was her compatriot, anarchist Emma GOLDMAN (1869–1940), who agitated for birth control. In her journal *Mother Earth*, Goldman published two important essays on religion, "The Failure of Christianity" (1913) and "The Philosophy of Atheism" (1916). Radical Lucy Parsons—widow of the freethinking martyr Albert Parsons, who was hanged as a scapegoat for the Haymarket riot—fought not only racism, but was a labor activist dogged by the FBI. Her journals, *Freedom* and *Liberator*, were peppered throughout with her freethought views.

Margaret SANGER began her crusade to bring contraception to women by launching a 1914 newspaper, the *Woman Rebel*, with the motto: "No Gods—No Masters." Arguably doing more than any other individual to free women, Sanger fought the power of the Roman Catholic Church in her lifelong campaign. In her 1938 autobiography, Sanger explained her goal to make every woman a rebellious Vashti, not an Esther (a wry reference to the Old Testament Book of Esther).

Charlotte Perkins GILMAN, an internationally known feminist, author, editor, and theorist, pulverized "death-based religions" with her highly original book, *His Religion and Hers: The Faith of Our Fathers and the Work of Our Mothers* (1923). Gilman noted that the human species was misdirecting its best efforts toward the sky. Rejecting the Genesis idea that work was a curse, Gilman believed work was humanizing, and would rescue women consigned by religion to be a servant class to men.

Among other important nineteenth-century American women freethinkers and critics of religion was Lydia Maria CHILD, author of *The Progress of Religious Ideas through Successive Ages* (1855). (Child was more antitheology than pro-freethought.) Margaret Fuller was a pioneering journalist, editor, and thinker whose motto was: "Give me truth; cheat me by no illusion." Ella E. GIBSON wrote for most of the nineteenth-century freethought publications, and produced the first book analyzing the Bible and women, *The Godly Women of the Bible, by an Ungodly Woman of the Nineteenth Century* (1878). Elmina D. SLENKER likewise wrote for freethought periodicals. Her book *Studying the Bible* was published in 1870. Etta SEMPLE, a progressive reformer, cofounded the Kansas Freethought Association, served as its president, and published *Freethought Ideal* from her parlor.

French Women Freethinkers. Olympe de Gouge, a political pamphleteer during the French Revolution, issued her short manifesto "Declaration of the Rights of Women" in 1791. The document referenced a supreme being in the deistic sense. Gouge wrote that "the tocsin of reason is being heard throughout the whole universe," dispersing "fanaticism, superstition." Gouge died by the guillotine. Despite her early cry for liberty, French women, like those in Germany and Britain, were a generation behind American women in organizing for their rights. A founding member of the feminist movement, Maria Deraismes was a comedic playwright. Deraismes welcomed participants to the first French Women's Congress, held in 1878, and was president of the Society for the Improvement of the Condition of Women. A rationalist, she was the first woman Freemason in France and directed several freethought societies. She was a copresider of the Anti-Clerical Congress in Paris in 1881 (see ANTICLERICALISM).

British Women Freethinkers. Among the British freethought movement's many women champions was Harriet MARTINEAU, the prominent author, abolitionist, reformer, feminist, and translator of Auguste COMTE into English. Martineau recoiled from theology. In her *Autobiography* (1877), she decried "the superstitions of the Christian mythology" and noted how "dogmatic faith compels the best minds and hearts to narrowness and insolence."

Emma MARTIN was an early lecturer and pamphleteer for freethought. A feminist and a friend of secularist George Jacob HOLYOAKE, she wrote an autobiographical pamphlet about rejecting religion titled "A Few Reasons for Renouncing Christianity and Professing and Disseminating Infidel Opinions." Martin's observation in "Renouncing Christianity" could summarize the leitmotif of feminine freethought: "Religion, with an upward glancing eye, asks what there is above. Philosophy looks around her and seeks to make a happy home of earth."

Barbara Leigh Smith Bodichon, another colleague of Holyoake, wrote a summary of laws concerning women in 1854. That work became a major catalyst of the British feminist movement and resulted in the adoption of the Married Women's Property Bill in 1857. Bodichon, who had met Elizabeth Cady Stanton, was inspired to petition Parliament for suffrage (though she did not succeed).

Harriet LAW worked for secular causes for thirty years and briefly edited the *Secular Chronicle*.

Annie BESANT, the professional partner of atheist leader Charles Bradlaugh in the NATIONAL SECULAR SOCIETY, was a famed freethought orator during the 1880s. Besant, with Bradlaugh, challenged the Obscene Publications Act by reprinting *The Fruits of Philosophy*, hastening the birth control movement (see KNOWLTON, CHARLES). Besant was a capable propagandist on freethought topics until her conversion to mysticism and THEOSOPHY in 1889.

Bradlaugh's daughter Hypatia Bradlaugh BONNER carried on after her father's death in 1891, starting a freethought publishing house, editing the *Reformer* (1897–1904), cofounding the RATIONALIST PRESS ASSOCIATION, and writing several freethought books, including *Christianity and Conduct* (1919). Bonner worked against the death penalty and BLASPHEMY laws, founded the Rationalist Peace Society in 1910, and was honored by London authorities for nearly half a century of public service.

Women and State/Church Advocacy. While Roger WILLIAMS is credited with the honors, it was in fact a woman, Anne Hutchinson, who was the first to found a colony establishing religious liberty in the New World. Hutchinson emigrated to the Massachusetts Bay Colony of Boston in 1634. Branded an "American Jezebel" for holding theological discussion groups in her home for women and attracting male followers to her Quaker-like opposition to Puritanism, Hutchinson was banished for sedition and heresy in 1637, then excommunicated. She and her doomed followers settled on an island in their short-lived Rhode Island colony, where they adopted the first declaration of religious freedom: "It is ordered that none shall be accounted a delinquent for doctrine." The colony was wiped out by an Indian tribe under Puritan influence.

An eccentric American defender of the Enlightenment, the outspoken Anne Newport ROYALL attacked the "Christian party in politics" and Sabbatarians (who sought to end postal delivery and force businesses to close on Sunday), who were coming to power in the 1820s. Royall, the first lobbyist to monitor the separation of church and state in Congress, fought to retain Sunday mail delivery, single-handedly destroyed Sunday school Union tracts left in the Library of Congress, and personally drove missionaries from the halls of Congress. The Baltimore-born deist was arrested and convicted of being a "common scold" in 1829. Undaunted, Royall launched the weekly watchdog journals *Paul Pry* (1831–36) and the *Huntress* (1836–54). Royall's motto: "Good works instead of long prayers."

In 1890 Matilda Joslyn Gage organized a short-lived women's organization to support church-state separation, the Woman's National Liberal Union, warning of the dangers to women and to liberty posed by "The Christian Party in Politics" seeking a union of church and state.

Vashti McCOLLUM won the first challenge against religious instruction in public schools in a US Supreme Court case handed down in 1948. She wrote *One Woman's Fight* (1951) about her family's ordeal in taking up the landmark challenge. Active in humanist and freethought groups, McCollum served two terms as president of the AMERICAN HUMANIST ASSOCIATION.

Contemporary Women Unbelievers. The two most prominent national US atheist/agnostic membership organizations in the late twentieth century were both founded by women.

American Atheists was launched by Madalyn Murray O'HAIR. O'Hair, born Madalyn Mays in Pittsburgh, came to prominence by winning a lawsuit challenging Bible reading and recitation in Baltimore's public schools. Her lawsuit, *Murray v. Curlett*, was joined to the major 1962 decision *Schempp v. Abington*, which ruled such religious rituals unconstitutional. O'Hair and the media concurred at the time that she had become "the most hated woman in America" for her outspoken, often vulgar attacks on religion. Controversial as she was, O'Hair was undeniably the best-known atheist in the United States. Her organization, headquartered in Austin, Texas, published periodicals, reissued a number of freethought books, and produced a radio series. She, her son Jon Garth, and granddaughter Robin were tragically murdered by a former employee/embezzler in 1995. The case was solved several years after their disappearance. Ellen Johnson, a New Jersey activist, now directs American Atheists from New Jersey.

Anne Nicol Gaylor established the Freedom From Religion Foundation as a national group in Madison, Wisconsin, in 1978, serving as its president through 2004. The foundation has grown to more than seventy-six hundred members nationwide, launched the newspaper *Freethought Today*, published several books and films, and has become a major litigator to keep church and state separate. Gaylor, a nontheist since childhood, followed the footsteps of many nineteenth-century predecessors by becoming a freethought activist after her interest in feminism made her aware that the root cause of women's oppression was religion. Belying the myth that atheists don't found charities, she has run the Women's Medical Fund as a volunteer since 1972. It is the longest-lived US abortion rights charity, and has helped more than sixteen thousand indigent women exercise their right to abortion despite constant attack by religionists.

Women's leadership has likewise been prominent in Great Britain. Psychologist Margaret KNIGHT became a national celebrity when she delivered a freethought lecture series over BBC radio in 1955, collected in book form as *Morals without Religion*. Barbara Smoker was president of the National Secular Society, founded by Charles Bradlaugh and Annie Besant, from 1971 to 1996.

Noted Women Unbelievers. Significant US freethought writers include Russian-born naturalized citizen Ayn RAND, an atheist, founder of the Objectivist movement, and a best-selling novelist; Ruth Hurmence Green, author of *The Born Again Skeptic's Guide to the Bible* (1979); Barbara G. Walker, author of *The Skeptical Feminist* (1987); writer and social critic Barbara Ehrenreich, an atheist who has written regularly for *Time* magazine; Katha Pollitt, atheist, poet, and columnist for the *Nation*; and Wendy Kaminer,

agnostic, social critic, and commentator. Mormon-turned-freethinker Sonia Johnson, author of *From Housewife to Heretic* (1983), became a freethinker after being excommunicated by the Mormon Church in 1979 for exposing that church's role in sabotaging the proposed Equal Rights Amendment to the US Constitution.

Freethinking novelists and playwrights include Margaret Atwood, Pearl S. Buck, Simone de BEAUVOIR, Isak Dinesen, George Eliot, Zona Gale, Zora Neale HURSTON, Lorraine HANSBERRY, Ursula K. LeGuin, Doris Lessing, Robin Morgan, Joyce Carol Oates, OUIDA, Olive Schreiner, Madame de Stael, Alice Walker, and Virginia Woolf.

Freethinking poets include Louise Victorine Ackermann, Amy Lowell, and Gertrude Stein.

Freethinking artists include Marie Bashkirtseff, Rosa Bonheur, Margaret Bourke-White, Isadora Duncan, Kate Greenaway, and Frida Kahlo.

Scientists include Marie Curie.

Entertainers include actress Marlene Dietrich, singer Ani DiFranco, actress Frances Farmer, actress Jodie Foster, actress Katharine Hepburn, actress Butterfly MCQUEEN, and actress/comedian Julia Sweeney.

Believers in This World. The history of women in freethought is singularly the history of activists working to improve conditions in this, the only known world. Proof of the continuing threat posed to women's liberty by fundamentalists is Bengali physician and author Taslima Nasrin. The outspoken atheist wrote of the plight of women in the Muslim world. She fled her country in 1994 and went into hiding after being condemned to death for BLASPHEMY by her country's "holy men." Nasrin is proof also of the new wave of feminism and freethought washing over non-Christian nations, as women find the courage to speak out against the greatest enemy of women and liberty under whatever guise: fundamentalism.

BIBLIOGRAPHY

Augur, Helen. *An American Jezebel: The Life of Anne Hutchinson.* New York: Brentano's, 1930.

Gaylor, Annie Laurie, ed. *Women without Superstition: "No Gods—No Masters." The Collected Writings of Women Freethinkers of the Nineteenth & Twentieth Centuries.* Madison, WI: Freedom From Religion Foundation, 1997.

Martineau, Harriet. *Autobiography.* 2 vols. Edited by Maria Weston Chapman. Boston: James R. Osgood and Company, 1877.

MCCABE, Joseph. *A Biographical Dictionary of Modern Rationalists.* London: Thoemmes Press, 1920.

Stanton, Elizabeth Cady, Susan B. Anthony, and Matilda Joslyn Gage, eds. *The History of Woman Suffrage, Vols. I–III.* Rochester, NY: Susan B. Anthony, 1881.

Stanton, Elizabeth Cady. Interview. *Chicago Record*, June 29, 1897.

ANNIE LAURIE GAYLOR

WOOLSTON, THOMAS (1669/1670–1731/1733), English deist. A passionate deist (see DEISM) critic of revealed religion, Thomas Woolston has been described by one contemporary apologist as an "evil genius." Thomas Woolston was born in Northampton, England. A studious young man, he studied theology at Sidney Sussex College, Cambridge, and embarked on a career in the Church of England. His studies of early Christianity led to an appreciation of the allegorical modes of biblical interpretation then frequently employed, particularly by the ancient church father Origen, whom Woolston particularly admired. But Woolston took this several steps further than Origen would have countenanced, and quickly moved to an advanced deist viewpoint.

His first significant work was *Old Apology for the Truth of the Christian Religion against the Jews and Gentiles Revived* (1705). From then on, Woolston was under suspicion for being dangerously unorthodox, which a new series of letters and pamphlets in 1720 and 1721 did nothing to ease. In 1721 he lost his fellowship at Sidney Sussex College and moved to London, where he survived on the support of his brother. In *The Moderator between an Infidel and an Apostate* (1725), Woolston entered controversial territory once more with a measured criticism of Anthony COLLINS (the infidel) and, more riskily, the established church (the apostate). In his role as the moderator, Woolston once more argued for the allegorical interpretation of scripture and against a literal reading of miracle stories and the resurrection of Christ. He developed his moderator device in a series of six *Discourses on the Miracles of Our Savior*, published between 1727 and 1730. As if the subject matter of the *Discourses* was not sufficiently incendiary, Woolston's notional moderator was a rabbi. The *Discourses* were devoted primarily to questioning the resurrection of Christ, miracles, and other supernatural elements of the gospels. The *Discourses* sold very well and attracted about sixty written replies.

This was too much for the church, which struck back late in 1729. Woolston was fined twenty-five pounds for each of the first four discourses and was to be imprisoned until the fines were paid. Not having access to that sort of money, and refusing to desist from further writing, Woolston remained incarcerated until his death. His date of death is uncertain, the most likely being January 21, 1731, though others have suggested January 21 or 27, 1733.

Woolston's posthumous reputation has been uneven. Friends and foes alike have long suspected a certain imbalance in his personality. His writing was pugnacious and sarcastic and he was unusually sensitive to criticism, of which he received a great deal. However, his conclusions were no more radical than most of his deist contemporaries.

BIBLIOGRAPHY

Redwood, John. *Reason, Ridicule and Religion: The Age of Enlightenment in England 1660–1750.* London: Thames and Hudson, 1996.
Stephen, Leslie. *History of English Thought in the Eighteenth Century.* 2 vols. New York: Harcourt Brace, 1962.

BILL COOKE

WRIGHT, ELIZUR (1804–1885), American atheist and abolitionist. Elizur Wright's emergence as a leading American freethought advocate during the 1870s was the logical outcome of his career as a radical abolitionist and life insurance reformer. His journey across the nineteenth century embodied the secularization and rationalism of the period, culminating in his rejection of church and creed.

Early Life. Born on February 12, 1804, in South Canaan, Connecticut, Wright was the eldest child of his father's second marriage. His yeoman parents, who moved to the Western Reserve of Ohio in 1810, were devout Congregationalists. His father was a Yale graduate, deacon, and frontier schoolmaster, while his mother, Clarissa (née Richards), stressed piety. Groomed for the ministry, Wight attended his father's alma mater from 1822 to 1826, where he displayed a paternal talent for mathematics and science.

Lack of funds, a love affair, and persistent qualms about a clerical calling led the young Wright to conflicted career choices. He resolved his quandary by marrying Susan Clark in 1829. In lieu of the ministry, he accepted a professorship of mathematics and natural philosophy at Western Reserve College in Hudson, Ohio. In 1832 and 1833 Wright and his colleagues Beriah Green and Charles B. Storrs transformed the college into a center of radical abolitionism. Convinced by the passionate arguments of William Lloyd Garrison, the Boston editor of the *Liberator*, the threesome denounced the moral expediency of repatriating African Americans to Liberia. Instead they demanded immediate emancipation and equal rights for blacks. (Fellow abolitionist minister John Ingersoll paid tribute to Beriah Green by making him the "middle-namesake" of his own son—the future orator and "Great Agnostic" Robert Green INGERSOLL, born in 1833.)

Reform Career. In 1833 Wright accepted the position of secretary of domestic correspondence of the American Anti-Slavery Society, a New York City posting that placed him in the vanguard of the movement. For the next six years, he displayed his organizational and literary talents, aided fugitive slaves, and argued for racial justice. A white backlash against abolitionism provoked Wright to caustic criticism of Christian hypocrisy. By 1840 factionalism among abolitionists found Wright in the forefront of political action in Boston, editing abolitionist papers such as *The Massachusetts Abolitionist* and *The Chronotype*. Caught in economic hard times and with a large family to support, Wright published a translation of La Fontaine's *Fables* (1841) and found gainful work consulting for life insurance companies. His mathematical talents and reformist zeal made him America's leading actuary at midcentury. He rationalized actuarial science and relentlessly ferreted out fraud as a pioneering commissioner of life insurance in Massachusetts from 1858 to 1867. Outraged by the repressive Comstock Act (1873) (see COMSTOCK, ANTHONY, AND UNBELIEF), Wright championed freethought along with Robert G. Ingersoll, Francis E. ABBOT, D. M. BENNETT, and Erza HEYWOOD. He served as president of the NATIONAL LIBERAL LEAGUE in 1879 and 1880. He died at Medford, Massachusetts, on November 21, 1885.

BIBLIOGRAPHY

Goodheart, Lawrence B. *Abolitionist, Actuary, Atheist: Elizur Wright and the Reform Impulse.* Kent, OH: Kent State University Press, 1990.

———. "The Ambiguity of Individualism: The National Liberal League's Challenge to the Comstock Law." In *American Chameleon: Individualism in Trans-National Context*, edited by Richard O. Curry and Lawrence B. Goodheart. Kent, OH: Kent State University Press, 1991.

LAWRENCE B. GOODHEART

WRIGHT, FRANCES (1795–1852), American freethinker, abolitionist, and sex radical. Born in Scotland of wealthy, intellectual parents, Frances Wright became one of the most despised women of the nineteenth century. Orphaned before she was three and raised by an aunt in southern England, Wright returned to Scotland when she turned eighteen. There, surrounded by supportive mother surrogates and brilliant men closely associated with the Scottish Enlightenment (see ENLIGHTENMENT, UNBELIEF DURING THE), Wright wrote tragic drama and a treatise on Greek philosophy.

In 1818 Wright and her sister Camilla traveled to America for a successful tour that inspired her to pen *Views of Society and Manners in America*, which would become her most popular book. Like her great-uncle James Mylne and her great-great-uncle John Millar, Wright advocated for the education of women and was fervently opposed to the slave trade. Seeing slavery for the first time on this trip, she brought the fresh perspective of a young woman's horror to this old American problem.

Returning to England in 1820, Wright, an attractive, well-connected, and outspoken young woman with a brilliant mind, formed friendships with two of the most important men in Europe—Jeremy BENTHAM and General Lafayette. Wright's relationship with Lafayette, much written about today, was complicated. From the moment she first met him—she went uninvited to his chateau in France—she encouraged a passionate relationship, much to the horror of his family. Wright proposed to him, then suggested that he adopt her as his legal daughter. Their intimacy, whether that of friends or lovers, helped give her more intellectual confidence as she imagined grand schemes for liberating the world.

Returning to the United States in 1824 to follow Lafayette as he traveled across the country, Wright was in Washington, DC, in February of 1825 when Robert OWEN spoke to Congress on his plan to create a "community of equality" in southwestern Indiana. This was New Harmony; visiting it twice in the spring of 1825, Wright decided to create an intentional community where slaves could "work out" their freedom, while at the same time they and their children could become educated and prepared for life as free men and women. Wright was not interested in plans she had heard of to simply send slaves to Haiti. Her fascination with Owen's notion of communal life was that it promised a way for poor, landless people to benefit from their own labor.

Encouraged by Lafayette, Wright advertised the community that would become Nashoba in the abolitionist journal the *Genius of Universal Emancipation* in October of 1825. Located outside of what is now Memphis, Tennessee, Nashoba spelled out women's rights and slaves' rights more explicitly than at any other nineteenth-century community. Yet the community was immediately plagued with too little money, too little food, and too much to do to maintain civilized life in the middle of "the west."

During her first summer in Tennessee in 1826, Wright became ill with fever—probably malaria—and her illness forced her to leave for Europe to convalesce the following year. As she was sailing to Europe, one of the white men in the community gave a copy of the "Nashoba Book" to a journalist to publish. It included a significant piece of information: that the while male member and a young, attractive black woman had begun living together. With the publishing of the "book," public outrage against Wright's "free-love colony" sprang up all over the country, destroying Wright's reputation.

In 1828 Wright realized that she cold not convert "the existing generation" to her plan and began to focus instead on writing and lecturing. Along with her friend Robert Dale OWEN, son of Robert Owen, Wright took over the editorship of the languishing *New Harmony Gazette*, renamed it the *FREE ENQUIRER*, and moved it and herself to New York City. From that base, Wright lectured and wrote on the importance of equal rights for women—and of how "priests," those "hired supporters of error," encouraged mental bondage for women. Wright's frank discussion of the "unnatural" sexual restraints upon women and the unnatural social limitations upon blacks inspired fury throughout the United Stated. Everyone criticized her, even her former friends.

In the midst of her writing and lecturing career, Wright decided to free the Nashoba slaves by removing them to Haiti. In October of 1829, she and William Phiquepal, another Owenite reformer who was familiar with the West Indies, sailed to Haiti with the slaves. During this trip, Wright became pregnant and the direction of her life changed forever. Wright married Phiquepal in 1831 when their daughter, Sylva, was over six months old, but domestic life (and a bad marriage) isolated Wright during the early 1830s. Returning to the United States in 1835, Wright attempted to regain her position as a public lecturer and writer, but could not. During the last years of her life, Frances Wright battled Phiquepal for her property and for her daughter, who, living with her father, primarily sided with him. Wright died in Cincinnati at age fifty-seven, alone and crippled from a fall that broke her hip.

The example of Frances Wright speaks powerfully to us today. Although her friends and colleagues all turned against her (even Robert Dale Owen summed up his work with her as "immature and extravagant"), Wright never stopped writing and speaking for women's equality and never stopped criticizing the society that created and perpetuated secondary citizenship for women. Whereas Robert Dale Owen "grew up" and denounced his former reform, Wright, to her credit, never repented.

CAROL KOLMERTEN

WRIGHT, RICHARD (1908–1960), American novelist and humanist. One of black America's greatest and most influential authors, Richard Wright was born on a plantation near Natchez, Mississippi. He and his family lived there for the first five years of his life. When he was six, the family moved to Memphis. Soon thereafter, his father abandoned the family for another woman. Later Richard and his mother moved to Jackson, Mississippi.

Wright's grandmother was a deeply religious Seventh-Day Adventist. She sent him to a Seventh-Day Adventist school near Jackson. He was later enrolled in a public school and developed a love of writing.

In 1927 Wright moved to Chicago. He met H. L. MENCKEN and read his material, as well as the works of Sinclair LEWIS and other religious skeptics. In 1937 he moved to New York City and became Harlem editor of the Communist publication the *Daily World.* In 1940 he wrote his masterpiece, *Native Son,* which became a best seller and international sensation. In 1944 he became disillusioned with the Communist Party and left it.

In 1945 he wrote his autobiography, *Black Boy: A Record of Childhood and Youth.* In 1946 he moved to France and became a friend of Albert CAMUS, Jean-Paul SARTRE, and Simone de BEAUVOIR. He read writings by such thinkers as Heidegger and became an existentialist (see EXISTENTIALISM). In 1953 he wrote his second novel, *The Outsider,* widely believed to be the first existentialist novel written by someone born in North America (not by an American, as Wright had become a naturalized French citizen in 1947).

The Outsider deals with a posttheistic world. However, Wright—like Sartre—did not believe that human beings could be trusted to produce a workable ethical system. Like C. L. R. JAMES, Wright did not believe in God, but he was also suspicious of human-centered belief systems. After all, both men had been disillusioned with atheistic communism.

Wright is generally recognized as one of the most important writers in American history. His brilliant ideas on the relationship of the individual to society and human destiny have made him one of the most talked-about writers of the twentieth century.

BIBLIOGRAPHY

Fabre, Michel. "Richard Wright: Beyond Naturalism?" In *African American Humanism: An Anthology,* edited by Norm R. Allen Jr. Amherst, NY: Prometheus Books, 1991.
Webb, Constance. *Richard Wright: A Biography.* New York: Putnam, 1968.
Wright, Richard. *Black Boy: A Record of Childhood and Youth.* New York: Harper, 1945.

NORM R. ALLEN JR.

XENOPHANES OF COLOPHON (ca. 560–ca. 478 BCE). Greek poet and thinker. Driven from his native city by a Persian invasion around 546, Xenophanes wandered Greece as an itinerant rhapsode, a poet in the Homeric mold who recited for his supper in a succession of royal courts. As a very old man, he settled in Elea on the western Italian coast. There he presumably composed his more philosophic works and laid early foundations for the Eleatic school of philosophy, whose actual founder is held to be Parmenides.

The works of Xenophanes survive only in fragments, the only sources for his life or his thought. Like his predecessors Thales, Anaximander, and Anaximenes, Xenophanes was a monist. He taught the absolute unity of all things, denying any distinction between matter on the one hand and spirit or the life principle on the other. He argued that God, too, was unitary—and moreover that God was one with the universe. While apologists portray him as an early monotheist, Xenophanes was more accurately a pantheist.

Such a view was equivalent to ATHEISM by the standards of the time; had Xenophanes resided in Athens like PROTAGORAS or, later, SOCRATES, he might have suffered exile or worse as they did. His travels and his sojourn in Elea offered Xenophanes more freedom. He relentlessly criticized Greek popular religion for its naive anthropomorphism: "Mortals suppose that the Gods are born, and wear a man's clothing, and have voice and body. But if cattle or lions had hands, so as to paint with their hands and make works of art as men do, they would paint their

Gods and give them bodies like their own—horses like horses, cattle like cattle." He ridiculed the immoral behavior of the gods of Olympus, claiming that Homer "attributed to the Gods all things that with men are of ill-fame and blame" and "told of them countless nefarious things." Prefiguring other traditions of interest to free-thinkers, Xenophanes denied the efficacy of divination and was the first Greek thinker to recognize fossils as historical records of bygone forms of life.

BIBLIOGRAPHY

Birx, H. James, "Evolution and Unbelief." In *The Encyclopedia of Unbelief*, edited by Gordon Stein. Amherst, NY: Prometheus Books, 1985.

Robertson, John M. *A Short History of Freethought, Ancient and Modern*. 3rd ed. London: Watts and Company, 1914.

TOM FLYNN

ZELENSKI, TADEUSZ (BOY; 1874–1941), Polish iconoclastic commentator, literary critic, theater critic, and translator of masterpieces of French literature. Tadeusz Zelenski's articles and columns appeared between World War I and World War II, mainly in the weekly *Wiadomosci Literackie* (Literary News). In 1928 he started his great campaign for modernization and secularization of traditional culture, opposing the aggresive clericalism that he described in his book *Nasi okupanci* (Our Occupiers, 1932). In *Dziewice konsystorskie* (Consistory Virgins, an ironic reference to wives declared unmarried by an ecclesiastical court, 1929), *Pieklo kobiet* (The Hell of Women, 1930) and *Jak skonczyc z pieklem kobiet* (How to End the Hell of Women, 1932), he described varied manifestations of sex discrimination and demanded women's right to abortion. While brutally attacked by the Catholic and nationalistic press, he enjoyed great prestige among the Polish liberal intelligentsia of this period.

BARBARA STANOSZ

GENERAL INDEX

(PERSONS, CONCEPTS, EVENTS, OBJECTS, AUTHORS CITED)

INDEX OF ORGANIZATIONS
AND INSTITUTIONS

INDEX OF PUBLISHED WORKS
(NON-PERIOIDICAL)

INDEX OF PERIODICALS